LIFE PICTORIAL ATLAS OF THE WORLD

LIFE PICTORIAL ATLAS OF THE WORLD

THE EDITORS OF LIFE
AND RAND McNALLY

TIME INCORPORATED
NEW YORK · 1961

OTHER BOOKS
BY THE EDITORS OF LIFE

LIFE'S PICTURE HISTORY OF WORLD WAR II

LIFE'S PICTURE HISTORY OF WESTERN MAN

THE WORLD WE LIVE IN
with LINCOLN BARNETT

THE WORLD'S GREAT RELIGIONS

AMERICA'S ARTS AND SKILLS

PICTURE COOK BOOK

THE SECOND WORLD WAR
with WINSTON S. CHURCHILL

THE WONDERS OF LIFE ON EARTH
with LINCOLN BARNETT

LIFE WORLD LIBRARY

LIFE NATURE LIBRARY

PUBLISHED SIMULTANEOUSLY IN CANADA.

LIFE

LIBRARY OF CONGRESS CATALOG CARD NUMBER: MAP 61-7
BOOK STORE DISTRIBUTION BY RAND McNALLY & COMPANY

TIME INC. BOOK DIVISION

Editor Norman P. Ross
Copy Director William Jay Gold
Chief of Research Beatrice T. Dobie

•

Publisher Jerome S. Hardy
General Manager John A. Watters

•

Editorial staffs of the *LIFE Pictorial Atlas of the World:*

FOR TIME INCORPORATED

Editor
Byron Dobell

Art Director
Charles Tudor

Associate Art Directors
Nina Rittenberg, Robert L. Young

Text by
Jay Brennan, *Senior Writer*
John Brick, Robert C. Christopher,
Walter Karp, Hillis Mills,
Richard Oulahan Jr.,
John Paul Porter,
Richard Seamon, Gerald Simons

Chief Researcher
Carlotta Kerwin

Text and Picture Research by
Linda Asher, Barbara Ballantine, Barbara J. Bennett,
Judith Bloom, Alice Bolocan,
Patricia Bowers, Iola Haverstick, Nancy Jones,
James Matthai, Pamela Painter,
Mary Elizabeth Serra, Linda Wolfe;
Margaret K. Goldsmith,
Deece Lesser, Joan Lynch

Production Coordinators
Robert E. Foy, James P. Menton

Art Production by
Albert J. Dunn, Arthur J. Dunn
Gretchen Weiffenbach, James D. Smith
Robert Fraser, Gennaro C. Esposito

Copy Staff
Marian Gordon Goldman, *Chief;*
Ann Shaw, Rebecca Chaitin, Suzanne Seixas,
Norma Stahl Rosen, Marguerite T. Scheips,
Dolores A. Littles,
Margaret Ramsay, Esther Kaplan, Clarice Garrison

FOR RAND McNALLY & COMPANY

Director
Sanford Cobb

Editorial Coordinator
Bruce C. Ogilvie, Ph.D.

Art Director
Chris J. Arvetis

Map Design and Illustration by
Gordon Hartshorne, Mario Pagliai,
Evelyn Mitchell, Dorothy Nelson, Ivan Barcaba,
Eugeniusz Melchert, Dean Wessel

Geo-Physical Globe Designed by
S. G. Berman *and* Kenneth S. Fagg

Director of Cartography
Russell L. Voisin
Adolph Bravi, Calvin H. Pratz, *Coordinators*

Cartographic Research Editor
Paul T. Tiddens

Editorial Research by
Douglas A. Judson, Joseph C. Smutnik, Luis Freile,
Richard L. Forstall, Laurence H. Nobles, Ph.D.

Cartographic Research by
Jerry G. Mason, Robert E. Krause,
Read C. Ross, John Fonda, Helmut Schaub, Donald R. Schultz,
Marcel R. Godfriaux, Esther Grene, John Isard

Cartographic Production by
Harry Bishop, *Chief;* Joseph H. Funke,
Jerome S. Krzywdzinski, Robert Mancic, Joseph Schillaci

Cartographers
Frank Baburek, Howard Gist, William Hajduk, William Karpa,
Roman Kobylesky, Gyula Pauer, Eugene Tiutko, John Zych

Most of the Terrain and Political Maps Originally Developed by Editors of
World Book Encyclopedia and Rand McNally

•

LIFE MAGAZINE

Managing Editor
Edward K. Thompson

Publisher
C. D. Jackson

CONTENTS

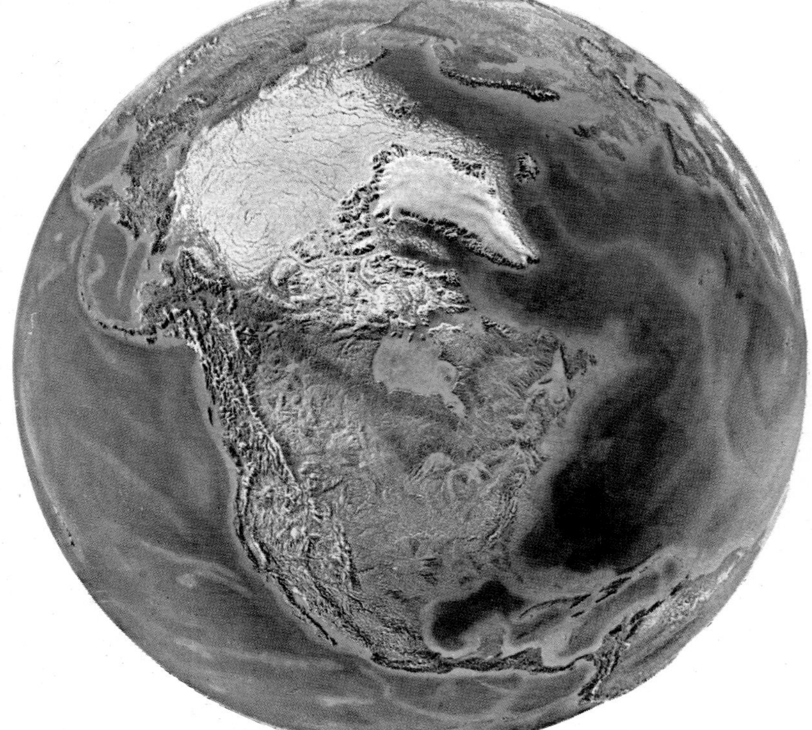

A HEMISPHERICAL VIEW OF THE GLOBE

FOREWORD:

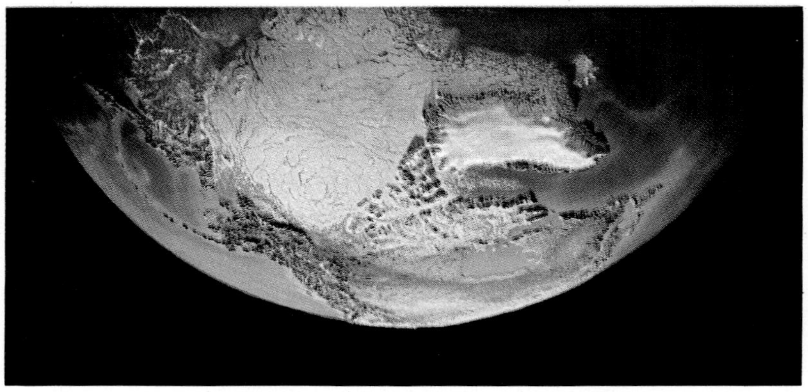

CANADA SEEN FROM ABOVE THE NORTH POLE

1. THE EARTH AS A PLANET IN SPACE

Ever since man first discovered that his world was round, he has fashioned replicas of the terrestrial sphere which is his home in the immensity of the universe. The most authentic replica ever made is the globe shown above in two photographs. Appearing in scores of views throughout the LIFE *Pictorial Atlas*, the globe is the first of many elements that make this a new and entirely different kind of atlas, one designed to be not only a valuable collection of reference maps but a provocative guide toward understanding man's world in the space age.

The finely sculptured terrain of this globe, through an exaggeration in the vertical scale, dramatically reveals the relative magnitude of the continents, the rise of mountain ranges, the sweep of plains and the arching of island chains. Its realistically colored land masses depict the hues of the earth's vegetation at the height of its seasonal growth, and the varying shades of blue indicate the relative depths of the seas. The globe was photographed from scores of different angles to obtain fresh close-ups of major regional areas. The view of Canada and Alaska above is an example. Here is the full span of a segment of the world that sweeps from Siberia, at upper left, far out into the Atlantic, at upper right. It was this kind of glimpse of the earth's grandeur that caused the first man to orbit the world to exclaim: "I saw for the first time the earth's shape."

Together with evocative photographs of real landscapes the world over and an interpretive text, these global views provide a new perspective for the human drama: the elemental earth—with its atmospheric cloak, its lands and seas and its living things—on which man plays out his role in an awesome stage setting provided by nature.

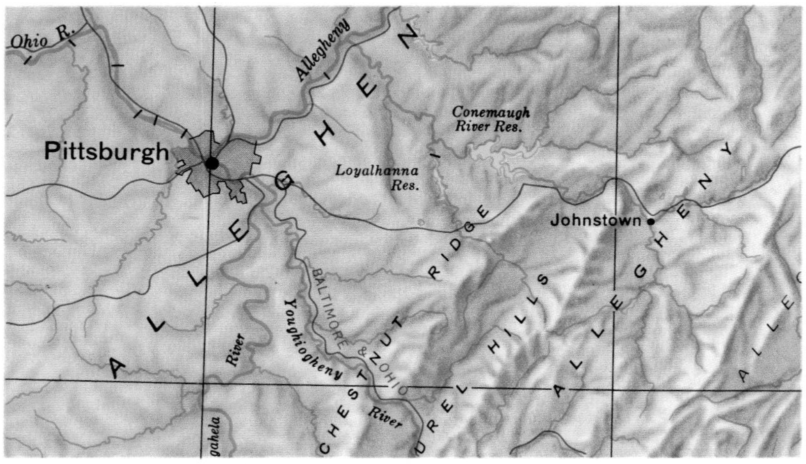

A TERRAIN MAP

A POLITICAL MAP

3. TWO KINDS OF MAPS AND WHAT THEY SHOW

The 16th Century Flemish geographer, Gerardus Mercator, was the first to use the word "atlas" for a volume of maps, and many early collections were embellished with an engraving of the Titan Atlas supporting a globe. In this ancient tradition, the *LIFE Pictorial Atlas* offers a set of reference maps of the world plus an index of some 75,000 place names.

The *LIFE Pictorial Atlas* uses two kinds of reference maps, sections of which appear above in detail. Both sections show the same 6,500-square-mile area around Pittsburgh, Pennsylvania. At the left is a terrain map, which gives a three-dimensional simulation of land forms and also shows the earth's vegetation by a naturalistic color code, the key to which is always provided with the map. This technique for terrain maps is employed here for the first time in any atlas. Like the photographs of the relief globe, the coloring of which was designed for the same purpose, the terrain maps represent a major advance in the portrayal of the earth's surface.

At right is a political map. Its chief purpose is to locate the names man has affixed to the land. In the pages devoted to the United States and Canada, where the two kinds of maps for each unit are printed together, usually on facing pages, the political map appears on a larger scale in order to encompass as many place names as possible. (Canadian and U.S. political maps also show principal highways, but only those which are major transport links between areas.) Where necessary to avoid overcrowding that would diminish the usefulness of a map, some place names have been omitted. Those which are retained represent, in the opinion of the editors, the places of the widest possible interest to the users of a contemporary world atlas.

A NEW KIND OF ATLAS

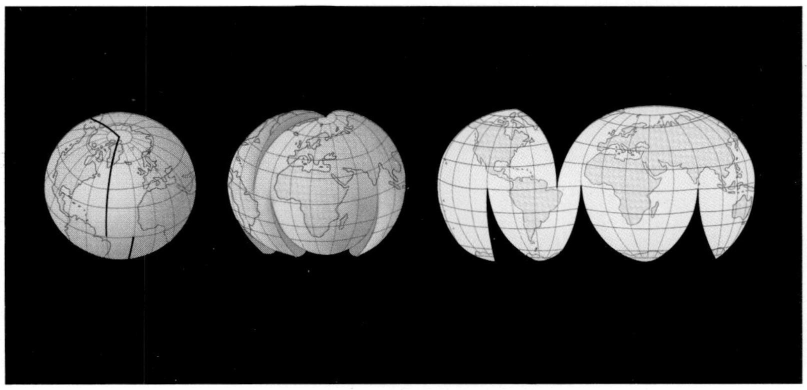

THE PROCESS OF PEELING THE GLOBE . . .

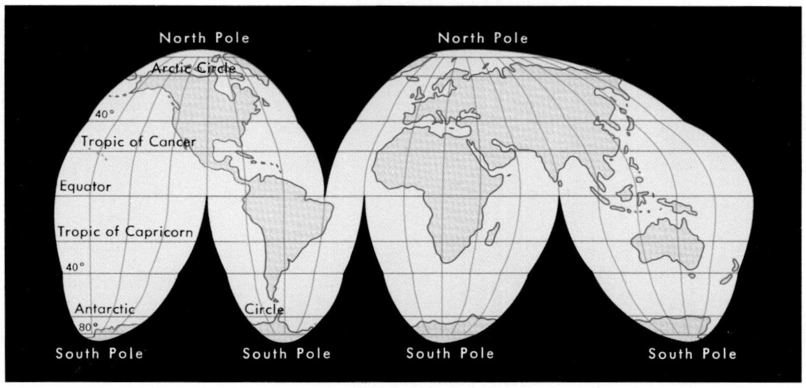

. . . TO CREATE A USEFUL MAP OF THE WORLD

2. THE ROUND WORLD MADE FLAT

Having designed a globe as a replica of the world, early cartographers struggled with the problem of projecting, or accurately depicting, its spherical surface on a flat map. They devised a variety of elaborate formulas for "peeling" the surface of the globe as one would peel a round fruit. Each solution was destined by the basically insolvable nature of the problem to contain distortions of one kind or another. One formula for "peeling" the earth's surface is shown above. As a beginning, the surface of the globe is cut along lines that intersect only the oceans and the polar regions, leaving the inhabited continents untouched *(left)*. When this is laid out flat *(right)*, the peelings form a "homolosine projection." One of several projections used in this *Atlas*, the homolosine is ideal for comparing the distribution of land areas on a world-wide basis. Though it divides the oceans, it leaves the continents correctly proportioned, and its odd shape serves as a reminder that a world map is no more than a stylized image of the spherical object it represents.

Here, as in all projections, the parallels of latitude *(red)* and meridians of longitude *(blue)* are transferred from the globe as lines on the flat surface of the map. Latitude measures the distance from the Equator to the North or South Pole—each degree of latitude representing about 69 miles. Longitude measures the distance east and west around the earth at right angles to the Equator—each degree of longitude at the Equator representing about 69 miles.

In maps that show smaller portions of the earth, other projections are used in this *Atlas*. These are less "radical" in nature than the homolosine projection because the area mapped needs less flattening.

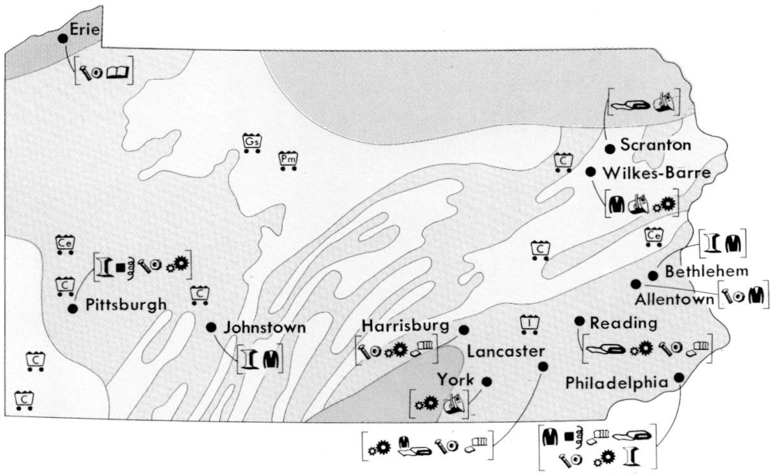

SYMBOLS OF A STATE'S ECONOMY

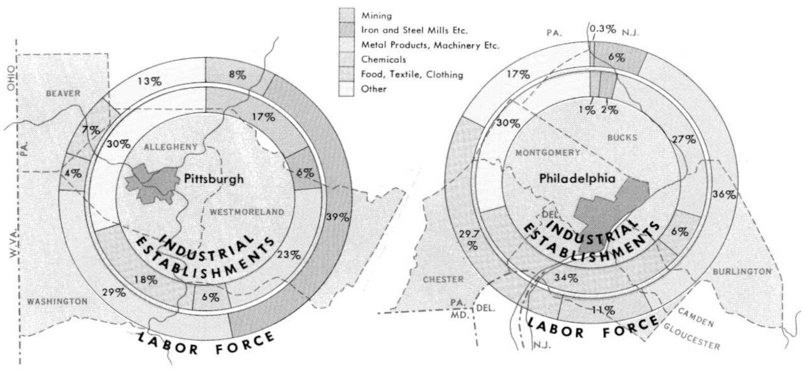

A CLOSE-UP OF TWO CITIES

4. FACTS AND DRAWINGS THAT MAKE MAPS LIVE

Shown above are two of the many special-purpose maps which add an extra dimension to this *Atlas*. At left is a map of Pennsylvania with symbols that summarize the economic activity of the state. At right is a close-up of the great industrial centers of Pittsburgh and Philadelphia, with a statistical diagram superimposed that is designed to demonstrate the widely dissimilar ways these two areas within the same state employ their labor forces and capital investment. These detail maps appear on the same pages with the basic reference maps devoted to Pennsylvania, together with other information in tables, and in a general introductory text. The LIFE *Pictorial Atlas* thus not only offers more information than is traditionally found in an atlas, but offers it in a more convenient plan of organization. All supplementary materials in the book are grouped with the reference maps to which they relate. And the maps themselves are grouped geographically according to continent and region.

Population figures and other data presented in this book are drawn from the latest figures available for every country in the world, including the 1960 United States decennial census report. Economic data are generally based on a four-year average. The reliability of the data varies, of course, from country to country. The figures for Gross National Product per capita, which represent the annual value per capita of all goods and services produced, must be based on figures supplied by governments. Where data are suspect, the figures have been adjusted by experts in each area. Statistics and all other source materials have been selected and evaluated by the editors with the aim of making the LIFE *Pictorial Atlas* a reliable and complete work of reference.

THE SOLAR SYSTEM

THE ELLIPTICAL ORBITS of planets around the sun are shown below in a stylized rendering (orbits and dimensions are not in scale). The average distances from the sun are: *(1)* Mercury, 37 million miles; *(2)* Venus, 67 million miles; *(3)* Earth, 93 million miles; *(4)* Mars, 142 million miles; *(5)* Jupiter, 483 million miles; *(6)* Saturn, 886 million miles; *(7)* Uranus, 1,780 million miles; *(8)* Neptune, 2,790 million miles; and *(9)* Pluto, 3,670 million miles.

From the seemingly motionless earth, the planets appear to be moving across the sky within a belt that the first astronomers called the zodiac. The reason for this apparent motion is that the planets revolve around the sun in orbits lying in the same plane as the earth's. The solar system comprises not only the nine planets, shown in true scale above, but also 31 moons or smaller satellites, 30,000 asteroids, thousands of comets and uncounted numbers of meteors. The planets revolve in elliptical orbits *(bottom, left)* at varying speeds and distances from the sun—moving fastest when closest to the sun, slower when

THE NINE PLANETS and their satellites are shown above in scale with the sun, whose unspeakably hot rim and surface of incandescent hydrogen arch across the painting. The planets are shown in their orbits. From the upper left they are: tiny Mercury; Venus; Earth with its moon; Mars with two satellites; Jupiter escorted by 12 satellites; ringed Saturn with its nine satellites; Uranus and Neptune with their satellites; and distant Pluto.

farther away. Their motions are governed by a precise balance between the planets' inertia and the gravitational pull of the sun, a balance which keeps them from flying off into space or from being drawn into the sun's luminous mass.

The solar system's dimensions are stupendous. The earth is 93 million miles from the sun and its diameter of 7,900 miles is less than one hundredth that of the sun's. If the sun were imagined as a six-inch ball, Earth would be 55 feet away from it, and the closest stars—Earth's neighbors in the vast Milky Way—would be 3,000 miles away.

THE EARTH'S ANNUAL ORBIT of the sun is shown in the painting below. Its axis is tilted 23.5 degrees to its orbital axis—away from the sun about January 4, toward the sun about July 4. The sun's direct rays shine alternately on the hemispheres—when it is winter in the Northern Hemisphere, it is summer in the Southern; when one polar region has 24 hours of sun, the other is dark for 24 hours. The sun's rays never shine directly on the poles.

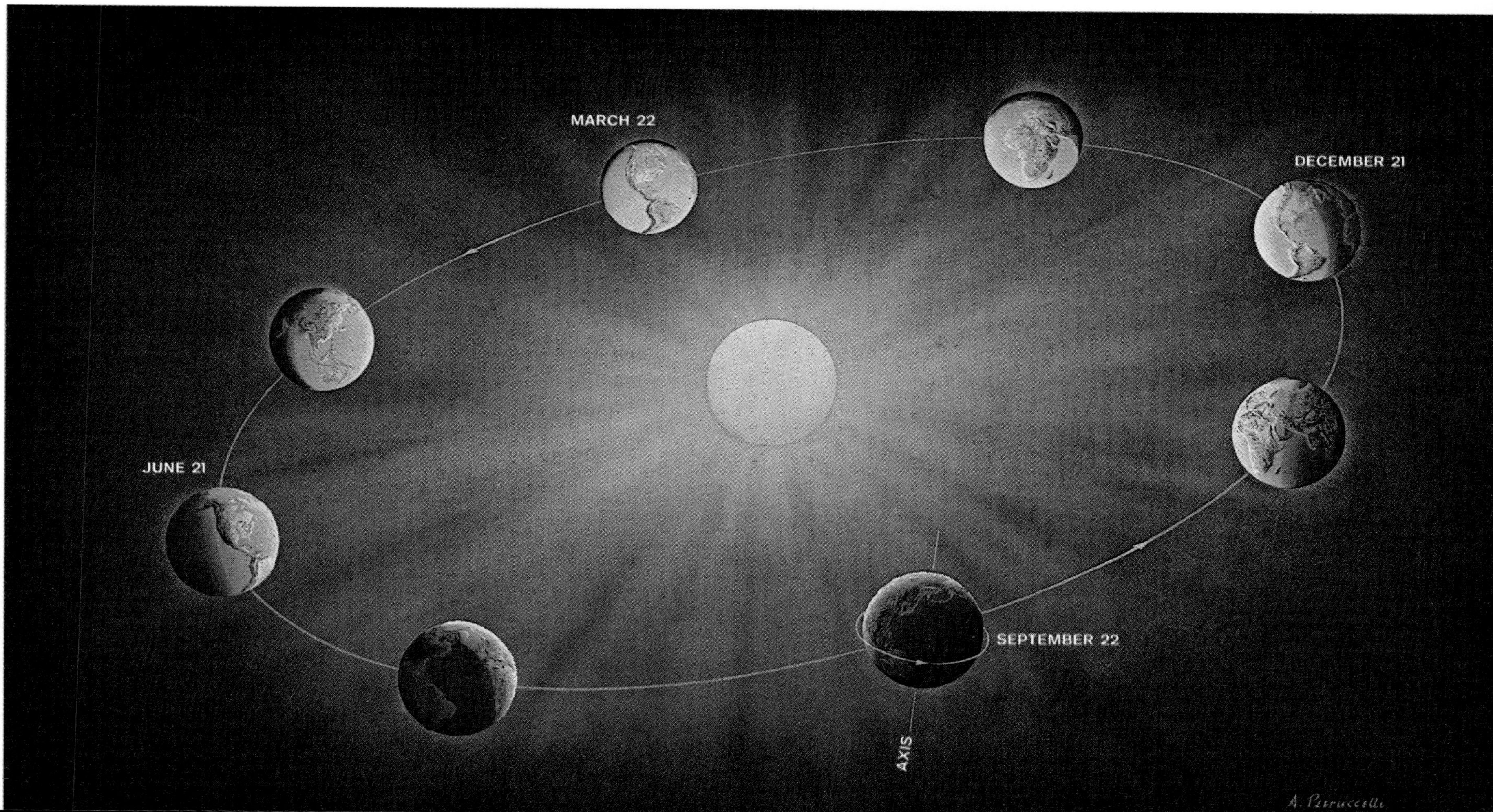

MARCH 22
DECEMBER 21
JUNE 21
SEPTEMBER 22
AXIS
A. Petruccelli

THE MOON: ECLIPSES, PHASES AND TIDES

The moon, a planet without an atmosphere, water or life, is held captive in space as the earth's satellite by mutual gravitational attraction. Its surface *(below)* is scarred by rugged mountains, some with peaks towering to 30,000 feet, as well as valleys and deep craters. Broad flat areas, called "seas" by early astronomers, are smooth plains lying between mountain ranges, valleys and deep craters. Second in brightness only to the sun, the moon as seen from the earth shines by the sun's reflected light. It revolves around the earth in an elliptical orbit *(painting on opposite page, bottom)* at an average speed of 2,287 miles per hour in a counterclockwise direction, the same direction as that in which the earth circles the sun. The moon takes a little over 29 earth days for a full circuit. Making a full rotation on its axis in almost exactly the same period that it takes to revolve around the earth, the moon exposes only one side of its surface to viewers of the night skies.

The distance of the moon from the earth averages 238,860 miles. The diameter of the moon is about one quarter that of the earth, its surface area about one thirteenth. Temperatures vary from a daytime high of 215°F. to a nighttime low of -250°F. Aside from eclipses *(opposite)*, the satellite's most dramatic manifestation on the earth is its effect on the tides of the earth's seas *(diagrams, center opposite)*.

A CRATERED PLANET, the moon *(below)* presents this surface to the earth. More than 30,000 craters have been charted. They range in width from 160 miles (Clavius crater) to one quarter mile. The dark plain *(left center)* is Oceanus Procellarum, largest of the "seas."

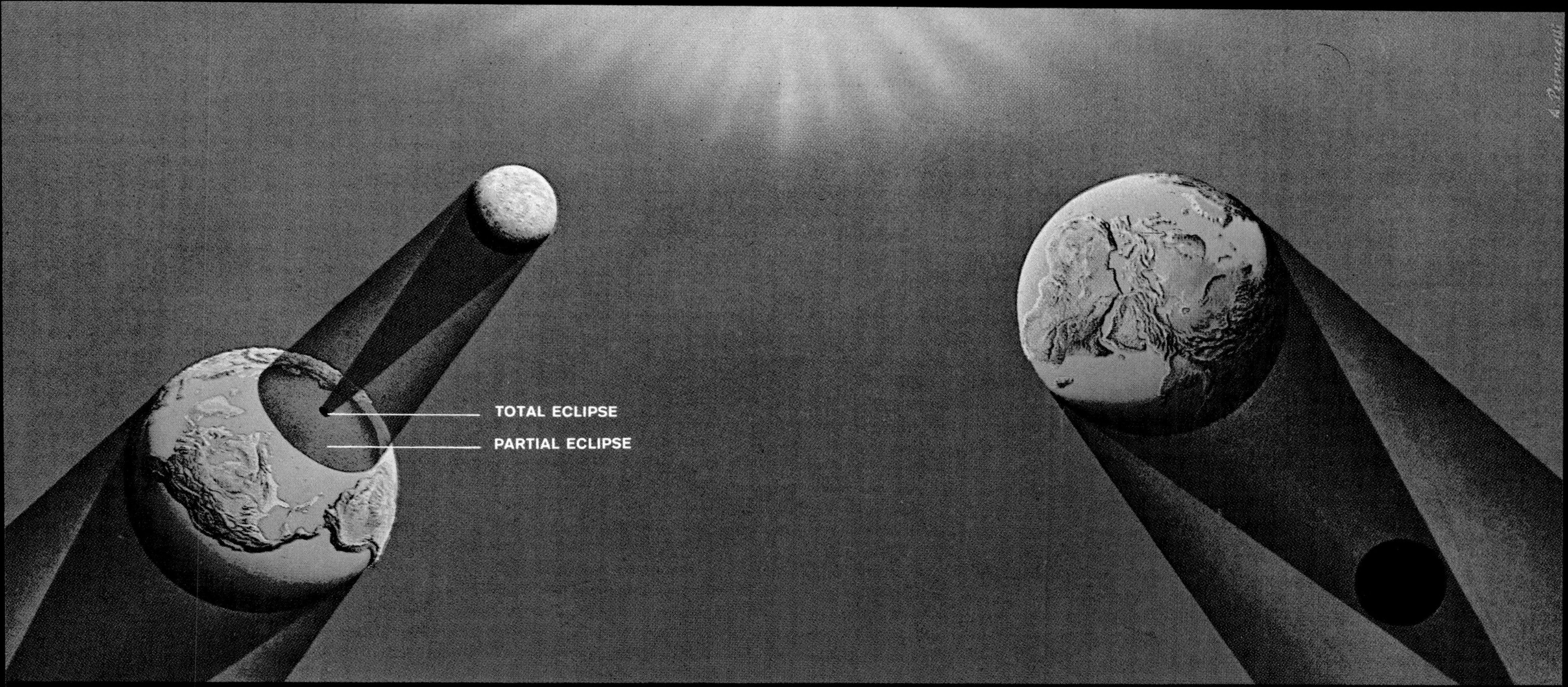

SOLAR AND LUNAR ECLIPSES are shown in the painting above. At the left is a solar eclipse, which occurs when the moon passes between the earth and the sun, blotting out the sun's image from a section of the earth. At the right is a lunar eclipse, which occurs when the earth comes between the sun and the moon, and the moon passes through the earth's shadow. As many as five solar eclipses may occur in one year. A lunar eclipse may occur as often as three times a year. During a lunar eclipse, the moon's bright color darkens to copper red.

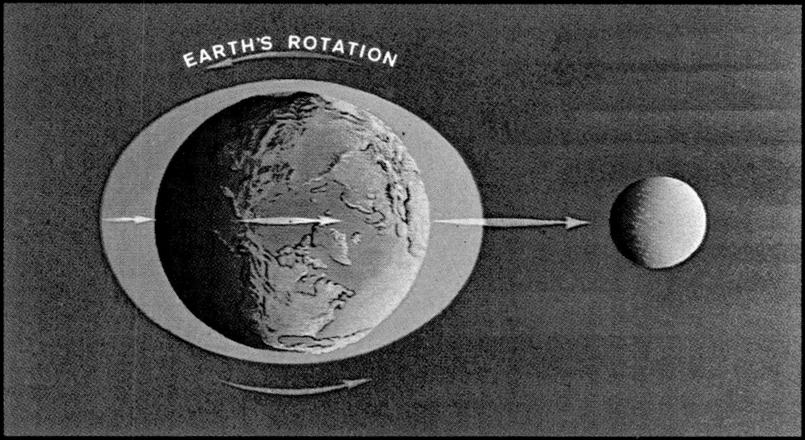

SPRING TIDES are created when the moon and sun line up on the same side of the earth, as shown above. The combined gravitational pull results in maximum-range tides. The same effect occurs when the sun and moon are in line but on opposite sides of the earth.

NEAP TIDES are created when the sun and moon are at right angles, as illustrated here. In this relationship, their gravitational pulls work against each other; the result is tides lower than average in range. Neap tides occur during the moon's first and third quarters.

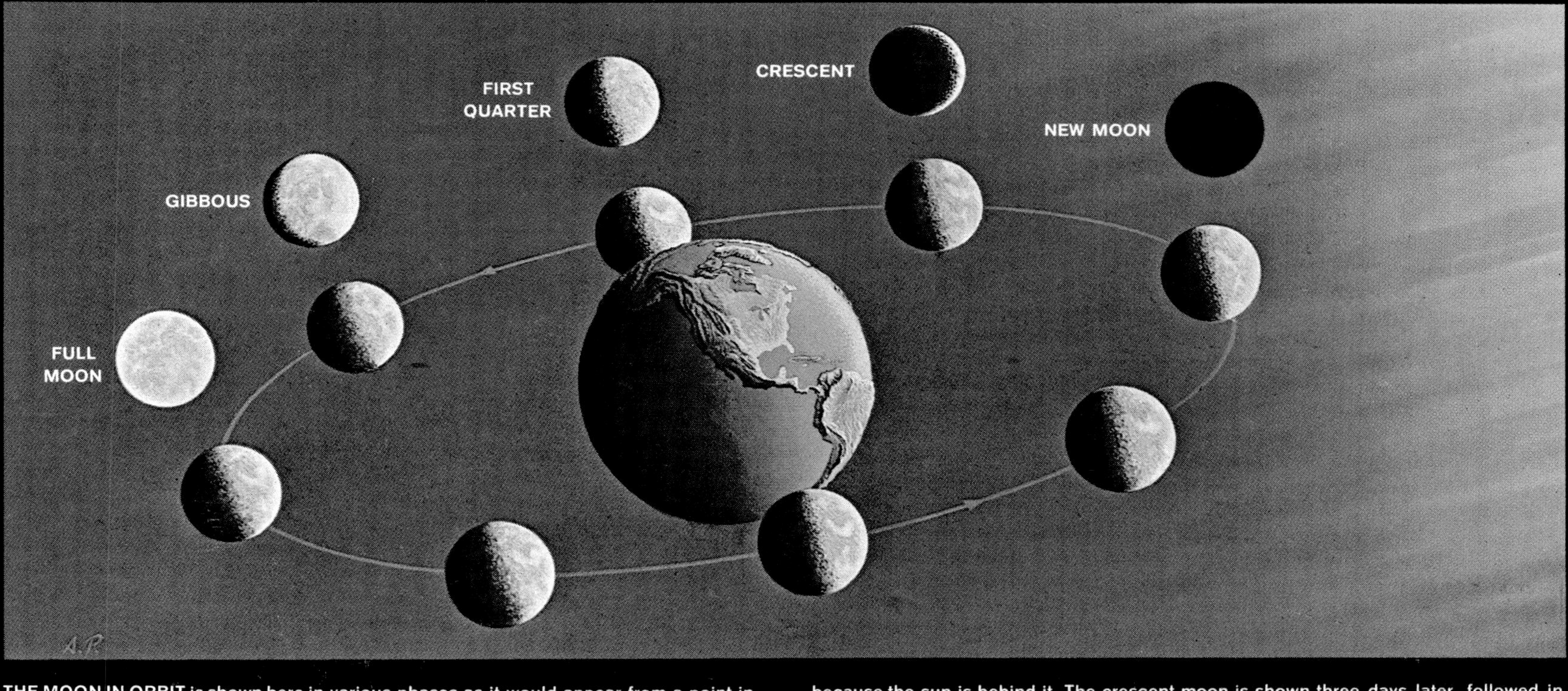

THE MOON IN ORBIT is shown here in various phases as it would appear from a point in space—the eight spheres connected by a line—and as it is seen from earth—the five upper spheres. The new moon appears as a dark disc, invisible against the heavens because the sun is behind it. The crescent moon is shown three days later, followed in seven and a half days by the first quarter and in eleven and three quarter days by the gibbous phase. The full moon phase is reached in about fourteen and three quarter days.

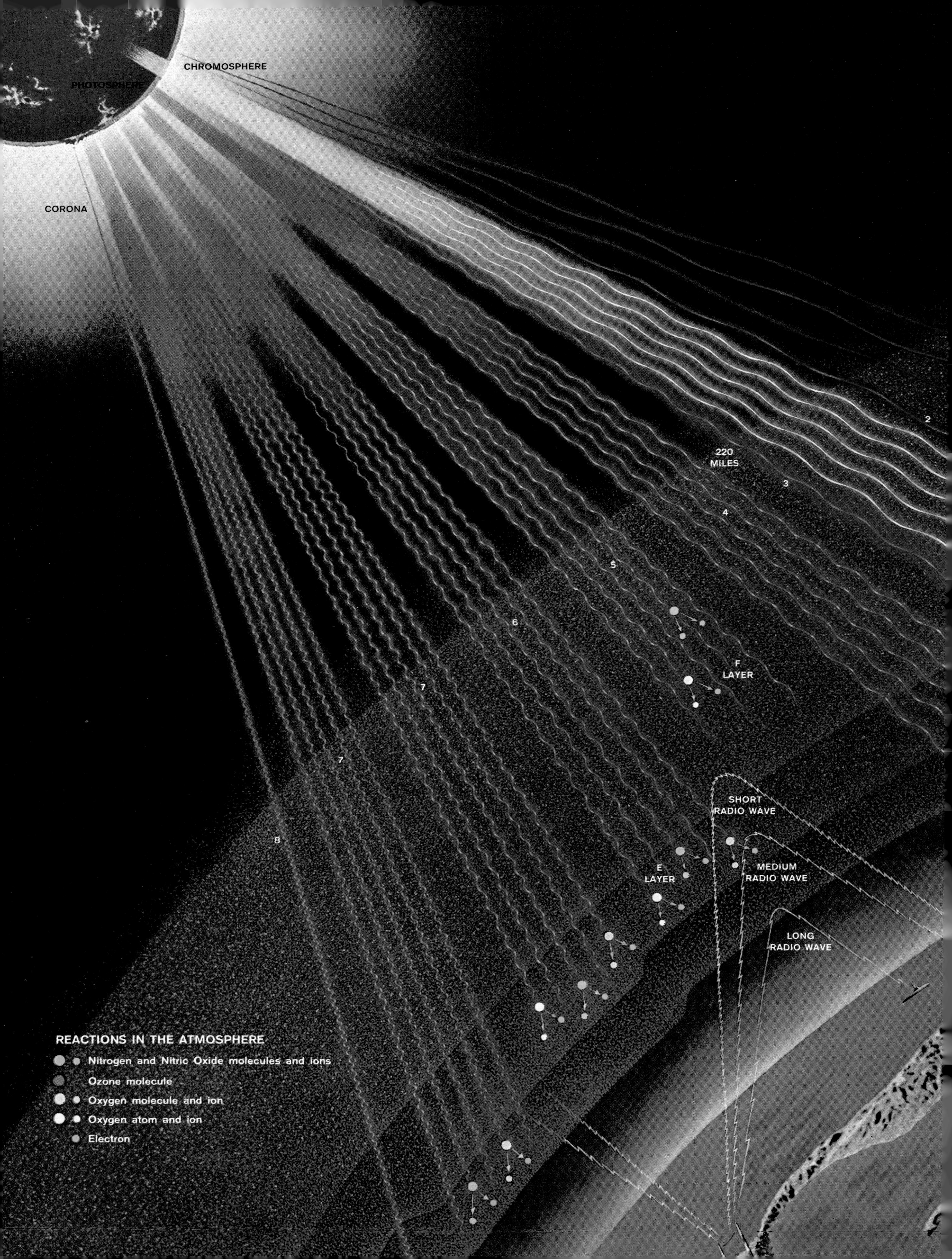

CHROMOSPHERE
PHOTOSPHERE
CORONA
2
220
MILES
3
4
5
6
F
LAYER
7
7
8
SHORT
RADIO WAVE
E
LAYER
MEDIUM
RADIO WAVE
LONG
RADIO WAVE
REACTIONS IN THE ATMOSPHERE
Nitrogen and Nitric Oxide molecules and ions
Ozone molecule
Oxygen molecule and ion
Oxygen atom and ion
Electron

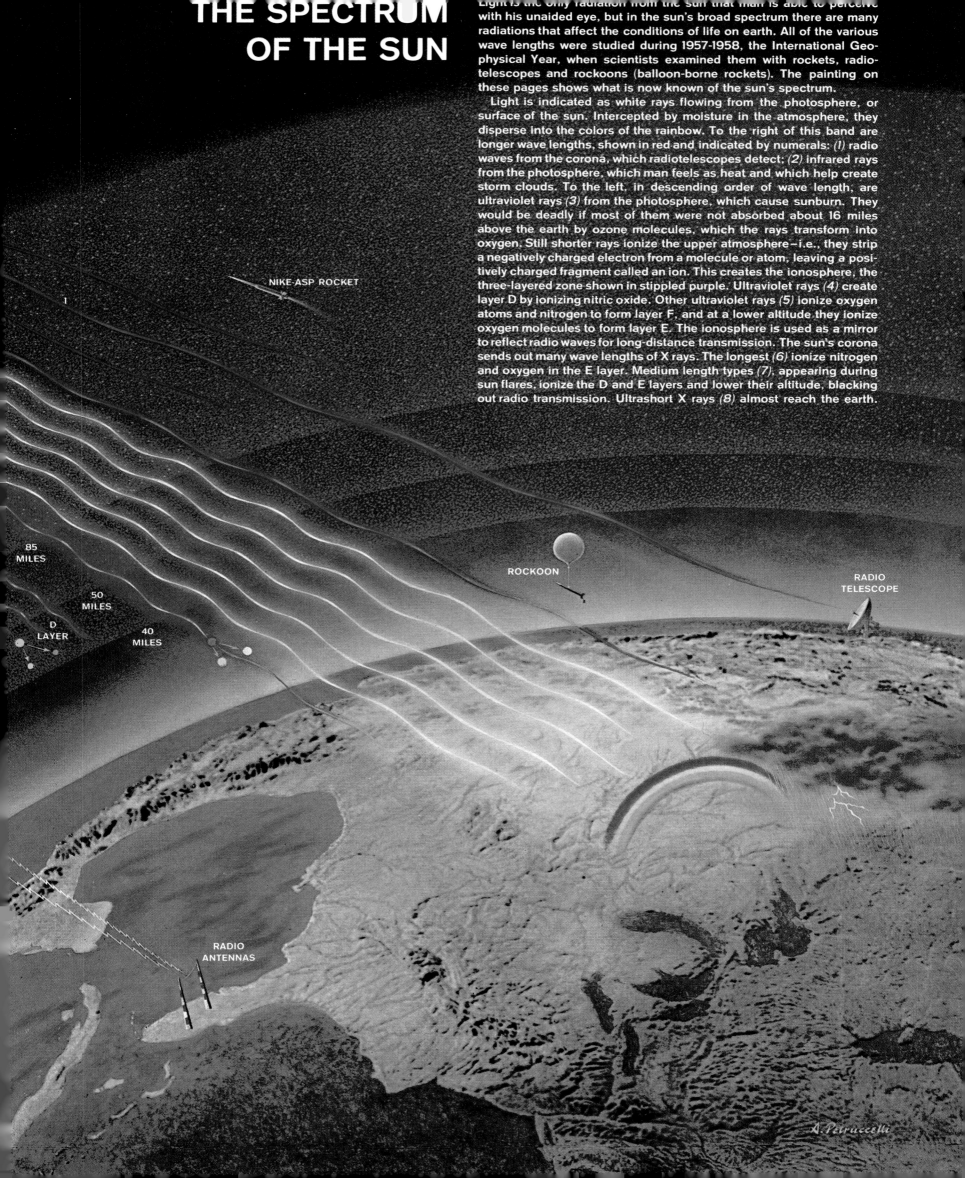

THE SPECTRUM OF THE SUN

Light is the only radiation from the sun that man is able to perceive with his unaided eye, but in the sun's broad spectrum there are many radiations that affect the conditions of life on earth. All of the various wave lengths were studied during 1957-1958, the International Geophysical Year, when scientists examined them with rockets, radiotelescopes and rockoons (balloon-borne rockets). The painting on these pages shows what is now known of the sun's spectrum.

Light is indicated as white rays flowing from the photosphere, or surface of the sun. Intercepted by moisture in the atmosphere, they disperse into the colors of the rainbow. To the right of this band are longer wave lengths, shown in red and indicated by numerals: *(1)* radio waves from the corona, which radiotelescopes detect; *(2)* infrared rays from the photosphere, which man feels as heat and which help create storm clouds. To the left, in descending order of wave length, are ultraviolet rays *(3)* from the photosphere, which cause sunburn. They would be deadly if most of them were not absorbed about 16 miles above the earth by ozone molecules, which the rays transform into oxygen. Still shorter rays ionize the upper atmosphere—i.e., they strip a negatively charged electron from a molecule or atom, leaving a positively charged fragment called an ion. This creates the ionosphere, the three-layered zone shown in stippled purple. Ultraviolet rays *(4)* create layer D by ionizing nitric oxide. Other ultraviolet rays *(5)* ionize oxygen atoms and nitrogen to form layer F, and at a lower altitude they ionize oxygen molecules to form layer E. The ionosphere is used as a mirror to reflect radio waves for long-distance transmission. The sun's corona sends out many wave lengths of X rays. The longest *(6)* ionize nitrogen and oxygen in the E layer. Medium length types *(7)*, appearing during sun flares, ionize the D and E layers and lower their altitude, blacking out radio transmission. Ultrashort X rays *(8)* almost reach the earth.

NIKE-ASP ROCKET
1
85
MILES
50
MILES
D
LAYER
40
MILES
ROCKOON
RADIO
TELESCOPE
RADIO
ANTENNAS
A. Petruccelli

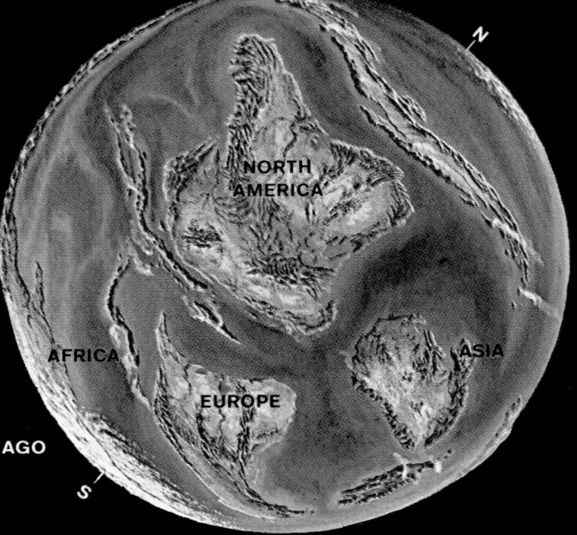

THE EARTH 500 MILLION YEARS AGO

THE CHANGING EARTH

The globes on this page illustrate one theory of the evolution of the continents. Graduated in size *(from top to bottom)* and dated from about 500 million years ago to the present, they also illustrate the theory that the earth itself has grown in size since the very beginning of its existence. The expanding-globe theory suggests that the earth began as a mass of cold radioactive dust which gradually warmed up over aeons. It began to expand, fracturing its relatively light crust and creating thousand-mile-long ridges that sundered existing land masses. The present-day shape of the continents seems to suggest that some of them were once joined together. It can be seen that South America and the west coast of Africa, for example, closely resemble related pieces of a gigantic jigsaw puzzle *(bottom globe)*. Evidence based on the nature of the earth's rock layers and shifts of the polar icecaps seems to confirm the theory that all of the present-day continents were in radically different relationships to each other in times past *(top three globes)*. In addition to the tremendous internal forces, the forces of erosion and weathering have played an important part in changing the whole face of the planet. Great mountains have been reduced to lowlands, and shallow areas that were once underwater have been lifted as towering peaks. The Mississippi valley of North America has been exposed and inundated and then exposed again in several geological cycles, just as the land beneath the Rocky Mountains and the Appalachians bears evidence of long submersion under forgotten seas. The forces making for change are still at work; the internal ones are shown in more detail on the opposite page.

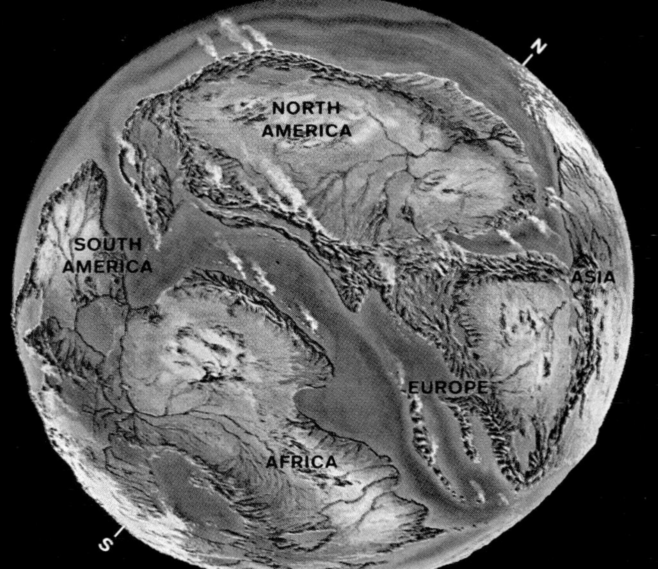

180 MILLION YEARS AGO

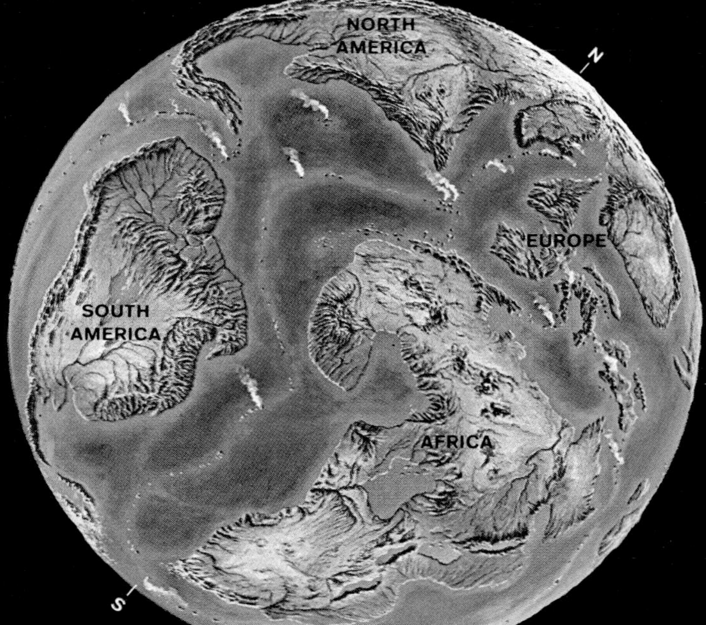

30 MILLION YEARS AGO

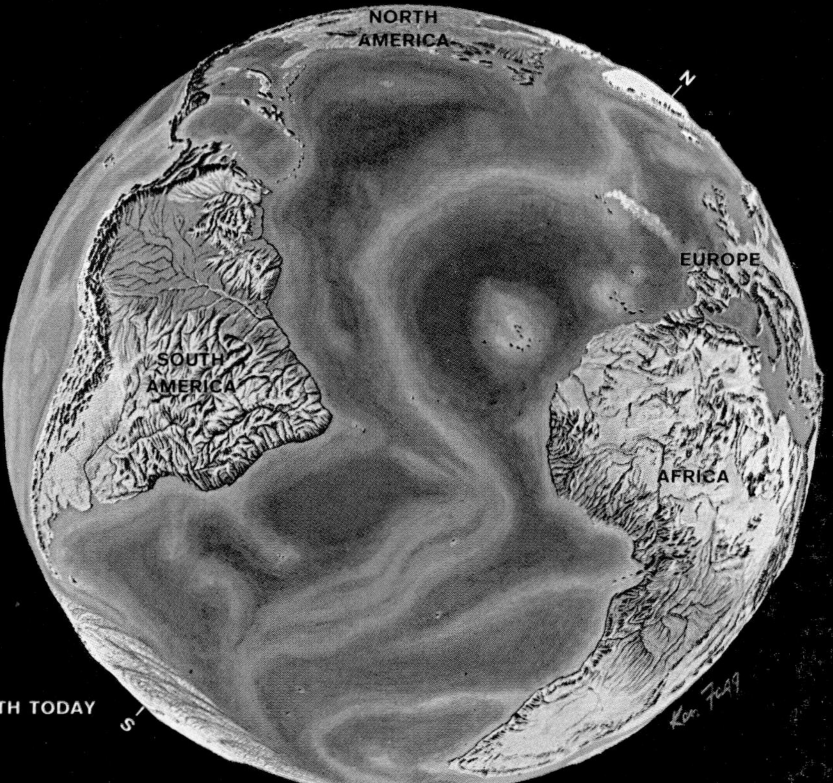

THE EARTH TODAY

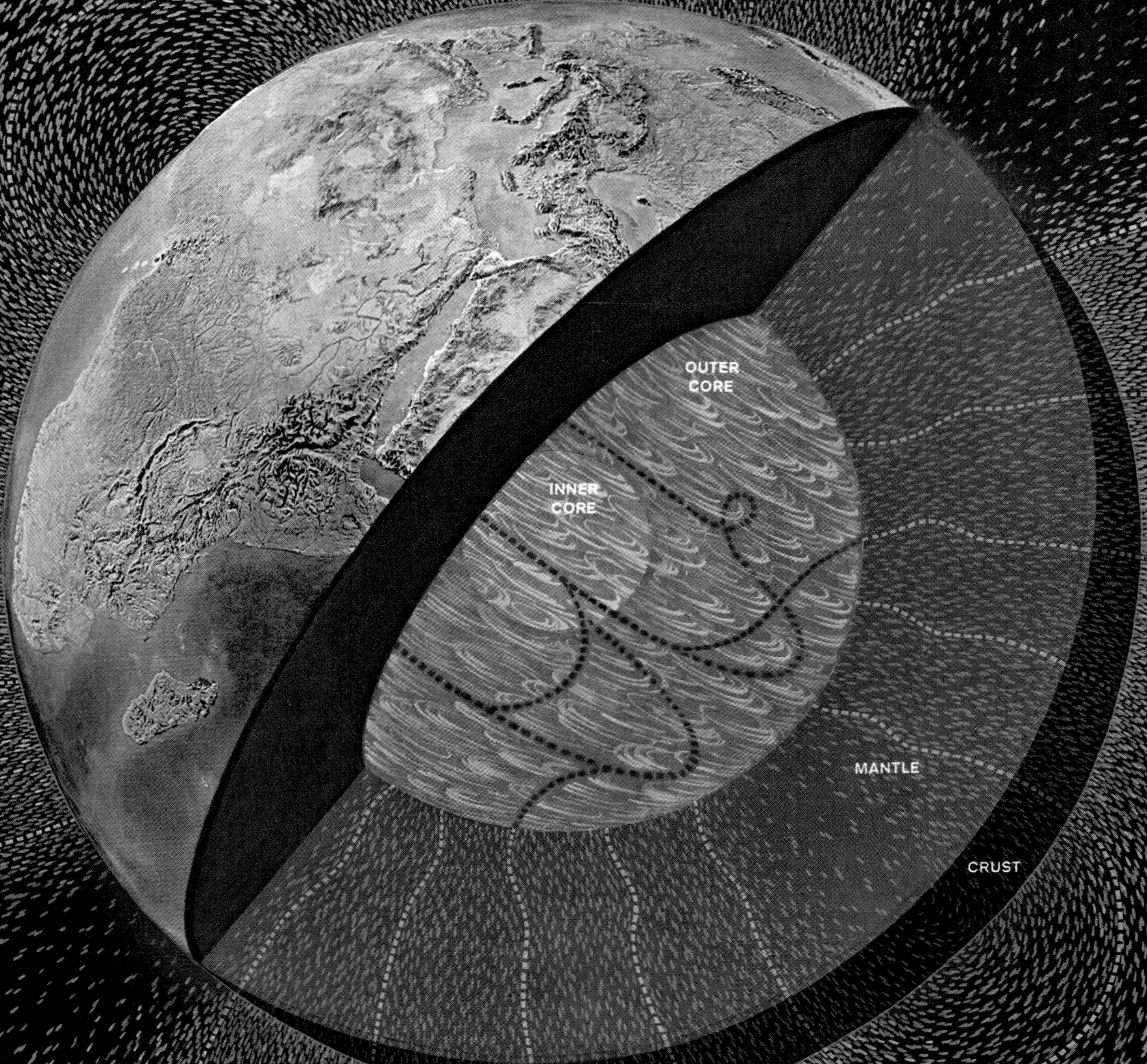

THE EARTH'S CORE

The great wedge cut out of the earth in the painting above reveals a hot core and the dense rock mantle on which the earth's crust is said by geologists to "float." Great forces of heat and pressure from within have kept the surface of the planet in a constant flux *(opposite page)*. The inner core of the earth is thought to be highly radioactive and able to heat the outer core. A new theory about the earth's magnetic field *(dotted lines)* states that it originates in the outer core. This magnetic field extends an average of eight earth radii out into space.

Probably composed of iron, the inner and outer cores together are about 4,300 miles in diameter. Around them lies the almost 1,800-mile-thick mantle of the earth, which consists of rock of unknown composition. The mantle supports the crust, which consists of basaltic ocean floors—3 to 4.5 miles thick—and the continents, which are composed of relatively light granites that average about 30 miles in depth.

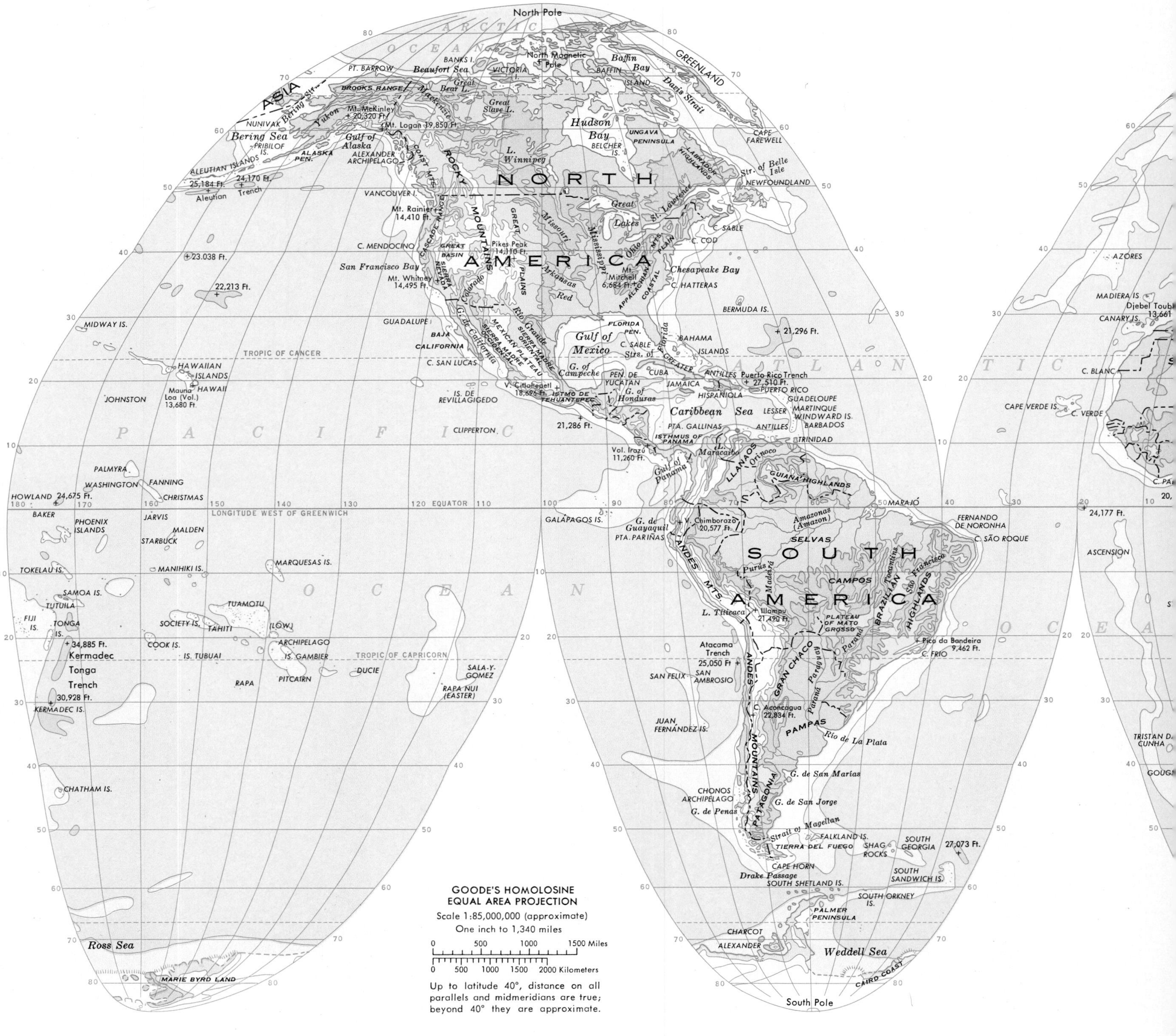

THE SURFACE OF THE EARTH

This map shows the mountains, plateaus, plains and lowlands which feature the earth's surface. A painting on pages 20 and 21 illustrates in detail the principal land forms of the earth, and the origins of the most important of these are explained here.

Block or *fault mountains* are created by the shift of great blocks of land along faults, or deep fractures, in the earth's crust. Faults often mark a chain of volcanic activity. Magma, or molten rock, finds exits along fault lines and often forms *volcanoes* as it forces its way to the surface. *Folded mountains* are created when the earth's crust buckles or doubles over on itself as a result of subterranean pressures. *Mountain glaciers*, great flows of moving ice which form from the massing of *snowfields* in cold wet regions, scoop out *U-shaped valleys* as they slide down the mountains. They carry earth and rock, which they later deposit as *moraines*. Glaciers also carve out bowl-shaped depressions called *cirques*, in which small lakes, or *tarns*, may collect. The junction

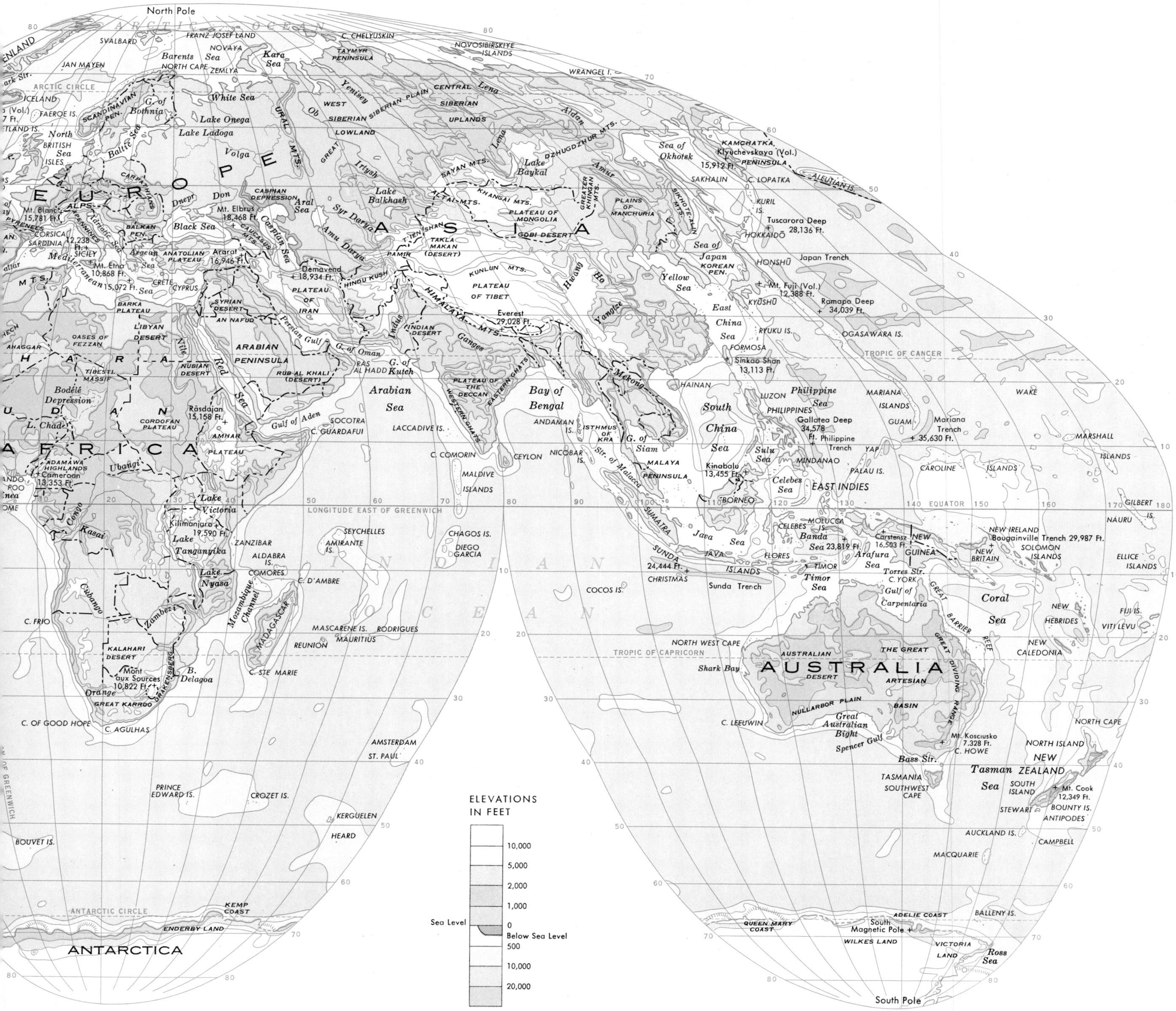

of the walls or troughs and cirques creates an *arête*, or sharp jagged ridge. *Horns* are mountain peaks formed by the intersection of three or more cirques.

V-shaped valleys are carved by streams pouring down from the mountain heights. Fast-moving streams cut deep, steep-walled valleys, or *canyons*, in some areas. *Badlands* result from the erosion of a *plateau* or upland area. The silt and stone carried by streams from higher slopes into low *basins* fan outward, creating *alluvial fans*. When a watercourse is choked with rock waste, it broadens and spreads its excess along the channel bottom, after which the stream divides and subdivides within its own channel, becoming a *braided stream*.

Mesas and *exfoliated dome mountains* are formations more resistant to the erosive forces of wind and water than the softer materials around them. A *butte* is a mesa in a later, worn-down state. Wind-blown sand forms dunes of many shapes, among them crescent-shaped *barchan dunes*. *Salt lakes*, sometimes called *playas*, are created when streams collect in low-lying areas and evaporation concentrates the salt content on the land's surface. *Karst regions* are created when water seeps through limestone bedrock, carving underground caverns.

A *meandering river* is an old stream that makes wide loops back and forth, frequently overflooding its banks to create *flood plains*. An *oxbow lake* results when the river changes course and cuts off one of its loops. Collections of silt brought downstream form at the many mouths or *distributaries* of such rivers to create an *arcuate delta*. *Submerged* or *drowned coastlines* result from the sea's rising and inundating river valleys. Cutting away at the slopes of submerged coastlines, the sea creates *wave-cut cliffs*. When material collects on a bar from both land and sea, a *complex spit* is built. Land rising slowly along ocean shores forms *emerged coastlines*. On such a coast, waves build bars of land parallel with the shore, called *barrier beaches*, which enclose *lagoons*.

HORN
SNOW FIELD
CIRQUE
VOLCANIC ISLAND
BLOCK OR FAULT MOUNTAIN
ARÊTE
TARN
U-SHAPED VALLEY
V-SHAPED VALLEY
ALLUVIAL FANS
KARST REGION
ESCARPMENT
SUBMERGED OR DROWNED COASTLINE
WAVE-CUT CLIFFS
COASTAL PLAIN
EMERGED COASTLINE
COMPLEX SPIT
DISTRIBUTARIES
LAGOON
BARRIER BEACH

LAND FORMS OF THE EARTH

In the imaginary landscape depicted on these pages, there is an example of most major land forms of the earth. This is a stylized rendering: such a variety of formations would not be found in nature in such proximity. The origin of most of the forms shown here is explained on pages 18 and 19.

Mountains dominate the scene. At upper center is a flat-topped block or fault mountain. A rolling range of folded mountains is at far right, ending in a wall-like escarpment. At upper left and lower right are craggy, complex mountains which are both folded and faulted. The hard granitic core of an eroded upland region forms an exfoliated dome at right center. In the distance an active volcano emits lava, gases and ash, building its cone higher and higher. Glaciers move down the highest peaks, turning V-shaped valleys into troughs with sharp divides, or arêtes, and creating cirques *(upper left)*. With them the glaciers carry cargoes of soil and stone which will be deposited as moraines in the valleys. Streams eroding both the block and folded mountains carry great quantities of rock, gravel and silt, depositing alluvial fans on the valley floor. At right center are roughly sculptured badlands, a circular mesa and a pinnacled butte. Coastal forms and various stream-erosion patterns are seen in the low-lying areas at left.

FOLDED MOUNTAINS
WATER GAP
ESCARPMENT
ALLUVIAL FANS
PLATEAU
CANYON
BADLANDS
MESA
BUTTE
BRAIDED STREAM
BASIN
PLAYA OR SALT LAKE
EXFOLIATED DOME MOUNTAIN
HORN
BARCHAN DUNES
FLOOD PLAIN
MEANDERING RIVER
OX-BOW LAKE
ARETE
MOUNTAIN GLACIER
ARCUATE DELTA
MORAINE

THE WORLD'S OUTSTANDING PHYSICAL FEATURES

CONTINENT	AREA SQ. MI.	POPULATION TOTAL	POPULATION PER SQ. MI.	ELEVATION IN FEET MEAN	ELEVATION IN FEET HIGHEST		ELEVATION IN FEET LOWEST		RECORDED TEMPERATURES (F.) HIGHEST		RECORDED TEMPERATURES (F.) LOWEST	
AFRICA	11,635,000	233,719,000	20	1,900	Mt. Kilimanjaro, Tanganyika	19,590	Quattara Depression, Egypt	-436	Azizia, Libya	136°	Port Etienne, Mauritania	3°
ANTARCTICA	5,100,000	Uninhabited		6,000	Mt. Fridtjof Nansen	18,953	Sea level		Little America	38°	Vostok	-125.3°
ASIA	17,035,000	1,691,328,000	99	3,000	Mt. Everest, Tibet-Nepal	29,028	Dead Sea, Israel-Jordan	-1,292	Baghdad, Iraq	123°	Verkhoyansk, Siberia	-90°
AUSTRALIA	2,974,581	10,050,000	3	1,000	Mt. Kosciusko	7,328	Lake Eyre	-39	Bourke, N.S.W.	127°	Mitchell, Queensland	19°
EUROPE	3,850,000	573,353,000	149	980	Mt. Elbrus, Soviet Union	18,468	Caspian Sea, Soviet Union	-92	Sevilla (Seville), Spain	124°	Ust-Tsilma, Soviet Union	-61°
NORTH AMERICA	9,435,000	251,054,000	27	2,000	Mt. McKinley, U.S.	20,320	Death Valley, U.S.	-282	Death Valley, U.S.	134°	Snag,Yukon, Canada	-81°
SOUTH AMERICA	6,860,000	137,847,000	20	1,800	Mt. Aconcagua, Argentina	22,834	Valde's Depression, Argentina	-131	Santiago del Estero, Arg.	115°	Colinia Sarmiento, Argentina	-27°

PRINCIPAL MOUNTAINS

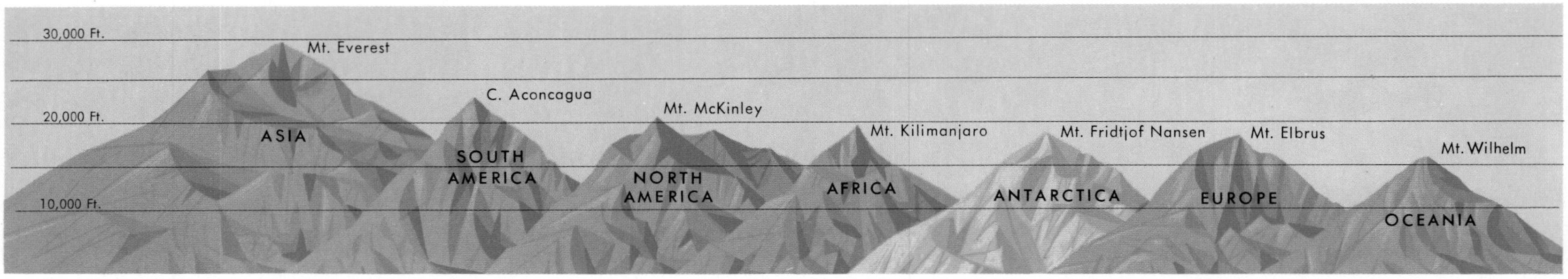

NORTH AMERICA

	HEIGHT (FEET)
McKinley, ▲Alaska, U.S. (▲North America)	20,320
Logan, ▲Canada (▲St. Elias Mts.)	19,850
Citlaltepetl (Orizaba), ▲Mexico	18,696
St. Elias, Alaska, U.S.-Canada	18,008
Popocatepetl, Mexico	17,887
Foraker, Alaska, U.S.	17,395
Ixtacihuatl, Mexico	17,343
Whitney, ▲California, U.S.	14,495
Elbert, ▲Colorado, U.S. (▲Rocky Mts.)	14,431
Massive, Colorado, U.S.	14,418
Harvard, Colorado, U.S.	14,414
Rainier, ▲Washington, U.S. (▲Cascade Range)	14,410
Williamson, California, U.S.	14,384
Blanca Peak, Colorado, U.S. (▲Sangre de Cristo Range)	14,317
Uncompahgre Peak, Colorado, U.S. (▲San Juan Mts.)	14,301
Grays Peak, Colorado, U.S. (▲Front Range)	14,274
Evans, Colorado, U.S.	14,260
Longs Peak, Colorado, U.S.	14,255
Colima, Nevado de, Mexico	14,235
Shasta, California, U.S.	14,162
Pikes Peak, Colorado, U.S.	14,110
Tajumulco, ▲Guatemala (▲Central America)	13,816
Gannett Peak, ▲Wyoming, U.S.	13,785
Grand Teton, Wyoming, U.S.	13,766
Kings Peak, ▲Utah, U.S.	13,498
Waddington, Canada (▲Coast Mts.)	13,260
Cloud Peak, Wyoming, U.S. (▲Big Horn Mts.)	13,175
Wheeler Peak, ▲New Mexico, U.S.	13,160
Boundary Peak, ▲Nevada, U.S.	13,145
Robson, Canada (▲Canadian Rockies)	12,972
Chirripó Grande, ▲Costa Rica	12,861
Granite Peak, ▲Montana, U.S.	12,799
Humphreys Peak, ▲Arizona, U.S.	12,670
Borah Peak, ▲Idaho, U.S.	12,662
Gunnbjörn, ▲Greenland	12,139
San Gorgonio, California, U.S.	11,485
Chiriquí, ▲Panama	11,410
Hood, ▲Oregon, U.S.	11,245
Lassen Peak, California, U.S.	10,466
Loma Rucilla (Pico Trujillo), ▲Dominican Rep.	10,249
Paricutín, Mexico	9,100
Selle, Massif de la, ▲Haiti	8,793
Guadalupe Peak, ▲Texas, U.S.	8,751
Olympus, Washington, U.S. (▲Olympic Mts.)	7,954
Santa Ana, ▲El Salvador	7,828

SOUTH AMERICA

	HEIGHT (FEET)
Aconcagua, ▲Argentina (▲Andes Mts.; ▲South America)	22,834
Ojos del Salado, Argentina-▲Chile	22,590
Pissis, Argentina	22,546
Tupungato, Argentina-Chile	22,310
Huascarán, ▲Peru	22,205
Tocorpuri, ▲Bolivia	22,162
Llullaillaco, Argentina-Chile	22,146
Mercedario, Argentina	21,885
Yerupaja, Peru	21,758
Incahuasi, Argentina-Chile	21,719
Illampú, Bolivia	21,490
Ancohuma, Bolivia	21,489
Sajama, Bolivia	21,391
Illimani, Bolivia	21,151
Chimborazo, ▲Ecuador	20,577
Cotopaxi, Ecuador	19,344
Misti, El, Peru	19,144
Cristóbal Colón, ▲Colombia	18,947
Huila, Colombia (▲Cordillera Central)	18,865
Columna, La, ▲Venezuela	16,411

EUROPE

	HEIGHT (FEET)
Elbrus, Soviet Union (▲Caucasus Mts.; ▲Europe)	18,468
Shkhara, Soviet Union	17,059
Dykh-Tau, Soviet Union	17,054
Kazbek, Soviet Union	16,554
Blanc, Mont, ▲France (▲Alps)	15,781
Rosa, Monte (Grenzgipfel), ▲Italy-Switzerland	15,200
Weisshorn, Switzerland	14,803
Matterhorn, Switzerland	14,685
Finsteraarhorn, Switzerland	14,026
Jungfrau, Switzerland	13,668
Gross Glockner, ▲Austria	12,461
Tenerife, Pico de, ▲Canary Is., ▲Spain	12,180
Mulhacén, ▲Spain (continental)	11,424
Aneto, Pico de, Spain (▲Pyrenees)	11,168
Perdido (Perdu), Spain	11,007
Etna, ▲Sicily, Italy	10,868
Zugspitze, ▲Germany	9,721
Stalin Peak (Musala), ▲Bulgaria	9,592
Corno, Italy (▲Apennines)	9,560
Olympus, ▲Greece	9,550
Djaravica, ▲Yugoslavia	9,524
Triglav, Yugoslavia	9,393
Korab, ▲Albania	9,068
Cinto, ▲Corsica, France	8,891
Stalin Peak (Gerlachovka), ▲Czechoslovakia (▲Carpathian Mts.)	8,737
Galdhöppigen, ▲Norway	8,400
Negoi, ▲Romania	8,346

ASIA

	HEIGHT (FEET)
Everest, ▲Tibet-▲Nepal (▲Himalaya Mts.; ▲Asia; ▲World)	29,028
Godwin Austen (K^2), ▲Jammu and Kashmir (▲Karakoram Range)	28,250
Kanchenjunga, Nepal-▲Sikkim	28,168
Makalu, Tibet-Nepal	27,790
Dhaulagiri, Nepal	26,810
Nanga Parbat, Jammu and Kashmir	26,660
Annapurna, Nepal	26,502
Gasherbrum, Jammu and Kashmir	26,470
Gosainthan, Tibet	26,291
Nanda Devi, India	25,645
Rakaposhi, Jammu and Kashmir	25,551
Kamet, India	25,447
Namcha Barwa, Tibet	25,445
Tirich Mir, ▲Pakistan (▲Hindu Kush)	25,426
Gurla Mandhata, Tibet	25,355
Ulugh Muztagh, China (▲Kunlun Mts.)	25,340
Minya Konka, China	24,900
Stalin Peak, ▲Soviet Union (▲Pamir-Alay Mts.)	24,590
Pobeda Peak, China-Soviet Union (▲Tien Shan)	24,409
Muztagh Ata, China	24,388
Lenin Peak, Soviet Union	23,382
Tengri Khan, China-Soviet Union	22,940
Kailas, Tibet	22,028
Demavend, ▲Iran	18,934
Ararat, ▲Turkey	16,946
Carstensz, ▲Neth. New Guinea (▲New Guinea)	16,503
Klyuchevskaya, ▲Kamchatka, Soviet Union	15,912
Wilhelmina, Neth. New Guinea	15,518
Tabun Bogdo (Khuitun), ▲Mongolia (▲Altai Mts.)	15,266
Belukha, Soviet Union	15,157
Kinabalu, ▲North Borneo (▲Borneo)	13,455
Hsinkao, ▲Formosa	13,113

AFRICA

	HEIGHT (FEET)
Kilimanjaro (Kibo), ▲Tanganyika (▲Africa)	19,590
Kenya, ▲Kenya	17,040
Margherita, ▲The Congo-▲Uganda	16,821
Rāsdajan, ▲Ethiopia	15,158
Elgon, Kenya-Uganda	14,178
Toubkal, Djebel, ▲Morocco (▲Atlas Mts.)	13,661
Cameroon, ▲Br. Cameroons	13,353
Thabantshonyana, ▲Basutoland (▲Southern Africa)	11,425
Emi Koussi, ▲Chad (▲Tibesti Mts.)	11,204

OCEANIA

	HEIGHT (FEET)
Wilhelm, New Guinea Ter.	15,400
Mauna Kea, ▲Hawaii I., ▲Hawaii, U.S.	13,796
Mauna Loa, Hawaii I., Hawaii, U.S.	13,680
Bangeta, New Guinea Ter.	13,434
Victoria, ▲Papua (▲Owen Stanley Range)	13,363
Cook, ▲South Island, ▲New Zealand	12,349
Balbi, ▲Bougainville, ▲Solomon Is.	10,170
Haleakala, ▲Maui, Hawaii, U.S.	10,025
Ruapehu, ▲North Island, New Zealand	9,175
Mauga Silisili, ▲Samoa, Western	8,000

ANTARCTICA

	HEIGHT (FEET)
Fridtjof Nansen (▲Antarctica)	18,953
Wade	16,146
Markham	15,100

▲Highest mountain in state, country, range or region named.

PRINCIPAL DESERTS

	ESTIMATED AREA (*SQ. MI.)
Sahara, Northern Africa	3,000,000
Libyan (part of Sahara Desert), Northeastern Africa	650,000
Australian, West and Central Australia	600,000
Arabian, Arabian Peninsula	500,000
Gobi, Mongolia	400,000
Rub'al Khali (part of Arabian Desert), Southeastern Saudi Arabia	250,000
Kalahari, Bechuanaland	200,000
Great Sandy (part of Australian Desert), Northwestern Australia	160,000
Great Victoria (part of Australian Desert), Southwestern Australia	125,000
Syrian (part of Arabian Desert), Northern Arabian Peninsula	125,000
Takla Makan, Southern Sinkiang, China	125,000
Arunta (part of Australian Desert), Central Australia	120,000
Karakum, Southern Turkestan, Soviet Union	105,000
Nubian (part of Sahara Desert), Northeastern Sudan	100,000
Thar (Great Indian), Northwestern India	100,000
Kyzylkum, Central Turkestan, Soviet Union	90,000
Gibson (part of Australian Desert), Western Australia	85,000
Atacama, Northern Chile	70,000
An Nafud (part of Arabian Desert), North and Central Saudi Arabia	50,000
Dasht-i-Lut, Eastern Iran	20,000
Dasht-i-Kavir, North Central Iran	18,000
Muyunkum, Eastern Turkestan, Soviet Union	17,000
Mojave, Southern California, U.S.	13,500
Sechura, Northwestern Peru	10,000
Vizcaino, Baja California, Mexico	6,000
Painted, Northeastern Arizona, U.S.	5,000
Great Salt Lake, Northwestern Utah, U.S.	4,000
Colorado, Southeastern California, U.S.	3,000

** Many areas given are based on boundaries not clearly defined.*

PRINCIPAL LAKES

	AREA (SQ. MI.)
*Caspian, Soviet Union-Iran	152,123
Superior, U.S.-Canada	31,820
Victoria, Kenya-Uganda-Tanganyika	26,828
*Aral, Soviet Union	26,525
Huron, U.S.-Canada	23,010
Michigan, U.S.	22,400
Tanganyika, Tanganyika-The Congo	12,355
Baykal, Soviet Union	12,162
Great Bear, Canada	12,000
Great Slave, Canada	11,170
Nyasa, Nyasaland	10,900
Erie, U.S.-Canada	9,940
Winnipeg, Canada	9,094
Chad, Chad-Niger	8,000
Ontario, U.S.-Canada	7,540
Ladoga, Soviet Union	7,104
Balkhash, Soviet Union	6,680
Onega, Soviet Union	3,822
*Eyre, Australia	3,700
*Rudolf, Kenya	3,500
Titicaca, Peru-Bolivia	3,261
Nicaragua, Nicaragua	3,060
Athabasca, Canada	3,058
Reindeer, Canada	2,440
*Torrens, Australia	2,400
*Ching Hai (Koko Nor), China	2,300
Issyk-Kul, Soviet Union	2,200
Vänern, Sweden	2,150
Winnipegosis, Canada	2,086
Bangweulu, Northern Rhodesia	2,000
*Urmia, Iran	1,900
Manitoba, Canada	1,817
Albert, Uganda-The Congo	1,750
*Great Salt, U.S.	1,700
Leopold II, The Congo	1,700
Khanka, Soviet Union-China	1,699
Dubawnt, Canada	1,650
Nipigon, Canada	1,640
*Gairdner, Australia	1,500
Lake of the Woods, U.S.-Canada	1,500
*Van, Turkey	1,450

* *Salt lakes*

PRINCIPAL WATERFALLS

	HEIGHT (FEET)
Angel, Venezuela	3,700
Tugela, South Africa	2,800
Yosemite (Upper, Central and Lower Falls), Yosemite National Park, California, U.S.	2,425
Kukenaam, Venezuela	2,000
Sutherland, New Zealand	1,904
Reichenbach, Switzerland	1,800
Kile, Norway	1,800
Wollomombie, Australia	1,700
Ribbon, Yosemite National Park, California, U.S.	1,612
Upper Yosemite, Yosemite National Park, California, U.S.	1,430
Gavarnie, France	1,385
Skjaeggedals, Norway	1,300
Krimml, Austria	1,250
King George VI, British Guiana	1,200
Takakkaw, British Columbia, Canada	1,200
Silver Strand, Yosemite National Park, California, U.S.	1,170
Giessbach, Switzerland	1,148
Staubbach, Switzerland	980
Trümmelbach, Switzerland	950
Middle Cascade, Yosemite National Park, California, U.S.	910
Chirombo, Northern Rhodesia	880
King Edward VIII, British Guiana	840
Gersoppa, India	829
Vetti, Norway	820
Kalambo, Northern Rhodesia	786
Kaieteur, British Guiana	741
Skykje, Norway	650
Maradals, Norway	650
Maletsunyane, Basutoland	630

PRINCIPAL RIVERS

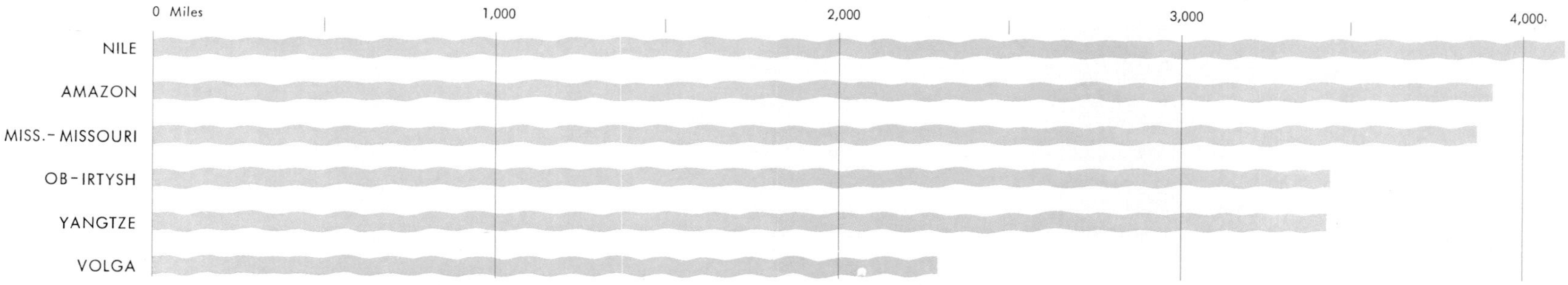
0 Miles
1,000
2,000
3,000
4,000
NILE
AMAZON
MISS.-MISSOURI
OB-IRTYSH
YANGTZE
VOLGA

	LENGTH (MILES)
Nile, Africa	4,132
Amazon, South America	3,900
Mississippi-Missouri-Red Rock, North America	3,860
Ob-Irtysh, Asia	3,461
Yangtze, Asia	3,430
Hwang Ho (Yellow), Asia	2,903
Congo, Africa	2,900
Amur, Asia	2,802
Lena, Asia	2,653
Mackenzie, North America	2,635
Mekong, Asia	2,600
Niger, Africa	2,590
Yenisey, Asia	2,566
Missouri, North America	2,466
Paraná, South America	2,450
Mississippi, North America	2,330
Irtysh, Asia	2,300
La Plata-Paraguay, South America	2,300
Volga, Europe	2,293
Ob, Asia	2,260
Madeira, South America	2,060
Indus, Asia	1,980
Purús, South America	1,900
St. Lawrence, North America	1,900
Rio Grande, North America	1,885
Brahmaputra, Asia	1,800
Orinoco, South America	1,800
São Francisco, South America	1,800
Yukon, North America	1,800
Danube, Europe	1,770
Darling, Australia	1,750
Salween, Asia	1,730
Euphrates, Asia	1,675
Syr Darya, Asia	1,653
Zambezi, Africa	1,650
Tocantins, South America	1,640
Araguaia, South America	1,630
Amu Darya, Asia	1,628
Kolyma, Asia	1,615
Murray, Australia	1,600
Angara, Asia	1,550
Ganges, Asia	1,550
Pilcomayo, South America	1,550
Ural, Asia	1,522
Vilyuy, Asia	1,513
Arkansas, North America	1,450
Colorado, North America	1,450
Irrawaddy, Asia	1,425
Dnepr, Europe	1,420
Aldan, Asia	1,392
Negro, South America	1,305
Paraguay, South America	1,290
Kama, Europe	1,261
Xingú, South America	1,230
Don, Europe	1,224
Ucayali, South America	1,220
Columbia, North America	1,214
Saskatchewan, North America	1,205
Juruá, South America	1,200
Peace, North America	1,195
Orange, Africa	1,155
Tigris, Asia	1,150
Pechora, Europe	1,118
Dvina, Europe	1,100
Tobol, Asia	1,093
Snake, North America	1,038
Uruguay, South America	1,025
Red, North America	1,018
Churchill, North America	1,000
Marañón, South America	1,000
Ohio, North America	981
Magdalena, South America	950
Roosevelt (River of Doubt), South America	950
Godavari, Asia	930
Si, Asia	930
Oka, Europe	920
Canadian, North America	906
Dnestr, Europe	876
Brazos, North America	870
Salado, South America	870
Fraser, North America	850
Parnaiba, South America	850
Colorado, North America	840
Rhine, Europe	820
Narbada, Asia	800
Athabasca, North America	765
Donets, Europe	735
Pecos, North America	735
Green, North America	730
Elbe, Europe	720
James, North America	710
Ottawa, North America	696
White, North America	690
Cumberland, North America	687
Gambia, Africa	680
Yellowstone, North America	671
Tennessee, North America	652
Gila, North America	630
Vistula, Europe	630

GREAT OCEANS AND SEAS

OCEANS AND SEAS	AREA SQ. MI.	DEPTH IN FEET AVERAGE	DEPTH IN FEET GREATEST
Pacific Ocean	63,985,000	14,040	35,630
Atlantic Ocean	31,529,000	12,880	27,510
Indian Ocean	28,357,000	13,000	24,444
Arctic Ocean	5,541,000	4,200	17,500
Mediterranean Sea	1,145,000	4,500	15,072
South China Sea	895,000	5,400	16,456
Bering Sea	878,000	1,665	13,420
Caribbean Sea	750,000	8,400	23,750
Gulf of Mexico	700,000	4,700	12,426

OCEANS AND SEAS	AREA SQ. MI.	DEPTH IN FEET AVERAGE	DEPTH IN FEET GREATEST
Okhotsk, Sea of	582,000	3,000	12,621
East China Sea	480,000	610	8,920
Yellow Sea	480,000	160	348
Hudson Bay	472,000	440	849
Japan, Sea of	405,000	4,835	13,241
North Sea	221,000	180	2,165
Red Sea	178,000	1,490	9,301
Black Sea	168,500	4,300	7,362
Baltic Sea	158,000	221	1,400

PRINCIPAL ISLANDS

	AREA (SQ. MI.)
Greenland, Arctic Region	840,000
New Guinea, Oceania	316,856
Borneo, East Indies	286,967
Madagascar, Indian Ocean	228,000
Baffin, Canadian Arctic	183,810
Sumatra, Indonesia	182,859
Honshū, Japan	88,930
Great Britain, North Atlantic Ocean	88,756
Ellesmere, Canadian Arctic	82,119
Victoria, Canadian Arctic	81,930
Celebes, Indonesia	72,986
South Island, New Zealand	58,897
Java, Indonesia	50,745
North Island, New Zealand	44,281
Cuba, Caribbean Sea	44,217
Newfoundland, North Atlantic Ocean	42,734
Luzon, Philippines	40,814
Iceland, North Atlantic Ocean	39,768
Mindanao, Philippines	36,906
Ireland, North Atlantic Ocean	32,596
Novaya Zemlya, Soviet Arctic	31,390
Hokkaidō, Japan	29,950
Hispaniola, Caribbean Sea	29,522
Sakhalin, Soviet Union	29,344
Tasmania, Australia	26,215
Ceylon, Indian Ocean	25,332
Banks, Canadian Arctic	23,230
Devon, Canadian Arctic	20,861
Tierra del Fuego, Argentina-Chile	18,600
Kyūshū, Japan	16,215
Melville, Canadian Arctic	16,141
Southampton, Hudson Bay, Canada	15,700
West Spitsbergen, Arctic Region	15,260
New Britain, Oceania	14,592
Formosa, China Sea	13,885
Hainan, South China Sea	13,127
Timor, Oceania	13,094
Prince of Wales, Canadian Arctic	12,830
Vancouver, Canada	12,408
Sicily, Mediterranean Sea	9,925
Somerset, Canadian Arctic	9,370
Sardinia, Mediterranean Sea	9,301
Shikoku, Japan	7,245
New Caledonia, Oceania	7,202
North East Island, Svalbard Group	6,350
Ceram, Indonesia	6,046
Flores, Indonesia	5,860
Samar, Philippines	5,124

ORIGINS OF WEATHER

The weather of the earth is determined by the interaction of many factors: ocean movements, temperatures, rainfall, humidity, atmospheric pressure, sunshine and winds. The painting at right – the Pacific and North America on a winter day – shows how the principal currents of sea and air are created by a great global interchange of heat. The process starts with the sun's radiation streaming to earth. About 65 per cent of the radiation which reaches the earth *(see below)* is absorbed by the planet and subsequently heats the atmosphere. At the Equator warm, light water and air begin to move poleward. They are replaced by colder, heavier water and air moving in beneath them from the north. Because the earth rotates, these north-south movements are shifted toward the east in the Northern Hemisphere and toward the west in the Southern Hemisphere.

At the Equator – the painting shows the globe cut in two, to reveal how ocean currents move in this region – the deepest layer *(1)* is cold water on the sea floor. Then comes a slow-moving current *(2)*. Above it is the swift, recently discovered Cromwell Current *(3)*, 100 to 1,000 feet below sea level. The surface currents *(4)* are quickened by easterly trade winds *(5)*. The stratosphere is swept by the erratic Berson Westerlies *(6)* at 60,000 feet and the strong Krakatoa Easterlies *(7)* at 80,000 feet. North of the Equator, surface winds *(8)* help produce tropical clouds and whirl into low-pressure storms. High above, the jet stream *(9)* spurts at 35,000 feet and the polar vortex *(10)* towers between 40,000 and 200,000 feet. The jet stream, formed where warm tropical air meets cold polar air, lashes around mid-latitudes at as much as 300 miles per hour. Its undulations affect the surface winds, which in turn affect surface currents at sea.

The planet's varied climates *(pages 26 and 27)* and its rainfall and vegetation *(pages 28 and 29)* are vitally affected by these surging patterns of air, wind and water that spread the sun's warmth over the earth.

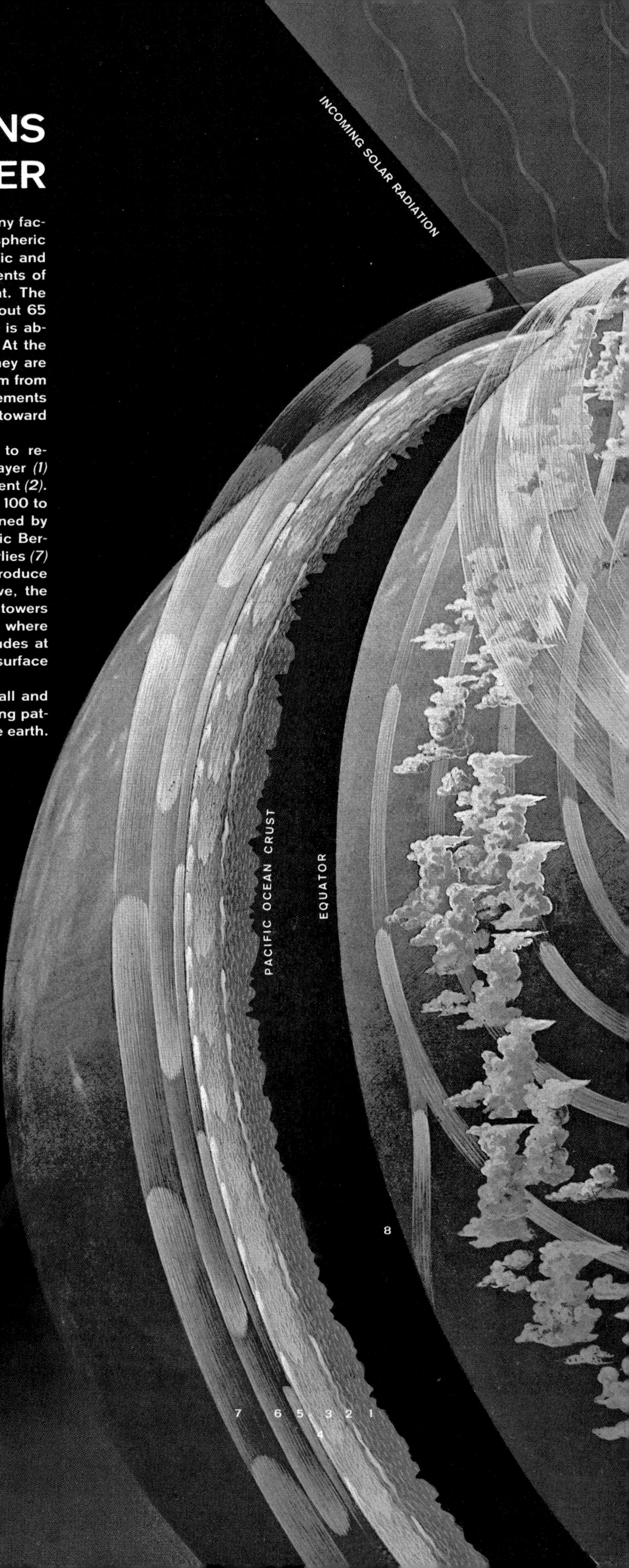
INCOMING SOLAR RADIATION
PACIFIC OCEAN CRUST
EQUATOR
8
7
6
5
4
3
2
1

RAYS FROM THE SUN stream to the earth. As the painting below shows, 35 per cent of the rays are reflected by clouds, dust and air, as well as by polar rock, ice and snow. The remaining 65 per cent of the sun's rays are absorbed – 15 per cent by clouds and moist air, 3 per cent by ozone and 47 per cent by the surface of the earth. This warmth is released as infrared rays to help create a system of currents, depicted in the painting at the right.

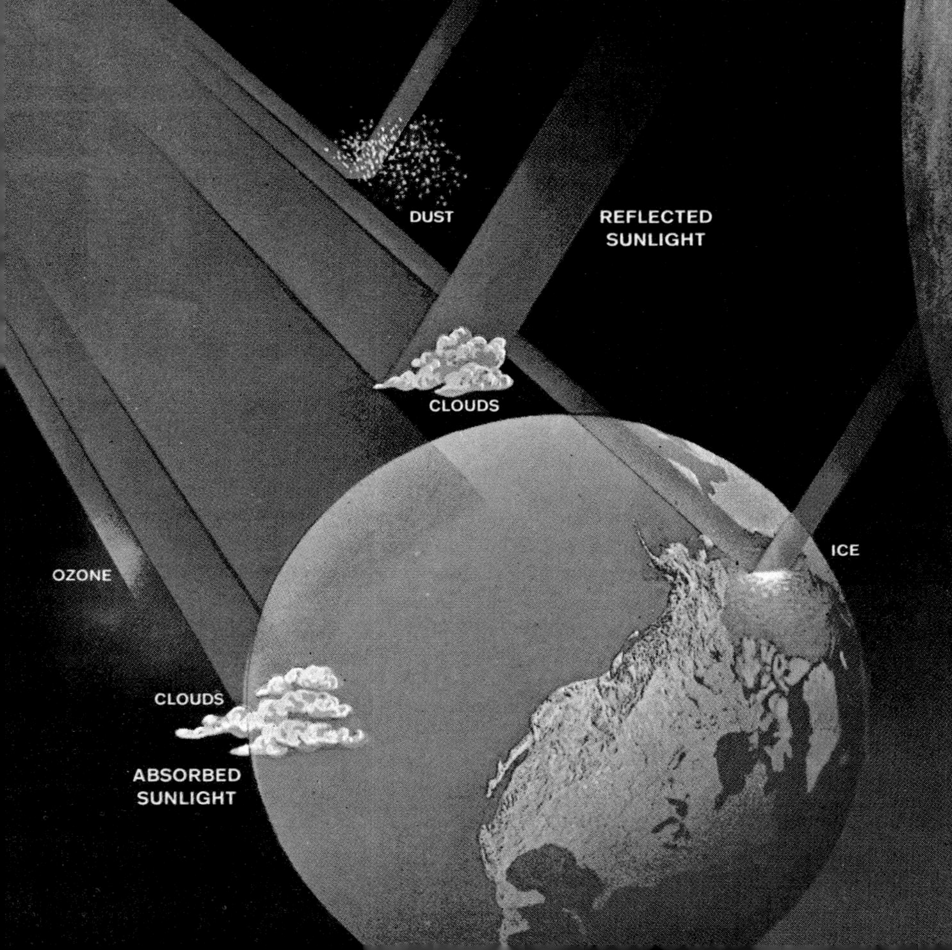
DUST
REFLECTED SUNLIGHT
CLOUDS
ICE
OZONE
CLOUDS
ABSORBED SUNLIGHT

OUTGOING INFRARED RADIATION
10
9
8
A. Petruccelli

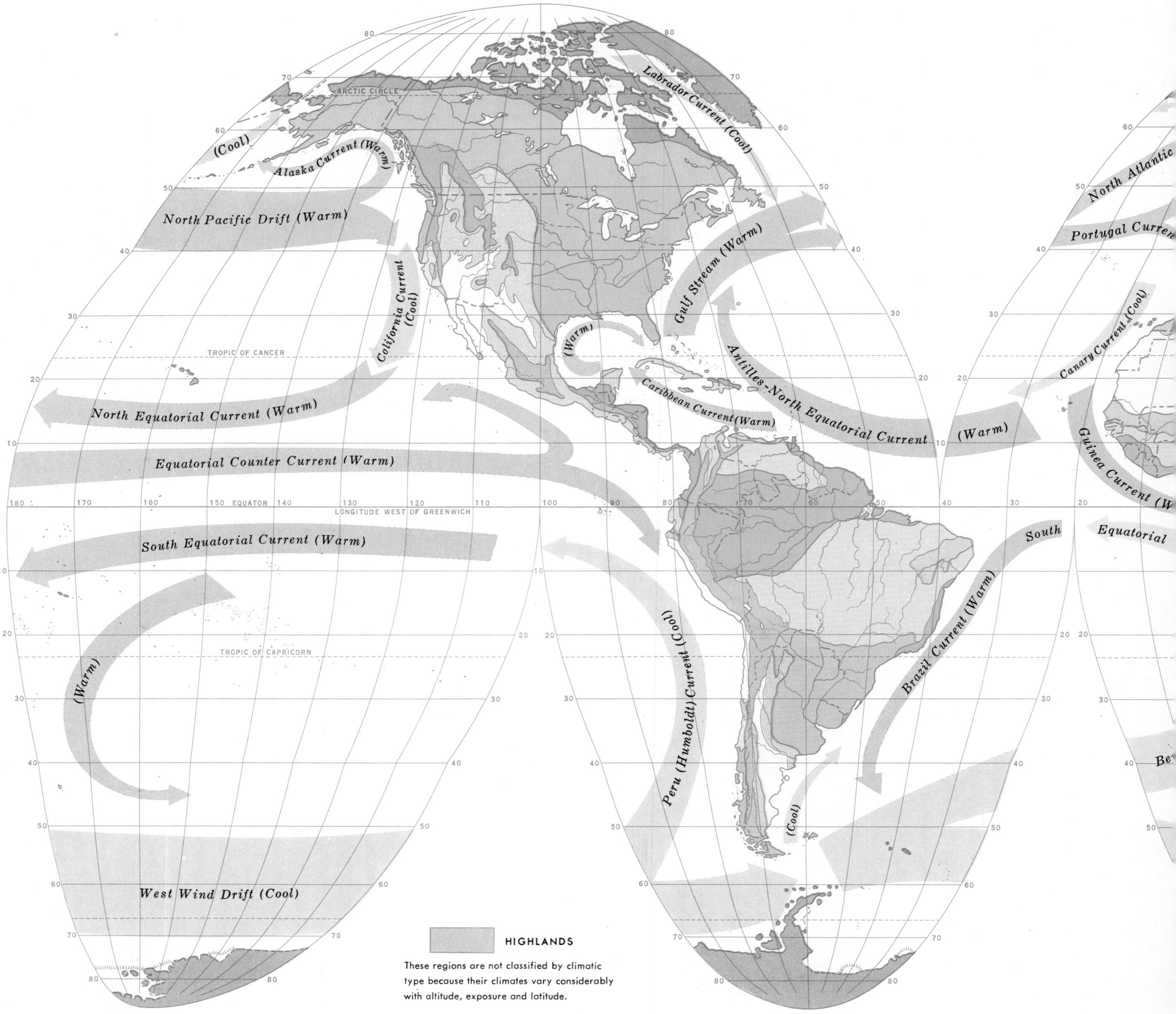

CLIMATE ZONES AND OCEAN CURRENTS

POLAR: The Polar climate is subdivided into the Tundra and the Icecap types. The Tundra climate has at least one month of the year with an average temperature above freezing (32°F.); the monthly average never rises above 50°F. There is no true summer and the low temperatures make cultivation nearly impossible, though mosses and coarse grasses grow. In Icecap climates, the average monthly temperature never rises above freezing, and snow and ice cover the ground throughout the year. Contrary to legend, the polar areas are not snowy; precipitation totals 10 inches or less annually.

HUMID CONTINENTAL: This is the climate of large areas of Europe, Asia and North America. The "warm summer" areas of the Humid Continental zone have at least one month with an average temperature over 71.6°F. and one cold month with an average below 26.6°F. Precipitation is heavier in summer and frequently occurs as thunderstorms. Favorable for corn, this is often called the "corn belt climate." In "cool summer" areas, at least one month averages over 50°F., but no month averages over 71.6°F. The coldest month averages below 26.6°F. Precipitation occurs throughout the year.

MARINE: Common to regions on the westward (windward) shores of continents lying between 40° and 60° north and south of the Equator, this climate is affected by the prevailing winds, the westerlies. Summer temperatures average above 50°F. but below 71.6°F. High temperatures may occur, although heat waves are rare. Freezing weather is unusual. There are few thundershowers. Precipitation is adequate throughout the year, with some increase in winter. The winters are usually mild, averaging above 26.6°F. A distinguishing feature of this climate is the large number of cloudy or rainy days.

CLIMATE ZONES AND OCEAN CURRENTS

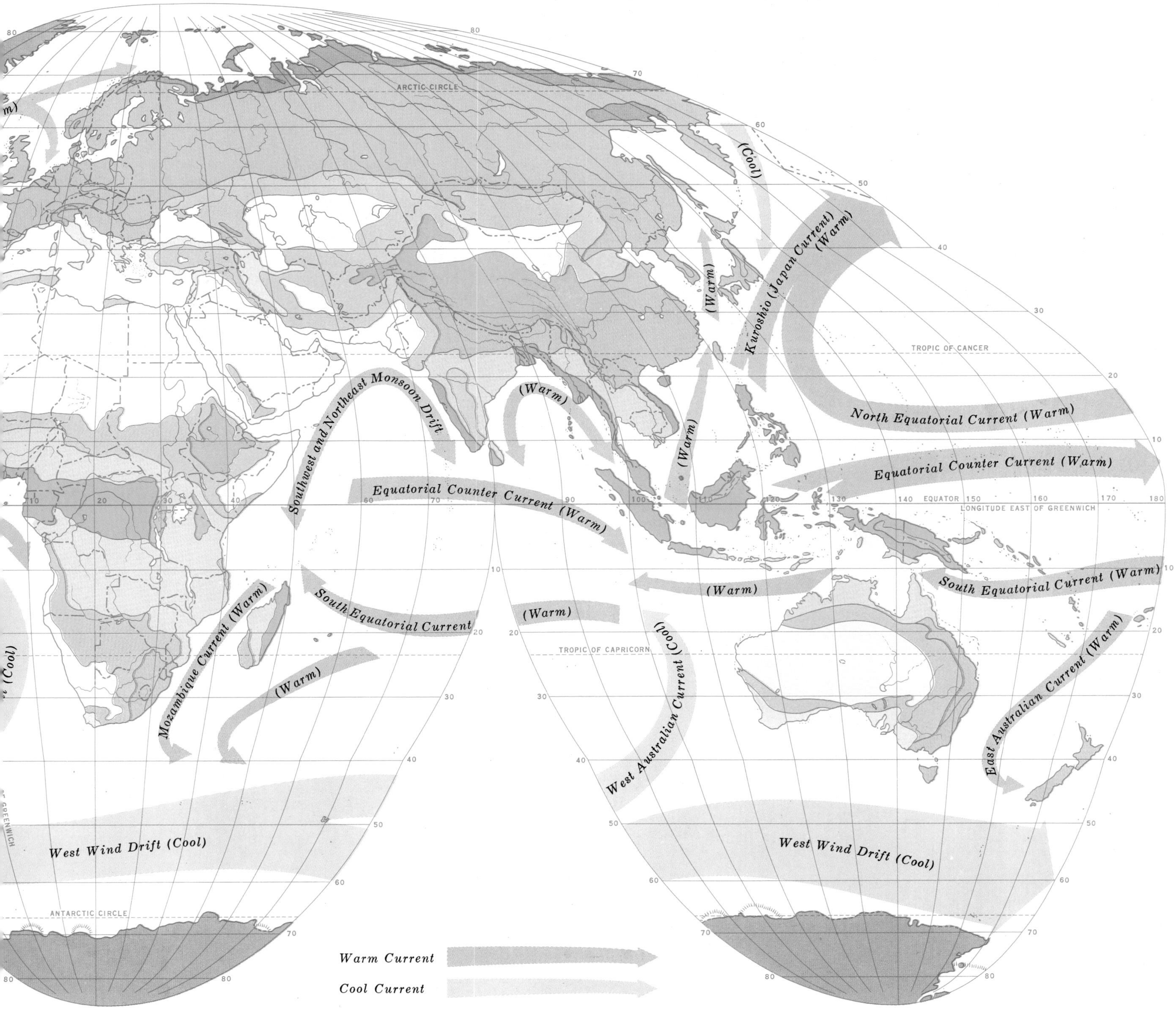

HUMID SUBTROPICAL: This climate is found on the eastern sides of continents lying between 25° and 40° north and south of the Equator. Temperatures in winter do not average below 26.6°F. and are higher than 71.6°F. in at least one summer month. Average summer temperatures are 75° to 82°F. Summer humidity makes the daytime uncomfortable. Winters are mild, freezing is infrequent. Rainfall is generally well distributed through the year, with infrequent summer drought, but some areas have dry winters. Tropical hurricanes add to the rainfall, especially in the U.S. and eastern Asia.

SUBTROPICAL DRY SUMMER: This is the "Mediterranean" climate that is found within latitudes 30° and 40° north and south of the Equator, on the western sides of continents. In winter, rain-producing fronts and cyclones caused by the westerlies prevail. Cold weather is almost entirely absent. In Mediterranean climate regions, the mild, frequently sunny winters average 40° to 50°F., summers average 70° to 80°F. During the nearly rainless summers, nighttime temperatures drop rapidly, as they do in the desert areas. An estimated 2 per cent of the earth's surface enjoys this balmy climate.

SEMIARID: Semiarid climates are found in two locations: the interiors of continents in the middle latitudes, and on western continental margins where cool ocean currents parallel the coast. These are transitional areas between deserts and humid regions. Often they surround desert areas. With low humidity and little cloud cover, semiarid lands usually have 10 to 20 inches of rainfall annually, but farming is hampered by the rapid evaporation of rain. Also, the rainfall is erratic; a year of adequate precipitation may be followed by several dry years. Temperatures have wide seasonal as well as daily ranges.

DESERT: What primarily characterizes deserts is their slight rainfall. Middle-latitude deserts occur in continental interiors walled off from moist air by mountains. Many deserts—the Atacama of South America and the Sahara of Africa—have less than five inches of rainfall annually. Evaporation of rainfall is so excessive, and so little rain which does fall is held by the soil, that agriculture is severely limited. Deserts are not universally hot, but often have wide daily and seasonal temperature ranges. They are frequently windy during the day. About 12 per cent of the world's land area is desert.

TROPICAL WET: Heat and heavy rainfall throughout the year mark the Tropical Wet climate zone, found within latitudes 5° to 10° north and south of the Equator. Annual temperatures average between 75° and 80°F., usually with less than five degrees' difference between the warmest and coolest months. Average monthly temperatures do not fall below 64.4°F. There are no long dry periods in Tropical Wet climates, only some periods that are less wet. Annual rainfall is seldom below 50 or 60 inches. The only relief from discomfort may be provided by squalls accompanying thundershowers.

TROPICAL WET AND DRY: Temperatures in this climate zone are constantly high, the coldest month averaging above 64.4°F., with the range between the warmest and coolest months about 15 degrees. There are two contrasting seasons. In the dry winter (June-September in the Southern Hemisphere, November-February in the Northern Hemisphere), temperatures may average above 90°F. In the hot, wet summer, temperatures are a little lower, but above 85°F. Toward the Equator, tropical Wet and Dry (Savanna) areas resemble rain forests; toward the poles, they resemble semiarid areas.

THE EARTH'S RAINFALL PATTERNS,

The maps below show the average rainfall throughout the world on a semiannual basis. Little or no rainfall (polar regions and deserts) or too much rainfall (the rain forests of the Amazon and Congo River basins) makes cultivation difficult, while dense populations can live in normally arid areas that are irrigated (southern California, the basins of the Tigris-Euphrates, the Nile and Indus Rivers).

Without moisture in a liquid form, there can be little or no vegetation. Most crops require an annual rainfall of at least 20 inches, well distributed throughout the growing season. Distribution is vital. West Syria, for example, has relatively abundant rainfall – but in the winter. Thus, instead of supporting a large population of farmers, the country has a sparse population of nomadic herdsmen. In other regions (the western Great Plains of the U.S., Sudan, the steppes of Asia), rain falls for so brief a period during the year that only quick-growing grasses can mature. In most dry areas of this kind, the population is relatively scanty because the only possible agricultural activity is grazing.

Rainfall is the common name for precipitation, a more precise term which includes rain, snow, sleet and hail. Rain is caused by the cooling of moist air – air with considerable water vapor (high humidity). Equatorial areas are generally among the wettest places on earth, polar regions generally among the driest. Air gets its water vapor by evaporation. Because evaporation takes place much more rapidly from warm water than from cold water, the major source of atmospheric moisture in the world is warm ocean water. Thus, rainfall is (1) usually greater over warm water and over continental margins bathed by warm water, and (2) low over cold water and the continental margins bordered by cold water, and in continental interiors far from warm ocean water.

The kind of vegetation in any region is determined to a large degree by rainfall and temperature. The key on the opposite page shows 12 of the colors used in the terrain maps of this *Atlas* to indicate the nature of land surfaces, which are also illustrated in photographs at the right of the page; 10 of these colors refer to types of vegetation.

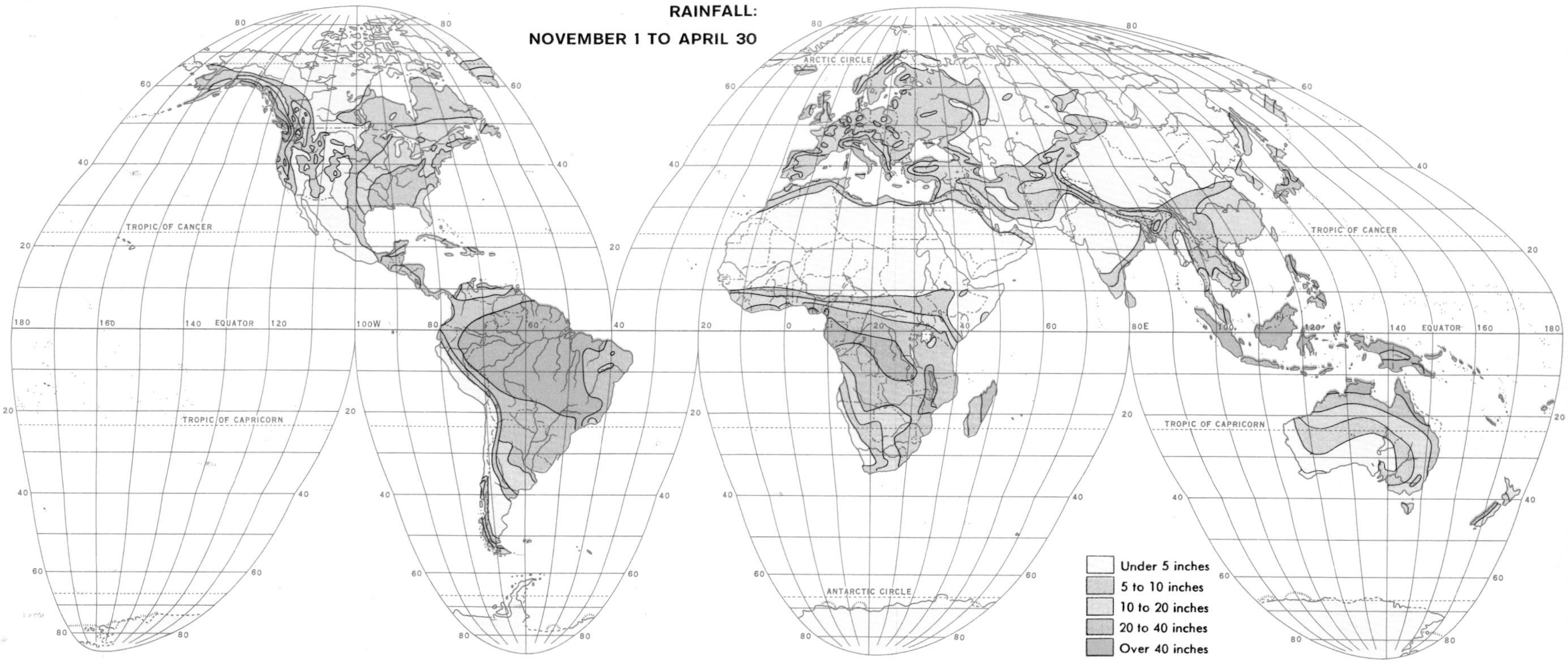
RAINFALL:
NOVEMBER 1 TO APRIL 30
ARCTIC CIRCLE
TROPIC OF CANCER
EQUATOR
TROPIC OF CAPRICORN
ANTARCTIC CIRCLE
Under 5 inches
5 to 10 inches
10 to 20 inches
20 to 40 inches
Over 40 inches

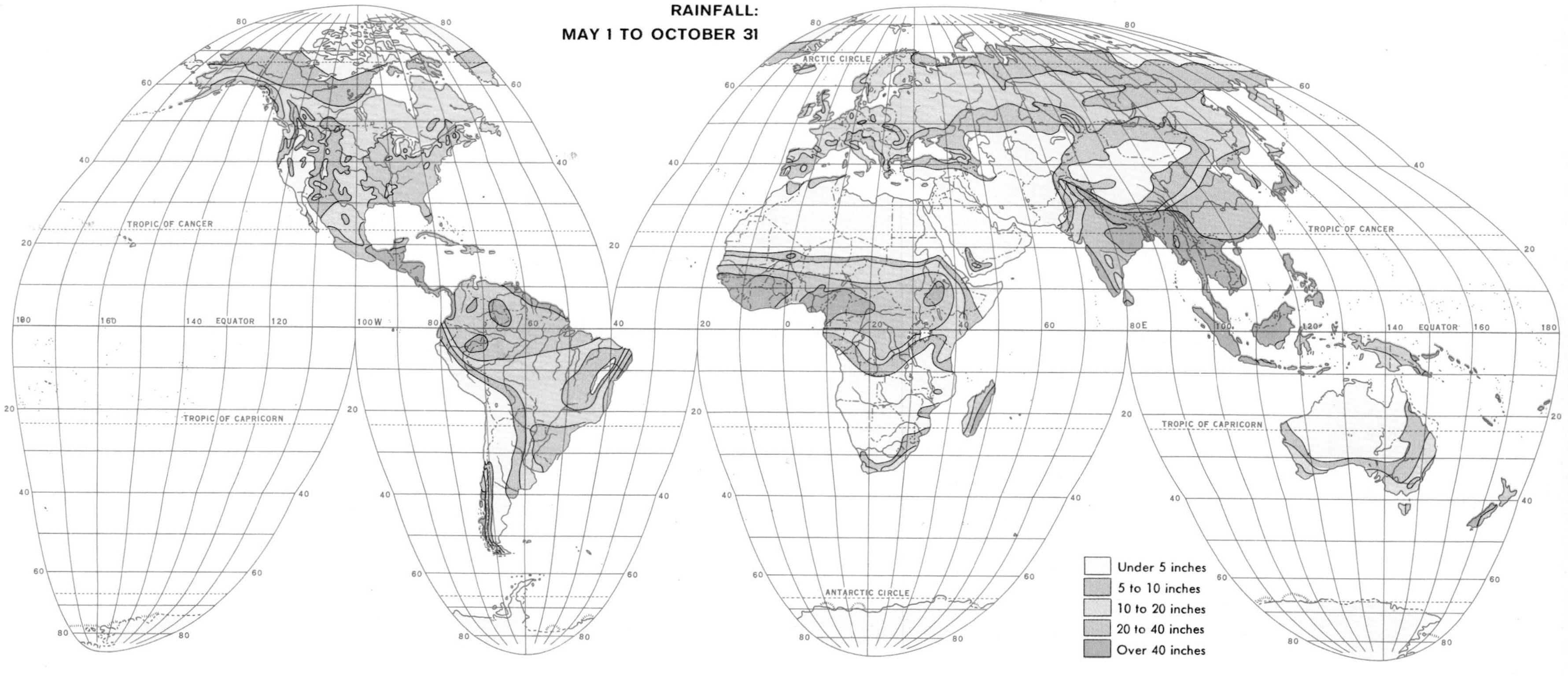
RAINFALL:
MAY 1 TO OCTOBER 31
ARCTIC CIRCLE
TROPIC OF CANCER
EQUATOR
TROPIC OF CAPRICORN
ANTARCTIC CIRCLE
Under 5 inches
5 to 10 inches
10 to 20 inches
20 to 40 inches
Over 40 inches

TERRAIN AND VEGETATION

KEY

BARREN ABOVE TIMBER: Mountain heights that rise above both the timber line and the zone of alpine meadows lack vegetation, except for scattered patches of moss. The heights have exposed rock and permanent snowfields on their surface. Shown at right is the Furka Pass in the Swiss Alps. Other examples are the high volcanic peaks of the Pacific Northwest, the Andes in South America, the Himalayas, and other peaks in the Alps.

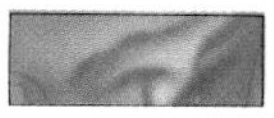

EVERGREEN: These areas are forested with trees that do not shed all their leaves in one season. Broadleaf evergreens grow densely in the tropics. Mid-latitude-zone evergreens are mostly needle-leaf and coniferous (pine, spruce, fir). At right is an evergreen coniferous forest in Switzerland. Broadleaf evergreens abound in the Congo and Amazon River basins. Needle-leaf conifers grow in North American and European forests.

MIXED EVERGREEN AND DECIDUOUS: These are regions forested with needle-leaf evergreens as well as broadleaf trees that shed all their foliage in season. Common types of broadleaf trees are beech, oak, hickory and chestnut. Forests of this kind are widespread in the U.S. (northeast, and southeastern piedmont regions), the Balkans and Central Europe, and southern Sweden. Shown at right is a forest in western North Carolina.

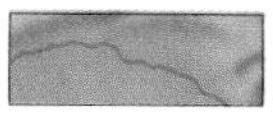

DECIDUOUS: The trees in these areas lose all their leaves in one season—during the winter in the middle and higher latitudes, during the dry season in tropical and low-latitude lands. Most deciduous trees are broadleaf, although they are generally smaller than tropical evergreens. Pictured here is a grove in Scotland. Deciduous forests are prevalent in the U.S., Western Europe, south central Africa and small areas of South America.

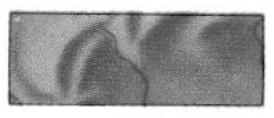

SHRUB: Associated with Mediterranean climates, shrub vegetation areas are dominated by woody plants, either evergreen or deciduous, that are generally smaller than trees. Trees such as olive and cork oak grow in moister sections of shrub areas. Shown is an expanse of shrub near Adelaide, Australia. Examples of shrub regions are portions of southern California, the Mediterranean Sea area and Africa's tip around Cape Town.

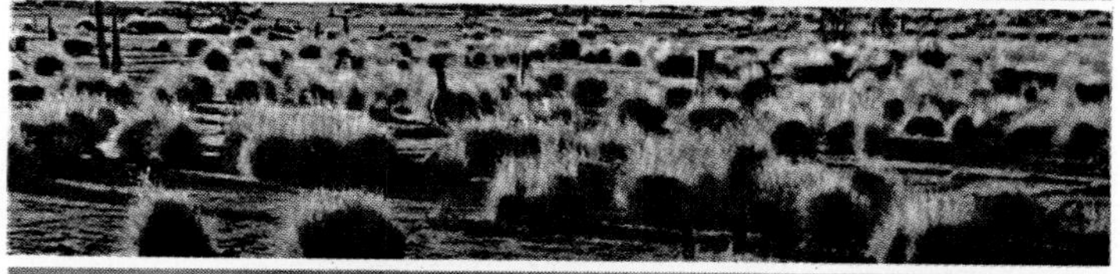

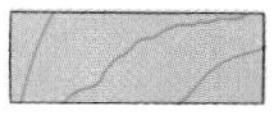

GRASS: These areas are free of trees except along streams and consist of grasses varying in height from a few inches in the dry steppe regions to as much as 10 to 12 feet on more humid prairies. The grasses are usually coarse and have varying degrees of green coloring, determined by local precipitation. The slopes of a Swiss valley are shown. Vast grassy areas are prevalent on the North American plains and on the Pampa of Argentina.

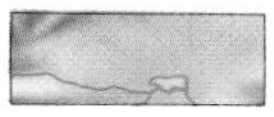

ALPINE VEGETATION: This is a zone of herbaceous plants growing above timber lines but below the exposed rocks and permanent snow of high mountains. The vegetation consists of small shrubs and grass, moss and lichens. Shown is a section of the Matterhorn on the Swiss-Italian border. Other Alpine examples are found in the Pacific Northwest of North America, Mexico's Sierra Madre, the Andes and areas of the Himalayas.

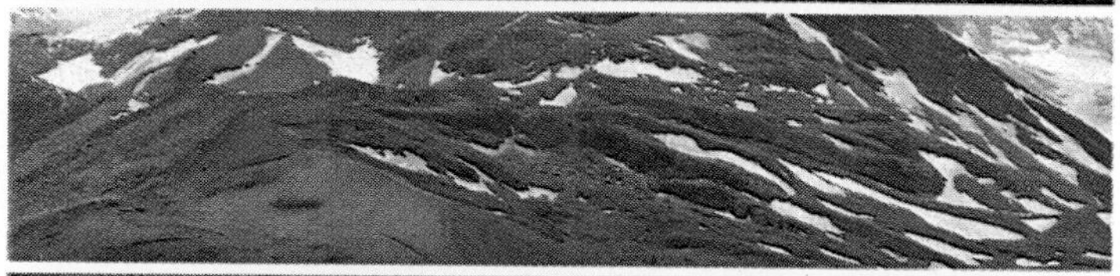

TUNDRA: Herbaceous plants (sedges, lichens, mosses) cover the ground in high latitudes from the timber line to the permanent snow zones. The vegetation decreases in height and density as the snow line is approached. Tundra is shown at right growing in the Northwest Territories of Canada. It is common to northern Canada and large areas of Alaska, the perimeters of Greenland and Iceland, and the northern sectors of the Soviet Union.

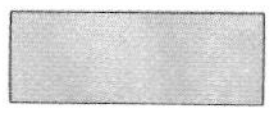

BARREN AND ARID: Desert regions with surfaces of sand, rock or soil are generally devoid of vegetation in their central dry cores, but may have some scattered areas of plant life suited to aridity. This vegetation normally has striking colors and sharp odors to attract insects that may enhance its chances of survival. At right are dunes of the Atacama Desert of northern Chile. Other examples are portions of the Sahara and the Gobi Desert.

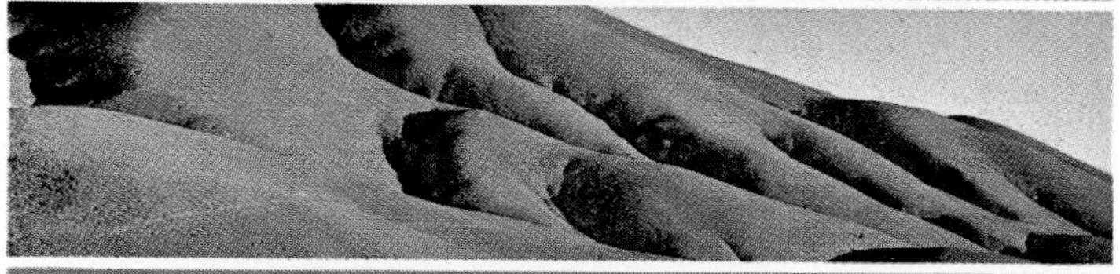

SNOW AND ICE: Permanent snow and ice cover large sections of the higher latitudes north and south, as well as high peaks above the snow line. In these cold lands, where minute amounts of soil may be exposed, the temperature so seldom rises above freezing that plant life has no chance to germinate even though there may be wind-borne seeds. At right is a part of Antarctica's icecap. Snow and ice also cover most of Greenland.

ICE PACK: This is permanently frozen sea water found in polar regions. When ice pack moves away from its origin in the high latitudes, it breaks up, forming an extensive floating mass called an ice floe. An example of an ice floe in the Arctic Ocean is shown at right. In shape and thickness, an ice floe differs from an iceberg, which is a mass of fresh-water ice that has been calved from a mountain or a continental glacier, as in Greenland.

VOLCANIC LAVA AREAS: Volcanic ash, distributed in light layers over large areas of countryside, serves as a moisture-preserving agent in semi-arid climates, increasing the productivity of soil surrounding volcanoes. At right are the great blue-purple lava fields beneath the Nyamlagira volcano in the Congo. Examples in the United States are the Craters of the Moon National Monument in Idaho and many parts of the Hawaiian Islands.

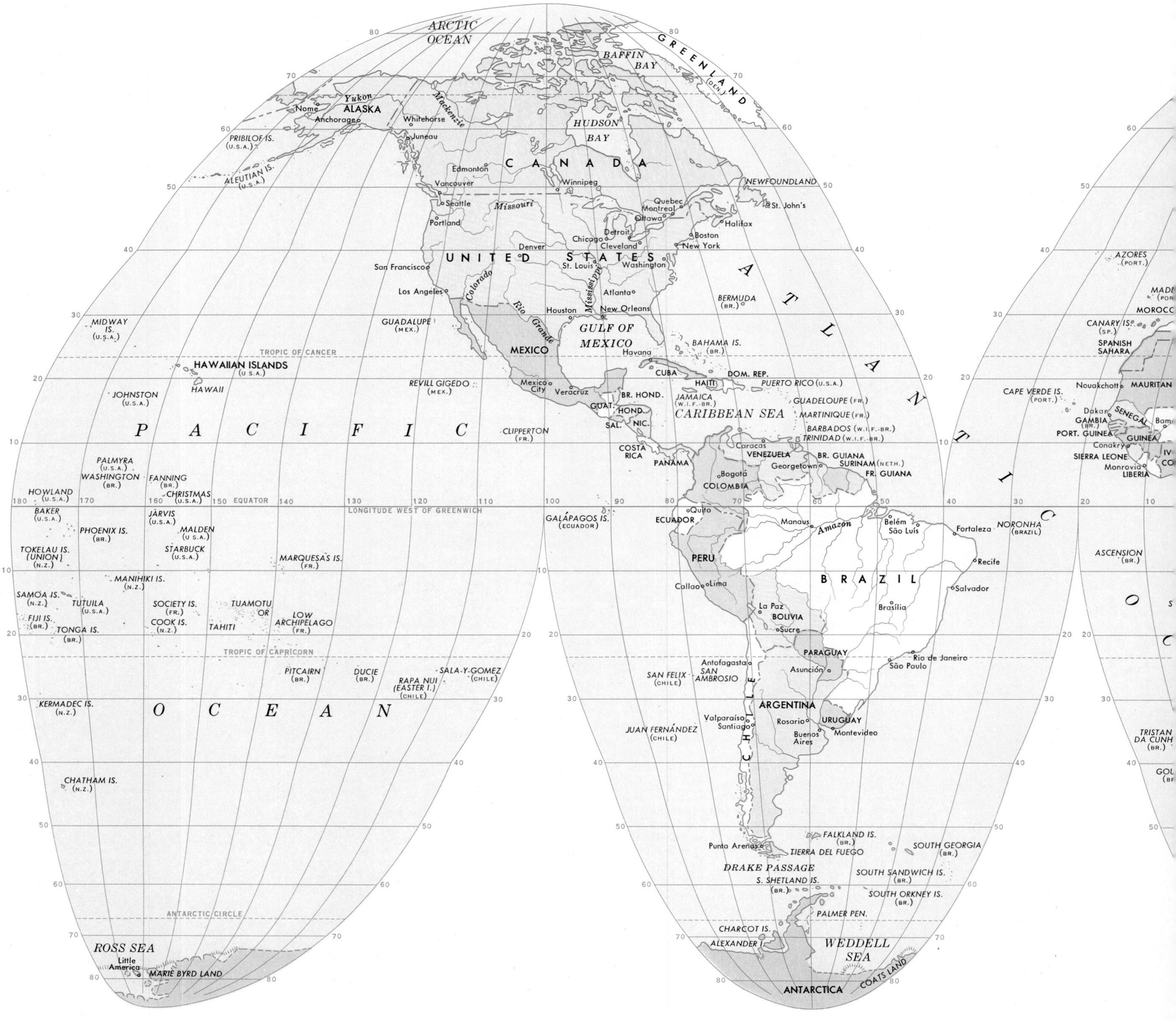

POLITICAL DIVISIONS OF THE WORLD

The preceding pages of this introductory section of the *Atlas* have dealt with the earth as a physical entity in the cosmos. The section beginning here deals with man, his relation to the earth and to the natural forces of his world.

The map on these pages shows the boundaries of the political divisions man has created. In the beginning, boundaries between peoples were vague. Early agricultural tribes might have considered their natural confines to be the ring of hills protecting a valley through which a vital stream ran. Today, a number of boundaries between nations still fall in part along natural barriers: a wide river (e.g., the Danube, which demarks Romania and Bulgaria; the Uruguay, which separates Uruguay from Argentina and Argentina from Brazil); a chain of high mountains (e.g., the Andes, which separate Chile and Argentina; the Pyrenees, which separate France from Spain); and lakes (e.g., the Great Lakes, which form part of the United States' boundary with

POLITICAL DIVISIONS OF THE WORLD

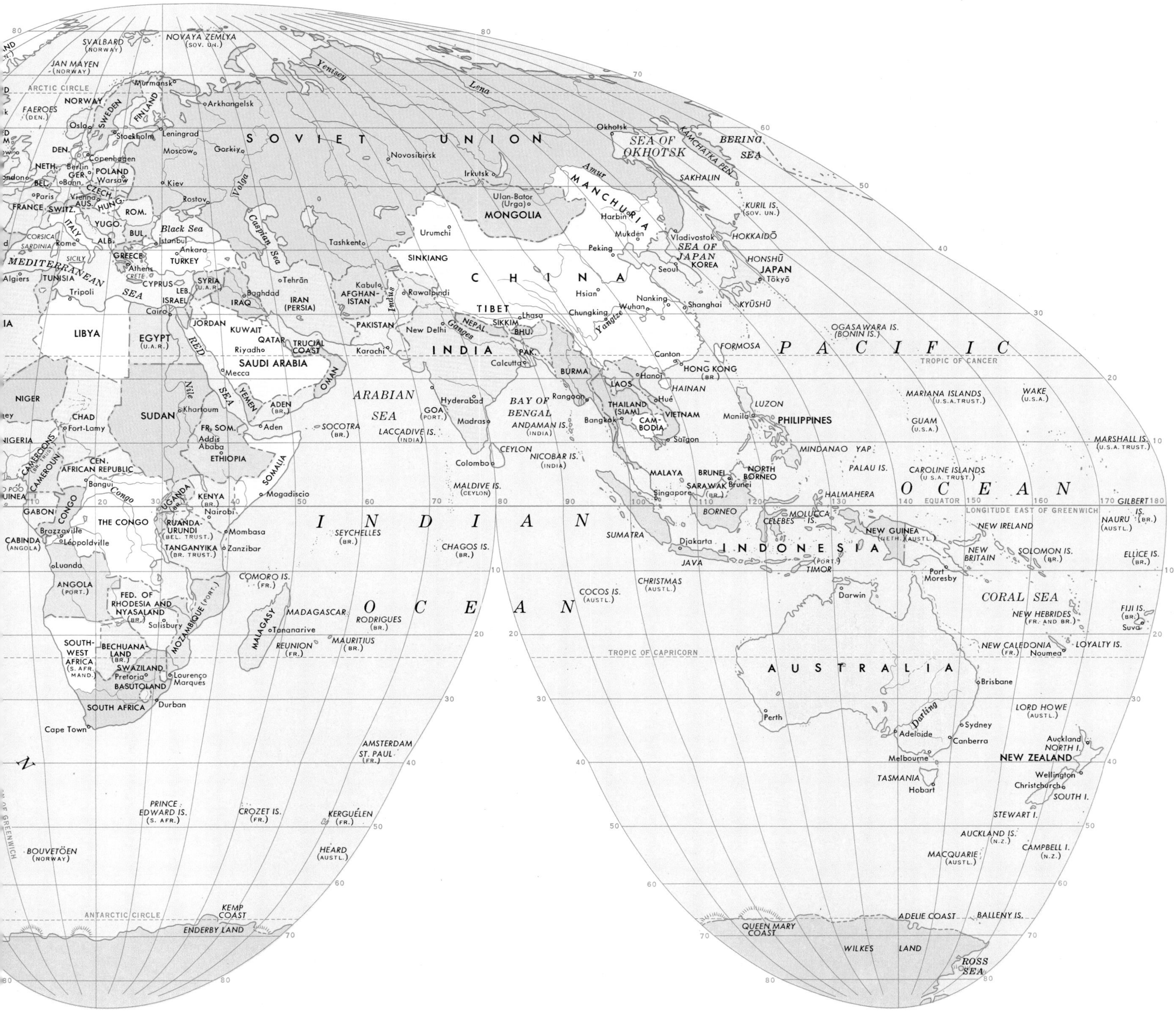

Canada). Only a handful of the more than 100 nations that now exist in the world are completely delimited by what early map makers used to call "natural frontiers." These are primarily insular countries, such as Australia, New Zealand, Japan, Ceylon and Cuba. Economic competition has accounted for some boundaries that have no relation to terrain: the Rhine River, for example, provides a natural border between France and Germany, with Germany on the east bank except where the border bulges westward beyond the river to encompass the coal-rich Saar basin. And religious and ethnic considerations sometimes lead to the creation of outlandishly shaped or economically unviable nations. An example is Pakistan, divided into an East and West Pakistan separated from each other by more than 900 miles of India.

In this century, a number of efforts have been made to reunite ethnic groups even though they had developed different customs and cultural patterns during years of separation and domination by foreign empires. Two examples are Czechoslovakia and Yugoslavia, both born after World War I. The former brought together Protestant and Catholic Czechs, Catholic Slovaks, and Greek Catholic and Greek Orthodox Ruthenians out of the disintegrated Austro-Hungarian Empire. The latter united Southern (Yugo) Slavs—Serbs, Croats, Slovenes, Bosnians and Macedonians—some of whom were Roman Catholics, some members of the Orthodox Eastern Church and some Moslems.

Boundary problems will continue to be severe for nations which have become independent in Africa since World War II. The old colonial lines these new nations have inherited were drawn without any regard for the ethnic or linguistic relationships of the people, with the result that some tribes now find themselves divided between two or more countries (the Hausa between Niger and Nigeria, for example), while hostile tribes (the Balubas and Luluas of the Congo, for example) find themselves locked within the boundaries of a common state.

THE WORLD'S DIETS

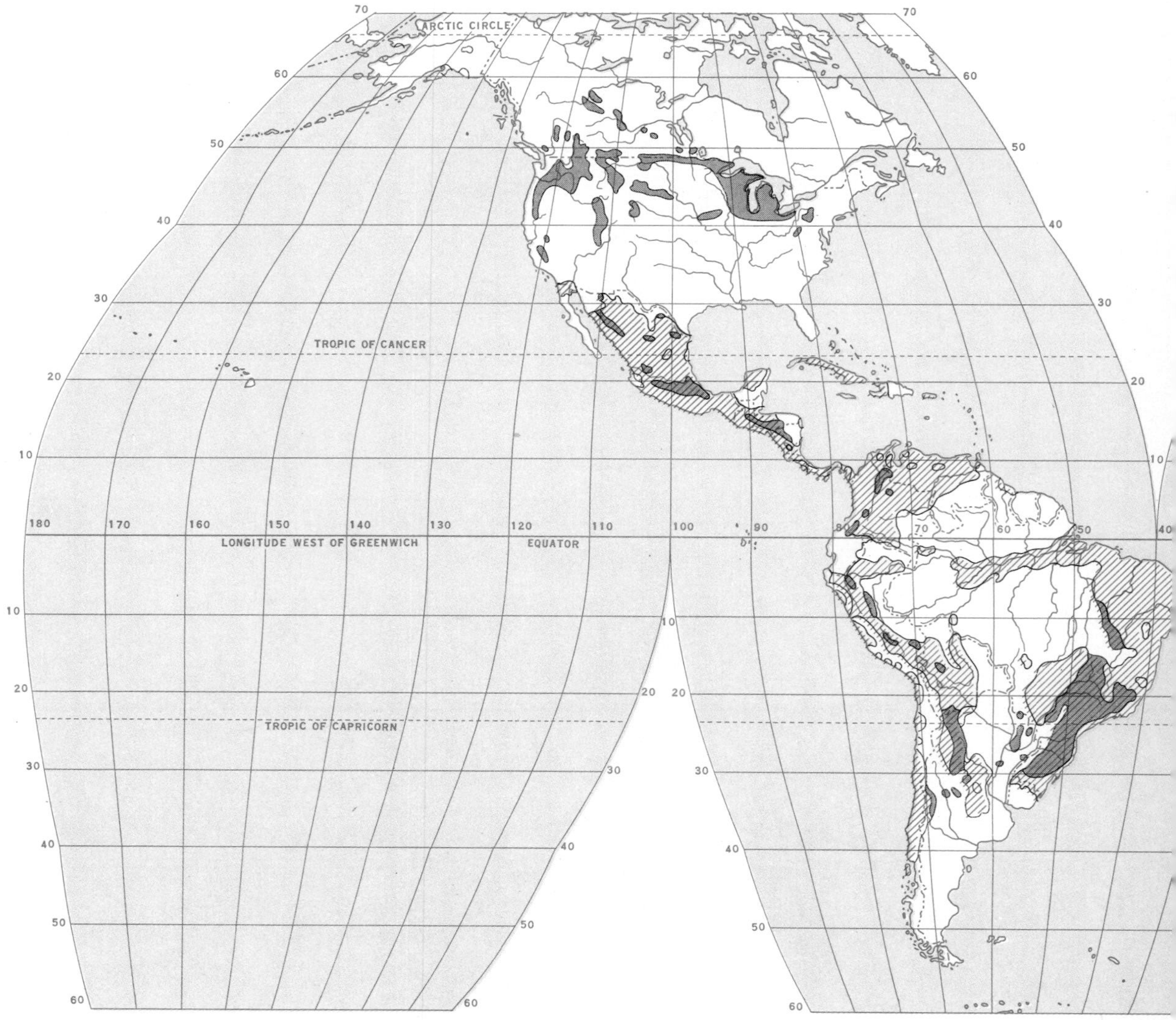

- Protein Deficiencies
- Multiple Vitamin Deficiencies
- Mineral Deficiencies (Iodine)

Areas of the world in which there are major diet deficiencies are shown at right. Lack of protein is the most severe diet problem. Protein deficiencies cause fatal diseases wherever production of cattle is inadequate (as in Africa) or where religious restrictions limit the amount of meat eaten (as in India). Peanuts and soybeans, inexpensive and protein-rich, can be substituted for meat. Vitamin deficiencies can be overcome by enriching available foods, such as rice. Mineral deficiencies – iodine, for example – are a minor problem in most of the world. Where they are detected, diets can be supplemented.

FOOD PRODUCTION

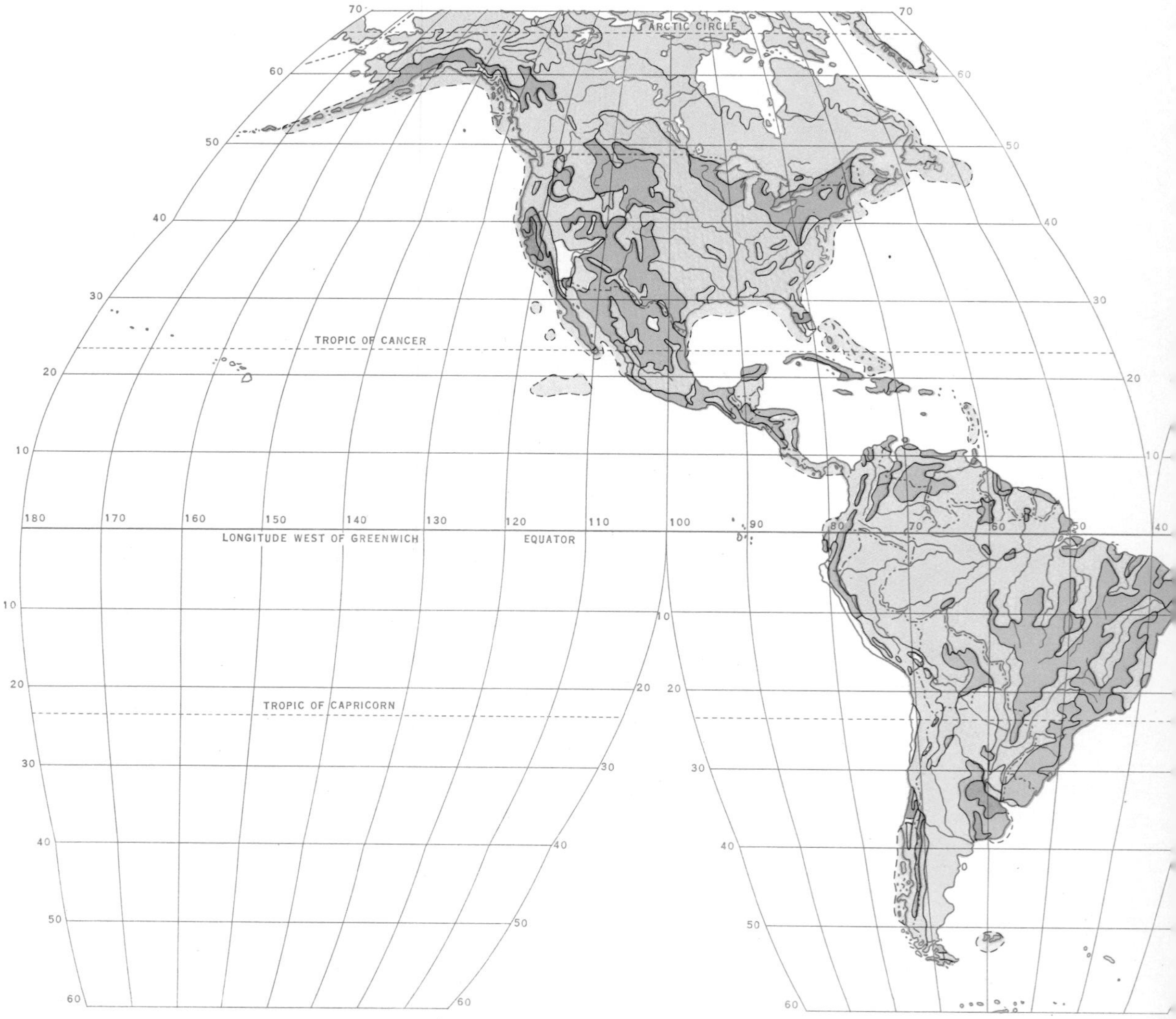

- General Agriculture
- Intensive Agriculture
- Plantation Agriculture
- Grazing
- Seasonal and Nomadic Herding
- Forest and Scattered Agriculture
- Non-Agricultural Areas
- Fishing

The major food-producing areas of the world are shown at right. *General Agriculture* areas yield mixed crops of grains, vegetables and fruits. *Intensive Agriculture* is practiced in those regions where every inch of arable land is precious. *Plantation Agriculture* is devoted to huge single crops like coffee and sugar. *Grazing* areas include dairy farming regions and land set aside for grazing animals. *Seasonal and Nomadic Herding* varies according to season or the availability of grasslands. In *Forest and Scattered Agriculture* areas there is some general farming as well as collecting of fruits and nuts.

DIETS AND FOOD PRODUCTION

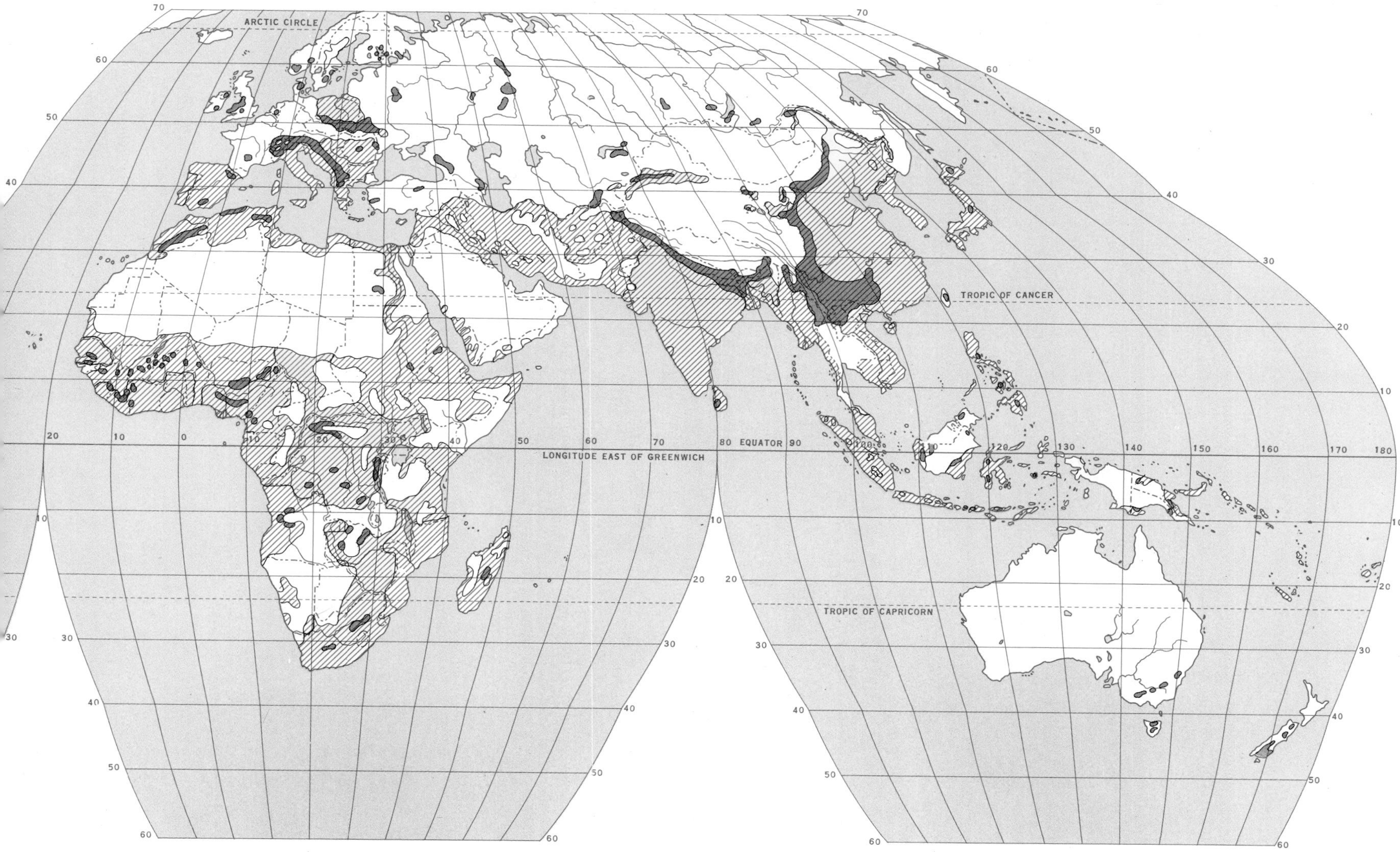

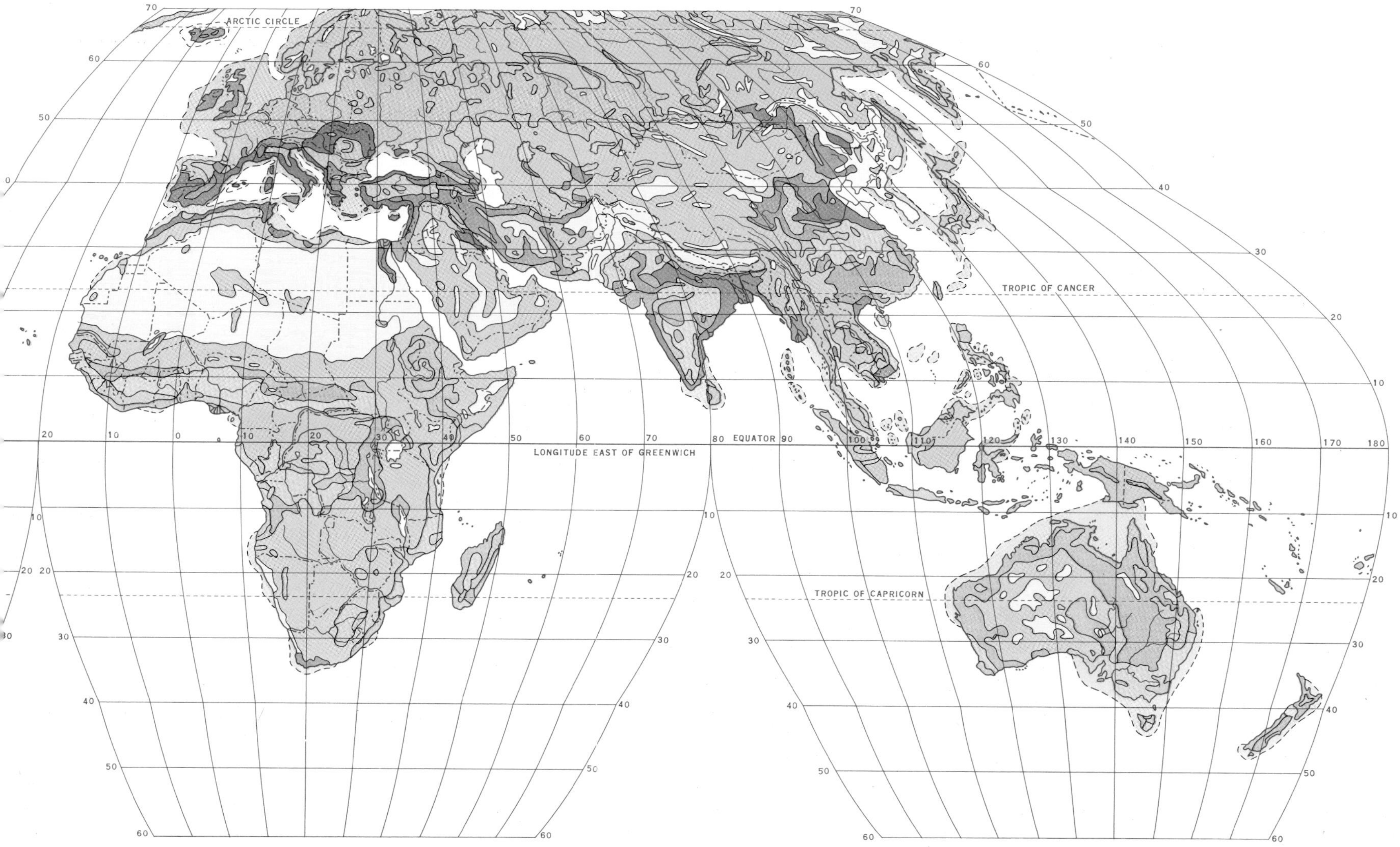

POPULATION OF THE WORLD

POPULATION DENSITY

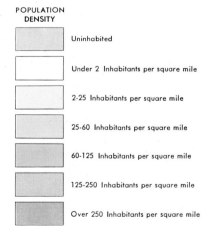

- Uninhabited
- Under 2 Inhabitants per square mile
- 2-25 Inhabitants per square mile
- 25-60 Inhabitants per square mile
- 60-125 Inhabitants per square mile
- 125-250 Inhabitants per square mile
- Over 250 Inhabitants per square mile

• City Over 1,000,000 Population

◦ City 500,000 to 1,000,000 Population

POPULATION OF THE WORLD

RURAL		URBAN
37.5%	Argentina	62.5%
31.1	Australia	68.9
63.8	Brazil	36.2
38.4	Canada	61.6
86.7	China	13.3
44.1	France	55.9
82.7	India	17.3
62.5	Japan	37.5
57.4	Mexico	42.6
52.0	Soviet Union	48.0
63.0	Spain	37.0
78.1	Turkey	21.9
57.4	South Africa	42.6
19.2	United Kingdom	80.8
36.0	United States	64.0

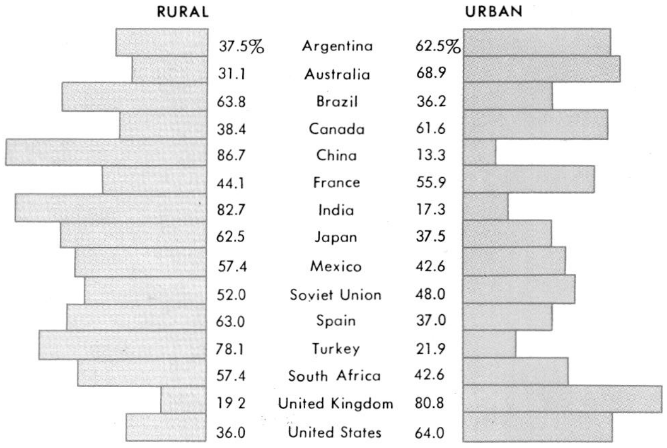

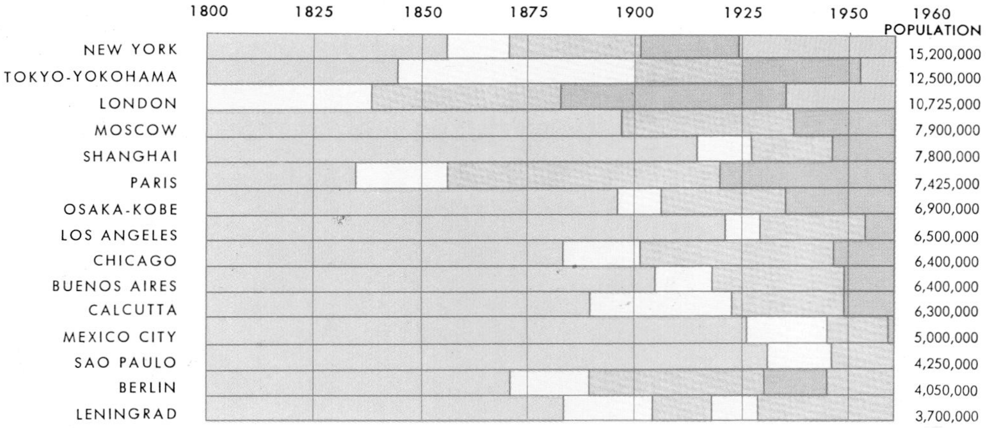

FARM VERSUS TOWN: A WORLD PERSPECTIVE

The ratio between city and rural dwellers varies widely from nation to nation, as this graph shows. Where urban dwellers greatly outnumber rural, as in the United Kingdom, the country is highly industrialized. But some agricultural nations, such as Australia and Argentina, where mechanization permits high farm yields with comparatively little labor, have more people in cities than on farms.

1800	1825	1850	1875	1900	1925	1950	1960 POPULATION
NEW YORK								15,200,000
TOKYO-YOKOHAMA								12,500,000
LONDON								10,725,000
MOSCOW								7,900,000
SHANGHAI								7,800,000
PARIS								7,425,000
OSAKA-KOBE								6,900,000
LOS ANGELES								6,500,000
CHICAGO								6,400,000
BUENOS AIRES								6,400,000
CALCUTTA								6,300,000
MEXICO CITY								5,000,000
SAO PAULO								4,250,000
BERLIN								4,050,000
LENINGRAD								3,700,000

1,000,000
2,000,000
5,000,000
10,000,000

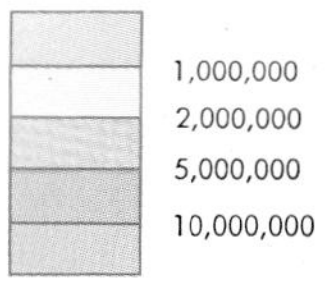

THE GROWING CITIES

The rapid growth of metropolitan areas since the Industrial Revolution, which led country workers to migrate to the cities in search of high wages, is shown on this chart. London became the first city to reach a population of two million in 1860, but did not pass the five million mark till more than 40 years after that. Cities which industrialized later grew faster. New York went from two million to five million in 30 years, Moscow did it in 12. About 125 cities now have a population of a million or more.

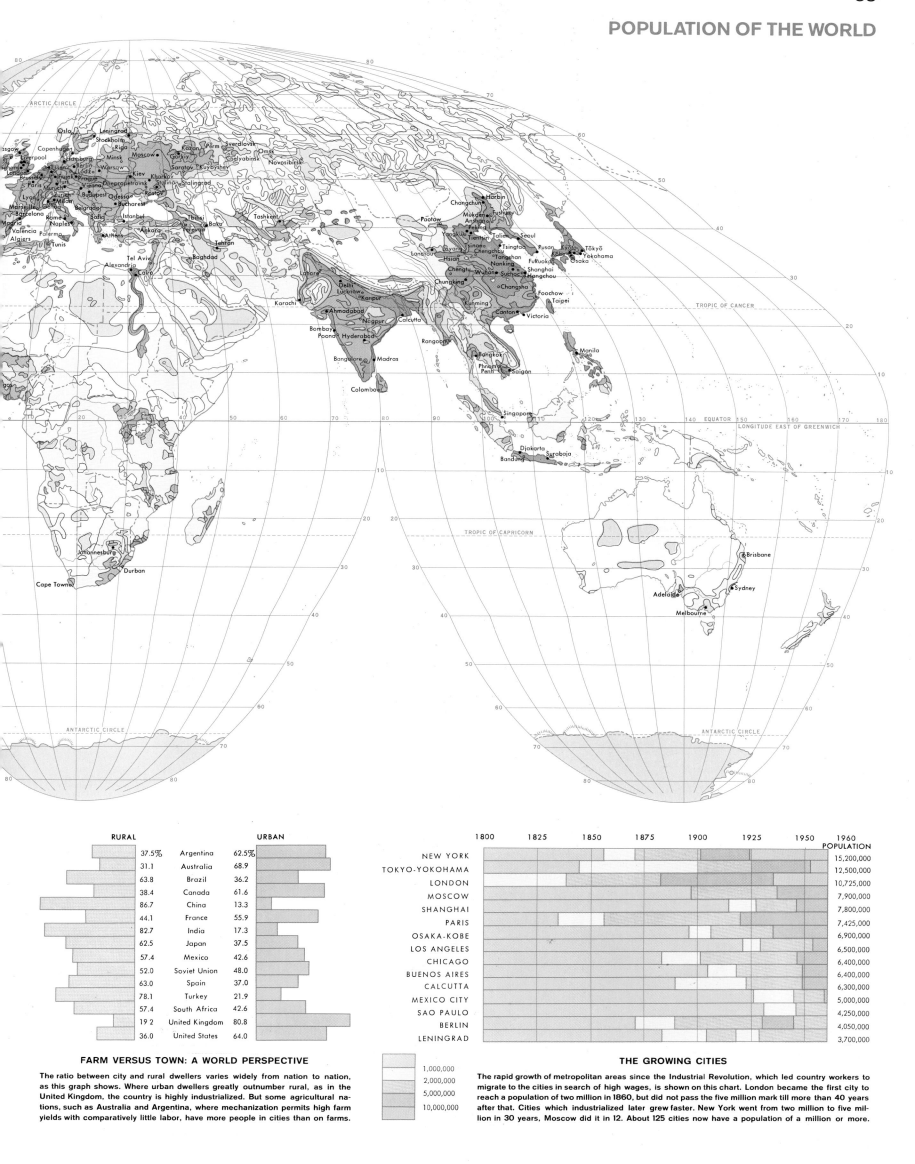

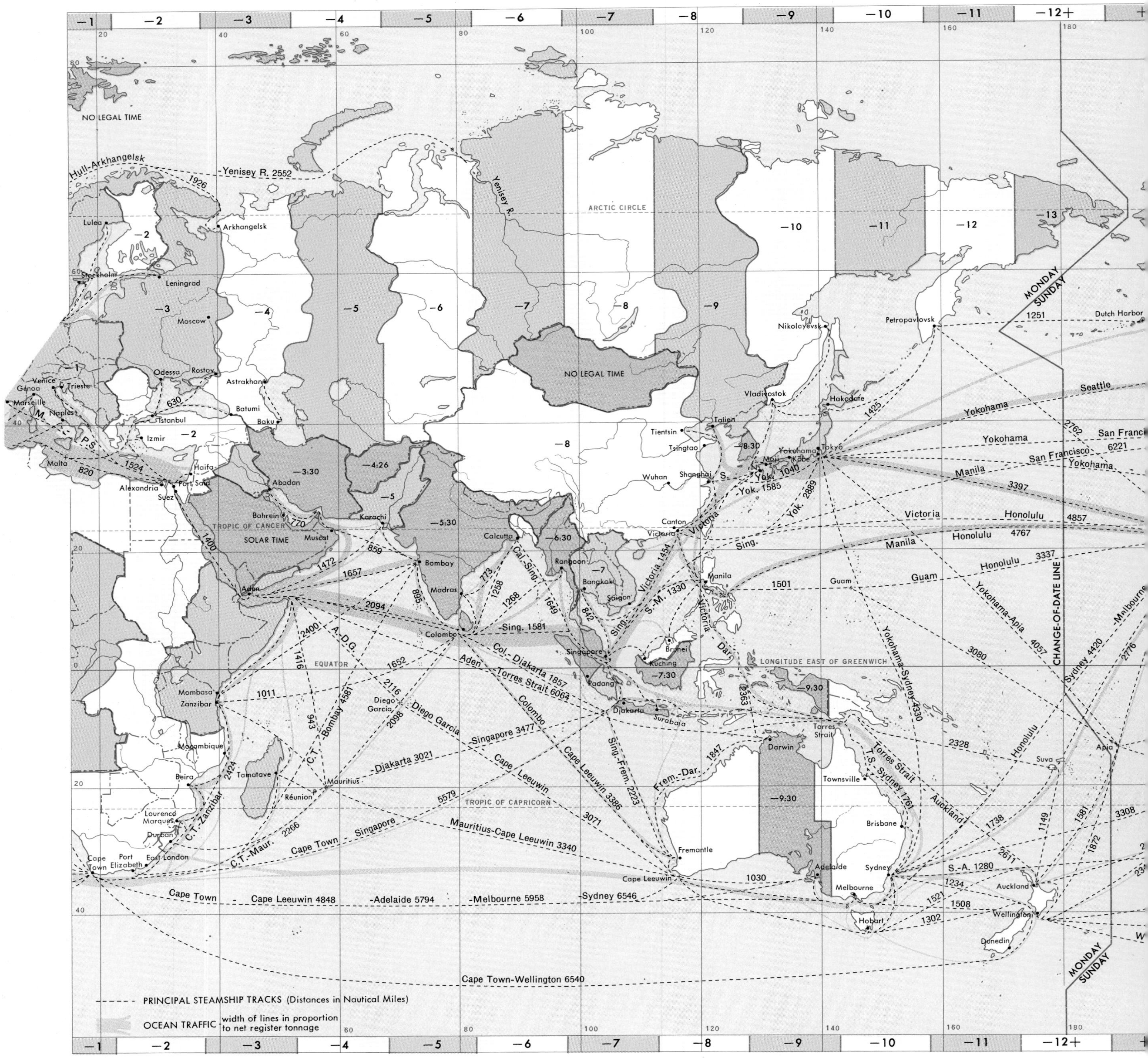

OCEAN ROUTES, AIR AND SEA DISTANCES, TIME ZONES

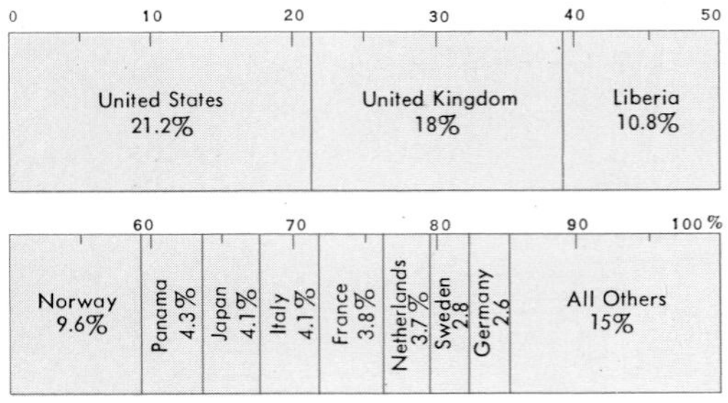

THE LEADING MERCHANT FLEETS

This graph shows cargo-ship tonnage percentages for the major maritime nations. World total for 1958 was 151,624,000 gross tons. Liberia and Panama rank high because of commercial gains they accord shipowners who register vessels with them.

OCEAN ROUTES, AIR AND SEA DISTANCES, TIME ZONES

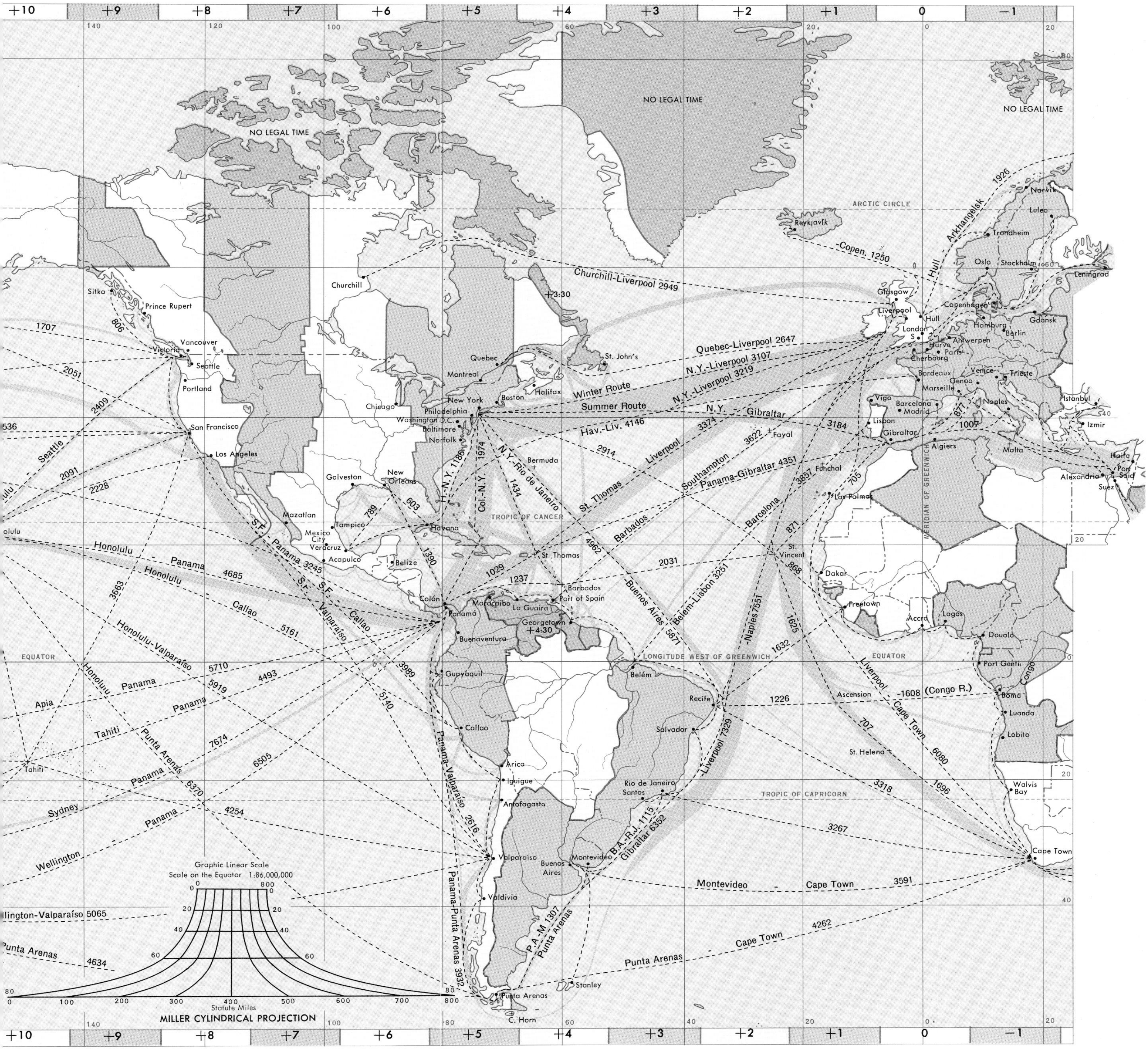

	Berlin	Buenos Aires	Calcutta	Chicago	Honolulu	London	Madrid	Mexico City	Moscow	New York	Paris	San Francisco	Shanghai	Sydney	Tokyo	Washington D.C.
Chicago	3825	4863	6935		3688	3432	3641	1454	4331	620	3591	1615	6129	8047	5477	514
London	499	6012	4305	3432	6279		686	4815	1346	3006	185	4653	4288	9194	5160	3185
Moscow	866	7278	2995	4331	6112	1346	1825	5812		4051	1339	5099	3680	7838	4041	4243
New York	3442	4603	6883	620	4309	3006	3094	1812	4051		3147	2234	6393	8685	5853	178
Paris	471	5976	4248	3591	6460	185	567	4958	1339	3147		4728	4998	9168	5243	3326
San Francisco	4916	5626	6786	1615	2079	4653	5044	1638	5099	2234	4728		5329	6465	4459	2122
Shanghai	4532	10599	1835	6129	4288	4962	5540	6986	3680	6393	4998	5329		4249	951	6467
Tokyo	4812	9906	2769	5477	3346	5160	5818	6113	4041	5853	5243	4459	951	4223		5882

INTERNATIONAL AIR DISTANCES

The graph above shows the air distances between eight major cities of the world *(vertical list, left)* and the other cities listed horizontally at the top of the graph. To use the graph to find the distance between New York and Paris, for example, follow the horizontal line of figures *(yellow column)* from New York until it meets the vertical line from Paris. All air distances listed on the graph are given in nautical miles; an international nautical mile is 6,076 feet.

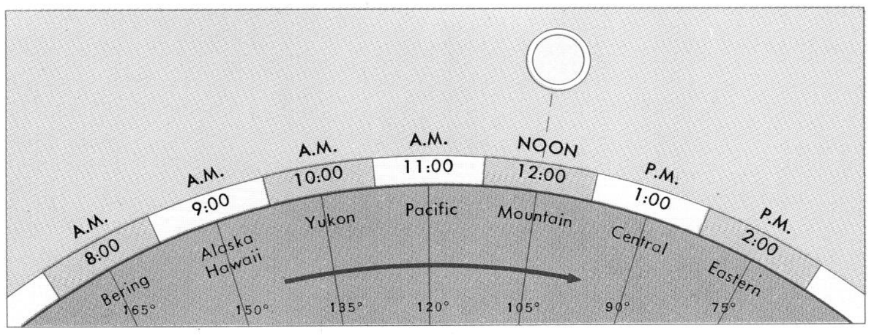

THE TIME ZONES

This drawing shows the seven U.S. standard time zones (world total: 24) with the sun at noon in the Mountain Time Zone, which puts it at longitude 105° W. As the earth turns *(arrow)*, 15° of longitude pass beneath the sun every hour. Each unit of 15° marks off one zone, which adds one hour to the time – ante meridiem (a.m.) before noon, post meridiem (p.m.) after noon.

THE WORLD'S LANGUAGES AND RELIGIONS

Religion, language and the ability to read and write are cultural forces that have historically operated to unite men—or divide them.

There are more than a dozen major religions and uncounted minor ones. As shown on the map below, Christianity predominates in North and South America. Approximately 74 million Protestants and 105 million Roman Catholics live in North America. Roman Catholicism is the chief religion in South America, which has 127 million Catholics and 2.5 million Protestants. Europe and parts of Australia and Southern Africa are also predominantly Christian.

Throughout the world there are 12 million Jews. Almost two million now live in Israel. Islam has some 430 million believers, most of them in Africa and western and southwest Asia. Hinduism has some 330 million adherents, most of them in India. Buddhism, Taoism, Confucianism and Shinto, together with fusions of parts of these faiths, are the principal religions of eastern Asia.

Man has evolved more than 2,790 languages. Included on the language map *(opposite page, bottom)* are the areas where nine major language families *(key outlined in black)* prevail. Because the Indo-European language family is so widespread, it has been divided into five groups, as shown in the key. English has a greater global distribution than any other current language; it is spoken by some 250 million people and belongs to the Germanic group. A non-Indo-European tongue, Chinese (Sino-Tibetan), in various dialects, outranks English in the total number of speakers—600 million. Third in rank is Hindi-Urdu (Indic), spoken by 200 million people. Russian (Slavic) has 150 million speakers. Spanish (Romance) is fifth, with 120 million.

Almost half the world's adult population cannot read and write. Illiterate adults in the world today are estimated at 700 million, or some 44 per cent of the total world population over 15 years old. In the U.S., Canada, most of Europe, the Soviet Union, Australia and New Zealand, more than 90 per cent of the population is literate. The level of literacy is much lower in most of South America and in China; it is lowest in southern Asia and large areas of Africa. The literacy map *(opposite page)* does not attempt to indicate areas of literacy within each country, but is calculated on the basis of the entire population.

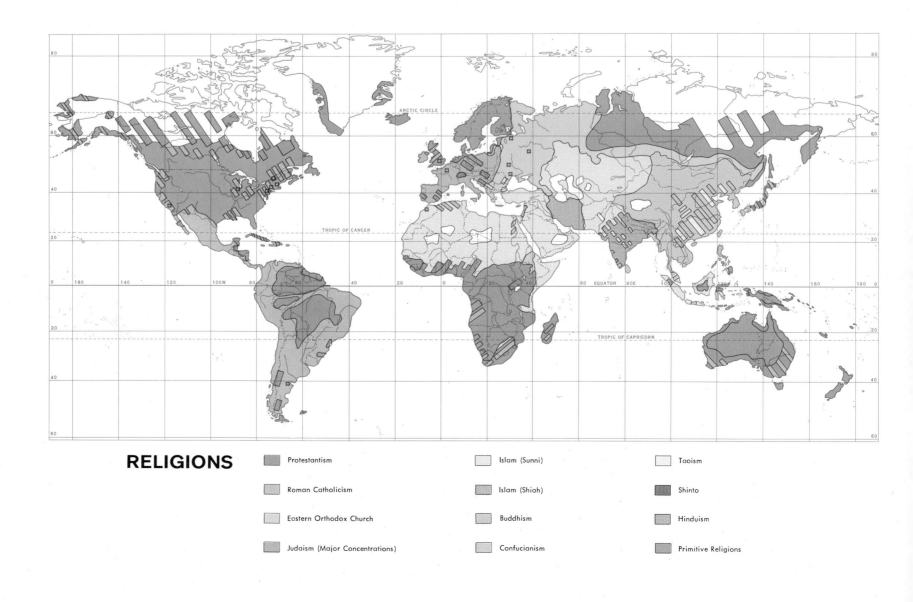

RELIGIONS

- Protestantism
- Roman Catholicism
- Eastern Orthodox Church
- Judaism (Major Concentrations)
- Islam (Sunni)
- Islam (Shiah)
- Buddhism
- Confucianism
- Taoism
- Shinto
- Hinduism
- Primitive Religions

THE WORLD'S LANGUAGES AND RELIGIONS

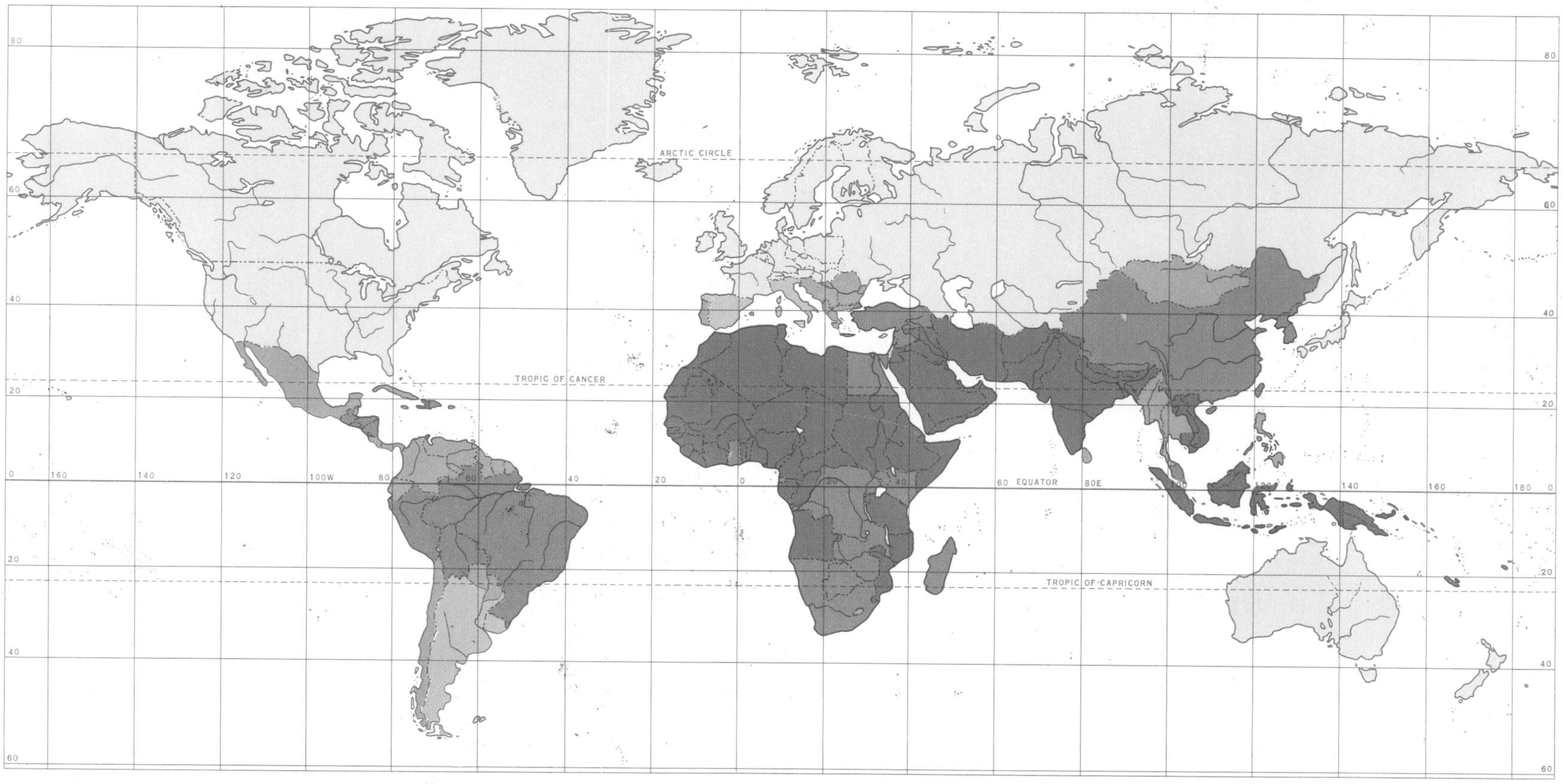

LITERACY

- 90%-100%
- 80%-90%
- 50%-80%
- 20%-50%
- 0-20%

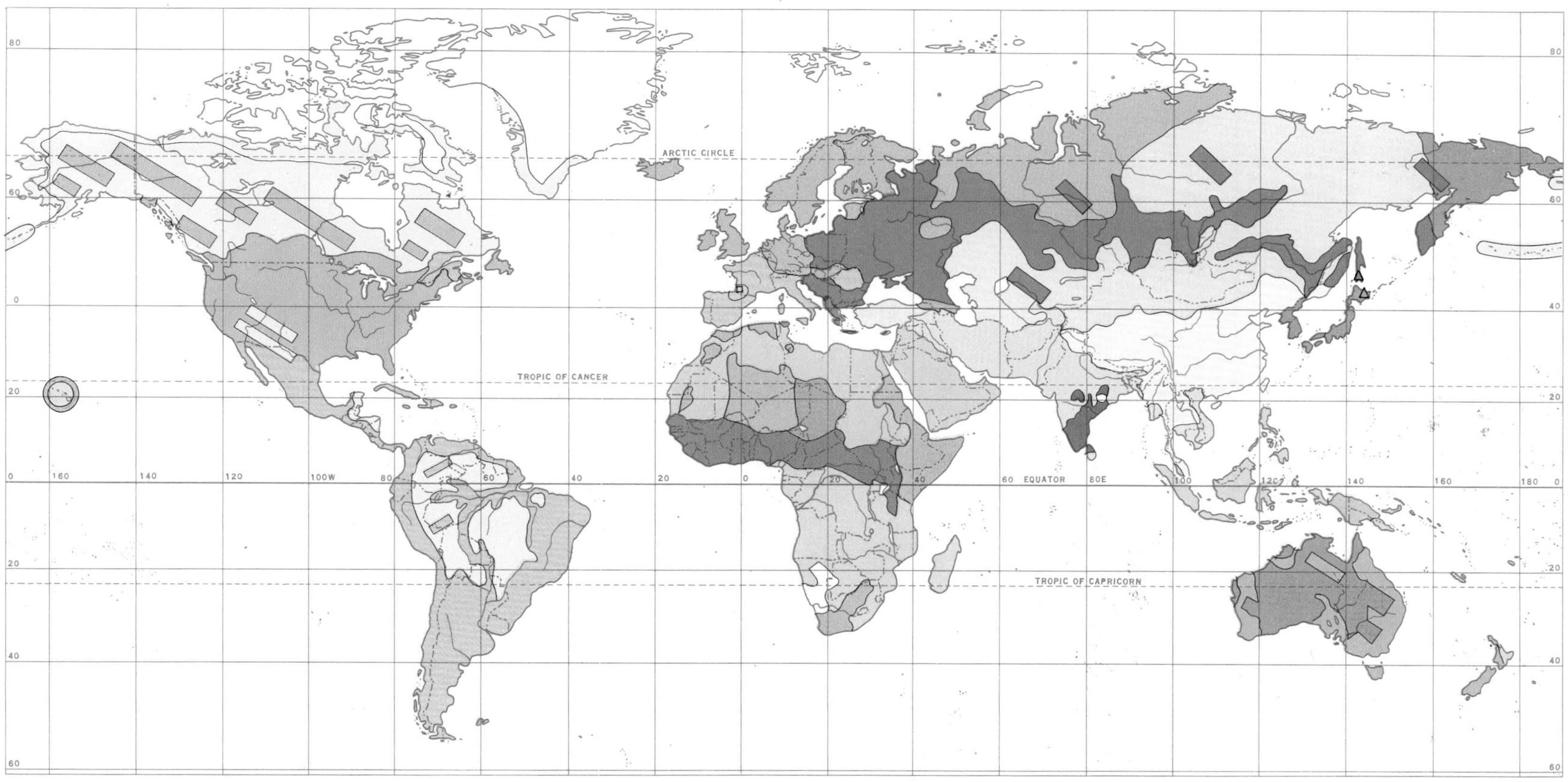

LANGUAGES

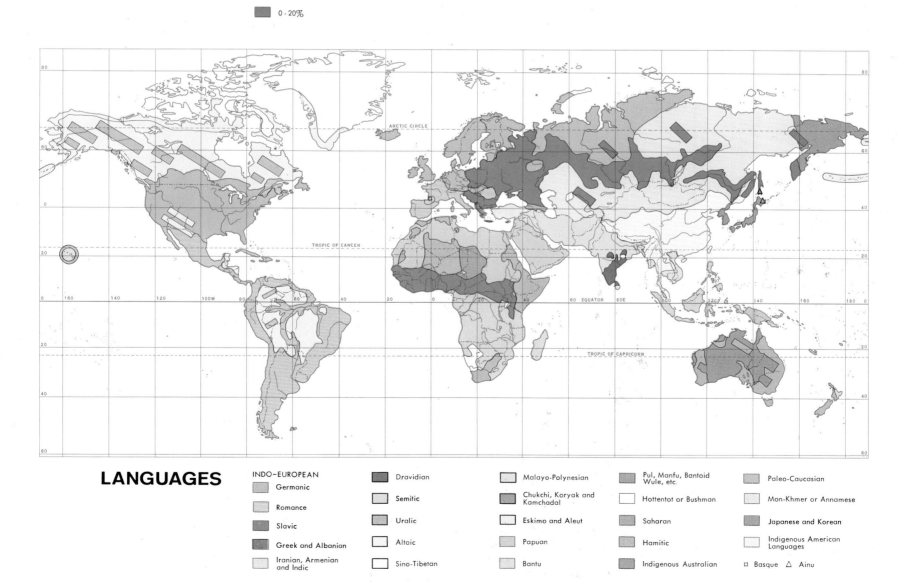

INDO-EUROPEAN
- Germanic
- Romance
- Slavic
- Greek and Albanian
- Iranian, Armenian and Indic

- Dravidian
- Semitic
- Uralic
- Altaic
- Sino-Tibetan
- Malayo-Polynesian
- Chukchi, Koryak and Kamchadal
- Eskimo and Aleut
- Papuan
- Bantu
- Pul, Manfu, Bantoid Wule, etc.
- Hottentot or Bushman
- Saharan
- Hamitic
- Indigenous Australian
- Paleo-Caucasian
- Mon-Khmer or Annamese
- Japanese and Korean
- Indigenous American Languages
- □ Basque △ Ainu

THE ARCTIC OCEAN'S BASIN is shown above as it would look without its thick covering of sea and ice. Thus exposed, the Arctic is seen to be a region of depressions *(red)* and ridges *(gray)* joining the continental shelves of Asia and North America. The deepest area is 14,700 feet below sea level.

THE ARCTIC

A challenge to adventurous men from the time of the early Vikings, the Arctic has been conquered often since Norway's Roald Amundsen completed his journey through the long-sought Northwest Passage in 1905 and U.S. Admiral Robert Peary reached the Pole itself in 1909. Today, although its resources—including gold, oil and coal—remain largely untapped, the Arctic has become a busy highroad for intercontinental jet airliners and an underwater corridor for U.S. nuclear submarines exploring the depths of the Northwest Passage. The DEW (Distant Early Warning) Line of radar stations, running 3,000 miles eastward across the Arctic from Cape Lisburne, Alaska, to Baffin Island in Canada, serves as a North American outpost.

The Arctic—all that region above the Arctic Circle, or 66°30'N.—is locked in frigidity most of the year. Drifting pack ice, averaging 10 feet in thickness, covers much of the 5,541,000 square miles of the Arctic Sea that surround the perpetually frozen Pole. Farther south, the winter temperatures, dropping to -50° F. and lower, congeal the land masses—the high, glacial peaks of Greenland, and the low, rolling tundra of Norway, Canada, Alaska and the U.S.S.R. During a short summer, the bleak land brightens with grass and flowering plants. Fish and animal life, ranging from plankton to polar bears, make it possible for the area to sustain inhabitants, mostly reindeer herdsmen in Europe and Asia, and Eskimos along the North American coasts. Unlike Antarctica, the Arctic has a few evergreen forests with trees that sometimes grow as high as 100 feet. These are found in Canada's river valleys and in Siberia.

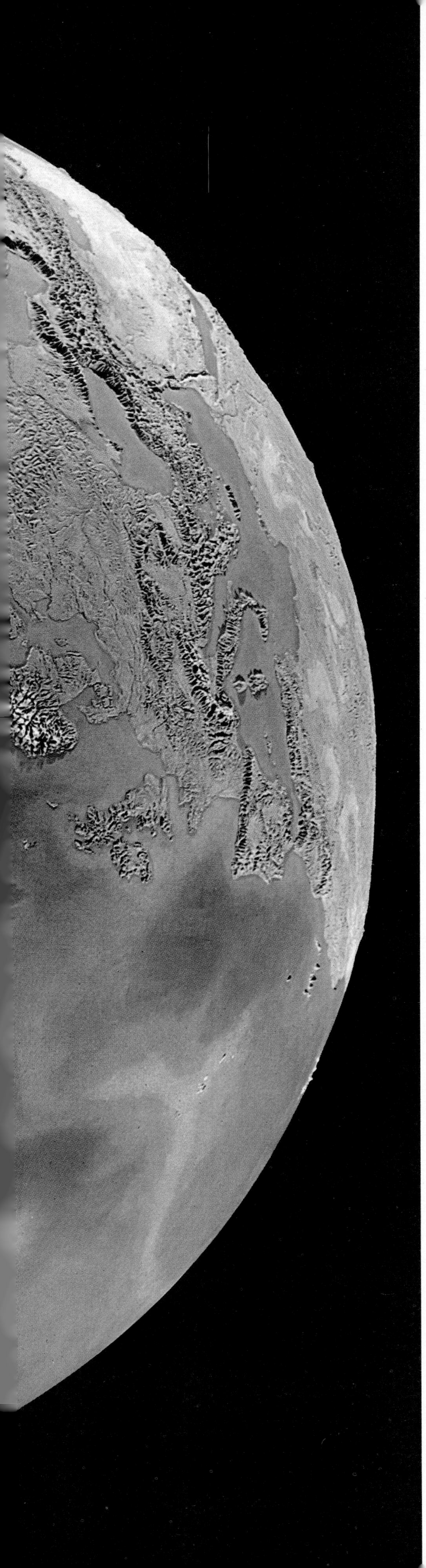

"THE TOP OF THE WORLD" is a large, almost landlocked sea centered on the perpetually frozen North Pole. At right center, the island mass of Greenland can be seen. Asian Siberia *(upper left)* is separated from Alaska *(lower left)* only by the narrow waters of Bering Strait.

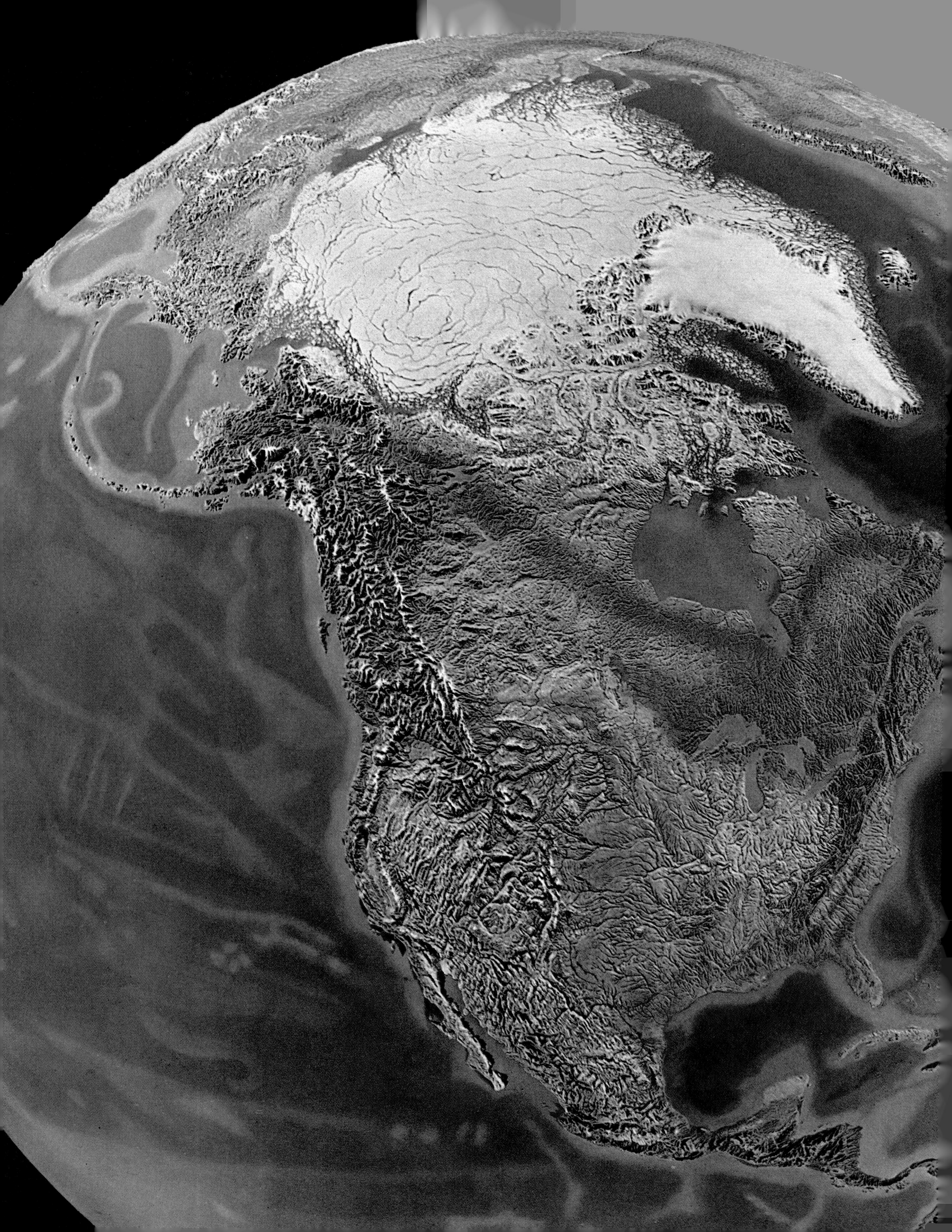

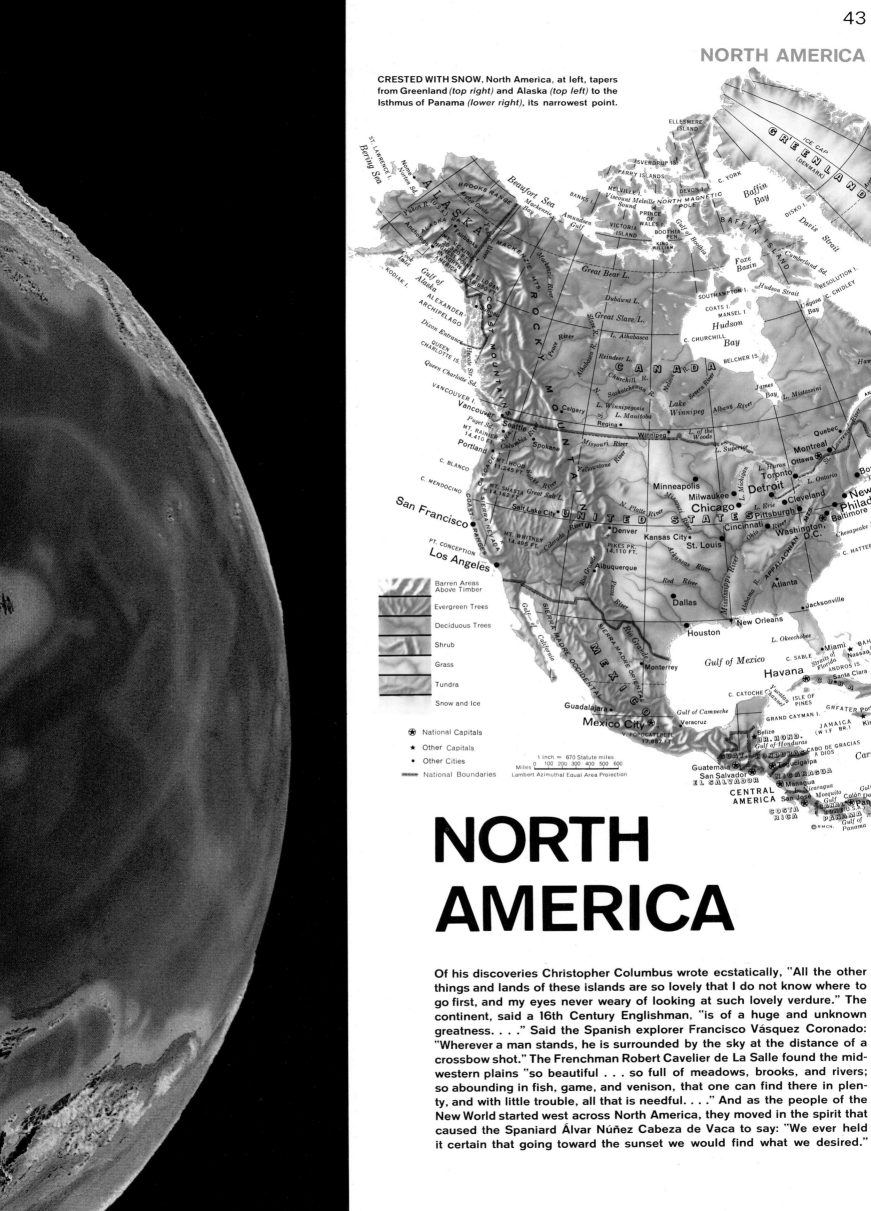

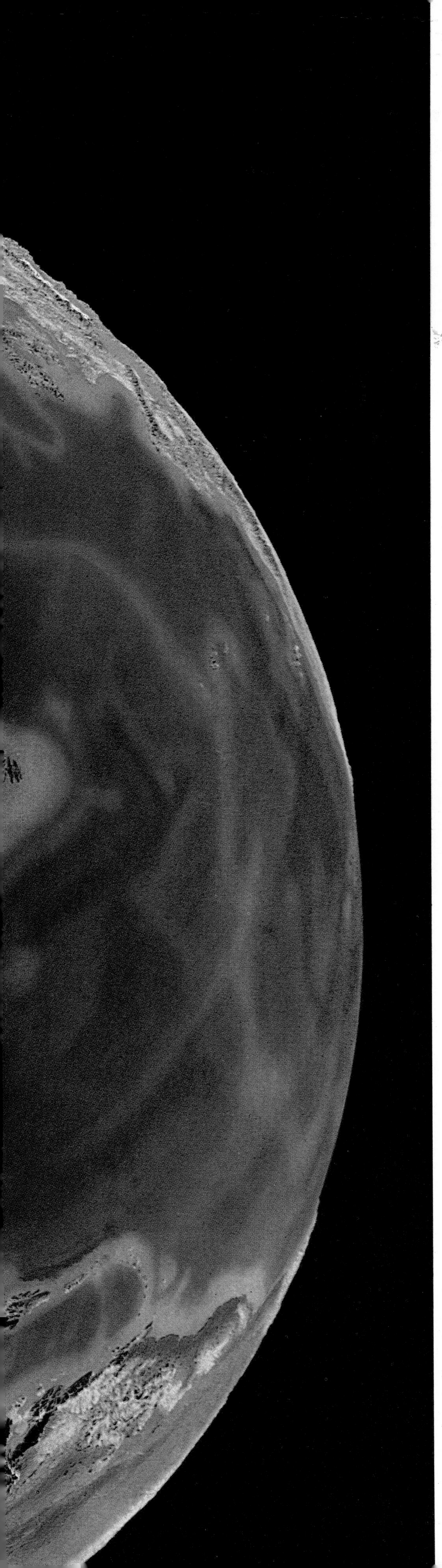

CRESTED WITH SNOW, North America, at left, tapers from Greenland *(top right)* and Alaska *(top left)* to the Isthmus of Panama *(lower right)*, its narrowest point.

NORTH AMERICA

Of his discoveries Christopher Columbus wrote ecstatically, "All the other things and lands of these islands are so lovely that I do not know where to go first, and my eyes never weary of looking at such lovely verdure." The continent, said a 16th Century Englishman, "is of a huge and unknown greatness. . . ." Said the Spanish explorer Francisco Vásquez Coronado: "Wherever a man stands, he is surrounded by the sky at the distance of a crossbow shot." The Frenchman Robert Cavelier de La Salle found the mid-western plains "so beautiful . . . so full of meadows, brooks, and rivers; so abounding in fish, game, and venison, that one can find there in plenty, and with little trouble, all that is needful. . . ." And as the people of the New World started west across North America, they moved in the spirit that caused the Spaniard Álvar Núñez Cabeza de Vaca to say: "We ever held it certain that going toward the sunset we would find what we desired."

NORTH AMERICA: "It had been there," the American biographer and historian Harold Lamb has written, "since the oceans themselves rose upon the earth." Over hundreds of millions of years the continent of North America was formed through volcanic explosion and the restless, often violent movement of the earth's crust. Its face was covered and uncovered, then recovered by ancient seas; it was altered by the erosion of ice, wind and water. Most prominent of the features formed at an early stage were the Canadian Shield, a great rockbound mass framing the northeast; the Appalachians, paralleling the eastern seaboard; the Cordilleran mountains, lining much of the west coast from Alaska to Mexico; the mountains hemming in and filling out the end of the continent as it narrows toward South America. Then the latest continental ice sheet came, grinding in the depressions for the northern lakes, diverting the flow of rivers, spreading the great central plains with rich topsoil from the north.

Afterwards, the continent waited. "Its only inhabitants," wrote the New England historian George Bancroft, "were a few scattered tribes of feeble barbarians. . . . The ax and the plowshare were unknown. The soil, which had been gathering fertility from the repose of centuries, was lavishing its strength in magnificent but useless vegetation." Then, late in the 15th Century, sails from Europe–"the Old World"–appeared in the east. The main thrust of civilization came from the commodious Atlantic coastal plain. Aided by a network of rivers, settlers broke through the densely forested Appalachians and spread west onto the prairies and plateau beyond. With the lure of gold added to their hunger for land, they rushed to the West Coast and opened the country in huge sections. To the north, development was retarded by the long northern winters that locked the rivers with ice and made overland travel difficult. To the south, progress was slowed in some places by excessive dryness, in other places by excessive rainfall and heat.

AREA: 9,435,000 sq. mi.
POPULATION: 251,054,000.
ALTITUDES: Mt. McKinley, Alaska, U.S., 20,320 ft. (highest); Death Valley, California, U.S., -282 ft. (lowest); Mt. Logan, Yukon Territory, Canada, 19,850 ft.

North America has been described as "the most successful and favored continent of historical times." The United States is the world's first industrial power, producing an endless variety of foodstuffs and goods for its highly urban and suburban population. At the current rate of use, however, several of its vital natural resources will be depleted in the not too distant future. Canada is second only to the U.S. in water power and exports one third of the world's wheat. But it is still underdeveloped and underpopulated. Mexico, only recently emerging from an economy based on partly exhausted mines and farms, is planting cotton and coffee for export on newly irrigated desert land, hoping by trade to balance out its shortage of food crops. The lands to the south have made little headway in industrializing: they still export food and raw materials and import manufactured goods.

The continent now looks to the south for new markets and it looks to the north for new resources. The U.S. state of Alaska is more than twice the size of giant Texas, but it supports only a fourth of the population of tiny Rhode Island. The thinly developed north of Canada constitutes four fifths of the Dominion's land area but accounts for less than a tenth of the population. Here, then, is the great developing future of the continent.

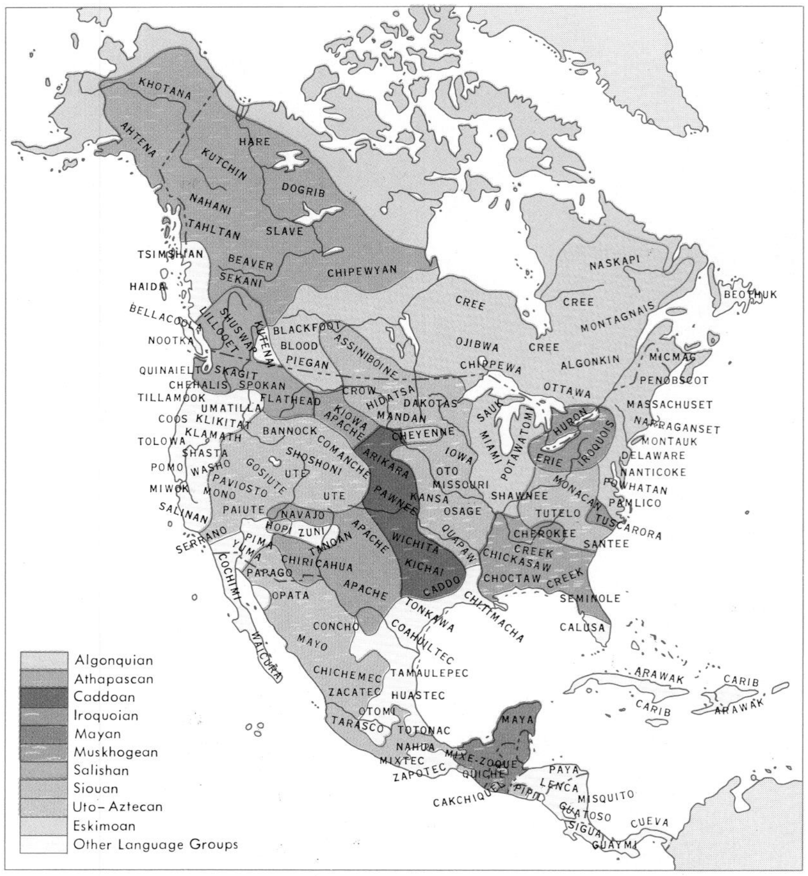

THE INDIAN TRIBES OF NORTH AMERICA

This map gives the location of the inhabitants of North America before the Europeans came and groups them (by color) according to language. Iroquoian was spoken by many tribes besides the Iroquois, an advanced political organization of six "nations" centered in what is now New York State. Algonquian-speaking tribes *(light green)* were primarily farmers, who held more land than any other group; they spread over a large part of the continent. The Siouan tribes *(light orange)* were hunters as well as farmers. The most advanced of all the North American Indian tribes were the Mayas and Aztecs of Mexico.

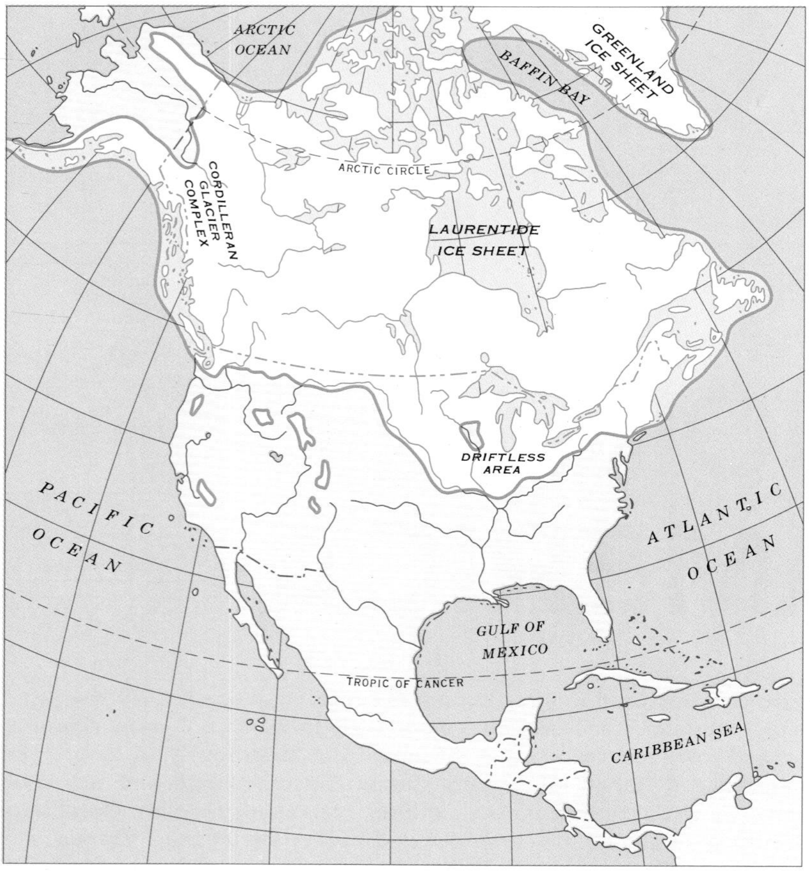

WHEN ICE CAME DOWN FROM THE NORTH

The map above shows, in white, the farthest reaches of glaciers on the North American continent during the great ice age–a period comprising several hundreds of thousands of years that came to an end about 11,000 years ago. Although the ice sheet, one to two miles thick, spread halfway down the continent and extended from ocean to ocean, it left untouched in the Midwest a "driftless area"–a section of land free of major glacial deposits. In the western U.S., glaciers formed in the Rockies and coastal ranges. Greenland's present icecap is the only large remnant of the ice age in the Northern Hemisphere.

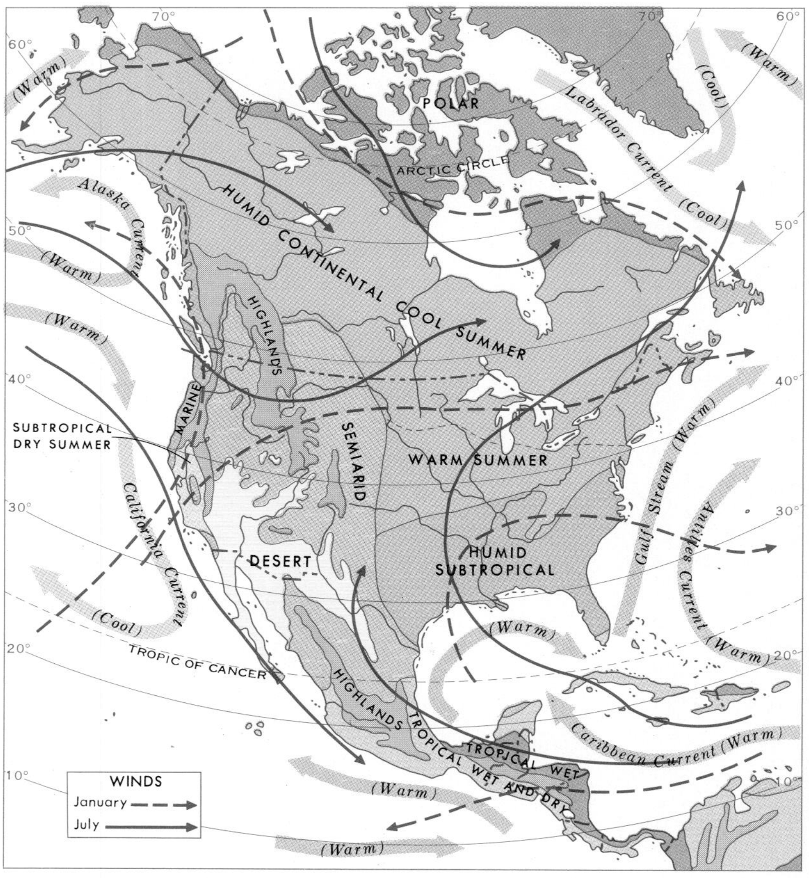

FROM POLAR TO TROPICAL CLIMATES

On the map above, each solid color represents one of North America's climate zones; ocean currents are shown in ribbons of red and blue, prevailing winds in solid lines (for summer) or broken lines (for winter). To the north the continent is subject to arctic air masses. These clash in the plains with warm air masses that come from the south. The "warm summer" section of the climate zone is the largest area of its kind on any continent. Western mountain ranges force precipitation from Pacific winds, creating a drier climate inland. One part of the west coast *(light green)* has a Mediterranean-like climate.

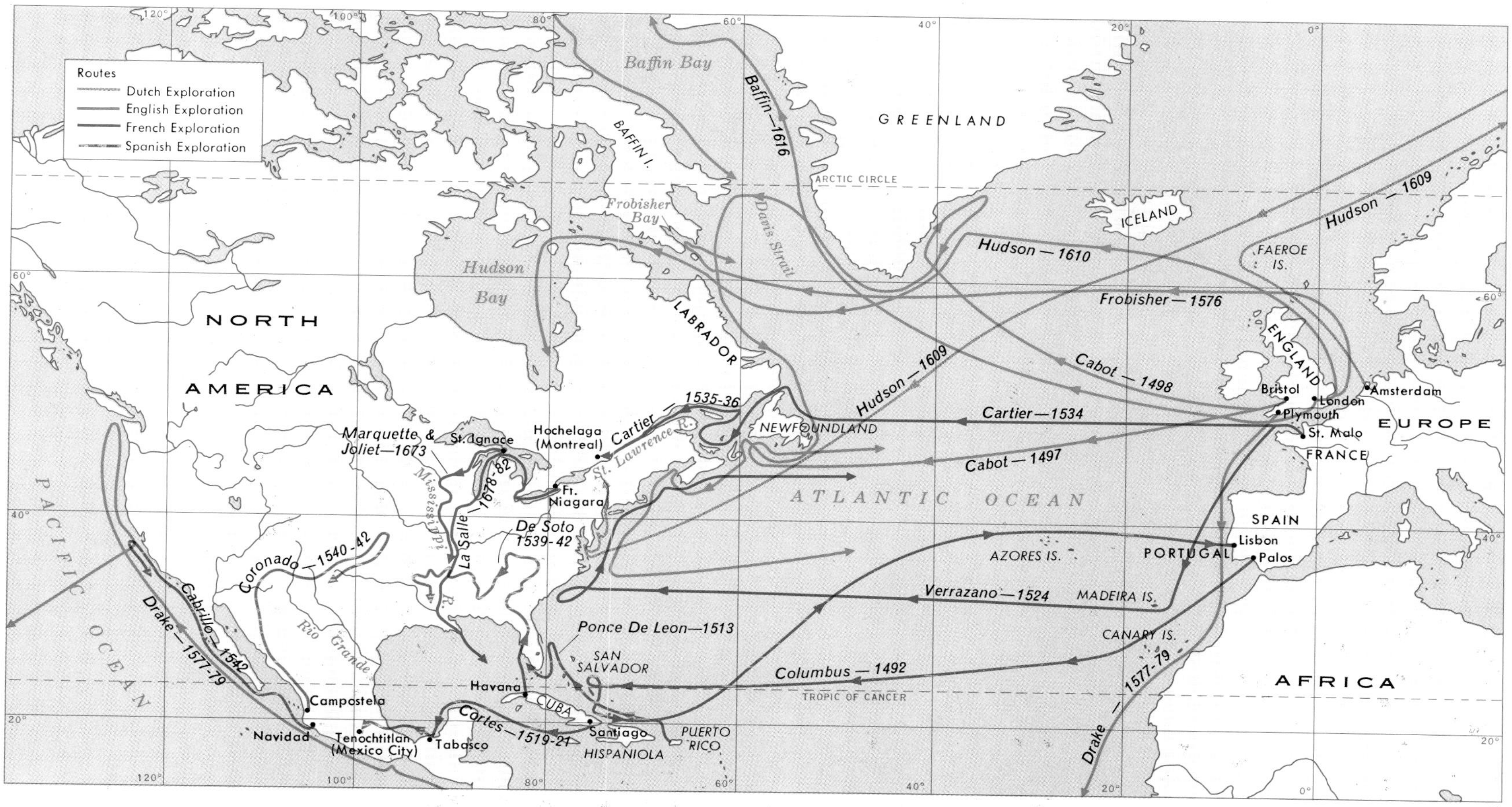

ROUTES OF EXPLORATION THAT TRACED THE SHAPE OF THE NEW WORLD

This map shows the routes and dates of major exploration by various European countries in the Northern Hemisphere of the New World. Sailing for Spain *(light red lines)*, Christopher Columbus was the first to touch North America, probably at San Salvador. England based its major territorial claims on John Cabot's first voyage in 1497 *(blue lines)*. Gold drew various conquistadors to the south: Hernando Cortes to conquests in Mexico, Hernando de Soto to the southeast, Francisco de Coronado's parties through the southwest to the Grand Canyon, Juan Cabrillo along the Pacific coast. Except for Sir Francis Drake, whose trip around the world was begun as a search for Spanish treasures in South America, the English voyagers ranged north. Three Englishmen–Sir Martin Frobisher, William Baffin and Henry Hudson–discovered large areas and bays that bear their names. Hudson, under the flag of Holland *(dark red lines)*, and Giovanni da Verrazano, under the flag of France *(gray lines)*, sailed the middle-Atlantic shores. The French staked out a riverside empire–Jacques Cartier along the St. Lawrence, Robert La Salle and Jacques Marquette along the Mississippi.

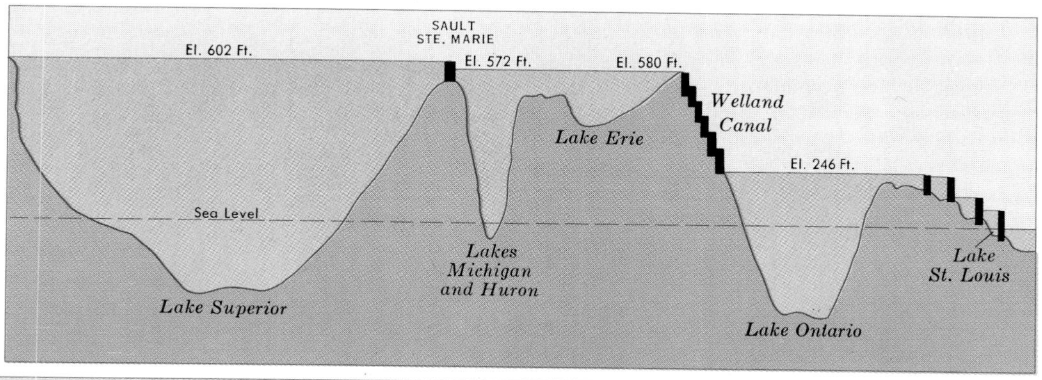

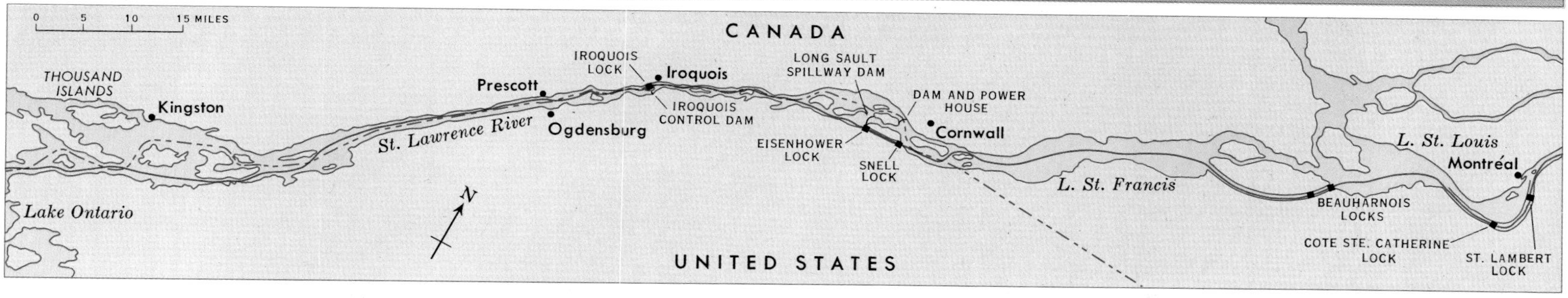

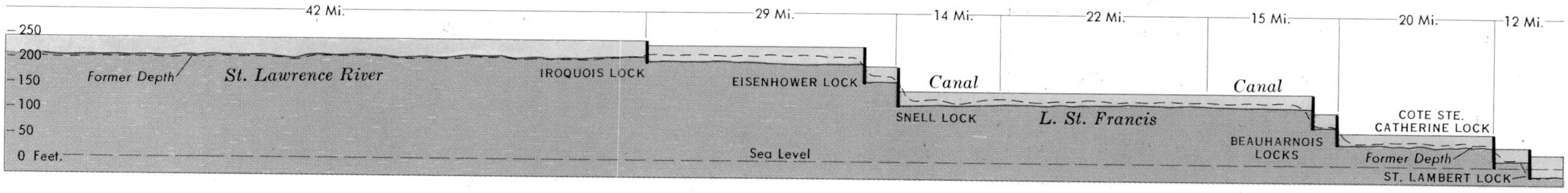

THE ST. LAWRENCE SEAWAY: NORTH AMERICA'S 'FIFTH COAST'

Shown on the map at top left is the Great Lakes-St. Lawrence area, opened to direct ocean-going traffic in 1958 by the St. Lawrence Seaway. Now, deep-sea shipping can dock at the Duluth-Superior port area in Minnesota and Wisconsin, 2,340 miles from the Atlantic coast. As the profile at top reveals, the Great Lakes are, in effect, a vast natural reservoir that drops steeply between Lakes Erie and Ontario, then lets down gradually to sea level. Harnessing the 81-foot drop in the international zone between Kingston and Cornwall *(center map)* are three newly built dams which produce 1.6 million kilowatts of electricity, shared equally by the United States and Canada. A system of seven locks and a 27-foot channel was built by the U.S. and Canada in collaboration to provide a deepwater route downstream from Iroquois Lock *(profile at bottom)*. In fulfilling its primary purpose–to provide cheaper transport for iron ore from Quebec and Labrador to the blast furnaces of the Midwest and for wheat from the Midwest to the ports of the lower St. Lawrence–the seaway has stimulated industry by bringing deep-sea shipping to the heart of the continent.

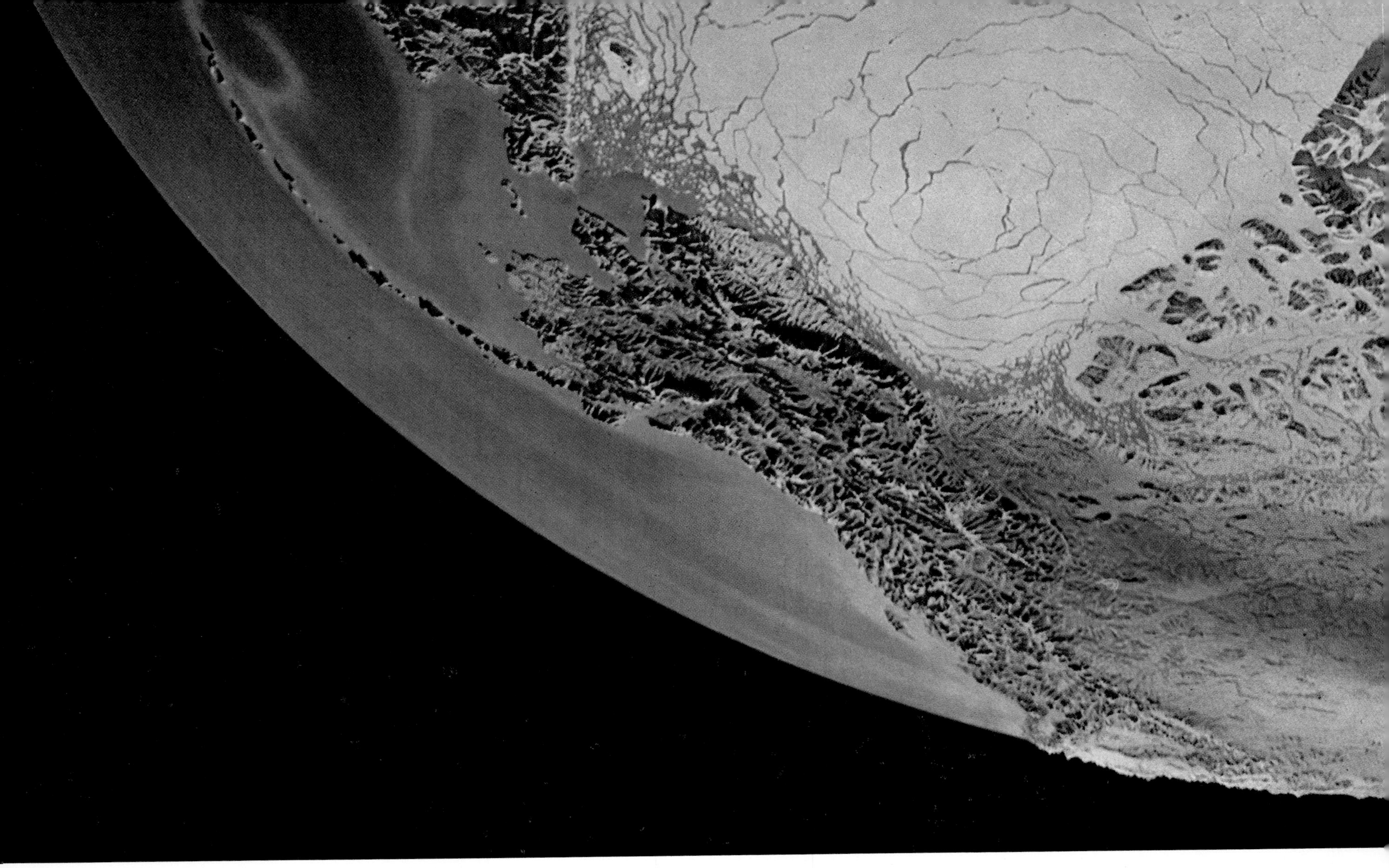

Barren Areas Above Timber
Evergreen Trees
Trees
Grass
Tundra
National Capitals
Provincial Capitals
Cities
Railroads
1 inch = 410 Statute Miles
Miles 0 50 100 150 200 250 300
Lambert Conformal Conic Projection
LANDS END
ELLESMERE ISLAND
Smith Sound
AXEL HEIBERG I.
BORDEN I.
ELLEF RINGNES
AMUND RINGNES
PRINCE PATRICK I.
CORNWALL I.
Craig Harbour
Jones Sound
PARRY ISLANDS
MELVILLE ISLAND
BATHURST I.
DEVON I.
Baffin Bay
C. WROTTESLEY
C. PRINCE ALBERT
M'Clure Str.
BANKS I.
CORNWALLIS I.
Viscount Melville Sound
Lancaster Sd.
BYLOT
NORTH MAGNETIC POLE
SOMERSET I.
Arctic Bay
C. ASTON
C. HENRY KATER
Davis Strait
Mackenzie Bay
Tuktoyaktuk
Amundsen Gulf
Ft. Collinson
VICTORIA ISLAND
PRINCE OF WALES I.
Prince Regent Inlet
BRODEUR PEN.
BAFFIN
PENNY HIGHLAND
C. WALSINGHAM
BOOTHIA PEN.
Gulf of Boothia
KING WILLIAM I.
Queen Maud Gulf
Foxe Basin
PRINCE CHARLES I.
Cumberland Sd.
ISLAND
L. Franklin
MELVILLE PEN.
Dawson
Arctic Circle
Coppermine
Great Bear L.
NORTHWEST TERRITORIES
Bathurst Inlet
Repulse Bay
Foxe Channel
FOXE PEN.
HALL PEN.
RESOLUTION I.
YUKON
MT. EDUNI 7,100 FT.
MT. SIR JAMES MC BRIEN 9,000 FT.
DOME PK. 9,000 FT.
MT. LOGAN 19,850 FT.
Whitehorse
ROCKY MOUNTAINS
L. de Gras
MacKay L.
Clinton Colden L.
Baker L.
SOUTHAMPTON ISLAND
Hudson Str.
C. CHIDLEY
Skagway
MT. FAIRWEATHER 15,300 FT.
Juneau
ADMIRALTY I.
Yellowknife
Great Slave Lake
Dubawnt L.
Chesterfield Inlet
Fisher Str.
COATS I.
MANSEL I.
Kovik
UNGAVA PENINSULA
Ungava Bay
Hebron
NEWFOUNDLAND
LABRADOR
ALEXANDER ARCHIPELAGO
Ft. Nelson
Nonacho L.
Kasba L.
Hudson Bay
Ft. Chimo
George R.
Hopedale
COAST MTS.
CARIBOU MTS.
Uranium City
Lake Athabasca
C. CHURCHILL
Churchill
L. Minto
Schefferville (Knob Lake)
HIGHLAND
Goose Bay
Str. of Belle Isle
Gander
Prince Rupert
QUEEN CHARLOTTE IS.
Peace River
BIRCH MTS.
Reindeer L.
York Factory
Clearwater L.
Hamilton
St. Johns
C. RACE
NEWFOUNDLAND
Pacific Ocean
Hecate Strait
BRITISH COLUMBIA
ALBERTA
SASKATCHEWAN
MANITOBA
Southern Indian L.
Ft. Severn
BELCHER IS.
James Bay
Ft. George
Ft. George R.
Sept Iles (Seven Islands)
ANTICOSTI I.
MT. WADDINGTON 13,260 FT.
Churchill R.
Nelson R.
AKIMISKI I.
QUEBEC
Gulf of St. Lawrence
PR. EDWARD ISLAND
BRETON ISLAND
Edmonton
Flin Flon
Island L.
ONTARIO
Broadback R.
L. Mistassini
Charlottetown
NOVA SCOTIA
VANCOUVER I.
Vancouver
Victoria
Kamloops
Calgary
Lethbridge
Saskatoon
L. Winnipegosis
Lake Winnipeg
Moosonee
Gouin Res.
Chicoutimi
Chatham
NEW BRUNSWICK
Fredericton
Halifax
Regina
Dauphin
Winnipeg
L. Manitoba
L. Seul
L. Nipigon
Timmins
Quebec
Trois-Rivières
Saint John
Bay of Fundy
C. SABLE
Lake of the Woods
Kenora
Ft. William
Lake Superior
Sault Ste. Marie
Montréal
OTTAWA
Toronto
Lake Huron
L. Ontario
L. Erie
©RMCN.

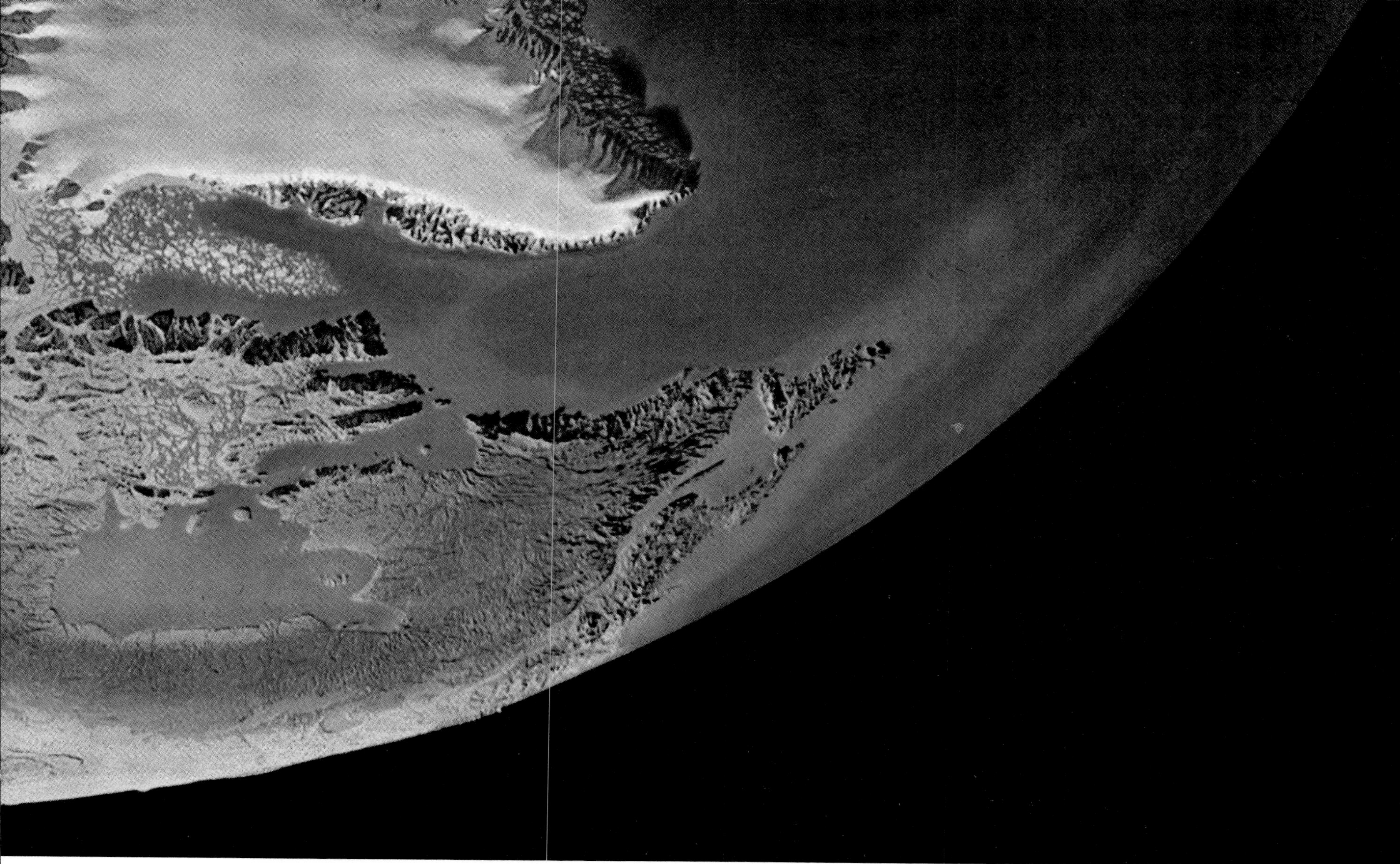

CANADA'S DOMINION covers 3.8 million square miles. It extends from the ice-covered "top of the world" to the Great Lakes *(bottom center)*, from Newfoundland and the other Atlantic provinces *(lower right)* to British Columbia on the Pacific *(lower left)*. This global view also shows a part of the continental U.S., including Alaska and the Aleutian Islands, as well as a part of the U.S.S.R.'s Siberia *(top left)* and Denmark's Greenland *(top right)*.

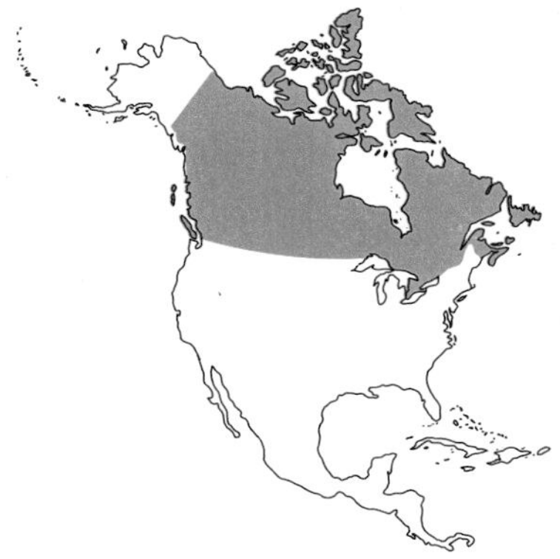

CANADA

The Vikings who strayed from their Greenland fishing grounds and happened upon the barren coast of Labrador about 1000 A.D. furnished man's first recorded impression of the region now called Canada. "Land of Stones," they named it, and hurriedly departed. Some 500 years later, other Europeans sailed toward the Arctic looking for a Northwest Passage to the Orient. Like the Vikings, they were repelled by the frozen barrens. "This was the land," wrote the French explorer Jacques Cartier on sighting the treeless coast of Quebec in 1534, "that God allotted to Cain." But explorers who were not deterred by their first sightings stayed to find another Canada. Cartier, for example, went on to Prince Edward Island and later declared he had discovered "the fairest land that could possibly be seen, full of goodly meadows and trees."

For a long time, however, the land remained fair only in what it promised. As recently as a hundred years ago an eminent British historian could still predict that, with a climate fit only "for the reindeer, the elk and the musk ox," seven eighths of Canada must be "doomed to eternal sterility." The immensity of the country—second only to the Soviet Union—and the harshness of climate and terrain kept much of Canada empty. A vast sheet of rock, the Canadian Shield, covered half of the total area. Distance made the remote central prairies inaccessible for three centuries, and massive mountain barriers limited the penetration of the west from the sea. Gradually the land yielded. The shield of rock that early settlers had cursed for its infertility turned out to be a treasure of mineral wealth. The Plains provinces became one of the great wheat-producing regions of the world as soon as railroads provided a way of getting the grain to market. And the vast stores of lead, zinc, copper and other metals that lay in British Columbia waited only for modern techniques to get them out of the mountains.

Part of the Pacific coast draws a mild climate from the warm ocean current which bathes its shores, but most of Canada is refrigerated during long winters by cold winds that blow in from the Arctic Ocean. However, Canadian farmers have developed fast-ripening crops to take advantage of the short, sunny growing season. The rich farms of the plains, together with a burgeoning industrial economy, combine to make the Dominion one of the most productive nations on earth.

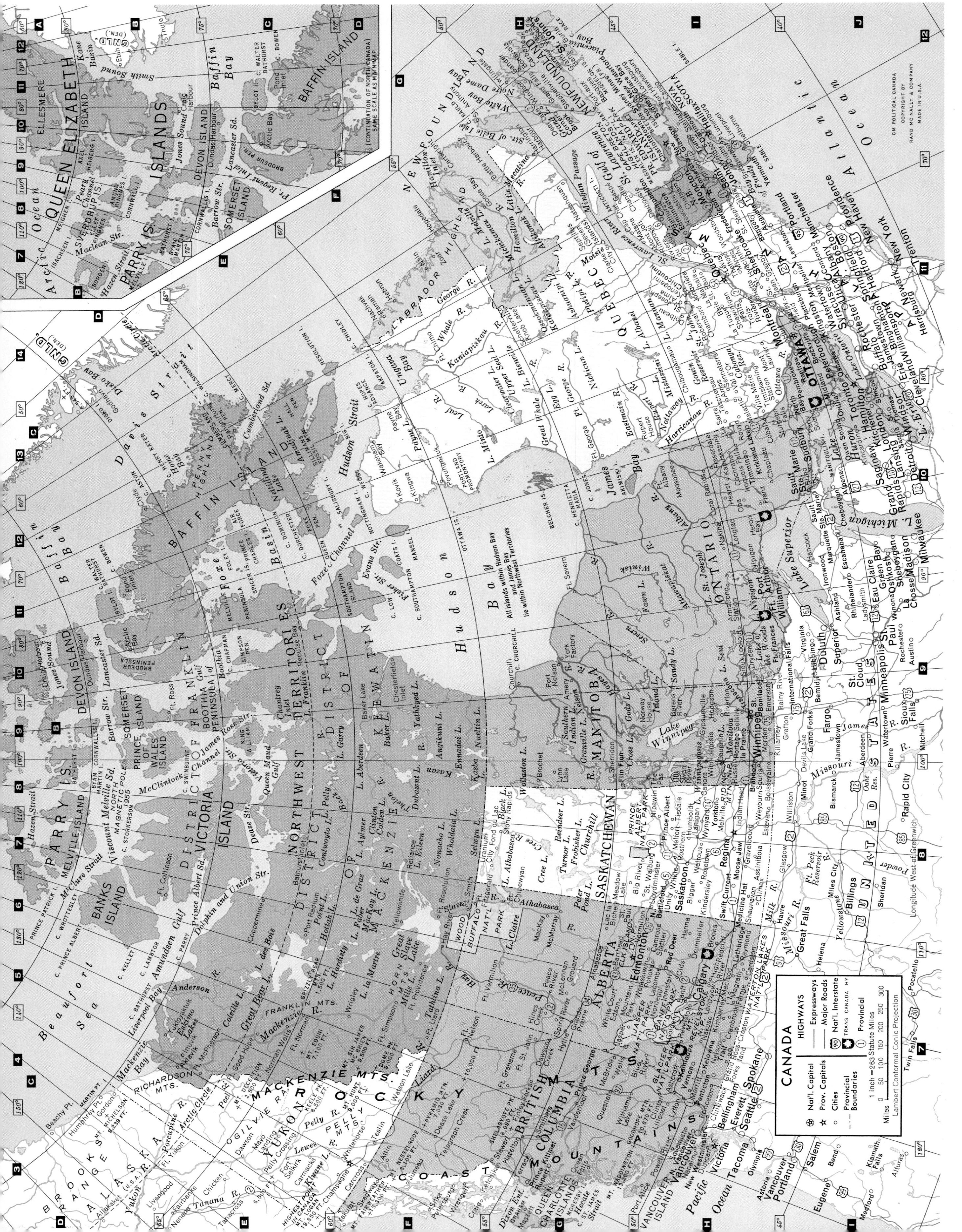
CANADA
HIGHWAYS
Nat'l. Capital
Prov. Capitals
Cities
Provincial Boundaries
Expressways
Major Roads
Nat'l. Interstate
TRANS CANADA HY
Provincial
1 inch = 263 Statute Miles
Miles 0 50 100 150 200 250 300
Lambert Conformal Conic Projection
Longitude West of Greenwich
CM POLITICAL CANADA
COPYRIGHT BY RAND McNALLY & COMPANY
MADE IN U.S.A.
(CONTINUATION OF NORTH CANADA)
SAME SCALE AS MAIN MAP
All islands within Hudson Bay and James Bay lie within Northwest Territories
QUEEN ELIZABETH ISLANDS
BAFFIN ISLAND
NORTHWEST TERRITORIES
DISTRICT OF FRANKLIN
DISTRICT OF KEEWATIN
DISTRICT OF MACKENZIE
YUKON
ALASKA
BRITISH COLUMBIA
ALBERTA
SASKATCHEWAN
MANITOBA
ONTARIO
QUEBEC
NEWFOUNDLAND
LABRADOR
NOVA SCOTIA
UNITED STATES
Hudson Bay
James Bay
Beaufort Sea
Baffin Bay
Davis Strait
Hudson Strait
Pacific Ocean
Atlantic Ocean
Gulf of St. Lawrence
OTTAWA
Edmonton
Calgary
Regina
Winnipeg
Toronto
Montreal
Quebec
Vancouver
Victoria
St. John's
Halifax
ROCKY MTS.
MACKENZIE MTS.

CANADA: At the beginning of the 1900s, the Canadian prime minister assayed the future of his country. "The new century," said Sir Wilfrid Laurier, "is Canada's."

Sir Wilfrid was not making a promise; he was issuing a challenge. How well the country has met that challenge is evident in the record at mid-century. Canada's population has more than tripled, from 5 million in 1901 to 17 million in 1960. In about the same span the value of its mineral production soared from $65 million to $2 billion. Total manufactured products went from $215 million to $10 billion.

At the start of the century the country had not touched its natural resources other than to scrape at some of its mineral wealth. Its waterfalls turned few turbines. Its forests supplied no pulp for paper mills. Today, Canada generates more hydroelectric power than any other nation except the U.S., and it produces enough paper to supply almost every other page of all the newspapers in the world. But the country has still hardly made a dent in its basic resources *(graph, below)*.

The principal agent in Canada's advance in the 20th Century was the railroad. Before the first transcontinental line was completed in 1886, the country was a loose collection of regions rather than a unified nation. The mid-continental plains lay empty, a weakening influence on the confederation that four of the provinces had established in 1867. For much of Canada the new capital at Ottawa was harder to get to than London. On the Pacific coast British Columbia might as well have been part of another country—and some Canadians talked of joining up with the United States. The completion of the Canadian Pacific Railway began to change all this. The empty plains became wheat farms, drawing in homesteaders and sending out grain. Canada became a seller of grain to the world. It built merchant ships and laid the foundations for factories.

Sir Wilfrid had predicted that the country would "grow up to its railroads." To make sure of the growth, the Canadian government advertised throughout Europe and the U.S. The message was that free land and new opportunity awaited immigrants in the land of the north. Imperial Germany entered a complaint. "The attempt to lure our fellow countrymen to this desolate, sub-arctic region," it said, "is to be denounced as criminal." But the Germans came, and founded New Prussia in Saskatchewan. Russians came, too, and Ukranians, Poles, Austrians. Between 1897 and 1914 three million people immigrated to Canada, and civilization moved across the continent.

AREA:	3,851,809 sq. mi.
POPULATION:	17,678,000.
	Largest city: Montreal, Quebec.
	Capital: Ottawa, Ontario.
GROSS NATIONAL	PRODUCT: $1,903 per capita.
HIGHEST POINT:	Mt. Logan, Yukon Territory, 19,850 ft.

Canada is now both an industrial power and an underdeveloped country. It is true that the land, as the official Canadian yearbook puts it, "imposes its own burdens and limitations." Immense areas of mountains, rocky plateaus, tundra and arctic wastes probably will never be settled. But many of these regions, particularly the northern territories *(diagram, below right)*, are treasure houses of mineral wealth, the lure of which is stronger than natural "burdens and limitations." In 1896 prospectors were drawn to the Yukon Territory, north of British Columbia, by the discovery of gold. Few stayed after the boom ended, and the total population of the Yukon and its neighbor, the Northwest Territories, is today only 34,000, including 6,000 Indians and 9,000 Eskimos. Though the two regions still produce more than $10 million worth of gold a year, other minerals are now more important. Silver, copper, nickel and lead are found throughout the territories. The ore from which the first atomic bomb was made came from Port Radium in the Mackenzie District. Fur pelts worth $850,000 are taken in the regions each year, and a $1.2 million fishing industry has been developed in Great Slave Lake.

Tremendous distances and the difficulties of mining in the Arctic have hampered mineral development in the Northwest Territories, but the tools and technology of the atomic age may make it easier to exploit these resources. Following their "polar star of destiny" toward the top of the world, Canadians can be certain, at least, of plenty of room in which to grow.

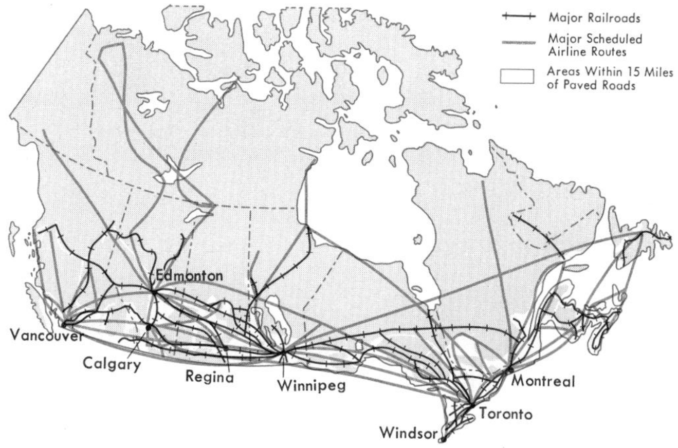
Major Railroads
Major Scheduled Airline Routes
Areas Within 15 Miles of Paved Roads
Vancouver
Calgary
Edmonton
Regina
Winnipeg
Montreal
Toronto
Windsor

TRANSPORTATION LINES

At left are shown the arteries of Canada's land and air transportation. The railroads, now totaling 59,319 miles in length, were the most important unifying agent of the sprawling nation. The first transcontinental line opened the way to the plains and carried the wheat out to market. Railroads also laid foundations for Canada's industrial growth.

The automobile era supplemented the rails with 401,887 miles of highways and rural roads. As the light yellow areas on the map show, virtually every settled part of Canada today is within at least 15 miles of a paved road.

Six domestic airlines have shrunk Canada's immense distances and have for the first time provided easy access to the increasingly important northern territories.

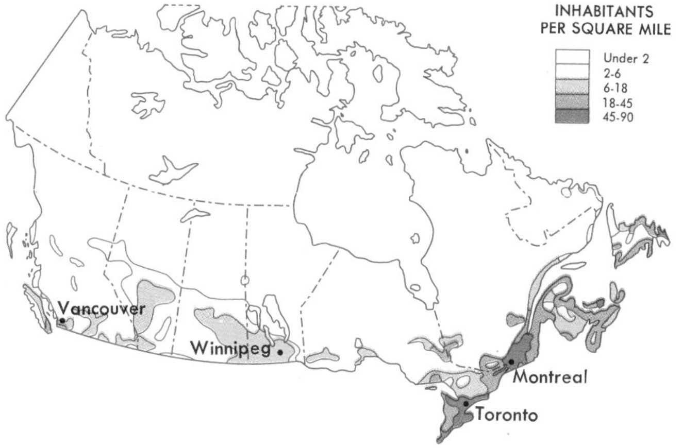
INHABITANTS PER SQUARE MILE
Under 2
2-6
6-18
18-45
45-90
Vancouver
Winnipeg
Montreal
Toronto

POPULATION ZONES

The bulk of Canada's population, as indicated in the map at left, lives in several intensely concentrated clusters along the country's southern border and on strips of coastline where the climate is moderated by the oceans. Most Canadians live within 200 miles of the U.S.

The lightly settled area extending westward from Winnipeg denotes the wheat belt, where fertile soil and climatic conditions make farming highly profitable. The sparsely settled area around Hudson Bay marks the non-arable soil of the Canadian Shield. Made up of heavily forested land in the south and scrubby forest and tundra in the north, the vast emptiness of the Shield and of the rest of the northern territories gives Canada an average population of only 4.5 people per square mile.

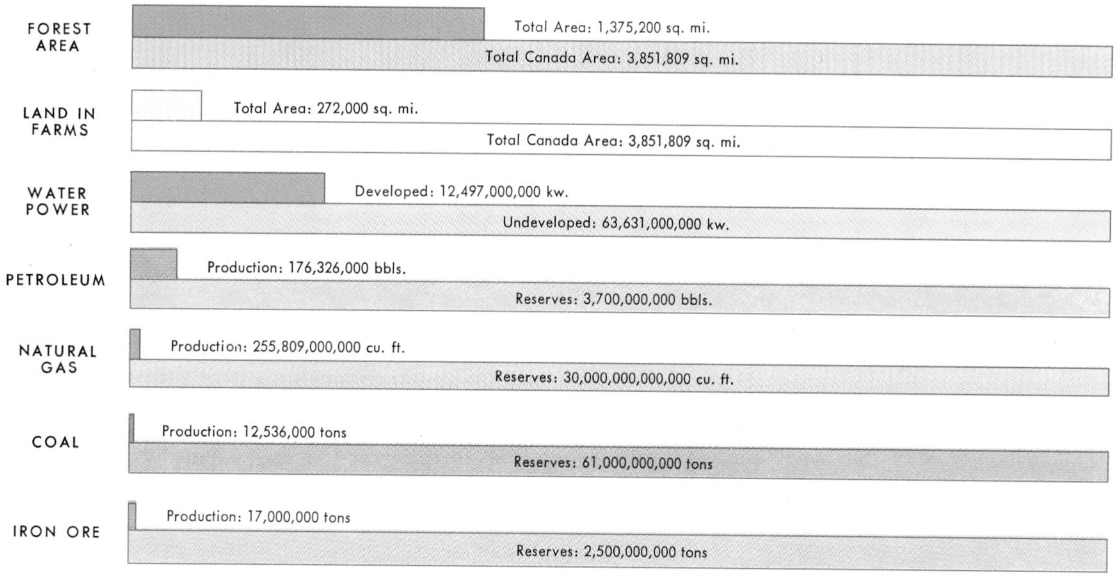
FOREST AREA
Total Area: 1,375,200 sq. mi.
Total Canada Area: 3,851,809 sq. mi.
LAND IN FARMS
Total Area: 272,000 sq. mi.
Total Canada Area: 3,851,809 sq. mi.
WATER POWER
Developed: 12,497,000,000 kw.
Undeveloped: 63,631,000,000 kw.
PETROLEUM
Production: 176,326,000 bbls.
Reserves: 3,700,000,000 bbls.
NATURAL GAS
Production: 255,809,000,000 cu. ft.
Reserves: 30,000,000,000,000 cu. ft.
COAL
Production: 12,536,000 tons
Reserves: 61,000,000,000 tons
IRON ORE
Production: 17,000,000 tons
Reserves: 2,500,000,000 tons

FOOD, FUEL AND METAL FOR TODAY AND THE FUTURE

The extent of Canada's reserves of natural resources is shown in the lower bars of each pair in the graph above. The upper bars of each pair show, from top to bottom: forest and farm lands in use; total water power developed for electricity; annual production of petroleum, natural gas, coal and iron ore. With this wide range of resources, the nation is more than amply endowed for major industrial development.

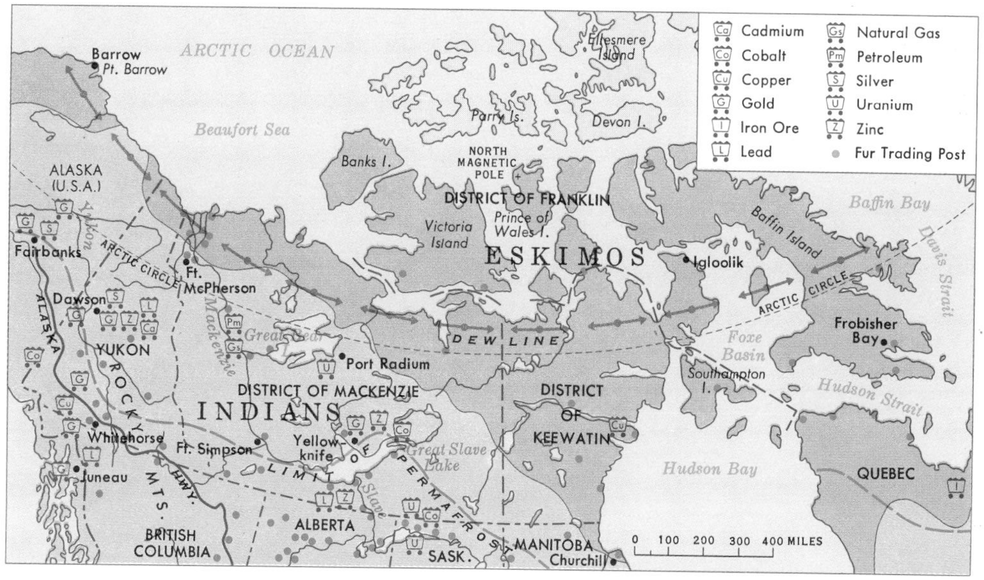
ARCTIC OCEAN
Barrow
Pt. Barrow
Beaufort Sea
ALASKA (U.S.A.)
Fairbanks
Dawson
YUKON
Whitehorse
Juneau
Ft. McPherson
ARCTIC CIRCLE
Banks I.
Victoria Island
Prince of Wales I.
Parry Is.
Ellesmere Island
Devon I.
NORTH MAGNETIC POLE
DISTRICT OF FRANKLIN
ESKIMOS
Igloolik
Baffin Island
Baffin Bay
Davis Strait
Frobisher Bay
Foxe Basin
Southampton I.
Hudson Strait
Hudson Bay
QUEBEC
DEW LINE
Port Radium
DISTRICT OF MACKENZIE
INDIANS
Ft. Simpson
Yellowknife
Great Slave Lake
LIMIT OF PERMAFROST
DISTRICT OF KEEWATIN
ROCKY MTS.
HWY.
BRITISH COLUMBIA
ALBERTA
SASK.
MANITOBA
Churchill
0 100 200 300 400 MILES
Cadmium
Cobalt
Copper
Gold
Iron Ore
Lead
Natural Gas
Petroleum
Silver
Uranium
Zinc
Fur Trading Post

THE ARCTIC STOREHOUSE OF THE NORTHWEST TERRITORIES

So lightly settled are Canada's harsh northern lands, shown in this map, that the white population only slightly outnumbers the Indians and Eskimos. But minerals are now luring men beyond the isolated posts where only fur trappers used to live *(blue dots)*. Other newcomers are soldiers manning the U.S.-Canada Distant Early Warning (DEW) radar defense line.

STRENGTH AND MAJESTY IN THE CANADIAN WEST

CREEPING ICE of the Athabaska glacier scoops out a U-shaped valley in Canada's Rockies. Breath-taking scenery such as this has made Alberta's nearby Banff-Jasper region a tourist paradise.

LUXURIANT FORESTS mantle northern British Columbia *(left)*, surrounding ice-age lakes which are storehouses of water power. Plans are being made to develop the region's natural resources.

SHORTHORN CATTLE graze on the plains of Alberta *(below)* near an Edmonton oil refinery. With twin resources of beef and petroleum, the province is sometimes called "Texas minus the twang."

BRITISH COLUMBIA
Provincial Capitals
Other Cities
City Limits
HIGHWAYS
Major Roads
Other Roads
Provincial
1 inch = 67 Statute Miles
Miles 0 5 10 20 30 40 50 60 70
Oblique Cylindrical Projection
Pacific Ocean
Queen Charlotte Sound
Hecate Strait
Dixon Entrance
QUEEN CHARLOTTE ISLANDS
VANCOUVER ISLAND
Prince Rupert
Prince George
Kamloops
Vancouver
VICTORIA
Edmonton
Calgary
ALBERTA
WASH.
IDA.
MONT.
ALASKA
CM POLITICAL BRITISH COLUMBIA
COPYRIGHT BY RAND McNALLY & COMPANY
MADE IN U.S.A.

BRITISH COLUMBIA: "This magnificent province," the essayist Stephen Leacock wrote, "with its happy climate, immense resources and its Pacific outlook, is an empire in itself." British Columbia must be reckoned as one of Canada's greatest potential sources of wealth. Massive geologic upheavals created a mountainous region with tremendous deposits of lead, zinc, copper, silver and gold, as well as some pockets of natural gas. The "happy climate," with its abundant rainfall, has produced luxuriant forests of virgin timber, including 260-foot-tall Douglas firs. From the Peace River valley—the most heavily populated area in northern Canada—comes a strain of disease-resistant wheat that is prized throughout North America. And from the Pacific, British Columbians harvest most of Canada's salmon.

AREA: 366,255 sq. mi. Rank: 3rd.
POPULATION: 1,594,000. Rank: 3rd. Largest city: Vancouver. Capital: Victoria.
CLIMATE: Cool winters, mild summers, heavy rainfall on coast; colder winters with heavy snow and short cool summers with light rainfall inland.
ALTITUDES: Mt. Fairweather, 15,300 ft. (highest); Vancouver, 38 ft.

In the late 1700s explorers sailed along the fjord-cut coastline of British Columbia but were deterred from going ashore by the sharply rising coastal ramparts. Not until 1858, when gold was discovered on the Fraser River, was there a movement inland. But the gold could not easily be panned, and the miners soon quit the area, leaving the treasure to the big machines of a later age. On July 4, 1886, the first trans-Canadian train chuffed into Port Moody—after a 136-hour journey from Montreal, 2,900 miles away. Slowly the province began to awaken to its new status as the nation's window on the west coast. During World War II the mineral storehouse of British Columbia was finally unlocked and a glimpse of its vast holdings was revealed. The power of lakes and rivers *(diagram, below)* was ingeniously harnessed for electricity. Accomplishments of this order, making a continued expansion of industry possible, have converted Vancouver into the fourth largest manufacturing center in Canada, and British Columbia into one of the fastest growing provinces.

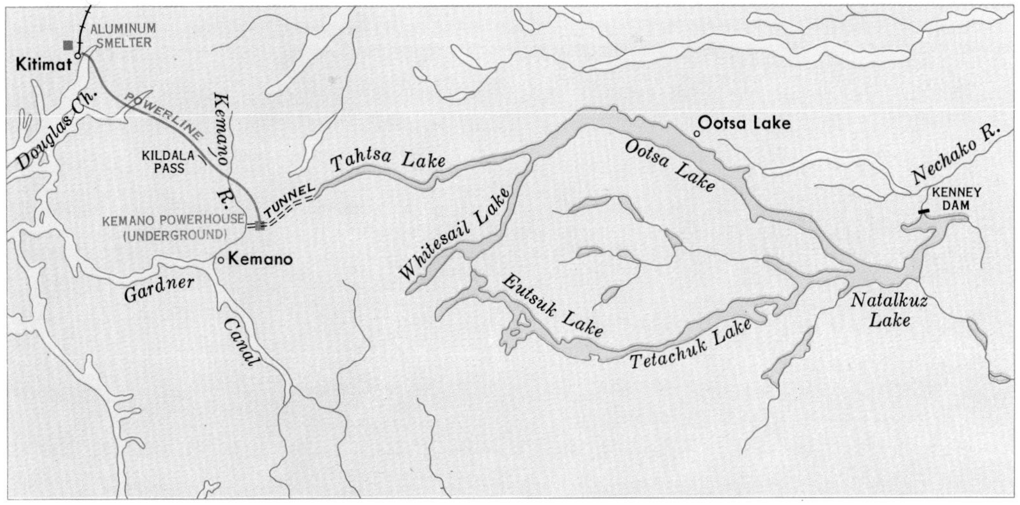

REVERSING THE WATERS FOR KITIMAT'S ALUMINUM

To harness the vast hydroelectric power potential in the coastal mountains of British Columbia, the Aluminum Company of Canada undertook the extensive Kitimat project, which is shown on the map at top. The three-year construction job began with the Kenney Dam *(right center)* at the easterly point of a chain of lakes more than a hundred miles long. Water had been flowing eastward in this chain; the dam forced it to reverse its course and flow west. As an outlet, a 10-mile-long mountain tunnel, shown in cross-section diagram, was dug at the western end of Tahtsa Lake *(left center)*. Through this tunnel, water pours with great force into turbines of the Kemano powerhouse, a huge underground plant. From there, cables carry the electricity to the city of Kitimat, where an aluminum-smelting plant has been built. Kitimat is at the head of Douglas Channel, a navigable inlet that reaches about 80 miles to the Pacific Ocean. This waterway is used to bring in bauxite, the raw material for aluminum-smelting.

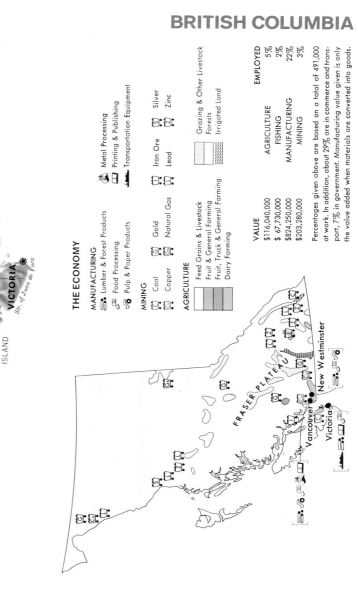

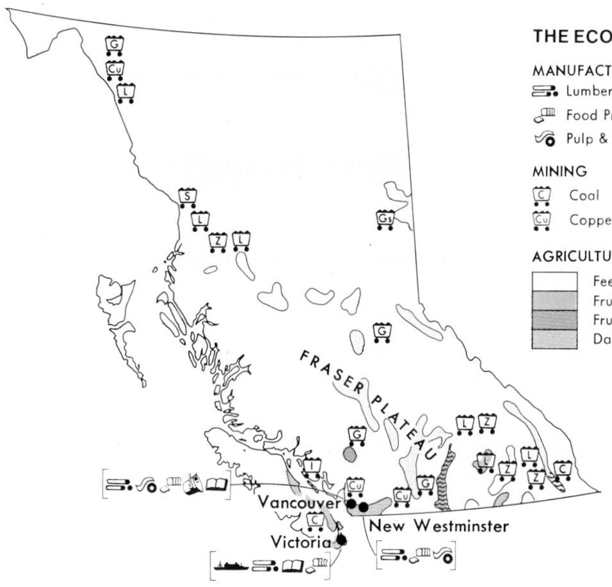

THE ECONOMY

MANUFACTURING
- Lumber & Forest Products
- Food Processing
- Pulp & Paper Products
- Metal Processing
- Printing & Publishing
- Transportation Equipment

MINING
- Coal
- Copper
- Gold
- Natural Gas
- Iron Ore
- Lead
- Silver
- Zinc

AGRICULTURE
- Feed Grains & Livestock
- Fruit & General Farming
- Fruit, Truck & General Farming
- Dairy Farming
- Grazing & Other Livestock
- Forests
- Irrigated Land

VALUE		EMPLOYED
$116,040,000	AGRICULTURE	5%
$ 67,730,000	FISHING	2%
$824,250,000	MANUFACTURING	22%
$203,280,000	MINING	3%

Percentages given above are based on a total of 491,000 at work. In addition, about 29% are in commerce and transport, 7% in government. Manufacturing value given is only the value added when materials are converted into goods.

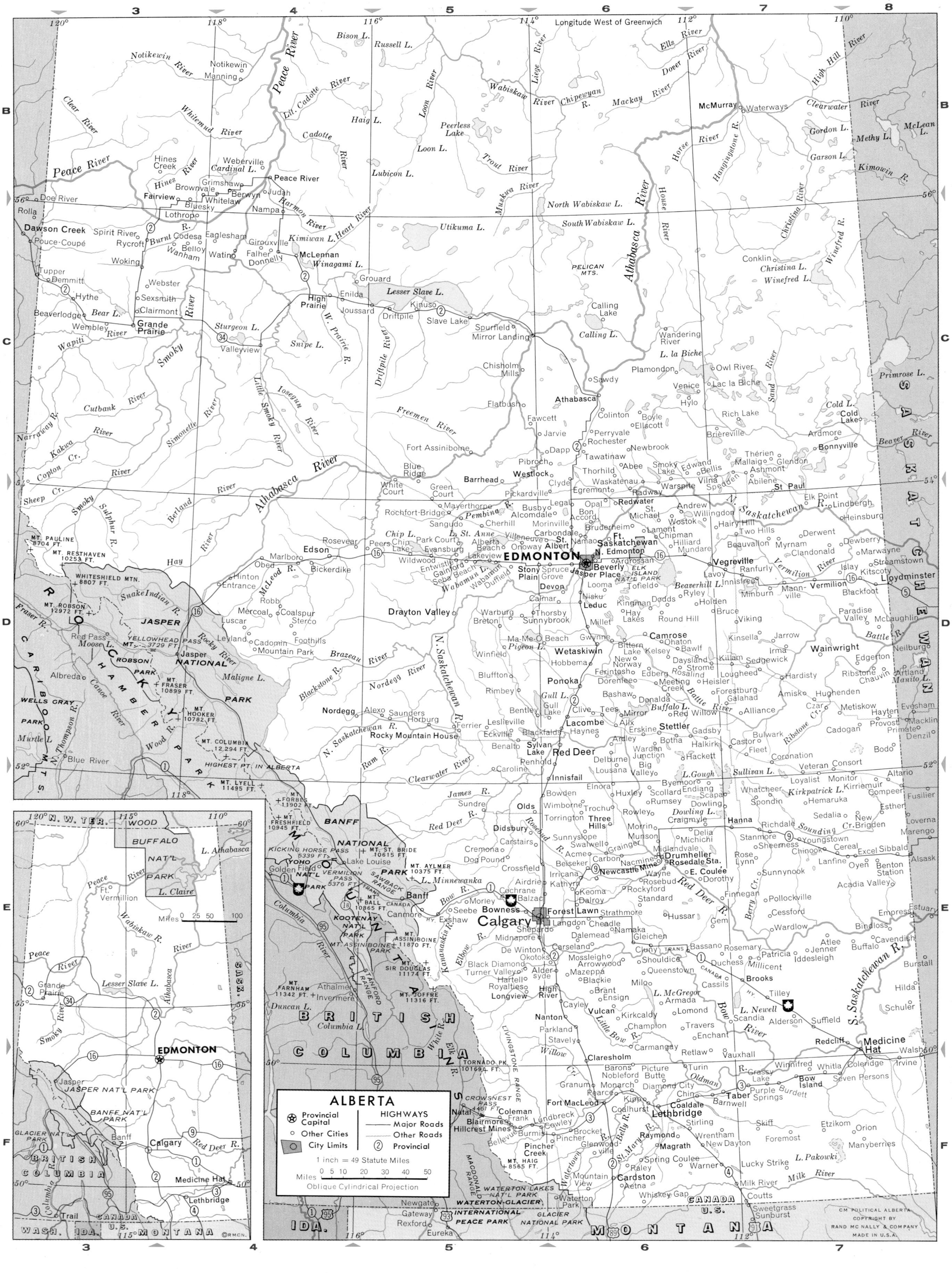
ALBERTA
Provincial Capital
Other Cities
City Limits
HIGHWAYS
Major Roads
Other Roads
Provincial
1 inch = 49 Statute Miles
Miles 0 5 10 20 30 40 50
Oblique Cylindrical Projection
Longitude West of Greenwich
EDMONTON
Calgary
Red Deer
Lethbridge
Medicine Hat
BRITISH COLUMBIA
SASKATCHEWAN
MONTANA
IDA.
WASH.
CANADA
U.S.
JASPER NATIONAL PARK
BANFF NATIONAL PARK
WATERTON LAKES NAT'L PARK
WATERTON-GLACIER INTERNATIONAL PEACE PARK
GLACIER NATIONAL PARK
Peace River
Athabasca River
N. Saskatchewan R.
S. Saskatchewan R.
Red Deer R.
Bow River
Milk River
Lesser Slave L.
MT. COLUMBIA 12,294 FT. HIGHEST PT. IN ALBERTA
CM POLITICAL ALBERTA
COPYRIGHT BY RAND MC NALLY & COMPANY
MADE IN U.S.A.

ALBERTA

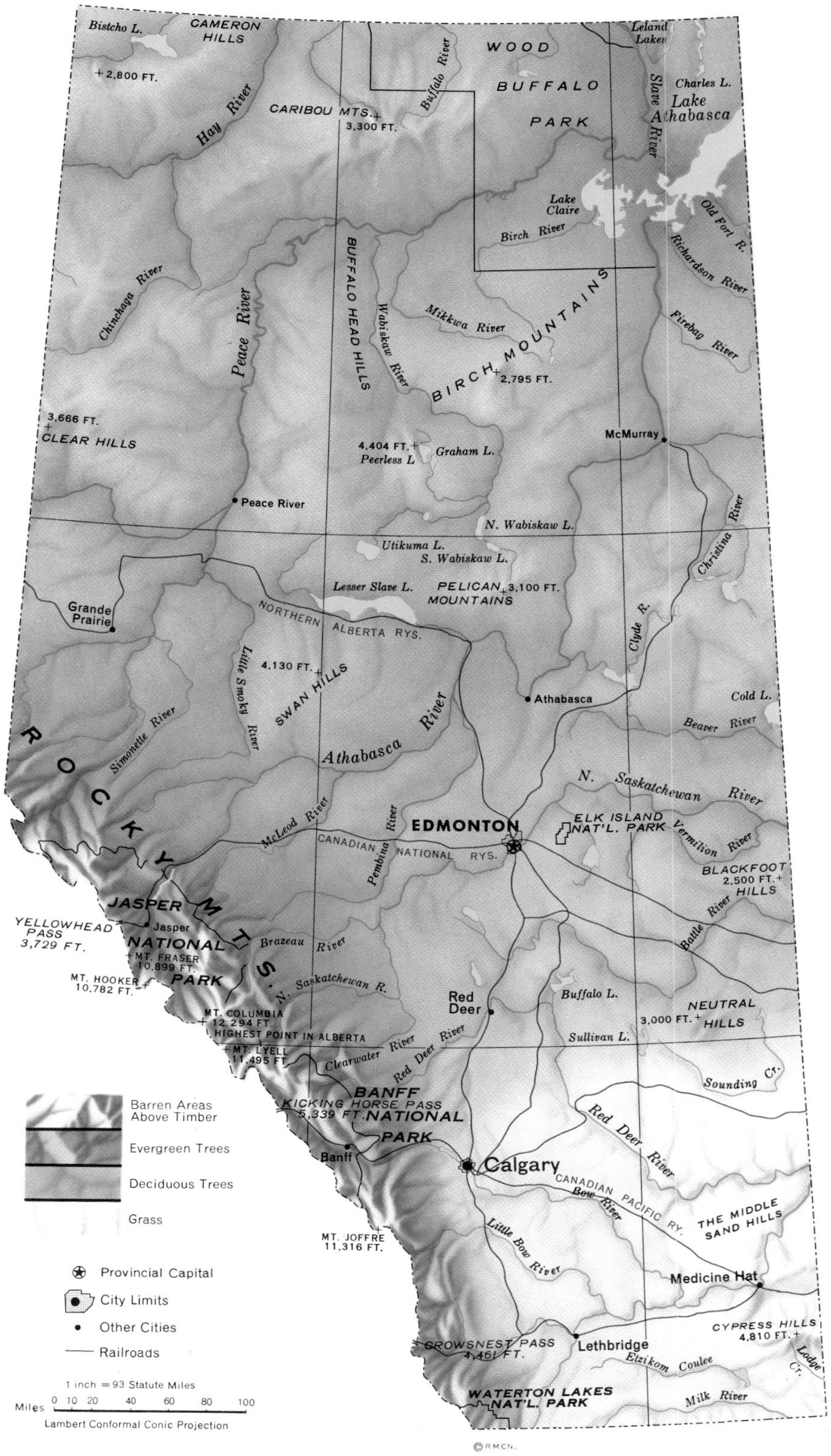

ALBERTA: Bounded by the nearly impenetrable Rockies on the west and a vast expanse of sparsely settled plains on the east, Alberta long defied all but the hardiest of pioneers. "This place would still belong to the Blackfoot," early arrivals said, "if it weren't for that cow path up from Texas." Indeed, the first settlers were cowboys who migrated up the cattle trails from Montana, Wyoming and Texas in the 1870s. They found Alberta familiar ground, for most of the province lies on a high plain—an extension of the Great Plains—that resembles the cattle country of the Texas Panhandle. After the cowboys came the farmers, brought by the trans-Canadian railroad, which was completed in 1885. They quickly transformed the land into golden fields of wheat.

AREA: 255,285 sq. mi. Rank: 4th.
POPULATION: 1,268,000. Rank: 4th.
Largest city and capital: Edmonton.
CLIMATE: Short cool summers with light rainfall; long cold winters. Heavy snow in mountains.
ALTITUDES: Mt. Columbia, 12,294 ft. (highest).

Between 1901 and 1911 homesteaders increased the population fivefold; nearly a quarter of them made their way up the cow trails. As the homesteading dust settled, the railroad bolstered the economy with tourist traffic by promoting the development of national parks (*diagram, below right*). Today, while the tourist business continues to thrive, the province produces 30 per cent of Canada's beef cattle and 25 per cent of its wheat. But leading all these sources of income is oil, which came in with the Leduc No. 1 well near Edmonton in 1947. The province now supplies most of Canada's oil and gas, requisites of a mighty industrial economy.

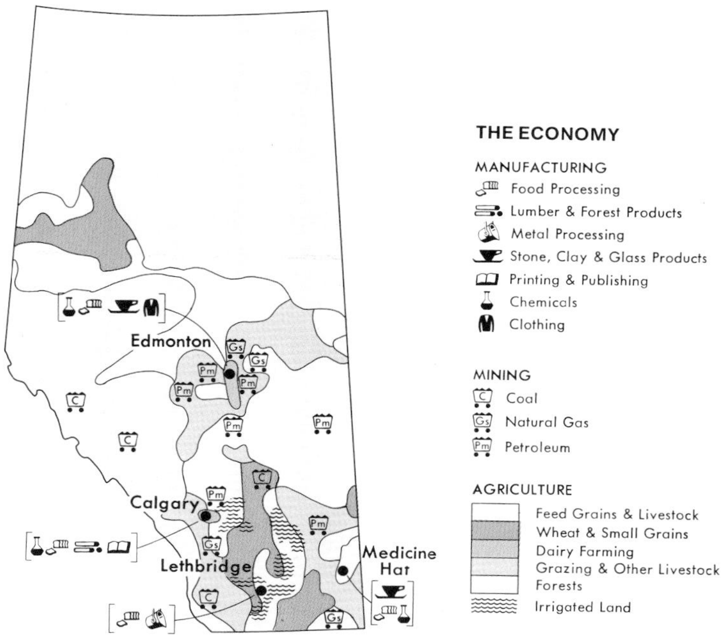

VALUE		EMPLOYED
$437,850,000	AGRICULTURE	30%
$285,830,000	MANUFACTURING	10%
$411,170,000	MINING	3%

Percentages given above are based on a total of 361,860 at work. In addition, about 24% are in commerce and transport, 6% in government. Manufacturing value given is only the value added when materials are converted into goods.

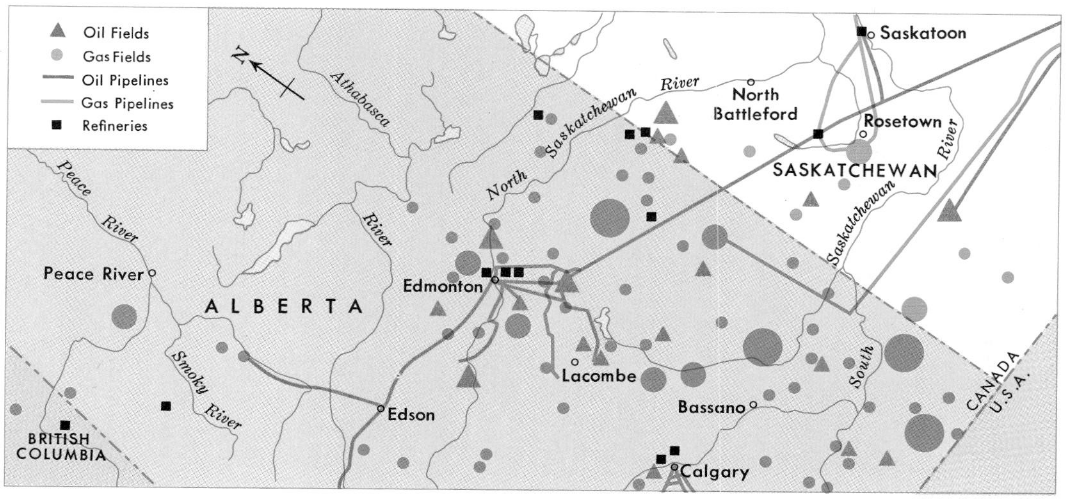

GREAT RESERVES OF OIL AND GAS

Alberta's wheat plains are crowded with oil and gas fields and dotted with refineries, as shown in the map above. Discovered in the 19th Century, Alberta's natural gas and oil were tapped in earnest only after World War II. Today, the province supplies Canada with 70 per cent of its oil and produces four times as much gas as any other province. In addition, potential reserves in the north of the province are still untapped. Provincial law requires that after oilmen finish drilling on farm land—and the settled portions of Alberta are mostly farm land—they must remove their rigs, gear and buildings, making the area fit again for agriculture.

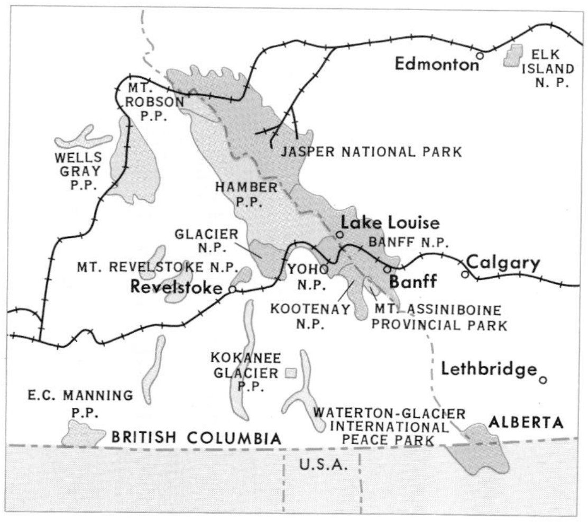

PARKS FOR THE MOUNTAIN PROVINCES

The national parks of Alberta and British Columbia, indicated on this map, are concentrated near the border line that separates the two provinces. The parks take up 8,713 square miles and annually attract more than 2.3 million visitors, who camp, fish and not infrequently bump into bears in the dense forests that blanket most of the mountainous area.

AN OCEAN OF WHEAT
FLOODING AN INLAND PLAIN

MAMMOTH STORAGE ELEVATORS edge the wheat fields at the railway town of Indian Head in southern Saskatchewan. Wheat brought the first settlers here and to the neighboring inland Canadian provinces of Manitoba and Alberta. In the early years the farmers experimented with many strains of wheat. Now Northern Manitoba No. 1 is the one planted most often. This strain of wheat was specially developed for Canada's relatively short growing season, during which the grain ripens quickly in the rich, dark brown soil.

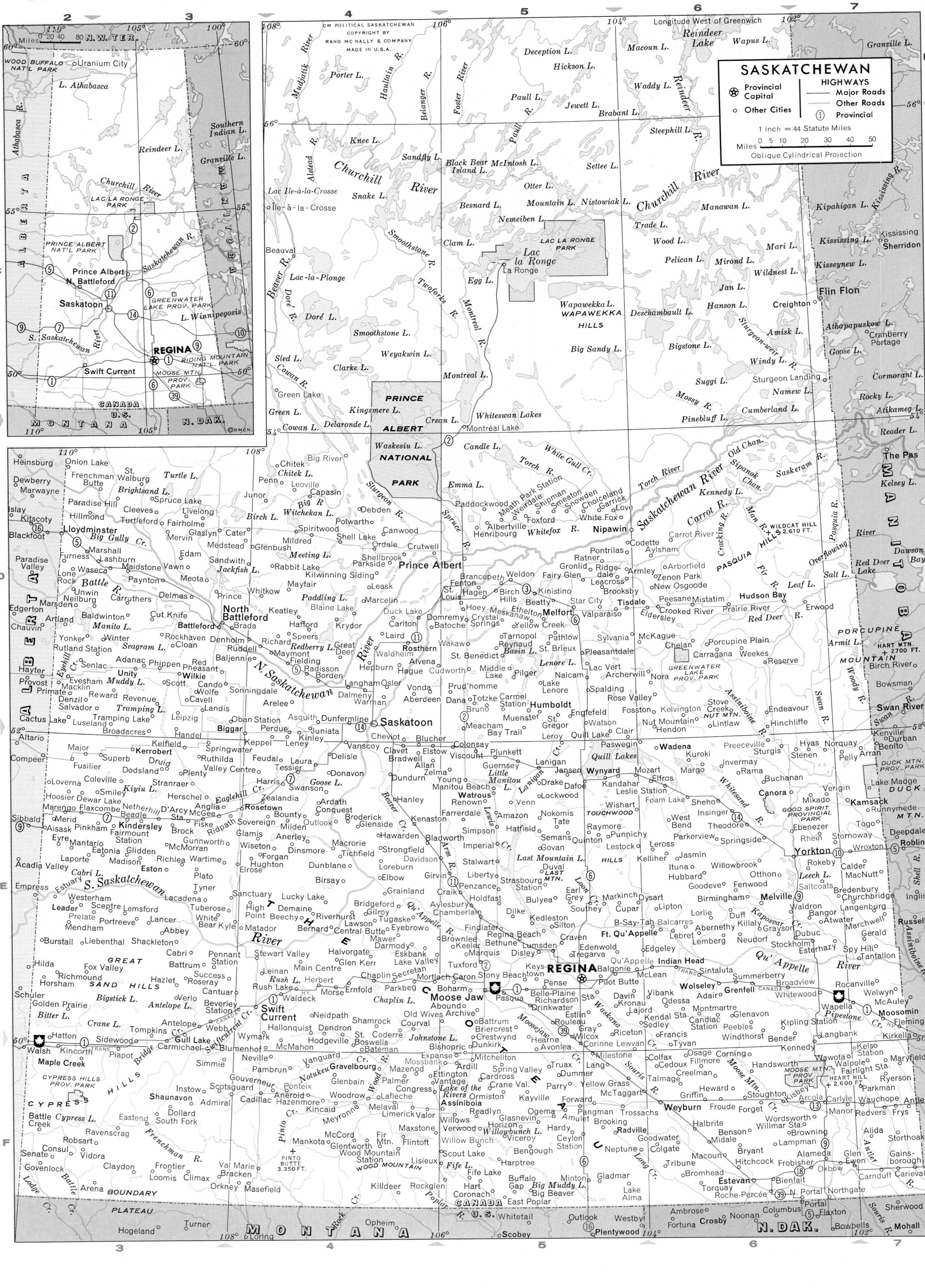
SASKATCHEWAN
Provincial Capital
Other Cities
HIGHWAYS
Major Roads
Other Roads
Provincial
1 inch = 44 Statute Miles
Miles 0 5 10 20 30 40 50
Oblique Cylindrical Projection
CM POLITICAL SASKATCHEWAN
COPYRIGHT BY
RAND MC NALLY & COMPANY
MADE IN U.S.A.
Longitude West of Greenwich
N.W. TER.
WOOD BUFFALO NAT'L PARK
Uranium City
L. Athabasca
Athabasca R.
Southern Indian L.
Reindeer L.
Granville L.
Churchill River
LAC LA RONGE PARK
PRINCE ALBERT NAT'L PARK
Prince Albert
N. Battleford
Saskatoon
GREENWATER LAKE PROV. PARK
L. Winnipegosis
S. Saskatchewan River
REGINA
RIDING MOUNTAIN NAT'L. PARK
Swift Current
MOOSE MTN. PROV. PARK
CANADA
U.S.
MONTANA
N. DAK.
ALBERTA
MANITOBA
Reindeer Lake
Wapus L.
Macoun L.
Deception L.
Hickson L.
Porter L.
Waddy L.
Paull L.
Jewett L.
Brabant L.
Steephill L.
Knee L.
Sandfly L.
Black Bear Island L.
McIntosh L.
Settee L.
Lac Ile-à-la-Crosse
Île-à-la Crosse
Snake L.
Otter L.
Mountain L.
Nistowiak L.
Besnard L.
Nemeiben L.
Trade L.
Manawan L.
Kipahigan L.
Kississing L.
Sherridon
Clam L.
Lac la Ronge
La Ronge
Beauval
Lac-la-Plonge
Egg L.
Wood L.
Pelican L.
Mirond L.
Mari L.
Flin Flon
Creighton
Wapawekka L.
WAPAWEKKA HILLS
Deschambault L.
Hanson L.
Athapapuskow L.
Cranberry Portage
Smoothstone L.
Weyakwin L.
Big Sandy L.
Bigstone L.
Amisk L.
Sled L.
Clarke L.
Montreal L.
Sturgeon Landing
Green Lake
Kingsmere L.
Namew L.
Cumberland L.
Cormorant L.
Green L.
Cowan L.
Delaronde L.
Crean L.
Whiteswan Lakes
Montréal Lake
Pinebluff L.
PRINCE ALBERT NATIONAL PARK
Waskesiu L.
Candle L.
Emma L.
The Pas
Heinsburg
Onion Lake
Big River
Chitek L.
Turtle L.
Lloydminster
Paddockwood
Nipawin
Carrot River
WILDCAT HILL 2,610 FT.
PASQUIA HILLS
Prince Albert
Tisdale
Hudson Bay
Melfort
North Battleford
Battleford
Red Deer L.
Rosthern
PORCUPINE
HART MTN. 2700 FT.
Humboldt
GREENWATER LAKE PROV. PARK
Saskatoon
Swan River
Kindersley
Wynyard
Quill Lakes
Wadena
DUCK MTN. PROV. PARK
Canora
Kamsack
Yorkton
Roblin
Melville
Last Mountain L.
Outlook
Watrous
Rosetown
GREAT SAND HILLS
Ft. Qu'Appelle
REGINA
Indian Head
Moose Jaw
Swift Current
Maple Creek
CYPRESS HILLS PROV. PARK
Gravelbourg
Assiniboia
Weyburn
Estevan
Moosomin
MOOSE MTN. PROV. PARK
HEART HILL 2,600 FT.
PINTO BUTTE 3,350 FT.
WOOD MOUNTAIN
Big Muddy L.
BOUNDARY PLATEAU
CANADA
U.S.
MONTANA
N. DAK.
Plentywood
Scobey

SASKATCHEWAN

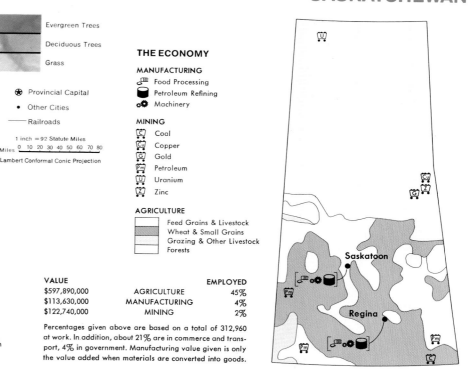

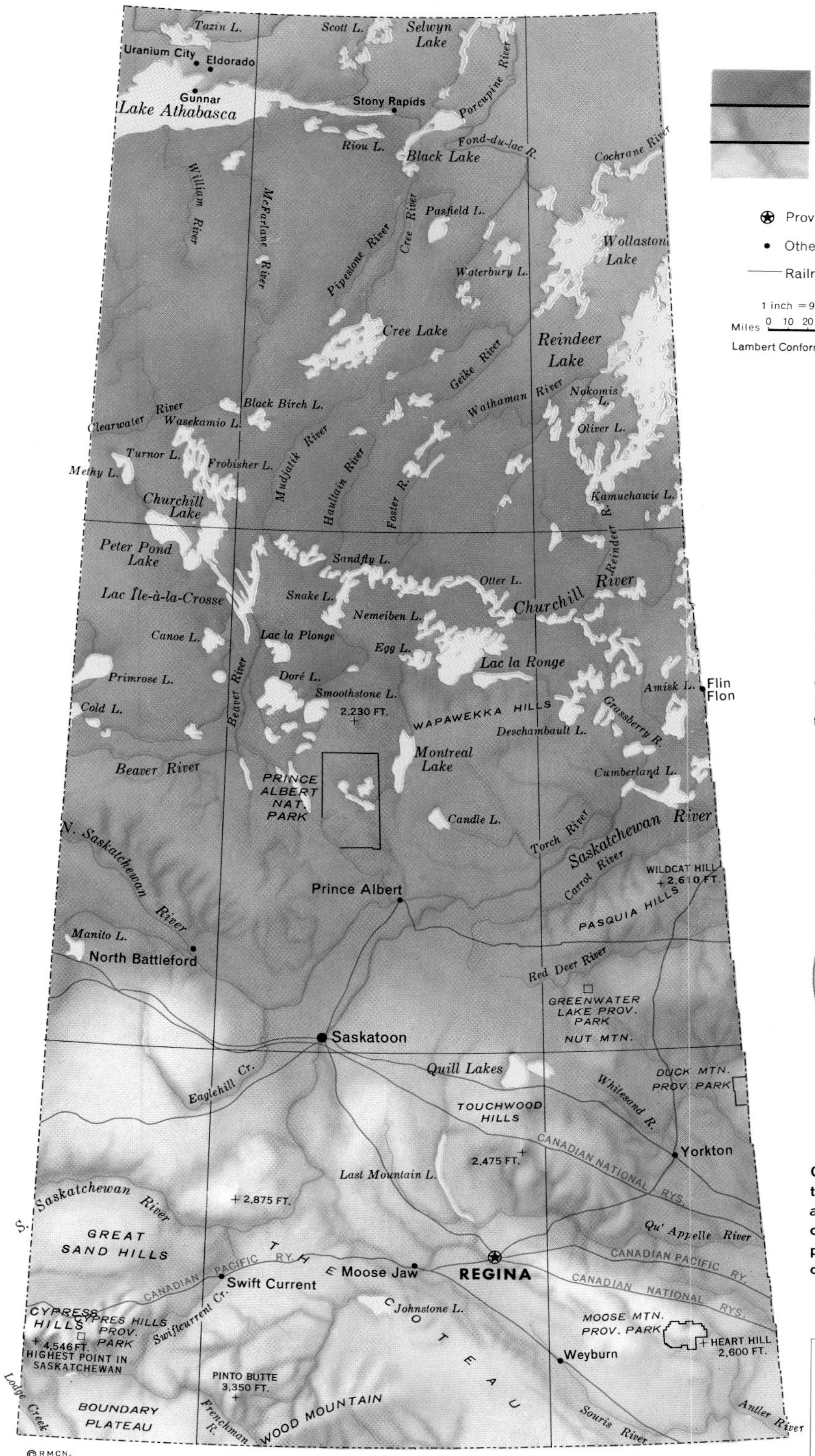

Evergreen Trees
Deciduous Trees
Grass

Provincial Capital
Other Cities
Railroads

1 inch = 92 Statute Miles
Miles 0 10 20 30 40 50 60 70 80
Lambert Conformal Conic Projection

THE ECONOMY

MANUFACTURING
- Food Processing
- Petroleum Refining
- Machinery

MINING
- Coal
- Copper
- Gold
- Petroleum
- Uranium
- Zinc

AGRICULTURE
- Feed Grains & Livestock
- Wheat & Small Grains
- Grazing & Other Livestock
- Forests

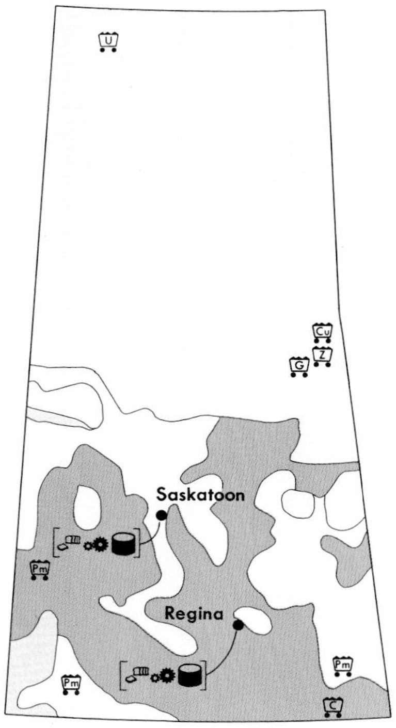

VALUE		EMPLOYED
$597,890,000	AGRICULTURE	45%
$113,630,000	MANUFACTURING	4%
$122,740,000	MINING	2%

Percentages given above are based on a total of 312,960 at work. In addition, about 21% are in commerce and transport, 4% in government. Manufacturing value given is only the value added when materials are converted into goods.

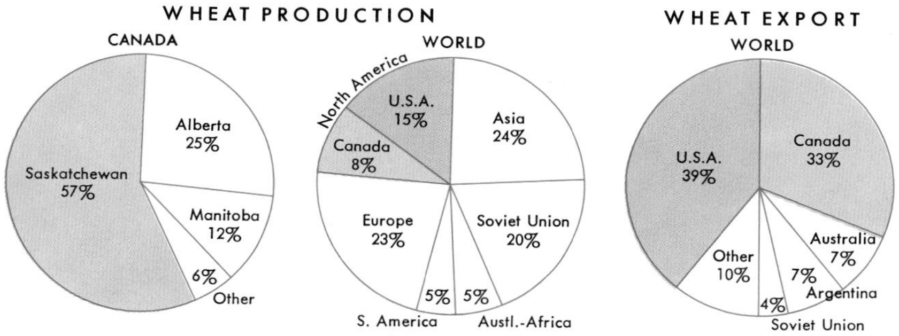

THE CANADIAN GIANT IN THE WORLD WHEAT MARKET

Canada's wheat bin is filled almost entirely by three provinces, as shown in the first diagram *(left, above)*. Saskatchewan alone grows more than half of the nation's crop. Although the total Canadian production is only a small fraction of world production *(center)*, Canadian wheat represents a big slice of the international market *(right)*. Canada manages the feat of supplying fully a third of the world market while growing only eight per cent of the world crop because it is, relatively speaking, a thinly populated country and—like the U.S.—produces more wheat than it can consume itself.

SASKATCHEWAN: There are times, says the novelist Hugh MacLennan, when "the Saskatchewan country can be so bleakly stern that it shrivels the soul," but "it can also intoxicate with a deluge of sheer loveliness." This monotonously flat province has varied moods, and people have damned it and sung its praises. But through both song and dirge runs one theme: wheat.

Saskatchewan's people, immigrants from many lands, came in one great tide of homesteaders at the turn of the century. They found an empty country. But with their arrival, the plains were filled almost overnight with the sound, as Stephen Leacock later said, of "people singing *Home Sweet Home* in all the tongues of Europe." They had been told this was wheat country, and that was what they all planted. Along with Manitoba and Alberta, Saskatchewan became one of the principal wheat provinces of Canada *(map, right)*.

AREA:	251,700 sq. mi. Rank: 5th.
POPULATION:	906,000. Rank: 5th.
	Largest city and capital: Regina.
CLIMATE:	Short cool summers, long cold winters.
	Light rainfall.
ALTITUDES:	Cypress Hills, 4,546 ft. (highest); Regina, 1,896.

Saskatchewan prospered until the wheat market collapsed shortly after World War I; drought and the depression of the 1930s added to the crisis. Determined never again to depend on a single commodity, the province began to diversify its crops, to develop rich mineral deposits and to encourage industry. Even the "Wheat Province" slogan was removed from Saskatchewan's auto license plates. Today, with more than 60 per cent of its income derived from sources other than wheat, the province has more security than it had in one-crop days.

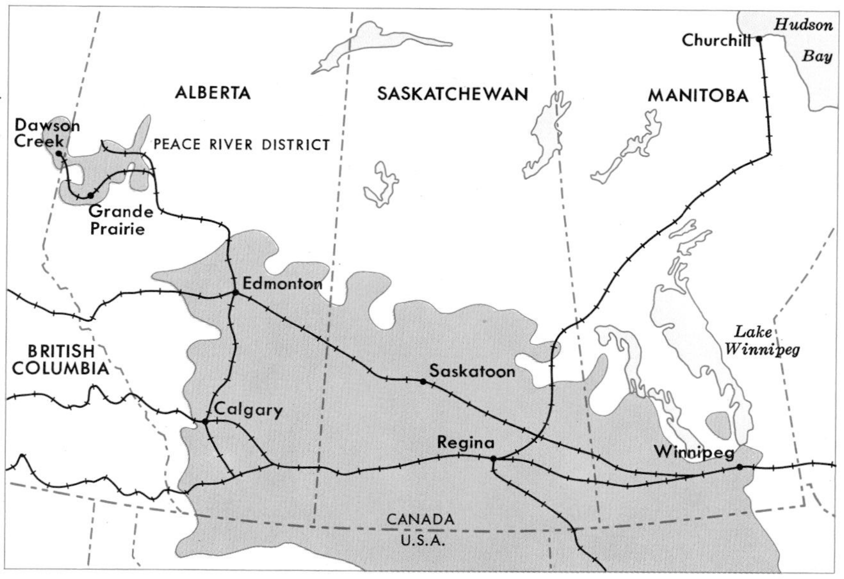

CANADA'S WHEAT BELT: 200,000 SQUARE MILES OF GRAIN

The Canadian wheat belt is centered in Saskatchewan, as shown in this map, but extends into Alberta and Manitoba. Wheat is the dominant crop of an area comprising 200,000 square miles. In this region the average summer rainfall is only eight to 10 inches, but the evaporation rate is low and the soil retains moisture. Long summer days compensate for the short growing season and the wheat matures quickly. The Chinook, a wind that comes down from the mountains to the west, can cause winter temperatures to soar high enough in a matter of hours to melt snow; thus early spring planting is possible. It was to bring the region's great crop to market that the building of a transcontinental railroad was pushed in the late 19th Century. Later, an important rail link was built to the Peace River District *(above left)*, a thriving wheat area 175 miles northwest of the main belt.

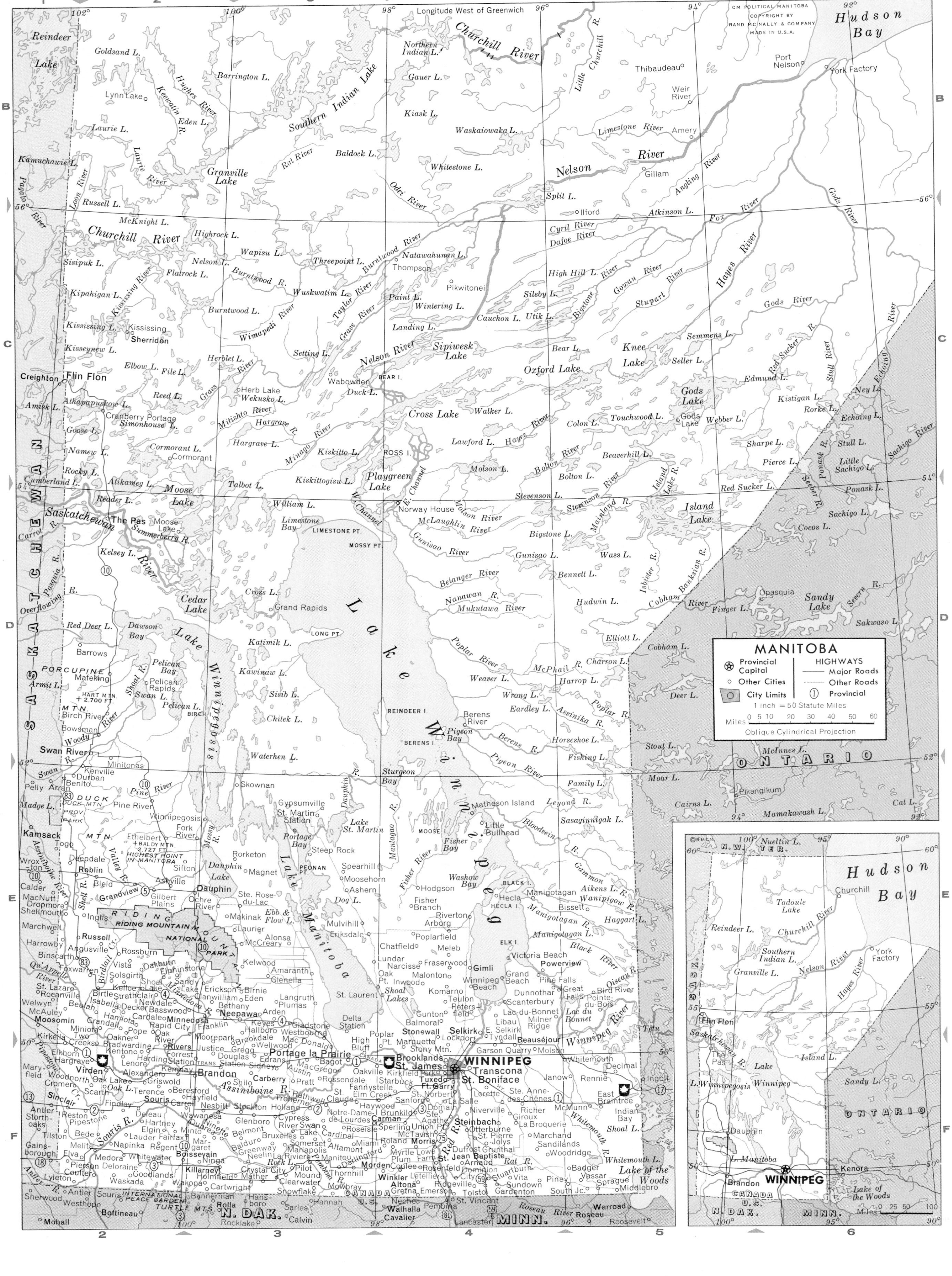
CM POLITICAL MANITOBA
COPYRIGHT BY
RAND McNALLY & COMPANY
MADE IN U.S.A.
Longitude West of Greenwich
MANITOBA
Provincial Capital
Other Cities
City Limits
HIGHWAYS
Major Roads
Other Roads
Provincial
1 inch = 50 Statute Miles
Miles 0 5 10 20 30 40 50 60
Oblique Cylindrical Projection
Hudson Bay
Lake Winnipeg
Lake Manitoba
Lake Winnipegosis
Cedar Lake
Nelson River
Churchill River
Hayes River
Southern Indian Lake
Island Lake
Gods Lake
SASKATCHEWAN
ONTARIO
N. DAK.
MINN.
WINNIPEG
St. James
St. Boniface
Transcona
Brandon
Portage la Prairie
Flin Flon
The Pas
Dauphin
Selkirk
Thompson
Churchill
Lake of the Woods
RIDING MOUNTAIN NATIONAL PARK
INTERNATIONAL PEACE GARDEN
N.W. TER.
Kenora
Miles 0 25 50 100

MANITOBA

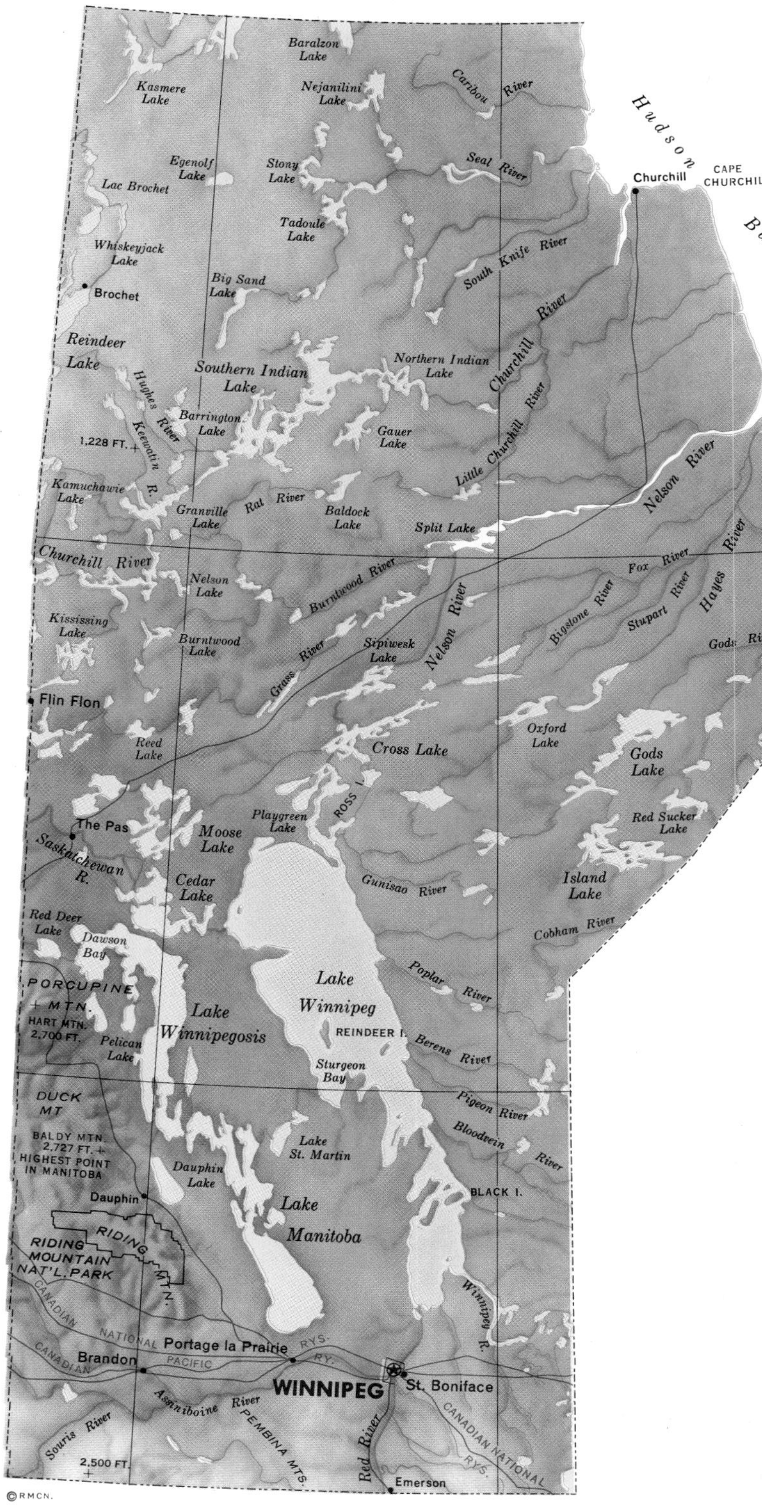

MANITOBA: Situated midway between the Atlantic and Pacific, the Plains province of Manitoba is the crossroads of the Dominion. Long before the first Scottish settlers moved into its fertile valley in 1812, Manitoba's rivers and lakes were passageways for the fur traders. At a junction of the Red River and the Assiniboine River, the Hudson's Bay Company, greatest of the trading companies, established the main base of a commercial empire that ruled 1.5 million square miles of wilderness. Its trading post became Winnipeg, Manitoba's leading city and a center of Canadian commerce and communications *(diagram, below)*.

AREA: 251,000 sq. mi. Rank: 6th.
POPULATION: 894,000. Rank: 6th.
Capital and largest city: Winnipeg.
CLIMATE: Short cool summers with long sunny days; long winters with heavy snow. Moderate rainfall.
ALTITUDES: Baldy Mountain, 2,727 ft. (highest); Winnipeg, 773 ft.

The ice age bequeathed fertile soil—"black as carbon paper"—to the valley of the Red River. It was in this valley that the Plains provinces were first settled. Homesteaders thrived by growing wheat as their predecessors had thrived by trapping beaver. In recent years, with a glut in the wheat market, Manitoba has exploited its petroleum, copper, zinc and gold, as well as the newly found deposits of nickel which now make it the second largest source of this metal in the world. The building of the town of Thompson, with a fully integrated nickel plant, and the construction of the Kelsey Generating Station on the Nelson River mark the beginning of the development of northern Manitoba's wilderness. In the populous south, the province has made extensive use of thermal and hydroelectric power to increase industrial production by more than 60 per cent in the last decade.

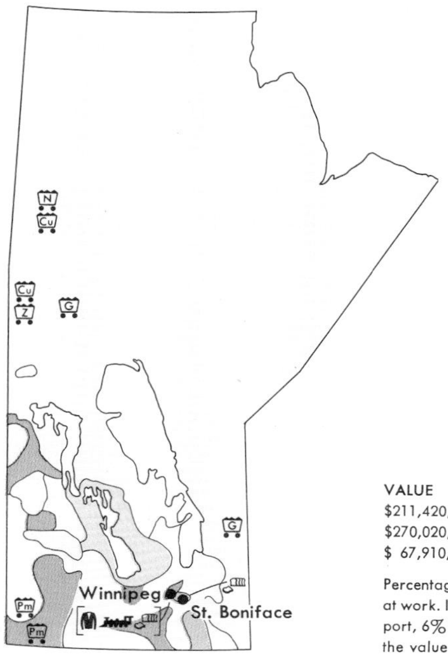

THE ECONOMY

MANUFACTURING
- Food Processing
- Transportation Equipment
- Clothing

MINING
- Copper
- Gold
- Nickel
- Petroleum
- Zinc

AGRICULTURE
- Feed Grains & Livestock
- Wheat & Small Grains
- Fruit, Truck & General Farming
- Dairy Farming
- Grazing & Other Livestock
- Forests

VALUE		EMPLOYED
$211,420,000	AGRICULTURE	23%
$270,020,000	MANUFACTURING	14%
$ 67,910,000	MINING	1%

Percentages given above are based on a total of 303,180 at work. In addition, about 30% are in commerce and transport, 6% in government. Manufacturing value given is only the value added when materials are converted into goods.

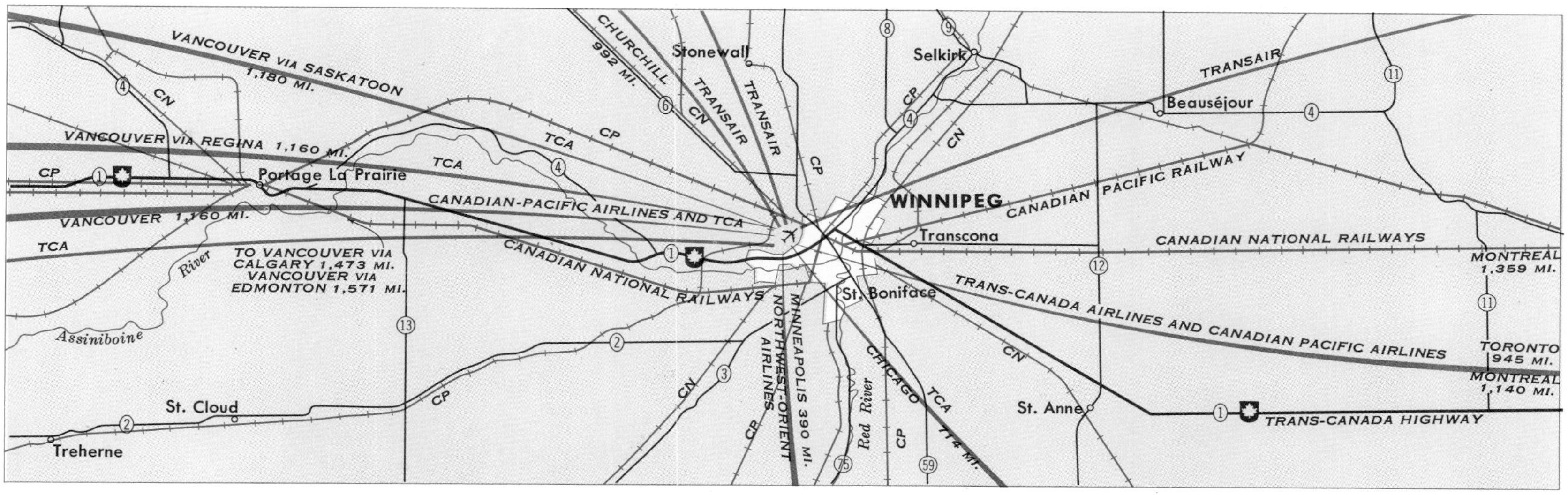

MID-CONTINENTAL WINNIPEG: WHERE ROUTES BEGIN AND END

This map shows how spokes of communication converge from all points of the compass on Winnipeg. A city of slaughterhouses, meat-packing establishments, machine shops and supply stores for farms and the oil industry, Winnipeg was founded in the heyday of the fur trade at a junction of two major rivers. With the coming of two trans-Canadian railroads *(heavy crosshatched lines)*—the Canadian Pacific and the Canadian National—the city's mid-continental location made it the focal point for shipping from both east and west, a position since reaffirmed by the Dominion's Trans-Canada Highway *(maple shield)*. In the air age Winnipeg has become a major terminal for Canada's main airlines *(red flight patterns)* and a take-off point to the north country *(single red lines)*.

A MAN-MADE PASSAGE, A NATURAL PRODIGY

A VITAL LINK in the St. Lawrence Seaway, the 29-year-old Welland Ship Canal connects Lake Ontario and Lake Erie. The 2,300-mile-long Seaway, which cost $470 million to build, carries ocean shipping into the heart of the North American continent. It opened in 1959.

A COLOSSUS OF POWER on the U.S.-Canada border is provided by Niagara Falls, one of the world's greatest tourist attractions. The Canadian, or "Horseshoe," half of the falls *(opposite page)* alone generates more than 12 billion kilowatt hours of electricity a year.

ONTARIO
Provincial Capitals
Other Cities
County Seat
City Limits
HIGHWAYS
Expressways
Major Roads
Other Roads
Provincial
Municipal County Line
1 inch = 35 Statute Miles
Miles 0 5 10 20 30 40
Oblique Cylindrical Projection
CM POLITICAL ONTARIO
COPYRIGHT BY RAND McNALLY & COMPANY
MADE IN U.S.A.
Lake Huron
Georgian Bay
Lake Ontario
Lake Erie
Lake St. Clair
QUEBEC
ALGONQUIN PROVINCIAL PARK
MANITOULIN ISLAND
OTTAWA
TORONTO
Hamilton
London
Windsor
Detroit
Buffalo
Kingston
Peterborough
Hudson Bay
James Bay
Lake Superior
Lake Winnipeg
Longitude West of Greenwich

ONTARIO: With all five of the Great Lakes in its front yard, a huge stand of timber and deposits of gold and other metals out back, and a bustling home workshop, Ontario is the richest house on the Canadian street. The province is first in population, commerce, manufacturing and mineral production. It has both the nation's political capital, Ottawa, and its financial capital, Toronto. This pre-eminence can be credited primarily to the province's location on the Great Lakes, the continent's busiest trade route *(map, below)*. The statesmen who separated Ontario from Quebec in 1791 and those who negotiated the boundary with the United States made certain that four of the lakes demarked Ontario's borders—an advantage which today brings to its ports one third of Canada's commerce.

AREA: 412,582 sq. mi. Rank: 2nd.
POPULATION: 6,040,000. Rank: 1st.
Largest city and capital: Toronto.
CLIMATE: Short cool summers, severe winters with lasting snow in north; warm summers, cold winters in south. Moderate rainfall throughout.
ALTITUDES: Tip Top Hill, 2,120 ft. (highest); Toronto, 254 ft. Ottawa, 214 ft.

Three quarters of northern Ontario is covered with the mineral-laden sheet of ancient rock called the Canadian Shield. From the Shield, Canadians now extract about 60 per cent of the country's gold, over 40 per cent of its copper and the major part of the world's nickel. In the southern peninsula, Ontario draws substantially on the abundant hydroelectric power of the Niagara, St. Lawrence and Ottawa Rivers and produces 50 per cent of Canada's manufactured goods, including virtually all of its motor vehicles, 90 per cent of its heavy electrical machinery, 80 per cent of its rubber products and 75 per cent of its primary iron and steel. Concentrated along the western end of Lake Ontario, this industrial complex constitutes a "Golden Horseshoe." One out of every seven Canadians lives here, on a 120-mile rim of lake shore between Oshawa and Niagara Falls. In the midst of the factories and mills—and gradually being engulfed by them—are some of Canada's finest fruit and dairy farms. Before industry became dominant, peninsular Ontario was called "the milch cow for the Provinces," and it is still an important producer of milk products. This region is also Canada's vineyard, growing most of the nation's grapes and making 90 per cent of its wine—more than five million gallons annually. With their bounty of both farm and factory, the residents of the Golden Horseshoe are the envy of their provincial neighbors.

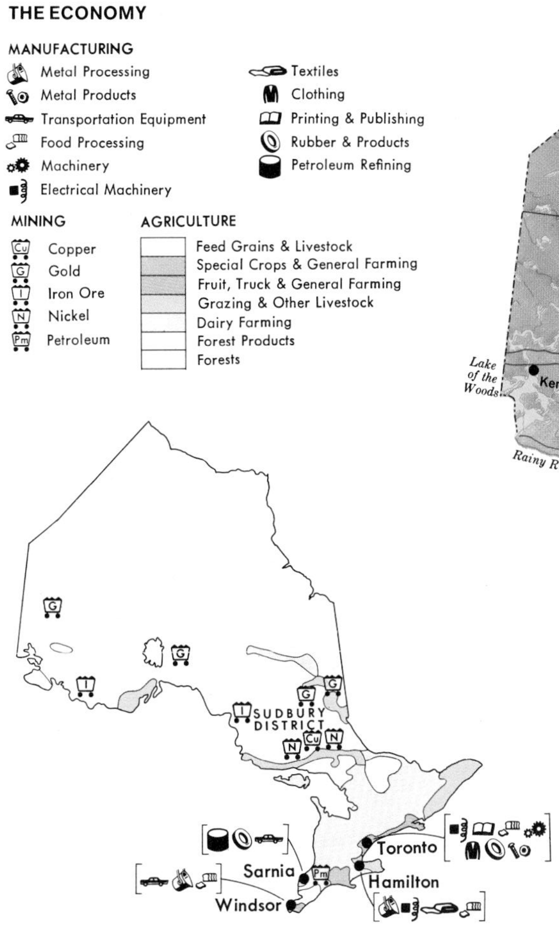

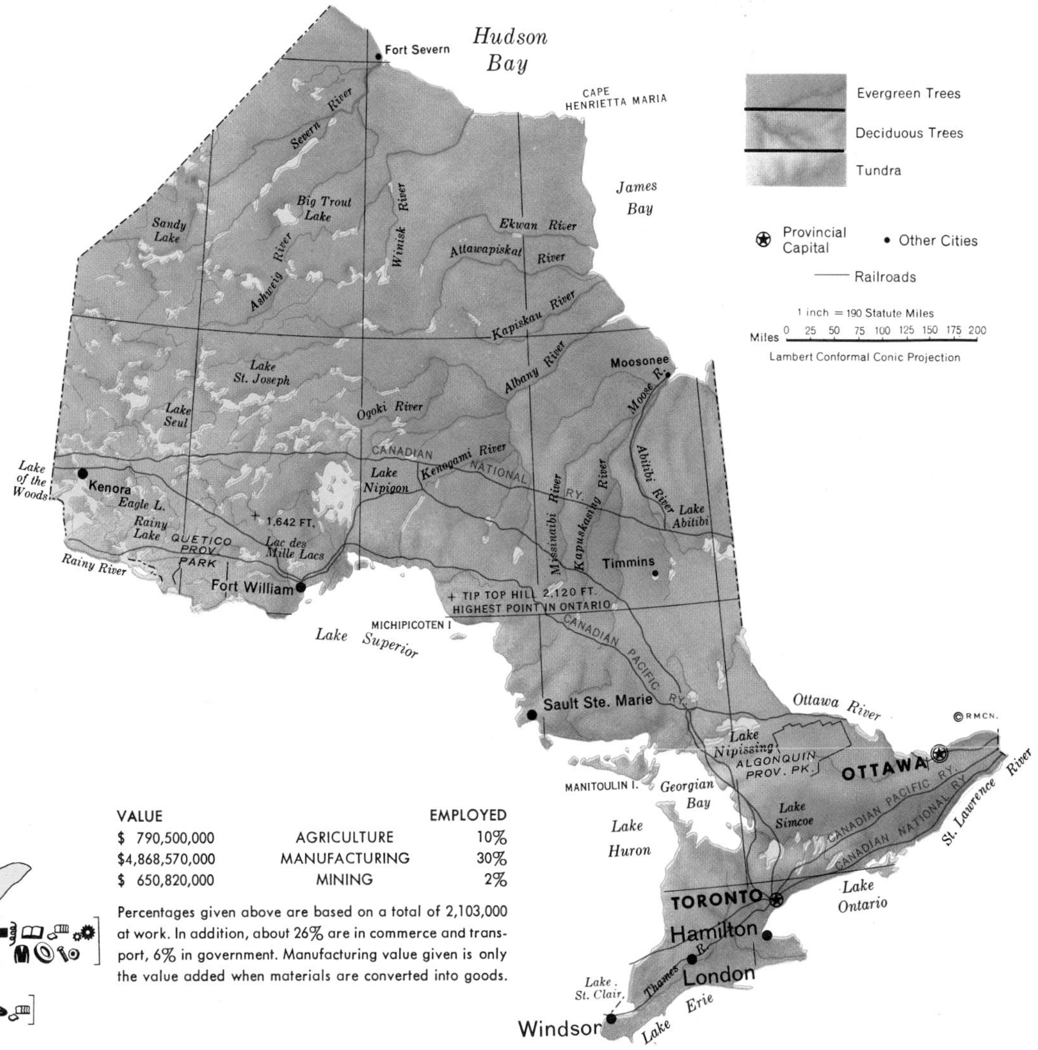

VALUE		EMPLOYED
$ 790,500,000	AGRICULTURE	10%
$4,868,570,000	MANUFACTURING	30%
$ 650,820,000	MINING	2%

Percentages given above are based on a total of 2,103,000 at work. In addition, about 26% are in commerce and transport, 6% in government. Manufacturing value given is only the value added when materials are converted into goods.

A COMPLEX OF INDUSTRIAL MIGHT ON THE ONTARIO PENINSULA

The peninsular area of Ontario, surrounded by the Ottawa River and Lakes Huron, Erie and Ontario, houses a mighty industrial complex. As indicated in the box graphs at the right of the map above, a majority of Canada's workers in a number of industries are employed in the province of Ontario. Readily available to the industries of the peninsula are these three essentials: raw materials, power and markets. To bring in iron ore and other materials and to ship out finished products, the Great Lakes provide relatively cheap seagoing shipping. Niagara Falls and other nearby water sources supply abundant hydroelectric power. And surrounding this industrial complex is a varied agricultural region that provides a rich larder *(key at upper left)* for Ontario's dense population.

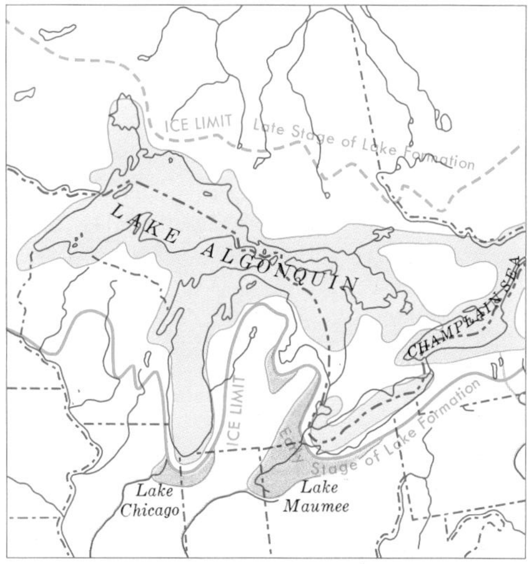

PREDECESSORS OF THE GREAT LAKES

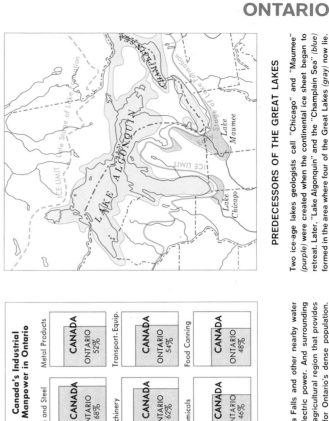

Two ice-age lakes geologists call "Chicago" and "Maumee" *(purple)* were created when the continental ice sheet began to retreat. Later, "Lake Algonquin" and the "Champlain Sea" *(blue)* formed in the area where four of the Great Lakes *(gray)* now lie.

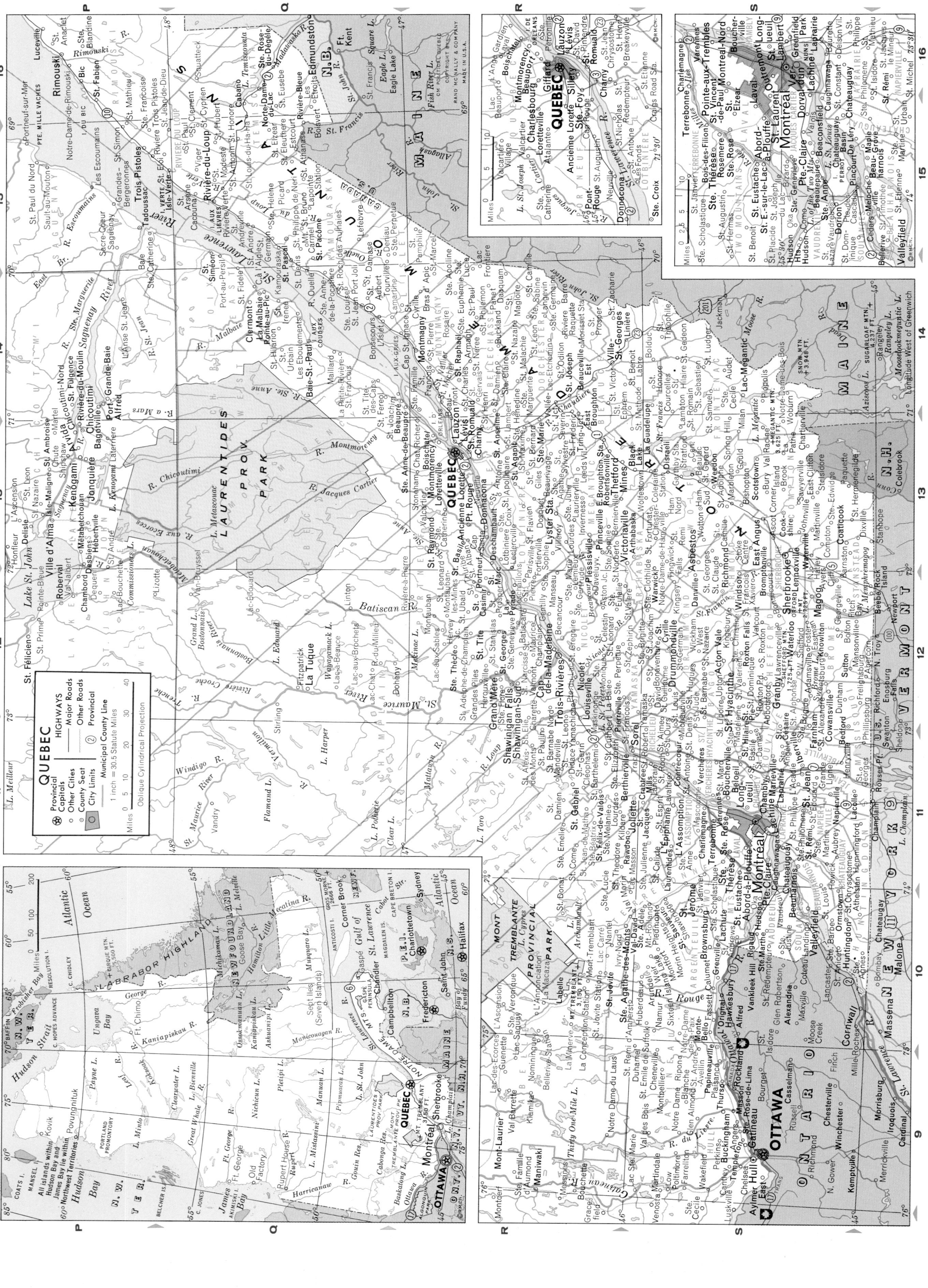
QUEBEC
Provincial Capitals
Other Cities
County Seat
City Limits
HIGHWAYS
Major Roads
Other Roads
Provincial
Municipal County Line
1 inch = 30.5 Statute Miles
Oblique Cylindrical Projection
LAURENTIDES PROV. PARK
MONT TREMBLANTE PROVINCIAL PARK

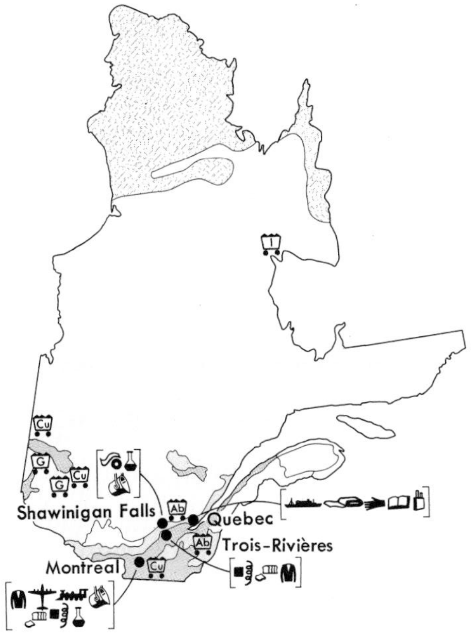

THE ECONOMY

MANUFACTURING
- Pulp & Paper Products
- Metal Processing
- Textiles
- Clothing
- Food Processing
- Chemicals
- Electrical Machinery
- Printing & Publishing
- Tobacco Products
- Leather Products
- Transportation Equipment

MINING
- Asbestos
- Copper
- Gold
- Iron Ore

AGRICULTURE
- Feed Grains & Livestock
- Dairy Farming
- Grazing & Other Livestock
- Forest Products
- Forests
- Tundra

VALUE		EMPLOYED
$ 389,500,000	AGRICULTURE	11%
$2,888,150,000	MANUFACTURING	29%
$ 422,460,000	MINING	2%

Percentages given above are based on a total of 1,538,000 at work. In addition, about 23% are in commerce and transport, 4% in government. Manufacturing value given is only the value added when materials are converted into goods.

AN ENCLAVE OF FIVE AND A HALF MILLION

The concentration of Canadians of French origin in eastern Canada is shown on the map at right. The French colonization of Canada ended officially in 1763 when the British took possession of what was then called New France and Acadia. At that time there were some 74,000 French colonists in the country. Now Canadians of French descent number more than 5.5 million, or nearly one third of the total population of Canada. The great majority of them live in Quebec. Other sizable groups of French Canadians live in Ontario and New Brunswick. In Canada as a whole, the Roman Catholic French Canadians constitute a political bloc and a tight-knit cultural enclave.

Evergreen Trees
Deciduous Trees
Tundra

- ⊛ Provincial Capital
- • Other Cities
- —— Railroads

1 inch = 172 Statute Miles
Miles 0 25 50 75 100 125 150
Lambert Conformal Conic Projection

QUEBEC: Largest of all the provinces, Quebec is "French Canada." Across nine tenths of the province lies the Canadian Shield, a sheet of Pre-Cambrian rock, centered on Hudson Bay, that covers much of Canada with a crescent-shaped plateau. The poor soil of the Shield offered Quebec's first settlers only a harsh life. These settlers were Frenchmen, who founded Quebec City on the St. Lawrence in 1608. The French population grew so slowly in inhospitable Quebec that the empire-building British were able to conquer the small colony of New France with little difficulty in 1760.

When the Treaty of Paris formally ended the French and Indian War in 1763, France ceded all of its holdings in Canada to Great Britain. But Quebec remained French in language and outlook. Today seven tenths of Quebec's population *(map, above)* are of French descent. And the Shield, which helped preserve the French nature of the settlement by discouraging British encroachment, still forces the majority of eastern Canada's population to hug a narrow zone bordering the St. Lawrence River—the only area where extensive agriculture is feasible.

AREA: 594,860 sq. mi. Rank: 1st.
POPULATION: 5,070,000. Rank: 2nd. Largest city: Montreal. Capital: Quebec.
CLIMATE: Long cold winters with lasting snow cover, short cool summers in north; milder winters, warm summers in south. Moderate rainfall.
ALTITUDES: Mt. Jacques Cartier, 4,160 ft. (highest); Montreal, 63 ft.

With the Industrial Revolution, Quebec's stone-blighted land proved to be a vast treasure chest of natural resources. The province now produces 38 per cent of Canada's copper and iron ore, and its forests provide the pulp for one fifth of the world's newsprint. With these assets, plus abundant hydroelectric power and a strategic location on the St. Lawrence gateway to the Atlantic, Quebec has become a great industrial province. Montreal is Canada's biggest city as well as the largest French-speaking city in the world after Paris.

FERTILE FARMLANDS
EMBRACED BY A SURROUNDING SEA

THE SCALLOPED SHORE is never far from the green farmlands of Prince Edward Island, the smallest but most fertile of all of Canada's salt-sprayed Atlantic Provinces. In their rich red soil Prince Edward Islanders grow potatoes, oats and hay and raise dairy cows and hogs. Seed potatoes that resist disease are a specialty of the island. In the other Atlantic Provinces of Newfoundland, New Brunswick and Nova Scotia, the land is less hospitable and many a family depends on its fishermen sons and husbands for its livelihood.

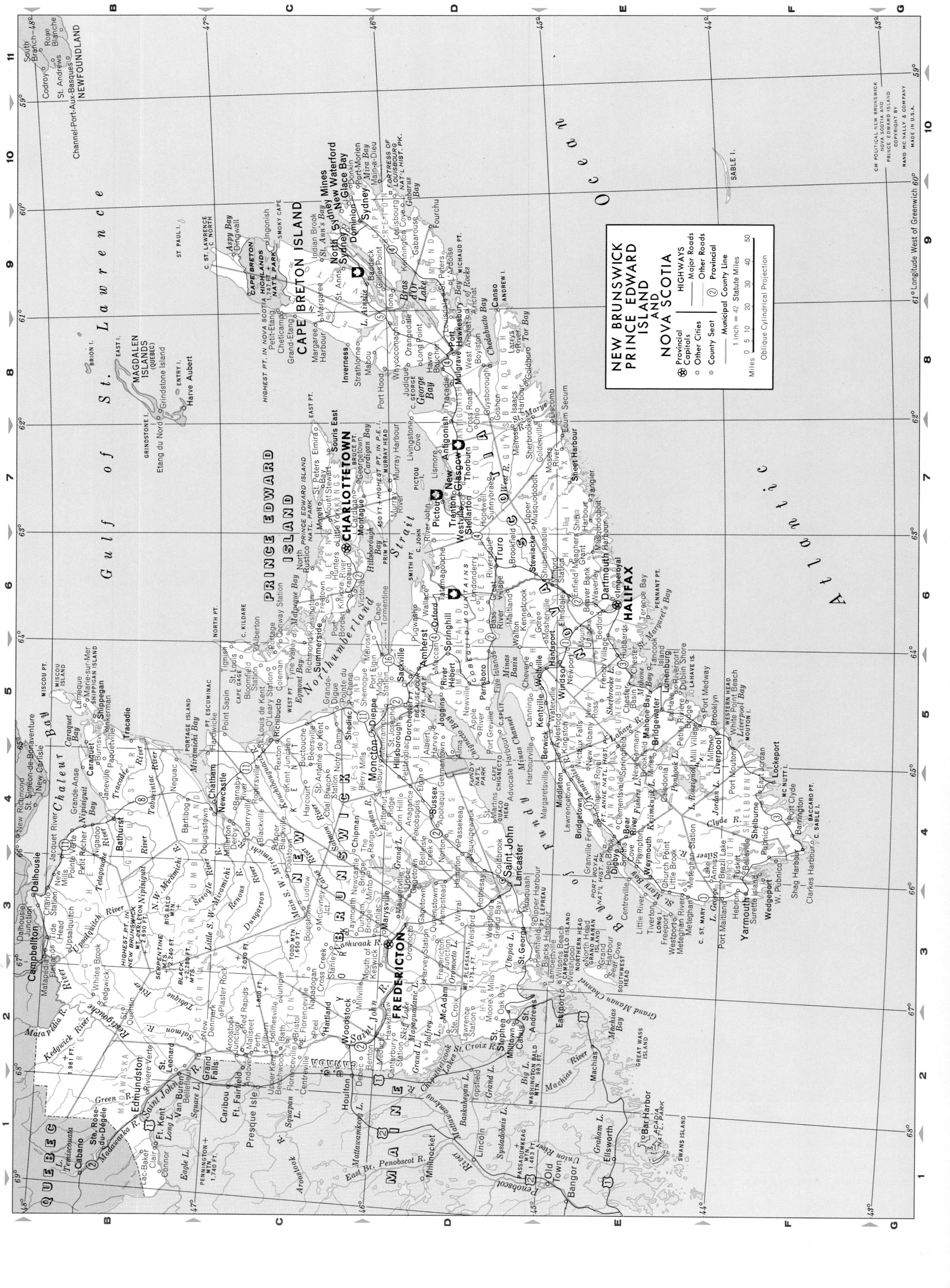

NEW BRUNSWICK
PRINCE EDWARD ISLAND
AND
NOVA SCOTIA
Provincial Capitals
Other Cities
County Seat
HIGHWAYS
Major Roads
Other Roads
Provincial
Municipal County Line
1 inch = 42 Statute Miles
Oblique Cylindrical Projection
CM POLITICAL NEW BRUNSWICK NOVA SCOTIA AND PRINCE EDWARD ISLAND
COPYRIGHT BY RAND MC NALLY & COMPANY
MADE IN U.S.A.
Longitude West of Greenwich
Gulf of St. Lawrence
Atlantic Ocean
Bay of Fundy
Northumberland Strait
PRINCE EDWARD ISLAND
CAPE BRETON ISLAND
NEW BRUNSWICK
NOVA SCOTIA
MAINE
QUEBEC
NEWFOUNDLAND
MAGDALEN ISLANDS (QUEBEC)
FREDERICTON
CHARLOTTETOWN
HALIFAX
Saint John
Moncton
Sydney
Dartmouth
Truro
Yarmouth

NEW BRUNSWICK, PRINCE EDWARD ISLAND AND NOVA SCOTIA

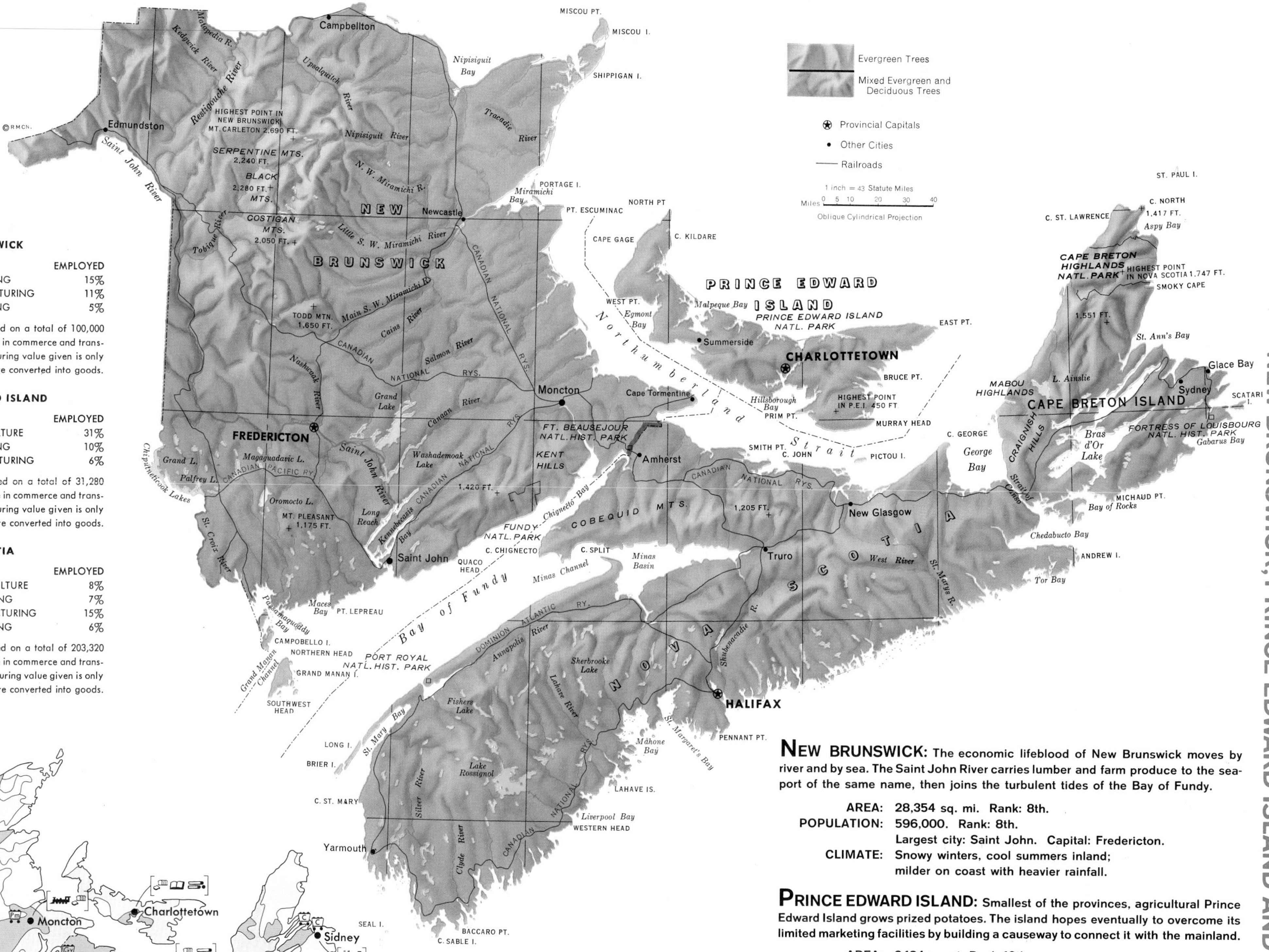

THE ECONOMY

NEW BRUNSWICK

VALUE		EMPLOYED
$29,370,000	FISHING	15%
$62,610,000	MANUFACTURING	11%
$84,350,000	MINING	5%

Percentages given above are based on a total of 100,000 at work. In addition, about 24% are in commerce and transport, 9% in government. Manufacturing value given is only the value added when materials are converted into goods.

PRINCE EDWARD ISLAND

VALUE		EMPLOYED
$26,630,000	AGRICULTURE	31%
$ 5,250,000	FISHING	10%
$ 6,160,000	MANUFACTURING	6%

Percentages given above are based on a total of 31,280 at work. In addition, about 19% are in commerce and transport, 7% in government. Manufacturing value given is only the value added when materials are converted into goods.

NOVA SCOTIA

VALUE		EMPLOYED
$ 44,420,000	AGRICULTURE	8%
$ 49,360,000	FISHING	7%
$159,820,000	MANUFACTURING	15%
$ 66,090,000	MINING	6%

Percentages given above are based on a total of 203,320 at work. In addition, about 25% are in commerce and transport, 10% in government. Manufacturing value given is only the value added when materials are converted into goods.

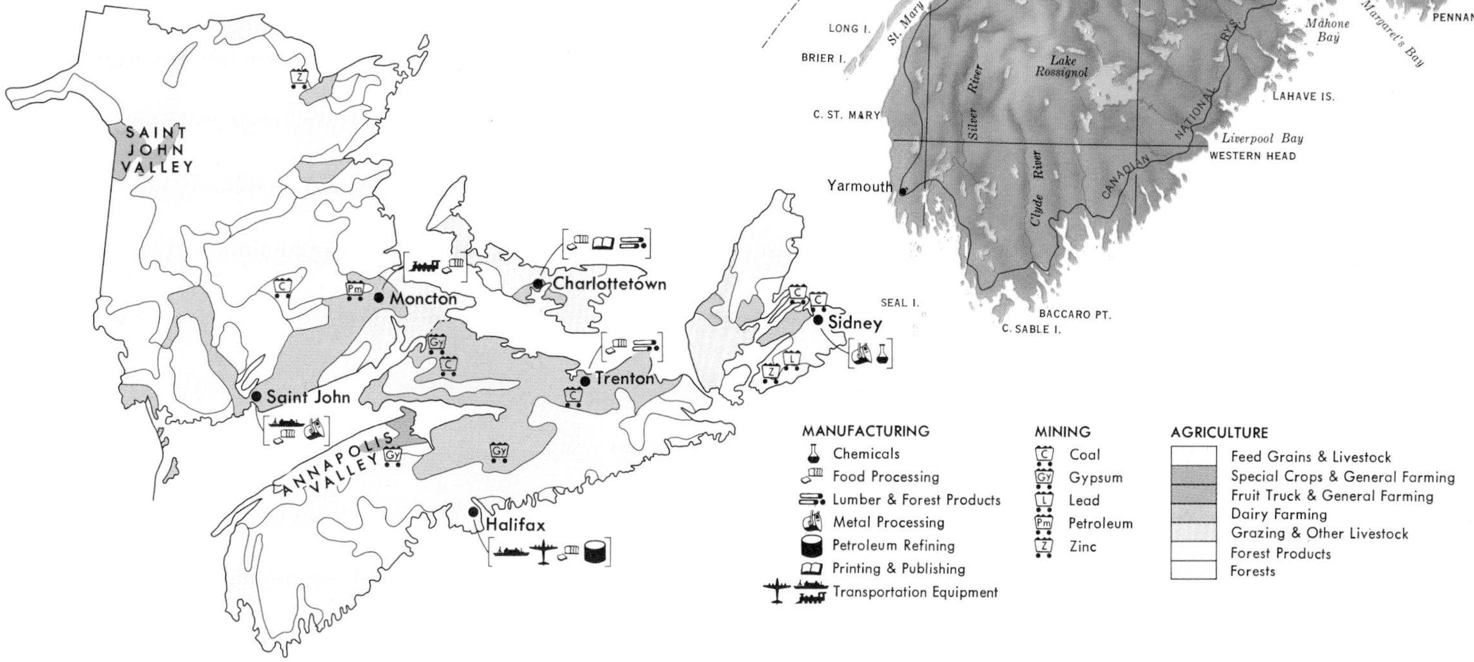

NEW BRUNSWICK: The economic lifeblood of New Brunswick moves by river and by sea. The Saint John River carries lumber and farm produce to the seaport of the same name, then joins the turbulent tides of the Bay of Fundy.

AREA: 28,354 sq. mi. Rank: 8th.
POPULATION: 596,000. Rank: 8th.
Largest city: Saint John. Capital: Fredericton.
CLIMATE: Snowy winters, cool summers inland; milder on coast with heavier rainfall.

PRINCE EDWARD ISLAND: Smallest of the provinces, agricultural Prince Edward Island grows prized potatoes. The island hopes eventually to overcome its limited marketing facilities by building a causeway to connect it with the mainland.

AREA: 2,184 sq. mi. Rank: 10th.
POPULATION: 103,000. Rank: 10th. Largest city and capital: Charlottetown.
CLIMATE: Cold winters, cool summers; adequate rainfall.

NOVA SCOTIA: A province with poor farmland, Nova Scotia looks to further growth of its pulp and paper industry, coal mines, and steel mills on Cape Breton Island. Halifax, an all-weather port, has long been a great naval garrison.

AREA: 21,425 sq. mi. Rank: 9th.
POPULATION: 719,000. Rank: 7th. Largest city and capital: Halifax.
CLIMATE: Cold winters, cool summers; ample rainfall decreasing inland.

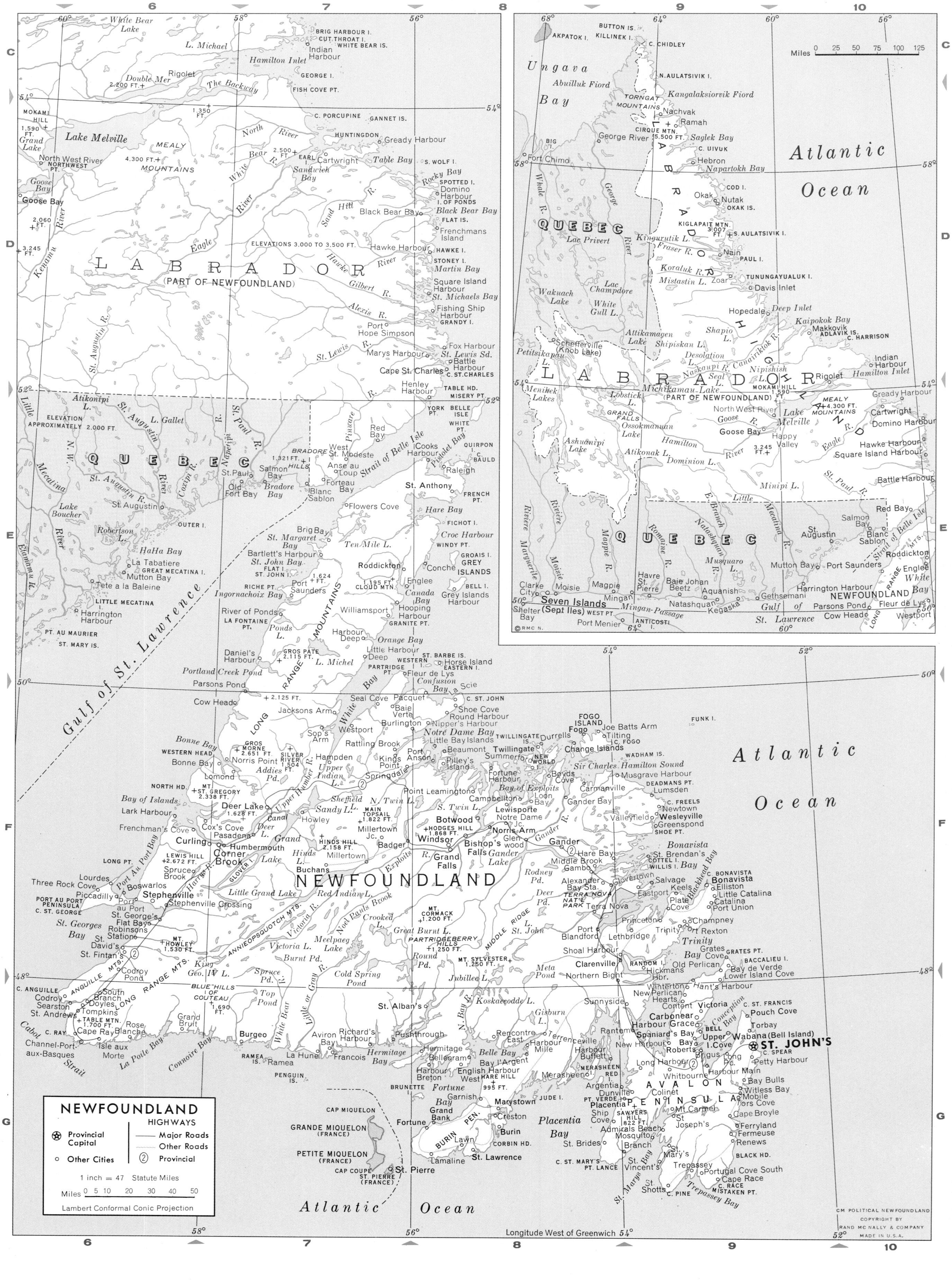

NEWFOUNDLAND
HIGHWAYS
Provincial Capital
Other Cities
Major Roads
Other Roads
Provincial
1 inch = 47 Statute Miles
Miles 0 5 10 20 30 40 50
Lambert Conformal Conic Projection
LABRADOR
(PART OF NEWFOUNDLAND)
QUEBEC
NEWFOUNDLAND
Lake Melville
MEALY MOUNTAINS
Hamilton Inlet
Goose Bay
North West River
Cartwright
Sandwich Bay
Table Bay
Black Bear Bay
Hawke Harbour
Square Island Harbour
St. Michaels Bay
Fishing Ship Harbour
Port Hope Simpson
Marys Harbour
Fox Harbour
St. Lewis Sd.
Battle Harbour
Cape St. Charles
Henley Harbour
Red Bay
West St. Modeste
Anse au Loup
Forteau Bay
Blanc Sablon
Strait of Belle Isle
Lourdes-de-Blanc-Sablon
St. Augustin
Harrington Harbour
La Tabatiere
Mutton Bay
Tete a la Baleine
Gulf of St. Lawrence
St. Anthony
Hare Bay
Croc Harbour
Conche
Englee
Canada Bay
Roddickton
Hooping Harbour
Williamsport
Orange Bay
Little Harbour Deep
Fleur de Lys
Confusion Bay
La Scie
Port Saunders
Ingornachoix Bay
River of Ponds
Daniel's Harbour
Portland Creek Pond
Parsons Pond
Cow Head
LONG RANGE MOUNTAINS
White Bay
Jacksons Arm
Baie Verte
Westport
Nippers Harbour
Round Harbour
Shoe Cove
Notre Dame Bay
Little Bay Islands
Rattling Brook
Hampden
Kings Point
Springdale
Port Anson
Beaumont
Pilley's Island
Twillingate
Fogo
Joe Batts Arm
Tilting
Change Islands
Sir Charles Hamilton Sound
Musgrave Harbour
Carmanville
Lumsden
Wesleyville
Newtown
Greenspond
Bonne Bay
Bay of Islands
Lark Harbour
Deer Lake
Humbermouth
Corner Brook
Pasadena
Cox's Cove
Curling
Grand Lake
Sandy L.
Howley
Millertown Jc.
Badger
Botwood
Bishop's Falls
Grand Falls
Windsor
Buchans
Norris Arm
Glenwood
Gander
Gander Lake
Lewisporte
Notre Dame Jc.
Campbellton
Port Au Port Bay
Stephenville
Stephenville Crossing
Piccadilly
Three Rock Cove
Boswarlos
Spruce Brook
St. Georges Bay
St. George's
Flat Bay
Robinsons Station
St. David's
St. Fintan's
Codroy Pond
South Branch
Doyles
Tompkins
St. Andrews
Codroy
Searston
Cape Ray
Channel-Port-aux-Basques
Isle aux Morte
Rose Blanche
Grand Bruit
La Poile Bay
Cabot Strait
Burgeo
Ramea
Connoire Bay
La Hune
Francois
Aviron Bay
Richard's Harbour
Hermitage Bay
Pushthrough
Hermitage
Belleoram
Harbour Breton
English Harbour West
St. Alban's
Red Indian L.
Victoria L.
Meelpaeg Lake
Burnt Pd.
Great Burnt L.
Cold Spring Pond
Round Pd.
Jubilee L.
Fortune Bay
Garnish
Grand Bank
Fortune
Marystown
Creston
Burin
Lawn
Lamaline
St. Lawrence
BURIN PEN.
Placentia Bay
Placentia
St. Brides
Argentia
Dunville
Ship Cove
Mosquito
Branch
St. Mary's
St. Vincent's
St. Shotts
Trepassey
Portugal Cove South
Cape Race
AVALON PENINSULA
ST. JOHN'S
Wabana (Bell Island)
Torbay
Pouch Cove
Petty Harbour
Bay Bulls
Witless Bay
Mobile
Tors Cove
Cape Broyle
Ferryland
Fermeuse
Renews
Holyrood
Avondale
Carbonear
Harbour Grace
Spaniard's Bay
Bay Roberts
Victoria
Heart's Content
Hant's Harbour
Sunnyside
Clarenville
Shoal Harbour
Northern Bight
Old Perlican
Bay de Verde
Grates Cove
Trinity Bay
Trinity
Port Rexton
Champney
Catalina
Little Catalina
Port Union
Elliston
Bonavista
Bonavista Bay
Plate Cove
Keels
Salvage
Eastport
Glovertown
Terra Nova
TERRA NOVA NAT'L PARK
Port Blandford
Lethbridge
Princeton
Gambo
Middle Brook
Hare Bay
GRANDE MIQUELON (FRANCE)
PETITE MIQUELON (FRANCE)
ST. PIERRE (FRANCE)
St. Pierre
Atlantic Ocean
Atlantic Ocean
Ungava Bay
Fort Chimo
George River
TORNGAT MOUNTAINS
Nachvak
Ramah
Saglek Bay
Hebron
Okak
Nutak
Nain
Davis Inlet
Hopedale
Makkovik
Rigolet
Cartwright
Goose Bay
Happy Valley
Schefferville (Knob Lake)
Michikamau Lake
Lobstick L.
Ossokmanuan Lake
Ashuanipi Lake
Atikonak L.
Dominion L.
Minipi L.
Seven Islands (Sept Iles)
Clarke City
Moisie
Magpie
Havre St. Pierre
Baie Johan Beetz
Aquanish
Natashquan
Kegaska
Gethsemani
Mingan-Passage
Port Menier
ANTICOSTI I.
Gulf of St. Lawrence
Longitude West of Greenwich
CM POLITICAL NEWFOUNDLAND
COPYRIGHT BY RAND MCNALLY & COMPANY
MADE IN U.S.A.

NEWFOUNDLAND

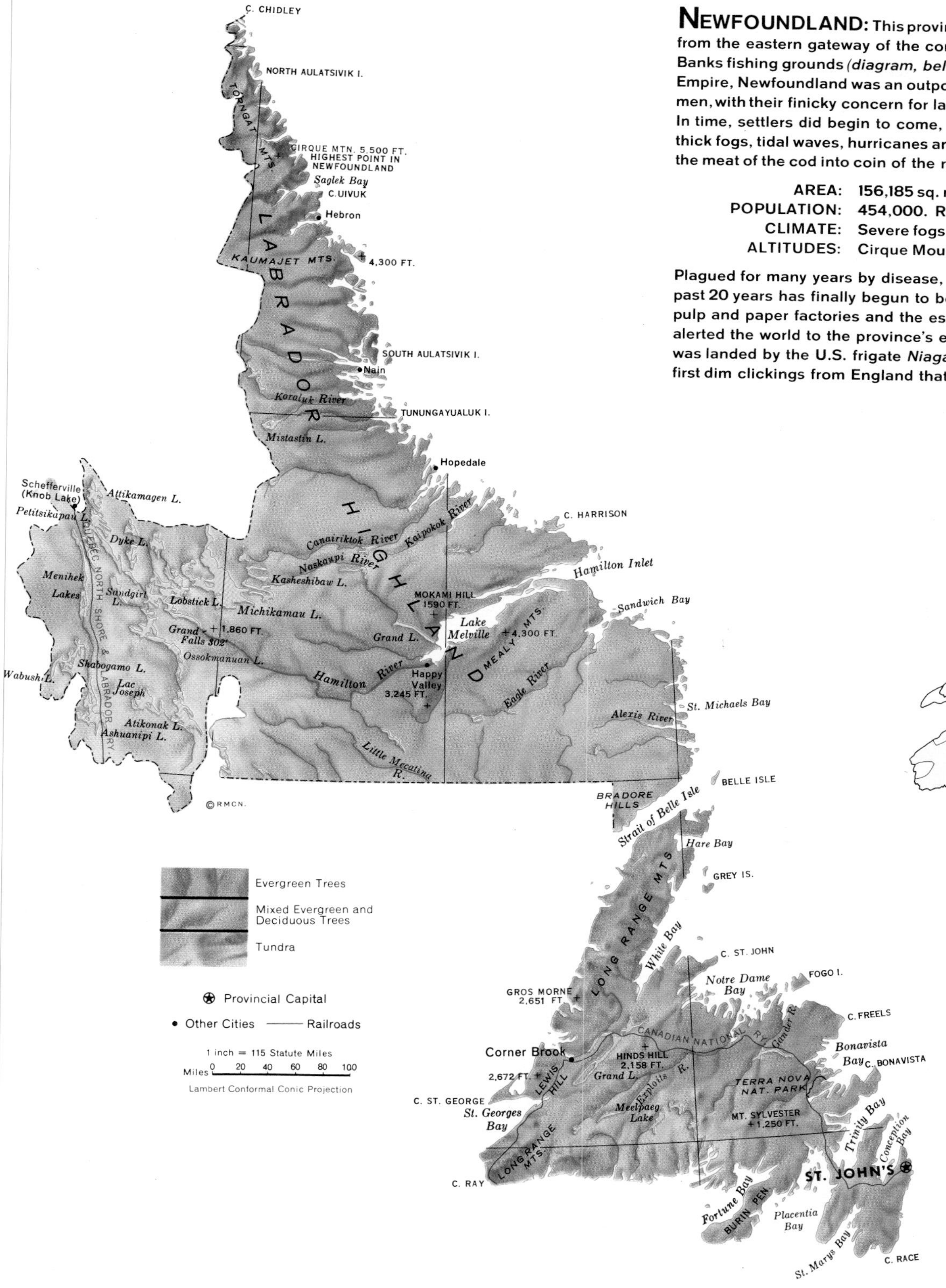

NEWFOUNDLAND: This province, once described as an "oddly shaped doorknocker hanging from the eastern gateway of the continent," dominates the cod-filled reaches of the great Grand Banks fishing grounds *(diagram, below)*. Claimed in 1583 as the very first possession of the British Empire, Newfoundland was an outpost specifically forbidden to settlers. England wanted no landsmen, with their finicky concern for law and order, to hamper the queen's favored "Fishing Admirals." In time, settlers did begin to come, but even they were forced to earn their living by braving the thick fogs, tidal waves, hurricanes and icebergs of the North Atlantic—all for the sake of converting the meat of the cod into coin of the realm in markets ranging from the Mediterranean to Brazil.

AREA: 156,185 sq. mi. Rank: 7th.
POPULATION: 454,000. Rank: 9th. Largest city and capital: St. John's.
CLIMATE: Severe fogs along the coast, much snow in winter; cool summers.
ALTITUDES: Cirque Mountain, 5,500 ft. (highest).

Plagued for many years by disease, poverty and a one-industry economy, Newfoundland in the past 20 years has finally begun to benefit from its rich ore deposits in Labrador, the growth of its pulp and paper factories and the establishment of important air bases. Modern communications alerted the world to the province's existence. In 1858 at Trinity Bay, the first transatlantic cable was landed by the U.S. frigate *Niagara*, and in 1901 on Signal Hill, Guglielmo Marconi heard the first dim clickings from England that announced the feasibility of long-range wireless telegraphy.

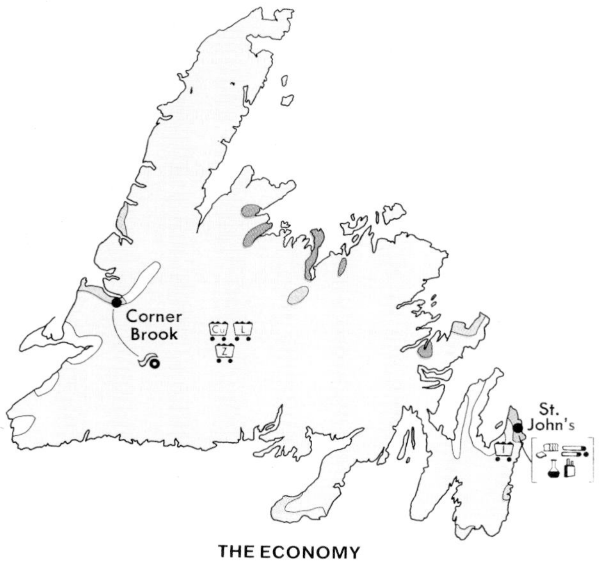

THE ECONOMY

MANUFACTURING
- Pulp & Paper Products
- Lumber & Forest Products
- Food Processing
- Chemicals
- Tobacco Products

MINING
- Copper
- Iron Ore
- Lead
- Zinc

AGRICULTURE
- Feed Grains & Livestock
- Special Crops & General Farming
- Dairy Farming
- Grazing & Other Livestock
- Forests

VALUE		EMPLOYED
$29,370,000	FISHING	15%
$62,610,000	MANUFACTURING	11%
$84,350,000	MINING	5%

Percentages given above are based on a total of 100,000 at work. In addition, about 24% are in commerce and transport, 9% in government. Manufacturing value given is only the value added when materials are converted into goods.

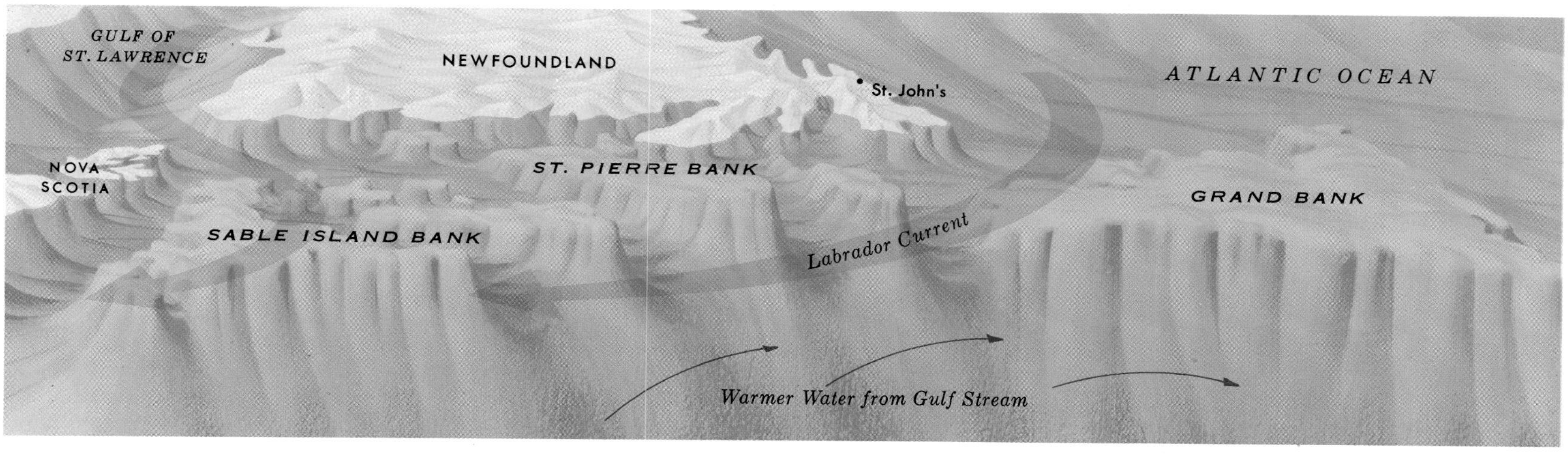

WHERE CURRENTS CLASH: A VAST AND FOGGY FISHING GROUND

In this drawing of the Grand Banks, part of the dark North Atlantic has been made transparent to show the position of underwater shelves off the coasts of Newfoundland and Nova Scotia. These shelves, thousands of feet above the deepest part of the sea, are the remains of land that once was higher than the water and was carved into its present shape by rivers and glaciers of an earlier epoch. The Banks are so near the surface of the sea that sunlight on them stimulates the growth of marine life attractive to fish. But the sunlight is fleeting. Lying at a juncture of the icy Labrador Current *(blue arrows, left and center)* and warmer waters from the Gulf Stream *(red arrows)*, the Grand Banks are subject to a clash of temperatures that creates extremely hazardous fogs.

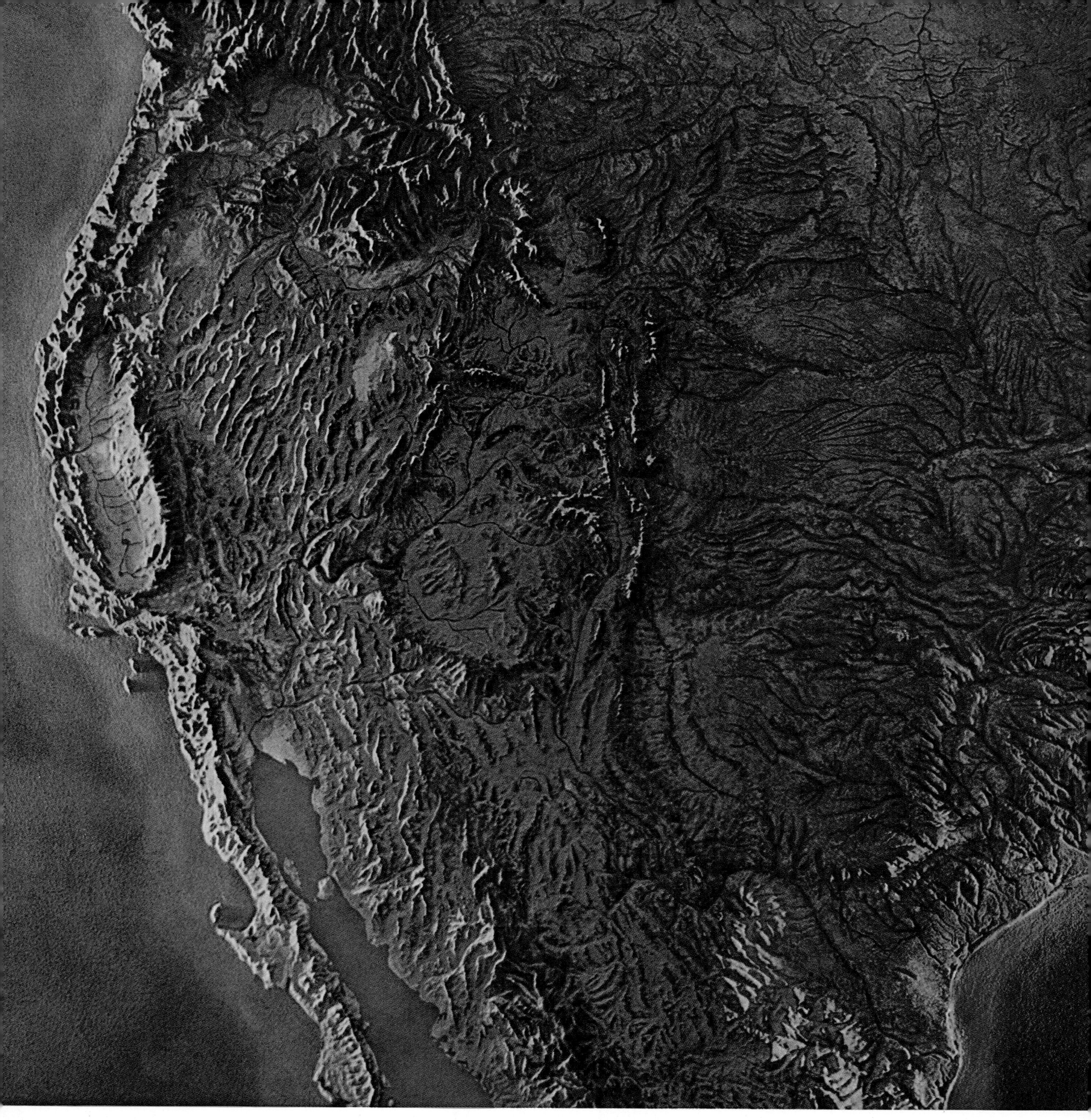

UNITED STATES

On a November morning in 1620, just 98 days out of England, the 180-ton *Mayflower* completed her rendezvous with history. She had arrived in America, bearing the bright hopes and meager possessions of the original Pilgrims, a resolute band of a hundred-odd men and women pursuing the dream of liberty. While the party paused at what is now Provincetown on Cape Cod, Captain Miles Standish went exploring in a large shallop and found a harbor across the bay. There at Plymouth the Pilgrims settled – and barely in time.

In the full fury of that first New England winter, half the settlers died. Yet those who survived sank their roots deep. And years later, looking back to the desperate times, their tough-minded governor, William

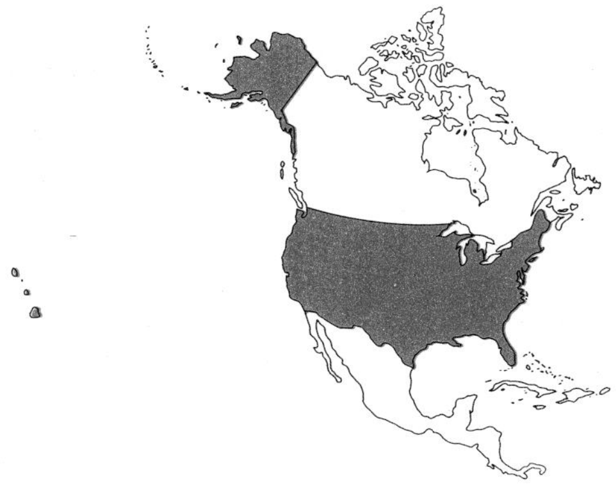

FROM SEA TO SEA stretch the 50 states of the United States. The youngest and westernmost of all are Hawaii and Alaska.

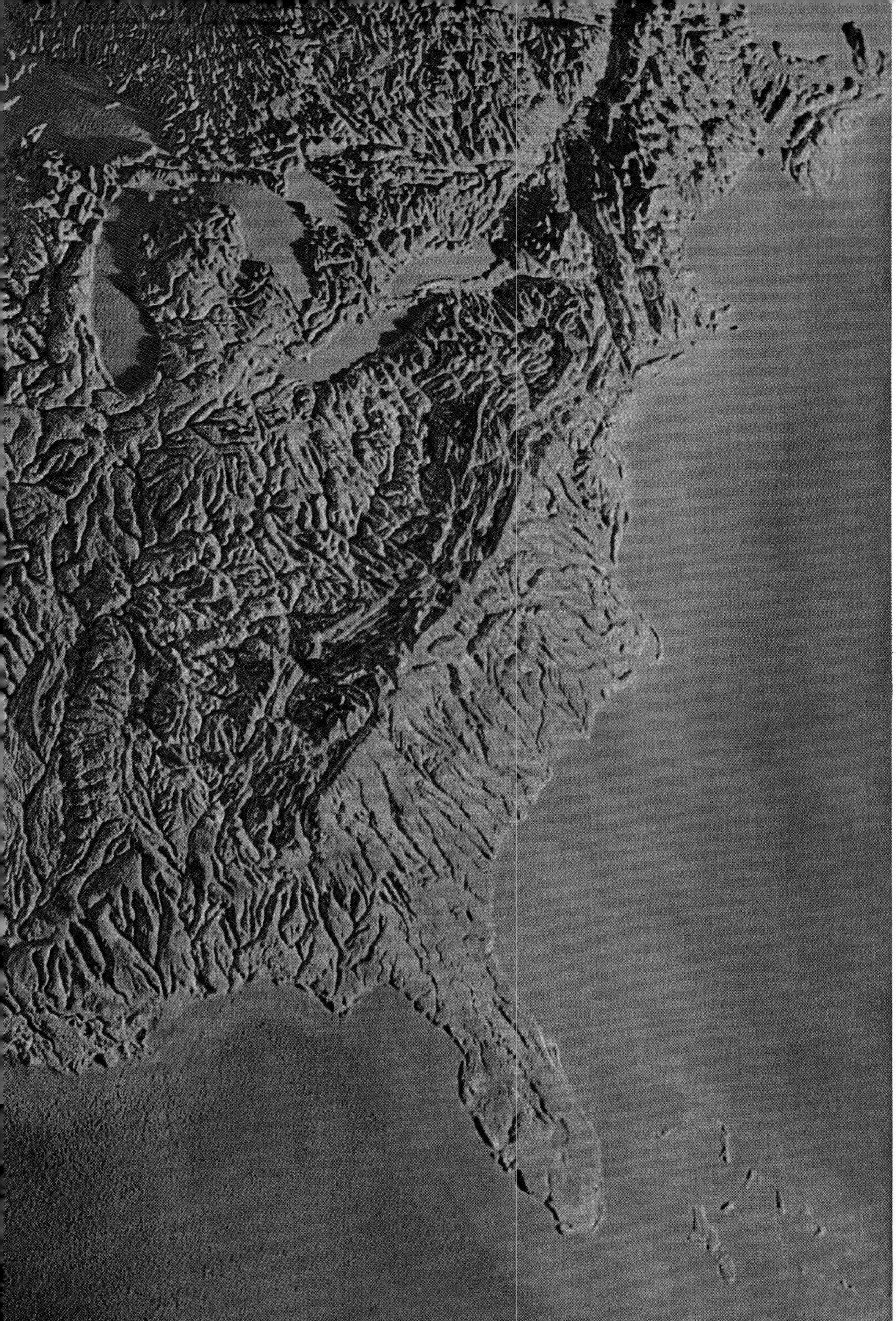

THE GLOWING COASTS of Washington, Oregon and California reflect the rays of the waning western sun *(left)*. Yet so vast is the U.S. that the Midwest already lies in the shadow of night. And the Atlantic seaboard, at right, is bathed in the light of the moon. From San Francisco to New York, the land is divided into four time zones: Pacific, Mountain, Central and Eastern.

Bradford, could write: "Thus out of small beginnings greater things have been produced by His hand that made all things of nothing . . . and, as one small candle may light a thousand, so the light here kindled hath shone unto many, yea in some sort to our whole nation."

Bradford and his Pilgrims had indeed kindled an extraordinary light on their barren coasts – a light that was eventually to illumine something more than the economic sinews of the most fabulously prolific land ever worked by man. "Those coasts," observed the prescient Frenchman Alexis de Tocqueville in 1835, "so admirably adapted for commerce and industry; those wide and deep rivers; that inexhaustible valley of the Mississippi . . . seemed prepared to be the abode of a great nation yet unborn. In that land the great experiment of the attempt to construct society upon a new basis was to be made . . . there, for the first time . . . theories hitherto unknown, or deemed impracticable, were to exhibit a spectacle for which the world had not been prepared."

Now the nation is full-grown, and the westward movement which brought it to fruition is over. But the Pilgrims' light nevertheless burns on. "No man," wrote the 20th Century American poet Archibald MacLeish, "can come to the Pacific coast of this continent . . . and feel that he has come to the *end* of anything. The American journey has not ended. America is never accomplished, America is always still to build; for men, as long as they are truly men, will dream of man's fulfillment."

UNITED STATES
Barren Areas Above Timber
Evergreen Trees
Deciduous Trees
Shrub
Medium Grass
Short Grass
Tundra
Barren Arid Areas
Below sea level areas are white. No vegetation is indicated.
National Capitals
State Capitals
Other Cities
State Boundaries
Railroads
1 inch = 220 Statute Miles
Lambert Conformal Conic Projection
Atlantic Ocean
Gulf of Mexico
Pacific Ocean
CANADA
MEXICO
HAWAIIAN ISLANDS
ALASKA
Bering Sea
Longitude West of Greenwich
COPYRIGHT BY RAND McNALLY & COMPANY MADE IN U.S.A.

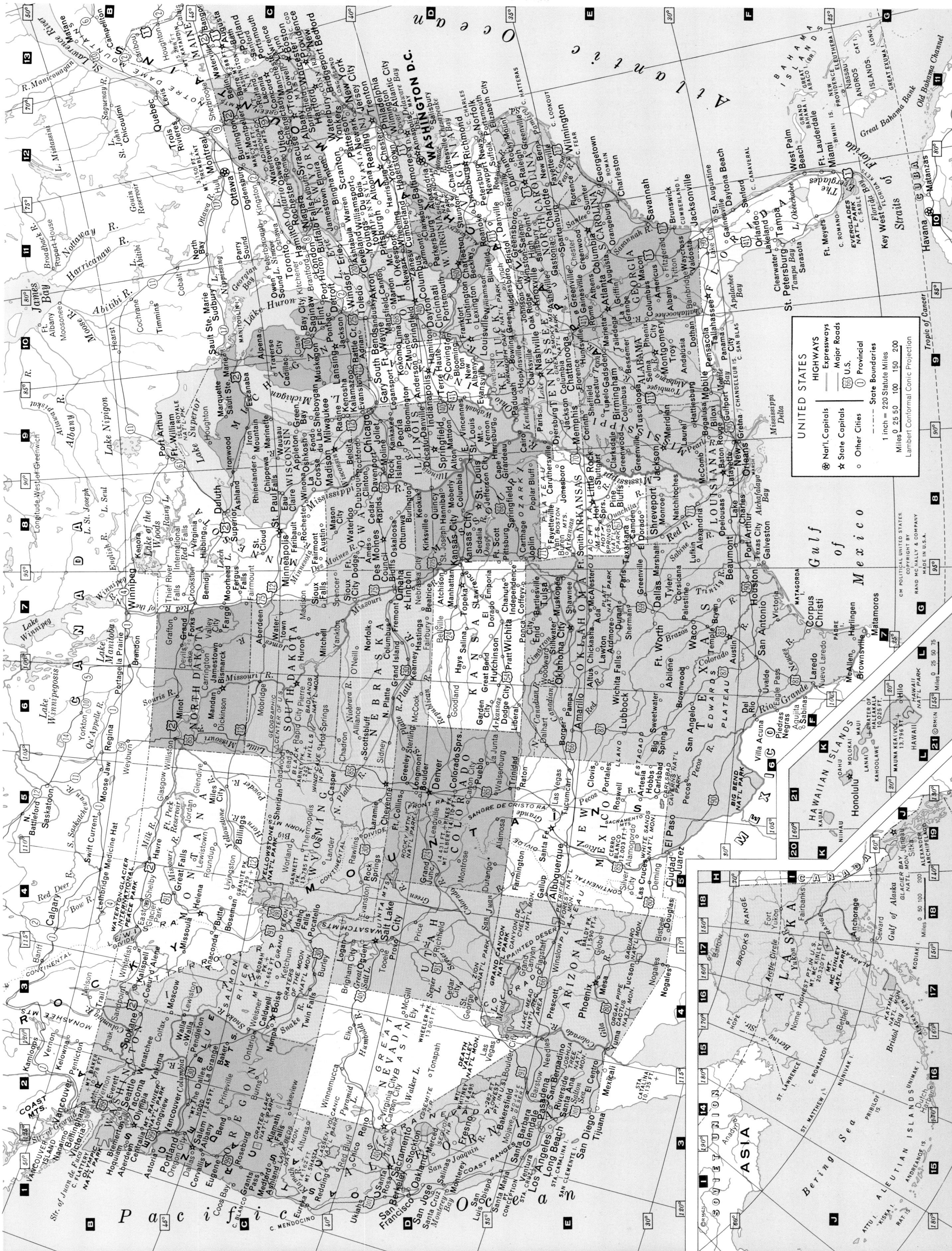
UNITED STATES
⊛ Nat'l. Capitals
★ State Capitals
○ Other Cities
HIGHWAYS
Expressways
Major Roads
U.S.
Provincial
State Boundaries
1 inch = 220 Statute Miles
Miles 0 25 50 100 150 200
Lambert Conformal Conic Projection
CM POLITICAL UNITED STATES
COPYRIGHT BY
RAND McNALLY & COMPANY
MADE IN U.S.A.
Atlantic Ocean
Pacific Ocean
Gulf of Mexico
CANADA
MEXICO
WASHINGTON D.C.
HAWAIIAN ISLANDS
ALASKA
Bering Sea
Gulf of Alaska
ASIA
Tropic of Cancer

UNITED STATES: More than 50 years ago the historian Henry Adams confidently predicted the coming of a "new American—the child of incalculable coal power, chemical power, electric power, and radiating energy, as well as of new forces yet undetermined." Today the bounty of the United States of America is staggering. Even without the energy of the atom, the nation now produces 831 billion kilowatt hours of energy annually, or 4,600 kilowatt hours each year for every one of the country's 179 million citizens. This is more than six times the total amount of power produced by Europeans, and more than 60 times the total produced by the inhabitants of Asia.

With this massive strength, the U.S. has become an unparalleled industrial colossus. It supplies more than one third of the world's steel, almost half of the radios, television sets and refrigerators, over three quarters of the airplanes and over one half of the trucks and automobiles. It has created the world's most elaborate transportation network and established a higher standard of living for more people than has ever been recorded in history.

The U.S. matches its productivity in industry with a stupendous performance in agriculture despite the fact that the land is anything but uniform in terrain or climate. There are dusty deserts, rain-soaked timberlands, sun-baked plains, glaciated northlands, subtropical forests, coastal lowlands and major mountain chains—the sharply peaked Cascade-Sierra Nevada ranges and Rockies of the West and the ancient, worn Appalachians of the East. Americans, using scientific farming and land conservation techniques, have so mastered this mixture of soils and climates that they produce $36 billion worth of food each year.

AREA:	3,675,630 sq. mi.
POPULATION:	179,323,175.
	Largest city: New York, N.Y.
	Capital: Washington, D.C.
GROSS NATIONAL PRODUCT:	$2,538 per capita.
HIGHEST POINT:	Mt. McKinley, Alaska, 20,320 ft.
LOWEST POINT:	Death Valley, Calif., −282 ft.

Abundance and affluence have created problems for which solutions have yet to be found. The rich harvests bring ever-growing and increasingly costly surpluses. The exploding populations of many cities have brought about a deterioration of urban facilities and living conditions. At the same time, in the sprawl of cities like New York, Chicago and Los Angeles, expanding suburbs have blended into each other to create extraordinary metropolitan complexes that outmode traditional forms of city government.

But these U.S. problems do not loom large to the underdeveloped nations of the world. Nearly all of them yearn to imitate the achievements of the U.S. They see that this country has set new standards of living that have forever changed man's relationship to the land and its resources. And the Americans themselves continue to press forward in the ebullient tradition of their forebears, one of whom, New England's Ralph Waldo Emerson, said a century ago: "We think our civilization is near its meridian, but we are yet only at the cockcrowing and the morning star."

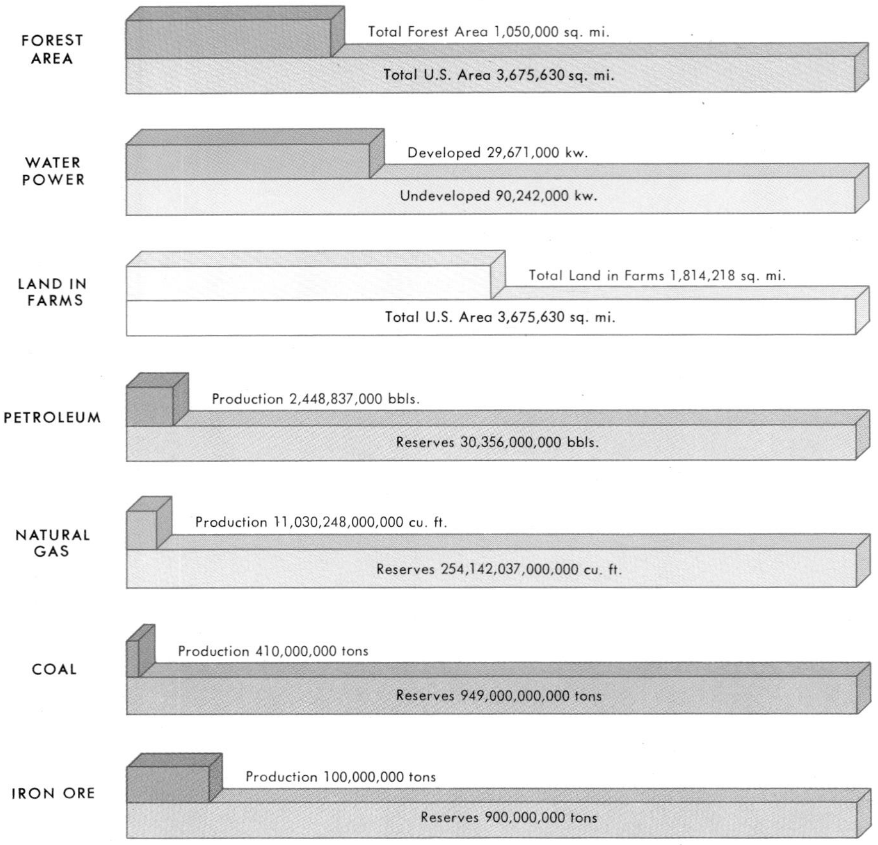

THE BUILDING BLOCKS OF THE ECONOMY

In this chart the lower of each pair of bars shows a known U.S. reserve while the upper bar shows how much of the reserve was utilized or consumed in a recent year. Farm and timberland and water power are resources that can be renewed or replenished, but iron ore, natural gas and petroleum can be increased only by the discovery of new fields or by the development of new mining or refining methods. In the last 50 years the U.S. has used up its best grades of copper, zinc, lead and iron ore. It is now working lower-grade deposits. In the far distant future, when the world's coal and oil reserves are exhausted, atomic energy may become a major source of power. But more important at present is the promise of small reactors now being used as a source of energy in areas with little or no water power or coal.

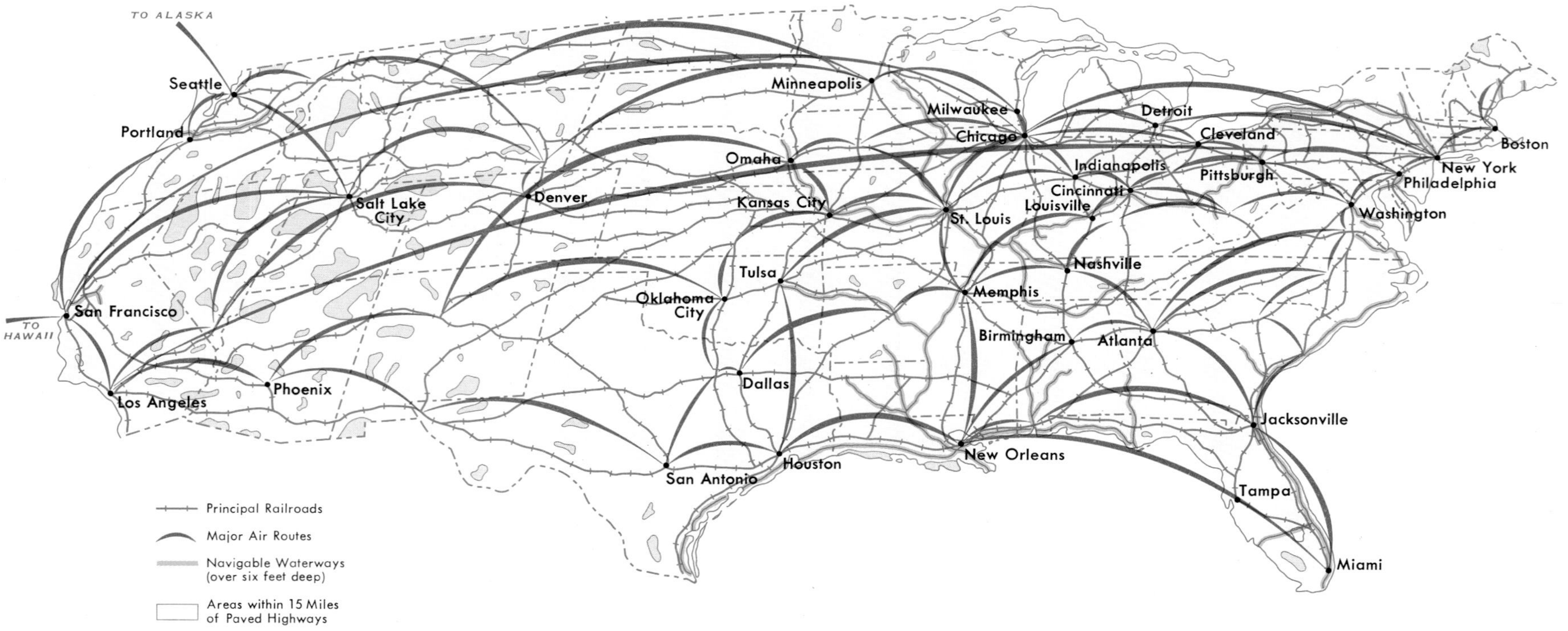

PEOPLE AND GOODS IN MOTION: THE TRANSPORTATION WEB THAT UNITES THE LAND

The intricate network of roads, railways, air routes and waterways that crisscrosses the U.S. is traced on this map. As indicated by the yellow tint, very few places lie farther than 15 miles from a paved highway. Over the country's 3.5 million miles of roads—more than any other nation's—some 68 million cars, trucks and buses travel 665 billion miles each year. The U.S. also has more rail trackage—385,264 miles—than any other country. Only major routes of this railroad system, which carries some 382 million passengers and 1.2 billion tons of freight a year, have been indicated here. Similarly, only the principal air routes are shown. Domestic airlines now carry over 55 million passengers and fly more than 29 billion passenger miles a year within the U.S. Air freight traffic, still relatively small at 343 million tons, is greater than any other nation's. Navigable inland waterways, with channel depths of six feet and over *(blue lines)*, stretch across the central and southern U.S.; also shown are the coastal waterways along the Gulf of Mexico and the Atlantic Ocean. Oldest of the country's transport links, rivers and canals are still important, carrying almost 190 billion tons of freight annually.

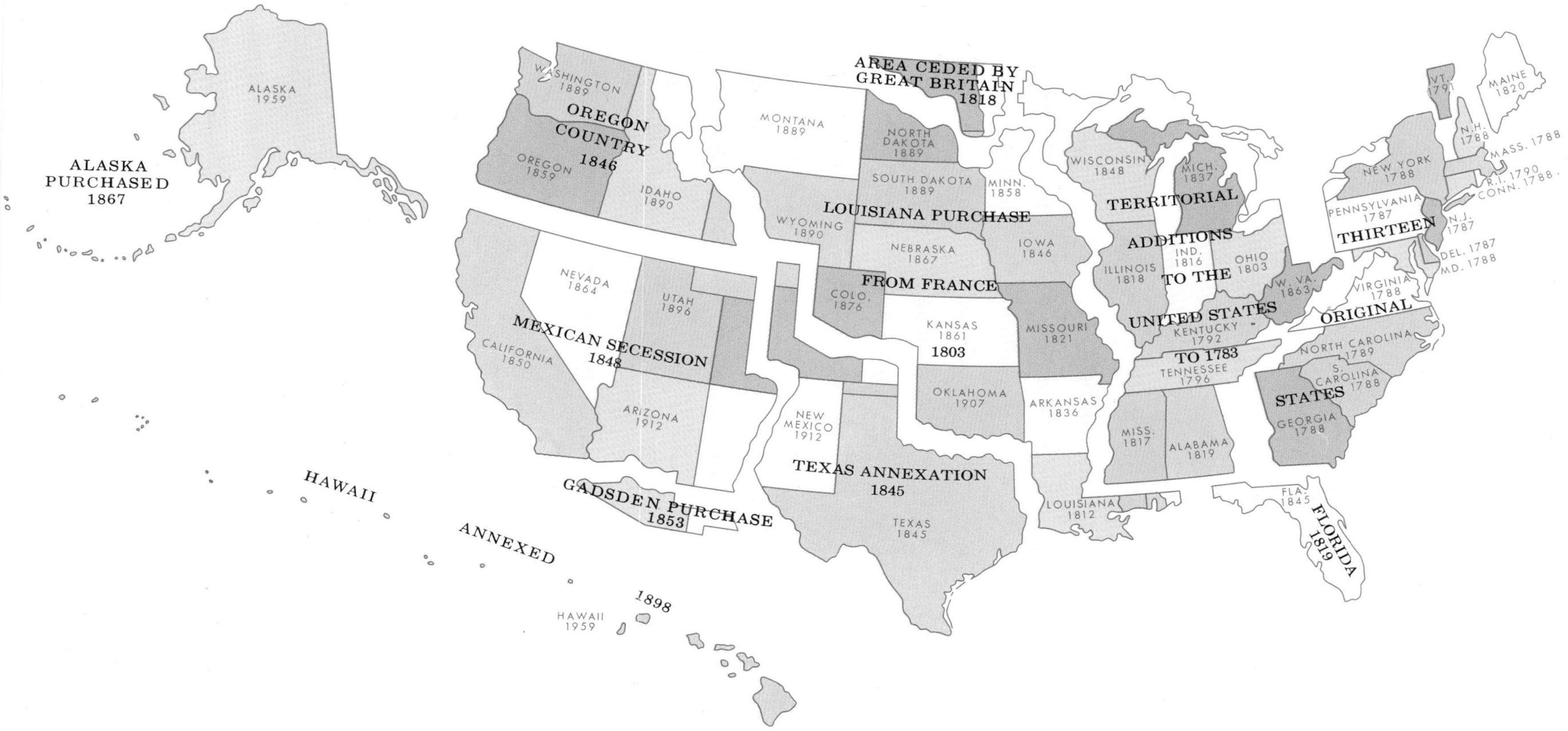

E PLURIBUS UNUM: HOW THE MANY PARTS WERE JOINED TOGETHER

The map above shows the major territorial additions to the U.S. and the dates of admission to the Union of states carved from them. Beginning with a core of 13 states *(present-day boundaries shown above)*, the young nation expanded by cession, purchase, unilateral annexation and war. By the Treaty of Paris, which officially ended the Revolution in 1783, Britain ceded to the new country the bulk of its lands lying between the Mississippi and the Appalachians. From France in 1803 the U.S. bought for $15 million the vast, mid-continental Louisiana Territory, which extended the public domain to the Rocky Mountains. (Sixteen states have been formed in part or in their entirety from the Louisiana Purchase.) A small region to the north of the area was ceded by Britain in 1818. Florida was purchased from Spain in 1819 for $5 million. The Republic of Texas, which had seceded from Mexico, was annexed in 1845. This led to war and the cession to the U.S. in 1848 of Mexico's northern territories. The Oregon Territory was ceded by Britain in 1846 after a bitter dispute between the two countries. The boundary was set along the 49th parallel, despite a belligerent American slogan, "Fifty-four forty or fight," which called for a boundary 400 miles to the north. To provide a railroad route to California, the southern portions of what are now Arizona and New Mexico were obtained from Mexico in the Gadsden Purchase of 1853, named after the diplomat who negotiated the sale. Last acquired were Alaska, by purchase from Russia in 1867, and Hawaii, by annexation in 1898.

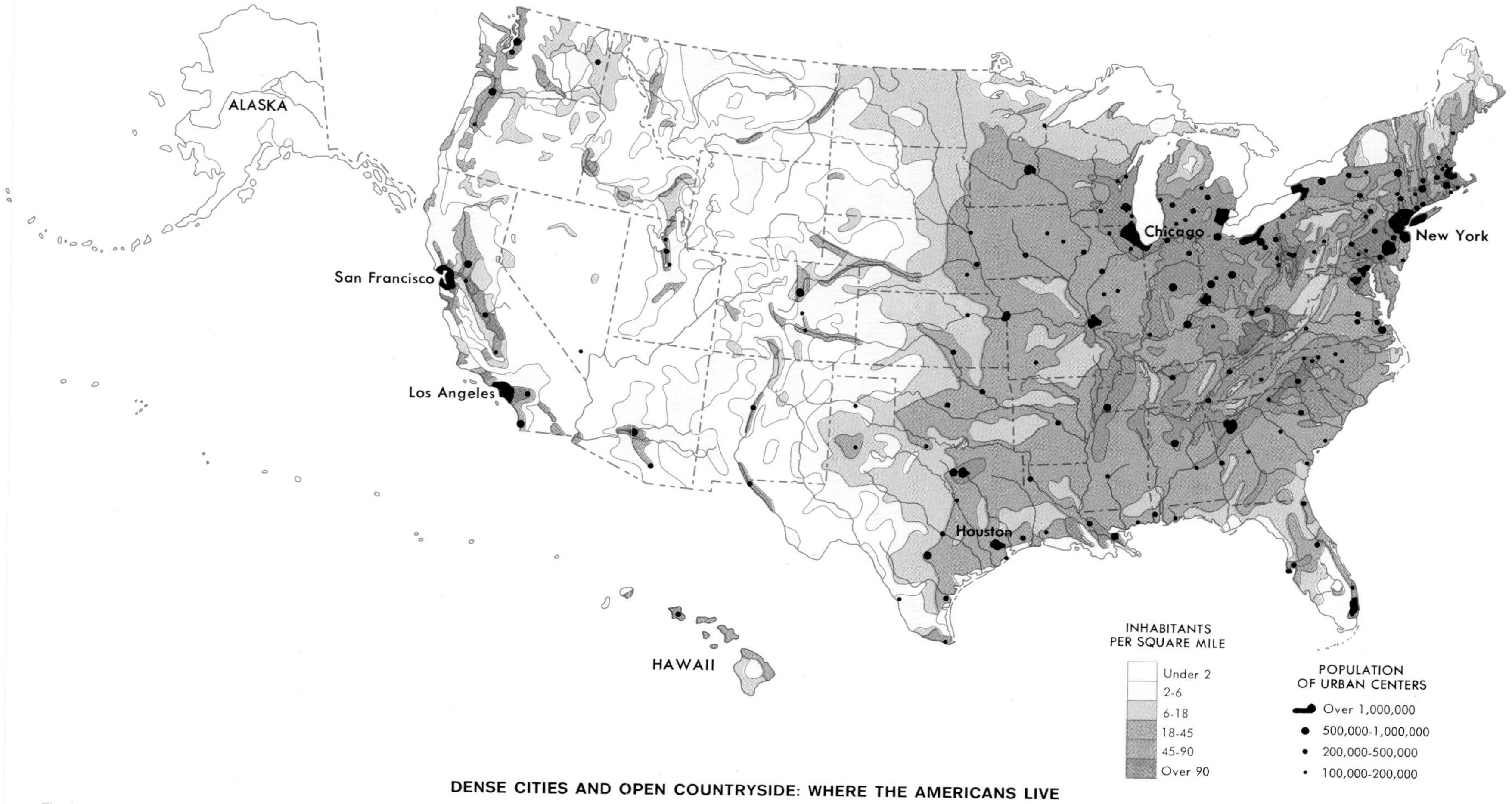

DENSE CITIES AND OPEN COUNTRYSIDE: WHERE THE AMERICANS LIVE

The historic movement of Americans toward open land has been reversed in the 20th Century. The darker hues of the map above show that 70 per cent of the country's 179 million persons now live in urban areas. Fewer workers are needed on the mechanized farms of today, and the higher wages offered by industry draw many people from rural areas to city life. In 1790, the year of the first census, the U.S. population was 3,929,000; by 1840 the expanding country contained 17,069,000 residents and by 1900, 76,212,000. Although some 40 million immigrants have entered the country since 1800, the population explosion is primarily the result of the preponderance of births over deaths and the lengthening of the life span. A dramatic illustration of the nation's great growth is the shift in location of the center of population. In 1790 it lay 23 miles east of Baltimore. Today it stands 700 miles to the west, at a point not far from St. Louis, and it continues to press westward. At the same time the northeast, the area first settled, has become the most crowded. In this region one metropolitan area now melts almost imperceptibly into the next, presaging the age of the "megalopolis."

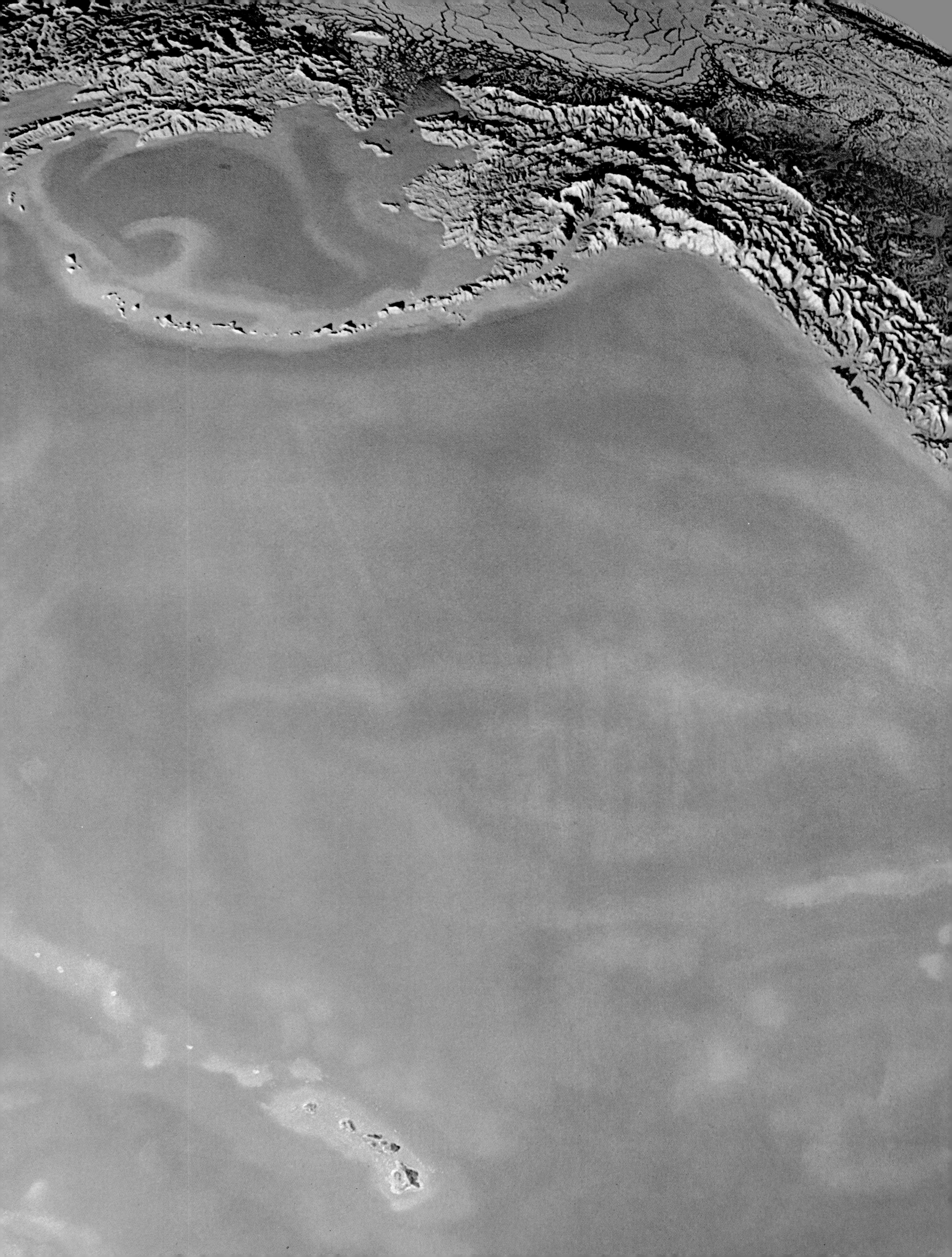

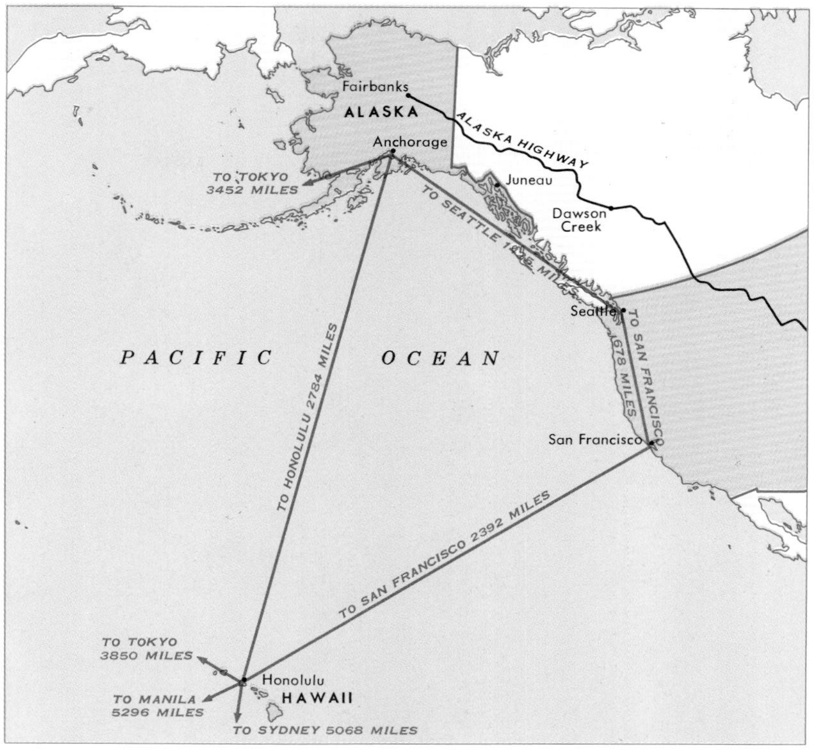

THE IMMENSE DISTANCES separating Alaska and Hawaii from the rest of the United States are shown above. But by jet, Honolulu is only five hours from San Francisco, Anchorage three hours from Seattle. The land route to Alaska through Canada is 1,982 miles.

PACIFIC FRONTIER STATES

"Take off the limit and I'll go you all," said the first poker player in *Burning Daylight,* a novel by Jack London about Alaskan gold prospectors. "Limit's the roof," said the second player. "Take off the roof," said the first. "The roof's off," said the second.

Today, in Alaska and in Hawaii – the two youngest of all the states – the sky is still the limit. But in climate, in the look of the land and the people, they are widely dissimilar. Hawaii is mild and highly developed, Alaska predominantly cold and untamed. The islands of Hawaii are volcanic. At times their highest peaks still erupt, mightily and noisily. Alaska is a land of crumpled mountains, some also born of volcanoes, all etched by glaciers. Its booming cities may echo to tunes like *Squaws Along the Yukon,* but more often the silence of the frozen tundra is broken only by the high-pitched whine of a jet taking the short cut to the other side of the world.

Yet both states share much. Throughout most of their history, they were known only to primitive peoples: Hawaii to far-ranging Polynesians, Alaska to Aleuts and Eskimos. Both were discovered by chance – Hawaii in 1778 by the British Captain James Cook, Alaska in 1741 by Vitus Bering, a Danish explorer in Russian employ. Both offered rich potentials, and both have become essential to U.S. security, as the attacks on Pearl Harbor and the Aleutians in World War II demonstrated.

FROM ABOVE THE PACIFIC, the rolling sea *(left)* both divides and connects the frontier states of Alaska, at top center, and Hawaii, in the left foreground. At far right is the rest of the United States. At upper left the Bering Strait separates Siberia from North America.

ON THE PACIFIC HORIZON: SLOPES OF FIRE

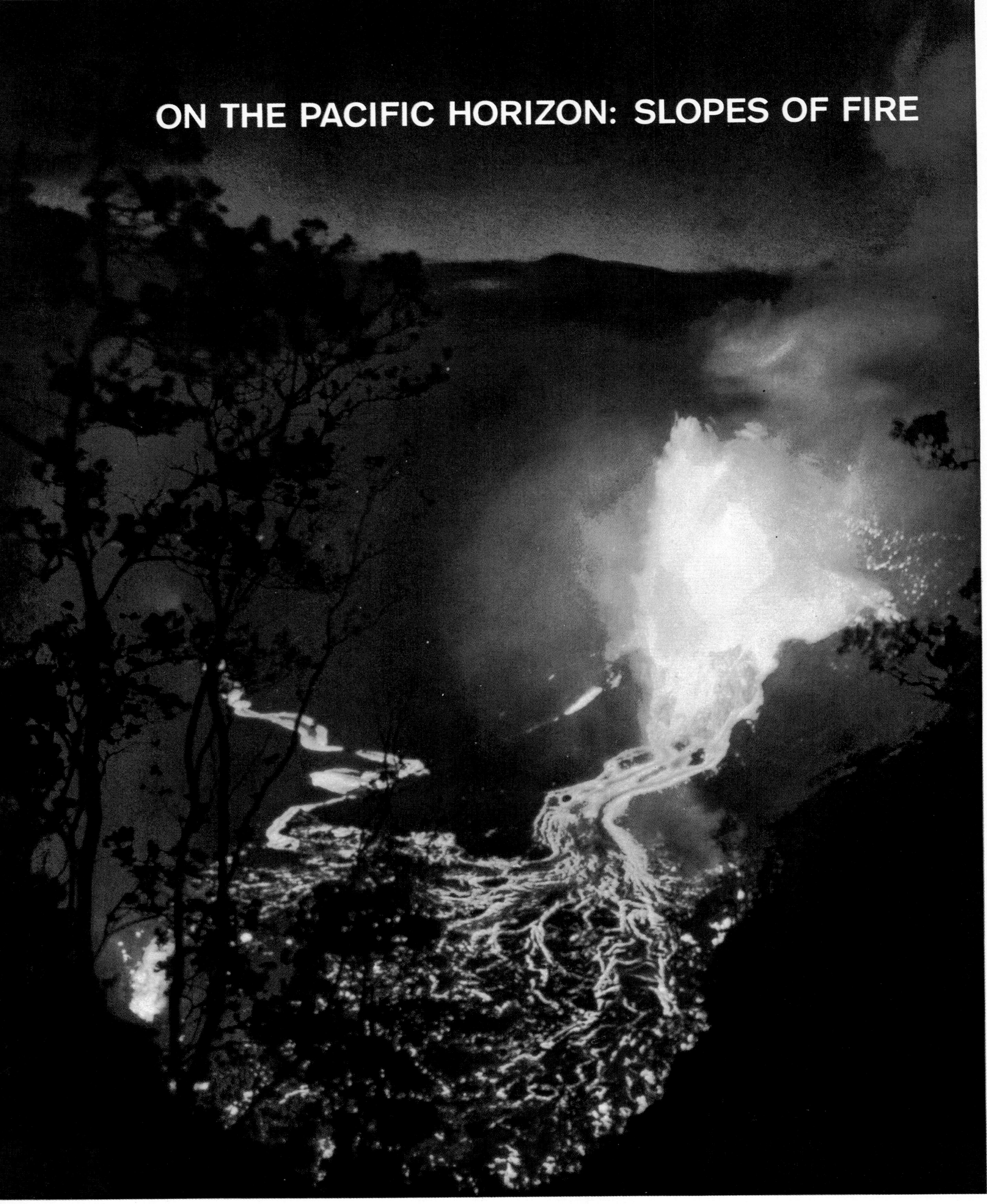

A HAWAIIAN VOLCANO, Kilauea Iki, spews fountains of incandescent lava through a wall fissure inside its crater. Kilauea Iki, a part of the larger volcano Kilauea, and Mauna Loa, a turbulent neighbor, are the only volcanoes in the islands which are still active.

. . . AND PEAKS OF ICE

AN ALASKAN SUMMIT, the 20,320-foot-high Mount McKinley, breaks into the blue sky through clouds drifting below its white-capped peak. Part of the towering Alaska Range in the center of the state, it is the highest mountain on the continent of North America.

ALASKA
HIGHWAYS
Major Roads
Other Roads
State Capital
Other Cities
State
1 inch = 151 Statute miles
Miles 0 25 50 75 100 125 150
Polyconic Projection
Longitude West of Greenwich
CM POLITICAL ALASKA
COPYRIGHT BY RAND MC NALLY & COMPANY
MADE IN U.S.A.
Arctic Ocean
Beaufort Sea
Chukchi Sea
Bering Sea
Bristol Bay
Gulf of Alaska
Pacific Ocean
Norton Sound
Kotzebue Sound
Prince William Sound
Cook Inlet
BROOKS RANGE
ALASKA RANGE
ALEUTIAN ISLANDS
ALASKA PENINSULA
SEWARD PENINSULA
ALEXANDER ARCHIPELAGO
BRITISH COLUMBIA
YUKON
CANADA
U.S.
U.S.S.R.
COAST MOUNTAINS
MT. MC KINLEY 20,320 FT. HIGHEST POINT IN NORTH AMERICA
JUNEAU
Anchorage
Fairbanks
Nome
Kotzebue
Barrow
Ketchikan
Sitka
Seward
Valdez
Cordova
Kodiak
Bethel
Prince Rupert
Dawson
Whitehorse
NUNIVAK ISLAND
ST. LAWRENCE ISLAND
PRIBILOF ISLANDS
KODIAK I.
RAT ISLANDS
NEAR ISLANDS
FOX IS.
SHUMAGIN IS.
Yukon R.
Kuskokwim R.
Tanana R.
Copper R.
Porcupine R.

ALASKA: Partly because of its forbidding size (it would almost touch all four boundaries if superimposed upon the rest of the continental U.S.) Alaska remains a largely untapped frontier region. Most of its frozen northern tundra, fog-enshrouded volcanic islands and moist panhandle are still public lands. Salmon, timber and gold are important sources of income. But all three are overshadowed by the size of federal expenditures on the area's defense. About one fourth of Alaska's residents are in uniform, in military posts scattered across the state—and for good reason. In the age of the airplane and intercontinental missiles, Fairbanks lies closer to Moscow (by 900 air miles) than does Chicago. Only the width of the Bering Strait, sometimes solid with ice during the winter, separates Alaska from Soviet Siberia *(map, below)*.

AREA:	586,400 sq. mi. Rank: 1st.
POPULATION:	226,167. Rank: 50th.
	Largest city: Anchorage. Capital: Juneau.
ENTERED UNION:	Jan. 3, 1959, as 49th state.
CLIMATE:	On the panhandle, relatively mild, with heavy rain; extremely cold winters inland, with cool summers, light rain.
ALTITUDES:	Mt. McKinley, 20,320 ft. (highest); Fairbanks, 512 ft.

Alaska is a land of promise, the last truly undeveloped region of the U.S. Here lie, still awaiting exploitation, rich petroleum reserves, as well as extensive gold and coal deposits. Here too are found all but two minerals (industrial diamonds and bauxite) of the 33 on the U.S. strategic list. The land's promise, moreover, is not far from reality, for a great asset of the nation's second youngest state is its people and their pride. "When I grow up," children are often heard to say, "I'm going to do something—for Alaska."

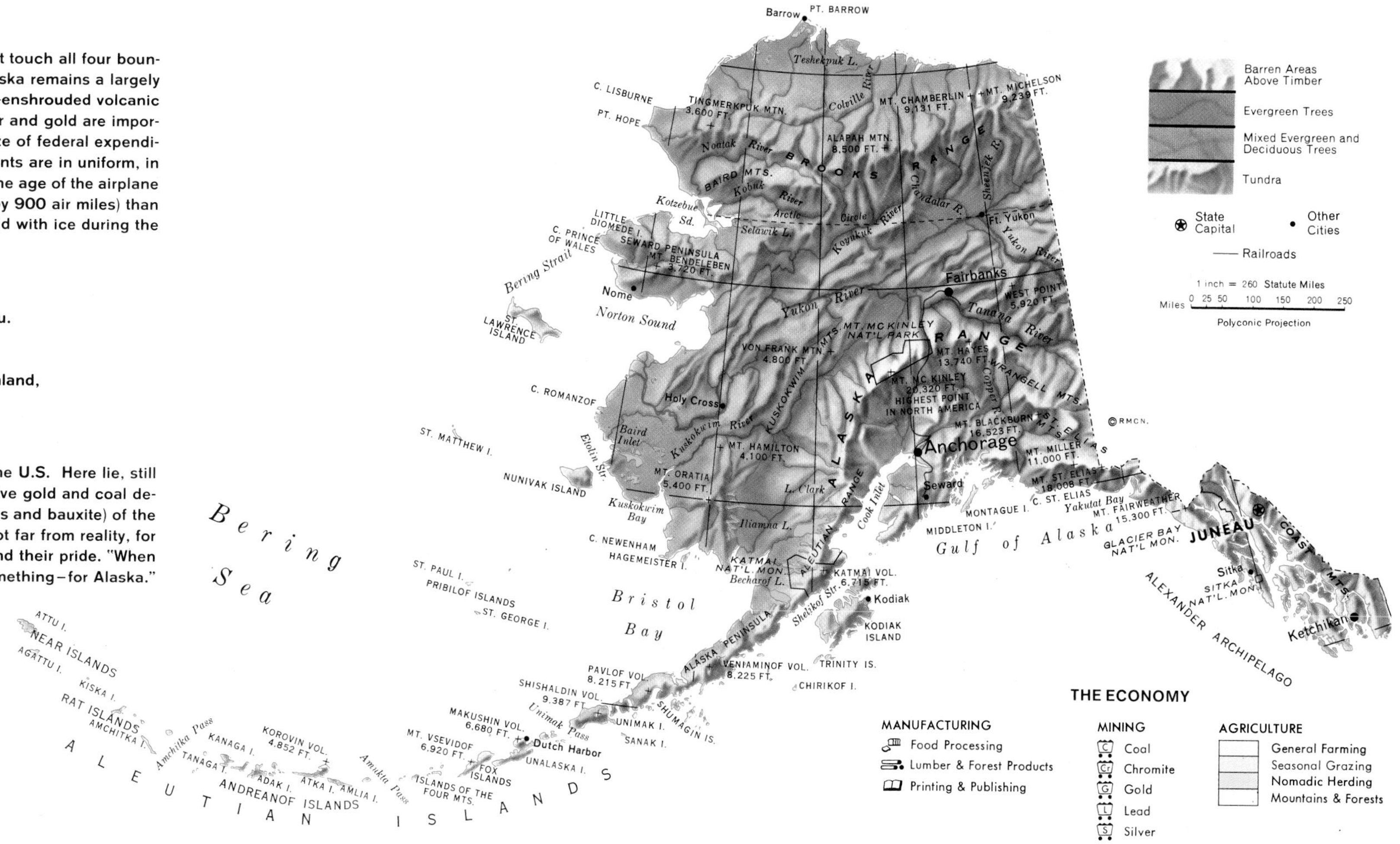
Barren Areas Above Timber
Evergreen Trees
Mixed Evergreen and Deciduous Trees
Tundra
State Capital
Other Cities
Railroads
1 inch = 260 Statute Miles
Miles 0 25 50 100 150 200 250
Polyconic Projection
Barrow
PT. BARROW
BROOKS RANGE
ALASKA RANGE
Fairbanks
Anchorage
JUNEAU
Nome
Kodiak
Seward
Sitka
Ketchikan
Dutch Harbor
Bering Sea
Gulf of Alaska
Bristol Bay
ALEXANDER ARCHIPELAGO
ALEUTIAN ISLANDS
MT. MC KINLEY 20,320 FT. HIGHEST POINT IN NORTH AMERICA
©RMCN.

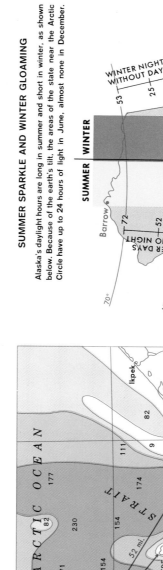

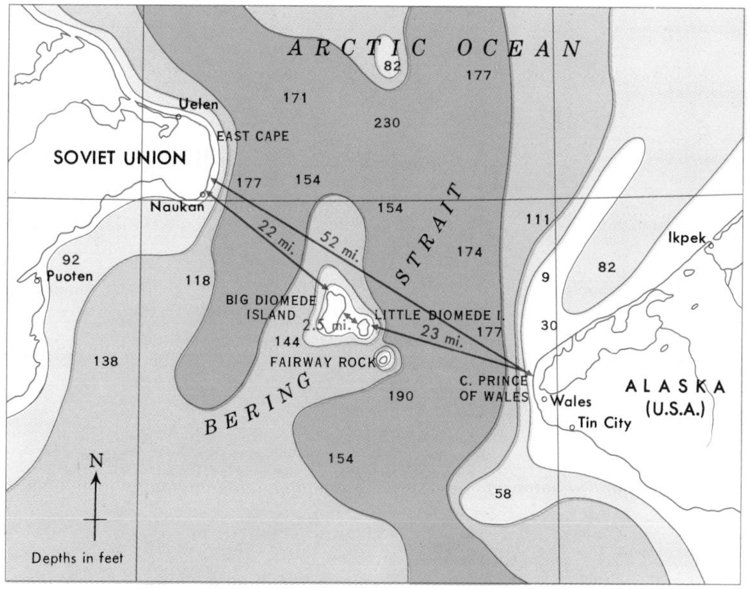
ARCTIC OCEAN
BERING STRAIT
SOVIET UNION
ALASKA (U.S.A.)
Uelen
EAST CAPE
Naukan
Puoten
BIG DIOMEDE ISLAND
LITTLE DIOMEDE I.
FAIRWAY ROCK
C. PRINCE OF WALES
Wales
Tin City
Ikpek
22 mi.
52 mi.
23 mi.
2.5 mi.
Depths in feet

HOW MEN MAY HAVE COME TO NORTH AMERICA

Depths of the Bering Strait, which separates the Soviet Union and Alaska by only 52 miles, are shown above. The shallowness suggests to some theorists that the Asian ancestors of American Indians could have made the voyage between the continents at this point, perhaps by an ancient land bridge.

SUMMER SPARKLE AND WINTER GLOAMING

Alaska's daylight hours are long in summer and short in winter, as shown below. Because of the earth's tilt, the areas of the state near the Arctic Circle have up to 24 hours of light in June, almost none in December.

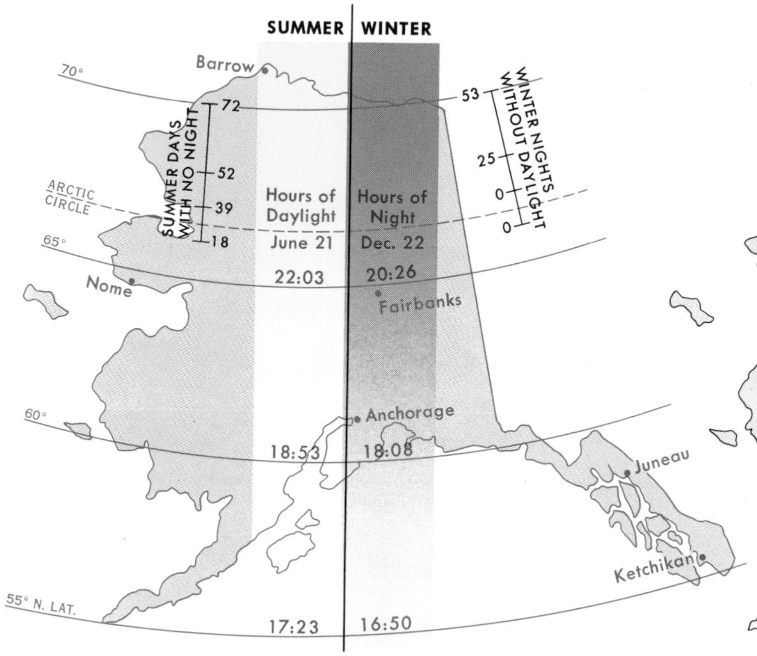
SUMMER
WINTER
Hours of Daylight June 21
Hours of Night Dec. 22
SUMMER DAYS WITH NO NIGHT
WINTER NIGHTS WITHOUT DAYLIGHT
Barrow
Nome
Fairbanks
Anchorage
Juneau
Ketchikan
ARCTIC CIRCLE
70°
65°
60°
55° N. LAT.
72
52
39
18
53
25
0
0
22:03
20:26
18:53
18:08
17:23
16:50

THE ECONOMY

MANUFACTURING	MINING	AGRICULTURE
Food Processing	Coal	General Farming
Lumber & Forest Products	Chromite	Seasonal Grazing
Printing & Publishing	Gold	Nomadic Herding
	Lead	Mountains & Forests
	Silver	

VALUE		EMPLOYED
$ 4,680,000	AGRICULTURE	1%
$40,240,000	MANUFACTURING	9%
$21,450,000	MINING	3%

Percentages are based on a total of 51,000 at work. In addition 25% are in commerce and transport, 40% in government, 22% in other areas. Manufacturing value is the value added when materials are converted into goods.

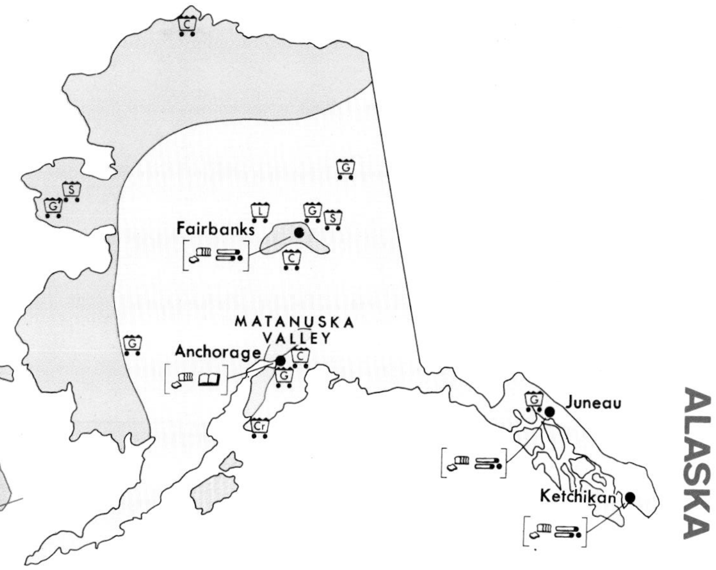
Fairbanks
MATANUSKA VALLEY
Anchorage
Juneau
Ketchikan

HAWAII
State Capital
Other Cities
County Seats
City Limits
HIGHWAYS
Major Roads
Other Roads
State
County Line
1 inch = 32 Statute Miles
Lambert Conformal Conic Projection
Longitude West of Greenwich
CM POLITICAL HAWAII
COPYRIGHT BY
RAND McNALLY & COMPANY
MADE IN U.S.A.
©RMCN.
Pacific Ocean
HAWAIIAN ISLANDS (UNITED STATES)
Tropic of Cancer
KURE
MIDWAY IS. (U.S.A.)
PEARL AND HERMES REEF
LISIANSKI I.
LAYSAN I.
MARO REEF
GARDNER PINNACLES
FRENCH FRIGATE SHOAL
NECKER
NIHOA
JOHNSTON (U.S.A.)
KRUSENSTERN ROCK
NIIHAU
KAUAI
OAHU
MOLOKAI
MAUI
HAWAII
HONOLULU
Hilo
KAUAI COUNTY
HONOLULU COUNTY
KALAWAO COUNTY
MAUI COUNTY
HAWAII COUNTY
Kauai Channel
Kaiwi Channel
Kaulakahi Channel
Alenuihaha Channel
Pailolo Channel
Kalohi Channel
Auau Channel
Kealaikahiki Channel
Hanalei Bay
Mamala Bay
Pearl Harbor
Kaneohe Bay
Maunalua Bay
Waimanalo Bay
Kailua
Kaneohe
Pearl City
Waipahu
Wahiawa
Schofield Barracks
Haleiwa
Waialua
Waianae
Nanakuli
Ewa
Ewa Beach
Aiea
Kaimuki
Waikiki
DIAMOND HEAD
KOKO HEAD
MAKAPUU PT.
KAENA PT.
KAHUKU PT.
BARBERS PT.
WAIANAE MTS.
KOOLAU RANGE
NUUANU PALI (PASS)
Lihue
Kapaa
Koloa
Waimea
Kekaha
Hanapepe
Wailuku
Kahului
Lahaina
Hana
Kaunakakai
Lanai City
KAHOOLAWE
LANAI
MOLOKAI
HAWAII NAT'L PARK
CRATER OF HALEAKALA 10,025 FT.
Kailua-kona
Captain Cook
Honokaa
Waimea
Pahala
Naalehu
Kurtistown
Pahoa
MAUNA KEA (VOL.) 13,796 FT.
MAUNA LOA (VOL.) 13,680 FT.
HUALALAI 8,251 FT.
KILAUEA CRATER 4,090 FT.
HAWAII NATIONAL PARK
KA LAE (SOUTH CAPE)
UPOLU PT.
CAPE KUMUKAHI
Kiholo Bay
Kawaihae Bay
Kealakekua Bay
Hilo Bay

HAWAII: "We came from Hawaiki-the-Great," runs the ancient Polynesian chant, "from Hawaiki-the-Long, from Hawaiki-the-Distant." So sang these far-roving South Pacific peoples as they sailed eastward, populating Samoa, Tonga, Bora-Bora, Tahiti and the Marquesas as they went. Sometime in the remote past, navigating by the stars in 70-foot, double-hulled canoes, they came upon a vast island chain. They named the major island "Hawaiki," as they had other islands at which they had paused en route.

Here was an ocean paradise. Gradually created by volcanic action over millenniums *(below, right)*, the eight main islands and a string of 20 coral-fringed islets sweep 1,600 miles across the Pacific. In their rich lava soil, the starchy taro plant flourished in the warm sun. In time Hawaiki became Hawaii, and other peoples came—missionaries and whalers from New England; entrepreneurs to service the whalers; Japanese, Filipinos and Chinese to work vast plantations of pineapple and sugar cane.

AREA:	6,421 sq. mi. Rank: 47th.
POPULATION:	632,772. Rank: 43rd. Largest city and capital: Honolulu.
ENTERED UNION:	Aug. 21, 1959, as 50th state.
CLIMATE:	Great variation in rainfall depending on trade winds. Windward slopes are wet, leeward slopes generally dry. Mild temperatures.
ALTITUDES:	Mauna Kea on Hawaii, 13,796 ft. (highest).

Hawaii's strategic location in the mid-Pacific dominates its economy. Twenty-five per cent of its labor force is employed on great military installations like the Navy's Pearl Harbor. Agriculture is now a declining industry, for the plantation operators find that rising costs make it difficult to compete with continental U.S. and Far Eastern growers. But the land itself—lulled by the northeast trades, its palm-clad slopes rising toward the Pacific sky—remains a paradise, recalling Mark Twain's description: ". . . the loveliest fleet of islands that lies anchored in any ocean."

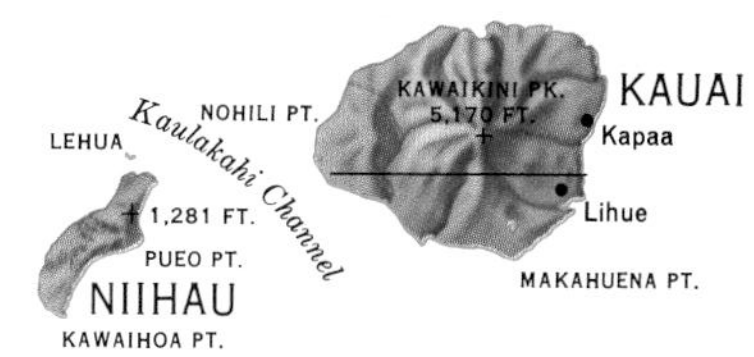
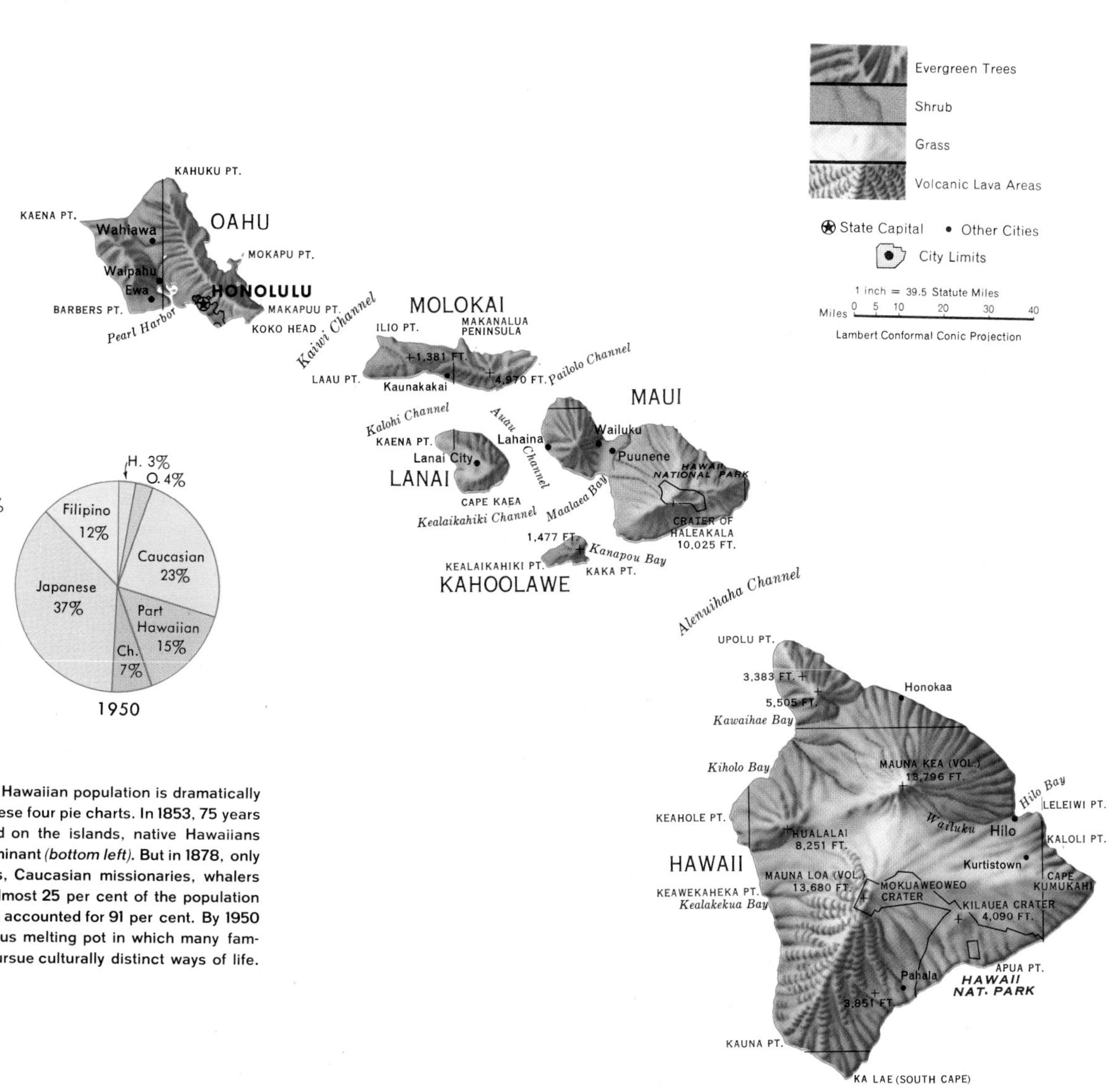

A MELTING POT IN MID-OCEAN

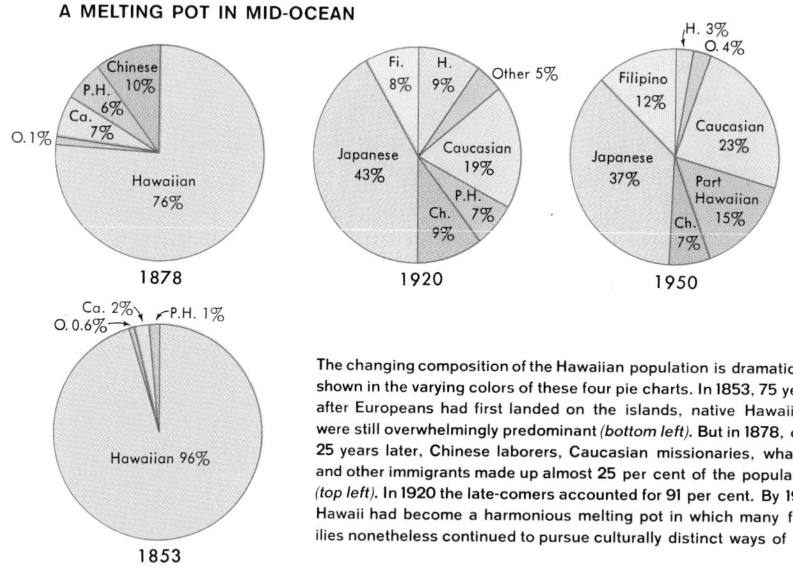

The changing composition of the Hawaiian population is dramatically shown in the varying colors of these four pie charts. In 1853, 75 years after Europeans had first landed on the islands, native Hawaiians were still overwhelmingly predominant *(bottom left)*. But in 1878, only 25 years later, Chinese laborers, Caucasian missionaries, whalers and other immigrants made up almost 25 per cent of the population *(top left)*. In 1920 the late-comers accounted for 91 per cent. By 1950 Hawaii had become a harmonious melting pot in which many families nonetheless continued to pursue culturally distinct ways of life.

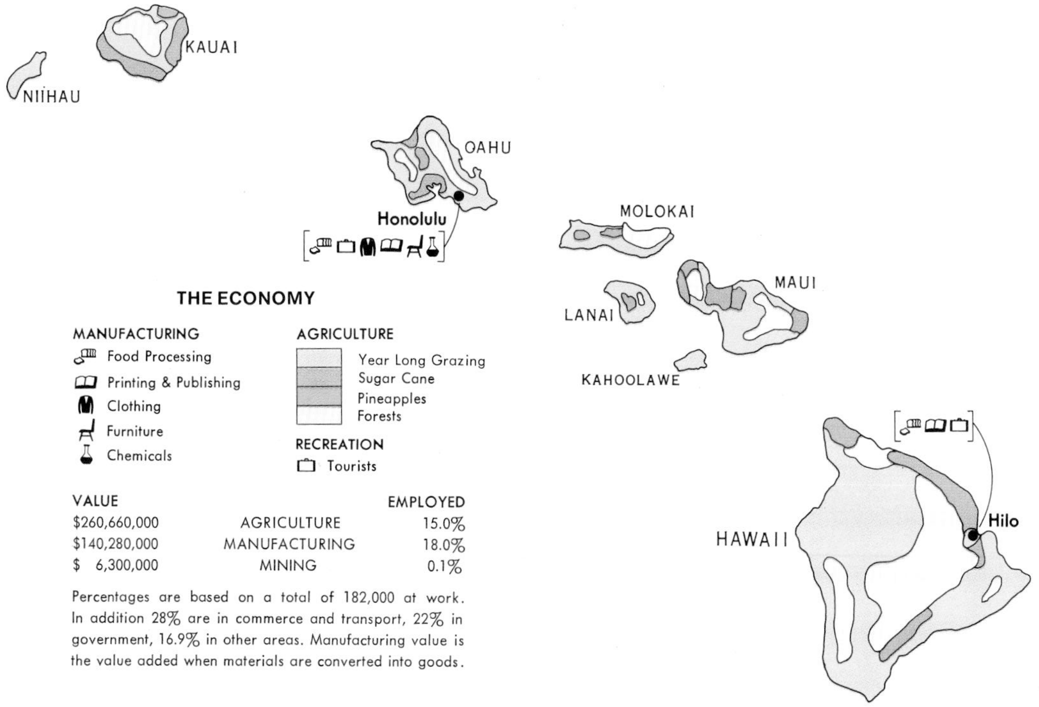

THE ECONOMY

MANUFACTURING	AGRICULTURE
Food Processing	Year Long Grazing
Printing & Publishing	Sugar Cane
Clothing	Pineapples
Furniture	Forests
Chemicals	RECREATION: Tourists

VALUE		EMPLOYED
$260,660,000	AGRICULTURE	15.0%
$140,280,000	MANUFACTURING	18.0%
$ 6,300,000	MINING	0.1%

Percentages are based on a total of 182,000 at work. In addition 28% are in commerce and transport, 22% in government, 16.9% in other areas. Manufacturing value is the value added when materials are converted into goods.

FROM THE PACIFIC FLOOR, A VOLCANO SLOWLY BUILDS TOWARD THE SKY

The formation of a representative volcanic Hawaiian island is shown in cross section above. On the Pacific floor a rift, or weakened zone in the earth's crust, has opened, permitting lava *(dark brown)* to erupt. Flowing up and out from the central vent, layers of lava, cinder and ash accumulate from successive eruptions over the centuries, piling the volcano higher and higher until it breaks the sea's surface. All the mountainous, fertile Hawaiian islands were born in this manner, although some smaller ones reached the surface only after coral growths piled up for centuries on their still-submerged bases. The larger islands contain some of the world's tallest peaks, measured from the ocean bottom. The highest formation, Mauna Kea on the island of Hawaii itself, is a dormant dome volcano thrusting over six miles from its underwater base to its top. Today the westernmost Hawaiian Islands, which were the first to form, are being worn away by the action of the Pacific waves.

PACIFIC COAST STATES

On November 7, 1805, 543 days out of St. Louis, Captains William Clark and Meriwether Lewis of the United States Army paused near the mouth of the Columbia to record a triumphant entry in their expedition logbook: "Great joy in camp we are in view of the Ocian, this great Pacific Octean . . . and the roreing or noise made by the waves brakeing on the rockey Shores . . . may be heard distictly." So began, as the historian Frederick Jackson Turner was to describe it a century later, "the age of the Pacific Ocean – mysterious and unfathomable in its meaning to our own future."

It was to this distant frontier that the spiritual heirs of the eastern seaboard pioneers first came. Some, like the forty-niners, were in search of the gold of Sutter's Creek. Some sought the parcel of Oregon Territory (640 acres to a married man) offered by a benevolent federal government conscious of the western tug of empire. Some came to Christianize the Indian; some to exploit him. And still others were

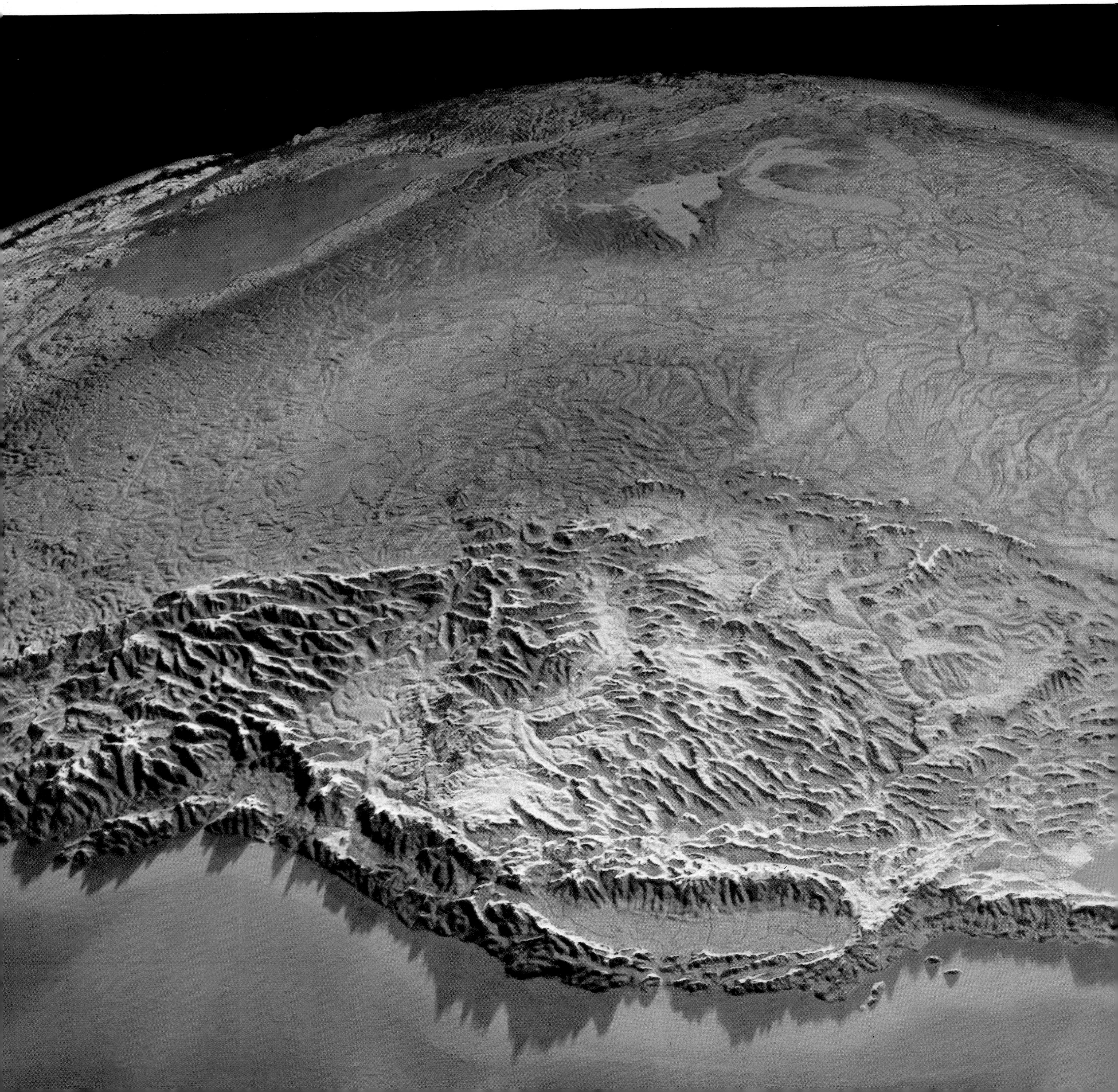

simply "a-westering," lured by the passionate belief that a man needed plenty of elbowroom and a clear view of the big sky.

Whatever impelled them across 2,000 miles of natural obstacles, the western pioneers found a lovely land – fantastic in its diversity, rich in its possibilities. When the trail forked in what is now Idaho, some turned northwest down the winding Snake and into Oregon Territory, where glacier-ground peaks stood white-capped against the Pacific, where virgin Douglas fir soared 200 feet and more into the air.

The southwest fork led to the drier land of California. There, with water from the mountains, men made the land rich beyond the dreams of those who came expecting the streets to be paved with yellow gold.

It was not easy, least of all for the pioneers who struggled through the first winters in Oregon's Willamette Valley and those who saw the bones of the unlucky in California's Donner Pass. But Manifest Destiny, the urge to span a continent, was done. And the West had begun.

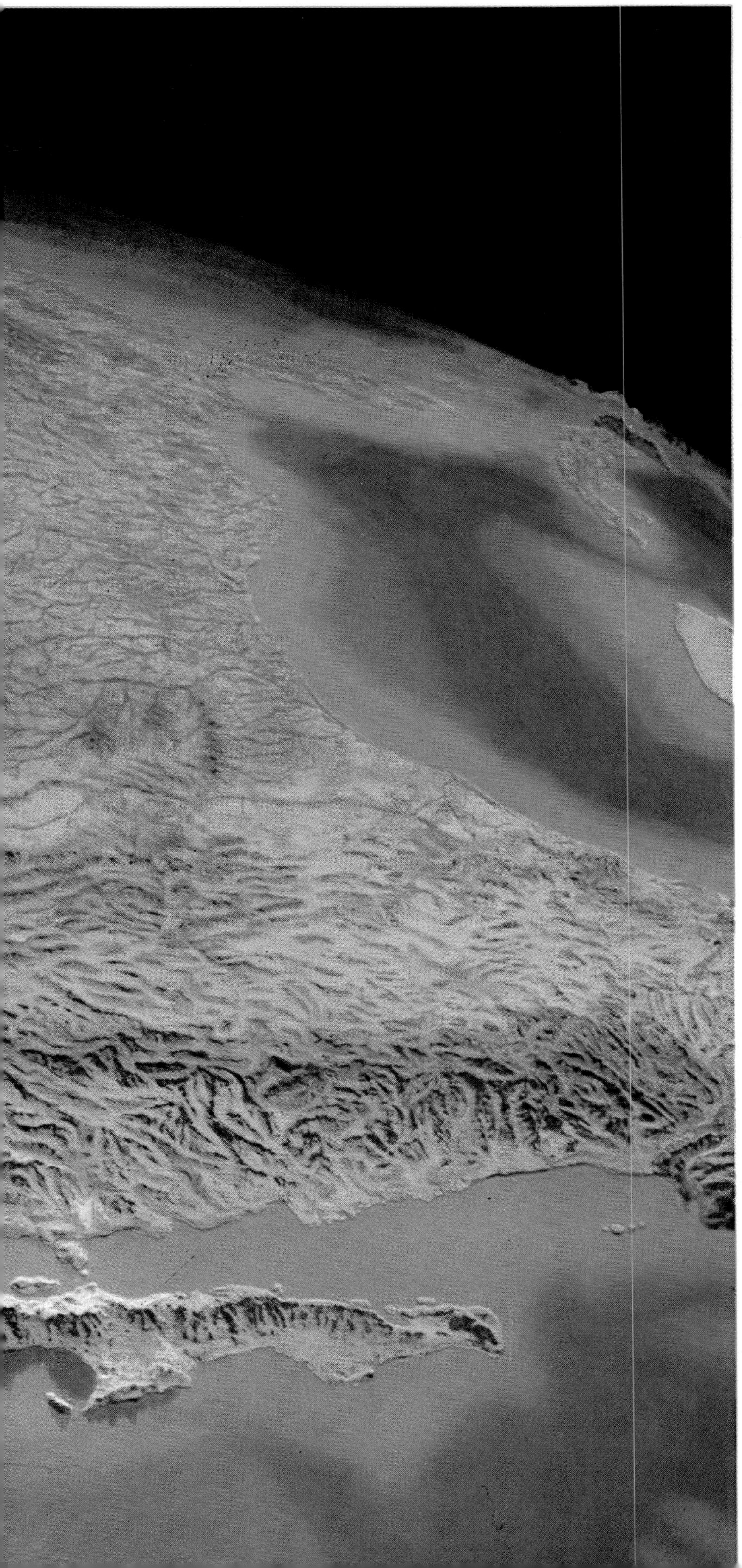

VIEWED FROM THE WEST, the mountains and plains of the U.S. *(left)* seem to roll relentlessly down to the Pacific. In the center foreground lies San Francisco, whose bay dents the west rim of California's Central Valley. At far left is Canada and at far right, Mexico.

A LAND TRANSFORMED

POWER OF THE WATERS pours through a spillway of the Belden Dam in northern California's $1.75 billion Feather River project. Together, the Pacific states produce more than 11.5 million kilowatts of hydroelectric power a year, some 40 per cent of the country's total.

REWARDS OF IRRIGATION line a lettuce field in California's 100-mile-long Salinas Valley. Despite a meager summer rainfall of less than five inches, the fertile soil of the valley is able to produce $40 million worth of lettuce and over $70 million worth of other truck farm

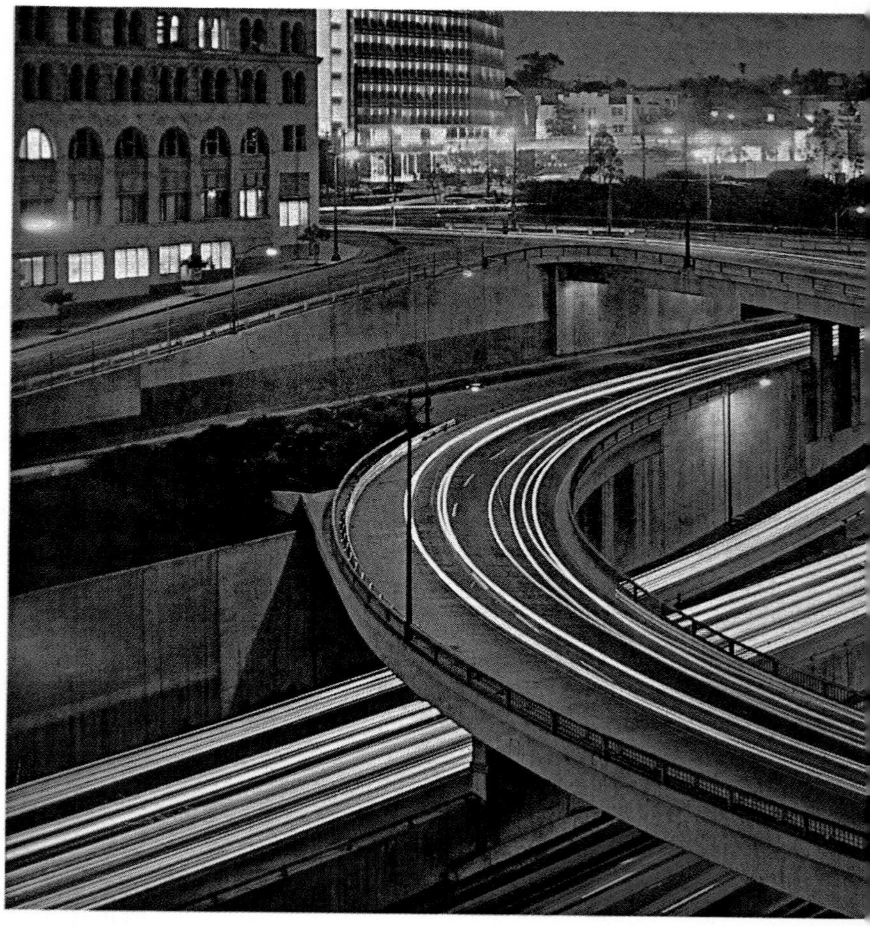

PATTERNS OF THE CITY are traced by the headlights of cars hurtling across the complex intersecting roadways of central Los Angeles. Here, where rapid transit facilities are overburdened, much of the area is devoted to freeways, turnpikes, parking facilities and

BY THE HAND OF MAN

products every year, thanks to the carefully channeled runoff of the region's abundant streams. To meet the ever-present problem of sparse rainfall, the state of California alone maintains more than one quarter of all the land now under irrigation in the United States.

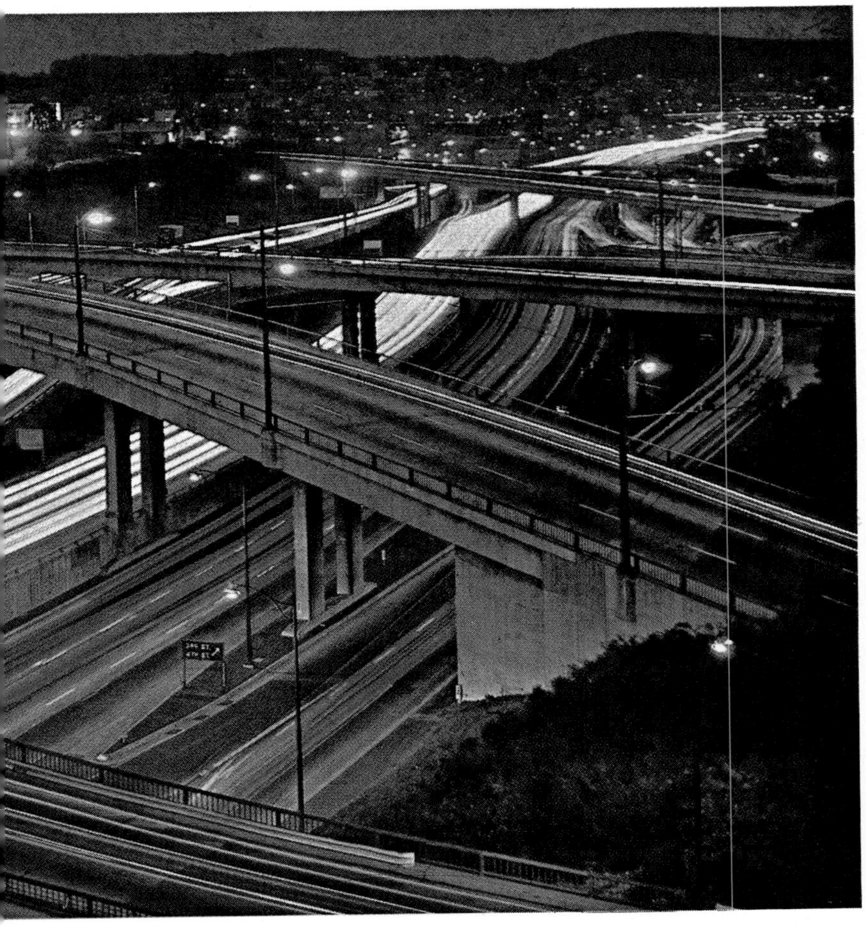

plain streets—barely sufficient to accommodate the two million automobiles which enter the metropolis daily. The largest city in area in the United States, fast-growing Los Angeles occupies a sprawling 458 square miles and anticipates a population of 10 million by 1980.

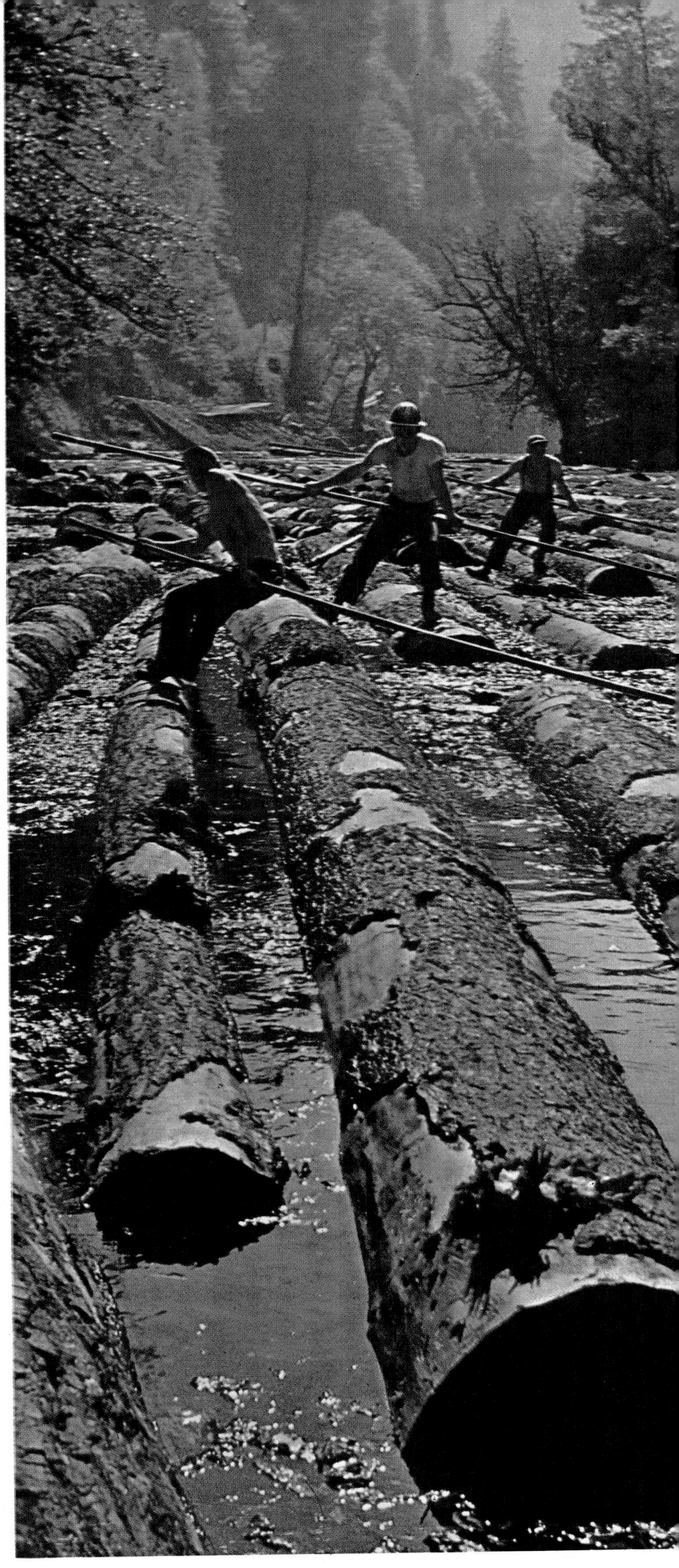

BOUNTY OF THE FOREST, logs of Douglas fir destined for a plywood mill are piked into position to pass downstream through a narrow tributary of the Coos River in northwest Oregon. The Pacific Coast states produce more than 40 per cent of the country's lumber.

SPECTACULAR YOSEMITE, its unspoiled beauty framed in a valley carved by glaciers more than a million years ago, lies 150 miles to the east of San Francisco. Its most awe-inspiring sight is Bridalveil Fall *(right)*, one of the eight misting cataracts which plunge to the valley floor. Today Yosemite ranks among the most popular of the seven national parks in the Pacific Coast states.

A GLORY PRESERVED IN A WILDERNESS VALLEY

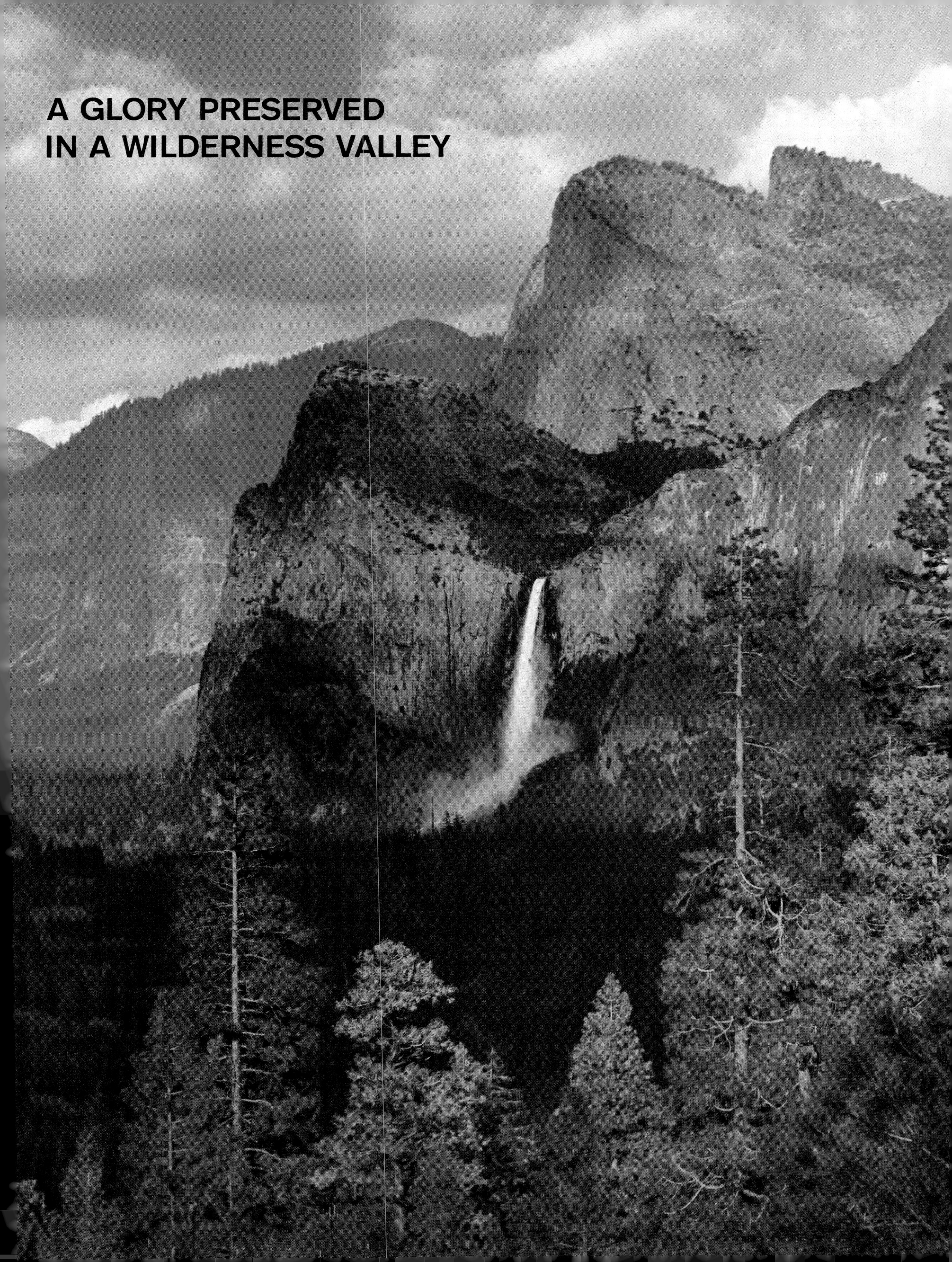

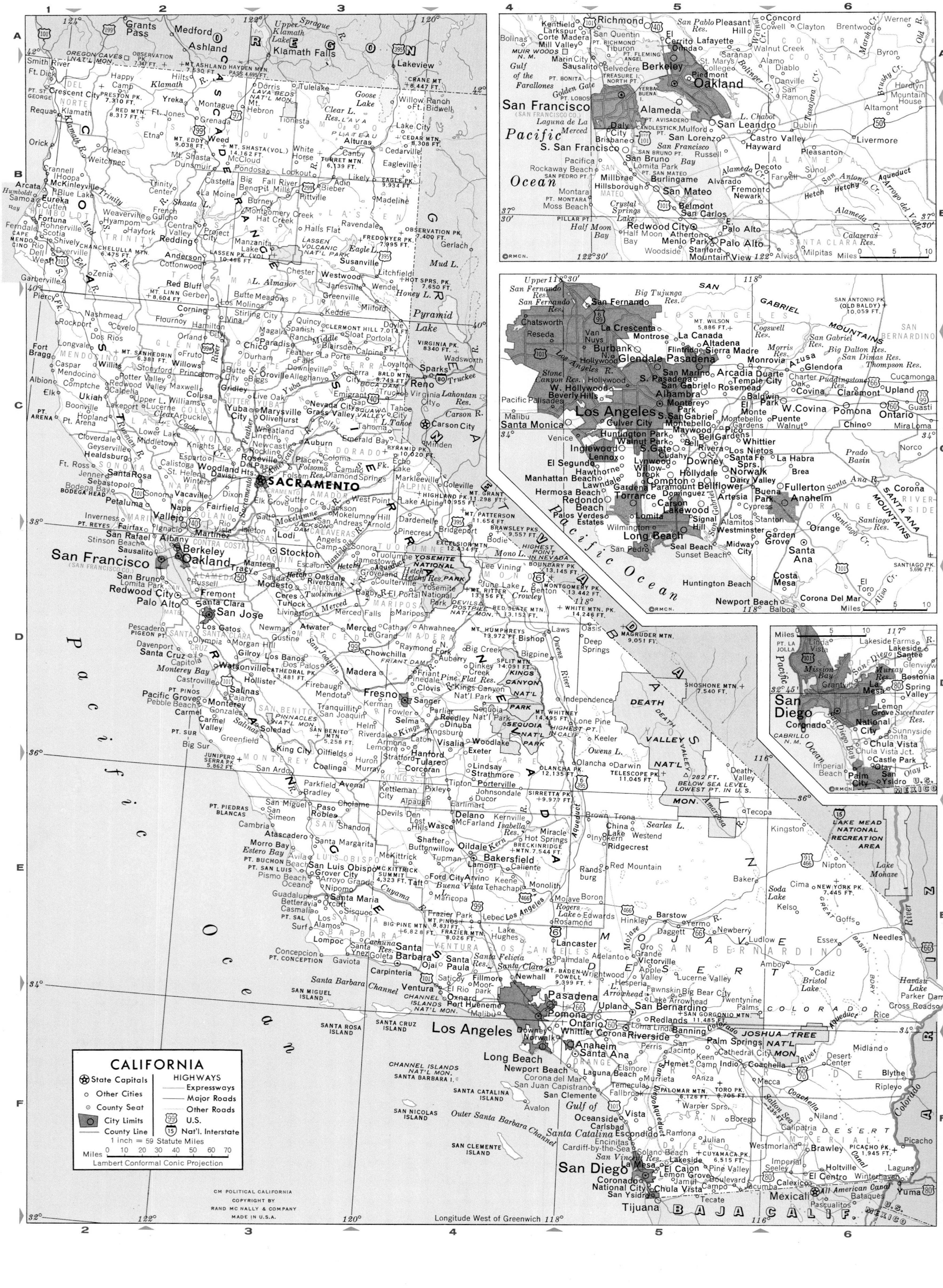
CALIFORNIA
State Capitals
Other Cities
County Seat
City Limits
County Line
HIGHWAYS
Expressways
Major Roads
Other Roads
U.S.
Nat'l. Interstate
1 inch = 59 Statute Miles
Miles 0 10 20 30 40 50 60 70
Lambert Conformal Conic Projection
CM POLITICAL CALIFORNIA
COPYRIGHT BY
RAND MC NALLY & COMPANY
MADE IN U.S.A.
Longitude West of Greenwich 118°
OREGON
NEVADA
ARIZONA
BAJA CALIF.
MEXICO
Pacific Ocean
SACRAMENTO
San Francisco
Oakland
Berkeley
San Jose
Fresno
Los Angeles
Long Beach
San Diego
Pasadena
Santa Ana
Anaheim
Bakersfield
Stockton
Modesto
Santa Barbara
San Bernardino
Riverside
Tijuana
Mexicali
Reno
Carson City
Lake Tahoe
Mono L.
Salton Sea
Death Valley Nat'l Mon.
Yosemite National Park
Sequoia Nat'l Park
Kings Canyon Nat'l Park
Lassen Volcanic Nat'l Park
Joshua Tree Nat'l Mon.
Lake Mead National Recreation Area
Channel Islands Nat'l Mon.
Santa Catalina Island
San Clemente Island
San Nicolas Island
Santa Cruz Island
Santa Rosa Island
San Miguel Island
Santa Barbara Channel
Gulf of Santa Catalina
Mojave Desert
Colorado Desert
Cascade Range
Coast Ranges
Sierra Nevada
Colorado R.
Sacramento R.
San Joaquin R.
Mt. Shasta (vol.) 14,162 ft.
Mt. Whitney 14,495 ft. Highest pt. in Calif.
282 ft. below sea level lowest pt. in U.S.
Pacific Ocean
San Francisco (San Francisco Co.)
Golden Gate
Gulf of the Farallones
Alameda
Daly City
Richmond
Hayward
San Mateo
Redwood City
Palo Alto
Livermore
Walnut Creek
Concord
San Leandro
Glendale
Burbank
Santa Monica
Torrance
Compton
Inglewood
Pomona
Whittier
Downey
Norwalk
Huntington Beach
Newport Beach
Costa Mesa
Orange
Fullerton
San Fernando
Van Nuys
Pacific Ocean
La Mesa
National City
Chula Vista
Coronado
Mission Bay
El Cajon

CALIFORNIA

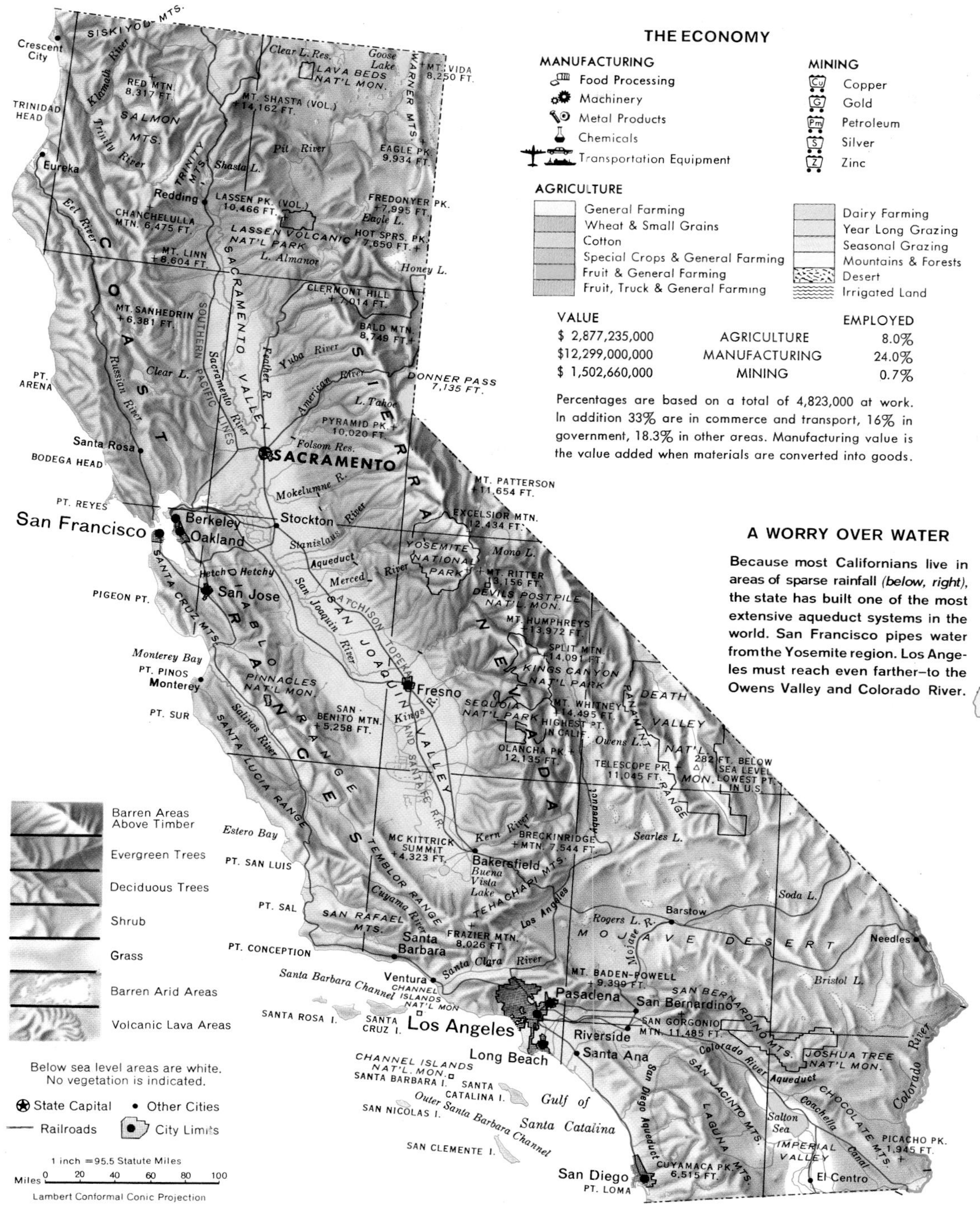

THE ECONOMY

MANUFACTURING
- Food Processing
- Machinery
- Metal Products
- Chemicals
- Transportation Equipment

MINING
- Cu Copper
- G Gold
- Pm Petroleum
- S Silver
- Z Zinc

AGRICULTURE
- General Farming
- Wheat & Small Grains
- Cotton
- Special Crops & General Farming
- Fruit & General Farming
- Fruit, Truck & General Farming
- Dairy Farming
- Year Long Grazing
- Seasonal Grazing
- Mountains & Forests
- Desert
- Irrigated Land

VALUE		EMPLOYED
$ 2,877,235,000	AGRICULTURE	8.0%
$12,299,000,000	MANUFACTURING	24.0%
$ 1,502,660,000	MINING	0.7%

Percentages are based on a total of 4,823,000 at work. In addition 33% are in commerce and transport, 16% in government, 18.3% in other areas. Manufacturing value is the value added when materials are converted into goods.

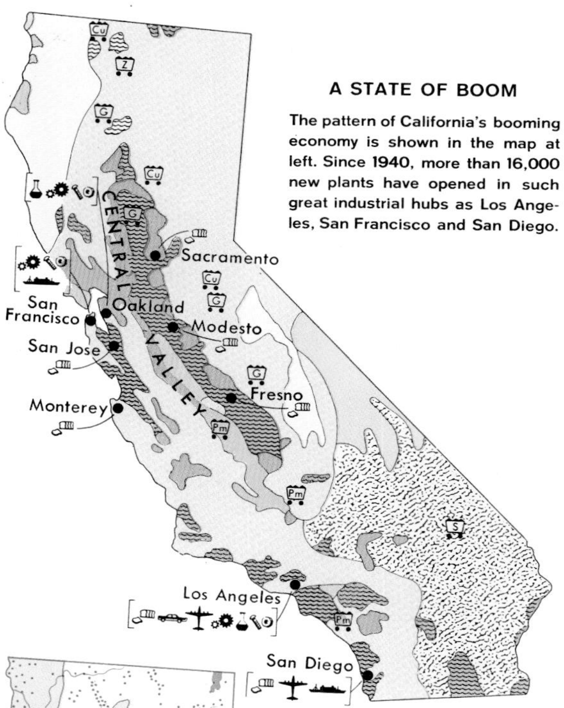

A STATE OF BOOM

The pattern of California's booming economy is shown in the map at left. Since 1940, more than 16,000 new plants have opened in such great industrial hubs as Los Angeles, San Francisco and San Diego.

A WORRY OVER WATER

Because most Californians live in areas of sparse rainfall *(below, right)*, the state has built one of the most extensive aqueduct systems in the world. San Francisco pipes water from the Yosemite region. Los Angeles must reach even farther—to the Owens Valley and Colorado River.

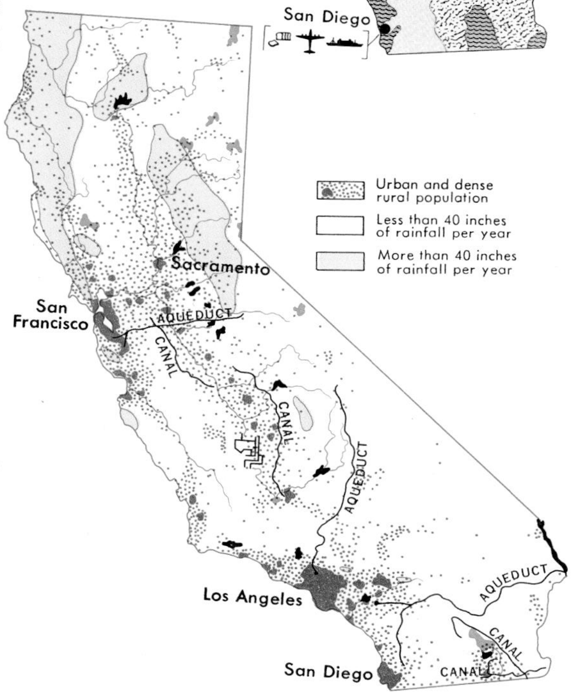

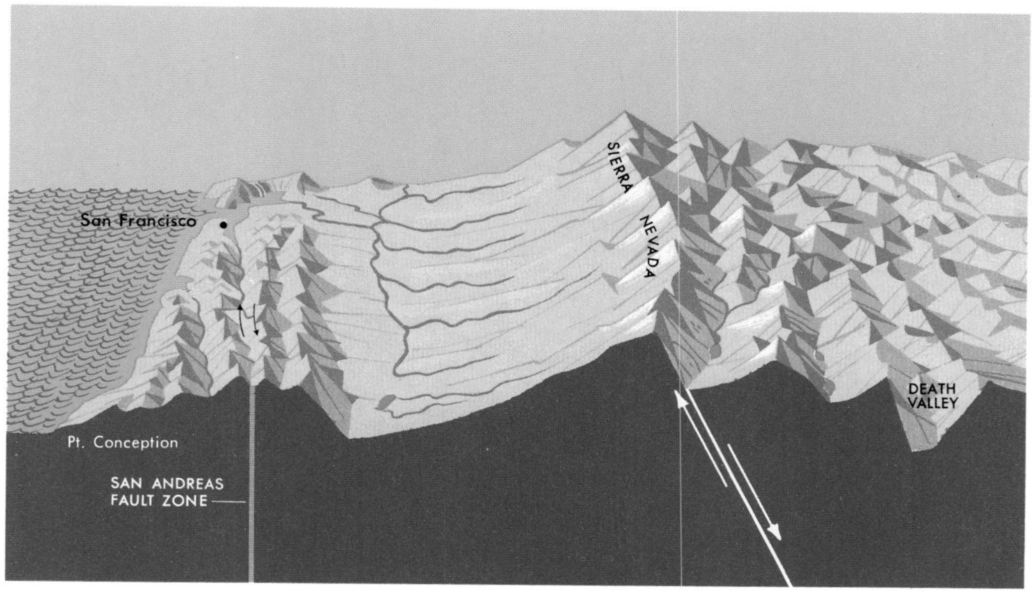

A HISTORIC FAULT BENEATH THE RUGGED MOUNTAINS

A cross section of California, from Point Conception to Death Valley, shows the great elevations and depressions that occur within a relatively short distance in the state. Extending deep beneath the surface are large faults, or planes of weakness created by movements in the earth's crust. A shift along the San Andreas fault caused San Francisco's 1906 earthquake.

CALIFORNIA: From the fir-clad Klamath Mountains at its northern borders to the scorching Mojave Desert in the south, California is a land of contrasts. In Mount Whitney it boasts the highest point of land in the United States except for Alaska; in Death Valley, only 90 miles away, the lowest. California's irrigated Central Valley, bounded by four major mountain ranges, is the nation's leading producer of fruits and vegetables. The valley drains west into the great bay of San Francisco, finance and distribution center of the Pacific Coast. To the south lies the highly urbanized Los Angeles basin, renowned for its diverse activities—ranging from oil-processing and aircraft-manufacturing to orange-growing, television and movie-making.

AREA:	158,693 sq. mi. Rank: 3rd.
POPULATION:	15,717,204. Rank: 2nd. Largest city: Los Angeles. Capital: Sacramento.
ENTERED UNION:	Sept. 9, 1850, as 31st state.
CLIMATE:	Rainless summers throughout. Cool foggy summers, mild winters on coast. Hot summers inland. Winter snows in the high mountains.
ALTITUDES:	Mt. Whitney, 14,495 ft. (highest); Lassen Peak, 10,466 ft.; Death Valley, -282 ft. (lowest).

In 1849, lured by the widely heralded discovery of gold in the creek at Sutter's Mill, nearly 40,000 would-be prospectors and their followers poured pell-mell into California. Today a seemingly endless tide of migrants (more than 300,000 yearly) travels to the West Coast for the golden sunshine—and for opportunity.

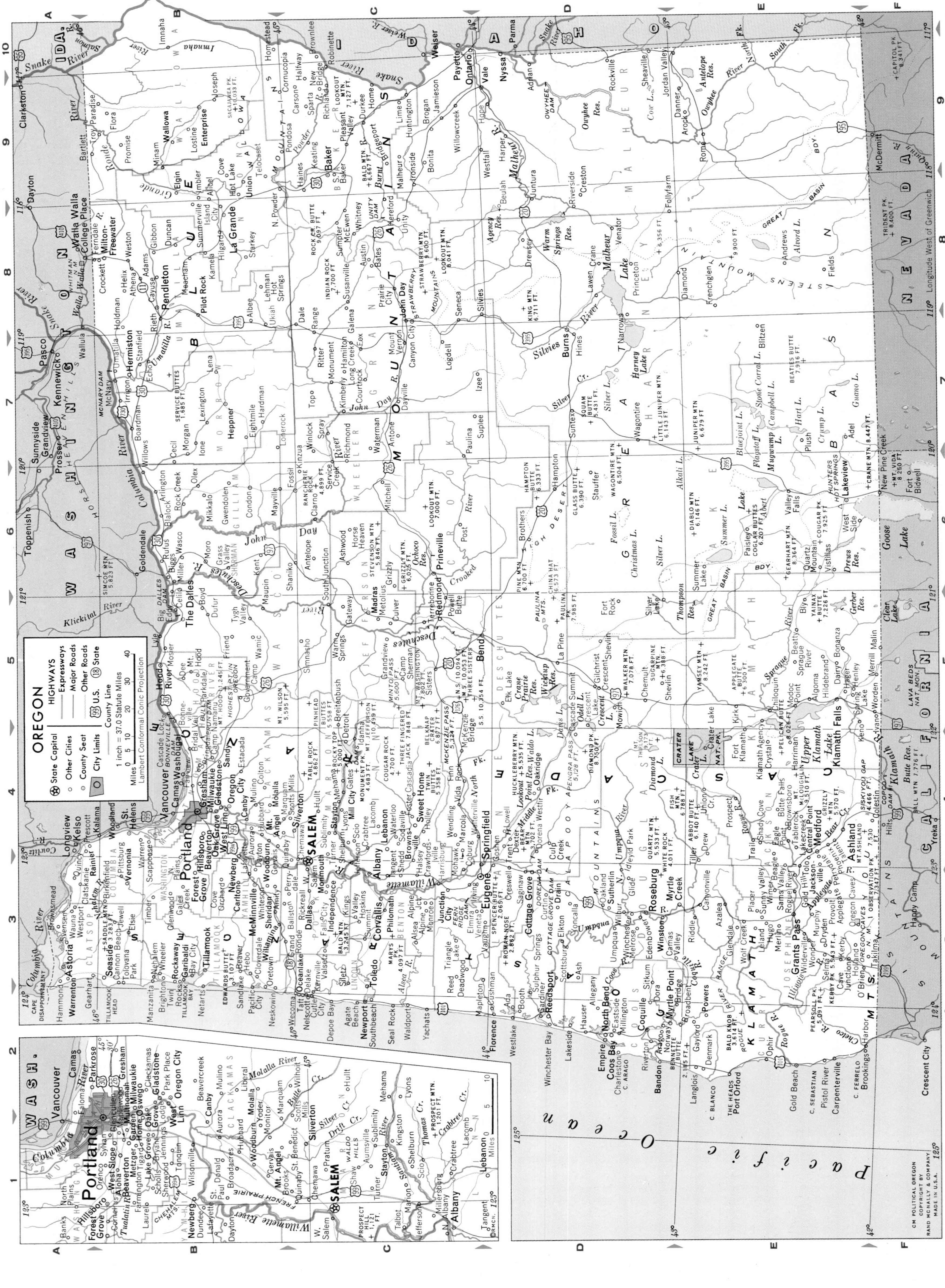
OREGON
HIGHWAYS
Expressways
Major Roads
Other Roads
U.S.
State
County Line
State Capital
Other Cities
County Seat
City Limits
1 inch = 37.0 Statute Miles
Miles
Lambert Conformal Conic Projection
Pacific Ocean
Longitude West of Greenwich
CM POLITICAL OREGON
COPYRIGHT BY RAND McNALLY & COMPANY
MADE IN U.S.A.

OREGON: Since the first pioneers pushed into the territory in the 1830s, most Oregonians have settled in the Willamette Valley, a fertile trough bounded by the wide Columbia River and the Coast and Cascade Ranges. To the northwest lies Portland, a major inland port which exercises commercial sway over the state's main industries: fruit, vegetable and fish canning; pulp and paper production; lumber.

AREA:	96,981 sq. mi. Rank: 10th.
POPULATION:	1,768,687. Rank: 32nd.
	Largest city: Portland. Capital: Salem.
ENTERED UNION:	Feb. 14, 1859, as 33rd state.
CLIMATE:	Cool summers, mild winters, heavy rain along coast and in Willamette Valley. Hot summers, cold winters in drier east.
ALTITUDES:	Mt. Hood, 11,245 ft. (highest).

Since the establishment of the state's first sawmill in 1832, the life of Oregon has been intertwined with its great forests of Douglas fir and western pine. Today, they contain 434 billion board feet of standing saw timber—more than a fifth of the current U.S. supply outside Alaska.

Barren Areas Above Timber
Evergreen Trees
Mixed Evergreen and Deciduous Trees
Shrub
Grass
Volcanic Lava Areas

State Capital • Other Cities
— Railroads City Limits

1 inch = 57.0 Statute Miles
Miles 0 5 10 20 30 40
Lambert Conformal Conic Projection

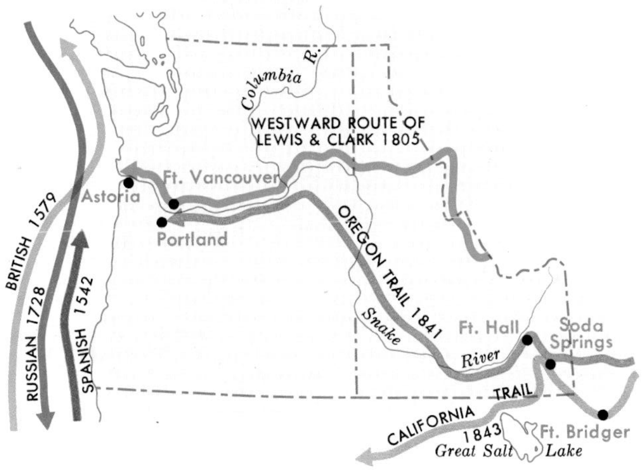

THE WAY WEST: OREGON TRAIL

For land-hungry pioneers in the 1840s, the Oregon Trail *(solid red line)* was the main route to the Pacific Coast after Dr. Elijah White's emigrant train traversed it in 1842. The trail, winding 2,000 miles from Independence, Missouri, partly paralleled the path of Lewis and Clark *(solid blue lines)*, the first to prove that the northwest coast, which had been explored from the sea *(arrows, left)*, could be reached overland.

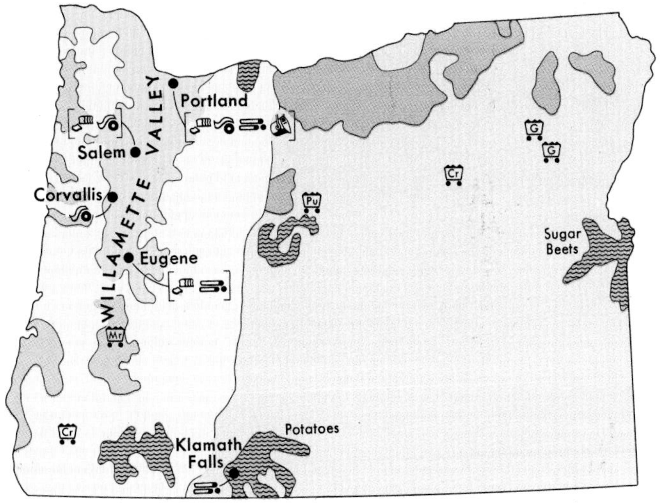

THE ECONOMY

MANUFACTURING
- Food Processing
- Pulp & Paper Products
- Lumber & Forest Products
- Metal Processing

MINING
- Cr Chromite
- G Gold
- Mr Mercury
- Pu Pumice

AGRICULTURE
- Wheat & Small Grains
- Special Crops & General Farming
- Fruit & General Farming
- Dairy Farming
- Dairy & General Farming
- Seasonal Grazing
- Mountains & Forests
- Irrigated Land

VALUE		EMPLOYED
$ 425,184,000	AGRICULTURE	17.0%
$1,216,000,000	MANUFACTURING	23.0%
$ 45,053,000	MINING	0.2%

Percentages are based on a total of 562,000 at work. In addition 30% are in commerce and transport, 16% in government, 13.8% in other areas. Manufacturing value is the value added when materials are converted into goods.

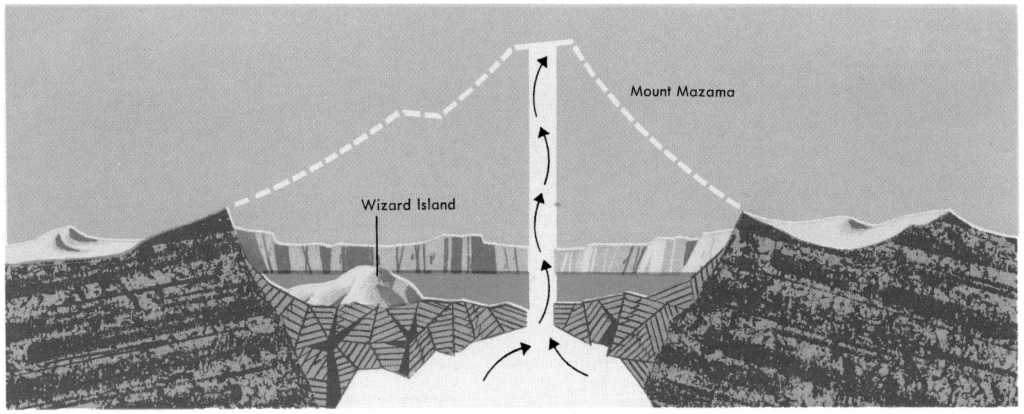

DEATH OF A MOUNTAIN, BIRTH OF A LAKE

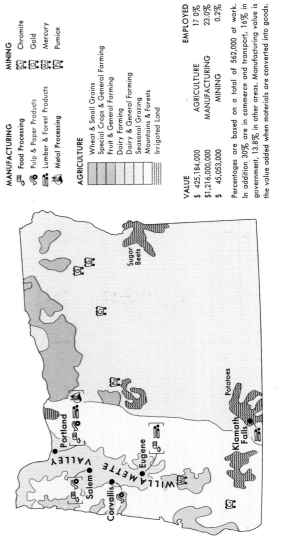

Crater Lake, whose startlingly blue waters reach a depth of 2,000 feet, lies high in the heart of the Cascade Range. A remarkable phenomenon of nature, it is cradled in the shattered hull of once-towering Mount Mazama, "the volcano that swallowed its head." When Mazama erupted some 6,500 years ago, it spewed millions of tons of incandescent lava and ashes up through its central vent *(black arrows)*, eating away the mountain's core. As the lava subsided, the walls *(dotted lines)* collapsed, forming a crater six miles across, which filled with water. Later the volcano pushed up another, smaller cone, today known as Wizard Island *(center)*.

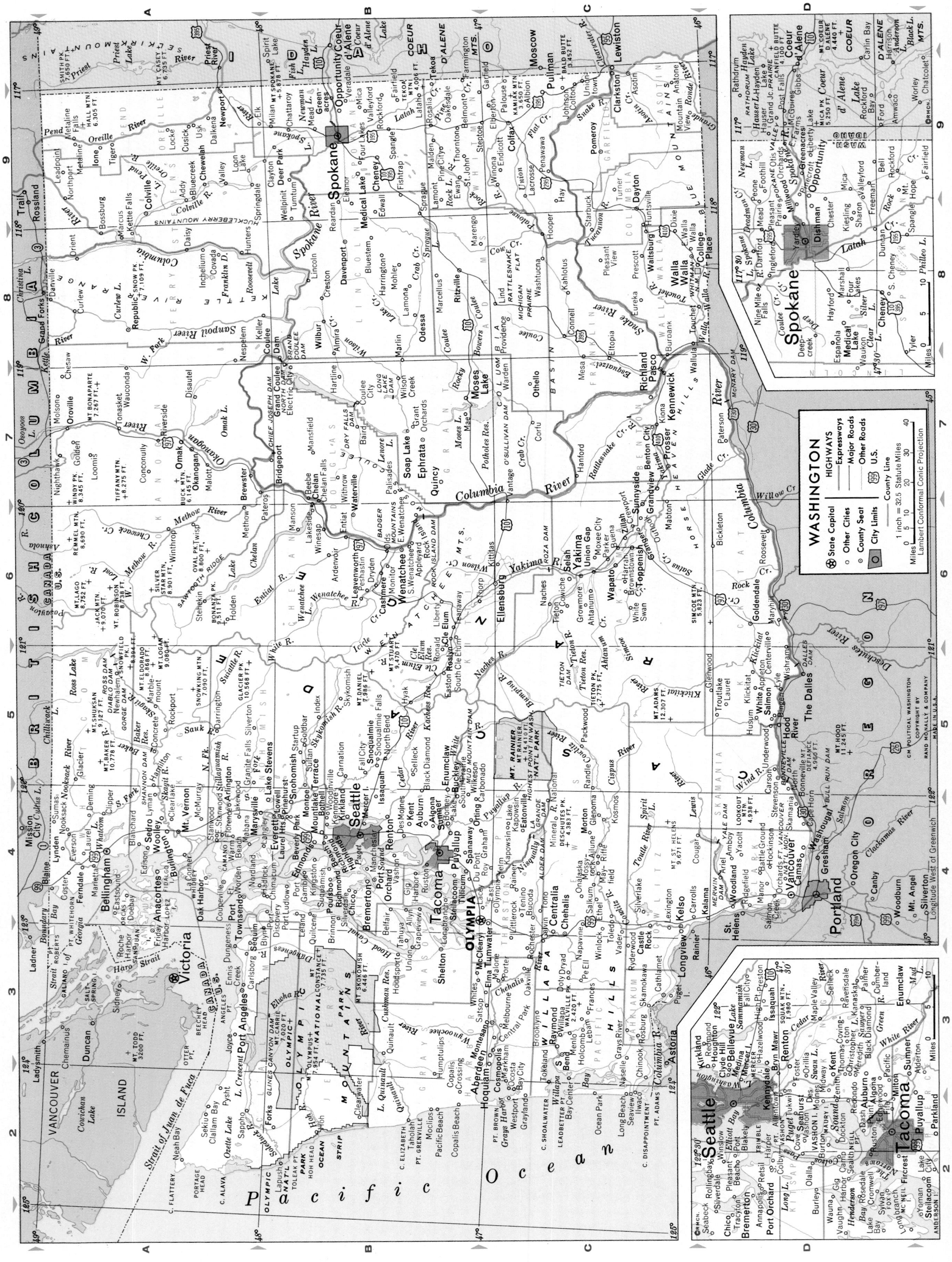
WASHINGTON
HIGHWAYS
Expressways
Major Roads
Other Roads
U.S.
State Capital
Other Cities
County Seat
City Limits
County Line
1 inch = 32.5 Statute Miles
Lambert Conformal Conic Projection
Longitude West of Greenwich
COPYRIGHT BY RAND McNALLY & COMPANY
MADE IN U.S.A.
BRITISH COLUMBIA
CANADA
U.S.
OREGON
IDAHO
Pacific Ocean
Strait of Juan de Fuca
VANCOUVER ISLAND
Victoria
OLYMPIA
Seattle
Tacoma
Spokane
Bellingham
Everett
Yakima
Wenatchee
Walla Walla
Richland
Pasco
Kennewick
Vancouver
Portland
Aberdeen
Hoquiam
Port Angeles
Bremerton
Ellensburg
Moses Lake
Pullman
Moscow
Lewiston
Columbia River
Snake River
Yakima R.
OLYMPIC MOUNTAINS
CASCADE
BLUE MOUNTAINS
WILLAPA HILLS
MT. RAINIER 14,410 FT.
MT. ADAMS 12,307 FT.
MT. ST. HELENS 9,671 FT.
MT. BAKER 10,778 FT.
MT. OLYMPUS 7,954 FT.
MT. HOOD 11,245 FT.
GRAND COULEE DAM
BONNEVILLE DAM
McNARY DAM
Franklin D. Roosevelt Lake
Lake Chelan
Puget Sound
Coeur d'Alene

WASHINGTON: The glaciated volcanic peaks of the Cascade Range form a great natural barrier between the moist valleys of the west and the dry inland plateaus of the east. In the west the Washingtonians run factories, fisheries and dairies, and manage timberland; in the eastern "Inland Empire" they grow fruit and wheat. The sea strongly influences the western economy: a 200-mile-long extension of the Pacific through Juan de Fuca Strait and Puget Sound gives many of the state's cities uniquely sheltered coastlines far inland.

On the semi-arid eastern plateau, the U.S. government has created a 151-mile-long body of water, Lake Roosevelt, which backs up from the mighty Grand Coulee Dam. One of the largest hydroelectric projects in the Western Hemisphere, Grand Coulee supplies power and water for irrigation throughout the vast Columbia Basin.

AREA:	68,192 sq. mi. Rank: 20th.
POPULATION:	2,853,214. Rank: 23rd.
	Largest city: Seattle. Capital: Olympia.
ENTERED UNION:	Nov. 11, 1889, as 42nd state.
CLIMATE:	Cool summers, mild winters along coast and Puget Sound; hot summers, cold winters on inland plateau. Heavy rainfall on windward slopes of the Olympics; dry on inland plateau.
ALTITUDES:	Mt. Rainier, 14,410 ft. (highest); Spokane, 1,890 ft.

First explored in 1792 by the British Captain George Vancouver, Washington still possesses areas of unspoiled beauty. Mount Rainier National Park contains 26 active glaciers. The moss-draped trees of Olympic National Park present a green luxuriance reminiscent of the rain forests of South America and Africa.

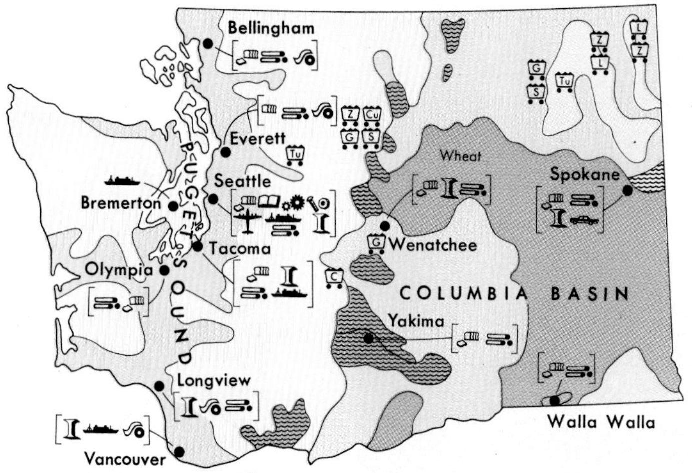

THE ECONOMY

MANUFACTURING
- Food Processing
- Transportation Equipment
- Lumber & Forest Products
- Primary Metals
- Printing & Publishing
- Machinery
- Metal Products
- Pulp & Paper Products

MINING
- Coal
- Copper
- Gold
- Lead
- Silver
- Tungsten
- Zinc

AGRICULTURE
- General Farming
- Wheat & Small Grains
- Special Crops & General Farming
- Fruit & General Farming
- Dairy & General Farming
- Seasonal Grazing
- Mountains & Forests
- Irrigated Land

VALUE		EMPLOYED
$ 598,153,000	AGRICULTURE	13.0%
$2,168,000,000	MANUFACTURING	24.0%
$ 60,897,000	MINING	0.2%

Percentages are based on a total of 900,000 at work. In addition 30% are in commerce and transport, 17% in government, 15.8% in other areas. Manufacturing value is the value added when materials are converted into goods.

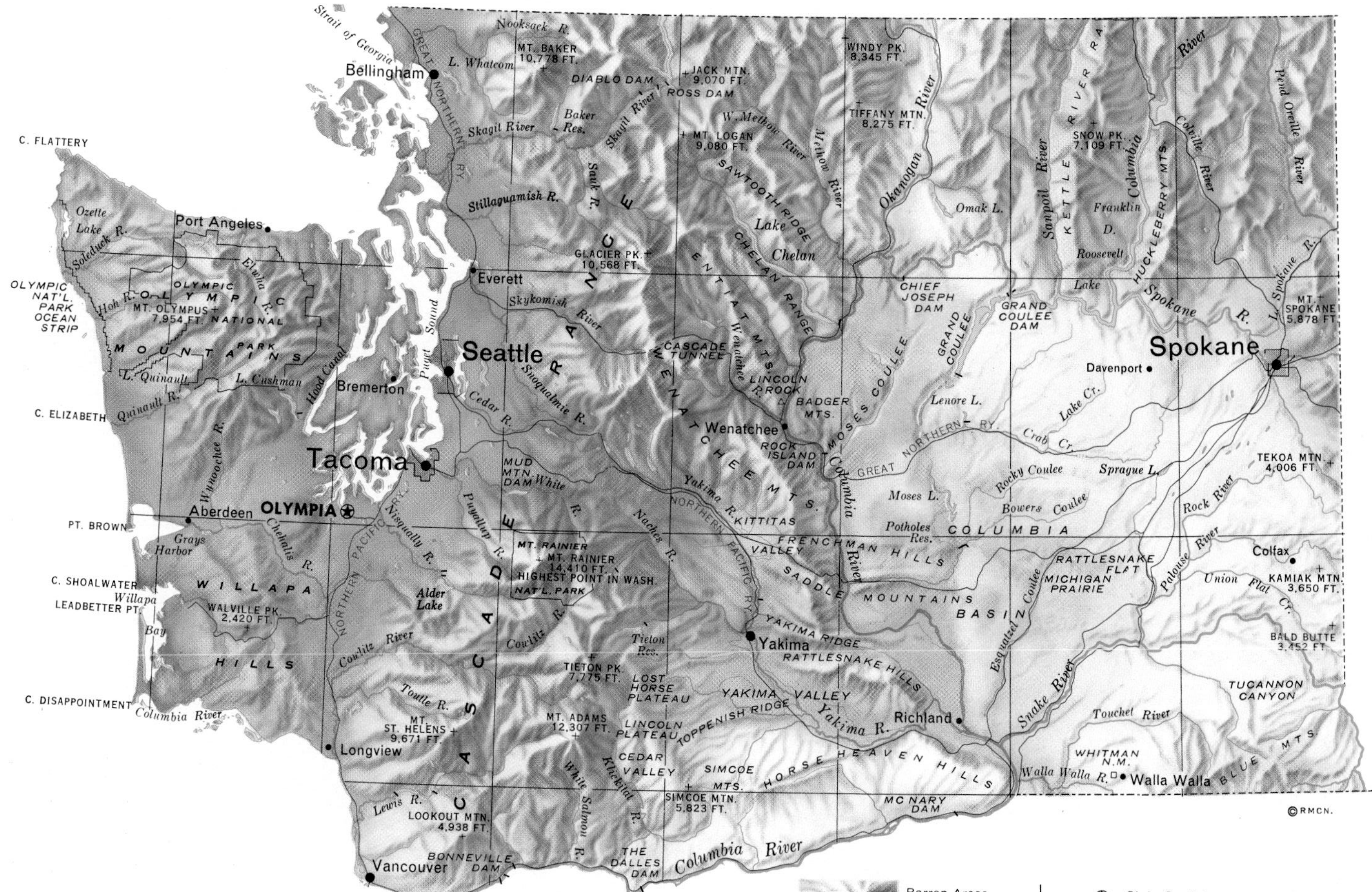

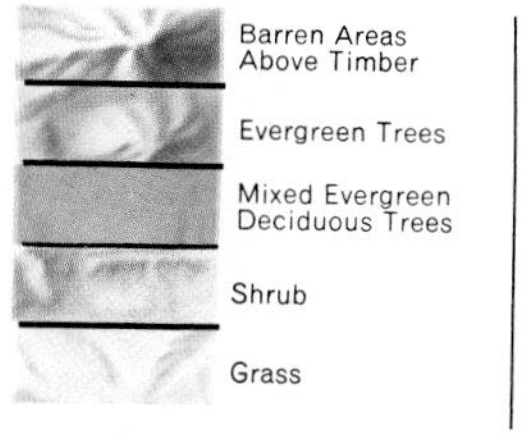

- State Capital
- City Limits
- Other Cities
- Railroads

1 inch = 50 Statute Miles
Miles 0 5 10 20 30 40
Lambert Conformal Conic Projection

A WETTER WEST, A DRIER EAST

The average annual precipitation in inches is shown below for six Washington locales. Prevailing westerly winds, heavily laden with water vapor after their passage over the Pacific *(left)*, rise to pass over the Olympic Range. Cooled at the higher altitudes, they drop heavy rains on the windward slopes. Warming as they descend the leeward slopes, they hold their moisture until they meet the Cascades *(right)* to repeat the wet-dry cycle.

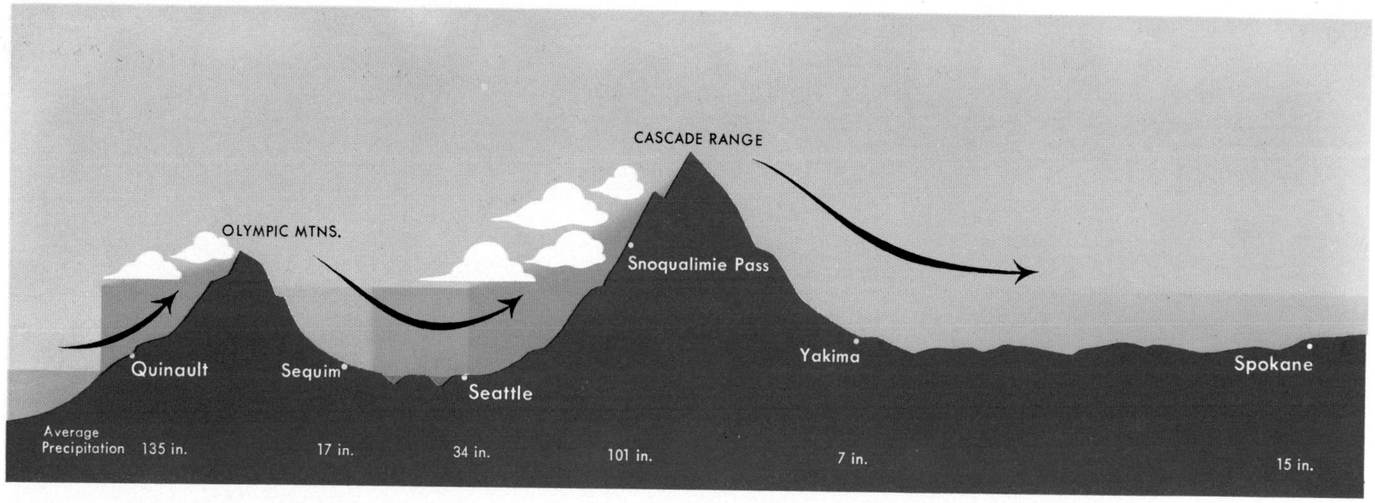

MOUNTAIN STATES

"All I knew was that it was pure delight to be where the land lifted in peaks and plunged in canyons, to sniff air that was thin, spray-cooled, full of the smells of pine and fir, to be so close-seeming to the improbable indigo sky," once wrote the novelist Wallace Stegner.

But for all this virgin beauty of the mountain states, no more formidable barrier to U.S. continental unity ever existed. Seared by the sun, their surface warped and cracked by the ponderous shifts and slidings of titanic subterranean forces, these states long harassed the 19th Century pioneers bound for California and Oregon. At the foothills of the Rockies, which touch all the mountain states except Nevada, the

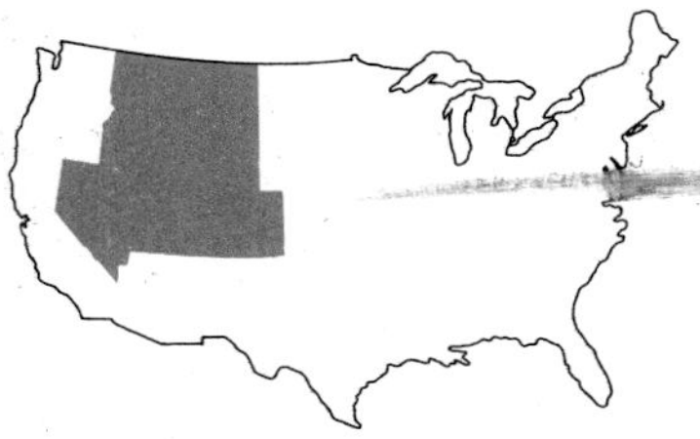

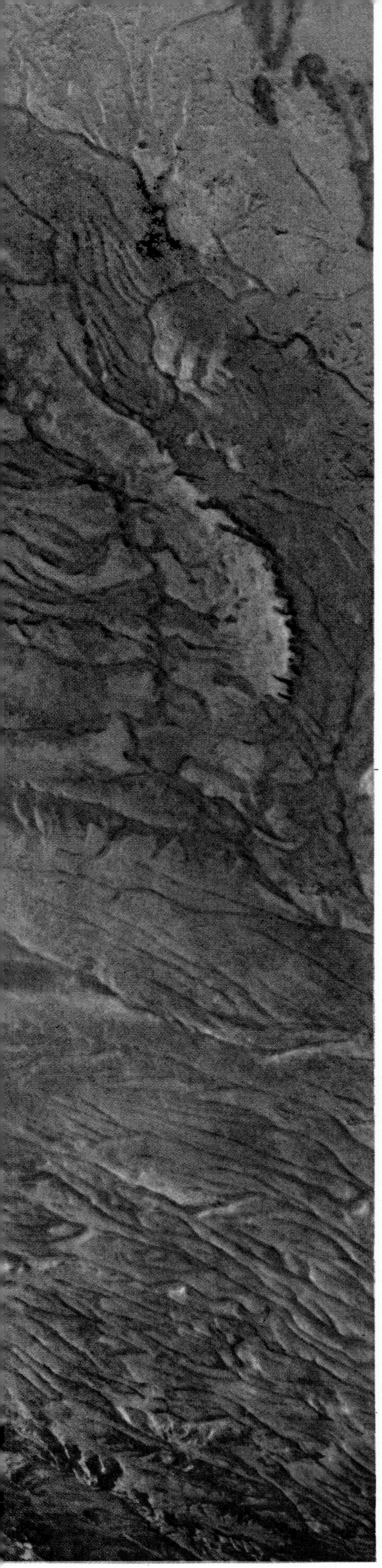

SWEEPING NORTHWARD ***(left)***, **the mountain ranges of the Continental Divide stretch across the Canadian border, at top. At the center is Great Salt Lake, lying in the region's Great Basin. At the left center, the desert lands of Nevada spread west to the Sierra Nevada and California. At the far right lie most of the Great Plains.**

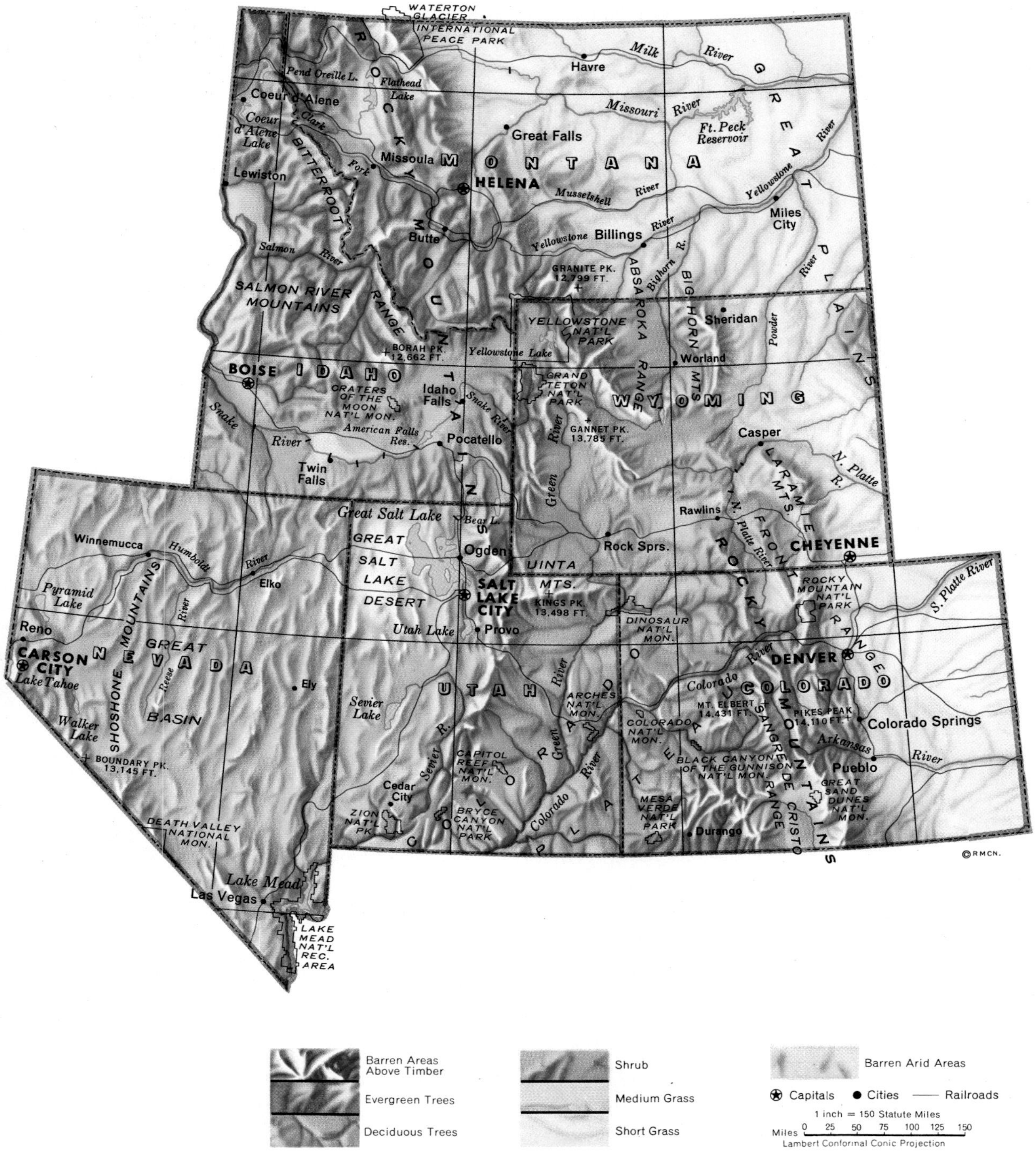

Conestoga wagons were abandoned and the burdens transferred to the backs of mules—or men. There to this day lie the cities of the mountain states, settled by men who decided it was easier to service those who kept heading west than to make the trek with them.

Ironically, the harsh Rockies themselves gave birth to the economy of the mountain states. The miners who went strikeless in California straggled back again, for they guessed that the faulted and folded land contained precious minerals. And it did. Today, Colorado's Bartlett Mountain supplies two thirds of the world's molybdenum; Montana's Butte is in effect a mountain of copper. And when power was needed, men harnessed the swift streams that tumbled down the mountainsides. Moreover, when the Mormons learned to irrigate with the mountain waters, the parched land proved fertile enough for the men of the West to plant vast fields of wheat, oats and barley.

What the area needed was transportation, noted the editor Samuel Bowles in 1865, to "open it to abundant labor, cheap capital, wood, water, science." Four years later at Promontory, Utah, the last spike (made of gold) was driven into the tie which knotted the Union Pacific Railway of the East to the Central Pacific of the West. All that now remained for a united country—and the mountain states—was to grow.

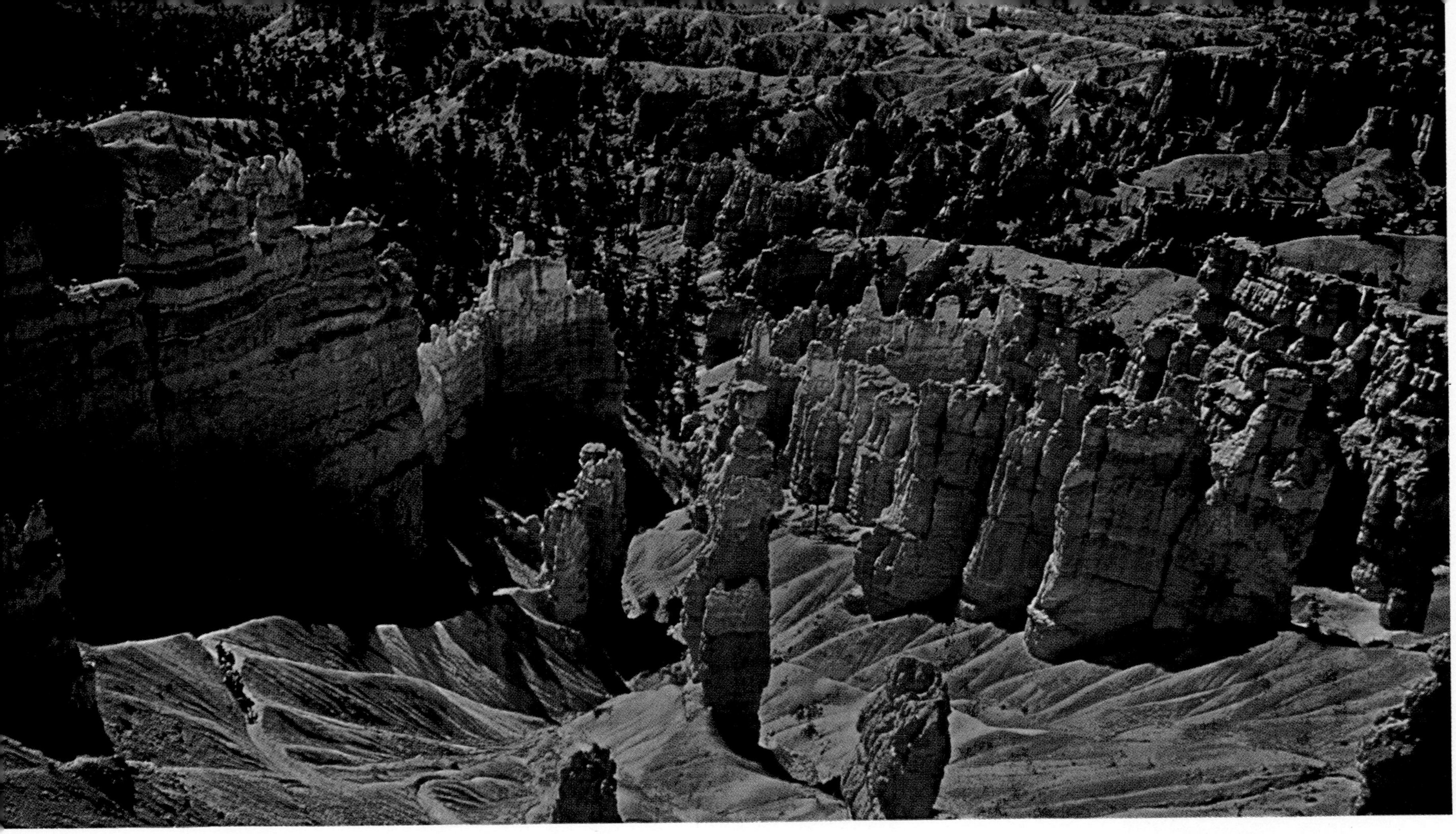

ERODED SPIRES of the Pink Cliffs loom over tourists *(far left)* in Bryce Canyon National Park in Utah. The vivid colors are caused by uneven oxidation of mineral deposits in the weathered rocks.

AN ARID LAND OF ROCK

EXPOSED SPINE of rocky Sheep Mountain *(opposite)* rises from the Wyoming plateau. Hard ridges that sweep around the base show the mountain's original extent before erosion cut it down.

ANCIENT HOMES of pre-Columbian Pueblo Indians, built of cut-stone blocks, stand beneath the protective overhang of rock in a rugged canyon of southwestern Colorado's Mesa Verde plateau.

A PATTERN OF PLENTY ON THE GREAT GOLDEN PLAINS

STRETCHING TO THE HORIZON, rows of golden wheat and brown fallow earth form a checkerboard pattern of plenty on the Great Plains of eastern Montana. Here, where rainfall is often scarce and unpredictable, early homesteaders found that their government grants of 160 acres would not sustain a family. Today Montana wheat farms average nearly 2,000 acres. By farming in alternate strips to husband the limited moisture, Montana in some years has pushed its wheat production to third place in the U.S.

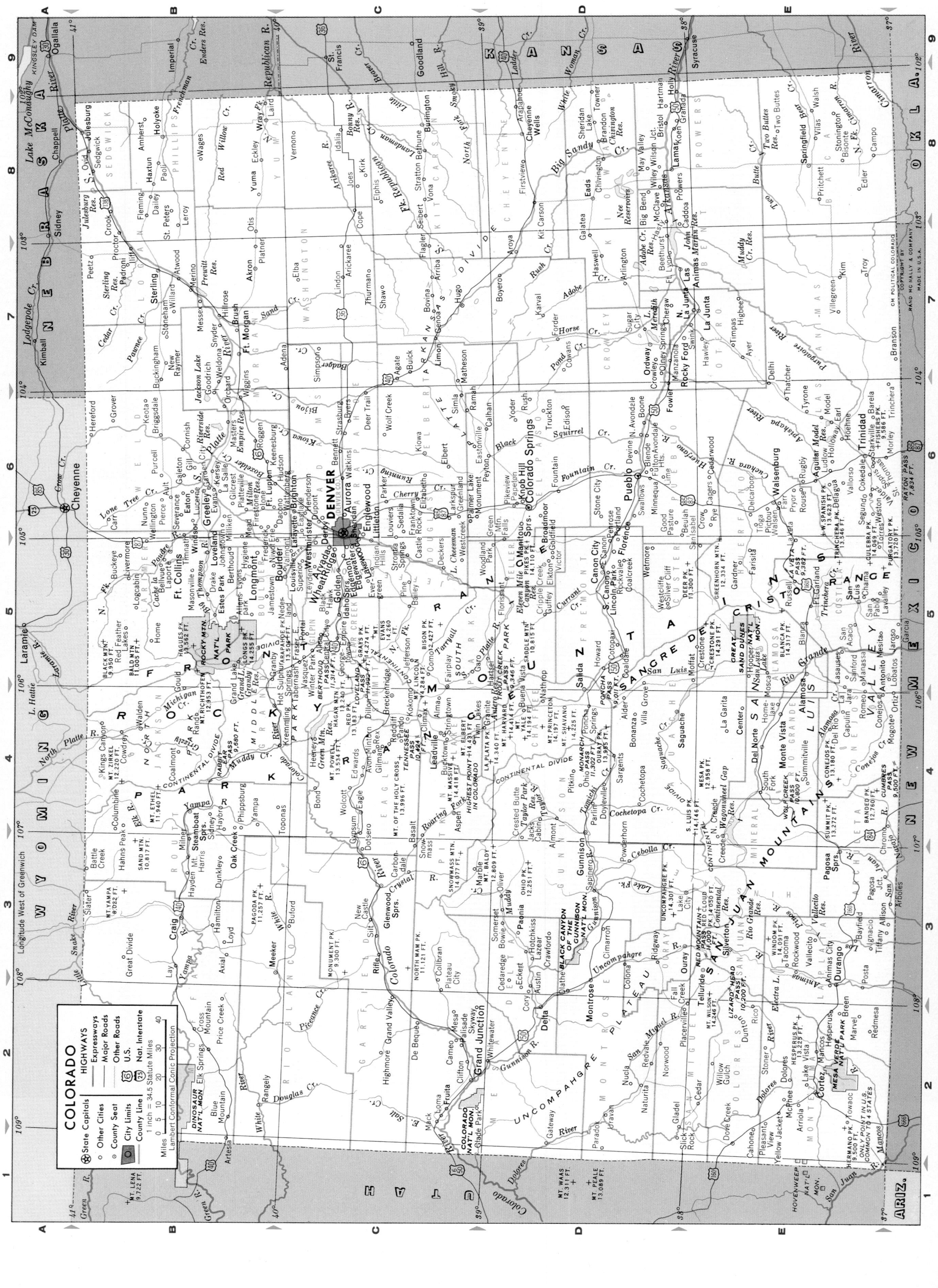
COLORADO
HIGHWAYS
Expressways
Major Roads
Other Roads
U.S.
Nat. Interstate
State Capitals
Other Cities
County Seat
City Limits
County Line
Miles 0 5 10 20 30 40
1 inch = 34.5 Statute Miles
Lambert Conformal Conic Projection
Longitude West of Greenwich
WYOMING
NEBRASKA
KANSAS
OKLAHOMA
NEW MEXICO
UTAH
ARIZ.
DENVER
Cheyenne
Colorado Springs
Pueblo
Grand Junction
Boulder
Ft. Collins
Greeley
Loveland
Longmont
Durango
Trinidad
Sterling
Lamar
La Junta
Walsenburg
Alamosa
Leadville
Gunnison
Montrose
Delta
Glenwood Sprs.
Craig
Meeker
Steamboat Sprs.
Salida
Canon City
Limon
Burlington
Julesburg
Holyoke
Ft. Morgan
Brush
Akron
Yuma
Wray
Cheyenne Wells
Eads
Las Animas
Springfield
Cortez
Telluride
Ouray
Silverton
Pagosa Sprs.
Monte Vista
Del Norte
ROCKY MTN. NAT'L PARK
DINOSAUR NAT'L MON.
COLORADO NAT'L MON.
BLACK CANYON OF THE GUNNISON NAT'L MON.
GREAT SAND DUNES NAT'L MON.
MESA VERDE NAT'L PARK
CONTINENTAL DIVIDE
SANGRE DE CRISTO MTS.
SAN JUAN MTS.
SAN LUIS VALLEY
UNCOMPAHGRE PLATEAU
NORTH PARK
MIDDLE PARK
SOUTH PARK
MT. ELBERT 14,433 FT. HIGHEST POINT IN COLORADO
PIKES PK. 14,110 FT.
LONGS PK. 14,255 FT.
ONLY POINT IN U.S. COMMON TO 4 STATES
Colorado R.
Rio Grande
Arkansas R.
South Platte R.
North Platte R.
Republican R.
Gunnison R.
Yampa R.
White R.
Dolores R.
San Juan R.
CM POLITICAL COLORADO
COPYRIGHT BY RAND McNALLY & COMPANY
MADE IN U.S.A.

Barren Areas Above Timber
Evergreen Trees
Mixed Evergreen and Deciduous Trees
Deciduous Trees
Shrub
Grass

State Capital • Other Cities
Railroads
City Limits

1 inch = 51.5 Statute Miles
Miles 0 10 20 30 40 50
Lambert Conformal Conic Projection

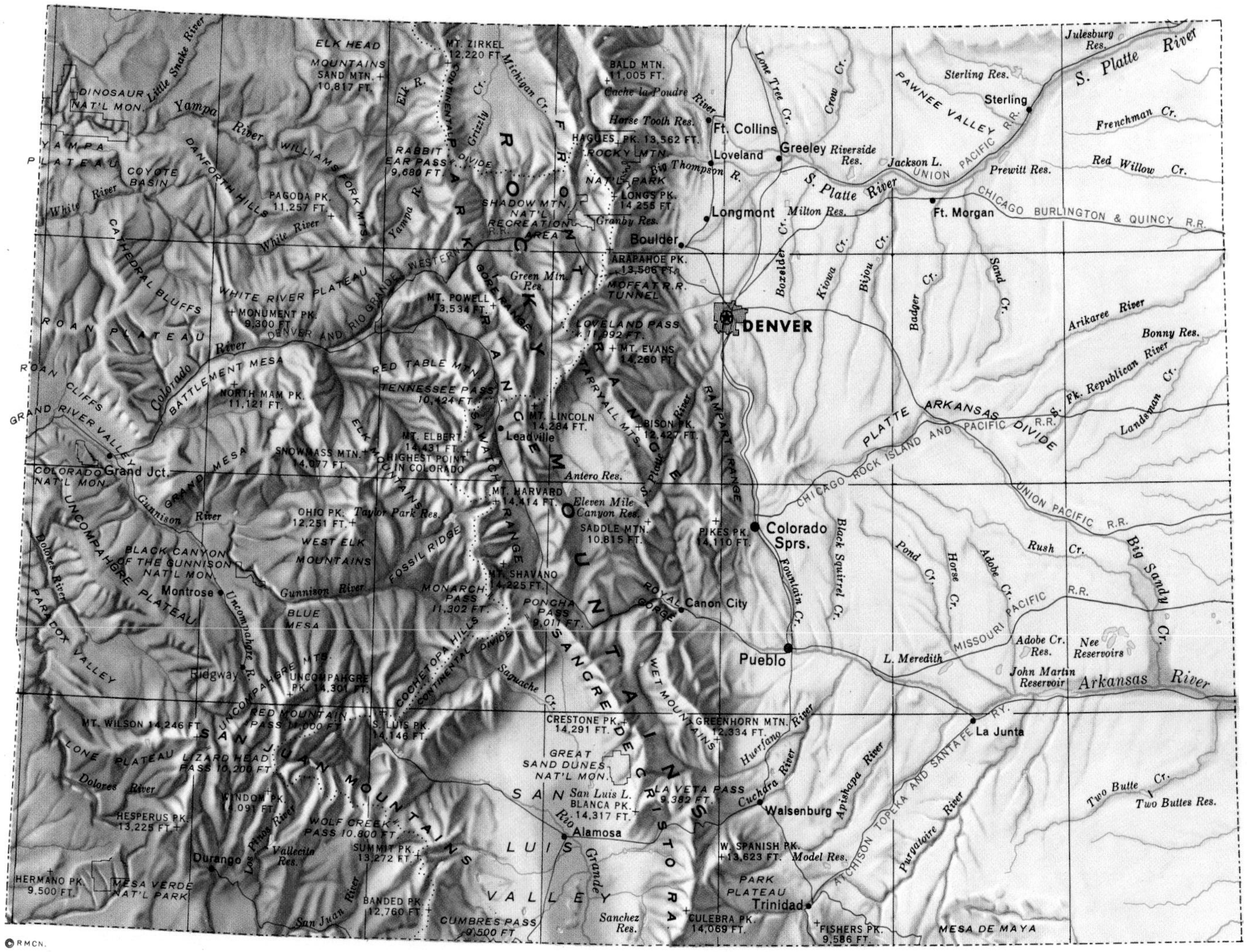

© RMCN.

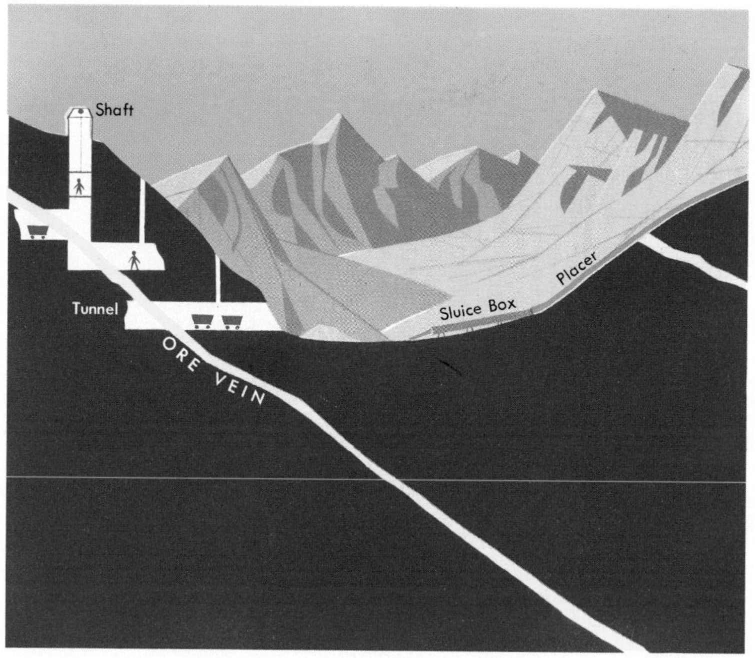

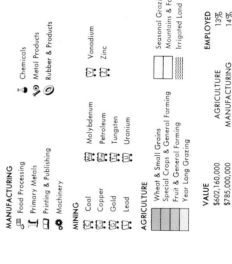

HOW GOLD IS TAKEN FROM THE EARTH

Gold veins in a Colorado mountain are shown in this illustration of two major mining methods. In shaft mining *(left)* deep veins are reached by vertical shafts and horizontal tunnels. In placer mining *(center)* gold is found on the surface, intermingled with sand and gravel. When the mixture is sluiced through an inclined trough, the heavier gold falls to the bottom as the sand and gravel wash away.

COLORADO: Here is a land of superlatives. With 40 peaks rising more than two and a half miles above sea level, Colorado has the highest average altitude of all the mountain states. Here too originate more major rivers than in any other state—the North and South Platte, the Arkansas, the Colorado and the storied Rio Grande—all of them flowing easterly or westerly down the opposing slopes of the Continental Divide, which zigzags on a rough north-south line through Colorado's middle, marking the boundary of the two major drainage areas of the United States.

Yet Colorado is one of the driest of states. West of the Divide stretch the semi-arid uplands of the Colorado Plateau, an area of stark beauty. Its spectacular gorges, abrupt escarpments and ancient cliff dwellings attract many thousands of tourists a year. But more important are the land's rich deposits of minerals, petroleum and natural gas.

AREA: 104,247 sq. mi. Rank: 8th.
POPULATION: 1,753,947. Rank: 33rd.
Largest city and capital: Denver.
ENTERED UNION: Aug. 1, 1876, as 38th state.
CLIMATE: Generally hot sunny summers, cold winters.
Light rainfall, varying at different altitudes;
heavy mountain snows.
ALTITUDES: Mt. Elbert, 14,431 ft. (highest);
Denver, 5,280 ft.

Colorado's dry climate and long periods of cloudless days have made it a center of air installations. Ten miles north of Colorado Springs lies the U.S. Air Force Academy. At Ent Air Force Base is the headquarters of the North American Air Defense Command.

THE ECONOMY

MANUFACTURING
Food Processing
Primary Metals
Printing & Publishing
Machinery
Chemicals
Metal Products
Rubber & Products

MINING
Coal
Copper
Gold
Lead
Molybdenum
Petroleum
Tungsten
Uranium
Vanadium
Zinc

AGRICULTURE
Wheat & Small Grains
Special Crops & General Farming
Fruit & General Farming
Year Long Grazing
Seasonal Grazing
Mountains & Forests
Irrigated Land

VALUE		EMPLOYED
$602,160,000	AGRICULTURE	13%
$785,000,000	MANUFACTURING	14%
$305,280,000	MINING	3%

Percentages are based on a total of 530,000 at work. In addition 35% are in commerce and transport, 18% in government, 17% in other areas. Manufacturing value is the value added when materials are converted into goods.

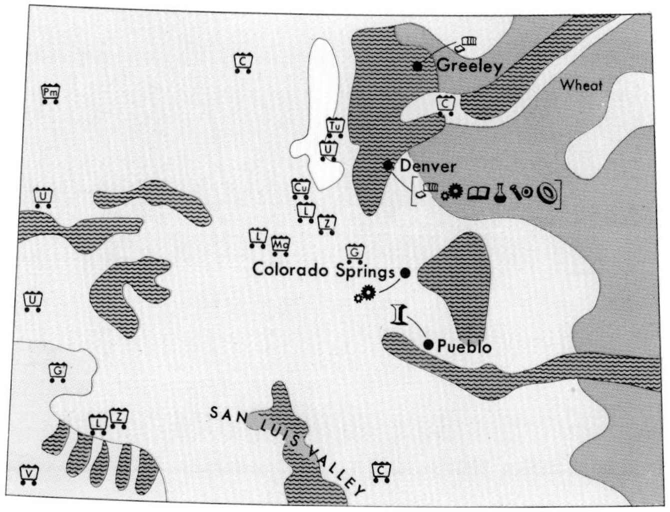

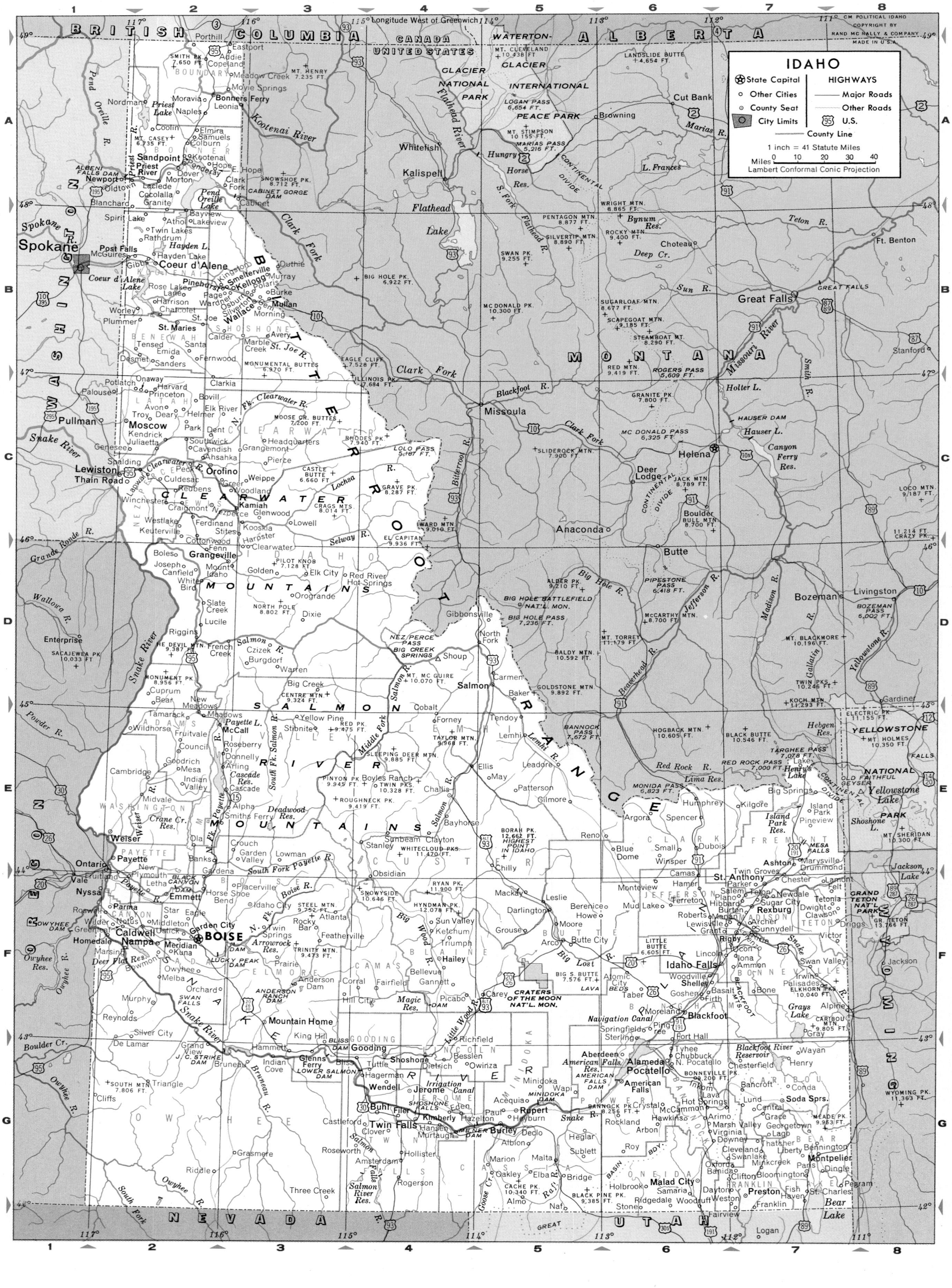
IDAHO
State Capital
Other Cities
County Seat
City Limits
HIGHWAYS
Major Roads
Other Roads
U.S.
County Line
1 inch = 41 Statute Miles
Miles 0 10 20 30 40
Lambert Conformal Conic Projection
CM POLITICAL IDAHO
COPYRIGHT BY
RAND MC NALLY & COMPANY
MADE IN U.S.A.
Longitude West of Greenwich
BRITISH COLUMBIA
ALBERTA
CANADA
UNITED STATES
WASHINGTON
OREGON
MONTANA
WYOMING
NEVADA
UTAH
BITTERROOT RANGE
CLEARWATER MOUNTAINS
SALMON RIVER MOUNTAINS
SNAKE RIVER
GLACIER NATIONAL PARK
WATERTON-GLACIER INTERNATIONAL PEACE PARK
YELLOWSTONE NATIONAL PARK
GRAND TETON NAT'L. PARK
CRATERS OF THE MOON NAT'L. MON.
BIG HOLE BATTLEFIELD NAT'L. MON.
BORAH PK. 12,662 FT. HIGHEST POINT IN IDAHO
BOISE
Spokane
Lewiston
Moscow
Pocatello
Idaho Falls
Twin Falls
Coeur d'Alene
Sandpoint
Bonners Ferry
Grangeville
Salmon
Nampa
Caldwell
Mountain Home
Burley
Rexburg
Blackfoot
Missoula
Helena
Butte
Great Falls
Kalispell
Bozeman
Anaconda

IDAHO

IDAHO: It was the buffalo-hunting Shoshone of the Great Plains who gave the land the name of Idaho, which means, "Behold the sun coming down the mountain." Nineteenth Century legislators created its panhandle conformation. In the north the "handle" reaches to the Canadian border. Folded, indented and crumpled as by the squeeze of a giant hand, it includes such mountain groups as the Coeur d'Alene, Clearwater, Salmon River and Sawtooth, and is edged on the east by the towering Bitterroot Range. To the south is attached the pan itself, the broad basin of the Snake River.

In neither area, north or south, is nature kind to man and his endeavors. Dry and sunny, the Snake River Plain *(diagram, below left)*, on which most Idahoans are concentrated, is a productive farming area—but mainly because of the technology of irrigation. Here the land yields a variety of special crops such as dry beans, alfalfa and sugar beets. Best known of all the state's products are Idaho potatoes, famous for their size, taste and baking qualities. The annual potato crop is valued at about $40 million.

The mountain region was, until recently, almost isolated from the Snake River Plain for lack of north-south highways and railroads (the transcontinental lines constructed in the 1880s run east-west). In this ruggedly beautiful area lies Sun Valley, to which skiers flock each winter. On the Oregon border is the spectacular gorge of Hell's Canyon, at 7,900 feet the deepest in North America.

AREA:	83,557 sq. mi. Rank: 13th.
POPULATION:	667,191. Rank: 42nd.
	Largest city and capital: Boise.
ENTERED UNION:	July 3, 1890, as 43rd state.
CLIMATE:	Cold winters, fairly cool summers. Light rainfall; heavy winter snows in the mountains.
ALTITUDES:	Borah Peak, 12,662 ft. (highest); Boise, 2,704 ft.

Mining is important to Idaho. Large amounts of lead, zinc, silver and other minerals are taken from the land each year. The state's hydroelectric power facilities and isolated areas have made it useful, too, to the Atomic Energy Commission. Idaho contains more experimental nuclear reactors than any other state. Arco, near Idaho Falls, was the first town to be lit by power derived from atomic energy.

THE ECONOMY

MANUFACTURING
- Food Processing
- Lumber & Forest Products
- Printing & Publishing

AGRICULTURE
- General Farming
- Wheat & Small Grains
- Special Crops & General Farming
- Dairy Farming
- Seasonal Grazing
- Mountains & Forests
- Irrigated Land

MINING
- Cu Copper
- G Gold
- L Lead
- Mr Mercury
- P Phosphate Rock
- S Silver
- Tu Tungsten
- V Vandadium
- Z Zinc

VALUE		EMPLOYED
$425,560,000	AGRICULTURE	32%
$246,000,000	MANUFACTURING	12%
$ 64,460,000	MINING	2%

Percentages are based on a total of 215,000 at work. In addition 26% are in commerce and transport, 14% in government, 14% in other areas. Manufacturing value is the value added when materials are converted into goods.

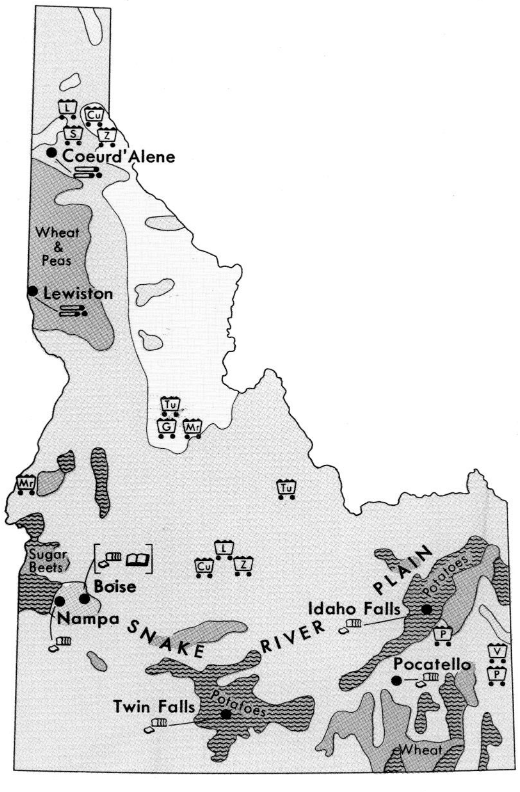

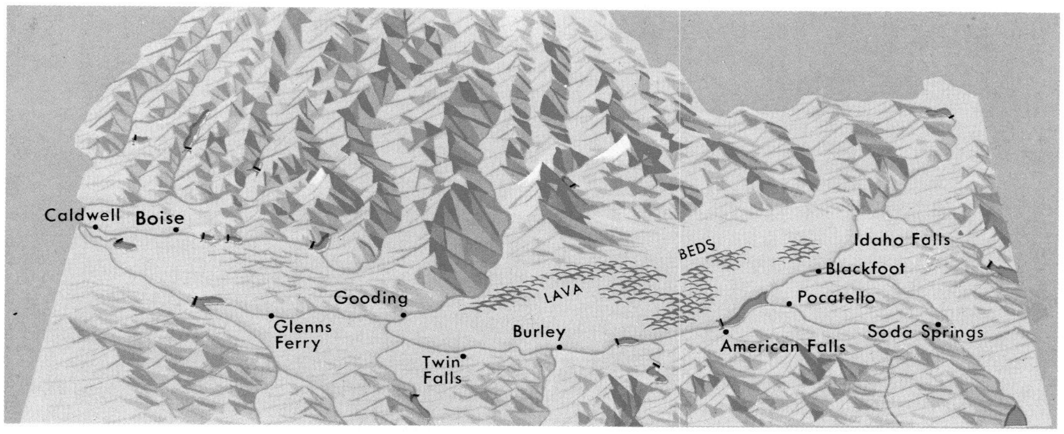

HOW MAN TURNED A VALLEY INTO A HOME

This bird's-eye view shows how man has converted the fertile but arid Snake River Plain of southern Idaho into a prosperous region of farms and cities. Irrigated by wells and dams *(black bars)* on the winding river, the volcanic lava soil permits intensive cultivation. Untillable corrugated lava beds *(red)* which once covered the entire region still lie exposed on the plateau above.

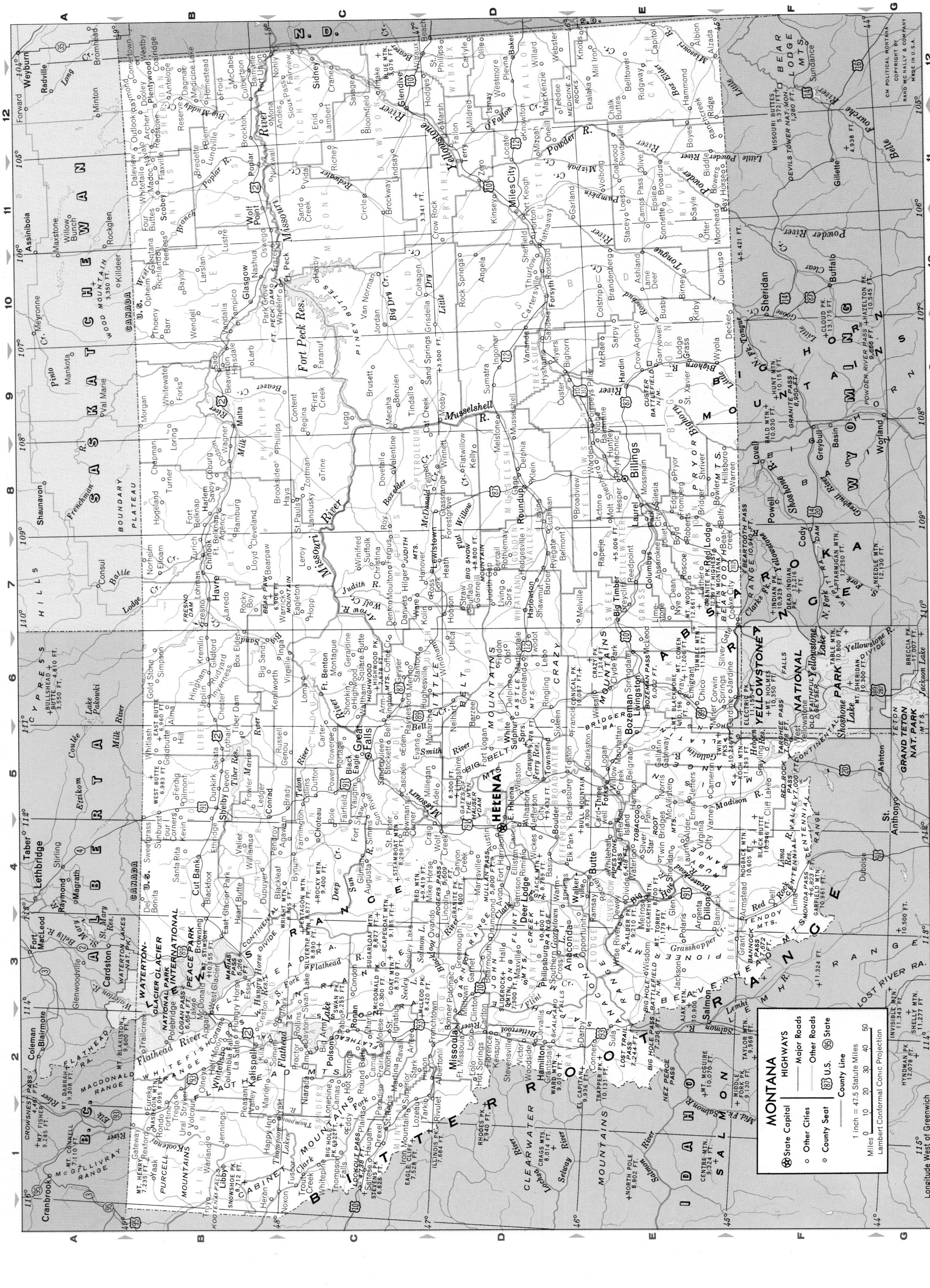
MONTANA
State Capital
Other Cities
County Seat
HIGHWAYS
Major Roads
Other Roads
U.S.
State
County Line
1 inch = 47.5 Statute Miles
Miles 0 10 20 30 40 50
Lambert Conformal Conic Projection
Longitude West of Greenwich
CM POLITICAL MONTANA
COPYRIGHT BY RAND McNALLY & COMPANY
MADE IN U.S.A.
SASKATCHEWAN
ALBERTA
BRITISH COLUMBIA
IDAHO
WYOMING
N. D.
CANADA
U.S.
HELENA
Billings
Great Falls
Missoula
Butte
Bozeman
Kalispell
Havre
Miles City
Glendive
Lewistown
YELLOWSTONE NATIONAL PARK
Fort Peck Res.
Missouri River
Yellowstone River

MONTANA: As inhabitants of an area large enough to accommodate either Germany or Japan, Montanans are said to be "so accustomed to vastness that anything less than huge seems trivial to them." Here, at Three Forks on the eastern slopes of the Rockies, originates one of the great rivers of America—the mighty Missouri, which drains an area of more than 500,000 square miles before joining the Mississippi.

It was up the Missouri in the early 1800s that the first Montanans came—fur traders and mountain men in search of beaver for the fashionable glossy hats of eastern dandies. Yet it was the Rockies which were to make Montana, for in them men of the mid-19th Century found gold and silver and, later, the copper of Butte, where lay "the richest hill on earth." But Indians roamed the mineral area. On June 25, 1876, George Armstrong Custer, the legendary general of the U.S. Seventh Cavalry, went in search of the Sioux and their Cheyenne allies, and found death near the Little Bighorn River.

AREA: 147,138 sq. mi. Rank: 4th.
POPULATION: 674,767. Rank: 41st. Largest city: Great Falls. Capital: Helena.
ENTERED UNION: Nov. 8, 1889, as 41st state.
CLIMATE: Cold winters, hot summers, light rain in east. Cooler summers, milder winters, more rain in west.
ALTITUDES: Granite Peak, 12,799 ft. (highest); Helena, 4,155 ft.

Cattle and wheat are the strength of Montana today. Dry farming—a technique by which the land is left fallow one season to allow it to absorb moisture for the next—produces an annual crop of some 100 million bushels on the eastern plain.

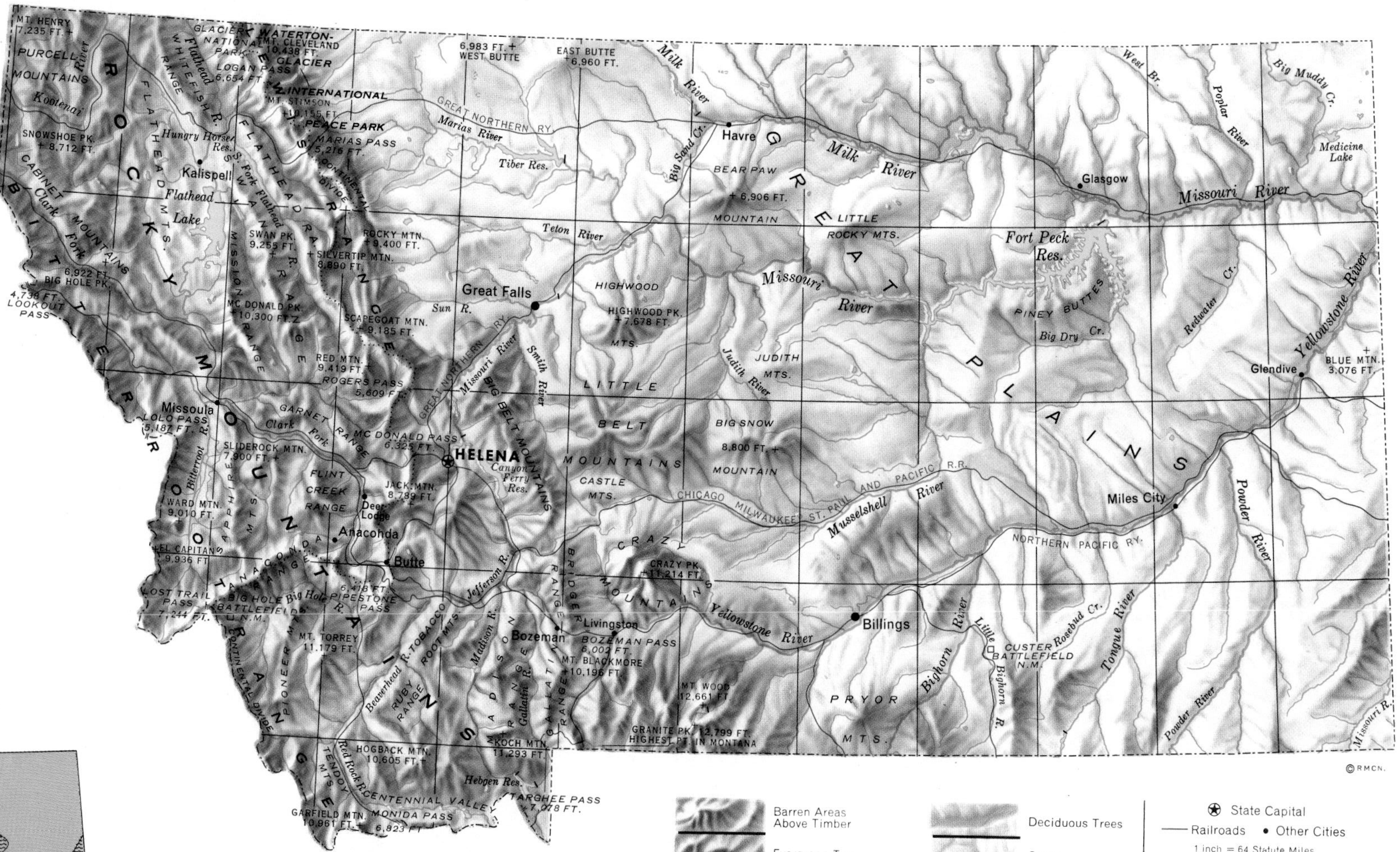

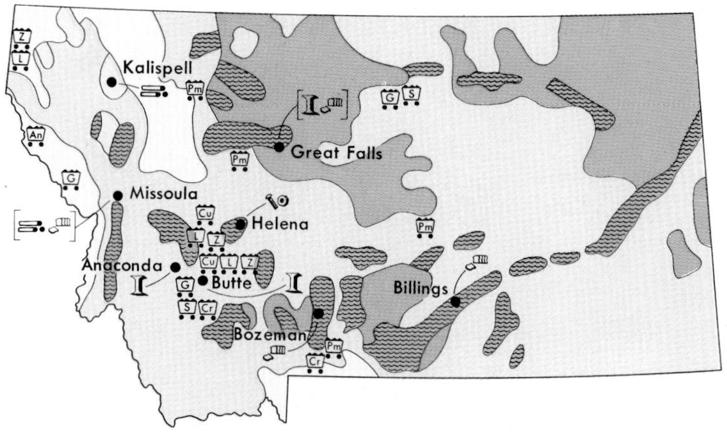

THE ECONOMY

MANUFACTURING
- Food Processing
- Lumber & Forest Products
- Primary Metals
- Metal Products

MINING
- Antimony
- Chromite
- Copper
- Gold
- Lead
- Petroleum
- Silver
- Zinc

AGRICULTURE
- General Farming
- Wheat & Small Grains
- Special Crops & General Farming
- Seasonal Grazing
- Mountains & Forest
- Irrigated Land

VALUE		EMPLOYED
$467,670,000	AGRICULTURE	25%
$191,000,000	MANUFACTURING	9%
$177,240,000	MINING	4%

Percentages are based on a total of 216,000 at work. In addition 31% are in commerce and transport, 15% in government, 16% in other areas. Manufacturing value is the value added when materials are converted into goods.

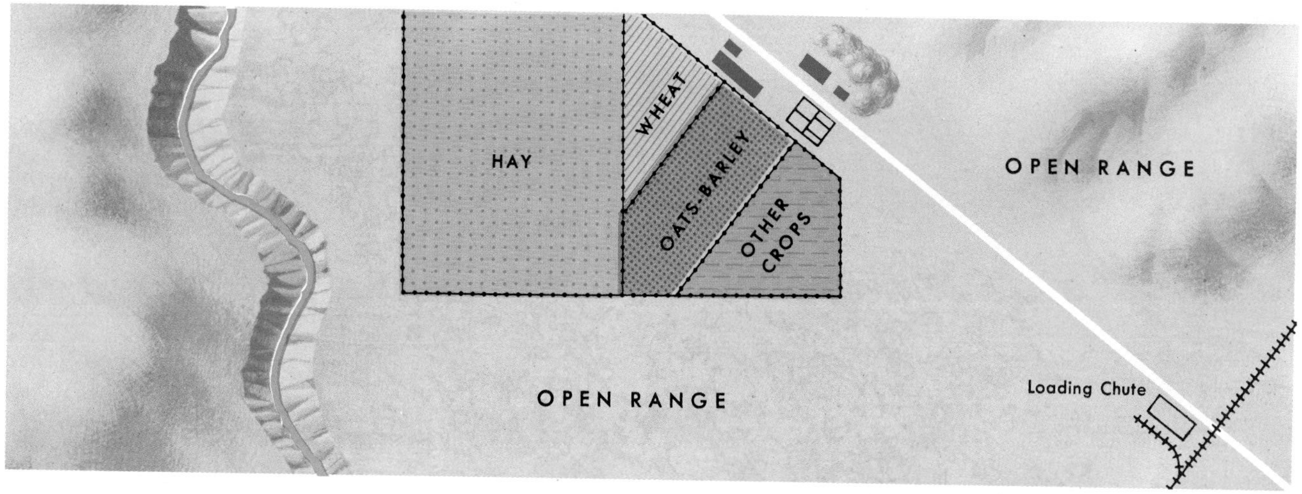

HOW A CATTLE RANCH SUSTAINS ITSELF

This plan of a representative ranch shows how cattle are raised in Montana and in other states on the Great Plains where livestock ranching is the primary occupation. Around the ranch buildings close by the roadside *(top)* stretch some 4,500 acres of open range, sparsely covered with short grasses. There the cattle graze during most of the year. Supplementary feed and some crops for sale or for the hands' own consumption are grown near the ranch. Cows, heifers and steers ready for market are cut out of the herd at yearly roundups and loaded aboard cattle cars at a nearby railroad siding *(right)* on the ranch. The animals are then transported to the Midwest for fattening and eventual slaughter. The key to the ranch's existence is the stream at left. In this semi-arid region, water is life for man and stock alike.

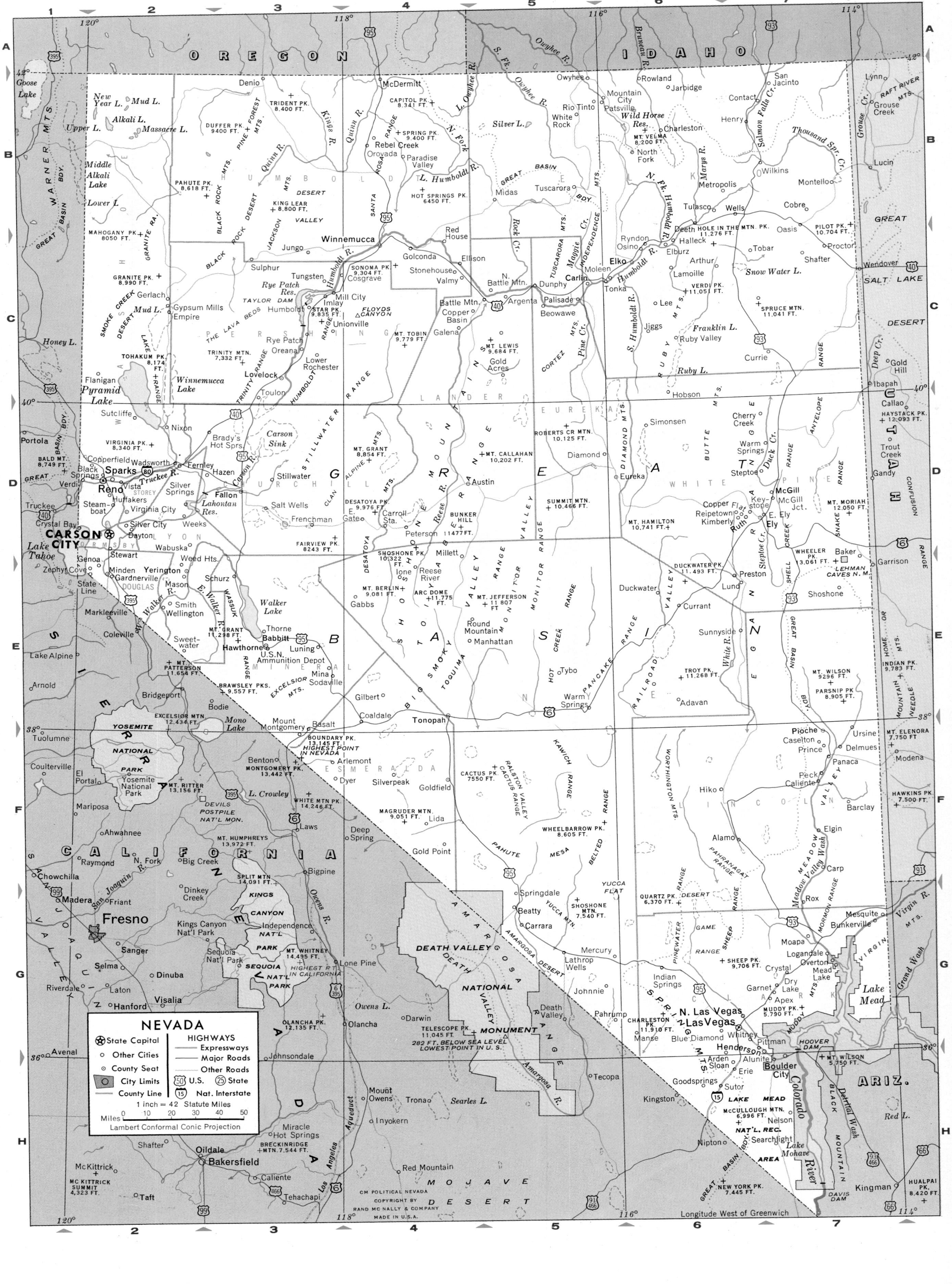

NEVADA
State Capital
Other Cities
County Seat
City Limits
County Line
HIGHWAYS
Expressways
Major Roads
Other Roads
U.S.
State
Nat. Interstate
1 inch = 42 Statute Miles
Miles 0 10 20 30 40 50
Lambert Conformal Conic Projection
CM POLITICAL NEVADA
COPYRIGHT BY RAND McNALLY & COMPANY
MADE IN U.S.A.
Longitude West of Greenwich
OREGON
IDAHO
UTAH
ARIZ.
CALIFORNIA
SIERRA NEVADA
CARSON CITY
Reno
Sparks
Las Vegas
N. Las Vegas
Henderson
Boulder City
Winnemucca
Elko
Ely
Tonopah
Hawthorne
Fallon
Lovelock
Eureka
Austin
Pioche
Goldfield
Yerington
Minden
Virginia City
Battle Mtn.
Carlin
Wells
McGill
Caliente
Beatty
Mesquite
Pyramid Lake
Walker Lake
Lake Tahoe
Lake Mead
Lake Mohave
Humboldt R.
Colorado River
Fresno
Bakersfield
Madera
Visalia
Mono Lake
HUMBOLDT
PERSHING
WASHOE
CHURCHILL
LANDER
EUREKA
ELKO
WHITE PINE
NYE
LINCOLN
CLARK
ESMERALDA
MINERAL
LYON
STOREY
DOUGLAS
ORMSBY
BOUNDARY PK. 13,145 FT. HIGHEST POINT IN NEVADA
282 FT. BELOW SEA LEVEL LOWEST POINT IN U.S.
MT. WHITNEY 14,495 FT. HIGHEST PT. IN CALIFORNIA
DEATH VALLEY NATIONAL MONUMENT
YOSEMITE NATIONAL PARK
KINGS CANYON NAT'L PARK
SEQUOIA NAT'L PARK
LAKE MEAD NAT'L REC. AREA
HOOVER DAM
DAVIS DAM
GREAT BASIN
GREAT SALT LAKE DESERT
MOJAVE DESERT
SAN JOAQUIN VALLEY
U.S.N. Ammunition Depot
LEHMAN CAVES N.M.

NEVADA

NEVADA: The driest state in the U.S., Nevada is a sun-scorched land of desert waste, sharply rising buttes and *playas* –evaporated lake beds filled with salty or alkaline deposits. It is, except for Alaska, the nation's most sparsely populated state. Had it not been for the discovery of the celebrated Comstock Lode at Virginia City in 1859, which was to yield more than $400 million in silver and other ore, Nevada might have remained simply a highway to California–and the pleasure domes of Las Vegas and Reno might never have come into existence.

AREA:	110,540 sq. mi. Rank: 7th.
POPULATION:	285,278. Rank: 49th. Largest city: Las Vegas. Capital: Carson City.
ENTERED UNION:	Oct. 31, 1864, as 36th state.
CLIMATE:	Dry and sunny with low humidity. Hot summers, cool winters. Light rainfall, deep mountain snows.
ALTITUDES:	Boundary Peak, 13,145 ft. (highest); Lake Tahoe, 6,229 ft.

Nevada's very handicaps–dryness and vast isolated spaces–have made it indispensable in the nuclear age. Yucca Flat, on the sprawling lands of the south, is a major atomic testing area.

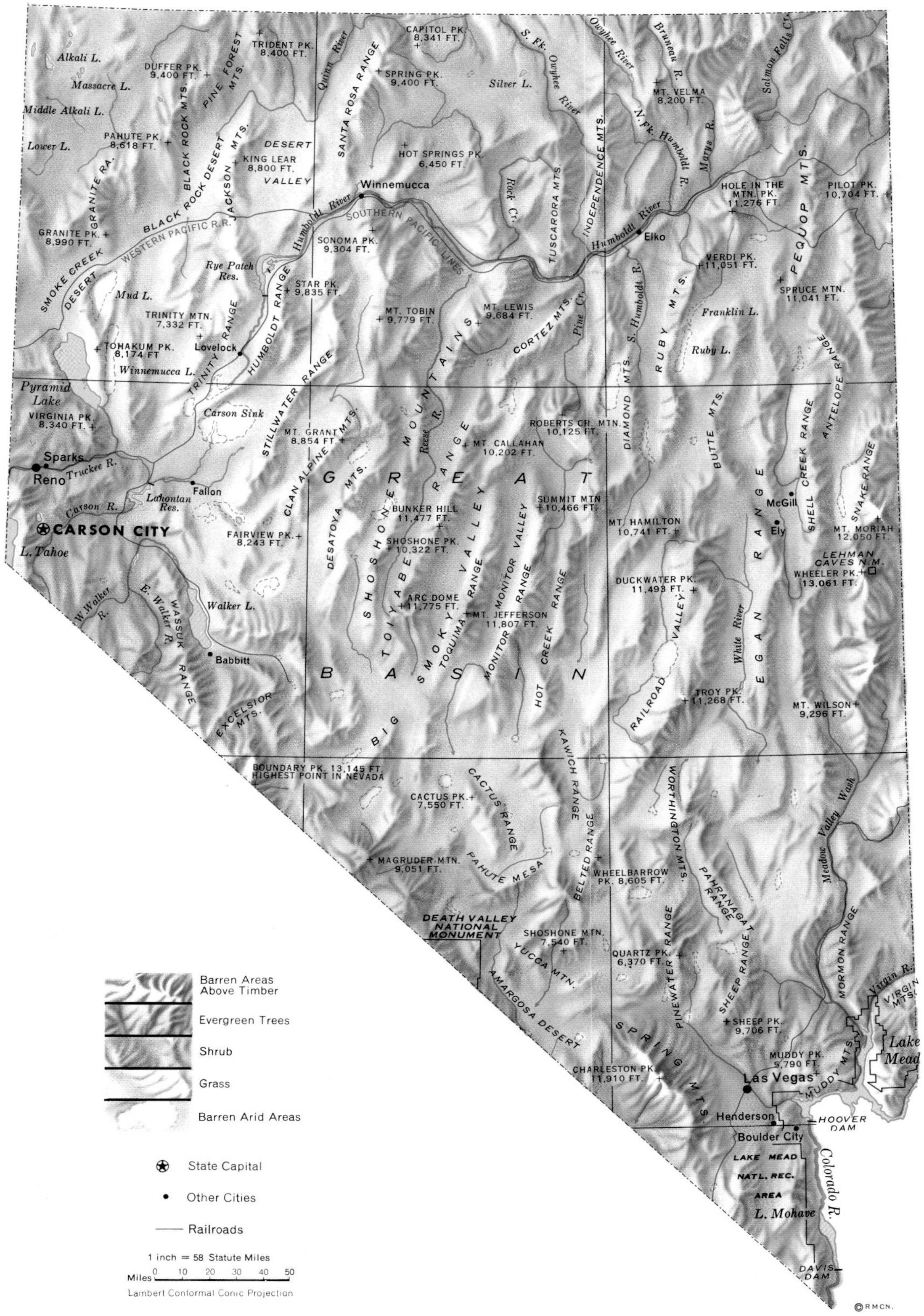

GREAT BASIN
Winnemucca
Elko
Lovelock
Sparks
Reno
Fallon
CARSON CITY
L. Tahoe
Babbitt
McGill
Ely
Las Vegas
Henderson
Boulder City
Pyramid Lake
Winnemucca L.
Carson Sink
Walker L.
Lake Mead
L. Mohave
Humboldt River
Colorado R.
HOOVER DAM
DAVIS DAM
DEATH VALLEY NATIONAL MONUMENT
LAKE MEAD NATL. REC. AREA
LEHMAN CAVES N.M.
BOUNDARY PK. 13,145 FT. HIGHEST POINT IN NEVADA
WHEELER PK. 13,061 FT.
CHARLESTON PK. 11,910 FT.
RUBY MTS.
TOIYABE RANGE
SHOSHONE MTS.
SNAKE RANGE
SPRING MTS.
Barren Areas Above Timber
Evergreen Trees
Shrub
Grass
Barren Arid Areas
State Capital
Other Cities
Railroads
1 inch = 58 Statute Miles
Miles 0 10 20 30 40 50
Lambert Conformal Conic Projection
©RMCN.

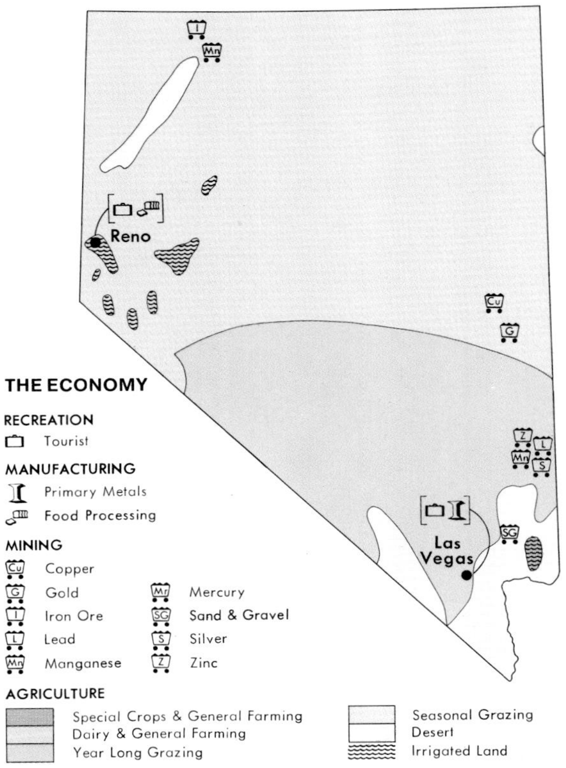

Reno
Las Vegas
THE ECONOMY
RECREATION
Tourist
MANUFACTURING
Primary Metals
Food Processing
MINING
Copper
Gold
Iron Ore
Lead
Manganese
Mercury
Sand & Gravel
Silver
Zinc
AGRICULTURE
Special Crops & General Farming
Dairy & General Farming
Year Long Grazing
Seasonal Grazing
Desert
Irrigated Land

VALUE		EMPLOYED
$55,240,000	AGRICULTURE	7%
$68,000,000	MANUFACTURING	5%
$68,290,000	MINING	3%

Percentages are based on a total of 91,000 at work. In addition 32% are in commerce and transport, 18% in government, 35% in other areas. Manufacturing value is the value added when materials are converted into goods.

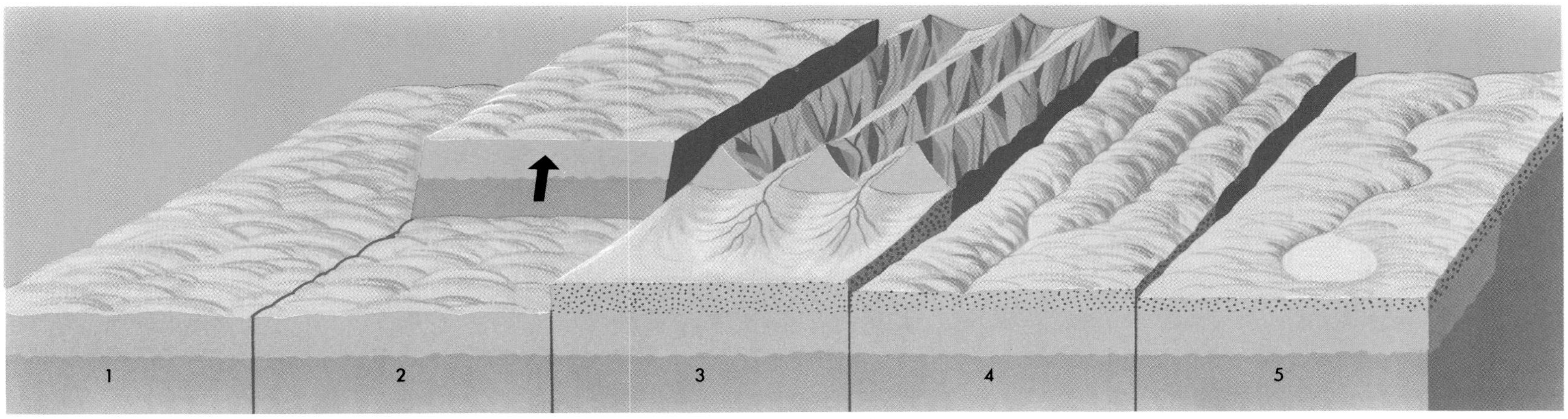

1
2
3
4
5

THE EVOLUTION OF A MOUNTAIN RANGE

The formation of "fault-block" mountains, the type common to Nevada and other mountain states, is shown above in this idealized rendering of typical stages from youth through maturity to old age. At far left, rolling land (1) is forced sharply upward (2) as slippage occurs along a "fault line," or plane of weakness in the earth. As wind, frost and streams roughen its angles, the land takes on a "youthful" shape (3). Millions of years of erosion smooth the mountain (4) to a gentle plain (5). But the earth's crust is never stable. Another uplifting of the surface may begin the cycle again.

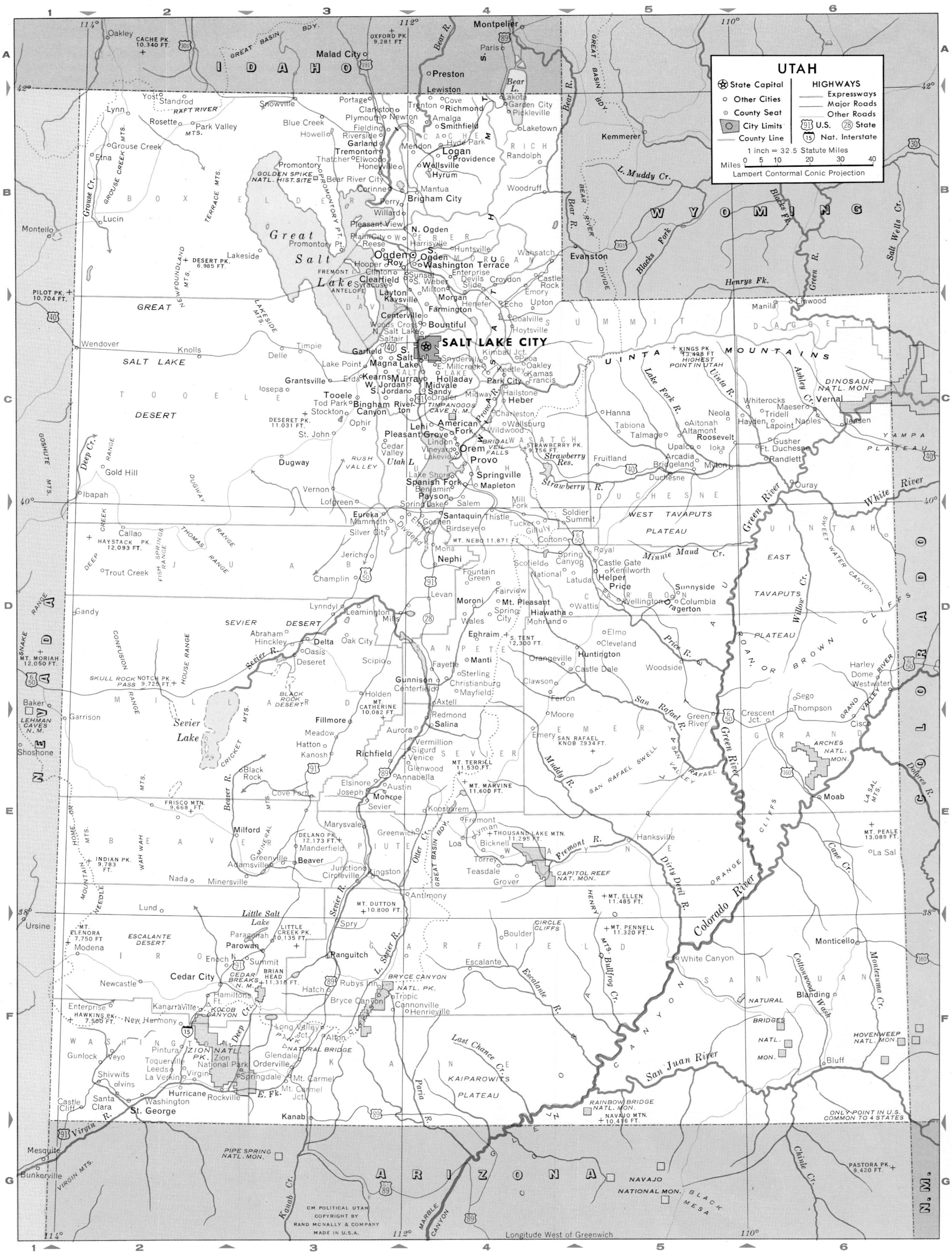

UTAH
State Capital
Other Cities
County Seat
City Limits
County Line
HIGHWAYS
Expressways
Major Roads
Other Roads
U.S.
State
Nat. Interstate
1 inch = 32.5 Statute Miles
Miles 0 5 10 20 30 40
Lambert Contormal Conic Projection
SALT LAKE CITY
IDAHO
WYOMING
COLORADO
ARIZONA
NEVADA
N. M.
Great Salt Lake
GREAT SALT LAKE DESERT
SEVIER DESERT
Sevier Lake
Utah L.
Bear L.
UINTA MOUNTAINS
KINGS PK. 13,498 FT. HIGHEST POINT IN UTAH
Ogden
Provo
Logan
Brigham City
Tooele
Nephi
Price
Vernal
Moab
Richfield
Cedar City
St. George
Kanab
Monticello
Blanding
Colorado River
Green River
San Juan River
DINOSAUR NATL. MON.
ARCHES NATL. MON.
CAPITOL REEF NAT. MON.
ZION NATL. PK.
BRYCE CANYON NATL. PK.
NATURAL BRIDGES NATL. MON.
RAINBOW BRIDGE NATL. MON.
HOVENWEEP NATL. MON.
TIMPANOGOS CAVE N.M.
GOLDEN SPIKE NATL. HIST. SITE
PIPE SPRING NATL. MON.
NAVAJO NATIONAL MON.
ONLY POINT IN U.S. COMMON TO 4 STATES
Longitude West of Greenwich
CM POLITICAL UTAH
COPYRIGHT BY
RAND McNALLY & COMPANY
MADE IN U.S.A.

UTAH

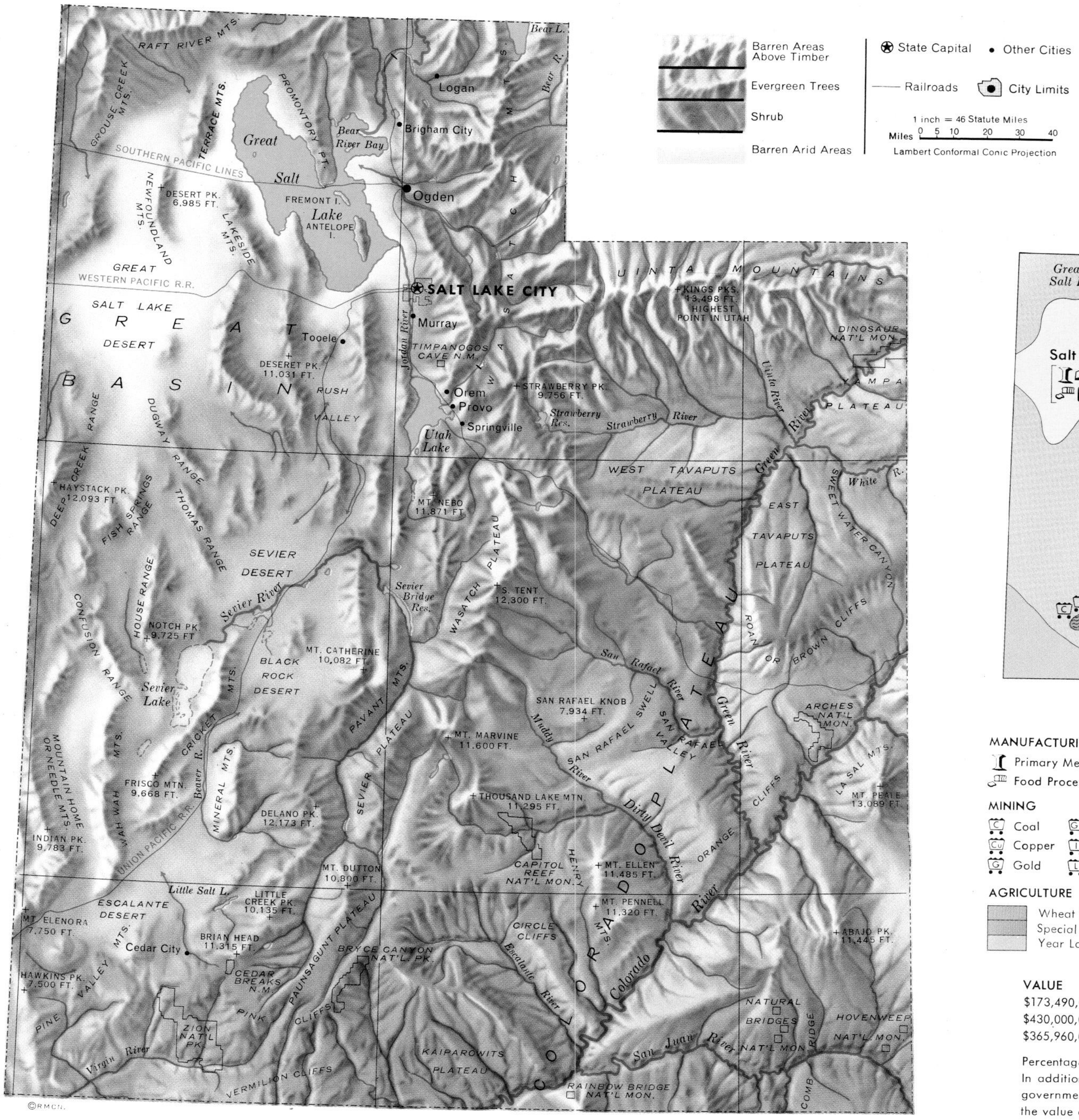

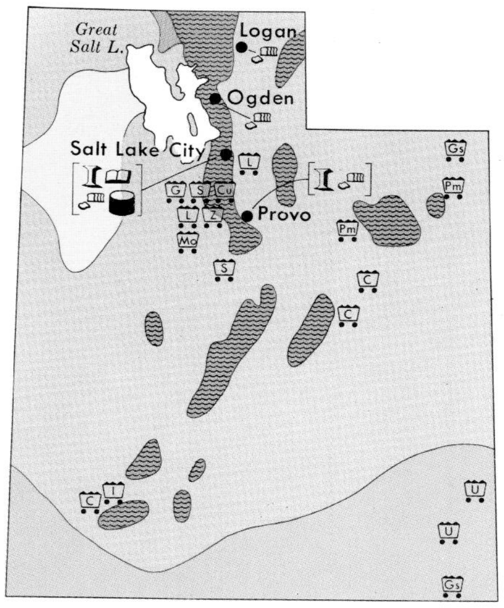

THE ECONOMY

VALUE		EMPLOYED
$173,490,000	AGRICULTURE	14%
$430,000,000	MANUFACTURING	13%
$365,960,000	MINING	5%

Percentages are based on a total of 275,000 at work. In addition 32% are in commerce and transport, 21% in government, 15% in other areas. Manufacturing value is the value added when materials are converted into goods.

UTAH: On July 23, 1847, while a wagon train of Mormons still labored across the plains behind him, Apostle Brigham Young of the Latter-day Saints came into the Salt Lake basin and spoke words that would gain lasting fame: "This is the place." Thus ended an epic exodus of some 1,500 miles from Illinois and Missouri. But many Mormons wondered at their leader's choice of the promised land. It was—and is—literally the hard earth. The settlers found that their wooden plows were broken by the sun-baked soil. To make the land easier to till, they flooded it with water drawn from the snow-fed streams running down the slopes of the nearby Wasatch Range. When hot summers disclosed there was insufficient rainfall to support crops, the mountain water proved providential. In this chance manner, the irrigation of the West began. Eventually, the practice spread into all the western states. It revolutionized traditional riparian water law, which declares that a downstream property holder is entitled to the same amount of water as an upstream owner. Today, the statutes of western states, following the lead of a law enacted by Utah in 1854, proclaim that whoever first uses the water of a stream for a beneficial purpose controls the water flow—"first in time, first in right."

AREA:	84,916 sq. mi. Rank: 11th.
POPULATION:	890,627. Rank: 38th. Largest city and capital: Salt Lake City.
ENTERED UNION:	Jan. 4, 1896, as 45th state.
CLIMATE:	Generally very dry. Warm summers, cold winters. Heaviest rain in mountains; winter snow.
ALTITUDES:	Kings Peak, 13,498 ft. (highest); Salt Lake City, 4,390 ft.

The eastern fringe of the Utah plateau is still watered by the runoff from the Wasatch Range, but manufacture and mining outrank agriculture. Utah mines almost one third of U.S. uranium ore; the 500-acre open-pit copper mine at Bingham Canyon is one of the world's most extensive.

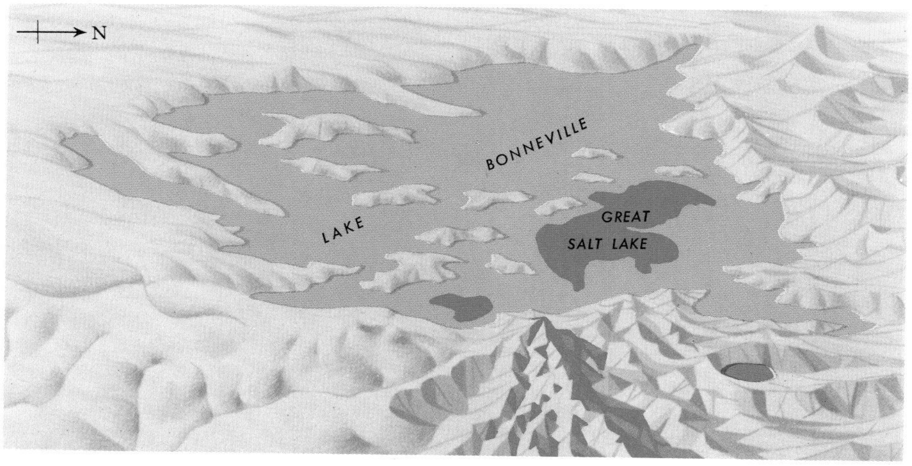

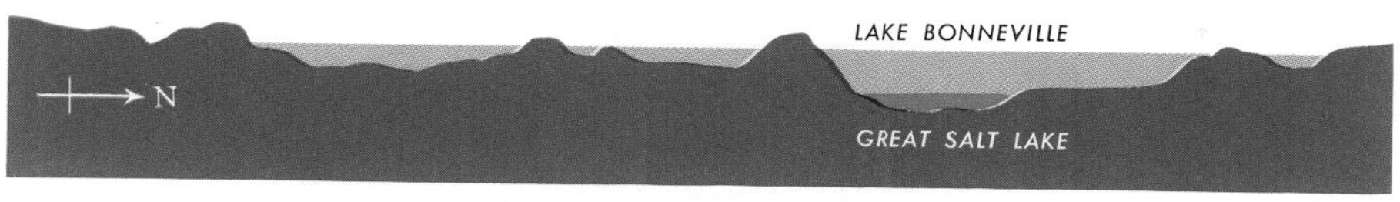

AN INLAND SEA SALTIER THAN THE OCEAN

Great Salt Lake is all that remains of Lake Bonneville *(top drawing)*, an ancient body of fresh water formed by melting glaciers and the heavy rains of an earlier climate period. Lake Bonneville's outlet became plugged when the flow cut down to resistant rock *(cross section)*. Evaporation shrank the lake to its present size, increasing its salinity so greatly that present-day Great Salt Lake is four to nine times saltier than the ocean.

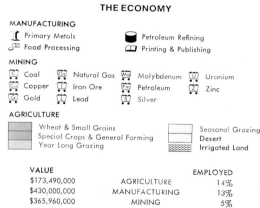

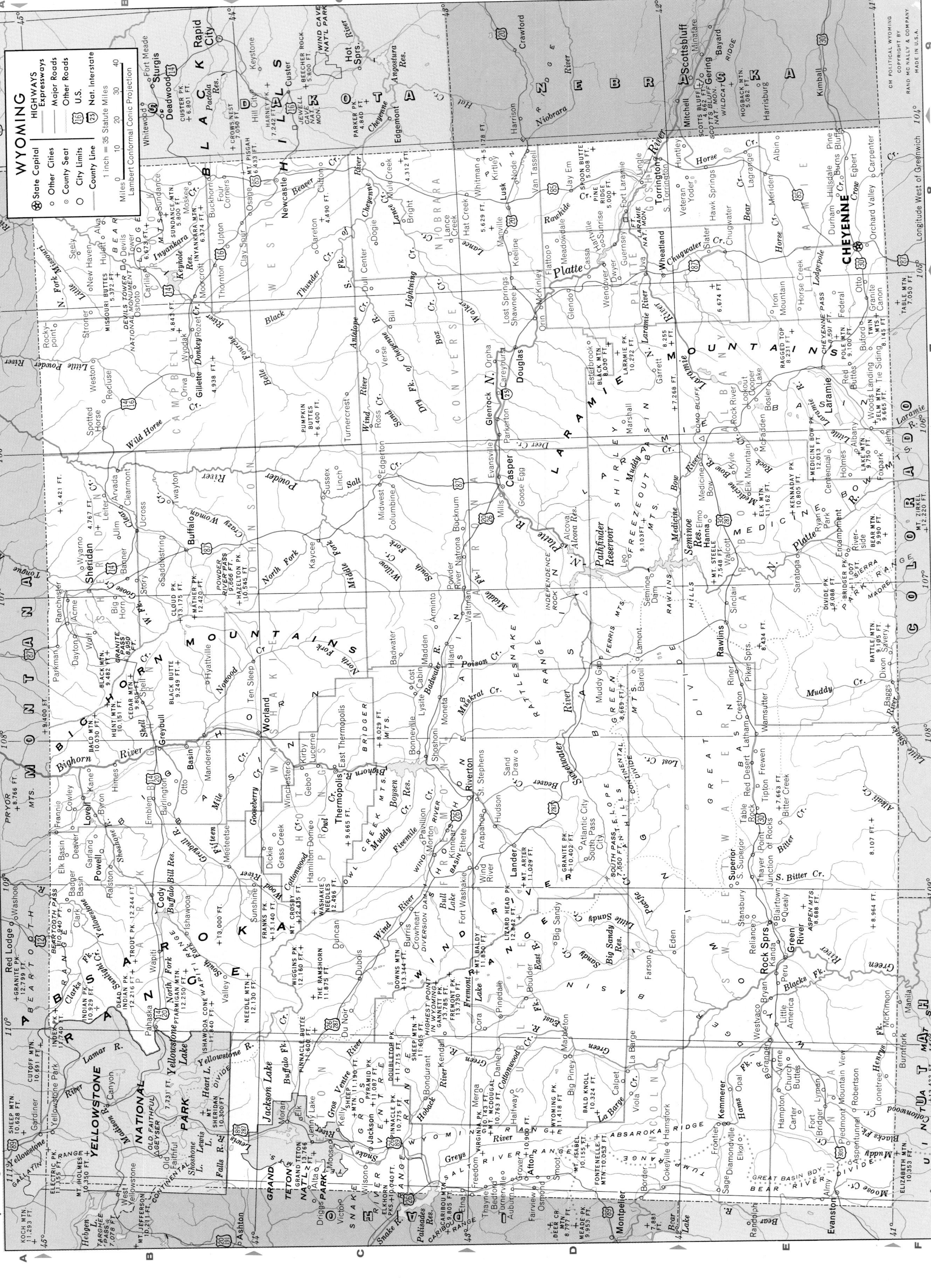
WYOMING
HIGHWAYS
Expressways
Major Roads
Other Roads
U.S.
Nat. Interstate
State Capital
Other Cities
County Seat
City Limits
County Line
Miles 0 10 20 30 40
1 inch = 35 Statute Miles
Lambert Conformal Conic Projection
CHEYENNE
Casper
Laramie
Rawlins
Rock Sprs.
Sheridan
Cody
Lander
Riverton
Douglas
Gillette
Evanston
Jackson
Worland
Buffalo
Torrington
YELLOWSTONE NATIONAL PARK
GRAND TETON NAT'L PARK
M O N T A N A
S O U T H D A K O T A
N E B R A S K A
C O L O R A D O
U T A H
I D A H O
Longitude West of Greenwich
CM POLITICAL WYOMING
COPYRIGHT BY
RAND McNALLY & COMPANY
MADE IN U.S.A.

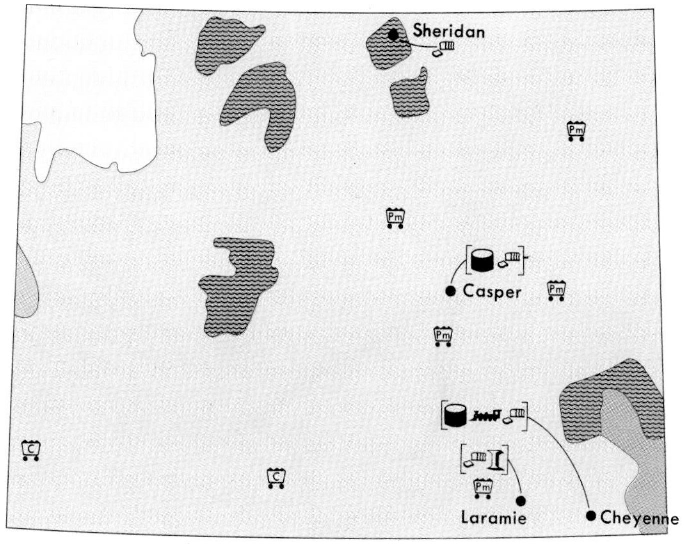

THE ECONOMY

MANUFACTURING
- Primary Metals
- Food Processing
- Petroleum Refining
- Transportation Equipment

MINING
- Coal
- Petroleum

AGRICULTURE
- Wheat & Small Grains
- Special Crops & General Farming
- Dairy Farming
- Seasonal Grazing
- Mountains & Forests
- Irrigated Land

VALUE		EMPLOYED
$178,690,000	AGRICULTURE	19%
$ 64,000,000	MANUFACTURING	6%
$369,940,000	MINING	8%

Percentages are based on a total of 106,000 at work. In addition 32% are in commerce and transport, 18% in government, 17% in other areas. Manufacturing value is the value added when materials are converted into goods.

Barren Areas Above Timber
Evergreen Trees
Mixed Evergreen and Deciduous Trees
Shrub
Grass

State Capital • Other Cities
—— Railroads

1 inch = 50 Statute Miles
Miles 0 10 20 30 40 50
Lambert Conformal Conic Projection

WYOMING

WYOMING: Here lay the great highway of the Old West. Much of the state is scrub and sage, a high land of thrusting mountain ranges, rolling plains and sloping basins. Past Rattlesnake Range and into legendary South Pass went the old Oregon and California trails. In some places, the deep ruts worn into the baked soil by the ironbound wheels of countless wagon trains can still be seen. Through Wyoming went the Pony Express, the first trans-continental telegraph line and the rails of the Union Pacific.

AREA: 97,914 sq. mi. Rank: 9th.
POPULATION: 330,066. Rank: 48th. Largest city and capital: Cheyenne.
ENTERED UNION: July 10, 1890, as 44th state.
CLIMATE: Mostly dry, with severe winters and fairly cool summers. Light summer rain.
ALTITUDES: Gannett Peak, 13,785 ft. (highest).

Although oil-refining, sugar-beet processing and coal mining are important to modern Wyoming, the state retains much of the atmosphere of the Old West. In Cheyenne in the late afternoon, cattle wranglers still idle by the Union Pacific depot. In the countryside graze more than two million sheep and a million head of cattle, creating a classic picture of the range. For tourists, Wyoming primarily means natural geysers *(right)*, protected wildlife, and the roaring cataracts of Yellowstone, oldest and largest national park in the U.S.

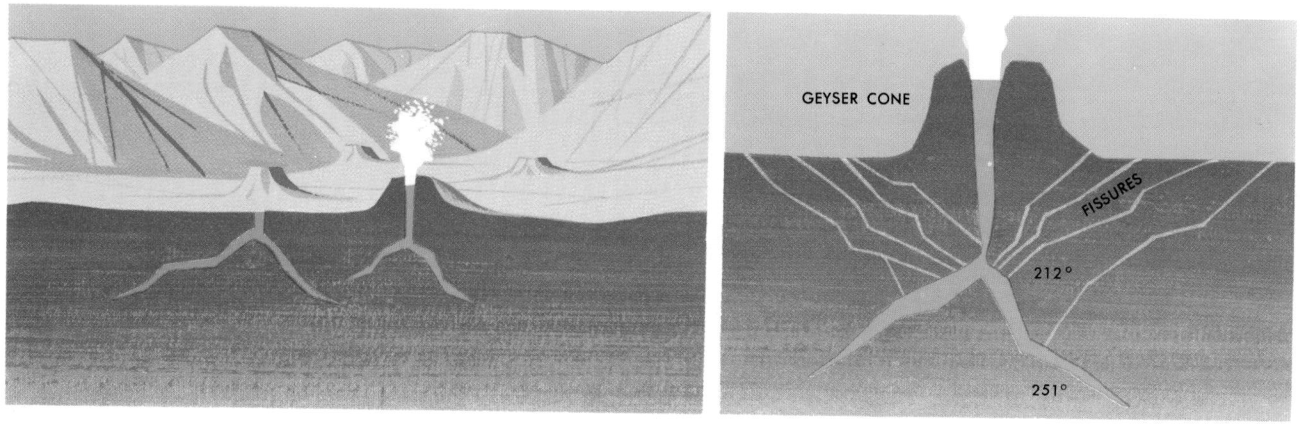

WHY GEYSERS ERUPT: A REALM OF UNDERGROUND POWER

A geyser basin like those at Yellowstone *(above left)* and a single geyser *(above right)* are shown here. Through fissures, water filters down to hot rock but, under pressure at that depth, cannot boil. Forced by expansion toward the surface, where pressure is lower, it turns to steam, allowing superheated water just below to erupt violently into the open. The process is repeated when more water seeps down. Surface cones are formed of minerals in the water deposited by successive eruptions.

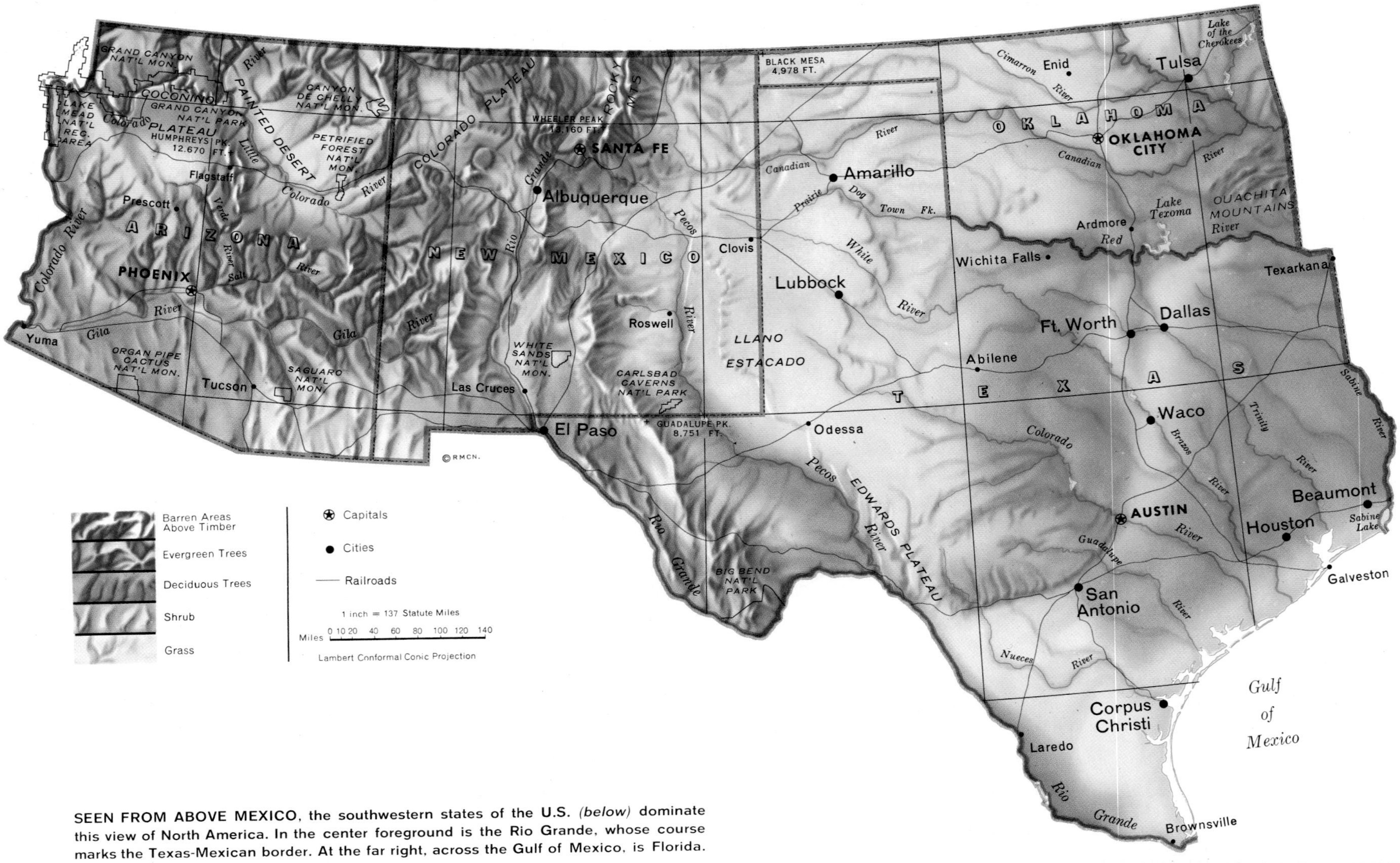

SEEN FROM ABOVE MEXICO, the southwestern states of the U.S. *(below)* dominate this view of North America. In the center foreground is the Rio Grande, whose course marks the Texas-Mexican border. At the far right, across the Gulf of Mexico, is Florida.

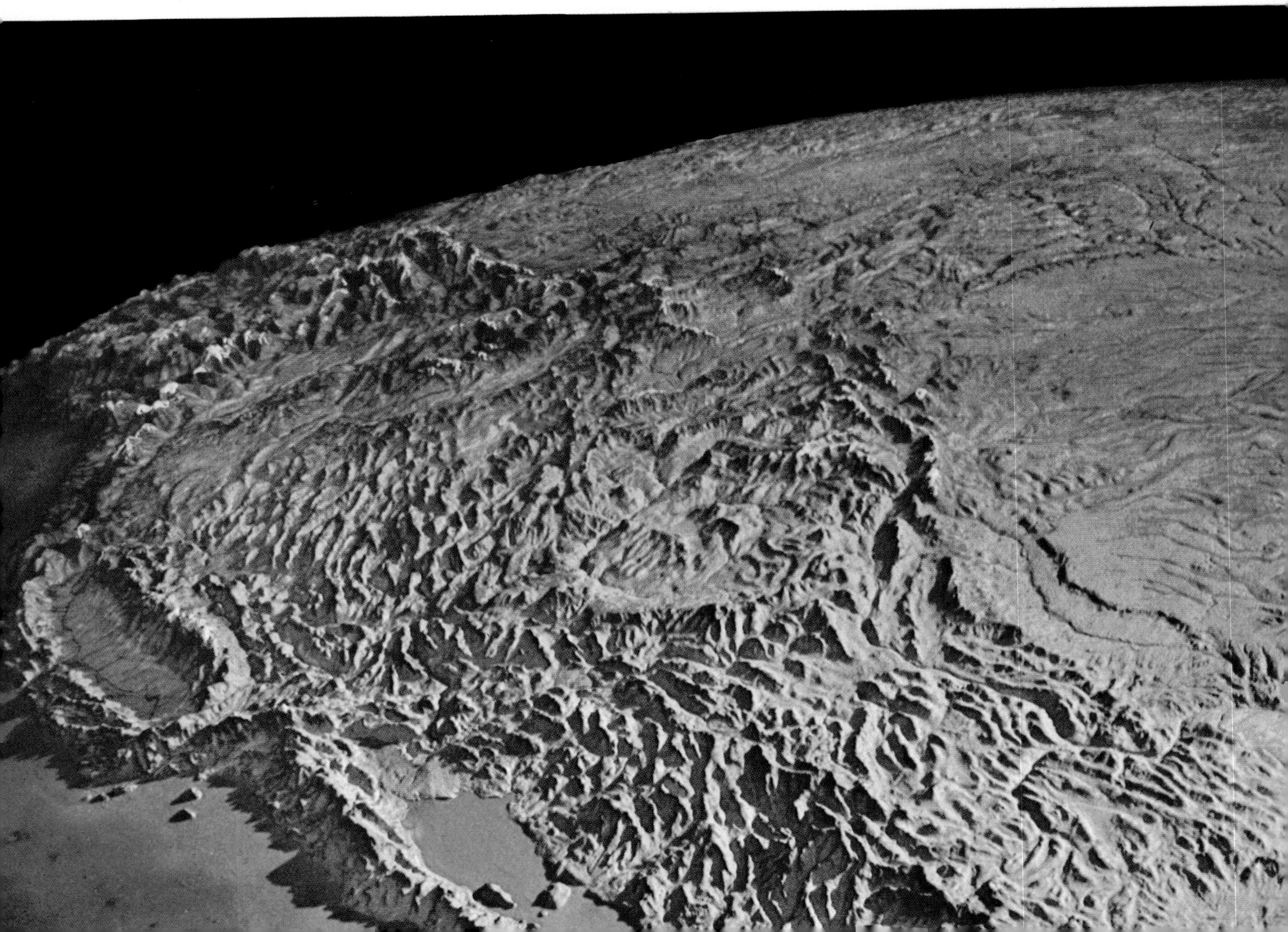

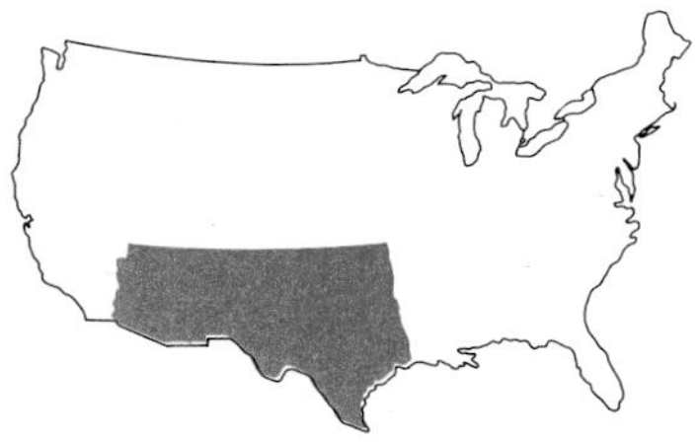

SOUTHWEST STATES

"The land lies flat, dry, and unending until the earth's gentle curvature is a subtle reality under the great arch of cloudless sky," wrote William Weber Johnson, a converted Texan. "Dusty red-and-white cattle are dots in the distance, moving slowly, searching for . . . grass on the seemingly barren earth."

Approached from the east, this is the familiar U.S. Southwest. Farther to the west the land divides in awesome canyons, then rises in bleak mesas toward mountain forests and snow-capped peaks shimmering above the desert heat. But most of it is so arid, so stark, that white men long thought it uninhabitable. Castañeda, the chronicler of Coronado's 1540 expedition, reported that *"no avian visto otra cosa sino vacas y cielo"* (They had seen nothing but cows and sky). But later men felt that if the sparse sage could support the buffalo that Castañeda called "cows," it might also maintain the wild Spanish cattle of the Rio Grande. By the late 1800s, much of the area was one enormous ranch. But the days of the open range were short-lived. With newly invented barbed wire, homesteaders cut the unwooded plains into rectangular fields. And with windmills for power, they pumped sufficient ground water to support modest farming.

There the dry land might have remained—good for cattle, for small-scale farming, for dispossessed eastern Indians and indigenous tribes. But underground lay vast deposits of copper, potash and sulphur, and, in Oklahoma and Texas, some of the world's most extensive petroleum reserves. The Indians who owned the land grew wealthy, and the white men who raised the derricks, wealthier still.

Today the Southwest produces more than one third of the U.S.'s cotton, and its vast areas of wheat and sorghum are interspersed with refineries, defense installations, booming cities and sun-seeking tourists. Of this region Walter Prescott Webb wrote: "The history of the white man is the history of . . . giving up an old way of life for a new way in order that there might be *a* way." Here Americans continued the long process of "moving from the forest-clad land into the treeless plain."

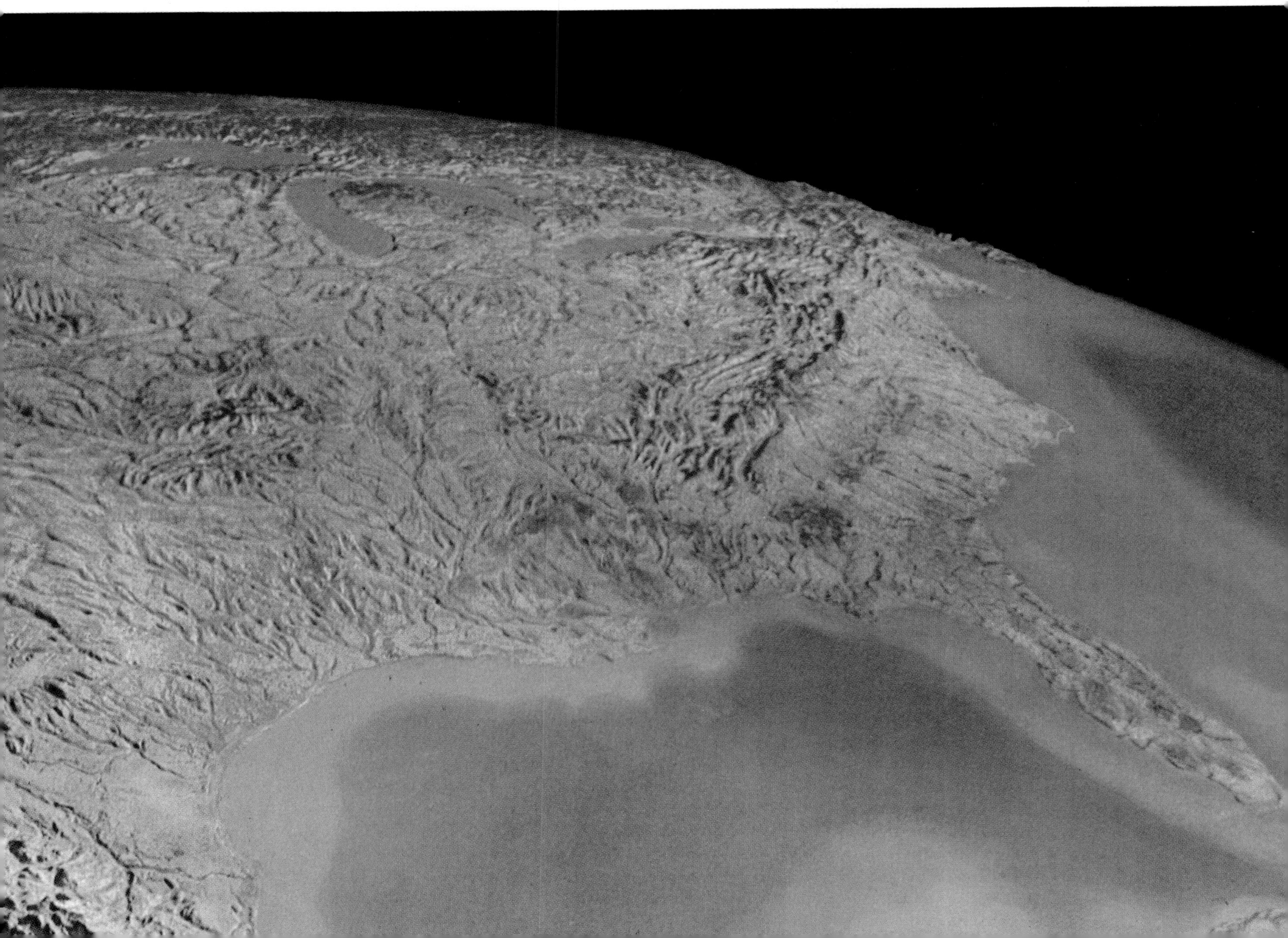

THE PAINTED CREATION OF A MILLION YEARS

GRAND CANYON, its iridescent walls aglow at sunset, paints the high plateaus of northern Arizona with glory. Carved deep into multiple layers of rock by the abrasive action of stones and sand rushing down the swift Colorado River, the canyon is 280 miles long and eight to 15 miles wide. In places the drop from rim to floor is more than a mile. Easily the Southwest's most popular attraction, the canyon offers tourists and geologists alike a spectacular view described as "millions of years of creation, all in one 10-second glance."

A SPRAWLING INDUSTRY BORN OF WIDE-OPEN SPACES

A HERD OF HEREFORDS, on the way to market, pauses for water during a drive across the White River in eastern Arizona. Here in the arid Southwest, where streams are dry much of the year and the soil is only sparsely covered with vegetation, it takes as many as 60 acres to support a single head. But thanks to an abundance of inexpensive range land, which permits ranches to become as large as 1,500 square miles, the southwestern states have been able to base a major part of their economy on the production of cattle.

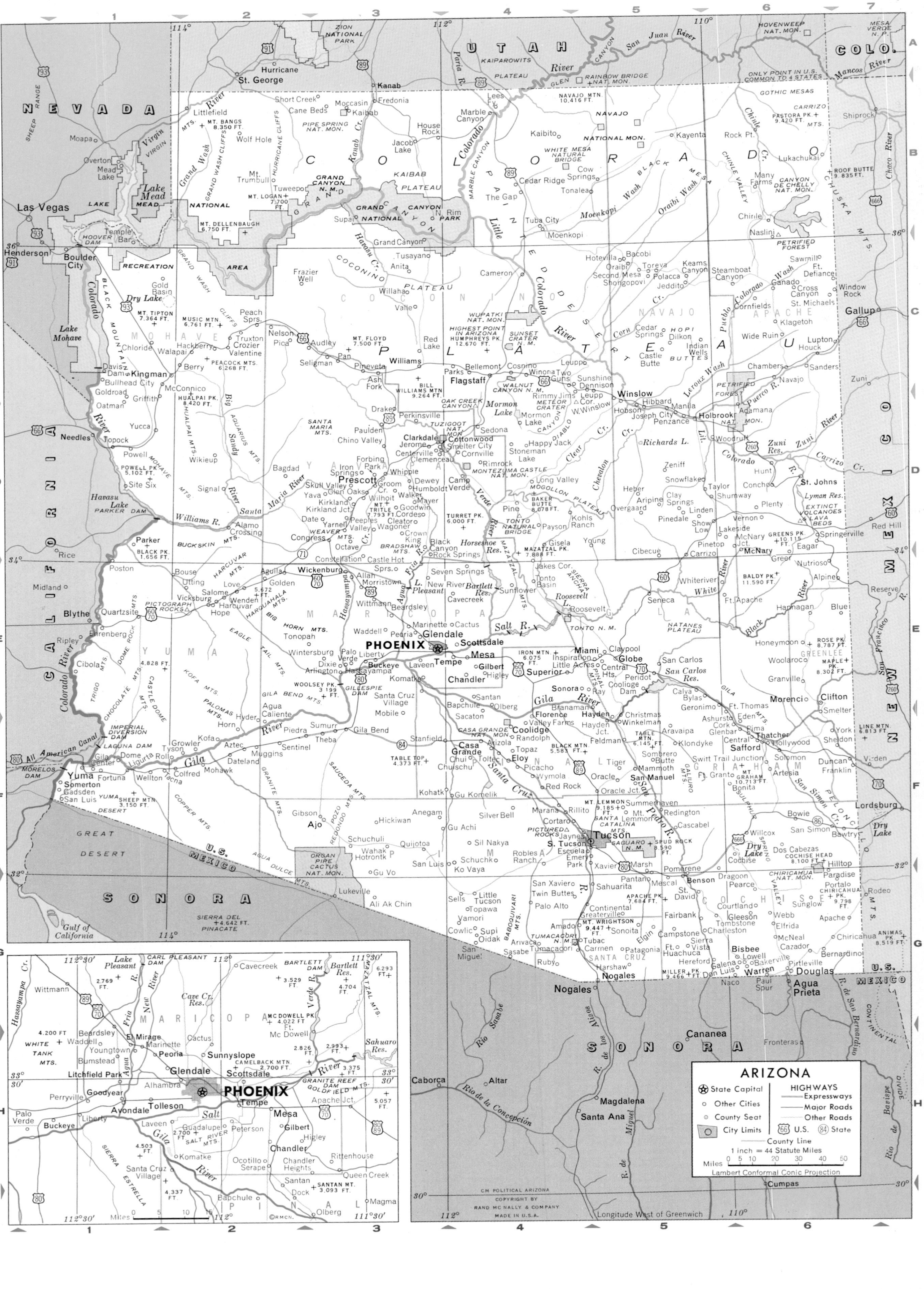
ARIZONA
State Capital
Other Cities
County Seat
City Limits
HIGHWAYS
Expressways
Major Roads
Other Roads
U.S.
State
County Line
1 inch = 44 Statute Miles
Miles 0 5 10 20 30 40 50
Lambert Conformal Conic Projection
CM POLITICAL ARIZONA
COPYRIGHT BY
RAND MC NALLY & COMPANY
MADE IN U.S.A.
Longitude West of Greenwich
UTAH
COLO.
NEVADA
CALIFORNIA
NEW MEXICO
SONORA
MEXICO
U.S.
COLORADO PLATEAU
GRAND CANYON
PAINTED DESERT
COCONINO PLATEAU
MOHAVE
YAVAPAI
MARICOPA
YUMA
PINAL
PIMA
GRAHAM
COCHISE
SANTA CRUZ
GILA
NAVAJO
APACHE
PHOENIX
Tucson
Flagstaff
Prescott
Yuma
Kingman
Winslow
Holbrook
Globe
Nogales
Douglas
Bisbee
Safford
Las Vegas
Gallup
Lordsburg
Needles
Blythe
St. George
Kanab
Lake Mead
Lake Mohave
Hoover Dam
Parker Dam
Gila River
Salt R.
Colorado River
Gulf of California
PHOENIX
Glendale
Tempe
Mesa
Scottsdale
Chandler
Gilbert
Peoria
Litchfield Park
Avondale
Tolleson
Buckeye
Sunnyslope

ARIZONA

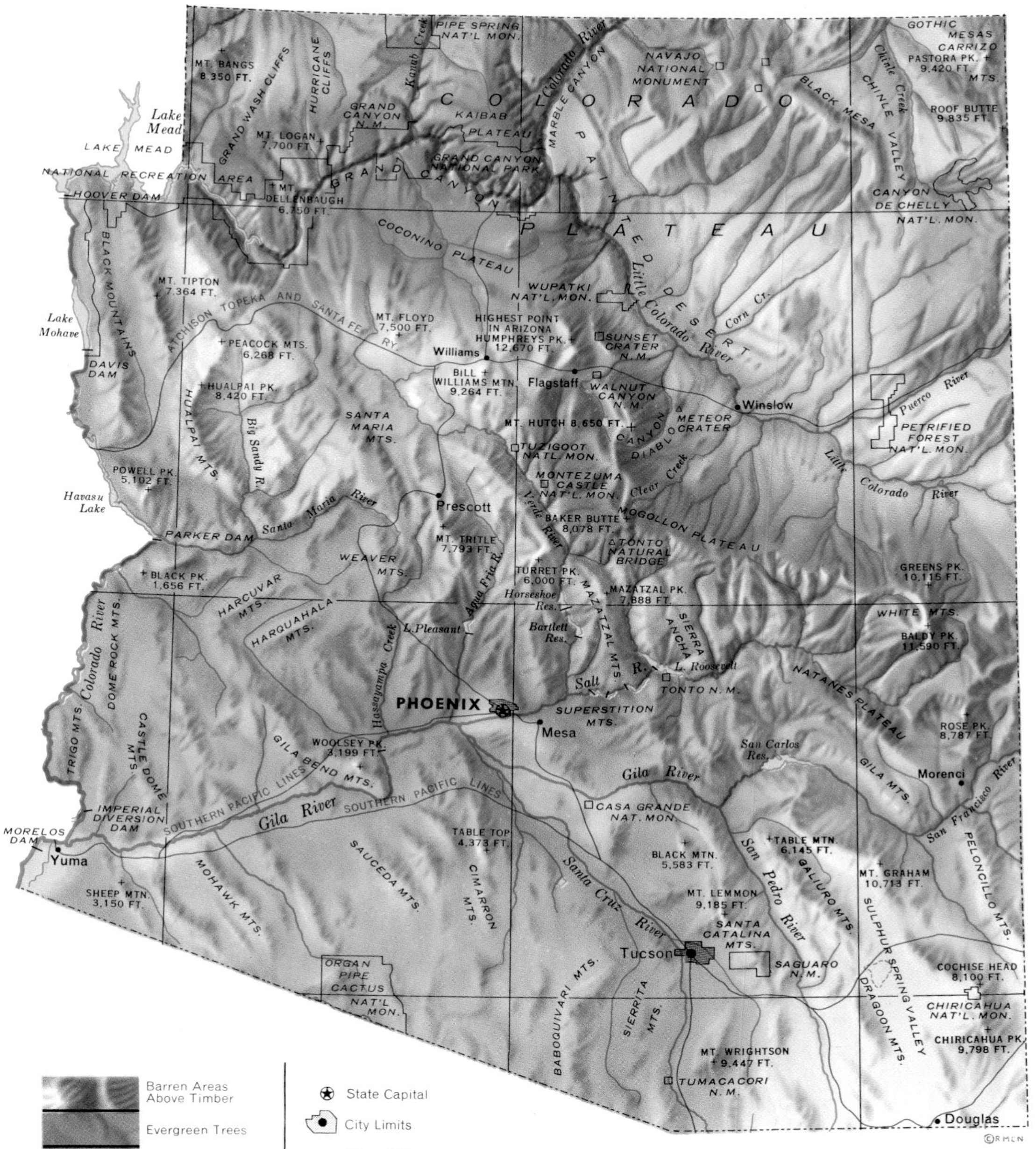

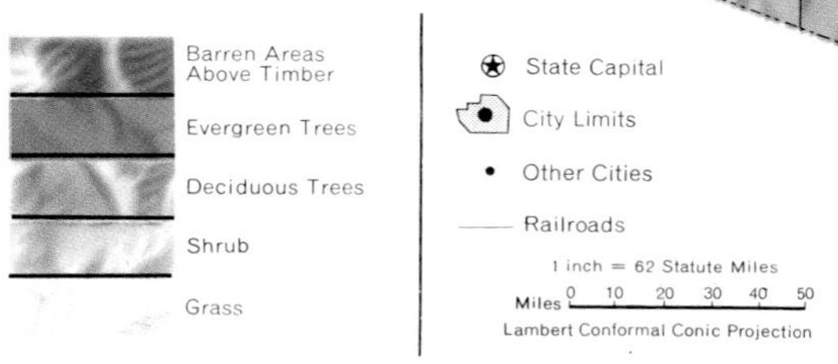

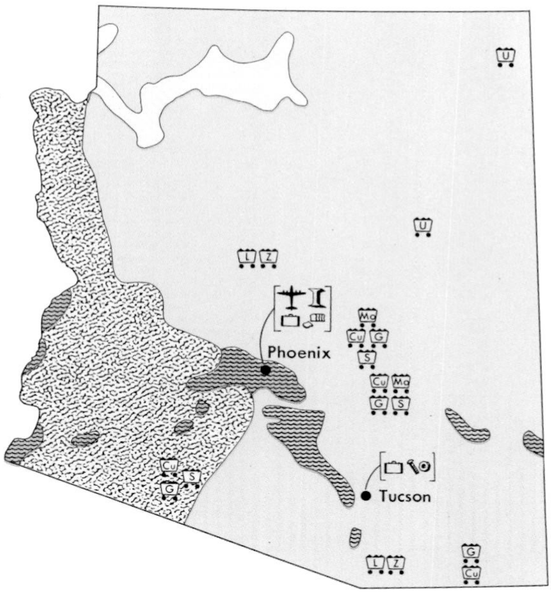

THE ECONOMY

MANUFACTURING
- Transportation Equipment
- Food Processing
- Primary Metals
- Metal Products

RECREATION
- Tourist

AGRICULTURE
- Cotton
- Special Crops & General Farming
- Fruit, Truck & General Farming
- Year Long Grazing
- Mountains & Forest
- Desert
- Irrigated Land

MINING
- Cu Copper
- G Gold
- L Lead
- Mo Molybdenum
- S Silver
- U Uranium
- Z Zinc

VALUE		EMPLOYED
$444,970,000	AGRICULTURE	15%
$438,000,000	MANUFACTURING	12%
$314,520,000	MINING	5%

Percentages are based on a total of 329,000 at work. In addition 31% are in commerce and transport, 18% in government, 19% in other areas. Manufacturing value is the value added when materials are converted into goods.

ARIZONA: "The region is altogether valueless," a report to Congress noted in 1858. "After entering it there is nothing to do but leave." An arid yet beautiful land of plunging gorges like Grand Canyon *(right)*, varicolored deserts, erosion-carved buttes, mountains and parched yellow sands nurturing only such desert life as Gila monsters and saguaro cactus, Arizona is, paradoxically, one of the fastest-growing areas of the nation.

Here, in "the land where time stands still," the population has more than doubled since 1940. The reason lies in Arizona's scenery, dry air and life-restoring sunshine. Drawn by such attractions as Tucson's resort pools and the pine-dotted ski slopes of nearby Mount Lemmon, health-seekers and vacationists add more than $250 million a year to the state's economy.

AREA: 113,909 sq. mi. Rank: 6th.
POPULATION: 1,302,161. Rank: 35th. Largest city and capital: Phoenix.
ENTERED UNION: Feb. 14, 1912, as 48th state.
CLIMATE: Clear air, nearly constant sunshine, low humidity, low rainfall. Hot summers; winters generally mild.
ALTITUDES: Humphreys Peak, 12,670 ft. (highest); Tucson, 2,390 ft.

Important sources of income in Arizona are the irrigated fields of long-staple cotton flourishing in the once dry desert east and south of Phoenix; the huge, terraced copper mines, among the most productive in the U.S.; and the herds of cattle which roam the vast ranges. More significantly, the endless sunshine and open spaces have lured hundreds of large and small manufacturers to the Phoenix and Tucson areas since the end of World War II, nourishing a highly promising industrial boom.

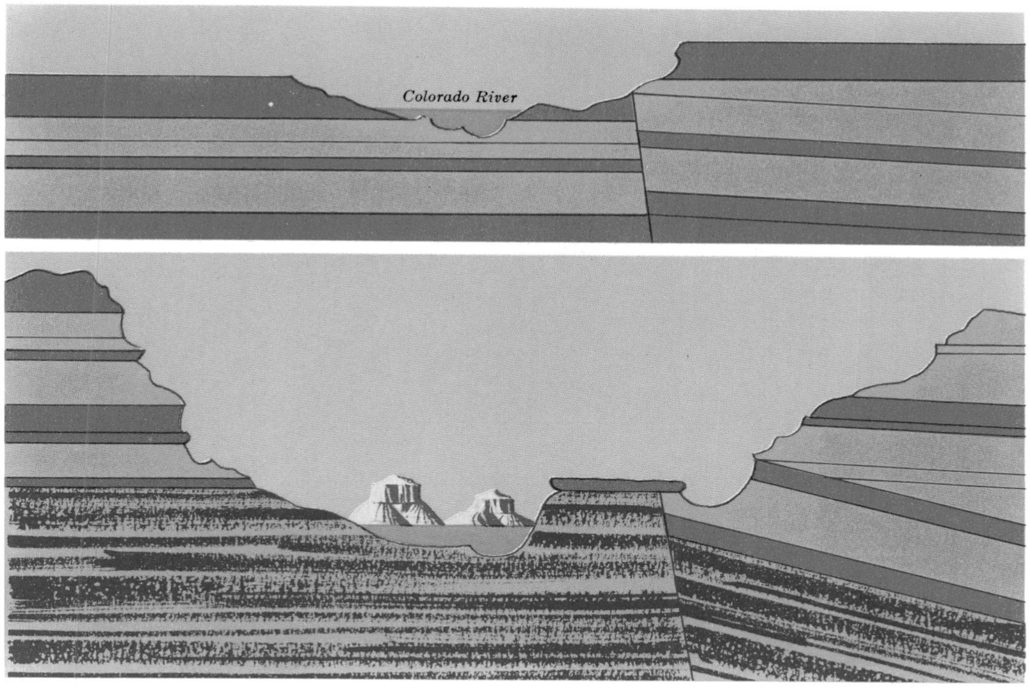

THE MAKING OF GRAND CANYON

Two stages in the development of Arizona's Grand Canyon are shown here in cross-section views. At top, the Colorado River has only begun its work of cutting away different rock strata. At bottom, some tens of thousands of years later, the surrounding land has been uplifted by pressures from deep within the earth. The river, loaded with abrasive stones, sand and silt, moves much more swiftly, cutting rapidly through the rock strata. Two "temples" capped with more resistant rock remain in the gorge.

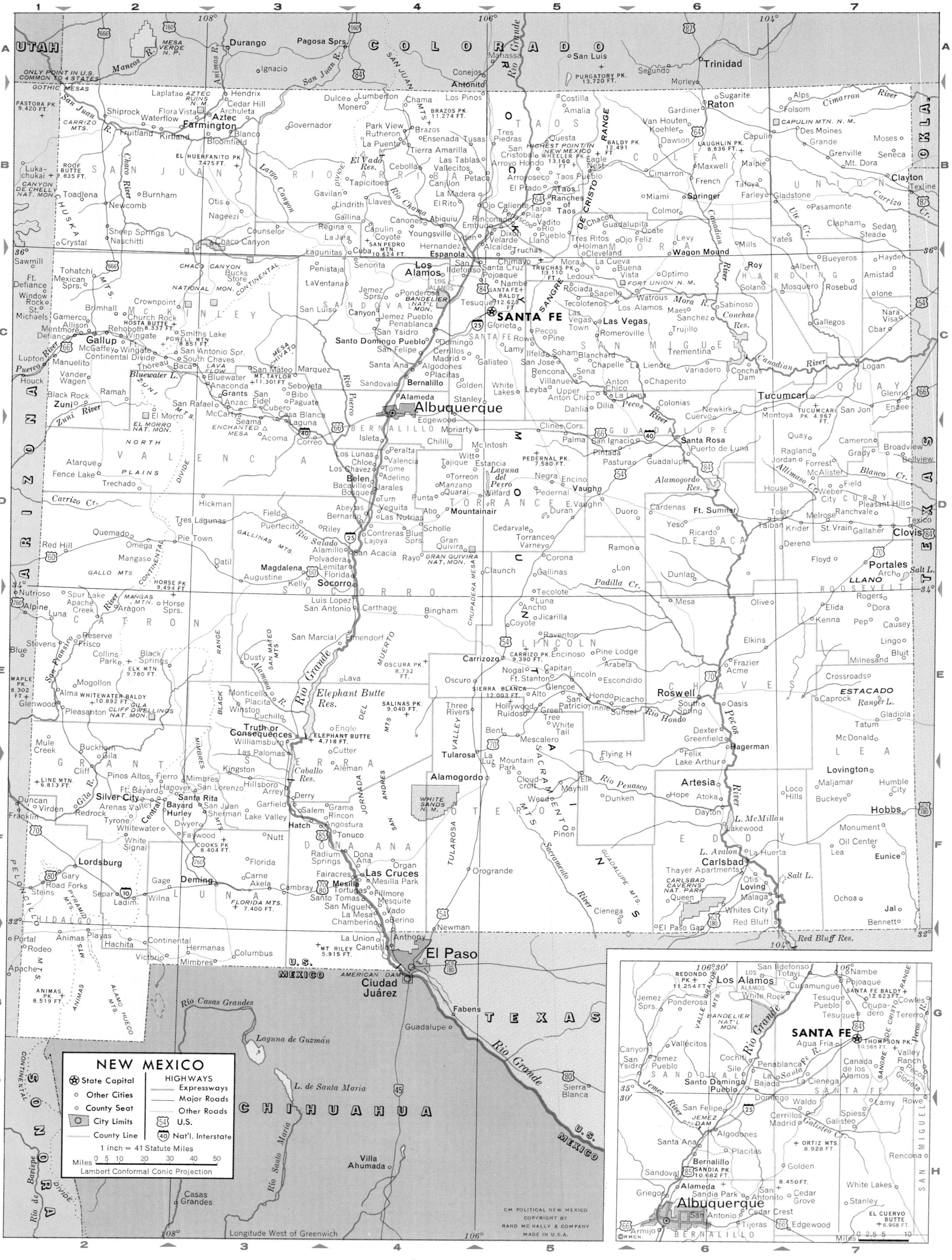
NEW MEXICO
State Capital
Other Cities
County Seat
City Limits
County Line
HIGHWAYS
Expressways
Major Roads
Other Roads
U.S.
Nat'l. Interstate
1 inch = 41 Statute Miles
Miles 0 5 10 20 30 40 50
Lambert Conformal Conic Projection
CM POLITICAL NEW MEXICO
COPYRIGHT BY RAND McNALLY & COMPANY
MADE IN U.S.A.
Longitude West of Greenwich
UTAH
COLORADO
ARIZONA
TEXAS
OKLA.
SONORA
CHIHUAHUA
U.S.
MEXICO
ONLY POINT IN U.S. COMMON TO 4 STATES
SANTA FE
Albuquerque
El Paso
Ciudad Juárez
Los Alamos
Las Cruces
Roswell
Carlsbad
Gallup
Farmington
Las Vegas
Tucumcari
Clovis
Hobbs
Socorro
Alamogordo
Deming
Silver City
Raton
Taos
Durango
Trinidad
Rio Grande
Pecos River
Canadian River
Elephant Butte Res.
HIGHEST POINT IN NEW MEXICO WHEELER PK. 13,160 FT.
SAN JUAN
RIO ARRIBA
TAOS
COLFAX
UNION
MORA
SANDOVAL
SANTA FE
SAN MIGUEL
HARDING
QUAY
MC KINLEY
VALENCIA
BERNALILLO
TORRANCE
GUADALUPE
DE BACA
CURRY
ROOSEVELT
SOCORRO
CATRON
LINCOLN
CHAVES
SIERRA
GRANT
OTERO
LEA
EDDY
DONA ANA
LUNA
HIDALGO
Pojoaque
Tesuque
Santo Domingo Pueblo
Bernalillo
Santa Ana
Sandia Park
Edgewood

NEW MEXICO

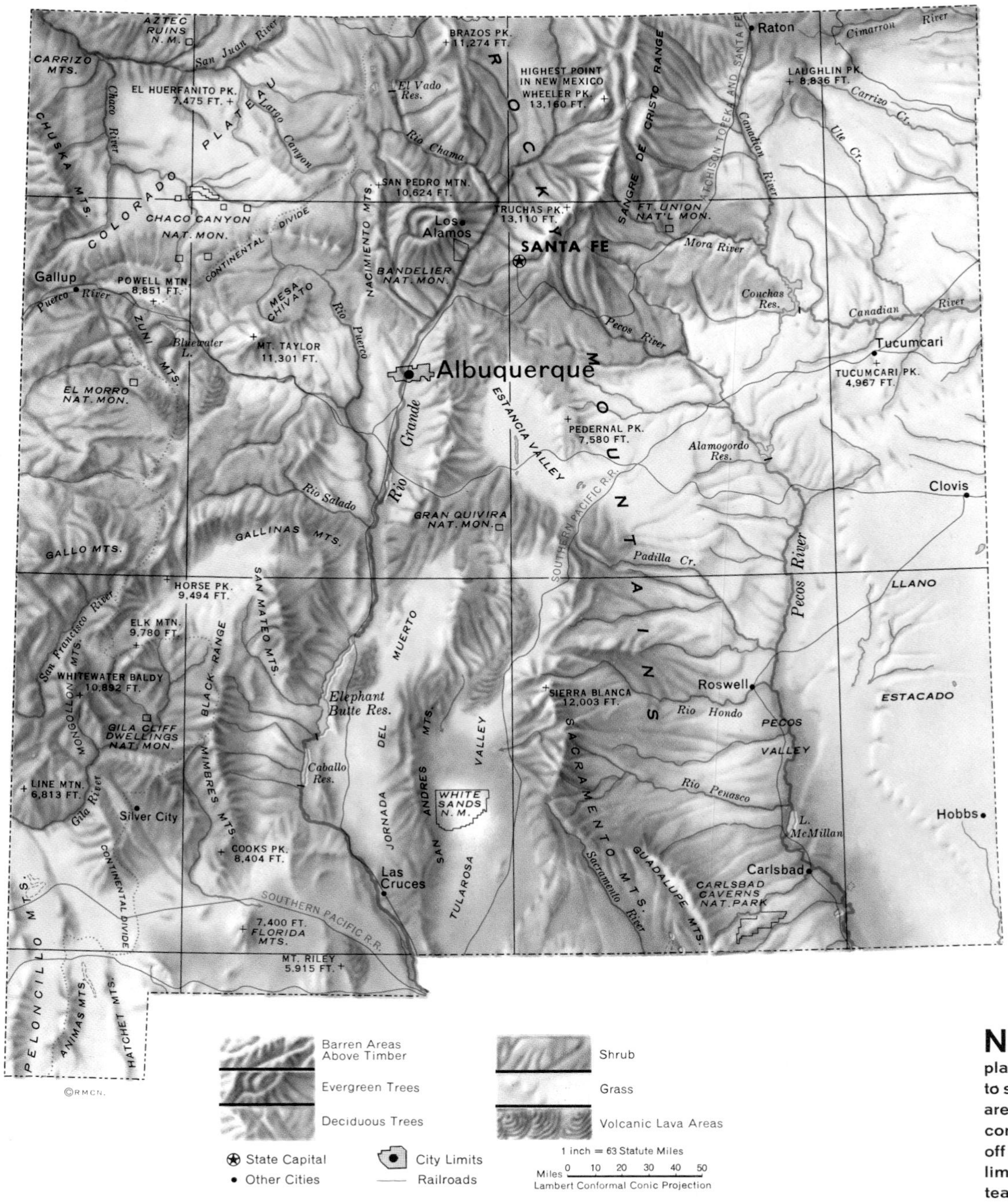

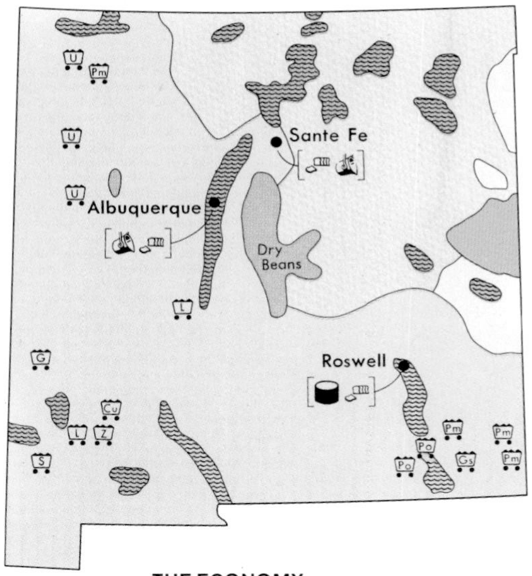

THE ECONOMY

MANUFACTURING
- Food Processing
- Petroleum Refining
- Metal Processing

MINING
- Copper
- Gold
- Natural Gas
- Lead
- Petroleum
- Potash
- Silver
- Uranium
- Zinc

AGRICULTURE
- General Farming
- Wheat & Small Grains
- Cotton
- Special Crops & General Farming
- Year Long Grazing
- Seasonal Grazing
- Irrigated Land

VALUE		EMPLOYED
$247,040,000	AGRICULTURE	20%
$221,000,000	MANUFACTURING	8%
$558,870,000	MINING	5%

Percentages are based on a total of 270,000 at work. In addition 28% are in commerce and transport, 21% in government, 18% in other areas. Manufacturing value is the value added when materials are converted into goods.

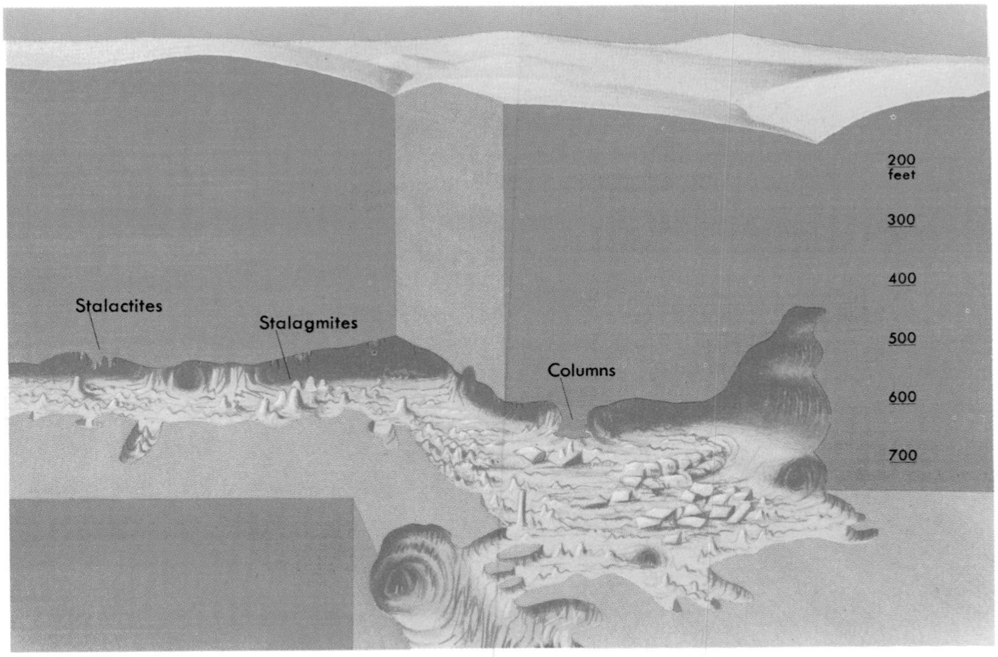

AN UNDERGROUND WONDER WROUGHT BY WATER

Shown here in cross section is a part of the giant Carlsbad Caverns of New Mexico, one of which plunges to a known depth of more than 1,100 feet. They are located in deep limestone beds, formed when ancient seas covered the region. Surface water seeping through cracks in the stone gradually hollowed out the caverns and slowly deposited varicolored lime in tiers of stalactites on the ceiling and stalagmites on the floor. Sometimes both formations join to form columns.

NEW MEXICO: A local booster once wrote, "New Mexico has plains so flat that the State Highway Department has to put up signs to show the water which way to run when it rains; yet the mountains are so steep that the bears which inhabit them have all developed corkscrew tails so they can sit down once in a while without sliding off into Texas." The proud state of New Mexico is a spacious land of limestone caverns *(drawing, left)*, mountain wilderness, high plateaus and sweeping deserts which can be made fruitful only by irrigation. Yet New Mexico has supported men longer than almost any other area of the United States.

Thousands of years before Francisco Coronado led his 16th Century Spanish conquistadors into the sun-scorched land in search of the gold and silver of the mythical Seven Cities of Cibola, a civilization of Indians known as the Basket Makers quietly flourished in northwestern New Mexico. Today, Pueblo Indians, who may be descendants of the Basket Makers, live atop a 357-foot sandstone mesa near Albuquerque in the "sky city" of Acoma, the oldest continuously inhabited spot in the United States. In Santa Fe is one of the oldest churches in North America, the handsome mission-style San Miguel, built by Spanish padres in 1636. And Santa Fe itself, inhabited at various times by Spaniards, Pueblos and Mexicans, is the oldest capital north of the Rio Grande.

AREA:	121,666 sq. mi. Rank: 5th.
POPULATION:	951,023. Rank: 37th. Largest city: Albuquerque. Capital: Santa Fe.
ENTERED UNION:	Jan. 6, 1912, as 47th state.
CLIMATE:	Clear air, nearly constant sunshine, low humidity and little rainfall. Hot summers; winters generally mild.
ALTITUDES:	Wheeler Peak, 13,160 ft. (highest); Santa Fe, 6,950 ft.

As in the rest of the Southwest, cattle, cotton, tourists and mining—mostly potash, uranium and petroleum—are major industries. But New Mexico has had an added spur to its economy. It was on the isolated mesa of Los Alamos, only 80 miles from old Acoma, that man assembled his first atomic bomb, and it was at equally isolated Alamogordo in the southern part of the state—in the region the Spanish called *Jornada del Muerto* (Dead Man's Journey)—that the bomb was exploded in 1945. The state is now dotted with subsidiary defense industries, missile-testing sites and government laboratories, which give New Mexicans one fifth of their income and help support a population that has increased by more than half since World War II.

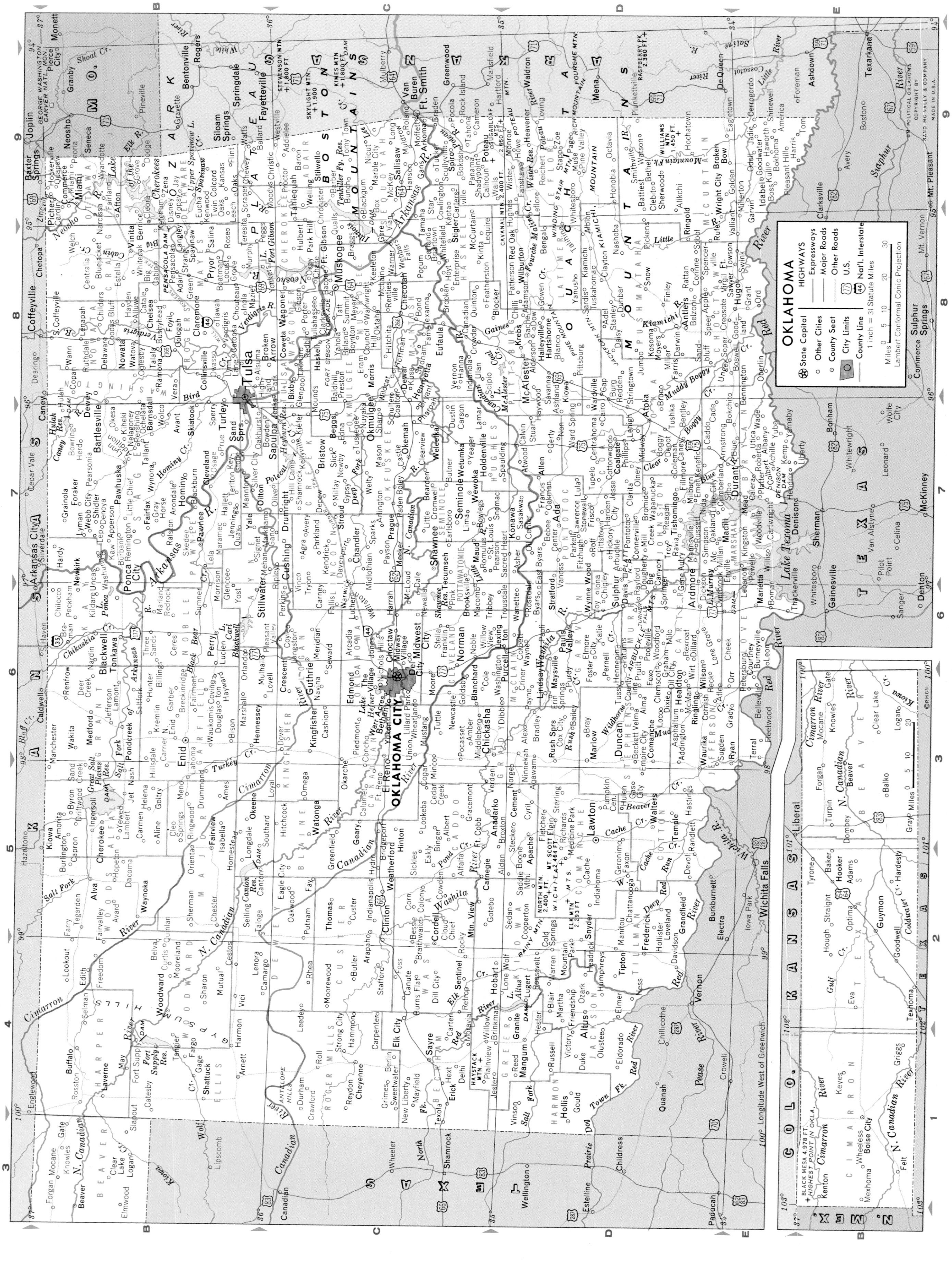
OKLAHOMA
HIGHWAYS
State Capital
Other Cities
County Seat
City Limits
County Line
Expressways
Major Roads
Other Roads
U.S.
Nat'l. Interstate
1 inch = 31 Statute Miles
Lambert Conformal Conic Projection
OKLAHOMA CITY
Tulsa
Lawton
TEXAS
KANSAS
COLO.
Longitude West of Greenwich

OKLAHOMA: Here the grassy lowlands of the central United States fade imperceptibly into the dry Great Plains of the West *(map, right)*. In the eastern part of the state, the moist winds of the Gulf of Mexico, rising and cooling as they meet cold air from the northwest, drop sufficient rainfall to permit Oklahoma farmers to grow cotton, fruit, nuts and the grain crops typical of the Midwest. But west of the 100th meridian, where the Gulf's humid winds seldom blow, rainfall gradually diminishes. There, even though men have learned to raise winter wheat on the dry land, cattle ranching remains predominant.

Farming on these plains is risky business. In the years when rain is plentiful, the land can be bountiful. But in the 1930s, when poor farming practices combined with the sun and wind to destroy the topsoil, the heavily mortgaged Oklahoma farmers packed up and headed toward California, giving their name—"Okies"—to a generation of westward-bound migrants.

AREA:	69,919 sq. mi. Rank: 18th.
POPULATION:	2,328,284. Rank: 27th. Largest city and capital: Oklahoma City.
ENTERED UNION:	Nov. 16, 1907, as 46th state.
CLIMATE:	Generally mild winters, hot summers, with great temperature fluctuations. Dry in the west.
ALTITUDES:	Black Mesa, 4,978 ft. (highest).

On the searing plains of Oklahoma, which were spurned by white men as seemingly worthless, Indian tribes were forcibly resettled *(below)* in the early 1800s. Ironically, the land which the U.S. government assigned to the red man "while grass should grow or waters run" was to prove among the nation's richest in oil reserves. Today over one fourth of the state's population depends upon the petroleum industry—and many an Osage, his land now studded with oil wells, lives in a wealthier, happier hunting ground.

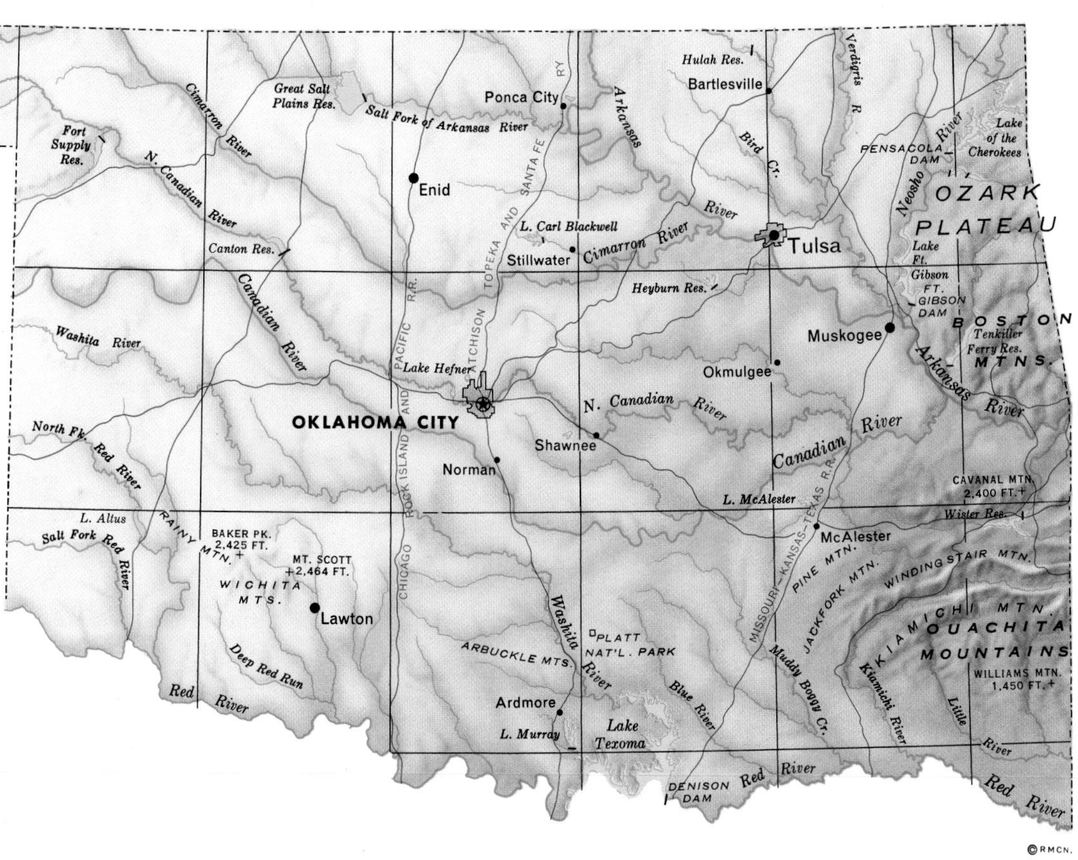
BLACK MESA 4,978 FT. HIGHEST POINT IN OKLAHOMA
Mixed Evergreen and Deciduous Trees
Deciduous Trees
Medium Grass
Short Grass
State Capital
Other Cities
Railroads
City Limits
1 inch = 53 Statute Miles
Miles 0 10 20 30 40 50
Lambert Conformal Conic Projection
OKLAHOMA CITY
Tulsa
Enid
Ponca City
Bartlesville
Stillwater
Muskogee
Okmulgee
Shawnee
Norman
Lawton
McAlester
Ardmore
OZARK PLATEAU
BOSTON MTNS.
OUACHITA MOUNTAINS
WICHITA MTS.
ARBUCKLE MTS.
PLATT NAT'L. PARK
CAVANAL MTN. 2,400 FT.
WILLIAMS MTN. 1,450 FT.
BAKER PK. 2,425 FT.
MT. SCOTT 2,464 FT.
©RMCN.

100°
Ten Wettest Years
20" Average
Ten Driest Years
100°

WHERE ARID WEST MEETS HUMID EAST

The 100th meridian generally parallels the transition zone between the semi-arid West and the more humid East. The broken lines show the way in which the zone's average annual rainfall of 20 inches shifts across the meridian. The West has less rain because of its relative isolation from moisture-laden winds.

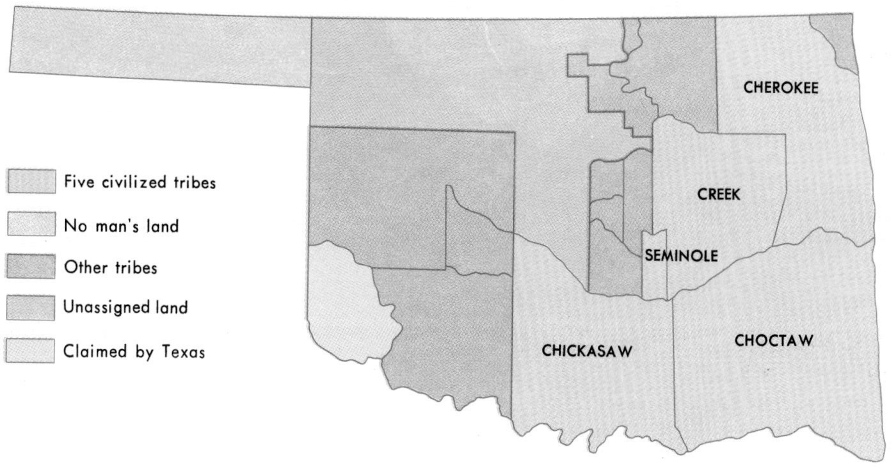
Five civilized tribes
No man's land
Other tribes
Unassigned land
Claimed by Texas
CHEROKEE
CREEK
SEMINOLE
CHICKASAW
CHOCTAW

WHERE THE SUN SET ON INDIAN POWER

This map of Oklahoma in the days before its statehood shows the area designated by the U.S. as Indian Territory for the "Five Civilized Tribes" driven from eastern ranges by an encircling civilization. In the 1820s they were assigned apparently worthless land *(green)*, but because they chose to support the Confederacy in the Civil War, some of their holdings were subsequently transferred to other Indians. All tribes were free to hunt and fish over unassigned land *(red)*. When major oil production began in 1901, many Indians moved out. Today there are no more official reservations.

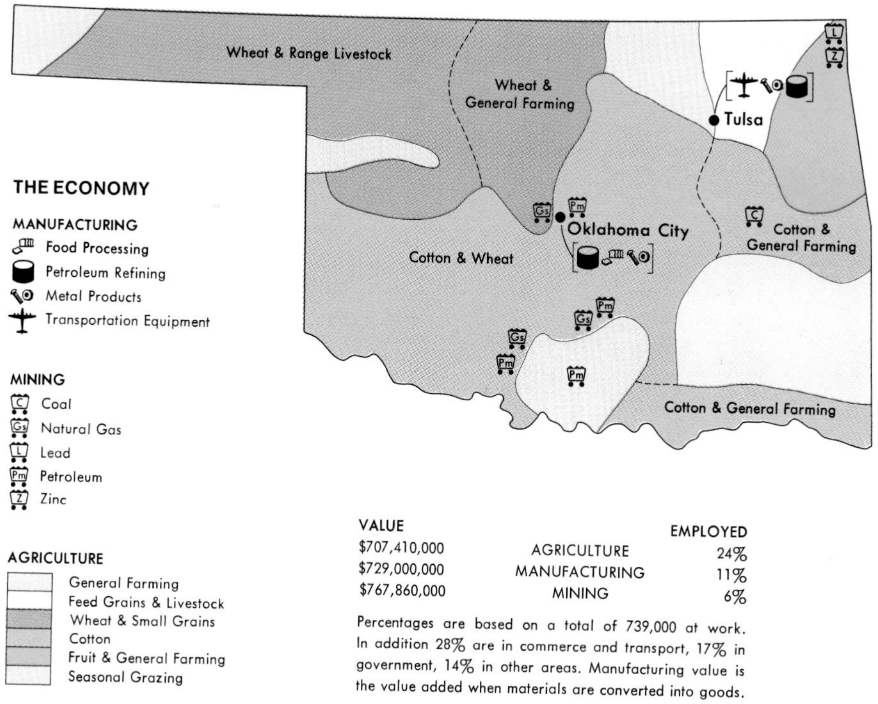
Wheat & Range Livestock
Wheat & General Farming
Tulsa
Oklahoma City
Cotton & Wheat
Cotton & General Farming
Cotton & General Farming
THE ECONOMY
MANUFACTURING
Food Processing
Petroleum Refining
Metal Products
Transportation Equipment
MINING
Coal
Natural Gas
Lead
Petroleum
Zinc
AGRICULTURE
General Farming
Feed Grains & Livestock
Wheat & Small Grains
Cotton
Fruit & General Farming
Seasonal Grazing

VALUE		EMPLOYED
$707,410,000	AGRICULTURE	24%
$729,000,000	MANUFACTURING	11%
$767,860,000	MINING	6%

Percentages are based on a total of 739,000 at work. In addition 28% are in commerce and transport, 17% in government, 14% in other areas. Manufacturing value is the value added when materials are converted into goods.

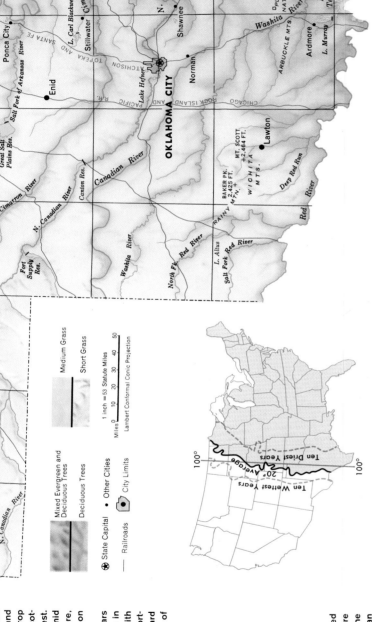

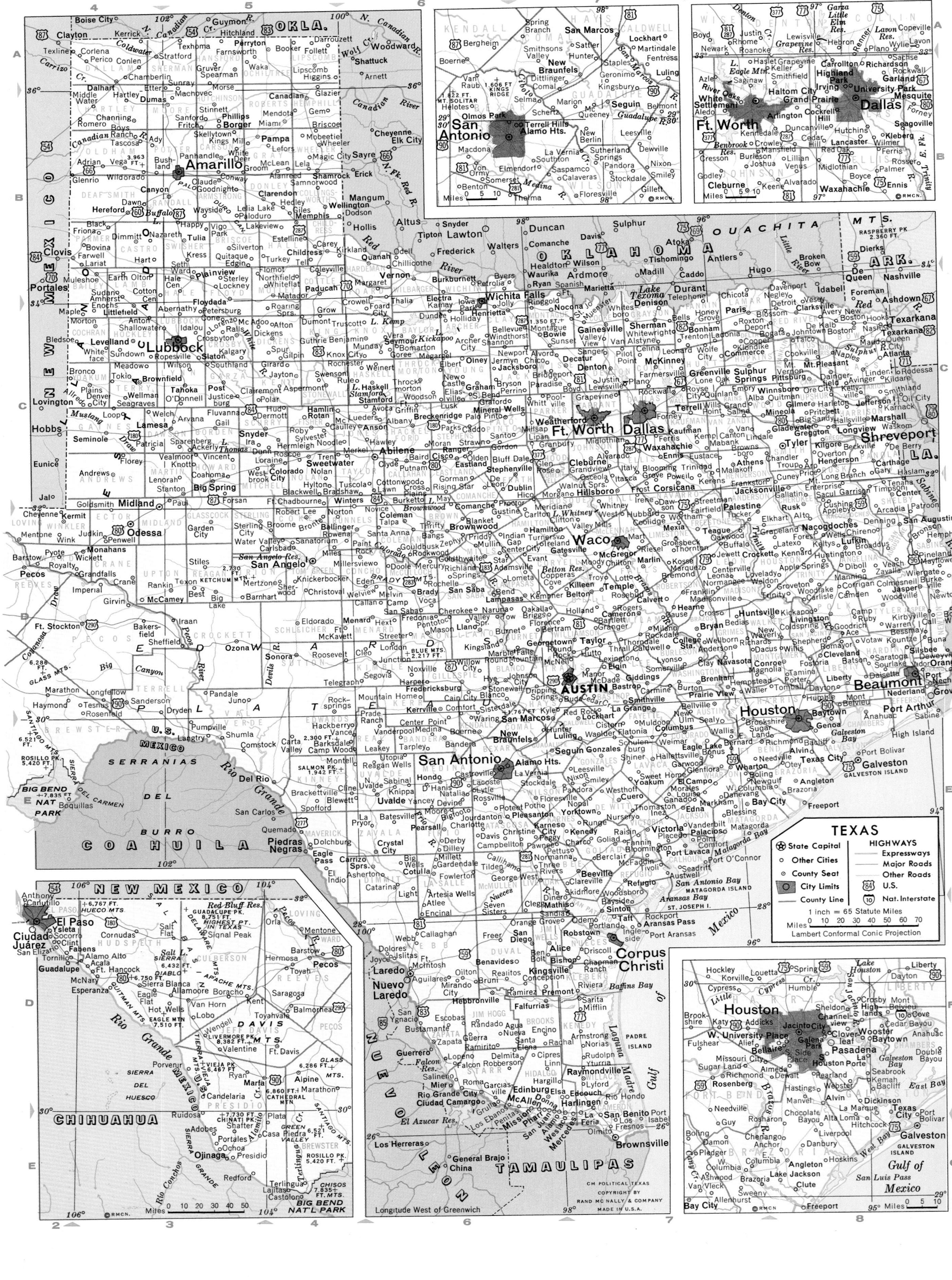
TEXAS
State Capital
Other Cities
County Seat
City Limits
County Line
HIGHWAYS
Expressways
Major Roads
Other Roads
U.S.
Nat. Interstate
1 inch = 65 Statute Miles
Miles 0 10 20 30 40 50 60 70
Lambert Conformal Conic Projection
AUSTIN
Amarillo
Lubbock
Odessa
Midland
San Angelo
Abilene
Wichita Falls
Ft. Worth
Dallas
Waco
San Antonio
Houston
Beaumont
Port Arthur
Galveston
Corpus Christi
Laredo
Nuevo Laredo
Brownsville
El Paso
Ciudad Juárez
Shreveport
Texarkana
OKLA.
OKLAHOMA
ARK.
LA.
NEW MEXICO
COAHUILA
CHIHUAHUA
NUEVO LEON
TAMAULIPAS
MEXICO
U.S.
Rio Grande
Red River
Gulf of Mexico
Galveston Bay
Matagorda Bay
PADRE ISLAND
OUACHITA MTS.
EDWARDS PLATEAU
BIG BEND NAT PARK
BIG BEND NAT'L PARK
Longitude West of Greenwich
CM POLITICAL TEXAS
COPYRIGHT BY RAND McNALLY & COMPANY
MADE IN U.S.A.

TEXAS

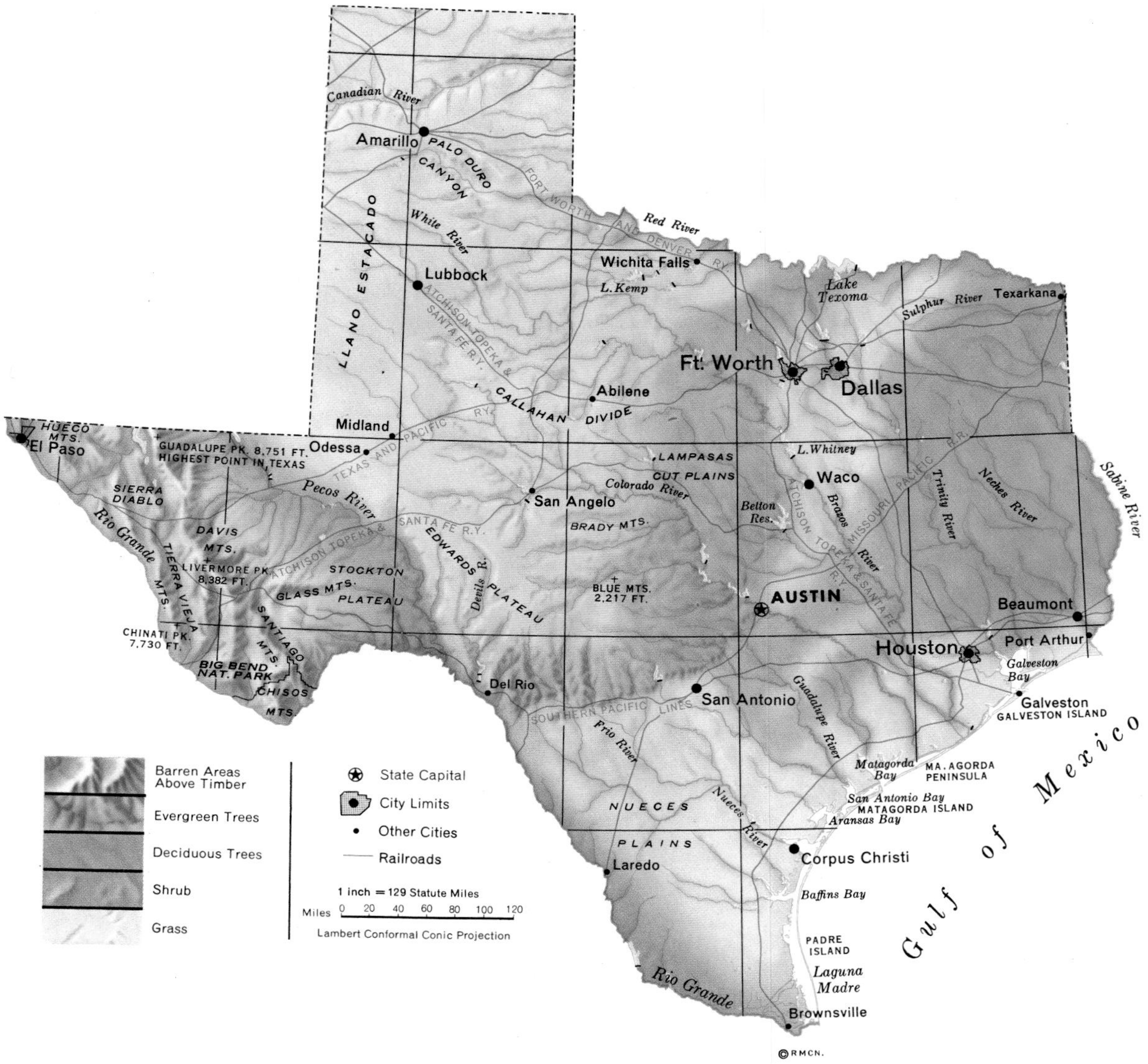

TEXAS: Here "big" is an adjective that never grows stale. Within its borders, Texas could accommodate all six states of New England—plus New York, Pennsylvania, Ohio and Illinois. No single characterization can apply equally to the moss-hung oak forests on its eastern borders, the bays and lagoons of the Gulf Coast, the black prairie soil extending from San Antonio to the Red River valley, the sandy lowlands of the Rio Grande, the rolling plains in the interior and the sharp canyons of the Pecos River valley. Moreover, almost any one of Texas' major industries would in itself be sufficient to make a smaller state wealthy. On the semi-arid high plains around Lubbock, artesian wells help make it possible for Texas to grow over four million bales of cotton each year, more than any other state. Under its land and coastal waters, Texas has almost half of the U.S.'s oil reserves *(map and diagram, below)*. The pecan is the state tree, and Texas orchards often produce the largest pecan crop in the United States. The northern panhandle supplies the world with most of its helium. Name something, and Texas probably has it: unexploited coal, hurricanes, drought, floods, sulphur, natural gas, potash, sheep and citrus crops.

AREA:	267,339 sq. mi. Rank: 2nd.
POPULATION:	9,579,677. Rank: 6th. Largest city: Houston. Capital: Austin.
ENTERED UNION:	Dec. 29, 1845, as 28th state.
CLIMATE:	Varies widely. Coastal areas and eastern interior humid, with mild winters, hot summers. West very dry, with greater temperature range.
ALTITUDES:	Guadalupe Peak, 8,751 ft. (highest); Austin, 505 ft.; Houston, 40 ft.

It was on the coastal plains south of San Antonio that the pioneers of the early 1800s founded the beef industry of the U.S. Later the yearly drives along the Chisholm Trail (which led to the railhead at Abilene, Kansas) became part of American lore. Today Texas produces 8.5 million head of cattle each year, easily maintaining a commanding lead as the United States' number one beef producer.

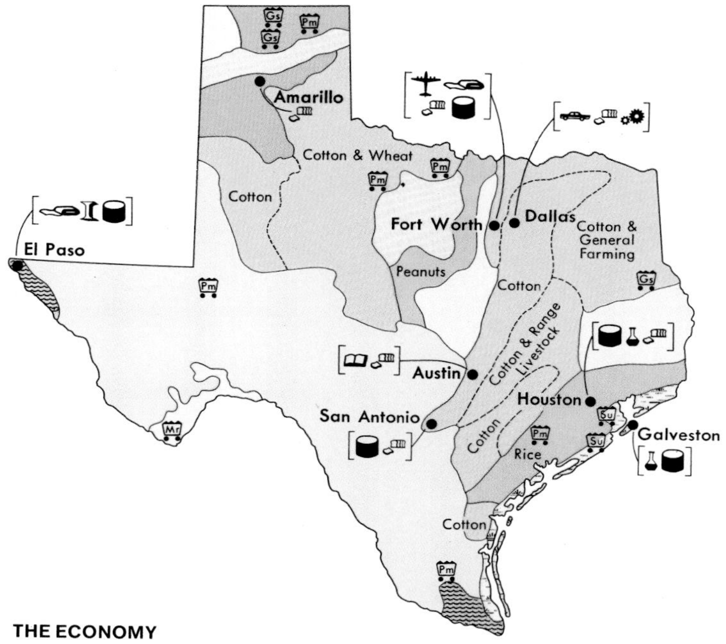

THE ECONOMY

MANUFACTURING
- Chemicals
- Food Processing
- Petroleum Refining
- Transportation Equipment
- Machinery
- Primary Metals
- Printing & Publishing
- Textiles

MINING
- Natural Gas
- Mercury
- Petroleum
- Sulphur

AGRICULTURE
- General Farming
- Wheat & Small Grains
- Cotton
- Special Crops & General Farming
- Fruit, Truck & General Farming
- Year Long Grazing
- Seasonal Grazing
- Mountains & Forest
- Marshland
- Irrigated Land

VALUE		EMPLOYED
$2,576,280,000	AGRICULTURE	16%
$5,133,000,000	MANUFACTURING	16%
$4,038,660,000	MINING	4%

Percentages are based on a total of 2,911,000 at work. In addition 35% are in commerce and transport, 13% in government, 16% in other areas. Manufacturing value is the value added when materials are converted into goods.

OIL LIFELINES OF A NATION

Routes from Texas of some seagoing oil tankers and some major continental crude and refined petroleum pipelines are traced on the map at right. Shipment of oil is less expensive per mile by tanker than by pipe, but the inland position of many refineries makes pipeline transport the cheaper over-all method. These lines were especially useful during World War II because they offered a secure and continuous flow at a time when coastal shipping was under enemy attack.

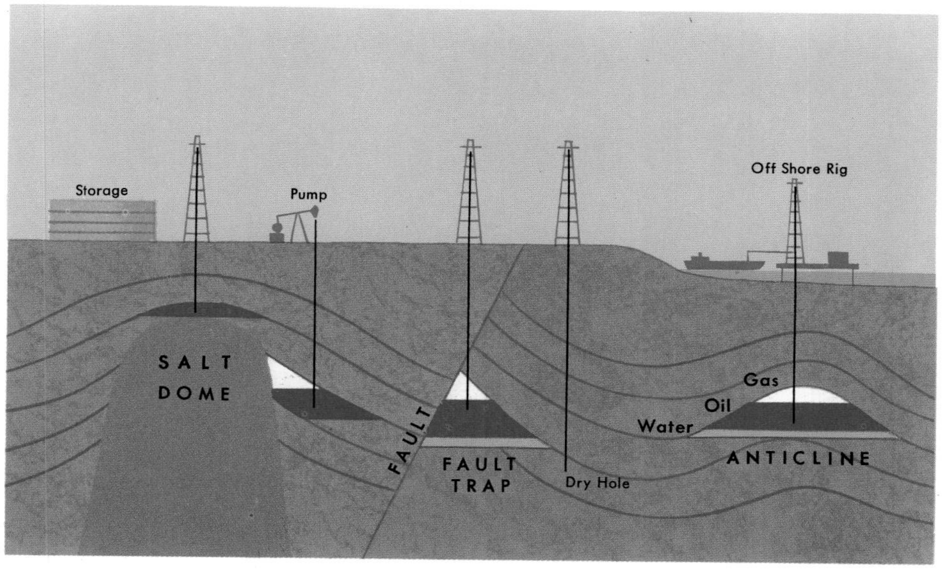

PROBING THE TRAPS AND DOMES OF TEXAN OIL

Typical subsurface formations in which oil occurs are shown in this cross section of Texas land and coastal waters. At far left, a well taps an oil pool *(brown)* trapped in layers of rock atop a salt dome. The well next to it taps a pool trapped in upthrust strata. A third well taps a trap created by earth slippage along a "fault line." Next to it is a "dry hole," a well that failed to reach an oil deposit. Offshore, firmly rooted in the Gulf of Mexico, a Texas Tower rig taps oil held in an anticline or sedimentary dome formation. Anticlines also occur under dry land.

THE BROAD PLAINS of the midwestern states stretch from the Rocky Mountains, at far left, to the Appalachians, at right. The Great Lakes are at upper right. At the center is the Mississippi, flowing in a southerly course to its outlet in the Gulf of Mexico, at bottom.

MIDWEST STATES

The Midwest "is a gift of the gods – the rain god, the sun god, the ice god, and the gods of geology," wrote geographer J. Russell Smith. Here lie lush and endless plains, flattened by aeons of erosion and imprinted with five great lakes by the pressure of ponderous glaciers. On this rich soil are 12 states so favored by climate that they are known collectively as the nation's breadbasket.

In the modern era, the Midwest constitutes one of the most extraordinary agricultural areas in the world. The sun-baked rectangular farms of this region, marching in orderly rows from the Appalachians to the Rockies, produce 60 per cent of the U.S.'s wheat, 80 per cent of its oats and soybeans, 70 per cent of its hogs and almost half of its cattle and dairy cows. Above all, they grow 80 per cent of the nation's most valuable single crop – corn. The Midwest's cornucopia is so golden that it creates the recurring problem of what to do with it all.

Ironically, the 18th Century pioneers who crossed the Appalachians into Ohio, Indiana and Illinois did not believe at first that the prairie lands, which had one third less rainfall than the East Coast, were fertile. They were understandably elated when they discovered that grains – first wheat and corn, and then rye, oats and barley – could flourish in the drier land. "The corn! The corn!" exulted Governor Richard James Oglesby of Illinois at the Harvest Home Festival in 1892. "Within those yellow hearts there is health and strength for all the nations. The corn triumphant!"

Today the undulating plains are not given over entirely to grain fields. The area is crosshatched by 90,000 miles of rails and 7,500 miles of waterways, which link the great distribution centers of St. Louis, Kansas City, Omaha and Chicago, and carry iron ore from Duluth, steel from Gary, tires from Akron, cars from Detroit, and countless other products from factories scattered across the whole mid-continental empire. The mighty Midwest is now second only to the Northeast as a manufacturing and distributing center.

But the build-up of the Midwest was long and arduous. "Men can say 'Dear old Kansas!'" wrote the American historian Carl Becker about the state which is often said to typify the midwestern spirit, "because the name symbolizes for them what the motto of the state so well expresses, *ad astra per aspera*" – through difficulties to the stars.

THE ENDLESS SINEWS OF THE PLAIN

WINDING WATERS of the Missouri cradle a towboat as it makes its slow way upstream near Jefferson City, Missouri, pushing barges laden with coal and other dry cargo like wheat and corn. The broad and generally tranquil rivers of the Midwest, linked by canals, form one of the most extensive networks of inland waterways in the world.

ARROW-STRAIGHT RAILS speed a crack passenger train, a Rock Island Rocket, through a cornfield in Illinois. The flatness of the prairies spurred the building of railroads, which today crisscross the region with 90,000 miles of track that tie together the inland waterway network and give the Midwest an unparalleled transportation system.

THE MARK OF MAN IN FIELD AND FACTORY

A SPRAWLING FARM prospers on the rich, dark earth of the Fox River valley in eastern Illinois. The bulk of the farm's income is derived from livestock and dairy products. Intensely green in this aerial view, the rolling fields are planted with corn, wheat and oats. Farther west, as the rainfall diminishes, farms are larger and tend to specialize in corn and wheat, the area's primary crops.

AN EXPANDING METROPOLIS, the inland port of Cleveland straddles the Cuyahoga River on Lake Erie, almost every foot of its surrounding area filled with factories and webbed with railroads, highways and power lines. Cleveland industry is diverse, like that of most midwestern cities. It makes machine tools, steel, electrical and freight-handling equipment and cement.

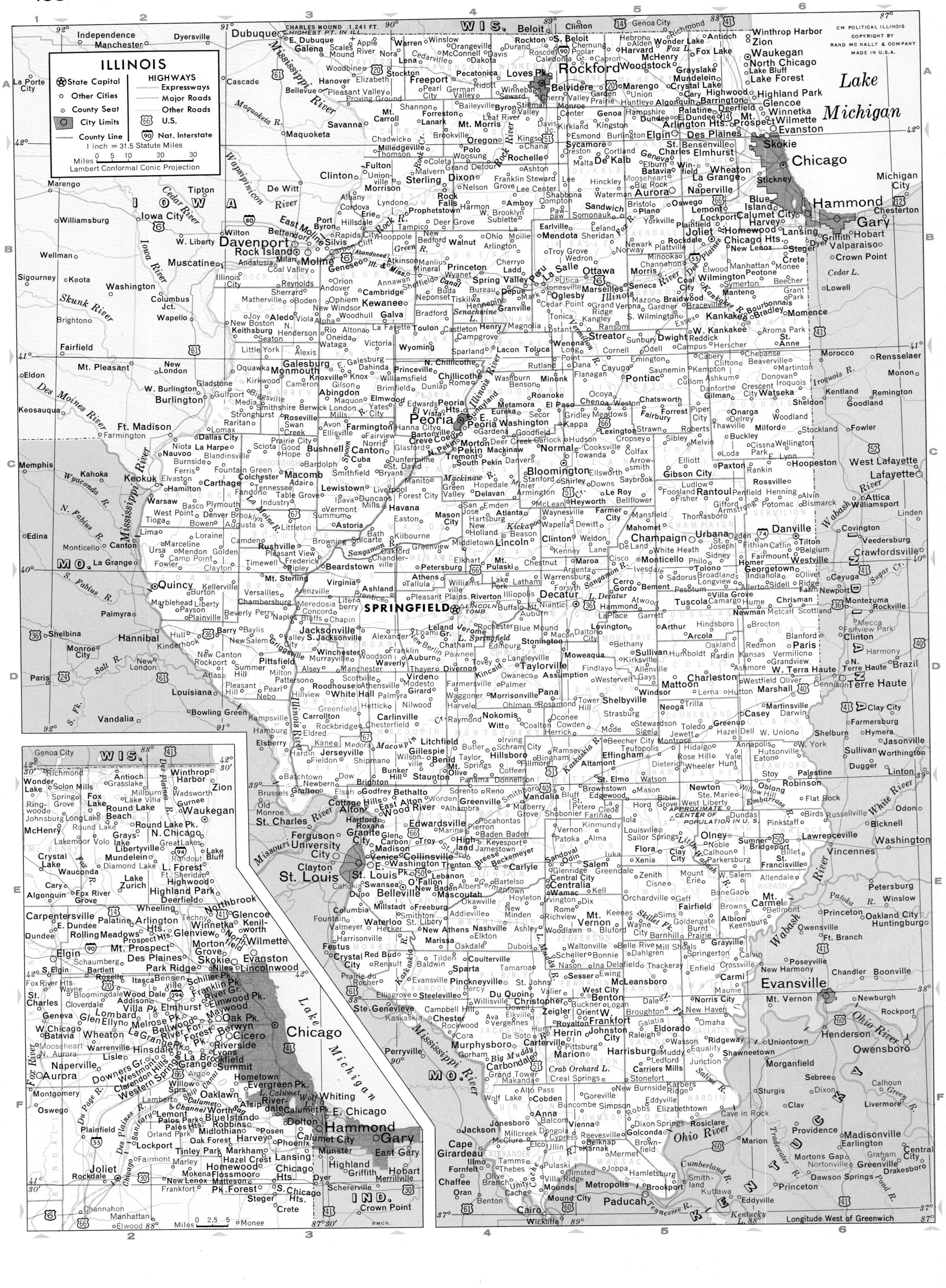
ILLINOIS
State Capital
Other Cities
County Seat
City Limits
County Line
HIGHWAYS
Expressways
Major Roads
Other Roads
U.S.
Nat. Interstate
1 inch = 31.5 Statute Miles
Miles
Lambert Conformal Conic Projection
CM POLITICAL ILLINOIS
COPYRIGHT BY
RAND MC NALLY & COMPANY
MADE IN U.S.A.
CHARLES MOUND 1,241 FT.
HIGHEST PT. IN ILL.
WIS.
IOWA
MO.
IND.
KENTUCKY
Lake Michigan
Chicago
Rockford
Peoria
SPRINGFIELD
Decatur
Champaign
Urbana
Bloomington
Normal
Joliet
Aurora
Elgin
Rock Island
Moline
Davenport
Quincy
Galesburg
Danville
Kankakee
St. Louis
East St. Louis
Belleville
Carbondale
Cairo
Paducah
Evansville
Terre Haute
Hammond
Gary
Mississippi River
Illinois River
Ohio River
Wabash River
Rock River
Kaskaskia R.
Sangamon R.
Longitude West of Greenwich

ILLINOIS

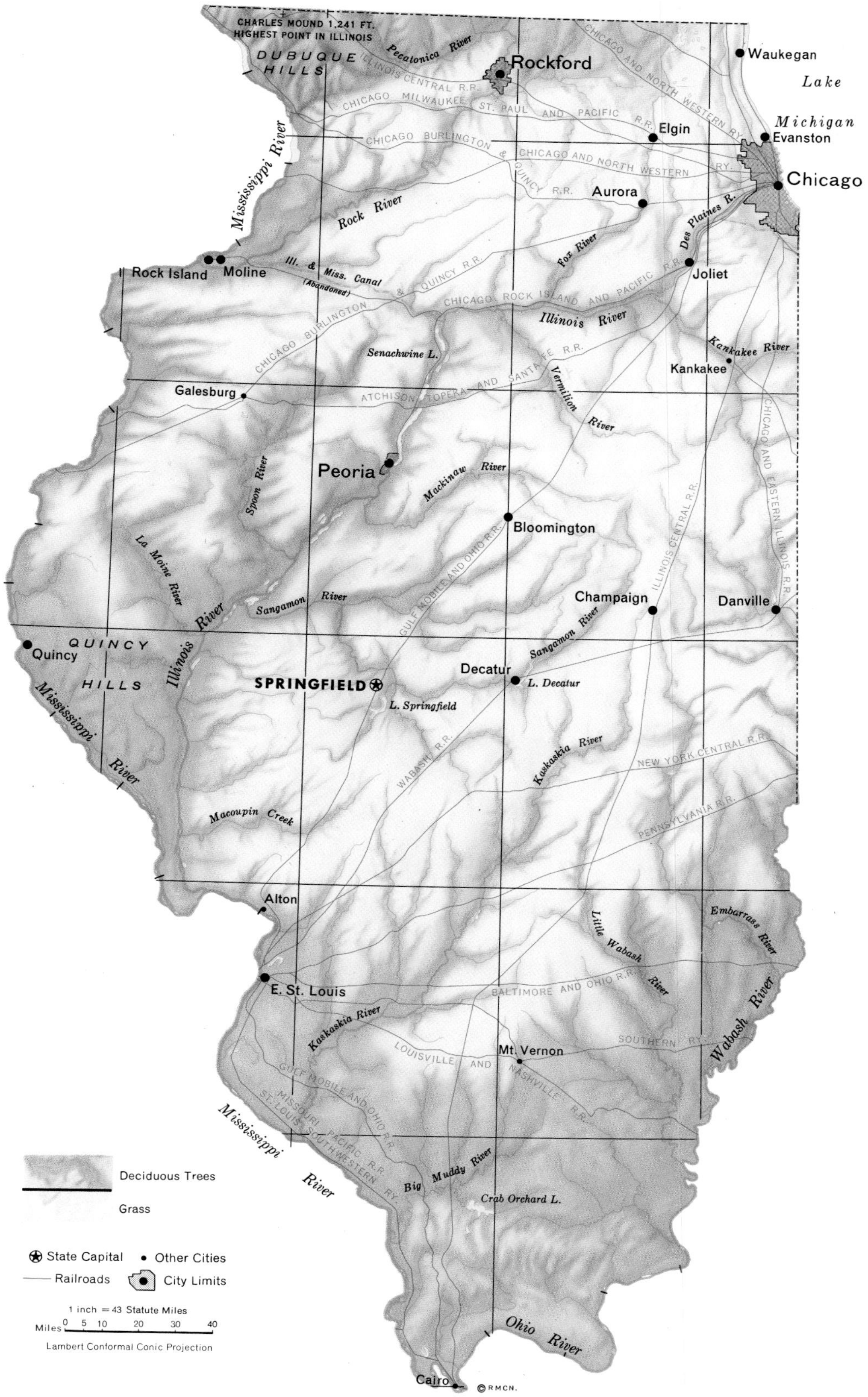
CHARLES MOUND 1,241 FT.
HIGHEST POINT IN ILLINOIS
DUBUQUE HILLS
Pecatonica River
Rockford
Waukegan
Lake Michigan
Elgin
Evanston
Chicago
Mississippi River
Rock River
Aurora
Des Plaines R.
Fox River
Rock Island
Moline
Ill. & Miss. Canal (Abandoned)
Joliet
Illinois River
Senachwine L.
Kankakee River
Kankakee
Galesburg
Vermilion River
Peoria
Spoon River
Mackinaw River
Bloomington
La Moine River
Sangamon River
Champaign
Danville
QUINCY HILLS
Quincy
Illinois River
SPRINGFIELD
Decatur
L. Decatur
L. Springfield
Sangamon River
Kaskaskia River
Macoupin Creek
Alton
Little Wabash River
Embarrass River
E. St. Louis
Kaskaskia River
Mt. Vernon
Wabash River
Mississippi River
Big Muddy River
Crab Orchard L.
Ohio River
Cairo
CHICAGO AND NORTH WESTERN RY.
ILLINOIS CENTRAL R.R.
CHICAGO MILWAUKEE ST. PAUL AND PACIFIC R.R.
CHICAGO BURLINGTON & QUINCY R.R.
CHICAGO ROCK ISLAND AND PACIFIC R.R.
ATCHISON TOPEKA AND SANTA FE R.R.
CHICAGO AND EASTERN ILLINOIS R.R.
GULF MOBILE AND OHIO R.R.
WABASH R.R.
NEW YORK CENTRAL R.R.
PENNSYLVANIA R.R.
BALTIMORE AND OHIO R.R.
SOUTHERN RY.
LOUISVILLE AND NASHVILLE R.R.
MISSOURI PACIFIC R.R.
ST. LOUIS SOUTHWESTERN RY.
Deciduous Trees
Grass
State Capital
Other Cities
Railroads
City Limits
1 inch = 43 Statute Miles
Miles 0 5 10 20 30 40
Lambert Conformal Conic Projection
© RMCN.

ILLINOIS: Served by no fewer than 25 railroads and 21 airlines, and enjoying 10,000 miles of primary highways as well as three important rivers and an outlet on Lake Michigan, Illinois is the transit hub of the nation. Chicago, its biggest city *(diagram, below)*, has been described by Carl Sandburg as "Tool-Maker, Stacker of Wheat, Player with Railroads and the Nation's Freight Handler."

As a growing meat-packing and grain center, Illinois early began to construct transportation arteries for the shipment of its products. One of the first major links to the eastern markets was a canal built to connect the Illinois River and the southern half of the state to the Great Lakes and, through the Erie Canal, to New York City. This was followed in the 1850s by the thundering arrival of the railroads, which—by bringing together raw materials, labor and market facilities—permitted heavy industry to thrive.

A state that has been called "a working model of the nation as a whole," Illinois has an impressive economic balance. It has large farms and profitable industries with hundreds of thousands of employees, as well as one-family dairy farms and small electronics workshops.

AREA:	56,400 sq. mi. Rank: 24th.
POPULATION:	10,081,158. Rank: 4th.
	Largest city: Chicago.
	Capital: Springfield.
ENTERED UNION:	Dec. 3, 1818, as 21st state.
CLIMATE:	Cold winters, hot summers; moderate rainfall.
ALTITUDES:	Charles Mound near Galena, 1,241 ft. (highest); Chicago, 595 ft.

It was in Illinois that the extraordinary sea of grass called the Big Prairie was first encountered by white settlers. Accustomed to a thickly forested countryside, the pioneers of the early 1800s hesitated to farm a land that seemed able to support only endless waves of six-foot-high grass. But beneath the tough sod their plows uncovered a deep treasure of mineral-laden soil left by the deposits of four continental ice sheets. The rolling prairies, stretching to the horizon with few obstructing outcrops of rock, were ideally suited to the use of harrows, cultivators and reapers, which eventually revolutionized food production.

In Illinois the 20th Century exodus from the fields to the city has been dramatic. Only seven per cent of all Illinoisans now live on farms. Nevertheless, with modern mechanized farming techniques, the land still yields enough to make the state rank fourth in farm income in the United States.

THE ECONOMY

MANUFACTURING
- Machinery
- Food Processing
- Electrical Machinery
- Metal Products
- Primary Metals
- Printing & Publishing
- Chemicals

MINING
- Coal
- Cement
- Petroleum
- Stone

AGRICULTURE
- General Farming
- Feed Grains & Livestock
- Dairy Farming

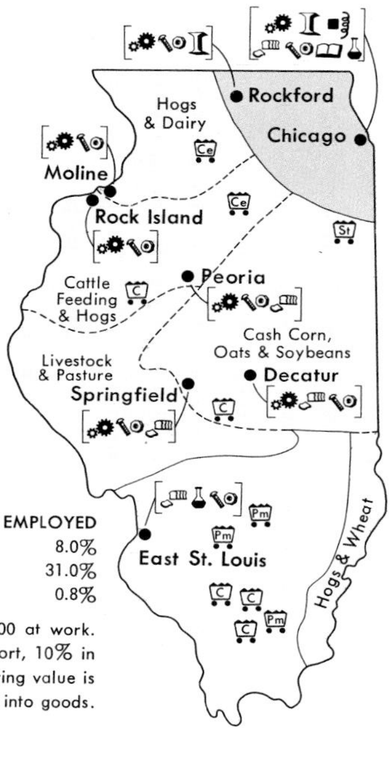
Rockford
Hogs & Dairy
Chicago
Moline
Rock Island
Peoria
Cattle Feeding & Hogs
Cash Corn, Oats & Soybeans
Decatur
Livestock & Pasture
Springfield
East St. Louis
Hogs & Wheat

VALUE		EMPLOYED
$ 2,178,450,000	AGRICULTURE	8.0%
$11,532,000,000	MANUFACTURING	31.0%
$ 582,410,000	MINING	0.8%

Percentages are based on a total of 3,583,000 at work. In addition 33% are in commerce and transport, 10% in government, 17.2% in other areas. Manufacturing value is the value added when materials are converted into goods.

WHERE THE SPOKES CONVERGE

The variety and volume of freight traffic pouring in and out of Chicago by rail, highway, pipeline and waterway are portrayed in the colored spokes at right. The widths of the spokes roughly indicate the relative proportions of net tonnage transported by each carrier. The numbers within the circle at the hub refer to millions of net tons.

Chicago has become the second largest city in the U.S. because of its strategic location as the transportation center of a great productive area. It lies on the northern routes of major east-west rail lines, and with more than 7,000 miles of track inside the metropolitan area, it is indisputably the nation's rail capital. Each day 30,000 freight cars are unloaded, and 1,000 trains carrying almost a third of a million persons pass into and through the city. Each year more than 100 million tons of freight move over its highways, and almost 60 million tons of crude oil, petroleum products and natural gas travel through the 25 pipelines that enter the city.

With the recent completion of the St. Lawrence Seaway, linking the Great Lakes by deep channel to the Atlantic trade routes, Chicago is well on its way to becoming one of North America's most important ports. Its waterways already handle almost 50 million tons of goods annually.

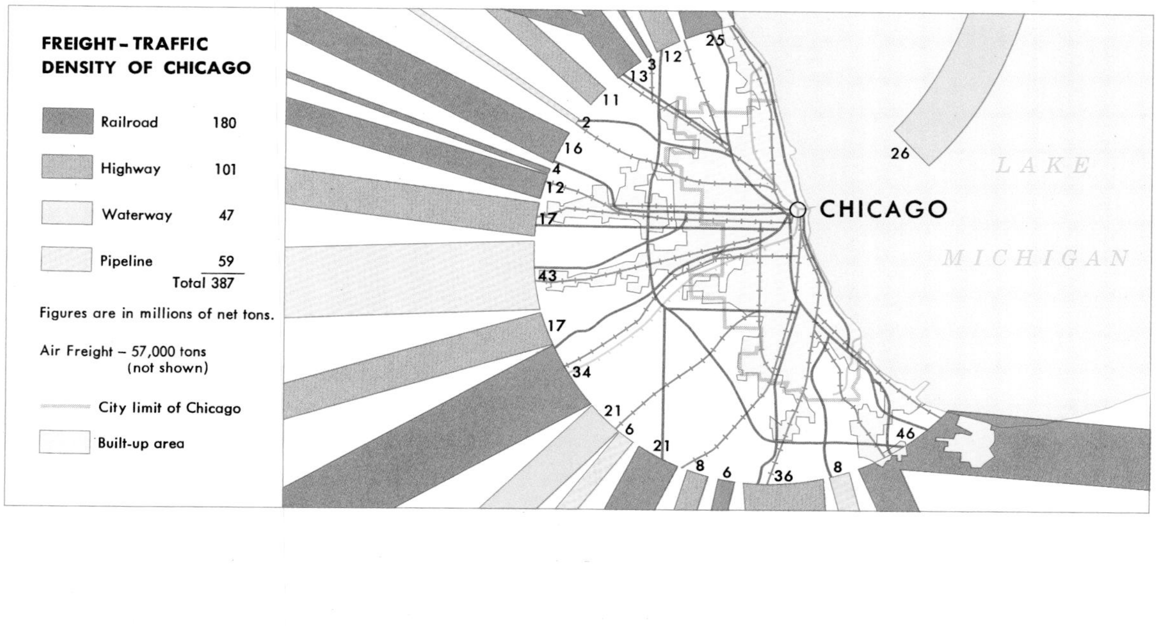
FREIGHT-TRAFFIC DENSITY OF CHICAGO
Railroad 180
Highway 101
Waterway 47
Pipeline 59
Total 387
Figures are in millions of net tons.
Air Freight – 57,000 tons (not shown)
City limit of Chicago
Built-up area
CHICAGO
LAKE MICHIGAN
25
12
13
3
11
2
16
4
12
17
43
17
34
21
6
21
8
6
36
8
46
26

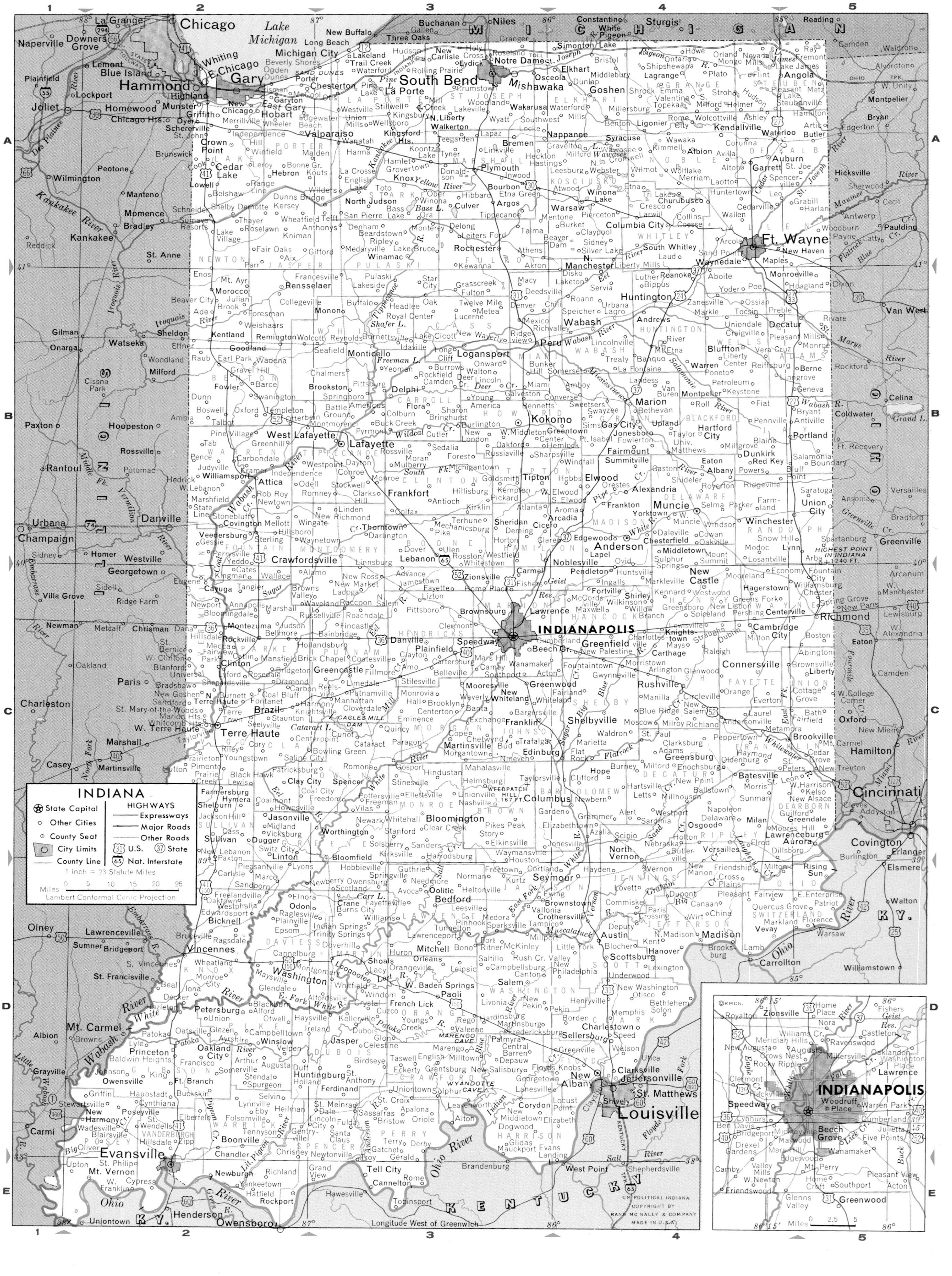

INDIANA
HIGHWAYS
State Capital
Other Cities
County Seat
City Limits
Expressways
Major Roads
Other Roads
U.S.
State
County Line
Nat. Interstate
1 inch = 23 Statute Miles
Miles 0 5 10 15 20 25
Lambert Conformal Conic Projection
INDIANAPOLIS
Longitude West of Greenwich
CM POLITICAL INDIANA
COPYRIGHT BY
RAND McNALLY & COMPANY
MADE IN U.S.A.
HIGHEST POINT IN INDIANA 1 240 FT.
Lake Michigan
MICHIGAN
OHIO
KENTUCKY
ILLINOIS
Chicago
Indianapolis
Louisville
Cincinnati
Evansville
Ft. Wayne
South Bend
Gary
Hammond
Terre Haute
Lafayette
Muncie
Anderson
Kokomo
Bloomington

INDIANA

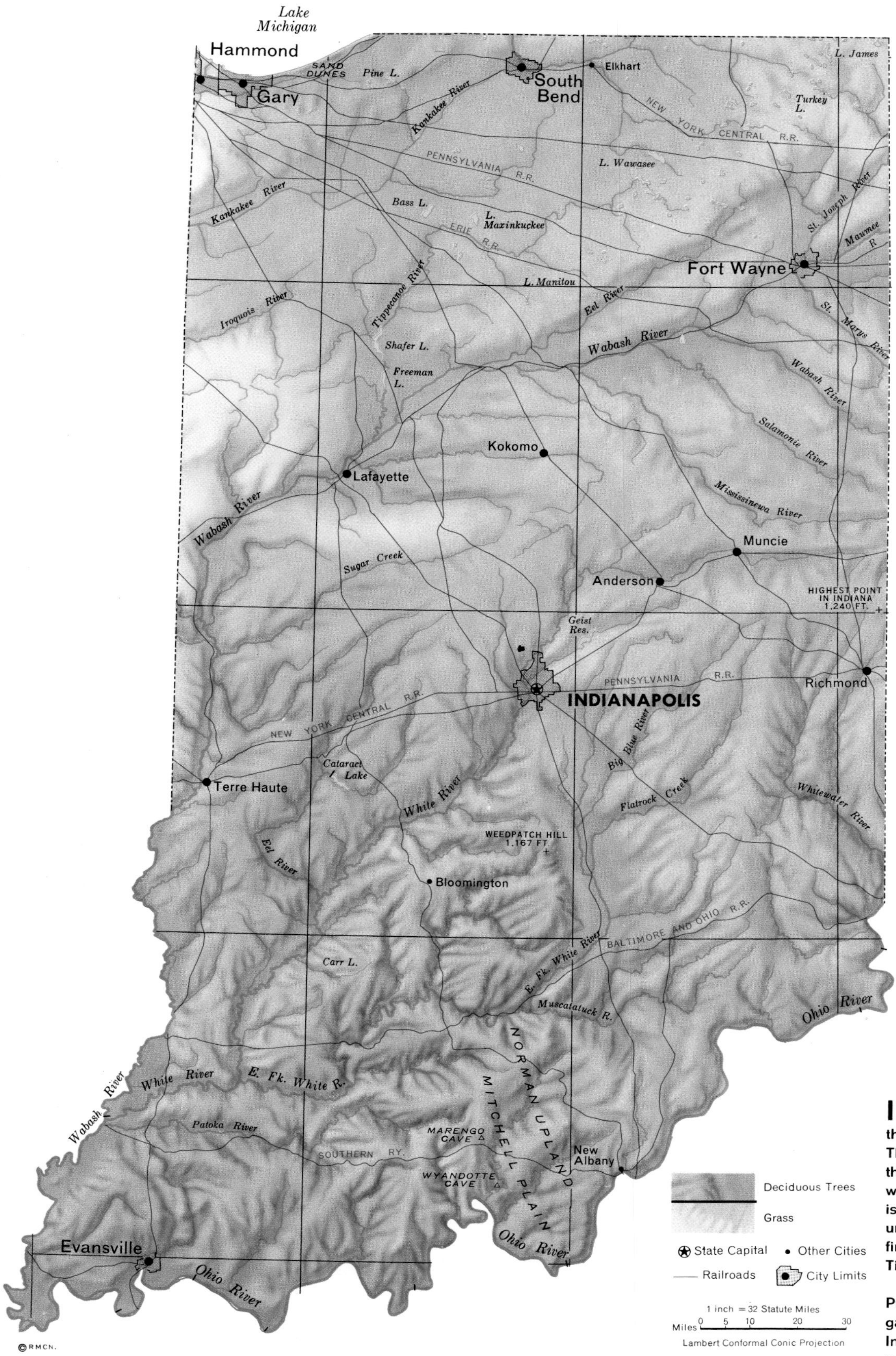

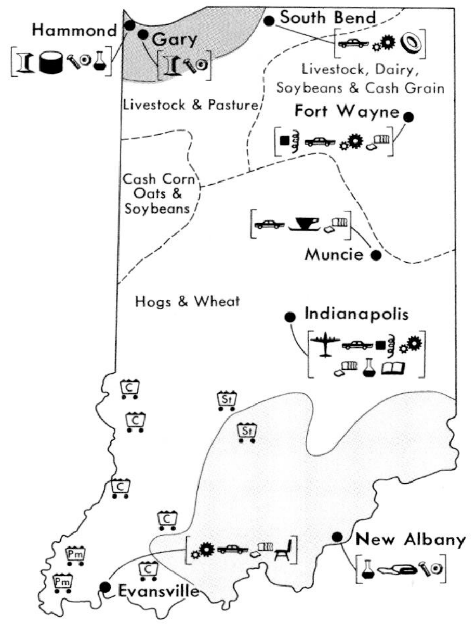

THE ECONOMY

MANUFACTURING
- Primary Metals
- Electrical Machinery
- Machinery
- Food Processing
- Chemicals
- Metal Products
- Petroleum Refining
- Printing & Publishing
- Textiles
- Stone, Clay & Glass Products
- Rubber & Products
- Furniture
- Transportation Equipment

MINING
- Coal
- Petroleum
- Stone

AGRICULTURE
- General Farming
- Feed Grains & Livestock
- Dairy Farming

VALUE		EMPLOYED
$1,170,280,000	AGRICULTURE	15.0%
$5,440,000,000	MANUFACTURING	34.0%
$ 197,680,000	MINING	0.6%

Percentages are based on a total of 1,557,000 at work. In addition 28% are in commerce and transport, 11% in government, 11.4% in other areas. Manufacturing value is the value added when materials are converted into goods.

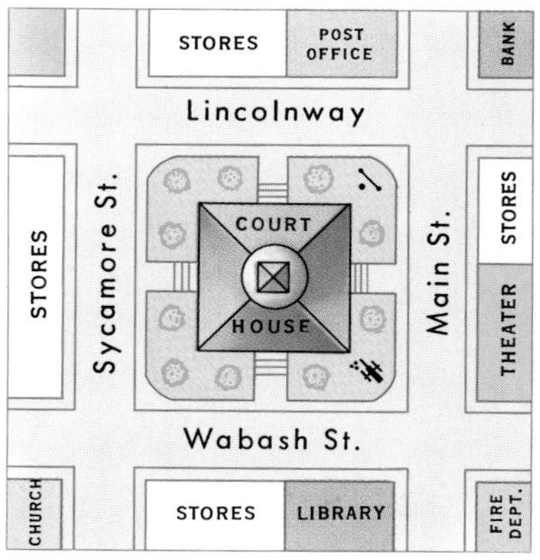

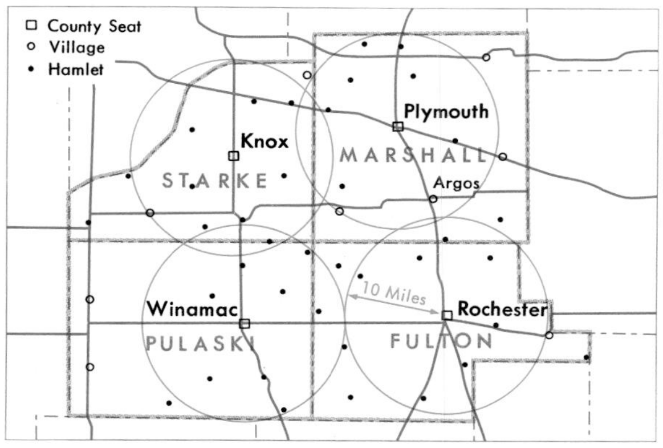

WHY THE TOWNS ARE WHERE THEY ARE

The pattern of settlement is much the same in all the counties of Indiana, as illustrated by the four above. Near the center of each lies the county seat with its town square (*left*), locus for such essentials as large stores, a library and theater—all centered around the county courthouse. Within a 10-mile radius of the county seat are smaller villages and hamlets, established in the horse-and-buggy era, when 20 miles was considered maximum for a round trip to market.

INDIANA: From the shores of Lake Michigan in the north to the curves of the Ohio River to the south, Indiana is a gentle land. The northern parts of the state were slow to bloom, for they lay off the westward route of the pioneers. Throughout its history Indiana was a battleground: Indians fought each other and fought the British; Indians and British fought French and Americans. It was not until 1811 that Indiana's territorial governor, William Henry Harrison, finally managed to put down the rebellious tribes at the battle of Tippecanoe, near what is now Lafayette.

It was a useful victory not only for Harrison (in 1840 he won the Presidency for himself and running mate John Tyler with the slogan "Tippecanoe and Tyler too") but for Indiana as well. With the Indians pacified, farmers poured onto the rich prairies. The railroads came in the 1840s. In time, steel men took advantage of cheap transport routes and the state's strategic location between iron and coal sources, and built the town of Gary on Lake Michigan. Today Indiana is the third largest producer of steel in the U.S.

AREA:	36,291 sq. mi. Rank: 38th.
POPULATION:	4,662,498. Rank: 11th. Largest city and capital: Indianapolis.
ENTERED UNION:	Dec. 11, 1816, as 19th state.
CLIMATE:	Hot, humid summers, cold winters; moderate rainfall.
ALTITUDES:	Greensfork Township, 1,240 ft. (highest); Indianapolis, 710 ft.

Like many midwestern states, Indiana has achieved an enviable economic balance. It produces heavy machinery, chemicals and more than 10 per cent of the nation's steel. From its quarries comes 80 per cent of the U.S.'s construction limestone. But more than one seventh of Indiana's population is still on farms, which cover 80 per cent of its area and are rich with corn, soybeans and oats.

Indiana remains essentially a quiet, rural state—the land of Booth Tarkington's fictional characters Penrod and Sam; of poet James Whitcomb Riley's "Old Swimmin' Hole"; of the nostalgic lyrics of Paul Dresser's state song: "From the fields there comes the breath of new-mown hay . . . On the banks of the Wabash, far away."

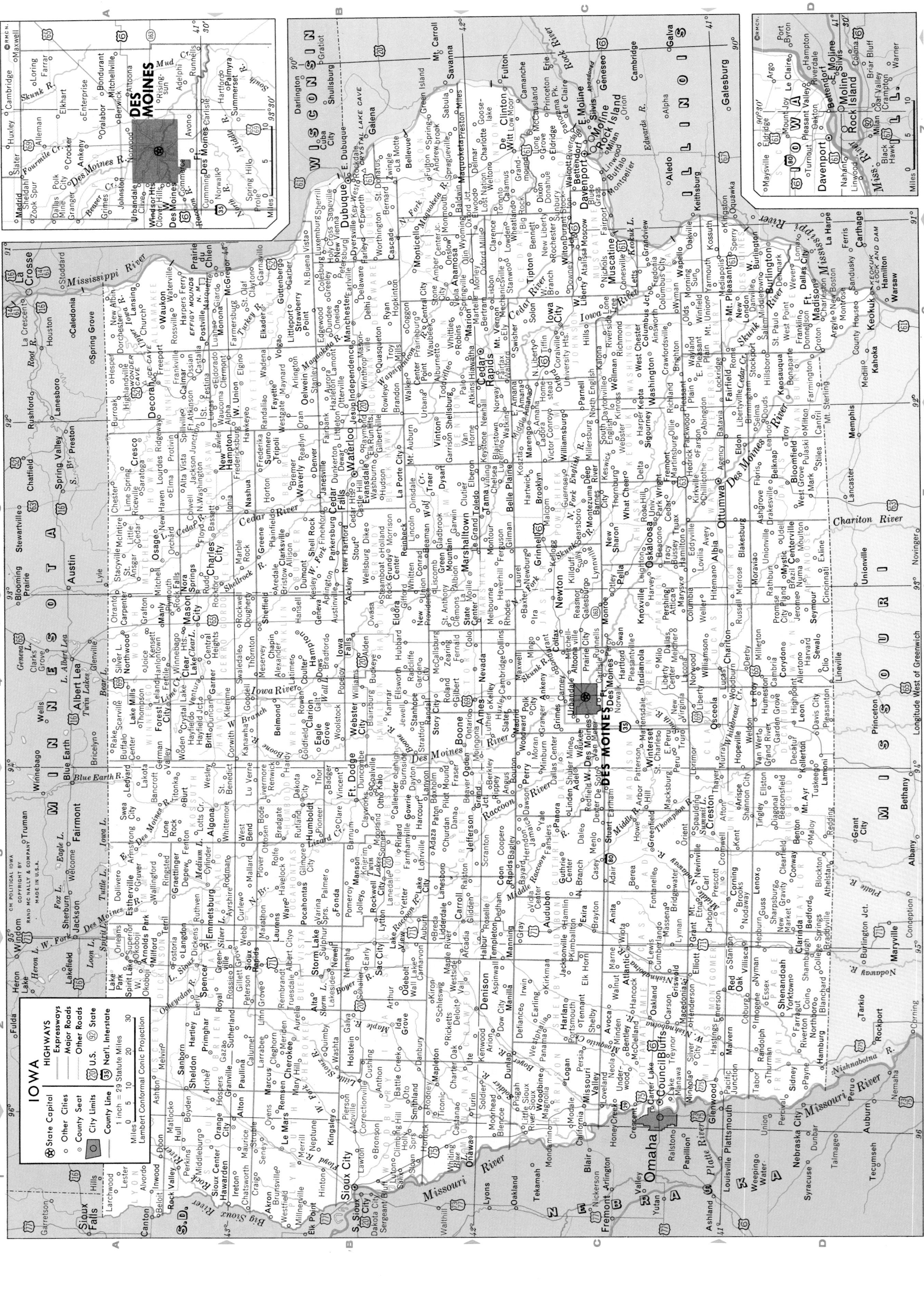
IOWA
HIGHWAYS
Expressways
Major Roads
Other Roads
U.S.
State
Nat'l. Interstate
State Capital
Other Cities
County Seat
City Limits
County Line
1 inch = 29 Statute Miles
Lambert Conformal Conic Projection
CM POLITICAL IOWA
COPYRIGHT BY RAND McNALLY & COMPANY
MADE IN U.S.A.

IOWA: Corn is the word for Iowa. "We're from Ioway, Ioway," they sing at the state fair in Des Moines, every hand rising symbolically on the last line: "That's where the tall corn grows." The high-yield hybrid corn of today is short–six to eight feet–but the "big fertile farm" which is Iowa grows more of it than any other state *(map, below)*. It is also first in pig and oat production, ranks high in the output of poultry, eggs and grain-fed cattle, and has rarely known a major crop failure. Iowa's agricultural success is due in large part to its deep mineral-laden topsoil, whose origin goes back to the ice-age glaciers. So concentrated is this fertile soil that Iowa has one fourth of all the grade A farmland in the United States.

AREA:	56,290 sq. mi. Rank: 25th.
POPULATION:	2,757,537. Rank: 24th. Largest city and capital: Des Moines.
ENTERED UNION:	Dec. 28, 1846, as 29th state.
CLIMATE:	Hot summers with ample rainfall; cold winters with some heavy snows.
ALTITUDES:	Ocheyedan Mound in the northwest, 1,675 ft. (highest); Des Moines, 805 ft.

Although 95 per cent of Iowa is farmland, industry also marks the plains. But its focus, too, is agricultural. Iowa brought a new word into the language when two Charles City mechanics built a strange vehicle called a "tractor" in 1906. Today the production of farm machinery and the processing of food are among Iowa's largest industries.

WHERE THE MOST CORN GROWS

Shown in red *(left)* is the vast area of the U.S. known as the Corn Belt. It blankets all of Iowa and touches almost every other midwestern state. Here exist all the requisites for a substantial corn crop–a mean summer temperature of at least 70 degrees, frequent summer showers and a growing season of more than 140 days. The Belt, where corn is the leading cash value crop, reaches north toward the Great Lakes, west to the drier Great Plains, east into Ohio and south to the rugged Ozark Plateau.

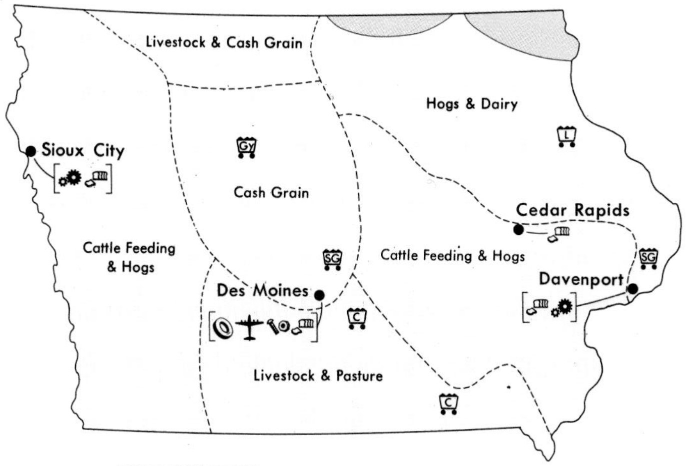

THE ECONOMY

MANUFACTURING
- Food Processing
- Machinery
- Metal Products
- Transportation Equipment
- Rubber & Products

MINING
- Coal
- Gypsum
- Lead
- Sand & Gravel

AGRICULTURE
- Feed Grains & Livestock
- Dairy Farming

VALUE		EMPLOYED
$2,695,230,000	AGRICULTURE	32.0%
$1,678,000,000	MANUFACTURING	17.0%
$ 85,360,000	MINING	0.3%

Percentages are based on a total of 931,000 at work. In addition 27% are in commerce and transport, 12% in government, 11.7% in other areas. Manufacturing value is the value added when materials are converted into goods.

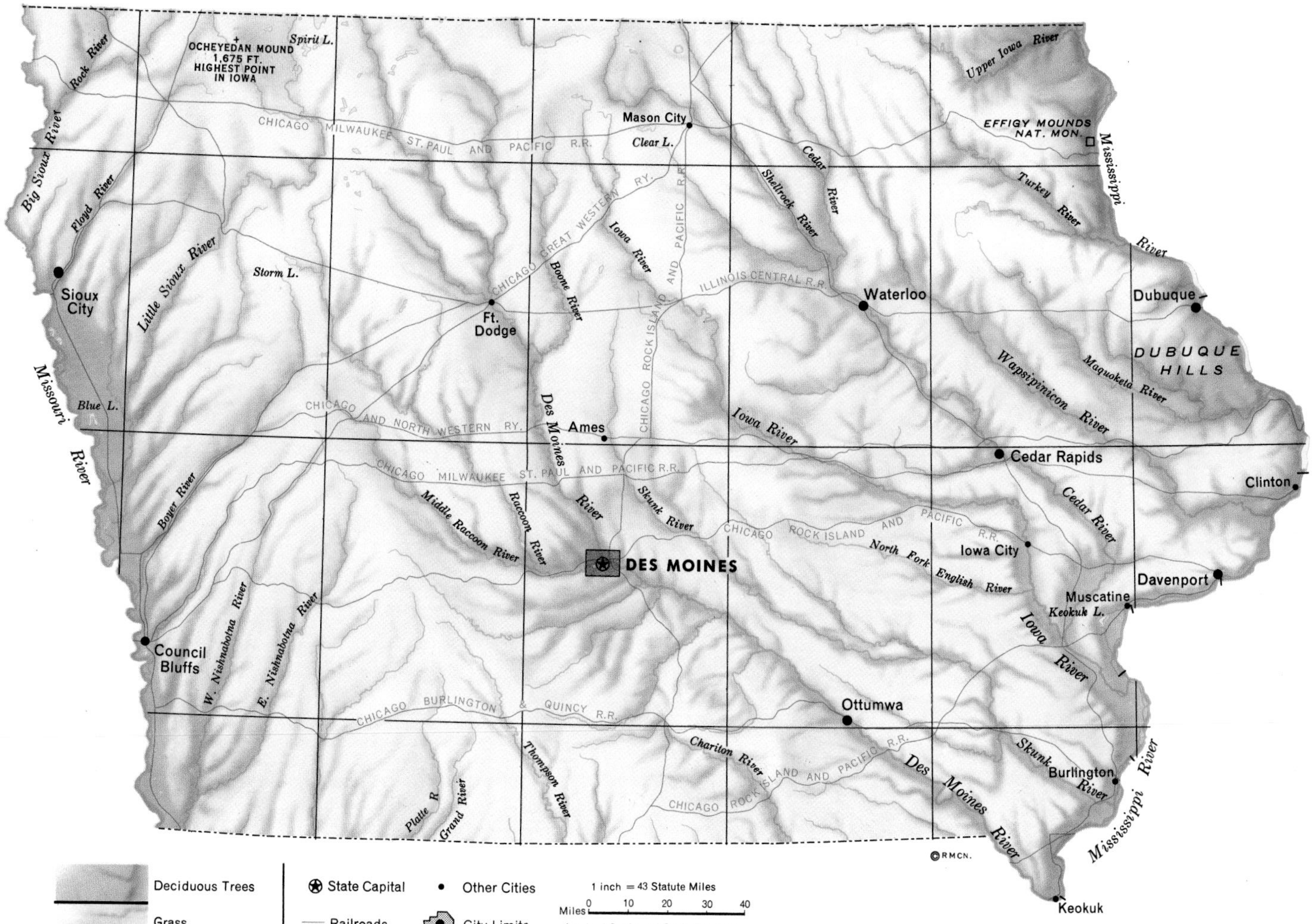

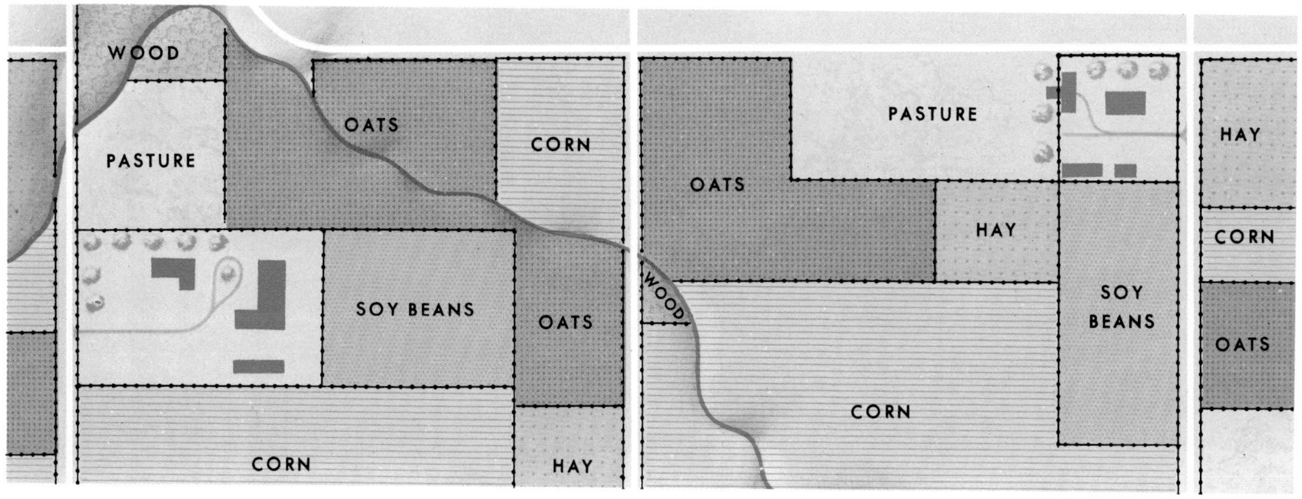

THE LOGIC OF AN IOWA FARM

The farms of Iowa, illustrated above, are characteristically rectangular in shape as a result of the surveying formula used by the federal government when it laid out public land for distribution to settlers in the 1800s. The average farm today devotes 35 per cent of its 177 acres to corn. Most of the corn harvest serves as feed for the farm's cattle and pigs; the rest is sold to be made into cereal and corn meal. The remaining acreage is given over to such crops as hay, oats and soybeans. To provide protection against the bitter winter northwesterlies of the plains, many farmers plant a copse of trees and shrubs as a windbreak, like the one shown at upper left.

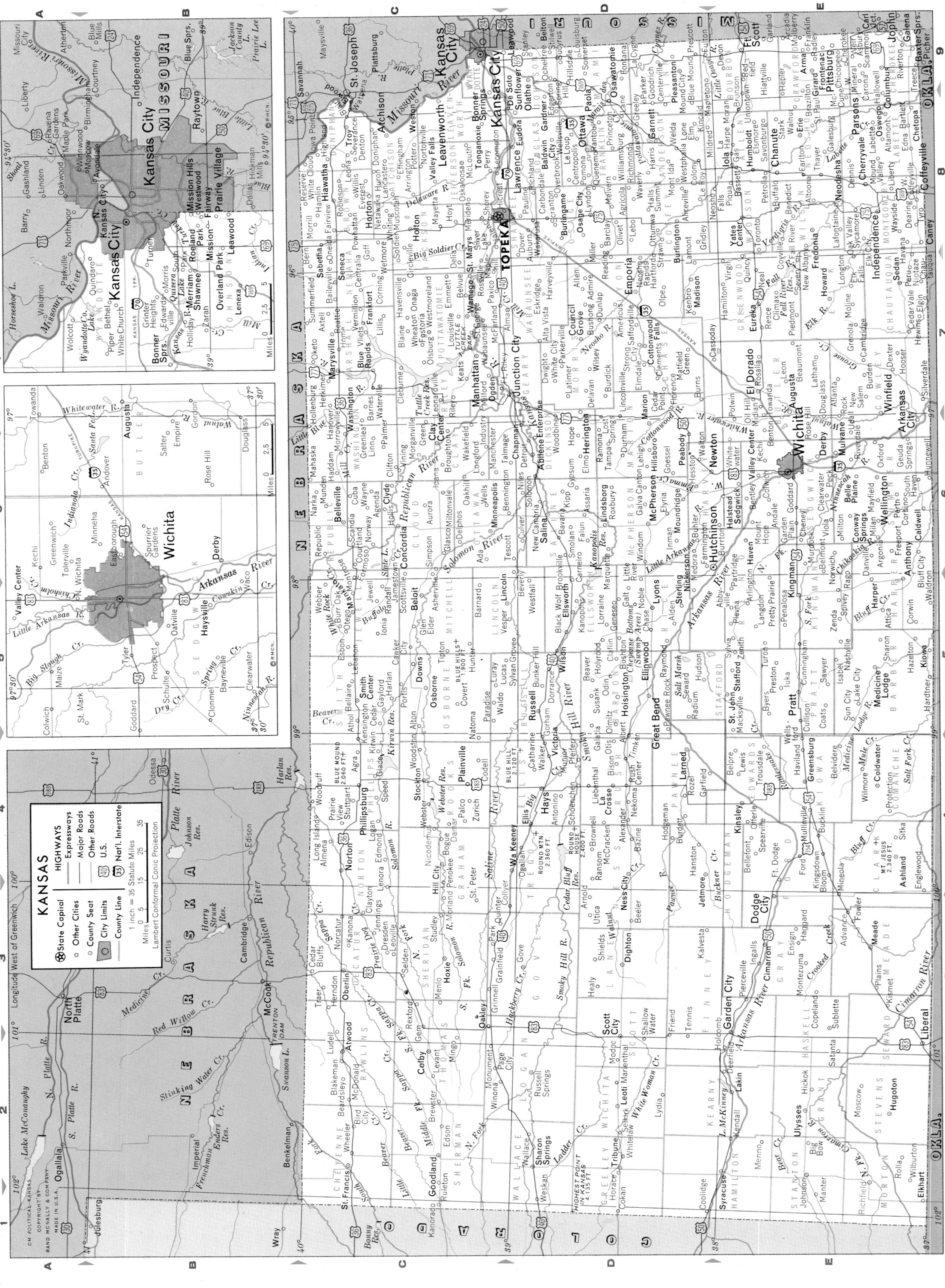
KANSAS
HIGHWAYS
State Capital
Other Cities
County Seat
City Limits
County Line
Expressways
Major Roads
Other Roads
U.S.
Nat'l. Interstate
1 inch = 35 Statute Miles
Miles 0 5 15 25 35
Lambert Conformal Conic Projection
Longitude West of Greenwich
CM POLITICAL-KANSAS
RAND McNALLY & COMPANY
MADE IN U.S.A.
NEBRASKA
OKLA.
MISSOURI
TOPEKA
Wichita
Kansas City
Lawrence
Salina
Hutchinson
Dodge City
Garden City
Liberal
Emporia
Manhattan
Hays
Great Bend
Junction City
Leavenworth
Atchison
Coffeyville
Pittsburg
Independence
Parsons

KANSAS: Like its neighboring landlocked states, far from the moderating, moisture-laden winds of the coasts, Kansas is either extremely hot or extremely cold. And it is forever at the mercy of the wind. Unprotected by peripheral mountain ranges, the land is swept by arctic gusts in winter and furnace-hot blasts in summer. When the wind is gentle, the effect is lovely: slender stalks of wheat, which march row upon row across the plains, rise and dip before the breeze like waves on the sea. But sometimes the wind blows so hard that the soil itself is removed. In the 1930s, before conservation methods were widespread, southwestern Kansas was part of the tragedy-strewn Dust Bowl.

AREA: 82,264 sq. mi. Rank: 14th.
POPULATION: 2,178,611. Rank: 28th. Largest city: Wichita. Capital: Topeka.
ENTERED UNION: Jan. 29, 1861, as 34th state.
CLIMATE: Cold winters, hot summers; moderate rainfall in east, diminishing in west.
ALTITUDES: In Wallace County, 4,135 ft. (highest); Topeka, 930 ft.

To early explorers, Kansas seemed "uninhabitable by a people depending on agriculture." But in 1874, when Mennonites from southern Russia planted Turkey red, a strain of wheat which had flourished on the Russian steppes, men discovered Kansas' destiny. Today, Kansas grows more than 165 million bushels of wheat each year, making it the nation's number one producer.

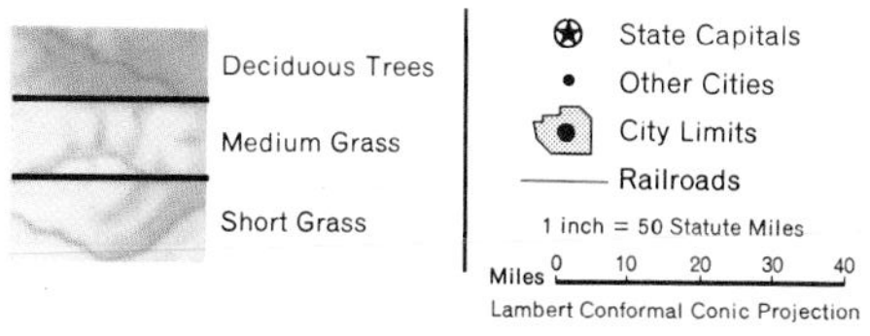

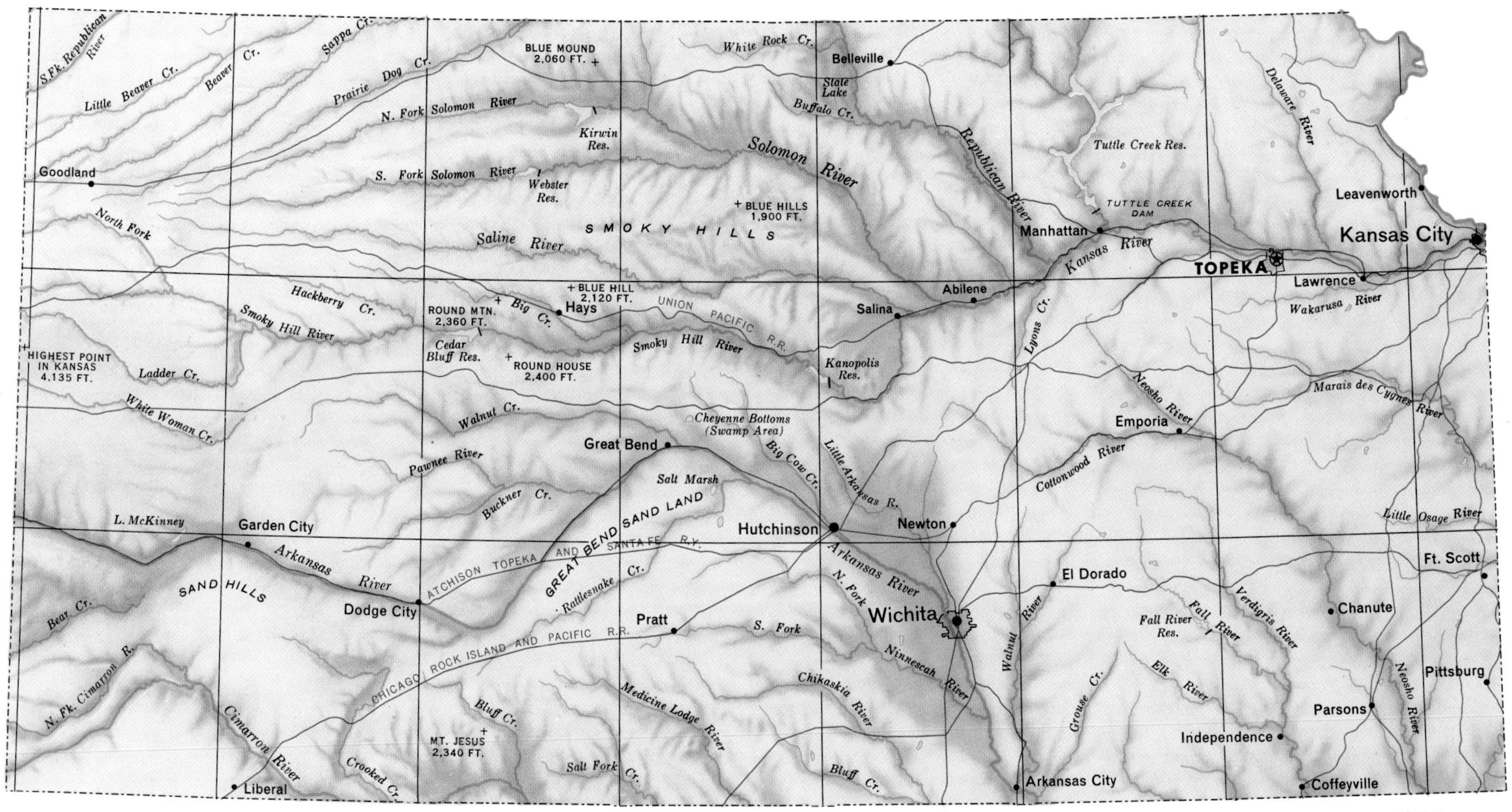

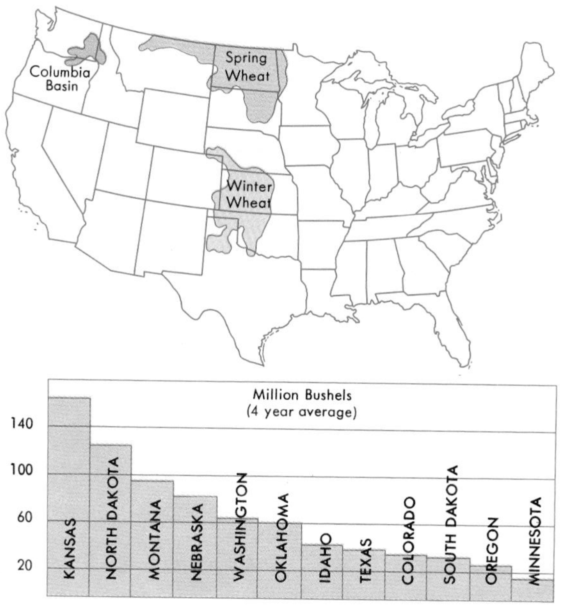

TWO KINDS OF WHEAT FOR TWO KINDS OF WEATHER

Shown here are areas of the U.S. where wheat is the major crop. Winter wheat, grown in an area centered in Kansas, is sown in the fall and reaped the next spring. In the Dakotas and Montana, where winter weather would destroy the crop, wheat is planted in the spring and harvested in late summer. On the Columbia Plateau *(top left)*, both varieties of wheat are grown.

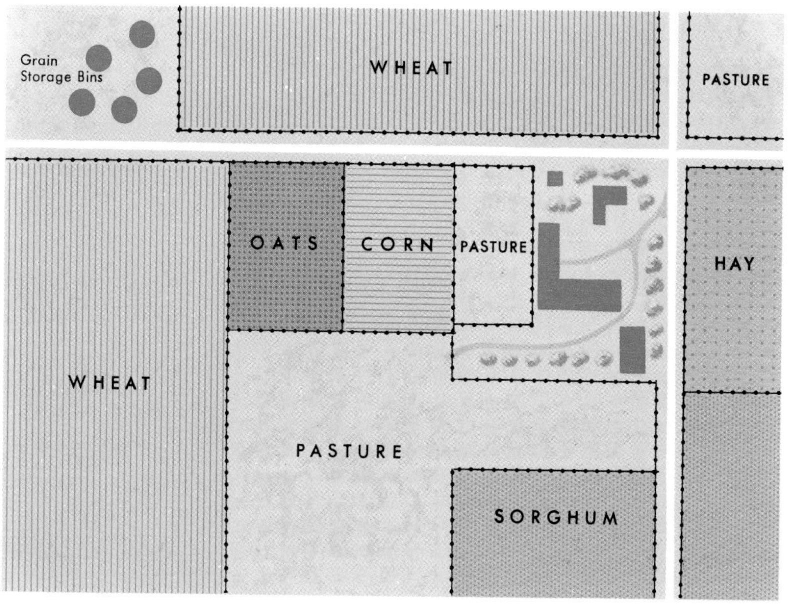

A FORMULA FOR FARMING

On a typical Kansas farm, whose layout is shown here, the chief crop is wheat. But as a protection against the hazards of searing summer heat and irregular rainfall, most farmers also raise cattle, using some acreage for pasture and some for feed crops like sorghum and hay. To be profitable in an area where the scarcity of rain may limit the yield per acre, and where a portion of the land must be left to lie fallow each year so that it can absorb moisture, Kansas farms are necessarily large. The average size is approximately 415 acres.

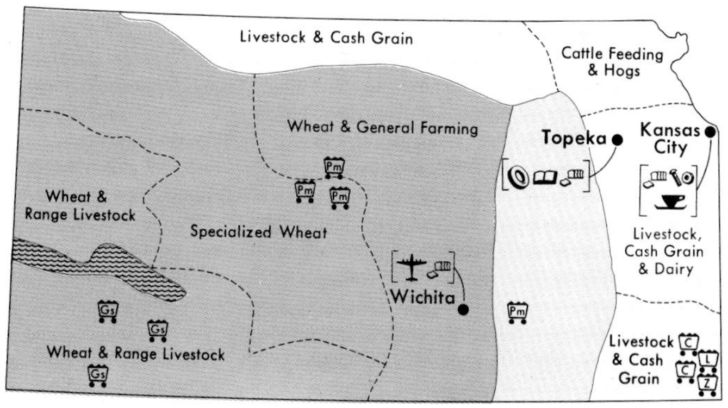

THE ECONOMY

MANUFACTURING
- Food Processing
- Metal Products
- Printing & Publishing
- Rubber & Products
- Stone, Clay & Glass Products
- Transportation Equipment

MINING
- Coal
- Natural Gas
- Lead
- Petroleum
- Zinc

AGRICULTURE
- Feed Grains & Livestock
- Wheat & Small Grains
- Special Crops & General Farming
- Seasonal Grazing
- Irrigated Land

VALUE		EMPLOYED
$1,254,670,000	AGRICULTURE	24%
$1,162,000,000	MANUFACTURING	16%
$ 498,530,000	MINING	2%

Percentages are based on a total of 711,000 at work. In addition 29% are in commerce and transport, 15% in government, 14% in other areas. Manufacturing value is the value added when materials are converted into goods.

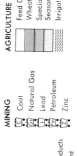

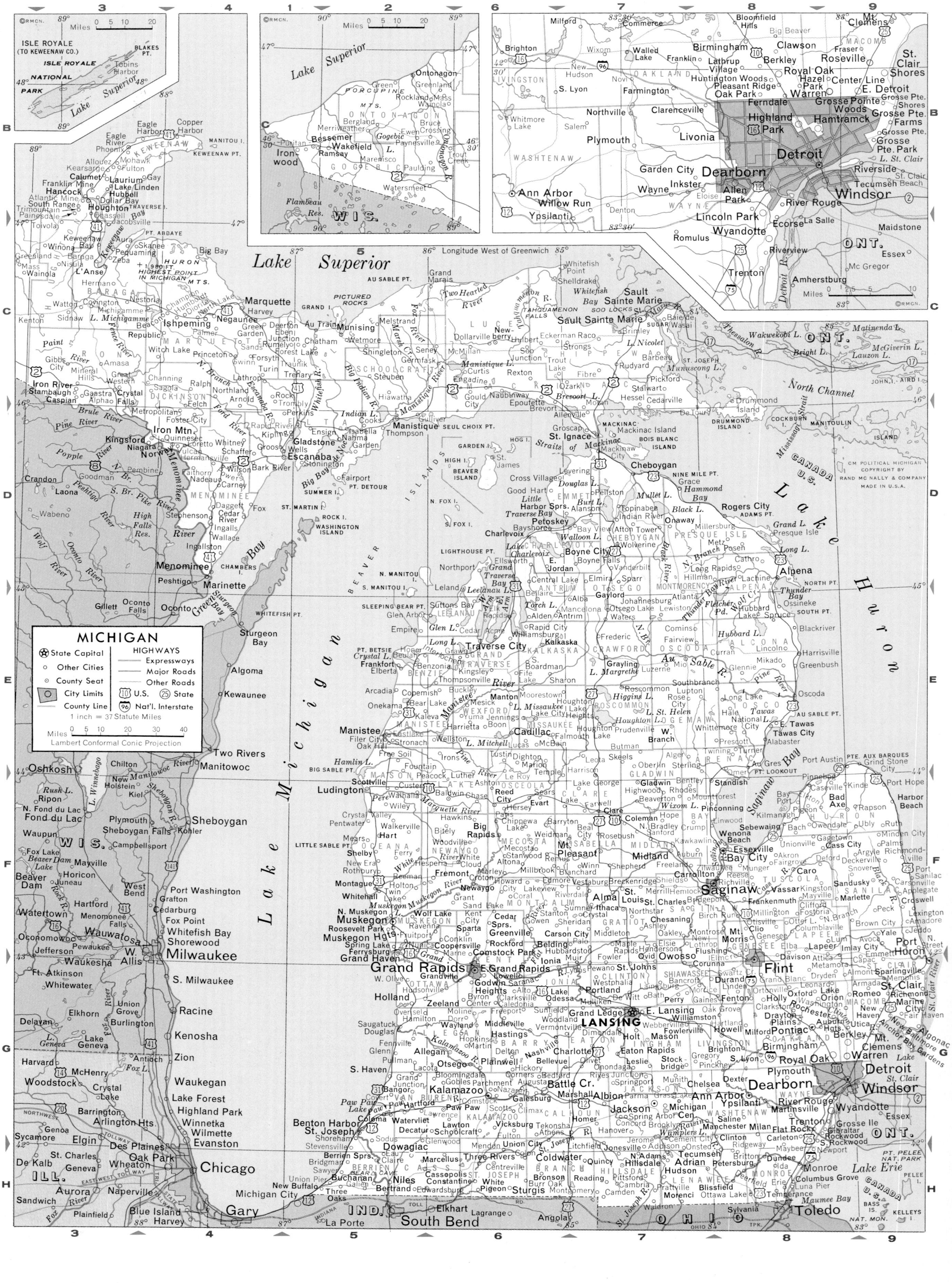
MICHIGAN
State Capital
Other Cities
County Seat
City Limits
County Line
HIGHWAYS
Expressways
Major Roads
Other Roads
U.S.
State
Nat'l. Interstate
1 inch = 37 Statute Miles
Lambert Conformal Conic Projection
ISLE ROYALE (TO KEWEENAW CO.)
ISLE ROYALE NATIONAL PARK
Lake Superior
Lake Michigan
Lake Huron
Lake Erie
Longitude West of Greenwich
W I S.
I L L.
I N D.
O H I O
O N T.
CANADA
U.S.
Marquette
Ishpeming
Negaunee
Sault Sainte Marie
St. Ignace
Mackinac Island
Cheboygan
Petoskey
Traverse City
Cadillac
Manistee
Ludington
Muskegon
Grand Rapids
Kalamazoo
Battle Cr.
Jackson
Ann Arbor
LANSING
Flint
Saginaw
Bay City
Midland
Alpena
Port Huron
Pontiac
Detroit
Dearborn
Windsor
Toledo
Benton Harbor
St. Joseph
South Bend
Gary
Chicago
Milwaukee
Green Bay
Escanaba
Menominee
Marinette
Iron Mtn.
Houghton
Hancock
Ironwood
Wyandotte
Royal Oak
Livonia
Hamtramck
Highland Park
Port Huron
Sheboygan
Manitowoc
Racine
Kenosha
Waukegan
Evanston
Elgin
Oak Park
Oshkosh

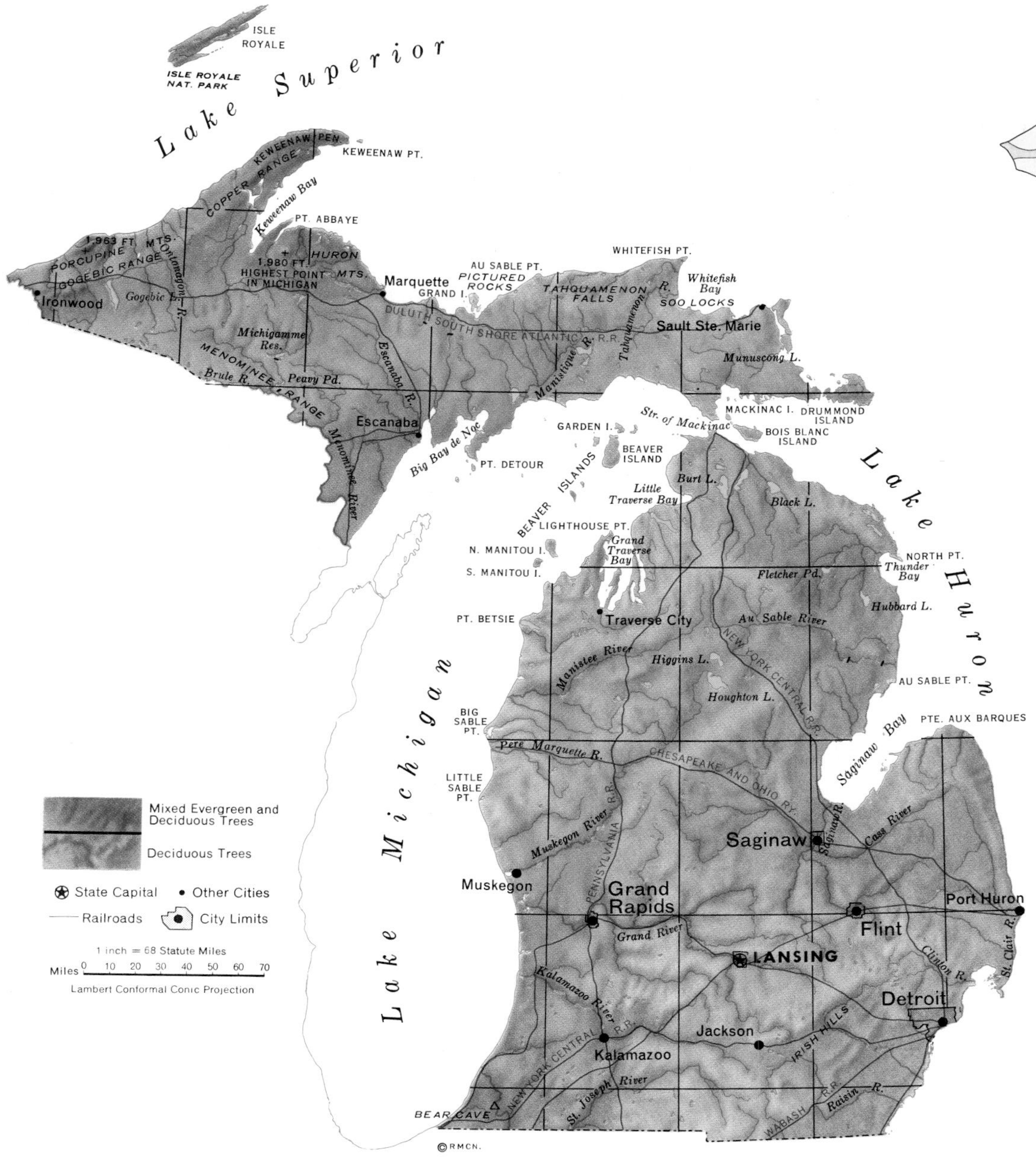

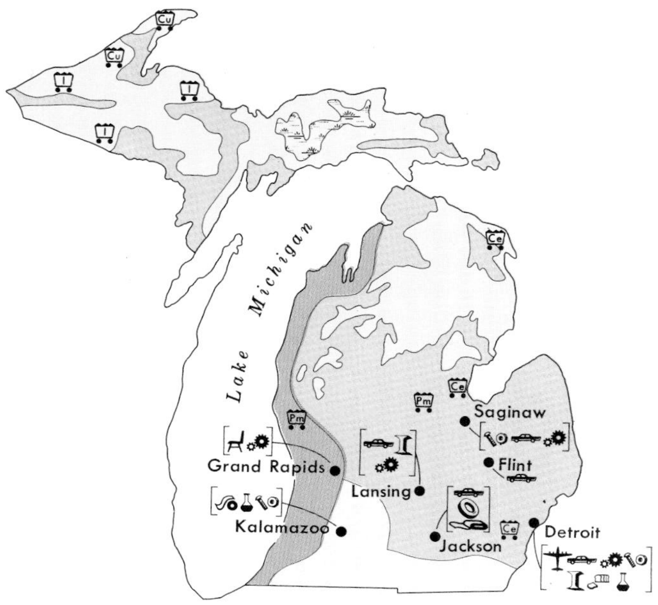

THE ECONOMY

MANUFACTURING

- Transportation Equipment
- Pulp & Paper Products
- Rubber & Products
- Food Processing
- Primary Metals
- Metal Products
- Machinery
- Chemicals
- Furniture
- Textiles

MINING

- Cement
- Copper
- Iron Ore
- Petroleum

AGRICULTURE

- Feed Grains & Livestock
- Fruit, Truck & General Farming
- Dairy & General Farming
- Forests
- Marshland

VALUE		EMPLOYED
$ 782,980,000	AGRICULTURE	10.0%
$8,683,000,000	MANUFACTURING	36.0%
$ 343,480,000	MINING	0.6%

Percentages are based on a total of 2,353,000 at work. In addition 28% are in commerce and transport, 12% in government, 13.4% in other areas. Manufacturing value is the value added when materials are converted into goods.

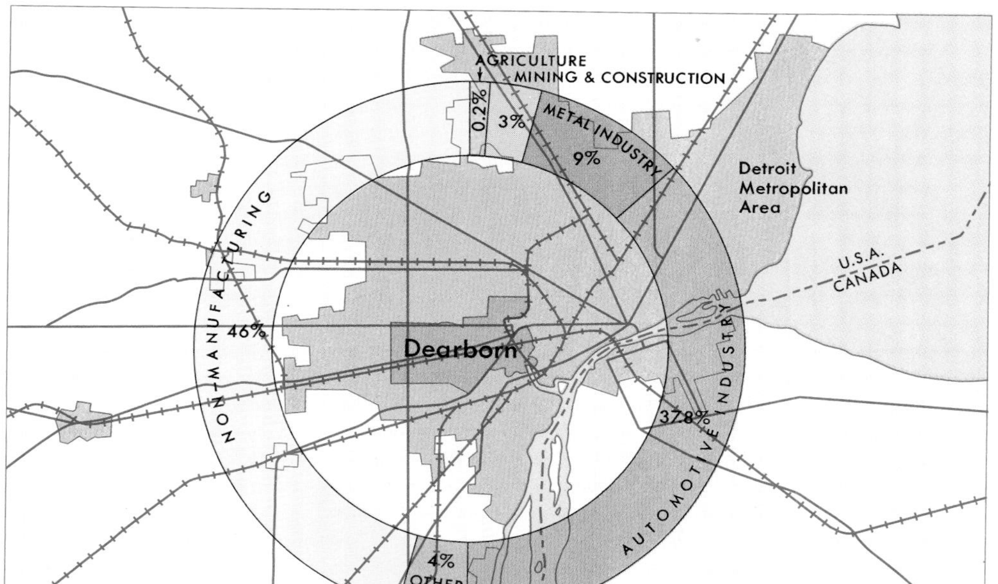

MODERN MODEL OF A ONE-INDUSTRY TOWN

The circle graph superimposed on the map above reveals how the youthful city of Dearborn owes its existence to the automobile industry of neighboring Detroit, sharing with it the prosperity and the problems of a one-product economy. In 1920, Dearborn was a village of only 2,500; 10 years later, it had grown to 50,000 and had become the home of the Ford Motor Company's giant Rouge plant. Since then, the city has mushroomed to more than 120,000 people. With nearly four out of every 10 people in its labor force employed at Ford and another five doing the community's other chores, Dearborn is a chrome-plated version of the old-time mill town, its livelihood depending almost entirely on a single industry.

MICHIGAN: The state the Algonquins called *Michi Gama,* "land of the great water," is divided by Lake Michigan into two great peninsulas which face each other across the narrow Straits of Mackinac. The Lower Peninsula forms the "Michigan mitten"—a land of wooded hills and resorts to the north, of fruit and dairy farms to the south, dotted with cities whose very names now evoke the industries located there. Detroit is, of course, automobiles *(map and diagram, left)*, just as Battle Creek is breakfast cereals and Grand Rapids is furniture. Less well known are Fremont, the nation's number one producer of canned baby foods; Traverse City, a packer of cherries; Grayling, which makes archery equipment, and Muskegon, a manufacturer of billiard tables and bowling equipment.

The Upper Peninsula, once rich in copper and iron, is a lovely wooded land with boisterous rivers hastening to the Great Lakes. Its widely scattered towns are thinly populated, but its trout streams, its game and scenic beauty lure thousands of sportsmen and tourists to the area each year. The Upper Peninsula provided the locale for Henry Wadsworth Longfellow's familiar poem, "The Song of Hiawatha."

AREA:	58,216 sq. mi. Rank: 23rd.
POPULATION:	7,823,194. Rank: 7th. Largest city: Detroit. Capital: Lansing.
ENTERED UNION:	Jan. 26, 1837, as 26th state.
CLIMATE:	Cold snowy winters, mild summers; adequate rainfall.
ALTITUDES:	Near L'Anse in northeast Baraga County, 1,980 ft. (highest); Lansing, 830 ft.; Detroit, 585 ft.

Some 10,000 to 30,000 years ago, glaciers gouged out the pattern of the Great Lakes and created the state's 3,100 miles of coastline, 11,000 inland lakes and 35,500 miles of streams and rivers. The Great Lakes—cooling the prevailing winds in summer and warming them in winter—make the shoreline of Michigan a unique fruit-growing region in the mid-continental Midwest.

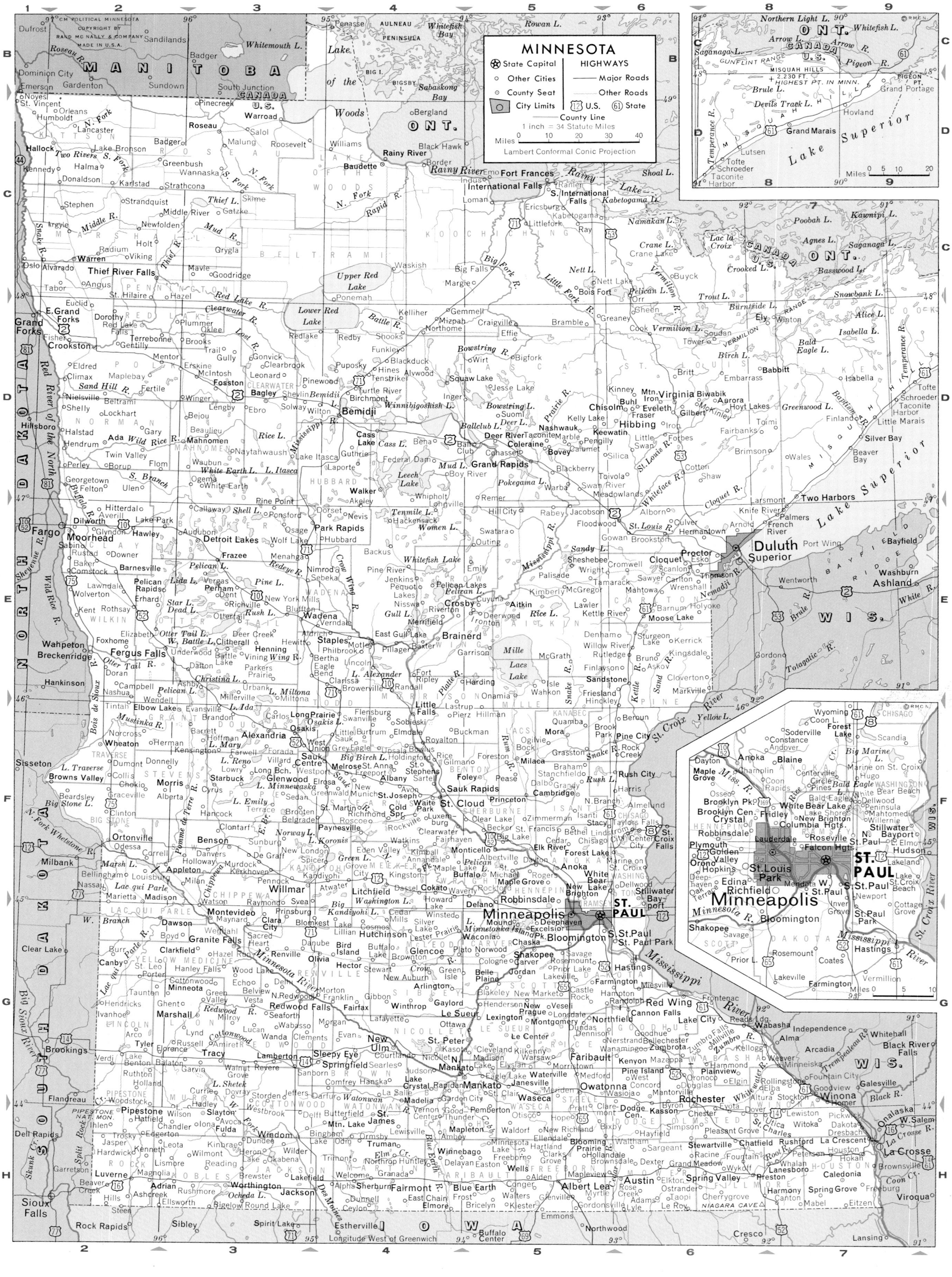
MINNESOTA
State Capital
Other Cities
County Seat
City Limits
HIGHWAYS
Major Roads
Other Roads
U.S.
State
County Line
1 inch = 34 Statute Miles
Miles 0 10 20 30 40
Lambert Conformal Conic Projection
CM POLITICAL MINNESOTA
COPYRIGHT BY RAND McNALLY & COMPANY
MADE IN U.S.A.
MANITOBA
ONT.
NORTH DAKOTA
SOUTH DAKOTA
IOWA
WIS.
Lake Superior
Duluth
Minneapolis
ST. PAUL
Longitude West of Greenwich

MINNESOTA

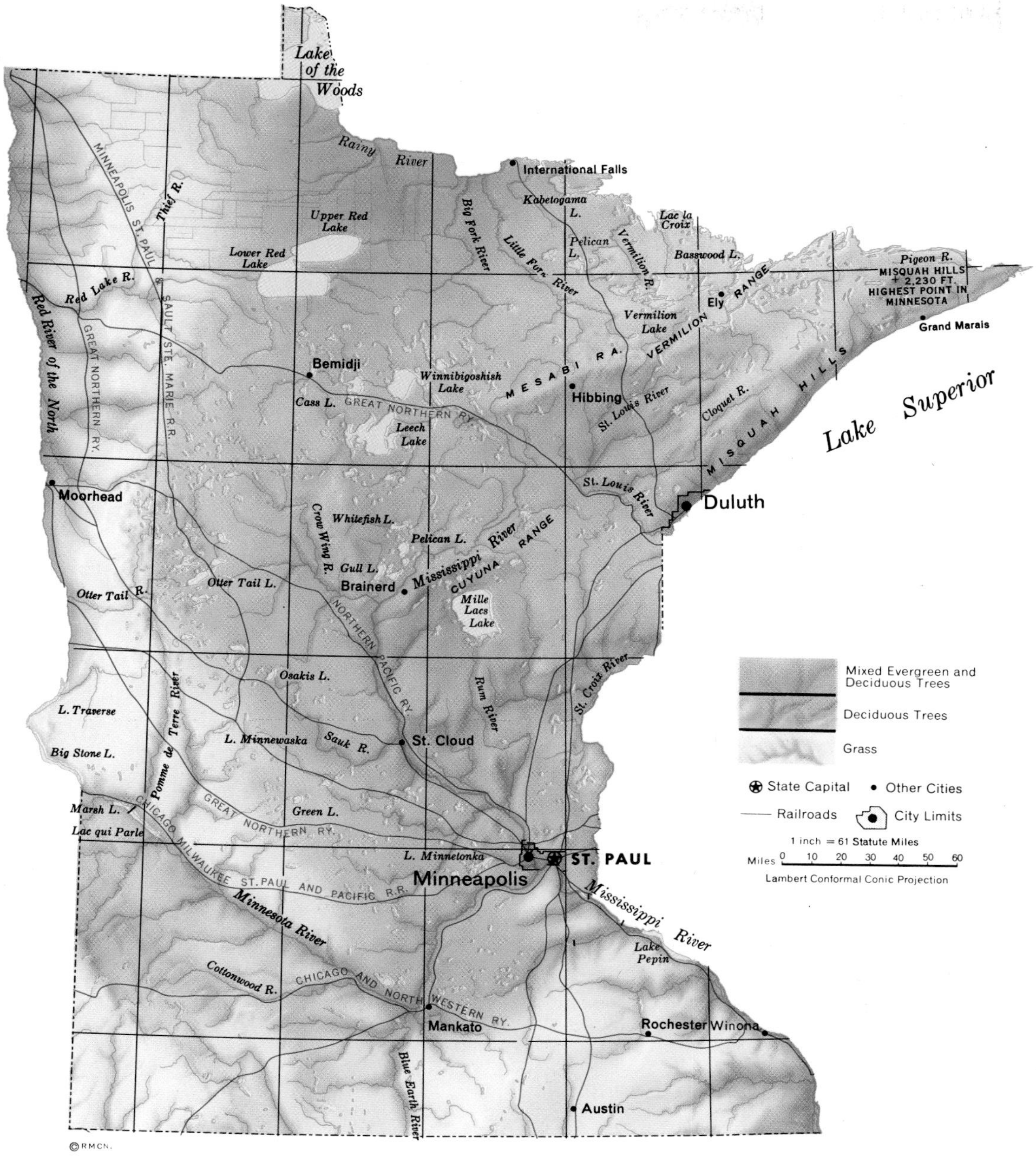

Lake of the Woods
Rainy River
International Falls
Kabetogama L.
Lac la Croix
Upper Red Lake
Lower Red Lake
Big Fork River
Little Fork River
Pelican L.
Vermilion R.
Basswood L.
Pigeon R.
MISQUAH HILLS + 2,230 FT. HIGHEST POINT IN MINNESOTA
Grand Marais
Ely
VERMILION RANGE
Vermilion Lake
MESABI RA.
Red Lake R.
Red River of the North
Thief R.
MINNEAPOLIS ST. PAUL & SAULT STE. MARIE R.R.
GREAT NORTHERN RY.
Bemidji
Winnibigoshish Lake
Cass L.
Leech Lake
Hibbing
St. Louis River
Cloquet R.
MISQUAH HILLS
Lake Superior
Duluth
Moorhead
Whitefish L.
Pelican L.
Mississippi River
CUYUNA RANGE
Crow Wing R.
Gull L.
Brainerd
Otter Tail R.
Otter Tail L.
Mille Lacs Lake
NORTHERN PACIFIC RY.
St. Croix River
Rum River
Osakis L.
L. Traverse
Big Stone L.
Pomme de Terre River
L. Minnewaska
Sauk R.
St. Cloud
Marsh L.
Lac qui Parle
Green L.
GREAT NORTHERN RY.
CHICAGO MILWAUKEE ST. PAUL AND PACIFIC R.R.
L. Minnetonka
ST. PAUL
Minneapolis
Mississippi River
Minnesota River
Lake Pepin
Cottonwood R.
CHICAGO AND NORTH WESTERN RY.
Mankato
Rochester
Winona
Blue Earth River
Austin
Mixed Evergreen and Deciduous Trees
Deciduous Trees
Grass
State Capital
Other Cities
Railroads
City Limits
1 inch = 61 Statute Miles
Miles 0 10 20 30 40 50 60
Lambert Conformal Conic Projection
© RMCN.

THE ECONOMY

MANUFACTURING
Food Processing
Printing & Publishing
Metal Products
Machinery
Textiles & Clothing

MINING
Iron Ore
Manganese
Stone

AGRICULTURE
Feed Grains & Livestock
Wheat & Small Grains
Dairy & General Farming

VALUE		EMPLOYED
$1,567,910,000	AGRICULTURE	24%
$2,035,000,000	MANUFACTURING	18%
$ 395,880,000	MINING	1%

Percentages are based on a total of 1,180,000 at work. In addition 30% are in commerce and transport, 12% in government, 15% in other areas. Manufacturing value is the value added when materials are converted into goods.

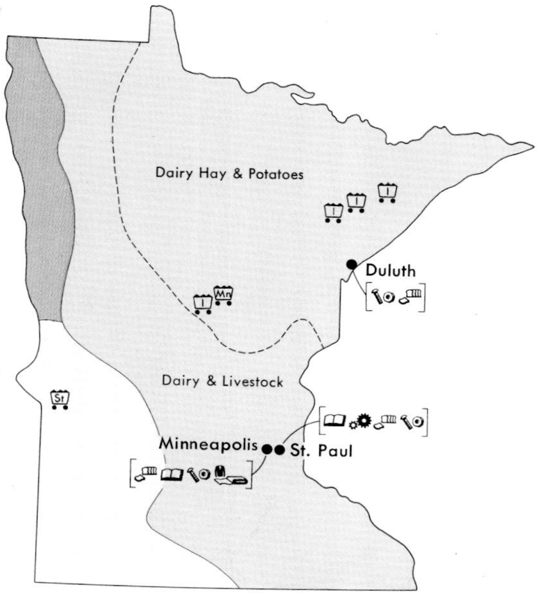

Dairy Hay & Potatoes
Duluth
Dairy & Livestock
Minneapolis
St. Paul

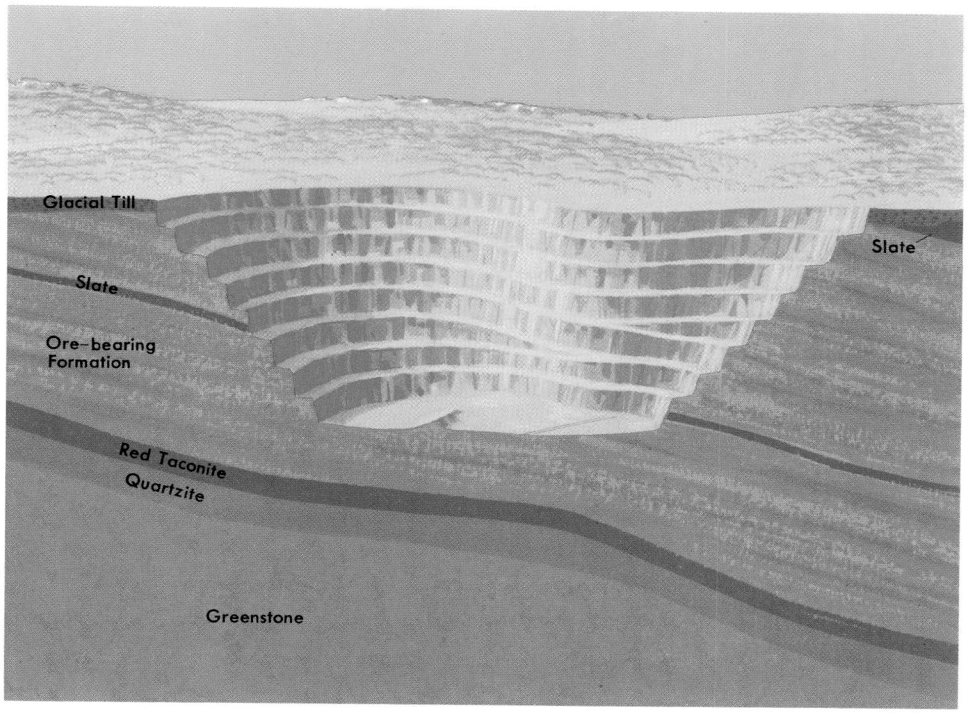

Glacial Till
Slate
Slate
Ore-bearing Formation
Red Taconite
Quartzite
Greenstone

MARVEL OF THE MESABI: MINES FOREVER OPEN TO THE SKY

Stadium-like tiers carve a Bunyanesque amphitheatre into the earth in this cross section of a typical iron mine in the Mesabi Range, revealing how the easy accessibility of the ore deposit makes possible mining in open pits. After a crust of glacial till—rock and clay—is scraped away, huge power shovels start at the surface and dig out the rich ore, leaving a sloping spiral path around the deepening pit as they work downward. The spiral then serves as a ramp for railroad ore cars. As the richer pay dirt is gradually depleted, red taconite, a lower-grade ore, takes on a new importance.

MINNESOTA: Here, Minnesotans like to say, is the land of the good life. With more than 11,000 clear blue lakes scattered through the state's level plains, rugged hills and valleys, nine out of every 10 people are within 10 miles of a body of water alive with wall-eyed pike, trout, bass and darting sloops. One of the most popular of the vacation states, Minnesota is a sportsman's paradise. According to legend, its lakes were created when Paul Bunyan, the giant of the woods, let his ax drag on the ground behind him. A more prosaic age attributes their formation to glacial action, but the vigorous outdoor tradition remains. During the Korean War, when more than a third of all American men were rejected for service, Minnesota rejected only a fifth of its men.

AREA:	84,068 sq. mi. Rank: 12th.
POPULATION:	3,413,864. Rank: 18th. Largest city: Minneapolis. Capital: St. Paul.
ENTERED UNION:	May 11, 1858, as 32nd state.
CLIMATE:	Long, cold winters, short summers; moderate rainfall.
ALTITUDES:	Misquah Hills, 2,230 ft. (highest); St. Paul, 780 ft.

Situated on the edge of the Corn Belt, Minnesota is primarily an agricultural state. The "bread-and-butter skyline" of the grain mills and creameries in Minneapolis bears testimony to the fact that the state is the nation's number one producer of creamery butter and a major source of milk, oats, corn, barley, spring wheat and hay. Buttressed by its sister city of St. Paul, just across the Mississippi, Minneapolis has become the upper Midwest's prime distributing center.

Minnesota has only one major metal, but it is a mighty one—iron. In the northeast, among the gentle hills of the glacier-leveled Mesabi Range *(drawing at left)*, lies "the biggest man-made hole" in the world—the open pits of the Hull-Rust-Mahoning mine, 458 feet deep and one mile across at its widest. From Mesabi and its associated ranges comes 60 per cent of all the iron ore mined in the U.S. Much of it moves through Duluth, which, together with the neighboring city of Superior in Wisconsin, sends 35 million tons of cargo a year across the Great Lakes toward the St. Lawrence Seaway and the Atlantic. Some 2,340 miles from the ocean, Duluth-Superior prospers as the greatest inland port area in the world.

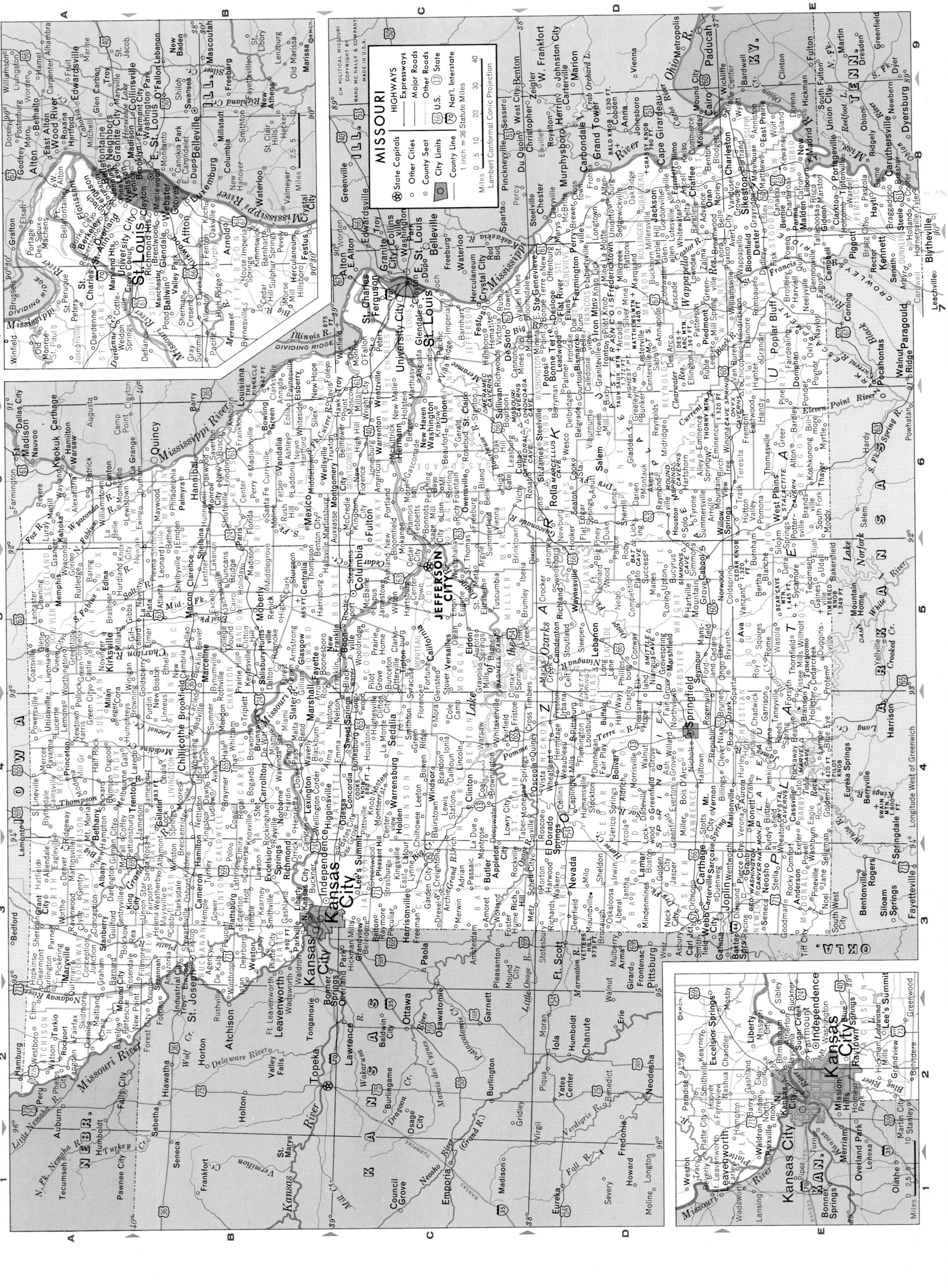
MISSOURI
State Capitals
Other Cities
County Seat
City Limits
County Line
HIGHWAYS
Expressways
Major Roads
Other Roads
U.S.
State
Nat'l. Interstate
Miles 0 5 10 20 30 40
1 inch = 36 Statute Miles
Lambert Conformal Conic Projection
CM POLITICAL MISSOURI
COPYRIGHT BY RAND McNALLY & COMPANY
MADE IN U.S.A.
JEFFERSON CITY
St. Louis
Kansas City
Springfield
IOWA
KANSAS
ARKANSAS
ILL.
KY.
TENN.
NEBR.
OKLA.
Mississippi River
Missouri River
Longitude West of Greenwich

MISSOURI: The first state west of the Mississippi to be admitted to the Union, Missouri was for many years both a jumping-off point to the West and a transportation center for an expanding U.S.–and so it remains. It is here that the country's two greatest rivers marry their waters. Above St. Louis, the swelling Mississippi is joined by the "Big Muddy," the Missouri, a voracious giant that western author Stanley Vestal once called "the hungriest river ever created . . . eating yellow clay banks and cornfields . . . winding up its banquet with a truck garden and picking its teeth with the timbers of a big red barn." It is indeed a mouthful of a river, and only in recent years have men begun to devise ways to harness its rampaging power *(map and diagram, below).*

AREA: 69,686 sq. mi. Rank: 19th.
POPULATION: 4,319,813. Rank: 13th.
Largest city: St. Louis.
Capital: Jefferson City.
ENTERED UNION: Aug. 10, 1821, as 24th state.
CLIMATE: Generally hot summers, cold winters; moderate rainfall.
ALTITUDES: Taum Sauk Mountain in the Ozarks, 1,772 ft. (highest).

In Missouri, the residents like to say, the East ends and the West begins. By way of example, they cite eastern-oriented St. Louis, an established manufacturing center with the second-oldest symphony orchestra in the U.S. For contrast, they turn to the younger metropolis of Kansas City, whose westward orientation is reflected in bawling stockyards, grain elevators and the meat-packing industry.

Physiographically, Missouri has equally great differences. The rugged Ozark uplands rise in the southern part of the state. East of them lies a flat land of abundant rain and rich black soil.

But the rest of the U.S. probably knows Missouri best for its "show-me" character, expressed by a now forgotten congressman named Willard Vandiver. "I come from a State that raises corn and cotton and cockleburs and Democrats," he said in 1899, "and frothy eloquence neither convinces nor satisfies me. I am from Missouri. You have got to show me."

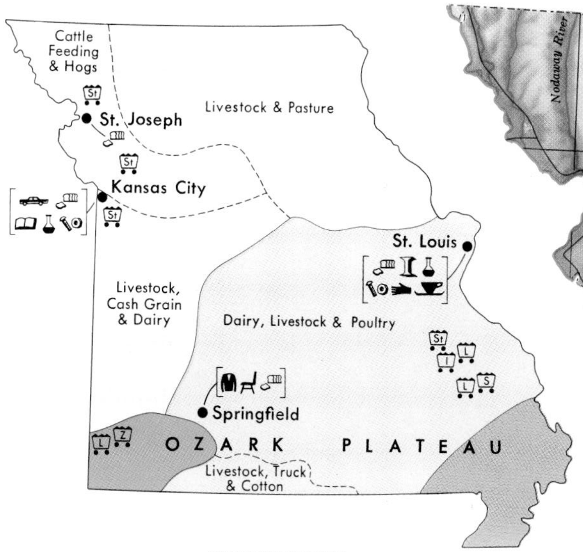

THE ECONOMY

MANUFACTURING: Clothing; Furniture; Chemicals; Metal Products; Primary Metals; Food Processing; Leather & Products; Printing & Publishing; Transportation Equipment; Stone, Clay & Glass Products

MINING: Iron Ore; Lead; Silver; Stone; Zinc

AGRICULTURE: General Farming; Feed Grains & Livestock; Cotton; Fruit & General Farming

VALUE		EMPLOYED
$1,229,840,000	AGRICULTURE	19.0%
$3,157,000,000	MANUFACTURING	24.0%
$ 144,010,000	MINING	0.5%

Percentages are based on a total of 1,559,000 at work. In addition 32% are in commerce and transport, 11% in government, 13.5% in other areas. Manufacturing value is the value added when materials are converted into goods.

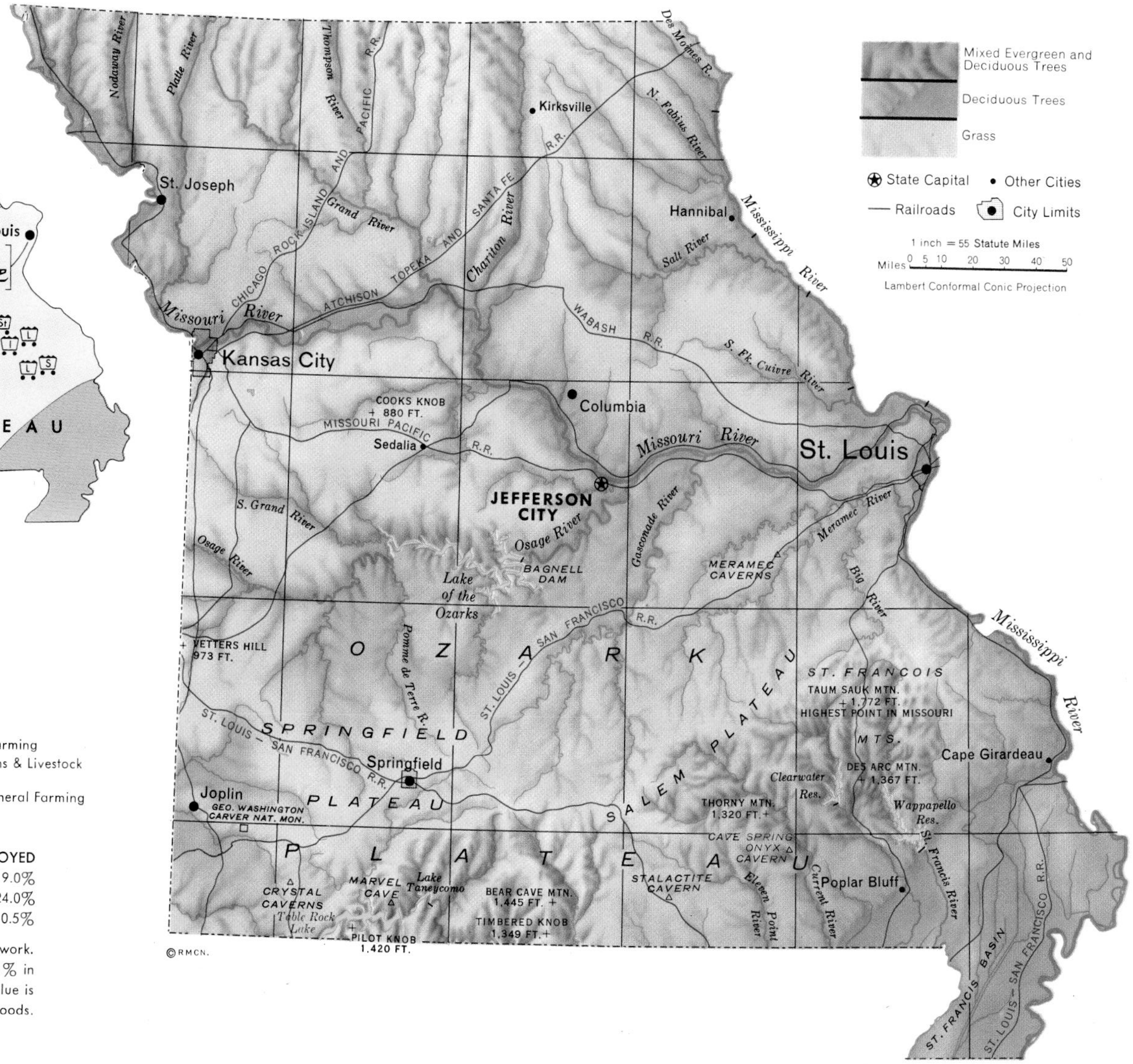

MASTERING THE 'BIG MO'

The Oahe Dam in South Dakota, shown in the drawing at right, is a major keystone in the vast Missouri River Basin project for flood control, irrigation and power *(map, far right).* When completed the system will have 137 dams, of which Oahe is the fifth major one to be built. Located near the city of Pierre and blocking the Missouri, Oahe is a typical earth-fill dam–a gigantic pile of dirt topped by rock and gravel *(center)*, 9,300 feet long and 242 feet high. During construction, the river was diverted from the dam site by an approach channel *(top left).* This later was converted into the spillway which now acts as a safety drain to keep the reservoir from overflowing at floodtime. To produce electricity, water is drawn into the intakes at both ends of the dam. Any excess is discharged into a "stilling basin" and the rest allowed to rush through tunnels to the powerhouse. There it spins the turbines and finally flows out the tailrace *(right center)* to continue down river.

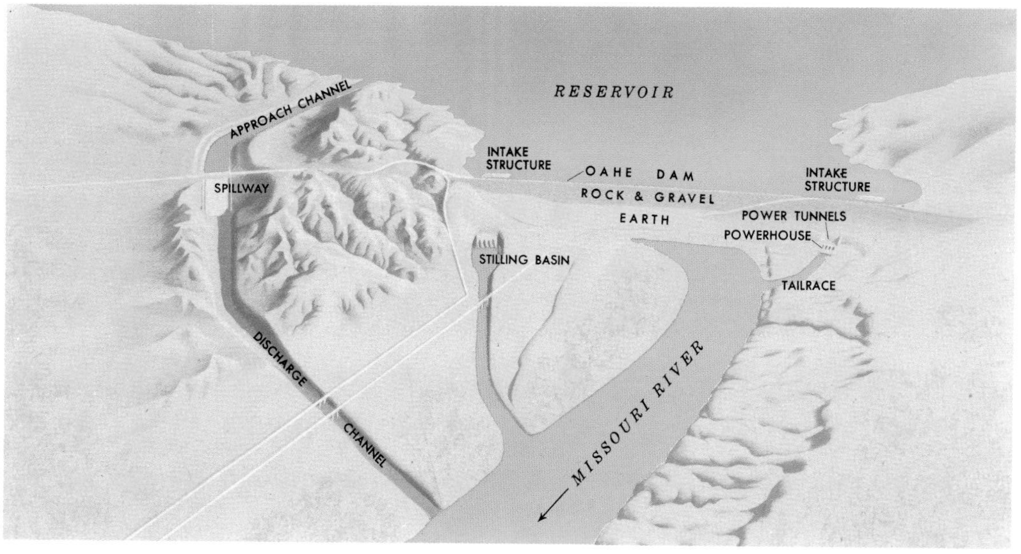

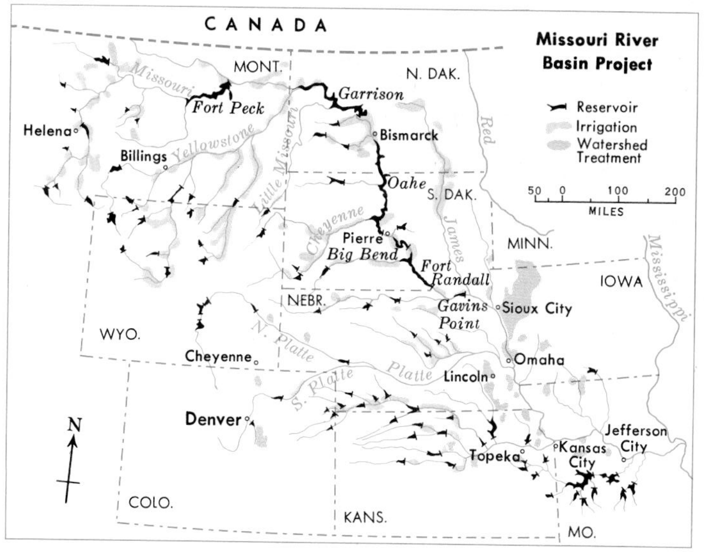

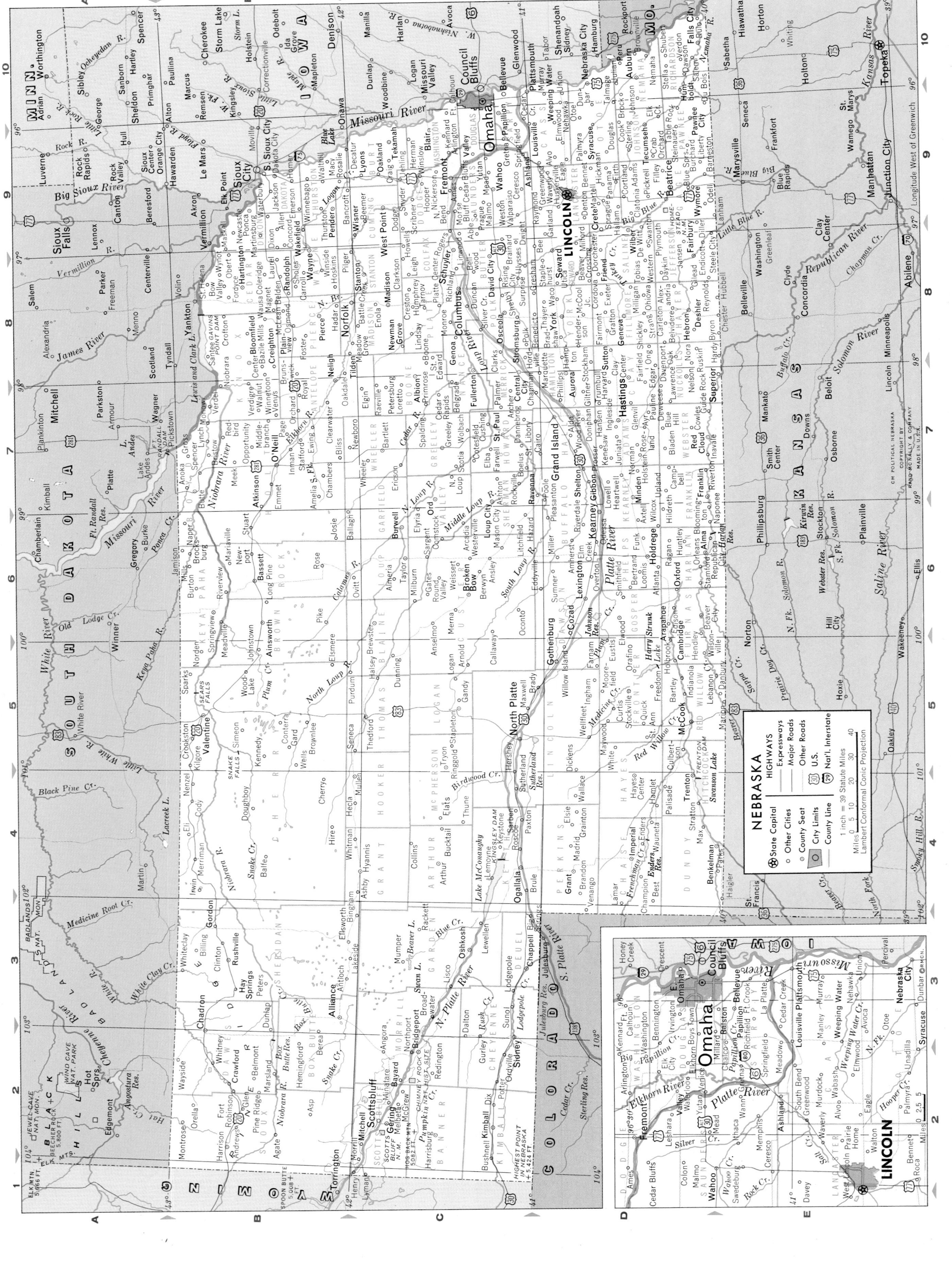
NEBRASKA
HIGHWAYS
Expressways
Major Roads
Other Roads
U.S.
Nat'l. Interstate
State Capital
Other Cities
County Seat
City Limits
County Line
1 inch = 39 Statute Miles
Miles 0 5 10 20 30 40
Lambert Conformal Conic Projection
Longitude West of Greenwich
CM POLITICAL NEBRASKA
COPYRIGHT BY RAND McNALLY & COMPANY
MADE IN U.S.A.
SOUTH DAKOTA
IOWA
MINN.
MO.
KANSAS
COLORADO
WYO.
LINCOLN
Omaha
Council Bluffs
Grand Island
Kearney
North Platte
Scottsbluff
Norfolk
Fremont
Hastings
Columbus
Sioux City
Sioux Falls
Yankton
Topeka
Missouri River
Platte River
Niobrara River
Loup River
Republican River
Big Sioux River
James River
White River
N. Platte River
S. Platte River
Elkhorn River
Lewis and Clark L.
Lake McConaughy
Harlan Co. Res.
Valentine
Chadron
Alliance
Sidney
Ogallala
McCook
Lexington
Beatrice
Nebraska City
Falls City
Plattsmouth
Bellevue
Papillion
Wahoo
Ashland
Crete
Seward
York
Aurora
Holdrege
Broken Bow
O'Neill
Ainsworth
Atkinson
Bassett
Burwell
Ord
Gering
Kimball
Imperial
Benkelman
Trenton
Superior
Red Cloud
Fairbury
Wymore
Pawnee City
Tecumseh
Auburn
Sterling
Syracuse
Wayne
West Point
Tekamah
Blair
Schuyler
David City
Wahoo
HIGHEST POINT IN NEBRASKA 5,424 FT.
SPOON BUTTE 5,008 FT.
BADLANDS NAT. MON.
WIND CAVE NAT. PARK
JEWEL CAVE NAT. MON.
BLACK HILLS
SCOTTS BLUFF N. M.
CHIMNEY ROCK NAT. HIST. SITE
KINGSLEY DAM
GAVINS POINT DAM
FT. RANDALL DAM

NEBRASKA: Here is the crucible in which the spirit of the western settlers received a severe test. With temperatures that soar to 110 degrees on the high dry plains of the west, Nebraska can be fearfully hot in summer. It can also be as icily cold as 30 below in winter on the sand hills of the north central region. Had it not been for the fact that its rolling central plains were chosen for the route of the Union Pacific, Nebraska might have long remained, as an Army Engineers' report described it in 1820, "the abode of perpetual desolation." But the railroad brought homesteaders to take up the free lands laid out by government surveyors *(maps, below right)*. Once there, the settlers found water in the Platte basin, and they managed to build homes of sod on the short-grass plain. But none of it was easy. In the 1870s the state was plagued by swarms of grasshoppers which stripped bare the grainfields of the Midwest. Escaping to the East, many a defeated pioneer sang a wry paean to Nebraska–"Land of the bedbug, grasshopper and flea. . . . I'll tell of its fame–while starving to death on my government claim."

AREA: 77,227 sq. mi. Rank: 15th.
POPULATION: 1,411,330. Rank: 34th. Largest city: Omaha. Capital: Lincoln.
ENTERED UNION: March 1, 1867, as 37th state.
CLIMATE: Hot summers, cold winters; semi-arid in the west, more rain in the east.
ALTITUDES: Peak in Kimball County, 5,424 ft. (highest); Omaha, 1,040 ft.

The earth itself is Nebraska's most valuable resource. "Loess" –topsoil deposited by hard-blowing winds–enriches the southern part of the state. On it Nebraska grows around $150 million worth of wheat each year. Beef cattle are raised in the west and fattened in the wetter east near the food-processing centers of Lincoln and Omaha, where corn and hogs flourish. Lying close to the center of the U.S., Omaha has attained a new importance as world headquarters of the Air Force's Strategic Air Command.

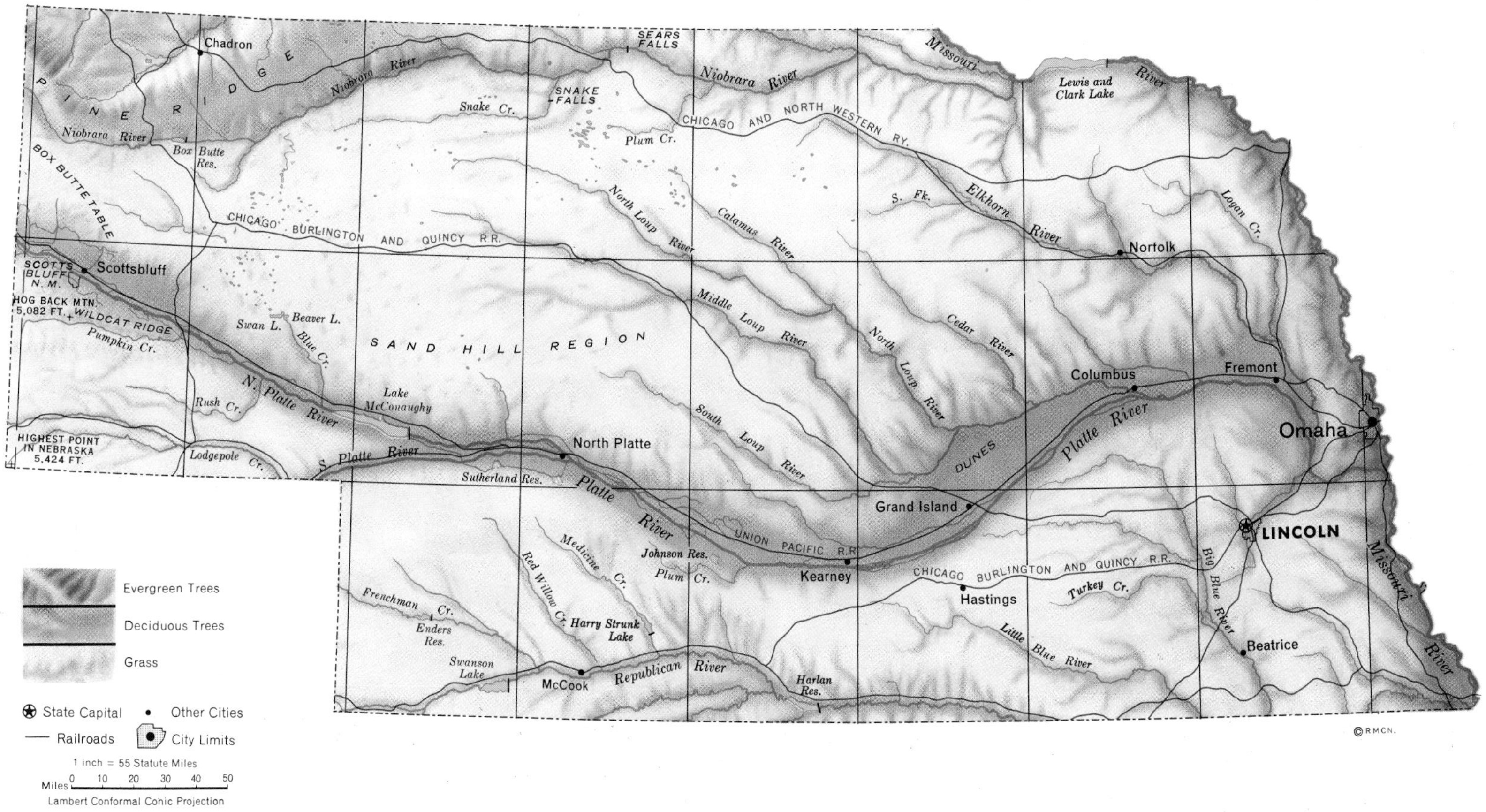
Chadron
PINE RIDGE
Niobrara River
Box Butte Res.
BOX BUTTE TABLE
Scottsbluff
SCOTTS BLUFF N. M.
HOG BACK MTN. 5,082 FT.
WILDCAT RIDGE
Pumpkin Cr.
HIGHEST POINT IN NEBRASKA 5,424 FT.
Rush Cr.
Lodgepole Cr.
CHICAGO BURLINGTON AND QUINCY R.R.
Swan L.
Beaver L.
Blue Cr.
N. Platte River
S. Platte River
Lake McConaughy
SAND HILL REGION
Snake Cr.
SNAKE FALLS
SEARS FALLS
Niobrara River
CHICAGO AND NORTH WESTERN RY.
Plum Cr.
North Loup River
Calamus River
Middle Loup River
South Loup River
North Platte
Sutherland Res.
Platte River
Medicine Cr.
Red Willow Cr.
Harry Strunk Lake
Frenchman Cr.
Enders Res.
Swanson Lake
McCook
Republican River
Harlan Res.
Johnson Res.
Plum Cr.
Kearney
UNION PACIFIC R.R.
DUNES
Grand Island
Hastings
CHICAGO BURLINGTON AND QUINCY R.R.
Turkey Cr.
Little Blue River
Big Blue River
Beatrice
LINCOLN
Missouri River
Omaha
Fremont
Columbus
Platte River
Cedar River
North Loup River
S. Fk.
Elkhorn River
Norfolk
Logan Cr.
Lewis and Clark Lake
Missouri
River
©RMCN.
Evergreen Trees
Deciduous Trees
Grass
State Capital
Other Cities
Railroads
City Limits
1 inch = 55 Statute Miles
Miles 0 10 20 30 40 50
Lambert Conformal Conic Projection

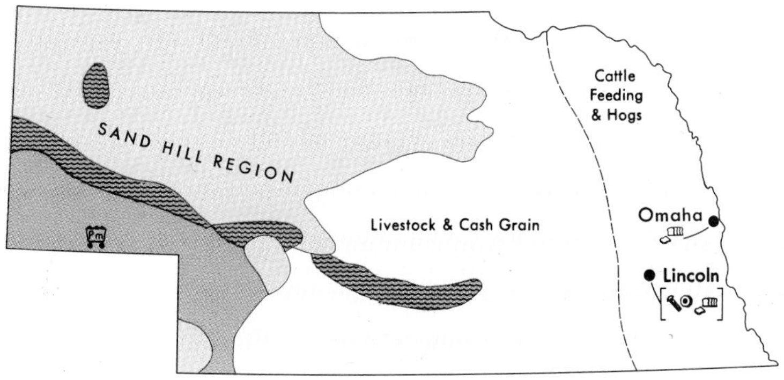
SAND HILL REGION
Livestock & Cash Grain
Cattle Feeding & Hogs
Omaha
Lincoln

THE ECONOMY

MANUFACTURING
Food Processing
Metal Products

MINING
Petroleum

AGRICULTURE
Feed Grains & Livestock
Wheat & Small Grains
Special Crops & General Farming
Seasonal Grazing
Irrigated Land

VALUE		EMPLOYED
$1,320,010,000	AGRICULTURE	31.0%
$ 536,000,000	MANUFACTURING	11.0%
$ 90,030,000	MINING	0.4%

Percentages are based on a total of 507,000 at work. In addition 30% are in commerce and transport, 14% in government, 13.6% in other areas. Manufacturing value is the value added when materials are converted into goods.

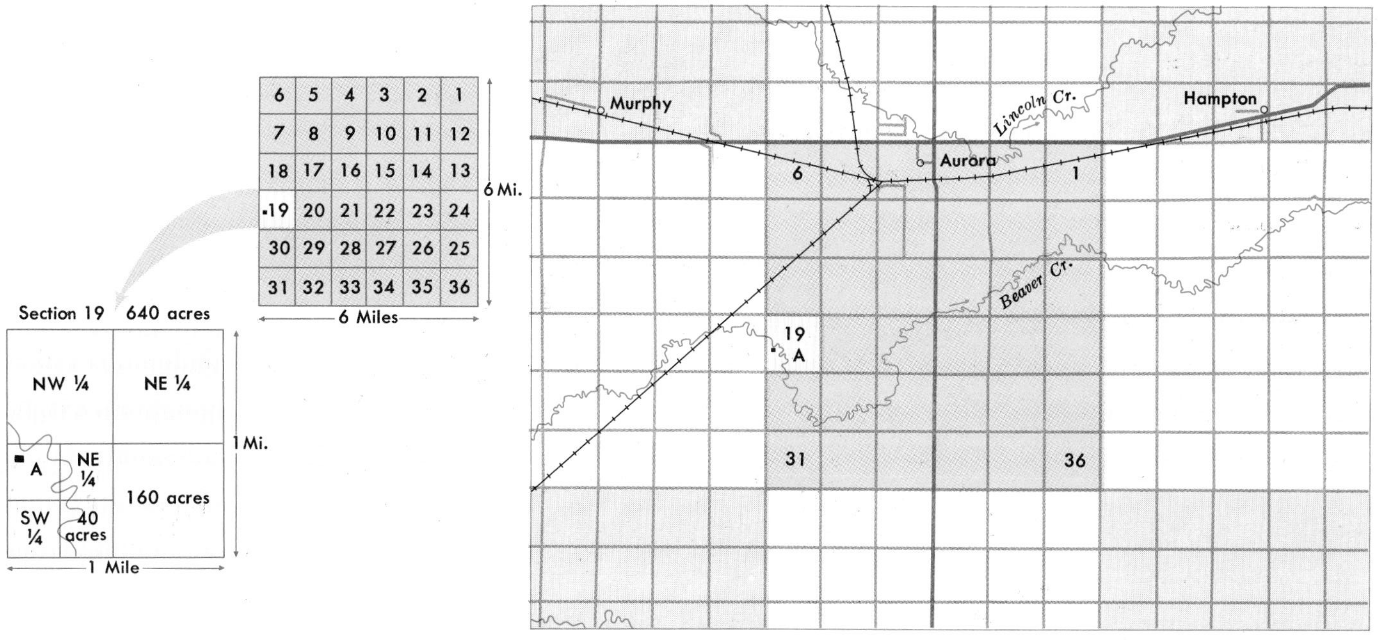
Section 19 640 acres
NW ¼
NE ¼
A
NE ¼
SW ¼
40 acres
160 acres
1 Mi.
1 Mile
6 5 4 3 2 1
7 8 9 10 11 12
18 17 16 15 14 13
19 20 21 22 23 24
30 29 28 27 26 25
31 32 33 34 35 36
6 Mi.
6 Miles
Murphy
Lincoln Cr.
Hampton
Aurora
6
1
Beaver Cr.
19
A
31
36

HOW THE WESTERN LAND WAS SQUARED AWAY

The division of Nebraska land shown here reflects the painstaking work of surveyors dispatched by the federal government in the 1800s to lay out "the Public Domain" under the Ordinance of 1785. Although boundaries within the eastern states were usually determined by the location of such natural features as rivers and mountains, more than 100 million acres west of the Appalachians were divided into geometric parcels "regardless of contour and relentless as fate." A 36-square-mile area called a "township" is shown in blue above. Section 19 of this township, in yellow at the left, is further subdivided into quarter sections of 160 acres each, and every quarter section is divided into four parcels of 40 acres each. To this day all sites in the area–such as the farmhouse labeled "A" in the northwest "forty"–are identified and located by this system, which is nearly 200 years old.

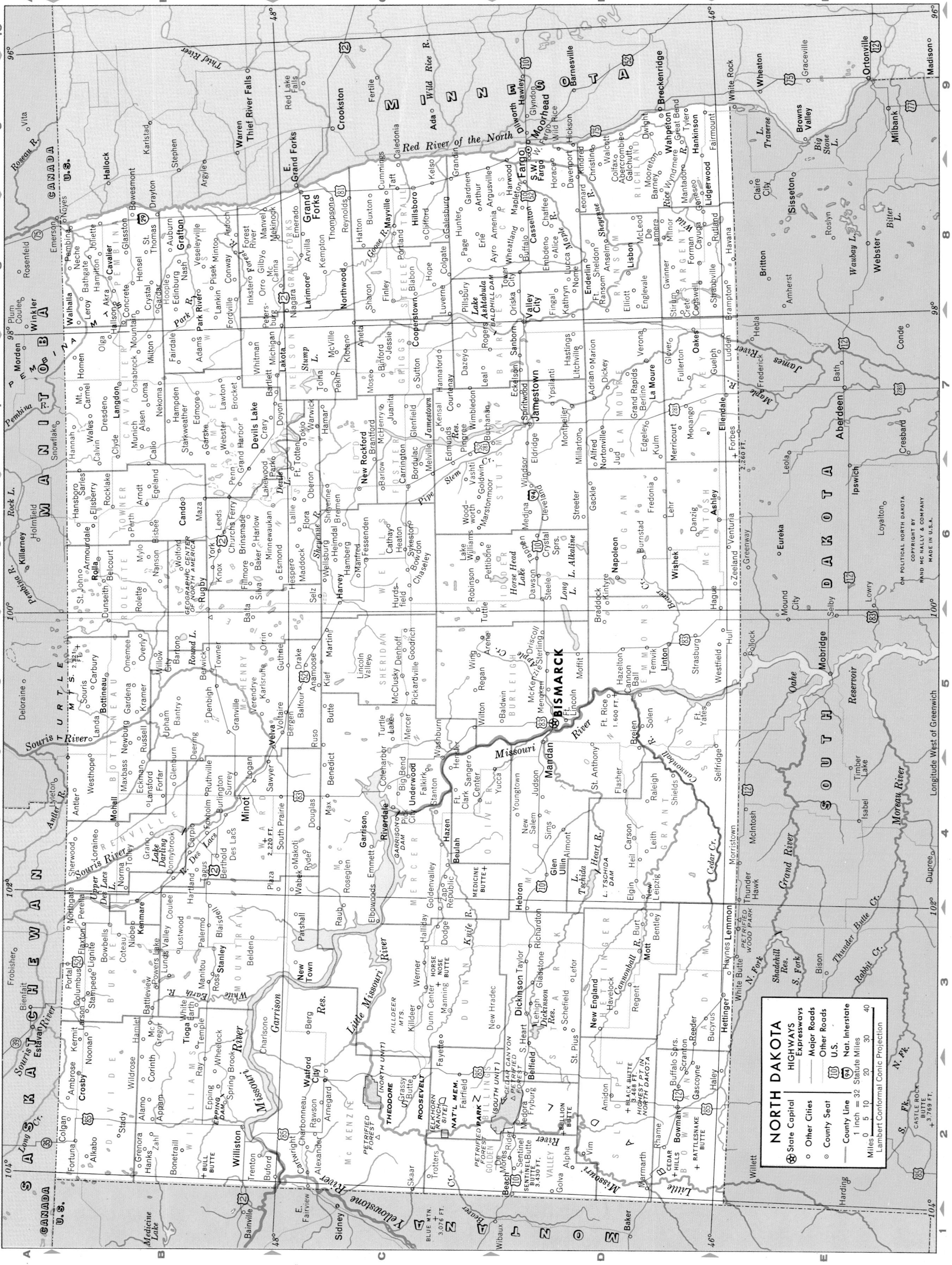
NORTH DAKOTA
State Capital
Other Cities
County Seat
County Line
HIGHWAYS
Expressways
Major Roads
Other Roads
U.S.
Nat. Interstate
1 inch = 32 Statute Miles
Miles 0 5 10 20 30 40
Lambert Conformal Conic Projection
Longitude West of Greenwich
OM POLITICAL NORTH DAKOTA
COPYRIGHT BY RAND McNALLY & COMPANY
MADE IN U.S.A.
SASKATCHEWAN
MANITOBA
CANADA
U.S.
MINNESOTA
SOUTH DAKOTA
MONTANA
BISMARCK
Fargo
Grand Forks
Minot
Jamestown
Devils Lake
Mandan
Dickinson
Williston
Valley City
Missouri River
Red River of the North
Souris River
Yellowstone River
Little Missouri River
Sheyenne R.
James River
Garrison Res.
Lake Sakakawea
Devils L.
TURTLE MTS.
KILLDEER MTS.
THEODORE ROOSEVELT NAT'L MEM. PARK

NORTH DAKOTA: The central point of North America lies in North Dakota–approximately 1,500 miles equidistant from the Atlantic, the Pacific, the Gulf of Mexico and the Arctic Archipelago. Here is a land of vivid colors and contrasting forms. The northern Red River valley, once the bed of an ancient glacial lake, is one of the most fertile agricultural regions in the nation. On the valley's rich black soil rolls a yellow ocean of spring wheat, speckled here and there with blue fields of flax, from which linseed oil is extracted. In the production of both crops, North Dakota ranks first in the nation. On the state's central drift plain, spotted with salt lakes, grain crops like barley, rye and durum wheat flourish. In the west are the Dakota badlands *(below, right)*, so called because they impeded early travelers with treacherously sandy soils and weirdly eroded sandstone buttes. But now the badlands have a symbolic value. They roof a part of the vast Williston Basin, an underground treasure house of almost untapped petroleum resources. This, said a prospector in 1952, shortly after oil was first discovered in the Basin, "is not just one oil field. It is an oil province."

AREA:	70,665 sq. mi. Rank: 17th.
POPULATION:	632,446. Rank: 44th. Largest city: Fargo. Capital: Bismarck.
ENTERED UNION:	Nov. 2, 1889, as 39th state.
CLIMATE:	Generally severe winters, short hot summers. Predominantly semi-arid and subject to droughts; moderate rainfall in the southeast.
ALTITUDES:	Black Butte, 3,468 ft. (highest); Fargo, 900 ft.

The shortage of water has always been North Dakota's major problem, for most of the state receives less than 20 inches of rainfall a year, and some areas as little as 10. Although the rich land can be extremely productive, it is so sensitive to variations in annual rainfall that the wheat harvest fluctuated dramatically between 19 million and 160 million bushels per year in the period from 1919 to 1952. The promise of North Dakota lies today in its rivers. As a participant in the vast Missouri River Basin Project, the state will eventually bring more than a million acres of marginal land under irrigation.

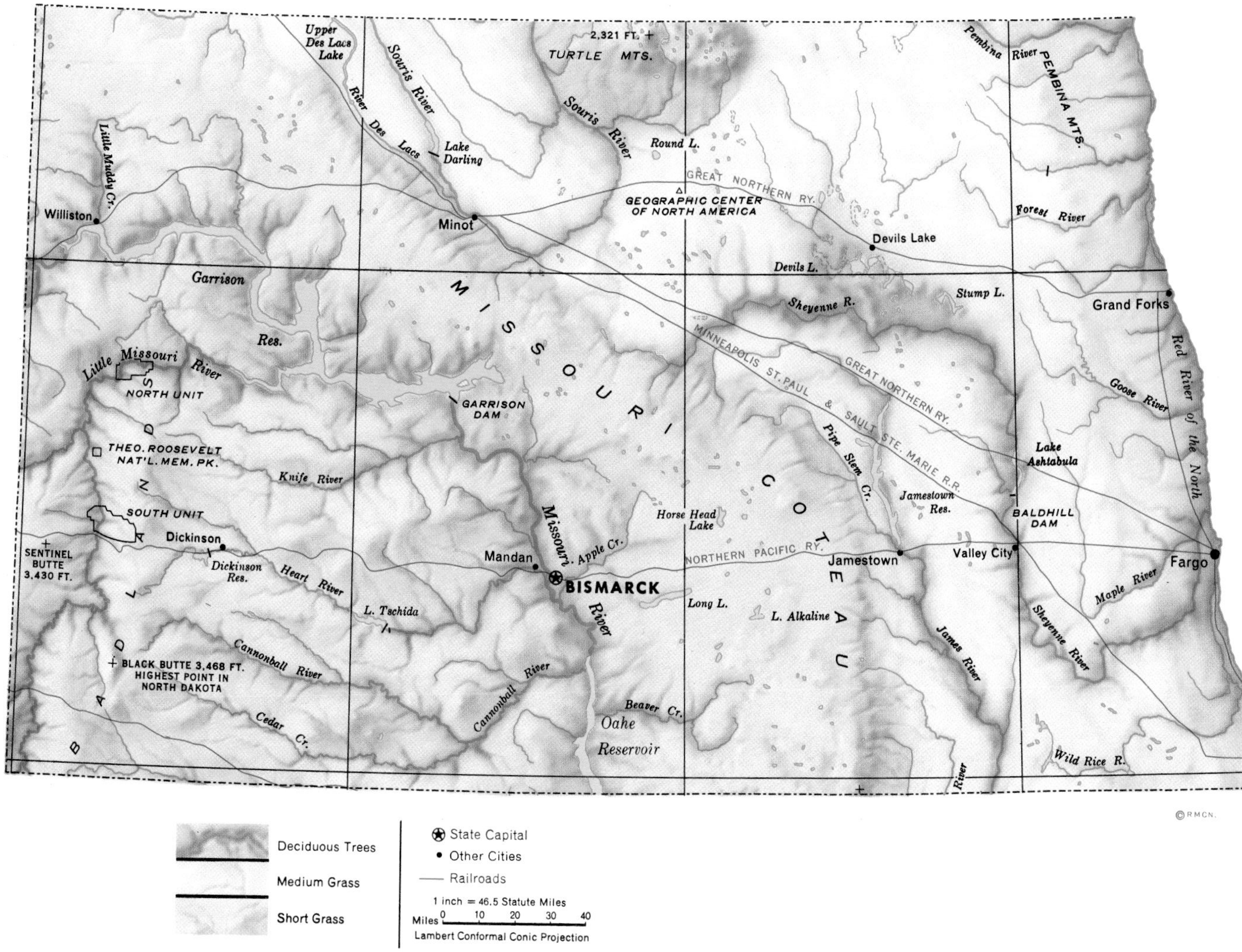

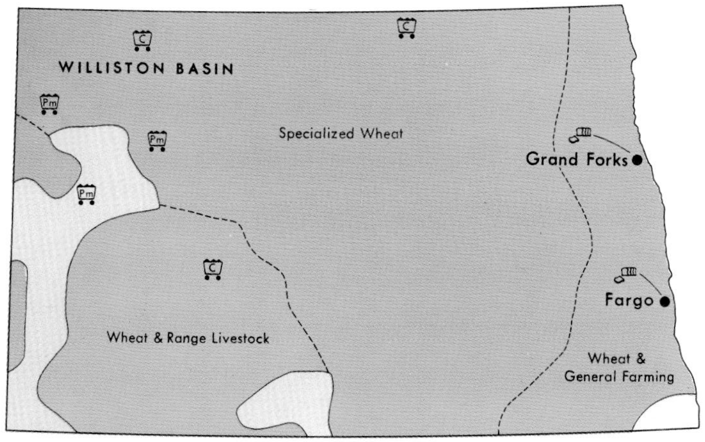

THE ECONOMY

MANUFACTURING: Food Processing

MINING: Coal; Petroleum

AGRICULTURE: Feed Grains & Livestock; Wheat & Small Grains; Seasonal Grazing

VALUE		EMPLOYED
$705,900,000	AGRICULTURE	46.0%
$ 61,000,000	MANUFACTURING	3.0%
$ 59,090,000	MINING	0.9%

Percentages are based on a total of 220,000 at work. In addition 26% are in commerce and transport, 13% in government, 11.1% in other areas. Manufacturing value is the value added when materials are converted into goods.

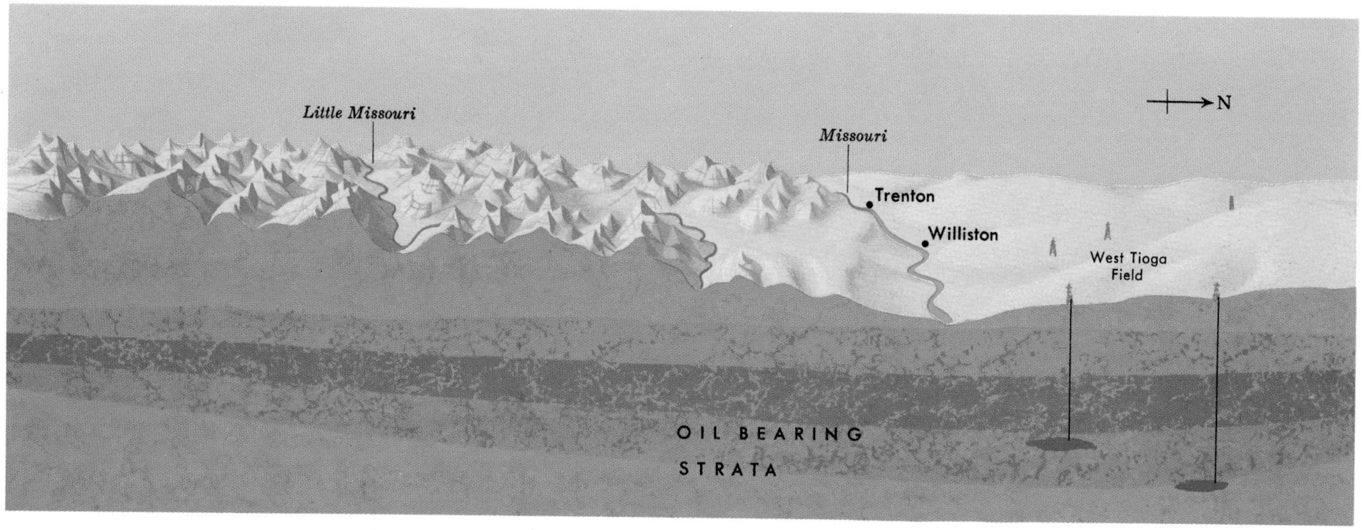

THE GOOD LAND THAT LIES BENEATH THE BADLANDS

A cross section of North Dakota's western edge, starting near the southernmost border *(left)* and running north toward Canada, reveals the grotesquely eroded region, carved by wind, rain and rivers, known today as the badlands. Deep underground, below the badlands, is a varicolored layer cake of soft shale and sandstone, which is part of the great Williston Basin. There, immense pressures over aeons transformed microscopic animal organisms and vegetable matter into pockets of oil *(right)* that form a vast field.

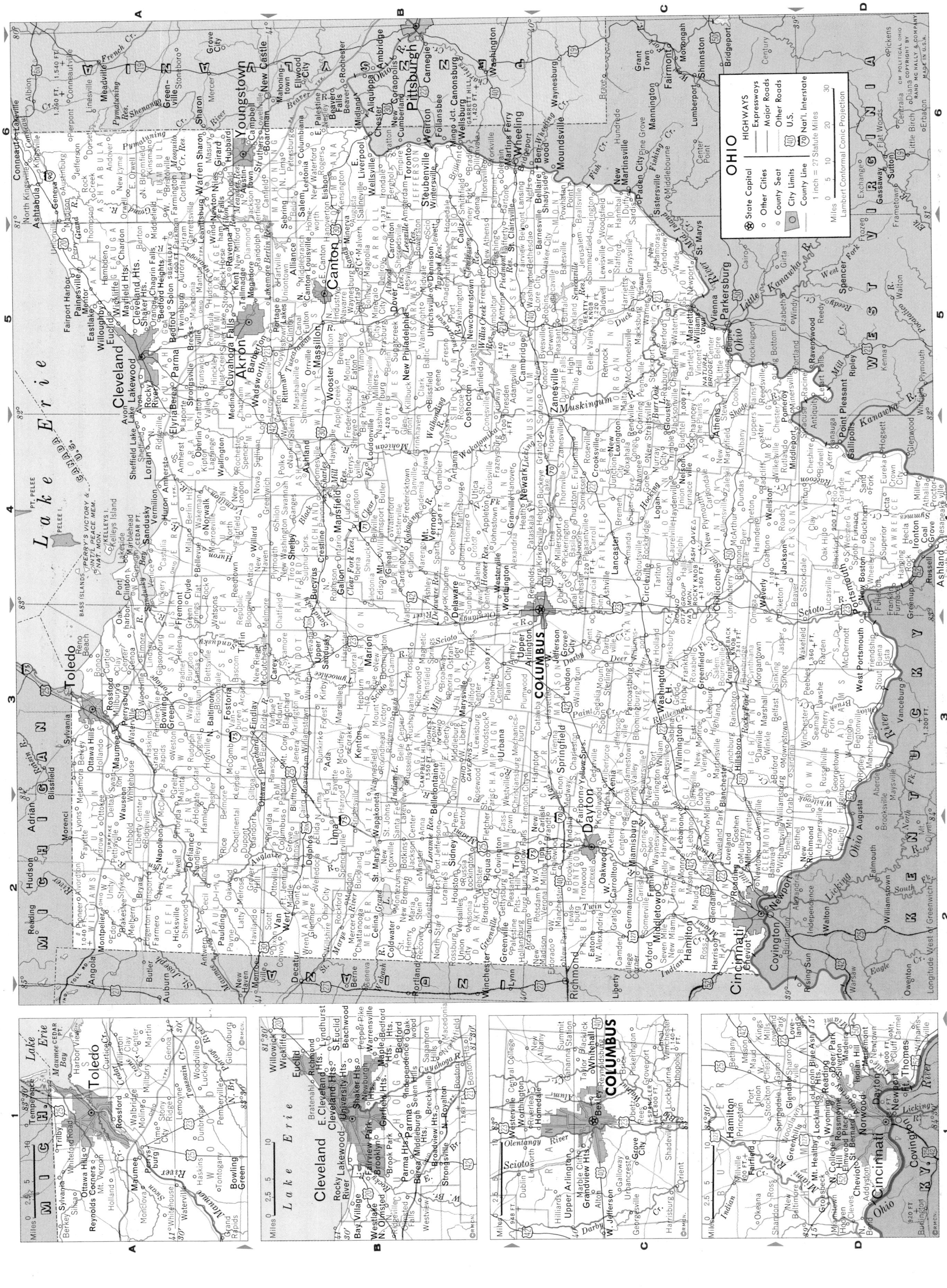

OHIO
State Capital
Other Cities
County Seat
City Limits
County Line
HIGHWAYS
Expressways
Major Roads
Other Roads
U.S.
Nat'l. Interstate
1 inch = 27 Statute Miles
Lambert Conformal Conic Projection
Lake Erie
MICHIGAN
INDIANA
KENTUCKY
WEST VIRGINIA
PENNSYLVANIA
Toledo
Cleveland
Akron
Youngstown
Canton
COLUMBUS
Dayton
Cincinnati
Pittsburgh
CM POLITICAL OHIO
COPYRIGHT BY RAND McNALLY & COMPANY
MADE IN U.S.A.

THE ECONOMY

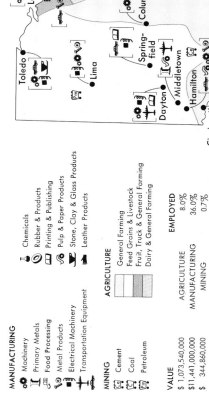

MANUFACTURING
- Machinery
- Primary Metals
- Food Processing
- Metal Products
- Electrical Machinery
- Transportation Equipment
- Chemicals
- Rubber & Products
- Printing & Publishing
- Pulp & Paper Products
- Stone, Clay & Glass Products
- Leather Products

MINING
- Cement
- Coal
- Petroleum

AGRICULTURE
- General Farming
- Feed Grains & Livestock
- Fruit, Truck & General Farming
- Dairy & General Farming

VALUE		EMPLOYED
$ 1,073,540,000	AGRICULTURE	8.0%
$11,441,000,000	MANUFACTURING	36.0%
$ 344,860,000	MINING	0.7%

Percentages are based on a total of 3,202,000 at work. In addition 29% are in commerce and transport, 11% in government, 15.3% in other areas. Manufacturing value is the value added when materials are converted into goods.

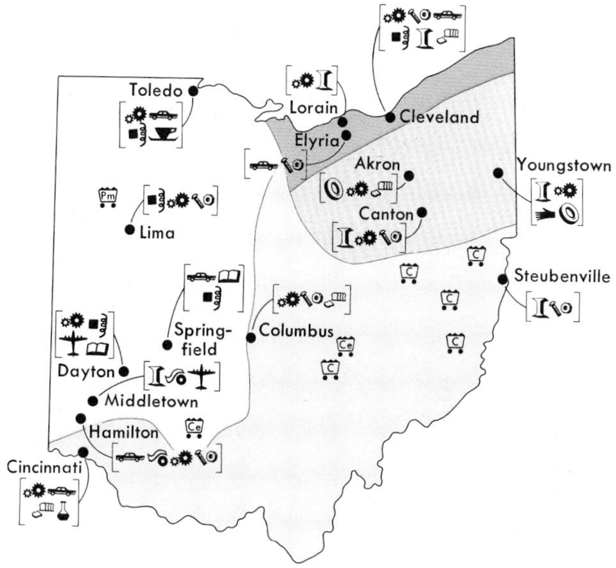

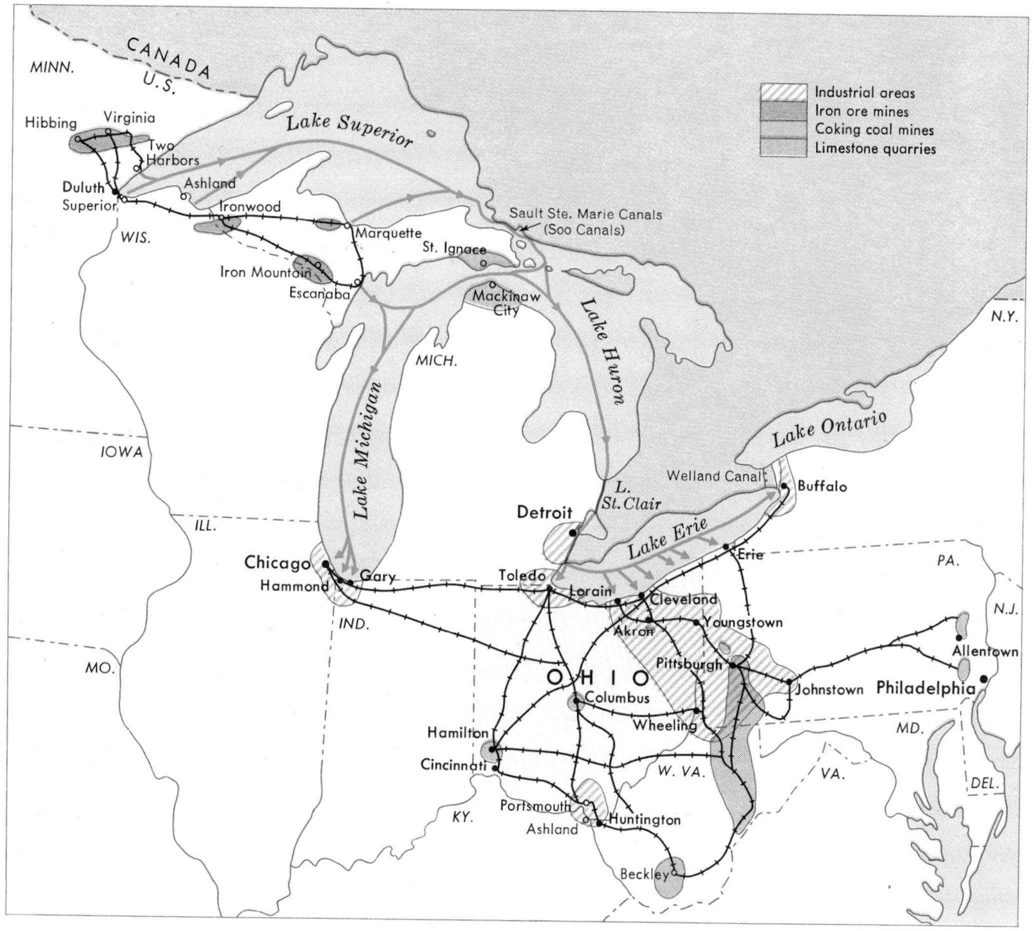

VIA LAKES AND RAILS, A MEETING OF MINERALS

The sprawling Great Lakes, forming the finest system of inland waterways in the world, give a unique unity to the economy of the Midwest. To Ohio, with its 230-mile shoreline on Lake Erie, come Great Lakes vessels, river barges and railroads, bringing together iron ore from Minnesota and Wisconsin, coal from West Virginia and Pennsylvania, and limestone from Michigan and Pennsylvania–all essential minerals in steel-making. Ohio, in turn, finds customers for its products in neighboring states, as well as throughout the nation. In this way the region generates an almost circular economy of raw materials to finished products.

OHIO: "As lovely a land as ever lay outdoors," was how a native son, author Sherwood Anderson, described his state. Ohio, whose rough easterly hills fade into the undulating western plains, matches its beauty with prosperity. It is a truism that Ohio makes everything from shoelace tips to blast furnaces, from machine tools and playing cards to Liederkranz (the world's only source is the western dairy town of Van Wert). And it was in a Dayton bicycle shop that Wilbur and Orville Wright designed the first airplane, fulfilling man's ancient dream of flight.

AREA: 41,222 sq. mi. Rank: 35th.
POPULATION: 9,706,397. Rank: 5th. Largest city: Cleveland. Capital: Columbus.
ENTERED UNION: March 1, 1803, as 17th state.
CLIMATE: Abundant rainfall. High but not oppressive summer temperatures; cool to cold winters.
ALTITUDES: Campbell Hill, 1,550 ft. (highest); Columbus, 780 ft.

Part of the bed of an ancient inland sea rose to form the Allegheny Plateau, which embraces eastern Ohio. This sea left the state rich in both fertile farmland and underground minerals. To this day intensively worked mines, mainly in the east, yield $130 million worth of soft coal a year. The glaciers which once moved across northern Ohio gave birth to Lake Erie and channeled many of the state's streams southward into the broad Ohio River. That great waterway, which curves first south, then west around the state, early made Ohio a key east-west corridor across the U.S. Located between the iron ore deposits to the northwest and the coal mines of the Alleghenies *(map, left)*, Ohio began its career as a great steelmaker in the 1890s. Today more coal is loaded in Toledo than in any other Great Lakes port, and the flare of blast furnaces lights the night sky above the mills of Youngstown and Cleveland. But around the great manufacturing centers which dominate the state, there still lie thousands of family-size farms. Their corn, dairy foods, hogs, cattle and other products give Ohio an agricultural income of more than one billion dollars a year.

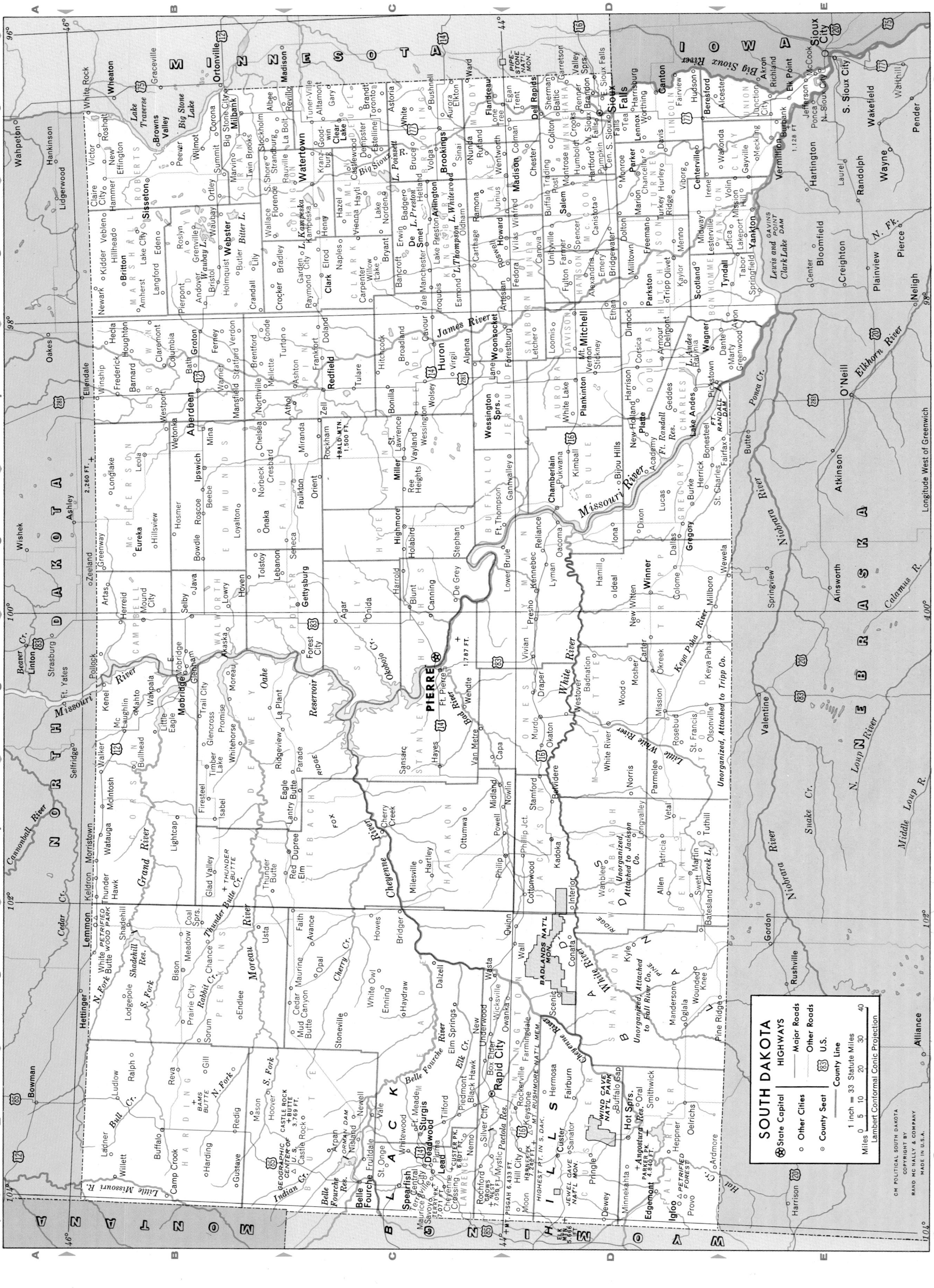
SOUTH DAKOTA
State Capital
Other Cities
County Seat
HIGHWAYS
Major Roads
Other Roads
U.S.
County Line
1 inch = 33 Statute Miles
Lambert Conformal Conic Projection
Longitude West of Greenwich
NORTH DAKOTA
MINNESOTA
IOWA
NEBRASKA
WYOMING
MONTANA
PIERRE
CM POLITICAL SOUTH DAKOTA
COPYRIGHT BY RAND MC NALLY & COMPANY
MADE IN U.S.A.

SOUTH DAKOTA: Divided by the mighty Missouri, the state of South Dakota contains four of the six major dams which will eventually control the river's relentless flow, providing massive flood protection in the vast valley basin and simultaneously distributing cheap power and water for irrigation. To the west of the Missouri, South Dakota is a land of short grass where herds of cattle thrive, while to the east stretches an expanse of fertile plains where oats, corn and spring wheat flourish. More than 90 per cent of South Dakota is farmland, and the state's prosperous farms earn an average of $12,000 a year, compared to an average of $8,000 throughout the rest of the country.

AREA:	77,047 sq. mi. Rank: 16th.
POPULATION:	680,514. Rank: 40th.
	Largest city: Sioux Falls.
	Capital: Pierre.
ENTERED UNION:	Nov. 2, 1889, as 40th state.
CLIMATE:	Hot summers, cold winters.
	Adequate rainfall during growing season; winter blizzards.
ALTITUDES:	Harney Peak, 7,242 ft. (highest);
	Pierre, 1,440 ft.

Mining is important to South Dakota. The mile-high city of Lead lies within "the richest 100 square miles on earth," an area dominated by the Homestake gold mine, the country's largest producer. First worked in 1876, Homestake veins still yield $20 million worth of gold a year. But most visitors to South Dakota know the state for the desolate pine-clad Black Hills rising from the western plains *(diagram, below right)*. In these hills, visited by one million tourists a year, stands 6,000-foot Mount Rushmore, on whose smooth granite walls a team of sculptors, led by Gutzon Borglum, labored for 14 years to blast and drill the faces of four U.S. Presidents–Washington, Jefferson, Lincoln and Theodore Roosevelt–each face measuring some 60 feet from chin to forehead.

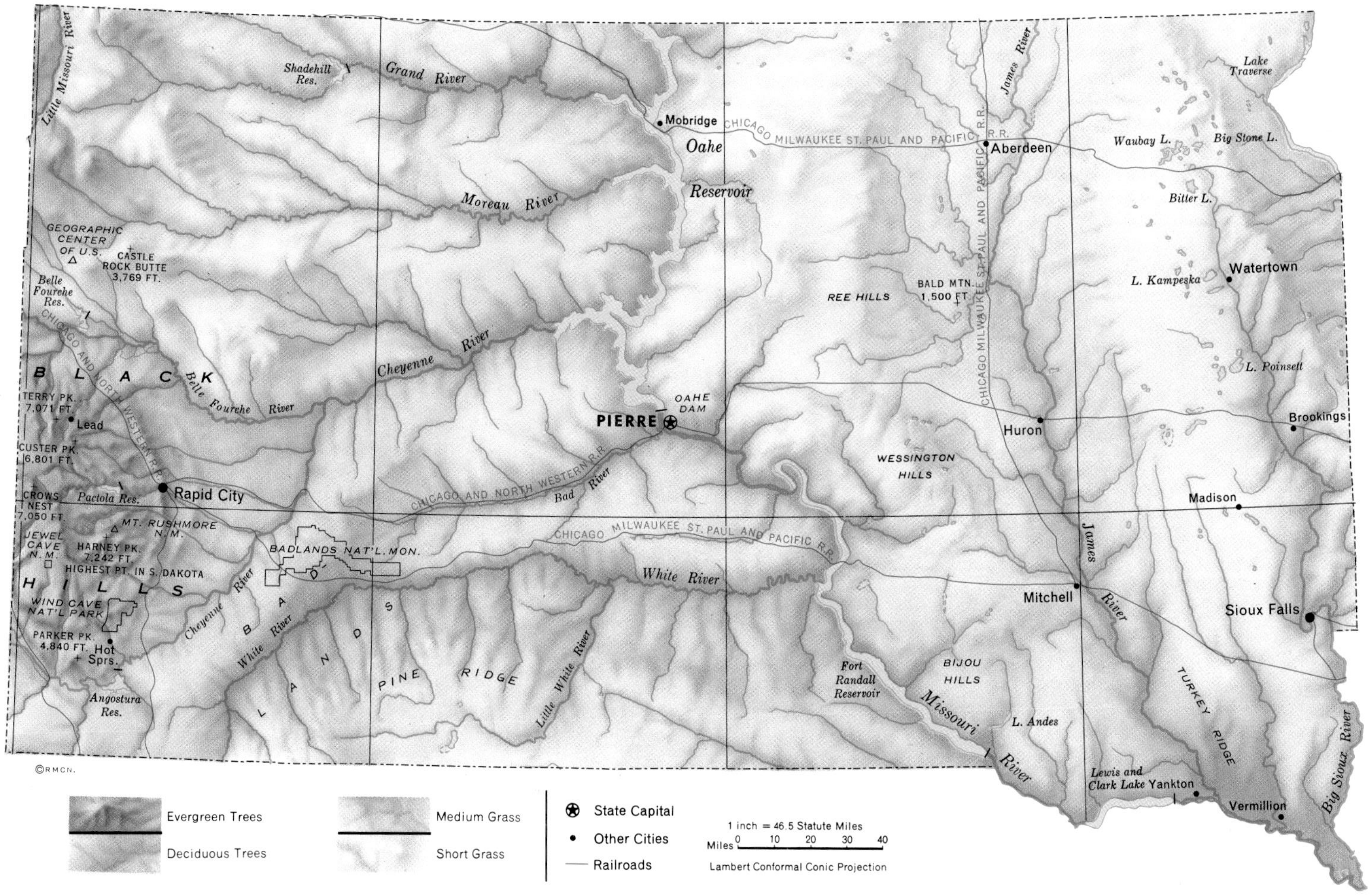

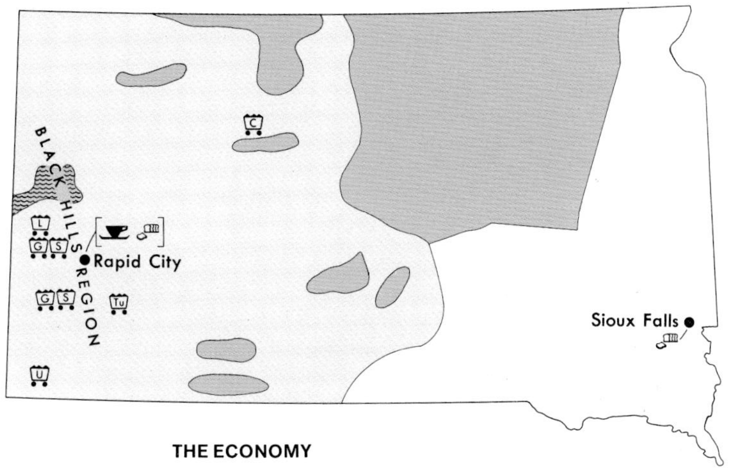

THE ECONOMY

MANUFACTURING
- Food Processing
- Stone, Clay & Glass Products

MINING
- Coal
- Gold
- Lead
- Silver
- Tungsten
- Uranium

AGRICULTURE
- Feed Grains & Livestock
- Wheat & Small Grains
- Special Crops & General Farming
- Seasonal Grazing
- Irrigated Land

VALUE		EMPLOYED
$729,550,000	AGRICULTURE	43%
$115,000,000	MANUFACTURING	5%
$ 41,530,000	MINING	1%

Percentages are based on a total of 229,000 at work. In addition 24% are in commerce and transport, 15% in government, 12% in other areas. Manufacturing value is the value added when materials are converted into goods.

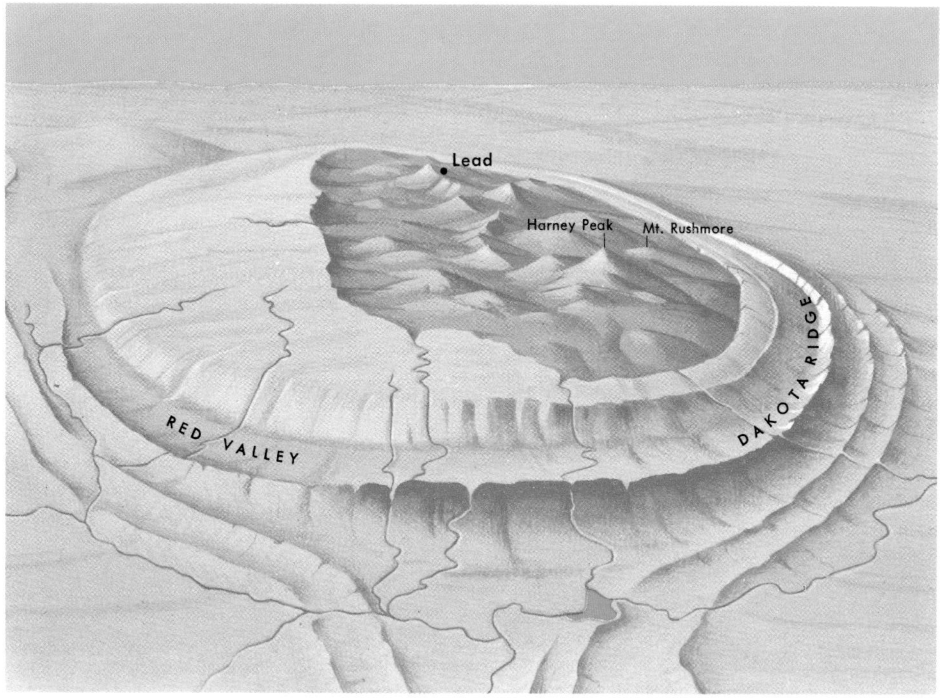

A DARKENED DOME ABOVE THE PLAIN

South Dakota's pine-clad Black Hills, shown at left in a three-dimensional view of their full extent, actually are a formidable mountain group. Towering 7,242-foot Harney Peak is the highest mountain east of the Rockies. Springing up suddenly from the plain, the Black Hills illustrate one of the ways mountains are formed: as a result of "domal uplift." This process simply creates a tremendous bulge of the earth's crust, heaved up by underground forces. Like a bride's first biscuits, the Black Hills dome started out with a smooth, elliptical shape. But with the passage of time, it got battered by the elements. High winds, heat, frost, rain and melting snow eroded part of the dome, carving soft limestone away from harder granite and leaving the roughly hewn shapes of individual mountains. Formations like these are often rich in minerals, and this one is especially famous for gold deposits, including the fabulous Homestake Mine at the town of Lead. Streams coursing down what is left of the dome have cut a wide circular swath, the Red Valley, which is aptly nicknamed the Race Track. Here, railroads and highways were easy to build and such towns as Rapid City, Spearfish and Sturgis were founded along the convenient, natural lines of transportation. Finally, forming a low railing along the valley at the dome's outer rim is Dakota Ridge. With its top and sides eroded unevenly–its height above the plain varies from 400 to 500 feet–this kind of bristling ridge is generally known as a "hogback."

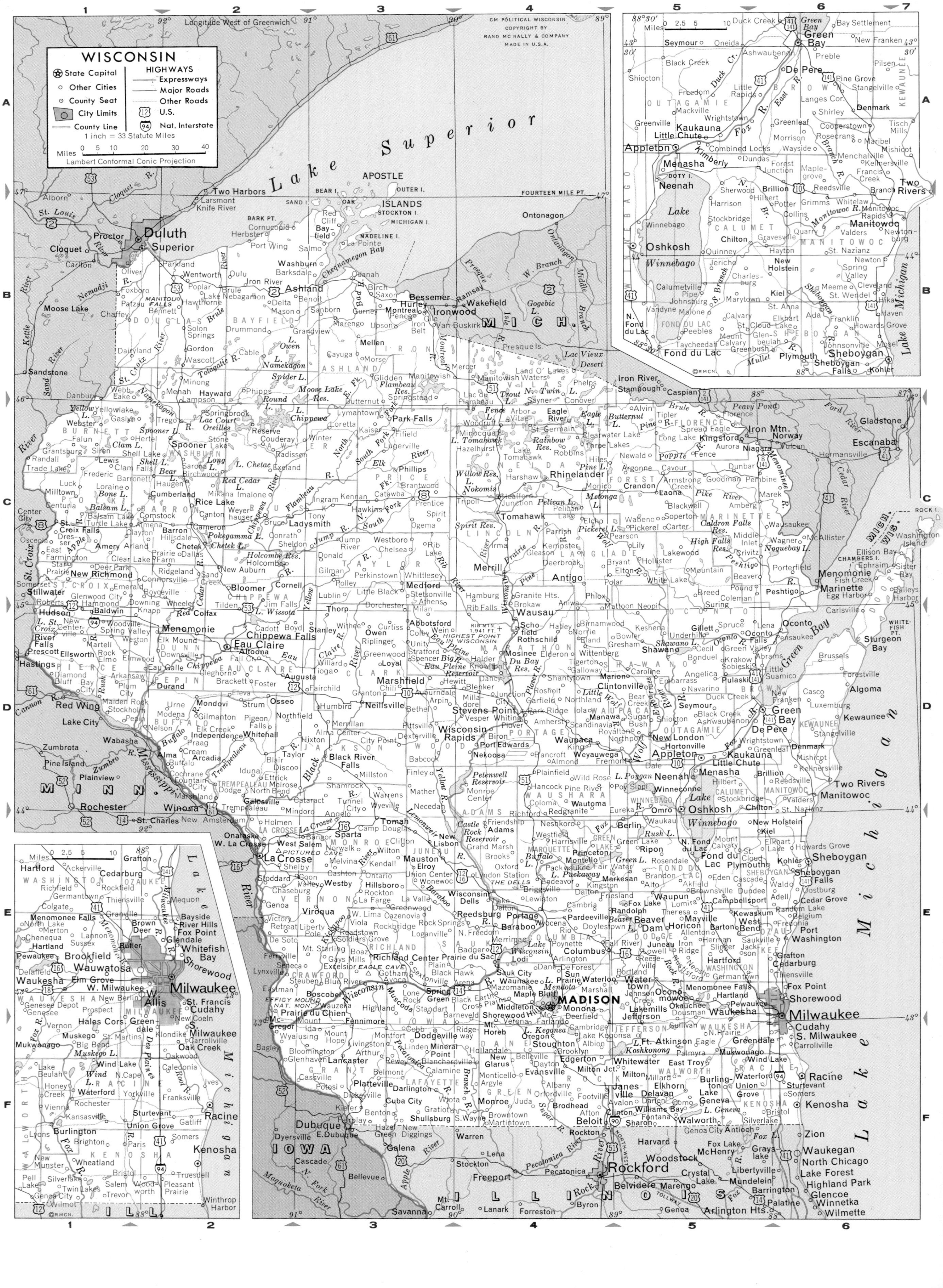
WISCONSIN
State Capital
Other Cities
County Seat
City Limits
County Line
HIGHWAYS
Expressways
Major Roads
Other Roads
U.S.
Nat. Interstate
1 inch = 33 Statute Miles
Miles 0 5 10 20 30 40
Lambert Conformal Conic Projection
Longitude West of Greenwich
CM POLITICAL WISCONSIN
COPYRIGHT BY
RAND MC NALLY & COMPANY
MADE IN U.S.A.
Lake Superior
APOSTLE ISLANDS
Lake Michigan
Green Bay
MICH.
MINN.
IOWA
ILLINOIS
Duluth
Superior
Ashland
Ironwood
Rhinelander
Wausau
Eau Claire
Chippewa Falls
La Crosse
Green Bay
Appleton
Oshkosh
Sheboygan
Manitowoc
MADISON
Milwaukee
Racine
Kenosha
Rockford
Dubuque
Rochester
Winona
Marinette
Menominee
Escanaba
Two Rivers
Fond du Lac
Janesville
Beloit
Waukegan

WISCONSIN

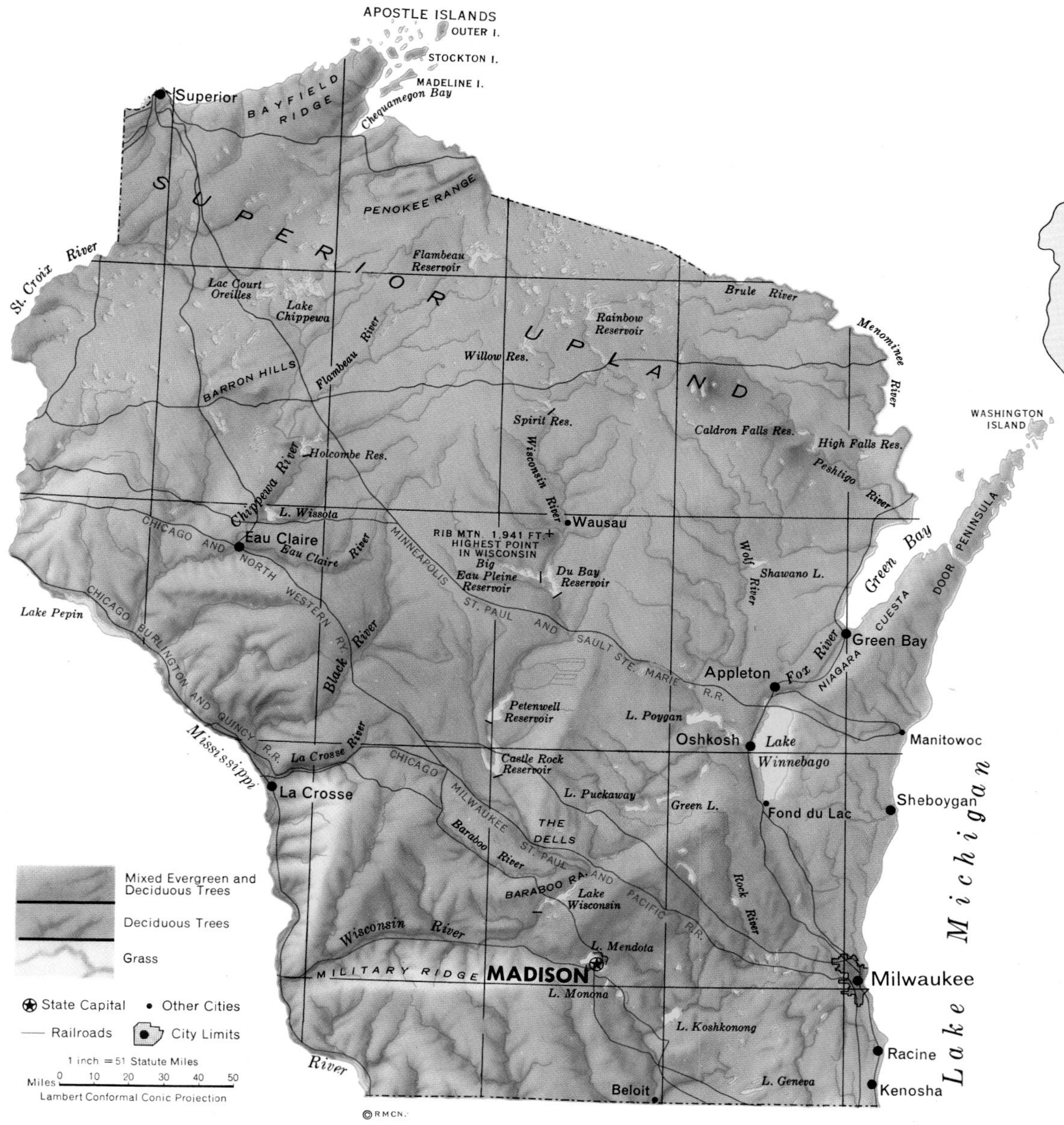

VALUE		EMPLOYED
$1,196,580,000	AGRICULTURE	22.0%
$3,997,000,000	MANUFACTURING	30.0%
$ 71,330,000	MINING	0.2%

Percentages are based on a total of 1,429,000 at work. In addition 26% are in commerce and transport, 10% in government, 11.8% in other areas. Manufacturing value is the value added when materials are converted into goods.

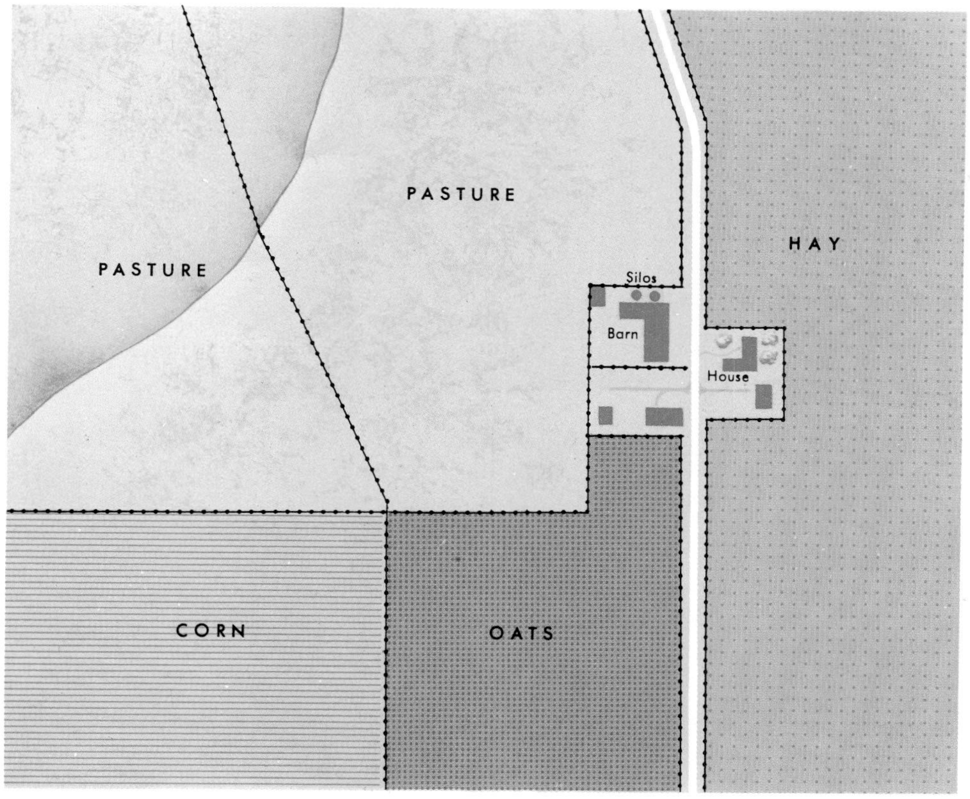

THE CARE AND FEEDING OF COWS

Pasture land for milk cows dominates the layout of a representative Wisconsin dairy farm, as shown in the drawing above. To provide year-round green fodder for the stock, farmers also plant their relatively small holdings – 147 acres is the average – with such crops as field corn, oats and alfalfa hay. Although some of the corn and oats are raised to maturity, most crops are chopped to bits while still green and blown into silos, familiar hallmarks of all dairy farms.

WISCONSIN: Wholly agricultural when it joined the Union in 1848, Wisconsin to this day appears predominantly rural. On the uplands of the interior and on the ridges and low hills of the east, the tillable soil left by the glacial ice sheet, combined with an annual rainfall of 30 to 35 inches and a growing season of 120 to 180 days, makes this region the dairy capital of the nation. Each year its farms *(diagram, left)* produce two billion gallons of milk, 14 per cent of the country's total output. Most of this is shipped to distant markets in the form of butter and cheese. (Wisconsin cheese accounts for nearly half of the U.S.'s total production.) The state is also a major grower of hay and corn, peas, beets and cranberries. Yet, like much of the Midwest, Wisconsin offsets the man on the land with the man in the city. For, despite agriculture's importance, less than one fifth of the people live on farms. Most of the population is concentrated in the southeast, whose rail lines, rivers and Great Lakes ports like Milwaukee help to make Wisconsin the nation's 11th most important industrial state. Milwaukee itself is a major manufacturer of heavy machinery and beer, Oshkosh of leather goods, Green Bay of paper, Kenosha of automobiles.

AREA:	56,154 sq. mi. Rank: 26th.
POPULATION:	3,951,777. Rank: 15th.
	Largest city: Milwaukee. Capital: Madison.
ENTERED UNION:	May 29, 1848, as 30th state.
CLIMATE:	Warm summers, cold winters, both marked by extremes of temperature. Moderate rainfall.
ALTITUDES:	Rib Mountain, 1,941 ft. (highest); Madison, 860 ft.

Of the states west of the Alleghenies, Wisconsin was among the first to be populated largely by immigrants who came directly from continental Europe after the political upheavals of 1848. Today many of the state's communities retain a distinctive European flavor. Swiss-Americans dominate the cheese-making town of New Glarus, near Madison. German-Americans brought their brewing skills to their new home in Milwaukee. Russians live around Lake Winnebago, while Icelanders have clustered on Washington Island. In addition there are groups of Poles, Norwegians and Austrians scattered about the state. "We are not a melting pot but a beef stew," John Rector Barton, the University of Wisconsin sociologist, has observed. "We were all thrown together in the same pot, but the beef remained the same and the carrots the same and the peas the same."

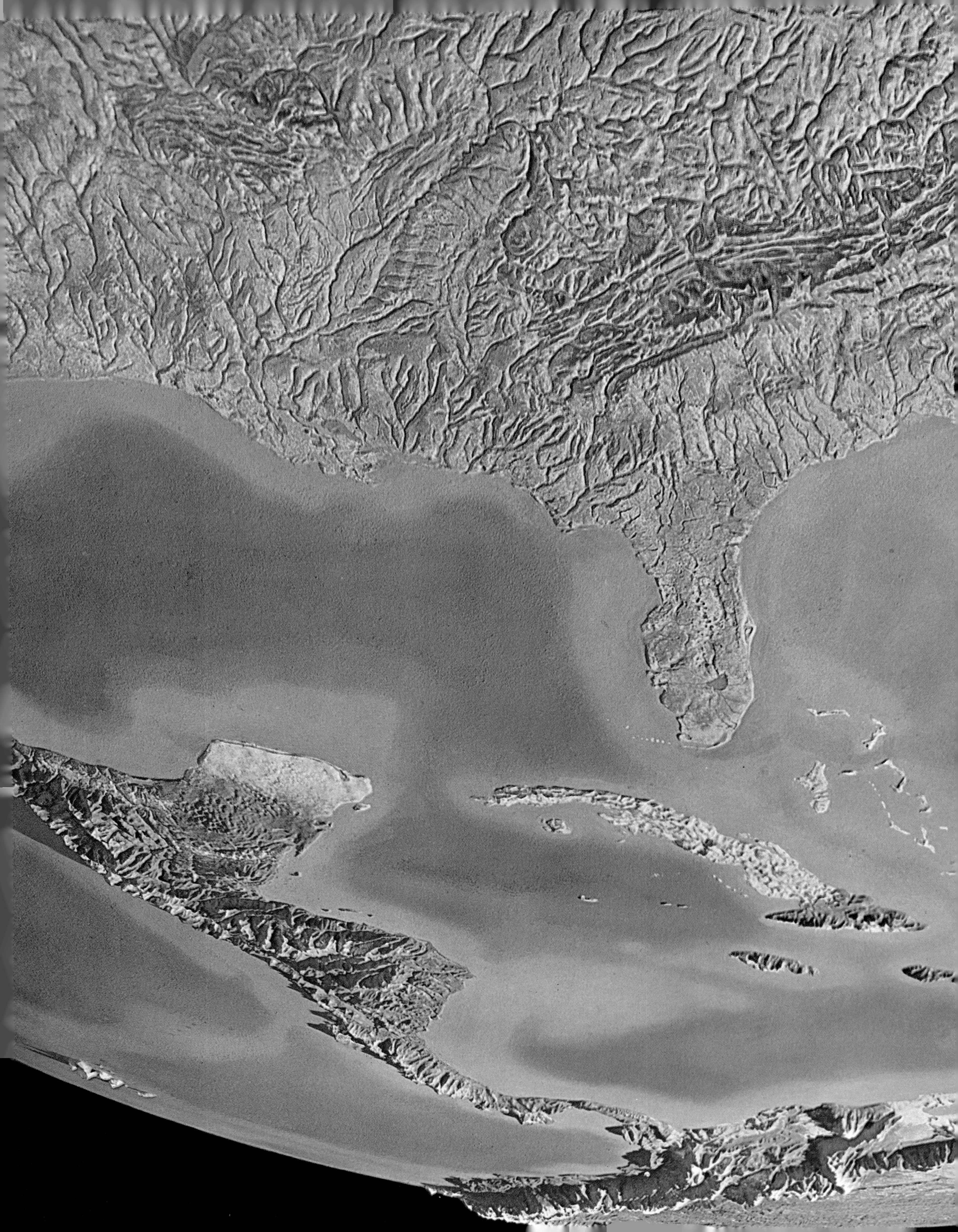

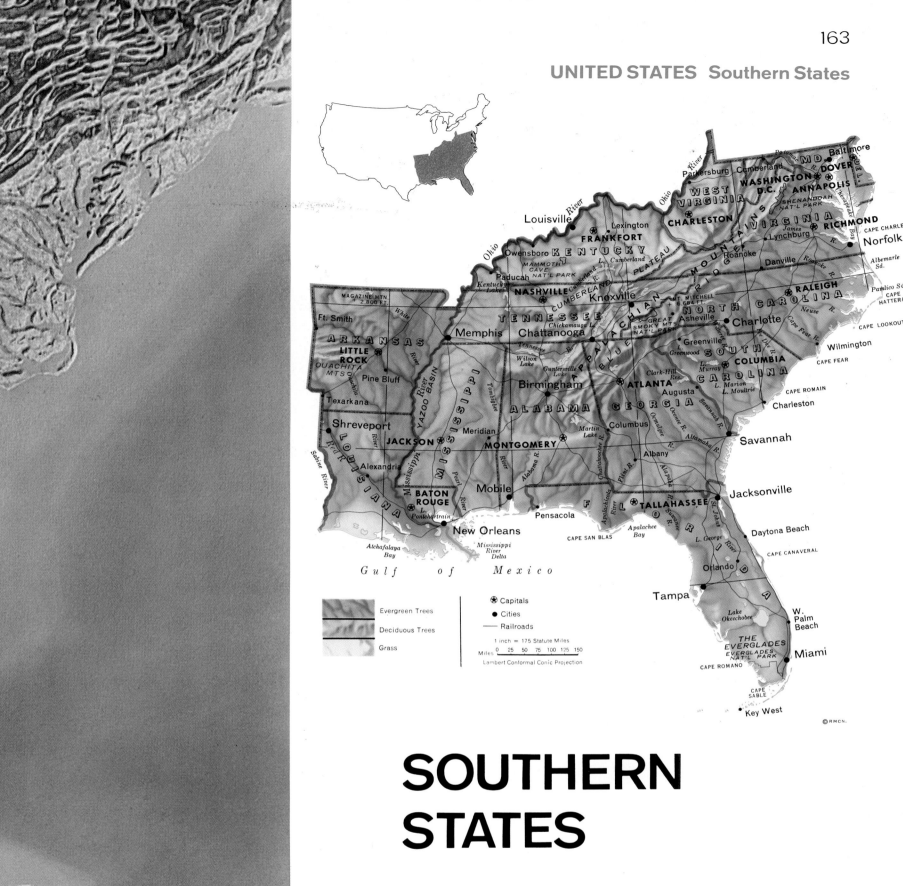

SOUTHERN STATES

More than three centuries ago, when Captain John Smith returned to England from the Virginia wilderness, he gave a remarkably prescient account of the land he had explored. "Wee . . . doubt not," he said, "but by Gods gracious assistance . . . to enjoy a Country, not onely exceeding pleasant for habitation, but also very profitable for comerce in generall." The land the Europeans found is today the warm and fertile American South.

To exploit this promising realm, white men were to enslave black, and in time the whole of the region came to echo the Indian word *kentucky*–"the dark and bloody ground." Here, in the South, the Union was struck a near-mortal blow–but here too it was forged. Today the South is no longer a land of cotton and kerchiefs. A variety of crops still flourish. But "comerce in generall" grows in importance. Its booming economy tied firmly to that of the whole nation, the South is helping the U.S. to fulfill yet another prophecy. "All the past we leave behind," said the poet Walt Whitman as he saw beyond the bitter sectionalism that erupted into Civil War. "We debouch upon a new and mightier world. . . ."

THE PENINSULA OF FLORIDA *(left)* points dramatically southward toward the Caribbean islands and the north coast of South America. The long line of the Appalachians, at top center, stretches from the Gulf coastal plain into the Northeast states, at upper right.

A BARRIER RANGE AND A RESTLESS RIVER

THE GREAT SMOKIES, their slopes reddened by the sinking sun, roll on the western border of North Carolina. A part of the Appalachians, which long held back the westward march, the Smokies still contain remote communities that seem to live in an earlier time.

THE SILT-LADEN MISSISSIPPI floods low-lying farmland near the city of Memphis. More than 30 years of planning by the U.S. Army Engineers have helped bring the restless river under partial control, but spring floods can still provoke emergency calls for sandbags.

IN GHOSTLY STRUCTURES, A CALDRON FOR NATURE'S FUELS

A LOUISIANA OIL REFINERY glows in the dusk, its lonely structures standing as symbols of the automation which permits the vast plant to be run by a handful of technicians. From its distillation columns *(left background)* and cat-crackers *(right)* to its storage spheres and drums *(foreground)*, this Lake Charles refinery typifies an industry which was one of the first to invest in automated equipment. Its raw material, petroleum, lends itself readily to processing by the complicated and costly paraphernalia of 20th Century technology.

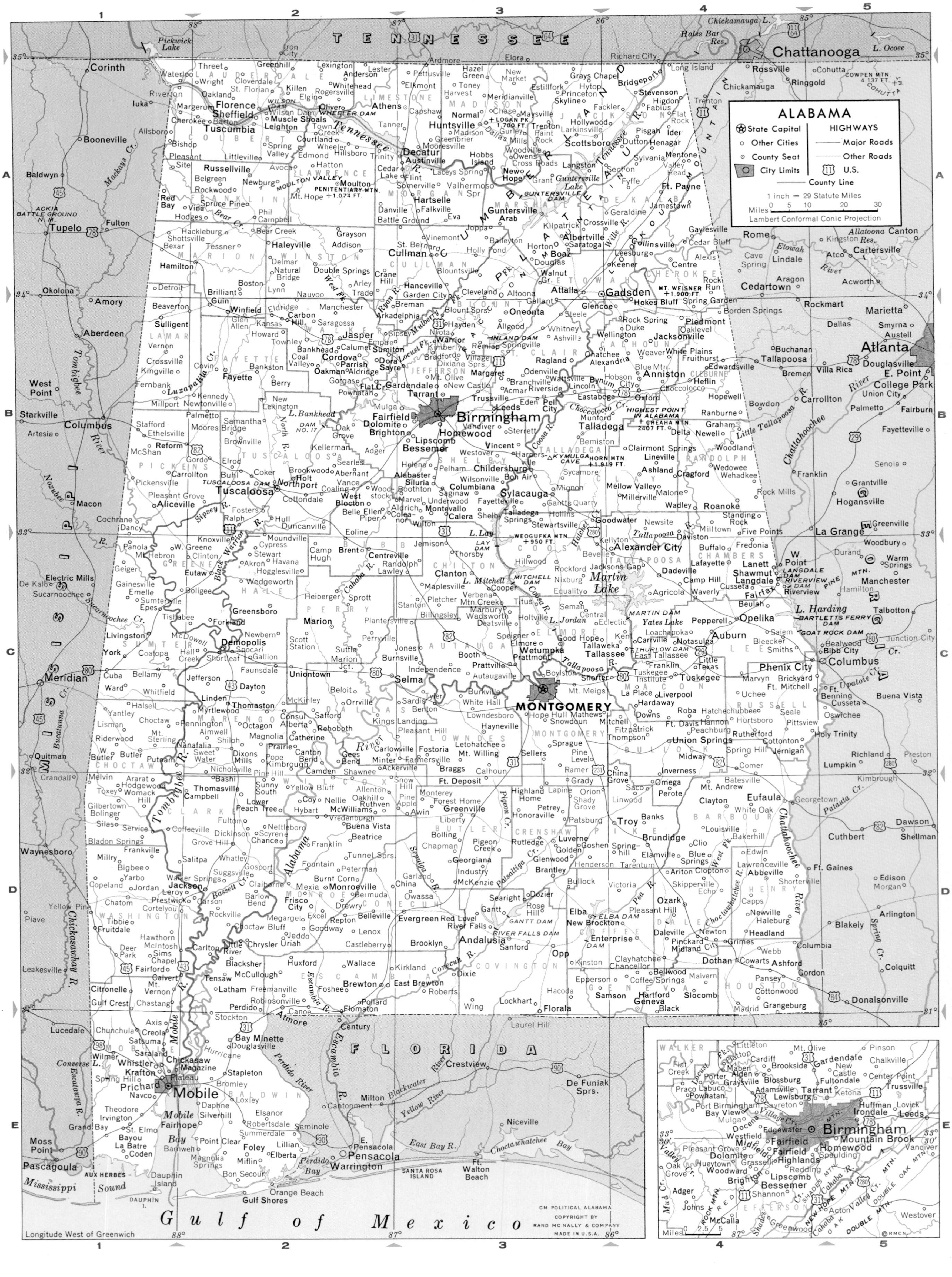
ALABAMA
State Capital
Other Cities
County Seat
City Limits
HIGHWAYS
Major Roads
Other Roads
U.S.
County Line
1 inch = 29 Statute Miles
Miles 0 5 10 20 30
Lambert Conformal Conic Projection
TENNESSEE
MISSISSIPPI
GEORGIA
FLORIDA
Gulf of Mexico
Birmingham
MONTGOMERY
Mobile
Huntsville
Tuscaloosa
Gadsden
Anniston
Decatur
Florence
Sheffield
Tuscumbia
Dothan
Selma
Opelika
Auburn
Phenix City
Columbus
Chattanooga
Atlanta
Meridian
Tupelo
Pensacola
Tennessee R.
Tombigbee R.
Alabama River
Coosa R.
Tallapoosa R.
Chattahoochee River
Black Warrior R.
Conecuh R.
Martin Lake
L. Harding
Guntersville Lake
Mississippi Sound
Mobile Bay
Longitude West of Greenwich
CM POLITICAL ALABAMA
COPYRIGHT BY RAND McNALLY & COMPANY
MADE IN U.S.A.
Birmingham
Fairfield
Bessemer
Homewood
Mountain Brook
Irondale
Leeds
Tarrant
Trussville

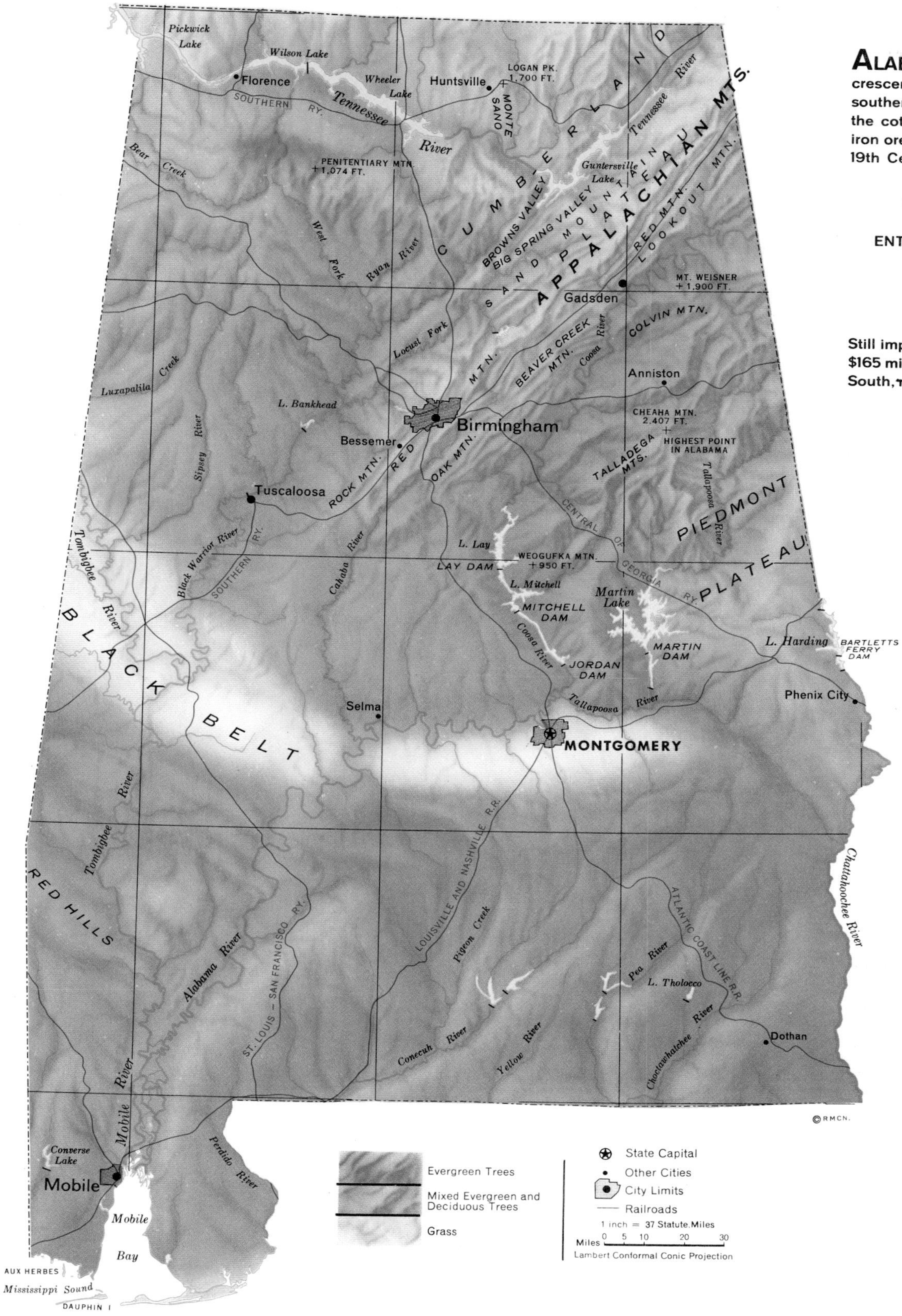

ALABAMA: Despite the once-fertile "Black Belt" of soil that forms a crescent shape across its middle, Alabama was one of the first of the southern states to develop industry. As erosion and the boll weevil ruined the cotton crops, Alabamans turned to the rich deposits of coal and iron ore in the rugged northern section of the state. By the end of the 19th Century, an industrial center had developed around Birmingham.

AREA:	51,609 sq. mi. Rank: 29th.
POPULATION:	3,266,740. Rank: 19th. Largest city: Birmingham. Capital: Montgomery.
ENTERED UNION:	Dec. 14, 1819, as 22nd state.
CLIMATE:	Humid, with long hot summers, short mild winters. Long growing season, heavy rainfall.
ALTITUDES:	Cheaha Mountain, 2,407 ft. (highest).

Still important in agriculture – its scientifically farmed cotton crop yields $165 million a year – Alabama ranks high as an industrial leader in the new South, making steel, textiles, chemicals and transportation equipment.

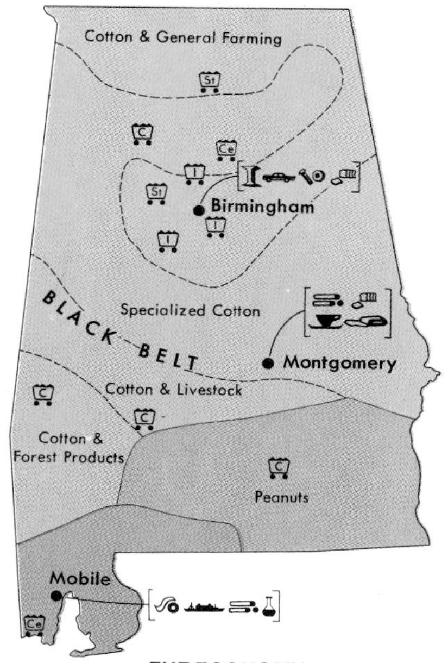

THE ECONOMY

MANUFACTURING
- Primary Metals
- Textiles
- Food Processing
- Lumber & Forest Products
- Chemicals
- Pulp & Paper Products
- Transportation Equipment
- Metal Products
- Stone, Clay & Glass Products

MINING
- Cement
- Coal
- Iron Ore
- Stone

AGRICULTURE
- Cotton
- Special Crops & General Farming
- Fruit, Truck, & General Farming

VALUE		EMPLOYED
$ 598,670,000	AGRICULTURE	18%
$1,751,000,000	MANUFACTURING	26%
$ 187,750,000	MINING	2%

Percentages are based on a total of 881,000 at work. In addition 26% are in commerce and transport, 16% in government, 12% in other areas. Manufacturing value is the value added when materials are converted into goods.

A GOOD STEEL LOCATION

The cross section at right is of the Appalachian foothills outside Birmingham. It shows the unusual combination of raw materials for steel that lies in close proximity to "the Pittsburgh of the South." Coal from the Warrior Basin *(left)* fires the Birmingham blast furnaces, which extract iron from the low-grade ore of Red Mountain *(far right)*. Also available nearby is the mineral dolomite *(center)*, used as a purifying agent in the refining process to remove foreign particles. The extracted iron is sent to neighboring steel mills for processing into finished plates, sheets and bars. By-products of the refining process include chemical fertilizers and slag for road building.

Birmingham is handicapped by its distance from the steel markets of the Midwest and Northeast, but its steelmaking costs are low, and it is the major supplier to the South. Another advantage for Alabama steelmakers is the climate, which eases handling and transportation tasks.

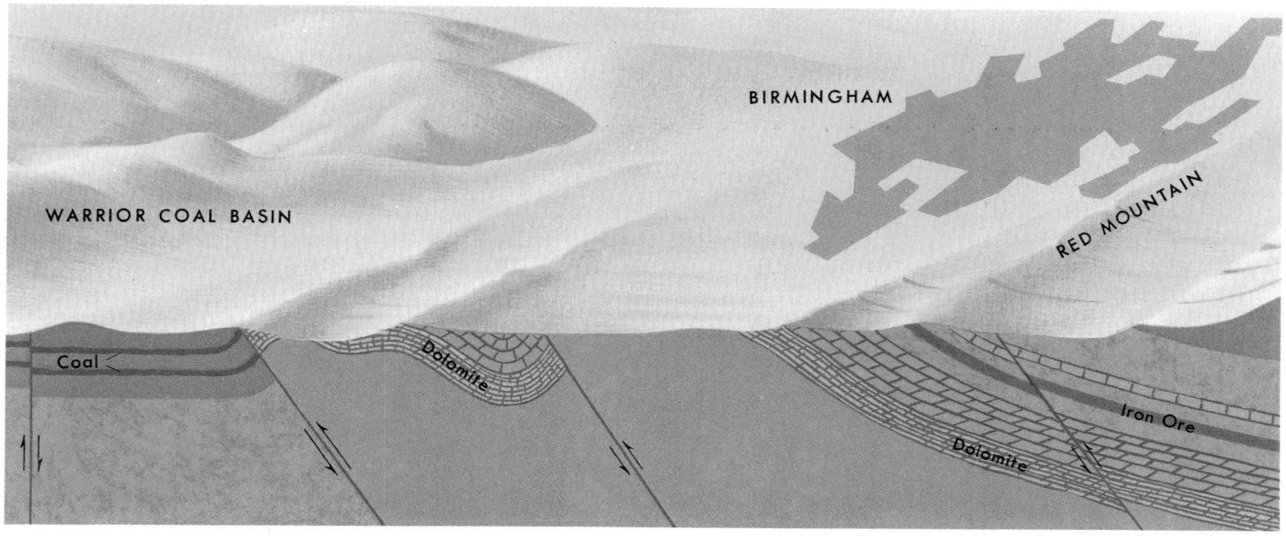

ARKANSAS
HIGHWAYS
Expressways
Major Roads
Other Roads
State Capital
Other Cities
County Seat
City Limits
County Line
Nat. Interstate
U.S.
1 inch = 29 Statute Miles
Lambert Conformal Conic Projection
Longitude West of Greenwich
LITTLE ROCK
Memphis
OM POLITICAL ARKANSAS
COPYRIGHT BY RAND McNALLY & COMPANY
MADE IN U.S.A.

ARKANSAS: This is a state divided in two by its physiography. Northwest Arkansas rises in mountainous ridges above the Ozark Plateau and the highlands of the Ouachita and Boston Mountains. To the south and east, the terrain slopes into the valley of the Mississippi and the lowlands of the coastal plain, which extends inland from the Gulf of Mexico. Here on the plain's river-enriched soil Arkansans cultivate enough rice to make the state the third largest producer in the nation *(diagram, below)*, and enough cotton to make it fourth in the nation. Ranging mile after mile throughout the state are magnificent forests – largely of pine and oak – which form the base for the state's lumber industry. A pioneer in scientific forestry, Arkansas discovered in the early 1900s that careful logging methods and fire control could result in the reproduction of commercially valuable forests within 20 years.

AREA:	53,104 sq. mi. Rank: 27th.
POPULATION:	1,786,272. Rank: 31st. Largest city and capital: Little Rock.
ENTERED UNION:	June 15, 1836, as 25th state.
CLIMATE:	Moderately long, hot summers; short, mild winters. Abundant rainfall.
ALTITUDES:	Blue Mountain and Magazine Mountain, 2,800 ft. (highest); Little Rock, 300 ft.

Having taken its name from an Indian tribe, the Akansea, the state has been embroiled in a controversy over its pronunciation ever since. "Bite a piece out of the moon . . . shake yourself and rumble the mountains," once rumbled a proud native Arkansan in a Senate debate over whether the name "Arkansas" rhymes with that of nearby Kansas. "But, sir, you will never change the name of Arkansaw!"

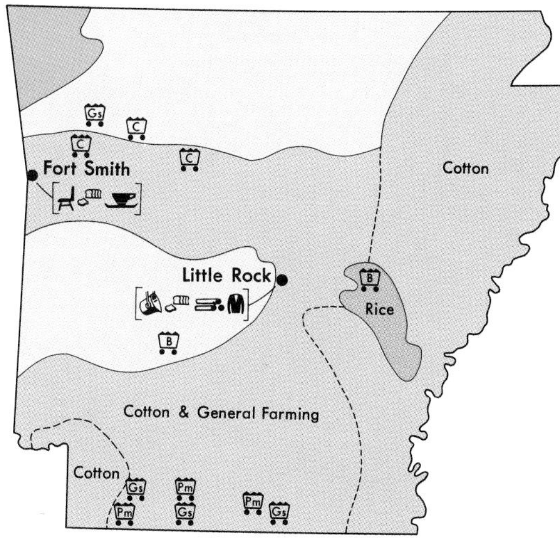

THE ECONOMY

MANUFACTURING
- Food Processing
- Lumber & Forest Products
- Furniture
- Metal Processing
- Clothing
- Stone, Clay & Glass Products

MINING
- Bauxite
- Coal
- Natural Gas
- Petroleum

AGRICULTURE
- General Farming
- Cotton
- Special Crops & General Farming
- Fruit & General Farming

VALUE		EMPLOYED
$671,680,000	AGRICULTURE	41%
$591,000,000	MANUFACTURING	15%
$131,600,000	MINING	1%

Percentages are based on a total of 563,000 at work. In addition 21% are in commerce and transport, 12% in government, 10% in other areas. Manufacturing value is the value added when materials are converted into goods

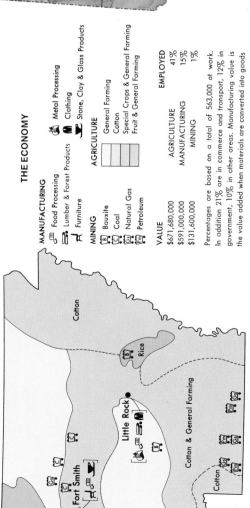

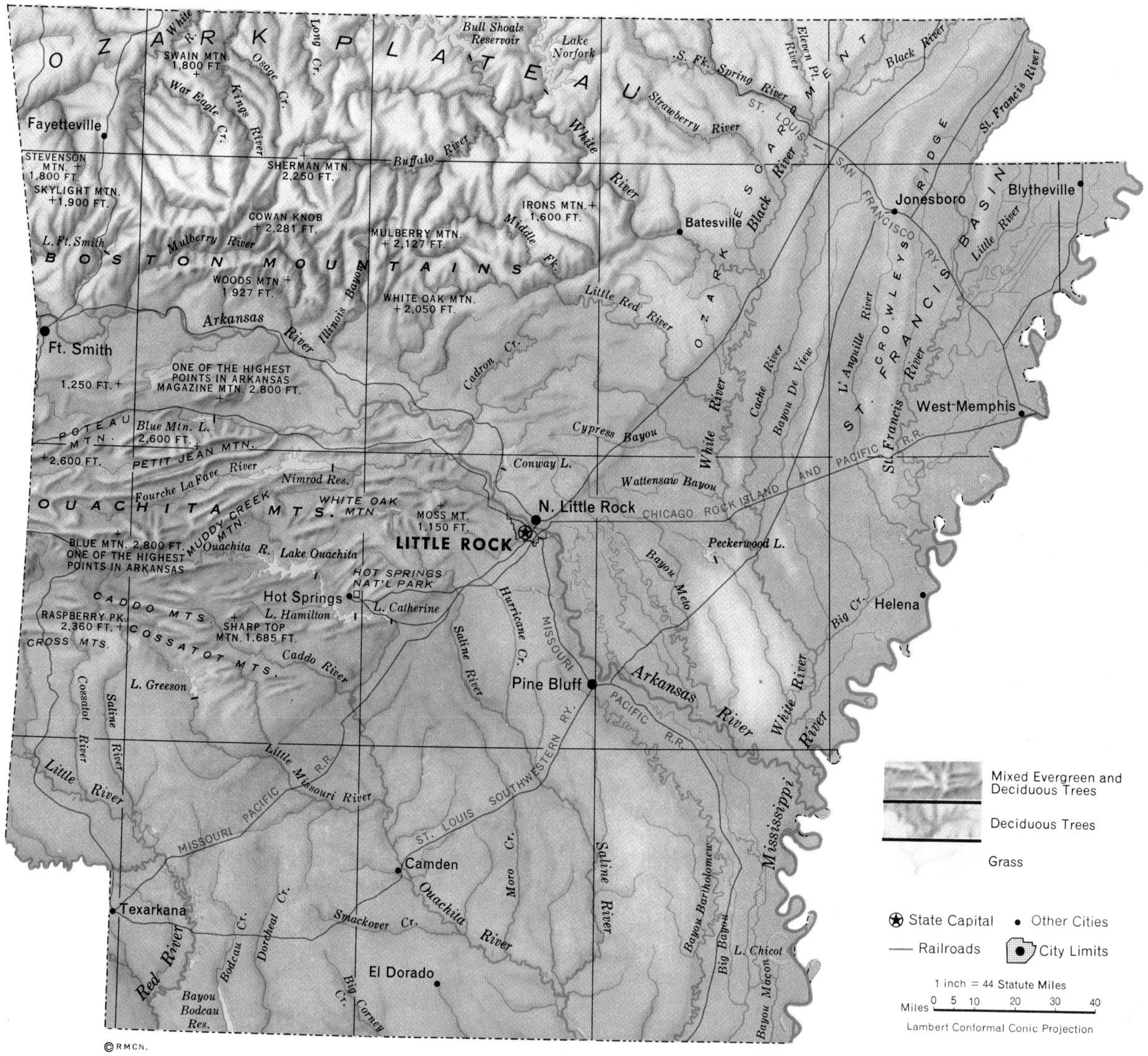

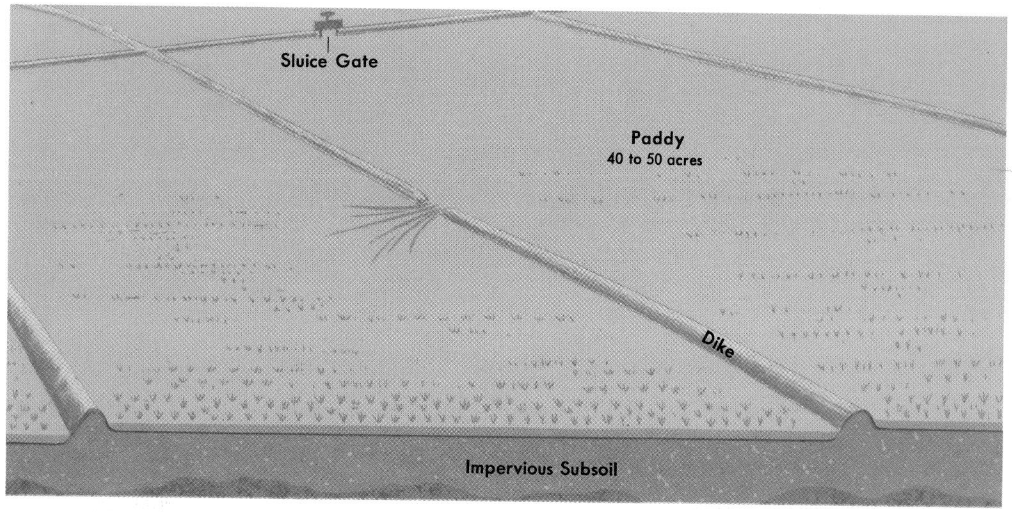

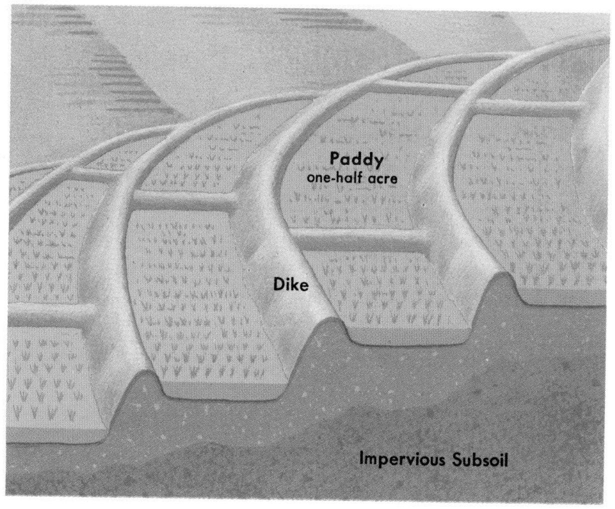

RICE CULTURE, EAST AND WEST

Two basic methods of growing rice are illustrated in the two diagrams at left. Mechanized, commercial production in Arkansas and other areas of the U.S. *(far left)* requires large, level fields ("paddies") in which dikes of earth can hold water at a level of six inches or so. This much water is necessary both for the nurture of the rice plants and for the control of weeds. Underlying clay or similarly dense soil minimizes the loss of water through seepage. Sluice gates which can be opened permit the fields to be drained so that combines can move in at harvest time. These techniques have made it possible for the U.S. to produce a surplus and become one of the leading exporters of rice in the world.

In Asia, paddies tend to be smaller. They are frequently terraced into hillsides whose steep slopes keep the water flowing from higher to lower fields *(right in diagram)*. Terracing and plowing are done with the help of water buffalo and oxen. Planting is done by hand. Scythes or sickles are used to mow the ripe grain, flails to thresh the grain from the straw. These ancient methods, employed by a huge labor force, produce high yields per acre, a low yield per worker. Most Asian rice-growing countries consume all of their own rice crops; only a few, such as Burma and Thailand, have a surplus for export.

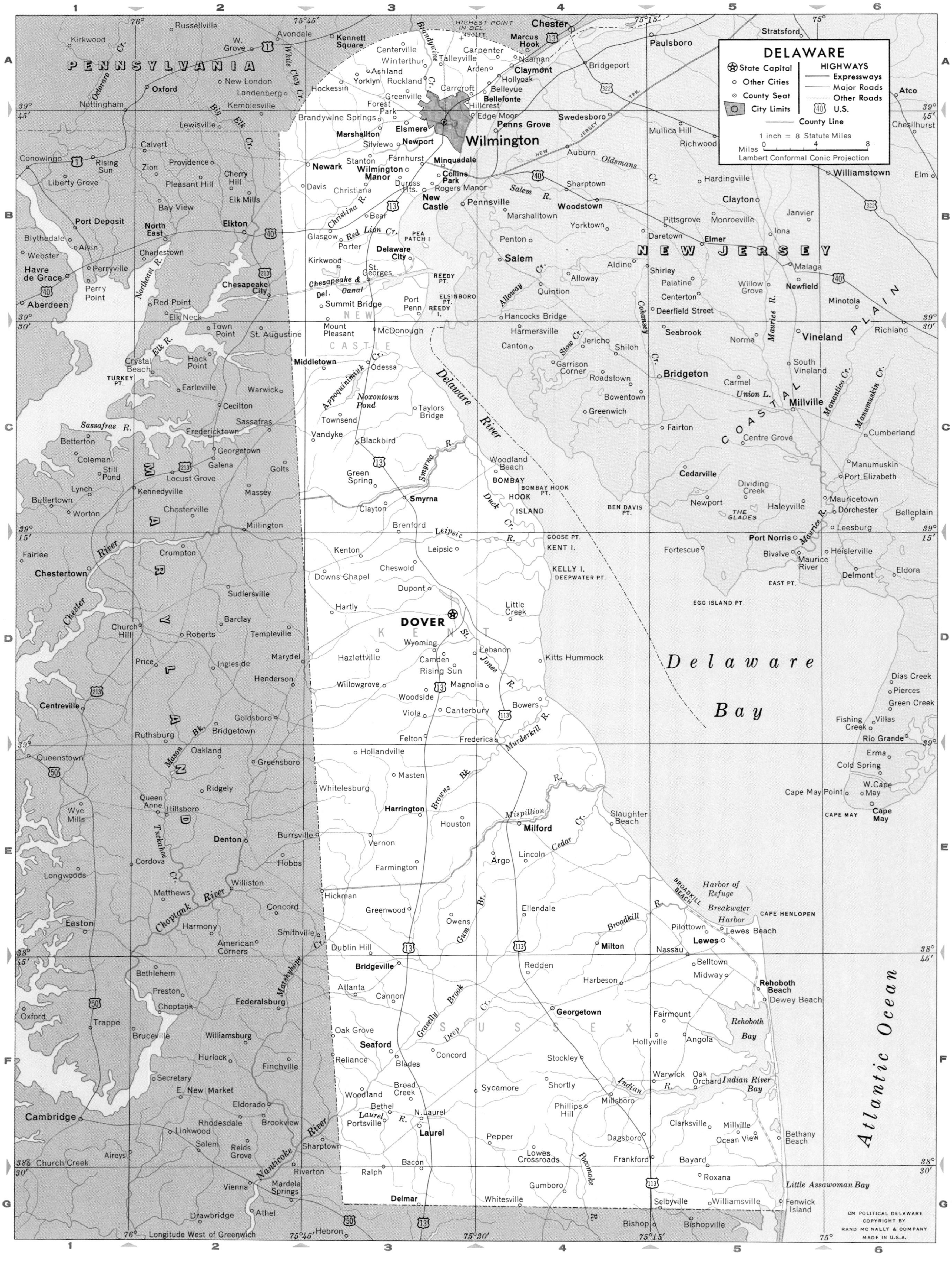
DELAWARE
State Capital
Other Cities
County Seat
City Limits
HIGHWAYS
Expressways
Major Roads
Other Roads
U.S.
County Line
1 inch = 8 Statute Miles
Miles
Lambert Conformal Conic Projection
PENNSYLVANIA
NEW JERSEY
MARYLAND
NEW CASTLE
KENT
SUSSEX
Delaware Bay
Atlantic Ocean
Delaware River
COASTAL PLAIN
Wilmington
DOVER
Chester
Marcus Hook
Claymont
Newark
New Castle
Elsmere
Newport
Middletown
Smyrna
Milford
Harrington
Seaford
Laurel
Georgetown
Lewes
Rehoboth Beach
Dewey Beach
Bethany Beach
Fenwick Island
Selbyville
Delmar
Bridgeville
Millsboro
Milton
Camden
Wyoming
Frederica
Felton
Delaware City
Salem
Pennsville
Penns Grove
Bridgeton
Vineland
Millville
Elkton
Chestertown
Centreville
Denton
Easton
Federalsburg
Cambridge
Havre de Grace
Aberdeen
Port Deposit
North East
Chesapeake City
Cape May
Cape May Point
Cape Henlopen
Harbor of Refuge
Breakwater Harbor
Rehoboth Bay
Indian River Bay
Little Assawoman Bay
Choptank River
Nanticoke River
Chester River
Sassafras R.
Elk R.
Christina R.
Chesapeake & Del. Canal
Mispillion R.
Broadkill R.
Indian R.
Pocomoke R.
Murderkill R.
St. Jones R.
Leipsic R.
Smyrna R.
Appoquinimink Cr.
Cedar Cr.
Bombay Hook Island
Kelly I.
Kent I.
Reedy Pt.
Pea Patch I.
Highest point in Del. 450 ft.
Longitude West of Greenwich
CM POLITICAL DELAWARE
COPYRIGHT BY RAND MC NALLY & COMPANY
MADE IN U.S.A.

DELAWARE

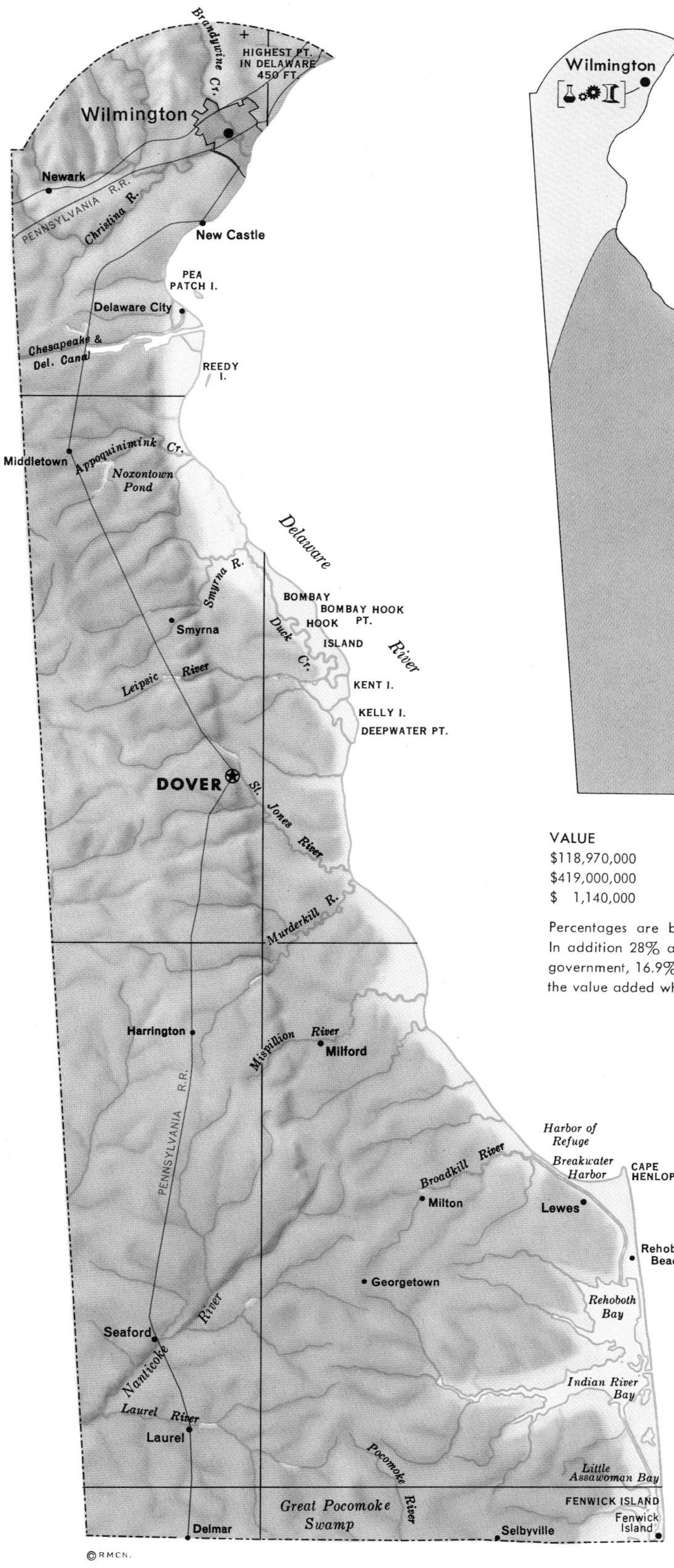

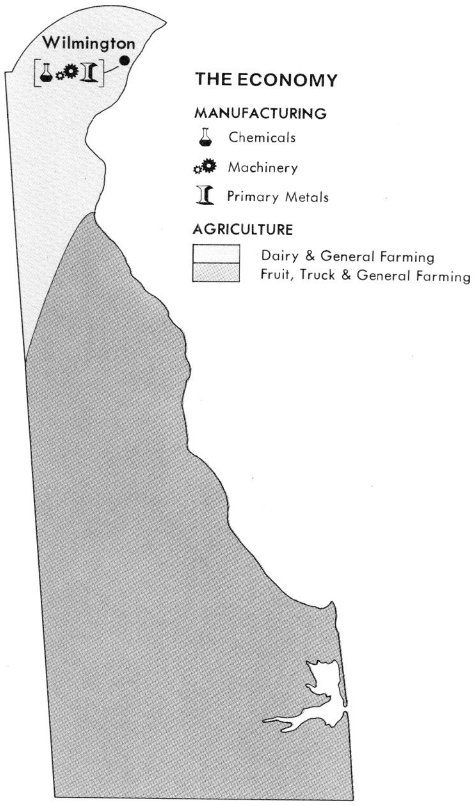

VALUE		EMPLOYED
$118,970,000	AGRICULTURE	8.0%
$419,000,000	MANUFACTURING	36.0%
$ 1,140,000	MINING	0.1%

Percentages are based on a total of 159,000 at work. In addition 28% are in commerce and transport, 11% in government, 16.9% in other areas. Manufacturing value is the value added when materials are converted into goods.

Mixed Evergreen and Deciduous Trees

Deciduous Trees

Grass

State Capital • Other Cities

Railroads City Limits

1 inch = 11 Statute Miles

Miles 0 5 10

Lambert Conformal Conic Projection

THE ORIGINS OF DELAWARE'S BORDERS

The borders of Delaware, shown above, are the result of compromise combined with a mistake that kept the second smallest state from being even smaller. After long dispute, its northern boundary was set as the arc of a circle centered on New Castle. In the west the arc was intersected by the Mason-Dixon Line. The southern boundary adjoining Maryland, originally supposed to be on a line with Cape Henlopen, was mistakenly placed about 25 miles south, at a "false" Cape Henlopen.

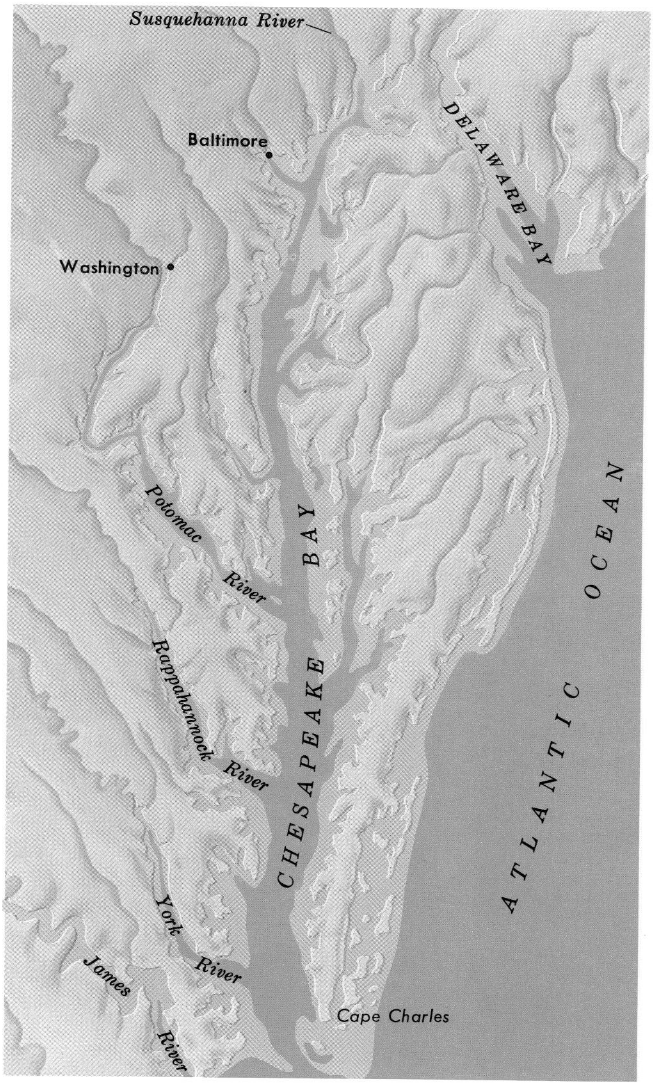

THE DROWNED ATLANTIC VALLEYS

How the great bays of the Atlantic Coast were formed is demonstrated on this map of the Chesapeake and Delaware Bays. In preglacial times rivers like the Susquehanna drained directly into the Atlantic. When the glaciers melted at the end of the ice age, the sea rose, pushing inland and drowning the low coastal valleys. The Susquehanna's former tributaries, including the Potomac and the York, became independent streams with their own outlets, and hills became islands.

DELAWARE: To a poet of a century ago, Delaware was "like a diamond, diminutive, but having within it inherent value." This tiny gem—only Rhode Island is smaller—rests almost entirely on the Atlantic coastal plain, a low-lying land of fertile loam and clay that is closely embraced by the long arm of Delaware Bay *(diagram, right)*. With a six-month-long growing season, the state has been cultivated for countless generations. Long before Henry Hudson piloted the *Half Moon* into the bay in 1609, Algonkin Indians were growing maize along the humid coast. To this day Delaware is a major producer of poultry, dairy products, fruits and vegetables. Corn—still a valuable crop—brings the state an impressive $10 million a year.

AREA:	2,057 sq. mi. Rank: 49th.
POPULATION:	446,292. Rank: 46th. Largest city: Wilmington. Capital: Dover.
ENTERED UNION:	Dec. 7, 1787, as 1st state.
CLIMATE:	Cool winters, hot summers; ample rainfall.
ALTITUDES:	Ebright Road, 450 ft. (highest); Dover, 55 ft.

Delaware's access to the sea and its routes to mineral-bearing areas inland through the Delaware River led to its early industrialization. Today the state produces heavy machinery and primary metals, and manufactures clothing, but most important is the chemical industry concentrated around Wilmington. This city is both a center of scientific thinking and a practical producer of such heavy industrial chemicals as carbon disulphide, used in the manufacture of viscose rayon and cellophane. Because of its location near the great cities of the eastern seaboard and its favorable corporation and tax laws, Delaware has become the titular headquarters of many of the largest U.S. corporations.

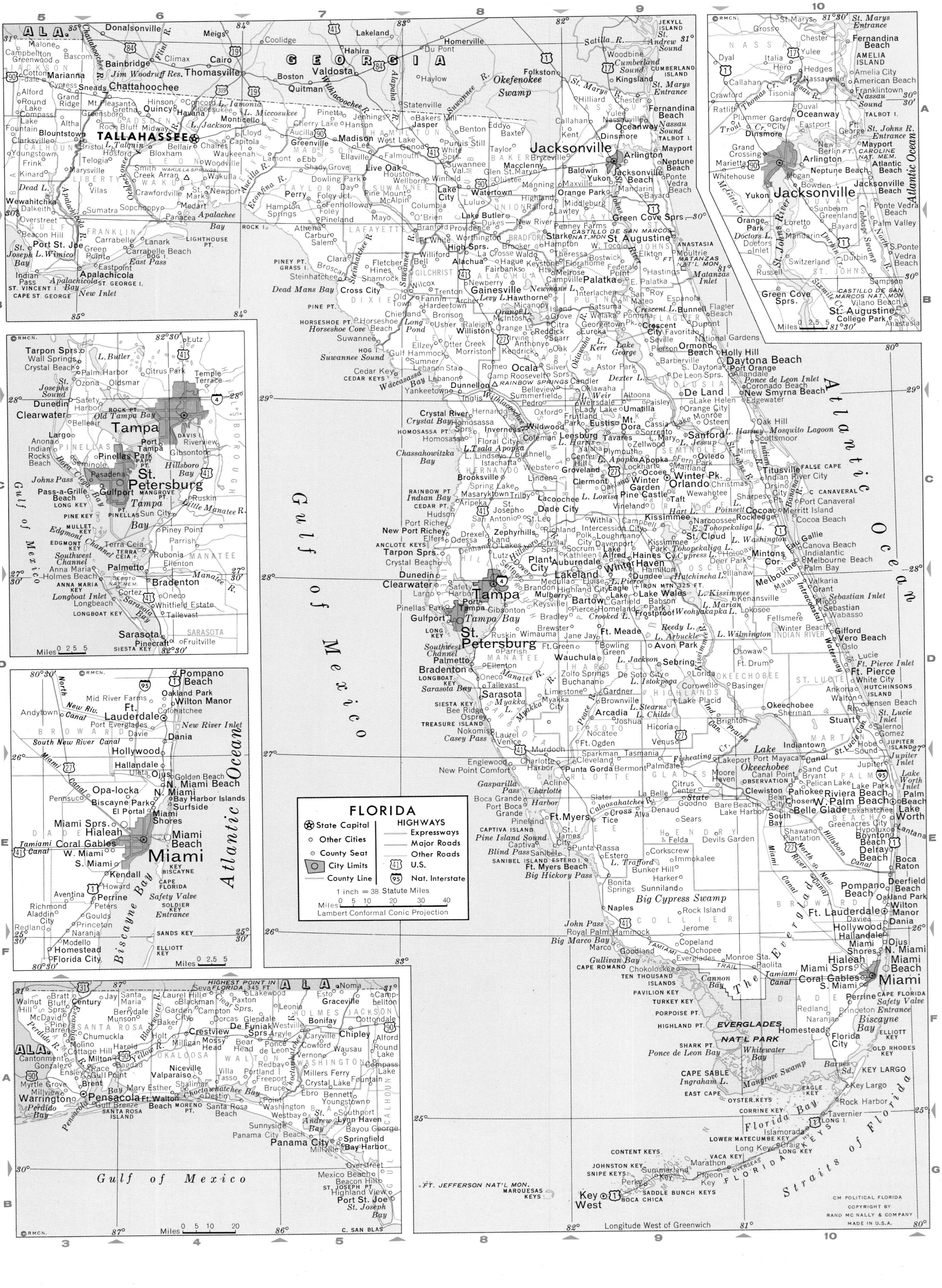
FLORIDA
State Capital
Other Cities
County Seat
City Limits
County Line
HIGHWAYS
Expressways
Major Roads
Other Roads
U.S.
Nat. Interstate
1 inch = 38 Statute Miles
Miles 0 5 10 20 30 40
Lambert Conformal Conic Projection
GEORGIA
ALA.
TALLAHASSEE
Jacksonville
St. Augustine
Gainesville
Ocala
Daytona Beach
Orlando
Tampa
St. Petersburg
Sarasota
Ft. Myers
Naples
W. Palm Beach
Ft. Lauderdale
Miami
Key West
Pensacola
Panama City
Gulf of Mexico
Atlantic Ocean
Straits of Florida
Florida Bay
Lake Okeechobee
Big Cypress Swamp
EVERGLADES NAT'L PARK
Okefenokee Swamp
Longitude West of Greenwich
CM POLITICAL FLORIDA
COPYRIGHT BY RAND McNALLY & COMPANY
MADE IN U.S.A.

FLORIDA

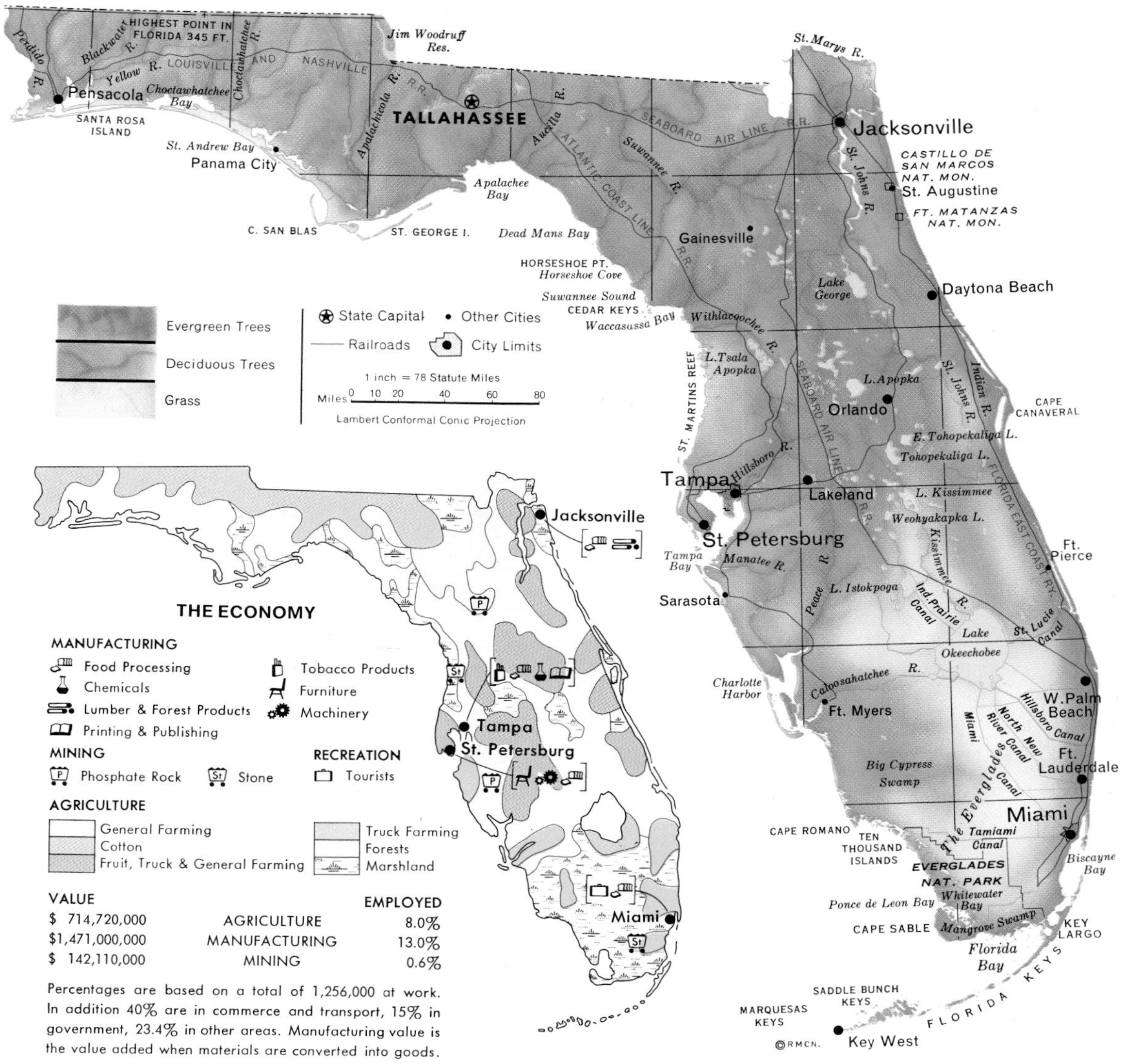

VALUE		EMPLOYED
$ 714,720,000	AGRICULTURE	8.0%
$1,471,000,000	MANUFACTURING	13.0%
$ 142,110,000	MINING	0.6%

Percentages are based on a total of 1,256,000 at work. In addition 40% are in commerce and transport, 15% in government, 23.4% in other areas. Manufacturing value is the value added when materials are converted into goods.

FLORIDA: A 400-mile-long peninsula with a coastline of nearly 1,200 miles, Florida has baffled men for more than four centuries–beginning with Juan Ponce de Leon, the Spaniard who landed here in 1513 and thought he was on an island. Though it lies entirely north of the Tropic of Cancer, Florida's southern tip has a tropical climate. The terrain varies from gently rolling, pine-covered hills in the north to the luxuriant, steaming Everglades in the south, where giant orchid plants sometimes live for hundreds of years. Around the peninsula's periphery, sand bars, coral reefs and keys are slowly creating new land out of the ocean *(diagrams, below left)*.

AREA:	58,560 sq. mi. Rank: 22nd.
POPULATION:	4,951,560. Rank: 10th. Largest city: Miami. Capital: Tallahassee.
ENTERED UNION:	March 3, 1845, as 27th state.
CLIMATE:	Hot humid summers; mild winters with occasional frost. Southern tip tropical. Heavy rains during hurricane season.
ALTITUDES:	Northern Walton County, 345 ft. (highest); Miami, 10 ft.

The early colonists were dismayed by this beautiful, balmy region. It had no precious metals; the land could not provide adequate food; and no white man was safe from the hostile Indians. After a slow, almost torpid development, the state underwent great changes at the beginning of the 20th Century, with the building of railroads and the draining of parts of the Everglades. Now, many square miles of the once useless swamps produce a variety of vegetables, notably sweet corn and snap beans. Farther north, citrus fruits thrive. Rich deposits of phosphate–an important component of fertilizer–have been found in central Florida; these supply most of the needs of the U.S., as well as enrich the soils of Florida itself. Phosphate also nurtures the grass which has helped make Florida an important producer of beef. The state raises a breed of Brahman hybrid cattle that is resistant to heat and many kinds of pests.

Above all else, Florida has found fortune in the vast number of people attracted by its climate *(diagram, below)*. To Florida now come throngs of vacationers, fleeing the intemperate winters of the North, and a multitude of elderly people seeking–if not Ponce de Leon's Fountain of Youth–at least a warm and comfortable "Isle of Flowers" for their quiet years.

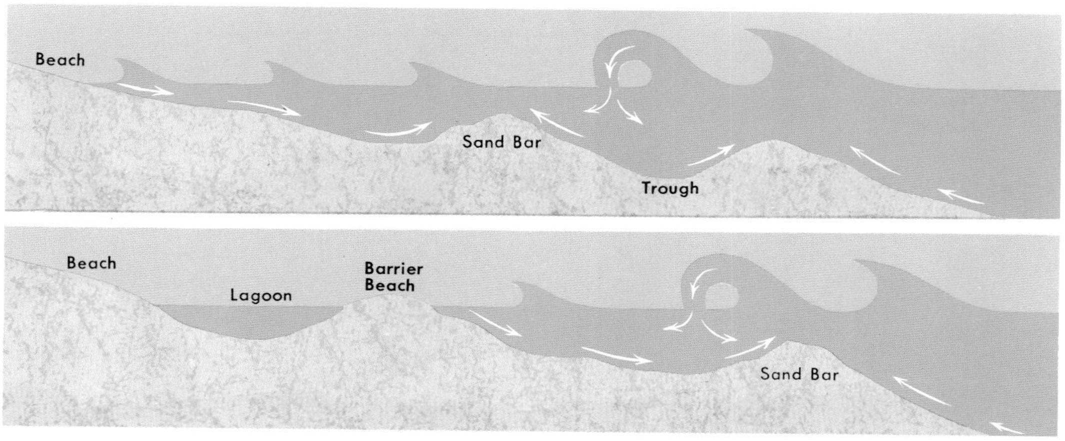

THE BIRTH OF A BARRIER BEACH

Two stages in the creation of an offshore barrier beach are shown above. Incoming waves *(top diagram)* break and churn on the shallows, depositing sand which forms underwater bars. When a bar reaches the surface *(bottom diagram, left)* it becomes a barrier beach. As barrier beaches grow and join together, they block off quiet bodies of water which are called lagoons.

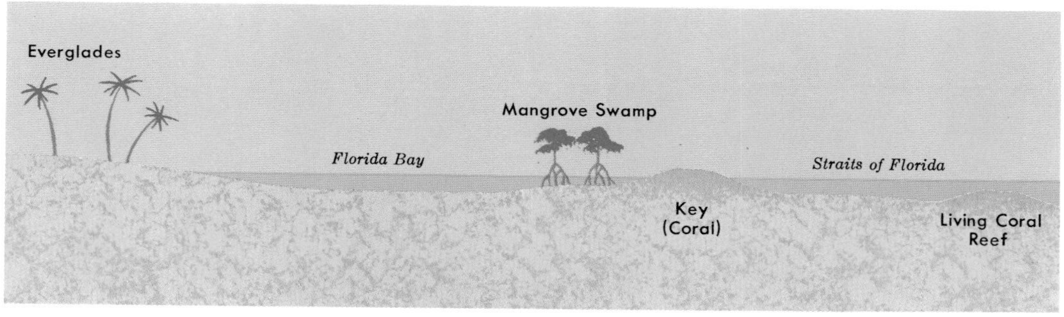

THE FLORIDA KEYS: ISLANDS BUILT BY LIVING ORGANISMS

The cross section above shows the southern tip of Florida *(left)*, a coral key and a living coral reef. The coral key was once part of a reef which became an island when the sea level dropped during the great ice age. Coral can live only in warm shallow water, and they are killed when a reef is exposed to the air. The accumulated skeletons of dead coral form the present-day keys.

RETIREMENT HAVEN AND SPACE BASE

The charts below show how Florida is expanding by attracting residents from various areas of the U.S. Newcomers drawn by climate and employment opportunities have helped swell the state's population by 78 per cent since 1950. Great numbers of older people *(pie chart)* come to Florida to retire, giving the state a greater percentage of people over age 59 than the national average.

Florida's glittering vacation spots, such as Miami Beach and Palm Beach, have created thousands of service jobs and small-business opportunities for younger people. The Space Age, too, has been a factor in providing jobs. The most recent Floridians have come to work in military installations as well as in the new avionics, electronics and chemical industries. Today the state's fastest-growing county is Brevard, on the east coast, where the Cape Canaveral missile base is situated.

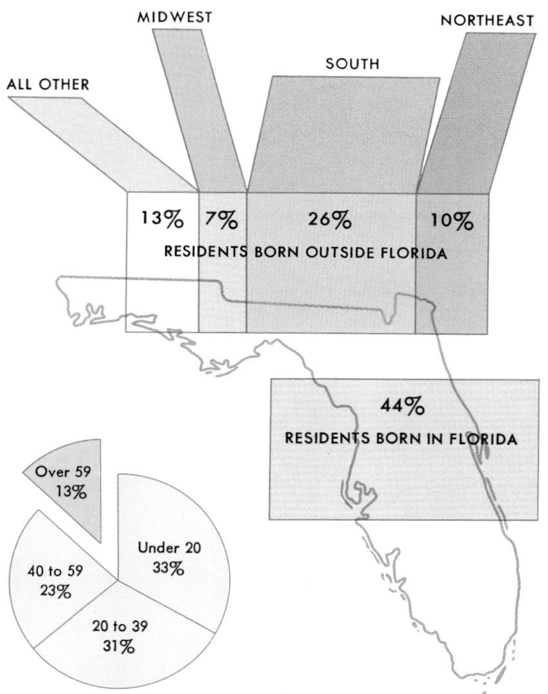

Florida's Population By Age Group

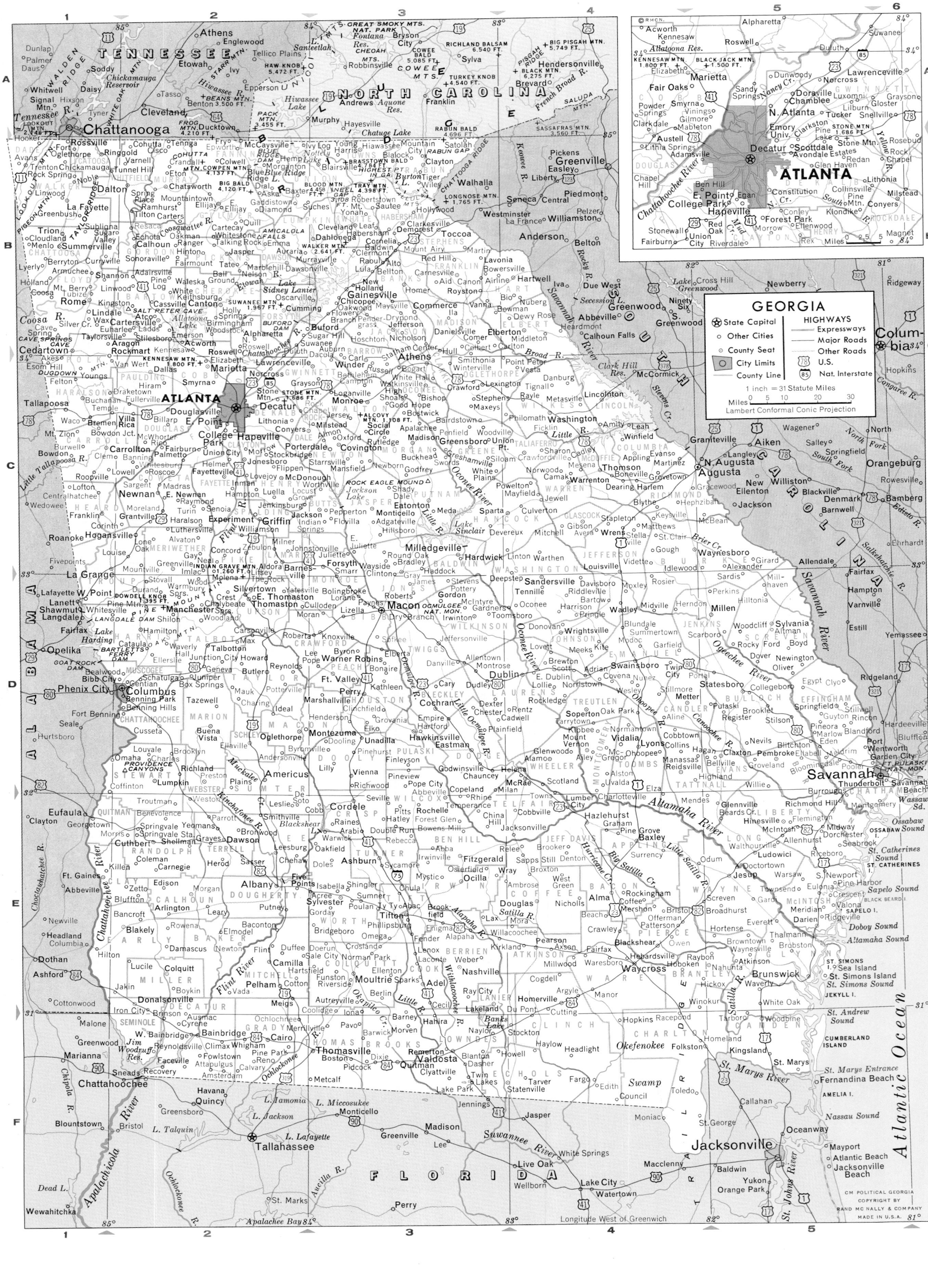

GEORGIA
State Capital
Other Cities
County Seat
City Limits
County Line
HIGHWAYS
Expressways
Major Roads
Other Roads
U.S.
Nat. Interstate
1 inch = 31 Statute Miles
Miles 0 5 10 20 30
Lambert Conformal Conic Projection
ATLANTA
TENNESSEE
NORTH CAROLINA
SOUTH CAROLINA
ALABAMA
FLORIDA
Atlantic Ocean
Chattanooga
Atlanta
Athens
Augusta
Macon
Columbus
Savannah
Albany
Valdosta
Tallahassee
Jacksonville
Columbia
Greenville
Brunswick
Waycross
Rome
Dalton
Gainesville
Milledgeville
Dublin
Americus
Thomasville
Okefenokee Swamp
Altamaha River
Savannah River
Chattahoochee River
Flint River
Ocmulgee R.
Oconee River
Ogeechee River
Apalachee Bay
Longitude West of Greenwich
CM POLITICAL GEORGIA
COPYRIGHT BY RAND MC NALLY & COMPANY
MADE IN U.S.A.

GEORGIA

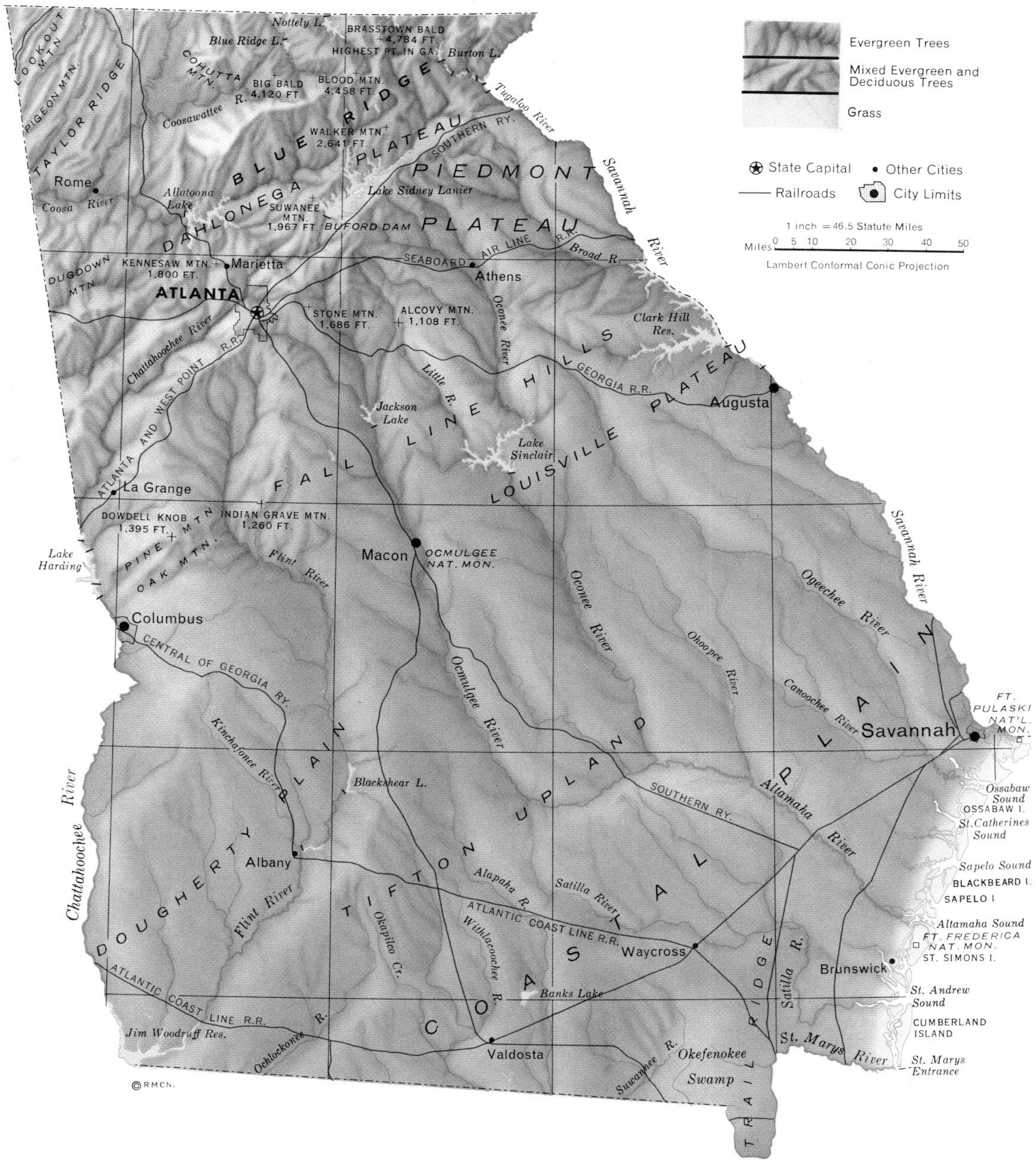

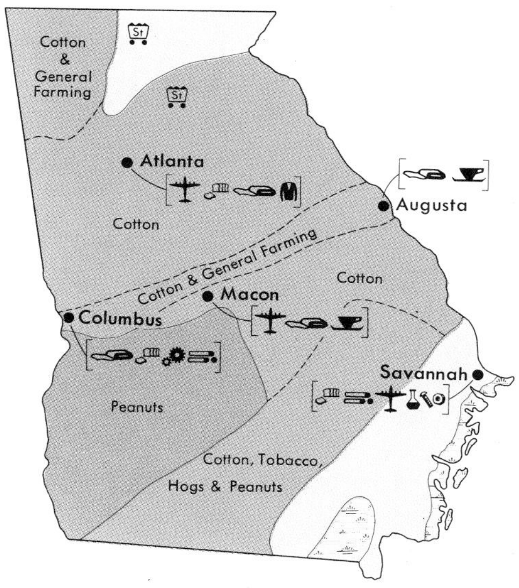

THE ECONOMY

MANUFACTURING
- Textiles
- Food Processing
- Transportation Equipment
- Clothing
- Lumber & Forest Products
- Chemicals
- Metal Products
- Machinery
- Stone, Clay & Glass Products

AGRICULTURE
- General Farming
- Cotton
- Special Crops & General Farming
- Marshland

MINING
- Stone

VALUE		EMPLOYED
$ 854,850,000	AGRICULTURE	17.0%
$2,088,000,000	MANUFACTURING	27.0%
$ 75,110,000	MINING	0.4%

Percentages are based on a total of 1,147,000 at work. In addition 29% are in commerce and transport, 14% in government, 12.6% in other areas. Manufacturing value is the value added when materials are converted into goods.

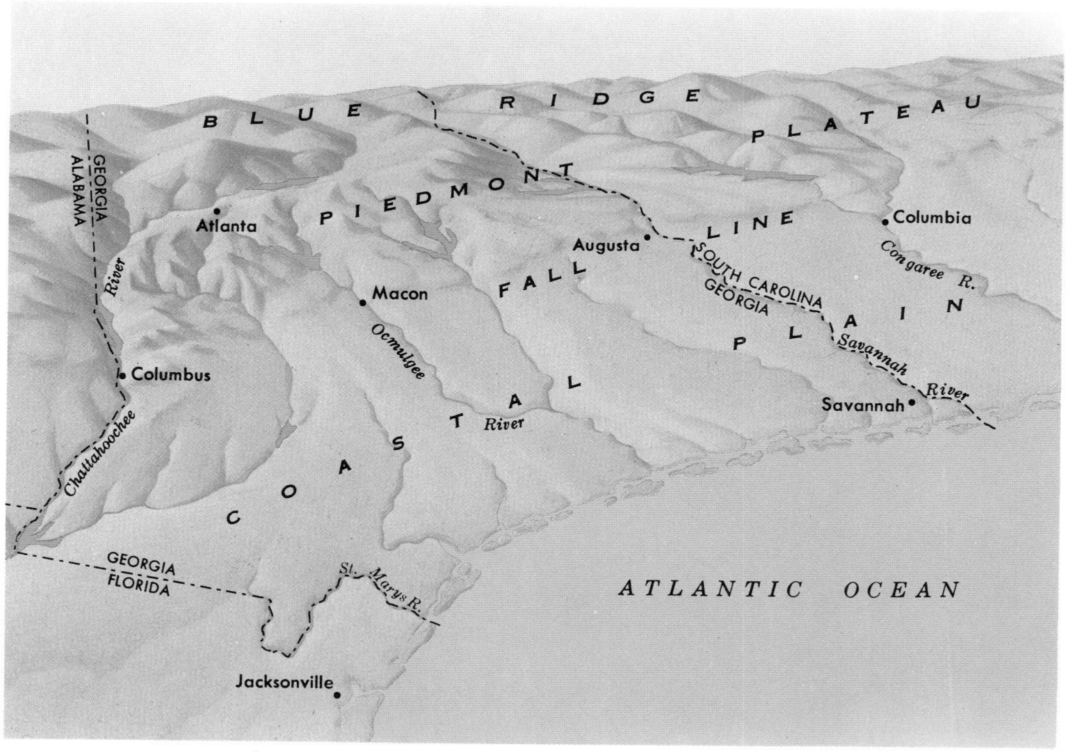

A FALL LINE BETWEEN PLATEAU AND PLAIN

There are two principal levels of terrain in Georgia and the division between them is known as the Fall Line. This separates Georgia's hilly upland region, the Piedmont Plateau, from the generally flat Coastal Plain that slopes gently down to the Atlantic. Underlying the Piedmont is a relatively resistant bedrock; the Coastal Plain, a softer area of sand, silt and gravel, is much more subject to erosion. Falls occur at the point where streams drop from the plateau to the plain. The water power thus created provided energy for some of Georgia's early industries. The Fall Line also marks the head of navigation on the rivers of Georgia.

GEORGIA: In 1732, when King George II chartered the American colony named for him, he ordered each settler to plant mulberry trees so Georgia could furnish England with all the silk she needed. Although silk turned out to be an uneconomic industry for the colony, the settlers very quickly discovered resources far more vital to a maritime empire: tar, pitch and other naval stores from the region's vast forests of pine. To this day Georgia furnishes a large part of the world's rosin—now used more for paper sizing, chemicals and plastics than for sealing ships. In recent decades the timber itself, supplying the raw material for pulp and paper mills, lumber and furniture, has become increasingly important.

The newly established state came into its first great prosperity after Eli Whitney invented the cotton gin in 1793. To run its cotton mills, Georgia needed power. Fortunately the shape of the land provided the means. Where the Coastal Plain met the Piedmont Plateau at the Fall Line, streams dropped rapidly enough to furnish water power for industry *(diagram, left)*. This natural phenomenon accounts for the location of some of the Southeast's leading manufacturing cities, such as Columbus and Augusta.

AREA:	58,876 sq. mi. Rank: 21st.
POPULATION:	3,943,116. Rank: 16th. Largest city and capital: Atlanta.
ENTERED UNION:	Jan. 2, 1788, as 4th state.
CLIMATE:	Humid. Hot summers, mild winters. Heavy rainfall in northeast.
ALTITUDES:	Brasstown Bald Mountain, 4,784 ft. (highest); Atlanta, 1,050 ft.

With the coming of the railroad, Georgia entered a new phase, for its position on the South Atlantic seaboard made it the logical distribution center for all of the South. As one railroad after another was built, Atlanta, founded in 1836, became a hub of trade and transportation. After many years of steady growth, the city attained its present position as a commercial, manufacturing and financial center for the entire Southeast.

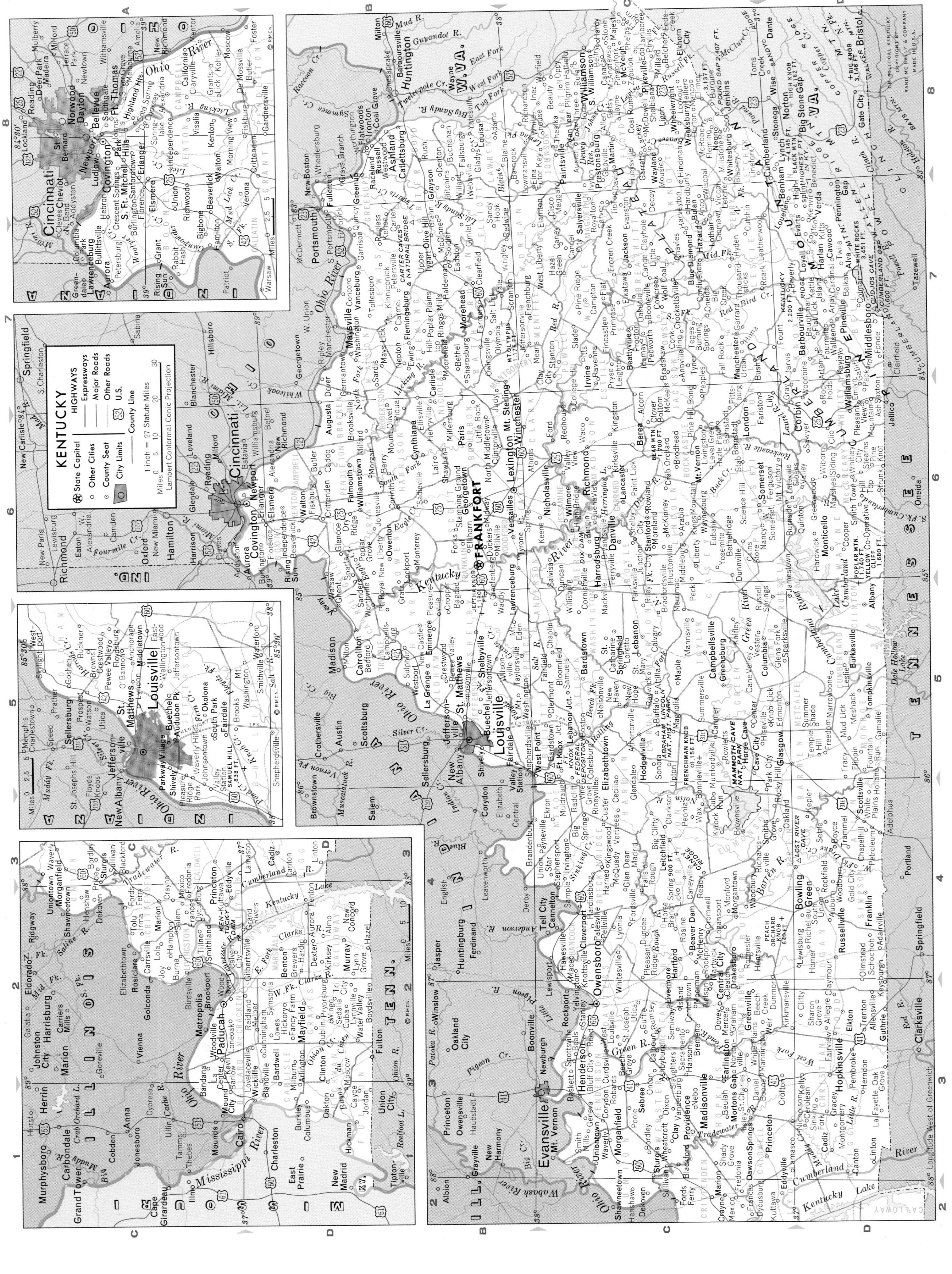
KENTUCKY
HIGHWAYS
Expressways
Major Roads
U.S.
County Line
State Capital
Other Cities
County Seat
City Limits
1 inch = 27 Statute Miles
Miles 0 5 10 20 30
Lambert Conformal Conic Projection
FRANKFORT
Louisville
Lexington
Cincinnati
Covington
Newport
Paducah
Owensboro
Evansville
Bowling Green
Ashland
Huntington
Hopkinsville
Henderson
Ohio River
Mississippi River
Kentucky Lake
Lake Cumberland
ILL.
IND.
OHIO
W. VA.
VA.
TENNESSEE
Longitude West of Greenwich

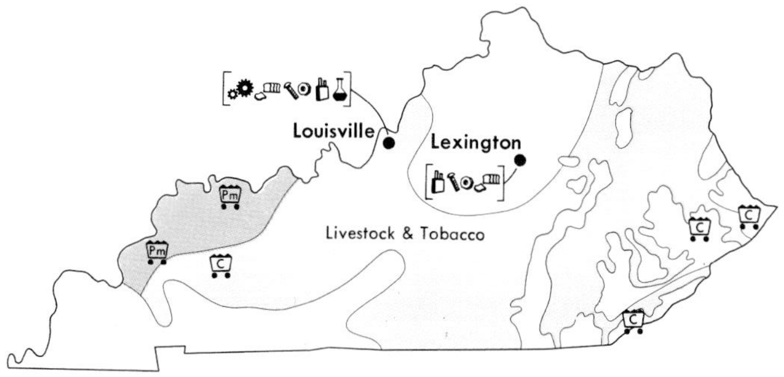

THE ECONOMY

MANUFACTURING
- Food Processing
- Machinery
- Tobacco Products
- Metal Products
- Chemicals

MINING
- Coal
- Petroleum

AGRICULTURE
- General Farming
- Feed Grains & Livestock
- Tobacco & General Farming
- Mountains & Forests

VALUE		EMPLOYED
$ 644,260,000	AGRICULTURE	28%
$1,768,000,000	MANUFACTURING	18%
$ 402,120,000	MINING	4%

Percentages are based on a total of 867,000 at work. In addition 26% are in commerce and transport, 12% in government, 12% in other areas. Manufacturing value is the value added when materials are converted into goods.

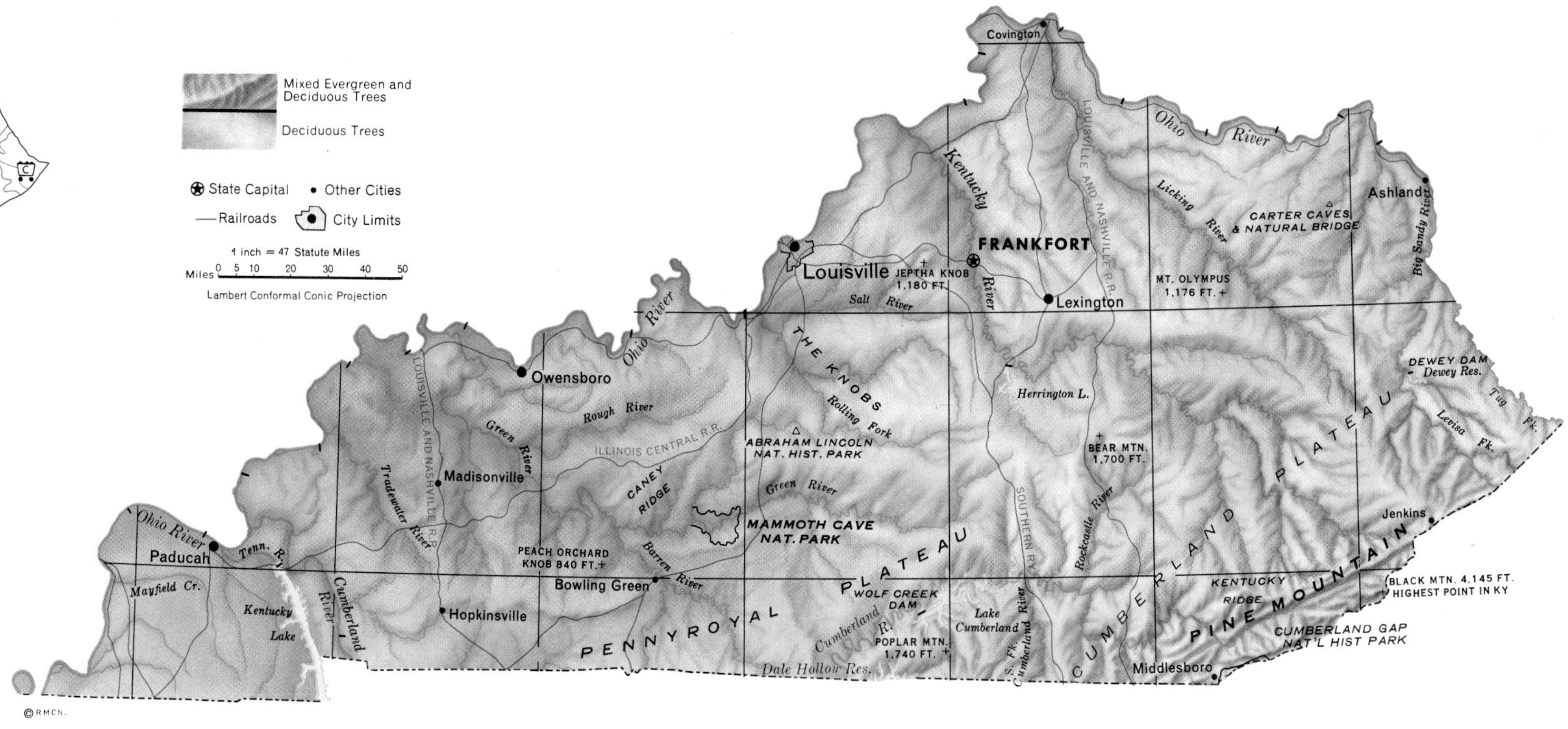

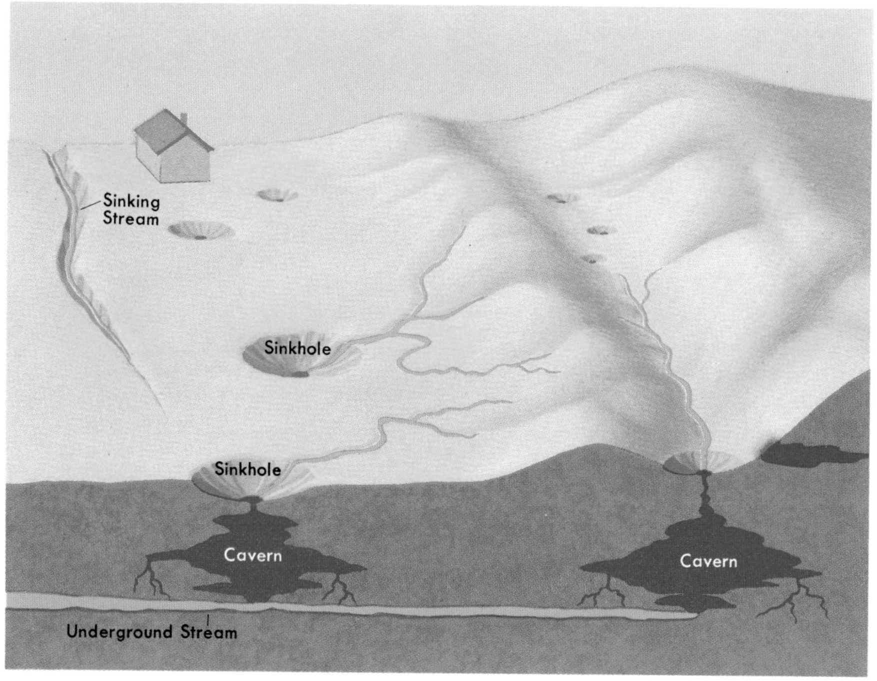

DISAPPEARING STREAMS AND UNDERGROUND CAVERNS

How streams and surface water go underground in Kentucky is shown in this cross-section diagram. At the surface of the land, or just underneath, lie deposits of soluble limestone. The surface water seeps underground and eventually creates a linked chain of caverns. As the caverns grow, their roofs collapse and form sinkholes on the surface. This process will continue as long as a climate of at least moderate rainfall exists. The pitted land formation that results is called "Karst," after a classic geologic region in Yugoslavia.

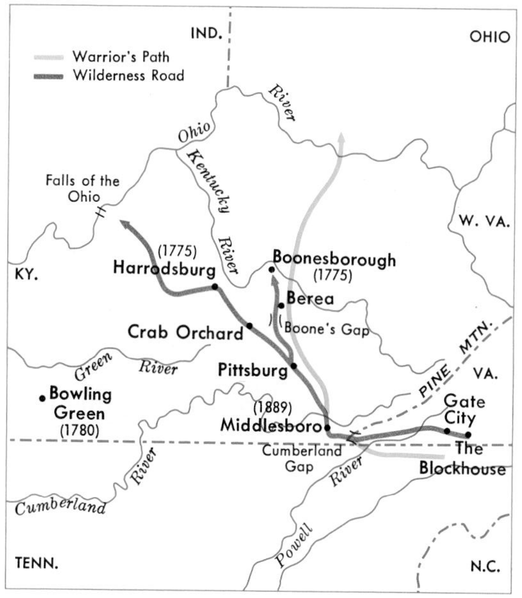

HISTORIC ROUTES ACROSS A WILDERNESS

The trails by which Indians and pioneers penetrated the Kentucky wilderness are traced on the map above. Rich in game attracted by its salt licks, Kentucky was a cherished hunting ground for the Iroquois and Cherokee tribes who opened the narrow "Warrior's Path" *(blue line)* into the region. It was Daniel Boone who first explored the land in 1767 and hacked out the "Wilderness Road" *(red line)*, a trail which ultimately ran west and north as far as the Falls of the Ohio at Louisville. Long a major westward route, the Wilderness Road is still followed along part of its course by U.S. 25–the busy Dixie Highway.

KENTUCKY: Because of a glimpse a great American pioneer caught through a niche in the Cumberland Mountains, Kentucky became the gateway and first stop in the march westward of the newborn American republic. "Nature was here a series of wonders and a fund of delight," reported Daniel Boone, who in 1775 led a party of early settlers over the Wilderness Road through Cumberland Gap to Boonesborough *(map, left)*. The wonders included highland forests of huge hardwood trees, fields of tall cane and a luxuriant growth of grass whose blossoms turned the land blue in spring. But the major natural wonder was the fertile soil of the Bluegrass Basin–formed in ancient times by erosion of the phosphate limestone strata that lie beneath Kentucky. The new settlers soon exploited the "fund of delight." They discovered that the high limestone content in the water and in the bluegrass soils enabled horses to develop strong tendons and "solid close-grained bones that take a polish like ivory," a fact since proved beyond challenge by thoroughbred Kentucky race horses like Man o' War, Whirlaway and Citation. Near the Bluegrass Basin some of the earliest Kentuckians found another delight: water which had percolated through the limestone ground produced a superior whisky in their mountain stills.

AREA:	40,395 sq. mi. Rank: 37th.
POPULATION:	3,038,156. Rank: 22nd.
	Largest city: Louisville.
	Capital: Frankfort.
ENTERED UNION:	June 1, 1792, as 15th state.
CLIMATE:	Hot summers, short winters with some snow; moderate rainfall.
ALTITUDES:	Black Mountain, 4,145 ft. (highest);
	Frankfort, 560 ft.; Louisville, 450 ft.

Far below the mountains and plains lies an incredible network of rooms and passages carved in the limestone by subterranean rivers *(diagram, far left)*. To resourceful Kentuckians, such wonders, seen best in Mammoth Cave National Park, have long provided a fund not only of delight but of millions of dollars from sightseers as well.

LOUISIANA
HIGHWAYS
Major Roads
Other Roads
U.S.
State Capital
Other Cities
County Seat
City Limits
County Line
1 inch = 33 Statute Miles
Lambert Conformal Conic Projection
Longitude West of Greenwich
ARKANSAS
MISSISSIPPI
ALA.
MISS.
Gulf of Mexico
Shreveport
BATON ROUGE
New Orleans
Lake Pontchartrain
CM POLITICAL LOUISIANA
COPYRIGHT BY RAND McNALLY & COMPANY
MADE IN U.S.A.

LOUISIANA: Shaped like a swashbuckler's boot, with a toe dipping into the Gulf of Mexico, Louisiana lies on a low coastal plain. Jean Lafitte found its coast a fine place from which to practice piracy in the 19th Century. In the inland bayou region, "a maze of sluggish and devious waters" darkened by moss-draped cypress forests, the Acadian settlers of Longfellow's *Evangeline* lived in an easygoing prosperity based on rich crops and cattle-raising. Their descendants, the "Cajuns," are still there.

Thanks to the bayou country, Louisiana leads the nation in wild muskrat and nutria trapping. The state is also first in shrimp fishing and sugar cane production and among the top three states in rice production. To the north the waterways are less kind, ceaselessly eroding the soil of the rolling "piney woods." But to the east, water has been benign, laying down a ribbon of exceptional fertility along the banks of the Mississippi. Here early planters turned the land into an Eden of cotton and cane.

AREA:	48,523 sq. mi. Rank: 31st.
POPULATION:	3,257,022. Rank: 20th.
	Largest city: New Orleans. Capital: Baton Rouge.
ENTERED UNION:	April 30, 1812, as 18th state.
CLIMATE:	Humid. Long hot summers, short mild winters.
	Moderately heavy rainfall.
ALTITUDES:	Driskill Mountain, 535 ft. (highest); New Orleans, 5 ft.

In the past four decades, mining and drilling in the area from New Orleans west to Texas have helped make Louisiana second in the U.S. in production of sulphur and natural gas, third in petroleum. Rich deposits of petroleum and sulphur are also being worked in the region south of New Orleans. This is delta country, where the Mississippi, coming to the end of its 2,330-mile journey, deposits its silt to create new land. Describing the delta, Mark Twain said it was "the youthfulest batch of country that lies around there anywhere."

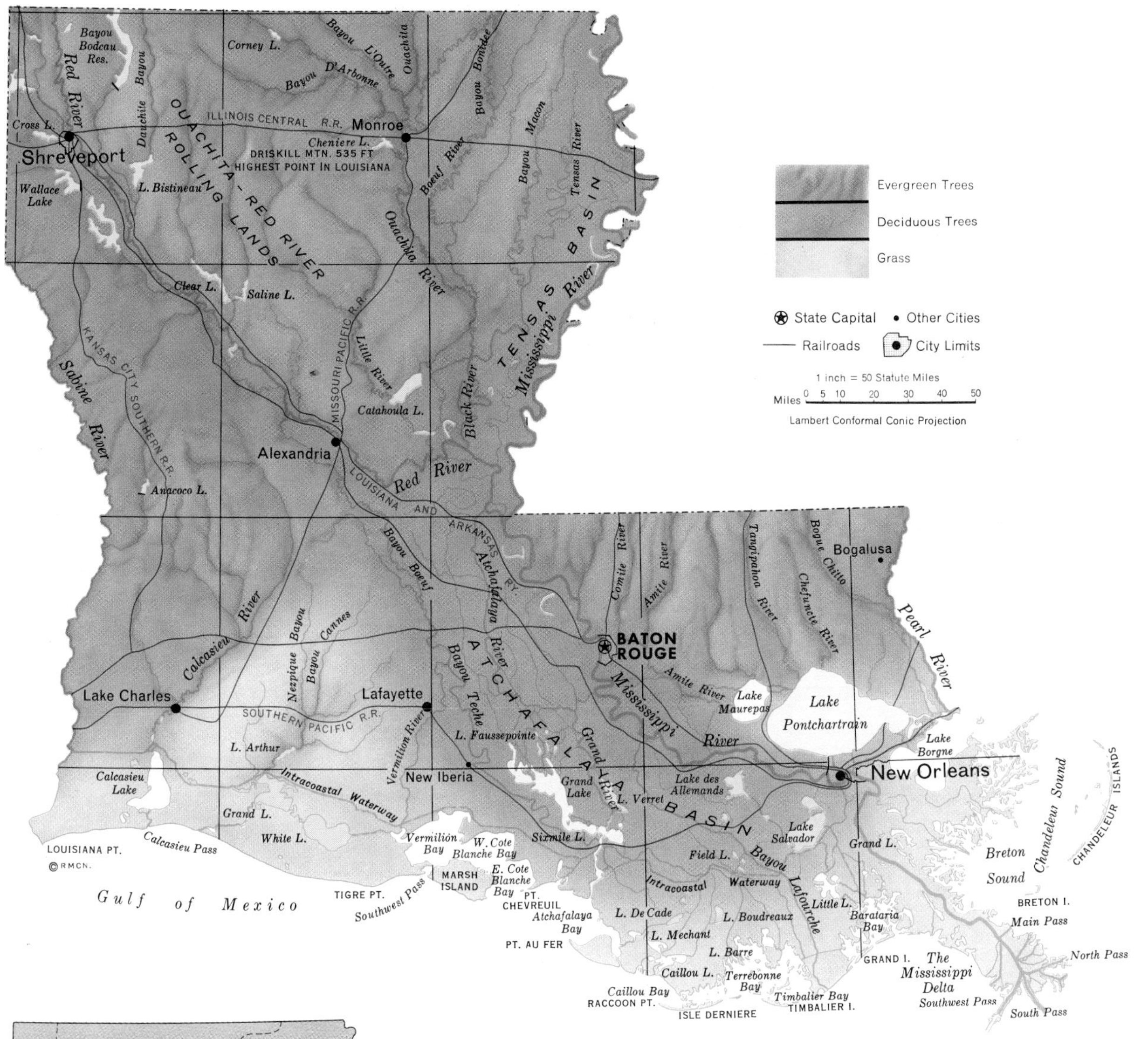

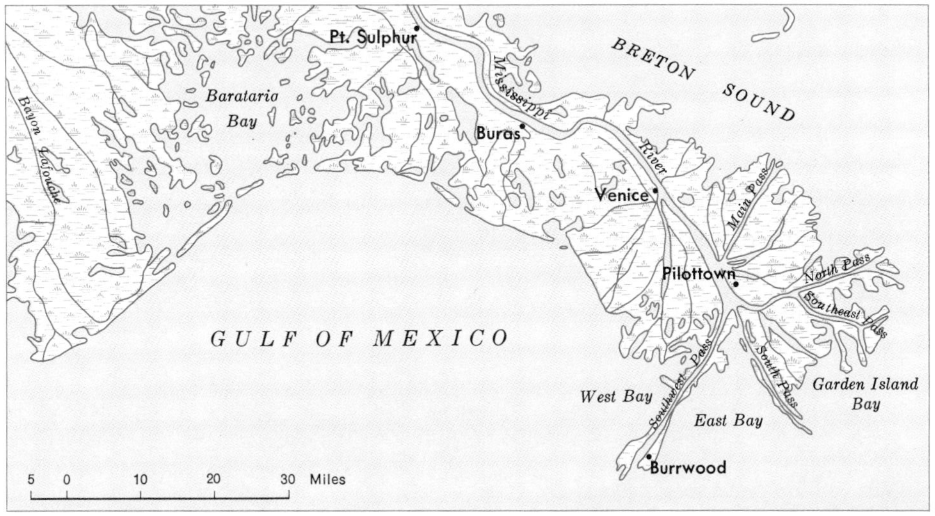

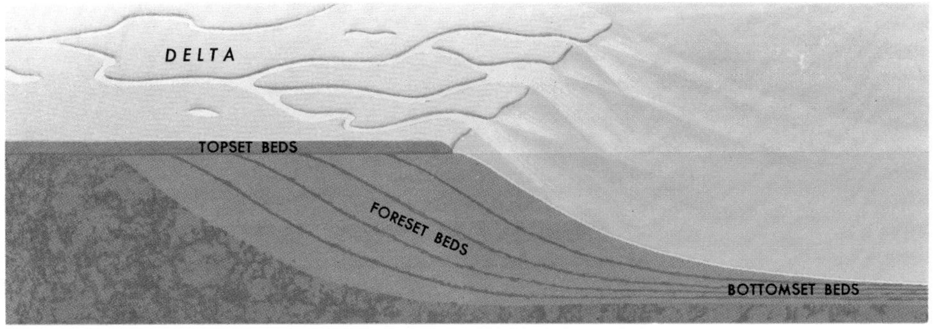

NEW LAND CREATED BY AN OLD RIVER

As it approaches the Gulf of Mexico, the Mississippi River divides into the bird-foot pattern that is shown on the map at the top. In the Gulf, with the silt picked up during its journey downstream, the river creates new land, or a delta. When it reaches the Gulf, the river is slowed down by its contact with the standing body of water and dumps its cargo of silt in successive stages, illustrated in the cross section directly above. Heavier sediments are deposited as topset beds while the river creates new side channels, or passes. Lighter particles come to rest in foreset beds, which constitute the advancing front of the delta. The finest silt is carried farthest, settling in the bottomset beds on the Gulf floor. The river's deposits have extended the delta into the Gulf at the rate of some 200 feet per year.

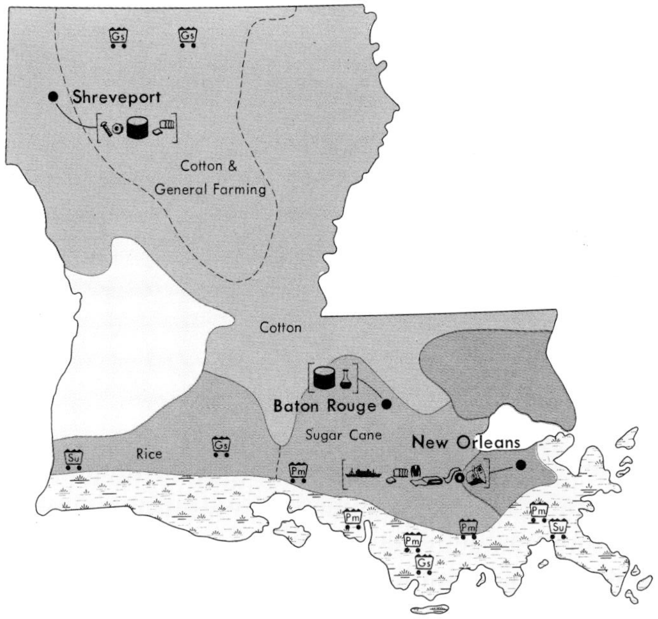

THE ECONOMY

MANUFACTURING
- Chemicals
- Food Processing
- Petroleum Refining
- Pulp & Paper Products
- Metal Products
- Transportation Equipment
- Textiles & Clothing
- Metal Processing

MINING
- Natural Gas
- Petroleum
- Sulfur

AGRICULTURE
- General Farming
- Cotton
- Special Crops & General Farming
- Fruit, Truck & General Farming
- Marshland

VALUE		EMPLOYED
$ 427,480,000	AGRICULTURE	17%
$1,435,000,000	MANUFACTURING	15%
$1,517,420,000	MINING	5%

Percentages are based on a total of 924,000 at work. In addition 33% are in commerce and transport, 14% in government, 16% in other areas. Manufacturing value is the value added when materials are converted into goods.

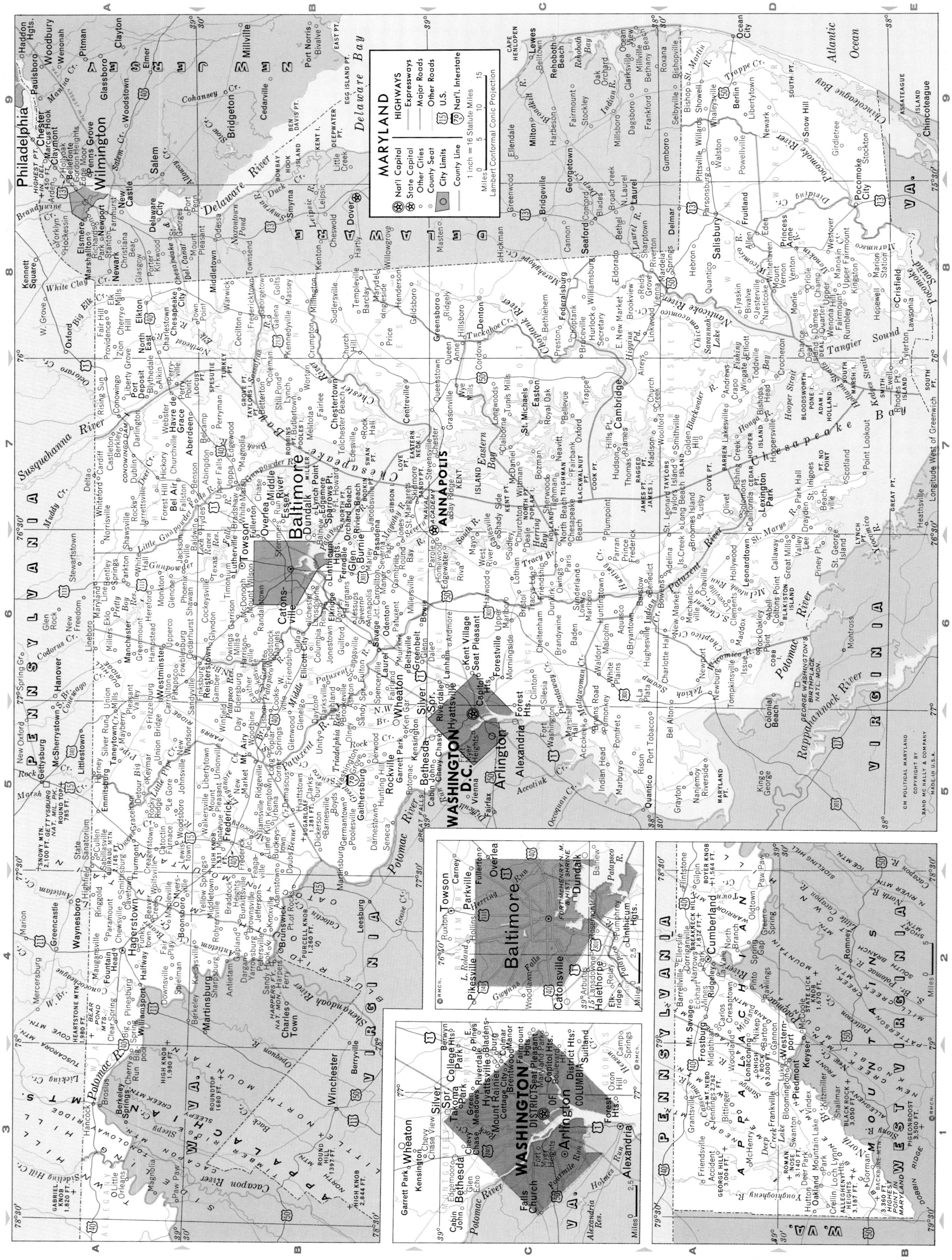
MARYLAND
Nat'l Capital
State Capital
Other Cities
County Seat
City Limits
County Line
HIGHWAYS
Expressways
Major Roads
Other Roads
U.S.
Nat'l. Interstate
1 inch = 16 Statute Miles
Miles 0 5 10 15
Lambert Conformal Conic Projection
PENNSYLVANIA
VIRGINIA
W. VA.
WASHINGTON D.C.
Baltimore
ANNAPOLIS
Philadelphia
Wilmington
Dover
Chesapeake Bay
Delaware Bay
Atlantic Ocean
Potomac River
Susquehanna River
Longitude West of Greenwich
CM POLITICAL MARYLAND
COPYRIGHT BY RAND MCNALLY & COMPANY
MADE IN U.S.A.

MARYLAND: With Chesapeake Bay penetrating it deeply, the colony of Maryland already had a natural division when in 1767 man created an artificial division that was to affect its history. This was the Mason-Dixon Line. Originally drawn to establish the boundary between lands granted to Lord Baltimore of Maryland and William Penn of Pennsylvania, the east-west line in time became the traditional dividing line between North and South. Though the state lies completely south of the line, Maryland's population suffered from divided loyalties during the Civil War, and even today vestiges of regional differences persist.

AREA:	10,577 sq. mi. Rank: 42nd.
POPULATION:	3,100,689. Rank: 21st. Largest city: Baltimore. Capital: Annapolis.
ENTERED UNION:	April 28, 1788, as 7th state.
CLIMATE:	Hot summers, cool winters in south and east; warm summers, cold winters in west. Ample rainfall.
ALTITUDES:	Backbone Mountain, 3,360 ft. (highest).

Chesapeake Bay, providing Maryland with an extensive fishing ground, produces more oysters than any other region of the U.S., and also contributes to the mild, humid climate which makes rich tobacco and truck crops and a valuable dairy industry possible. On a northwest inlet of the bay is Baltimore, the third largest port in the nation and a major manufacturing center. Baltimore has the second largest steel plant in the world. Accounting for four fifths of the value of the state's manufacture, the city is also active in chemicals, copper and petroleum refining, as well as shipbuilding.

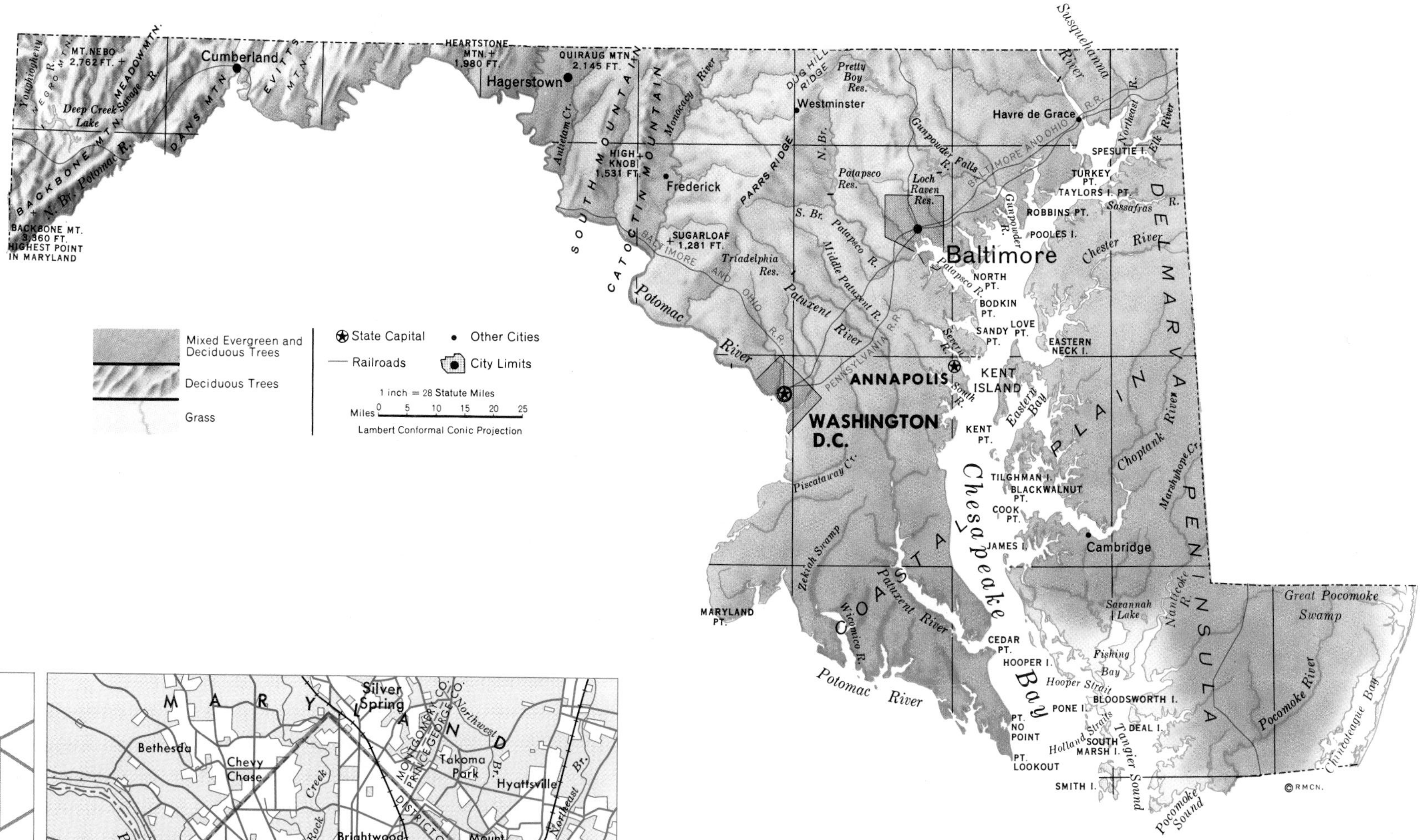

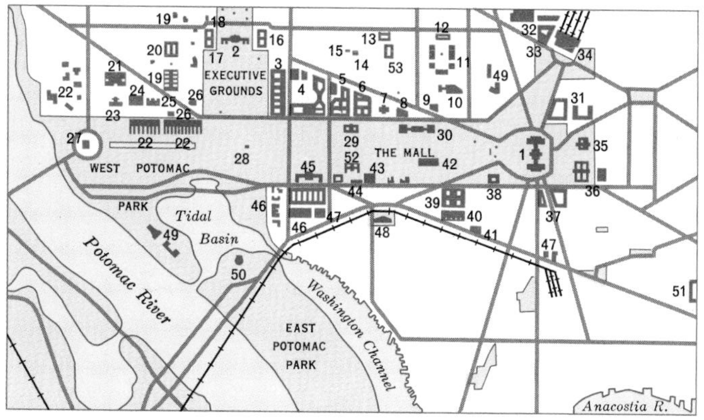

GOVERNMENT BUILDINGS AND POINTS OF INTEREST

1. The Capitol
2. White House
3. Commerce Department
4. Post Office
5. Internal Revenue Bureau
6. Justice Department
7. Archives
8. Federal Trade Commission
9. Unemployment Compensation
10. Municipal Building
11. Judiciary Sq. (Municipal Court, Police Court, Juvenile Court, Court of Appeals)
12. Accounting Office
13. Civil Service Commission
14. Lincoln Museum
15. Peterson House
16. Treasury Department
17. Executive Offices
18. Court of Claims
19. Interior Department Buildings
20. General Services Adm. Building
21. State Department
22. Navy Department
23. National Academy of Sciences
24. Federal Reserve Board
25. Public Health Service
26. Pan American Union
27. Lincoln Memorial
28. Washington Monument
29. National Museum
30. National Art Gallery
31. Senate Office Buildings
32. Government Printing Office
33. Post Office
34. Union Station
35. Supreme Court
36. Library of Congress and Annex
37. House Office Buildings
38. Botanic Gardens
39. Health, Education, Welfare Department
40. Railroad Retirement Board Building
41. F.B.I. Identification Division
42. Army Institute of Pathology
43. Arts Industries Building
44. Museums
45. Department of Agriculture
46. Bureau of Engraving and Printing
47. Capitol Heating and Power Plant
48. Federal Warehouse
49. Federal Office Building
50. Thomas Jefferson National Memorial
51. Marine Barracks
52. Smithsonian Institution
53. Tariff Commission

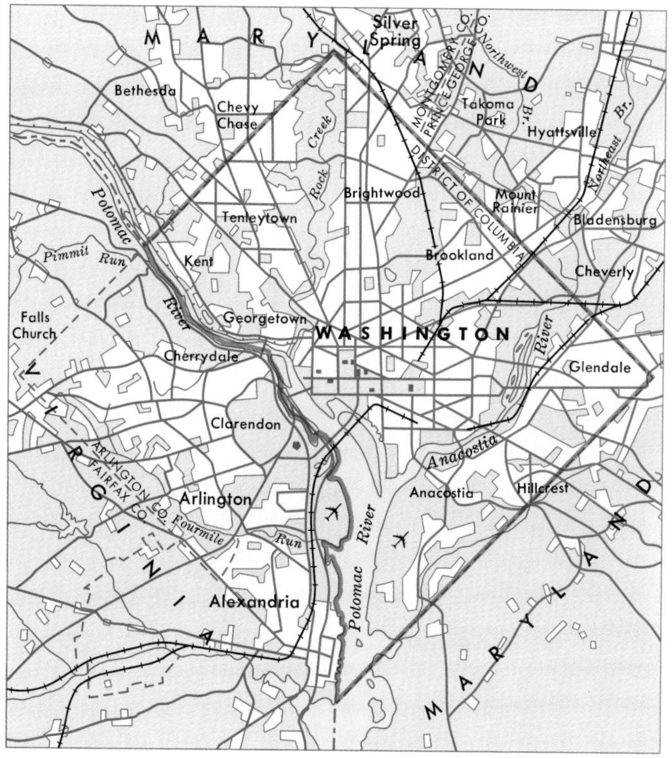

A GIFT FROM MARYLAND FOR THE 'FEDERAL CITY' OF A NEW NATION

After long arguments over the location of the national capital, Congress in 1790 accepted a joint offer of land from Maryland and Virginia. President George Washington himself chose a site 10 miles square, shown on the map at the right above *(red line and gray dashes)*, on which to build a "Federal City." During the first decades it appeared that not all of the land would be required for federal offices. Accordingly, the portion given by Virginia was returned to the state in 1846. The present District of Columbia comprises about 70 square miles, all of it ceded by Maryland. Central Washington, with its broad diagonal avenues converging on the Capitol *(left, above)*, owes its plan to Pierre L'Enfant, the French architect who designed the city in 1791 under the direction of Washington and Jefferson. L'Enfant took his inspiration from the avenues and parks of Paris. On both of these maps, the yellow areas indicate heavily built up sections; green areas are either parks or less populated areas.

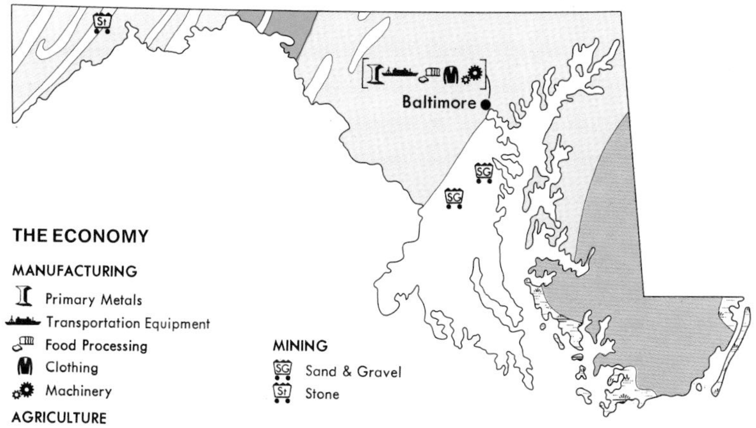

THE ECONOMY

MANUFACTURING
- Primary Metals
- Transportation Equipment
- Food Processing
- Clothing
- Machinery

MINING
- Sand & Gravel
- Stone

AGRICULTURE
- Tobacco & General Farming
- Fruit & General Farming
- Fruit, Truck & General Farming
- Dairy & General Farming
- Mountains & Forests
- Marshland

VALUE		EMPLOYED
$ 277,470,000	AGRICULTURE	7.0%
$2,451,000,000	MANUFACTURING	27.0%
$ 44,680,000	MINING	0.3%

Percentages are based on a total of 918,000 at work. In addition 33% are in commerce and transport, 15% in government, 17.7% in other areas. Manufacturing value is the value added when materials are converted into goods.

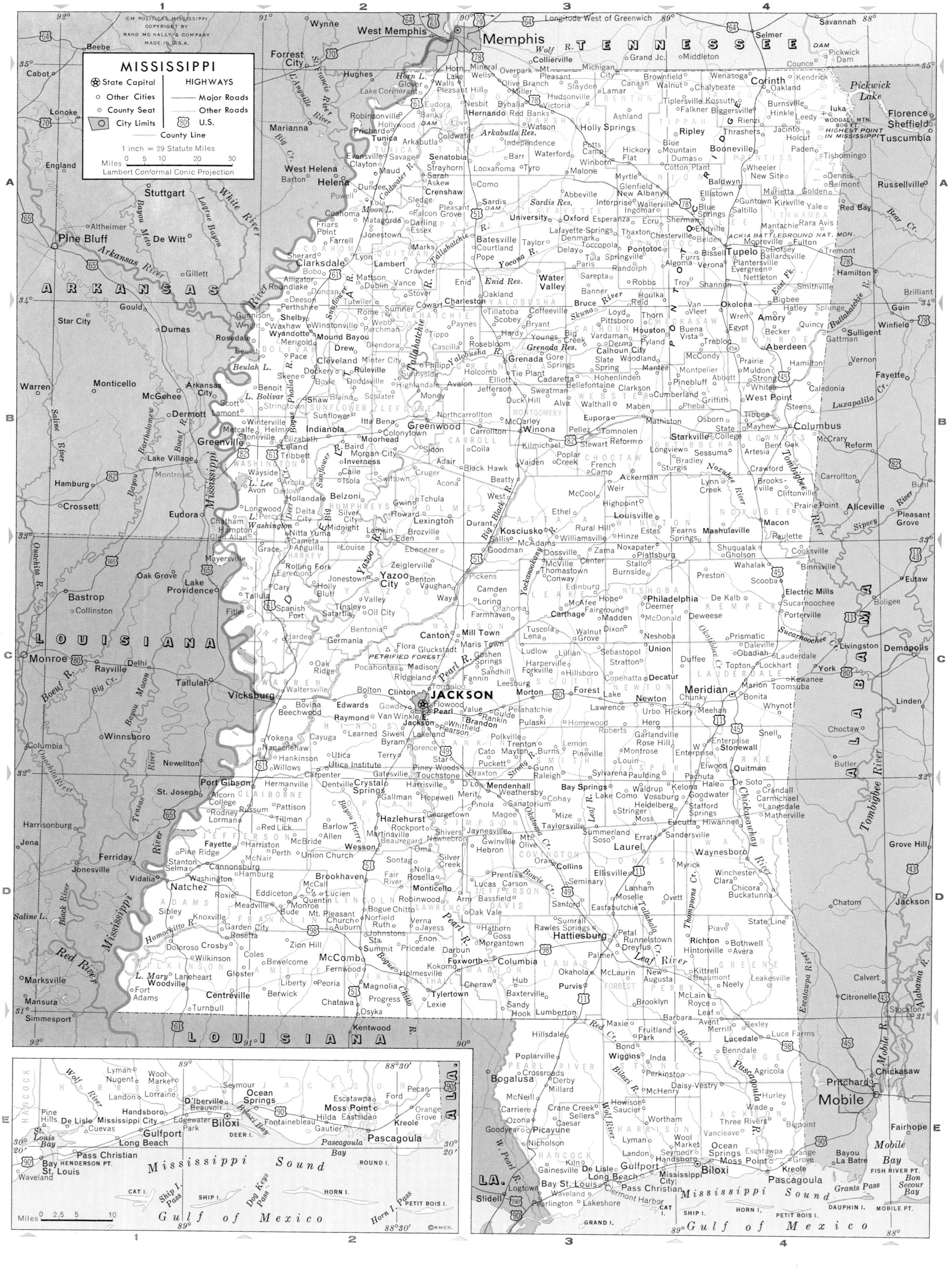
MISSISSIPPI
State Capital
Other Cities
County Seat
City Limits
HIGHWAYS
Major Roads
Other Roads
U.S.
County Line
1 inch = 29 Statute Miles
Miles 0 5 10 20 30
Lambert Conformal Conic Projection
CM POLITICAL MISSISSIPPI
COPYRIGHT BY
RAND MC NALLY & COMPANY
MADE IN U.S.A.
Longitude West of Greenwich
TENNESSEE
ARKANSAS
LOUISIANA
ALABAMA
LA.
ALA.
Memphis
West Memphis
JACKSON
Vicksburg
Greenville
Meridian
Hattiesburg
Tupelo
Columbus
Natchez
McComb
Laurel
Biloxi
Gulfport
Pascagoula
Mobile
Monroe
Pine Bluff
Mississippi River
Pearl R.
Yazoo R.
Tombigbee River
Mississippi Sound
Gulf of Mexico
PETRIFIED FOREST
ACKIA BATTLEGROUND NAT. MON.
WOODALL MTN. 806 FT. HIGHEST POINT IN MISSISSIPPI
©RMCN.

MISSISSIPPI

MISSISSIPPI: This is where cotton was once king, and it is still the heart of the traditional Cotton Belt *(map, bottom right)*. But here, too, as elsewhere in the South, the breakup of the vast semifeudal plantations and the depredations of the boll weevil, as well as of erosion, have forced Mississippi into a diversity of crops–notably tung nuts and soybeans. Cotton continues to be the most valuable crop, however, accounting for more than one fourth of the state's total production. (Only Texas and California lead Mississippi in this commodity.) The agricultural staple of the Old South grows in vast fields stretching from the fertile plains along the great Mississippi, across the Pontotoc Ridge to the east, and far south through the Pine Hills.

AREA:	47,716 sq. mi. Rank: 32nd.
POPULATION:	2,178,141. Rank: 29th. Largest city and capital: Jackson.
ENTERED UNION:	Dec. 10, 1817, as 20th state.
CLIMATE:	Long, hot, humid summers with many thundershowers; short, mild winters.
ALTITUDES:	Woodall Mountain, 806 ft. (highest); Jackson, 298 ft.; Greenville, 125 ft.

Like its sister states in the South, Mississippi is turning toward industry. The old order–whose gradual disintegration is portrayed in the novels of Mississippian William Faulkner–is giving way to a new industrial society. There is a boom in the pulp and paper industries, growth in food processing and textile factories and a new air of bustle in the ports of Biloxi and Gulfport. As the countryside empties and the cities grow, the state is surging ahead at a much faster rate than the U.S. as a whole. But Mississippians' acceptance of the economic realities of the 20th Century has not diminished the homage they pay to an earlier, heroic era. In this state are the sites of such famous and hard-fought battles as Vicksburg, Jackson and Corinth–and "old times . . . are not forgotten."

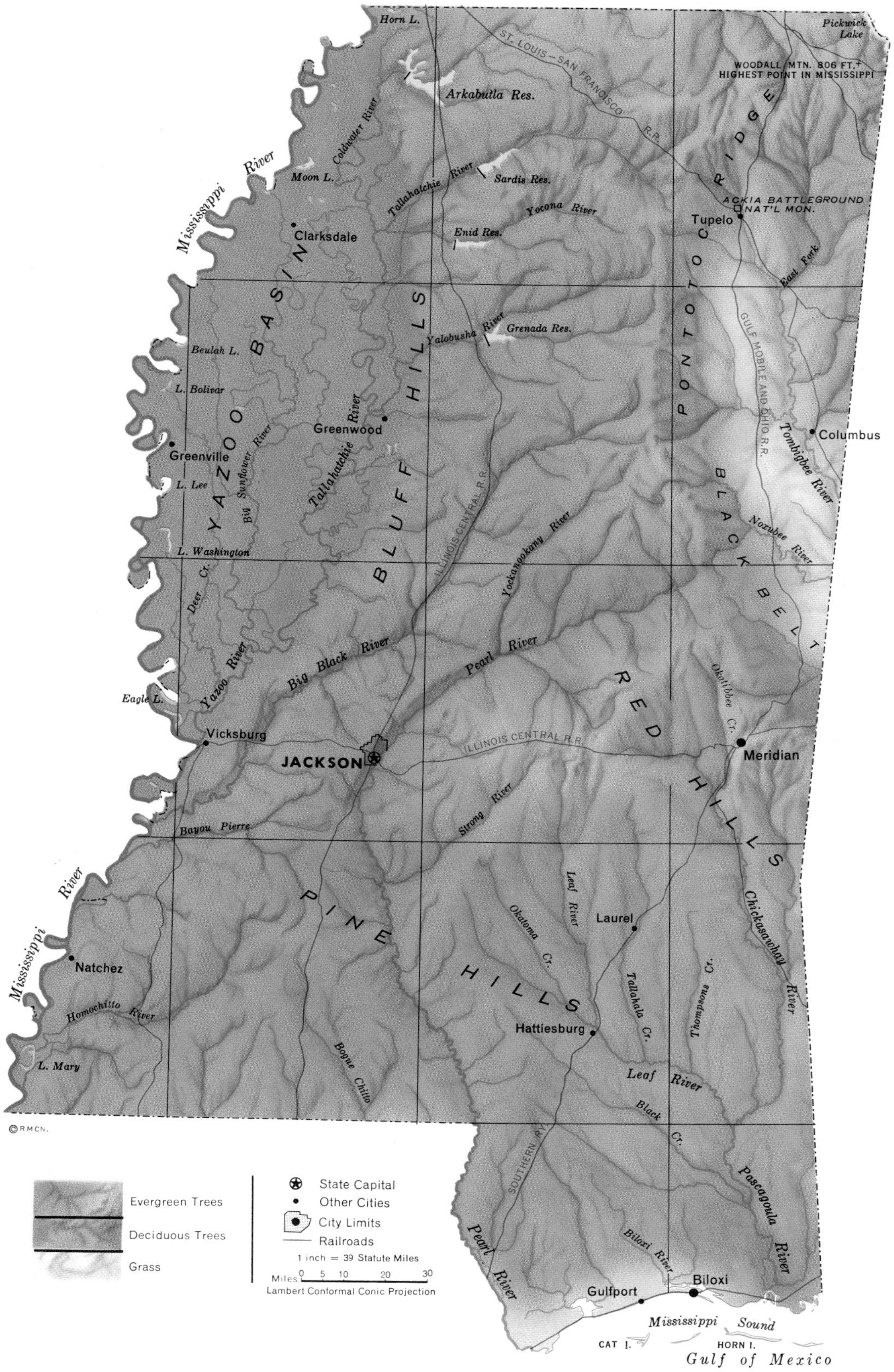

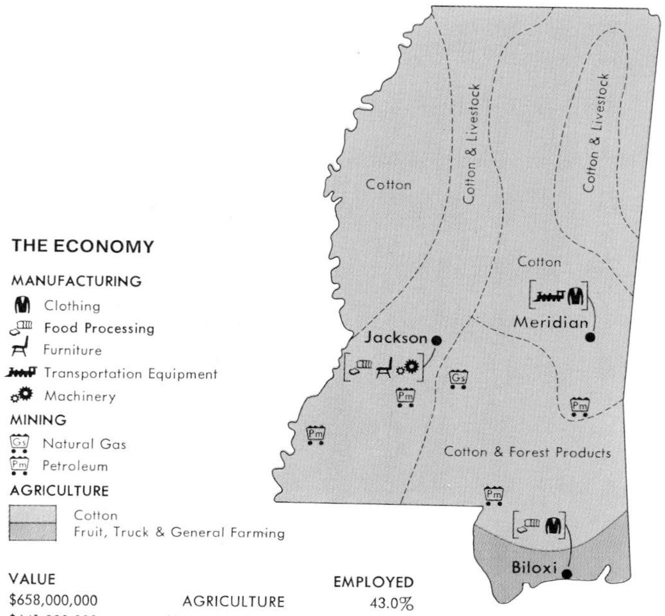

VALUE		EMPLOYED
$658,000,000	AGRICULTURE	43.0%
$641,000,000	MANUFACTURING	17.0%
$148,660,000	MINING	0.8%

Percentages are based on a total of 643,000 at work. In addition 19% are in commerce and transport, 12% in government, 8.2% in other areas. Manufacturing value is the value added when materials are converted into goods.

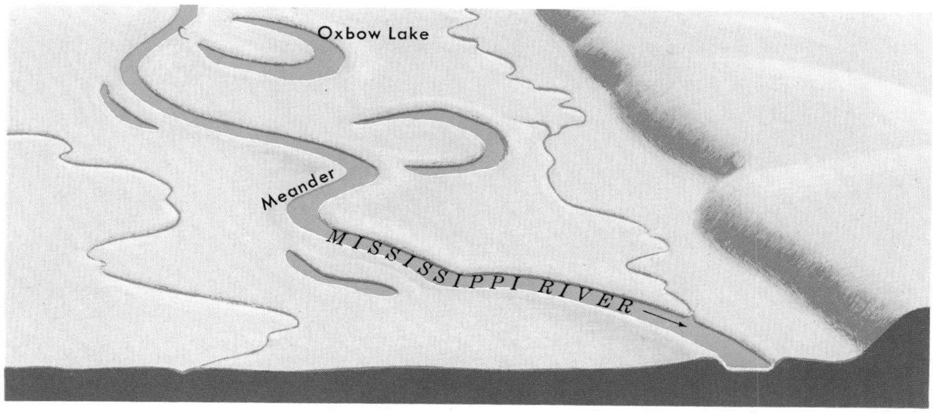

FROM A MEANDER TO AN OXBOW LAKE

"Meander" is the term given to a loop of a river like the Mississippi, shown above at a point near Vicksburg, that is old or "mature" enough to have eroded a very flat valley. With no steep walls left to channel its course, the river pushes harder against one bank than the other. Eventually a great loop is formed. Later, a new channel cuts through the neck of the loop, leaving behind an "oxbow" lake, so-called because of its yoke-like shape.

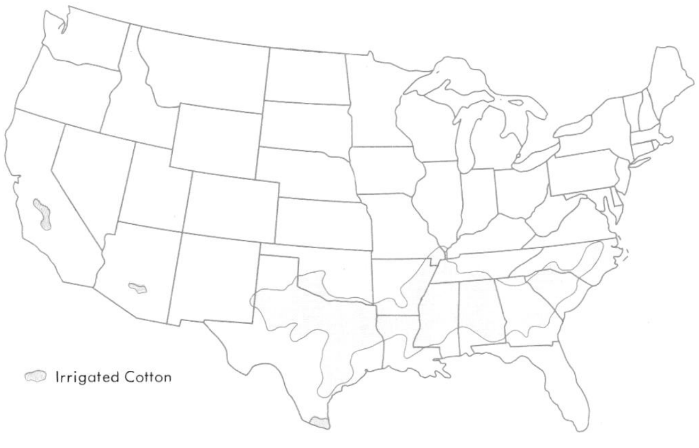

COTTON'S OLD-TIME KINGDOM AND ITS NEW COLONIES

Boundaries of the Cotton Belt show the main regions in the South where a hot, humid climate has permitted the crop to be grown naturally. But irrigated fields in California, Arizona and Texas *(blue areas)* have made cotton increasingly valuable in these states. Here the drier atmosphere is useful: in it the boll weevil cannot live.

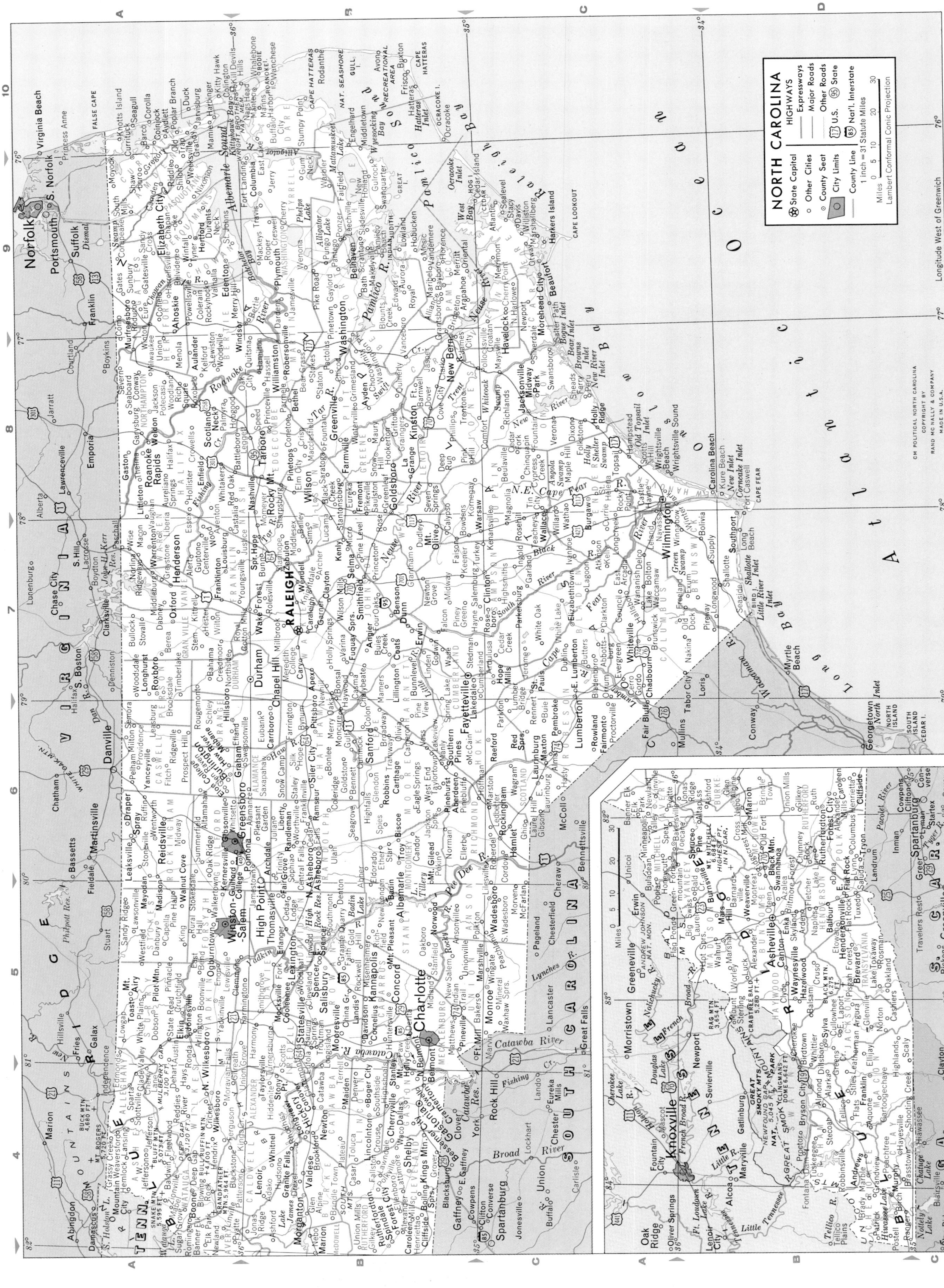
NORTH CAROLINA
State Capital
Other Cities
County Seat
City Limits
County Line
HIGHWAYS
Expressways
Major Roads
Other Roads
Nat'l. Interstate
U.S.
State
1 inch = 31 Statute Miles
Lambert Conformal Conic Projection
Longitude West of Greenwich
CM POLITICAL NORTH CAROLINA
COPYRIGHT BY
RAND MC NALLY & COMPANY
MADE IN U.S.A.

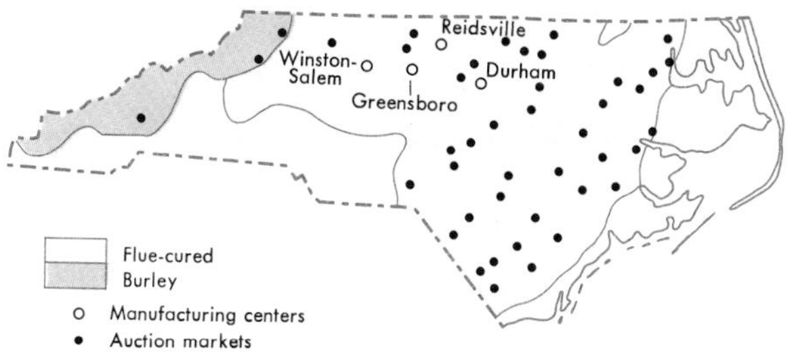
Reidsville
Winston-Salem
Greensboro
Durham
Flue-cured
Burley
Manufacturing centers
Auction markets

TOBACCO IN NORTH CAROLINA

North Carolina's big crop, cigarette tobacco *(yellow)*, is grown throughout the Piedmont section. Burley *(green)* is grown in the west; it is blended with other tobaccos for various products, including cigarette and pipe mixtures.

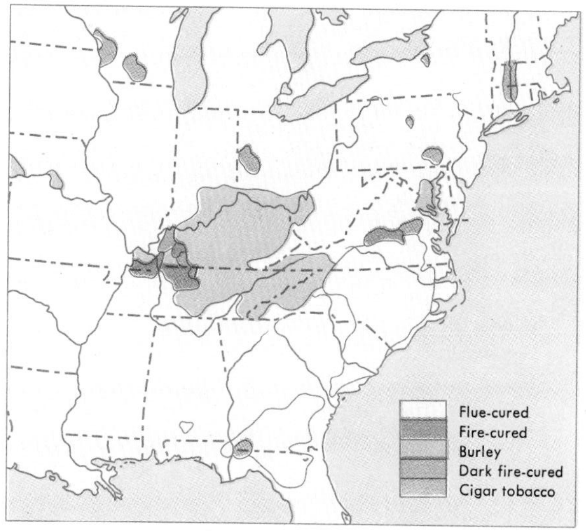
Flue-cured
Fire-cured
Burley
Dark fire-cured
Cigar tobacco

THE TOBACCO BELT OF THE U.S.

Tobacco is grown commercially in 18 states in addition to North Carolina. The color key on the map above shows the regions which specialize in the five basic types. Tobacco is classified according to both curing and use.

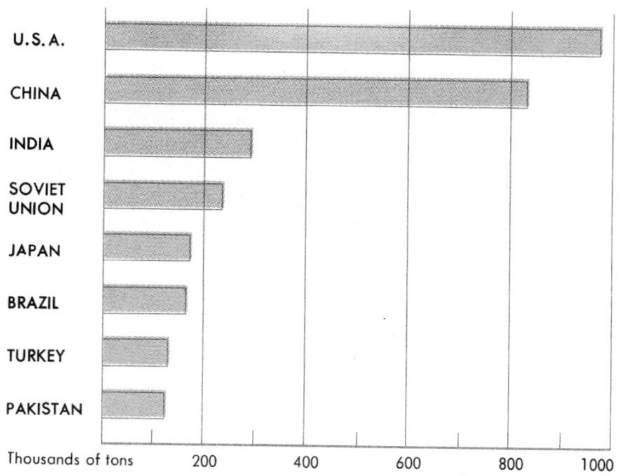
U.S.A.
CHINA
INDIA
SOVIET UNION
JAPAN
BRAZIL
TURKEY
PAKISTAN
Thousands of tons
200
400
600
800
1000

THE WORLD'S TOBACCO CROPS

As the bar graph above shows, the U.S. leads all other nations in tobacco production. The U.S. is also the world's leading tobacco exporter. China, the second leading tobacco producer, consumes most of its own tobacco.

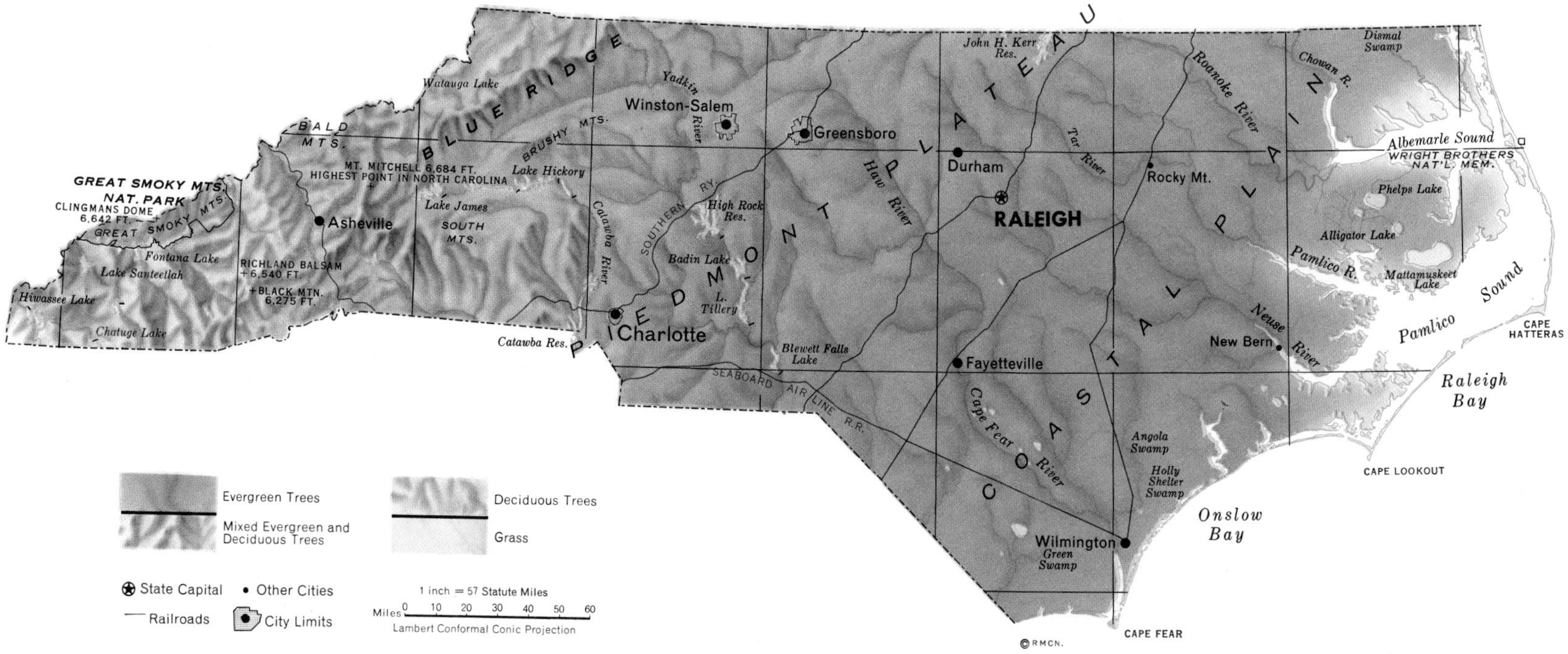
BLUE RIDGE
PIEDMONT
PLATEAU
COASTAL PLAIN
GREAT SMOKY MTS. NAT. PARK
CLINGMANS DOME 6,642 FT.
MT. MITCHELL 6,684 FT. HIGHEST POINT IN NORTH CAROLINA
RICHLAND BALSAM 6,540 FT.
BLACK MTN. 6,275 FT.
Asheville
Winston-Salem
Greensboro
Durham
RALEIGH
Charlotte
Rocky Mt.
Fayetteville
New Bern
Wilmington
Albemarle Sound
Pamlico Sound
WRIGHT BROTHERS NAT'L. MEM.
CAPE HATTERAS
Raleigh Bay
CAPE LOOKOUT
Onslow Bay
CAPE FEAR
Evergreen Trees
Mixed Evergreen and Deciduous Trees
Deciduous Trees
Grass
State Capital
Other Cities
Railroads
City Limits
1 inch = 57 Statute Miles
Lambert Conformal Conic Projection
© RMCN.

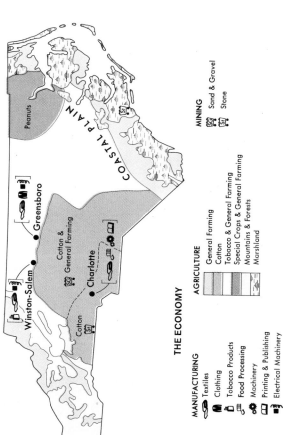

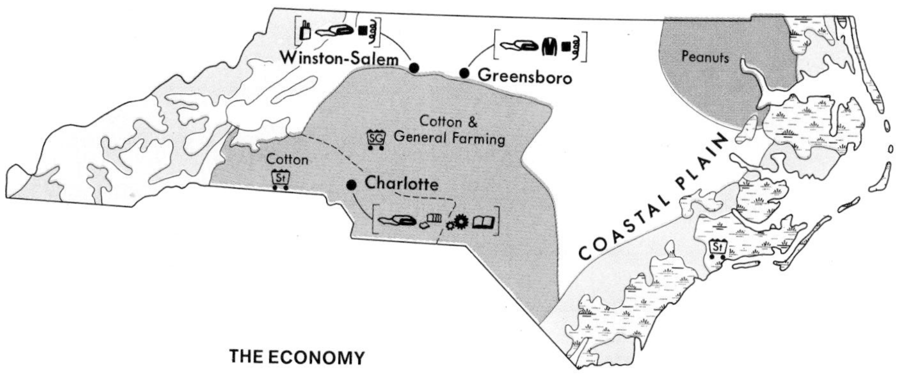
Winston-Salem
Greensboro
Charlotte
Cotton
Cotton & General Farming
Peanuts
COASTAL PLAIN

THE ECONOMY

MANUFACTURING
- Textiles
- Clothing
- Tobacco Products
- Food Processing
- Machinery
- Printing & Publishing
- Electrical Machinery

AGRICULTURE
- General Farming
- Cotton
- Tobacco & General Farming
- Special Crops & General Farming
- Mountains & Forests
- Marshland

MINING
- Sand & Gravel
- Stone

VALUE		EMPLOYED
$1,188,080,000	AGRICULTURE	29.0%
$3,095,000,000	MANUFACTURING	30.0%
$ 39,890,000	MINING	0.2%

Percentages are based on a total of 1,508,000 at work. In addition 21% are in commerce and transport, 10% in government, 9.8% in other areas. Manufacturing value is the value added when materials are converted into goods.

NORTH CAROLINA: In the west of this state rise the highest peaks of the Appalachian range. Along the Atlantic Coast in the east lie swamplands accurately known as "dismals." And sprawling into the sea off the coast are the forbidding Outer Banks, around whose sandy shores and often tempestuous capes–Fear, Hatteras, and Lookout–rot the carcasses of uncounted wrecks. Some of the isolated Outer Banks families trace their ancestry to sailors and colonists who were shipwrecked many generations ago. They speak in old English dialects and celebrate Christmas on Epiphany.

Between the extremes of west and east are the rolling hills of the Piedmont and the coastal plains. North Carolina has more farms than any state but Texas, and its total cash receipts from crops are fourth in the nation. Cigarette tobacco outstripped cotton as the state's most important crop in the 1920s; today North Carolina grows over two thirds of the nation's flue-cured output *(maps and chart, far left)*. It is also the second largest producer of peanuts and a principal grower of corn and hay.

AREA: 52,712 sq. mi. Rank: 28th.
POPULATION: 4,556,155. Rank: 12th. Largest city: Charlotte. Capital: Raleigh.
ENTERED UNION: Nov. 21, 1789, as 12th state.
CLIMATE: Hot humid summers, mild winters in east; cool summers, cold winters, heavy rainfall in mountainous west.
ALTITUDES: Mt. Mitchell, 6,684 ft. (highest); Asheville, 1,985 ft.; Charlotte, 720 ft.

In industrial as well as in agricultural output North Carolina heads the southeastern states. The state has at its disposal ample hydro-electric power generated by the rivers of the Piedmont region as they fall from the heights of the Appalachians. It is the leading manufacturer of textile goods in the United States. With extensive forests of pine, oak, poplar, hickory, fir and maple, North Carolina is the second largest lumber-producing state in the South and fifth in the nation. It is also an important manufacturer of household furniture.

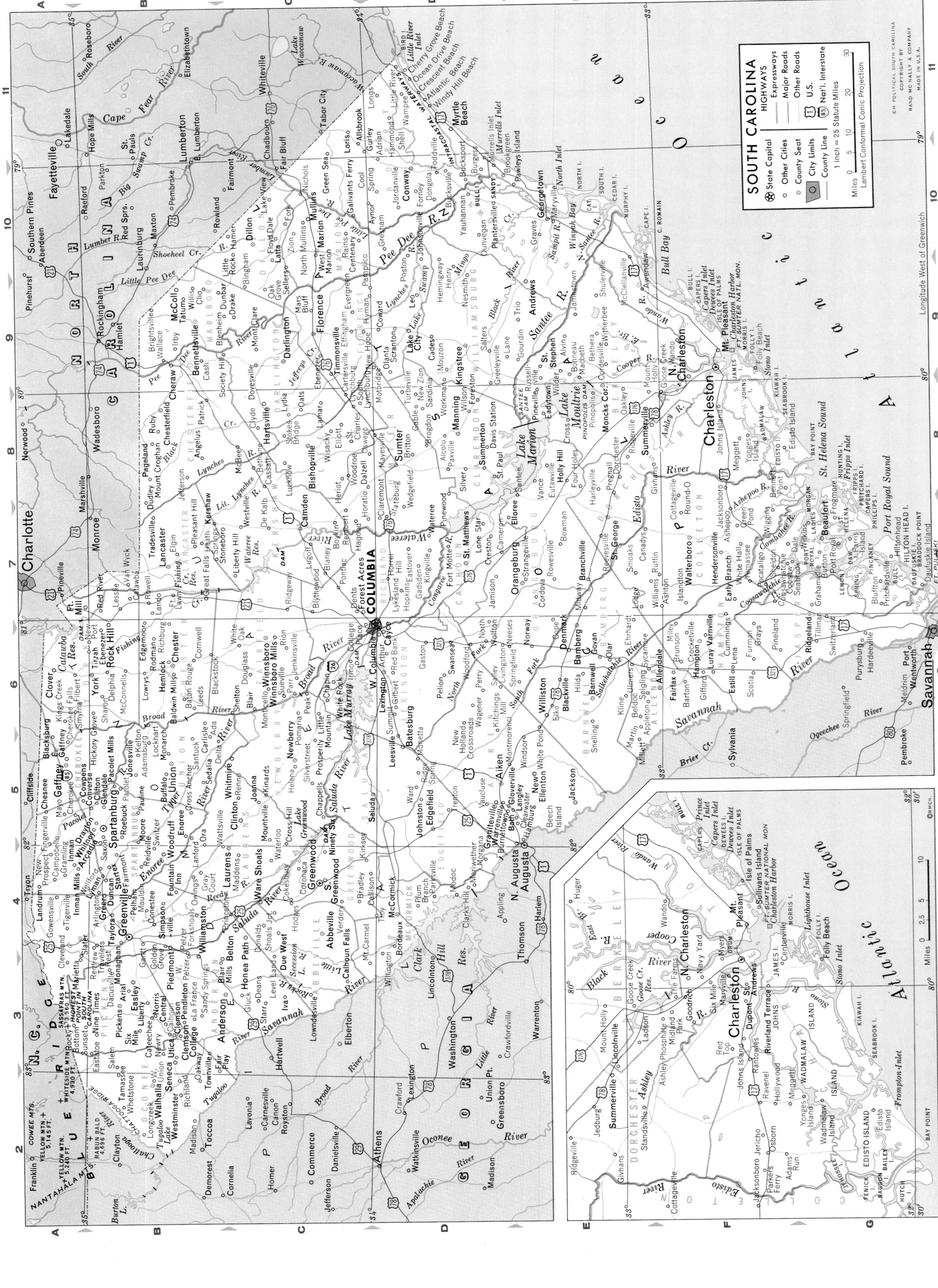
SOUTH CAROLINA
HIGHWAYS
Expressways
Major Roads
Other Roads
Nat'l. Interstate
U.S.
State Capital
Other Cities
County Seat
City Limits
County Line
1 inch = 25 Statute Miles
Miles 0 5 10 20 30
Lambert Conformal Conic Projection
Longitude West of Greenwich
CM POLITICAL SOUTH CAROLINA
COPYRIGHT BY RAND MC NALLY & COMPANY
MADE IN U.S.A.
NORTH CAROLINA
GEORGIA
Atlantic Ocean
COLUMBIA
Charleston
Charlotte
Savannah
Augusta
Greenville
Spartanburg
Florence
Sumter
Myrtle Beach
Rock Hill
Anderson
Orangeburg
Aiken
Beaufort
Georgetown
Lake Marion
Lake Moultrie
Lake Murray
Savannah River
Santee R.
Pee Dee R.
Broad River
Saluda River
Edisto River
Port Royal Sound
St. Helena Sound
Bull Bay
Winyah Bay

SOUTH CAROLINA: "The Palmetto State" acquired its nickname from the luxuriantly fringed trees that shadow Fort Sumter in Charleston Harbor. Along the island-studded coast, cypresses soar, gum and bay trees tower and spiky reeds jut up from acres of swamps. On the higher areas of the Coastal Plain, water oaks and longleaf pines arch against the soft skies. Far inland, the "up country" of the Piedmont Plateau boasts a timberland of yellow poplars, black walnuts, sycamores and other soft and hard woods. On the western border, in the highest part of the state, the Appalachian ridges are adorned with laurel, hemlock and majestic oak. South Carolina's profusion of trees makes the state a leader in the South's growing forest industry *(diagram and map, below)*, which is rising to challenge that of the Pacific Northwest.

AREA:	31,055 sq. mi. Rank: 40th.
POPULATION:	2,382,594. Rank: 26th. Largest city and capital: Columbia.
ENTERED UNION:	May 23, 1788, as 8th state.
CLIMATE:	Humid. Long hot summers, short mild winters. Some snow in mountains and upper Piedmont.
ALTITUDES:	Sassafras Mountain, 3,560 ft. (highest); Columbia, 190 ft.

Spaniards sailing from Santo Domingo in 1521 were the first Europeans to sight the virgin splendor of South Carolina. But the English, in 1670, founded the first permanent white settlement in the colony. One hundred years of defending themselves against sporadic attacks by the Spanish, as well as the French, Indians and pirates, gave the colonists a sturdy sense of independence. Inevitably, South Carolina was a leader in the American Revolution. And in 1860, maintaining what it considered its tradition of self-determination, South Carolina became the first state to secede from the Union.

Agricultural distress blighted the state from the time of the Civil War, and the fortunes of the economy remained low until after World War II. Now the Savannah River Plant, a 250,000-acre atomic production complex, creates new jobs while hydroelectric power from the state's many rivers draws textile and other industries in quantity. Industrial development is proceeding rapidly; three fourths of South Carolina's production is in manufacturing, with textiles and chemicals at the head of the list. At the same time, the state is one of the nation's important producers of tobacco. But there is still more than enough open land in South Carolina for the sport of quail-hunting, which remains a favorite pastime on the plantations of the "low country."

THE ECONOMY

MANUFACTURING
- Textiles & Clothing
- Textiles
- Chemicals
- Transportation Equipment
- Pulp & Paper Products
- Lumber & Forest Products
- Food Processing
- Machinery
- Stone, Clay & Glass Products

MINING
- Clay
- Sand & Gravel
- Stone

AGRICULTURE
- General Farming
- Cotton
- Mountains & Forests
- Marshland

VALUE		EMPLOYED
$ 417,080,000	AGRICULTURE	28.0%
$1,367,000,000	MANUFACTURING	30.0%
$ 22,410,000	MINING	0.1%

Percentages are based on a total of 730,000 at work. In addition 20% are in commerce and transport, 12% in government, 9.9% in other areas. Manufacturing value is the value added when materials are converted into goods.

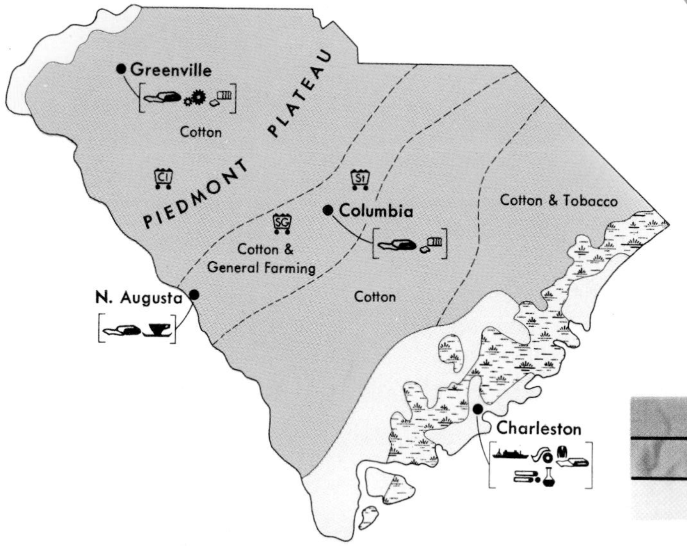
Greenville
Cotton
PIEDMONT PLATEAU
Columbia
Cotton & General Farming
N. Augusta
Cotton
Cotton & Tobacco
Charleston

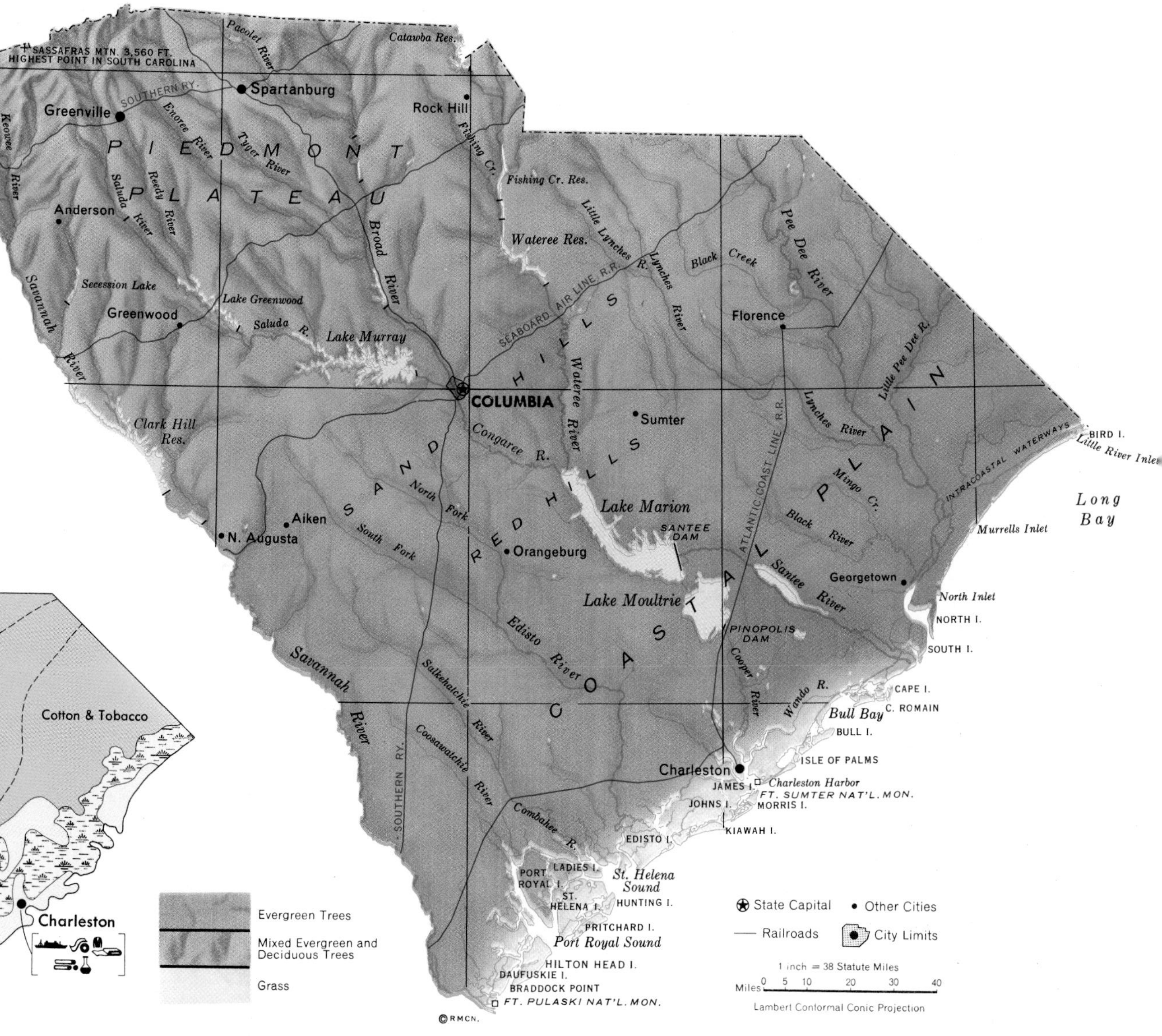
SASSAFRAS MTN. 3,560 FT. HIGHEST POINT IN SOUTH CAROLINA
Chattooga River
CHATTOOGA RIDGE
Tugaloo River
Keowee River
Savannah River
Greenville
SOUTHERN RY.
Spartanburg
Pacolet River
Enoree River
Tyger River
Reedy River
Saluda River
Anderson
Rock Hill
Catawba Res.
Fishing Cr.
Fishing Cr. Res.
P I E D M O N T
P L A T E A U
Broad River
Secession Lake
Greenwood
Lake Greenwood
Saluda R.
Lake Murray
Wateree Res.
Little Lynches R.
Lynches River
SEABOARD AIR LINE R.R.
COLUMBIA
Wateree River
Congaree R.
Sumter
Clark Hill Res.
Aiken
N. Augusta
North Fork
South Fork
Orangeburg
S A N D H I L L S
Lake Marion
SANTEE DAM
Lake Moultrie
PINOPOLIS DAM
Black Creek
Pee Dee River
Florence
Little Pee Dee R.
Lynches River
ATLANTIC COAST LINE R.R.
Black River
Mingo Cr.
Santee River
Georgetown
INTRACOASTAL WATERWAYS
BIRD I.
Little River Inlet
Long Bay
Murrells Inlet
North Inlet
NORTH I.
SOUTH I.
C O A S T A L P L A I N
Edisto River
Savannah River
Salkehatchie River
Coosawatchie River
Combahee R.
SOUTHERN RY.
Cooper River
Wando R.
CAPE I.
C. ROMAIN
Bull Bay
BULL I.
ISLE OF PALMS
Charleston
Charleston Harbor
FT. SUMTER NAT'L. MON.
JAMES I.
JOHNS I.
MORRIS I.
KIAWAH I.
EDISTO I.
LADIES I.
PORT ROYAL I.
ST. HELENA I.
St. Helena Sound
HUNTING I.
PRITCHARD I.
Port Royal Sound
HILTON HEAD I.
DAUFUSKIE I.
BRADDOCK POINT
FT. PULASKI NAT'L. MON.
Evergreen Trees
Mixed Evergreen and Deciduous Trees
Grass
State Capital
Other Cities
Railroads
City Limits
1 inch = 38 Statute Miles
Miles 0 5 10 20 30 40
Lambert Conformal Conic Projection
©RMCN.

WOODLAND WEALTH OF THE SOUTHEAST

Rich stands of oak and pine, shown on the map at right, make the Southeast the nation's second-ranking commercial forestry area. The oak, a hardwood used mainly in making furniture, grows in clay soils from southwest Mississippi to North Carolina. The softwood pine–including the loblolly, slash and longleaf varieties–thrives throughout the sandy Gulf and Atlantic Coastal Plains.

Much of the Southeast's great forest was once cleared by farmers, but with long growing seasons and heavy rains, pine trees quickly shot up in abandoned fields. Such a rapid rate of regrowth puts some southeastern forestry on a schedule as regular as harvest time on the farm.

The split log at the far right shows what happens to pine harvested in the Southeast. The slice labeled "logging residues" (tops, limbs and branches of trees) shows the percentage of all cut pines left in the forest. Sawmilling residues are wood scraps and sawdust, half of which are recovered for pulpwood. Pulpwood is used mostly in the manufacture of packaging and insulating materials, cardboard and newsprint.

One precious product of the living pine not shown on the graph is the oozing pitch, which furnishes rosins, turpentine and pine tars. These were called naval stores in the days when seamen used much of the supply to make their wooden ships watertight. Pitch products, of which the Southeast is the world's chief supplier, have since found their way into such modern industries as plastics, jet lubricants, synthetic rubber and detergents.

ARK.
MISS.
TENN.
ALA.
GA.
N.C.
S.C.
LA.
FLA.
Mississippi R.
Jackson
BLACK BELT
Montgomery
Atlanta
Macon
Columbus
Augusta
Charleston
Charlotte
Savannah
Mobile
New Orleans
Tallahassee
Jacksonville
Atlantic
Ocean
Gulf of Mexico
Pine
Oak-Pine
Tidal Marsh
Swamp
Farm Land

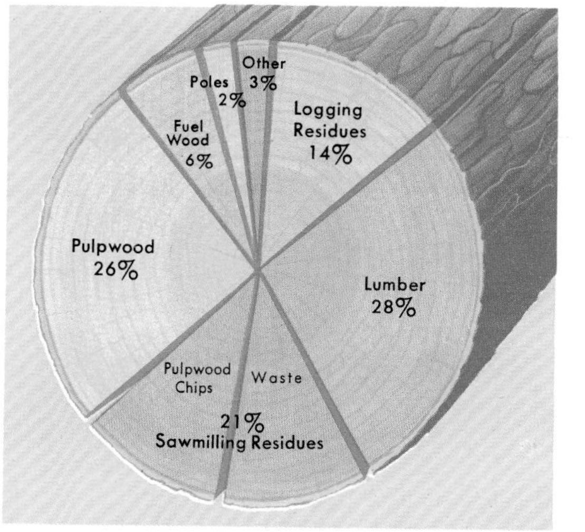
Other 3%
Poles 2%
Fuel Wood 6%
Logging Residues 14%
Pulpwood 26%
Lumber 28%
Pulpwood Chips
Waste
21%
Sawmilling Residues

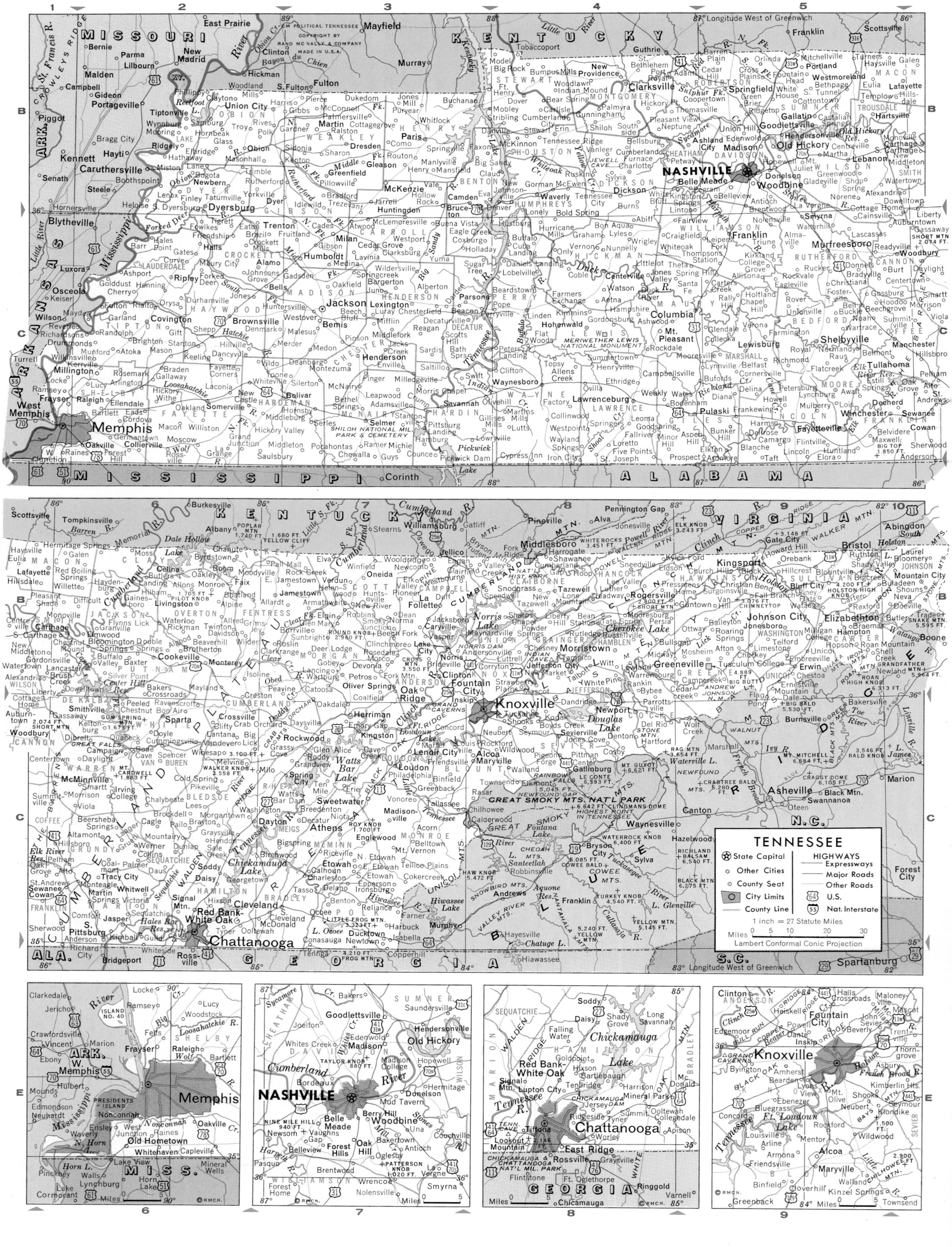
TENNESSEE
State Capital
Other Cities
County Seat
City Limits
County Line
HIGHWAYS
Expressways
Major Roads
Other Roads
U.S.
Nat. Interstate
1 inch = 27 Statute Miles
Lambert Conformal Conic Projection
CM POLITICAL TENNESSEE COPYRIGHT BY RAND McNALLY & COMPANY MADE IN U.S.A.
MISSOURI
KENTUCKY
ARKANSAS
MISSISSIPPI
ALABAMA
VIRGINIA
GEORGIA
N.C.
S.C.
NASHVILLE
Memphis
Knoxville
Chattanooga
Jackson
Clarksville
Johnson City
Kingsport
Bristol
Asheville
GREAT SMOKY MTS. NAT'L PARK
CUMBERLAND PLATEAU
Longitude West of Greenwich

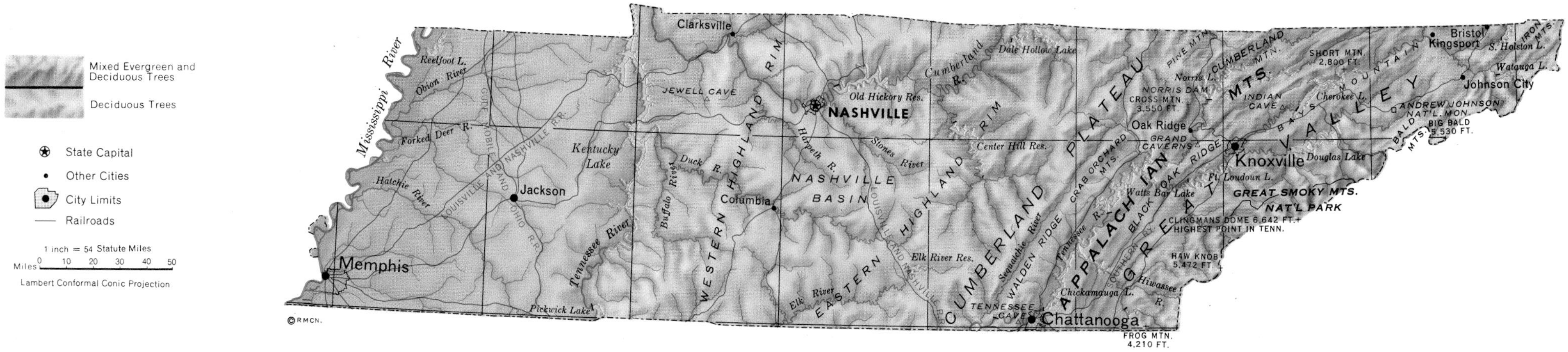

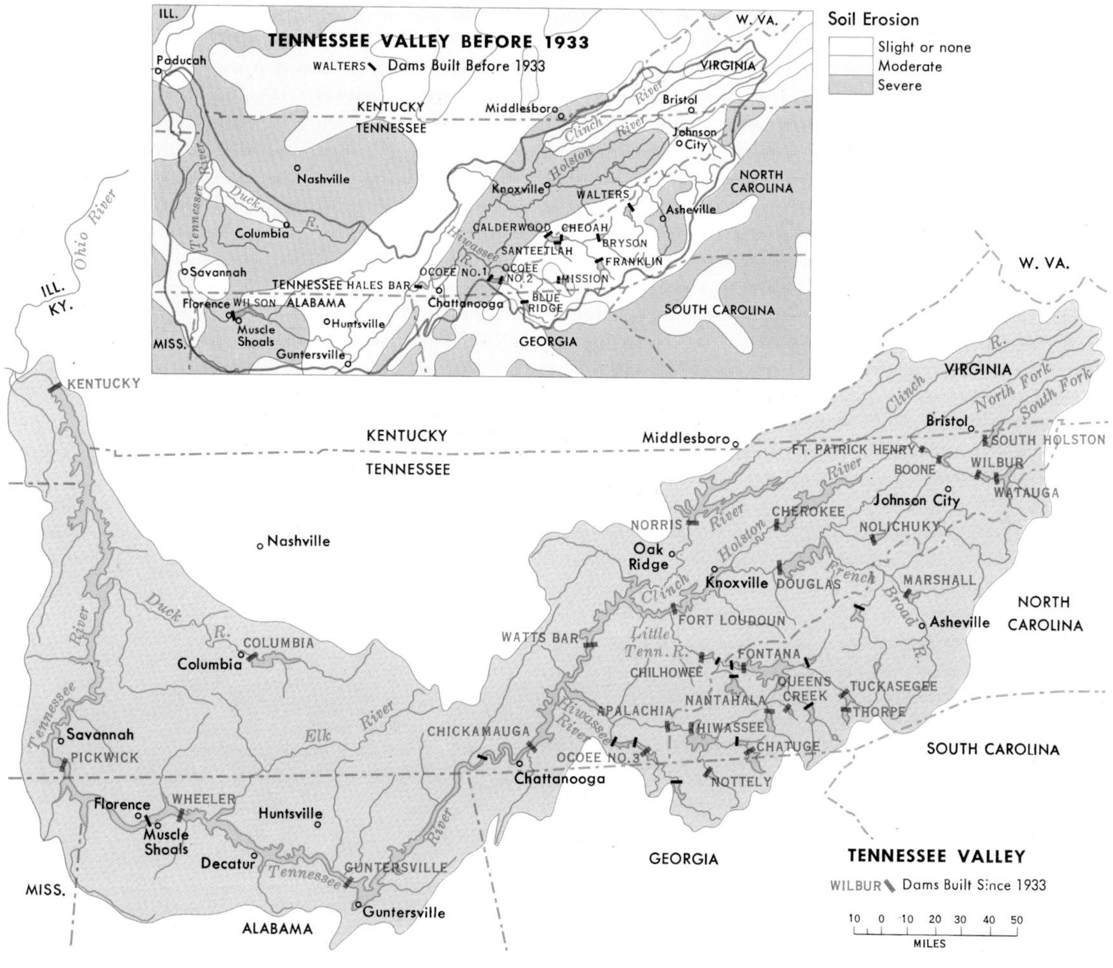

HOW TVA'S THERAPY REVIVED A SICK VALLEY

The case history of a miraculous recovery, these maps show part of the erosion-splotched region into which the Tennessee Valley Authority moved in 1933 *(inset)* and the same area restored to health some thirty years later. Established by the U.S. government to develop the natural resources of the Tennessee Basin, the agency's coordinated program has become a classic model for conservation and land rejuvenation. The first step was to build dams for flood control, which greatly reduced erosion; this effort was reinforced by reforestation and an education program for farmers. With its huge power output–one tenth of the nation's total–and with its dams and locks providing year-round river navigation, TVA attracted industry which has further improved the valley's economy. Serving an 80,000-square-mile area, twice the size of the drainage basin, TVA's power is sold to cities, industries and federal agencies for national defense, including two atomic energy plants.

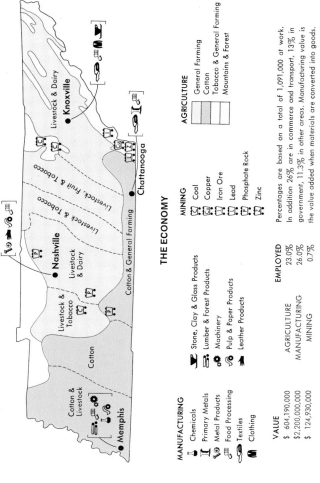

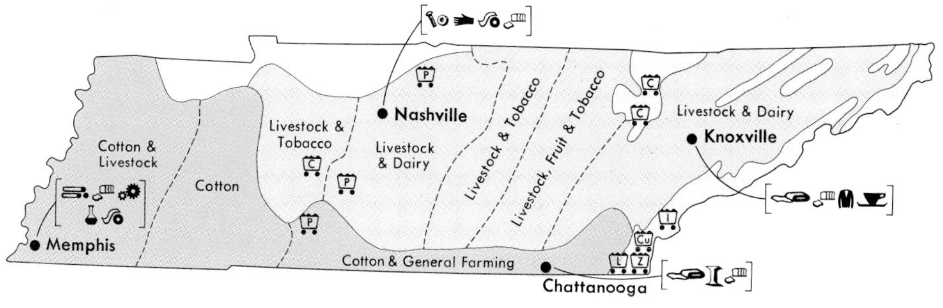

THE ECONOMY

MANUFACTURING: Chemicals; Primary Metals; Metal Products; Food Processing; Textiles; Clothing; Stone, Clay & Glass Products; Lumber & Forest Products; Machinery; Pulp & Paper Products; Leather Products

MINING: Coal; Copper; Iron Ore; Lead; Phosphate Rock; Zinc

AGRICULTURE: General Farming; Cotton; Tobacco & General Farming; Mountains & Forest

VALUE		EMPLOYED
$ 604,190,000	AGRICULTURE	23.0%
$2,200,000,000	MANUFACTURING	26.0%
$ 124,930,000	MINING	0.7%

Percentages are based on a total of 1,091,000 at work. In addition 26% are in commerce and transport, 13% in government, 11.3% in other areas. Manufacturing value is the value added when materials are converted into goods.

TENNESSEE: From its rich bottom lands bordering the Mississippi in the west to its stony uplands in the east, Tennessee has in the last three decades gone through a period of revolutionary transformation. Chiefly and initially responsible has been the Tennessee Valley Authority *(map, left)*. Once one of the poorest southern states, Tennessee was plagued by backward farming methods that allowed rampaging rivers to wash away the topsoil. But today, thanks to TVA's effective flood control system and agricultural education program, the state is able to produce valuable crops of corn, cotton and tobacco and to nurture dairy herds. At the same time, Tennessee's economy has been shifting its emphasis from farming to manufacturing, which now accounts for about three fourths of the state's total production. The power for this manufacturing–chemicals, metal-processing and textiles–is supplied by TVA's great thermal and hydroelectric plants, which also fuel government installations throughout the South.

AREA: 42,244 sq. mi. Rank: 34th.
POPULATION: 3,567,089. Rank: 17th. Largest city: Memphis. Capital: Nashville.
ENTERED UNION: June 1, 1796, as 16th state.
CLIMATE: Hot summers; short and generally mild winters. Moderate rainfall; some mountain snow.
ALTITUDES: Clingmans Dome, 6,642 ft. (highest); Nashville, 546 ft.

Although known to the Indians as "the land of Peaceful Hunting," Tennessee was to become one of the great battlegrounds of the Civil War. Five of the war's bloodiest battles were fought here–Shiloh, Murfreesboro, Chattanooga, Franklin and Nashville–leaving the state with memories of a proud but tragic past.

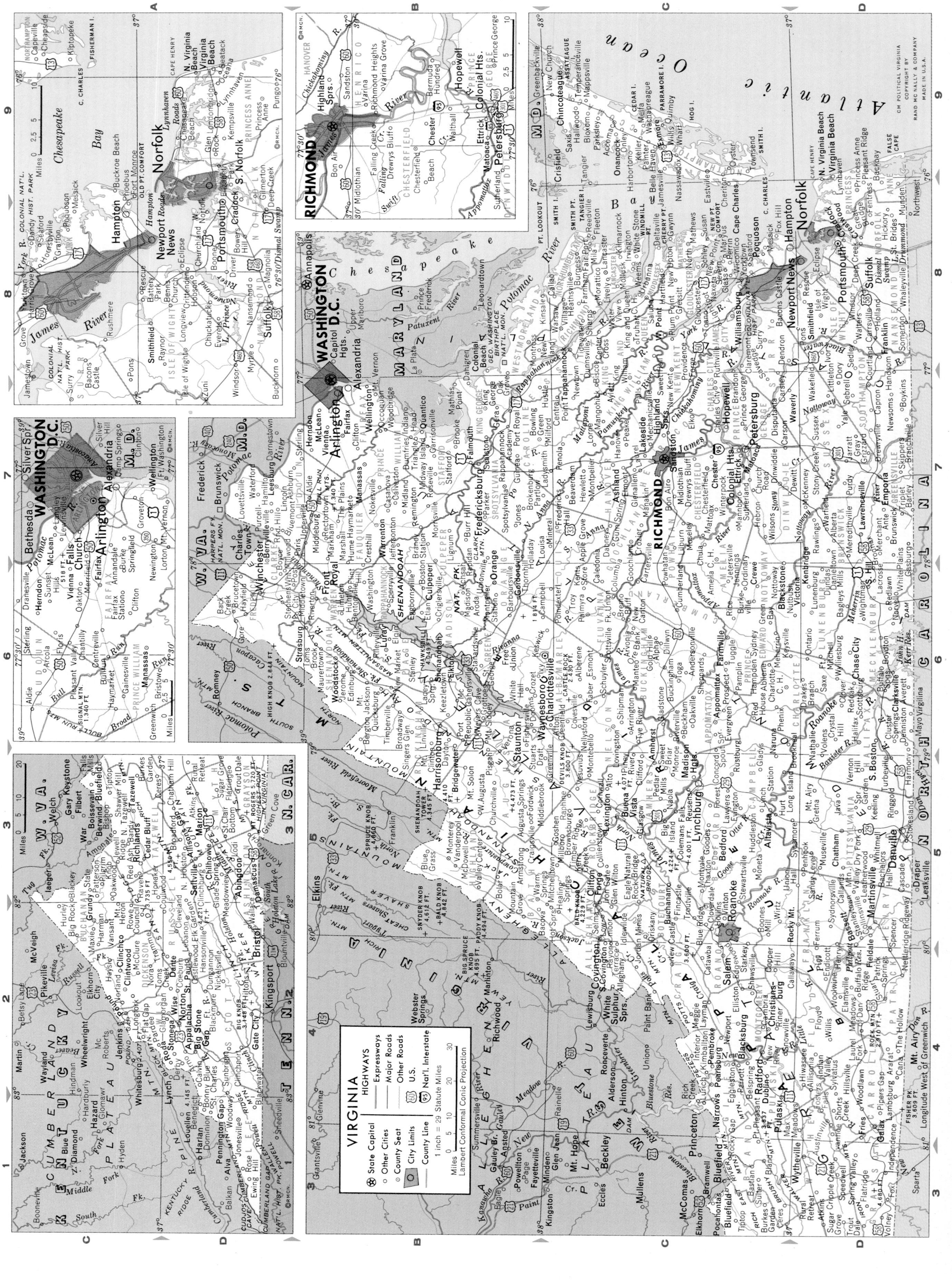
VIRGINIA
State Capital
Other Cities
County Seat
City Limits
County Line
HIGHWAYS
Expressways
Major Roads
Other Roads
U.S.
Nat'l. Interstate
1 inch = 29 Statute Miles
Lambert Conformal Conic Projection
RICHMOND
WASHINGTON D.C.
Norfolk
Atlantic Ocean
CM POLITICAL VIRGINIA
COPYRIGHT BY
RAND MCNALLY & COMPANY
MADE IN U.S.A.

VIRGINIA: The land the English colonists came upon in 1607 stirred feelings of wonder. Green pines stood high by the sea. Cedars looked as impressive as those of Biblical Lebanon. Wild grapes were abundant and the streams pure and cool.

To this day the state retains much of the pristine beauty that led settlers to name the colony in honor of their Virgin Queen, Elizabeth I. The Old Dominion rises slowly from the placid tidewater lowlands by the Atlantic, through the rounded hills of the Piedmont Plateau, to the crowning Blue Ridge Mountains. In the Shenandoah National Park, which straddles the Blue Ridge, Virginia rejoices in one of America's natural wonders. From the park's 105-mile-long Skyline Drive, visitors can look west toward a horizon that evokes a sense of the wilderness that confronted the pioneers.

AREA:	40,815 sq. mi. Rank: 36th.
POPULATION:	3,966,949. Rank: 14th. Largest city: Norfolk. Capital: Richmond.
ENTERED UNION:	June 25, 1788, as 10th state.
CLIMATE:	Hot summers, short winters with some snow. Moderate rainfall.
ALTITUDES:	Mt. Rogers, 5,720 ft. (highest); Norfolk, 10 ft.; Richmond, 164 ft.

The land remains as prolific as it is beautiful. Here tobacco was first cultivated by white men in North America, and today it is the state's largest cash crop. Fruits and forests are important too: Virginia ranks third among apple-growing states and is a major producer of paper and furniture. From the state's industrial centers—Norfolk, Richmond, Newport News and Roanoke—come such products as chemicals, cigarettes, textiles and transport equipment, notably ships.

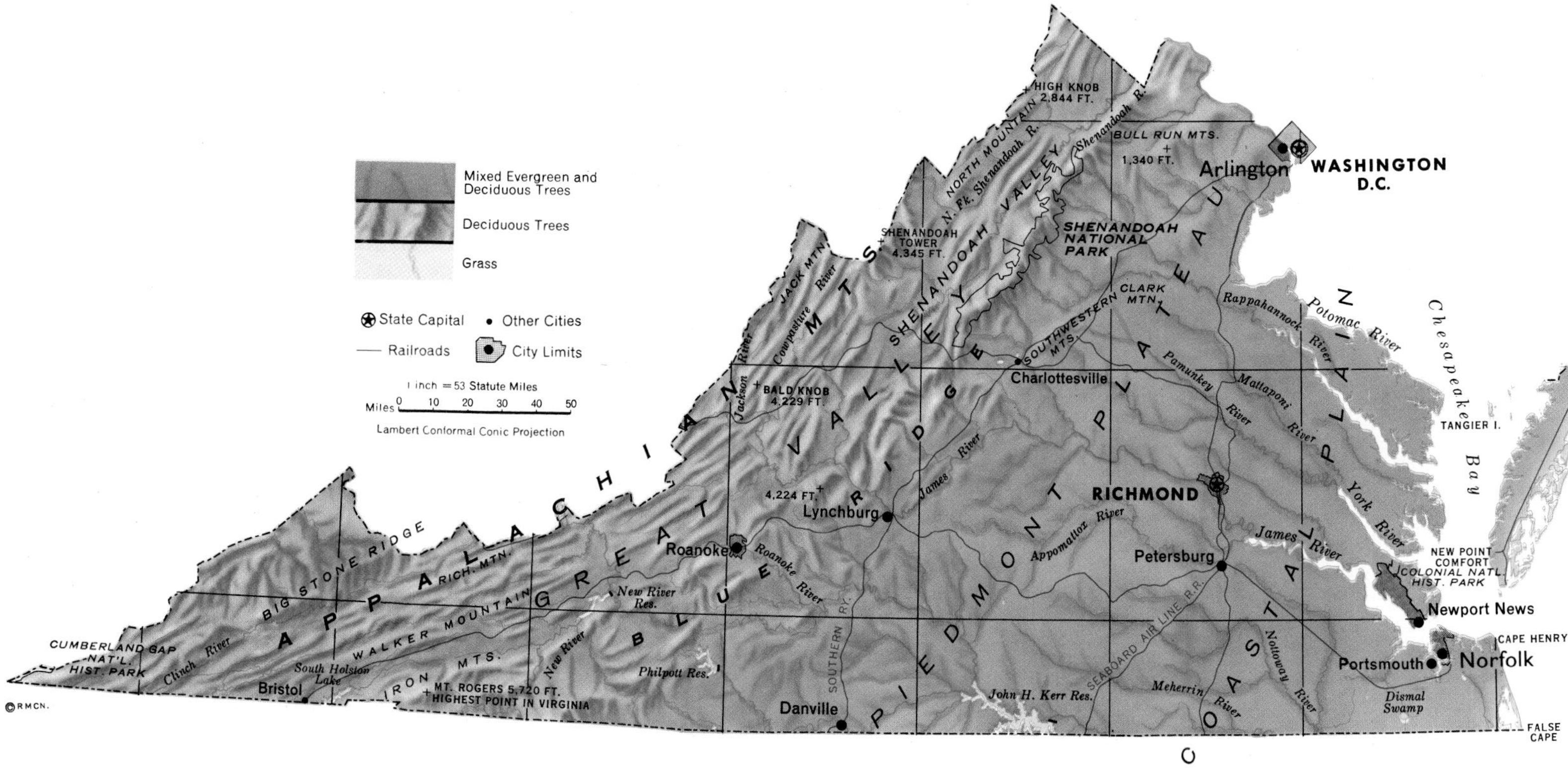
Mixed Evergreen and Deciduous Trees
Deciduous Trees
Grass
State Capital
Other Cities
Railroads
City Limits
1 inch = 53 Statute Miles
Miles 0 10 20 30 40 50
Lambert Conformal Conic Projection
WASHINGTON D.C.
Arlington
RICHMOND
Charlottesville
Lynchburg
Roanoke
Petersburg
Danville
Bristol
Newport News
Portsmouth
Norfolk
SHENANDOAH NATIONAL PARK
MT. ROGERS 5,720 FT. HIGHEST POINT IN VIRGINIA
Chesapeake Bay
©RMCN.

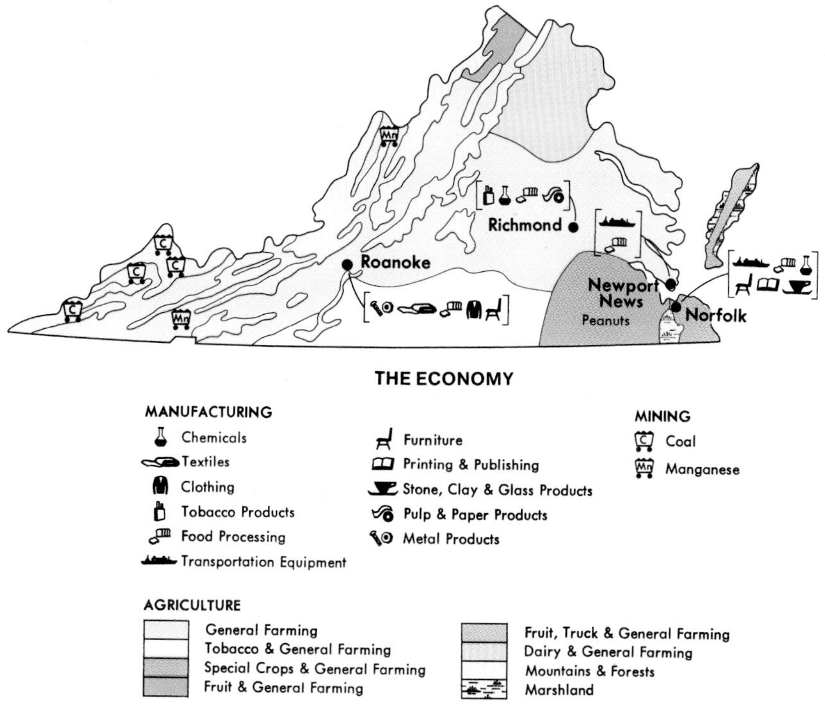
Richmond
Roanoke
Newport News
Peanuts
Norfolk
THE ECONOMY
MANUFACTURING
Chemicals
Textiles
Clothing
Tobacco Products
Food Processing
Transportation Equipment
Furniture
Printing & Publishing
Stone, Clay & Glass Products
Pulp & Paper Products
Metal Products
MINING
Coal
Manganese
AGRICULTURE
General Farming
Tobacco & General Farming
Special Crops & General Farming
Fruit & General Farming
Fruit, Truck & General Farming
Dairy & General Farming
Mountains & Forests
Marshland

VALUE		EMPLOYED
$ 553,420,000	AGRICULTURE	18%
$2,161,000,000	MANUFACTURING	21%
$ 203,230,000	MINING	2%

Percentages are based on a total of 1,208,000 at work. In addition 30% are in commerce and transport, 15% in government, 14% in other areas. Manufacturing value is the value added when materials are converted into goods.

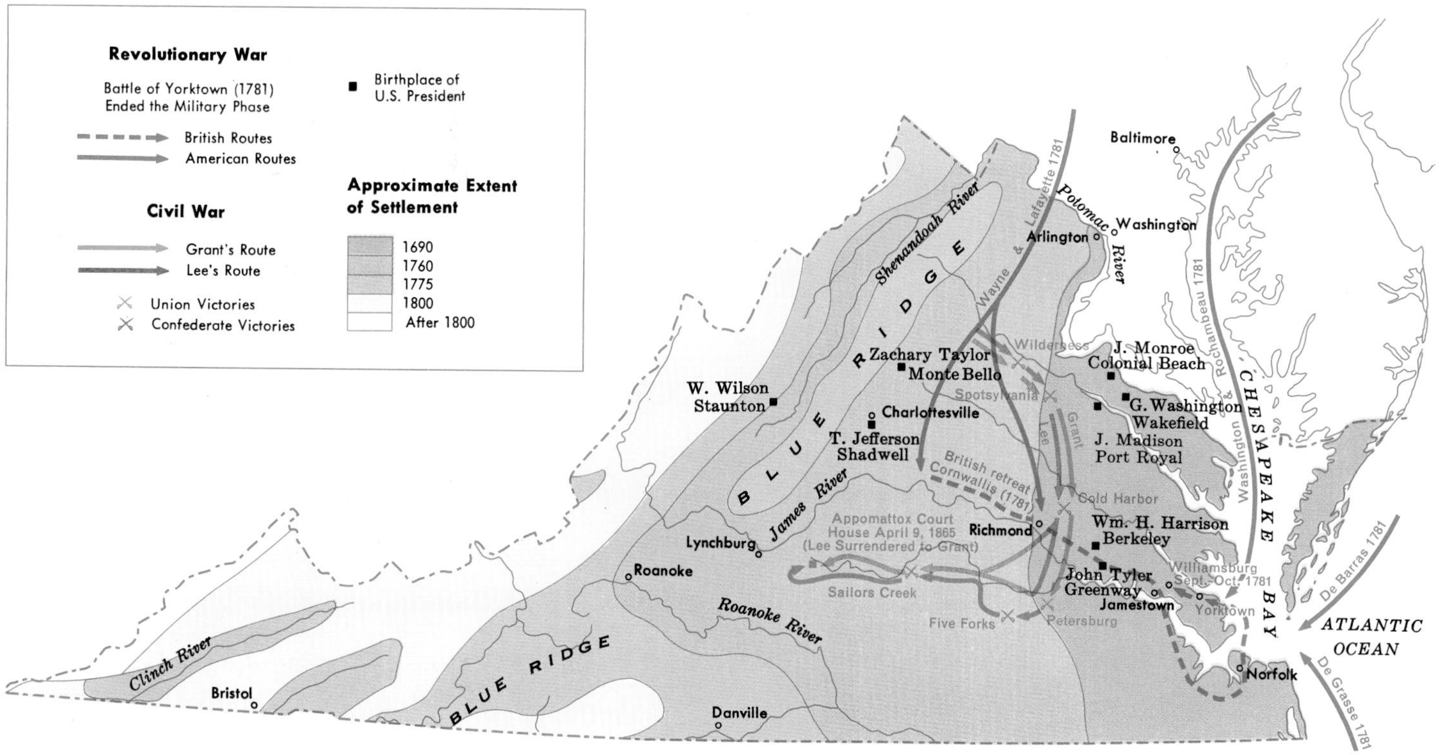
Revolutionary War
Battle of Yorktown (1781) Ended the Military Phase
British Routes
American Routes
Birthplace of U.S. President
Civil War
Grant's Route
Lee's Route
Union Victories
Confederate Victories
Approximate Extent of Settlement
1690
1760
1775
1800
After 1800
W. Wilson Staunton
Zachary Taylor Monte Bello
T. Jefferson Shadwell
J. Monroe Colonial Beach
G. Washington Wakefield
J. Madison Port Royal
Wm. H. Harrison Berkeley
John Tyler Greenway
Appomattox Court House April 9, 1865 (Lee Surrendered to Grant)
CHESAPEAKE BAY
ATLANTIC OCEAN

IN OLD VIRGINIA: PATHS OF PAIN AND GLORY THAT SHAPED AMERICA'S DESTINY

The slow tides of settlement and darting lines of war, shown on the map above, are testimony to the rich history of this state, which Virginians proudly call "the Old Dominion." The first permanent English colony, Jamestown, was founded in 1607, and most of present-day Virginia was settled well before the U.S. became a nation. A cradle of American political thought, the state was the birthplace of eight presidents. Here Jefferson wrote: "I have sworn upon the altar of God eternal hostility against every form of tyranny over the mind of man." It was in Virginia that two military surrenders took place which decided the nation's destiny. When Lafayette, Washington and two French fleets converged upon Cornwallis at Yorktown in 1781, the American Revolution was won. When the Confederate General Robert E. Lee offered Ulysses S. Grant his sword at Appomattox Court House one afternoon in 1865, the Union was preserved.

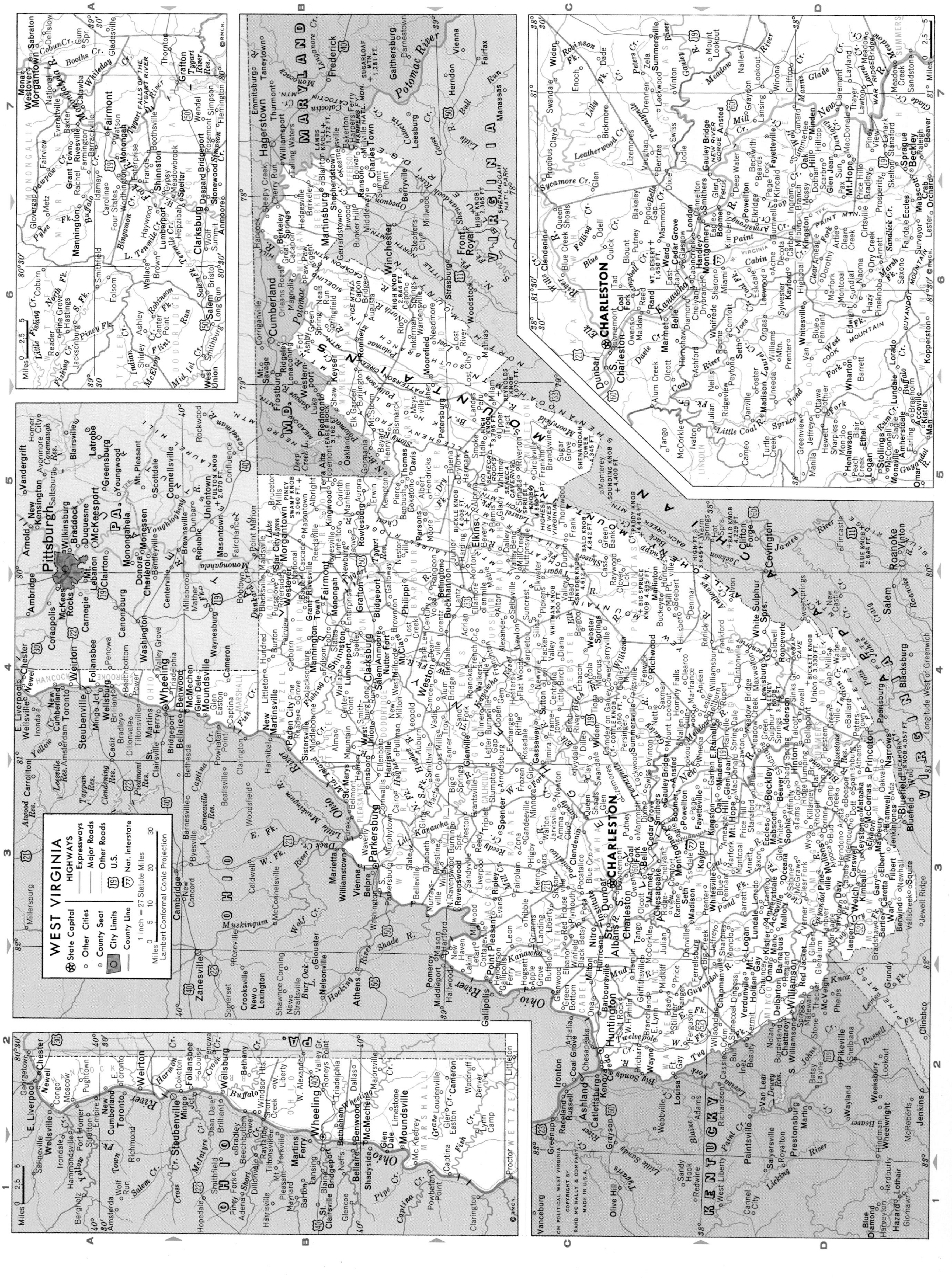
WEST VIRGINIA
HIGHWAYS
State Capital
Other Cities
County Seat
City Limits
County Line
Expressways
Major Roads
Other Roads
U.S.
Nat. Interstate
1 inch = 27 Statute Miles
Lambert Conformal Conic Projection
MARYLAND
VIRGINIA
KENTUCKY
OHIO
PA.
CHARLESTON
Pittsburgh
Wheeling
Parkersburg
Huntington
Morgantown
Clarksburg
Fairmont
CM POLITICAL WEST VIRGINIA
COPYRIGHT BY RAND McNALLY & COMPANY
MADE IN U.S.A.
Longitude West of Greenwich

WEST VIRGINIA: "It's a wonderful place to work," runs a local joke. "When you get tired in West Virginia, you lean up against it." Two thirds of craggy West Virginia lies on the rough, uplifted Allegheny Plateau, an area intricately eroded by streams hurrying through a maze of V-shaped valleys and sharply angled hills. The eastern third, dominated by the Appalachians, is a land of rocky ridges separated by parallel valleys.

In consequence the hilly state was only a hunting ground–and hence a battleground–for Indian tribes until the seaboard colonists came to know it. Only the most hardy of the pioneers had dared settle in its wilderness when the young Virginian surveyor George Washington plied his trade in the eastern uplands. To this day, despite ample rainfall and four frost-free months each year, there is not sufficient flat land to make agriculture important to the state. But with almost 70 per cent of its slopes and gorges still covered with towering oaks, maples and other trees, West Virginia is one of the chief sources of American hardwoods.

AREA:	24,181 sq. mi. Rank: 41st.
POPULATION:	1,860,421. Rank: 30th. Largest city and capital: Charleston.
ENTERED UNION:	June 20, 1863, as 35th state.
CLIMATE:	Hot summers in valleys, mild in mountains; cool winters. Ample rainfall.
ALTITUDES:	Spruce Knob, 4,860 ft. (highest); Charleston, 601 ft.

"Mountaineers–Always Free" is the state's motto, and West Virginians have always believed that their mountain isolation breeds an independent folk. Thousands of colonists had settled in western Virginia before the Revolutionary War, in defiance of a royal law forbidding settlement west of the Alleghenies. Descendants of these settlers broke from Virginia during the Civil War and led their region into statehood.

In the sharply folded Appalachians lie many of the state's most valuable resources. Since the 1930s West Virginia has been the nation's leading producer of bituminous coal *(diagram, below)*. The bedrock also yields petroleum, natural gases and lime. In the northern panhandle are almost 2,500 square miles of salt deposits, important to the chemical plants at central Charleston.

West Virginia's economy has been plagued in recent years by a decreased demand for coal. But with a skilled labor supply, ready access to markets and power aplenty available from its swift rivers, the state still maintains an important place in the U.S. economy.

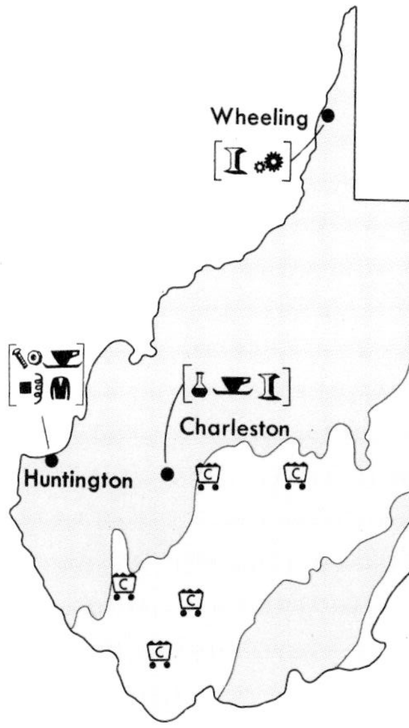

THE ECONOMY

MANUFACTURING: Chemicals; Metal Products; Primary Metals; Stone, Clay & Glass Products; Electrical Machinery; Clothing; Machinery

MINING: Coal

AGRICULTURE: General Farming; Fruit & General Farming; Mountains & Forests

VALUE		EMPLOYED
$ 146,500,000	AGRICULTURE	14%
$1,216,000,000	MANUFACTURING	22%
$ 749,780,000	MINING	13%

Percentages are based on a total of 547,000 at work. In addition 27% are in commerce and transport. 11% in government, 13% in other areas. Manufacturing value is the value added when materials are converted into goods.

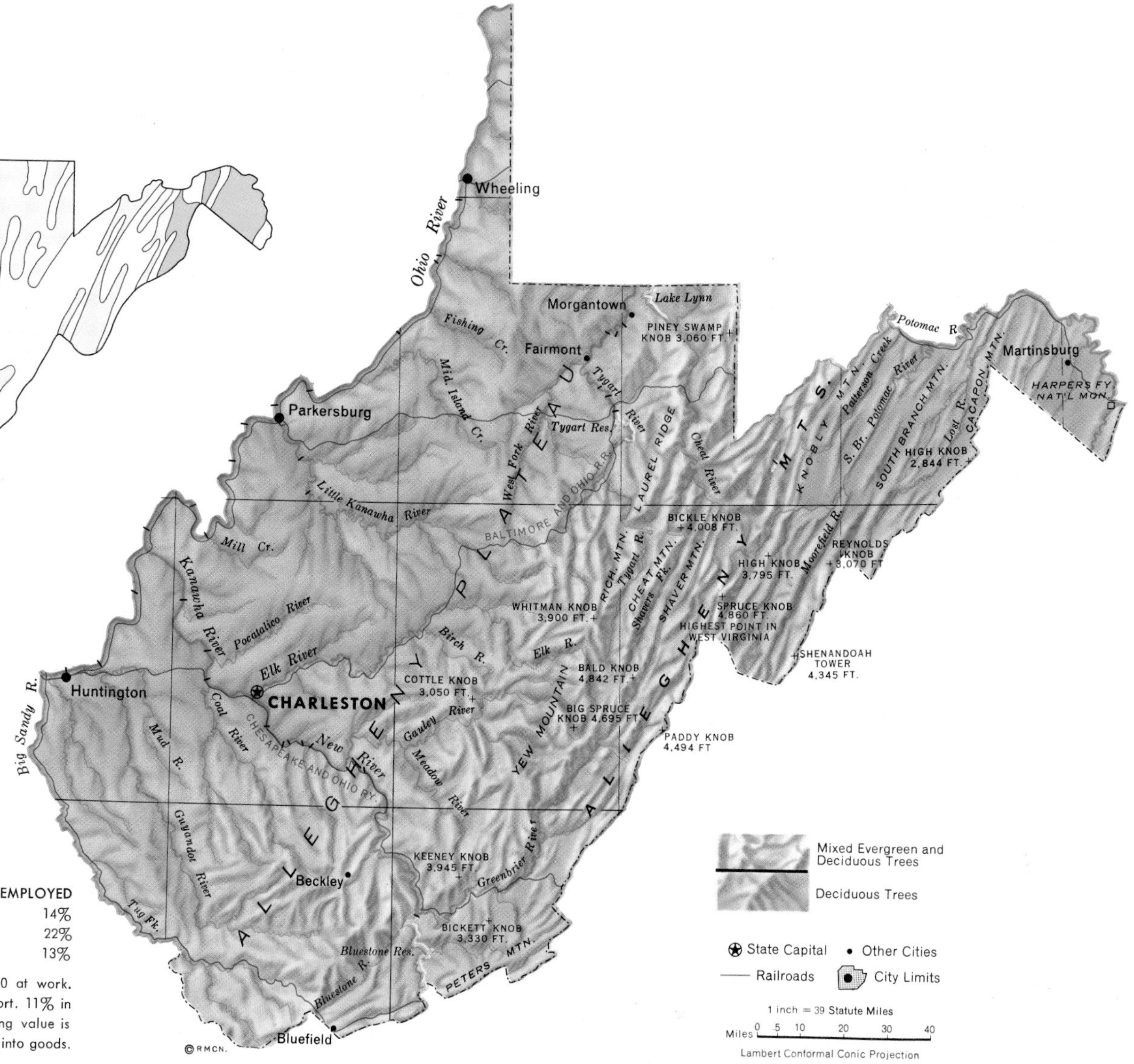

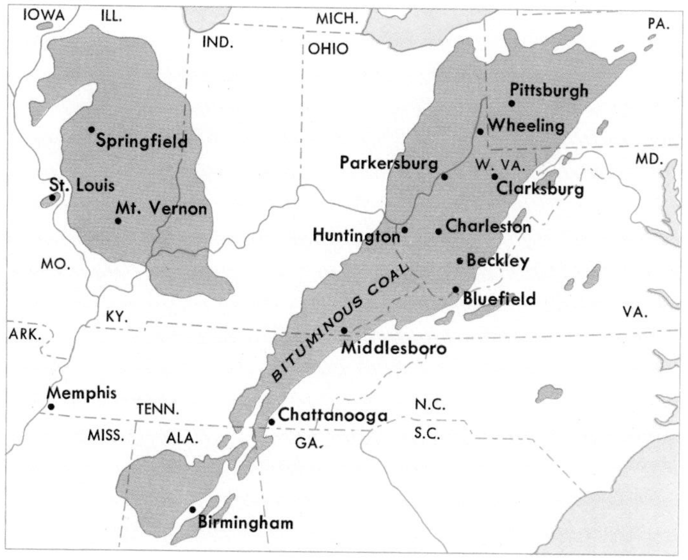

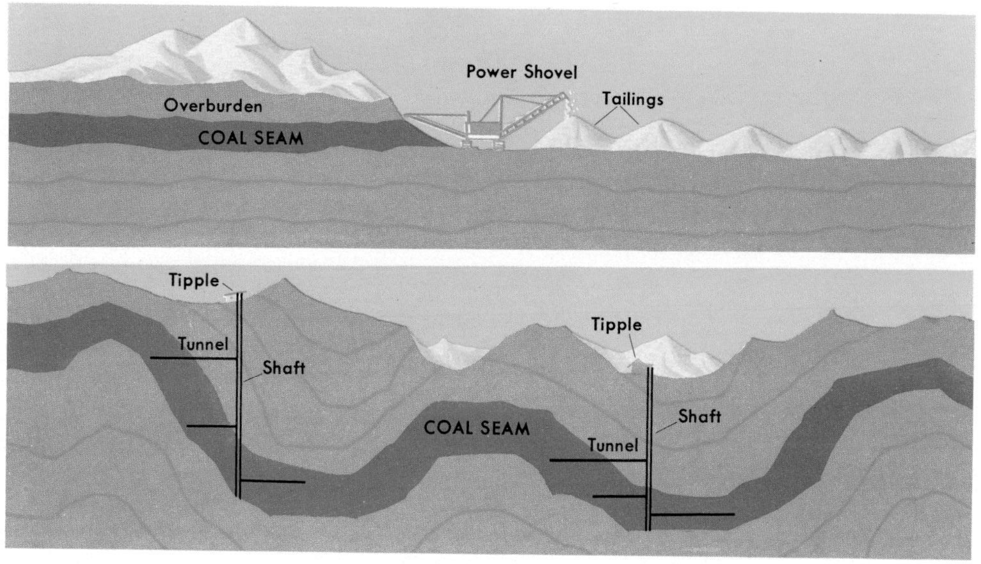

COAL: ON TOP AND FAR BELOW

From the Appalachian Highlands *(map, far left)* comes almost three fourths of the U.S. production of bituminous coal. Another great deposit of this valuable fuel lies in the Eastern Interior fields centering in Illinois, seen on the left edge of the map. Bituminous, or soft, coal is used in the production of electric power and in the manufacture of iron and steel. Anthracite, a hard coal mined in significant quantities only in northeastern Pennsylvania *(not shown)*, is of limited industrial importance and is used mainly for heating.

In surface, or strip, mining *(top diagram)* power shovels remove surface layers of earth, rock and vegetation, called the "overburden," and deposit them in huge dumps called "tailings." The coal thus exposed is broken up and hauled to preparation plants for washing, grading and sizing.

In underground mining *(bottom diagram)* shafts and tunnels are dug and coal is removed from the seams by electric slicing or drilling machines. Coal is then broken loose with explosives or a compressed-air charge. A familiar landmark in regions of deep-shaft mining is the surface "tipple," which houses ventilating, lighting and elevator machinery.

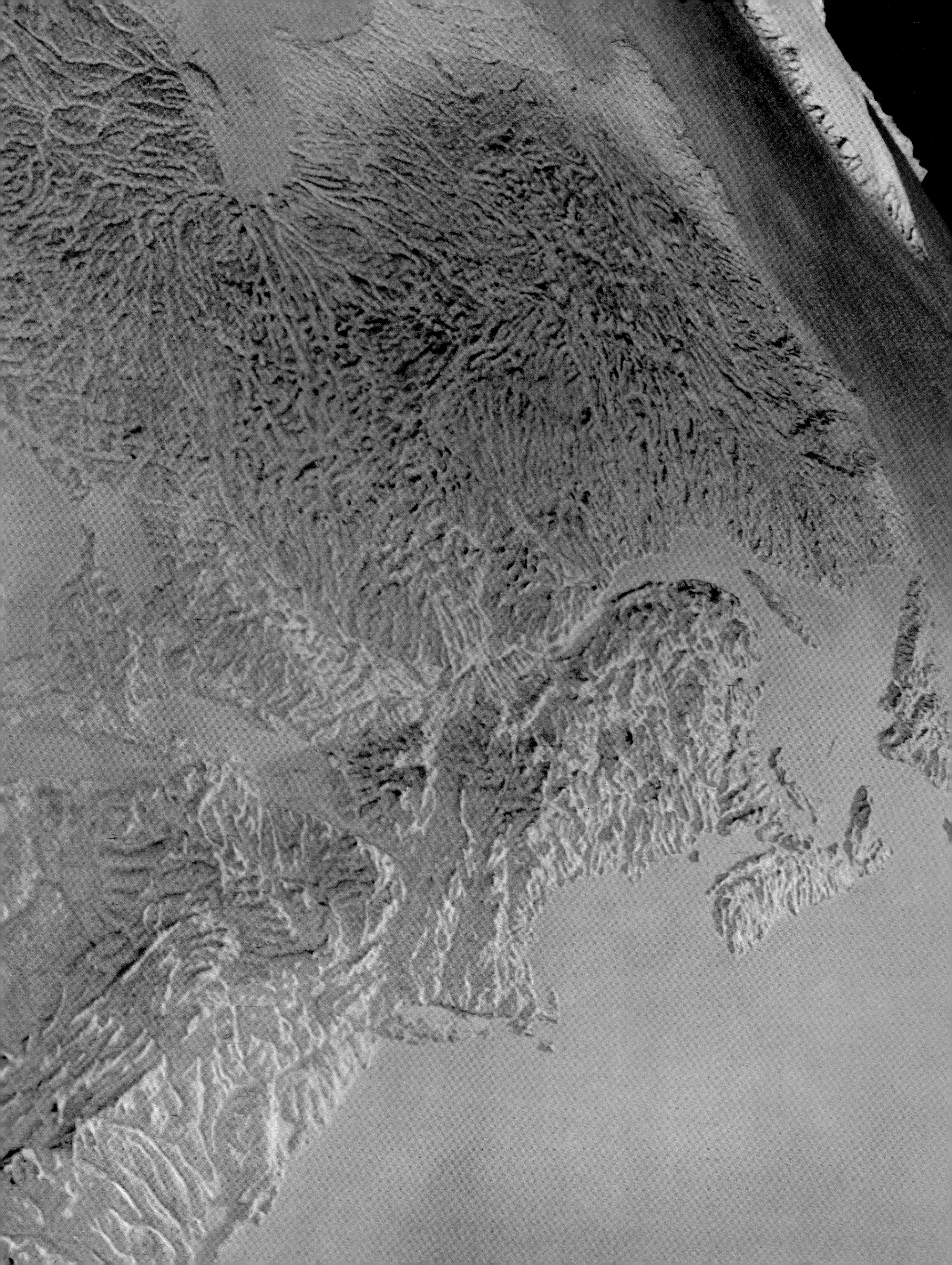

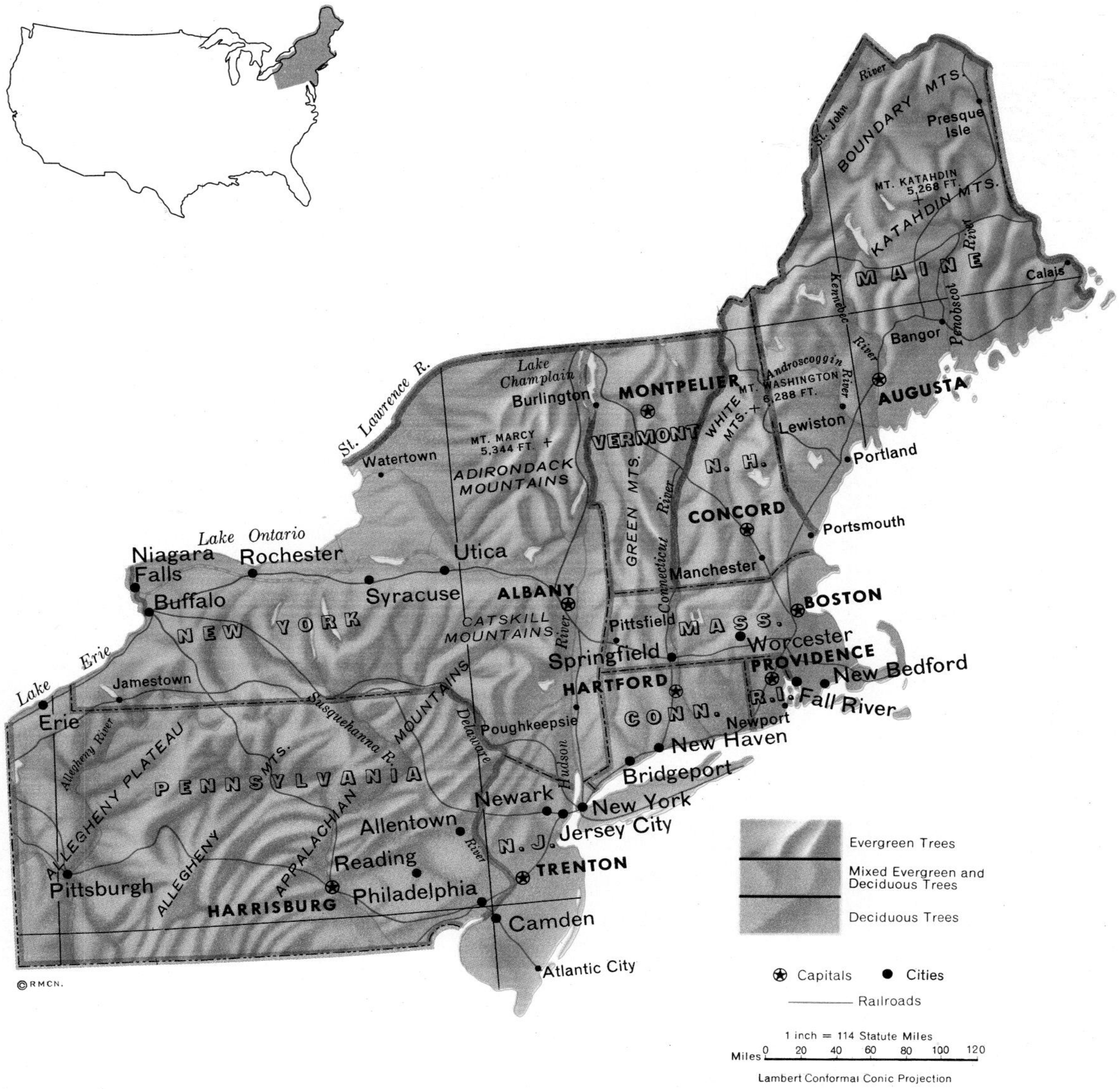

NORTHEAST STATES

"We are a people of cultivators . . . all animated with the spirit of industry," reported the Frenchman Hector St. John de Crèvecoeur in 1782, after 17 years of farming in New York.

Today, nearly two centuries later, intensively farmed soils still make the nine states of the Northeast a major region of "cultivators." But it is primarily the spirit of industry that animates the people. Here men of the 18th and 19th Centuries turned from their rocky land and fish-filled waters to yoke the tumbling streams of the Appalachians with fast-spinning wheels. When water power proved insufficient for the growing factories, they built steam engines and ran them with coal extracted from the mountains. Here in the Northeast they tested the world's first steamboat, patented the first cotton gin, perfected the sewing machine, pioneered the intricacies of the blast furnace and developed some of the first high-speed rotary presses to meet the demands of a growing reading public for news about the world it was reshaping.

Here, too, on the island of Manhattan, man built a mighty city, capable of inspiring both awe and love. "One hears the hoarse notes of the great ships in the river," wrote the novelist Thomas Wolfe, "and one remembers suddenly the princely girdle of proud, potent tides that bind the city, and suddenly New York blazes like a magnificent jewel in its fit setting of sea, and earth and stars."

ALONG THE ATLANTIC SHORE lie the nine northeast states. At the far left, Lake Erie and Lake Ontario mark the northwest boundaries of Pennsylvania and New York. On the coast, the finger of Long Island points northeast along the air and sea routes to Europe.

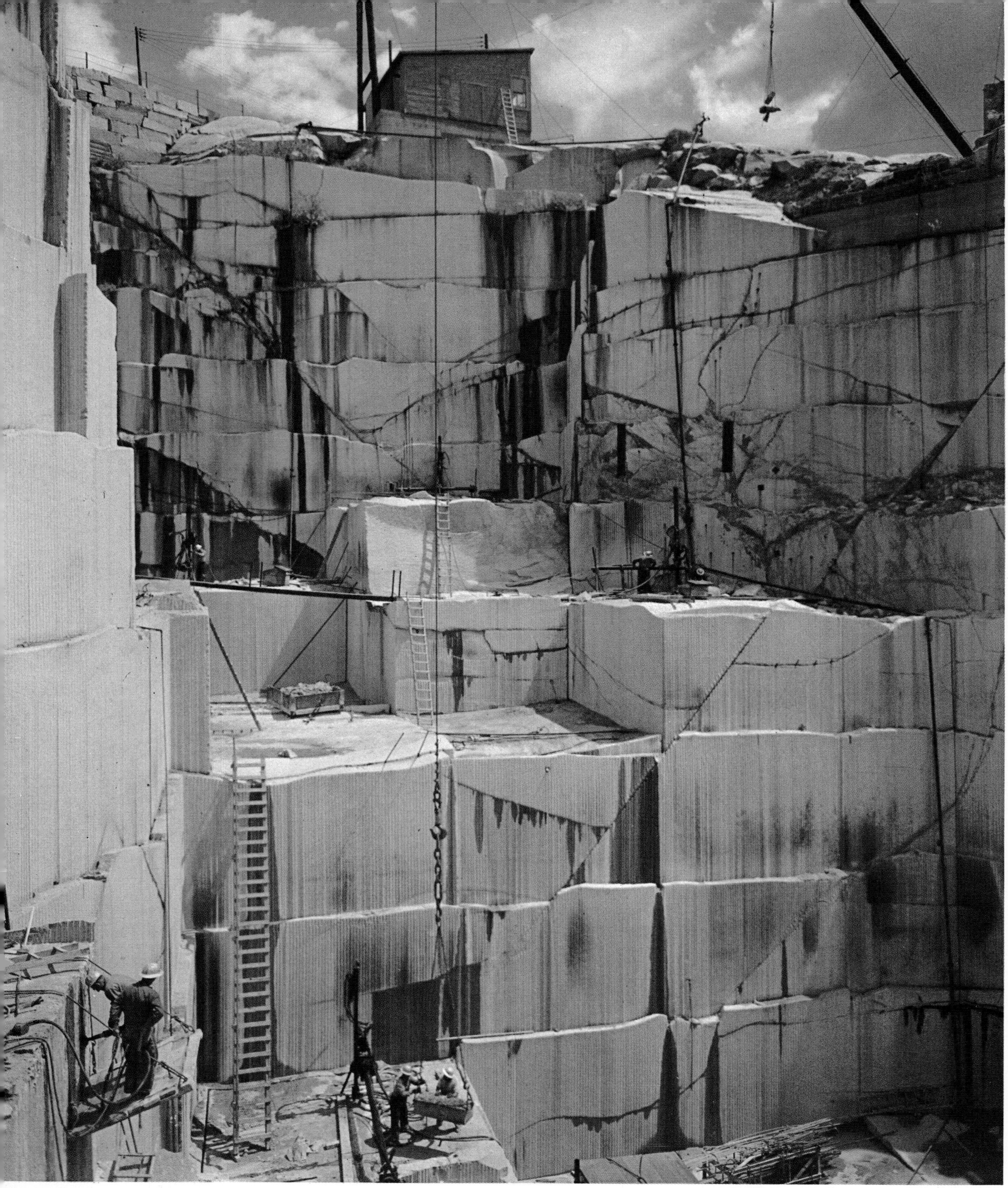

A REGION ROOTED IN STONE

TERRACES OF STONE tower above workmen inside a quarry at Barre, Vermont, one of the main granite centers of the Northeast. Formed millenniums ago, granite is a hard crystalline building stone, durable in climates with great temperature changes. In quarrying granite, man leaves behind tiered forms strikingly similar to the ones he eventually constructs from this material.

TERRACES OF STEEL, faced with brick and stone, rise in New York City against the background of the East River. Such weighty skyscrapers are possible only because of the underlying support of Manhattan Island's thick, unyielding, mica-bearing bedrock. This foundation stone, called Manhattan schist, is rooted in one of the regions of the globe least subject to severe earthquakes.

MOBILITY ON THE LAND AND DEFIANCE OF THE SEA

THE SWEEP OF A HIGHWAY, Massachusetts Route 128, arcs in a great semicircle around Boston, bearing through traffic away from the choked city. Here, in the thickly settled Northeast, highway engineers pioneered the uninterrupted turnpike and cloverleaf intersection. Highways like these have helped 20th Century Americans to retain their mobility in an age of urban congestion.

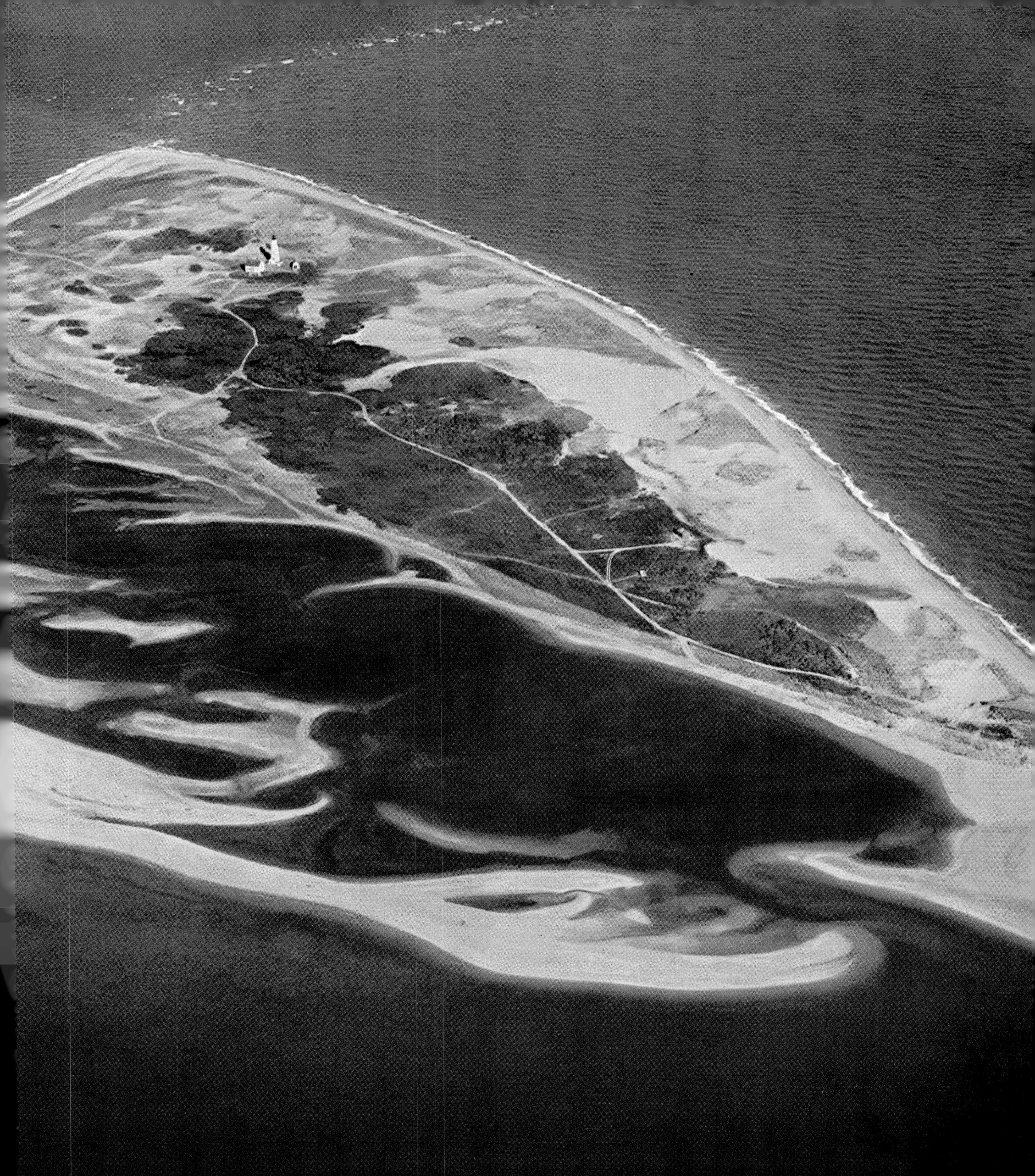

THE WORK OF THE OCEAN is revealed in the filigreed shore line of Nantucket, a 50-square-mile island off the Massachusetts coast. In the 18th Century, Nantucket sailors built a major industry out of whaling and made their island world-famous. Now the island's main income derives from tourists, but its defiance of the sea lives on as a memorable chapter of United States history.

CONNECTICUT
State Capital
Other Cities
City With Courthouse
City Limits
County Line
HIGHWAYS
Expressways
Major Roads
Other Roads
U.S.
State
Nat'l. Interstate
1 inch = 8.5 Statute Miles
Lambert Conformal Conic Projection
Longitude West of Greenwich
CM POLITICAL CONNECTICUT
COPYRIGHT BY RAND MCNALLY & COMPANY
MADE IN U.S.A.
MASSACHUSETTS
RHODE ISLAND
NEW YORK
LONG ISLAND N.Y.
Long Island Sound
Block Island Sound
Atlantic Ocean
HARTFORD
New Haven
Bridgeport
Waterbury
Stamford
Norwich
New London
Danbury
Greenwich
Norwalk
Meriden
New Britain

CONNECTICUT: In 1633, the Dutch purchased the area now occupied by Connecticut's capital, Hartford, from the Pequots for one piece of heavy wool, six axes, six kettles, 18 knives, a pair of shears, toys and a sword blade. Today, the old Indian crop of tobacco still covers much of the valley of the Connecticut River. But far more important are the factories which make Connecticut's part of the valley one of the nation's prime manufacturing regions of such items as aircraft engines, typewriters and propeller blades *(map, below)*. From the fur of the rabbit Connecticut manufactures more men's hats than any other state. It is also first in the production of small arms, ammunition and helicopters.

AREA: 5,009 sq. mi. Rank: 48th.
POPULATION: 2,535,234. Rank: 25th. Largest city and capital: Hartford.
ENTERED UNION: Jan. 9, 1788, as 5th state.
CLIMATE: Cold winters, warm summers; moderate rainfall.
ALTITUDES: South slope of Mt. Frissell, 2,380 ft. (highest); Hartford, 40 ft.

Connecticut still symbolizes old New England in the white clapboard houses that ring its village greens, but, as a builder of nuclear submarines, it is also an integral part of the atomic age. On the waters of Long Island Sound to the south, the state boasts one of the sailing centers of the nation. To many, however, Connecticut is best known as a sophisticated outpost of New York City, bedroom for commuting executives who work in finance, commerce and the communications industry.

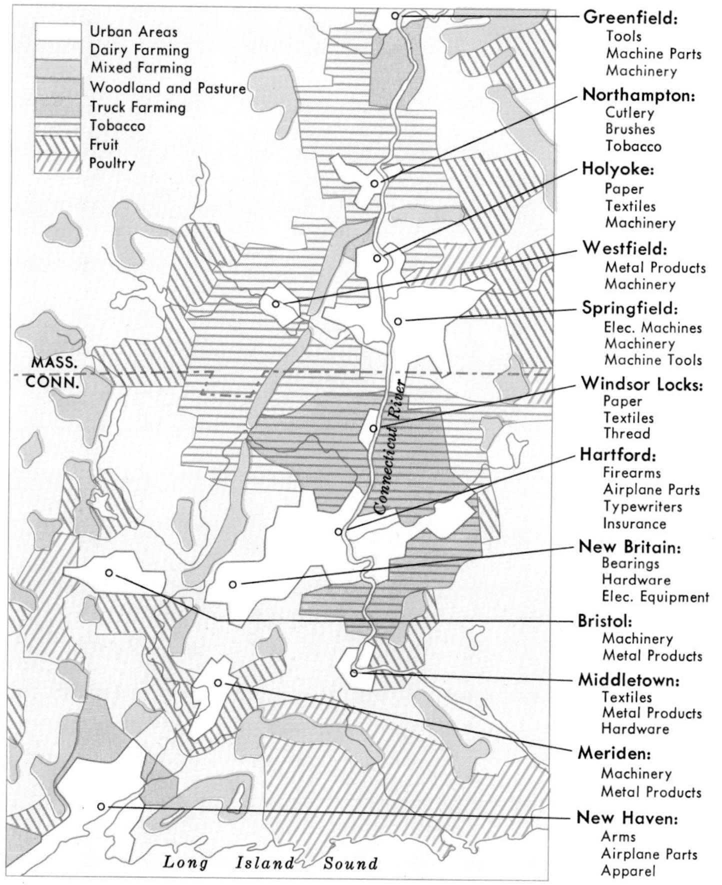

DIVERSIFICATION IN A WELL-EXPLOITED REGION

The Connecticut Valley is a patchwork of farm and foundry, as shown on the map above. Here is an economy that makes prudent use of natural advantages and limitations. The alluvial lowland yields a valuable cash crop of tobacco, and farmers also prosper by selling perishables such as dairy products, fruits and vegetables to nearby big cities. Though the valley itself is poor in raw materials, the Connecticut River and its tributaries provide abundant water for use in many industrial processes. Manufacturers specialize in light metal goods demanding precision crafting.

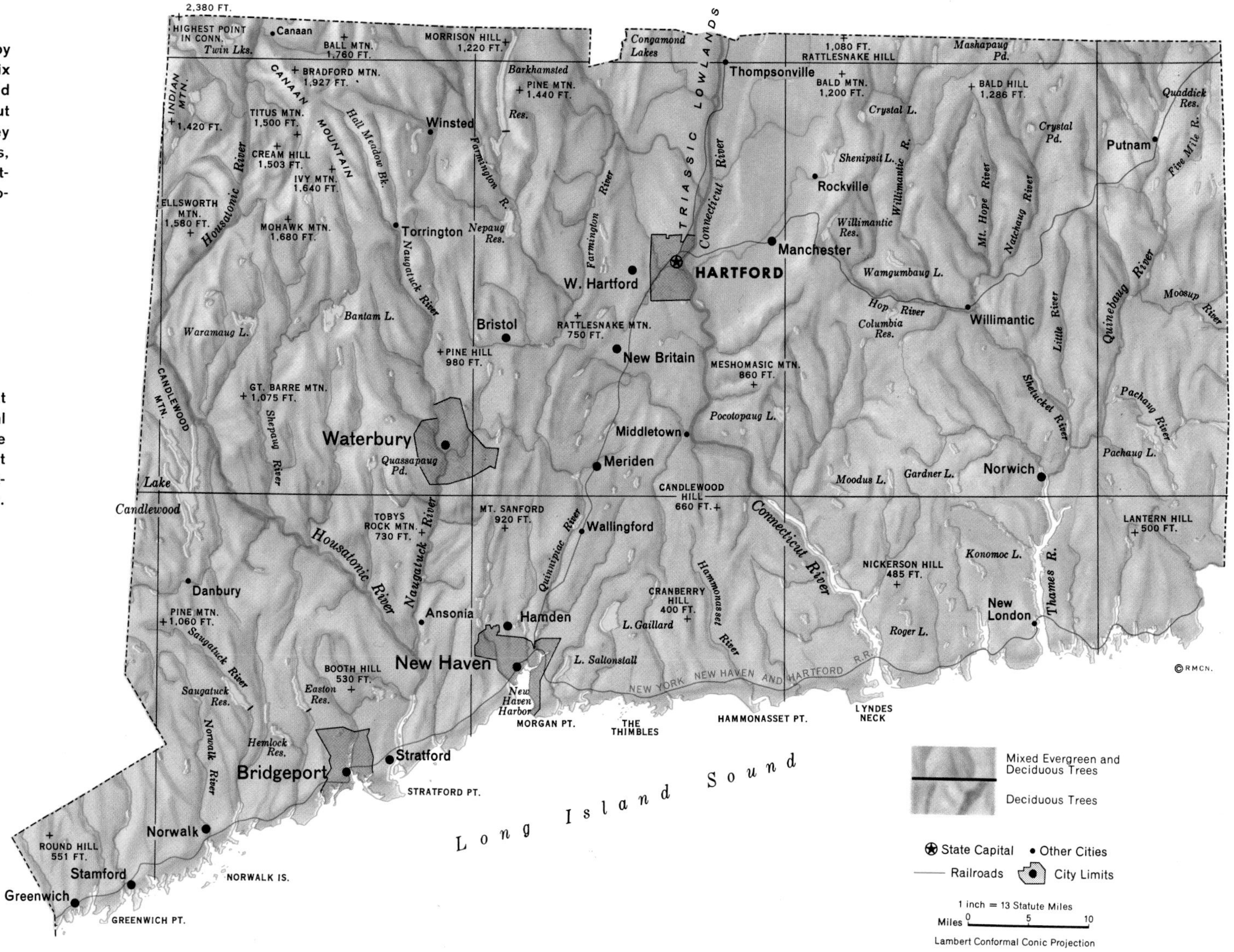

THE ECONOMY

MANUFACTURING
- Machinery
- Transportation Equipment
- Metal Products
- Electrical Machinery
- Primary Metals
- Textiles & Clothing
- Food Processing

MINING
- Mica
- Stone

AGRICULTURE
- Dairy Farming
- Dairy & General Farming

VALUE		EMPLOYED
$ 173,660,000	AGRICULTURE	3.0%
$3,148,000,000	MANUFACTURING	43.0%
$ 13,130,000	MINING	0.1%

Percentages are based on a total of 897,000 at work. In addition 28% are in commerce and transport, 10% in government, 15.9% in other areas. Manufacturing value is the value added when materials are converted into goods.

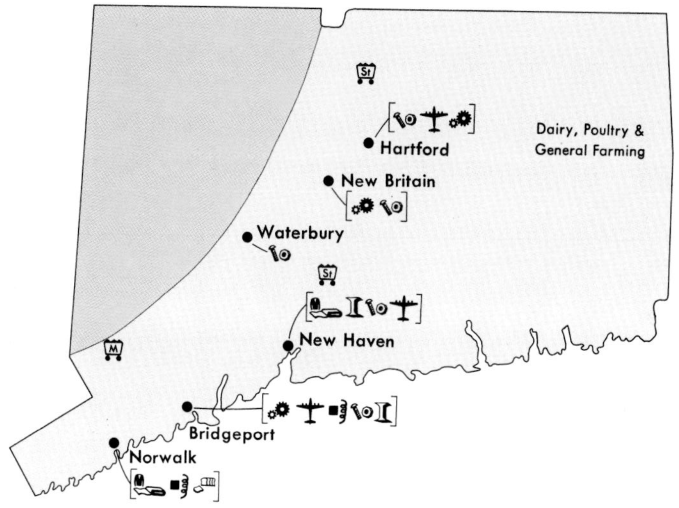

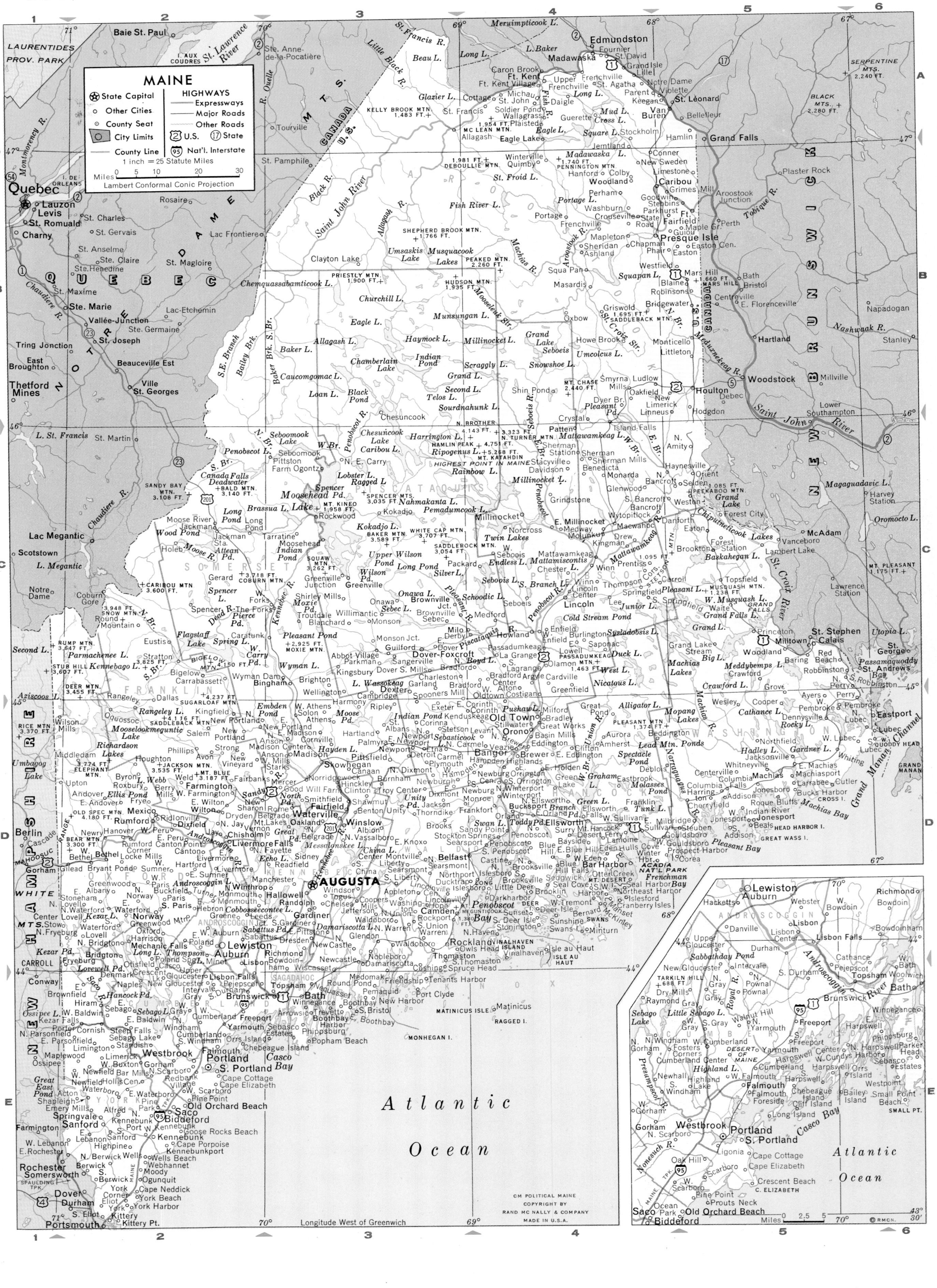
MAINE
State Capital
Other Cities
County Seat
City Limits
County Line
HIGHWAYS
Expressways
Major Roads
Other Roads
U.S.
State
Nat'l. Interstate
1 inch = 25 Statute Miles
Miles 0 5 10 20 30
Lambert Conformal Conic Projection
LAURENTIDES PROV. PARK
Baie St. Paul
St. Lawrence River
Edmundston
Madawaska
Quebec
Lauzon
Levis
St. Romuald
Charny
QUEBEC
NOTRE DAME MTS.
CANADA U.S.
NEW BRUNSWICK
Saint John River
Allagash
Fort Kent
Caribou
Presque Isle
Houlton
Woodstock
Millinocket
Moosehead Lake
Greenville
Rockwood
Mt. Katahdin
Highest Point in Maine 5,268 FT.
Bangor
Old Town
Orono
Brewer
Lincoln
Calais
St. Stephen
Eastport
Lubec
Machias
Ellsworth
Bar Harbor
Belfast
Camden
Rockland
Waterville
Skowhegan
AUGUSTA
Gardiner
Lewiston
Auburn
Brunswick
Bath
Portland
S. Portland
Westbrook
Saco
Biddeford
Old Orchard Beach
Sanford
Kennebunk
Kittery
Portsmouth
Dover
Rochester
Berlin
Rumford
Farmington
Rangeley
Lac Megantic
Thetford Mines
Penobscot Bay
Casco Bay
Atlantic Ocean
Grand Manan Channel
Passamaquoddy Bay
MONHEGAN I.
MATINICUS ISLE
Longitude West of Greenwich
CM POLITICAL MAINE
COPYRIGHT BY
RAND MC NALLY & COMPANY
MADE IN U.S.A.
Lewiston
Auburn
Portland
S. Portland
Westbrook
Freeport
Yarmouth
Falmouth
Cape Elizabeth
Scarboro
Saco
Biddeford
Old Orchard Beach
Atlantic Ocean
Casco Bay
Miles 0 2.5 5
RMCN.

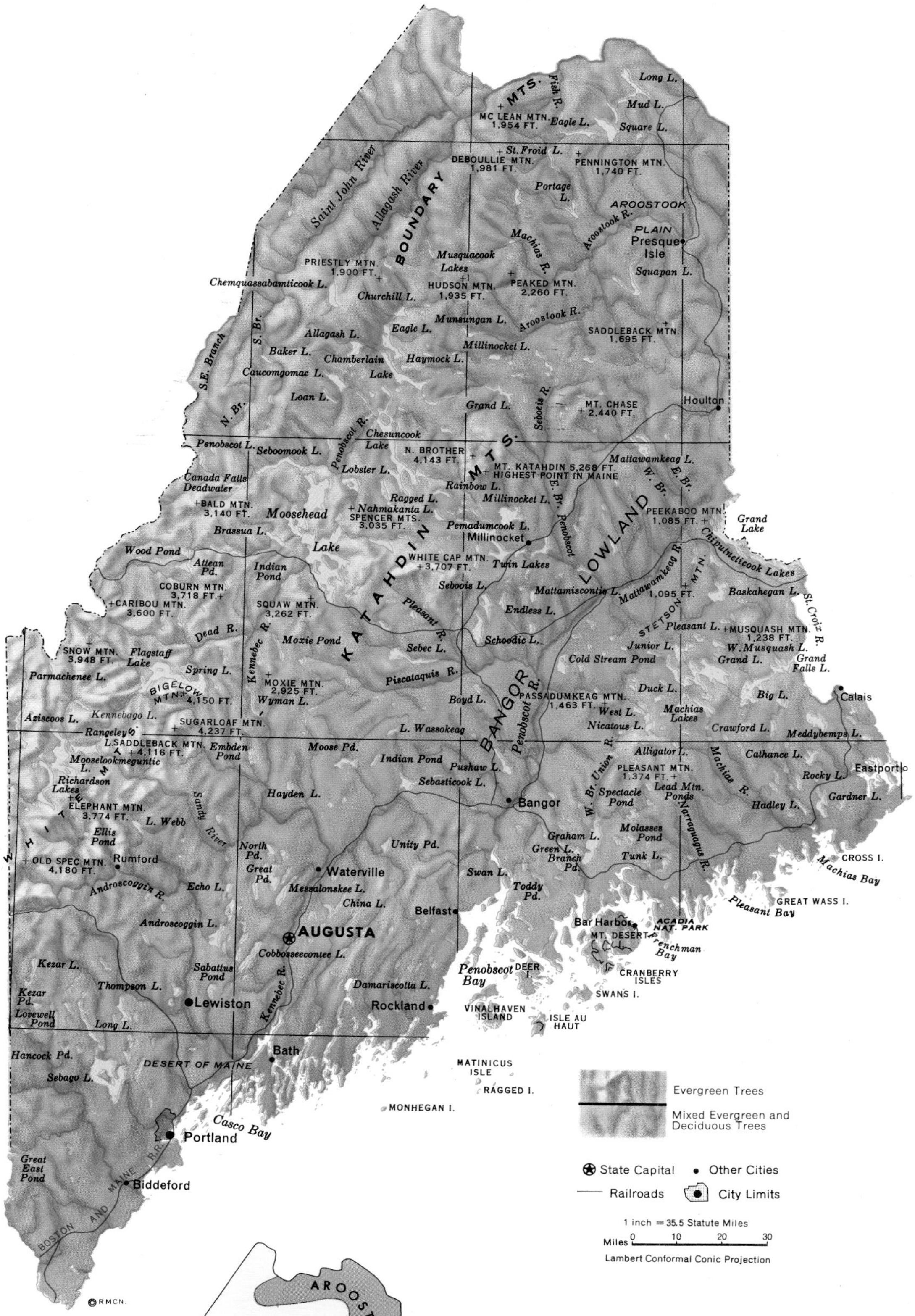

MAINE: By airline the distance along the Maine coast from the New Hampshire boundary in the south to the Canadian border in the north is only 248 miles. But so irregularly does the coastline run along the bays and inlets that it would be 3,478 miles long if stretched out straight. Offshore, patient Maine fishermen probe the Atlantic for sardines, lobster and ocean perch. Inland, sportsmen find serene seclusion in the state's more than 5,000 streams and 2,500 lakes. Around the waters, a rustling splendor of forests shelters partridge and woodcock, deer and bear.

While tourism is the state's major source of income—some $280 million each year—Maine also depends heavily upon its pulp and paper industry. More than $160 million worth of everything from fine writing paper to coarse binding and chip board is made yearly from softwoods of the forests. From its hardwoods, Maine manufactures a range of products from toothpicks to yacht hulls. Despite extensive cutting, timber is more than plentiful. In the northwest of the state stretches one of the few remaining preserves of primeval forest in the United States.

AREA:	33,215 sq. mi. Rank: 39th.
POPULATION:	969,265. Rank: 36th. Largest city: Portland. Capital: Augusta.
ENTERED UNION:	March 15, 1820, as 23rd state.
CLIMATE:	Long cold winters, short cool summers; moderate rainfall.
ALTITUDES:	Mt. Katahdin, 5,268 ft. (highest).

Progress in attracting new industry to Maine has been slow, and the bulk of manufacturing is still concentrated in paper, leather and textile mills. But developers have an eye on the 1.8 billion kilowatt hours of power produced yearly by the state's harnessed rivers. They predict that power demands by new and established industries will increase enormously in the next decade.

For farming, too, the future seems assured. Aroostook County in the north grows so many potatoes that Maine is second only to Idaho in potato production. And farther south, in the Atlantic coastal area, Maine grows the bulk of the nation's blueberry crop.

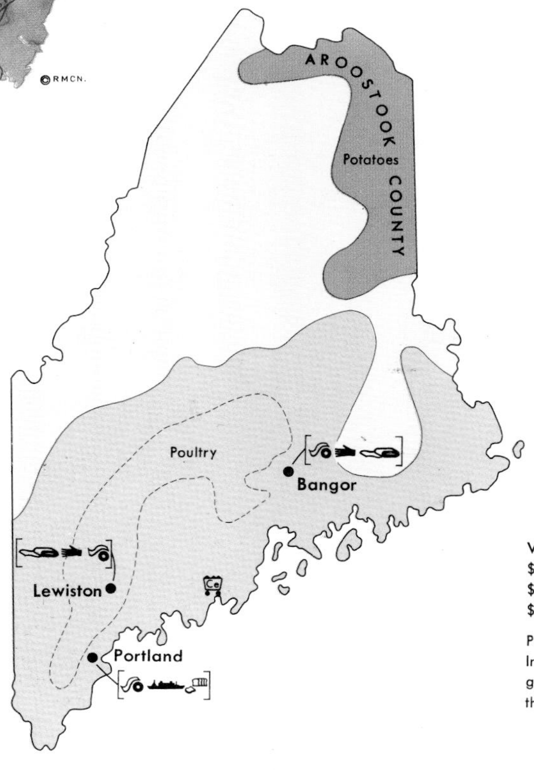

THE ECONOMY

MANUFACTURING
- Pulp & Paper Products
- Textiles
- Leather Products
- Food Processing
- Transportation Equipment

MINING
- Cement

AGRICULTURE
- Special Crops & General Farming
- Dairy & General Farming
- Mountains & Forests

VALUE		EMPLOYED
$220,420,000	AGRICULTURE	19.0%
$653,000,000	MANUFACTURING	31.0%
$ 12,570,000	MINING	0.3%

Percentages are based on a total of 328,000 at work. In addition 25% are in commerce and transport, 13% in government, 11.7% in other areas. Manufacturing value is the value added when materials are converted into goods.

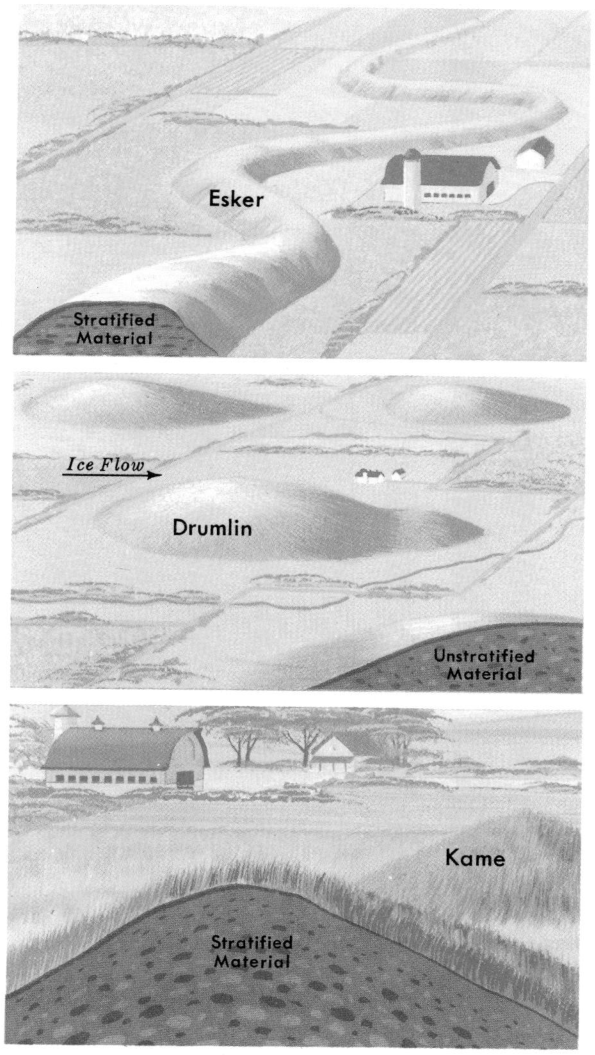

THE SCULPTURED DEBRIS OF AN ICE AGE

Odd lumps of land deposited during the ice age are widespread in Maine. The serpentine esker *(top)* was formed when a stream flowing under a glacier filled with sand and gravel. The egg-shaped drumlins *(center)* are hills or ridges of clay and rock molded by moving glaciers. The knobby kames *(bottom)* are deposits on the valley floor left by glacial streams. Generally too rocky to plow, Maine pasture lands often have formations like these.

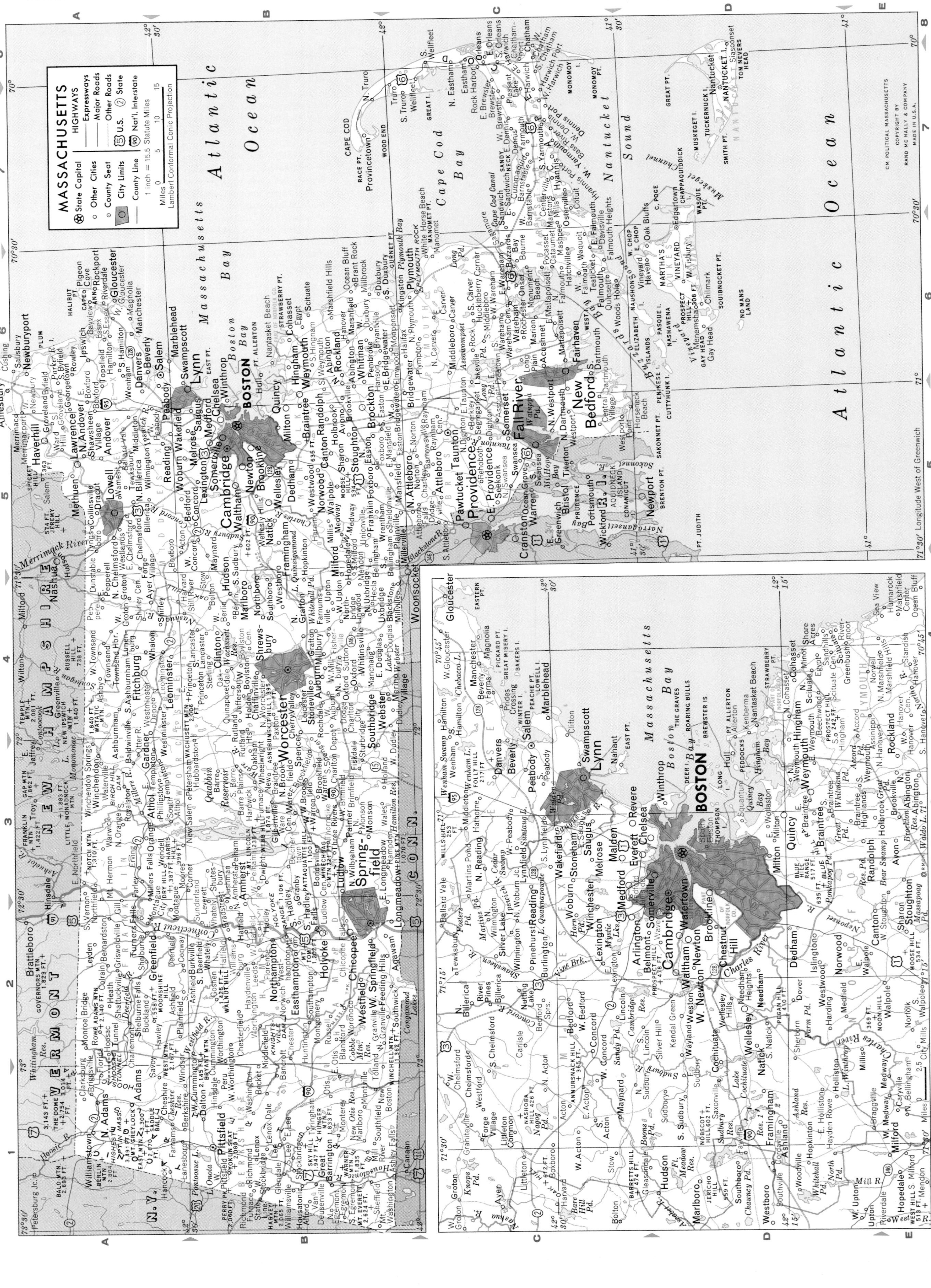
MASSACHUSETTS
HIGHWAYS
Expressways
Major Roads
Other Roads
U.S.
State
Nat'l. Interstate
State Capital
Other Cities
County Seat
City Limits
County Line
1 inch = 15.5 Statute Miles
Miles 0 5 10 15
Lambert Conformal Conic Projection
Atlantic Ocean
Massachusetts Bay
Cape Cod Bay
Nantucket Sound
BOSTON
Worcester
Springfield
Longitude West of Greenwich
CM POLITICAL MASSACHUSETTS
COPYRIGHT BY
RAND McNALLY & COMPANY
MADE IN U.S.A.

MASSACHUSETTS: Here is the cradle of the American nation, endlessly rocked by the ebb and flood of the powerful Atlantic. It was from the sea, past the beckoning finger of Cape Cod *(diagram, below right)*, that the Pilgrim Fathers came, and it was to the cod-crowded sea that Massachusetts was to turn for livelihood when the rock-strewn, sandy soil proved infertile for other than subsistence farming.

By the 18th Century, firmly established in their new-found land, the colonists were quick to respond to voices which rang out for independence. One was that of stormy Sam Adams of Boston, who wished that "a just sense of liberty . . . be transmitted to posterity." Another was that of quiet John Parker, captain of the Lexington militia, who on a dew-sprinkled Massachusetts morning called the order: "Stand your ground. Don't fire unless fired upon. But if they mean to have a war, let it begin here." And so it began. Here on April 19, 1775, was fired the shot heard round the world.

AREA:	8,257 sq. mi. Rank: 45th.
POPULATION:	5,148,578. Rank: 9th. Largest city and capital: Boston.
ENTERED UNION:	Feb. 6, 1788, as 6th state.
CLIMATE:	Long cold winters, warm summers; moderate rainfall.
ALTITUDES:	Mt. Greylock, 3,491 ft. (highest); Pittsfield, 1,015 ft.

As Massachusetts had led the way in the American Revolution, so it led the way in the Industrial Revolution. Enterprising men used the rapid rivers to turn the wheels of textile mills and sawmills. Technical skills learned in these early industries laid the groundwork for the state's present efficiency. With some 95 per cent of its income derived from manufacture, Massachusetts is a leader in the production of clothing, textiles, shoes and electrical machinery, in the processing of foods, and in printing and publishing. The fishing industry is still important to Gloucester and Boston. But today Boston takes only a small portion of its total wealth from the sea. Ringed by the research laboratories of great electronics companies, which are able to draw upon the resources of Harvard and the Massachusetts Institute of Technology, New England's largest city now stands on the threshold of space.

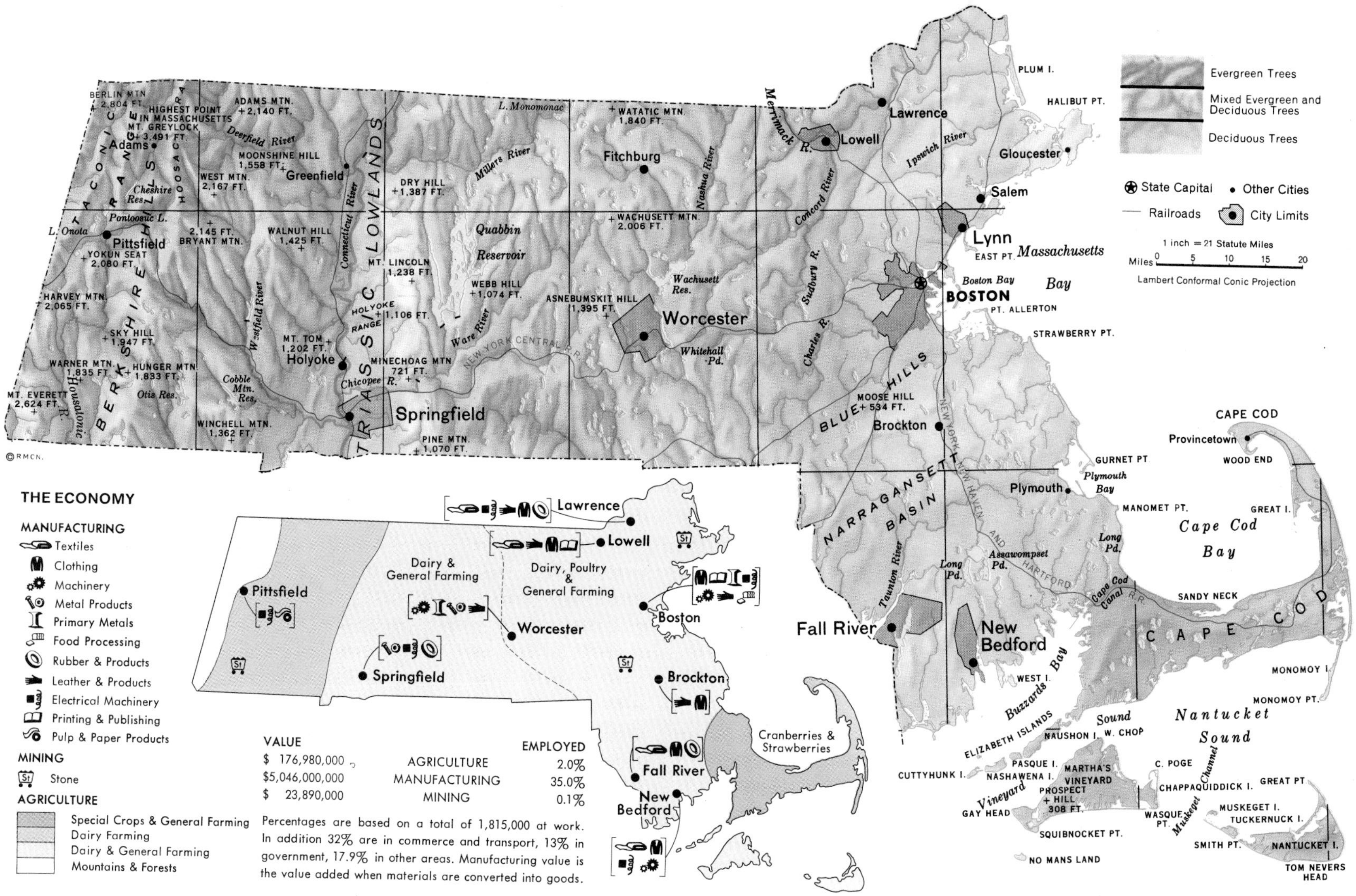

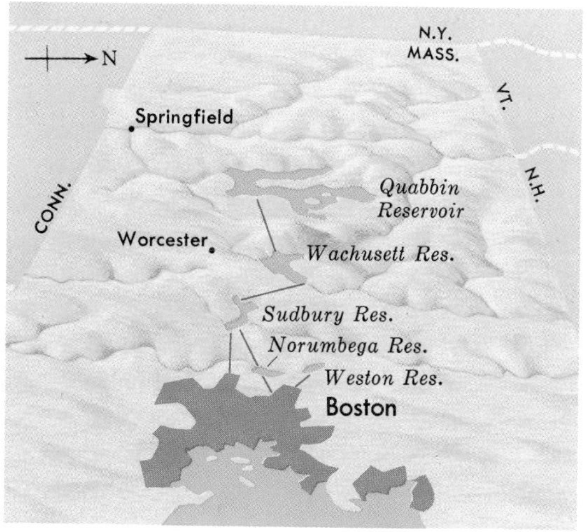

WATER FOR A THIRSTY METROPOLIS

Although rainfall in New England is ample, the aqueducts that sustain life in Boston must reach westward to reservoirs more than halfway across Massachusetts. Each day the city consumes 216 million gallons of water, and the thirst of the metropolitan area continues to increase.

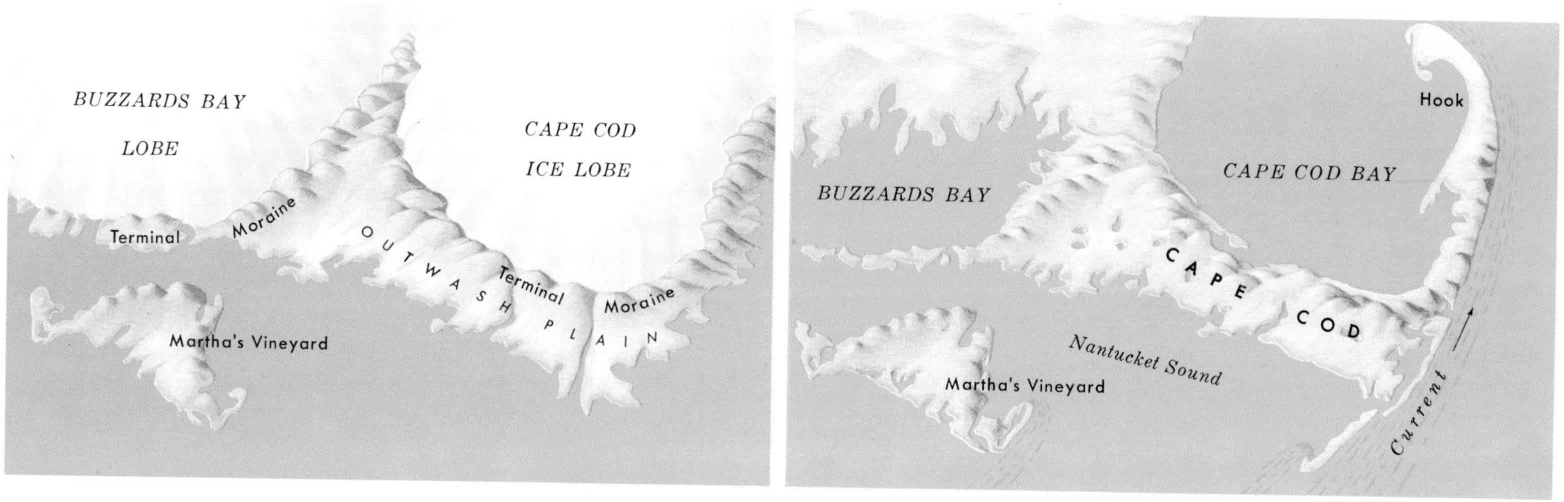

WHERE THE GLACIERS HALTED: A REGION OF BAYS AND BEACHES

The creation of Cape Cod at the edge of a continental ice sheet is illustrated in these before-and-after drawings. Some 10,000 to 30,000 years ago ice-age glaciers *(left)*, bearing millions of tons of crushed rock, sand and clay, halted in Massachusetts, depositing much of their load as "terminal moraines" to form the base of what is now Cape Cod. Streams of melted ice carried lighter materials forward to form the sandy "outwash plains" of the southern slopes that border Nantucket Sound. After the glaciers retreated *(right)*, the sea rose, inundating areas scooped out by the glaciers and depositing its own burden of sand and sediment. Thus were created the manifold bays and beaches of the area as well as the 65-mile-long hook of the Cape itself.

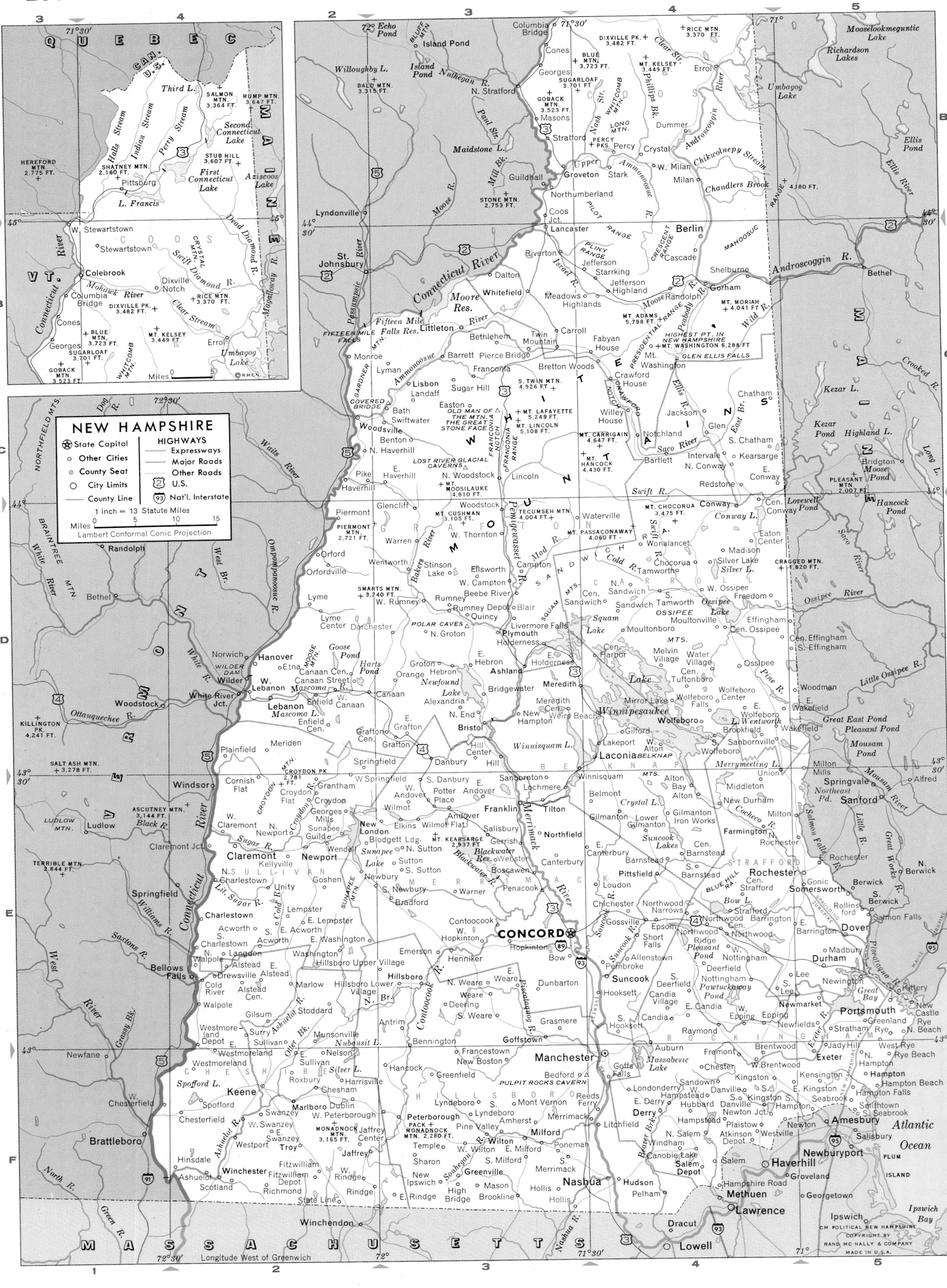

NEW HAMPSHIRE
State Capital
Other Cities
County Seat
City Limits
County Line
HIGHWAYS
Expressways
Major Roads
Other Roads
U.S.
Nat'l. Interstate
1 inch = 13 Statute Miles
Miles 0 5 10 15
Lambert Conformal Conic Projection
QUEBEC
CAN.
U.S.
MAINE
VT.
VERMONT
MASSACHUSETTS
COOS
GRAFTON
CARROLL
BELKNAP
SULLIVAN
MERRIMACK
STRAFFORD
CHESHIRE
HILLSBORO
ROCKINGHAM
WHITE MOUNTAINS
SANDWICH RANGE
PRESIDENTIAL RANGE
HIGHEST PT. IN NEW HAMPSHIRE MT. WASHINGTON 6,288 FT.
Third L.
Second Connecticut Lake
First Connecticut Lake
Pittsburg
L. Francis
Colebrook
Dixville Notch
Errol
Umbagog Lake
Berlin
Gorham
Lancaster
Littleton
Whitefield
Woodsville
Plymouth
Hanover
Lebanon
Laconia
Wolfeboro
Winnipesaukee
Franklin
Claremont
Newport
CONCORD
Manchester
Nashua
Keene
Peterborough
Milford
Derry
Exeter
Portsmouth
Dover
Rochester
Somersworth
Durham
Hampton
Salem
Conway
Haverhill
Lawrence
Lowell
Newburyport
Amesbury
Brattleboro
Bellows Falls
Windsor
Atlantic Ocean
Connecticut River
Merrimack River
Androscoggin R.
Longitude West of Greenwich
CM POLITICAL NEW HAMPSHIRE
COPYRIGHT BY RAND MCNALLY & COMPANY
MADE IN U.S.A.

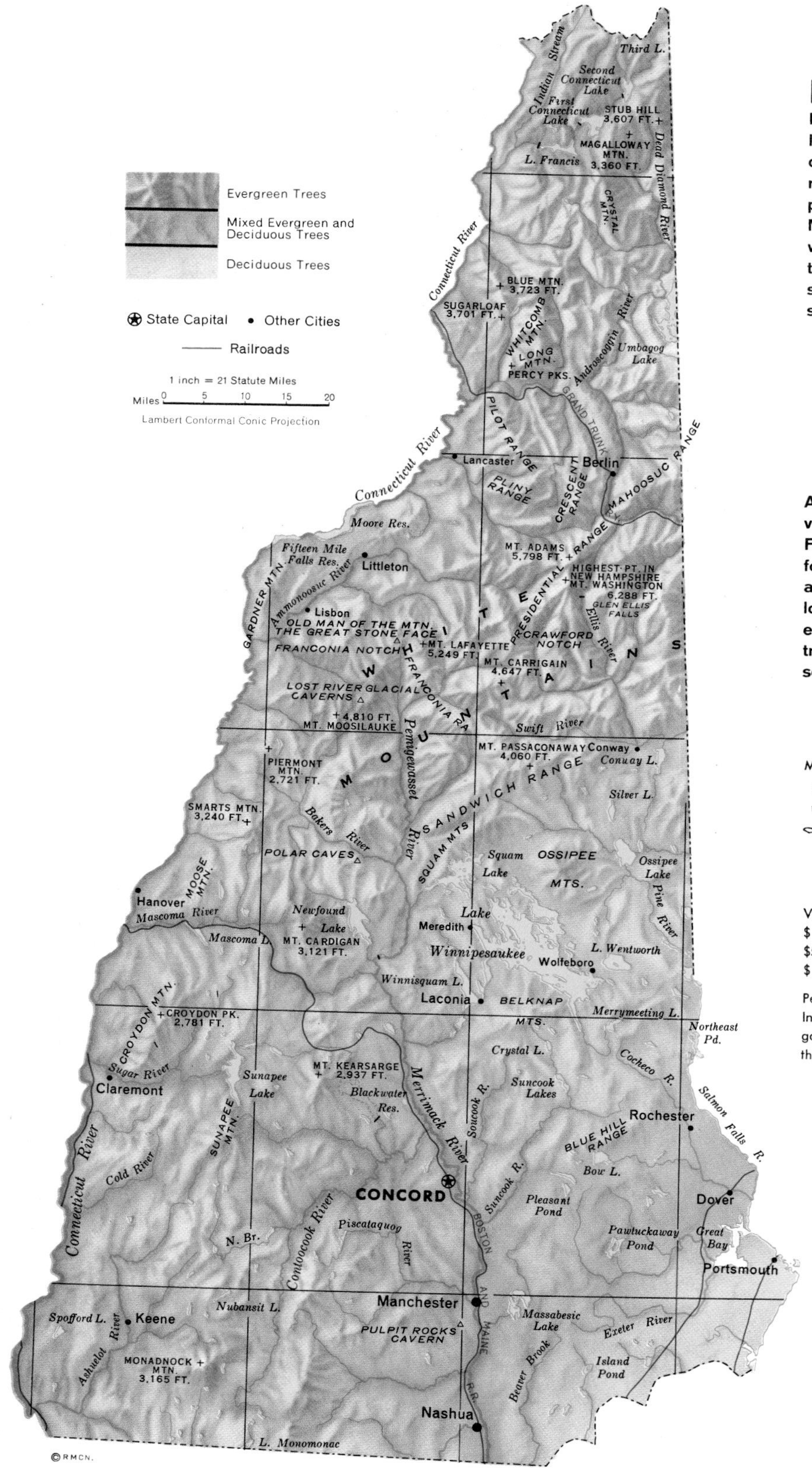

NEW HAMPSHIRE: Inspired by New Hampshire's granite-ribbed ranges, Nathaniel Hawthorne once wrote: "Mountains are earth's undecaying monuments." But his poetic line overlooks the fact that the state's mountains, middle-aged by the timetable of geology, have been decaying for aeons. Once rising in sharply pointed towers like today's relatively young Rockies, they have been ground down by glaciation and erosion to their present rounded shapes. But monumental they are nonetheless. The sculptured White Mountains, pierced by sheer gorges like Franconia and Crawford Notches, dominate the whole of New England and also play an important role in New Hampshire's economy. More than 10 per cent of the state's income from retail trade is derived from skiers who seek the snowbound slopes in winter and from tourists and hay fever sufferers who are lured by sweeping vistas and relatively pollen-free air in summer.

AREA:	9,304 sq. mi. Rank: 44th.
POPULATION:	606,921. Rank: 45th.
	Largest city: Manchester. Capital: Concord.
ENTERED UNION:	June 21, 1788, as 9th state.
CLIMATE:	Short mild summers, cold winters;
	moderate rainfall, heavy mountain snows.
ALTITUDES:	Mt. Washington, 6,288 ft. (highest); Concord, 290 ft.

Although New Hampshire has many dairy and truck farms—most of them in the fertile valleys south of the mountains—manufacturing provides the bulk of the state's income. Fast-falling rivers, notably the Connecticut and the Merrimack, supply hydroelectric power for major industries—leather products, textiles and machinery. New Hampshire's pine and hemlock forests, cut in the 18th Century to supply masts for the British Navy and logged off by the pulp industry in the 20th, have grown back with the application of modern forestry techniques. The state's forests have not only been conserved for use by industry but also for their sheer beauty. Some 5,000 acres in the White Mountains have been set aside as a wilderness tract, forever safeguarded against any form of commercial use.

THE ECONOMY

MANUFACTURING
- Machinery
- Leather Products
- Textiles

AGRICULTURE
- Dairy Farming
- Dairy & General Farming
- Mountains & Forests

MINING
- Stone

VALUE		EMPLOYED
$ 67,220,000	AGRICULTURE	8.0%
$509,000,000	MANUFACTURING	40.0%
$ 3,880,000	MINING	0.1%

Percentages are based on a total of 195,000 at work. In addition 26% are in commerce and transport, 11% in government, 14.9% in other areas. Manufacturing value is the value added when materials are converted into goods.

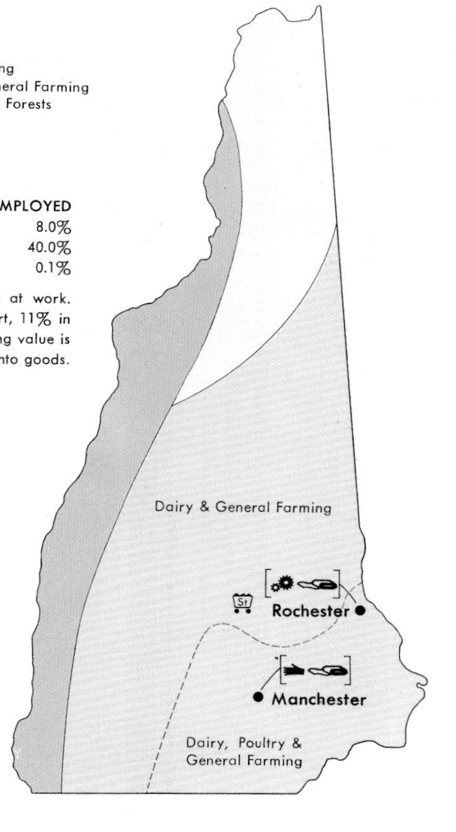

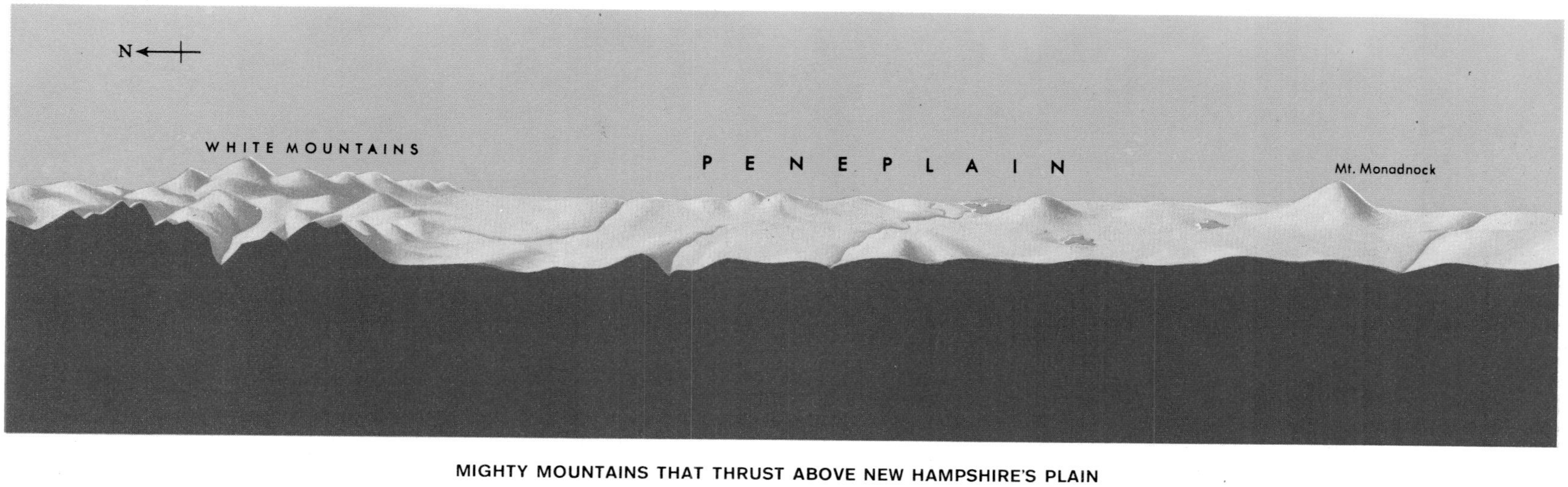

MIGHTY MOUNTAINS THAT THRUST ABOVE NEW HAMPSHIRE'S PLAIN

The White Mountains *(above left)* are the resistant roots of a once mighty range cut down by aeons of rain, ice and scouring streams. The complex structure of the tallest peaks indicates that they once lay beneath the crushing pressure of at least five miles of rock. Part of New Hampshire consists of an eroded plain called a "peneplain" by geologists. It is a region which was leveled by erosion, then uplifted by gigantic earth pressures that started another cycle of erosion. "Monadnocks," remnants of the early stage of the plain, are rocky promontories named for Mount Monadnock *(far right)*.

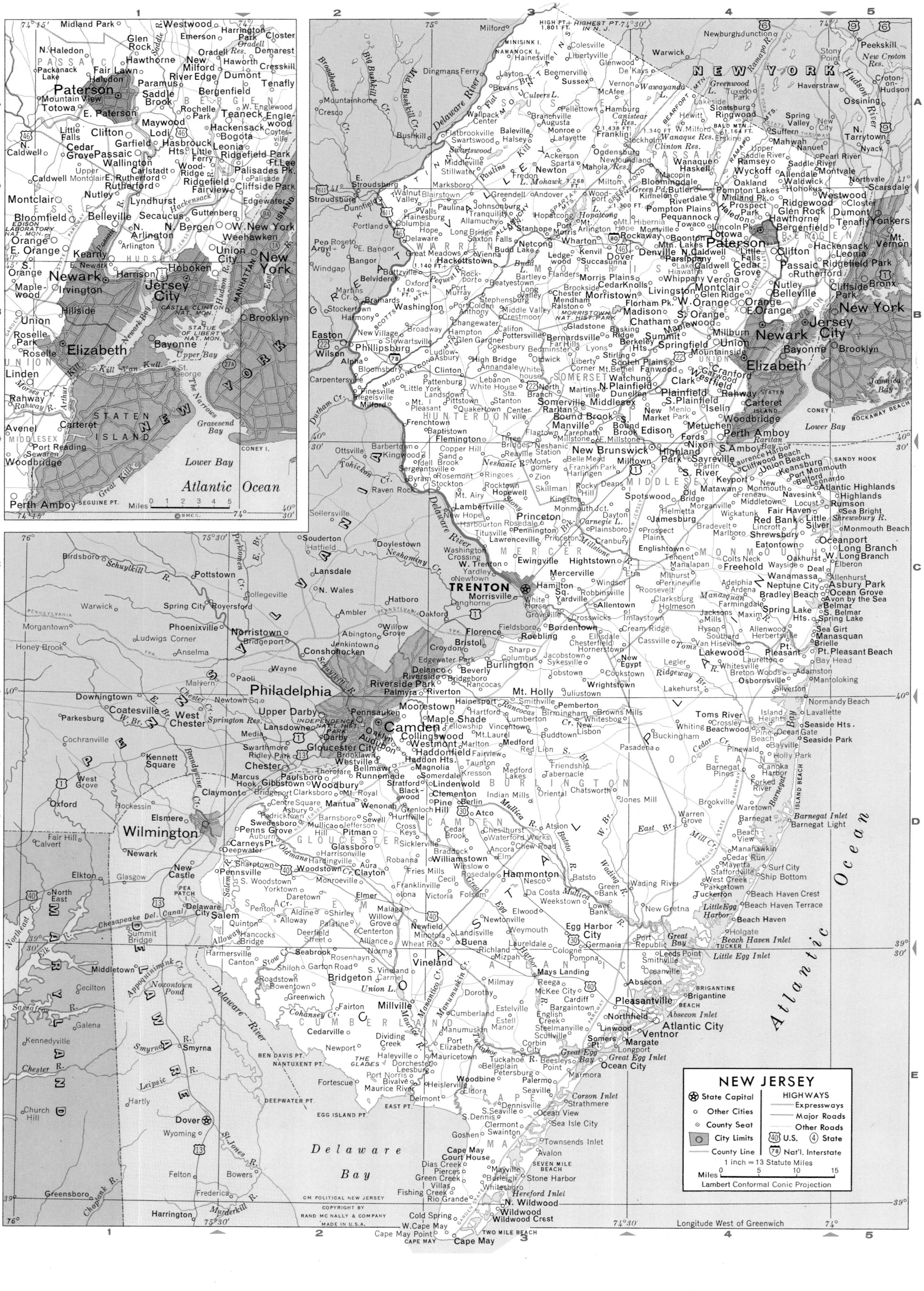

NEW JERSEY
State Capital
Other Cities
County Seat
City Limits
County Line
HIGHWAYS
Expressways
Major Roads
Other Roads
U.S.
State
Nat'l. Interstate
1 inch = 13 Statute Miles
Miles 0 5 10 15
Lambert Conformal Conic Projection
Longitude West of Greenwich
CM POLITICAL NEW JERSEY
COPYRIGHT BY RAND McNALLY & COMPANY MADE IN U.S.A.
NEW YORK
PENNSYLVANIA
DELAWARE
MARYLAND
Atlantic Ocean
Delaware Bay
Delaware River
Lower Bay
Upper Bay
TRENTON
Newark
Jersey City
Paterson
Elizabeth
Camden
Philadelphia
Wilmington
Atlantic City
New Brunswick
Princeton
New York
Brooklyn
Staten Island
SUSSEX
PASSAIC
BERGEN
WARREN
MORRIS
ESSEX
HUDSON
UNION
SOMERSET
HUNTERDON
MIDDLESEX
MERCER
MONMOUTH
OCEAN
BURLINGTON
CAMDEN
GLOUCESTER
SALEM
CUMBERLAND
ATLANTIC
CAPE MAY
HIGH PT. HIGHEST PT. IN N.J. 1,801 FT.
Cape May

NEW JERSEY: Long before it became a state, New Jersey served as a well-trodden corridor for the march of history. For centuries, Iroquois and Delaware hunting and war parties roamed its inner lowlands; in the early 1770s, Paul Revere galloped across the same lowlands to Philadelphia with the news of the Boston Tea Party. Today, New Jersey is a primary transportation center. Newark Airport, a pioneer commercial airport which opened in 1928, is still one of the nation's busiest air terminals. New Jersey is overlaid with more railroad trackage per square mile than any other state. And the 15-mile-wide strip between New York and Philadelphia *(map, below)* is the most heavily traveled section of land in the United States.

AREA:	7,836 sq. mi. Rank: 46th.
POPULATION:	6,066,782. Rank: 8th. Largest city: Newark. Capital: Trenton.
ENTERED UNION:	Dec. 18, 1787, as 3rd state.
CLIMATE:	Warm summers, cool winters along seacoast; considerable snow in highlands. Ample rainfall.
ALTITUDES:	1,801 ft. (highest) in Kittatinny Mountains.

After the American Revolution, the water power of the Passaic River was harnessed near Paterson, which became the country's first planned industrial city. Once the silk capital of the nation and still a great textile center, Paterson is today renowned—like most New Jersey cities—for its diversity of products (metal and rubber goods, furniture, plastics). The state has made its name for quantity as well as for variety. It ranks first in chemical products in the U.S., refines more than $161 million worth of petroleum and coal products each year and produces $864 million worth of electrical machinery. One of the richest industrial regions in the world, New Jersey uses enormous quantities of power to turn its machinery and light its skies. The poet William Carlos Williams, a native of New Jersey, was being both literal and poetic when he exclaimed, "Everywhere the Electric!"

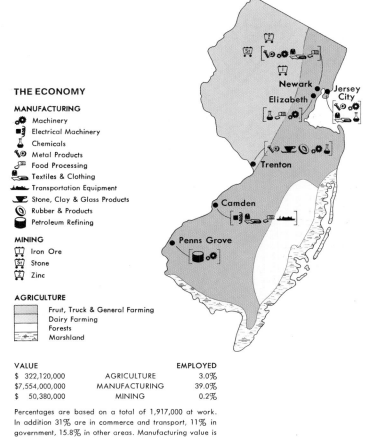

THE ECONOMY

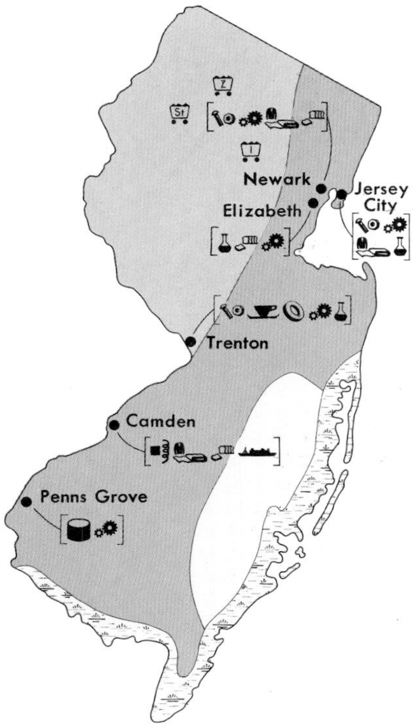

MANUFACTURING
- Machinery
- Electrical Machinery
- Chemicals
- Metal Products
- Food Processing
- Textiles & Clothing
- Transportation Equipment
- Stone, Clay & Glass Products
- Rubber & Products
- Petroleum Refining

MINING
- Iron Ore
- Stone
- Zinc

AGRICULTURE
- Fruit, Truck & General Farming
- Dairy Farming
- Forests
- Marshland

VALUE		EMPLOYED
$ 322,120,000	AGRICULTURE	3.0%
$7,554,000,000	MANUFACTURING	39.0%
$ 50,380,000	MINING	0.2%

Percentages are based on a total of 1,917,000 at work. In addition 31% are in commerce and transport, 11% in government, 15.8% in other areas. Manufacturing value is the value added when materials are converted into goods.

THE CORE OF A SUPERCITY

From Boston to Washington the northeast coast of the U.S. today is dominated by an almost unbroken urban belt constituting a kind of single supercity which sociologists call a megalopolis. While all the states in this area have been greatly affected, nowhere has the growth of the urban belt blotted out so much of the countryside as in New Jersey. There, as shown in the maps at right, greater New York and metropolitan Philadelphia merge with the Jersey lowland in a vast complex of cities, suburbs, shopping centers and factory districts that comprise the core of an East Coast megalopolis.

In the 13 metropolitan areas making up this complex live some 20 million people. To transport goods and men in and out of the region, 29,132 miles of highway and 5,191 miles of railroad track form a latticework across the tiny state; some 32,000 motor vehicles travel the New York-Philadelphia route each day. In terms of dollar value added by manufacture, 17 per cent of all U.S. manufacturing is concentrated in the small area shown on the map at the far right.

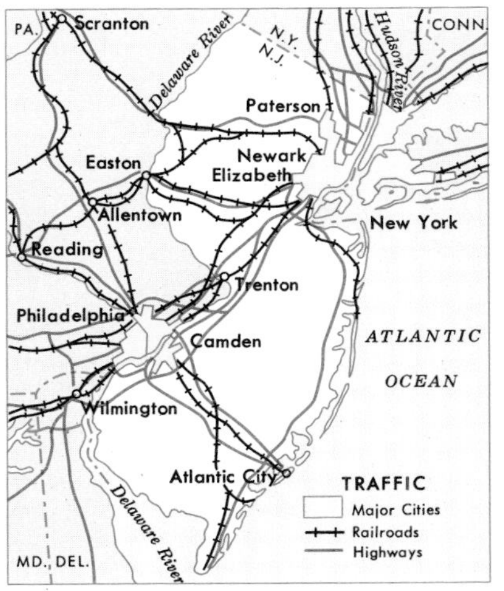

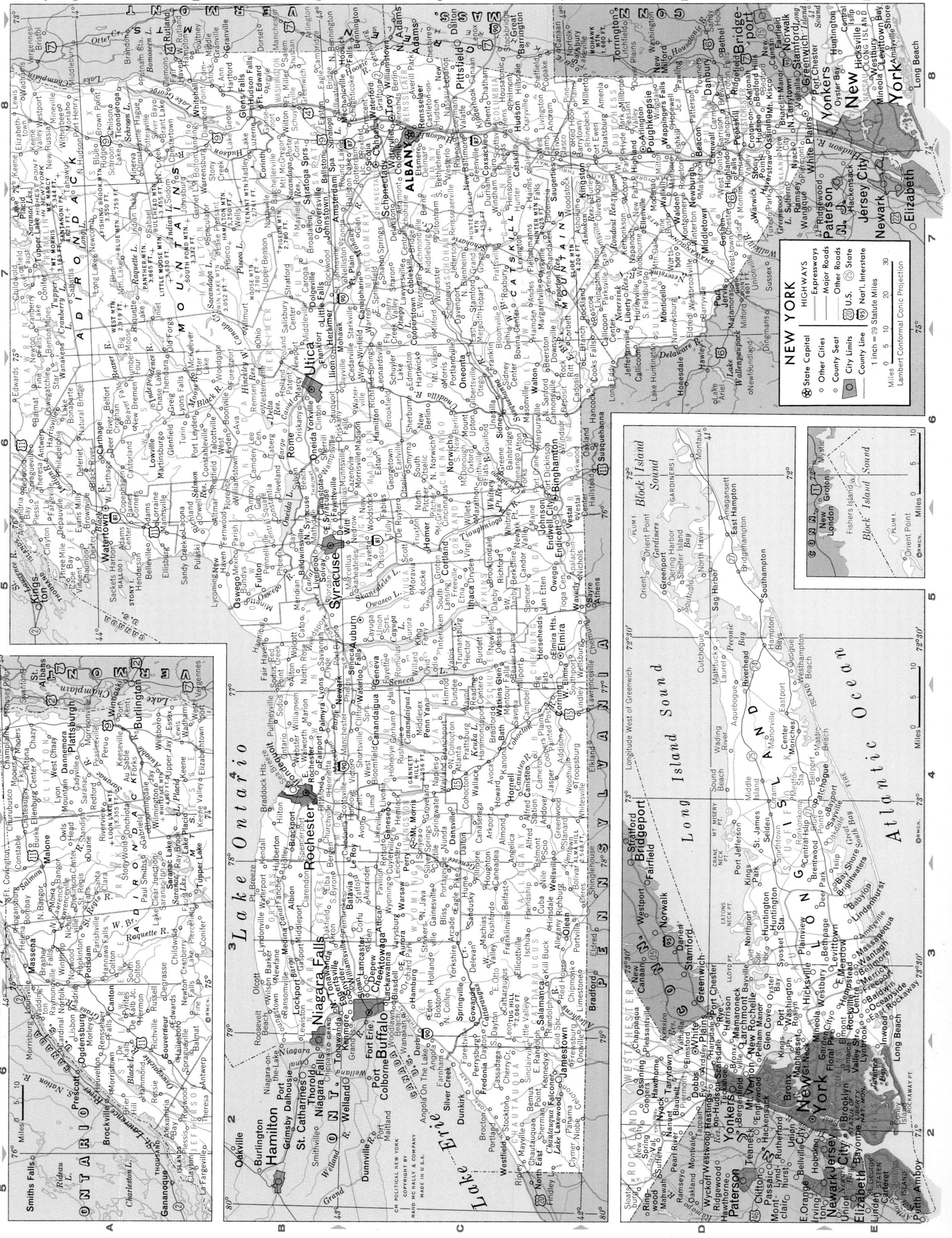
NEW YORK
State Capital
Other Cities
County Seat
City Limits
County Line
HIGHWAYS
Expressways
Major Roads
Other Roads
U.S.
State
Nat'l. Interstate
1 inch = 29 Statute Miles
Lambert Conformal Conic Projection
Lake Ontario
Lake Erie
Long Island Sound
Atlantic Ocean
Block Island Sound
CM POLITICAL NEW YORK
COPYRIGHT BY RAND McNALLY & COMPANY
MADE IN U.S.A.
DWIGHT D. EISENHOWER LOCK
ADIRONDACK MOUNTAINS
CATSKILL MOUNTAINS
PENNSYLVANIA
ALBANY
New York
Buffalo
Rochester
Syracuse
Utica
Binghamton

NEW YORK: This state, George Washington predicted, would become the "seat of empire." The center of an industrial empire it has certainly become. The most populous state in the union, New York also leads in the number of manufacturing establishments, with about 48,000. They produce over $16 billion worth of goods each year, a total which exceeds the production of any other state by approximately $4 billion a year. In western New York a new hydroelectric project on the short, swift Niagara River will in the next few years produce 13 billion kilowatt hours per year, which will make it the largest hydroelectric project in the United States.

Cutting through the fertile Mohawk Valley, the Erie Canal in 1825 linked the Great Lakes with the vast harbor of New York City by way of the Hudson River. Thus New York City in the middle of the 19th Century became the outlet for the beef, wheat and corn of the Midwest. To the farmers of that rapidly developing region the city shipped manufactures of its own as well as products of foreign countries.

AREA: 49,576 sq. mi. Rank: 30th.
POPULATION: 16,782,304. Rank: 1st.
Largest city: New York. Capital: Albany.
ENTERED UNION: July 26, 1788, as 11th state.
CLIMATE: Cool winters, hot summers in south; cold winters with heavy snow, short summers in north and west. Moderate rainfall.
ALTITUDES: Mt. Marcy, 5,344 ft. (highest); New York City, 55 ft.

The harbor of New York City remains a major bulwark of the state's economy. More than 40 per cent of the nation's $23 billion worth of ocean-borne imports and exports is handled at the Port of New York's piers. The city itself *(maps below)* is not only the cultural, financial and communications center of the nation, but an industrial center too. It is the headquarters for a $1.8 billion apparel industry, and more than $1.2 billion worth of books, magazines and newspapers are published here each year. Electrical and other machinery, chemicals and metals amount to some $975 million annually.

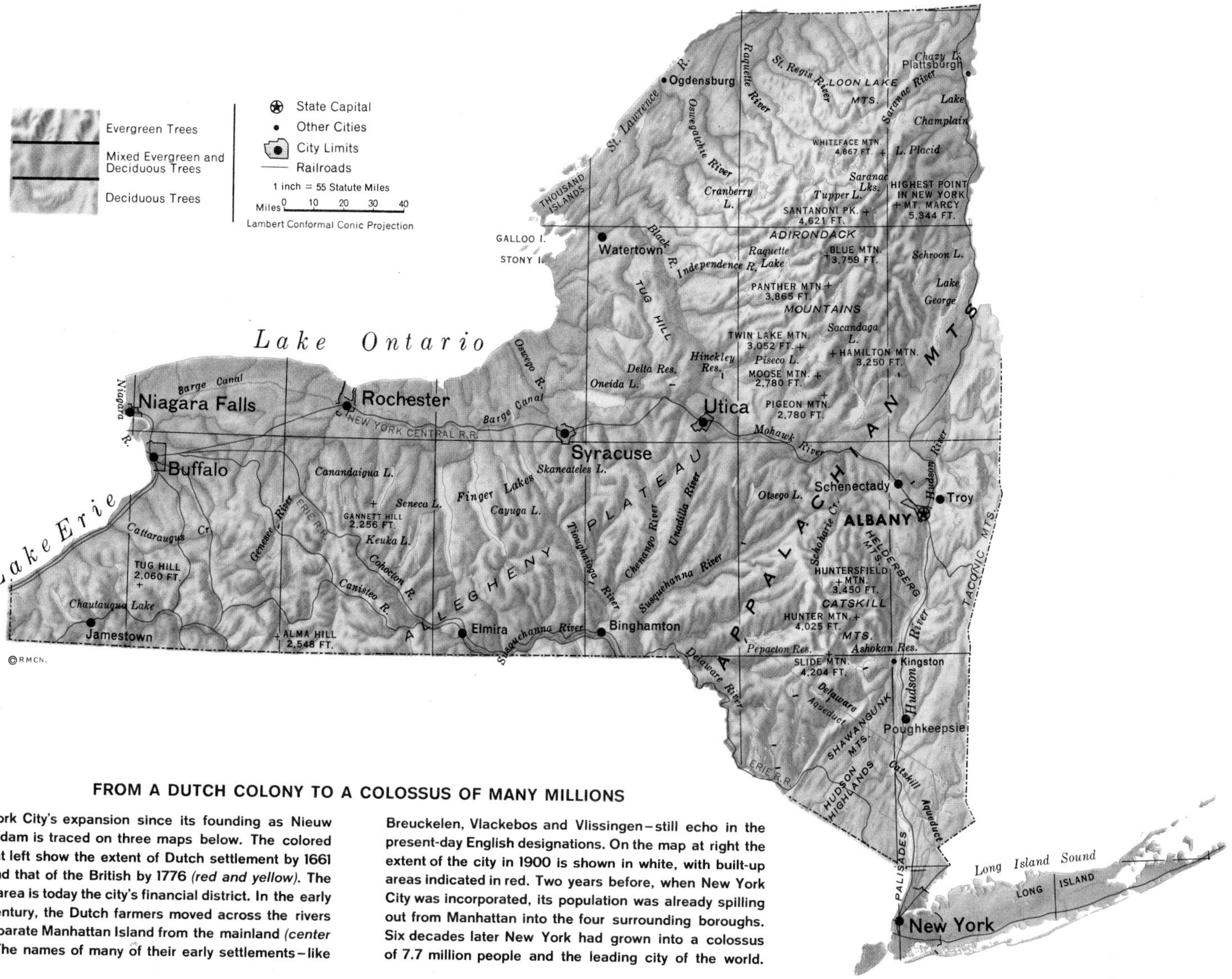

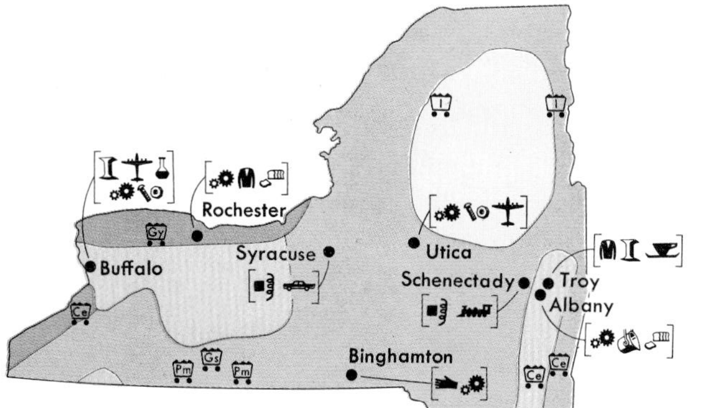

THE ECONOMY

MANUFACTURING
Metal Processing
Food Processing
Metal Products
Primary Metals
Machinery
Chemicals
Clothing
Stone, Clay & Glass Products
Textiles & Clothing
Leather & Products
Electrical Machinery
Printing & Publishing
Transportation Equipment

MINING
Cement
Natural Gas
Gypsum
Iron Ore
Petroleum
Stone

AGRICULTURE
Fruit, Truck & General Farming
Dairy Farming
Dairy & General Farming
Mountains & Forests

VALUE		EMPLOYED
$ 893,670,000	AGRICULTURE	3.0%
$16,062,000,000	MANUFACTURING	28.0%
$ 204,920,000	MINING	0.2%

Percentages are based on a total of 6,200,000 at work. In addition 38% are in commerce and transport, 13% in government, 17.8% in other areas. Manufacturing value is the value added when materials are converted into goods.

FROM A DUTCH COLONY TO A COLOSSUS OF MANY MILLIONS

New York City's expansion since its founding as Nieuw Amsterdam is traced on three maps below. The colored areas at left show the extent of Dutch settlement by 1661 *(red)* and that of the British by 1776 *(red and yellow)*. The Dutch area is today the city's financial district. In the early 17th Century, the Dutch farmers moved across the rivers that separate Manhattan Island from the mainland *(center map)*. The names of many of their early settlements—like Breuckelen, Vlackebos and Vlissingen—still echo in the present-day English designations. On the map at right the extent of the city in 1900 is shown in white, with built-up areas indicated in red. Two years before, when New York City was incorporated, its population was already spilling out from Manhattan into the four surrounding boroughs. Six decades later New York had grown into a colossus of 7.7 million people and the leading city of the world.

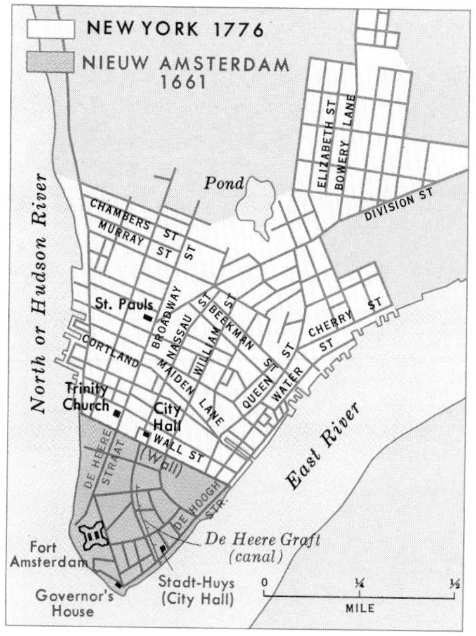

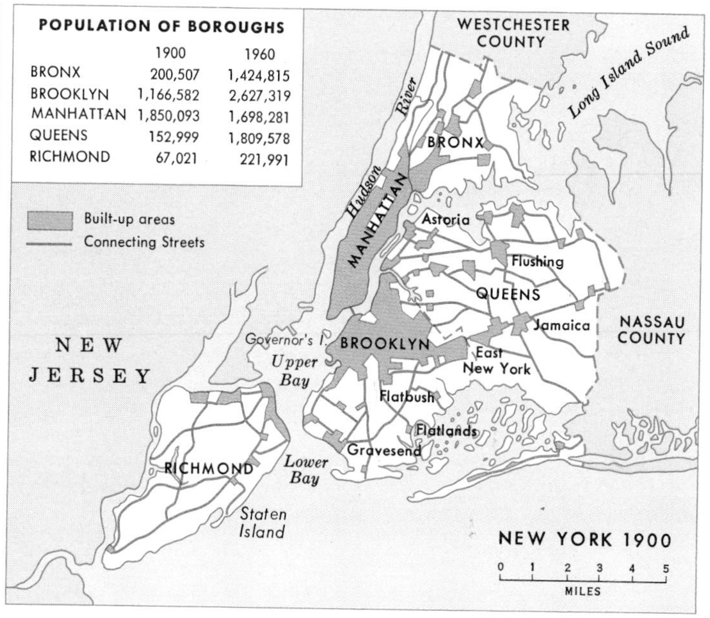

POPULATION OF BOROUGHS

	1900	1960
BRONX	200,507	1,424,815
BROOKLYN	1,166,582	2,627,319
MANHATTAN	1,850,093	1,698,281
QUEENS	152,999	1,809,578
RICHMOND	67,021	221,991

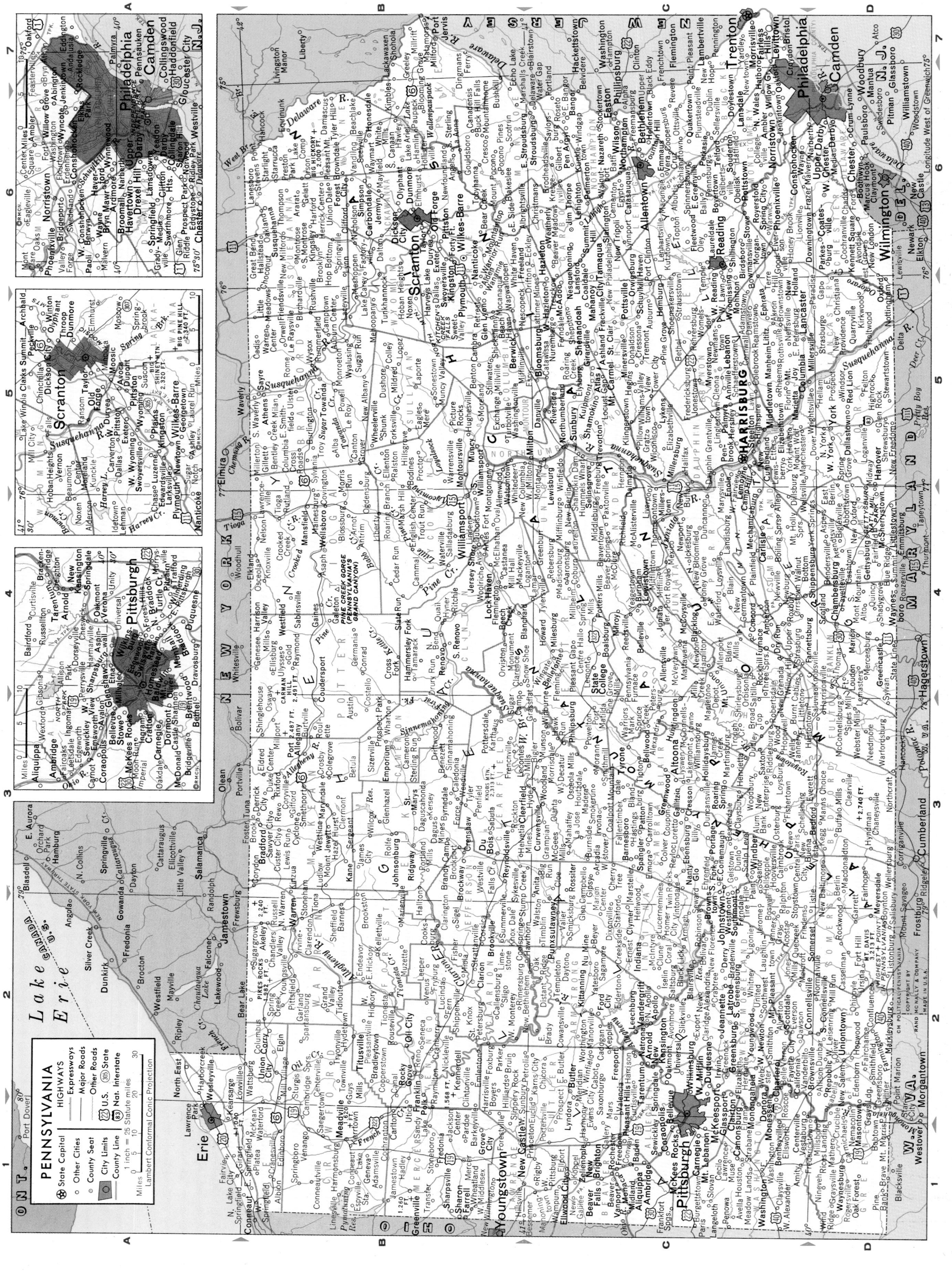
PENNSYLVANIA
HIGHWAYS
State Capital
Other Cities
County Seat
City Limits
County Line
Expressways
Major Roads
Other Roads
U.S.
State
Nat. Interstate
1 inch = 25 Statute miles
Lambert Conformal Conic Projection
Lake Erie
NEW YORK
NEW JERSEY
MARYLAND
DEL.
W. VA.
OHIO
ONT.
CANADA
U.S.
Pittsburgh
Philadelphia
Scranton
Harrisburg
Erie
Allentown
Reading
Wilkes-Barre
Camden
Trenton
Wilmington
Longitude West of Greenwich
COPYRIGHT BY RAND McNALLY & COMPANY
MADE IN U.S.A.
CM POLITICAL/PENNSYLVANIA

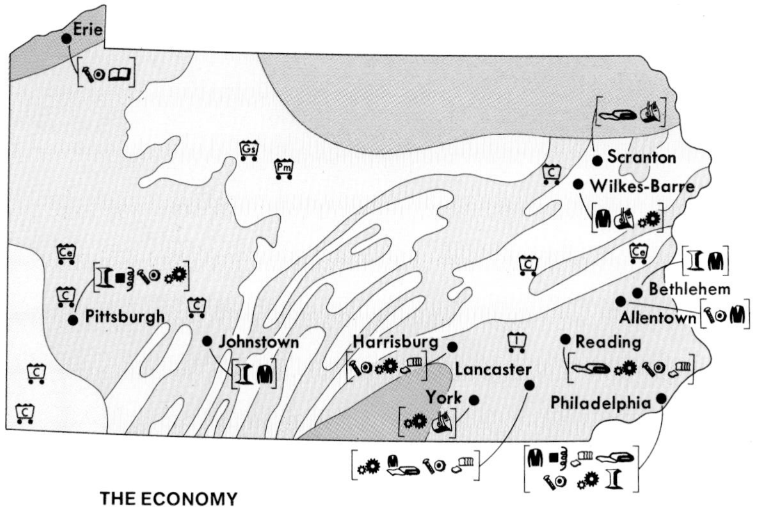

THE ECONOMY

MANUFACTURING
- Metal Processing
- Primary Metals
- Metal Products
- Textiles & Clothing
- Clothing
- Textiles
- Machinery
- Electrical Machinery
- Food Processing
- Printing & Publishing

MINING
- Coal
- Cement
- Iron Ore
- Natural Gas
- Petroleum

AGRICULTURE
- General Farming
- Fruit & General Farming
- Fruit, Truck & General Farming
- Dairy Farming
- Dairy & General Farming
- Mountains & Forests

VALUE		EMPLOYED
$ 851,610,000	AGRICULTURE	6%
$11,461,000,000	MANUFACTURING	36%
$ 881,180,000	MINING	2%

Percentages are based on a total of 3,824,000 at work. In addition 30% are in commerce and transport, 11% in government, 15% in other areas. Manufacturing value is the value added when materials are converted into goods.

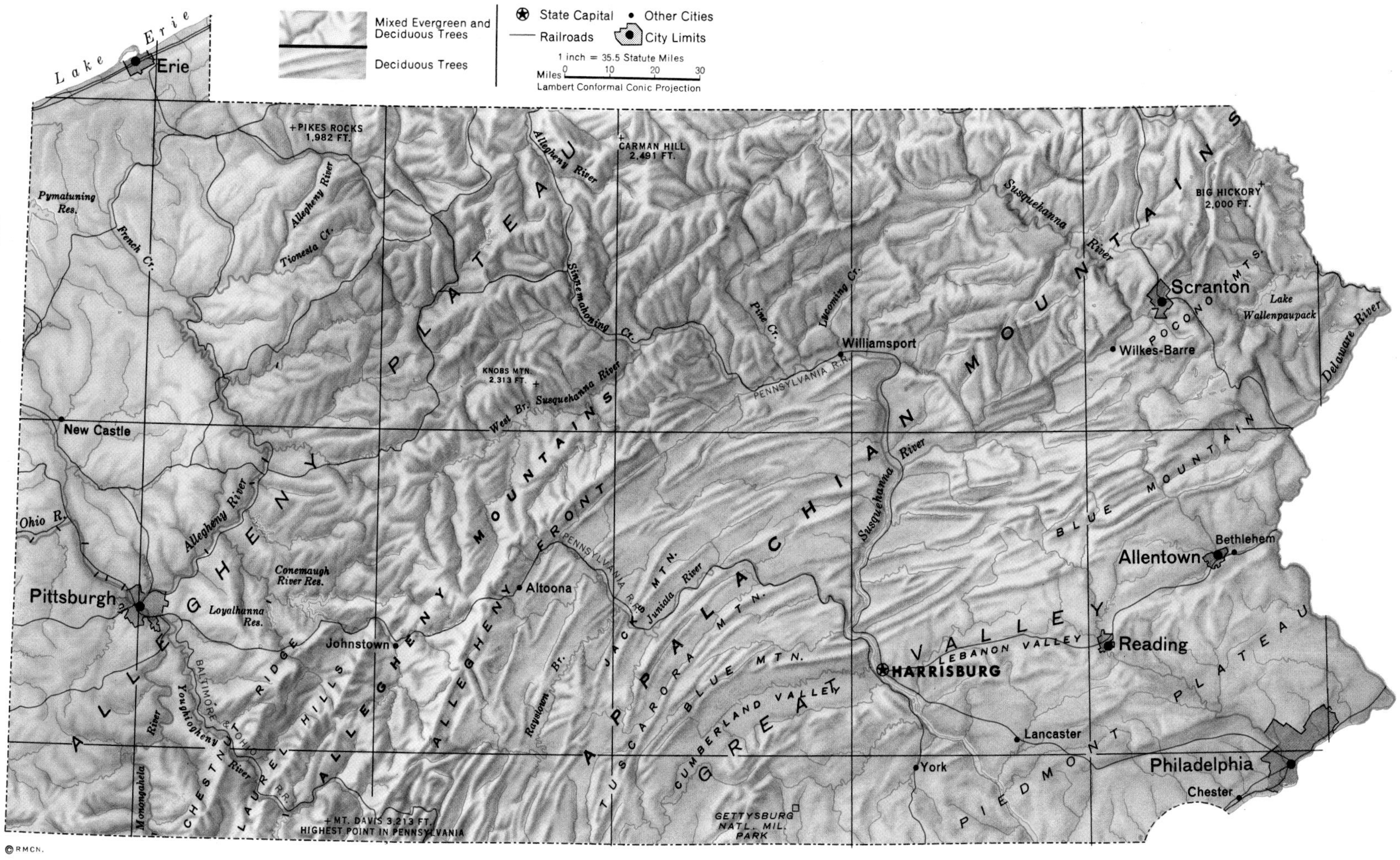

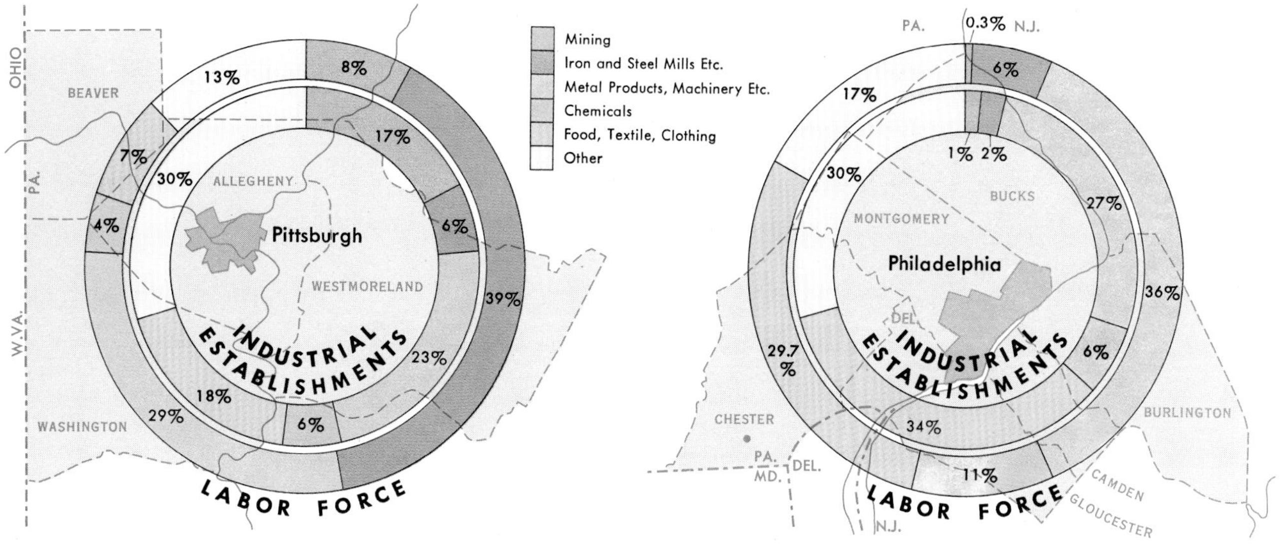

DIVISION OF LABOR AND PLANTS IN TWO INDUSTRIAL REGIONS

These double rings around Pittsburgh and Philadelphia show how the local labor force in each region is divided among industries *(outer rings)*, and what percentage of the total number of manufacturing establishments each industry accounts for *(inner rings)*. In Philadelphia, more than a third of the labor force works in the metal products and machinery industries. In Pittsburgh, iron and steel account for 39 per cent of the total labor force.

PENNSYLVANIA: Founder William Penn's "good and fruitful land" was in ancient times almost blanketed with vast stretches of forests and immense fields of ferns and shrubs. Some 250 million years ago the forests and fields were flooded with sea water. Later, the folding of the Appalachian Mountains compressed the trees and shrubs into coal—hard, smokeless anthracite in the northeastern part of the state, soft bituminous in the west. Pennsylvania's coal has been mined since the late 18th Century. The state still has almost all of the nation's anthracite reserves as well as extensive veins of bituminous coal in its rocky hills.

In addition to coal, Pennsylvania once contained great deposits of iron ore, so industrialization came early to the state. Today ore is brought in from the Great Lakes region and other areas to be processed in the giant mills clustered around Pittsburgh and in the steel cities of the east. To move raw materials and finished products efficiently, Pennsylvanians have built spectacular highways and an elaborate railroad system.

AREA:	45,333 sq. mi. Rank: 33rd.
POPULATION:	11,319,366. Rank: 3rd. Largest city: Philadelphia. Capital: Harrisburg.
ENTERED UNION:	Dec. 12, 1787, as 2nd state.
CLIMATE:	Warm summers, cold winters; moderate rainfall, heavy snow in mountains.
ALTITUDES:	Mt. Davis, 3,213 ft. (highest); Harrisburg, 365 ft.

It was at Philadelphia in 1751 that the Provincial Assembly of Pennsylvania ordered a bell from England emblazoned with these words from Leviticus: "Proclaim Liberty Throughout All the Land unto All the Inhabitants Thereof." On July 8, 1776, from the tower atop Philadelphia's Independence Hall, the bell proclaimed the news that the Declaration of Independence had been signed four days earlier in the same building.

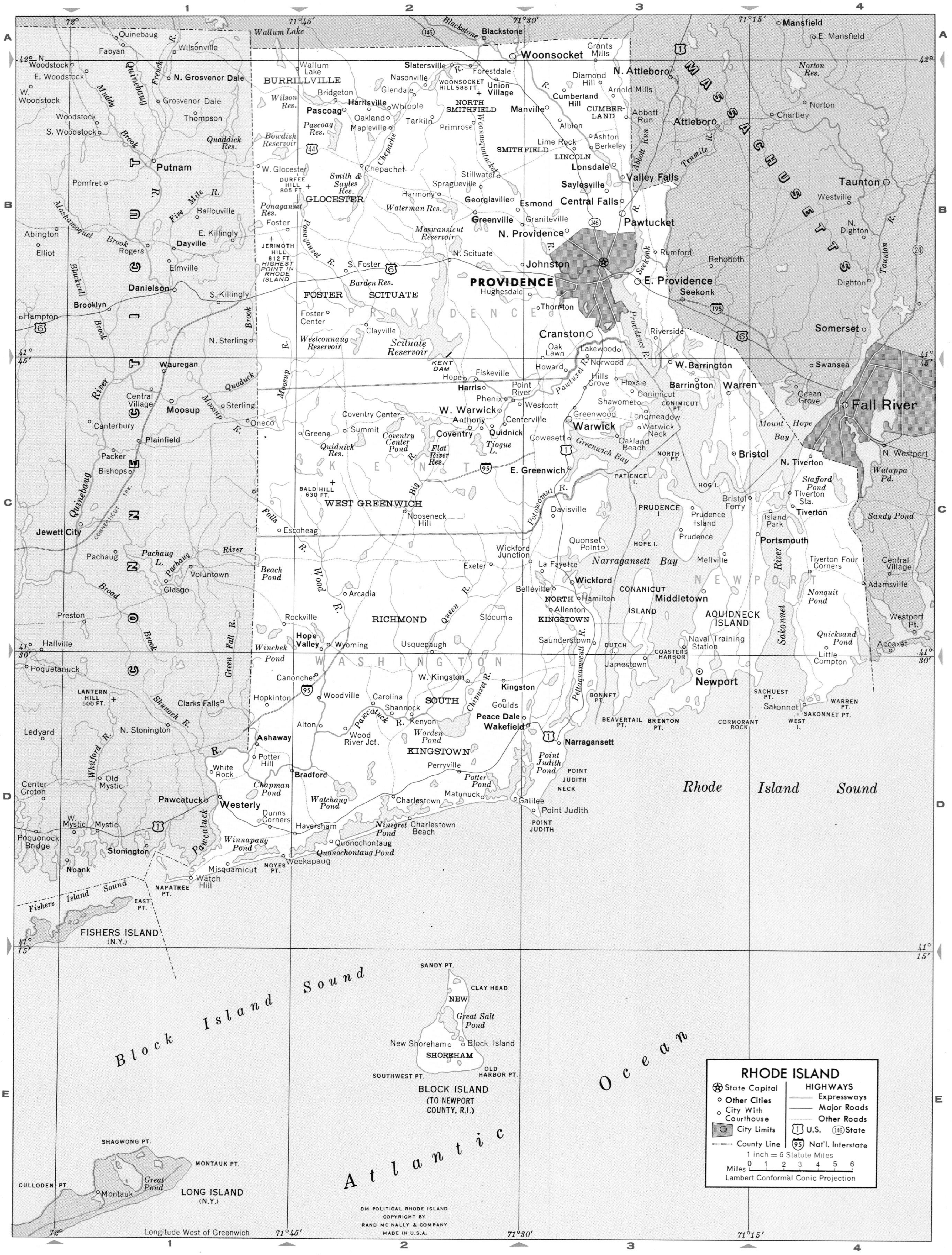
RHODE ISLAND
State Capital
Other Cities
City With Courthouse
City Limits
County Line
HIGHWAYS
Expressways
Major Roads
Other Roads
U.S.
State
Nat'l. Interstate
1 inch = 6 Statute Miles
Miles 0 1 2 3 4 5 6
Lambert Conformal Conic Projection
PROVIDENCE
Woonsocket
Pawtucket
Central Falls
Cranston
Warwick
E. Providence
Newport
Westerly
Bristol
Johnston
N. Providence
Fall River
Taunton
Attleboro
N. Attleboro
Somerset
M A S S A C H U S E T T S
C O N N E C T I C U T
P R O V I D E N C E
K E N T
W A S H I N G T O N
N E W P O R T
BURRILLVILLE
GLOCESTER
FOSTER
SCITUATE
NORTH SMITHFIELD
SMITHFIELD
LINCOLN
CUMBERLAND
WEST GREENWICH
RICHMOND
SOUTH KINGSTOWN
NORTH KINGSTOWN
Narragansett Bay
Rhode Island Sound
Block Island Sound
Atlantic Ocean
Fishers Island Sound
FISHERS ISLAND (N.Y.)
BLOCK ISLAND (TO NEWPORT COUNTY, R.I.)
LONG ISLAND (N.Y.)
PRUDENCE I.
CONANICUT ISLAND
AQUIDNECK ISLAND
HOPE I.
PATIENCE I.
Scituate Reservoir
JERIMOTH HILL 812 FT. HIGHEST POINT IN RHODE ISLAND
DURFEE HILL 805 FT.
WOONSOCKET HILL 588 FT.
BALD HILL 630 FT.
LANTERN HILL 500 FT.
Longitude West of Greenwich
CM POLITICAL RHODE ISLAND
COPYRIGHT BY RAND McNALLY & COMPANY
MADE IN U.S.A.

RHODE ISLAND

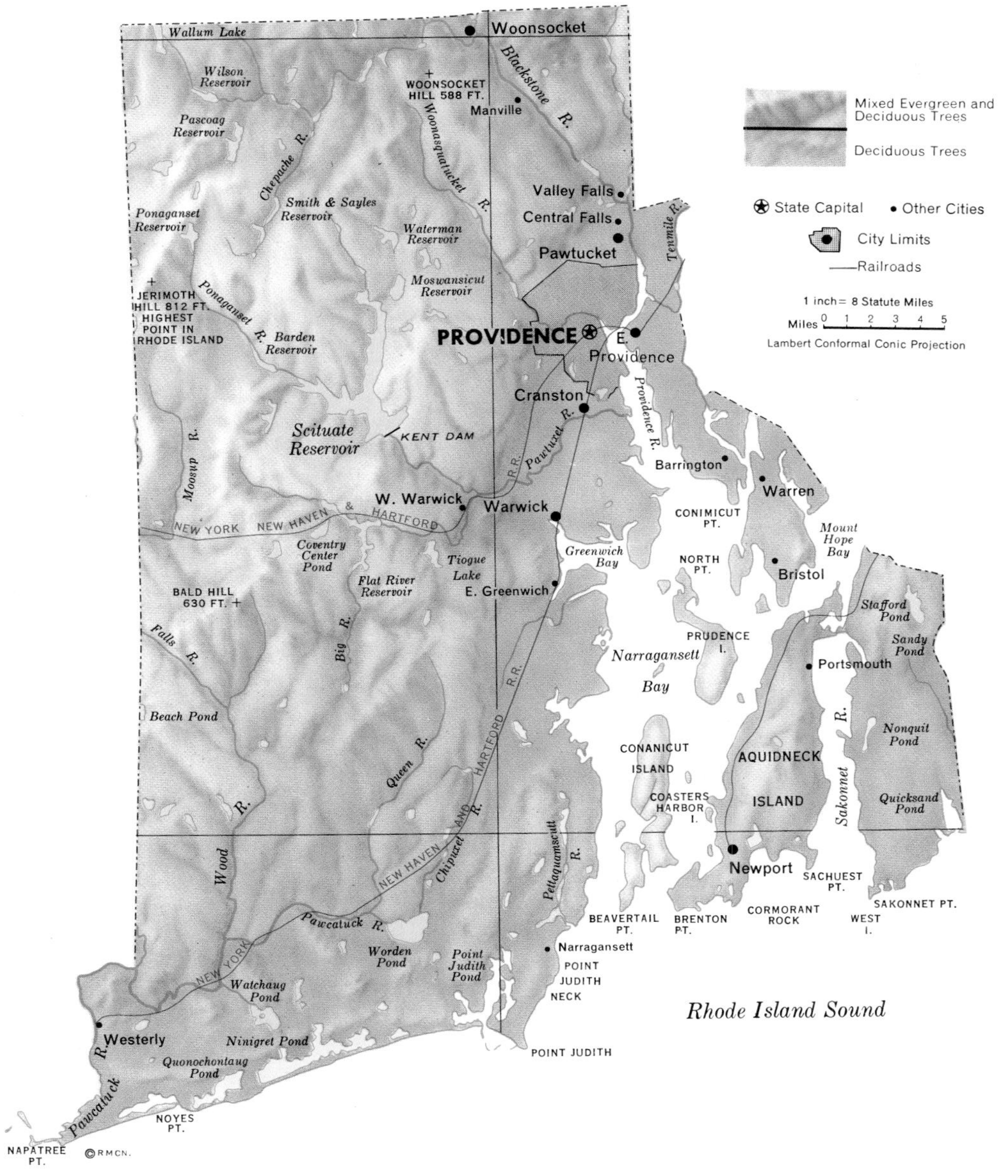

THE ECONOMY

MANUFACTURING
- Textiles & Apparel
- Machinery
- Metal Processing

AGRICULTURE
- Dairy & General Farming

VALUE		EMPLOYED
$ 22,680,000	AGRICULTURE	1.0%
$759,000,000	MANUFACTURING	40.0%
$ 2,250,000	MINING	0.1%

Percentages are based on a total of 275,000 at work. In addition 29% are in commerce and transport, 13% in government, 16.9% in other areas. Manufacturing value is the value added when materials are converted into goods.

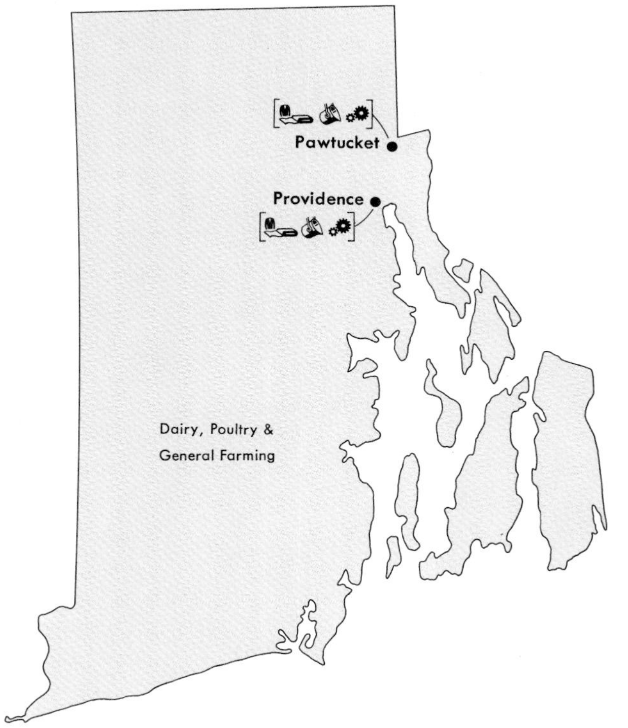

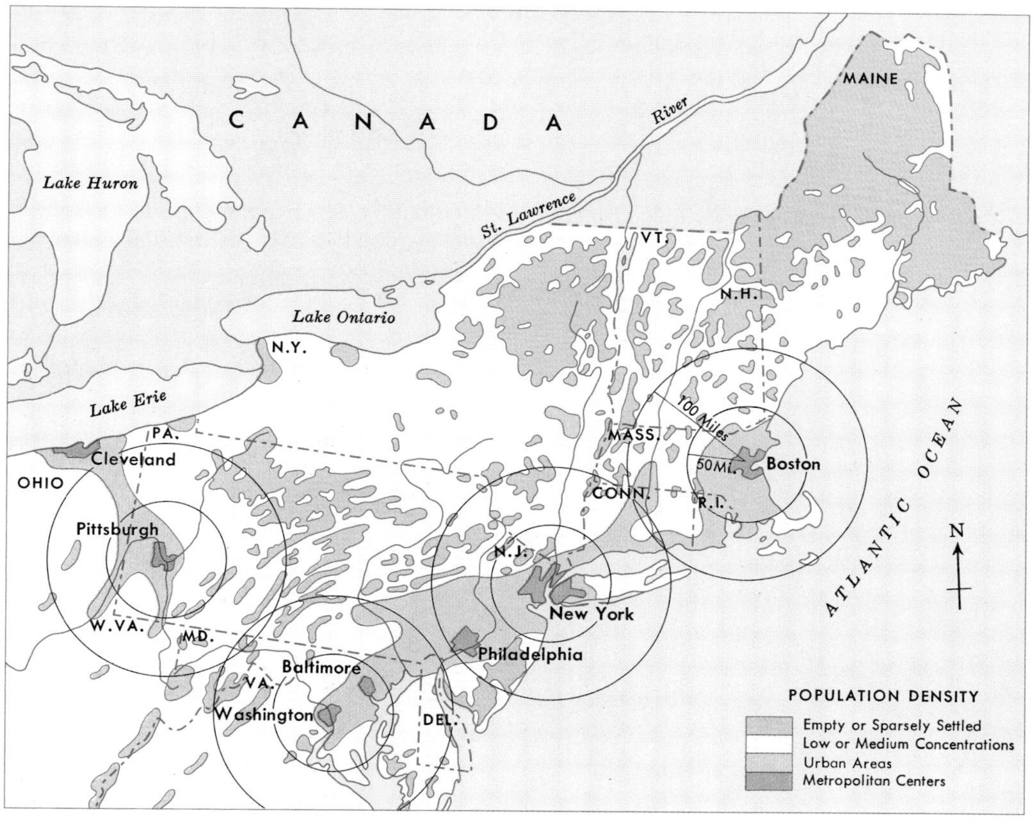

URBAN SPRAWL IN THE NORTHEAST

More than one quarter of the total U.S. population is jammed into the northeastern U.S., shown above, although large areas of open country *(green)* still exist here. The crowded urban areas *(light red)* have merged into each other, forming a broad strip along U.S. Highway 1, which runs from Boston to Washington, D.C. There is urban sprawl, too, between Pittsburgh and Cleveland. Away from main routes, as the concentric circles around cities show, population density falls off radically.

RHODE ISLAND: The most densely populated state in the nation, Rhode Island is also the smallest. The state is actually smaller than its boundaries would indicate, for Narragansett Bay and numerous reservoirs and lakes drown one eighth of its total area. On the land that remains there are some 800 people to the square mile, compared to a national average of about 50.

The textile industry of Rhode Island goes back to 1790, when Slater's cotton mill—the first successful mill in the nation—was built at Pawtucket. A state that has few raw materials, Rhode Island nevertheless has advantages to offer industry: an abundant supply of water power, ready access to markets and a large pool of highly skilled workers. Although the 19th Century industries of jewelry, silverware, machinery, metal products and rubber goods are still important, plastics and electronics have been emerging as new sources of income.

AREA:	1,214 sq. mi. Rank: 50th.
POPULATION:	859,488. Rank: 39th. Largest city and capital: Providence.
ENTERED UNION:	May 29, 1790, as 13th state.
CLIMATE:	Cold winters, warm summers; temperature range modified by proximity to ocean. Moderate rainfall.
ALTITUDES:	Jerimoth Hill, 812 ft. (highest).

Rhode Island is not an island. It received its name in the 16th Century when the Italian navigator Giovanni da Verrazano entered Narragansett Bay. His account notes that an island, probably present-day Block Island, reminded him of historic Rhodes in the Aegean. Later, after Roger Williams had broken away from the Puritan intolerance of Massachusetts and set up a colony called Providence Plantations, Rhode Island became the name of the island on which Newport, the famous summer resort, is situated. In 1776 the state officially called itself the State of Rhode Island and Providence Plantations.

The state's history has always been linked with the sea and seafarers. Rhode Islanders fitted out John Paul Jones' first fighting sloop, the *Providence*, and later furnished the nation with two great naval heroes—Commodore Oliver Hazard Perry, who won the Battle of Lake Erie in the War of 1812, and Commodore Matthew Perry, who in 1854 opened Japan to the world.

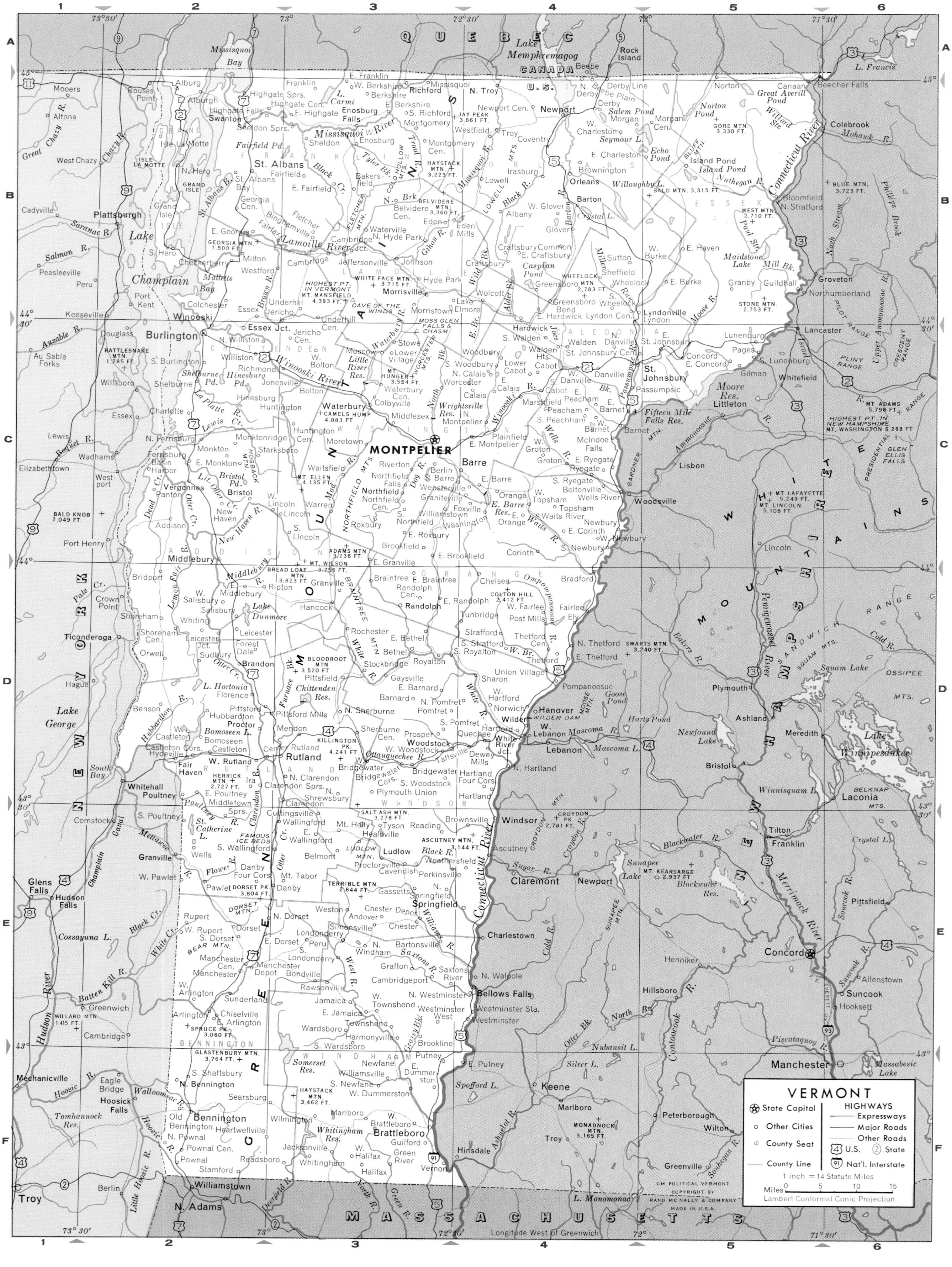
VERMONT
State Capital
Other Cities
County Seat
County Line
HIGHWAYS
Expressways
Major Roads
Other Roads
U.S.
State
Nat'l. Interstate
1 inch = 14 Statute Miles
Miles 0 5 10 15
Lambert Conformal Conic Projection
CM POLITICAL VERMONT
COPYRIGHT BY
RAND MCNALLY & COMPANY
MADE IN U.S.A.
Longitude West of Greenwich
1
2
3
4
5
6
A
B
C
D
E
F
73°30′
73°
72°30′
72°
71°30′
45°
44° 30′
44°
43° 30′
43°
QUEBEC
CANADA
U.S.
NEW YORK
NEW HAMPSHIRE
MASSACHUSETTS
WHITE MOUNTAINS
GREEN MOUNTAINS
MONTPELIER
Burlington
Rutland
Barre
St. Albans
St. Johnsbury
Bennington
Brattleboro
Springfield
Bellows Falls
Windsor
Middlebury
Newport
Lake Champlain
Lake Memphremagog
Lake George
Lake Winnipesaukee
Connecticut River
Concord
Manchester
Keene
Laconia
Plattsburgh
Claremont
Lebanon
HIGHEST PT. IN VERMONT MT. MANSFIELD 4,393 FT.
HIGHEST PT. IN NEW HAMPSHIRE MT. WASHINGTON 6,288 FT.

VERMONT

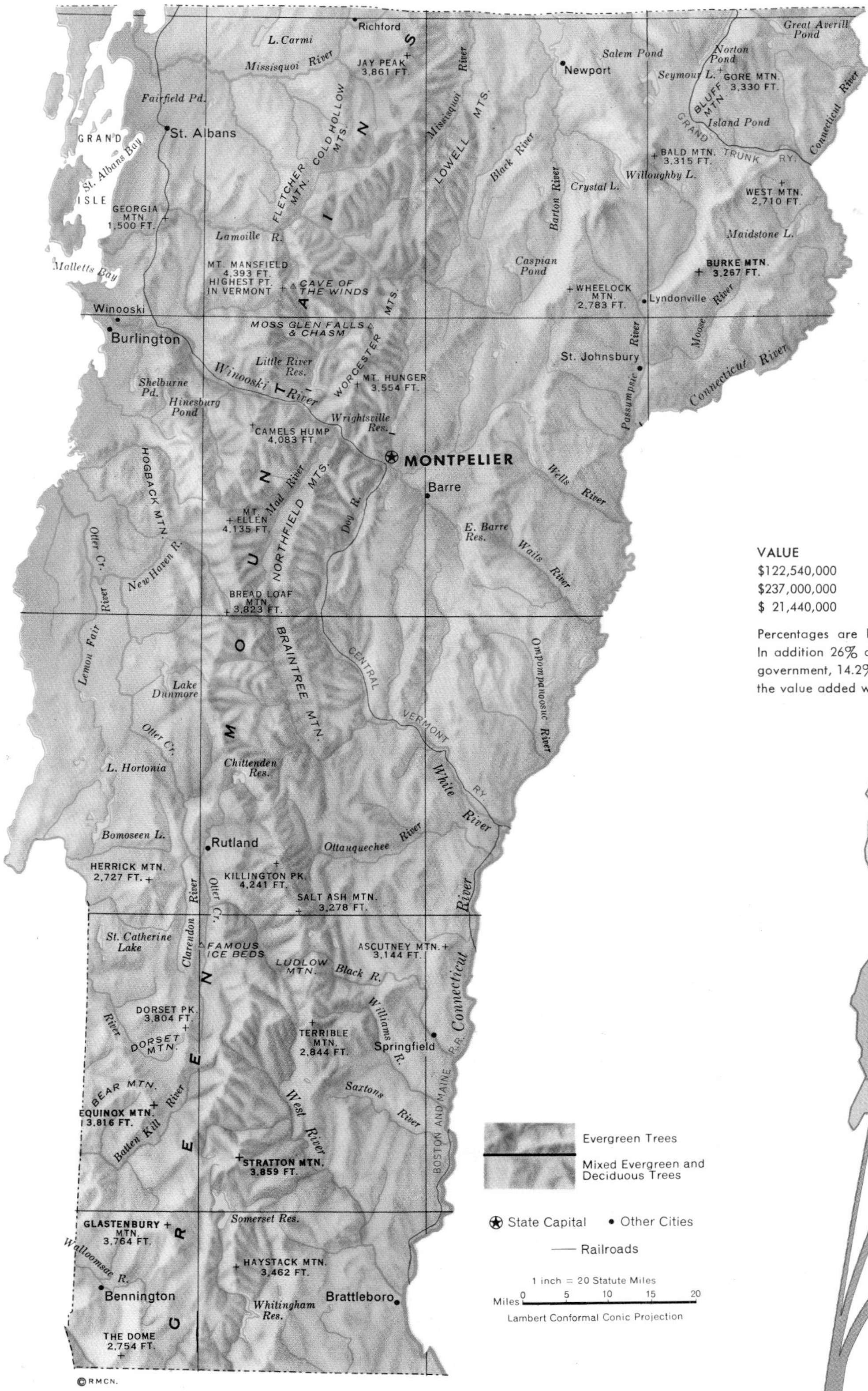

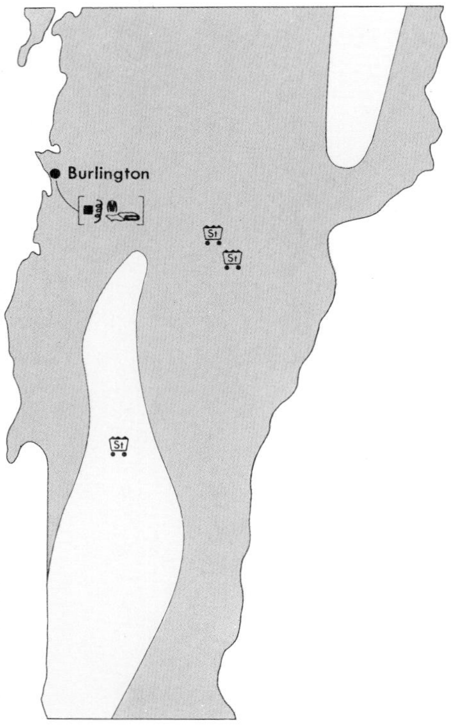

THE ECONOMY

MANUFACTURING
- Electrical Machinery
- Textiles & Clothing

MINING
- Stone

AGRICULTURE
- Dairy Farming
- Mountains & Forests

VALUE		EMPLOYED
$122,540,000	AGRICULTURE	21.0%
$237,000,000	MANUFACTURING	26.0%
$ 21,440,000	MINING	0.8%

Percentages are based on a total of 128,000 at work. In addition 26% are in commerce and transport, 12% in government, 14.2% in other areas. Manufacturing value is the value added when materials are converted into goods.

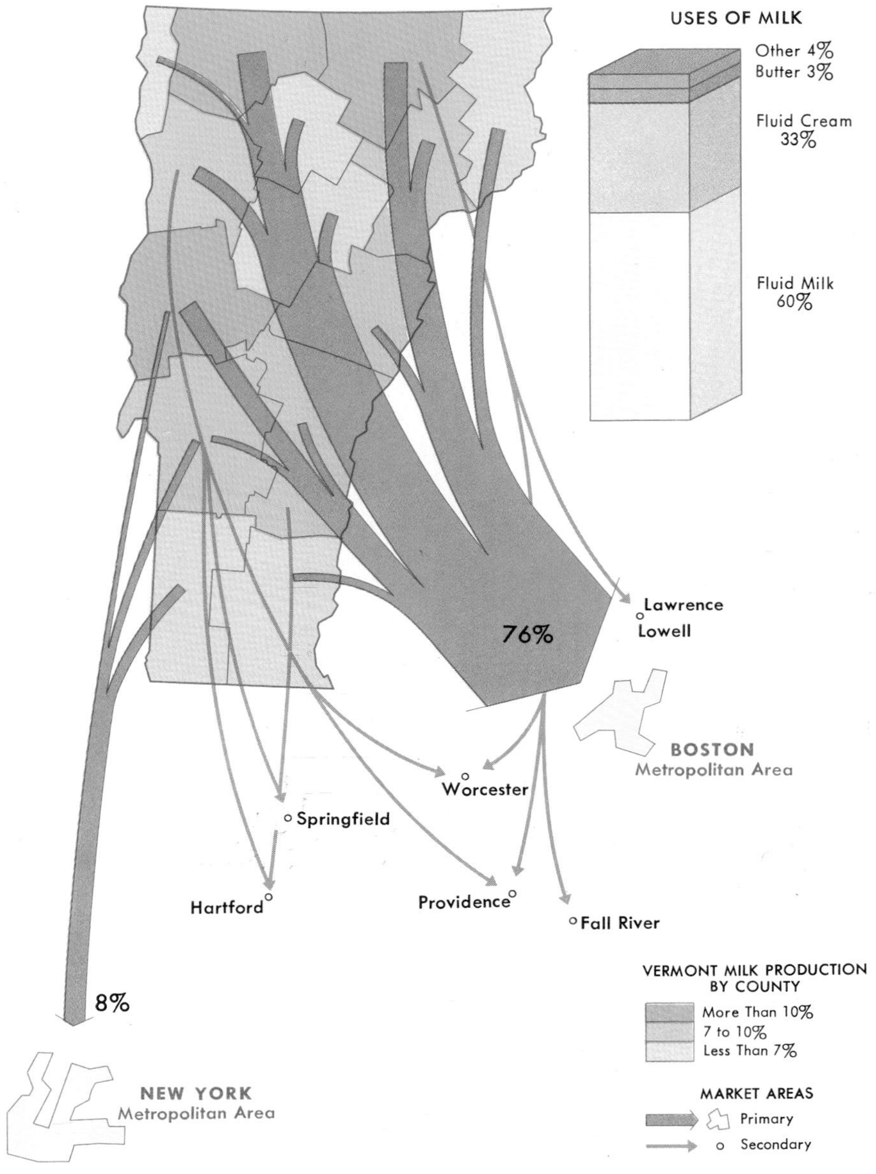

A SMALL STATE, A GIANT MILKSHED

The flow of milk from Vermont to the various cities of the Eastern Seaboard is shown above. With over 60 per cent of its farms devoted to dairying and with more cattle and calves than people, Vermont ships 94 per cent of its total fluid-milk production out of the state. The biggest market is Boston, which takes more than three quarters of the annual production of 190 million gallons. Until the turn of the century, Vermont dairymen used to turn most of their milk into butter and cheese, just as Wisconsin dairymen still do. Then, seeing the expanding market possibilities for fresh milk among city dwellers, Vermont took advantage of its proximity to big eastern cities and switched to profitable fluid-milk shipping.

VERMONT: "The Vermont mountains stretch extending straight," the poet Robert Frost has written. The rounded, rocky mass of the state's Green Mountains seems poised to slide off into the Champlain Lowland to the west and the valley of the Connecticut River to the east. Vermont has never been more than thinly populated. It is a vacationer's delight: trout, bass, pickerel and landlocked salmon flourish in more than 400 glacial lakes and ponds; rabbit and deer abound in the fir, maple and birch forests; the snow-covered mountains offer superb ski slopes.

AREA:	9,609 sq. mi. Rank: 43rd.
POPULATION:	389,881. Rank: 47th. Largest city: Burlington. Capital: Montpelier.
ENTERED UNION:	March 4, 1791, as 14th state.
CLIMATE:	Long cold winters with heavy snows; short mild summers. Moderate rainfall.
ALTITUDES:	Mt. Mansfield, 4,393 ft. (highest).

The Vermonters make modest livings from dairying *(diagram, right)* and other agricultural pursuits. About a fourth of the labor force is engaged in manufacturing: machinery, lumber and furniture. This small state leads the nation in producing asbestos for brake linings and clutch facings and in granite and marble quarrying. The quarrying has been carried on ever since American pioneers first began using Vermont marble for fireplaces and tombstones. The seemingly inexhaustible quarries of one small hamlet, Proctor, on the western slopes of the Green Mountains, have provided the marble for the Supreme Court Building in Washington, D.C., the Secretariat of the United Nations and dozens of other major buildings throughout the U.S.

MIDDLE AMERICA

Bracketed between continents, Middle America is a meeting ground of mountain ranges, the benign Atlantic trade winds and wild hurricanes. At a point near Mexico City, the north-to-south mountains of North America come to a halt at a line of east-to-west mountains. This Middle American range of volcanic peaks, some of them still active, plunges into the Caribbean Sea and emerges farther east as islands of the Antilles. The tropical region of Middle America has been one of the world's great melting pots. It was here that the New World's densest Indian population met and mingled with the heaviest wave of invading Spanish conquistadors and tens of thousands of West Africans brought in to work as slaves on plantations of sugar cane and tobacco. Out of this mixture of races and cultures has come an astonishingly varied civilization—developed in what the Spanish explorer Vasco Núñez de Balboa called a land of "great secrets and marvelous riches."

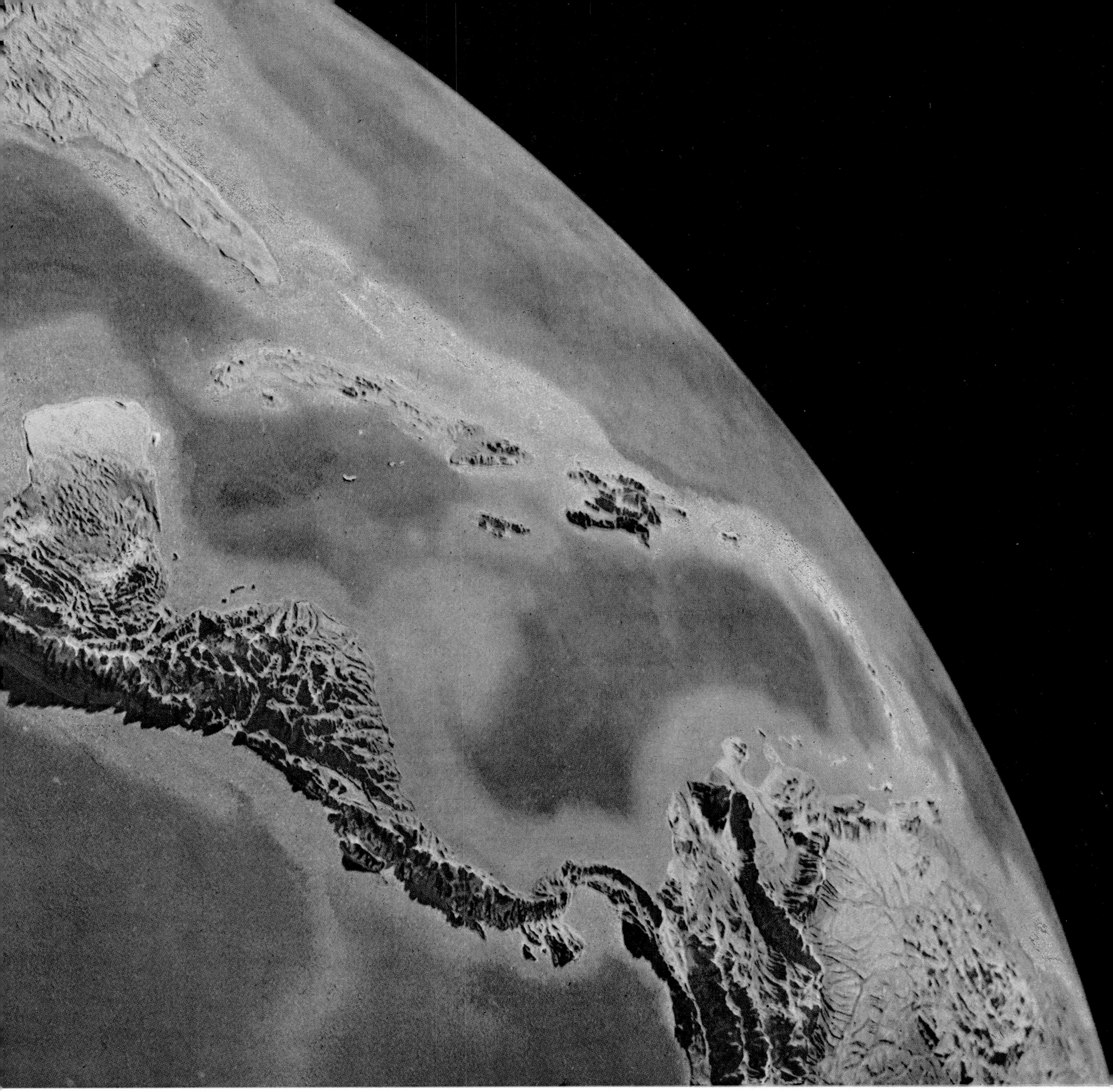

SOUTH OF THE RIO GRANDE lies Middle America, reaching from the U.S. to South America, at bottom right, and stretching out to include the Caribbean Islands, right. The countries below Mexico are called Central America. It was from Panama, the narrowest of these countries, that Balboa caught his first glimpse of the Pacific Ocean in 1513.

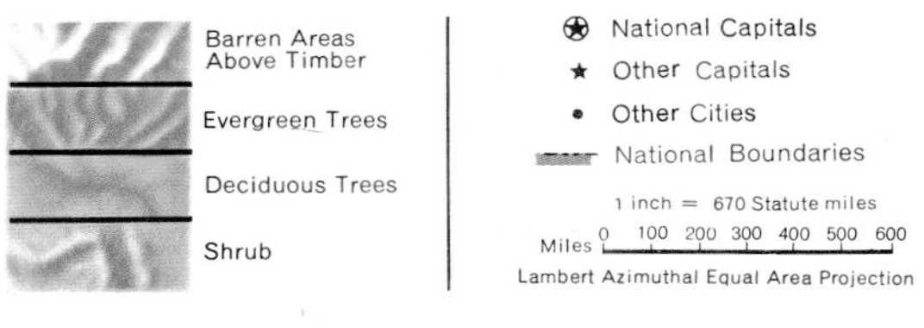

THE SUN-BLESSED SPLENDORS OF

MIDDLE AMERICA

A FASHIONABLE RESORT, the Mexican city of Acapulco encircles a bay of the Pacific with high cliffs and crescent beaches. For centuries its principal visitors were Spanish captains who put into its harbor with oriental spices. Today, galleons have been replaced by luxury yachts, and the visitors are tourists for whom Acapulco has been made into a luxurious watering place.

AN AWESOME RELIC, a pyramid more than eight centuries old *(left)* rises from the flat floor of the Valley of Mexico, cradle of ancient Indian civilizations. This 216-foot monument, called the Pyramid of the Sun, and the nearby Pyramid of the Moon *(left, background)* were part of the great ceremonial center of Teotihuacan, built by the Toltecs before the coming of the Aztecs.

LOADS OF BANANAS leave Guanaja Island off the Caribbean coast of Honduras for a rendezvous with a banana schooner which will take the cargoes to the mainland. From their hot and steamy lowlands, four countries of Middle America—the small "Banana Republics" of Panama, Honduras, Guatemala and Costa Rica—export one half of the world's supply of this fruit.

MEXICO
Barren Areas Above Timber
Evergreen Trees
Mixed Evergreen and Deciduous Trees
Deciduous Trees
Shrub
Grass
Volcanic Lava Areas
Below sea level areas are white. No vegetation is indicated.
National Capitals
Cities
State Capitals
Railroads
State Boundaries
Dry Stream
1 inch = 115 Statute Miles
Miles 0 20 40 60 80 100 120
Oblique Conformal Conic Projection
CALIF.
ARIZONA
NEW MEXICO
SONORA
CHIHUAHUA
DURANGO
NAYARIT
JALISCO
BAJA CALIFORNIA
BAJA CALIFORNIA SUR (TER.)
SIERRA MADRE OCCIDENTAL
SIERRA MADRE OCCIDENTAL
SIERRA S. PEDRO MARTIR
SIERRA COLUMBIA
SIERRA DE LA GIGANTA
Golfo de California
Pacific Ocean
Tropic of Cancer
San Diego
Tijuana
Mexicali
Ensenada
Yuma
Phoenix
Tucson
Nogales
Hermosillo
Guaymas
Ciudad Obregón
Ciudad Juárez
El Paso
Chihuahua
Culiacán
Mazatlán
Durango
Tepic
Guadalajara
La Paz
San Lucas
Santa Rosalia
Mulegé
Loreto
Topolobampo
Los Mochis
Navojoa
Puerto Vallarta
Manzanillo
Colima
GUADALOUPE (MEX.)
I. DE CEDROS
Bahía de Sebastián Vizcaíno
B. de Ballenas
B. de La Paz
ISLA TIBURÓN
ISLA ÁNGEL DE LA GUARDA
ISLAS TRES MARÍAS
CABO SAN LUCAS
CABO CORRIENTES
Longitude West of Greenwich
Tlalnepantla
Atzcapotzalco
Colonia Gustavo A. Madero
San Juan de Aragón
L. de Texcoco (Almost Dry)
MEXICO CITY
Chapultepec
Tacubaya
Santa Anita
Ixtacalco
Ixtapalapa
Coyoacán
Villa Obregón
San Ángel
Tizapán
DISTRITO FEDERAL
Xochimilco
Tlalpan
Tepepan
Chimalhuacán
Santa Fe
San Jerónimo
La Magdalena Contreras
San Nicolás
Santa Úrsula
Zapotitlán
Tlaltenco
Tláhuac
Tulyehualco
Santiago Tepalcatlalpan
San Gregorio Atlapulco
C. PETLALCATL 8,882 FT.
C. XOCHITEPETL 8,184 FT.
C. XALTEPETL 8,230 FT.
C. XITLE 10,237
Miles 0 1 2 3 4

SAN LUIS POTOSI
ZACATECAS
AGUASCALIENTES
JALISCO
GUANAJUATO
QUERÉTARO
HIDALGO
MICHOACÁN
MÉXICO
MORELOS
PUEBLA
TLAXCALA
GUERRERO
OAXACA
VERACRUZ
MEXICO CITY
San Luis Potosí
Aguascalientes
Guadalajara
Tlaquepaque
León
Guanajuato
Irapuato
Salamanca
Celaya
Querétaro
Morelia
Uruapan
Toluca
Pachuca
Puebla
Tlaxcala
Cuernavaca
Xochimilco
Coyoacán
Tampico
Tuxpan
Veracruz
Jalapa Enríquez
Orizaba
Córdoba
L. de Chapala
L. de Pátzcuaro
PARICUTIN (VOL.) 9,100 FT.
PICO DE TANCITARO 12,660 FT.
NEVADO DE TOLUCA 15,016 FT.
IXTACIHUATL 17,343 FT.
V. POPOCATEPETL 17,887 FT.
CERRO LA MALINCHE 14,636 FT
V. CITLALTEPETL 18,696 FT.
SIERRA MADRE ORIENTAL
Laguna de Tamiahua
CABO ROJO
Gulf of Mexico
Miles 0 10 20 30 40 50
Tropic of Cancer
TEXAS
NUEVO LEON
TAMAULIPAS
Monterrey
Saltillo
Laredo
Nuevo Laredo
Brownsville
Matamoros
Ciudad Victoria
Lubbock
Big Spring
San Angelo
Del Rio
Eagle Pass
Rio Grande
Golfo de Campeche
YUCATÁN
CAMPECHE
QUINTANA ROO (TER.)
TABASCO
CHIAPAS
Mérida
Progreso
Campeche
Villahermosa
Coatzacoalcos
Oaxaca
Acapulco de Juárez
Chilpancingo
Tuxtla Gutiérrez
Salina Cruz
Golfo de Tehuantepec
ISTMO DE TEHUANTEPEC
SIERRA MADRE
CHICHÉN ITZÁ (RUINS)
UXMAL (RUINS)
TIKAL (RUINS)
Cozumel
ISLA DE COZUMEL
ISLA MUJERES
CABO CATOCHE
Yucatán Channel
CUBA
Golfo de Guanahacabibes
C. SAN ANTONIO
C. CORRIENTES
Caribbean Sea
Bahía Chetumal
Ciudad Chetumal
Belize
BR. HOND.
Stann Creek
TURNEFFE IS.
Gulf of Honduras
GUATEMALA
Guatemala
HONDURAS
Tegucigalpa
EL SAL.
San Salvador
Puerto Barrios
Puerto Cortés
La Ceiba
ISLAS DE LA BAHÍA
CABO DE HONDURAS
Tapachula
Quezaltenango
CM TERRAIN MEXICO
COPYRIGHT BY RAND MC NALLY & COMPANY
MADE IN U.S.A.

MEXICO: When he was asked what his newly won empire looked like, Spanish conquistador Hernando Cortes crumpled a piece of parchment and said, "This is a map of Mexico." Two thirds of this country, dominated by the spines of the Sierra Madre Oriental and the Sierra Madre Occidental, consist of steep mountains or highlands. Only the narrow coastal fringes and the Yucatán Peninsula are flat.

The northern half of the country is harshly dry and the dense tropical Gulf Coast forests are drenched by some 100 inches of rain. It is hot in the lowlands, cool in the heights above 8,000 feet and temperate in the tablelands of the central region.

A large indigenous population remains in Mexico: there are some six million Indians speaking 50 different native languages. In formerly isolated regions like Yucatán, cut off by mountains, the proud descendants of the Mayas still refuse to call themselves Mexicans.

The historic heartland of the country is the Valley of Mexico and the neighboring tablelands *(diagram, bottom of page)*. Here corn grew well enough to convert nomadic hunters into builders of cities, pyramids and empires. Corn is still the staple food of Mexico, and the center of the ancient civilization is also the center of modern Mexico. But what seemed fertile land to tribesmen wandering south from the arid north is not fertile enough to support a modern nation. Today Mexico's farmers are slowly pushing out from the overworked fields in the crowded central region. Cotton for export now grows in irrigated districts in the north, coffee is produced in the Chiapas and sugar in the Sonora region.

AREA:	758,061 sq. mi.
POPULATION:	33,954,000. Largest city and capital: Mexico City.
CLIMATE:	Hot, wet on coast; milder winters, hot summers in the dry north; mild dry winters on Central Plateau.
ALTITUDES:	Volcan Citlaltepetl, 18,696 ft. (highest); Mexico City, 7,349 ft.

With its non-agricultural assets largely confined to minerals such as silver, lead, copper and petroleum, Mexico has traditionally been a poor land. It is now trying to reshape itself by shifting from the mining which has been its dominant industry to commercial farming and diversified manufacturing. To open markets for the produce of isolated peasant villages, over 4,000 miles of rough roads have been built in areas where two decades ago there were none. Though Mexico is changing, the pyramids, adobe villages, Spanish towns and churches of old Mexico remain to draw half a million visitors and half a billion U.S. dollars into Mexico each year.

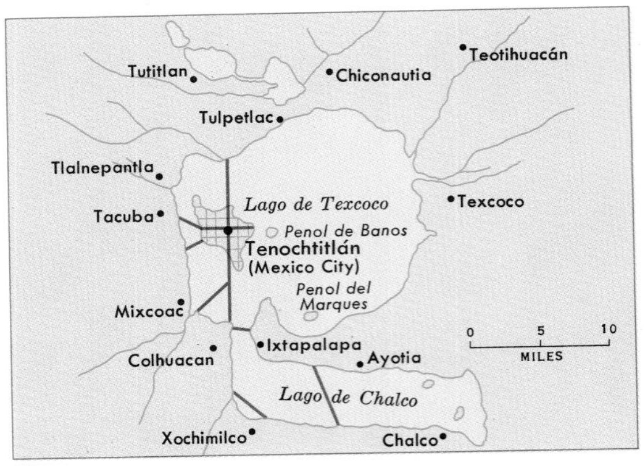

AN AZTEC CITY'S ENDURING LIFE

Mexico City, then called Tenochtitlan, was the island capital of the Aztecs *(map, top)* when Cortes first saw its pyramids in 1520. Now this ancient capital of modern Mexico *(map, bottom)* blends skyscrapers and boulevards with the narrow streets and compact plazas built by the Spanish conquerors on the drained site of the Aztecs' lake city.

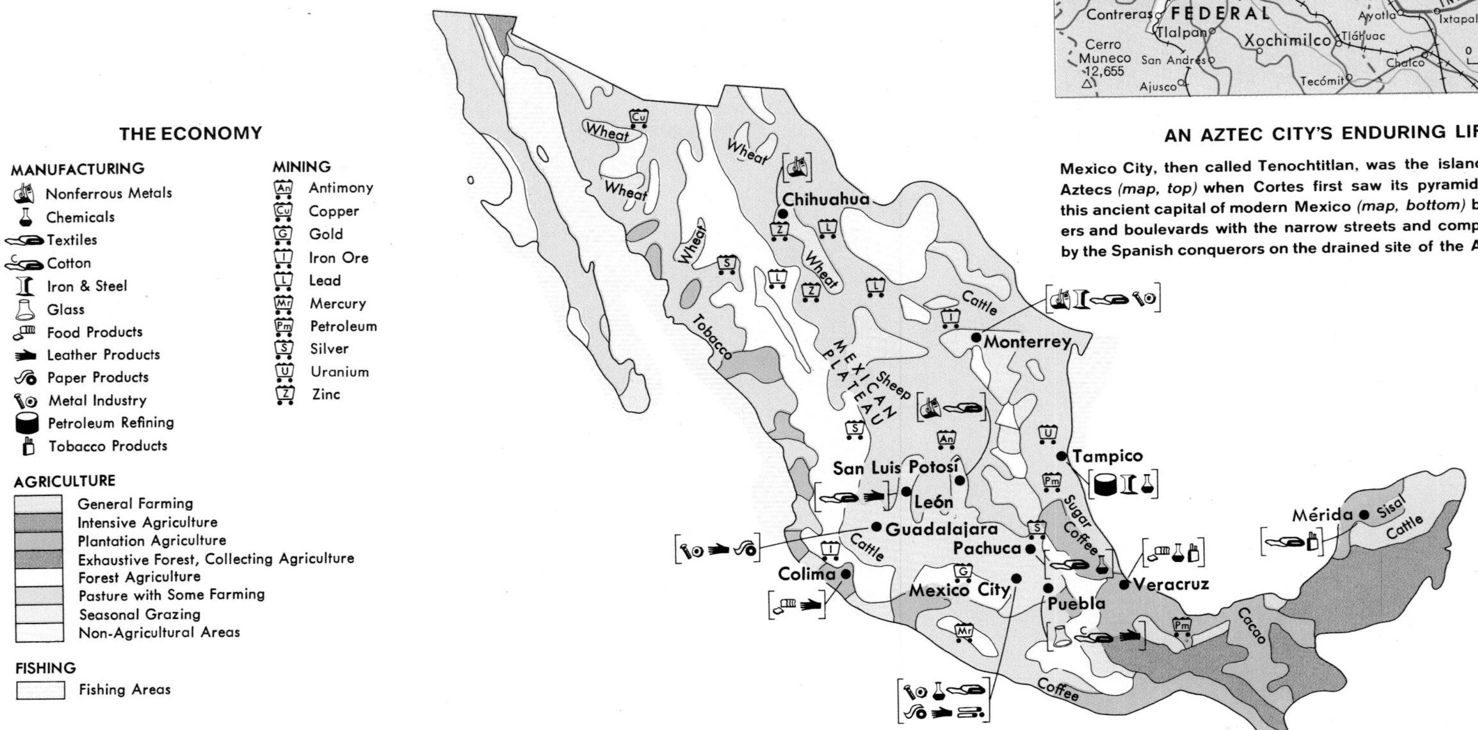

GROSS NATIONAL PRODUCT PER CAPITA $282

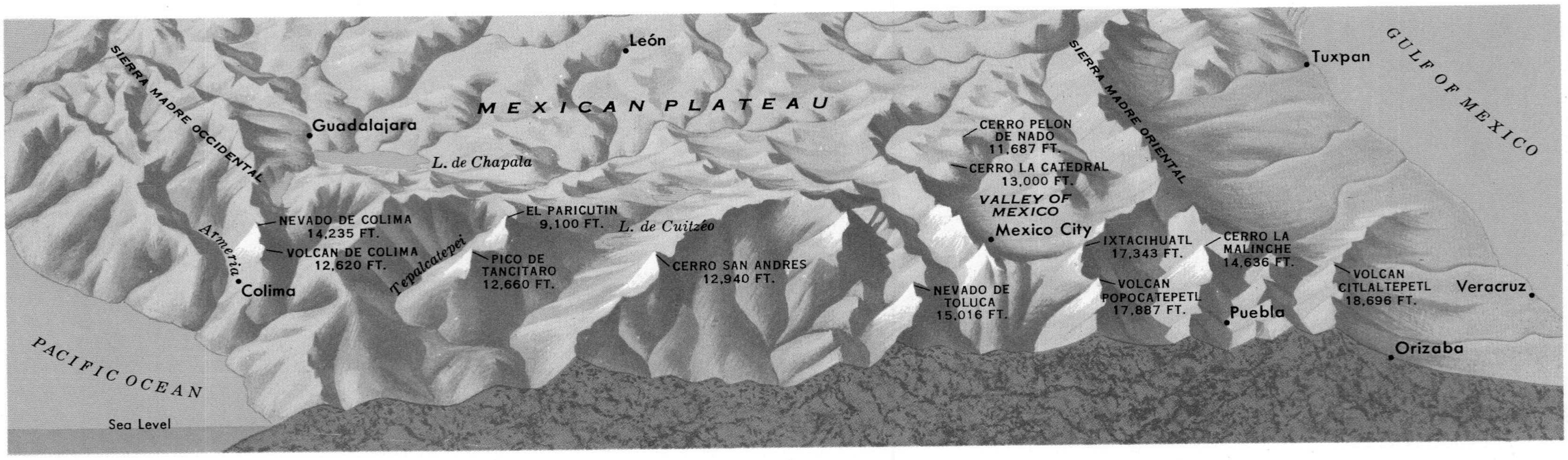

A PROFILE OF MEXICO: MOUNTAINS LEFT, RIGHT AND CENTER

Here, in cross section, is a view of central Mexico from the Pacific Ocean to the Gulf of Mexico. At the left is the Sierra Madre Occidental, rising from the Pacific coastal plain, which is barely a few miles wide. With its steep narrow gorges and peaks more than 10,000 feet high, the Occidental range forms one of the great mountain barriers of the hemisphere. At right, rising from the Gulf Coast plain on the east, is the narrower and less rugged Sierra Madre Oriental. Between these steep ranges lies the Mexican Plateau. Gradually increasing in altitude as it extends southward from the U.S. border, the plateau meets a third range of peaks in the center foreground of the view shown above. The mountains of this third range impound Lake Chapala, Mexico's largest lake, and cut the plateau into separate walled-in basins, which include Puebla, Guadalajara and the Valley of Mexico. Most of Mexico's population lives on these six-to-eight-thousand-foot-high tablelands.

MEXICO

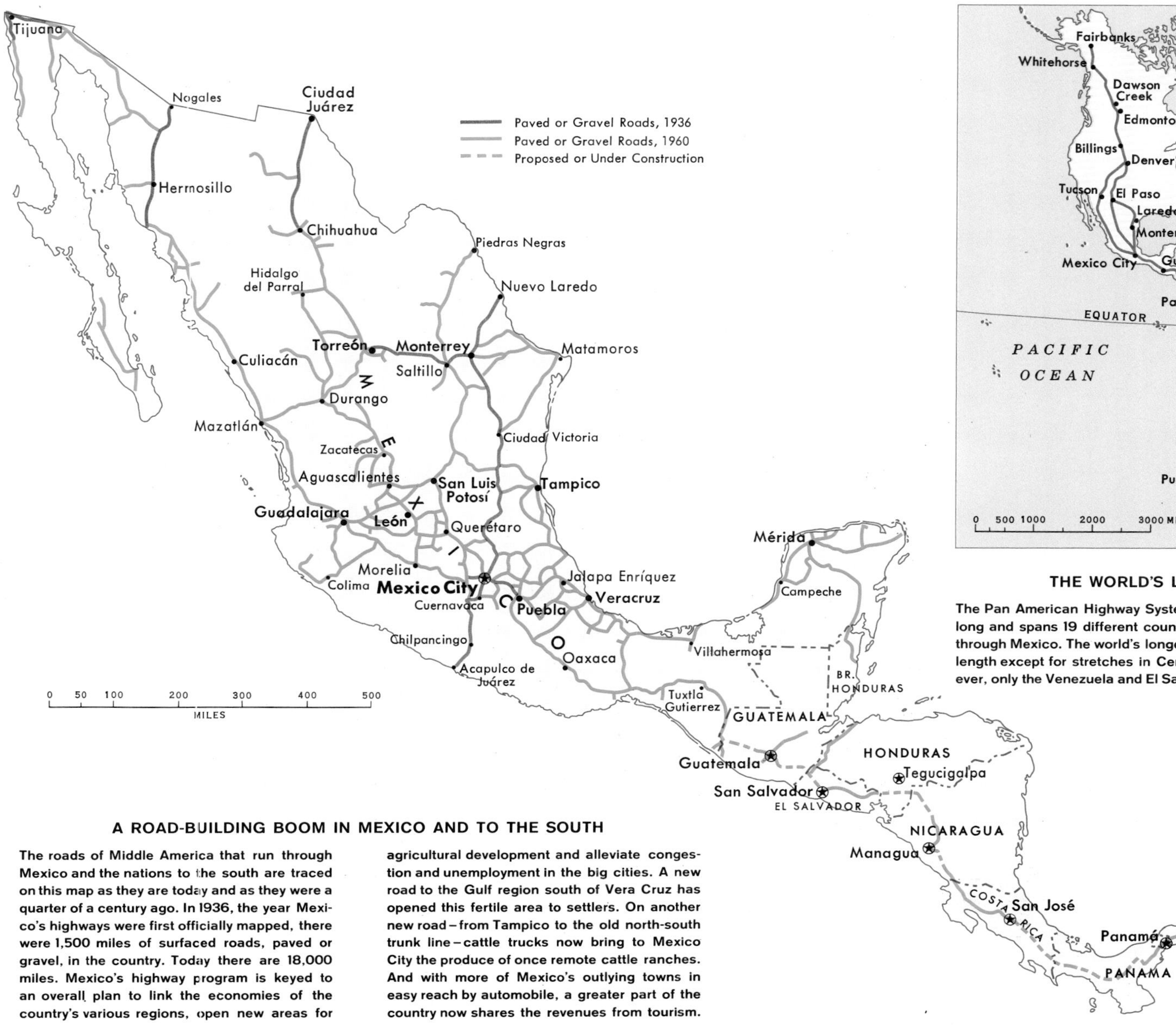

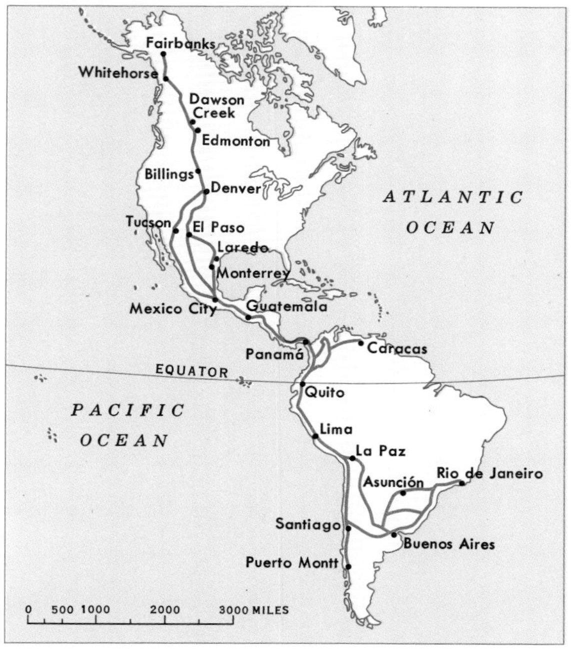

THE WORLD'S LONGEST HIGHWAY

The Pan American Highway System shown here is some 26,000 miles long and spans 19 different countries. More than 4,000 miles of it run through Mexico. The world's longest highway, it is passable over its full length except for stretches in Central America. South of the U.S., however, only the Venezuela and El Salvador sections are completely paved.

A ROAD-BUILDING BOOM IN MEXICO AND TO THE SOUTH

The roads of Middle America that run through Mexico and the nations to the south are traced on this map as they are today and as they were a quarter of a century ago. In 1936, the year Mexico's highways were first officially mapped, there were 1,500 miles of surfaced roads, paved or gravel, in the country. Today there are 18,000 miles. Mexico's highway program is keyed to an overall plan to link the economies of the country's various regions, open new areas for agricultural development and alleviate congestion and unemployment in the big cities. A new road to the Gulf region south of Vera Cruz has opened this fertile area to settlers. On another new road—from Tampico to the old north-south trunk line—cattle trucks now bring to Mexico City the produce of once remote cattle ranches. And with more of Mexico's outlying towns in easy reach by automobile, a greater part of the country now shares the revenues from tourism.

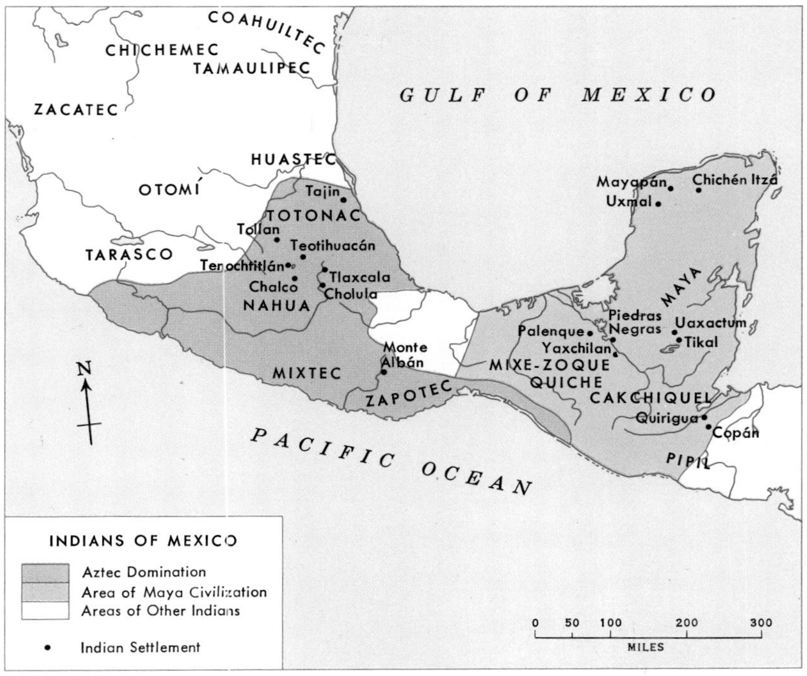

MEXICO'S PEOPLE BEFORE CORTES

Before the Spanish Conquest, Mexico had an indigenous population that has been conservatively estimated at three million, or three times as many Indians as there were then in all of the rest of North America. This map shows where the many primitive Indian tribes and petty kingdoms were located. Two of the largest groups were advanced builders of pyramids: the Nahuas (including the Aztecs) of the highlands, and the Mayas, who lived in the Yucatán Peninsula and farther south in what is now Guatemala.

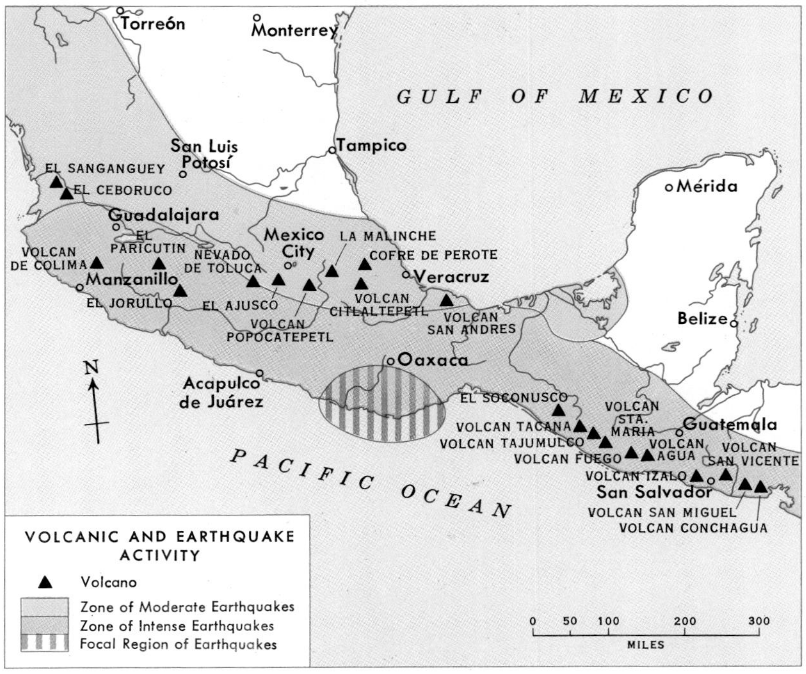

A REGION OF SEISMIC VIOLENCE

Mexico is constantly under the threat of earthquakes and volcanic eruption because it rests on an area of weakness in the earth's crust. Most of Mexico's earthquakes and some of the most severe shocks in the Western Hemisphere originate around Oaxaca, the "focal" region shown in red stripes on the map. Tremors may be felt hundreds of miles away from the point of origin of earthquakes. A dozen peaks over 15,000 feet high have been built in Mexico by eruptions, including 18,696-foot Citlaltepetl.

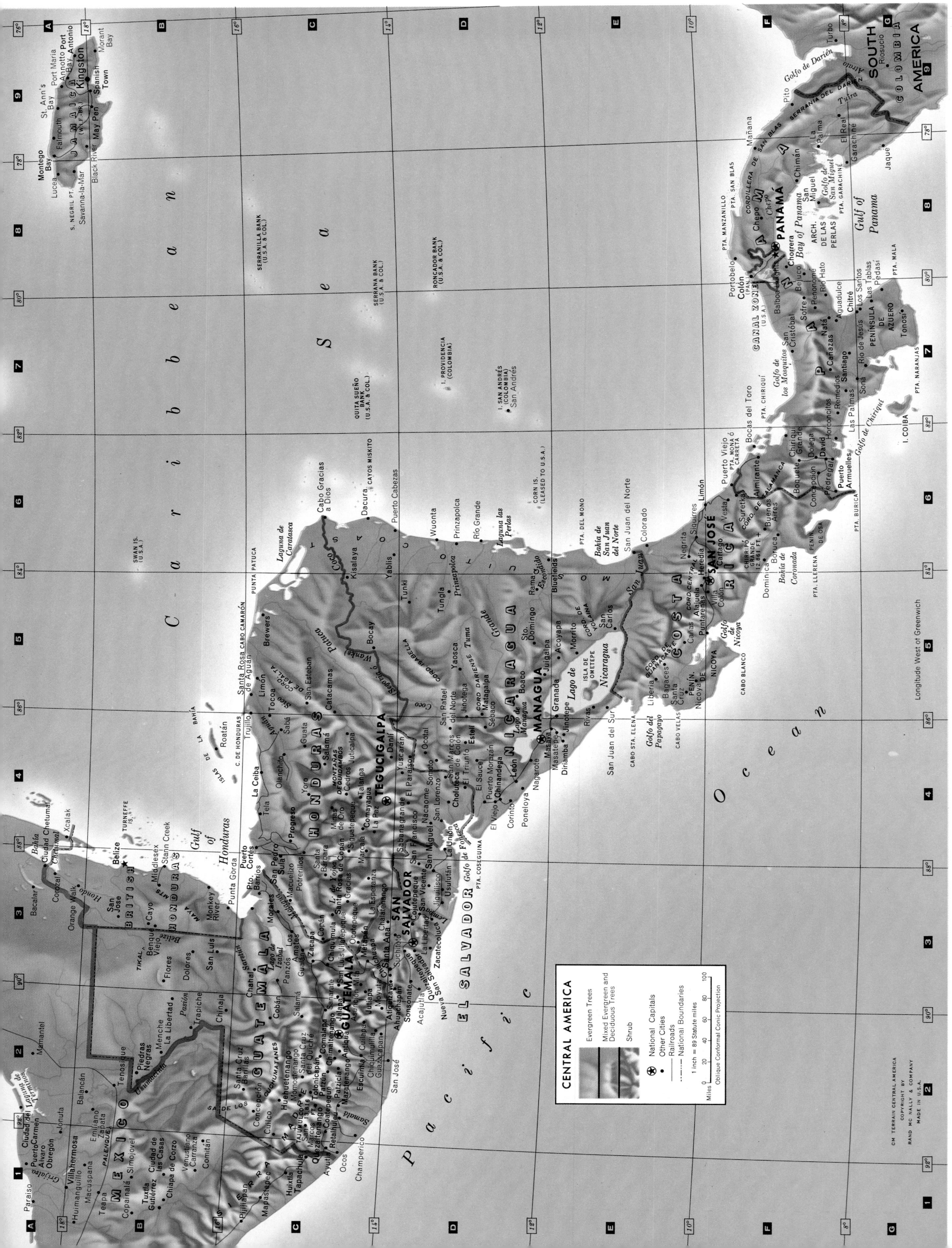
CENTRAL AMERICA
Evergreen Trees
Mixed Evergreen and Deciduous Trees
Shrub
National Capitals
Other Cities
Railroads
National Boundaries
1 inch = 89 Statute miles
Oblique Conformal Conic Projection
Longitude West of Greenwich
CM TERRAIN CENTRAL AMERICA
COPYRIGHT BY
RAND MC NALLY & COMPANY
MADE IN U.S.A.
Caribbean Sea
Pacific Ocean
MEXICO
GUATEMALA
BRITISH HONDURAS
HONDURAS
EL SALVADOR
NICARAGUA
COSTA RICA
PANAMÁ
COLOMBIA
SOUTH AMERICA
JAMAICA
Kingston
Spanish Town
Montego Bay
Belize
TEGUCIGALPA
SAN SALVADOR
MANAGUA
SAN JOSÉ
Gulf of Honduras
Golfo de Fonseca
Lago de Nicaragua
Lago de Managua
Gulf of Panama
Golfo de Darién
Golfo de Chiriquí
Golfo de Nicoya
Golfo del Papagayo
Laguna de Caratasca
Laguna de Chiriquí
SWAN IS. (U.S.A.)
SERRANILLA BANK (U.S.A. & COL.)
SERRANA BANK (U.S.A. & COL.)
RONCADOR BANK (U.S.A. & COL.)
QUITA SUEÑO BANK (U.S.A. & COL.)
I. PROVIDENCIA (COLOMBIA)
I. SAN ANDRÉS (COLOMBIA)
CORN IS. (LEASED TO U.S.A.)
CANAL ZONE (U.S.A.)
Colón
Puerto Cortés
La Ceiba
San Pedro Sula
Santa Ana
León
Granada
Limón
Puntarenas
David
Portobelo

CENTRAL AMERICA: The tightly pinched waistline of the Western Hemisphere, Central America is far from being a homogeneous unit, geographically, politically or socially. This zigzagging land bridge between continents is made up of two separate mountain ranges which are themselves barely bridged by the lowlands of Nicaragua. The densely forested and mountainous isthmus is known for treacherous mangrove swamps, trackless rain forests and many active volcanoes. Some Central American countries are peopled mostly by Indians who speak no Spanish—the official language of all the republics of the isthmus. One country, Costa Rica, has almost no trace of the indigenous race. Central America has primitive adobe villages built by Maya Indians and modern hygienic towns laid out by U.S. fruit companies. Poor in minerals and other essentials for industry, most of the republics depend on coffee and bananas *(map, below right)* as the staples of their economy.

CLIMATE: Coastal lowlands are generally hot and rainy. Cooler temperatures prevail in the central upland valleys, where most people live.
ALTITUDES: Tajumulco, Guatemala, 13,816 ft. (highest); Guatemala (city), 4,850 ft.

BRITISH HONDURAS: This rain-soaked part of the Yucatán Peninsula is heavily forested. The crown colony draws much of its income from wood products, sugar and citrus fruits.

AREA: 8,864 sq. mi.
POPULATION: 91,000. Capital: Belize.

GUATEMALA: An undeveloped country, Guatemala needs labor for coffee and banana plantations, but two thirds of its people are Mayas who will not leave their ancient cornfields.

AREA: 42,031 sq. mi.
POPULATION: 2,584,000. Capital: Guatemala.

EL SALVADOR: Tiny and crowded, El Salvador grows coffee, cotton and corn on a land area too small for its population.

AREA: 8,260 sq. mi.
POPULATION: 2,556,000. Capital: San Salvador.

HONDURAS: A great banana exporter, Honduras has 1,000 miles of railroad, 900 of which belong to U.S. fruit companies.

AREA: 43,266 sq. mi.
POPULATION: 1,915,000. Capital: Tegucigalpa.

NICARAGUA: Nicaragua has cotton, gold and cattle for export as well as coffee and bananas. Its stretch of lakes and lowlands was once considered for an Atlantic-Pacific canal.

AREA: 57,128 sq. mi.
POPULATION: 1,489,000. Capital: Managua.

COSTA RICA: A plateau region with great banana plantations and many small coffee farms, stable Costa Rica enjoys a higher level of living than her Central American neighbors.

AREA: 19,647 sq. mi.
POPULATION: 1,194,000. Capital: San José.

PANAMA: Although Panama is the world's second leading banana exporter, wages paid Panamanians for work on the Panama Canal supply the nation with over half its total income.

AREA: 28,745 sq. mi.
POPULATION: 1,040,000. Capital: Panamá.

CANAL ZONE: A narrow ribbon of U.S. sovereignty rented from Panama *(diagram, below)*, the Canal Zone is a residence for U.S. military personnel and canal and railway employees.

AREA: 553 sq. mi.
POPULATION: 60,000.

THE ECONOMY

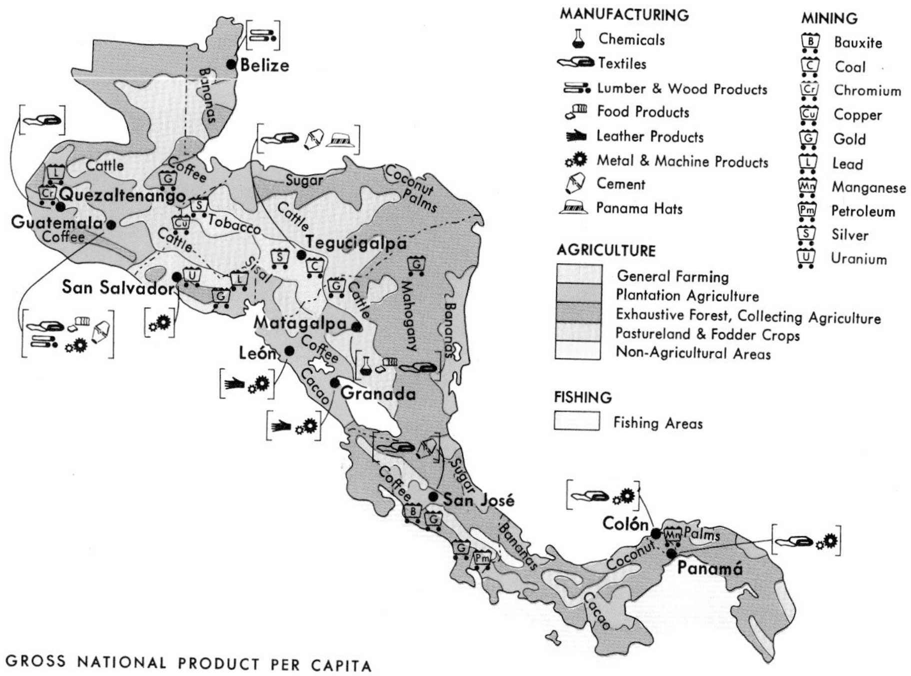

GROSS NATIONAL PRODUCT PER CAPITA

Costa Rica $412	El Salvador $214
Guatemala $189	Honduras $206
Nicaragua $218	Panama $327

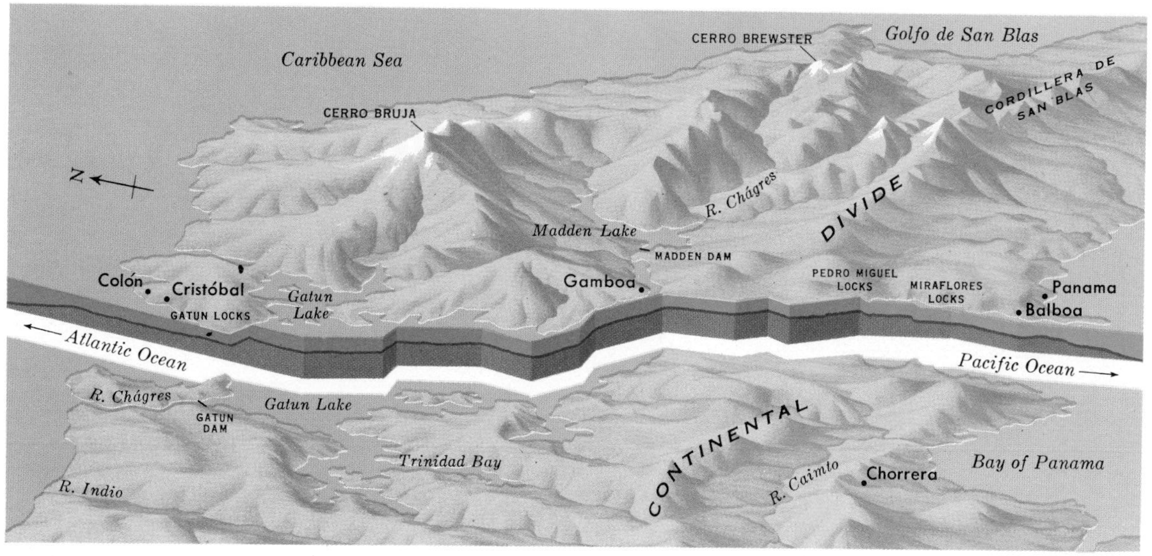

A NARROW STEPLADDER OF WATER CONNECTING TWO OCEANS

In this cross-section view, the Panama Canal is seen in its full 50-mile length as it cuts across Central America from the Atlantic Ocean to the Pacific in a northwest to southeast direction. There are six pairs of locks, each a 1,000-foot-long section in which the water level can be raised or lowered to act as an elevator for ships floating inside it. Locks are built in pairs to allow ships to pass in both directions. A ship heading for the Pacific is raised up in three successive stages in the Gatun locks *(left)* before entering Gatun Lake, which lies 85 feet above the Atlantic. It rides through a narrow channel known as Gaillard Cut and is then lowered through the three locks at Pedro Miguel and Miraflores before entering the Pacific. Opened in 1914, the canal cost $380,000,000 and took 10 years to build. Today, some 10,000 ships pass through annually.

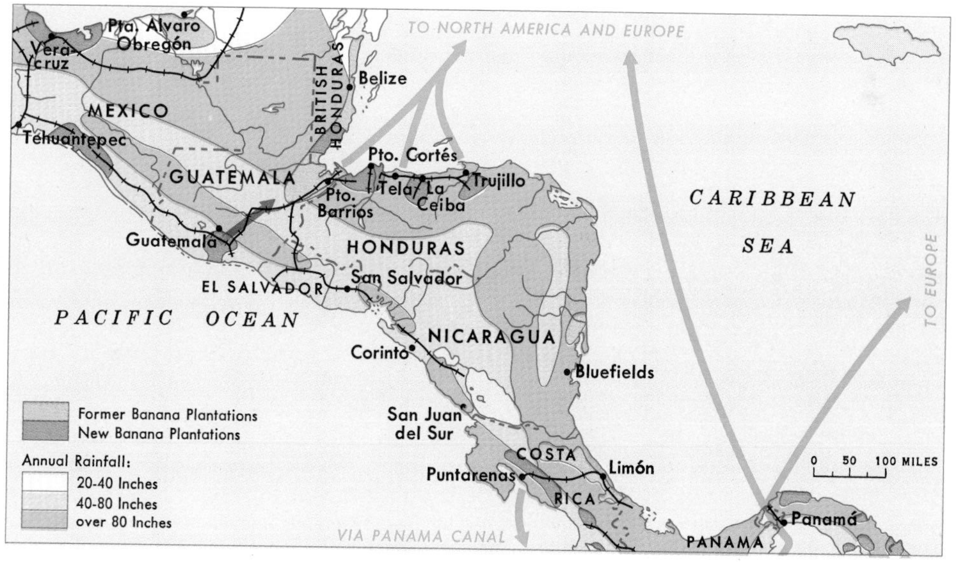

THE MIGRATION OF THE BANANA PLANTATIONS

The Caribbean lowlands of Central America seemed to provide ideal conditions for the early banana plantations *(light orange, above)*. In this region of heavy rainfall and hot sunshine between showers, the fruit thrived in the volcanic ash soil. But the onset of two plant diseases, plus exhaustion of the soil and the menace of hurricane winds, forced a movement to the drier west, as indicated by the location of later plantations *(deep orange)*. Since World War II effective sprays against the diseases have been developed and some new plantations have been established in the east. Rail lines *(red arrow)* take the fruit from the west to the east coast for shipment to North America and Europe.

DARK STRUCTURES IN AN EMERALD SEA

THE CREATIVE SEA built these dark ridges of coral visible below the green shallows of the Great Bahama Bank, just as it formed the 3,000 coral islands of the Bahamas and the reefs ringing most of the Caribbean's volcanic islands. In the silt-free waters of this region, land is constructed when the accumulated skeletons of coral polyps and other sea organisms solidify into rock.

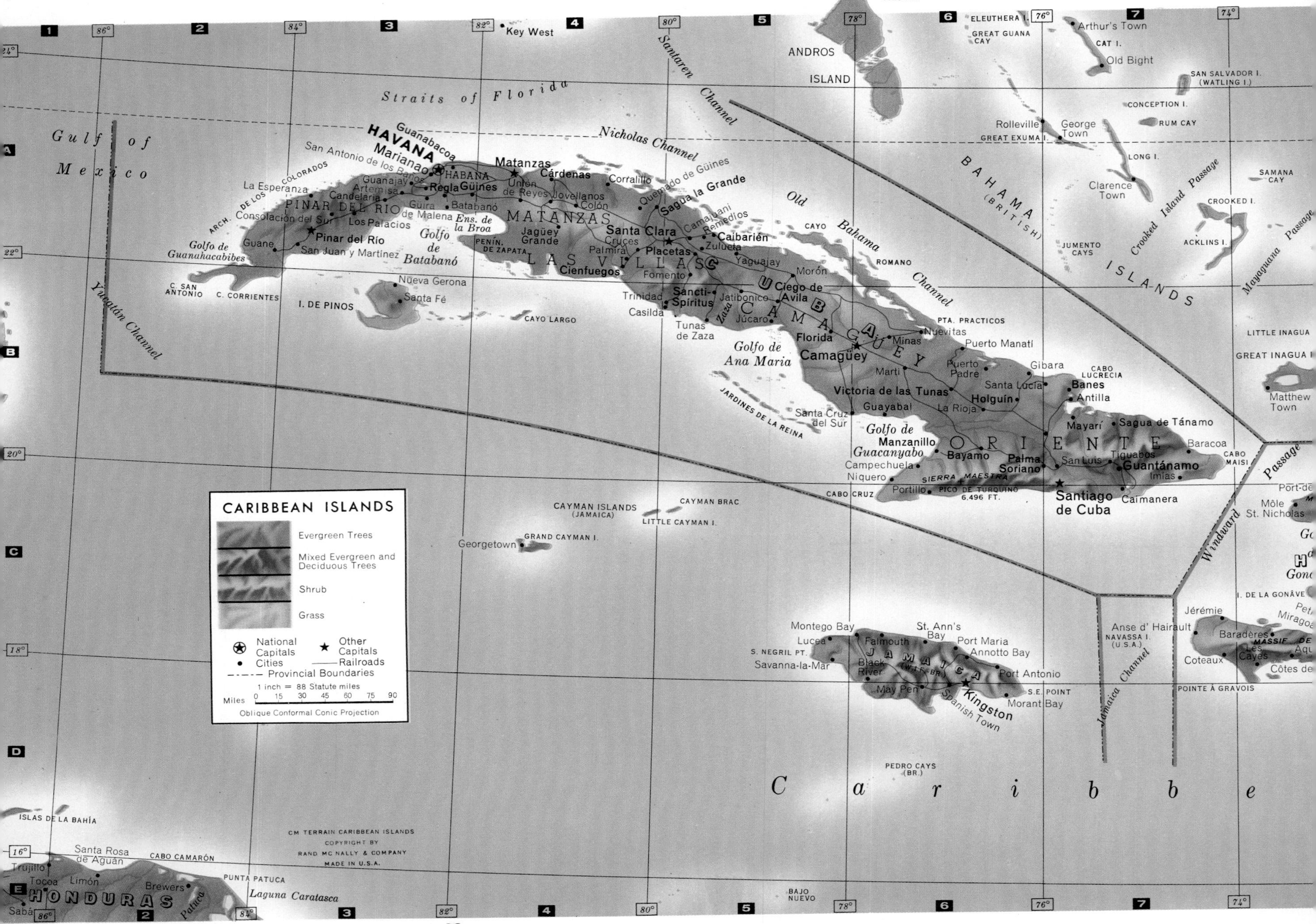

THE ECONOMY

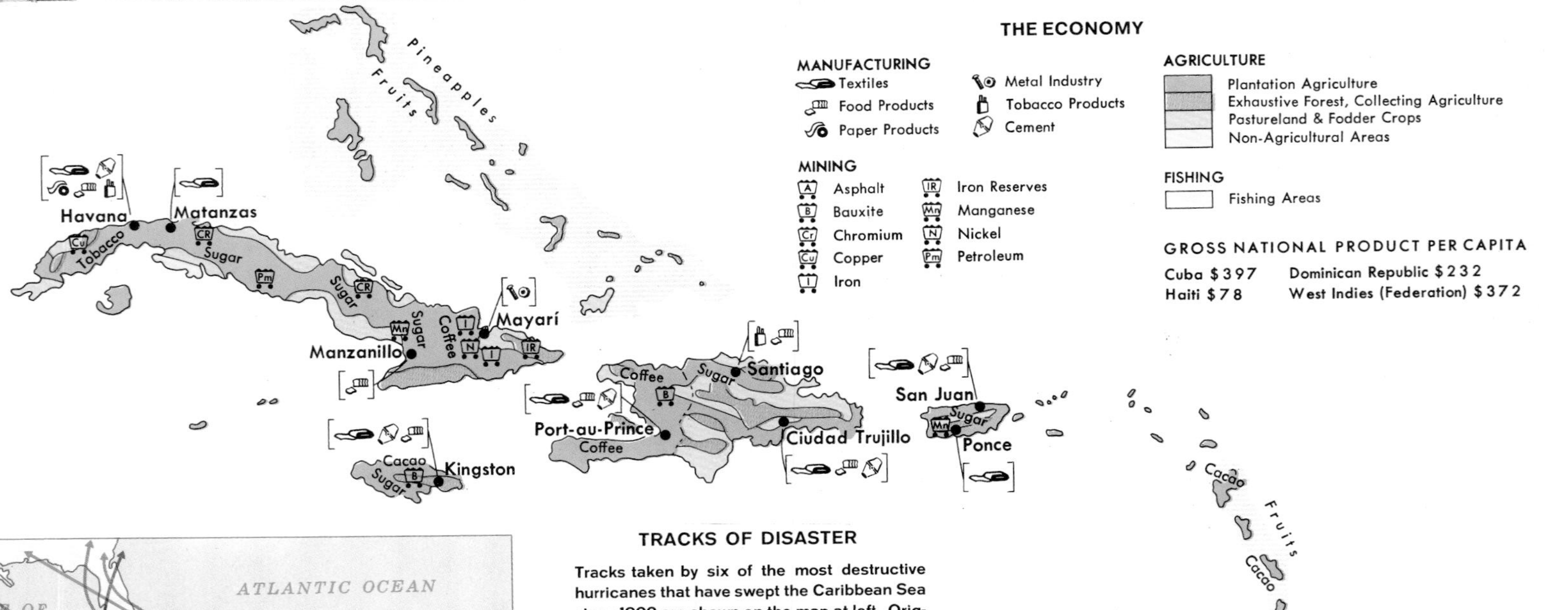

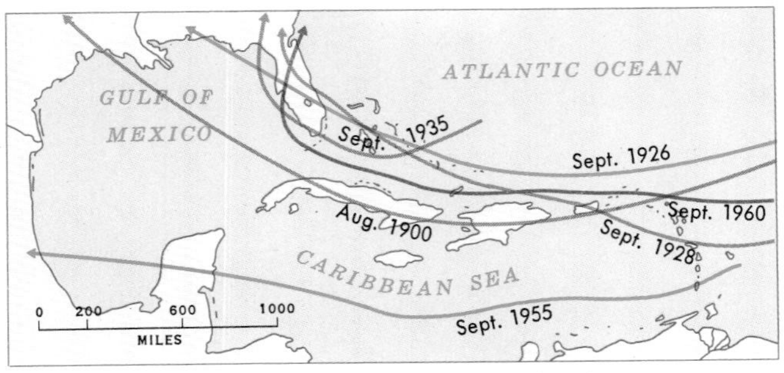

TRACKS OF DISASTER

Tracks taken by six of the most destructive hurricanes that have swept the Caribbean Sea since 1900 are shown on the map at left. Originating over the Atlantic Ocean near the point where the trade winds from the Northern and Southern Hemispheres converge, these tropical storms, with winds up to 200 miles an hour, make the Caribbean Sea one of the world's worst hurricane regions. Sometimes they drive into the North American mainland as far north as Labrador, creating havoc with high tides and drowning rains. The hurricane "season" runs from June to November.

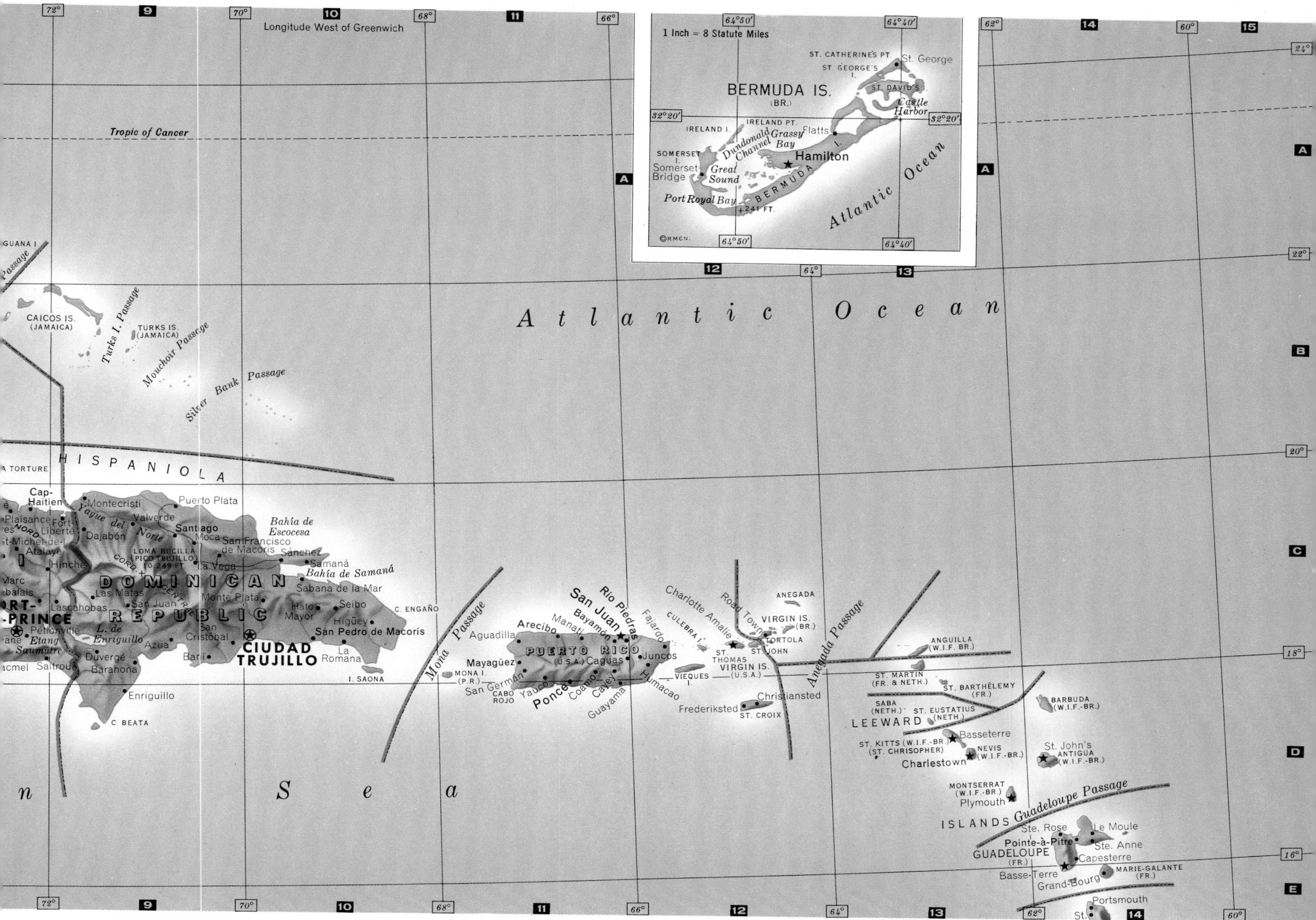

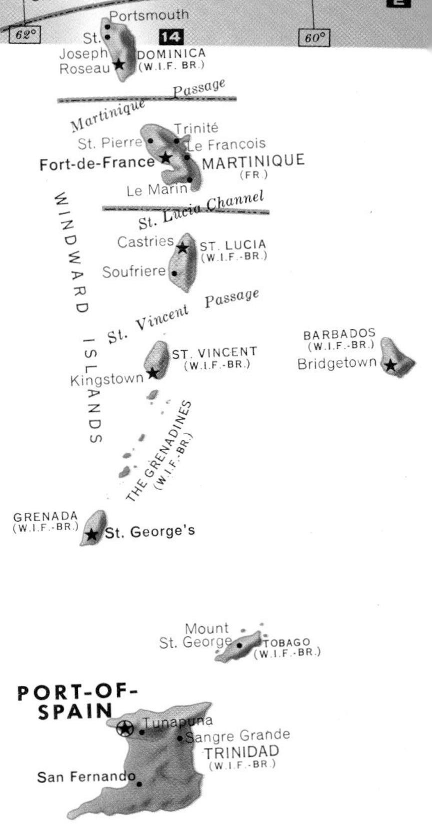

CARIBBEAN ISLANDS: The Antilles, hundreds of islands in the Caribbean Sea, form an almost continuous breakwater 2,500 miles long that provides a homeland for 19,650,000 people. By origin, many of the islets are volcanic cones; others are coral structures. Puerto Rico, Hispaniola and Jamaica are extensions of the Central American highlands.

The Caribbean Islands have calm lagoons, velvety air and palm-fringed shores. Prevailing Atlantic trade winds and warm seas keep the average temperatures moderately high and almost constant, making the region ideal for the sugar-cane plantations that are the islands' dominant economic institution.

Sugar cane was introduced here in the latter part of the 17th Century. To work the plantations, colonists came from half a dozen European countries, and hundreds of thousands of Africans were brought as slaves. Today, Caribbean Islanders speak a number of languages including Spanish, English, Dutch and French.

CLIMATE: Tropical. Little daily or seasonal temperature range. Moderate rainfall, heaviest on windward side of islands.

ALTITUDES: Loma Rucilla, Dominican Republic, 10,249 ft. (highest); Mt. Pelée, Martinique, 4,800 ft.

CUBA: The "Pearl of the Antilles" is the largest of the Caribbean Islands. Sugar and its by-products—rum and molasses—supply more than 80 per cent of Cuba's exports. The largest sugar producer in the world, Cuba also grows world-famous cigar tobaccos on the plains of the Pinar del Rio and mines nickel, manganese and iron ore in the mountains.

AREA: 44,217 sq. mi.
POPULATION: 6,627,000.

DOMINICAN REPUBLIC: Covering almost two thirds of the island of Hispaniola, this nation is developing light industry to bolster a weak sugar, coffee and cacao economy.

AREA: 18,811 sq. mi.
POPULATION: 2,929,000.

HAITI: A French-speaking Negro republic on the western third of Hispaniola, Haiti has one of the lowest per capita incomes in Latin America. It raises coffee, sugar and sisal.

AREA: 10,711 sq. mi.
POPULATION: 3,492,000.

WEST INDIES: A federation of 13 major islands and many islets, this British Commonwealth nation lives on sugar and cacao exports, oil wells at Trinidad and tourist dollars.

AREA: 8,005 sq. mi.
POPULATION: 3,279,000.

CARIBBEAN DEPENDENCIES: Two hundred years ago every Caribbean island was a European colony. Today, the one major nonsovereign island is Puerto Rico, linked to the U.S. since the Spanish-American War of 1898. Twice the size of all the other dependencies combined, Puerto Rico has an area of 3,435 square miles and a population of 2,403,000. A densely crowded rectangle of rugged hills, the island is achieving relative prosperity by improving its agriculture and by using hydroelectric power to develop light industries.

Other dependencies include the U.S. Virgin Islands of St. Thomas, St. Croix and St. John, which are growing tourist meccas; the British Virgin Islands; the Windward and Leeward Islands of the Netherlands Antilles; and the French islands of Martinique and Guadaloupe.

BAHAMAS: A 700-mile-long strand of islands and reefs 40 miles off the Florida coast, the British Bahamas cater to 200,000 vacationers who come annually to its limpid waters.

AREA: 4,404 sq. mi.
POPULATION: 136,000.

BERMUDA: Three hundred and sixty British coral islands lying 570 miles east of North Carolina, Bermuda adds to its tourist income by exporting lily bulbs and cut flowers.

AREA: 22 sq. mi.
POPULATION: 46,000.

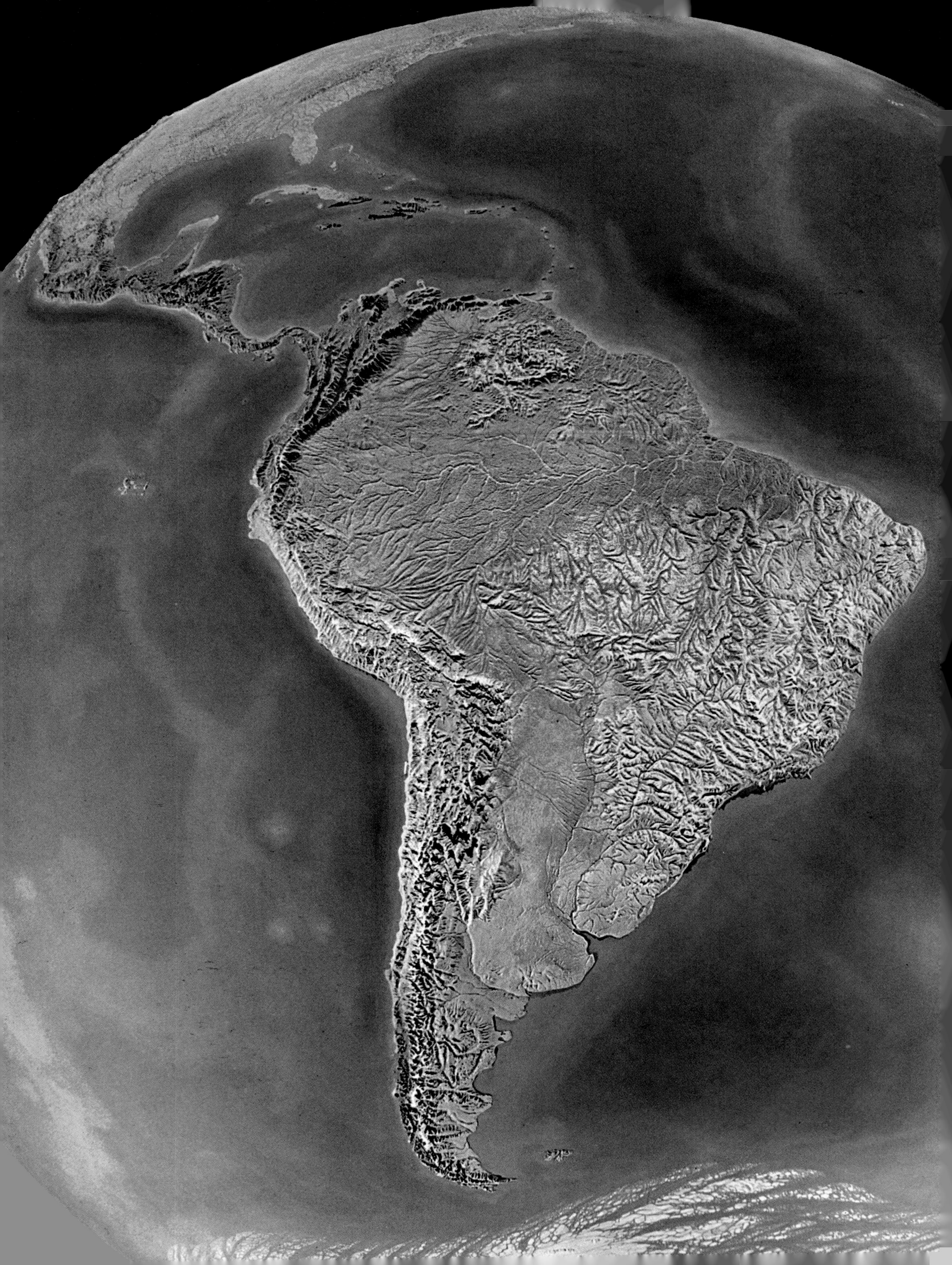

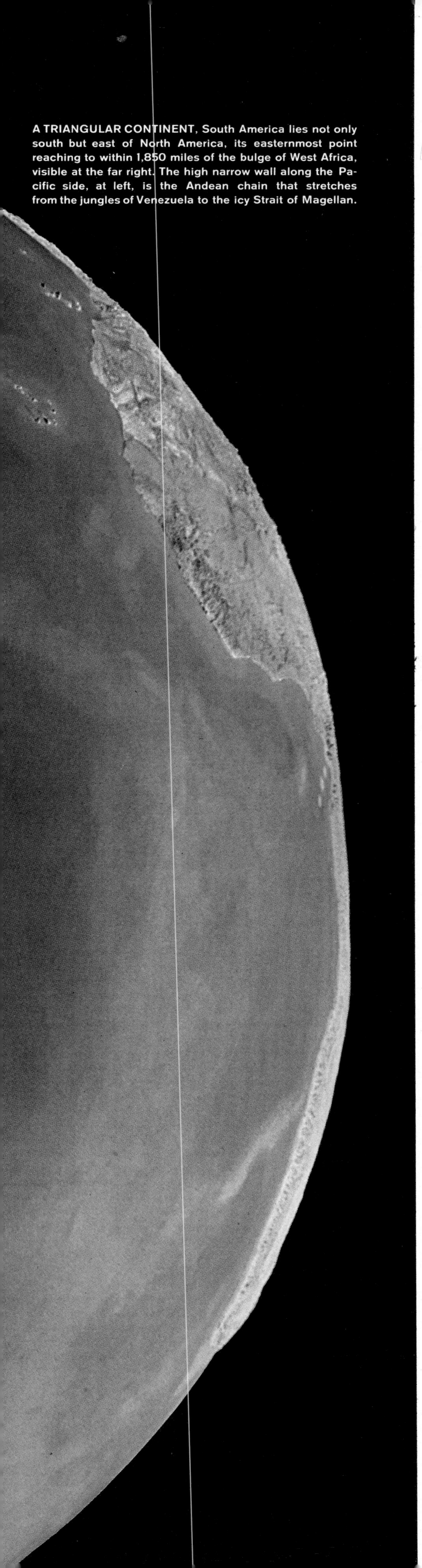

A TRIANGULAR CONTINENT, South America lies not only south but east of North America, its easternmost point reaching to within 1,850 miles of the bulge of West Africa, visible at the far right. The high narrow wall along the Pacific side, at left, is the Andean chain that stretches from the jungles of Venezuela to the icy Strait of Magellan.

SOUTH AMERICA

Nothing plods the middle way in South America. The lands and peoples of this continent run to extremes. Here are the world's longest mountain chain (the Andes), the greatest of rivers (the Amazon), the driest of deserts (the Atacama), the broadest of rain forests (in Brazil and elsewhere). Most of South America is either near-empty countryside or teeming metropolis. It has patricians and peasants but few people in between. It was colonized by Spanish and Portuguese treasure hunters, and by cavaliers with a taste for lordly estates. A continent dotted with rotting, short-lived boom towns, it has always attracted men haunted by *El Dorado*—the dream of quick fortune. But today, as industry and the stabilizing force of a middle class begin to change the lives of its inhabitants, a maturing South America is challenging the traditional ways. Now the continent is writing a realistic epilogue to the gaudy melodrama begun by the conquistadors, those "kinglets of a day."

SOUTH AMERICA
National Capitals
Other Capitals
Other Cities
National Boundaries
1 inch = 430 Statute Miles
Miles 0 100 200 300 400
Sinusoidal Projection
CM POLITICAL SOUTH AMERICA
COPYRIGHT BY
RAND MC NALLY & COMPANY
MADE IN U.S.A.
Longitude West of Greenwich
Equator
Tropic of Capricorn
Atlantic Ocean
Pacific Ocean
Caribbean Sea
WEST INDIES
GREATER ANTILLES
LESSER ANTILLES
LEEWARD IS.
WINDWARD IS.
CENTRAL AMERICA
MEXICO
BR. HOND.
GUAT.
HONDURAS
EL SALVADOR
NICARAGUA
COSTA RICA
PANAMA
CANAL ZONE (U.S.A.)
CUBA
HAITI
DOM. REP.
PUERTO RICO (U.S.A.)
VENEZUELA
COLOMBIA
ECUADOR
PERU
BOLIVIA
BRAZIL
BR. GUIANA
SURINAM (NETH. GUIANA)
FR. GUIANA
PARAGUAY
URUGUAY
CHILE
ARGENTINA
PATAGONIA
ANDES MOUNTAINS
SELVAS
BRAZILIAN PLATEAU
HIGHLANDS
GUIANA HIGHLANDS
GRAN CHACO
PAMPA
MATO GROSSO
SERRA DOS PARECIS
Amazonas (Amazon)
Orinoco
Paraná
Uruguay
Rio de La Plata
Havana
Kingston
Port-au-Prince
Ciudad Trujillo
San Juan
Port-of-Spain
Caracas
Bogotá
Quito
Lima
La Paz
Sucre
Asunción
Montevideo
Buenos Aires
Santiago
Georgetown
Paramaribo
Cayenne
Brasília
Rio de Janeiro
São Paulo
Salvador
Recife
Belém
Manaus
Pôrto Alegre
Córdoba
Rosario
Valparaíso
Mendoza
Tucumán
Bahía Blanca
Mar del Plata
Guayaquil
Medellín
Cali
Barranquilla
Maracaibo
Arequipa
Cusco
Antofagasta
Concepción
Punta Arenas
Strait of Magellan
TIERRA DEL FUEGO
CAPE HORN
FALKLAND ISLANDS (GREAT BRITAIN)
Port Stanley
SOUTH GEORGIA (BR.)
SHAG ROCKS
GALÁPAGOS ISLANDS (ECUADOR)
JUAN FERNÁNDEZ (CHILE)
SAN FELIX
SAN AMBROSIO (CHILE)
COCOS (COSTA RICA)
MALPELO (COL.)
ACONCAGUA 22,834 FT. HIGHEST POINT IN SO. AM.
CHIMBORAZO 20,577 FT.
HUASCARÁN 22,205 FT.
YERUPAJA 21,758 FT.
EL MISTI (VOL.) 19,144 FT.
VOLCÁN LLULLAILLACO 22,146 FT.
MT. FITZ ROY 11,600 FT.
MT. SAN VALENTIN 13,314 FT.
MONTE SARMIENTO 7,546 FT.

SOUTH AMERICA: For a long time this was the "forgotten continent"; now it is a misunderstood one. Though two thirds of it lies in the tropics, it is not entirely a sultry area *(diagram, bottom right)*. Though sparsely populated, it is not a virgin land but one that has long been settled and is now partly exhausted *(diagram, right)*. The countries of the continent, lumped together as "Latin America," differ radically from one another.

Running close to the west coast of South America for 4,500 miles, the narrow Andes form the world's longest continuous mountain system. They impose on an equatorial region a variety of altitude zones in which anything from bananas to barley can be grown. With its strategic passes over 10,000 feet high, the Andes also close off the bulk of the continent from the Pacific coast. To the east, the older and deeply eroded highlands, which rarely average above 5,000 feet, make up large sections of Venezuela, the Guianas and Brazil. Lying between these two mountain areas are South America's plains. Here are the three great river systems of the continent: Venezuela's 1,800-mile-long Orinoco River; the shifting, flooding Paraná-Paraguay-Plata System; and the majestic Amazon. With five tributaries over a thousand miles long, the 3,900-mile-long Amazon carries five times the Mississippi's volume of water and drains two fifths of the entire continent. Here too is the world's largest tropical rain forest, covering an area two thirds the size of Canada.

AREA:	6,860,000 sq. mi.
POPULATION:	137,847,000.
ALTITUDES:	Mt. Aconcagua, Argentina, 22,834 ft. (highest in the Western Hemisphere); La Paz, 12,792 ft. (highest city in South America); Valdés Depression, Argentina, –131 ft. (lowest in South America).

Although half the population is engaged in farming, most of South America's people inhabit the rim of the continent *(diagram at bottom)* in a series of scattered urban clusters. Advances into the hinterland have been slow because most of the interior is poor for farming or too far away from markets. Tropical forests make poor farmland. When the trees are cleared, the heavy rains quickly leach away the soil's nutrients and cause severe erosion. Despite the great rivers, natural transportation is poor in South America *(diagram, below)*. Many rivers like the Paraguay and the Magdalena are difficult to navigate; others are not in the right places for man's purposes. A productive center like Rio de Janeiro, for instance, has no river reaching the interior.

South America has a long catalogue of minerals: oil, iron, copper, tin, tungsten, bauxite and lead. But coal, that vital ingredient of heavy industry, is almost nonexistent. Despite this handicap, South America has increased its industrial output by an estimated 50 per cent in the past 10 years. Further advances in South America may depend more on political reform in various countries than on the potential of the land's natural resources.

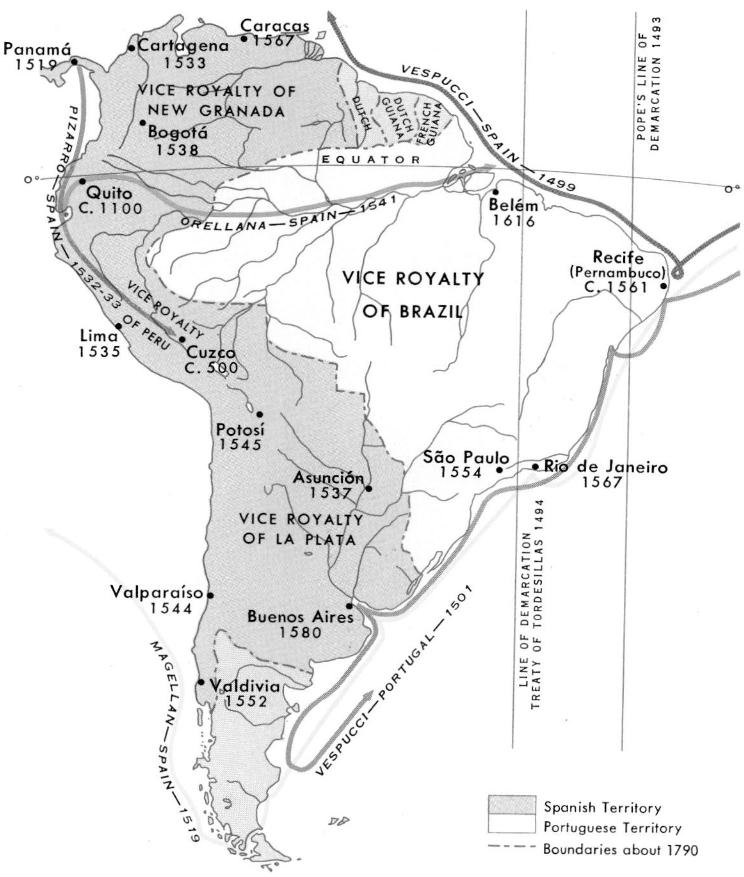

THE SLICED-UP PRIZE OF TWO OLD EMPIRES

Portuguese and Spanish explorations of South America and the continent's former colonial divisions are shown here. Explorers seeking gold, glory, landed estates and Christian converts founded all of South America's major cities before the end of the 16th Century. Viceroyalties were administrative divisions of the colonial empire, each governed by a representative of the crown. The treaty lines on the map were two attempts to divide the world between the mighty Iberian empires. Spain was to get all the unclaimed lands lying west of the line and Portugal all the lands to the east. The Guianas *(gray, at top)* were the only territories that the English, French and Dutch empires could establish on the continent.

A CONTINENT'S LIMITED TRANSPORTATION

South America's railroads, shown in red on this map, barely penetrate the interior except across the productive La Pampa region of Argentina. Roads through tropical lowlands are hard to maintain because of the density of forests. The Andes Mountains *(purple)* are the greatest barrier to east-west transport.

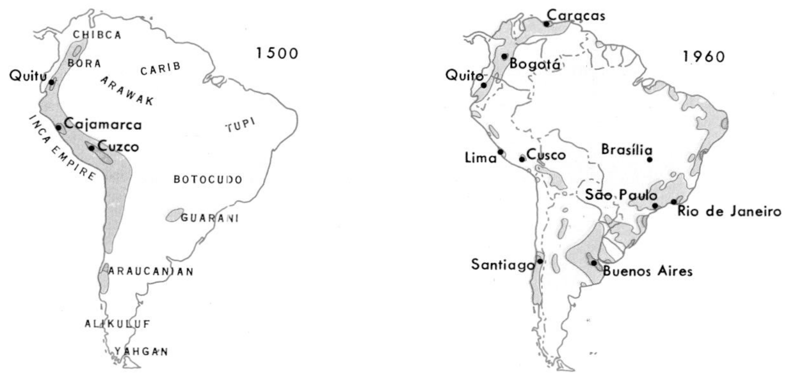

THE POPULOUS RIM OF A SPARSELY SETTLED LAND

The two maps above show the distribution of South America's people in 1500 and 1960. The red areas have a heavy concentration of population; the orange, moderate density; and the yellow, a sparse population. Early settlement, shown in the map at left, centered on the Inca and other Indian territories. The centers of population shifted to the east *(right)* with the rise of sugar cane and coffee planting on the Brazil coast and cattle raising in Argentina. The inhospitable interior still remains sparsely settled.

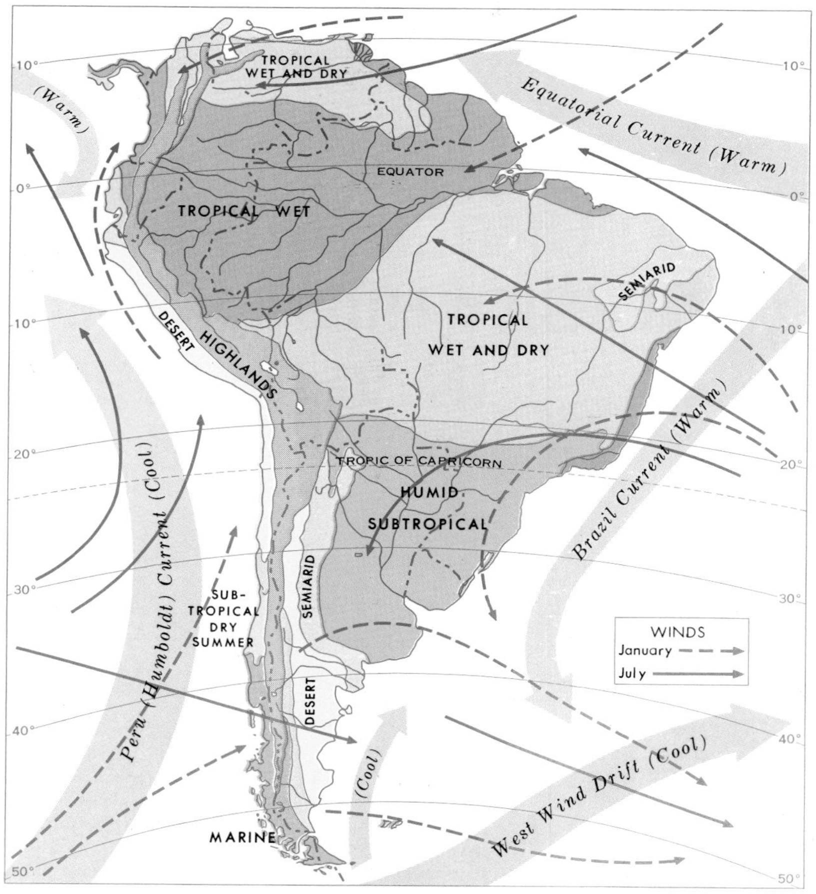

WINDS, CURRENTS AND RAINS

Here are South America's climate zones, the prevailing winds *(gray arrows)* and ocean currents *(color arrows)*. In the central areas, it is generally wet because winds crossing above the warm Atlantic currents *(right)* pick up moisture and carry rain inland. In the Pacific, winds encounter a cool current *(left)* and become dry. The coastal lowlands they blow over are a desert. Further south, winds bring heavy precipitation to the Andes' western flanks. East of the Andes, the winds, their moisture gone, create deserts.

A FOREST OF DERRICKS rooted in the oil-rich waters of Venezuela's Lake Maracaibo stretches across the sunset-inflamed horizon. Before World War I, the abundant oil was regarded by the local Indians as a nuisance that contaminated the 130-mile-long lake and fouled the nets of the fishermen. Today oil has transformed the lakeside villages into boom towns and provides Venezuela with 65 per cent of its annual income. Since 1955 Venezuela has had the highest per capita income in all of South America. The country exports more oil than any other country in the world, with the United States as its most important market.

UNDERWATER OIL AND SKY-HIGH ROADS IN VENEZUELA

A TRIUMPH OF ROAD BUILDING, Venezuela's new four-lane *autopista (right)* spans gorges, slices off hillsides and tunnels through mountains to speed transportation between the highland city of Caracas and its seaport, La Guaira, 10 rugged miles away. Conforming more to the landscape but twice as long, the old highway had 311 curves along its 21-mile route. With new wealth, new industry and a growing urban population, the pace has quickened in Venezuela. Since 1950 the country has launched a highway program making Caracas the center of a nationwide network of roads and opening up the isolated interior.

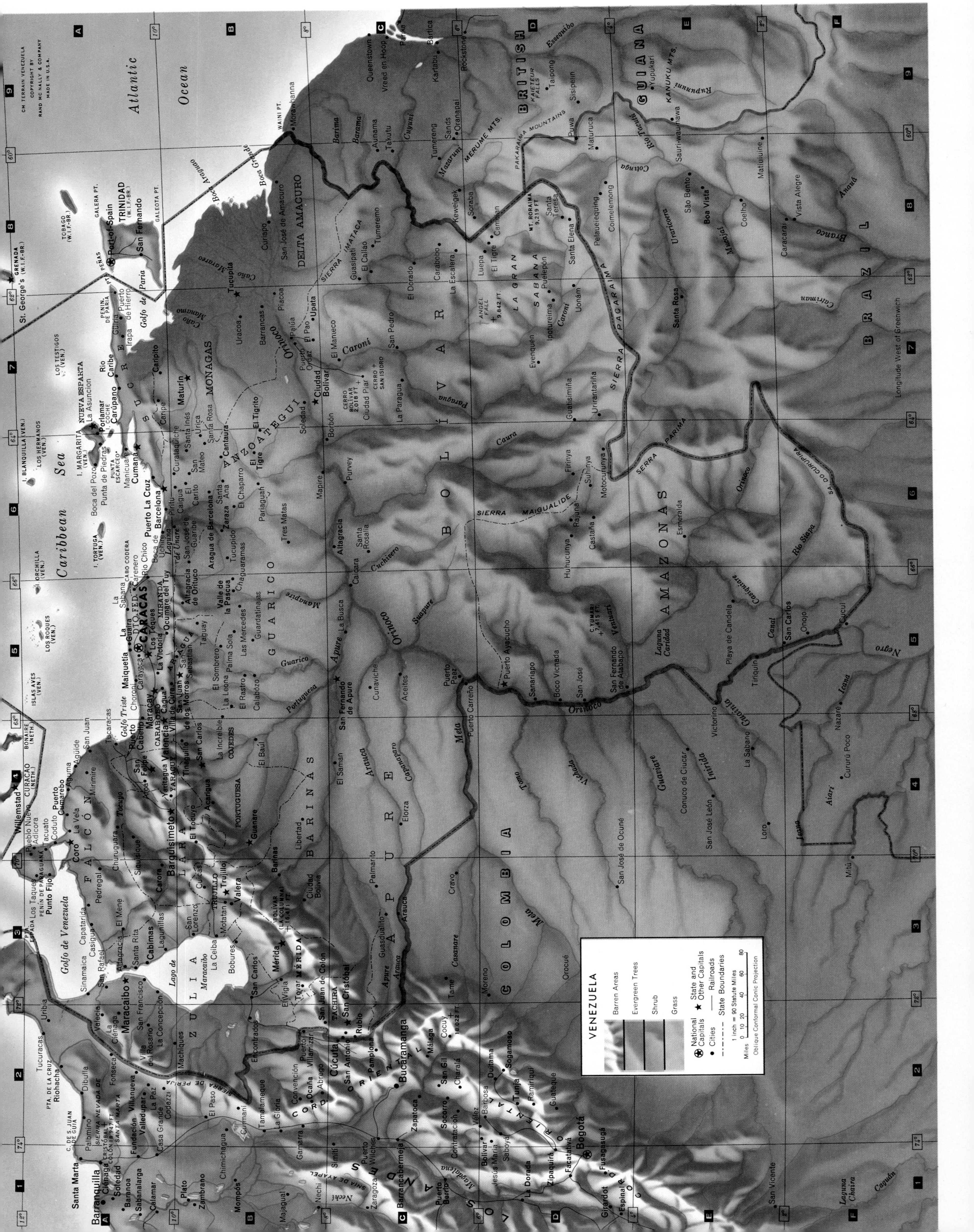
VENEZUELA
Barren Areas
Evergreen Trees
Shrub
Grass
National Capitals
State and Other Capitals
Cities
Railroads
State Boundaries
1 inch = 90 Statute Miles
Miles 0 10 20 40 60 80
Oblique Conformal Conic Projection
CM TERRAIN VENEZUELA
COPYRIGHT BY RAND MC NALLY & COMPANY
MADE IN U.S.A.
Longitude West of Greenwich
Caribbean Sea
Atlantic Ocean
Golfo de Venezuela
Lago de Maracaibo
Golfo de Paria
Golfo Triste
CARACAS
Bogotá
Maracaibo
Valencia
Barquisimeto
Maracay
Ciudad Bolívar
Port-of-Spain
TRINIDAD
TOBAGO (W.I.F.-BR.)
GRENADA
St. George's
CURAÇAO (NETH.)
BONAIRE (NETH.)
Willemstad
I. MARGARITA (VEN.)
ZULIA
FALCÓN
LARA
TRUJILLO
MÉRIDA
TACHIRA
BARINAS
PORTUGUESA
COJEDES
YARACUY
CARABOBO
ARAGUA
MIRANDA
GUARICO
APURE
ANZOATEGUI
MONAGAS
SUCRE
DELTA AMACURO
BOLÍVAR
AMAZONAS
COLOMBIA
BRITISH GUIANA
BRAZIL
LA GRAN SABANA
SIERRA PACARAIMA
SIERRA PARIMA
SIERRA MAIGUALIDE
SIERRA IMATACA
PAKARAIMA MOUNTAINS
MERUME MTS.
KANUKU MTS.
SIERRA DE PERIJA
SIERRA NEVADA DE SANTA MARTA
Orinoco
Apure
Meta
Caroni
Caura
Arauca
Ventuari
Guaviare
Negro
Essequibo
Cuyuni
Mazaruni
Rupununi
Branco
ANGEL FALL 9,842 FT.
MT. RORAIMA 9,219 FT.
KAIETEUR FALLS
PICO BOLIVAR (LA COLUMNA) 16,411 FT.
CERRO BOLIVAR 2,018 FT.

VENEZUELA: Lying close to the equator, Venezuela is hot and humid throughout most of its territory. The southern half is a tropical forest covering the rounded hills of the Guiana Highlands where Angel Falls, the world's highest, is found. The basin of the Orinoco River is a 120,000-square-mile treeless grassland ravaged by floods and droughts and swarming with flies. The Maracaibo lowlands in the northwest are a windless pocket of stifling heat and malaria. As a result, the national life has always been cramped into the relatively cool Venezuela Highlands, a Caribbean wing of the Andes. Here three quarters of the population lives.

Venezuela's tightly circumscribed economy was burst open after 1914 by a gush of oil from soupy Lake Maracaibo, and the country is now being further transformed by the four billion tons of iron ore found mostly in the rock of the Guiana Highlands *(diagram, lower right)*. The oil fields at Maracaibo are among the world's most productive, making Venezuela second only to the U.S. in oil production and first in oil exports *(diagrams, right)*. Working its iron ore deposits by cheap open-pit methods, Venezuela has become one of the great iron producers of the world. Together, iron and oil account for 68 per cent of the national income.

AREA: 352,051 sq. mi.
POPULATION: 6,622,000. Capital: Caracas.
CLIMATE: Generally hot wet summers and hot dry winters in the lowlands; highland climates vary with altitude from warm to cold, very wet to dry.
ALTITUDES: Bolivar (La Columna), 16,411 ft. (highest); Caracas, 3,164 ft.

Modern Venezuela is energetically using its oil and iron profits to transform an economy in which 75 per cent of the population is still rural. In recent years plants manufacturing pharmaceuticals and cement and processing sugar, rubber and textiles have sprung up around Caracas, Maracay and Valencia. Caracas, now a city of 1,022,000, has been building large and boldly designed suburbs in the hillsides surrounding the old colonial city. A great highway system is under construction *(diagram, below)*. In 1953 the clogged Orinoco River was opened for shipping. Venezuela has no significant coal deposits, but it has the capital to pay for hydroelectric and other kinds of power to run steel mills. Today, the steel mill near Puerto Ordaz on the Orinoco is only a "seed" industry but may become the core of a new Pittsburgh rising in the Venezuelan forests.

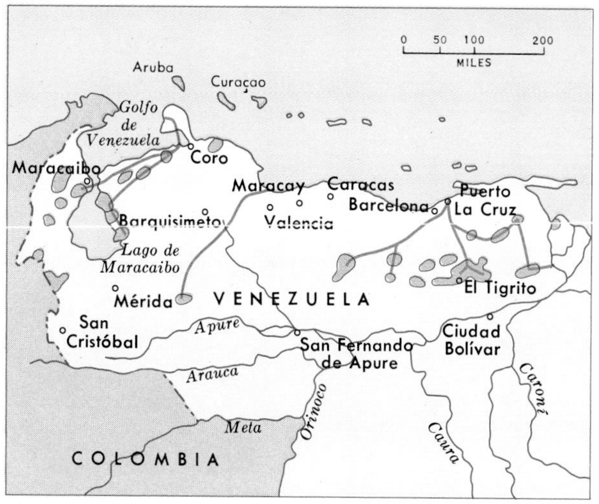
0 50 100 200
MILES
Aruba
Curaçao
Golfo de Venezuela
Maracaibo
Coro
Maracay
Caracas
Barcelona
Puerto La Cruz
Barquisimeto
Valencia
Lago de Maracaibo
El Tigrito
Mérida
VENEZUELA
San Cristóbal
Apure
San Fernando de Apure
Ciudad Bolívar
Arauca
Orinoco
Caroní
Caura
Meta
COLOMBIA

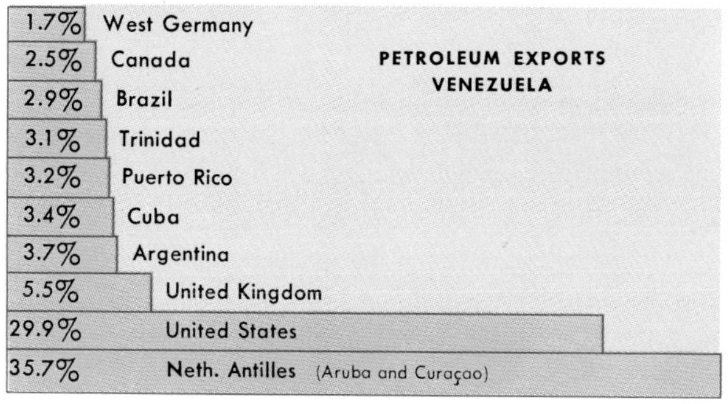
PETROLEUM EXPORTS VENEZUELA
1.7% West Germany
2.5% Canada
2.9% Brazil
3.1% Trinidad
3.2% Puerto Rico
3.4% Cuba
3.7% Argentina
5.5% United Kingdom
29.9% United States
35.7% Neth. Antilles (Aruba and Curaçao)

OIL FOR WORLD MARKETS

A wide swath of oil fields, shown in orange on the map *(top)*, covers 62 million acres of Venezuelan land. More than 2,000 miles of pipelines *(red lines)* carry oil to Caribbean ports. Two tiny islands of the Netherlands Antilles take 35 per cent of Venezuela's oil *(graph, bottom)* for refining and then re-export it, mainly to the United States and countries of Western Europe. Directly and indirectly, the U.S. gets about 40 per cent of Venezuela's total oil exports.

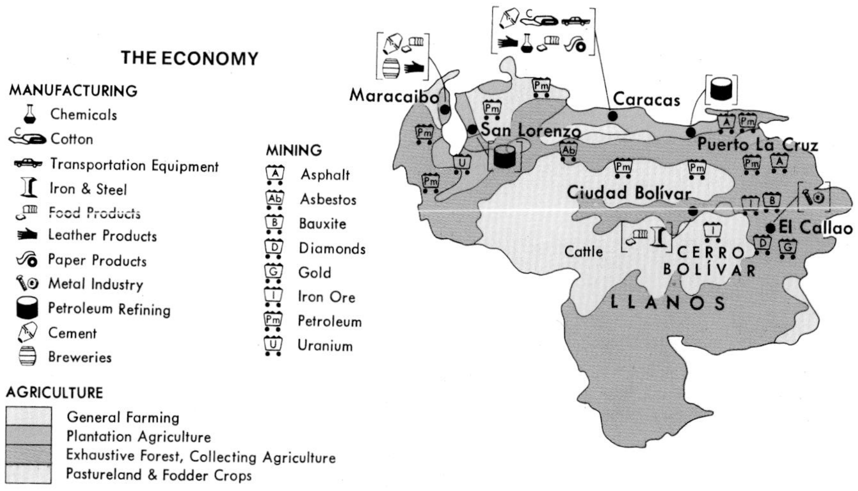
THE ECONOMY
MANUFACTURING
Chemicals
Cotton
Transportation Equipment
Iron & Steel
Food Products
Leather Products
Paper Products
Metal Industry
Petroleum Refining
Cement
Breweries
MINING
Asphalt
Asbestos
Bauxite
Diamonds
Gold
Iron Ore
Petroleum
Uranium
AGRICULTURE
General Farming
Plantation Agriculture
Exhaustive Forest, Collecting Agriculture
Pastureland & Fodder Crops
Maracaibo
San Lorenzo
Caracas
Puerto La Cruz
Ciudad Bolívar
El Callao
Cattle
CERRO BOLÍVAR
LLANOS

GROSS NATIONAL PRODUCT PER CAPITA $1,019

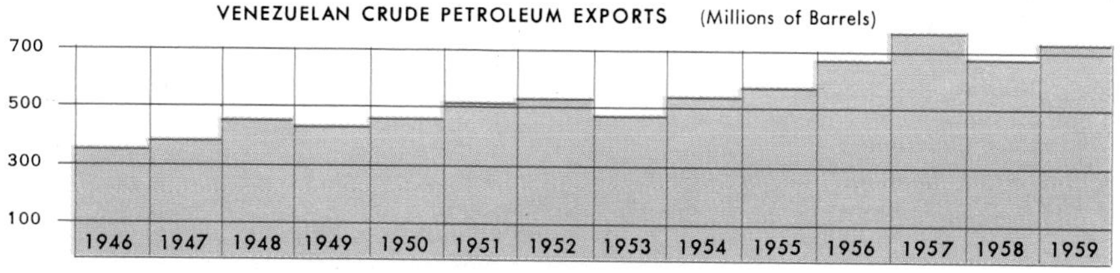
VENEZUELAN CRUDE PETROLEUM EXPORTS (Millions of Barrels)
700
500
300
100
1946 1947 1948 1949 1950 1951 1952 1953 1954 1955 1956 1957 1958 1959

UP AND UP, TOWARD A BILLION BARRELS A YEAR

Venezuela's petroleum exports, shown in the bar graph above, have risen about 50 per cent since World War II. Venezuela entered the international oil market in 1914, when the first successful commercial well was drilled by Royal Dutch Shell on the hot, sticky shores of Lake Maracaibo. Well ahead of Saudi Arabia, its nearest competitor, Venezuela is the world's leading oil exporter. In 1957 the Suez crisis helped boost its oil export total to a record high of 758,758,000 barrels as Western European countries began buying more Venezuelan oil to offset a threatened cut-off in their regular Middle East oil supply.

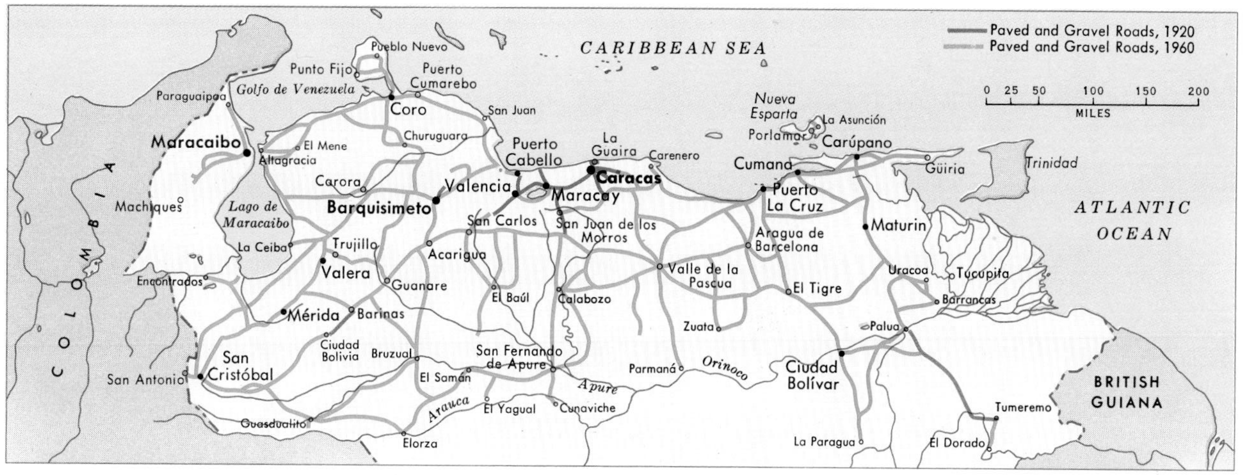
CARIBBEAN SEA
Paved and Gravel Roads, 1920
Paved and Gravel Roads, 1960
0 25 50 100 150 200
MILES
ATLANTIC OCEAN
BRITISH GUIANA
COLOMBIA
Trinidad
Maracaibo
Coro
Valencia
Caracas
Barquisimeto
Maracay
Puerto Cabello
Cumaná
Carúpano
Puerto La Cruz
Maturín
Valera
Mérida
San Cristóbal
Ciudad Bolívar
El Tigre
Tumeremo
El Dorado
Palua

VENEZUELA'S ROADS: THREE DECADES OF GROWTH

A network of new roads is beginning to bind together the northern regions of developing Venezuela, as shown in this map. In 1920 an automobile was almost completely useless in the country: most of Venezuela's 1,654 miles of roads were narrow gravel lanes used by ox carts. By 1960 the nation had 15,520 miles of modern highway usable all year round. Today, for the first time, a major highway crosses the Venezuela-Colombia border. The pre-1920 road from Tumeremo to Palua *(right)*, used to transport gold, remains the deepest penetration into Venezuela's southland, which is still not completely mapped.

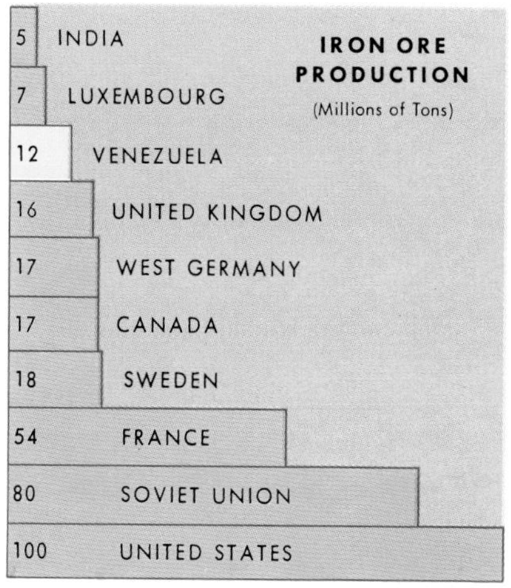
IRON ORE PRODUCTION
(Millions of Tons)
5 INDIA
7 LUXEMBOURG
12 VENEZUELA
16 UNITED KINGDOM
17 WEST GERMANY
17 CANADA
18 SWEDEN
54 FRANCE
80 SOVIET UNION
100 UNITED STATES

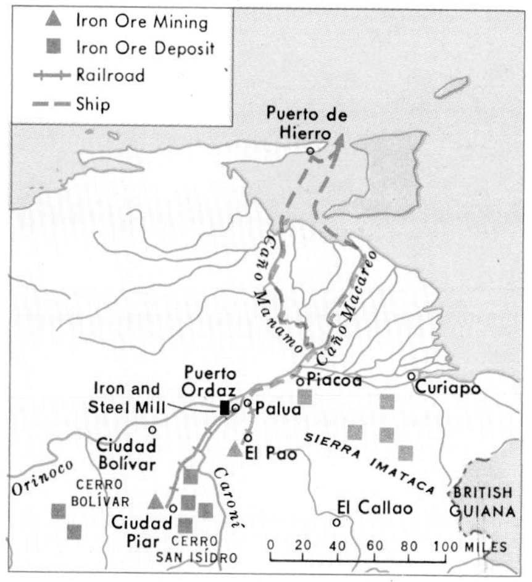
Iron Ore Mining
Iron Ore Deposit
Railroad
Ship
Puerto de Hierro
Caño Macareo
Caño Manamo
Iron and Steel Mill
Puerto Ordaz
Palua
Piacoa
Curiapo
Ciudad Bolívar
El Pao
SIERRA IMATACA
BRITISH GUIANA
El Callao
CERRO BOLÍVAR
Ciudad Piar
CERRO SAN ISIDRO
Orinoco
Caroní
0 20 40 60 80 100 MILES

AN IRON BANK FOR U.S. INDUSTRY

Eighth among the world's iron producers, as shown in the graph at the left, Venezuela started extracting ore only in 1951. But since then, mining operations, including construction of the railroads, ports and towns indicated on the map, have been carried on by two large U.S. subsidiaries. Of Venezuela's exported iron ore, 80 per cent goes to supplement the fast dwindling U.S. reserves of high-grade iron ore.

THE WORKS OF MAN IN THE

HIGH ANDES

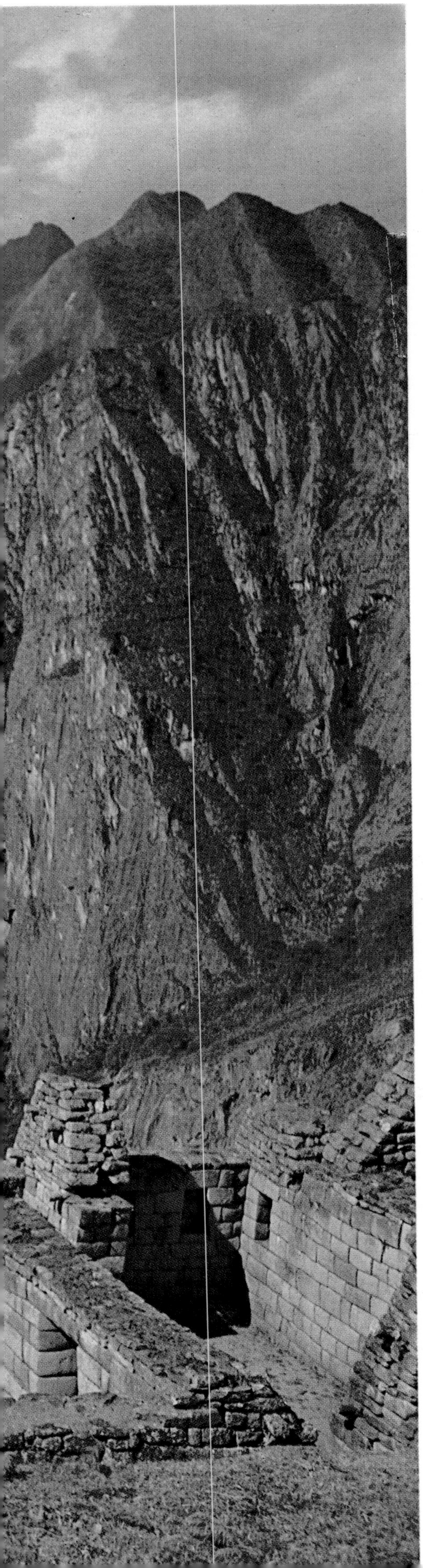

A GOLDEN FIELD, 11,000 feet above sea level, yields barley for Ecuador's Indian farmers, who have kept to their highland huts and their own language while the empires of both the Incas and the Spaniards prospered and passed on. These Indians grow corn, wheat, barley, quinoa and potatoes in highland basins ringed by towering mountains like 20,577-foot Mount Chimborazo, seen here looming on the horizon.

A DEAD MOUNTAIN TOWN lying in the Andean sun, the ancient Inca city of Machu Picchu was abandoned and forgotten when the Inca Empire was conquered by the Spanish in the 16th Century. Rediscovered in 1911, the superbly crafted masonry buildings of this Peruvian relic bear witness to the Andean people's Olympian drive to sustain an urban way of life amid the most remote and forbidding mountain peaks.

A BOUNTIFUL HEAP OF TIN, Bolivia's Cerro Rico Mountain rises above the 13,600-foot-high town of Potosí. Located in a steep and barren region, where water is scarce, the air thin and vegetation nonexistent, Potosí's mountain of tin, together with deposits in neighboring districts in the eastern Andes, provides the world with 13 per cent of its tin supply. Low-grade tin ore makes up 55 per cent of Bolivia's total exports.

COLOMBIA: The northwestern corner of South America, Colombia is settled only in the narrow region that lies between the coast and the eastern foothills of the Andes. In this area Colombians have adapted their farming to the climatic belts that occur at different levels of the Andes *(diagram, below)*.

AREA: 439,405 sq. mi.
POPULATION: 14,105,000. Capital: Bogotá.
CLIMATE: Lowlands are generally hot with heavy rainfall; highland climates vary with altitude from warm to cold, very wet to dry.
ALTITUDES: Cristóbal Colón, 18,947 ft. (highest); Bogotá, 8,659 ft.

The wet lowlands and the Andean foothills yield such tropical crops as sugar cane and cacao. In the 3,000-to-6,500-foot zone Colombians grow the second largest coffee crop in the world. Above this belt, in chilly but very densely populated mountain basins, wheat and barley are raised, and sheep are herded in the alpine meadows. Colombia has a textile industry in the Antioquia valley and makes steel in the iron and coal area near Sogamoso. But most Colombians depend directly on income from coffee.

THE ECONOMY

MANUFACTURING
- Chemicals
- Transportation Equipment
- Textiles
- Iron & Steel
- Food Products
- Leather Products
- Tobacco Products
- Cement
- Wineries, Distilleries, Breweries

MINING
- Coal
- Gold
- Platinum
- Petroleum

AGRICULTURE
- General Farming
- Plantation Agriculture
- Exhaustive Forest, Collecting Agriculture
- Pastureland & Stock Farming
- Non-Agricultural Areas

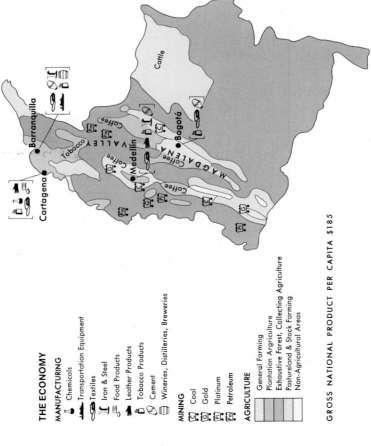

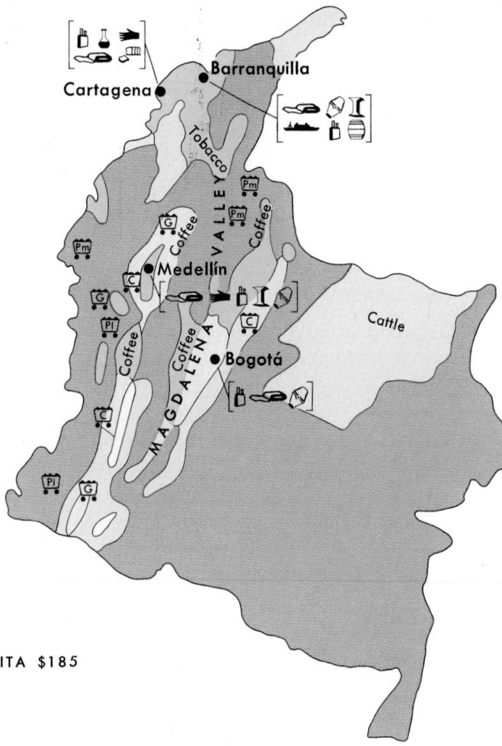

GROSS NATIONAL PRODUCT PER CAPITA $185

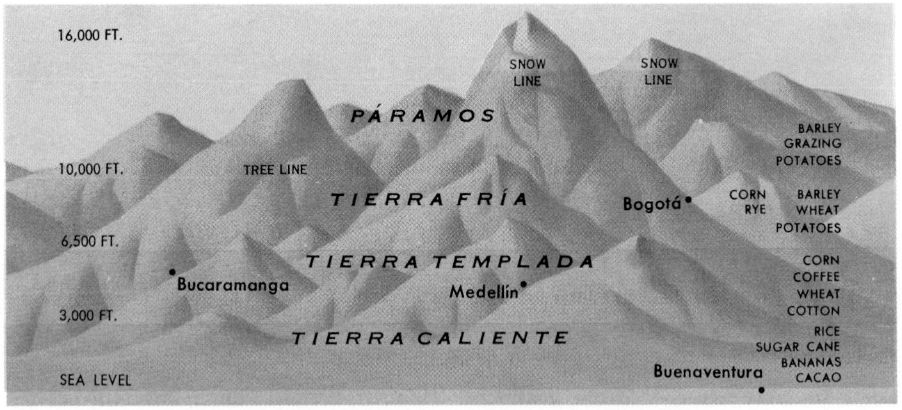

THE VERTICAL AGRICULTURE OF THE ANDES

This profile of the Colombian Andes shows the remarkably wide range of climatic conditions and natural vegetation that can exist at the Equator. As the mountains rise from sea level to 17,000 feet, they pass through four temperature zones, ranging from a hot, humid equatorial climate at the base to a cold polar climate at the peaks. Because of the equatorial position, the temperature within each zone varies little from month to month.

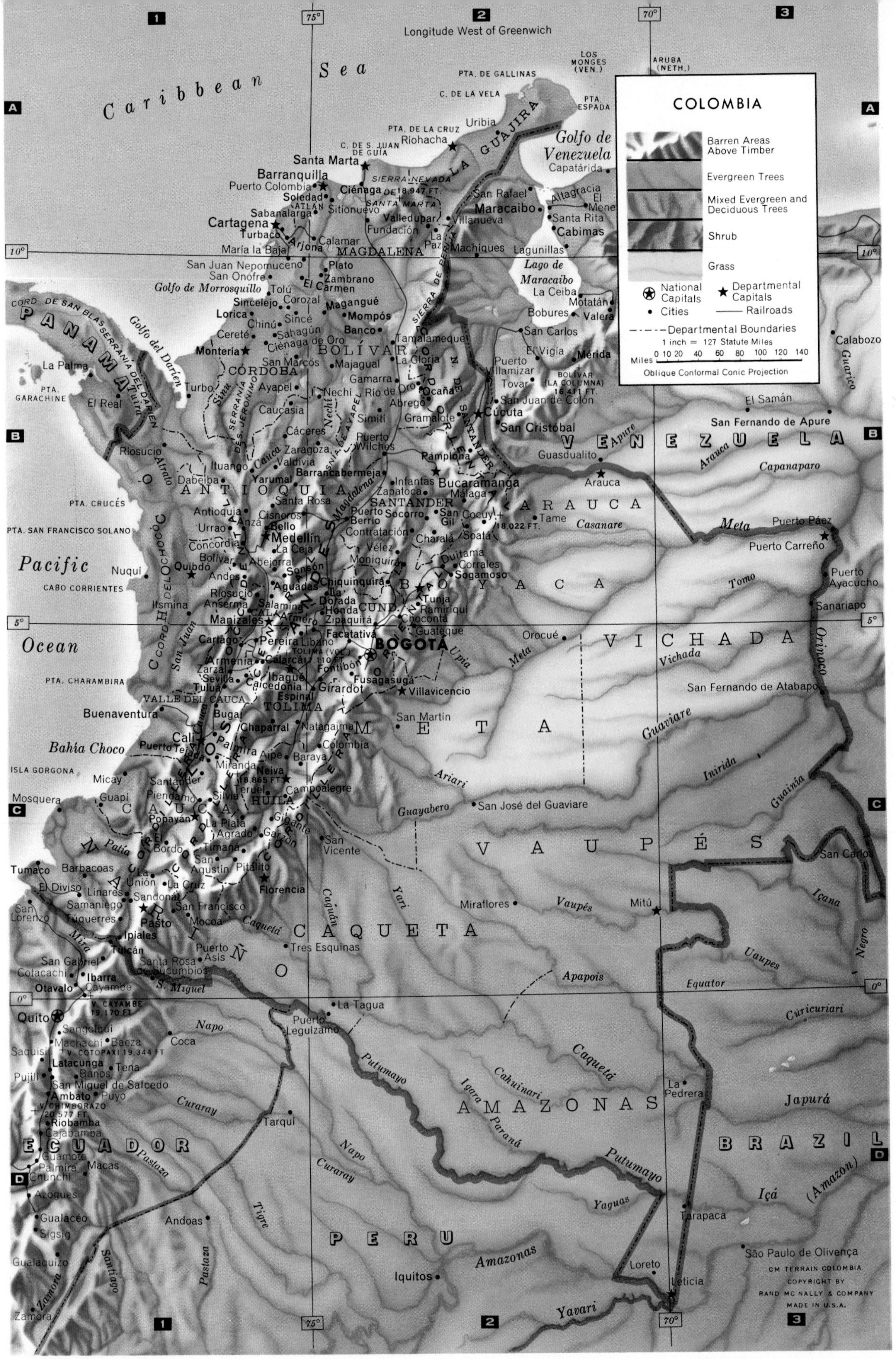

PERU: The ancient home of the Incas *(diagram, below)*, Peru's Andean highlands provide limited areas for profitable commercial agriculture. Here, where mountain basins are often located well above 10,000 feet, the Incas' heirs grow corn and barley and hold themselves apart from the national life.

AREA: 482,133 sq. mi.
POPULATION: 10,640,000. Capital: Lima
CLIMATE: Eastern lowlands, hot and wet; coast, very dry and mild; highland climate variable.
ALTITUDES: Huascarán, 22,205 ft. (highest); Lima, 501 ft.

Peru's coastal region, where the major cities are located, is a desert dissected by seasonal mountain streams. At some 40 of these oases, Peruvians raise their two chief exports—sugar cane and cotton.

ECUADOR: Underdeveloped Ecuador is split by the Andes, which wall off extensive coastal lowlands from the interior forests and provide a lofty homeland for a large Indian population. Source of the "Panama" hat, Ecuador also exports the world's largest banana crop. But total export revenue is small.

AREA: 104,479 sq. mi.
POPULATION: 4,191,000. Capital: Quito.
CLIMATE: Eastern lowlands, hot and wet; coastal plains, seasonal rainfall; highland climate variable.
ALTITUDES: Mt. Chimborazo, 20,577 ft. (highest); Quito, 9,320 ft.

THE ECONOMY

MANUFACTURING
- Chemicals
- Textiles
- Food Products
- Leather Products
- Metal Industry
- Petroleum Refining
- Tobacco Products
- Cement
- Panama Hats
- Breweries

MINING
- Copper
- Gold
- Iron Ore
- Lead
- Manganese
- Molybdenum
- Petroleum
- Silver
- Tungsten
- Vanadium
- Zinc

AGRICULTURE
- General Farming
- Plantation Agriculture
- Exhaustive Forest, Collecting Agriculture
- Pastureland & Fodder Crops
- Seasonal Grazing
- Non-Agricultural Areas

GROSS NATIONAL PRODUCT PER CAPITA
Peru $126 Ecuador $198

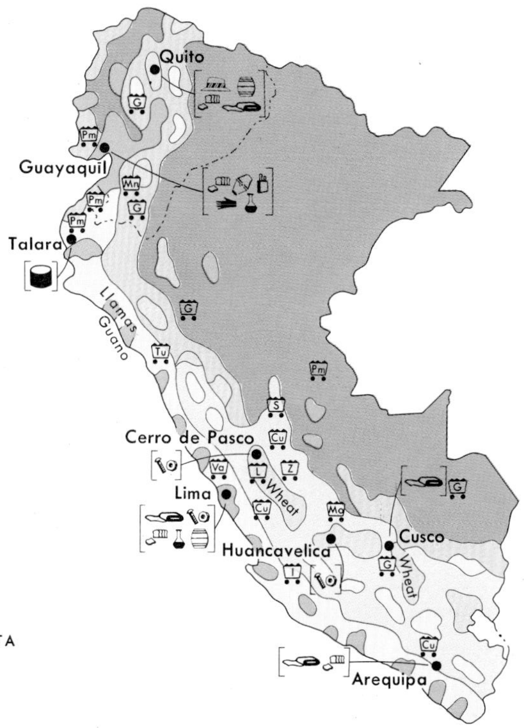
Quito
Guayaquil
Talara
Llamas
Guano
Cerro de Pasco
Lima
Wheat
Huancavelica
Cusco
Wheat
Arequipa

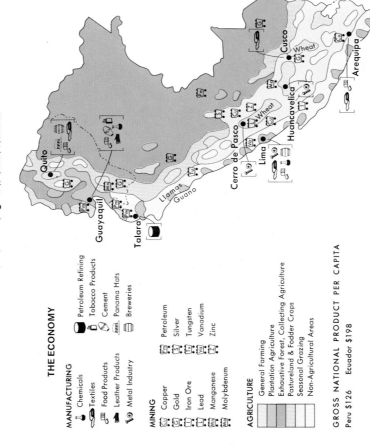

AN EMPIRE'S GOOD ROADS

The portion of the Inca Empire that covers today's Ecuador and Peru is shown in green at right. Traced in red is the intricate roadway system built by the Incas to consolidate their vast holdings. Carved out of solid rock by enforced communal labor, the roads spanned mile-high gorges with suspension bridges. Over these narrow pathways relays of swift runners traveled quickly from Quitu (Quito) in the north to Cuzco (Cusco) in the south. Ironically, the Inca roads also served the Spanish when they attacked the Incas in 1532. Four centuries later, some of the roads were used as a base for the Pan American Highway.

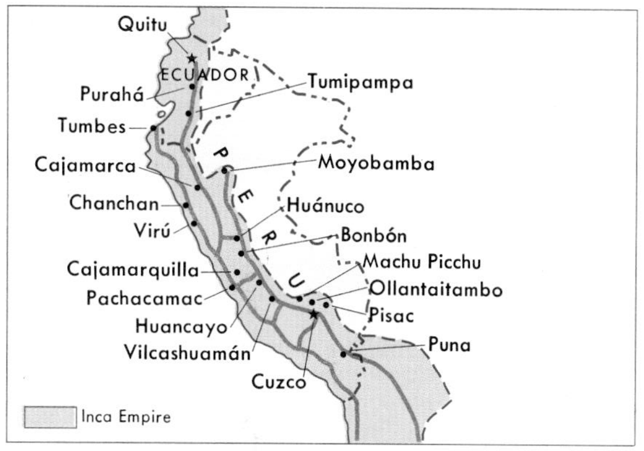
Quitu
Puruhá
Tumbes
Cajamarca
Chanchan
Virú
Cajamarquilla
Pachacamac
Huancayo
Vilcashuamán
Cuzco
ECUADOR
PERU
Tumipampa
Moyobamba
Huánuco
Bonbón
Machu Picchu
Ollantaitambo
Pisac
Puna
Inca Empire

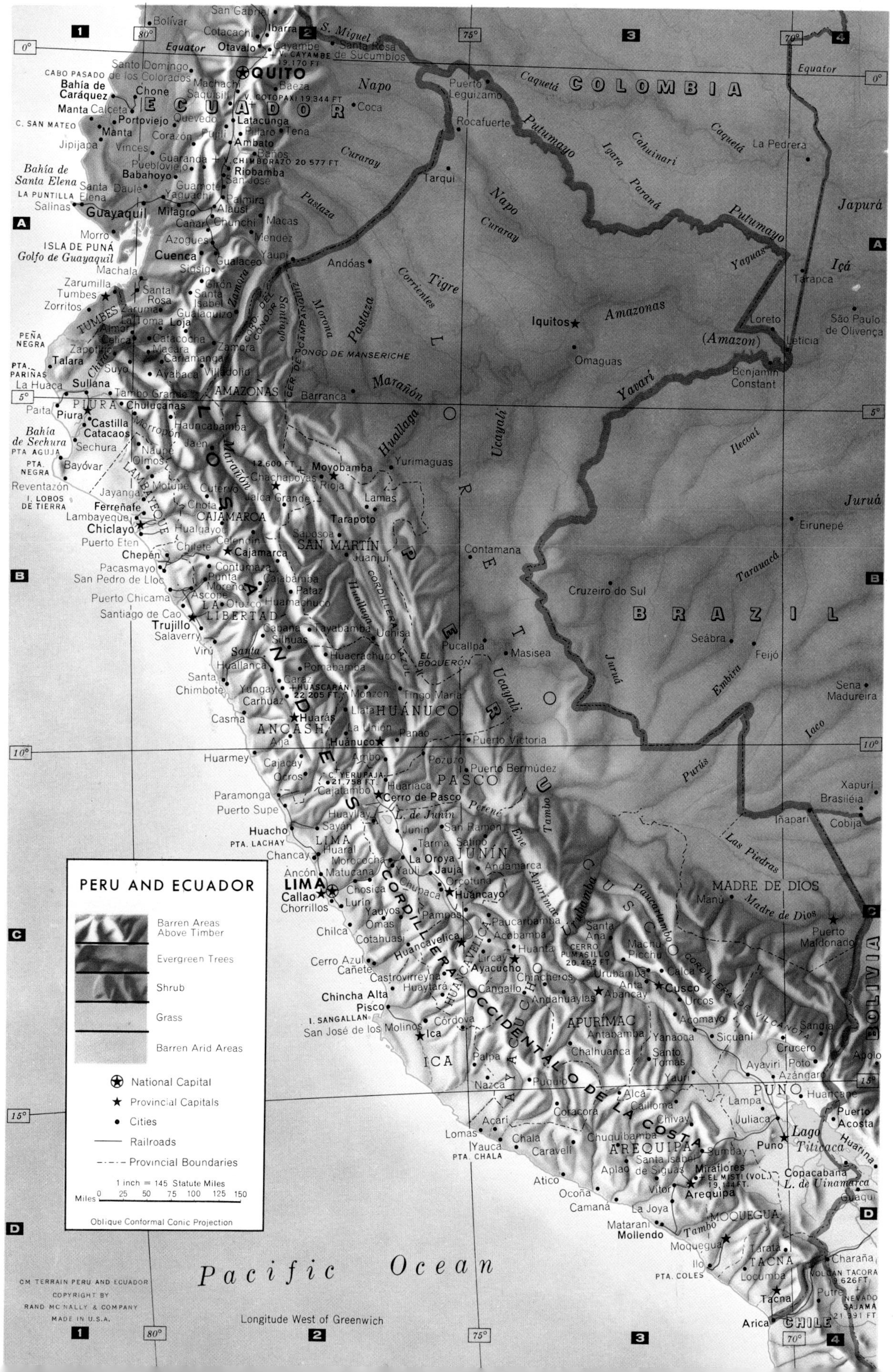
PERU AND ECUADOR
Barren Areas Above Timber
Evergreen Trees
Shrub
Grass
Barren Arid Areas
National Capital
Provincial Capitals
Cities
Railroads
Provincial Boundaries
1 inch = 145 Statute Miles
Miles 0 25 50 75 100 125 150
Oblique Conformal Conic Projection
COLOMBIA
ECUADOR
PERU
BRAZIL
BOLIVIA
CHILE
QUITO
LIMA
Guayaquil
Iquitos
Cusco
Arequipa
Callao
Pacific Ocean
Longitude West of Greenwich
CM TERRAIN PERU AND ECUADOR
COPYRIGHT BY
RAND MCNALLY & COMPANY
MADE IN U.S.A.

BOLIVIA: Landlocked Bolivia is the most sparsely settled country in South America. The plateau of the Andean highlands, where most of the population lives, is some 12,000 feet above sea level, a height at which few crops other than potatoes and barley can grow. As a result, most Bolivian farms are located along the valleys of rivers that flow into the Amazon Basin. Here farmers grow corn, barley, alfalfa, fruit and, on the wetter northerly slopes, coffee and cacao. Because rail transportation across the Andes to the Pacific coast is costly, few agricultural products are exported. With mainly local demand to satisfy, Bolivians farm only .3 per cent of their land, the lowest percentage in South America.

AREA: 424,052 sq. mi.
POPULATION: 3,366,000. Capital: La Paz and Sucre.
CLIMATE: Eastern lowlands hot year round; wet, November through March; dry, May through September. Highland climate varies greatly with altitude.
ALTITUDES: Tocorpuri, 22,162 ft. (highest); La Paz, 12,795 ft.

A mineral belt 60 miles wide and 450 miles long extends south from Lake Titicaca. Four centuries ago one of the richest silver mines in the world was found here and, later, one of the richest tin mines. The largest producer of tungsten and antimony in the Western Hemisphere, Bolivia is also the second largest producer of lead and zinc in South America. The nation mines copper and gold and is self-sufficient in petroleum. This mineral wealth accounts for more than 90 per cent of Bolivia's entire export wealth.

THE ECONOMY

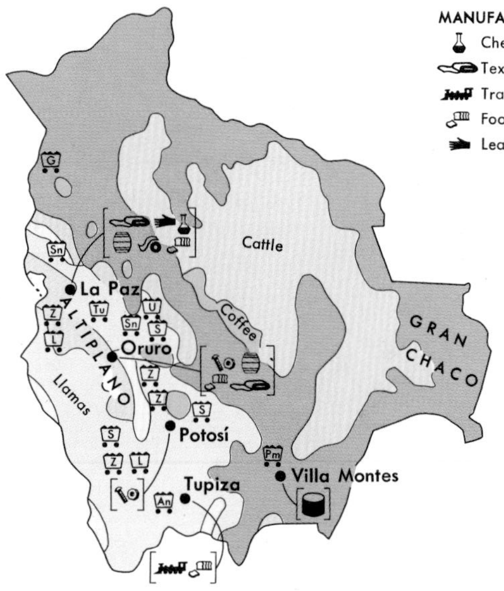
Cattle
Coffee
GRAN CHACO
La Paz
ALTIPLANO
Oruro
Llamas
Potosí
Tupiza
Villa Montes

MANUFACTURING
- Chemicals
- Textiles
- Transportation Equipment
- Food Products
- Leather Products
- Paper Products
- Metal Industry
- Petroleum Refining
- Wineries, Distilleries, Breweries

MINING
- Antimony
- Copper
- Gold
- Lead
- Petroleum
- Silver
- Tin
- Tungsten
- Uranium
- Zinc

AGRICULTURE
- General Farming
- Plantation Agriculture
- Exhaustive Forest, Collecting Agriculture
- Pastureland & Fodder Crops
- Alpine Herding
- Non-Agricultural Areas

GROSS NATIONAL PRODUCT PER CAPITA $60

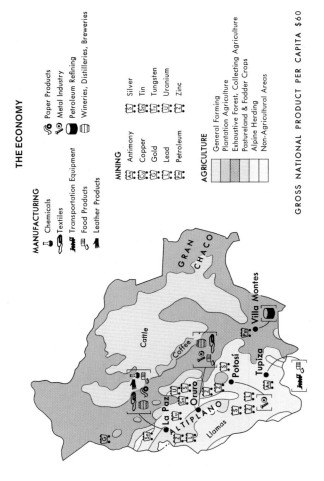

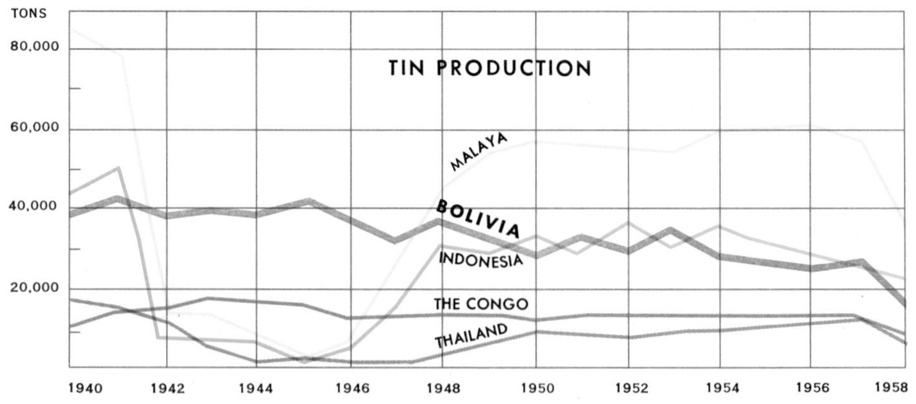
TONS
80,000
60,000
40,000
20,000
TIN PRODUCTION
MALAYA
BOLIVIA
INDONESIA
THE CONGO
THAILAND
1940
1942
1944
1946
1948
1950
1952
1954
1956
1958

THE UPS AND DOWNS OF BOLIVIAN TIN

Bolivia's fluctuating position in the world tin market is traced here. From 1940 to 1945, when Japan kept Asian tin off international markets, Bolivia became the world's leading supplier. But the lead was lost in 1948 when Malaya's tin once more became available. With mines at the nearly inaccessible heights of 12,000 feet and up, and mining methods that are costly and often primitive, Bolivia faces a continuing decline in income from tin.

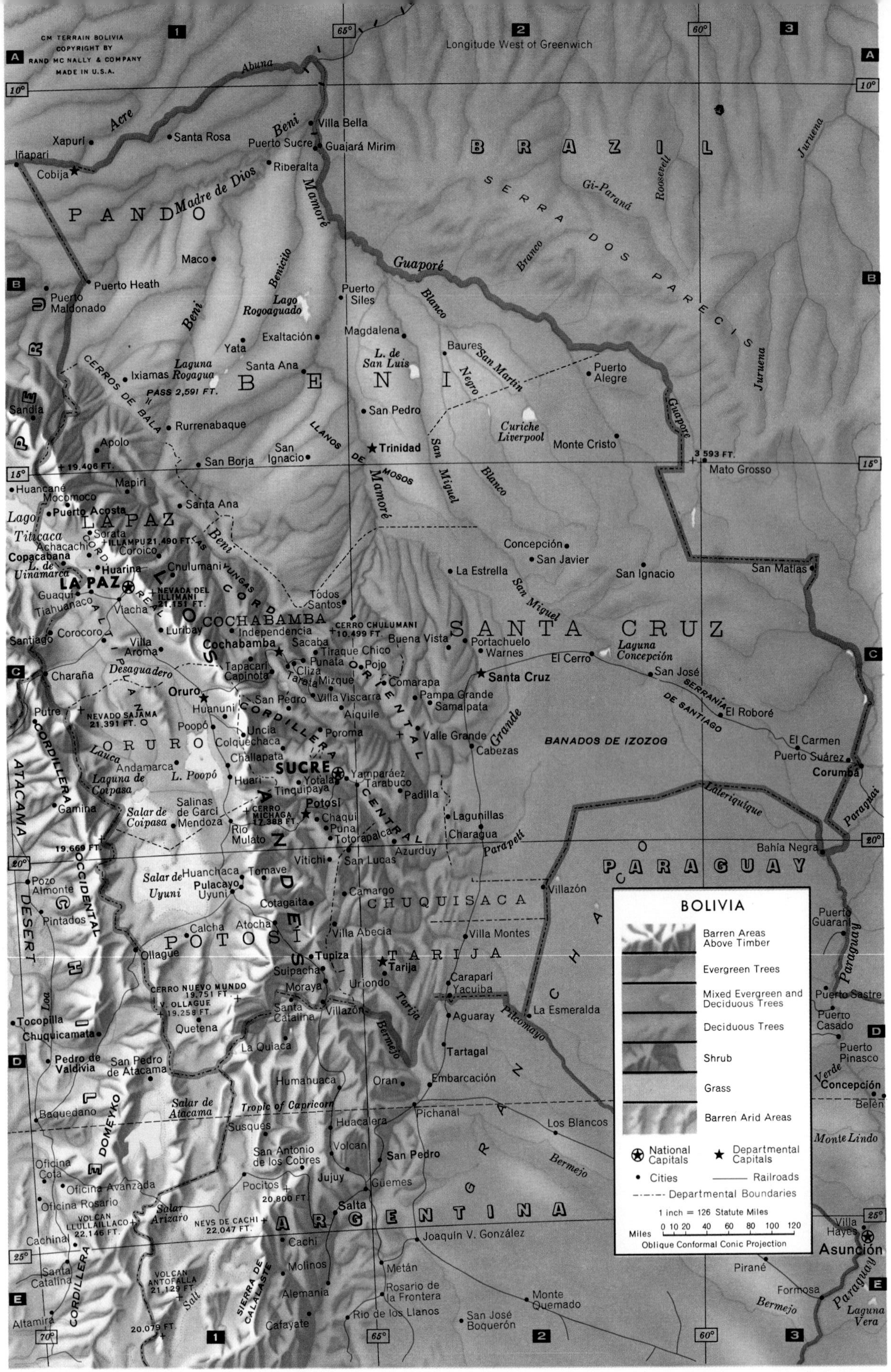
CM TERRAIN BOLIVIA
COPYRIGHT BY
RAND MCNALLY & COMPANY
MADE IN U.S.A.
Longitude West of Greenwich
BRAZIL
SERRA DOS PARECIS
PANDO
BENI
LA PAZ
COCHABAMBA
SANTA CRUZ
ORURO
POTOSÍ
CHUQUISACA
TARIJA
PARAGUAY
ARGENTINA
CHACO
ATACAMA DESERT
CORDILLERA OCCIDENTAL
CORDILLERA ORIENTAL
CORDILLERA CENTRAL
BANADOS DE IZOZOG
LLANOS DE MOSOS
Lago Titicaca
L. Poopó
Salar de Uyuni
Salar de Coipasa
Salar de Atacama
Tropic of Capricorn
LA PAZ
SUCRE
Asunción
Cochabamba
Oruro
Potosí
Santa Cruz
Trinidad
Tarija
Cobija
Riberalta
Villa Montes
Tupiza
Puerto Suárez
Corumbá
Guaporé
Mamoré
Beni
Madre de Dios
Pilcomayo
Bermejo
Paraguay
BOLIVIA
Barren Areas Above Timber
Evergreen Trees
Mixed Evergreen and Deciduous Trees
Deciduous Trees
Shrub
Grass
Barren Arid Areas
National Capitals
Departmental Capitals
Cities
Railroads
Departmental Boundaries
1 inch = 126 Statute Miles
Miles 0 10 20 40 60 80 100 120
Oblique Conformal Conic Projection

PARAGUAY: The Paraguay River divides this small nation into two geographic regions that have little in common. The eastern third, where the bulk of the population lives, has a moderate and mild climate, abundant rains, gently rolling hills, open pasture lands, and low tablelands covered with forests. The bounteous soil yields corn, yerba maté, beans, cotton and rice; cattle thrive on the grasslands. The western two thirds of Paraguay is part of the Gran Chaco—a "green hell" of swamps and grassy prairies dotted with thickets—and is practically devoid of population. From the quebracho trees that grow in this region Paraguay extracts tannin, the leather-processing acid which is one of the country's chief exports.

AREA: 157,006 sq. mi.
POPULATION: 1,736,000. Capital: Asunción.
CLIMATE: Warm all year round. Heaviest rainfall, November through April. Less rain, May through October.
ALTITUDES: Ibyturuzú, 2,297 ft. (highest); Asunción, 246 ft.

Devastating wars *(map and diagram, below)* and a lack of access to markets have blocked Paraguay's growth. Her main link to the Atlantic coast is the shifting Paraguay River, which winds loosely through the plain, making shipping slow and expensive. With few mineral assets, Paraguay has little money to build the roads and rails that might raise her per capita income, one of the lowest in South America.

THE ECONOMY

MANUFACTURING
- Cotton
- Food Products
- Leather Products
- Breweries

MINING
- Copper
- Iron Ore
- Manganese

AGRICULTURE
- Plantation Agriculture
- Exhaustive Forest, Collecting Agriculture
- Pastureland & Fodder Crops
- Seasonal Grazing

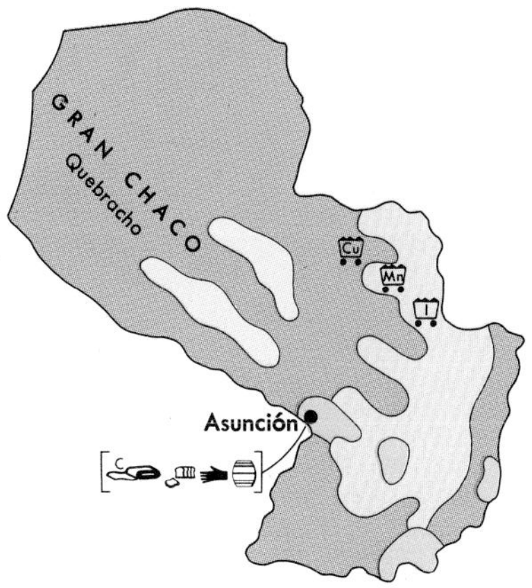

GROSS NATIONAL PRODUCT PER CAPITA $133

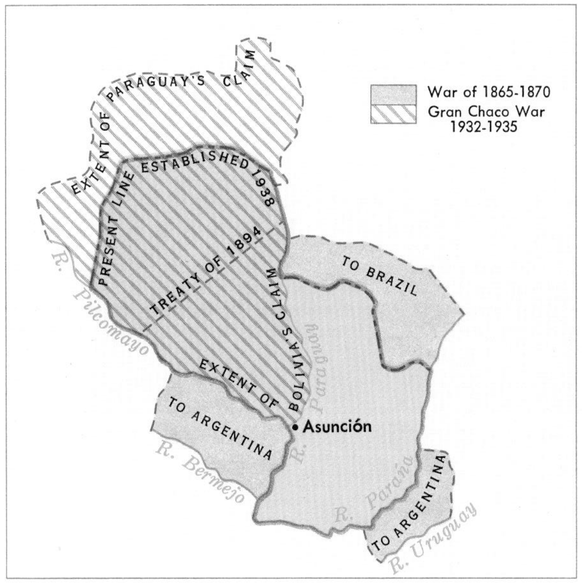

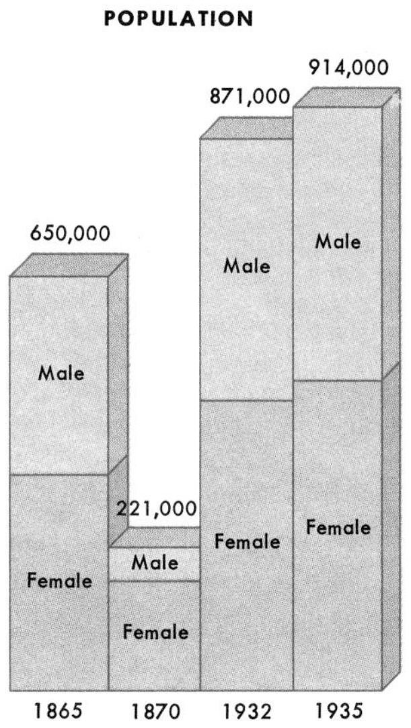

THE BLOODY WARS OF TINY PARAGUAY

Paraguay's borders *(outlined in red on map)* are the result of two bloody wars. For access to the sea, the tiny nation fought Brazil, Uruguay and Argentina in 1865, but lost 400,000 lives *(graph, right)* and much territory *(in orange on map)*. Disputing her vague 1894 borders with Bo..via and seeking access to oil in the Gran Chaco area, Paraguay went to war again in 1932. The war, costing 10,000 lives, gained her new territory but no oil land.

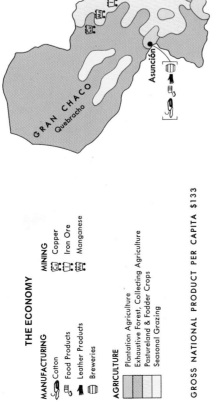

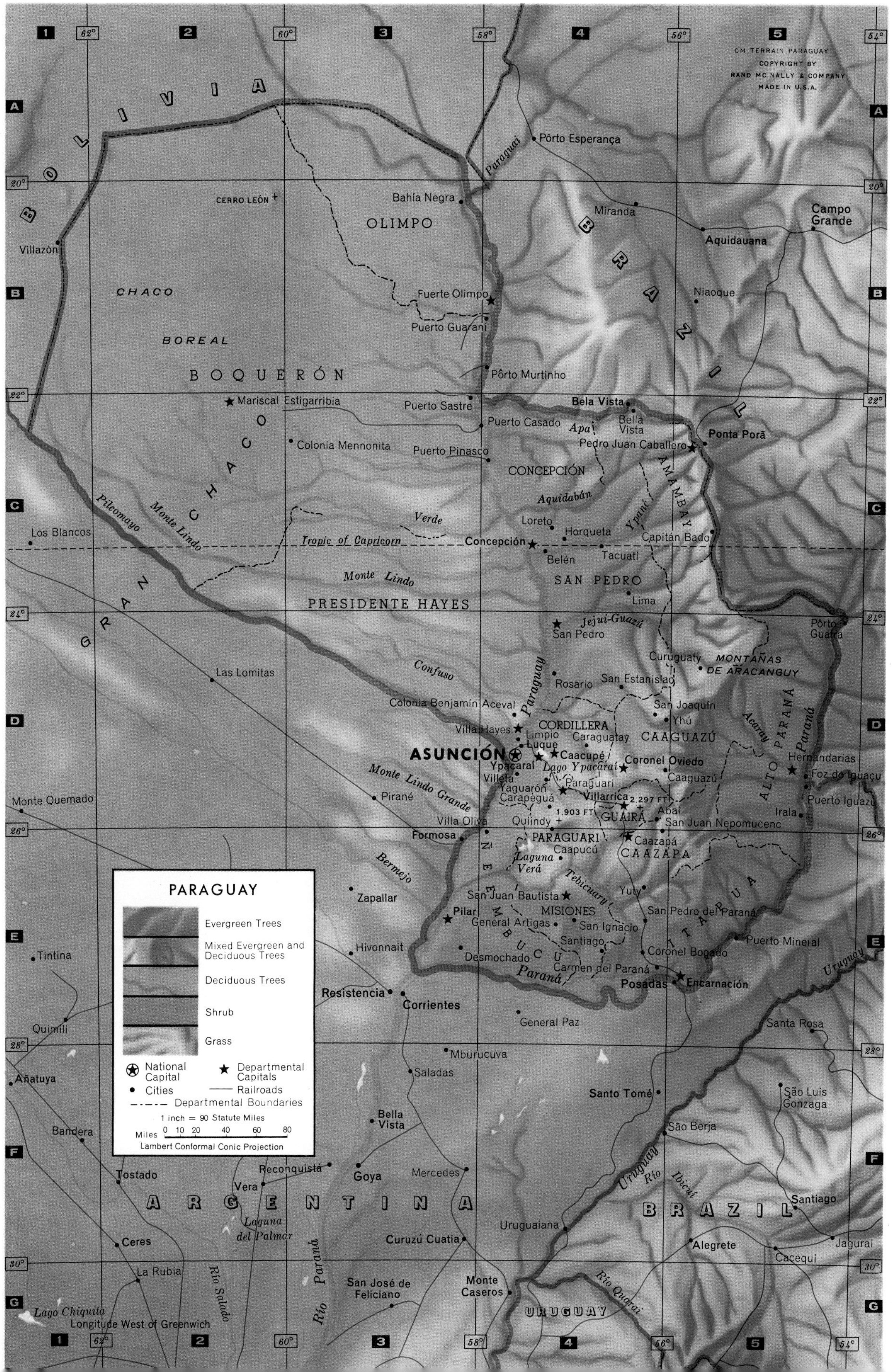

THE WEALTH OF SOUTHERNMOST AMERICA

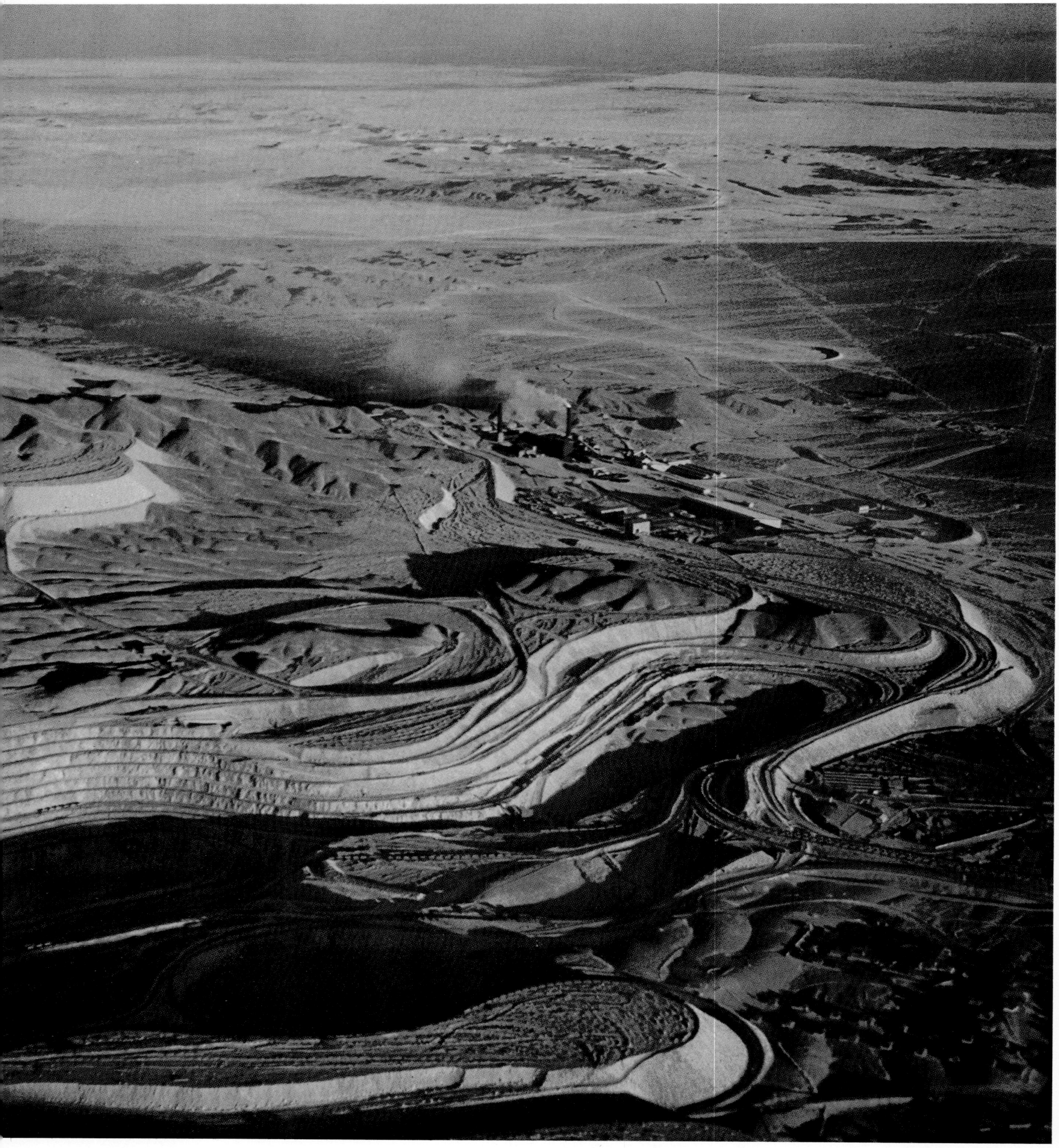

COPPER BENEATH A DESERT is mined in a swirling pattern of open-pit terraces at Chuquicamata in Chile. Here the searing Atacama desert surrounds the largest deposit of copper ore being worked in the world. Chile is second only to the U.S. as a producer of the ore.

WATER FOR BEEF is pumped from a well into a trough *(opposite)* that serves three adjoining cattle ranches on Argentina's wide grazing land. Fattened on the Pampas' rich grass, Argentina's livestock makes up some 20 per cent of the world's exported beef and veal.

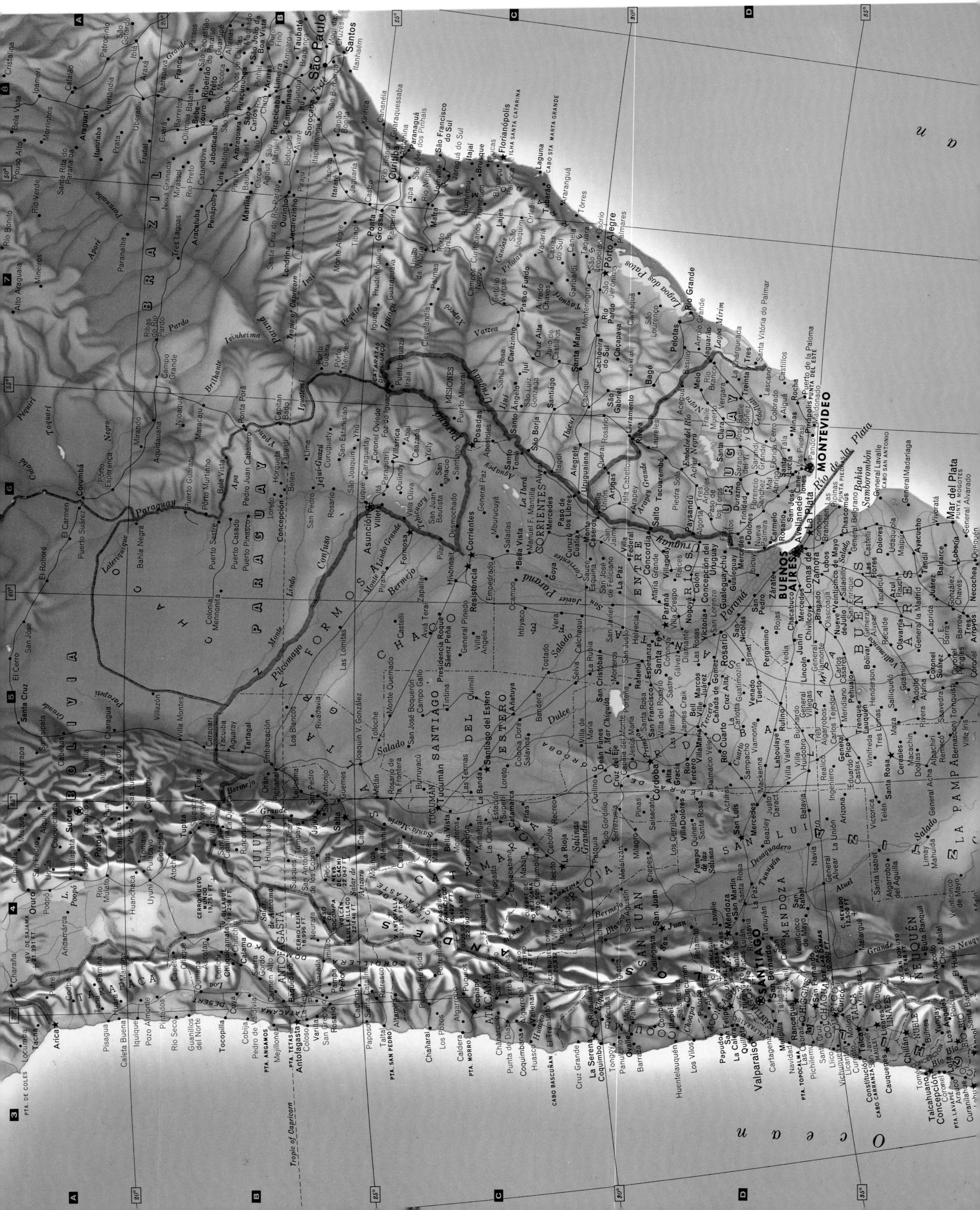
BRAZIL
BOLIVIA
PARAGUAY
URUGUAY
CHACO
FORMOSA
SANTIAGO DEL ESTERO
TUCUMÁN
CORRIENTES
MISIONES
ENTRE RIOS
SANTA FE
CÓRDOBA
BUENOS AIRES
LA PAMPA
SAN LUIS
MENDOZA
SAN JUAN
LA RIOJA
CATAMARCA
SALTA
JUJUY
ANTOFAGASTA
ATACAMA
COQUIMBO
NEUQUÉN
TARAPACÁ
Tropic of Capricorn
São Paulo
Santos
Curitiba
Florianópolis
Pôrto Alegre
Asunción
Montevideo
Buenos Aires
La Plata
Rosario
Córdoba
Mendoza
Santiago
Valparaíso
Concepción
Antofagasta
Sucre
Rio de la Plata
Mar del Plata
Ocean

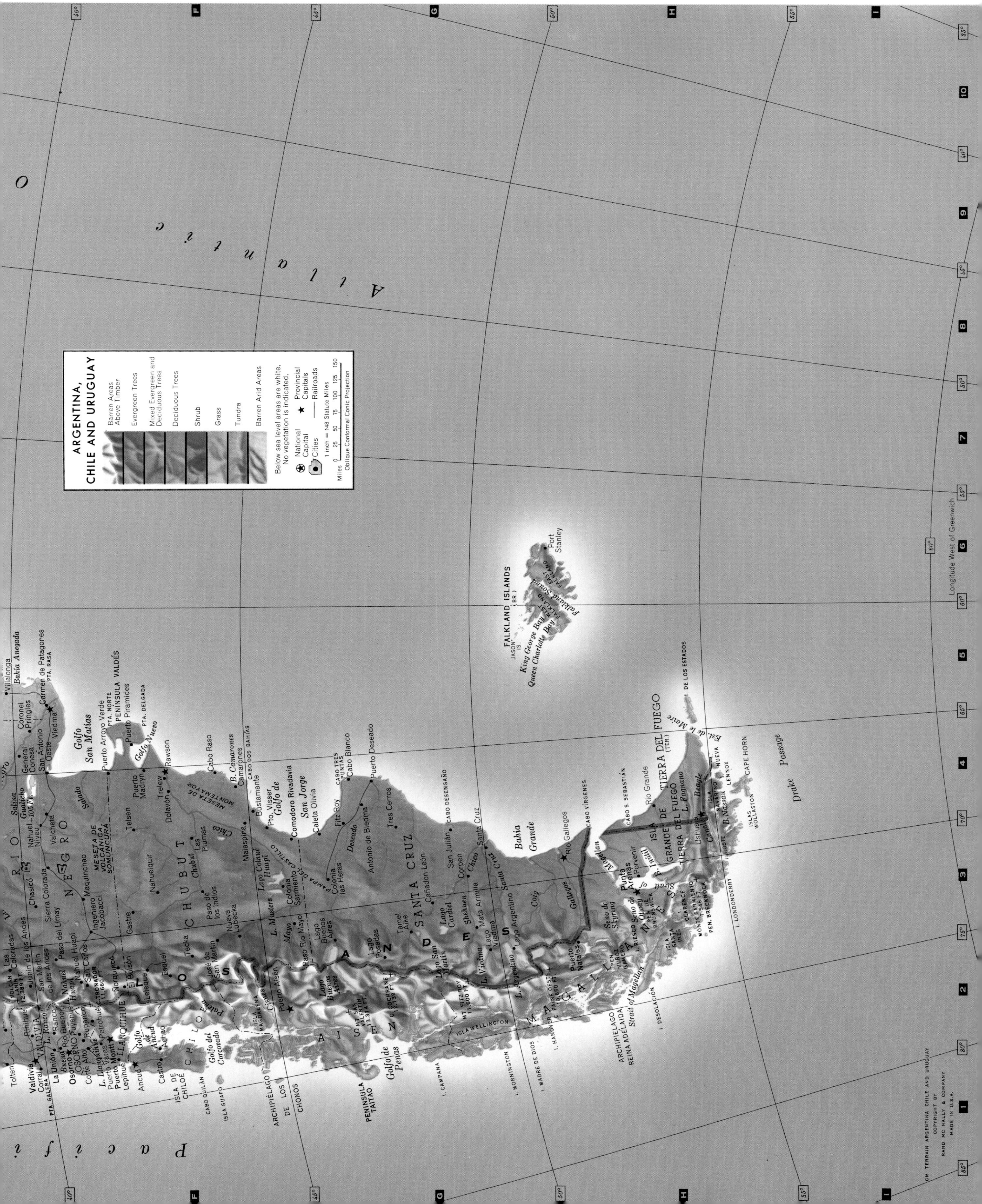
ARGENTINA, CHILE AND URUGUAY
Barren Areas Above Timber
Evergreen Trees
Mixed Evergreen and Deciduous Trees
Deciduous Trees
Shrub
Grass
Tundra
Barren Arid Areas
Below sea level areas are white. No vegetation is indicated.
National Capital
Provincial Capitals
Cities
Railroads
1 inch = 148 Statute Miles
Miles 0 25 50 75 100 125 150
Oblique Conformal Conic Projection
Atlantic
Pacific
FALKLAND ISLANDS (BR.)
Port Stanley
Falkland Sound
King George Bay
Queen Charlotte Bay
JASON IS.
TIERRA DEL FUEGO (TER.)
ISLA GRANDE DE TIERRA DEL FUEGO
I. DE LOS ESTADOS
Est. de le Maire
Beagle
CAPE HORN
ISLAS WOLLASTON
Drake Passage
Strait of Magellan
Punta Arenas
Porvenir
Ushuaia
Rio Grande
Rio Gallegos
CABO VÍRGENES
Bahía Grande
Santa Cruz
San Julián
CABO DESENGAÑO
Puerto Deseado
Cabo Blanco
Golfo de San Jorge
Comodoro Rivadavia
Caleta Olivia
SANTA CRUZ
CHUBUT
Rawson
Trelew
Puerto Madryn
Golfo Nuevo
PENÍNSULA VALDÉS
Golfo San Matías
San Antonio Oeste
Viedma
Carmen de Patagones
Bahía Anegada
RIO NEGRO
MAGALLANES
AISÉN
CHILOÉ
LLANQUIHUE
OSORNO
VALDIVIA
Puerto Montt
Puerto Aisén
Puerto Natales
Golfo de Penas
PENÍNSULA TAITAO
ARCHIPIÉLAGO DE LOS CHONOS
ISLA DE CHILOÉ
Golfo del Corcovado
ISLA WELLINGTON
I. DESOLACIÓN
ARCHIPIÉLAGO REINA ADELAIDA
L. Argentino
L. Viedma
Lago Buenos Aires
Longitude West of Greenwich
CM TERRAIN ARGENTINA CHILE AND URUGUAY
COPYRIGHT BY RAND MC NALLY & COMPANY
MADE IN U.S.A.

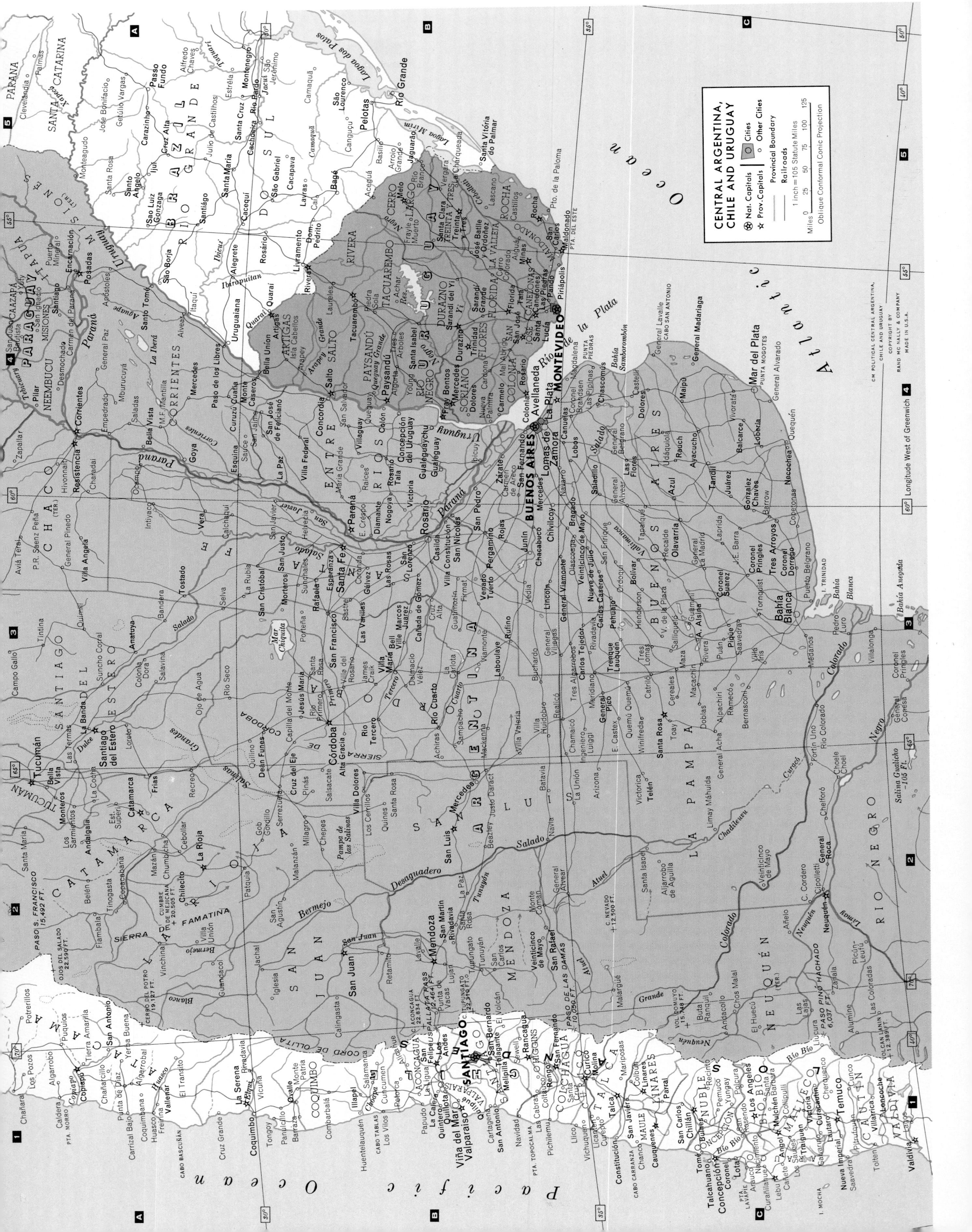
CENTRAL ARGENTINA, CHILE AND URUGUAY
Nat. Capitals
Prov. Capitals
Cities
Other Cities
Provincial Boundary
Railroads
1 inch = 105 Statute Miles
Miles 0 25 50 75 100 125
Oblique Conformal Conic Projection
CM POLITICAL CENTRAL ARGENTINA, CHILE AND URUGUAY
COPYRIGHT BY RAND McNALLY & COMPANY
MADE IN U.S.A.
Longitude West of Greenwich
Atlantic Ocean
Pacific Ocean
Río de la Plata
BUENOS AIRES
MONTEVIDEO
SANTIAGO
URUGUAY
BRAZIL
RIO GRANDE DO SUL
SANTA CATARINA
PARANÁ
PARAGUAY
CHACO
CORRIENTES
MISIONES
ENTRE RIOS
SANTA FE
CÓRDOBA
SANTIAGO DEL ESTERO
TUCUMÁN
CATAMARCA
LA RIOJA
SAN JUAN
SAN LUIS
MENDOZA
LA PAMPA
NEUQUÉN
RIO NEGRO
ATACAMA
COQUIMBO
ACONCAGUA
VALPARAISO
O'HIGGINS
COLCHAGUA
CURICÓ
TALCA
MAULE
LINARES
ÑUBLE
CONCEPCIÓN
BIO-BIO
ARAUCO
MALLECO
CAUTÍN
VALDIVIA
Córdoba
Rosario
Santa Fe
Paraná
Mendoza
San Juan
Tucumán
Corrientes
Resistencia
Bahía Blanca
Mar del Plata
La Plata
Valparaiso
Viña del Mar
Concepción
Temuco
Talca
Porto Alegre
Pelotas
Rio Grande
Lagoa dos Patos
Lagoa Mirim
C. ACONCAGUA 22,834 FT.
Salina Gualicho -105 Ft.

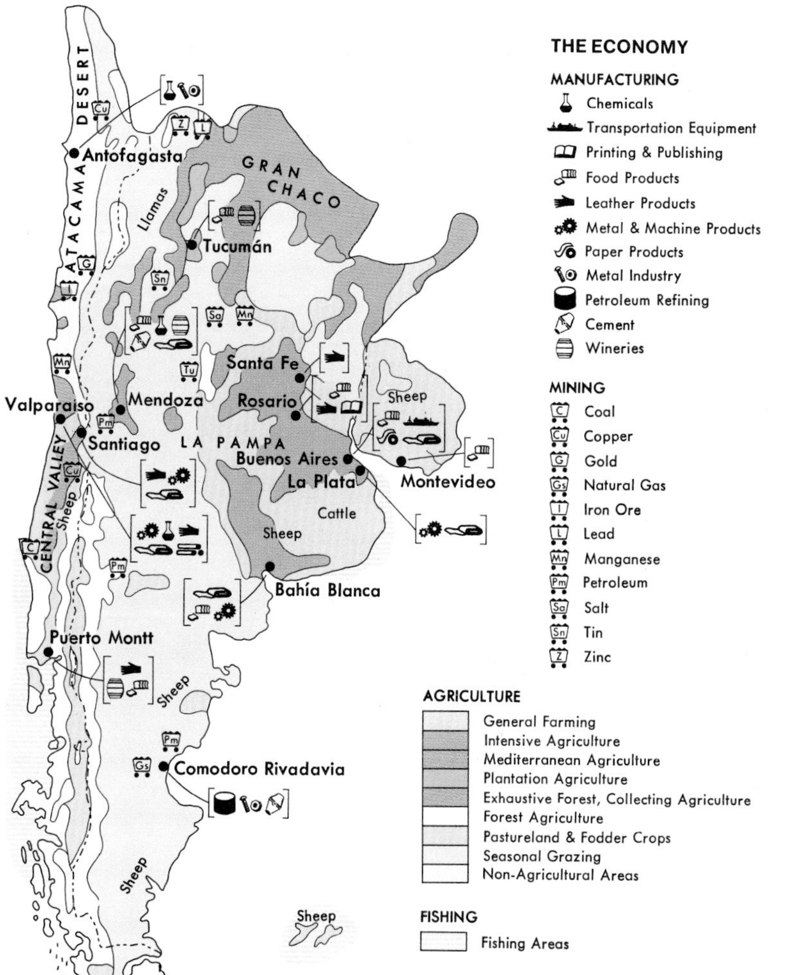

GROSS NATIONAL PRODUCT PER CAPITA
Argentina $185 Chile $386 Uruguay $559

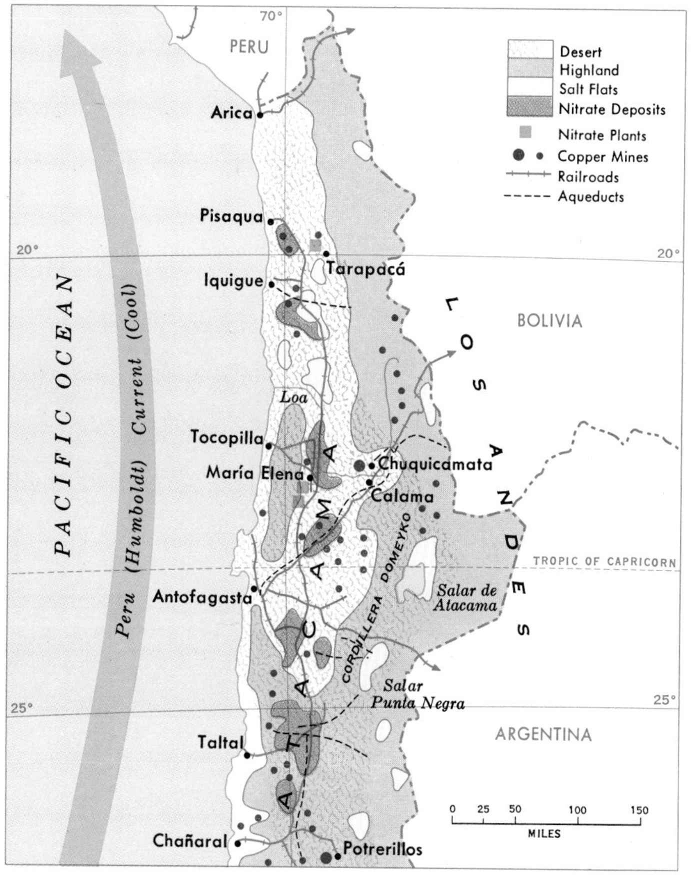

A RICH DESERT IN NORTHERN CHILE

The valuable resources of Chile's Atacama Desert, one of the earth's most barren regions, are shown on the map above. In some parts of this 600-mile-long wasteland, rain has never been recorded. Atacama supplies more than 50 per cent of Chile's low-grade copper and is the sole source of natural sodium nitrate, used in making explosives. Towns in Atacama have to bring in everything: food, building materials and water (moved in via aqueduct).

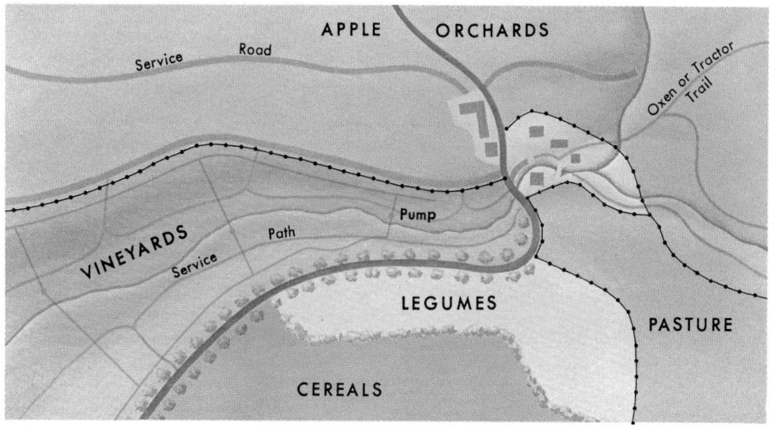

FARMING FOR EXPORT IN CENTRAL CHILE

Though Chile has to import food, it does have farms that grow crops for export and for local markets. A typical commercial farm of the Central Valley is seen here. It usually comprises 600 acres and is smaller than Chile's livestock haciendas farther north. As much as 38 per cent of the farm is in orchards and vineyards, the two major sources of income. Built along a motor highway *(red line)*, the farm also produces for sale locally small crops of beans, peas or lentils and such cereals as wheat, barley and corn.

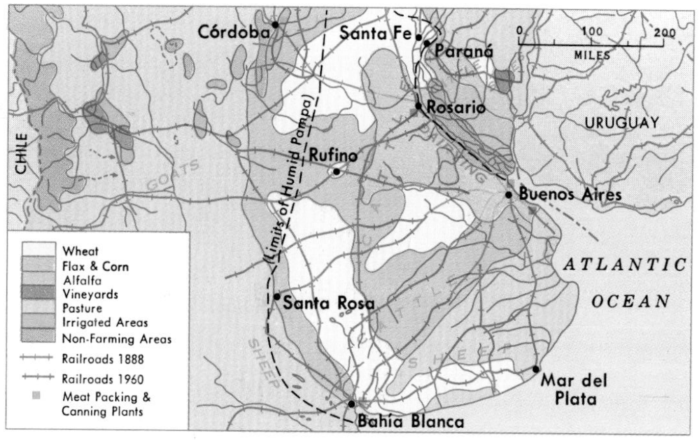

THE BOUNTIFUL PAMPA OF ARGENTINA

The western Pampa of Argentina is too dry for agriculture, but its grasses, as indicated on this map, support sheep and goats. In the wetter eastern half, cattle grow fat on alfalfa *(dark green)*, and farmers raise the world's second largest export crop of corn. The humid Pampa, covering 30,000 square miles, is favored by a long growing season. It has thousands of miles of railroads, more than enough to provide efficient shipping for its food products.

ARGENTINA: The Argentinian Pampa is one of the great food-producing regions of the world, and Argentina is among the leading suppliers of beef, wool, mutton, wheat, corn, hides, wine, cheese and flax. Ringed by the Patagonian Plateau, the Andes and the northern tropical plains, the vast prairie that is the Pampa *(diagram, below left)* was a wasteland until the mid-19th Century. Then the rapid growth of cities all over the world and the subsequent expansion of commercial markets for food spurred the settlement of new arable lands such as the Pampa.

AREA: 1,072,467 sq. mi.
POPULATION: 20,737,000. Largest city and capital: Buenos Aires.
CLIMATE: Hot wet northern plains; temperate central regions with moderate rainfall; dry southern coastal plains; wet and cool in extreme south; highlands variable.
ALTITUDES: Aconcagua, 22,834 ft. (highest).

Despite a lack of coal, iron and water power, Argentina is today the only Latin American country with more people working in factories than on the land. The principal industries are textiles, meat packing, food processing and chemicals—all producing for export. The majority are centered in the area of sprawling Buenos Aires, the largest and most cosmopolitan city in South America.

CHILE: The most elongated country in the world, Chile is 2,600 miles long, but only 221 miles at its widest point. Its length takes it from latitude 17°S., not far from the Equator, to 56°S., about 2,400 miles from the South Pole. The country has great variations in climate, duplicating almost the full gamut of climatic zones of the North American west coast. Northern Chile, like Baja California, is a desert—the Atacama, shown in the diagram at left. South of Concepción, Chile is like the Pacific Northwest, a cool, rainy region where dense forests give way to storm-battered fjords and islands. Central Chile enjoys the warm summers and mild winters of California, and 70 per cent of the population lives here.

AREA: 286,322 sq. mi.
POPULATION: 7,560,000. Capital: Santiago.
CLIMATE: Northern coastal lowlands very hot and dry; Central Valley warm and dry October through April, mild and damp May through September; southern regions wet and cool.
ALTITUDES: Ojos del Salado, 22,590 ft. (highest).

Iron and coal deposits are mined near Concepción. Copper, of which Chile is the world's second largest producer, brings in 78 per cent of the country's export revenue. With 60 per cent of its people now living in cities, Chile must import most of its food.

URUGUAY: Second only to big Argentina in the export of meat and wool in South America, the continent's smallest republic has built a prospering society around the livestock industry. On its superb grazing lands, Uruguay raises more sheep and cattle per person than any other country in the world.

AREA: 72,150 sq. mi.
POPULATION: 2,709,000. Capital: Montevideo.
CLIMATE: Moderate year round. Hot November through April, mild May through October. Moderate, evenly distributed rainfall.
ALTITUDES: Mirador Nacional, 1,644 ft. (highest), 24 miles northwest of Maldonado.

The country did not begin to prosper until England came looking for new sources of raw materials for its textile mills. In the latter part of the 19th Century Great Britain built railroads in Uruguay, protected Uruguayan sovereignty and introduced high-quality cattle and sheep onto its ranges. With high-grade wool and meat production geared to international markets, the Uruguayans now enjoy the second highest per capita income in all of Latin America.

BRAZIL: A WORLD WITHIN A NATION

A MIGHTY WATERCOURSE, the Amazon makes its way for 3,900 miles through forest and jungle from the Andes to the ocean. Fed by hundreds of tributaries, it carries more water than any other river in the world.

A BOTANICAL EXUBERANCE, the Amazon rain forest *(right)* has a sunless floor littered with fungi, molds and ferns. This still-unmapped wilderness owes its growth to heavy rains that fall throughout the year.

A COFFEE PLANTATION *(above)* is planted with garden-patch neatness in Brazil's purple soil region. One tree yields about one pound of beans a year. Half the world's coffee normally comes from Brazil.

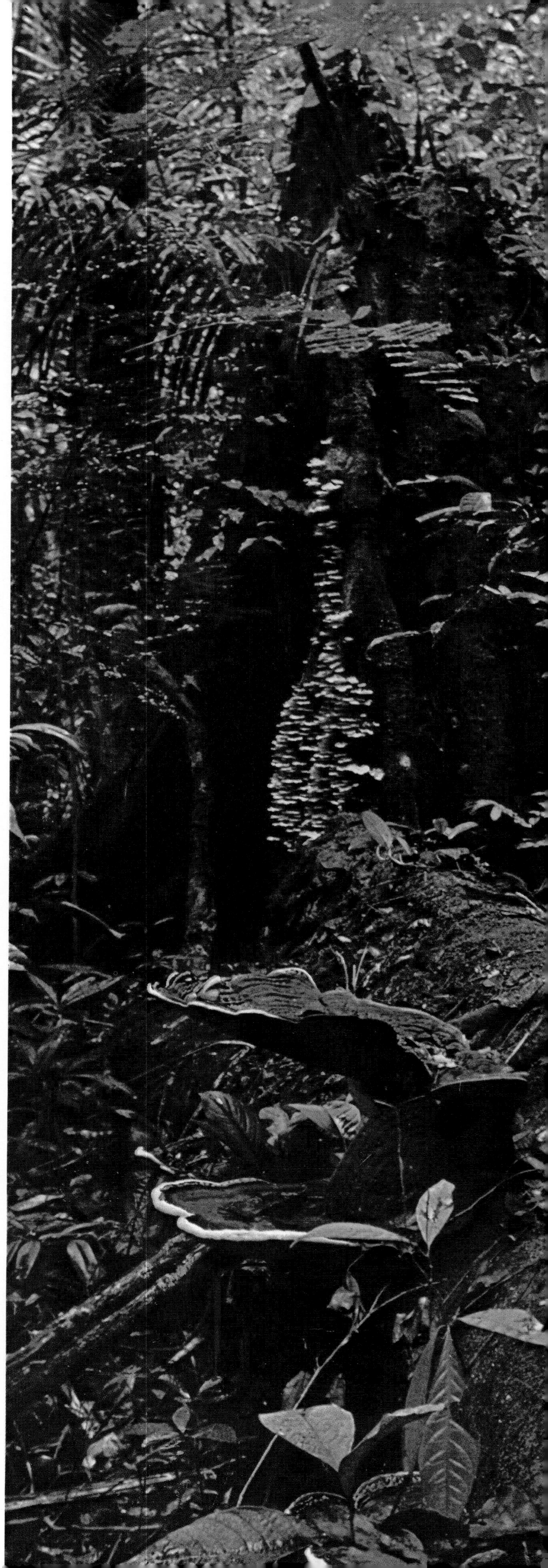

A FOREST HIGHWAY runs due north from Brazil's new capital, Brasília, to the Atlantic port of Belém 1,400 miles away. This road through wilderness may eventually help open up the interior's "forgotten lands."

CM TERRAIN BRAZIL THE GUIANAS
COPYRIGHT BY
RAND MC NALLY & COMPANY
MADE IN U.S.A.
Atlantic Ocean
Caribbean Sea
Equator
GEORGETOWN
PARAMARIBO
CAYENNE
BRITISH GUIANA
SURINAM (NETH. GUIANA)
FRENCH GUIANA
GUIANA HIGHLANDS
VENEZUELA
COLOMBIA
BRAZIL
RIO BRANCO (TER.)
AMAPÁ (TER.)
AMAZONAS
PARÁ
MARANHÃO
CEARÁ
PIAUÍ
PERNAMBUCO
PARAÍBA
ACRE
SELVAS
LEEWARD ISLANDS
WINDWARD ISLANDS
DOMINICAN REP.
HAITI
PUERTO RICO
Caracas
Bogotá
Maracaibo
Barquisimeto
Valencia
Maracay
Cumana
Barcelona
Ciudad Bolívar
Port-of-Spain
San Fernando
Bridgetown
Fort-de-France
Castries
Kingstown
St. George's
Roseau
Pointe-à-Pitre
Basse-Terre
St. John's
San Juan
Ponce
Mayagüez
Ciudad Trujillo
Port-au-Prince
Santa Marta
Cúcuta
Bucaramanga
Tunja
Sogamoso
Villavicencio
Mérida
San Cristóbal
Manaus
Santarém
Belém
Macapá
São Luís
Teresina
Fortaleza
Natal
João Pessoa
Recife
Olinda
Campina Grande
Mossoró
Sobral
Iquitos
Leticia
Benjamin Constant
Boca do Acre
Pôrto Velho
Humaitá
Orinoco
Amazonas
Negro
Tocantins
Xingu
Tapajós
Madeira
Purus
Juruá
Trombetas
Essequibo
Courantyne
Maroni
Caroní
Meta
Apure
Guaviare
Caquetá
Putumayo
Napo
Magdalena
Marajó
Golfo de Venezuela
Golfo Triste
G. de Paria
Boca Grande
Mona Passage
Equator

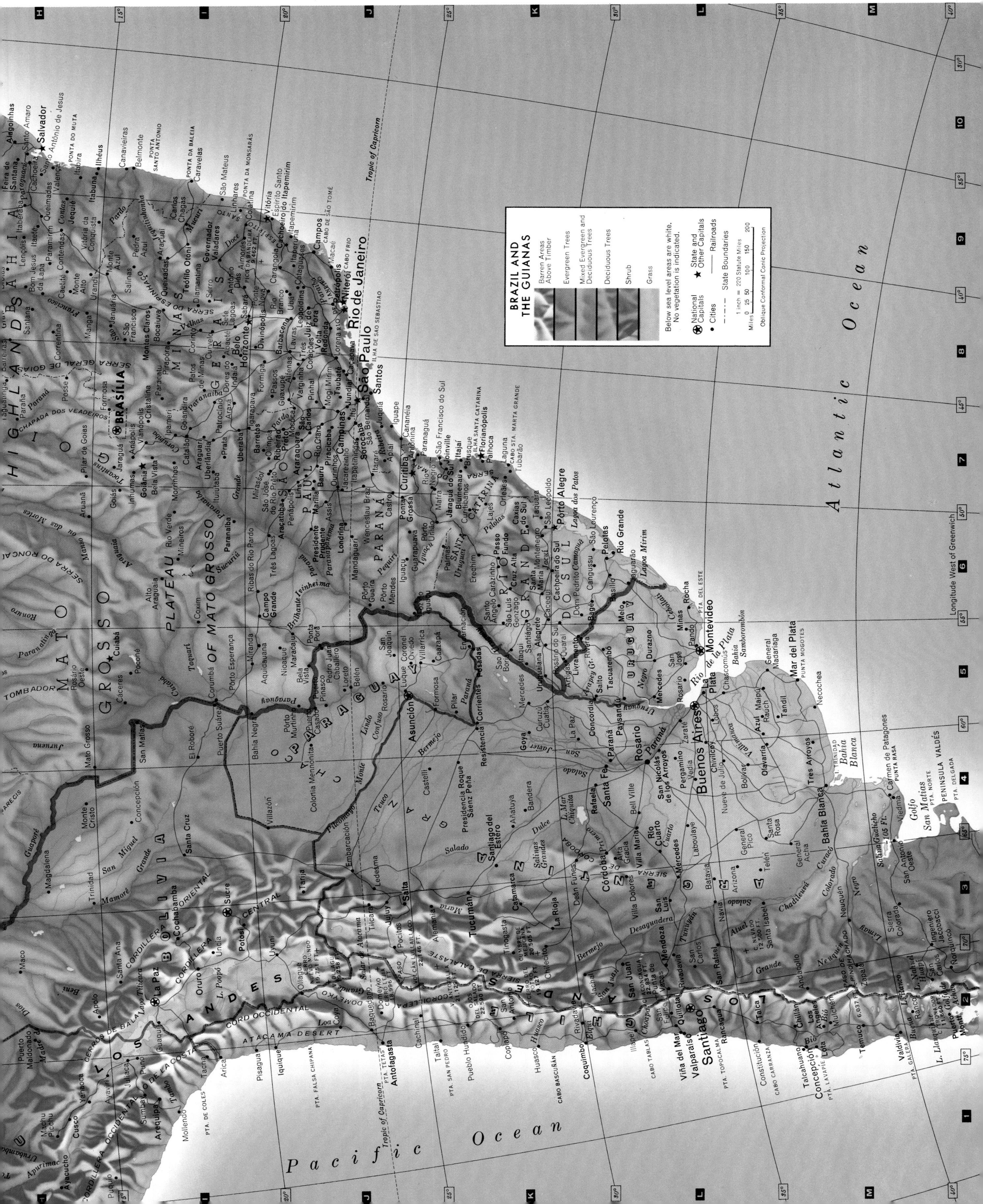
BRAZIL AND THE GUIANAS
Barren Areas Above Timber
Evergreen Trees
Mixed Evergreen and Deciduous Trees
Deciduous Trees
Shrub
Grass
Below sea level areas are white. No vegetation is indicated.
National Capitals
State and Other Capitals
Cities
State Boundaries
Railroads
1 inch = 220 Statute Miles
Miles 0 25 50 100 150 200
Oblique Conformal Conic Projection
Atlantic Ocean
Pacific Ocean
Tropic of Capricorn
Longitude West of Greenwich

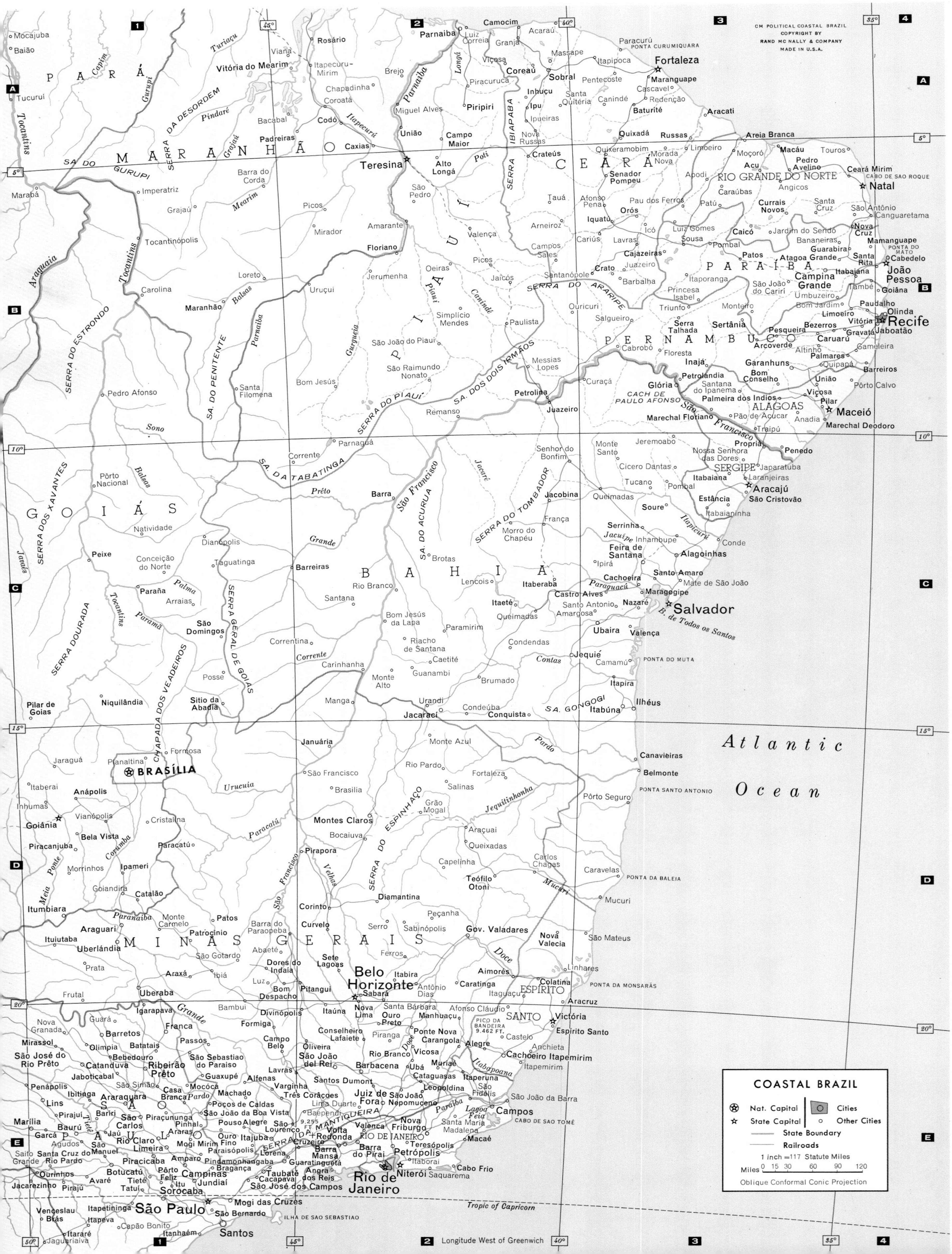
CM POLITICAL COASTAL BRAZIL
COPYRIGHT BY
RAND MC NALLY & COMPANY
MADE IN U.S.A.
COASTAL BRAZIL
Nat. Capital
State Capital
Cities
Other Cities
State Boundary
Railroads
1 inch = 117 Statute Miles
Miles 0 15 30 60 90 120
Oblique Conformal Conic Projection
Longitude West of Greenwich
Atlantic
Ocean
PARÁ
MARANHÃO
CEARÁ
RIO GRANDE DO NORTE
PARAÍBA
PERNAMBUCO
ALAGOAS
SERGIPE
PIAUÍ
BAHIA
GOIÁS
MINAS GERAIS
ESPÍRITO SANTO
SÃO PAULO
RIO DE JANEIRO
BRASÍLIA
Fortaleza
Natal
João Pessoa
Recife
Maceió
Aracajú
Salvador
Teresina
Belo Horizonte
Vitória
Rio de Janeiro
Niterói
São Paulo
Santos
Goiânia
Campina Grande
Tropic of Capricorn
B. de Todos os Santos
São Francisco
PICO DA BANDEIRA 9.462 FT.
CABO DE SAO ROQUE
PONTA DO MUTA
PONTA SANTO ANTONIO
PONTA DA BALEIA
PONTA DA MONSARÁS
CABO DE SAO TOMÉ
ILHA DE SAO SEBASTIAO
SERRA DA MANTIQUEIRA
SERRA DO ESPINHAÇO
SERRA GERAL DE GOIAS
CHAPADA DOS VEADEIROS
SERRA DO ARARIPE
SERRA IBIAPABA

BRAZIL AND THE GUIANAS

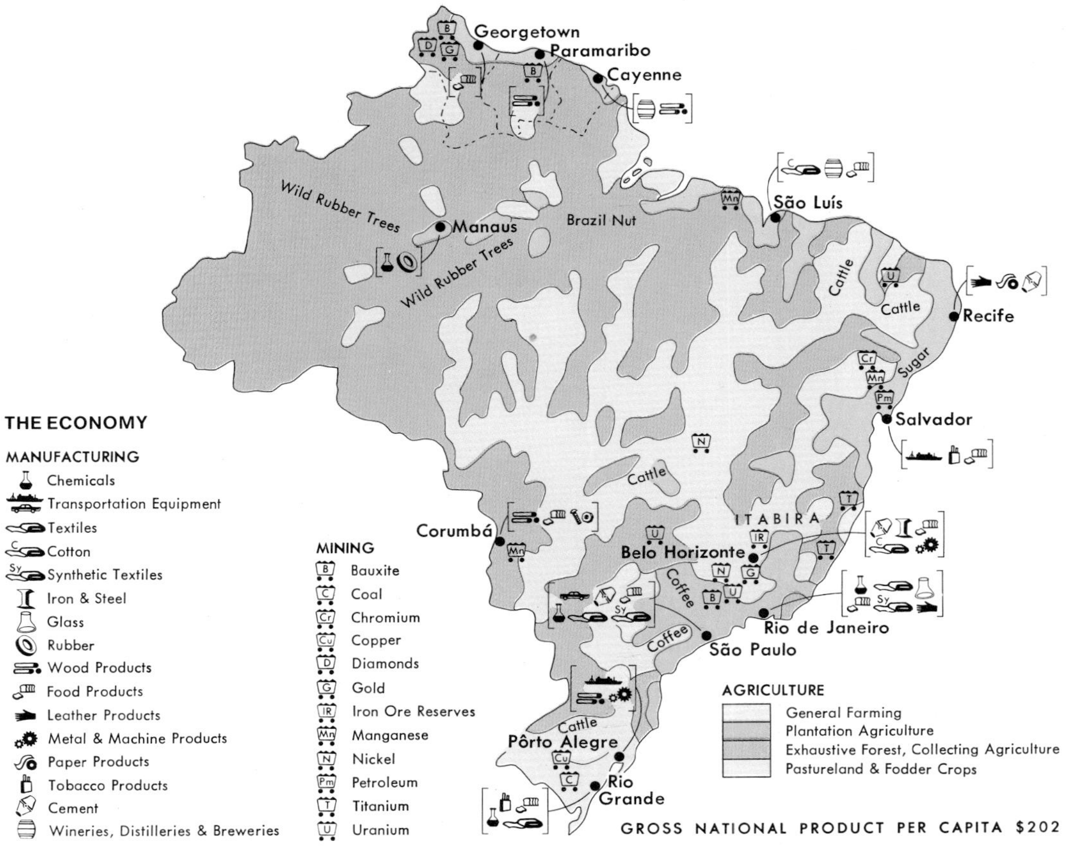

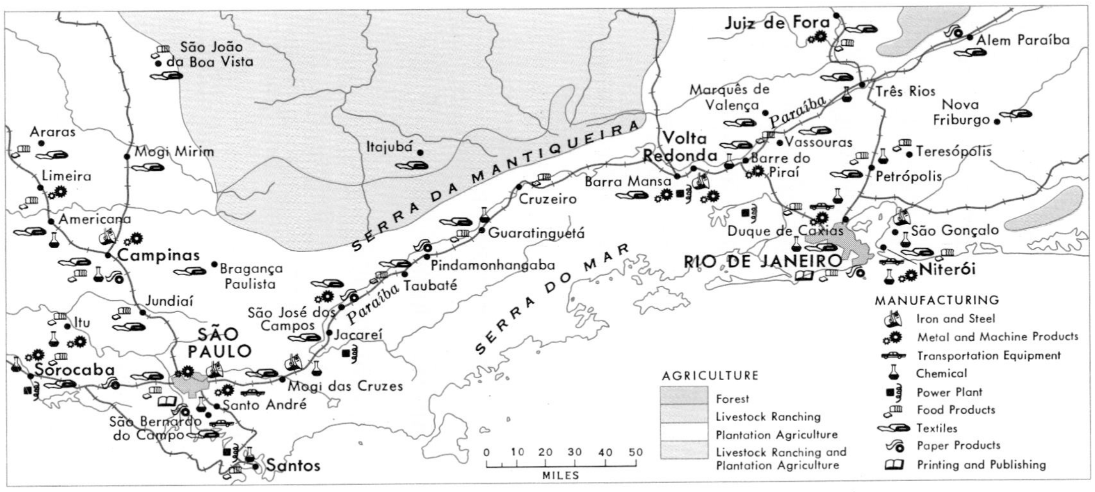

A COMPACT PRODUCTIVE CORE

Brazil's major industries, as well as most of its commercial agriculture, are concentrated in the area shown on this map. The manufacturing establishments of the region include South America's largest steel mill and its biggest automobile factories. Cotton is grown here, and some coffee, sugar cane and rice as well. Lands abandoned by coffee growers are now used as livestock pasture.

BRAZIL: The fifth largest country in the world, this onetime prize of the Portuguese empire is mostly undeveloped land. The dense Amazon rain forest and the highland zone of tropical grass and scrub make up the major part of Brazil's area, but these regions are inhabited by fewer than three persons per square mile. Most Brazilians are clustered in several large urban centers located along the 4,600-mile coast on the Atlantic. And there is at present little prospect of a westward advance of any great dimensions. Much of Brazil, including the savanna of tall, coarse grass surrounding the rain forest, is low-grade agricultural or pastoral land.

Nevertheless, Brazil's interior is not a virgin land. In the past 400 years, thousands of men have been lured inland by hopes of getting rich quick – in gold, sugar, rubber or coffee. Many who went in as prospectors or speculative farmers stayed on to raise cattle and live in the tiny villages that now dot the hinterland.

The hinterland has been opened for the nation's new capital, Brasília, built in the rugged interior of Goiás State, 570 miles from the old and famous capital, Rio de Janeiro. Begun in 1956 and costing many millions of dollars so far, this ambitious city of modern glass buildings and still-empty lots is expected someday to encourage the settlement of the surrounding regions.

AREA:	3,286,344 sq. mi.
POPULATION:	64,837,000. Capital: Brasília.
CLIMATE:	Northern lowlands generally hot, with heavy rainfall; central and northeastern regions drier. Southern regions have moderate rainfall and temperatures.
ALTITUDES:	Pico da Bandeira, 9,462 ft. (highest); Brasília, 3,075 ft.

Coffee – a source of quick, speculative profits with low investments in time and money – has long been an important crop in Brazil *(diagram, below)*. The world's leading producer, Brazil gets over half its export revenues from coffee beans. Investment of income from this source in capital equipment has made the region of São Paulo *(diagram, left)* the largest single industrial center in Latin America. The biggest handicap to a growing industry in Brazil is the scarcity of cheap coal and the remoteness of the most abundant sources of hydroelectric power.

THE GUIANAS: The last colonial holdings in South America – British Guiana, Netherlands Guiana (Surinam) and French Guiana – comprise a very poor region, with one of the highest average annual temperatures in the Western Hemisphere. Lying in an area called the "Heat Equator," the rainy Guianas have an average annual temperature above 80 degrees and no cool season.

British Guiana has an area of 82,978 square miles and a population of 558,000, including a number of descendants of runaway slaves who live in the forests. The Netherlands colony, which has an area of 55,198 square miles and a population of 254,000, is the world's second leading supplier of bauxite, from which aluminum is made. French Guiana, with 35,126 square miles and a population of only 31,000, has only 11 square miles under cultivation.

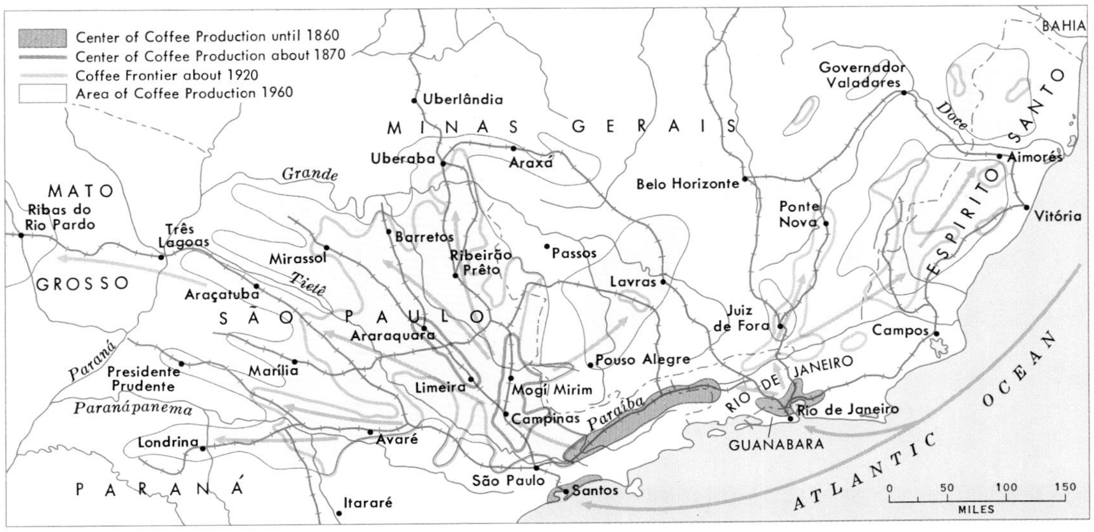

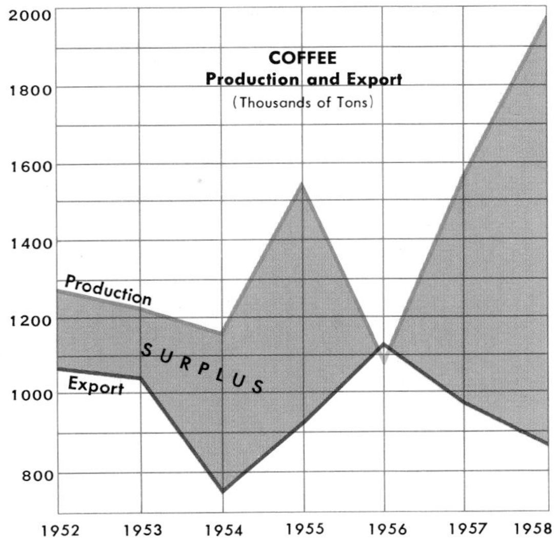

BOOM AND GLUT IN COFFEE, BRAZIL'S MOST VALUABLE CROP

The rapid spread of coffee cultivation in Brazil, as shown in the map above, has in recent years been accompanied by a mounting surplus, indicated in the graph at the right of the map. Introduced to Brazil in 1774, coffee growing began to expand rapidly in the years after 1860. Before World War I, the country provided 75 per cent of the world's coffee. Since World War II, competition from Colombia, Central America and Africa has cut Brazil's share to 50 per cent. Except in years like 1956, when rain and frost ruined the crop, Brazil cannot sell all its coffee without deflating world prices.

NORTH ATLANTIC

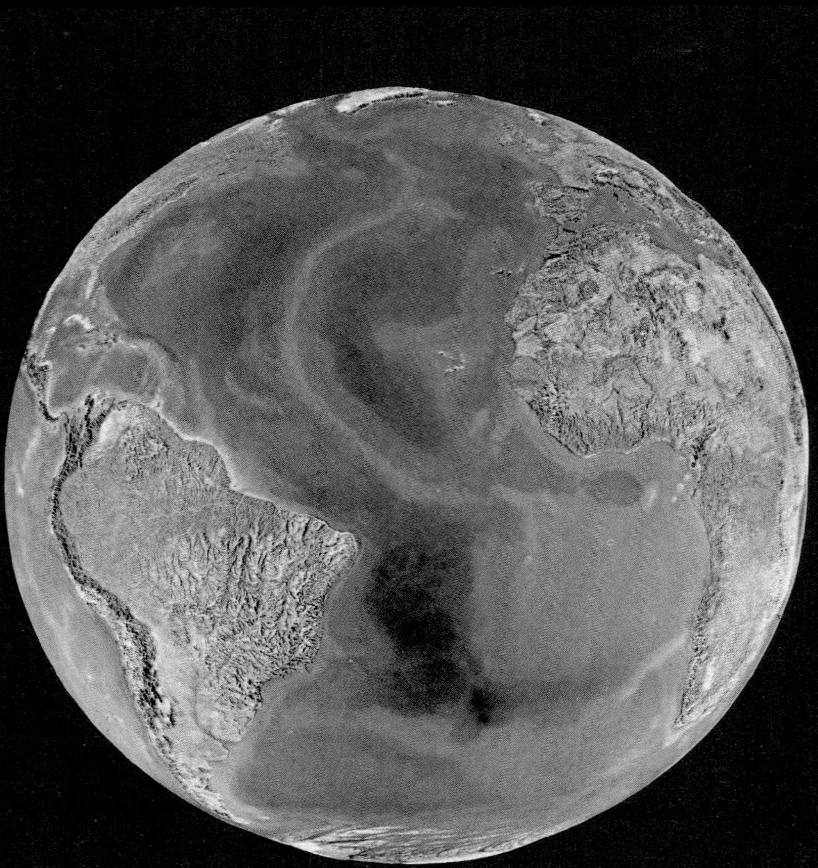

FROM ARCTIC TO ANTARCTIC the Atlantic Ocean stretches like a broad S with ragged edges. In the view above, North and South America are at the left, Europe and Africa at the right.

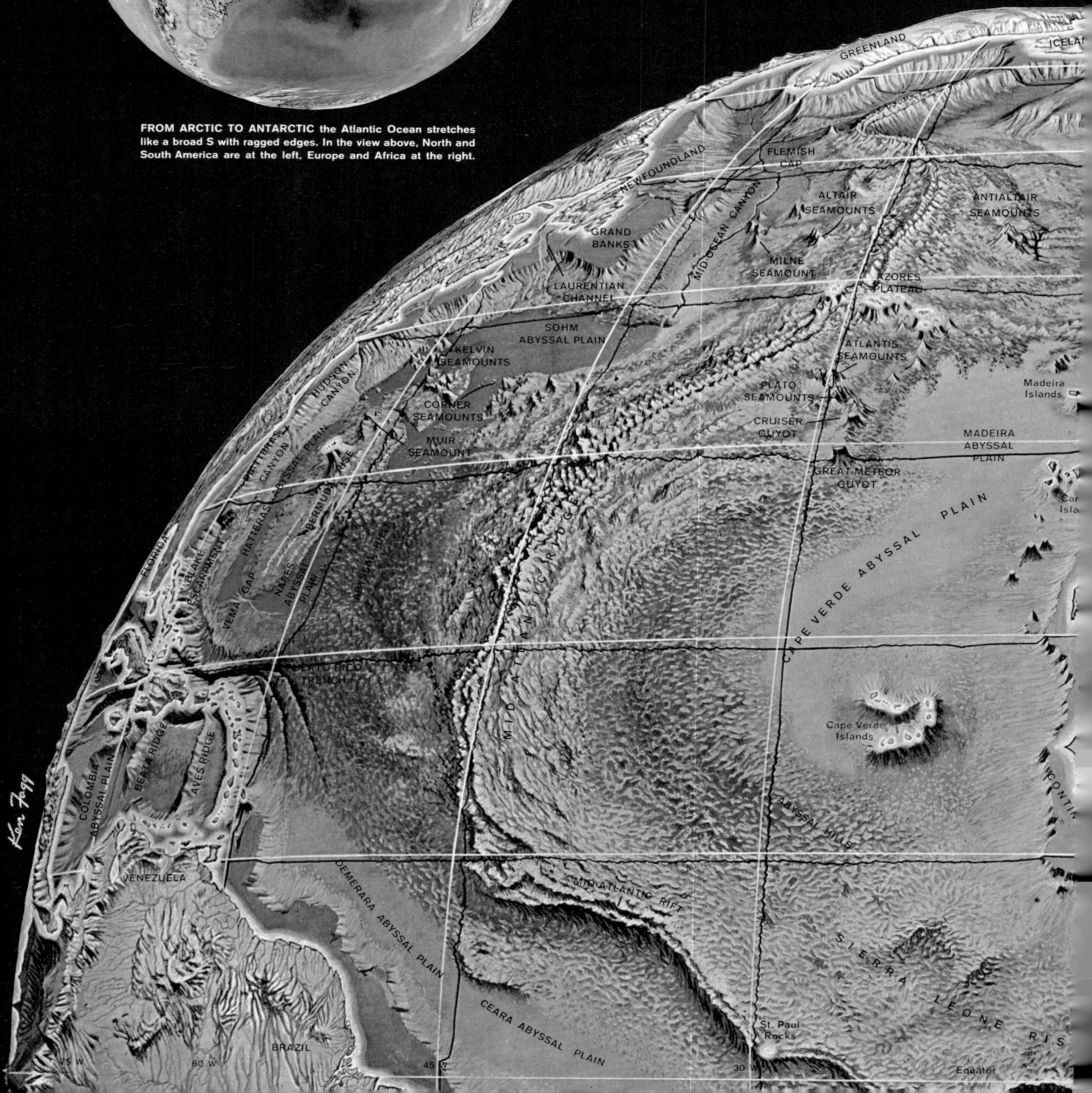
GREENLAND
FLEMISH CAP
NEWFOUNDLAND
ALTAIR SEAMOUNTS
ANTIALTAIR SEAMOUNTS
MID-OCEAN CANYON
GRAND BANKS
MILNE SEAMOUNT
AZORES PLATEAU
LAURENTIAN CHANNEL
SOHM ABYSSAL PLAIN
KELVIN SEAMOUNTS
ATLANTIS SEAMOUNTS
HUDSON CANYON
Madeira Islands
PLATO SEAMOUNTS
CORNER SEAMOUNTS
CRUISER GUYOT
MUIR SEAMOUNT
MADEIRA ABYSSAL PLAIN
HATTERAS CANYON
HATTERAS ABYSSAL PLAIN
BERMUDA RISE
GREAT METEOR GUYOT
CAPE VERDE ABYSSAL PLAIN
FLORIDA
BLAKE ESCARPMENT
VEMA GAP
NARES ABYSSAL PLAIN
ABYSSAL HILLS
MID-ATLANTIC RIDGE
PUERTO RICO TRENCH
Cape Verde Islands
COLOMBIA ABYSSAL PLAIN
BEATA RIDGE
AVES RIDGE
Ken Fagg
ABYSSAL HILLS
VENEZUELA
MID-ATLANTIC RIFT
DEMERARA ABYSSAL PLAIN
SIERRA LEONE
CEARA ABYSSAL PLAIN
St. Paul Rocks
BRAZIL
75 W
60 W
45 W
30 W
Equator

Man had long been able to map in fairly accurate detail the land areas of his globe before he was able to ascertain the configuration of the bottom of the tremendous oceans that occupied 139,434,000 square miles of his world's surfaces. It was not until 1957-1958–the International Geophysical Year–that scientists of many nations worked together as a tremendous team to compile a comprehensive portrait of the oceans' floors. The maps here and on the following pages incorporate their findings.

Below is the North Atlantic as it would look without water. The most startling feature is the Mid-Atlantic Ridge, part of a globe-girdling mountain range two to three miles high. It is split down its crestline by the Mid-Atlantic Rift, a giant fissure two miles deep and up to 30 miles wide. The ridge swings south from Iceland, following the center of the ocean bed. It widens to 1,200 miles, narrows to 300 miles, as though expanding or contracting to match the continental shores it faces. East and west the ridge descends to bumpy, so-called abyssal hills, then to abyssal plains thickly mantled in silt and organic ooze. Seamounts (submerged pinnacles) and guyots (flat-topped seamounts) poke up from the three-mile depths. The level plains give way to the gentle continental rise, then to the steeper continental slope. The slope gives way to the massive, cliff-sided continental shelf. The shelf reaches landward–sometimes for 200 miles–and is often gouged by vast canyons and channels.

Many of the North Atlantic's islands are continental–rising, like Great Britain, from the continental shelf. A few, like the Cape Verde Islands, are oceanic–rising from the ocean floor. The Azores, an oceanic plateau, have hot springs created by the volcanic action that is frequent all along the ridge.

The deepest part of the Atlantic is the 27,510-foot Puerto Rico Trench, seen as a black groove above the West Indies *(at far left).*

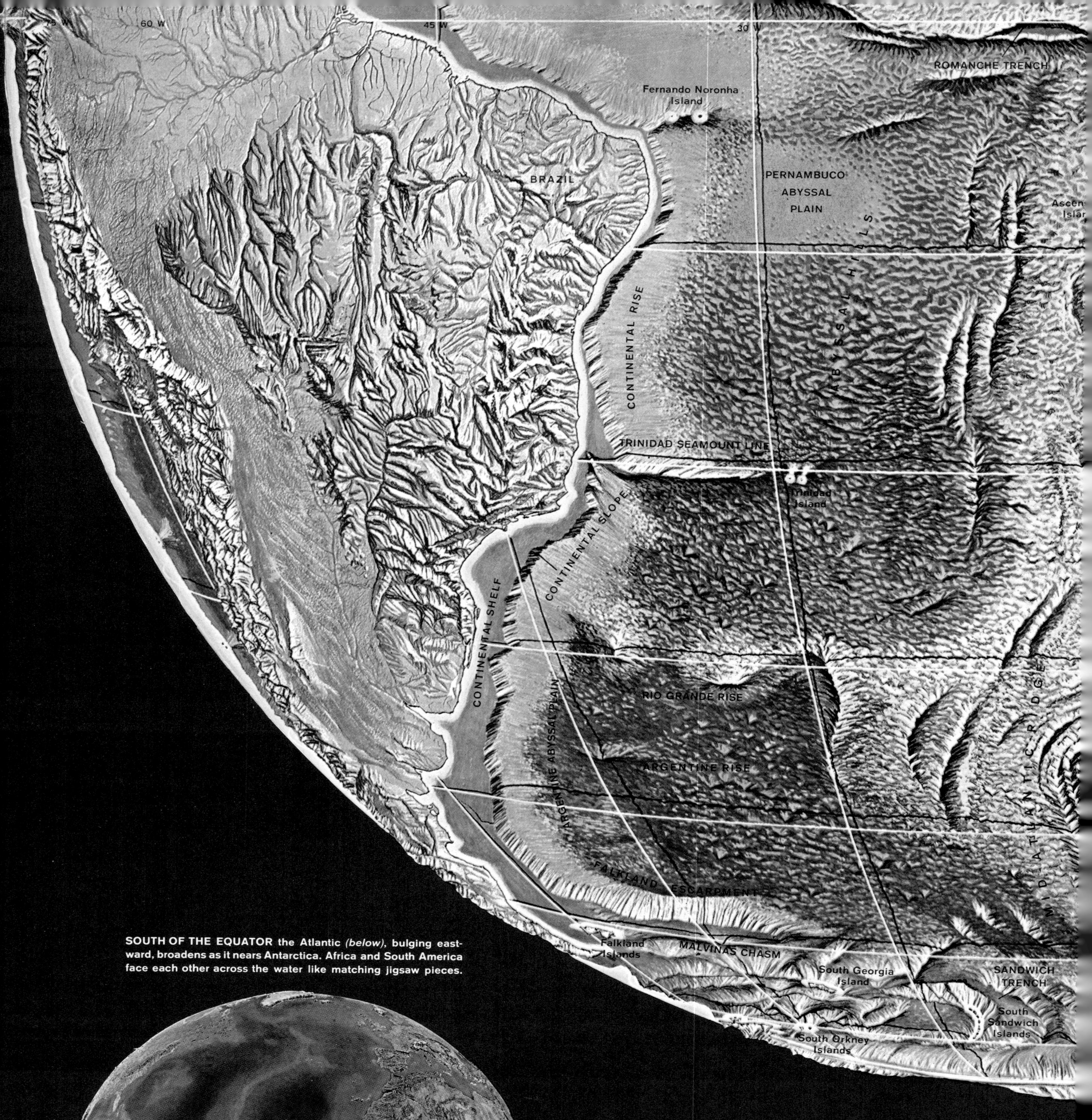
60 W
45 W
30 W
ROMANCHE TRENCH
Fernando Noronha
Island
BRAZIL
PERNAMBUCO
ABYSSAL
PLAIN
CONTINENTAL RISE
TRINIDAD SEAMOUNT LINE
Trinidad
Island
CONTINENTAL SLOPE
CONTINENTAL SHELF
RIO GRANDE RISE
ARGENTINE ABYSSAL PLAIN
ARGENTINE RISE
FALKLAND ESCARPMENT
Falkland
Islands
MALVINAS CHASM
South Georgia
Island
SANDWICH
TRENCH
South
Sandwich
Islands
South Orkney
Islands

SOUTH OF THE EQUATOR the Atlantic *(below)*, bulging eastward, broadens as it nears Antarctica. Africa and South America face each other across the water like matching jigsaw pieces.

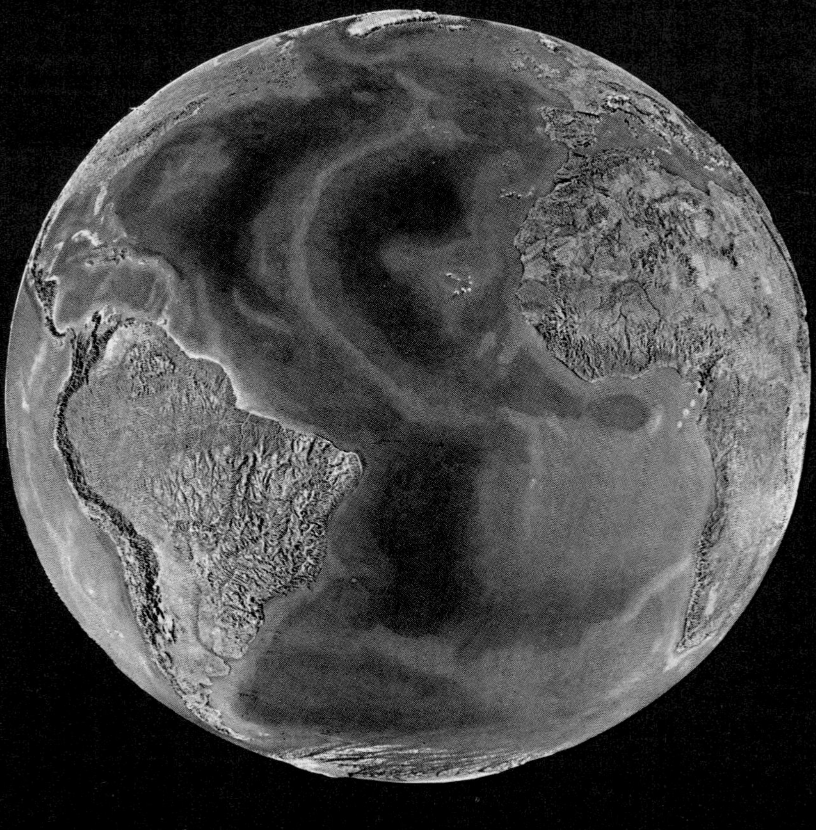

SOUTH ATLANTIC

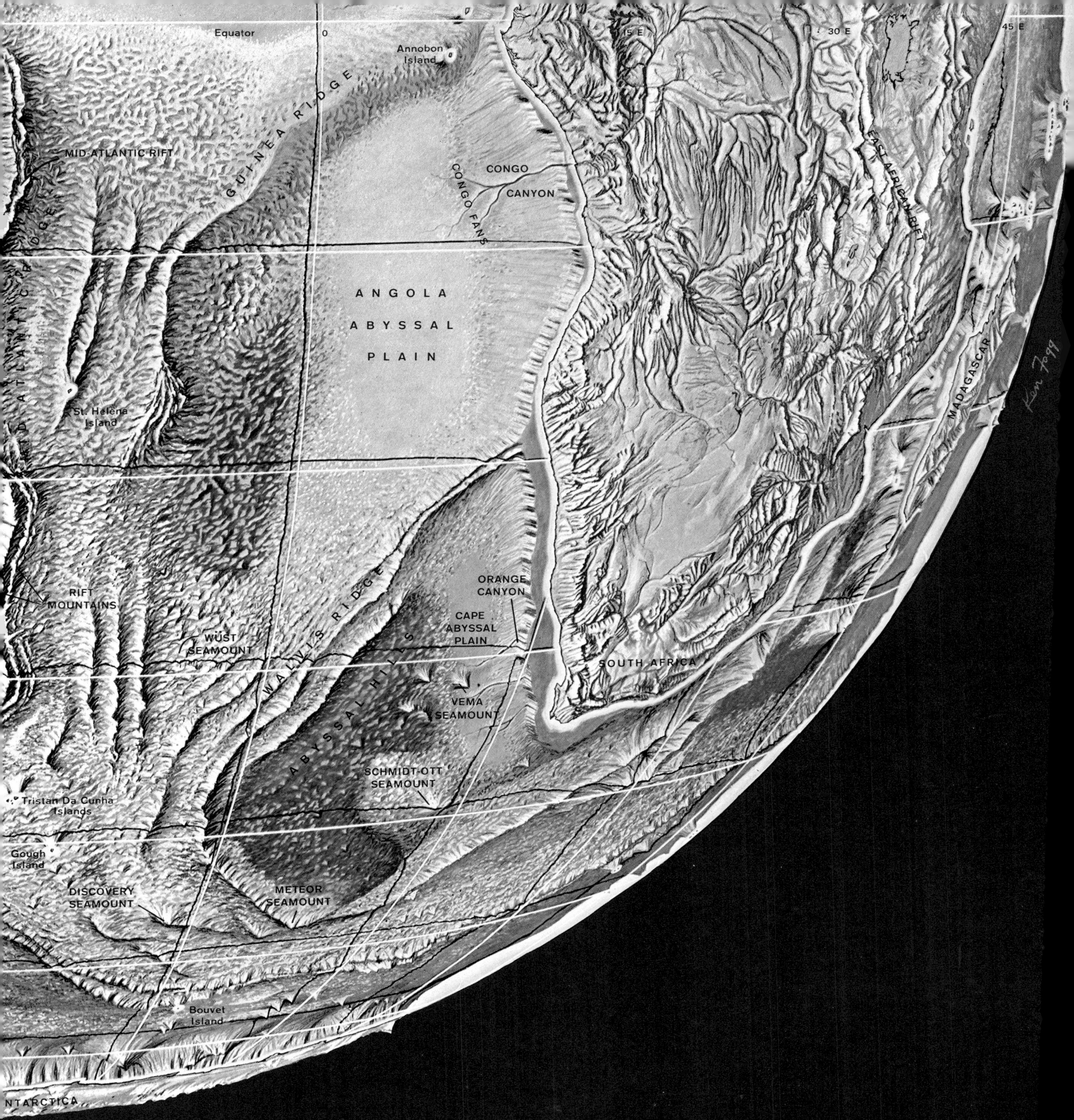
Equator
0
Annobon Island
15 E
30 E
45 E
GUINEA RIDGE
MID-ATLANTIC RIFT
CONGO
CANYON
CONGO FANS
EAST AFRICAN RIFT
ANGOLA
ABYSSAL
PLAIN
MADAGASCAR
St. Helena Island
ORANGE CANYON
CAPE ABYSSAL PLAIN
RIFT MOUNTAINS
WUST SEAMOUNT
WALVIS RIDGE
SOUTH AFRICA
VEMA SEAMOUNT
ABYSSAL HILLS
SCHMIDT-OTT SEAMOUNT
Tristan Da Cunha Islands
Gough Island
DISCOVERY SEAMOUNT
METEOR SEAMOUNT
Bouvet Island
NTARCTICA

Compared to the North Atlantic, the South Atlantic has regular and smoothly indented coastlines. It has few islands, and they are minor ones. The subsea terrain, too, is simpler.

As it crosses the Equator, the prodigious Mid-Atlantic Ridge bends sharply to the east, paralleling the coastal bulges of Africa and South America. Still split by the Mid-Atlantic Rift, the crest of this easterly section of the ridge parts to become the Romanche Trench, a cut 25,748 feet deep. Then the ridge plunges south, broadening as it goes, with lesser mountain ranges rising north and south in its foothills. Extending out of the continental slope off Brazil is the knifelike Trinidad Seamount Line. Further south, the ridge bulks out to fully half the ocean's width. It twists east to skirt the ice-impacted land mass of Antarctica, and then circles the tip of South Africa on its way to the Pacific.

There are two other important ridges in the South Atlantic: the Guinea and the Walvis. The Guinea Ridge rises to the east of Napoleon's island of exile, St. Helena, and flares out toward Africa. The Walvis Ridge extends from the foothills of the Mid-Atlantic Ridge in a northeasterly direction to Africa. There is also Rio Grande Rise, a winglike projection that branches to the west of the Mid-Atlantic Ridge south of the Trinidad Seamount Line.

Between Antarctica and the fringed tip of South America runs a looping, faulted rise that surfaces as several island groups—including, most prominently, the South Sandwich Islands. Outside the island arc lies the Sandwich Trench, 27,114 feet deep, deeper than any in this ocean—except the Puerto Rico Trench in the North Atlantic. This region, heavy in earthquake action, may be a mountain range in the making. The South Atlantic has steeper slopes than the North Atlantic, as in the case of the Falkland Escarpment to the north, and fewer seamounts. Sea avalanches on the rugged slopes dump tons of silt on the abyssal plains; silt-laden currents add more and help form huge deltas

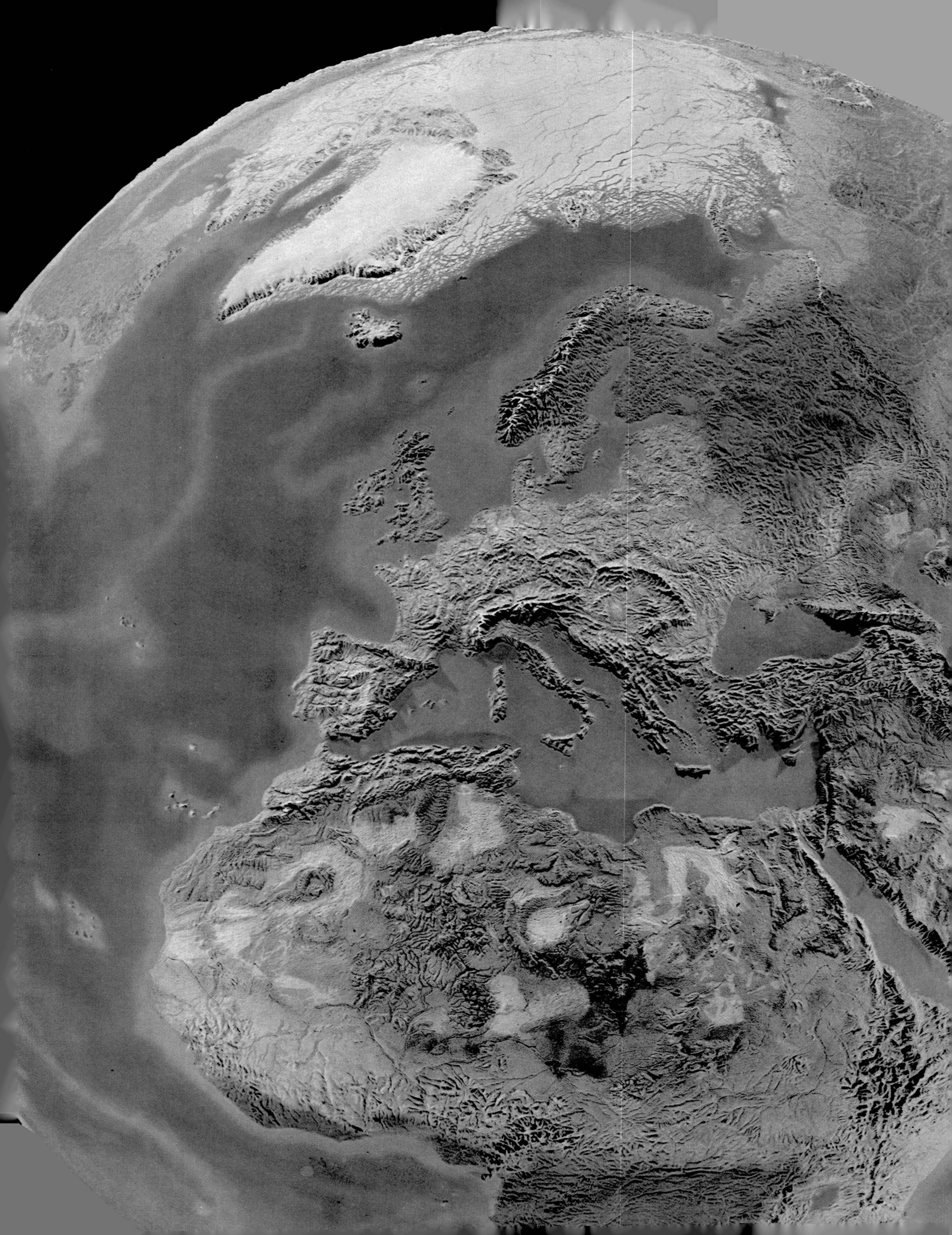

EUROPE

"But how bountiful is nature," exclaimed an early European, Marcus Tullius Cicero. Writing in the First Century B.C., he marveled that man was provided with "such an abundance of various and delicious food; and this varying with the different seasons, so that we may be constantly pleased with change, and satisfied with abundance! How seasonable and useful to man, to beasts, and even to vegetables, are the . . . winds she has bestowed, which moderate intemperate heat, and render navigation more sure and speedy! . . . it is impossible to relate the great utility of rivers, the flux and reflux of the sea, the mountains clothed with grass and trees . . . the earth replete with salutary medicines, or, in short, the innumerable designs of nature necessary for sustenance and the enjoyment of life."

On this continent, still beneficent in the 20th Century A.D., man mastered many of the skills he needed to cope with his environment and to create an enduring civilization. On the fertile rolling hills of Europe's northern plains he learned to rotate crops and to renew the fertility of his soil by the use of fertilizer, and so built a stable, predictable agricultural economy. In areas of North-Central Europe and in Britain he learned how to release the locked energy of coal and to substitute its power for that of his own muscles and those of his animals. In Europe he proved that his planet revolved around the sun. Here he fashioned tremendous and elaborate structures of stone. And, early in his experience in the foothills surrounding the Mediterranean, he evolved two of his most consequential concepts: the Roman ideal of law and the Greek spirit of scientific inquiry.

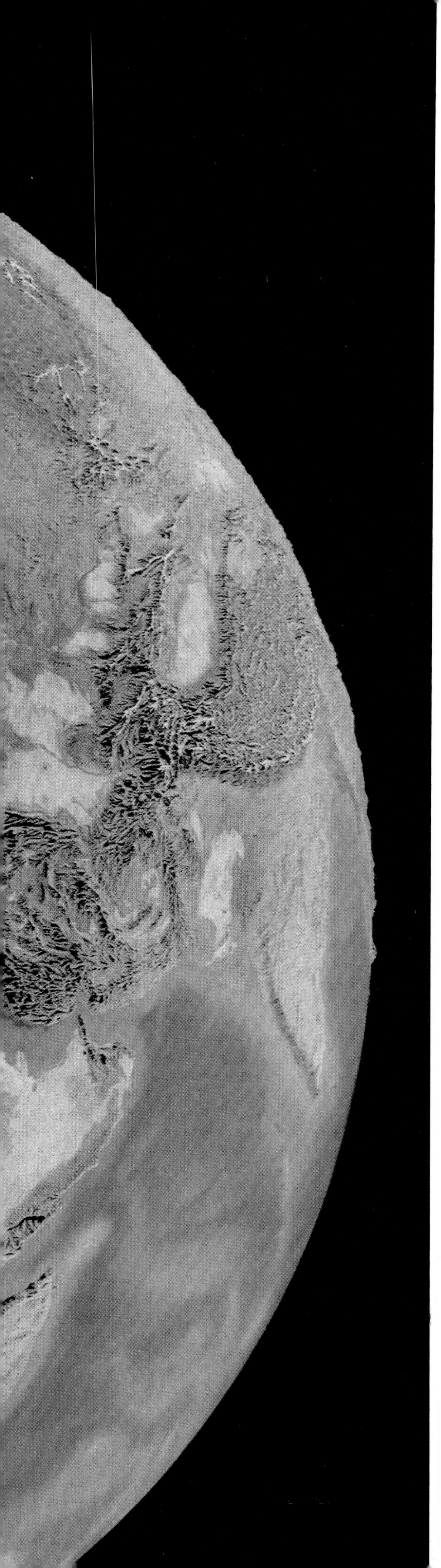

THE CENTRAL CONTINENT of Europe is poised between the vast land mass of Asia at the right and Africa. The dark lushness of much of Europe's vegetation contrasts strongly with the brown, baked deserts of North Africa, at bottom, and the bleak Arctic icecap, at top.

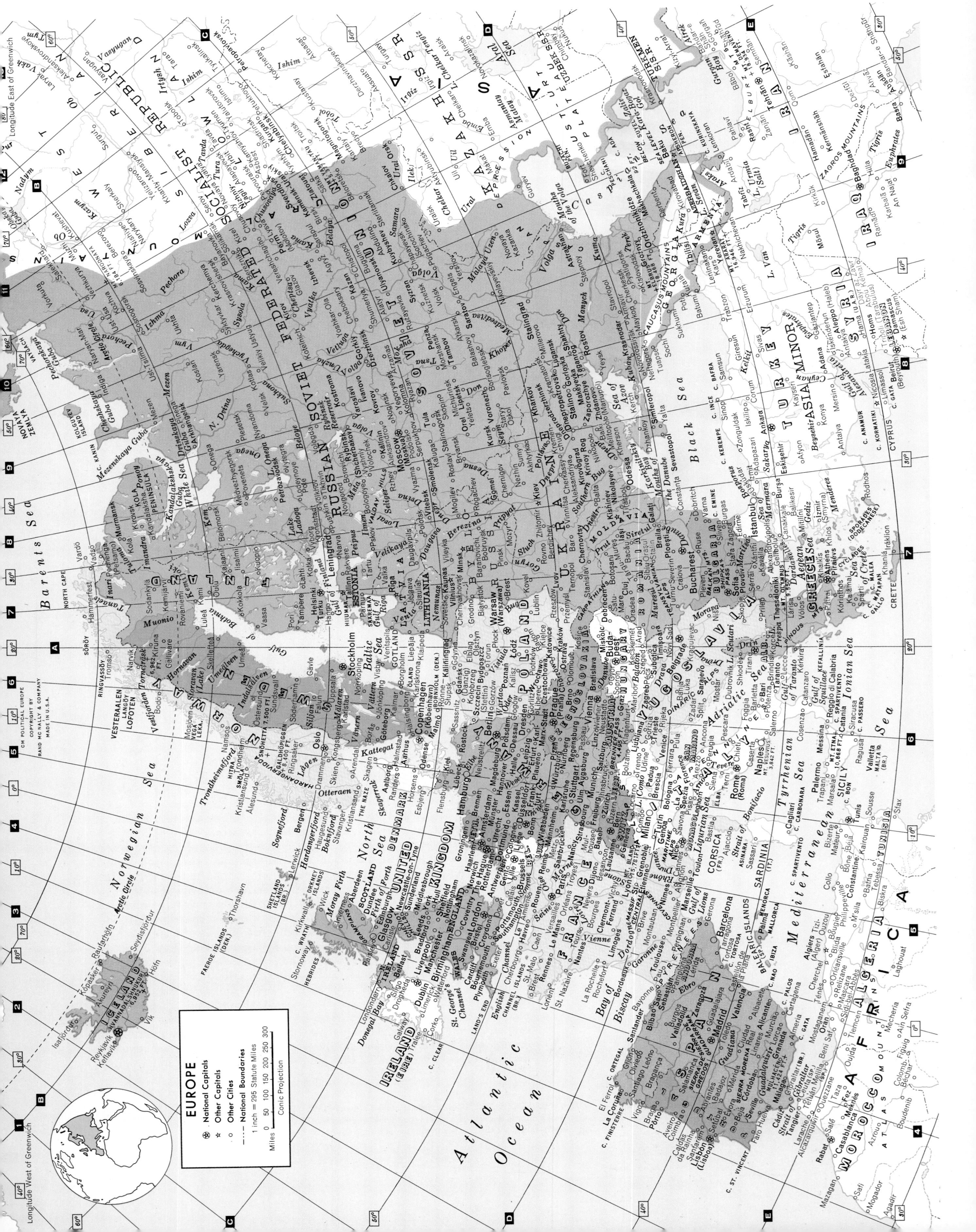
EUROPE
National Capitals
Other Capitals
Other Cities
National Boundaries
1 inch = 295 Statute Miles
Miles 0 50 100 150 200 250 300
Conic Projection
CM POLITICAL EUROPE
COPYRIGHT BY
RAND McNALLY & COMPANY
MADE IN U.S.A.
Longitude West of Greenwich
Longitude East of Greenwich
Atlantic Ocean
Norwegian Sea
Barents Sea
North Sea
Baltic Sea
Black Sea
Mediterranean Sea
Tyrrhenian Sea
Ionian Sea
Adriatic Sea
Aegean Sea
Bay of Biscay
Caspian Sea
Aral Sea
ICELAND
IRELAND (EIRE)
UNITED KINGDOM
FRANCE
SPAIN
PORTUGAL
NORWAY
SWEDEN
FINLAND
DENMARK
POLAND
HUNGARY
ROMANIA
YUGOSLAVIA
BULGARIA
GREECE
ALBANIA
ITALY
TURKEY
SYRIA
IRAQ
IRAN
CYPRUS
ALGERIA
MOROCCO
TUNISIA
AFRICA
ASIA MINOR
UNION OF SOVIET SOCIALIST REPUBLICS
RUSSIAN SOVIET FEDERATED SOCIALIST REPUBLIC
UKRAINE
KAZAKH S.S.R.
WEST SIBERIAN LOWLAND
CAUCASUS MOUNTAINS
ZAGROS MOUNTAINS

EUROPE: A phoenix among continents, Europe has been ravaged time after time during its long history by war and pestilence, and it has always revived, forging ahead to greater achievement. "I take Europe to be worn out," wrote the English author Horace Walpole in 1774. Since that time it has survived the devastation of seven major wars and more than 10 smaller conflicts and revolutions.

Today, short years after a holocaust of global war which killed or maimed millions of Europeans, demolished or heavily damaged thousands of the continent's factories and gutted many of its cities, Europe has staged a remarkable renaissance. Here are some production figures, with Russia excluded: In the 20 years between 1938 (the last full pre-World War II year) and 1958, European hydroelectric and thermal power was increased by more than 200 per cent. In automobile production during the same period, the increase was a little over 300 per cent. And in the production of radios and television sets, the increase approached 800 per cent. The continent's exports now exceed $47 billion a year, a rise of nearly $40 billion from 1938 levels. Imports, which in 1938 were a little over $13 billion, have risen to more than $50 billion. New buildings in the prewar period totaled some 900,000 each year. In recent years the number has reached 1.7 million.

Only part of this vigorous resurgence can be attributed to U.S. aid channeled into the area since the war. Europe has always been a region of great natural advantages, and Europeans are unsurpassed in a great range of skills. For centuries Europe has tilled some of the most productive soils in the world—the glacial deposits of the great northern plains *(map, center below)*, the polder of the lowlands, the loess deposited by the wind in the Paris Basin and the alluvium of Hungary. The mild, moist winds which stream in from the Atlantic *(map, right)* bear ample rainfall to almost all of the region, and they also serve to temper the European winters.

There are few formidable physical barriers to trade in Europe. Except in Russia, no point on the continent is more than 400 miles from a seacoast, and almost every nation is traversed by a major river. Few countries lack direct access to the sea. Even the Alps, mightiest of the continent's mountains, are cut by natural passes. So it developed that centuries before their continent became the trading center of the world, Europeans were exchanging among themselves the minerals of their islands and central hills, the mutton and fruits of the southlands, the grains and fabrics of the north.

AREA: 3,850,000 sq. mi. (including the Soviet Union in Europe).
POPULATION: 573,353,000 (including the Soviet Union in Europe).
ALTITUDES: Mt. Elbrus, Soviet Union, 18,468 ft. (highest);
Mont Blanc, France, 15,781 ft.;
Mt. Vesuvius, Italy, 3,842 ft.

"This noble continent," Winston Churchill observed in 1946, had been reduced to "a vast quivering mass of tormented, hungry, care-worn and bewildered human beings. . . . Yet all the while there is a remedy. . . . We must build a kind of United States of Europe." Nearly a decade passed before any significant progress was made in this direction, but in 1957 Belgium, France, West Germany, Italy, Luxembourg and The Netherlands formed the European Economic Community. The Common Market—also known as the "Inner Six"—is eliminating tariff barriers between its members. In 1959 a trade group was formed by Austria, Denmark, the United Kingdom, Norway, Portugal, Sweden and Switzerland; this is the European Free Trade Association, or the "Outer Seven." The unifying work of these organizations is supplemented by other associations with specific programs. The European Coal and Steel Community facilitates the exchange of materials and workers among France, Belgium, The Netherlands, Germany, Italy and Luxembourg. Euratom seeks to develop atomic energy for industry.

Not all of Europe is prospering equally. Nations plagued by a lack of resources lag in economic as well as social progress. But in much of the old continent, steps toward a unified, progressive community are slowly being taken.

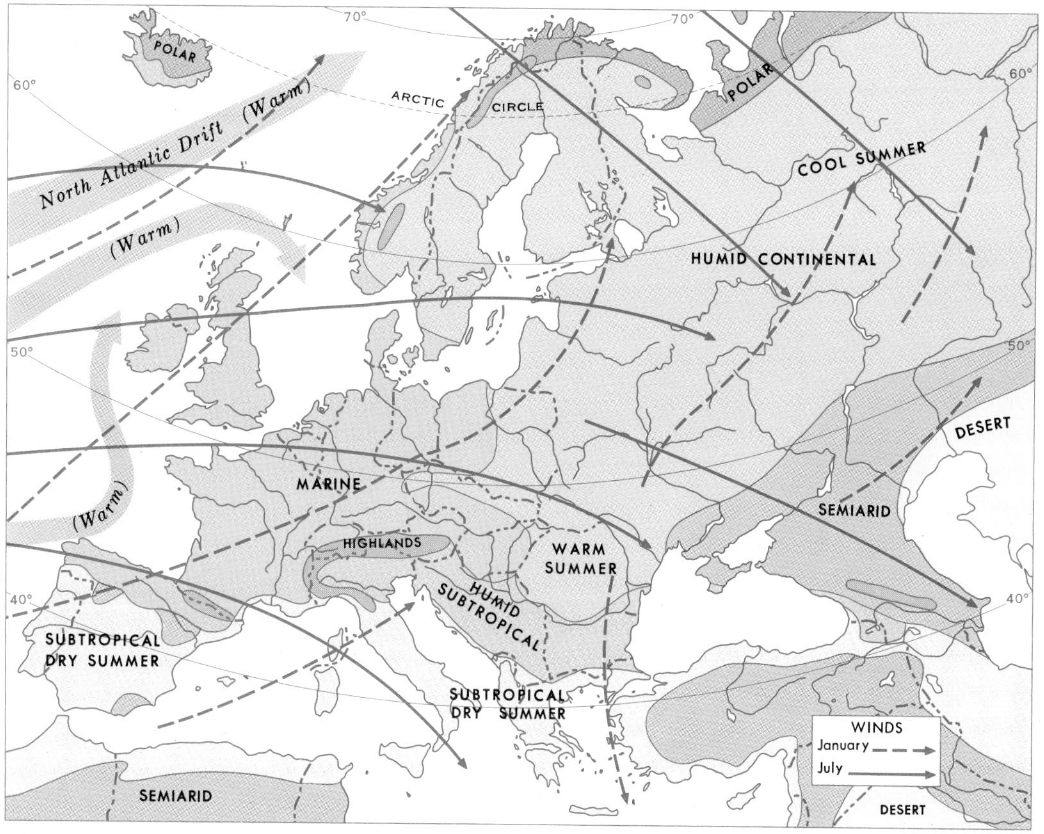

WINDS, CURRENTS AND CLIMATE IN EUROPE

The winds and ocean currents that determine Europe's climate are shown above. Warmed by Atlantic currents, westerly winds carry moisture deep into Western Europe, giving it a mild climate with well-distributed rainfall *(dark green areas)*. Farther east *(blue area)*, the winds lose much of their moisture. Here, away from the ocean's moderating influence, the temperature ranges are greater. Rain is carried to the Mediterranean areas *(light green)* only during the winters; in the dry summers brilliant sunshine prevails.

EURASIA: A GEOGRAPHER'S CONTINENT

Modern geographers prefer to think of Europe and Asia together, as a single land mass forming a single continent they call "Eurasia," shown in the map above. In their view, because no formidable barrier separates the two, Europe is really only an extension (3.8 million square miles) of vast Asia (17 million square miles). According to the traditional concept of Europe as a continent *(shown here in red)*, its eastern boundary is a line that extends north-south along the Urals and east-west along the Caucasus Mountains of Russia.

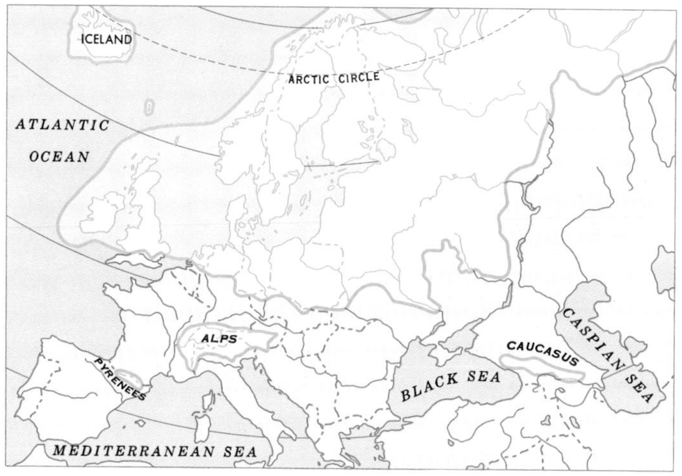

THE GLACIATION OF EUROPE

Glaciers invaded and retreated from Europe 15,000 to 20,000 years ago. The white area on this map shows their farthest penetration to the south. In the British Isles *(left)* they rounded out the floors of valleys and removed the top layers of earth, making minerals more accessible. Soil carried by glaciers from Scandinavia *(top center)* helped make the north European plain one of the world's most productive areas. Glaciers in the Alps *(left center)*, and in the Caucasus *(right)*, remnants of which are still extant, were independent formations.

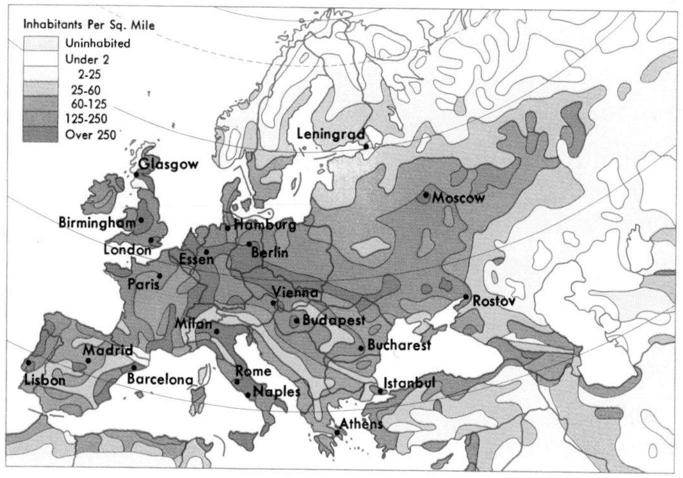

WHERE THE EUROPEANS LIVE AND WORK

The concentrations of European population, shown on this map, are greatest in those areas with an industrial or an advanced agricultural economy *(purple)*. These areas are frequently located on coasts and inland plains. Nearness to water transportation and mineral deposits provides a powerful stimulus to industrial growth. Some examples: Essen in Germany, Birmingham in England, and Milan in Italy. Climate is a factor too: much of the dry Mediterranean and the cold northerly regions of Europe are sparsely populated.

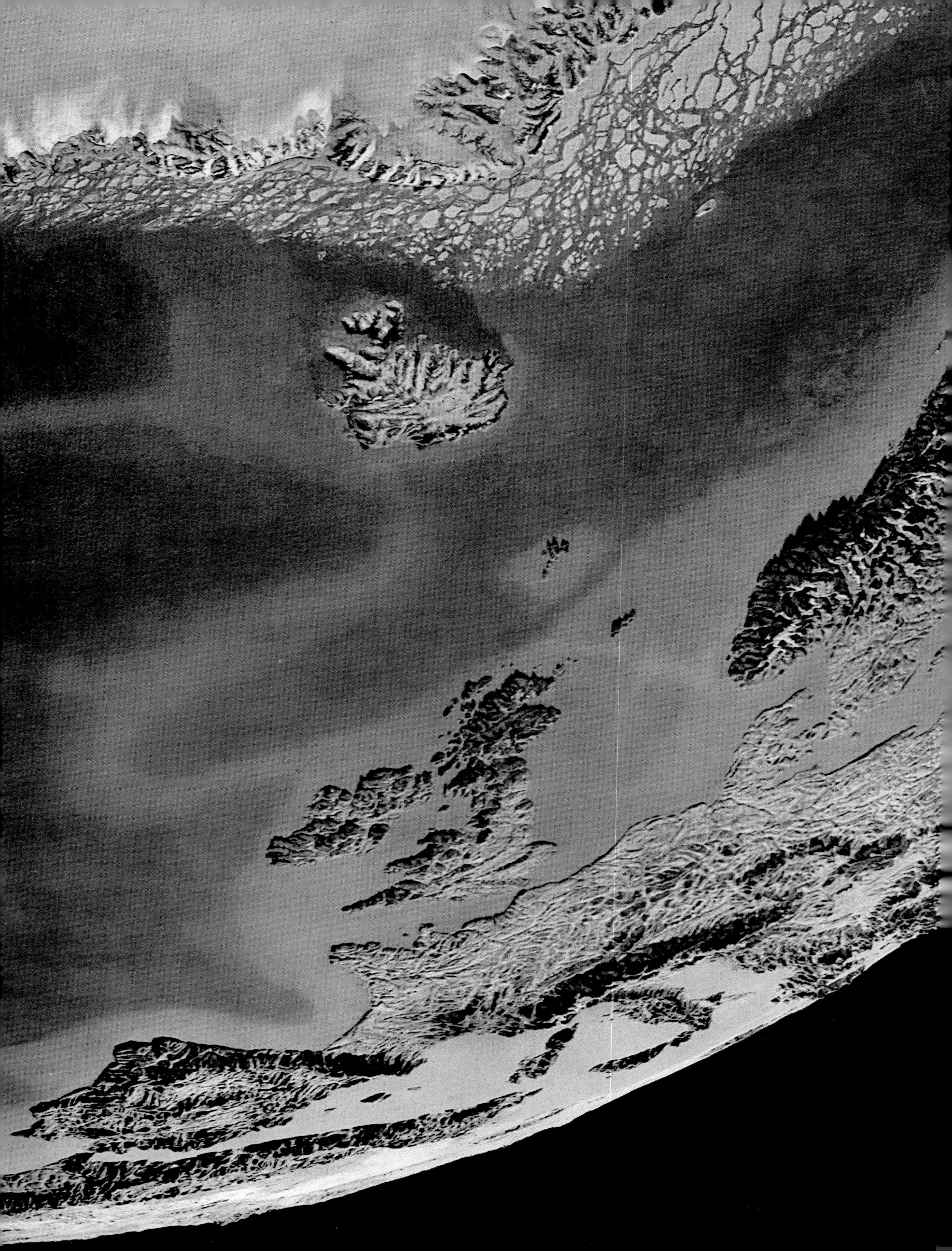

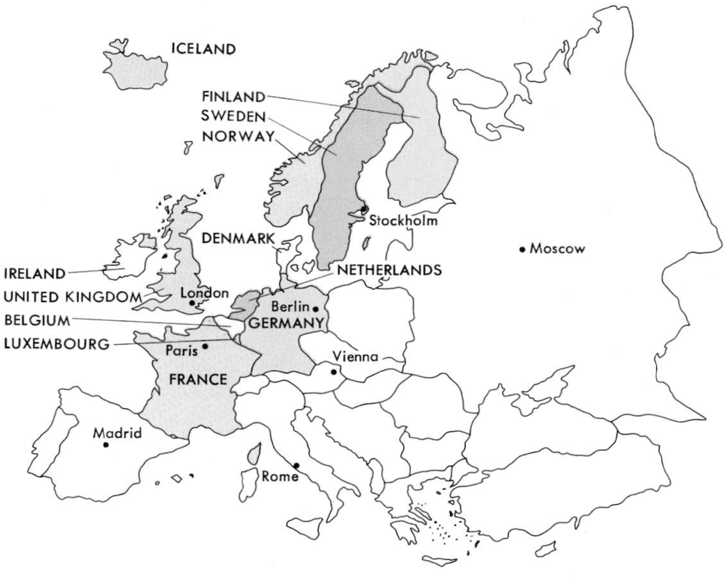

WESTERN EUROPE

The French philosopher Montesquieu called Western Europe "the workshop of the human race." Close to the Atlantic, men found ample rainfall, productive soils and one of the milder climates in the world – moderate in winter, cool in summer. The sea was there for transportation, of goods as well as people, and it became an avenue to the markets of the rest of the world. Few coasts are as favored as Western Europe's with sheltered coves and harbors and broad rivers which lead far inland. And few areas occupy a more central position. The nations of Western Europe lie close to the great land masses of Africa, Asia and North America. Prevailing winds and favorable currents gave their trading ships relatively easy sailing routes. And the aggressive, enterprising spirit of Europeans impelled them to exploit their favorable geographic resources. One of the results was the development of the kind of business sense which has been defined as "an urgent sense of the necessity of the moment."

In the 16th Century, Western Europe was already launched as a manufacturing center. Great Britain was brewing beer, smelting tin, and producing glass, cast iron, gunpowder and textiles; Germany and the Low Countries were manufacturing pewter and silver; France was renowned for its soap and silk industries. In this workshop of the human race erupted the Industrial Revolution, which changed the world forever. It began in Britain in the early 1700s when steam power was first set to work pumping underground water from coal mines. The great breakthrough in the application of man-made power came in 1765 when James Watt perfected a steam engine that could generate energy in the factories, turning the looms and spindles of the burgeoning textile industry and putting sources of mechanical power in any place that man chose. Throughout the continent, all kinds of factories began to operate with steam power. Dredges deepened canals and waterways, steel mills turned out rails on which the newly invented railroads could run swiftly and safely, and eventually steamships were built that carried the products of Western Europe throughout the world with a regularity and efficiency that transformed international patterns of transport and communication. "Never before," observes the geographer Margaret Shackleton, "had the world seen such a brilliant outpouring of inventive genius."

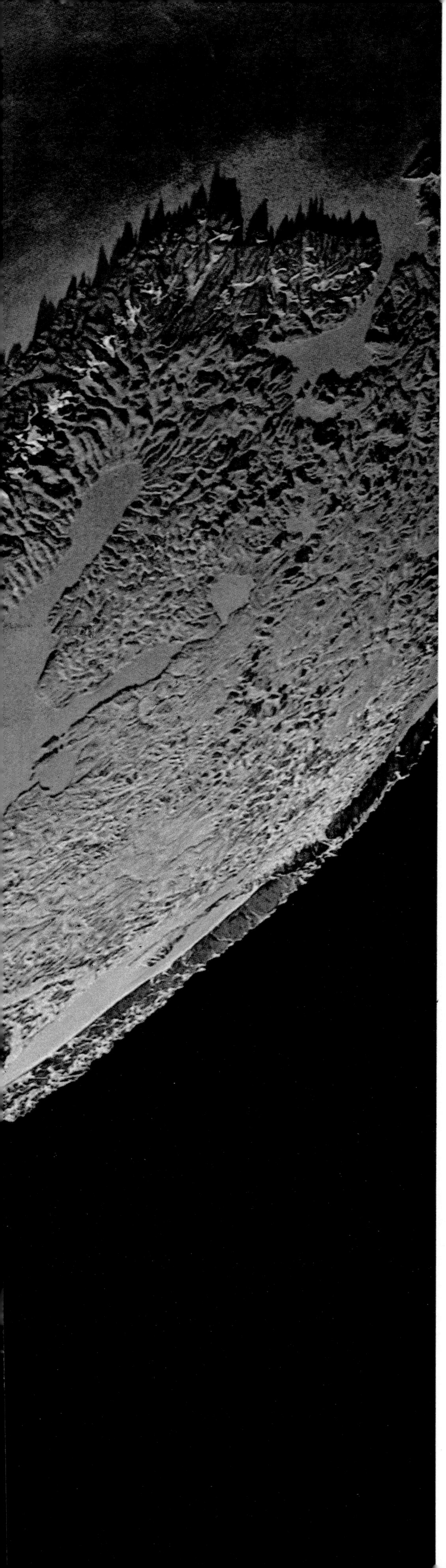

WASHED BY THE NORTH ATLANTIC, Western Europe includes Ireland and the United Kingdom, at center. On the continent, Western Europe begins with France, just below Britain, and extends to Germany's eastern boundary, as shown on the inset map at top of page.

A MARITIME LIFELINE IN THE HEART OF LONDON

RIVER CRAFT AND OCEAN-GOING VESSELS throng the lower Thames of the Port of London. Queen Victoria's Tower Bridge is seen at the left. At the far right are the St. Katharine and the London Western Docks. These are "enclosed docks"; ships must enter and leave them through gates. The practice of enclosing docks was first instituted in London in the early 19th Century as a protection against pilfering. The enclosed docks were constructed on dry land, and water was afterwards brought in from the Thames.

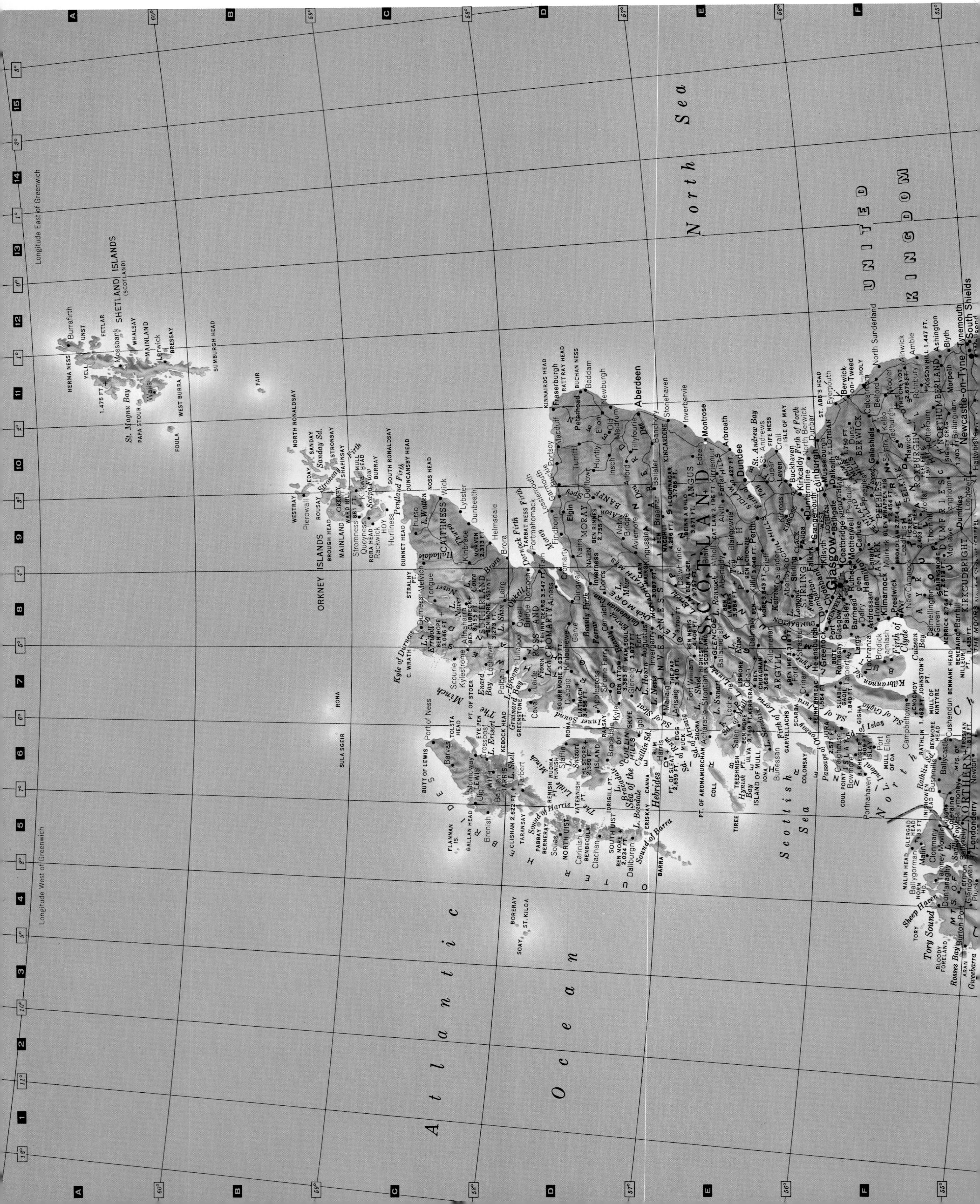
Longitude East of Greenwich
Longitude West of Greenwich
North Sea
Atlantic Ocean
UNITED KINGDOM
SCOTLAND
SHETLAND ISLANDS
(SCOTLAND)
ORKNEY ISLANDS
Scottish Sea
Hebrides
CAITHNESS
SUTHERLAND
ROSS AND CROMARTY
INVERNESS
MORAY
BANFF
ABERDEEN
ANGUS
PERTH
ARGYLL
STIRLING
FIFE
LANARK
AYR
DUMFRIES
KIRKCUDBRIGHT
PEEBLES
SELKIRK
ROXBURGH
BERWICK
NORTHUMBERLAND
Aberdeen
Dundee
Edinburgh
Glasgow
Inverness
Perth
Newcastle-on-Tyne
South Shields
Londonderry
Fair Isle
Foula
Rona
Sula Sgeir
St. Kilda
North Channel
Pentland Firth
Moray Firth
Firth of Forth
Firth of Clyde
Firth of Lorne
The Minch
Little Minch
Sea of the Hebrides
Sound of Harris
Sound of Barra

BRITISH ISLES: UNITED KINGDOM AND IRELAND

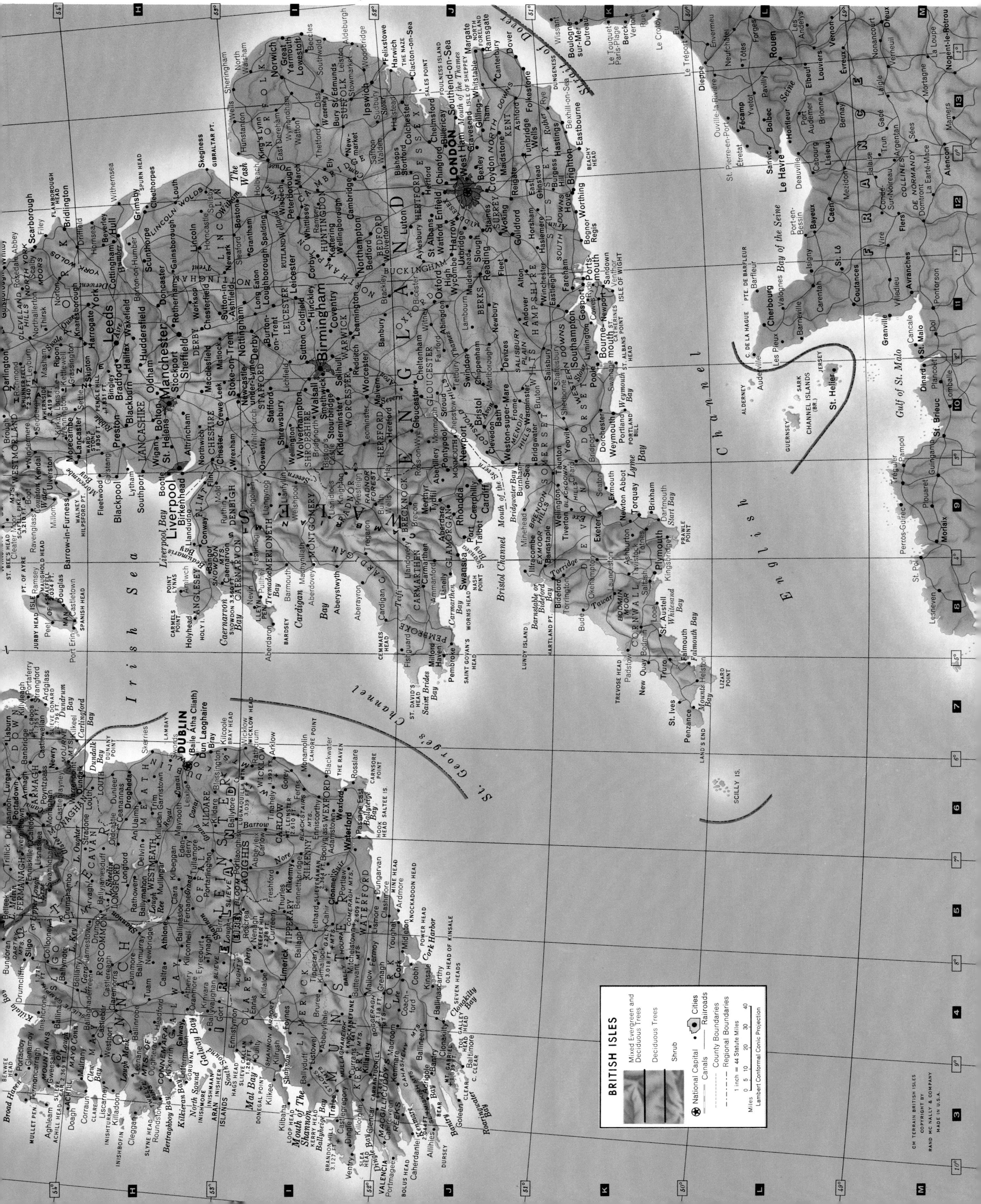
BRITISH ISLES
Mixed Evergreen and Deciduous Trees
Deciduous Trees
Shrub
National Capital
Cities
Canals
Railroads
County Boundaries
Regional Boundaries
1 inch = 44 Statute Miles
Miles 0 5 10 20 30 40
Lambert Conformal Conic Projection
Irish Sea
St. George's Channel
Bristol Channel
English Channel
Strait of Dover
CM TERRAIN BRITISH ISLES
COPYRIGHT BY RAND MC NALLY & COMPANY
MADE IN U.S.A.

THE UNITED KINGDOM: "This fortress built by Nature . . . This blessed plot . . . England, bound in with the triumphant sea." Thus William Shakespeare hailed his country's insularity. The land that once connected Great Britain to the continent was covered by the water of melting glaciers. The channel which resulted *(diagram, opposite page)* performed the function of a protective moat for the island. In secure isolation "this scepter'd isle" could become the fountainhead of the English-speaking world, which covers about one fifth of the land area of the globe. The island is bathed by the North Atlantic Drift, an ocean current with a warm even temperature all year. Southwesterly winds crossing this current give Great Britain a climate much milder than would be expected of its latitude, which is the same as that of Labrador.

Ages ago Great Britain was luxuriant swampland. Its rich vegetation in time became the rich deposits of coal found in Wales, Scotland and England *(diagram, below right)*. The deposits were laid down along inland waters and the coasts, where they were readily accessible. Here cities grew, and during the Industrial Revolution they became coaling stations and manufacturing centers for a great overseas empire. At its height, the British Empire had no rival in area, population, wealth, power or endurance. The empire has now given way to a voluntary association of free nations bound together in the Commonwealth of Nations *(map, at bottom of opposite page)*.

AREA: 94,214 sq. mi.
POPULATION: 58,591,000. Largest city and capital: London.
CLIMATE: Cool summers, mild winters; rainfall in all seasons.
ALTITUDES: Ben Nevis, Scotland, 4,406 ft. (highest); London, 80 ft.

The United Kingdom—comprising Great Britain (England, Scotland and Wales) and Northern Ireland—is the focal point of the Commonwealth. Located on the Great Circle route between Northern Europe and North America, with easy access to the populous markets of both continents, Britain retains a leading position in commerce. It is one of the most highly industrialized countries of the world, outstanding in shipbuilding and in the production of heavy industrial machinery, automobiles, bicycles, aircraft, textiles, clothing, leather goods and chemicals. And the numerous banking firms of "the City" make London an important international financial center.

IRELAND (EIRE): The stormy westerlies that drench the coasts and fields of Ireland throughout the year are largely responsible for the famous emerald green grass of the island. In the 1840s the excessive rains brought rot and ruin to the potato crops, causing a million Irishmen to die of starvation or disease and hundreds of thousands more to emigrate. The disaster revolutionized the farming life of the country. Today dairying, pig raising and horse breeding predominate. There is light industry: glass, brewing, linens, lace and woolens.

AREA: 27,137 sq. mi.
POPULATION: 2,893,000. Largest city and capital: Dublin.
CLIMATE: Cool summers, mild winters; rainfall, all seasons.
ALTITUDES: Carrantuohill, 3,414 ft. (highest); Dublin, 35 ft.

Ireland was governed by British administrators for hundreds of years, and its troubles were usually blamed, whether justly or not, on the lords and landlords of the larger island. It was in the 12th Century that the English King Henry II was granted sovereignty over Ireland by Pope Adrian IV, but English rule did not sit well with the Irish. Conflict between the two peoples grew in the 16th Century when England left the Roman Catholic Church. Economic pressures on the Irish added to the conflict. Finally, after a bitterly fought revolutionary war, the 26 counties of Catholic southern Ireland in 1921 became the Irish Free State and, in 1949, the Republic of Ireland.

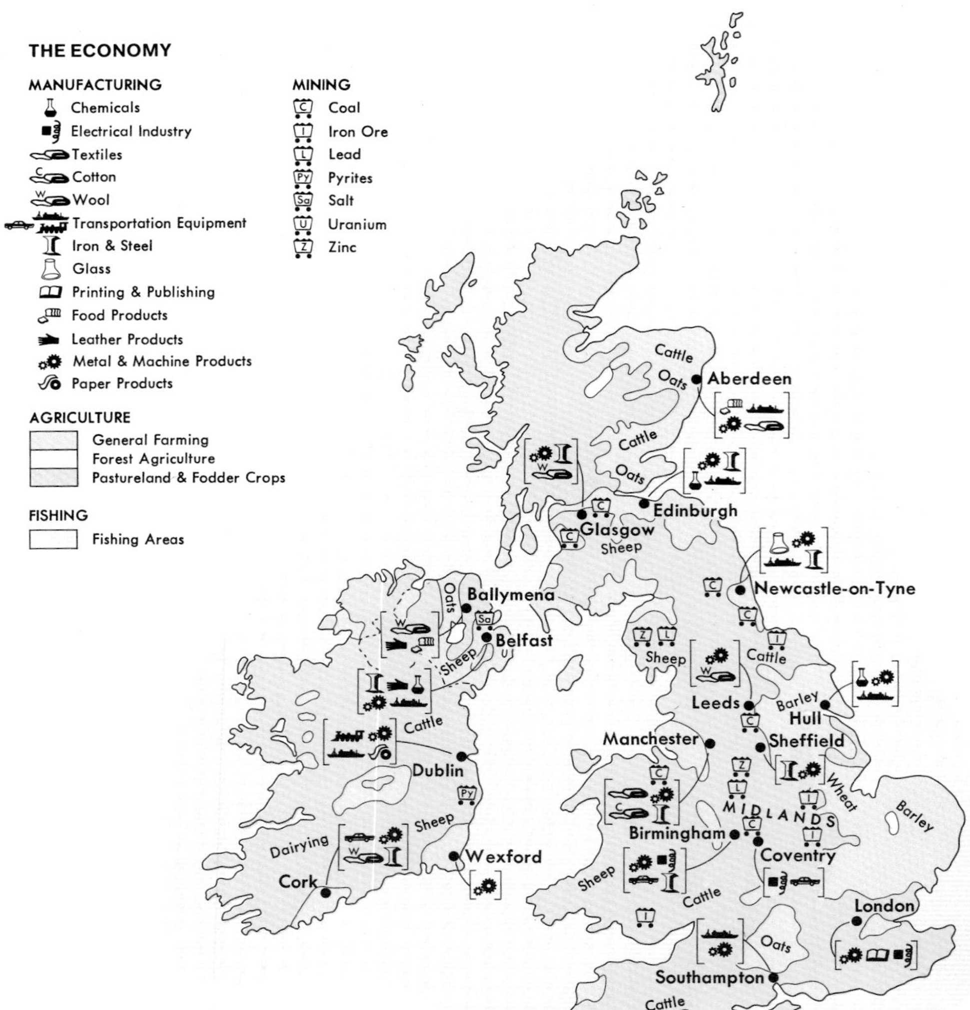

GROSS NATIONAL PRODUCT PER CAPITA
Ireland $571 United Kingdom $1,224

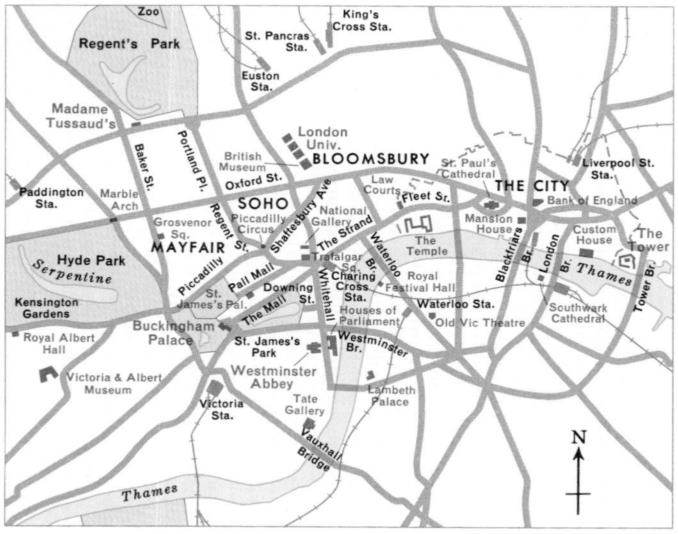

LONDON: CENTER OF THE COMMONWEALTH

The map above shows the center of the world's third largest city (total population, 10,450,000). London's history began in what is called "the City," a single square mile, at right, that has long been a world financial center. Government buildings are in Whitehall. Directly south are the Houses of Parliament and Westminster Abbey, where English monarchs are crowned. At left is Buckingham Palace, principal residence of the ruling sovereign. Other public buildings, squares and landmarks are shown in red.

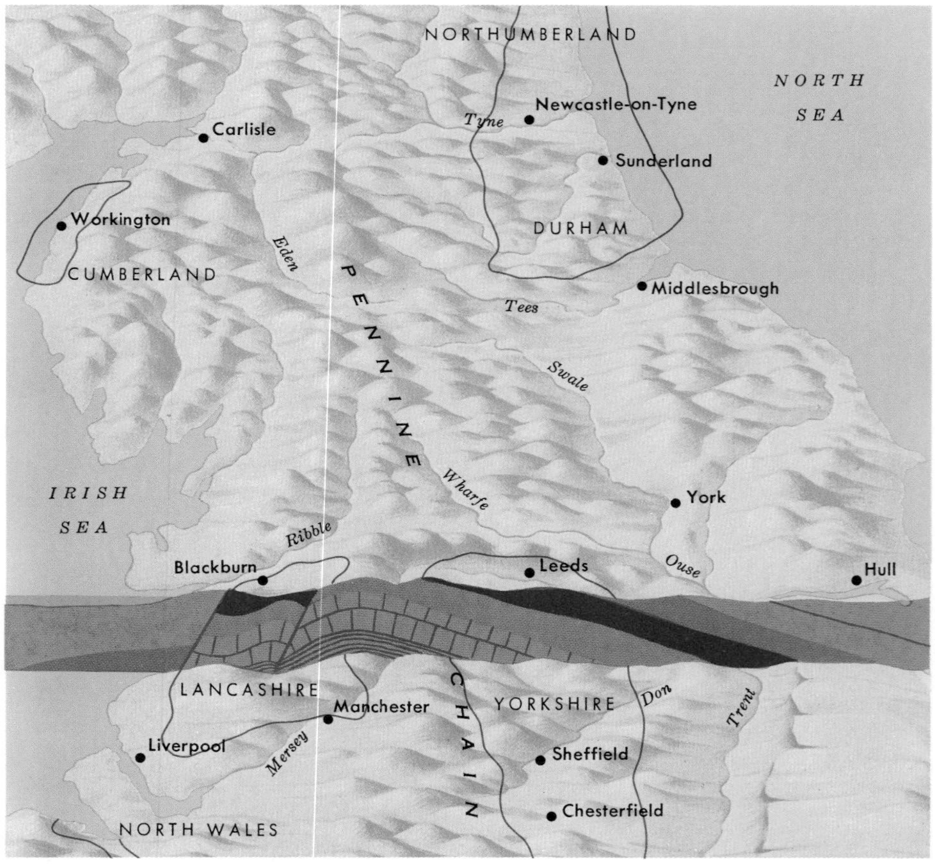

COAL TO FUEL ENGLAND'S FACTORIES

Some of England's major coal deposits, such as those outlined in red on the map above, are easily reached because they lie on coasts or along inland waterways. The deposits were formed here because the region was once swampland which gradually sank, pressing layers of vegetation between layers of rock and soil. Folding and faulting occurred ages afterwards, as seen in the cross section above, and the vegetation slowly turned to coal. Later uplifting caused some coal *(dark brown)* to be pushed up to the surface, while other seams stayed deep underground. Some coal deposits under the sea are mined through tunnels that lead from inland shafts.

BRITISH ISLES: UNITED KINGDOM AND IRELAND

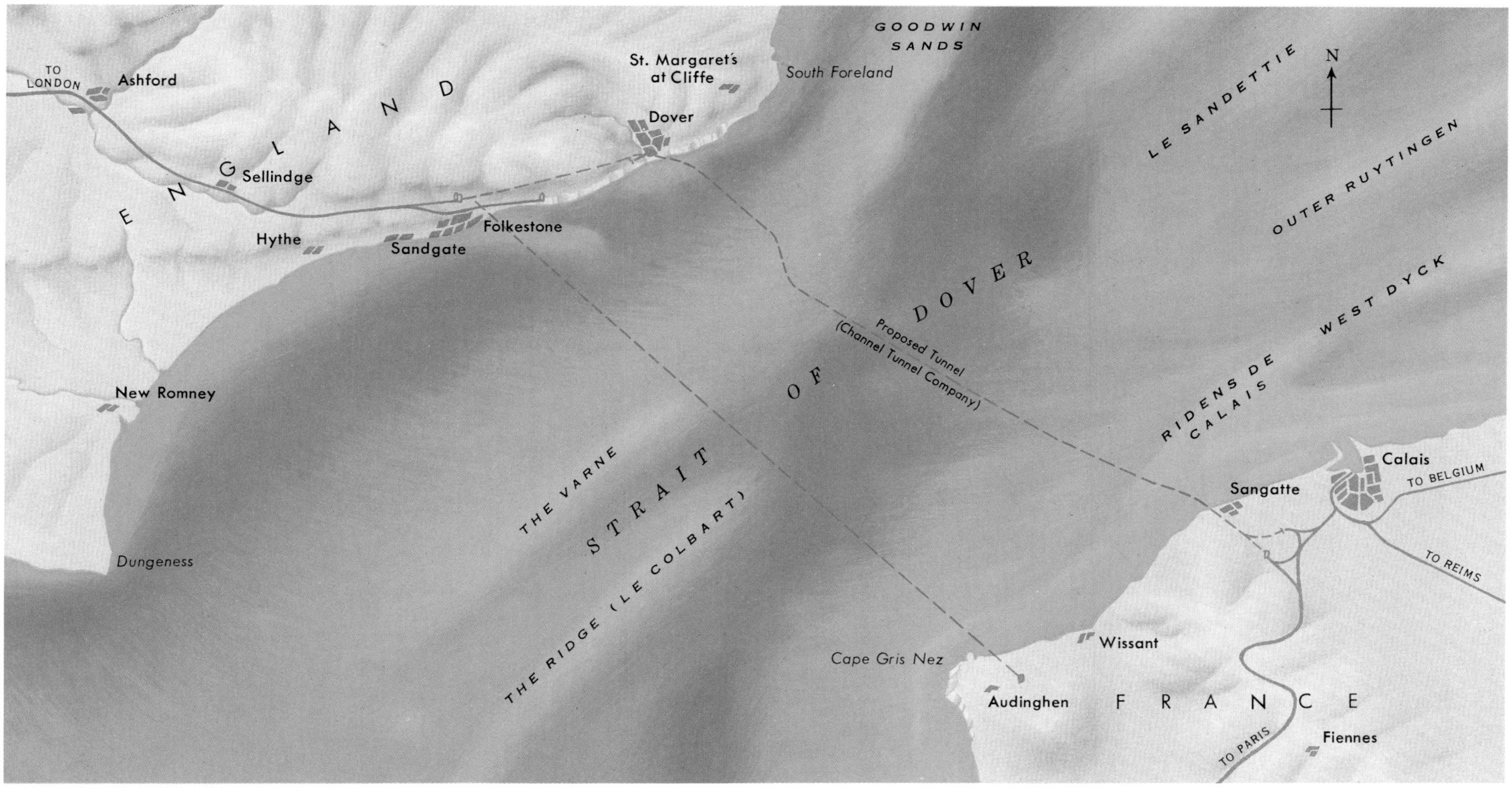

A LINK BETWEEN GREAT BRITAIN AND THE CONTINENT AT THE STRAIT OF DOVER

The 22-mile-wide Strait of Dover has for centuries been part of England's natural fortress. Now, a tunnel under the floor of the channel, shown on the drawing above, has been proposed to link the island with Europe. Such a tunnel has long been an engineering dream. Most plans for digging under the channel floor have proposed a route at the strait's narrowest point *(lower dotted line)*; these have been deemed impracticable because the earth under the channel at this point is too porous for this kind of construction. Alternate plans for a tube built on the channel bottom here are ruled out by high submerged ridges such as The Varne and Le Colbart. The latest proposal for a tunnel, made by French, British and American engineers, is based on a route chosen after a three-year study *(upper dotted line)*. This calls for a railroad tunnel to be bored through a layer of chalk which starts in France. The chalk extends under the channel and crops up again as the White Cliffs of Dover. The tunnel would take five years to build, cost an estimated £130 million and cut the time for surface travel between London and Paris from nearly eight hours to less than four and a half.

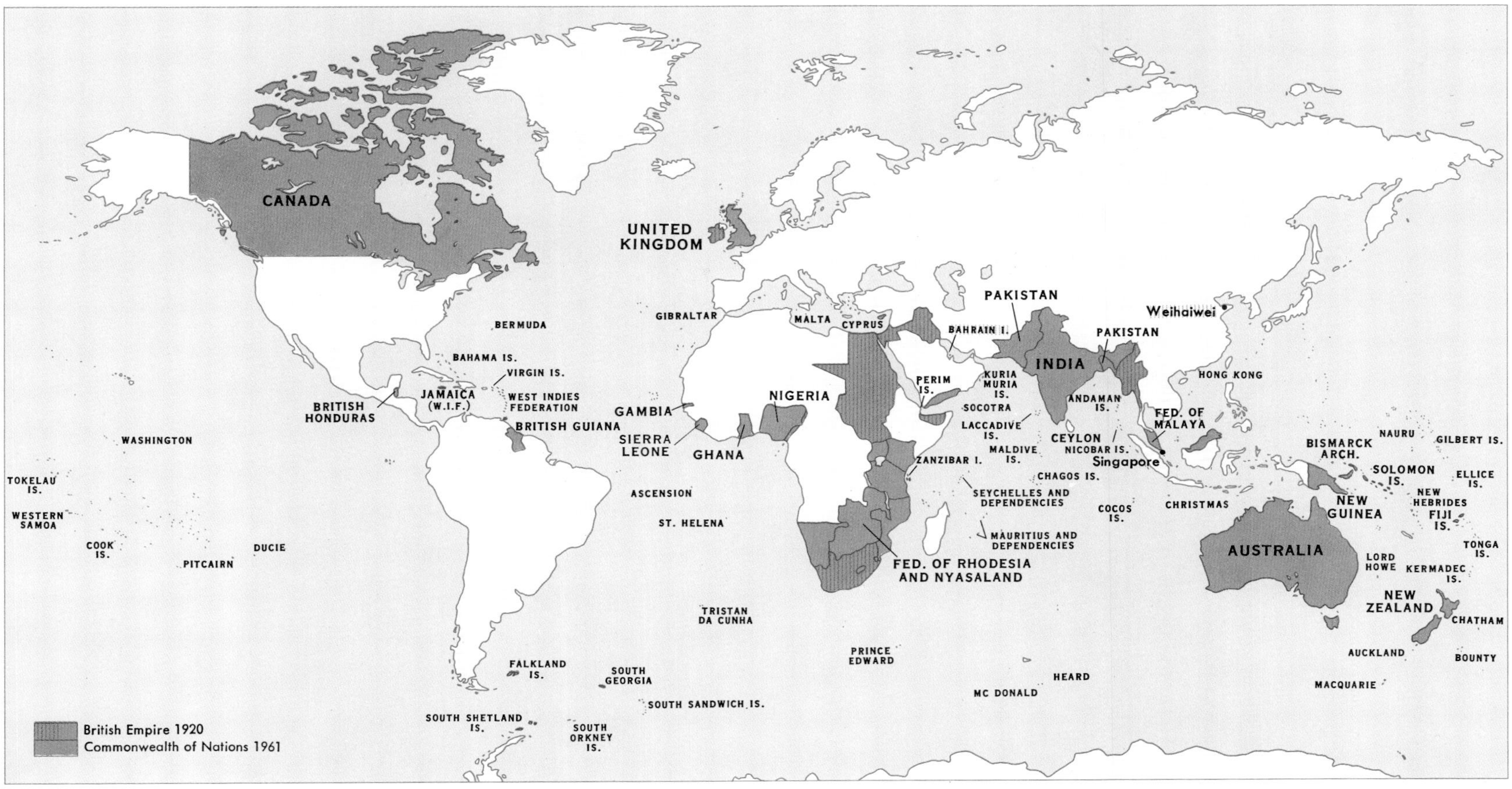

THE BRITISH REALM: FROM COLONIAL EMPIRE TO A COMMONWEALTH OF NATIONS

The map shows the British Empire which existed in 1920 when George V was sovereign and its transformation in the course of four decades into the Commonwealth of Nations under Queen Elizabeth II. Place names on the map indicate current members of the Commonwealth: nations, federations, colonies, protectorates and trusteeships. There are 12 member nations, including the United Kingdom, all of them autonomous. They are joined through a symbolic allegiance to the Crown. They have economic ties through "imperial preference," a series of trade agreements between Commonwealth nations. In addition, British overseas investment provides much of the development capital of Commonwealth nations. All members of the Commonwealth except Canada belong to the sterling area system, which provides them with international banking services including insurance, foreign exchange, shipping and credits. In addition to the nations of the Commonwealth, there are other political units with varying degrees of autonomy, governed partially or completely by the United Kingdom. The shaded areas are former British lands no longer under British influence.

PAST AND PRESENT GLORIES OF FRANCE

A FORTIFIED ABBEY built on a rock off the Normandy coast, Mont-Saint-Michel is shown at low tide *(opposite)*. At the flood, tides here advance at up to eight miles per hour, very quickly turning the abbey into an island connected to the mainland only by causeway.

A LAVENDER-LADEN FIELD, ruffled by a Mediterranean breeze, blooms near the town of Grasse, major supplier of flower essences to the French perfume industry. On these sun-baked hills behind the Riviera, growers also produce roses, jasmine and orange blossoms.

FRANCE
Barren Areas Above Timber
Evergreen Trees
Mixed Evergreen and Deciduous Trees
Deciduous Trees
Grass
Below sea level areas are white. No vegetation is indicated.
National Capitals
Cities
Canals
Railroads
1 inch = 63 Statute Miles
Miles 0 5 10 20 30 40 50 60 70
Conic Projection
PARIS
North Sea
GREAT BRITAIN
NETHERLANDS
BELGIUM
LUX.
GERMANY
SWITZ.
ITALY
SPAIN
ANDORRA
MONACO
English Channel
CHANNEL ISLANDS (BR.)
Bay of Biscay
Gulf of Lions
Mediterranean Sea
NORMANDY
BRITTANY
PICARDY
ARTOIS
FLANDERS
ILE-DE-FRANCE
CHAMPAGNE
LORRAINE
ALSACE
MAINE
ANJOU
ORLÉANAIS
TOURAINE
BERRY
POITOU
NIVERNAIS
BURGUNDY
FRANCHE-COMTÉ
BOURBONNAIS
MARCHE
LIMOUSIN
AUVERGNE
LYONNAIS
SAVOY
DAUPHINÉ
GUYENNE
GASCONY
LANGUEDOC
PROVENCE
BÉARN
ROUSSILLON
PYRENEES
Longitude West of Greenwich
Longitude East of Greenwich
CM TERRAIN FRANCE
COPYRIGHT BY RAND MC NALLY & COMPANY
MADE IN U.S.A.

FRANCE: Except for the low plains of Picardy in the northwest and the uplands adjoining Belgium and Luxembourg in the north, France's borders are clearly set by natural barriers: the Rhine River, the Jura Mountains, the Alps, the Mediterranean, the Pyrenees, the Atlantic Ocean and the English Channel. But these imposing borders have seldom isolated or protected the country during its long history.

Inside France, converging valleys and rivers form great east-west and north-south corridors that make the nation "an Atlantic bridgehead and a Mediterranean balcony." The Rhone-Sâone Valley, which provides the only direct land route between the North Sea and the Mediterranean, runs into the central basin of France, known as the Paris Basin. It was from here that the monarchs of France rode out in ancient times, spring after spring, to expand the realm until they reached what Louis XIV called "the natural frontiers" which roughly outline modern France.

AREA:	212,766 sq. mi.
POPULATION:	44,927,000. Largest city and capital: Paris.
CLIMATE:	Generally humid, with cool winters and mild summers. Greater temperature range in eastern and central regions; milder winters and hot dry summers on southern coast.
ALTITUDES:	Mt. Blanc, 15,781 ft. (highest).

France is the only European nation virtually self-sufficient in food. In Normandy and Brittany fat dairy cattle graze. The Paris Basin grows sugar beets, oats, rye and barley. Wheat grows on the central plains (France produces 20 per cent of Europe's supply, exclusive of Russia), vegetables and fruits grow in the sundrenched south and rich wine grapes almost everywhere.

Under the tablelands of eastern Lorraine are some of the most extensive iron ore deposits in Europe. France processes enough of this ore in the Moselle Valley and in St. Etienne and Lille to rank it third among European steel producers (Russia excluded). Power for industry is provided by massive hydroelectric projects and by steam generators that use coal imported primarily from Germany and Great Britain and oil brought from the Middle East.

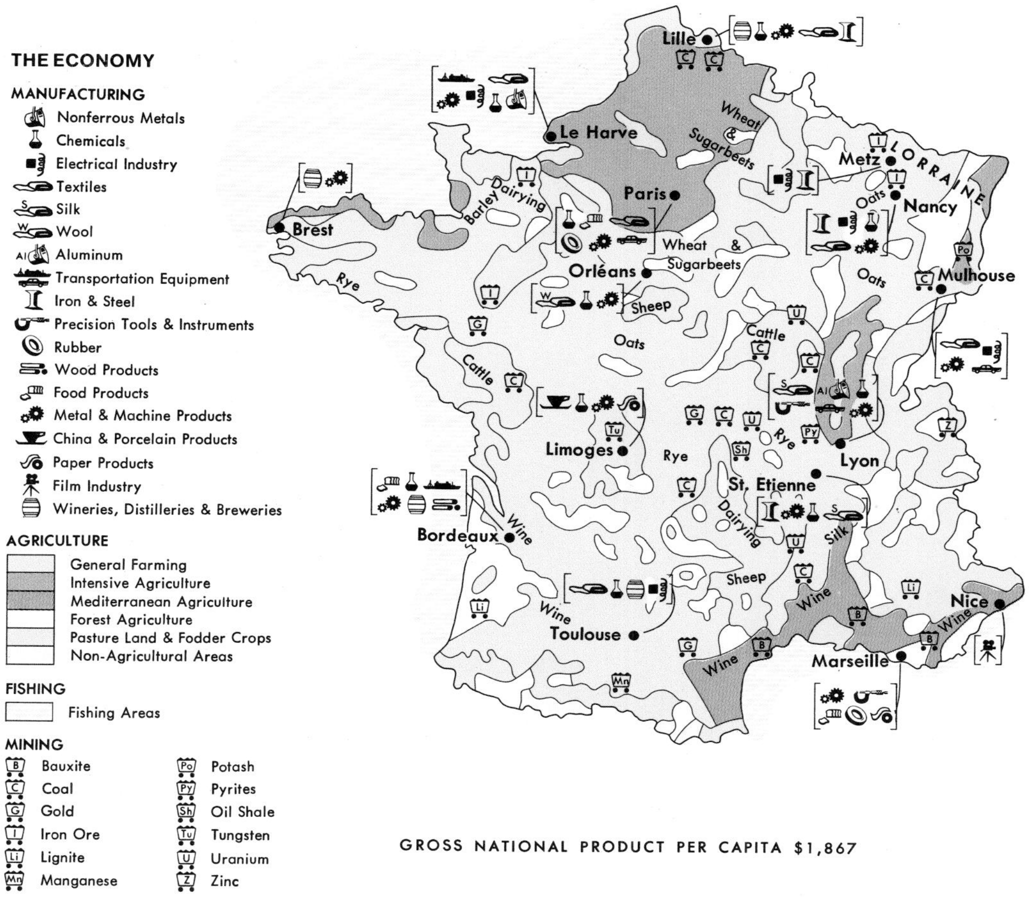

GROSS NATIONAL PRODUCT PER CAPITA $1,867

PRODUCTS OF THE GRAPES OF FRANCE

The wines and liqueurs of France take their names from the administrative districts *(capital letters, map above)* and famous wine regions in which they are produced. French law forbids misrepresenting their origin. Grapes grow well everywhere but in the extreme northwest (only the most prominent wine areas are shown here). France produces some 16 billion gallons of wine a year; the per capita consumption is estimated at 34 gallons.

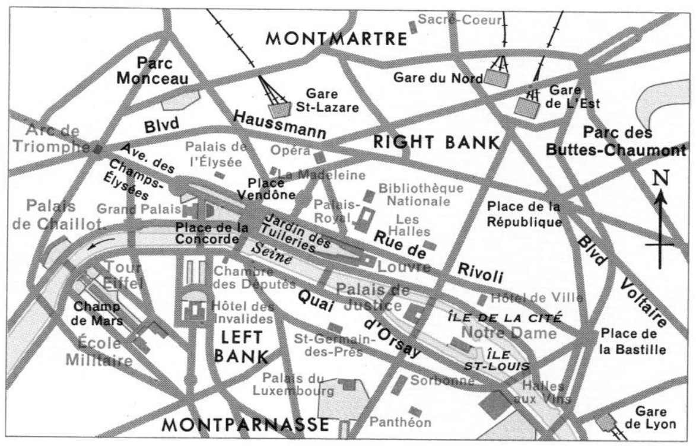

THE HEART OF PARIS

The largest city in France (6.6 million people live in the greater metropolitan area), Paris developed from a nucleus on the Ile de la Cité *(center right)*, an island in the Seine. Only the center of the present city is shown here. Historic sites, buildings and other points of interest are in red. At the top of the map lies the Right Bank (of the Seine), a district of business and fashionable residences. The Left Bank is the traditional home of artists, intellectuals and students, and is also the site of many government offices.

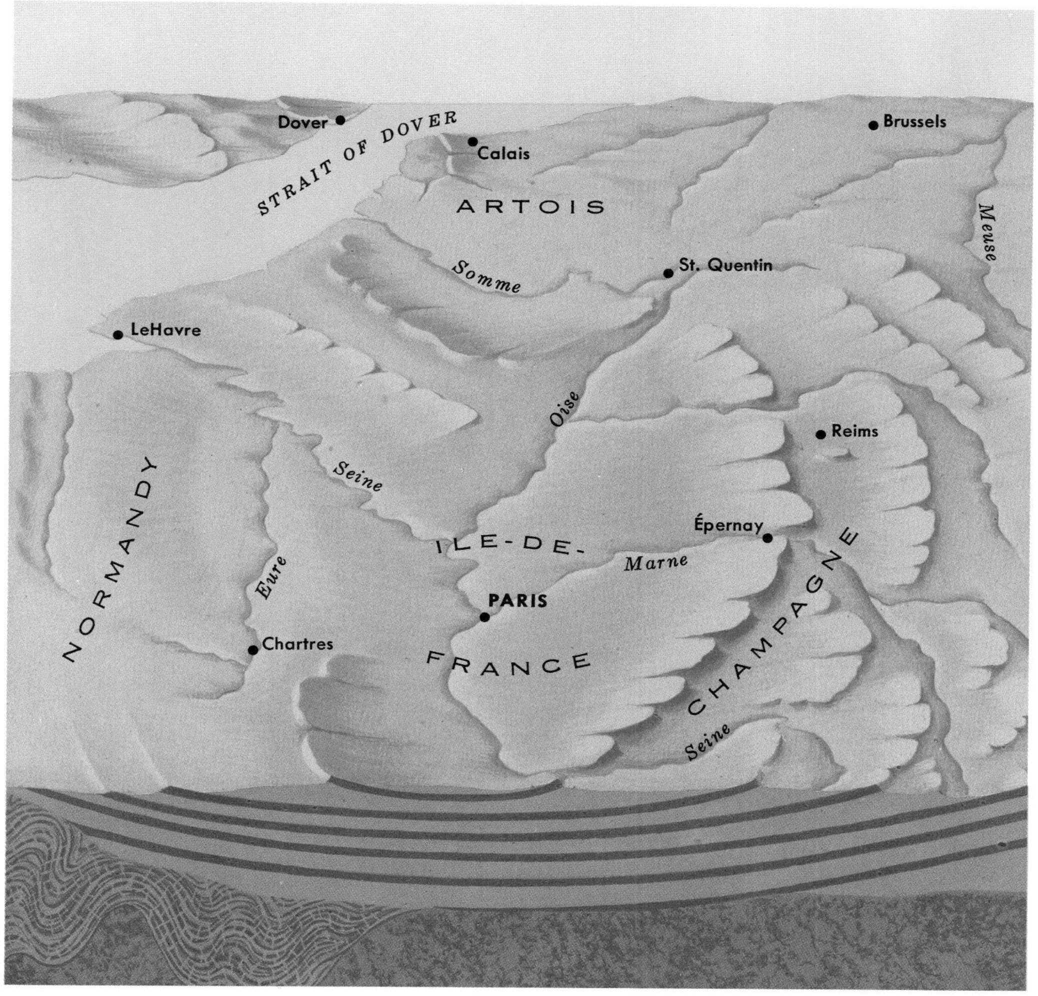

THE LIMESTONE ESCARPMENTS OF THE PARIS BASIN

The Paris Basin, covering an area of more than 20,000 square miles, was formed by the warping of the earth's surface into a broad, shallow depression, as shown in this cross section. The structure of the basin resembles a stack of saucers, each one smaller than the one beneath it. The city of Paris stands in the smallest, uppermost "dish." The saucers themselves are composed of thick limestone layers *(brown)* with underlayers of clay and some outcroppings of sandstone. Rivers in the basin have eroded these different materials irregularly—eating away most voraciously at the softer clay and leaving behind on the surface concentric bands of outward-facing limestone escarpments, once considered the natural fortifications of Paris. Because of the basin's shape, streams here appear to converge on Paris as the spokes of a wheel converge on its hub.

THE LOWLANDS: RICH SOIL WRESTED

FROM THE SEA

ACROSS A FLOWERING CARPET of crimson Darwin tulips, blooming luxuriantly in a Netherlands field, a worker carries a basket of pink petals gathered from adjoining rows. The blooms are removed to make the bulbs hardier before they are dug up and prepared for sale. Because these flowers need well-drained, fertile soil, they grow splendidly in the loamy sands of Holland.

RISING WATERS of the North Sea *(left)* crest over dikes and inundate the Overflakkee Island village of Nieuwe Tonge. This happened during the 1953 floods, when the water rose three feet above previous levels. More than one third of The Netherlands was once sea bottom. A series of reclamation projects begun in 1920 will give Hollanders another half-million acres by 1978.

DRYING FLAX, piled in shocks, stands in the bright Belgian sun *(below)*. In the background barges in the River Lys wait to carry the flax to linen-spinning mills. The flax has already been saturated in water to facilitate separation of the fiber from the woody core of the stem. Linens have been a specialty of the lowlands since the textile industry began here in the early Middle Ages.

BELGIUM, THE NETHERLANDS AND LUXEMBOURG
Mixed Evergreen and Deciduous Trees
Grass
Below sea level areas are white. No vegetation is indicated.
National Capitals
Cities
Railroads
Canals
Provincial Boundaries
1 inch = 23 Statute miles
Miles 0 5 10 15 20 25
Lambert Conformal Conic Projection
CM TERRAIN BELGIUM THE NETHERLANDS AND LUXEMBOURG COPYRIGHT BY RAND MC NALLY & COMPANY MADE IN U.S.A.
Longitude East of Greenwich
North Sea
WEST FRISIAN ISLANDS
EAST FRISIAN ISLANDS
Wadden Zee
IJsselmeer (Zuider Zee)
NOORD-OOST POLDER
GRONINGEN
FRIESLAND
DRENTE
NOORD-HOLLAND
OVERIJSSEL
GELDERLAND
UTRECHT
ZUID-HOLLAND
ZEELAND
NOORD-BRABANT
LIMBURG
OOST VLAANDEREN
WEST VLAANDEREN
BRABANT
ANTWERPEN
HAINAUT
NAMUR
LIÈGE
LUXEMBOURG
BELGIUM
FRANCE
ARDENNES
HOHE VENN
AMSTERDAM
THE HAGUE ('s Gravenhage)
BRUSSELS
LUXEMBOURG
Rotterdam
Antwerpen (Antwerp)
Gent (Ghent)
Brugge (Bruges)
Oostende (Ostend)
Liège
Namur
Charleroi
Lille
Roubaix
Tourcoing
Aachen
Köln (Cologne)
Düsseldorf
Essen
Duisburg
Utrecht
Haarlem
Leiden
Delft
Dordrecht
Eindhoven
Tilburg
Breda
's Hertogenbosch
Nijmegen
Arnhem
Apeldoorn
Zwolle
Deventer
Enschede
Hengelo
Groningen
Leeuwarden
Maastricht
Heerlen
Hasselt
Mechelen
Leuven (Louvain)
Kortrijk (Courtrai)
Mons
Tournai
Verviers
Trier
Emden
Den Helder
Hilversum
Amersfoort
Vlissingen
Middelburg
Texel
Vlieland
Terschelling
Ameland
Schiermonnikoog
Borkum
Maas
Rhein (Rhine)
Waal
Neder Rijn
Lek
IJssel
Schelde
Wester Schelde
Meuse
Sambre
Ourthe
Semois
Moselle
Sûre
Roer
Ems
Vechte
Lippe
Erft
Kyll
Oise
Aisne
Afsluitdijk
Albert Canal
Juliana Canal
Dollart

BELGIUM, THE NETHERLANDS AND LUXEMBOURG

BELGIUM: A line of ethnic and linguistic differences roughly divides the north of Belgium from the south. On the plains stretching down from the North Sea live the Belgians who call themselves Flemings and who speak Flemish, a variant of the language of their Dutch neighbors to the north. To the south and east, where the land rises toward the Ardennes uplands, is the area inhabited by French-speaking Walloons. At the country's heart lies bilingual Brussels, capital and manufacturing center.

It was in Flanders (Vlaanderen) that the first great European trading center arose, initially basing its prosperity on lace handcrafting by Flemish women and, later, on the manufacture of textiles from imported British wool. Today, with an economy utilizing the rich coal fields of the Sambre-Meuse valley, Belgium is one of the most intensely industrialized nations in Europe.

AREA: 11,775 sq. mi.
POPULATION: 9,117,000. Capital: Brussels.
CLIMATE: Cool winters, mild summers; moderate, well-distributed rainfall.
ALTITUDES: Botrange, north of Malmédy, 2,274 ft. (highest).

THE NETHERLANDS: "God having created the land and the sea, the Dutch took care of the coast," a Dutch author has written. Holland is an area, partly salvaged from the sea *(diagram, upper right)*, on which a major commercial and financial center has been built. The country has an intricate system of internal waterways, the chief of which are the Rhine (Rijn) and Meuse (Maas) Rivers, and it also has Europe's major seaport, Rotterdam. Over 90 million tons of shipping enter and leave the country annually. Dutch farmers, using mechanized farm equipment, have made the country a major producer of dairy products.

AREA: 12,526 sq. mi.
POPULATION: 11,389,000. Capital: Amsterdam and The Hague.
CLIMATE: Same as above.
ALTITUDES: The Hague, -4 ft. to 25 ft.

LUXEMBOURG: Perched in part on the Ardennes uplands, tiny Luxembourg is dissected by deep valleys. Only about a third of its area—the southern lowlands of Lorraine—has good soil. But the country produces oats, potatoes and wheat in quantity. Extensive iron ore deposits in the foothills of the Ardennes have made Luxembourg Europe's sixth largest producer of steel.

AREA: 998 sq. mi.
POPULATION: 320,000. Capital: Luxembourg.
CLIMATE: Same as above.
ALTITUDES: Bourgplatz, north of Troisvierges, 1,846 ft. (highest).

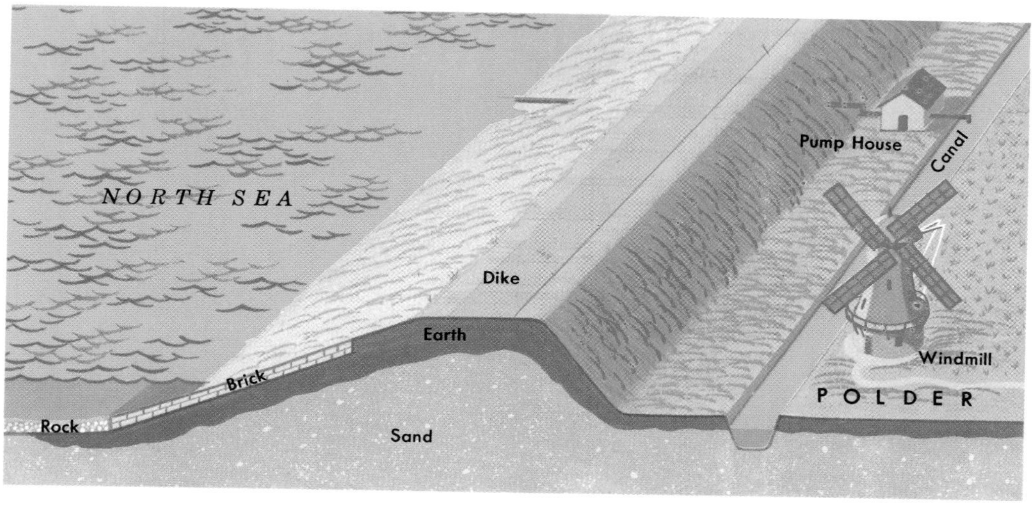

HOW DIKING CREATES HOLLAND'S PRODUCTIVE POLDER LAND

Construction of the dikes of Holland, shown in cross section above, begins with the dumping of tons of sand in the water at low tide. Later, the seaward slope *(left)* is reinforced with crushed rock, brick and mixtures of clay and earth. After the dike has been completed, it is frequently topped with a road. Then the sea water trapped behind the dike is pumped out.

The land thus gained is known as "polder"—a Dutch term for drained and diked lowlands. After the polder has been treated with chemicals to remove salt, it becomes highly productive agricultural land. Rain water and seepage which collect in small ditches *(right)* were once pumped out into drainage canals by windmills; today the pumps are powered by electricity.

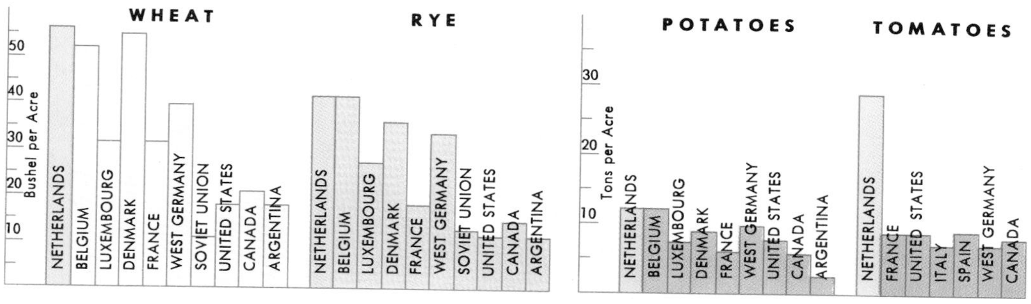

THE BOUNTIFUL CROPS OF A CROWDED COUNTRY

As these graphs indicate, The Netherlands leads the world in the yield per acre of wheat and tomatoes, and it is equaled only by Belgium in its yield of rye and potatoes. With an area of only 12,526 miles and a population of well over 10 million, The Netherlands must practice intensive agriculture, fertilizing its soils heavily to achieve very high productivity. In neighboring Belgium—which also obtains high yields from well-worked farms—soil, climate and topography are similar.

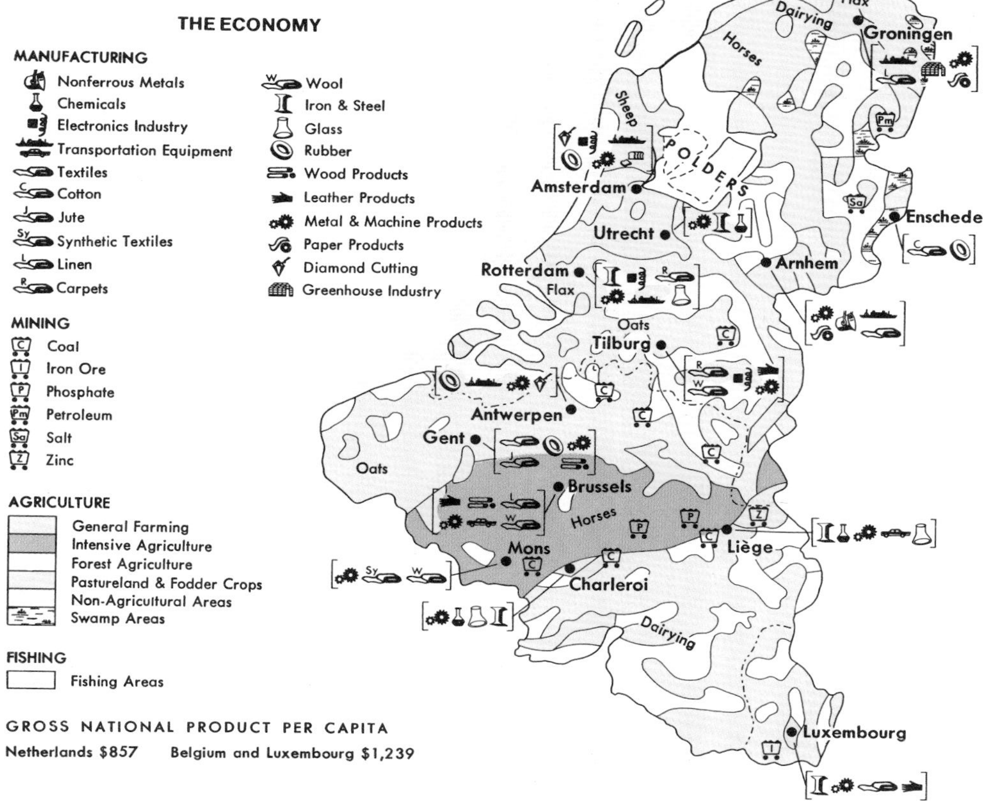

GROSS NATIONAL PRODUCT PER CAPITA
Netherlands $857   Belgium and Luxembourg $1,239

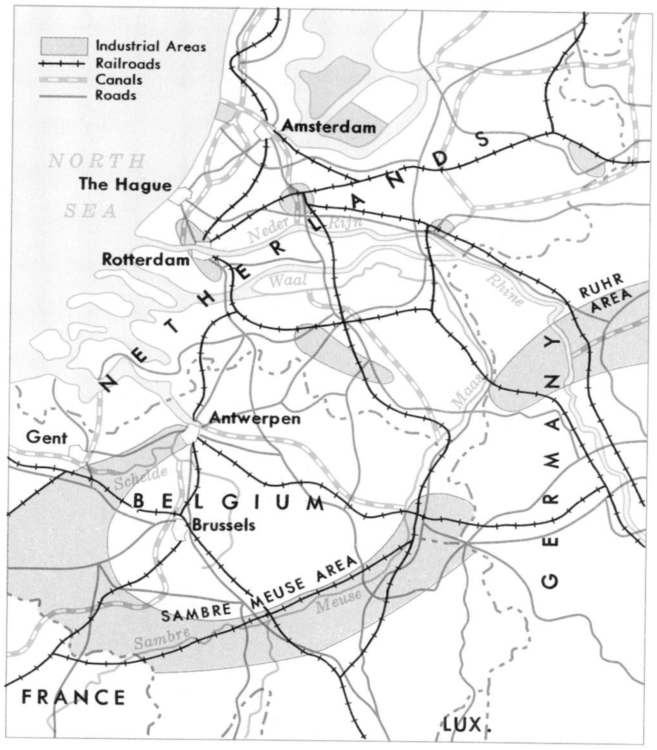

CROSSROADS OF A GREAT TRADING AREA

A complex transport network—highways, railways, rivers and canals—crosses and recrosses Belgium and The Netherlands, as shown in the map above, making these countries the commercial crossroads of Western Europe. Situated at the mouths of the Schelde, Maas and Rijn Rivers and lying directly opposite England's Thames River, the area is ideally located to receive and ship raw materials and manufactured products. It services a number of major industrial regions, including the Ruhr and the Sambre-Meuse. Holland's Rotterdam is the second largest port in tonnage in the world; Belgium's Antwerp ranks among the top 10.

THE PRODUCTIVE VALLEYS OF GERMANY

A GREAT RIVER PORT, Hamburg is also an industrial giant of Germany. The Zollkanal links Hamburg to the Elbe River *(top)*, which in turn empties into the North Sea. Germany's river ports played a central role in the birth and growth of modern merchant capitalism.

A TERRACED HILLSIDE in the valley of the Moselle bears row upon row of stakes erected to hold grape vines *(opposite)*. Only the slopes facing in a southerly direction are used for viniculture in this valley. The vineyard pictured here has already been harvested.

GERMANY
Barren Areas Above Timber
Evergreen Trees
Mixed Evergreen and Deciduous Trees
Deciduous Trees
Grass
Below sea level areas are white. No vegetation is indicated.
National Capitals
Cities
Canals
Railroads
1 inch = 47 Statute Miles
Miles 0 5 10 20 30 40 50
Lambert Conformal Conic Projection
Longitude East of Greenwich
CM TERRAIN GERMANY
COPYRIGHT BY RAND MC NALLY & COMPANY MADE IN U.S.A.
North Sea
Baltic Sea
NORTH FRISIAN ISLANDS
EAST FRISIAN ISLANDS
JUTLAND
DENMARK
Copenhagen (København)
Malmö
SWEDEN
BORNHOLM (DEN.)
SJAELLAND
FYN
LOLLAND
FALSTER
RÜGEN
FEHMARN
Kiel Bay
Kadet Channel
SCHLESWIG
HOLSTEIN
MECKLENBURG
HANOVER
WESTPHALIA
WEST GERMANY
EAST GERMANY
BRANDENBURG
SAXONY
THURINGIA
HESSE
BAVARIA
WÜRTTEMBERG
BADEN
SAAR
POLAND
CZECHOSLOVAKIA
BOHEMIA
AUSTRIA
SWITZERLAND
LIECHTENSTEIN
LUX.
BELGIUM
NETHERLANDS
FRANCE
Hamburg
Bremen
Hannover
BERLIN
BONN
Köln (Cologne)
Düsseldorf
Dortmund
Essen
Frankfurt
Stuttgart
München (Munich)
Nürnberg
Leipzig
Dresden
Magdeburg
Karl-Marx-Stadt (Chemnitz)
Prague (Praha)
Szczecin (Stettin)
Strasbourg
Basel
Zurich
Salzburg
Linz
Innsbruck
Rhine
Elbe
Weser
Main
Donau (Danube)
Oder
Ems
Mosel
BROCKEN 3,747 FT.
GREAT ARBER 4,777 FT.
FELDBERG 4,898 FT.
ZUGSPITZE 9,721 FT.
GROSS GLOCKNER 12,461 FT.
KEILBERG 4,078 FT.
GUEBWILLER 4,672 FT.
BLACK FOREST
HARZ MTS.
THÜRINGER WALD
ERZGEBIRGE
BOHEMIAN FOREST
Constance L.
Chiem L.

THE CHANGING BORDERS OF THE REICH

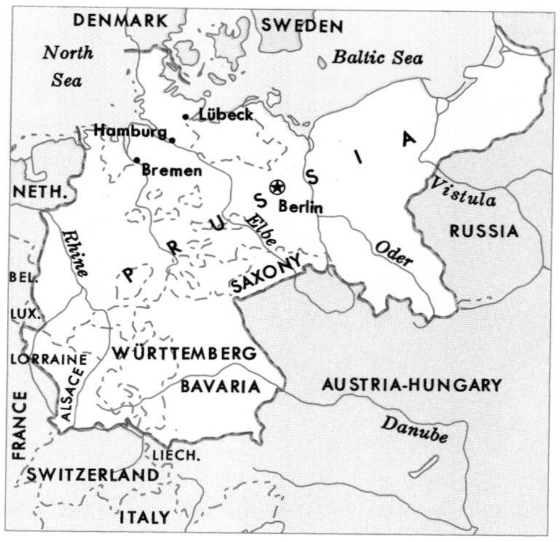

1871: THE FIRST UNITED GERMANY

Before 1871 there were separate German kingdoms – Prussia, Bavaria, Württemberg and Saxony; Hamburg, Bremen and Lübeck were free cities; and there were also a number of other smaller states. In 1871, under Prussian leadership, all were united as the "Deutsches Reich," shown in this map, with Wilhelm I of Prussia as emperor. Alsace and Lorraine *(left)*, territories Prussia had acquired in war with France, were included.

1919-1933: THE GERMAN REPUBLIC

The Treaty of Versailles that ended World War I redrew the borders of Germany on the lines shown above. Alsace and Lorraine were returned to France. Most of Poznan, West Prussia and parts of Upper Silesia went to Poland, isolating East Prussia. A plebiscite restored north Schleswig to Denmark. These borders remained until Adolf Hitler's Third Reich, founded in 1933, began its expansion by annexing Austria in 1938.

1945: GERMANY DIVIDED

After World War II, the western Allies and the Soviet Union set Germany's eastern boundary on the Oder and Neisse Rivers, pending a final peace treaty. This shrank Germany to the shape shown here. West Germany, formerly divided into U.S., British and French zones, became the German Federal Republic in 1949, and East Germany, the Russian zone, was established as the German Democratic Republic the same year.

WEST GERMANY: The mountains and forests of West Germany have traditionally been formidable divisive barriers. On the North European Plain, the intensively cultivated rolling fields are separated from the forested Alps of the south by the hills of central Germany. The forces which created these old central German uplands also helped to form the valuable mineral deposits of coal and now nearly depleted iron ore that provided the basis for Germany's modern industry. In the Ruhr-Rhine valley lies a 2,000-square-mile industrial region *(map below, right)*. In the southwest the rich Rhine River valley nurtures vineyards, fruits and cereals.

AREA:	95,885 sq. mi.
POPULATION:	55,746,000.
	Largest city: West Berlin.
	Capital: Bonn.
CLIMATE:	Cold winters and cool summers; moderate, well-distributed rainfall.
ALTITUDES:	Zugspitze, 9,721 ft. (highest).

Only short years after World War II leveled many of its cities, the country re-established itself as one of the most productive manufacturing economies in Europe, leading in iron and steel and chemical production. In automobiles and textiles, too, it is an important producer. As a trading nation it is third greatest in the world (after the U.S. and Great Britain) and has one of the highest levels of living in Europe.

EAST GERMANY: Almost all of East Germany lies within the great North European Plain, an historic east-west path for invading armies and a prodigious producer of food. In the Baltic Sea area, the sandy soil of the plain grows fodder for dairy cattle. Farther south is a region of important food crops: potatoes and rye. To the east, in the fertile Magdeburg Basin, is an extensive beet region that supports a prosperous sugar industry. Barley and wheat are also grown here. In the far south, the plain merges with forested uplands like the Thüringer Wald, traditional home of commercial wood carvers, and with the Erzgebirge (Ore Mountains) in the industrial province of Saxony.

AREA:	41,634 sq. mi.
POPULATION:	16,403,000.
	Largest city and capital: East Berlin.
CLIMATE:	Like West Germany; slightly drier, greater temperature range.
ALTITUDES:	Keilberg, 4,078 ft. (highest).

East Germany has fewer raw materials than West Germany. Only lignite exists in quantity. However, by importing raw materials, East Germany is expanding its industry. Among the most important products are chemicals, many of which come from the large plants in the Leipzig area, optical equipment and machines. Light industrial products include textiles, clothing, woodwork, leather and shoes.

THE ECONOMY

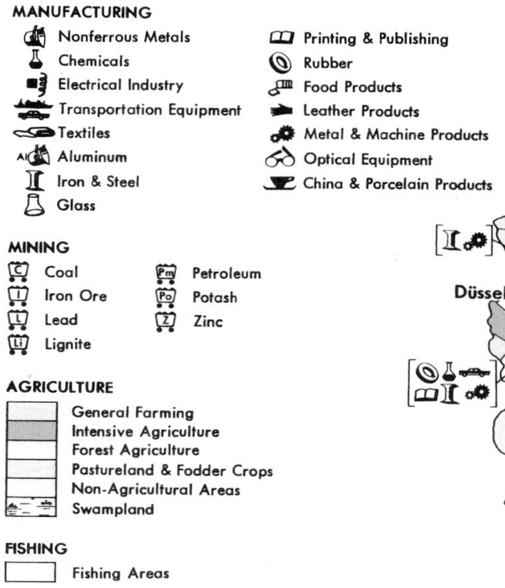

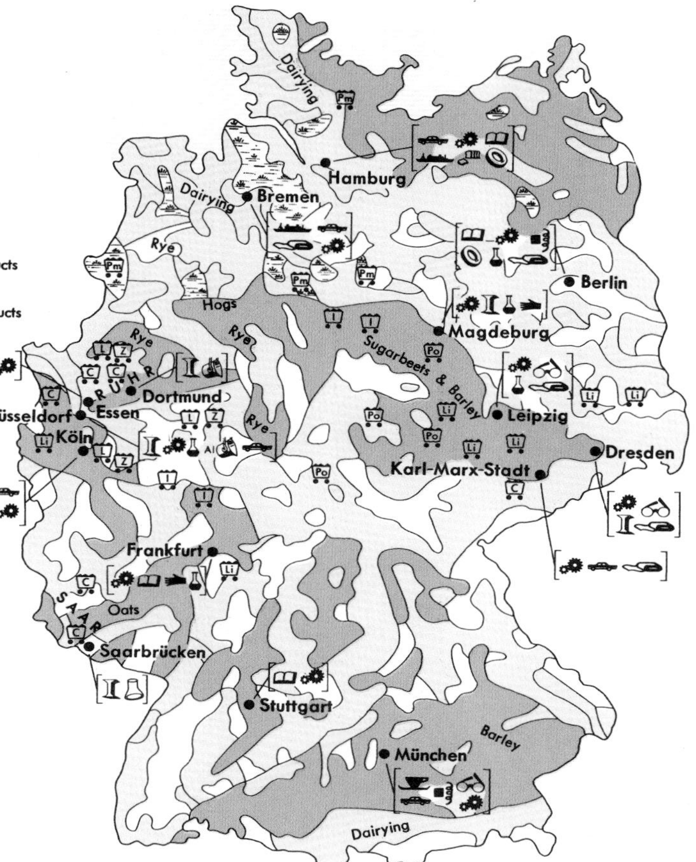

GROSS NATIONAL PRODUCT PER CAPITA

West Germany $1,035 East Germany Not Available

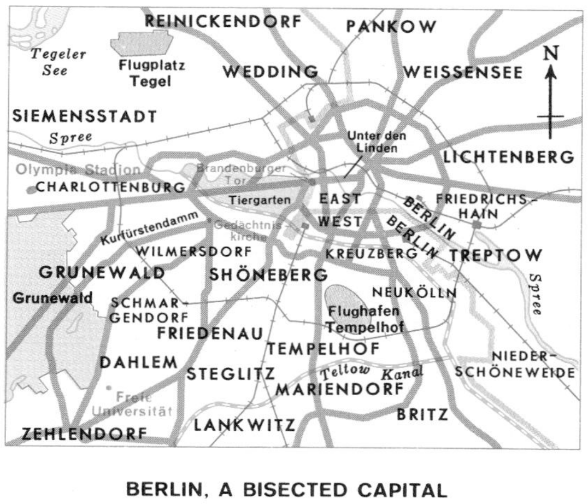

BERLIN, A BISECTED CAPITAL

The red line that wanders through this map of Berlin marks the division of the former capital of Germany into West and East Berlin. Drawn by the victorious Allies in 1945, it roughly parallels major transportation routes, curving sharply in the center of the city to make the zones approximately equal in area. Until this split, Berlin was the artistic center of Germany, the leading commercial and industrial city on the continent and the sixth largest city in the world.

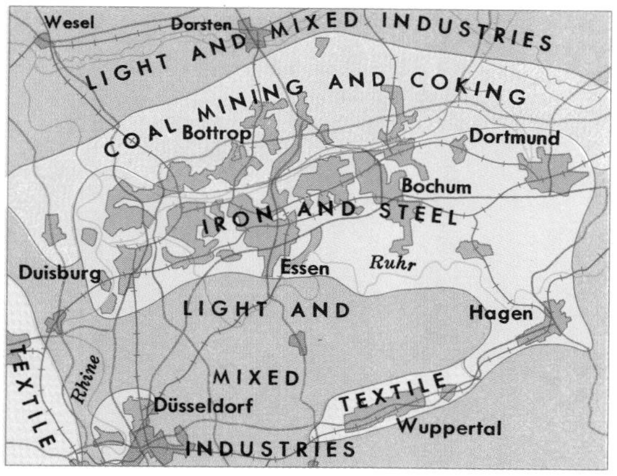

GERMANY'S INDUSTRIAL HEART

The colored areas on this map show where various kinds of manufacturing – chiefly steel, heavy machinery and chemicals – are concentrated in the Ruhr, West Germany's vast industrial region. Coal reserves here are approximated at 490 billion tons. The Ruhr's iron ore deposits are almost exhausted, but ores brought largely from Sweden and France over river and rail networks enable the region to produce an average of 18,700,000 tons of crude steel per year.

A LAND WELL HUSBANDED

ON THE SCANDINAVIAN COAST

DANISH FIELDS AND VILLAGES are laid out in geometric patterns in the Jutland region along the North Sea coast. The intensely cultivated fields radiate out from cozy villages. The rest of Scandinavia does not have Denmark's fertile soils, but all Scandinavian countries share the Danish tradition of painstakingly frugal employment of the land to raise quality livestock and dairy cattle, grains and vegetables. Much of the Danish produce is exported, particularly to the United Kingdom, Germany and the United States.

Barents Sea
Norwegian Sea
Gulf of Bothnia
Atlantic Ocean
Greenland Sea
Denmark Strait
Davis Strait
Baffin Bay
ICELAND
GREENLAND (DEN.)
REYKJAVÍK
LAPLAND
Longitude East of Greenwich
CM. TERRAIN NORWAY, SWEDEN, FINLAND DENMARK AND ICELAND
COPYRIGHT BY RAND MC NALLY & COMPANY
MADE IN U.S.A.

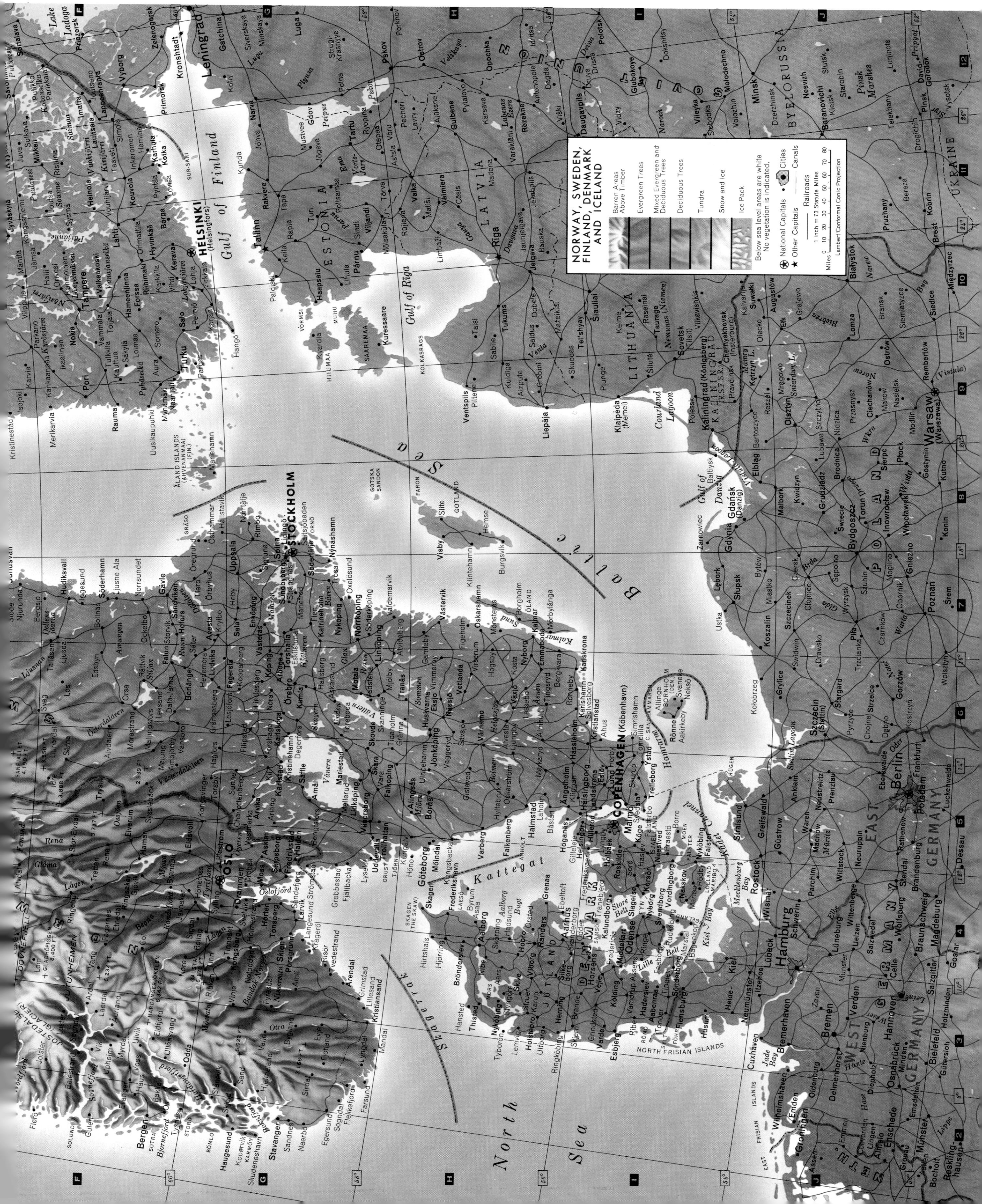
NORWAY, SWEDEN, FINLAND, DENMARK AND ICELAND
Barren Areas Above Timber
Evergreen Trees
Mixed Evergreen and Deciduous Trees
Deciduous Trees
Tundra
Snow and Ice
Ice Pack
Below sea level areas are white
No vegetation is indicated.
National Capitals
Other Capitals
Cities
Railroads
Canals
1 inch = 73 Statute Miles
Lambert Conformal Conic Projection
North Sea
Skagerrak
Kattegat
Baltic Sea
Gulf of Finland
Gulf of Riga
OSLO
STOCKHOLM
HELSINKI (Helsingfors)
COPENHAGEN (København)
Leningrad
Riga
Warsaw (Warszawa)
Berlin

SOUTHERN SCANDINAVIA
Nat. Capitals
Other Cities
Railroads
Ferries
National Boundaries
County Boundaries
1 inch = 40 Statute Miles
Miles 0 5 10 20 30 40
Lambert Conformal Conic Projection
CM POLITICAL
SOUTHERN SWEDEN
COPYRIGHT BY
RAND MC NALLY & COMPANY
MADE IN U.S.A.
Longitude East of Greenwich
NORWAY
SWEDEN
DENMARK
WEST GERMANY
EAST GERMANY
POLAND
OSLO
STOCKHOLM
COPENHAGEN (København)
Skagerrak
Kattegat
Gulf of Bothnia
Alands Hav
Baltic Sea
Gulf of Danzig
Vistula Lagoon
Pomeranian Bay
Mecklenburg Bay
Kiel Bay
Fehmarn Strait
Kadet Channel
Hanöbukten
Kalmar Sund
Södra Kvarken
ÅLAND ISLANDS (AHVENANMAA) (FINLAND)
Mariehamn
OPPLAND
HEDMARK
BUSKERUD
AKERSHUS
VESTFOLD
ØSTFOLD
VÄRMLAND
KOPPARBERG
GÄVLEBORG
UPPSALA
VÄSTMANLAND
STOCKHOLM
ÖREBRO
SÖDERMANLAND
SKARABORG
ÖSTERGÖTLAND
GÖTEBORG OCH BOHUS
ÄLVSBORG
JÖNKÖPING
KALMAR
HALLAND
KRONOBERG
BLEKINGE
KRISTIANSTAD
MALMÖHUS
GOTLAND
ÖLAND
BORNHOLM (DENMARK)
HJÖRRING
AALBORG
RANDERS
FYN
SVENDBORG
MARIBO
PRAESTO
SORÖ
HOLBAEK
FREDERIKSBORG
KÖBENHAVN
ROSKILDE
Vänern
Vättern
Siljan
Mälaren
Hjälmaren
Göteborg
Malmö
Helsingborg
Uppsala
Västerås
Örebro
Norrköping
Linköping
Jönköping
Karlstad
Gävle
Kalmar
Karlskrona
Växjö
Halmstad
Borås
Trollhättan
Uddevalla
Visby
Ronne
Odense
Aalborg
Frederikshavn
Gdańsk (Danzig)
Gdynia
Sopot
Stralsund
Rostock
Koszalin
Elbląg
Lubeck

NORWAY, SWEDEN, FINLAND, DENMARK AND ICELAND

NORWAY: Rising up abruptly from the fjord-indented coast *(diagram, below right)*, Norway's mountains have always turned the faces of the people toward the sea. Despite a scanty population, Norway leads the world in whaling and mans the third largest merchant fleet. Farmers who till small grain and vegetable plots along the coast often turn to cod fishing in the winter. Agricultural land is limited, but there are rich forests to exploit and hydroelectric power to run sawmills. Almost one fourth of the country's exports are wood products.

AREA: 125,032 sq. mi.
POPULATION: 3,574,000. Capital: Oslo.
CLIMATE: Wet and mild along the coast; cold snowy winters and cool summers in the interior and uplands.
ALTITUDES: Galdhöpiggen, 8,400 ft. (highest).

SWEDEN: Despite an unsettled northland that is the last great frontier of Western Europe, Sweden has the most advanced economy of Scandinavia. The nation enjoys a high level of living as a result of careful exploitation of key resources: high-grade iron ore, numerous waterfalls and widespread forests. With hydroelectric power plentiful, Sweden's steel and wood industries are dispersed over a score of smokeless cities. Dairy farming, livestock and intensive cultivation supply the country with 85 per cent of its food needs.

AREA: 173,577 sq. mi.
POPULATION: 7,468,000. Capital: Stockholm.
CLIMATE: Cold snowy winters and cool summers, with milder winters in the southern regions; most rain in late summer.
ALTITUDES: Sarektjåkko, 6,972 ft. (highest).

FINLAND: Fifty thousand lakes and a land surface blanketed with rich forests of pine and fir combine to make Finland one of the world's leading exporters of wood pulp. Finnish loggers, many of whom farm during the summer months, use the country's great linkage of lakes and rivers as a cheap and convenient chute to move logs from the interior to coastal towns.

AREA: 130,085 sq. mi.
POPULATION: 4,435,000. Capital: Helsinki.
CLIMATE: Long, cold, snowy winters and cool summers, with less severe winters in the south; most rain in summer.
ALTITUDES: Mt. Haltia, 4,344 ft. (highest).

DENMARK: A flat thumb jutting out of the fertile plain of Northern Europe, Denmark has built her snug prosperity around efficient small-scale farming meticulously geared to European markets. Two thirds of the national revenue comes from dairy products, sugar beets, bacon and ham, making it possible for mineral-poor Denmark to buy raw materials for table-service manufacturing and the shipbuilding and diesel engine industries. One thousand three hundred and twenty-five miles off the Danish coast is Greenland—an 840,000-square-mile island, nine tenths covered by a polar icecap—which is considered a county of the mother country.

AREA: 16,614 sq. mi.
POPULATION: 4,580,000. Capital: Copenhagen.
CLIMATE: Fairly cold winters and damp cool summers; most rain in late summer.
ALTITUDES: Ejer Bavnehöj, 568 ft. (highest).

ICELAND: This rocky island, the western outpost of Europe, has ponderous glaciers, violent earthquakes, erupting volcanoes and geysers. Where the lava has not yet been weathered into soil, much of the land is rubble-strewn and treeless. Only about one fourth of the country is inhabited. Iceland has some inland pasturage, but most Icelanders live on the coast. Fishing, primarily for cod and herring, and the manufacture of such fish by-products as cod-liver oil provide the island with almost 80 per cent of its exports.

AREA: 39,750 sq. mi.
POPULATION: 171,000. Capital: Reykjavik.
CLIMATE: Long cold winters and cool summers; rainfall in all seasons and often heavy winter snowfall.
ALTITUDES: Hvannadalshnukur, 6,952 ft. (highest).

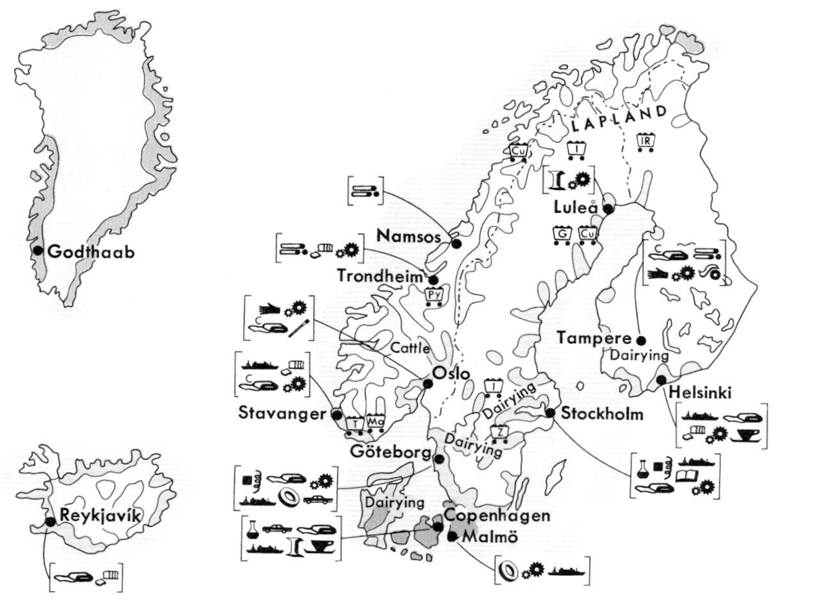

THE ECONOMY

MANUFACTURING
- Chemicals
- Electrical Industry
- Transportation Equipment
- Textiles
- Cotton
- Iron & Steel
- Printing & Publishing
- Rubber
- Wood Products
- Food Products
- Leather Products
- Metal & Machine Products
- Paper Products
- China & Porcelain Products
- Match Industry

AGRICULTURE
- General Farming
- Intensive Agriculture
- Forest Agriculture
- Forest Agriculture, Wood Crops Dominant
- Pastureland & Fodder Crops
- Nomadic Herding
- Non-Agricultural Areas

FISHING
- Fishing Areas

MINING
- Copper
- Gold
- Iron Ore
- Iron Ore Reserves
- Lead
- Molybdenum
- Nickel
- Pyrites
- Silver
- Oil Shale
- Zinc

GROSS NATIONAL PRODUCT PER CAPITA

Norway $1,104
Finland $843
Denmark $1,074
Sweden $1,433
Iceland $1,237

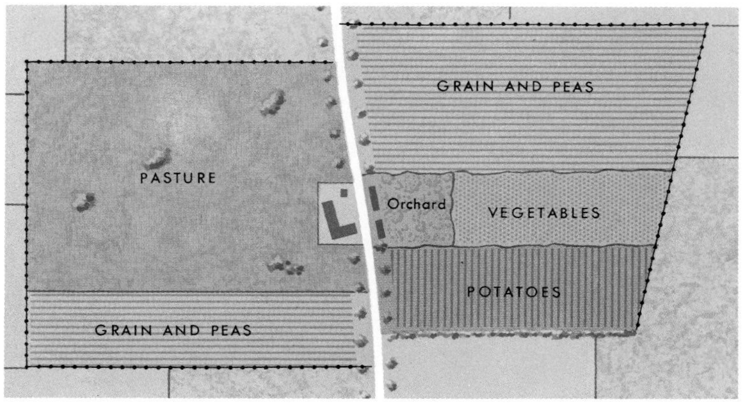

THE LAYOUT OF A NORWEGIAN FARM

A typical 60-acre Norwegian farm is laid out in the manner shown in this drawing. Because so much of the country is rugged upland with thin stony soil, dairying is important and pasture land dominates the farm. An area almost as large is planted with grains, peas and other vegetables, the bulk of which is used as fodder for the cows. The Norwegian farmer shelters his dairy herd in a huge, two-story barn like the L-shaped one visible in the center here. The barn dwarfs both the farmhouse next to it and the turf-roofed storage sheds across the road that divides the farm.

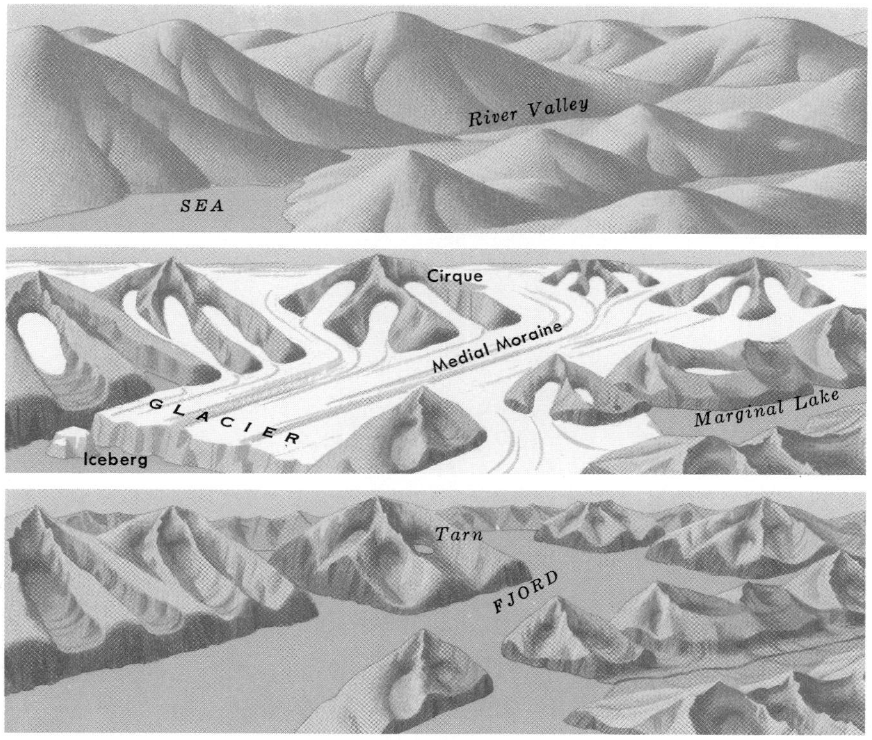

HOW FJORDS WERE CUT INTO SCANDINAVIA'S COAST

Three stages in the formation of a fjord are shown in these drawings. Before the glacial period *(top)* the mountains were smooth and the river had eroded a V-shaped valley. When the ice moved in *(middle drawing)* mountains were worn by frost and glacial erosion into sharp pinnacles. Amphitheater-shaped "cirques" were gouged out of mountain sides and the valley became U-shaped. At a much later stage, when the ice began to melt, temporary, or marginal, lakes were formed. As the glacier retreated, the sea flooded the valley, forming a fjord *(bottom)*. Cirques that retain water become tarns or permanent lakes.

SOUTHERN EUROPE

The biographer-historian Emil Ludwig said that the Mediterranean Sea, which has for centuries dominated the life of Southern Europe, "is the Helen among oceans; like her it was desired by all who saw it." In the lands bordering on Homer's "wine-dark, sounding sea" the great Greek, Roman, Byzantine and Renaissance cultures flowered and western civilization was shaped.

Some 2,000 years before Christ, Asian peoples made their way to the Mediterranean and discovered that the land would support olive and citrus trees, grapevines and sheep. These are still staples of Mediterranean agriculture. The mountains girding the great intercontinental sea not only provided protection against invasion from the north, they also kept the Mediterranean people clustered close to their shorelines. The sea was there for the use of a trading people, and wood for ships was at hand in the forests of European Turkey and northern Greece. From Athens to the ancient trading center of Izmir in Turkey the distance was 1,194 miles by land, by water 284; from Rome to Cartagena in Spain it was 1,251 miles through the Alps and Pyrenees, 515 by sea. So it came about that in the Mediterranean, man evolved the techniques of navigation. In the Third Century B.C. a Mediterranean philosopher, a Greek by the name of Eratosthenes,

THE MEDITERRANEAN SEA *(below)* sweeps 2,400 miles from the Straits of Gibraltar at left to the coast of Turkey at far right. The countries of Southern Europe border the sea's north shore. At center the Italian boot points its toe toward the island of Sicily and the coast of North Africa. In the Atlantic Ocean, at upper left, are the British Isles. At upper right the Soviet Union stretches into the huge land mass of Asia.

demonstrated mathematically that the earth was round. And 1,800 years later Christopher Columbus set forth from Spain to prove that the theory was a fact.

Man's exploitation of this lovely, sunny region diminished its usefulness to him. In his greed and ignorance, he deforested the mountain slopes. Crude farming methods brought on cycles of erosion that continue to plague the lands of Southern Europe. With the forests cut down, with the soil plowed every year, with herds of sheep overgrazing the pasture lands, the streams that tumbled down the sides of the mountains grew swifter, carrying away the topsoil.

Today, although modern farming methods and scientific use of fertilizers produce more food on its eroded lands than in ancient times, populous Southern Europe cannot nourish itself adequately. And most of the countries that border the historic Mediterranean have been left in the backwash of the western civilization which they helped mold. Virtually without coal and iron ore, and with very little oil and hydroelectric power potential, the countries of the Mediterranean are still beckoning lands of blue water and sky. But with the notable exception of northern Italy, they lack the means to give their people a high standard of living in the industrial 20th Century.

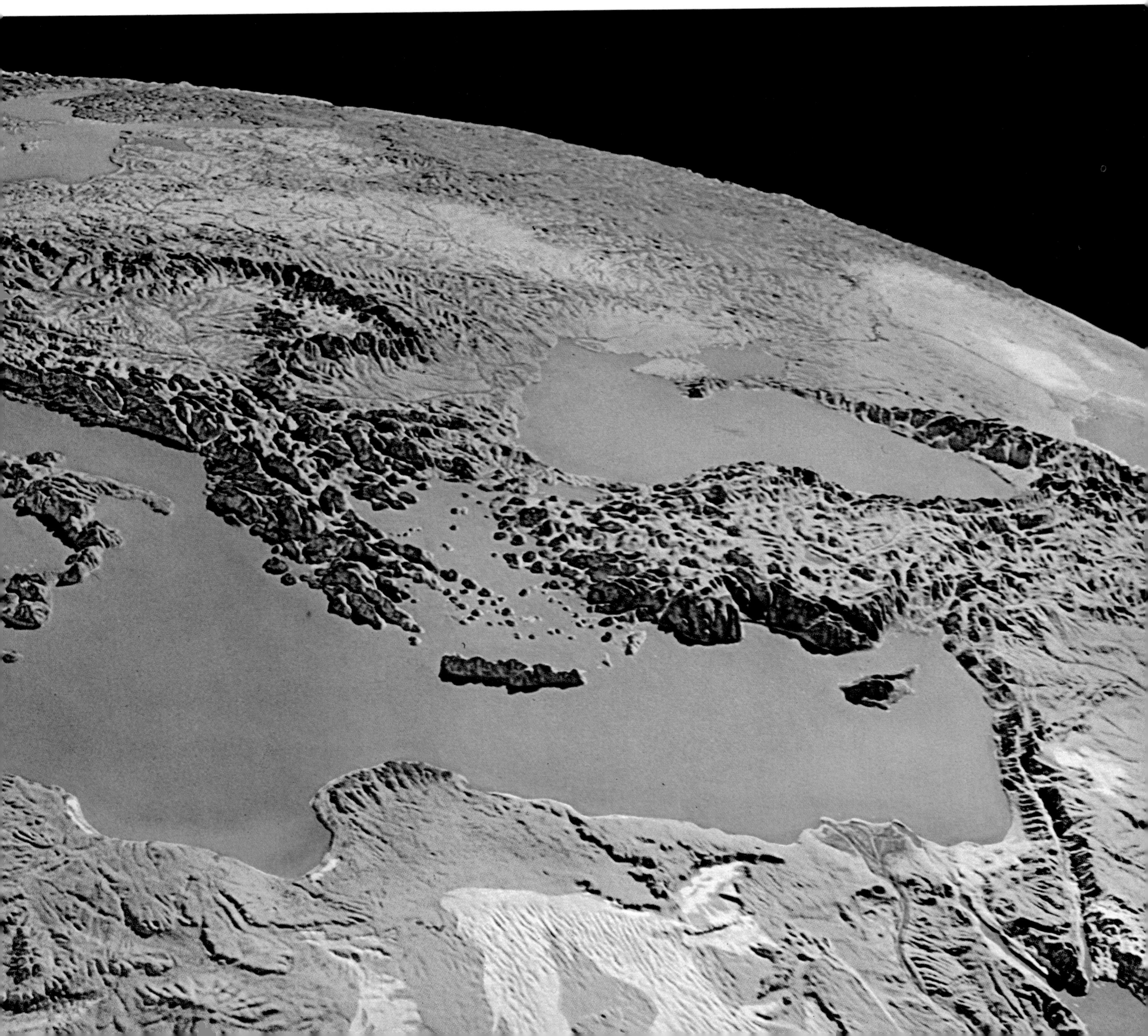

THE RED EARTH OF SPAIN

OLIVE TREES, gnarled and bent by the wind, add their soft green to the rolling red hills of Spain near Sevilla. The color of the soil here is in part determined by iron compounds. Common in the Mediterranean countries, where it is known as "terra rossa," this soil is easily tilled. In southern Spain three fourths of the total agricultural area is given over to olive groves and some 20 varieties are grown. Spain is the world's largest producer of olives, most of which are pressed for oil.

SPAIN AND PORTUGAL
Evergreen Trees
Deciduous Trees
Shrub
Grass
National Capitals
Cities
Canals
Railroads
1 inch = 63 Statute Miles
Conic Projection
Longitude East of Greenwich
Longitude West of Greenwich
Bay of Biscay
Atlantic Ocean
Mediterranean Sea
Gulf of Lions
BALEARIC ISLANDS
CANARY ISLANDS (SPAIN)
ALGERIA
AFRICA
FRANCE
PYRENEES
MADRID
LISBON (Lisboa)
Barcelona
Valencia
Sevilla
Pôrto
Strait of Gibraltar
Gibraltar (BR.)
Marseille
Toulouse
CM TERRAIN SPAIN AND PORTUGAL
COPYRIGHT BY RAND McNALLY & COMPANY
MADE IN U.S.A.

SPAIN: Mountains not only separate Spain from the rest of Europe, they stretch like the fingers of a giant hand across the country itself. Extending from the Atlantic to the Mediterranean, the high Pyrenees merge with the lower Cantábrica Mountains in the northwest. A succession of lesser ranges in central Spain–the Sierra de Gredos, the Sierra de Guadarrama and the Sierra de Gata, which runs into Portugal–divide the country. In the southwest is the Sierra Morena. The Mediterranean coastline is guarded by still another chain–the high, snow-capped Sierra Nevada, where the mountains of Spain reach their highest point. Between the ranges, there is some level land, notably the tableland, or *meseta,* of central Spain, the fruitful Andalusian plains of the southwest and the Ebro River valley of the northeast.

Because much of Spain is relatively dry, some of its agricultural products are drought-resistant crops. These include olives, in which it leads the world, and grapes, from which come the classic wines of Spain. Also important are oranges and other citrus fruits from the Mediterranean coast of Valencia, wheat, barley, oats and rye.

AREA: 194,345 sq. mi.
POPULATION: 30,090,000.
Largest city and capital: Madrid.
CLIMATE: Generally hot dry summers and mild damp winters, with cooler winters due to altitude in the interior highlands.
ALTITUDES: Mulhacén, 11,424 ft. (highest); Madrid, 2,150 ft.

Despite numerous mineral resources–its ranges contain copper, lead, iron ore, zinc and mercury–Spain has never developed extensive manufacturing. Metal and machine products, textiles and chemicals are manufactured near Barcelona. Additional chemicals, iron and steel, and food products come from Santander. In Cartagena, cork products, glassware and transportation equipment are made.

This peninsular country was once the greatest empire in recorded history. Under Isabella and Ferdinand, the united Spain which routed the Moors *(map, below center)* financed the discovery of America in 1492. Its "Golden Age" during the 16th Century followed, when it held lands of great wealth in Europe, the Pacific, Asia, Africa and the Americas.

PORTUGAL: Made up primarily of coastal and valley lowlands, Portugal is blessed with a milder climate than Spain, in part because of its extended Atlantic coast location and the protecting mountains of the north and east. In the north, grapevines flourish in the upper Douro River valley, the famous *pais do vinho,* or "wine country." Here port wine is produced, and much of it is exported through the city of Pôrto. In the center of the country are Portugal's highest mountains, the Serra da Estrêla. In the south, in orchards near the Guadiana River, grow most of the drought-resistant cork oak trees from which comes the country's primary export–one half the world's supply of cork. Sunny southern Portugal also grows cereals, olives, grapes and other fruits. Pôrto and Lisbon produce both textiles and transportation equipment.

AREA: 35,589 sq. mi.
POPULATION: 9,108,000. Largest city and capital: Lisbon.
CLIMATE: Hot dry summers and mild damp winters, tempered along the coast by the Atlantic.
ALTITUDES: Malhão, 6,532 ft. (highest); Lisbon, 285 ft.

Portugal, like Spain, was for a time a mighty empire. The Portuguese early discovered and claimed the islands of the Azores, and they were also the first Europeans to round the tip of Africa. Today Portugal's overseas empire, which once ranged through Asia, America and Africa, has largely disappeared, but the experienced Portuguese sailors still roam the world. The canning and salting of fish–including tuna caught off the Río de Oro of Africa–is one of Portugal's valuable industries.

ANDORRA: A circuit of mountain valleys in the Pyrenees, 175-square-mile Andorra is one of the smallest states in Europe. Flocks of sheep and herds of goats, horses, mules and cattle roam the slopes of the country, and tobacco is an important crop.

Andorra sends annual tributary dues to its joint rulers, the Republic of France and the Spanish bishops of Urgel. It has no taxes and no national budget, and both French and Spanish currencies are used.

AREA: 175 sq. mi.
POPULATION: 6,500. Capital: Andorra.
ALTITUDES: Coma Pedrosa, 9,665 ft. (highest).

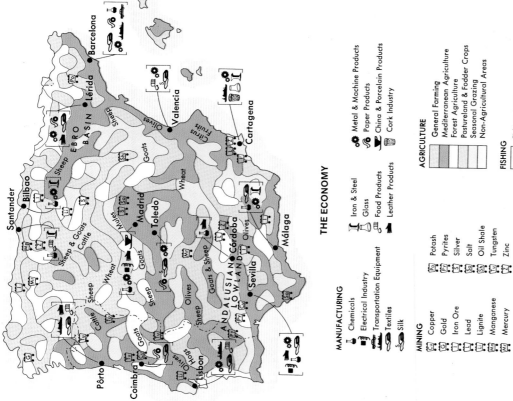

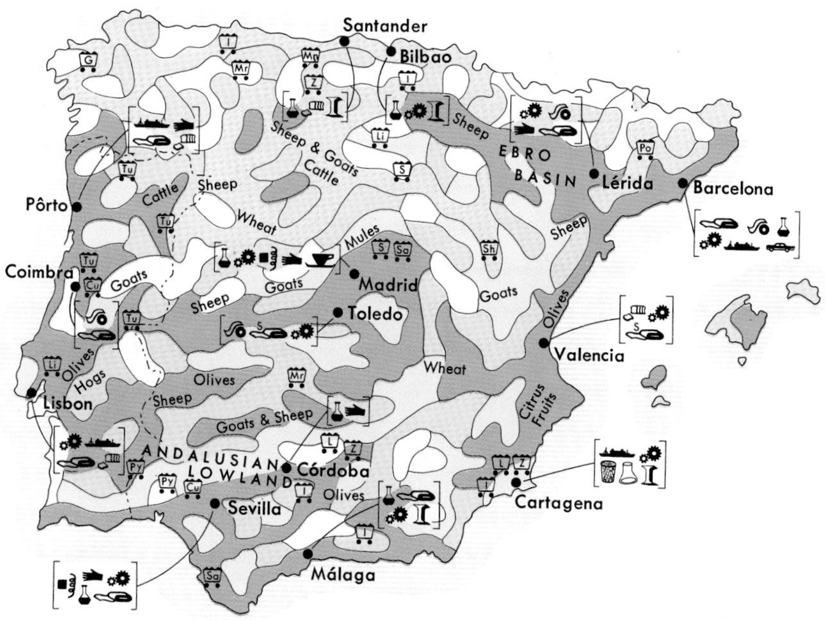

THE ECONOMY

MANUFACTURING
Chemicals
Electrical Industry
Transportation Equipment
Textiles
Silk
Iron & Steel
Glass
Food Products
Leather Products
Metal & Machine Products
Paper Products
China & Porcelain Products
Cork Industry

MINING
Copper
Gold
Iron Ore
Lead
Lignite
Manganese
Mercury
Potash
Pyrites
Silver
Salt
Oil Shale
Tungsten
Zinc

AGRICULTURE
General Farming
Mediterranean Agriculture
Forest Agriculture
Pastureland & Fodder Crops
Seasonal Grazing
Non-Agricultural Areas

FISHING
Fishing Areas

GROSS NATIONAL PRODUCT PER CAPITA
Spain $295 Portugal $230

THE WET AND THE DRY OF IBERIA

The green areas on this map show where the Atlantic's moist winds drop most of the rainfall that the Iberian Peninsula gets. Throughout the peninsula the population *(red dots)* tends to concentrate near rivers and coasts. Madrid, in a dry area *(yellow),* is heavily populated because of its politically important central location.

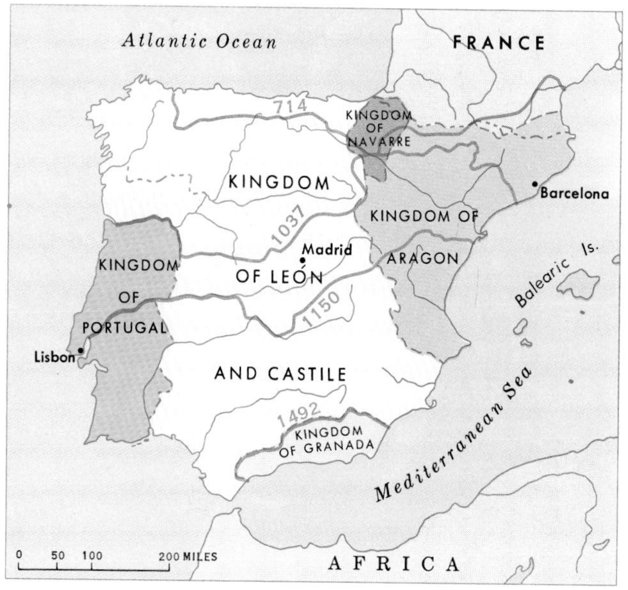

EXPULSION OF MOORS

The Moors crossed into Europe from Africa in 711 A.D., and it took eight centuries to expel them. Stages of their expulsion are shown by the dated red lines on the map above. By 714 the Moors controlled most of the peninsula. In 1492 the united Spanish kingdoms conquered the last Mohammedan kingdom, Granada *(bottom).*

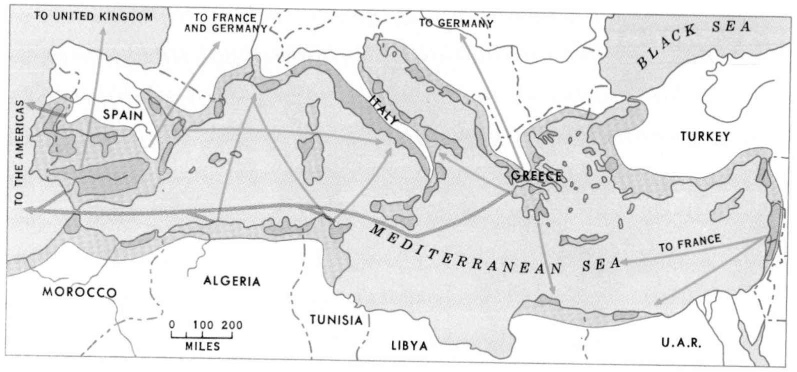

OLIVES IN THE MEDITERRANEAN BASIN

Because olive trees penetrate deep into the soil to reach low-lying moisture, they flourish in dry Mediterranean lands. In this map, olive-growing areas are indicated in shades of green, with the areas of highest production shown in dark green. The leading olive-producing countries of the world are Spain, Italy and Greece. Blue arrows indicate local routes of olive export; red arrows show export routes to the Americas.

IN THE ROUNDED HILLS of the province of Latium in central Italy, a shepherd tends his flock. In ancient times Italy was covered with forests and grasses, but the soil has for centuries been subjected to massive erosion. So poor has the soil become that the slopes of the predominantly hilly countryside of central Italy can grow little but sparse fodder. Goats and sheep can subsist on this fare, but both are close-cropping feeders. Allowed to overgraze, the flocks tear out the roots of grass that hold the soil and water. Thus Italy's difficulties with erosion continue to be compounded.

IN CLASSIC ITALY: SOFT HILLS, LUSTROUS MARBLE

IN JAGGED QUARRIES beneath a storm-swept Tuscan sky lie blocks of the marble with which sculptors and architects have created works of art for over 2,000 years. The Renaissance—an age that in thought and deed exulted in an awareness of mankind's environment—was shaped in this province north of Rome. From the quarries of Carrara, which lie in the foothills of the Apennines, Michelangelo chose the block for his *Moses*. Of this great stone he said, "Shapes that seem alive, wrought in hard mountain marble, will survive their maker, whom the years to dust return!"

ITALY
Barren Areas Above Timber
Evergreen Trees
Mixed Evergreen and Deciduous Trees
Deciduous Trees
Shrub
Grass
National Capitals
Canals
Cities
Railroads
1 inch = 67 Statute Miles
Miles 0 10 20 30 40 50 60 70
Conic Projection
Ligurian Sea
Adriatic Sea
Tyrrhenian Sea
Mediterranean Sea
Gulf of Venice
Gulf of Genoa
Gulf of Taranto
Strait of Bonifacio
CORSICA (FR.)
SARDINIA (IT.)
SICILY
CALABRIA
BASILICATA
TUSCANY
UMBRIA
LATIUM
ABRUZZI
MOLISE
LOMBARDY
PIEDMONT
EMILIA
MARCHES
APENNINES
ALPS
SWITZERLAND
AUSTRIA
GERMANY
YUGOSLAVIA
TUNISIA
ALGERIA (FR.)
LIECHTENSTEIN
MONACO
SAN MARINO
VATICAN CITY
ROME (Roma)
Milano (Milan)
Torino (Turin)
Venezia (Venice)
Firenze (Florence)
Napoli (Naples)
Genova (Genoa)
Palermo
Bologna
Bari
Messina
Catania
Cagliari
Vienna (Wien)
München (Munich)
Budapest
Zagreb
Ljubljana
Tunis
Longitude East of Greenwich
CM TERRAIN ITALY
COPYRIGHT BY
RAND MC NALLY & COMPANY
MADE IN U.S.A.

ITALY: "Italia! O Italia!" cried Lord Byron. "Thou who hast the fatal gift of beauty!" Here are the treasures of time: the historic monuments of Rome *(map, below)*, the breath-taking sweep of the Amalfi Drive around the Bay of Naples and Gulf of Salerno, the canals of Venice, the multi-hued grottoes of Capri, the art masterpieces of Florence and the ancient archeological treasures of Palermo on the volcanic island of Sicily. Each year more than 15 million tourists view the splendors of ancient Italy, bringing $450 million to the economy. But Italy lives largely on the produce of the plains of the Po River valley in the far north. In this region, occupying only some 15 per cent of the country's total surface, lives roughly a third of the population, growing some 60 per cent of the land's corn and 40 per cent of its wheat. In both crops Italy ranks as a major European producer. The valley also raises most of Italy's sugar beets and rice and most of its horses, cattle and swine; it provides impressive quantities of grapes, peas, beans, milk and cheese. The fertile soils deposited by the Po and its tributaries and irrigated by an intricate canal system make this the most important agricultural area in Southern Europe. In the south of Italy, however, poor soils and erosion have crippled agricultural enterprise. The food here is inadequate for the growing population, and the farmers are chronically impoverished.

AREA:	116,273 sq. mi.
POPULATION:	49,363,000.
	Largest city and capital: Rome.
CLIMATE:	Warm summers, cool winters, abundant rainfall in the north.
	Dry hot summers, mild rainy winters elsewhere.
ALTITUDES:	Monte Rosa, 15,200 ft. (highest); Rome, 66 ft.;
	Milan, 397 ft.; Mt. Etna in Sicily, 10,868 ft.

With more than 20 billion kilowatt hours taken annually from the dams in the Po River valley area, Italy is the greatest producer of hydroelectric power in Europe and its power capacity continues to expand. From the factories in the industrial triangle that centers on Genoa, Turin and Milan and a scattering of factories in the agricultural south come each year 6.7 million tons of steel, 2.2 million tons of pig iron, textiles, vehicles and chemicals.

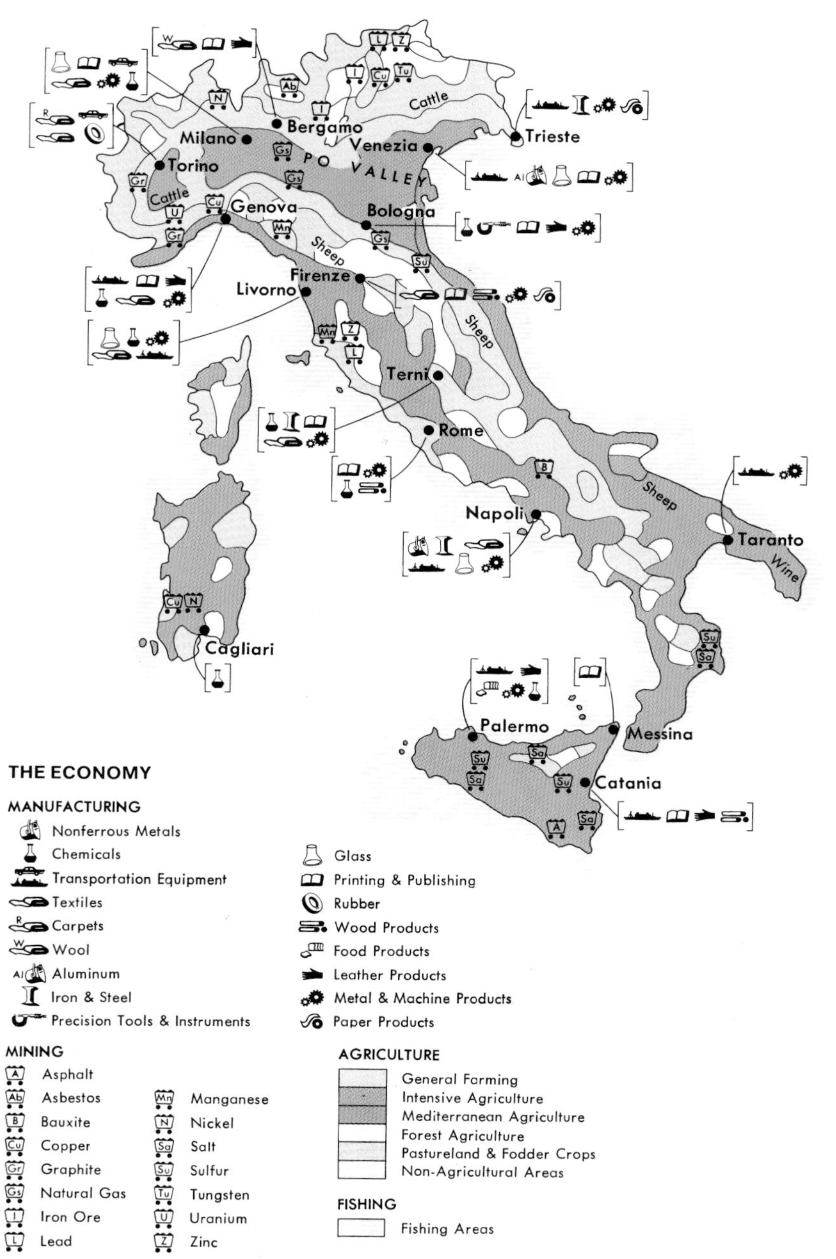

GROSS NATIONAL PRODUCT PER CAPITA $548

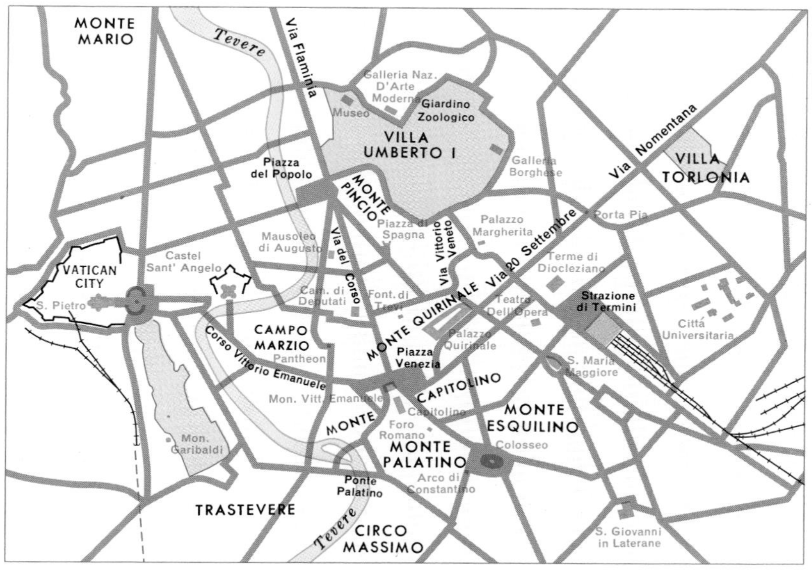

THE CITY OF CLASSICAL SPLENDOR

The streets of modern Rome *(above)* are studded with centuries-old monuments *(red)*. Constructed on high ground for protection against both human enemies and the mosquitoes of low marshes nearby, the capital now occupies nine square miles. Vatican City, enclosing St. Peter's Cathedral, is at the left.

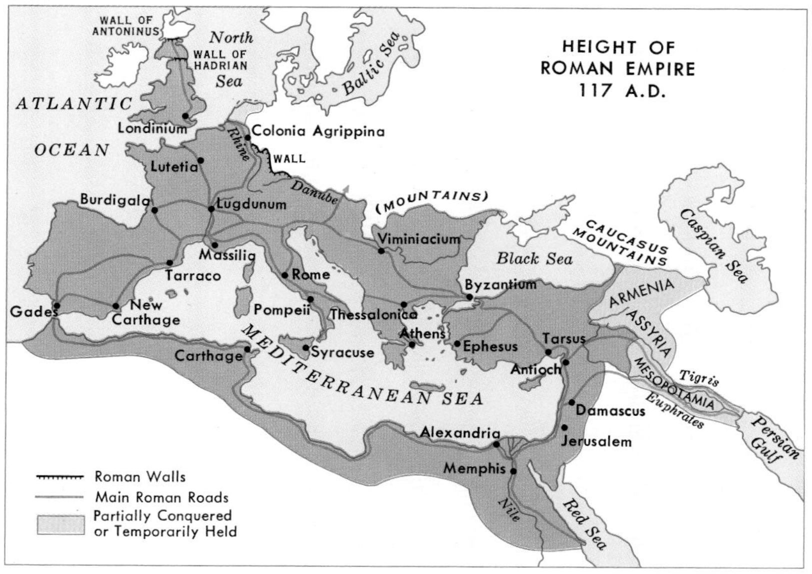

THE WIDE WORLD OF IMPERIAL ROME

Ancient Rome, its outposts connected by some 3,700 miles of brilliantly executed roads of stone slabs, controlled some 2.5 million square miles of territory at its height in the Second Century A.D. The Empire shown on this map stretched from the Red Sea to Scotland. The areas in orange were held only briefly.

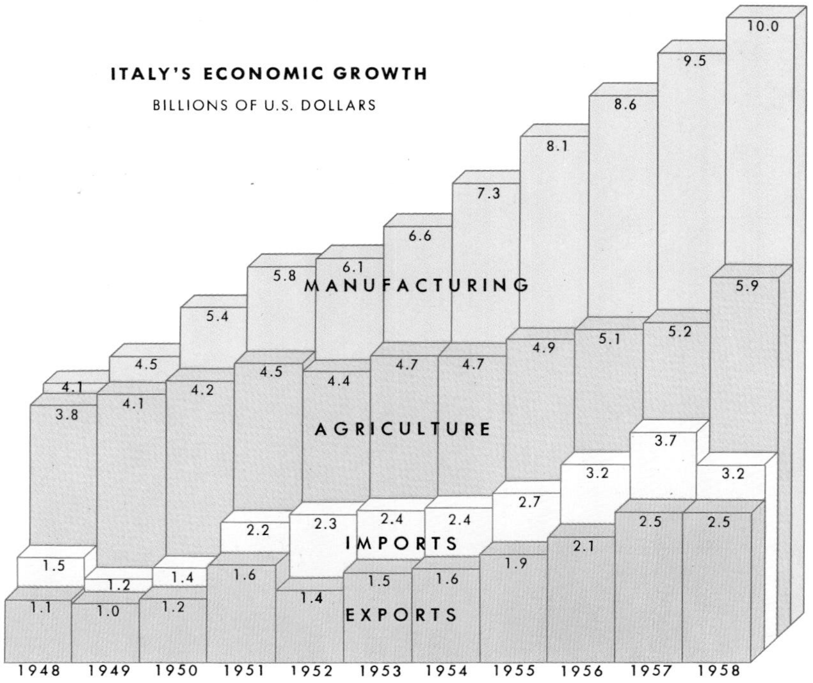

THE UPWARD MOVEMENT OF INDUSTRY

A decade of growth is seen in the ascending steps of this graph. Agricultural values *(green)* have stayed relatively stable largely because of a shortage of cropland. Italy compensates for an imbalance between exports and imports *(orange and yellow bars)* with its income from tourism and its foreign investments.

THE ENDURANCE OF STONE AND GREATNESS OF MIND

CLASSIC COLUMNS of the Parthenon in Athens frame a glimpse of the harsh and stony land where western civilization began. With access to sea routes of the Mediterranean, the ancient Greeks naturally turned to commerce. Stimulated by their contact with people and ideas of the East, they fashioned 2,500 years ago a culture whose timeless perfection is embodied in this great hilltop temple.

NATURAL MONOLITHS on a remote plateau in central Turkey provide crude dwellings for farmers and herdsmen. Erosion sculpted the monoliths into their odd shapes because the underlying rock was softer than the rock that now roofs the cones. The current inhabitants, shut off from the rest of the world by the desolate terrain, lead a primitive life little changed from that of their ancestors.

GREECE

GREECE: Like ruins of an Athenian temple, the land of Greece lies fragmented at the base of the Balkan Peninsula. The resulting jagged coastline provided shelter for the tiny vessels of the ancient world, and each valley, sheltered by mountains, was a sanctuary in which small states like Athens could prosper and build a great culture.

AREA:	51,169 sq. mi.
POPULATION:	8,319,000. Largest city: Athens Capital: Athens.
CLIMATE:	Hot, dry summers; mild, rainy winters.
ALTITUDES:	Mt. Olympus, 9,550 ft. (highest); Athens, 300 ft.

The Greeks of today are the heirs of almost 2,000 years of depredation: resources stolen or squandered, and land so rugged and eroded that only a fourth of it is arable. Greece has few minerals, but it does have hydroelectric resources. With foreign technical and financial help these are being developed and industrial plants are being built. Meanwhile, Greece can count on an expanding merchant marine and a continued influx of tourists.

ALBANIA: Isolated by mountains to the north and east and bounded by the Adriatic Sea on the west, Albania is a primitive land with few resources.

AREA:	11,097 sq. mi.
POPULATION:	1,562,000. Largest city and capital: Tiranë.

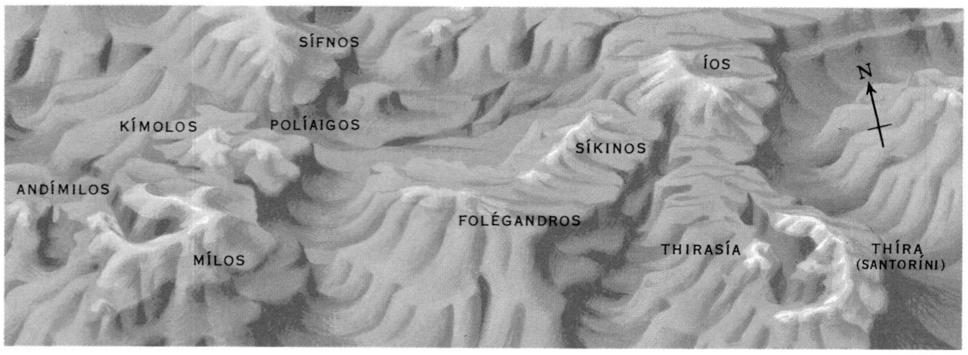

THE ISLANDS OF A SINKING COASTLINE

This drawing of the bottom of the Aegean Sea reveals the Greek islands of the Cyclades *(yellow)* to be peaks of mountains. Some of the mountains were once part of the mainland and were inundated when the Mediterranean seacoast sank during a late geologic era. Other islands later emerged from the sea because of volcanic action.

GROSS NATIONAL PRODUCT PER CAPITA
Greece $ 3 4 2 Albania Not Available

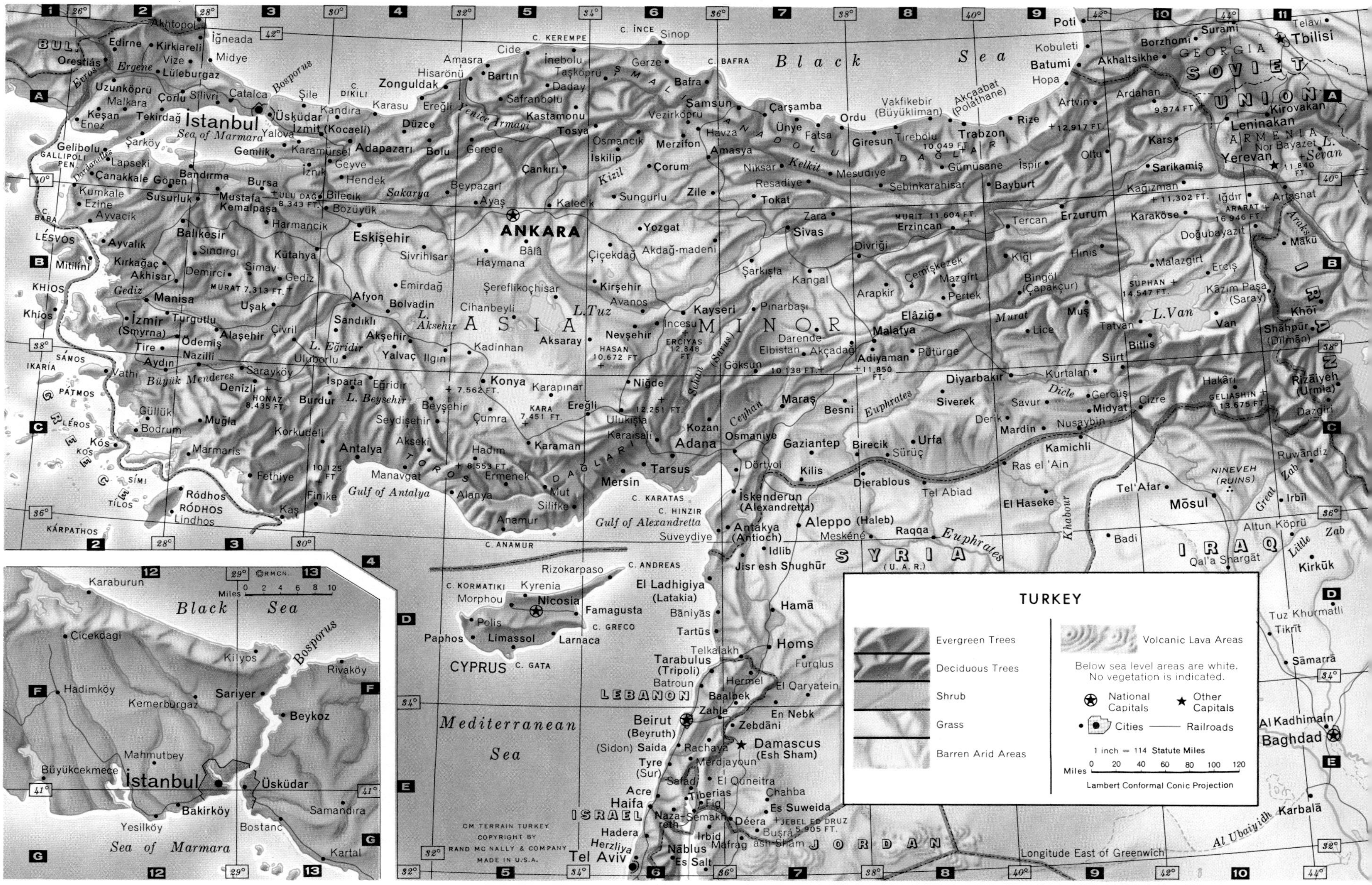

TURKEY: "A marriage of East and West," Turkey lies partly in Europe, mostly in Asia, occupying a rectangle between the Black Sea and the Mediterranean. In the European segment is the country's principal port, Istanbul, built on the site of the ancient Greek city of Byzantium. The "Golden Horn," Istanbul's crowded harbor, has for centuries been the great trading center of the eastern Mediterranean. Asian Turkey, called Anatolia, is largely a high plateau surrounded by rough-textured mountains that converge in the east. The highest of these, Mount Ararat, is where legend says Noah's Ark came to rest after the Flood.

AREA:	296,108 sq. mi.
POPULATION:	26,494,000. Largest city: Istanbul. Capital: Ankara.
CLIMATE:	Hot summers, mild winters, with greater temperature extremes on interior plateau.
ALTITUDES:	Mt. Ararat, 16,946 ft. (highest); Ankara, 2,250 ft.

Despite its eastern heritage and its preponderantly Asian location, Turkey has western goals. Stultified for hundreds of years under Ottoman rule, the country began to make advances in technology and education after World War I. Today Turkey is on its way to becoming a modern state in government and outlook. Eighty per cent of the Turkish labor force is engaged in agriculture, but great efforts are being made to exploit forests and other natural resources. An important share of the world's chrome ore comes from Turkey, and diversified industry is being developed with assistance from European countries and the United States.

CYPRUS: An independent nation since 1960, Cyprus is an island with a stable economy. It produces adequate food for its own needs and mines deposits of copper, iron ore, chrome and asbestos in small quantities for export.

AREA:	3,572 sq. mi.
POPULATION:	559,000. Capital: Nicosia.

THE ECONOMY

MANUFACTURING
- Nonferrous Metals
- Chemicals
- Transportation Equipment
- Textiles
- Cotton
- Silk
- Wool
- Iron & Steel
- Glass
- Printing & Publishing
- Rubber
- Food Products
- Metal & Machine Products
- China & Porcelain Products
- Cement

MINING
- Asphalt
- Antimony
- Bauxite
- Coal
- Chromium
- Copper
- Iron Ore
- Lead
- Lignite
- Petroleum
- Zinc

AGRICULTURE
- General Farming
- Mediterranean Agriculture
- Plantation Agriculture
- Forest Agriculture
- Pastureland & Fodder Crops
- Seasonal Grazing
- Non-Agricultural Areas

FISHING
- Fishing Areas

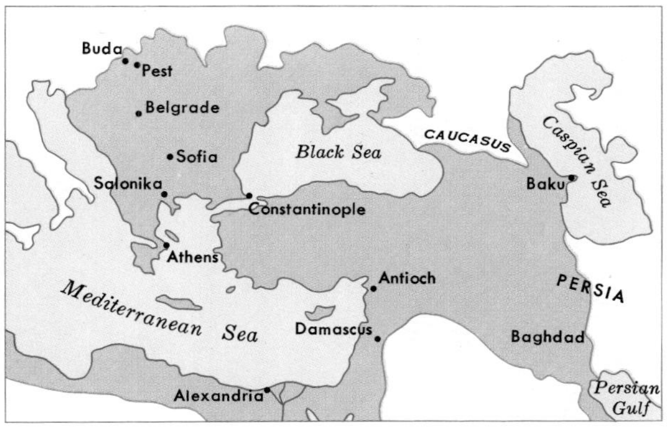

THE EMPIRE OF THE OTTOMAN TURKS

At its height the Ottoman Empire *(purple)* ranged across southeast Europe, the Near East and North Africa. The Ottoman Turks began their expansion from eastern Anatolia at the end of the 14th Century, conquering Constantinople in 1453. Despotic and ingrown, the empire began to decline about 1683. It came to an end in 1923 with the establishment of the Republic of Turkey.

GROSS NATIONAL PRODUCT PER CAPITA $151

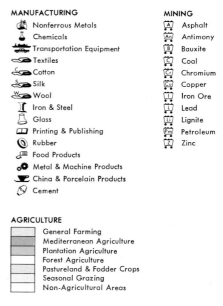

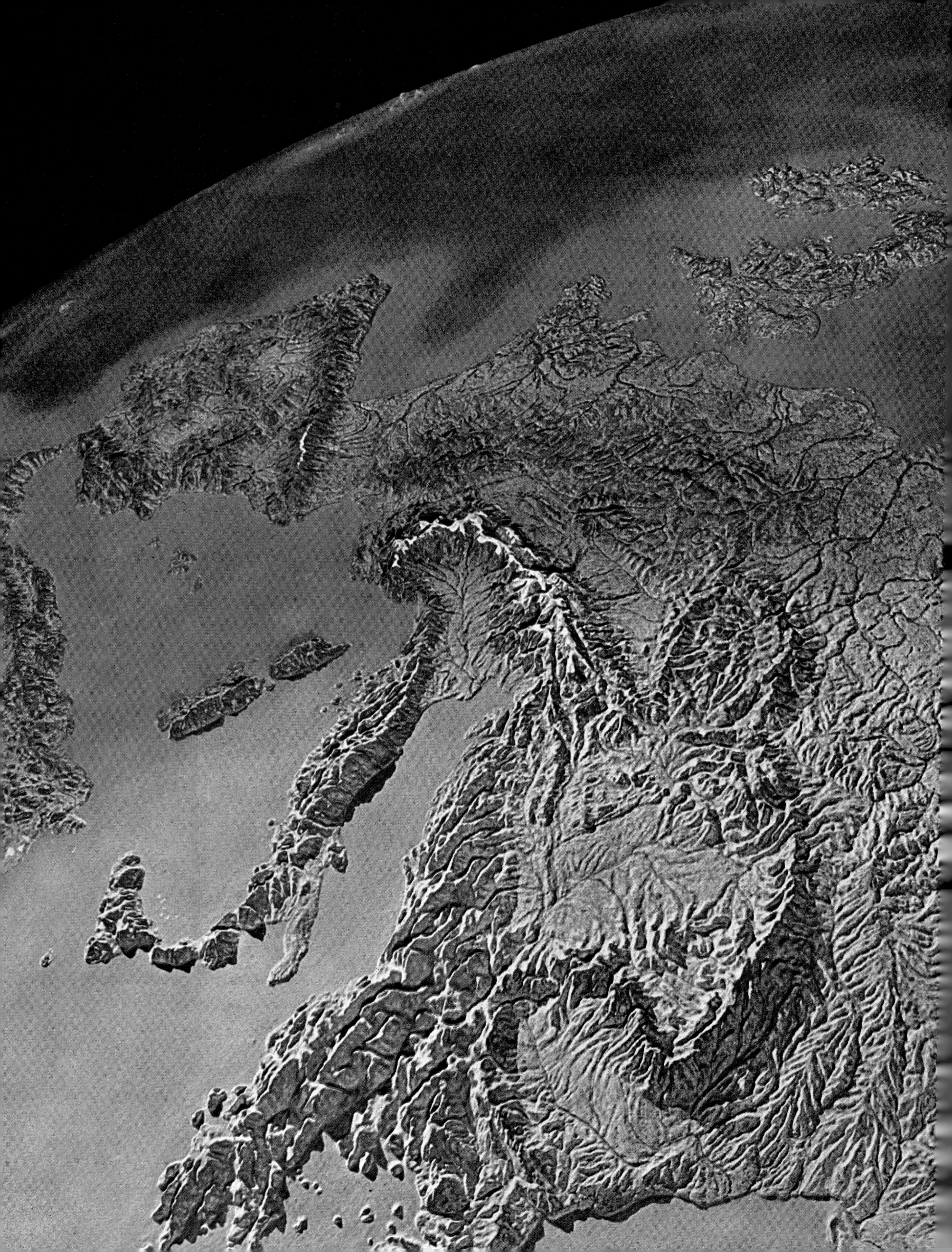

CENTRAL AND EASTERN EUROPE

The 487,342-square-mile area of Eastern and Central Europe spans the continent from the Baltic to the Black and Adriatic Seas and from the Franco-Swiss Jura Mountains to the rolling lands of the Soviet Ukraine. To geographers it is known as a "shatter belt," embodying most of the geographic and social features found in all of the European continent. It has young jagged peaks and old rounded mountains, pine-covered lowlands and rich fertile plains. Here are political units that have pronounced geographic boundaries, and artificial states with a history of fluctuating frontiers. The people of Central and Eastern Europe belong to many ethnic groups and speak scores of languages. They live in historically cosmopolitan cities such as Vienna and Budapest, as well as in backward villages still clinging to Moslem customs that are a legacy from earlier eras of Turkish rule. Christianity is the predominant religion today, but many different forms of it are practiced.

Eastern and Central Europe have rarely known peace or stability. In the 14th Century, Slavic tribes that had drifted in from the East were caught here between the advancing Moslem Ottoman and retreating Christian Byzantine Empires. The clash of cultures fostered sectionalism and hampered social and commercial intercourse among tribes.

Only in recent decades have large-scale efforts been made to exploit Eastern Europe's deposits of coal, iron, pitchblende, bauxite and oil. But now industrialization is playing an increasingly important role in the economies of all these countries. Considerable effort is going into the production of raw mineral materials and the manufacture of heavy industrial goods.

In many of the folk songs that are sung in the more than 150 dialects of the area, a poignant theme is voiced. This is love of country and pride in national identity. But toward the end of the 19th Century, driven by despotic governments or seeking broader opportunities, millions of Central and East Europeans left their homelands for the cities and prairies of the United States and Canada. And so Slovenes, Croats, Bulgars, Serbs, Slovaks, Bohemians and many other old peoples of Europe helped to settle a New World.

AN ENORMOUS EXPANSE, Eastern and Central Europe are here seen from a vantage point high above the Black Sea *(bottom center)*. The region runs from the Baltic *(right)* to the Adriatic *(left)*. In the distance, beyond the Alps, are Western Europe and the Atlantic.

A SPARKLING LAKE, Lugano reflects the lights of the resort hotels that line its shores. Lying between Italy and Switzerland, Lugano is fed by the glacial streams of the surrounding Alps.

LORDLY ALPINE LANDS

A FLOWING GLACIER, Switzerland's deep Aletsch *(opposite)* is formed by the juncture of ice masses. Cargoes of rock and earth are seen as dark tracks. The Jungfrau is second from left at top.

A MEANDERING RIVER, the Danube is seen from an Austrian hilltop at sunset. An artery fed by more than 300 tributaries, the Danube at close range looks muddy. It is blue only in legend.

SWITZERLAND

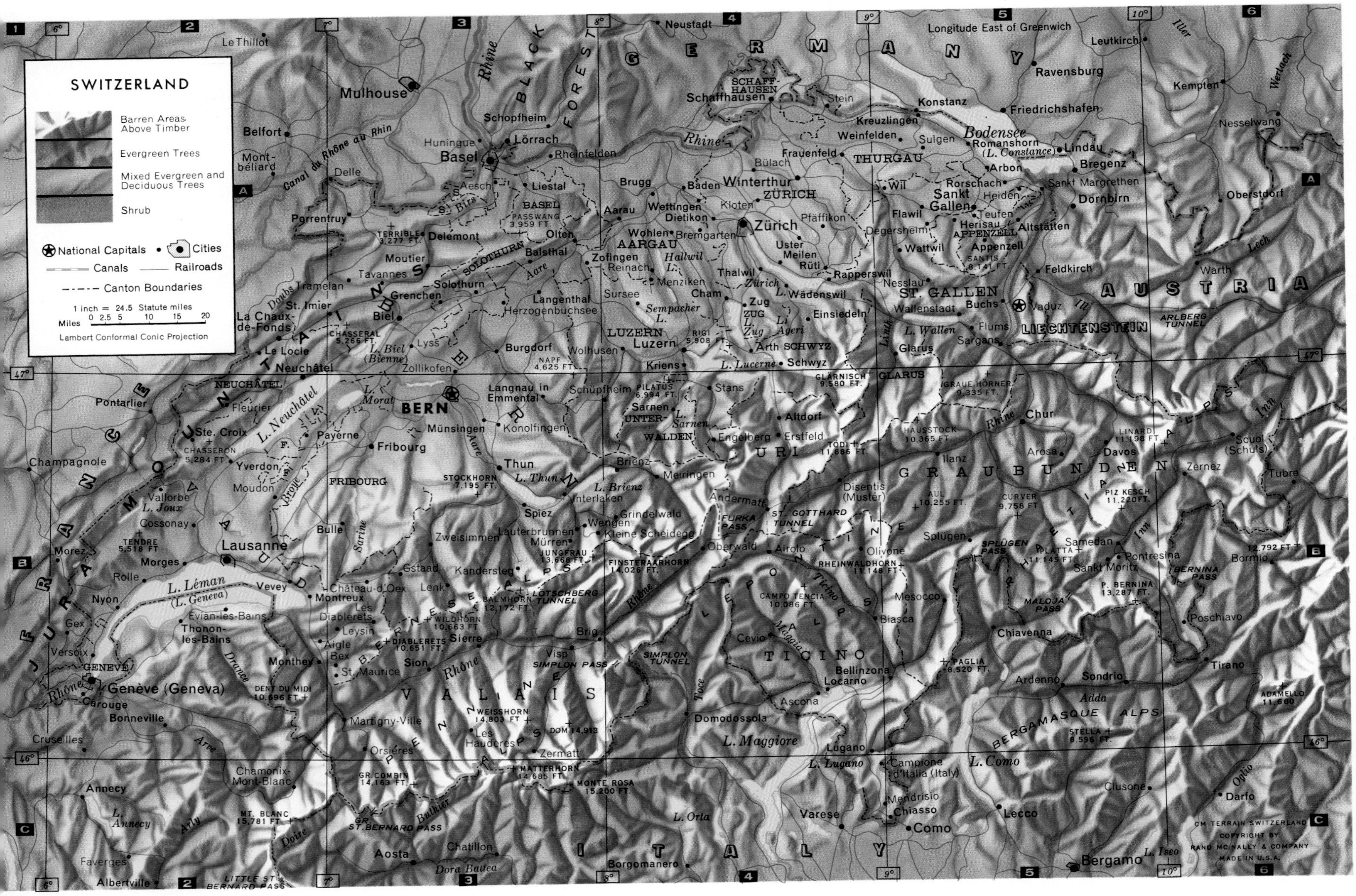

SWITZERLAND: Here is the roof of Europe. On the French border rise the 3,000-foot-high ridges of the Jura Mountains, geological cousins to the Alps which range across the southern half of the country and soar to heights of 13,000 feet and more. Climbers were attracted to Swiss slopes a century ago, and today 27 million vacationers a year make the hotel and resort business the fourth largest industry in Switzerland.

The Mittelland, a 30-mile-wide plateau that stretches between the Jura and the Alps from Lake Geneva to Lake Constance, is where 70 per cent of the Swiss live. Here, utilizing ancient grazing methods *(diagram below, right)*, the Swiss annually produce 67,000 tons of cheese for an export market of 50 countries. Small quantities of cereals and potatoes are grown throughout the north.

AREA: 15,937 sq. mi.
POPULATION: 5,246,000. Largest city: Zürich. Capital: Bern.
CLIMATE: Cool summers, cold winters north of Alps; warm summers, mild winters south of Alps. Great variation of temperature and rainfall in the mountains.
ALTITUDES: Pointe Dufour near Monte Rosa, 15,217 ft. (highest); The Matterhorn, 14,685 ft.

To pay for the food they are forced to import and to compensate for the lack of raw materials necessary for heavy manufacturing, the Swiss long ago turned to the production of small quality goods. The renowned Swiss watches have been made in the workshops and factories of the Jura foothills and the Mittelland since the late 16th Century. Today 25 million watches are exported annually. Precision tools and engine parts, chemicals and fabrics are other Swiss products. Shipped from the river port of Basel down the Rhine into Germany and through the long Alpine tunnels that bore south toward Italy, Swiss exports bring the nation an income of $1.7 billion a year.

THE ECONOMY

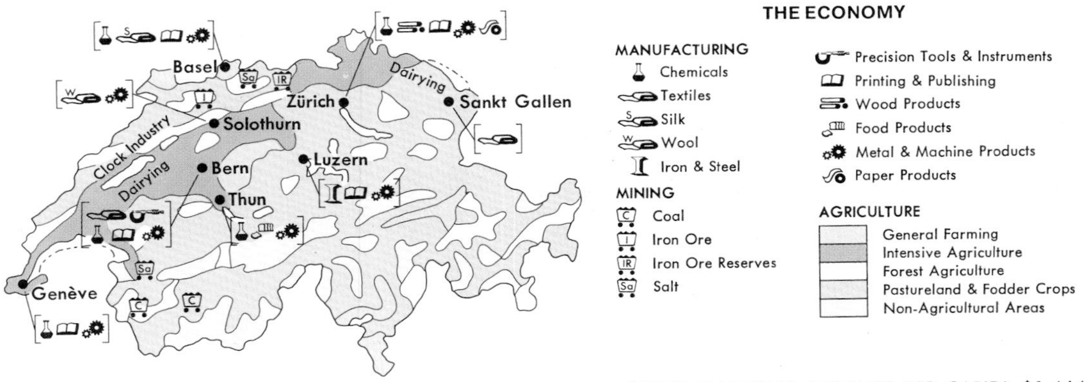

GROSS NATIONAL PRODUCT PER CAPITA $1,464

GRAZING PATTERNS BY THE SEASONS

The cycle of the grazing season in Switzerland and other areas with limited flatland is illustrated by the dated arrows in the drawing above. Starting in late spring, livestock are grazed on lower slopes *(center)*, then gradually driven upward into the mountains as pasturage is cropped off and the sun brings grass to higher meadows. This system, called vertical transhumance, is reversed in the fall.

AUSTRIA

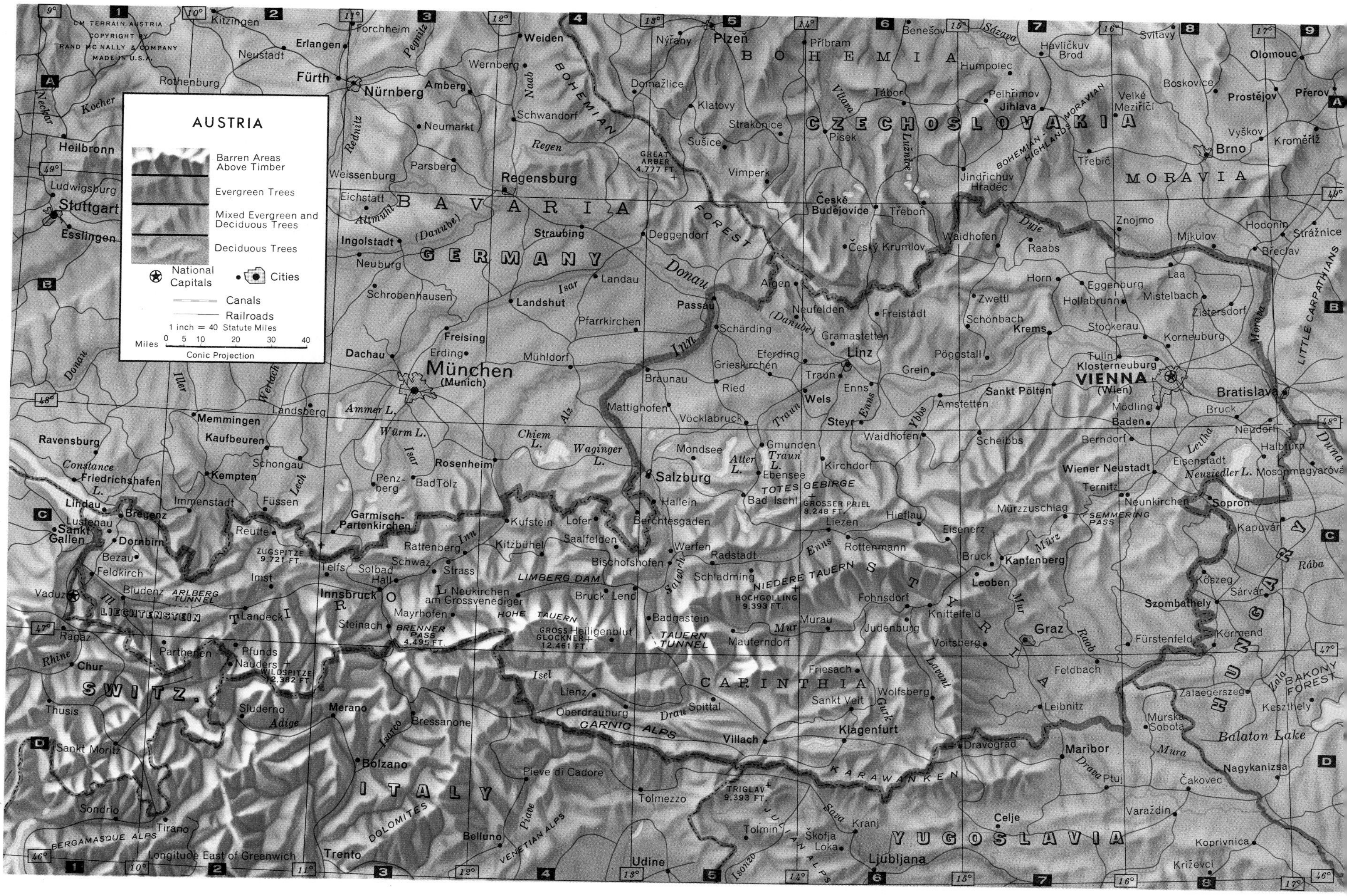

AUSTRIA: "We live at an ethnographic crossroads," wrote Austrian Count Ferdinand Czernin, "where the Latin world meets the Teuton and the Slav meets them both." At the eastern end of Austria is located the only break in Central Europe between the Alps and the Bohemian highlands. Southward, the Brenner Pass leads through the Alps to the rich Po valley of Italy.

The high isolated valleys of the Alps favor neither industry nor agriculture; tourism is the major occupation here. And in the northwest, where the Bohemian highlands descend from Czechoslovakia, the land supports few crops. But the Danubian plains are rich in loess and produce large quantities of potatoes, rye and oats. Altogether, Austrian farmers supply their industrialized country with almost 80 per cent of its food.

AREA: 32,365 sq. mi.
POPULATION: 7,082,000. Largest city and capital: Vienna.
CLIMATE: Cool summers, cold winters; temperature and rainfall vary with altitude and location.
ALTITUDES: Gross Glockner, 12,461 ft. (highest); Vienna, 550 ft.

The Danubian plains support an economy whose total value of manufactured products is two billion dollars. The area has minerals too, as attested by the names of cities and mountains. In the west, Salzburg (salt castle) is a center of the chemical industry. Iron and steel mills are located along the Mürz River close to Eisenerz (iron ore). Near Zistersdorf lie the petroleum reserves that rank Austria the fourth largest oil producer in Europe.

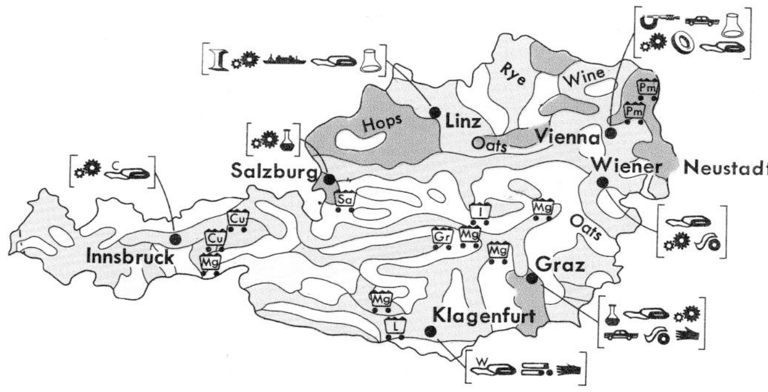

THE ECONOMY

MANUFACTURING
- Chemicals
- Transportation Equipment
- Textiles
- Cotton
- Wool
- Iron & Steel
- Precision Tools & Instruments
- Glass
- Rubber
- Wood Products
- Leather Products
- Metal & Machine Products
- Paper Products

MINING
- Cu Copper
- Gr Graphite
- Iron Ore
- Lead
- Mg Magnesium
- Pm Petroleum
- Sa Salt

AGRICULTURE
- General Farming
- Intensive Agriculture
- Forest Agriculture
- Pastureland & Fodder Crops
- Non-Agricultural Areas

GROSS NATIONAL PRODUCT PER CAPITA $703

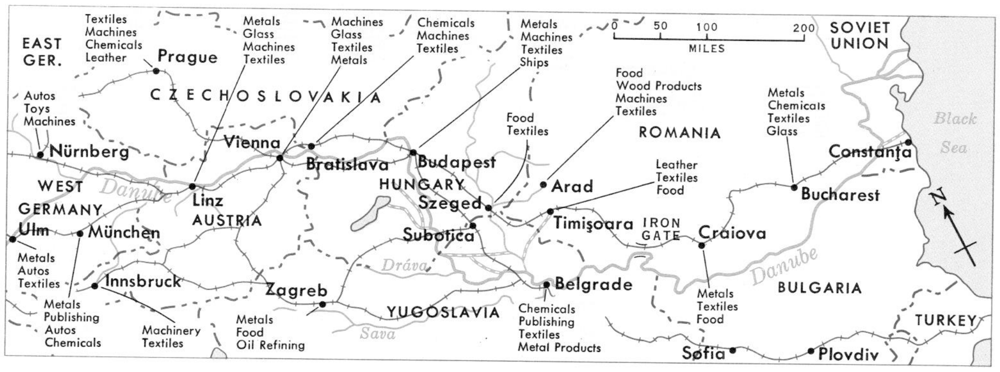

A LONG RIVER SHORT ON TRAFFIC

The Danube makes an 1,800-mile voyage through or bordering on eight countries, from West Germany to the Black Sea. Despite widespread manufacturing in the cities of this basin (as indicated on the map above), river traffic is limited by the fact that sources of bulky raw materials are downstream and it is costly to have them shipped upstream to factories.

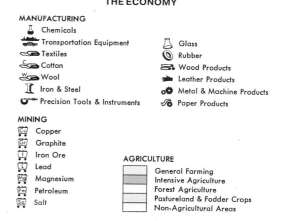

THE SPARSE EARTH OF THE BALKANS

GREEN PASTURES clothe the steep pine-forested slopes of the Rhodope Mountains which rise above a country village in southern Bulgaria *(opposite)*. Limited level land in mountainous Bulgaria makes grazing and forestry the only important pursuits in this area.

WHITE LIMESTONE outcroppings on the surface of the soil in Yugoslavia surround the small, cleared plots being plowed by a Dalmatian farmer. Farmland here is fertile, but the ever-present rock and primitive methods of farming hamper extensive cultivation.

YUGOSLAVIA

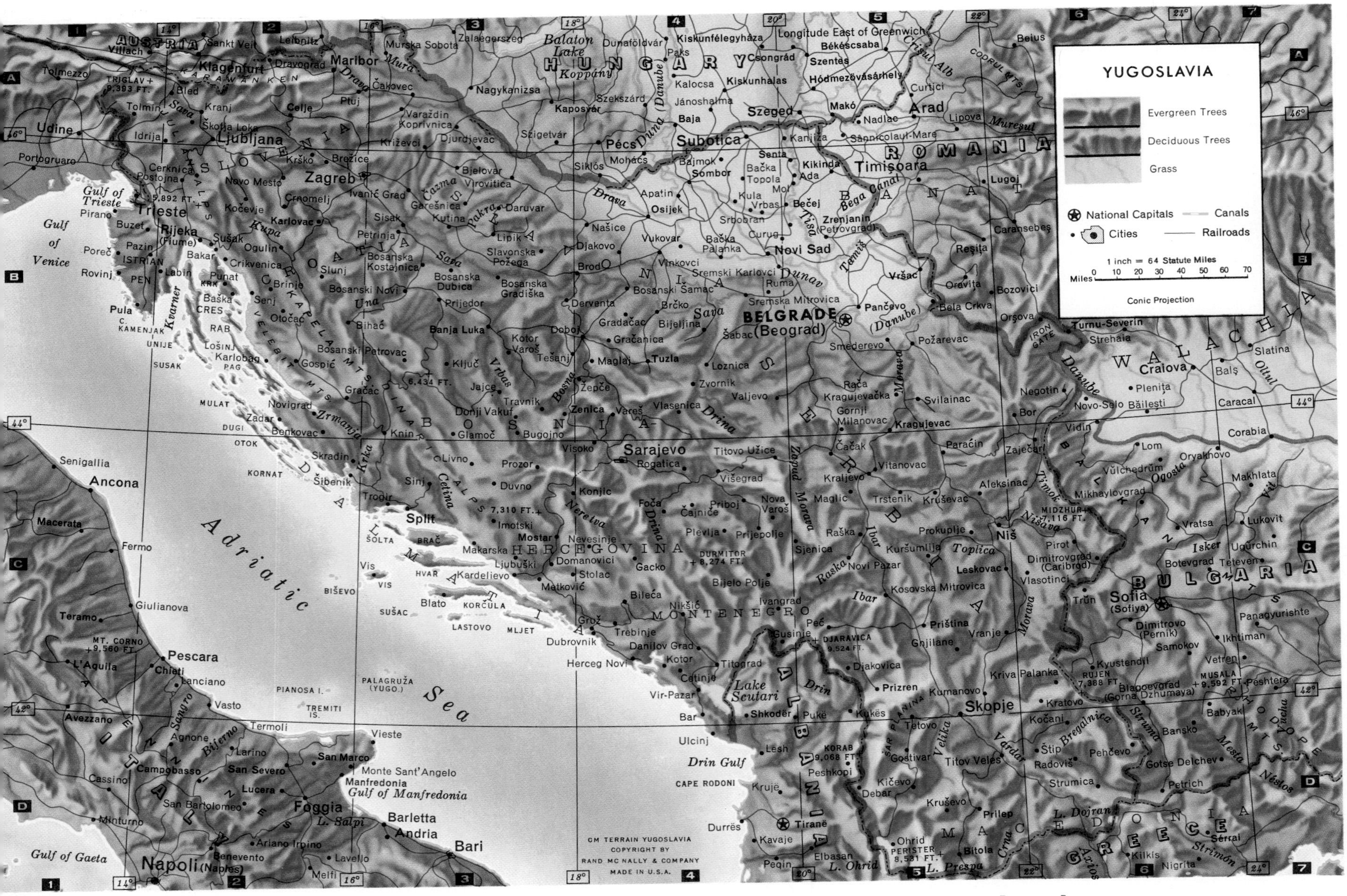

YUGOSLAVIA: Eighty per cent of Yugoslavia is rough hill and mountain area. Wooded uplands and eroded plateaus stretching from Austria to Greece descend to the narrow Adriatic Coast, which has a spectacularly irregular shore line broken by numerous gulfs, bays, coves and channels. Yugoslavia's only large lowland–the fertile Pannonian Plain–lies in the northeast and is drained by the Danubian river system.

AREA:	98,740 sq. mi.
POPULATION:	18,796,000. Largest city and capital: Belgrade.
CLIMATE:	Hot dry summers and mild damp winters along the coast; cooler winters and heavier rainfall in the interior.
ALTITUDES:	Djaravica, 9,524 ft. (highest); Belgrade, 433 ft.

In the mountain pastures the Yugoslavs graze sheep and cows. In the valleys they plant cereals, hemp, cotton and sugar beets. As the country began to recover from World War II, a major effort at industrialization was launched. Today, heavy and light industry, including textiles, steel, chemicals and wood products, is replacing agriculture as the basis of the economy. And in the mountain areas that had once isolated its people, Yugoslavia mines enough antimony and bauxite to put it among Europe's important producers of these ores.

GROSS NATIONAL PRODUCT PER CAPITA $203

HOW YUGOSLAVIA WAS PUT TOGETHER

Yugoslavia *(outlined in red, above)* first came into being in 1918, when parts of Austria-Hungary *(yellow)* were united with the states of Montenegro and Serbia as the Kingdom of Serbs, Croats and Slovenes. In 1929 it was renamed the Kingdom of Yugoslavia, meaning "land of Southern Slavs." In 1945 the country became a Federal People's Republic.

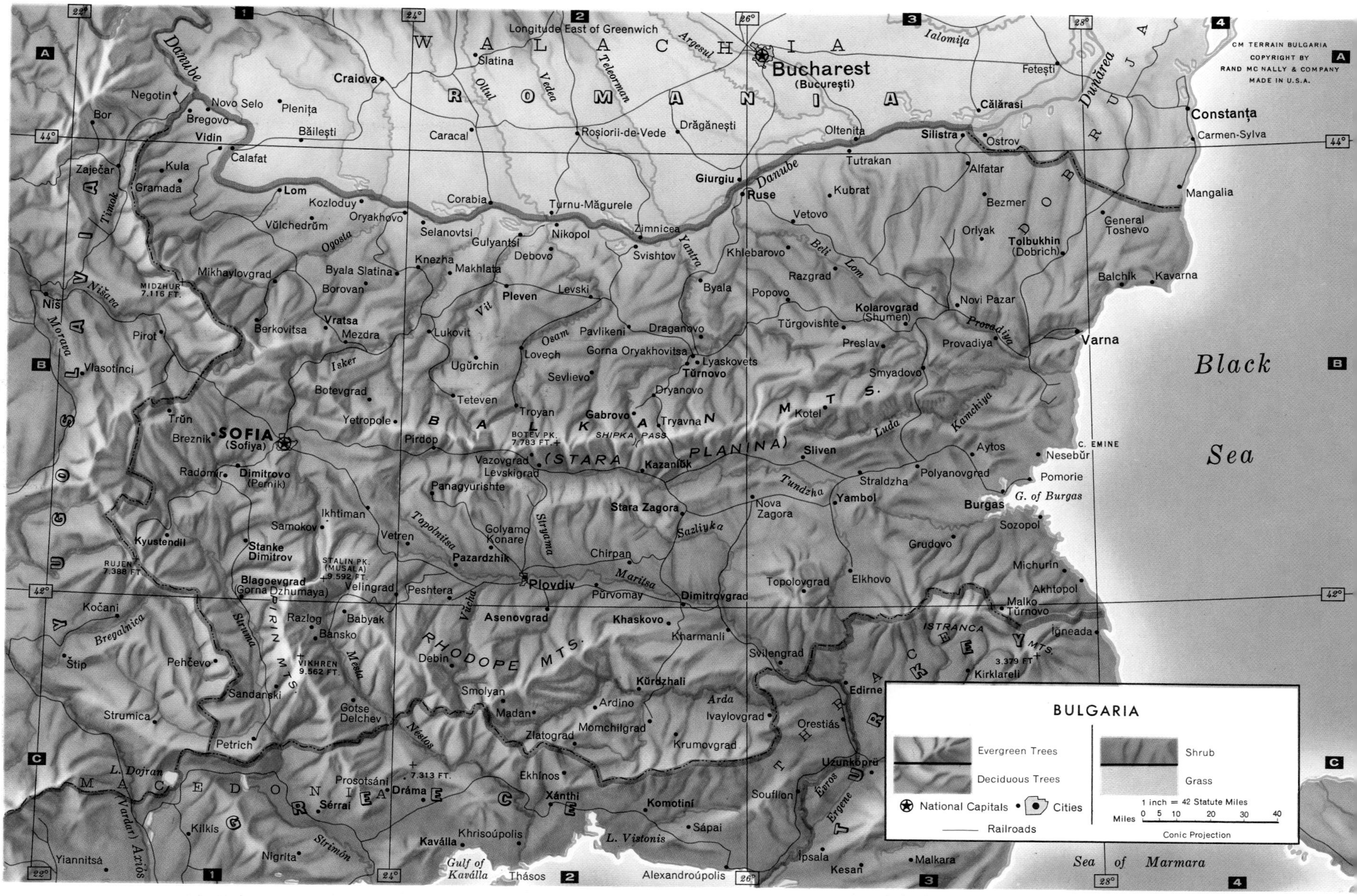

BULGARIA: The northern part of Bulgaria, extending from the Balkan Mountains to the Danube, which marks most of the border with Romania, is known as the Balkan Plateau. The uplands here are planted to wheat, the deep valleys to corn. The farmers live in villages in the valleys and make a long trek to their upland fields each day. Abutting the plateau is the Balkan range, a mountainous region in which sheep and cattle are raised. Here there are small deposits of coal and metals, and potential sources of water power. At the base of the mountains thousands of acres are given to the cultivation of roses for the extraction of attar, used in perfume. Between the Balkans and the Rhodope range to the south is the Maritsa Valley—"Bulgaria's California"—noted for its diversity of crops. Among these are wheat, cotton, fruit, aromatic tobacco and rice.

The Balkan Mountains are called *Stara Planina* (old mountain) in Bulgarian. The local name is apt, for the Balkans have rounded summits, with almost no rocky peaks or glaciers, and permanent snow can be found only in a few sheltered crevices. The Rhodope Mountains in the south are higher and more rugged.

AREA:	43,036 sq. mi.
POPULATION:	7,859,000. Largest city and capital: Sofia.
CLIMATE:	Warm summers, cold winters; lowest temperatures in the interior highlands; most rain in summer.
ALTITUDES:	Stalin Peak (formerly Musala), 9,592 ft. (highest).

In 1939 Bulgaria's economy was 70 per cent agricultural; now it is well over 50 per cent industrial. Much of Bulgarian industry is devoted to processing cereal grains and specialty crops. But there are also mills and plants turning out machine tools, and production of chemicals and steel has been steadily increased.

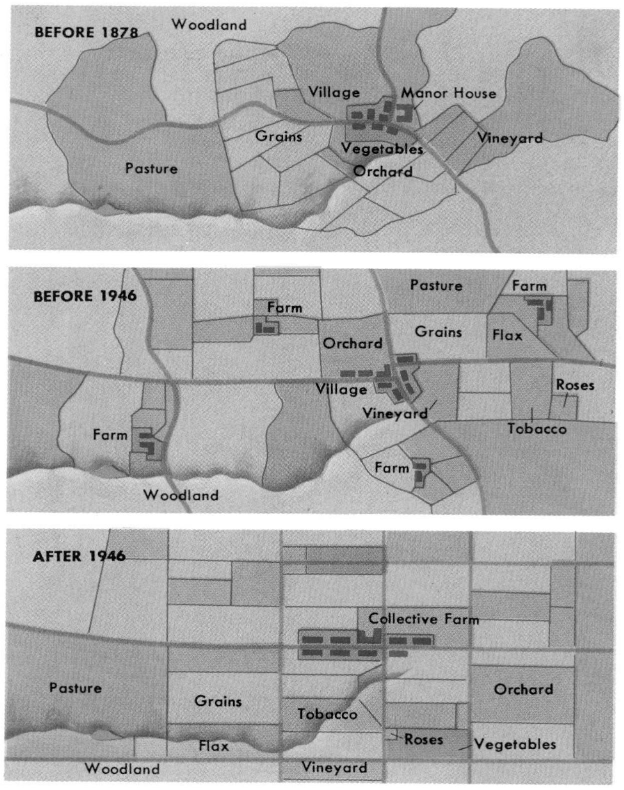

FROM FEUDAL MANOR TO COLLECTIVE

Before its liberation from Turkish rule *(top drawing)*, Bulgaria had big farms centered about a manor. Manorial rights were ended in 1878 and peasants became small landowners. In 1946 collectivization brought back large units.

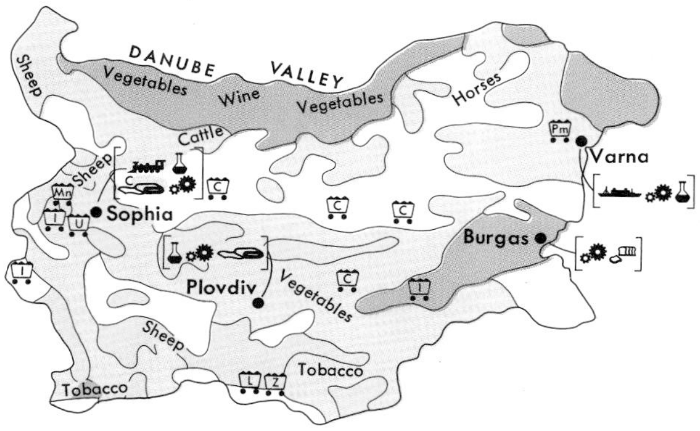

THE ECONOMY

MANUFACTURING
- Chemicals
- Transportation Equipment
- Textiles
- Cotton
- Food Products
- Metal & Machine Products

MINING
- Coal
- Iron Ore
- Lead
- Manganese
- Petroleum
- Zinc
- Uranium

AGRICULTURE
- General Farming
- Intensive Agriculture
- Plantation Agriculture
- Forest Agriculture
- Pastureland & Fodder Crops

GROSS NATIONAL PRODUCT PER CAPITA $285

THE COLLECTIVES OF HUNGARY AND ROMANIA

THE "GOLD OF HUNGARY," its wheat harvest, is fed into a thresher by field hands on a collective farm near Eger. The farm is at the northern edge of the Great Plain, which is called the Alföld. Corn and wheat account for more than 60 per cent of Hungary's cultivated land, but Hungarian grain yields have been hampered by shortages of fertilizers and modern farm machinery.

A ROMANIAN COOPERATIVE spreads itself across the broad, fertile uplands of Transylvania *(opposite)*. This cooperative combines vegetable and dairy farming with the production of cereals, notably corn and oats. On the slope in the foreground are fruit trees. There are fields of tall corn ready for harvest behind the trees and near the low buildings *(center)*, which are dairy sheds.

A MIXED FLOCK of sheep and goats on a Moldavian country road is shepherded home after grazing on high pasture land. Romania has more than 11 million sheep and goats. Sheep like those seen here are bred for their wool, the goats for milk and cheese. The hillsides visible in the distance are thickly wooded and help make forestry one of the country's most important industries.

HUNGARY

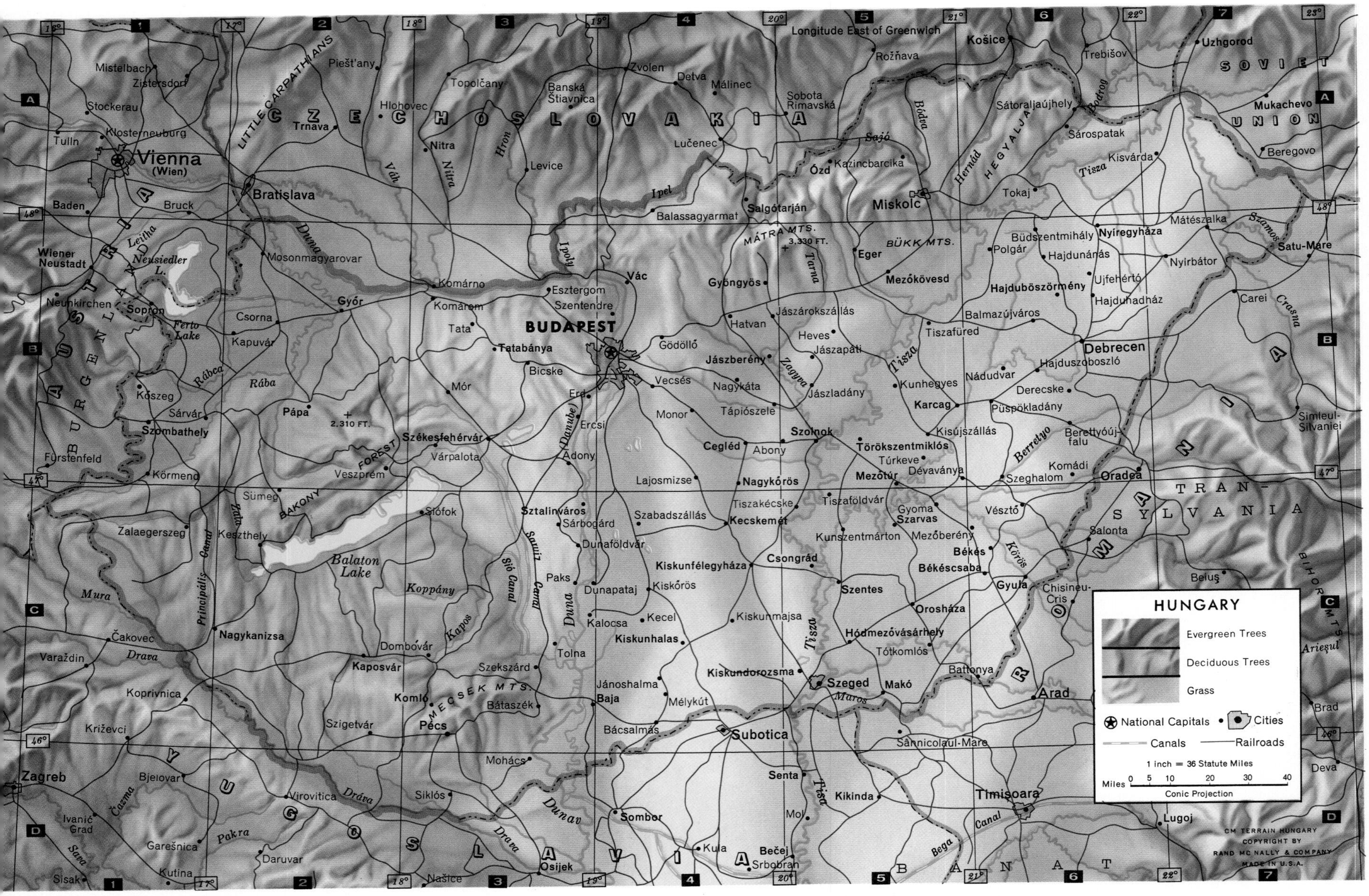

HUNGARY: A pivotal area between East and West, Hungary has been called "Asia's westernmost outpost" as well as "one of the earliest sites of Western culture." The country owes its beginning in the late Ninth Century to the Magyars, descendants of Finno-Ugrian tribesmen who made their way to Central Europe from the far side of the Ural Mountains. Hungary's position astride the productive Danube basin made it a natural battleground between eastern and western European countries. From 1867 on, the country was a proud partner of the Dual Monarchy of Austria-Hungary. In the breakup of the Austro-Hungarian Empire after World War I, Hungary lost about two thirds of its territory and population.

Hungary has fertile soil, but its agriculture is periodically depressed by severe summer drought. The country is poor in power and natural resources, although industry has increased considerably since World War II and now provides nearly half of the national income. The most important mineral deposit is bauxite.

AREA: 35,909 sq. mi.
POPULATION: 9,943,000. Largest city and capital: Budapest.
CLIMATE: Warm summers, cold winters; most rain in summer.
ALTITUDES: Mt. Kekes in Mátra Mts., 3,330 ft. (highest); Budapest, 370 ft.

At Budapest, the Danube, which cuts through the country from north to south, intersects a belt of hills that angles from northeast to southwest, thus roughly dividing Hungary into four regions. The northeastern quadrant dominated by hilly ranges has timber, and there are iron ore and coal near Miskolc. In the northwestern quadrant, the Kis Alföld (little plain) descends to Fertö Lake from a hilly belt which includes the heights of Buda and the forested Bakony ridge. This region has lignite and major deposits of bauxite. The southwestern quadrant is a rich, rolling land bracketed by 48-mile-long Balaton Lake and the coal-bearing Mecsek massif. Filling the big southeastern quadrant is the Nagy Alföld (great plain), which consists of miles of black earth, sand and marshy flood-plains, flat as a floor, along the meandering Tisza. A rich farming area is located near Debrecen.

THE ECONOMY

MANUFACTURING
- Chemicals
- Transportation Equipment
- Textiles
- Wool
- Iron & Steel
- Wood Products
- Food Products
- Leather Products
- Metal & Machine Products

MINING
- Bauxite
- Iron Ore
- Lignite
- Petroleum
- Uranium

AGRICULTURE
- General Farming
- Intensive Agriculture
- Forest Agriculture
- Pastureland & Fodder Crops

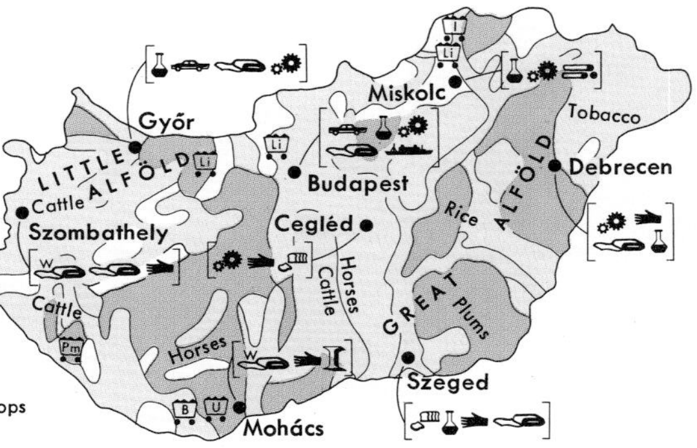

GROSS NATIONAL PRODUCT PER CAPITA $387

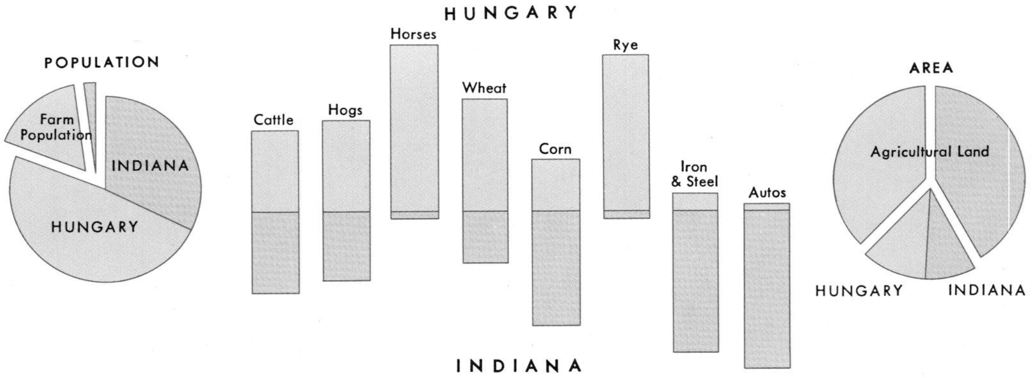

TWO WAYS OF LIFE: HUNGARY VERSUS INDIANA, U.S.A.

The Hungarian economy is shown here in comparison with Indiana's. The two are similar in farm area *(circle at right)* and climate. With twice Indiana's population *(circle at left)*, Hungary employs 12 times as many workers to grow two thirds as big a cereal crop. The bar graph contrasts Hungary's agricultural economy with the mixed economy of the U.S. state.

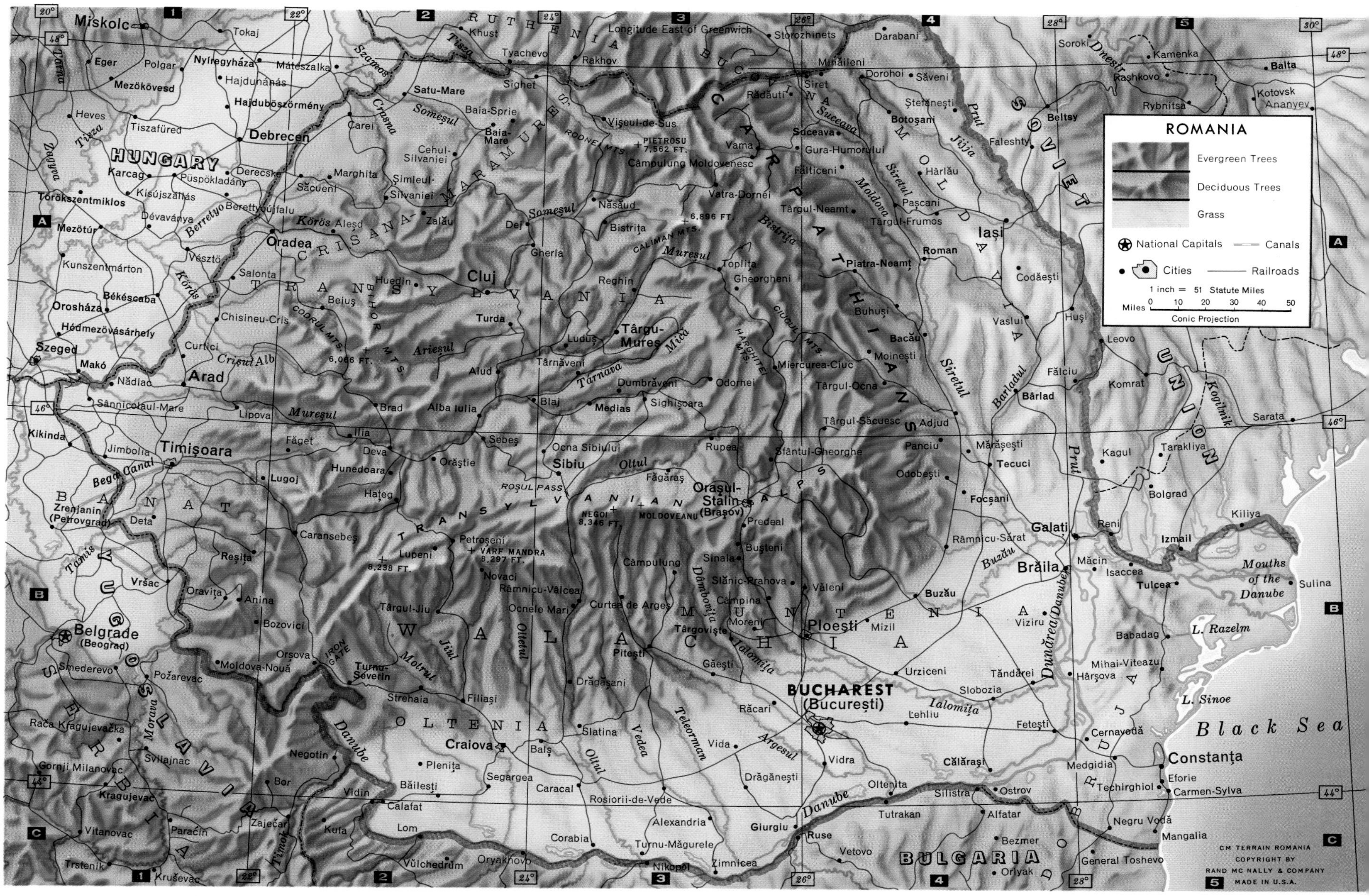

ROMANIA:

The mountain ridges in the center of Romania appear to constitute an impregnable redoubt, but they are heavily dissected by rivers and by easily traversed passes: the apparent citadel has served throughout history as a pathway for invaders.

Below the mountains, in the west of Transylvania and in the crescent-shaped river valley of the Danube and the Prut Rivers, are the great cereal-producing regions of Romania. Some 75 per cent of the Romanian labor force is engaged in agriculture. Agricultural output supplies more than one third of the nation's income despite widespread erosion and the ever-present threat of drought in a climate of erratic rainfall and blistering hot summers. Romanian farmers still observe the old rites of the soil, and folk magic of pre-Christian faiths echoes in the sowing and harvest ceremonies that are enacted yearly in the smaller villages.

AREA:	91,675 sq. mi.
POPULATION:	18,398,000. Largest city and capital: Bucharest.
CLIMATE:	Warm summers, cold winters; warmer temperatures in plain areas. Most rain in summer.
ALTITUDES:	Mt. Negoi, 8,346 ft. (highest); Bucharest, 276 ft.; Cluj, 1,150 ft.

In the last decade, the bulk of Romania's capital investment has been made in industry. Some changes are now taking place: textiles and rolling stock are being produced in Arad, iron and steel products in Orasul-Stalin; scattered chemical plants are using the natural gas of Transylvania; and a complex of industry encircles Bucharest. The most important natural resource is oil, extracted commercially since 1854 from pools in the Carpathian and Transylvanian foothills. Some oil fields, like those of Ploesti and Câmpina, once thought depleted, are now producing with the use of deeper drilling techniques. New discoveries of oil help maintain Romania's lead as the largest producer in Europe, excluding the U.S.S.R.

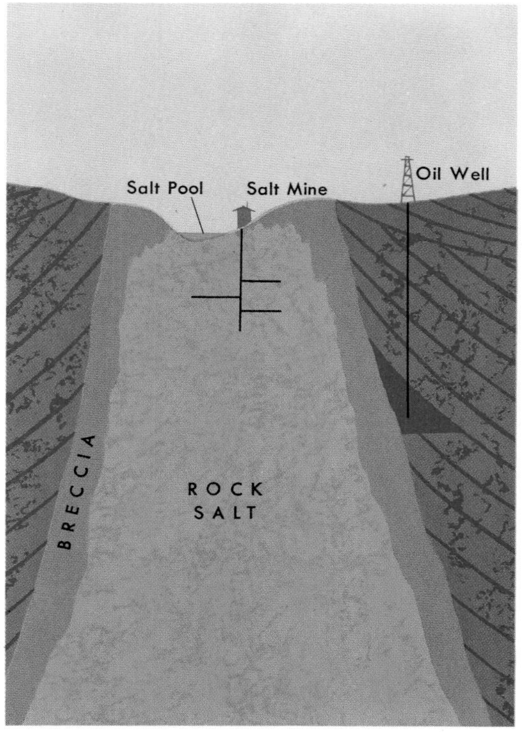

PILLARS OF SALT AND POOLS OF OIL

Salt pillars rising from beds deep beneath the Carpathian foothills reach the earth's surface, where the mineral is exposed, as shown in the cross section above. Pushing to the surface, the pillar fractures surrounding rock layers to form breccia *(red)*, or impermeable zones of angular rock. Oil is often trapped against brecciated zones, and so these salt formations are likely sites for drilling.

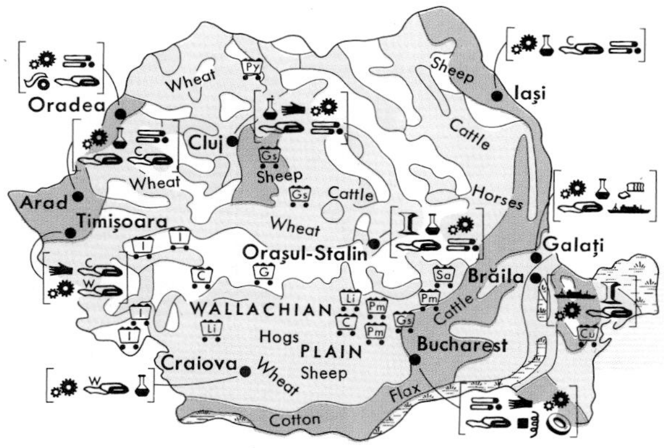

THE ECONOMY

MANUFACTURING
- Chemicals
- Electrical Industry
- Transportation Equipment
- Textiles
- Cotton
- Wool
- Iron & Steel
- Rubber
- Wood Products
- Food Products
- Leather Products
- Metal & Machine Products
- Paper Products

MINING
- C Coal
- Cu Copper
- G Gold
- Gs Natural Gas
- I Iron Ore
- Li Lignite
- Pm Petroleum
- Py Pyrites
- Sa Salt

AGRICULTURE
- General Farming
- Intensive Agriculture
- Forest Agriculture
- Pastureland & Fodder Crops
- Swamp Land

FISHING
- Fishing Areas

GROSS NATIONAL PRODUCT PER CAPITA $320

TWO TRADITIONS OF CENTRAL EUROPE

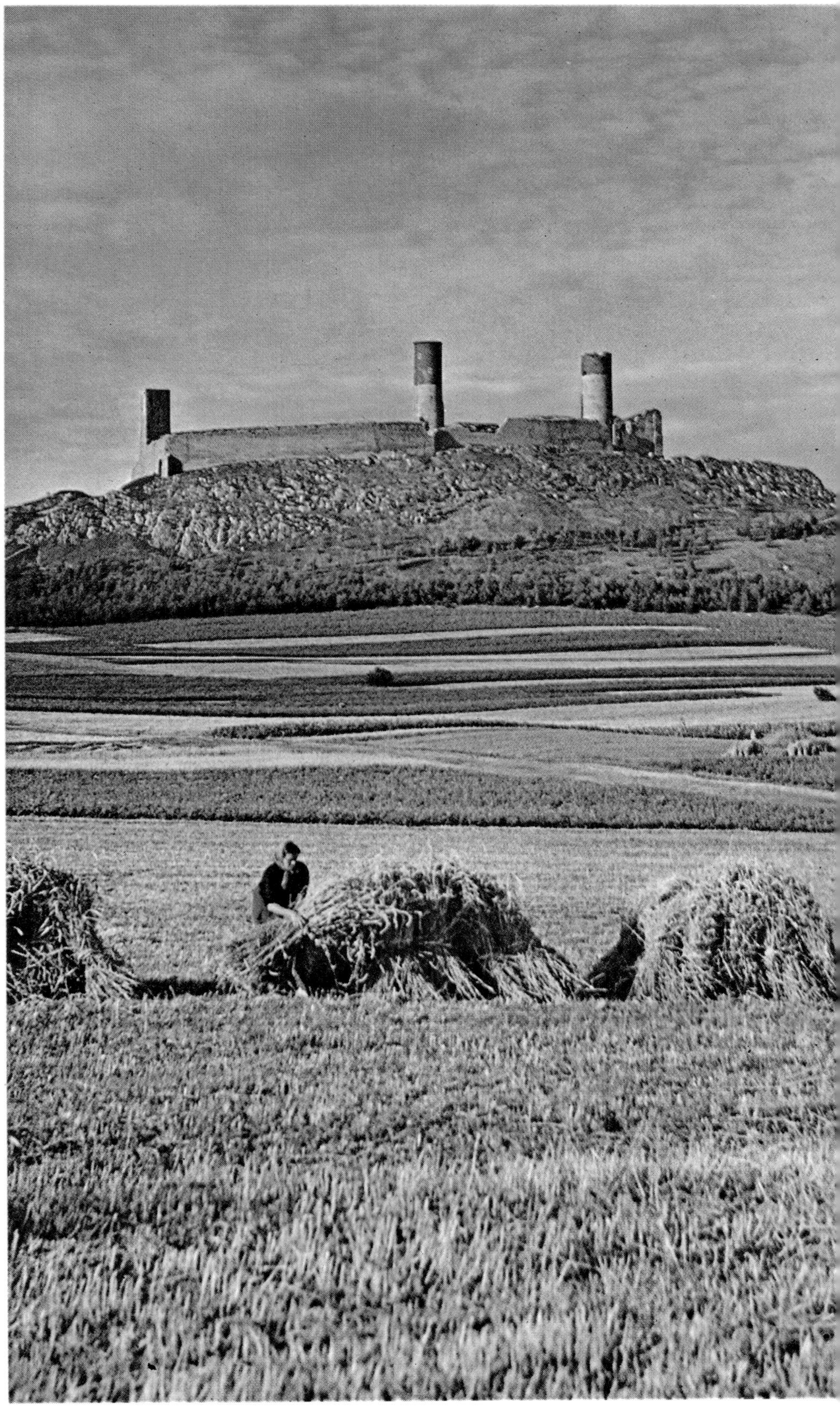

IN A POLISH FIELD near Kielce, this peasant woman gathers sheaves of rye in the fashion of her ancestors. Behind her are the ruins of an ancient castle. Forty per cent of Poland's population are farmers, who cultivate about two thirds of the land. Unless fertilized, the soil tends to be poor, but the cool and moist climate is favorable to the production of rye and potatoes.

A CZECH SPA, Karlovy Vary carries on a tradition that predates the time of the Austro-Hungarian Empire, when the city was known as Karlsbad. Now, many of the hotels of this old resort, famous for the waters of its hot springs, have been converted into rest homes for Czechoslovakia's workers. The Tepla River, at left center, divides the beflagged main promenade of the city.

CZECHOSLOVAKIA

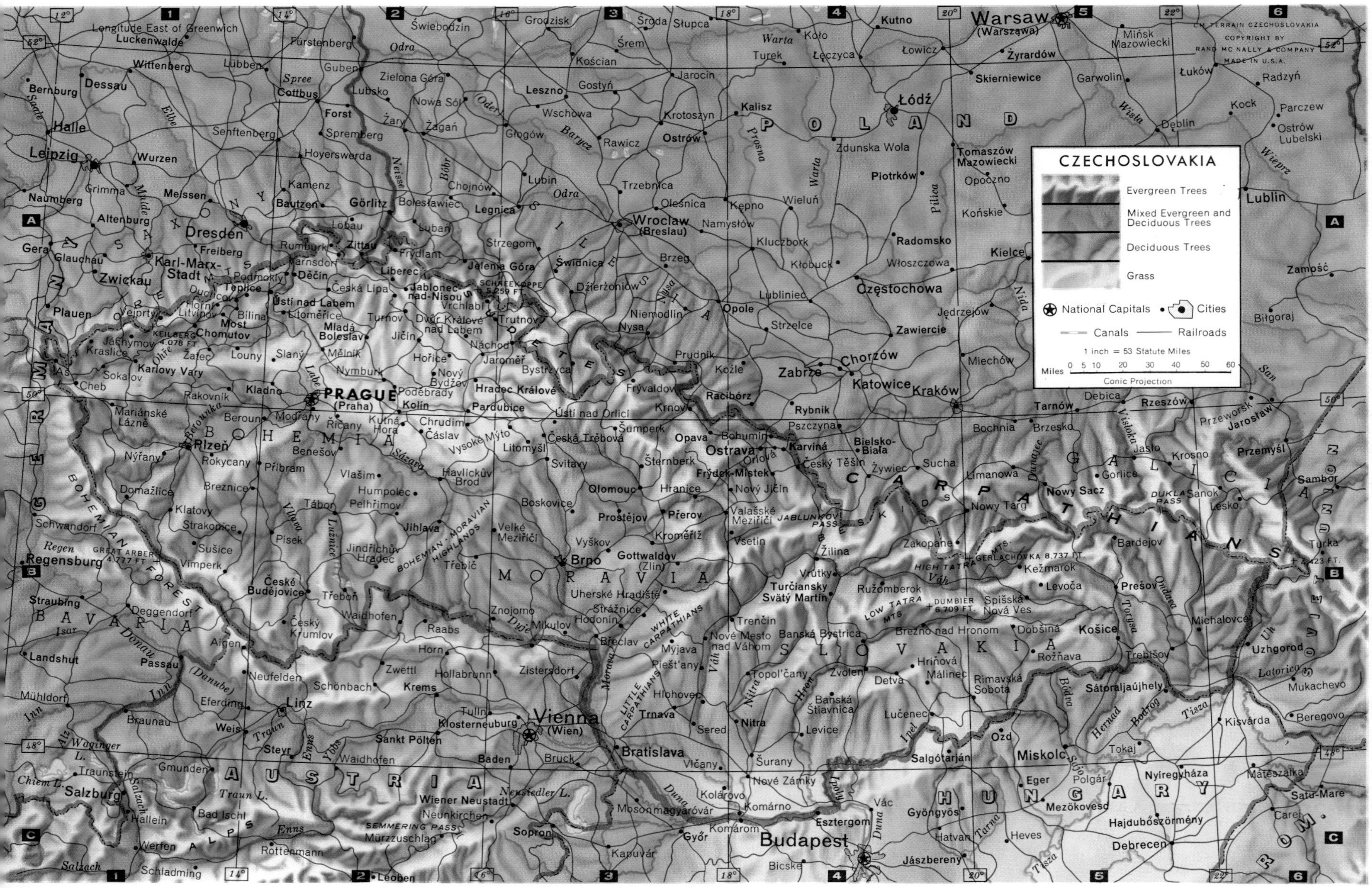

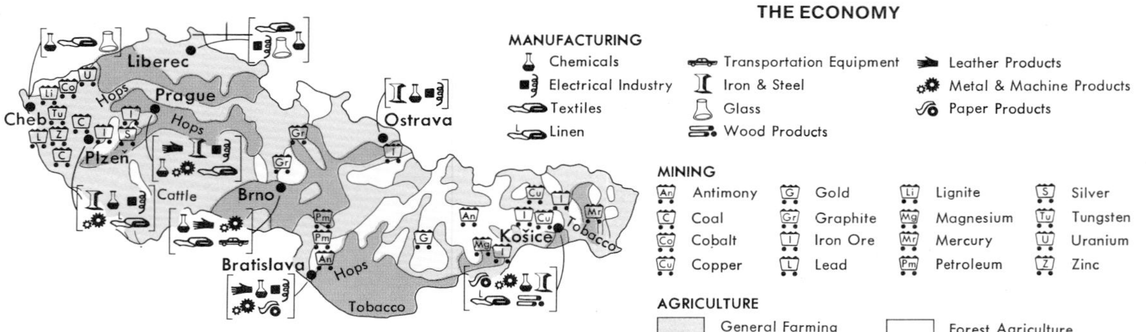

GROSS NATIONAL PRODUCT PER CAPITA $543

CZECHOSLOVAKIA: A composite of national cultures, Czechoslovakia was assembled in 1918 from some of the remnants of the Austro-Hungarian Empire (Bohemia, Moravia-Silesia, Slovakia and Ruthenia). West of the wide Moravian Depression—a low plateau that cuts the country in two—the enterprising, urbanized Czechs reflect their heritage from Austrian rule in the old empire. To the east, the agricultural Slovaks reflect the long years of Hungarian control.

Set in the middle of Europe, little Czechoslovakia was trimmed still further in 1945 when the Soviet Union annexed Ruthenia. The landlocked country is more than 200 miles away from Baltic ports to the northwest and from Trieste on the Adriatic in the south. The meandering route of the Danube River to the Black Sea requires a voyage of more than 915 miles.

AREA:	49,353 sq. mi.
POPULATION:	13,639,000. Largest city and capital: Prague.
CLIMATE:	Cold winters, mild summers; most rainfall in summer.
ALTITUDES:	Mt. Gerlachovka, 8,737 ft. (highest); Prague, 575 ft.

The high mountain areas are snow-covered and cold for five months of the year, but many parts of the country have black, fertile soil. Agriculture is highly diversified. Cereal grains—wheat, rye, barley and oats—flourish in the rich Danube valley and in Moravia and Bohemia. Sugar beets and potatoes are grown almost everywhere. Before World War II, Czechoslovakia could easily feed all of its people. Now, however, food imports have become essential to the Czechoslovak economy.

In Bohemia-Moravia, armaments, locomotives and autos are produced, mainly for export; shoes, beer and power-plant and food-processing machinery are shipped to foreign markets in steadily increasing quantities. The country has coal and some minerals, but iron, petroleum and other vital raw materials for industry must be imported.

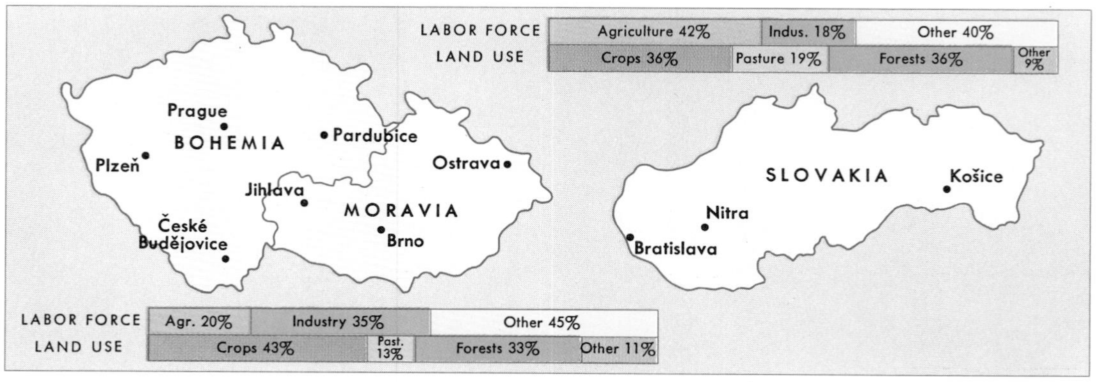

CZECHOSLOVAKIA'S TWO ECONOMIES

This map illustrates the division of Czechoslovakia into two contrasting economies: an industrialized Bohemia-Moravia in the west *(left)* and an agricultural Slovakia to the east *(right)*. The graphs show what proportion of the labor force of each division works in agriculture and in industry; they also show the relative amounts of land each division puts into use as forest, pasture and farm.

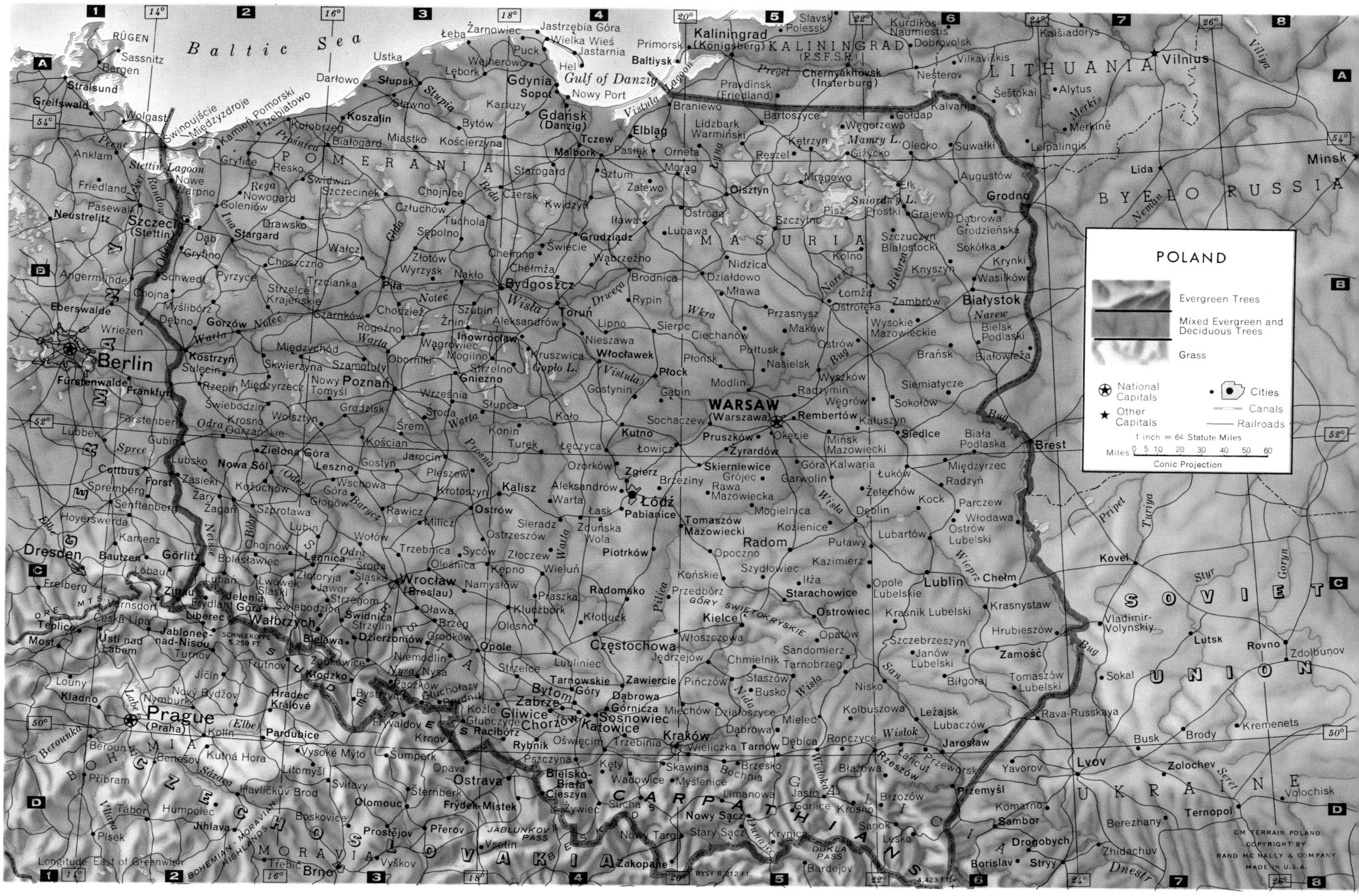

POLAND: Itself once a far-ranging invader, Poland has been divided, destroyed, restored. Its history is a long record of turmoil. With no natural boundaries on the east or west – there are mountains only to the south – Poland has been a highway of history, trampled by the armies of Europe and Asia. The mere fact of Poland's survival, wrote the English essayist Hilaire Belloc, makes it "the hope of the half-defeated."

The word *pole*, from which the country takes its name, means "field" – and indeed much of Poland is flat and open. Along the southeast border is the farmland of the rich Silesian region. The principal crop grown here is wheat. The great plain which tilts northward toward the Baltic from the mountains in the south and which occupies two thirds of the country is less favored, but it supports swine and cattle, raises potatoes and rye. The northern plain also has extensive forests.

AREA:	120,327 sq. mi.
POPULATION:	29,550,000. Largest city and capital: Warsaw.
CLIMATE:	Cold winters, warm summers; most rain in spring and summer.
ALTITUDES:	Czerwone, near Zakopane, 6,965 ft. (highest).

Today, the country that stubborn Poles have constantly rebuilt is turning away from its traditional agricultural economy. The products of a new and growing industrial complex include rolling stock, autos and machine tools. Petroleum from Galician wells is no longer sufficient to satisfy the expanding needs of the many new factories.

Fuel to stoke the fires of industry comes mainly from Upper Silesia. Near Katowice and Walbrzych, coal mines that once belonged to Germany are capable of producing some 90 million tons a year, and have more than 100 billion tons in reserve. Lignites are mined along the bank of the Neisse River near the German frontier. New cities have grown up around the larger coal fields to house the miners and workers employed in the new steel plants.

THE MANY SHAPES OF POLAND

The changing shape and dimensions of Poland since 1772 appear on the maps above. On both maps a red line designates the 1918 frontiers. The top map shows the various annexations by Russia, Prussia and Austria. The bottom map shows post-World War II border realignments involving Poland and the U.S.S.R.

THE ECONOMY

MANUFACTURING

- Chemicals
- Electrical Industry
- Transportation Equipment
- Cotton
- Jute
- Synthetic Textiles
- Silk
- Wool
- Iron & Steel
- Precision Tools & Instruments
- Printing & Publishing
- Wood Products
- Leather Products
- Metal & Machine Products
- Paper Products

MINING

- Coal
- Copper
- Iron Ore
- Lead
- Lignite
- Magnesium
- Petroleum
- Pyrites
- Zinc

AGRICULTURE

- General Farming
- Intensive Agriculture
- Forest Agriculture
- Pastureland & Fodder Crops

FISHING

- Fishing Areas

GROSS NATIONAL PRODUCT PER CAPITA $468

SOVIET UNION

"There are at the present time two great nations in the world which . . . have grown up unnoticed. . . . They are proceeding with ease and with celerity along a path to which no limit can be perceived. . . . Their starting point is different and their courses are not the same; yet each of them seems marked out by the will of Heaven to sway the destinies of half the globe." Thus, in 1835, the French historian, writer and social philosopher Alexis de Tocqueville accurately prophesied the future of the United States and Russia.

Few nations so plainly destined for power have been isolated by more natural barriers than the great sprawling area which is today the Union of Soviet Socialist Republics. Curving along Arctic seas, the Soviet's northern coast has only a scattering of ports, most of which are choked with polar ice for a large part of the year. In Siberia, the major rivers flow into the Arctic. They silt up the harbors in summer and pile up against the ice in spring, flooding the land. They are all but impassable routes to the frozen interior. To the south, the Elburz, Tien Shan and Sayan Mountains are rugged sentinels on the border.

Locked in its own immensity, prerevolutionary Russia turned inward to follow a course of autocracy and isolation. "The extent of the Dominion," said Catherine the Great in 1767, "requires the person who rules it to be vested with absolute power." Although some of the czars and some members of the aristocracy were oriented toward the West, Russia was long a backward country. Improved agricultural methods familiar in Europe in the 14th Century did not reach Russia until the 20th; its peasants were not freed from serfdom until 1861, some 300 years behind their fellows in Western Europe. The Industrial Revolution did not arrive until the turn of the century.

The Soviet Union is now rapidly transforming itself. In the vastness of Siberia, modern cities and giant hydroelectric dams now rise where there were once only forest and steppe. Icebreakers keep northern ports open long into the fall; and Soviet engineers talk of reversing rivers to make it easier to move cargo into the interior. No longer locked in, the Soviet Union is marshaling an expanding population to the task of ameliorating an environment that is generally harsh.

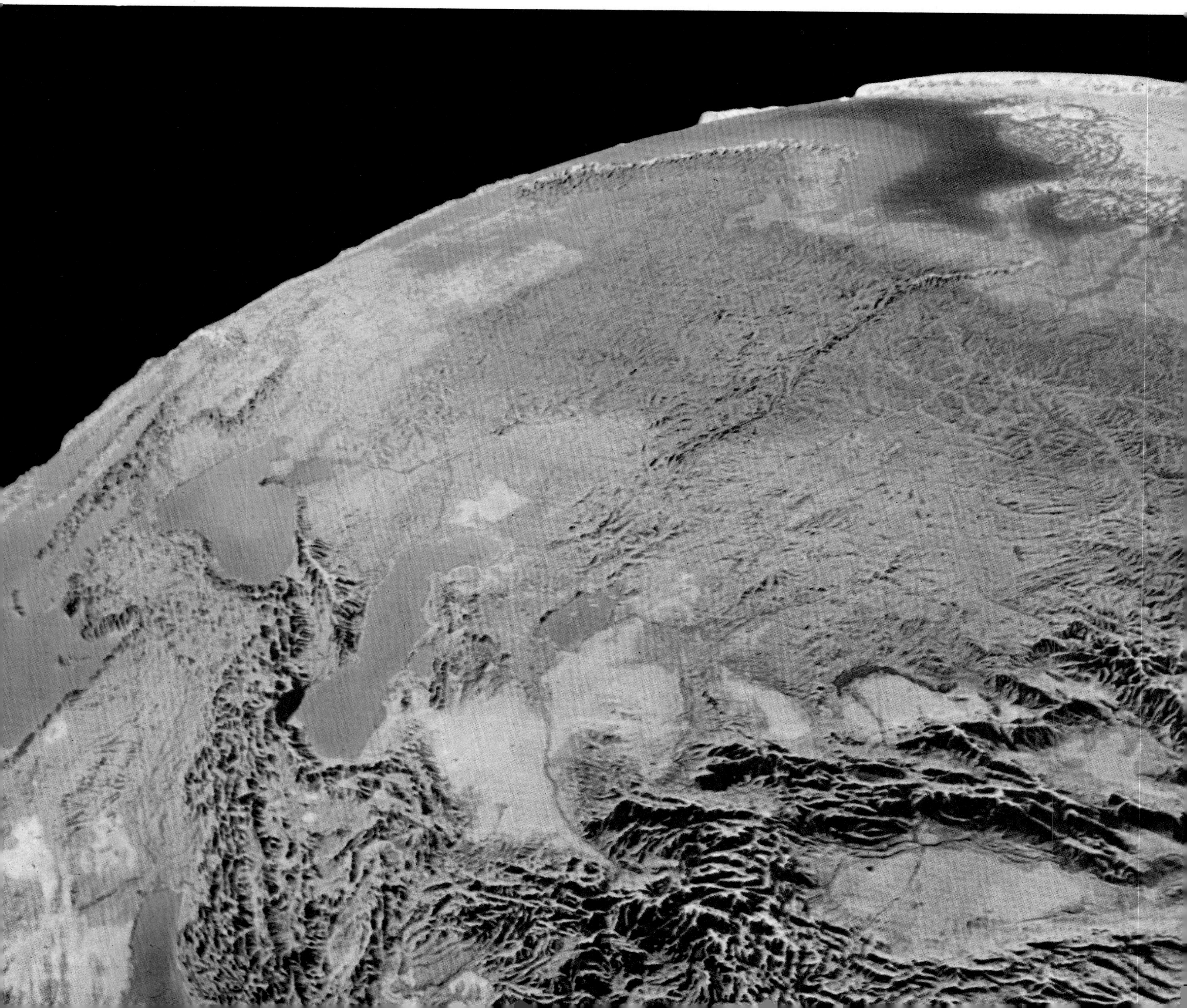

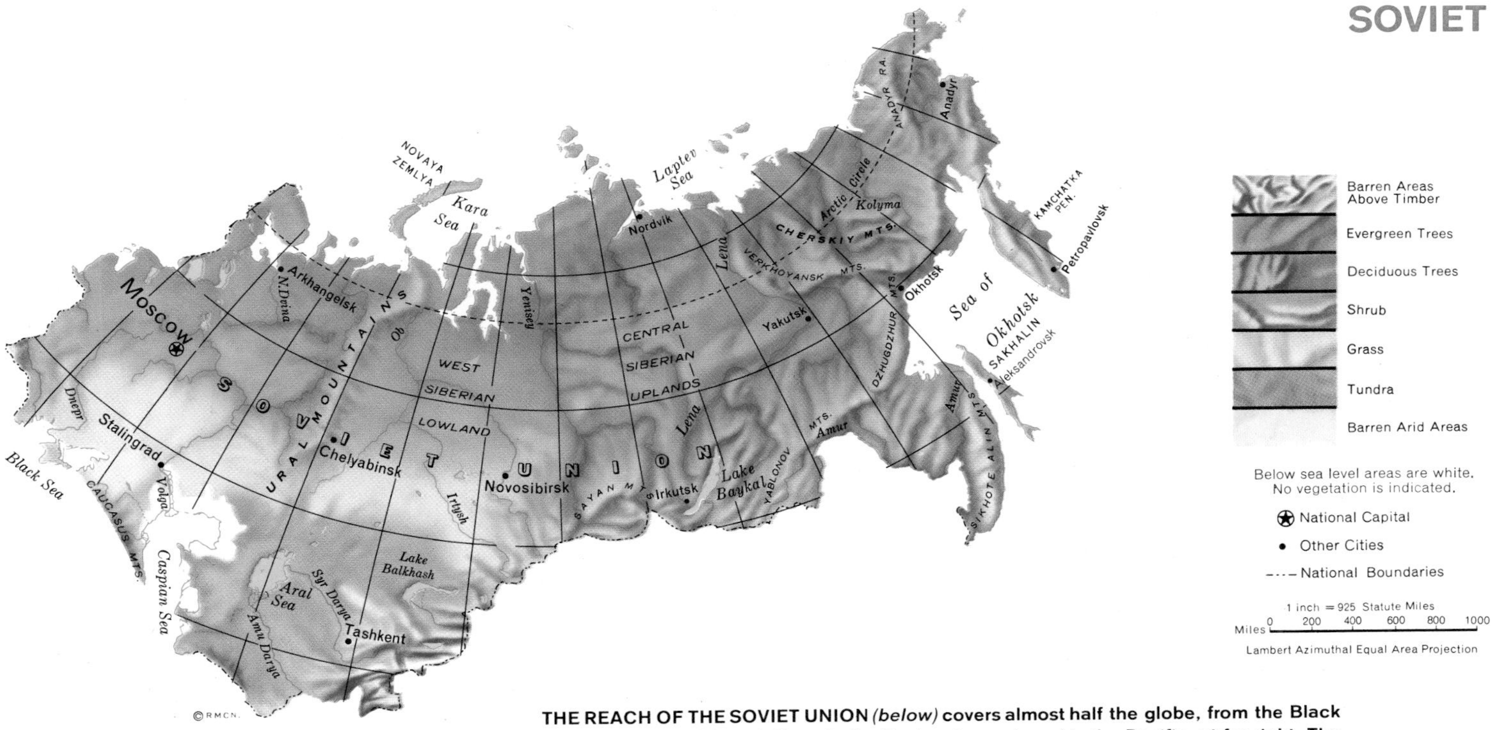

THE REACH OF THE SOVIET UNION ***(below)*** **covers almost half the globe, from the Black Sea, at far left, to Siberia's Kamchatka Peninsula, anchored in the Pacific, at far right. The ridge of the Ural Mountains, at middle left, extends 1,300 miles from north to south.**

CM TERRAIN SOVIET UNION
COPYRIGHT BY
RAND MC NALLY & COMPANY
MADE IN U.S.A.
Longitude West of Greenwich
Atlantic Ocean
Norwegian Sea
Arctic Circle
Greenland Sea
Barents Sea
Kara Sea
Arctic
Queen Victoria Sea
FRANZ JOSEF LAND
JAN MAYEN (NOR.)
FAEROE IS. (DEN.)
SHETLAND IS. (BR.)
BEAR I. (NOR.)
WEST SPITSBERGEN
SVALBARD (SPITSBERGEN) (NOR.)
NORTH EAST I.
HOPE I.
NOVAYA ZEMLYA
C. ZHELANIYA
Arkangelskoye
Lagernoye
Karmakuly
KOLGUYEV I.
VAYGACH
Cheshskaya Bay
C. KANIN
BELYY I.
YAMAL PEN.
GYDANSKIY PEN.
Obskaya Guba
IRELAND
Dublin
Belfast
Londonderry
Glasgow
Edinburgh
Aberdeen
UNITED KINGDOM
Liverpool
Leeds
York
Newcastle-on-Tyne
Nottingham
Birmingham
Norwich
North Sea
DENMARK
Copenhagen
Esbjerg
Aarhus
Aalborg
Rotterdam
Amsterdam
Hamburg
Kiel
Rostock
Berlin
Hannover
Essen
Bonn
Frankfurt
Leipzig
GERMANY
Bergen
Haugesund
Ålesund
Trondheim
Namsos
Bodø
Narvik
Tromsø
Hammerfest
NORTH CAPE
Vardø
NORWAY
SWEDEN
Oslo
Larvik
Arendal
Göteborg
Malmö
Jönköping
Kalmar
Norrköping
Stockholm
Uppsala
Gävle
Sundsvall
Östersund
Umeå
Skellefteå
Luleå
Kiruna
Gällivare
LAPLAND
Gulf of Bothnia
Baltic Sea
FINLAND
Oulu
Vaasa
Pori
Tampere
Turku
Helsinki
Kuopio
Tallinn
ESTONIA
Riga
LATVIA
LITHUANIA
Kaunas
Kaliningrad
Gdańsk
Szczecin
Poznań
POLAND
Warsaw
Lodz
Częstochowa
Kraków
Katowice
Prague
CZECH.
Vienna
Brno
Bratislava
Budapest
HUNG.
Szeged
Cluj
Sibiu
RUMANIA
Bucharest
BUL.
Constanța
Kishinev
MOLD.
Odessa
Nikolayev
Kherson
Simferopol
Sevastopol
Kerch
Black Sea
Sea of Azov
Istanbul
Üsküdar
Zonguldak
Sinop
Samsun
Trabzon
Ankara
Kayseri
Sivas
Erzurum
Malatya
Adana
TURKEY
Leningrad
Petrozavodsk
KARELIAN A.S.S.R.
White Sea
Murmansk
KOLA PEN.
Kandalaksha
Belomorsk
Arkhangelsk
Mezen
Vologda
Yaroslavl
Rybinsk
Kalinin
MOSCOW
Smolensk
Minsk
Vitebsk
Vilnius
BYELORUSSIA
Pinsk
Brest
Gomel
Mogilev
Bryansk
Kaluga
Tula
Ryazan
Kursk
Orel
Voronezh
Kharkov
Kiev
UKRAINE
Zhitomir
Vinnitsa
Chernovtsy
Poltava
Dnepropetrovsk
Krivoy Rog
Zaporozhye
Stalino
Zhdanov
Lugansk
Makeyevka
Rostov
Krasnodar
Novorossiysk
Armavir
Stavropol
Grozny
Ordzhonikidze
CAUCASUS MTS.
GEORGIA
Tbilisi
Batumi
Poti
Yerevan
ARMENIA
AZERBAYDZHAN
Baku
Kirovabad
Makhachkala
Astrakhan
Stalingrad
Saratov
Engels
Penza
Tambov
Kuybyshev
Ulyanovsk
Syzran
Kazan
TATAR A.S.S.R.
Gorkiy
Ivanovo
Kostroma
Kirov
Izhevsk
Perm
Ufa
BASHKIR A.S.S.R.
Sterlitamak
Orenburg
Magnitogorsk
Chelyabinsk
Sverdlovsk
Nizhniy Tagil
Zlatoust
Kurgan
Tyumen
Tobolsk
KOMI A.S.S.R.
Syktyvkar
Ukhta
Pechora
Vorkuta
Salekhard
Labytnangi
Naryan-Mar
URAL MOUNTAINS
RUSSIAN SOVIET FE
WEST SIBERIAN LOWLAND
Ob
Irtysh
Omsk
Petropavlovsk
Novosibirsk
Barnaul
Tomsk
Kemerovo
Prokopyevsk
Biysk
Semipalatinsk
Ust-Kamenogorsk
Pavlodar
Akmolinsk
Karaganda
KAZAKH S.S.R.
Kustanay
Aktyubinsk
Orsk
Uralsk
Guryev
CASPIAN DEPRESSION
Caspian Sea
Fort Shevchenko
USTURT PLATEAU
Aral Sea
Aralsk
Kzyl-Orda
Lake Balkhash
Balkhash
Turkestan
Dzhambul
Chimkent
Tashkent
Frunze
Alma-Ata
KIRGHIZ S.S.R.
Issyk-Kul
Namangan
Andizhan
Kokand
Fergana
Osh
Samarkand
Bukhara
Chardzhou
UZBEK S.S.R.
KYZYLKUM DESERT
KARAKUM DESERT
TURKMEN S.S.R.
Krasnovodsk
Ashkhabad
Mary
Stalinabad
TADZHIK S.S.R.
PAMIR
TIEN SHAN
SINKIANG
TAKLA MAKAN (DESERT)
Kashgar
Yarkand
AFGHAN.
IRAN
Tehran
Tabriz
Rasht
Mashhad
Esfahan
Hamadan
Kermanshah
IRAQ
Baghdad
Mosul
Kirkuk
SYRIA (U.A.R.)
Aleppo
Hama
Homs
SAUDI ARABIA
MT. ARARAT 16,946 FT.
MT. BELUKHA 14,783 FT.
TENGRI KHAN 22,940 FT.
STALIN PK. 24,590 FT.
MT. NARODNAYA 6,184 FT.

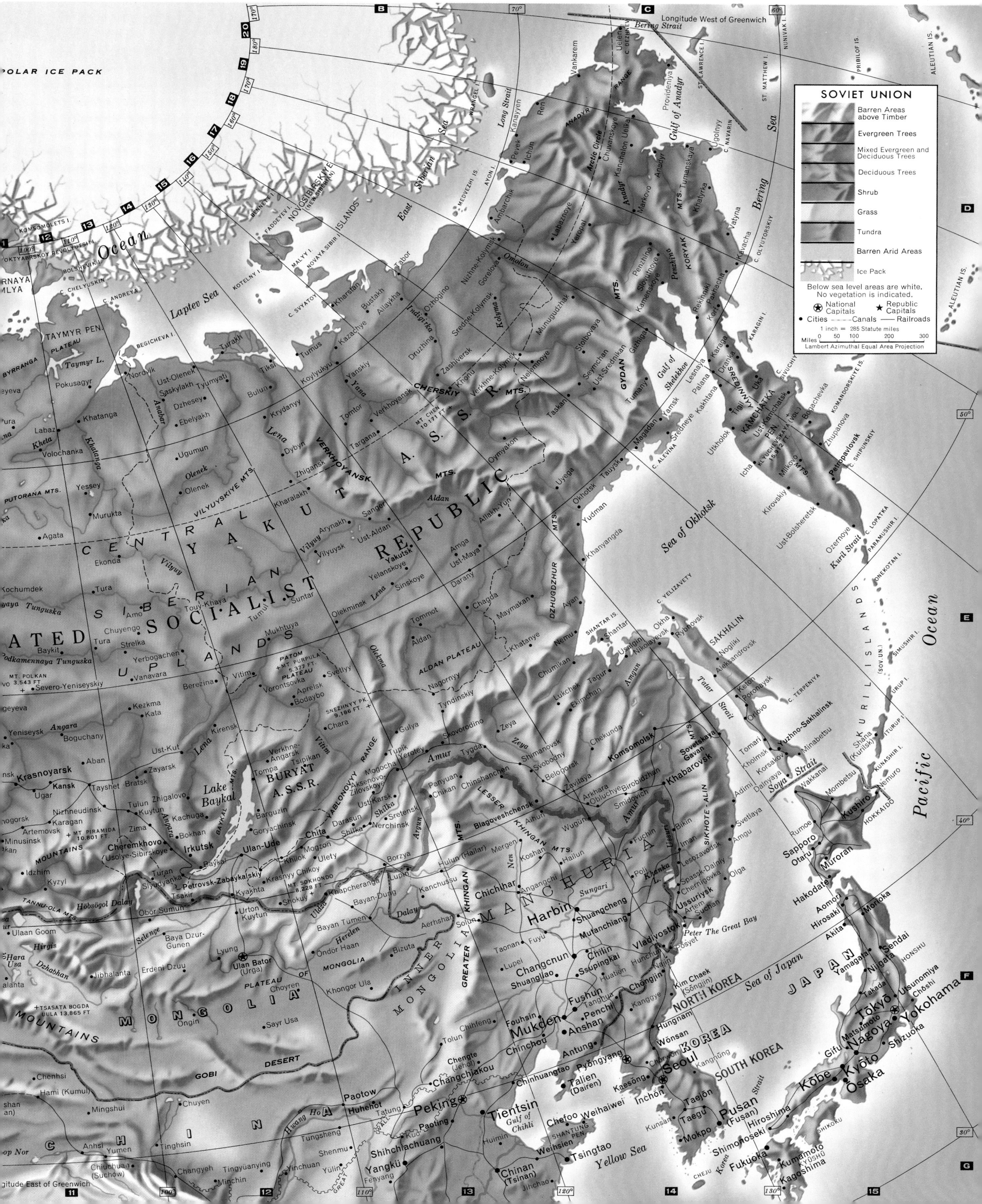
SOVIET UNION
Barren Areas above Timber
Evergreen Trees
Mixed Evergreen and Deciduous Trees
Deciduous Trees
Shrub
Grass
Tundra
Barren Arid Areas
Ice Pack
Below sea level areas are white.
No vegetation is indicated.
National Capitals
Republic Capitals
Cities
Canals
Railroads
1 inch = 285 Statute miles
Miles 0 50 100 200 300
Lambert Azimuthal Equal Area Projection
Longitude West of Greenwich
Longitude East of Greenwich
POLAR ICE PACK
Ocean
Laptev Sea
East Siberian Sea
Bering Strait
Bering Sea
Gulf of Anadyr
Sea of Okhotsk
Pacific Ocean
Sea of Japan
Yellow Sea
Gulf of Chihli
Kuril Strait
Soya Strait
Tatar Strait
Korea Strait
Long Strait
Gulf of Shelekhov
NOVOSIBIRSKIYE (NEW SIBERIAN) ISLANDS
SAKHALIN
KURIL ISLANDS
KAMCHATKA PEN.
TAYMYR PEN.
CENTRAL SIBERIAN UPLANDS
YAKUT A. S. S. R.
YAKUT AUTONOMOUS SOVIET SOCIALIST REPUBLIC
BURYAT A.S.S.R.
VERKHOYANSK MTS.
CHERSKIY MTS.
KORYAK MTS.
ANADYR RANGE
GYDAN MTS.
DZHUGDZHUR MTS.
ALDAN PLATEAU
PATOM PLATEAU
YABLONOVYY RANGE
SIKHOTE ALIN
LESSER KHINGAN MTS.
GREATER KHINGAN MTS.
SAYAN MOUNTAINS
MANCHURIA
MONGOLIA
INNER MONGOLIA
MONGOLIA PLATEAU
GOBI DESERT
CHINA
JAPAN
HOKKAIDO
HONSHU
SHIKOKU
KYUSHU
NORTH KOREA
SOUTH KOREA
KOREA
Lake Baykal
Lena
Amur
Kolyma
Indigirka
Yana
Aldan
Vilyuy
Olenek
Sungari
Yakutsk
Irkutsk
Ulan-Ude
Chita
Khabarovsk
Komsomolsk
Vladivostok
Magadan
Petropavlovsk
Yuzhno-Sakhalinsk
Harbin
Mukden
Peking
Tientsin
Seoul
Pyŏngyang
Pusan
Tokyo
Yokohama
Nagoya
Kyoto
Osaka
Kobe
Sapporo
Hakodate
Sendai
Ulan Bator (Urga)
Krasnoyarsk
Blagoveshchensk
Dairen
Tsingtao
MT. CHEN 10,171 FT.
MT. PURPULA 5,377 FT.
SNEZHNYY PK. 9,186 FT.
MT. PIRAMIDA 10,801 FT.
MT. SOKHONDO 8,228 FT.
MT. POLKAN 3,543 FT.
TSASATA BOGDA ULA 13,865 FT.
KLYUCHEVSKAYA (VOL.) 15,912 FT.

THE BLACK STEPPE OF THE WIDE UKRAINE

A UKRAINIAN PASTURE, where peasant women pause for gossip on their way to market, is part of the rich agricultural area—one of the oldest farming regions of Europe—that yields the Soviet Union two thirds of its sugar and one fifth of its grain. The Ukrainian steppe, or grassland, has black, fertile soil, warm summers and usually adequate rainfall. In addition to wheat and sugar beets, the farmers of the Ukraine raise herds of cattle and sheep on the grassy plains and produce meat and dairy products in quantity.

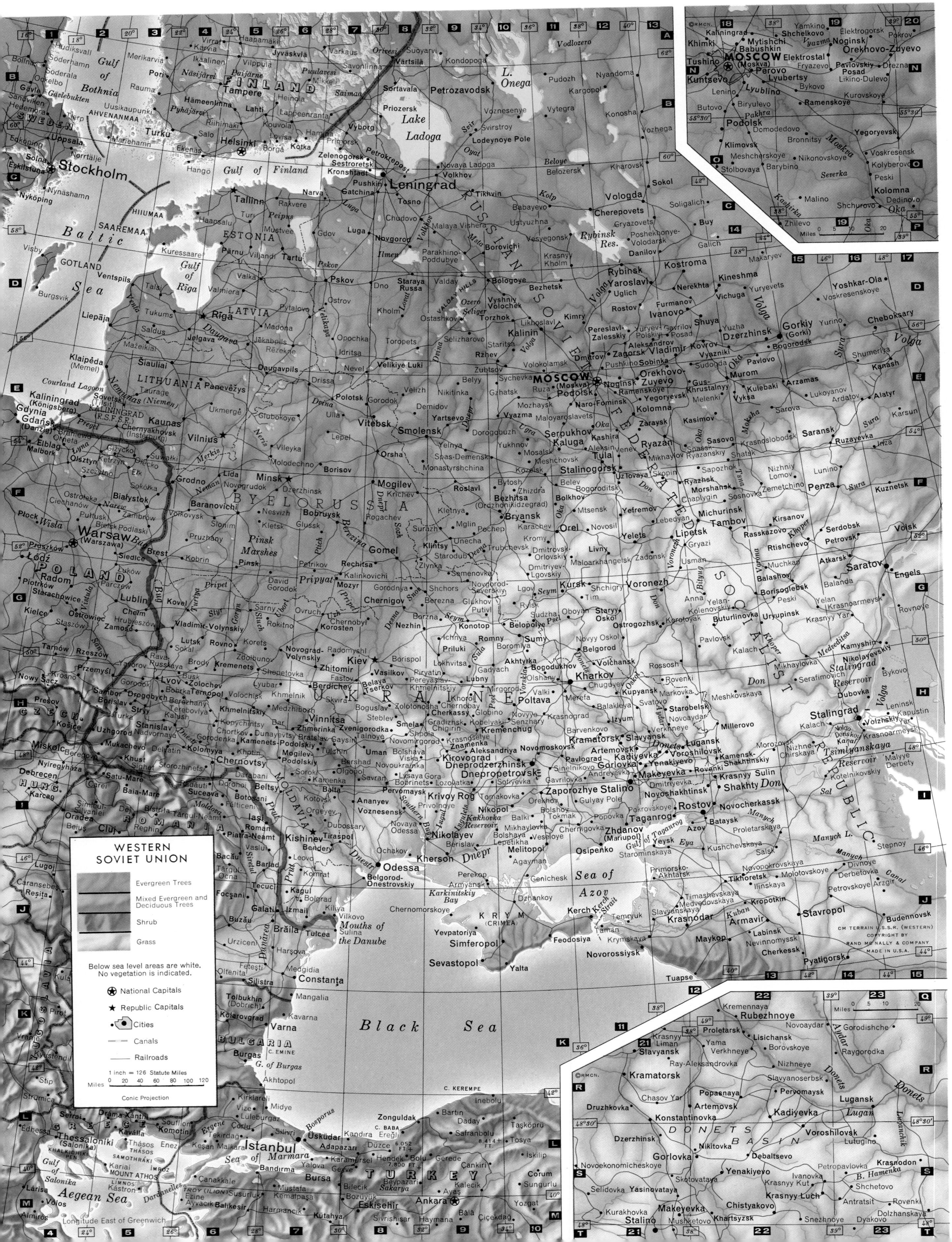
WESTERN SOVIET UNION
Evergreen Trees
Mixed Evergreen and Deciduous Trees
Shrub
Grass
Below sea level areas are white. No vegetation is indicated.
National Capitals
Republic Capitals
Cities
Canals
Railroads
1 inch = 126 Statute Miles
Miles 0 20 40 60 80 100 120
Conic Projection
CM TERRAIN U.S.S.R. (WESTERN)
COPYRIGHT BY RAND McNALLY & COMPANY
MADE IN U.S.A.
Longitude East of Greenwich
MOSCOW
Leningrad
Stockholm
Helsinki
Warsaw (Warszawa)
Kiev
Kharkov
Stalingrad
Odessa
Istanbul
Ankara
FINLAND
ESTONIA
LATVIA
LITHUANIA
BYELORUSSIA
UKRAINE
MOLDAVIA
POLAND
ROMANIA
BULGARIA
TURKEY
RUSSIAN SOVIET FEDERATED SOCIALIST REPUBLIC
Baltic Sea
Gulf of Bothnia
Gulf of Finland
Gulf of Riga
Lake Ladoga
L. Onega
Black Sea
Sea of Azov
Sea of Marmara
Aegean Sea
KRYM (CRIMEA)
Mouths of the Danube
Pripet Marshes
DONETS BASIN
Volga
Don
Dnepr

SOVIET UNION: "Russia," runs an old Czarist proverb, "is not a state, but a world." It is a world as vital as its great western cities, as rude and inhospitable as Siberia's Verkhoyansk Mountains. It is a world as rich and green as the "fertile triangle" rolling from Leningrad and Odessa to Lake Baykal, as empty as Uzbek's parched Kyzylkum Desert. It is as varied as its Union Republics, as monotonous as the tundra of Siberia.

Traditionally called Russia, after the people who have dominated it through history, the Soviet Union is the largest nation on the globe – more than twice as large as the United States *(map, left)*. Prevailing winds carry rain as far inland as the fertile triangle, where Russia grows most of its food. The Soviet Union (according to Soviet statistics) gathers such rich harvests that it ranks among the world's six largest producers of wheat, oats, barley and rye. Even so, one of the country's greatest challenges in the foreseeable future will be to feed a population growing at the rate of 3.5 million a year, a population which, like that of the U.S., is deserting the farms and moving steadily into the cities.

To the south, the winds are drier and in the virgin lands of Kazakh, irrigation is a stubborn problem. Northward, the terrain does little to temper the arctic air rolling down on the country from the Pole. Almost half the nation's land mass is covered by frozen soil. Only a smattering of root crops can grow in the thin layers of this permafrost which thaw briefly during the summer.

AREA: 8,650,140 sq. mi.
POPULATION: 212,810,000.
Largest city and capital: Moscow.
ALTITUDES: Stalin Peak, Tadzhik, 24,590 ft. (highest); Caspian Sea, −92 ft. (lowest).

Despite efforts at dispersal of industry into Siberia *(page 337)*, the roots of Soviet strength remain in the west. Industrial minerals are mined close to the farms of the fertile triangle. The Urals, a center of Soviet metallurgy, contain a variety of ores: high-quality iron, coal, manganese, bauxite and at least a dozen others. In the Ukraine to the south, the Donbas coal fields spread across nearly 9,000 square miles, hold reserves estimated in the billions of tons. Only 200 miles to the west are the iron mines of Krivoy Rog with some billion tons of reserve. On the Sea of Azov lie the iron mines of Kerch, and to the north, those of the Kursk area.

In the center of the western region, the metropolis of Moscow dominates the northern plain. Throughout most of Russia's history, Moscow has been the hub of its transport. Rivers and railroads converge on the city. A modern network of canals makes such an improvement on the natural waterways that today, by barge and river boat, Moscow handles cargo from the ships of five different seas – the Baltic, the Caspian, the White, the Black and the Sea of Azov. The factories of Moscow, also the largest manufacturing center in the U.S.S.R., turn out machine tools, cars, chemicals, textiles and electrical equipment.

NORTH POLE
80°
Murmansk
Leningrad
Moscow
Kiev
Fairbanks
ALASKA
ARCTIC CIRCLE
Yakutsk
Petropavlovsk
Sverdlovsk
60°
Novosibirsk
Irkutsk
Vladivostok
Boston
New York
Baku
Seattle
Chicago
Washington
Tashkent
St. Louis
Denver
40°
San Francisco
Los Angeles
New Orleans
Miami
Honolulu
HAWAII
TROPIC OF CANCER
20°
0 200 400 800 1200 MILES

THE U.S.S.R. AND THE U.S.: A GEOGRAPHIC COMPARISON

On this map the United States is shown superimposed upon the Soviet Union, with both countries drawn to the same scale and occupying their actual latitudinal locations. The bulk of the Soviet Union lies much closer to the Arctic than the U.S. does. In winter Moscow temperatures drop as low as 43° below zero, an extreme regularly rivaled in the U.S. only by Alaska and the most northerly of the midwestern states. The Soviet Union has more than twice the area of the United States. From its western European border *(far left)* to the coast of Kamchatka *(far right)* it stretches 4,785 miles. The greatest distance between the two coasts in the continental U.S., from West Quoddy Head, Maine, to Point Arena, California, is only 2,897 miles.

THE ECONOMY
MANUFACTURING
Nonferrous Metals
Chemicals
Electrical Industry
Transportation Equipment
Textiles
Cotton
Wool
Iron & Steel
Metal & Machine Products
Wood Products
Food Products
Leather Products
Glass
Petroleum Refining
MINING
Antimony
Coal
Chromium
Copper
Gold
Iron Ore
Lead
Lignite
Magnesium
Manganese
Molybdenum
Mercury
Phosphate
Platinum
Petroleum
Silver
Sulfur
Uranium
Zinc
AGRICULTURE
General Farming
Intensive Agriculture
Mediterranean Agriculture
Plantation Agriculture
Forest Agriculture
Forest Agriculture, Wood Crops Dominant
Pastureland & Fodder Crops
Pastureland with Sparse Vegetation
Nomadic Herding
Seasonal Grazing
Non-Agricultural Areas
FISHING
Fishing Areas
Tallinn
Murmansk
Dairying
Flax
Leningrad
Minsk
Dairying
UKRAINE
Kiev
Wheat
Odessa
Moscow
Dnepropetrovsk
Kharkov
Gorkiy
Stalino
Reindeer
Reindeer
Rostov
Wheat
Kuybyshev
Sverdlovsk
Stalingrad
Rye
Wheat
Cattle
Chelyabinsk
Magnitogorsk
Tbilisi
Camels
Dairying
Novosibirsk
Baku
Horses
Sheep
Stalinsk
Oats
Tashkent
Irkutsk
Ulan-Ude
Cattle
Stalinabad
Vladivostok

GROSS NATIONAL PRODUCT PER CAPITA $682

KAZAKH PINE FORESTS climb toward mountain snows near the city of Alma-Ata (Father of Apples) in Central Asia. A lumber camp is at the left. The region has orchards, vineyards and health spas.

THREE SOVIET OUTPOSTS

A SIBERIAN RAIL CENTER *(opposite)* clings to the shore of Lake Baykal, the deepest fresh-water lake in the world. The Trans-Siberian Railroad links the town with the rest of the Soviet Union.

UZBEK MARKET BUILDINGS stand near the ruins of an ancient mosque in Samarkand. One of the oldest cities in Central Asia, Samarkand was a station on the overland silk route from China.

CENTRAL SOVIET UNION
Barren Areas Above Timber
Evergreen Trees
Mixed Evergreen and Deciduous Trees
Shrub
Grass
Barren Arid Areas
Below sea level areas are white. No vegetation is indicated.
National Capitals
Cities
Republic Capitals
Canals
Railroads
1 inch = 162 Statute Miles
Miles 0 25 50 75 100 150
Conic Projection
CM TERRAIN CENTRAL SOVIET UNION
COPYRIGHT BY RAND McNALLY & COMPANY
MADE IN U.S.A.
WEST SIBERIAN LOWLAND
RUSSIAN SOVIET FEDERATED SOCIALIST REPUBLIC
KAZAKH S.S.R.
KAZAKH HILLS
UZBEK S.S.R.
TURKMEN S.S.R.
KIRGHIZ S.S.R.
Caspian Sea
Aral Sea
Lake Balkhash
CASPIAN DEPRESSION
URAL MOUNTAINS
VOLGA PLATEAU
TURAN LOWLAND
KYZYLKUM DESERT
KARAKUM DESERT
USTURT PLATEAU
BETPAK-DALA (GOLODNAYA STEPPE)
TIEN SHAN
CAUCASUS MTS.
TAKLA MAKAN (DESERT)
MOSCOW (Moskva)
Longitude East of Greenwich

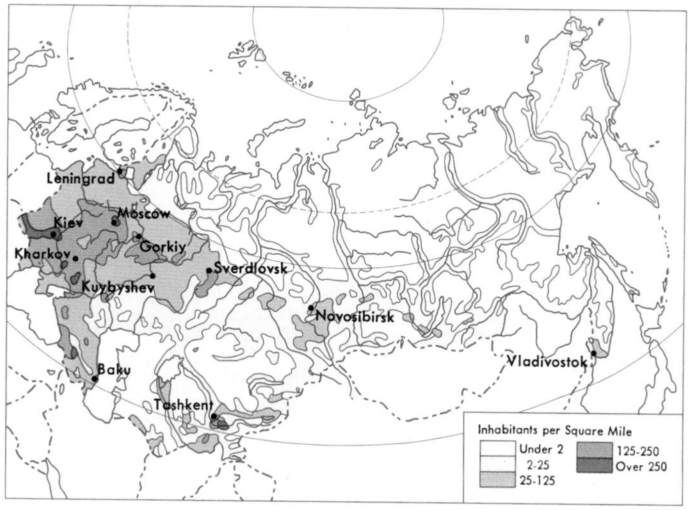

SOVIET POPULATION CENTERS

Although still concentrated around Russia's historic cities in the west, as shown at the left on the map above, the Soviet population is increasing in the east. For instance, Novosibirsk *(center)*, a hamlet only 50 years ago, is now a major machinery producer and scientific research station with a population of 900,000. The bulk of the population in areas of the east that were once empty lives beside rivers and along the Trans-Siberian railroad. Vladivostok, at far right, is the road's eastern terminus, some 5,800 miles from Moscow.

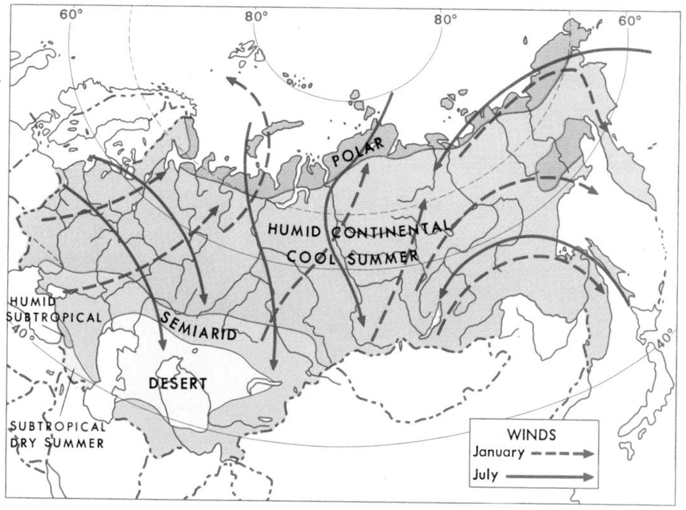

THE GEOGRAPHY OF SOVIET CLIMATE

The Soviet Union's climate, as shown on this map, is controlled by two factors: the country's distance from the Equator and its remoteness from the winds of the Atlantic *(arrows, left)*. After a long journey across Northern Europe, the sea winds are no longer heavy with moisture. Almost everywhere in the U.S.S.R., annual rainfall is less than 20 inches. It is even lower in the extensive deserts of Central Asia *(yellow and orange areas, left)* because of the mountain barriers to the south and the greater distance from the Atlantic.

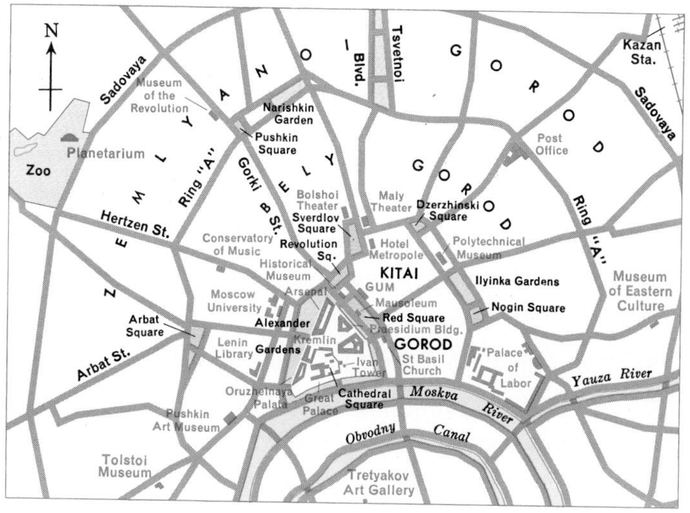

CAPITAL CITY OF THE SOVIETS

The Soviet capital, the center of which is seen here, lies along the banks of the narrow Moskva, where it was founded as a river trading post in 1147. Moscow's central section was fortified in the 15th Century by the massive stone walls of the Kremlin *(red, center)*. The wheel-like pattern of the city's major avenues is reminiscent of the layout of Paris. Adjoining the Kremlin is Red Square, which contains the tombs of the Soviet heroes Lenin and Stalin. Other historical sites, major public buildings and museums are shown in red.

THE SOVIET TRANSPORTATION NET

The Soviet transportation network, shown above, is barely equal to the country's enormous distances. As indicated by yellow shading, only limited areas lie within 15 miles of all-weather roads. In the Soviet Union, the category of "all-weather roads" includes those paved with asphalt or, in Siberia, with logs, plus roads made of hard-packed dirt or of pressed gravel. The rail system, unevenly distributed, contains only some 75,000 miles of track. Soviet air routes primarily service the west. Only major segments of the extensive waterways network, which carries about 160 million tons of cargo each year, are indicated on the map. This system, tying lakes, canals and rivers together, is the realization of an elaborate plan originally envisioned by Peter the Great.

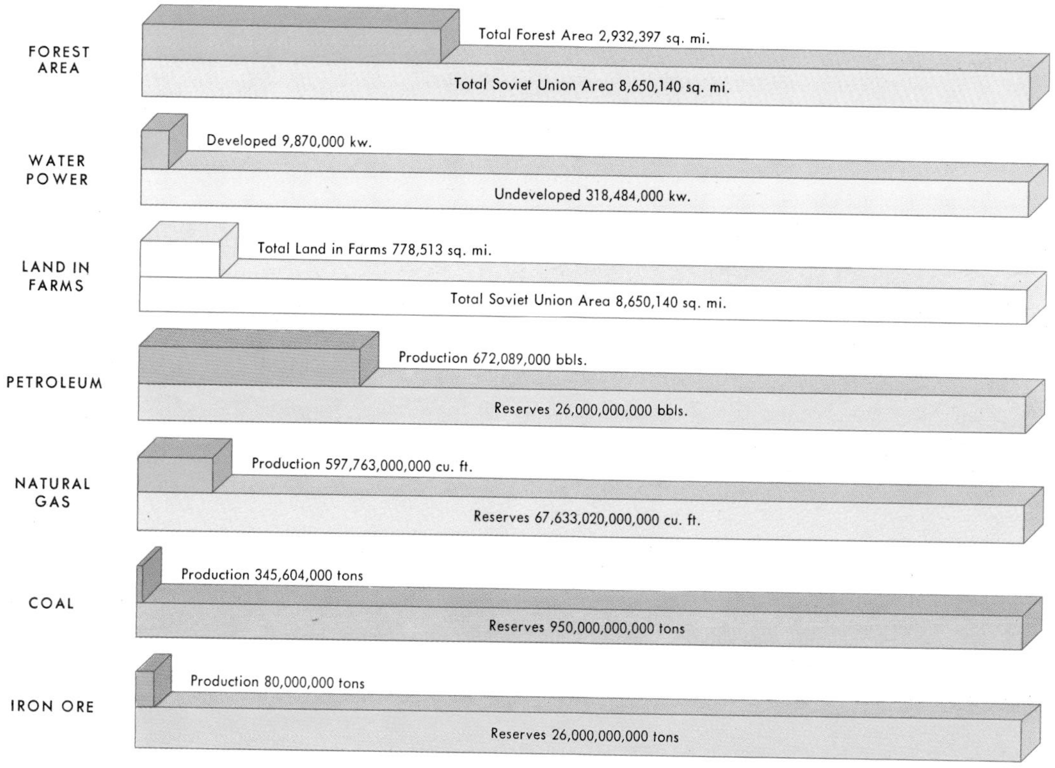

BASIS OF THE SOVIET ECONOMY

Each pair of bars on the graph above indicates the reserves of a basic Soviet natural resource *(lower bar)* and the amount in use or consumed annually *(upper bar)*. All of the figures are estimates, based in part on claims made by the Soviet Union. While the reserves appear to be great, additional exploitation of many of them is limited by various factors. For example, heavily forested and burdened with a rigorous climate, the Soviet Union has little land that can readily be added to its agricultural areas currently under cultivation. Much of the undeveloped hydroelectric power is located in inaccessible parts of Siberia remote from manufacturing centers and means of transportation. This is true also of some of the important mineral reserves: coal, iron ore and petroleum.

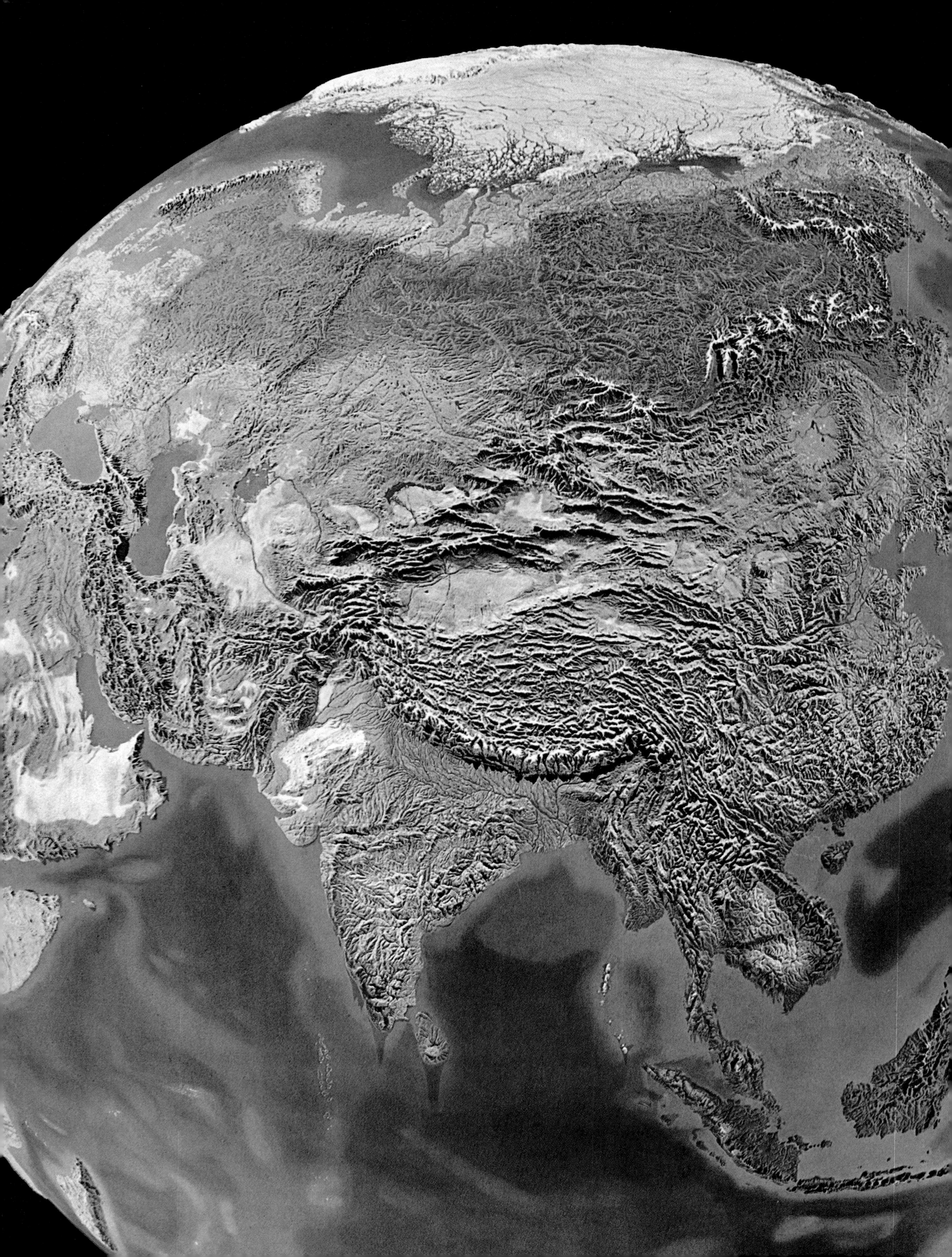

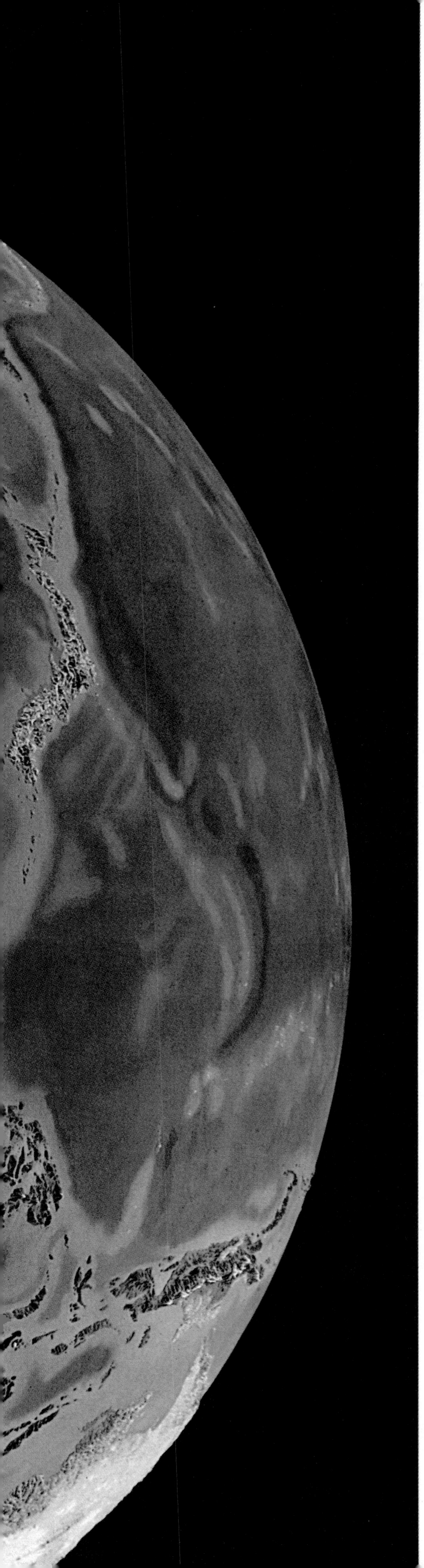

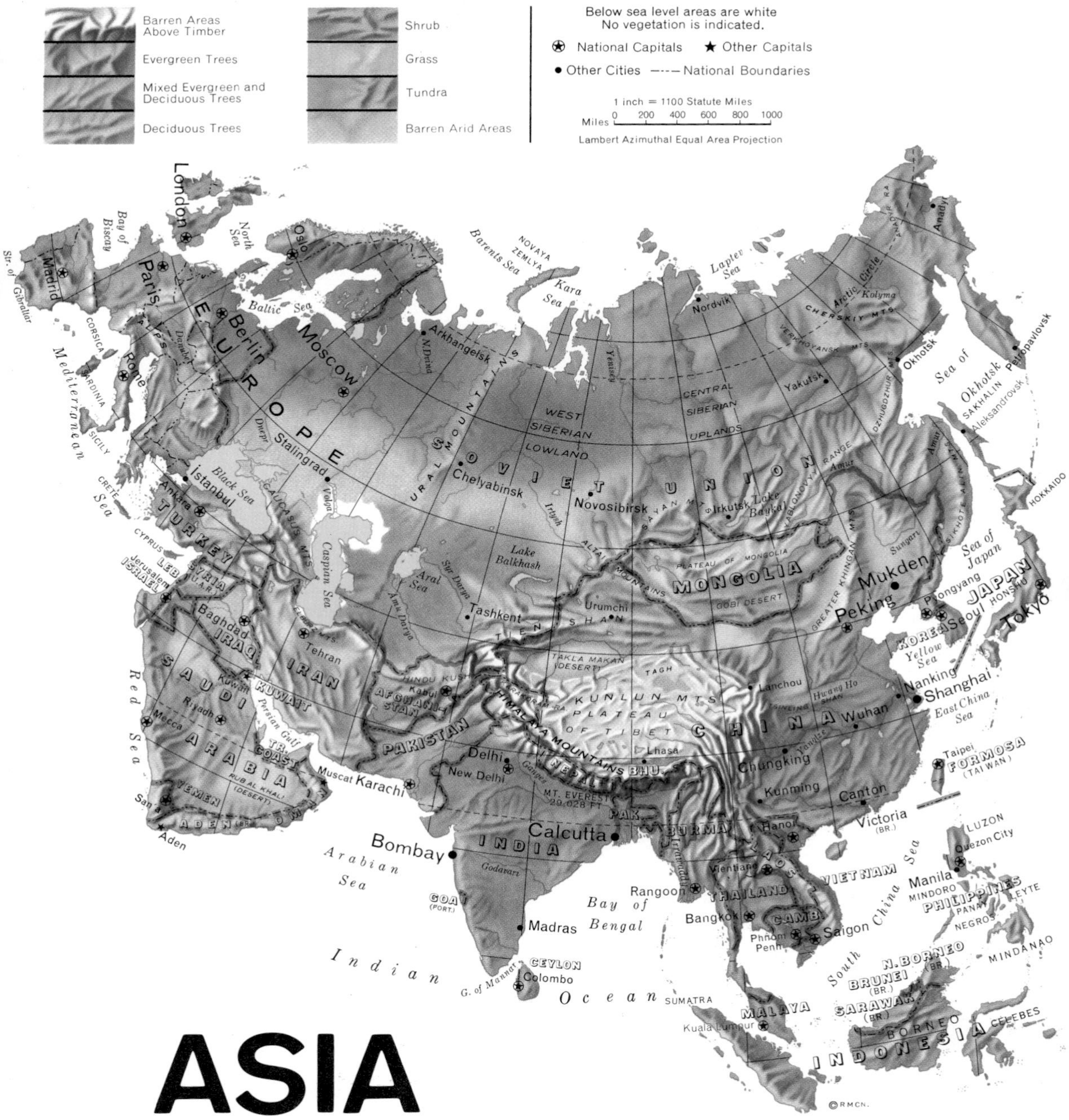

ASIA

The greatest of the continents, Asia covers fully a third of the world's land surface – 17 million square miles – and has two thirds of the world's people. There are many Asias: the sparsely settled desert of the Kingdom of Jordan and the teeming, green-clad island of Java; the virgin Siberian lands now being plowed for wheat and the ancient rice paddies of Indonesia; the industrialized society of Japan and the nomadic tribes of Iraq; the highest land in the world, the Himalayas, and the lowest, the basin of the Dead Sea; the carefree islands of the Pacific north of Borneo and the oppressive streets of India's cities, crammed with beggars.

Highly developed civilizations flourished in Asia for thousands of years while Europe was still in the Stone Age. The great religions of Judaism, Christianity, Islam, Buddhism and Hinduism were all founded in Asia. But while Asian cultures grew and declined, the huge mass of the people went on through the centuries illiterate, poverty-stricken and pestilence-ridden. Today the inhabitants of many Asian countries still depend on primitive farming methods for their livelihoods. And much of the land of Asia is useless to farmers: the frozen tundra in the north, the tangled jungle in the south, immense areas of deserts and mountains in the continent's interior. On this continent there has always been too little arable land for too many people.

The past two decades have brought a spectacular transformation in Asia. There are new independent nations, from Israel to Pakistan to Indonesia to the Philippines. Both new and old nations are beginning to use technical skills of the scientific revolution to improve their farming methods, develop their natural resources and utilize their tremendous supply of manpower.

A SPRAWLING GIANT with many peninsulas, bays and islands, Asia girdles almost one half of the globe. The Black Sea is at left center, Japan at right center. From north to south, the continent extends from Siberia to the equatorial island of Sumatra at bottom right.

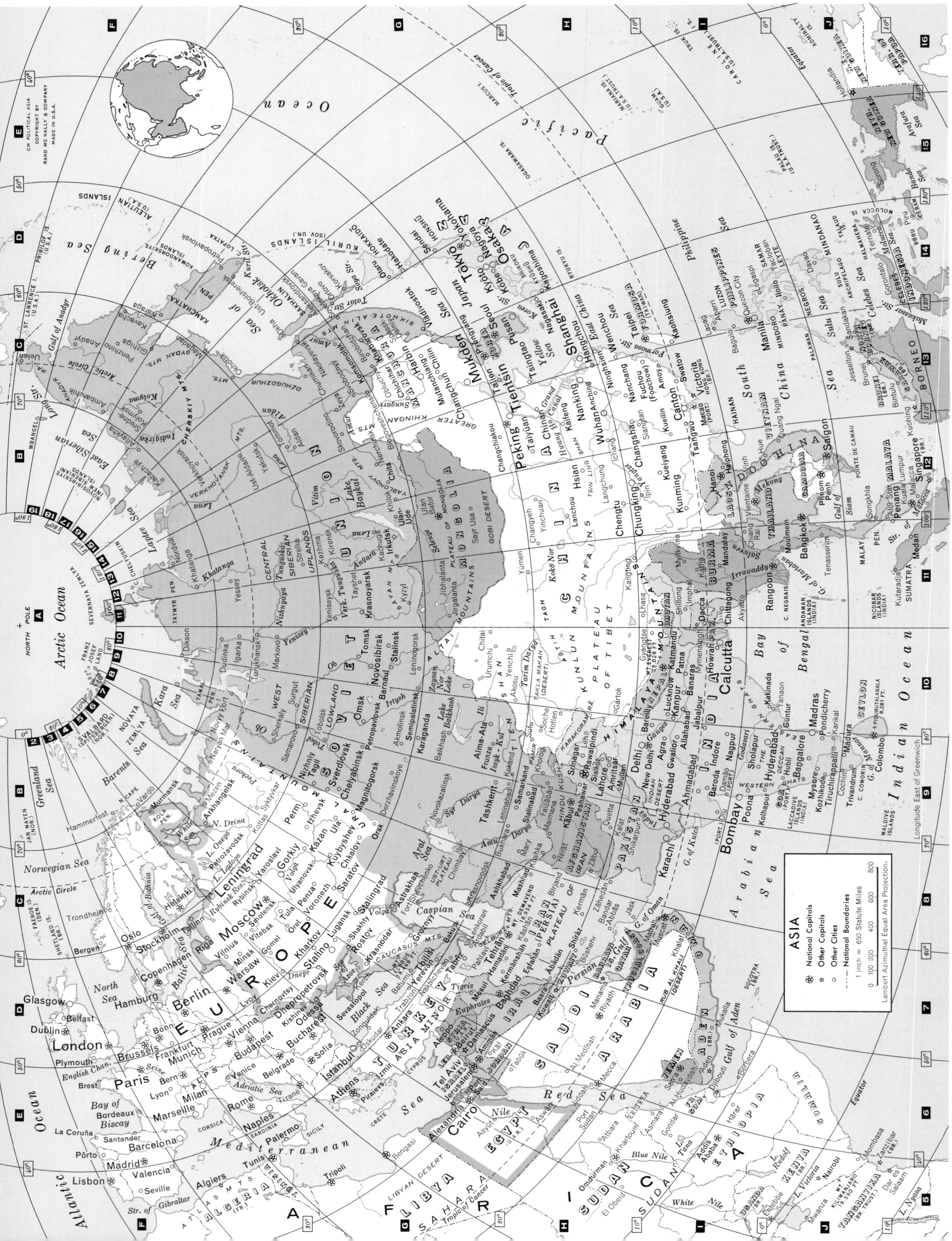
ASIA
National Capitals
Other Capitals
Other Cities
National Boundaries
1 inch = 650 Statute Miles
0 100 200 400 600 800
Lambert Azimuthal Equal Area Projection.
CM POLITICAL ASIA
COPYRIGHT BY
RAND MC NALLY & COMPANY
MADE IN U.S.A.
Arctic Ocean
Pacific Ocean
Indian Ocean
Atlantic Ocean
Arabian Sea
Bay of Bengal
South China Sea
Philippine Sea
Bering Sea
Sea of Okhotsk
Sea of Japan
East China Sea
Yellow Sea
Mediterranean Sea
Red Sea
Black Sea
Caspian Sea
Aral Sea
Kara Sea
Barents Sea
Laptev Sea
East Siberian Sea
Norwegian Sea
North Sea
Tropic of Cancer
Arctic Circle
Equator
EUROPE
AFRICA
Longitude East of Greenwich

ASIA: "On no other continent," according to the geographer Norton S. Ginsburg, "are such densely settled areas separated by such enormous negative areas. But out of the mountain-hearted highlands, sterile in themselves, flows Asia's lifeblood–its major rivers." The highest and most rugged mountains on earth form a vast welt north of India. Mountain chains radiate in all directions from the Pamir Knot, dividing the continent into compartments, isolating peoples in cultural pockets, impeding commerce and communication, and making a large part of Asia's natural resources inaccessible.

The mountains are land lost to constructive use, and the loss is great. The Plateau of Tibet alone accounts for a half million square miles over two miles high. Even greater areas are covered by mountain chains that stretch 5,000 miles from the Mediterranean to the Bering Sea. In addition to the mountains, there are immense reaches of desert, tundra, jungle and Arctic ice that reduce Asia's arable land to a meager 11 per cent of the total area *(map, below)*. The continent of Asia has only .7 of an acre of arable land per person as opposed to 2.5 acres of arable land per person in North America.

Asia has a number of great rivers, but not many of them alleviate the aridity of the continent or make its interior more accessible. Nearly all of Russia's rivers flow northward into the desolate Arctic. Many Asian rivers end uselessly by emptying into brackish lakes in the interior or by disappearing into underground channels. Except for the Tigris and Euphrates in Southwest Asia, most of the important rivers rise in the highland core around Tibet. They come cascading east and south to the sea: the Indus and Ganges of India; the Irrawaddy of Burma; the Hwang Ho (Yellow River) and the Yangtze of China; and the mighty Mekong emptying from Vietnam. In the river valleys *(map, below right)* the population reaches a crushing density–close to 2,000 people per square mile in some places. Virtually all of the valley multitudes live by farming or fishing. But they have too little land and too little water, and they are handicapped by primitive methods. At best their lot is a fraction of the food they need. On the coast, where the density of population is as great, the degree of poverty is as high.

AREA:	17,035,000 sq. mi.
POPULATION:	1,691,328,000.
ALTITUDES:	Mt. Everest, Tibet-Nepal, 29,028 ft. (highest); Dead Sea, Israel-Jordan, -1,292 ft. (lowest).

Asia has a goodly share of the world's timber, water power, fuels and minerals. Many of the resources, however, are not readily accessible, or they are present where they cannot be used. Southwest Asia has about half of the world's oil, but practically no other raw materials for building industries based on oil. Southeast Asia has tin and tungsten, but is deficient in coal to refine them. Japan has coal, but not enough iron. The Philippines have valuable teak and lauan mahogany, but the timber is difficult to bring out of the dense jungles. The northeastern region of India has both coal and iron and here huge steel works are being built, but the country employs less than one per cent of its population in modern industry. Flood and famine frequently cancel out advances made in China's nationalized industries as well as on its collectivized farms.

An explosive birth rate puts even greater stress on Asia's economy. To feed its next generations, the continent must learn to develop its barely touched resources and employ its enormous fund of manpower in industry.

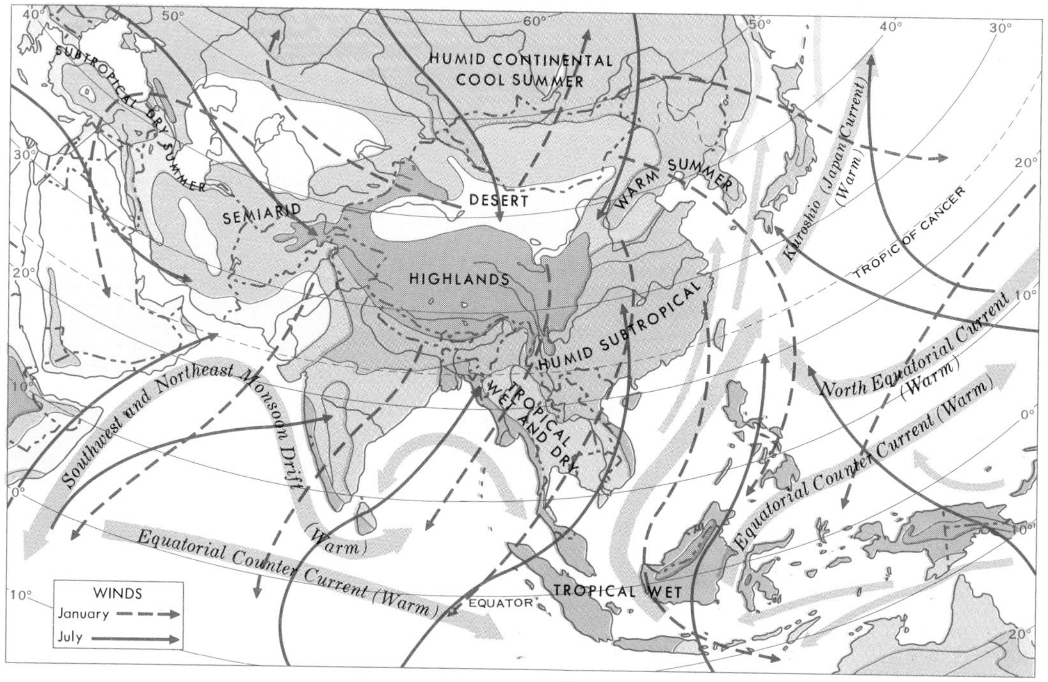

THE CLIMATE ZONES OF ASIA

On this map, Asia's climate zones are shown in solid colors. Ocean currents are indicated by broad arrows (red for warm, blue for cold), and the direction of the seasonal winds by thin arrows, solid and broken. The east coast has climates similar to those of the east coast of the United States. Great heat and long rainy seasons prevail in the tropics farther south. The summer monsoons begin in the south when warm moisture-laden air is drawn north by the existence of low pressure beyond the mountains.

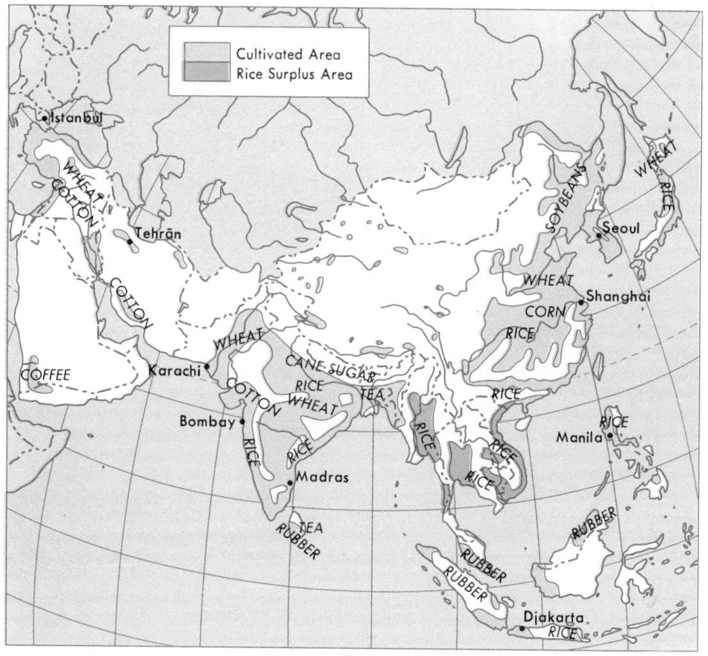

THE USES OF ASIAN LAND

The green areas on this map indicate the location of cultivatable land in Asia (excluding the Soviet Union) and show what crops are grown. Farming is widespread in the rainy coastal areas and in irrigated river valleys. Those ricelands of Southeast Asia shown in dark green produce a surplus. The interior of the continent is barren except for scattered fertile spots.

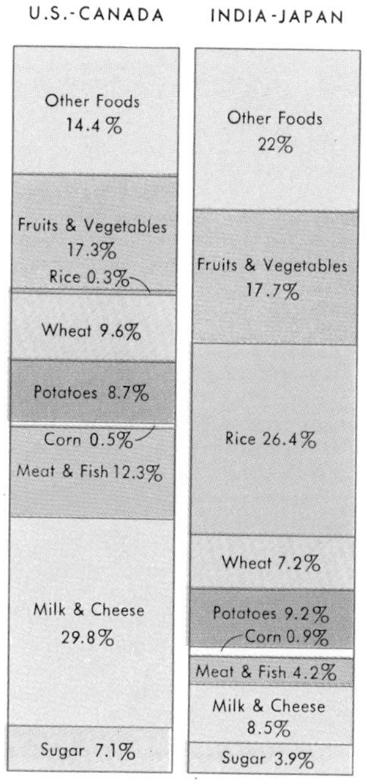

EASTERN AND WESTERN DIETS

In consumption of cereals, the rice-eating Indians and Japanese, as shown by the graph above, outdistance by far the citizens of the U.S. and Canada.

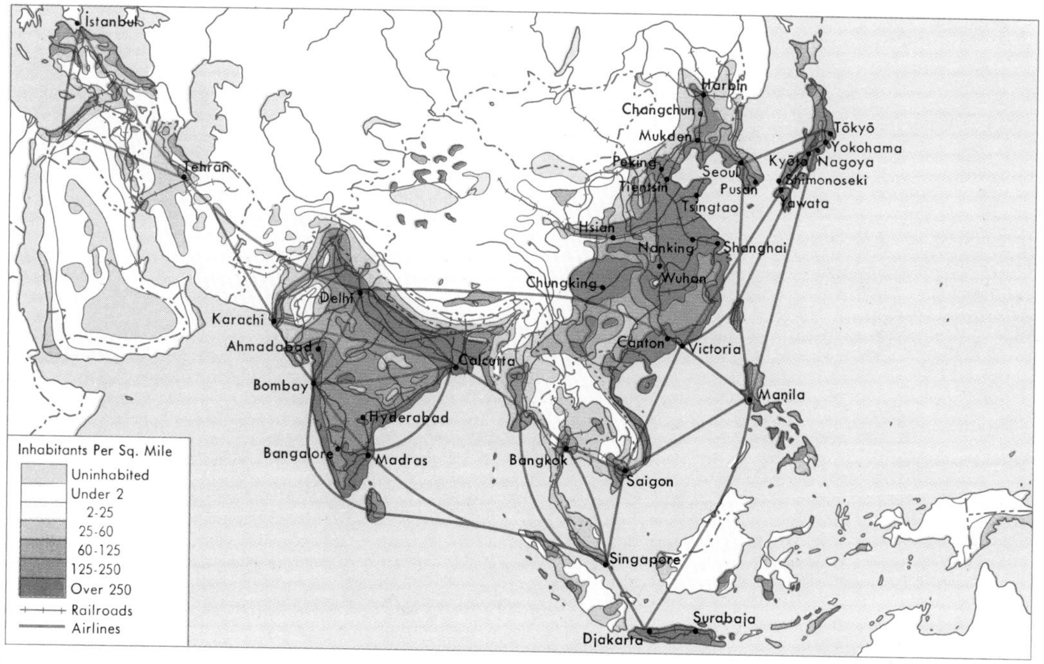

POPULATION AND TRANSPORTATION IN ASIA

The distribution of Asia's people and their main transportation routes are shown on this map. Except for scattered oases in the interior, the densest concentrations of population *(in dark purple)* occur on the coasts and along big navigable rivers where soil and water permit intensive agriculture and raw materials can be easily transported for industrial use. Most of the rail lines connect coastal cities with productive inland valleys. Air transport is available mostly along the coasts and between islands.

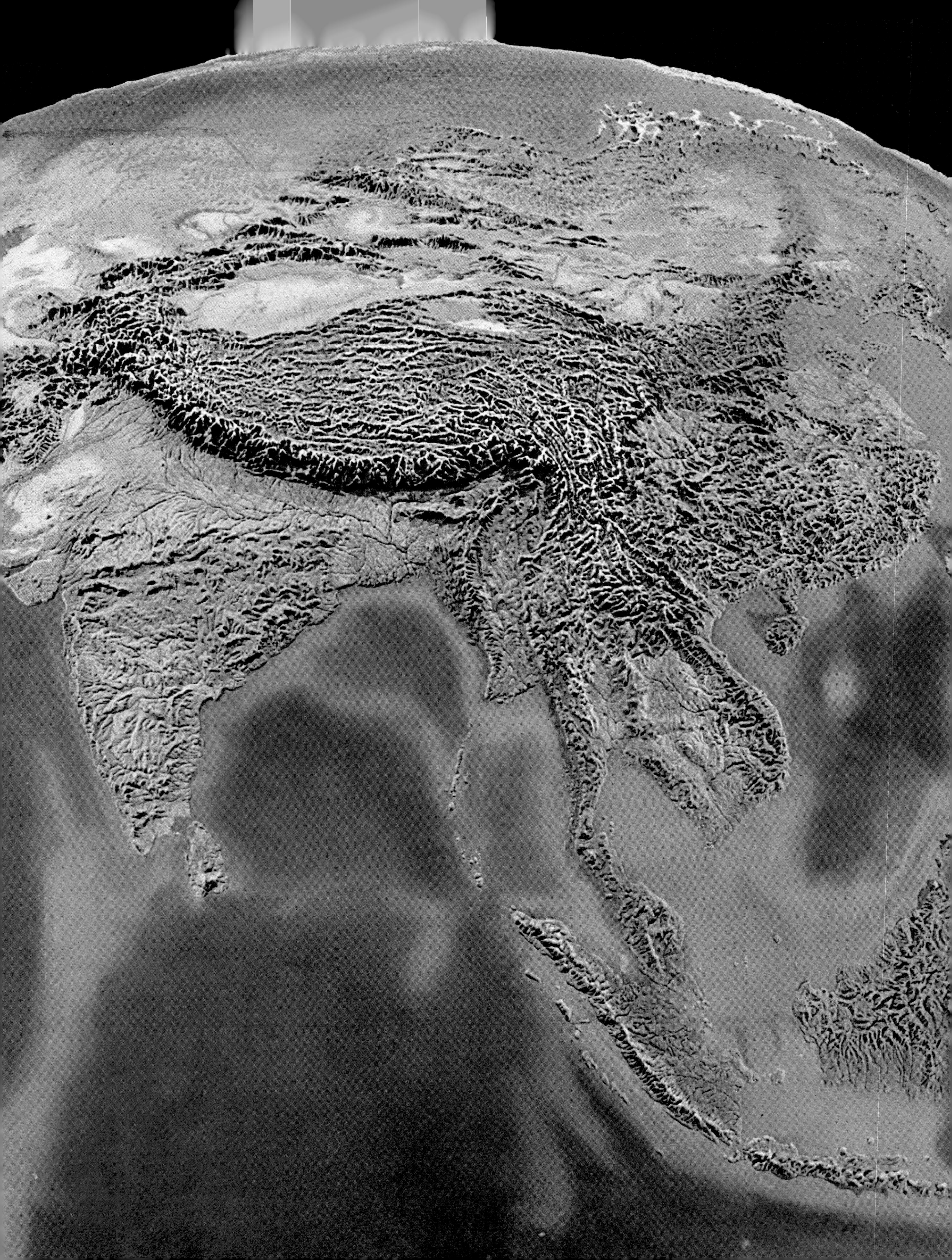

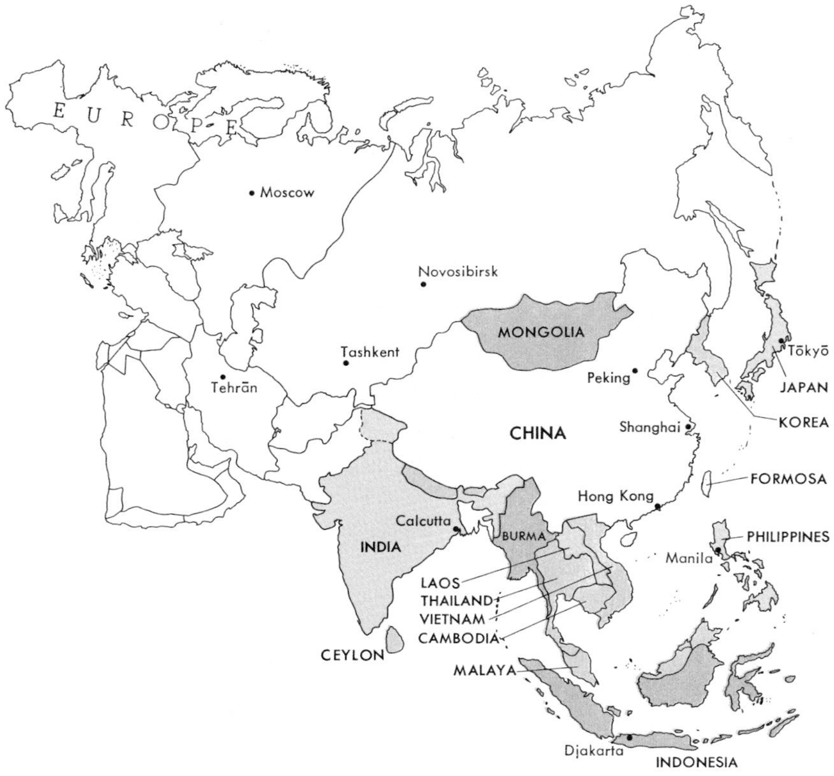

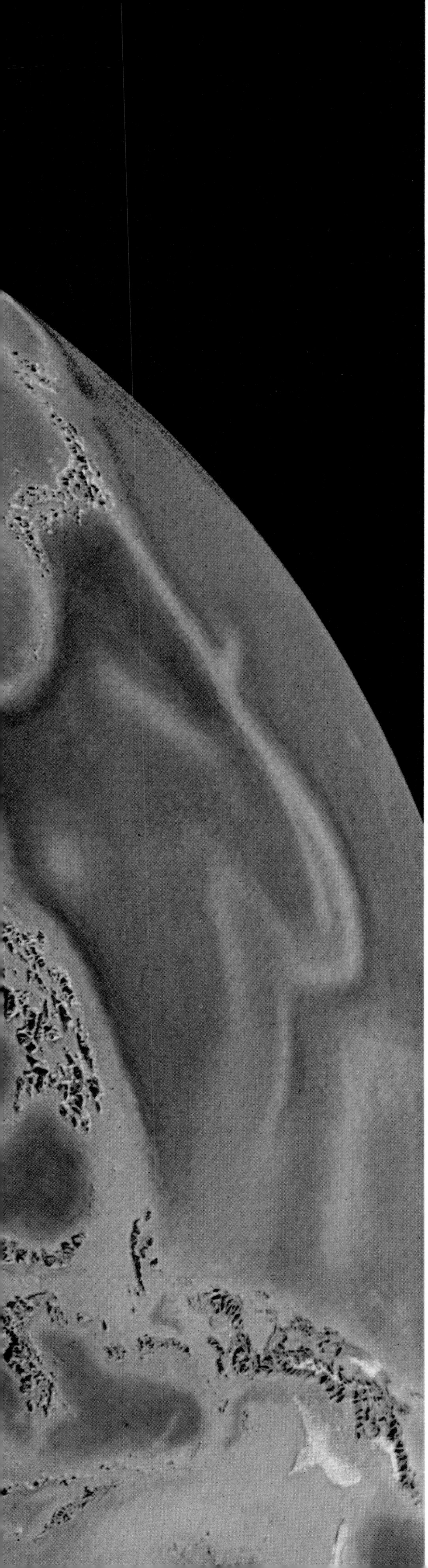

EAST AND SOUTH ASIA

In what has been called "Asian Asia," almost half the world's people remain in the condition geography first imposed on them – cut off from each other and from the outside world. As early as the Third Century B.C., China was building the Great Wall along the weakest stretch of its natural inland barrier of mountains and deserts. As late as the 19th Century, China and Japan were resisting trade with the West. But Asia's raw materials and the handiwork of its craftsmen had long since become Europe's luxuries. The names of Asian products often bespoke their origin: china for porcelain ware, japanning for lacquer work, Java for coffee, Shantung for silk.

Until very recently the people of East and South Asia changed little in their relation to the land and to each other. Agriculture continues to occupy about three quarters of the population. In deltas and river valleys, farmers swarm industriously over tiny, mosaic-like plots that have been tilled for countless generations. The farmers are so numerous that rice is said to grow half of the time in the earth, half in the farmer's hand. Yet few of these nations grow enough food. And none is fully self-sufficient in mineral resources.

Contact with the West has left unifying as well as modernizing influences. Ports founded or developed by outsiders have opened ocean highways to an expanding intra-Asia trade. In India and the Philippines, English continues to be a common tongue among peoples separated by many dialects. A hundred years of western methods have made Japan the busiest industrial nation of the Orient. The peninsula and islands of Southeast Asia have economic development plans on the western pattern. But for tens of millions, day-to-day life remains a struggle to subsist. As nutritionist Dr. Josue de Castro has written, "No other social factor anywhere has molded human conduct with such despotic control as the collective hunger in the Far East."

BETWEEN TWO OCEANS, the Malay peninsula trails its island arm, Indonesia, at bottom center. China and Japan face each other across Korea, at the upper right. At the far left, the subcontinent of India, tipped by Ceylon, pokes southward into the Indian Ocean.

A GREAT WALL, A LONG VALLEY

A SLUGGISH RIVER, the Naktong makes its way for more than 300 miles in South Korea to Pusan on the coast, its course slowed by sand deposited along the edges by its tributary streams. The river's water is used to irrigate the rice paddies of the Naktong valley.

A HISTORIC REDOUBT, the Great Wall of China *(opposite)* stretches 1,500 miles across the country's northern plains. Construction of the wall was begun some 2,000 years ago to keep out raiders from the north. Now it serves as a source of building stone.

CHINA AND MONGOLIA
Barren Areas Above Timber
Evergreen Trees
Mixed Evergreen and Deciduous Trees
Shrub
Grass
Alpine Vegetation
Barren Arid Areas
Below sea level areas are white. No vegetation is indicated.
National Capitals
Provincial and Other Capitals
Cities
Railroads
Canals
1 inch = 270 Statute Miles
Polyconic Projection
CM TERRAIN CHINA, MONGOLIA COPYRIGHT BY RAND MC NALLY & COMPANY MADE IN U.S.A.
Longitude East of Greenwich
PEKING
Shanghai
Sea of Japan
Yellow Sea
South China Sea
Bay of Bengal
GOBI DESERT
TAKLA MAKAN (DESERT)
PLATEAU OF TIBET
Yangtze

CHINA AND MONGOLIA

CHINA: Here lives the world's largest population, growing at the rate of 15 million a year. If the present trend continues, China should have a billion inhabitants in another 20 years. "Even though the topography is more rugged than that of any other nation of comparable size and importance," Dr. Gerald F. Winfield, an American student of China, has written, "no valley is too remote to be inhabited. Human feet have worn trails across every hill and mountain. . . . Every foot of available soil is patiently cultivated. Everywhere, one can hear the call of human voices."

AREA: 3,767,751 sq. mi.
POPULATION: 699,966,000. Largest city: Shanghai. Capital: Peking.
CLIMATE: Northern regions–warm summers, cold winters; moderate summer rainfall, dry winters. Southern regions–warmer winters, heavier rainfall. Western regions–hot summers, cold winters; very dry. Highlands vary from warm to cold, wet to dry.
ALTITUDES: Minya Konka, 24,900 ft.; Peking, 165 ft.

Isolated for centuries from the outside world, China developed culture, art, literature and religions predating the ancient civilization of the Greeks by more than a thousand years. The soaring Himalayas in the southwest, the Pacific Ocean on the east, the pestilential jungles of the southeast and the deserts of the west and north have provided forbidding frontiers for China. The Emperor Shih Hwang-ti attempted to complete a continuous Great Wall across the country's most vulnerable boundary in the northwest more than 2,000 years ago. Like other wall-builders, he failed, and Mongol horsemen and other invaders in succeeding centuries swarmed down into the plains of north China.

Agricultural China cultivates only 12 per cent of the land, but is trying to increase total production with the institution of communal farms. In the flat, semiarid north, cereals and other dry crops are raised; in the tropical and subtropical south, which has abundant rainfall, rice and tea are the staples. Industrially, China is still a fast-growing infant; with plentiful resources of coal, plus recently discovered reserves of iron, uranium and other minerals, it has an industrial potential as promising as that of any nation on earth.

The north Chinese, speaking Mandarin, are generally taller than their brothers south of the Yangtze River, who speak various other dialects of Chinese. Despite the linguistic and physical variations between inhabitants of the north and south, the Chinese are a homogeneous people.

MONGOLIA: This is a desolate, wind-swept land, where horses outnumber humans two to one. Mongolia is part desert, part grassland. The sparse population is concentrated in the northern half of the country; in the south is the forbidding Gobi Desert, a huge and empty gravel pit. In the 13th and 14th Centuries, under Genghis Khan and his grandson Kublai Khan, the Mongols ruled an empire that stretched from the China Sea to Budapest.

AREA: 590,966 sq. mi.
POPULATION: 1,056,000. Largest city and capital: Ulan Bator.
CLIMATE: Arid; warm summers, cold winters.
ALTITUDES: Turgun Uula, 14,052 ft. (highest).

More than 80 per cent of the people are nomads who live in tents and subsist entirely on a diet of meat and milk. But there has been a trend toward industrialization in the past decade: a factory has been built to process sheepskins, and the country's coal mine operations have been expanding.

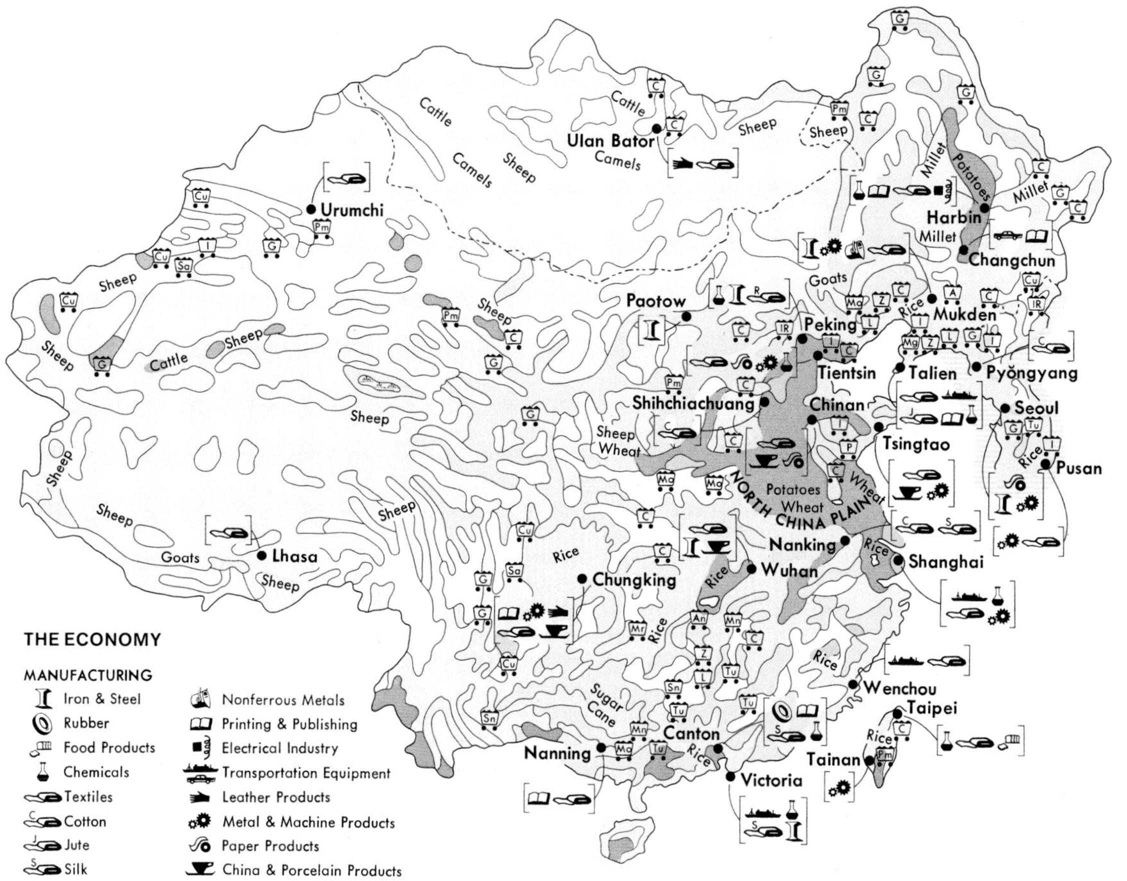

THE ECONOMY

MANUFACTURING: Iron & Steel; Rubber; Food Products; Chemicals; Textiles; Cotton; Jute; Silk; Carpets; Nonferrous Metals; Printing & Publishing; Electrical Industry; Transportation Equipment; Leather Products; Metal & Machine Products; Paper Products; China & Porcelain Products

MINING: Asphalt; Antimony; Coal; Copper; Gold; Iron Ore; Iron Ore Reserves; Lead; Magnesium; Manganese; Molybdenum; Mercury; Phosphate; Petroleum; Salt; Tin; Tungsten; Zinc

AGRICULTURE: General Farming; Intensive Agriculture; Plantation Agriculture; Exhaustive Forest, Collecting Agriculture; Forest Agriculture; Pastureland with Sparse Vegetation; Seasonal Grazing; Non-Agricultural Areas; Swamp Areas

FISHING: Fishing Areas

GROSS NATIONAL PRODUCT PER CAPITA
China $56 Formosa $104 Korea $99 Mongolia—not available

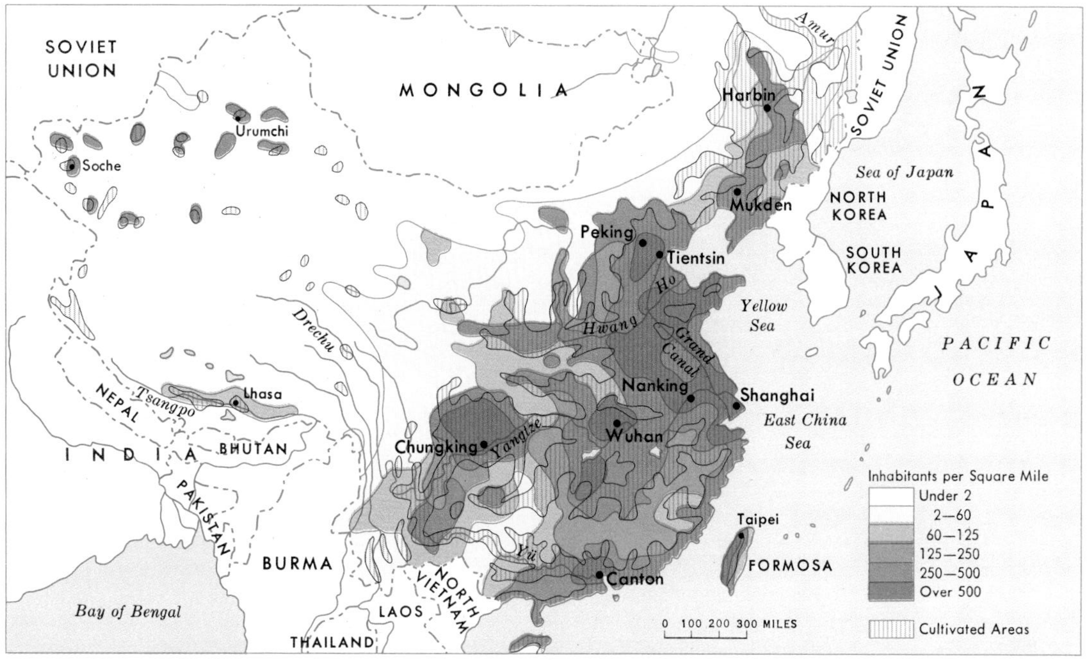

THE THRONGS OF CHINA

The map above shows how China's dense population *(purple areas)*, cultivated lands *(gray vertical lines)* and major cities are concentrated in the river valleys and coastal plains of the eastern half of the country. The interior of China, like all of Mongolia, has only a sparse population, with some thick clusters near water in the northwest. There is less than half an acre of farm land per capita in China.

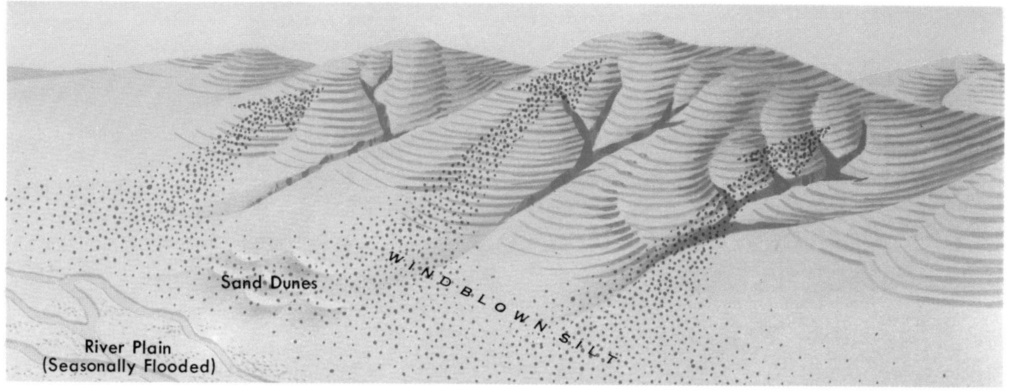

LOESS-COVERED HILLS OF CHINA

This diagram shows how loess (fine particles of earth or sand) is carried by wind from river plains or distant deserts and deposited on the slopes of hills in China. Some deposits here are 500 feet deep. Terracing permits cultivation of the fertile loess on hillsides and keeps it from washing out in gullies *(dark areas)*. Loess areas are also present in the U.S. and in Europe.

SOVIET UNION
MANCHURIA
HEILUNGKIANG
KIRIN
LIAONING
MONGOLIA
INNER MONGOLIA
GOBI DESERT
PLATEAU OF MONGOLIA
NORTH KOREA
SOUTH KOREA
HOPEI
SHANSI
SHANTUNG
HONAN
KANSU
SHENSI
ORDOS
Sea of Japan
Yellow Sea
Korea Bay
Gulf of Chihli (Pohai)
Korea Strait
Tsushima Strait
Liaotung Bay
Laichow Bay
Haichow Bay
Tongjosŏn Bay
Kanghwa Bay
Huang Ho (Yellow R.)
Amur
Sungari
Nen
Yalu
GREATER KHINGAN MTS.
LESSER KHINGAN MTS.
CHANGPAI MTS.
GREAT WALL
Grand Canal
PEKING (Peiping)
Tientsin
Mukden (Shenyang)
Harbin (Pinchiang)
Changchun (Hsinking)
Kirin
Dairen
Lüshun (Port Arthur)
Tsingtao (Tsingtao)
Chefoo
Chinan (Tsinan)
Kaifeng
Chengchou
Hsian (Sian)
Yangkü (Taiyüan)
Tatung
Huhehot (Kueisui)
Paotow
Yinchuan (Ningsia)
Ulan Bator (Urga)
Choybalsan
PYŎNGYANG (Heijō)
SEOUL (Keijō)
Pusan (Fusan)
Taegu (Taikyū)
Wŏnsan (Gensan)
Hamhŭng (Kanko)
Chŏngjin (Seishin)
Antung
Anshan
Fushun
Chichihar
Mutanchiang
Tangshan
Shihchiachuang
Paoting
Changchiakou (Kalgan)
Chengte (Jehol)
Chinhuangtao
Loyang
Lanchow

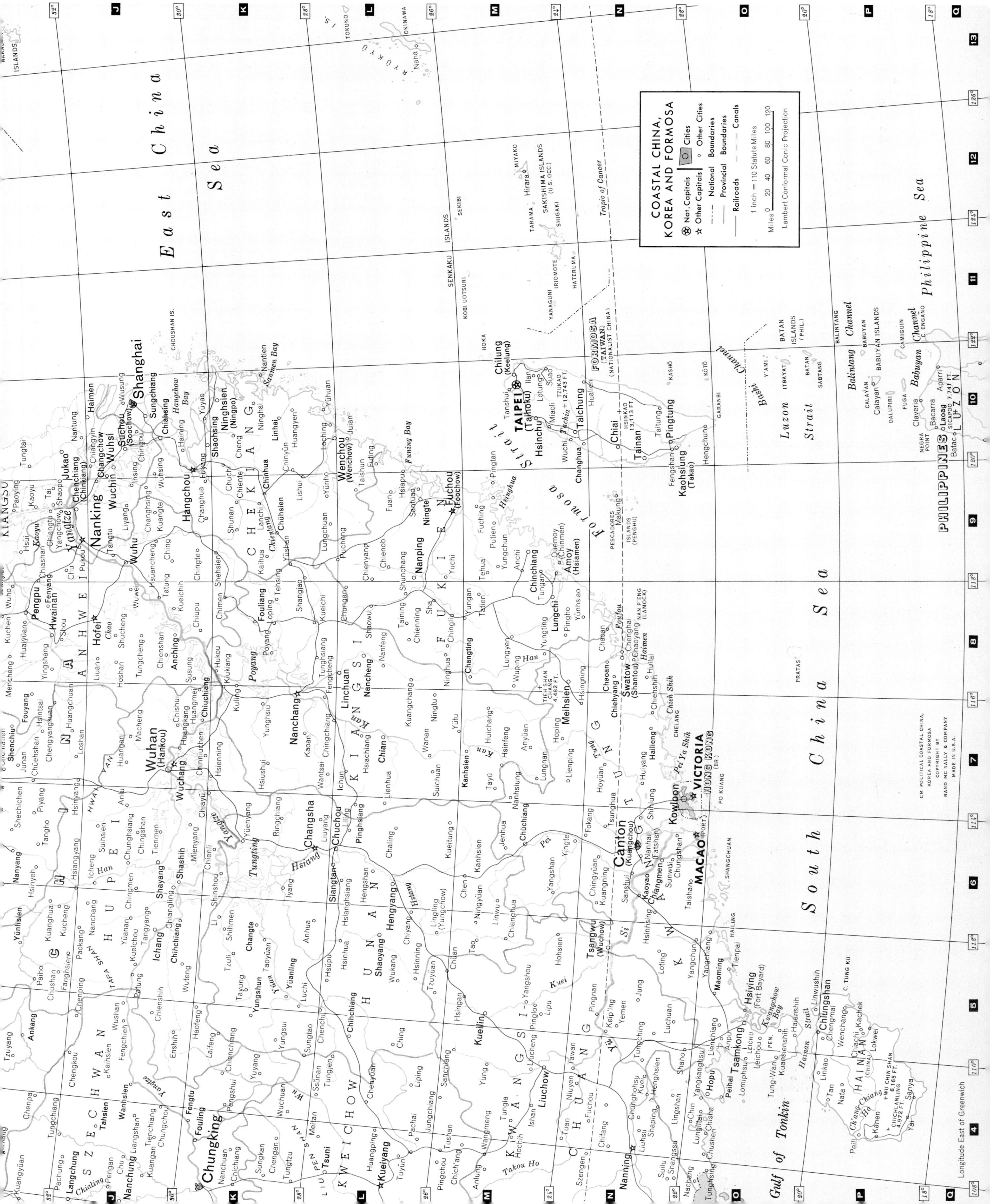
COASTAL CHINA, KOREA AND FORMOSA
Nat. Capitals
Cities
Other Capitals
Other Cities
National Boundaries
Provincial Boundaries
Railroads
Canals
1 inch = 110 Statute Miles
Miles 0 20 40 60 80 100 120
Lambert Conformal Conic Projection
CM POLITICAL COASTAL CHINA, KOREA AND FORMOSA
COPYRIGHT BY RAND MC NALLY & COMPANY
MADE IN U.S.A.
East China Sea
South China Sea
Philippine Sea
Formosa Strait
Luzon Strait
Gulf of Tonkin
FORMOSA (TAIWAN) (NATIONALIST CHINA)
TAIPEI
VICTORIA
HONG KONG (BR.)
MACAO
PHILIPPINES
Shanghai
Nanking
Canton
Wuhan
Chungking
Tropic of Cancer
Longitude East of Greenwich

FORMOSA (NATIONALIST CHINA): Rugged mountains cover two thirds of Formosa, which is about 100 miles off the Fukien coast of mainland China. Also known by its Chinese name, Taiwan, the island has few natural harbors and a coastline partly fringed with reefs. It lies in the path of Pacific typhoons *(map below)* and is subject to frequent earthquakes, although few are severe. Formosa has a humid, subtropical climate with an average annual rainfall of 101 inches that permits two rice crops a season. These crops help feed the dense population (more than 740 people per square mile). The population increase is 3.5 per cent annually. The island's limited arable land, most of it in a strip on the east coast and a broad plain in the west, grows rice, sweet potatoes, sugar cane, bananas, pineapples, citrus fruits and tea.

AREA: 13,885 sq. mi.
POPULATION: 10,323,000. Largest city and capital: Taipei.
CLIMATE: Hot summers, warm winters; heavy summer rainfall. Variations in highlands.
ALTITUDES: Hsinkao, 13,113 ft. (highest); Taipei, 26 ft.

Formosa's industries include rice and sugar milling, pineapple canning and other agricultural processing. Industrial output rose 80 per cent between 1952 and 1959, chiefly in such light industries as textiles. Formosa has launched a program to become self-sufficient in hydroelectric power by means of a large-scale project in the Tachia River Valley in the northwest. To make the valley accessible, a 250-mile-long $10 million highway has been built from east to west across the mountains, linking Taichung in the west with Hualien and Ilan on the east coast.

NORTH KOREA: As the American journalist John Gunther has noted, the Koreans are a "stubborn, emotional, strongly individualistic race perpetually tortured by invasion, the gloomy mark of the conqueror and enforced partition." The documented history of Korea goes back to about the 12th Century B.C. In the 15th Century, Korean artisans invented a movable metal type 50 years before Gutenberg. Historically, "the land of the morning calm" has been anything but calm, and the largely mountainous Korean peninsula, roughly 150 miles wide and 600 miles long, is now divided into two nations. The Korean climate is much like that of the middle to northern U.S. Atlantic seabord. North Korea concentrates on heavy industry. It has been building textile mills, hydroelectric plants steel works, refineries, and fertilizer and cement plants. The country has a good power potential and such important natural resources as coal, iron, tungsten, gold, molybdenum, copper, lead, zinc and silver.

AREA: 47,811 sq. mi.
POPULATION: 8,083,000. Largest city and capital: Pyŏngyang.
CLIMATE: Dry cold winters, warm summers; moderate summer rainfall. Variations in highlands.
ALTITUDES: Peak in Changpai Mountains, 9,003 ft. (highest).

SOUTH KOREA: With a population approaching three times that of its neighbor to the north, South Korea's chief crop is rice, but wheat, barley, beans, potatoes and cotton are also grown. However, as in all of the peninsula, the arable land in South Korea is limited and fish is the staple diet. Thousands of islands, most of them rocky and uninhabited, lie off the Korean shores, the largest being Chejū in the Korean Strait. The chief mineral resources are gold, silver, copper, tungsten and lead. During the past decade South Korea's war-shattered industries have been reviving. Centered at Seoul and Pusan, they include cotton manufacturing, food processing, ceramics, paper and leather goods.

Most of the country's trade is with the U.S. and with Japan and other Asian countries, and consists of an exchange of minerals and fishery products for machinery, medical supplies, fertilizer and food.

AREA: 37,414 sq. mi.
POPULATION: 22,834,000. Largest city and capital: Seoul.
CLIMATE: Dry cool winters, hot summers; moderate to heavy summer rainfall. Variations in highlands.
ALTITUDES: Halla-San, 6,398 ft. (highest); Seoul, 75 ft.

HONG KONG AND MACAO: An estimated three million people crowd tiny Hong Kong *(map below)*, the British crown colony on China's coast. A major center of Chinese trade, Hong Kong—meaning "fragrant harbor"—is regarded by travelers as one of the world's most beautiful cities. It specializes in light industry, chiefly clothing and textiles. The United States has replaced Britain as Hong Kong's best customer: 20 per cent of Hong Kong's exports now go to the U.S.

Macao, a Portuguese city at the mouth of the Canton River in China, was once an important transit center for Chinese trade. Fishing, light industry (firecrackers) and the narcotics trade provide a livelihood for 228,000 people living on 6.2 square miles of land. It is one of the oldest European settlements in the Orient, dating from 1557.

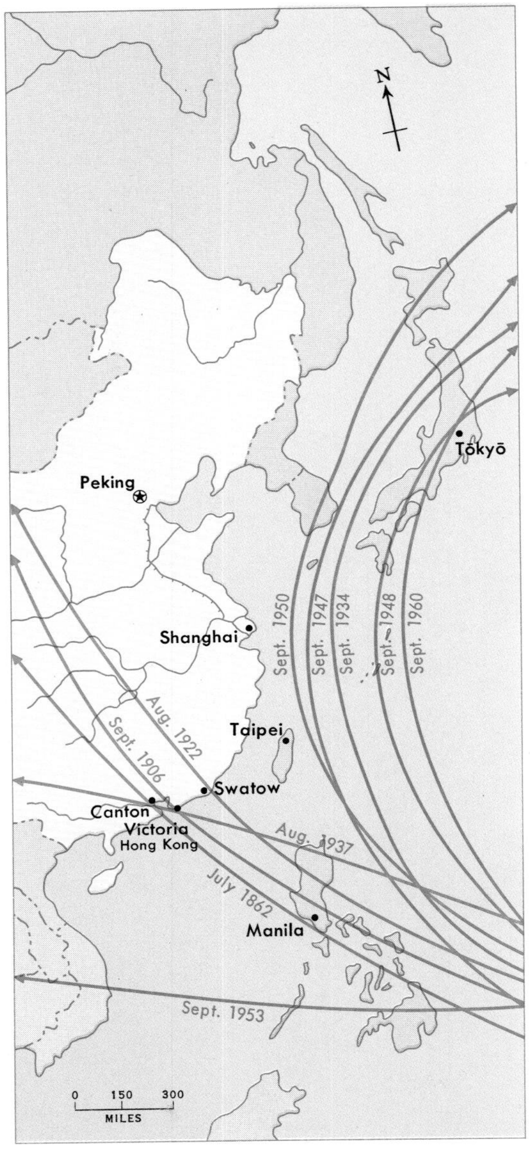

TYPHOON TRACKS IN THE PACIFIC

This map traces the paths of 10 typhoons (tropical storms) that occurred in Asia in the last 100 years. Like hurricanes, typhoons form over warm seas in the trade-wind belt. High winds and rains during the storm of August 1922 killed 50,000 people at Swatow, China.

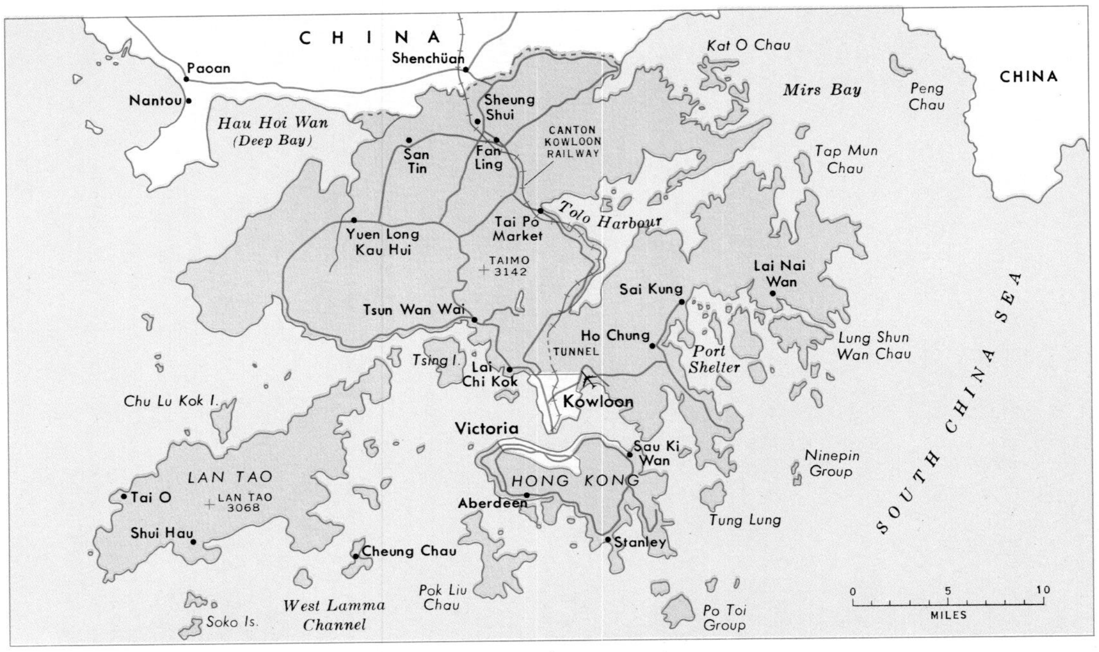

HONG KONG: BUSTLING TRADE CENTER

A fine deepwater harbor makes British Hong Kong *(green, map above)* a great commercial port on the southeast coast of China. The Canton-Kowloon Railway *(center)* and roads *(red)* converge on Kowloon on the mainland, which is connected by ferry with the governmental city of Victoria on the island of Hong Kong itself. The colony has an area of 391 square miles, 12 of them urban and only 50 cultivated, with most of the land forming the hillsides of the New Territories *(upper center)*. Kowloon is the industrial region.

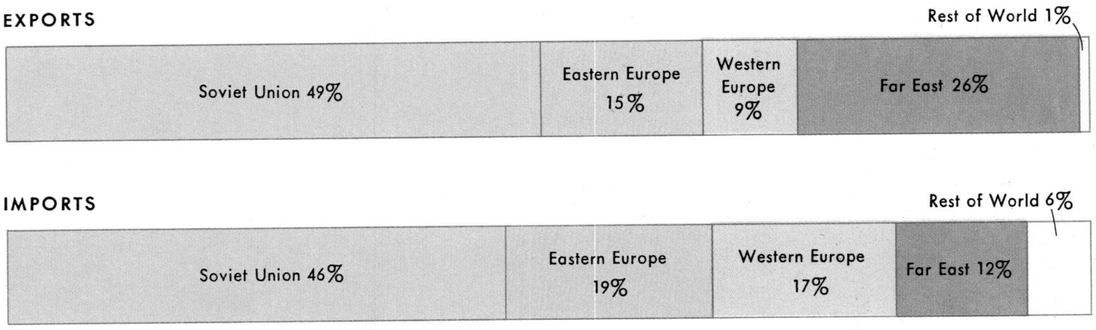

MAINLAND CHINA'S EXPORTS AND IMPORTS

The two graphs above show where mainland China buys and sells in world markets, according to statistics published by the countries with which it trades regularly. The heaviest trade is with the Soviet Union and the countries of Eastern Europe. China exports 64 per cent of its goods to the Soviet Union and Eastern European nations, while importing 65 per cent of its needs from the same countries. Western Europe accounts for only 9 per cent of China's exports and provides 17 per cent of China's purchases abroad.

FORMOSA, KOREA AND HONG KONG

CHINA IN 1930

The map above shows China in 1930, when it was ruled by the Nationalist Party, or Kuomintang, from the capital at Nanking. Tibet, Sinkiang, Mongolia and Manchuria *(orange, left to right)* were under varying degrees of Chinese influence. Although Tibet was a dependency of China, civil and religious administration of the state was under the leadership of the Dalai Lama. Formosa (Taiwan) belonged to Japan.

CHINA IN 1960

Three decades of change are reflected on this map of the autonomous regions *(shown in orange)* dominated by mainland China. The capital is Peking. A vast expanse of Mongolia *(upper center)* is a separate political unit. Inner Mongolia, Sinkiang and Tibet are called "autonomous regions" of China, and Manchuria has been absorbed by China. The island of Formosa *(lower right)* is held by Nationalist China.

THE YELLOW RIVER'S CHANNELS

Many courses of the shifting Hwang Ho (Yellow River) are shown above at seven different periods in its history, dating from 600 B.C. Floodings of the river have left rich soils *(green)* both north and south of the Shantung Peninsula *(upper right)*. These fertile basins are crossed by China's Grand Canal *(blue, center)*. In 1947 the course of the Hwang Ho was diverted with United Nations aid to its present channel.

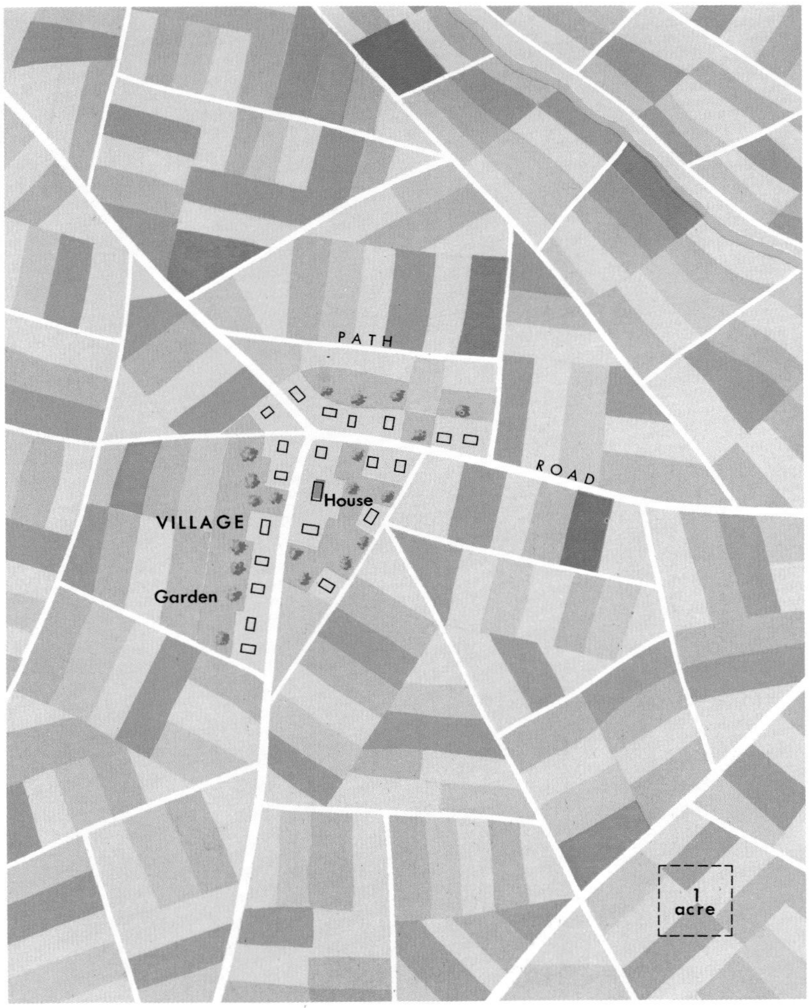

AN ANCIENT AGRICULTURAL PATTERN

A traditional farm hamlet in central China is shown in the drawing above. Usually these settlements were situated along a well-traveled road, near a stream. The separated plots in shades of red around the village are the holdings of one family *(red house, center)*, broken up this way by old inheritance customs. Recently such scattered holdings have been consolidated by the government into large collective farms.

BETWEEN HEAVEN AND EARTH ON FUJIYAMA

SHROUDED IN CLOUDS, Fujiyama, Japan's highest peak (12,388 feet), has alpine flowers blooming in the rich volcanic soil along a path. At an altitude of 8,000 feet, just above the timber line, this path is called "the border between heaven and earth." Pilgrims often come to pray at the Shinto shrines located on the slopes of Mount Fuji. A dormant volcano, it has been shaped into an almost perfect cone by many eruptions, the last of which occurred in 1707, spreading lava and ashes smoothly over two older mountains.

JAPAN
Evergreen Trees
Mixed Evergreen and Deciduous Trees
Deciduous Trees
National Capital
Cities
Railroads
1 inch = 102 Statute Miles
Miles 0 10 20 40 60 80 100
Lambert Conformal Conic Projection
CHINA
SOVIET UNION
SIKHOTE ALIN MOUNTAINS
SAKHALIN (SOV. UN.)
HOKKAIDŌ
HONSHŪ
SHIKOKU
KYŪSHŪ
NORTH KOREA
KOREA
SOUTH KOREA
Sea of Japan
Pacific Ocean
Chingcheng
Suileng
Suihua
Suipin
Fuchin
Sungari
Vyazemskaya
Jaoho (Tuanshantzu)
Bikin
Paoching
Hulin
Iman
Ivanovichi
Muleng
Mishan
Lesozavodsk
Khanka L.
Turiy Rog
Lishukou
Acheng
Wuchang
Shulan
Suifenho
Spassk-Dalniy
Chernigovka
Uborka
Tungning
Ussuriysk
Olga
Tetyukhe-Pristan
Plastun
Terney
Amgu
Svetlaya
Samarga
C. ZOLOTOY
Tantsanza
Chiaoho
Sungari Reservoir
Wangching
Yenchi
Onsong
Hunchun
Artem
Shkotovo
Vladivostok
Suchan
Dunay
Nakhodka
Vladimiro Aleksandrovskoye
C. POVOROTNYY
C. NIZMENNYY
Peter The Great Bay
Chongsong
Hoeryong
Fusung
CHANGPAI MTS (PAEKTU-SAN)
Tumen
Musan
Puryong
Unggi
Aojidong
Najin (Rashin)
Kyongsong
Chongjin (Seishin)
Hyesanjin
Yongan
Kapsan
Hapsu
Pungsan
Kilchu
Kim Chaek (Songjin)
Iwon
Pukchong
Hamhung
Tongjoson Bay
Kosong
Kansong
Yangyang
Kangnung
Pyongchang
Chechon
Ulchin
Naesong
Pungsan
Andong
Sangju
Hunghae
Pohang
Yongil Bay
Taegu (Taikyu)
Kyongju (Keishu)
Hyopchon
Ulsan
Masan
Chinhae
Pusan (Fusan)
ULLUNG (UTSURYO-TO)
TAKE
Korea Strait
Tsushima Strait
TSU-SHIMA
KOJE
Izuhara
KAMI
SHIMO
IKI
Dolinsk (Ochiai)
Yuzhno-Sakhalinsk
C. SVOBODNYY
Tunaicha
Kholmsk (Maoka)
Nevelsk (Honto)
KRILON PEN.
Korsakov (Otomari)
Muravyevo
Aniva Bay
Minabetsu
Chikatomari
C. ANIVA
KAIBA
Kuznetsovo
Dalnyaya
C. KRILON
Soya Strait
C. SOYA
Wakkanai
REBUN
RISHIRI
Senhoshi
Sarufutsu
Hamatombetsu
Esashi
Teshio
Embetsu
YANGESHIRI
TEURE
Haboro
Piuka
Nayoro
Shibetsu
Engaru
Mombetsu
C. SHIRETOKO
RAUSU-DAKE 5,449 FT.
C. RURUI
Nemuro Strait
Abashiri
Kitami
Shari
Rumoe
Asahigawa
ASAHI-DAKE 7,513 FT.
Sunagawa
Otaru Bay
Otaru
Bibai
Furano
SHIBETSU-DAKE 5,666 FT.
C. SHAKOTAN
Yoichi
Sapporo
Iwamisawa
Yubari
Obihiro
Pombetsu
Kushiro
Akkeshi
Akkeshi Bay
Nemuro
Iwanai
Suttsu
Atsuma
POROSHIRI-DAKE 6,732 FT.
KARIBA-YAMA 4,987 FT.
Oshamambe
Tomakomai
Setana
Noboribetsu
Uchiura Bay
Muroran
Urakawa
C. ERIMO
OKUSHIRI
Tsurikake
Mori
Esashi
C. ESAN
Hakodate
Matsumae
OSHIMA
KO
Tsugaru Strait
C. SHIRIYA
Ominato
Mutsu Bay
Noheji
Ajigasawa
Aomori
Towada
Hachinohe
KYUROKU
Hirosaki
Fukuoka
Kuji
Noshiro
OGA PEN.
Oga (Funakawa)
GANJU-SAN 6,696 FT.
Morioka
Akita
HAYACHINE-SAN 6,279 FT.
Miyako
C. TODOGA
Yokote
Kamaishi
TOBI
CHOKAI-SAN 7,700 FT.
Ofunato
Ichinoseki
Kesennuma
Shinjo
Sakata
Tsuruoka
AWA
Ishinomaki
Shiogama
Yamagata
Sendai
Sendai Bay
C. HAJIKI
SADO
KINPOKU 3,848 FT.
Aikawa
Murakami
Yonezawa
HEKURA
Niigata
IIDE-SAN 6,906 FT.
Fukushima
Sanjo
Wakamatsu
NANATSU
C. SUZU
Wajima
Nagaoka
Takata
Koriyama
Kashiwazaki
NOTO PEN.
Toyama Bay
NASU-DAKE 6,283 FT.
Nanao
Takada
Taira
C. SHIOYA
Nikko
Ashio
Hitachi
Takaoka
Nagano
Toyama
Utsunomiya
Kanazawa
Komatsu
YARIGA-TAKE 10,466 FT.
Maebashi
Kiryu
Ueda
Tochigi
Mito
Furukawa
Takasaki
Ashikaga
Isezaki
Tsuchiura
HIGASHI (DOGO)
Saigo
OKI ISLANDS
Matsumoto
Kasumiga-Ura
Fukui
Takayama
Okaya
YATSUGA-TAKE 9,511 FT.
Omiya
Urawa
TOKYO
Choshi
C. INUBO
Chiba
Kasumi
C. KYOGA
Wakasa Bay
Kinosaki
Fukushima
Kofu
Hachioji
Kawasaki
Yokohama
Yokosuka
Matsue
Tottori
Fukuchiyama
Tsuruga
Maizuru
Gifu
Mitake
Iida
Izumo
Yonago
MT. FUJI 12,388 FT.
Tajimi
Ogaki
Seto
Numazu
Hiratsuka
Odawara
Tateyama
C. NOJIMA
Tsuyama
Kyoto
Yokkaichi
Nagoya
Shimizu
Shizuoka
Mishima
Hamada
Niimi
Himeji
Kobe
Amagasaki
Hamamatsu
O-SHIMA
KAMURI-YAMA 4,393 FT.
Okayama
Kurashiki
Akashi
Fuse
Tsu
Matsuzaka
Toyohashi
MI
Masuda
Hagi
Fukuyama
Tamano
Osaka
Ujiyamada
C. IRO
TO
NII
KOZU
MIYAKE
MIKURA
Hiroshima
Kure
Onomichi
AWAJI
Sumoto
Wakayama
C. DAIO
Yamaguchi
Iwakuni
Marugame
Takamatsu
Shimonoseki
Ube
Tokuyama
Imabari
Tokushima
Kainan
HAKKEN SAN 6,283 FT.
Yawata
Moji
Kokura
Hofu
Suo Sea
Matsuyama
Niihama
Komatsushima
Kii Strait
Tanabe
Fukuoka
Kochi
Aki
Shingu
HIRADO
Karatsu
Yawatahama
TSURUGI SAN 6,414 FT.
C. SHIO
GOTO ISLANDS
Sasebo
Saga
Kurume
Beppu
Oita
Ozu
KASATORI-YAMA 5,126 FT.
C. MUROTO
Isahaya
Omuta
Shimabara
KUJU-SAN 5,866 FT.
Uwajima
Nakamura
Nagasaki
Kumamoto
Saeki
Bungo Strait
C. ASHIZURI
Amakusa Sea
Yatsushiro
KUNIMI-DAKE 5,705 FT.
Nobeoka
SHIMO
Hitoyoshi
DANJO
Yatsushiro Sea
Minamata
Miyazaki
KOSHIKI
Sendai
Kagoshima
Miyakonojo
C. NOMA
Kanoya
UJI
Makurazaki
Ariake Bay
Kagoshima Bay
Osumi Strait (Van Diemen Strait)
KUSAKAKI
KURO
OSUMI IS.
TANEGA
KUCHINO ERABU
YAKU
Tanega Strait
KUCHINO
NAKANO
Tokara Strait
SUWANOSE
AKUSEKI
TOKARA ISLANDS
TOKARA
YOKOATE
AMAMI
KAKAIGA
Longitude East of Greenwich
CM TERRAIN JAPAN
COPYRIGHT BY RAND MCNALLY & COMPANY
MADE IN U.S.A.
©RMCN.
YARIGA-TAKE 10,466 FT.
Furukawa
Takayama
HAKU-SAN 8,865 FT.
Katsuyama
NORIKURA-DAKE 9,928 FT.
Shiojiri
Ueda
Iwamurada
Matsumoto
Takasaki
Matsuida
Kiryu
Maebashi
Isezaki
Kumagaya
Tochigi
Ashikaga
Koga
Mito
Shishido
Minato
Shimodate
Ishioka
Hokota
Tsuchiura
Kasumiga-Ura
Kasukabe
Okaya
Suwa
Mamba
Kitamaki
Shimo
Kuki
Ono
Osaka
Narai
Fukushima
YATSUGA-TAKE 9,511 FT.
Chichibu
Kawagoe
Omiya
Toride
Kashima
Omigawa
Takefu
ONTAKE-SAN 10,049 FT.
Ina
Urawa
Kawaguchi
Narita
Gero
Agematsu
Takato
TOKYO
Ichikawa
Choshi
Wakasa Bay
KAMURI-YAMA 5,304 FT.
Hachiman
Enzan
Tachikawa
Funabashi
Ine
Tsuruga
Kanayama
Sakashita
Nirasaki
Kofu
Hachioji
Chiba
Yokoshiba
Miyazu
Kinomoto
Mino
Ena
Kajikazawa
Kawasaki
Tokyo Bay
Maizuru
Obama
Gifu
Mitake
Iida
Yokohama
Oami
Fukuchiyama
Ogaki
Minokamo
Tajimi
ENA-SAN 7,185 FT.
Fujiyoshida
Atsugi
Mobara
Imazu
Ichinomiya
Akechi
MT. FUJI 12,388 FT.
Hiratsuka
Kamakura
Otaki
Ayabe
Biwa
Hikone
Nagoya
Neba
Gotemba
Yokosuka
Ohara
Hiraya
Echigawa
Tsushima
Seto
Asuke
Misakubo
Fujinomiya
Odawara
Minato
Sonobe
Katata
Kuwana
Koromo
Yoshiwara
Mishima
Miura (Misaki)
Kominato
Kuge
Kyoto
Kusatsu
Taguchi
Senzu
Atami
Kameoka
Yokkaichi
Okazaki
Shimizu
Numazu
Tateyama
Chikura
Otsu
Handa
Anjo
Shinshiro
Shimada
Shizuoka
Ito
C. NOJIMA
Sanda
Ikeda
Takatsuki
Seki
Yaizu
Shuzenji
Itami
Toyonaka
Suzuka
Kowa
Gamagori
Futamata
Ukusu
Inatori
Oshima (Moto)
Kobe
Amagasaki
Ueno
Atsumi Bay
Arai
Kakegawa
Suruga Bay
Matsuzaki
O-SHIMA
Fuse
Nara
Aho
Tsu
Toyohashi
Yokosuka
Sagara
Shimoda
Iwaya
Sakai
Matsuzaka
Hamamatsu
C. OMAE
C. IRO
TO
Osaka
Osaka Bay
Kishiwada
Yagi
Ujiyamada
Fukue
Kaizuka
Toba
Hashimoto
Gojo
Takihara
Totomi Sea
Niijimahon
NII
Wakayama
HAKKEN SAN 6,283 FT.
Kainan
Nakiri
KOZU
Miles 0 5 10 20 30 40

JAPAN

GROSS NATIONAL PRODUCT PER CAPITA $302

JAPAN: This is a country of pastel-print beauty, where mountains are formed in the perfect symmetry of Mount Fuji, the sea gurgles in every cranny of the islands, and the fragile beauties of blossoms and snowflakes and flickering dragonflies are savored by the humblest peasant. It is also a country of extravagantly tortured mountain landscapes, many of them scarred by volcanoes that are periodically still active. Made up of geologically young land forms, Japan's coastline ranges from gentle lowlands with fine harbors to precipitous cliffs against which the sea beats mercilessly. Beneath the beauty and the scars runs the constant threat of earthquakes; there are more than 7,000 recorded tremors a year. Now and then, as in the great shock of 1923, widespread devastation results.

With a population of over 93 million crammed into an area smaller than California and a terrain that is as inhospitable as it is beautiful, Japan is hard pressed to support its people. Rice paddies are squeezed into every available crevice between the steep mountains and the omnipresent sea. By clever and energetic agricultural practices—intricate terracing of the hills and mountainsides, multiple cropping, intensive fertilization and transplanting—Japanese farmers exact one of the world's greatest rice yields from the limited soil. And where there is no land, truck farmers use water: the science of water gardening, or hydroponics, is highly developed in Japan. Forestry, a major source of fuel and trade, occupies 1.5 million people. Japan is also one of the leading fishing nations; some 630,000 Japanese make their living from the sea.

AREA: 142,773 sq. mi.
POPULATION: 93,406,445. Largest city and capital: Tōkyō.
CLIMATE: Warm summers and mild winters in the southern regions; cooler summers and colder winters in the north. Summer rainfall, decreasing from south to north.
ALTITUDES: Mt. Fuji, 12,388 ft. (highest); Yokohama, 110 ft.; Tōkyō, 45 ft.

Only about 15 per cent of Japan's land is arable, and 20 per cent of the total imports are foodstuffs. To balance its economy and feed its people the country has turned with tremendous vigor and great ingenuity to industry. World War II cost Japan 52 per cent of its prewar land area, 80 per cent of its shipping and 30 per cent of its industrial capacity. Since 1945, the hard-working nation has made an industrial comeback that has been called "one of the economic miracles of the world." Today Japan is the world's largest producer of ships, rayon, cameras, sewing machines and transistor radios, the biggest exporter of textiles, textile machines, cement, ceramics, toys and plywood. In 1959, after years of unfavorable trade balances, Japan was able for the first time to show a profit in its trade with the U.S., its biggest customer. In international trade Japan ranks seventh.

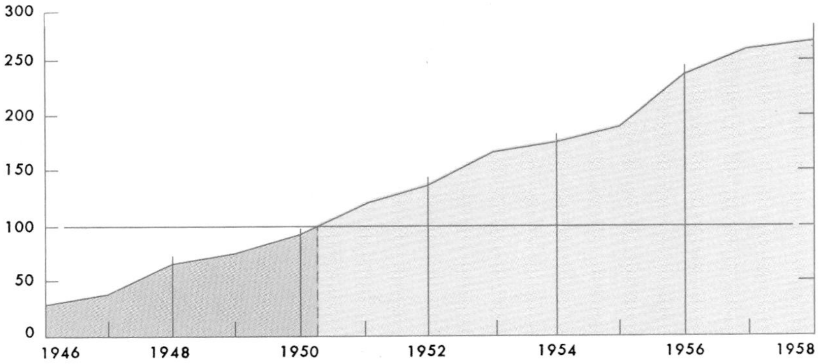

AN INDUSTRIAL COMEBACK

The enormous industrial growth of Japan since the end of World War II is shown on this graph. A base value of 100 is assigned to the pre-World War II peak of 1934-1936. In 1946, the first postwar year, Japan's industrial production index was only 33, or 67 per cent below the 1934-1936 peak. But Japan has rebuilt rapidly. With such industries as shipbuilding and iron and steel production leading the way, Japan's manufactured goods reached the prewar level in 1950 and increased more than one and a half times by 1958. Electronics products and optical equipment have also been important in this comeback.

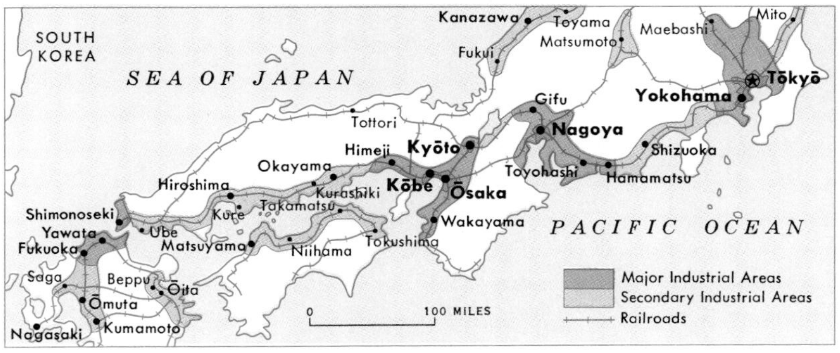

THE INDUSTRIAL ISLAND

The concentration of Japanese industry is shown on this map of Japan's major and secondary industrial areas on Honshū, the main island. Largest of the manufacturing centers, the Tōkyō-Yokohama area benefits from its location on a spreading, populous plain served by Yokohama's excellent harbor facilities. The Ōsaka-Kōbe area, second in importance, must import coal because it lacks hydroelectric power. Nagoya, though situated on a large plain served by rail lines, has grown slowly because its harbor does not equal Yokohama's. The Fukuoka-Yawata area owes its importance largely to nearby coal.

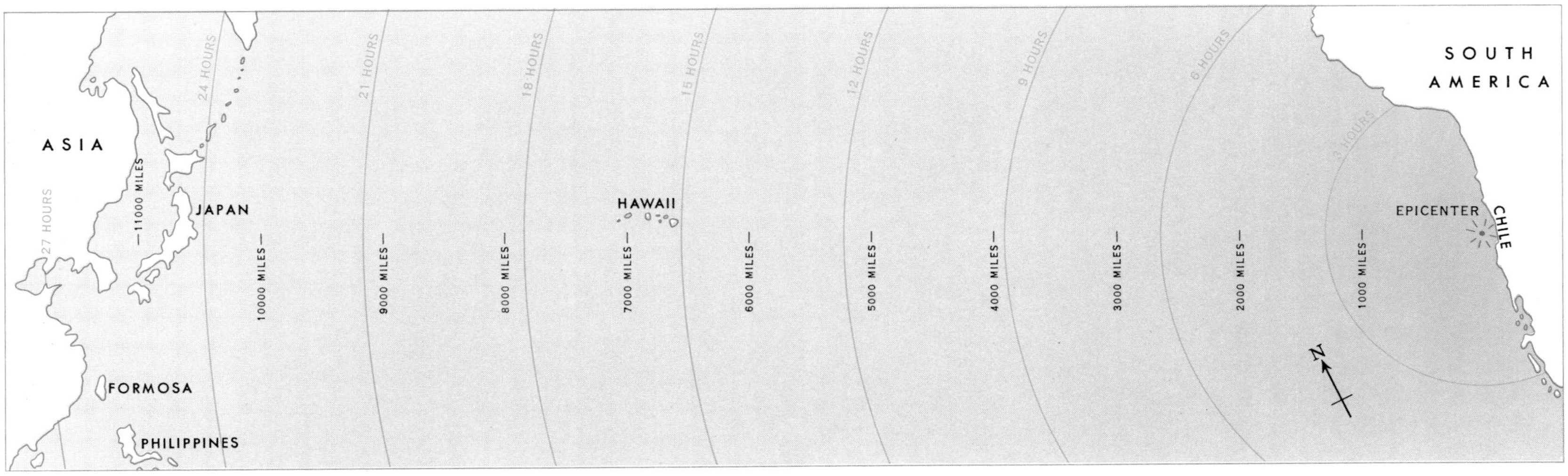

EARTHQUAKE IN CHILE, HAVOC IN JAPAN

The path of a Pacific Ocean *tsunami* (erroneously called a "tidal wave" in common parlance) is shown on the map above. One particular wave was started by an earthquake off the coast of Chile in 1960 *(far right)*. It moved with jet speed—300 to 500 miles per hour—hitting the Hawaiian Islands *(center)*, 7,000 miles away, in 15 hours and striking the Japanese coast *(far left)*, almost 11,000 miles away, in about 24 hours. The wave killed 150 and crushed houses, leaving 150,000 homeless. *Tsunamis,* which have nothing to do with tides, are thought to be caused by earthquakes or volcanic eruptions that result in displacements of the ocean bottom. The first visual warning of an approaching *tsunami* may come when coastal waters suddenly ebb; this is followed by their return in a smashing wave or series of waves. The depth of the ocean bottoms determines the height of the seismic wave; in shallower depths, the *tsunami* is likely to have great height when it hits the land. An international warning system pinpoints earthquakes and measures unusual sea activity in the Pacific Ocean with a chain of seismograph and tide stations. It also alerts endangered areas.

FOOD FOR THE PHILIPPINES ON GIANT STEPS

THE FERTILE SLOPES of the mountains of Luzon, which were terraced for rice paddies by Malays between 3,000 and 4,000 years ago, are weeded by Filipino women. Instead of sowing the seeds directly in the field, the Filipinos start seedlings in flats or boxes, sometimes indoors, and then transplant them to the paddies. This tedious hand labor produces high yields: more than a ton of rice per acre. The soils are loam and heavy clay, both of which retain water. These elaborate terraces in Luzon cover over 150 square miles.

THE PHILIPPINES: The first European in the Philippine Sea was Ferdinand Magellan, circumnavigator of the world. Magellan planted the Spanish king's cross on the island of Limasawa and then died on the scimitars of fierce Mactan tribesmen. The islands, named for King Philip II, remained under Spanish rule for more than 300 years. As a result the Philippines became the first—and only—predominantly Christian nation in the Orient.

In the Philippine archipelago are some 7,000 islands, most of them volcanic in origin, which are actually the peaks of partly submerged mountains. High mountains, some with active volcanoes, and placid lakes dramatize the landscape of the larger islands. One of the finest harbors in the Far East is Manila Bay.

The Filipinos are a racial conglomeration, mainly Malayan, speaking no fewer than 87 dialects and languages. The country has one of the highest birth rates in the world, but there are many large, sparsely settled islands which offer generous room for expansion.

AREA:	115,600 sq. mi.
POPULATION:	23,721,000. Largest city: Manila. Capital: Quezon City.
CLIMATE:	Hot summers, warm winters; heavy summer rainfall.
ALTITUDES:	Mt. Apo, 9,690 ft. (highest); Manila, 30 ft.

After the havoc of World War II, the Philippines made a swift economic recovery. In the last decade agricultural production of the country has doubled, manufacturing and mining have nearly tripled. Employment has gone up by 30 per cent, the gross national product by 75 per cent.

INDONESIA: The original spice islands, objective of the early European explorers, resemble the scattered pieces of a jigsaw puzzle, flung capriciously over 3,000 miles of tropic seas. The islands occupy a land area one quarter as large as that of the U.S. They are as rich as the legends about them that wafted back to Europe in the Middle Ages. Fertile soils and monsoon rains enable the Indonesians to produce quantities of such commercial plantation crops as coffee, tea, rubber, sugar and tobacco. Minerals are scarce, but those which exist are high in export value. There are petroleum deposits in Sumatra, Borneo and Java; tin and bauxite are present on several of the smaller islands.

Indonesia has a number of active volcanoes which make life hazardous. The eruption of Krakatoa in 1883 blew the tiny, uninhabited island to bits, launched waves

THE PHILIPPINES AND INDONESIA

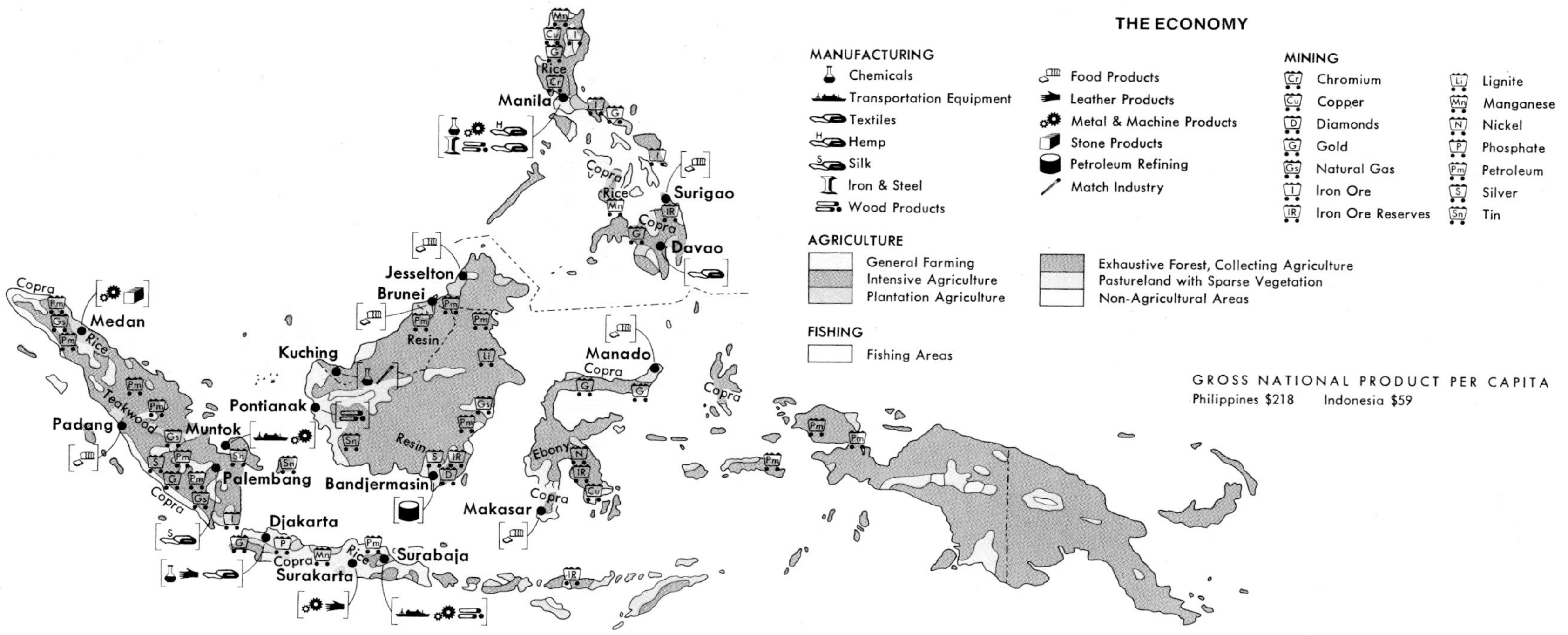

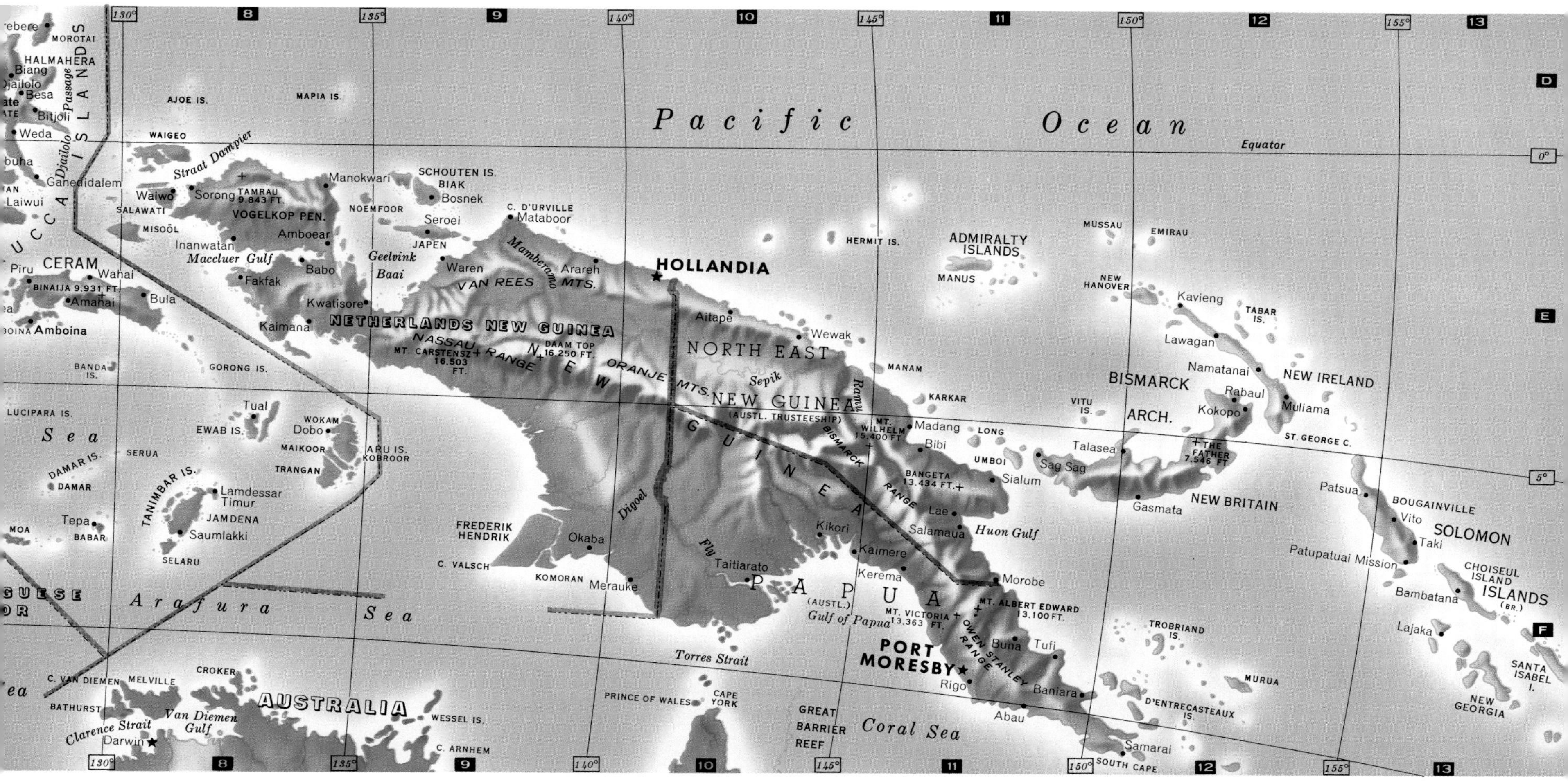

that killed 36,000 in neighboring Java and Sumatra, and threw a pall of dust around the world.

AREA: 575,893 sq. mi.
POPULATION: 87,802,000.
Largest city and capital: Djakarta.
CLIMATE: Hot summers and winters; heavy annual rainfall (summer maximum in the eastern regions).
ALTITUDES: Kerintji, 12,484 ft. (highest point); Rindjani, 12,225 ft.

The Indonesians are a small, lithe people of Malay stock. Insularity has given them the opportunity to develop a vivid and distinctive culture. The graceful, stylized dances of Bali, the temples and music of Java, and the art and the fiery cuisine of the outer islands are world famous.

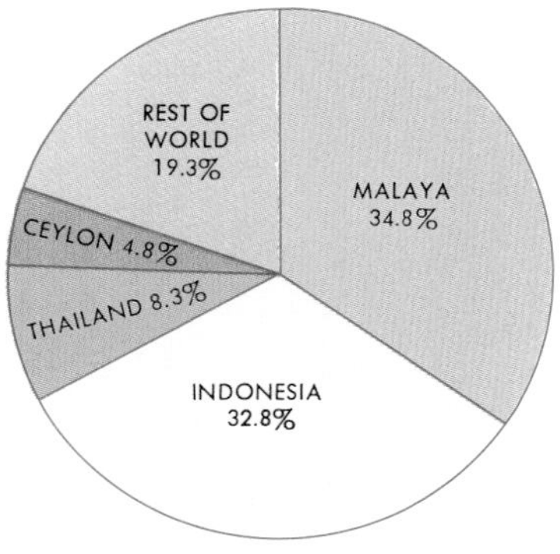

NATURAL RUBBER PRODUCTION

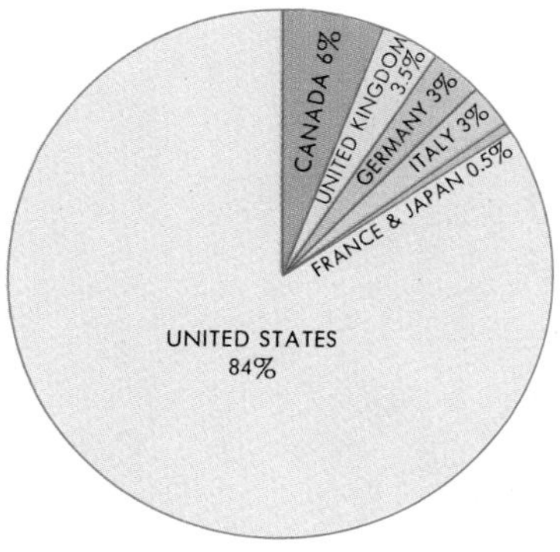

SYNTHETIC RUBBER PRODUCTION

COMPETITION IN RUBBER

Wild rubber was for many years a jealously guarded monopoly of Brazil. British entrepreneurs planted seedlings in Southeast Asia, and their success can be measured in the pie charts at the left. Together Malaya and Indonesia now produce almost 70 per cent of the world's natural rubber *(far left)*.

World War II cut the U.S. off from Southeast Asian supplies of natural rubber, so a crash program of synthetic rubber production was started. In recent years, the production of artificial rubber has expanded rapidly *(near left)*.

WORSHIP IN SOUTHEAST ASIA

BUDDHIST TEMPLES built in the last century surround the Kuthodaw Pagoda shrine *(below)* near Mandalay Hill in Burma. The covered staircase is of teak, one of Burma's principal products.

PROTECTIVE STATUES line a bridge across the drained bed of a Cambodian irrigation canal *(above)* which is being regraded. Irrigation is vital in Cambodia because the rains are seasonal.

A RELIGIOUS CAVE, carved from limestone deposits by underground streams near the city of Phet Buri in Thailand *(below)*, has an assemblage of statues of the Buddha and his acolytes.

BURMA, THAILAND, MALAYA, CAMBODIA, LAOS AND VIETNAM
Barren Areas Above Timber
Evergreen Trees
Mixed Evergreen and Deciduous Trees
Shrub
Alpine Vegetation
National Capitals
Cities
Railroads
1 inch = 148 Statute Miles
Miles 0 25 50 100 150
Lambert Conformal Conic Projection
CM TERRAIN
BURMA, THAILAND, MALAYA, CAMBODIA, LAOS AND VIETNAM
COPYRIGHT BY
RAND MC NALLY & COMPANY
MADE IN U.S.A.
Longitude East of Greenwich
INDIA
BHUTAN
HIMALAYA MOUNTAINS
PAKISTAN
BURMA
CHINA
PLATEAU OF YÜNAN
LAOS
NORTH VIETNAM
SOUTH VIETNAM
THAILAND
(SIAM)
CAMBODIA
MALAY PENINSULA
MALAYA
SUMATRA
INDONESIA
RANGOON
BANGKOK (Krung Thep)
VIENTIANE
HANOI
PHNOM PENH
SAIGON
KUALA LUMPUR
SINGAPORE
Mandalay
Moulmein
Chiang Mai
Kunming
Haiphong
Hue
Tourane
Penang
Medan
Kweiyang
Nanning
Kweilin
Luichow
Wuchow
Bay of Bengal
Andaman Sea
Gulf of Martaban
Gulf of Siam
Gulf of Tonkin
South China Sea
Indian Ocean
Strait of Malacca
Mouths of the Ganges
Mouths of the Irrawaddy
Mouths of the Mekong
Ten Degree Channel
Great Channel
Sombrero Channel
Tropic of Cancer
HAINAN (CHINA)
ANDAMAN ISLANDS (INDIA)
NICOBAR ISLANDS (INDIA)
ISTHMUS OF KRA
MERGUI ARCHIPELAGO
ANAMBAS ISLANDS
NATUNA ISLANDS
SARAWAK (BR.)
BORNEO
Kuching
Mekong
Salween
Irrawaddy
Chindwin
Sittang
Red
Black
Menam
Chao Phraya
Tonle Sap
Hainan Strait
Singapore Str.

BURMA, THAILAND, MALAYA, CAMBODIA, LAOS AND VIETNAM

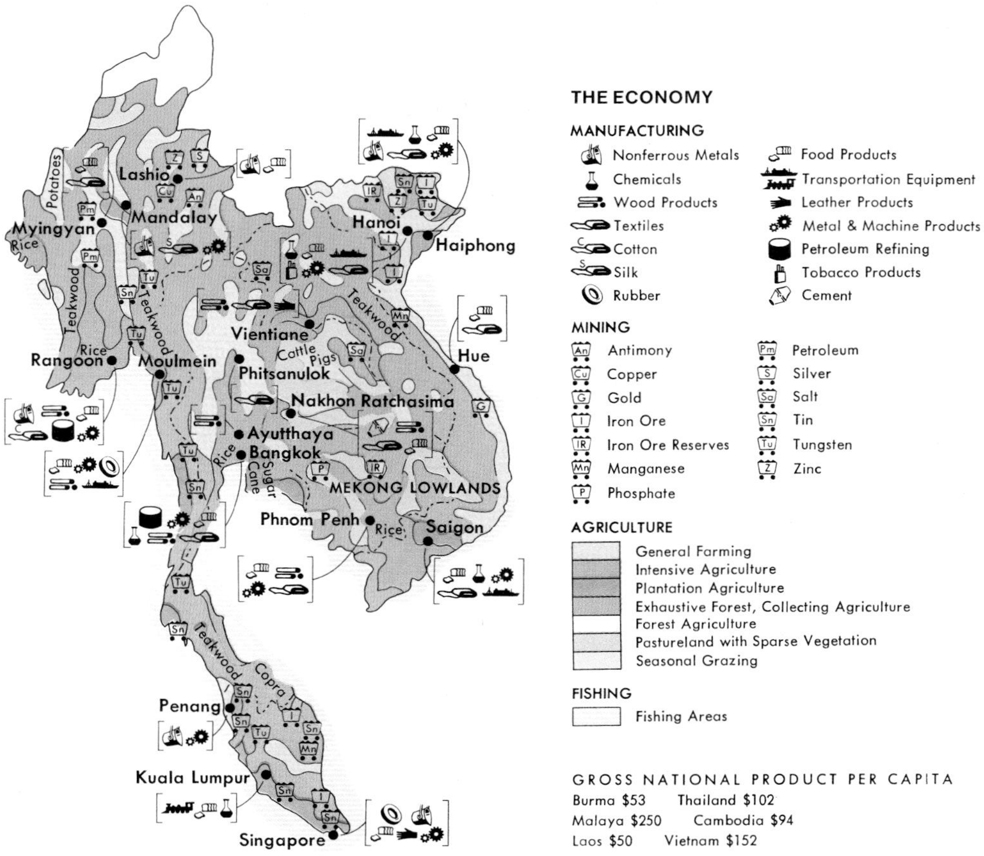

SOUTHEAST ASIA'S RICE BOWLS

Southeast Asia's most productive ricelands, pictured in orange on the map above, are located in the great river basins indicated by gray lines: the Irrawaddy in Burma *(left)*; the Menam in Thailand; the Mekong, which winds through Laos, Cambodia and South Vietnam; and the Red River in North Vietnam. Not quite as productive, but good, are the coastal regions of South Vietnam and the Malay Peninsula. Rice flourishes in those parts of the river basins which are low and level. The crosshatching of smaller streams and canals permits easy flooding and draining of the paddies. Southeast Asia harvests 8 per cent of the world's rice and exports over 60 per cent to rice-deficient areas.

BURMA: Once one of the most romantic outposts of the old British Empire, Burma has been independent since 1948. It is a devoutly Buddhist land with thousands of many-storied temples called pagodas. The country is fenced off by mountains; the highest rise to over 19,000 feet.

AREA: 261,689 sq. mi.
POPULATION: 20,303,000. Largest city and capital: Rangoon.
CLIMATE: Little seasonal change in temperature, cooler in mountains; heavy summer rainfall, dry winters.
ALTITUDES: Hkakabo Razi, 19,296 ft. (highest).

THAILAND: Eighty per cent of Thailand's arable land is planted in rice, and most farmers own their own land. (The average farm comprises 10 acres.) The northern uplands yield one third of the world's supply of teakwood, and the lacework of canals in the central plain supplies the country not only with transportation but with fish to complete a well-balanced diet of rice, fruit and vegetables, poultry and pork.

AREA: 198,404 sq. mi.
POPULATION: 22,003,000. Largest city and capital: Bangkok.
CLIMATE: Same as above.
ALTITUDES: Doi Angka, 8,452 ft. (highest); Bangkok, 10 ft.

MALAYA: A prosperous federation of nine sultanates and two former British settlements (Penang and Malacca), Malaya has an export economy based firmly on rubber and tin. Four fifths of the peninsular country is covered with jungle, swampland and mountain; 65 per cent of the remainder is given over to the plantations that make Malaya the world's leading producer of rubber.

AREA: 50,677 sq. mi.
POPULATION: 6,809,000. Largest city: Penang. Capital: Kuala Lumpur.
CLIMATE: Hot summers and winters; heavy summer rainfall, moderate winter rainfall.
ALTITUDES: Tahan, 7,186 ft. (highest).

CAMBODIA: Six months of the year, Cambodia is a land of waterlogged plains; this is the time when the Mekong River overflows its banks and the Great Lake, or Tonle Sap, grows from 100 to 770 square miles in area. Cambodia has some industry: fish, rice and rubber processing, palm sugar refining, silk and cotton weaving and pottery.

AREA: 67,550 sq. mi.
POPULATION: 5,056,000. Largest city and capital: Phnom Penh.
CLIMATE: Hot summers and winters; heavy summer rainfall, moderately dry winters.
ALTITUDES: Peak of Elephant Range, 5,750 ft. (highest).

LAOS: The landlocked kingdom of Laos is wholly dependent on the Mekong River and its many tributaries, which have gouged fertile valleys and alluvial plains from the mountains. On the small amount of cultivated land, barely enough rice is grown to feed the people of Laos. The country has less than 1,800 miles of all-weather roads and there is not a mile of railroad within its cramped borders.

AREA: 91,482 sq. mi.
POPULATION: 1,754,000. Largest city and capital: Vientiane.
CLIMATE: Hot, with little seasonal change in temperature; cooler in mountains; heavy summer rainfall, dry winters.
ALTITUDES: Phu Bia, 9,242 ft. (highest).

NORTH VIETNAM: The densely populated delta of the Red River in the north (a region formerly known as Tonkin) has been called a "basket of rice." North Vietnam has substantial deposits of coal and iron as well as other minerals that give the promise of future industrial development. So far, however, the minerals remain unexploited and the state remains essentially agricultural.

AREA: 61,516 sq. mi.
POPULATION: 14,788,000. Largest city and capital: Hanoi.
CLIMATE: Same as above.
ALTITUDES: Fan Si Pan, 10,308 ft. (highest); Hanoi, 30 ft.

SOUTH VIETNAM: In sharp contrast to the north, South Vietnam lacks the potential for expansion of manufacture. Struggling with an unfavorable trade balance and overpopulation in the coastal and delta rice areas, it has now opened for development parts of the Moi Plateau, about 25,000 square miles in its south-central region, formerly a great estate. Here each settler is given a maximum of 12 acres, and is also taught to make rattan furniture, baskets and matting.

AREA: 65,709 sq. mi.
POPULATION: 12,988,000. Largest city and capital: Saigon.
CLIMATE: Same as above.
ALTITUDES: Quang Ngai, 10,761 ft. (highest); Saigon, 26 ft.

SINGAPORE: A tropical island just a stone's throw from the tip of Malaya, Singapore is connected with the mainland by a causeway. This modern, skyscrapered city, strategically situated at the confluence of the sea lanes between East and West, thrives on its bustling commerce.

CEYLON TEA PICKERS with deep baskets trudge down a hillside to work at the dark green bushes. They pick only the "flush," the tender young shoots of the plant, 3,000 of which make one pound of cured tea. Cultivated on estates of 100 acres or more, tea is agricultural Ceylon's most important export. The tea that comes from highland slopes like this one is generally the best.

WORKERS OF SOUTH ASIA

INDIAN FISHERMEN work with *jals,* nets that are made of jute and hemp, in an artificial lake created by the construction of Maithon Dam in the northeastern state of Bihar. Irrigation projects are essential in this area of unevenly distributed rainfall. The reservoirs are stocked with fish so that they do double duty by providing a cheap food not often available to inland dwellers.

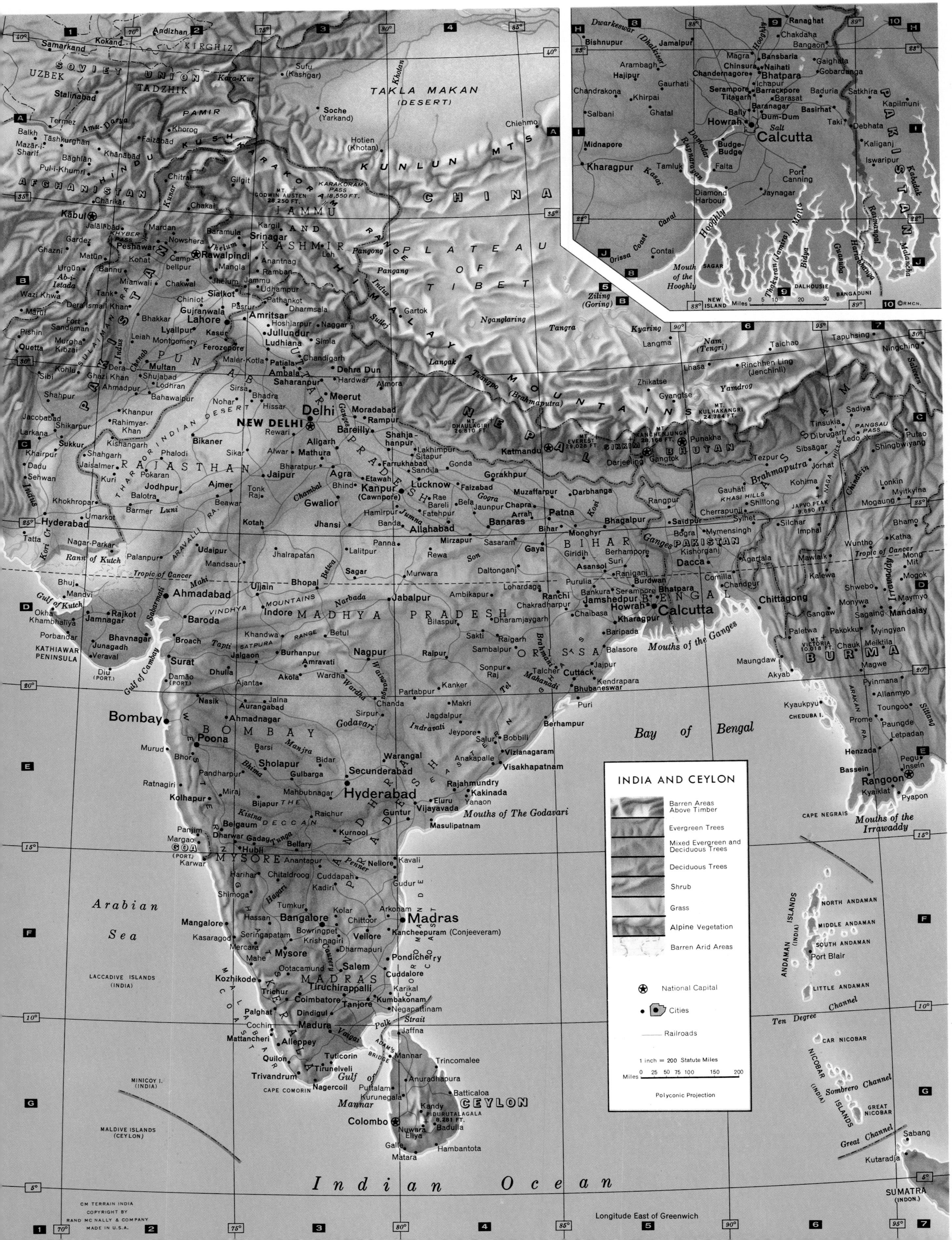
INDIA AND CEYLON
Barren Areas Above Timber
Evergreen Trees
Mixed Evergreen and Deciduous Trees
Deciduous Trees
Shrub
Grass
Alpine Vegetation
Barren Arid Areas
National Capital
Cities
Railroads
1 inch = 200 Statute Miles
Miles 0 25 50 75 100 150 200
Polyconic Projection
Longitude East of Greenwich
CM TERRAIN INDIA
COPYRIGHT BY
RAND McNALLY & COMPANY
MADE IN U.S.A.
©RMCN.
Samarkand
Kokand
Andizhan
KIRGHIZ
SOVIET UNION
UZBEK
TADZHIK
Stalinabad
PAMIR
Termez
Amu-Darya
Balkh
Mazar-i-Sharif
Khorog
Faizābād
HINDU KUSH
AFGHANISTAN
Chitral
Gilgit
Chārikār
Kabul
Jalalabad
KHYBER PASS
Peshawar
Mardan
Nowshera
Rawalpindi
Kohat
Bannu
Gardez
Ghazni
Matūn
KARAKORAM PASS 18,550 FT.
MT. GODWIN AUSTEN 28,250 FT.
JAMMU AND KASHMIR
Srinagar
Baramula
Jhelum
Leh
Kargil
Anantnag
Jammu
Sialkot
Chakwal
Mianwali
Wazi Khwa
Dera Ismail Khan
Fort Sandeman
Quetta
Pishin
Murgha Kibzai
Kohlu
Sibi
Dera Ghazi Khan
Multan
Shujabad
Lodhran
Bahawalpur
Ahmadpur
Shahpur
Jacobabad
Shikarpur
Larkana
Sukkur
Khairpur
Dadu
Sehwan
Hyderabad
Tatta
Umarkot
Khokhropar
Nagar-Parkar
Rann of Kutch
Bhuj
Mandvi
Gulf of Kutch
Okha
Jamnagar
Rajkot
Porbandar
KATHIAWAR PENINSULA
Junagadh
Bhavnagar
Veraval
Diu (PORT.)
Gulf of Cambay
Daman (PORT.)
Surat
Broach
Baroda
Ahmadabad
Palanpur
Tropic of Cancer
Lahore
Gujranwala
Amritsar
Jullundur
Ludhiana
Ferozepore
Kasur
Montgomery
Lyallpur
Chiniot
Leiah
Bhakkar
PUNJAB
Patiala
Ambala
Simla
Saharanpur
Hardwar
Dehra Dun
Chandigarh
Sirsa
Hissar
Bhadra
Bikaner
NEW DELHI
Delhi
Meerut
Moradabad
Rampur
Bareilly
Shahjahanpur
Aligarh
Mathura
Agra
Bharatpur
Jaipur
Ajmer
Beawar
Jodhpur
Pokaran
Jaisalmer
Shahgarh
Barmer
Balotra
Luni
RAJASTHAN
THAR OR INDIAN DESERT
ARAVALLI RA.
Udaipur
Kotah
Tonk
Gwalior
Jhansi
Chambal
Etawah
Kanpur (Cawnpore)
Lucknow
Faizabad
Gorakhpur
Allahabad
Banaras
Mirzapur
Rewa
Banda
Panna
Lalitpur
Jhalrapatan
Mandsaur
Ujjain
Bhopal
Indore
Sagar
Jabalpur
MADHYA PRADESH
VINDHYA MOUNTAINS
Narbada
SATPURA RANGE
Tapti
Khandwa
Burhanpur
Jalgaon
Dhulia
Ajanta
Akola
Amravati
Nagpur
Wardha
Raipur
Bilaspur
Sambalpur
Raigarh
Nasik
Jalna
Aurangabad
Ahmadnagar
Bombay
BOMBAY
Poona
Murud
Bhor
Barsi
Sholapur
Bidar
Gulbarga
Ratnagiri
Kolhapur
Miraj
Bijapur
Belgaum
Panjim
Margao
GOA (PORT.)
Karwar
Dharwar
Gadag
Hubli
Bellary
Kurnool
Raichur
THE DECCAN
Kistna
Mahbubnagar
Hyderabad
Secunderabad
Warangal
Godavari
Chanda
Jagdalpur
Indravati
Jeypore
Salur
Bobbili
Vizianagaram
Visakhapatnam
Anakapalle
Rajahmundry
Kakinada
Yanaon
Eluru
Vijayavada
Guntur
Masulipatnam
Mouths of The Godavari
ANDHRA PRADESH
Nellore
Kavali
Penner
Anantapur
MYSORE
Harihar
Chitaldroog
Cuddapah
Kadiri
Shimoga
Tumkur
Kolar
Hassan
Bangalore
Chittoor
Arkonam
Madras
Kancheepuram (Conjeeveram)
Vellore
Mangalore
Kasaragod
Seringapatam
Mercara
Mysore
Mahe
Krishnagiri
Dharmapuri
Salem
Pondicherry
Cuddalore
Kozhikode
Ootacamund
Tiruchirappalli
MADRAS
Karikal
Trichur
Coimbatore
Tanjore
Kumbakonam
Negapattinam
Palghat
Dindigul
Cochin
Madura
Mattancheri
Alleppey
KERALA
Quilon
Trivandrum
Tuticorin
Tirunelveli
Nagercoil
CAPE COMORIN
Palk Strait
Jaffna
ADAM'S BRIDGE
Mannar
Gulf of Mannar
Trincomalee
Anuradhapura
Puttalam
Kurunegala
Batticaloa
Kandy
CEYLON
Colombo
PIDURUTALAGALA 8,281 FT.
Nuwara Eliya
Badulla
Galle
Matara
Hambantota
Arabian Sea
LACCADIVE ISLANDS (INDIA)
MINICOY I. (INDIA)
MALDIVE ISLANDS (CEYLON)
Indian Ocean
Bay of Bengal
TAKLA MAKAN (DESERT)
Sufu (Kashgar)
Soche (Yarkand)
Hotien (Khotan)
Chiehmo
KUNLUN MTS
CHINA
PLATEAU OF TIBET
Pangong
Gartok
Nganglaring
Tangra
Kyaring
Nam (Tengri)
Lhasa
Rinchhen Ling (Jenchinli)
Zhikatse
Gyangtse
Yamdrog
Langma
Taichao
Tapuhsing
Ningching
Salween
Ziling (Goring)
HIMALAYA MOUNTAINS
Tsangpo (Brahmaputra)
Langak
Almora
NEPAL
MT. DHAULAGIRI 26,810 FT.
MT. EVEREST 29,028 FT.
MT. KANCHENJUNGA 28,168 FT.
MT. KULHAKANGRI 24,784 FT.
Katmandu
SIKKIM
Gangtok
Darjeeling
BHUTAN
Punakha
ASSAM
Sadiya
Tinsukia
Dibrugarh
Ledo
PANGSAU PASS
Putao
Shingbwiyang
Sibsāgar
Tezpur
Jorhat
Brahmaputra
NAGA HILLS
Kohima
Gauhāti
KHASI HILLS
Shillong
JAPVO PEAK 9,890 FT.
Cherrapunji
Sylhet
Silchar
Imphal
Lonkin
Myitkyina
Mogaung
Bhamo
Katha
Chindwin
Muzaffarpur
Darbhanga
Chapra
Arrah
Patna
Kosi
Bhagalpur
Monghyr
Bihar
BIHAR
Gaya
Sasaram
Son
Daltonganj
Giridih
Berhampore
Suri
Asansol
Raniganj
Burdwan
Purulia
Lohardaga
Ranchi
Bankura
Serampore
Bhatpara
Jamshedpur
Howrah
Calcutta
BENGAL
Chaibasa
Kharagpur
Baripada
Balasore
Chakradharpur
Dharamjaygarh
Mouths of the Ganges
Sakti
ORISSA
Brahmani
Mahanadi
Talcher
Cuttack
Jajpur
Kendrapara
Bhubaneswar
Puri
Berhampur
Sonpur Raj
Kanker
Partabpur
Makri
Rangpur
Saidpur
Bogra
Mymensingh
Kishorganj
PAKISTAN
Dacca
Agartala
Comilla
Chandpur
Chittagong
Akyab
Maungdaw
Mawlaik
Kalewa
Wuntho
Shwebo
Monywa
Sagaing
Mandalay
Maymyo
Mogok
Mong Mit
Irrawaddy
Gangaw
Paletwa
Pakokku
Myingyan
Meiktila
Chauk
MT. VICTORIA 10,018 FT.
BURMA
Magwe
Pyinmana
Allanmyo
Toungoo
Sittang
Kyaukpyu
CHEDUBA I.
ARAKAN RA.
Prome
Paungde
Letpadan
Henzada
Bassein
Pegu
Insein
Rangoon
Kyaiklat
Pyapon
CAPE NEGRAIS
Mouths of the Irrawaddy
ANDAMAN ISLANDS (INDIA)
NORTH ANDAMAN
MIDDLE ANDAMAN
SOUTH ANDAMAN
Port Blair
LITTLE ANDAMAN
Ten Degree Channel
CAR NICOBAR
NICOBAR ISLANDS (INDIA)
Sombrero Channel
GREAT NICOBAR
Great Channel
Sabang
Kutaradja
SUMATRA (INDON.)
Dwarkeswar (Dhalkisor)
Bishnupur
Jamalpur
Ranaghat
Chakdaha
Bangaon
Magra
Bansbaria
Gaighata
Gobardanga
Arambagh
Chinsura
Naihati
Hajipur
Chandernagore
Bhatpara
Ichapur
Chandrakona
Gaurhati
Serampore
Barrackpore
Baduria
Satkhira
Khirpai
Titagarh
Barasat
Kapilmuni
Salbani
Ghatal
Baranagar
Basirhat
Bally
Dum-Dum
Taki
Howrah
Salt Lake
Debhata
Midnapore
Damodar
Rupnarayan
Budge-Budge
Kaliganj
Iswaripur
Kharagpur
Kasai
Tamluk
Falta
Port Canning
Kabadak
Diamond Harbour
Jaynagar
Canal
Raimangal
Hooghly
Matla
Orissa Coast
Contai
Thakuran (Jamira)
Bidya
Gosaba
Harinbhanga
Malancha
SAGAR
Mouth of the Hooghly
DALHOUSIE
BANGADUNI
NEW ISLAND

INDIA AND CEYLON

INDIA: The riches of India were the indirect cause of the discovery that the world is round. Long before Columbus' search for a westward passage to India, however, the vast subcontinent attracted adventurers and would-be conquerors, from Alexander the Great to Marco Polo. About one third the size of the U.S., India ranks seventh in area among the nations of the world, but with its 438 million people (and a birth rate of over seven million more every year) it is second only to China in population. In the state of West Bengal alone, an area that is the size of Maine, live 35 million people. Throughout India, Hindus, Moslems, Sikhs, Jains, Buddhists, Christians, Jews, Zoroastrians – men of many different colors, sects, languages, backgrounds and temperaments – live side by side. People are, so to speak, India's principal commodity, as they are its greatest problem, and its promise for the future.

AREA: 1,269,506 sq. mi.
POPULATION: 438,000,000. Largest city: Bombay.
Capital: New Delhi.
CLIMATE: Hot wet summers, warm dry winters in the lowlands;
highland climates vary with altitude
from warm to cool, very wet to dry.
ALTITUDES: Mt. Godwin Austen in Jammu and Kashmir,
28,250 ft. (highest); New Delhi, 760 ft.

The cloud-crowned Himalayas, the highest mountains in the world, provided a natural deterrent to conquerors, enabling India to establish an insulated religion and a unique culture that have withstood many invaders, from the Aryans to the British. The land is divided into three physical zones: the Himalayas, with three ranges surrounding beautiful fertile valleys and plateaus (the Vale of Kashmir is the most famous); the rich, densely populated alluvial plain, which stretches 1,500 miles from West Pakistan to the Bay of Bengal; and the Deccan Peninsula, divided from the plain by a series of hills and mountains (1,500 to 4,000 ft.), the habitat of tigers and elephants and the home of millions of cotton and tobacco workers. India grows the world's largest crop of tea, mainly in the Assam hills. Flowing through the heart of the nation like a muddy aorta is the Ganges River, which is holy to Hindus.

India has long been represented to the world outside as a land of vivid color, serene architecture, gentle philosophy and oriental splendor. But along with its great culture and folkways, there is the India of mud huts, poverty and 76 per cent illiteracy, the land of the bullock and the spinning wheel *(page 369)*. An agricultural nation, India suffers from annual floods and frequent famines and, in most parts of the country, wretched weather for six months of the year – the temperature can rise to 118° in Delhi in the summer. Industrialization got off to a good start under the British, who ruled India for two centuries. Since it became independent in 1947, India has pumped $21 billion of fresh investment into the national economy, created six million new jobs (still not enough to keep pace with the sprinting population) and raised the national income by 42 per cent, the per capita income by 20 per cent. Steel capacity has quadrupled and coal production nearly doubled. At the same time, four million acres of wasteland have been brought under the plow, and irrigated land has increased from 51.5 million acres to 70 million acres.

CEYLON: The island of Ceylon in the Indian Ocean has long been a popular port of call. Arabian traders made Ceylon an important commercial center before Europeans found the passage to India around the tip of Africa.

AREA: 25,332 sq. mi.
POPULATION: 9,643,000. Largest city and capital: Colombo.
CLIMATE: Hot summers, warm winters; heavy rainfall in southwest,
moderate rainfall elsewhere.
ALTITUDES: Pidurutalagala, near Kandy, 8,281 ft. (highest); Colombo, 15 ft.

The world's finest tea is grown on the highlands in the southwest of Ceylon. Rubber and coconut products are the other principal agricultural exports. Singhalese rubies have long been famous, and the island is the world's leading producer of high-grade graphite.

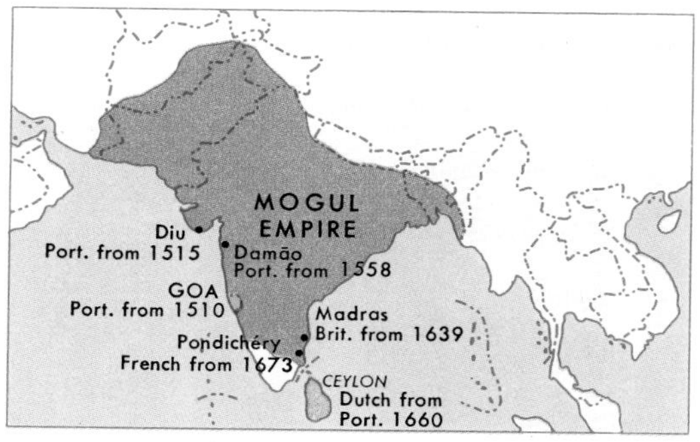

INDIA UNDER THE MOGULS: 1700

The Moguls ruled nearly all of India at the height of their power, but the Hindus retained the southernmost tip, as shown on the map above. The dates refer to the first European footholds in India.

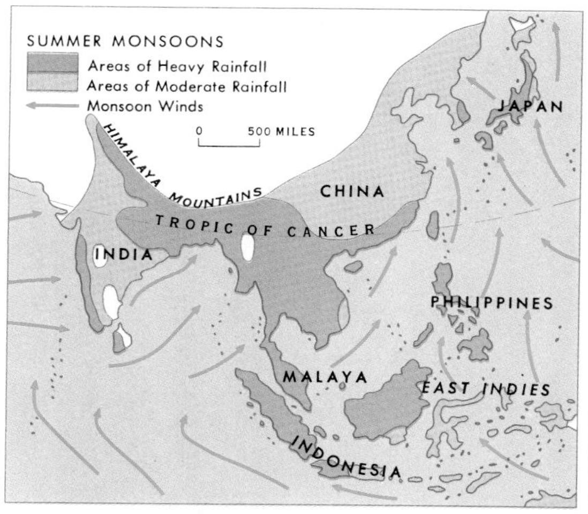

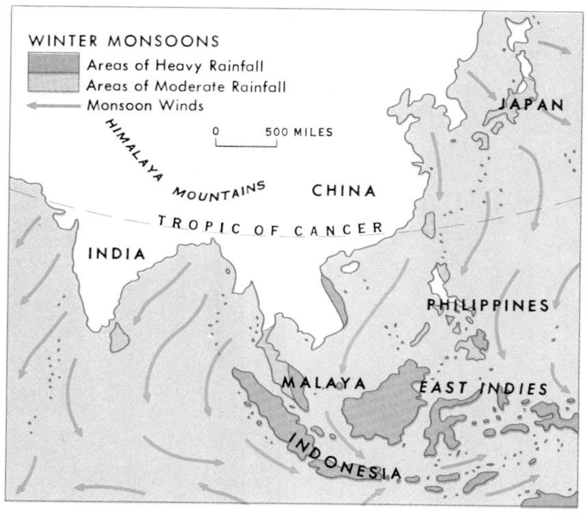

THE WET AND THE DRY MONSOONS

These maps show how winds, by switching directions with the seasons, make much of Southeast Asia rainy in the summer *(left)*, dry in the winter *(right)*. The winds are called monsoons, after an Arabic word meaning "season," because of their annual shift in direction. From late April to mid-October, warm winds blow in from the Indian Ocean, where they pick up heavy loads of moisture. When they reverse and come from Asia's arid interior, they are desiccating and pick up moisture only after they reach the ocean.

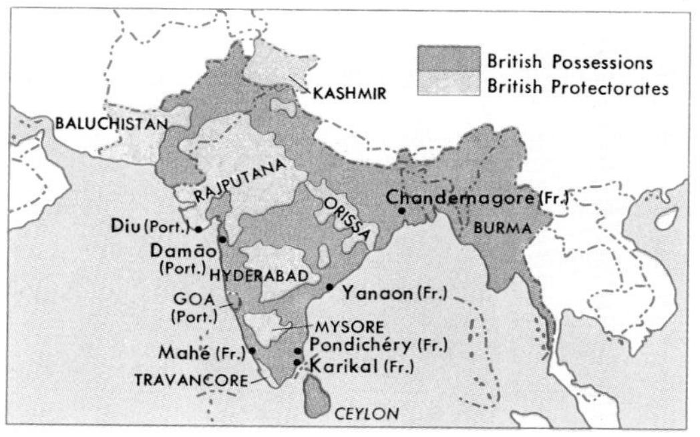

THE BRITISH IN INDIA: 1900

This map shows British possessions *(red)* and protectorates *(pink)* in India and Burma at the turn of the century, when the empire was at its height. Other European nations had only small enclaves.

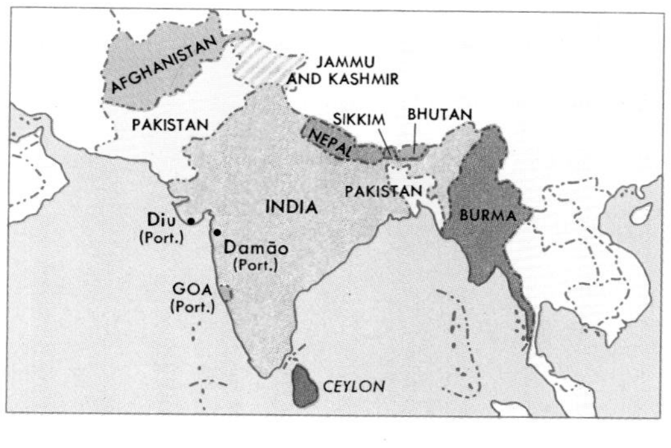

INDEPENDENT INDIA: 1947

The new India *(orange)* shown here emerged in 1947 from British rule together with a divided Pakistan. Ceylon and Burma became independent in 1948. The striped area is Kashmir, still in dispute.

THE ECONOMY

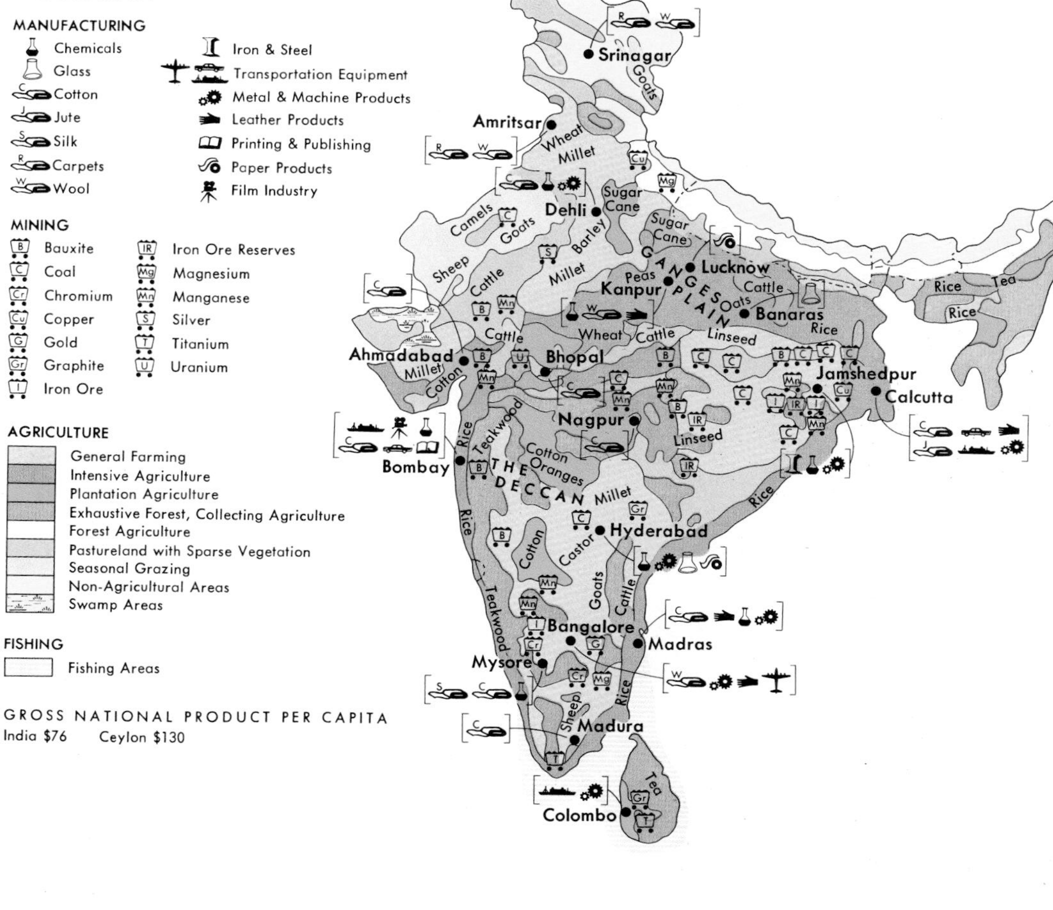

GROSS NATIONAL PRODUCT PER CAPITA
India $76 Ceylon $130

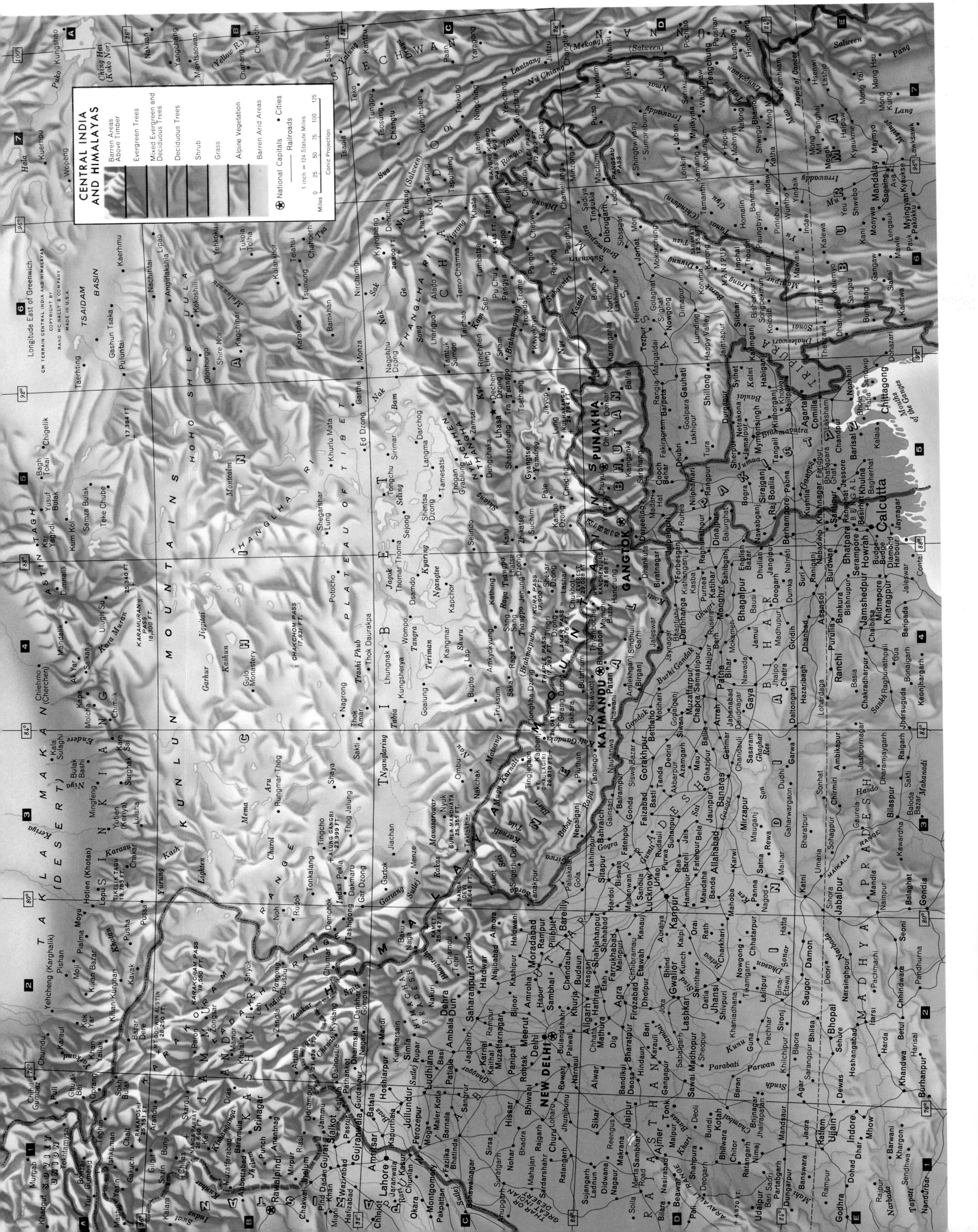
CENTRAL INDIA AND HIMALAYAS
Barren Areas Above Timber
Evergreen Trees
Mixed Evergreen and Deciduous Trees
Deciduous Trees
Shrub
Grass
Alpine Vegetation
Barren Arid Areas
National Capitals
Cities
Railroads
1 inch = 124 Statute Miles
Conic Projection
Longitude East of Greenwich
CM TERRAIN CENTRAL INDIA AND HIMALAYAS
COPYRIGHT BY RAND McNALLY & COMPANY
MADE IN U.S.A.

TIBET: Climbing to an average altitude of nearly 15,000 feet along four major mountain chains—the Himalayan, Ladakh, Karakoram and Kunlun—Tibet has the highest average altitude of any region in the world. Few crops thrive in the short growing season of its cold heights and arid valleys *(drawings, right)*. Iron ore has been found in the eastern mountains, and there are deposits of coal and perhaps of copper and uranium elsewhere in the country. Traces of gold have been discovered. But Tibet remains primitive, and the hardy long-haired yak, a species of cattle which can live on sparse vegetation, is the mainstay of the pastoral Tibetan economy.

AREA: 469,194 sq. mi.
POPULATION: 1,699,000. Largest city and capital: Lhasa.
CLIMATE: Cold winters, relatively warm summers; very low annual rainfall; violent winds in all seasons.
ALTITUDES: Mt. Everest (Tibet-Nepal border), 29,028 ft. (highest).

NEPAL: Northern Nepal contains some of the mightiest mountains in the world, including Everest, the mightiest of all. Most Nepalese earn meager livings as rice and grain farmers in the major river valleys.

AREA: 54,330 sq. mi.
POPULATION: 8,978,000. Largest city and capital: Katmandu.
CLIMATE: Warm summers, mild winters in the lowlands; cooler temperatures in the highlands. Most rainfall in the summer.
ALTITUDES: Mt. Everest (Nepal-Tibet border), 29,028 ft. (highest); Katmandu, 4,223 ft.

SIKKIM: Perched in the eastern Himalayas, primitive Sikkim survives on the maize and rice grown on narrow terraces dug into the lower slopes of the mountains. Since 1950, the tiny state has been a protectorate of India.

AREA: 2,745 sq. mi.
POPULATION: 152,000. Largest city and capital: Gangtok.
CLIMATE: Warm summers, mild winters in the lowlands; cooler temperatures in the highlands. Most rainfall in the summer.
ALTITUDES: Mt. Kanchenjunga, 28,168 ft. (highest); Gangtok, 5,000 ft.

BHUTAN: Lying between Sikkim, India and Tibet, lonely Bhutan is inhabited by a peaceful people with a talent for metal working. The higher valleys are planted to maize, barley and wheat; rice grows in winter in the lower valleys.

AREA: 19,300 sq. mi.
POPULATION: 670,000. Largest city and capital: Punakha.
CLIMATE: Warm summers, mild winters in the lowlands; cooler temperatures in the highlands. Most rainfall in the summer.
ALTITUDES: Chomo Lhari, 35 mi. northwest of Punakha, 23,997 ft. (highest); Punakha, 6,000 ft.

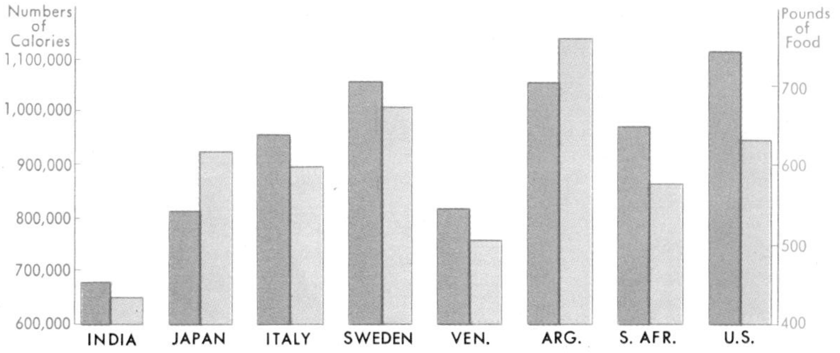

DIETS OF THE WORLD

A comparison of the world's diets on the graph above shows that the average Indian gets far less food *(blue columns)* and fewer calories *(red)* annually than the average citizen of other major countries. The Indian diet is limited not only by an inadequate food supply, but by religious restrictions on the eating of meat, a high-protein food. Caloric intake in the U.S. is among the highest in the world.

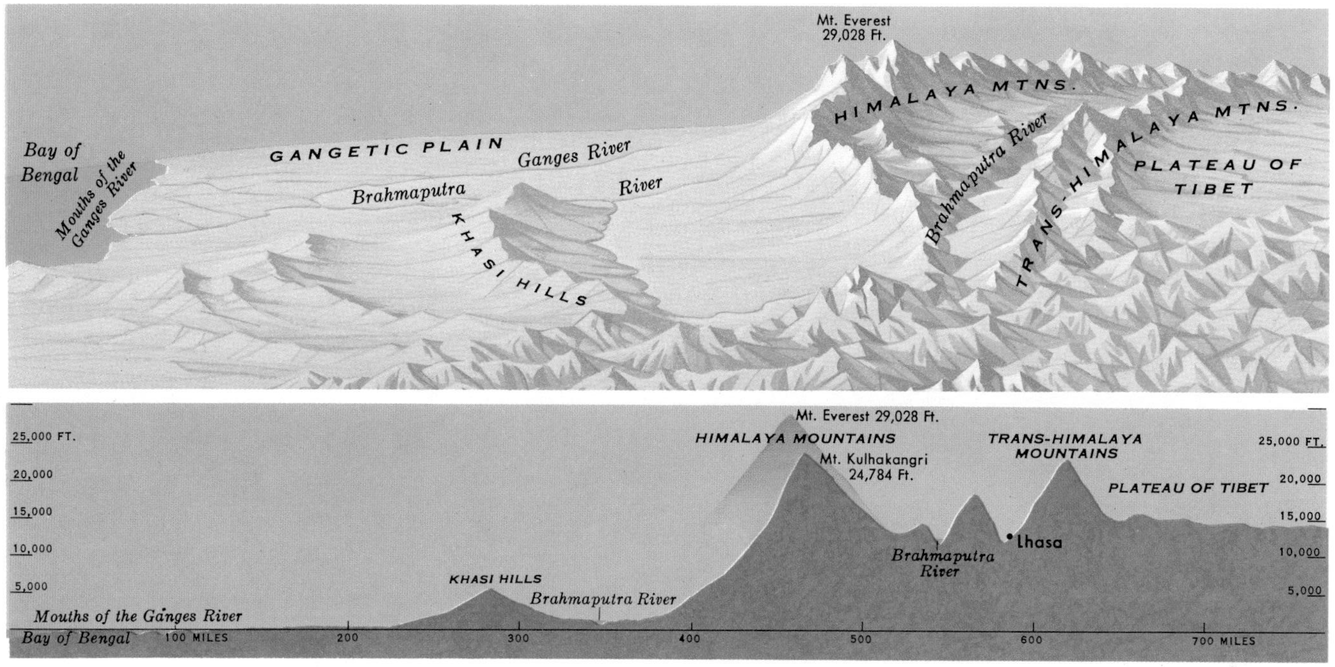

HOW THE HIGH HIMALAYAS DOMINATE LIFE ON THE PLAINS AND SLOPES

The rugged terrain of northeastern India, including the high Himalayas which separate the country from Tibet, is shown above in a drawing *(top)* and in profile *(bottom)*. The mountains help make the Indian plains of the Brahmaputra and Ganges Rivers among the wettest in the world when the snow melts and causes the rivers to flood.

The river plains are also inundated by the rains of the hot summer monsoons that blow in from the Bay of Bengal *(left)*. The Indian plains produce large crops of rice, jute and sugar cane. The mountains block off the rains from Tibet. With cool summers and little rainfall, Tibet can produce only such hardy crops as barley and wheat.

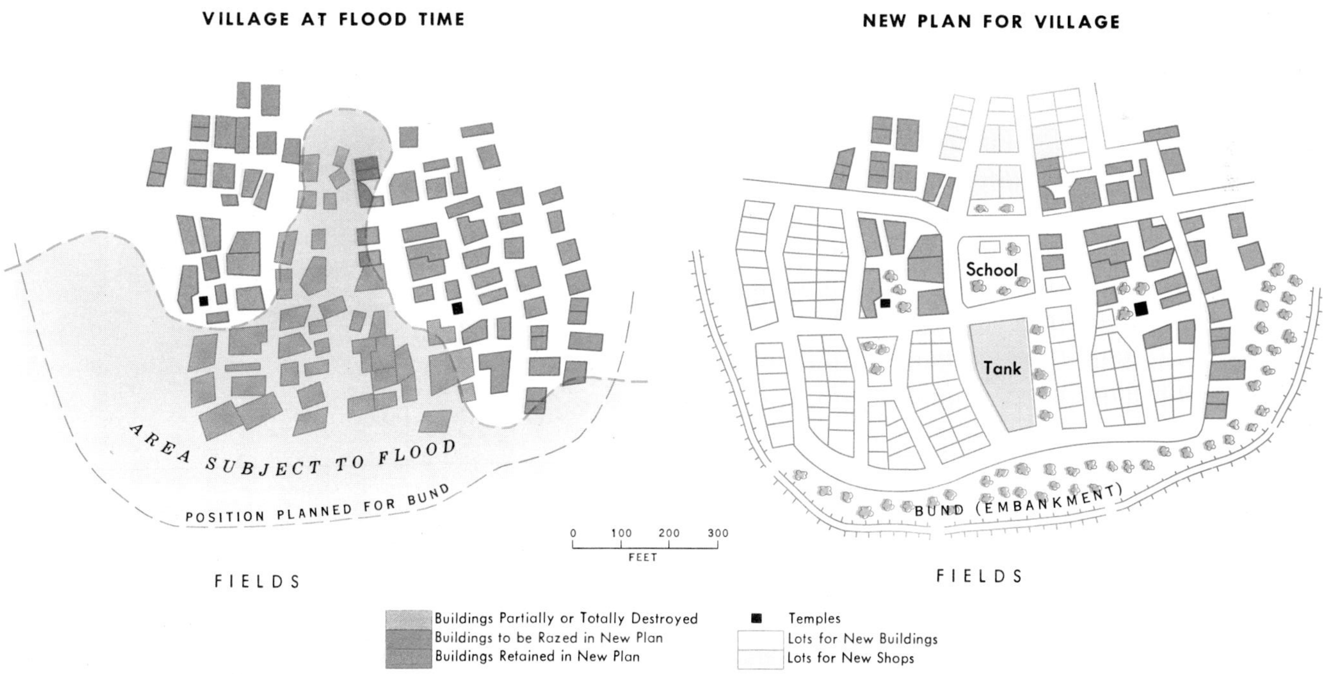

FLOOD CONTROL FOR LOWLAND VILLAGES: A MODERN SOLUTION FOR AN ANCIENT PROBLEM

The clustered villages of India's lowlands have always been harassed by recurring floods. The diagram at the right above shows how villages are being reorganized to control this old problem. In the past, when floods came *(left)*, they swept unchecked through the center of the settlements, washing over the mud brick buildings. Now a mud embankment, or bund, separates the village from the fields and keeps water out of the area. Trees and shrubs *(green)* are planted behind the bund. Excavation for the banks of the bund leaves a drainage area *(blue)*. Protected by the bund, villagers have been moved to modernize their schools and build parks and wider streets.

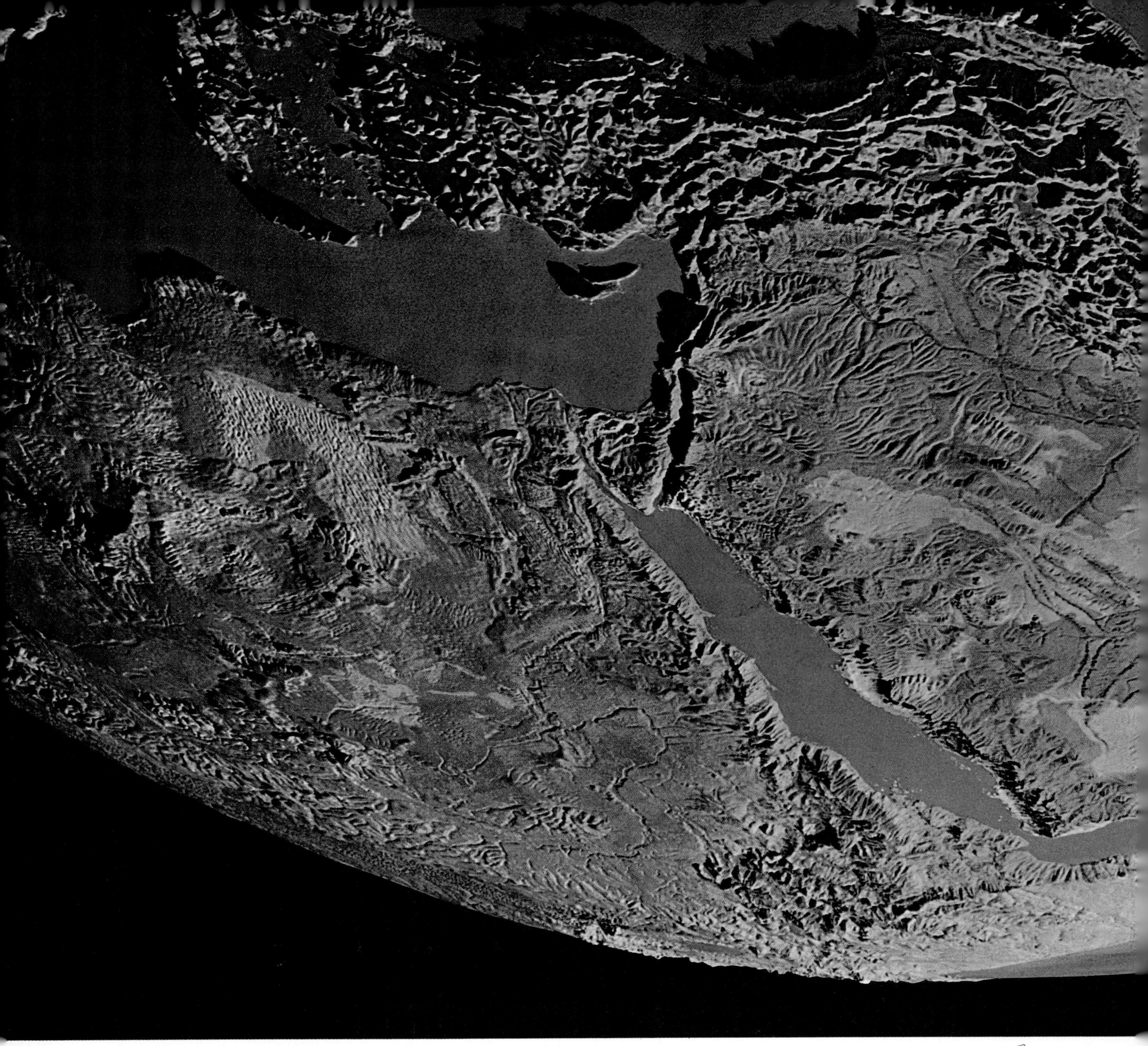

BROWN LANDSCAPES dominate Southwest Asia, which is framed by seas around the Arabian Peninsula *(center)*. At the upper left is the Mediterranean Sea. The Red Sea cuts diagonally across left center, the Caspian is at top center and the Arabian Sea at lower right.

SOUTHWEST ASIA

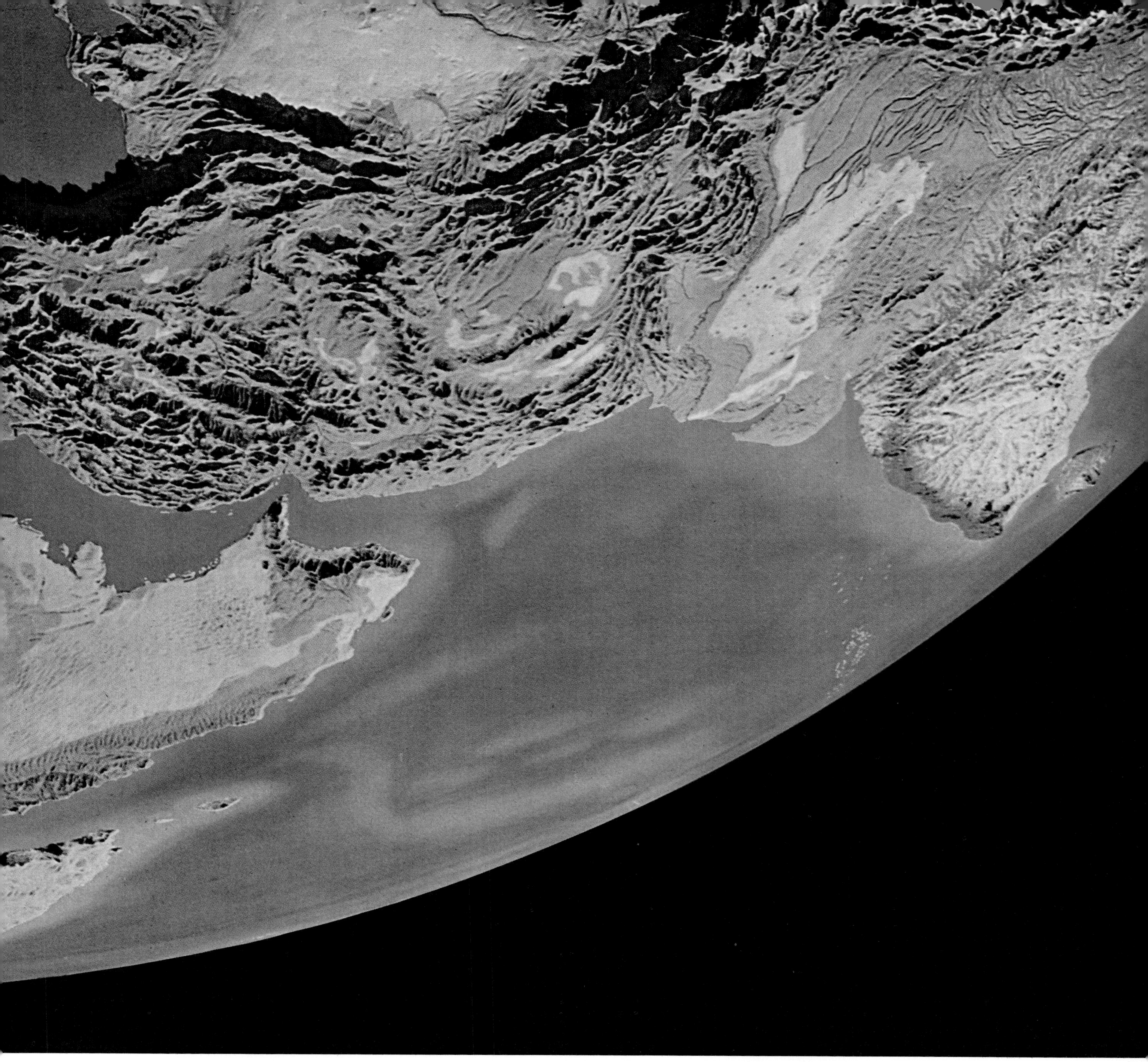

"A cloud gathers, the rain falls, men live; the cloud disperses without rain, and men and animals die. In the deserts of southern Arabia there is no rhythm of the seasons, no rise and fall of sap, but empty wastes where only the changing temperature marks the passage of the years." These are the somber reflections of an Englishman, Wilfred Thesiger, who lived for years as an Arab in the barren mountains and burned deserts of Southwest Asia. In this arid corner of a huge continent, management of water has been the key to man's livelihood ever since the time of the Sumerians, who had irrigation systems in 3500 B.C. Agriculture furnishes the main livelihood of the peoples of Southwest Asia, and some irrigation is required for one third of the region's 250,000 square miles of arable land.

But there are islands of fertility. Well-watered lands form the Fertile Crescent that links the head of the Persian Gulf and the eastern Mediterranean. The Fertile Crescent has a congested population of more than 100 per square mile. In contrast, the largely waterless deserts of the Arabian Peninsula, western Iraq, eastern Jordan and eastern Syria have less than 25 people per square mile, most of them nomads. The salt deserts of Iran and the Empty Quarter of Saudi Arabia are virtually uninhabitable. Land reclamation and irrigation projects in some sectors of Southwest Asia now offer the promise of increasing the land available for cultivation.

Oil fields are present in only a small fraction of the Southwest Asian land mass, but oil produces great wealth for several nations in the area. Oil and gas seeps have been known here for thousands of years – the Biblical fiery furnace may well have been the "eternal" fire still burning near Kirkūk in Iraq. However, petroleum production was not begun in Iran until shortly before World War I, and many of the great fields of the Arabian Peninsula were not even discovered until after World War II. The income that many governments of Southwest Asia currently obtain from oil royalties has already begun to make a number of startling changes in the lives of the people. Foreign oil companies have built hundreds of miles of modern highways and have helped train Southwest Asia's young people in modern technical skills. One important result, after many centuries of an unchanging social structure, has been the emergence of a new middle class.

A BUDDHIST SANCTUARY IN AFGHANISTAN'S HEIGHTS

JAGGED PEAKS of the Hindu Kush range, one of the main mountain systems in Central Asia, tower above the village of Bamian, set in a valley in northern Afghanistan. The side of the cliff which rises behind the village is pierced with openings for the cave cells of Buddhist monks and a niche for a religious statue that is 173 feet tall. This is an isolated area about 80 miles northwest of Kābul, now infrequently traveled but once a major route for Indian and Chinese silk caravans using the Khyber Pass, about 200 miles to the south.

AFGHANISTAN

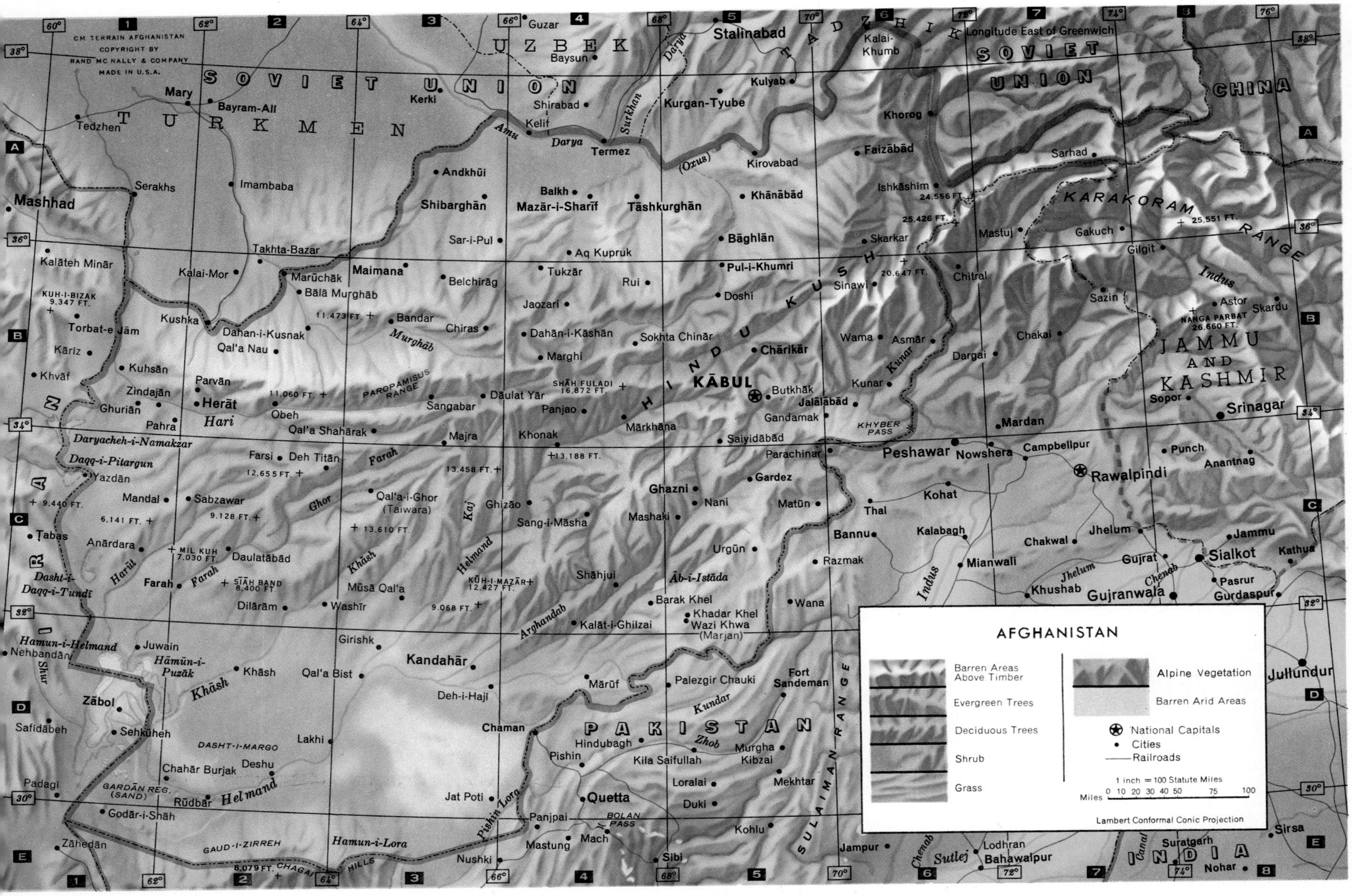

AFGHANISTAN: This mountain-locked country lies high and dry on the rooftop of the world. The great range of the Hindu Kush, with a hundred peaks soaring more than four miles high, rams across the center of Afghanistan like a huge fist 150 miles wide. Its melting snows make up for scanty rainfall by feeding four rivers—the Helmand, Kābul, Oxus and Hari Rud. Only the Kābul eventually reaches the sea, via the Indus; the others lose themselves in deserts, swamps and the inland Caspian Sea. Deserts alternate with grassy plains and with fertile valleys like the flower-strewn Vale of Jalālābād, where camel caravans used to pass on the ancient Silk Road from China to Europe.

The mountain barrier to the southeast is pierced by the Khyber Pass, the traditional funnel for invaders into the Indian subcontinent. Greeks, Huns, Arabs, Turks and Mongols have ruled the land. Some Afghans are red-haired and blue-eyed, others have basically Mongolian features. Afghans still usually live in mud-walled villages perched on hilltops for defense. Pantalooned men with rifles mount guard over flocks of karakul sheep; the women, except for the "emancipated" ones, are shrouded in sacklike *burkhas*.

AREA:	250,900 sq. mi.
POPULATION:	13,310,000. Largest city and capital: Kābul.
CLIMATE:	Hot summers, cold winters; little annual rainfall. Climate varies in mountains according to elevation.
ALTITUDES:	Peak of Hindu Kush, 24,556 ft. (highest); Kābul, 5,890 ft.

Despite the presence of coal, oil, lead, chromium, copper and sulphur, Afghanistan remains primarily an agricultural country; the principal export is hides and skins. There are no railroads or navigable streams.

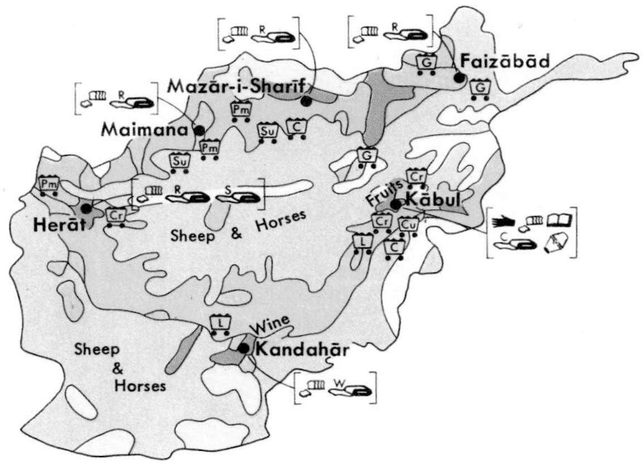

THE ECONOMY

MANUFACTURING
- Cotton
- Silk
- Carpets
- Wool
- Printing & Publishing
- Food Products
- Leather Products
- Cement

MINING
- Coal
- Chromium
- Copper
- Gold
- Lead
- Petroleum
- Sulfur

AGRICULTURE
- General Farming
- Intensive Agriculture
- Forest Agriculture
- Pastureland with Sparse Vegetation
- Seasonal Grazing
- Non-Agricultural Areas

GROSS NATIONAL PRODUCT PER CAPITA $48

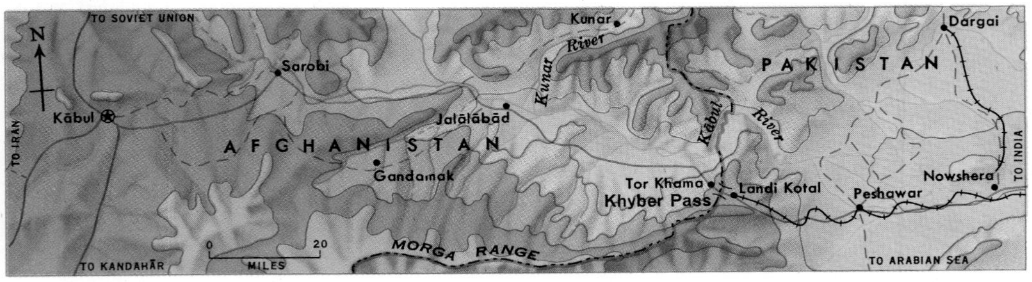

THE HISTORIC PASS OF THE KHYBER

On the map above, the harsh Afghan terrain near the Khyber Pass (*right center*) is shown in shaded relief. The historic road (*solid red line*) through the pass is a sector of the old land route between India and Russia. Mountain settlements are linked by trails (*broken red lines*) that use high passes instead of valleys to avoid deep gorges and torrential currents.

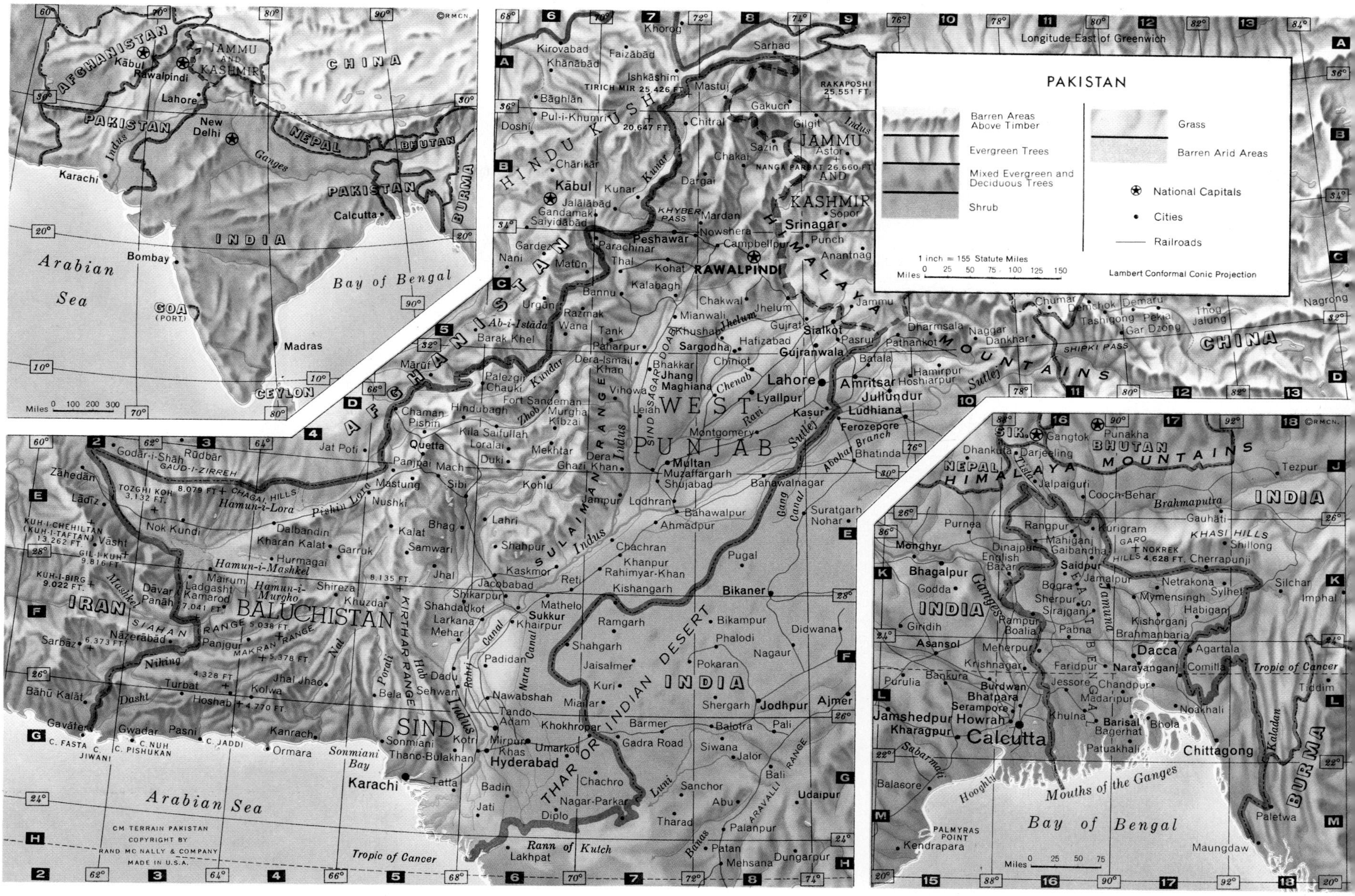

PAKISTAN:

Mohammed Ali Jinnah, the founder of Pakistan, complained in 1947 of the "mutilated, truncated, moth-eaten" country granted him as a result of the partition of British India. Instead of being separated *from* India, the new Moslem nation of Pakistan was separated *by* India into two unequal parts. West Pakistan is big, arid, mountainous and scantily populated. Nearly a thousand miles away by land and 3,000 by sea, East Pakistan is small, waterlogged, jammed with people and flat. In the west, Urdu is spoken; in the east, Bengali. The only adequate bridge between the two regions is the airplane.

AREA: 364,702 sq. mi.

POPULATION: 93,812,000. Largest city: Karachi. Temporary capital: Rawalpindi.

CLIMATE: West: hot summers, warm dry winters; limited rainfall; cooler with heavier rainfall in the highlands. East: hot summers, warm winters; heavy rain in summer.

ALTITUDES: Tirich Mir, 25,426 ft. (highest); Karachi, 60 ft.; Dacca, 26 ft.

West Pakistan is rimmed in the north by mountains whose valleys contain the semi-independent domains of such rulers as the Wali of Swat and the Nawabs of Dir and Amb. The land descends to forest-clad hills and desert plateaus. The twisting Indus River gives life to the parched earth and is supplemented by irrigation canals for wheat and cotton. In vast, sun-baked Baluchistan (thought to be the original home of the world's gypsies) there is natural gas. East Pakistan is veined with rivers, wandering streams and mile on mile of rice paddies. Natural gas has also been found at Sylhet. Jute is the principal export crop.

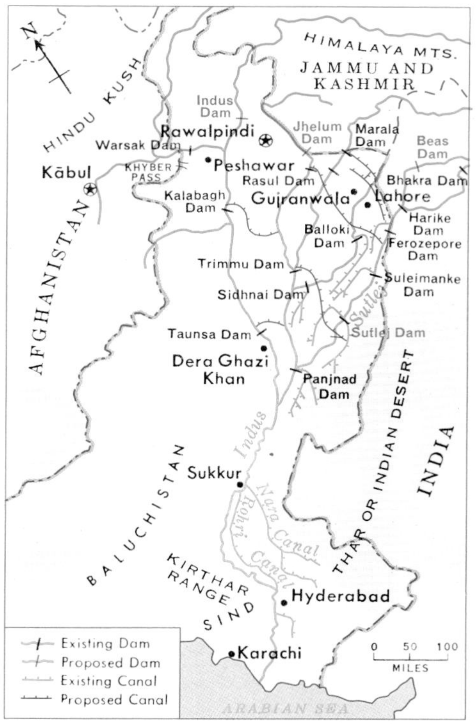

THE INDUS WATER BASIN

This map of the Indus River basin in West Pakistan *(above)* shows where new dams *(red)* and new canals *(gray)* will be added to help store the water of the river and to provide irrigation for dry areas bordering the desert wastelands *(yellow)*. The new dams and canals, to be ready by 1970, will also help control floods caused by the heavy monsoon rains.

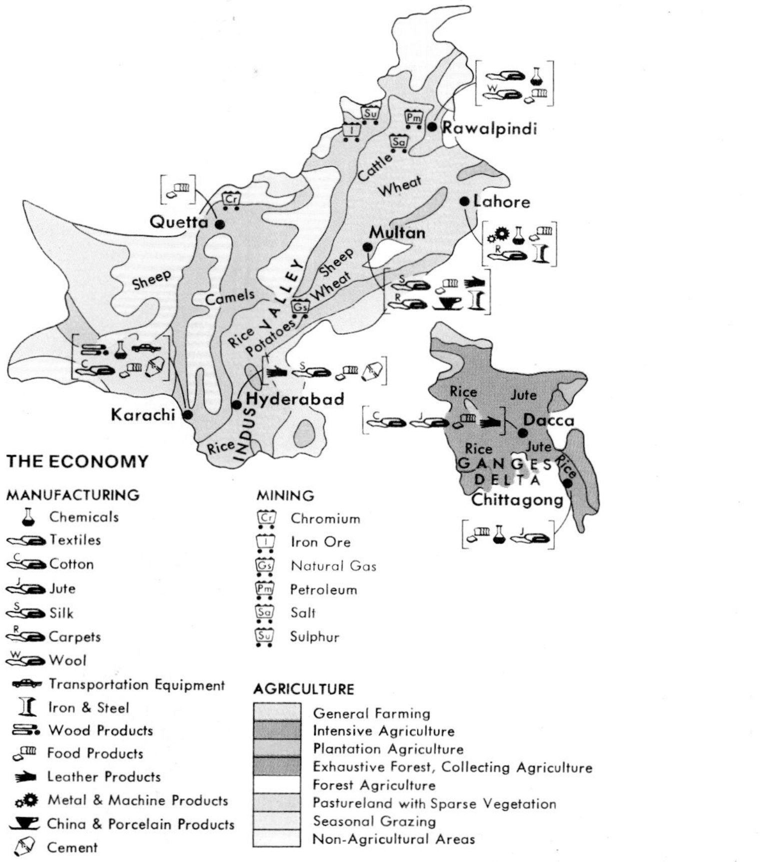

GROSS NATIONAL PRODUCT PER CAPITA $66

FLAMING TOWERS separate natural gas from petroleum at Kirkuk *(above)* in the oil fields of Iraq's mountainous northeast. The oil is then piped to Mediterranean ports and to refineries at Baghdad, Basrah and Khanaqin. Most of the gas is "flared"—enough being burned off each day to heat a city of 420,000—but Iraq is now preparing to use part of it. The Kirkuk field produced 261.4 million barrels of Iraq's total of 346.5 million barrels in 1960. Oil brings the country $250 million in revenue each year.

AN ANCIENT ROUTE in Iran, once used by nomads and traders, is now followed by a multiple oil pipeline *(left)* near Ahwāz. A shepherd with a flock of sheep is crossing the pipes which carry oil to the great refineries and shipping docks at Abādān, 70 miles to the south on the Persian Gulf. With 120 oil wells in operation and 2,600 miles of pipelines, Iran now produces almost 400 million barrels of oil a year. Most of this petroleum is exported, bringing a total income of roughly $280 million a year.

CRUMBLING COLUMNS IN SYRIA are all that is left of Palmyra *(right)*, once one of the world's great trade cities. Situated at a crossroads of caravan routes in the Syrian Desert, the city is called "Tadmor" in the Bible. In the First Century B.C. it came under Roman rule, and for nearly three centuries (14-270 A.D.) it was a buffer state between Rome and Parthia. Spectacular columns of rosy-white limestone lined its avenues. The fortress-castle on the summit of the hill was built much later by the Turks.

TIME'S CHANGES ON THE DESERT SANDS

SYRIA, LEBANON, JORDAN AND IRAQ

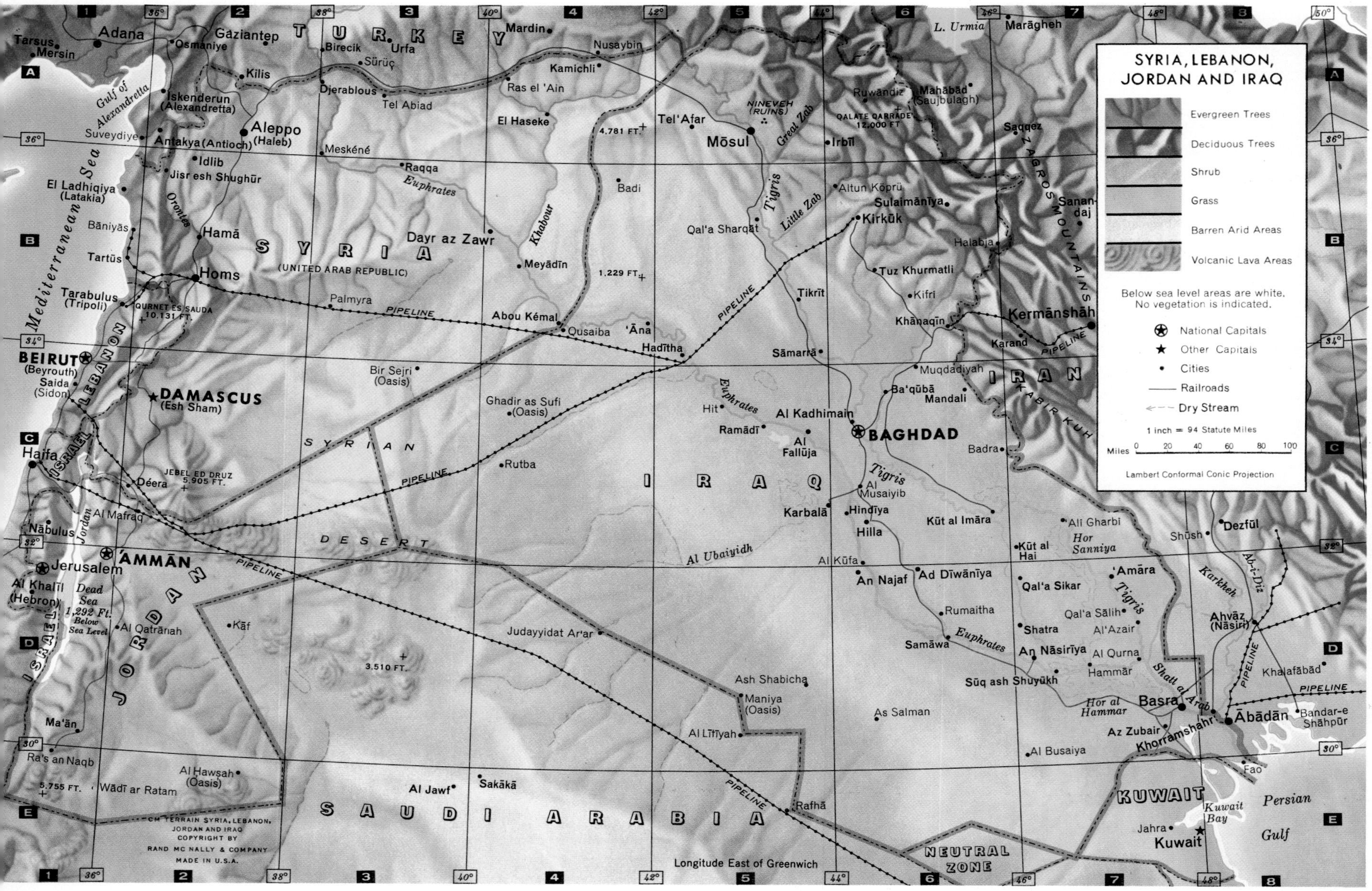

SYRIA (U.A.R.): Over the centuries a corridor for trade caravans and contending armies, Syria has often known foreign rule. In 1958, it joined with Egypt to become part of the United Arab Republic. Despite mountains and deserts, modern Syria is a pastoral and agricultural country, and irrigation produces a wheat crop often large enough for export. Completion of reclamation projects, such as the draining of the Orontes River marshes, will not only limit the spread of malaria but add precious farmland to the nation.

AREA: 71,209 sq. mi.
POPULATION: 4,556,000.
Capital: Damascus.
U.A.R. capital: Cairo.
CLIMATE: Dry summers; winter rain along coast, arid inland.
ALTITUDES: Jebel Chaqif, near Damascus, 8,077 ft. (highest).

LEBANON: Half-Christian and half-Moslem Lebanon is a tourist center. Along its narrow coast, rugged, resort-dotted mountains rise to 5,000 feet only 12 to 15 miles away from sunny Mediterranean beaches. Some regions enjoy such varied temperatures that apples, olives and bananas all grow within a 10-mile radius. Cotton is a staple crop and there is a growing textile industry. Heirs to the traditions of the ancient Phoenicians, the Lebanese also carry on a thriving trade through the port city of Beirut.

AREA: 4,014 sq. mi.
POPULATION: 1,719,000.
Capital: Beirut.
CLIMATE: Hot dry summers, mild wet winters; cooler and wetter in mountains.
ALTITUDES: Qurnet es Sauda, 10,131 ft. (highest); Beirut, 200 ft.

JORDAN: Created by the British after World War I, the Emirate of Trans-Jordan became the Hashemite Kingdom of Jordan when it annexed areas of Arab Palestine in 1949. On the west bank of the Jordan River are the religious shrines of Jerusalem's Old City and Bethlehem. Jordanians grow wheat, barley and grapes, and some eke out a living by raising livestock. The east bank of the Jordan is largely a desert roamed by nomadic camel herders. There are phosphates in the desert and mineral salts in the Dead Sea.

AREA: 37,291 sq. mi.
POPULATION: 1,702,000.
Capital: 'Ammān.
CLIMATE: Hot, very dry summers; mild winters; little rainfall.
ALTITUDES: Jebel Ram, near Ra's an Naqb, 5,755 ft. (highest); Dead Sea, -1,292 ft.

IRAQ: The fertile valley of the Tigris and Euphrates Rivers, said to be the site of the Biblical Garden of Eden, was once the granary of the great Babylonian empire. Iraq's population still clusters along the twin rivers, which sometimes surge over their banks. Most of the rest of the land is sun-scorched, except after winter rains. Less than one fifth of Iraq's area is cultivated. The country gets more than 50 per cent of its national income from its oil deposits, worked principally by European and American companies.

AREA: 171,554 sq. mi.
POPULATION: 6,784,000.
Capital: Baghdad.
CLIMATE: Very hot, very dry summers; mild winters; little rainfall.
ALTITUDES: Qalate Qarrade, 12,000 ft. (highest); Baghdad, 112 ft.

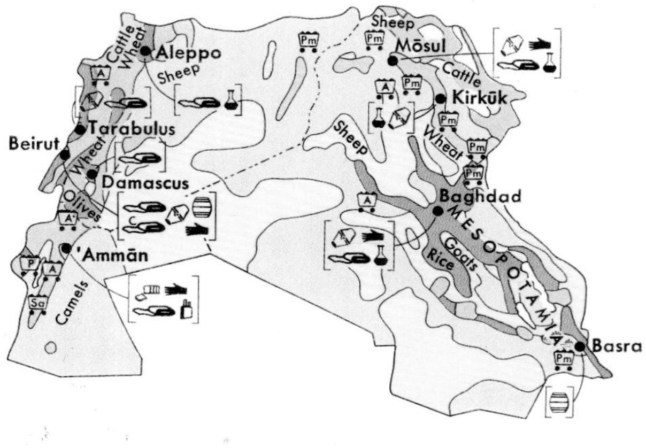

THE ECONOMY

MANUFACTURING
- Chemicals
- Textiles
- Cotton
- Food Products
- Leather Products
- Tobacco Products
- Cement
- Wineries, Distilleries & Breweries

MINING
- Asphalt
- Petroleum
- Phosphate
- Salt

AGRICULTURE
- General Farming
- Mediterranean Agriculture
- Forest Agriculture
- Pastureland with sparse vegetation
- Seasonal Grazing
- Non-Agricultural Areas
- Swamp Areas

GROSS NATIONAL PRODUCT PER CAPITA

Syria $142 Lebanon $358 Jordan $111 Iraq $160

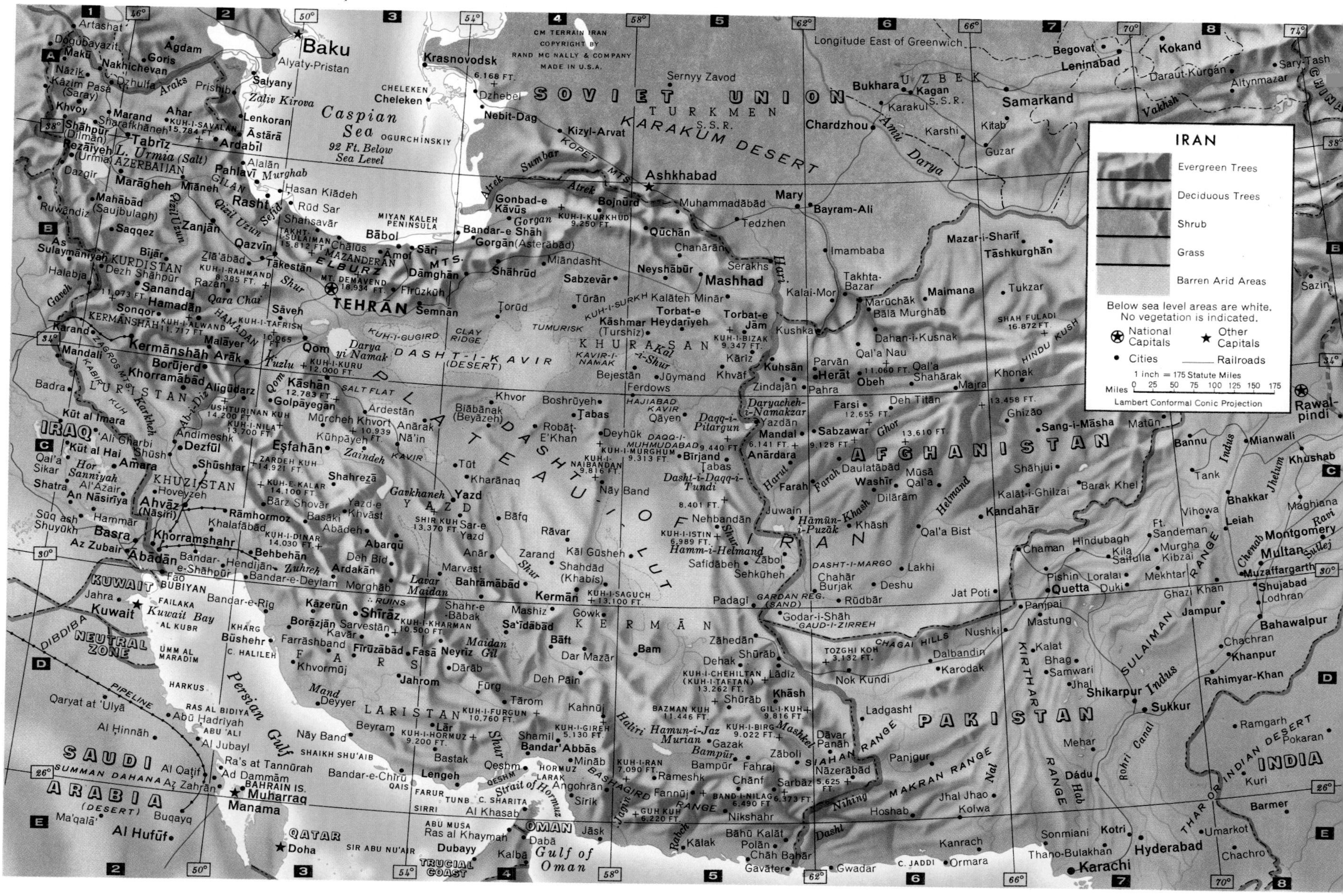

IRAN: Over 2,400 years ago, the Persian King Darius I ordered his majestic tomb inscribed: "I am Darius, the great King, King of Kings . . . King of this great earth far and wide. . . ." Now the pomp and glory of the Persian empire are buried in the poverty of present-day Iran. Second largest country of the Middle East, Iran has little agriculture or industry.

AREA:	629,180 sq. mi.
POPULATION:	20,577,000. Capital: Tehrān.
CLIMATE:	Hot summers, mild winters along coasts; cooler in interior and mountains. Little rainfall except along Caspian coast and in mountains.
ALTITUDES:	Demavend, 18,934 ft. (highest).

Oil deposits, mainly around Ābādān at the head of the Persian Gulf, provide Iran with more than half of its foreign exchange. In an effort to raise the living standards, some oil revenues are now being used for land reclamation projects. A notable example is the project to build a dam across the Ab-i-Diz River. This will furnish power and provide irrigation to more than 150 villages scattered over a large region in Iran's southwest Khuzistan province, near the oil fields on the Persian Gulf.

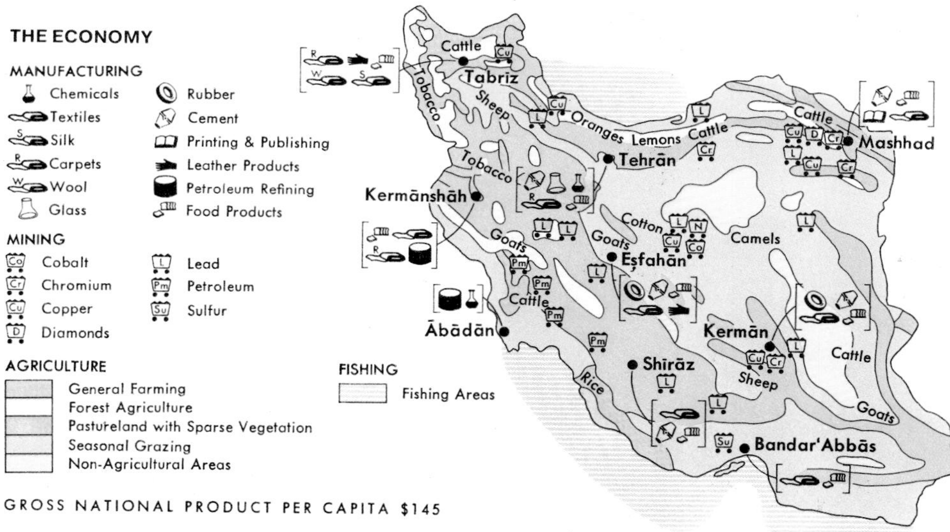

GROSS NATIONAL PRODUCT PER CAPITA $145

TRANSHUMANCE IN IRAN

The drawing at left shows how Iran's herds move *(red arrows)* among the pastures of lowland oases which stay green during the late fall, winter and early spring. This pastoral pattern is called horizontal transhumance (vertical transhumance is practiced in predominantly mountainous lands like Switzerland, where livestock summer in the heights and winter in the valleys). Iran also has summer ranges on its mountains *(background)*, and the herds are taken there when the grass withers in the lowlands. The herds sometimes make treks of as much as 300 miles from pasture to pasture.

MIDDLE EAST FARMLAND AND WASTELAND

A RECLAIMED MARSHLAND, the fertile Jezreel Valley lies at the foot of the storied hills of Galilee in northern Israel. Now the country's most important agricultural region, the valley supports a variety of crops, including sugar beets, cotton, peanuts and citrus fruits.

A DIMPLED DESERT of dunes and depressions, Saudi Arabia's Rub' al Khali, "The Empty Quarter," stretches desolately across an area larger than Texas. Still being explored, this wasteland, one of the largest expanses of sand in the world, may contain oil deposits.

ISRAEL

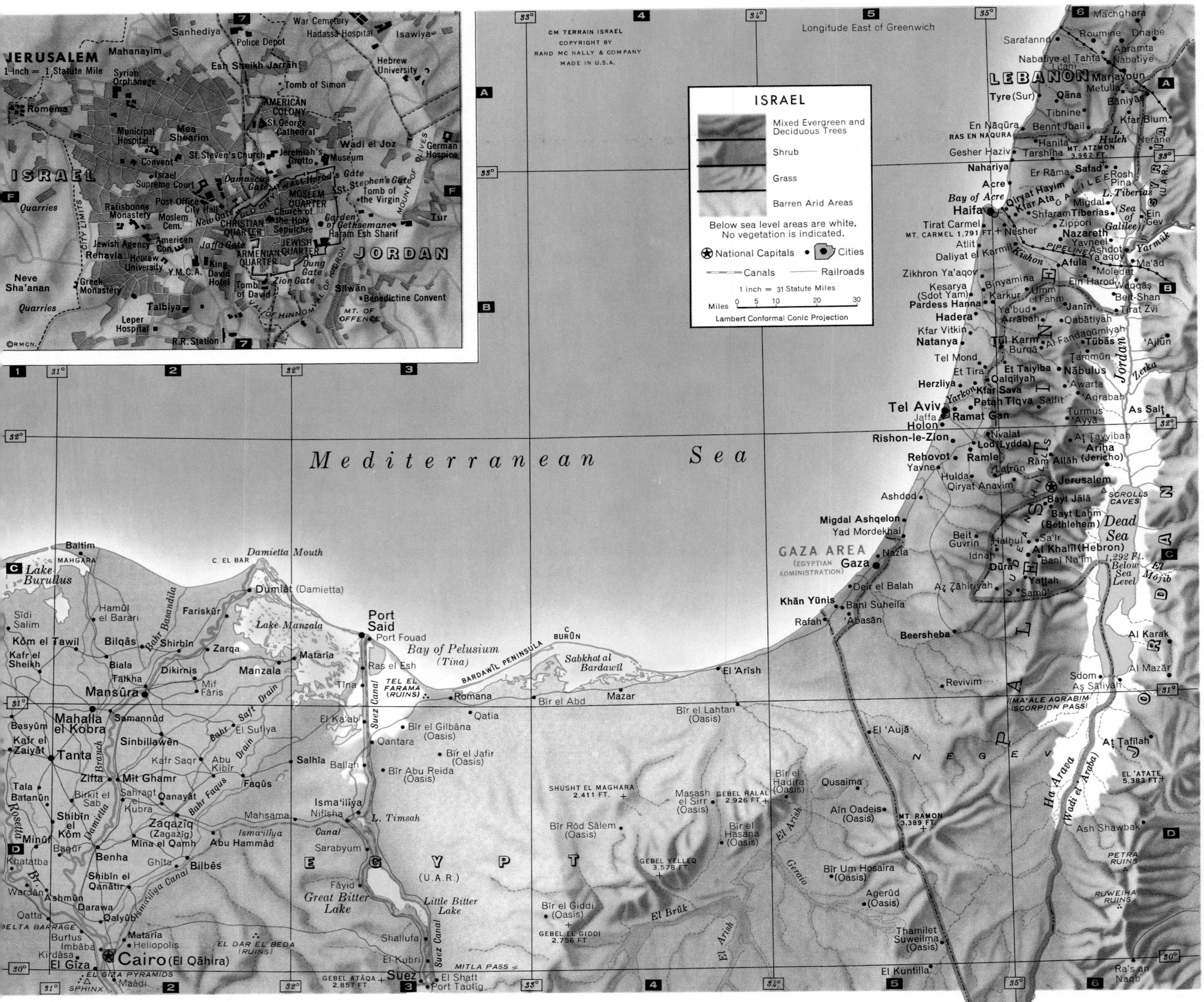

ISRAEL: Within the cramped borders of Israel, established in 1948, the look of the land offers an astonishing variety: from the tinted cliffs of the Negev Desert to the flat white beaches of the Mediterranean, from the dry green of the Jordan Valley to the brown of the Judean Hills to the snow-covered peaks of Mount Atzmon. At any season of the year, the climate ranges from the searing heat of the Dead Sea to the fresh breeziness of Galilee in the temperate northern highlands only 60 miles away.

AREA:	7,990 sq. mi.
POPULATION:	2,111,000. Largest city: Tel Aviv-Jaffa. Capital: Jerusalem.
CLIMATE:	Hot summers, mild winters; winter rainfall along the coast, low annual rainfall inland.
ALTITUDES:	Mt. Atzmon, 3,962 ft. (highest); Dead Sea, -1,292 ft.

Although the desert has been made to bloom and giant irrigation projects have more than doubled Israel's cultivated area, some food must still be imported. The country's natural resources are far from sufficient to supply its growing industry. Potash and bromides are extracted from the Dead Sea and copper is mined from the site in the Negev where King Solomon's workers dug 3,000 years ago. Crude oil, iron ore and other essentials, however, must be bought abroad, and Israel is dependent on outside economic aid as it organizes the technical skills of its people to increase the output of high-value manufactured goods. Heavy industries, such as metal production and machinery, are booming in Haifa and Tel Aviv. Processed foods and textiles are shipped to world markets. But Israel's best money-making export is the citrus crop from irrigated orchards throughout the country.

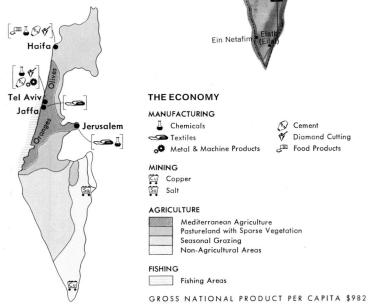

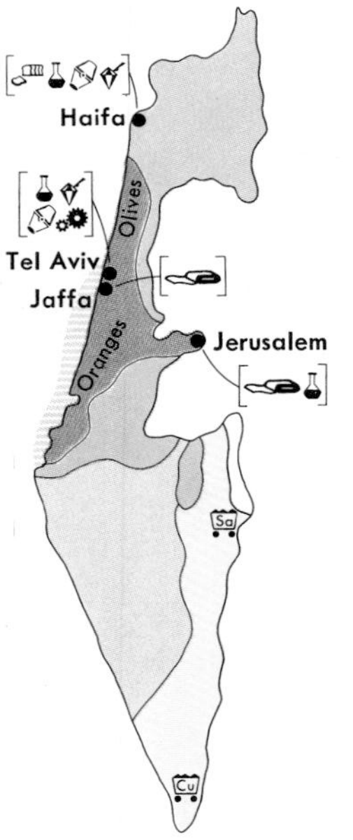

THE ECONOMY

MANUFACTURING
- Chemicals
- Textiles
- Metal & Machine Products
- Cement
- Diamond Cutting
- Food Products

MINING
- Copper
- Salt

AGRICULTURE
- Mediterranean Agriculture
- Pastureland with Sparse Vegetation
- Seasonal Grazing
- Non-Agricultural Areas

FISHING
- Fishing Areas

GROSS NATIONAL PRODUCT PER CAPITA $982

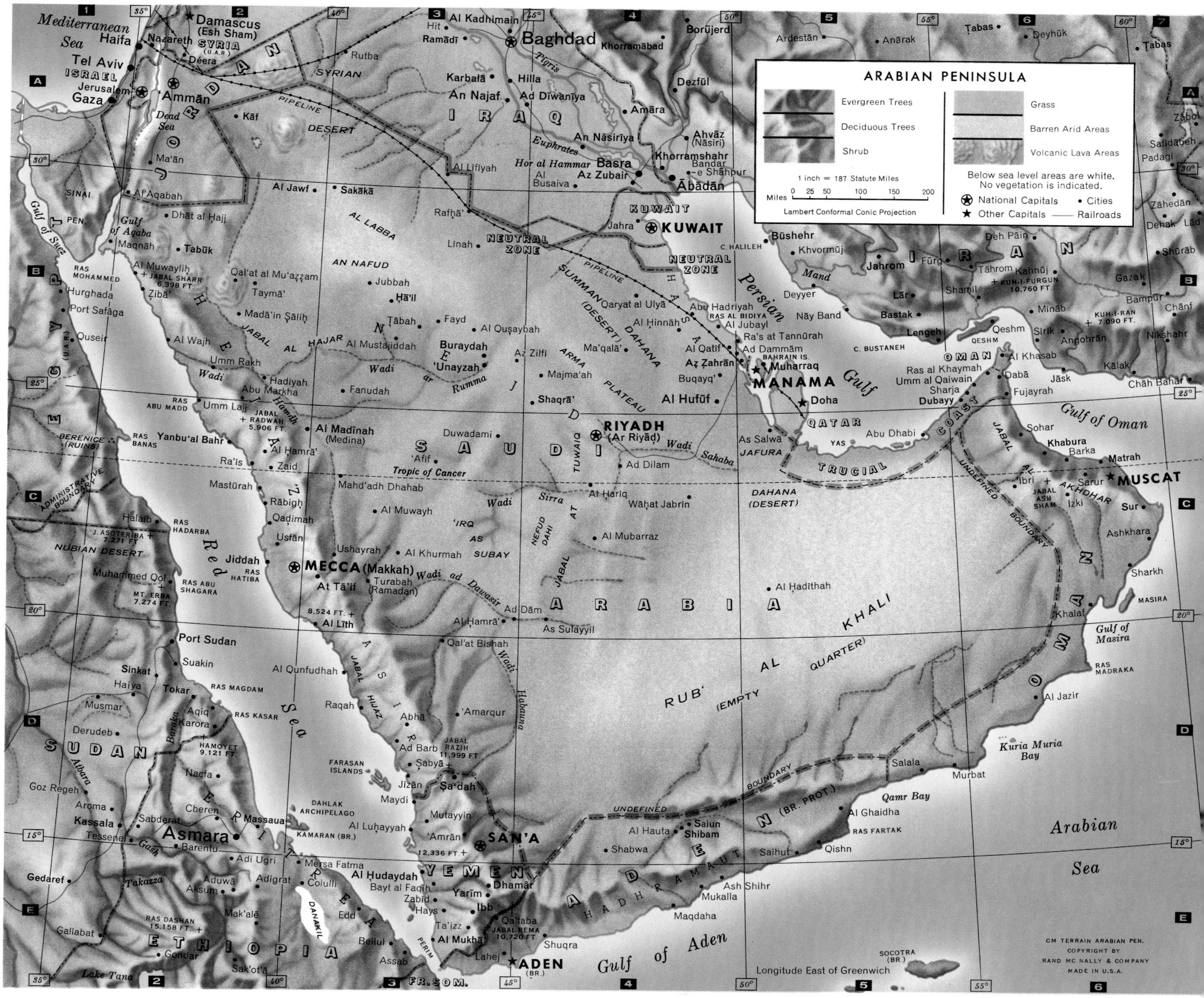

SAUDI ARABIA: Tremendous deposits of petroleum under Saudi Arabia's coastal lowland along the Persian Gulf have brought wealth but few modern ways to Saudi Arabia, the world's fifth largest producer of crude oil. Oil furnishes 80 per cent of governmental revenue. Oil-producing areas now boast new schools, health centers and whole new towns, but one half of the people still live as nomadic or seminomadic herdsmen on a basic diet of dates (the country's chief agricultural export) and camel milk. The present Kingdom of Saudi Arabia was first unified by Mohammed in 630 A.D., and his birthplace, Mecca, remains the sacred city of Islam. The most populated area is in the Western Mountains, where rain and irrigation make agriculture possible and the farmers cling to techniques as ancient as their holy book, the Koran.

AREA:	600,000 sq. mi.
POPULATION:	6,159,000. Largest city: Mecca. Capitals: Riyadh and Mecca.
CLIMATE:	Hot summers, mild to warm winters; dry all year.
ALTITUDES:	Mt. Jabal Razih, 11,999 ft. (highest); Riyadh, 1,897 ft.; Mecca, 919 ft.

SULTANATES AND SHEIKDOMS: A number of small states fringe the Arabian Peninsula. The Sheikdoms of Kuwait and Qatar have great oil wealth—Kuwait ranking second in the world (after Venezuela) as an exporter of crude oil. The island Sheikdom of Bahrain, a refining center, also shares in the petroleum prosperity. The Kingdom of Yemen has the best farmland on the peninsula. Seven sheikdoms form the Trucial Oman States, where pearling and fishing are carried on. Other principal areas: the Sultanate of Muscat and Oman, the British Crown Colony of Aden and the Protectorate of Aden.

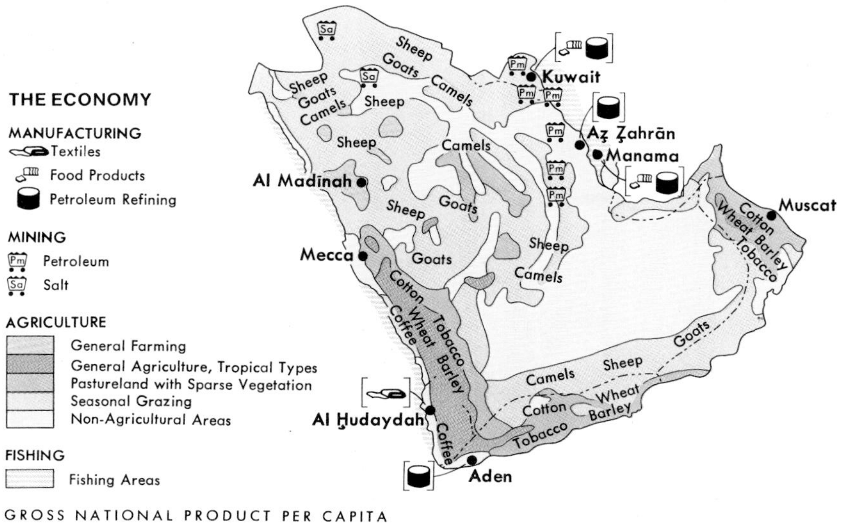

GROSS NATIONAL PRODUCT PER CAPITA
Saudi Arabia $169   Yemen $75

MIDDLE EAST
National Capitals
Other Capitals
Cities
Railroads
Canals
1 inch = 200 Statute Miles
Miles 0 25 50 75 100 150 200
Lambert Conformal Conic Projection
CM POLITICAL MIDDLE EAST
COPYRIGHT BY
RAND MC NALLY & COMPANY
MADE IN U.S.A.
Longitude East of Greenwich
A
B
C
D
E
F
1
2
3
4
5
6
7
8
9
Mediterranean Sea
Aegean Sea
Caspian Sea
Persian Gulf
Gulf of Oman
Gulf of Aden
Arabian Sea
Red Sea
Tropic of Cancer
TURKEY
SYRIA
LEBANON
ISRAEL
JORDAN
IRAQ
IRAN
PLATEAU OF IRAN
AFGHANISTAN
PAKISTAN
SOV. UNION
SAUDI ARABIA
KUWAIT
QATAR
TRUCIAL OMAN
MUSCAT AND OMAN
YEMEN
ADEN
EGYPT
SUDAN
ETHIOPIA
ERITREA
CYPRUS
GREECE
NEUTRAL ZONE
RUB' AL KHALI (EMPTY QUARTER)
NEJD
HEJAZ
HASA
Cairo
Tehrān
Baghdad
Damascus
Beirut
Ammān
Jerusalem
Riyadh
Mecca (Makkah)
Kuwait
Doha
Manama
Muscat
San'a
Aden
Khartoum
Nicosia
Asmara

MIDDLE EAST: This segment of the world is redolent of human history. Indeed, British scientist Julian Huxley has said that it represents "solid history": for here, he explains, "civilization began. Everywhere else . . . civilization diffused in from somewhere else. Only in the Middle East . . . are to be found the first spontaneous developments of that novel form of human organization we call civilized society." Among the notable civilizations that originated in the Middle East were the Egyptian, before 4000 B.C.; the Sumerian, which developed in the delta of the Tigris and Euphrates before 3500 B.C.; the Babylonian, which also developed along these rivers about 2000 B.C.; and the Hittite, which flourished in Turkey and Syria from around 2000 to 1200 B.C.

As a regional entity the Middle East does not, however, fit neatly into commonly accepted geographical concepts, and the result has been confusion in nomenclature. For many years part of it was called "Asia Minor," a term first used in the Fifth Century A.D. for the Roman province of what is now Turkey in Asia. In recent times the designation "Near East" was used for the area. During World War II the term preferred in British usage, "Middle East," gained wider acceptance and is now generally endorsed by American as well as British geographers.

In the Middle East—where Europe and Africa converge upon Asia—there are two land bridges: the narrow neck of desert traversed by the Suez Canal and the wide bridge that links the Arabian Peninsula to the Asian mainland. Two nations transcend continental divisions here: the United Arab Republic joins Egypt and Syria to form an Afro-Asian political unit, and Turkey is Eurasian.

For many centuries the Middle East has been the main transit route between East and West, with such famed travelers and conquerors as Herodotus, Cyrus, Alexander the Great and Marco Polo using its routes and way stations. Rich and exotic cargoes have filled the ships that sailed Middle Eastern seas, and great treasure has crossed the deserts in camel caravans. The English poet John Masefield described the sea-borne commerce:

> Quinquireme of Nineveh from distant Ophir,
> Rowing home to haven in sunny Palestine,
> With a cargo of ivory,
> And apes and peacocks,
> Sandalwood, cedarwood, and sweet white wine.

A modern addition to the traditional Middle Eastern economy is in the vast reserves of oil *(map, lower right)*, estimated at about half the world's total and apparently increasing in potential.

An inhospitable natural environment and the resultant rigorous struggle for survival are common to nearly all Middle Eastern countries. More important as unifying factors throughout the area are the cultural, social and legal systems that developed over many centuries under Arabic and Moslem influences *(map, right)*. The Middle East is the Arab world. The Arabic language crosses most of the political frontiers. It is estimated that 52 million people live in Middle Eastern countries where Arabic is the prevailing language, and the Islamic faith unites many millions more, like the populations of Iran and Turkey, which have entered the Middle Eastern pattern even though they have no Arab heritage or language.

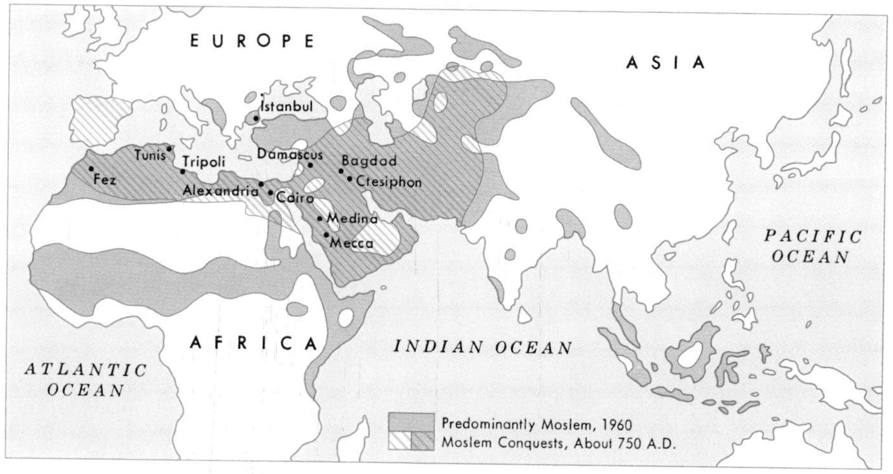

AN EMPIRE CARVED OUT BY THE SWORD OF ISLAM

Moslem conquests in the Seventh and Eighth Centuries *(diagonal lines over red and yellow)* that extended through Africa, Asia and Europe are mapped above. Also shown are those areas *(red)* that are now predominantly Moslem. The Arab caliphs who succeeded Mohammed spread Islam (meaning submission to God's will) by conquest. The new faith spread rapidly, but the conquerors tolerated nonbelievers who paid tribute. Unrest in the vast domains gradually undermined Moslem temporal power, but the faith of Islam endured and prospered, journeying far and wide on three continents, wherever Moslems migrated, traveled and traded.

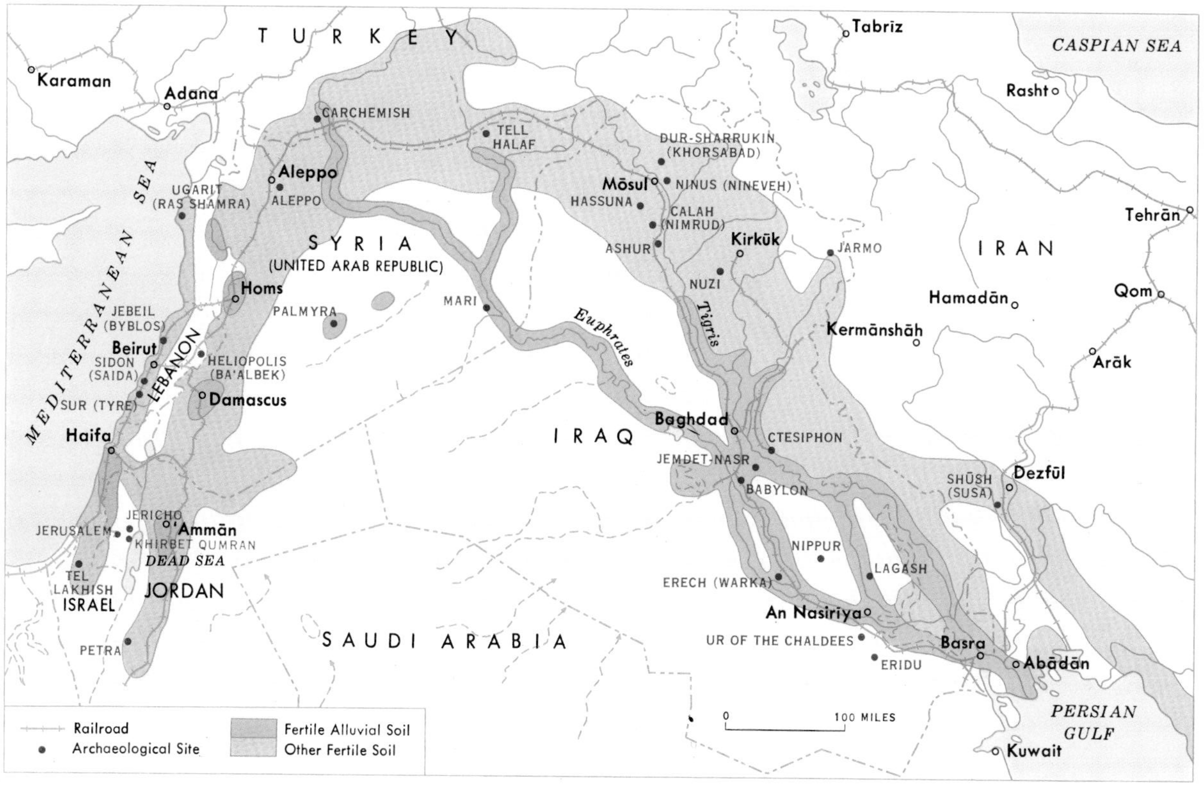

THE SPAN OF THE FERTILE CRESCENT

The map above shows the Fertile Crescent of the Middle East, the arc of grassland bordering the Tigris-Euphrates river area and linking the Persian Gulf to the Mediterranean. The arable heart of the Middle East, it has been called "the world's first great international highway." The crescent forms a rich, level land "bridge," as geographers describe it, between Southwest Asia's mountains and deserts. From before the time of the Old Testament, man has been tilling the productive alluvial soil here *(dark green)* and its surrounding good farmland *(light green)*. The Tigris-Euphrates delta *(lower right)* is subject to recurring floods that often deposit ruinous salt crusts. The crescent is dotted with rich archaeological sites *(names in red)*. Jericho *(lower left)* is thought to be one of the oldest of man's settlements in the area, with Carbon-14 dating suggesting that it existed in 6800 B.C.

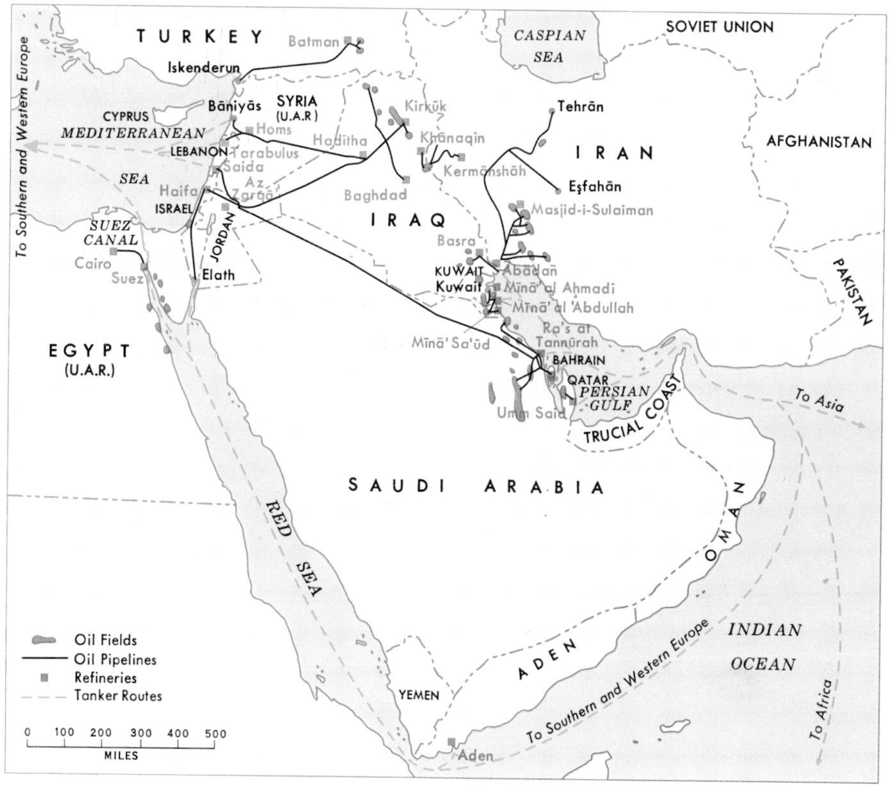

OIL FIELDS AND ROUTES OF THE MIDDLE EAST

Shown here are the major oil centers of the Middle East. The heaviest concentrations of fields *(purple)* and refineries *(red)* are near the coast of the Persian Gulf *(center)* and farther north. Pipelines, shown in solid black lines, run from fields across deserts to reach the chief tanker routes, shown in broken lines. Most oil destined for Europe goes by tanker around the Arabian Peninsula to the Suez Canal, or by pipeline to Mediterranean ports. Kuwait *(center)* ranks first in production in the area, fourth in the world. Saudi Arabia comes next, then Iran and Iraq. American and European companies dominate the oil industry in the Middle East.

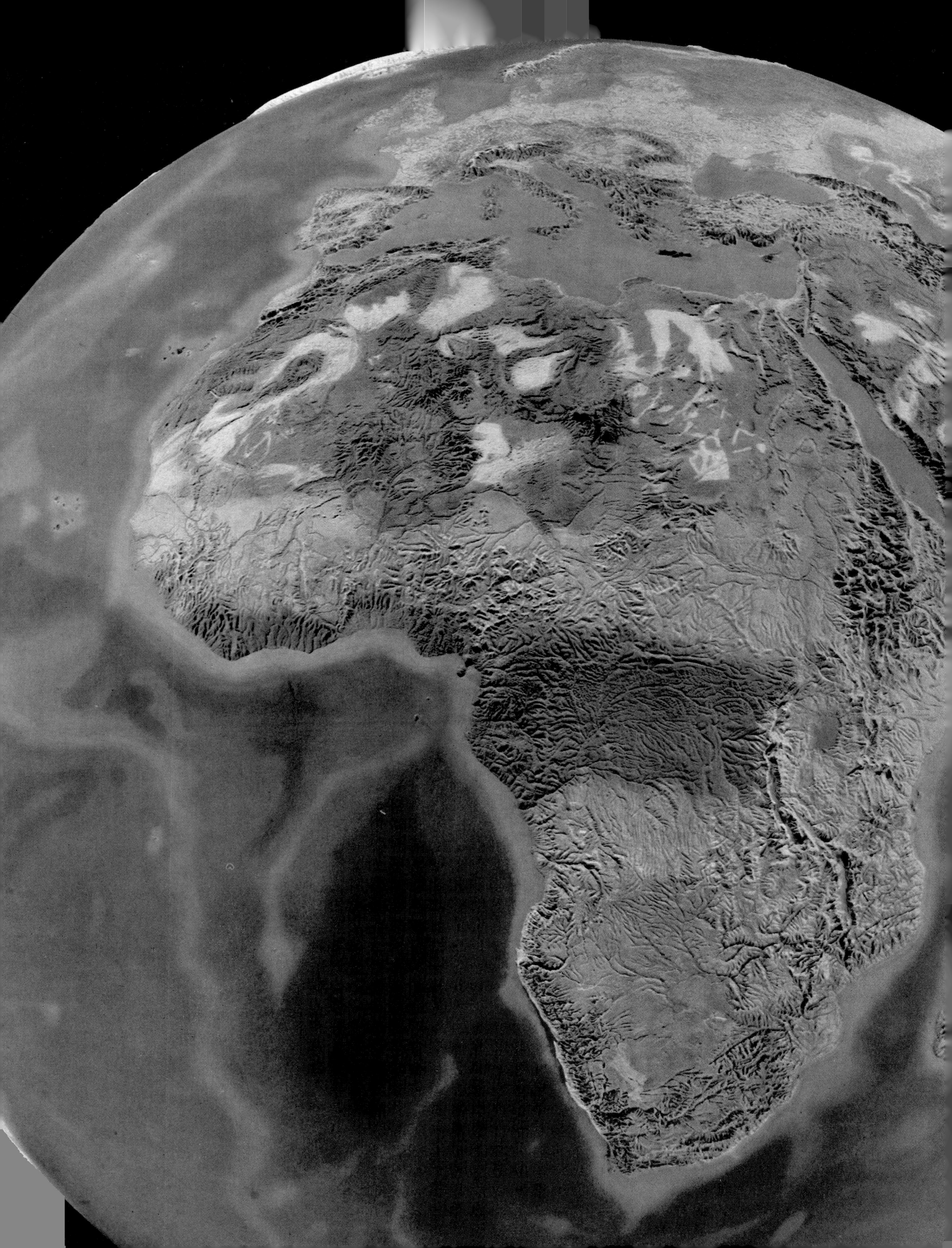

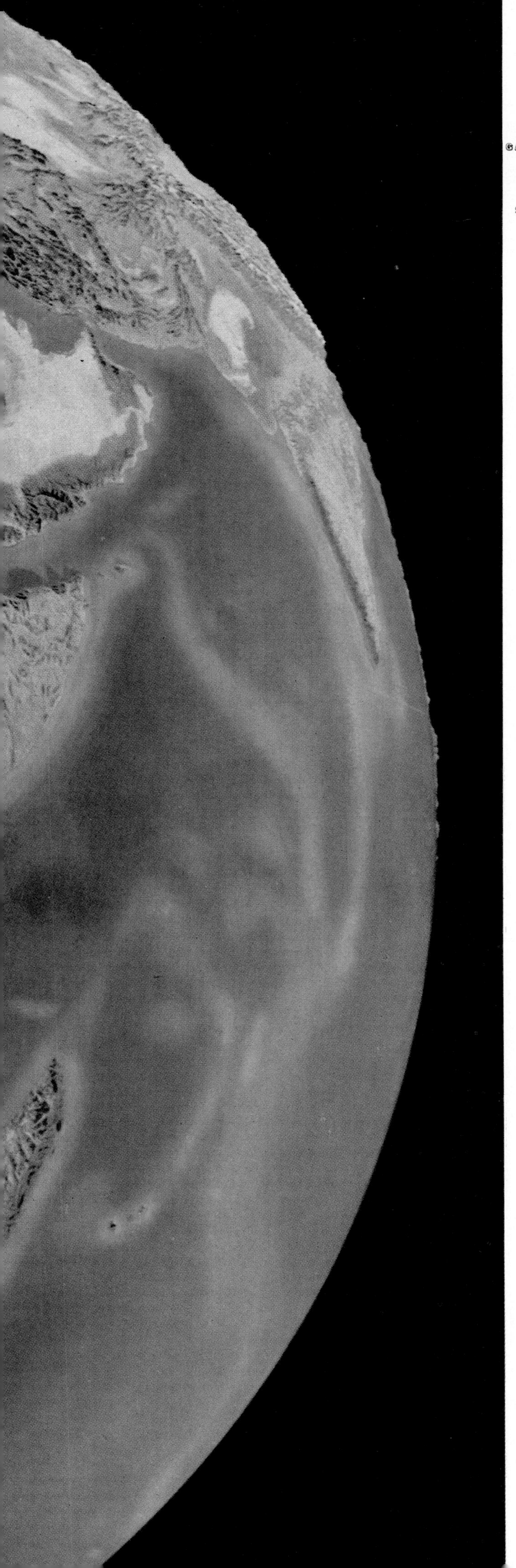

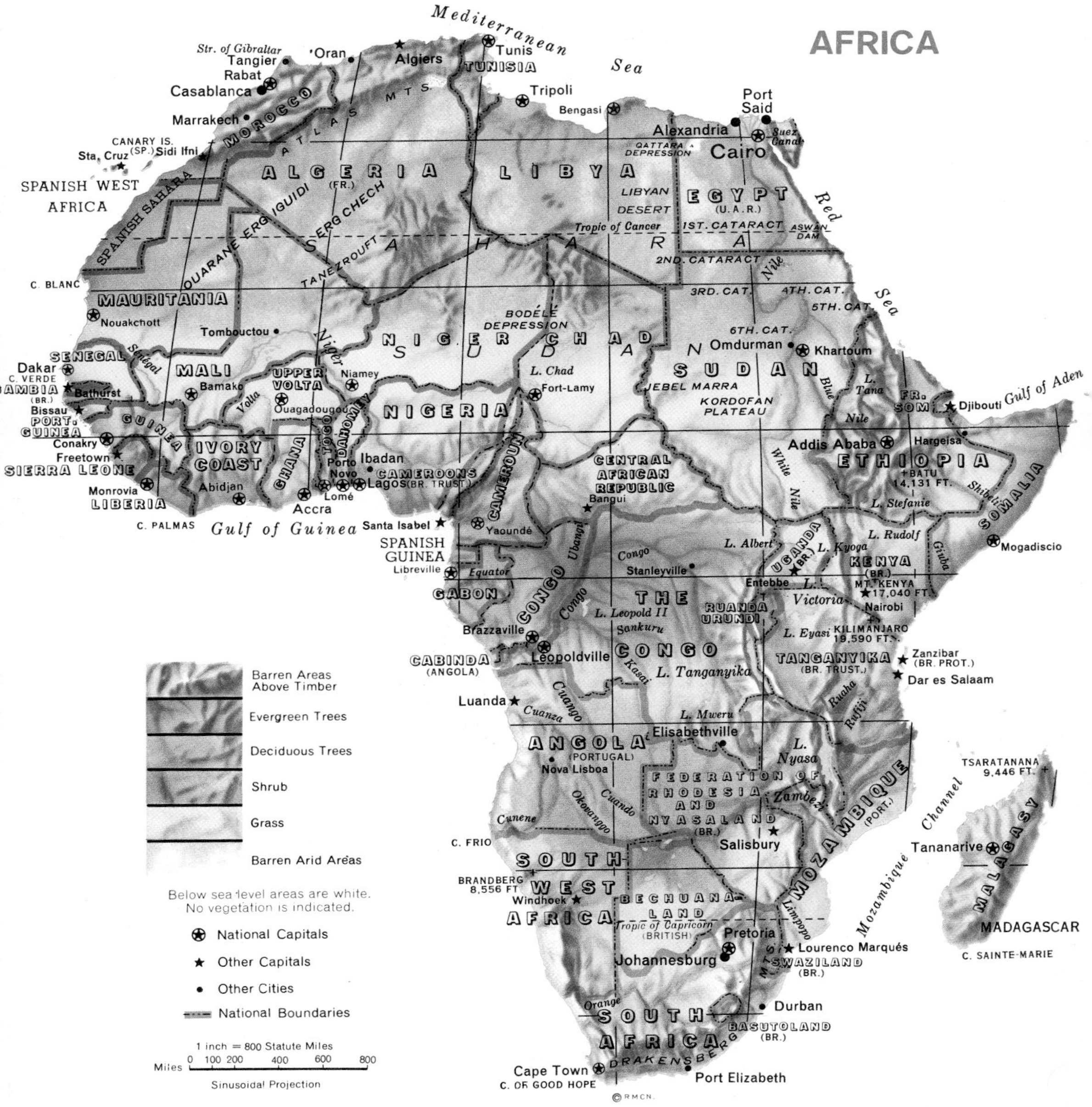

AFRICA

"One's eyes and limbs ache with the sight and the bulk of it," Laurens van der Post, a contemporary explorer of Africa, has written. He found himself "dazzled by this inexhaustible repetition of desert, lake, escarpment, plateau, plain, snow-capped mountain." For over 50 centuries, the eye-filling sight of Africa was denied to outsiders. Maps showed nothing more than a vast coastline; the second largest land mass on earth was an unexplored continent. The northern littoral was invaded by Phoenicians, Greeks, Romans and Turks, and it remains a Mediterranean Africa, altogether different from the violent, primitive land that lies south of the Sahara Desert. In the 15th Century, the caravels of Dias and da Gama sailed around the tip of Africa, but many natural barriers, as stubborn as the Sahara, prevented penetration of the interior. Fevers and steaming climate repelled Europeans as much as the tales of cannibals and dreadful animals. Only in the past century, with the epic explorations of Livingstone, Stanley and Speke, has Africa finally begun to disclose its secrets to the world.

For 70 years the awakening continent was largely held by half a dozen European powers, but by the end of World War II Africa was moving toward independence. Since the war more than 20 new African nations have been established, and Africa is hesitantly entering a world that is in many ways just as mysterious to Africans as their own land was to the early explorers.

AFRICA'S VAST BULK stretches 5,300 miles, from the Strait of Gibraltar *(top, left)* to the Cape of Good Hope in the south. To the east, the scimitar of Somalia cuts under the Arabian Peninsula, and to the west, Cape Verde bulges far out into the Atlantic Ocean.

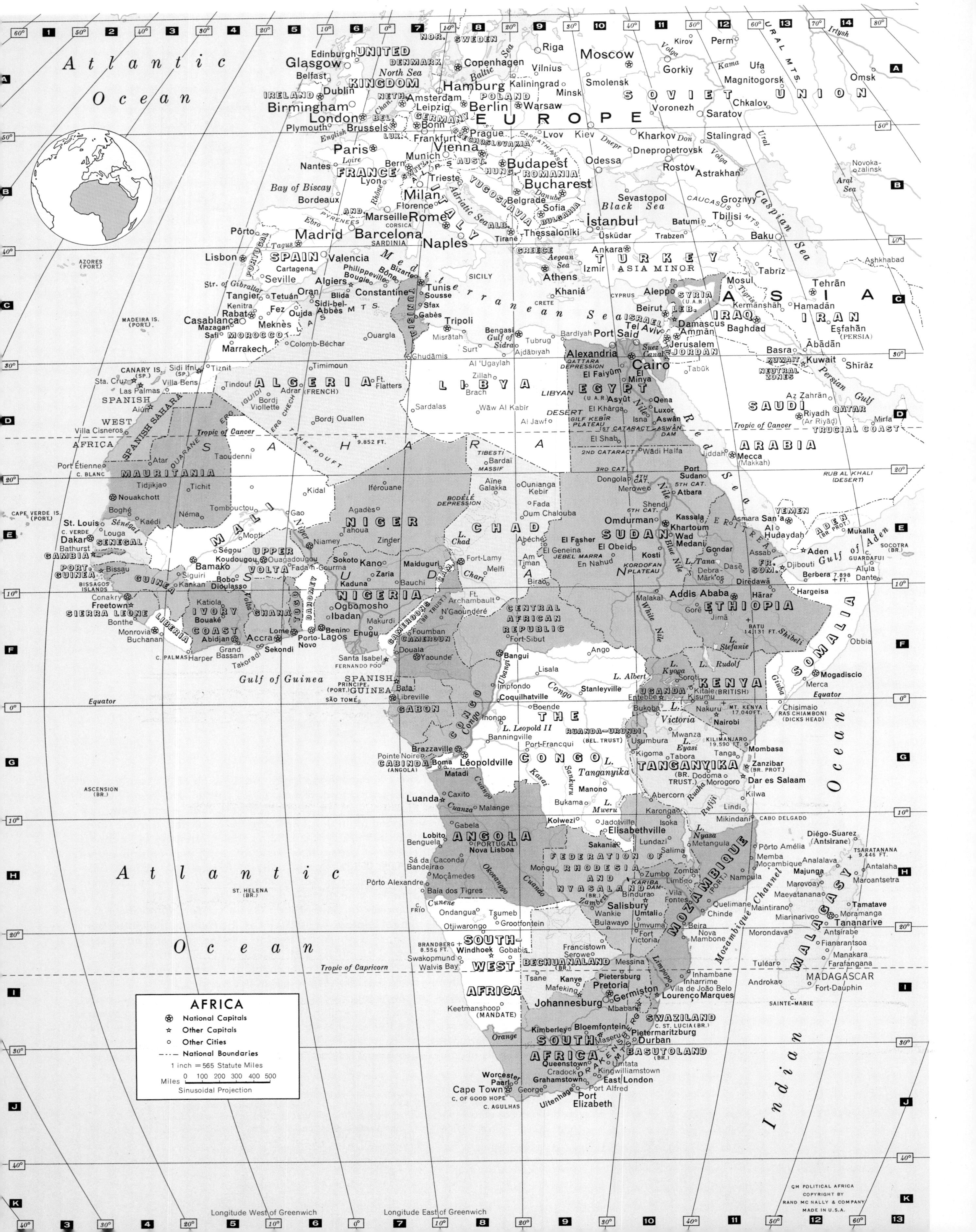
Atlantic Ocean
EUROPE
ASIA
SOVIET UNION
UNITED KINGDOM
IRELAND
FRANCE
SPAIN
ITALY
GERMANY
POLAND
TURKEY
ASIA MINOR
Mediterranean Sea
Black Sea
Caspian Sea
Red Sea
Persian Gulf
Gulf of Aden
Gulf of Guinea
ALGERIA
LIBYA
EGYPT
MOROCCO
TUNISIA
SAHARA
LIBYAN DESERT
SPANISH SAHARA
MAURITANIA
MALI
NIGER
CHAD
SUDAN
ETHIOPIA
SOMALIA
KENYA
UGANDA
TANGANYIKA
NIGERIA
GHANA
IVORY COAST
LIBERIA
SIERRA LEONE
GUINEA
SENEGAL
GAMBIA
UPPER VOLTA
DAHOMEY
TOGO
CAMEROUN
CENTRAL AFRICAN REPUBLIC
GABON
CONGO
THE CONGO
ANGOLA
FEDERATION OF RHODESIA AND NYASALAND
MOZAMBIQUE
MALAGASY
SOUTH-WEST AFRICA
BECHUANALAND
SOUTH AFRICA
BASUTOLAND
SWAZILAND
ARABIA
SAUDI ARABIA
YEMEN
IRAQ
IRAN
SYRIA
JORDAN
ISRAEL
Indian Ocean
Tropic of Cancer
Equator
Tropic of Capricorn
Cairo
Alexandria
Addis Ababa
Khartoum
Nairobi
Léopoldville
Johannesburg
Cape Town
Algiers
Tunis
Tripoli
Dakar
Lagos
Accra
Mogadiscio
Dar es Salaam
Tananarive
Madrid
Paris
London
Rome
Moscow
AFRICA
National Capitals
Other Capitals
Other Cities
National Boundaries
1 inch = 565 Statute Miles
Miles 0 100 200 300 400 500
Sinusoidal Projection
Longitude West of Greenwich
Longitude East of Greenwich
CM POLITICAL AFRICA
COPYRIGHT BY
RAND MC NALLY & COMPANY
MADE IN U.S.A.

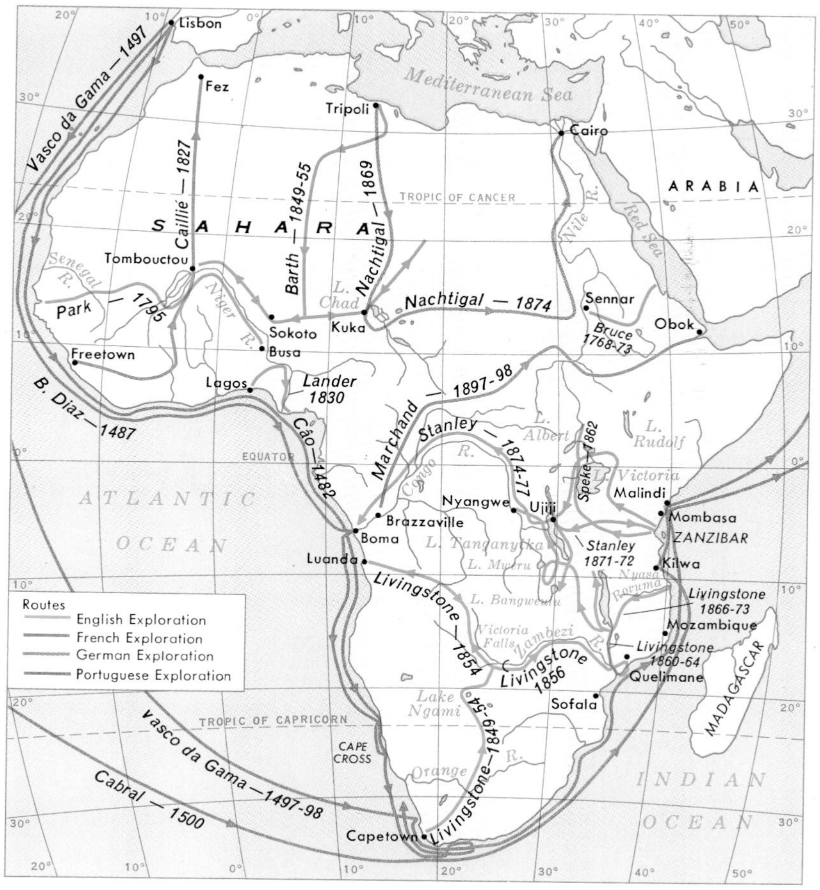

EXPLORATIONS THAT OPENED A CONTINENT

The Mediterranean coast of Africa was explored and settled by the ancient Greeks, Romans and Phoenicians, but the land south of the Sahara, as indicated on this map, was unknown to outsiders until the 15th Century. The Portuguese were the first to circumnavigate the continent. The travels of Mungo Park and James Bruce in the late 18th Century aroused Europe's interest in the Dark Continent. The first methodical probing of the interior got under way in the 19th Century. René Caillié and Heinrich Barth crossed the Sahara, and Livingstone, Nachtigal, Stanley and Speke reached the heart of the continent.

AFRICA: In the Kenya highlands, English gentlemen hunt leopards and elephants under the shadow of snow-mantled Mount Kilimanjaro. In Addis Ababa, tame lions crouch by the throne of an emperor who counts the Queen of Sheba among his ancestors. At the First Cataract of the Nile, perspiring Egyptians labor over the great Aswân High Dam, as their forefathers labored to build the Great Pyramid of Khufu. Platter-lipped matrons gossip in the marketplace of Fort Archambault, in Chad, while 2,288 miles away in the *Médina* of Casablanca, Arab women in veils whisper to each other. A Cairo-bound airliner casts its fleeting shadow on a procession of camels laboring over the dunes of the mid-Sahara. And all of these are Africa.

Africa's 233,719,000 citizens are as variegated as any people on earth. Berbers and Arabs, sons of the wind and sun, predominate in the north; copper-skinned Hamites dwell in the high fastnesses of Ethiopia; medium-height, solemn Bantu cattlemen occupy most of the southern third of the continent; Pygmies live in the vaporous rain forests. The European latecomers to the African scene are a small minority. Population density changes with the land and the climate; it ranges from a teeming 2,000 per square mile in the fruitful Valley of the Nile to lunar emptiness in barren Tanezrouft in the Algerian Sahara. Most of the people live by the soil, though cattle raising is an important livelihood in the grassy uplands and mining predominates in the south. The Industrial Revolution, like the incursion of western civilization, is just beginning to make itself felt.

There are still reminders to be seen of a primitive, barbarous past in Africa, but they are now fading. Cannibalism, widely practiced among certain tribes not long ago, has nearly vanished. The diseases that have immemorially crippled great numbers of Africa's people and kept some of its richest land sparsely populated are yielding to modern medicine. The specters of illiteracy, poverty and superstition that endured over the centuries are now retreating.

AREA: 11,635,000 sq. mi.
POPULATION: 233,719,000.
ALTITUDES: Mt. Kilimanjaro, Tanganyika, 19,590 ft. (highest);
Qattara Depression, Egypt, -436 ft. (lowest);
Mt. Kenya, Kenya, 17,040 ft.;
Mont Tahat in Ahaggar Mountains, Algerian Sahara, 9,852 ft.; Johannesburg, South Africa, 5,689 ft.;
Tombouctou (Timbuktu), Mali, 938 ft.

The land is an almost endless plateau, bounded by narrow, fever-ridden coasts, rain forests and steeply rising grasslands, and occasionally seamed by the valleys of great sluggish rivers. Africa has the world's largest desert, the longest river, the third biggest inland lake. Plunging 350 feet over Victoria Falls, the mighty Zambezi River sends up a plume of mist several hundreds of feet high—the Africans call it "The Smoke Which Sounds"—that can be seen 70 miles away. The largest diamonds ever known have been plucked from the African earth. Birds and beasts that seem fantastic outside Africa inhabit the thick forests and rolling savannas.

Jan Christiaan Smuts, the prescient South African statesman, once characterized his native continent in these eloquent words: "Africa, in spite of all change, will remain Africa, and its most distinctive features among the continents will continue to be its untamed wildness, its aloofness and solitude, and its mysterious, eerie, brooding spirit."

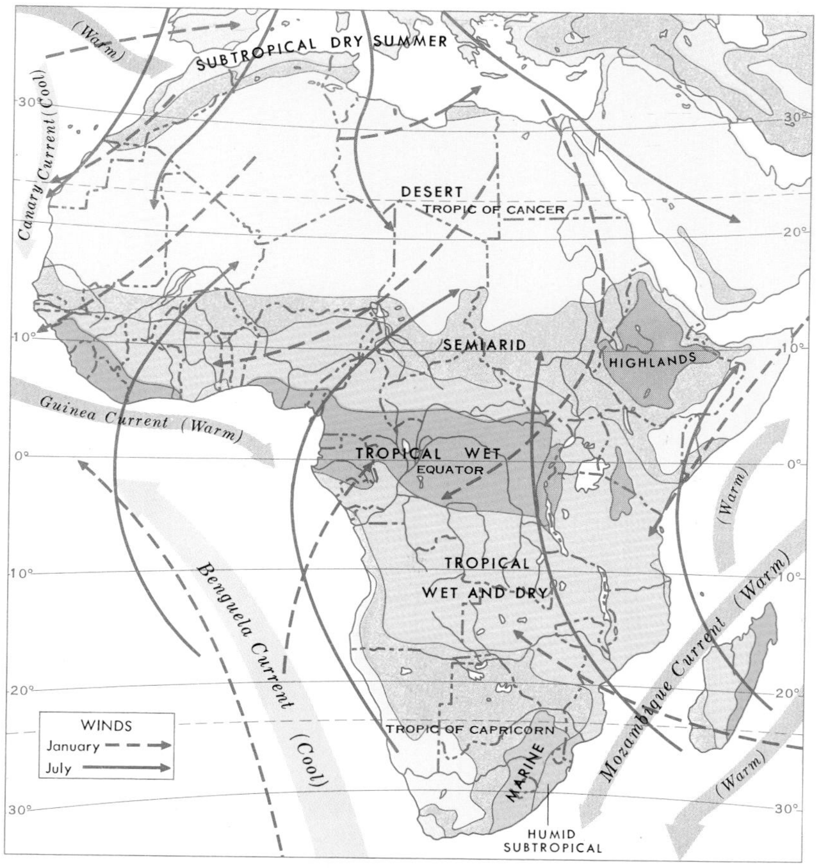

THE CLIMATIC BANDS OF AFRICA

The dunes of the Sahara cover the northern third of Africa; other desert outcroppings, as shown on the map above, exist along the southwest coast and on the horn of Somalia. Surrounding the deserts are wide bands of semiarid land—tufted-grass and scrub country. From Senegal to Zanzibar there is a belt of moist tropical areas, with rain forests along the Congo and the Guinea coast and mixed forests in South Africa. The highlands of Kenya and Ethiopia offer temperate climates, and regions of North Africa—mainly in Morocco and Algeria—and of the Cape of Good Hope are "Mediterranean" areas.

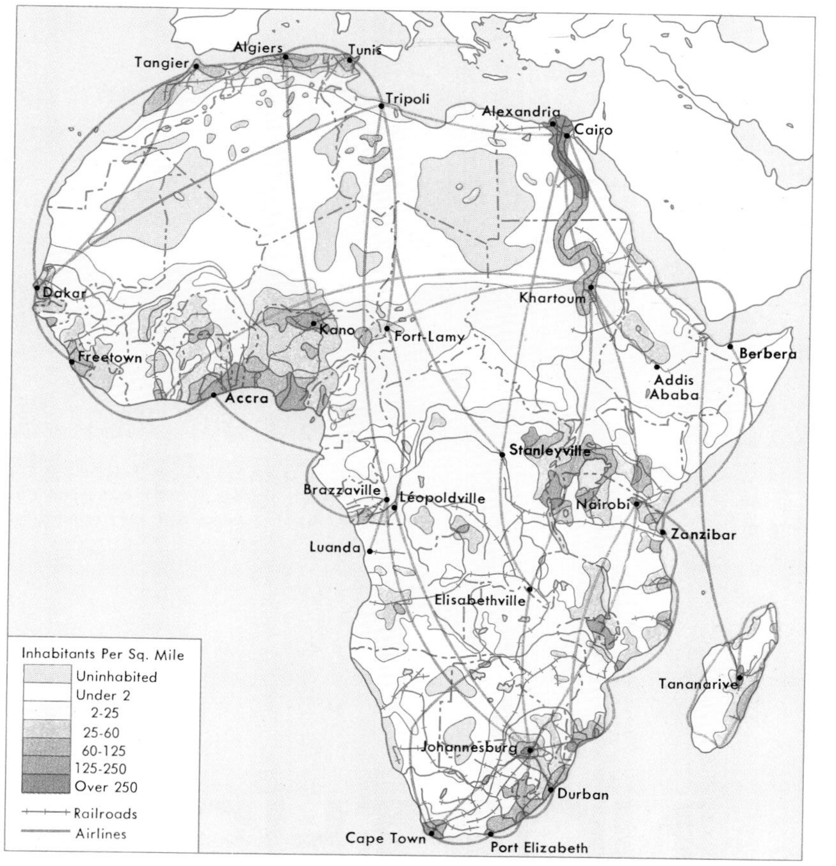

POPULATION AND TRANSPORTATION

As the map above shows, the main centers of population in Africa cluster on the coastal regions of the north, in the Nile valley, around the Niger delta and in the healthy highlands of eastern Africa. The lower Nile valley (near Cairo) is one of the earth's most densely populated regions. Large patches of the Sahara and southwestern Africa are uninhabitable, and the population in the belt across the continent's waist has been held down by the humid climate and the tsetse fly, carrier of sleeping sickness. Railroads *(crosshatched lines)* were introduced by the European colonists. Airlines now connect all leading cities.

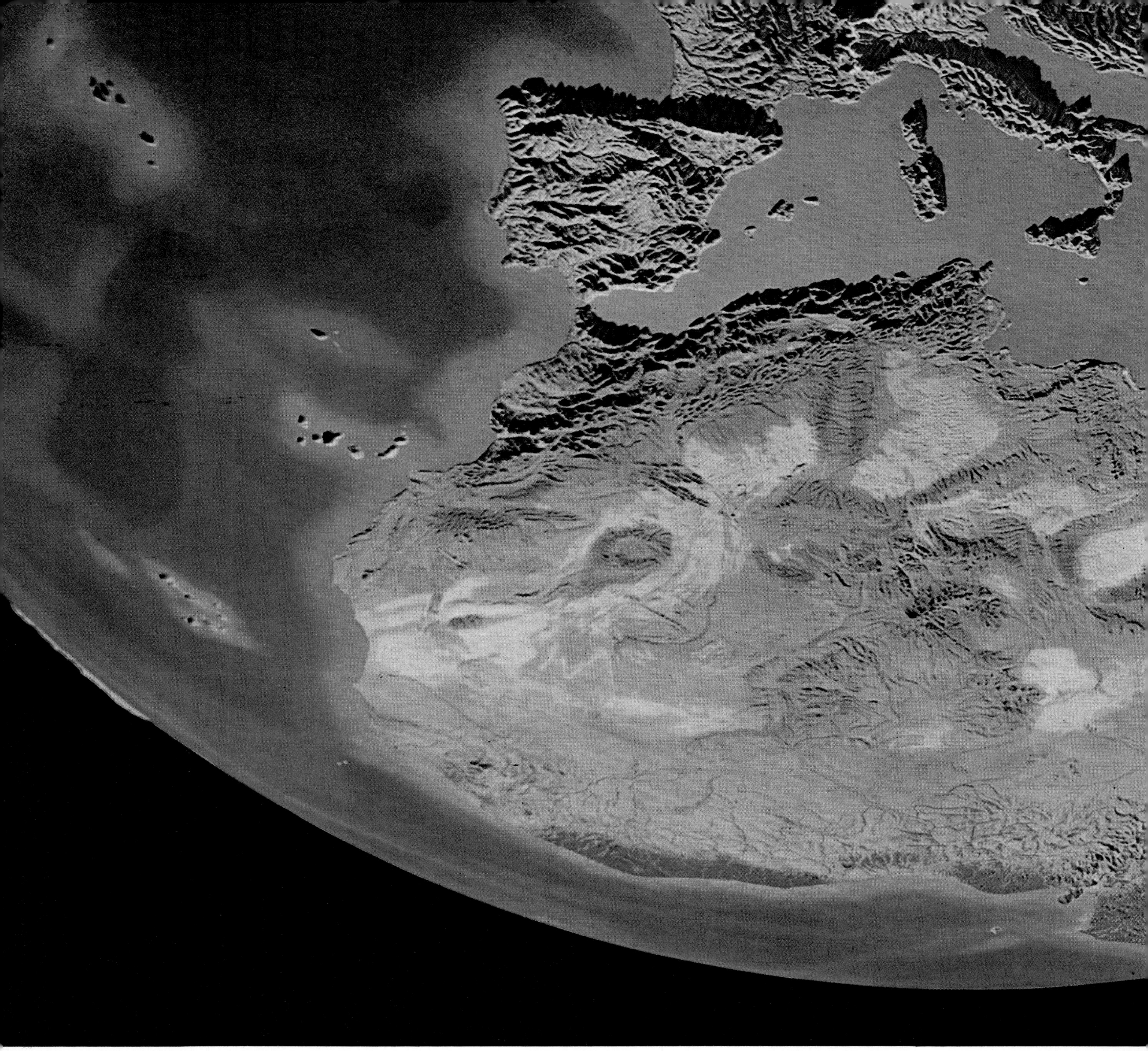

THE AWESOME SAHARA stretches across the width of Northern Africa. The serpentine coastline of the Mediterranean *(top, center)* is the northern border of the region. The Red Sea, at right, marks the beginning of Asia. The Somali peninsula is at the extreme right.

NORTHERN AFRICA

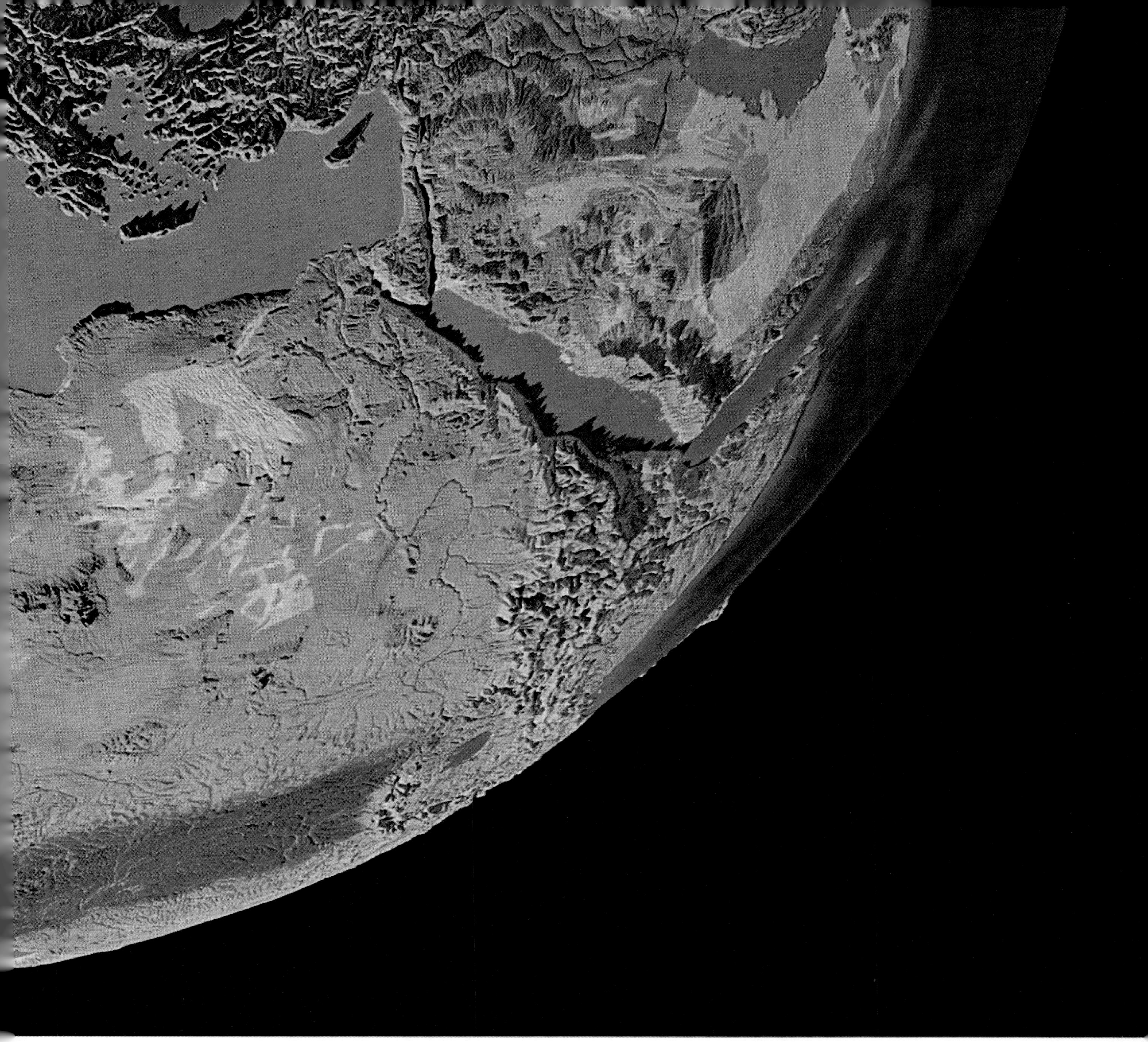

From the Atlantic beaches of Morocco, Northern Africa fans out close to 3,000 miles along the length of the Mediterranean Sea and then along the Red Sea to steaming Somalia on the Indian Ocean, where Cape Guardafui points to the Orient. With the exception of Ethiopia, which is about one half Christian, the nations of Northern Africa are Mohammedan: the western frontier of Islam begins in Morocco at the Pillars of Hercules, which flank the Strait of Gibraltar.

One awesome natural phenomenon dominates all Northern Africa: the vast, empty Sahara, a burning wasteland as large as Australia. Less than a fifth of the Sahara is made up of sand or sand dune *(erg)*; the rest is exposed bedrock *(hamada)* or gravel and small stones *(reg)*. The Sahara affects the lives of all who inhabit its fringes. The world's largest desert forms an immense curtain of sand and stone between Northern Africa and the rest of the continent. At the eastern limit of the Sahara, the Nile–the world's longest river and a geographical wonder as impressive as the Sahara–has carved out a fertile valley that sustains over 25 million people. The lofty Atlas range of Morocco and Algeria at the northwestern extremity of the region, the Ethiopian highlands in the southeast, and the Ahaggar and Tibesti Mountains of the Sahara are the only mountains of Northern Africa. Between them lies a huge, barren plateau.

But Northern Africa is not all wasteland. Many of the continent's great cities are here: Alexandria, Cairo, Algiers, Casablanca and Tunis. The land throbs with history, and the names–Carthage, Thebes, El Alamein, the Barbary Coast, Tangier–conjure up the spectacle of a colorful, often tragic past. All of the countries are accessible from the sea–an invitation to invasion–and over the centuries Northern Africa has heard the cadenced beat of marching feet, from Caesar's legions to the troops of Napoleon; more recently, its soil has shuddered under the motorized columns of Rommel's Afrika Korps and of the Americans from across the Atlantic. The North Africans themselves have been invaders, too. The Alpine adventures of the Carthaginian Hannibal and his elephants and the invasion of Spain by the Berber leader Tarik, which led to the domination of Spain for nearly 800 years, were military epics. But through most of its history Northern Africa has been the battleground rather than the springboard for invasion.

MAN-MADE MOUNTAINS AGAINST THE EGYPTIAN SKY

IN THE PURPLISH DUSK, the pyramids of El Giza rise from a rocky plateau of the Western (Libyan) Desert of Egypt. These tremendous tombs were built nearly 5,000 years ago by three pharaohs: Khufu, Khaf-Re and Men-kau-Re. In the foreground, shadowy in the fading light, lies the great commercial and financial center of modern Cairo, built on the ancient farmlands of the Nile delta. The dome of the University of Cairo is at the center. With 2.5 million inhabitants, Cairo is the largest Arab city and the largest African metropolis.

LIBYA

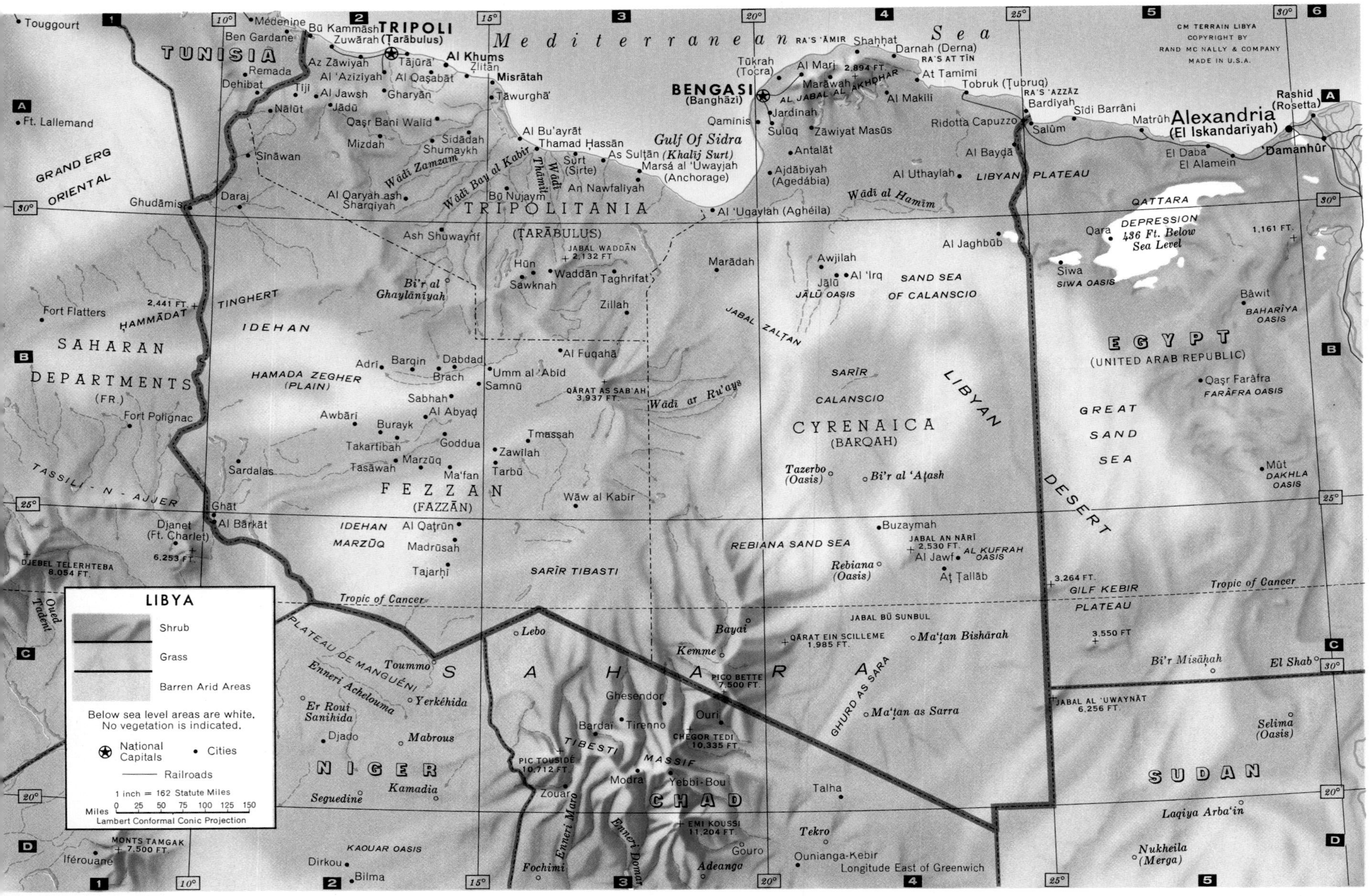

LIBYA: Most of Libya is a sun-scorched wasteland. The countryside around Tripoli, one of the two capitals of Libya, is a dazzling vivid green, but scarcely 25 miles from the city limits temperatures have been recorded as high as 136°F., the highest in Africa. The gibleh, the killing wind that blows in from the Sahara, withers all growth except olive trees and date palms. Only in the two constricted coastal strips of Tripolitania and Cyrenaica and in a few widely scattered oases of the Fezzan and the Libyan Desert is life supportable. One fourth of the people are nomads or seminomads; the others are clustered around Tripoli and Bengasi. Since 1959, oil has been discovered at several inland sites and production is under way.

AREA: 679,358 sq. mi.
POPULATION: 1,200,000.
Largest city: Tripoli. Capitals: Tripoli, Bengasi.
CLIMATE: Hot summers, mild winters; dry all year.
ALTITUDES: Picco Bette, 7,500 ft. (highest); Tripoli, 35 ft.; Bengasi, 45 ft.

The two fertile coastal areas of Libya differ in their historical heritage: Tripolitania was once a Phoenician stronghold; Cyrenaica was an outpost of Greece. The separation of the two is perpetuated by 300 miles of trackless desert which stretches along the shores of the Gulf of Sidra.

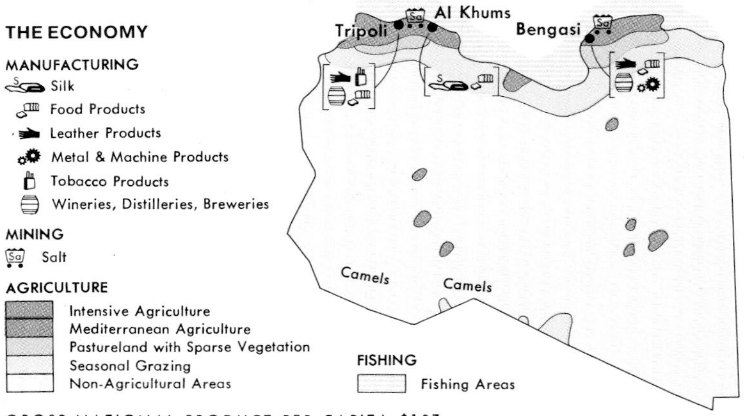

GROSS NATIONAL PRODUCT PER CAPITA $107

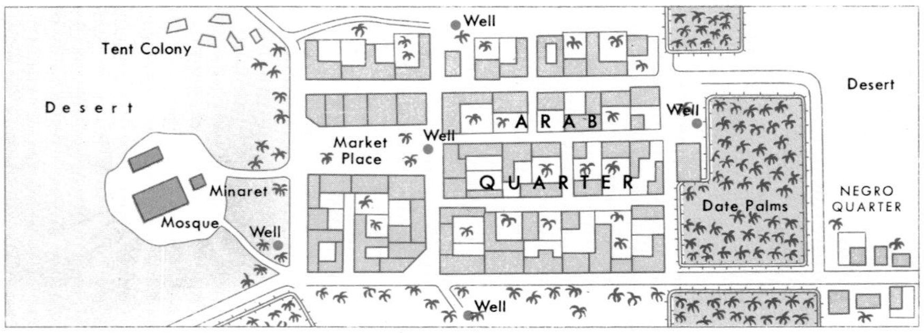

A WALLED TOWN IN THE DESERT

The layout of a Libyan village is shown in this drawing. In the outskirts are the tents of nomadic shepherds *(top left)*. The Mohammedan mosque and the Arab quarter are separated from the Negro quarter *(right)* by date palm groves *(green)*. Wells are the key to life in this settlement adjacent to the desert.

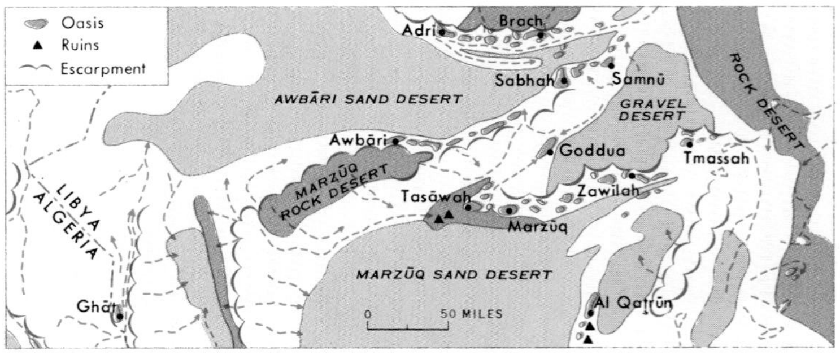

GREEN LINES IN WASTES OF ROCK AND SAND

This map shows oases which are the centers of life in Fezzan, Libya's arid southwestern province. They are strung along the dry river beds into which the rare desert rains flow *(dotted arrows)*. Ruins nearby indicate that the watercourse pattern has been the same for centuries.

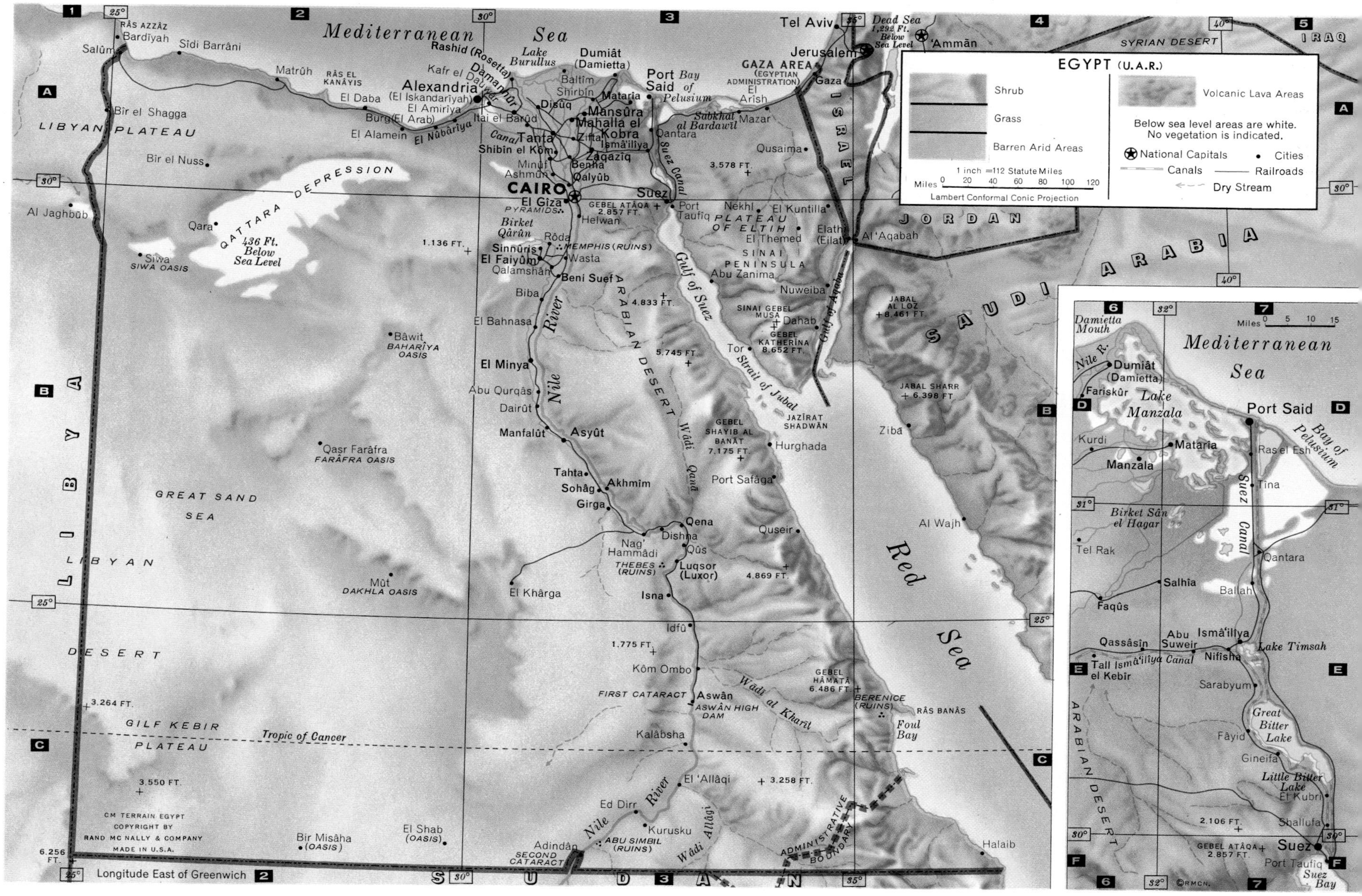

EGYPT (U.A.R.): "There, an arid waste, lies a desert: on either hand it rises, and between the heights lies wonderland. To the west, the range forms a chain of sand hills; to the east, it looks like the belly of a lean horse or a camel's back. This, O Ruler of the Faithful, is Egypt. But all its wealth comes from the blessed river that moves through it with the dignity of a caliph." Thus the Arab general Amr ibn el As described Egypt in the Seventh Century. The description would have been appropriate for Egypt 3,000 years earlier—and 1,300 years later. The Nile River *is* Egypt. Ninety-five per cent of the people live on the banks of the Nile; the ancient Nilotic civilization, the splendor of Egypt's past and the aspirations of the future are all closely associated with this great stream.

Modern Egypt, major partner in the United Arab Republic, has a limited industrial potential, though there is some oil along the shores of the Red Sea and iron ore at Aswân. Long-staple cotton and rice are grown for export. The Aswân Dam, built in 1902, permits perennial irrigation, but it also prevents the nourishing silting that once came with the spring floods, and the land grows less productive. A new Aswân High Dam, to be completed around 1970, will increase Egypt's arable land by 30 per cent.

AREA: 386,100 sq. mi.
POPULATION: 25,313,000. Largest city and capital: Cairo. U.A.R. capital: Cairo.
CLIMATE: Hot summers, mild winters; dry all year.
ALTITUDES: Gebel Katherina, 8,652 ft. (highest); Cairo, 98 ft.

The Suez Canal is another waterway that has played a vital role both in world history and in recent Egyptian history. Built by Europeans nearly a century ago and nationalized in 1956, the "big ditch" is still an indispensable short cut for sea-borne commerce between Europe and the Far East.

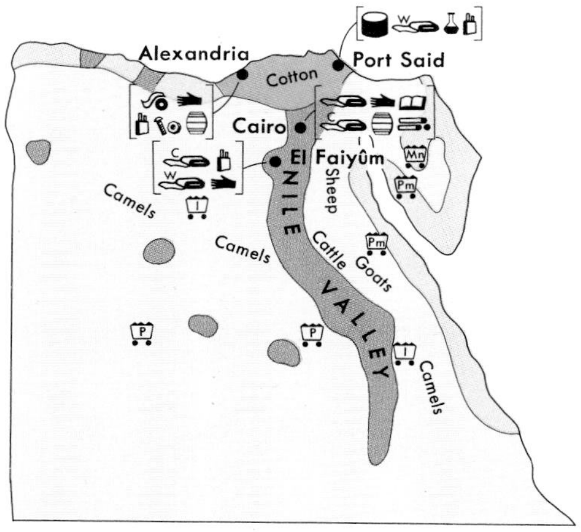

THE ECONOMY

MANUFACTURING
- Chemicals
- Textiles
- Cotton
- Wool
- Printing & Publishing
- Wood Products
- Leather Products
- Paper Products
- Metal Products
- Petroleum Refining
- Tobacco Products
- Wineries, Distilleries, Breweries

MINING
- Iron Ore
- Manganese
- Phosphate
- Petroleum

AGRICULTURE
- Intensive Agriculture
- Mediterranean Agriculture
- Plantation Agriculture
- Seasonal Grazing
- Non-Agricultural Areas

GROSS NATIONAL PRODUCT PER CAPITA $136

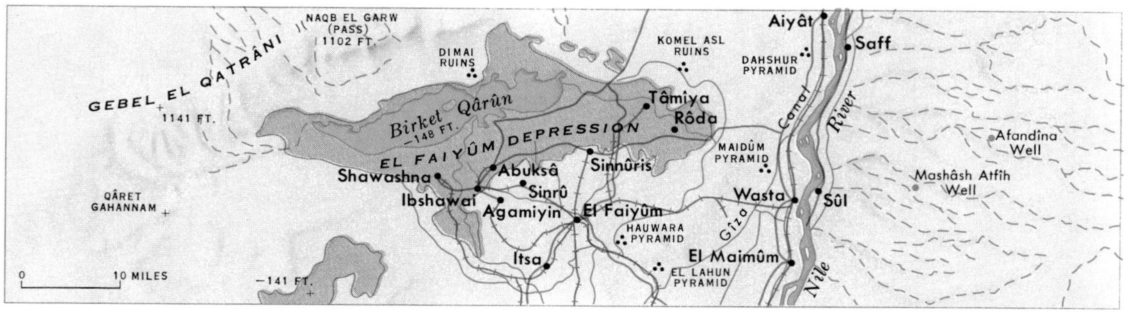

A FERTILE VALLEY FED BY THE NILE

Lying far below sea level, Egypt's El Faiyûm area *(map above)* is enriched by soil carried by Nile floods. The central lake of Birket Qârûn was used as a reservoir for flood waters, which were redistributed through canals in drought times. Modernized, some of the canals are still used in the El Faiyûm irrigation system *(solid blue lines)*. The area is an important producer of cotton, wheat, corn and rice.

VOLCANIC LAKES IN ETHIOPIA

THE COLLAPSED CONES of a volcanic range encircle lakes and swamps in Ethiopia. At the upper right is the 9,808-foot volcano of Zik'Wala. This region, not far from the capital of Addis Ababa, is in the central highlands, where farmers grow cereal crops in a primitive patchwork pattern of shifting cultivation. As their methods overwork the ground and erode it, the Ethiopians simply abandon the worn-out fields and move.

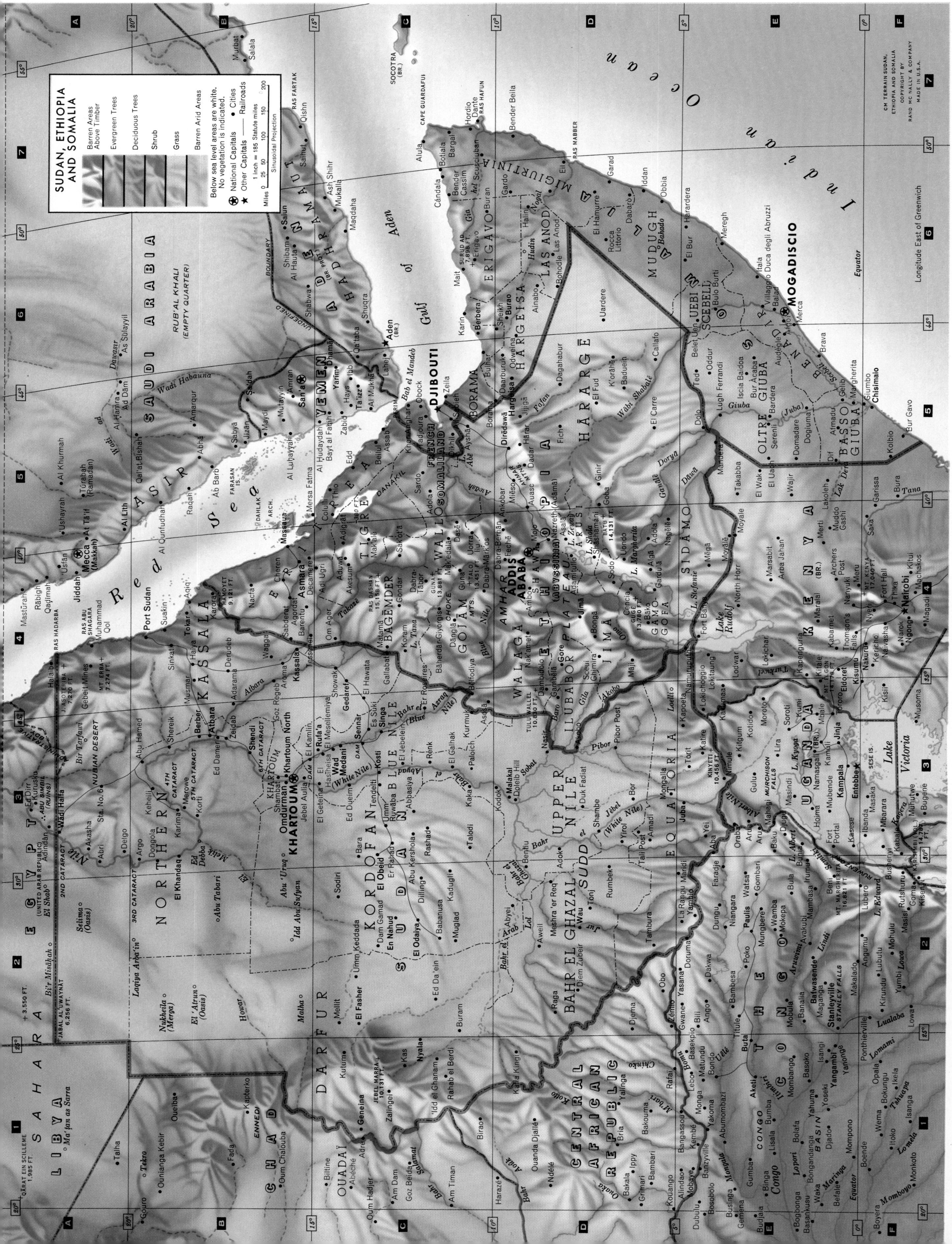
SUDAN, ETHIOPIA AND SOMALIA
Barren Areas Above Timber
Evergreen Trees
Deciduous Trees
Shrub
Grass
Barren Arid Areas
Below sea level areas are white.
No vegetation is indicated.
National Capitals
Cities
Other Capitals
Railroads
1 Inch = 185 Statute miles
Sinusoidal Projection
Longitude East of Greenwich
CM TERRAIN SUDAN, ETHIOPIA AND SOMALIA
COPYRIGHT BY RAND MC NALLY & COMPANY
MADE IN U.S.A.

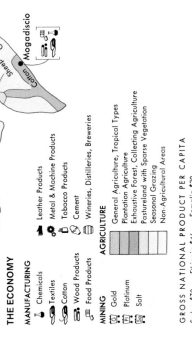

SUDAN: ". . . the north is dry, while the south is wet; the north is yellow, while the south is green." Thus a onetime British governor describes this transition area between the north and south of the Sahara. A clay plain bounded by uplands, with a huge desert to the north, Sudan covers nearly 10 per cent of the land surface of Africa. From the Egyptian border almost to Khartoum, the capital, it is desert. Here, Arab-speaking Moslem nomads drive their camels across the ancient trade routes. South of the meeting point of two rivers (the White and Blue Nile), the farmers raise cotton, millet, corn and peanuts. In the dry north there are gazelles, jackals, foxes, hyenas, sand grouse and vultures. Southward, beyond Khartoum, there are crocodiles, hippopotamuses, buffaloes, elephants, antelopes and giraffes.

Sudan's big industry is the Gezira irrigation project, which got under way in 1925. Watered by canals fed by the dammed reservoir at Sennar, Gezira produces a million acres of cotton, millet and beans. Gezira provides more than half of the government's total revenue; the Sudan Railways, which transport the cotton crop to the coast, provide most of the rest.

From the acacia trees of Kordofan province, west of Khartoum, comes most (over 85 per cent) of the world's gum arabic. Much of Sudan's land in the deep south is infested with the tsetse fly and is liable to flooding. However, a reservoir created by Egypt's Aswân High Dam will extend down to the third cataract on the Nile—roughly 150 miles into Sudan—and will double the area the country will be able to put under cultivation.

AREA: 967,248 sq. mi.
POPULATION: 11,549,000. Largest city and capital: Khartoum.
CLIMATE: Hot throughout year; generally dry throughout year in northern regions, summer rainfall in south.
ALTITUDES: Kinyeti, 10,456 ft. (highest); Khartoum, 1,252 ft.

ETHIOPIA: Mountainous Ethiopia, inhabited by a practical and independent people, has been isolated from outside influences for centuries by deserts to the north, east and west. The land divides into three distinct climatic regions, each with its own agricultural uses. The *dega*—steep, chilly (50°-61°F.) slopes of over 8,000 feet—is mostly grassland used for livestock and production of cereal grains. The *voina dega*—from 6,000 to 8,000 feet in altitude and with temperatures of 61°-68°F.—contains most of the country's population and produces the major cash crop, coffee, as well as cotton, tobacco, grapes and olives. The *quolla*—everything below 6,000 feet—includes such arid spots as the Danikil lowlands, a sea of yellow sand stretching northeast into Eritrea beside the Red Sea, and the lower reaches of the Ogaden Plateau in Hārargē province. Amid withered thorn trees and scorched stream beds in the *quolla*, nomads wander with sheep, goats and camels.

With few minerals discovered and none developed to any extent, Ethiopia's main export is one that produces no direct cash income—the waters of the Blue Nile, which sweep in a great curve from the river's source at Lake Tana, tumble down plateau after plateau and flow west to provide rich, well-irrigated soil for the farmers of Sudan and Egypt.

AREA: 457,147 sq. mi.
POPULATION: 21,351,000. Largest city and capital: Addis Ababa.
CLIMATE: Generally hot throughout year, cooler in highlands; dry winters, moderately wet summers throughout.
ALTITUDES: Rāsdajan, 15,158 ft. (highest); Addis Ababa, 7,749 ft.

SOMALIA: Somalia has an average annual rainfall of only 11 inches. It has a strategic location on the eastern hook of Africa, south of the Red Sea, but the main harbor, at Mogadiscio, is so blocked by sandbars that even coastal vessels must lighter their cargoes to shore through a crashing surf. Roughly 75 per cent of the people are pastoral nomads. Between the Juba and Wābi Shabalē Rivers a tiny export crop of bananas is grown, in addition to some cotton, millet and sugar cane. Somalia supplies 60 per cent of the world's frankincense and myrrh.

AREA: 246,137 sq. mi.
POPULATION: 2,047,000. Largest city and capital: Mogadiscio.
CLIMATE: Hot and dry throughout year.
ALTITUDES: Surud Ad, 7,898 ft. (highest); Mogadiscio, 27 ft.

FRENCH SOMALILAND: The most valuable asset of French Somaliland, the bulk of which is an extension of Ethiopia's Danakil desert, is its port, Djibouti, but the only product available for export in commercial quantity is salt.

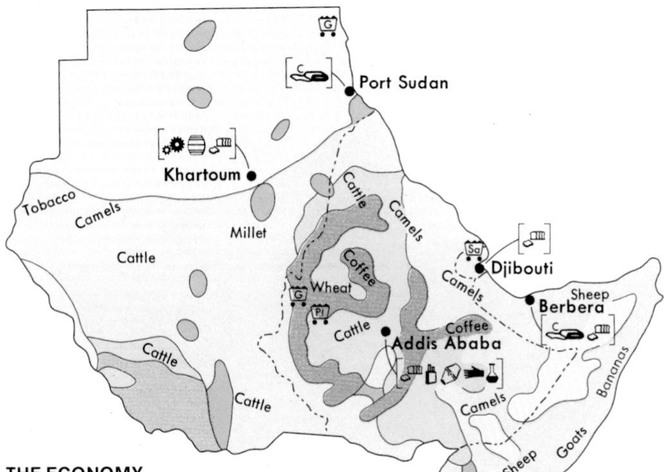

THE ECONOMY

MANUFACTURING
Chemicals
Textiles
Cotton
Wood Products
Food Products
Leather Products
Metal & Machine Products
Tobacco Products
Cement
Wineries, Distilleries, Breweries

MINING
Gold
Platinum
Salt

AGRICULTURE
General Agriculture, Tropical Types
Plantation Agriculture
Exhaustive Forest, Collecting Agriculture
Pastureland with Sparse Vegetation
Seasonal Grazing
Non-Agricultural Areas

GROSS NATIONAL PRODUCT PER CAPITA
Sudan $70 Ethiopia $46 Somalia $39

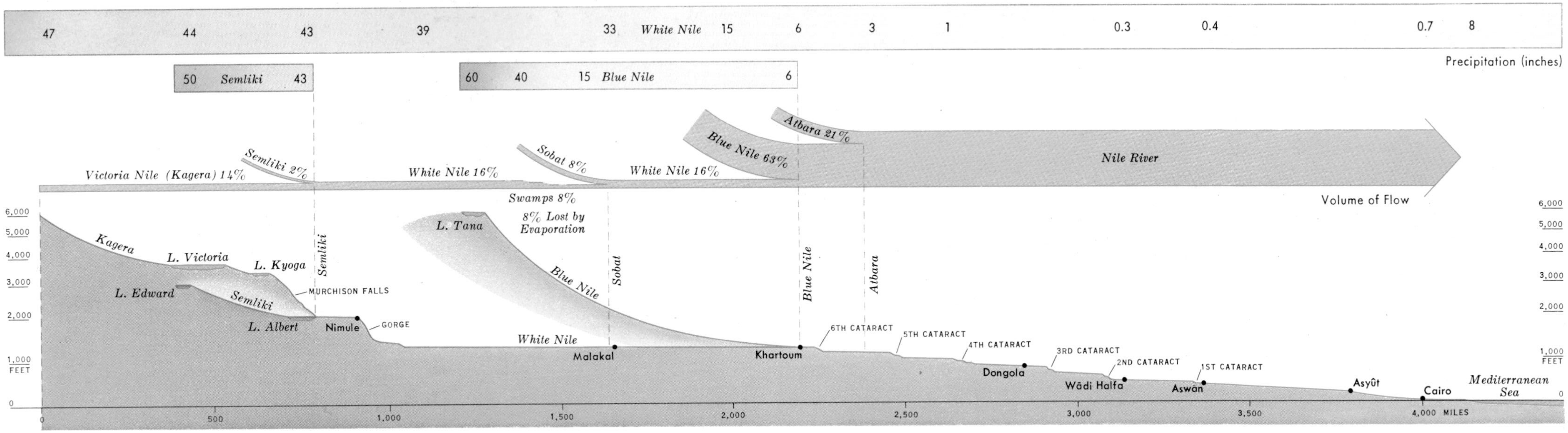

THE NILE'S LONG JOURNEY

The path of the Nile, longest river in the world (4,132 miles), is traced in the diagram above. For 40 per cent of its length the Nile has no tributaries, so its water level and rate of flow are largely determined by the rainfall in the highlands of Ethiopia, where the Blue Nile originates *(center left)*. The blue band at top gives the average annual rainfall along the river's course. The green band at the middle of the diagram shows the principal tributaries and how much water they supply. The blue and gray sketch at bottom is a cross section showing how the river steps down from 6,000 feet to sea level. The White Nile, one of the two main branches, begins in Lake Victoria *(far left)*, which has three big tributaries, including the Kagera River. Fed by the Semliki River, the White Nile drops nearly a thousand feet in 750 miles before it is joined by the Sobat near Malakal. Here the rivers overflow their banks in the rainy season, backwashing and replenishing the swamps created by earlier floodings. As much as 8 per cent of the water evaporates in this area, in effect canceling out the Sobat's contribution. Below Khartoum *(center)*, the river is joined by its other major branch, the Blue Nile, which rises in Lake Tana in Ethiopia. Floodwaters originating in this region are the chief source for the Egyptian-Sudan irrigation system. In addition to being indispensable as a provider of irrigation waters, the Nile for centuries has been an important highway. It is navigable for 960 miles inland from the Mediterranean, up to the second of its six tumbling cataracts.

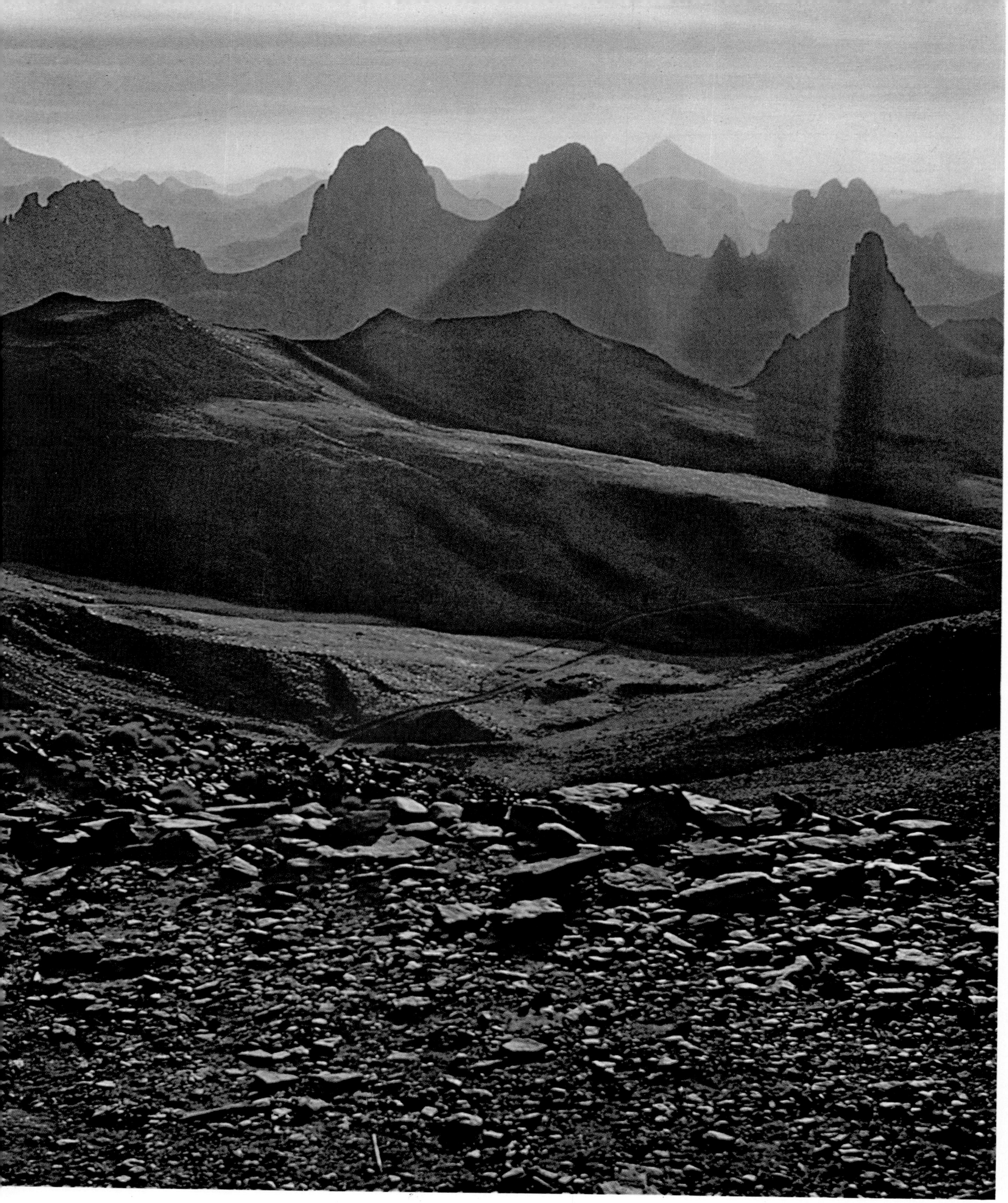

FANTASY AND FUNCTION IN NORTH AFRICA

A GEOLOGIC NIGHTMARE, the Ahaggar massif in the Sahara region of southeast Algeria is a volcanic upland that rises to almost 10,000 feet. It consists of large areas of broken ground, massive boulders and bare outcrops of rock carved by wind and sand into weird pinnacles and parapets. In parts of this most unpromising landscape, hardy Tuareg nomads raise livestock.

A CUBISTIC MAZE, the old Arab quarter of Sousse in Tunisia borders the modern port area built by the French along the peerlessly blue Mediterranean. The thick walls, the small windows and the narrow, blue-painted courts of the Arab buildings all have a function: to offset the withering heat of North Africa. Sousse's principal industry is the milling of olive oil for export.

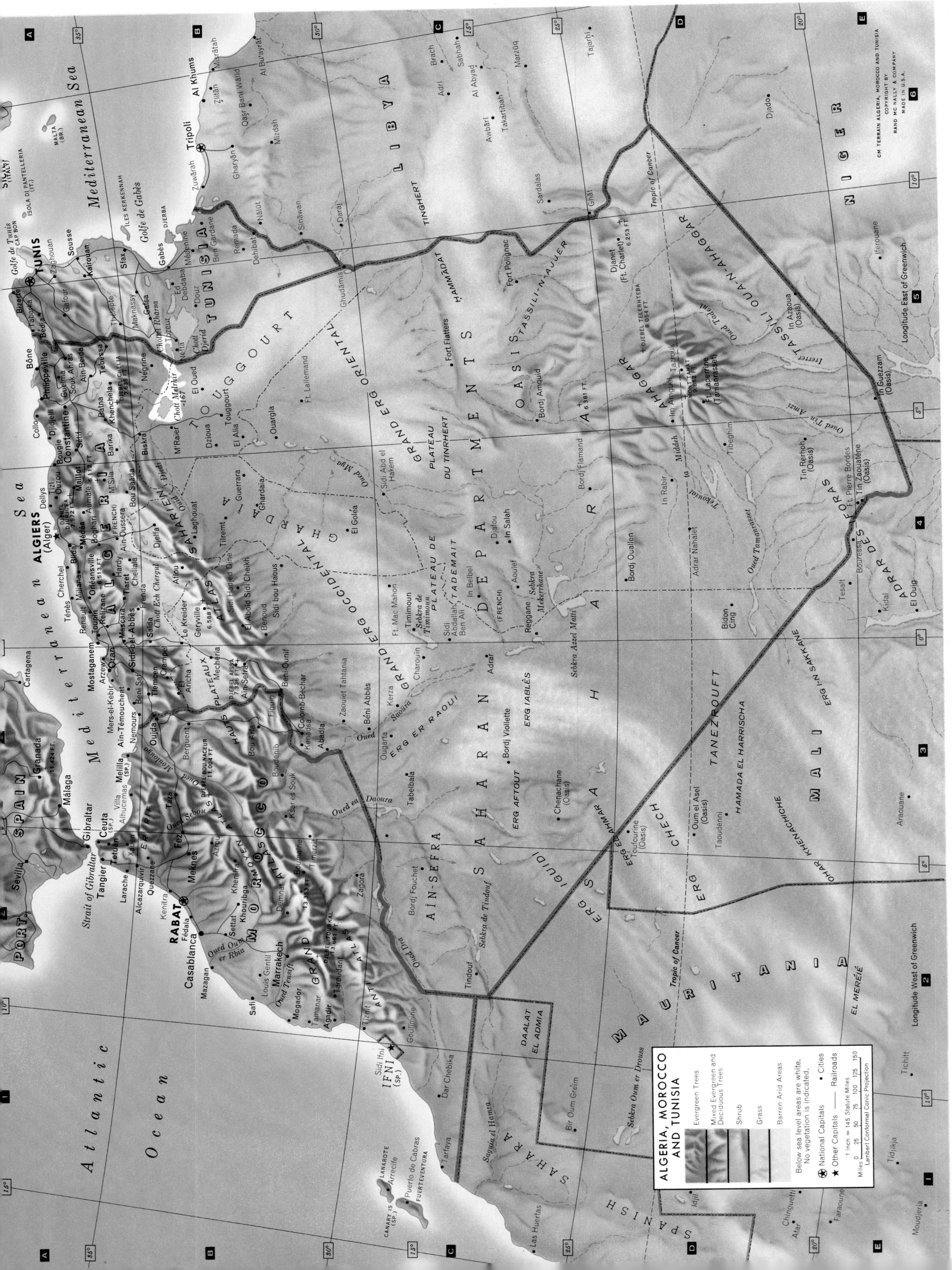

ALGERIA, MOROCCO AND TUNISIA
Evergreen Trees
Mixed Evergreen and Deciduous Trees
Shrub
Grass
Barren Arid Areas
Below sea level areas are white. No vegetation is indicated.
National Capitals
Other Capitals
Cities
Railroads
1 inch = 145 Statute Miles
Miles 0 25 50 75 100 125 150
Lambert Conformal Conic Projection
CM TERRAIN ALGERIA, MOROCCO AND TUNISIA
COPYRIGHT BY RAND MC NALLY & COMPANY
MADE IN U.S.A.
Longitude West of Greenwich
Longitude East of Greenwich
Tropic of Cancer
Atlantic Ocean
Mediterranean Sea
SPAIN
PORT.
MOROCCO
ALGERIA
TUNISIA
LIBYA
NIGER
MALI
MAURITANIA
SPANISH SAHARA
IFNI (SP.)
SAHARAN DEPARTMENTS (FRENCH)
CANARY IS. (SP.)
LANAROTE
FUERTEVENTURA
Arrecife
Puerto de Cabras
MALTA (BR.)
ISOLA DI PANTELLERIA (IT.)
Strait of Gibraltar
Golfe de Tunis
Golfe de Gabès
ILES KERKENNAH
DJERBA
ALGIERS (Alger)
RABAT
TUNIS
Tripoli
Casablanca
Marrakech
Fez
Meknes
Tangier
Gibraltar
Ceuta (SP.)
Melilla (SP.)
Oran
Constantine
Bône
Bizerte
Sousse
Sfax
Gabès
Al Khums
Misrātah
Sevilla
Málaga
Granada
Cartagena
GRAND ATLAS
ANTI ATLAS
MOYEN ATLAS
ER RIF
HAUTS PLATEAUX
SAHARIEN ATLAS
GRAND ERG OCCIDENTAL
GRAND ERG ORIENTAL
ERG ER RAOUI
ERG IGUIDI
ERG CHECH
TANEZROUFT
AHAGGAR
TASSILI-N-AJJER
TASSILI OUAN-AHAGGAR
ADRAR DES IFORAS
PLATEAU DU TINRHERT
PLATEAU DU TADEMAIT
HAMADA EL HARRISCHA
HAMMĀDAT TINGHERT
AÏN-SEFRA
OASIS
TOUGGOURT
GHARDAÏA
EL MEREÏÉ
DAALAT EL ADMIA
Saguia el Hamra
Tindouf
Colomb-Bechar
Ouargla
El Goléa
Laghouat
Biskra
Adrar
In Salah
Reggane
Timimoun
Tamanrasset
Djanet
Fort Polignac
Ghudāmis
Ghāt
Bordj Flamand
Taoudenni
Araouane
Tichitt
Tarfaya
Atar
JEBEL TOUBKAL 13,661 FT.

ALGERIA: The ranges of the Atlas Mountains divide northern Algeria into the Tell, a sun-dappled coastal strip, and the steppes, a high, dry plateau. The valleys and hillsides of the Tell are filled with vineyards, orange groves and orchards of fig and olive trees. In the more arid steppes, esparto grass, used to make fine paper, is grown, and goats, sheep and camels are bred.

Algiers, the capital, is a dazzling white city and a busy seaport. This cosmopolitan crossroads of east and west is, much like San Francisco, perched on hills; the scent of Paris lingers in its boulevards, shops and cafes, and mingles with the mysteries of Arabia in the tortured byways of the famous Casbah.

Agriculture and stock raising are the foundations of the Algerian economy. Rich deposits of iron are mined in the hills near the Tunisian border, but other essential minerals are of poor quality and the outlook for industrialization is dim.

The Saharan Departments are a desolate stretch of desert from cultivated Algeria to the savanna belt of North Africa. This desert is the home of nomads who live on oases in the midst of fierce heat and misty mirages. Since World War II, it has been extensively developed by France both for its oil fields and as an atomic testing site.

AREA: 919,352 sq. mi.
POPULATION: 10,648,000. Capital: Algiers.
CLIMATE: Hot summers, mild winters; interior dry all year, moderate winter rainfall along coast.
ALTITUDES: Mt. Tahat, 9,852 ft. (highest); Djebel Djurjura, 7,572 ft.

MOROCCO: Homeland of the proud and independent Berbers and the westernmost outpost of Islam, Morocco has had a turbulent history. Across the Strait of Gibraltar lies Europe, and Morocco has served as a staging area for two major assaults on that continent: the Moorish invasion of Spain in the Eighth Century and the Allied landings in World War II. In the south the desert intrudes, but the Atlantic coastal valleys resemble California; and the green wheat and barley fields of the northwest could fit comfortably into the Great Plains of the United States. The Atlas Mountains dominate most of the country, their snowy peaks rising over 13,000 feet. The Riff Mountains, the immemorial refuge of pirates, bandits and rebels, plunge to the Mediterranean shore.

Diverse crops–cereals, citrus fruit, cork, olives–provide a livelihood for two thirds of Morocco's people. Some of the world's largest phosphate reserves and the most important hard coal deposits in the Mediterranean area are in Morocco. Sardine fishing now provides a more lucrative income for the country's seagoing men than piracy did for their Barbary ancestors.

AREA: 170,382 sq. mi.
POPULATION: 10,165,000. Capital: Rabat.
CLIMATE: Hot summers, mild winters; moderate winter rainfall along the coast, interior dry all year.
ALTITUDES: Djebel Toubkal, 13,661 ft. (highest).

TUNISIA: The Romans called the place Africa, and in time the name was applied to the entire continent. Under another name, Tunisia was a world power, but all that remains of mighty Carthage today are some broken columns and rubble near the modern city of Tunis. Situated midway between Gibraltar and Suez, Tunisia is divided by the Atlas Mountains. The southern two fifths of the country is a burning plain that joins the Sahara. The north is an extension of the Algerian panorama: a dry plateau where livestock graze, merging into fertile valleys near the coast. Tunisia became an independent republic in 1957.

AREA: 48,319 sq. mi.
POPULATION: 3,987,000. Capital: Tunis.
CLIMATE: Hot summers, mild winters; dry all year except for coast, which has moderate winter rainfall.
ALTITUDES: Djebel Chambi, near Gafsa, 5,138 ft. (highest); Tunis, 30 ft.

DESERTS: SAND AND 'PAVEMENT'

Two major types of deserts are shown in the drawings above. Deserts occur in areas where there is insufficient rainfall to permit the growth of vegetation, the roots of which hold soil in place. Sand deserts *(top)* are formed when winds pick up particles of soil and heap them in dunes against high points of the landscape. The slopes of the dunes are gradual on the windward side and fall away steeply on the leeward. A "desert pavement," or rock desert *(bottom)*, results when the wind removes the covering of sand, leaving buttes and stone behind.

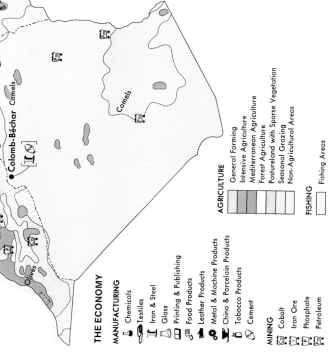

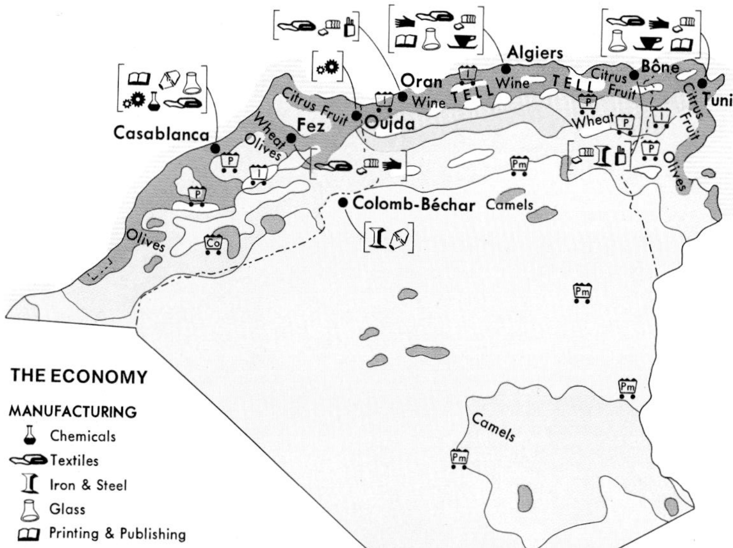

THE ECONOMY

MANUFACTURING
- Chemicals
- Textiles
- Iron & Steel
- Glass
- Printing & Publishing
- Food Products
- Leather Products
- Metal & Machine Products
- China & Porcelain Products
- Tobacco Products
- Cement

MINING
- Cobalt
- Iron Ore
- Phosphate
- Petroleum

AGRICULTURE
- General Farming
- Intensive Agriculture
- Mediterranean Agriculture
- Forest Agriculture
- Pastureland with Sparse Vegetation
- Seasonal Grazing
- Non-Agricultural Areas

FISHING
- Fishing Areas

GROSS NATIONAL PRODUCT PER CAPITA
Algeria $217 Morocco $169 Tunisia $190

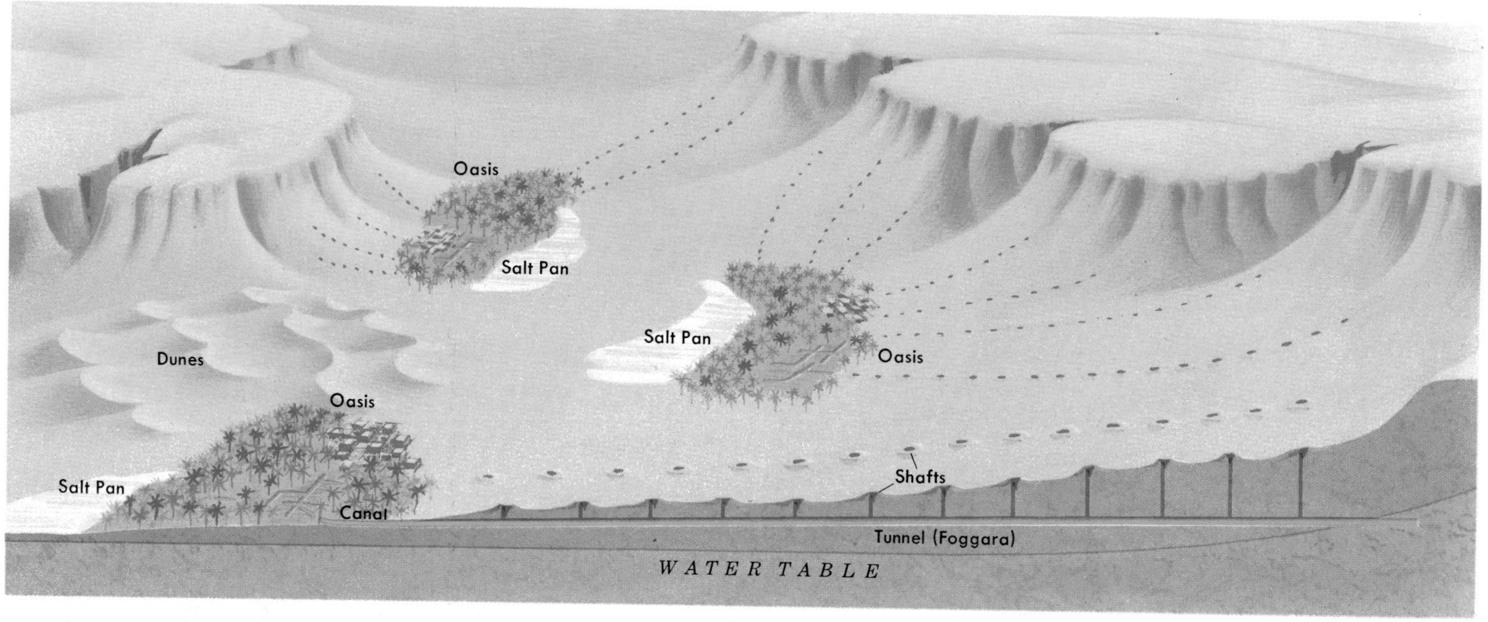

A 'FOGGARA,' OR HORIZONTAL WELL, IN DESERT COUNTRY

The construction of a *foggara*, an underground water tunnel in desert country, is shown in this cross section. A tunnel is dug to reach water that has collected underground from occasional rains on the plateaus. Vertical shafts are sunk for access to the tunnel. The incline assures a continuous flow of fresh water into the canals of the low-lying oases *(left)*. If a shaft were dug to the water table directly below an oasis, it would reach saline water, as shown by the salt pans, or dried water basins, that frequently come to the surface.

AN ENORMOUS BULGE, West Africa juts some 2,000 miles into the Atlantic, at the extreme left. Changing bands of color mark the continent. The yellow Sahara *(top)* gives way to West Africa's vast grasslands, which yield to the deep green of the equatorial forest.

WEST AND CENTRAL AFRICA

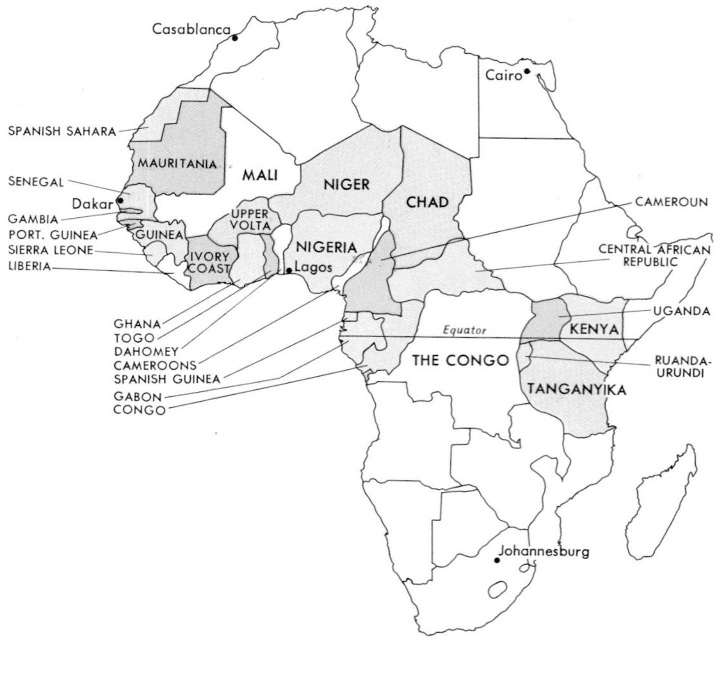

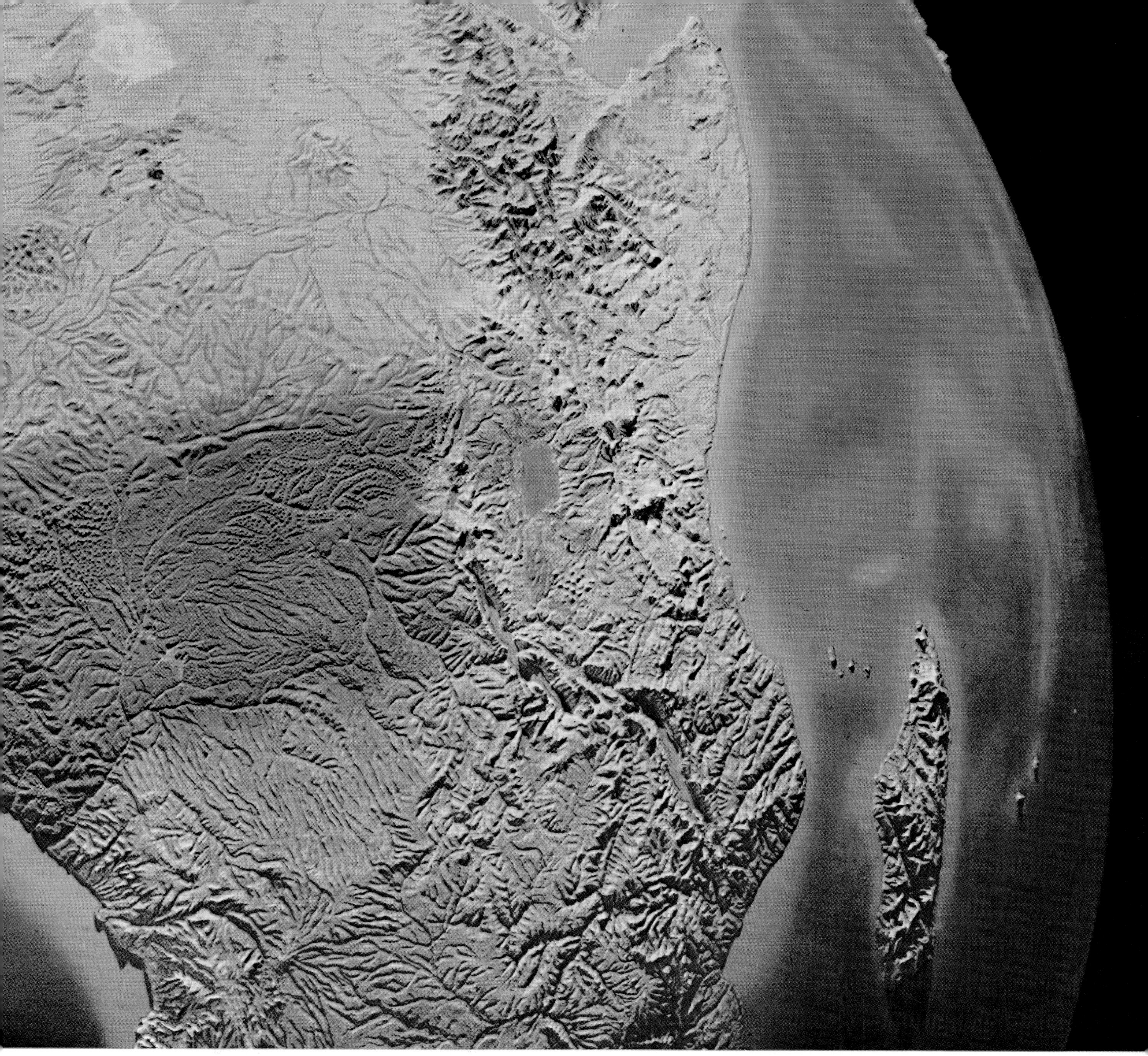

While Europe drifted through the Middle Ages, great empires flourished in West and Central Africa. But European history books did not tell of the glories of ancient Mali or Ghana, and Europeans could only conjecture over the tales of the wonders of Timbuktu, the cultured capital of the vast Gao Empire. The great empires prospered on trade with the trans-Sahara caravans, but Westerners knew of them only from the ivory and spices and the stories the desert traders brought back. The empires were succeeded by coastal kingdoms with such romantic names as Zanzibar, Benin and Dahomey. After the first Portuguese landings in 1446, these places began to be better known to Europeans who came to trade in gold and ivory and human beings. In three centuries of the lucrative slave trade, as many as 18 to 24 million people were shipped to the plantations of the New World. One American in every 10 can claim Africa as the land of his ancestors.

Although this part of Africa was better known than any area south of the Sahara, western contacts ended at the dockside or the safari trading post. The interior remained a vast unknown, curtained off by the Sahara and by the forest-fringed seacoast. Until the latter part of the 19th Century, when the rush for colonies reached its crest, the region was left undisturbed. Wrote the English satirist Jonathan Swift:

> So Geographers in *Afric*-Maps
> With Savage-Pictures fill their Gaps;
> And o'er unhabitable Downs
> Place Elephants for want of Towns.

When the colonial powers of Europe divided West and Central Africa among themselves, they found a land supporting more than one third of the continental population, with hundreds of tribes and languages. It was a land of well-defined geographical zones: tropical rain forests, mountains and highlands, a chain of lakes, deciduous forests, grasslands, scrub and desert. The tribes, customs, cultures and economies of the region differed as sharply as the vegetational zones.

Many new nations have been created here since World War II. The drive for national independence in this region, British historian Lord Hailey has noted, means that "the African has come in person onto the stage, and he . . . takes an effective share in the action of the play."

RICE LAND AND DESERT LAND IN WEST AFRICA

A WATERY LANDSCAPE is being readied in the Ivory Coast for "wet rice" production. The irrigation ditches, like the one shown here, near Abidjan, are being dug by hand. The Ivory Coast has the dense vegetation and hot, moist climate of Africa's equatorial zone.

THE FEATURELESS WASTES of the Sahara Desert in the Chad Republic are reddened by an annular eclipse which leaves only a crescent of the sun visible. The desert is scorching by day, freezing by night. Because there is no haze, it is possible to see for great distances.

WEST AFRICA
Barren Areas Above Timber
Evergreen Trees
Deciduous Trees
Shrub
Grass
Barren Arid Areas
National Capitals
Other Capitals
Cities
Railroads
1 inch = 182 Statute Miles
Miles 0 25 50 75 100 150 200
Sinusoidal Projection
Atlantic Ocean
SPANISH WEST AFRICA
SAGUIA EL-HAMRA
SPANISH SAHARA
RÍO DE ORO
CABO BOJADOR
Aiún
Smara
Ain Ben Tili
Hasi Duaiheb
Fort Trinquet
Tindouf
Tropic of Cancer
Villa Cisneros
PUNTA DURNFORD
Timkerdat
Aou Hofrit
Togba
Fort-Gouraud
Atoui
Zoug
Char
Rallaouia
MAKTEÏR
Port Étienne
CAP BLANC
Atar
Chinguetti
AKCHAR
ADRAR
OUARANE
EL DJOUF
El Memrhar
Akjoujt
Aguelt Nemadi
MAURITANIA
Bourjeïmat
AMECHTIL
Tichit
Aratane
NOUAKCHOTT
Tichinane
Tidjikja
Moudjéria
Boutilimit
In Ahmar
Tagouranet
Tamchakett
Méderdra
Aleg
Podor
Rosso
Boghé
Kaédi
Kiffa
Oualata
Aïoun el Atrous
Néma
Timbédra
Saint Louis
Dagana
Mbout
Bassikounou
Louga
Linguère
Matam
Sénégal
Kolimbine
Yélimané
Nioro
Ballé
Nara
Nampala
Selibaby
Rufisque
C. VERDE
DAKAR
Thiès
Tivaouane
Touba
Tiel
Bakel
Mbour
Diourbel
SENEGAL
Kidira
Kayes
Dioka
Kaolack
Kaffrine
Goudiri
Kalabana
Baoulé
Nioro
BATHURST
GAMBIA (BR.)
Georgetown
Tambacounda
Mansa Konko
Kolda
Vélingara
Gambia
Bignona
Sédhiou
Ziguinchor
Bafata
PORT. GUINEA
BISSAU
Youkounkoun
MT. TAMGUE 4,970 FT.
Mali
Bafoulabé
Badoumbé
Kéniéba
Falémé
Kédougou
Bakoy
Kita
Banamba
Kolokani
Koulikoro
Niger
Ségou
BAMAKO
Douna
Bani
San
Fari
FOUTA DJALLON
Labé
Pita
Buba
Bensané
Gaoual
Télimélé
Boké
Dalaba
Dabola
Boffa
Kindia
GUINEA
Mamou
Farana
Tinkisso
Dinguiraye
Siguiri
Kouroussa
Tiriro
Kankan
Sankarani
Kourémalé
Bougouni
Yanfolila
Ouakoro
Sikasso
Dioila
Koutiala
Bagoe
CONAKRY
Forékaria
Kabala
Baga
Batkanu
Rokkel
LOMA MTS.
Port Loko
SIERRA LEONE
FREETOWN
Waterloo
Makump
Moyamba
Bo
Kenema
Pendembu
Bonthe
Pujehun
Sefadu
Kissidougou
Guékédou
Macenta
PIC DE TIBÉ 4,734 FT.
Beyla
Bako
NIMBA MTS.
N'Zérékoré
NZÉRÉKORÉ 5,760 FT.
Touba
Danané
Man
Ganta
Sakripé
Bellivela
Boporo
LIBERIA
St. Paul
Roysville
Tapi Town
Robertsport
MONROVIA
Careysburg
Marshall
Buchanan
River Cess
Cess
Cavalla
Sangwin
NIETE 2,297 FT.
Greenville
Grand Cess
Harper
Plebo
Tabou
CAPE PALMAS
Duékoué
Toulépleu
Guiglo
Taï
Sassandra
Odienné
Boundiali
Korhogo
Kani
Mankono
Séguéla
Vavoua
Béoumi
Zuénoula
Bouaflé
Daloa
Issia
Gagnoa
Soubré
Divo
Bandama
Grand-Lahou
Fresko
IVORY COAST
Tengrela
KONG
Katiola
Bouaké
Dabakala
Bondoukou
Bouna
Ouellé
Bokanda
Dimbokro
Adzopé
Agboville
Comoé
ABIDJAN
Aboisso
Assinie
Grand-Bassam
Sassandra
Sierra
Tindouf
IGUIDI
REG AFTOUT
Chenachane (Oasis)
ERG
ERG EL AHMAR
Toufourine (Oasis)
ERG CHECH
El Mreïti
Aguéraktem
Oum el Asel (Oasis)
Taoudenni
Sobti
Bir Zreigat
El Mreyer
Bir el Ksaib
BASIN
Bir Ounane
Achourat
Arebeb
SAHARA
Bordj Viollette
ERG IABLES
Reggane
Aoulef
Djafou
In Salah
Sebkra Mekerrhane
Sebkra Azzel Matti
Bordj Amguid
Bordj Flamand
Bordj Ouallen
SAHARAN DEPART(MENTS)
(FRENCH)
In-Rabit
TANEZROUFT
Adrar Nahalet
MONT TAHAT 9,852 FT.
Tibeghim
AHAGGAR
Bidon Cinq
Tin Rerhoh (Oasis)
Tessalit
ADRAR DES IFORAS
Ft. Pierre Bordes
Tin Zaouatène (Oasis)
In Guezzam (Oasis)
Agueloc
El Ouig
AZAOUAD
In Beriem
El Mraïti
Araouane
Bou Djébena
VALLÉE DU TILEMSI
Kidal
Anéfis
Anou Mellène
Sédérog
Ouchina
In Alay
Bamba
Bourem
L. Faguibine
Tombouctou (Timbuktu)
Goundam
Niafounké
Gourma-Rarous
Gao
Azaouak
Assakari
Mantas
L. Garou
Ansongo
Ménaka
L. Debo
MALI
Boré
L. Korarou
Hombori
Fada
Tlemcès
Baniloudi
Tahoua
Douenza
Mopti
Bandiagara
Sokolo
Ké-Macina
Djenné
Bankasse
Djibo
Dori
Ouallam
Tillabéri
Téra
Filingue
Birni-Nkoni
Dogondoutchi
NIAMEY
Ouahigouya
Kaya
Bogandé
Boulsa
Tougan
Nouna
Dédougou
OUAGADOUGOU
Koudougou
Matiakouali
Fada-Ngourma
Diapaga
Say
Magou
Dosso
Gaya
Birnin Kebbi
Argungu
Sokoto
Kaura Namoda
Gusau
Kalmalo
Sabon Birni
Faramana
UPPER VOLTA
Boromo
Tenkodogo
Volta
Houndé
Bobo-Dioulasso
Noire
Léo
Pô
Pama
Kandi
Kebbi
Koko
Zuru
Anka
Illo
Yelwa
Banfora
Gaoua
Tumu
Lawra
Navrongo
Bawku
Gambaga
Tanguiéta
Sansanné-Mango
Natitingou
Babana
Bussa
Koton Karifi
Kontagora
Batié
Wa
NORTHERN REGION
Damongo
Yendi
Tamale
Bole
White Volta
Black Volta
Salaga
TRANS VOLTA TOGOLAND
Lama-Kara
Djougou
Parakou
Nikki
Kaiama
Kishi
Jebba
Zungeru
Lafiagi
Bida
Kintampo
Wenchi
GHANA
ASHANTI
Sunyani
Kumasi
Mampong
Juaso
EASTERN REGION
Obuasi
Kade
Koforidua
Oda
Nsawam
Ada
Keta
ACCRA
Winneba
Saltpond
Cape Coast
Sekondi
Takoradi
C. THREE POINTS
Tarkwa
Axim
WESTERN REGION
Dunkwa
Enchi
Abengourou
TOGO
Blita
Atakpamé
Palimé
Lokossa
Ouidah
Cotonou
LOMÉ
PORTO-NOVO
DAHOMEY
Savalou
Abomey
Pobé
Allada
Abeokuta
Shaki
Iseyin
Oyo
Ilorin
Ogbomosho
Iwo
Oshogbo
Ilesha
Ibadan
Ife
Ondo
Owo
Akure
Ijebu Ode
WESTERN REGION
LAGOS
Kabba
Lokoja
Benin
Agbor
Sapele
Warri
Kwale
Forcados
Ubiaja
Port Harcourt
Brass
Bonny
Mouths of the Niger
Bight of Benin
Gulf of Guinea
Equator
SÃO TOMÉ (PORT.)
ANNOBÓN (SP. GUI.)
Longitude West of Greenwich
Longitude East of Greenwich
20° 15° 10° 5° 0° 5°
25° 20° 15° 10° 5° 0°
A B C D E F G
1 2 3 4 5

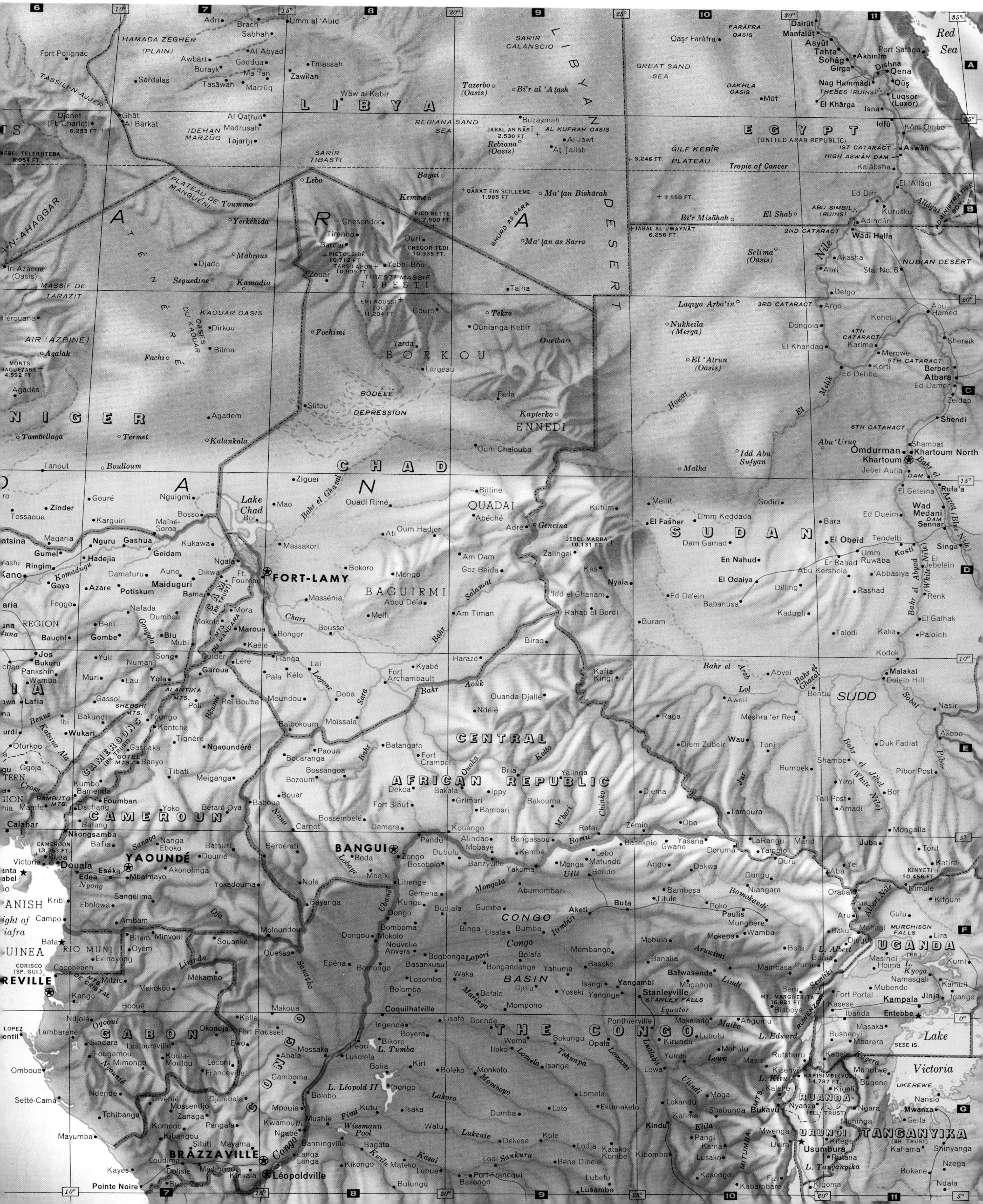
L I B Y A
E G Y P T
(UNITED ARAB REPUBLIC)
C H A D
S U D A N
N I G E R
CENTRAL AFRICAN REPUBLIC
CAMEROUN
GABON
THE CONGO
UGANDA
RUANDA-URUNDI
TANGANYIKA
LIBYAN DESERT
NUBIAN DESERT
Red Sea
Lake Victoria
Lake Chad
Tropic of Cancer
TIBESTI
BORKOU
ENNEDI
QUADAI
BAGUIRMI
BODÉLÉ DEPRESSION
SUDD
CONGO BASIN
FORT-LAMY
Khartoum
Omdurman
BANGUI
YAOUNDÉ
BRAZZAVILLE
Léopoldville
Kampala
Stanleyville
Coquilhatville
Wādī Halfa
Aswān
Asyūt
Fort Polignac
Ghāt
Djanet
Bilma
Agadem
Zinder
Maiduguri
Kano
Jos
Garoua
Douala
Libreville
Pointe Noire
Port Gentil
El Obeid
Kosti
Wau
Juba
Malakal
Atbara
Dongola
Nile
Congo
Ubangi
Bahr el Ghazal
Chari
Logone
Benue
Uele
Kasai
L. Léopold II
L. Albert
L. Edward
L. Kivu
L. Tanganyika
Entebbe
Usumbura
Bukavu
Kindu
Lusambo

WEST AFRICA: The new and old political divisions of West Africa have inherited a legacy of confusion from the European powers that once dominated the region. The English, French, German and Portuguese drew the boundaries of their West African colonial possessions late in the 19th Century without regard to ethnic, religious or geographic unities or divisions. As a result, to cite one example, the Niger-Nigeria boundary divides the Hausa people, and these Moslem cultivators of the northern Nigerian savannas find themselves in a common nation with the Christian-influenced Yoruba farmers of the southwest, with whom they have virtually nothing in common. There are no rail communications and few roads between countries formerly ruled by rival powers, making this a region of isolated as well as fledgling nations. In spite of the toll taken by slavery and disease, West Africa is densely populated. It contains over 30 per cent of the population of the entire continent.

The Europeans often named a region for the outstanding local product, and so there are inevitable confusions about the designations of new political units. The Gold Coast took the name of ancient Ghana on becoming independent (although the old empire of Ghana was some 400 miles to the north of the modern state), but its neighbor elected to keep another old name of the area – the Ivory Coast.

CLIMATE: Southern regions very hot throughout the year; heavy summer rainfall; heavy to moderate winter rainfall along the coast, decreasing northward. Northern regions have hot summers, warm winters; moderate summer rainfall, dry winters.

ALTITUDES: Cameroon Mountain, Cameroons (British), 13,353 ft. (highest).

West Africa is an agricultural region, with cattle raising an important supplement to farming in the northern savannas. The economy rests squarely on four main export crops: peanuts, cacao, coffee and palm products. Many of the new countries that have leaned heavily on single crops (cacao in Ghana, cottonseed in Chad, peanuts in Senegal) have learned the perils of a fluctuating market.

For a great many West African farmers in the humid tropical area, bare subsistence on harvests of yams and cassavas is the goal of their primitive methods. But these methods are extraordinarily well adapted to the environment. Around the village homesteads, women maintain vegetable and fruit gardens which often boast a scattering of palm-oil trees. Surrounding the villages are fields cultivated by "bush fallowing." A field is planted for a year or two, then is allowed to be run over by wild vegetation, or bush, for a few years in order to regenerate its fertility. The fact that fields are small limits the danger of erosion. But as the population increases, the period of rest is being reduced, raising a threat to the continued productivity of the land.

A few of the countries are converting to more diversified economies, notably rubber-rich Liberia, which is gradually building up an export trade in cacao, coffee, piassava and palm kernels. Substantial mineral reserves have been discovered: manganese in Gabon and Ghana, bauxite in Guinea and Ghana, iron in Sierra Leone, Liberia and Mauritania, oil in Gabon and Nigeria.

The Europeans left behind handsome modern capitals at Conakry, Dakar, Accra and their sister cities along the coast. And though disease still takes an appalling toll, modern medicine has made heartening progress, especially against the twin curses of the region, sleeping sickness and malaria. In Lagos, Nigeria, infant mortality was reduced from 105.8 to 79 children per thousand births between 1949 and 1958 (in the U.S. during the same period, infant deaths declined from 31.3 to 26.9 per thousand). The thirst for education has become insatiable: in Ghana the number of primary schools increased from 1,000 to 3,713 between 1951 and 1959, and in Nigeria *(see graph, opposite page)* primary-school enrollments rocketed from 1,252,000 in 1954 to 2,595,000 in 1958. The religions of the outside world have won increasing acceptance: Mohammedanism, brought in by the desert caravans from Northern Africa, and Christianity, introduced by generations of missionaries, are now the faiths of almost half of West Africa's inhabitants.

POLITICAL UNITS	AREA In sq. mi.	POPULATION
CAMEROONS (BRITISH)	34,080	1,613,000
CAMEROUN	166,752	3,303,000
CENTRAL AFRICAN REPUBLIC	227,118	1,224,000
CHAD	446,640	2,541,000
CONGO	125,890	816,000
DAHOMEY	44,713	1,750,000
FERNANDO POO	785	44,000
GABON	98,283	434,400
GAMBIA	3,978	307,000
GHANA	91,819	4,847,000
GUINEA	94,945	2,667,000
IVORY COAST	124,550	3,145,000
LIBERIA	42,989	1,350,000
MALI	465,050	3,748,000
MAURITANIA	419,390	685,000
NIGER	459,180	2,515,000
NIGERIA	350,291	33,441,000
PORTUGUESE GUINEA	13,944	563,000
RIO MUNI	10,043	172,000
SENEGAL	76,153	2,337,000
SIERRA LEONE	27,925	2,185,000
SPANISH SAHARA	102,676	13,000
TOGO	22,002	1,136,000
UPPER VOLTA	105,879	3,516,000

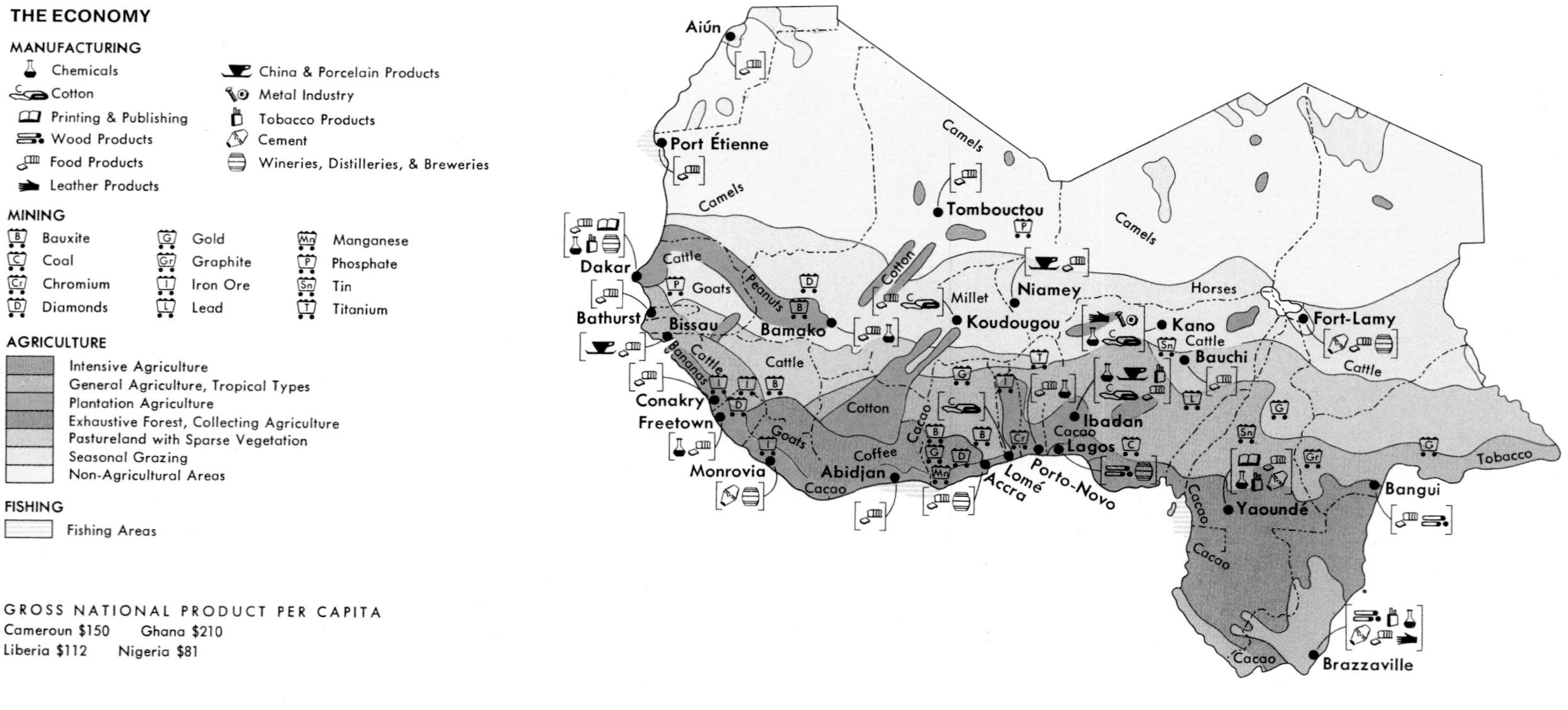

THE ECONOMY
MANUFACTURING
Chemicals
Cotton
Printing & Publishing
Wood Products
Food Products
Leather Products
China & Porcelain Products
Metal Industry
Tobacco Products
Cement
Wineries, Distilleries, & Breweries
MINING
Bauxite
Coal
Chromium
Diamonds
Gold
Graphite
Iron Ore
Lead
Manganese
Phosphate
Tin
Titanium
AGRICULTURE
Intensive Agriculture
General Agriculture, Tropical Types
Plantation Agriculture
Exhaustive Forest, Collecting Agriculture
Pastureland with Sparse Vegetation
Seasonal Grazing
Non-Agricultural Areas
FISHING
Fishing Areas
Aiún
Port Étienne
Camels
Tombouctou
Dakar
Bathurst
Bissau
Bamako
Cattle
Goats
Peanuts
Cotton
Millet
Niamey
Koudougou
Horses
Kano
Bauchi
Fort-Lamy
Conakry
Freetown
Monrovia
Bananas
Coffee
Cacao
Abidjan
Accra
Lomé
Porto-Novo
Lagos
Ibadan
Yaoundé
Bangui
Tobacco
Brazzaville

GROSS NATIONAL PRODUCT PER CAPITA
Cameroun $150 Ghana $210
Liberia $112 Nigeria $81

NIGERIA: AN INDEX TO WEST AFRICA

In West Africa, a remarkably close-knit land, the variants of people, topography, climate and natural resources are striking, but in country after country the same variations recur. The problems of the Ivory Coast, for example, are similar to the problems of Gabon. Most of the countries have an over-all transportation problem, a river that is navigable only in season, a one-crop economy and a yearning for education. In Nigeria, the most populous of the West African lands and a country situated in the heart of the region, the socio-economic picture, as shown on the maps and graphs of this page, can be magnified to include all of West Africa, or condensed to apply to any of the other, smaller countries of the area.

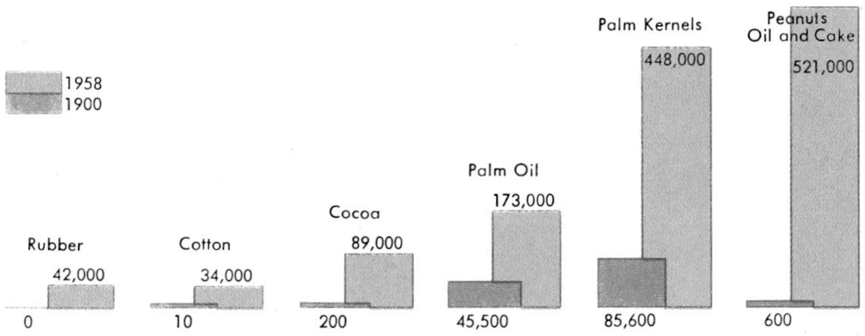

AN ECONOMY BASED ON PALMS AND PEANUTS

Three quarters of Nigeria's people are peasant farmers, who produce most of the country's food requirements and 85 per cent of the exports. Palm products and peanuts, as shown in the graph above, are the big export crops: Nigeria is the world's largest exporter of both. Cacao was introduced in Nigeria some years ago, and cotton is planted in the fertile northern plains. Rubber, which is grown mainly in the western region, is only a minor export crop.

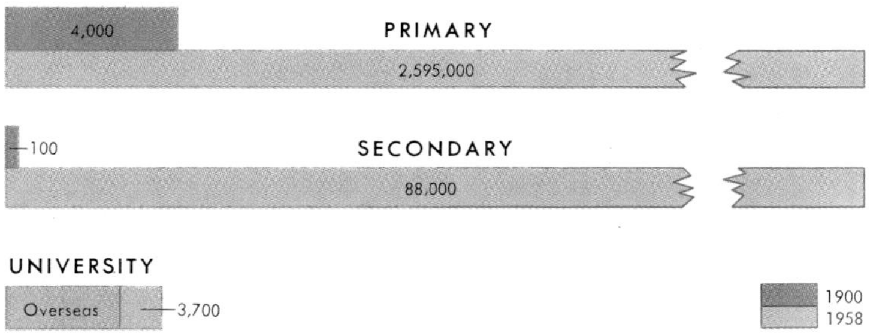

THE RISING TIDE OF EDUCATION

The clamor for education is heard all over West Africa, and nowhere is it stronger than in Nigeria. As this chart shows, the country has taken giant strides toward literacy. The first government school was opened in 1899. Today, the University College at Ibadan, the Nigeria College of Arts, Science and Technology, and the University of Nigeria at Nsukka offer higher educations to young Nigerians, and many go to college in the United Kingdom or in the U.S.

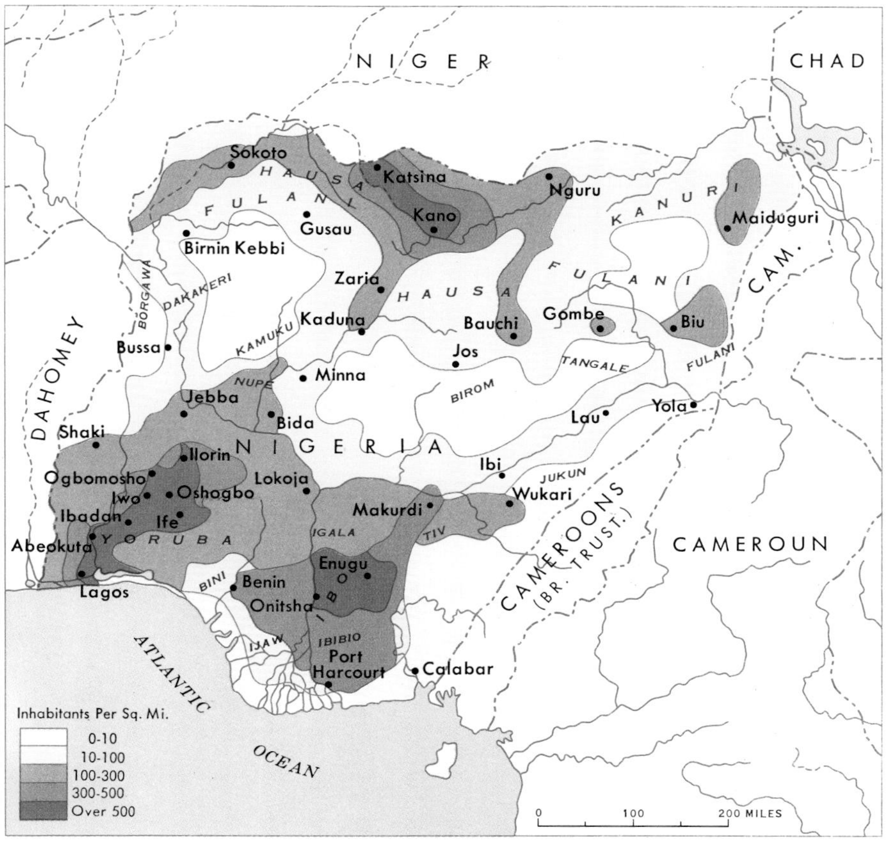

A RICHLY VARIED TAPESTRY OF HUMANITY

With 33,441,000 inhabitants, Nigeria is, by a large margin, the biggest nation in West Africa. Some 300 tribes and more than 300 languages and dialects *(map above)* make the country a tapestry of humanity, differing as widely from community to community as the terrain does. Five major tribal groups predominate. In the north live the Fulani and the Hausa, two distinct but interrelated groups of Moslems. To the northeast, near the shores of Lake Chad, are Moslems of Berber origin, the aloof Kanuri. Among the most advanced of African tribes are the tall Yoruba, who live in the southwest, and the Ibo, in the southeast, a tribe from which the early slave traders obtained a large percentage of their human cargo.

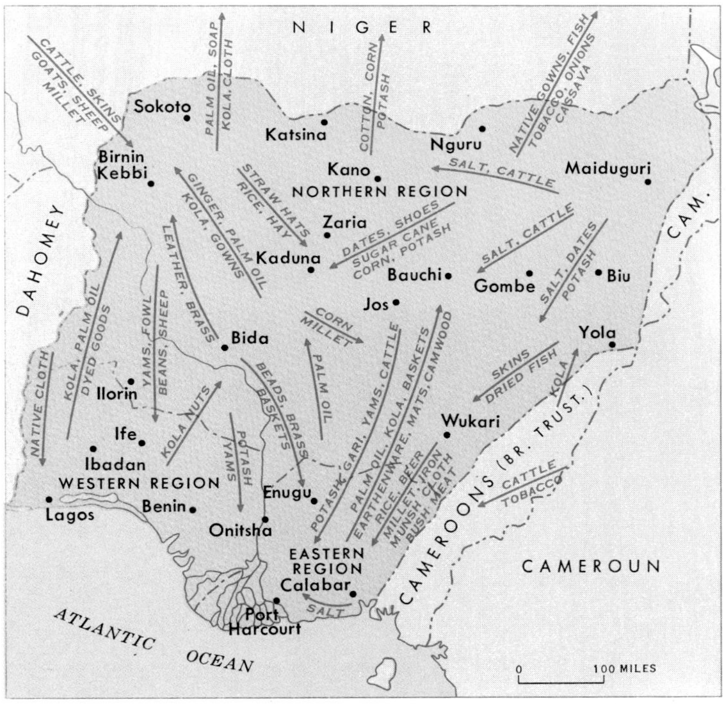

A VERTICAL PATTERN OF TRADE ROUTES

The movement of trade in Nigeria, illustrated on the map above, follows two well-established patterns, both of them predominantly north and south. Some exports leave the country overland to the north, following the centuries-old caravan routes to the desert. But most trade flows to and from the port cities on what was once called the Slave Coast. The British colonists followed the rigid system prevailing throughout West Africa and discouraged east-west traffic between Nigeria and its neighbors. There is still almost no trade with nearby Dahomey or Cameroun—a condition that will probably change as roads and communications improve.

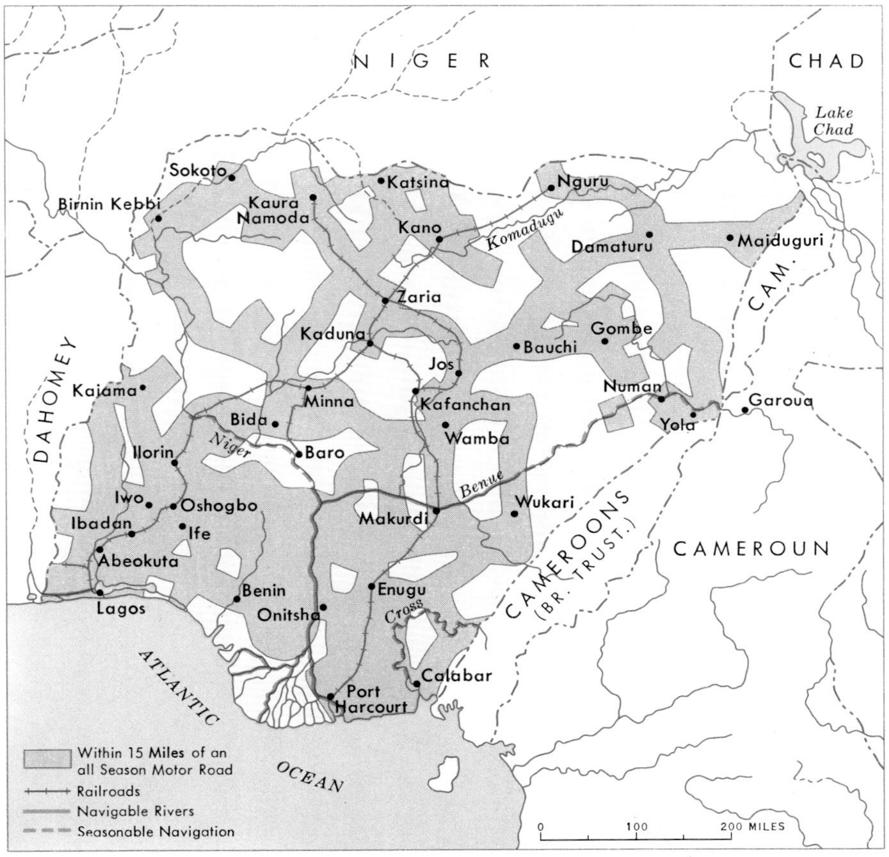

TRANSPORTATION

As in most of West Africa, the roads and rails of Nigeria lead from the coastline inland to the north. Communication between east and west, and with neighboring countries, is slight, but much of the country is within 15 miles of an all-purpose road, as the map above shows. The two main rail lines, totaling 1,270 miles, go from Lagos to Kano and from Port Harcourt to Kaduna; a third rail line will open up the northeast. The Niger River is commercially navigable for slightly more than half its 2,590-mile length, but only 362 miles within Nigeria are navigable for nine months of the year; the Benue River, a tributary of the Niger, is seasonably navigable as far as Garoua, in Cameroun, but only for six to 10 weeks of the year.

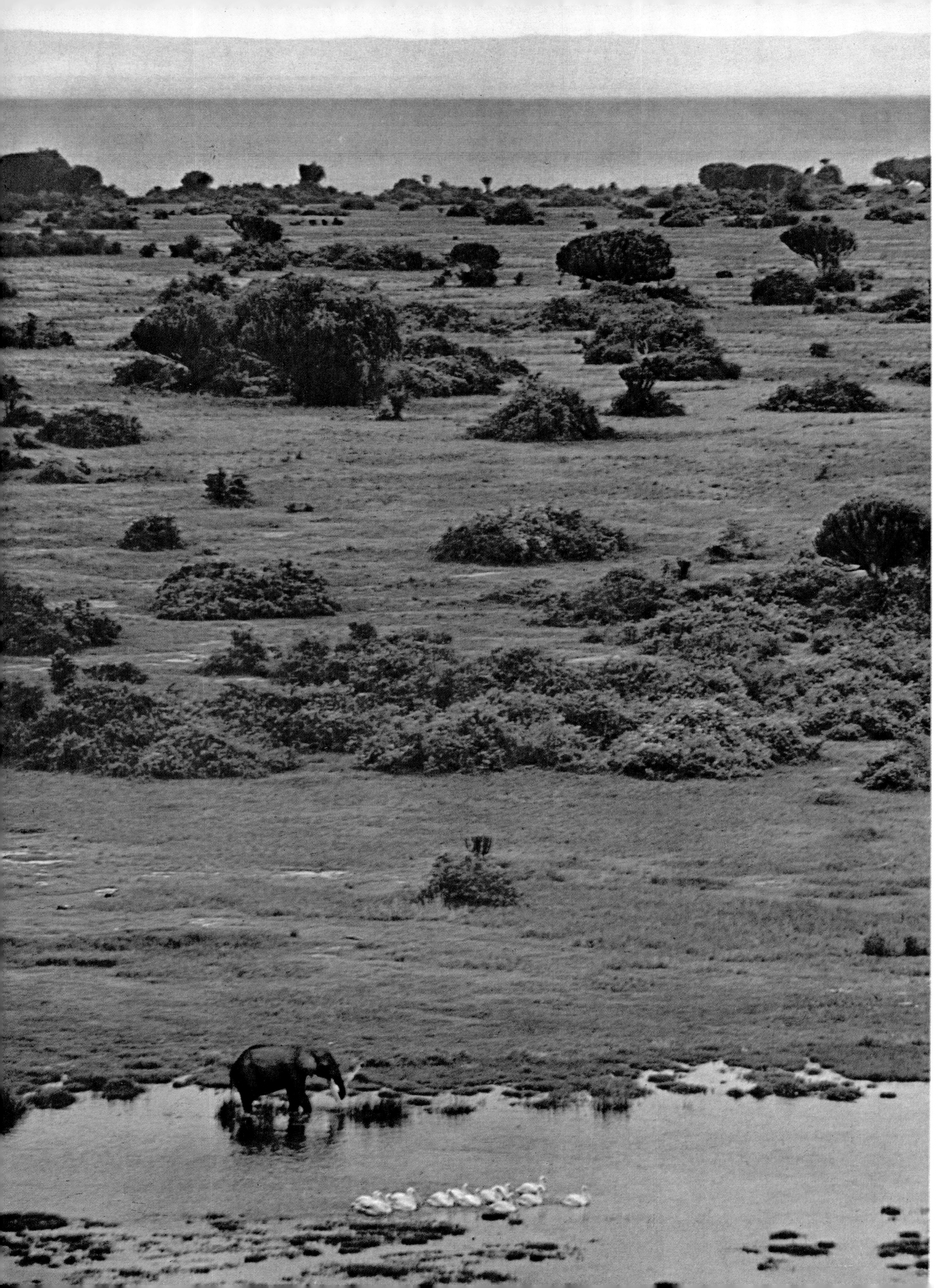

HEATH AND GRASSLAND IN THE CONGO

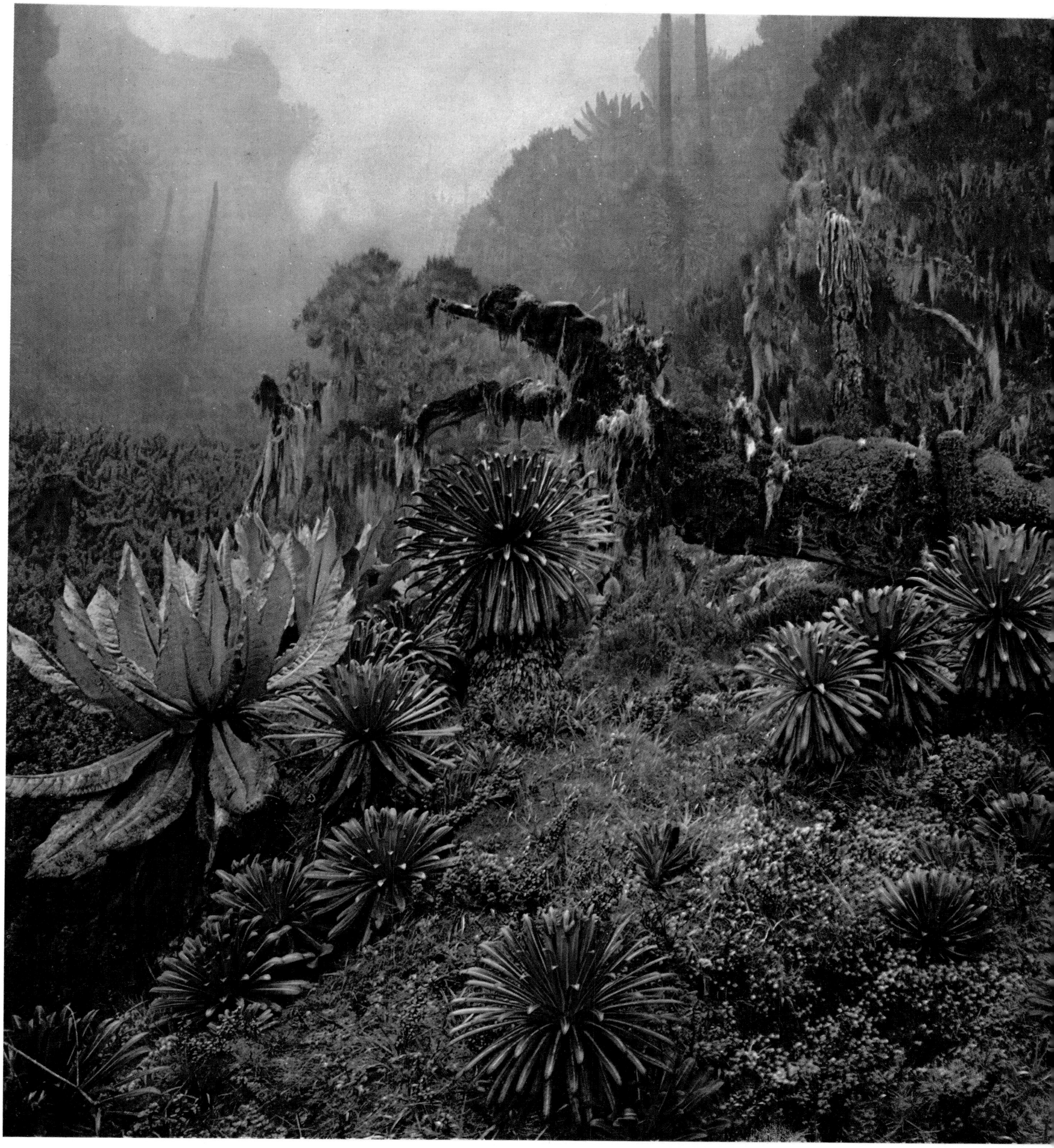

A THICKETED GRASSLAND lying between the Rutshuru River and Lake Edward in the Congo *(opposite page)* provides a natural and peaceful sanctuary for animals in Albert National Park. Grassland, like that seen here, and scrub forest cover almost half of Africa.

A MISTY HEATH of orange and yellow mosses and spiky plants grows 12,000 feet above sea level on the slopes of Mount Ruwenzori in the eastern Congo. Lush flora thrives in this area, where rain falls 10 months of the year. Higher up, the mountain is capped with snow.

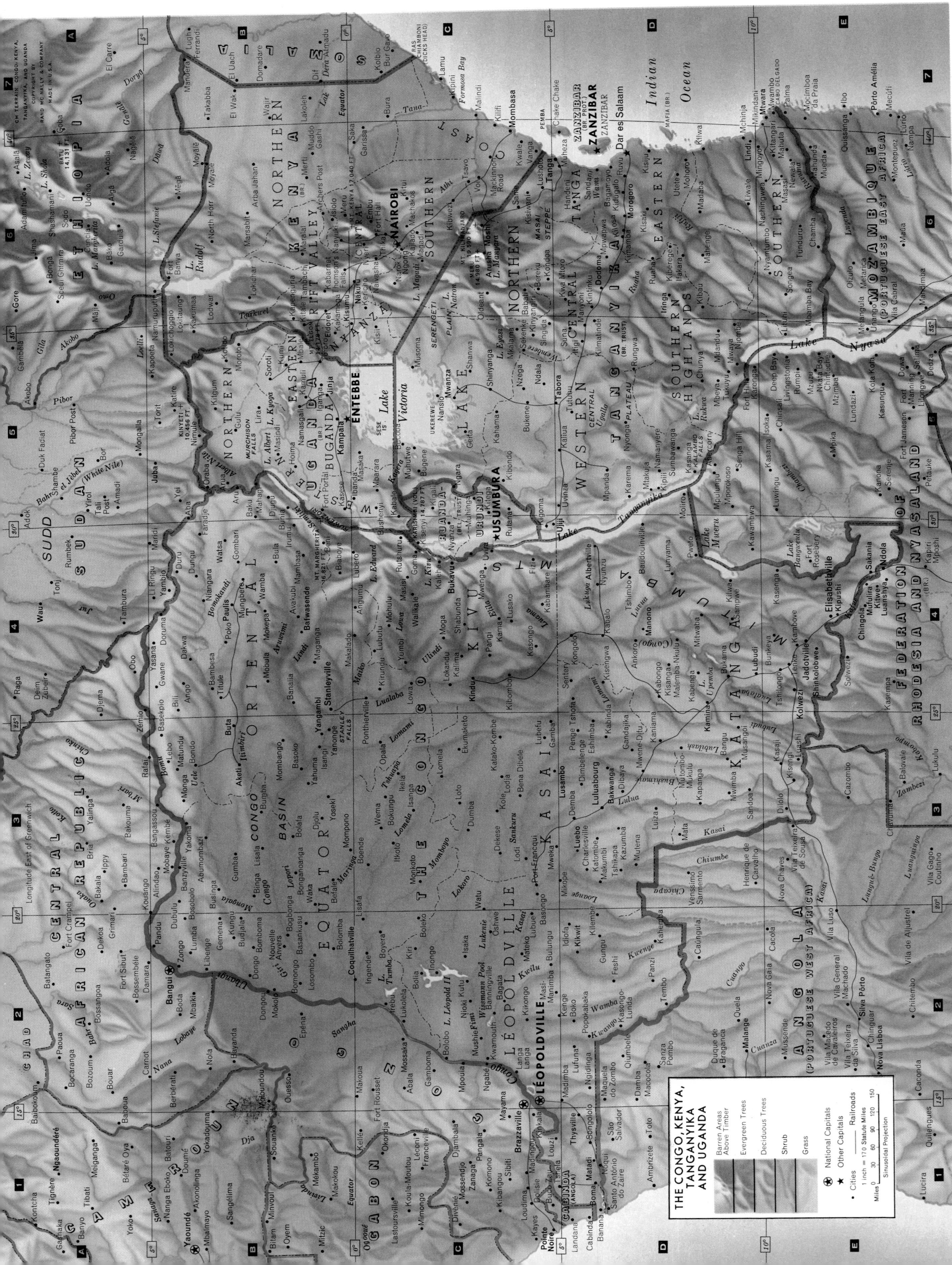
THE CONGO, KENYA, TANGANYIKA AND UGANDA
Barren Areas Above Timber
Evergreen Trees
Deciduous Trees
Shrub
Grass
National Capitals
Other Capitals
Cities
Railroads
1 inch = 170 Statute Miles
Miles 0 30 60 90 120 150
Sinusoidal Projection
CM TERRAIN, CONGO, KENYA, TANGANYIKA AND UGANDA
COPYRIGHT BY RAND McNALLY & COMPANY
MADE IN U.S.A.

THE CONGO: Carved out of a still-raw Africa by the ambition of King Leopold II of Belgium and the daring of explorer Henry M. Stanley in the 19th Century, the Congo is nearly 80 times the size of Belgium itself. Most of the land is a plateau of equatorial rain forests, but snow-capped ranges rise in the east. On uplands in the north and south the land is covered by the tall grass of savannas.

Under Leopold's personal ownership of the region, rubber and ivory were the major exports. After Belgium annexed the territory in 1908, additional treasures flowed down the rivers of the Congo Basin toward Matadi, the main port on the country's pinched, 25-mile-long coastline on the Atlantic.

The Congo, granted independence in 1960, still has an export economy based mainly on agriculture and mining. Palm oil and rubber come from its tropical forests. Copper comes from the mines of Katanga, and industrial diamonds are dug in Kasai. Coffee, tea and cinchona are grown in the eastern highlands.

AREA: 905,329 sq. mi.
POPULATION: 13,732,000.
Largest city and capital: Léopoldville.
CLIMATE: Hot with heavy rainfall in lowlands, cooler temperatures in highlands.
Most rain, Nov.-April.
ALTITUDES: Mt. Margherita, 16,821 ft. (highest);
Léopoldville, 1,045 ft.

KENYA: Britons took control of Kenya in the late 19th Century. Avoiding the arid northern three fifths of the country, they concentrated in the fertile 16,500-square-mile "White Highlands" in the southwest. In this pleasant region, plantations today raise coffee and cattle. In the wetter climate of the west, tea plantations flourish and native farmers grow cotton crops near the shores of Lake Victoria.

AREA: 224,960 sq. mi.
POPULATION: 6,444,000.
Largest city and capital: Nairobi.
CLIMATE: Hot all year, with cooler temperatures in interior highlands. Most rain, Feb.-May.
ALTITUDES: Mt. Kenya, 17,040 ft. (highest).

TANGANYIKA: On the northern border of Tanganyika, Mount Kilimanjaro, the "Shining Mountain," is the tallest in Africa, reaching more than 19,000 feet into the clouds that water the thick forests and the green and fertile acres along its slopes. About two thirds of the country is wasteland, hot and infested with the tsetse fly. Tanganyika produces hardwood, sisal and diamonds.

AREA: 362,688 sq. mi.
POPULATION: 9,052,000.
Largest city and capital: Dar es Salaam.
CLIMATE: Hot all year, cooler in highlands.
Most rainfall, Nov.-April; dry, May-Oct.
ALTITUDES: Mt. Kilimanjaro, 19,590 ft. (highest).

UGANDA: This basically agricultural country is being transformed by the Owens Falls Dam, completed in 1954. The dam, which funnels the White Nile away from Lake Victoria, has created an industrial potential. Electricity is exported on transmission lines reaching out to Kenya, and the growth of copper mines and textile mills inside Uganda has been stimulated.

AREA: 93,981 sq. mi.
POPULATION: 5,892,000.
Largest city: Kampala. Capital: Entebbe.
CLIMATE: Hot all year; moderate rainfall.
ALTITUDES: Mt. Elgon, 14,178 ft. (highest).

RUANDA-URUNDI: With a population of nearly five million living on its 20,916 square miles, Ruanda-Urundi is one of the most densely settled areas of Africa. It raises crops of cotton and coffee and mines quantities of gold, tin ores and tungsten.

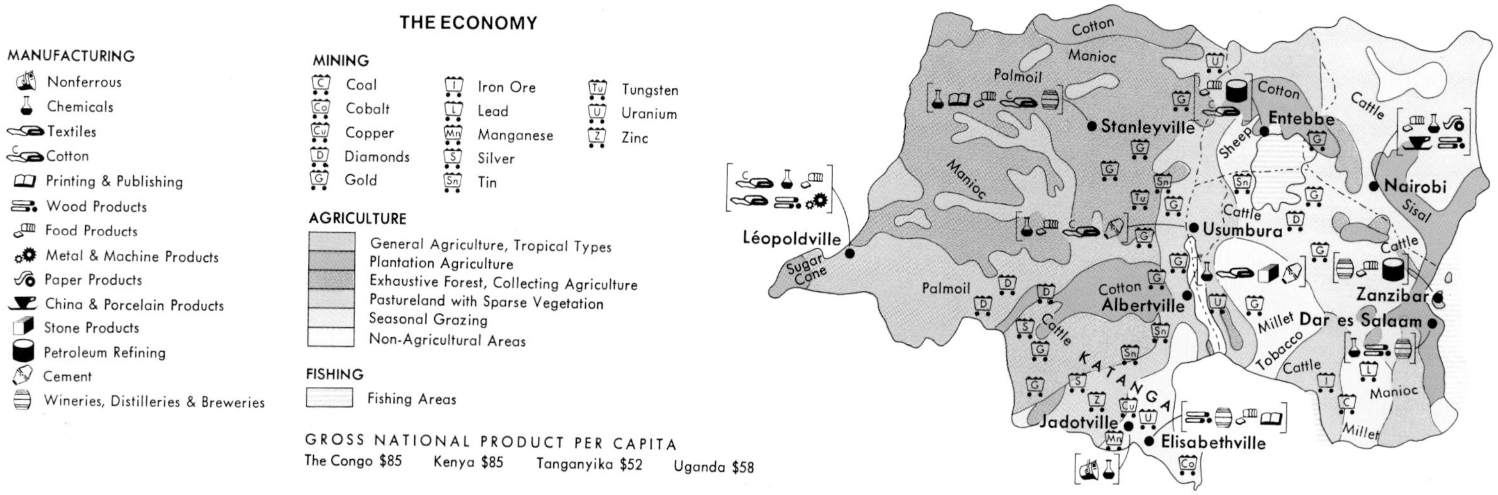
THE ECONOMY
MANUFACTURING
Nonferrous
Chemicals
Textiles
Cotton
Printing & Publishing
Wood Products
Food Products
Metal & Machine Products
Paper Products
China & Porcelain Products
Stone Products
Petroleum Refining
Cement
Wineries, Distilleries & Breweries
MINING
Coal
Cobalt
Copper
Diamonds
Gold
Iron Ore
Lead
Manganese
Silver
Tin
Tungsten
Uranium
Zinc
AGRICULTURE
General Agriculture, Tropical Types
Plantation Agriculture
Exhaustive Forest, Collecting Agriculture
Pastureland with Sparse Vegetation
Seasonal Grazing
Non-Agricultural Areas
FISHING
Fishing Areas
GROSS NATIONAL PRODUCT PER CAPITA
The Congo $85
Kenya $85
Tanganyika $52
Uganda $58
Léopoldville
Stanleyville
Entebbe
Nairobi
Usumbura
Albertville
Zanzibar
Dar es Salaam
Jadotville
Elisabethville
KATANGA
Cotton
Manioc
Palmoil
Cattle
Sheep
Sisal
Sugar Cane
Millet
Tobacco

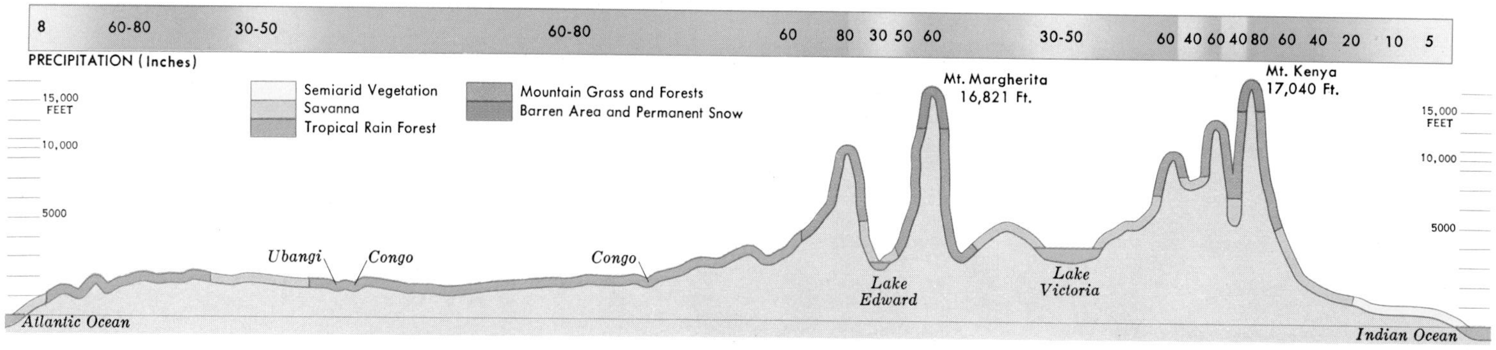
PRECIPITATION (Inches)
8
60-80
30-50
60-80
60
80
30
50
60
30-50
60
40
60
40
80
60
40
20
10
5
15,000 FEET
10,000
5000
Semiarid Vegetation
Savanna
Tropical Rain Forest
Mountain Grass and Forests
Barren Area and Permanent Snow
Mt. Margherita 16,821 Ft.
Mt. Kenya 17,040 Ft.
Ubangi
Congo
Congo
Lake Edward
Lake Victoria
Atlantic Ocean
Indian Ocean

RAINFALL AND VEGETATION ALONG THE EQUATOR IN AFRICA

Fluctuations in rainfall in Equatorial Africa *(bar graph at top)* produce a wide range of vegetation at various altitudes, shown here in a continental cross section. The savannas *(orange)*, areas of tall grasses and low forests, occur wherever moderate seasonal rains prevail. Dense tropical forests *(green)* flourish under constant rains and high humidity. Where the land climbs *(red)*, mountain grasses and open forests grow. Above them loom Mount Margherita and Mount Kenya. The east coast *(far right)*, with little rain and hot temperatures, has desert grass and shrubs *(yellow)*.

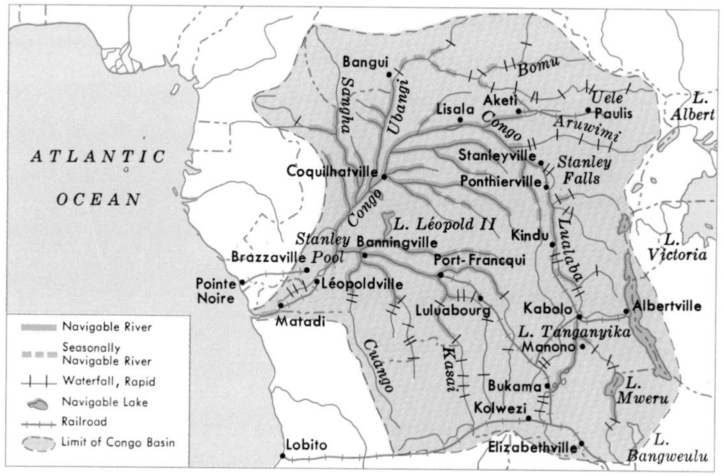
ATLANTIC OCEAN
Bangui
Sangha
Ubangi
Bomu
Lisala
Aketi
Congo
Uele
Paulis
Aruwimi
L. Albert
Stanleyville
Stanley Falls
Ponthierville
Coquilhatville
L. Léopold II
Kindu
Lualaba
L. Victoria
Stanley Pool
Banningville
Brazzaville
Port-Francqui
Pointe Noire
Léopoldville
Matadi
Luluabourg
Kabolo
Albertville
L. Tanganyika
Manono
Cuango
Kasai
Bukama
L. Mweru
Kolwezi
Lobito
Elizabethville
L. Bangweulu
Navigable River
Seasonally Navigable River
Waterfall, Rapid
Navigable Lake
Railroad
Limit of Congo Basin

THE CONGO'S UNIQUE TRANSPORT COMPLEX

The Congo Basin of Equatorial Africa *(green, in map above)* is a vast tropical plateau of low elevation where rivers and railroads together provide a unique transportation complex through dense rain forests. The railroads are stepchildren of river traffic, born of the necessity to bypass the numerous rapids and waterfalls *(black bars)* on the Congo River and its tributaries. Altogether the basin has 8,500 miles of navigable water, but the natural barriers occur so frequently that freight can reach its destination only after portage from boat to railroad boxcar and back to boat again.

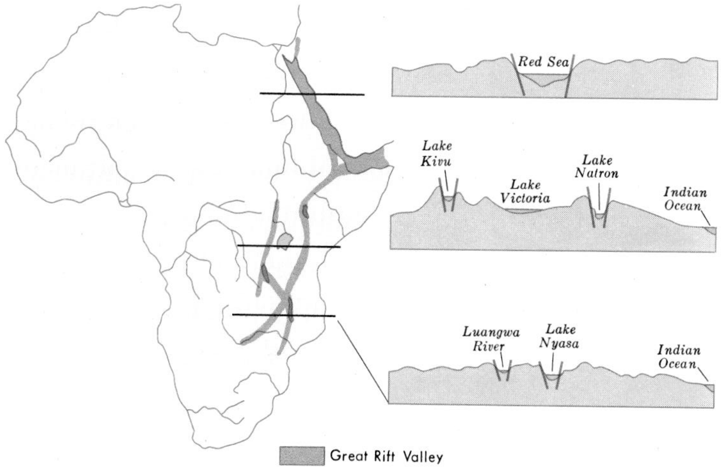
Red Sea
Lake Kivu
Lake Victoria
Lake Natron
Indian Ocean
Luangwa River
Lake Nyasa
Indian Ocean
Great Rift Valley

THE GREAT RIFT OF AFRICA

The Great Rift Valley, a 4,000-mile north-south gash across Africa, is shown on the map at left above, alongside cross sections *(right)* of the rift at three separate points. One of the most spectacular of the earth's land features, it was formed ages ago when a great strip of land sank between parallel faults in the earth's crust. The rift forms the 1,500-mile-long basin of the Red Sea *(upper cross section)*, as well as the narrow troughs of Lake Kivu and Lake Natron *(middle)*. Cliffs that rim Lake Nyasa and the Luangwa River *(bottom)* are also part of the rift formation.

SOUTHERN AFRICA

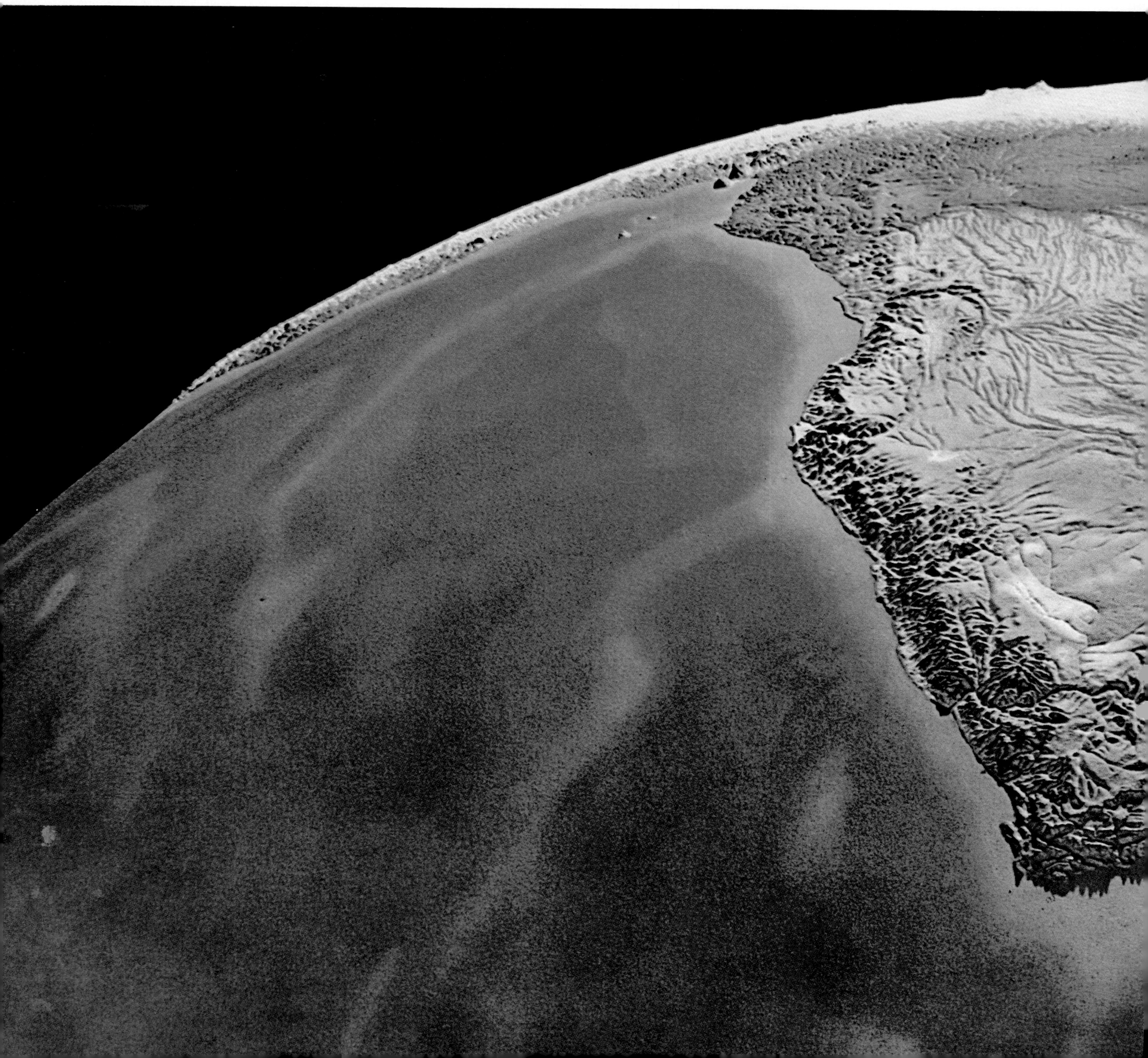

UNDER THE BULGE of the continent juts the stubby southern stem of Africa. At right, the island of Madagascar looms out of the Indian Ocean. At the upper left can be seen the southern coast of the bulge, looking westward over the sea toward South America.

SOUTHERN AFRICA

The great African explorer Dr. David Livingstone wrote: "The flat uniformities over which we had roamed made me feel as if buried alive." Livingstone's long treks, made at the middle of the 19th Century, had taken him across the southern portion of the continent, across the enormous tableland, nearly twice the size of India, that stretches from fever-ridden Congo rain forests to a "Mediterranean" littoral near the Cape of Good Hope, 1,800 miles away.

There is little to break the monotony of the great plateau that stifled Dr. Livingstone. Only on its eastern edge does the gradually rising tableland tilt upward into steep peaks where rivers tumble into magnificent waterfalls or rapids. Vegetation varies gradually, without abrupt contrast, from tufted grasses and low shrub in the dry west to grassy parkland and low trees in the east. Only the pattern of rainfall shows a marked change across the longitudes. The warm, moisture-laden summer winds from the Indian Ocean are forced to rise when they encounter the heights of the east coast, and so they release their moisture. The Atlantic winds that blow across the cold Benguela Current along the west coast are not forced to climb as high when they encounter the land, and so they provide much less rainfall. As a result, throughout much of the year the midland veld and the west thirst for water.

The high, grassy tableland of the east with its scattered scrub trees is cool and pleasant. It is known as "white settlers' territory." Many of Southern Africa's tiny minority of Europeans moved there to farm or mine or start frontier businesses, and the descendants of these settlers form cohesive pockets of European culture among the Africans.

Among the many tribes who inhabit this region, three linguistic groups predominate. The Bushmen, most primitive of all the peoples in Africa, are hunters in the Kalahari Desert and in South-West Africa. The pastoral, nomadic Hottentots live in South-West Africa and in the Cape Province of South Africa. Most numerous of all are the Bantus, who are cattle herders; they total 10 million in South Africa alone. For many years the presence of Europeans in their land had little impact on the traditional African way of life, with its communal lands, its barter economy and hereditary chiefs. But as more and more Africans move to the larger cities—Johannesburg, Cape Town, Pretoria and Durban—their old tribal organizations are finally breaking up.

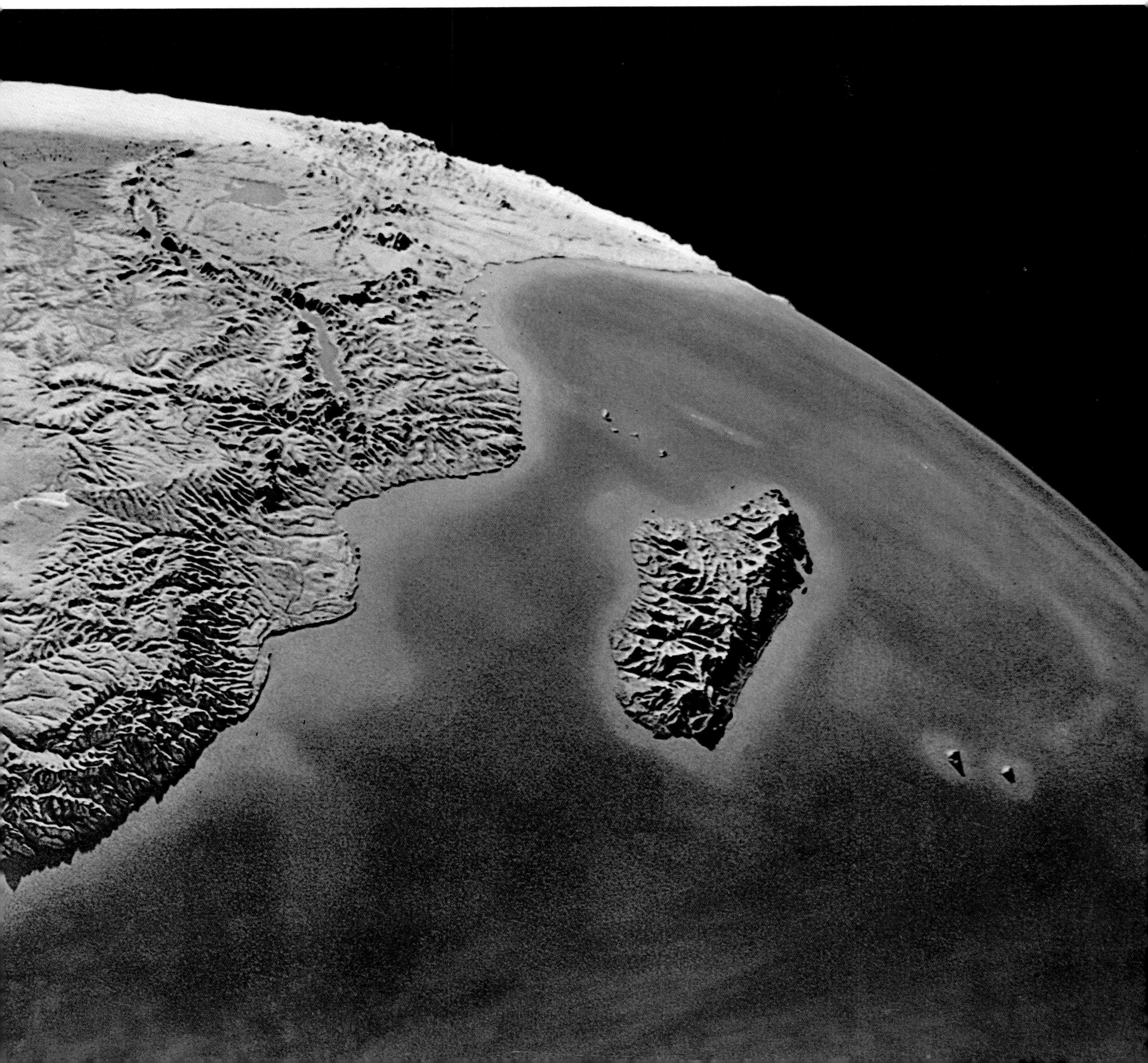

SOUTH AFRICA:
DRY PEAKS AND A SCARRED VELD

A THIRSTY FARM on the veld, or grassland, below the Drakensberg Mountains is scarred by the erosion which has carried away much of the soil of South Africa's plateau. This region is afflicted by erratic rainfall—severe periods of drought alternating with heavy rains that cut gullies in the land. The bare mountains provide a poor watershed, and overgrazing has added to the erosion. Only 15 per cent of South Africa is arable, so even marginal farms in this relatively dry country must be worked to feed the growing population.

SOUTHERN AFRICA
Barren Areas Above Timber
Evergreen Trees
Deciduous Trees
Shrub
Grass
National Capitals
Other Capitals
Other Cities
Railroads
Canals
1 inch = 162 Statute Miles
Miles 0 25 50 75 100 125 150 175
Sinusoidal Projection
Atlantic Ocean
Tropic of Capricorn
ANGOLA (PORTUGUESE WEST AFRICA)
SOUTH-WEST AFRICA (SOUTH AFRICA MANDATE)
BECHUANALAND (BRITISH PROTECTORATE)
THE CONGO
FEDERATION OF RHODESIA AND NYASALAND
NORTHERN RHODESIA
SOUTHERN RHODESIA
UNION OF SOUTH AFRICA
BASUTOLAND (BR.)
BAROTSELAND PROTECTORATE
LUANDA
WINDHOEK
CAPE TOWN
PRETORIA
MASERU
MAFEKING
KALAHARI DESERT
NAMIB DESERT
CAPE OF GOOD HOPE
ORANGE FREE STATE
TRANSVAAL
Cabinda
Banana
Boma
Matadi
Nóqui
Santo António do Zaire
São Salvador
Ambrizete
Ambriz
Caxito
Catete
Muxima
Dondo
Malange
Pôrto Amboim
Novo Redondo
Lobito
Benguela
Dombe Grande
Lucira
Sá da Bandeira
Moçâmedes
Pôrto Alexandre
Baía dos Tigres
PENINSULA DOS TIGRES
Nova Lisboa
Silva Pôrto
Vila Luso
Etosha Pan
Tsumeb
Grootfontein
Otavi
Outjo
Otjiwarongo
Omaruru
Okahandja
Swakopmund
Walvis Bay (SOUTH AFRICA)
Rehoboth
Gobabis
Mariental
Gibeon
Keetmanshoop
Lüderitz
Lüderitz Bay
Bethanie
Aus
Seeheim
Karasburg
Warmbad
Oranjemund
Alexander Bay
Port Nolloth
Springbok
Upington
Kimberley
Bloemfontein
Vryburg
Johannesburg
Germiston
Vereeniging
Krugersdorp
Potchefstroom
Klerksdorp
Lichtenburg
Zeerust
Lobatsi
Kanye
Molepolole
Mochudi
Gaberones
Mahalapye
Serowe
Palapye
Francistown
Bulawayo
Wankie
Livingstone
Victoria Falls
Kariba Reservoir
Maun
Lake Ngami
Ghanzi
Tsau
Toteng
Sesheke
Mulobezi
Kalomo
Choma
Lusaka
Broken Hill
Mumbwa
Kafue
Mazabuka
Ndola
Kitwe
Luanshya
Chingola
Solwezi
Kasempa
Mwinilunga
Balovale
Chavuma
Kalabo
Mongu
Senanga
Kolwezi
Jadotville
Elisabethville
Kamina
Luluabourg
Dilolo
Sandoa
Kapanga
Manono
Lake Mweru
Beaufort West
Graaff-Reinet
Cradock
Queenstown
Umtata
East London
King William's Town
Grahamstown
Port Elizabeth
Algoa Bay
Port Alfred
Uitenhage
Humansdorp
Knysna
George
Mossel Bay
Oudtshoorn
Worcester
Paarl
Stellenbosch
Malmesbury
Table Bay
False Bay
Saldanha
St. Helena Bay
Piketberg
Clanwilliam
Calvinia
Vanrhynsdorp
Bitterfontein
Garies
Carnarvon
Victoria West
De Aar
Colesberg
Middelburg
Burgersdorp
Aliwal North
Bredasdorp
CAPE AGULHAS
GREAT KARROO
Drakensberg
Orange
Vaal
Molopo
Cunene
Cubango
Okovanggo
Zambezi
Kasai
Cuanza
Congo

Indian Ocean
Zanzibar
Dar es Salaam
Dodoma
Morogoro
TANGANYIKA
(BR. TRUST)
Iringa
MAFIA (BR.)
Kilwa
Lindi
Mikindani
Mtwara
CABO DELGADO
Mocimboa da Praia
Ibo
Pôrto Amélia
Lake Nyasa
NYASALAND
NORTHERN RHODESIA
Zomba
Blantyre
MOÇAMBIQUE
Moçambique
António Enes
Quelimane
ZAMBÉZIA
NIASSA
MANICA E SOFALA
Beira
Nova Sofala
Vila de Manica
Umtali
SALISBURY
INHAMBANE
GAZA
Inhambane
Inharrime
Vila de João Belo
LOURENÇO MARQUES
B. Delagoa
MBABANE
Mozambique Channel
ALDABRA IS. (BR.)
COSMOLEDO IS. (BR.)
GRANDE COMORE
ARCHIPEL DES COMORES (FR.)
Moroni
Fomboni
MOHELI
ANJOUAN
Dzaoudzi
MAYOTTE
IS. GLORIEUSES (FR.)
BASSAS DA INDIA (FR.)
EUROPA (FR.)
C. D'AMBRE
Diégo-Suarez (Antsirane)
DIÉGO-SUAREZ
Majunga
MAJUNGA
Maroantsetra
B. d'Antongil
SAINTE MARIE
Tamatave
TANANARIVE
MADAGASCAR
MALAGASY REPUBLIC
Antsirabe
Fianarantsoa
FIANARANTSOA
Morondava
Tuléar
Manakara
Farafangana
Fort-Dauphin
CAP SAINTE MARIE
CAP ANDAVAKA
Tropic of Capricorn
Indian Ocean
Longitude East of Greenwich
CM TERRAIN SOUTHERN AFRICA
COPYRIGHT BY
RAND MC NALLY & COMPANY
MADE IN U.S.A.

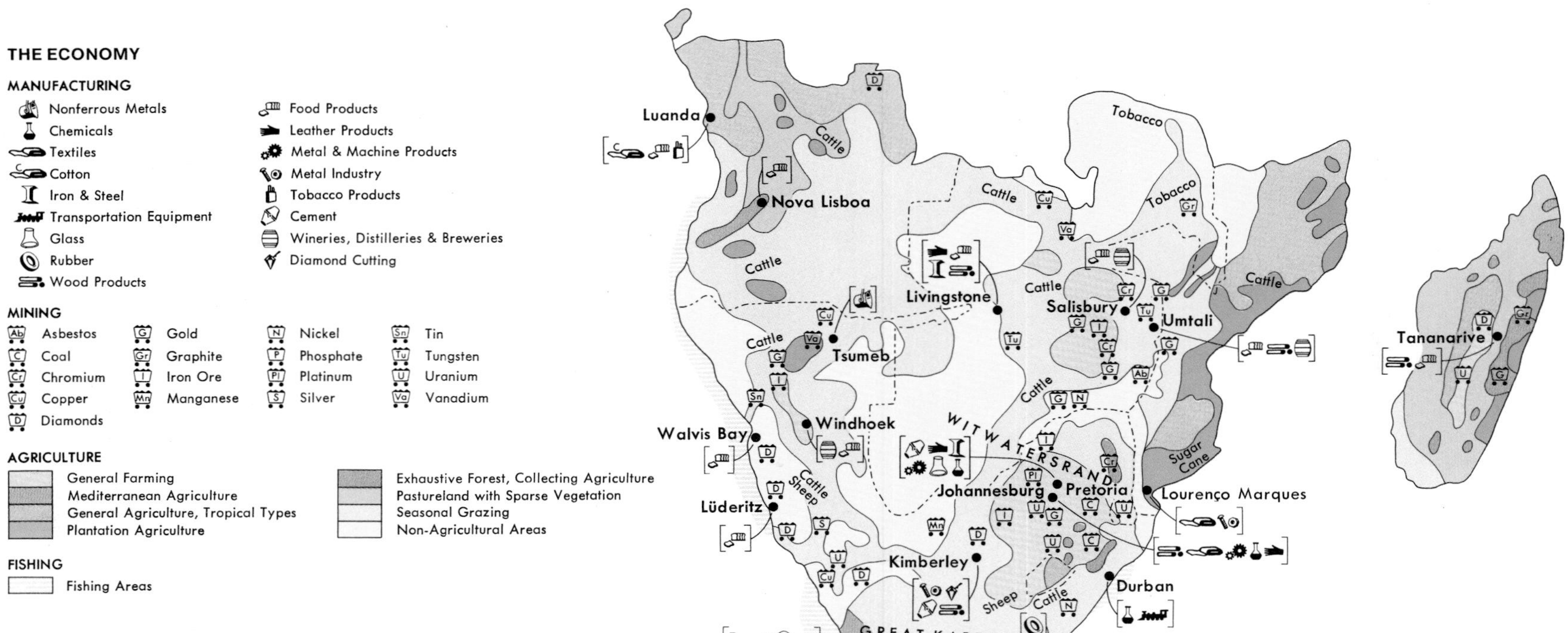
THE ECONOMY
MANUFACTURING
Nonferrous Metals
Chemicals
Textiles
Cotton
Iron & Steel
Transportation Equipment
Glass
Rubber
Wood Products
Food Products
Leather Products
Metal & Machine Products
Metal Industry
Tobacco Products
Cement
Wineries, Distilleries & Breweries
Diamond Cutting
MINING
Asbestos
Coal
Chromium
Copper
Diamonds
Gold
Graphite
Iron Ore
Manganese
Nickel
Phosphate
Platinum
Silver
Tin
Tungsten
Uranium
Vanadium
AGRICULTURE
General Farming
Mediterranean Agriculture
General Agriculture, Tropical Types
Plantation Agriculture
Exhaustive Forest, Collecting Agriculture
Pastureland with Sparse Vegetation
Seasonal Grazing
Non-Agricultural Areas
FISHING
Fishing Areas
Luanda
Nova Lisboa
Livingstone
Salisbury
Umtali
Tananarive
Tsumeb
Windhoek
Walvis Bay
Lüderitz
WITWATERSRAND
Johannesburg
Pretoria
Lourenço Marques
Kimberley
Durban
GREAT KARROO
East London
Cape Town
Port Elizabeth
Tobacco
Cattle
Sheep
Sugar Cane

GROSS NATIONAL PRODUCT PER CAPITA
Federation of Rhodesia and Nyasaland $155   South Africa $398*
*Includes Basutoland, Bechuanaland, South West Africa and Swaziland.

SOUTH AFRICA:

In his biography of Cecil Rhodes, the man who brought a large segment of Southern Africa into the British Empire, André Maurois writes: "All the wealth of the Arabian Nights was there; diamonds and gold, the fantastic fruitfulness of Natal and the vast grazing grounds of the Transvaal." Cooled by the Benguela Current, and washed by sporadic rains sweeping down from the Indian Ocean, the high tableland of the Republic of South Africa offers a relatively dry climate. Even along the warm northern rim of the nation, the climate is not oppressive. After 300 years of settlement, three million Europeans call this land home.

Farmers from The Netherlands made up the first great wave of European settlers. These men, the Boers, laid the groundwork for the present-day agriculture that supplies most of the country's needs. Fine wine grapes flourish on terraced slopes and fields along the southwest coast near Cape Town; wheat and citrus fruit thrive in the irrigated valleys despite the destruction of occasional flash floods. Inland, the rolling plains of the High Veld cover a vast triangle stretching across the Orange Free State and into southern Transvaal and Cape Province. In this triangle the descendants of the pioneer Dutch farmers, who made the Great Trek of 1836 northward from Cape Province, grow corn on widely scattered, sprawling farms.

Along the east coast, on the hills of Natal Province, the summer winds spill most of their rain. "The grass is rich and matted," says novelist Alan Paton, "you cannot see the soil . . . the ground is holy, being even as it came from the Creator." On the green slopes Indians provide the muscle for plantations of sugar cane. And just as their ancestors did generations ago, millions of natives raise cattle and corn in the country's tribal reserves and in the territories of Swaziland and Basutoland.

AREA: 472,550 sq. mi.
POPULATION: 14,435,000.
Largest city: Johannesburg.
Capital: Pretoria, Cape Town.
CLIMATE: Generally mild all year, cooler in highlands; moderate rainfall decreasing from east to west.
ALTITUDES: Injasuti, 11,182 ft. (highest).

Despite the continued emphasis on agriculture, the Republic of South Africa has changed from a static, rural community into the wealthiest and most industrialized nation on the continent. Diamonds, discovered in 1866, are now mined mainly around Kimberley and Pretoria *(diagram, opposite page)*. Gold, discovered in 1884, is taken in great quantities from the 225-mile "golden arc" of the Witwatersrand (Ridge of White Waters) in the Transvaal and in the gold fields of the Orange Free State. More than 40 per cent of the world's gold supply comes from the Rand's surface outcroppings of Pre-Cambrian rock and from deep veins buried under younger stone. The mining and refining industries absorb large quantities of the output of the nearby coal fields. The nation's steel industry is concentrated at Pretoria and near Vereeniging, while Johannesburg, the largest city, is the commercial and industrial metropolis of all of Southern Africa.

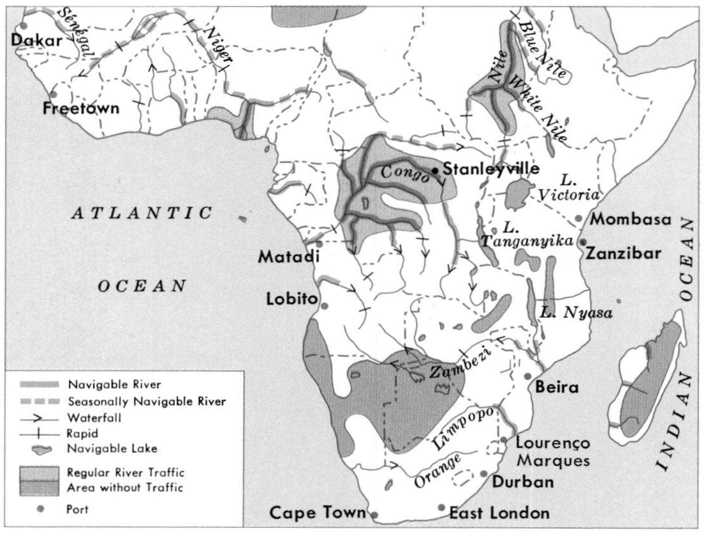
Dakar
Sénégal
Niger
Freetown
Blue Nile
White Nile
Nile
Congo
Stanleyville
L. Victoria
ATLANTIC
OCEAN
Mombasa
L. Tanganyika
Zanzibar
Matadi
Lobito
L. Nyasa
Zambezi
Beira
Limpopo
Lourenço Marques
Orange
Durban
Cape Town
East London
INDIAN
OCEAN
Navigable River
Seasonally Navigable River
Waterfall
Rapid
Navigable Lake
Regular River Traffic Area without Traffic
Port

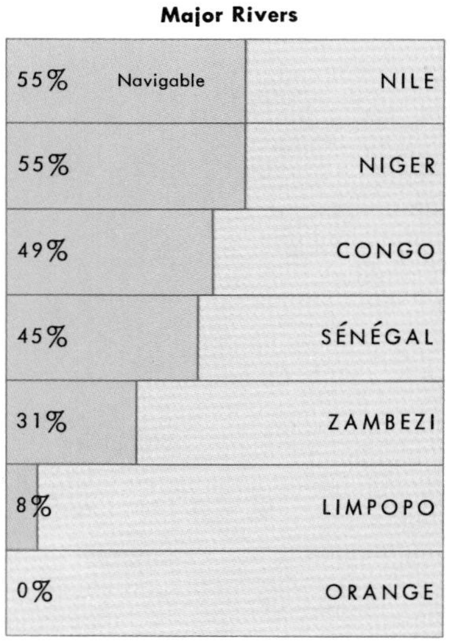
Major Rivers
55% Navigable NILE
55% NIGER
49% CONGO
45% SÉNÉGAL
31% ZAMBEZI
8% LIMPOPO
0% ORANGE

BLOCKED RIVER ROUTES TO THE SEA

The usefulness of Southern Africa's rivers as avenues to and from the coast, shown on the map at left above, is limited by terrain and rainfall. The tableland of the interior drops steeply to the coast, and river traffic is blocked by waterfalls and rapids. The climate alternates between droughts that dry up rivers and rainy-season floods that send them rampaging over their banks. The bar graph at right illustrates how little of the continent's large network of rivers and lakes is actually navigable, even under ideal conditions.

BECHUANALAND:

Bleak and backward, dusty Bechuanaland suffers from an almost constant shortage of water. Most of the southern region is occupied by the Kalahari Desert, a level plateau broken by undulating sand hills, large stretches of tufted grass and scrubby bushes. Lakes that once studded the Kalahari are dry now, but every so often great gully-washing rains fall heavily to moisten seeds that have long lain dormant. Then patches of tsama melons sprout to provide a brief feast for antelopes, lions and hyenas. In the northwest, the Okovanggo River flows into a 4,000-square-mile depression to create the malaria-infested Okovanggo Swamp and shallow, reed-choked Lake Ngami.

AREA: 274,928 sq. mi.
POPULATION: 368,000. Largest city: Kanye. Capital: Mafeking.
CLIMATE: Hot summers (Nov.-April), warm winters (May-Oct.); very dry except in extreme north, which has moderate summer rainfall.

The population, which is 99 per cent Negro, is divided into eight tribes and is concentrated in the better grazing lands to the east. Cattle are Bechuanaland's most valuable export. In the desolate west a few Bushmen survive, eking out an existence as hunters. Rent from the Rhodesia railroad, which runs from Cape Town to Bulawayo through Bechuanaland, and the export of labor for Rhodesian mines are other important sources of income.

SOUTH-WEST AFRICA:

South-West Africa supports only two people per square mile. Along the narrow Atlantic coastal lowlands, the Namib Desert is an empty stretch of sand. The remainder of the territory is a plateau which begins some 60 miles from the coast. The plateau increases in elevation inland, reaching heights of more than 6,000 feet. Most of this region of tufted grass and low shrub wilts under less than 20 inches of rain a year. The only farming is marginal, but cattle and sheep graze throughout the highlands. In the parched south, karakul sheep, brought to the country by German settlers at the turn of the century, are the world's prime source of Persian lamb coats.

AREA: 317,725 sq. mi.
POPULATION: 608,000. Largest city and capital: Windhoek.
CLIMATE: Hot summers (Nov.-April), warm winters (May-Oct.); very dry along coast, some summer rain inland, very dry winters.

Along a 300-mile stretch of the Atlantic shore north of the mouth of the Orange River, diamonds brought down the Orange River are washed up by the cold Benguela Current. Lüderitz, the chief diamond port, is also the location of a fishing industry, which includes canning factories for the native rock lobster. At Tsumeb, copper, zinc and lead are mined. In the wetter and greener area of the far north, some 316,000 tribesmen subsist on corn and cattle.

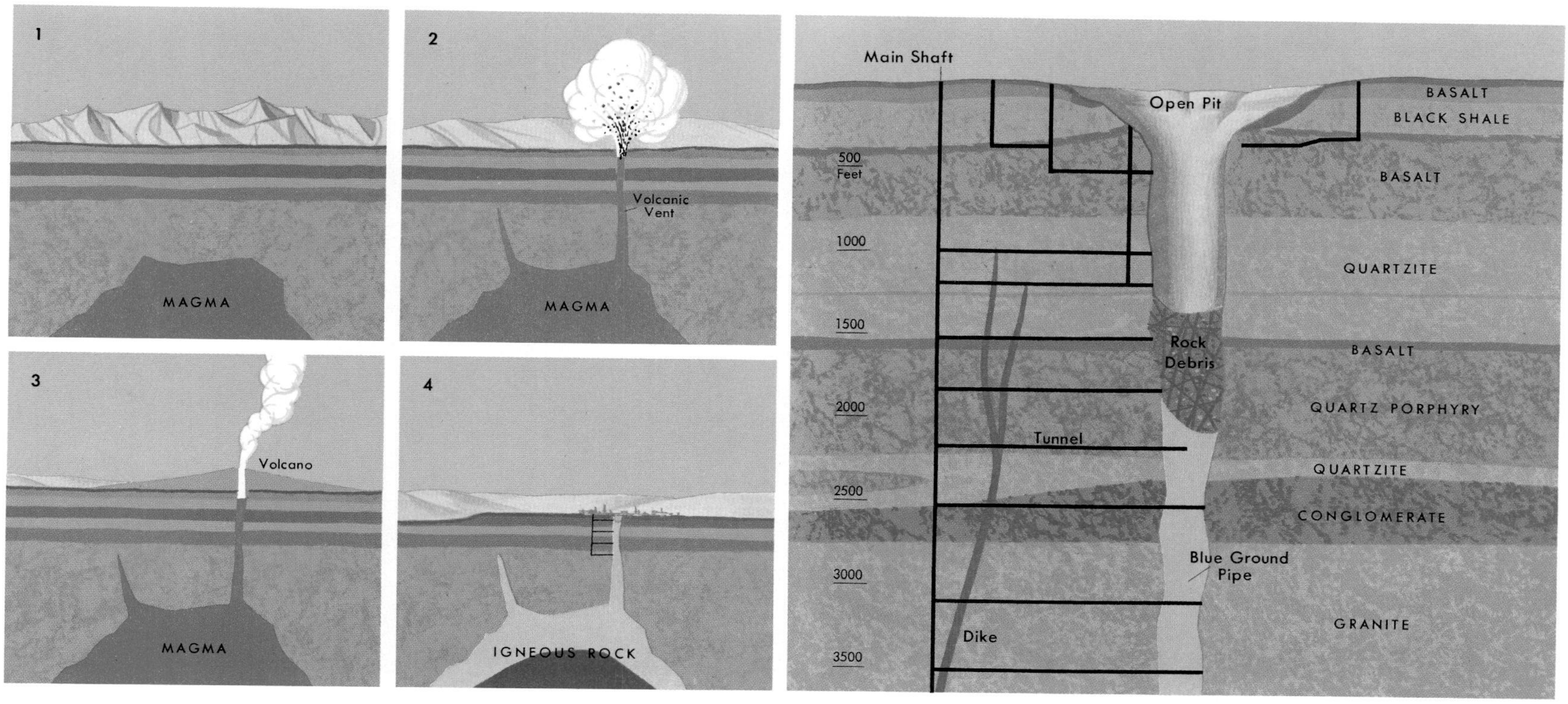

DIAMONDS FROM CREATION TO MINE SHAFT

The formation of diamonds and procedures used to mine them are illustrated here. Millions of years ago minute particles of carbon were crystallized into diamonds by intense heat and pressure in pools of magma (molten rock) beneath the surface of the earth *(cross section 1, at left above)*. The magma was forced upward through a weakness in the earth's crust, which formed a volcanic vent *(2)*. Rising through the vent, the magma erupted at the surface as a volcano *(3)* and then cooled to blue-tinged igneous rock *(4)*. Miners work the "blue ground" inside the vents, or "pipes." Until cave-ins stop them, the miners work in an open pit above the pipe *(cross section at right)*. Later, shafts are sunk parallel to the pipe, and tunnels are cut to the blue ground. Good mines produce four carats of diamonds from 35 tons of rock.

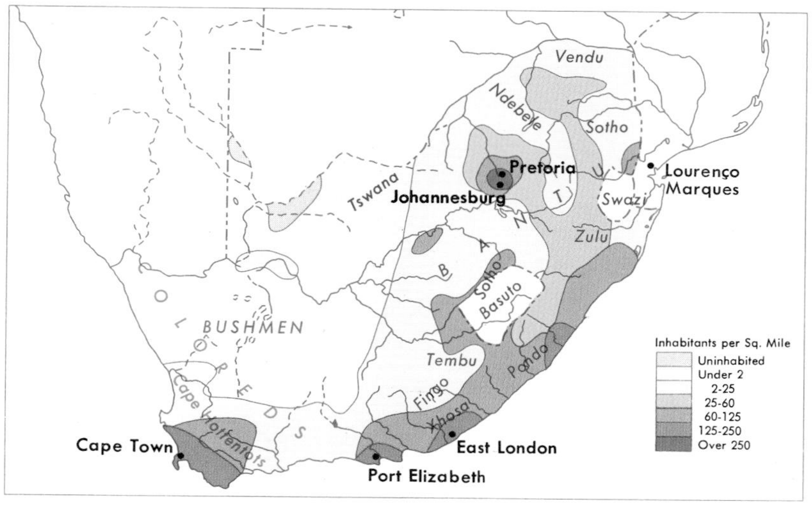

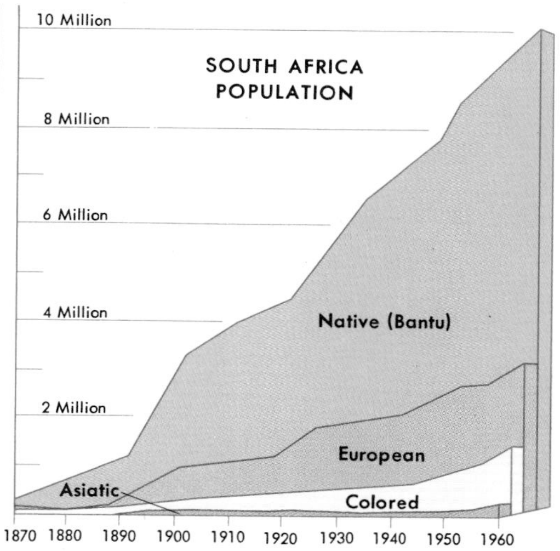

SOUTH AFRICA'S RACES

In South Africa all nonwhite individuals and tribes have official designations. The principal locations of the people who bear various designations are shown on the map at far left. "Natives" include the many subdivisions of Bantu-speaking Negroes, found mainly in the eastern half of the country. "Coloreds" are descendants of early European sailors and settlers who intermarried with imported slaves and with the Hottentots living near Cape Town when the Dutch arrived. Not shown are the white "Europeans," so called whether from Europe or not, and the "Asiatics," descendants of the Chinese brought around the turn of the century to work in the gold fields, and of the Indians imported to work on the sugar plantations. The growth of each of these groups, particularly the rapid increase in the Bantus, is shown on the graph *(right)*.

RHODESIA AND NYASALAND: Nearly twice the size of Texas, the Federation of Rhodesia and Nyasaland is being swiftly transformed into a modern commercial economy. Some 300,000 Europeans, most of them British, make their home in the grassy parkland of the Federation's plateau. The settlers' large commercial farms, mechanized mines, factories and towns are enclaves of European culture in a region that was first opened up for colonists by Cecil Rhodes in 1890.

The Federation is outstanding as a preserve for the animals that the white man once tried to exterminate in order to eliminate the tsetse fly: elephants, buffaloes, zebras, giraffes, kudu, wildebeest, antelopes, lions and leopards.

AREA: 487,639 sq. mi.
POPULATION: 7,805,000. Largest city and capital: Salisbury.
CLIMATE: Hot summers (Nov.-April), warm winters (May-Oct.); moderate summer rainfall, winters very dry.

The Federation has a number of assets. Plentiful rains water large areas and make farming profitable. The second largest exporter of tobacco in the world, the Federation also exports some tea, maize and peanuts. Its varied mines produce 45 different minerals. Copper, the most important, is mined in the Northern Rhodesian Copperbelt, which is the world's fourth largest producer and supplies the country with nearly 60 per cent of its export revenue. For Southern Rhodesia's steel and textile industries, there are numerous potential power sites, including the greatest of all, 350-foot-high Victoria Falls. At Kariba, where the broad Zambezi River churns through a narrow gorge of rocks, a 420-foot-high dam is already in place.

ANGOLA: The central section of Angola is an upland region where the African Plateau rises more than 6,000 feet. Here, plentiful rainfall and moderate temperatures combine to provide a climate that attracts most of Angola's 200,000 Europeans and its densest population of Africans. More than 90 per cent of Angola's corn crop is grown here, much of it for export to Western Europe.

AREA: 481,226 sq. mi.
POPULATION: 4,496,000. Largest city and capital: Luanda.
CLIMATE: Coastal regions hot and dry; interior uplands milder, with moderate rainfall in summer (Nov.-April).

Diamond fields in the northeast and recently discovered oil deposits in the Cuanza basin are Angola's most significant mineral resources. Industry is small-scale; most of it consists of processing food for local needs. In the south, the Portuguese colonists carry on their traditional trades of cattle raising and fishing. Fishing fleets bring in rich hauls of sardines, mackerel and tuna for canning plants and for the fish-meal factories along the coast.

MOZAMBIQUE: Lying mostly to the east of the African Plateau, Mozambique's lowlands are plagued with malaria. Most of the year the country is a hot, humid home for mosquitoes and the tsetse fly. Largely undeveloped, Mozambique is a rural land with only one per cent of its potentially arable acreage under cultivation.

AREA: 297,654 sq. mi.
POPULATION: 6,253,000. Largest city and capital: Lourenço Marques.
CLIMATE: Hot summers (Nov.-April), warm winters (May-Oct.); rainy summers, dry winters.

The busy ports of Beira and Lourenço Marques handle imports and exports of the Federation and South Africa.

MALAGASY REPUBLIC: The republic occupies Madagascar, the world's fourth largest island, which became a home for migrating Indonesians and Malayans long before the first white man arrived.

AREA: 228,510 sq. mi.
POPULATION: 5,225,000. Largest city and capital: Tananarive.
CLIMATE: Hot along coast, cool highlands; rain decreases from east to west.

Rice is grown on the lowlands adjacent to the island's high eastern plateau. In the western grasslands cattle, sheep and goats are herded. The main export is coffee.

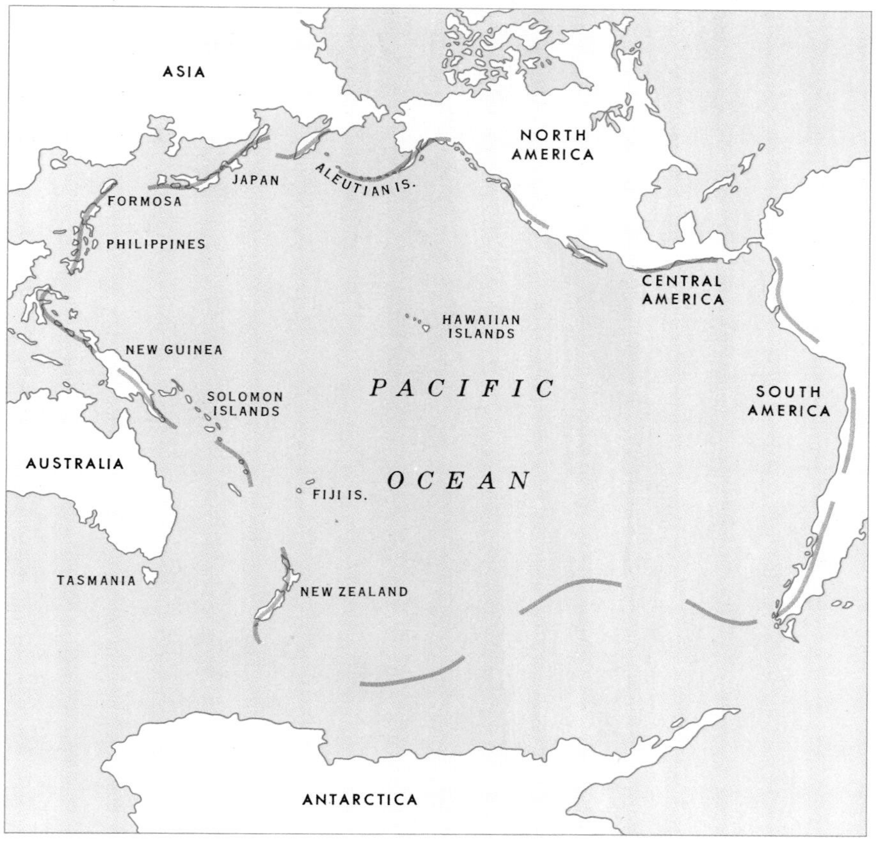

A RING OF FIRE created by a chain of volcanoes runs around the rim of the largest ocean in the world. More than three fifths of the earth's active volcanoes rise along the edge of the Pacific, and most earthquakes rumble on the shallow curve reaching from New Guinea to New Zealand.

THE PACIFIC

"The Mediterranean is the ocean of the past," wrote U.S. Secretary of State John Hay at the turn of the century. "The Atlantic is the ocean of the present, and the Pacific is the ocean of the future." Several generations later, history vindicated Hay's vision. The high tides of World War II washed ashore on far islands. Names of distant places in this huge ocean—Choiseul, Palau, Kolombangara, Guadalcanal, Kwajalein, Bougainville, Tarawa, Eniwetok, Saipan, Iwo Jima and Okinawa—sounded suddenly familiar everywhere in the world. Soldiers, airmen and sailors, home from obscure battlegrounds, remembered the ominous silence of the rain forest and the steady passage of trade winds over curving, palm-lined beaches.

In western man's imagination, the Pacific is still the South Seas, and the far islands are still the islands of desire and languid ease. Little has changed since the first European explorers came ashore on Pacific isles seeking gold, spices and the expansion of empire. The dark-skinned Melanesians, their teeth blackened by betel nut, still squat in spindly villages, making carvings of their ancestor gods and hacking fitfully at the encroaching jungle. Brown-skinned Micronesians fish from outriggers and wrest meager crops of taro from their coral strands. Golden-brown Polynesians maintain their leisurely ways despite increasing contact with the West.

Jet planes have destroyed the vast distances that once set these peoples apart from most of the world. Some of their atolls have been made into testing grounds for nuclear bombs. Tourists now fly in to visit islands that used to see ships only rarely, or they stop in passage between continents. But Oceania still seems as remote as it was when the first waves of migration pushed out from the Asian mainland ages ago, when the first settlers sailed into 64,000,000 square miles of ocean, homing on an unknown shore.

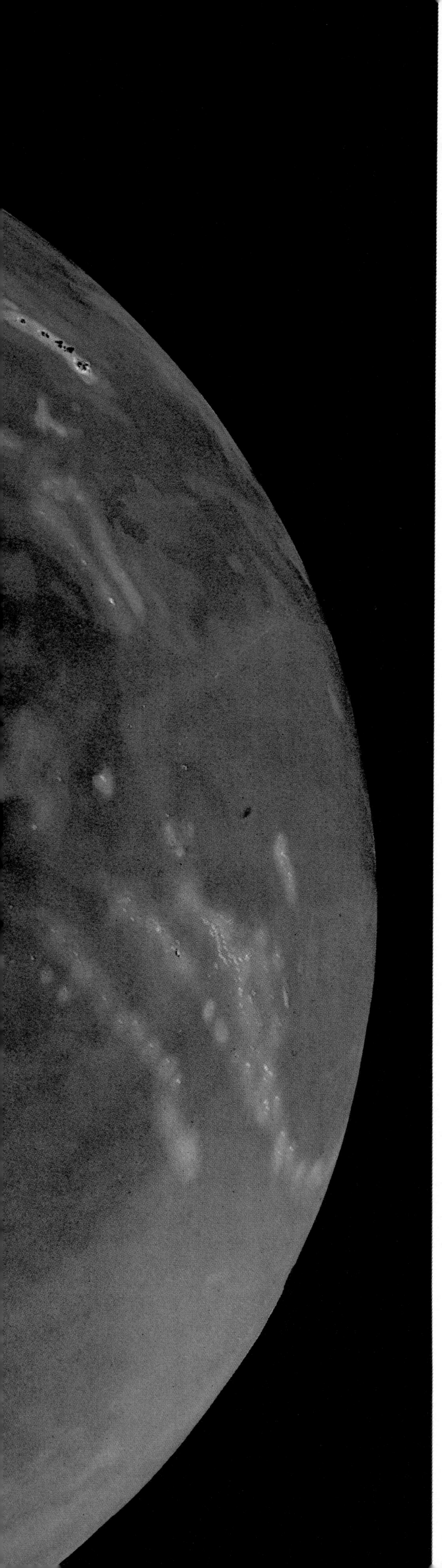

A THIRD OF THE WORLD belongs to the Pacific. From Australia *(lower left)* it arcs north past Indonesia to the thin line of the Aleutians *(upper left)*. Northeast toward the Hawaiian Islands *(upper right)*, an emptiness of water is dotted by the archipelagoes of Oceania.

NORTH PACIFIC

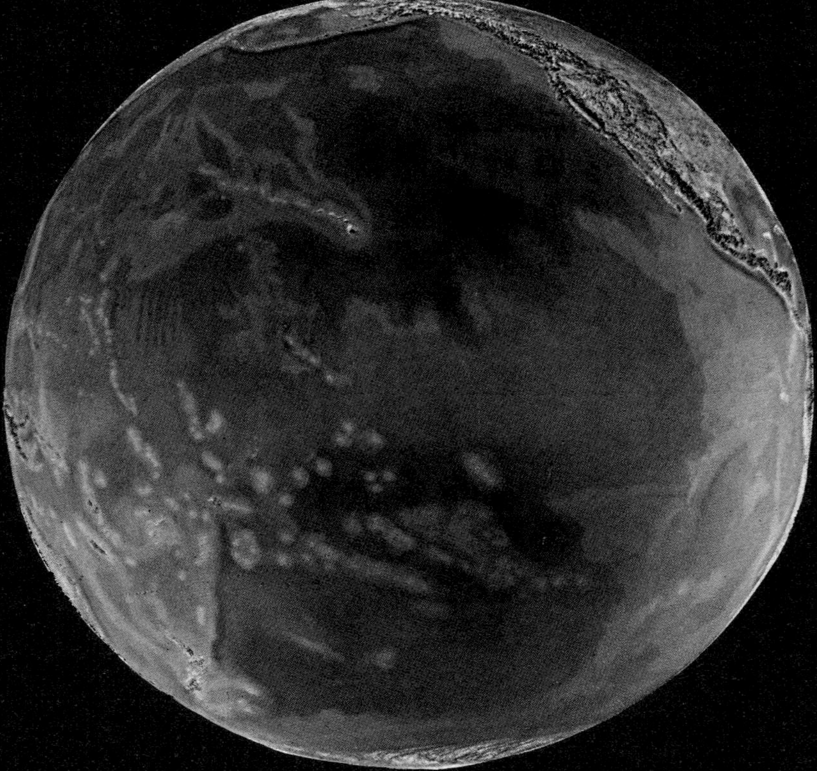

THE LARGEST OCEAN IN THE WORLD, the Pacific *(above)* is almost a perfect hemisphere in shape. North America is at upper right. The Aleutian Islands trail across the top of the globe.

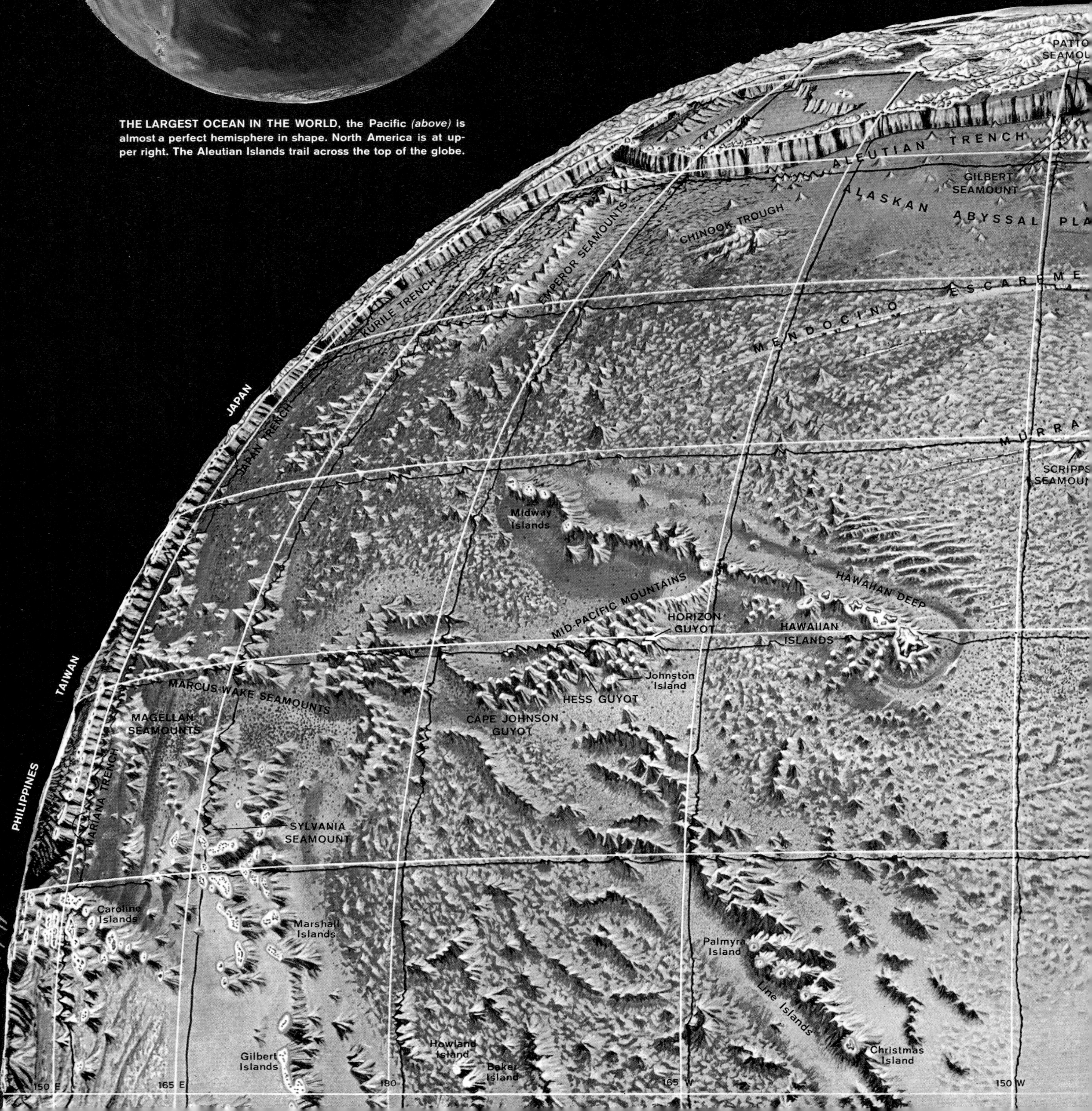

PATTO
SEAMOU
ALEUTIAN TRENCH
GILBERT SEAMOUNT
ALASKAN ABYSSAL PLA
CHINOOK TROUGH
EMPEROR SEAMOUNTS
KURILE TRENCH
ESCARPME
MENDOCINO
JAPAN
JAPAN TRENCH
MURRA
SCRIPPS SEAMOUN
Midway Islands
HAWAIIAN DEEP
MID-PACIFIC MOUNTAINS
HORIZON GUYOT
HAWAIIAN ISLANDS
Johnston Island
HESS GUYOT
TAIWAN
MARCUS-WAKE SEAMOUNTS
MAGELLAN SEAMOUNTS
CAPE JOHNSON GUYOT
PHILIPPINES
MARIANA TRENCH
SYLVANIA SEAMOUNT
Caroline Islands
Marshall Islands
Palmyra Island
Line Islands
Christmas Island
Howland Island
Baker Island
Gilbert Islands
150 E
165 E
180
165 W
150 W
Ken Fagg

Emptied of water, the tremendous North Pacific would expose as wild and rugged a landscape as can be found anywhere in the world. The maps on these and the following pages, drawn from International Geophysical Year findings, show how the Pacific is fashioned. For 3,600 miles from the Bering Sea to the Equator, for 10,600 miles from Central America to Mindanao, the ocean floor is wrinkled and scarred. There is no mid-ocean ridge, as in the Atlantic, no north-south flaw like the great valley of the Mid-Atlantic Rift, but four gigantic fissures slice east and west in parallel flaws that are up to 30 miles wide, 3,300 miles long and 10,500 feet deep. These fissures are the Mendocino Escarpment and the Murray, Clarion and Clipperton Fracture Zones. Off the Philippines *(extreme lower left)*, the Mariana Trench descends 35,630 feet, the greatest depth plumbed by man. At the same latitude, a peak of the Hawaiian Islands *(center)* reaches from its subsea base to a height of 32,024 feet, the highest recorded in the world.

The continental shelves of the Pacific fall away into steep-sided abysses. Almost everywhere there are submerged pinnacles of seamounts, guyots (flat-topped seamounts) and undersea mountains. The East Pacific Rise makes a long run down the west coast of the Americas, extending into the South Pacific. In the western segment of the ocean, many mountain peaks and ranges thrust themselves up high enough to form islands.

Only rarely is this corrugated bottom of the Pacific relieved by flat plains such as those that spread across thousands of miles of the Atlantic. South of the Aleutian Trench an abyssal plain stretches toward the Mendocino Escarpment. Silt fans out from California in a relatively smooth run to the guyots at the eastern end of the Murray Fracture. And strands of sediment flatten around the base of Pacific archipelagoes – along the run of islands from Midway to Hawaii and the Line Islands, a portion of which, from Palmyra to Christmas, is visible here.

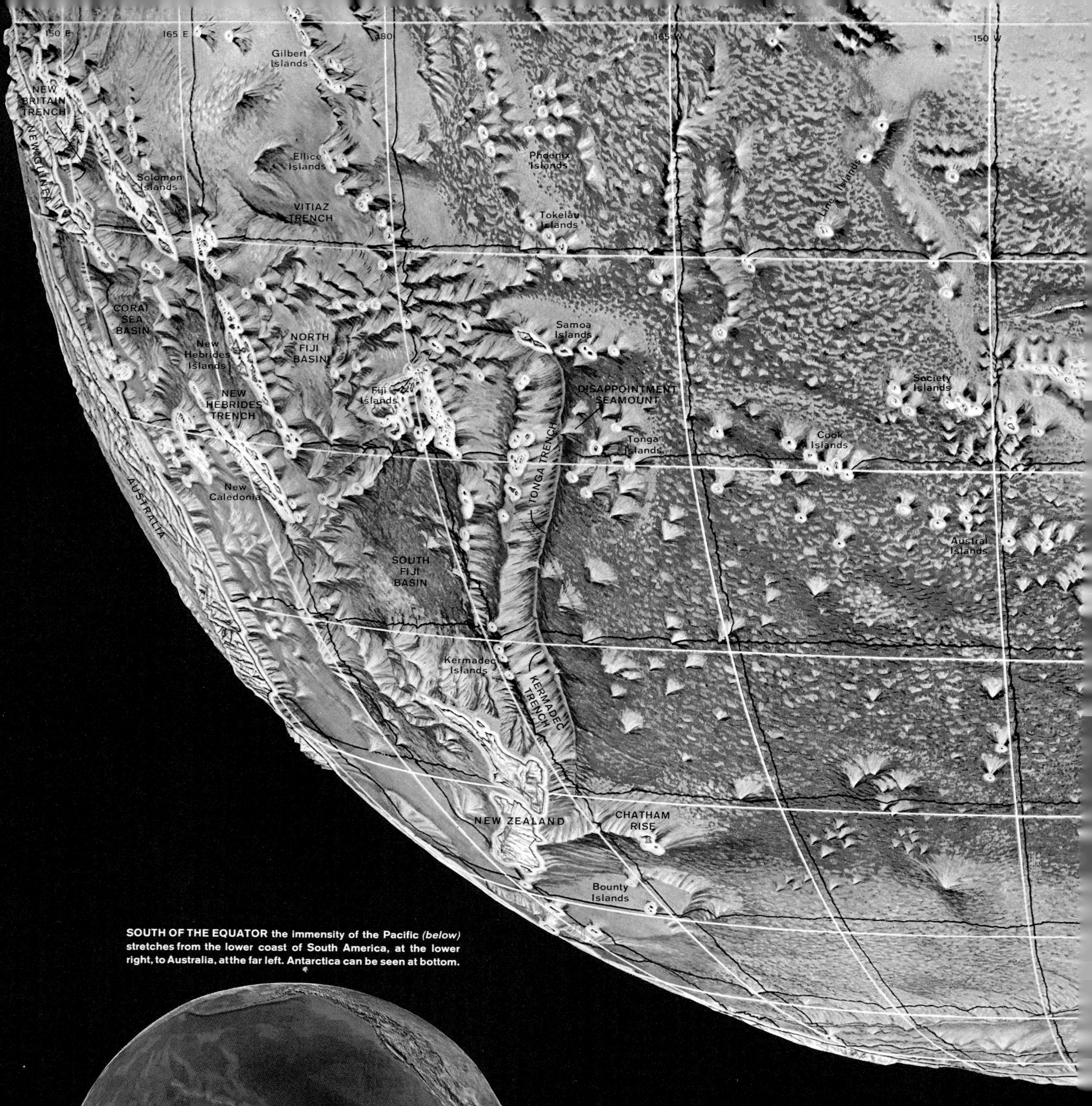

150 E
165 E
180
165 W
150 W
Gilbert Islands
NEW BRITAIN TRENCH
NEW GUINEA
Ellice Islands
Phoenix Islands
Solomon Islands
VITIAZ TRENCH
Tokelau Islands
Line Islands
CORAL SEA BASIN
New Hebrides Islands
NORTH FIJI BASIN
Samoa Islands
Fiji Islands
NEW HEBRIDES TRENCH
DISAPPOINTMENT SEAMOUNT
Society Islands
TONGA TRENCH
Tonga Islands
Cook Islands
AUSTRALIA
New Caledonia
Austral Islands
SOUTH FIJI BASIN
Kermadec Islands
KERMADEC TRENCH
NEW ZEALAND
CHATHAM RISE
Bounty Islands

SOUTH OF THE EQUATOR the immensity of the Pacific *(below)* stretches from the lower coast of South America, at the lower right, to Australia, at the far left. Antarctica can be seen at bottom.

SOUTH PACIFIC

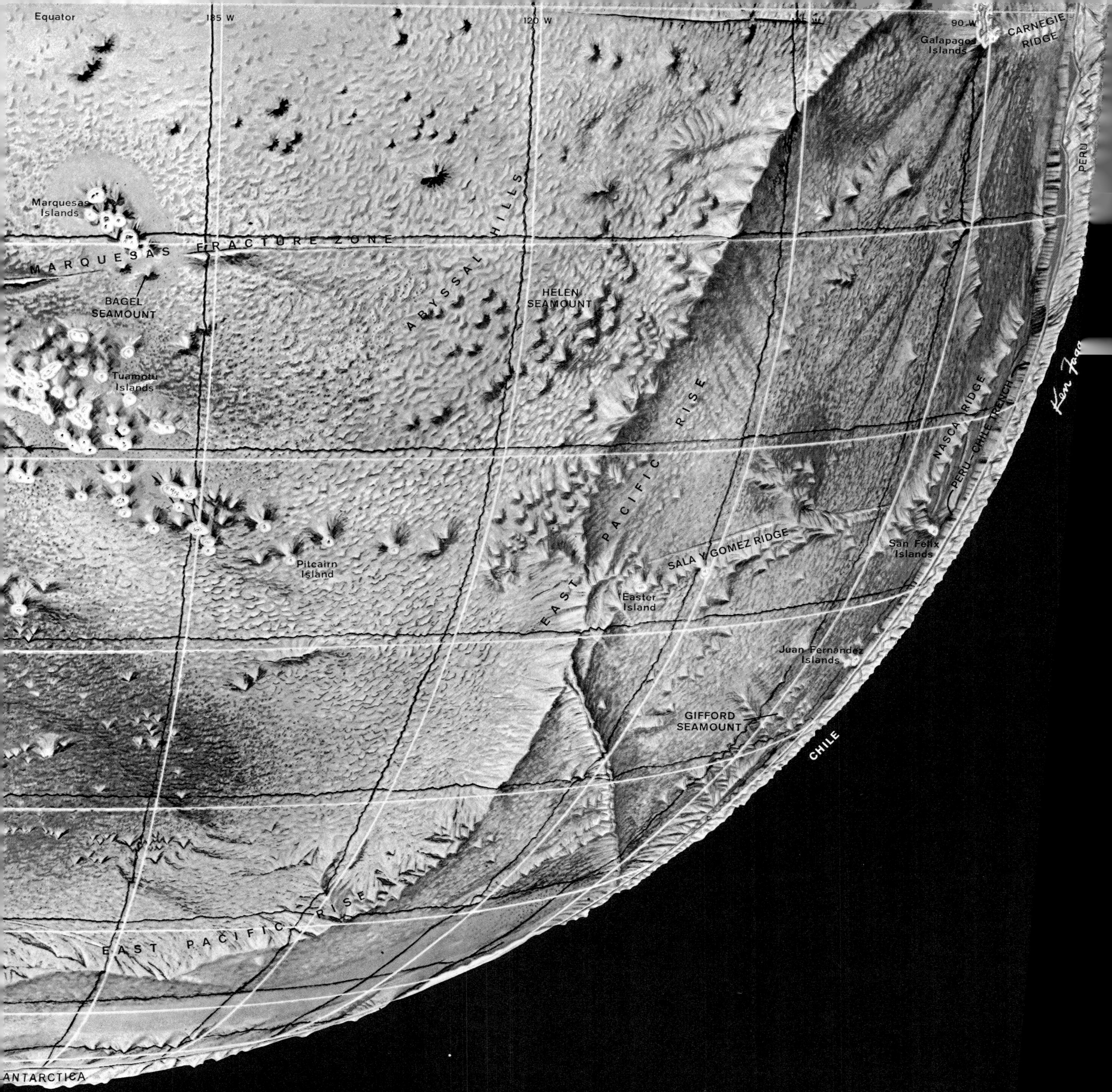
Equator
135 W
120 W
90 W
Galapagos Islands
CARNEGIE RIDGE
PERU
Marquesas Islands
MARQUESAS FRACTURE ZONE
ABYSSAL HILLS
HELEN SEAMOUNT
BAGEL SEAMOUNT
Tuamotu Islands
EAST PACIFIC RISE
NASCA RIDGE
PERU-CHILE TRENCH
San Felix Islands
SALA Y GOMEZ RIDGE
Pitcairn Island
Easter Island
Juan Fernández Islands
GIFFORD SEAMOUNT
CHILE
EAST PACIFIC RISE
ANTARCTICA

In the 36 million square miles of sea bottom encompassed by the southern segment of the Pacific Ocean there is only one major fissure – the Marquesas Fracture Zone – as against the four which slash deeply into the floor of the North Pacific. The Marquesas Fracture Zone *(top center, above)* runs about 1,500 miles east and west, is 30 miles across at its widest point, goes 4,000 feet down. The greatest depth in the South Pacific – 34,876 feet – is located in the Tonga-Kermadec Trench, which extends for 1,600 miles north and south between New Zealand and the Samoa Islands *(left center)*.

In the South Pacific the peaks of the East Pacific Rise were found by International Geophysical Year determinations to lie as much as 10,000 feet below sea level in most places. The rise loops from South America around Australia and joins the Mid-Atlantic Ridge to make up a world-circling submarine range. The amount of heat radiating from the crust of the rise near Easter Island *(lower right)* is seven times as great as the heat that emanates from the earth's crust elsewhere. T discovery has led to the theory that molten rock is welling up from depths far inside the planet. If the action continues, the rise some day in the distant future become dry land.

The region between New Zealand, Tonga and New Guinea is most active earthquake zone in the world. Other bad earthquake z are the continental mountains which rim the South Pacific in the and the trenches which cut into the ocean floor there. Severe m ments in the earth's crust have been created in these areas by combination of a northward shift of the ocean floor and a south slide of the continent. The result has been disastrous earthquak Chile and the movement of great masses of sediment shake underwater cliffs. The movement of the sediment has created waves that sweep unchecked clear across the Pacific to caus mendous damage on the coasts of Japan, almost 11,000 miles

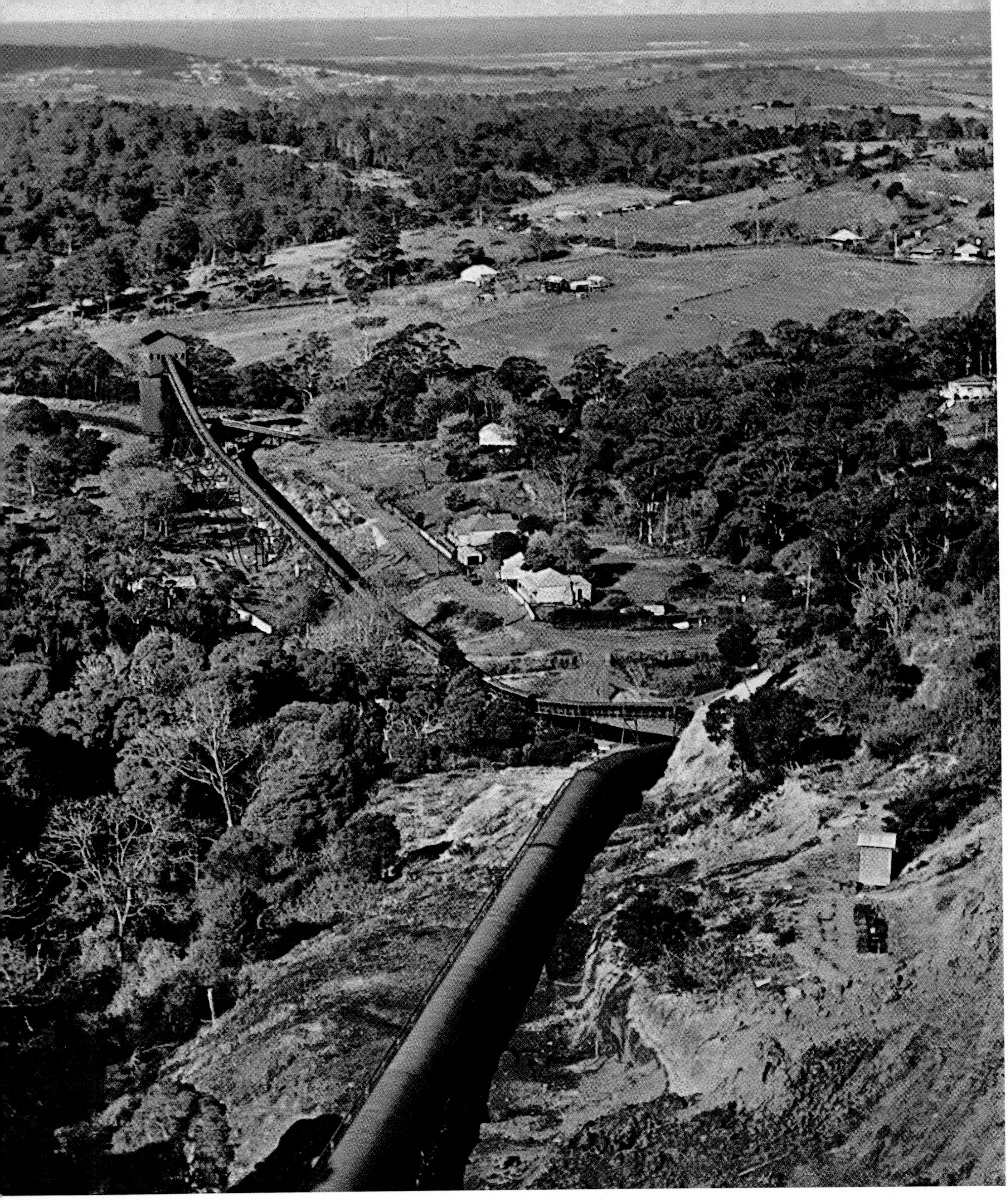

THE AUSTRALIAN LANDS

HOSPITABLE HILLS at the edge of Australia's eastern agricultural lands in New South Wales stretch almost to the Pacific. In the foreground, coming down from upland mines, is a closed conveyor belt carrying coal towards Port Kembla, a thriving iron and steel community not far from Sydney. The most important Australian coal mining districts are located in New South Wales.

INHOSPITABLE RIDGES, these worn relics of a mountain chain form the southern end of the Macdonnell Range in Australia's Northern Territory. Hot and barren, with sparse vegetation, much of the center of Australia consists of the aptly named "Dead Heart"—land so desiccated that, except for the town of Alice Springs, there are only isolated mining camps and cattle ranches.

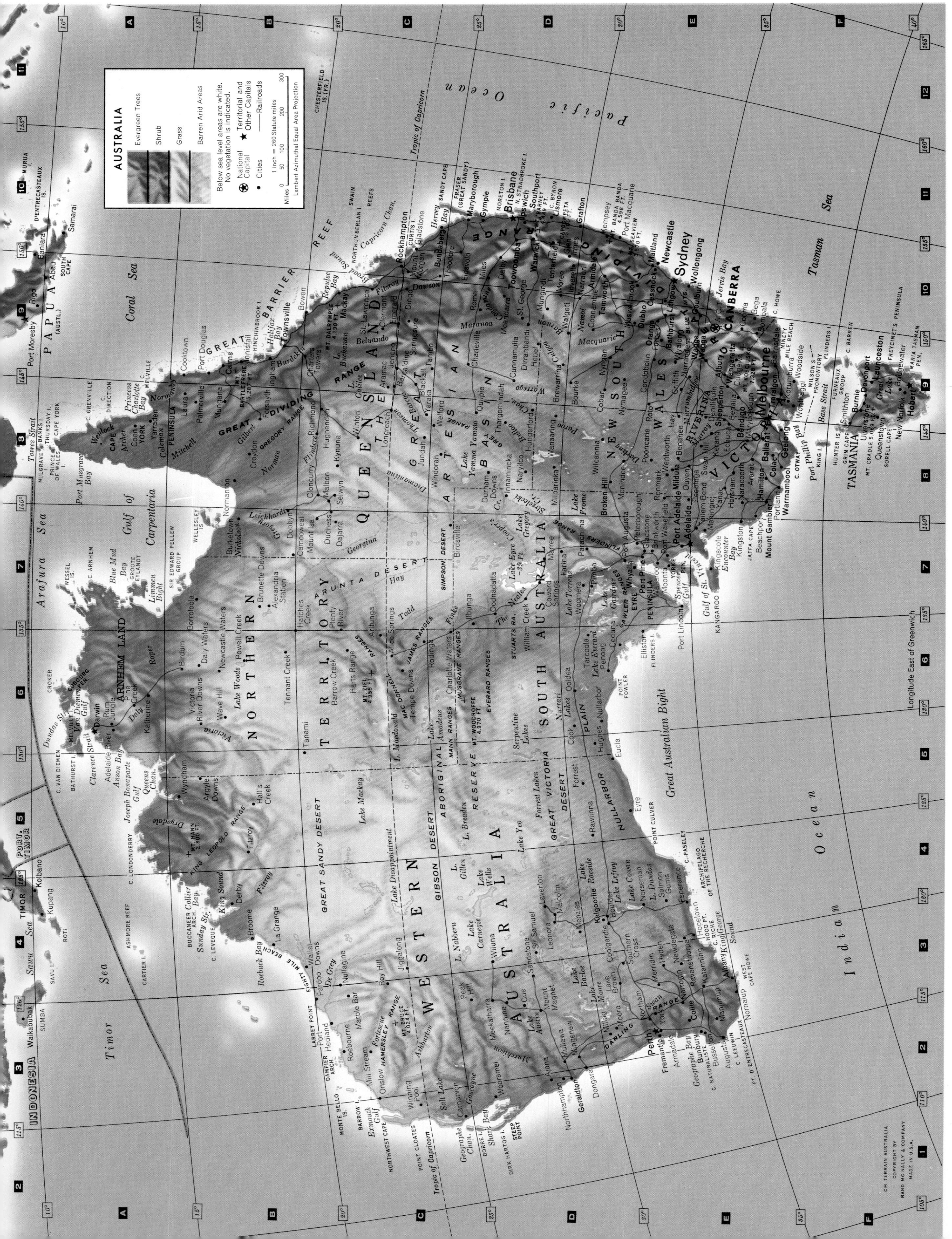
AUSTRALIA
Evergreen Trees
Shrub
Grass
Barren Arid Areas
Below sea level areas are white. No vegetation is indicated.
National Capital
Territorial and Other Capitals
Cities
Railroads
1 inch = 260 Statute miles
Miles 0 50 100 200 300
Lambert Azimuthal Equal Area Projection
Coral Sea
Arafura Sea
Timor Sea
Gulf of Carpentaria
Great Australian Bight
Indian Ocean
Pacific Ocean
Tasman Sea
Torres Strait
Bass Strait
Tropic of Capricorn
GREAT BARRIER REEF
GREAT DIVIDING RANGE
ARNHEM LAND
NORTHERN TERRITORY
QUEENSLAND
WESTERN AUSTRALIA
SOUTH AUSTRALIA
NEW SOUTH WALES
VICTORIA
TASMANIA
GREAT SANDY DESERT
GIBSON DESERT
GREAT VICTORIA DESERT
NULLARBOR PLAIN
SIMPSON DESERT
GREAT ARTESIAN BASIN
INDONESIA
PAPUA (AUSTL.)
Port Moresby
Darwin
Perth
Adelaide
Melbourne
CANBERRA
Sydney
Brisbane
Hobart
Alice Springs
Lake Eyre -39 Ft.
Longitude East of Greenwich
CM. TERRAIN AUSTRALIA
COPYRIGHT BY RAND MC NALLY & COMPANY
MADE IN U.S.A.

Darwin
Cattle
Sheep
Rockhampton
Brisbane
Wheat
Newcastle
Sydney
Perth
Cattle
Wheat
KALGOORLIE
Port Pirie
Adelaide
BROKEN HILL
MURRAY BASIN
Melbourne
Hobart
THE ECONOMY
MANUFACTURING
Chemicals
Transportation Equipment
Textiles
Wool
Iron & Steel
Food Products
Leather Products
Metal & Machine Products
Paper Products
MINING
Antimony
Coal
Copper
Gold
Iron Ore
Iron Ore Reserves
Lead
Magnesium
Silver
Tin
Uranium
Zinc
AGRICULTURE
General Farming
Intensive Agriculture
Plantation Agriculture
Exhaustive Forest, Collecting Agriculture
Forest Agriculture
Pastureland & Fodder Crops
Seasonal Grazing
Non-Agricultural Areas
FISHING
Fishing Areas

GROSS NATIONAL PRODUCT PER CAPITA $1,351

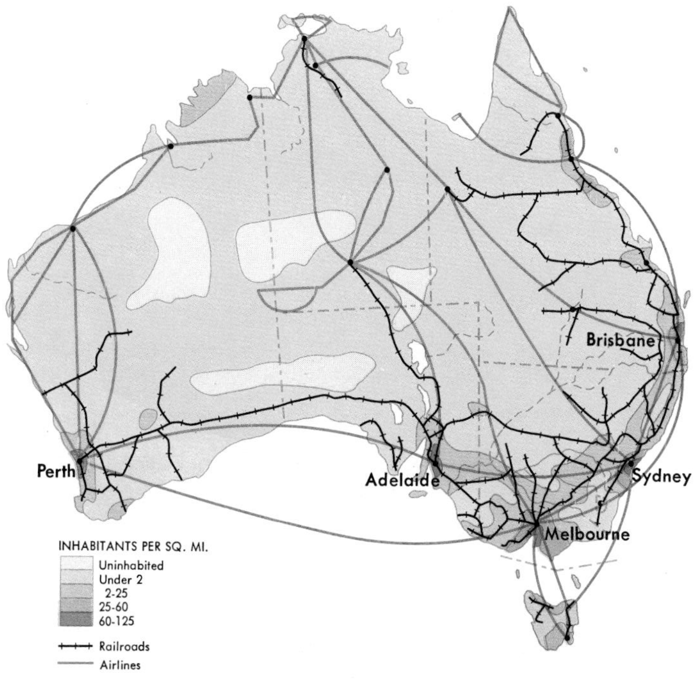
Brisbane
Perth
Adelaide
Sydney
Melbourne
INHABITANTS PER SQ. MI.
Uninhabited
Under 2
2-25
25-60
60-125
Railroads
Airlines

LONG DISTANCES, CLUSTERS OF PEOPLE

Most Australians live in the southeast of their island continent, and fully a third of them live in the Sydney-Melbourne area. The Perth area has only 4.3 per cent of the population. Australia's settled regions are served by 26,478 miles of railroads, 392,130 miles of roads and 13 airlines.

AUSTRALIA

AUSTRALIA: By one definition Australia is the smallest continent in the world; by another it is the largest island. It is surrounded by two oceans and four seas—and its main problem is water. A third of the country has inadequate rainfall and much of the area is sparsely inhabited desert. A narrow strip along the eastern coast sometimes has too much rain.

Beset by periodic floods, among other hardships, Captain Arthur Phillip, who founded the British settlement of Sydney in 1788, cried in amazement, "No other country offers less assistance to first settlers." The fact that these first settlers were "indolent" and "disordered" convicts from the overcrowded jails of Britain did not make the captain's task easier. But Phillip was an optimist and predicted that Australia would prove "the most valuable acquisition Great Britain ever made." It is true that Australians today enjoy one of the world's highest standards of living. But in a country virtually the same size as the United States *(map, below)*, there are only one eighteenth as many people, and nearly all of these live along the southeastern coast *(map, left)*. The rest of the continent has not justified the captain's ebullient expectations.

AREA: 2,974,581 sq. mi.
POPULATION: 10,050,000. Largest city: Sydney. Capital: Canberra.
ALTITUDES: Mt. Kosciusko, 7,328 ft. (highest).

Much of the east coast of Australia lies in the path of the warm southeast trade winds. They bring rainfall during Australia's summer months. The stormy westerlies, however, bring rainfall throughout the year to the southeast coast below Sydney. As a result, this is the most intensively cultivated region in Australia.

The vast interior of Australia is a semiarid or desert region exceeded in size only by the Sahara of Africa. The winds that reach the interior from the east coast have lost their moisture in rising over the East Australian Highlands, or Great Dividing Range; the southeast trade winds are another drying influence in the interior. In addition, Australia's proximity to the Equator puts the sun almost directly overhead during the summer. Hot temperatures evaporate what little moisture does find its way inland. One section of the interior—the Great Artesian Basin—can be irrigated from underground streams, and plans are also being made to irrigate the dry valleys west of Canberra, but most of the inland region is probably beyond reclamation.

A wide belt around most of Australia's arid areas is excellent for grazing sheep, and the country is the world's biggest wool producer. Iron ore and coal deposits are located near Melbourne and Sydney. These and other resources have helped make Australia the biggest manufacturing nation—automobiles are an important product—in the Southern Hemisphere.

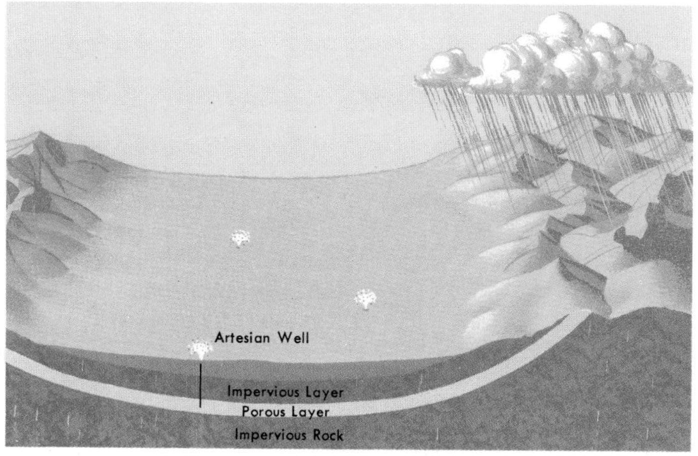
Artesian Well
Impervious Layer
Porous Layer
Impervious Rock

NATURAL FOUNTAINS FROM POROUS ROCK

In natural-flowing wells, like those of Australia's Great Artesian Basin *(cross section, above)*, water seeps into porous rock which is sandwiched between nonporous layers. Trapped in the porous layer, water accumulates under pressure and gushes upward when tapped by wells.

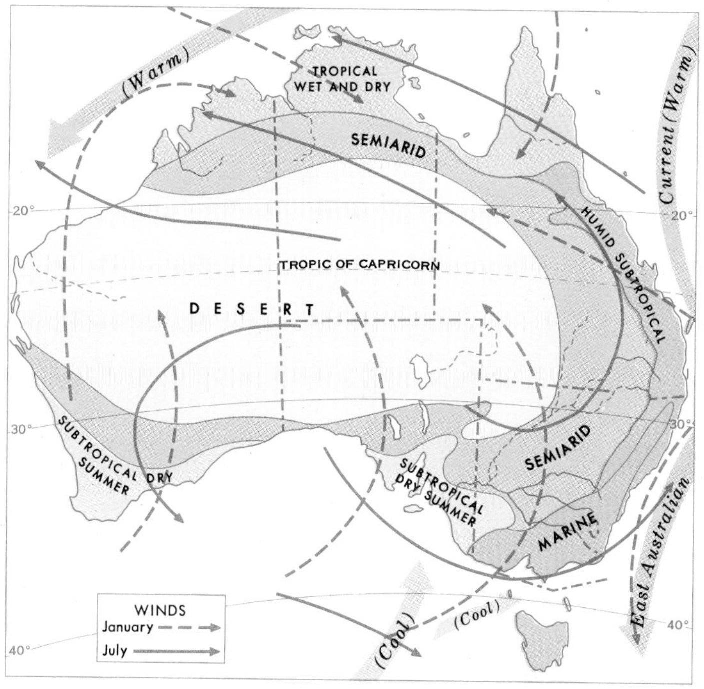
(Warm)
TROPICAL WET AND DRY
SEMIARID
Current (Warm)
HUMID SUBTROPICAL
20°
TROPIC OF CAPRICORN
D E S E R T
30°
SUBTROPICAL DRY SUMMER
SUBTROPICAL DRY SUMMER
SEMIARID
MARINE
East Australian
WINDS
January
July
(Cool)
(Cool)
40°

THE CLIMATES OF AUSTRALIA

Ocean currents and winds which influence Australia's climate are shown here. Because of the continent's latitude, the climate is tropical and subtropical. Much of the interior is desert, but winds crossing the warm East Australian Current *(right)* bring rain to the east coast.

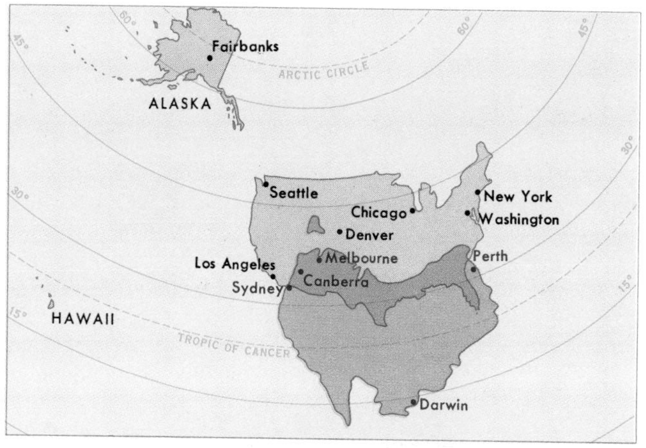
Fairbanks
ALASKA
ARCTIC CIRCLE
Seattle
Chicago
Denver
New York
Washington
Melbourne
Canberra
Los Angeles
Sydney
Perth
HAWAII
TROPIC OF CANCER
Darwin

A MIRROR IMAGE OF THE U.S.

To compare size, shape and climate zones, Australia is here shown superimposed, upside down, on the United States. In this way the tropic lines of both hemispheres coincide, putting the polar direction for both countries at the top of the diagram.

IN LATE AFTERNOON the South Pacific, seen from Tahiti, justifies the tribute of the American novelist Herman Melville: "To any meditative . . . rover, this serene Pacific, once beheld, must ever after be the sea of his adoption." A rain squall passes overhead while a Polynesian fisherman skims across the dappled water in an outrigger canoe to one of the Society Islands, the coral and volcanic group to which Tahiti belongs.

ISLANDS OF AN IMMENSE OCEAN

EARLY IN THE MORNING on North Island, a mounted shepherd and his dog keep a flock of New Zealand sheep moving. When the first European settlers arrived here, much of North Island was covered with forest and wild grasses. The land was laboriously cleared and sown with rich pasture grasses. When top-dressed —a job now often done by airplane—the best pasture land can accommodate six or more sheep to an acre.

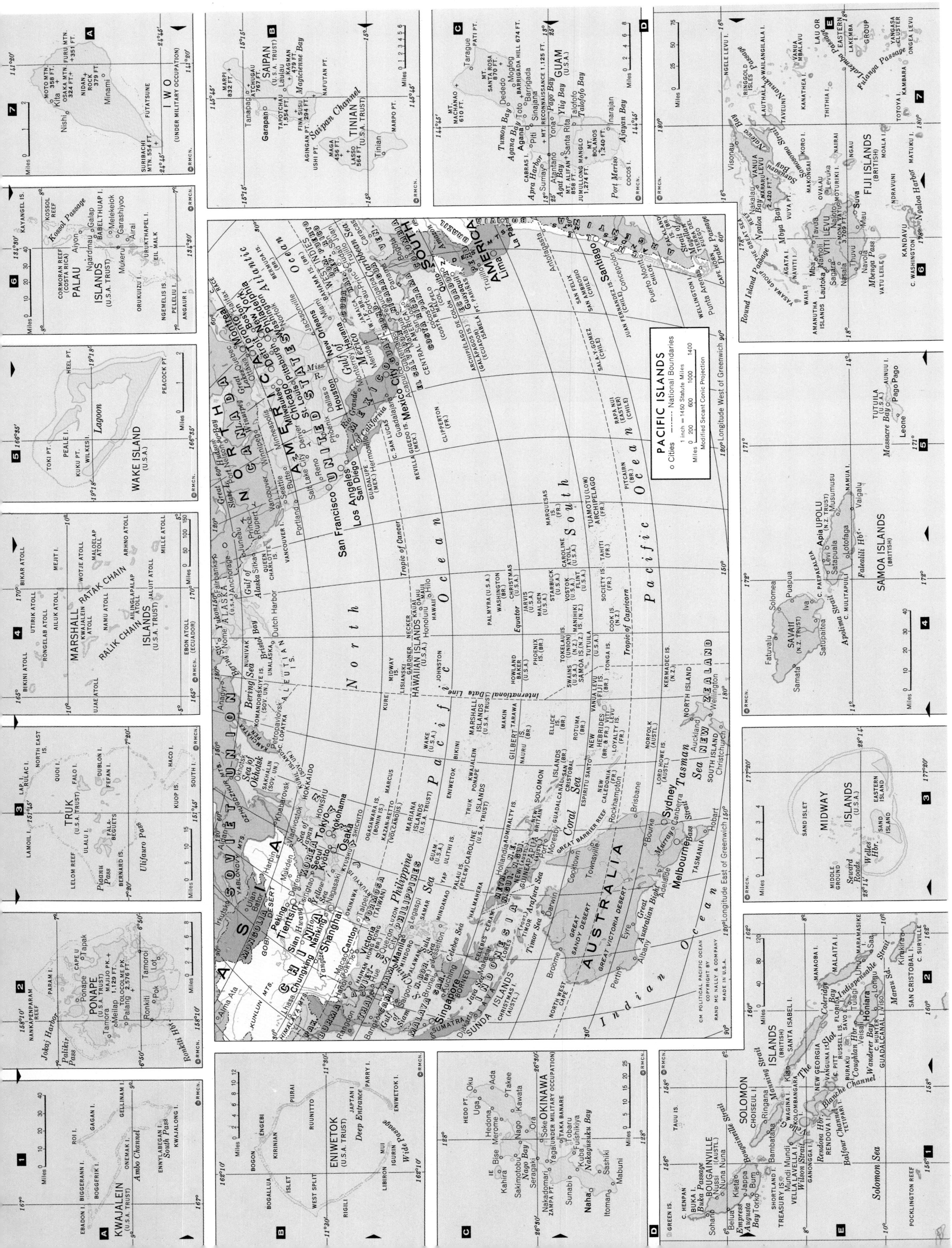
PACIFIC ISLANDS
o Cities
National Boundaries
1 inch = 1450 Statute Miles
Modified Secant Conic Projection
CM POLITICAL PACIFIC OCEAN
COPYRIGHT BY
RAND MC NALLY & COMPANY
MADE IN U.S.A.
KWAJALEIN (U.S.A. TRUST)
PONAPE (U.S.A. TRUST)
TRUK (U.S.A. TRUST)
MARSHALL ISLANDS (U.S.A. TRUST)
WAKE ISLAND (U.S.A.)
PALAU ISLANDS (U.S.A. TRUST)
IWO (UNDER MILITARY OCCUPATION)
ENIWETOK (U.S.A. TRUST)
OKINAWA (UNDER MILITARY OCCUPATION)
SOLOMON ISLANDS (BRITISH)
MIDWAY ISLANDS (U.S.A.)
SAMOA ISLANDS (BRITISH)
FIJI ISLANDS (BRITISH)
SAIPAN (U.S.A. TRUST)
TINIAN (U.S.A. TRUST)
GUAM (U.S.A.)

NEW ZEALAND: The most out-of-the-way nation on earth, this member of the British Commonwealth of Nations is a thousand miles from its nearest big neighbor, Australia, and 11,700 shipping miles from England, its principal market. Tall glacier-studded mountains cover much of South Island and still-active volcanoes rumble on North Island. Nevertheless, New Zealand boasts some of the world's finest pasture lands and one of the best climates for grazing sheep and cattle. With these natural advantages, New Zealand ranks first in the export of butter and second in cheese, and is one of the giants in world wool production *(chart at bottom)*.

AREA: 103,736 sq. mi.
POPULATION: 2,332,000. Largest city: Auckland. Capital: Wellington.
CLIMATE: Warm summers, mild winters; moderately heavy rainfall, well distributed throughout the year.
ALTITUDES: Mt. Cook, 12,349 ft. (highest).

Although its wool-based economy is vulnerable to the fluctuations of world markets, New Zealand has prospered. The country has mineral resources—there is coal on South Island and iron ore on both islands—and is now beginning to develop industry. Inevitably, New Zealanders, including the proud Maori natives *(population map, below)*, are gradually being transformed from a pastoral to an urban people.

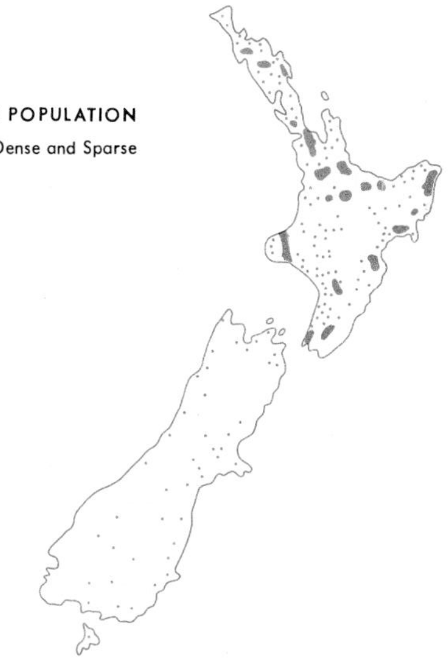
MAORI POPULATION
Dense and Sparse

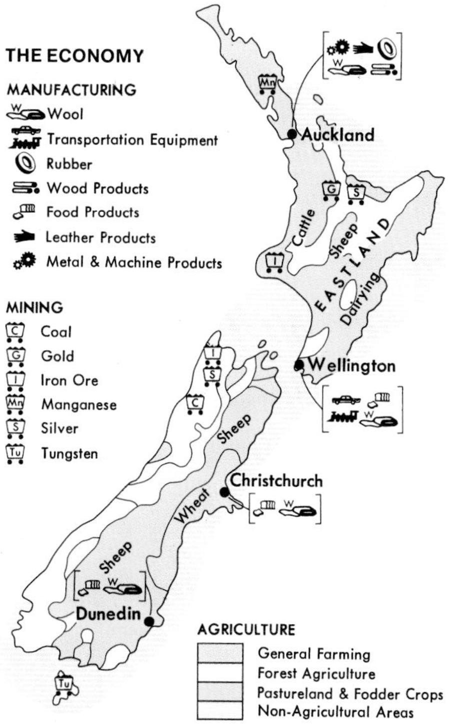
THE ECONOMY
MANUFACTURING
Wool
Transportation Equipment
Rubber
Wood Products
Food Products
Leather Products
Metal & Machine Products
MINING
Coal
Gold
Iron Ore
Manganese
Silver
Tungsten
AGRICULTURE
General Farming
Forest Agriculture
Pastureland & Fodder Crops
Non-Agricultural Areas
FISHING
Fishing Areas
Auckland
Wellington
Christchurch
Dunedin
EASTLAND
Cattle
Sheep
Dairying
Wheat

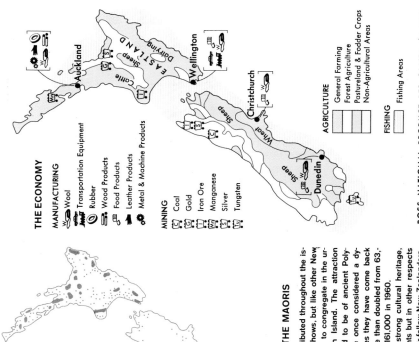

ROSS NATIONAL PRODUCT PER CAPITA $1,395

COMEBACK OF THE MAORIS

New Zealand's Maoris are distributed throughout the islands, as this population map shows, but like other New Zealanders they are beginning to congregate in the urban centers located on North Island. The attraction here is new industry. Believed to be of ancient Polynesian origin, the Maoris were once considered a dying race. But in recent decades they have come back strongly. Their population more than doubled from 63,670 in 1926 to an estimated 161,000 in 1960.

An intelligent people with a strong cultural heritage, Maoris have limited voting rights but in other respects have equal citizenship with their fellow New Zealanders.

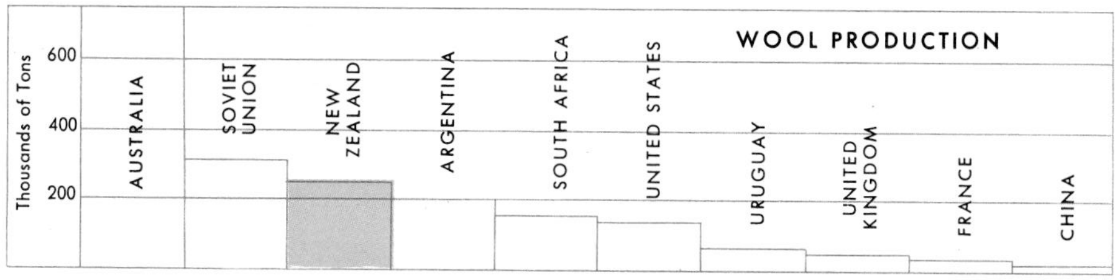
WOOL PRODUCTION
Thousands of Tons
600
400
200
AUSTRALIA
SOVIET UNION
NEW ZEALAND
ARGENTINA
SOUTH AFRICA
UNITED STATES
URUGUAY
UNITED KINGDOM
FRANCE
CHINA

A GIANT IN THE WORLD'S WOOL MARKET

As shown on this chart of the world's 10 leading producers of raw wool, tiny New Zealand *(blue)* presses the Soviet Union for second place and shears almost one third as much as the world leader, Australia. New Zealand also ranks second as an exporter of wool, and it ships more mutton and lamb than any other nation.

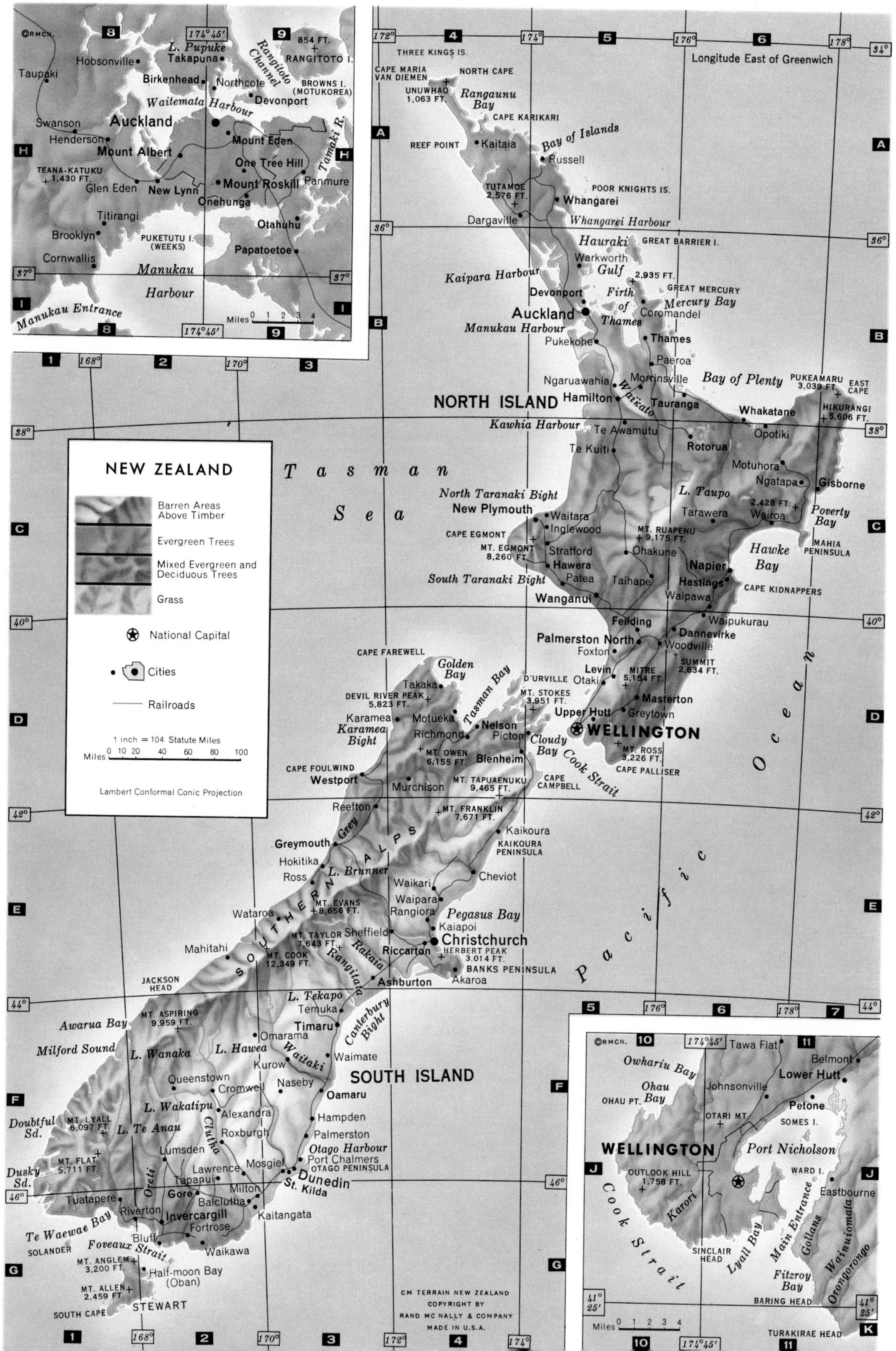
NEW ZEALAND
Barren Areas Above Timber
Evergreen Trees
Mixed Evergreen and Deciduous Trees
Grass
National Capital
Cities
Railroads
1 inch = 104 Statute Miles
Lambert Conformal Conic Projection
Longitude East of Greenwich
NORTH ISLAND
SOUTH ISLAND
Tasman Sea
Pacific Ocean
Auckland
WELLINGTON
Christchurch
Dunedin
Cook Strait
Foveaux Strait
STEWART
SOUTHERN ALPS
CM TERRAIN NEW ZEALAND
COPYRIGHT BY
RAND MC NALLY & COMPANY
MADE IN U.S.A.

ANTARCTICA'S LAND MASS is portrayed on this map as it would look stripped of ice and snow. The continent was once thought to encompass the entire area within the dotted line. But recent theories suggest that part of the land has sunk below sea level under the enormous weight of ice.

ANTARCTICA

The Antarctic has been called a "gigantic refrigerator with a leak" because of its chilling influence on the weather to the north. It bears over 90 per cent of the ice on the earth at any time and supports no land-animal life. Winds up to 200 miles per hour, temperatures down to 125 degrees below zero, plains of ice up to two miles thick, vast ice shelves that "calve" giant-size icebergs and choke the surrounding sea with milky rubble—these phenomena make the continent as desolate as the moon, and for centuries as inaccessible.

The first man to sight the Antarctic mainland was the American Captain Nathaniel Brown Palmer in 1820. The first expedition to winter upon it was that of Norwegian-born Carsten Borchgrevink for Great Britain in 1899. The mainland yielded its mysteries grudgingly. In 1951, forty years after Roald Amundsen planted the flag of Norway at the South Pole, nearly two thirds of its five million square miles—almost one and a half times the size of the United States—remained unexplored. But during the International Geophysical Year—an unprecedented example of cooperation between nations—scientists of 12 countries crisscrossed and honeycombed the enormous wasteland, adding richly to man's knowledge of it. It is known that Antarctica has iron, graphite, pitchblende and other minerals, and is in a key strategic location. Nevertheless, the likeliest uses of Antarctica for the near future are as a receiving station for seismic vibrations and information from satellites, as a launching base for manned space flights, and as an icebound laboratory for the long-term study of climate, cosmic rays, the water level of oceans, and the earth's past.

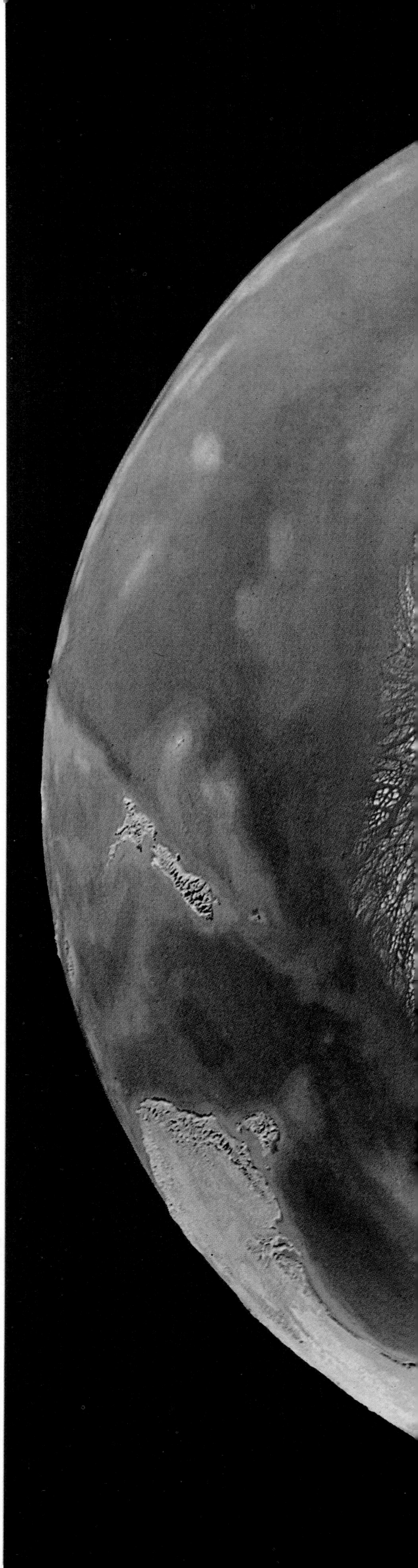

"THE BOTTOM OF THE WORLD," Antarctica is a vast continent entirely covered by ice. At the upper right is the southern portion of South America; at the lower right, the tip of Africa. Australia is at the lower left. At the left are New Zealand and the Pacific Ocean.

INDEX, SYMBOLS AND ABBREVIATIONS

All the important names that appear on the maps of the LIFE *Pictorial Atlas of the World* are included in the index that begins on the opposite page.

NAMES OF CITIES AND TOWNS: The name of each United States city and town is followed by its county, state, population, map index key and page number:

Barre, Washington, Vt. 10,387 C4 218

Here, Barre is the city, Washington the county, Vt. (Vermont) the state, 10,387 the population, C4 the map index key and 218 the page. Provincial locations are given for all cities and towns in Canada. All other place name entries show only country locations.

NAMES OF OTHER POLITICAL DIVISIONS: The names of political divisions other than those of cities and towns are followed by a term describing the division (county, district, region, province, department, state, etc.) and by the name of the country in which it is located. Major political units, such as countries or colonies, are located by continent.

KEYS TO THE MAPS: The index reference key – a letter-and-figure combination such as E3 – and the map page number are the last items in each entry. To find a place turn to the page indicated, find the key letter along one edge of the map and the key number along another edge. Where the two meet inside the map is the approximate location of the name being sought. Because some places are shown on both a main map and on an inset map, more than one index key may be given for a single map page:

Clay, Clay, W.Va. 486 C3 194
C7

When the index refers to more than one main map, both the reference key and additional page number, in that order, will always be included:

French Broad, riv., N.C., Tenn. B2 186
C9 190

POPULATIONS: Population figures given in the index are based on the latest available official census figures and estimates. Absence of a population figure indicates that no trustworthy statistic is available. For some larger cities, a second population figure is given on the line following the first one and is marked with a star (*). The starred figure indicates the population of the city's entire metropolitan area including suburbs:

Chicago, Cook, Ill. 3,550,404
(*6,517,600)

For some other towns, a second population figure is given, marked with a triangle (▲). This population figure is for an entire township, municipality or other minor civil division, including its rural areas.

PHYSICAL NAMES AND POINTS OF INTEREST: Each entry for a physical feature is printed in *italics*, and is followed by a descriptive term (bay, hill, range, river, basin, national park, mountain, island, etc.):

Donets, basin, Sov.Un.

Some place names included in the *Atlas* index have been omitted from the maps because of lack of space. These entries are identified by an asterisk (*), and a map index key indicates their approximate location:

Paxtang, Dauphin, Pa. 1,916 *C5 214

Some long names appear on the map in a shortened form. The part of the name not shown on the map appears in the index in brackets:

Laval [des Rapides]

When several names with the same spelling are listed in the index, the sequence always is: place names, political divisions and physical features.

Afg.	Afghanistan
Afr.	Africa
Ala.	Alabama
Alb.	Albania
Alg.	Algeria
Alsk.	Alaska
Alta.	Alberta
Am.	American
And.	Andorra
Ang.	Angola
Ant.	Antarctica
Arc.	Arctic
arch.	archipelago
Arg.	Argentina
Ariz.	Arizona
Ark.	Arkansas
A.S.S.R.	Autonomous Soviet Socialist Republic
Atl. O.	Atlantic Ocean
Aus.	Austria
Austl.	Australia, Australian
auton.	autonomous
Ba. Is.	Bahama Islands
Barb.	Barbados
Bas.	Basutoland
B.C.	British Columbia
Bech.	Bechuanaland
Bel.	Belgium, Belgian
Bhu.	Bhutan
Bis. Arch.	Bismarck Archipelago
Bol.	Bolivia
Br.	British
Braz.	Brazil
Br. Cam.	British Cameroons
Br. Gu.	British Guiana
Br. Hond.	British Honduras
Bru.	Brunei
Bul.	Bulgaria
Bur.	Burma
Calif.	California
Cam.	Cameroun
Camb.	Cambodia
Can.	Canada
Can. Is.	Canary Islands
Can. Z.	Canal Zone
Cen. Afr. Rep.	Central African Republic
Cey.	Ceylon
C.H.	Court House
chan.	channel
co.	county
Col.	Colombia
Colo.	Colorado
Con. B.	Congo, Brazzaville
Con. L.	Congo, The, Léopoldville
Conn.	Connecticut
cont.	continent
C.R.	Costa Rica
C.V. Is.	Cape Verde Islands
Cyp.	Cyprus
Czech.	Czechoslovakia
Dah.	Dahomey
Dan.	Danish
D.C.	District of Columbia
Del.	Delaware
Den.	Denmark
dept.	department
des.	desert
dist.	district
div.	division
Dom. Rep.	Dominican Republic
Ec.	Ecuador
Eg.	Egypt
Eng.	England
Eth.	Ethiopia
Eur.	Europe
Fed.	Federation
Fin.	Finland
Fla.	Florida
For.	Formosa
Fr.	France, French
Fr. Gu.	French Guiana
Fr. Som.	French Somaliland
Ga.	Georgia
Gam.	Gambia
Ger.	Germany
Gib.	Gibraltar
Grc.	Greece
Grnld.	Greenland
Guad.	Guadeloupe
Guat.	Guatemala
Hai.	Haiti
Haw.	Hawaii
hbr.	harbor
Hond.	Honduras
Hung.	Hungary
I.	Island
I.C.	Ivory Coast
Ice.	Iceland
Ill.	Illinois
Ind.	Indiana
Indon.	Indonesia
I. of Man	Isle of Man
Ire.	Ireland
is.	islands
isl.	island
Isr.	Israel
isth.	isthmus
It.	Italy, Italian
Jam.	Jamaica
Jap.	Japan
Kans.	Kansas
Ken.	Kenya
Kor.	Korea
Kuw.	Kuwait
Ky.	Kentucky
La.	Louisiana
Leb.	Lebanon
Le. Is.	Leeward Islands
Lib.	Liberia
Liech.	Liechtenstein
Lux.	Luxembourg
Mala.	Malaya
Malag.	Malagasy
Man.	Manitoba
Mart.	Martinique
Mass.	Massachusetts
Maur.	Mauritania
Md.	Maryland
Medit.	Mediterranean
Mex.	Mexico
Mich.	Michigan
Minn.	Minnesota
Miss.	Mississippi
Mo.	Missouri
Mong.	Mongolia
Mont.	Montana
Mor.	Morocco
Moz.	Mozambique
mtn.	mount, mountain
mts.	mountains
mun.	municipality
N.A.	North America
natl. mon.	national monument
natl. park	national park
N.B.	New Brunswick
N. Bor.	North Borneo
N.C.	North Carolina
N. Cal.	New Caledonia
N. Dak.	North Dakota
Nebr.	Nebraska
Nep.	Nepal
Neth.	Netherlands
Neth. N. Gui.	Netherlands New Guinea
Neth. W.I.	Netherlands West Indies
Nev.	Nevada
Newf.	Newfoundland
N. Gui.	New Guinea
N.H.	New Hampshire
Nic.	Nicaragua
Nig.	Nigeria
N. Ire.	Northern Ireland
N.J.	New Jersey
N. Mex.	New Mexico
Nor.	Norway, Norwegian
N.S.	Nova Scotia
N.W. Ter.	Northwest Territories
N.Y.	New York
N.Z.	New Zealand
occ.	occupied area
Om.	Oman
Ont.	Ontario
Oreg.	Oregon
Pa.	Pennsylvania
Pac. O.	Pacific Ocean
Pak.	Pakistan
Pan.	Panama
Pap.	Papua
Par.	Paraguay
par.	parish
P.E.I.	Prince Edward Island
pen.	peninsula
Phil.	Philippines
plat.	plateau
Pol.	Poland
pol. dist.	political district
pop.	population
Port.	Portugal, Portuguese
Port. Gui.	Portuguese Guinea
Port. Timor	Portuguese Timor
poss.	possession
P.R.	Puerto Rico
pref.	prefecture
prot.	protectorate
prov.	province
pt.	point
Que.	Quebec
reg.	region
rep.	republic
res.	reservoir
Rh. & Nya.	Rhodesia and Nyasaland
R.I.	Rhode Island
riv.	river
Rom.	Romania
S.A.	South America
Sal.	El Salvador
Sam.	Samoa
Sar.	Sarawak
Sask.	Saskatchewan
Sau. Ar.	Saudi Arabia
S.C.	South Carolina
S. Dak.	South Dakota
Sen.	Senegal
S.L.	Sierra Leone
Som.	Somalia
Sov. Un.	Soviet Union
Sp.	Spain
S.S.R.	Soviet Socialist Republic
St., Ste.	Saint, Sainte
Sud.	Sudan
Sur.	Surinam
S.W. Afr.	South-West Africa
Swaz.	Swaziland
Swe.	Sweden
Switz.	Switzerland
Syr.	Syria
Tan.	Tanganyika
Tenn.	Tennessee
ter.	territory
Tex.	Texas
Thai.	Thailand
Trin.	Trinidad
Tr. Coast	Trucial Coast
trust.	trusteeship
Tun.	Tunisia
Tur.	Turkey
U.A.R.	United Arab Republic
Ug.	Uganda
Ur.	Uruguay
U.S.	United States
U.S. Afr.	South Africa (formerly Union of South Africa)
Va.	Virginia
val.	valley
Ven.	Venezuela
Viet.	Vietnam
Vir. Is.	Virgin Islands
vol.	volcano
Vt.	Vermont
Wash.	Washington
W.I.	West Indies
W.I. Fed.	West Indies Federation
Win. Is.	Windward Islands
Wis.	Wisconsin
W. Va.	West Virginia
Wyo.	Wyoming
Yugo.	Yugoslavia
Zan.	Zanzibar

A

Aabenraa, Den.	13,704	I3	291
Aabenraa, co., Den.	48,676	*I3	291
Aachen, Ger.	151,000	C2	286
Aakirkeby, Den.	1,574	F5	292
Aalbaek, Den.	776	D1	292
Aalbaek, bay, Den.		D1	292
Aalborg, Den.	81,954	H3	291
Aalborg, co., Den.	232,885	*H3	291
Aalborg, bay, Den.		E1	292
Aalen, Ger.	28,700	D4	286
Aalsmeer, Neth.	4,800	B3	282
Aalst, Bel.	44,179	D3	282
Aalten, Neth.	6,600	C5	282
Äänekoski, Fin.	5,948	E11	290
Aarau, Switz.	14,800	A4	312
	(*19,300)		
Aare, riv., Switz.		A3	312
Aargau (Argovie), canton, Switz.	330,000	A4	312
Aarhus, Den.	118,888	H4	291
Aarhus, co., Den.	210,409	*H4	291
Aarhus, bay, Den.		E1	292
Aars, Den.	2,875	H3	291
Aarschot, Bel.	11,787	D3	282
Aba, Con.L.		B5	414
Aba, Nig.	57,787	E6	408
Abac, Tift, Ga.	500	E3	176
Ābādān, Iran	226,083	C2	379
Ābādeh, Iran	7,448	C3	379
Abadla, Alg.		B3	402
Abaete, Braz.	3,828	D1	258
Abaetetuba, Braz.	5,449	F7	256
Abai, Par.		D4	247
Abakan, Sov.Un.	56,000	D11	329
Abala, Con.B.		G8	409
Aban, Sov.Un.		D11	329
Abancay, Peru	8,100	C3	245
Abanilla, Sp.	3,144	C6	298
Abarqū, Iran	16,000	C3	379
Abashiri, Jap.	42,961	B10	354
Abau, Pap.		F11	359
Abbasiya, Sud.	2,846	C3	398
Abbaye, pt., Mich.		C3	146
Abbeville, Henry, Ala.	2,524	D4	168
Abbeville, Fr.	19,502	B4	278
Abbeville, Wilcox, Ga.	872	E3	176
Abbeville, Vermilion, La.	10,414	E3	180
Abbeville, Lafayette, Miss.	275	A3	184
Abbeville, Abbeville, S.C.	5,436	C4	188
Abbeville, co., S.C.	21,417	C3	188
Abbey, Sask., Can.	305	E3	58
Abbeyfeale, Ire.	1,170	I3	273
Abbeyleix, Ire.	1,118	I5	273
Abbiategrasso, It.	15,100	*C2	302
Abbot, Clay, Miss.	50	B4	184
Abbot, butte, Oreg.		E4	96
Abbotsford, B.C., Can.	830	C16	52
Abbotsford, Que., Can.	500	S12	66
Abbotsford, Clark, Wis.	1,171	D3	160
Abbott, Scott, Ark.	150	B2	170
Abbott Run, Providence, R.I.	20	B3	216
Abbot Village, Piscataquis, Maine	100	C3	204
	(404*)		
Abbyville, Reno, Kans.	118	E5	144
Abco, Hot Spring, Ark.	100	*C4	170
Abé, lake, Eth.		C5	398
Abéché, Chad		D9	409
Abee, Alta., Can.	75	C6	54
Abejorral, Col.	5,129	B1	244
Abell, St. Marys, Md.	10	D6	182
Abengourou, I.C.	2,350	E4	408
Abeokuta, Nig.	84,451	E5	408
Aberayron, Wales		I8	273
Abercorn, Que., Can.	405	S12	66
Abercorn, Rh.&Nya.	2,300	A6	421
Abercrombie, Richland, N.Dak.	244	D9	154
Aberdare, Wales	40,200	J9	273
Aberdaron, Wales		I8	273
Aberdeen, Sask., Can.	284	D4	58
Aberdeen, Bingham, Idaho	1,484	G6	108
Aberdeen, Harford, Md.	9,679	A7	182
Aberdeen, Monroe, Miss.	6,450	B4	184
Aberdeen, Moore, N.C.	1,531	B6	186
Aberdeen, Brown, Ohio	774	D3	156
Aberdeen, Scot.	186,400	D10	272
Aberdeen, Brown, S.Dak.	23,073	B7	158
Aberdeen, U.S.Afr.		F4	420
Aberdeen, Grays Harbor, Wash.	18,741	C3	98
Aberdeen, co., Scot.	328,800	D9	272
Aberdeen, lake, N.W.Ter., Can.		E8	48
Aberdovey, Wales		I8	273
Aberfeldy, Scot.	1,500	E9	272
Aberfoyle, Scot.	1,133	E8	272
Abernant, Tuscaloosa, Ala.	250	B2	168
Abernathy, Hale and Lubbock, Tex.	2,491	C5	130
Abernethy, Sask., Can.	290	E6	58
Abert, lake, Oreg.		E6	96
Abertillery, Wales	26,800	J9	273
Aberystwyth, Wales	10,400	I8	273
Abez, Sov.Un.		C8	328
Abhā, Sau.Ar.		D3	383
Ab-i-Diz, riv., Iran		C2	379
Abidjan, I.C.	127,585	E4	408
Abiff, Dickson, Tenn.		C4	190
Āb-i-Istāda, lake, Afg.		C5	374
Abilene, Alta., Can.	25	C7	54
Abilene, Dickinson, Kans.	6,746	D6	144
Abilene, Taylor, Tex.	90,368	C6	130
Abilene, Charlotte, Va.	60	C6	192
Abingdon, Eng.	12,800	J11	273
Abingdon, Knox, Ill.	3,469	C3	138
Abingdon, Jefferson, Iowa	140	C5	142
Abingdon, Harford, Md.	400	B7	182
Abingdon, Washington, Va.	4,758	D3	192
Abington, Windham, Conn.	130	B7	202
Abington, Wayne, Ind.	250	C5	140
Abington, Plymouth, Mass.	4,500	B6	206
	(10,607*)	E3	
Abington, Montgomery, Pa.	8,000	A6	214
Abiquiu, Rio Arriba, N.Mex.	200	B4	126
Abisko, Swe.		B8	290
Abita Springs, St. Tammany, La.	655	B7	180
		D5	
Abitibi, co., Que., Can.	99,578	*Q8	66
Abitibi, lake, Ont., Can.		R25	64
Abitibi, riv., Ont., Can.		R25	64
Able, Butler, Nebr.	117	C9	152
Ablon, Fr.		J10	278
Åbo, see Turku, Fin.			
Aboisso, I.C.	2,000	E4	408
Abomey, Dah.	16,700	E5	408
Abony, Hung.	10,544	B5	320
Abord-à-Plouffe, Que., Can.	8,099	S11	66
		S15	
Aboriginal, reserve, Austl.		C5	432
Abou Deïa, Chad		D8	409
Abou Kémal, Syr., U.A.R.	5,580	B4	378
Abound, Sask., Can.	25	E5	58
Abraham, Millard, Utah		D3	114
Abraham Lincoln, natl. historical park, Ky.		C5	178
Abrams, Oconto, Wis.	230	D5	160
Abrantes, Port.	3,507	C2	298
Abrego, Col.	2,250	B2	244
Abreojos, pt., Mex.		B3	224
Abri, Sud.		A3	398
Abruzzi and Molise (Abruzzi e Molise), reg., It.	1,700,000	D4	302
Absaroka, range, Wyo.		B3	116
Absaroka, ridge, Wyo.		D2	116
Absarokee, Stillwater, Mont.	600	E7	110
Absecon, Atlantic, N.J.	4,320	E3	210
Absecon, inlet, N.J.		E4	210
Abu Dhabi, Tr. Coast		C5	383
Abū Hadriyah, Sau. Ar.		B4	383
Abu Hamed, Sud.	1,450	B3	398
Abu Hammād, Eg., U.A.R.	7,685	D2	382
Abu Hummus, Eg., U.A.R.	6,525	*A3	395
Abuja, Nig.		E6	408
Abu Kershola, Sud.	4,154	C3	398
Abu Kibir, Eg., U.A.R.		D2	382
Abu Madd, cape, Sau. Ar.		C2	383
Abu Markha, Sau. Ar.		B2	383
Abumombazi, Con. L.		B3	414
Abuna, riv., Bol.		A1	246
Abu Qir, Eg., U.A.R.	7,086	*A3	395
Abu Qurqâs, Eg., U.A.R.	7,285	B3	395
Abu Shagara, cape, Sud.		A4	398
Abu Simbel, ruins, Eg., U.A.R.		C3	395
Abu Suweir, Eg., U.A.R.		E7	395
Abu Tabari, Sud.		B2	398
Abu 'Uruq, Sud.		B3	398
Abu Zanima, Eg., U.A.R.		B3	395
Aby, Swe.	2,217	C7	292
Abyei, Sud.		D2	398
Åbyn, Swe.		D9	290
Academy, Charles Mix, S.Dak.	25	D6	158
Acadia, par., La.	49,931	D3	180
Acadia, natl. park, Maine		D4	204
Acadia Valley, Alta., Can.	75	E7	54
Acajutla, Sal.	2,018	D3	228
Acámbaro, Mex.	23,016	C5	225
		K13	
Acaponeta, Mex.	7,592	C4	224
Acapulco de Juarez, Mex.	27,913	D6	225
Acarai, mts., Braz.		E5	256
Acaraú, Braz.	1,807	A2	258
Acaray, riv., Par.		D5	247
Acari, Peru	561	D3	245
Acarigua, Ven.	16,542	B4	240
Acatlán, Mex.	7,569	D6	225
		L14	
Acayucan, Mex.	7,094	D7	225
Accident, Garrett, Md.	237	A1	182
Accokeek, Prince Georges, Md.	250	C5	182
Accomac, Accomack, Va.	414	C9	192
Accomack, co., Va.	30,635	C9	192
Accord, Plymouth, Mass.	75	D3	206
Accord, Ulster, N.Y.	400	D7	212
Accord, pond, Mass.		D3	206
Accoville, Logan, W.Va.	800	D3	194
		D5	
Accra, Ghana	165,000	E4	408
Acebuches, Mex.		B5	224
Aceguá, Ur.		B5	252
Aceites, Ven.		C5	240
Acequia, Minidoka, Idaho	107	G5	108
Achacachi, Bol.	3,621	C1	246
Achaea, see Akhaia, prov., Grc.			
Achao, Chile	707	F3	251
Achar, Ur.		B4	252
Acharacle, Scot.		E6	272
Acheng, China	5,000	C13	348
Achill, head, Ire.		G2	273
Achill, isl., Ire.		H2	273
Achille, Bryan, Okla.	294	E7	128
Achinsk, Sov.Un.	39,100	A12	336
Achiotepec, Mex.		K14	225
Achiras, Arg.		B3	252
Achourat, well, Mali		B4	408
Achsah, Madison, Va.	35	B6	192
Acireale, It.	24,400	G5	302
Ackerman, Choctaw, Miss.	1,382	B3	184
Ackerson, Sussex, N.J.		A3	210
Ackerville, Wilcox, Ala.		C2	168
Ackerville, Washington, Wis.	40	E1	160
Ackia Battleground, natl. mon., Miss.		A4	184
Ackley, Hardin, Iowa	1,731	B4	142
Acklins, isl., W.I.		A7	232
Ackworth, Warren, Iowa	77	*C4	142
Acline, Charlotte, Fla.	100	E8	174
Acmar, St. Clair, Ala.	250	B3	168
Acme, Alta., Can.	292	E6	54
Acme, Dickinson, Kans.	7	*D6	144
Acme, Concordia, La.	50	C4	180
Acme, Grand Traverse, Mich.	120	E6	146
Acme, Whatcom, Wash.	275	*A4	98
Acme, Kanawha, W.Va.	500	D6	194
Acme, Sheridan, Wyo.	125	B5	116
Acmetonia, Allegheny, Pa.	1,500	*C1	214
Acobamba, Peru	1,912	C3	245
Acomaya, Peru	2,120	C3	245
Acomita, Valencia, N.Mex.	500	*C3	126
Acona, Holmes, Miss.		B2	184
Aconcagua, prov., Chile	128,378	D3	250
Aconcagua, mtn., Arg.		B2	252
Açores (Azores) (Archipelago), prov., Port.	318,558	*C4	388
Acorn, Polk, Ark.		C2	170
Acorn, Monroe, Tenn.		C7	190
Acosta, Somerset, Pa.	975	C2	214
Acoyapa, Nic.	1,146	E5	228
Acqui, It.	12,200	C2	302
Acre, Isr.	19,000	B6	382
Acre, ter., Braz.	143,000	G2	256
Acre, bay, Isr.		B6	382
Acre, riv., Bol.		B1	246
Acredale, Princess Anne, Va.	1,022	*D8	192
Acree, Dougherty, Ga.	125	E3	176
Acres, Clark, Kans.	35	*E4	144
Actinolite, Ont., Can.		P23	64
Acton, Shelby, Ala.	50	E5	168
Acton, Ont., Can.	3,578	Q20	64
Acton, Marion, Ind.	650	C4	140
		E5	
Acton, York, Maine	65	E2	204
	(501*)		
Acton, Middlesex, Mass.	400	B5	206
	(7,238*)	C1	
Acton, Yellowstone, Mont.	15	E8	110
Acton Vale, Que., Can.	3,547	S12	66
Actopan, Mex.	4,830	K14	225
Acu, Braz.	5,071	B3	258
Acurua, mts., Braz.		C2	258
Acushnet, Bristol, Mass.	3,000	C6	206
	(5,755*)		
Acworth, Cobb, Ga.	2,359	A4	176
		B2	
Acworth, Sullivan, N.H.	(371*)	E2	208
Acy, Ascension, La.	30	B6	180
Ada, Ghana	2,327	E5	408
Ada, Ottawa, Kans.	155	C6	144
Ada, Bienville, La.	495	B2	180
Ada, Norman, Minn.	2,064	D2	148
Ada, Hardin, Ohio	3,918	B3	156
Ada, Pontotoc, Okla.	14,347	D7	128
Ada, Lane, Oreg.		D2	96
Ada, Union, S.C.		B5	188
Ada, Mercer, W.Va.	300	D3	194
Ada, Sheboygan, Wis.	75	B6	160
Ada, Yugo.	11,010	B5	316
Ada, co., Idaho	93,460	F2	108
Adair, Adair, Iowa	742	C3	142
Adair, Carroll, Miss.		B2	184
Adair, Mayes, Okla.	434	B8	128
Adair, Madison, Tenn.	53	*C3	190
Adair, co., Iowa	10,893	C3	142
Adair, co., Ky.	14,699	C5	178
Adair, co., Mo.	20,105	A5	150
Adair, co., Okla.	13,112	C9	128
Adairsville, Bartow, Ga.	1,026	B2	176
Adairville, Logan, Ky.	848	D4	178
Adak, Alsk.	89	E4	84
Adak, isl., Alsk.		E4	84
Adam, isl., Md.		D7	182
Adamana, Apache, Ariz.	30	D6	124
Adamitullo, Eth.		D4	398
Adams, Decatur, Ind.	350	C4	140
Adams, Kingman, Kans.	42	*E5	144
Adams, Kenton, Ky.	350	B8	178
Adams, Berkshire, Mass.	12,391	A1	206
Adams, Mower, Minn.	806	H6	148
Adams, Gage, Nebr.	387	D9	152
Adams, Jefferson, N.Y.	1,914	B5	212
Adams, Walsh, N.Dak.	360	B7	154
Adams, Texas, Okla.	165	B2	128
Adams, Umatilla, Oreg.	192	B8	96
Adams, Robertson, Tenn.	500	B4	190
Adams, Adams, Wis.	1,301	E4	160
Adams, co., Colo.	120,296	C6	106
Adams, co., Idaho	2,978	E2	108
Adams, co., Ill.	68,467	D2	138
Adams, co., Ind.	24,643	B5	140
Adams, co., Iowa	7,468	C3	142
Adams, co., Miss.	37,730	D1	184
Adams, co., Nebr.	28,944	D7	152
Adams, co., N.Dak.	4,449	D3	154
Adams, co., Ohio	19,982	D3	156
Adams, co., Pa.	51,906	D4	214
Adams, co., Wash.	9,929	B8	98
Adams, co., Wis.	7,566	D4	160
Adams, mtn., Mass.		A2	206
Adams, mtn., N.H.		C4	208
Adams, mtn., Vt.		C3	218
Adams, mtn., Wash.		C5	98
Adams, pt., Mich.		D8	146
Adam's Bridge, shoals, India		G3	366
Adamsburg, Union, S.C.	155	B5	188
Adams Center, Jefferson, N.Y.	850	B5	212
Adamson, Pittsburg, Okla.	160	D8	128
Adams Run, Charleston, S.C.	250	F2	188
Adamston, Ocean, N.J.	500	C4	210
Adamstown, Ire.	156	I6	273
Adamstown, Frederick, Md.	310	B5	182
Adamstown, Lancaster and Berks, Pa.	1,190	C5	214
Adamsville, Jefferson, Ala.	2,095	E4	168
Adamsville, Que., Can.	387	S12	66
Adamsville, McNairy, Tenn.	1,046	C3	190
Adamsville, Beaver, Utah		E3	114
Adana, Tur.	172,465	C6	307
Adana, prov., Tur.	633,225	*C6	307
Adanac, Sask., Can.	47	D3	58
Adapazari, Tur.	55,116	A4	307
Adarama, Sud.	981	B3	398
Ad Barb, Sau.Ar.		D3	383
Ad Dām, Sau.Ar.		C3	383
Ad Dammām, Sau.Ar.		B5	383
Addie, Boundary, Idaho		A2	108
Addies, pond, Newf., Can.		F7	72
Ad Dilam, Sau.Ar.		C4	383
Addington, Jefferson, Okla.	144	D6	128
Addis, West Baton Rouge, La.	590	D4	180
Addis Ababa, Eth.	401,915	D4	398
Addison, Winston, Ala.	343	A2	168
Addison, Du Page, Ill.	6,741	F2	138
Addison, Washington, Maine	350	D5	204
	(744*)		
Addison, Lenawee, Mich.	575	G7	146
Addison, Steuben, N.Y.	2,185	C4	212
Addison, Addison, Vt.	60	C2	218
	(645*)		
Addison, see Webster Springs, W.Va.			
Addison, co., Vt.	20,076	C2	218
Ad Dīwānīya, Iraq	27,839	D6	378
Addy, Stevens, Wash.	245	A9	98
Addyston, Hamilton, Ohio	1,376	D1	156
Adel, Cook, Ga.	4,321	E3	176
Adel, Dallas, Iowa	2,060	C3	142
Adel, Cascade, Mont.	40	C5	110
Adel, Lake, Oreg.	100	E7	96
Adelaide, Austl.	75,100	E7	432
Adelaide River, Austl.	112	A6	432
Adelanto, San Bernardino, Calif.	1,500	E5	94
Adelina, Calvert, Md.	100	D6	182
Adell, Sheboygan, Wis.	398	E6	160
Adelphi, Prince Georges, Md.	8,000	*C6	182
Adelphi, Ross, Ohio	441	C4	156
Adelphia, Monmouth, N.J.	300	C4	210
Aden, Aden	99,285	E4	383
	(*138,441)		
Aden, Br. prot., Asia	150,000	H6	340
			383
Aden (Prot.), Br. poss., Asia	650,000	H6	340
			383
Aden, gulf, Afr.		E4	383
Adena, Jefferson, Ohio	1,317	B6	156
Adger, Jefferson, Ala.	150	B2	168
		E4	
Adicora, Ven.		A4	240
Adige, riv., It.		C3	302
Adigrät, Eth.		C4	398
Adimi, Sov.Un.		E15	329
Adin, Modoc, Calif.	175	B3	94
Adindān, Eg., U.A.R.		C3	395
Adirondack, mts., N.Y.		B7	212
Adi Ugri, Eth.	5,000	C4	398
Adiyaman, Tur.	14,017	B8	307
Adiyaman, prov., Tur.	211,002	*C8	307
Adjud, Rom.	6,119	A4	321
Adlavik, is., Newf., Can.		D10	72
Admaston, Ont., Can.	75	O24	64
Admiral, Sask., Can.	152	F3	58
Admirals Beach, Newf., Can.	31	G9	72
Admiralty, isl., Alsk.		J14	84
Admiralty, is., Pac.O.		C3	436
Admire, Lyon, Kans.	149	D7	144
Adobe, creek, Colo.		D7	106
Adobe Creek, res., Colo.		D7	106
Adok, Sud.		D3	398
Adola, Eth.		C5	398
Adola, Eth.		D4	398
Adolfo Alsina, Arg.	5,836	C3	252
Adolphus, Allen, Ky.	300	D4	178
Adona, Perry, Ark.	154	B4	170
Adony, Hung.	3,437	B3	320
Adra, Sp.	7,923	D5	298
Adrano, It.	27,700	G5	302
Adrar, Alg.	1,865	C3	402
Adrar, sand dunes, Maur.		B2	408
Adrar des Iforas, reg., Mali		B5	408
Adrar Nahalet, Alg.		D4	402
Adré, Chad		D9	409
Adri, Libya	935	B2	394
Adria, It.	12,100	C4	302
Adrian, Emanuel and Johnson, Ga.	568	D4	176
Adrian, Lenawee, Mich.	20,347	H7	146
Adrian, Nobles, Minn.	1,215	H3	148
Adrian, Bates, Mo.	1,082	C3	150
Adrian, La Moure, N.Dak.	64	D7	154
Adrian, Malheur, Oreg.	300	D9	96
Adrian, Horry, S.C.		D10	188
Adrian, Upshur, W.Va.	600	C4	194
Adriatic, sea, It.		D6	266
Adrigole, Ire.	73	J3	273
Adújar, Sp.	21,900	C4	298
Aduwā, Eth.	5,000	C4	398
Advance, Boone, Ind.	463	C3	140
Advance, Meade, Kans.		E3	144
Advance, Stoddard, Mo.	692	D8	150
Advance, Davie, N.C.	197	*B5	186
Advocate Harbour, N.S., Can.	175	D5	70
Adzopé, I.C.	3,350	E4	408
Aegean, sea, Grc.		E7	266
Aegean Islands (Nésoi Aiyaions), reg., Grc.	528,766	*C5	306
Aegina, see Aiyina, isl., Grc.			
Aerhshan (Wenchuan), China		B9	348
Aerö, isl., Den.		G1	292
Aesch, Switz.	3,149	A3	312
Aetna, Alta., Can.	50	F6	54
Aetna, Barber, Kans.	50	*E5	144
Aetna, Hickman, Tenn.	50	C4	190
Aetolia and Acarnania, see Aitolia Kai Akarnania, prov., Grc.			
Affinity, Raleigh, W.Va.	400	D3	194
Afghanistan, country, Asia	13,000,000	F8	340
			374
Afgoi, Som.	3,000	E6	398
	(14,400*)		
Afif, Sau.Ar.		C3	383
Afjord, Nor.		E4	290
Aflou, Alg.	3,370	B4	402
Afmadu, Som.	1,700	E5	398
Afognak, Alsk.	158	D6	84
Afognak, isl., Alsk.		D6	84
Afonso Cláudio, Braz.	1,583	E2	258
Afonso Pena, Braz.		B3	258
Africa, cont.	233,719,000		19
			388
Afsluitdijk, dam, Neth.		B4	282
Afton, Union, Iowa	773	C3	142
Afton, Cheboygan, Mich.	100	D7	146
Afton, Washington, Minn.	158	*F8	148
Afton, Chenango, N.Y.	956	C6	212
Afton, Ottawa, Okla.	1,111	B9	128
Afton, Greene, Tenn.	125	B9	190
Afton, Nelson, Va.	75	B6	192
Afton, Rock, Wis.	175	F4	160
Afton, Lincoln, Wyo.	1,337	D2	116
Afula, Isr.	10,000	B6	382
Afyon, Tur.	31,385	B4	307
Afyonkarahisar, prov., Tur.	407,126	*B4	307
Agadem, Niger		C7	409
Agadès, Niger	4,250	C6	409
Agadir, Mor.	30,111	B2	402
Agalak, well, Niger		C6	409
Agalta, mts., Hond.		C5	228
Agaman, Sov.Un.		I10	332
Agamiaure, mts., Braz.		E6	256
Agana, Guam	1,330	C7	436
	(*11,000)		
Agana, bay, Guam		C7	436
Agar, India		E1	368
Agar, Sully, S.Dak.	139	C5	158
Agartala, India	42,595	E5	368
Agassiz, B.C., Can.	500	B16	52
		F12	
Agat, bay, Guam		D7	436
Agata, Sov.Un.		C11	329
Agata, isl., Fiji		E6	436
Agate, Elbert, Colo.	150	C7	106
Agate, Sioux, Nebr.	11	B2	152

Aldie, Loudoun, Va.	100	A6	192
		B7	
Aldine, Salem, N.J.		D2	210
Aldora, Lamar, Ga.	535	C2	176
Aldrich, Shelby, Ala.	800	B3	168
Aldrich, Wadena, Minn.	90	E4	148
Aldrich, Polk, Mo.	181	D4	150
Aldridge, Walker, Ala.	150	B2	168
Aledo, Mercer, Ill.	3,080	B3	138
Aleg, Maur.		C2	408
Alegre, Braz.	5,159	E2	258
Alegrete, Braz.	19,560	K5	257
Aleknagik, Alsk.	153	D6	84
Aleknagik, lake, Alsk.		D5	84
Aleksandriya, Sov.Un.	43,300	H9	332
Aleksandrov, Sov.Un.	30,600	D12	332
Aleksandrov-Gay, Sov.Un.		B3	336
Aleksandrovsk, Sov.Un.	39,400	D16	329
Aleksandrovskoye, Sov.Un.		A9	336
Aleksandrów, Pol.	7,577	B4	325
Aleksandrów, Pol.	6,926	C4	325
Aleksin, Sov.Un.	9,300	E11	332
Aleksinac, Yugo.	6,735	C5	316
Alemania, Arg.		C4	250
Aleppo (Haleb), Syr., U.A.R.	407,613	A2	378
Alençon, Fr.	21,893	C3	278
Alentejo, reg., Port.	713,335	C3	298
Alenuihaha, channel, Haw.		C5	86
Aleppa, Sedgwick, Kans.	20	*E6	144
Alert, Decatur, Ind.	80	C4	140
Alert Bay, B.C., Can.	695	E9	52
Alès, Fr.	36,893	E6	278
Alessandria, It.	55,400 (83,600▲)	C2	302
Alessandria, prov., It.	481,000	*C2	302
Ålesund, Nor.	18,845 (*26,200)	E2	290
Aleutian, is., Alsk.		E4	84
Aleutian, range, Alsk.		D6	84
Alevina, cape, Sov.Un.		D17	329
Alex, Grady, Okla.	545	D6	128
Alexander, Alsk.	15	*C7	84
Alexander, Pulaski and Saline, Ark.	177	C4	170
		D6	
Alexander, Man., Can.	450	F2	60
Alexander, Burke, Ga.	150	C5	176
Alexander, Franklin, Iowa	294	B4	142
Alexander, Rush, Kans.	153	D4	144
Alexander, Washington, Maine	40 (220▲)	*C5	204
Alexander, Buncombe, N.C.	75	B3	186
Alexander, McKenzie, N.Dak.	269	C2	154
Alexander, Upshur, W.Va.	150	C4	194
Alexander, co., Ill.	16,061	F4	138
Alexander, co., N.C.	15,625	B4	186
Alexander, arch., Alsk.		D8	84
Alexander, lake, Minn.		E4	148
Alexander Bay Station, Newf., Can.	20	F8	72
Alexander City, Tallapoosa, Ala.	13,140	C4	168
Alexander Mills, Rutherford, N.C.	947	B4	186
Alexandra, N.Z.	1,823	F2	437
Alexandretta, see İskenderun, Tur.			
Alexandretta, gulf, Tur.		C6	307
Alexandria, Calhoun, Ala.	200	B4	168
Alexandria, B.C., Can.		D11	52
Alexandria, Ont., Can.	2,487	O26	64
Alexandria, Madison, Ind.	5,582	B4	140
Alexandria, Campbell, Ky.	1,307	A8	178
		B6	
Alexandria, Rapides, La.	40,279	C3	180
Alexandria, Douglas, Minn.	6,713	F3	148
Alexandria, Clark, Mo.	452	A6	150
Alexandria, Thayer, Nebr.	257	D8	152
Alexandria, Grafton, N.H.	75 (370▲)	D3	208
Alexandria, Licking, Ohio	452	B4	156
Alexandria, Rom.	19,294	C3	321
Alexandria, Hanson, S.Dak.	614	D8	158
Alexandria, De Kalb, Tenn.	599	B5	190
Alexandria (El Iskandarīyah), Eg., U.A.R.	919,024	A2	395
Alexandria (Independent City), Va.	91,023	A7	192
		B7	
Alexandria Bay, Jefferson, N.Y.	1,583	A6	212
Alexandria Station, Austl.	50	B7	432
Alexandria Southwest, Rapides, La.	2,782	*C3	180
Alexandroúpolis, Grc.	16,632	A5	306
Alexis, Cherokee, Ala.	90	A4	168
Alexis, Warren, Ill.	878	B3	138
Alexis, riv., Newf., Can.		D7	72
Alexis Creek, B.C., Can.	10	D11	52
Alexo, Alta., Can.		D5	54
Aleysk, Sov.Un.	10,000	B10	336
Alfalfa, Caddo, Okla.	80	C5	128
Alfalfa, co., Okla.	8,445	B5	128
Alfalfa Center, Mississippi, Mo.	115	E8	150
Al Falluja, Iraq	15,930	C5	378
Al Fandaqūmīyah, Jordan	3,000	B6	382
Alfaro, Sp.	8,097	A6	298
Alfatar, Bul.	3,446	B3	317
Alfenas, Braz.	9,052	E1	258
Alfiós, riv., Grc.		C3	306
Alford, Jackson, Fla.	380	A5	174
Alford, Berkshire, Mass.	30 (256▲)	B1	206
Alford, Scot.	1,248	D10	272
Alfordsville, Daviess, Ind.	121	D3	140
Alfortville, Fr.	30,195	I10	278
Alfred, Ont., Can.	1,257	O26	64
Alfred, York, Maine	300 (1,201▲)	E2	204
Alfred, Allegany, N.Y.	2,807	C4	212
Alfred, La Moure, N.Dak.	150	D7	154
Alfred Station, Allegany, N.Y.	200	C4	212
Alftanes, Ice.		L18	290
Al Fuqahā, Libya		B3	394
Algā, Eth.		D4	398
Algarrobal, Chile		A1	252
Algarrobo, Chile		A1	252
Algarve, prov., Port.	328,231	*D2	298
Algarve, reg., Port.	328,231	D2	298
Algeciras, Sp.	42,728	D4	298
Algemesí, Sp.	17,789	C6	298
Alger, see Algiers, Alg.			
Alger, Arenac, Mich.	60	E7	146
Alger, Hardin, Ohio	1,068	B3	156
Alger, co., Mich.	9,250	C5	146
Algeria, Fr. poss., Afr.	10,265,000	D7	388
			402
Algers Corners Junction, Bristol, Mass.	130	*B5	206
Algete, Sp.	1,204	*B5	298
Al Ghaidha, Aden		D5	383
Alghero, It.	20,100	E2	302
Algiers (Alger), Alg.	361,285	A4	402
Algoa, bay, U.S.Afr.		F5	420
Algodones, Sandoval, N.Mex.	150	C4	126
		H6	
Algoma, Bonner, Idaho		*A2	108
Algoma, Pontotoc, Miss.	100	A3	184
Algoma, Klamath, Oreg.		E5	96
Algoma, McDowell, W.Va.	400	*D3	194
Algoma, Kewaunee, Wis.	3,855	D6	160
Algoma, dist., Ont., Can.	82,059	R24	64
Algona, Kossuth, Iowa	5,702	A3	142
Algona, King, Wash.	1,311	B4	98
		D3	
Algonac, St. Clair, Mich.	3,190	G9	146
Algonquin, Ont., Can.	165	P25	64
Algonquin, McHenry, Ill.	2,014	A5	138
		E2	
Algonquin, prov. park, Ont., Can.		O22	64
		S25	
Algonquin Park, Ont., Can.	110	O22	64
Algood, Putnam, Tenn.	886	B6	190
Algorta, Ur.		B4	252
Al Ḥadīthah, Sau.Ar.		C5	383
Alhama, Sp.	7,835	D5	298
Alhama, Sp.	6,442	D6	298
Alhambra, Maricopa, Ariz.	200	H2	124
Alhambra, Los Angeles, Calif.	54,807	C5	94
Alhambra, Madison, Ill.	537	E4	138
Alhambra, Jefferson, Mont.	40	D5	110
Al Ḥamrā', Sau.Ar.		C2	383
Al Ḥariq, Sau.Ar.	5,000	C4	383
Alhaurín el Grande, Sp.	11,710	D4	298
Al Ḥauṭa, Aden	4,500	D4	383
Al Ḥawṣah (Oasis), Jordan		E2	378
Al Hinnah, Sau.Ar.		B4	383
Al Ḥudaydah, Yemen	30,000	E3	383
Al Hufūf, Sau.Ar.	90,000	B4	383
Al Ḥumaymah, Jordan		E6	382
Ali Ak Chin, Pima, Ariz.	40	G3	124
Aliákmon, riv., Grc.		A3	306
Alicahue, Chile		B1	252
Alicante, Sp.	109,399	C6	298
Alicante, prov., Sp.	634,632	*C6	298
Alicante, gulf, Sp.		C6	298
Alice, Ont., Can.	35	O23	64
Alice, Cass, N.Dak.	124	D8	154
Alice, Jim Wells, Tex.	20,861	F6	130
Alice, lake, Minn.		D7	148
Alicel, Union, Oreg.	35	B9	96
Alice Southwest, Jim Wells, Tex.	1,813	*F6	130
Alice Springs, Austl.	2,785	C6	432
Aliceville, Pickens, Ala.	3,194	B1	168
Aliceville, Coffey, Kans.	100	D8	144
Alicia, Lawrence, Ark.	236	B5	170
Alicudi, isl., It.		F5	302
Alida, Sask., Can.	168	F7	58
Alifan, mtn., Guam		D7	436
Aligarh, India	141,618	D2	368
Ali Gharbī, Iran	3,377	C7	378
Ali-gūdarz, Iran	8,459	C2	379
Alikchi, McCurtain, Okla.		D9	128
Alindao, Cen.Afr.Rep.		F9	409
Aline, Alfalfa, Okla.	314	B5	128
Alingsås, Swe.	16,665	D3	292
Aliquippa, Beaver, Pa.	26,369	A3	214
		C1	
Al 'Irq, Libya		B4	394
Ali Sabieh, Fr.Som.		C5	398
Alisal, Monterey, Calif.	16,473	*D3	94
Aliso, creek, Calif.		D6	94
Alistráti, Grc.	4,951	A4	306
Alitak, Alsk.	72	D6	84
Aliwal North, U.S.Afr.	9,717	F5	420
Alix, Franklin, Ark.	350	B3	170
Alix, Alta., Can.	517	D6	54
Al Jaghbūb, Libya	196	B4	394
Aljarrobo de Aguilla, Arg.		C2	252
Al Jawf, Libya		C4	394
Al Jawf, Sau.Ar.	10,000	B2	383
Al Jawsh, Libya	2,680	A2	394
Al Jazin, Om.		D6	383
Aljezur, Port.	5,286	D2	298
Al Jubayl, Sau.Ar.		B4	383
Aljustrel, Port.	5,844	D2	298
Alkabo, Divide, N.Dak.	70	B2	154
Al Kadhimain, Iraq	48,678	C6	378
Alkali, creek, Wyo.		E4	116
Alkali, lake, Nev.		B2	112
Alkali, lake, Oreg.		E6	96
Alkaline, lake, N.Dak.		D6	154
Al Karak, Jordan	5,539	C6	382
Al Khalil (Hebron), Jordan	35,983	C6	382
Al Khasab, Om.		B6	383
Al Khums, Libya	62,272	A2	394
Al Khurmah, Sau.Ar.		C3	383
Alkmaar, Neth.	41,126	B3	282
Al Kūfa, Iraq	17,717	C6	378
Al Kufrah, oasis, Libya, Eg., U.A.R.		C4	394
Allada, Dah.	4,700	E5	408
Allagash, Aroostook, Maine	500 (557▲)	A3	204
Allagash, lake, Maine		B3	204
Allagi, riv., Eg., U.A.R.		C3	395
Allah, Maricopa, Ariz.	100	E3	124
Allahabad, India	312,259 (*332,295)	D3	368
Allakaket, Alsk.	79	B6	84
Allakh-Yun, Sov.Un.		C15	329
Allamakee, co., Iowa	15,982	A6	142
Allamuchy, Warren, N.J.	150	B3	210
Allamuchy, mtn., N.J.		B3	210
Allan, Sask., Can.	337	E4	58
Allandale, Volusia, Fla.	400	B10	174
Allanmyo, Bur.	15,580	C2	362
Allardt, Fentress, Tenn.	650	B7	190
Allariz, Sp.	1,936	A3	298
Allatoona, lake, Ga.		B2	176
Allaykha, Sov.Un.	800	B16	329
Alleene, Little River, Ark.	120	D2	170
Allegan, Allegan, Mich.	4,822	G6	146
Allegan, co., Mich.	57,729	G5	146
Allegany, Cattaraugus, N.Y.	2,064	C3	212
Allegany, Coos, Oreg.	40	D2	96
Allegany, co., Md.	84,169	A2	182
Allegany, co., N.Y.	43,978	C3	212
Alleghany, Sierra, Calif.	200	C3	94
Alleghany, Alleghany, Va.	150	C4	192
Alleghany, co., N.C.	7,734	A4	186
Alleghany, co., Va.	12,128	C4	192
Allegheny, co., Pa.	1,628,587	C1	214
Allegheny, mts., U.S.		D10	77
Allegheny, plat., Pa., W.Va.		C1	214
		C3	194
Allegheny, riv., Pa.		C2	214
Allegheny Front, uplands, W.Va.		B5	194
Allegheny Heights, mtn., Md.		B1	182
Allegre, Todd, Ky.	60	D3	178
Allemands, St. Charles, La.	1,167	C6	180
		E5	
Allen, Lyon, Kans.	205	D7	144
Allen, Floyd, Ky.	370	C8	178
Allen, Wicomico, Md.	175	D8	182
Allen, Hillsdale, Mich.	325	*H7	146
Allen, Copiah, Miss.		D2	184
Allen, Dixon, Nebr.	350	B9	152
Allen, Pontotoc, Okla.	1,005	D7	128
Allen, Bennett, S.Dak.	100	D4	158
Allen, Collin, Tex.	659	*C7	130
Allen, Skagit, Wash.	300	*A4	98
Allen, co., Ind.	232,196	A4	140
Allen, co., Kans.	16,369	E8	144
Allen, co., Ky.	12,269	D4	178
Allen, co., Ohio	103,691	B2	156
Allen, par., La.	19,867	D3	180
Allen, mtn., N.Z.		G1	437
Allendale, Wabash, Ill.	465	E6	138
Allendale, Worth, Mo.	136	A3	150
Allendale, Bergen, N.J.	4,092	A4	210
Allendale, Allendale, S.C.	3,114	E6	188
Allendale, co., S.C.	11,362	E6	188
Allende, Mex.	7,076	B5	225
Allenford, Ont., Can.	175	P19	64
Allenhurst, Liberty, Ga.	200	E5	176
Allenhurst, Monmouth, N.J.	795	C4	210
Allen Junction, Wyoming, W. Va.	300	*D3	194
Allen Park, Wayne, Mich.	37,052	B8	146
Allens Creek, Wayne, Tenn.		C4	190
Allenspark, Boulder, Colo.	40	B5	106
Allenstein, see Olsztyn, Pol.			
Allenstown (Town of), Merrimack, N.H.	(1,789▲)	E4	208
Allensville, Todd, Ky.	286	D3	178
Allenton, Wilcox, Ala.	150	D2	168
Allenton, St. Louis, Mo.	350	B7	150
Allenton, Washington, R.I.		C3	216
Allenton, Washington, Wis.	350	E5	160
Allentown, Wilkinson, Ga.	450	D3	176
Allentown, Monmouth, N.J.	1,393	C3	210
Allentown, Allegany, N.Y.	400	C3	212
Allentown, Lehigh, Pa.	108,347 (*299,700)	C6	214
Allenwood, King, Wash.	600	D2	98
Allenville, Mackinac, Mich.	35	D7	146
Allenville, Cape Girardeau, Mo.	190	D8	150
Allenwood, Monmouth, N.J.	350	C4	210
Alleppey, India	116,278	G3	366
Aller, Sp.	828	A4	298
Aller, riv., Ger.		B3	286
Allerton, Wayne, Iowa	692	D4	142
Allerton, Plymouth, Mass.		D3	206
Allerton, pt., Mass.		B6	206
Allgood, Blount, Ala.	147	B3	168
Allgunnen, lake, Swe.		D5	292
Allgunnen, lake, Swe.		D7	292
Alliance, Alta., Can.	313	D7	54
Alliance, Box Butte, Nebr.	7,845	B3	152
Alliance, Salem, N.J.		D2	210
Alliance, Pamlico, N.C.	200	B9	186
Alliance, Stark, Ohio	28,362	B5	156
Allier, dept., Fr.	372,689	*D5	278
Allier, riv., Fr.		D5	278
Al Lifiyah (Oasis), Sau.Ar.		A3	383
Alligator, Bolivar, Miss.	227	A2	184
Alligator, lake, Maine		D4	204
Alligator, lake, N.C.		B9	186
Alligator, riv., N.C.		B9	186
Allihies, Ire.	85	J2	273
Allimaso, creek, N.Mex.		D7	126
Allinge, Den.	1,503	F5	292
Allison, La Plata, Colo.	125	E3	106
Allison, Butler, Iowa	952	B5	142
Allison, McKinley, N.Mex.	25	C2	126
Allison, Fayette, Pa.	1,285	D2	214
Allisona, Williamson and Rutherford, Tenn.	100	C5	190
Allison Harbour, B.C., Can.		E9	52
Allisonia, Pulaski, Va.	160	D4	192
Allison Park, Allegheny, Pa.	5,000	A4	214
Allisons Gap, Smyth, Va.	600	D3	192
Alliston, Ont., Can.	2,426	P21	64
Al Līth, Sau.Ar.	10,000	C3	383
Alloa, Scot.	13,900	E9	272
Allock, Perry, Ky.	100	*C7	178
Allons, Overton, Tenn.	270	B6	190
Allouez, Keweenaw, Mich.	175	B3	146
Allouez, Brown, Wis.	9,557	*D6	160
Alloway, Salem, N.J.	800	D2	210
Alloway, creek, N.J.		D2	210
Allred, Overton, Tenn.	100	B6	190
Allsboro, Colbert, Ala.	125	A1	168
Allsbrook, Horry, S.C.		C11	188
Al Luhayyah, Yemen	5,000	D3	383
Allumette, lake, Ont., Can.		O23	64
Alluwe, Nowata, Okla.	100	B8	128
Allyn, Mason, Wash.	600	B4	98
Allyns Point, New London, Conn.	75	D7	202
Alma, Crawford, Ark.	1,370	B2	170
Alma, N.B., Can.	475	D5	70
Alma, Ont., Can.	210	Q20	64
Alma, Park, Colo.	107	C4	106
Alma, Bacon, Ga.	3,515	E4	176
Alma, Marion, Ill.	358	E5	138
Alma, Wabaunsee, Kans.	838	C7	144
Alma, Gratiot, Mich.	8,978	F7	146
Alma, Lafayette, Mo.	390	B4	150
Alma, Liberty, Mont.	35	B6	110
Alma, Harlan, Nebr.	1,342	D6	152
Alma, Stephens, Okla.	120	D6	128
Alma, Tyler, W.Va.	152	B4	194
Alma, Buffalo, Wis.	1,008	D2	160
Alma, hill, N.Y.		C3	212
Alma-Ata, Sov.Un.	455,000	D9	336
Alma Center, Jackson, Wis.	464	D3	160
Al Madīnah (Medina), Sau.Ar.	50,000	C2	383
Al Mafraq, Jordan		C2	378
Almagro, Sp.	9,939	C5	298
Al Makīlī, Libya		A4	394
Almanor, lake, Calif.		B3	94
Almansa, Sp.	16,087	C6	298
Almanzora, riv., Sp.		D5	298
Al Marj, Libya	9,992	A4	394
Almazán, Sp.	3,819	B5	298
Al Mazār, Jordan		C6	382
Almeirim, Braz.	742	F6	256
Almeirim, Port.	7,104	C2	298
Almelo, Neth.	45,336	B5	282
Almelund, Chisago, Minn.	150	F6	148
Almena, Norton, Kans.	555	C4	144
Almena, Barron, Wis.	398	C1	160
Almendralejo, Sp.	21,418	C3	298
Almeria, Loup, Nebr.	18	C6	152
Almería, Sp.	67,091	D5	298
Almería, prov., Sp.	361,769	*D5	298
Almería, gulf, Sp.		D5	298
Almería, riv., Sp.		D5	298
Älmhult, Swe.	4,581	E5	292
Almira, Lincoln, Wash.	414	B8	98
Almirante, Pan.	2,341	F6	228
Almirós, Grc.	7,034	B4	306
Almo, Cassia, Idaho	100	G5	108
Almo, Calloway, Ky.	150	D2	178
Almodóvar, Port.	4,390	D2	298
Almodóvar, Sp.	7,609	C4	298
Almogía, Sp.	2,741	D4	298
Almon, Newton, Ga.	300	C3	176
Almonaster, Sp.	998	D3	298
Almond, Allegany, N.Y.	696	C4	212
Almond, Portage, Wis.	391	D4	160
Almonesson, Gloucester, N.J.	1,500	*D2	210
Almont, Gunnison, Colo.	11	D4	106
Almont, Lapeer, Mich.	1,279	G8	146
Almont, Morton, N.Dak.	190	D4	154
Almonte, Ont., Can.	2,960	O24	64
Almonte, Sp.	9,981	D3	298
Almonte, riv., Sp.		C4	298
Almor, Ec.		A1	245
Almora, India	12,116	C2	368
Almoradí, Sp.	3,998	C6	298
Al Mubarraz, Sau.Ar.		C4	383
Al Mukhā, Yemen	5,000	E3	383
Almundsryd, Swe.	4,347	E5	292
Almuñécar, Sp.	6,235	D5	298
Al Musaiyib, Iraq		C6	378
Al Muwayh, Sau.Ar.		C3	383
Al Muwaylih, Sau.Ar.		B2	383
Almy, Uinta, Wyo.	25	E1	116
Almyra, Arkansas, Ark.	240	C5	170
Alna, Lincoln, Maine	130 (347▲)	*D3	204
Alness, Scot.	1,019	D8	272
Alnwick, Eng.	7,300	F11	272
Aloha, Washington, Oreg.	4,000	B1	96
Along, bay, Viet.		B5	362
Alonsa, Man., Can.	125	E3	60
Alor, isl., Indon.		F6	358
Alora, Sp.	5,960	D4	298
Alor Star, Mala.	52,772	F4	362
Alorton, St. Clair, Ill.	3,282	*E3	138
Alosno, Sp.	2,617	D3	298
Aloys, Cuming, Nebr.	10	*C9	152
Alpachiri, Arg.		C3	252
Alpaugh, Tulare, Calif.	638	E4	94
Alpena, Boone, Ark.	283	A3	170
Alpena, Alpena, Mich.	14,682	D8	146
Alpena, Jerauld, S.Dak.	407	C7	158
Alpena, Randolph, W.Va.	75	C5	194
Alpena, co., Mich.	28,556	D8	146
Alpers, Carter, Okla.	60	*D6	128
Alpes-Maritimes, dept., Fr.	515,484	*F7	278
Alpha, Valley, Idaho		E2	108
Alpha, Henry, Ill.	637	B3	138
Alpha, Iron, Mich.	317	C3	146
Alpha, Jackson, Minn.	207	H4	148
Alpha, Warren, N.J.	2,406	B2	210
Alpha, Greene, Ohio	350	C2	156
Alpha, Buckingham, Va.		C6	192
Alpharetta, Fulton, Ga.	1,349	A5	176
		B2	
Alphen aan den Rijn, Neth.	15,500	B3	282
Alpheus, McDowell, W.Va.	500	*D3	194
Alpine, Apache, Ariz.	300	E6	124
Alpine, Clark, Ark.	75	C3	170
Alpine, San Diego, Calif.	1,044	*F5	94
Alpine, Bonneville, Idaho	50	F7	108
Alpine, Bergen, N.J.	921	*B5	210
Alpine, Benton, Oreg.	115	C3	96
Alpine, Overton, Tenn.	200	B6	190
Alpine, Brewster, Tex.	4,740	D4	130
Alpine, Utah, Utah	775	*C4	114
Alpine, Lincoln, Wyo.	25	*D2	116
Alpine, co., Calif.	397	C4	94
Alpine Junction, Benton, Oreg.		C3	96
Alpoca, Wyoming, W.Va.	400	D3	194
Alps, mts., Fr.		E7	278
Alps, mts., It.		B2	302
Al Qaryah ash Sharqīyah, Libya		A2	394
Al Qasabāt, Libya	3,190	A2	394
Al Qatīf, Sau.Ar.	5,000	C4	383
Al Qatrānah, Jordan		D2	378
Al Qaṭrūn, Libya	1,674	C2	394
Al Qunfudhah, Sau.Ar.		D3	383
Al Qurna, Iraq	3,156	D7	378
Al Quṣaybah, Sau.Ar.		B3	383
Als, Den.	610	E1	292
Alsace, former prov., Fr.	1,317,000	D7	278
Alsask, Sask., Can.	232	E3	58
Alsea, Benton, Oreg.	200	C3	96
Alsea, riv., Oreg.		C3	96
Alşed, Rom.		A2	321
Alsek, riv., Alsk., Can.		C8	84
Alsen, East Baton Rouge, La.	500	*D4	180
Alsen, Cavalier, N.Dak.	228	B7	154
Alsfeld, Ger.	9,000	C3	286
Alsip, Cook, Ill.	3,770	F3	138
Alstead, Cheshire, N.H.	325 (843▲)	E2	208
Alstead, riv., Sask., Can.		C4	58
Alston, Eng.		G10	272
Alston, Montgomery, Ga.	154	D4	176

Alsuma, Tulsa, Okla. 500 B8 128
Alta, Buena Vista, Iowa 1,393 B2 142
Alta, Teton, Wyo. C1 116
Altadena, Los Angeles, Calif. 40,568 C5 94
Altaelv, riv., Nor. B10 290
Altafjord, fjord, Nor. A10 290
Alta Gracia, Arg. 11,570 B3 252
Altagracia, Ven. 3,959 A1 240
Altagracia de Orituco, Ven. 7,413 B5 240
Altai, mts., Asia E10 340
Alta Loma, Galveston, Tex. 1,020 F8 130
Altamaha, riv., Ga. E4 176
Altamaha, sound, Ga. E5 176
Altamahaw, Alamance, N.C. 625 A6 186
Altamira, Braz. 1,809 F6 256
Altamira, Chile C4 250
Altamira, Mex. 1,348 C6 225
Altamont, Man., Can. 100 F3 60
Altamont, Effingham, Ill. 1,656 D5 138
Altamont, Labette, Kans. 672 E8 144
Altamont, Daviess, Mo. 190 B3 150
Altamont, Albany, N.Y. 1,365 C7 212
Altamont, Klamath, Oreg. 10,811 *E5 96
Altamont, Deuel, S.Dak. 77 C9 158
Altamont, Grundy, Tenn. 552 C6 190
Altamont, Duchesne, Utah 102 C5 114
Altamont, Uinta, Wyo. 25 *E2 116
Altamonte Springs, Seminole, Fla. 1,202 *C9 174
Altamura, It. 41,500 E6 302
Altamura, isl., Mex. C4 224
Altan Bulag, Mong. 10,000 A9 346
Altar, Mex. 1,116 A3 224
Altario, Alta., Can. 75 E7 54
Alta Vista, Chickasaw, Iowa 276 A5 142
Alta Vista, Wabaunsee, Kans. 400 D7 144
Alta Vista, Richland, S.C. 500 *C6 188
Altavista, Campbell, Va. 3,299 C5 192
Altdorf, Switz. 6,576 B4 312
Altenburg, Ger. 48,300 C5 286
Altenburg, Perry, Mo. 260 D8 150
Alter do Chão, Port. 4,633 C3 298
Altha, Calhoun, Fla. 413 A5 174
Altheimer, Jefferson, Ark. 979 C5 170
Altinho, Braz. 2,880 B3 258
Altiplano, upland, Bol. C1 246
Altman, Screven, Ga. 100 D5 176
Altmühl, riv., Ger. D4 286
Altnaharra, Scot. C8 272
Alto, Habersham and Banks, Ga. 275 B3 176
Alto, Richland, La. 100 B4 180
Alto, Kent, Mich. 250 G6 146
Alto, Franklin, Tenn. 85 C6 190
Alto, Cherokee, Tex. 869 D8 130
Alto, Amherst, Va. C5 192
Alto, Fond du Lac, Wis. 150 E5 160
Alto Alentejo, prov., Port. 400,374 *C3 298
Alto Araguaia, Braz. 972 I6 257
Alto Longá, Braz. B2 258
Alto Lucero, Mex. L15 225
Alto Molocuè, Moz. C7 421
Alton, Ont., Can. 515 Q20 64
Alton, Eng. 8,700 J12 273
Alton, Madison, Ill. 43,047 E3 138
Alton, Crawford, Ind. 57 D3 140
Alton, Sioux, Iowa 1,048 B1 142
Alton, Osborne, Kans. 299 C5 144
Alton, St. Tammany, La. 60 B8 180
Alton (Town of), Penobscot, Maine (303▲) C4 204
Alton, Oregon, Mo. 677 E6 150
Alton, Belknap, N.H. 300 E4 208
(1,241▲)
Alton, Washington, R.I. 300 D2 216
Alton, Kane, Utah 116 F3 114
Alton, Upshur, W.Va. 176 C4 194
Altona, Man., Can. 1,698 F4 60
Altona, Knox, Ill. 505 B3 138
Altona, De Kalb, Ind. 313 A4 140
Altona, Mecosta, Mich. 150 F6 146
Altona, Wayne, Nebr. 10 *B9 152
Altona, Clinton, N.Y. 400 A8 212
Altonah, Duchesne, Utah 10 C5 114
Alton Bay, Belknap, N.H. 100 E4 208
Altoona, Etowah, Ala. 744 A3 168
Altoona, Lake, Fla. 600 B9 174
Altoona, Polk, Iowa 1,458 A7 142
C4
Altoona, Wilson, Kans. 490 E8 144
Altoona, Blair, Pa. 69,407 C3 214
(*104,500)
Altoona, Eau Claire, Wis. 2,114 D2 160
Alto Paraná, dept., Par. 9,531 D5 247
Alto Park, Floyd, Ga. 500 *B1 176
Alto Pass, Union, Ill. 323 F4 138
Alto Trombetas, riv., Braz. E5 256
Altrincham, Eng. 40,400 H10 273
Altstätten, Switz. 8,603 A5 312
Altun Köprü, Iraq 3,744 B6 378
Altura, Winona, Minn. 320 G7 148
Alturas, Modoc, Calif. 2,819 B3 94
Altus, Franklin, Ark. 392 B3 170
Altus, Jackson, Okla. 21,225 D4 128
Altus, lake, Okla. D4 128
Al Ubaiyidh, riv., Iraq C5 378
Alula, Som. 1,300 C7 398
Alum, creek, Ohio C1 156
Alum Bridge, Lewis, W.Va. 120 B4 194
Alum Creek, Kanawha, W.Va. 300 C5 194
Alumine, Arg. C1 252
Alunite, Clark, Nev. 20 H7 112
Al 'Uqaylah (Aghéila), Libya 734 A3 394
Al Uthaylah, Libya A4 394
Alva, Lee, Fla. 200 E9 174
Alva, Harlan, Ky. 700 D7 178
Alva, Webster, Miss. 45 B3 184
Alva, Woods, Okla. 6,258 B5 128
Alva, Crook, Wyo. 60 B8 116
Alva, cape, Wash. A2 98
Alvadore, Lane, Oreg. 130 *C3 96
Alvangen, Swe. D3 292
Alvarado, Alameda, Calif. (part of Union City) B5 94
Alvarado, Mex. 8,820 D6 225
Alvarado, Marshall, Minn. 282 C2 148
Alvarado, Johnson, Tex. 1,907 B8 130
C7
Alvarez, Mex. L13 225
Alvaro Obregón, Mex. D8 225
Alvaro Obregón, Mex. 1,906 K13 225
Alvdal, Nor. E4 291
Älvdalen, Swe. 1,206 F6 291
Alvear, Arg. 3,544 A4 252
Älve Fjorden, fjord, Swe. D2 292
Alvena, Sask., Can. 176 D4 58
Alvesta, Swe. 5,815 E5 292
Alvin, Berkeley, S.C. 100 E9 188
Alvin, Brazoria, Tex. 5,643 E8 130
F8
Alvin, Forest, Wis. 150 C5 160
Alvinston, Ont., Can. 652 R19 64
Alviso, Santa Clara, Calif. 1,174 B6 94
Alvkarleby, Swe. 9,141 A8 292
Alvo, Cass, Nebr. 159 D9 152
E2
Alvon, Greenbrier, W.Va. 80 D4 194
Alvord, Lyon, Iowa 238 A1 142
Alvord, Wise, Tex. 694 C7 130
Alvord, lake, Oreg. E8 96
Alvordton, Williams, Ohio 388 A2 156
Alvsborg, co., Swe. 368,068 C3 292
Älvsbyn, Swe. D9 290
Alvsered, Swe. D3 292
Al Wajh, Sau.Ar. B2 383
Alwar, India 57,868 D2 368
Aly, Yell, Ark. 35 C3 170
Alyaty-Pristan, Sov.Un. 500 E3 336
Alyth, Scot. 2,000 E9 272
Alz, riv., Ger. D5 286
Alzada, Carter, Mont. 60 E12 110
Ama, St. Charles, La. 600 C7 180
Amadeus, lake, Austl. C6 432
Amadi, Sud. D3 398
Amadjuak, lake, N.W.Ter., Can. E11 48
Amado, Santa Cruz, Ariz. 40 G4 124
Amador, co., Calif. 9,990 C3 94
Amadore, Sanilac, Mich. F9 146
Amagansett, Suffolk, N.Y. 1,095 D5 212
Amagasaki, Jap. 335,513 G5 354
M11
Amagon, Jackson, Ark. 234 B5 170
Amahai, Indon. E7 359
Amakusa, sea, Jap. H2 354
Åmål, Swe. 8,573 B3 292
Amalfi, It. 4,700 *E4 302
Amalga, Alsk. 20 *D8 84
Amalga, Cache, Utah 198 B4 114
Amaliás, Grc. 15,189 C3 306
Amambay, dept., Par. 18,160 C4 247
Amami, isl., Jap. J2 354
Amana, Iowa, Iowa 465 C6 142
Amanda, Fairfield, Ohio 732 C4 156
Amandaville, Kanawha, W.Va. 225 *C3 194
Amangeldy, Sov.Un. B7 336
Amantea, It. 5,822 F6 302
Amapá, Braz. 1,163 E6 256
Amapá, ter., Braz. 53,000 E6 256
'Amära, Iraq 44,064 D7 378
Amarante, Braz. 2,355 B2 258
Amaranth, Man., Can. 108 E3 60
Amargosa, Braz. 4,744 C3 258
Amargosa, des., Nev. G5 112
Amargosa, riv., Calif. E5 94
Amarillo, Potter and Randall, Tex. 137,969 B5 130
(*142,500)
Amaro, mtn., It. D5 302
'Amarqur, Sau.Ar. D3 383
Amasa, Iron, Mich. 500 C3 146
Amasra, Tur. 1,379 A5 307
Amasya, Tur. 17,549 A6 307
Amazon, Sask., Can. 75 E5 58
Amazonas, comisaría, Col. 13,450 D2 244
Amazonas, dept., Peru 96,444 A2 245
Amazonas, state, Braz. 579,000 F3 256
Amazonas, state, Ven. 10,582 E5 240
Amazonas (Amazon), riv., Braz. F4 256
Amazonas (Amazon), riv., Peru A3 245
Amazonia, Andrew, Mo. 326 B3 150
Ambala, India 52,685 C2 368
(*146,128)
Ambalavao, Malag. 4,000 D9 421
Ambam, Cam. F7 409
Ambanja, Malag. B9 421
Ambarchik, Sov.Un. 800 C18 329
Ambato, Ec. 31,312 A2 245
Ambato-Boeni, Malag. C9 421
Ambatondrazaka, Malag. C9 421
Ambatosorata, Malag. C9 421
Amber, Grady, Okla. 300 C6 128
Amberg, Ger. 43,100 D4 286
Amberg, Marinette, Wis. 220 C6 160
Ambérieu [-en-Bugey], Fr. 5,333 E6 278
Amberley, Hamilton, Ohio 2,951 D1 156
Ambia, Benton, Ind. 351 B2 140
Ambikapur, India 8,517 E3 368
Ambilobe, Malag. B9 421
Ambjörby, Swe. A4 292
Amble, Eng. 4,800 F11 272
Ambler, Montgomery, Pa. 6,765 A6 214
C6
Ambo, Eth. D4 398
Ambo, Peru 1,243 C2 245
Ambo, chan., Kwajalein A1 436
Amboear, Neth. N.Gui. E8 359
Amboina, Indon. 31,600 E7 359
Amboina, isl., Indon. E7 359
Amboise, Fr. 5,904 D4 278
Ambositra, Malag. 4,636 D9 421
Amboy, San Bernardino, Calif. 125 E6 94
Amboy, Lee, Ill. 2,067 B4 138
Amboy, Miami, Ind. 446 B4 140
Amboy, Blue Earth, Minn. 629 H4 148
Amboy, Clark, Wash. 150 D4 98
Ambridge, Beaver, Pa. 13,865 A3 214
C1
Ambriz, Ang. 2,196 A2 420
Ambrizete, Ang. 1,147 A2 420
Ambrose, Coffee, Ga. 244 E3 176
Ambrose, Divide, N.Dak. 220 B2 154
Amchitka, isl., Alsk. E3 84
Amchitka, pass, Alsk. E4 84
Am Dam, Chad D9 409
Amderma, Sov.Un. 12,000 C8 328
Ameagle, Raleigh, W.Va. 500 D3 194
D6
Ameca, Mex. 13,589 C5 224
Amecameca, Mex. 9,629 D6 225
L14
Amecameca [de Juárez], Mex. 9,626 L14 225
Amechtil, sand dunes, Maur. C2 408
Ameland, isl., Neth. A4 282
Amelia, St. Mary, La. 950 C5 180
Amelia, Holt, Nebr. 62 B7 152
Amelia, Clermont, Ohio 913 C2 156
Amelia, co., Va. 7,815 C7 192
Amelia, isl., Fla. A10 174
Amelia City, Nassau, Fla. 125 A10 174
Amelia Court House, Amelia, Va. 800 C7 192
Amendolara, It. 1,947 F6 302
Amenia, Dutchess, N.Y. 600 D8 212
Amenia, Cass, N.Dak. 117 C8 154
America, McCurtain, Okla. E9 128
American, riv., Calif. C3 94
American Beach, Nassau, Fla. 75 A10 174
American Falls, Power, Idaho 2,123 G6 108
American Falls, dam and res., Idaho G6 108
American Fork, Utah, Utah 6,373 C4 114
American Samoa, see Samoa, U.S. poss., Pac.O.
Americus Sumter, Ga. 13,472 D2 176
Americus, Lyon, Kans. 300 D7 144
Amersfoort, Neth. 62,362 B4 282
Amery, Man., Can. 35 B5 60
Amery, Polk, Wis. 1,769 C1 160
Ames, Story, Iowa 27,003 B4 142
Ames, Dodge, Nebr. 65 C9 152
D2
Ames, Major, Okla. 211 B5 128
Amesbury, Essex, Mass. 10,787 A6 206
Ámfissa, Grc. 5,553 B4 306
Amga, Sov.Un. 800 C15 329
Amgu, Sov.Un. E15 329
Amgun, riv., Sov.Un. D15 329
Amherst, N.S., Can. 10,301 D5 70
Amherst, Phillips, Colo. 106 B8 106
Amherst, Hancock, Maine 140 D4 204
(168▲)
Amherst, Hampshire, Mass. 10,306 B2 206
(13,718▲)
Amherst, Hillsboro, N.H. 500 F3 208
(2,051▲)
Amherst, Lorain, Ohio 6,750 A4 156
Amherst, Marshall, S.Dak. 75 B8 158
Amherst, Knox, Tenn. 400 E9 190
Amherst, Lamb, Tex. 883 B4 130
Amherst, Amherst, Va. 1,200 C5 192
Amherst, Portage, Wis. 596 D4 160
Amherst, co., Va. 22,953 C5 192
Amherstburg, Ont., Can. 4,099 R18 64
Amherstdale, Logan, W.Va. 900 D3 194
D5
Amherst Junction, Portage, Wis. 131 *D4 160
Amiata, mtn., It. D3 302
Amicalola, falls, Ga. B2 176
Amidon, Slope, N.Dak. 84 D2 154
Amiens, Fr. 92,506 C5 278
Aminuis, S.W.Afr. D3 420
'Āmir, cape, Libya A4 394
Amisk, Alta., Can. 151 D7 54
Amisk, lake, Sask., Can. C6 58
Amistad, Union, N.Mex. 35 C7 126
Amite, Tangipahoa, La. 3,316 D5 180
Amite, co., Miss. 15,573 D2 184
Amite, riv., La. D5 180
Amity, Clark, Ark. 543 C3 170
Amity, Lincoln, Ga. 300 C4 176
Amity, Yamhill, Oreg. 620 B3 96
Amityville, Suffolk, N.Y. 8,318 E3 212
E8
Amlekhganj, Nep. D4 368
Amli, Nor. G3 291
Amlia, isl., Alsk. E4 84
Amlwch, Wales 3,000 H8 273
Amma, Roane, W.Va. 300 C3 194
Ammān, Jordan 202,000 D1 378
Ammanford, Wales 6,700 J8 273
Ammarfjället, mtn., Swe. C6 290
Ammer, lake, Ger. E4 286
Ammon, Bonneville, Idaho 1,882 F7 108
Ammonoosuc, riv., N.H. C3 208
Amne Machin, mts., China E7 346
Amo, Hendricks, Ind. 437 C3 140
Amo, Sov.Un. C12 329
Āmol, Iran 14,166 B3 379
Amoles, Mex. K14 225
Amonate, Tazewell, Va. 875 C3 192
Amoret, Bates, Mo. 261 C3 150
Amorgós, isl., Grc. C5 306
Amorita, Alfalfa, Okla. 74 B5 128
Amory, Monroe, Miss. 6,474 B4 184
Åmotfors, Swe. B3 292
Amoy (Hsiamen), China 224,300 M9 349
Ampanihy, Malag. D8 421
Amparo, Braz. 10,482 E1 258
Amposta, Sp. 9,802 B7 298
Amqui, Que., Can. 3,247 *Q10 66
'Amrān, Yemen 20,000 D3 383
Amravati, India 87,099 D3 366
Amritsar, India 325,747 C1 368
Amroha, India 59,105 C2 368
Amrum, isl., Ger. A3 286
Amsterdam, Decatur, Ga. 511 F2 176
Amsterdam, Twin Falls, Idaho G4 108
Amsterdam, Bates, Mo. 118 C3 150
Amsterdam, Gallatin, Mont. 55 *E5 110
Amsterdam, Neth. 858,702 B3 282
(*1,150,000)
Amsterdam, Montgomery, N.Y. 28,772 C7 212
Amsterdam, Jefferson, Ohio 931 B6 156
Amstetten, Aus. 11,344 B6 313
Amston, Tolland, Conn. 300 C6 202
Am Timan, Chad D9 409
Amu Darya (Oxus), riv., Afg. A3 374
Amu Darya, riv., Sov.Un. D6 336
Amukta, pass, Alsk. E4 84
Amund Ringnes, isl., N.W.Ter., Can. B9 48
Amundsen, gulf, N.W.Ter., Can. C6 48
Amungen, lake, Swe. F6 291
Amur, riv., Sov.Un. E15 329
Amvrakia, gulf, Grc. B3 306
Āna, Iraq 5,860 B4 378
Anabar, riv., Sov.Un. B13 329
Anacoco, Vernon, La. 300 C2 180
Anacoco, lake, La. C2 180
Anaconda, Deer Lodge, Mont. 12,054 D4 110
Anaconda, Valencia, N.Mex. 350 C3 126
Anaconda, range, Mont. E3 110
Anacortes, Skagit, Wash. 8,414 A4 98
Anadarko, Caddo, Okla. 6,299 C5 128
Anadia, Braz. 2,306 B3 258
Anadyr, Sov.Un. 5,000 C19 329
Anadyr, gulf, Sov.Un. C20 329
Anadyr, range, Sov.Un. C19 329
Anadyr, riv., Sov.Un. C18 329
Anáfi, isl., Grc. C5 306
Anagance, N.B., Can. 145 D4 70
Anaheim, Orange, Calif. 104,184 C6 94
F5
Anahim Lake, B.C., Can. D10 52
Anahola, Kauai, Haw. 326 A2 86
Anahuac, Chambers, Tex. 1,985 E8 130
F8
Anahulu, riv., Haw. F9 86
Anajás, Braz. 143 F7 256
Anakapalle, India 40,102 E4 366
Anaktuvuk Pass, Alsk. 66 B6 84
Analava, Malag. B9 42
Analco, Mex. M15 225
Ana Maria, gulf, Cuba B5 232
Anambas, is., Indon. D3 358
Anamoose, McHenry, N.Dak. 503 C5 154
Anamosa, Jones, Iowa 4,616 B6 142
Anamur, Tur. 2,982 C5 307
Anamur, cape, Tur. C5 307
Anandale, Rapides, La. 2,827 *C3 180
Anantapur, India 31,952 F3 366
Anantnag, India 11,985 B1 368
Ananyev, Sov.Un. 40,500 I7 332
Anápolis, Braz. 18,350 D1 258
Anār, Iran C4 379
Anārak, Iran 1,270 C3 379
Anārdara, Afg. 10,000 C1 374
Anastasia, St. Johns, Fla. 300 B10 174
Anastasia, isl., Fla. B9 174
Anatone, Asotin, Wash. 90 C9 98
Anatuya, Arg. 9,310 A3 252
Anawalt, McDowell, W.Va. 1,062 *D3 194
Ancash, dept., Peru 644,418 B2 245
Ancell, Scott, Mo. D8 150
Ancenis, Fr. 5,050 D3 278
Anchi, China 5,000 M9 349
Anchieta, Braz. 1,179 E2 258
Anching, China 105,300 J8 349
Anchor, pt., Alsk. H10 84
Anchorage, Alsk. 44,237 C7 84
(*80,000) G11
Anchorage, Jefferson, Ky. 1,170 A5 178
Anchorage, see Marsá al 'Uwayjah, Libya
Anchor Bay Gardens, Macomb, Mich. 1,830 G9 146
Anchor Point, Alsk. 196 *D6 84
Ancienne Lorette, Que., Can. 3,464 R13 66
R15
Anclote, keys, Fla. C8 174
Anco, Knott, Ky. 396 C7 178
Ancón, Peru 1,097 C2 245
Ancona, It. 64,800 D4 302
(89,800▲)
Ancona, prov., It. 406,700 *D4 302
Ancora, Camden, N.J. D3 210
Ancud, Chile 6,410 F3 251
Ancud, gulf, Chile F3 251
Andacollo, Arg. C1 252
Andahuaylas, Peru 2,309 C2 245
Andale, Sedgwick, Kans. 432 E6 144
Andalgala, Arg. A2 252
Åndalsnes, Nor. 1,943 E2 290
Andalusia, Covington, Ala. 10,263 D3 168
Andalusia, Rock Island, Ill. 560 B3 138
Andalusia, Bucks, Pa. (part of Cornwell Heights) A7 214
Andalusia (Andalucía), reg., Sp. 5,647,244 D4 298
Andaman, is., India F6 366
Andaman, sea, Indian O. E2 362
Andaman and Nicobar Islands, ter., India 30,971 F6 366
Andamarca, Bol. C1 246
Andamarca, Peru 1,576 C3 245
Andapa, Malag. B9 421
Andavaka, cape, Malag. E9 421
Andenne, Bel. 7,829 D4 282
Anderlecht, Bel. 92,642 D3 282
Andermatt, Switz. 1,231 B4 312
Andernach, Ger. 18,000 C2 286
Anderson, Lauderdale, Ala. 450 A2 168
Anderson, Shasta, Calif. 4,492 B2 94
Anderson, Madison, Ind. 49,061 B4 140
Anderson, McDonald, Mo. 992 E3 150
Anderson, Anderson, S.C. 41,316 B3 188
Anderson, Franklin, Tenn. 40 C6 190
Anderson, Grimes, Tex. 500 D8 130
Anderson, co., Kans. 9,035 D8 144
Anderson, co., Ky. 8,618 C5 178
Anderson, co., S.C. 98,478 B3 188
Anderson, co., Tenn. 60,032 B7 190
Anderson, co., Tex. 28,162 D8 130
Anderson, isl., Wash. D2 98
Anderson, riv., N.W.Ter., Can. D6 48
Anderson, riv., Ind. D3 140
Anderson Dam, Elmore, Idaho 35 F3 108
Anderson East Side, Madison, Ind. 3,778 *B4 140
Anderson Ranch, dam and res., Idaho F3 108
Andersonville, Sumter, Ga. 263 D2 176
Andersonville, Franklin, Ind. 250 C4 140
Andersonville, Anderson, Tenn. 500 B7 190
Andersonville, Buckingham, Va. 65 C6 192
Andes, Col. 6,905 B1 244
Andes, Richland, Mont. 5 C12 110
Andes, Delaware, N.Y. 399 C7 212
Andes, lake, S.Dak. D7 158
Andes, mts., Arg. F3 251
Andes, mts., S.A. D4 236
H4
Andhra Pradesh, state, India 31,260,133 E3 366
Andikithira, isl., Grc. D4 306
Andilamena, Malag. C9 421
Andīmeshk, Iran 7,324 C2 379
Andizhan, Sov.Un. 129,000 D8 336
Andkhüi, Afg. 18,438 A3 374
Andóas, Peru 189 A2 245
Andorra, And. 600 A7 298
Andorra, country, Eur. 6,500 D5 266
278
Andover, N.B., Can. 315 C2 70

Andover, Tolland, Conn. 200 C6 202
(1,771*)
Andover, Eng. 15,900 J11 273
Andover, Clinton, Iowa 91 *C7 142
Andover, Butler, Kans. 171 B6 144
Andover, Oxford, Maine 300 D2 204
(762*)
Andover, Essex, Mass. 10,000 A5 206
(15,878*)
Andover, Merrimack, N.H. 350 E3 208
(955*)
Andover, Sussex, N.J. 734 B3 210
Andover, Allegany, N.Y. 1,247 C4 212
Andover, Ashtabula, Ohio 1,116 A6 156
Andover, Day, S.Dak. 224 B8 158
Andover, Windsor, Vt. (215*) E3 218
Andraitx, Sp. 2,922 C8 298
Andreafski, see St. Marys, Alsk.
Andreanof, is., Alsk. E4 84
Andreas, cape, Cyp. D6 307
Andrew, Alta., Can. 602 D6 54
Andrew, Jackson, Iowa 349 B7 142
Andrew, co., Mo. 11,062 B3 150
Andrew, isl., N.S., Can. D9 70
Andrew Johnson, natl. mon., Tenn. B9 190
Andrews, Huntington, Ind. 1,132 B4 140
Andrews, Dorchester, Md. 150 D7 182
Andrews, Cherokee, N.C. 1,404 B2 186
Andrews, Sioux, Nebr. 6 B2 152
Andrews, Harney, Oreg. 5 E8 96
Andrews, Georgetown, S.C. 2,995 E9 188
Andrews, Andrews, Tex. 11,135 C4 130
Andrews, co., Tex. 13,450 C4 130
Andreya, cape, Sov.Un. B13 329
Andreyevka, Sov.Un. H11 332
Andria, It. 67,900 E6 302
Androka, Malag. D8 421
Ándros, Grc. 2,236 C5 306
Ándros, isl., Grc. C5 306
Andros, isl., W.I. A5 232
Androscoggin, co., Maine 86,312 D2 204
Androscoggin, lake, Maine D2 204
Androscoggin, riv., Maine, N.H. D2 204
B4 208
Andytown, Broward, Fla. 50 D5 174
Aneby, Swe. D5 292
Anécho, Togo E5 408
Anéfis, Mali C5 408
Anegada, bay, Arg. F5 251
Anegada, isl., Vir.Is. C12 233
Anegada, passage, W.I. C12 233
Anegam, Pima, Ariz. 35 F3 124
Añelo, Arg. C2 252
Anerley, Sask., Can. 25 E4 58
Aneroid, Sask., Can. 350 F4 58
Aneta, Nelson, N.Dak. 451 C8 154
Aneto, peak, Sp. A7 298
Angamos, pt., Chile B3 250
Angara, riv., Sov.Un. D12 329
Angaur, isl., Palau B6 436
Ånge, Swe. E6 291
Angel, falls, Ven. D7 240
Angel, isl., Calif. A5 94
Angela, Rosebud, Mont. 6 D10 110
Angeles, pt., Wash. A3 98
Ängelholm, Swe. 11,463 E3 292
Angelica, Allegany, N.Y. 898 C3 212
Angelica, Shawano, Wis. 30 D5 160
Angelina, co., Tex. 39,814 D8 130
Angelo, Monroe, Wis. 150 E3 160
Ängelsberg, Swe. B7 292
Angels Camp, Calaveras, Calif. 1,121 C3 94
Angelus, Chesterfield, S.C. 65 B8 188
Ångermanälven, riv., Swe. E7 290
Ångermanland, prov., Swe. 192,060 *E7 290
Angermünde, Ger. 12,000 B5 286
Angers, Que., Can. 487 S9 66
Angers, Fr. 102,142 D3 278
Ängesön, isl., Swe. E9 290
Angicos, Braz. 1,355 B3 258
Angie, Washington, La. 254 D6 180
Angier, Harnett, N.C. 1,249 B7 186
Angikuni, lake, N.W.Ter., Can. E9 48
Angkor, ruins, Camb. D4 362
Anglem, mtn., N.Z. G1 437
Anglesey, co., Wales 51,660 H8 273
Anglet, Fr. 12,603 F3 278
Angleton, Brazoria, Tex. 7,312 E8 130
G8
Anglia, Sask., Can. 100 E3 58
Angmagssalik, Grnld. 277 Q31 290
Ango, Con.L. B4 414
Angohrān, Iran D4 379
Angol, Chile 14,292 C1 252
Angola, Sussex, Del. F5 172
Angola, Steuben, Ind. 4,746 A5 140
Angola, Erie, N.Y. 2,499 C2 212
Angola, Port. poss., Afr. 4,508,000 H8 388
421
Angola, swamp, N.C. C8 186
Angola On The Lake, Erie, N.Y. (part of Lake Erie Beach) C2 212
Angoon, Alsk. 429 D8 84
J14
Angora, Morrill, Nebr. 80 C2 152
Angostura, Dona Ana, N.Mex. F3 126
Angostura, res., S.Dak. D2 158
Angoulême, Fr. 43,170 E4 278
Angoumois, former prov., Fr. 292,000 E3 278
Angra dos Reis, Braz. 5,277 E2 258
Angren, Sov.Un. D7 336
Ang Thong, prov., Thai. 150,304 *D3 362
Anguilla, Sharkey, Miss. 580 C2 184
Anguilla, ter., W.I.Fed. 7,895 C13 233
Anguillara, It. 2,419 *D4 302
Anguille, cape, Newf., Can. G6 72
Anguille, mts., Newf., Can. G6 72
Angumu, Con.L. C4 414
Angus, Ont., Can. 350 P21 64
Angus, Nuckolls, Nebr. 35 *D7 152
Angus, co., Scot. 275,900 E9 272
Angusville, Man., Can. 450 E2 60
Anhalt, reg., Ger. *C5 286
Anholt, isl., Den. E2 292
Anhsi, China 25,000 C7 346
Anhua, China 5,000 K5 349
Anhwei, prov., China 33,560,000 E11 346
Aniak, Alsk. 142 C6 84
Anikeyeva, Sov.Un. B11 329
Animas City, La Plata, Colo. (part of Durango) E3 106
Animas, Hidalgo, N.Mex. 40 G2 126
Animas, mts., N.Mex. G2 126
Animas, peak, N.Mex. G2 126
Animas, riv., Colo. E3 106
Anina, Rom. 11,837 B1 321
Anita, Cass, Iowa 1,233 C3 142
Aniwa, Shawano, Wis. 247 C4 160
Anjean, Greenbrier, W.Va. 400 C4 194
Anjō, Jap. 52,820 M13 354
Anjou, Que., Can. 2,140 *S16 66
Anjou, former prov., Fr. 631,000 D3 278
Anjouan, isl., Afr. B8 421
Anju, Kor. 21,861 F12 348
Anjum, Neth. 1,002 A5 282
Ankang, China I4 349
Ankara, Tur. 453,151 B5 307
Ankara, prov., Tur. 1,120,622 *B5 307
Ankaratra, mts., Malag. C9 421
Ankarsrum, Swe. D7 292
Ankavandra, Malag. C9 421
Ankazoabo, Malag. 1,800 D8 421
Ankeny, Polk, Iowa 2,964 A7 142
C4
An Khe, Viet. D6 362
Anklam, Ger. 20,200 B5 286
Ankobar, Eth. D4 398
Ankona, Saint Lucie, Fla. 89 D10 174
Ankoro, Con.L. D4 414
Ankuang, China 15,000 C11 348
Anlu, China 20,000 J6 349
Anlung, China 8,700 M3 349
Anmoore, Harrison, W.Va. 1,050 B4 194
B6
Ann, cape, Mass. A6 206
Ann, lake, Swe. E5 290
Anna, Union, Ill. 4,280 F4 138
Anna, Shelby, Ohio 701 B2 156
Anna, Sov.Un. 8,000 G13 332
Anna, Collin, Tex. 639 *C7 130
Annabella, Sevier, Utah 177 E3 114
An Najaf, Iraq 74,089 D6 378
Annalee Heights, Fairfax, Va. 2,000 *B7 192
Anna Maria, Manatee, Fla. 690 C6 174
Anna Maria, key, Fla. D6 174
Annandale, Wright, Minn. 984 F4 148
Annandale, Hunterdon, N.J. 500 B3 210
Annandale, Fairfax, Va. 5,000 A7 192
Annapolis, Parke, Ind. 100 C2 140
Annapolis, Anne Arundel, Md. 23,385 C7 182
Annapolis, Iron, Mo. 334 D7 150
Annapolis, Kitsap, Wash. 600 D2 98
Annapolis, co., N.S., Can. 21,682 E4 70
Annapolis, riv., N.S., Can. E4 70
Annapolis Junction, Howard, Md. 525 B6 182
Annapolis Royal, N.S., Can. 765 E4 70
Ann Arbor, Washtenaw, Mich. 67,340 B6 146
G8
An Nāsirīya, Iraq 25,515 D7 378
Annawan, Henry, Ill. 701 B4 138
Anne Arundel, co., Md. 206,634 B6 182
Annecy, Fr. 33,114 E7 278
Annemasse, Fr. 10,209 D7 278
Annette, Alsk. 302 *K15 84
Annette, isl., Alsk. K15 84
Annieopsquotch, mts., Newf., Can. F7 72
Anniston, Calhoun, Ala. 33,657 B4 168
Anniston, Mississippi, Mo. 307 E8 150
Annobón, isl., Afr. G6 408
Annonay, Fr. 13,005 E6 278
Annotto Bay, Jam. 25,000 C6 232
Annursnack, hill, Mass. C1 206
Annville, Jackson, Ky. 400 C7 178
Annville, Lebanon, Pa. 4,264 C5 214
Anogoche, Moz. C7 421
Anoka, Anoka, Minn. 10,562 F5 148
Anoka, Boyd, Nebr. 32 B7 152
Anoka, co., Minn. 85,916 F5 148
Anona, Pinellas, Fla. 120 C5 174
Áno Theológos, Grc. 2,320 A5 306
Anou Mellène, well, Mali C5 408
Áno Viánnos, Grc. 1,961 D5 306
Anóyia, Grc. 3,072 D5 306
Anpei, China 4,000 E4 348
Anping, China 20,000 F7 348
Anrep, Jefferson, Ark C5 170
Ansbach, Ger. 33,600 D4 286
Anse au Loup, Newf., Can. E7 72
Anse d'Hainault, Hai. 2,270 C7 232
Anselmo, Custer, Nebr. 269 C6 152
Anserma, Col. 7,767 B1 244
Anshan, China 548,900 E11 348
Ansley, Jackson, La. 400 B3 180
Ansley, Custer, Nebr. 714 C6 152
Anson, Somerset, Maine 900 D3 204
(2,252*)
Anson, Jones, Tex. 2,890 C6 130
Anson, co., N.C. 24,962 B5 186
Anson, bay, Austl. A5 432
Ansŏng, Kor. 19,356 G13 348
Ansongo, Mali 400 C5 408
Ansonia, New Haven, Conn. 19,819 D3 202
Ansonia, Darke, Ohio 1,002 B2 156
Ansonville, Anson, N.C. 558 B5 186
Ansted, Fayette, W.Va. 1,511 C3 194
D7
Anta, China 35,000 B12 348
Anta, Peru 1,542 C3 245
Antakya (Antioch), Tur. 37,484 C7 307
Antalāt, Libya A4 394
Antalya, Tur. 35,923 C4 307
Antalya, prov., Tur. 357,919 *C4 307
Antalya, gulf, Tur. C4 307
Antarctica, cont. 19
Ante, Brunswick, Va. 20 D7 192
Antelope, Sask., Can. 100 E3 58
Antelope, Sheridan, Mont. 150 B12 110
Antelope, Wasco, Oreg. 46 C6 96
Antelope, co., Nebr. 10,176 B7 152
Antelope, creek, Wyo. C7 116
Antelope, hills, Wyo. D4 116
Antelope, isl., Utah B3 114
Antelope, lake, Sask., Can. E3 58
Antelope, range, Nev. D7 112
Antelope, res., Oreg. E9 96
Antelope Mine, Rh. & Nya. D5 420
Antequera, Sp. 29,855 D4 298
Antero, res., Colo. C5 106
Antes Fort, Lycoming, Pa. 390 B4 214
Anthon, Woodbury, Iowa 681 B2 142
Anthony, Hempstead, Ark. 120 D3 170
Anthony, Marion, Fla. 500 B8 174
Anthony, Harper, Kans. 2,744 E5 144
Anthony, Hunterdon, N.J. B3 210
Anthony, Dona Ana, N.Mex. 916 G4 126
Anthony, Kent, R.I. 2,800 C2 216
Anthony, El Paso, Tex. 1,082 D2 130
Anthonys, creek, W.Va. D4 194
Anthony-Williams Spur, Union, Ark. D4 170
Anti Atlas, mts., Mor. C2 402
Antibes, Fr. 27,064 F7 278
Anticosti, isl., Que., Can. Q10 66
Antietam, Washington, Md. 300 B4 182
Antietam, creek, Md. B4 182
Antigo, Langlade, Wis. 9,691 C4 160
Antigonish, N.S., Can. 3,592 D8 70
Antigonish, co., N.S., Can. 13,076 D8 70
Antigua, ter., W.I.Fed. 50,000 D14 233
Antigua [Guatemala], Guat. 10,744 C2 228
Antilla, Cuba 6,481 B7 232
Antimony, Garfield, Utah 161 E4 114
Anting, China G4 348
Antioch, Contra Costa, Calif. 17,305 *D3 94
Antioch, Lake, Ill. 2,268 A5 138
D2
Antioch, Clinton, Ind. 75 B3 140
Antioch, Sheridan, Nebr. 30 B3 152
Antioch, Davidson, Tenn. 250 B5 190
E7
Antioch, see Antakya, Tur.
Antioquia, Col. 3,998 B1 244
Antioquia, dept., Col. 1,747,580 B1 244
Antler, Sask., Can. 143 F7 58
Antler, Bottineau, N.Dak. 210 B4 154
Antler, riv., Man., Can. F2 60
Antler, riv., Sask., Can. F7 58
Antlers, Pushmataha, Okla. 2,085 D8 128
Antofagasta, Chile 62,272 B3 250
Antofagasta, prov., Chile 184,824 B4 250
Antofalla, vol., Arg. C4 250
Antoine, Pike, Ark. 163 C3 170
Anton, Hockley, Tex. 1,068 C4 130
Anton Chico, Guadalupe, N.Mex. 560 C5 126
Antone, Wheeler, Oreg. C7 96
Antongil, bay, Malag. C9 421
Antonina, Braz. 5,151 K7 257
Antonino, Ellis, Kans. 50 D4 144
Antonio de Biedma, Arg. G4 251
Antônio Dias, Braz. 1,100 D2 258
Antônio Enes, Moz. 11,628 C7 421
Antonito, Conejos, Colo. 1,045 E4 106
Antony, Fr. 24,512 I10 278
Antratsit, Sov.Un. S23 332
Antrim, Antrim, Mich. 200 E6 146
Antrim, Hillsboro, N.H. 850 E3 208
(1,121*)
Antrim, co., Mich. 10,373 D6 146
Antrim, co., N.Ire. 232,700 G6 272
Antrim, mts., N.Ire. G6 272
Antsalova, Malag. 1,000 C8 421
Antsirabe, Malag. 14,600 C9 421
Antsirane, see Diégo-Suarez, Malag.
Antung, China 360,000 E12 348
Antwerp, see Antwerpen, Bel.
Antwerp, Jefferson, N.Y. 881 A6 212
Antwerp, Paulding, Ohio 1,465 A2 156
Antwerpen (Antwerp), Bel. 256,126 C3 282
(*895,000)
Antwerpen, prov., Bel. 1,389,860 C3 282
An Uaimh, Ire. 3,643 H6 273
Anupgarh, India C1 368
Anuradhapura, Cey. 18,390 G4 366
Anutt, Dent, Mo. 150 D6 150
Anvik, Alsk. 99 C5 84
Anyang, China 124,900 G7 348
Anyi, China H5 348
Anyüan, China M7 349
Anza, Riverside, Calif. 220 F5 94
Anzá, Col. 610 B1 244
Anzhero-Sudzhensk, Sov.Un. 116,000 A11 336
Anzio, It. 10,000 E4 302
Anzoátegui, state, Ven. 242,058 B6 240
Aojidong, Kor. 39,616 D15 348
Aomori, Jap. 183,747 D8 354
Aosta, It. 26,500 C1 302
Aou Hofrit, well, Sp. Sahara B2 408
Aoulef, Alg. C4 402
Apa, riv., Par. C4 247
Apache, Cochise, Ariz. 15 G6 124
Apache, Caddo, Okla. 1,455 D5 128
Apache, co., Ariz. 30,438 C6 124
Apache, mts., Tex. D3 130
Apache, peak, Ariz. G5 124
Apache Creek, Catron, N.Mex. 40 E2 126
Apache Junction, Pinal, Ariz. 200 H3 124
Apalachee, Morgan, Ga. 158 C3 176
Apalachee, bay, Fla. A6 174
Apalachicola, Franklin, Fla. 3,099 B6 174
Apalachicola, bay, Fla. B5 174
Apalachicola, riv., Fla. A5 174
Apam, Mex. 6,645 L14 225
Apaporis, riv., Col. C2 244
Aparri, Phil. 10,125 A6 358
Apatin, Yugo. 15,088 B4 316
Apatzingán, Mex. 8,372 D5 225
L12
Apeldoorn, Neth. 70,100 B4 282
Apennine, tunnel, It. C3 302
Apennines, mts., It. C2 302
Apex, Wake, N.C. 1,368 B7 186
Apgar, Flathead, Mont. 100 B2 110
Apia, Samoa 16,000 E4 436
Apiaí, Braz. 1,172 J7 257
Apíranthos, Grc. 2,438 C5 306
Apishapa, riv., Colo. E6 106
Apison, Hamilton, Tenn. 375 E8 190
Apizaco, Mex. 12,717 L14 225
Aplin, Perry, Ark. 100 C4 170
Aplington, Butler, Iowa 840 B5 142
Apo, mtn., Phil. C7 358
Apodi, Braz. 1,094 B3 258
Apohaqui, N.B., Can. 210 D4 70
Apolda, Ger. 31,100 C4 286
Apolima, strait, Samoa E4 436
Apollo, Armstrong, Pa. 2,694 C2 214
Apolo, Bol. 1,043 B1 246
Apopka, Orange, Fla. 3,578 C9 174
Apopka, lake, Fla. C9 174
Apostle, is., Wis. A3 160
Apóstoles, Arg. 3,385 A4 252
Apozol, Mex. K12 225
Appalachia, Pawnee, Okla. 260 *B7 128
Appalachia, Wise, Va. 2,456 D2 192
Appalachian, mts., U.S. D10 77
Appam, Williams, N.Dak. 60 B2 154
Appanoose, co., Iowa 16,015 D5 142
Appenzell, Switz. 5,001 A5 312
Appenzell, canton, Switz. 62,400 A5 312
Apperson, Osage, Okla. 21 B7 128
Appingedam, Neth. 7,000 A5 282
Apple, Choctaw, Okla. D8 128
Apple, creek, N.Dak. D5 154
Apple, riv., Wis. C1 160
Appleby, Eng. 1,700 G10 273
Apple Creek, Wayne, Ohio 722 B5 156
Applecross, Scot. 735 D7 272
Applegate, Sanilac, Mich. 252 F9 146
Applegate, Jackson, Oreg. 350 E3 96
Applegate, butte, Oreg. E5 96
Applegate, riv., Oreg. E3 96
Apple Grove, Louisa, Va. 25 C7 192
Apple Grove, Mason, W.Va. 600 C2 194
Apple Hill, Ont., Can. 410 O26 64
Apple River, N.S., Can. 400 D5 70
Apple River, Jo Daviess, Ill. 477 A3 138
Appleton, Pope, Ark. 150 B4 170
Appleton, Knox, Maine 160 D3 204
(672*)
Appleton, Swift, Minn. 2,172 F2 148
Appleton, Allendale, S.C. 198 E6 188
Appleton, Klickitat, Wash. 10 D5 98
Appleton, Outagamie, Wis. 48,411 A5 160
(*123,200) D5
Appleton City, St. Clair, Mo. 1,075 C3 150
Apple Valley, San Bernardino, Calif. 1,800 E5 94
Apple Valley, Canyon, Idaho *F2 108
Appleyard (South Wenatchee), Chelan, Wash. 950 B6 98
Appling, Columbia, Ga. 250 C4 176
Appling, co., Ga. 13,246 E4 176
Appomattox, Appomattox, Va. 1,184 C6 192
Appomattox, co., Va. 9,148 C6 192
Appomattox, riv., Va. C6 192
Appoquinimink, creek, Del. C3 172
Approuague, Fr.Gu. 407 E6 256
Apra, hbr., Guam C7 436
Aprelsk, Sov.Un. 800 D13 329
Araduey, riv., Sp. B4 298
Arafura, sea, Indon. F8 359
Arago, Coos, Oreg. 140 D2 96
Aragon, Polk, Ga. 1,023 B1 176
Aragon, Catron, N.Mex. 63 E2 126
Aragon (Aragón), reg., Sp. 1,090,343 B6 298
Aprilia, It. 1,753 E4 302
Apsley, Ont., Can. 170 P22 64
Apt, Fr. 5,521 F6 278
Apua, pt., Haw. D6 86
Apulia (Puglia), reg., It. 3,413,000 E5 302
Apure, state, Ven. 88,939 C3 240
Apure, riv., Ven. C5 240
Apurimac, dept., Peru 388,630 C3 245
Apurimac, riv., Peru C3 245
Aqaba, gulf, Sau.Ar. B1 383
Aqiq, Sud. B4 398
Aq Kupruk, Afg. 5,000 A4 374
Āqrabah, Jordan B6 382
Aquarius, mts., Ariz. D2 124
Aquasco, Prince Georges, Md. 400 C6 182
Aquebogue, Suffolk, N.Y. 791 D5 212
Aquidabán, riv., Par. C4 247
Aquidauana, Braz. 7,472 J5 257
Aquidneck, isl., R.I. C3 216
Aquila, see L'Aquila, It.
Aquiles Serdán, Mex. 3,927 B4 224
Aquilla, Geauga, Ohio 459 *A5 156
Aquin, Hai. 2,649 C8 232
Arab, Marshall, Ala. 2,989 A3 168
Arab, riv., Sud. D2 398
Arabela, Lincoln, N.Mex. 20 E5 126
Arabi, Crisp, Ga. 303 E3 176
Arabi, St. Bernard, La. 5,000 C7 180
Arabia, Lincoln, Ky. 50 C6 178
Arabian, des., Eg., U.A.R. B3 395
Arabian, sea, Asia F2 366
Aracajú, Braz. 67,539 C3 258
Aracanguy, mts., Par. D5 247
Aracati, Braz. 8,952 A3 258
Araçatuba, Braz. 26,862 J6 257
Aracoma, Logan, W.Va. 350 *D3 194
Aracruz, Braz. 404 D2 258
Araçuai, Braz. 4,822 D2 258
Arad, Rom. 106,460 A1 321
Aragón, riv., Sp. A6 298
Aragon Mills, York, S.C. 655 *B6 188
Aragua, state, Ven. 241,481 A5 240
Aragua de Barcelona, Ven. 5,286 B6 240
Araguaia, riv., Braz. B1 258
Araguao, riv. mouth, Ven. B8 240
Araguari, Braz. 24,619 D1 258
Araguari, riv., Braz. E6 256
Arai, Jap. 12,901 M13 354
Arāk, Iran 58,998 B2 379
Arakan, range, Bur. B2 362
Arakhthos, riv., Grc. B3 306
Araks, riv., Iran A2 379
Aral, sea, Sov.Un. C5 336
Aral Karkum, des., Sov.Un. C6 336
Aralsk, Sov.Un. 18,600 C6 336
Aramac, Austl. 532 C9 432
Arambagh, India I8 366
Aran, isl., Ire. G4 272
Aran, is., Ire. H3 273
Aranda de Duero, Sp. 10,420 B5 298
Arandas, Mex. 9,318 K12 225
Arandu, India B1 368
Aranjuez, Sp. 21,910 B5 298
Aransas, co., Tex. 7,006 E7 130
Aransas, bay, Tex. E7 130
Aransas Pass, San Patricio and Aransas, Tex. 6,956 F7 130
Aranyaprathet, Thai. 25,000 D4 362
Arao, Jap. 67,504 *H3 354
Araouane, Mali C4 408
Arapaho, Custer, Okla. 351 C5 128
Arapahoe, Cheyenne, Colo. 125 D8 106

Arapahoe, Furnas, Nebr.	1,084	D6	152
Arapahoe, Pamlico, N.C.	274	B9	186
Arapahoe, Fremont, Wyo.	30	D4	116
Arapahoe, co., Colo.	113,426	C6	106
Arapahoe, peak, Colo.		B5	106
Arapey, Ur.		B4	252
Arapey Grande, riv., Ur.		B4	252
Arapkir, Tur.	6,745	B8	307
Araraquara, Braz.	34,114	E1	258
Araras, Braz.	12,331	E1	258
Ararat, Choctaw, Ala.	50	D1	168
Ararat, Austl.	7,414	F8	432
Ararat, Patrick, Va.	300	D4	192
Ararat, mt., Tur.		B11	307
Arareh, Neth. N.Gui.		E9	359
Araripe, mts., Braz.		B2	258
Aratane, well, Maur.		C3	408
Arauca, Col.	9,310	B2	244
Arauca, intendencia, Col.	14,080	B2	244
Arauca, riv., Ven.		C4	240
Arauco, Chile	2,707	C1	252
Arauco, prov., Chile	72,289	E3	250
Aravalli, range, India		D2	366
Araxá, Braz.	14,375	D1	258
Arba, Randolph, Ind.	100	B5	140
Arba Jahan, Ken.		B6	414
Arbaugh, Newton, Ark.		B3	170
Arboga, Swe.	10,586	B6	292
Arbogaån, riv., Swe.		B7	292
Arbois, Fr.		D6	278
Arboles, Archuleta, Colo.	100	E3	106
Arbon, Power, Idaho	10	G6	108
Arbon, Switz.	8,816	A5	312
Arbor, Middlesex, N.J.	2,000	*B4	210
Arborea, It.	908	F2	302
Arborfield, Sask., Can.	557	D6	58
Arborg, Man., Can.	400	E4	60
Arbor Terrace, St. Louis, Mo.	1,225	*C7	150
Arbor Vitae, Vilas, Wis.	150	C4	160
Arbroath, Scot.	19,900	E10	272
Arbuckle, Colusa, Calif.	950	C2	94
Arbuckle, Murray, Okla.		D7	128
Arbuckle, lake, Fla.		D9	174
Arbuckle, mts., Okla.		D6	128
Arbutus, Baltimore, Md. (part of Halethorpe)		C4	182
Arbyrd, Dunklin, Mo.	667	E7	150
Arcachon, Fr.	14,985	E3	278
Arcade, Jackson, Ga.	108	*B3	176
Arcade, Wyoming, N.Y.	1,930	C3	212
Arcadia, Los Angeles, Calif.	41,005	C5	94
Arcadia, De Soto, Fla.	5,889	D9	174
Arcadia, Hamilton, Ind.	1,271	B3	140
Arcadia, Carroll, Iowa	437	B2	142
Arcadia, Crawford, Kans.	507	E9	144
Arcadia, Bienville, La.	2,547	B3	180
Arcadia, Manistee, Mich.	600	E5	146
Arcadia, Iron, Mo.	489	D7	150
Arcadia, Valley, Nebr.	446	C6	152
Arcadia, Hancock, Ohio	610	A3	156
Arcadia, Oklahoma, Okla.	400	C6	128
Arcadia, Washington, R.I.	75	C2	216
Arcadia, Spartanburg, S.C.	2,458	B5	188
Arcadia, Duchesne, Utah	10	C5	114
Arcadia, Botetourt, Va.	25	*C5	192
Arcadia, Trempealeau, Wis.	2,084	D2	160
Arcadia, see Arkadhia, prov., Grc.			
Arcadia Lakes, Richland, S.C.	316	*C6	188
Arcanum, Darke, Ohio	1,678	C2	156
Arcata, Humboldt, Calif.	5,235	B1	94
Arcelia, Mex.	5,688	L13	225
Arcena, Sp.	5,830	D3	298
Arch, Roosevelt, N.Mex.	20	D7	126
Archambault, lake, Que., Can.		R10	66
Archbald, Lackawanna, Pa.	5,471	A5	214
Archbold, Fulton, Ohio	2,348	A2	156
Archdale, Randolph, N.C.	1,520	B6	186
Archer, Alachua, Fla.	707	B8	174
Archer, Madison, Idaho	50	F7	108
Archer, O'Brien, Iowa	209	A2	142
Archer, Sheridan, Mont.	5	B12	110
Archer, Merrick, Nebr.	80	C7	152
Archer, Laramie, Wyo.	20	*E8	116
Archer, co., Tex.	6,110	C6	130
Archer, riv., Austl.		A8	432
Archer City, Archer, Tex.	1,974	C6	130
Archers Post, Ken.		B6	414
Archerwill, Sask., Can.	230	D6	58
Arches, natl. mon., Utah		E6	114
Archibald, Richland, La.	140	B4	180
Archidona, Sp.	7,962	D4	298
Archie, Cass, Mo.	348	C3	150
Archuleta, co., Colo.	2,629	E3	106
Arco, Glynn, Ga.	1,500	*E5	176
Arco, Butte, Idaho	1,562	F5	108
Arco, Lincoln, Minn.	140	G2	148
Arcola, Sask., Can.	609	F6	58
Arcola, Douglas, Ill.	2,273	D5	138
Arcola, Allen, Ind.	275	A4	140
Arcola, Washington, Miss.	366	B2	184
Arcola, Dade, Mo.	105	D4	150
Arcola, Loudoun, Va.	40	A6	192
Arcola, Webster, W.Va.	100	C4	194
Arcos de la Frontera, Sp.	11,585	D4	298
Arcoverde, Braz.	9,599	B3	258
Arctic, Alsk.	53	B7	84
Arctic, ocean			329
Arctic Bay, N.W.Ter., Can.		C10	48
Arcturus, Fairfax, Va.	40	*B7	192
Arcueil, Fr.	18,067	I10	278
Arda, riv., Bul.		C2	317
Ardabil, Iran	65,742	A2	379
Ardahan, Tur.	4,768	A10	307
Ardakān, Iran	8,490	C3	379
Ardal, Nor.		F2	291
Ardara, Ire.	514	G4	272
Ardath, Sask., Can.	68	E4	58
Ardatov, Sov.Un.	12,800	E16	332
Ardbeg, Ont., Can.	95	O20	64
Ardea, It.	857	*E4	302
Ardèche, dept., Fr.	249,077	*E6	278
Arden, Little River, Ark.	25	D2	170
Arden, Man., Can.	275	E3	60
Arden, Ont., Can.	315	P24	64
Arden, New Castle, Del.	1,500	A4	172
Arden, Clark, Nev.	35	G6	112
Arden, Buncombe, N.C.	800	B3	186
Ardena, Monmouth, N.J.		C4	210
Arden Hills, Ramsey, Minn.	3,930	*F5	148
Ardennes, dept., Fr.	280,490	*C6	278
Ardennes, mts., Bel.		E4	282
Ardenvoir, Chelan, Wash.	200	B6	98
Ardestan, Iran	5,669	C3	379
Ardglass, N.Ire.	673	G7	273
Ardila, riv., Port.		C3	298
Ardill, Sask., Can.	34	F5	58
Ardincaple, Richland, S.C.	729	*C6	188
Ardino, Bul.	1,469	C2	317
Ardley, Alta., Can.	100	D6	54
Ardmore, Limestone, Ala.	439	A3	168
Ardmore, Alta., Can.	100	C7	54
Ardmore, Ire.	250	J5	273
Ardmore, Prince Georges, Md.	750	C6	182
Ardmore, Carter, Okla.	20,184	D6	128
Ardmore, Delaware, Pa.	15,000	A6	214
Ardmore, Fall River, S.Dak.	73	D2	158
Ardmore, Giles, Tenn.	195	C5	190
Ardnamurchan, pt., Scot.		E6	272
Ardoch, Walsh, N.Dak.	106	B8	154
Ardrossan, Alta., Can.	50	D6	54
Ardrossan, Scot.	9,400	F8	272
Ardsley, Westchester, N.Y.	3,991	D2	212
Ardulusa, Cumberland, N.C.		C7	186
Åre, Swe.		E5	290
Arebeb, well, Mali		B5	408
Arecibo, P.R.	28,659	C11	233
Aredale, Butler, Iowa	153	B4	142
Areia Branca, Braz.	7,665	B3	258
Arelee, Sask., Can.	124	D4	58
Arena, Iowa, Wis.	309	E4	160
Arena, pt., Calif.		C2	94
Arena, pt., Mex.		C4	224
Arenac, co., Mich.	9,860	E8	146
Arenas de San Pedro, Sp.	5,263	D4	298
Arenas Valley, Grant, N.Mex.	150	F2	126
Arendal, Nor.	11,708 (*19,000)	G3	291
Arendonk, Bel.	8,576	C4	282
Arendsee, Ger.		B4	286
Arenzville, Cass, Ill.	417	D3	138
Areópolis, Grc.	1,217	C4	306
Arequipa, dept., Peru	375,126	D3	245
Arezzo, It.	31,200 (68,500▲)	D3	302
Arezzo, prov., It.	327,000	*D3	302
Arga, riv., Sp.		A6	298
Argalastí, Grc.	3,021	B4	306
Argangchi, China		B11	348
Argenta, Macon, Ill.	860	D5	138
Argenta, It.	4,600	C3	302
Argenta, Beaverhead, Mont.	10	E4	110
Argenta, Lander, Nev.	10	C5	112
Argentan, Fr.	7,168	C3	278
Argenteuil, Fr.	63,316	I10	278
Argenteuil, co., Que., Can.	28,474	S10	66
Argentia, Newf., Can.	750	G9	72
Argentina, country, S.A.	20,433,000	G5	236, 251
Argentino, lake, Arg.		H3	251
Argenton [-sur-Creuse], Fr.	6,109	D4	278
Argesul, riv., Rom.		B3	321
Arghandab, riv., Afg.		C4	374
Argle Downs, Austl.	99	B5	432
Argo, Sussex, Del.		E4	172
Argo, Sud.	2,389	B3	398
Argolis, prov., Grc.	85,389	*C4	306
Argolis, gulf, Grc.		C4	306
Argonia, Sumner, Kans.	553	E6	144
Argonne, Forest, Wis.	150	C5	160
Argonne, plat., Fr.		C6	278
Argora, Clark, Idaho		E6	108
Árgos, Grc.	13,163	C4	306
Argos, Marshall, Ind.	1,339	A3	140
Árgos, Orestikón, Grc.	4,292	A3	306
Argostólion, Grc.	8,724	B3	306
Argun, riv., Sov.Un.		D13	329
Argunda, Sp.	5,076	*B5	298
Argungu, Nig.		D5	408
Argusville, Cass., N.Dak.	118	C9	154
Argyle, Walton, Fla.	200	A4	174
Argyle, Clinch, Ga.	225	E4	176
Argyle (Town of), Penobscot, Maine	(133▲)	C4	204
Argyle, Sanilac, Mich.	150	F9	146
Argyle, Marshall, Minn.	789	C2	148
Argyle, Osage, Mo.	99	C5	150
Argyle, Lafayette, Wis.	786	F4	160
Argyll, co., Scot.	57,800	E7	272
Arhno, atoll, Marshall		A4	436
Ariake, bay, Jap.		I3	354
Arial, Pickens, S.C.	950	B3	188
Ariano Irpino, It.	11,300	E5	302
Ariari, riv., Col.		C2	244
Arica, Chile	18,947	A3	250
Arichat, N.S., Can.	675	D8	70
Arickaree, Washington, Colo.		C7	106
Ariège, dept., Fr.	140,010	*F4	278
Ariel, Cowlitz, Wash.	75	D4	98
Arieșul, riv., Rom.		A2	321
Arīḥa (Jericho), Jordan		C6	382
Arikaree, riv., Colo.		C8	106
Arimo, Bannock, Idaho	303	G6	108
Arinos, riv., Braz.		H5	257
Ario de Rosales, Mex.	6,651	D5, L13	225
Arion, Crawford, Iowa	201	C2	142
Aripeka, Pasco, Fla.	160	C8	174
Aripuān, riv., Braz.		G4	256
Arisaig, Scot.	1,002	E7	272
Arisaig, sound, Scot.		E7	272
Arispe, Union, Iowa	125	D3	142
Arista, Mercer, W.Va.	300	D3	194
Aristazabal, isl., B.C., Can.		D8	52
Ariton, Dale, Ala.	687	D4	168
Arivaca, Pima, Ariz.	26	G4	124
Arivonimamo, Malag.		C9	421
Arizaro, salt flat, Arg.		B4	250
Arizola, Pinal, Ariz.	20	F4	124
Arizona, Arg.		C2	252
Arizona, Claiborne, La.	50	B3	180
Arizona, state, U.S.	1,302,161	E4	77, 124
Arizpe, Mex.	1,403	A3	224
Årjäng, Swe.	2,893	B3	292
Arjay, Bell, Ky.	890	D7	178
Arjeplog, Swe.	1,222	C8	290
Arjona, Col.	12,361	A1	244
Arjona, Sp.	5,076	D4	298
Ark, Gloucester, Va.	75	*C8	192
Arkabutla, Tate, Miss.	175	A2	184
Arkabutla, res., Miss.		A3	184
Arkadelphia, Cullman, Ala.	298	B3	168
Arkadelphia, Clark, Ark.	8,069	C3	170
Arkadhia (Arcadia), prov., Grc.	154,361	*C4	306
Arkangelskoye, Sov.Un.		B7	328
Arkansas, state, U.S.	1,786,272	D8	77, 170
Arkansas, riv., U.S.		D6	77
Arkansas City, Desha, Ark.	783	D5	170
Arkansas City, Cowley, Kans.	14,262	E6	144
Arkansas Post, Arkansas, Ark.	25	C5	170
Arkansas, co., Ark.	23,355	C5	170
Arkansaw, Pepin, Wis.	400	D1	160
Arkhangelsk, Sov.Un.	256,000	C6	328
Arkhara, Sov.Un.	5,300	E15	329
Arkinda, Little River, Ark.	80	D2	170
Arklow, Ire.	5,292	I6	273
Arkoma, Le Flore, Okla.	1,862	C9	128
Arkona, Ont., Can.	447	Q19	64
Arkonam, India	23,032	F3	366
Arkösund, Swe.		C7	292
Arkport, Steuben, N.Y.	837	C4	212
Arkville, Delaware, N.Y.	500	C7	212
Arkwright, Spartanburg, S.C.	1,656	*B6	188
Arland, Barron, Wis.	50	C1	160
Arlanza, riv., Sp.		A5	298
Arlanzón, riv., Sp.		A4	298
Arlberg, tunnel, Aus.		C2	313
Arlee, Lake, Mont.	300	C2	110
Arlemont, Esmeralda, Nev.	10	F3	112
Arles, Fr.	23,776	F6	278
Arley, Winston, Ala.	300	A2	168
Arline, Blount, Tenn.		E9	190
Arling, Valley, Idaho		E2	108
Arlington, Maricopa, Ariz.	25	E3	124
Arlington, Kiowa, Colo.	5	D7	106
Arlington, Duval, Fla.	4,200	A9, A10	174
Arlington, Calhoun and Early, Ga.	1,462	E2	176
Arlington, Rush, Ind.	470	C4	140
Arlington, Fayette, Iowa	614	B6	142
Arlington, Reno, Kans.	466	E5	144
Arlington, Carlisle, Ky.	584	D1	178
Arlington, Middlesex, Mass.	49,953	C2	206
Arlington, Sibley, Minn.	1,601	G4	148
Arlington, Washington, Nebr.	740	C9, D2	152
Arlington, Hudson, N.J.		B1	210
Arlington, Dutchess, N.Y.	8,317	D8	212
Arlington, Yadkin, N.C.	590	A5	186
Arlington, Hancock, Ohio	955	B3	156
Arlington, Lincoln, Okla.	40	C7	128
Arlington, Gilliam, Oreg.	643	B6	96
Arlington, Spartanburg, S.C.	500	B4	188
Arlington, Kingsbury, S.Dak.	996	C8	158
Arlington, Shelby, Tenn.	620	C2	190
Arlington, Tarrant, Tex.	44,775	B8	130
Arlington, Bennington, Vt.	1,111 (1,605▲)	E2	218
Arlington, Arlington, Va.	163,401	A7, B7	192
Arlington, Snohomish, Wash.	2,025	A4	98
Arlington, Columbia, Wis.	349	E4	160
Arlington, co., Va.	163,401	A7	192
Arlington Heights, Cook, Ill.	27,878	A6, E2	138
Arlington Heights, Hamilton, Ohio	1,325	*C2	156
Arlon, Bel.	12,724	E4	282
Arltunga, Austl.		C6	432
Arm, Lawrence, Miss.	75	D2	184
Arm, riv., Sask., Can.		E5	58
Arma, Crawford, Kans.	1,296	E9	144
Arma, plat., Sau.Ar.		B4	383
Armada, Alta., Can.	75	E6	54
Armada, Macomb, Mich.	1,111	G9	146
Armadale, Austl.	1,496	E3	432
Armagh, Que., Can.	839	R14	66
Armagh, N.Ire.	9,279	G6	273
Armagh, co., N. Ire.	113,900	G6	273
Armathwaite, Fentress, Tenn.	150	B7	190
Armavir, Sov.Un.	111,000	J13	332
Armenia, Col.	57,098	C1	244
Armenia, rep., Sov.Un.	1,768,000	E6	328
Armeria, Mex.		D5	224
Armero, Col.	10,258	B1	244
Armidale, Austl.	8,661	E10	432
Armijo, Bernalillo, N.Mex.	2,500	H6	126
Armington, Cascade, Mont.	168	C6	110
Arminto, Natrona, Wyo.	15	C5	116
Armley, Sask., Can.	75	D5	58
Armona, Kings, Calif.	1,302	D4	94
Armonk, Westchester, N.Y.	2,000	*D8	212
Armorel, Mississippi, Ark.	150	B7	170
Armour, Douglas, S.Dak.	875	D7	158
Armstead, Beaverhead, Mont.	250	F4	110
Armstrong, B.C., Can.	1,197	E13	52
Armstrong, Emmet, Iowa	958	A3	142
Armstrong, Howard, Mo.	387	B5	150
Armstrong, Bryan, Okla.		D7	128
Armstrong, Bath, Va.		B5	192
Armstrong, co., Pa.	79,524	C2	214
Armstrong, co., Tex.	1,966	B5	130
Armstrong, creek, W.Va.		D6	194
Armstrong Creek, Forest, Wis.	250	C5	160
Armstrong Station, Ont., Can.	410	R24	64
Armuchee, Floyd, Ga.	200	B1	176
Armyansk, Sov.Un.	5,800	I9	332
Arnar, fjord, Ice.		L17	290
Arnaud, Man., Can.	500	F4	60
Arnaudville, St. Landry and St. Martin, La.	1,184	D4	180
Arnedo, Sp.	7,072	A5	298
Arnegard, McKenzie, N.Dak.	228	C2	154
Arneiroz, Braz.		B2	258
Arnes, Ice.		K19	290
Arnes, Nor.		A2	292
Arnett, Ellis, Okla.	547	B4	128
Arnett, Raleigh, W.Va.	250	D3, D6	194
Arnhem, Neth.	114,002 (*175,000)	C4	282
Arnhem, cape, Austl.		A7	432
Arnhem Land, reg., Austl.		A6	432
Árnissa, Grc.	2,915	A3	306
Arno, Wise, Va.		D2	192
Arno, riv., It.		D3	302
Arnold, Calaveras, Calif.	375	C3	94
Arnold, Ness, Kans.	120	D3	144
Arnold, Marquette, Mich.	45	C4	146
Arnold, St. Louis, Minn.	200	E6	148
Arnold, Custer, Nebr.	844	C5	152
Arnold, Westmoreland, Pa.	9,437	A4, C2	214
Arnold City, Fayette, Pa.	500	*D2	214
Arnold Mills, Providence, R.I.	250	B3	216
Arnoldsburg, Calhoun, W.Va.	200	C3	194
Arnolds Park, Dickinson, Iowa	953	A2	142
Arnöy, isl., Nor.		A9	290
Arnprior, Ont., Can.	5,137	O24	64
Arnsberg, Ger.	20,500	C3	286
Arnstadt, Ger.	27,400	C4	286
Arnstein, Ont., Can.	200	O21	64
Aroa, Ven.	4,209	A4	240
Aroab, S.W.Afr.		E3	420
Arock, Malheur, Oreg.	25	E9	96
Aroda, Madison, Va.	80	B6	192
Aroma, Sud.	3,451	B4	398
Aroma Park, Kankakee, Ill.	744	B6	138
Arondale, Osage, Okla.		B7	128
Aroostook, co., Maine	106,064	B3	204
Aroostook, plain, Maine		B4	204
Aroostook, riv., Maine		B4	204
Aroostook Junction, N.B., Can.	320	C2	70
Arosa, Switz.		B5	312
Aroya, Cheyenne, Colo.	24	D7	106
Arp, Smith, Tex.	812	C8	130
Arpin, Wood, Wis.	350	D3	160
'Arrābah, Jordan	4,000	B6	382
Arrah, India	64,205	D4	368
Arraias, Braz.	830	C1	258
Arraiján, Can.Zone	1,857	*F8	228
Arran, Sask., Can.	183	E7	58
Arran, Wakulla, Fla.	200	A6	174
Arrandale, B.C., Can.		C7	52
Arras, Fr.	36,242	B5	278
Arrecife, Mor.		C1	402
Arrecife, Sp.	8,929	F13	298
Arriaga, Mex.	8,734	D7	225
Arriaga, Mex.	2,094	K13	225
Arriba, Lincoln, Colo.	296	C7	106
Arrington, Atchison, Kans.	100	C8	144
Arrington, Nelson, Va.	250	C6	192
Arriola, Montezuma, Colo.		E2	106
Ar Riyād, see Riyadh, Sau.Ar.			
Arrow, riv., Mont.		C7	110
Arrowhead, B.C., Can.	180	E14	52
Arrowhead, lake, Calif.		E5	94
Arrow Rock, Saline, Mo.	245	B5	150
Arrowrock, res., Idaho		F3	108
Arrowsic, Sagadahoc, Maine	35 (177▲)	E3	204
Arrowwood, Alta., Can.	240	E6	54
Arroyo de la Luz, Sp.	10,515	C3	298
Arroyo del Valle, riv., Calif.		B6	94
Arroyo Grande, San Luis Obispo, Calif.	3,291	E3	94
Arroyo Hondo, Taos, N.Mex.	541	B5	126
Arroyoseco, Taos, N.Mex.	50	B5	126
Ar Rumma, wadi, Sau.Ar.		B3	383
Árta, Grc.	12,947	B3	306
Árta, prov., Grc.	72,717	*B3	306
Artas, Campbell, S.Dak.	87	B6	158
Artem, Sov.Un.	55,000	E15	329
Artemisa, Cuba	17,461	A3	232
Artemovsk, Sov.Un.	61,000	H12, R21	332
Artemovskiy, Sov.Un.	31,900	A6	336
Artemus, Knox, Ky.	950	D7	178
Artena, It.	4,027	*E4	302
Arter, mtn., Wyo.		D4	116
Artern, Ger.	7,601	C4	286
Artesia, Graham, Ariz.	10	F6	124
Artesia, Bech.		D5	420
Artesia, Los Angeles, Calif.	9,993	C5	94
Artesia, Moffat, Colo.	318	B1	106
Artesia, Lowndes, Miss.	469	B4	184
Artesia, Eddy, N.Mex.	12,000	F6	126
Artesian, Alsk.	381	*C7	84
Artesian, Sanborn, S.Dak.	330	C8	158
Arth, Switz.	5,816	A4	312
Arthabaska, Que., Can.	2,399	R13	66
Arthabaska, co., Que., Can.	41,422	R12	66
Arthal, India		B2	368
Arthur, Ont., Can.	1,124	Q20	64
Arthur, Moultrie, Ill.	2,120	D5	138
Arthur, Pike, Ind.	150	D2	140
Arthur, Ida, Iowa	265	B2	142
Arthur, Arthur, Nebr.	165	C4	152
Arthur, Cass. N.Dak.	325	C8	154
Arthur, Lexington, S.C.	649	D6	188
Arthur, Grant, Wis.	75	F3	160
Arthur, co., Nebr.	680	C4	152
Arthur, lake, La.		D3	180
Arthur Kill, riv., N.J.		B1	210
Arthur's Town, Cat Island	385	A7	232
Arthurtown, Richland, S.C.	800	*C6	188
Artie, Raleigh, W.Va.	900	D6	194
Artigas, Ur.	16,500	B4	252
Artigas, dept., Ur.	56,423	B4	252
Artland, Sask., Can.	70	D3	58
Artois, former prov., Fr.	1,010,000	B5	278
Artvin, Tur.	4,547	A9	307
Artvin, prov., Tur.	176,888	*A9	307
Aru, Con. L.		B5	414
Aru, is., Indon.		F8	359
Arua, Ug.		B5	414
Aruanã, Braz.	432	H6	257
Aruba Island, Neth.poss., Neth.W.I.		*B5	236
Arucas, Sp.	9,597	F12	298
Arundel, Que., Can.	370	S10	66
Arundel (Town of), York, Maine	(907▲)	*E2	204
Arundel Village, Anne Arundel, Md.	1,600	*B6	182
Arunta, desert, Austl.		C7	432
Arusha, Tan.	10,038	C6	414
Arusi, prov., Eth.	1,000,000	D4	398
Aruwimi, riv., Con.L.		B4	414
Arvada, Jefferson, Colo.	19,242	C5	106
Arvada, Sheridan, Wyo.	100	B6	116
Arvagh, Ire.		H5	273
Arvida, Que., Can.	12,919	P13	66
Arvidsjaur, Swe.	2,643	D8	290
Arvilla, Grand Forks, N.Dak.	100	C8	154
Arvin, Kern, Calif.	5,310	E4	94
Arvonia, Osage, Kans.	40	*D8	144
Arvonia, Buckingham, Va.	700	C6	192
Arynakh, Sov.Un.		C14	329

Arys, Sov.Un. D7 336
Arzamas, Sov.Un. 39,000 A2 336
Arzgir, Sov.Un. J15 332
Arzúa, Sp. 1,368 A2 298
Aš, Czech. 10,524 A1 324
Asaa, Den. 1,221 D1 292
Asab, S.W.Afr. E3 420
Asahi-Dake, peak, Jap. C9 354
Asahigawa, Jap. 164,971 C9 354
Asalä, Eth. D4 398
Asansol, India 76,277 E4 368
Asarum, Swe. 8,511 E5 292
Asbest, Sov.Un. 60,000 A6 336
Asbestos, Que., Can. 8,969 S13 66
Asbury, Dubuque, Iowa 71 *B7 142
Asbury, Jasper, Mo. 186 D3 150
Asbury, Gloucester, N.J. D2 210
Asbury, Knox, Tenn. 300 E9 190
Asbury Park, Monmouth, N.J. 17,366 C4 210
Ascensión, Mex. 1,591 A4 224
Ascension, par., La. 27,927 D5 180
Aschaffenburg, Ger. 53,100 D3 286
Aschersleben, Ger. 36,400 C4 286
Ascoli Piceno, It. 26,600 D4 302
Ascoli Piceno, prov., It. 332,100 *D4 302
Ascona, Switz. 2,923 B4 312
Ascotan, Chile B4 250
Ascot Corner, Que., Can. 325 S13 66
Ascutney, Windsor, Vt. 150 E4 218
Ascutney, mtn., Vt. E4 218
Aseda, Swe. 1,569 D6 292
Asele, Swe. 1,906 D7 290
Asenovgrad, Bul. 25,319 C2 317
Asensbruk, Swe. C3 292
Aserbeidshan-O, prov., Iran 2,474,146 *A2 379
Aserbeidshan-W, prov., Iran 792,371 *B1 379
Asgardstrand, Nor. B1 292
Ash, Douglas, Oreg. D3 96
Ash, cave, Ohio C4 156
Asha, Sov.Un. 32,000 A5 336
Ashanti, ter., Ghana E4 408
Ashaway, Washington, R.I. 1,298 D1 216
Ashburn, Turner, Ga. 3,291 E3 176
Ashburn, Pike, Mo. 124 B6 150
Ashburn, Loudoun, Va. 200 A7 192
Ashburnham, Worcester, Mass. 1,000 A4 206
(2,758▲)
Ashburton, Eng. 2,700 K9 273
Ashburton, N.Z. 10,176 E3 437
Ashburton, riv., Austl. C3 432
Ashby, Middlesex, Mass. 500 A4 206
(1,883▲)
Ashby, Grant, Minn. 426 E3 148
Ashby, Grant, Nebr. 175 B4 152
Ashbyburg, Hopkins, Ky. 150 C3 178
Ashcreek, Rock, Minn. 100 H2 148
Ashcroft, B.C., Can. 805 E12 52
Ashdod, Isr. C5 382
Ashdod, Plymouth, Mass. 120 *B6 206
Ashdot Ya'aqov, Isr. 1,393 B6 382
Ashdown, Little River, Ark. 2,725 D2 170
Ashe, co., N.C. 19,768 A4 186
Asheboro, Randolph, N.C. 9,449 B6 186
Asheboro South, Randolph, N.C. 1,515 *B6 186
Asheboro West, Randolph, N.C. 1,228 *B6 186
Ashepoo, Colleton, S.C. 150 F7 188
Ashepoo, riv., S.C. F7 188
Asher, Pottawatomie, Okla. 343 D7 128
Ashern, Man., Can. 300 E3 60
Asherton, Dimmit, Tex. 1,890 E6 130
Asherville, Mitchell, Kans. 105 C6 144
Asheville, Buncombe, N.C. 60,192 B3 186
(*105,000)
Ashfield, Franklin, Mass. 350 A2 206
(1,131▲)
Ash Flat, Sharp, Ark. 192 A5 170
Ashford, Houston, Ala. 1,511 D4 168
Ashford, Windham, Conn. 50 B7 202
(1,315▲)
Ashford, Eng. 26,000 J13 273
Ashford, Boone, W.Va. 300 C6 194
Ash Fork, Yavapai, Ariz. 681 C3 124
Ash Grove, Greene, Mo. 886 D4 150
Ashibetsu, Jap. 68,091 *C9 354
Ashibetsu-Dake, peak, Jap. C9 354
Ashikaga, Jap. 102,078 F7 354
K15
Ashington, Eng. 28,400 F11 272
Ashio, Jap. 18,510 F7 354
Ashizuri, cape, Jap. H4 354
Ashkhabad, Sov. Un. 170,000 F7 328
Ashkhara, Om. C6 383
Ashkum, Iroquois, Ill. 601 C6 138
Ashland, Clay, Ala. 1,610 B4 168
Ashland, New Castle, Del. A3 172
Ashland, Cass, Ill. 1,064 D3 138
Ashland, Clark, Kans. 1,312 E4 144
Ashland, Boyd, Ky. 31,283 B8 178
Ashland, Natchitoches, La. 300 B2 180
Ashland, Terrebonne, La. 200 E5 180
Ashland, Aroostook, Maine 900 B4 204
(1,980▲)
Ashland, Middlesex, Mass. 7,779 D1 206
Ashland, Benton, Miss. 309 A3 184
Ashland, Boone, Mo. 495 C5 150
Ashland, Rosebud, Mont. 120 E10 110
Ashland, Saunders, Nebr. 1,989 C9 152
E2
Ashland, Grafton, N.H. 1,237 D3 208
(1,473▲)
Ashland, Camden, N.J. 2,000 *D2 210
Ashland, Ashland, Ohio 17,419 B4 156
Ashland, Pittsburg, Okla. 87 D7 128
Ashland, Jackson, Oreg. 9,119 E4 96
Ashland, Schuylkill and Columbia, Pa. 5,237 C5 214
Ashland, Hanover, Va. 2,773 C7 192
Ashland, McDowell, W.Va. 450 *D3 194
Ashland, Ashland, Wis. 10,132 B3 160
Ashland, co., Ohio 38,771 B4 156
Ashland, co., Wis. 17,375 B3 160
Ashland, mtn., Oreg. E4 96
Ashland, res., Mass. D1 206
Ashland City, Cheatham, Tenn. 1,400 B4 190
Ashley, Honolulu, Haw. *F9 86
Ashley, Washington, Ill. 662 E4 138
Ashley, De Kalb and Steuben, Ind. 721 A4 140
Ashley, Gratiot, Mich. 448 F7 146
Ashley, Pike, Mo. 350 B6 150
Ashley, McIntosh, N.Dak. 1,419 D6 154
Ashley, Delaware, Ohio 907 B4 156
Ashley, Luzerne, Pa. 4,258 A5 214
Ashley, Doddridge, W.Va. 50 A6 194
Ashley, co., Ark. 24,220 D5 170
Ashley, creek, Utah C6 114
Ashley, riv., S.C. F8 188
Ashley Falls, Berkshire, Mass. 300 B1 206
Ashley Phosphate, Charleston, S.C. F3 188
Ashmont, Alta., Can. 100 C7 54
Ashmore, Coles, Ill. 447 D5 138
Ashmore, reef, Austl. A4 432
Ashmūn, Eg., U.A.R. 19,229 A3 395
Ashnola, riv., Wash. A6 98
Ashokan, res., N.Y. D7 212
Ashport, Lauderdale, Tenn. 150 C2 190
Ash Shabicha, Iraq D5 378
Ash Shallāl *C3 395
Ash Sham, mtn., Om. C6 383
Ash Shawbak, Jordan D6 382
Ash Shihr, Aden E4 383
Ash Shuwayrif, Libya B2 394
Ashtabula, Ashtabula, Ohio 24,559 A6 156
Ashtabula, co., Ohio 93,067 A6 156
Ashton, Ont., Can. 185 O24 64
Ashton, Fremont, Idaho 1,242 E7 108
Ashton, Lee, Ill. 1,024 B4 138
Ashton, Osceola, Iowa 615 A2 142
Ashton, Sumner, Kans. 40 *E6 144
Ashton, Montgomery, Md. 157 B5 182
Ashton, Osceola, Mich. 125 F6 146
Ashton, Sherman, Nebr. 320 C7 152
Ashton, Providence, R.I. 2,000 B3 216
Ashton, Spink, S.Dak. 182 B7 158
Ashuanipi, lake, Newf., Can. E8 72
Ashuelot, Cheshire, N.H. 300 F2 208
Ashuelot, riv., N.H. F2 208
Ashville, St. Clair, Ala. 973 B3 168
Ashville, Man., Can. 42 E2 60
Ashville, Pickaway, Ohio 1,639 C4 156
Ashwaubenon, Brown, Wis. 2,657 A6 160
D5
Ashwood, Jefferson, Oreg. 15 C6 96
Ashwood, Maury, Tenn. 100 C4 190
Asia, cont. 1,691,328,000 19
340
Asinara, gulf, It. E2 302
Asinara, isl., It. E2 302
Asino, Sov.Un. A11 336
Asir, reg., Sau.Ar. D3 383
Aska, Fannin, Ga. 135 B2 176
Askam, Luzerne, Pa. 1,500 *B5 214
Asker, Nor. 13,923 B1 292
Askersund, Swe. 4,325 C5 292
Askew, Panola, Miss. 100 A2 184
Askim, Nor. 8,764 B2 292
Askot, India C3 368
Askov, Pine, Minn. 331 E6 148
Asmār, Afg. 5,000 B6 374
Asmara, Eth. 120,000 B4 398
Asnebumskit, hill, Mass. B4 206
Åsnen, lake, Swe. E5 292
Asnières [-sur-Seine], Fr. 77,838 I10 278
Asosā, Eth. C3 398
Asoteriba, mtn., Sud. A4 398
Asotin, Asotin, Wash. 745 C9 98
Asotin, co., Wash. 12,909 C9 98
Asotin, creek, Wash. C9 98
Asp, Sioux, Nebr. 4 B2 152
Aspe, Sp. 7,810 C6 298
Aspen, Pitkin, Colo. 1,101 C4 106
Aspen, mts., Wyo. E3 116
Aspen Hill, Giles, Tenn. 200 C4 190
Aspentunnel, Uinta, Wyo. 45 E2 116
Aspermont, Stonewall, Tex. 1,286 C5 130
Aspetuck, Fairfield, Conn. 125 E2 202
Aspinwall, Crawford, Iowa 95 C2 142
Aspinwall, Allegheny, Pa. 3,727 A4 214
Aspiring, mtn., N.Z. F2 437
Aspy, bay, N.S., Can. C9 70
Asquith, Sask., Can. 288 D4 58
Assab, Eth. C5 398
Assabet, riv., Mass. D1 206
Aş Şāfiyah, Jordan 1,000 C6 382
As Salman, Iraq D6 378
As Salt, Jordan 15,478 B6 382
As Salwā, Sau.Ar. C5 383
Assam, state, India 9,043,707 C6 366
Assaria, Saline, Kans. 322 D6 144
Assateague, isl., Va. C9 192
Assawompsett, pond, Mass. C6 206
Asseh, Neth. 22,600 B5 282
Assens, Den. 5,075 I3 291
Assens, co., Den. 58,005 *I3 291
Assiniboia, Sask., Can. 2,027 F5 58
Assiniboine, mtn., B.C., Can. E15 52
Assiniboine, riv., Man., Can. F3 60
Assinie, I.C. E4 408
Assinika, riv., Man., Can. D5 60
Assinippi, Plymouth, Mass. 105 D4 206
Assinniboine, Hill, Mont. 50 *B7 110
Assis, Braz. 16,675 J6 257
Assisi, It. 5,200 D4 302
Assonet, Bristol, Mass. 630 C5 206
As Sulayyil, Sau.Ar. C4 383
As Sultan, Libya A3 394
Assumption, Christian, Ill. 1,439 D4 138
Assumption, Adams, Nebr. 40 *D7 152
Assumption, par., La. 17,991 E4 180
Astakós, Grc. 2,992 B3 306
Astārā, Iran 8,425 A2 379
Astatula, Lake, Fla. 357 *C9 174
Asten, Neth. 4,199 C4 282
Asterābād, see Gorgān, Iran
Asti, It. 36,000 C2 302
Asti, prov., It. 222,300 *C2 302
Astintagh, mts., China D5 346
Astipálaia, isl., Grc. C6 306
Aston, Delaware, Pa. 1,200 *D6 214
Aston, cape, N.W.Ter., Can. C12 48
Aston Junction, Que., Can. 403 R12 66
Astorga, Sp. 9,032 A3 298
Astoria, Fulton, Ill. 1,206 C3 138
Astoria, Clatsop, Oreg. 11,239 A3 96
Astoria, Deuel, S.Dak. 176 C9 158
Astorp, Swe. 6,446 E3 292
Astor Park, Lake, Fla. 60 B9 174
Astrakhan, Sov.Un. 294,000 C3 336
Asturias, reg., Sp. 895,804 A3 298
Asuke, Jap. 16,820 L13 354
Asunción, Par. 201,340 D4 247
Asunción Mita, Guat. 4,015 C3 228
Åsunden, lake, Swe. C6 292
Åsunden, lake, Swe. D4 292
Aswān, Eg., U.A.R. 26,343 C3 395
Aswān, dam, Eg., U.A.R. C3 395
Asyūt, Eg., U.A.R. 90,103 B3 395
Atacama, prov., Chile 80,113 C3 250
Atacama, des., Chile B3 250
Atacama, salt flat, Chile B4 250
Atagoa Grande, Braz. B3 258
Atakpamé, Togo 6,005 E5 408
Atalándi, Grc. 4,277 B4 306
Atalissa, Muscatine, Iowa 212 C6 142
Atami, Jap. 39,812 L15 354
Atantano, Guam C7 437
Atāqa, mtn., Eg., U.A.R. B3 395
Atar, Maur. 4,000 B2 408
Atascadero, San Luis Obispo, Calif. 5,983 E3 94
Atascosa, co., Tex. 18,828 E6 130
Atash, well, Libya B4 394
Atasuskiy, Sov.Un. 2,800 C8 336
Ataúro, isl., Port. Timor F7 359
Atavus, Fin. E10 290
Atbara, Sud. 36,298 B3 398
Atbara, riv., Sud. B3 398
Atbasar, Sov.Un. 22,300 B7 336
Atchafalaya, Saint Martin, La. 10 D4 180
Atchafalaya, basin, La. D4 180
Atchafalaya, bay, La. E4 180
Atchafalaya, riv., La. D4 180
Atchison, Atchison, Kans. 12,529 C8 144
Atchison, co., Kans. 20,898 C8 144
Atchison, co., Mo. 9,213 A2 150
Atchugau, mtn., Saipan B7 436
Atco, Bartow, Ga. B2 176
Atco, Camden, N.J. 2,400 D3 210
Aten, Cedar, Nebr. 35 *B8 152
Atenango, riv., Mex. L14 225
Atenango del Rio, Mex. L14 225
Ath, Bel. 10,560 D2 282
Athabasca, Alta., Can. 1,293 C6 54
Athabasca, lake, Can. F8 48
Athabasca, riv., Alta., Can. C4 54
Athalia, Lawrence, Ohio 341 D4 156
Athalmer, B.C., Can. 200 E14 52
Athapapuskow, lake, Man., Can. C2 60
Atha Road, Ont., Can. R22 64
Athelstan, Que., Can. 300 S10 66
Athelstan, Taylor, Iowa 75 D3 142
Athena, Umatilla, Oreg. 950 B8 96
Athenry, Ire. 1,287 H4 273
Athens, Limestone, Ala. 9,330 A3 168
Athens, Howard, Ark. 67 C3 170
Athens, Ont., Can. 935 P25 64
Athens, Clarke, Ga. 31,355 C3 176
Athens (Athinai), Grc. 565,084 B4 306
(*1,378,586)
Athens, Menard, Ill. 1,035 D4 138
Athens, Fulton, Ind. 100 A3 140
Athens, Fayette, Ky. 225 C6 178
Athens, Claiborne, La. 406 B2 180
Athens, Somerset, Maine 225 D3 204
(602▲)
Athens, Calhoun, Mich. 966 G6 146
Athens, Greene, N.Y. 1,754 C8 212
Athens, Athens, Ohio 16,470 C4 156
Athens, Bradford, Pa. 4,515 B5 214
Athens, McMinn, Tenn. 12,103 C7 190
Athens, Henderson, Tex. 7,086 C8 130
Athens, Windham, Vt. 35 *E3 218
(142▲)
Athens, Mercer, W.Va. 1,086 D3 194
Athens, Marathon, Wis. 770 C3 160
Athens, co., Ohio 46,998 C4 156
Atherley, Ont., Can. 265 P21 64
Atherton, San Mateo, Calif. 7,717 B5 94
Athertonville, Larue, Ky. 200 C5 178
Athi, riv., Ken. C6 414
Athinai, see Athens, Grc.
Athis-Mons, Fr. 14,120 J10 278
Athlone, Ire. 9,393 H5 273
Athok, Bur. 4,770 C2 362
Athol, Kootenai, Idaho 214 B2 108
Athol, Smith, Kans. 140 C5 144
Athol, Worcester, Mass. 11,637 A3 206
Athol, Spink, S.Dak. 100 B7 158
Athos, mtn., Grc. A5 306
Ati, Chad D8 409
Atikameg, lake, Man., Can. C2 60
Atikokan, Ont., Can. 2,500 R23 64
Atikonak, lake, Newf., Can. E9 72
Atiquizaya, Sal. 5,276 D2 228
Atka, Alsk. 85 E4 84
Atka, isl., Alsk. E4 84
Atkarsk, Sov.Un. 39,800 G15 332
Atkins, Pope, Ark. 1,391 B4 170
Atkins, Benton, Iowa 527 C6 142
Atkins, Smyth, Va. 400 D3 192
Atkinson, Henry, Ill. 944 B3 138
Atkinson (Town of), Piscataquis, Maine (280▲) *C3 204
Atkinson, Holt, Nebr. 1,324 B7 152
Atkinson, see Atkinson Depot, N.H.
Atkinson, Pender, N.C. 302 C7 186
Atkinson, co., Ga. 6,188 E4 176
Atkinson, lake, Man., Can. B5 60
Atkinson Depot (Atkinson), Rockingham, N.H. 700 F4 208
(1,017▲)
Atlacomulco, Mex. 2,525 L14 225
Atlanta, Columbia, Ark. 50 D3 170
Atlanta, Sussex, Del. 65 F3 172
Atlanta, Fulton and De Kalb, Ga. 487,455 B5 176
(*1,011,100) C2
Atlanta, Elmore, Idaho 50 F3 108
Atlanta, Logan, Ill. 1,568 C4 138
Atlanta, Hamilton, Ind. 602 B3 140
Atlanta, Cowley, Kans. 267 E7 144
Atlanta, Winn, La. 300 C3 180
Atlanta, Montmorency, Mich. 450 D7 146
Atlanta, Macon, Mo. 386 B5 150
Atlanta, Phelps, Nebr. 107 D6 152
Atlanta, Steuben, N.Y. 500 C4 212
Atlanta, Cass, Tex. 4,076 C8 130
Atlantic, Cass, Iowa 6,890 C2 142
Atlantic, Carteret, N.C. 850 C9 186
Atlantic, co., N.J. 160,880 E3 210
Atlantic, ocean 18
Atlantic Beach, Duval, Fla. 3,125 A10 174
Atlantic Beach, Nassau, N.Y. 1,500 *E8 212
Atlantic Beach, Horry, S.C. 200 D11 188
Atlantic City, Atlantic, N.J. 59,544 E4 210
(*129,800)
Atlantic City, Fremont, Wyo. 25 D4 116
Atlantic Highlands, Monmouth, N.J. 4,119 C4 210
Atlantic Mine, Houghton, Mich. 400 B3 146
Atlántico, dept., Col. 514,490 A1 244
Atlas, Northumberland, Pa. 1,574 C5 214
Atlas Saharien, mts., Alg. B4 402
Atlee, Alta., Can. 50 E7 54
Atlee, Jefferson, Okla. D6 128
Atlit, Isr. 397 B5 382
Atlixco, Mex. 15,603 D6 225
L14
Atmore, Escambia, Ala. 8,173 D2 168
Atna, mts., B.C., Can. B9 52
Atna, peak, B.C., Can. D8 52
Atocha, Bol. D1 246
Atoka, Eddy, N.Mex. 30 F6 126
Atoka, Atoka, Okla. 2,877 D7 128
Atoka, Tipton, Tenn. 357 C2 190
Atoka, co., Okla. 10,352 D7 128
Atomic City, Bingham, Idaho 141 F6 108
Atotonilco, Mex. 803 K12 225
Atotonilco El Alto, Mex. 11,037 K12 225
Atotonilco El Grande, Mex. 3,152 K14 225
Atoui, wadi, Maur. B1 408
Atoyac, riv., Mex. L14 225
Åtran, riv., Swe. D4 292
Atrato, riv., Col. B1 244
Atrek, riv., Iran B4 379
Atrisco, Bernalillo, N.Mex. 3,000 *C4 126
Atsion, Burlington, N.J. D3 210
Atsugi, Jap. 39,409 L15 354
Atsukeshi, bay, Jap. C10 354
Atsuma, Jap. C8 354
Atsumi, bay, Jap. M13 354
Attachie, B.C., Can. B12 52
At Tafilah, Jordan D6 382
At Ta'if, Sau.Ar. 25,000 C3 383
Attala, co., Miss. 21,335 B3 184
Attalla, Etowah, Ala. 8,257 A3 168
At Tallāb, Libya C4 394
At Tamimi, Libya A4 394
Attapulgus, Decatur, Ga. 567 F2 176
Attawapiskat, Ont., Can. R25 64
Attawapiskat, riv., Ont., Can. Q24 64
Attawaugan, Windham, Conn. 350 B8 202
At Tayyibah, Jordan C6 382
Attean, pond, Maine C2 204
Atter, lake, Aus. C5 313
Attica, Randolph, Ark. A6 170
Attica, Fountain, Ind. 4,341 B2 140
Attica, Harper, Kans. 845 E5 144
Attica, Lapeer, Mich. 250 F8 146
Attica, Wyoming, N.Y. 2,758 C3 212
Attica, Seneca, Ohio 965 A4 156
Attica, see Attici, prov., Grc.
Attici (Attica), prov., Grc. 1,553,815 *B4 306
Attikamagen, lake, Newf., Can. D9 72
Attilla, Larue, Ky. 25 C5 178
Attleboro, Bristol, Mass. 27,118 C5 206
Attleboro Falls, Bristol, Mass. C5 206
Attopeu, Laos D5 362
Attow, mtn., Scot. D7 272
Attu, isl., Alsk. E3 84
Atuel, riv., Arg. C2 252
Atuntzu, China F7 346
Atvidaberg, Swe. 7,156 C7 292
Atwater, Merced, Calif. 7,318 D3 94
Atwater, Sask., Can. 106 E6 58
Atwater, Kandiyohi, Minn. 899 F4 148
Atwood, Ont., Can. 525 Q19 64
Atwood, Logan, Colo. 55 B7 106
Atwood, Piatt, Ill. 1,258 D5 138
Atwood, Kosciusko, Ind. 250 A4 140
Atwood, Rawlins, Kans. 1,906 C2 144
Atwood, Hughes, Okla. 200 D7 128
Atwood, Carroll, Tenn. 461 C3 190
Atzcapotzalco, Mex. 49,617 L14 225
G10
Atzmon, mtn., Isr. A6 382
Auasc, Eth. D5 398
Auau, chan., Haw. C5 86
Auaz, mts., S.W.Afr. D3 420
Aubagne, Fr. 9,196 F6 278
Aube, dept., Fr. 240,797 *C6 278
Aubenas, Fr. 5,774 E6 278
Auberry, Fresno, Calif. 400 D4 94
Aubervilliers, Fr. 58,740 I10 278
Aubière, Fr. E5 278
Aubigny-sur-Nère, Fr. D5 278
Aubin, Fr. 8,275 E5 278
Aubrey, Lee, Ark. 400 C6 170
Aubrey, Que., Can. 230 S11 66
Auburn, Lee, Ala. 16,261 C4 168
Auburn, Placer, Calif. 5,586 C3 94
Auburn, Ont., Can. 125 Q19 64
Auburn, Barrow, Ga. 374 B3 176
Auburn, Sangamon, Ill. 2,209 D4 138
Auburn, De Kalb, Ind. 6,350 A4 140
Auburn, Sac, Iowa 367 B3 142
Auburn, Shawnee, Kans. 110 D8 144
Auburn, Logan, Ky. 1,013 D4 178
Auburn, Androscoggin, Maine 24,449 D2 204
D5
Auburn, Worcester, Mass. 14,047 B4 206
Auburn, Bay, Mich. 1,497 F7 146
Auburn, Lincoln, Miss. 250 D2 184
Auburn, Nemaha, Nebr. 3,229 D10 152
Auburn, Rockingham, N.H. 150 E4 208
(1,292▲)
Auburn, Salem, N.J. 200 D2 210
Auburn, Cayuga, N.Y. 35,249 C5 212
Auburn, Walsh, N.Dak. 60 B8 154
Auburn, Schuylkill, Pa. 936 C5 214
Auburn, King, Wash. 11,933 B4 98
D3
Auburn, Ritchie, W.Va. 139 B4 194
Auburn, Lincoln, Wyo. 100 D2 116
Auburndale, Polk, Fla. 5,595 C9 174

Auburndale

Auburndale, Wood, Wis. 396 D3 160
Auburn Heights, Oakland, Mich. 2,500 G8 146
Auburntown, Cannon, Tenn. 256 C5 190
Aubusson, Fr. 5,595 E5 278
Auch, Fr. 14,315 F4 278
Aucilla, Jefferson, Fla. 300 A7 174
Aucilla, riv., Fla. A7 174
Auckland, N.Z. 136,540 (*381,100) B5 437 H9
Aude, dept., Fr. 268,254 *F5 278
Aude, riv., Fr. F5 278
Audègle, Som. 2,000 (7,800*) E5 398
Audet, Que., Can. 350 S14 66
Audierne, Fr. C1 278
Audincourt, Fr. 10,282 D7 278
Audley, Yavapai, Ariz. 10 C3 124
Audrain, co., Mo. 26,079 B6 150
Audsholt, Ice. M19 290
Audubon, Audubon, Iowa 2,928 C3 142
Audubon, Becker, Minn. 245 E3 148
Audubon, Camden, N.J. 10,440 D2 210
Audubon, co., Iowa 10,919 C3 142
Audubon Park, Jefferson, Ky. 1,867 A5 178
Audubon Park, Camden, N.J. 1,713 *D3 210
Aue, Ger. 32,800 C5 286
Au Fer, pt., La. E4 180
Auglaize, co., Ohio 36,147 B2 156
Auglaize, riv., Ohio A2 156
Au Gres, Arenac, Mich. 584 E8 146
Augsburg, Ger. 202,700 D4 286
Augusta, Woodruff, Ark. 2,272 B5 170
Augusta, Austl. 217 E3 432
Augusta, Richmond, Ga. 70,626 (*160,600) C5 176
Augusta, Hancock, Ill. 915 C3 138
Augusta, Marion, Ind. 150 D4 140
Augusta, It. 24,700 G5 302
Augusta, Butler, Kans. 6,434 B7 144 E7
Augusta, Bracken, Ky. 1,458 B6 178
Augusta, Kennebec, Maine 21,680 D3 204
Augusta, Kalamazoo, Mich. 972 G6 146
Augusta, St. Charles, Mo. 206 C7 150
Augusta, Lewis and Clark, Mont. 400 C4 110
Augusta, Sussex, N.J. 70 A3 210
Augusta, Carroll, Ohio 360 B5 156
Augusta, Hampshire, W.Va. 250 B6 194
Augusta, Eau Claire, Wis. 1,338 D2 160
Augusta, co., Va. 37,363 B5 192
Augusta Springs, Augusta, Va. 300 B5 192
Augustow, Pol. 12,700 B6 325
Auke Bay, Alsk. 295 D8 84 I14
Aulander, Bertie, N.C. 1,083 A8 186
Aulnay-sous-Bois, Fr. 38,534 I11 278
Aulne, riv., Fr. C1 278
Ault, Weld, Colo. 799 B6 106
Aultsville, Ont., Can. 400 P25 64
Aumale, Alg. 4,460 (9,229*) A4 402
Aumsville, Marion, Oreg. 300 C1 96
Aunis, former prov., Fr. 167,000 *D3 278
Auno, Nig. D7 409
Aunuu, isl., Samoa E5 436
Aur, isl., Mala. G5 362
Aura, Fin. F10 291
Aura, Baraga, Mich. 40 C3 146
Aura, Gloucester, N.J. D2 210
Auraiya, India D2 368
Aurangabad, India 66,636 E3 366
Auray, Fr. 8,159 D2 278
Aurelia, Cherokee, Iowa 904 B2 142
Aurich, Ger. 9,600 B2 286
Aurillac, Fr. 22,224 E5 278
Aurland, Nor. F2 291
Aurora, Br. Gu. 290 D5 256
Aurora, Ont., Can. 3,957 P21 64
Aurora, Arapahoe and Adams, Colo. 48,548 C6 106
Aurora, Kane, Ill. 63,715 B5 138 F1
Aurora, Dearborn, Ind. 4,119 C5 140
Aurora, Buchanan, Iowa 223 B6 142
Aurora, Cloud, Kans. 150 C6 144
Aurora, Marshall, Ky. 40 D2 178
Aurora, Hancock, Maine 70 (75*) D4 204
Aurora, St. Louis, Minn. 2,799 D6 148
Aurora, Lawrence, Mo. 4,683 E4 150
Aurora, Hamilton, Nebr. 2,576 D7 152
Aurora, Cayuga, N.Y. 834 C5 212
Aurora, Beaufort, N.C. 449 B9 186
Aurora, Portage, Ohio 4,049 A5 156
Aurora, Marion, Oreg. 274 B1 96 B4
Aurora, Brookings, S.Dak. 232 C9 158
Aurora, Sevier, Utah 465 E4 114
Aurora, Preston, W.Va. 350 B5 194
Aurora, co., S.Dak. 4,749 D7 158
Aurora Lodge, Alsk. 50 *C7 84
Aurora Springs, Miller, Mo. 150 C5 150
Aus, S.W.Afr. 529 E3 420
Au Sable, pt., Mich. C5 146
Au Sable, pt., Mich. E8 146
Au Sable, riv., Mich. E7 146
Ausable, riv., N.Y. A8 212
Au Sable Forks, Essex, N.Y. 2,026 A8 212
Ausmac, Decatur, Ga. 100 F2 176
Ausser Rhoden (Rhodes Exterieures), sub canton, Switz. 48,800 *A5 312
Aust-Agder, co., Nor. 76,332 *G2 291
Austell, Cobb, Ga. 1,867 B4 176
Austin, Lonoke, Ark. 210 C5 170
Austin, Man., Can. 264 F3 60
Austin, Delta, Colo. (part of Eckert) D3 106
Austin, Scott, Ind. 3,838 D4 140
Austin, Mower, Minn. 27,908 H6 148
Austin, Lewis and Clark, Mont. 20 D4 110
Austin, Lander, Nev. 400 D4 112
Austin, Grant, Oreg. 35 C8 96
Austin, Potter, Pa. 721 B3 214
Austin, Travis, Tex. 186,545 (*210,000) D7 130
Austin, Sevier, Utah 100 E3 114
Austin, co., Tex. 13,777 E7 130
Austin, lake, Austl. D3 432
Austinburg, Ashtabula, Ohio 350 A6 156
Austin Lake, Kalamazoo, Mich. 3,520 *G6 146
Austintown, Mahoning, Ohio 5,000 A6 156
Austinville, Morgan, Ala. A3 168
Austinville, Wythe, Va. 750 D4 192
Australia, country 10,050,000 19 432
Australian Capital Territory, ter., Austl. 37,865 F9 432
Austria, country, Eur. 7,021,000 D6 266 313
Autauga, co., Ala. 18,739 C3 168
Autaugaville, Autauga, Ala. 440 C3 168
Autlán de Navarro, Mex. 11,355 D5 224
Au Train, Alger, Mich. 100 C5 146
Autun, Fr. 14,399 D6 278
Auvergne, Jackson, Ark. 100 B5 170
Auvergne, former prov., Fr. 838,000 E5 278
Auvergne, mts., Fr. E5 278
Aux Barques, pt., Mich. E9 146
Aux Chene, riv., La. C8 180
Auxerre, Fr. 26,583 D5 278
Aux Herbes, isl., Ala. E1 168
Auxier, Floyd, Ky. 649 C8 178
Auxonne, Fr. 5,657 D6 278
Aux Pins, pt., Ont., Can. R19 64
Auxvasse, Callaway, Mo. 534 B6 150
Ava, Jackson, Ill. 665 F4 138
Ava, Douglas, Mo. 1,581 E5 150
Avakubi, Con. L. B4 414
Avallon, Fr. 5,497 D5 278
Avalon, Los Angeles, Calif. 1,536 F4 94
Avalon, Stephens, Ga. 194 *B3 176
Avalon, Carroll, Miss. 200 B2 184
Avalon, Cape May, N.J. 695 E3 210
Avalon, Allegheny, Pa. 6,859 A3 214
Avalon, Rock, Wis. 110 F5 160
Avalon, pen., Newf., Can. G9 72
Avamonte, Sp. 8,908 D3 298
Avanos, Tur. 5,240 B6 307
Avans, Dade, Ga. 990 B1 176
Avant, Osage, Okla. 381 B7 128
Avanzada, Chile B4 250
Avard, Woods, Okla. 56 B5 128
Avaré, Braz. 12,061 E1 258
Aveiro, Port. 13,423 B2 298
Avella, Washington, Pa. 1,310 C1 214
Avellaneda, Arg. B4 252
Avellino, It. 27,100 E5 302
Avellino, prov., It. 501,200 *E5 302
Avenal, Kings, Calif. 3,147 E3 94
Avenel, Middlesex, N.J. 9,000 B1 210
Avening, Ont., Can. 75 P20 64
Avent, Greene, Miss. 150 E4 184
Avera, Jefferson, Ga. 197 C4 176
Avera, Greene, Miss. 150 D4 184
Averett, Mecklenburg, Va. 25 D6 192
Averill Park, Rensselaer, N.Y. 900 C8 212
Averöy, isl., Nor. E2 290
Aversa, It. 35,800 E5 302
Avery, Shoshone, Idaho 450 B3 108
Avery, Monroe, Iowa 200 C5 142
Avery, Lincoln, Okla. 30 C7 128
Avery, co., N.C. 12,009 A4 186
Avery Island, Iberia, La. 650 E4 180
Aves, is., Ven. A5 240
Avesta, Swe. 9,609 A7 292
Aveyron, dept., Fr. 292,727 *E5 278
Avezzano, It. 22,100 D4 302
Aviá Teral, Arg. A3 252
Aviemore, Scot. D9 272
Avigliano, It. 4,554 E5 302
Avignon, Fr. 62,768 F6 278
Ávila, Sp. 21,262 B4 298
Ávila, prov., Sp. 259,534 *B4 298
Avila Beach, San Luis Obispo, Calif. 300 E3 94
Avilés, Sp. 13,060 A4 298
Avilla, Noble, Ind. 919 A4 140
Avinger, Cass, Tex. 730 C8 130
Aviron Bay, Newf., Can. G7 72
Avis, Clinton, Pa. 1,262 B4 214
Avisadero, pt., Calif. B5 94
Aviston, Clinton, Ill. 717 *E4 138
Avoca, Lawrence, Ala. 400 A2 168
Avoca, Benton, Ark. 90 A2 170
Avoca, Lawrence, Ind. 400 D3 140
Avoca, Pottawattamie, Iowa 1,540 C2 142
Avoca, St. Clair, Mich. 300 F9 146
Avoca, Murray, Minn. 226 H3 148
Avoca, Cass, Nebr. 218 E3 152
Avoca, Steuben, N.Y. 1,086 C4 212
Avoca, Luzerne, Pa. 3,562 A5 214
Avoca, Iowa, Wis. 363 E3 160
Avola, B.C., Can. 110 E13 52
Avola, It. 25,100 G5 302
Avon, Houston, Ala. 132 *D4 168
Avon, Ont., Can. 140 R20 64
Avon, Eagle, Colo. 5 C4 106
Avon, Hartford, Conn. 5,273 B4 202
Avon, Latah, Idaho C2 108
Avon, Fulton, Ill. 996 C3 138
Avon (Town of), Franklin, Maine (436*) D2 204
Avon, Norfolk, Mass. 4,301 B5 206 E3
Avon, Stearns, Minn. 443 F4 148
Avon, Washington, Miss. 110 B1 184
Avon, Powell, Mont. 175 D4 110
Avon, Livingston, N.Y. 2,772 C4 212
Avon, Dare, N.C. 300 B10 186
Avon, Lorain, Ohio 754 A4 156
Avon, Lebanon, Pa. 1,212 *C5 214
Avon, Bon Homme, S.Dak. 637 E7 158
Avon, riv., Eng. I10 273
Avon, riv., Scot. D9 272
Avon by the Sea, Monmouth, N.J. 1,707 C4 210
Avondale, Maricopa, Ariz. 6,151 H1 124
Avondale, Pueblo, Colo. 300 D6 106
Avondale, Tensas, La. 100 C4 180
Avondale, Prince Georges, Md. 2,000 *C6 182
Avondale, Clay, Mo. 663 E2 150
Avondale, Rutherford, N.C. 800 *B4 186
Avondale, Chester, Pa. 1,016 D6 214
Avondale, McDowell, W.Va. 450 *D3 194
Avondale Estates, De Kalb, Ga. 1,646 B5 176
Avon Lake, Lorain, Ohio 9,403 A4 156
Avonlea, Sask., Can. 342 E5 58
Avonmore, Westmoreland, Pa. 1,351 C2 214
Avon Park, Highlands, Fla. 6,073 D9 174
Avoyelles, par., La. 37,606 C3 180
Avranches, Fr. 8,004 C3 278
Avrika, Swe. B3 292
Awa, isl., Jap. E7 354
Awaji, isl., Jap. G5 354
'Awarta, Jordan 2,000 B6 382
Awarua, bay, N.Z. F2 437
Awāsh, riv., Eth. C5 398
Awbāri, Libya B2 394
Aweil, Sud. 2,438 D2 398
Awendaw, Charleston, S.C. 50 E9 188
Awin, Wilcox, Ala. D3 168
Awjilah, Libya B4 394
Axar, fjord, Ice. K21 290
Axel, Neth. 5,100 C2 282
Axel Heiberg, isl., N.W.Ter., Can. B9 48
Axial, Moffat, Colo. 5 B3 106
Axim, Ghana 4,647 F4 408
Axiós, riv., Grc. A4 306
Axis, Mobile, Ala. 125 E1 168
Axmar, Swe. A8 292
Axson, Atkinson, Ga. 320 E4 176
Axtell, Marshall, Kans. 493 C7 144
Axtell, Kearney, Nebr. 477 D6 152
Axtell, Sanpete, Utah 10 D4 114
Ay, Fr. 6,806 C5 278
Ay, riv., Sov.Un. A5 336
Ayabe, Jap. 52,310 L11 354
Ayacucho, Arg. 9,220 C4 252
Ayacucho, Peru 25,400 C3 245
Ayacucho, dept., Peru 546,556 C3 245
Ayaguz, Sov.Un. 52,400 C10 336
Ayan, Sov.Un. 9,300 D15 329
Ayapel, Col. 2,436 B1 244
Ayapel, mts., Col. B2 244
Ayaş, Tur. 3,303 A5 307
Ayaviri, Peru 6,586 C3 245
Aycock, Claiborne, La. B3 180
Aydar, riv., Sov.Un. H12 332 R23
Ayden, Pitt, N.C. 3,108 B8 186
Aydin, Tur. 27,706 C2 307
Aydin, prov., Tur. 415,352 *C3 307
Ayer, Middlesex, Mass. 14,927 A4 206 C1
Ayers Cliff, Que., Can. 718 S12 66
Ayersville, Que., Can. 2,348 *S10 66
Ayiá, Grc. 2,826 B4 306
Ayia Paraskevi, Grc. 4,357 B6 306
Ayiassos, Grc. 5,692 B6 306
Áyion Óros (Mount Athos), prov., Grc. 3,086 *A5 306
Ayios Nikólaos, Grc. 3,321 D5 306
Aylen, lake, Ont., Can. O23 64
Aylesbury, Sask., Can. 180 E5 58
Aylesbury, Eng. 21,800 J12 273
Aylesford, N.S., Can. 525 D5 70
Aylett, King William, Va. 60 C7 192
Aylmer, lake, N.W.Ter., Can. E8 48
Aylmer, mtn., Alta., Can. E5 54
Aylmer East, Que., Can. 5,294 S9 66
Aylmer West, Ont., Can. 4,201 R20 64
Aylsham, Sask., Can. 320 D6 58
Aynor, Horry, S.C. 635 D10 188
Ayon, isl., Sov.Un. B18 329
Ayora, Sp. 6,067 C6 298
Ayr, Adams, Nebr. 116 D7 152
Ayr, Cass, N.Dak. 81 C8 154
Ayr, Scot. 43,400 F8 272
Ayr, co., Scot. 331,700 F8 272
Ayre, pt., Isle of Man G8 273
Ayrshire, Pike, Ind. 100 D2 140
Ayrshire, Palo Alto, Iowa 298 A3 142
Aysén, prov., Chile 26,262 G3 251
Ayton, Ont., Can. 310 P20 64
Aytos, Bul. 14,003 B3 317
Ayutla, Guat. 1,653 C1 228
Ayutla, Mex. 2,688 D6 225
Ayutthaya, Thai. 25,000 D4 362
Ayutthaya, prov., Thai. 363,060 *D4 362
Ayvacik, Tur. 1,441 B2 307
Ayvalik, Tur. 16,755 B2 307
Ayyā, Jordan B6 382
Ayzew, Alg. 4,276 A3 402
Azalea, Douglas, Oreg. 30 E3 96
Azalia, Bartholomew, Ind. 100 C4 140
Azamgarh, India D3 368
Azángaro, Peru 2,619 C3 245
Azaouad, sand dunes, Mali C4 408
Azaouak Assakari, wadi, Niger C5 408
Azare, Nig. 10,000 D7 409
Azerbaidzhan, rep., Sov.Un. 3,700,000 E6 328
Azerbaijan, reg., Iran B1 379
Azilek, well, Niger C6 408
Aziscoos, lake, Maine C1 204
Azle, Parker and Tarrant, Tex. 2,969 B8 130
Azogues, Ec. 6,588 A2 245
Azores Islands, Port. poss., Atl.O. 338,000 C4 388
Azov, Sov.Un. 42,300 I12 332
Azov, sea, Sov.Un. I11 332
Azrou, Mor. B2 402
Aztec, Yuma, Ariz. 65 F2 124
Aztec, San Juan, N.Mex. 4,137 B3 126
Aztec Ruins, nat. mon., N.Mex. B2 126
Azua, Dom.Rep. 7,419 C9 233
Azuaga, Sp. 16,453 C4 298
Azuero, pen., Pan. G7 228
Azul, Arg. 28,609 C4 252
Azul, range, Peru B2 245
Azurduy, Bol. 1,234 C2 246
Azusa, Los Angeles, Calif. 20,497 C6 94
Az Zahiriyah, Jordan C5 382
Az Zahrān, Sau.Ar. 75,000 B4 383
Az Zawiyah, Libya 8,428 A2 394
Azzāz, cape, Eg., U.A.R. A2 395
Azzaz, cape, Libya A5 394
Azzel Matti, lake, Alg. C4 402
Az Zubair, Iraq 23,582 D7 378

B

Baarle-Hertog, Bel. 1,947 C3 282
Baba, cape, Tur. B2 307
Babadag, Rom. 5,549 B5 321
Babahoyo, Ec. 9,181 A2 245
Babai, riv., Nep. C3 368
Babana, Nig. D5 408
Babanusa, Sud. C2 398
Babar, isl., Indon. F7 359
Babati, Tan. C6 414
Babayevo, Sov.Un. 4,000 C11 332
Babb, Glacier, Mont. 50 *B3 110
Babb, creek, Pa. B4 214
Babbie, Covington, Ala. 60 *D3 168
Babbitt, St. Louis, Minn. 2,587 D7 148
Babbitt, Mineral, Nev. 2,159 E3 112
Babcock, Wood, Wis. 125 D3 160
Babelthaup, isl., Palau A6 436
Babine, lake, B.C., Can. C9 52
Babine, riv., B.C., Can. C9 52
Babo, Neth.N.Gui. E8 359
Bābol, Iran 36,194 B3 379
Baboquivari, mts., Ariz. G4 124
Baboua, Cen.Afr.Rep. E7 409
Babson Park, Polk, Fla. 950 D9 174
Babushkin, Sov.Un. 112,000 N18 332
Babyak, Bul. 6,211 C1 317
Babylon, Suffolk, N.Y. 11,062 E3 212
Baca, co., Colo. 6,310 E8 106
Bacabal, Braz. 4,857 A2 258
Bacalar, Mex. 744 D8 225
Bacarra, Phil. 6,566 A6 358
Bacău, Rom. 54,138 A4 321
Bacaville, Valencia, N.Mex. 30 D4 126
Baccalieu, isl., Newf., Can. F9 72
Baccarat, Fr. 6,024 C7 278
Baccaro, pt., N.S., Can. F4 70
Bacerac, Mex. 1,016 A4 224
Bach, Huron, Mich. 100 F8 146
Bache, Pittsburg, Okla. 100 D8 128
Bachelors Hall, Pittsylvania, Va. 50 D5 192
Bachurka, Sov.Un. C7 328
Back, riv., N.W.Ter., Can. D8 48
Bac Kan, Viet. 10,000 B5 362
Bačka Planka, Yugo. 12,830 B4 316
Bačka Topola, Yugo. 13,924 B4 316
Backbay, Princess Anne, Va. 500 D8 192
Backbone, mtn., Md. B1 182
Back Creek, Frederick, Va. A6 192
Backus, Cass, Minn. 317 E4 148
Bac Lieu, Viet. 58,920 E5 362
Bacliff, Galveston, Tex. 1,707 E8 130 F8
Bac Ninh, Viet. 10,000 B5 362
Bacobi, Navajo, Ariz. 100 C5 124
Bacolod, Phil. 42,820 B6 358
Bacon, Sussex, Del. 26 F3 172
Bacon, co., Ga. 8,359 E4 176
Bacone, Muskogee, Okla. 250 C8 128
Bacons Castle, Surry, Va. A8 192 C8
Baconton, Mitchell, Ga. 564 E2 176
Bacova, Bath, Va. 175 B5 192
Bac Quang, Viet. B5 362
Bácsalmás, Hung. 8,014 C4 320
Bács-Kiskun, co., Hung. 580,000 *C4 320
Bácum, Mex. 1,509 B3 224
Bad, riv., S.Dak. C5 158
Bad, riv., Wis. B3 160
Badajoz, Sp. 82,800 (99,554*) C2 298
Badajoz, prov., Sp. 817,703 *C3 298
Badakhshan, prov., Afg. *A6 374
Badalona, Sp. 40,983 B8 298
Bad Axe, Huron, Mich. 2,998 F8 146
Baddeck, N.S., Can. 635 C9 70
Bad Doberan, Ger. 12,200 A4 286
Baden, Aus. 21,312 B8 313
Baden, Ont., Can. 920 Q20 64
Baden, Prince Georges, Md. 12 C6 182
Baden, Beaver, Pa. 6,109 C1 214
Baden, Switz. 12,000 (*27,900) A4 312
Baden, reg., Ger. D3 286
Baden-Baden, Ger. 40,800 D3 286
Baden-Powell, mtn., Calif. E5 94
Baden-Württemberg, state, Ger. 7,156,700 *D3 286
Bad Freienwalde [an der Oder], Ger. 12,600 B6 286
Badgastein, Aus. 5,048 C5 313
Badger, Man., Can. F5 60
Badger, Newf., Can. 988 F7 72
Badger, Webster, Iowa 340 B3 142
Badger, Roseau, Minn. 338 C2 148
Badger, Kingsbury, S.Dak. 117 C8 158
Badger, Sauk, Wis. 700 E4 160
Badger, creek, Colo. C7 106
Badger, mts., Wash. B6 98
Badger Basin, Park, Wyo. B3 116
Bad Godesberg, Ger. 58,800 *C2 286
Bad Hersfeld, see Hersfeld, Ger.
Bad Homburg [vor der Höhe], Ger. 33,900 C3 286
Badi, Iraq B4 378
Badin, Stanly, N.C. 1,905 B5 186
Badin, Pak. G6 375
Badin, lake, N.C. B5 186
Badirahuato, Mex. B4 224
Bad Ischl, Aus. 13,422 C5 313
Bad Kissingen, Ger. 13,300 C4 286
Bad Kreuznach, Ger. 35,400 D2 286
Badlands, reg., N.Dak. D2 154
Badlands, reg., S.Dak. D3 158
Badlands, natl. mon., S.Dak. D3 158
Bad Mergentheim, Ger. 10,870 D3 286
Bad Oldesloe, Ger. 15,000 B4 286
Badon, Viet. C5 362
Badoumbé, Mali D2 408
Badra, Iraq 3,638 C6 378
Bad Reichenhall, Ger. 13,700 E5 286
Bad Salzungen, Ger. 10,000 C4 286
Bad Segeberg, Ger. 11,635 B4 286
Bad Tölz, Ger. 12,800 E4 286
Baduein, Eth. D5 398
Badulla, Cey. 17,043 G4 366
Baduria, India I9 366
Badwater, Natrona, Wyo. C5 116
Badwater, riv., Wyo. C5 116
Baena, Sp. 17,761 D4 298
Baependi, Braz. 2,864 E2 258
Baeza, Ec. A2 245
Baeza, Sp. 15,176 D5 298
Bafang, Cam. 3,022 E7 409
Bafata, Port.Gui. D2 408
Baffin, bay, Can. C12 48
Baffin, isl., N.W.Ter., Can. D11 48
Baffins, bay, Tex. F7 130

Bafia, Cam. 4,537 F7 409
Bafoulabé, Mali 1,000 D2 408
Bafq, Iran 6,000 C4 379
Bafra, Tur. 17,588 A6 307
Bafra, cape, Tur. A6 307
Bāft, Iran 8,693 D4 379
Bafwasende, Con.L. B4 414
Baga, S.L. E2 408
Bagaces, C.R. 706 E5 228
Bagamoyo, Tan. 3,861 D6 414
Bagana, Nig. E6 409
Bagan Siapiapi, Indon. 15,321 D2 358
Bagata, Con.L. C2 414
Bagdad, Yavapai, Ariz. 1,462 D2 124
Bagdad, Santa Rosa, Fla. 763 A3 174
Bagdad, Shelby, Ky. 500 B5 178
Bagé, Braz. 34,525 L6 257
Bagemder, prov., Eth. 1,800,000 C4 398
Bagenkop, Den. 654 G1 292
Bagerhat, Pak. 7,431 L16 375
Baggs, Carbon, Wyo. 199 E5 116
Baghdad, Iraq 730,549 C6 378
Bagheria, It. 32,500 F4 302
Baghlān, Afg. 24,410 A5 374
Bagley, Guthrie, Iowa 406 C3 142
Bagley, Clearwater, Minn. 1,385 D3 148
Bagley, Grant, Wis. 275 F2 160
Bagleys Mills, Lunenburg, Va. 10 D6 192
Bagnara [Calabra], It. 10,000 F5 302
Bagnell, dam, Mo. C5 150
Bagnères-de-Bigorre, Fr. 9,795 F4 278
Bagnères-de-Luchon, Fr. F4 278
Bagnolet, Fr. 26,779 I10 278
Bagnols [-sur-Cèze], Fr. E6 278
Bagoé, riv., Mali D3 408
Bagot, Man., Can. 75 F3 60
Bagot, co., Que., Can. 20,213 S12 66
Bagotville, Que., Can. 4,822 P14 66
Bagrash, lake, China C5 346
Baguezane, mtn., Niger C6 409
Baguio, Phil. 29,262 A6 358
Baguirmi, reg., Chad D8 409
Bagūr, Eg., U.A.R. 4,756 D2 382
Bahado, Som. D6 398
Bahama Islands, Br. poss., N.A. 131,000 A6 232
Bahariya, oasis, Eg., U.A.R. B2 395
Bahawalnagar, Pak. 18,373 E8 375
Bahawalpur, Pak. 40,698 (41,646▲) E7 375
Bāherdār-Giyorgis, Eth. C4 398
Bahia, see Salvador, Braz.
Bahia, state, Braz. 5,496,000 H8 257
Bahia, is., Hond. B4 228
Bahia Blanca, Arg. 112,597 C3 252
Bahia de Caráquez, Ec. 9,316 A1 245
Bahia Kino, Mex. B3 224
Bahia Negra, Par. B3 247
Bahias, cape, Arg. G4 251
Bahraich, India D3 368
Bahrain, country, Asia 139,000 B5 383
G7 340
Bahrain, is., Asia B5 383
Bahrāmābād, Iran 14,867 C4 379
Bahr Aoūk, riv., Cen. Afr. Rep. E8 409
Bahr Basandila, canal, Eg., U.A.R. C2 382
Bahr el Abyad (White Nile), riv., Sud. C3 398
Bahr el Azraq (Blue Nile), riv., Sud. C3 398
Bahr el Ghazal, prov., Sud. 991,002 D2 398
Bahr el Ghazal, riv., Chad D8 409
Bahr el Jebel (White Nile), riv., Sud. D3 398
Bahr Faqus, drain, Eg., U.A.R. D2 382
Bahr Saft, drain, Eg., U.A.R. D2 382
Bahr Salamat, riv., Chad D8 409
Bahr Sara, riv., Chad E8 409
Bāhū Kalāt, Iran E5 379
Baia dos Tigres, Ang. C2 420
Baia-Mare, Rom. 35,920 A2 321
Baião, Braz. 1,580 A1 258
Baia-Sprie, Rom. 8,134 A2 321
Baïbokoum, Chad E8 409
Baidarik, riv., Mong. B7 346
Baie Comeau, Que., Can. 4,332 *Q10 66
Baie de Wasai, Chippewa, Mich. 30 C7 146
Baie-St.-Paul, Que., Can. 4,052 Q14 66
Baie Verte, Newf., Can. 250 F7 72
Baile Átha Cliath, see Dublin, Ire.
Bailén, Sp. 10,045 C5 298
Băilești, Rom. 15,932 B2 321
Bailey, Park, Colo. 100 C5 106
Bailey, Nash, N.C. 795 B7 186
Bailey, co., Tex. 9,090 B4 130
Bailey, brook, Maine B2 204
Bailey, isl., S.C. G2 188
Bailey Island, Cumberland, Maine 250 E6 204
Baileys Harbor, Door, Wis. 300 C6 160
Baileyton, Cullman, Ala. 200 A3 168
Baileyton, Greene, Tenn. 206 B9 190
Baileyville, Nemaha, Kans. 200 C7 144
Baileyville (Town of), Washington, Maine (1,863▲) *C5 204
Bainbridge, Decatur, Ga. 12,714 F2 176
Bainbridge, Putnam, Ind. 603 C3 140
Bainbridge, Chenango, N.Y. 1,712 C6 212
Bainbridge, Ross, Ohio 1,001 C3 156
Bains, West Feliciana, La. 85 D4 180
Baintree, mtn., Vt. D3 218
Bainville, Roosevelt, Mont. 285 B12 110
Baird, Sunflower, Miss. 175 B2 184
Baird, Callahan, Tex. 1,633 C6 130
Baird, Douglas, Wash. B7 98
Baird, inlet, Alsk. C5 84
Baird, mts., Alsk. B5 84
Bairdford, Allegheny, Pa. 950 A4 214
Bairdstown, Oglethorpe, Ga. 200 C3 176
Bairnsdale, Austl. 5,718 F9 432
Bairoil, Sweetwater, Wyo. 300 D5 116
Baise, riv., Fr. F4 278
Bait, mts., B.C., Can. C9 52
Baixo Altentejo, prov., Port. 380,236 *C3 298
Baixo Longa, Ang. C3 420
Baja, Hung. 31,000 C3 320
Baja California, state, Mex. 226,965 A2 224
Baja California Sur., ter., Mex. 60,864 B3 224
Bajmok, Yugo. B4 316
Bakala, Cen. Afr. Rep. E9 409
Bakar, Yugo. 1,759 B2 316
Bakel, Sen. 2,400 D2 408
Baker, San Bernardino, Calif. 200 E5 94
Baker, Okaloosa, Fla. 1,000 A4 174
Baker, Lemhi, Idaho 200 D5 108
Baker, Brown, Kans. 16 *C8 144
Baker, East Baton Rouge, La. 4,823 D4 180
Baker, Fallon, Mont. 2,365 D12 110
Baker, White Pine, Nev. 120 D7 112
Baker, Texas, Okla. 70 B2 128
Baker, Baker, Oreg. 9,986 C9 96
Baker, co., Fla. 7,363 A8 174
Baker, co., Ga. 4,543 E2 176
Baker, co., Oreg. 17,295 C9 96
Baker, brook, Maine B3 204
Baker, butte, Ariz. D4 124
Baker, isl., Pac. O. C4 436
Baker, lake, N.W.Ter., Can. E9 48
Baker, lake, Maine B3 204
Baker, mtn., Maine C3 204
Baker, mtn., Wash. A5 98
Baker, riv., Wash. A5 98
Bakerhill, Barbour, Ala. 100 D4 168
Baker Lake, N.W.Ter., Can. E9 48
Bakers, Franklin, La. B4 180
Bakers, Davidson, Tenn. E7 190
Bakers, bayou, Ark. D7 170
Bakers, isl., Mass. C4 206
Bakers, riv., N.H. D3 208
Bakersfield, Kern, Calif. 56,848 (*158,000) E4 94
Bakersfield, Ozark, Mo. 177 E5 150
Bakersfield, Franklin, Vt. 225 (664▲) B3 218
Bakers Mill, Hamilton, Fla. 50 A8 174
Bakersville, Litchfield, Conn. 150 B3 202
Bakersville, Mitchell, N.C. 393 A3 186
Bakerton, Jefferson, W.Va. 225 B7 194
Bakertown, Davidson, Tenn. 200 E7 190
Bakerville, Cochise, Ariz. 500 G6 124
Bakhta, Sov.Un. C10 328
Bakirköy, Tur. G12 307
Bakka, Nor. F1 291
Bakkagerdhi, Ice. L23 290
Bako, Eth. D4 398
Bako, I.C. E3 408
Bakony Forest, mts., Hung. C2 320
Bakouma, Cen.Afr.Rep. E9 409
Bakoy, riv., Mali D3 408
Baku, Con.L. B5 414
Baku, Sov.Un. 636,000 (*1,060,000) D3 336
Bakundi, Nig. E7 409
Bakwanga, Con.L. D3 414
Bala, Ont., Can. 452 O21 64
Bālā, Tur. 1,756 B5 307
Bala, mts., Bol. B1 246
Balabac, isl., Phil. C5 358
Balad, Som. E6 398
Balaghat, India E3 368
Balaguer, Sp. 6,031 B7 298
Balaka, Rh. & Nya. 560 C7 421
Balakleya, Sov.Un. 10,000 H11 332
Balallan, Scot. C6 272
Bālā Murghāb, Afg. 5,000 B2 374
Balancán, Mex. 1,980 D7 225
Balanda, Sov.Un. 25,200 G15 332
Balanga, Phil. 5,061 B6 358
Balashov, Sov.Un. 64,000 B2 336
Balasore, India 22,851 D5 366
Balassagyarmat, Hung. 12,000 A4 320
Balaton, Lyon, Minn. 723 G3 148
Balaton, lake, Hung. C2 320
Balcarce, Arg. 15,210 C4 252
Balcarres, Sask., Can. 640 E6 58
Balch, Jackson, Ark. 100 B5 170
Balchik, Bul. 7,990 B4 317
Balch Springs, Dallas, Tex. 6,821 *C7 130
Balclutha, N.Z. 3,326 G2 437
Balcones Heights, Bexar, Tex. 950 *E6 130
Bald, butte, Wash. C9 98
Bald, hill, Conn. B7 202
Bald, hill, R.I. C2 216
Bald, mtn., Calif. C3 94
Bald, mtn., Colo. B5 106
Bald, mtn., Conn. B6 202
Bald, mtn., Maine C2 204
Bald, mtn., N.J. A4 210
Bald, mtn., Oreg. C3 96
Bald, mtn., Oreg. C9 96
Bald, mtn., S.Dak. C7 158
Bald, mtn., Vt. B5 218
Bald, mtn., Wyo. B5 116
Bald, mts., N.C., Tenn. A3 186
B9 190
Bald Creek, Yancey, N.C. 600 B3 186
Bald Eagle, Ramsey, Minn. 1,200 F7 148
Bald Eagle, lake, Minn. D7 148
Bald Eagle, lake, Minn. F7 148
Baldhill, dam, N. Dak. C7 154
Bald Knob, White, Ark. 1,705 B5 170
Bald Knob, mtn., Oreg. E2 96
Bald Knob, mtn., Va. C5 192
Bald Knob, mtn., W. Va. C5 194
Bald Knoll, mtn., Wyo. D2 116
Baldock, lake, Man., Can. B4 60
Baldur, Man., Can. 427 F3 60
Baldwin, Duval, Fla. 1,272 A9 174
Baldwin, Banks and Habersham, Ga. 698 B3 176
Baldwin, Randolph, Ill. 336 E4 138
Baldwin, Jackson, Iowa 228 B7 142
Baldwin, St. Mary, La. 1,548 E4 180
Baldwin (Town of), Cumberland, Maine (773▲) *E2 204
Baldwin, Baltimore, Md. 100 A7 182
Baldwin, Lake, Mich. 835 F6 146
Baldwin, Nassau, N.Y. 30,204 E3 212
Baldwin, Burleigh, N. Dak. 60 C5 154
Baldwin, Allegheny, Pa. 24,489 A4 214
Baldwin, St. Croix, Wis. 1,184 D1 160
Baldwin, co., Ala. 49,088 E2 168
Baldwin, co., Ga. 34,064 C3 176
Baldwin City, Douglas, Kans. 1,877 D8 144
Baldwin Heights, Gibson, Ind. 200 D2 140
Baldwin Mills, Chester, S.C. 1,201 B6 188
Baldwin Park, Los Angeles, Calif. 33,951 C5 94
Baldwinsville, Onondaga, N.Y. 5,985 B5 212
Baldwinton, Sask., Can. 130 D3 58
Baldwinville, Worcester, Mass. 1,631 A3 206
Baldwyn, Lee and Prentiss, Miss. 2,023 A4 184
Baldy, mtn., B.C., Can. E12 52
Baldy, mtn., Man., Can. E2 60
Baldy, mtn., Colo. C3 106
Baldy, mtn., Wyo. D3 116
Baldy, peak, Ariz. E6 124
Baldy, peak, N. Mex. B5 126
Bâle, see Basel, Switz.
Baleares, prov., Sp. 419,628 *C8 298
Balearic, is., Sp. C7 298
Balearic Islands (Baleares), reg., Sp. 419,628 C7 298
Baleia, pt., Braz. D3 258
Balestrand, Nor. F2 291
Baleville, Sussex, N.J. 75 A3 210
Balfai, Bhu. D5 368
Balfe, Cherry, Nebr. B4 152
Balfour, Henderson, N.C. 1,106 B3 186
Balfour, McHenry, N.Dak. 159 C5 154
Balfour, chan., Solomon E1 436
Balfours, see North Asheboro, N.C.
Balgonie, Sask., Can. 215 E5 58
Bal Harbour, Dade, Fla. 727 *E6 174
Bali, isl., Indon. F5 358
Balikesir, Tur. 46,556 B2 307
Balikesir, prov., Tur. 613,447 *B2 307
Balikpapan, Indon. 29,843 E5 358
Balje, Ger. 1,900 B3 286
Balkan, Bell, Ky. 676 D7 178
Balkan (Stara Planina), mts., Bul. B2 317
Balkh, Afg. 12,466 A4 374
Balkhash, Sov.Un. 53,000 C9 336
Balkhash, lake, Sov.Un. C9 336
Balki, Sov.Un. I10 332
Balko, Beaver, Okla. 100 B3 128
Ball, Rapides, La. 350 C3 180
Ball, mtn., Alta., Can. E5 54
Ball, mtn., Conn. A3 202
Ballachulish, Scot. 2,960 E7 272
Ballagh, Ire. I5 273
Ballagh, Garfield, Nebr. B6 152
Ballaghaderreen, Ire. 1,374 H4 273
Ballah, Eg., U.A.R. D3 382
Ballah, Eg., U.A.R. E7 395
Ballantine, Yellowstone, Mont. 250 E8 110
Ballarat, Austl. 39,945 (*48,030) F8 432
Ballard, Adair, Okla. 40 B9 128
Ballard, Monroe, W.Va. 400 D4 194
Ballard, co., Ky. 8,291 C1 178
Ballardsville, Itawamba, Miss. 125 A4 184
Ballard Vale, Essex, Mass. 1,000 A5 206
C2
Ballater, Scot. 1,200 D9 272
Ballclub, lake, Minn. D5 148
Balle, Mali C3 408
Ballenas, bay, Mex. B3 224
Balleza, Mex. B4 224
Ball Ground, Cherokee, Ga. 707 B2 176
Ballia, India D4 368
Ballina, Ire. 6,091 G3 273
Ballinascarthy, Ire. J4 273
Ballinasloe, Ire. 5,489 H4 273
Ballineen, Ire. J4 273
Ballinger, Runnels, Tex. 5,043 D6 130
Ballinrobe, Ire. 1,218 H3 273
Ballintra, Ire. 275 G4 273
Ballouville, Windham, Conn. 125 B8 202
Ballston, Polk, Oreg. 200 B3 96
Ballston Spa, Saratoga, N.Y. 4,991 B8 212
Balltown, Dubuque, Iowa 43 *B7 142
Ballville, Sandusky, Ohio 1,424 *A3 156
Ballwin, St. Louis, Mo. 5,710 B7 150
Bally, India 63,138 I9 366
Bally, Berks, Pa. 1,033 C6 214
Ballycastle, N.Ire. 2,558 F6 272
Ballyduff, Ire. 312 I3 273
Ballygorman, Ire. F5 272
Ballyheige, bay, Ire. I3 273
Bally Houra, mts., Ire. I4 273
Ballyjamesduff, Ire. 636 H5 273
Ballykelly, N.Ire. 2,558 F5 272
Ballymahon, Ire. 835 H5 273
Ballymena, N.Ire. 14,165 G7 272
Ballymoney, N.Ire. 3,306 F6 272
Ballymote, Ire. 991 G4 273
Ballymurray, Ire. H4 273
Ballyteige, bay, Ire. I6 273
Ballytore, Ire. H6 273
Ballyvaughan, Ire. 160 H3 273
Balmazújváros, Hung. 13,730 B6 320
Balmoral, Man., Can. 180 E4 60
Balmorhea, Reeves, Tex. 604 D4 130
Balmville, Orange, N.Y. 1,538 *D7 212
Balnew, Baltimore, Md. (part of Dundalk) B6 182
Baloda Bazar, India E3 368
Balotra, India 9,637 C2 366
Balovale, Rh.&Nya. 1,110 B4 420
Balrampur, India D3 368
Balș, Rom. 6,956 B3 321
Balsam, Jackson, N.C. 300 B2 186
Balsam, lake, Ont., Can. P22 64
Balsam, lake, Wis. C1 160
Balsam Lake, Polk, Wis. 541 C1 160
Balsas, riv., Braz. B1 258
Balsas, riv., Braz. C1 258
Balsas, riv., Mex. D5 225
L13
Balsfjord, Nor. B8 290
Balsthal, Switz. 5,107 A3 312
Balta, Pierce, N.Dak. 165 B5 154
Balta, Sov.Un. 47,400 I7 332
Baltic, New London, Conn. 1,366 C7 202
Baltic, Tuscarawas, Ohio 537 B5 156
Baltic, Minnehaha, S.Dak. 278 D9 158
Baltic, sea, Sov.Un. C2 332
Baltim, Eg., U.A.R. 8,862 A3 395
Baltimore, Ont., Can. 280 P22 64
Baltimore, Ire. 217 J3 273
Baltimore (Independent City), Md. 939,024 (*1,636,500) B6 182
C4
Baltimore, Fairfield, Ohio 2,116 C4 156
Baltimore, Windsor, Vt. (90▲) *E3 218
Baltimore, co., Md. 492,428 B6 182
Balurghat, India D5 368
Balzac, Alta., Can. E6 54
Bam, Iran 13,938 D5 379
Bama, Br. Cam. D7 409
Bamako, Mali 100,433 D3 408
Bamba, Mali C4 408
Bambari, Cen.Afr.Rep. E9 409
Bambatana, Solomon Is. F13 359
Bamberg, Ger. 76,400 D4 286
Bamberg, Bamberg, S.C. 3,081 E6 188
Bamberg, co., S.C. 16,274 E6 188
Bambesa, Con.L. B4 414
Bambuí, Braz. 4,114 E1 258
Bambuto, mts., Br.Cam. E6 409
Bamenda, Br.Cam. 2,264 E7 409
Bampūr, Iran D5 379
Bampūr, riv., Iran D5 379
Bams, butte, S.Dak. B2 158
Banalia, Con.L. B4 414
Banamba, Mali D3 408
Banana, Con.L. D1 414
Banana, riv., Fla. C10 174
Bananal, isl., Braz. H6 257
Bananeiras, Braz. 2,825 B3 258
Banaras, India 341,811 (*355,777) D3 368
Banas, cape, Eg., U.A.R. C4 395
Banas, riv., India D1 368
Banat, prov., Rom. 948,596 *C5 321
Banat, reg., Rom. B1 321
Ban Bangsaphan Yai, Thai. E3 362
Banbridge, N.Ire. 6,098 G6 273
Banbury, Eng. 19,300 I11 273
Banchory, Scot. 1,900 D10 272
Banco, Col. 9,636 B2 244
Bancroft, Ont., Can. 1,669 O23 64
S25
Bancroft, Caribou, Idaho 416 G7 108
Bancroft, Kossuth, Iowa 1,000 A3 142
Bancroft, Nemaha, Kans. 40 *C8 144
Bancroft, Beauregard, La. 100 D2 180
Bancroft, Aroostook, Maine 50 (94▲) C4 204
Bancroft, Hampshire, Mass. 60 B1 206
Bancroft, Shiawassee, Mich. 636 G7 146
Bancroft, Cuming, Nebr. 496 B9 152
Bancroft, Kingsbury, S.Dak. 86 C8 158
Bancroft, Putnam, W.Va. 469 *C3 194
Bancroft, Portage, Wis. 250 D4 160
Banda, India 30,327 D3 368
Banda, is., Indon. E7 359
Banda, sea, Indon. F7 358
Banda Banda, mtn., Austl. E10 432
Bandak Norsjo, riv., Nor. G3 291
Bandama, riv., I.C. E3 408
Bandana, Ballard, Ky. 400 C2 178
Bandar, Afg. 5,000 B3 374
Bandar 'Abbas, Iran 14,278 D4 379
Bandar Bahru, Mala. 1,188 F4 362
Bandar-e Chīrū, Iran D3 379
Bandar-e Deylam, Iran 3,130 C3 379
Bandar-e Rīg, Iran 2,250 D3 379
Bandar-e Shāh, Iran 8,284 B4 379
Bandar-e Shahpūr, Iran C2 379
Bandar Maharani (Muar), Mala. 39,137 G4 362
Bandar Penggaram, see Batu Pahat, Mala.
Bande, Sp. 946 A3 298
Banded, peak, Colo. E4 106
Bandeira, peak, Braz. E2 258
Bandelier, natl. mon., N.Mex. C4 126
G6
Bandera, Arg. A3 252
Bandera, Bandera, Tex. 950 E6 130
Bandera, co., Tex. 3,892 E6 130
Bandiagara, Mali 3,700 D4 408
Bandikui, India D2 368
Band-i-Nilag, mtn., Iran D5 379
Bandirma, Tur. 25,515 A2 307
Bandjermasin, Indon. 176,800 E4 358
Bandon, Coos, Oreg. 1,653 D2 96
Bandung, Indon. 839,200 F3 358
Bandy, Tazewell, Va. 800 C3 192
Bandytown, Boone, W.Va. 300 *D3 194
Banes, Cuba 20,257 B7 232
Banff, Alta., Can. 2,518 E5 54
F3
Banff, co., Scot. 50,900 D9 272
Banff, natl. park, Alta., Can. E4 54
Banfora, Upper Volta 2,100 D4 408
Bangaduni, isl., India J9 366
Bangalore, India 778,977 F3 366
Bangaon, India 23,364 H9 366
Bangassou, Cen.Afr.Rep. F9 409
Banggai, Indon. E6 358
Banghāzī, see Bengasi, Libya
Bangka, isl., Indon. E3 358
Bangkalan, Indon. 12,359 F4 358
Bangkok (Krung Thep), Thai. 1,202,000 D4 362
Bangor, Sask., Can. 104 E6 58
Bangor, N.Ire. 20,615 G7 273
Bangor, Penobscot, Maine 38,912 D4 204
Bangor, Van Buren, Mich. 2,109 G5 146
Bangor, Northampton, Pa. 5,766 C6 214
Bangor, Wales 13,700 H8 273
Bangor, La Crosse, Wis. 928 E3 160
Bangor, lowland, Maine C4 204
Bangs, Brown, Tex. 967 D6 130
Bangs, mtn., Ariz. B2 124
Bangu, Con.L. D3 414
Bangued, Phil. 5,663 A6 358
Banguey, isl., N.Bor. C5 358
Bangui, Cen.Afr.Rep. 41,085 F8 409
Bangweulu, lake, Rh.&Nya. B5 420
Ban Houei Sai, Laos B4 362
Bani, Dom.Rep. 10,210 C9 233
Bani, riv., Mali D3 408
Baniara, Pap. F11 359
Banida, Franklin, Idaho 100 G7 108
Baniloudi, Niger C5 408
Bani Na'im, Jordan 3,000 C6 382
Bāniyās, Syr., U.A.R. 5,184 B1 378

Banjak, is., Indon. D1 358
Banja Luka, Yugo. 38,600 B3 316
Banjuwangi, Indon. 25,185 F4 358
Bankasse, Mali D4 408
Bankhead, Walker, Ala. B2 168
Bankhead, lake, Ala. B2 168
Banks, Pike, Ala. 201 D4 168
Banks, Bradley, Ark. 233 D4 170
Banks, Boise, Idaho 50 E2 108
Banks, Tunica, Miss. A2 184
Banks, Washington, Oreg. 347 A1 96
Banks, co., Ga. 6,497 B3 176
Banks, isl., Austl. A8 432
Banks, isl., B.C., Can. D7 52
Banks, isl., N.W.Ter., Can. C6 48
Banks, lake, Ga. F3 176
Banks, pen., N.Z. E4 437
Banksian, riv., Man., Can. D5 60
Bankston, Fayette, Ala. 300 B2 168
Bankston, Dubuque, Iowa 36 *B7 142
Bankura, India 49,369 E4 368
Ban Me Thuot, Viet. D6 362
Bannack, Beaverhead, Mont. E4 110
Banner, Calhoun, Miss. 75 A3 184
Banner, Sheridan, Wyo. 10 B6 116
Banner, co., Nebr. 1,269 C2 152
Banner Elk, Avery, N.C. 564 A4 186
Banner Hill, Unicoi, Tenn. 2,132 *B9 190
Bannerman, Man., Can. 100 F3 60
Bannertown, Surry, N.C. 1,096 *A5 186
Banning, Riverside, Calif. 10,250 F5 94
Banning, Carroll, Ga. 150 C2 176
Banningville, Con.L. 4,753 C2 414
Bannock, co., Idaho 49,342 G6 108
Bannock, pass, Idaho, Mont. E5 108
F3 110
Bannock, peak, Idaho G6 108
Bannockburn, Ont., Can. 210 P23 64
Bannockburn, Lake, Ill. 466 *A6 138
Bannu, Pak. 20,509 C7 375
(27,516▲)
Bañolas, Sp. 6,338 A8 298
Baños, Ec. 2,691 A2 245
Banquo, Huntington, Ind. 75 B4 140
Bansbaria, India 30,622 I9 366
Banská Bystrica, Czech. 18,806 B4 324
Banská Štiavnica, Czech. 10,381 B4 324
Bansko, Bul. 6,842 C1 317
Banskobystrický, co., Czech. 525,072 *B4 324
Bantam, Litchfield, Conn. 833 C3 202
Bantam, lake, Conn. C3 202
Bantam, riv., Conn. B3 202
Bantry, Ire. 2,211 J3 273
Bantry, McHenry, N.Dak. 66 B5 154
Bantry, bay, Ire. J3 273
Banyo, Cam. 2,606 E7 409
Banzyville, Con.L. B3 414
Baoulé, riv., Mali D3 408
Bapchule, Pinal, Ariz. 100 E4 124
H2
Baptiste, Ont., Can. 95 O23 64
Baptistown, Hunterdon, N.J. 350 B2 210
Ba'quba, Iraq 13,203 C6 378
Baquedano, Chile B4 250
Bar, Sov.Un. 22,100 H6 332
Bar, Yugo. 1,113 C4 316
Bara, Sud. 4,885 C3 398
Barabinsk, Sov.Un. 38,900 A9 336
Baraboo, Sauk, Wis. 6,672 E4 160
Baraboo, riv., Wis. E3 160
Baracaldo, Sp. 36,165 A5 298
Baracoa, Cuba 11,459 B7 232
Barada, Richardson, Nebr. 58 *D9 152
Baradères, Hai. 902 C8 232
Baraga, Baraga, Mich. 991 C3 146
Baraga, co., Mich. 7,151 C3 146
Barahona, Dom.Rep. 14,654 C9 233
Barak, riv., India D6 368
Barak Khel, Afg. 5,000 C4 374
Baramula, India 12,724 B1 368
Baran, India D2 368
Baranagar, India 77,126 I9 366
Baranof, Alsk. 16 J14 84
Baranof, isl., Alsk. J14 84
Baranovichi, Sov.Un. 58,000 F5 332
Baranya, co., Hung. 300,000 *C3 320
Barasat, India I9 366
Barataria, Jefferson, La. 900 C7 180
E5
Barataria, bay, La. E6 180
Barataria, bayou, La. C7 180
Baraya, Col. 1,736 C1 244
Barbacena, Braz. 24,718 E2 258
Barbacoas, Col. 3,349 C1 244
Barbados, ter., W.I.Fed. 227,000 E14 233
Barbalha, Braz. 4,165 B3 258
Barbara, Perry, Miss. E4 184
Barbastro, Sp. 8,144 A7 298
Barbate, Sp. 10,660 D4 298
Barbeau, Chippewa, Mich. 20 C7 146
Barber, Golden Valley, Mont. 35 D7 110
Barber, Cherokee, Okla. C9 128
Barber, co., Kans. 8,713 E5 144
Barbers, pt., Haw. B3 86
Barberton, Summit, Ohio 33,805 A5 156
Barberton, U.S.Afr. 6,430 E6 421
Barberville, Volusia, Fla. 350 B9 174
Barbour, co., Ala. 24,700 D4 168
Barbour, co., W.Va. 15,474 B4 194
Barboursville, Orange, Va. 150 B6 192
Barboursville, Cabell, W.Va. 2,331 C2 194
Barbourville, Knox, Ky. 3,211 D7 178
Barbuda, isl., W.I. D14 233
Barby, Ger. 7,788 C4 286
Barcaldine, Austl. 1,705 C9 432
Barcarrota, Sp. 8,020 C3 298
Barcellona, It. 20,000 F5 302
Barcelona, Sp. 1,428,777 B8 298
(*1,750,000)
Barcelona, Ven. 38,000 A6 240
Barcelona, prov., Sp. 2,215,901 *B8 298
Barcelos, Braz. 812 F4 256
Barclay, Osage, Kans. 50 D8 144
Barclay, Queen Annes, Md. 142 B8 182
Barclay, Lincoln, Nev. 10 F7 112
Barco, Currituck, N.C. 250 A10 186
Barcoo, riv., Austl. C8 432
Bard, Greene, Ark. 25 *A6 170
Bardaï, Chad B8 409
Bardawīl, pen., Eg., U.A.R. C3 382
Bardejov, Czech. 6,572 B5 324
Barden, res., R.I. B2 216
Bardera, Som. 1,500 E5 398
(4,900▲)
Bardīyah, Libya A5 394
Bardīyah, Eg., U.A.R. A2 395
Bardo, Harlan, Ky. 250 *D7 178
Bardsey, isl., Wales I8 273
Bardstown, Mississippi, Ark. 75 B6 170
Bardstown, Nelson, Ky. 4,798 C5 178
Bardstown Junction, Bullitt, Ky. 150 C5 178
Bardswell Group, is., B.C., Can. D8 52
Bardwell, Carlisle, Ky. 1,067 D1 178
Bare Beach, Hendry, Fla. 70 E10 174
Bare Hill, pond, Mass. C1 206
Bareilly, India 194,679 C2 368
(*208,083)
Barela, Las Animas, Colo. E6 106
Barentin, Fr. 6,371 C4 278
Barentu, Eth. B4 398
Baresville, York, Pa. 1,700 *D5 214
Barfield, Mississippi, Ark. 40 B7 170
Barfleur, pt., Fr. C3 278
Bargaintown, Atlantic, N.J. E3 210
Bargal, Som. 2,200 C7 398
Bargersville, Johnson, Ind. 586 C3 140
Barguzin, Sov.Un. 5,600 D12 329
Barh, India D4 368
Bar Harbor, Hancock, Maine 2,444 D4 204
(3,807▲)
Bari, India D2 368
Bari, It. 287,700 E6 302
Bari, prov., It. 1,243,800 *E6 302
Baria, Viet. 7,660 E5 362
Barika, Alg. 2,945 A5 402
(71,235▲)
Barinas, Ven. 17,000 B3 240
Barinas, state, Ven. 79,944 B4 240
Baring, Washington, Maine 130 C5 204
(157▲)
Baring, Knox, Mo. 213 A5 150
Baring Head, cape, N.Z. J11 437
Baripada, India 9,277 E4 368
Bariri, Braz. 5,145 E1 258
Bari Sadri, India D1 368
Barisal, Pak. 89,694 L17 375
Barisan, mts., Indon. E2 358
Barito, riv., Indon. E4 358
Barium Springs, Iredell, N.C. 300 B5 186
Bark, lake, Ont., Can. O23 64
Bark, pt., Wis. B2 160
Barka, Om. C6 383
Barken, lake, Swe. A6 292
Barker, Niagara, N.Y. 528 B3 212
Barker Heights, Henderson, N.C. 300 *B3 186
Barkerville, B.C., Can. 250 D12 52
Barkhamsted, Litchfield, Conn. 60 B4 202
(1,370▲)
Barkhamsted, res., Conn. B4 202
Barkley, sound, B.C., Can. F10 52
Barkly East, U.S.Afr. F5 420
Barköl, see Chenhsi, China
Bark River, Delta, Mich. 200 D4 146
Barksdale, Bayfield, Wis. 75 B3 160
Bârlad (Birlad), Rom. 32,043 A4 321
Barladul, riv., Rom. A4 321
Bar-le-Duc, Fr. 16,609 C6 278
Barlee, lake, Austl. D3 432
Barletta, It. 67,200 E6 302
Barley, Greenville, Va. 50 D7 192
Barling, Sebastian, Ark. 770 B2 170
Barlow, Ballard, Ky. 731 C1 178
Barlow, Copiah, Miss. D2 184
Barlow, Foster, N.Dak. 50 C6 154
Barlow, Clackamas, Oreg. 85 *B4 96
Barlow Bend, Clarke, Ala. 300 D2 168
Barmer, India 20,812 C2 366
Bar Mills, York, Maine 400 E2 204
Barmouth, Wales 2,300 I8 273
Barnabus, Logan, W.Va. 600 D2 194
Barnaby River, N.B., Can. 290 C4 70
Barnard, Lincoln, Kans. 205 C5 144
Barnard, Nodaway, Mo. 237 A3 150
Barnard, Brown, S.Dak. 82 B7 158
Barnard, Windsor, Vt. 75 D3 218
(435▲)
Barnardsville, Buncombe, N.C. 199 B3 186
Barnaul, Sov.Un. 320,000 B10 336
Barnegat, Ocean, N.J. 287 D4 210
Barnegat, bay, N.J. D4 210
Barnegat, inlet, N.J. D4 210
Barnegat Light, Ocean, N.J. 227 D4 210
Barnegat Pines, Ocean, N.J. 200 D4 210
Barnes, Washington, Kans. 247 C7 144
Barnes, Douglas, Oreg. 5,076 *D3 96
Barnes, co., N.Dak. 16,719 C7 154
Barnes, sound, Fla. F10 174
Barnesboro, Cambria, Pa. 3,035 C3 214
Barnes City, Mahaska, Iowa 273 C5 142
Barnes Corners, Lewis, N.Y. 100 B6 212
Barnesdale, Ont., Can. 85 O21 64
Barneston, Gage, Nebr. 177 D9 152
Barnesville, Lamar, Ga. 4,919 C2 176
Barnesville, Montgomery, Md. 145 B5 182
Barnesville, Clay, Minn. 1,632 E2 148
Barnesville, Belmont, Ohio 4,425 C5 156
Barnet, Caledonia, Vt. 250 C4 218
(1,445▲)
Barnett, Morgan, Mo. 200 *C5 150
Barneveld, Neth. 6,200 B4 282
Barneveld, Iowa, Wis. 420 E4 160
Barney, Brooks, Ga. 165 E3 176
Barney, Richland, N.Dak. 115 D8 154
Barney, mtn., Austl. D10 432
Barnhart, Jefferson, Mo. 400 B8 150
C7
Barnhart, Irion, Tex. 250 D5 130
Barnhill, Tuscarawas, Ohio 350 *B5 156
Barnrock, Johnson, Ky. 189 C8 178
Barnsboro, Gloucester, N.J. 600 D2 210
Barnsdall, Osage, Okla. 1,663 B7 128
Barnstable, Barnstable, Mass. 800 C7 206
(13,465▲)
Barnstable, co., Mass. 70,286 C6 206
Barnstaple, Eng. 15,800 J8 273
Barnstaple, bay, Eng. J8 273
Barnstead, Belknap, N.H. 200 E4 208
(850▲)
Barnum, Webster, Iowa 154 B3 142
Barnum, Carlton, Minn. 417 E6 148
Barnwell, Baldwin, Ala. 175 E2 168
Barnwell, Alta., Can. 150 F6 54
Barnwell, Barnwell, S.C. 4,568 E6 188
Barnwell, co., S.C. 17,659 E6 188
Baro, Nig. 217 E6 408
Baro, riv., Eth. D3 398
Baroda, India 211,407 D2 366
Baroda, Berrien, Mich. 488 *H5 146
Baron, Adair, Okla. 100 C9 128
Barons, Alta., Can. 352 F6 54
Barotseland Protectorate, prov., Rh. & Nya. C4 420
Barotseland, prot., Rh. & Nya. C4 420
Barpeta, India D5 368
Barqah, see Cyrenaica, Libya
Barqin, Libya B2 394
Barquisimeto, Ven. 200,000 A4 240
Barr, Fr. C7 278
Barr, Tate, Miss. 275 A3 184
Barr, Valley, Mont. B10 110
Barr, Lauderdale, Tenn. C2 190
Barra, Braz. 5,580 C2 258
Barra, isl., Scot. E5 272
Barra, sound, Scot. D5 272
Barrackpore, India 42,639 I9 366
Barrackville, Marion, W.Va. 950 A7 194
Barra do Corda, Braz. 2,851 B1 258
Barra do Paraopeba, Braz. D1 258
Barra do Pirai, Braz. E2 258
Barra Mansa, Braz. 20,893 E2 258
Barranca, Peru 192 A2 245
Barrancabermeja, Col. 25,046 B2 244
Barrancas, Ven. 1,982 B7 240
Barranquilla, Col. 356,920 A2 244
Barraza, Chile B1 252
Barre, Worcester, Mass. 1,065 B3 206
(3,479▲)
Barre, Washington, Vt. 10,387 C4 218
Barre (Town of), Washington, Vt. (4,580▲) *C4 218
Barre, lake, La. E5 180
Barre des Écrins, mtn., Fr. E7 278
Barreiras, Braz. 5,802 C1 258
Barreiro, Port. 22,190 C2 298
Barreiros, Braz. 7,666 B3 258
Barrellville, Allegany, Md. 300 A2 182
Barren, co., Ky. 28,303 D4 178
Barren, cape, Austl. G9 432
Barren, isl., Alsk. H10 84
Barren, isl., Md. D7 182
Barren, is., Malag. C8 421
Barren, riv., Ky. C4 178
Barren Plain, Robertson, Tenn. 100 B5 190
Barrens, plat., Tenn. C5 190
Barre Plains, Worcester, Mass. 300 B3 206
Barretos, Braz. 22,689 E1 258
Barrett, Grant, Minn. 345 F3 148
Barrett, Harris, Tex. 2,364 *E8 130
Barrett, Boone, W. Va. 800 D3 194
D6
Barretts, hill, Mass. C1 206
Barrhead, Alta., Can. 1,610 C5 54
Barrhead, Scot. 13,700 F8 272
Barrhill, Scot. F8 272
Barrie, Ont., Can. 16,851 P21 64
Barrie, isl., Ont., Can. O18 64
Barrière, B.C., Can. 25 E12 52
Barrigada, Guam 1,666 C7 436
Barrigada, hill, Guam C7 436
Barringer, Clark, Ark. 50 D3 170
Barrington, N.S., Can. 385 F4 70
Barrington, Lake, Ill. 5,434 A5 138
Barrington, Strafford, N.H. 70 E4 208
(1,036▲)
Barrington, Camden, N.J. 7,943 *D3 210
Barrington, Bristol, R.I. 9,800 C3 216
(13,826▲)
Barrington, lake, Man., Can. B2 60
Barrington Hills, Cook, Ill. 1,391 *A5 138
Barron, Barron, Wis. 2,338 C2 160
Barron, co., Wis. 34,270 C2 160
Barronett, Barron, Wis. 100 C1 160
Barrow, Alsk. 1,314 A6 84
Barrow, co., Ga. 14,485 B3 176
Barrow, isl., Austl. C3 432
Barrow, pt., Alsk. A6 84
Barrow, riv., Ire. I6 273
Barrow, strait, N.W. Ter., Can. C9 48
Barrow Creek, Austl. C6 432
Barrow-in-Furness, Eng. 64,900 G9 273
Barrows, Man., Can. 25 D2 60
Barrowsville, Bristol, Mass. 500 C5 206
Barruelo de Santullán, Sp. 4,702 A4 298
Barry, Pike, Ill. 1,422 D2 138
Barry, co., Mich. 31,738 G6 146
Barry, co., Mo. 18,921 E4 150
Barrys Bay, Ont., Can. 1,366 O23 64
Barryton, Mecosta, Mich. 418 F6 146
Barryville, Sullivan, N.Y. 400 D7 212
Barsi, India 41,849 E3 366
Barstow, San Bernardino, Calif. 11,644 E5 94
Barstow, Calvert, Md. 117 C6 182
Barstow, Ward, Tex. 707 D4 130
Bar-sur-Aube, Fr. 4,387 C6 278
Barth, Ger. 13,000 A5 286
Bartholomew, co., Ind. 48,198 C4 140
Bartibog, N.B., Can. B4 70
Bartica, Br.Gu. 2,352 D5 256
Bartin, Tur. 10,057 A5 307
Bartlebaugh, Hamilton, Tenn. 200 E8 190
Bartle Frere, mtn., Austl. B8 432
Bartlesville, Washington, Okla. 27,893 B8 128
Bartlett, Cook, Ill. 1,540 E2 138
Bartlett, Labette, Kans. 137 E8 144
Bartlett, Wheeler, Nebr. 125 C7 152
Bartlett, Carroll, N.H. 550 C4 208
(1,013▲)
Bartlett, Ramsey, N.Dak. 39 B7 154
Bartlett, Wallowa, Oreg. B9 96
Bartlett, Shelby, Tenn. 508 C2 190
E6
Bartlett, Bell and Williamson, Tex. 1,540 D7 130
Bartlett, dam, Ariz. G3 124
Bartlett, res., Ariz. E4 124
Bartletts Ferry, dam, Ala., Ga. C4 168
D1 176
Bartlett's Harbour, Newf., Can. 80 E7 72
Bartley, Red Willow, Nebr. 308 D5 152
Bartley, Morris, N.J. 90 B3 210
Bartley, McDowell, W.Va. 900 D3 194
Bartolomeu Dias, Moz. D7 421
Barton, Colbert, Ala. 300 A2 168
Barton, Phillips, Ark. 250 C6 170
Barton, Ascension, La. 200 B5 180
Barton, Allegany, Md. 731 A1 182
Barton, Pierce, N.Dak. 80 B5 154
Barton, Belmont, Ohio 966 B6 156
Barton, Allendale, S.C. F6 188
Barton, Orleans, Vt. 1,169 B4 218
(3,066▲)
Barton, Washington, Wis. 1,569 E5 160
Barton, co., Kans. 32,368 D5 144
Barton, co., Mo. 11,113 D3 150
Barton, riv., Vt. B4 218
Barton-on-Humber, Eng. 6,400 H12 273
Bartonsville, Windham, Vt. 70 E3 218
Bartonville, Peoria, Ill. 7,253 C4 138
Bartonwoods, De Kalb, Ga. 3,000 *C2 176
Bartoszyce, Pol. 3,449 A5 325
Bartow, Polk, Fla. 12,849 D9 174
Bartow, Jefferson, Ga. 366 D4 176
Bartow, co., Ga. 28,267 B2 176
Barvas, Scot. C6 272
Barvenkovo, Sov.Un. 26,800 H11 332
Barview District, Coos, Oreg. 450 *D2 96
Barwani, India E1 368
Barwick, Brooks and Thomas, Ga. 400 F3 176
Barwon, riv., Austl. D9 432
Barybino, Sov.Un. O18 332
Barzee, Meagher, Mont. D6 110
Bärz Shovär, Iran C3 379
Basāki, Iran C3 379
Basalt, Eagle, Colo. 213 C3 106
Basalt, Bingham, Idaho 275 F6 108
Basankusu, Con.L. B2 414
Basbulak, Sov.Un. D6 336
Bascom, Jackson, Fla. 250 A5 174
Bascom, Seneca, Ohio 400 A3 156
Bascuñan, cape, Chile A1 252
Basekpio, Con.L. B3 414
Basel, Switz. 192,000 A3 312
(*305,000)
Basel (Bâle), canton, Switz. 335,600 A3 312
Basel-Land (Bâle-Campagne), sub canton, Switz. 122,400 *A3 312
Basel-Stadt (Bâle-Ville), sub canton, Switz. 213,200 *A4 312
Bashagird, range, Iran D5 379
Bashaw, Alta., Can. 597 D6 54
Bashi, Clarke, Ala. 300 D2 168
Bashi, chan., For. O10 349
Bashkir A.S.S.R., Sov.Un. 3,335,000 D8 328
Basi, India C2 368
Basil, Fairfield, Ohio 800 C4 156
Basilan, isl., Phil. C6 358
Basile, Evangeline, La. 1,932 D3 180
Basilicata (Lucania), reg., It. 658,000 E5 302
Basilio, Braz. 297 L6 257
Basin, Jefferson, Mont. 300 D4 110
Basin, Big Horn, Wyo. 1,319 B4 116
Basin, lake, Sask., Can. D5 58
Basinger, Okeechobee, Fla. 100 D9 174
Basirhat, India 34,823 I9 366
Baška, Yugo. 1,016 B2 316
Baskahegan, lake, Maine C5 204
Baskatong, lake, Que., Can. R9 66
Baskett, Henderson, Ky. 300 C3 178
Baskin, Franklin, La. 238 B4 180
Basking Ridge, Somerset, N.J. 2,438 B3 210
Basoko, Con.L. B3 414
Basongo, Con.L. C3 414
Basque Provinces (Vascongadas), reg., Sp. 1,039,465 A5 298
Basra, Iraq 159,355 D7 378
Bas-Rhin, dept., Fr. 707,934 *C7 278
Bass, Newton, Ark. 30 *B3 170
Bass, is., Ohio A4 156
Bass, lake, Ind. A3 140
Bass, strait, Austl. F9 432
Bassac, Laos 5,000 D5 362
Bassano, Alta., Can. 753 E6 54
Bassano del Grappa, It. 18,100 C3 302
Bassas da India, isl., Afr. D7 421
Bassein, Bur. 77,905 C2 362
Basses-Alpes, dept., Fr. 84,335 *E7 278
Basses-Pyrénées, dept., Fr. 420,019 *F3 278
Basse-Terre, Guad. 9,124 E14 233
Basseterre, St. Kitts 12,453 D13 233
Bassett, Mississippi, Ark. 250 B6 170
Bassett, Chickasaw, Iowa 130 A5 142
Bassett, Allen, Kans. 67 E8 144
Bassett, Rock, Nebr. 1,023 B6 152
Bassett, Henry, Va. 3,148 D5 192
Bassett, creek, Ala. D2 168
Bassfield, Jefferson Davis, Miss. 295 D3 184
Bassikounou, Maur. C3 408
Basso Giuba, pol. dist., Som. 113,449 E5 398
Bass River, N.S., Can. 430 D6 70
Bass River, Barnstable, Mass. 200 C7 206
Bassum, Ger. B3 286
Basswood, Man., Can. 125 E2 60
Båstad, Swe. 2,271 E3 292
Bastak, Iran 7,500 D4 379
Bastelica, Fr. E2 302
Basti, India D3 368
Bastia, Fr. 40,000 D2 302
Bastian, Bland, Va. 700 C3 192
Bastogne, Bel. 5,927 D4 282
Bastrop, Morehouse, La. 15,193 B4 180
Bastrop, Bastrop, Tex. 3,001 D7 130
Bastrop, co., Tex. 16,925 D7 130
Baskuträsk, Swe. 705 D9 290
Basutoland, Br. poss., Afr. 658,000 I9 388
420
Basyūm, Eg., U.A.R. 11,952 D1 382
Bat, cave, Mo. D5 150
Bata, Rio Muni 842 F6 409
Batabanó, Cuba 5,075 A3 232
Batabanó, gulf, Cuba A3 232
Batala, India 55,850 C1 368
Batangafo, Cen.Afr.Rep. E8 409
Batangas, Phil. 10,326 B6 358
Batanūn, Eg., U.A.R. 18,925 D1 382
Bátaszék, Hung. 7,555 C3 320
Batatais, Braz. 9,735 E1 258
Batavia, Boone, Ark. 40 A3 170

Batavia, Arg.		B2	252
Batavia, Kane, Ill.	7,496	B5	138
		F1	
Batavia, Jefferson, Iowa	533	D5	142
Batavia, Genesee, N.Y.	18,210	C3	212
Batavia, Clermont, Ohio	1,729	C2	156
Bataysk, Sov.Un.	52,000	I12	332
Batchelor, bay, N.C.		B9	186
Bateman, Sask., Can.	161	E4	58
Bates, Scott, Ark.	106	C2	170
Bates, Grant, Oreg.	200	C8	96
Bates, co., Mo.	15,905	C3	150
Batesburg, Lexington, S.C.	3,806	D5	188
Batesland, Shannon, S.Dak.	95	D3	158
Batesville, Barbour, Ala.	25	C4	168
Batesville, Independence, Ark.	6,207	B5	170
Batesville, Ripley, Ind.	3,349	C4	140
Batesville, Panola, Miss.	3,284	A3	184
Bath, N.B., Can.	395	C2	70
Bath, Ont., Can.	637	P24	64
Bath, Eng.	79,800	J10	273
Bath, Mason, Ill.	398	C3	138
Bath, Franklin, Ind.	100	C5	140
Bath, Sagadahoc, Maine	10,717	E3	204
		E6	
Bath, Clinton, Mich.	500	G7	146
Bath, Grafton, N.H.	160 (604▴)	C3	208
Bath, Steuben, N.Y.	6,166	C4	212
Bath, Beaufort, N.C.	346	B9	186
Bath, Northampton, Pa.	1,736	C6	214
Bath, Aiken, S.C.	1,419	D5	188
Bath, Brown, S.Dak.	80	B7	158
Bath, see Berkeley Springs, W.Va.			
Bath, co., Ky.	9,114	B7	178
Bath, co., Va.	5,335	B5	192
Bathgate, Scot.	11,900	F9	272
Bathgate, Pembina, N.Dak.	175	B8	154
Bath Springs, Decatur, Tenn.	50	C3	190
Bathurst, Austl.	16,089	E9	432
Bathurst, N.B., Can.	5,267	B4	70
Bathurst, Gam.	21,022	D1	408
Bathurst Inlet, N.W.Ter., Can.		D8	48
Bathurst, cape, N.W.Ter., Can.		C5	48
Bathurst, isl., Austl.		A6	432
Bathurst, isl., N.W.Ter., Can.		B8	48
Batié, Upper Volta		E4	408
Batiscan, Que., Can.	730	R12	66
Batiscan, riv., Que., Can.		Q12	66
Batjan, isl., Indon.		E7	359
Batkanu, S.L.		E2	408
Batna, Alg.	14,732 (26,413▴)	A5	402
Batoche, Sask., Can.	165	D4	58
Baton Rouge, East Baton Rouge, La.	152,419 (*248,700)	B5	180
		D4	
Baton Rouge, Chester, S.C.	50	B6	188
Batouri, Cam.	6,044	F7	409
Båtsfjord, Nor.		A13	290
Batson, Hardin, Tex.	650	D8	130
Batsto, Atlantic, N.J.	50	D3	210
Batsto, riv., N.J.		D3	210
Battambang, Camb.	16,000	D4	362
Batten Kill, riv., Vt.		E2	218
Battery Park, Isle of Wight, Va.	240	A8	192
Batticaloa, Cey.	17,439	G4	366
Battiest, McCurtain, Okla.	50	D9	128
Battle, creek, Mont.		A7	110
Battle, creek, Sask., Can.		F3	58
Battle, mtn., Wyo.		E5	116
Battle, riv., Minn.		D4	148
Battle, riv., Sask., Can.		D3	58
Battleboro, Nash and Edgecombe, N.C.	364	A8	186
Battle Creek, Sask., Can.	20	F3	58
Battle Creek, Routt, Colo.		B3	106
Battle Creek, Ida, Iowa	786	B2	142
Battle Creek, Calhoun, Mich.	44,169 (*107,300)	G6	146
Battle Creek, Madison, Nebr.	587	C8	152
Battleford, Sask., Can.	1,498	D3	58
Battle Ground, Cullman, Ala.	200	A3	168
Battle Ground, Tippecanoe, Ind.	804	B3	140
Battle Ground, Clark, Wash.	888	D4	98
Battle Harbour, Newf., Can.	100	D8	72
		E10	
Battle Lake, Otter Tail, Minn.	733	E3	148
Battle Mountain, Lander, Nev.	1,050	C5	112
Battles Wharf, Baldwin, Ala.	400	*E2	168
Battleview, Burke, N.Dak.	55	B3	154
Battonya, Hung.	9,051	C6	320
Battrum, Sask., Can.	35	E3	58
Batu, is., Indon.		E1	358
Batu, mtn., Eth.		D4	398
Batuc, Mex.	1,267	B4	224
Batumi, Sov.Un.	82,000	E6	328
Batu Pahat, Mala.	39,308	G4	362
Baturadja, Indon.	2,955	E2	358
Baturino, Sov.Un.		A11	336
Baturité, Braz.	5,194	A3	258
Bauang, Phil.	3,188	A6	358
Baubau, Indon.	10,000	F6	358
Bauchi, Nig.	13,440	D6	409
Baudette, Lake of the Woods, Minn.	1,597	C4	148
Baudouinville, Con.L.		D4	414
Baugé, Fr.		D3	278
Baughman, Knox, Ky.	500	D7	178
Bauld, cape, Newf., Can.		E8	72
Baunei, It.	4,000	E2	302
Baures, Bol.	592	B2	246
Baurú, Braz.	51,734	E1	258
Bausi, India		D4	368
Bautzen, Ger.	42,000	C6	286
Bauxite, Saline, Ark.	950	C4	170
		D6	
Bavaria (Bayern), reg., Ger.		D4	286
Bavaria, Saline, Kans.	76	D6	144
Bavispe, Mex.	923	A4	224
Bawcomville, Ouachita, La.	1,500	B3	180
Bawean, isl., Indon.		F4	358
Bāwīt, Eg., U.A.R.	2,039	B2	395
Bawku, Ghana		D4	408
Bawlf, Alta., Can.	287	D6	54
Baxley, Appling, Ga.	4,268	E4	176
Baxter, Drew, Ark.		D5	170
Baxter, Baker, Fla.	125	A8	174
Baxter, Union, Ga.	120	B2	176
Baxter, Jasper, Iowa	681	C4	142

Baxter, Harlan, Ky.	900	*D7	178
Baxter, Crow Wing, Minn.	1,037	E4	148
Baxter, Putnam, Tenn.	853	B6	190
Baxter, Marion, W.Va.	574	A7	194
		B4	
Baxter, co., Ark.	9,943	A4	170
Baxter Springs, Cherokee, Kans.	4,498	E9	144
Baxterville, Lamar, Miss.		D3	184
Bay, Craighead, Ark.	627	B6	170
Bay, co., Fla.	67,131	A5	174
Bay, co., Mich.	107,042	F7	146
Bay, pt., S.C.		G8	188
Baya Dzur-Gunen, Mong.	5,000	B8	346
Bayai, well, Libya		C3	394
Bay al Kabir, wadi, Libya		A2	394
Bayamo, Cuba	20,178	B6	232
Bayamón, P.R.	20,171	C11	233
Bayan-Aul, Sov.Un.	2,600	B9	336
Bayan Dung, Mong.		B10	346
Bayanga, Cen.Afr.Rep.		F8	409
Bayan Tümen, Mong.		B10	346
Bayard, Sussex, Del.		F5	172
Bayard, Duval, Fla.	300	A9	174
		B10	
Bayard, Guthrie, Iowa	597	C3	142
Bayard, Morrill, Nebr.	1,519	C2	152
Bayard, Grant, N.Mex.	2,327	F2	126
Bayard, Grant, W.Va.	484	B5	194
Bayboro, Pamlico, N.C.	545	B9	186
Bay Bulls, Newf., Can.	650	G9	72
Bayburt, Tur.	13,332	A9	307
Bay Center, Pacific, Wash.	600	C3	98
Bay City, Bay, Mich.	53,604	F8	146
Bay City, Tillamook, Oreg.	996	B3	96
Bay City, Matagorda, Tex.	11,656	E8	130
		G7	
Bay City, Grays Harbor, Wash.		C2	98
Bay City, Pierce, Wis.	327	D1	160
Bay Colony, Princess Anne, Va.	850	*D8	192
Bay de Verde, Newf., Can.	906	F9	72
Bayern (Bavaria), state, Ger.	9,176,600	*D4	286
Bayeux, Fr.	10,077	C3	278
Bayfield, Ont., Can.	300	Q19	64
Bayfield, La Plata, Colo.	322	E3	106
Bayfield, Bayfield, Wis.	969	B3	160
Bayfield, co., Wis.	11,910	B2	160
Bay Harbor, Bay, Fla. (part of Springfield)		A5	174
Bay Harbor Islands, Dade, Fla.	3,249	E6	174
Bay Head, Ocean, N.J.	824	C4	210
Bayhorse, Custer, Idaho		E4	108
Bay Horse, Powder River, Mont.	4	E11	110
Baykal, Sov.Un.		D12	329
Baykal, lake, Sov.Un.		D12	329
Baykal, mts., Sov.Un.		D12	329
Baykit, Sov.Un.		C11	329
Bay l'Argent, Newf., Can.	200	G8	72
Baylor, Valley, Mont.	66	B10	110
Baylor, co., Tex.	5,893	C6	130
Baymak, Sov.Un.	10,000	B5	336
Bay Minette, Baldwin, Ala.	5,197	E2	168
Bayneville, Sedgwick, Kans.	15	B5	144
Bay of Islands, bay, Newf., Can.		F6	72
Bayonne, Fr.	32,575	F3	278
Bayonne, Hudson, N.J.	74,215	B1	210
		B4	
Bayou Bodcau, res., Ark.		D3	170
Bayou Cane, Terrebonne, La.	3,173	*E5	180
Bayou Chene, St. Martin, La.		D4	180
Bayou Chicot, Evangeline, La.	50	D3	180
Bayou Current, St. Landry, La.	75	D4	180
Bayou George, Bay, Fla.	100	A5	174
Bayou Goula, Iberville, La.	750	B5	180
		D4	
Bayou La Batre, Mobile, Ala.	2,572	E1	168
Bayou Meto, Arkansas, Ark.	20	C5	170
Bayou Sorrel, Iberville, La.	300	*D4	180
Bayóvar, Peru		B1	245
Bay Park, Nassau, N.Y.	1,500	*E3	212
Bay Port, Huron, Mich.	400	F8	146
Bayport, Washington, Minn.	3,205	F6	148
		F8	
Bayport, Suffolk, N.Y.	3,000	D4	212
Bayram-Ali, Sov.Un.	28,800	F8	328
Bayreuth, Ger.	60,600	D4	286
Bay Ridge, Anne Arundel, Md.	100	C7	182
Bay Roberts, Newf., Can.	1,306	G9	72
Bays, lake, Ont., Can.		O21	64
Bays, mts., Tenn.		B8	190
Bay St. Louis, Hancock, Miss.	5,073	E1	184
		E3	
Bay Settlement, Brown, Wis.	25	A6	160
Bayshore, Charlevoix, Mich.	160	D6	146
Bay Shore, Suffolk, N.Y.	20,000	E3	212
		E8	
Bayshore Gardens, Manatee, Fla.	2,297	*D8	174
Bayside, Hancock, Maine	70	D4	204
Bayside, Princess Anne, Va.	6,000	*D8	192
Bayside, Milwaukee, Wis.	3,181	E2	160
Bayside Garden, Tillamook, Oreg.	140	*B3	96
Bay Springs, Jasper, Miss.	1,544	D3	184
Bayt al Faqīh, Yemen		E3	383
Bayt Jālā, Jordan		C6	382
Bayt Laḥm (Bethlehem), Jordan	19,155	C6	382
Baytown, Harris, Tex.	28,159	E8	130
		F8	
Bay View, Jefferson, Ala.	1,081	E4	168
Bayview, New Haven, Conn.	300	E3	202
Bayview, Bay, Fla.	422	*A5	174
Bayview, Kootenai, Idaho	250	B2	108
Bayview, Essex, Mass.		A6	206
Bay View, Emmet, Mich.		D7	146
Bay View, Erie, Ohio	802	*A4	156
Bay View, Richland, S.C.	600	*C6	188
Bay Village, Cross, Ark.	150	B6	170
Bay Village, Cuyahoga, Ohio	14,489	B1	156
Bayville, Ocean, N.J.	700	D4	210
Bayville, Nassau, N.Y.	3,962	D3	212
Baywood, East Baton Rouge, La.		D5	180
Baza, Sp.	14,880	D5	298
Bazaar, Chase, Kans.	60	*D7	144
Bazajas de Madrid, Sp. (part of Madrid)		*B5	298
Bazar Dere, India		A2	368
Bazaruto, isl., Moz.		D7	421

Bazile Mills, Knox, Nebr.	45	B8	152
Bazine, Ness, Kans.	429	D4	144
Bazman Kuh, mtn., Iran		D5	379
Baztán, Sp.	1,534	A6	298
Beach (Dunes Park), Lake, Ill.	1,800	*A6	138
Beach, Golden Valley, N.Dak.	1,460	D1	154
Beach, Chesterfield, Va.	70	B9	192
Beach, pond, Conn.		C8	202
Beachburg, Ont., Can.	500	O24	64
Beach City, Stark, Ohio	1,151	B5	156
Beach Haven, Ocean, N.J.	1,041	D4	210
Beach Haven, inlet, N.J.		D4	210
Beach Haven Crest, Ocean, N.J.	60	D4	210
Beach Haven Terrace, Ocean, N.J.	100	D4	210
Beachport, Austl.	382	F8	432
Beach View, Ocean, N.J.		D4	210
Beachville, Ont., Can.	650	Q20	64
Beachville, St. Marys, Md.	350	D7	182
Beachwood, Ocean, N.J.	2,765	D4	210
Beachwood, Cuyahoga, Ohio	6,089	B1	156
Beachy, head, Eng.		J13	273
Beacon, Mahaska, Iowa	718	C5	142
Beacon, Dutchess, N.Y.	13,922	D8	212
Beacon, Decatur, Tenn.	300	C3	190
Beacon Falls, New Haven, Conn.	2,886	D3	202
Beacon Hill, Gulf, Fla.	100	B5	174
Beacon Hill, Cowlitz, Wash.	1,019	*C4	98
Beaconsfield, Que., Can.	5,496	S15	66
Beaconsfield, Ringgold, Iowa	71	D3	142
Beadle, Sask., Can.	50	E3	58
Beadle, co., S.Dak.	21,682	C7	158
Beadling, Allegheny, Pa.	1,500	*C1	214
Beagle, Jackson, Oreg.		E4	96
Beagle, chan., Arg.		H4	251
Beal, Knox, Ind.	75	D2	140
Bealanana, Malag.		B9	421
Beal City, Isabella, Mich.	150	F7	146
Beale, cape, B.C., Can.		F10	52
Beallsville, Monroe, Ohio	441	C5	156
Beals, Henderson, Ky.	100	C3	178
Beals, Washington, Maine	400 (640▴)	D5	204
Beaman, Grundy, Iowa	247	B5	142
Beamsville, Ont., Can.	2,198	Q21	64
Bean City, Palm Beach, Fla.	100	E10	174
Bean Station, Grainger, Tenn.	100	B8	190
Bear, New Castle, Del.	65	B3	172
Bear, Adams, Idaho	5	D2	108
Bear, cave, Mich.		H5	146
Bear, creek, Ala.		A2	168
Bear, creek, Colo., Kans.		E8	106
		E2	144
Bear, creek, Oreg.		E4	96
Bear, creek, Wyo.		E8	116
Bear, inlet, N.C.		C8	186
Bear, isl., Man., Can.		C3	60
Bear, isl., Ire.		J3	273
Bear, lake, Alta., Can.		C3	54
Bear, lake, B.C., Can.		B9	52
Bear, lake, Man., Can.		C5	60
Bear, lake, Idaho, Utah		G7	108
		A4	114
Bear, lake, Wis.		C2	160
Bear, mtn., Ark.		C6	170
Bear, mtn., Ky.		C6	178
Bear, mtn., Maine		D2	204
Bear, mtn., Oreg.		D4	96
Bear, mtn., Vt.		E2	218
Bear, mtn., Wyo.		E6	116
Bear, riv., Utah		B4	114
Bear, swamp, Mass.		E3	206
Bear Cave, mtn., Mo.		E5	150
Bear Creek, Marion, Ala.	243	A2	168
Bearcreek, Carbon, Mont.	61	E7	110
Bear Creek, Outagamie, Wis.	455	D5	160
Bearden, Ouachita, Ark.	1,268	D4	170
Bearden, Okfuskee, Okla.	150	C7	128
Bearden, Knox, Tenn.	3,600	E9	190
Beards Fork, Fayette, W.Va.	800	D7	194
Beardsley, Maricopa, Ariz.	12	E3	124
Beardsley, Rawlins, Kans.	50	C2	144
Beardsley, Big Stone, Minn.	410	F2	148
Beardstown, Cass, Ill.	6,294	C3	138
Beardstown, Perry, Tenn.	50	C4	190
Bearfort, mtn., N.J.		A4	210
Bear Head, Walton, Fla.	50	A4	174
Bear Lake, Manistee, Mich.	323	E5	146
Bear Lake, co., Idaho	7,148	G7	108
Bear Lodge, mts., Wyo.		B8	116
Bearmouth, Granite, Mont.	10	D3	110
Béarn, former prov., Fr.	275,000	F3	278
Bearpaw, Blaine, Mont.		B7	110
Bear Paw, mtn., Mont.		B7	110
Bear Pond, mts., Md.		A4	182
Bear River, N.S., Can.	1,150	E4	70
Bear River, divide, Wyo.		E2	116
Bear River City, Box Elder, Utah	447	B3	114
Bear Spring, Stewart, Tenn.	50	B4	190
Beartooth, pass, Wyo.		B3	116
Beartooth, range, Mont., Wyo.		E7	110
		A3	116
Bear Town, Pike, Miss.	1,865	*D2	184
Beas, riv., India		C1	368
Beas de Segura, Sp.	9,251	C5	298
Beata, cape, Dom. Rep.		D9	233
Beaties, butte, Oreg.		E7	96
Beaton, B.C., Can.	100	E14	52
Beatrice, Monroe, Ala.	506	D2	168
Beatrice, Gage, Nebr.	12,132	D9	152
Beattie, Marshall, Kans.	314	C7	144
Beatton, riv., B.C., Can.		B12	52
Beatty, Sask., Can.	141	D5	58
Beatty, Carroll, Miss.	50	B3	184
Beatty, Nye, Nev.	450	G5	112
Beatty, Klamath, Oreg.	200	E5	96
Beatty Knob, hill, Ohio		C5	156
Beattyville, Lee, Ky.	1,048	C7	178
Beatyestown, Warren, N.J.	100	B3	210
Beau, lake, Maine		A3	204
Beaucaire, Fr.	7,983	F6	278
Beauce, co., Que., Can.	59,957	R14	66
Beauceville Est, Que., Can.	1,740	R14	66
Beauceville Ouest, Que., Can.	1,459	*R14	66
Beaucourt, Fr.		D7	278
Beaudry, Garland, Ark.		C4	170
Beaufort, Franklin, Mo.	100	C6	150

Beaufort, N.Bor.	2,000	C5	358
Beaufort, Carteret, N.C.	2,922	C9	186
Beaufort, Beaufort, S.C.	6,298	G7	188
Beaufort, co., N.C.	36,014	B8	186
Beaufort, co., S.C.	44,187	G7	188
Beaufort, sea, N.A.		C4	48
Beaufort West, U.S. Afr.	11,809	F4	420
Beaugency, Fr.		D4	278
Beauharnois, Que., Can.	6,774	S11	66
		S15	
Beauharnois, co., Que., Can.	42,691	S10	66
		S15	
Beauly, firth, Scot.		D8	272
Beauly, riv., Scot.		D8	272
Beaumaris, bay, Wales		H8	273
Beaumont, Bel.	1,744	D3	282
Beaumont, Riverside, Calif.	4,288	*F5	94
Beaumont, Newf., Can.	350	F8	72
Beaumont, Que., Can.	500	R13	66
Beaumont, Butler, Kans.	150	E7	144
Beaumont, Perry, Miss.	926	D4	184
Beaumont, Jefferson, Tex.	119,175 (*266,600)	D8	130
Beaune, Fr.	13,175	D6	278
Beauport, Que., Can.	6,735	R16	66
Beauport Est, Que., Can.	1,417	*R16	66
Beaupré, Que., Can.	2,381	Q14	66
Beauraing, Bel.	2,343	D3	282
Beauregard, Copiah, Miss.	193	D2	184
Beauregard, par., La.	19,191	D2	180
Beaurepaire, Que., Can.	2,000	S15	66
Beaurivage, Que., Can.	405	R13	66
Beauséjour, Man., Can.	1,523	E4	60
Beauty, Martin, Ky.	300	C8	178
Beauvais, Fr.	26,756	C5	278
Beauvallon, Alta., Can.	200	D7	54
Beauvoir, Harrison, Miss.	50	E1	184
Beaux Arts, King, Wash.	351	*D3	98
Beaver, Alsk.	101	B7	84
Beaver, Carroll, Ark.	24	A3	170
Beaver, Boone, Iowa	115	B3	142
Beaver, Barton, Kans.	125	D5	144
Beaver, Pike, Ohio	341	C4	156
Beaver, Beaver, Okla.	2,087	B3	128
Beaver, Tillamook, Oreg.	200	B3	96
Beaver, Beaver, Pa.	6,160	C1	214
Beaver, Beaver, Utah	1,548	E3	114
Beaver (Glen Hedrick), Raleigh, W.Va.	1,230	D3	194
		D7	
Beaver, Marinette, Wis.	75	C5	160
Beaver, co., Okla.	6,965	B3	128
Beaver, co., Pa.	206,948	C1	214
Beaver, co., Utah	4,331	E2	114
Beaver, brook, N.H.		F4	208
Beaver, creek, Iowa		A7	142
Beaver, creek, Kans.		C2	144
Beaver, creek, Kans.		C5	144
Beaver, creek, Ky.		C8	178
Beaver, creek, Md.		A4	182
Beaver, creek, Mo.		E5	150
Beaver, creek, Mont.		B9	110
Beaver, creek, Mont., N.Dak.		C12	110
		D6	154
Beaver, creek, Okla.		D5	128
Beaver, creek, Sask., Can.		E4	58
Beaver, creek, Wyo.		C8	116
Beaver, creek, Wyo.		D4	116
Beaver, isl., Mich.		D6	146
Beaver, lake, Nebr.		C3	152
Beaver, lake, Wis.		E5	160
Beaver, riv., N.Y.		B6	212
Beaver, riv., Sask., Can.		C4	58
Beaver, riv., Utah		E2	114
Beaver Bank, N.S., Can.	265	E6	70
Beaver Bay, Lake, Minn.	287	D7	148
Beaver City, Furnas, Nebr.	818	D6	152
Beaver Creek, Washington, Md.	150	A4	182
Beaver Creek, Rock, Minn.	250	H2	148
Beavercreek, Clackamas, Oreg.	100	B2	96
Beaver Crossing, Seward, Nebr.	439	D8	152
Beaverdale, Cambria, Pa.	1,000	C3	214
Beaver Dam, Kosciusko, Ind.	100	A3	140
Beaver Dam, Ohio, Ky.	1,648	C4	178
Beaverdam, Allen, Ohio	514	B3	156
Beaverdam, Hanover, Va.	50	C7	192
Beaver Dam, Dodge, Wis.	13,118	E5	160
Beaverdell, B.C., Can.	75	F13	52
Beaver Falls, Lewis, N.Y.	640	B6	212
Beaver Falls, Beaver, Pa.	16,240	C1	214
Beaverhead, co., Mont.	7,194	E3	110
Beaverhead, mts., Mont.		E3	110
Beaverhead, riv., Mont.		E4	110
Beaverhill, Overton, Tenn.		B6	190
Beaverhill, lake, Alta., Can.		D6	54
Beaverhill, lake, Man., Can.		C5	60
Beaverlick, Boone, Ky.	175	A8	178
		B6	
Beaverlodge, Alta., Can.	768	C3	54
Beaver Meadows, Carbon, Pa.	1,392	C6	214
Beavermouth, B.C., Can.		E14	52
Beavertail, pt., R.I.		D3	216
Beaverton, Ont., Can.	1,099	P21	64
Beaverton, Lamar, Ala.	162	B1	168
Beaverton, Gladwin, Mich.	926	F7	146
Beaverton, Valley, Mont.		B9	110
Beaverton, Washington, Oreg.	5,937	B1	96
		B4	
Beaverville, Iroquois, Ill.	430	C6	138
Beawar, India	51,054	D1	368
Beazley, Arg.		B2	252
Bebedouro, Braz.	11,360	E1	258
Bécancour, Que., Can.	320	R12	66
Bécancour, riv., Que., Can.		R12	66
Beccles, Eng.	7,100	I14	273
Bečej, Yugo.	23,322	B5	316
Becerreá, Sp.	749	A3	298
Becharof, lake, Alsk.		D6	84
Bechuanaland, Br. poss., Afr.	337,000	I9	388
			421
Beckemeyer, Clinton, Ill.	1,056	E4	138
Becker, Sherburne, Minn.	279	F5	148
Becker, Monroe, Miss.	141	B4	184
Becker, co., Minn.	23,959	E3	148
Becket, Berkshire, Mass.	350 (770▴)	B1	206
Beckett, Stephens, Okla.	125	D6	128
Beckham, Appomattox, Va.		C6	192

Beckham

Beckham, co., Okla. 17,782 C4 128
Beckley, Raleigh, W.Va. 18,642 D3 194
D7
Beckleys, Hartford, Conn. 150 C5 202
Beckville, Panola, Tex. 632 C8 130
Beckwith, Fayette, W.Va. 500 D7 194
Beckwith, creek, La. D2 180
Bédarieux, Fr. 7,416 F5 278
Beddington, Washington, Maine (14▲) D4 204
Bede, Man., Can. F2 60
Bedford, N.S., Can. 910 E6 70
Bedford, Que., Can. 2,272 S12 66
Bedford, Eng. 56,500 I12 273
Bedford, Lawrence, Ind. 13,024 D3 140
Bedford, Taylor, Iowa 1,807 D3 142
Bedford, Trimble, Ky. 717 B5 178
Bedford, Middlesex, Mass. 10,969 B5 206
C2
Bedford, Calhoun, Mich. 150 G6 146
Bedford, Hillsboro, N.H. 175 F3 208
(3,636▲)
Bedford, Westchester, N.Y. 893 D8 212
Bedford, Cuyahoga, Ohio 15,223 A5 156
B1
Bedford, Bedford, Pa. 3,696 C3 214
Bedford, Tarrant, Tex. 2,706 *C7 130
Bedford, Bedford, Va. 5,921 C5 192
Bedford, Lincoln, Wyo. 75 D2 116
Bedford, co., Eng. 329,900 I12 273
Bedford, co., Pa. 42,451 D3 214
Bedford, co., Tenn. 23,150 C5 190
Bedford, co., Va. 31,028 C5 192
Bedford Heights, Cuyahoga, Ohio 5,275 A5 156
B1
Bedford Hills, Westchester, N.Y. 3,000 D8 212
Bedford Park, Cook, Ill. 737 *F2 138
Bedford Springs, Middlesex, Mass. C2 206
Bédja, Tun. 34,645 A5 402
Bedminster, Somerset, N.J. 300 B3 210
Bee, Seward, Nebr. 149 C8 152
Bee, co., Tex. 23,755 E7 130
Beebe, White, Ark. 1,697 B5 170
Beebe, Que., Can. 1,363 S12 66
Beebe Plain, Orleans, Vt. 140 A4 218
Beebe River, Grafton, N.H. 250 D3 208
Bee Branch, Van Buren, Ark. 63 B4 170
Beech, fork, Ky. C5 178
Beech Bluff, Madison, Tenn. 150 C3 190
Beechbottom, Brooke, W.Va. 506 A4 194
B2
Beech Creek, Muhlenberg, Ky. 788 C3 178
Beecher, Will, Ill. 1,367 B6 138
Beecher City, Effingham, Ill. 452 D5 138
Beecher Falls, Essex, Vt. 350 A5 218
Beechey, head, B.C., Can. C14 52
Beech Fork, Campbell, Tenn. B7 190
Beech Grove, Greene, Ark. 60 A6 170
Beech Grove, Marion, Ind. 10,973 C3 140
D5
Beech Grove, McLean, Ky. 159 C3 178
Beechgrove, Coffee, Tenn. 150 C5 190
Beech Island, Aiken, S.C. 900 E5 188
Beechwood, N.B., Can. C2 70
Beechwood, Norfolk, Mass. 505 D4 206
Beechwood, Ottawa, Mich. 2,323 *G5 146
Beechwood, Warren, Miss. 50 C2 184
Beechwood Village, Jefferson, Ky. 1,903 *B5 178
Beechy, Sask., Can. 358 E4 58
Beedeville, Jackson, Ark. 150 B5 170
Beek, Neth. 5,100 D4 282
Beeler, Ness, Kans. 100 D3 144
Beelick Knob, Fayette, W.Va. 250 *D4 194
Beemer, Cuming, Nebr. 667 C9 152
Beemerville, Sussex, N.J. 70 A3 210
Bee Ridge, Sarasota, Fla. 2,043 D8 174
Beersheba, Isr. 21,000 C5 382
Beersheba Springs, Grundy, Tenn. 577 C6 190
Beersville, N.B., Can. 90 C4 70
Beeskow, Ger. 7,571 B5 286
Beesleys Point, Cape May, N.J. 200 E3 210
Beeson, Mercer, W.Va. 300 D3 194
Beethurst, Bent, Colo. 165 D7 106
Beeton, Ont., Can. 675 P21 64
Beeville, Bee, Tex. 13,811 E7 130
Befale, Con.L. B3 414
Bega, Austl. 3,518 F9 432
Bega, canal, Rom. B1 321
Bega, canal, Yugo. B5 316
Beggs, Okmulgee, Okla. 1,114 C7 128
Begicheva, isl., Sov.Un. B13 329
Bègles, Fr. 23,176 E3 278
Begna, riv., Nor. F3 291
Behbehān, Iran 22,610 C3 379
Behm, canal, Alsk. K15 84
Beilul, Eth. C5 398
Beira, Moz. 25,000 C6 421
Beira, reg., Port. 2,048,956 B2 298
Beira Alta, prov., Port. 703,231 *B3 298
Beira Baixa, prov., Port. 361,191 *C3 298
Beira Litoral, prov., Port. 985,135 *B2 298
Beirne, Clark, Ark. 300 D3 170
Beirut (Beyrouth), Leb. 233,000 C1 378
Beiseker, Alta., Can. 321 E6 54
Beitbridge, Rh.&Nya. 395 D6 421
Beit Guvrin, Isr. 1,000 C5 382
Beit-Shan, Isr. 2,875 B6 382
Beiuş, Rom. 6,467 A2 321
Beja, Port. 14,058 C3 298
Béjar, Sp. 12,518 B4 298
Bejestan, Iran B5 379
Bejou, Mahnomen, Minn. 164 D3 148
Bejuco, Pan. 780 F8 228
Bekdash, Sov.Un. D4 336
Békés, Hung. 17,044 C6 320
Békés, co., Hung. 470,000 *C5 320
Békéscsaba, Hung. 40,000 C6 320
(50,000▲)
Bekily, Malag. D9 421
Bela, India 15,026 D3 368
Bela, Pak. 3,063 F5 375
Belacázar, Sp. 9,471 C4 298
Bela Crkva, Yugo. 9,803 B5 316
Belaga, Sar. 258 D4 358
Bel Air, Harford, Md. 4,300 A7 182
Bel Alton, Charles, Md. 175 D6 182
Beland, Muskogee, Okla. 65 C8 128
Belanger, riv., Man., Can. D4 60
Belanger, riv., Sask., Can. B4 58
Bela Vista, Braz. 6,090 D1 258
Bela Vista, Moz. E6 421
Belawan, Indon. D1 358
Belaya, riv., Sov.Un. A4 336
Belaya Tserkov, Sov.Un. 71,000 H8 332
Belcamp, Harford, Md. 225 B7 182
Belcher, White, Ark. B5 170
Belcher, Pike, Ky. 591 C8 178
Belcher, Caddo, La. 400 B2 180
Belcher, is., N.W.Ter., Can. F10 48
Belchertown, Hampshire, Mass. 900 B3 206
(5,186▲)
Belchirāg, Afg. 5,000 B3 374
Belcourt, Rolette, N.Dak. 200 B6 154
Belden, Lee, Miss. 250 A4 184
Belden, Cedar, Nebr. 157 B8 152
Belding, Ionia, Mich. 4,887 F6 146
Beldoc, Allendale, S.C. E6 188
Belém, Braz. 225,218 F7 256
Belén, Arg. 4,342 A2 252
Belén, Par. C4 247
Belen, Valencia, N.Mex. 5,031 D4 126
Belet Uen, Som. 7,800 E6 398
Belev, Sov.Un. 32,500 F11 332
Belfair, Mason, Wash. 400 B4 98
Belfast, Grant, Ark. 60 *C4 170
Belfast, Waldo, Maine 6,140 D3 204
Belfast, Allegany, N.Y. 788 C3 212
Belfast, N.Ire. 450,800 G7 273
Belfast, Marshall, Tenn. 200 C5 190
Belfield, Stark, N.Dak. 1,064 D2 154
Bëlfodiyo, Eth. C3 398
Belford, Eng. F11 272
Belford, Monmouth, N.J. 3,500 C4 210
Belforest, Baldwin, Ala. 300 *E2 168
Belfort, Fr. 43,434 D7 278
Belfort, dept., Fr. 99,427 *D7 278
Belfry, Pike, Ky. 950 C8 178
Belfry, Carbon, Mont. 250 E7 110
Belgard, see Białogard, Pol.
Belgaum, India 85,988 E2 366
(*102,705)
Belgium, Vermilion, Ill. 494 C6 138
Belgium, Ozaukee, Wis. 643 E6 160
Belgium, country, Eur. 9,053,000 C5 266
282
Belgorod, Sov.Un. 71,000 G11 332
Belgorod-Dnestrovskiy, Sov.Un. 38,600 I8 332
Belgrade, Kennebec, Maine 250 *D3 204
(1,102▲)
Belgrade, Stearns, Minn. 666 F4 148
Belgrade, Washington, Mo. 187 D6 150
Belgrade, Gallatin, Mont. 1,057 E5 110
Belgrade, Nance, Nebr. 224 C7 152
Belgrade (Beograd), Yugo. 470,172 B5 316
Belgrade Lakes, Kennebec, Maine 300 D3 204
Belgreen, Franklin, Ala. 350 A2 168
Belhaven, Beaufort, N.C. 2,386 B9 186
Beli Lom, riv., Bul. B3 317
Belington, Barbour, W.Va. 1,528 B5 194
Belingwe, Rh. & Nya. 1,100 D5 420
Belitung, isl., Indon. E3 358
Belize, Br. Hond. 21,886 B3 228
Belize, riv., Br. Hond. B3 228
Belknap, co., N.H. 28,912 D4 208
Belknap, crater, Oreg. C5 96
Belknap, mts., N.H. D4 208
Belkofski (Balkofski), Alsk. 119 D5 84
Bell, Los Angeles, Calif. 19,450 C5 94
Bell, Gilchrist, Fla. 134 B8 174
Bell, Spokane, Wash. D9 98
Bell, co., Ky. 35,336 D7 178
Bell, co., Tex. 94,097 D7 130
Bell, isl., Newf., Can. G9 72
Bella Bella, B.C., Can. D8 52
Bella Coola, B.C., Can. 50 D9 52
Bella Coola, riv., B.C., Can. D9 52
Bellahy, Ire. 741 H4 273
Bellaire, Smith, Kans. 50 C5 144
Bellaire, Antrim, Mich. 689 E6 146
Bellaire, Belmont, Ohio 11,502 B6 156
Bellaire, Harris, Tex. 19,872 F8 130
Bellamy, Sumter, Ala. 615 C1 168
Bellarthur, Pitt, N.C. 204 *B8 186
Bellary, India 70,322 E3 366
Bella Unión, Ur. 5,000 B4 252
Bella Vista, Arg. 7,922 A4 252
Bella Vista, Arg. 8,352 A2 252
Bella Vista, Par. C4 247
Bellbrook, Greene, Ohio 941 C2 156
Bell Buckle, Bedford, Tenn. 318 C5 190
Bellburn, Greenbrier, W.Va. 250 C4 194
Bell Center, Crawford, Wis. 155 *E3 160
Bell City, Calcasieu, La. 250 D3 180
Bell City, Stoddard, Mo. 409 D8 150
Belle, Maries, Mo. 1,016 C6 150
Belle, Kanawha, W.Va. 5,000 C3 194
C6
Belle, bay, Newf., Can. G8 72
Belle, isl., Newf., Can. E8 72
Belle, isl., Fr. D2 278
Belle, riv., La. C5 180
Belleair, Pinellas, Fla. 2,456 C5 174
Belleair Beach, Pinellas, Fla. 563 *D8 174
Belle Alliance, Assumption, La. 100 B5 180
Belle Center, Logan, Ohio 949 B3 156
Belle Chasse, Plaquemines, La. 700 C7 180
E6
Bellechasse, co., Que., Can. 26,203 R14 66
Bellechester, Goodhue, Minn. 184 G6 148
Belleek, N.Ire. 162 G4 273
Belle Ellen, Bibb, Ala. 200 B2 168
Bellefleur, N.B., Can. B2 70
Bellefont, Ford, Kans. 25 E4 144
Bellefontaine, Logan, Ohio 11,424 B3 156
Bellefontaine Neighbors, St. Louis, Mo. 13,650 A8 150
Bellefonte, Boone, Ark. 100 A3 170
Bellefonte, New Castle, Del. 1,536 A4 172
Bellefonte, Boyd, Ky. 337 *B8 178
Bellefonte, Centre, Pa. 6,088 C4 214
Belle Fourche, Butte, S. Dak. 4,087 C2 158
Belle Fourche, res., S. Dak. C2 158
Belle Fourche, riv., S.Dak., Wyo. C2 158
C7 116
Bellegarde [-sur-Valserine], Fr. 5,743 D6 278
Belle Glade, Palm Beach, Fla. 11,273 E10 174
Belle Haven, Accomack, Va. 371 C9 192
Belle Isle, Orange, Fla. 2,344 *C9 174
Belle Isle, strait, Newf., Can. E7 72
Belleisle Creek, N.B., Can. 120 D4 70
Bellemead, Prince Georges, Md. 1,400 *C6 182
Belle Mead, Somerset, N.J. 150 C3 210
Bellemeade, Jefferson, Ky. 438 *B5 178
Belle Meade, Davidson, Tenn. 3,082 B5 190
E7
Belle Mina, Limestone, Ala. 250 *A3 168
Bellemont, Coconino, Ariz. 25 C4 124
Belleoram, Newf., Can. 570 G8 72
Belleplain, Cape May, N.J. 400 E3 210
Belle-Plaine, Sask., Can. 81 E5 58
Belle Plaine, Benton, Iowa 2,923 C5 142
Belle Plaine, Sumner, Kans. 1,579 E6 144
Belle Plaine, Scott, Minn. 1,931 G5 148
Bellepoint, Summers, W.Va. 900 D4 194
Bellerive, Que., Can. 1,000 S15 66
Bellerive, St. Louis, Mo. 314 *C7 150
Belle River, Ont., Can. 1,814 R18 64
Bellerose, Assumption, La. 300 B5 180
D4
Bellerose, Nassau, N.Y. 1,083 *E8 212
Belle Valley, Noble, Ohio 438 C5 156
Belle Vernon, Washington, Pa. 1,784 C2 214
Belleview, Marion, Fla. 864 B8 174
Belleview, Iron, Mo. 300 D7 150
Belleview, Davidson, Tenn. 100 B5 190
E7
Belle View, Fairfax, Va. 3,500 *B7 192
Belleville, Conecuh, Ala. 273 D2 168
Belleville, Yell, Ark. 273 B3 170
Belleville, N.S., Can. 100 F4 70
Belleville, Ont., Can. 20,605 P23 64
Belleville, St. Clair, Ill. 37,264 E4 138
Belleville, Hendricks, Ind. 350 C3 140
Belleville, Republic, Kans. 2,940 C6 144
Belleville, Wayne, Mich. 1,921 *G8 146
Belleville, Essex, N.J. 35,005 B1 210
B4
Belleville, Mifflin, Pa. 1,539 C4 214
Belleville, Washington, R.I. C3 216
Belleville, Wood, W.Va. B3 194
Belleville, Dane, Wis. 844 F4 160
Belleville North, Wayne, Mich. 1,128 *G8 146
Bellevue, Alta., Can. 850 F5 54
Bellevue, New Castle, Del. A4 172
Bellevue, Blaine, Idaho 384 F4 108
Bellevue, Peoria, Ill. 1,561 *C4 138
Bellevue, Jackson, Iowa 2,181 B7 142
Bellevue, Campbell, Ky. 9,336 A8 178
Bellevue, Talbot, Md. 267 C7 182
Bellevue, Eaton, Mich. 1,277 G6 146
Bellevue, Sarpy, Nebr. 8,831 C9 152
E3
Bellevue, Huron, Ohio 8,286 A4 156
Bellevue, Allegheny, Pa. 11,412 A3 214
C1
Bellevue, King, Wash. 12,809 D3 98
Bellewood, Jefferson, Ky. 426 *B5 178
Belley, Fr. 4,609 E6 278
Bellflower, Los Angeles, Calif. 44,846 C5 94
Bellflower, McLean, Ill. 389 C5 138
Bellflower, Montgomery, Mo. 245 B6 150
Bellfountain, Benton, Oreg. 110 *C3 96
Bell Gardens, Los Angeles, Calif. 26,467 C5 94
Bellglade Camp, Palm Beach, Fla. 1,658 *E10 174
Bellingham, Eng. 1,242 F10 272
Bellingham, Norfolk, Mass. 700 B5 206
(6,774▲)
Bellingham, Lac qui Parle, Minn. 327 F2 148
Bellingham, Whatcom, Wash. 34,688 A4 98
Bellinzona, Switz. 12,600 B5 312
Bell Irving, riv., B.C., Can. B8 52
Bellis, Alta., Can. 135 C6 54
Bell Island, see Wabana, Newf., Can.
Bellivela, Lib. E3 408
Bellmawr, Camden, N.J. 11,853 D2 210
Bellmead, McLennan, Tex. 5,127 *D7 130
Bellmont, Wabash, Ill. 320 E6 138
Bellmore, Parke, Ind. 75 C2 140
Bellmore, Nassau, N.Y. 12,784 E3 212
Bello, Col. 28,398 B1 244
Bellows Falls, Windham, Vt. 3,831 E4 218
Belloy, Alta., Can. 75 C3 54
Bellport, Suffolk, N.Y. 2,461 D4 212
Bells, Crockett, Tenn. 1,232 C2 190
Bells, Grayson, Tex. 707 C7 130
Bells, creek, W.Va. C6 194
Bellsburg, Dickson, Tenn. 75 B4 190
Bells Corners, Ont., Can. 175 Q25 64
Bellton, Hall and Banks, Ga. B3 176
Belltower, Carter, Mont. E12 110
Belltown, Sussex, Del. 300 F5 172
Belltown, Polk, Tenn. 50 C7 190
Belluno, It. 12,800 B4 302
Belluno, prov., It. 242,100 *B4 302
Bellview, Curry, N.Mex. 50 D7 126
Bell Ville, Arg. 15,796 B3 252
Bellville, Evans, Ga. 300 D5 176
Bellville, Richland, Ohio 1,621 B4 156
Bellville, Austin, Tex. 2,218 E7 130
Bellvue, Larimer, Colo. 150 B5 106
Bellwood, Geneva, Ala. 263 D4 168
Bellwood, Cook, Ill. 20,729 F2 138
Bellwood, Butler, Nebr. 361 C8 152
Bellwood, Blair, Pa. 2,330 C3 214
Bellwood, Fayette, W.Va. 300 *D4 194
Belly, riv., Alta., Can. F6 54
Belmar, Monmouth, N.J. 5,190 C4 210
Bélmez, Sp. 8,068 C4 298
Belmond, Wright, Iowa 2,506 B4 142
Belmont, San Mateo, Calif. 15,996 B5 94
Belmont, Man., Can. 325 F3 60
Belmont, Ont., Can. 495 R19 64
Belmont, Pinellas, Fla. 2,000 *D8 174
Belmont, Kingman, Kans. 200 E6 144
Belmont, Sabine, La. 50 C2 180
Belmont, Waldo, Maine 80 *D3 204
(295▲)
Belmont, Middlesex, Mass. 28,715 C2 206
Belmont, Tishomingo, Miss. 901 A4 184
Belmont, Golden Valley, Mont. 30 D7 110
Belmont, Dawes, Nebr. B2 152
Belmont, Belknap, N.H. 600 E4 208
(1,953▲)
Belmont, Allegany, N.Y. 1,146 C3 212
Belmont, N.Z. 536 J11 437
Belmont, Gaston, N.C. 5,007 B4 186
Belmont, Belmont, Ohio 563 B5 156
Belmont, Rutland, Vt. 65 E3 218
Belmont, Whitman, Wash. 50 B9 98
Belmont, Pleasants, W.Va. 454 B3 194
Belmont, Lafayette, Wis. 616 F3 160
Belmont, co., Ohio 83,864 C5 156
Belmonte, Braz. 5,204 D3 258
Belmont Hills, see W.Manayunk, Pa.
Bel-Nor, St. Louis, Mo. 2,388 *C7 150
Belo, Malag. 3,278 C8 421
Beloeil [Village], Que., Can. 3,966 S11 66
Belo Horizonte, Braz. 507,852 D2 258
Beloit, Dallas, Ala. 500 C2 168
Beloit, Mitchell, Kans. 3,837 C5 144
Beloit, Mahoning, Ohio 877 B6 156
Beloit, Rock, Wis. 32,846 F4 160
Beloit West, Rock, Wis. 2,160 *F4 160
Belomorsk, Sov.Un. 17,400 C5 328
Belopolye, Sov.Un. 39,300 G10 332
Beloretsk, Sov.Un. 59,000 B5 336
Beloye, lake, Sov.Un. B11 332
Belozersk, Sov.Un. 16,800 C11 332
Belpre, Edwards, Kans. 211 E4 144
Belpre, Washington, Ohio 5,418 C5 156
Bel-Ridge, St. Louis, Mo. 4,395 *C7 150
Belspring, Pulaski, Va. 400 C4 192
Belt, Cascade, Mont. 757 C6 110
Belt, creek, Mont. C6 110
Belted, range, Nev. F5 112
Belterra, Braz. 3,556 F6 256
Belton, Cass, Mo. 4,897 C3 150
Belton, Anderson, S.C. 5,106 B4 188
Belton, Bell, Tex. 8,163 D7 130
Belton, res., Tex. D7 130
Beltrami, Polk, Minn. 186 D2 148
Beltrami, co., Minn. 23,425 C3 148
Beltsville, Prince Georges, Md. 3,500 B6 182
Beltsy, Sov.Un. 67,000 I6 332
Belua, Solomon D1 436
Belukha, mtn., Sov.Un. C11 336
Beluran, N.Bor. 50 C5 358
Belva, Woodward, Okla. 35 B4 128
Belva, Nicholas, W.Va. 250 *C3 194
Belvedere, Marin, Calif. 2,148 A5 94
Belvedere, Aiken, S.C. 500 *E5 188
Belvedere, Fairfax, Va. 1,100 *B7 192
Belvedere Marittimo, It. 1,981 F5 302
Belvidere, New Castle, Del. 1,000 *B3 172
Belvidere, Boone, Ill. 11,223 A5 138
Belvidere, Kiowa, Kans. 125 E4 144
Belvidere, Jackson, Mo. 350 C3 150
E2
Belvidere, Thayer, Nebr. 185 D8 152
Belvidere, Warren, N.J. 2,636 B2 210
Belvidere, Jackson, S.Dak. 232 D4 158
Belvidere, Franklin, Tenn. 125 C5 190
Belvidere, mtn., Vt. B3 218
Belvidere Center (Belvidere), Lamoille, Vt. 75 B3 218
(155▲)
Belview, Redwood, Minn. 400 G3 148
Belvue, Pottawatomie, Kans. 179 C7 144
Belwood, Ont., Can. 225 Q20 64
Belyando, riv., Austl. C9 432
Belyy, Sov.Un. 17,200 E9 332
Belyy, isl., Sov.Un. B9 328
Belzig, Ger. 7,597 B5 286
Belzoni, Humphreys, Miss. 4,142 B2 184
Belzoni, Pushmataha, Okla. D8 128
Bement, Piatt, Ill. 1,558 D5 138
Bemidji, Beltrami, Minn. 9,958 D4 148
Bemidji, lake, Minn. D4 148
Bemis, Madison, Tenn. 3,127 C3 190
Bemis, Randolph, W.Va. 60 C5 194
Bemiston, Talladega, Ala. B3 168
Bemus Point, Chautauqua, N.Y. 443 C2 212
Bena, Cass, Minn. 286 D4 148
Benabarre, Sp. 1,358 A7 298
Bena Dibele, Con.L. C3 414
Benadir, pol. dist., Som. 387,600 E5 398
Benalla, Austl. 6,045 F9 432
Benalto, Alta., Can. 115 D5 54
Benanee, Austl. E8 432
Benares, see Banaras, India
Benátky nad Jizerou, Czech. 4,266 *A2 324
Benavente, Sp. 7,884 A4 298
Benavides, Duval, Tex. 2,459 F6 130
Ben Avon, Indiana, Pa. 2,553 *C2 214
Ben Avon, Spartanburg, S.C. 600 *B5 188
Benbecula, isl., Scot. D5 272
Benbrook, Tarrant, Tex. 3,254 *C7 130
Benbrook, res., Tex. B8 130
Benbush, Tucker, W.Va. 107 B5 194
Ben Cat, Viet. E5 362
Benchland, Judith Basin, Mont. 85 *C6 110
Bend, B.C., Can. D12 52
Bend, Deschutes, Oreg. 11,936 C5 96
Bendale, Richland, S.C. 1,544 *C6 188
Bendale, Lewis, W.Va. B4 194
Ben Davis, Marion, Ind. 900 D4 140
Ben Davis, pt., N.J. E2 210
Bendeleben, mtn., Alsk. B5 84
Bendena, Doniphan, Kans. 90 *C8 144
Bender, Sask., Can. 25 E6 58
Bender Beila, Som. 1,900 D7 398
Bender Cassim (Bosaso), Som. 5,200 C6 398
Bendery, Sov.Un. 38,000 I7 332
Bendigo, Austl. 28,726 F8 432
(*36,918)
Benebairo, Scot. F8 272
Benedict, Wilson, Kans. 128 E8 144
Benedict, Charles, Md. 460 C6 182
Benedict, York, Nebr. 170 C8 152
Benedict, McLean, N.Dak. 129 C4 154
Benedict, Lee, Va. 30 D1 192
Benedicta, Aroostook, Maine 50 C4 204
(200▲)
Benenitra, Malag. D9 421
Benešov, Czech. 8,241 B2 324
Benevento, It. 36,800 E5 302
Benevento, prov., It. 334,400 *E5 302
Benevolence, Randolph, Ga. 123 E2 176
Benewah, co., Idaho 6,036 B2 108

Bengal, Latimer, Okla. 40 D8 128
Bengal, bay, Asia H10 340
Ben Gardane, Tun. 2,100 B6 402
Bengasi (Banghāzī), Libya 69,718 A4 394
Bengkalis, Indon. 3,291 D2 358
Bengkulu, Indon. 16,800 E2 358
Ben Goi, bay, Viet. D6 362
Bengough, Sask., Can. 573 F5 58
Bengtsfors, Swe. 3,327 C3 292
Benguela, Ang. 15,399 B2 420
Benguela, dist., Ang. 328,765 B2 420
Benha, Eg., U.A.R. 35,880 A3 395
Benham, Harlan, Ky. 1,874 D8 178
Ben Hill, co., Ga. 13,633 E3 176
Ben Hur, Newton, Ark. 30 B4 170
Beni, Con.L. B4 414
Beni, Nig. D7 409
Beni, dept., Bol. B1 246
Beni, riv., Bol. B1 246
Béni Abbès, Alg. 1,427 B3 402
(12,418▲)
Benicarló, Sp. 9,491 B7 298
Benicia, Solano, Calif. 6,070 *C2 94
Benicito, riv., Bol. B1 246
Benin, Nig. 53,753 E6 408
Benin, bight, Afr. E5 408
Béni Ounif, Alg. 877 B3 402
Benisa, Sp. 3,479 C7 298
Beni Saf, Alg. 10,934 A3 402
(21,098▲)
Beni Suef, Eg., U.A.R. 57,106 B3 395
Benito, Man., Can. 487 E2 60
Benjamin, Utah, Utah 100 C4 114
Benjamin Constant, Braz. 1,540 F2 256
Benkelman, Dundy, Nebr. 1,400 D4 152
Benkovac, Yugo. 1,367 B2 316
Benld, Macoupin, Ill. 1,848 D4 138
Ben Lomond, Sevier, Ark. 157 D2 170
Ben Lomond, Santa Cruz, Calif. 1,814 *D2 94
Benmore, head, N.Ire. F6 272
Bennane, head, Scot. F7 272
Benndale, George, Miss. 450 E4 184
Bennet, Lancaster, Nebr. 381 D9 152
E2
Bennett, Adams, Colo. 287 C6 106
Bennett, Cedar, Iowa 374 C7 142
Bennett, Lea, N.Mex. 150 F7 126
Bennett, Chatham, N.C. 222 B6 186
Bennett, Douglas, Wis. 50 B2 160
Bennett, co., S.Dak. 3,053 D4 158
Bennett, creek, Md. B5 182
Bennett, isl., Sov.Un. B16 329
Bennett, lake, Man., Can. D4 60
Bennette, butte, Oreg. E2 96
Bennetts, Miami, Ind. 130 B3 140
Bennettsbridge, Ire. 280 I5 273
Bennetts Point, Colleton, S.C. 130 F8 188
Bennettsville, Marlboro, S.C. 6,963 B9 188
Bennettsville Southwest, Marlboro, S.C. 1,022 *B9 188
Benning Hills, Muscogee, Ga. 500 D2 176
Benning Park, Muscogee, Ga. 1,100 D2 176
Bennington, Bear Lake, Idaho 100 G7 108
Bennington, Ottawa, Kans. 535 C6 144
Bennington, Douglas, Nebr. 341 D3 152
Bennington, Hillsboro, N.H. 400 E3 208
(591▲)
Bennington, Bryan, Okla. 226 D7 128
Bennington, Bennington, Vt. 8,023 F2 218
(13,002▲)
Bennington, co., Vt. 25,088 E2 218
Bennion, Salt Lake, Utah 200 *C4 114
Benns Church, Isle of Wight, Va. A8 192
Benoit, Bolivar, Miss. 453 B1 184
Benoit, Bayfield, Wis. 30 B2 160
Benoud, Alg. B4 402
Bénoue, riv., Cam. E7 409
Benque Viejo, Br. Hond. 1,264 B3 228
Bensané, Guinea D2 408
Bensenville, Du Page, Ill. 9,141 B6 138
E2
Bensheim, Ger. 23,400 D3 286
Benson, Cochise, Ariz. 2,494 G5 124
Benson, Sask., Can. 164 F6 58
Benson, Woodford, Ill. 427 C4 138
Benson, De Soto, La. 100 C2 180
Benson, Harford, Md. 195 A7 182
Benson, Swift, Minn. 3,678 F3 148
Benson, Johnston, N.C. 2,355 B7 186
Benson, Rutland, Vt. 60 D2 218
(549▲)
Benson, co., N.Dak. 9,435 B6 154
Benson Gardens, Douglas, Nebr. 800 *C9 152
Bent, co., Colo. 7,419 E7 106
Bentiu, Sud. D2 398
Bentley, Alta., Can. 536 D5 54
Bentley, Sedgwick, Kans. 204 E6 144
Bentley, Grant, La. 200 C3 180
Bentley, Bay, Mich. 100 F7 146
Bentley, Hettinger, N.Dak. 70 D3 154
Bentley, Atoka, Okla. 100 D7 128
Bentley Springs, Baltimore, Md. 120 A6 182
Bentleyville, Cuyahoga, Ohio 301 *A4 156
Bentleyville, Washington, Pa. 3,160 C1 214
Bent Oak, Lowndes, Miss. B4 184
Benton, Lowndes, Ala. 300 C3 168
Benton, Saline, Ark. 10,399 C4 170
D6
Benton, Mono, Calif. 100 D4 94
Benton, N.B., Can. 115 C2 70
Benton, Otero, Colo. 10 *E7 106
Benton, Franklin, Ill. 7,023 E5 138
Benton, Elkhart, Ind. 250 A4 140
Benton, Ringgold, Iowa 84 D3 142
Benton, Butler, Kans. 452 A6 144
E6
Benton, Marshall, Ky. 3,074 D2 178
Benton, Bossier, La. 1,336 B2 180
Benton, Kennebec, Maine 100 D3 204
(1,521▲)
Benton, Yazoo, Miss. 250 C2 184
Benton, Scott, Mo. 554 D8 150
Benton, Grafton, N.H. 35 C3 208
(172▲)
Benton, Columbia, Pa. 981 B5 214
Benton, Polk, Tenn. 638 C7 190
Benton, Milwaukee, Wis. 837 F3 160
Benton, co., Ark. 36,272 A2 170
Benton, co., Ind. 11,912 B2 140
Benton, co., Iowa 23,422 B5 142
Benton, co., Minn. 17,287 F4 148
Benton, co., Miss. 7,723 A3 184
Benton, co., Mo. 8,737 C4 150
Benton, co., Oreg. 39,165 C3 96
Benton, co., Tenn. 10,662 B3 190
Benton, co., Wash. 62,070 C7 98
Benton City, Audrain, Mo. 155 B6 150
Benton City, Benton, Wash. 1,210 C7 98
Benton Harbor, Berrien, Mich. 19,136 G5 146
Benton Heights, Berrien, Mich. 6,112 *G5 146
Bentonia, Yazoo, Miss. 511 C2 184
Benton Ridge, Hancock, Ohio 325 A3 156
Benton Station, Alta., Can. 100 E7 54
Benton Station, Kennebec, Maine 600 *D3 204
Bentonville, Benton, Ark. 3,649 A2 170
Bentonville, Adams, Ohio 300 D3 156
Bentonville, Warren, Va. 350 B6 192
Bentree, Nicholas, W.Va. 350 C7 194
Benue, riv., Nig. E6 409
Benwee, head, Ire. G3 273
Benwood, Marshall, W.Va. 2,850 A4 194
B2
Benzie, co., Mich. 7,834 E5 146
Benzien, Garfield, Mont. C9 110
Benzonia, Benzie, Mich. 407 E5 146
Beo, Indon. D7 358
Beograd, see Belgrade, Yugo.
Béoumi, I.C. E3 408
Beowawe, Eureka, Nev. 60 C5 112
Beppu, Jap. 102,330 H3 354
Berat, Alb. 14,374 A2 306
Berat, pref., Alb. 176,000 *D4 316
Berber, Sud. 10,977 B3 398
Berbera, Som. 20,000 C6 398
Berbera, pol. dist., Som. *C6 398
Berbérati, Cen. Afr. Rep. F8 409
Bercail, Wheatland, Mont. D7 110
Berchogur, Sov.Un. C5 336
Berchtesgaden, Ger. 5,100 E5 286
Berck, Fr. 14,285 B4 278
Berdell Hills, St. Louis, Mo. 533 *C7 150
Berdichev, Sov.Un. 53,000 H7 332
Berea, Madison, Ky. 4,302 C6 178
Berea, Box Butte, Nebr. 23 B3 152
Berea, Cuyahoga, Ohio 16,516 A5 156
B1
Berebere, Indon. D7 359
Beregovo, Sov.Un. 27,900 H4 332
Bereku, Tan. C6 414
Berenice, Butte, Idaho F6 108
Berenice, ruins, Eg., U.A.R. C4 395
Berens, isl., Man., Can. D4 60
Berens, riv., Man., Can. D4 60
Berens River, Man., Can. 175 D4 60
Beresford, Man., Can. 50 F2 60
Beresford, Union and Lincoln, S.Dak. 1,794 D9 158
Berettyóújfalu, Hung. 11,670 B6 320
Berezhany, Sov.Un. 23,800 H5 332
Berezina, Sov.Un. D12 329
Berezina, riv., Sov.Un. F7 332
Berezna, Sov.Un. 23,300 G8 332
Berezniki, Sov.Un. 106,000 A5 336
Berezovo, Sov.Un. 4,000 C8 328
Berg, Nor. B7 290
Berga, Sp. 6,468 A7 298
Berga, Swe. 3,496 E7 292
Bergamasque Alps, mts., It. B2 302
Bergamo, It. 107,600 C2 302
Bergamo, prov., It. 717,000 *C2 302
Bergby, Swe. A8 292
Bergedorf, Ger. (part of Hamburg) B4 286
Bergen [auf Rügen], Ger. 10,100 A5 286
Bergen, Genesee, N.Y. 964 B4 212
Bergen, McHenry, N.Dak. 52 B5 154
Bergen, Nor. 113,243 F1 291
(*150,000)
Bergen, co., N.J. 780,255 B4 210
Bergen, co., Nor. 113,243 *F1 291
Bergen aan Zee, Neth. 221 B3 282
Bergenfield, Bergen, N.J. 27,203 A2 210
B5
Bergen op Zoom, Neth. 31,917 C3 282
Bergen Park, Jefferson, Colo. 25 *C5 106
Berger, Franklin, Mo. 187 C6 150
Bergerac, Fr. 19,070 E4 278
Bergholz, Jefferson, Ohio 955 B6 156
Bergisch Gladbach, Ger. 35,800 C2 286
Bergkvara, Swe. E7 292
Bergland, Ontonagon, Mich. 600 C2 146
Bergman, Boone, Ark. 100 A3 170
Bergoo, Webster, W.Va. 900 C4 194
Bergsjö, Swe. F7 291
Bergton, Rockingham, Va. 100 B6 192
Berguent, Mor. B3 402
Berhampore, India 55,613 D5 368
Berhampur, India 62,343 E4 366
Bering, sea, Alsk. D4 84
Bering, strait, Alsk. C4 84
Berislav, Sov.Un. 17,600 I9 332
Berja, Sp. 6,425 D5 298
Berkeley, Alameda, Calif. 111,268 A5 94
D2
Berkeley, Ont., Can. 175 P20 64
Berkeley, Cook, Ill. 5,792 *B6 138
Berkeley, St. Louis, Mo. 18,676 A8 150
Berkeley, Providence, R.I. 1,000 B3 216
Berkeley, Berkeley, W.Va. 100 B7 194
Berkeley, co., S.C. 38,196 E9 188
Berkeley, co., W.Va. 33,791 B6 194
Berkeley Heights, Union, N.J. 8,721 B4 210
Berkeley Springs (Bath), Morgan, W.Va. 1,138 B6 194
Berkley, Boone, Iowa 58 C3 142
Berkley, Harford, Md. 48 A7 182
Berkley, Bristol, Mass. 130 C5 206
(1,609▲)
Berkley, Oakland, Mich. 23,275 B8 146
G8
Berkovitsa, Bul. 9,059 B1 317
Berks, co., Eng. 454,900 J11 273
Berks, co., Pa. 275,414 C5 214
Berkshire, Prince Georges, Md. 1,200 *C6 182
Berkshire, Berkshire, Mass. 330 A1 206
Berkshire, Tioga, N.Y. 450 C5 212
Berkshire, Franklin, Vt. 35 B3 218
(965▲)
Berkshire, co., Mass. 142,135 B1 206
Berkshire, hills, Mass. B1 206
Berland, riv., Alta., Can. D3 54
Berlengas, is., Port. C2 298
Berlin, Hartford, Conn. 3,500 C5 202
(11,250▲)
Berlin, Colquitt, Ga. 419 E3 176
Berlin, Ger. 3,343,200 B5 286
(*3,900,000)
Berlin, East, Ger. 1,139,900 B5 286
Berlin, West, Ger. 2,203,300 B5 286
Berlin, Worcester, Md. 2,046 D9 182
Berlin, Worcester, Mass. 450 B4 206
(1,742▲)
Berlin, Coos, N.H. 17,821 C4 208
Berlin, Camden, N.J. 3,578 D3 210
Berlin, Rensselaer, N.Y. 900 C8 212
Berlin, La Moure, N.Dak. 78 D7 154
Berlin, Roger Mills, Okla. 50 C4 128
Berlin, Somerset, Pa. 1,600 D3 214
Berlin, Washington, Vt. 100 C3 218
(1,306▲)
Berlin, Green Lake, Wis. 4,838 E5 160
Berlin, West, state, Ger. 2,203,300 *B5 286
Berlin, mtn., Mass. A1 206
Berlin, res., Ohio A5 156
Berlin Heights, Erie, Ohio 721 A4 156
Berlin Township, see W. Berlin, N.J.
Bermejo, riv., Bol. D2 246
Bermeo, Sp. 11,739 A5 298
Bermijillo, Mex. B5 224
Bermuda, Monroe, Ala. 200 D2 168
Bermuda, isl., W.I. A12 233
Bermuda Hundred, Chesterfield, Va. 30 B9 192
Bermuda Islands, Br. poss., N.A. 43,500 A12 233
Bern, Bear Lake, Idaho 20 *G7 108
Bern, Nemaha, Kans. 206 C8 144
Bern, Switz. 155,600 B3 312
(*199,200)
Bern (Berne), canton, Switz. 848,600 B3 312
Bernalillo, Sandoval, N.Mex. 2,574 C4 126
H6
Bernalillo, co., N.Mex. 262,199 D4 126
Bernard, Dubuque, Iowa 173 B7 142
Bernard, Hancock, Maine 200 D4 204
Bernard, is., Truk A3 436
Bernard, lake, Ont., Can. O21 64
Bernardino, Cochise, Ariz. 25 G6 124
Bernardston, Franklin, Mass. 600 A2 206
(1,370▲)
Bernardsville, Somerset, N.J. 5,515 B3 210
Bernasconi, Arg. 2,094 C3 252
Bernau [bei Berlin], Ger. 13,900 B5 286
Bernay, Fr. 7,418 C4 278
Bernburg, Ger. 46,700 C4 286
Berndorf, Aus. 9,541 C8 313
Berne, Adams, Ind. 2,644 B5 140
Berne, see Bern, Switz.
Bernese Alps, mts., Switz. B3 312
Bernice, Union, La. 1,641 B3 180
Bernice, Delaware, Okla. 100 B9 128
Bernie, Stoddard, Mo. 1,578 E8 150
Bernina, pass, Switz. B6 312
Bernina, peak, Switz. B5 312
Bernstadt, Laurel, Ky. 425 C6 178
Beroroha, Malag. D9 421
Beroun, Czech. 15,473 B2 324
Beroun, Pine, Minn. 128 F6 148
Berre [l'Etang], Fr. 6,216 F6 278
Berretyo, riv., Hung. B6 320
Berrien, co., Ga. 12,038 E3 176
Berrien, co., Mich. 149,865 H5 146
Berrien Springs, Berrien, Mich. 1,953 H5 146
Berry, Fayette, Ala. 645 B2 168
Berry, Alsk. 103 *C7 84
Berry, Mohave, Ariz. 20 C2 124
Berry, Baxter, Ark. A4 170
Berry, creek, Alta., Can. E7 54
Berry, former prov., Fr. 464,000 D4 278
Berry, Harrison, Ky. 279 B6 178
Berrydale, Santa Rosa, Fla. 100 A4 174
Berry Hill, Davidson, Tenn. 1,551 E7 190
Berryman, Crawford, Mo. 150 D6 150
Berry Mills, N.B., Can. C5 70
Berry Mills, Franklin, Maine 75 D2 204
Berryton, Chattooga, Ga. 600 B1 176
Berryton, Shawnee, Kans. 70 *D8 144
Berryville, Carroll, Ark. 1,999 A3 170
Berryville, Clarke, Va. 1,645 A7 192
Bershad, Sov. Un. 24,600 H7 332
Bertha, Todd, Minn. 562 E3 148
Berthier, co., Que., Can. 26,359 R11 66
Berthierville, Que., Can. 3,504 R11 66
Berthold, Ward, N.Dak. 431 B4 154
Berthoud, Larimer, Colo. 867 B5 106
Berthoud, pass, Colo. C5 106
Bertie, Bertie, N.C. 303 B9 186
Bertie, co., N.C. 24,350 A8 186
Bertram, Ont., Can. 342 R24 64
Bertram, Linn, Iowa 170 C6 142
Bertrand, Berrien, Mich. 3,500 H5 146
Bertrand, Mississippi, Mo. 465 E8 150
Bertrand, Phelps, Nebr. 691 D6 152
Bertrandville, Plaquemines, La. 100 C7 180
E6
Bertrix, Bel. 4,489 E4 282
Berwick, N.S., Can. 1,134 D5 70
Berwick, Polk, Iowa 150 A7 142
Berwick, St. Mary, La. 3,880 C5 180
E4
Berwick, York, Maine 1,557 E2 204
(2,738▲)
Berwick, Amite, Miss. 100 D2 184
Berwick, McHenry, N.Dak. 56 B5 154
Berwick, Columbia, Pa. 13,353 B5 214
Berwick, co., Scot. 24,300 F10 272
Berwick-on-Tweed, Eng. 12,700 F10 272
Berwind, McDowell, W.Va. 950 D3 194
Berwyn, Alta., Can. 342 B4 54
Berwyn, Cook, Ill. 54,224 F2 138
Berwyn, Custer, Nebr. 104 C6 152
Berwyn, Chester, Pa. 5,000 A6 214
Berwyn Heights, Prince Georges, Md. 2,376 C4 182
Beryl, Mineral, W. Va. 400 *D5 194
Besa, Indon. D7 359
Besalampy, Malag. C8 421
Besançon, Fr. 73,445 D7 278
Besar, mtn., Mala. G4 362
Besar Hantu, mtn., Mala. G4 362
Beskids, mts., Czech., Pol. B4 324
D4 325
Besnard, lake, Sask., Can. C5 58
Besni, Tur. 11,452 C7 307
Besoco, Raleigh, W.Va. 400 *D3 194
Bessèges, Fr. 5,823 E6 278
Bessemer, Jefferson, Ala. 33,054 B3 168
E4
Bessemer, Gogebic, Mich. 3,304 C1 146
Bessemer, Lawrence, Pa. 1,491 C1 214
Bessemer City, Gaston, N.C. 4,017 B4 186
Bessie, Washita, Okla. 226 C5 128
Besslen, Lincoln, Idaho G4 108
Best, Chase, Nebr. D4 152
Bestobe, Sov.Un. B8 336
Bestwater, Benton, Ark. A2 170
Betafo, Malag. C9 421
Betanzos, Sp. 7,561 A2 298
Bétaré-Oya, Cam. 4,033 E7 409
Bethaine, S.W.Afr. 554 E3 420
Bethalto, Madison, Ill. 3,235 E3 138
Bethany, Man., Can. 130 E3 60
Bethany, Ont., Can. 310 P22 64
Bethany, New Haven, Conn. 2,384 D4 202
Bethany, Moultrie, Ill. 1,118 D5 138
Bethany (Bethany Park), Morgan, Ind. 119 *C3 140
Bethany, Caddo, La. 160 B1 180
Bethany, Harrison, Mo. 2,771 A3 150
Bethany, Oklahoma, Okla. 12,342 C6 128
Bethany, Brooke, W.Va. 992 B2 194
Bethany Beach, Sussex, Del. 170 F5 172
Bethel, Alsk. 1,258 C5 84
Bethel, Fairfield, Conn. 8,200 D2 202
Bethel, Sussex, Del. 236 F3 172
Bethel, Wyandotte, Kans. 100 B7 144
Bethel, Bath, Ky. 200 B7 178
Bethel, Oxford, Maine 1,117 D2 204
(2,408▲)
Bethel, Anoka, Minn. 302 F5 148
Bethel, Shelby, Mo. 152 B5 150
Bethel, Pitt, N.C. 1,578 B8 186
Bethel, Clermont, Ohio 2,019 D2 156
Bethel, McCurtain, Okla. 150 D9 128
Bethel, Lane, Oreg. 1,500 *C3 96
Bethel, Allegheny, Pa. 23,650 A3 214
Bethel, Windsor, Vt. 100 D3 218
(1,356▲)
Bethel, Kitsap, Wash. 300 *B4 98
Bethel, Wood, Wis. 150 D3 160
Bethelridge, Casey, Ky. 50 C6 178
Bethel Springs, McNairy, Tenn. 533 C3 190
Bethera, Berkeley, S.C. 165 E9 188
Bethesda, Independence, Ark. 115 B5 170
Bethesda, Montgomery, Md. 56,527 C3 182
C5
Bethesda, Belmont, Ohio 1,178 B5 156
Bethlehem, Litchfield, Conn. 600 C3 202
(1,486▲)
Bethlehem, Barrow, Ga. 297 C3 176
Bethlehem, Clark, Ind. 150 D4 140
Bethlehem, Caroline, Md. 85 C8 182
Bethlehem, Grafton, N.H. 450 C3 208
(898▲)
Bethlehem, Northampton and Lehigh, Pa. 75,408 C6 214
Bethlehem, Ohio, W.Va. 2,308 B2 194
Bethlehem, U.S.Afr. 18,574 E5 420
Bethpage, Nassau, N.Y. 30,000 D3 212
Bethpage, Sumner, Tenn. 400 B5 190
Bethune, Sask., Can. 288 E5 58
Bethune, Kit Carson, Colo. 70 C8 106
Bethune, Kershaw, S.C. 579 C8 188
Betioky, Malag. 755 D8 421
Betpak-Dala, Sov.Un. C8 336
Betroka, Malag. 2,524 D9 421
Betsiboka, riv., Malag. C9 421
Betsie, pt., Mich. E5 146
Betsy Layne, Floyd, Ky. 912 C8 178
Bette, peak, Libya C3 394
Bettendorf, Scott, Iowa 11,534 C7 142
D7
Betteravia, Santa Barbara, Calif. 335 E3 94
Betterton, Kent, Md. 328 B7 182
Bettiah, India D4 368
Bettles, Alsk. 47 B6 84
Bettsville, Seneca, Ohio 776 A3 156
Betul, India 11,841 E2 368
Betwa, riv., India D2 368
Between, Walton, Ga. 80 *C3 176
Beulah, Lee, Ala. 200 C4 168
Beulah, Prairie, Ark. 100 C5 170
Beulah, Man., Can. 80 E2 60
Beulah, Pueblo, Colo. 275 D6 106
Beulah, Hopkins, Ky. 100 C3 178
Beulah, Benzie, Mich. 436 E5 146
Beulah, Bolivar, Miss. 421 B2 184
Beulah, Mercer, N.Dak. 1,318 C4 154
Beulah, Malheur, Oreg. D8 96
Beulah, Crook, Wyo. 45 *B8 116
Beulah, lake, Miss. B1 184
Beulaville, Duplin, N.C. 1,062 C8 186
Beuthen, see Bytom, Pol.
Bevans, Sussex, N.J. 75 A3 210
Bevelle, Tallapoosa, Ala. 809 C4 168
Beverley, Eng. 15,600 H12 273
Beverley Station, Sask., Can. 50 E4 58
Beverly, Alta., Can. 4,602 D6 54
Beverly, Lincoln, Kans. 199 C6 144
Beverly, Bell, Ky. 306 D7 178
Beverly, Essex, Mass. 36,108 A6 206
C3
Beverly, Burlington, N.J. 3,400 C3 210
Beverly, Washington, Ohio 1,194 C5 156
Beverly, Knox, Tenn. 30 E9 190
Beverly, McLennan, Tex. 1,728 *D7 130
Beverly, Randolph, W.Va. 441 C5 194
Beverly Farms, Essex, Mass. (part of Beverly) C4 206
Beverly Gardens, Montgomery, Ohio 2,200 *C2 156
Beverly Hills, Los Angeles, Calif. 30,817 C5 94
Beverly Hills, Marquette, Mich. 8,633 *C4 146
Beverly Hills, St. Louis, Mo. 849 *C7 150

Beverly Park, Snohomish, Wash. 950 B4 98
Beverly Shores, Porter, Ind. 773 A3 140
Beverwijk, Neth. 29,729 B3 282
Bevier, Macon, Mo. 781 B5 150
Bevington, Madison and Warren, Iowa 55 *C4 142
Bewdley, Ont., Can. 125 P22 64
Bewelcome, Amite, Miss. 50 D2 184
Bex, Switz. 4,762 B3 312
Bexar, Marion, Ala. 300 A1 168
Bexar, co., Tex. 687,151 E6 130
Bexley, Eng. 89,300 J13 273
Bexley, George, Miss. 157 E4 184
Bexley, Franklin, Ohio 14,319 C1 156
Beyazeh, see Biābanak, Iran
Beykoz, Tur. F13 307
Beyla, Guinea 3,700 E3 408
Beypazari, Tur. 5,930 A4 307
Beyram, Iran D3 379
Beyrouth, see Beirut, Leb.
Beyşehir, Tur. 3,189 C4 307
Beyşehir, lake, Tur. C4 307
Bezau, Aus. 1,468 C1 313
Bezerros, Braz. 7,737 B3 258
Bezhetsk, Sov.Un. 25,000 D11 332
Bezhitsa (Ordzhonikidzegrad), Sov. Un. 74,000 F10 332
Béziers, Fr. 64,929 F5 278
Bezmer, Bul. 2,452 B3 317
Bezons, Fr. 16,993 I9 278
Bhadgaon, Nep. 32,320 D4 368
Bhadra, India 6,708 C1 368
Bhag, Pak. E5 375
Bhagalpur, India 114,530 D4 368
Bhagirathi, riv., India C2 368
Bhakkar, Pak. 12,397 D7 375
Bhamo, Bur. 9,817 A3 362
Bhaptiahi, India D4 368
Bharatpur, India 37,321 D2 368
Bharatpur, India E3 368
Bhatinda, India C1 368
Bhatpara, India 134,916 E5 368
Bhavnagar, India 137,951 D2 366
Bheigeir, mtn., Scot. F6 272
Bheri, riv., Nep. C3 368
Bhilsa, India E2 368
Bhilwara, India D1 368
Bhima, riv., India E3 366
Bhind, India 13,244 D2 368
Bhiwani, India 52,183 C2 368
Bhola, Pak. 6,198 L17 375
Bhopal, India 102,333 E2 368
Bhor, India 7,393 E2 366
Bhreac, mtn., Scot. E7 272
Bhubaneswar, India D5 366
Bhuj, India 30,985 D1 366
Bhutan, country, Asia 650,000 G11 340, 368
Biābanak (Beyazeh), Iran 6,000 C4 379
Biaboye, Con.L. B4 414
Biafra, bight, Afr. F6 409
Biak, is., Neth. N. Gui. E9 359
Biala, Eg., U.A.R. 10,005 C2 382
Biała Podlaska, Pol. 15,300 B6 325
Białogard, Pol. 15,200 A3 325
Białystok, Pol. 95,000 B6 325
Białystok, pol. div., Pol. 1,038,000 *B6 325
Bianco, It. 3,524 F6 302
Biang, Indon. D7 359
Biaora, India E2 368
Biarritz, Fr. 22,922 F3 278
Biasca, Switz. 2,882 B4 312
Biba, Eg., U.A.R. 15,971 B3 395
Bibai, Jap. 15,000 (88,667*) C8 354
Bibb, co., Ala. 14,357 C2 168
Bibb, co., Ga. 141,249 D3 176
Bibb City, Muscogee, Ga. 1,213 D2 176
Biberach [an der Riss], Ger. 17,900 D3 286
Bic, Que., Can. 1,142 P16 66
Bic, isl., Que., Can. P16 66
Bicester, Eng. 5,100 J11 273
Bickerdike, Alta., Can. 210 D4 54
Bickett Knob, mtn., W.Va. D4 194
Bickleton, Klickitat, Wash. 100 D6 98
Bickmore, Clay, W.Va. 200 C7 194
Bicknell, Knox, Ind. 3,878 D2 140
Bicknell, Wayne, Utah 366 E4 114
Bicske, Hung. 8,018 B3 320
Bida, Nig. 19,346 E6 408
Bidar, India 31,341 E3 366
Biddeford, York, Maine 19,255 E2 204, E4
Biddle, Powder River, Mont. 14 E11 110
Bideford, Eng. 10,200 J8 273
Bideford, bay, Eng. J8 273
Bidiya, cape, Sau. Ar. B4 383
Bidon Cinq (Oasis), Alg. 2 D4 402
Bidwell, Gallia, Ohio 350 D4 156
Bidya, riv., India J9 366
Bieber, Lassen, Calif. 300 B3 94
Biel, Switz. 52,300 (*58,900) A3 312
Biel (Bienne), lake, Switz. A3 312
Bielawa, Pol. 24,700 C3 325
Bield, Man., Can. 35 E2 60
Bielefeld, Ger. 172,700 (*351,000) B3 286
Biella, It. 44,000 C2 302
Bielsko-Biała, Pol. 67,000 D4 325
Bielsk Podlaski, Pol. 6,203 B6 325
Biem, Roosevelt, Mont. B12 110
Bienfait, Sask., Can. 802 F6 58
Bien Hoa, Viet. 39,500 E5 362
Bienne, see Biel, Switz.
Bienville, Bienville, La. 305 B3 180
Bienville, par., La. 16,726 B2 180
Bienville, lake, Que., Can. Q9 66
Bièvre, riv., Fr. I9 278
Biferno, riv., It. E5 302
Big, bayou, Ark. D5 170
Big, creek, Ark. C6 170
Big, creek, B.C., Can. E11 52
Big, creek, Ind. D2 140
Big, creek, Ind. D4 140
Big, creek, Kans. D4 144
Big, creek, La. B4 180
Big, creek, Mo. A3 150
Big, creek, Mo. C3 150
Big, creek, Tenn. E6 190
Big, isl., N.W.Ter., Can. E11 48
Big, lake, Maine C5 204
Big, riv., Sask., Can. D4 58
Big, riv., Mo. C7 150
Big, riv., R.I. C2 216
Big Arm, Lake, Mont. 60 C2 110
Big Bald, mtn., N.B., Can. B3 70
Big Bald, mtn., Ga. B2 176
Big Bald, mtn., Tenn. C9 190
Big Bay, Marquette, Mich. 250 C4 146
Big Bay de Noc, bay, Mich. D5 146
Big Bear City, San Bernardino, Calif. 400 E5 94
Big Bear Lake, San Bernardino, Calif. 1,562 *E5 94
Big Beaver, Sask., Can. 60 F5 58
Big Beaver House, Ont., Can. Q24 64
Bigbee, Washington, Ala. 25 D1 168
Bigbee, Monroe, Miss. 150 A4 184
Big Belt, mts., Mont. D5 110
Big Bend, Shasta, Calif. 230 B3 94
Big Bend, Bent, Colo. 10 D8 106
Big Bend, McLean, N.Dak. 39 C4 154
Big Bend, Waukesha, Wis. 797 F1 160
Big Bend, natl. park, Tex. E4 130
Big Birch, lake, Minn. F4 148
Big Black, riv., Miss. B3 184
Big Blue, riv., Ind. C4 140
Big Blue, riv., Nebr. D9 152
Bigbone, Boone, Ky. 50 A7 178
Big Bow, Stanton, Kans. 100 E2 144
Big Butt, mtn., Tenn. B9 190
Big Cabin, Craig, Okla. 228 B8 128
Big Cabin, creek, Okla. B8 128
Big Cane, St. Landry, La. 100 D4 180
Big Canyon, Murray, Okla. 175 D6 128
Big Canyon, creek, Tex. D4 130
Big Chimney, Kanawha, W.Va. 300 *C3 194
Big Clifty, Grayson, Ky. 550 C4 178
Big Corney, creek, Ark. D3 170
Big Corney, creek, La. B3 180
Big Creek, Fresno, Calif. 400 D4 94
Big Creek, B.C., Can. 25 E11 52
Big Creek, Valley, Idaho 34 D3 108
Big Creek, Clay, Ky. 250 C7 178
Big Creek, Calhoun, Miss. 100 B3 184
Big Creek, Logan, W.Va. 450 C2 194
Big Creek, springs, Idaho D4 108
Big Cypress, swamp, Fla. E9 174
Big Dalton, res., Calif. C6 94
Big Delta, Alsk. 155 C7 84
Big Dry, creek, Mont. C10 110
Big Eau Pleine, res., Wis. D4 160
Big Eddy, Wasco, Oreg. B5 96
Big Elk, creek, Md. A8 182
Bigelow, Perry, Ark. 231 B4 170
Bigelow, Marshall, Kans. 120 *C7 144
Bigelow, Franklin, Maine 10 C2 204
Bigelow, Nobles, Minn. 256 H3 148
Bigelow, Holt, Mo. 100 A2 150
Bigelow, mtn., Maine C2 204
Big Falls, Koochiching, Minn. 526 C5 148
Big Falls, Waupaca, Wis. 119 *D5 160
Bigflat, Baxter, Ark. 217 A4 170
Big Flats, Chemung, N.Y. 900 C5 212
Bigfork, Itasca, Minn. 464 D5 148
Bigfork, Flathead, Mont. 400 B2 110
Big Fork, riv., Minn. C5 148
Biggar, Sask., Can. 2,424 D3 58
Biggerann, isl., Kwajalein A1 436
Biggers, Randolph, Ark. 274 A6 170
Biggersville, Alcorn, Miss. 135 A4 184
Biggs, Butte, Calif. 831 C3 94
Biggs, Sherman, Oreg. 10 B6 96
Biggsville, Henderson, Ill. 345 C3 138
Big Gully, creek, Sask., Can. D3 58
Big Hickory, mtn., Pa. B6 214
Big Hickory, pass, Fla. E9 174
Big Hole Battlefield, natl. mon., Mont. E3 110
Big Hole, pass, Idaho, Mont. D5 108, E3 110
Big Hole, peak, Mont. C1 110
Big Hole, riv., Mont. E4 110
Bighorn, Treasure, Mont. 100 D9 110
Big Horn, Sheridan, Wyo. 100 B5 116
Big Horn, co., Mont. 10,007 E9 110
Big Horn, co., Wyo. 11,897 B4 116
Big Horn, basin, Wyo. B4 116
Big Horn, mts., Ariz. E2 124
Big Horn, mts., Wyo. B5 116
Bighorn, riv., Mont., Wyo. E9 110, B4 116
Big Hurricane, cavern, Ark. A4 170
Big Indian, riv., Mich. C5 146
Big Island, Bedford, Va. 500 C5 192
Big Kandiyohi, lake, Minn. G4 148
Big Lake, Ont., Can. Q24 64
Big Lake, Sherburne, Minn. 610 F5 148
Big Lake, Reagan, Tex. 2,668 D5 130
Big Lake, Skagit, Wash. 300 *A4 98
Biglerville, Adams, Pa. 923 D4 214
Big Marco, bay, Fla. F9 174
Big Marine, lake, Minn. F7 148
Big Muddy, creek, Mont. B12 110
Big Muddy, lake, Sask., Can. F5 58
Big Muddy, riv., Ill. F4 138
Bignona, Sen. 2,450 D1 408
Bigonville, Lux. 421 E4 282
Bigpine, Inyo, Calif. 556 D4 94
Big Pine, hill, Pa. A5 214
Big Pine, mtn., Calif. E4 94
Big Piney, Sublette, Wyo. 663 D2 116
Big Pipe, creek, Md. A5 182
Bigpoint, Jackson, Miss. 200 E4 184
Bigpool, Washington, Md. 50 A3 182
Big Port Walter, Alsk. 10 J14 84
Big Rapids, Mecosta, Mich. 8,686 F6 146
Big River, Sask., Can. 904 D4 58
Big Rock, Stewart, Tenn. 220 B4 190
Big Rock, Buchanan, Va. 300 C2 192
Big Rock, mtn., Ark. D7 170
Big Run, Jefferson, Pa. 857 C3 214
Big Sable, pt., Mich. E5 146
Big Sand, creek, Mont. B6 110
Big Sandy, Chouteau, Mont. 954 B6 110
Big Sandy, Benton, Tenn. 492 B3 190
Big Sandy, Upshur, Tex. 848 C8 130
Big Sandy, Sublette, Wyo. D3 116
Big Sandy, creek, Colo. D8 106
Big Sandy, lake, Sask., Can. C5 58
Big Sandy, res., Wyo. D3 116
Big Sandy, riv., Ariz. D2 124
Big Sandy, riv., Ky., W.Va. B8 178, C2 194
Big Sandy, riv., Tenn. C3 190
Big Satilla, creek, Ga. E4 176
Big Savage, mtn., Md. A1 182
Big Shiney, mtn., Pa. A5 214
Big Sioux, riv., Iowa, S.Dak. B1 142, E9 158
Big Slough, creek, Kans. A5 144
Big Smoky, valley, Nev. E4 112
Big Snow, mtn., Mont. D7 110
Big Soldier, creek, Kans. C8 144
Big South, butte, Idaho F5 108
Big Spring, Breckinridge, Ky. 150 C4 178
Big Spring, Washington, Md. 110 A4 182
Bigspring, Meigs, Tenn. C7 190
Big Spring, Howard, Tex. 31,230 C5 130
Big Springs, Fremont, Idaho E7 108
Big Springs, Deuel, Nebr. 506 C3 152
Big Springs, Calhoun, W.Va. 225 C3 194
Big Spruce Knob, mtn., W.Va. C4 194
Bigstick, lake, Sask., Can. E3 58
Big Stone, co., Minn. 8,954 F2 148
Bigstone, lake, Man., Can. D5 60
Bigstone, lake, Sask., Can. C6 58
Big Stone, lake, Minn. F2 148
Big Stone, lake, S.Dak. B9 158
Bigstone, riv., Man., Can. C5 60
Big Stone City, Grant, S.Dak. 718 B9 158
Big Stone Gap, Wise, Va. 4,688 D2 192
Big Sunflower, riv., Miss. B2 184
Big Sur, Monterey, Calif. 125 D3 94
Big Thompson, riv., Colo. B5 106
Big Timber, Sweet Grass, Mont. 1,660 E7 110
Big Top, mtn., Tenn. C5 190
Big Trout, lake, Ont., Can. Q24 64
Big Tujunga, res., Calif. B5 94
Big Valley, Alta., Can. 354 D6 54
Big Walnut, creek, Ohio C1 156
Big Wells, Dimmit, Tex. 801 E6 130
Bigwood, Ont., Can. 70 O20 64
Big Wood, riv., Idaho F4 108
Bihać, Yugo. 10,956 B2 316
Bihar, India 63,124 D4 368
Bihar, state, India 38,784,172 D5 366
Bihor, mts., Rom. A2 321
Bijapur, India 65,734 E3 366
Bijār, Iran 12,928 B2 379
Bijeljina, Yugo. 15,682 B4 316
Bijelo Polje, Yugo. 4,029 C4 316
Bijnor, India C2 368
Bijou, creek, Colo. C6 106
Bijou Hills, Brule, S.Dak. D6 158
Bikaner, India 117,113 C1 368
Bikar, atoll, Marshall A4 436
Bikin, Sov.Un. 14,000 E15 329
Bikini, atoll, Marshall A4 436
Bikini, isl., Pac.O. C3 436
Bikita, Rh.&Nya. D6 421
Bilara, India D1 368
Bilaspur, India 39,099 E3 368
Bilauktaung, range, Thai. D3 362
Bilbao, Sp. 254,672 (*425,000) A5 298
Bilbês, Eg., U.A.R. 29,200 D2 382
Bileća, Yugo. 1,547 C4 316
Bilecik, Tur. 4,886 A3 307
Bilecik, prov., Tur. 139,532 *A4 307
Biłgoraj, Pol. 4,745 C6 325
Bili, Con.L. B4 414
Bilin, Bur. 5,265 C3 362
Bílina, Czech. 8,551 A1 324
Bill, Converse, Wyo. 10 C7 116
Billarp, Douglas, Ga. 350 C2 176
Billerica, Middlesex, Mass. 1,600 (17,867*) A5 206, C2
Billing, Sheridan, Nebr. B3 152
Billingen, mts., Swe. C4 292
Billings, Christian, Mo. 602 D4 150
Billings, Yellowstone, Mont. 52,851 E8 110
Billings, Noble, Okla. 510 B6 128
Billings, co., N.Dak. 1,513 C2 154
Billings Bench, Yellowstone, Mont. 1,500 *E8 110
Billings Heights, Yellowstone, Mont. 2,500 *E8 110
Billingsley, Autauga, Ala. 179 C3 168
Bill Williams, mtn., Ariz. C3 124
Bilma, Niger 1,100 C7 409
Biloxi, Harrison, Miss. 44,053 E1 184, E4
Biloxi, bay, Miss. E2 184
Biloxi, riv., Miss. E3 184
Bilqās, Eg., U.A.R. 43,200 C2 382
Biltine, Chad D9 409
Biltmore Forest, Buncombe, N.C. 1,004 B3 186
Bilzen, Bel. 6,003 D4 282
Bim, Boone, W.Va. 300 *C3 194
Bina-Etawa, India D2 368
Binaija, mtn., Indon. E7 359
Bindal, Nor. D5 290
Bindloss, Alta., Can. 119 E7 54
Bindura, Rh.&Nya. 2,500 C6 421
Binfield, Blount, Tenn. 100 E9 190
Binford, Griggs, N.Dak. 261 C7 154
Binga, Con.L. B3 414
Bingamon, creek, W.Va. A6 194
Bingen, Hempstead, Ark. 150 D3 170
Bingen, Ger. 18,700 D2 286
Bingen, Klickitat, Wash. 636 D5 98
Binger, Caddo, Okla. 603 C5 128
Bingham, Somerset, Maine 1,180 (1,308*) C3 204
Bingham, Sheridan, Nebr. 100 B3 152
Bingham, Dillon, S.C. 95 C9 188
Bingham, co., Idaho 28,218 F6 108
Bingham Canyon, Salt Lake, Utah 1,516 C3 114
Bingham Farms, Oakland, Mich. 394 *G8 146
Bingham Lake, Cottonwood, Minn. 254 H3 148
Binghamton, Broome, N.Y. 75,941 (*212,600) C6 212
Binghamville, Franklin, Vt. 115 B3 218
Bingley, Eng. H11 273
Bingöl (Çapakçur), Tur. 3,728 B9 307
Bingöl, prov., Tur. 114,997 *B9 307
Binh Dinh, Viet. D6 362
Binnsville, Kemper, Miss. 75 C4 184
Binscarth, Man., Can. 452 E2 60
Bintang, mtn., Mala F4 362
Bintuhan, Indon. E2 358
Bintulu, Sar. 3,957 D4 358
Binyamina, Isr. 2,850 B5 382
Bio, Hart, Ga. 300 B4 176
Bio Bio, prov., Chile 138,292 E3 250
Bio Bio, riv., Chile C1 252
Biola Junction, Fresno, Calif. *D4 94
Bippus, Huntington, Ind. 275 B4 140
Bir Abu Reida (Oasis), Eg., U.A.R. D3 382
Birao, Cen.Afr.Rep. D9 409
Biratnagar, Nep. 8,060 D4 368
Birch, isl., Man., Can. D3 60
Birch, lake, Sask., Can. D3 58
Birch, lake, Minn. D6 148
Birch, riv., W.Va. C4 194
Birch Bay, Whatcom, Wash. 350 *A4 98
Birch Cliff, Ont., Can. 960 Q21 64, R22
Birch Hill, Litchfield, Conn. 60 C2 202
Birch Hills, Sask., Can. 562 D5 58
Birch Island, B.C., Can. 75 E13 52
Birch River, Man., Can. 200 D2 60
Birch River, Nicholas, W.Va. 200 C4 194
Birch Run, Saginaw, Mich. 844 F8 146
Birch Tree, Shannon, Mo. 420 E6 150
Birchwood, Washington, Minn. 598 *F6 148
Birchwood, Hamilton, Tenn. 250 C7 190
Birchwood, Washburn, Wis. 433 C2 160
Bird, creek, Okla. B8 128
Bird, isl., S.C. D11 188
Bird City, Cheyenne, Kans. 678 C2 144
Bird Creek, Ont., Can. 45 O23 64
Birdeye, Cross, Ark. 100 *B6 170
Bird Island, Renville, Minn. 1,384 G4 148
Bird River, Man., Can. E5 60
Birdsboro, Berks, Pa. 3,025 C6 214
Birdseye, Dubois, Ind. 366 D3 140
Birdseye, Utah, Utah 25 D4 114
Birdsnest, Northampton, Va. 125 *C9 192
Birdsong, Mississippi, Ark. 100 B6 170
Birdsville, Austl. D8 432
Birdsville, Livingston, Ky. 92 C2 178
Birdtail, creek, Man., Can. E2 60
Birdum, Austl. B6 432
Birdwood, creek, Nebr. C4 152
Birecik, Tur. 10,421 C7 307
Bir el Abd, Eg., U.A.R. 1,001 C4 382
Bir el Giddi (Oasis), Eg., U.A.R. D4 382
Bir el Gilbâna (Oasis), Eg., U.A.R. D3 382
Bir el Hadira (Oasis), Eg., U.A.R. D5 382
Bir el Hasana (Oasis), Eg., U.A.R. D4 382
Bir el Jafir (Oasis), Eg., U.A.R. D3 382
Bir el Ksaib, well, Mali B3 408
Bir el Lahtan (Oasis), Eg., U.A.R. D4 382
Bir el Nuss, Eg., U.A.R. A2 395
Bir Gameil (Oasis), Eg., U.A.R. D4 382
Birganj, Nep. 10,037 D4 368
Birilyussy, Sov.Un. A12 336
Birjand, Iran 23,488 C5 379
Birkenfield, Columbia, Oreg. 100 B3 96
Birkenhead, Eng. 141,600 H9 273
Birkenhead, N.Z. 5,644 H8 437
Birkeröd, Den. F3 292
Birket Qârûn, lake, Eg., U.A.R. B3 395
Birket San el Hagar, lake, Eg., U.A.R. E6 395
Birmingham, Jefferson, Ala. 340,887 (*624,000) B3 168, E4
Birmingham, Sask., Can. 50 E6 58
Birmingham, Eng. 1,110,800 (*2,450,000) I11 273
Birmingham, Fulton, Ga. 120 B2 176
Birmingham, Van Buren, Iowa 441 D6 142
Birmingham, Oakland, Mich. 25,525 B8 146, G8
Birmingham, Clay, Mo. 201 E2 150
Birmingham, Burlington, N.J. 25 D3 210
Bir Misâha (Oasis), Eg., U.A.R. C2 395
Birnamwood, Shawano, Wis. 568 D4 160
Birney, Rosebud, Mont. 27 E10 110
Birnie, Man., Can. 100 E3 60
Birnin Kebbi, Nig. 12,270 D5 408
Birni-Nkoni, Niger 6,000 D6 408
Birohidzhan, Sov.Un. 41,000 E15 329
Biron, Wood, Wis. 726 D4 160
Bir Ounane, well, Mali B4 408
Birr, Ire. 3,257 H5 273
Bir Rôd Sâlem (Oasis), Eg., U.A.R. D4 382
Birs, riv., Switz. A3 312
Birsay, Sask., Can. 142 E4 58
Bir Sejri (Oasis), Syr., U.A.R. C3 378
Birta, Yell, Ark. 52 *B3 170
Bir Tarfawi, Sud. A3 398
Birtle, Man., Can. 806 E2 60
Bir Um Hosaira (Oasis), Eg., U.A.R. D5 382
Biryulevo, Sov.Un. 33,400 N18 332
Bir Zreigat, well, Maur. B3 408
Bisbee, Cochise, Ariz. 9,914 G6 124
Bisbee, Towner, N.Dak. 388 B6 154
Biscay, bay, Fr. E2 278
Biscay, bay, Sp. A4 298
Biscayne, bay, Fla. F10 174
Biscayne, key, Fla. E6 174
Biscayne Park, Dade, Fla. 2,911 E6 174
Bisceglie, It. 40,900 E6 302
Bischofshofen, Aus. 7,921 C5 313
Biscoe, see Fredonia, Ark.
Biscoe, Montgomery, N.C. 1,053 B6 186
Biscoe, King and Queen, Va. 75 C7 192
Bise, Okinawa C1 436
Biševo, isl., Yugo. C2 316
Bishārah, well, Libya C4 394
Bishenpur, India D6 368
Bishnupur, India 23,981 H8 366
Bishop, Colbert, Ala. A1 168
Bishop, Inyo, Calif. 2,875 D4 94
Bishop, Oconee, Ga. 214 C3 176
Bishop, Worcester, Md. 5 D9 182
Bishop, Nueces, Tex. 3,722 F7 130
Bishop, Tazewell, Va. 900 C3 192
Bishop Auckland, Eng. 35,300 G11 273
Bishopric, Sask., Can. 95 E5 58
Bishop's Castle, Eng. 1,300 I10 273
Bishop's Falls, Newf., Can. 2,500 F8 72
Bishops Head, Dorchester, Md. 327 D7 182
Bishops Mills, Ont., Can. 110 P25 64
Bishop's Stortford, Eng. 14,600 J13 273

Bishopton, Que., Can.	378	S13	66
Bishopville, Worcester, Md.	100	D9	182
Bishopville, Lee, S.C.	3,586	C8	188
Biskra, Alg.	52,511	B5	402
Bismarck, Hot Spring, Ark.	250	D6	170
Bismarck, Vermilion, Ill.	400	C6	138
Bismarck, St. Francois, Mo.	1,237	D7	150
Bismarck, Burleigh, N.Dak.	27,670	D5	154
Bismarck, Grant, W.Va.	113	B5	194
Bismarck Archipelago, N.Gui.	157,000	E12	358
Bismarck, arch., N.Gui.		E11	358
Bison, Rush, Kans.	291	D4	144
Bison, Garfield, Okla.	200	B6	128
Bison, Perkins, S.Dak.	457	B3	158
Bison, lake, Alta., Can.		B4	54
Bison, peak, Colo.		C5	106
Bisonte, Baca, Colo.	10	E8	106
Bispberg Klack, mtn., Swe.		A7	292
Bispgarden, Swe.		E7	290
Bissau, Port. Gui.	18,309	D1	408
Bissell, Lee, Miss.	200	A4	184
Bissett, Man., Can.	200	E5	60
Bistineau, lake, La.		B2	180
Bistrița, Rom.	20,292	A3	321
Bistrița, riv., Rom.		A3	321
Biswan, India		D3	368
Bitam, Gabon		F7	409
Bitely, Newaygo, Mich.	200	F6	146
Bithlo, Orange, Fla.	168	*C9	174
Bitjoli, Indon.		D7	359
Bitlis, Tur.	14,022	B10	307
Bitlis, prov., Tur.	111,789	*B10	307
Bitola, Yugo.	37,564	D5	316
Bitonto, It.	32,400	E6	302
Bitter, creek, Wyo.		E4	116
Bitter, lake, Sask., Can.		E3	58
Bitter, lake, S.Dak.		B8	158
Bitter Creek, Sweetwater, Wyo.	70	E4	116
Bitterfeld, Ger.	32,500	C5	286
Bitterfontein, U.S.Afr.		F3	420
Bittern Lake, Alta., Can.	45	D6	54
Bitterroot, range, U.S.		B3	77
Bitterroot, riv., Mont.		D2	110
Bittinger, Garrett, Md.	20	A1	182
Bityug, riv., Sov.Un.		G13	332
Biu, Nig.		D7	409
Bivalve, Wicomico, Md.	230	D8	182
Bivalve, Cumberland, N.J.	600	E2	210
Biwa, lake, Jap.		L12	354
Biwabik, St. Louis, Minn.	1,836	D6	148
Bixby, Tulsa, Okla.	1,711	C8	128
Biya, riv., Sov.Un.		B11	336
Biysk, Sov.Un.	146,000	B11	336
Bizerte, Tun.	44,721	A5	402
Bizuta, Mong.	10,000	B11	346
Bjelovar, Yugo.	13,569	B3	316
Björbo, Swe.		A5	292
Björkö, isl., Swe.		B10	292
Bjornefjord, fjord, Nor.		F1	291
Björneröd, Swe.		B2	292
Björnör, Nor.		D4	290
Bjurholm, Swe.		E8	290
Bjuv, Swe.	4,000	E3	292
Blåbärskullen, mtn., Swe.		B3	292
Black, Geneva, Ala.	133	D4	168
Black, bayou, La.		E5	180
Black, butte, Mont.		F5	110
Black, butte, N.Dak.		D2	154
Black, butte, Wyo.		B5	116
Black, creek, Miss.		E4	184
Black, creek, S.C.		B8	188
Black, creek, Vt.		B3	218
Black, fork, Ohio		B4	156
Black, head, Newf., Can.		G9	72
Black, hills, S.Dak.		C2	158
Black, isl., Man., Can.		E4	60
Black, lake, La.		C2	180
Black, lake, Mich.		D7	146
Black, lake, N.Y.		A6	212
Black, mesa, Ariz.		B5	124
Black, mesa, Okla.		B1	128
Black, mtn., Ariz.		F4	124
Black, mtn., Colo.		B5	106
Black, mtn., Ky.		D8	178
Black, mtn., N.C.		B3	186
Black, mtn., Wyo.		D7	116
Black, mtn., Wyo.		B5	116
Black, mts., Ariz.		C1	124
Black, mts., N.B., Can.		B2	70
Black, peak, Ariz.		D1	124
Black, pond, Maine		B3	204
Black, range, N.Mex.		E3	126
Black, riv., Ariz.		E6	124
Black, riv., Ark., Mo.		B5	170
		E7	150
Black, riv., Man., Can.		E5	60
Black, riv., Maine		B3	204
Black, riv., Mich.		D7	146
Black, riv., Mich.		F9	146
Black, riv., N.J.		*B3	210
Black, riv., N.Y.		B6	212
Black, riv., N.C.		C7	186
Black, riv., S.C.		D9	188
Black, riv., S.C.		E3	188
Black, riv., Vt.		B4	218
Black, riv., Vt.		E3	218
Black, riv., Viet.		B4	362
Black, riv., Wis.		D3	160
Black, sea, Europe		D8	266
Blackall, Austl.	1,885	C9	432
Black Bear, bay, Newf., Can.		D8	72
Black Bear, creek, Okla.		B6	128
Black Bear Bay, Newf., Can.	8	D8	72
Black Bear Island, lake, Sask., Can.		C5	58
Blackberry City, Mingo, W.Va.	300	*D2	194
Black Betsy, Putnam, W.Va.	100	C3	194
Blackbird, New Castle, Del.	39	C3	172
Black Bottom, Harlan, Ky.	300	*D7	178
Blackburn, Eng.	107,900	H10	273
Blackburn, Saline, Mo.	310	B4	150
Blackburn, Pawnee, Okla.	129	B7	128
Blackburn, mtn., Alsk.		C7	84
Black Buttes, Sweetwater, Wyo.	20	*E4	116
Black Canyon, Yavapai, Ariz.	100	D3	124
Black Canyon, dam, Idaho		F2	108
Black Canyon of the Gunnison, natl. mon., Colo.		D3	106
Black Cloud, Shoshone, Idaho	100	*B3	108
Black Creek, Wilson, N.C.	310	B8	186
Black Creek, Outagamie, Wis.	707	A5	160
		D5	
Black Diamond, Jefferson, Ala.	250	*B2	168
Black Diamond, Alta., Can.	991	E5	54
Black Diamond, King, Wash.	1,026	B4	98
		D3	
Black Dome, mtn., B.C., Can.		D9	52
Blackdown, hills, Eng.		K9	273
Blackduck, Beltrami, Minn.	765	D4	148
Black Eagle, Cascade, Mont.	2,000	C5	110
Black Earth, Dane, Wis.	784	E4	160
Blackey, Letcher, Ky.	300	C8	178
Blackey, Buchanan, Va.	200	C3	192
Blackfalds, Alta., Can.	340	D6	54
Blackfoot, Alta., Can.	75	D7	54
Blackfoot, Bingham, Idaho	7,378	F6	108
Blackfoot, Glacier, Mont.	80	B4	110
Blackfoot, mts., Idaho		F7	108
Blackfoot, riv., Mont.		C3	110
Blackfoot River, res., Idaho		G7	108
Blackford, Webster, Ky.	175	C3	178
Blackford, co., Ind.	14,792	B4	140
Black Forest (Schwarzwald), mts., Ger.		E2	286
Black Fork, Scott, Ark.	30	C2	170
Blackfork, Lawrence, Ohio	624	D4	156
Blackgum, Sequoyah, Okla.	35	C9	128
Black Hawk, Gilpin, Colo.	171	C5	106
Black Hawk, Vigo, Ind.	100	C2	140
Black Hawk, Carroll, Miss.	100	B2	184
Black Hawk, Meade, S.Dak.	200	C2	158
Black Hawk, Sauk, Wis.	85	E4	160
Black Hawk, co., Iowa	122,482	B5	142
Blackhead, bay, Newf., Can.		F9	72
Black Horse, Portage, Ohio	900	A5	156
Blackie, Alta., Can.	198	E6	54
Black Jack, mtn., Ga.		A5	176
Black Lake, Que., Can.	3,685	R13	66
Black Lake, bayou, La.		B2	180
Blackleaf, Teton, Mont.		B4	110
Blackman, Okaloosa, Fla.	45	A4	174
Blackmore, mtn., Mont.		E6	110
Black Mountain, Buncombe, N.C.	1,313	B3	186
Black Oak, Craighead, Ark.	220	B6	170
Black Oak, ridge, Tenn.		C7	190
Black Pine, peak, Idaho		G5	108
Blackpool, Eng.	146,500	H9	273
Black River, Alsk.	30	*C5	84
Black River, Jam.	1,500	C5	232
Blackriver, Alcona, Mich.	90	E8	146
Black River, Jefferson, N.Y.	1,237	A6	212
Black River Falls, Jackson, Wis.	3,195	D3	160
Black Rock, Lawrence, Ark.	554	A5	170
Black Rock, Norfolk, Mass.	500	*D5	206
Black Rock, McKinley, N.Mex.	35	C2	126
Black Rock, Millard, Utah	30	E3	114
Black Rock, des., Nev.		C3	112
Black Rock, des., Utah		D3	114
Black Rock, mts., Nev.		B3	112
Blacks, fork, Wyo.		E3	116
Blacksburg, Cherokee, S.C.	2,174	A5	188
Blacksburg, Montgomery, Va.	7,070	C4	192
Blacks Harbour, N.B., Can.	585	D3	70
Blackshear, Pierce, Ga.	2,482	E4	176
Blackshear, lake, Ga.		E3	176
Blacksher, Baldwin, Ala.	200	D2	168
Black Springs, Montgomery, Ark.	75	C3	170
Black Springs, Washoe, Nev.	200	D2	112
Black Squirrel, creek, Colo.		D6	106
Blackstairs, mts., Ire.		I6	273
Blackstock, Ont., Can.	285	P22	64
Blackstock, Fairfield, S.C.	175	B6	188
Blackstone, Worcester, Mass.	2,000 (5,130▲)	B4	206
Blackstone, Nottoway, Va.	3,659	C6	192
Blackstone, riv., Alta., Can.		D4	54
Blackstone, riv., Mass.		C5	206
Blackstone, riv., R.I.		A2	216
Blacksville, Monongalia, W.Va.	211	B4	194
Black Thunder, creek, Wyo.		C7	116
Blackton, Monroe, Ark.	50	C5	170
Blackville, N.B., Can.	515	C4	70
Blackville, Barnwell, S.C.	1,901	E6	188
Black Volta, riv., Ghana		E4	408
Blackwalnut, pt., Md.		C7	182
Black Warrior, riv., Ala.		C2	168
Blackwater, Ire.	208	I6	273
Blackwater, Cooper, Mo.	284	C5	150
Blackwater, Lee, Va.	50	D1	192
Blackwater, res., N.H.		E3	208
Blackwater, riv., Fla.		A4	174
Blackwater, riv., Md.		D7	182
Blackwater, riv., Va.		D8	192
Blackwell, Conway, Ark.	75	B4	170
Blackwell, Kay, Okla.	9,588	B6	128
Blackwell, Forest, Wis.	100	C5	160
Black Wolf, Ellsworth, Kans.	32	D5	144
Blackwood, Camden, N.J.	3,000	D2	210
Bladen, Webster, Nebr.	322	D7	152
Bladen, co., N.C.	28,881	C7	186
Bladenboro, Bladen, N.C.	774	C7	186
Bladensburg, Prince Georges, Md.	3,103	C4	182
Blades, Sussex, Del.	729	F3	172
Bladon Springs, Choctaw, Ala.	400	D1	168
Bladworth, Sask., Can.	178	E4	58
Blaenga, mtn., Nor.		A2	292
Blagodarnoye, Sov.Un.	29,500	C2	336
Blagoevgrad (Gorna Dzhumaya), Bul.	21,936	B1	317
Blagoevgradski, prov., Bul.		*C1	317
Blaine, Pottawatomie, Kans.	78	C7	144
Blaine, Lawrence, Ky.	124	B8	178
Blaine, Aroostook, Maine	375 (945▲)	B5	204
Blaine, Anoka, Minn.	7,570	F7	148
Blaine, Sunflower, Miss.	125	B2	184
Blaine, Whatcom, Wash.	1,735	A4	98
Blaine, co., Idaho	4,598	F4	108
Blaine, co., Mont.	8,091	B7	110
Blaine, co., Nebr.	1,016	C5	152
Blaine, co., Okla.	12,077	C5	128
Blaine, creek, Ky.		B8	178
Blaine Lake, Sask., Can.	638	D4	58
Blaineville, Page, Va.	40	*B6	192
Blair, Doniphan, Kans.	75	C8	144
Blair, Washington, Nebr.	4,931	C9	152
Blair, Jackson, Okla.	893	D4	128
Blair, Fairfield, S.C.	75	C6	188
Blair, Logan, W.Va.	350	D5	194
Blair, Trempealeau, Wis.	909	D2	160
Blair, co., Pa.	137,270	C3	214
Blair-Atholl, Scot.	1,868	E9	272
Blairgowrie [& Rattray], Scot.	5,300	E9	272
Blair Mills, Anderson, S.C.	75	B3	188
Blairmore, Alta., Can.	1,973	F5	54
Blairsden, Plumas, Calif.	90	C3	94
Blairstown, Benton, Iowa	583	C5	142
Blairstown, Henry, Mo.	177	C4	150
Blairstown, Warren, N.J.	550	B3	210
Blairsville, Union, Ga.	437	B3	176
Blairsville, Posey, Ind.	100	D2	140
Blairsville, Indiana, Pa.	4,930	C2	214
Blairton, Berkeley, W.Va.	200	B7	194
Blairtown, Sweetwater, Wyo.		E3	116
Blaisdell, Mountrail, N.Dak.	62	B3	154
Blaj, Rom.	8,731	A2	321
Blakeley, Kanawha, W.Va.	600	C6	194
Blakely, Garland, Ark.	250	*C3	170
Blakely, Early, Ga.	3,580	E2	176
Blakely, see Peckville, Pa.			
Blakeman, Rawlins, Kans.	12	C2	144
Blakes, pt., Mich.		B3	146
Blakesburg, Wapello, Iowa	401	D5	142
Blalock, Rabun, Ga.	150	B3	176
Blalock, Gilliam, Oreg.	20	B6	96
Blanc, cape, Maur.		B1	408
Blanc, mtn., Fr.		E7	278
Blanc, mtn., It.		C1	302
Blanca, Costilla, Colo.	233	E5	106
Blanca, bay, Arg.		C3	252
Blanca, peak, Colo.		E5	106
Blanca, pt., Mex.		B3	224
Blanchard, Bonner, Idaho	100	A2	108
Blanchard, Page, Iowa	174	D2	142
Blanchard, Caddo, La.	500	B2	180
Blanchard, Piscataquis, Maine	10 (57▲)	C3	204
Blanchard, Isabella, Mich.	275	F6	146
Blanchard, McClain, Okla.	1,377	C6	128
Blanchard, Skagit, Wash.	200	A4	98
Blanchard, riv., Ohio		A3	156
Blanchardville, Lafayette, Wis.	632	F4	160
Blanche, Que., Can.	208	S9	66
Blanche, Lincoln, Tenn.	150	C5	190
Blanche, chan., Solomon		E1	436
Blanchester, Clinton, Ohio	2,944	C3	156
Blanco, San Juan, N.Mex.	100	B3	126
Blanco, Pittsburg, Okla.	200	D8	128
Blanco, Blanco, Tex.	789	D6	130
Blanco, co., Tex.	3,657	D6	130
Blanco, cape, C.R.		F5	228
Blanco, cape, Oreg.		E2	96
Blanco, creek, N.Mex.		D7	126
Blanco, riv., Arg.		A2	252
Blanco, riv., Bol.		B2	246
Blanco, riv., Mex.		L15	225
Bland, Gasconade, Mo.	654	C6	150
Bland, Bland, Va.	500	C3	192
Bland, co., Va.	5,982	C3	192
Blandford, Hampden, Mass.	600 (636▲)	B2	206
Blanding, San Juan, Utah	1,805	F6	114
Blandinsville, McDonough, Ill.	883	C3	138
Blandville, Ballard, Ky.	133	D2	178
Blaney, Kershaw, S.C.	329	C7	188
Blanford, Vermillion, Ind.	800	C2	140
Blankenberge, Bel.	10,013	C2	282
Blankenburg [im Harz], Ger.	19,700	C4	286
Blanquilla, isl., Ven.		A6	240
Blanton, Lowndes, Ga.	125	F3	176
Blantyre, Rh. & Nya.	52,110	C6	421
Blasdell, Erie, N.Y.	3,909	C3	212
Blato, Yugo.	5,676	C3	316
Blauvelt, Rockland, N.Y.	3,000	D2	212
Blawnox, Allegheny, Pa.	2,085	*C1	214
Blaye [-et-Ste.-Luce], Fr.		E3	278
Blażowa, Pol.	4,002	D6	325
Bleckley, co., Ga.	9,642	D3	176
Bled, Yugo.	1,193	A2	316
Bledsoe, co., Tenn.	7,811	C6	190
Bleecker, Lee, Ala.	157	C4	168
Blekinge, co., Swe.	145,387	E6	292
Blekinge, reg., Swe.	145,387	*H6	291
Blencoe, Monona, Iowa	286	C1	142
Blende, Pueblo, Colo.	600	D6	106
Blenheim, Ont., Can.	2,844	R18	64
Blenheim, N.Z.	9,219	D4	437
Blenheim, Marlboro, S.C.	185	B9	188
Blenker, Wood, Wis.	100	D4	160
Blesetsk, Sov.Un.		C6	328
Blessing, Matagorda, Tex.	700	E7	130
Blessington, Ire.	478	H6	273
Blevins, Hempstead, Ark.	198	D3	170
Blida, Alg.	67,913	A4	402
Blija, Neth.	784	A4	282
Blind, pass, Fla.		E8	174
Blind, riv., La.		B6	180
Blind River, Ont., Can.	3,633	S25	64
Bliss, Gooding, Idaho	91	G4	108
Bliss, Holt, Nebr.	5	B7	152
Bliss, Wyoming, N.Y.	400	C3	212
Bliss, dam, Idaho		G3	108
Blissfield, Lenawee, Mich.	2,653	H8	146
Blita, Togo		E5	408
Blitzen, Harney, Oreg.		E7	96
Blocher, Scott, Ind.	250	D4	140
Block, isl., R.I.		E2	216
Block City, Hawkins, Tenn.	350	B9	190
Blocker, Pittsburg, Okla.	85	C8	128
Block Island (New Shoreham), Newport, R.I.	400 (486▲)	E2	216
Block Island, sound, N.Y.		D6	212
Block Island, sound, R.I.		E1	216
Blockton, Taylor, Iowa	343	D3	142
Blodgett, Scott, Mo.	203	D8	150
Bloedel, B.C., Can.		E10	52
Bloemfontein, U.S.Afr.	112,406 (*141,600)	E5	420
Blois, Fr.	28,190	D4	278
Blomkest, Kandiyohi, Minn.	171	G3	148
Blomstermåla, Swe.		E7	292
Blönduós, Ice.	529	L19	290
Blood, mtn., Ga.		B3	176
Bloodroot, mtn., Vt.		D3	218
Bloodsworth, isl., Md.		D7	182
Bloodvein, riv., Man., Can.		E4	60
Bloody Foreland, pt., Ire.		F4	272
Bloom, Ford, Kans.	100	E4	144
Bloomdale, Wood, Ohio	669	A3	156
Bloomer, Sebastian, Ark.	150	B2	170
Bloomer, Chippewa, Wis.	2,834	C2	160
Bloomfield, Ont., Can.	769	Q23	64
Bloomfield, Hartford, Conn.	5,000 (13,613▲)	B5	202
Bloomfield, Bibb, Ga.	4,381	*D3	176
Bloomfield, Greene, Ind.	2,224	C3	140
Bloomfield, Davis, Iowa	2,771	D5	142
Bloomfield, Nelson, Ky.	916	C5	178
Bloomfield, Dawson, Mont.	50	C12	110
Bloomfield, Stoddard, Mo.	1,330	E8	150
Bloomfield, Knox, Nebr.	1,349	B8	152
Bloomfield, Essex, N.J.	51,867	B1	210
Bloomfield, San Juan, N.Mex.	1,292	B3	126
Bloomfield, Essex, Vt.	120 (212▲)	B5	218
Bloomfield, Loudoun, Va.	25	*A7	192
Bloomfield Highlands, Oakland, Mich.	900	*G8	146
Bloomfield Hills, Oakland, Mich.	2,378	B8	146
Bloomfield Station, P.E.I., Can.	80	C5	70
Bloomfield Village, Oakland, Mich.	3,500	*B8	146
Bloomingburg, Fayette, Ohio	719	C3	156
Bloomingdale, Chatham, Ga.	1,000	D5	176
Bloomingdale, DuPage, Ill.	1,262	E2	138
Bloomingdale, Parke, Ind.	455	C2	140
Bloomingdale, Van Buren, Mich.	471	G6	146
Bloomingdale, Passaic, N.J.	5,293	A4	210
Bloomingdale, Essex, N.Y.	490	A7	212
Bloomingdale, Sullivan, Tenn.	950	*B9	190
Blooming Grove, Navarro, Tex.	725	C7	130
Blooming Grove, Dane, Wis.	8,500	*E4	160
Blooming Prairie, Steele, Minn.	1,778	H5	148
Bloomington, Bear Lake, Idaho	254	G7	108
Bloomington, McLean, Ill.	36,271	C4	138
Bloomington, Monroe, Ind.	31,357	C3	140
Bloomington, Garrett, Md.	338	A1	182
Bloomington, Hennepin, Minn.	50,498	G5	148
		G7	
Bloomington, Franklin, Nebr.	176	D6	152
Bloomington, Victoria, Tex.	1,756	E7	130
Bloomington, Grant, Wis.	735	F3	160
Bloomington Springs, Putnam, Tenn.	200	B6	190
Bloomsburg, Columbia, Pa.	10,655	C5	214
Bloomsbury, Hunterdon, N.J.	838	B2	210
Bloomsdale, Ste. Genevieve, Mo.	400	C7	150
Bloomville, Seneca, Ohio	836	A3	156
Blossburg, Jefferson, Ala.	500	E4	168
Blossburg, Tioga, Pa.	1,956	B4	214
Blossom, Lamar, Tex.	545	C8	130
Blossom Hill, Lancaster, Pa.	1,000	*D5	214
Blount, Kanawha, W.Va.	200	C6	194
Blount, co., Ala.	25,449	B3	168
Blount, co., Tenn.	57,525	C8	190
Blount Hills, Blount, Tenn.	500	*C8	190
Blount Springs, Blount, Ala.	75	B3	168
Blountstown, Calhoun, Fla.	2,375	A5	174
Blountsville, Blount, Ala.	672	A3	168
Blountsville, Henry, Ind.	218	*C4	140
Blountville, Sullivan, Tenn.	650	B9	190
Blowing Rock, Watauga and Caldwell, N.C.	711	A4	186
Bloxham, Leon, Fla.	100	A6	174
Bloxom, Accomack, Va.	349	C9	192
Blucher, Sask., Can.	45	E4	58
Bludenz, Aus.	10,178	C1	313
Blue, Bryan, Okla.	150	D7	128
Blue, bayou, La.		E5	180
Blue, creek, W.Va.		C6	194
Blue, hill, Kans.		D4	144
Blue, hills, Kans.		C5	144
Blue, lake, Iowa		B1	142
Blue, mound, Kans.		C4	144
Blue, mtn., Ark.		C2	170
Blue, mtn., Maine		D2	204
Blue, mtn., Mont.		C12	110
Blue, mtn., N.H.		B4	208
Blue, mtn., N.Y.		B7	212
Blue, mtn., Pa.		C4	214
Blue, mts., Austl.		E9	432
Blue, mts., Oreg., Wash.		B8	96
		C9	98
Blue, mts., Tex.		D6	130
Blue, riv., Ind.		D3	140
Blue, riv., Mo.		E2	150
Blue, riv., Okla.		D7	128
Blue Ash, Hamilton, Ohio	8,341	D1	156
Blue Ball, Montgomery, Pa.	1,000	*C6	214
Bluebell, Duchesne, Utah	250	*C5	114
Blueberry, riv., B.C., Can.		B12	52
Blue Buck, pt., La.		E2	180
Bluecreek, Stevens, Wash.	45	A9	98
Blue Creek, Kanawha, W.Va.	310	C3	194
		C6	
Blue Creek, Box Elder, Utah		B3	114
Blue Diamond, Perry, Ky.	300	C7	178
Blue Diamond, Clark, Nev.	250	G6	112
Blue Dome, Clark, Idaho		E6	108
Blue Earth, Faribault, Minn.	4,200	H4	148
Blue Earth, co., Minn.	44,385	G4	148
Blue Earth, riv., Minn.		H4	148
Blue Eye, Carroll, Ark.	69	*A3	170
Blue Eye, Stone, Mo.	74	E4	150
Bluefield, Tazewell, Va.	4,235	C3	192
Bluefield, Mercer, W.Va.	19,256	D3	194
Bluefields, Nic.	8,016	D6	228
Blue Grass, Scott, Iowa	568	C7	142
Bluegrass, Knox, Tenn.		E9	190
Blue Grass, Highland, Va.	75	B5	192
Blue Hill, Hancock, Maine	500 (1,270▲)	D4	204
Blue Hill, Webster, Nebr.	723	D7	152
Blue Hill, range, N.H.		E4	208
Blue Hill Falls, Hancock, Maine	100	D4	204
Blue Hills, Hartford, Conn.	4,000	B5	202
Blue Hills, range, Mass.		D3	206
Blue Hills of Couteau, hills, Newf., Can.		G7	72

Blue Island, Cook, Ill. 19,618 B6 138
F3
Bluejacket, Craig, Okla. 245 B8 128
Blue Jay, Raleigh, W.Va. 300 *D3 194
Bluejoint, lake, Oreg. E7 96
Blue Lake, Humboldt, Calif. 1,234 B2 94
Bluemont, Loudoun, Va. 225 A7 192
Blue Mound, Macon, Ill. 1,038 D4 138
Blue Mound, Linn, Kans. 319 D8 144
Blue Mound, Tarrant, Tex. 1,253 *C7 130
Blue Mounds, Dane, Wis. 227 *E4 160
Blue Mountain, Calhoun, Ala. 446 B4 168
Blue Mountain, Logan, Ark. 94 B3 170
Blue Mountain, Moffat, Colo. 30 B2 106
Blue Mountain, Tippah, Miss. 741 A3 184
Blue Mountain, lake, Ark. B3 170
Blue Mud, bay, Austl. A7 432
Blue Nile, prov., Sud. 2,069,646 C3 398
Blue Nile, riv., Eth. C4 398
Blue Nile, riv., Sud. C3 398
Blue Pennant, Boone, W.Va. 350 D3 194
D6
Blue Point, Suffolk, N.Y. 2,300 D4 212
Blue Rapids, Marshall, Kans. 1,426 C7 144
Blue Ridge, Alta., Can. C5 54
Blue Ridge, Fannin, Ga. 1,406 B2 176
Blue Ridge, Shelby, Ind. 150 C4 140
Blue Ridge, Botetourt, Va. 900 C5 192
Blue Ridge, dam, Ga. B2 176
Blue Ridge, lake, Ga. B2 176
Blue Ridge, mts., U.S. D10 77
Blue Ridge Summit,
Franklin, Pa. 650 D4 214
Blue River, B.C., Can. 410 D13 52
Blue River, Lane, Oreg. 250 *C4 96
Blue River, Grant, Wis. 356 E3 160
Bluesky, Alta., Can. 300 B3 54
Blue Springs, Barbour, Ala. 94 D4 168
Blue Springs, Union, Miss. 99 A4 184
Blue Springs, Jackson, Mo. 2,555 E2 150
Blue Springs, Gage, Nebr. 509 D9 152
Blue Stack, mts., Ire. G4 272
Bluestem, Lincoln, Wash. B8 98
Bluestone, res., W.Va. D4 194
Bluestone, riv., W.Va. D3 194
Bluevale, Ont., Can. 250 Q19 64
Blueville, Taylor, W.Va. 900 *B4 194
Bluewater, Valencia, N.Mex. 250 C3 126
Bluewater, lake, N.Mex. C2 126
Bluff, Alsk. C5 84
Bluff, N.Z. 2,693 G2 437
Bluff, San Juan, Utah 100 F6 114
Bluff, creek, Kans. E4 144
Bluff, creek, Kans. E5 144
Bluff, mtn., N.C. A4 186
Bluff, mtn., Vt. B5 218
Bluff City, Nevada, Ark. 140 D3 170
Bluff City, Harper, Kans. 152 E6 144
Bluff City, Henderson, Ky. 250 C3 178
Bluff City, Sullivan, Tenn. 948 B9 190
Bluff Park, Jefferson, Ala. 3,000 *B3 168
Bluffs, Scott, Ill. 779 D3 138
Bluff Springs, Escambia, Fla. 50 A3 174
Bluffton, Yell, Ark. 50 C3 170
Bluffton, Alta., Can. D5 54
Bluffton, Clay, Ga. 176 E2 176
Bluffton, Wells, Ind. 6,238 B4 140
Bluffton, Otter Tail, Minn. 211 E3 148
Bluffton, Allen, Ohio 2,591 B3 156
Bluffton, Beaufort, S.C. 356 G7 188
Bluford, Jefferson, Ill. 388 E5 138
Blumenau, Braz. 22,627 K7 257
Blumenhof, Sask., Can. 135 E4 58
Blumenthal, Ger. (part
of Bremen) B3 286
Blumut, mtn., Mala. G4 362
Blunt, Hughes, S.Dak. 532 C6 158
Bly, Riverside, Calif. 1,554 *E5 94
Bly, Klamath, Oreg. 600 E5 96
Blyn, Clallam, Wash. 50 A4 98
Blyth, Ont., Can. 757 Q19 64
Blyth, Eng. 34,500 F11 272
Blythe, Riverside, Calif. 6,023 F6 94
Blythe, Richmond and
Burke, Ga. 172 C4 176
Blythedale, Cecil, Md. 125 A7 182
Blythedale, Harrison, Mo. 179 A4 150
Blytheville, Mississippi, Ark. 20,797 B7 170
Blythewood, Richland, S.C. 300 C7 188
Bo, S.L. E2 408
Boac, Phil. 3,262 B6 358
Boaco, Nic. 3,073 D5 228
Boakview, Ont., Can. 165 O20 64
Board Camp, Polk, Ark. 70 C2 170
Boardman, Mahoning, Ohio 20,000 A6 156
Boardman, Morrow, Oreg. 153 B7 96
Boardmans Bridge,
Litchfield, Conn. 165 C2 202
Boatland, Fentress, Tenn. B6 190
Boatman, Mayes, Okla. 180 B8 128
Boa Vista, Braz. 5,132 E4 256
Boaz, Marshall, Ala. 4,654 A3 168
Boaz, Christian, Mo. 125 D4 150
Boaz, Richland, Wis. 117 E3 160
Bobbili, India 23,102 E4 366
Bobcaygeon, Ont., Can. 1,242 P22 64
Bobigny, Fr. 18,521 I10 278
Bobo, Coahoma, Miss. 150 A2 184
Bobo-Dioulasso, Upper Volta 38,131 D4 408
Bobrinets, Sov.Un. 25,300 H9 332
Bobrka, Sov.Un. 11,400 H5 332
Bobruysk, Sov.Un. 97,000 F7 332
Bobtown, Greene, Pa. 1,167 D2 214
Bobures, Ven. 1,525 B3 240
Boca, dam, Calif. C3 94
Boca Chica, is., Fla. G9 174
Boca Ciega, bay, Fla. C5 174
Boca de Uchire, Ven. A6 240
Bôca do Acre, Braz. 1,702 G3 256
Boca Grande, Lee, Fla. 300 E8 174
Bocaiúva, Braz. 3,474 D2 258
Bocaranga, Cen.Afr.Rep. E8 409
Boca Raton, Palm Beach, Fla. 6,961 E10 174
Bocas del Toro, Pan. 2,160 F6 228
Bocay, Nic. C5 228
Boccea (Buxus), It.
(part of Rome) *E4 302
Bochnia, Pol. 11,000 D5 325
Bocholt, Ger. 39,742 C2 286
Bochum, Ger. 342,400 C2 286
Bock, Mille Lacs, Minn. 91 F5 148
Boco Vicnada, Ven. D5 240
Bocock, Campbell, Va. 65 *C5 192
Boda, Cen.Afr.Rep. F8 409
Böda, Swe. 1,928 D8 292
Bodaybo, Sov.Un. 14,700 D13 329
Bodcaw, Nevada, Ark. 100 D3 170
Boddam, Scot. D11 272
Bode, Humboldt, Iowa 430 B3 142
Bodega, head, Calif. C2 94
Bodega Bay, Sonoma, Calif. 350 C2 94
Bodélé, depression, Nig., Chad C8 409
Bodem, Swe. 12,301 D9 290
Bodenham, Giles, Tenn. C4 190
Bodensee (Constance), lake, Switz. A5 312
Bodie, isl., N.C. B10 186
Bodine, mtn., B.C., Can. C10 52
Bodkin, pt., Md. B7 182
Bodmin, Eng. 6,000 K8 273
Bodmin, moor, Eng. K8 273
Bodo, Alta., Can. D7 54
Bodo, Nor. 8,221 C6 290
Bodrog, riv., Hung. A6 320
Bodrum, Tur. 4,742 C2 307
Bodva, riv., Hung. A5 320
Boelus, Howard, Nebr. 181 C7 152
Boende, Con.L. C3 414
Boeotia, see Voiotia, prov., Grc.
Boerne, Kendall, Tex. 2,169 A6 130
E6
Boeuf, bayou, La. D3 180
Boeuf, lake, La. E5 180
Boeuf, riv., La. B4 180
Boffa, Guinea 600 D2 408
Bogachevka, Sov.Un. D18 329
Bogallua, isl., Eniwetok B1 436
Bogalusa, Washington, La. 21,423 D6 180
Bogandé, Upper Volta D5 408
Bogard, Carroll, Mo. 277 B4 150
Bogart, Oconee and Clark, Ga. 403 C3 176
Bogata, Red River, Tex. 1,112 C8 130
Bogbonga, Con.L. B2 414
Bogenfels, S.W.Afr. E3 420
Boger City, Lincoln, N.C. 2,200 *B4 186
Boggeragh, mts., Ire. I3 273
Boggerik, isl., Kwajalein A1 436
Boggy Depot, Atoka, Okla. 40 D7 128
Boghari, Alg. 10,166 A4 402
(11,518▲)
Boghé, Maur. 1,200 C2 408
Bognor Regis, Eng. 25,700 K12 273
Bogodukhov, Sov.Un. 33,700 G10 332
Bogon, isl., Eniwetok B1 436
Bogor, Indon. 123,800 F3 358
Bogoroditsk, Sov.Un. 15,000 F12 332
Bogorodsk, Sov.Un. 36,200 D14 332
Bogotá, Col. 954,120 C2 244
Bogota, Bergen, N.J. 7,965 A1 210
Bogota, Dyer, Tenn. 250 B2 190
Bogotol, Sov.Un. 26,500 A11 336
Bogra, Pak. 25,303 K16 375
Boguchany, Sov.Un. 3,600 D11 329
Bogue, Graham, Kans. 234 C4 144
Bogue Chitto, Lincoln, Miss. 400 D2 184
Bogue Chitto, riv., La., Miss. D5 180
D2 184
Bogue, inlet, N.C. C8 186
Bogue Phalia, riv., Miss. B2 184
Boguslav, Sov.Un. 27,800 H8 332
Bohain [-en-Vermandois], Fr. 6,151 C5 278
Boharm, Sask., Can. 100 E5 58
Bohemia, Suffolk, N.Y. 2,000 *D4 212
Bohemia (Cechy), reg., Czech. B2 324
Bohemian Forest, mts., Ger. D5 286
*Bohemian-Moravian,
highlands, Czech.* B2 324
Bohodle, Som. D6 398
Bohol, isl., Phil. C6 358
Bohumin, Czech. 19,218 B4 324
Bohuslän, reg., Swe. 158,781 *G4 291
Boiestown, N.B., Can. 235 C3 70
Boiling Springs,
Cleveland, N.C. 1,311 B4 186
Boiling Springs,
Cumberland, Pa. 1,182 C4 214
Bois, lake, N.W.Ter., Can. D6 48
Bois Blanc, isl., Mich. D7 146
Boischatel, Que., Can. 1,461 R13 66
R16
Bois-Colombes, Fr. 27,899 I10 278
Boisdale, inlet, Scot. D5 272
Bois D'Arc, Greene, Mo. 152 D4 150
Bois D'Arc, Kay, Okla. 150 *B6 128
Bois-des-Filion, Que., Can. 1,648 S15 66
Bois de Sioux, riv., Minn. F2 148
Boise, Ada, Idaho 34,481 F2 108
Boise, co., Idaho 1,646 F3 108
Boise City, Cimarron, Okla. 1,978 B1 128
Bois Fort, Koochiching, Minn. 400 C5 148
Boissevain, Man., Can. 1,115 F2 60
Boissevain, Tazewell, Va. 600 C3 192
Bojador, cape, Sp.Sahara A2 408
Bojnūrd, Iran 15,293 B4 379
Bokanda, I.C. E4 408
Bokchito, Bryan, Okla. 620 D7 128
Boké, Guinea 5,700 D2 408
Bokhan, Sov.Un. D12 329
Bokhoma, McCurtain, Okla. 200 E9 128
Boko, Con.L. D2 414
Bokoro, Chad D8 409
Bokoshe, LeFlore, Okla. 431 C9 128
Bokungu, Con.L. C3 414
Bol, Chad D7 409
Bolafa, Con.L. B3 414
Bolama, Port.Gui. D1 408
Bolanos, mtn., Guam D7 436
Bolar, Bath, Va. 45 B5 192
Bolbec, Fr. 11,716 C4 278
Bolckow, Andrew, Mo. 232 A3 150
Bolding, Union, Ark. 75 D4 170
Bold Spring, Humphreys, Tenn. 125 B4 190
Bole, Ghana 1,813 E4 408
Bole, Teton, Mont. C4 110
Boleko, Con.L. C2 414
Boles, Scott, Ark. 120 C2 170
Boles, Idaho, Idaho D2 108
Bolesławiec, Pol. 16,300 C2 325
Boley, Okfuskee, Okla. 573 C7 128
Bolgrad, Sov.Un. 18,300 J7 332
Bolia, Con.L. C2 414
Boliden, Swe. D9 290
Boligee, Greene, Ala. 134 C1 168
Bolinas, Marin, Calif. 400 A4 94
Boling, Wharton, Tex. 950 E8 130
G7
Bolinger, Choctaw, Ala. 100 D1 168
Bolinger, Bossier, La. 100 B2 180
Bolívar, Arg. 14,010 C3 252
Bolívar, Col. 6,121 B1 244
Bolivar, Polk, Mo. 3,512 D4 150
Bolivar, Allegany, N.Y. 1,405 C3 212
Bolivar, Tuscarawas, Ohio 932 B5 156
Bolivar, Westmoreland, Pa. 716 C2 214
Bolivar, Hardeman, Tenn. 3,338 C3 190
Bolivar, Jefferson, W.Va. 754 B7 194
Bolivar, co., Miss. 54,464 B2 184
Bolívar, dept., Col. 737,890 B2 244
Bolívar, state, Ven. 127,436 C6 240
Bolivar, lake, Miss. B1 184
Bolívar (La Columna), mt., Ven. B3 240
Bolívar, mt., Ven. C7 240
Bolivia, Brunswick, N.C. 201 C7 186
Bolivia, country, S.A. 3,349,000 E5 236
246
Bolkhov, Sov.Un. 36,800 F11 332
Bolling, Butler, Ala. 300 D3 168
Bollinger, co., Mo. 9,167 D7 150
Bollnäs, Swe. 5,897 F7 291
Bollullos, Sp. 9,706 D3 298
Bolmen, lake, Swe. E4 292
Bolobo, Con.L. C2 414
Bologna, It. 364,100 C3 302
Bologna, prov., It. 787,000 *C3 302
Bologoye, Sov.Un. 22,000 D10 332
Bolomba, Con.L. B2 414
Bolotnoye, Sov.Un. 26,500 A10 336
Bolovens, plat., Laos D5 362
Bolsena, lake, It. D3 302
Bolshava Viska, Sov.Un. 16,200 H8 332
Bolshaya Lepetikha,
Sov.Un. 29,300 I10 332
Bolshaya Irgiz, riv., Sov.Un. B3 336
Bolshaya Uzen, riv., Sov.Un. C3 336
Bolshaya Yugan, riv., Sov.Un. A8 336
Bolshevik, is., Sov.Un. B12 329
Bolshoya Hamenka, riv., Sov.Un. S23 332
Bolshoy Tokmak, Sov.Un. 17,900 I10 332
Bolsward, Neth. 8,014 A4 282
Bolt, Raleigh, W.Va. 300 *D3 194
Bolton, Ont., Can. 1,093 Q21 64
Bolton, Tolland, Conn. 500 B6 202
(2,933▲)
Bolton, Eng. 163,800 H10 273
Bolton, Worcester, Mass. 150 B4 206
(1,264▲) C1
Bolton, Hinds, Miss. 797 C2 184
Bolton, Columbus, N.C. 617 C7 186
Bolton, Chittenden, Vt. 40 C3 218
(237▲)
Bolton, lake, Man., Can. C5 60
Bolton, riv., Man., Can. C4 60
Bolton Landing, Warren, N.Y. 600 B8 212
Bolton Notch, Tolland, Conn. 250 B6 202
Boltonville, Orange, Vt. 105 C4 218
Bolu, Tur. 11,884 A4 307
Bolu, prov., Tur. 318,612 *A4 307
Bolus, head, Ire. J2 273
Bolvadin, Tur. 12,604 B4 307
Bolzano, It. 76,900 B3 302
Bolzano, prov., It. 350,200 *B3 302
Boma, Con.L. 24,700 D1 414
Bomar, Lee, Va. 50 *D1 192
Bombala, Austl. 1,258 F9 432
Bombay, India 2,839,270 E2 366
Bombay, Franklin, N.Y. 400 A7 212
Bombay, state, India 48,265,221 E2 366
Bombay Hook, isl., Del. C4 172
Bombay Hook, pt., Del. C4 172
Bombetoka, Malag. C9 421
Bom Conselho, Braz. B3 258
Bom Despacho, Braz. 7,976 D1 258
Bom Jardim, Braz. 2,500 B3 258
Bom Jesús, Braz. B2 258
Bom Jesús da Lapa, Braz. 4,740 C2 258
Bömlo, isl., Nor. G1 291
Bomokandi, riv., Con.L. B4 414
Bomongo, Con.L. B2 414
Bomoseen, Rutland, Vt. 85 D2 218
Bomoseen, lake, Vt. D2 218
Bomu, riv., Afr. B3 414
Bon, cape, Tun. A6 402
Bon Accord, Alta., Can. 142 D6 54
Bonaigarh, India E4 368
Bon Air, Talladega, Ala. 297 B3 168
Bon Air, Delaware, Pa. 1,000 *D6 214
Bon Air, Chesterfield, Va. 1,500 B9 192
C7
Bonaire, Houston, Ga. 200 D3 176
Bonaire Island, Neth. poss.,
Neth. W.I. 5,218 *B5 236
Bonanza, Sebastian, Ark. 247 B2 170
Bonanza, Saguache, Colo. 19 D4 106
Bonanza, Klamath, Oreg. 297 E5 96
Bonanza, Uintah, Utah 60 *D6 114
Bonanza, peak, Wash. A6 98
Bonaparte, Van Buren, Iowa 574 D6 142
Bonaparte, mtn., Wash. A7 98
Bonaparte, riv., B.C., Can. E12 52
Bon Aqua, Hickman, Tenn. 150 C4 190
Boñar, Sp. 1,788 A4 298
Bonarlaw, Ont., Can. 82 P23 64
Bonaventure, Que., Can. 2,100 *Q10 66
Bonaventure, co.,
Que., Can. 43,240 *Q10 66
Bonavista, Newf., Can. 4,078 F9 72
Bonavista, bay, Newf., Can. F9 72
Bonavista, cape, Newf., Can. F9 72
Bond, Eagle, Colo. 150 C4 106
Bond, Leon, Fla. 750 *A6 174
Bond, Jackson, Ky. 600 C6 178
Bond, Stone, Miss. 500 E3 184
Bond, McIntosh, Okla. 50 C8 128
Bond, co., Ill. 14,060 E4 138
Bondoukon, I.C. 5,400 E4 408
Bondsville, Hampden and
Hampshire, Mass. 950 B3 206
Bonduel, Shawano, Wis. 876 D5 160
Bondurant, Polk, Iowa 389 A7 142
C4
Bondurant, Sublette, Wyo. 35 C2 116
Bondy, Fr. 22,411 I10 278
Bône, Alg. 114,068 A5 402
Bone, Bonneville, Idaho F7 108
Bone, gulf, Indon. E6 358
Bone, lake, Wis. C1 160
Bone Cave, Van Buren, Tenn. 50 C6 190
Bonesteel, Gregory, S.Dak. 452 D7 158
Boneville, McDuffie, Ga. 100 C4 176
Bonfouca, St. Tammany, La. 60 B8 180
Bonga, Eth. D4 398
Bonganoanga, Con.L. B3 414
Bongor, Chad D8 409
Bong Son, Viet. D6 362
Bonham, Fannin, Tex. 7,357 C7 130
Bon Homme, co., S.Dak. 9,229 D7 158
Bonidee, bayou, La. B4 180
Bonifacio, strait, It. E2 302
Bonifay, Holmes, Fla. 2,222 A5 174
Bonilla, Beadle, S.Dak. 75 C7 158
Bonin, see Ogasawara
Islands, Pac.O.
Bonita, San Diego, Calif. 2,000 D6 94
Bonita, Morehouse, La. 574 B4 180
Bonita, Lauderdale, Miss. 500 C4 184
Bonita, Malheur, Oreg. C9 96
Bonita, pt., Calif. A4 94
Bonita Springs, Lee, Fla. 356 E9 174
Bonn, Ger. 140,800 C2 286
(*255,000)
Bonne, bay, Newf., Can. F6 72
Bonneau, Berkeley, S.C. 402 E9 188
Bonne Bay, Newf., Can. F7 72
Bonner, Missoula, Mont. 150 D3 110
Bonner, co., Idaho 15,587 A2 108
Bonnerdale, Hot Spring, Ark. 40 C3 170
Bonners Ferry, Boundary,
Idaho 1,921 A2 108
Bonner Springs, Wyandotte,
Kans. 3,171 B7 144
C9
Bonnet, pt., R.I. D3 216
*Bonnet Carré, spillway and
floodway, La.* B7 180
Bonne Terre, St.
Francois, Mo. 3,219 D7 150
Bonneville, Multnomah, Oreg. 150 B5 96
Bonneville, Fremont, Wyo. 50 C4 116
Bonneville, co., Idaho 46,906 F7 108
Bonneville, dam, Oreg., Wash. B5 96
D5 98
Bonneville, peak, Idaho G6 108
Bonney Lake, Pierce, Wash. 645 B4 98
Bonnie Doone,
Cumberland, N.C. 4,481 *B7 186
Bonnieville, Hart, Ky. 376 C5 178
Bonnots Mill, Osage, Mo. 210 C6 150
Bonny, Nig. 8,690 F6 408
Bonny Blue, Lee, Va. 504 D1 192
Bonny Slope,
Multnomah, Oreg. 200 *B4 96
Bonnyville, Alta., Can. 1,495 C7 54
Bono, Craighead, Ark. 339 B6 170
Bono, Lawrence, Ind. 75 D3 140
Bono, Lucas, Ohio 450 A3 156
Bonorva, It. 7,500 E2 302
Bon Secour, Baldwin, Ala. 500 E2 168
Bonsecours, Que., Can. 350 S12 66
Bonthain, Indon. 6,711 F5 358
Bonthe, S.L. E2 408
Bonwood, Madison, Tenn. 75 *C3 190
Book, Catahoula, La. 20 C4 180
Booker, Lipscomb and
Ochiltree, Tex. 817 A5 130
Boolyglass, Ire. I5 273
Boom, Pickett, Tenn. 50 B6 190
Boomer, Fayette, W.Va. 1,657 C3 194
D6
Boon, Wexford, Mich. 150 E6 146
Boone, Pueblo, Colo. 548 D6 106
Boone, Boone, Iowa 12,468 B4 142
Boone, Boone, Nebr. 60 C8 152
Boone, Watauga, N.C. 3,686 A4 186
Boone, Norfolk, Va. 30 A8 192
Boone, co., Ark. 16,116 A3 170
Boone, co., Ill. 20,326 A5 138
Boone, co., Ind. 27,543 B3 140
Boone, co., Iowa 28,037 B4 142
Boone, co., Ky. 21,940 B6 178
Boone, co., Mo. 55,202 B5 150
Boone, co., Nebr. 9,134 C7 152
Boone, co., W.Va. 28,764 C3 194
Boone, riv., Iowa B4 142
Boone Grove, Porter, Ind. 175 A2 140
Boones Mill, Franklin, Va. 371 C5 192
Booneville, Logan, Ark. 2,690 B3 170
Booneville, Owsley, Ky. 143 C7 178
Booneville, Prentiss, Miss. 3,480 A4 184
Boons, pond, Mass. C1 206
Boonsboro, Washington, Md. 1,211 A4 182
Boon Terrace,
Washington, Pa. 1,100 *C1 214
Boonton, Morris, N.J. B4 210
Boonville, Mendocino, Calif. 950 C2 94
Boonville, Warrick, Ind. 4,801 D2 140
Boonville, Cooper, Mo. 7,090 C5 150
Boonville, Oneida, N.Y. 2,403 B6 212
Boonville, Yadkin, N.C. 539 A5 186
Boot, Eng. G9 273
Booth, Autauga, Ala. 250 C3 168
Booth, Douglas, Oreg. D2 96
Booth, Monongalia, W.Va. 400 *B4 194
Booth, hill, Conn. D3 202
Boothbay, Lincoln, Maine 600 E3 204
(1,617▲)
Boothbay Harbor, Lincoln,
Maine 1,850 E3 204
(2,252▲)
Boothia, gulf, N.W.Ter., Can. D10 48
Boothia, pen., N.W.Ter., Can. C9 48
Booths, creek, W.Va. A7 194
Boothspoint, Dyer, Tenn. 30 B2 190
Boothsville, Marion, W.Va. 200 A7 194
Boothton, Shelby, Ala. B3 168
Boothville, Plaquemines, La. 550 E6 180
Boothwyn, Delaware, Pa. 5,000 D6 214
Bootle, Eng. 79,400 H9 273
Booué, Gabon F7 409
Boporo, Lib. E2 408
Boppard, Ger. 8,700 C2 286
Boquerón, dept., Par. 28,082 B2 247
Boquete, Pan. 1,967 F6 228
Bor, Sud. 1,632 D3 398
Bor, Yugo. 14,244 B6 316
Borah, peak, Idaho E5 108

Borama, Som.		C5	398
Borama, pol. dist., Som.		C5	398
Borås, Swe.	62,728	D3	292
Borāzjān, Iran	8,543	D3	379
Borba, Braz.	1,037	F5	256
Borculo, Neth.	2,596	B5	282
Bordeaux, Fr.	257,946	E3	278
Bordeaux, McCormick, S.C.		D4	188
Bordeaux, Davidson, Tenn.	500	E7	190
Bordelonville, Avoyelles, La.	420	C4	180
Borden, Sask., Can.	208	D4	58
Borden (New Providence), Clark, Ind.	327	D4	140
Borden, co., Tex.	1,076	C5	130
Borden, isl., N.W.Ter., Can.		B7	48
Borden, lake, Swe.		C6	292
Borden Springs, Cleburne, Ala.	500	B4	168
Bordentown, Burlington, N.J.	4,974	C3	210
Border, Koochiching, Minn.	125	C4	148
Border, Lincoln, Wyo.		D1	116
Borderland, Mingo, W.Va.	300	D2	194
Bordheyri, Ice.		L19	290
Bordighera, It.	7,135	D1	302
Bordj Amquid, Alg.		D5	402
Bordj Flamand, Alg.		C4	402
Bordj Fouchet, Alg.		C2	402
Bordj Ouallen, Alg.		D4	402
Bordj Viollette, Alg.		C3	402
Bordley, Union, Ky.	150	C3	178
Bordulac, Foster, N.Dak.	200	C7	154
Bordzon, China		D2	348
Boré, Mali		C4	408
Borensberg, Swe.	1,157	C6	292
Boreray, isl., Scot.		D4	272
Borg, Ice.		L19	290
Borga, Fin.	8,446	F11	291
Borger, Neth.	1,411	B5	282
Borger, Hutchinson, Tex.	20,911	B5	130
Borgholm, Swe.	2,563	E7	292
Borghorst, Ger.	15,074	B2	286
Borgne, lake, La.		D6	180
Borgomanero, It.	1,900	C2	302
Borgo Piave, It.		*E4	302
Borgo Val di Taro, It.	3,882	C2	302
Borikhane, Laos		C4	362
Boring, Clackamas, Oreg.	800	*B2	96
Borislav, Sov. Un.	47,500	H4	332
Borisoglebsk, Sov. Un.	54,000	B2	336
Borisov, Sov. Un.	59,000	E7	332
Borispol, Sov.Un.	27,800	G8	332
Borja, Sp.	5,024	B6	298
Borjas Blancas, Sp.	4,240	B7	298
Borkou, reg., Chad		C8	409
Borkum, isl., Ger.		B2	286
Borlänge, Swe.	24,482	A6	292
Borne, Neth.	9,100	B5	282
Borneo, reg., Indon.	3,700,000	D4	358
Borneo, isl., Indon.		D4	358
Bornholm, co., Den.	48,632	*I6	291
Bornholm, reg., Den.	48,254	*I6	291
Bornholm, isl., Den.		F5	292
Bornos, Sp.	6,351	D4	298
Boromlya, Sov.Un.	33,900	G10	332
Boromo, Upper Volta		D4	408
Boron, Kern, Calif.	592	E5	94
Borovan, Bul.	5,644	B1	317
Borovichi, Sov.Un.	47,100	C9	332
Borovskoye, Sov.Un.	12,800	R22	332
Borrby, Swe.	3,815	F5	292
Borre, Den.		G3	292
Borroloola, Austl.		B7	432
Borsod-Abaúj-Zemplén, co., Hung.	560,000	*A5	320
Bort-les-Orgues, Fr.		E5	278
Boruca, C.R.	300	F6	228
Borūjerd, Iran	49,186	C2	379
Borup, Norman, Minn.	145	D2	148
Borzna, Sov.Un.	26,800	G9	332
Borzya, Sov.Un.	31,500	D13	329
Bosa, It.	8,100	E2	302
Bosanska Dubica, Yugo.	5,579	B3	316
Bosanska Gradiška, Yugo.	9,932	B3	316
Bosanska Kostajnica, Yugo.	2,171	B3	316
Bosanski Novi, Yugo.	4,884	B3	316
Bosanski Petrovac, Yugo.	3,250	B3	316
Bosanski Samac, Yugo.	2,950	B4	316
Boscawen, Merrimack, N.H.	350 (2,181▲)	E3	208
Bosco, Ouachita, La.	100	B3	180
Boscobel, Grant, Wis.	2,608	E3	160
Boshrūyeh, Iran		C4	379
Boskovice, Czech.	6,396	B3	324
Bosler, Albany, Wyo.	75	E7	116
Bosna, riv., Yugo.		B3	316
Bosnek, Neth. N.Gui.		E9	359
Bosnia-Hercegovina (Bosna i Hercegovina), rep., Yugo.	2,847,790	B3	316
Bosobolo, Con.L.		B2	414
Bosö-Fjärden, fjord, Swe.		C7	292
Bosporus, strait, Tur.		A3	307
Bosque, Valencia, N.Mex.	20	D4	126
Bosque, co., Tex.	10,809	D7	130
Boss, McCurtain, Okla.		E9	128
Bossangoa, Cen. Afr. Rep.		E8	409
Bossburg, Stevens, Wash.		A8	98
Bossembélé, Cen.Afr.Rep.		E8	409
Bossier, par., La.	57,622	B2	180
Bossier City, Bossier, La.	32,776	B2	180
Bostanc, Tur.		G13	307
Bostic, Rutherford, N.C.	274	*B4	186
Boston, Marion, Ala. (part of Brilliant)		A2	168
Boston, Eng.	24,200	I12	273
Boston, Thomas, Ga.	1,357	F3	176
Boston, Wayne, Ind.	240	C5	140
Boston, Nelson, Ky.	500	C5	178
Boston, Suffolk, Mass.	697,197 (*2,913,500)	D3	206
Boston, Summit, Ohio	450	B1	156
Boston, Allegheny, Pa.	2,300	*C1	214
Boston, Culpeper, Va.	40	B6	192
Boston, bay, Mass.		B6	206
Boston, mts., Ark., Okla.		B3 C9	170 128
Boston Bar, B.C., Can.	125	F12	52
Boston Heights, Summit, Ohio	831	B1	156
Bostonia, San Diego, Calif. (part of El Cajon)		D6	94
Bostonnais, riv., Que., Can.		Q12	66
Bostwick, Putnam, Fla.	400	B9	174
Bostwick, Morgan, Ga.	272	C3	176
Bostwick, Nuckolls, Nebr.	50	*D7	152
Boswarlos, Newf., Can.	200	F6	72
Boswell, Izard, Ark.	10	A4	170
Boswell, B.C., Can.	25	F14	52
Boswell, Benton, Ind.	957	B2	140
Boswell, Choctaw, Okla.	753	D8	128
Boswell, Somerset, Pa.	1,508	C2	214
Bosworth, Carroll, Mo.	465	B4	150
Botang, Indon.		D5	358
Botetourt, co., Va.	16,715	C5	192
Botev, peak, Bul.		B2	317
Botevgrad, Bul.	8,683	B1	317
Botha, Alta., Can.	102	D6	54
Bothell, King, Wash.	2,237	B4	98
Bothnia, gulf, Swe.		A9	292
Bothwell, Ont., Can.	765	R19	64
Bothwell, Greene, Miss.	75	D4	184
Bothwell, Box Elder, Utah	302	*B3	114
Botiala, Som.		C6	398
Botkinburg, Van Buren, Ark.	175	B4	170
Botkins, Shelby, Ohio	854	B2	156
Botoşani, Rom.	29,569	A4	321
Botsford, Fairfield, Conn.	150	D2	202
Bottineau, Bottineau, N.Dak.	2,613	B5	154
Bottineau, co., N.Dak.	11,315	B5	154
Bottrop, Ger.	105,700	*C2	286
Botucatú, Braz.	23,099	E1	258
Botwood, Newf., Can.	2,800	F8	72
Bouaflé, I.C.	800	E3	408
Bouaké, I.C.	30,753	E3	408
Bouar, Cen. Afr. Rep.		E8	409
Bou Arfa, Mor.		B3	402
Boucau, Fr.	5,400	F3	278
Boucherville, Que., Can.	3,911	S11 S16	66
Bouches-du-Rhône, dept., Fr.	1,048,762	*F6	278
Bouchette, Que., Can.	415	R9	66
Bou Djébena, well, Mali		C4	408
Boudreaux, Terrebonne, La.	300	E5	180
Boudreaux, lake, La.		*E5	180
Bougainville, isl., Solomon		D1	437
Bougainville, strait, Solomon		D1	437
Bougie, Alg.	43,934	A5	402
Bougival, Fr.		I9	278
Bougouni, Mali	2,250	D3	408
Bouillon, Bel.	3,088	E4	282
Boulder, Austl.	6,279	E4	432
Boulder, Boulder, Colo.	37,718	B5	106
Boulder, Jefferson, Mont.	1,394	D4	110
Boulder, Garfield, Utah	150	F4	114
Boulder, Sublette, Wyo.	30	D3	116
Boulder, co., Colo.	74,254	B5	106
Boulder, creek, Idaho		G1	108
Boulder City, Clark, Nev.	4,059	H7	112
Boulder Creek, Santa Cruz, Calif.	1,306	*D2	94
Boulevard Heights, Prince Georges, Md.	384	C4	182
Boulloum, well, Niger		C7	409
Boulogne-Billancourt, Fr.	93,998	C5 I9	278
Boulogne [-sur-Mer], Fr.	41,870	B4	278
Boumaine, Mor.		B2	402
Bouna, I.C.	2,600	E4	408
Boundary, co., Idaho	5,809	A2	108
Boundary, bay, Wash.		A3	98
Boundary, peak, Nev.		F3	112
Boundary, plat., Sask., Can.		F3	58
Bound Brook, Somerset, N.J.	10,263	B3	210
Boundiali, I.C.	2,200	E3	408
Bountiful, Davis, Utah	17,039	C4	114
Bounty, Sask., Can.	87	E4	58
Bourbeuse, riv., Mo.		C6	150
Bourbon, Marshall, Ind.	1,522	A3	140
Bourbon, Crawford, Mo.	779	C6	150
Bourbon, co., Kans.	16,090	E9	144
Bourbon, co., Ky.	18,178	B6	178
Bourbonnais, Kankakee, Ill.	3,336	B6	138
Bourbonnais, former prov., Fr.	318,000	D5	278
Bourem, Mali	1,700	C4	408
Bourg [-en-Bresse], Fr.	26,699	D6	278
Bourg, Terrebonne, La.	900	E5	180
Bourg-de-Péage, Fr.	7,151	E6	278
Bourges, Fr.	53,879	D5	278
Bourget, Ont., Can.	600	O25	64
Bourg-la-Reine, Fr.	11,708	I10	278
Bourgoin, Fr.	8,153	E6	278
Bourjeïmat, well, Maur.		C1	408
Bourke, Austl.	2,642	E9	432
Bourne, Barnstable, Mass.	750 (14,001▲)	C6	206
Bournedale, Barnstable, Mass.	130	*C6	206
Bournemouth, Eng.	142,600	K11	273
Bou Saâda, Alg.	11,661	A4	402
Bouse, Yuma, Ariz.	100	E2	124
Bousso, Chad		D8	409
Boutilimit, Maur.		C2	408
Bouton, Dallas, Iowa	145	C4	142
Boutte, St. Charles, La.	155	C6	180
Bovey, Itasca, Minn.	1,086	D5	148
Bovill, Latah, Idaho	357	C2	108
Bovina, Lincoln, Colo.	25	C7	106
Bovina, Warren, Miss.	100	C2	184
Bovina, Parmer, Tex.	1,029	B4	130
Bow (Bow Mills), Merrimack, N.H.	300 (1,340▲)	E3	208
Bow, Skagit, Wash.	300	*A4	98
Bow, lake, N.H.		E4	208
Bow, riv., Alta., Can.		E6	54
Bowbells, Burke, N.Dak.	687	B3	154
Bowden, Alta., Can.	296	E6	54
Bowden, Duval, Fla.	100	A10	174
Bowden, Creek, Okla.	35	B7	128
Bowdens, Duplin, N.C.	300	B7	186
Bowdish, res., R.I.		B1	216
Bowdle, Edmunds, S.Dak.	673	B6	158
Bowdoin, Sagadahoc, Maine	(668▲)	D6	204
Bowdoinham, Sagadahoc, Maine	375 (1,131▲)	D3 D6	204
Bowdon, Carroll, Ga.	1,155	C1	176
Bowdon, Wells, N.Dak.	259	C6	154
Bowdon Junction, Carroll, Ga.	150	C1	176
Bowen, Austl.	3,660	C9	432
Bowen, Hancock, Ill.	559	C2	138
Bowens, Calvert, Md.	100	D6	182
Bowentown, Cumberland, N.J.		E2	210
Bowers, Kent, Del.	324	D4	172
Bowers, Carbon, Mont.	6	E11	110
Bowers, coulee, Wash.		B8	98
Bowers Hill, Norfolk, Va.	800	A8	192
Bowerston, Harrison, Ohio	463	B5	156
Bowersville, Hart, Ga.	293	B3	176
Bowersville, Greene, Ohio	327	C3	156
Bowesmont, Pembina, N.Dak.	175	B8	154
Bowie, Cochise, Ariz.	650	F6	124
Bowie, Delta, Colo.	100	D3	106
Bowie, Prince Georges, Md.	1,489	B6	182
Bowie, Montague, Tex.	4,566	C7	130
Bowie, co., Tex.	59,971	C8	130
Bowie, creek, Miss.		D3	184
Bow Island, Alta., Can.	1,001	F7	54
Bowlegs, Seminole, Okla.	200	C7	128
Bowler, Carbon, Mont.		E8	110
Bowler, Shawano, Wis.	274	D5	160
Bowling Green, Hardee, Fla.	1,171	D9	174
Bowling Green, Clay, Ind.	229	C2	140
Bowling Green, Warren, Ky.	28,338	D4	178
Bowling Green, Pike, Mo.	2,650	B6	150
Bowling Green, Wood, Ohio	13,574	A1 A3	156
Bowling Green, Caroline, Va.	528	B7	192
Bowlus, Morrison, Minn.	263	F4	148
Bowman, Elbert, Ga.	654	B3	176
Bowman, Bowman, N.Dak.	1,730	D2	154
Bowman, Orangeburg, S.C.	1,106	E7	188
Bowman, co., N.Dak.	4,154	D2	154
Bowman, creek, Pa.		A4	214
Bowman, mtn., B.C., Can.		E12	52
Bowman's Corner, Lewis and Clark, Mont.	5	C4	110
Bowmanville, Ont., Can.	6,544	Q22	64
Bow Mar, Arapahoe and Jefferson, Colo.	748	*C5	106
Bow Mills, see Bow, N.H.			
Bowmont, Canyon, Idaho	25	F2	108
Bownemont, Kanawha, W.Va.	900	C3 C6	194
Bowness, Alta., Can.	6,217	E5	54
Bowokan, is., Indon.		E6	358
Bowring, Osage, Okla.	100	B7	128
Bowringpet, India	7,515	F3	366
Bowron, riv., B.C., Can.		D12	52
Bowser, lake, B.C., Can.		B8	52
Bowsman, Man., Can.	519	D2	60
Bowstring, lake, Minn.		D5	148
Bowstring, riv., Minn.		D5	148
Bow Valley, Cedar, Nebr.	75	B8	152
Box, creek, Wyo.		C7	116
Boxboro, Middlesex, Mass.	100 (744▲)	A5 C1	206
Box Butte, co., Nebr.	11,688	B2	152
Box Butte, creek, Nebr.		B3	152
Box Butte, res., Nebr.		B2	152
Box Elder, Hill, Mont.	230	B6	110
Box Elder, Pennington, S.Dak.	56	C3	158
Box Elder, co., Utah	25,061	B2	114
Boxelder, creek, Colo.		B6	106
Box Elder, creek, Mont.		E12	110
Boxelder, creek, Mont.		C8	110
Boxford, Essex, Mass.	300 (2,010▲)	A6	206
Boxholm, Boone, Iowa	250	B3	142
Boxholm, Swe.	4,162	C5	292
Boxmeer, Neth.	4,900	C4	282
Box Springs, Talbot, Ga.	300	D2	176
Boxtel, Neth.	9,700	C4	282
Boyaca, dept., Col.	737,890	B2	244
Boyce, Warren, Ky.	250	D4	178
Boyce, Rapides, La.	1,094	C3	180
Boyce, Clarke, Va.	384	A6	192
Boyceville, Dunn, Wis.	660	C1	160
Boyd, Lafayette, Ark.	25	D3	170
Boyd, Screven, Ga.	450	D5	176
Boyd, Lac qui Parle, Minn.	419	G3	148
Boyd, Carbon, Mont.	30	E7	110
Boyd, Wasco, Oreg.	30	B5	96
Boyd, Chippewa, Wis.	622	D2	160
Boyd, co., Ky.	52,163	B8	178
Boyd, co., Nebr.	4,513	B6	152
Boydell, Ashley, Ark.	85	D5	170
Boyden, Sioux, Iowa	562	A2	142
Boyden Arbor, Richland, S.C.	271	*C6	188
Boyd Hill, York, S.C.	950	*B6	188
Boyds, Montgomery, Md.	85	B5	182
Boyds Cove, Newf., Can.	300	F8	72
Boyds Creek, Sevier, Tenn.		C8	190
Boydsville, Clay, Ark.	25	A6	170
Boydsville, Graves, Ky.	80	D2	178
Boydton, Mecklenburg, Va.	449	D6	192
Boyera, Con.L.		C2	414
Boyer Knob, mtn., Md.		A2	182
Boyero, Lincoln, Colo.	66	D7	106
Boyertown, Berks, Pa.	4,067	C6	214
Boyes, Carter, Mont.	15	E11	110
Boykin, Miller, Ga.	601	E2	176
Boykin, Kershaw, S.C.	665	C7	188
Boykins, Southampton, Va.	710	D7	192
Boyle, Alta., Can.	304	C6	54
Boyle, Bolivar, Miss.	848	B2	184
Boyle, co., Ky.	21,257	C6	178
Boyles Ranch, Custer, Idaho		E4	108
Boylston, Montgomery, Ala.	1,300	C3	168
Boylston, N.S., Can.	460	D8	70
Boylston Center, Worcester, Mass.	400 (2,367▲)	B4	206
Boyne City, Charlevoix, Mich.	2,797	D6	146
Boyne Falls, Charlevoix, Mich.	260	D7	146
Boynton, Muskogee, Okla.	604	C8	128
Boynton, Somerset, Pa.	800	D2	214
Boynton Beach, Palm Beach, Fla.	10,467	E10	174
Boysen, Fremont, Wyo.	50	*C4	116
Boysen, res., Wyo.		C4	116
Boys Town, Douglas, Nebr.	997	D3	152
Bozeman, Gallatin, Mont.	13,361	E5	110
Bozeman, pass, Mont.		E6	110
Bozman, Talbot, Md.	150	C7	182
Bozoum, Cen.Afr.Rep.		E8	409
Bozovici, Rom.	3,431	B1	321
Bozrah (Town of), New London, Conn.	(1,590▲)	C7	202
Bozüyük, Tur.	7,618	B4	307
Bra, It.	13,100	C1	302
Braås, Swe.	3,170	D6	292
Brabant, prov., Bel.	1,919,837	D3	282
Brabant, lake, Sask., Can.		B6	58
Brač, isl., Yugo.		C3	316
Bracadale, Scot.	969	D6	272
Bracadale, bay, Scot.		D6	272
Bracciano, It.	5,432	*D4	302
Bracciano, lake, It.		D4	302
Bracebridge, Ont., Can.	2,849	O21	64
Braceville, Grundy, Ill.	558	B5	138
Brach, Libya	3,874	B2	394
Bräcke, Swe.		E6	290
Bracken, Sask., Can.	107	F3	58
Bracken, co., Ky.	7,422	B6	178
Brackenridge, Allegheny, Pa.	5,697	A4	214
Brackett, Eau Claire, Wis.	100	D2	160
Brackettville, Kinney, Tex.	1,662	E5	130
Brackley, Eng.	3,100	I11	273
Braco Maior, riv., Braz.		H6	257
Braco Menor, riv., Braz.		H6	257
Brad, Rom.	9,963	A2	321
Bradano, riv., It.		E6	302
Bradbury Heights, Prince Georges, Md.	1,100	*C6	182
Braddock, Camden, N.J.	300	D3	210
Braddock, Emmons, N.Dak.	141	D5	154
Braddock, Allegheny, Pa.	12,337	A4	214
Braddock, pt., S.C.		G7	188
Braddock Heights, Frederick, Md.	600	B4	182
Braddock Hills, Allegheny, Pa.	2,414	*C2	214
Braddyville, Page, Iowa	176	D2	142
Braden, LeFlore, Okla.	40	C9	128
Braden, Fayette, Tenn.	500	C2	190
Bradenton, Manatee, Fla.	19,380	D6 D8	174
Bradenton Beach, Manatee, Fla.	1,124	*D8	174
Bradenton South, Manatee, Fla.	3,400	*D8	174
Bradenville, Westmoreland, Pa.	1,000	C2	214
Bradford, White, Ark.	779	B5	170
Bradford, Ont., Can.	2,010	P21	64
Bradford, Eng.	286,400	H11	273
Bradford, Stark, Ill.	857	B4	138
Bradford, Franklin, Iowa	200	B4	142
Bradford, Penobscot, Maine	150 (690▲)	C4	204
Bradford, Merrimack, N.H.	300 (508▲)	E3	208
Bradford, Darke and Miami, Ohio	2,148	B2	156
Bradford, McKean, Pa.	15,061	B3	214
Bradford, Washington, R.I.	950	D2	216
Bradford, Gibson, Tenn.	763	B3	190
Bradford, Orange, Vt.	760 (1,619▲)	D4	218
Bradford, co., Fla.	12,446	B8	174
Bradford, co., Pa.	54,925	B5	214
Bradford, mtn., Conn.		B2	202
Bradford Center, Penobscot, Maine	175	C4	204
Bradfordsville, Marion, Ky.	387	C5	178
Bradgate, Humboldt, Iowa	166	B3	142
Bradley, Lafayette, Ark.	712	D3	170
Bradley, Monterey, Calif.	60	E3	94
Bradley, Polk, Fla.	1,035	D9	174
Bradley, Jones, Ga.	100	C3	176
Bradley, Kankakee, Ill.	8,082	B6	138
Bradley, Penobscot, Maine	500 (951▲)	D4	204
Bradley, Oktibbeha, Miss.	150	B4	184
Bradley, Jefferson, Ohio	500	B6	156
Bradley, Grady, Okla.	294	D6	128
Bradley, Greenwood, S.C.	135	C4	188
Bradley, Clark, S.Dak.	188	B8	158
Bradley, Raleigh, W.Va.	800	D7	194
Bradley, co., Ark.	14,029	D4	170
Bradley, co., Tenn.	38,324	C7	190
Bradley Beach, Monmouth, N.J.	4,204	C4	210
Bradley Gardens, Somerset, N.J.	1,800	*B3	210
Bradner, Wood, Ohio	994	A3	156
Bradore, hills, Newf., Can.		E7	72
Bradshaw, Vigo, Ind.	150	C2	140
Bradshaw, Jackson, Ky.	35	C7	178
Bradshaw, Baltimore, Md.	547	B7	182
Bradshaw, York, Nebr.	306	D8	152
Bradshaw, McDowell, W.Va.	950	D3	194
Bradshaw, mts., Ariz.		D3	124
Bradstreet, Hampshire, Mass.	250	B2	206
Bradwardine, Man., Can.	175	F2	60
Bradwell, Sask., Can.	134	E4	58
Bradwood, Clatsop, Oreg.	150	*A3	96
Brady, Pondera, Mont.	180	B5	110
Brady, Lincoln, Nebr.	273	C5	152
Brady, McCulloch, Tex.	5,338	D6	130
Brady, Lincoln, W.Va.	190	C2	194
Brady, mts., Tex.		D6	130
Brady Lake, Portage, Ohio	544	*A5	156
Bradyville, Cannon, Tenn.	75	C5	190
Braeholm, Logan, W.Va.	300	D5	194
Braemar, Scot.	1,291	E9	272
Braemar, Carter, Tenn.	800	B9	190
Braeside, Ont., Can.	506	O24	64
Braga, Port.	32,153	B2	298
Bragado, Arg.	16,104	C3	252
Bragança, Braz.	5,495	E1	258
Bragança, Port.	8,245	B3	298
Bragg, Raleigh, W.Va.	250	*D4	194
Braggadocio, Pemiscot, Mo.	450	E8	150
Bragg City, Pemiscot, Mo.	274	E8	150
Braggs, Lowndes, Ala.	300	C3	168
Braggs, Muskogee, Okla.	279	C8	128
Braggville, Middlesex, Mass.	150	D1	206
Braham, Isanti, Minn.	728	F5	148
Brahmanbaria, Pak.	38,042	L17	375
Brahmani, riv., India		D4	366
Brahmaputra, riv., India		D6	368
Braidwood, Will, Ill.	1,944	B5	138
Brăila, Rom.	102,500	B4	321
Brainard, Butler, Nebr.	300	C9	152
Brainards, Warren, N.J.		B2	210
Braine-le-Comte, Bel.	10,608	D3	282
Brainerd, Crow Wing, Minn.	12,898	E4	148
Brain Head, mtn., Utah		F3	114
Braintree, Norfolk, Mass.	31,069	B5 D3	206
Braintree, Orange, Vt.	100 (536▲)	D3	218
Braintree Highlands, Norfolk, Mass.		D3	206

Braithwaite, Plaquemines, La. 375 C7 180
Brakel, Ger. 6,137 C3 286
Brakpan, U.S.Afr. 85,102 E5 420
Brålanda, Swe. 3,978 C3 292
Braleys, Bristol, Mass. 200 *C6 206
Bralorne, B.C., Can. 425 E11 52
Braman, Kay, Okla. 336 B6 128
Brampton, Ont., Can. 12,587 Q21 64
R21
Brampton, Sargent, N.Dak. 70 E8 154
Bramwell, Mercer, W.Va. 1,195 D3 194
Branbgt, mtn., Swe. A3 292
Branch, Franklin, Ark. 257 B3 170
Branch, Newf., Can. 400 G9 72
Branch, Acadia, La. 100 D3 180
Branch, Manitowoc, Wis. 190 B6 160
Branch, co., Mich. 34,903 H6 146
Branch, riv., Wis. A6 160
Branch, riv., Wis. F4 160
Branchburg Park, Somerset, N.J. 200 *B3 202
Branchland, Lincoln, W.Va. 518 C2 194
Branchville, St. Clair, Ala. 250 B3 168
Branchville, Fairfield, Conn. 200 D2 202
Branchville, Sussex, N.J. 963 A3 210
Branchville, Orangeburg, S.C. 1,182 E7 188
Branchville, Southampton, Va. 158 D7 192
Branco, riv., Braz. E4 256
Brandbu, Nor. F4 291
Brande, Den. 3,585 I3 291
Brandenberg, Rosebud, Mont. 5 E10 110
Brandenburg [an der Havel], Ger. 87,100 B5 286
Brandenburg, Meade, Ky. 1,542 C4 178
Brandenburg, reg., Ger. B5 286
Brandenburg, mtn., S.W.Afr. D2 420
Brandon, Man., Can. 24,796 F3 60
F5
Brandon, Kiowa, Colo. 75 D8 106
Brandon, Hillsborough, Fla. 1,665 D8 174
Brandon, Buchanan, Iowa 322 B6 142
Brandon, Douglas, Minn. 353 F3 148
Brandon, Rankin, Miss. 2,139 C3 184
Brandon, Perkins, Nebr. 35 D4 152
Brandon, Greenville, S.C. 1,000 *B4 188
Brandon, Minnehaha, S.Dak. 200 D9 158
Brandon, Rutland, Vt. 1,675 D2 218
(3,329▲)
Brandon, Prince George, Va. C8 192
Brandon, Fond du Lac, Wis. 758 E5 160
Brandon, hill, Ire. I2 273
Brandonville, Preston, W.Va. 109 *B5 194
Brandsville, Howell, Mo. 128 E6 150
Brandt, Miami, Ohio 450 C2 156
Brandt, Deuel, S.Dak. 148 C9 158
Brandvlei, U.S.Afr. F4 420
Brandýs nad Labem, Czech. 6,904 *A2 324
Brandy Station, Culpeper, Va. 200 B7 192
Brandywine, Prince Georges, Md. 80 C6 182
Brandywine, Pendleton, W.Va. 125 C5 194
Brandywine, creek, Del. A3 172
Brandywine Springs, New Castle, Del. 400 B3 172
Branford, New Haven, Conn. 2,371 D4 202
(16,610▲)
Branford, Suwannee, Fla. 663 B8 174
Branford Point, New Haven, Conn. 300 D4 202
Braniewo, Pol. 1,373 A4 325
Brańsk, Pol. 2,542 B6 325
Branson, Las Animas, Colo. 124 E7 106
Branson, Taney, Mo. 1,887 E4 150
Brant, Alta., Can. 72 E6 54
Brant, co., Ont., Can. 77,992 Q20 64
Brantevik, Swe. F5 292
Brantford, Ont., Can. 51,869 Q20 64
Brantford, Eddy, N.Dak. 55 C7 154
Brantley, Crenshaw, Ala. 1,014 D3 168
Brantley, co., Ga. 5,891 E4 176
Brant Rock, Plymouth, Mass. 75 B6 206
Brantwood, Price, Wis. 40 C3 160
Bras d'Or, lake, N.S., Can. D9 70
Braselton, Jackson, Ga. 255 *B3 176
Brasfield, Prairie, Ark. 200 C5 170
Brashear, Adair, Mo. 309 A5 150
Brasher, Pemiscot, Mo. 135 E8 150
Brasher Falls, St. Lawrence, N.Y. 750 A7 212
Brasiléia, Braz. 1,634 H3 257
Brasília, Braz. 48,100 D1 258
Brasília, Braz. 1,828 D2 258
Brasília, fed. dist., Braz. 118,000 I7 257
Brașov, see Orașul-Stalin, Rom.
Brass, Nig. F6 408
Brasstown Bald, mtn., Ga. B3 176
Brassua, lake, Maine C3 204
Bratenahl, Cuyahoga, Ohio 1,332 B1 156
Bratislava, Czech. 246,695 B3 324
Bratislavský, co., Czech. 970,285 *B3 324
Bratsk, Sov.Un. 51,000 D12 329
Bratslav, Sov.Un. 18,100 H7 332
Bratt, Escambia, Fla. 150 A3 174
Brattleboro, Windham, Vt. 11,734 F3 218
Braunau [am Inn], Aus. 11,608 B5 313
Braunschweig, Ger. 244,500 B4 286
Brava, Som. 3,000 E5 398
(7,000▲)
Bråviken, lake, Swe. C7 292
Brawley, Imperial, Calif. 12,703 F6 94
Brawsley, peaks, Calif. C4 94
Braxton, Simpson, Miss. 191 C3 184
Braxton, co., W.Va. 15,152 C4 194
Bray, Ire. 10,856 H6 273
Bray, Stephens, Okla. 50 D6 128
Bray, head, Ire. H7 273
Braymer, Caldwell, Mo. 874 B4 150
Brayton, Audubon, Iowa 229 C3 142
Brayton, Bledsoe, Tenn. C6 190
Brazeau, riv., Alta., Can. D4 54
Brazil, Clay, Ind. 8,853 C2 140
Brazil, Appanoose, Iowa 300 D5 142
Brazil, Gibson, Tenn. 200 C2 190
Brazil, country, S.A. 64,216,000 D6 236
257
Brazil Lake, N.S., Can. 85 F4 70
Brazilton, Crawford, Kans. 250 E9 144
Brazoria, Brazoria, Tex. 1,291 E8 130
G7
Brazoria, co., Tex. 76,204 E8 130
Brazos, co., Tex. 44,895 D7 130
Brazos, peak, N.Mex. B4 126
Brazos, riv., Tex. D7 130
Brazzaville, Con.B. 99,002 G8 409
Brčko, Yugo. 12,290 B4 316
Brea, Orange, Calif. 8,487 C6 94
Breaden, lake, Austl. D5 432
Bread Loaf, mtn., Vt. C3 218
Breakenridge, mtn., B.C., Can. F11 52
Breakeyville, Que., Can. 460 R16 66
Breakneck, hill, Md. A2 182
Breared, Swe. E4 292
Breathitt, co., Ky. 15,490 C7 178
Breaux Bridge, St. Martin, La. 3,303 D4 180
Brechin, Ont., Can. 240 P21 64
Breckenridge, Summit, Colo. 393 C4 106
Breckenridge, Gratiot, Mich. 1,131 *F7 146
Breckenridge, Wilkin, Minn. 4,335 E2 148
Breckenridge, Caldwell, Mo. 605 B4 150
Breckenridge, Stephens, Tex. 6,273 C6 130
Breckenridge Hills, St. Louis, Mo. 6,299 *C7 150
Breckinridge, Garfield, Okla. 42 B6 128
Breckinridge, co., Ky. 14,734 C4 178
Breckinridge, mtn., Calif. E4 94
Brecknock, co., Wales 56,300 J9 273
Brecknock, pen., Chile H3 251
Brecksville, Cuyahoga, Ohio 5,435 A5 156
B1
Břeclav, Czech. 11,462 B3 324
Brecon, Wales 6,200 J9 273
Breda, Carroll, Iowa 543 B3 142
Breda, Neth. 96,317 C3 282
Bredasdorp, U.S.Afr. 3,995 F4 420
Bredenbury, Sask., Can. 456 E6 58
Bree, Bel. 6,825 C4 282
Breed, Oconto, Wis. 30 C5 160
Breedsville, Van Buren, Mich. 245 *G5 146
Breen, La Plata, Colo. 50 E2 106
Breese, Clinton, Ill. 2,461 E4 138
Bregalnica, riv., Yugo. D6 316
Bregenz, Aus. 20,277 C1 313
Bregovo, Bul. 5,271 A1 317
Breidha, fjord, Ice. L18 290
Breidhavik, Ice. L17 290
Breitenbush, Marion, Oreg. 50 C5 96
Brejo, Braz. 2,551 A2 258
Breman, Cullman, Ala. 65 B2 168
Bremangerland, isl., Nor. F1 291
Bremen, Haralson, Ga. 3,132 C1 176
Bremen, Ger. 508,600 B3 286
Bremen, Marshall, Ind. 3,062 A3 140
Bremen, Muhlenberg, Ky. 328 C3 178
Bremen (Town of), Lincoln, Maine (438▲) *D3 204
Bremen, Wells, N.Dak. 87 C6 154
Bremen, Fairfield, Ohio 1,417 C4 156
Bremen, state, Ger. 639,600 *B3 286
Bremer, co., Iowa 21,108 B5 142
Bremerhaven, Ger. 131,000 B3 286
Bremerton, Kitsap, Wash. 28,922 B4 98
D2
Bremerton East (Enetal), Kitsap, Wash. 2,539 *B4 98
Bremgarten, Switz. 3,469 A4 312
Bremo Bluff, Fluvanna, Va. 100 C6 192
Bremond, Robertson, Tex. 803 D7 130
Brendon, hills, Eng. J9 273
Brenford, Kent, Del. C3 172
Brenham, Washington, Tex. 7,740 D7 130
Brenish, Scot. C5 272
Brenner, pass, Eur. D6 266
Brent, Bibb, Ala. 1,879 C2 168
Brent, Ont., Can. 50 O22 64
Brent, Escambia, Fla. 7,000 A3 174
Brentford, Spink, S.Dak. 96 B7 158
Brenton, Wyoming, W.Va. 500 *D3 194
Brenton, pt., R.I. D3 216
Brentwood, Contra Costa, Calif. 2,487 A6 94
Brentwood, Prince Georges, Md. 3,693 C3 182
Brentwood, St. Louis, Mo. 12,250 B8 150
Brentwood, Rockingham, N.H. 75 F4 208
(1,072▲)
Brentwood, Suffolk, N.Y. 15,387 D3 212
Brentwood, Allegheny, Pa. 13,706 A4 214
Brentwood, Williamson, Tenn. 300 B5 190
E7
Brescia, It. 146,800 C3 302
Brescia, prov., It. 871,900 *C3 302
Breskens, Neth. 2,193 C2 282
Breslau, see Wroclaw, Pol.
Bressanone, It. 9,100 B3 302
Bressay, isl., Scot. A11 272
Bressler, Dauphin, Pa. 1,000 *C5 214
Bressuire, Fr. 6,206 D3 278
Brest, Fr. 110,713 C1 278
Brest, Sov.Un. 73,000 F4 332
Breton, Alta., Can. D5 54
Breton, isl., La. E6 180
Breton, sound, La. E6 180
Breton, strait, Fr. D3 278
Breton Woods, Ocean, N.J. 1,292 C4 210
Brettingsstadhir, Ice. K20 290
Bretton Woods, Eaton, Mich. 1,500 *G7 146
Brevard, Transylvania, N.C. 4,857 B3 186
Brevard, co., Fla. 111,435 C10 174
Breves, Braz. 1,234 F6 256
Břevnov, Czech. (part of Prague) *A2 324
Brevoort, lake, Mich. C7 146
Brevort, Mackinac, Mich. 75 C6 146
Brewarrina, Austl. 905 D9 432
Brewer, Penobscot, Maine 9,009 D4 204
Brewer, Perry, Mo. 200 D8 150
Brewers, Hond. C5 228
Brewers, Marshall, Ky. 60 D2 178
Brewster, Polk, Fla. 890 D9 174
Brewster, Thomas, Kans. 317 C2 144
Brewster, Barnstable, Mass. 500 C7 206
(1,236▲)
Brewster, Nobles, Minn. 500 H3 148
Brewster, Blaine, Nebr. 44 C6 152
Brewster, Putnam, N.Y. 1,714 D8 212
Brewster, Stark, Ohio 2,025 B5 156
Brewster, Okanogan, Wash. 940 A7 98
Brewster, co., Tex. 6,434 E4 130
Brewster, cape, Grnld. P34 290
Brewster, is., Mass. D3 206
Brewton, Escambia, Ala. 6,309 D2 168
Brewton, Laurens, Ga. 100 D4 176
Brežice, Yugo. 1,823 B2 316
Breznice, Czech. 2,385 B1 324
Breznik, Bul. 3,486 B1 317
Brezno nad Hronom, Czech. B4 324
Bria, Cen.Afr.Rep. E9 409
Brian Boru, peak, B.C., Can. C9 52
Briançon, Fr. 6,252 E7 278
Briarcliff Manor, Westchester, N.Y. 5,105 D8 212
Briare, Fr. D5 278
Briartown, Muskogee, Okla. 100 C8 128
Briarwood, Jefferson, Ky. 428 *B5 178
Briarwood, Clackamas, Oreg. 150 *B2 96
Briarwood Beach, Medina, Ohio 359 *B5 156
Bricelyn, Faribault, Minn. 542 H5 148
Briceville, Anderson, Tenn. 1,217 B7 190
Brickaville, Malag. C9 421
Brickeys, Lee, Ark. 62 C6 170
Brickyard, Russell, Ala. 800 C4 168
Bridal Veil, Multnomah, Oreg. 60 B4 96
Bridal Veil, falls, Alsk. G12 84
Bridal Veil, falls, Utah C4 114
Bridesville, B.C., Can. 108 F13 52
Bridge, Cassia, Idaho 10 G5 108
Bridge, Coos, Oreg. 200 D2 96
Bridge, creek, Sask., Can. F3 58
Bridge, riv., B.C., Can. E11 52
Bridgeboro, Worth, Ga. 250 E3 176
Bridgeboro, Burlington, N.J. 500 C3 210
Bridge City, Jefferson, La. 2,500 C7 180
Bridge City, Orange, Tex. 4,677 *D9 130
Bridgedale, Jefferson, La. (part of Metairie) C7 180
Bridgeford, Sask., Can. 42 E4 58
Bridgehampton, Suffolk, N.Y. 906 D5 212
Bridge Lake, B.C., Can. E12 52
Bridgeland, Duchesne, Utah 10 C5 114
Bridgeport, Jackson, Ala. 2,906 A4 168
Bridgeport, Mono, Calif. 300 C4 94
Bridgeport, Ont., Can. 1,402 Q20 64
Bridgeport, Mesa, Colo. 10 *D2 106
Bridgeport, Fairfield, Conn. 156,748 E3 202
(*322,800)
Bridgeport, Lawrence, Ill. 2,260 E6 138
Bridgeport, Marion, Ind. 700 D4 140
Bridgeport, Saginaw, Mich. 1,326 F8 146
Bridgeport, Morrill, Nebr. 1,645 C2 152
Bridgeport, Gloucester, N.J. 500 D2 210
Bridgeport, Belmont, Ohio 3,824 B6 156
Bridgeport, Caddo, Okla. 139 C5 128
Bridgeport, Baker, Oreg. 10 C9 96
Bridgeport, Montgomery, Pa. 5,306 A6 214
Bridgeport, Wise, Tex. 3,218 C7 130
Bridgeport, Douglas, Wash. 876 A7 98
Bridgeport, Harrison, W.Va. 4,199 B4 194
B7
Bridger, Carbon, Mont. 824 E8 110
Bridger, basin, Wyo. E2 116
Bridger, mts., Wyo. C4 116
Bridger, peak, Wyo. E5 116
Bridger, range, Mont. E6 110
Bridgeton, Parke, Ind. 350 C2 140
Bridgeton, St. Louis, Mo. 7,820 *C7 150
Bridgeton, Cumberland, N.J. 20,966 E2 210
Bridgeton, Craven, N.C. 638 B8 186
Bridgeton, Multnomah, Oreg. 300 *B4 96
Bridgeton, Providence, R.I. B2 216
Bridgeton Terrace, St. Louis, Mo. 625 *C7 150
Bridgetown, Barb. 13,345 E14 233
Bridgetown, N.S., Can. 1,041 E4 70
Bridgetown, Caroline, Md. 39 *B8 182
Bridge View, Cook, Ill. 7,334 *B6 138
Bridgeville, Sussex, Del. 1,469 F3 172
Bridgeville, Allegheny, Pa. 7,112 A3 214
Bridgewater, Austl. 329 G9 432
Bridgewater, N.S., Can. 4,445 E5 70
Bridgewater, Litchfield, Conn. 250 C2 202
(898▲)
Bridgewater, Adair, Iowa 225 C3 142
Bridgewater, Aroostook, Maine 700 B5 204
(999▲)
Bridgewater, Grafton, N.H. 40 D3 208
(293▲)
Bridgewater, see W.Bridgewater, Pa.
Bridgewater, McCook, S.Dak. 694 D8 158
Bridgewater, Windsor, Vt. 175 D3 218
(776▲)
Bridgewater, Rockingham, Va. 1,815 B6 192
Bridgewater Corners, Windsor, Vt. 100 D3 218
Bridgman, Berrien, Mich. 1,454 H5 146
Bridgnorth, Eng. 6,300 I10 273
Bridgton, Cumberland, Maine 1,715 D2 204
(2,707▲)
Bridgwater, Eng. 24,100 J10 273
Bridgwater, Plymouth, Mass. 4,296 C6 206
(10,276▲)
Bridgwater, bay, Eng. J9 273
Bridlington, Eng. 24,600 G12 273
Bridport, Eng. 6,700 K10 273
Bridport, Addison, Vt. 100 D2 218
(653▲)
Brieg, see Brzeg, Pol.
Brielle, Monmouth, N.J. 2,619 C4 210
Brienz, Switz. 2,861 B4 312
Brienz, lake, Switz. B3 312
Brier, creek, Ga. C5 176
Briercrest, Sask., Can. 171 E5 58
Brièreville, Alta., Can. C7 54
Brier Hill, St. Lawrence, N.Y. 400 A6 212
Brig, Switz. 3,854 B3 312
Brigantine, Atlantic, N.J. 4,201 E4 210
Brigantine, beach, N.J. E4 210
Brig Bay, Newf., Can. 80 E7 72
Brigden, Ont., Can. 485 R18 64
Briggsdale, Weld, Colo. 120 B6 106
Briggsville, Yell, Ark. 60 C3 170
Briggsville, Berkshire, Mass. 300 A1 206
Briggsville, Marquette, Wis. 200 E4 160
Brigham City, Box Elder, Utah 11,728 B3 114
Brighouse, B.C., Can. 750 B14 52
Bright, Ont., Can. 300 Q20 64
Bright, Niobrara, Wyo. C8 116
Brighton, Jefferson, Ala. 2,884 B3 168
E4
Brighton, Ont., Can. 2,182 P23 64
Brighton, Adams, Colo. 7,055 C6 106
Brighton, Eng. 158,700 K12 273
Brighton, Highlands, Fla. 50 D9 174
Brighton, Macoupin, Ill. 1,248 D3 138
Brighton, Washington, Iowa 724 C6 142
Brighton (Town of), Somerset, Maine (62▲) C3 204
Brighton, Livingston, Mich. 2,282 B6 146
G8
Brighton, Tillamook, Oreg. 100 B3 96
Brighton, Tipton, Tenn. 652 C2 190
Brighton (Town of), Essex, Vt. (1,545▲) *B5 218
Brighton, Kenosha, Wis. 35 F1 160
Brightsand, lake, Sask., Can. D3 58
Brightsville, Marlboro, S.C. B9 188
Brightwaters, Suffolk, N.Y. 3,193 E3 212
Brightwood, Clackamas, Oreg. 150 *B4 96
Brignoles, Fr. 5,347 F7 278
Brigus, Newf., Can. 850 G9 72
Brihuega, Sp. 2,123 B5 298
Brijnagar, India D2 368
Brilhante, riv., Braz. J6 257
Brilliant, Marion, Ala. 749 A2 168
Brilliant, B.C., Can. 500 F14 52
Brilliant, Jefferson, Ohio 2,174 B6 156
Brillion, Calumet, Wis. 1,783 A6 160
D5
Brilon, Ger. 10,340 C3 286
Brimfield, Peoria, Ill. 656 C4 138
Brimfield, Hampden, Mass. 350 B3 206
(1,414▲)
Brimhall, McKinley, N.Mex. 200 C2 126
Brimley, Chippewa, Mich. 400 C7 146
Brimson, Grundy, Mo. 107 A4 150
Brindisi, It. 55,500 E6 302
(62,500▲)
Brindisi, prov., It. 326,500 *E6 302
Bringhurst, Carroll, Ind. 275 B3 140
Brinje, Yugo. 997 B2 316
Brinkley, Monroe, Ark. 4,636 C5 170
Brinkman, Greer, Okla. 14 C4 128
Brinktown, Maries, Mo. 375 C5 150
Brinkworth, Austl. 457 E7 432
Brinnon, Jefferson, Wash. 100 B4 98
Brinsmade, Benson, N.Dak. 110 B6 154
Brinson, Decatur, Ga. 246 F2 176
Brintbodarne, Swe. A5 292
Brioude, Fr. 5,687 E5 278
Brisbane, Austl. 555,000 D10 432
Brisbane, San Mateo, Calif. 5,000 B5 94
Briscoe, co., Tex. 3,577 B5 130
Bristol, N.B., Can. 290 C2 70
Bristol, Prowers, Colo. 250 D8 106
Bristol, Hartford, Conn. 45,499 C4 202
Bristol, Eng. 440,500 J10 273
Bristol, Liberty, Fla. 614 A6 174
Bristol, Pierce, Ga. 162 E4 176
Bristol, Kendall, Ill. (part of Yorkville) B5 138
Bristol, Elkhart, Ind. 991 A4 140
Bristol, St.Landry, La. 65 D3 180
Bristol (Town of), Lincoln, Maine (1,441▲) *D3 204
Bristol, Anne Arundel, Md. 39 C6 182
Bristol, Grafton, N.H. 1,054 D3 208
(1,470▲)
Bristol, Bucks, Pa. 12,364 C7 214
Bristol, Bristol, R.I. 14,570 C3 216
Bristol, Day, S.Dak. 562 B8 158
Bristol, Sullivan, Tenn. 17,582 B9 190
Bristol, Addison, Vt. 1,421 C2 218
(2,159▲)
Bristol (Independent City), Va. 17,144 D2 192
Bristol, Harrison, W.Va. 300 B6 194
Bristol, Kenosha, Wis. 350 F1 160
F5
Bristol, co., Mass. 398,488 C5 206
Bristol, co., R.I. 37,146 C3 216
Bristol, bay, Alsk. D5 84
Bristol, chan., Eng. J9 273
Bristol, pond, Vt. C2 218
Bristol Ferry, Newport, R.I. 175 C3 216
Bristol Terrace No.2, Bucks, Pa. 1,300 *C6 214
Bristolville, Trumbull, Ohio 900 A6 156
Bristow, Perry, Ind. 100 D3 140
Bristow, Butler, Iowa 268 B5 142
Bristow, Boyd, Nebr. 153 B7 152
Bristow, Creek, Okla. 4,795 C7 128
Bristow, Prince William, Va. 50 A6 192
Britannia Bay, Ont., Can. 270 Q25 64
Britannia Beach, B.C., Can. 1,250 F11 52
British Columbia, prov., Can. 1,594,000 F6 48
52
British Guiana, poss., S.A. 541,000 C6 236
257
British Honduras, poss., N.A. 88,000 B3 228
Britstown, U.S.Afr. 2,384 F4 420
Britt, Ont., Can. 215 O20 64
Britt, Hancock, Iowa 2,042 A4 142
Britt, St.Louis, Minn. 150 D6 148
Brittany (Bretagne), former prov., Fr. 3,072,000 C2 278
Brittany, Ascension, La. 20 B6 180
Brittany, hills, Fr. D2 278
Britton, Lenawee, Mich. 622 H8 146
Britton, Marshall, S.Dak. 1,442 B8 158
Brive [-la-Gaillarde], Fr. 36,088 E4 278
Briviesca, Sp. 3,587 A5 298
Brixham, Eng. 9,100 K9 273
Brněnský, co., Czech. 1,001,091 *B3 324
Brno, Czech. 306,371 B3 324
Broa, gulf, Cuba A3 232
Broach, India 62,729 D2 366
Broad, riv., Ga. B4 176
Broad, riv., S.C. C6 188
Broad, sound, Austl. C10 432
Broadacres, Sask., Can. 30 D3 58
Broadacres, Marion, Oreg. 65 B1 96
Broadalbin, Fulton, N.Y. 1,438 B7 212
Broadbent, Coos, Oreg. 300 D2 96
Broad Brook, Hartford, Conn. 1,389 B5 202
Broad Creek, Sussex, Del. F3 172
Broaddus, San Augustine, Tex. 200 D8 130
Broad Fields, Jefferson, Ky. 515 *B5 178
Broadford, Smyth, Va. 600 D3 192
Broad Haven, bay, Ire. G3 273
Broadhurst, Wayne, Ga. 200 E5 176
Broadkill, beach, Del. E5 172
Broadkill, riv., Del. E4 172
Broadland, Beadle, S.Dak. 33 C7 158
Broad Law, mtn., Scot. F9 272
Broadmead, Polk, Oreg. 15 *B3 96
Broadmoor, Jefferson, Ala. 800 *B3 168

Broadmoor, El Paso, Colo.	1,585	D6	106
Broadmoor, Orleans, La.	650	*D4	180
Broad Pass, Alsk.	10	*C7	84
Broad Run, riv., Va.		A6	192
Broadus, Powder River, Mont.	628	E11	110
Broadview, Sask., Can.	978	E6	58
Broadview, Cook, Ill.	8,588	*B6	138
Broadview, Monroe, Ind.	1,865	*C3	140
Broadview, Yellowstone, Mont.	160	D8	110
Broadview, Curry, N.Mex.	70	D7	126
Broadview Heights, Cuyahoga, Ohio	6,209	B1	156
Broadwater, Morrill, Nebr.	235	C3	152
Broadwater, co., Mont.	2,804	D5	110
Broadway, Warren, N.J.	250	B2	210
Broadway, Lee, N.C.	466	B6	186
Broadway, Rockingham, Va.	646	B6	192
Broby, Swe.	3,451	E5	292
Brochet, Man., Can.		*E5	60
Brock, Sask., Can.	240	E3	58
Brock, Nemaha, Nebr.	213	D10	152
Brockdell, Bledsoe, Tenn.		C6	190
Brocken, mtn., Ger.		C4	286
Brocket, Alta., Can.	75	F6	54
Brocket, Ramsey, N.Dak.	153	B7	154
Brockport, Monroe, N.Y.	5,256	B4	212
Brocksburg, Keya Paha, Nebr.	13	B6	152
Brockton, Plymouth, Mass.	72,813	B5	206
Brockton, Roosevelt, Mont.	367	B12	110
Brockton, res., Mass.		E3	206
Brockville, Ont., Can.	13,885	P25	64
Brockway, McCone, Mont.	185	C11	110
Brockway, Jefferson, Pa.	2,563	B3	214
Brockwell, Izard, Ark.	30	A5	170
Brocton, Edgar, Ill.	380	D6	138
Brocton, Chautauqua, N.Y.	1,416	C2	212
Brod, Yugo.	21,858	B4	316
Broderick, Sask., Can.	130	E4	58
Brodeur, pen., N.W.Ter., Can.		C10	48
Brodhead, Rockcastle, Ky.	762	C6	178
Brodhead, Green, Wis.	2,444	F4	160
Brodick, Scot.		F7	272
Brodnax, Brunswick and Mecklenburg, Va.	561	D6	192
Brodnica, Pol.	12,600	B4	325
Brody, Sov.Un.	26,900	G5	332
Brogan, Malheur, Oreg.	100	C9	96
Brokaw, Marathon, Wis.	319	C4	160
Broken Arrow, Tulsa, Okla.	5,928	B8	128
Broken Bow, Custer, Nebr.	3,482	C6	152
Broken Bow, McCurtain, Okla.	2,087	D9	128
Brokenburg, Spotsylvania, Va.	100	B7	192
Broken Hill, Austl.	31,351	E8	432
Broken Hill, Rh. & Nya.	17,000	B5	420
	(*27,000)		
Brokind, Swe.		C6	292
Brome, co., Que., Can.	13,790	S12	66
Brome, lake, Que., Can.		S12	66
Bromhead, Sask., Can.	117	F6	58
Bromide, Coal and Johnston, Okla.	264	D7	128
Bromley, Baldwin, Ala.	350	E2	168
Bromley, Kenton, Ky.	998	*B6	178
Bromolla, Swe.	4,422	E5	292
Bromptonville, Que., Can.	2,316	S13	66
Bronaugh, Vernon, Mo.	173	D3	150
Brönderslev, Den.	8,466	H3	291
Bronnitsy, Sov.Un.	9,400	O19	332
Brönnöysund, Nor.	1,564	D5	290
Bronson, Levy, Fla.	707	B8	174
Bronson, see Losantville, Ind.			
Bronson, Woodbury, Iowa	250	B1	142
Bronson, Bourbon, Kans.	354	E8	144
Bronson, Branch, Mich.	2,267	H6	146
Bronte, Ont., Can.	2,024	Q21	64
Bronte, Coke, Tex.	999	D5	130
Bronwood, Terrell, Ga.	400	E2	176
Bronx, Bronx, N.Y.		D2	212
Bronx, co., N.Y.	1,424,815	D2	212
Bronxville, Westchester, N.Y.	6,744	D2	212
Brook, Newton, Ind.	845	B2	140
Brookdale, Man., Can.	95	E3	60
Brooke, Stafford, Va.	100	B7	192
Brooke, co., W.Va.	28,940	A4	194
Brooken, Haskell, Okla.	75	C8	128
Brooker, Bradford, Fla.	292	B8	174
Brookeville, Montgomery, Md.	140	B5	182
Brookfield, N.S., Can.	200	D6	70
Brookfield, Fairfield, Conn.	500	D2	202
	(3,405▲)		
Brookfield, Tift, Ga.	990	E3	176
Brookfield, Cook, Ill.	20,429	F2	138
Brookfield, Worcester, Mass.	950	B3	206
	(1,751▲)		
Brookfield, Linn, Mo.	5,694	B4	150
Brookfield, Carroll, N.H.	40	D4	208
	(145▲)		
Brookfield, Madison, N.Y.	425	C6	212
Brookfield, Orange, Vt.	35	C3	218
	(597▲)		
Brookfield, Waukesha, Wis.	19,812	E1	160
Brookfield Center, Fairfield, Conn.	400	D2	202
Brookfield Mines, N.S., Can.	130	E5	70
Brookford, Catawba, N.C.	596	B4	186
Brookgreen, Georgetown, S.C.	100	D10	188
Brookhaven, De Kalb, Ga.	8,000	*C2	176
Brookhaven, Lincoln, Miss.	9,885	D2	184
Brooking, Sask., Can.	110	F5	58
Brookings, Clay, Ark.	100	A6	170
Brookings, Curry, Oreg.	2,637	E2	96
Brookings, Brookings, S.Dak.	10,558	C9	158
Brookings, co., S.Dak.	20,046	C8	158
Brookland, Craighead, Ark.	301	B6	170
Brooklands, Man., Can.	3,941	F4	60
Brooklands, Oakland, Mich.	1,800	*G8	146
Brookland Terrace, New Castle, Del.	900	*A1	172
Brooklawn, Camden, N.J.	2,504	D2	210
Brooklet, Bulloch, Ga.	557	D5	176
Brooklin, Ont., Can.	640	Q22	64
Brooklin, Hancock, Maine	400	D4	204
	(525▲)		
Brookline, Norfolk, Mass.	54,044	B5	206
		D2	
Brookline, Jackson, Mich.	1,600	*G7	146
Brookline, Hillsboro, N.H.	300	F3	208
	(795▲)		
Brookline, Windham, Vt.	89	E3	218
	(127▲)		
Brooklyn, Conecuh, Ala.	300	D3	168
Brooklyn, N.S., Can.	300	E5	70
Brooklyn, Windham, Conn.	900	B8	202
	(3,312▲)		
Brooklyn (Lovejoy), St. Clair, Ill.	1,922	*E3	138
Brooklyn, Morgan, Ind.	866	C3	140
Brooklyn, Poweshiek, Iowa	1,415	C5	142
Brooklyn, Jackson, Mich.	986	G7	146
Brooklyn, Forrest, Miss.	500	D3	184
Brooklyn, Kings, N.Y.		E2	212
Brooklyn, N.Z.	292	H8	437
Brooklyn, Cuyahoga, Ohio	10,733	B1	156
Brooklyn, Pacific, Wash.	25	C3	98
Brooklyn, Green, Wis.	590	F4	160
Brooklyn Center, Hennepin, Minn.	24,356	F6	148
Brooklyn Heights, Cuyahoga, Ohio	1,449	*A5	156
Brooklyn Park, Anne Arundel, Md.	1,800	*B6	182
Brooklyn Park, Hennepin, Minn.	10,197	F6	148
Brookmere, B.C., Can.	100	F12	52
Brookneal, Campbell, Va.	1,070	C6	192
Brook Park, Pine, Minn.	108	F5	148
Brook Park, Cuyahoga, Ohio	12,856	B1	156
Brookport, Massac, Ill.	1,154	F5	138
Brooks, Alta., Can.	2,320	E7	54
Brooks, Fayette, Ga.	158	*C2	176
Brooks, Adams, Iowa	185	D3	142
Brooks, Bullitt, Ky.	150	A5	178
Brooks, Waldo, Maine	550	D3	204
	(758▲)		
Brooks, Red Lake, Minn.	148	D3	148
Brooks, Marion, Oreg.	250	C1	96
Brooks, Adams, Wis.	130	E4	160
Brooks, co., Ga.	15,292	F3	176
Brooks, co., Tex.	8,609	F6	130
Brooks, pen., B.C., Can.		E9	52
Brooks, range, Alsk.		B6	84
Brooksburg, Jefferson, Ind.	129	D4	140
Brooksby, Sask., Can.	200	D5	58
Brookshire, Waller, Tex.	1,339	E8	130
		F7	
Brookside, Jefferson, Ala.	999	E4	168
Brookside, Fremont, Colo.	163	*D5	106
Brookside, New Castle, Del.	4,500	*A1	172
Brookside, Harlan, Ky.	400	*D7	178
Brookside, Phillips, Mont.		B8	110
Brookside, Morris, N.J.	300	B3	210
Brookside, Belmont, Ohio	831	*B6	156
Brookston, White, Ind.	1,202	B3	140
Brookston, St. Louis, Minn.	144	E6	148
Brooksville, Hernando, Fla.	3,301	C8	174
Brooksville, Bracken, Ky.	601	B6	178
Brooksville, Hancock, Maine	120	*D4	204
	(603▲)		
Brooksville, Noxubee, Miss.	857	B4	184
Brooksville, Pottawatomie, Okla.	200	C7	128
Brookton, Washington, Maine	160	C5	204
	(206▲)		
Brookview, Dorchester, Md.	83	C8	182
Brookville, Franklin, Ind.	2,596	C4	140
Brookville, Saline, Kans.	246	D6	144
Brookville, Norfolk, Mass.	3,000	B6	206
		E3	
Brookville, Ocean, N.J.		D4	210
Brookville, Montgomery, Ohio	3,184	C2	156
Brookville, Jefferson, Pa.	4,620	B2	214
Brookwood, Tuscaloosa, Ala.	500	B2	168
Brookwood, Caddo, La.	750	*B2	180
Broom, bay, Scot.		D7	272
Broomall, Delaware, Pa.	19,722	A6	214
Broome, Austl.	1,095	B4	432
Broome, co., N.Y.	212,661	C6	212
Broomes Island, Calvert, Md.	450	D6	182
Broomfield Heights, Boulder, Colo.	4,535	*C5	106
Brooten, Stearns, Minn.	661	F3	148
Brora, Scot.		C9	272
Brora, riv., Scot.		C8	272
Broscan, Dixie, Fla.	250	B7	174
Broseley, Butler, Mo.	200	E7	150
Brotas [de Macaúbas], Braz.	1,083	C2	258
Broten, Bonner, Idaho		*A2	108
Brothers, Deschutes, Oreg.	10	D6	96
Brothers, is., Thai.		F3	362
Brotherton, Putnam, Tenn.	65	B6	190
Brough, head, Scot.		B9	272
Broughton, Clay, Kans.	90	C6	144
Brounland, Kanawha, W.Va.	300	*C3	194
Broussard, Lafayette, La.	1,600	D4	180
Broward, co., Fla.	333,946	E10	174
Browerville, Todd, Minn.	744	E4	148
Brown, Harrison, W.Va.	300	A6	194
Brown, co., Ill.	6,210	D3	138
Brown, co., Ind.	7,024	C3	140
Brown, co., Kans.	13,229	C8	144
Brown, co., Minn.	27,676	G4	148
Brown, co., Nebr.	4,436	B5	152
Brown, co., Ohio	25,178	D3	156
Brown, co., S.Dak.	34,106	B7	158
Brown, co., Tex.	24,728	D6	130
Brown, co., Wis.	125,082	D6	160
Brown, lake, Austl.		E3	432
Brown, pt., Wash.		C2	98
Brown, riv., Vt.		B2	218
Brown City, Sanilac, Mich.	993	F9	146
Brown Deer, Milwaukee, Wis.	11,280	E2	160
Brownell, Ness, Kans.	118	D4	144
Brownfield, Oxford, Maine	130	*E2	204
	(538▲)		
Brownfield, Tippah, Miss.	75	A4	184
Brownfield, Terry, Tex.	10,286	C4	130
Brownfields, East Baton Rouge, La.	750	*D4	180
Browning, Sask., Can.	50	F6	58
Browning, Linn and Sullivan, Mo.	412	A4	150
Browning, Glacier, Mont.	2,011	B3	110
Browning, entrance, B.C., Can.		D7	52
Brownington, Henry, Mo.	130	C4	150
Brownington, Orleans, Vt.	50	B4	218
	(599▲)		
Brownlee, Sask., Can.	115	E4	58
Brownlee, Jackson, Colo.	4	*B4	106
Brownlee Park, Calhoun, Mich.	3,307	*G6	146
Brownlee, Cherry, Nebr.	36	B5	152
Brownlee, Baker, Oreg.	800	C10	96
Browns, Oldham, Ky.	300	A5	178
Browns, brook, Del.		E3	172
Browns, inlet, N.C.		C8	186
Browns (Motukorea), isl., N.Z.		H9	437
Brownsboro, Jackson, Oreg.		E4	96
Brownsboro Village, Jefferson, Ky.	598	*B5	178
Brownsburg, Que., Can.	3,412	S10	66
Brownsburg, Hendricks, Ind.	4,478	C3	140
Brownsburg, Rockbridge, Va.	300	C5	192
Brownsdale, Mower, Minn.	622	H6	148
Brownsmead, Clatsop, Oreg.	140	A3	96
Browns Mills, Burlington, N.J.	792	D3	210
Brownson, Cheyenne, Nebr.	50	*C2	152
Browns Point, Pierce, Wash.	600	*B4	98
Brownstown, Fayette, Ill.	659	E5	138
Brownstown, Jackson, Ind.	2,140	D3	140
Brownstown, Cambria, Pa.	1,379	C3	214
Brownstown, Yakima, Wash.	60	C6	98
Browns Valley, Montgomery, Ind.	75	C3	140
Browns Valley, Traverse, Minn.	1,033	F2	148
Brownsville, Union, Ind.	250	C4	140
Brownsville, see West Pensacola, Fla.			
Brownsville, Edmonson, Ky.	473	C4	178
Brownsville, Ouachita, La.	3,000	*B3	180
Brownsville, Washington, Md.	170	B4	182
Brownsville, Houston, Minn.	382	H7	148
Brownsville, Linn, Oreg.	875	C4	96
Brownsville, Fayette, Pa.	6,055	C2	214
Brownsville, Haywood, Tenn.	5,424	C2	190
Brownsville, Cameron, Tex.	48,040	G7	130
	(*49,500)		
Brownsville, Windsor, Vt.	70	E4	218
Brownsville, Dodge, Wis.	276	E5	160
Brownsville Township, Fayette, Pa.	1,365	*D2	214
Brownton, McLeod, Minn.	698	G4	148
Brownton, Barbour, W.Va.	745	B4	194
Browntown, Green, Wis.	263	F4	160
Brownvale, Alta., Can.	177	B3	54
Brownville, Jefferson, Ala.	534	*B3	168
Brownville, Tuscaloosa, Ala.	400	B2	168
Brownville, Piscataquis, Maine	700	C3	204
	(1,641▲)		
Brownville, Nemaha, Nebr.	243	D10	152
Brownville, Jefferson, N.Y.	1,082	A6	212
Brownville Junction, Piscataquis, Maine	900	C3	204
Brownwood, Stoddard, Mo.	150	D8	150
Brownwood, Brown, Tex.	16,974	D6	130
Brownwood, Orange, Tex.	1,286	*D9	130
Brownwood, lake, Tex.		D6	130
Broxton, Coffee, Ga.	907	E4	176
Broye, riv., Switz.		B2	312
Brozas, Sp.	6,076	C3	298
Brozville, Holmes, Miss.		B2	184
Bruay[-en-Artois], Fr.	31,923	B5	278
Bruce, Alta., Can.	150	D6	54
Bruce, Walton, Fla.	300	A5	174
Bruce, Calhoun, Miss.	1,698	B3	184
Bruce, Brookings, S.Dak.	272	C9	158
Bruce, Rusk, Wis.	815	C2	160
Bruce, co., Ont., Can.	42,070	P19	64
Bruce, mtn., Austl.		C3	432
Bruce, pt., P.E.I., Can.		C7	70
Bruce Crossing, Ontonagon, Mich.	130	C2	146
Brucefield, Ont., Can.	190	Q19	64
Bruceton, Carroll, Tenn.	1,158	B3	190
Bruceton Mills, Preston, W.Va.	209	B5	194
Brucetown, Frederick, Va.	200	A6	192
Bruceville, Knox, Ind.	623	D2	140
Bruceville, Talbot, Md.	75	C8	182
Bruchsal, Ger.	18,900	D3	286
Bruck [an der Grossglockner-strasse], Aus.		C4	313
Bruck [an der Leitha], Aus.	6,663	B8	313
Bruck [an der Mur], Aus.	14,731	C7	313
Brückenau, Ger.		C3	286
Bruderheim, Alta., Can.	290	D6	54
Bruges, see Brugge, Bel.			
Brugg, Switz.	5,508	A4	312
Brugge (Bruges), Bel.	52,278	C2	282
Bruini, India		C7	368
Brule, Keith, Nebr.	370	C4	152
Brule, Douglas, Wis.	100	B2	160
Brule, co., S.Dak.	6,319	D6	158
Brule, lake, Minn.		D8	148
Brule, riv., Mich., Wis.		D3	146
		C5	160
Brule riv., Wis.		B2	160
Brûle Lake Station, Ont., Can.	50	O22	64
Brumado, Braz.	3,012	C2	258
Brumath, Fr.	6,273	C7	278
Brundidge, Pike, Ala.	2,523	D4	168
Bruneau, Owyhee, Idaho	200	G3	108
Bruneau, riv., Idaho, Nev.		G3	108
		A6	112
Brunei, Bru.	16,000	D5	358
Brunei, Br. poss., Asia	40,657	I13	340
			359
Brunei, bay, Bru.		C5	358
Brunete, Sp.	678	*B5	298
Brunette, isl., Newf., Can.		G7	72
Brunette Downs, Austl.		B7	432
Bruning, Thayer, Nebr.	289	*D8	152
Brunkild, Man., Can.	80	F4	60
Brunner, lake, N.Z.		E3	437
Bruno, Sask., Can.	646	D5	58
Bruno, Pine, Minn.	116	E6	148
Bruno, Atoka, Okla.	30	D7	128
Brunson, Hampton, S.C.	603	F6	188
Brunsville, Plymouth, Iowa	128	B1	142
Brunswick, Glynn, Ga.	21,703	E5	176
Brunswick, see Braunschweig, Ger.			
Brunswick, Cumberland, Maine	12,500	E3	204
	(15,797▲)	E5	
Brunswick, Frederick, Md.	3,555	B4	182
Brunswick, Chariton, Mo.	1,493	B4	150
Brunswick, Antelope, Nebr.	254	B8	152
Brunswick, Medina, Ohio	6,453	A5	156
Brunswick, Essex, Vt.	(62▲)	*B5	218
Brunswick, Brunswick, Va.		D7	192
Brunswick, co., N.C.	20,278	C7	186
Brunswick, co., Va.	17,779	D7	192
Brunswick (Braunschweig), reg., Ger.		*B4	286
Brunswick, pen., Chile		H3	251
Bruree, Ire.	329	I4	273
Brusett, Garfield, Mont.	12	C9	110
Brush, Morgan, Colo.	3,621	B7	106
Brush Creek, Smith, Tenn.	200	B5	190
Brushy, mts., N.C.		B4	186
Brusly Landing, West Baton Rouge, La.	544	B5	180
Brusque, Braz.	11,011	K7	257
Brussels (Bruxelles), Bel.	171,020	D3	282
	(*1,360,000)		
Brussels, Ont., Can.	782	Q19	64
Brussels, Door, Wis.	200	D6	160
Bruton, Eng.	1,614	J10	273
Bruxelles, see Brussels, Bel.			
Bruxelles, Man., Can.	100	F3	60
Bryan, Williams, Ohio	7,361	A2	156
Bryan, Brazos, Tex.	27,542	D7	130
Bryan, Sweetwater, Wyo.	10	E3	116
Bryan, co., Ga.	6,226	D5	176
Bryan, co., Okla.	24,252	E7	128
Bryansk, Sov.Un.	206,000	F10	332
Bryans Road, Charles, Md.	50	C5	182
Bryant, Saline, Ark.	737	C4	170
		D6	
Bryant, Sask., Can.	45	F6	58
Bryant, Palm Beach, Fla.	450	E10	174
Bryant, Fulton, Ill.	346	C3	138
Bryant, Jay, Ind.	316	B5	140
Bryant, Yalobusha, Miss.		B3	184
Bryant, Okmulgee, Okla.	72	C7	128
Bryant, Clackamas, Oreg.		B1	96
Bryant, Hamlin, S.Dak.	522	C8	158
Bryant, Langlade, Wis.	100	C4	160
Bryant, mtn., Mass.		B2	206
Bryant Pond, Oxford, Maine	600	D2	204
Bryantsville, Garrard, Ky.	73	C6	178
Bryantville, Plymouth, Mass.	500	B6	206
Bryce Canyon, Garfield, Utah	5	F3	114
Bryce Canyon, natl. park, Utah		F3	114
Bryceland, Bienville, La.	89	B3	180
Bryceville, Nassau, Fla.	75	A9	174
Bryn Athyn, Montgomery, Pa.	1,057	A7	214
Bryn Mawr, Montgomery and Delaware, Pa.	9,000	A6	214
Bryn Mawr, King, Wash.	10,000	D3	98
Bryson City, Swain, N.C.	1,084	B2	186
Bryson Mountain, Claiborne, Tenn.	100	B8	190
Brzeg, Pol.	18,000	C3	325
Brzesko, Pol.	2,684	D5	325
Brzeziny, Pol.	6,008	C4	325
Brzozów, Pol.	3,725	D6	325
B-Say-Tah, Sask., Can.	21	E6	58
Buba, Port. Gui.		D1	408
Bucaramanga, Col.	153,790	B2	244
Buccaneer, arch., Austl.		B4	432
Buchanan, Sask., Can.	460	E6	58
Buchanan, Haralson, Ga.	753	C1	176
Buchanan, Lawrence, Ky.	125	B8	178
Buchanan, Lib.		E2	408
Buchanan, Berrien, Mich.	5,341	H5	146
Buchanan, Westchester, N.Y.	2,019	*D8	212
Buchanan, Stutsman, N.Dak.	76	C7	154
Buchanan, Henry, Tenn.	50	B3	190
Buchanan, Botetourt, Va.	1,349	C5	192
Buchanan, co., Iowa	22,293	B6	142
Buchanan, co., Mo.	90,581	B3	150
Buchanan, co., Va.	36,724	C2	192
Buchanan, lake, Austl.		C9	432
Buchan Ness, cape, Scot.		D11	272
Buchans, Newf., Can.	1,600	F7	72
Buchardo, Arg.		B3	252
Bucharest (București), Rom.	1,236,908	B4	231
	(*1,570,959)		
Buchloe, Ger.	5,400	D4	286
Buchon, pt., Calif.		E3	94
Buchs, Switz.	5,204	A5	312
Buchtel, Athens, Ohio	499	C4	156
Buck, creek, Ind.		D5	140
Buck, creek, Ky.		C6	178
Buck, mtn., Wash.		A7	98
Buckatunna, Wayne, Miss.	300	D4	184
Buck Creek, Tippecanoe, Ind.	270	B3	140
Buckeye, Maricopa, Ariz.	2,286	E3	124
		H1	
Buckeye, Larimer, Colo.	5	B5	106
Buckeye, Hardin, Iowa	190	B4	142
Buckeye, Lea, N.Mex.	225	F7	126
Buckeye, Pocahontas, W.Va.	350	C4	194
Buckeye Lake, Licking, Ohio	2,129	C4	156
Buckeystown, Frederick, Md.	400	B5	182
Buckfield, Oxford, Maine	400	D2	204
	(982▲)		
Buck Grove, Crawford, Iowa	40	*C2	142
Buckhannon, Upshur, W.Va.	6,389	C4	194
Buckhaven [& Methil], Scot.	21,300	E9	272
Buckhead, Morgan, Ga.	169	C3	176
Buckhorn, Madison, Mo.	100	D7	150
Buckhorn, Grant, N.Mex.	87	E2	126
Buckhorn, Weston, Wyo.		B8	116
Buckhorn Knob, mtn., W.Va.		D4	194
Buckie, Scot.	7,800	D10	272
Buckingham, Que., Can.	6,781	S9	66
Buckingham, Weld, Colo.	50	B7	106
Buckingham, Ocean, N.J.		D4	210
Buckingham, Buckingham, Va.	218	C6	192
Buckingham, co., Eng.	419,100	J12	273
Buckingham, co., Va.	10,877	C6	192
Buckland (Elephant Point), Alsk.	108	B5	84
Buckland, Que., Can.	615	R14	66
Buckland, Franklin, Mass.	150	A2	206
	(1,664▲)		
Buckland, Auglaize, Ohio	300	B2	156
Buckley, Iroquois, Ill.	690	C5	138
Buckley, Wexford, Mich.	247	E6	146
Buckley, Pierce, Wash.	3,538	B4	98
Bucklin, Ford, Kans.	752	E4	144
Bucklin, Linn, Mo.	639	B5	150
Buckman, Morrison, Minn.	166	F4	148
Bucknell Manor, Fairfax, Va.	2,000	*B7	192
Buckner, Lafayette, Ark.	289	D3	170
Buckner, Franklin, Ill.	610	F4	138
Buckner, Oldham, Ky.	200	A5	178
Buckner, Jackson, Mo.	1,198	B3	150
		E3	
Buckner, creek, Kans.		D4	144
Bucknum, Natrona, Wyo.		C6	116
Buckroe Beach, Va. (part of Hampton)		A9	192

Bucks, co., Pa.	308,567	C6	214
Bucks Harbor, Washington, Maine	150	D5	204
Buckskin, Gibson, Ind.	280	D2	140
Buckskin, mts., Ariz.		D2	124
Bucksport, Hancock, Maine	2,327 (3,466▲)	D4	204
Bucksport, Horry, S.C.	50	D10	188
Bucksville, Horry, S.C.	50	D10	188
Bucktail, Arthur, Nebr.	10	C4	152
Bucktown, Lake, Colo.	100	C4	106
Buckville, Garland, Ark.	75	C3	170
Bucoda, Thurston, Wash.	390	C4	98
Bucovina, prov., Rom.	300,751	*B7	321
Bucovina, reg., Rom.		A3	321
Buco Zau, Ang.		C1	414
Buctouche, N.B., Can.	790	C5	70
Bucyrus, Miami, Kans.	125	D9	144
Bucyrus, Adams, N.Dak.	60	D3	154
Bucyrus, Crawford, Ohio	12,276	B4	156
Bud, Wyoming, W.Va.	400	D3	194
Buda, Bureau, Ill.	732	B4	138
Budapest, Hung.	1,850,000 (*2,120,000)	B4	320
Budapest, co., Hung.	1,850,000	B4	320
Budaun, India	53,521	C2	368
Budd, lake, N.J.		B3	210
Budd Lake, Morris, N.J.	1,520	B3	210
Buddtown, Burlington, N.J.	100	D3	210
Bude [-Stratton], Eng.	5,200	K8	273
Bude, Franklin, Miss.	1,185	D2	184
Budennovsk, Sov.Un.		J15	332
Budge-Budge, India	32,196	I9	366
Budhareyri, Ice.		L23	290
Budhir, Ice.		L22	290
Budjala, Con.L.		B2	414
Budňany, Czech.	690	*B2	324
Budrio, It.	3,259	C3	302
Büdszentmihály, Hung.	11,996	B6	320
Buechel, Jefferson, Ky.	8,000	A5 B5	178
Buena, Atlantic, N.J.	3,243	D3	210
Buena, Yakima, Wash.	670	C6	98
Buena, Tucker, W.Va.	156	B5	194
Buena Park, Orange, Calif.	46,401	C5	94
Buenaventura, Col.	35,087	C1	244
Buenaventura, Mex.	2,613	B4	224
Buena Vista, Monroe, Ala.	300	D2	168
Buena Vista, Bol.	435	C2	246
Buena Vista, Chaffee, Colo.	1,806	D4	106
Buena Vista, Marion, Ga.	1,574	D2	176
Buena Vista, Garrard, Ky.	500	C6	178
Buenavista, Mex.	426	C5	224
Buenavista, Mex.	235	A5	224
Buena Vista, Chickasaw, Miss.	150	B4	184
Buena Vista, Carroll, Tenn.	200	C3	190
Buena Vista, Salt Lake, Utah	200	*C4	114
Buena Vista (Independent City), Va.	6,300	C5	192
Buena Vista, co., Iowa	21,189	B2	142
Buena Vista, lake, Calif.		E4	94
Bueno, riv., Chile		F3	251
Buenos Aires, Arg.	3,673,575 (*5,850,000)	B4	252
Buenos Aires, C.R.	750	F6	228
Buenos Aires, prov., Arg.	5,244,800	E5	250
Buenos Aires, lake, Chile		G3	251
Bueyeros, Harding, N.Mex.	12	C7	126
Buffalo, Chambers, Ala.	90	C4	168
Buffalo, Alta., Can.	100	E7	54
Buffalo, Sangamon, Ill.	356	D4	138
Buffalo, White, Ind.	250	B3	140
Buffalo, Scott, Iowa	1,088	C7	142
Buffalo, Wilson, Kans.	422	E8	144
Buffalo, Larue, Ky.	201	C5	178
Buffalo, Wright, Minn.	2,322	F5	148
Buffalo, Dallas, Mo.	1,477	D4	150
Buffalo, Fergus, Mont.	150	D7	110
Buffalo, Erie, N.Y.	532,759 (*1,244,200)	C3	212
Buffalo, Cass, N.Dak.	234	D8	154
Buffalo, Guernsey, Ohio	800	C5	156
Buffalo, Harper, Okla.	1,618	B4	128
Buffalo, Union, S.C.	1,209	B5	188
Buffalo, Harding, S.Dak.	652	B2	158
Buffalo, Humphreys, Tenn.		C4	190
Buffalo, Leon, Tex.	1,108	D7	130
Buffalo, Putnam, W.Va.	396	C3	194
Buffalo, Buffalo, Wis.	484	D2	160
Buffalo, Johnson, Wyo.	2,907	B6	116
Buffalo, co., Nebr.	26,236	D6	152
Buffalo, co., S.Dak.	1,547	C6	158
Buffalo, co., Wis.	14,202	D2	160
Buffalo, creek, Kans.		C5	144
Buffalo, creek, W.Va.		A6	194
Buffalo, creek, W.Va.		B2	194
Buffalo, creek, W.Va.		D5	194
Buffalo, lake, Alta., Can.		D6	54
Buffalo, lake, Tex.		B4	130
Buffalo, lake, Wis.		E4	160
Buffalo, riv., Ark.		B4	170
Buffalo, riv., Minn.		D2	148
Buffalo, riv., Tenn.		C4	190
Buffalo, riv., Wis.		D2	160
Buffalo Bill, res., Wyo.		B3	116
Buffalo Center, Winnebago, Iowa	1,140	A4	142
Buffalo Fork, creek, Wyo.		C2	116
Buffalo Gap, Sask., Can.	60	F5	58
Buffalo Gap, Custer, S.Dak.	194	D2	158
Buffalo Grove, Cook, Ill.	1,492	*E2	138
Buffalo Lake, Renville, Minn.	707	G4	148
Buffalo Ridge, Patrick, Va.		D4	192
Buffalo Springs, Mecklenburg, Va.	50	D6	192
Buffalo Valley, Putnam, Tenn.	175	B6	190
Buford, Rio Blanco, Colo.	10	C3	106
Buford, Gwinnett, Ga.	4,168	B2	176
Buford, Williams, N.Dak.	65	B2	154
Buford, Albany, Wyo.	20	E7	116
Buford, dam, Ga.		B2	176
Bug, riv., Pol.		B5	325
Bug, riv., Sov. Un.		G4	332
Buga, Col.	32,016	C1	244
Buganda, prov., Ug.		B5	414
Bugene, Tan.		C5	414
Bugojno, Yugo.	3,950	B3	316
Bugulma, Sov. Un.	61,000	B4	336
Buguruslan, Sov. Un.	35,700	B4	336
Buha, India		D6	368
Buhl, Tuscaloosa, Ala.	200	B2	168
Buhl, Twin Falls, Idaho	3,059	G4	108
Buhl, St. Louis, Minn.	1,526	D6	148
Buhler, Reno, Kans.	888	D6	144
Buhuşi, Rom.	12,382	A4	321
Buick, Elbert, Colo.	20	C7	106
Buies Creek, Harnett, N.C.	435	B7	186
Buitenpost, Neth.	1,515	A5	282
Buith Wells, Wales	1,600	I9	273
Bujalance, Sp.	14,022	D4	298
Buka, isl., Solomon		D1	436
Buka, passage, Solomon		D1	436
Bukama, Con.L.		D4	414
Bü Kammāsh, Libya		A2	394
Bukavu, Con.L.		C4	414
Bukene, Tan.		C5	414
Bukit Panjang, dist., Singapore	62,088	*G4	362
Bükk, mts., Hung.		B5	320
Bukollen, mtn., Nor.		A1	292
Bukuru, Nig.	8,450	E6	409
Bula, Con.L.		B4	414
Bula, Indon.		E8	359
Bülach, Switz.	4,634	A4	312
Buladean, Mitchell, N.C.	200	A3	186
Buladeen, Carter, Tenn.	100	B9	190
Bulan, Perry, Ky.	700	C7	178
Bulandshahr, India		C2	368
Bulawayo, Rh.&Nya.	120,000 (*145,000)	D5	420
Bulfontein, U.S.Afr.		E5	420
Bulgaria, country, Eur.	7,766,000	D7	266, 317
Bulhar, Som.		C5	398
Bulkley, mts., B.C., Can.		C9	52
Bulkley, riv., B.C., Can.		C9	52
Bull, Wayne, W.Va.		D2	194
Bull, bay, S.C.		F9	188
Bull, butte, N.Dak.		B2	154
Bull, creek, S.Dak.		B2	158
Bull, isl., S.C.		D10	188
Bull, isl., S.C.		F9	188
Bull, isl., S.C.		G7	188
Bull, mtn., Mont.		D4	110
Bullange, Bel.	2,205	D5	282
Bullaque, riv., Sp.		C4	298
Bullas, Sp.	7,790	C6	298
Bulle, Switz.	5,255	B3	312
Bullfrog, creek, Utah		F5	114
Bullhead, Corson, S.Dak.	200	B4	158
Bullhead, mtn., N.Y.		B7	212
Bullhead City, Mohave, Ariz.	250	C1	124
Bullion, butte, N.Dak.		D2	154
Bullitt, co., Ky.	15,726	C5	178
Bullittsville, Boone, Ky.	100	A7	178
Bullmoose, mtn., B.C., Can.		C12	52
Bulloch, co., Ga.	24,263	D5	176
Bullock, Crenshaw, Ala.	40	D3	168
Bullock, co., Ala.	13,462	C4	168
Bulloo, riv., Austl.		D8	432
Bull River, B.C., Can.	125	F15	52
Bull Ruffin, mtn., N.C.		A4	186
Bullrun, Loudoun, Va.		A6	192
Bull Run, dam, Oreg.		B4	96
Bull Run, mts., Va.		B7	192
Bull Run, ridge, Tenn.		E9	190
Bull Run, riv., Va.		A6	192
Bullsgap, Hawkins, Tenn.	682	B8	190
Bull Shoals, Marion, Ark.	268	A4	170
Bull Shoals, res., Ark.		A4	170
Bulnes, Chile	5,147	C1	252
Bulo Burti, Som.	3,300	E6	398
Buluan, Phil.	3,296	C6	358
Bulun, Sov.Un.	800	B14	329
Bulungu, Con.L.		C2	414
Bulwark, Alta., Can.	50	D7	54
Bulyea, Sask., Can.	172	E5	58
Bum, Solomon		E1	436
Bumba, Con.L.		B3	414
Bumping, riv., Wash.		C5	98
Bumpus Mills, Stewart, Tenn.	200	B4	190
Buna, Pap.		F11	359
Buna, Jasper, Tex.	950	D9	130
Bunbury, Austl.	9,869	E3	432
Bunceton, Cooper, Mo.	468	C5	150
Bunch, Adair, Okla.	80	C9	128
Buncombe, co., N.C.	130,074	B3	186
Bundaberg, Austl.	22,200	C10	432
Bundi, India		D1	368
Bundick, creek, La.		D2	180
Bundoran, Ire.	1,413	G4	273
Bunessan, Scot.		E6	272
Bungo, strait, Jap.		H4	354
Bungtlang, India		E6	368
Bunia, Con.L.		B5	414
Bunji, India		B1	368
Bunker, Reynolds, Mo.	250	D6	150
Bunker Hill, Macoupin, Ill.	1,524	D4	138
Bunker Hill, Miami, Ind.	1,049	B3	140
Bunker Hill, Russell, Kans.	200	D5	144
Bunker Hill, Coos, Oreg.	1,655	*D2	96
Bunker Hill, Harris, Tex.	2,216	*E8	130
Bunker Hill, Berkeley, W.Va.	246	B6	194
Bunkerville, Clark, Nev.	200	G7	112
Bunkeya, Con.L.		E4	414
Bunkie, Avoyelles, La.	5,188	D3	180
Bunn, Dallas, Ark.	25	C4	170
Bunn, Franklin, N.C.	332	B7	186
Bunnell, Flagler, Fla.	1,860	B9	174
Bunny Run, Oakland, Mich.	1,058	*G8	146
Bü Nujaym, Libya		A3	394
Buo Ha, Viet.	10,000	B5	362
Buqayo, Sau.Ar.		B4	383
Bura, Ken.		C7	414
Bur Acaba, Som.	2,500 (10,600▲)	E5	398
Buraku, isl., Solomon		E1	436
Buram, Sud.		C2	398
Buran, Som.		C6	398
Burao, Som.	10,000	D6	398
Buras, Plaquemines, La.	4,000	E6	180
Burathum, Nep.		C4	368
Buraydah, Sau.Ar.	20,000	B3	383
Burayk, Libya,	683	B2	394
Burbank, Los Angeles, Calif.	90,155	C5	94
Burbank, Wayne, Ohio	324	*B5	156
Burbank, Osage, Okla.	238	B7	128
Burbank, Clay, S.Dak.	112	E9	158
Burbank, Walla Walla, Wash.	600	C8	98
Burchard, Pawnee, Nebr.	132	D9	152
Burdekin, riv., Austl.		B9	432
Burden, Cowley, Kans.	580	E7	144
Burdett, Alta., Can.	225	F7	54
Burdett, Pawnee, Kans.	250	D4	144
Burdett, Schuyler, N.Y.	420	C5	212
Burdette, Mississippi, Ark.	115	B7	170
Burdick, Morris, Kans.	100	D7	144
Burdine, Letcher, Ky. (part of Jenkins)		C8	178
Burdur, Tur.	19,235	C4	307
Burdur, prov., Tur.	158,302	*C4	307
Burdwan, India	75,376	E4	368
Bureå, Swe.		D9	290
Bureau, Bureau, Ill.	401	B4	138
Bureau, co., Ill.	37,594	B4	138
Büren, Ger.	6,058	C3	286
Burford, Ont., Can.	675	Q20	64
Burg, Ger.	30,000	B4	286
Burg, Atoka, Okla.	60	D8	128
Burg (El Arab), Eg., U.A.R.		A2	395
Burgas, Bul.	72,795	B3	317
Burgas, gulf, Bul.		B3	317
Burgaski, prov., Bul.		*B3	317
Bur Gavo, Som.		F5	398
Burgaw, Pender, N.C.	1,750	C8	186
Burgdorf, Idaho, Idaho		D3	108
Burgdorf, Switz.	12,500 (*15,300)	A3	312
Burgenland, state, Aus.	276,136	*C8	313
Burgeo, Newf., Can.	1,138	G7	72
Burgesdorp, U.S.Afr.	6,184	F5	420
Burgess, Horry, S.C.	100	D10	188
Burgess, Northumberland, Va.	570	C8	192
Burgess Hill, Eng.	12,200	K12	273
Burgess Junction, Sheridan, Wyo.	15	*B5	116
Burgettstown, Washington, Pa.	2,383	C1	214
Burgin, Mercer, Ky.	879	C6	178
Burgos, Mex.		C6	225
Burgos, Sp.	61,789	A5	298
Burgos, prov., Sp.	390,058	*A5	298
Burgreuland, Bel.	1,985	D5	282
Burgsuiken, bay, Swe.		D9	292
Burgsvik, Swe.	312	D9	292
Burgundy (Bourgogne), former prov., Fr.	1,264,000	D5	278
Burhanpur, India	70,066	E2	368
Burhara, Sov.Un.		F7	328
Burhi Gandak, riv., India		D4	368
Burica, pt., C.R.		F6	228
Burien, King, Wash.	10,000	*B4	98
Burin, Newf., Can.	1,116	G8	72
Burin, pen., Newf., Can.		G8	72
Buriram, Thai.	189,000	D4	362
Buriram, prov., Thai.	339,480	*D4	362
Burkburnett, Wichita, Tex.	7,621	B6	130
Burke, Shoshone, Idaho	300	B3	108
Burke, Gregory, S.Dak.	811	D6	158
Burke, Caledonia, Vt.	50 (922▲)	*B5	218
Burke, Fairfax, Va.	150	A6	192
Burke, co., Ga.	20,596	C4	176
Burke, co., N.C.	52,701	B4	186
Burke, co., N.Dak.	5,886	B3	154
Burke, chan., B.C., Can.		D9	52
Burke City, St. Louis, Mo.	150	A8	150
Burkes Garden, Tazewell, Va.	100	C3	192
Burkesville, Cumberland, Ky.	1,688	D5	178
Burket, Kosciusko, Ind.	259	A4	140
Burketon Station, Ont., Can.	160	P22	64
Burketown, Austl.	79	B7	432
Burkettsville, Mercer and Darke, Ohio	290	B2	156
Burkeville, Nottoway, Va.	705	C6	192
Burkittsville, Frederick, Md.	208	B4	182
Burkley, Carlisle, Ky.	300	D1	178
Burks Falls, Ont., Can.	902	O21	64
Burkville, Lowndes, Ala.	150	C3	168
Burkville, Franklin, Mass.	154	A2	206
Burleigh, Cape May, N.J.	100	E3	210
Burleigh, co., N.Dak.	34,016	D5	154
Burleson, Johnson, Tex.	2,345	B8	130
Burleson, co., Tex.	11,177	D7	130
Burley, Cassia, Idaho	7,508	G5	108
Burley, Kitsap, Wash.	250	D2	98
Burlingame, San Mateo, Calif.	24,036	B5	94
Burlingame, Osage, Kans.	1,151	D8	144
Burlington, Newf., Can.	277	F7	72
Burlington, Ont., Can.	9,127	Q21	64
Burlington, Kit Carson, Colo.	2,090	C8	106
Burlington, Hartford, Conn.	700 (2,790▲)	B4	202
Burlington, Carroll, Ind.	500	B3	140
Burlington, Des Moines, Iowa	32,430	D6	142
Burlington, Coffey, Kans.	2,113	D8	144
Burlington, Boone, Ky.	350	A6 A7	178
Burlington, Penobscot, Maine	150 (353▲)	C4	204
Burlington, Middlesex, Mass.	12,852	C2	206
Burlington, Calhoun, Mich.	329	*G6	146
Burlington, Burlington, N.J.	12,687	C3	210
Burlington, Alamance, N.C.	33,199	A6	186
Burlington, Ward, N.Dak.	262	B4	154
Burlington, Alfalfa, Okla.	174	B5	128
Burlington, Chittenden, Vt.	35,531	C2	218
Burlington, Skagit, Wash.	2,968	A4	98
Burlington, Mineral, W.Va.	400	B6	194
Burlington, Racine, Wis.	5,856	F1 F5	160
Burlington, Big Horn, Wyo.	100	B4	116
Burlington, co., N.J.	224,499	D3	210
Burlington Beach, Ont., Can.	3,314	Q21	64
Burlington Junction, Nodaway, Mo.	650	A2	150
Burli-Tyube, Sov.Un.		C9	336
Burma, country, Asia	20,457,000	G11	340, 362
Burmah, Lincoln, Idaho		*F4	108
Burmis, Alta., Can.	175	F5	54
Burna, Livingston, Ky.	300	C2	178
Burnaby, isl., B.C., Can.		D7	52
Burnet, Burnet, Tex.	2,214	D6	130
Burnet, co., Tex.	9,265	D6	130
Burnett, Vigo, Ind.	270	C2	140
Burnett, co., Wis.	9,214	C1	160
Burnettown, Aiken, S.C.	578	D5	188
Burnettsville, White, Ind.	452	B3	140
Burney, Shasta, Calif.	1,294	B3	94
Burney, Decatur, Ind.	250	C4	140
Burneyville, Love, Okla.	30	E6	128
Burnham, Cook, Ill.	2,478	*B6	138
Burnham, Waldo, Maine	100 (755▲)	D3	204
Burnham, Mifflin, Pa.	2,755	C4	214
Burnham-on-Sea, Eng.	9,700	J10	273
Burnie, Austl.	11,193	G9	432
Burning Springs, Clay, Ky.	350	C7	178
Burning Springs, Wirt, W.Va.	200	C3	194
Burns, Marion, Kans.	314	D7	144
Burns, Smith, Miss.	100	C3	184
Burns, Harney, Oreg.	3,523	D7	96
Burns, Dickson, Tenn.	386	B4	190
Burns, Laramie, Wyo.	225	E8	116
Burns City, Martin, Ind.	180	D3	140
Burns Flat, Washita, Okla.	2,280	C4	128
Burnside, Pulaski, Ky.	575	D6	178
Burnside, Ascension, La.	20	B5	180
Burnside, Neshoba, Miss.	100	C3	184
Burns Lake, B.C., Can.	1,016	C10	52
Burnstad, Logan, N.Dak.	50	D6	154
Burnsville, Dallas, Ala.	200	C3	168
Burnsville, N.B., Can.	115	B4	70
Burnsville, Tishomingo, Miss.	416	A4	184
Burnsville, Yancey, N.C.	1,388	B3	186
Burnsville, Braxton, W.Va.	728	C4	194
Burnt, pond, Newf., Can.		F7	72
Burnt, riv., Oreg.		C9	96
Burnt Corn, Monroe, Ala.	300	D2	168
Burnt River, Ont., Can.	200	P22	64
Burntroot, lake, Ont., Can.		O22	64
Burntside, lake, Minn.		D6	148
Burntwood, lake, Man., Can.		C2	60
Burntwood, riv., Man., Can.		C3	60
Burnwell, Walker, Ala.	500	*B2	168
Burnwell, Kanawha, W.Va.	699	D6	194
Burqa, Jordan	3,000	B6	382
Burr, Otoe, Nebr.	81	*D9	152
Burrafirth, Scot.		A12	272
Burrage, Plymouth, Mass.	150	*B6	206
Burray, isl., Scot.		C10	272
Burr Ferry, Vernon, La.	100	C2	180
Burr Hill, Orange, Va.	100	B7	192
Burriana, Sp.	15,154	C6	298
Burrillville (Town of), Providence, R.I.	(9,119▲)	B2	216
Burris, Fremont, Wyo.	10	C3	116
Burroak, Winneshiek, Iowa	200	A6	142
Burr Oak, Jewell, Kans.	473	C5	144
Burr Oak, St. Joseph, Mich.	867	H6	146
Burr Oak, lake, Ohio		C4	156
Burrow, head, Scot.		G8	273
Burrows, Carroll, Ind.	200	B3	140
Burrton, Harvey, Kans.	774	D6	144
Burruyacú, Arg.	3,034	C5	250
Burrville, Morgan, Tenn.	150	B7	190
Burrwood, Plaquemines, La.	400	F6	180
Bursa, Tur.	131,336	A3	307
Bursa, prov., Tur.	613,263	*A3	307
Burstall, Sask., Can.	222	E3	58
Burt, Kossuth, Iowa	620	A3	142
Burt, Hettinger, N.Dak.	75	D3	154
Burt, co., Nebr.	10,192	C9	152
Burt, lake, Mich.		D7	146
Burton, Tulare, Calif.	4,635	*D4	94
Burton, B.C., Can.		F14	52
Burton, Madison, Idaho		F7	108
Burton, Floyd, Ky.	504	*C8	178
Burton, Keya Paha, Nebr.	17	B6	152
Burton, Geauga, Ohio	1,085	A5	156
Burton, Beaufort, S.C.	400	G7	188
Burton, King, Wash.	400	D2	98
Burton, Wetzel, W.Va.	160	B4	194
Burton, lake, Ga.		B3	176
Burton-on-Trent, Eng.	48,900	I11	273
Burton Port, Ire.	219	G4	272
Burträsk, Swe.	1,240	D9	290
Burtrum, Todd, Minn.	160	F4	148
Burtus, Eg., U.A.R.		D2	382
Buru, isl., Indon.		E7	358
Burullus, lake, Eg., U.A.R.		A3	395
Burūn, cape, Eg., U.A.R.		C4	382
Burwell, Carroll, Ga.	175	C1	176
Burwell, Garfield, Nebr.	1,425	C6	152
Bury, Que., Can.	575	S13	66
Buryat A.S.S.R., Sov.Un.	671,000	D13	329
Burynshik, Sov. Un.		C4	336
Bury St. Edmunds, Eng.	20,900	I13	273
Busby, Alta., Can.	130	D6	54
Busby, Big Horn, Mont.	100	E10	110
Bush, Williamson, Ill.	459	*F4	138
Bush, Laurel, Ky.	20	C7	178
Bush, riv., Md.		B7	182
Būshehr, Iran.	27,317	D3	379
Bushenyi, Ug.		C5	414
Bushimaie, riv., Con.L.		D3	414
Bushmills, N.Ire.	947	F6	272
Bushnell, Sumter, Fla.	644	C8	174
Bushnell, McDonough, Ill.	3,710	C3	138
Bushnell, Kimball, Nebr.	266	C2	152
Bushnell, Brookings, S.Dak.	92	C9	158
Bushong, Lyon, Kans.	51	D7	144
Bushton, Rice, Kans.	499	D5	144
Bushyhead, Rogers, Okla.	30	B8	128
Businga, Con.L.		B3	414
Busk, Sov.Un.	13,900	H5	332
Buskerud, co., Nor.	158,681	*F3	291
Busko, Pol.	5,975	C5	325
Bussa, Nig.		D5	408
Busselton, Austl.	2,449	E3	432
Bussey, Columbia, Ark.	50	D3	170
Bussey, Marion, Iowa	557	C5	142
Bussum, Neth.	36,741	B4	282
Bustakh, Sov.Un.		B16	329
Bustamante, Arg.		G4	251
Buşteni, Rom.	8,591	B3	321
Busto Arsizio, It.	54,900	C2	302
Bu Sunbul, hills, Libya		C4	394
Buta, Con.L.		B3	414
Buta Ranquil, Arg.		C2	252
Bute, co., Scot.	17,300	F7	272
Bute, inlet, B.C., Can.		E10	52
Bute, isl., Scot.		F7	272
Butedale, B.C., Can.	15	D8	52
Butkhāk, Afg.	10,000	B5	374

Camacho

Camacho, Mex. 1,692 C5 225
Camagüey, Cuba 110,388 B6 232
Camagüey, prov., Cuba 618,256 B5 232
Camajuani, Cuba 11,339 A5 232
Camak, Warren, Ga. 285 C4 176
Camambe, vol., Ec. A2 245
Camamu, Braz. 2,248 C3 258
Camaná, Peru 2,253 D3 245
Camanche, Clinton, Iowa 2,225 C7 142
Camano, isl., Wash. A4 98
Camaquã, riv., Braz. L6 257
Camargo, Bol. 1,609 D1 246
Camargo, Dewey, Okla. 254 B4 128
Camarillo, Ventura, Calif. 2,359 *E4 94
Camarillo Heights, Ventura, Calif. 1,704 *E4 94
Camarón, cape, Hond. B5 228
Camarones, Arg. F4 251
Camarones, bay, Arg. F4 251
Camas, Jefferson, Idaho 5 E6 108
Camas, Sanders, Mont. 80 C2 110
Camas, Clark, Wash. 5,666 D4 98
Camas, co., Idaho 917 F4 108
Camas Valley, Douglas, Ore. 130 D3 96
Camau, pt., Viet. E5 362
Cambay, gulf, India D2 366
Cambodia, country, Asia 4,845,000 H12 340, 362
Cambrai, Fr. 29,567 B5 278
Cambria, San Luis Obispo, Calif. 700 E3 94
Cambria, Williamson, Ill. 568 *F4 138
Cambria, Hillsdale, Mich. 250 H7 146
Cambria, Latimer, Okla. 40 *D8 128
Cambria, Montgomery, Va. 722 C4 192
Cambria, Columbia, Wis. 589 E4 160
Cambria, co., Pa. 203,283 C3 214
Cambrian, mts., Wales I9 273
Cambridge, Eng. 91,800 I13 273
Cambridge, Washington, Idaho 473 E2 108
Cambridge, Henry, Ill. 1,665 B3 138
Cambridge, Story, Iowa 587 A7 142, C4
Cambridge, Cowley, Kans. 140 E7 144
Cambridge, Jefferson, Ky. 288 *B5 178
Cambridge, Middlesex, Mass. 107,716 B5 206, D2
Cambridge, Somerset, Maine 150 (354▲) C3 204
Cambridge, Dorchester, Md. 12,239 C7 182
Cambridge, Isanti, Minn. 2,728 F5 148
Cambridge, Furnas, Nebr. 1,090 D5 152
Cambridge, Burlington, N.J. 1,900 *C3 210
Cambridge, Washington, N.Y. 1,748 B8 212
Cambridge, Guernsey, Ohio 14,562 B5 156
Cambridge, Lamoille, Vt. 217 (1,295▲) B3 218
Cambridge, Dane, Wis. 605 E4 160
Cambridge, co., Eng. 270,000 I13 273
Cambridge, res., Mass. C2 206
Cambridge City, Wayne, Ind. 2,569 C4 140
Cambridgeport, Windham, Vt. 100 E3 218
Cambridge Springs, Crawford, Pa. 2,031 B1 214
Camby, Marion, Ind. 400 C3 140, E4
Camden, Wilcox, Ala. 1,121 D2 168
Camden, Ouachita, Ark. 15,823 D4 170
Camden, Kent, Del. 1,125 D3 172
Camden, Carroll, Ind. 601 B3 140
Camden, Knox, Maine 3,523 (3,988▲) D3 204
Camden, Hillsdale, Mich. 434 H7 146
Camden, Ray, Mo. 310 B3 150
Camden, Camden, N.J. 117,159 D2 210
Camden, Oneida, N.Y. 2,694 B6 212
Camden, Camden, N.C. 300 A9 186
Camden, Preble, Ohio 1,308 C2 156
Camden, Kershaw, S.C. 6,842 C7 188
Camden, Benton, Tenn. 2,774 B3 190
Camden, Polk, Tex. 1,131 D8 130
Camden, Lewis, W.Va. 125 B4 194
Camden, co., Ga. 9,975 F5 176
Camden, co., Mo. 9,116 C5 150
Camden, co., N.J. 392,035 D3 210
Camden, co., N.C. 5,598 A9 186
Camden on Gauley, Webster, W.Va. 301 C4 194
Camden Point, Platte, Mo. 171 *B3 150
Camdenton, Camden, Mo. 1,405 D5 150
Camelback, mtn., Ariz. H2 124
Camels Hump, mtn., Vt. C3 218
Cameo, Mesa, Colo. 50 C2 106
Cameo, Boone, W.Va. 250 D5 194
Camerino, It. 4,200 D4 302
Cameron, Coconino, Ariz. 20 C4 124
Cameron, Teller, Colo. 7 *D5 106
Cameron, Cameron, La. 950 E2 180
Cameron, Clinton and De Kalb, Mo. 3,674 B3 150
Cameron, Madison, Mont. 10 E5 110
Cameron, Le Flore, Okla. 211 C9 128
Cameron, Calhoun, S.C. 607 D7 188
Cameron, Milam, Tex. 5,640 D7 130
Cameron, Marshall, W.Va. 1,625 B4 194, C2
Cameron, Barron, Wis. 982 C2 160
Cameron, co., Pa. 7,586 B3 214
Cameron, co., Tex. 151,098 F7 130
Cameron, par., La. 6,909 E2 180
Cameroon, mtn., Cam. F6 409
Cameroons, Br. trust., Afr. 1,400,000 E7 409, F7 388
Cameroun, country, Afr. 3,187,000 F8 388, 409
Cametá, Braz. 3,538 F7 256
Cameta, Sharkey, Miss. B2 184
Camilla, Mitchell, Ga. 4,753 E2 176
Camillus, Onondaga, N.Y. 1,416 *C5 212
Caminha, Port. 2,190 C2 298
Camino, El Dorado, Calif. 700 C3 94
Camlachie, Ont., Can. 155 Q18 64
Cammack Village, Pulaski, Ark. 1,355 C4 170, D6
Camocim, Braz. 8,299 A2 258
Camoian, Ven. D8 240
Camooweal, Austl. 178 B7 432
Camp, co., Tex. 7,849 C8 130
Campaign, Warren, Tenn. 500 C6 190
Campana, isl., Chile G2 251
Campanario, Sp. 9,340 C4 298
Campania, reg., It. 4,628,000 E5 302
Campania, isl., B.C., Can. D8 52
Campanquiz, mts., Peru A2 245
Campbell, Clarke, Ala. 100 D2 168
Campbell, Santa Clara, Calif. 11,863 *D2 94
Campbell, Osceola, Fla. 160 C9 174
Campbell, Wilkin, Minn. 365 E2 148
Campbell, Dunklin, Mo. 1,964 E7 150
Campbell, Franklin, Nebr. 424 D7 152
Campbell, Steuben, N.Y. 650 C4 212
Campbell, Mahoning, Ohio 13,406 A6 156
Campbell, Albemarle, Va. 40 B6 192
Campbell, co., Ky. 86,803 B6 178
Campbell, co., S.Dak. 3,531 B5 158
Campbell, co., Tenn. 27,936 B7 190
Campbell, co., Va. 32,958 C5 192
Campbell, co., Wyo. 5,861 B7 116
Campbell, cape, N.Z. D5 437
Campbell, creek, W.Va. C6 194
Campbell, hill, Ohio B3 156
Campbell, isl., B.C., Can. D8 52
Campbell, lake, Oreg. E7 96
Campbellford, Ont., Can. 3,425 P23 64
Campbell Island, B.C., Can. 150 D8 52
Campbellpur, Pak. 10,135 (17,689▲) C8 375
Campbell River, B.C., Can. 3,069 E10 52
Campbellsburg, Washington, Ind. 612 D3 140
Campbellsburg, Henry, Ky. 348 B5 178
Campbellsport, Fond du Lac, Wis. 1,472 E5 160
Campbell Station, Jackson, Ark. 140 *B5 170
Campbellsville, Taylor, Ky. 6,966 C5 178
Campbellsville, Giles, Tenn. 150 C4 190
Campbellton, N.B., Can. 8,389 A3 70
Campbellton, Newf., Can. 400 F8 72
Campbellton, Jackson, Fla. 309 A5 174
Campbelltown, Pike, Ind. 175 D2 140
Campbelltown, Lebanon, Pa. 1,061 *C5 214
Campbeltown, Scot. 7,000 F7 272
Campbird, Ouray, Colo. 40 *D3 106
Camp Borden, Ont., Can. P21 64
Camp Creek, Mercer, W.Va. 300 D3 194
Camp Crook, Harding, S.Dak. 90 B2 158
Camp Douglas, Juneau, Wis. 489 E3 160
Campeche, Mex. 31,279 D7 225
Campeche, state, Mex. 122,098 D7 225
Campeche, gulf, Mex. D7 225
Campechuela, Cuba 5,536 B6 232
Camp Hill, Tallapoosa, Ala. 1,270 C4 168
Camp Hill, Cumberland, Pa. 8,559 C5 214
Camp Hugh, Bibb, Ala. 60 C2 168
Campiglia Marittima, It. 2,716 D3 302
Câmpina, Rom. 18,680 B3 321
Campina Grande, Braz. 75,464 B3 258
Campinas, Braz. 99,156 E1 258
Campione d'Italia, It. *C2 302
Camp Namanu, Clackamas, Oreg. B4 96
Campo, San Diego, Calif. 300 F5 94
Campo, Cam. 2,001 F6 409
Campo, Baca, Colo. 235 E8 106
Campoalegre, Col. 5,997 C1 244
Campobasso, It. 22,900 E5 302
Campobasso, prov., It. 407,100 *E5 302
Campobello, Spartanburg, S.C. 420 A4 188
Campobello, isl., N.B., Can. E3 70
Campo Belo, Braz. 10,449 E1 258
Campo de Criptana, Sp. 15,427 C5 298
Campo Gallo, Arg. A3 252
Campo Grande, Braz. 31,708 J6 257
Campo Maior, Braz. 6,992 A2 258
Campo Maior, Port. 8,086 C3 298
Campo Real, Sp. 1,557 *B5 298
Campos, Braz. 61,633 E2 258
Campos, Mex. K13 225
Campos Sales, Braz. 2,641 B2 258
Camp Point, Adams, Ill. 1,092 C2 138
Camp Sealth, King, Wash. D2 98
Camp Sherman, Jefferson, Oreg. 25 C5 96
Camps Pass, Powder River, Mont. 3 E10 110
Camp Springs, Prince Georges, Md. 50 C4 182
Campstone, Cochise, Ariz. 600 G5 124
Campti, Natchitoches, La. 1,045 C2 180
Campton, Okaloosa, Fla. 40 A4 174
Campton, Walton, Ga. 200 C3 176
Campton, Wolfe, Ky. 484 C7 178
Campton, Grafton, N.H. 350 (1,058▲) D3 208
Camp Twelve, Lincoln, Oreg. 150 *C3 96
Câmpulung, Rom. 18,880 B3 321
Câmpulung Moldovenesc, Rom. 13,627 A3 321
Camp Verde, Yavapai, Ariz. 285 D4 124
Campville, Alachua, Fla. 150 B8 174
Camp Wood, Real, Tex. 879 E5 130
Camrose, Alta., Can. 5,817 D6 54
Cana, Carroll, Va. 65 D4 192
Canaan, Litchfield, Conn. 1,146 A2 202
Canaan (Town of), Litchfield, Conn. (790▲) B2 202
Canaan, Seminole, Fla. 400 *C9 174
Canaan, Jefferson, Ind. 100 D4 140
Canaan, Somerset, Maine 130 (800▲) D3 204
Canaan, Benton, Miss. 150 A3 184
Canaan, Grafton, N.H. 450 (1,507▲) D2 208
Canaan, Columbia, N.Y. 500 C8 212
Canaan, Essex, Vt. 275 (1,094▲) B5 218
Canaan, riv., N.B., Can. C4 70
Canaan Center, Grafton, N.H. 140 D2 208
Canaan Street, Grafton, N.H. 150 D2 208
Canada, Pike, Ky. 900 C8 178
Canada, country, N.A. 17,678,000 48
Canada, bay, Newf., Can. E8 72
Cañada de Gómez, Arg. 12,354 B3 252
Canada de los Alamos, Santa Fe, N. Mex. 40 G7 126
Canada Falls Deadwater, lake, Maine C2 204
Canadian, Pittsburg, Okla. 255 C8 128
Canadian, Hemphill, Tex. 2,239 B5 130
Canadian, co., Okla. 24,727 C5 128
Canadian, riv., U.S. D6 77
Cañadon León, Arg. G3 251
Canadys, Colleton, S.C. 150 E7 188
Canairiktok, riv., Newf., Can. D9 72
Canajoharie, Montgomery, N.Y. 2,681 C7 212
Çanakkale, Tur. 16,074 A2 307
Çanakkale, prov., Tur. 312,679 *A2 307
Canal, riv., Ven. E5 240
Canal Fulton, Stark, Ohio 1,555 B5 156
Canalou, New Madrid, Mo. 447 E8 150
Canal Point, Palm Beach, Fla. 900 E10 174
Canal Winchester, Fairfield, Ohio 1,976 C1 156, C4
Canal Zone, U.S. poss., N.A. 52,822 F7 228
Canandaigua, Ontario, N.Y. 9,370 C4 212
Canandaigua, lake, N.Y. C4 212
Cananea, Mex. 17,914 A3 224
Cananéia, Braz. 1,037 K7 257
Cañar, Ec. 4,415 A2 245
Canary, is., Atl.O. D5 388
Canary Islands (Canarias), reg., Sp. 807,773 F11 298
Cañas, C.R. 1,459 E5 228
Canaseraga, Allegany, N.Y. 730 C4 212
Canastota, Madison, N.Y. 4,896 B6 212
Canatlán, Mex. C5 224
Canaveral, cape, Fla. C10 174
Canavieiras, Braz. 6,579 D3 258
Cañazas, Pan. 840 F7 228
Canberra, Austl. 35,827 F9 432
Canby, Modoc, Calif. 500 B3 94
Canby, Yellow Medicine, Minn. 2,146 G2 148
Canby, Clackamas, Oreg. 2,168 B2 96, B4
Cancale, Fr. C3 278
Cancienne, Assumption, La. 25 C5 180
Cándala, Som. 1,800 (2,800▲) C6 398
Candelaria, Cuba 3,461 A3 232
Candeleda, Sp. 5,874 B4 298
Candia, see Iráklion, Grc.
Candia, Rockingham, N.H. 200 (1,490▲) E4 208
Candiac Station, Sask., Can. 55 E6 58
Candle, Alsk. 105 B5 84
Candle, lake, Sask., Can. D5 58
Candler, Marion, Fla. 200 B9 174
Candler, co., Ga. 6,672 D4 176
Candlestick, pt., Calif. B5 94
Candlewood, hill, Conn. D5 202
Candlewood, lake, Conn. C2 202
Candlewood, mtn., Conn. C2 202
Candlewood Isle, Fairfield, Conn. 200 D2 202
Cando, Sask., Can. 130 D3 58
Cando, Towner, N.Dak. 1,566 B6 154
Candor, Tioga, N.Y. 956 C5 212
Candor, Montgomery, N.C. 593 B6 186
Candy, Perry, Ky. 500 *C7 178
Cane, creek, Tenn. C5 190
Cane, creek, Utah E6 114
Canea, see Khaniá, Grc.
Canea, see Khaniá, prov., Grc.
Canelones, Ur. 15,000 B4 252
Canelones, dept., Ur. 200,308 B4 252
Cañete, Chile 3,137 C1 252
Cañete, Peru 4,794 C2 245
Cane Valley, Adair, Ky. 300 C5 178
Caney, Montgomery, Kans. 2,682 E8 144
Caney, Morgan, Ky. 400 C7 178
Caney, Atoka, Okla. 128 D7 128
Caney, fork, Tenn. B6 190
Caney, ridge, Ky. C4 178
Caney, riv., Okla. B7 128
Caneyville, Grayson, Ky. 278 C4 178
Canfield, Lafayette, Ark. 200 D3 170
Canfield, Idaho, Idaho D2 108
Canfield, Mahoning, Ohio 3,252 A6 156
Cangallo, Peru 902 C3 245
Cangamba, Ang. 269 B3 420
Cangas, Sp. 4,008 A2 298
Cangas de Narcea, Sp. 2,528 A3 298
Cangas de Onis, Sp. 3,517 A4 298
Canguaretama, Braz. 3,009 B3 258
Cangussu, Braz. 2,438 L6 257
Caniçado, Moz. D6 421
Canicatti, It. 31,800 G4 302
Caniles, Sp. 5,183 D5 298
Canim, lake, B.C., Can. E12 52
Canim Lake, B.C., Can. E12 52
Canindé, Braz. 3,965 A3 258
Canindé, riv., Braz. B2 258
Canistear, res., N.J. A4 210
Canisteo, Steuben, N.Y. 2,731 C4 212
Canisteo, riv., N.Y. C4 212
Canistota, McCook, S.Dak. 627 D8 158
Cañitas, Mex. C5 224
Canjilon, Rio Arriba, N.Mex. 100 B4 126
Çankiri, Tur. 18,084 A5 307
Çankiri, prov., Tur. 228,777 *A5 307
Canmer, Hart, Ky. 500 C5 178
Canmore, Alta., Can. 700 E5 54
Canna, isl., Scot. D6 272
Cannelburg, Daviess, Ind. 124 D3 140
Cannel City, Morgan, Ky. 300 C7 178
Cannelton, Perry, Ind. 1,829 E3 140
Cannelton, Fayette, W.Va. 400 C6 194
Cannes, Fr. 50,192 F7 278
Cannes, bayou, La. D3 180
Cannich, Scot. D8 272
Canning, N.S., Can. 775 D5 70
Canning, Hughes, S.Dak. 50 C5 158
Cannington, Ont., Can. 926 P21 64
Cannon, Sussex, Del. 150 F3 172
Cannon, co., Tenn. 8,537 C5 190
Cannon, bay, Fla. F9 174
Cannon Ball, Sioux, N.Dak. 200 D5 154
Cannonball, riv., N.Dak. D3 154
Cannon Beach, Clatsop, Oreg. 495 B3 96
Cannondale, Fairfield, Conn. 300 E2 202
Cannon Falls, Goodhue, Minn. 2,055 G6 148
Cannonsburg, Jefferson, Miss. 250 D1 184
Cannonsville, Delaware, N.Y. 400 C6 212
Cannonville, Garfield, Utah 153 F3 114
Canobie Lake, Rockingham, N.H. 250 F4 208
Canoe, Escambia, Ala. 500 D2 168
Canoe, B.C., Can. 100 E13 52
Canoe, Breathitt, Ky. 500 C7 178
Canoe, riv., B.C., Can. D13 52
Canoe Lake, Ont., Can. 25 O22 64
Canon, Franklin and Hart, Ga. 626 B3 176
Canonchet, Washington, R.I. 100 D2 216
Canon City, Fremont, Colo. 8,973 D5 106
Canones, Rio Arriba, N.Mex. 90 B4 126
Canonsburg, Washington, Pa. 11,877 C1 214
Canoochee, riv., Ga. D5 176
Canora, Sask., Can. 1,873 E6 58
Canosa [di Puglia], It. 35,600 E6 302
Canova, Miner, S.Dak. 247 D8 158
Canova Beach, Brevard, Fla. 100 C10 174
Canso, N.S., Can. 1,261 D8 70
Cantábrica, mts., Sp. A4 298
Cantal, dept., Fr. 177,065 *E5 278
Cantaura, Ven. 6,562 B6 240
Canterbury, Windham, Conn. 175 (1,857▲) C8 202
Canterbury, Kent, Del. 23 D3 172
Canterbury, Eng. 30,000 J14 273
Canterbury, Merrimack, N.H. 100 (674▲) E3 208
Canterbury, bight, N.Z. F3 437
Canterbury Station, N.B., Can. 375 D2 70
Can Tho, Viet. 75,630 E5 362
Cantley, Que., Can. 300 S9 66
Canton (Kuangchou), China 1,820,523 N6 349
Canton, Hartford, Conn. 400 (4,783▲) B4 202
Canton, Cherokee, Ga. 2,411 B2 176
Canton, Fulton, Ill. 13,588 C3 138
Canton, Washington, Ind. 75 D3 140
Canton, McPherson, Kans. 784 D6 144
Canton, Trigg, Ky. 350 D3 178
Canton, Oxford, Maine 400 (728▲) D2 204
Canton, Norfolk, Mass. 12,771 B5 206, D2
Canton, Fillmore, Minn. 467 H7 148
Canton, Madison, Miss. 9,707 C2 184
Canton, Lewis, Mo. 2,562 A6 150
Canton, Salem, N.J. 500 E2 210
Canton, St. Lawrence, N.Y. 5,046 A6 212
Canton, Haywood, N.C. 5,068 B3 186
Canton, Stark, Ohio 113,631 (*281,900) B5 156
Canton, Blaine, Okla. 887 B5 128
Canton, Bradford, Pa. 2,102 B5 214
Canton, Lincoln, S.Dak. 2,511 D9 158
Canton, Van Zandt, Tex. 1,114 C8 130
Canton, Barron, Wis. 100 C2 160
Canton, res., Okla. B5 128
Canton Bend, Wilcox, Ala. 300 C2 168
Canton Center, Hartford, Conn. 175 B4 202
Cantonment, Escambia, Fla. 2,499 A3 174
Cantril, Van Buren, Iowa 299 D5 142
Cantuar, Sask., Can. 50 E3 58
Cantwell, Alsk. 67 C7 84
Canuelas, Arg. 5,614 C4 252
Canutama, Braz. 940 G4 256
Canute, Washita, Okla. 370 C4 128
Canutillo, El Paso, Tex. 1,377 D2 130
Canwood, Sask., Can. 310 D4 58
Cany, creek, Tex. G7 130
Canyon, Randall, Tex. 5,864 B5 130
Canyon, Yellowstone Natl. Park, Wyo. B2 116
Canyon, co., Idaho 57,662 F2 108
Canyon City, Grant, Oreg. 654 C8 96
Canyon Creek, Lewis and Clark, Mont. 10 D4 110
Canyon de Chelly, natl. mon., Ariz. B6 124
Canyon Ferry, res., Mont. D5 110
Canyonville, Douglas, Oreg. 1,089 E3 96
Cao Bang, Viet. 9,000 B5 362
Capa, Jones, S.Dak. 39 C5 158
Capac, St. Clair, Mich. 1,235 F9 146
Çapakçur, see Bingöl, Tur.
Cap à l'Aigle, Que., Can. 595 Q14 66
Capanaparo, riv., Ven. C4 240
Capão Bonito, Braz. 4,287 E1 258
Capatárida, Ven. 1,104 A3 240
Capbreton, Fr. F3 278
Cap Chat, Que., Can. 1,954 *Q10 66
Cap-de-la-Madeleine, Que., Can. 22,943 R12 66
Cape, isl., S.C. E10 188
Cape Breton, co., N.S., Can. 125,478 C9 70
Cape Breton, isl., N.S., Can. C9 70
Cape Breton Highlands, natl. park, N.S., Can. C9 70
Cape Broyle, Newf., Can. 450 G9 72
Cape Charles, Northampton, Va. 2,041 C8 192
Cape Coast, Ghana 23,346 E4 408
Cape Cod, bay, Mass. C7 206
Cape Cod, canal, Mass. C6 206
Cape Cottage, Cumberland, Maine 400 E2 204, E5
Cape Elizabeth, Cumberland, Maine 5,505 E2 204, E5
Cape Fear, riv., N.C. C7 186
Cape Girardeau, Cape Girardeau, Mo. 24,947 D8 150
Cape Girardeau, co., Mo. 42,020 D8 150
Cape Hatteras, natl. seashore recreational area, N.C. B10 186
Cape Horn, Skamania, Wash. D4 98
Capelinha, Braz. 2,249 D2 258
Capels, McDowell, W.Va. 800 D3 194
Cape May, Cape May, N.J. 4,477 E3 210
Cape May, co., N.J. 48,555 E3 210
Cape May Court House, Cape May, N.J. 1,749 E3 210
Cape May Point, Cape May, N.J. 263 E3 210
Cape Neddick, York, Maine 600 E2 204
Cape of Good Hope, prov., U.S.Afr. 4,426,726 F3 420
Cape Porpoise, York, Maine 400 E2 204
Cape Race, Newf., Can. 25 G9 72

Carver, co., Minn. 21,358 G5 148
Carverton, Luzerne, Pa. 970 A5 214
Carville, Iberville, La. 950 B5 180
Cary, McHenry, Ill. 2,530 A5 138
E2
Cary, Aroostook, Maine 25 *C5 204
(208▲)
Cary, Sharkey, Miss. 428 C2 184
Cary, Wake, N.C. 3,356 B7 186
Caryville, Washington, Fla. 730 A5 174
Caryville, Norfolk, Mass. 500 E1 206
Caryville, Campbell, Tenn. 950 B7 190
Casa, Perry, Ark. 184 B3 170
Casa Adobes, Pima, Ariz. 5,000 *F4 124
Casablanca, Mor. 742,000 B2 402
Casa Blanca, Valencia, N.Mex. 135 C3 126
Casa Branca, Braz. 7,373 E1 258
Casa Grande, Pinal, Ariz. 8,311 F4 124
Casa Grande, natl. mon., Ariz. F4 124
Casale Monferrato, It. 27,200 C2 302
Casalmaggiore, It. 5,656 C3 302
Casanare, riv., Col. B2 244
Casanova, Fauquier, Va. 100 B7 192
Casape, It. 1,300 *E4 302
Casar, Cleveland, N.C. 310 B4 186
Casarano, It. 14,100 E7 302
Cascade, B.C., Can. 210 F13 52
Cascade, Valley, Idaho 923 E2 108
Cascade, Dubuque, Iowa 1,601 B6 142
Cascade, Cascade, Mont. 604 C5 110
Cascade, Coos, N.H. 500 C4 208
Cascade, Pittsylvania, Va. 500 D5 192
Cascade, Preston, W.Va. 200 B5 194
Cascade, Sheboygan, Wis. 449 E5 160
Cascade, co., Mont. 73,418 C5 110
Cascade, range, U.S. C2 77
Cascade, res., Idaho E3 108
Cascade Locks, Hood River, Oreg. 660 B5 96
Cascade Summit, Klamath, Oreg. 25 D4 96
Cascadia, Linn, Oreg. 100 C4 96
Cascavel, Braz. 2,752 A3 258
Casco, Cumberland, Maine 300 D2 204
(947▲)
Casco, Kewaunee, Wis. 460 D6 160
Casco, bay, Maine E3 204
Caserta, It. 31,200 E5 302
Caserta, prov., It. 623,400 *E5 302
Caseville, Huron, Mich. 659 F8 146
Casey, Clark, Ill. 2,890 D6 138
Casey, Guthrie, Iowa 589 C3 142
Casey, co., Ky. 14,327 C5 178
Casey, mtn., Idaho A2 108
Casey, pass, Fla. D8 174
Caseyville, St. Clair, Ill. 2,455 *E3 138
Caseyville, Union, Ky. 53 *C3 178
Cash, Craighead, Ark. 141 B6 170
Cash, Chesterfield, S.C. 100 B9 188
Cashiers, Jackson, N.C. 342 B2 186
Cashion, Kingfisher, Okla. 221 C6 128
Cashmere, Chelan, Wash. 1,891 B6 98
Cashton, Monroe, Wis. 828 E3 160
Casigua, Ven. A3 240
Casilda, Arg. 11,023 B3 252
Casilda, Cuba 1,986 B5 232
Casiquiare, riv., Ven. E5 240
Čáslav, Czech. 8,773 B2 324
Casma, Peru 2,676 B2 245
Casmalia, Santa Barbara, Calif. 200 E3 94
Casnovia, Kent and Muskegon, Mich. 371 *F6 146
Caspar, Mendocino, Calif. 250 C2 94
Caspe, Sp. 490 B6 298
Casper, Natrona, Wyo. 38,930 D6 116
Caspian, Iron, Mich. 1,493 C3 146
Caspian, depression, Sov.Un. C3 336
Caspian, pond, Vt. B4 218
Caspian, sea, Asia D3 336
Caspiana, Caddo, La. 250 B2 180
Cass, Sullivan, Ind. 350 C2 140
Cass, Pocahontas, W.Va. 327 C5 194
Cass, co., Ill. 14,539 D3 138
Cass, co., Ind. 40,931 B3 140
Cass, co., Iowa 17,919 C3 142
Cass, co., Mich. 36,932 H5 146
Cass, co., Minn. 16,720 E4 148
Cass, co., Mo. 29,702 C3 150
Cass, co., Nebr. 17,821 D9 152
Cass, co., N.Dak. 66,947 C8 154
Cass, co., Tex. 23,496 C8 130
Cass, lake, Minn. D4 148
Cass, riv., Mich. F8 146
Cassá, Sp. 4,760 B8 298
Cassa, Platte, Wyo. 5 D8 116
Cassadaga, Chautauqua, N.Y. 820 C2 212
Cassatt, Kershaw, S.C. 50 C8 188
Cass City, Tuscola, Mich. 1,945 F8 146
Cassel, see Kassel, Ger.
Casselberry, Seminole, Fla. 2,463 *C9 174
Casselman, Ont., Can. 1,241 025 64
Casselman, riv., Md. A1 182
Casselton, Cass, N.Dak. 1,394 D8 154
Cassia, Lake, Fla. 400 C9 174
Cassia, co., Idaho 16,121 G5 108
Cassidy, B.C., Can. B14 52
Cassie, Wayne, W.Va. 25 D2 194
Cassils, Alta., Can. 25 E6 54
Cassino, It. 8,000 E4 302
Cassiporé, cape, Braz. E6 256
Cass Lake, Cass, Minn. 1,586 D4 148
Cassoday, Butler, Kans. 180 D7 144
Cassopolis, Cass, Mich. 2,027 H5 146
Casstown, Miami, Ohio 366 B2 156
Cassville, Bartow, Ga. 200 B2 176
Cassville, Barry, Mo. 1,451 E4 150
Cassville, Ocean, N.J. 205 C4 210
Cassville, Monongalia, W.Va. 800 *B4 194
Cassville, Grant, Wis. 1,290 F3 160
Castalia, Winneshiek, Iowa 216 A6 142
Castalia, Nash, N.C. 267 A7 186
Castalia, Erie, Ohio 954 A4 156
Castalian Springs, Sumner, Tenn. 150 B5 190
Castana, Monona, Iowa 230 B2 142
Castaña, Ven. D6 240
Castanea, Clinton, Pa. 1,218 *B4 214
Castaños, Mex. 2,607 B5 225
Castel di Guido, It. (part of Rome) *E4 302
Castel Gandolfo, It. 2,600 *E4 302
Castel Giuliano, It. *D4 302
Casteljaloux, Fr. E4 278
Castella, Shasta, Calif. 300 B2 94
Castelli, Arg. 3,263 C4 252
Castelli, Arg. C5 250
Castellón, prov., Sp. 330,257 *C6 298
Castellón de la Plana, Sp. 49,300 C6 298
(57,998▲)
Castel Madama, It. 4,400 *E4 302
Castelnaudary, Fr. 7,584 F4 278
Castelo, Braz. 3,623 E2 258
Castelo Branco, Port. 13,056 C3 298
Castelo de Vide, Port. 3,379 C3 298
Castelsarrasin, Fr. 6,639 E4 278
Castelvetrano, It. 31,000 G4 302
Castile, Wyoming, N.Y. 1,146 C3 212
Castille, Acadia, La. D3 180
Castillo, pampa, Arg. G4 251
Castillo de San Marcos, natl. mon., Fla. B9 174
Castillos, Ur. B5 252
Castine, Hancock, Maine 550 D4 204
(824▲)
Castle, Alsk. 23 *C6 84
Castle, Okfuskee, Okla. 149 C7 128
Castle, butte, Idaho C3 108
Castle, harbor, Bermuda A13 233
Castle, mtn., Alsk. J14 84
Castle, mts., Mont. D6 110
Castlebar, Ire. 5,321 H3 273
Castleberry, Conecuh, Ala. 669 D2 168
Castleblayney, Ire. 2,143 G6 273
Castle Butte, Navajo, Ariz. 15 C5 124
Castle Cliff, Washington, Utah 4 F2 114
Castle Clinton, natl. mon., N.J. B1 210
Castle Dale, Emery, Utah 617 D4 114
Castle Dome, mts., Ariz. E1 124
Castlefinn, Ire. 574 F5 272
Castleford, Twin Falls, Idaho 274 G4 108
Castlegar, B.C., Can. 1,705 F14 52
Castle Gate, Carbon, Utah 321 D5 114
Castlegregory, Ire. 258 I2 273
Castle Hayne, New Hanover, N.C. 500 C8 186
Castle Hill, Black Hawk, Iowa 932 B5 142
Castle Hill (Town of), Aroostook, Maine (554▲) *B4 204
Castle Hot Springs, Maricopa, Ariz. 25 E3 124
Castle Park, San Diego, Calif. 1,800 D6 94
Castlereagh, Ire. 1,647 H4 273
Castle Rock, Douglas, Colo. 1,152 C6 106
Castle Rock, Butte, S.Dak. 15 C2 158
Castle Rock, Summit, Utah 15 B4 114
Castle Rock, Cowlitz, Wash. 1,424 C4 98
Castle Rock, butte, S.Dak. C2 158
Castle Rock, mtn., Va. C6 192
Castle Rock, res., Wis. E4 160
Castle Shannon, Allegheny, Pa. 11,836 A3 214
Castleton, Ont., Can. 430 P23 64
Castleton, Marion, Ind. 267 D5 140
Castleton, Harford, Md. 95 A7 182
Castleton, Rutland, Vt. 375 D2 218
(1,902▲)
Castleton Corners, Rutland, Vt. 140 D2 218
Castleton-on-the-Hudson, Rensselaer, N.Y. 1,752 C8 212
Castletown, Isle of Man 1,755 G8 273
Castlewellan, N.Ire. 801 G7 273
Castlewood, Hamlin, S.Dak. 500 C8 158
Castlewood, Russell, Va. 500 D2 192
Castor, Alta., Can. 958 D7 54
Castor, Bienville, La. 142 B2 180
Castor, creek, La. B3 180
Castor, riv., Mo. D7 150
Castres, Fr. 28,982 F5 278
Castries, St. Lucia 7,146 E14 233
(*16,579)
Castro, Braz. 6,316 J6 257
Castro, Chile 6,283 F3 251
Castro [del Río], Sp. 16,173 *D4 298
Castro, co., Tex. 8,923 B4 130
Castro Alves, Braz. 6,479 C3 258
Castro Marim, Port. 4,613 D3 298
Castrop-Rauxel, Ger. 83,600 *C2 286
Castropol, Sp. 528 A3 298
Castro Urdiales, Sp. 6,222 A5 298
Castro Valley, Alameda, Calif. 37,120 B5 94
Castro Verde, Port. 2,794 D2 298
Castrovillari, It. 12,500 F6 302
Castroville, Monterey, Calif. 2,838 D3 94
Castroville, Medina, Tex. 1,508 E6 130
Castrovirreyna, Peru 872 C2 245
Castuera, Sp. 10,169 C4 298
Caswell (Plantation of), Aroostook, Maine (853▲) *B5 204
Caswell, co., N.C. 19,912 A6 186
Cat, isl., Miss. E3 184
Cat, isl., S.C. E10 188
Cat, isl., W.I. A7 232
Catacamas, Hond. 2,412 C5 228
Catacaos, Peru 8,526 B1 245
Catacocha, Ec. 2,755 A2 245
Cataguases, Braz. 12,837 E2 258
Catahoula, St. Martin, La. 600 D4 180
Catahoula, lake, La. C3 180
Catahoula, par., La. 11,421 C4 180
Catalão, Braz. 6,088 D1 258
Catalca, Tur. 3,842 A3 307
Cataldo, Kootenai, Idaho 100 *B2 108
Catalina, Newf., Can. 800 F9 72
Catalonia (Cataluña), reg., Sp. 3,218,596 B7 298
Catamarca, Arg. 31,067 A2 252
Catamarca, prov., Arg. 177,700 C4 250
Catanduanes, isl., Phil. B6 358
Catanduva, Braz. 21,604 E1 258
Catania, It. 321,000 G5 302
Catania, prov., It. 834,100 *G5 302
Catania, gulf, It. G5 302
Catanzaro, It. 40,300 F6 302
(65,000▲)
Catanzaro, prov., It. 747,000 *F6 302
Cataouatche, lake, La. C7 180
Cataract, Monroe, Wis. 200 D3 160
Cataract, lake, Ind. C3 140
Catarroja, Sp. 10,437 C6 298
Catasauqua, Lehigh, Pa. 5,062 C6 214
Catáula, Harris, Ga. 350 D2 176
Cataumet, Barnstable, Mass. 300 C6 206
Catawba, Catawba, N.C. 504 B4 186
Catawba, Clark, Ohio 355 C3 156
Catawba, York, S.C. 575 B7 188
Catawba, Roanoke, Va. 25 C4 192
Catawba, Marion, W.Va. 150 A7 194
Catawba, Price, Wis. 230 C3 160
Catawba, co., N.C. 73,191 B4 186
Catawba, res., N.C., S.C. B4 188
A6 188
Catawba, riv., N.C. B5 186
Catawissa, Columbia, Pa. 1,824 C5 214
Catbalogan, Phil. 10,757 B6 358
Cat Creek, Petroleum, Mont. 200 C8 110
Cateechee, Pickens, S.C. 600 B3 188
Cates, Fountain, Ind. 150 C2 140
Catesby, Ellis, Okla. 5 B4 128
Catete, Ang. 716 A2 420
Cathance, lake, Maine D5 204
Catharine, Ellis, Kans. 225 D4 144
Cathay, Mariposa, Calif. 100 D3 94
Cathay, Wells, N.Dak. 110 C6 154
Cathedral, cave, Mo. D6 150
Cathedral, mtn., Tex. D4 130
Cathedral, peak, Calif. D3 94
Cathedral City, Riverside, Calif. 1,855 F5 94
Catherine, Wilcox, Ala. 150 C2 168
Catherine, lake, Ark. C4 170
Catherine, mtn., Utah E3 114
Cathlamet, Wahkiakum, Wash. 615 C3 98
Cat Law, mtn., Scot. E9 272
Catlettsburg, Boyd, Ky. 3,874 B8 178
Catlin, Vermilion, Ill. 1,263 C6 138
Catlin, Parke, Ind. 150 C2 140
Cato, Faulkner, Ark. 50 C4 170
Cato, Rankin, Miss. C3 184
Cato, Barry, Mo. 100 E4 150
Cato, Cayuga, N.Y. 476 B5 212
Catoche, cape, Mex. C8 225
Catoctin, mtn., Md. B4 182
Catoctin Furnace, Frederick, Md. 150 A5 182
Catonsville, Baltimore, Md. 37,372 B6 182
C4
Catoosa, Rogers, Okla. 638 B8 128
Catoosa, co., Ga. 21,101 B1 176
Catriló, Arg. C3 252
Catron, New Madrid, Mo. 177 E8 150
Catron, co., N.Mex. 2,773 E2 126
Catskill, Greene, N.Y. 5,825 C8 212
Catskill, mts., N.Y. C7 212
Catt, mtn.; B.C., Can. C8 52
Cattaraugus, Cattaraugus, N.Y. 1,258 C3 212
Cattaraugus, co., N.Y. 80,187 C3 212
Cattaraugus, creek, N.Y. C3 212
Cattolica, It. 9,800 D4 302
Catumbela, riv., Ang. B2 420
Cauca, dept., Col. 481,980 C1 244
Cauca, riv., Col. B1 244
Caucasia, Col. 897 B1 244
Caucasus, mts., Sov.Un. D2 336
Cauchon, lake, Man., Can. C4 60
Caucomgomac, lake, Maine B3 204
Caudebec [-lès-Elbeuf], Fr. 9,429 C4 278
Caudéran, Fr. 26,548 E3 278
Caudete, Sp. 7,442 C6 298
Caudry, Fr. 12,173 B5 278
Caughnawaga, Que., Can. 2,200 S11 66
S16
Caúngula, Ang. A3 420
Cauquenes, Chile 14,849 C1 252
Caura, riv., Ven. D6 240
Causapscal, Que., Can. 2,957 *Q10 66
Causses, plat., Fr. E4 278
Cauthron, Scott, Ark. 60 C2 170
Cautín, prov., Chile 365,072 E3 251
Caution, cape, B.C., Can. E9 52
Cauvery, riv., India F3 366
Cavado, riv., Port. B2 298
Cavaillon, Fr. 9,825 F6 278
Cavalier, Pembina, N.Dak. 1,423 B8 154
Cavalier, co., N.Dak. 10,064 B7 154
Cavalli, riv., Lib. E3 408
Cavan, co., Ire. 61,740 H5 273
Cavanal, mtn., Okla. C9 128
Cavanaugh, Sebastian, Ark. 250 B2 170
Cavarzere, It. 5,600 C4 302
Cave, It. 4,890 *E4 302
Cave City, Sharp, Ark. 540 B5 170
Cave City, Barren, Ky. 1,418 C5 178
Cavecreek, Maricopa, Ariz. 250 E4 124
G2
Cavecreek, Newton, Ark. 10 B4 170
Cave Creek, Roane, Tenn. C7 190
Cave Creek, res., Ariz. G2 124
Cave in Rock, Hardin, Ill. 495 F5 138
Cave Junction, Josephine, Oreg. 248 E3 96
Cavell, Sask., Can. 25 D3 58
Cavendish, Alta., Can. 75 E7 54
Cavendish, Clearwater, Idaho 25 C2 108
Cavendish, Windsor, Vt. 250 E3 218
(1,223▲)
Cave of the Winds, cave, Vt. B3 218
Cave Spring, Floyd, Ga. 1,153 B1 176
Cave Springs, Benton, Ark. 281 A2 170
Cave Springs, cave, Ga. B1 176
Cave Spring Onyx, caverns, Mo. E6 150
Cavetown, Washington, Md. 282 A4 182
Cavour, Beadle, S.Dak. 140 C7 158
Cavour, Forest, Wis. 130 C5 160
Cawker City, Mitchell, Kans. 686 C5 144
Cawnpore, see Kanpur, India
Cawood, Harlan, Ky. 800 D7 178
Caxias, Braz. 14,445 A2 258
Caxias do Sul, Braz. 31,561 K6 257
Caxito, Ang. 8,690 A2 420
Cayambe, Ec. 7,409 A2 245
Cayce, Fulton, Ky. 175 D1 178
Cayce, Lexington, S.C. 8,517 D6 188
Cayenne, Fr.Gu. 13,346 E6 256
Cayey, P.R. 18,429 C11 233
Cayley, Alta., Can. 146 E6 54
Cayman Islands (with Turks and Caicos Islands), ter., W.I.Fed. 15,000 C4 232
Cayman Brac, isl., Cayman Is. C5 232
Cayo, Br.Hond. 1,548 B3 228
Cayo, isl., Cuba A5 232
Cayo Largo, isl., Cuba B4 232
Cayuga, Ont., Can. 772 R21 64
Cayuga, Vermillion, Ind. 904 C2 140
Cayuga, Hinds, Miss. 50 C2 184
Cayuga, Cayuga, N.Y. 621 C5 212
Cayuga, Sargent, N.Dak. 195 D8 154
Cayuga, co., N.Y. 73,942 C5 212
Cayuga, lake, N.Y. C5 212
Cayuga Heights, Tompkins, N.Y. 2,788 *C5 212
Cayuse, Umatilla, Oreg. 80 B8 96
Cazador, Cochise, Ariz. 10 G6 124
Cazalla de la Sierra, Sp. 9,284 D4 298
Cazaux, lagoon, Fr. E3 278
Cazenovia, Madison, N.Y. 2,584 C6 212
Cazenovia, Richland, Wis. 351 E3 160
Čazma, riv., Yugo. B3 316
Cazombo, Ang. 2,212 B4 420
Cazorla, Sp. 8,699 D5 298
C.D. Hidalgo, Mex. E7 225
Céa, riv., Sp. A4 298
Ceanannas, Ire. 2,162 H6 273
Ceara, state, Braz. 3,147,000 G9 256
Ceará Mirim, Braz. 5,092 B3 258
Ceballos, Mex. B5 224
Cebolla, Rio Arriba, N. Mex. 100 B4 126
Cebolla, creek, Colo. D3 106
Cebollar, Arg. A2 252
Cebollati, riv., Ur. B5 252
Cebreros, Sp. 3,995 B4 298
Cebu, Phil. 77,411 B6 358
(*120,000)
Cebu, isl., Phil. B6 358
Cecil, Franklin, Ark. 150 B3 170
Cecil, Cook, Ga. 279 E3 176
Cecil, Gloucester, N.J. D3 210
Cecil, Morrow, Oreg. 5 B7 96
Cecil, Shawano, Wis. 357 D5 160
Cecil, co., Md. 48,408 A7 182
Cecilia, Hardin, Ky. 500 C5 178
Cecilia, Saint Martin, La. 400 D4 180
Cecilton, Cecil, Md. 596 B8 182
Cecina, It. 6,741 D3 302
Cecir de Mer, isl., Viet. E6 362
Cedar, San Miguel, Colo. E2 106
Cedar, Mahaska, Iowa 185 C5 142
Cedar, Smith, Kans. 73 C5 144
Cedar, Leelanau, Mich. 150 E6 146
Cedar, co., Iowa 17,791 C6 142
Cedar, co., Mo. 9,185 D4 150
Cedar, co., Nebr. 13,368 B8 152
Cedar, creek, Colo. B7 106
Cedar, creek, Del. E4 172
Cedar, creek, Ind. A4 140
Cedar, creek, Iowa D6 142
Cedar, creek, Mo. C5 150
Cedar, creek, N.J. D4 210
Cedar, creek, N. Dak. D4 154
Cedar, creek, Ohio A1 156
Cedar, hills, N. Dak. D2 154
Cedar, isl., N.C. C9 186
Cedar, isl., S.C. E10 188
Cedar, isl., Va. C9 192
Cedar, keys, Fla. B7 174
Cedar, knob, Mo. E5 150
Cedar, lake, Man., Can. D2 60
Cedar, lake, Ont., Can. 022 64
Cedar, mtn., Calif. B3 94
Cedar, mtn., Wyo. B5 116
Cedar, pt., Fla. C8 174
Cedar, pt., Md. D7 182
Cedar, riv., Iowa C6 142
Cedar, riv., Minn. H6 148
Cedar, riv., Nebr. C7 152
Cedar, swamp, Mass. C3 206
Cedar Bayou, Harris, Tex. (part of Baytown) F8 130
Cedar Bluff, Cherokee, Ala. 687 A4 168
Cedar Bluff, Tazewell, Va. 995 C3 192
Cedar Bluff, res., Kans. D4 144
Cedar Bluffs, Decatur, Kans. 60 C3 144
Cedar Bluffs, Saunders, Nebr. 585 C9 152
D2
Cedar Breaks, natl. mon., Utah F3 114
Cedar Brook, Camden, N.J. 400 D3 210
Cedarburg, Ozaukee, Wis. 5,191 E1 160
E6
Cedar Canyon, petrified forest, N.Dak. D2 154
Cedar City, Calloway, Mo. 600 C5 150
Cedar City, Iron, Utah 7,543 F2 114
Cedar Creek, Scott, Ark. 120 C3 170
Cedarcreek, Taney, Mo. 200 E5 150
Cedar Creek, Cass, Nebr. 101 C9 152
E3
Cedarcreek, Greene, Tenn. 120 B9 190
Cedar Crest, Bernalillo, N.Mex. 100 H6 126
Cedaredge, Delta, Colo. 549 D3 106
Cedar Falls, Black Hawk, Iowa 21,195 B5 142
Cedar Falls, Randolph, N.C. 500 B6 186
Cedar Fork, Duplin, N.C. C8 186
Cedar Grove, Bay, Fla. 676 *A5 174
Cedar Grove, Franklin, Ind. 232 C5 140
Cedar Grove, Essex, N.J. 14,603 A1 210
B4
Cedar Grove, Carroll, Tenn. 125 C3 190
Cedar Grove, Kanawha, W.Va. 1,569 C3 194
C6
Cedar Grove, Sheboygan, Wis. 1,175 E6 160
Cedar Hammock, Manatee, Fla. 3,089 *D8 174
Cedar Heights, Prince Georges, Md. 1,900 *C6 182
Cedar Hill, Jefferson, Mo. 300 B7 150
Cedar Hill, Robertson, Tenn. 530 B5 190
Cedar Hill, Dallas, Tex. 1,848 B8 130
Cedar Hills, Washington, Oreg. 4,000 *A1 96
Cedarhurst, Carroll, Md. 115 A6 182
Cedarhurst, Nassau, N.Y. 6,954 *E3 212
Cedar Key, Levy, Fla. 668 B7 174
Cedar Knolls, Morris, N.J. 2,800 B4 210
Cedar Lake, Morgan, Ala. 250 A3 168
Cedar Lake, Lake, Ind. 5,766 A2 140
Cedar Lodge, Davidson (part of Fair Grove), N.C. 2,323 B5 186
Cedar Mills, Meeker, Minn. 96 G4 148

Cedar Point, Chase, Kans. 87 D7 144
Cedar Rapids, Linn, Iowa 92,035 C6 142
(*119,600)
Cedar Rapids, Boone, Nebr. 512 C7 152
Cedar River, Menominee, Mich. 50 D4 146
Cedar Run, Ocean, N.J. 350 D4 210
Cedars, Que., Can. 385 S15 66
Cedar Springs, Ont., Can. 110 R18 64
Cedar Springs, Kent, Mich. 1,768 F6 146
Cedar Terrace, Richland, S.C. 1,000 *C6 188
Cedartown, Polk, Ga. 9,340 B1 176
Cedarvale, B.C., Can. 15 C8 52
Cedar Vale, Chautauqua, Kans. 859 E7 144
Cedarvale, Torrance, N.Mex. 20 D5 126
Cedar Valley, Utah, Utah 150 C3 114
Cedarville, Crawford, Ark. 52 B2 170
Cedarville,Modoc, Calif. 750 B3 94
Cedarville, Stephenson, Ill. 570 A4 138
Cedarville, Allen, Ind. 240 A4 140
Cedarville, Plymouth, Mass. 300 *C6 206
Cedarville, Mackinac, Mich. 300 C7 146
Cedarville, Cumberland, N.J. 1,095 E2 210
Cedarville, Greene, Ohio 1,702 C3 156
Cedarwood, Pueblo, Colo. 20 E6 106
Cedarwood Park, Ocean, N.J. 1,052 *C4 210
Cedoux, Sask., Can. 72 F6 58
Cedros, Hond. 1,313 C4 228
Cedros, isl., Mex. B2 224
Ceduna, Austl. 609 E6 432
Ceepeecee, B.C., Can. 85 F9 52
Cefalù, It. 10,700 F5 302
Cega, riv., Sp. B5 298
Cegléd, Hung. 28,000 B4 320
(39,000▲)
Ceglie Messapico, It. 16,500 E6 302
Cehegin, Sp. 7,084 C6 298
Cehul-Silvaniei, Rom. A2 321
Cela, Ang. B3 420
Čelákovice, Czech. 6,041 *A2 324
Celanese Village, Floyd, Ga. 1,500 *B1 176
Celaya, Mex. 34,426 C5 225
K13
Celebes, reg., Indon. 6,100,000 E5 358
Celebes, isl., Indon. E5 358
Celebes, sea, Asia I14 340
Celendin, Peru 4,045 B2 245
Celestine, Dubois, Ind. 150 D3 140
Celica, Ec. 1,553 A2 245
Celilo, Wasco, Oreg. 15 B6 96
Celina, Mercer, Ohio 7,659 B2 156
Celina, Clay, Tenn. 1,228 B6 190
Celina, Collin, Tex. 1,204 C7 130
Celje, Yugo. 27,000 A2 316
Celle, Ger. 59,900 B4 286
Celoron, Chautauqua, N.Y. 1,507 C2 212
Celriver, see Red River, S.C.
Cement, Caddo, Okla. 959 D5 128
Cement City, Lenawee, Mich. 471 G7 146
Cementon, Lehigh, Pa. 1,800 *C6 214
Çemişkezek, Tur. 1,821 B8 307
Cemmaes, head, Wales I8 273
Cencia, Eth. D4 398
Cendradillas, Mex. B4 224
Cenon, Fr. 10,747 E3 278
Centenary, Marion, S.C. 300 C10 188
Centennial, Albany, Wyo. 50 E6 116
Centennial, range, Mont. F4 110
Centennial, valley, Mont. F4 110
Center, Saguache, Colo. 1,600 E4 106
Center, Jackson, Ga. 137 B3 176
Center, Howard, Ind. 250 B3 140
Center, Metcalfe, Ky. 115 C5 178
Center, Attala, Miss. C3 184
Center, Ralls, Mo. 484 B6 150
Center, Knox, Nebr. 147 B8 152
Center, Oliver, N.Dak. 476 C4 154
Center, Pontotoc, Okla. 150 D7 128
Center, Shelby, Tex. 4,510 D8 130
Center Barnstead, Belknap, N.H. 150 E4 208
Centerbrook, Middlesex, Conn. 600 D6 202
Centerburg, Knox, Ohio 963 B4 156
Center City, Chisago, Minn. 293 F6 148
Center Conway, Carroll, N.H. 200 D4 208
Center Cross, Essex, Va. 200 C8 192
Centereach, Suffolk, N.Y. 8,524 *D4 212
Centerfield, Sanpete, Utah 475 D4 114
Center Groton, New London, Conn. 150 D7 202
Center Harbor, Belknap, N.H. 200 D4 208
(511▲)
Center Hill, White, Ark. 50 B5 170
Center Hill, Sumter, Fla. 529 C9 174
Center Hill, res., Tenn. B6 190
Center Junction, Jones, Iowa 201 B6 142
Center Line, Macomb, Mich. 10,164 B9 146
Center Lovell, Oxford, Maine 100 D2 204
Center Montville (Montville), Waldo, Maine 15 D3 204
(366▲)
Center Moriches, Suffolk, N.Y. 2,521 D4 212
Center Ossipee, Carroll, N.H. 500 D4 208
Center Point, Jefferson, Ala. 7,500 E5 168
Center Point, Howard, Ark. 136 C3 170
Centerpoint, Clay, Ind. 268 C2 140
Center Point, Linn, Iowa 1,236 B6 142
Center Point, Avoyelles, La. 250 C3 180
Center Point, Kerr, Tex. 1,000 E6 130
Center Point, Doddridge, W.Va. 125 A6 194
B4
Centerport, Suffolk, N.Y. 3,628 *E8 212
Center Ridge, Conway, Ark. B4 170
Center Rutland, Rutland, Vt. 225 D2 218
Center Sandwich, Carroll, N.H. 250 D4 208
Center Star, Lauderdale, Ala. 200 *A2 168
Centerton, Benton, Ark. 177 A2 170
Centerton, Morgan, Ind. 500 C3 140
Centerton, Salem, N.J. 100 D2 210
Centertown, Ohio, Ky. 327 C4 178
Centertown, Cole, Mo. 190 C5 150
Centertown, Warren, Tenn. 169 C6 190
Center Tuftonboro, Carroll, N.H. 100 D4 208
Centerview, Johnson, Mo. 208 C4 150
Centerville, Yavapai, Ariz. 50 D3 124
Centerville, Yell, Ark. 200 B3 170
Centerville, New Castle, Del. 42 A3 172
Centerville, Houston, Ga. 290 *D3 176
Centerville, St. Clair, Ill. 12,769 *E3 138
Centerville, Wayne, Ind. 2,378 C5 140
Centerville, Appanoose, Iowa 6,629 D5 142
Centerville, Linn, Kans. 250 D8 144
Centerville, St. Mary, La. 537 E4 180
Centerville, Washington, Maine 40 D5 204
(47▲)
Centerville, Barnstable, Mass. 544 C7 206
Centerville, Anoka, Minn. 338 F7 148
Centerville, Reynolds, Mo. 163 D7 150
Centerville, Silver Bow, Mont. 950 *D4 110
Centerville, Hunterdon, N.J. 120 B3 210
Centerville, Montgomery, Ohio 3,490 C2 156
Centerville, Washington, Pa. 5,088 C2 214
Centerville, Kent, R.I. (part of West Warwick) C2 216
Centerville, Charleston, S.C. 500 F4 188
Centerville, Turner, S.Dak. 887 D9 158
Centerville, Hickman, Tenn. 1,678 C4 190
Centerville, Leon, Tex. 836 D8 130
Centerville, Davis, Utah 2,361 C4 114
Centerville, Klickitat, Wash. 100 D6 98
Centrahoma, Coal, Okla. 148 D7 128
Central, Elmore, Ala. 250 C3 168
Central, Alsk. 41 B7 84
Central, Hot Spring, Ark. 150 D7 170
Central, Graham, Ariz. 100 F6 124
Central, Caribou, Idaho 10 G7 108
Central, Grant, N.Mex. 1,075 F2 126
Central, Pickens, S.C. 1,473 B3 188
Central, dist., Isr. 365,736 *C5 382
Central, prov., Ken. C6 414
Central, prov., Lib. *E3 408
Central (N.Rh.), prov., Rh.&Nya. 185,000 B5 420
Central (Nya.), prov., Rh.&Nya. B6 421
Central, prov., Tan. 886,306 D5 414
Central, plat., Tan. D5 414
Central, range, Dom.Rep. C9 233
Central African Republic, country, Afr. 1,177,000 F9 388
409
Central America, reg., N.A. 10,929,000 288
Central Barren, Harrison, Ind. 100 D3 140
Central Bridge, Schoharie, N.Y. 400 C7 212
Central Butte, Sask., Can. 318 E4 58
Central City, Gilpin, Colo. 250 C5 106
Central City, Marion, Ill. 1,422 E4 138
Central City, Linn, Iowa 1,087 B6 142
Central City, Muhlenberg, Ky. 3,694 C3 178
Central City, Merrick, Nebr. 2,406 C8 152
Central City, Somerset, Pa. 1,604 C3 214
Central City, Lawrence, S.Dak. 784 C2 158
Central Falls, Providence, R.I. 19,858 B3 216
Central Greece and Euboea (Stereá Ellás kai Évvoia) reg., Grc. 2,284,805 *B4 306
Centralhatchee, Heard, Ga. 174 C1 176
Central Heights, Gila, Ariz. 2,486 E5 124
Central Heights, Cerro Gordo, Iowa 900 A4 142
Centralia, Ont., Can. 220 Q19 64
Centralia, Marion, Ill. 13,904 E4 138
Centralia, Dubuque, Iowa 85 *B7 142
Centralia, Nemaha, Kans. 527 C7 144
Centralia, Boone, Mo. 3,200 B5 150
Centralia, Craig, Okla. 80 B8 128
Centralia, Columbia, Pa. 1,435 *B5 214
Centralia, Lewis, Wash. 8,586 C4 98
Centralia, Braxton, W.Va. 300 C4 194
Central Islip, Suffolk, N.Y. 10,000 D3 212
E8
Central Lake, Antrim, Mich. 692 D6 146
Central Pacolet, Spartanburg, S.C. 333 *B5 188
Central Park, Vermilion, Ill. 2,676 *C6 138
Central Park, Grays Harbor, Wash. 1,622 C3 98
Central Point, Jackson, Oreg. 2,289 E4 96
Central Point, Caroline, Va. 200 C7 192
Central Siberian, plat., Sov.Un. C12 329
Central Square, Oswego, N.Y. 935 B5 212
Central Valley, Shasta, Calif. 2,854 B2 94
Central Valley, Orange, N.Y. 950 D7 212
Central Village, Windham, Conn. 800 C8 202
Central Village, Bristol, Mass. 500 C5 206
Centre, Cherokee, Ala. 2,392 A4 168
Centre, co., Pa. 78,580 C3 214
Centre Hall, Centre, Pa. 1,109 C4 214
Centre Square, Gloucester, N.J. D2 210
Centreville, Bibb, Ala. 1,981 C2 168
Centreville, N.B., Can. 265 C2 70
Centreville, N.S., Can. 230 E3 70
Centreville, Queen Annes, Md. 1,863 B7 182
Centreville, St. Joseph, Mich. 971 H6 146
Centreville, Wilkinson and Amite, Miss. 1,229 D1 184
Centreville, Fairfax, Va. 600 A6 192
Centropolis, Franklin, Kans. 100 D8 144
Centuria, Polk, Wis. 551 C1 160
Century, Escambia, Fla. 2,046 A3 174
Century, Barbour, W.Va. 700 B4 194
Cephalonia, see Kefallinia, prov., Grc.
Ceram, isl., Indon. E7 359
Čerčany, Czech. 1,261 *B2 325
Cereal, Alta., Can. 154 E7 54
Cereales, Arg. C3 252
Ceredo, Wayne, W.Va. 1,387 C2 194
Ceres, Stanislaus, Calif. 4,406 D3 94
Ceres, Allegany, N.Y. 450 C3 212
Ceres, Bland, Va. 75 C3 192
Ceresco, Saunders, Nebr. 429 C9 152
E2
Ceres Northwest, Stanislaus, Calif. 1,126 *D3 94
Céret, Fr. 4,548 F5 278
Cereté, Col. 6,161 B1 244
Cerignola, It. 53,800 E5 302
Cerknica, Yugo. 1,404 B2 316
Cernavodă, Rom. 8,802 B5 321
Cernay, Fr. 6,645 D7 278
Cerralvo, Mex. 3,050 B6 225
Cerralvo, isl., Mex. C4 224
Cerrillos, Sante Fe, N.Mex. 148 C4 126
H7
Cerritos, Mex. 8,755 C5 225
Cerro Azul, Peru 1,372 C2 245
Cerro Colorado, Ur. B4 252
Cerro de Pasco, Peru 26,900 C2 245
Cerrogordo, Little River, Ark. D2 170
Cerro Gordo, Piatt, Ill. 1,067 D5 138
Cerro Gordo, Columbus, N.C. 306 C7 186
Cerrogordo, McCurtain, Okla. 60 E9 128
Cerro Gordo, co., Iowa 49,894 A4 142
Cerro Largo, dept., Ur. 97,256 B5 252
Cerulean, Trigg, Ky. 206 D3 178
Cervantes, Sp. 664 A3 298
Cervera del Rio Alhama, Sp. 4,905 A6 298
Cerveteri, It. 2,610 *E4 302
Cesena, It. 25,800 C4 302
(72,900▲)
Cesenatico, It. 5,935 C4 302
Česká Lipa, Czech. 12,621 A2 324
Česká Třebová, Czech. 12,840 B3 324
České Budějovice, Czech. 64,104 B2 324
Českobudějovický, co., Czech. 521,894 *B2 324
Český Brod, Czech. 5,754 *A2 324
Český Krumlov, Czech. 11,724 B2 324
Český Těšín, Czech. 14,243 B4 324
Cess, riv., Lib. E3 408
Cessford, Alta., Can. 160 E7 54
Cessnock, Austl. 14,417 E10 432
Cestos, Dewey, Okla. 10 B4 128
Cetina, riv., Yugo. C3 316
Cetinje, Yugo. 9,102 C4 316
Cetraro, It. 2,822 F5 302
Cévennes, mts., Fr. F5 278
Cevio, Switz. 504 B4 312
Ceyhan, riv., Tur. C7 307
Ceylon, Ont., Can. 145 P20 64
Ceylon, Martin, Minn. 554 H4 148
Ceylon, country, Asia 8,929,000 I10 340
368
Ceylon Station, Sask., Can. 355 F5 58
Chabot, lake, Calif. B5 94
Chacabuco, Arg. 12,530 B3 252
Chacahoula, Terrebonne, La. 50 C5 180
E5
Chachapoyas, Peru 7,700 B2 245
Chachoengsao, Thai. D4 362
Chachoengsao, prov., Thai. 240,565 *D4 362
Chachran, Pak. 2,954 E7 375
Chaco, prov., Arg. 650,600 C5 250
Chaco, riv., N.Mex. B2 126
Chaco Boreal, plains, Par. B2 247
Chaco Canyon, San Juan, N.Mex. 100 B3 126
Chaco Canyon, nat. mon., N.Mex. C2 126
Chad, country, Afr. 2,600,000 E8 388
409
Chad, lake, Chad D7 409
Chadbourn, Columbus, N.C. 2,323 C7 186
Chadileuvu, riv., Arg. C2 252
Chadiza, Rh. & Nya. B6 421
Chadron, Dawes, Nebr. 5,079 B3 152
Chadwick, Carroll, Ill. 602 A4 138
Chadwick, Christian, Mo. 175 E4 150
Chaerhsen, China B10 348
Chaffee, Scott, Mo. 2,862 D8 150
Chaffee, Cass, N.Dak. 106 D8 154
Chaffee, co., Colo. 8,298 D4 106
Chaffey, Douglas, Wis. 100 B1 160
Chaffinville, Worcester, Mass. 3,500 B4 206
Chagai, hills, Pak. E3 375
Chagda, Sov.Un. D15 329
Chagl, Sov.Un. D5 336
Chagny, Fr. D6 278
Chagrin Falls, Cuyahoga, Ohio 3,458 A5 156
Chahār Burjak, Afg. 5,000 D2 374
Chahal, Guat. 329 C3 228
Chāh Bahār, Iran 5,189 E5 379
Chaibasa, India 13,052 E4 368
Chainat, prov., Thai. 173,413 *D4 362
Chaires, Leon, Fla. 70 A6 174
Chaiyaphum, prov., Thai. 293,745 *D4 362
Chakai, Pak. B8 375
Chakdaha, India H9 366
Chakradharpur, India 14,807 E4 368
Chakwal, Pak. 13,319 C8 375
Chala, Peru 721 D3 245
Chala, pt., Peru D3 245
Chalatenango, Sal. 4,128 C3 228
Chalchuapa, Sal. 9,855 C3 228
Chalcidice, see Khalkidhik, prov., Grc.
Chalco, Sarpy, Nebr. E2 152
Chalco, riv., Mex. G10 224
Chaleur, bay, N.B., Can. B4 70
Chalfant, Allegheny, Pa. 1,414 *C2 214
Chalfont, Bucks, Pa. 1,410 *C6 214
Chalhuanca, Peru 2,538 C3 245
Chaling, China 15,000 L6 349
Chaling, lake, China E7 346
Chalk Buttes, Carter, Mont. E12 110
Chalk River, Ont., Can. 986 O23 64
Chalkville, Jefferson, Ala. 1,000 E5 168
Challapata, Bol. 2,529 C1 246
Challis, Custer, Idaho 732 E4 108
Chalmers, White, Ind. 548 B3 140
Chalmette, St. Bernard, La. 10,000 C7 180
E6
Chalmette, natl. hist. park and cem., La. C7 180
Châlons-sur-Marne, Fr. 36,834 C6 278
Chalon-sur-Saône, Fr. 37,399 D6 278
Chalt, India A1 368
Chālūs, Iran B3 379
Chalybeate, Tippah, Miss. 199 A4 184
Chalybeate, Van Buren, Tenn. 175 C6 190
Chalybeate Springs, Meriwether, Ga. 295 D2 176
Cham, Switz. 5,486 A4 312
Chama, Costilla, Colo. 500 E5 106
Chama, Rio Arriba, N.Mex. 791 B4 126
Chama, riv., N.Mex. B4 126
Chamaicó, Arg. C3 252
Chaman, Pak. 7,161 D5 375
Chamba, Tan. E6 414
Chambal, riv., India D2 368
Chamberlain, Sask., Can. 154 E5 58
Chamberlain, Brule, S.Dak. 2,598 D6 158
Chamberlain, lake, Maine B3 204
Chamberlayne Heights, Henrico, Va. 1,000 *C7 192
Chamberlin, mtn., Alsk. B7 84
Chambers, Apache, Ariz. 150 C6 124
Chambers, Bolivar, Miss. 322 *B2 184
Chambers, Holt, Nebr. 396 B7 152
Chambers, co., Ala. 37,828 C4 168
Chambers, co., Tex. 10,379 E8 130
Chambers, isl., Wis. C6 160
Chambersburg, Franklin, Pa. 17,670 D4 214
Chambéry, Fr. 32,139 E6 278
Chambezi, riv., Rh. & Nya. B6 421
Chamblee, De Kalb, Ga. 6,635 A5 176
Chambly, Que., Can. 2,817 S11 66
Chambly, co., Que., Can. 111,979 S11 66
S16
Chambly Canton, Que., Can. 1,885 *S11 66
Chambord, Que., Can. 1,091 P12 66
Chamela, Mex. D5 224
Chamois, Osage, Mo. 658 C6 150
Chamoli, India C2 368
Chamonix [-Mont-Blanc], Fr. E7 278
Champ, Somerset, Md. 100 D8 182
Champagne, Yukon, Can. E5 48
Champagne, former prov., Fr. 1,504,000 C5 278
Champagnole, Fr. 5,862 D6 278
Champaign, Champaign, Ill. 49,583 C5 138
Champaign, co., Ill. 132,436 C5 138
Champaign, co., Ohio 29,714 B3 156
Champerico, Guat. 982 C2 228
Champigny-sur-Marne, Fr. 36,903 I11 278
Champion, Alta., Can. 402 E6 54
Champion, Marquette, Mich. 750 C4 146
Champion, Chase, Nebr. 140 D4 152
Champlain, Que., Can. 710 R12 66
Champlain, Clinton, N.Y. 1,549 A8 212
Champlain, co., Que., Can. 102,674 Q11 66
Champlain, lake, N.Y., Vt. A8 212
B2 218
Champlin, Hennepin, Minn. 1,271 F6 148
Champlin, Juab, Utah D3 114
Champney, Newf., Can. 350 F9 72
Champotón, Mex. 2,853 D7 225
Chan, isl., Thai. E3 362
Chan, riv., Austl. D9 432
Chañaral, Chile 2,980 A1 252
Chanārān, Iran B5 379
Chañarcillo, Chile A1 252
Chanca, riv., Port. D3 298
Chancay, Peru 2,761 C2 245
Chance, Clarke, Ala. 300 D2 168
Chance, Somerset, Md. 275 D8 182
Chance, Perkins, S.Dak. 31 B3 158
Chancellor, Geneva, Ala. 150 D4 168
Chancellor, Turner, S.Dak. 214 D9 158
Chanchelulla, mtn., Calif. B2 94
Chanco, Chile 1,931 C1 252
Chanda, India 40,744 E3 366
Chandalar, riv., Alsk. B7 84
Chandauli, India D3 368
Chandausi, India C2 368
Chandeleur, isl., La. E7 180
Chandeleur, sound, La. E6 180
Chandernagore, India 49,909 I9 366
Chandler, Maricopa, Ariz. 9,531 E4 124
H2
Chandler, Que., Can. 3,338 Q10 66
Chandler, Warrick, Ind. 1,784 D2 140
Chandler, Murray, Minn. 338 H3 148
Chandler, Lincoln, Okla. 2,524 C7 128
Chandler Heights, Maricopa, Ariz. 75 H3 124
Chandlerville, Cass, Ill. 718 C3 138
Chandos, lake, Ont., Can. P22 64
Chandpur, Pak. 32,048 L17 375
Chandrakona, India I8 366
Chaneliak, Alsk. 100 *C5 84
Chanf, Iran D5 379
Chang, isl., Thai. D4 362
Changchiakou (Kalgan), China 229,300 E7 348
Ch'ang-Chiang, riv., China P4 349
Changchih, China 97,800 G6 348
Changchow, China 296,500 J10 349
Changchui, China G8 348
Changchun (Hsinking), China 855,200 D12 348
Change Islands, Newf., Can. 804 F8 72
Changewater, Warren, N.J. 100 B3 210
Changhsing, China 10,000 J9 349
Changhua, China 5,000 J9 349
Changhua, For. 40,980 M10 349
Changli, China 45,000 F9 348
Changling, China 5,000 C11 348
Changoing, China E8 348
Changpei, China E7 348
Changsha, China 650,600 K6 349
Changte, China 94,800 K5 349
Changting, China 25,000 M8 349
Changtu, China 25,000 E7 346
Changü, China C11 348
Changwu, China 5,000 D11 348
Changwu, China 10,000 H3 348
Changyeh, China D8 346
Changyön, Kor. 18,072 F12 348
Chanhassen, Carver, Minn. 244 *G5 148
Channahon, Will, Ill. 400 B5 138
F2
Channel (Channel Lake), Lake, Ill. 1,969 *A5 138
Channel, isl., Eur. L10 273
Channel Islands, Br.poss., Eur. 101,000 D4 266
Channel Islands, natl. mon., Calif. E4 94
Channel Lake, see Channel, Ill.
Channel-Port-aux-Basques, Newf., Can. 3,320 G6 72
Channelview, Harris, Tex. 7,500 F8 130
Channing, Dickinson, Mich. 600 C3 146
Chantada, Sp. 64,485 A3 298
Chanthaburi, Thai. 25,000 D4 362
Chanthaburi, prov., Thai. 110,808 *D4 362
Chantilly, Fr. 7,065 C5 278
Chantilly, Fairfax, Va. 400 A6 192
Chantrey, inlet, N.W.Ter., Can. D9 48
Chanute, Neosho, Kans. 10,849 E8 144
Chany, lake, Sov.Un. B9 336
Chao, lake, China J8 349
Chaoan, China 101,300 N8 349
Chaoan, China N8 349
Chaochou, China 15,000 C12 348

Chao Phraya (Menam), riv., Thai. D4 362
Chaotung, China 40,000 B12 348
Chaotung, China F8 346
Chaoyang, China 25,000 N8 349
Chaoyang (Foshan), China 16,000 E10 348
Chapadinha, Braz. 1,700 A2 258
Chapala, lake, Mex. K12 225
Chaparral, Col. 11,705 C1 244
Chapayevsk, Sov.Un. 83,000 B4 336
Chapelhill, Allen, Ky. 300 D4 178
Chapel Hill, Orange, N.C. 12,573 B6 186
Chapel Hill, Marshall, Tenn. 630 C5 190
Chapin, Morgan, Ill. 477 D3 138
Chapin, Franklin, Iowa 200 B4 142
Chapin, Lexington, S.C. 358 C6 188
Chapleau, Ont., Can. 2,800 R25 64
Chaplin, Sask., Can. 488 E4 58
Chaplin, Windham, Conn. 130 (1,230▲) B7 202
Chaplin, Nelson, Ky. 187 C5 178
Chaplin, lake, Sask., Can. E4 58
Chaplygin, Sov.Un. 21,400 F12 332
Chapman, Butler, Ala. 617 D3 168
Chapman, Dickinson, Kans. 1,095 D6 144
Chapman, Aroostook, Maine 40 (376▲) B4 204
Chapman, Phillips, Mont. B8 110
Chapman, Merrick, Nebr. 303 C7 152
Chapman, cape, N.W.Ter., Can. D10 48
Chapman, pond, R.I. D1 216
Chapman Camp, B.C., Can. 567 F15 52
Chapmanville, Logan, W.Va. 1,241 D2 194
Chappaqua, Westchester, N.Y. 6,000 D2 212
Chappaquiddick, isl., Mass. D7 206
Chappell, Deuel, Nebr. 1,280 C3 152
Chappells, Newberry, S.C. 128 C5 188
Chapra, India 64,309 D4 368
Chaptico, creek, Md. D6 182
Chapultepec, Mex. G10 224
Chaqui, Bol. 291 C1 246
Char, well, Maur. B2 408
Chara, Sov.Un. D13 329
Charadai, Arg. A4 252
Charagua, Bol. 1,185 C2 246
Charalá, Col. 3,309 B2 244
Charambira, pt., Col. C1 244
Charaña, Bol. 794 C1 246
Charcas, Mex. 9,318 C5 225
Chard, Eng. K10 273
Chardon, Geauga, Ohio 3,154 A5 156
Chardzhou, Sov.Un. 66,000 F8 328
Charente, dept., Fr. 313,635 *E4 278
Charente, riv., Fr. E3 278
Charente-Maritime, dept., Fr. 447,973 *D3 278
Charenton, St. Mary, La. 650 E4 180
Charenton-le-Pont, Fr. 22,079 I10 278
Charette, Que., Can. 785 R12 66
Chārikar, Afg. 21,070 B5 374
Charing, Taylor, Ga. 100 D2 176
Chariton, Lucas, Iowa 5,042 C4 142
Chariton, co., Mo. 12,720 B4 150
Chariton, riv., Iowa D5 142
Chariton, riv., Mo. B5 150
Charity, Dallas, Mo. 100 D4 150
Charkhari, India D2 368
Charklik, see Erhchiang, China
Charlack, St. Louis, Mo. 1,493 *C7 150
Charlemagne, Que., Can. 2,428 S11 S16 66
Charlemont, Franklin, Mass. 500 (897▲) A2 206
Charleroi, Bel. 26,433 (*124,400) D3 282
Charleroi, Washington, Pa. 8,148 C2 214
Charles, Stewart, Ga. 50 D2 176
Charles, co., Md. 32,572 C5 182
Charles, cape, Va. C9 192
Charles, mound, Ill. A3 138
Charles, riv., Mass. B5 206
Charlesbourg, Que., Can. 8,202 R16 66
Charlesburg, Calumet, Wis. 100 B5 160
Charles City, Floyd, Iowa 9,964 A5 142
Charles City, Charles City, Va. 20 C7 192
Charles City, co., Va. 5,492 C7 192
Charles Mill, res., Ohio B4 156
Charles Mix, co., S.Dak. 11,785 D7 158
Charleston, Cochise, Ariz. 15 G5 124
Charleston, Franklin, Ark. 1,036 B2 170
Charleston, Coles, Ill. 10,505 D5 138
Charleston, Penobscot, Maine 175 (750▲) C3 204
Charleston, Tallahatchie, Miss. 2,528 A2 184
Charleston, Mississippi, Mo. 5,911 E8 150
Charleston, Coos, Oreg. 500 D2 96
Charleston, Charleston, S.C. 65,925 (*203,100) F9 F4 188
Charleston, Bradley, Tenn. 764 C7 190
Charleston, Wasatch, Utah 223 C4 114
Charleston, Orleans, Vt. (668▲) *B4 218
Charleston, Kanawha, W.Va. 85,796 (*213,900) C3 C6 194
Charleston, co., S.C. 216,382 F9 188
Charleston, harbor, S.C. F9 188
Charleston Heights, Charleston, S.C. 19,000 *F9 188
Charlestown, Clark, Ind. 5,726 D4 140
Charlestown, Cecil, Md. 711 A8 182
Charlestown, Nevis 1,556 D13 233
Charlestown, Sullivan, N.H. 1,173 (2,576▲) E2 208
Charlestown, Washington, R.I. 300 (1,966▲) D2 216
Charles Town, Jefferson, W.Va. 3,329 B7 194
Charlestown Beach, Washington, R.I. 100 D2 216
Charlesville, Con.L. D3 414
Charleville, Austl. 4,900 D9 432
Charleville, Fr. 22,536 C6 278
Charlevoix, Charlevoix, Mich. 2,751 D6 146
Charlevoix, co., Mich. 13,421 D6 146
Charlevoix, lake, Mich. D6 146
Charlevoix East, co., Que., Can. 15,706 Q14 66
Charlevoix West, co., Que., Can. 14,557 Q14 66
Charlieu, Fr. 5,069 D6 278
Charlie Lake, B.C., Can. B12 52
Charlo, Lake, Mont. 380 C2 110
Charlo Station, N.B., Can. 200 B3 70
Charlotte, Independence, Ark. 75 B5 170
Charlotte, Clinton, Iowa 417 C7 142
Charlotte (Town of), Washington, Maine (260▲) *D5 204
Charlotte, Eaton, Mich. 7,657 G7 146
Charlotte, Mecklenburg, N.C. 201,564 (*272,700) B5 186
Charlotte, Dickson, Tenn. 551 B4 190
Charlotte, Atascosa, Tex. 1,465 E6 130
Charlotte, Chittenden, Vt. 160 (1,271▲) C2 218
Charlotte, co., N.B., Can. 24,497 D3 70
Charlotte, co., Fla. 12,594 E8 174
Charlotte, co., Va. 13,368 C6 192
Charlotte, hbr., Fla. E8 174
Charlotte Amalie, Vir.Is. 11,469 C12 233
Charlotte Court House, Charlotte, Va. 555 C6 192
Charlotte Hall, St. Marys, Md. 82 D6 182
Charlotte Harbor, Charlotte, Fla. 200 E8 174
Charlottenberg, Swe. B3 292
Charlottesville, Hancock, Ind. 500 C4 140
Charlottesville (Independent City), Va. 29,427 B6 192
Charlottetown, P.E.I., Can. 16,707 C6 70
Charlotteville, Montgomery, Ga. 150 D4 176
Charlotte Waters, Austl. D6 432
Charlton, Worcester, Mass. 200 (3,685▲) *B4 206
Charlton, co., Ga. 5,313 F4 176
Charlton City, Worcester, Mass. 750 B4 206
Charlton Depot, Worcester, Mass. 200 B4 206
Charlton Heights, Fayette, W.Va. 600 *C3 194
Charmes, Fr. C7 278
Charny, Que., Can. 3,639 R13 R16 66
Charouïn, Alg. C3 402
Charron, lake, Man., Can. D5 60
Charter Oak, Crawford, Iowa 665 B2 142
Charters Towers, Austl. 6,780 C9 432
Chartley, Bristol, Mass. 500 C5 206
Chartrand, Ont., Can. 210 P26 64
Chartres, Fr. 28,750 C4 278
Charysh, riv., Sov.Un. B10 336
Chascomús, Arg. 9,105 C4 252
Chase, Madison, Ala. 550 A3 168
Chase, B.C., Can. 550 E13 52
Chase, Rice, Kans. 922 D5 144
Chase, Franklin, La. 65 B4 180
Chase, Baltimore, Md. 950 B7 182
Chase, Lake, Mich. 185 F6 146
Chase, Chase, Nebr. 140 *D4 152
Chase, Muskogee, Okla. 50 C8 128
Chase, co., Kans. 3,921 D7 144
Chase, co., Nebr. 4,317 D4 152
Chase, mtn., Maine B4 204
Chaseburg, Vernon, Wis. 242 E2 160
Chase City, Mecklenburg, Va. 3,207 D6 192
Chaseley, Wells, N.Dak. 72 C6 154
Chasicó, Arg. F4 251
Chaska, Carver, Minn. 2,501 G5 148
Chasŏng, Kor. E13 348
Chasov Yar, Sov.Un. 19,200 R21 332
Chassahowitzka, bay, Fla. C8 174
Chassell, Houghton, Mich. 500 B3 146
Chasseral, mtn., Switz. A3 312
Chastang, Mobile, Ala. 175 D1 168
Chataignier, Evangeline, La. 550 D3 180
Chatanika, Alsk. 30 B7 84
Chatawa, Pike, Miss. 300 D2 184
Chatcolet, Benewah, Idaho 101 B2 108
Châteaubriant, Fr. 9,284 D3 278
Château-d'Oex, Switz. 3,381 B3 312
Château-du-Loir, Fr. 4,530 D4 278
Châteaudun, Fr. 9,687 D4 278
Chateaugay, Franklin, N.Y. 1,097 A7 212
Château-Gontier, Fr. 6,729 D3 278
Chateauguay, Que., Can. 1,100 S11 S15 66
Chateauguay, co., Que., Can. 22,588 S11 S15 66
Chateauguay Basin, Que., Can. 1,146 S15 66
Chateauguay Station, Que., Can. 3,265 *S15 66
Châteauneuf [-sur-Loire], Fr. D5 278
Château-Renault, Fr. 4,035 D4 278
Chateau Richer, Que., Can. 685 R13 66
Châteauroux, Fr. 36,420 D4 278
Château-Thierry, Fr. 8,841 C5 278
Châtellerault, Fr. 23,583 D4 278
Chatfield, Crittenden, Ark. 100 B6 170
Chatfield, Man., Can. 110 E4 60
Chatfield, Fillmore, Minn. 1,841 H6 148
Chatham, N.B., Can. 6,332 B4 70
Chatham, Ont., Can. 22,262 R18 64
Chatham, Sangamon, Ill. 1,069 D4 138
Chatham, Jackson, La. 758 B3 180
Chatham, Barnstable, Mass. 1,479 (3,273▲) C8 206
Chatham, Alger, Mich. 175 C5 146
Chatham, Washington, Miss. 50 B1 184
Chatham, Carroll, N.H. 30 (150▲) C4 208
Chatham, Morris, N.J. 9,517 B4 210
Chatham, Columbia, N.Y. 2,426 C8 212
Chatham, Pittsylvania, Va. 1,822 D5 192
Chatham, co., Ga. 188,299 E5 176
Chatham, co., N.C. 26,785 B6 186
Chatham, is., Pac.O. D4 436
Chatham, strait, Alsk. J14 84
Chatham City, see Garden City, Ga.
Chatham Hill, Smyth, Va. 75 D3 192
Chathamport, Barnstable, Mass. 150 C8 206
Châtillon-sur-Seine, Fr. D6 278
Chatkal, range, Sov.Un. D8 336
Chatom, Washington, Ala. 993 D1 168
Chatra, India D4 368
Chatsworth, Ont., Can. 410 P20 64
Chatsworth, Murray, Ga. 1,184 B2 176
Chatsworth, Livingston, Ill. 1,330 C5 138
Chatsworth, Sioux, Iowa 84 B1 142
Chatsworth, Burlington, N.J. 295 D3 210
Chattahoochee, Gadsden, Fla. 9,699 A6 174
Chattahoochee, co., Ga. 13,011 D2 176
Chattahoochee, riv., U.S. E10 77
Chattanooga, Comanche, Okla. 356 D5 128
Chattanooga, Hamilton, Tenn. 130,009 (*286,700) C6 E8 190
Chattaroy, Spokane, Wash. 150 B9 98
Chattaroy, Mingo, W.Va. 950 D2 194
Chattel Rharsa, lake, Tun. B5 402
Chattooga, co., Ga. 19,954 B1 176
Chattooga, ridge, S.C. B2 188
Chattooga, riv., S.C. B2 188
Chatuge, lake, N.C. C2 186
Chatwood, Chester, Pa. 3,621 *D6 214
Chau Doc, Viet. 35,500 E5 362
Chaudiere, riv., Que., Can. R14 66
Chauk, Bur. 24,466 B2 362
Chaumont, Fr. 19,346 C6 278
Chaumont, Jefferson, N.Y. 523 A5 212
Chauncey, Athens, Ohio 996 C4 156
Chauncey, Logan, W.Va. 800 D3 194
Chauncey, Dodge, Ga. 330 D3 176
Chauncy, pond, Mass. D1 206
Chauny, Fr. 10,544 C5 278
Chautauqua, Chautauqua, Kans. 205 E7 144
Chautauqua, co., Kans. 5,956 E7 144
Chautauqua, co., N.Y. 145,377 C2 212
Chautauqua, lake, N.Y. C2 212
Chauvigny, Fr. 4,024 D4 278
Chauvin, Alta., Can. 353 D7 54
Chauvin, Terrebonne, La. 950 E5 180
Chaves, Braz. 448 F7 256
Chaves, Port. 11,286 B3 298
Chaves, co., N.Mex. 57,649 E6 126
Chavies, Perry, Ky. 294 C7 178
Chavinda, Mex. 5,418 K12 225
Chavuma, Rh.&Nya. B4 420
Chazelles [-sur-Lyon], Fr. 5,076 E6 278
Chazy, Clinton, N.Y. 600 A8 212
Cheadle, Alta., Can. 64 E6 54
Cheaha, mtn., Ala. B4 168
Cheapside, Northampton, Va. 150 A9 192
Cheat, mtn., W.Va. C5 194
Cheat, riv., W.Va. B5 194
Cheatham, co., Tenn. 9,428 B4 190
Cheb, Czech. 20,136 A1 324
Chebacco, lake, Mass. C4 206
Chebanse, Iroquois and Kankakee, Ill. 995 C6 138
Chebeague Island, Cumberland, Maine 300 E2 E5 204
Cheboksary, Sov.Un. 83,000 A3 336
Cheboygan, Cheboygan, Mich. 5,859 D7 146
Cheboygan, co., Mich. 14,550 D7 146
Chech, sand dunes, Maur., Mali B3 408
Checheng, China 12,000 H7 348
Chechŏn, Kor. 28,391 G14 348
Checkerberry, Chittenden, Vt. 80 B2 218
Checotah, McIntosh, Okla. 2,614 C8 128
Chedabucto, bay, N.S., Can. D8 70
Cheduba, isl., Bur. C2 362
Cheek, Carter, Okla. D6 128
Cheektowaga Southwest, Erie, N.Y. 12,766 *C3 212
Cheektowaga, Erie, N.Y. 52,362 C3 212
Chefoo, China 116,000 G10 348
Chefornak, Alsk. 106 C5 84
Chefuncte, riv., La. D5 180
Chegor Tedi, mtn., Chad B8 409
Chehalem, mts., Oreg. B1 96
Chehalis, Lewis, Wash. 5,199 C4 98
Cheju, Kor. 60,180 I13 348
Cheju (Saishū), isl., Kor. I13 348
Chekiang, prov., China 25,280,000 F11 346
Chekunda, Sov.Un. D15 329
Chela, mtn., Ang. C2 420
Chelan, Sask., Can. 135 D6 58
Chelan, Chelan, Wash. 2,402 B7 98
Chelan, co., Wash. 40,744 B6 98
Chelan, lake, Wash. A6 98
Chelan Falls, Chelan, Wash. 150 B7 98
Chelang, cape, China N7 349
Chelforó, Arg. C2 252
Cheli, China G8 346
Chelia, mtn., Alg. A5 402
Chelkar, Sov.Un. 19,300 C5 336
Chelkar, lake, Sov.Un. B4 336
Chelkar-Tengiz, lake, Sov.Un. C6 336
Chellala, Alg. 5,196 A4 402
Chełm [Lubelski], Pol. 27,000 C6 325
Chełmno, Pol. 14,400 B4 325
Chelmsford, Ont., Can. 2,142 S25 64
Chelmsford, Eng. 41,420 J13 273
Chelmsford, Middlesex, Mass. 3,500 (15,130▲) A5 C2 206
Chełmża, Pol. 12,200 B4 325
Chelsea, Que., Can. 300 S9 66
Chelsea, Tama, Iowa 453 C5 142
Chelsea, Kennebec, Maine 125 (1,893▲) D3 204
Chelsea, Suffolk, Mass. 33,749 B5 D3 206
Chelsea, Washtenaw, Mich. 3,355 G7 146
Chelsea, Rogers, Okla. 1,541 B8 128
Chelsea, Faulk, S.Dak. 53 B7 158
Chelsea, Orange, Vt. 500 (957▲) D4 218
Chelsea, Taylor, Wis. 110 C3 160
Cheltenham, Eng. 68,000 J10 273
Cheltenham, Prince Georges, Md. 900 C6 182
Chelva, Sp. 3,554 C6 298
Chelyabinsk, Sov.Un. 688,000 (*860,000) A6 336
Chelyan, Kanawha, W.Va. 500 C3 C6 194
Chelyuskin, cape, Sov.Un. B12 329
Chemainus, B.C., Can. 2,000 C14 F11 52
Chemawa, Marion, Oreg. C1 C4 96
Chemnitz, see Karl-Marx-Stadt, Ger.
Chemquassabamticook, lake, Maine B3 204
Chemult, Klamath, Oreg. 150 D5 96
Chemung, Chemung, N.Y. 585 C5 212
Chemung, co., N.Y. 98,706 C5 212
Chen, China 25,000 M6 349
Chen, mtn., Sov.Un. C15 329
Chenab, riv., India, Pak. B2 368, D8 375
Chenachane (Oasis), Alg. C3 402
Chenan, China 5,000 I4 348
Chenango, co., N.Y. 43,243 C6 212
Chenango, riv., N.Y. C6 212
Chenango Bridge, Broome, N.Y. 2,000 *C6 212
Chenango Forks, Broome, N.Y. 510 C6 212
Chenchi, China 2,000 L5 349
Chenchiachen, China I18 346
Chenchiang (Chinkiang), China 179,000 I9 349
Chene, bayou, La. C5 180
Chenega, Alsk. 91 C7 G11 84
Chenequa, Waukesha, Wis. 445 E1 160
Cheneville, Que., Can. 706 S9 66
Cheney, Sedgwick, Kans. 1,101 E6 144
Cheney, Spokane, Wash. 3,173 B9 D8 98
Cheneys, Lancaster, Nebr. 85 *D9 152
Cheneyville, Rapides, La. 1,037 C3 180
Cheng, China 15,000 K10 349
Chengan, China 5,000 K3 349
Chengane, riv., Moz. D6 421
Chengchow, China 594,700 H6 348
Chenghai, China N8 349
Chenghua, China 25,000 B5 346
Chengkou, China J4 349
Chengku, China 10,000 I3 349
Chengmal, China P5 349
Chengte (Jehol), China 92,900 E8 348
Chengting, China F7 348
Chengtu, China 1,107,000 E8 346
Chengyangkuan, China 25,000 I7 349
Chenhsi (Barkŏl), China 10,000 C6 346
Cheniere, lake, La. *B3 180
Chenkang, China G7 346
Chennan, China F8 346
Chenoa, McLean, Ill. 1,523 C5 138
Chenoweth, Wasco, Oreg. 950 *B5 96
Chenpa, China 2,000 I3 349
Chenping, China 500 J4 349
Chentung, China 10,000 C11 348
Chenyüan, China 15,000 L4 349
Cheo Reo, Viet. D6 362
Chepache, riv., R.I. B2 216
Chepachet, Providence, R.I. 800 B2 216
Chepén, Peru 8,214 B2 245
Chepes, Arg. 2,131 B2 252
Chepo, Pan. 1,300 F8 228
Chepo, riv., Pan. F8 228
Chepstow, Wales 5,900 J10 273
Chepwe, India C6 368
Chequamegon, bay, Wis. B3 160
Cher, dept., Fr. 284,376 *D5 278
Cheraw, Otero, Colo. 173 D7 106
Cheraw, Marion, Miss. 100 D3 184
Cheraw, Chesterfield, S.C. 5,171 B9 188
Cherbourg, Fr. 38,262 C3 278
Cherchel, Alg. 8,332 (16,929▲) A4 402
Cherdyn, Sov.Un. A5 336
Cheremkhovo, Sov.Un. 123,000 D12 329
Cheren, Eth. 2,700 B4 398
Cherepanovo, Sov.Un. 23,100 B10 336
Cherepovets, Sov.Un. 92,000 A1 336
Cherhill, Alta., Can. 120 D5 54
Cheriton, Northampton, Va. 761 C8 192
Cherkassy, Sov.Un. 83,000 H9 332
Cherkessk, Sov.Un. 41,000 J13 332
Chernigov, Sov.Un. 89,000 G8 332
Chernigovka, Sov.Un. 3,300 I11 332
Chernobay, Sov.Un. 16,400 H9 332
Chernobyl, Sov.Un. 20,200 G8 332
Chernofski, Alsk. 4 *E5 84
Chernogorsk, Sov.Un. 51,000 D11 329
Chernomorskoye, Sov.Un. 3,800 J9 332
Chernovtsy, Sov.Un. 145,000 H5 332
Chernyakhovsk (Insterburg), Sov.Un. 33,000 E3 332
Chernyy Irtysh, riv., Sov.Un. C10 336
Cherokee, Colbert, Ala. 1,349 A2 168
Cherokee, Cherokee, Iowa 7,724 B2 142
Cherokee, Crawford, Kans. 797 E9 144
Cherokee, Swain, N.C. 500 B2 186
Cherokee, Alfalfa, Okla. 2,410 B5 128
Cherokee, Spartanburg, S.C. 100 A5 188
Cherokee, co., Ala. 16,303 A4 168
Cherokee, co., Ga. 23,001 B2 176
Cherokee, co., Iowa 18,598 B2 142
Cherokee, co., Kans. 22,279 E9 144
Cherokee, co., N.C. 16,335 B1 186
Cherokee, co., Okla. 17,762 C8 128
Cherokee, co., S.C. 35,205 A5 188
Cherokee, co., Tex. 33,120 D8 130
Cherokee, lake, Okla. B9 128
Cherokee, lake, Tenn. B8 190
Cherokee Ranch, Wayne, Pa. 1,200 *B6 214
Cherquenco, Chile 1,677 C1 252
Cherry, Bureau, Ill. 501 B4 138
Cherry, Cherry, Nebr. B4 152
Cherry, Lauderdale, Tenn. 75 C2 190
Cherry, co., Nebr. 8,218 B4 152
Cherry, creek, Colo. C6 106
Cherry, creek, S.Dak. C3 158
Cherry, pt., Va. C8 192
Cherry Creek, Oneida, Idaho *G6 108
Cherry Creek, White Pine, Nev. 50 D7 112
Cherry Creek, Chautauqua, N.Y. 649 C2 212
Cherry Creek, Ziebach, S.Dak. 150 C4 158
Cherryfield, Washington, Maine 750 (780▲) D5 204
Cherry Grove, Washington, Oreg. 300 *B3 96
Cherry Grove Beach, Horry, S.C. 208 D11 188
Cherry Hill, Polk, Ark. 150 C2 170
Cherry Hill, Cecil, Md. 150 A8 182
Cherry Hills Village, Arapahoe, Colo. 1,931 *C6 106
Cherry Lake, Madison, Fla. 400 A7 174
Cherry Point (Marine Corps Air Base), Craven, N.C. C9 186

Cherry Run, Morgan, W.Va. 100 B6 194
Cherryvale, Montgomery, Kans. 2,783 E8 144
Cherry Valley, Cross, Ark. 455 B6 170
Cherry Valley, Ont., Can. 225 Q23 64
Cherry Valley, Winnebago, Ill. 875 A5 138
Cherry Valley, Worcester, Mass. 1,500 B4 206
Cherry Valley, Otsego, N.Y. 668 C7 212
Cherryville, Gaston, N.C. 3,607 B4 186
Cherrywood Village, Jefferson, Ky. 531 *B5 178
Cherskiy, mts., Sov.Un. C16 329
Chesaning, Saginaw, Mich. 2,770 F7 146
Chesapeake, Lawrence, Ohio 1,396 D4 156
Chesapeake, Kanawha, W.Va. 2,699 C3 194
Chesapeake, bay, U.S. D11 77
Chesapeake Beach, Calvert, Md. 504 C6 182
Chesapeake Beach, Princess Anne, Va. (part of Bayside) A9 192
Chesapeake City, Cecil, Md. 1,104 A8 182
Chesapeake and Delaware, canal, Del. B3 172
Chesaw, Okanogan, Wash. 50 A7 98
Chesconessex, Accomack, Va. 60 *C9 192
Chesham, Cheshire, N.H. 150 F2 208
Cheshire, New Haven, Conn. 4,072 (13,383▲) D4 202
Cheshire, Berkshire, Mass. 1,078 (2,472▲) A1 206
Cheshire, Gallia, Ohio 369 D4 156
Cheshire, co., Eng. 1,294,000 H10 273
Cheshire, co., N.H. 43,342 F2 208
Cheshire, res., Mass. A1 206
Cheshskaya, bay, Sov.Un. C6 328
Chesilhurst, Camden, N.J. 384 D3 210
Chesley, Ont., Can. 1,629 P19 64
Chesnee, Spartanburg, S.C. 1,045 A5 188
Chester, Crawford, Ark. 99 B2 170
Chester, Plumas, Calif. 1,553 B3 94
Chester, N.S., Can. 975 E5 70
Chester, Middlesex, Conn. 1,414 (2,520▲) D6 202
Chester, Eng. 58,800 H10 273
Chester, Nassau, Fla. 200 A9 A10 174
Chester, Dodge, Ga. 377 D3 176
Chester, Fremont, Idaho 100 F7 108
Chester, Randolph, Ill. 4,460 F4 138
Chester, Wayne, Ind. 130 C5 140
Chester, Howard, Iowa 211 A5 142
Chester, Penobscot, Maine 75 (261▲) C4 204
Chester, Queen Annes, Md. 900 C7 182
Chester, Hampden, Mass. 950 (1,155▲) B2 206
Chester, Liberty, Mont. 1,158 B6 110
Chester, Thayer, Nebr. 480 D8 152
Chester, Rockingham, N.H. 400 (1,053▲) F4 208
Chester, Morris, N.J. 1,074 B3 210
Chester, Orange, N.Y. 1,492 D7 212
Chester, Delaware, Pa. 63,658 A6 D6 214
Chester, Chester, S.C. 6,906 B6 188
Chester, Lake, S.Dak. 200 D9 158
Chester, Windsor, Vt. 923 (2,318▲) E3 218
Chester, Chesterfield, Va. 2,000 B9 C7 192
Chester, Spokane, Wash. D9 98
Chester, Hancock, W.Va. 3,787 A2 A4 194
Chester, co., Pa. 210,608 D6 214
Chester, co., S.C. 30,888 B6 188
Chester, co., Tenn. 9,569 C3 190
Chester, riv., Md. B7 182
Chester Basin, N.S., Can. 275 E5 70
Chester Depot, Windsor, Vt. 350 E3 218
Chesterfield, New London, Conn. 100 D7 202
Chesterfield, Eng. 67,200 H11 273
Chesterfield, Caribou, Idaho G7 108
Chesterfield, Madison, Ind. 2,588 B4 140
Chesterfield, Hampshire, Mass. 180 (556▲) B2 206
Chesterfield, Cheshire, N.H. 90 (1,405▲) F2 208
Chesterfield, Burlington, N.J. 150 C3 210
Chesterfield, Chesterfield, S.C. 1,532 B8 188
Chesterfield, Henderson, Tenn. 200 C3 190
Chesterfield, Salt Lake, Utah 500 *C4 114
Chesterfield, Chesterfield, Va. 135 B9 C7 192
Chesterfield, co., S.C. 33,717 B8 188
Chesterfield, co., Va. 71,197 C7 192
Chesterfield, is., Pac.O. B11 432
Chesterfield Inlet, N.W.Ter., Can. E9 48
Chesterhill, Morgan, Ohio 876 C5 156
Chesterton, Porter, Ind. 4,335 A2 140
Chestertown, Kent, Md. 3,602 B7 182
Chester Township, Delaware, Pa. 3,602 *D6 214
Chesterville, Ont., Can. 1,169 O25 64
Chesterville, Franklin, Maine 100 (505▲) *D2 204
Chesterville, Pontotoc, Miss. 125 A4 184
Chestnut, Natchitoches, La. 50 B2 180
Chestnut, ridge, Pa. B5 194
Chestnut Mound, Smith, Tenn. 125 B6 190
Chestoa, Unicoi, Tenn. 150 B9 190
Chesuncook, Piscataquis, Maine 10 B3 204
Chesuncook, lake, Maine C3 204
Cheswick, Allegheny, Pa. 2,734 A4 214
Cheswold, Kent, Del. 281 D3 172
Chetac, lake, Wis. C2 160
Chetco, riv., Oreg. E2 96
Chetek, Barron, Wis. 1,729 C2 160
Chetek, lake, Wis. C2 160
Cheticamp, N.S., Can. 580 C8 70
Chetopa, Labette, Kans. 1,538 E8 144
Chetumal, bay, Mex. D8 225
Chevak, Alsk. 230 C5 84
Chevalon, creek, Ariz. D5 124
Cheverie, N.S., Can. 180 D5 70
Cheverly, Prince Georges, Md. 5,223 *C6 182
Cheviot, Sask., Can. 23 D4 58
Cheviot, N.Z. 440 E4 437
Cheviot, Hamilton, Ohio 10,701 C2 D1 156
Cheviot, hills, Eng. F10 272
Cheviot, mtn., Eng. F10 272
Chevreuil, bayou, La. C6 180
Chevreuil, pt., La. E4 180
Chevy Chase, Montgomery, Md. 2,405 C3 C5 182
Chevy Chase Heights, Indiana, Pa. 1,160 *C2 214
Chevy Chase Lake, Montgomery, Md. 2,500 *C5 182
Chevy Chase Section Four, Montgomery, Md. 2,243 *C4 182
Chevy Chase View, Montgomery, Md. 1,000 C3 182
Chewack, creek, Wash. A6 98
Chewalla, McNairy, Tenn. 150 C3 190
Chewelah, Stevens, Wash. 1,525 A9 98
Chewey, Adair, Okla. 30 B9 128
Chew Road, Camden, N.J. D3 210
Chews (Chews Landing), Camden, N.J. 1,500 *D2 210
Chews Landing, see Chews, N.J.
Chewsville, Washington, Md. 250 A4 182
Cheyenne, Roger Mills, Okla. 930 C4 128
Cheyenne, Laramie, Wyo. 43,505 E8 116
Cheyenne, co., Colo. 2,789 D8 106
Cheyenne, co., Kans. 4,708 C2 144
Cheyenne, co., Nebr. 14,828 C2 152
Cheyenne, pass, Wyo. E7 116
Cheyenne, riv., S.Dak., Wyo. C4 C8 158 116
Cheyenne Agency, Dewey, S.Dak. 300 B5 158
Cheyenne Bottoms, swamp, Kans. D5 144
Cheyenne Wells, Cheyenne, Colo. 1,020 D8 106
Chhata, India D2 368
Chhatarpur, India D2 368
Chhibramau, India D2 368
Chhindwara, India E2 368
Chi, China 21,000 H7 348
Chi, riv., Thai. C4 362
Chia, China 4,000 F5 358
Chiachi, China P5 349
Chiahsing, China 78,300 J10 349
Chiai, For. 124,000 N10 349
Chialing, riv., China J3 349
Chiamboni (Dicks Head), cape, Ken., Som. C7 414
Chiamussu, China 146,000 B15 348
Chian, China 10,000 E13 348
Chian, China 52,800 L7 349
Chianghua, China 2,000 M5 349
Chiang Kham, Thai. 10,000 C4 362
Chiang Khong, Thai. 10,000 B4 362
Chiangling, China 15,500 J6 349
Chiang Mai, Thai. 25,000 C3 362
Chiang Mai, prov., Thai. 534,628 *C3 362
Chiangmen, China N6 349
Chiang Rai, Thai. 25,000 C3 362
Chiang Rai, prov., Thai. 481,621 *C3 362
Chiangtu, China I9 349
Chiangwan, China I16 346
Chiangyin, China 90,000 J10 349
Chiangyu, China E8 346
Chiao, bay, China H10 348
Chiaochia, China F8 346
Chiaochou, China G10 348
Chiaoho, China 10,000 D13 348
Chiaotso, China 20,000 H6 348
Chiapa de Corzo, Mex. 6,745 D7 225
Chiapas, state, Mex. 907,026 D7 225
Chiapo, China J16 346
Chiari, It. 9,000 C2 302
Chiashan, China 5,000 I9 349
Chiasso, Switz. 5,744 C5 312
Chiating, China 110,000 I16 346
Chiautla de Tapia, Mex. 3,554 L14 225
Chiavari, It. 21,200 C2 302
Chiayü, China 10,000 J6 349
Chiba, Jap. 197,962 G8 L16 354
Chibemba, Ang. 354 C2 420
Chibuni, India C7 368
Chibuto, Moz. D6 421
Chicago, Cook, Ill. 3,550,404 (*6,517,600) B6 F3 138
Chicago Heights, Cook, Ill. 34,331 B6 F3 138
Chicago Ridge, Cook, Ill. 5,748 *F3 138
Chicago Sanitary and Ship, canal, Ill. F2 138
Chicamacomico, creek, Md. D8 182
Chicapa, riv., Ang. A4 420
Chichagof, Alsk. 20 J13 84
Chichagof, isl., Alsk. J14 84
Chich'ang, China M3 349
Chichén-Itzá, ruins, Mex. C8 225
Chichester, Merrimack, N.H. 130 (821▲) E4 208
Chichiang, China 35,000 K3 349
Chichibu, Jap. 44,671 L15 354
Chichihar, China 344,700 B12 348
Chichlanling, mtn., China P4 349
Chickahominy, riv., Va. C7 192
Chickaloon, Alsk. 10 C7 G11 84
Chickamauga, Walker, Ga. 1,824 B1 176
Chickamauga, dam, Tenn. E8 190
Chickamauga, lake, Tenn. C6 190
Chickasaw, Mobile, Ala. 10,002 E1 168
Chickasaw, co., Iowa 15,034 A5 142
Chickasaw, co., Miss. 16,891 B3 184
Chickasawhay, riv., Miss. D4 184
Chickasha, Grady, Okla. 14,866 C6 128
Chicken, Alsk. 34 C7 84
Chiclana, Sp. 16,241 D3 298
Chiclayo, Peru 49,600 B2 245
Chico, Butte, Calif. 14,757 C3 94
Chico, Park, Mont. 24 E6 110
Chico, Wise, Tex. 654 C7 130
Chico, Kitsap, Wash. 300 B4 D2 98
Chico, riv., Arg. G4 251
Chico, riv., Arg. F4 251
Chicoa, Moz. C6 421
Chicomo, Moz. D6 421
Chicontepec, Mex. 2,859 C6 K14 225
Chicopee, Hall, Ga. 900 B3 176
Chicopee, Crawford, Kans. 200 E9 144
Chicopee, Hampden, Mass. 61,553 B2 206
Chicora, Wayne, Miss. 150 D4 184
Chicora, Butler, Pa. 1,156 C2 214
Chicot, Chicot, Ark. 25 D5 170
Chicot, co., Ark. 18,990 D5 170
Chicot, isl., La. E6 180
Chicot, lake, Ark. D5 170
Chicot, pt., La. E6 180
Chicoutimi, Que., Can. 24,878 P13 66
Chicoutimi, co., Que., Can. 137,999 P13 66
Chicoutimi, riv., Que., Can. P13 66
Chicoutimi-Nord, Que., Can. 6,446 P13 66
Chico Vecino, Butte, Calif. 4,688 *C3 94
Chidester, Ouachita, Ark. 348 D3 170
Chidley, cape, Can. E12 48
Chieh, China 5,000 H5 349
Chief Joseph, dam, Wash. A7 98
Chiefland, Levy, Fla. 1,459 B8 174
Chiefs, pt., Ont., Can. P19 64
Chieh Shih, bay, China N7 349
Chiehhsiu, China 5,000 G6 348
Chiehmo, China 5,000 D5 346
Chiehyang, China 54,000 N8 349
Chiem, lake, Ger. E5 286
Chien, China 5,000 H4 348
Chienan, China 5,000 E9 348
Chienchang, China 5,000 E12 348
Chienchiang, China 5,000 K4 349
Chieng Dao, mtn., Thai. C3 362
Chienli, China 8,000 K6 349
Chienning, China L8 349
Chienob, China L9 349
Chienping, China E9 348
Chienshan, China 7,000 J8 349
Chienshih, China 10,000 J4 349
Chienshin, China N7 349
Chienshui, China G8 346
Chientang, riv., China K9 349
Chiente, China 3,000 K10 349
Chienyang, China 5,000 L9 349
Chierhkalang, China 5,000 D11 348
Chieri, It. 11,900 C1 302
Chieti, It. 27,200 D5 302
Chieti, prov., It. 404,700 *D5 302
Chietla, Mex. 3,676 L14 225
Chigasaki, Jap. 56,895 *L15 354
Chigirin, Sov.Un. 18,200 H9 332
Chignahuapan, Mex. 3,873 L14 225
Chignecto, bay, N.S., Can. D5 70
Chignecto, cape, N.S., Can. D4 70
Chignik, Alsk. 253 D6 84
Chigubo, Moz. D6 421
Chihchiang, China 2,000 J5 349
Chihchiang, China 20,000 L4 349
Chihfeng (Wulanhata), China 40,000 D9 348
Chihli (Pohai), gulf, China F9 348
Chihsi, China 50,000 C15 348
Chihuahua, Mex. 86,961 B4 224
Chihuahua, state, Mex. 846,414 B4 224
Chiili, Sov.Un. D7 336
Chikard, India B1 368
Chikaskia, creek, Okla. B6 128
Chikaskia, riv., Kans. E6 144
Chikura, Jap. M15 354
Chikwolnepy, stream, N.H. B4 208
Chilapa, Mex. 7,333 D6 M14 225
Chilas, India B1 368
Chilca, Peru 1,341 C2 245
Chilco, Kootenai, Idaho *B2 108
Chilcotin, riv., B.C., Can. D11 52
Childers, Nowata, Okla. B8 128
Childersburg, Talladega, Ala. 4,884 B3 168
Childress, Childress, Tex. 6,399 B5 130
Childress, co., Tex. 8,421 B5 130
Childs, lake, Fla. D9 174
Chile, country, S.A. 7,394,000 G4 236 251
Chilecito, Arg. 6,121 A2 252
Chilesburg, Caroline, Va. 85 *B7 192
Chilete, Peru 476 B2 245
Chilhowee, Johnson, Mo. 339 C4 150
Chilhowee, Blount, Tenn. C7 190
Chilhowee, mtn., Tenn. E9 190
Chilhowie, Smyth, Va. 1,169 D3 192
Chili, Miami, Ind. 145 B3 140
Chili, Clark, Wis. 225 D3 160
Chilili, Bernalillo, N.Mex. 100 D4 126
Chilin (Kirin), China D13 348
Chilko, lake, B.C., Can. E10 52
Chilko, riv., B.C., Can. E11 52
Chilkoot, see Port Chilkoot, Alsk.
Chillán, Chile 52,576 C1 252
Chilli, Latimer, Okla. D8 128
Chillicothe, Peoria, Ill. 3,054 C4 138
Chillicothe, Wapello, Iowa 148 C5 142
Chillicothe, Livingston, Mo. 9,236 B4 150
Chillicothe, Ross, Ohio 24,957 C4 156
Chillicothe, Hardeman, Tex. 1,161 B6 130
Chilliwack, B.C., Can. 7,297 C16 F12 52
Chillum, Prince Georges, Md. 10,000 *C6 182
Chilly, Custer, Idaho E5 108
Chilmark, Dukes, Mass. 150 (238▲) D6 206
Chilocco, Kay, Okla. 80 B6 128
Chiloé, prov., Chile 100,687 F3 251
Chiloé, isl., Chile F3 251
Chiloquin, Klamath, Oreg. 945 E5 96
Chilpancingo, Mex. 12,662 D6 M14 225
Chilton, Calumet, Wis. 2,578 B5 D5 160
Chilton, co., Ala. 25,693 C3 168
Chilung (Keelung), For. 181,140 M10 349
Chilwa, lake, Moz. C7 421
Chimacum, Jefferson, Wash. 100 A4 98
Chimalhuacán, Mex. 2,433 G11 224
Chimalpan, Mex. G9 224
Chimaltenago, Guat. 6,136 C2 228
Chimán, Pan. 448 F8 228
Chimay, Bel. 3,212 D3 282
Chimayo, Rio Arriba, N.Mex. 800 B5 126
Chimbay, Sov.Un. 16,100 D5 336
Chimborazo, vol., Ec. A2 245
Chimbote, Peru 4,243 B2 245
Chimen, China 5,000 K8 349
Chimkent, Sov.Un. 153,000 D7 336
Chimney Rock, Archuleta, Colo. 2 *E3 106
Chimney Rock, Rutherford, N.C. 150 B3 186
Chimneytop, mtn., Tenn. B9 190
Chimo, China 10,000 G10 348
Chin, Alta., Can. 50 F6 54
Chin, China G6 348
Chin, China 10,000 O4 349
Chin, cape, Ont., Can. O19 64
Chin, riv., China H6 348
China, Conecuh, Ala. 50 D2 168
China, Kennebec, Maine 200 (1,561▲) *D3 204
China, Mex. 2,496 B6 225
China, country, Asia 699,966,000 F12 340 346
China, lake, Maine D3 204
China Grove, Pike, Ala. 150 C4 168
China Grove, Rowan, N.C. 1,500 B5 186
China Hat, mtn., Oreg. D5 96
Chinaja, Guat. B2 228
China Lake, Kern, Calif. 5,000 E5 94
Chinan (Tsinan), China 680,000 G8 348
Chinandega, Nic. 13,146 D4 228
Chincha Alta, Peru 18,386 C2 245
Chincheng, China 10,000 H6 348
Chincheros, Peru 1,330 C3 245
Chinchilla, Lackawanna, Pa. 1,100 *B6 214
Chinchilla, Sp. 3,231 C6 298
Chinchiang, China 107,700 M9 349
Chinchou, China 352,200 E10 348
Chin Chuck, Hawaii, Haw. 209 *D6 86
Chincoteague, Accomack, Va. 2,131 C9 192
Chincoteague, bay, Md. D9 182
Chinde, Moz. 5,000 C7 421
Chindo, Kor. H13 348
Chindwin, riv., Bur. B2 362
Ching, China 594,700 J9 349
Ching, China 15,000 L4 349
Ching, riv., China H4 348
Chingcheng, China 10,000 B13 348
Chingchiang, China 77,000 K7 349
Chingchien, China 2,000 G5 348
Chingchuan, China 4,000 H3 348
Chingford, Eng. 46,800 J13 273
Chinghai, China D8 346
Chinghsing, China 15,000 B11 348
Chingliu, China 10,000 L8 349
Chingmen, China 8,000 J6 349
Chingning, China 20,000 H2 348
Chingola, Rh. & Nya. 6,410 B5 420
Chingpeng, China 5,000 D8 348
Chingpien, China 3,000 G4 348
Chingpu, China 45,000 J10 349
Chingshan, China 3,000 J6 349
Chingtai, China E6 348
Chingtao, see Tsingtao, China
Chingte, China 2,000 J9 349
Chingtzukuan, China I5 349
Chinguar, Ang. 1,675 B3 420
Chinguetti, Maur. B2 408
Chingyang, China 5,000 G3 348
Chingyüan, China 14,000 D12 348
Chingyüan, China 55,000 N6 349
Chingyün, China 5,000 G8 348
Chinhsi, China 3,000 E10 348
Chinhsien, China 20,000 F10 348
Chinhua, China 46,200 K9 349
Chinhuangtao, China 100,000 F9 348
Chining, China 40,000 E6 348
Chining, China 20,000 H8 348
Chiniot, Pak. 39,070 D8 375
Chinipas, Mex. 474 B4 224
Chinitna, pt., Alsk. H10 84
Chinju, Kor. 78,295 H14 348
Chinkiang, see Chenchiang, China
Chinko, riv., Cen.Afr.Rep. E9 409
Chinle, Apache, Ariz. 150 B6 124
Chinle, creek, Ariz. B6 124
Chinle, val., Ariz. B6 124
Chinmen, see Quemoy, China
Chinnampo, see Nampo, Kor.
Chinniuchen, China J7 349
Chino, San Bernardino, Calif. 10,305 C6 94
Chinon, Fr. 4,872 D4 278
Chinook, Alta., Can. 154 E7 54
Chinook, Blaine, Mont. 2,326 B7 110
Chinook, Pacific, Wash. 350 C3 98
Chinook Cove, B.C., Can. E12 52
Chino Valley, Yavapai, Ariz. 50 D3 124
Chinquapin, Duplin, N.C. 800 C8 186
Chinsali, Rh. & Nya. 169 B6 421
Chinsha, see Drechu, riv., China
Chinsura, India 56,805 I9 366
Chinta, China C7 346
Chinteche, Rh. & Nya. B6 421
Chinú, Col. 4,987 B1 244
Chinyang, China H6 348
Chinyün, China 10,000 K10 349
Chioco, Moz. C6 421
Chioggia, It. 26,700 C4 302
Chios, see Khios, prov., Grc.
Chip, lake, Alta., Can. D5 54
Chipinga, Rh. & Nya. 1,400 D6 421
Chip Lake, Alta., Can. D5 54
Chipley, Washington, Fla. 3,159 A5 174
Chipman, Alta., Can. 192 D6 54
Chipman, N.B., Can. 1,250 C4 70
Chippawa, Ont., Can. 2,039 Q21 64
Chippawa Hill, Ont., Can. 230 P19 64
Chippenham, Eng. 15,300 J10 273
Chippewa, co., Mich. 32,655 C7 146
Chippewa, co., Minn. 16,320 F3 148
Chippewa, co., Wis. 45,096 C2 160
Chippewa, lake, Wis. C2 160
Chippewa, riv., Minn. F3 148
Chippewa, riv., Wis. D2 160
Chippewa Falls, Chippewa, Wis. 11,708 D2 160
Chippewa Lake, Mecosta, Mich. 150 F6 146
Chipewyan, riv., Alta., Can. B6 54
Chiputneticook, lakes, Maine C5 204
Chipuxet, riv., R.I. D2 216

Clarissa, Todd, Minn. 569 E4 148
Clarita, Coal, Okla. 125 D7 128
Clark, Routt, Colo. 5 *B4 106
Clark, Randolph, Mo. 260 B5 150
Clark, Union, N.J. 12,195 B4 210
Clark, Clark, S.Dak. 1,484 C8 158
Clark, Park, Wyo. 10 B3 116
Clark, co., Ark. 20,950 C3 170
Clark, co., Idaho 915 E6 108
Clark, co., Ill. 16,546 D6 138
Clark, co., Ind. 62,795 D4 140
Clark, co., Kans. 3,396 E4 144
Clark, co., Ky. 21,075 C6 178
Clark, co., Mo. 8,725 A6 150
Clark, co., Nev. 127,016 G6 112
Clark, co., Ohio 131,440 C3 156
Clark, co., S.Dak. 7,134 C8 158
Clark, co., Wash. 93,809 D4 98
Clark, co., Wis. 31,527 D3 160
Clark, lake, Alsk. C6 84
Clark, mtn., Va. B7 192
Clark, pt., Ont., Can. P19 64
Clarkdale, Yavapai, Ariz. 1,095 D3 124
Clarkdale, Cobb, Ga. 750 A4 176
Clarke, co., Ala. 25,738 D2 168
Clarke, co., Ga. 45,363 C3 176
Clarke, co., Iowa 8,222 D4 142
Clarke, co., Miss. 16,493 C4 184
Clarke, co., Va. 7,942 A6 192
Clarke, lake, Sask., Can. C4 58
Clarkes Harbour, N.S., Can. 945 F4 70
Clarkesville, Habersham, Ga. 1,352 B3 176
Clarkfield, Yellow Medicine, Minn. 1,100 G3 148
Clark Fork, Bonner, Idaho 452 A2 108
Clark Fork, riv., Idaho, Mont. B3 108
C1 110
Clark Hill, res., Ga., S.C. C4 176
D4 188
Clarkia, Shoshone, Idaho 200 B2 108
Clarkrange, Fentress, Tenn. 150 B6 190
Clarks, Caldwell, La. 940 B3 180
Clarks, Merrick, Nebr. 439 C8 152
Clarks, riv., Ky. D2 178
Clarksboro, Gloucester, N.J. 500 D2 210
Clarksburg, Ont., Can. 450 P20 64
Clarksburg, Decatur, Ind. 300 C4 140
Clarksburg, Montgomery, Md. 900 B5 182
Clarksburg, Berkshire, Mass. 120 A1 206
(1,741▲)
Clarksburg, Moniteau, Mo. 357 C5 150
Clarksburg, Monmouth, N.J. 300 C4 210
Clarksburg, Ross, Ohio 438 C3 156
Clarksburg, Carroll, Tenn. 250 C3 190
Clarksburg, Harrison, W.Va. 28,112 B4 194
B6
Clarksdale, Coahoma, Miss. 21,105 A2 184
Clarksdale, De Kalb, Mo. 242 B3 150
Clarks Falls, New London, Conn. 100 D8 202
Clarks Fork of the Yellowstone, riv., Mont., Wyo. F7 110
B3 116
Clarks Green, Lackawanna, Pa. 1,256 *B6 214
Clarks Grove, Freeborn, Minn. 353 H5 148
Clarks Hill, Tippecanoe, Ind. 654 B3 140
Clarks Hill, McCormick, S.C. 25 D4 188
Clarkson, Ont., Can. 1,400 Q21 64
Clarkson, Grayson, Ky. 645 C4 178
Clarkson, Webster, Miss. 100 B3 184
Clarkson, Colfax, Nebr. 797 C8 152
Clarks Point, Alsk. 128 D6 84
Clarks Summit, Lackawanna, Pa. 3,693 A5 214
Clarkston, De Kalb, Ga. 1,524 B5 176
Clarkston, Oakland, Mich. 769 G8 146
Clarkston, Gallatin, Mont. 5 D5 110
Clarkston, Cache, Utah 490 B3 114
Clarkston, Asotin, Wash. 6,209 C9 98
Clarksville, Johnson, Ark. 3,919 B3 170
Clarksville, Sussex, Del. 200 F5 172
Clarksville, Calhoun, Fla. 150 A5 174
Clarksville, Kootenai, Idaho 44 *B2 108
Clarksville, Clark, Ind. 8,088 D4 140
Clarksville, Butler, Iowa 1,328 B5 142
Clarksville, Howard, Md. 180 B6 182
Clarksville, Ionia, Mich. 371 G6 146
Clarksville, Pike, Mo. 638 B7 150
Clarksville, Coos, N.H. (179▲) *A4 208
Clarksville, Clinton, Ohio 583 C3 156
Clarksville, Wagoner, Okla. 145 C8 128
Clarksville, Montgomery, Tenn. 22,021 B4 190
Clarksville, Red River, Tex. 3,851 C8 130
Clarksville, Mecklenburg, Va. 1,530 D6 192
Clarkton, Dunklin, Mo. 1,049 E8 150
Clarkton, Bladen, N.C. 662 C7 186
Clarno, Wheeler, Oreg. C6 96
Claryville, Campbell, Ky. 20 A8 178
Clashmore, Ire. 154 I5 273
Clatonia, Gage, Nebr. 203 D9 152
Clatskanie, Columbia, Oreg. 797 A3 96
Clatsop, co., Oreg. 27,380 A3 96
Claude, Armstrong, Tex. 895 B5 130
Claudell, Smith, Kans. 40 *C5 144
Claudy, N.Ire. 237 G5 272
Claunch, Socorro, N.Mex. 80 D5 126
Clausthal-Zellerfeld, Ger. 15,800 C4 286
Claveria, Phil. 5,046 A6 358
Clavet, Sask., Can. 60 E4 58
Clawson, Teton, Idaho F7 108
Clawson, Oakland, Mich. 14,795 B8 146
Clawson, Emery, Utah 130 D4 114
Claxton, Evans, Ga. 2,672 D5 176
Clay, Webster, Ky. 1,343 C3 178
Clay, Jackson, La. 150 B3 180
Clay, Onondaga, N.Y. 500 B5 212
Clay, Clay, W.Va. 486 C3 194
C7
Clay, co., Ala. 12,400 B4 168
Clay, co., Ark. 21,258 A6 170
Clay, co., Fla. 19,535 A9 174
Clay, co., Ga. 4,551 E2 176
Clay, co., Ill. 15,815 E5 138
Clay, co., Ind. 24,207 C2 140
Clay, co., Iowa 18,504 A2 142
Clay, co., Kans. 10,675 C6 144
Clay, co., Ky. 20,748 C7 178
Clay, co., Minn. 39,080 E2 148
Clay, co., Miss. 18,933 B4 184
Clay, co., Mo. 87,474 B3 150
Clay, co., Nebr. 8,717 D7 152
Clay, co., N.C. 5,526 B2 186
Clay, co., S.Dak. 10,810 E8 158
Clay, co., Tenn. 7,289 B6 190
Clay, co., Tex. 8,351 C6 130
Clay, co., W.Va. 11,942 C3 194
Clay, head, R.I. E2 216
Clayburn, B.C., Can. C15 52
F11
Clay Center, Clay, Kans. 4,613 C6 144
Clay Center, Clay, Nebr. 792 D7 152
Clay Center, Ottawa, Ohio 446 A1 156
A3
Clay City, Clay, Ill. 1,144 E5 138
Clay City, Clay, Ind. 950 C2 140
Clay City, Powell, Ky. 764 C7 178
Claycomo, Clay, Mo. 1,423 E2 150
Claydon, Sask., Can. 105 F3 58
Clayhatchee, Dale, Ala. 300 D4 168
Clayhole, Breathitt, Ky. 850 C7 178
Claymont, New Castle, Del. 10,000 A4 172
Claymour, Todd, Ky. 35 D3 178
Clayoquot, sound, B.C., Can. F9 52
Claypool, Gila, Ariz. 1,800 E5 124
Claypool, Kosciusko, Ind. 452 A4 140
Claysburg, Blair, Pa. 1,439 C3 214
Clay Springs, Navajo, Ariz. 150 D5 124
Clay Spur, Weston, Wyo. 15 B8 116
Claysville, Washington, Pa. 986 C1 214
Clayton, Barbour, Ala. 1,313 D4 168
Clayton, Contra Costa, Calif. 140 A6 94
Clayton, Ont., Can. 175 O24 64
Clayton, Kent, Del. 1,028 C3 172
Clayton, Rabun, Ga. 1,507 B3 176
Clayton, Custer, Idaho 125 E4 108
Clayton, Adams, Ill. 774 C3 138
Clayton, Hendricks, Ind. 653 C3 140
Clayton, Clayton, Iowa 130 B6 142
Clayton, Norton and Decatur, Kans. 161 C3 144
Clayton, Concordia, La. 882 C4 180
Clayton, Lenawee, Mich. 470 *H7 146
Clayton, Tunica, Miss. 25 A2 184
Clayton, St. Louis, Mo. 15,245 B8 150
C7
Clayton, Gloucester, N.J. 4,711 D2 210
Clayton, Union, N.Mex. 3,314 B7 126
Clayton, Jefferson, N.Y. 1,996 A5 212
Clayton, Johnston, N.C. 3,302 B7 186
Clayton, Montgomery, Ohio 550 *C2 156
Clayton, Pushmataha, Okla. 615 D8 128
Clayton, Stevens, Wash. 240 B9 98
Clayton, Polk, Wis. 324 C1 160
Clayton, co., Ga. 46,365 C2 176
Clayton, co., Iowa 21,962 B6 142
Clayville, Oneida, N.Y. 686 C6 212
Clayville, Providence, R.I. 150 B2 216
Clayworks, Webster, Iowa 200 B3 142
Clear, Alsk. 20 C7 84
Clear, cape, Ire. J3 273
Clear, creek, Ariz. D4 124
Clear, creek, Tenn. B7 190
Clear, creek, Wyo. B6 116
Clear, fork, Tenn. B7 190
Clear, fork, W.Va. D3 194
Clear, fork, W.Va. D6 194
Clear, isl., Ire. J3 273
Clear, lake, Calif. C2 94
Clear, lake, Ont., Can. O23 64
Clear, lake, Que., Can. Q11 66
Clear, lake, Iowa A4 142
Clear, lake, La. C2 180
Clear, lake, Wash. D8 98
Clear, riv., Alta., Can. B3 54
Clear, stream, N.H. B4 208
Clear Boggy, creek, Okla. D7 128
Clearbrook, Clearwater, Minn. 589 D3 148
Clearco, Greenbrier, W.Va. 150 C4 194
Clear Creek, Monroe, Ind. 250 C3 140
Clearcreek, Carbon, Utah 145 *D4 114
Clear Creek, Raleigh, W.Va. 204 D6 194
Clear Creek, co., Colo. 2,793 C5 106
Clearfield, Taylor, Iowa 504 D3 142
Clearfield, Douglas, Kans. 50 *D8 144
Clearfield, Rowan, Ky. 550 B7 178
Clearfield, Clearfield, Pa. 9,270 B3 214
Clearfield, Davis, Utah 8,833 B3 114
Clearfield, co., Pa. 81,534 B3 214
Clear Fork, Wyoming, W.Va. 425 D3 194
Clear Fork, res., Ohio B4 156
Clear Lake, Steuben, Ind. 147 *A5 140
Clearlake, Cerro Gordo, Iowa 6,158 A4 142
Clear Lake, Sherburne, Minn. 316 F5 148
Clear Lake, Deuel, S.Dak. 1,137 C9 158
Clearlake, Skagit, Wash. 600 A4 98
Clear Lake, Polk, Wis. 724 C1 160
Clear Lake, res., Calif. B3 94
Clearmont, Nodaway, Mo. 292 A2 150
Clearmont, Sheridan, Wyo. 154 B6 116
Clear Spring, Washington, Md. 488 A4 182
Clear Springs, Walton, Fla. 200 A4 174
Clearview, Okfuskee, Okla. 500 C7 128
Clearview, Ohio, W.Va. 520 *A4 194
Clearwater, Man., Can. 475 F3 60
Clearwater, Pinellas, Fla. 34,653 C5 174
D8
Clearwater, Idaho, Idaho 40 D3 108
Clearwater, Sedgwick, Kans. 1,073 B5 144
E6
Clearwater, Wright, Minn. 274 F4 148
Clearwater, Antelope, Nebr. 418 B7 152
Clearwater, Aiken, S.C. 1,450 D5 188
Clearwater, Jefferson, Wash. 70 B2 98
Clearwater, co., Idaho 8,548 C3 108
Clearwater, co., Minn. 8,864 D3 148
Clearwater, lake, B.C., Can. D12 52
Clearwater, lake, Que., Can. Q9 66
Clearwater, mts., Idaho C2 108
Clearwater, res., Mo. D7 150
Clearwater, riv., Alta., Can. B7 54
Clearwater, riv., Alta., Can. D5 54
Clearwater, riv., B.C., Can. E12 52
Clearwater, riv., Idaho C2 108
Clearwater, riv., Minn. D3 148
Clearwater, riv., Wash. C10 98
Clearwater Lake, Oneida, Wis. 200 C4 160
Clearwater Station, B.C., Can. E12 52
Cleater Moor, Eng. 6,411 G9 273
Cleaton, Muhlenberg, Ky. 700 C3 178
Cleator, Yavapai, Ariz. 15 D3 124
Clebit, McCurtain, Okla. 250 D9 128
Cleburne, Riley, Kans. 150 C7 144
Cleburne, Johnson, Tex. 15,381 B8 130
C7
Cleburne, co., Ala. 10,911 B4 168
Cleburne, co., Ark. 9,059 B4 170
Cle Elum, Kittitas, Wash. 1,816 B6 98
Cle Elum, res., Wash. B5 98
Cle Elum, riv., Wash. B5 98
Cleethorpes, Eng. 30,300 H12 273
Cleeves, Sask., Can. 50 D3 58
Cleggan, Ire. H2 273
Cleghorn, Cherokee, Iowa 228 B2 142
Cleghorn, Eau Claire, Wis. 80 D2 160
Clem, Carroll, Ga. 180 C1 176
Clementon, Camden, N.J. 3,766 D3 210
Clements, Chase, Kans. 50 D7 144
Clements, St. Marys, Md. 150 D6 182
Clements, Redwood, Minn. 269 G3 148
Clementsvale, N.S., Can. 525 E4 70
Clemons, Marshall, Iowa 198 B4 142
Clemons, Washington, N.Y. 500 B8 212
Clemscot, Carter, Okla. 250 D6 128
Clemson, Pickens, S.C. 1,587 B3 188
Clemson College, Oconee, S.C. 3,500 B3 188
Clendenin, Kanawha, W.Va. 1,510 C3 194
C6
Clendening, res., Ohio B5 156
Cleona, Lebanon, Pa. 1,988 C5 214
Cleo Springs, Major, Okla. 236 B5 128
Clermont, Austl. 1,587 C9 432
Clermont, Que., Can. 2,628 Q14 66
Clermont, Lake, Fla. 3,313 C9 174
Clermont-Ferrand, Fr. 113,391 E5 278
Clermont, Hall, Ga. 268 B3 176
Clermont, Marion, Ind. 1,058 C3 140
D4
Clermont, Fayette, Iowa 570 A6 142
Clermont, Bullitt, Ky. 100 C5 178
Clermont, Cape May, N.J. 250 E3 210
Clermont, co., Ohio 80,530 C2 156
Clermont, hill, Calif. C3 94
Clermont Harbor, Hancock, Miss. 300 E3 184
Clermont-l'Hérault, Fr. 5,314 F5 278
Clervaux, Lux. 996 D5 282
Cleve, see Kleve, Ger.
Clevedon, Eng. 9,700 J10 273
Cleveland, Blount, Ala. 300 A3 168
Cleveland, Conway, Ark. 79 B4 170
Cleveland, Charlotte, Fla. 100 E9 174
Cleveland, White, Ga. 657 B3 176
Cleveland, Franklin, Idaho G7 108
Cleveland, Le Sueur, Minn. 389 G5 148
Cleveland, Bolivar, Miss. 10,172 B2 184
Cleveland, Cass, Mo. 216 *C3 150
Cleveland, Blaine, Mont. 15 B7 110
Cleveland, Oswego, N.Y. 732 B6 212
Cleveland, Rowan, N.C. 594 B5 186
Cleveland, Stutsman, N.Dak. 169 D6 154
Cleveland, Cuyahoga, Ohio 876,050 A5 156
(*2,090,800) B1
Cleveland, Pawnee, Okla. 2,519 B7 128
Cleveland, Greenville, S.C. 250 A3 188
Cleveland, Bradley, Tenn. 16,196 C7 190
Cleveland, Liberty, Tex. 5,838 D8 130
Cleveland, Emery, Utah 261 D5 114
Cleveland, Russell, Va. 415 D2 192
Cleveland, Manitowoc, Wis. 687 B6 160
Cleveland, co., Ark. 6,944 D4 170
Cleveland, co., N.C. 66,048 B4 186
Cleveland, co., Okla. 47,600 C6 128
Cleveland, hills, Eng. G11 273
Cleveland Heights, Cuyahoga, Ohio 61,813 A5 156
B1
Clever, Christian, Mo. 283 D4 150
Cleves, Hamilton, Ohio 2,076 D1 156
Clew, bay, Ire. H3 273
Clewiston, Hendry, Fla. 3,114 E10 174
Clibreck, mtn., Scot. C8 272
Clichy [-la-Garenne], Fr. 55,591 I10 278
Cliff, Grant, N.Mex. 175 F2 126
Cliff Lake, Madison, Mont. 4 F5 110
Clifford, Ont., Can. 533 Q20 64
Clifford, Bartholomew, Ind. 241 C4 140
Clifford, Lapeer, Mich. 389 F8 146
Clifford, Traill, N.Dak. 109 C8 154
Clifford, Amherst, Va. 135 C5 192
Cliffside, B.C., Can. C14 52
Cliffside, Rutherford, N.C. 1,275 B4 186
Cliffside Park, Bergen, N.J. 17,642 B2 210
B5
Clifftop, Fayette, W.Va. 250 D7 194
Cliffview, Carroll, Va. 150 *D4 192
Cliffwood, Monmouth, N.J. 3,000 *C4 210
Cliffwood Beach, Middlesex and Monmouth, N.J. 3,000 C4 210
Clifton, Greenlee, Ariz. 4,191 E6 124
Clifton, Mesa, Colo. 300 C2 106
Clifton, Franklin, Idaho 150 G6 108
Clifton, Iroquois, Ill. 1,018 C6 138
Clifton, Washington and Clay, Kans. 746 C6 144
Clifton, Penobscot, Maine 85 D4 204
(227▲)
Clifton, Essex, Mass. C3 206
Clifton, Passaic, N.J. 82,084 A1 210
B4
Clifton, Spartanburg, S.C. 1,249 B5 188
Clifton, Wayne, Tenn. 708 C4 190
Clifton, Bosque, Tex. 2,335 D7 130
Clifton, Fairfax, Va. 230 A6 192
B7
Clifton, Monroe, Wis. 60 E3 160
Clifton, Weston, Wyo. C8 116
Clifton City, Cooper, Mo. 117 C4 150
Clifton Forge (Independent City), Va. 5,268 C5 192
Clifton Heights, Delaware, Pa. 8,005 A6 214
Clifton Hill, Randolph, Mo. 207 B5 150
Clifton Springs, Ontario, N.Y. 1,953 C4 212
Cliftonville, Noxubee, Miss. 250 B4 184
Clifty, Todd, Ky. 100 D3 178
Clifty, White and Cumberland, Tenn. 75 C6 190
Climax, Sask., Can. 402 F3 58
Climax, Lake, Colo. 1,609 C4 106
Climax, Decatur, Ga. 329 F2 176
Climax, Greenwood, Kans. 81 E7 144
Climax, Kalamazoo, Mich. 587 G6 146
Climax, Polk, Minn. 310 D2 148
Climax Springs, Camden, Mo. 93 C4 150
Climbing Hill, Woodbury, Iowa 140 B1 142
Clinch, co., Ga. 6,545 F4 176
Clinch, mtn., Tenn., Va. B8 190
D2 192
Clinch, riv., Tenn. C7 190
Clinchburg, Washington, Va. 450 D3 192
Clinchco, Dickenson, Va. 975 C2 192
Clinchfield, Houston, Ga. 250 D3 176
Clinchfield, McDowell, N.C. 950 *B4 186
Clinchmore, Campbell, Tenn. 250 B7 190
Clinchport, Scott, Va. 302 D2 192
Clingmans Dome, mtn., Tenn. C8 190
Clint, El Paso, Tex. 802 D2 130
Clinton, Greene, Ala. 150 C2 168
Clinton, Van Buren, Ark. 744 B4 170
Clinton, B.C., Can. 250 E12 52
Clinton, Ont., Can. 2,896 Q19 64
Clinton, Middlesex, Conn. 4,166 D5 202
Clinton, De Witt, Ill. 7,355 C5 138
Clinton, Vermillion, Ind. 5,843 C2 140
Clinton, Clinton, Iowa 33,589 C7 142
Clinton, Hickman, Ky. 1,647 D2 178
Clinton, East Feliciana, La. 1,568 D4 180
Clinton, Kennebec, Maine 800 D3 204
(1,729▲)
Clinton, Prince Georges, Md. 1,578 C6 182
Clinton, Essex, Mass. 12,848 B4 206
Clinton, Lenawee, Mich. 1,481 G8 146
Clinton, Big Stone, Minn. 565 F2 148
Clinton, Hinds, Miss. 3,438 C2 184
Clinton, Henry, Mo. 6,925 C4 150
Clinton, Missoula, Mont. 3 D3 110
Clinton, Sheridan, Nebr. 46 B3 152
Clinton, Hunterdon, N.J. 1,158 B3 210
Clinton, Oneida, N.Y. 1,855 B6 212
Clinton, Sampson, N.C. 7,461 C7 186
Clinton, Summit, Ohio 924 B5 156
Clinton, Custer, Okla. 9,617 C5 128
Clinton, Laurens, S.C. 7,937 C5 188
Clinton, Anderson, Tenn. 4,943 B7 190
E9
Clinton, Davis, Utah 1,025 B3 114
Clinton, Island, Wash. 800 *B4 98
Clinton, Rock, Wis. 1,274 F5 160
Clinton, co., Ill. 24,029 E4 138
Clinton, co., Ind. 30,765 B3 140
Clinton, co., Iowa 55,060 C7 142
Clinton, co., Ky. 8,886 D5 178
Clinton, co., Mich. 37,969 G7 146
Clinton, co., Mo. 11,588 B3 150
Clinton, co., N.Y. 72,722 A8 212
Clinton, co., Ohio 30,004 C3 156
Clinton, co., Pa. 37,619 B4 214
Clinton, riv., Mich. G8 146
Clinton Colden, lake, N.W.Ter., Can. E8 48
Clintonville, Bourbon, Ky. 250 B6 178
Clintonville, Greenbrier, W.Va. D4 194
Clintonville, Waupaca, Wis. 4,778 D5 160
Clintwood, Dickenson, Va. 1,400 C2 192
Clio, Barbour, Ala. 929 D4 168
Clio, Wayne, Iowa 120 D4 142
Clio, Whitley, Ky. 700 D6 178
Clio, Genesee, Mich. 2,212 F8 146
Clio, Marlboro, S.C. 847 B9 188
Clio, Roane, W.Va. 400 C3 194
Clipper, Whatcom, Wash. 65 A4 98
Clipperton, isl., Pac.O. C5 436
Clisham, mtn., Scot. D6 272
Clitherall, Otter Tail, Minn. 138 E3 148
Clive, Alta., Can. 249 D6 54
Clive, Polk, Iowa 752 A7 142
Cliza, Bol. 3,121 C1 246
Cloates, point, Austl. C2 432
Clonakilty, bay, Ire. J4 273
Cloncurry, Austl. 1,955 C8 432
Clonmany, Ire. 239 F5 272
Clonmel, Sedgwick, Kans. 50 B5 144
Clonmel, Ire. 10,697 I5 273
Clontarf, Swift, Minn. 139 F3 148
Clo-oose, B.C., Can. F10 52
Cloppenburg, Ger. B3 286
Clopton, Dale, Ala. 75 D4 168
Cloquet, Carlton, Minn. 9,013 E6 148
Cloquet, riv., Minn. D6 148
Closplint, Harlan, Ky. 400 *D7 178
Closter, Bergen, N.J. 7,767 A2 210
B5
Clothier, Logan, W.Va. 392 D5 194
Cloud, co., Kans. 14,407 C6 144
Cloud, mtn., Newf., Can. E7 72
Cloud, peak, Wyo. B5 116
Cloud Chief, Washita, Okla. 75 C5 128
Cloudcroft, Otero, N.Mex. 464 F5 126
Cloud Lake, Palm Beach, Fla. 148 *E10 174
Cloudland, Chattooga, Ga. 150 B1 176
Cloudy, bay, N.Z. D5 437
Cloutierville, Natchitoches, La. 225 C3 180
Clover, Twin Falls, Idaho G4 108
Clover, York, S.C. 3,500 A6 188
Clover, Halifax, Va. 261 D6 192
Clover Bottom, Jackson, Ky. 190 C6 178
Cloverdale, Lauderdale, Ala. 500 A2 168
Cloverdale, Sonoma, Calif. 2,848 C2 94
Cloverdale, B.C., Can. 1,100 B15 52
Cloverdale, Ada, Idaho 75 *F2 108
Cloverdale, Tazewell, Ill. 600 *C4 138
Cloverdale, Putnam, Ind. 741 C3 140
Cloverdale, Chautauqua, Kans. 850 *E5 144
Cloverdale, Tillamook, Oreg. 200 B3 96
Cloverdale, Botetourt, Va. 500 C5 192
Clover Hills, Polk, Iowa 408 A7 142
Cloverhill, Blount, Tenn. E9 190
Cloverleaf, Harris, Tex. 3,000 F8 130
Clover Lick, Pocahontas, W.Va. 350 C5 194
Cloverport, Breckinridge, Ky. 1,334 C4 178
Cloverton, Pine, Minn. 150 E6 148
Clovis, Fresno, Calif. 5,546 D4 94
Clovis, Curry, N.Mex. 23,713 D7 126
Cluj, Rom. 154,752 A2 321
Cluny, Alta., Can. 197 E6 54
Cluny, Fr. 4,032 D6 278
Cluster Springs, Halifax, Va. 150 D6 192
Clute, Brazoria, Tex. 4,501 G8 130

Clutha, riv., N.Z.		F2	437
Clutier, Tama, Iowa	292	B5	142
Clyattville, Lowndes, Ga.	150	F3	176
Clyde, Alta., Can.	221	C6	54
Clyde, N.W.Ter., Can.		C12	48
Clyde, Cloud, Kans.	1,025	C6	144
Clyde, Nodaway, Mo.	90	A3	150
Clyde, Wayne, N.Y.	2,693	B5	212
Clyde, Haywood, N.C.	680	B3	186
Clyde, Cavalier, N. Dak.	100	B7	154
Clyde, Sandusky, Ohio	4,826	A4	156
Clyde, Darlington, S.C.	200	C8	188
Clyde, Callahan, Tex.	1,116	C6	130
Clyde, firth, Scot.		F8	272
Clyde, riv., Alta., Can.		*C7	54
Clyde, riv., N.S., Can.		E4	70
Clydebank, Scot.	48,800	F8	272
Clyde Hill, King, Wash.	1,871	D3	98
Clyde Park, Park, Mont.	253	E6	110
Clyman, Dodge, Wis.	259	*E5	160
Clymer, Chautauqua, N.Y.	400	C2	212
Clymer, Indiana, Pa.	2,251	C2	214
Clyo, Effingham, Ga.	250	D5	176
Cnocmoy, mtn., Scot.		F7	272
Cnossus, ruins, Grc.		D5	306
Coa, riv., Port.		B3	298
Coachella, Riverside, Calif.	4,854	F5	94
Coachella, canal, Calif.		F6	94
Coachford, Ire.	267	J4	273
Coahoma, Coahoma, Miss.	300	A2	184
Coahoma, Howard, Tex.	1,239	C5	130
Coahoma, co., Miss.	46,212	A2	184
Coahuayutla, Mex.	521	L13	225
Coahuila, state, Mex.	720,619	B5	225
Coal, co., Okla.	5,546	D7	128
Coal, creek, Ind.		C2	140
Coal, creek, Okla.		C8	128
Coal, fork, W.Va.		D6	194
Coal Bluff, Vigo, Ind.	100	C2	140
Coal Branch Station, N.B., Can.	195	C4	70
Coalburg, Kanawha, W.Va.	450	*C3	194
Coal City, Grundy, Ill.	2,852	B5	138
Coal City, Owen, Ind.	235	C2	140
Coal City, Raleigh, W.Va.	750	*D3	194
Coalcomán, Mex.	3,642	D5	224
Coal Creek, B.C., Can.	130	F15	52
Coalcreek, Fremont, Colo.	206	D5	106
Coaldale, Alta., Can.	2,327	F6	54
Coaldale, Fremont, Colo.	15	D5	106
Coaldale, Esmeralda, Nev.	15	E4	112
Coaldale, Schuylkill, Pa.	3,949	C6	214
Coalfield, Morgan, Tenn.	250	B7	190
Coal Fork, Kanawha, W.Va.	1,000	C3 C6	194
Coalgate, Coal, Okla.	1,689	D7	128
Coalgood, Harlan, Ky.	800	*D7	178
Coal Grove, Lawrence, Ohio	2,961	D4	156
Coal Harbour, B.C., Can.		E9	52
Coal Hill, Johnson, Ark.	704	B3	170
Coalhurst, Alta., Can.	125	F6	54
Coaling, Tuscaloosa, Ala.	410	B2	168
Coalinga, Fresno, Calif.	5,965	D3	94
Coalmont, B.C., Can.	215	F12	52
Coalmont, Jackson, Colo.	8	B4	106
Coalmont, Clay, Ind.	500	C2	140
Coalmont, Grundy, Tenn.	458	C6	190
Coalport, Clearfield, Pa.	821	C3	214
Coalridge, Sheridan, Mont.	36	B12	110
Coal Run, Pike, Ky.	250	C8	178
Coalspur, Alta., Can.	75	D4	54
Coalton, Montgomery, Ill.	352	D4	138
Coalton, Jackson, Ohio	648	C4	156
Coalton, Okmulgee, Okla.	150	C8	128
Coalton (Womelsdorf), Randolph, W.Va.	354	*C5	194
Coaltown, Lawrence, Pa.	1,033	*B1	214
Coal Valley, Walker, Ala.	653	B2	168
Coal Valley, Rock Island, Ill.	435	B3	138
Coalville, Webster, Iowa	300	B3	142
Coalville, Summit, Utah	907	C4	114
Coalwood, Powder River, Mont.	21	E11	110
Coalwood, McDowell, W.Va.	1,199	*D3	194
Coamo, P.R.	11,592	C11	233
Coari, Braz.	3,019	F4	256
Coast, mts., Alsk.		D8	84
Coast, mts., Can.		F5	48
Coast, prov., Ken.		C6	414
Coast, ranges, U.S.		C2	77
Coastal, plain, N.C., S.C., Va.		C7 / E8 / D7	186 / 188 / 192
Coasters Harbor, isl., R.I.		C3	216
Coatbridge, Scot.	51,000	F8	272
Coatepec, Mex.	13,755	L15	225
Coatepeque, Guat.	6,272	C2	228
Coates, Dakota, Minn.	202	G7	148
Coatesville, Hendricks, Ind.	497	C3	140
Coatesville, Chester, Pa.	12,971	D6	214
Coaticook, Que., Can.	6,492	S13	66
Coatopa, Sumter, Ala.	150	C1	168
Coatopin, Mex.		D5	225
Coats, Pratt, Kans.	152	E5	144
Coats, Harnett, N.C.	1,049	B7	186
Coats, isl., N.W.Ter., Can.		E10	48
Coatsville, Schuyler, Mo.	100	A5	150
Coatzacoalcos, Mex.	19,503	D7	225
Cobalt, Ont., Can.	2,367	R25	64
Cobalt, Middlesex, Conn.	200	C5	202
Cobalt, Lemhi, Idaho	250	D4	108
Cobalt City, Madison, Mo.	434	*D7	150
Cobán, Guat.	7,917	C2	228
Cobar, Austl.	2,224	E9	432
Cobb, Sumter, Ga.	90	E3	176
Cobb, Iowa, Wis.	387	F3	160
Cobb, co., Ga.	114,174	C2	176
Cobb, isl., Md.		D6	182
Cobb, riv., Minn.		H5	148
Cobble Hill, B.C., Can.	315	C14	52
Cobbosseecontee, lake, Maine		D3	204
Cobbtown, Tattnall, Ga.	280	D4	176
Cobden, Ont., Can.	913	O24	64
Cobden, Brown, Minn.	114	*G4	148
Cobden, Union, Ill.	918	F4	138
Cobequid, mts., N.S., Can.		D5	70
Cobh, Ire.	5,169	J4	273
Cobham, riv., Man., Can.		D5	60
Cobija, Bol.	1,726	B1	246
Cobija, Chile		B3	250
Coble, Hickman, Tenn.	100	C4	190
Coblence, see Koblenz, Ger.			
Cobleskill, Schoharie, N.Y.	3,471	C7	212
Coboconk, Ont., Can.	495	P22	64
Cobourg, Ont., Can.	9,399	Q22	64
Cobre, Elko, Nev.	20	B7	112
Cobun, creek, W.Va.		A7	194
Coburg, Ger.	45,800	C4	286
Coburg, Montgomery, Iowa	54	D2	142
Coburg, Blaine, Mont.	7	B8	110
Coburg, Lane, Oreg.	754	C3	96
Coburg, pen., Austl.		A6	432
Coburn, Wetzel, W.Va.	75	A6 B4	194
Coburn, mtn., Maine		C2	204
Coburn Gore, Franklin, Maine	80 (105▲)	C2	204
Coca, Ec.		A2	245
Cocentaina, Sp.	6,590	C6	298
Cochabamba, Bol.	80,795	C1	246
Cochabamba, dept., Bol.		C1	246
Coche, isl., Ven.		A7	240
Cocheco, riv., N.H.		E4	208
Cochesett, Plymouth, Mass.	300	*B5	206
Cochetopa, creek, Colo.		D4	106
Cochin, India	29,881 (*175,000)	G3	366
Cochise, Cochise, Ariz.	85	F6	124
Cochise, co., Ariz.	55,039	G6	124
Cochise Head, mtn., Ariz.		F6	124
Cochiti, Sandoval, N.Mex.	25	G6	126
Cochituate, Middlesex, Mass.	4,000	D1	200
Cochituate, lake, Mass.		D1	206
Cochran, Bleckley, Ga.	4,714	D3	176
Cochran, co., Tex.	6,417	C4	130
Cochrane, Pickens, Ala.	100	B1	168
Cochrane, Alta., Can.	707	E5	54
Cochrane, Ont., Can.	3,695	R25	64
Cochrane, Buffalo, Wis.	455	D2	160
Cochrane, dist., Ont., Can.	86,768	R24	64
Cochrane, mtn., Chile		G3	251
Cochranton, Crawford, Pa.	1,139	B1	214
Cocke, co., Tenn.	23,390	C8	190
Cockerill, Crawford, Kans.	35	*E9	144
Cockeysville, Baltimore, Md.	2,582	B6	182
Cockrell Hill, Dallas, Tex.	3,104	B8	130
Coco (Segovia or Wanks), riv., Nic.		D5	228
Cocoa, Brevard, Fla.	12,294	C10	174
Cocoa Beach, Brevard, Fla.	3,475	C10	174
Cocoa West, Brevard, Fla.	3,975	*C10	174
Cocobeach, Gabon		F6	409
Cocolalla, Bonner, Idaho	20	A2	108
Coconino, co., Ariz.	41,857	C3	124
Coconino, plat., Ariz.		C3	124
Cocos, isl., Guam		D7	436
Cocula, Mex.	7,859	C5	224
Cocuy, Col.	2,793	B2	244
Cod, cape, Mass.		B7	206
Cod, isl., Newf., Can.		D9	72
Codaeşti, Rom.	3,650	A4	321
Codajás, Braz.	1,248	F4	256
Codell, Rooks, Kans.	100	C4	144
Coden, Mobile, Ala.	950	E1	168
Codera, cape, Ven.		A5	240
Coderre, Sask., Can.	132	E4	58
Codesa, Alta., Can.	65	C3	54
Codette, Sask., Can.	194	D5	58
Codington, co., S.Dak.	20,220	C8	158
Codó, Braz.	6,027	A2	258
Codogno, It.	10,500	C2	302
Codpa, Chile		A4	250
Codroy, Newf., Can.	300	G6	72
Codroy Pond, Newf., Can.	40	F6	72
Codrul, mts., Rom.		A2	321
Coduto, Ven.		A4	240
Cody, Cherry, Nebr.	230	B4	152
Cody, Park, Wyo.	4,838	B3	116
Coe Hill, Ont., Can.	310	P23	64
Coeburn, Wise, Va.	2,471	D2	192
Coen, Austl.	77	A8	432
Coesfeld, Ger.	17,900	C2	286
Coesse, Whitley, Ind.	225	A4	140
Coeur d'Alene, Kootenai, Idaho	14,291	B2	108
Coeur d'Alene, lake, Idaho		B2	108
Coeur d'Alene, mts., Idaho		B9	98
Coevorden, Neth.	5,400	B5	282
Coeymans, Albany, N.Y.	950	C8	212
Coffee, Bacon, Ga.	150	E4	176
Coffee, co., Ala.	30,583	D3	168
Coffee, co., Ga.	21,593	E4	176
Coffee, co., Tenn.	28,603	C5	190
Coffee Creek, Fergus, Mont.	100	C6	110
Coffeen, Montgomery, Ill.	502	D4	138
Coffee Springs, Geneva, Ala.	205	D4	168
Coffeeville, Clarke, Ala.	250	D1	168
Coffeeville, Yalobusha, Miss.	813	B3	184
Coffey, Daviess, Mo.	190	A3	150
Coffey, co., Kans.	8,403	D8	144
Coffeyville, Montgomery, Kans.	17,382	E8	144
Cofield, Hertford, N.C.	350	A9	186
Cofradía, Mex.		L13	225
Cogar, Caddo, Okla.		C5	128
Cogdell, Clinch, Ga.	210	E4	176
Coggon, Linn, Iowa	672	B6	142
Coghinas, riv., It.		E2	302
Coglar, buttes, Oreg.		E6	96
Cognac, Fr.	19,026	E3	278
Cogswell, Sargent, N.Dak.	305	D8	154
Cogswell, res., Calif.		B5	94
Cohagen, Garfield, Mont.	42	C10	110
Cohansey, creek, N.J.		E2	210
Cohasset, Norfolk, Mass.	2,748 (5,840▲)	B6 D4	206
Cohasset, Itasca, Minn.	605	D5	148
Cohay, Smith, Miss.	50	D3	184
Cohocton, Steuben, N.Y.	929	C4	212
Cohocton, riv., N.Y.		C4	212
Cohoe, Alsk.	36	G10	84
Cohoes, Albany, N.Y.	20,129	C8	212
Cohutta, Whitfield, Ga.	325	B2	176
Cohutta, mtn., Ga.		B2	176
Coiba, isl., Pan.		G7	228
Coig, riv., Arg.		H3	251
Coila, Carroll, Miss.	200	B3	184
Coimbatore, India	197,755	F3	366
Coimbra, Port.	41,977	B2	298
Coin, Page, Iowa	346	D2	142
Coin, Sp.	11,828	D4	298
Coipasa, lake, Bol.		C1	246
Coipasa, salt flat, Bol.		C1	246
Coire, riv., Scot.		C8	272
Coire, see Chur, Switz.			
Coixtlahuaca, Mex.	1,604	M15	225
Cojedes, state, Ven.	54,097	B4	240
Cojutepeque, Sal.	10,015	D3	228
Cokan, Greeley, Kans.		D1	144
Cokato, Wright, Minn.	1,356	F4	148
Coke, co., Tex.	3,589	D5	130
Cokedale, Las Animas, Colo.	219	E6	106
Coker, Tuscaloosa, Ala.	200	B2	168
Cokercreek, Monroe, Tenn.	60	C7	190
Cokesbury, Hunterdon, N.J.	100	B3	210
Cokesbury, Greenwood, S.C.		C4	188
Coketon, Brooke, W.Va.	80	B2	194
Coketon, Tucker, W.Va.	156	B5	194
Cokeville, Lincoln, Wyo.	545	D2	116
Colac, Austl.	8,032	F8	432
Colalla, Bonner, Idaho		*A2	108
Colatina, Braz.	6,451	D2	258
Colbert, Madison, Ga.	425	B3	176
Colbert, Bryan, Okla.	671	E7	128
Colbert, co., Ala.	46,506	A2	168
Colbert Heights, Colbert, Ala.	400	*A2	168
Colborne, Ont., Can.	1,240	P23	64
Colbún, Chile		C1	252
Colburn, Bonner, Idaho	50	A2	108
Colburn, Tippecanoe, Ind.	280	B3	140
Colby, Thomas, Kans.	4,210	C2	144
Colby, Aroostook, Maine	200	B4	204
Colby, Clark, Wis.	1,085	D3	160
Colbyville, Washington, Vt.	120	C3	218
Colchagua, prov., Chile	139,531	D3	250
Colchester, New London, Conn.	2,260 (4,648▲)	C6	202
Colchester, Eng.	61,900	J13	273
Colchester, McDonough, Ill.	1,495	C3	138
Colchester, Chittenden, Vt.	225 (4,718▲)	B2	218
Colchester, co., N.S., Can.	34,640	D6	70
Colcord, Delaware, Okla.	173	B9	128
Colcord, Raleigh, W.Va.	500	*D3	194
Cold, lake, Alta., Can.		C7	54
Cold, riv., N.H.		D4	208
Cold, riv., N.H.		E2	208
Cold Bay, Alsk.	100	*D5	84
Coldbrook, N.B., Can.	525	D3	70
Cold Fell, mtn., Eng.		G10	272
Cold Hollow, mts., Vt.		B3	218
Cold Lake, Alta., Can.	1,097	C7	54
Cold Spring, Campbell, Ky.	1,095	A8	178
Cold Spring, Stearns, Minn.	1,760	F4	148
Cold Spring, Cape May, N.J.	350	E3	210
Cold Spring, Putnam, N.Y.	2,083	*D8	212
Cold Spring, pond, Newf., Can.		F7	72
Cold Spring Harbor, Suffolk, N.Y.	1,705	D3	212
Cold Springs, Kiowa, Okla.	75	D5	128
Coldstream, Eng.		F10	272
Cold Stream, pond, Maine		C4	204
Coldwater, Calhoun, Ala.	350	*B4	168
Coldwater, Ont., Can.	693	P21	64
Coldwater, Comanche, Kans.	1,164	E4	144
Coldwater, Branch, Mich.	8,880	H6	146
Coldwater, Tate, Miss.	1,264	A3	184
Coldwater, Mercer, Ohio	2,766	B2	156
Coldwater, creek, Okla., Tex.		B2 / A4	128 / 130
Coldwater, riv., Miss.		A2	184
Cole, McClain, Okla.	100	C6	128
Cole, co., Mo.	40,761	C5	150
Coleanor, Bibb, Ala.		B2	168
Colebrook, Litchfield, Conn.	125 (791▲)	B3	202
Colebrook, Coos, N.H.	1,550	B4	208
Cole Camp, Benton, Mo.	853	C4	150
Coleharbor, McLean, N.Dak.	210	C4	154
Cole Lake, Ont., Can.		P24	64
Coleman, Alta., Can.	1,566	F5	54
Coleman, P.E.I., Can.	90	C5	70
Coleman, Sumter, Fla.	921	C8	174
Coleman, Randolph, Ga.	220	E2	176
Coleman, Kent, Md.	275	B7	182
Coleman, Midland, Mich.	1,264	F7	146
Coleman, Johnston, Okla.	150	D7	128
Coleman, Coleman, Tex.	6,371	D6	130
Coleman, Marinette, Wis.	718	C5	160
Coleman, co., Tex.	12,458	D6	130
Coleman, riv., Austl.		A8	432
Colemans Falls, Bedford, Va.	180	C5	192
Colerain, Bertie, N.C.	340	A9	186
Colerain, Belmont, Ohio	885	B6	156
Coleraine, Itasca, Minn.	1,346	D5	148
Coleraine, N.Ire.	10,748	F5	272
Coleraine Station, Que., Can.	310	S13	66
Coleridge, Alta., Can.	160	F7	54
Coleridge, Cedar, Nebr.	604	B8	152
Coleridge, Randolph, N.C.	500	B6	186
Coleridge, bay, Solomon		E2	436
Coles, Amite, Miss.	225	D1	184
Coles, co., Ill.	42,860	D5	138
Colesberg, U.S.Afr.	3,667	F5	420
Colesburg, Delaware, Iowa	365	B6	142
Colesburg, Hardin, Ky.	150	C5	178
Colestin, Jackson, Oreg.		E4	96
Colesville, Sussex, N.J.	100	A3	210
Coleville, Mono, Calif.	275	C4	94
Coleville, Sask., Can.	472	E3	58
Coleyville, Cottle, Tex.	100	B5	130
Colfax, Placer, Calif.	915	C3	94
Colfax, Sask., Can.	85	F6	58
Colfax, McLean, Ill.	894	C5	138
Colfax, Clinton, Ind.	725	B3	140
Colfax, Jasper, Iowa	2,331	C4	142
Colfax, Grant, La.	1,934	C3	180
Colfax, Richland, N.Dak.	98	D9	154
Colfax, Whitman, Wash.	2,860	C9	98
Colfax, Dunn, Wis.	885	D2	160
Colfax, co., Nebr.	9,595	C8	152
Colfax, co., N.Mex.	13,806	B6	126
Colfer, Dundy, Nebr.	34	*D4	152
Colfred, Yuma, Ariz.	15	F2	124
Colgate, Sask., Can.	103	F6	58
Colgate, Washington, Wis.	60	E1	160
Colhuré Huapi, lake, Arg.		G4	251
Colijnsplaat, Neth.	1,686	C2	282
Colima, Mex.	28,658	D5	224
Colima, state, Mex.	112,321	D5	224
Colinet, Newf., Can.	150	G9	72
Colinton, Alta., Can.	185	C6	54
Coll, isl., Scot.		E6	272
Collbran, Mesa, Colo.	310	C3	106
College, Alsk.	1,755	C7	84
Collegeboro, Bulloch, Ga.	900	D5	176
College City, Lawrence, Ark.	358	A6	170
College Corner, Butler and Preble, Ohio	439	C2	156
Collegedale, Hamilton, Tenn.	1,500	E8	190
College Grove, Williamson, Tenn.	200	C5	190
College Heights, Drew, Ark.	1,000	D5	170
College Heights, Darlington, S.C.	1,330	*C9	188
College Hill, Madison, Ky.	700	C6	178
College Park, Saint Johns, Fla.	1,200	B10	174
College Park, Fulton and Clayton, Ga.	23,469	B5 C2	176
College Park, Saline, Ill.	300	*F5	138
College Park, Prince Georges, Md.	18,482	C4	182
College Place, Richland, S.C.		C6	188
College Place, Walla Walla, Wash.	4,031	C8	98
College Springs, Page, Iowa	290	D2	142
College Station, Brazos, Tex.	11,396	D7	130
Collegeville, Jasper, Ind.	1,400	B2	140
Collegeville, Montgomery, Pa.	2,254	C6	214
Colleton, co., S.C.	27,816	F7	188
Colleyville, Tarrant, Tex.	1,491	*C7	130
Collie, Austl.	8,667	E3	432
Collier, co., Fla.	15,753	E9	174
Collier, bay, Austl.		B4	432
Colliers, Brooke, W.Va.	900	*A4	194
Collierstown, Rockbridge, Va.	150	C5	192
Collierville, Shelby, Tenn.	2,020	C2	190
Collin, co., Tex.	41,247	C7	130
Collingdale, Delaware, Pa.	10,268	A6	214
Collingswood, Camden, N.J.	17,370	D2	210
Collingsworth, co., Tex.	6,276	B5	130
Collingwood, Ont., Can.	7,978	P20	64
Collins, Drew, Ark.	107	D5	170
Collins, Ont., Can.	80	R24	64
Collins, Tattnall, Ga.	565	D4	176
Collins, Whitley, Ind.	95	A4	140
Collins, Story, Iowa	435	C4	142
Collins, Covington, Miss.	1,537	D3	184
Collins, St.Clair, Mo.	177	D4	150
Collins, Teton, Mont.	15	C5	110
Collins, Arthur, Nebr.		C4	152
Collins, Grundy, Tenn.	400	C6	190
Collins, Manitowoc, Wis.	190	B6	160
Collins Park, New Castle, Del.	2,500	B3	172
Collins Park, Catron, N.Mex.	100	E2	126
Collinston, Morehouse, La.	497	B4	180
Collinston, Box Elder, Utah	75	*B3	114
Collins View, Multnomah, Oreg.	1,500	*B2	96
Collinsville, De Kalb, Ala.	1,199	A4	168
Collinsville, Hartford, Conn.	1,682	B4	202
Collinsville, De Kalb, Ga.	120	B5	176
Collinsville, Madison, Ill.	14,217	E4	138
Collinsville, Middlesex, Mass. (part of Dracut)		A5	206
Collinsville, Tulsa, Okla.	2,526	B8	128
Collinsville, Henry, Va.	3,586	D5	192
Collinwood, Wayne, Tenn.	596	C4	190
Collipulli, Chile	4,057	C1	252
Collister, Ada, Idaho	5,436	*F2	108
Collo, Alg.	4,518 (6,960▲)	A5	402
Collooney, Ire.	536	G4	273
Collyer, Trego, Kans.	233	C3	144
Colman, Moody, S.Dak.	505	D9	158
Colmar, Bell, Ky.	500	D7	178
Colmar, Fr.	47,305	C7	278
Colmar Manor, Prince Georges, Md.	1,772	C3	182
Colmenar de Oreja, Sp.	5,740	B5	298
Colmenar Viejo, Sp.	7,951	B5	298
Colmor, Colfax, N.Mex.	35	B6	126
Colo, Story, Iowa	574	B4	142
Cologne, see Köln, Ger.			
Cologne, Carver, Minn.	454	G5	148
Cologne, Atlantic, N.J.	600	D3	210
Colohatchee, Broward, Fla.	400	D6	174
Coloma, El Dorado, Calif.	280	C3	94
Coloma, Berrien, Mich.	1,473	G5	146
Coloma, Waushara, Wis.	312	D4	160
Colomb-Béchar, Alg.	18,090 (43,250▲)	B3	402
Colombes, Fr.	67,909	I10	278
Colombia, Col.	1,217	C2	244
Colombia, country, S.A.	13,824,000	C4	236 244
Colombo, Cey.	426,127 (*610,000)	G3	366
Colome, Tripp, S.Dak.	398	D6	158
Colón, Arg.	8,335	B4	252
Colón, Cuba	15,755	A4	232
Colon, St. Joseph, Mich.	1,055	H6	146
Colón, Mex.	2,247	K13	225
Colon, Saunders, Nebr.	110	D2	152
Colon, Lee, N.C.	350	B6	186
Colón, Pan.	52,204	F8	228
Colon, lake, Man., Can.		C5	60
Colona, Ouray, Colo.	75	D3	106
Colona, Henry, Ill.	491	*B3	138
Colonia, Middlesex, N.J.	6,000	*B4	210
Colonia, Ur.	7,700	B4	252
Colonia, dept., Ur.	130,325	B4	252
Colonia Benjamin Aceval, Par.	2,416	D3	247
Colonia Dora, Arg.	2,183	A3	252
Colonia Gustavo A. Madero, Mex.	60,239	G10	224
Colonial, natl. hist. park, Va.		C8	192
Colonial Beach, Westmoreland, Va.	1,769	B8	192
Colonial Heights, Kingsport, Tenn.	2,312	*B9	190
Colonial Heights (Independent City), Va.	9,587	B9 C7	192
Colonial Manor, Gloucester, N.J.	1,300	*D2	210
Colonia Mennonita, Par.		C3	247
Colonia Sarmiento, Arg.	3,648	G3	251
Colonie, Albany, N.Y.	6,992	C8	212
Colonna, It.	1,244	*E4	302
Colonne, cape, It.		F6	302

Colonsay, Sask., Can. 295 E5 58
Colonsay, isl., Scot. E6 272
Colony, Anderson, Kans. 419 D8 144
Colony, Washita, Okla. 200 C5 128
Colonytown, Leflore, Miss. 125 B2 184
Colorado, C.R. E6 228
Colorado, co., Tex. 18,463 E7 130
Colorado, desert, Calif. E6 94
Colorado, natl. mon., Colo. C2 106
Colorado, plat., U.S. D4 77
Colorado, riv., Arg. C2 252
Colorado, riv., Tex. D6 130
Colorado, riv., U.S. E4 77
Colorado, state, U.S. 1,753,947 D5 77, 106
Colorado City, Mitchell, Tex. 6,457 C5 130
Colorado River, aqueduct, Calif. F5 94
Colorados, arch., Cuba A2 232
Colorado Springs, El Paso, Colo. 70,194 (*139,500) D6 106
Colored Hill, Mercer, W.Va. 1,115 *D3 194
Coloso, Chile B3 250
Colotepec, Mex. 455 D6 225
Colotlán, Mex. 5,119 C5 224, J12
Colquechaca, Bol. 1,070 C1 246
Colquitt, Miller, Ga. 1,556 E2 176
Colquitt, Claiborne, La. 40 B3 180
Colquitt, co., Ga. 34,048 E3 176
Colrain, Franklin, Mass. 180 (1,426▲) A2 206
Colstrip, Rosebud, Mont. 200 E10 110
Colt, St. Francis, Ark. 394 B6 170
Coltauco, Chile B1 252
Colton, San Bernardino, Calif. 18,666 *E5 94
Colton, Cheyenne, Nebr. 17 *C3 152
Colton, Clackamas, Oreg. 150 B4 96
Colton, Minnehaha, S.Dak. 593 D9 158
Colton, Utah, Utah 12 D4 114
Colton, Whitman, Wash. 253 C9 98
Colton, hill, Vt. D4 218
Coltons Point, St. Marys, Md. 118 D6 182
Colts Neck, Monmouth, N.J. 400 C4 210
Colulli, Eth. C5 398
Columbia, Houston, Ala. 783 D4 168
Columbia, Tolland, Conn. 200 (2,163▲) C6 202
Columbia, Columbia, Fla. 85 A8 174
Columbia, Monroe, Ill. 3,174 E3 138
Columbia, Marion, Iowa 150 C4 142
Columbia, Adair, Ky. 2,255 C5 178
Columbia, Caldwell, La. 1,021 B3 180
Columbia, Washington, Maine 40 (219▲) D5 204
Columbia, Howard, Md. 70 B6 182
Columbia, Marion, Miss. 7,117 D3 184
Columbia, Boone, Mo. 36,650 C5 150
Columbia, Coos, N.H. (457▲) *B3 208
Columbia, Warren, N.J. 400 B2 210
Columbia, Tyrrell, N.C. 1,099 B9 186
Columbia, Lancaster, Pa. 12,075 C5 214
Columbia, Richland, S.C. 97,433 (*213,400) C6 188
Columbia, Brown, S.Dak. 272 B7 158
Columbia, Maury, Tenn. 17,624 C4 190
Columbia, Fluvanna, Va. 86 C6 192
Columbia, Carbon, Utah 300 D5 114
Columbia, co., Ark. 26,400 D3 170
Columbia, co., Fla. 20,077 A8 174
Columbia, co., Ga. 13,423 C4 176
Columbia, co., N.Y. 47,322 C8 212
Columbia, co., Oreg. 22,379 B3 96
Columbia, co., Pa. 53,489 B5 214
Columbia, co., Wash. 4,569 C8 98
Columbia, co., Wis. 36,708 E4 160
Columbia, basin, Wash. C7 98
Columbia, lake, B.C., Can. E15 52
Columbia, mtn., Alta., Can. D4 54
Columbia, mts., Mex. B3 224
Columbia, riv., U.S. B2 77
Columbia City, Whitley, Ind. 4,803 A4 140
Columbia City, Columbia, Oreg. 423 *B4 96
Columbia Falls, Flathead, Mont. 2,132 B2 110
Columbia Falls, Washington, Maine 300 (442▲) D5 204
Columbia Gardens, Silver Bow, Mont. 50 *D4 110
Columbia Heights, Anoka, Minn. 17,533 F7 148
Columbia Heights, Flathead, Mont. 50 *B2 110
Columbia Heights, Cowlitz, Wash. 2,227 *C4 98
Columbiana, Shelby, Ala. 2,264 B3 168
Columbiana, Columbiana, Ohio 4,164 B6 156
Columbiana, co., Ohio 107,004 B6 156
Columbiaville, Lapeer, Mich. 878 F8 146
Columbine, Natrona, Wyo. 20 C6 116
Columbus, Hempstead, Ark. 275 D3 170
Columbus, Muscogee, Ga. 116,779 (*201,500) D2 176
Columbus, Bartholomew, Ind. 20,778 C4 140
Columbus, Cherokee, Kans. 3,395 E9 144
Columbus, Hickman, Ky. 357 D1 178
Columbus, Sabine, La. C2 180
Columbus, Lowndes, Miss. 24,771 B4 184
Columbus, Stillwater, Mont. 1,281 E7 110
Columbus, Platte, Nebr. 12,476 C8 152
Columbus, Burlington, N.J. 600 C3 210
Columbus, Luna, N.Mex. 307 G3 126
Columbus, Polk, N.C. 725 B3 186
Columbus, Burke, N.Dak. 672 B3 154
Columbus, Franklin, Ohio 471,316 (*715,400) C1 156, C3
Columbus, Colorado, Tex. 3,656 E7 130
Columbus, Columbia, Wis. 3,467 E4 160
Columbus, co., N.C. 48,973 C7 186
Columbus City, Louisa, Iowa 327 C6 142
Columbus Grove, Monroe, Mich. (part of Luna Pier) H8 146
Columbus Grove, Putnam, Ohio 2,104 B2 156
Columbus Junction, Louisa, Iowa 1,016 C6 142
Colusa, Colusa, Calif. 3,518 C2 94
Colusa, co., Calif. 12,075 C2 94
Colver, Cambria, Pa. 1,261 C3 214
Colville, Stevens, Wash. 3,806 A9 98
Colville, lake, N.W.Ter., Can. D6 48
Colville, riv., Alsk. B6 84
Colville, riv., Wash. A9 98
Colvos, pass, Wash. D2 98
Colwell, Floyd, Iowa 119 *A5 142
Colwich, Sedgwick, Kans. 703 A5 144, E6
Colwyn, Delaware, Pa. 3,074 *D6 214
Colyell, creek, La. B6 180
Comacchio, It. 10,200 C4 302
Comal, co., Tex. 19,844 E6 130
Comalapa, Guat. 7,768 C2 228
Comanche, Stephens, Okla. 2,082 D6 128
Comanche, Comanche, Tex. 3,415 D6 130
Comanche, co., Kans. 3,271 E4 144
Comanche, co., Okla. 90,803 D5 128
Comanche, co., Tex. 11,865 C6 130
Comanjilla, Mex. K13 225
Comarapa, Bol. 1,096 C2 246
Comayagua, Hond. 5,192 C4 228
Combarbalá, Chile 2,134 B1 252
Comber, Ont., Can. 615 R18 64
Combermere, Ont., Can. 145 O23 64
Combermere, bay, Bur. C2 362
Combes, Cameron, Tex. 605 *F7 130
Combined Locks, Outagamie, Wis. 1,421 A5 160
Combomune, Moz. D6 421
Combs, Madison, Ark. 200 B3 170
Combs, Perry, Ky. 900 *C7 178
Comer, Barbour, Ala. 200 C4 168
Comer, Madison, Ga. 882 B3 176
Comeragh, mts., Ire. I5 273
Comertown, Sheridan, Mont. B12 110
Comfort, Jones, N.C. 400 B8 186
Comfort, Marion, Tenn. 35 C6 190
Comfort, Kendall, Tex. 950 E6 130
Comfort, Boone, W.Va. 160 C3 194, C6
Comfort, pt., La. E6 180
Comfrey, Brown, Minn. 616 G4 148
Comilla, Pak. 47,526 L17 375
Comines, Bel. 8,369 D1 282
Comino, cape, It. E2 302
Comins, Oscoda, Mich. 80 E7 146
Comiso, It. 24,900 G5 302
Comitán, Mex. 11,760 D7 225
Comite, riv., La. D4 180
Commack, Suffolk, N.Y. 9,613 *D3 212
Commentry, Fr. 7,167 D5 278
Commerce, Los Angeles, Calif. 9,555 *E4 94
Commerce, Jackson, Ga. 3,551 B3 176
Commerce, Oakland, Mich. 1,200 B7 146
Commerce, Scott, Mo. 247 D8 150
Commerce, Hunt, Texas 5,789 C8 130
Commerce Town, Adams, Colo. 8,970 *C6 106
Commercial Point, Pickaway, Ohio 308 C3 156
Commercy, Fr. 7,028 C6 278
Commiskey, Jennings, Ind. 100 D4 140
Commissioners, lake, Que., Can. P12 66
Como, Que., Can. 780 S15 66
Como, Park, Colo. 30 C5 106
Como, It. 72,100 C2 302
Como, Panola, Miss. 789 A3 184
Como, Henry, Tenn. 160 B3 190
Como, prov., It. 577,300 *C2 302
Como, lake, It. B2 302
Comodoro Rivadavia, Arg. 25,651 G4 251
Comores, Archipel des, Fr. poss., Afr. 176,000 B8 421
Comores, is., Afr. B8 421
Comorin, cape, India G3 366
Comox, B.C., Can. 1,151 F10 52
Compass Lake, Jackson, Fla. 300 A5 174
Compeer, Alta., Can. 170 E7 54
Compiègne, Fr. 22,325 C5 278
Comptche, Mendocino, Calif. 175 C2 94
Compton, Los Angeles, Calif. 71,812 C5 94
Compton, Que., Can. 481 S13 66
Compton, co., Que., Can. 25,057 S13 66
Comstock, Kalamazoo, Mich. 3,000 G6 146
Comstock, Clay, Minn. 138 E2 148
Comstock, Custer, Nebr. 235 C6 152
Comstock, Barron, Wis. 60 C1 160
Comstock Park, Kent, Mich. 2,500 F6 146
Comtat Venaissin, former prov., Fr. 211,000 *F6 278
Conakry, Guinea 52,521 E2 408
Conanicut, isl., R.I. C3 216
Conasauga, Polk, Tenn. 150 C7 190
Conca, Mex. K14 225
Concarneau, Fr. 8,507 D2 278
Conceição do Norte, Braz. C1 258
Concepción, Arg. 12,479 C4 250
Concepción, Bol. 1,056 C2 246
Concepcion, Santa Barbara, Calif. 50 E3 94
Concepción, Chile 134,549 C1 252
Concepción, Guat. 1,855 C2 228
Concepción, Mex. L12 225
Concepción, Pan. 3,063 F6 228
Concepción, Par. 14,640 C4 247
Concepción, dept., Par. 62,326 C4 247
Concepción, prov., Chile 411,566 E3 250
Concepción, lake, Bol. C2 246
Concepción del Oro, Mex. 5,427 C5 225
Concepción del Uruguay, Arg. 31,498 B4 252
Conception, Nodaway, Mo. 450 A3 150
Conception, bay, Newf., Can. G9 72
Conception, isl., W.I. A7 232
Conception, pt., Calif. E3 94
Conception Junction, Nodaway, Mo. 253 A3 150
Conchas, res., N.Mex. C6 126
Conchas Dam, San Miguel, N.Mex. 40 C6 126
Conche, Newf., Can. 15 E8 72
Conchi, Chile B4 250
Concho, Apache, Ariz. 150 D6 124
Concho, Canadian, Okla. 500 C6 128
Concho, co., Tex. 3,672 D6 130
Conchos, riv., Mex. B4 224
Conconully, Okanogan, Wash. 108 A7 98
Concord, Jefferson, Ala. 900 *B3 168
Concord, Cleburne, Ark. 300 B5 170
Concord, Contra Costa, Calif. 36,208 *D2 94
Concord, Sussex, Del. 400 F3 172
Concord, Gadsden, Fla. 300 A6 174
Concord, Pike, Ga. 333 C2 176
Concord, Lewis, Ky. 83 B7 178
Concord, Middlesex, Mass. 3,188 (12,517▲) B5 206, C2
Concord, Jackson, Mich. 990 G7 146
Concord, Dixon, Nebr. 150 B9 152
Concord, Merrimack, N.H. 28,991 E3 208
Concord, Cabarrus, N.C. 17,799 B5 186
Concord, Knox, Tenn. 250 C7 190, E9
Concord, Essex, Vt. 388 (956▲) C5 218
Concord, Campbell, Va. 400 C6 192
Concord, riv., Mass. B5 206
Concordia, Arg. 52,213 B4 252
Concordia, Col. 3,906 B1 244
Concordia, Cloud, Kans. 7,022 C6 144
Concordia, Mex. 2,801 C4 224
Concordia, Lafayette, Mo. 1,471 C4 150
Concordia, par., La. 20,467 C4 180
Concrete, Pembina, N.Dak. 125 B8 154
Concrete, Skagit, Wash. 840 A5 98
Conda, Caribou, Idaho 200 G7 108
Conde, Braz. 2,953 C3 258
Conde, Spink, S.Dak. 388 B7 158
Condendas, Braz. C2 258
Condé-sur-Noireau, Fr. C3 278
Condeúba, Braz. 1,440 C2 258
Condobolin, Austl. 2,840 E9 432
Condom, Fr. F4 278
Condon, Missoula, Mont. 25 C3 110
Condon, Gilliam, Oreg. 1,149 B6 96
Cóndor, range, Peru A2 245
Conecuh, co., Ala. 17,762 D2 168
Conecuh, riv., Ala. D3 168
Conegliano [Veneto], It. 11,300 C4 302
Conehatta, Newton, Miss. 50 C3 184
Conejos, Conejos, Colo. 175 E4 106
Conejos, co., Colo. 8,428 E4 106
Conejos, creek, Colo. E4 106
Conejos, peak, Colo. E4 106
Conemaugh (East Conemaugh), Cambria, Pa. 3,334 C3 214
Conemaugh River, res., Pa. *C2 214
Conestee, Greenville, S.C. 750 B4 188
Conesville, Muscatine, Iowa 248 C6 142
Conesville, Coshocton, Ohio 451 B5 156
Confluence, Leslie, Ky. 175 C7 178
Confluence, Somerset, Pa. 938 D2 214
Confusion, bay, Newf., Can. E8 72
Confusion, range, Utah D2 114
Confuso, riv., Par. D3 247
Congamond, Hampden, Mass. 500 *B2 206
Congamond, lakes, Conn., Mass. A4 202, B2 206
Congaree, riv., S.C. D7 188
Conger, Freeborn, Minn. 694 H5 148
Congers, Rockland, N.Y. 3,000 D2 212
Congo, Mex. D7 225
Congo, Hancock, W.Va. A2 194
Congo, dist., Ang. 400,153 A2 420
Congo (Republic of Congo; capital Brazzaville), country, Afr. 795,000 G8 388, 409
Congo, The (Republic of the Congo; capital Léopoldville), country, Afr. 12,117,400 G9 388, 414
Congo, basin, Con.L. B3 414
Congo, riv., Afr. C2 414
Congress, Yavapai, Ariz. 150 D3 124
Congress, Sask., Can. 75 F4 58
Conical, peak, Mont. D6 110
Conicville, Shenandoah, Va. 45 *B6 192
Conil, Sp. 4,730 D3 298
Conimicut, Kent, R.I. (part of Warwick) C3 216
Conimicut, pt., R.I. C3 216
Coniston, Ont., Can. 2,478 S25 64
Coniston Water, lake, Eng. G9 273
Conjeeveram, see Kancheepuram, India
Conklin, Alta., Can. 10 C7 54
Conklin, Ottawa, Mich. 270 F6 146
Conkling, Owsley, Ky. 400 C7 178
Conley, Clayton, Ga. 200 B5 176
Conn, lake, Ire. G3 273
Connacht, prov., Ire. 70,290 H3 273
Conneaut, Ashtabula, Ohio 10,557 A6 156
Conneaut, creek, Ohio A6 156
Conneautville, Crawford, Pa. 1,100 B1 214
Connecticut, state, U.S. 2,535,234 C12 77, 202
Connecticut, riv., Conn., Mass. C5 202, B2 206
Connell, Franklin, Wash. 906 C8 98
Connellsville, Fayette, Pa. 12,814 C2 214
Connelsville, Adair, Mo. 113 A5 150
Connemara, mts., Ire. H3 273
Conner, Aroostook, Maine 180 (630▲) B4 204
Conner, Ravalli, Mont. 5 E2 110
Connersville, Fayette, Ind 17,698 C4 140
Connerville, Johnston, Okla. 200 D7 128
Conning Towers, New London, Conn. 3,457 *D7 202
Connorsville, Dunn, Wis. 100 C1 160
Conococheague, creek, Md. A4 182
Conover, Catawba, N.C. 2,281 B4 186
Conover, Vilas, Wis. 80 B4 160
Conowingo, Cecil, Md. 25 A7 182
Conowingo, dam, Md. A7 182
Conquest, Sask., Can. 292 E4 58
Conquista, Braz. C2 258
Conrad, Grundy, Iowa 799 B5 142
Conrad, Pondera, Mont. 2,665 B5 110
Conrath, Rusk, Wis. 121 C2 160
Conroe, Montgomery, Tex. 9,192 D8 130
Conroy, Iowa, Iowa 160 C5 142
Consecon, Ont., Can. 510 Q23 64
Conselheiro Lafaiete, Braz. 18,042 E2 258
Conser, Le Flore, Okla. 100 *D9 128
Consett, Eng. 38,800 G11 272
Conshohocken, Montgomery, Pa. 10,259 A6 214, C6
Consolación del Sur, Cuba 6,146 A3 232
Consort, Alta., Can. 434 D7 54
Constableville, Lewis, N.Y. 439 B6 212
Constance, see Konstanz, Ger.
Constance (Bodensee), lake, Ger. E3 286
Constance, see Bodensee, lake, Ger., Switz.
Constance, mtn., Wash. B3 98
Constanta, Rom. 99,690 B5 321
Constantia, Oswego, N.Y. 800 B5 212
Constantina, Sp. 11,910 D4 298
Constantine, Alg. 148,725 A5 402
Constantine, St. Joseph, Mich. 1,710 H6 146
Constitución, Chile 8,285 C1 252
Constitution, DeKalb, Ga. 900 B5 176
Consuegra, Sp. 9,332 C5 298
Consul, Marengo, Ala. 50 C2 168
Consul, Sask., Can. 166 F3 58
Contact, Elko, Nev. 30 B7 112
Contamana, Peru 2,860 B3 245
Contas, riv., Braz. C2 258
Content, keys, Fla. G9 174
Content, Phillips, Mont. B9 110
Conterra, Cherry, Nebr. B5 152
Continental, Pima, Ariz. 10 G5 124
Continental, Grant, N.Mex. 12 G2 126
Continental, Putnam, Ohio 1,147 A2 156
Continental, divide, U.S. C5 77
Continental, res., Colo. E3 106
Contoocook, Merrimack, N.H. 900 E3 208
Contoocook, riv., N.H. E3 208
Contraalmirante Cordero, Arg. C2 252
Contra Costa, co., Calif. 409,030 D3 94
Contratación, Col. 3,303 B2 244
Contrecoeur, Que., Can. 1,662 S11 66
Contreras, Socorro, N.Mex. 70 D4 126
Contumaza, Peru 1,911 B2 245
Contwoyto, lake, N.W.Ter., Can. D7 48
Convent, St. James, La. 400 B6 180, D5
Converse, Miami, Ind. 1,044 B4 140
Converse, Sabine, La. 291 C2 180
Converse, Spartanburg, S.C. 950 B5 188
Converse, co., Wyo. 6,366 C7 116
Converse, lake, Ala. E1 168
Convoy, Van Wert, Ohio 976 B2 156
Conway, Faulkner, Ark. 9,791 B4 170
Conway, Taylor, Iowa 82 D3 142
Conway, Franklin, Mass. 600 (875▲) A2 206
Conway, Leake, Miss. 96 C3 184
Conway, Laclede, Mo. 500 D5 150
Conway, Carroll, N.H. 1,143 (4,298▲) D4 208
Conway, Northampton, N.C. 662 A8 186
Conway, Walsh, N.Dak. 67 B8 154
Conway, Beaver, Pa. 1,926 C1 214
Conway, Horry, S.C. 8,563 D10 188
Conway, Wales 10,500 H9 273
Conway, co., Ark. 15,430 B4 170
Conway, lake, Ark. B4 170
Conway, lake, N.H. D4 208
Conway Springs, Sumner, Kans. 1,057 E6 144
Conway Station, P.E.I., Can. 110 C6 70
Conyers, Rockdale, Ga. 2,881 B6 176, C2
Conyngham, Luzerne, Pa. 1,163 *B5 214
Cooch Behar, India D5 368
Coodys Bluff, Nowata, Okla. 50 B8 128
Cook, Austl. 132 E6 432
Cook, Lake, Ind. 250 A2 140
Cook, St. Louis, Minn. 527 D6 148
Cook, Johnson, Nebr. 313 D9 152
Cook, co., Ga. 11,822 E3 176
Cook, co., Ill. 5,129,725 A6 138
Cook, co., Minn. 3,377 D8 148
Cook, cape, B.C., Can. E9 52
Cook, inlet, Alsk. D6 84
Cook, is., Pac.O. D4 436
Cook, mtn., N.Z. E3 437
Cook, mtn., W.Va D6 194
Cook, pt., Md. C7 182
Cook, strait, N.Z. D5 437
Cooke, co., Tex. 22,560 C7 130
Cooke City, Park, Mont. 100 E7 110
Cookeville, Putnam, Tenn. 7,805 B6 190
Cook Islands, N.Z. poss., Pac.O. 15,079 D4 436
Cooks, Schoolcraft, Mich. 60 D5 146
Cooks, peak, N.Mex. F3 126
Cooks Harbour, Newf., Can. 300 E8 72
Cookshire, Que., Can. 1,315 S13 66
Cook Springs, St. Clair, Ala. 300 *B3 168
Cookstown, Ont., Can. 585 P21 64
Cookstown, Burlington, N.J. 75 C3 210
Cooksville, Ont., Can. 1,750 Q21 64
Cooksville, Howard, Md. 200 B5 182
Cooksville, Noxubee, Miss. 40 C4 184
Cooktown, Austl. 448 B9 432
Cooleemee, Davie, N.C. 1,609 B5 186
Coolgardie, Austl. 952 E4 432
Coolidge, Pinal, Ariz. 4,990 F4 124
Coolidge, Thomas, Ga. 679 E3 176
Coolidge, Hamilton, Kans. 117 D1 144
Coolidge, Limestone, Tex. 913 D7 130
Coolidge Dam, Gila, Ariz. 18 E5 124
Coolin, Bonner, Idaho 100 A2 108
Cool Ridge, Raleigh, W.Va. 400 D3 194
Cool Ridge Heights, Richland, Ohio 800 *B4 156
Cool Spring, Horry, S.C. 75 D10 188
Coolville, Athens, Ohio 443 C5 156
Cooma, Austl. 6,506 F9 432
Coonamble, Austl. 2,910 E9 432
Coon Lake Beach, Anoka, Minn. 180 F7 148
Coon Rapids, Carroll, Iowa 1,560 C3 142
Coon Rapids, Anoka, Minn. 14,931 F7 148
Coon Valley, Vernon, Wis. 536 E2 160
Cooper, Chilton, Ala. 300 C3 168
Cooper, Broward, Fla. 550 *E10 174
Cooper, Wayne, Ky. 250 D6 178
Cooper, Washington, Maine 65 (106▲) D5 204
Cooper, Delta, Tex. 2,213 C8 130

Cooper, co., Mo. 15,448 C5 150
Cooper, riv., S.C. E9 188
Co-Operative, McCreary, Ky. 350 D6 178
Cooper Lake, Albany, Wyo. 20 E7 116
Cooper's, creek, Austl. D8 432
Coopersburg, Lehigh, Pa. 1,800 C6 214
Coopers Mills, Lincoln, Maine 150 D3 204
Coopers Plains, Steuben, N.Y. 400 C4 212
Cooperstown, Otsego, N.Y. 2,553 C7 212
Cooperstown, Griggs, N. Dak. 1,424 C7 154
Cooperstown, Manitowoc, Wis. 100 A6 160
Coopersville, Ottawa, Mich. 1,584 F6 146
Cooperton, Kiowa, Okla. 106 D5 128
Coopertown, Robertson, Tenn. 50 B5 190
Cooper Village, Gloucester, N.J. 1,500 *D2 210
Coos, co., N.H. 37,140 B4 208
Coos, co., Oreg. 54,955 D2 96
Coos, riv., Oreg. D3 96
Coosa, Floyd, Ga. 150 B1 176
Coosa, co., Ala. 10,726 C3 168
Coosa, riv., Ala., Ga. C3 168 / B1 176
Coosada, Elmore, Ala. 235 *C3 168
Coosaw, Beaufort, S.C. 400 F7 188
Coosawattee, riv., Ga. B2 176
Coosawhatchie, Jasper, S.C. 160 F7 188
Coosawhatchie, riv., S.C. F7 188
Coos Bay, Coos, Oreg. 7,084 D2 96
Cooter, Pemiscot, Mo. 477 E8 150
Copacabana, Arg. A2 252
Copacabana, Bol. 1,981 C1 246
Copainalá, Mex. 2,019 D7 225
Copalis Beach, Grays Harbor, Wash. 350 B2 98
Copalis Crossing, Grays Harbor, Wash. 100 B2 98
Copán, Hond. 977 C3 228
Copan, Washington, Okla. 617 B8 128
Cope, Washington, Colo. 125 C8 106
Cope, Orangeburg, S.C. 227 E6 188
Copeland, Washington, Ala. 250 D1 168
Copeland, Collier, Fla. 800 F9 174
Copeland, Boundary, Idaho 25 A2 108
Copeland, Gray, Kans. 247 E3 144
Copemish, Manistee, Mich. 232 E6 146
Copen, Braxton, W.Va. 30 C4 194
Copenhagen (Köbenhavn), Den. 760,820 (*1,189,177) F3 292
Copenhagen, Lewis, N.Y. 673 B6 212
Copetonas, Arg. C3 252
Copiague, Suffolk, N.Y. 14,081 *E3 212
Copiah, co., Miss. 27,051 D2 184
Copiapó, Chile 19,535 A1 252
Copiapó, riv., Chile A1 252
Coplay, Lehigh, Pa. 3,701 *C6 214
Copparo, It. 5,800 C3 302
Copper, mts., Ariz. F2 124
Copper, ridge, Tenn. E9 190
Copper, riv., Alsk. C7 84
Copperas Cove, Coryell, Tex. 4,567 D7 130
Copper Center, Alsk. 90 C7 84 / G12
Copper City, Houghton, Mich. 293 *B3 146
Copper Cliff, Ont., Can. 3,801 *S25 64
Copperfield, Washoe, Nev. 150 D2 112
Copper Harbor, Keweenaw, Mich. 60 B4 146
Copperhill, Polk, Tenn. 631 C7 190
Copper Hill, Floyd, Va. 40 C4 192
Coppermine, N.W.Ter., Can. 100 D7 48
Copper Mountain, B.C., Can. 185 F12 52
Copperton, Salt Lake, Utah 850 *C3 114
Coppock, Henry, Jefferson and Washington, Iowa 61 *C6 142
Copton, creek, Alta., Can. C3 54
Coquilhatville, Con.L. 26,600 B2 414
Coquille, Coos, Oreg. 4,730 D2 96
Coquille, riv., Oreg. E3 96
Coquimbana, Chile A1 252
Coquimbo, Chile 24,962 A1 252
Coquimbo, prov., Chile 262,169 D3 250
Cora, Logan, W.Va. 500 *D2 194
Cora, Sublette, Wyo. 5 D3 116
Corabia, Rom. 11,502 C3 321
Coracora, Peru 3,671 D3 245
Coral, Montcalm, Mich. 225 F6 146
Coral, sea, Austl. B10 432
Coral Gables, Dade, Fla. 34,793 E6 174 / F10
Coral Gardens, Honolulu, Haw. (part of Kaneohe) 300 G10 86
Coral Rapids, Ont., Can. 60 R25 64
Coralville, Johnson, Iowa 2,357 C6 142
Coram, Flathead, Mont. 450 B2 110
Coram, Suffolk, N.Y. 400 D4 212
Coraopolis, Allegheny, Pa. 9,643 A3 214 / C1
Corato, It. 45,300 E6 302
Corazón, Ec. 1,057 A2 245
Corbeil [-Essonnes], Fr. 22,891 C5 278
Corbett, Cleveland, Okla. 25 D6 128
Corbett, Multnomah, Oreg. 140 *B4 96
Corbetton, Ont., Can. 125 P20 64
Corbie, Fr. C5 278
Corbin, B.C., Can. F15 52
Corbin, Sumner, Kans. 100 E6 144
Corbin, Whitley, Ky. 7,119 D6 178
Corbin, Livingston, La. 100 A6 180
Corbin, head, Newf., Can. G8 72
Corbin City, Atlantic, N.J. 271 E3 210
Corby, Eng. 26,200 I12 273
Corcoran, Kings, Calif. 4,976 D4 94
Corcoran, Hennepin, Minn. 1,237 *F5 148
Corcovado, gulf, Chile F3 251
Corcyra, see Kérkira, prov., Grc.
Cord, Independence, Ark. 100 B5 170
Cordaville, Worcester, Mass. 250 D1 206
Cordele, Crisp, Ga. 10,609 E3 176
Cordell (New Cordell), Washita, Okla. 3,589 C5 128
Corder, Lafayette, Mo. 506 B4 150
Cordesville, Berkeley, S.C. 500 E9 188
Cordillera, dept., Par. 145,232 D4 247
Cordillera Central, range, Col. C1 244
Cordillera Occidental, range, Col. C1 244
Cordillera Occidental o de la Costa, range, Peru C2 245
Cordillera Oriental, range, Bol. C2 246
Cordillera Oriental, range, Col. B2 244
Córdoba, Arg. 369,886 B3 252
Córdoba, Mex. 32,733 L15 225
Córdoba, Sp. 160,347 D4 298
Córdoba, dept., Col. 357,000 B1 244
Córdoba, prov., Arg. 1,880,700 D5 250
Córdoba, prov., Sp. 790,242 *D4 298
Córdoba, mts., Arg. B3 252
Cordova, Walker, Ala. 3,184 B2 168
Cordova, Alsk. 1,128 C7 84 / G12
Cordova, Rock Island, Ill. 502 B3 138
Cordova, Talbot, Md. 245 C8 182
Cordova, Seward, Nebr. 152 D8 152
Cordova, Richmond, N.C. 950 C6 186
Córdova, Peru 534 C2 245
Cordova, Orangeburg, S.C. 209 E7 188
Cordova, Shelby, Tenn. 350 C2 190
Cordova Mines, Ont., Can. 575 P23 64
Corea, Hancock, Maine 160 D5 204
Coreaú, Braz. 1,286 A2 258
Corella, Sp. 5,748 A6 298
Corfu, Genesee, N.Y. 616 C3 212
Corfu, Grant, Wash. C7 98
Corfu, see Kérkira, prov., Grc.
Cori, It. 7,179 *E4 302
Coria, Sp. 5,211 B3 298
Corigliano [Calabro], It. 16,300 F6 302
Corinna, Penobscot, Maine 650 (1,895▲) D3 204
Corinne, Pushmataha, Okla. 50 D8 128
Corinne, Box Elder, Utah 510 B3 114
Corinne, Wyoming, W.Va. 1,273 D3 194
Corinth, Heard, Ga. 105 C2 176
Corinth, see Kórinthos, Grc.
Corinth, Grant, Ky. 238 B6 178
Corinth (Town of), Penobscot, Maine (1,138▲) D4 204
Corinth, Alcorn, Miss. 11,453 A4 184
Corinth, Saratoga, N.Y. 3,193 B8 212
Corinth, Orange, Vt. 25 (775▲) C4 218
Corinth, Preston, W.Va. 115 B5 194
Corinth, gulf, Grc. B4 306
Corinthia, see Korinthia, prov., Grc.
Corinto, Braz. 6,678 D2 258
Corinto, Nic. 4,765 D4 228
Corisco, isl., Afr. F6 409
Cork, Ire. 80,011 (*114,428) J4 273
Cork, co., Ire. 336,663 J4 273
Cork, hbr., Ire. J4 273
Corkscrew, Collier, Fla. 150 E9 174
Corleone, It. 16,600 G4 302
Çorlu, Tur. 17,025 A12 307
Cormack, mtn., Newf., Can. F8 72
Cormoran, reef, Palau A6 436
Cormorant, Man., Can. C2 60
Cormorant, lake, Man., Can. C2 60
Cormorant, rock, R.I. D3 216
Corn, Washita, Okla. 317 C5 128
Corn, creek, Ariz. C5 124
Corn, is., Cen.Am. D6 228
Cornelia, Habersham, Ga. 2,936 B3 176
Cornelius, Mecklenburg, N.C. 1,444 B5 186
Cornelius, Washington, Oreg. 1,146 B1 96
Cornell, Livingston, Ill. 524 C5 138
Cornell, Chippewa, Wis. 1,685 C2 160
Corner Brook, Newf., Can. 23,225 F7 72
Cornersville, Marshall, Tenn. 315 C5 190
Cornerville, Lincoln, Ark. 100 D5 170
Corney, lake, La. B3 180
Cornfield, pt., Conn. D6 202
Corn Hill, N.B., Can. 120 D4 70
Corning, Clay, Ark. 2,192 A6 170
Corning, Tehama, Calif. 3,006 C2 94
Corning, Sask., Can. 130 F6 58
Corning, Adams, Iowa 2,041 D3 142
Corning, Nemaha, Kans. 240 C7 144
Corning, Holt, Mo. 128 A2 150
Corning, Steuben, N.Y. 17,085 C4 212
Corning, Perry, Ohio 1,065 C4 156
Cornish, Weld, Colo. 5 B6 106
Cornish, York, Maine 600 (816▲) E2 204
Cornish (Town of), Sullivan, N.H. (1,106▲) *E2 208
Cornish, Jefferson, Okla. 127 D6 128
Cornish, Cache, Utah 157 *B4 114
Cornish Flat, Sullivan, N.H. 90 E2 208
Cornishville, Mercer, Ky. 250 C6 178
Cornlea, Platte, Nebr. 44 *C8 152
Corno, mtn., It. D4 302
Cornucopia, Baker, Oreg. 355 C9 96
Cornucopia, Bayfield, Wis. 200 B2 160
Cornville, Somerset, Maine 150 (585▲) D3 204
Cornville, Yavapai, Ariz. 22 D4 124
Cornwall, Ont., Can. 18,158 (*42,000) O26 64
Cornwall, Litchfield, Conn. 150 (1,051▲) B2 202
Cornwall, Orange, N.Y. 2,824 D7 212
Cornwall, Lebanon, Pa. 1,934 C5 214
Cornwall, Rockbridge, Va. 100 C5 192
Cornwall, Addison, Vt. 40 (756▲) *D2 218
Cornwall, co., Eng. 340,600 K8 273
Cornwall, isl., N.W.Ter., Can. B9 48
Cornwall Bridge, Litchfield, Conn. 200 B2 202
Cornwallis, N.Z. 42 H8 437
Cornwallis, Ritchie, W.Va. 106 B3 194
Cornwallis, isl., N.W.Ter., Can. C9 48
Cornwell, Highlands, Fla. 92 D9 174
Cornwell, Chester, S.C. 80 B6 188
Coro, Ven. 39,000 A4 240
Coroatá, Braz. 4,970 A2 258
Corocoro, Bol. 4,431 C1 246
Coroico, Bol. 2,235 C1 246
Coromandel, N.Z. 709 B5 437
Corona, Riverside, Calif. 13,336 C6 94 / F5
Corona, Lincoln, N.Mex. 420 D5 126
Corona, Roberts, S.Dak. 150 B9 158
Coronaca, Greenwood, S.C. 200 C4 188
Coronach, Sask., Can. 358 F5 58
Coronada, bay, C.R. F6 228
Coronado, San Diego, Calif. 18,039 D6 94 / F5
Coronation, Alta., Can. 784 D7 54
Coronda, Arg. B3 252
Coronel, Chile 17,372 C1 252
Coronel Bogado, Par. 3,758 E4 247
Coronel Brandsen, Arg. 3,803 C4 252
Coronel Dorrego, Arg. 7,245 C3 252
Coronel Oviedo, Par. 5,804 D4 247
Coronel Pringles, Arg. 12,844 C3 252
Coronel Pringles, Arg. D3 252
Coronel Suárez, Arg. 11,133 C3 252
Coronie, Sur. D5 256
Corozal, Br.Hond. 2,190 A3 228
Corozal, Col. 7,240 B1 244
Corpen, Arg. G4 251
Corpus Christi, Nueces, Tex. 167,690 (*195,200) F7 130
Corral, Camas, Idaho 20 F4 108
Corral de Almaguer, Sp. 10,920 C5 298
Corrales, Col. 1,226 B2 244
Corralillo, Cuba 1,073 A4 232
Corraun, Ire. H3 273
Correctionville, Woodbury, Iowa 912 B2 142
Correll, Big Stone, Minn. 101 F2 148
Corrente, Braz. 1,386 C2 258
Corrente, riv., Braz. C2 258
Correntina, Braz. 1,927 C2 258
Correo, Valencia, N.Mex. 35 D3 126
Corrèze, dept., Fr. 242,798 *E4 278
Corrientes, Arg. 56,544 A4 252
Corrientes, prov., Arg. 645,500 C6 250
Corrientes, cape, Col. B1 244
Corrientes, cape, Cuba B2 232
Corrientes, cape, Mex. C4 224
Corrientes, riv., Arg. A4 252
Corrientes, riv., Peru A2 245
Corrigan, Polk, Tex. 986 D8 130
Corriganville, Allegany, Md. 602 A2 182
Corry, Erie, Pa. 7,744 B2 214
Corryton, Knox, Tenn. 300 B8 190
Corse (Corsica), dept., Fr. 246,995 *D2 302
Corsica, Douglas, S.Dak. 479 D7 158
Corsica (Corse), former prov., Fr. 244,000 *D2 302
Corsica, isl., Medit. Sea *D2 302
Corsicana, Navarro, Tex. 20,344 C7 130
Corson, co., S.Dak. 5,798 B4 158
Corson, inlet, N.J. E3 210
Cortaro, Pima, Ariz. 50 F4 124
Cortazar, Mex. 12,142 K13 225
Corte, Fr. D2 302
Corte Alto, Chile F3 251
Cortegana, Sp. 5,099 D3 298
Cortelyou, Washington, Ala. 225 D1 168
Corte Madera, Marin, Calif. 5,962 A4 94
Cortes, Sp. 2,230 D4 298
Cortez, Montezuma, Colo. 6,764 E2 106
Cortez, Manatee, Fla. 468 D6 174
Cortina d'Ampezzo, It. 3,900 *B4 302
Cortland, De Kalb, Ill. 461 B5 138
Cortland, Jackson, Ind. 170 D4 140
Cortland, Gage, Nebr. 285 D9 152
Cortland, Cortland, N.Y. 19,181 C5 212
Cortland, Trumbull, Ohio 1,957 A6 156
Cortland, co., N.Y. 41,113 C5 212
Cortona, It. 4,000 D3 302
Coruche, Port. 2,925 C2 298
Çorum, Tur. 25,827 A6 307
Çorum, prov., Tur. 403,527 *A6 307
Corumbá, Braz. 18,725 I5 257
Corumbá, riv., Braz. D1 258
Coruña, prov., Sp. 971,641 *A2 298
Corunna, Ont., Can. 245 R18 64
Corunna, De Kalb, Ind. 361 A4 140
Corunna, Shiawassee, Mich. 2,764 G7 146
Corvallis, Ravalli, Mont. 390 D2 110
Corvallis, Benton, Oreg. 20,669 C3 96
Corwin, Harper, Kans. 40 E5 144
Corwin Springs, Park, Mont. 12 E6 110
Corwith, Hancock, Iowa 488 B4 142
Cory, Delta, Colo. (part of Eckert) 100 D3 106
Cory, Clay, Ind. 200 C2 140
Corydon, Harrison, Ind. 2,701 D3 140
Corydon, Wayne, Iowa 1,687 D4 142
Corydon, Henderson, Ky. 746 C3 178
Coryell, co., Tex. 23,961 D7 130
Cosalá, Mex. 1,694 C4 224
Cosby, Andrew, Mo. 119 B3 150
Cosby, Cocke, Tenn. 50 C8 190
Coscomatepec, Mex. 5,649 L15 225
Cosenza, It. 49,500 (62,200▲) F6 302
Cosenza, prov., It. 710,000 *F6 302
Coshocton, Coshocton, Ohio 13,106 B5 156
Coshocton, co., Ohio 32,224 B4 156
Coskakat, Alsk. 15 C6 84
Cosmoledo, isl., Afr. A9 421
Cosmopolis, Grays Harbor, Wash. 1,312 C3 98
Cosmos, Meeker, Minn. 487 G4 148
Cosne [-sur-Loire], Fr. 7,827 D5 278
Cosnino, Coconino, Ariz. 15 C4 124
Cossatot, mts., Ark. C3 170
Cossatot, riv., Ark. C2 170
Cossonay, Switz. 1,214 B2 312
Costa Mesa, Orange, Calif. 37,550 D6 94
Costa Rica, country, N.A. 1,124,000 E5 228
Costigan, Penobscot, Maine 70 C4 204
Costilla, Taos, N.Mex. 475 B5 126
Costilla, co., Colo. 4,219 E5 106
Cotabato, Phil. 8,909 C6 358
Cotacachi, Ec. 4,354 A2 245
Cotagaita, Bol. 1,353 D1 246
Cotahuasi, Peru 1,354 C2 245
Cotati, Sonoma, Calif. 1,852 *C2 94
Cotaxtla, Mex. 351 L15 225
Coteau, Terrebonne, La. 500 *E5 180
Coteau, Burke, N.Dak. 100 B3 154
Coteau Landing, Que., Can. 551 S10 66
Coteaux, Hai. 2,893 C7 232
Côte-d'Or, dept., Fr. 356,839 *D6 278
Côtes de Fer, Hai. 736 C8 232
Côtes-du-Nord, dept., Fr. 503,178 *C2 278
Cotesfield, Howard, Nebr. 81 C7 152
Côte St. Luc, Que., Can. 5,914 *S16 66
Côte St. Michel, Que., Can. 24,706 *S16 66
Cotija, Mex. 5,672 L12 225
Cotonou, Dah. 21,140 E5 408
Cotopaxi, Fremont, Colo. 120 D5 106
Cotopaxi, vol., Ec. A2 245
Cotswold, hills, Eng. J10 273
Cottage, Aroostook, Maine 15 A4 204
Cottage City, Prince Georges, Md. 1,099 C3 182
Cottage Grove, Union, Ind. 100 C5 140
Cottage Grove, Washington, Minn. 160 G7 148
Cottage Grove, Lane, Oreg. 3,895 D3 96
Cottagegrove, Henry, Tenn. 130 B3 190
Cottage Grove, Dane, Wis. 568 *E4 160
Cottage Grove, dam, Oreg. D3 96
Cottage Hill, Escambia, Fla. 500 A3 174
Cottage Hills, Madison, Ill. 3,976 E3 138
Cottageville, Colleton, S.C. 520 F8 188 / F2
Cottageville, Jackson, W.Va. 300 C3 194
Cottam, Ont., Can. 410 R18 64
Cottbus, Ger. 64,500 C6 286
Cotter, Baxter, Ark. 683 A4 170
Cotter, Louisa, Iowa 52 *C6 142
Cottian Alps, mts., Fr. E7 278
Cottingham, Eng. 39,000 H12 273
Cottle, Nicholas, W.Va. 500 *C4 194
Cottle, co., Tex. 4,207 B5 130
Cottle Knob, mtn., W.Va. C4 194
Cottleville, St. Charles, Mo. 200 A7 150
Cotton, Mitchell, Ga. 108 E2 176
Cotton, co., Okla. 8,031 D5 128
Cottondale, Tuscaloosa, Ala. 900 B2 168
Cottondale, Jackson, Fla. 849 A5 174
Cotton Mill (Mills), Grayson, Tex. 950 *C7 130
Cotton Plant, Woodruff, Ark. 1,704 B5 170
Cotton Plant, Tippah, Miss. 75 A3 184
Cottonport, Avoyelles, La. 1,581 D3 180
Cottonton, Russell, Ala. 950 C4 168
Cotton Town, Yell, Ark. 40 B3 170
Cottontown, Sumner, Tenn. 50 B5 190
Cotton Valley, Webster, La. 1,145 B2 180
Cottonwood, Houston, Ala. 953 D4 168
Cottonwood, Yavapai, Ariz. 1,879 D3 124
Cottonwood, Shasta, Calif. 700 B2 94
Cottonwood, Idaho, Idaho 1,081 C2 108
Cottonwood, Lyon, Minn. 717 G3 148
Cottonwood, Coal, Okla. 100 D7 128
Cottonwood, Jackson, S.Dak. 38 D4 158
Cottonwood, co., Minn. 16,166 G3 148
Cottonwood, creek, Wyo. C4 116
Cottonwood, creek, Wyo. D2 116
Cottonwood, creek, Wyo. E2 116
Cottonwood, riv., Kans. D6 144
Cottonwood, riv., Minn. G3 148
Cottonwood, wash, Utah F6 114
Cottonwood Falls, Chase, Kans. 971 D7 144
Cotuit, Barnstable, Mass. 850 C7 206
Cotulla, La Salle, Tex. 3,960 E6 130
Couchiching, lake, Ont., Can. P21 64
Couchville, Davidson, Tenn. E7 190
Couchwood, Webster, La. 200 B2 180
Coudekerque-Branche, Fr. 15,334 B5 278
Couderay, Sawyer, Wis. 113 C2 160
Coudersport, Potter, Pa. 2,889 B3 214
Coudres, isl., Que., Can. Q14 66
Couëron, Fr. 5,077 D3 278
Cougar, Cowlitz, Wash. 300 C4 98
Cougar, peak, Oreg. E6 96
Cougar, rock, Oreg. C4 96
Coughlan, harbor, Solomon E2 436
Coul, pt., Scot. F6 272
Coulee, Mountrail, N.Dak. 68 B3 154
Coulee, creek, Wash. D8 98
Coulee City, Grant, Wash. 654 B7 98
Coulee Dam, Douglas, Wash. 1,344 B8 98
Coulommiers, Fr. 8,561 C5 278
Coulter, Man., Can. 50 F2 60
Coulter, Franklin, Iowa 315 B4 142
Coulterville, Mariposa, Calif. 180 D3 94
Coulterville, Randolph, Ill. 1,022 E4 138
Coulwood, Russell, Va. 125 D2 192
Counce, Hardin, Tenn. 500 C3 190
Council, Alsk. 41 C5 84
Council, Adams, Idaho 827 E2 108
Council, Buchanan, Va. 50 C2 192
Council Bluffs, Pottawattamie, Iowa 55,641 C2 142
Council Grove, Morris, Kans. 2,664 D7 144
Council Hill, Muskogee, Okla. 130 C8 128
Country Club Hills, Cook, Ill. 3,421 *F3 138
Country Club Hills, St. Louis, Mo. 1,763 *C7 150
Country Club Village, Andrew, Mo. 395 *B3 150
Country Homes, Spokane, Wash. 1,600 *B9 98
Countryside, Johnson, Kans. 428 *D9 144
County Line, Pike, Ala. 278 *D3 168
Countyline, Carter and Stephens, Okla. 500 D6 128
Coupe, cape, Miquelon Isl. G7 72
Coupeville, Island, Wash. 740 A4 98
Courbevoie, Fr. 59,730 I10 278
Courcelles, Que., Can. 610 S14 66
Courland, lagoon, Sov.Un. E3 332
Coursan, Fr. F5 278
Courtenay, B.C., Can. 3,025 F10 52
Courtenay, Stutsman, N.Dak. 168 C7 154
Courtland, Lawrence, Ala. 495 A2 168
Courtland, Cochise, Ariz. 11 G6 124
Courtland, Ont., Can. 350 R20 64
Courtland, Republic, Kans. 384 C6 144
Courtland, Nicollet, Minn. 239 G4 148
Courtland, Panola, Miss. 242 A3 184
Courtland, Southampton, Va. 855 D7 192
Courtney, Love, Okla. 40 E6 128
Courtrai, see Kortrijk, Bel.
Courtright, Ont., Can. 581 R18 64
Courtrock, Grant, Oreg. 60 C7 96
Courval, Sask., Can. 110 E4 58
Courville, Que., Can. 3,772 *R16 66
Coushatta, Red River, La. 1,663 B2 180
Coutances, Fr. 8,216 C3 278
Coutras, Fr. E3 278
Coutts, Alta., Can. 300 F7 54
Couvin, Bel. 3,626 D3 282
Covada, Ferry, Wash. A8 98
Cove, Polk, Ark. 320 C2 170
Cove, Union, Oreg. 311 B9 96
Cove, Scot. D3 272
Cove, Cache, Utah B4 114
Cove, King, Wash. 150 D2 98
Cove, isl., Ont., Can. O19 64

Cove, pt., Md. D7 182
Cove City, Craven, N.C. 551 B8 186
Cove City, Orange, Tex. 1,749 *D9 130
Cove Fort, Millard, Utah E3 114
Covelo, Mendocino, Calif. 348 C2 94
Covena, Emanuel, Ga. 105 D4 176
Coventry (South Coventry), Tolland, Conn. 3,568 (6,356▴) B6 202
Coventry, Eng. 272,600 I11 273
Coventry, Kent, R.I. 4,500 (15,432▴) C2 216
Coventry, Orleans, Vt. 130 (458▴) B4 218
Coventry Center, Kent, R.I. 125 C2 216
Coventry Center, pond, R.I. C2 216
Cove Orchard, Yamhill, Oreg. B3 96
Covered, bridge, N.H. C3 208
Covert, Osborne, Kans. 50 C5 144
Covert, Van Buren, Mich. 500 G5 146
Covesville, Albemarle, Va. 150 C6 192
Covilhã, Port. 20,423 B3 298
Covin, Fayette, Ala. 100 B2 168
Covina, Los Angeles, Calif. 20,124 C6 94
Covington, Newton, Ga. 8,167 C3 176
Covington, Fountain, Ind. 2,759 B2 140
Covington, Kenton, Ky. 60,376 A6 A8 178
Covington, St. Tammany, La. 6,754 B7 D5 180
Covington, Baraga, Mich. 200 C3 146
Covington, Miami, Ohio 2,473 B2 156
Covington, Garfield, Okla. 687 B6 128
Covington, Tipton, Tenn. 5,298 C2 190
Covington (Independent City), Va. 11,062 C5 192
Covington, King, Wash. 50 D3 98
Covington, co., Ala. 35,631 D3 168
Covington, co., Miss. 13,637 D3 184
Cow, creek, Wash. C8 98
Cow, lake, Oreg. D9 96
Cowan, Delaware, Ind. 250 B4 140
Cowan, Franklin, Tenn. 1,979 C5 190
Cowan, lake, Austl. E4 432
Cowan, lake, Sask., Can. C4 58
Cowan, riv., Sask., Can. C4 58
Cowan Knob, mtn., Ark. B3 170
Cowans, Lincoln, Colo. D7 106
Cowansville, Que., Can. 5,242 S12 66
Coward, Florence, S.C. 150 D9 188
Coward Springs, Austl. D7 432
Cowarts, Houston, Ala. 920 D4 168
Cowcreek, Owsley, Ky. 320 C7 178
Cowden, Shelby, Ill. 575 D5 138
Cowden, Washita, Okla. 40 C5 128
Cowdrey, Jackson, Colo. 100 B4 106
Cowell, Newton, Ark. 35 B3 170
Cowell, Contra Costa, Calif. 200 A5 94
Cowen, Webster, W.Va. 475 C4 194
Cowen, mtn., Mont. E6 110
Cowesett, Kent, R.I. (part of Warwick) C3 216
Coweta, Wagoner, Okla. 1,858 C8 128
Coweta, co., Ga. 28,893 C2 176
Cowford, Washington, Fla. 300 A5 174
Cowgill, Caldwell, Mo. 259 B4 150
Cow Head, Newf., Can. 325 F7 E10 72
Cowichan, lake, B.C., Can. F10 52
Cowichan Station, B.C., Can. 185 C14 52
Cowiche, Yakima, Wash. 175 C6 98
Cowles, Webster, Nebr. 55 D7 152
Cowles, San Miguel, N.Mex. 300 G7 126
Cowley, Alta., Can. 92 F5 54
Cowley, Big Horn, Wyo. 459 B4 116
Cowley, co., Kans. 37,861 E7 144
Cowlington, Le Flore, Okla. 74 C9 128
Cowlitz, co., Wash. 57,801 C4 98
Cowlitz, riv., Wash. C4 98
Cowpasture, riv., Va. B5 192
Cowpen, mtn., Ga. B2 176
Cowpens, Spartanburg, S.C. 2,038 A5 188
Cowskin, creek, Kans. B5 144
Cox City, Grady, Okla. 150 D6 128
Coxim, Braz. 855 I6 257
Coxsackie, Greene, N.Y. 2,849 C8 212
Cox's Cove, Newf., Can. 450 F6 72
Coxs Mills, Gilmer, W.Va. 50 B4 194
Coxton, Harlan, Ky. 950 D7 178
Coy, Wilcox, Ala. 100 D2 168
Coy, Lonoke, Ark. 206 C5 170
Coyame, Mex. 790 B4 224
Coyanosa, draw, Tex. D4 130
Coyle, Logan, Okla. 292 C6 128
Coyoacán, Mex. 46,031 L14 G10 225
Coyote, Lincoln, N.Mex. 50 E5 126
Coytesville, Bergen, N.J. A2 210
Coyuca de Benítez, Mex. 3,597 D6 225
Coyville, Wilson, Kans. 133 E8 144
Cozad, Dawson, Nebr. 3,184 D6 152
Cozahome, Searcy, Ark. 50 A4 170
Cozumel, Mex. 2,330 C8 225
Cozumel, isl., Mex. C8 225
Crab, creek, Wash. B8 98
Crab Orchard, Lincoln, Ky. 808 C6 178
Crab Orchard, Johnson, Nebr. 103 D9 152
Crab Orchard, Cumberland, Tenn. 700 C7 190
Crab Orchard, Raleigh, W.Va. 1,953 D7 194
Crab Orchard, lake, Ill. F4 138
Crab Orchard, mts., Tenn. C7 190
Crabtree, Van Buren, Ark. B4 170
Crabtree, Linn, Oreg. 250 C1 C4 96
Crabtree, Westmoreland, Pa. 950 C2 214
Crabtree, creek, Oreg. C2 96
Crabtree Bald, mtn., N.C. B3 186
Crabtree Mills, Que., Can. 1,103 S11 66
Cracking, riv., Sask., Can. D6 58
Cradle, mtn., Austl. G8 432
Cradock, U.S.Afr. 14,866 F5 420
Cradock, Norfolk, Va. (part of Portsmouth) A8 D8 192
Crafton, Allegheny, Pa. 8,418 A3 214
Craftsbury, Orleans, Vt. 175 (674▴) B4 218
Craftsbury Common, Orleans, Vt. 90 B4 218
Cragford, Clay, Ala. 114 B4 168
Cragged, mtn., N.H. D4 208
Crags, mts., Idaho C3 108
Craig, Alsk. 273 D8 K14 84
Craig, Moffat, Colo. 3,984 B3 106
Craig, Plymouth, Iowa 117 B1 142
Craig, Lewis and Clark, Mont. 66 C5 110
Craig, Holt, Mo. 488 A2 150
Craig, Burt, Nebr. 378 C9 152
Craig, co., Okla. 16,303 B8 128
Craig, co., Va. 3,356 C4 192
Craig, creek, Va. C4 192
Craig Beach, Mahoning, Ohio 1,139 *A6 156
Craigellachie, B.C., Can. E13 52
Craigfield, Williamson, Tenn. C4 190
Craig Harbour, N.W.Ter., Can. B10 48
Craighead, co., Ark. 47,253 B6 170
Craighouse, Scot. F7 272
Craighurst, Ont., Can. 210 P21 64
Craigmyle, Alta., Can. 138 E6 54
Craigsville, Augusta, Va. 978 B5 192
Craigsville, Nicholas, W.Va. 175 C4 194
Craigville, Wells, Ind. 190 B4 140
Craigville, Barnstable, Mass. 300 *C7 206
Craik, Sask., Can. 607 E5 58
Crail, Scot. 1,200 E10 272
Crailsheim, Ger. 12,700 D4 286
Crainville, Williamson, Ill. 421 *F4 138
Craiova, Rom. 96,929 B2 321
Cram, Calhoun, Ark. D4 170
Cramerton, Gaston, N.C. 3,123 B4 186
Crampel, Alg. 161 B3 402
Cranberry, hill, Conn. D5 202
Cranberry, is., Maine *D4 204
Cranberry Isles, Hancock, Maine 135 (181▴) D4 204
Cranberry Lake (part of Powell River), B.C., Can. F10 52
Cranberry Portage, Man., Can. 250 C2 60
Cranbrook, B.C., Can. 4,562 F15 52
Cranbury, Middlesex, N.J. 1,038 C3 210
Crandall, Man., Can. 200 E2 60
Crandall, Murray, Ga. 208 B2 176
Crandall, Harrison, Ind. 166 *D3 140
Crandall, Clarke, Miss. 75 D4 184
Crandall, Day, S.Dak. 30 B8 158
Crandall, Kaufman, Tex. 640 *C7 130
Crandon, Forest, Wis. 1,679 C5 160
Crane, Martin, Ind. 750 D3 140
Crane, Stone, Mo. 954 E4 150
Crane, Richland, Mont. 85 C12 110
Crane, Harney, Oreg. 75 D8 96
Crane, Crane, Tex. 3,796 D4 130
Crane, co., Tex. 4,699 D4 130
Crane, creek, Ohio A1 156
Crane, lake, Sask., Can. E3 58
Crane, lake, Minn. C6 148
Crane, mtn., Oreg. E6 96
Craneco, Logan, W.Va. (part of Lundale) D3 194
Crane Creek, Hancock, Miss. 150 E3 184
Crane Creek, res., Idaho E2 108
Crane Hill, Cullman, Ala. 200 A2 168
Crane Lake, St. Louis, Minn. 100 C6 148
Crane Neck, pt., N.Y. D4 212
Crane Prairie, res., Oreg. D5 96
Crane Valley, Sask., Can. 105 F5 58
Cranford, Union, N.J. 26,424 B4 210
Crannell, Humboldt, Calif. 437 B1 94
Cransac, Fr. 4,765 E5 278
Cranston, Providence, R.I. 66,766 B3 216
Crapaud, P.E.I., Can. C6 70
Crapo, Dorchester, Md. 40 D7 182
Crary, Ramsey, N.Dak. 195 B7 154
Crater Lake, Klamath, Oreg. 50 E4 96
Crater, lake, Oreg. E4 96
Crater Lake, natl. park, Oreg. E4 96
Craters of the Moon, natl. mon., Idaho F5 108
Crateús, Braz. 7,391 B2 258
Crato, Braz. 15,464 B3 258
Craven, Sask., Can. 189 E5 58
Craven, co., N.C. 58,773 B8 186
Craver, Stillwater, Mont. 60 *E7 110
Crawford, Delta, Colo. 147 D3 106
Crawford, Oglethorpe, Ga. 541 C3 176
Crawford (Town of), Washington, Maine (83▴) C5 204
Crawford, Lowndes, Miss. 317 B4 184
Crawford, Dawes, Nebr. 1,588 B2 152
Crawford, Roger Mills, Okla. 50 C4 128
Crawford, co., Ark. 21,318 B2 170
Crawford, co., Ga. 5,816 D2 176
Crawford, co., Ill. 20,751 D6 138
Crawford, co., Ind. 8,379 D3 140
Crawford, co., Iowa 18,569 B2 142
Crawford, co., Kans. 37,032 E8 144
Crawford, co., Mich. 4,971 E7 146
Crawford, co., Mo. 12,647 D6 150
Crawford, co., Ohio 46,775 B4 156
Crawford, co., Pa. 77,956 B1 214
Crawford, co., Wis. 16,351 E3 160
Crawford, lake, Maine C5 204
Crawford Bay, B.C., Can. F14 52
Crawfordsville, Crittenden, Ark. 744 B6 170
Crawfordsville, Montgomery, Ind. 14,231 B3 140
Crawfordsville, Washington, Iowa 317 C6 142
Crawfordsville, Linn, Oreg. 170 C4 96
Crawfordville, Wakulla, Fla. 600 A6 174
Crawfordville, Taliaferro, Ga. 786 C4 176
Crayne, Crittenden, Ky. 125 C2 178
Crazy, peak, Mont. D6 110
Crazy Woman, creek, Wyo. B6 116
Creagerstown, Frederick, Md. 75 A5 182
Creal Springs, Williamson, Ill. 784 F5 138
Cream, Buffalo, Wis. 20 D2 160
Cream, hill, Conn. B2 202
Cream Ridge, Monmouth, N.J. 50 C3 210
Crean, lake, Sask., Can. C4 58
Crediton, Ont., Can. 490 Q19 64
Creede, Mineral, Colo. 350 E4 106
Creedmoor, Granville, N.C. 862 A7 186
Creek, co., Okla. 40,495 C7 128
Creelman, Sask., Can. 215 F6 58
Creemore, Ont., Can. 838 P20 64
Creggan, N.Ire. G5 273
Creighton, Ont., Can. S25 64
Creighton, Sask., Can. 1,659 C7 58
Creighton, Cass, Mo. 228 C3 150
Creighton, Knox, Nebr. 1,388 B8 152
Creighton, Allegheny, Pa. 2,865 A4 214
Creil, Fr. 13,500 C5 278
Crellin, Garrett, Md. 425 B1 182
Crema, It. 18,200 C2 302
Cremona, Alta., Can. 192 E5 54
Cremona, It. 56,200 (68,900▴) C3 302
Cremona, prov., It. 378,200 *C2 302
Crenshaw, Panola, Miss. 1,382 A2 184
Crenshaw, co., Ala. 14,909 D3 168
Creola, Mobile, Ala. 500 E1 168
Creole, Cameron, La. 150 E2 180
Creosote, Choctaw, Okla. 250 D8 128
Cres, isl., Yugo. B2 316
Cresaptown, Allegany, Md. 1,680 A2 182
Cresbard, Faulk, S.Dak. 229 B7 158
Crescent, McIntosh, Ga. 300 E5 176
Crescent, Pottawattamie, Iowa 296 C2 142
Crescent, Logan, Okla. 1,264 C6 128
Crescent, Klamath, Oreg. 350 D5 96
Crescent, lake, Fla. B9 174
Crescent, lake, Oreg. D5 96
Crescent, lake, Wash. A3 98
Crescent Beach, Cumberland, Maine 80 E5 204
Crescent Beach, Horry, S.C. 440 D11 188
Crescent City, Del Norte, Calif. 2,958 B1 94
Crescent City, Putnam, Fla. 1,629 B9 174
Crescent City Northwest, Del Norte, Calif. 3,086 *B1 94
Crescent Junction, Grand, Utah 12 E6 114
Crescent Lake, Cumberland, Maine 175 E2 204
Crescent Lake, Klamath, Oreg. 175 D5 96
Crescent Park, Kenton, Ky. 564 *A6 178
Crescent Springs, Kenton, Ky. 946 A8 178
Cresco, Howard, Iowa 3,809 A5 142
Cresskill, Bergen, N.J. 7,290 A2 210
Cresson, Cambria, Pa. 2,659 C3 214
Cressona, Schuylkill, Pa. 1,854 C5 214
Crest, Fr. E6 278
Crest, Upson, Ga. 125 D2 176
Crested Butte, Gunnison, Colo. 289 D4 106
Cresthill, Fauquier, Va. 50 B6 192
Crestlawn, Madison, Ind. 2,194 *B4 140
Crestline, Crawford, Ohio 5,521 B4 156
Crestmoor, Morris, N.J. 30 B3 210
Creston, B.C., Can. 1,844 F14 52
Creston, Newf., Can. 550 G8 72
Creston, Ogle, Ill. 454 B5 138
Creston, Union, Iowa 7,667 C3 142
Creston, Natchitoches, La. 110 C2 180
Creston, Flathead, Mont. 25 B2 110
Creston, Platte, Nebr. 177 C8 152
Creston, Wayne, Ohio 1,522 B5 156
Creston, Calhoun, S.C. 250 D7 188
Creston, Cumberland, Tenn. 25 B6 190
Creston, Lincoln, Wash. 317 B8 98
Creston, Wirt, W.Va. 225 C3 194
Creston, Sweetwater, Wyo. 15 E5 116
Crestone, Saguache, Colo. 51 E5 106
Crestone, peak, Colo. E5 106
Crestview, Okaloosa, Fla. 7,467 A4 174
Crestview, Campbell, Ky. 616 *A6 178
Crestview Hills, Kenton, Ky. 15 *A6 178
Crestwood, Cook, Ill. 1,213 *B6 138
Crestwood, Oldham, Ky. 600 A5 B5 178
Crestwood, St. Louis, Mo. 11,106 *C7 150
Crestwood, Norfolk, Va. 2,200 D8 192
Crestwynd, Sask., Can. 42 E5 58
Creswell, Washington, N.C. 402 B9 186
Creswell, Lane, Oreg. 760 D3 96
Crete (Kriti), reg., Grc. 462,124 D5 306
Crete, Will, Ill. 3,463 B6 F3 138
Crete, Saline, Nebr. 3,546 D9 152
Crete, Sargent, N. Dak. 200 D8 154
Crete, isl., Grc. D5 306
Crete, sea, Europe E7 266
Cretone, It. 578 *D4 302
Creus, cape, Sp. A8 298
Creuse, dept., Fr. 172,702 *D4 278
Creutzwald [-la-Croix], Fr. 10,183 C7 278
Creve Coeur, Tazewell, Ill. 6,684 C4 138
Creve Coeur, St. Louis, Mo. 5,122 A8 150
Crevillente, Sp. 11,403 C6 298
Crewe, Eng. 51,500 H10 273
Crewe, Nottoway, Va. 2,012 C6 192
Crewport, Yakima, Wash. 750 C6 98
Cricket, Wilkes, N.C. 950 A4 186
Cricket, mts., Utah E2 114
Cridersville, Auglaize, Ohio 1,053 B2 156
Crieff, Scot. 5,400 E9 272
Criffel, mtn., Scot. G9 272
Crigler, Lincoln, Ark. 50 D5 170
Criglersville, Madison, Va. 45 B6 192
Crikvenica, Yugo. 3,060 B2 316
Crimea, see Krym, pen., Sov.Un.
Crimmitschau, Ger. 33,400 C5 286
Crinan, Scot. E7 272
Cripple, Alsk. 2 C6 84
Cripple Creek, Teller, Colo. 614 D5 106
Cripple Creek, Wythe, Va. 300 D3 192
Crişana-Maramures, prov., Rom. 1,391,672 *B6 321
Crişana-Maramures, reg., Rom. A1 321
Crisfield, Somerset, Md. 3,540 E8 182
Crisman, Boulder, Colo. 25 *C5 106
Crisman, Porter, Ind. (part of Portage) A2 140
Crisp, co., Ga. 17,768 E3 176
Criss Creek, B.C., Can. E12 52
Cristal, mts., Gabon F6 409
Cristalina, Braz. 1,719 D1 258
Crişul Alb, riv., Rom. A1 321
Crittenden, Grant, Ky. 287 B6 B8 178
Crittenden, Nansemond, Va. 250 A8 192
Crittenden, co., Ark. 47,564 B6 170
Crittenden, co., Ky. 8,648 C2 178
Crivitz, Marinette, Wis. 650 C6 160
Crna, riv., Yugo. D5 316
Črnomelj, Yugo. 1,920 B2 316
Croatia (Hrvatska), rep., Yugo. 3,918,817 B2 316
Croc, hbr., Newf., Can. E8 72
Croche, riv., Que., Can. Q12 66
Crocheron, Dorchester, Md. 125 D7 182
Crocker, Pulaski, Mo. 821 D5 150
Crocker, Clark, S.Dak. 77 B8 158
Crockett, Umatilla, Oreg. B8 96
Crockett, Houston, Tex. 5,356 D8 130
Crockett, co., Tenn. 14,594 C2 190
Crockett, co., Tex. 4,209 D5 130
Crockett Mills, Crockett, Tenn. 125 C2 190
Crockettsville, Breathitt, Ky. 50 C7 178
Crocketville, Hampton, S.C. 75 F6 188
Crofton, Christian, Ky. 892 C3 178
Crofton, Knox, Nebr. 604 B8 152
Croghan, Lewis, N.Y. 821 B6 212
Croker, cape, Ont., Can. P20 64
Croker, isl., Austl. A6 432
Cromarty, Scot. 700 D8 272
Cromer, Man., Can. 95 F2 60
Cromona, Letcher, Ky. 950 *C8 178
Cromwell, Middlesex, Conn. 6,780 C5 202
Cromwell, Noble, Ind. 451 A4 140
Cromwell, Union, Iowa 138 C3 142
Cromwell, Ohio, Ky. 200 C4 178
Cromwell, Carlton, Minn. 187 E6 148
Cromwell, N.Z. 885 F2 437
Cromwell, Seminole, Okla. 269 C7 128
Cromwell, Pierce, Wash. D2 98
Crook, Logan, Colo. 209 B8 106
Crook [& Willington], Eng. 26,800 G11 273
Crook, co., Oreg. 9,430 C6 96
Crook, co., Wyo. 4,691 B8 116
Crooked, creek, Ark. A4 170
Crooked, creek, Kans. E3 144
Crooked, creek, Pa. B4 214
Crooked, isl., W.I. A7 232
Crooked, lake, Fla. D9 174
Crooked, lake, Minn. C6 148
Crooked, lake, Newf., Can. F7 72
Crooked, riv., B.C., Can. C11 52
Crooked, riv., Oreg. C6 96
Crooked Creek, Alsk. 43 C6 84
Crooked Island, passage, W.I. A7 232
Crooked River, Sask., Can. 200 D6 58
Crooks, Minnehaha, S. Dak. 135 D9 158
Crookston, Polk, Minn. 8,546 D2 148
Crookston, Cherry, Nebr. 139 B5 152
Crooksville, Perry, Ohio 2,958 C4 156
Cropper, Shelby, Ky. 250 B5 178
Crosby, Crow Wing, Minn. 2,629 E5 148
Crosby, Amite and Wilkinson, Miss. 705 D1 184
Crosby, Divide, N.Dak. 1,759 B2 154
Crosby, Harris, Tex. 1,500 F8 130
Crosby, co., Tex. 10,347 C5 130
Crosby, mtn., Wyo. C3 116
Crosbyton, Crosby, Tex. 2,088 C5 130
Crosland, Colquitt, Ga. 95 E3 176
Cross, Berkeley, S.C. 50 E8 188
Cross, co., Ark. 19,551 B6 170
Cross, creek, W.Va. B2 194
Cross, isl., Maine D5 204
Cross, lake, La. B2 180
Cross, lake, Maine A4 204
Cross, lake, Man., Can. C4 60
Cross, lake, Man., Can. D3 60
Cross, mtn., Tenn. B7 190
Cross, mts., Ark. C2 170
Cross, riv., Nig. E6 409
Cross, sound, Alsk. I13 84
Cross Anchor, Spartanburg, S.C. 500 B5 188
Crossbost, Scot. C6 272
Cross City, Dixie, Fla. 1,857 B7 174
Cross Creek, N.B., Can. 190 C3 70
Crossett, Ashley, Ark. 5,370 D5 170
Cross Fell, mtn., Eng. G10 273
Crossfell Edge, mts., Eng. G10 273
Crossfield, Alta., Can. 459 E5 54
Cross Hill, Laurens, S.C. 441 C5 188
Cross Keys, Bibb, Ga. 1,000 *D3 176
Cross Keys, Gloucester, N.J. 140 D2 210
Crosslake, Crow Wing, Minn. 165 *E4 148
Cross Lanes, Kanawha, W.Va. 950 *C3 194
Crossley, Ocean, N.J. D4 210
Cross Mill, McDowell, N.C. 700 B3 186
Crossnore, Avery, N.C. 277 *A4 186
Cross Plains, Ripley, Ind. 160 D4 140
Cross Plains, Robertson, Tenn. 200 B5 190
Cross Plains, Callahan, Tex. 1,168 C6 130
Cross Plains, Dane, Wis. 1,066 E4 160
Cross Roads, San Bernardino, Calif. 150 E6 94
Cross Roads Ohio, N.S., Can. 175 D7 70
Crossroads, Pearl River, Miss. 100 E3 184
Cross Timbers, Hickory, Mo. 186 C4 150
Cross Village, Emmet, Mich. 50 D6 146
Crossville, De Kalb, Ala. 579 A4 168
Crossville, Lamar, Ala. 45 B1 168
Crossville, White, Ill. 874 E5 138
Crossville, Cumberland, Tenn. 4,668 C6 190
Crosswicks, Burlington, N.J. 550 C3 210
Croswell, Sanilac, Mich. 1,817 F9 146
Crothersville, Jackson, Ind. 1,449 D4 140
Croton, see Crotone, It.
Croton, Licking, Ohio 397 B4 156
Crotone, It. 31,200 F6 302
Croton-on-Hudson, Westchester, N.Y. 6,812 D8 212
Crouch, Boise, Idaho 89 E3 108
Crouse, Lincoln, N.C. 901 B4 186
Crouseville, Aroostook, Maine 230 B4 204
Crow, creek, Colo. A6 106
Crow, creek, Wyo. E8 116
Crow, riv., Minn. G4 148
Crow Agency, Big Horn, Mont. 600 E9 110
Crowder, Newton, Mo. 115 E8 150
Crowder, Quitman and Panola, Miss. 528 A2 184
Crowder, Pittsburg, Okla. 254 C8 128
Crowell, Dodge, Nebr. 25 *C9 152
Crowell, Foard, Tex. 1,703 C6 130
Crowheart, Fremont, Wyo. 5 C3 116
Crowley, Tulare, Calif. 3,950 *D4 94
Crowley, Crowley, Colo. 265 D7 106
Crowley, Acadia, La. 15,617 D3 180
Crowley, co., Colo. 3,978 D7 106
Crowley, lake, Calif. D4 94
Crowleys, ridge, Mo. E7 150
Crown, Logan, W.Va. 450 *D3 194
Crown City, Gallia, Ohio 323 D4 156
Crown Hill, Kanawha, W.Va. 600 *C3 194
Crown King, Yavapai, Ariz. 50 D3 124
Crown Point, Lake, Ind. 8,443 A2 140

Crown Point, Jefferson, La. 175 C7 180
Crownpoint, McKinley, N.Mex. 300 C2 126
Crown Point, Essex, N.Y. 900 B8 212
Crow Rock, Prairie, Mont. D10 110
Crows Nest, B.C., Can. 180 F15 52
Crows Nest, Marion, Ind. 122 D5 140
Crows Nest, mtn., S.Dak. C2 158
Crowsnest, pass, Alta., Can. F5 54
Crowville, Franklin, La. 165 B4 180
Crow Wing, co., Minn. 32,134 E4 148
Crow Wing, riv., Minn. E4 148
Croydon, Austl. 127 B8 432
Croydon, Eng. 249,300 J12 273
Croydon, Sullivan, N.H. 100 (312▲) E2 208
Croydon, Bucks, Pa. 9,000 C7 214
Croydon, Morgan, Utah 91 B4 114
Croydon, mtn., N.H. E2 208
Croydon, peak, N.H. E2 208
Croydon, riv., N.H. E2 208
Croydon Flat, Sullivan, N.H. 130 E2 208
Crozet, Albemarle, Va. 900 B6 192
Crozier, Mohave, Ariz. 50 C2 124
Crozier, Terrebonne, La. 100 E5 180
Crozier, Goochland, Va. 100 C7 192
Crucero, Peru 226 C3 245
Cruces, Cuba 10,704 A4 232
Cruces, pt., Col. B1 244
Crucible, Greene, Pa. 1,064 D2 214
Cruger, Holmes, Miss. 362 B2 184
Crum, Wayne, W.Va. 300 D2 194
Crum Lynne, Delaware, Pa. 3,500 D6 214
Crump, Bay, Mich. 50 F7 146
Crump, Hardin, Tenn. 250 C3 190
Crump, lake, Oreg. E7 96
Crumpler, McDowell, W.Va. 800 *D3 194
Crumpton, Queen Annes, Md. 300 B8 182
Crumrod, Phillips, Ark. 40 C6 170
Crumstown, St. Joseph, Ind. 250 A3 140
Cruz, cape, Cuba C5 232
Cruz, pt., Col. A2 244
Cruz Alta, Arg. B3 252
Cruz Alta, Braz. 19,375 K6 257
Cruz del Eje, Arg. 15,563 B3 252
Cruzeiro, Braz. 14,169 E2 258
Cruzeiro do Sul, Braz. 3,709 G2 256
Cruz Grande, Chile A1 252
Crysler, Ont., Can. 350 O25 64
Crystal, Power, Idaho G6 108
Crystal, Aroostook, Maine 50 (285▲) B4 204
Crystal, Montcalm, Mich. 400 F7 146
Crystal, Hennepin, Minn. 24,283 F6 148
Crystal, Pembina, N.Dak. 372 B8 154
Crystal, Klamath, Oreg. E4 96
Crystal, Mercer, W.Va. 500 *D3 194
Crystal, bay, Fla. C8 174
Crystal, caverns, Mo. E4 150
Crystal, lake, Conn. B6 202
Crystal, lake, Mich. E5 146
Crystal, lake, N.H. E4 208
Crystal, lake, Vt. B4 218
Crystal, mtn., N.H. B4 208
Crystal, pond, Conn. B7 202
Crystal, riv., Colo. C3 106
Crystal Bay, Washoe, Nev. 400 D2 112
Crystal Beach, Ont., Can. 1,850 R21 64
Crystal Beach, Pinellas, Fla. 600 C8 174
B5
Crystal City, Man., Can. 505 F3 60
Crystal City, Jefferson, Mo. 3,678 B8 150
C7
Crystal City, Zavala, Tex. 9,101 E6 130
Crystal Falls, Iron, Mich. 2,203 C3 146
Crystal Hill, Halifax, Va. 150 D6 192
Crystal Lake, Tolland, Conn. 640 B6 202
Crystal Lake, Washington, Fla. 100 A5 174
Crystal Lake, McHenry, Ill. 8,314 A5 138
E1
Crystal Lake, Hancock, Iowa 267 A4 142
Crystal Lake, cave, Iowa B7 142
Crystal Lake Park, St. Louis, Mo. 307 *C7 150
Crystal Lakes, Clark, Ohio 1,569 *C3 156
Crystal River, Citrus, Fla. 1,423 C8 174
Crystal Springs, Garland, Ark. 100 C3 170
C6
Crystal Springs, Sask., Can. 146 D5 58
Crystal Springs, Pasco, Fla. 100 C8 174
Crystal Springs, Copiah, Miss. 4,496 D2 184
Crystal Springs, lake, Calif. B5 94
Crystal Valley, Oceana, Mich. 100 F5 146
Csongrád, Hung. 16,000 C5 320
Csongrád, co., Hung. 330,000 *C5 320
Csorna, Hung. 7,425 B2 320
Cuajimalpa, Mex. 3,504 G9 224
Cuando, riv., Ang. C4 420
Cuando Cubango, dist., Ang. 475,956 B3 420
Cuangar, Ang. 136 C3 420
Cuango, riv., Ang. A3 420
Cuanza Norte, dist., Ang. 216,463 A2 420
Cuanza Sul, dist., Ang. 296,610 B2 420
Cua Rao, Viet. C5 362
Cuarenta, Mex. K13 225
Cuarto, riv., Arg. B3 252
Cuasquipula, Mex. L12 225
Cuatrociénegas, Mex. B5 225
Cuauhtémoc, Mex. 6,402 B4 224
Cuautepec, Mex. 3,609 F10 224
Cuautla, Mex. 9,779 L14 225
Cuba, Sumter, Ala. 390 C1 168
Cuba, Fulton, Ill. 1,380 C3 138
Cuba, Republic, Kans. 336 C6 144
Cuba, Graves, Ky. 100 D2 178
Cuba, Crawford, Mo. 1,672 C6 150
Cuba, Sandoval, N.Mex. 733 B4 126
Cuba, Allegany, N.Y. 1,949 C3 212
Cuba, country, N.A. 5,829,029 A5 232
Cuba City, Grant, Wis. 1,673 F3 160
Cubal, Ang. B2 420
Cuba Landing, Humphreys, Tenn. C4 190
Cubango, riv., Ang. C3 420
Cubero, Valencia, N.Mex. 225 C3 126
Cubia, Ang. C4 420
Cub Run, Hart, Ky. 250 C4 178
Cucamonga, San Bernardino, Calif. 2,500 C6 94
Cuchara, Huerfano, Colo. 10 *E6 106
Cuchara, riv., Colo. E6 106
Cuchillo, Sierra, N.Mex. 200 E3 126
Cuchivero, riv., Ven. C6 240
Cuchumatanes, mts., Guat. C2 228
Cucumber, McDowell, W.Va. 300 *D3 194
Cudahy, Los Angeles, Calif. 12,000 C5 94
Cudahy, Milwaukee, Wis. 17,975 E2 160
F6
Cuddalore, India 69,084 F3 366
Cuddapah, India 37,438 F3 366
Cuddy, Allegheny, Pa. 1,400 *C1 214
Cudgewa, Austl. 257 F9 432
Cudjos, cave, Ky. D7 178
Cudworth, Sask., Can. 582 D5 58
Cue, Austl. 467 D3 432
Cuéllar, Sp. 5,284 B4 298
Cuenca, Ec. 39,983 A2 245
Cuenca, Sp. 23,305 B5 298
Cuenca, prov., Sp. 344,033 *B5 298
Cuenca, mts., Sp. B5 298
Cuencamé, Mex. 2,321 C5 224
Cuernavaca, Mex. 30,597 D6 225
L14
Cuero, De Witt, Tex. 7,338 E7 130
Cuervo, Guadalupe, N.Mex. 160 C6 126
Cuetzalan, Mex. 4,006 K15 225
Cuevas, Harrison, Miss. 500 E1 184
Cuevas, Sp. 2,974 D6 298
Cuglieri, It. 4,700 E2 302
Cuiabá, Braz. 23,745 I5 257
Cuiabá, riv., Braz. I5 257
Cuicas, Ven. 706 B3 240
Cuicatlán, Mex. 1,986 D6 225
M15
Cuilapa, Guat. 2,685 C2 228
Cuillin, hills, Scot. D6 272
Cuillin, sound, Scot. D6 272
Cuilo, Guat. 519 C2 228
Cuito Cuanavale, Ang. C3 420
Cuito, riv., Ang. C3 420
Cuitzéo, lake, Mex. L13 225
Cuivre, riv., Mo. B6 150
Culberson, co., Tex. 2,794 D3 130
Culbertson, Roosevelt, Mont. 919 B12 110
Culbertson, Hitchcock, Nebr. 803 D5 152
Culdesac, Nez Perce, Idaho 209 C2 108
Culebra, isl., P.R. C12 233
Culebra, peak, Colo. E5 106
Culgoa, riv., Austl. D9 432
Culhuacán, Mex. 2,087 G10 224
Culiacan, Mex. 48,963 C4 224
Culion, Phil. 3,279 B6 358
Cúllar de Baza, Sp. 4,851 D5 298
Cullen, Webster, La. 2,194 B2 180
Cullen, Frederick, Md. 550 A5 182
Cullendale, Ouachita, Ark. (part of Camden) D4 170
Culleoka, Maury, Tenn. 300 C5 190
Cullera, Sp. 15,005 C6 298
Cullion, N.Ire. G5 272
Cullison, Pratt, Kans. 129 E5 144
Cullman, Cullman, Ala. 10,883 A3 168
Cullman, co., Ala. 45,572 A3 168
Culloden, Monroe, Ga. 260 D2 176
Culloden, Cabell, W.Va. 700 *C2 194
Cullom, Livingston, Ill. 555 C5 138
Cullomburg, Choctaw, Ala. 300 *D1 168
Cullowhee, Jackson, N.C. 1,500 B2 186
Culmore, Fairfax, Va. 1,700 *B7 192
Culp Creek, Lane, Oreg. 100 D4 96
Culpeper, Van Buren, Ark. B4 170
Culpeper, Culpeper, Va. 2,412 B6 192
Culpeper, co., Va. 15,088 B7 192
Culver, Marshall, Ind. 1,558 A3 140
Culver, Ottawa, Kans. 200 D6 144
Culver, Jefferson, Oreg. 301 C5 96
Culver, point, Austl. E4 432
Culver City, Los Angeles, Calif. 32,163 C5 94
Culvers, lake, N.J. A3 210
Culzean, bay, Scot. F8 272
Cumaná, Ven. 64,000 A6 240
Cumberland, B.C., Can. 1,039 F10 52
Cumberland, Marion, Ind. 872 C4 140
D5
Cumberland, Cass, Iowa 425 C3 142
Cumberland, Harlan, Ky. 4,271 D8 178
Cumberland, see Cumberland Center, Maine
Cumberland, Allegany, Md. 33,415 A2 182
Cumberland, Webster, Miss. 145 B3 184
Cumberland, Cumberland, N.J. E3 210
Cumberland, Cumberland, N.C. 500 B7 186
Cumberland, Guernsey, Ohio 493 C5 156
Cumberland, Marshall, Okla. 250 D7 128
Cumberland, Providence, R.I. 8,800 (18,792▲) B3 216
Cumberland, Cumberland, Va. 250 C6 192
Cumberland, King, Wash. 160 D3 98
Cumberland, Barron, Wis. 1,860 C1 160
Cumberland, co., N.S., Can. 39,598 D5 70
Cumberland, co., Eng. 285,900 G9 272
Cumberland, co., Ill. 9,936 D5 138
Cumberland, co., Ky. 7,835 D5 178
Cumberland, co., Maine 182,751 E2 204
Cumberland, co., N.J. 106,850 E2 210
Cumberland, co., N.C. 148,418 B7 186
Cumberland, co., Pa. 124,816 C4 214
Cumberland, co., Tenn. 19,135 C6 190
Cumberland, co., Va. 6,360 C6 192
Cumberland, gap, Ky. D7 178
Cumberland, isl., Ga. F5 176
Cumberland, lake, Ky. D5 178
Cumberland, lake, Sask., Can. C6 58
Cumberland, mtn., Ky., Tenn., Va. D7 178
B7 190
D1 192
Cumberland, pen., N.W.Ter., Can. D12 48
Cumberland, plat., Ala., Ky., Tenn. A3 168
D6 178
C6 190
Cumberland, riv., Ky., Tenn. D5 178
B6 190
Cumberland, sound, N.W.Ter., Can. D12 48
Cumberland Center (Cumberland), Cumberland, Maine 600 (2,765▲) E5 204
Cumberland City, Stewart, Tenn. 314 B4 190
Cumberland Foreside, Cumberland, Maine 600 *E5 204
Cumberland Furnace, Dickson, Tenn. 250 B4 190
Cumberland Gap, Claiborne, Tenn. 291 B8 190
Cumberland Gap, natl. hist. park, Va. D1 192
Cumberland Hill, Providence, R.I. B3 216
Cumbres, pass, Colo. E4 106
Cumbrian, mts., Eng. G9 273
Cuming, co., Nebr. 12,435 C9 152
Cummaquid, Barnstable, Mass. 95 C7 206
Cumming, Forsyth, Ga. 1,561 B2 176
Cumming, Warren, Iowa 148 *C4 142
Cummings, Traill, N.Dak. 51 C8 154
Cummings, Hampton, S.C. 200 F6 188
Cummington, Hampshire, Mass. 200 (550▲) B2 206
Cumpas, Mex. 2,314 A4 224
Cumra, Tur. 6,589 C5 307
Cunard, Fayette, W.Va. 450 D7 194
Cunaviche, Ven. C5 240
Cunco, Chile 2,728 C1 252
Cuncumen, Chile B1 252
Cundinamarca, dept., Col. 1,840,890 B2 244
Cundys Harbor, Cumberland, Maine 125 E6 204
Cunene, riv., S.W.Afr. C2 420
Cuneo, It. 26,600 C1 302
Cuneo, prov., It. 570,300 *C1 302
Cunnamulla, Austl. 1,955 D9 432
Cunningham, Kingman, Kans. 618 E5 144
Cunningham, Carlisle, Ky. 300 D2 178
Cunningham, Montgomery, Tenn. 40 B4 190
Cupar, Sask., Can. 519 E5 58
Cupar, Scot. 5,700 E10 272
Cupertino, Santa Clara, Calif. 3,664 *D2 94
Cuprum, Adams, Idaho 20 D2 108
Curaçá, Braz. 1,046 B3 258
Curaçao Island, Neth. poss., Neth.W.I. B5 236
Curacautin, Chile 9,201 C1 252
Curacó, riv., Arg. C2 252
Curañilahue, Chile 3,995 C1 252
Curaray, riv., Ec. A2 245
Curaray, riv., Peru A3 245
Curataquiche, Ven. B6 240
Curdsville, Daviess, Ky. 175 C3 178
Curepto, Chile 1,739 C1 252
Curiapo, Ven. 403 B8 240
Curicó, Chile 26,773 C1 252
Curicó, prov., Chile 89,432 D3 250
Curitiba, Braz. 138,178 K7 257
Curitibanos, Braz. 2,059 K6 257
Curlew, Palo Alto, Iowa 134 B3 142
Curlew, Ferry, Wash. 100 A8 98
Curlew, lake, Wash. A8 98
Curling (part of Corner Brook), Newf., Can. F6 72
Currais Novos, Braz. 5,179 B3 258
Curran, Ont., Can. 225 O26 64
Curran, Alcona, Mich. 50 E8 146
Currans, Ire. I3 273
Currant, Nye, Nev. 25 E6 112
Currant, creek, Colo. D5 106
Curreeny, Ire. I4 273
Current, riv., Ark., Mo. A6 170
D6 150
Currie, Murray, Minn. 438 G3 148
Currie, Elko, Nev. 25 C7 112
Currituck, Currituck, N.C. 250 A9 186
Currituck, co., N.C. 6,601 A9 186
Curry, Alsk. 183 C7 84
F11
Curry, Twin Falls, Idaho *G4 108
Curry, co., N.Mex. 32,691 D7 126
Curry, co., Oreg. 13,983 E2 96
Curryville, Pike, Mo. 287 B6 150
Curtea de Argeș, Rom. 10,764 B3 321
Curtice, Ottawa, Ohio 475 A1 156
A3
Curtici, Rom. 8,050 A1 321
Curtin, Douglas, Oreg. 40 D3 96
Curtis, Clark, Ark. D3 170
Curtis, Mackinac, Mich. C6 146
Curtis, Frontier, Nebr. 868 D5 152
Curtis, Woodward, Okla. 25 B4 128
Curtis, isl., Austl. C10 432
Curtiss, Clark, Wis. 147 D3 160
Curtisville, Allegheny, Pa. 1,376 A4 214
C2
Curuá, riv., Braz. G6 256
Ćurug, Yugo. 8,466 B4 316
Curuguaty, Par. D5 247
Curumiquara, pt., Braz. A3 258
Curupira, mts., Ven. F6 240
Curuzú Cuatia, Arg. 15,440 A4 252
Curve, Lauderdale, Tenn. 40 C2 190
Curvelo, Braz. 13,633 D2 258
Curwensville, Clearfield, Pa. 3,231 C3 214
Cusco, Peru 64,100 C3 245
Cusco, dept., Peru 749,903 C3 245
Cushendun, N.Ire. 504 F6 272
Cushing, Woodbury, Iowa 261 B2 142
Cushing, Knox, Maine 130 (479▲) D3 204
Cushing, Essex, Mass. 385 A6 206
Cushing, Howard, Nebr. 56 C7 152
Cushing, Payne, Okla. 8,619 C7 128
Cushman, Independence, Ark. 241 B5 170
Cushman, Hampshire, Mass. 250 B2 206
Cushman, Golden Valley, Mont. 47 D7 110
Cushman, Lane, Oreg. 150 D2 96
Cushman, mtn., N.H. D3 208
Cushman, res., Wash. B3 98
Cusick, Pend Oreille, Wash. 299 A9 98
Cusihuiráchic, Mex. 380 B4 224
Cusset, Fr. 10,405 D5 278
Cusseta, Chambers, Ala. 300 C4 168
Cusseta, Chattahoochee, Ga. 768 D2 176
Custer, Breckinridge, Ky. 650 C4 178
Custer, Mason, Mich. 365 F5 146
Custer, Yellowstone, Mont. 275 D9 110
Custer, Custer, Okla. 448 C5 128
Custer, Custer, S.Dak. 2,105 D2 158
Custer, Whatcom, Wash. 400 A4 98
Custer, co., Colo. 1,305 D5 106
Custer, co., Idaho 2,996 E4 108
Custer, co., Mont. 13,227 D11 110
Custer, co., Nebr. 16,517 C6 152
Custer, co., Okla. 21,040 C4 128
Custer, co., S.Dak. 4,906 D2 158
Custer, peak, S.Dak. C2 158
Custer Battlefield, natl. mon., Mont. E9 110
Cut Bank, Glacier, Mont. 4,539 B4 110
Cutbank, riv., Alta., Can. C3 54
Cutchogue, Suffolk, N.Y. 950 D5 212
Cutervo, Peru 3,481 B2 245
Cuthbert, Randolph, Ga. 4,300 E2 176
Cut Knife, Sask., Can. 453 D3 58
Cutler, Tulare, Calif. 2,191 *D4 94
Cutler, Perry, Ill. 445 *E4 138
Cutler, Carroll, Ind. 200 B3 140
Cutler, Washington, Maine 200 (654▲) D5 204
Cutler City, Lincoln, Oreg. 525 C2 96
Cutler Ridge, Dade, Fla. 7,005 *F10 174
Cut Off, Lafourche, La. (part of New Orleans) E5 180
Cutshin, Leslie, Ky. 450 C7 178
Cuttack, India 102,505 D5 366
Cutten, Humboldt, Calif. 1,572 B1 94
Cutter, Sierra, N.Mex. 20 E4 126
Cut Throat, isl., Newf., Can. C7 72
Cuttingsville, Rutland, Vt. 100 E3 218
Cuttyhunk, isl., Mass. D6 206
Cuvo, riv., Ang. B2 420
Cuxhaven, Ger. 44,400 B3 286
Cuyahoga, co., Ohio 1,647,895 A5 156
Cuyahoga, riv., Ohio A5 156
Cuyahoga Falls, Summit, Ohio 47,922 A5 156
Cuyama, riv., Calif. E4 94
Cuyamaca, peak, Calif. F5 94
Cuyamungue, Santa Fe, N.Mex. 120 G7 126
Cuyo, is., Phil. B6 358
Cuyuna, Crow Wing, Minn. 86 E5 148
Cuyuni, riv., Br.Gu. D5 256
Cyclades, see Kikládhes, prov., Grc.
Cyclades, is., Grc. C5 306
Cygnet, Wood, Ohio 593 A3 156
Cylinder, Palo Alto, Iowa 161 A3 142
Cynthiana, Posey, Ind. 663 D2 140
Cynthiana, Harrison, Ky. 5,641 B6 178
Cypress, Hale, Ala. 150 C2 168
Cypress, Orange, Calif. 1,753 C5 94
Cypress, Jackson, Fla. 260 A5 174
Cypress, Johnson, Ill. 264 F4 138
Cypress, Natchitoches, La. 200 C2 180
Cypress, bayou, Ark. B4 170
Cypress, hills, Sask., Can. F3 58
Cypress, lake, Fla. C9 174
Cypress, lake, Sask., Can. F3 58
Cypress Creek, Duplin, N.C. C8 186
Cypress Hills, prov. park, Sask., Can. F3 58
Cypress Inn, Wayne, Tenn. 250 C4 190
Cypress River, Man., Can. 430 F3 60
Cyprus, country, Asia 528,618 F5 340
307
Cyr (Plantation of), Aroostook, Maine (233▲) *A5 204
Cyrenaica (Barqah), prov., Libya B4 394
Cyrene, Decatur, Ga. 200 F2 176
Cyril, Caddo, Okla. 1,284 D5 128
Cyrus, Pope, Minn. 362 F3 148
Cythera, see Kithira, isl., Grc.
Czar, Alta., Can. 153 D7 54
Czarnków, Pol. 4,394 B3 325
Czechoslovakia, country, Eur. 13,538,000 D6 266
324
Czersk, Pol. 7,092 B3 325
Częstochowa, Pol. 148,000 C4 325
Czizek, Idaho, Idaho D3 108
Cztuchów, Pol. 3,711 B3 325

D

Daam Top, mtn., Neth. N.Gui. E9 359
Daaquam, Que., Can. 230 R14 66
Daarburuk, Som. D5 398
Dabā, Tr. Coast B6 383
Dabakala, I.C. 1,600 E4 408
Dabaro, Som. D6 398
Dabdab, Libya B2 394
Dabeiba, Col. 2,832 B1 244
Dáblice, Czech. 5,378 *A2 324
Dabney, Van Buren, Ark. B4 170
Dabney, Logan, W.Va. 200 *D3 194
Dabneys, Louisa, Va. 15 C7 192
Dabola, Guinea 3,800 D2 408
Dabra-Berhān, Eth. D4 398
Dabra-Mārk'os, Eth. C4 398
Dabra-Tābor, Eth. C4 398
Dąbrowa, Pol. 4,520 C5 325
Dąbrowa Górnicza, Pol. 41,000 C4 325
Dacca, Pak. 276,033 (*411,279) L17 375
Dachau, Ger. 25,700 D4 286
Dacoma, Woods, Okla. 219 B5 128
Dacono, Weld, Colo. 302 B6 106
Da Costa, Atlantic, N.J. D3 210
Dacula, Gwinnett, Ga. 440 C3 176
Dacura, Nic. C6 228
Dacusville, Pickens, S.C. 175 B3 188
Dadar, Eth. D5 398
Daday, Tur. 1,398 A5 307
Daddy, creek, Tenn. C7 190
Dade, Nicholas, W.Va. 50 C7 194
Dade, co., Fla. 935,047 F10 174
Dade, co., Ga. 8,666 B1 176
Dade, co., Mo. 7,577 D4 150
Dade City, Pasco, Fla. 4,759 C8 174
Dadeville, Tallapoosa, Ala. 2,940 C4 168
Dadeville, Dade, Mo. 142 D4 150
Dadu, Pak. 13,716 F5 375
Dafoe, Sask., Can. 95 E5 58
Dafoe, riv., Man., Can. C5 60
Dagahabur, Eth. D5 398
Dagana, Sen. 4,100 C1 408
Daggett, San Bernardino, Calif. 800 E5 94
Daggett, Menominee, Mich. 296 D4 146
Daggett, co., Utah 1,164 C6 114
Dagmar, Sheridan, Mont. 61 B12 110
Dagsboro, Sussex, Del. 477 F4 172
Dahab, Eg., U.A.R. B3 395
Dahana, des., Sau.Ar. C5 383
Dahān-i-Kāshān, Afg. 5,000 B4 374
Dahan-i-Kusnak, Afg. 5,000 B2 374
Dahlak, arch., Afr. B5 398
Dahlgren, Hamilton, Ill. 480 E5 138
Dahlgren, King George, Va. 475 B7 192
Dahlia, Guadalupe, N.Mex. 25 C5 126
Dahlonega, Lumpkin, Ga. 2,604 B3 176
Dahme, Ger. 6,391 C5 286

Dahomey, country, Afr.	1,725,000	E7	388
			409
Daigle, Aroostook, Maine	150	A4	204
Daigleville, Terrebonne, La.	5,906	*E5	180
Dailey, Logan, Colo.	10	B8	106
Dailey, Randolph, W.Va.	800	C5	194
Daimiel, Sp.	19,759	C5	298
Daingerfield, Morris, Tex.	3,133	C8	130
Daiō, cape, Jap.		G6	354
Dairût, Eg., U.A.R.	14,001	B3	395
	(*32,000)		
Dairy, Klamath, Oreg.	50	E5	96
Dairyland, Orange, Calif.	622	*F5	94
Dairyland, Douglas, Wis.	25	B1	160
Dairy Valley, Los Angeles, Calif.	3,508	C5	94
Daisetta, Liberty, Tex.	1,500	D8	130
Daisy, Pike, Ark.	86	C3	170
Daisy, Evans, Ga.	229	*D5	176
Daisy, Atoka, Okla.	25	D8	128
Daisy, Hamilton, Tenn.	1,508	C6	190
		E8	
Daisy, Stevens, Wash.	30	A8	98
Daisy-Vestry, Jackson, Miss.	100	E4	184
Dajabón, Dom.Rep.	1,691	C9	233
Dajarra, Austl.	199	C7	432
Dakar, Sen.	230,887	D1	408
Dakhla, oasis, Eg., U.A.R.		B2	395
Dakoro, Niger		D6	409
Dakota, Winona, Minn.	339	H7	148
Dakota, Marion, W.Va.	750	*B4	194
Dakota, co., Minn.	78,303	G5	148
Dakota, co., Nebr.	12,168	B9	152
Dakota City, Humboldt, Iowa	706	B3	142
Dakota City, Dakota, Nebr.	928	B9	152
Dakwa, Con.L.		B4	414
Dalaba, Guinea		D2	408
Dala-Jarna, Swe.		F6	291
Dalälven, riv., Swe.		A5	292
Dalark, Dallas, Ark.	123	C4	170
Dalarna, prov., Swe.	280,738	*F6	291
Dalarö, Swe.	595	B9	292
Dalat, Viet.	25,041	E6	362
Dalay, riv., China		A8	348
Dalbandin, Pak.		E4	375
Dalbeattie, Scot.	3,400	G9	272
Dalbosjön Vänern, lake, Swe.		C3	292
Dalby, Austl.	6,900	D10	432
Dalby, Madison, Idaho	9	*F7	108
Dalbyn, Swe.		A6	292
Dalcour, Plaquemines, La.		C7	180
Dale, Spencer, Ind.	900	D3	140
Dale, Guthrie, Iowa	850	C3	142
Dale, Pottawatomie, Okla.	400	C6	128
Dale, Grant, Oreg.	5	C8	96
Dale, Cambria, Pa.	2,807	*C3	214
Dale, Beaufort, S.C.	160	F7	188
Dale, Outagamie, Wis.	350	D5	160
Dale, co., Ala.	31,066	D4	168
Dale Hollow, Clay, Tenn.	15	*B6	190
Dale Hollow, lake, Ky., Tenn.		D5	178
		B6	190
Dalemead, Alta., Can.	50	E6	54
Daleville, Dale, Ala.	693	D4	168
Daleville, Delaware, Ind.	1,548	B4	140
Daleville, Lauderdale, Miss.	125	C4	184
Dalhart, Dallam and Hartley, Tex.	5,160	A4	130
Dalhousie, N.B., Can.	5,468	A3	70
Dalhousie, India		B2	368
Dalhousie, isl., India		J9	366
Dalhousie Junction, N.B., Can.	125	A3	70
Dalias, Sp.	3,540	D5	298
Daliburgh, Scot.		D5	272
Daliyat el Karmil, Isr.	2,769	B6	382
Dalkeith, Scot.	9,100	F9	272
Dalkena, Pend Oreille, Wash.	30	A9	98
Dall, isl., Alsk.		K14	84
Dall, mtn., Alsk.		F10	84
Dallam, co., Tex.	6,302	A4	130
Dallas, Paulding, Ga.	2,065	C2	176
Dallas, Marion, Iowa	392	C4	142
Dallas, Franklin, Maine	50	D2	204
	(77▲)		
Dallas, Gaston, N.C.	3,270	B4	186
Dallas, Polk, Oreg.	5,072	C3	96
Dallas, Luzerne, Pa.	2,586	A5	214
		B6	
Dallas, Gregory, S.Dak.	212	D6	158
Dallas, Dallas, Tex.	679,684	B8	130
	(*1,022,300)	C7	
Dallas, Marshall, W.Va.	135	B2	194
Dallas, Barron, Wis.	401	C2	160
Dallas, co., Ala.	56,667	C2	168
Dallas, co., Ark.	10,522	D4	170
Dallas, co., Iowa	24,123	C3	142
Dallas, co., Mo.	9,314	D4	150
Dallas, co., Tex.	951,527	C7	130
Dallas Center, Dallas, Iowa	1,083	C4	142
Dallas City, Hancock, Ill.	1,276	C2	138
Dallas Mills, Madison, Ala.		A3	168
Dallas Mine, Dallas, Iowa	165	A7	142
Dallastown, York, Pa.	3,615	D5	214
Dalles, dam, Oreg.		B5	96
Dalmacio Vélez, Arg.		B3	252
Dalmally, Scot.	876	E8	272
Dalmatia, reg., Yugo.		C2	316
Dalmellington, Scot.	4,702	F8	272
Dalmeny, Sask., Can.	352	D4	58
Dalnyaya, Sov.Un.		E16	329
Daloa, I.C.	5,100	E3	408
Dalroy, Alta., Can.	50	E6	54
Dalry, Scot.	6,764	F8	272
Dalrymple, mtn., Austl.		C9	432
Dalsland, reg., Swe.	61,593	*G5	291
Dals Långed, Swe.		C3	292
Dalton, Randolph, Ark.	25	A5	170
Dalton, Whitfield, Ga.	17,868	B2	176
Dalton, Sumner, Kans.	35	*E6	144
Dalton, Berkshire, Mass.	6,436	B1	206
Dalton, Otter Tail, Minn.	239	E3	148
Dalton, Chariton, Mo.	197	B5	150
Dalton, Cheyenne, Nebr.	503	C3	152
Dalton, Coos, N.H.	50	C3	208
	(567▲)		
Dalton, Livingston, N.Y.	500	C4	212
Dalton, Wayne, Ohio	1,067	B5	156
Dalton, Lackawanna, Pa.	1,227	B6	214
Dalton, Green Lake, Wis.	350	E4	160
Dalton City, Moultrie, Ill.	386	D5	138
Daltonganj, India	13,943	D4	368
Dalwhinnie, Scot.		E8	272
Daly, riv., Austl.		A6	432
Daly City, San Mateo, Calif.	44,791	B5	94
Daly Waters, Austl.		B6	432
Dalzell, Bureau, Ill.	496	*B4	138
Dalzell, Sumter, S.C.	80	C8	188
Dam, Sud.		B3	398
		C3	
Dam, Sur.		E6	256
Dama, is., Viet.		E5	362
Damanhûr, Eg., U.A.R.	84,352	A3	395
Damão (Port. India), poss., Asia	82,800	D2	366
		G9	340
Damar, Rooks, Kans.	361	C4	144
Damar, isl., Indon.		F7	359
Damara, Cen.Afr.Rep.		E8	409
Damaraland, reg., S.W.Afr.		*D3	420
Damariscotta, Lincoln, Maine	800	D3	204
	(1,093▲)		
Damariscotta, lake, Maine		D3	204
Damas, pass, Arg.		B1	252
Damascus, Faulkner and Van Buren, Ark.	400	B4	170
Damascus, Early, Ga.	297	E2	176
Damascus, Montgomery, Md.	1,500	B5	182
Damascus (Esh Sham), Syr., U.A.R.	408,774	C2	378
Damascus, Washington, Va.	1,485	D3	192
Damaturu, Nig.	2,379	D7	409
Damba, Ang.	1,367	A3	420
Dambidolo, Eth.		D3	398
Dâmbovița, riv., Rom.		B3	321
D'Ambre, cape, Malag.		B9	421
Dames Quarter, Somerset, Md.	330	D8	182
Dam Gamad, Sud.		C2	398
Dāmghān, Iran	12,235	B4	379
Damietta, see Dumiât, Eg., U.A.R.			
Damietta, riv. mouth, Eg., U.A.R.		D6	395
Damietta Branch, riv., Eg., U.A.R.		D2	382
Damodar, riv., India		I9	366
Damoh, India		E2	368
Damongo, Ghana		E4	408
Dampier, arch., Austl.		C3	432
Dampier, strait, Neth.N.Gui.		D8	359
Damyanovka, Sov.Un.		B7	336
Dan, riv., Va.		D5	192
Dana, Sask., Can.	68	D5	58
Dana, Vermillion, Ind.	811	C2	140
Dana, Greene, Iowa	123	B3	142
Dana, Henderson, N.C.	200	B3	186
Danakil, depression, Eth.		C5	398
Danané, I.C.		E3	408
Dana Point, Orange, Calif.	1,186	*F5	94
Danburg, Wilkes, Ga.	108	C4	176
Danbury, Fairfield, Conn.	22,928	D2	202
	(39,382▲)		
Danbury, Woodbury, Iowa	510	B2	142
Danbury, Red Willow, Nebr.	185	D5	152
Danbury, Merrimack, N.H.	200	D3	208
	(435▲)		
Danbury, Stokes, N.C.	175	A5	186
Danbury, Brazoria, Tex.	600	G8	130
Danbury, Burnett, Wis.	300	B1	160
Danby, Rutland, Vt.	250	E3	218
	(891▲)		
Dancy, Pickens, Ala.	150	B1	168
Dancy, Marathon, Wis.	100	D4	160
Dande, riv., Ang.		A2	420
Dandridge, Jefferson, Tenn.	829	B8	190
Dandy, York, Va.	400	A8	192
Dane, Dane, Wis.	394	E4	160
Dane, co., Wis.	222,095	F4	160
Danebo, Lane, Oreg.	900	*C3	96
Danforth, Ont., Can.	450	R22	64
Danforth, Iroquois, Ill.	394	C6	138
Danforth, Washington, Maine	800	C5	204
	(821▲)		
Dänglä, Eth.		C4	398
Dangrek, mts., Thai.		D5	362
Dania, Broward, Fla.	7,065	D6	174
		E10	
Daniel, Sublette, Wyo.	110	D2	116
Daniel, mtn., Wash.		B5	98
Daniel Boone, Hopkins, Ky.	300	C3	178
Daniels, Howard, Md.	750	B6	182
Daniels, Lincoln, N.C.	640	*B4	186
Daniels, Raleigh, W.Va.	950	*D3	194
Daniels, co., Mont.	3,755	B11	110
Daniel's Harbour, Newf., Can.	250	E7	72
Danielson, Windham, Conn.	4,642	B8	202
Danielsville, Madison, Ga.	362	B3	176
Danieltown, Brunswick, Va.	40	D7	192
Danilov, Sov.Un.	16,600	A2	336
Danilov Grad, Yugo.	1,373	C4	316
Danjo, isl., Jap.		H2	354
Dankhar Gompa, India		B2	368
Danlí, Hond.	4,207	C4	228
Dannebrog, Howard, Nebr.	277	C7	152
Dannemora, Clinton, N.Y.	4,835	A8	212
Dannenberg, Ger.	3,327	B4	286
Danner, Malheur, Oreg.		E9	96
Dans, mtn., Md.		A2	182
Dansville, Ingham, Mich.	453	*G7	146
Dansville, Livingston, N.Y.	5,460	C4	212
Dante, Som.		C7	398
Dante, Charles Mix, S.Dak.	102	D7	158
Dante, Knox, Tenn.	600	E9	190
Dante, Russell, Va.	1,436	D2	192
Danube, Renville, Minn.	494	G3	148
Danube, riv., Eur.		D6	266
Danube, riv. mouths, Eur.		D7	266
Danubyu, Bur.		C2	362
Danvers, McLean, Ill.	783	C4	138
Danvers, Essex, Mass.	21,926	A6	206
		C3	
Danvers, Swift, Minn.	132	F3	148
Danvers, Fergus, Mont.	23	C7	110
Dannevirke, N.Z.	5,294	D6	437
Danville, Morgan, Ala.	300	A2	168
Danville, Yell, Ark.	955	B3	170
Danville, Contra Costa, Calif.	3,585	A6	94
Danville, Que., Can.	2,296	S12	66
Danville, Twiggs and Wilkinson, Ga.	264	D3	176
Danville, Vermilion, Ill.	41,856	C6	138
Danville, Hendricks, Ind.	3,287	C3	140
Danville, Des Moines, Iowa	579	D6	142
Danville, Harper, Kans.	118	E6	144
Danville, Boyle, Ky.	9,010	C6	178
Danville, Bienville, La.	75	B3	180
Danville, Androscoggin, Maine		D5	204
Danville, Rockingham, N.H.	175	F4	208
	(605▲)		
Danville, Knox, Ohio	926	B4	156
Danville, Montour, Pa.	6,889	C5	214
Danville, Caledonia, Vt.	300	C4	218
	(1,368▲)		
Danville (Independent City), Va.	46,577	D5	192
Danville, Ferry, Wash.	80	A8	98
Danville, Boone, W.Va.	507	C3	194
		D5	
Danville East (Mechanicsville), Montour, Pa.	1,758	*B5	214
Danzig, see Gdansk, Pol.			
Danzig, gulf, Pol.		A4	325
Daosa, India		D2	368
Daphne, Baldwin, Ala.	1,527	E2	168
Dapp, Alta., Can.	130	C6	54
Daqq-i-Muhmudabad, salt lake, Iran		C5	379
Daqq-i-Pitargun, lake, Iran		C5	379
Dārāb, Iran	7,403	D4	379
Darabani, Rom.	11,379	A4	321
Daraj, Libya		A2	394
Darany, Sov.Un.		D15	329
Darasun, Sov.Un.	18,000	D13	329
Darawa, Eg., U.A.R.	9,322	D2	382
Darbhanga, India	84,816	D4	368
D'Arbonne, Union, La.		B3	180
D'Arbonne, bayou, La.		B3	180
Darbun, Walthall, Miss.	300	D2	184
Darby, Ravalli, Mont.	398	D2	110
Darby, Delaware, Pa.	14,059	A6	214
		D6	
Darby, creek, Ohio		C3	156
Darbydale, Franklin, Ohio	740	*C3	156
Dar Chebika, Mor.		C1	402
D'Arcy Station, Sask., Can.	201	E3	58
Dardanelle, Yell, Ark.	2,098	B3	170
Darden, Henderson, Tenn.	250	C3	190
Dare, co., N.C.	5,936	B10	186
Darende, Tur.	6,485	B7	307
Dar es Salaam, Tan.	128,742	D6	414
Daretown, Salem, N.J.	75	D2	210
Darfur, Watonwan, Minn.	191	G4	148
Darfur, reg., Sud.	1,328,765	C2	398
Dargai, Pak.		B8	375
Dargan, Washington, Md.	150	B4	182
Dargan-Ata, Sov.Un.		D6	336
Dargaville, N.Z.	3,306	A4	437
Darien (Talien), China	595,000	F10	348
Darien, Fairfield, Conn.	18,437	E2	202
Darien, McIntosh, Ga.	1,569	E5	176
Darien, Dent, Mo.	100	D6	150
Darien, Walworth, Wis.	805	F5	160
Darien, gulf, Col.		B1	244
Darien, mts., Pan.		F9	228
Dariense, mts., Nic.		D5	228
Darjeeling, India	33,605	D5	368
Darke, co., Ohio	45,612	B2	156
Darkharbor, Waldo, Maine	100	D4	204
Darling, Quitman, Miss.	250	A2	184
Darling, lake, N.Dak.		B4	154
Darling, range, Austl.		E3	432
Darling, riv., Austl.		E8	432
Darlington, Eng.	83,400	G11	273
Darlington, Butte, Idaho	10	F5	108
Darlington, Montgomery, Ind.	668	B3	140
Darlington, Harford, Md.	250	A7	182
Darlington, Gentry, Mo.	169	A3	150
Darlington, Darlington, S.C.	6,710	C9	188
Darlington, Lafayette, Wis.	2,349	F3	160
Darlington, co., S.C.	52,928	C9	188
Darlove, Washington, Miss.	100	B2	184
Darłowo, Pol.	5,262	A3	325
Dar Mazār, Iran		D4	379
Darmody, Sask., Can.	39	E4	58
Darmstadt, Ger.	124,400	D3	286
Darnah (Derna), Libya	15,891	A4	394
Darnell, West Carroll, La.	65	B4	180
Darnestown, Montgomery, Md.	150	B5	182
Daroca, Sp.	3,786	B6	298
Darr, Dawson, Nebr.	11	*D6	152
Darrington, Snohomish, Wash.	1,272	A5	98
Darrow, Ascension, La.	400	B5	180
Dartford, Spokane, Wash.	30	D8	98
Dartmouth, N.S., Can.	21,093	E6	70
Dartmouth, Eng.	6,000	K9	273
Dartmouth, Bristol, Mass.	700	C5	206
	(14,607▲)		
Dartry, mts., Ire.		G4	273
Daruvar, Yugo.	5,367	B3	316
Darvel, bay, N.Bor.		D5	358
Darwin, Austl.	9,395	A6	432
Darwin, Inyo, Calif.	450	D5	94
Darwin, Meeker, Minn.	273	*F4	148
Daryacheh-i-Namakzar, salt lake, Afg., Iran		C1	374
Darya yi Namak, lake, Iran		B3	379
Dase, Eth.	40,000	C4	398
Dasher, Lowndes, Ga.	200	F3	176
Dash Point, Pierce, Wash.	300	D2	98
Dasht, riv., Pak.		G3	375
Dasht-i-Daqq-i-Tundī, desp Afg.		C1	374
Dasht-i-Kavir, des., Iran		B3	379
Dasht-i-Lut, plain, Iran		C4	379
Dasht-i-Margo, des., Afg.		D2	374
Dashwood, Ont., Can.	560	Q19	64
Dassel, Meeker, Minn.	863	F4	148
Date, Yavapai, Ariz.	25	D3	124
Dateland, Yuma, Ariz.	30	F2	124
Datia, India		D2	368
Datil, Catron, N.Mex.	50	D3	126
Datto, Clay, Ark.	167	A6	170
Datu, cape, Indon., Sar.		D3	358
Dauchite, bayou, La.		B2	180
Daudnagar, India		D4	368
Daufuskie Island, Beaufort, S.C.	225	G7	188
Daufuskie, isl., S.C.		G7	188
Daugava, riv., Sov.Un.		D5	328
Daugavpils, Sov.Un.	65,000	E6	332
Daulatābād, Afg.	5,000	C2	374
Däulat Yār, Afg.	5,000	B3	374
Daule, Ec.	4,501	A2	245
Dauphin, Man., Can.	6,190	E2	60
		F5	
Dauphin, co., Pa.	220,255	C5	214
Dauphin, isl., Ala.		E1	168
Dauphin, lake, Man., Can.		E3	60
Dauphin, riv., Man., Can.		E3	60
Dauphiné, former prov., Fr.	1,016,000	E6	278
Dauphin Island, Mobile, Ala.	250	E1	168
Daus, Sequatchie, Tenn.	250	C6	190
Davant, Plaquemines, La.	415	C8	180
		E6	
Davao, Phil.	47,486	C7	358
Davao, gulf, Phil.		C7	358
Dävar Panāh, Iran		D6	379
Daveluyville, Que., Can.	591	R12	66
Davenport, Santa Cruz, Calif.	500	D2	94
Davenport, Polk, Fla.	1,209	C9	174
Davenport, Scott, Iowa	88,981	C7	142
	(*260,300)	D7	
Davenport, Thayer, Nebr.	416	D8	152
Davenport, Delaware, N.Y.	260	C7	212
Davenport, Cass, N.Dak.	143	D8	154
Davenport, Lincoln, Okla.	813	C7	128
Davenport, Lincoln, Wash.	1,494	B8	98
Davey, Lancaster, Nebr.	121	E2	152
David, Floyd, Ky.	800	C8	178
David, Pan.	14,847	F6	228
David City, Butler, Nebr.	2,304	C8	152
David-Gorodok, Sov.Un.		F6	332
Davidson, Sask., Can.	851	E4	58
Davidson, Mecklenburg, N.C.	2,573	B5	186
Davidson, Tillman, Okla.	429	D4	128
Davidson, Fentress, Tenn.	200	B6	190
Davidson, co., N.C.	79,493	B5	186
Davidson, co., Tenn.	399,743	B5	190
Davie, Broward, Fla.	950	D6	174
		E10	
Davie, co., N.C.	16,728	B5	186
Daviess, co., Ind.	26,636	D2	140
Daviess, co., Ky.	70,588	C3	178
Daviess, co., Mo.	9,502	B3	150
Davin, Sask., Can.	96	E5	58
Davis, Yolo, Calif.	8,910	C3	94
Davis, New Castle, Del.		B2	172
Davis, Stephenson, Ill.	434	A4	138
Davis, Carteret, N.C.	500	C9	186
Davis, Murray, Okla.	2,203	D6	128
Davis, Turner, S.Dak.	124	D9	158
Davis, Tucker, W.Va.	898	B5	194
Davis, co., Iowa	9,199	D5	142
Davis, co., Utah	64,760	C3	114
Davis, creek, W.Va.		C6	194
Davis, dam, Ariz.		C1	124
Davis, isl., Fla.		C6	174
Davis, lake, Oreg.		D5	96
Davis, mtn., Pa.		D2	214
Davis, mts., Tex.		D3	130
Davis, strait, Can.		D13	48
Davisboro, Washington, Ga.	417	D4	176
Davis City, Decatur, Iowa	346	D4	142
Davis Dam, Mohave, Ariz.	150	C1	124
Davis Inlet, Newf., Can.	120	D9	72
Davison, Genesee, Mich.	3,761	F8	146
Davison, co., S.Dak.	16,681	D7	158
Davis Station, Clarendon, S.C.	60	D8	188
Daviston, Tallapoosa, Ala.	129	B4	168
Davisville, Barnstable, Mass.	250	C6	206
Davisville, Washington, R.I.	1,800	C3	216
Davle, Czech.	1,490	B2	324
Davos, Switz.	10,700	B5	312
Davy, McDowell, W.Va.	1,331	D3	194
Däwä, riv., Eth.		E4	398
Dawasir, wadi, Sau.Ar.		C3	383
Dawes, Kanawha, W.Va.	400	*C3	194
Dawes, co., Nebr.	9,536	B2	152
Dawn, Livingston, Mo.	200	B4	150
Dawros, head, Ire.		G4	272
Dawson, Yukon, Can.	851	E5	48
Dawson, Terrell, Ga.	5,062	E2	176
Dawson, Dallas, Iowa	257	C3	142
Dawson, Lac qui Parle, Minn.	1,766	G2	148
Dawson, Richardson, Nebr.	263	D10	152
Dawson, Kidder, N.Dak.	206	D6	154
Dawson, Navarro, Tex.	911	D7	130
Dawson, co., Ga.	3,590	B2	176
Dawson, co., Mont.	12,314	C11	110
Dawson, co., Nebr.	19,405	D6	152
Dawson, co., Tex.	19,185	C4	130
Dawson, bay, Man., Can.		D2	60
Dawson, mtn., B.C., Can.		E14	52
Dawson, riv., Austl.		C9	432
Dawson Creek, B.C., Can.	7,531	C12	52
		F8	
Dawson Springs, Hopkins, Ky.	3,002	C3	178
Dawsonville, Dawson, Ga.	307	B2	176
Dax, Fr.	14,557	F3	278
Day, Lafayette, Fla.	150	A7	174
Day, Carroll, Md.	130	B5	182
Day, co., S.Dak.	10,516	B8	158
Dayang Bunting, isl., Thai.		F3	362
Day Island, Pierce, Wash.	500	*B4	98
Daykin, Jefferson, Nebr.	144	D8	152
Daylight, Warren, Tenn.	20	C6	190
Dayr az Zawr, Syr., U.A.R.	73,805	B4	378
Days Creek, Douglas, Oreg.	225	*E3	96
Daysland, Alta., Can.	499	D6	54
Daysville, Cumberland, Tenn.	100	C7	190
Dayton, Marengo, Ala.	99	C2	168
Dayton, Franklin, Idaho	212	G7	108
Dayton, Tippecanoe, Ind.	700	B3	140
Dayton, Webster, Iowa	820	B3	142
Dayton, Campbell, Ky.	9,050	A8	178
Dayton (Town of), York, Maine	(451▲)	*E2	204
Dayton, Howard, Md.	200	B6	182
Dayton, Hennepin and Wright, Minn.	456	F5	148
		F6	
Dayton, Lake, Mont.	57	C2	110
Dayton, Lyon, Nev.	200	D2	112
Dayton, Middlesex, N.J.	500	C3	210
Dayton, Montgomery, Ohio	262,332	C2	156
	(*648,600)		
Dayton, Yamhill, Oreg.	673	B1	96
		B3	
Dayton, Armstrong, Pa.	769	C2	214
Dayton, Rhea, Tenn.	3,500	C6	190
Dayton, Liberty, Tex.	3,367	D8	130
		F8	
Dayton, Rockingham, Va.	930	B6	192
Dayton, Columbia, Wash.	2,913	C9	98
Dayton, Green, Wis.	100	F4	160
Dayton, Sheridan, Wyo.	333	B5	116

Daytona Beach, Volusia, Fla. 37,395 B9 174
Daytona Beach Shores, Volusia, Fla. 3,741 *B9 174
Dayville, Alsk. 54 C7 84
G11
Dayville, Windham, Conn. 900 B8 202
Dayville, Grant, Oreg. 234 C7 96
Dazey, Barnes, N.Dak. 226 C7 154
Dazgir, Iran B1 379
De Aar, U.S.Afr. 11,075 F4 420
Dead, creek, Vt. C2 218
Dead, lake, Fla. A5 174
Dead, lake, Minn. E3 148
Dead, riv., Maine C2 204
Dead, sea, Isr., Jordan D1 378
Dead Diamond, riv., N.H. B4 208
Dead Indian, peak, Wyo. B3 116
Deadman, creek, Wash. D8 98
Dead Mans, bay, Fla. B7 174
Deadmans, pass, Oreg. *B8 96
Deadmans, pt., Newf., Can. F9 72
Deadwood, Lane, Oreg. 200 C3 96
Deadwood, Lawrence, S.Dak. 3,045 C2 158
Deadwood, res., Idaho E3 108
Deaf Smith, co., Tex. 13,187 B4 130
Deal, Monmouth, N.J. 1,889 C4 210
Deal, isl., Md. D8 182
Deale, Anne Arundel, Md. 526 C6 182
Deal Island, Somerset, Md. 516 D8 182
Dean, Stillwater, Mont. E7 110
Dean (Roach Creek), Scott, Tenn. 50 B7 190
Dean, chan., B.C., Can. D9 52
Dean, riv., B.C., Can. D9 52
Deán Funes, Arg. B3 252
Deans, Middlesex, N.J. 300 C3 210
Deans, Anderson, S.C. 125 C3 188
Dean Spring, Crawford, Ark. B2 170
Deanville, Lewis, W.Va. 175 B4 194
Dearborn, Wayne, Mich. 112,007 B8 146
G8
Dearborn, Platte, Mo. 444 B3 150
Dearborn, co., Ind. 28,674 C5 140
Dearg, mtn., Scot. D8 272
Dearing, McDuffie, Ga. 403 C4 176
Dearing, Montgomery, Kans. 249 E8 144
De Armanville, Calhoun, Ala. 250 *B4 168
Deary, Latah, Idaho 349 C2 108
Dease, strait, N.W.Ter., Can. D8 48
Death, valley, Calif. D5 94
Death Valley, Inyo, Calif. 75 D5 94
Death Valley, natl. mon., Calif. D5 94
Deatsville, Elmore, Ala. 210 C3 168
Deauville, Fr. 5,211 C4 278
Deaver, Big Horn, Wyo. 121 B4 116
De Baca, co., N.Mex. 2,991 D6 126
Debaltsevo, Sov.Un. 33,800 S22 332
Debar, Yugo. 5,520 D5 316
De Bary, Volusia, Fla. 2,362 *C9 174
Debden, Sask., Can. 379 D4 58
Debec, N.B., Can. 145 C2 70
De Beque, Mesa, Colo. 172 C2 106
Dębica, Pol. 19,000 C5 325
Debin, Bul. 3,602 C2 317
Deblois, Washington, Maine 20 (26▲) D4 204
Dębno, Pol. 3,341 B2 325
Debo, lake, Mali C4 408
De Borgia, Mineral, Mont. 100 *C1 110
Deboullie, mtn., Maine B4 204
Debovo, Bul. 2,113 B2 317
Debrecen, Hung. 130,000 B6 320
De Cade, lake, La. E5 180
Decamere, Eth. C4 398
Decatur, Morgan, Ala. 29,217 A3 168
Decatur, Benton, Ark. 415 A2 170
Decatur, De Kalb, Ga. 22,026 B5 176
C2
Decatur, Macon, Ill. 78,004 (*111,300) D5 138
Decatur, Adams, Ind. 8,327 B5 140
Decatur, Decatur, Iowa 203 D4 142
Decatur, Van Buren, Mich. 1,827 G6 146
Decatur, Newton, Miss. 1,340 C3 184
Decatur, Burt, Nebr. 786 B9 152
Decatur, Meigs, Tenn. 681 C7 190
Decatur, Wise, Tex. 3,563 C7 130
Decatur, co., Ga. 25,203 E2 176
Decatur, co., Ind. 20,019 C4 140
Decatur, co., Iowa 10,539 D4 142
Decatur, co., Kans. 5,778 C3 144
Decatur, co., Tenn. 8,324 C3 190
Decatur, lake, Ill. D5 138
Decaturville, Decatur, Tenn. 571 C3 190
Decazeville, Fr. 11,510 E5 278
Deccan, plain, India E3 366
Deception, lake, Sask., Can. B5 58
Deception, mtn., Yukon, Can. D5 48
Decherd, Franklin, Tenn. 1,704 C5 190
Decimal, Man., Can. F5 60
Děčín, Czech. 34,930 A2 324
Decize, Fr. D5 278
Decker, Man., Can. 100 E2 60
Decker, Knox, Ind. 317 D2 140
Decker, Big Horn, Mont. 15 E10 110
Deckers, Douglas, Colo. 50 C5 106
Deckerville, Poinsett, Ark. 27 *B6 170
Deckerville, Sanilac, Mich. 798 F9 146
Declo, Cassia, Idaho 237 G5 108
De Cocksdorp, Neth. 347 A3 282
Decorah, Winneshiek, Iowa 6,435 A6 142
Decota, Kanawha, W.Va. 350 D6 194
Decoto, Alameda, Calif. (part of Union City) B5 94
De Coursey, Kenton, Ky. 250 A8 178
Decoy, Knott, Ky. 300 C7 178
Dededo, Guam 997 C7 436
Dedemsvaart, Neth. 5,800 B5 282
Dedham, Carroll, Iowa 322 C3 142
Dedham, Hancock, Maine 65 (438▲) *D4 204
Dedham, Norfolk, Mass. 23,869 B5 206
D2
Dedinovo, Sov.Un. 4,000 O20 332
Dédougou, Upper Volta 2,700 D4 408
Dedza, Rh.&Nya. 2,325 B6 421
Dee, Hood River, Oreg. 50 B5 96
Dee, riv., Scot. D10 272
Deedsville, Miami, Ind. 120 B3 140
Deemer, Neshoba, Miss. 300 C3 184
Deep, creek, Del. F3 172
Deep, creek, Mont. C4 110
Deep, creek, Utah F3 114
Deep, creek, Wash. D8 98
Deep, entrance, Eniwetok B1 436
Deep, fork, Okla. C7 128
Deep, gap, N.C. A4 186
Deep, inlet, Newf., Can. D10 72
Deep Bay, Rh.&Nya. B6 421
Deep Brook, N.S., Can. 425 E4 70
Deep Creek, Norfolk, Va. 350 A8 192
D8
Deepcreek, Spokane, Wash. 100 D8 98
Deep Creek, lake, Md. A1 182
Deep Creek, range, Utah D2 114
Deepdale, Man., Can. 80 E2 60
Deep Gap, Watauga, N.C. 130 A4 186
Deephaven, Hennepin, Minn. 3,286 F6 148
G5
Deep Red, run, Okla. D5 128
Deep River, Ont., Can. O23 64
Deep River, Middlesex, Conn. 2,166 (2,968▲) D6 202
Deep River, Poweshiek, Iowa 329 C5 142
Deepstep, Washington, Ga. 139 C4 176
Deepwater, Henry, Mo. 712 C4 150
Deepwater, Salem, N.J. 700 D1 210
Deep Water, Fayette, W.Va. 900 D6 194
Deepwater, pt., Del. D4 172
Deer, Newton, Ark. 150 B3 170
Deer, creek, Ind. B3 140
Deer, creek, Md. A7 182
Deer, creek, Miss. B2 184
Deer, creek, Ohio C3 156
Deer, isl., Maine D4 204
Deer, isl., Mass. D3 206
Deer, isl., Miss. E2 184
Deer, lake, Newf., Can. F7 72
Deer, lake, Minn. D5 148
Deer, mtn., Maine C2 204
Deer, peak, Colo. D5 106
Deer, pond, Newf., Can. F8 72
Deera, Syr., U.A.R. 15,635 C2 378
Deerbrook, Langlade, Wis. 25 C4 160
Deer Creek, Tazewell, Ill. 583 C4 138
Deer Creek, Carroll, Ind. 200 B3 140
Deer Creek, Freeborn, Minn. 312 E3 148
Deer Creek, Grant, Okla. 215 B6 128
Deerfield, Lake, Ill. 11,786 A6 138
E2
Deerfield, Kearny, Kans. 442 E2 144
Deerfield, Franklin, Mass. 500 (3,338▲) A2 206
Deerfield, Lenawee, Mich. 866 H8 146
Deerfield, Henry, Mo. 200 D3 150
Deerfield, Rockingham, N.H. 75 (714▲) E4 208
Deerfield, Portage, Ohio 500 A5 156
Deerfield, Dane, Wis. 795 E4 160
Deerfield, riv., Mass. A2 206
Deerfield, riv., Vt. F3 218
Deerfield Beach, Broward, Fla. 9,573 E10 174
Deerfield Street, Cumberland, N.J. 400 D2 210
Deer Flat, res., Idaho F2 108
Deering, Alsk. 174 B5 84
Deering, Hillsboro, N.H. 30 (345▲) E3 208
Deering, McHenry, N.Dak. 117 B4 154
Deer Isle, Hancock, Maine 600 (1,129▲) D4 204
Deer Lake, Newf., Can. 3,481 F7 72
Deer Lake, Ont., Can. Q23 64
Deer Lodge, Powell, Mont. 4,681 D4 110
Deer Lodge, Morgan, Tenn. 250 B7 190
Deer Lodge, co., Mont. 18,640 D3 110
Deer Park, Washington, Ala. 200 D1 168
Deer Park, Garrett, Md. 379 B1 182
Deer Park, Suffolk, N.Y. 11,725 D3 212
Deer Park, Hamilton, Ohio 8,423 D1 156
Deer Park, Harris, Tex. 4,865 *E8 130
Deer Park, Spokane, Wash. 1,333 B9 98
Deer Park, St. Croix, Wis. 221 C1 160
Deer River, Itasca, Minn. 992 D5 148
Deer River, Lewis, N.Y. 170 B6 212
Deerton, Alger, Mich. 50 C4 146
Deer Trail, Arapahoe, Colo. 764 C6 106
Deerwood, Crow Wing, Minn. 527 E5 148
Deeson, Bolivar, Miss. 300 A2 184
Deeth, Elko, Nev. 25 B6 112
Deferiet, Jefferson, N.Y. 470 A6 212
Defiance, Shelby, Iowa 386 C2 142
Defiance, St. Charles, Mo. 110 B7 150
Defiance, McKinley, N.Mex. 12 C2 126
Defiance, Defiance, Ohio 14,553 A2 156
Defiance, co., Ohio 31,508 A2 156
Deford, Tuscola, Mich. 150 F8 146
De Forest, Dane, Wis. 1,223 E4 160
De Funiak Springs, Walton, Fla. 5,282 A4 174
Degerfors, Swe. 1,597 B5 292
Degersheim, Switz. 3,186 A5 312
Deggendorf, Ger. 16,600 D5 286
De Graff, Swift, Minn. 196 F3 148
De Graff, Logan, Ohio 996 B3 156
Degrasse, St. Lawrence, N.Y. 250 A6 212
De Grey, riv., Austl. C3 432
Dehak, Iran D5 379
Deh Bid, Iran C3 379
Dehibat, Tun. 1,579 B6 402
Deh-i-Haji, Afg. D3 374
Deh Pāin, Iran D4 379
Dehra Dun, India 116,404 (*144,216) C2 368
Deh Titān, Afg. 5,000 C2 374
Dehue, Logan, W.Va. 750 *D3 194
Deim Zubeir, Sud. D2 398
Deinze, Bel. 5,863 D2 282
Dej, Rom. 19,281 A2 321
Deje, Swe. B4 292
Dejvice, Czech. (part of Prague) *A2 324
De Kalb, De Kalb, Ill. 18,486 B5 138
De Kalb, Kemper, Miss. 880 C4 184
De Kalb, Buchanan, Mo. 300 B3 150
De Kalb, Kershaw, S.C. 125 C7 188
De Kalb, Bowie, Tex. 2,042 C8 130
De Kalb, co., Ala. 41,417 A4 168
De Kalb, co., Ga. 256,782 C2 176
De Kalb, co., Ill. 51,714 B5 138
De Kalb, co., Ind. 28,271 A4 140
De Kalb, co., Mo. 7,226 B3 150
De Kalb, co., Tenn. 10,774 C6 190
De Kalb Junction, St. Lawrence, N.Y. 260 A6 212
De Kays, Sussex, N.J. A4 210
Dekese, Con.L. C3 414
Dekoa, Cen.Afr.Rep. E8 409
Dekoven, Union, Ky. 296 C2 178
Delacroix, St. Bernard, La. 650 C8 180
Delafield, Waukesha, Wis. 2,334 E1 160
Delagoa, bay, Moz. E6 421
Delagua, Las Animas, Colo. E6 106
Delake, Lincoln, Oreg. 803 C2 96
De Lamar, Owyhee, Idaho F2 108
De Lamere, Sargent, N.Dak. 170 D8 154
Delanco, Burlington, N.J. 4,011 C3 210
De Land, Volusia, Fla. 10,775 B9 174
De Land, Piatt, Ill. 422 C5 138
Delaney, Madison, Ark. 75 B3 170
Delano, Kern, Calif. 11,913 E4 94
Delano, Wright, Minn. 1,612 F5 148
Delano, Polk, Tenn. 200 C7 190
Delano, peak, Utah E3 114
Delanson, Schenectady, N.Y. 398 C7 212
Delaplaine, Greene, Ark. 186 A6 170
Delaronde, lake, Sask., Can. C4 58
Delavan, Tazewell, Ill. 1,377 C4 138
Delavan, Morris, Kans. 200 D7 144
Delavan, Faribault, Minn. 322 H4 148
Delavan, Walworth, Wis. 4,846 F5 160
Delavan Lake, Walworth, Wis. 1,884 *F5 160
Delaware, Logan, Ark. 300 B3 170
Delaware, Ont., Can. 310 R19 64
Delaware, Ripley, Ind. 155 C4 140
Delaware, Delaware, Iowa 167 B6 142
Delaware, Warren, N.J. 275 B2 210
Delaware, Delaware, Ohio 13,282 B3 156
Delaware, Nowata, Okla. 540 B8 128
Delaware, co., Ind. 110,938 B4 140
Delaware, co., Iowa 18,483 B6 142
Delaware, co., N.Y. 43,540 C6 212
Delaware, co., Ohio 36,107 B3 156
Delaware, co., Okla. 13,198 B9 128
Delaware, co., Pa. 553,154 D6 214
Delaware, state, U.S. 446,292 D11 77
172
Delaware, bay, U.S. D12 77
Delaware, mts., Tex. D3 130
Delaware, res., Ohio B3 156
Delaware, riv., Del. C3 172
Delaware, riv., Kans. C8 144
Delaware, riv., N.J., Pa. D6 214
Delaware City, New Castle, Del. 1,658 B3 172
Delaware Water Gap, Monroe, Pa. 554 C6 214
Delay, Lafayette, Miss. 150 A3 184
Delbarton, Mingo, W.Va. 1,122 D2 194
Del Bonita, Glacier, Mont. B4 110
Delburne, Alta., Can. 429 D6 54
Delcambre, Vermilion and Iberia, La. 1,857 E4 180
Delcarbon, Huerfano, Colo. 5 E6 106
Del City, Oklahoma, Okla. 12,934 C6 128
Deleau, Man., Can. 200 F2 60
Delémont, Switz. 7,504 A3 312
De Leon, Comanche, Tex. 2,022 C6 130
De Leon Springs, Volusia, Fla. 708 B9 174
De Léry, Que., Can. 1,573 S15 66
Delevan, Cattaraugus, N.Y. 777 C3 212
Delft, Cottonwood, Minn. 125 H3 148
Delft, Neth. 67,758 B3 282
Delfzijl, Neth. 8,700 A5 282
Delgada, pt., Arg. F5 251
Delgo, Sud. A3 398
Delhi, Merced, Calif. 1,175 *D3 94
Delhi, Ont., Can. 3,002 R20 64
Delhi, Las Animas, Colo. 25 E6 106
Delhi, India 914,790 (*1,039,013) C2 368
Delhi, Delaware, Iowa 464 B6 142
Delhi, Richland, La. 2,514 B4 180
Delhi, Redwood, Minn. 124 G3 148
Delhi, Delaware, N.Y. 2,307 C7 212
Delhi, Beckham, Okla. 50 C4 128
Delhi, ter., India 1,744,072 *C3 366
Delia, Alta., Can. 282 E6 54
Delia, Jackson, Kans. 163 C8 144
Delight, Pike, Ark. 446 C3 170
Delisle, Que., Can. 1,282 P13 66
Delisle, Sask., Can. 482 E4 58
De Lisle, Harrison, Miss. 800 E1 184
E3
Delitzsch, Ger. 23,700 C5 286
Dell, Mississippi, Ark. 383 B6 170
Dell, Beaverhead, Mont. 30 F4 110
Dell' Alice, pt., It. F6 302
Delle, Tooele, Utah 25 C3 114
Dellenbaugh, mtn., Ariz. B2 124
Dellensjöarna, lake, Swe. F7 291
Dell Rapids, Minnehaha, S.Dak. 1,863 D9 158
Dellrose, Lincoln, Tenn. 175 C5 190
Dellroy, Carroll, Ohio 391 B5 156
Dellslow, Monongalia, W.Va. 800 A7 194
Dellwood, Washington, Minn. 310 F6 148
F7
Dellwood, St. Louis, Mo. 4,720 *C7 150
Dellwood, Yamhill, Oreg. 50 *B3 96
Dellys, Alg. 5,774 (21,591▲) A4 402
Delmar, Winston, Ala. 300 A2 168
Del Mar, San Diego, Calif. 3,124 *F5 94
Delmar, Sussex, Del. 934 G3 172
Delmar, Clinton, Iowa 556 C7 142
Delmar, Wicomico, Md. 1,291 D8 182
Delmar, Albany, N.Y. 7,000 C8 212
Delmas, Sask., Can. 145 D3 58
Delmenhorst, Ger. 55,500 B3 286
Del Mono, pt., Nic. E6 228
Delmont, Cumberland, N.J. 300 E3 210
Delmont (New Salem), Westmoreland, Pa. 1,313 *C2 214
Delmont, Douglas, S.Dak. 363 D7 158
Del Monte Heights, Monterey, Calif. 1,174 *D3 94
Del Monte Park, Monterey, Calif. 2,177 *D3 94
Del Norte, Rio Grande, Colo. 1,856 E4 106
Del Norte, co., Calif. 17,771 B2 94
Deloit, Crawford, Iowa 222 B2 142
Delong, Fulton, Ind. 130 A3 140
Deloraine, Man., Can. 900 F2 60
Deloro, Ont., Can. 253 P23 64
Del Paso Heights, Sacramento, Calif. 11,495 C3 94
Delphi, Carroll, Ind. 2,517 B3 140
Delphia, Musselshell, Mont. 10 D8 110
Delphia, York, S.C. 100 B6 188
Delphine, Meagher, Mont. D6 110
Delphos, Ringgold, Iowa 48 *D3 142
Delphos, Ottawa, Kans. 619 C6 144
Delphos, Allen and Van Wert, Ohio 6,961 B2 156
Delray Beach, Palm Beach, Fla. 12,230 E10 174
Del Rey Oaks, Monterey, Calif. 1,831 *D3 94
Del Rio, Conejos, Colo. E4 106
Del Rio, Cocke, Tenn. 25 C8 190
Del Rio, Val Verde, Tex. 18,612 E5 130
Delson Village, Que., Can. 816 S16 66
Delta, Clay, Ala. 150 B4 168
Delta, Ont., Can. 540 P24 64
Delta, Delta, Colo. 3,832 D2 106
Delta, Keokuk, Iowa 514 C5 142
Delta, Madison, La. 111 B5 180
Delta, Cape Girardeau, Mo. 416 D8 150
Delta, Fulton, Ohio 2,376 A2 156
Delta, York, Pa. 822 D5 214
Delta, Union, S.C. 300 B5 188
Delta, Millard, Utah 1,576 D3 114
Delta, Bayfield, Wis. 150 B2 160
Delta, co., Colo. 15,602 D3 106
Delta, co., Mich. 34,298 D4 146
Delta, co., Tex. 5,860 C8 130
Delta, res., N.Y. B6 212
Delta Amacuro, state, Ven. 33,648 B8 240
Delta Barrage, dam, Eg., U.A.R. D1 382
Delta City, Sharkey, Miss. 300 B2 184
Delta Station, Man., Can. E3 60
Deltaville, Middlesex, Va. 800 C8 192
Delton, Barry, Mich. 250 G6 146
Delvin, Ire. 295 H5 273
Delyatin, Sov.Un. 14,000 H5 332
Demaine, Sask., Can. 130 E4 58
Demanda, mts., Sp. A5 298
Demarest, Bergen, N.J. 4,231 A2 210
Demavend, mtn., Iran B3 379
Demba, Con.L. D3 414
Demidov, Sov.Un. 14,700 E8 332
Deming, Luna, N.Mex. 6,764 F3 126
Deming, Whatcom, Wash. 250 A4 98
Demirci, Tur. 6,501 B3 307
Demmin, Ger. 17,100 B5 286
Demmitt, Alta., Can. C3 54
Demnat, Mor. 6,896 B2 402
Demopolis, Marengo, Ala. 7,377 C2 168
Demorest, Habersham, Ga. 1,029 B3 176
Demorestville, Ont., Can. 225 P23 64
De Mossville, Pendleton, Ky. 90 A8 178
Demotte, Jasper, Ind. 700 A2 140
Dempo, mtn., Indon. E2 358
Dempster, Hamlin, S. Dak. 95 C9 158
Demyanka, riv., Sov.Un. A8 336
Denain, Fr. 27,449 B5 278
Denali, Alsk. 4 C7 84
Denaud, Hendry, Fla. 250 E9 174
Denbigh, co., Wales 170,700 H9 273
Den Burg, Neth. 2,888 A3 282
Dendermonde, Bel. 9,464 C3 282
Dendron, Surry, Va. 403 C8 192
Denezhkin Kamen, mtn., Sov.Un. A5 336
Denham, Pasco, Fla. 175 C8 174
Denham, Pulaski, Ind. 180 A3 140
Denham, Pine, Minn. 71 E6 148
Denham Springs, Livingston, La. 5,991 A5 180
D5
Den Helder, Neth. 41,546 B3 282
Denhoff, Sheridan, N. Dak. 164 C5 154
Denholm, Sask., Can. 104 D3 58
Den Hoorn, Neth. 454 A3 282
Denia, Sp. 7,875 C7 298
Deniau, Que., Can. 215 Q15 66
Deniliquin, Austl. 4,704 F8 432
Denio, Humboldt, Nev. 30 B3 112
Denison, Crawford, Iowa 4,930 B2 142
Denison, Jackson, Kans. 184 *C8 144
Denison, Grayson, Tex. 22,748 C7 130
Denison, dam, Okla. E7 128
Denizli, Tur. 29,934 C3 307
Denizli, prov., Tur. 368,853 *C3 307
Denman, Buffalo, Nebr. 17 *D7 152
Denmar, Pocahontas, W.Va. 180 C4 194
Denmark, Jackson, Ark. B5 170
Denmark, Lee, Iowa 635 D6 142
Denmark, Lincoln, Kans. 50 *C5 144
Denmark, Oxford, Maine 160 (376▲) E2 204
Denmark, Lafayette, Miss. 150 A3 184
Denmark, Curry, Oreg. 25 E2 96
Denmark, Bamberg, S.C. 3,221 E6 188
Denmark, Madison, Tenn. 58 C2 190
Denmark, Brown, Wis. 1,106 A6 160
D6
Denmark, country, Eur. 4,515,000 C5 266
291
Denmark, strait, Arc.O. R32 290
Dennard, Van Buren, Ark. 100 B4 170
Denning, Franklin, Ark. 227 B3 170
Dennis, Labette, Kans. 150 E8 144
Dennis, Barnstable, Mass. 550 (3,769▲) C7 206
Dennis, Tishomingo, Miss. 125 A4 184
Dennis, Delaware, Okla. 100 *B9 128
Dennison, Goodhue, Minn. 179 G5 148
Dennison, Tuscarawas, Ohio 4,158 B5 156
Dennis Port, Barnstable, Mass. 1,271 C7 206
Denniston, Halifax, Va. 50 D6 192
Dennisville, Cape May, N.J. 500 E3 210
Dennysville, Washington, Maine 250 (303▲) D5 204
Denny Terrace, Richland, S.C. 2,000 *D6 188
Den Oever, Neth. 1,497 B4 282
Denpasar, Indon. 16,639 F5 358
Densmore, Norton, Kans. 65 *C4 144
Dent, Clearwater, Idaho C2 108

Dent, Otter Tail, Minn. 176 E3 148
Dent, co., Mo. 10,445 D6 150
Dent du Midi, mtn., Switz. B2 312
Denton, Jeff Davis, Ga. 1,726 E4 176
Denton, Doniphan, Kans. 161 C8 144
Denton, Carter, Ky. 100 B8 178
Denton, Caroline, Md. 1,938 C8 182
Denton, Wayne, Mich. 200 B7 146
Denton, Fergus, Mont. 410 C7 110
Denton, Lancaster, Nebr. 94 D9 152
Denton, Davidson, N.C. 852 B5 186
Denton, Cocke, Tenn. 100 C8 190
Denton, Denton, Tex. 26,844 C7 130
Denton, co., Tex. 47,432 C7 130
Denton, creek, Tex. A8 130
Dentons Point, Deer Lodge, Mont. 40 *D4 110
D'Entrecasteaux, point, Austl. E2 432
Dents, Richland, S.C. 100 C7 188
Dentville, Copiah, Miss. 75 D2 184
Denver, Denver, Colo. 493,887 (*858,300) C6 106
Denver, Miami, Ind. 565 B3 140
Denver, Bremer, Iowa 831 B5 142
Denver, Worth, Mo. 116 A3 150
Denver, Lincoln, N.C. 113 B4 186
Denver, Lancaster, Pa. 1,875 C5 214
Denver, Humphreys, Tenn. 100 B4 190
Denver, Marshall, W.Va. 75 C2 194
Denver, Preston, W.Va. 150 B5 194
Denver, co., Colo. 493,887 C6 106
Denver City, Yoakum, Tex. 4,302 C4 130
Denville, Morris, N.J. 10,632 B4 210
Denzil, Sask., Can. 259 D3 58
Deogarh, India 25,510 D4 368
Deoli, India D1 368
Deora, Baca, Colo. 4 *E8 106
Deori, India E2 368
Deoria, India D3 368
De Panne, Bel. 5,873 C1 282
Depauw, Harrison, Ind. 120 D3 140
Dependencias Federales (Los Roques) (Dependency), state, Ven. 779 A5 240
De Pere, Brown, Wis. 10,045 A6 160
D5
Depew, Erie, N.Y. 13,580 C3 212
Depew, Creek, Okla. 686 C7 128
Depoe Bay, Lincoln, Oreg. 600 C2 96
Deport, Lamar and Red River, Tex. 639 C8 130
Deposit, Broome, N.Y. 2,025 C6 212
Depot Harbour, Ont., Can. 480 O20 64
Depue, Bureau, Ill. 1,920 B4 138
Deputy, Jefferson, Ind. 300 D4 140
De Queen, Sevier, Ark. 2,859 C2 170
Dequidambos, mts., Hond. C4 228
De Quincy, Calcasieu, La. 3,928 D2 180
Dera Ghazi Khan, Pak. 36,239 D7 375
Dera Ismail Khan, Pak. 39,846 (41,663▲) D7 375
Derbent, Sov.Un. 38,000 D3 336
Derbetovka, Sov.Un. 13,400 J14 332
Derby, Austl. 478 B4 432
Derby, N.B., Can. 115 C4 70
Derby, Adams, Colo. 10,124 C6 106
Derby, New Haven, Conn. 12,132 D3 202
Derby, Eng. 137,500 I11 273
Derby, Lucas, Iowa 151 D4 142
Derby, Sedgwick, Kans. 6,458 B6 144
E6
Derby, Piscataquis, Maine 500 C4 204
Derby, Pearl River, Miss. 100 E3 184
Derby, Erie, N.Y. 3,500 C3 212
Derby, Pickaway, Ohio 325 C3 156
Derby, Orleans, Vt. 433 (2,506▲) B4 218
Derby, Wise, Va. 800 D2 192
Derby, co., Eng. 848,100 H11 273
Derby Line, Orleans, Vt. 849 A4 218
Derecske, Hung. 9,479 B6 320
Derg, lake, Ire. I4 273
De Ridder, Beauregard, La. 7,188 D2 180
Derik, Tur. 3,842 C9 307
Derita, Mecklenburg, N.C. 1,500 B5 186
Derma, Calhoun, Miss. 578 B3 184
Dermott, Chicot, Ark. 3,665 D5 170
Derna, see Darnah, Libya
Derniere, isl., La. E5 180
Derry, Natchitoches, La. 75 C3 180
Derry, Westmoreland, Pa. 3,426 C2 214
Derry (West Derry), Rockingham, N.H. 4,468 (6,987▲) F4 208
Derudeb, Sud. B4 398
De Ruyter, Madison, N.Y. 627 C6 212
Derventa, Yugo. 9,133 B3 316
Derwent, Alta., Can. 289 D7 54
Derwent, Guernsey, Ohio 350 C5 156
Derwent, riv., Eng. H12 273
Derwood, Montgomery, Md. 110 B5 182
Desaguadero, riv., Arg. B2 252
Desaguadero, riv., Bol. C1 246
Des Allemands, bayou, La. C6 180
Des Allemands, lake, La. E5 180
Des Arc, Prairie, Ark. 1,482 C5 170
Des Arc, Iron, Mo. 275 D7 150
Des Arc, bayou, Ark. B5 170
Des Arc, mtn., Mo. D7 150
Desbiens, Que., Can. 2,014 P13 66
Desboro, Ont., Can. 85 P19 64
Deschaillons, Que., Can. 493 R12 66
Deschaillons sur St. Laurent, Que., Can. 1,266 *R12 66
Deschambault, Que., Can. 1,002 R13 66
Deschambault, lake, Sask., Can. C6 58
Deschutes, co., Oreg. 23,100 D5 96
Deschutes, peak, Wash. C4 98
Deschutes, riv., Oreg. B6 96
Deseado, riv., Arg. G4 251
Desengaño, cape, Arg. G4 251
Deseret, Millard, Utah 310 D3 114
Deseret, peak, Utah C3 114
Deseronto, Ont., Can. 1,729 P23 64
Desert, mtn., W.Va. C6 194
Desert, peak, Utah B2 114
Desert, val., Nev. B3 112
Desert Center, Riverside, Calif. 200 F6 94
Desert Hot Springs, Riverside, Calif. 1,472 *F5 94
Desha, Independence, Ark. 350 B5 170
Desha, co., Ark. 20,770 D5 170
Deshler, Thayer, Nebr. 956 D8 152
Deshler, Henry, Ohio 1,824 A3 156
Deshu, Afg. 5,000 D2 374
Des Lacs, Ward, N.Dak. 185 B4 154
Des Lacs, riv., N.Dak. B4 154
Desloge, St. Francois, Mo. 2,308 D7 150
Desmet, Benewah, Idaho 100 B2 108
De Smet, Kingsbury, S.Dak. 1,324 C8 158
Desmochado, Par. E3 247
Des Moines, Polk, Iowa 208,982 (*261,900) A7 142
C4
Des Moines, Union, N.Mex. 207 B7 126
Des Moines, King, Wash. 1,987 B4 98
D2
Des Moines, co., Iowa 44,605 D6 142
Des Moines, riv., Iowa D5 142
Des Moines, riv., Minn. H3 148
Desna, riv., Sov.Un. G8 332
Desolación, isl., Chile H3 251
Desolation, lake, Newf., Can. D9 72
Desordem, mts., Braz. A1 258
De Soto, Sumter, Ga. 282 E2 176
De Soto, Jackson, Ill. 723 F4 138
De Soto, Dallas, Iowa 273 C3 142
De Soto, Johnson, Kans. 1,271 D9 144
De Soto, Clarke, Miss. 185 D4 184
De Soto, Jefferson, Mo. 5,804 C7 150
De Soto, Dallas, Tex. 1,969 *C7 130
De Soto, Vernon, Wis. 357 E2 160
De Soto, co., Fla. 11,683 E9 174
De Soto, co., Miss. 23,891 A2 184
De Soto, par., La. 24,248 B2 180
De Soto City, Highlands, Fla. 245 D9 174
De Soto Park, Floyd, Ga. 700 *B1 176
Despard, Harrison, W.Va. 1,763 B6 194
Des Peres, St. Louis, Mo. 4,362 *C7 150
Des Plaines, riv., Ill. B5 138
Des Plaines, riv., Wis. F2 160
Dessau, Ger. 94,300 C5 286
Destin, Okaloosa, Fla. 1,000 A4 174
Destrehan, St. Charles, La. 330 C7 180
E5
Deta, Rom. B1 321
Detlor, Ont., Can. 110 O23 64
Detmold, Ger. 32,300 C3 286
Detour, Carroll, Md. 100 A5 182
De Tour, Chippewa, Mich. 669 D8 146
Detour, pt., Mich. D5 146
Detroit, Lamar, Ala. 113 A1 168
Detroit, Dickinson, Kans. 100 D6 144
Detroit, Somerset, Maine 250 (564▲) D3 204
Detroit, Wayne, Mich. 1,670,144 (*3,838,500) B8 146
G8
Detroit, Marion, Oreg. 206 C4 96
Detroit, riv., Mich. C8 146
Detroit Beach, Monroe, Mich. 1,571 *H8 146
Detroit Lakes, Becker, Minn. 5,633 E3 148
Dett, Rh.&Nya. 820 C5 420
Detva, Czech. 7,786 B4 324
Deuel, co., Nebr. 3,125 C3 152
Deuel, co., S.Dak. 6,782 C9 158
Deurne, Bel. 63,184 C3 282
Deux Frères, isl., Viet. E5 362
Deux-Sèvres, dept., Fr. 312,842 *D3 278
Deva, Rom. 16,879 B2 321
De Valls Bluff, Prairie, Ark. 654 C5 170
Dévaványa, Hung. 10,127 B5 320
Deventer, Neth. 49,942 B5 282
Devereux, Hancock, Ga. 200 C3 176
De View, bayou, Ark. B5 170
Devil River, peak, N.Z. D4 437
Devils, lake, N.Dak. B6 154
Devils, riv., Tex. D5 130
Devils Den, Kern, Calif. 150 E4 94
Devils Knob, mtn., Va. C6 192
Devils Lake, Ramsey, N.Dak. 6,299 B7 154
Devils Postpile, natl. mon., Calif. D4 94
Devils Slide, Morgan, Utah 250 B4 114
Devils Tower, Crook, Wyo. 10 B8 116
Devils Tower, natl. mon., Wyo. B8 116
Devils Track, lake, Minn. D8 148
Devine, Pueblo, Colo. 10 D6 106
Devine, Medina, Tex. 2,522 E6 130
Devizes, Eng. 8,200 J11 273
Devol, Cotton, Okla. 117 D5 128
Devolt, riv., Alb. A3 306
Devon, Alta., Can. 1,429 D6 54
Devon, New Haven, Conn. (part of Milford) E3 202
Devon, Bourbon, Kans. 125 E9 144
Devon, Toole, Mont. 43 B5 110
Devon, Chester, Pa. 1,500 *D6 214
Devon, co., Eng. 805,900 K9 273
Devon, isl., N.W.Ter., Can. B10 48
Devondale, Jefferson, Ky. 477 *B5 178
Devonia, Anderson, Tenn. 150 B7 190
Devonport, Austl. 10,624 G9 432
Devonport, N.Z. 11,179 B5 437
H9
Dewar, Okmulgee, Okla. 817 C8 128
Dewar Lake, Sask., Can. 75 E3 58
Dewas, India E2 368
Dewberry, Alta., Can. 135 D7 54
Dew Drop, see Leitner, Ark.
Dewees, inlet, S.C. F9 188
Dewees, isl., S.C. F5 188
Deweese, Neshoba, Miss. 250 C4 184
Deweese, Clay, Nebr. 100 D7 152
Dewey, Yavapai, Ariz. 50 D3 124
Dewey, Beaverhead, Mont. 35 E4 110
Dewey, Washington, Okla. 3,994 B8 128
Dewey, Custer, S.Dak. 55 D2 158
Dewey, co., Okla. 6,051 C4 128
Dewey, co., S.Dak. 5,257 B4 158
Dewey, res., Ky. C8 178
Dewey Beach, Sussex, Del. 150 F5 172
Dewey Mills, Windsor, Vt. 100 D4 218
Deweyville, Box Elder, Utah 265 *B3 114
De Winton, Alta., Can. 75 E5 54
De Witt, Arkansas, Ark. 3,019 C5 170
De Witt, Clinton, Iowa 3,224 C7 142
De Witt, Clinton, Mich. 1,238 G7 146
De Witt, Carroll, Mo. 174 B4 150
De Witt, Saline, Nebr. 504 D9 152
De Witt, Onondaga, N.Y. 3,500 B5 212
Dewitt, Dinwiddie, Va. 100 C7 192
De Witt, co., Ill. 17,253 C4 138
De Witt, co., Tex. 20,683 E7 130
Dewright, Seminole, Okla. 100 *C7 128
Dewy Rose, Elbert, Ga. 150 B4 176
Dexter, Laurens, Ga. 359 D3 176
Dexter, Dallas, Iowa 670 C3 142
Dexter, Cowley, Kans. 291 E7 144
Dexter, Calloway, Ky. 250 D2 178
Dexter, Penobscot, Maine 2,720 (3,951▲) C3 204
Dexter, Washtenaw, Mich. 1,702 G8 146
Dexter, Mower, Minn. 313 H6 148
Dexter, Stoddard, Mo. 5,519 E8 150
Dexter, Chaves, N.Mex. 885 E6 126
Dexter, Jefferson, N.Y. 1,009 A5 212
Dexter, Lane, Oreg. 200 D4 96
Dexter, lake, Fla. B9 174
Dexterville, Wood, Wis. 75 D3 160
Deyhuk, Iran C4 379
Deyyer, Iran D3 379
Dezful, Iran 52,121 C2 379
Dezhnev, cape, Sov.Un. C20 329
Dezh Shāhpur, Iran B2 379
Dhaleswari, riv., India E6 368
Dhamar, Yemen 20,000 E3 383
Dhanbad, India E4 368
D'Hanis, Medina, Tex. 850 E6 130
Dhankuta, Nep. 4,194 D4 368
Dhanuoak, India E6 368
Dhar, India E1 368
Dharamjaygarh, India E3 368
Dharmapuri, India 24,094 F3 366
Dharmsala, India 9,653 B2 368
Dharwar, India 66,571 E3 366
Dhasan, riv., India D2 368
Dhāt al Hajj, Sau.Ar. B2 383
Dhaulagiri, mtn., Nep. C3 368
Dhenousa, isl., Grc. C5 306
Dhidhimótikhon, Grc. 8,136 A6 306
Dhilos, isl., Grc. C5 360
Dhimitsána, Grc. 1,710 C4 306
Dhodhekánisos (Dodecanese), prov., Grc. 121,480 *C6 306
Dholpur, India D2 368
Dhrépanon, cape, Grc. B5 306
Dhubri, India D5 368
Dhulia, India 76,880 D2 366
Dhulian, India D4 368
Dhur, Bhu. D5 368
Dia, isl., Grc. D5 306
Diabaig, Scot. D7 272
Diable (Devils Island), isl., Fr.Gu. D6 257
Diablerets, mtn., Switz. B3 312
Diablo, Contra Costa, Calif. 2,096 A6 94
Diablo, canyon, Ariz. D4 124
Diablo, dam, Wash. A5 98
Diablo, mtn., Oreg. E6 96
Diagonal, Ringgold, Iowa 443 D3 142
Dial, Howard, Ark. C2 170
Dial, Fannin, Ga. 800 B2 176
Diamante, Arg. B3 252
Diamantina, Braz. 9,837 D2 258
Diamantina, riv., Austl. C8 432
Diamond, Plaquemines, La. 200 E6 180
Diamond, Newton, Mo. 453 E3 150
Diamond, Harney, Oreg. 10 D8 96
Diamond, Kanawha, W.Va. 900 C6 194
Diamond, cave, Ark. B3 170
Diamond, head, Haw. G10 86
Diamond, lake, Oreg. D4 96
Diamond, mts., Nev. D6 112
Diamond, peak, Oreg. D4 96
Diamond, pt., Indon. C1 358
Diamond Bluff, Pierce, Wis. 150 D1 160
Diamond City, Alta., Can. 165 F6 54
Diamond Harbour, India I9 366
Diamond Hill, Providence, R.I. 300 B3 216
Diamond Lake, Lake, Ill. 400 E2 138
Diamond Point, Warren, N.Y. 400 B8 212
Diamond Springs, Eldorado, Calif. 617 C3 94
Diamond Springs, Princess Anne, Va. 1,500 *D8 192
Diamondville, Lincoln, Wyo. 398 E2 116
Diana, Giles, Tenn. 100 C5 190
Diana, Webster, W.Va. 180 C4 194
Dianópolis, Braz. 804 C1 258
Diapaga, Upper Volta 2,800 D5 408
Dias Creek, Cape May, N.J. E3 210
Diaz, Jackson, Ark. 348 B5 170
Dibang, riv., India C6 368
Dibaya, Con.L. D3 414
Dibble, McClain, Okla. 127 C6 128
Dibër, pref., Alb. 96,000 *A3 306
D'Iberville, Harrison, Miss. 3,005 E1 184
Diboll, Angelina, Tex. 2,506 D8 130
Dibrell, Warren, Tenn. 90 C6 190
Dibrugarh, India 37,991 D6 368
Dickens, Clay, Iowa 241 A2 142
Dickens, Lincoln, Nebr. 25 D5 152
Dickens, co., Tex. 4,963 C5 130
Dickenson, co., Va. 20,211 C2 192
Dickerson, Montgomery, Md. 246 B5 182
Dickey, Calhoun, Ga. 76 *E2 176
Dickey, La Moure, N.Dak. 143 D7 154
Dickey, co., N.Dak. 8,147 D7 154
Dickeyville, Grant, Wis. 671 F3 160
Dickie, Hot Springs, Wyo. 15 C4 116
Dickinson, Clarke, Ala. 200 D2 168
Dickinson, Stark, N.Dak. 9,971 D3 154
Dickinson, Galveston, Tex. 4,715 F8 130
Dickinson, co., Iowa 12,574 A2 142
Dickinson, co., Kans. 21,572 D6 144
Dickinson, co., Mich. 23,917 C3 146
Dickinson, res., N.Dak. D3 154
Dicks Head, see Chiamboni, cape, Ken., Som.
Dickson, Carter, Okla. 125 D7 128
Dickson, Dickson, Tenn. 5,028 B4 190
Dickson, co., Tenn. 18,839 B4 190
Dickson City, Lackawanna, Pa. 7,738 A5 214
B6
Dicle, riv., Tur. C9 307
Didsbury, Alta., Can. 1,227 E5 54
Didwana, India D1 368
Diégo-Suarez (Antsirane), Malag. 23,900 B9 421
Diégo-Suarez, prov., Malag. B9 421
Diekirch, Lux. 3,809 E5 282
Dien Bien Phu, Viet. 10,000 B4 362
Diepholz, Ger. 9,100 B3 286
Dieppe, N.B., Can. 3,876 C5 70
Dieppe, Fr. 26,427 C4 278
Dierks, Howard, Ark. 1,276 C2 170
Diest, Bel. 9,547 D4 282
Dieterich, Effingham, Ill. 591 D5 138
Dietikon, Switz. 7,132 A4 312
Dietrich, Lincoln, Idaho 118 G4 108
Diever, Neth. 857 B5 282
Dif, Som. E5 398
Differdange, Lux. 15,179 E4 282
Difficult, Smith, Tenn. 150 B6 190
Dig, India D2 368
Digby, N.S., Can. 2,145 E4 70
Digby, co., N.S., Can. 19,869 E4 70
Digerbgt, mtn., Swe. A4 292
Dighton, Lane, Kans. 1,526 D3 144
Dighton, Bristol, Mass. 700 (3,769▲) C5 206
Dighton, Osceola, Mich. 75 E6 146
Digne, Fr. 9,084 E7 278
Digoel, riv., Neth. N.Gui. F10 359
Digoin, Fr. 5,904 D5 278
Dijon, Fr. 112,844 D6 278
Dikanas, Swe. D6 290
Dike, Grundy, Iowa 630 B5 142
Dikhil, Fr. Som. 500 C5 398
Dikili, cape, Tur. A4 307
Dikirnis, Eg., U.A.R. 10,681 C2 382
Diksmuide, Bel. 3,825 C1 282
Dikson, Sov.Un. B10 328
Dikwa, Br.Cam. 5,242 D7 409
Dilārām, Afg. 5,000 C2 374
Dili, Port. Timor 1,795 F7 358
Dilingāt, Eg., U.A.R. 10,636 *A3 395
Dilke, Sask., Can. 168 E5 58
Dillard, Rabun, Ga. 204 *B3 176
Dillard, Carter, Okla. 125 D6 128
Dillard, Douglas, Oreg. 400 *D3 96
Dill City, Washita, Okla. 623 C4 128
Dille, Clay, W.Va. 500 C4 194
Dillenburg, Ger. 10,155 C3 286
Dillengen (an der Donau), Ger. 9,900 D4 286
Diller, Jefferson, Nebr. 286 D9 152
Dilley, Washington, Oreg. 250 *B1 96
Dilley, Frio, Tex. 2,118 E6 130
Dilling, Sud. 5,295 C2 398
Dillingham, Alsk. 400 D6 84
Dillon, Summit, Colo. 814 C4 106
Dillon, Phelps, Mo. 100 D6 150
Dillon, Beaverhead, Mont. 3,690 E4 110
Dillon, Dillon, S.C. 6,173 C10 188
Dillon, co., S.C. 30,584 C10 188
Dillonvale, Jefferson, Ohio 1,232 B6 156
Dillsboro, Dearborn, Ind. 745 C4 140
Dillsburg, York, Pa. 1,322 C4 214
Dillwyn, Buckingham, Va. 515 C6 192
Dilmān, see Shāhpūr, Iran
Dilolo, Con.L. E3 414
Dilworth, Clay, Minn. 2,102 E2 148
Dimapur, India D6 368
Dimas, Mex. C4 224
Dimbelenge, Con.L. D3 414
Dimbokro, I.C. 1,200 E4 408
Dimitrovgrad, Bul. 34,389 B2 317
Dimitrovgrad (Caribod), Yugo. 2,891 C6 316
Dimitrovo (Pernik), Bul. 59,721 B1 317
Dimitrovski, prov., Bul. *B1 317
Dimmit, co., Tex. 10,095 E6 130
Dimmitt, Castro, Tex. 2,935 B4 130
Dimock, Hutchinson, S.Dak. 150 D8 158
Dimondale, Eaton, Mich. 866 G7 146
Dinagat, isl., Phil. B7 358
Dinajpur, Pak. 35,687 K16 375
Dinan, Fr. 13,844 C2 278
Dinant, Bel. 6,726 D3 282
Dinapore, India D4 368
Dinard (-St. Enogat), Fr. 8,540 C2 278
Dinaric Alps, mts., Yugo. B3 316
Dindigul, India 78,361 F3 366
Dingess, Mingo, W.Va. 300 D2 194
Dingle, Bear Lake, Idaho 100 G7 108
Dingle, Ire. 1,453 I2 273
Dingle, bay, Ire. I2 273
Dingo, Austl. 147 C9 432
Dinguiraye, Guinea 2,900 D2 408
Dingwall, N.S., Can. 145 C9 70
Dingwall, Scot. 3,500 D8 272
Dinh Lap, Viet. 10,000 B5 362
Dinkey Creek, Fresno, Calif. 300 D4 94
Dinosaur, natl. mon., Colo., Utah B2 106
C6 114
Dinsmore, Sask., Can. 388 E4 58
Dinsmore, Duval, Fla. 2,000 A9 174
A10
Dinuba, Tulare, Calif. 6,103 D4 94
Dinwiddie, Dinwiddie, Va. 200 C7 192
Dinwiddie, co., Va. 22,183 C7 192
Dioïla, Mali D3 408
Dioka, Mali D2 408
Diomede, Alsk. 103 *B5 84
Diorite, Marquette, Mich. 120 C4 146
Diósgyőr, Hung. (pop. incl. in Miskolc) *A5 320
Dioura, Mali D3 408
Diourbel, Sen. 15,300 D1 408
Diplo, Pak. G6 375
Dipper Harbour, N.B., Can. 200 D3 70
Direction, cape, Austl. A8 432
Diredawa, Eth. 30,000 D5 398
Diriamba, Nic. 7,561 E4 228
Dirico, Ang. C4 420
Dirk Hartog, isl., Austl. D2 432
Dirkou, Niger C7 409
Dirranbandi, Austl. 870 D9 432
Dirty Devil, riv., Utah E5 114
Disappointment, cape, Wash. C2 98
Disappointment, lake, Austl. C4 432
Disautel, Okanogan, Wash. 50 A7 98
Disentis (Mustér), Switz. 2,330 B4 312
Dishman, Spokane, Wash. 5,000 D8 98
Dishna, Eg., U.A.R. 16,336 B3 395
Disko, Fulton, Ind. 140 B4 140
Disko, bay, Grnld. Q28 290
Disko, isl., Grnld. P28 290
Disley, Sask., Can. 78 E5 58
Dismal, swamp, N.C., Va. A9 186
D8 192

Disney, Mayes, Okla.	224	B8	128
Disputanta, Prince George, Va.	350	C7	192
Disraeli, Que., Can.	2,473	S13	66
Diss, Eng.	3,600	I14	273
Disston, Lane, Oreg.	130	*D4	96
District Heights, Prince Georges, Md.	7,524	C4	182
District of Columbia, U.S.	763,956	D11	77
Distrito Federal, dist., Mex.	3,050,442	D6	225
Distrito Federal (Federal District), state, Ven.	1,167,618	A5	240
Disûq, Eg., U.A.R.	23,992	A3	395
Diu (Port. India), poss., Asia	30,000	D2	366
		G9	340
Divènié, Con.B.		G7	409
Divernon, Sangamon, Ill.	997	D4	138
Dives [-sur-Mer], Fr.	5,893	C3	278
Divide, Silver Bow, Mont.	5	E4	110
Divide, co., N.Dak.	5,566	B2	154
Divide, peak, Wyo.		E5	116
Dividend, Utah, Utah	10	D3	114
Dividing, creek, Md.		D8	182
Dividing Creek, Cumberland, N.J.	600	E2	210
Divinópolis, Braz.	19,701	E2	258
Divišov, Czech.	904	*B2	324
Divnoye, Sov.Un.	17,300	C2	336
Divo, I.C.	2,200	E3	408
Divriği, Tur.	6,271	B8	307
Dix, Kimball, Nebr.	420	C2	152
Dix, dam, Ky.		C6	178
Dix, riv., Ky.		C6	178
Dixfield, Oxford, Maine	1,298 (2,323▴)	D2	204
Dixiana, Jefferson, Ala.	500	B3	168
Dixie, Escambia, Ala.	100	D3	168
Dixie, Maricopa, Ariz.	10	E3	124
Dixie, Woodruff, Ark.	40	B5	170
Dixie, Ont., Can.	350	Q21	64
Dixie, Brooks, Ga.	220	F3	176
Dixie, Idaho, Idaho	25	D3	108
Dixie, Caddo, La.	250	B2	180
Dixie, Stephens, Okla.		D6	128
Dixie, Walla Walla, Wash.	250	C8	98
Dixie, Nicholas, W.Va.	850	C3	194
		C7	
Dixie, co., Fla.	4,479	B7	174
Dixie Gardens, Caddo, La.	400	*B2	180
Dixie Inn, Webster, La.	399	B2	180
Dixmont, Penobscot, Maine	130 (551▴)	*D3	204
Dixmoor, Cook, Ill.	3,076	*B6	138
Dixon, Solano, Calif.	2,970	C3	94
Dixon, Lee, Ill.	19,565	B4	138
Dixon, Scott, Iowa	280	C7	142
Dixon, Webster, Ky.	541	C3	178
Dixon, Neshoba, Miss.	120	C3	184
Dixon, Pulaski, Mo.	1,473	D5	150
Dixon, Sanders, Mont.	132	C2	110
Dixon, Dixon, Nebr.	139	B9	152
Dixon, Rio Arriba, N.Mex.	600	B5	126
Dixon, Gregory, S.Dak.	26	D6	158
Dixon, Carbon, Wyo.	108	E5	116
Dixon, co., Nebr.	8,106	B9	152
Dixon, entrance, Alsk.		E8	84
Dixon, entrance, B.C., Can.		C6	52
Dixons Mills, Marengo, Ala.	150	C2	168
Dixonville, Escambia, Ala.	200	*D2	168
Dixonville, Indiana, Pa.	868	C2	214
Dixville, Que., Can.	458	S13	66
Dixville, peak, N.H.		B4	208
Diyarbakir, Tur.	63,180	C9	307
Diyarbakir, prov., Tur.	345,247	*B9	307
Diyung, riv., India		D6	368
Dja, riv., Cam.		F7	409
Djado, Niger		B7	409
Djafou, Alg.		C4	402
Djailolo, Indon.		D7	359
Djailolo, passage, Indon.		E7	359
Djakarta, Indon.	1,492,100 (*1,871,200)	F3	358
Djakovica, Yugo.	17,065	C5	316
Djakovo, Yugo.	9,573	B4	316
Djambala, Con.B.		G7	409
Djambi, Indon.	63,200	E2	358
Djanet (Ft. Charlet), Alg.		D5	402
Djaravica, mtn., Yugo.		C5	316
Djebel Bou Naceur, mtn., Mor.		B3	402
Djebel Toubkâl, mtn., Mor.		B2	402
Djelfa, Alg.	10,070 (110,681▴)	B4	402
Djema, Cen.Afr.Rep.		E10	409
Djenné, Mali	5,000	D4	408
Djerablous, Syr., U.A.R.	8,521	A3	378
Djerba, isl., Tun.		B6	402
Djibo, Upper Volta		D4	408
Djibouti, Fr. Som.	31,000	C5	398
Djidjelli, Alg.	31,580	A5	402
Djiring, Viet.		E6	362
Djolu, Con.L.		B3	414
Djouf, basin, Maur.		B3	408
Djougou, Dah.	5,400	E5	408
Djugu, Con.L.		B5	414
Djupivogur, Ice.		L22	290
Djurdjevac, Yugo.	6,397	A3	316
Djurjura, mtn. Alg.		A4	402
Djursholm, Swe.	7,770	B9	292
D'Lo, Simpson, Miss.	428	D3	184
Dmitriyevka, Sov.Un.		I12	332
Dmitriyev-Lgovskiy, Sov.Un.	5,000	F10	332
Dmitrov, Sov.Un.	31,000	D11	332
Dmitrovsk-Orlovskiy, Sov.Un.	11,600	F10	332
Dnepr, riv., Sov.Un		I9	332
Dneprodzerzhinsk, Sov.Un.	194,000	H10	332
Dnepropetrovsk, Sov.Un.	658,000	H10	332
Dnestr, riv., Sov.Un.		I8	332
Dno, Sov.Un.	18,000	D7	332
Doagh, Ire.		H2	273
Doaktown, N.B., Can.	280	C3	70
Doba, Chad		E8	409
Dobbinton, Ont., Can.	110	P19	64
Dobbs Ferry, Westchester, N.Y.	9,260	D2	212
Dobbyn, Austl.		B7	432
Döbeln, Ger.	30,300	C5	286
Doblas, Arg.		C3	252
Dobo, Indon.		F8	359
Doboj, Yugo.	8,997	B4	316
Doboy, sound, Ga.		E5	176
Dobřejovice, Czech.	2,188	*B2	324
Dobrich, see Tolbukhin, Bul.			
Dobříš, Czech.	4,130	*B2	324
Dobrogea, prov., Rom.	503,217	*C9	321
Dobrovice, Czech.	2,137	*A2	324
Dobruja, reg., Bul.		B3	317
Dobruja (Dobrogea), reg., Rom.		B5	321
Dobšiná, Czech.	4,215	B5	324
Dobson, Surry, N.C.	684	A5	186
Doce, riv., Braz.		D2	258
Docena, Jefferson, Ala.	1,400	E4	168
Dock, Pinal, Ariz.	10	H2	124
Dockery, Sunflower, Miss.		B2	184
Dock Junction, Glynn, Ga.	3,920	*E5	176
Dockton, King, Wash.	400	D2	98
Doctor Arroyo, Mex.	3,055	C5	225
Doctors Inlet, Clay, Fla.	600	B10	174
Doctors, lake, Fla.		B10	174
Doctortown, Wayne, Ga.	350	E5	176
Doddridge, Miller, Ark.	500	D3	170
Doddridge, co., W.Va.	6,970	B4	194
Dodds, Alta., Can.		D6	54
Doddsville, Sunflower, Miss.	190	B2	184
Dodecanese, see Dhodhekánisos, prov., Grc.			
Dodge, Worcester, Mass.	450	B4	206
Dodge, Dodge, Nebr.	649	C9	152
Dodge, Dunn, N.Dak.	226	C3	154
Dodge, Delaware, Okla.		B9	128
Dodge, Trempealeau, Wis.	130	D2	160
Dodge, co., Ga.	16,483	D3	176
Dodge, co., Minn.	13,259	H6	148
Dodge, co., Nebr.	32,471	C9	152
Dodge, co., Wis.	63,170	E5	160
Dodge Center, Dodge, Minn.	1,441	G6	148
Dodge City, Ford, Kans.	13,520	E3	144
Dodgeville, Bristol, Mass.		C5	206
Dodgeville, Iowa, Wis.	2,911	F3	160
Dodoma, Tan.	13,435	D6	414
Dodsland, Sask., Can.	323	E3	58
Dodson, Winn, La.	512	B3	180
Dodson, Phillips, Mont.	313	B8	110
Doebay, San Juan, Wash.	50	A4	98
Doe River, B.C., Can.	275	C12	52
Doerun, Colquitt, Ga.	1,037	E3	176
Doe Run, St. Francois, Mo.	600	D7	150
Doetinchem, Neth.	15,300	C5	282
Doeville, Johnson, Tenn.		B10	190
Dog, isl., Fla.		B6	174
Dog, lake, Man., Can.		E3	60
Dog, riv., Vt.		C3	218
Dog Creek, B.C., Can.		E11	52
Dogie, Niobrara, Wyo.		C8	116
Dogiuma, Som.		E5	398
Dog Keys, pass, Miss.		E2	184
Dogondoutchi, Niger	4,000	D5	408
Dog Pound, Alta., Can.	26	E5	54
Dogtooth, mts., B.C., Can.		E14	52
Doğubayazit, Tur.	5,723	B11	307
Doha, Qatar		B5	383
Dohad, India		E1	368
Doi Angka, mtn., Thai.		C3	362
Dois Irmaos, mts., Braz.		B2	258
Dojran, lake, Yugo.		D6	316
Dokka, Nor.		A1	292
Dokkum, Neth.	6,194	A4	282
Doland, Spink, S.Dak.	481	C7	158
Dolavón, Arg.		F4	251
Dolcedorme, mtn., It.		F6	302
Dol[-de-Bretagne], Fr.		C3	278
Dôle, Fr.	22,022	D6	278
Dolega, Pan.	732	F6	228
Doleib Hill, Sud.		D3	398
Dolgeville, Herkimer, N.Y.	3,058	B7	212
Dolisie, Con.B.		G7	409
Dollar Bay, Houghton, Mich.	500	B3	146
Dollard, Sask., Can.	193	F3	58
Dollart, bay, Neth.		A5	282
Dollarville, Luce, Mich.	100	C6	146
Dolliver, Emmet, Iowa	122	A3	142
Dolo, Eth.		E5	398
Dolomite, Jefferson, Ala.	1,300	B3	168
		E4	
Dolomites, mts., It.		B3	302
Dolores, Arg.	14,438	C4	252
Dolores, Montezuma, Colo.	805	E2	106
Dolores, Guat.	512	B3	228
Dolores, Mex.	137	B4	224
Dolores, Ur.	11,500	B4	252
Dolores, co., Colo.	2,196	E2	106
Dolores, riv., Colo., Utah		D1	106
		E6	114
Dolores Hidalgo, Mex.	9,296	C5	225
		K13	
Doloroso, Wilkinson, Miss.	200	D1	184
Dolphin and Union, strait, N.W.Ter., Can.		D7	48
Dolton, Cook, Ill.	18,746	F3	138
Dolton, Turner, S.Dak.	71	D8	158
Dolzhanskaya, Sov.Un.		S23	332
Dom, mtn., Switz.		B3	312
Domadare, Som.		E5	398
Domain, Man., Can.	50	F4	60
Domanovići, Yugo.	2,172	C3	316
Domažlice, Czech.	7,228	B1	324
Dombarovskiy, Sov.Un.		B5	366
Dombe Grande, Ang.		B2	420
Domboma, Con.L.		B2	414
Dombóvár, Hung.	13,542	C3	320
Domburg, Neth.	1,419	C2	282
Dome, Yuma, Ariz.	50	F1	124
Dome, peak, N.W.Ter., Can.		E6	48
Domel, isl., Bur.		E3	362
Dome Rock, mts., Ariz.		E1	124
Domeyko, range, Chile		C4	250
Domingo, Sandoval, N.Mex.	75	C4	126
		G6	
Dominguez, Los Angeles, Calif.	5,000	C5	94
Dominica, C.R.		F6	228
Dominica, ter., W.I.Fed.	60,000	E14	233
Dominica, isl., Wind. Is.		E14	233
Dominican Republic, country, N.A.	2,135,872	C9	233
Dominion, N.S., Can.	2,964	C9	70
Dominion, Lee, Va.		D1	192
Dominion, cape, N.W.Ter., Can.		D11	48
Dominion, lake, Newf., Can.		E9	72
Dominion City, Man., Can.	600	F4	60
Domino Harbour, Newf., Can.		D8	72
		E10	
Dömitz, Ger.	4,585	B4	286
Dommel, riv., Neth.		C4	282
Domo, Solomon Is.		F13	359
Domodedovo, Sov.Un.	17,600	O18	332
Domodossola, It.	14,400	B2	302
Dom Pedrito, Braz.	11,124	L6	257
Domremy, Sask., Can.	226	D5	58
Domuyo, mtn., Arg.		C1	252
Don, pen., B.C., Can.		D8	52
Don, riv., Scot.		D9	272
Don, riv., Sov.Un.		H13	332
Don, riv., Sov.Un.		C2	336
Dona Ana, Dona Ana, N.Mex.	100	F4	126
Dona Ana, co., N.Mex.	59,948	F3	126
Donaghadee, N.Ire.	3,398	*G6	273
Donahue, Scott, Iowa	133	C7	142
Donald, Ont., Can.	450	P22	64
Donald, Marion, Oreg.	201	B1	96
Donalda, Alta., Can.	256	D6	54
Donalds, Abbeville, S.C.	416	C4	188
Donaldson, Hot Spring, Ark.	500	C4	170
Donaldson, Marshall, Ind.	120	A3	140
Donaldson, Kittson, Minn.	64	C2	148
Donaldson, Schuylkill, Pa.	637	C5	214
Donaldsonville, Ascension, La.	6,082	B5	180
		D5	
Donalsonville, Seminole, Ga.	2,621	E2	176
Donau (Danube), riv., Aus.		B5	313
Donau (Danube), riv., Ger.		D5	286
Donauwörth, Ger.	9,625	D4	286
Donavon, Sask., Can.	70	E4	58
Don Benito, Sp.	20,931	C4	298
Doncaster, Eng.	83,200	H11	273
Dondo, Ang.	645	A2	420
Dondo, Moz.		C6	421
Donegal, Ire.	1,413	G4	273
Donegal, co., Ire.	122,059	G5	273
Donegal, bay, Ire.		G4	273
Donegal, mts., Ire.		G5	272
Donegal, pt., Ire.		I3	273
Donelson, Davidson, Tenn.	17,195	B5	190
		E7	
Doneraile, Darlington, S.C.	1,043	*C9	188
Donets, basin, Sov.Un.		S22	332
Donets, riv., Sov.Un.		H12	332
		R23	
Dongara, Austl.	381	D2	432
Donggala, Indon.	3,821	E5	358
Dong Hoi, Viet.	21,850	C5	362
Dongo, Con.L.		B2	414
Dongola, Union, Ill.	757	F4	138
Dongola, Horry, S.C.	150	D10	188
Dongola, Sud.	3,350	B3	398
Dongou, Con.B.		F8	409
Doniphan, White, Ark.	150	B5	170
Doniphan, Doniphan, Kans.	150	C8	144
Doniphan, Ripley, Mo.	1,421	E7	150
Doniphan, Hall, Nebr.	390	D7	152
Doniphan, co., Kans.	9,574	C8	144
Donji Vakuf, Yugo.	2,583	B3	316
Donkar, Bhu.		D5	368
Donkey, creek, Wyo.		B7	116
Donkin, N.S., Can.	785	C10	70
Donley, co., Tex.	4,449	B5	130
Don Luis, Cochise, Ariz.	200	G6	124
Don Martin, lake, Mex.		B5	225
Donna, Hidalgo, Tex.	7,522	F6	130
Donnacona, Que., Can.	4,147	R13	66
		R15	
Donnan, Fayette, Iowa	32	*B6	142
Donnellson, Lee, Iowa	709	D6	142
Donnelly, Alta., Can.	265	C4	54
Donnelly, Valley, Idaho	161	E2	108
Donnelly, Stevens, Minn.	358	F2	148
Donner, Terrebonne, La.	300	C5	180
		E5	
Donnybrook, Ward, N.Dak.	196	B4	154
Donora, Washington, Pa.	11,131	C2	214
Donovan, Johnson, Ga.	125	D4	176
Donovan, Iroquois, Ill.	320	C6	138
Dooley, Sheridan, Mont.	9	B12	110
Dooling, Dooly, Ga.	300	D3	176
Doolittle, Phelps, Mo.	499	*D6	150
Dooly, co., Ga.	11,474	D3	176
Dooms, Augusta, Va.	200	B6	192
Doon, Lyon, Iowa	436	A1	142
Door, co., Wis.	20,685	D6	160
Dora, Walker, Ala.	1,776	B2	168
Dora, Crawford, Ark.	60	B2	170
Dora, Roosevelt, N.Mex.	200	E7	126
Dora, Coos, Oreg.	100	D2	96
Dora Baltea, riv., It.		C1	302
Dorada, Col.		B2	244
Doran, Wilkin, Minn.	136	E2	148
Doraville, De Kalb, Ga.	4,437	A5	176
Dorcas, Okaloosa, Fla.	100	A4	174
Dorcheat, creek, Ark.		D3	170
Dorchester, N.B., Can.	1,000	D5	70
Dorchester, Eng.	11,400	K10	273
Dorchester, Saline, Nebr.	460	D8	152
Dorchester, Grafton, N.H.	10 (91▴)	D3	208
Dorchester, Cumberland, N.J.	250	E3	210
Dorchester, Dorchester, S.C.	400	E8	188
Dorchester, Wise, Va.	150	*D2	192
Dorchester, Clark, Wis.	504	C3	160
Dorchester, co., Que., Can.	34,692	R14	66
Dorchester, co., Md.	29,666	D7	182
Dorchester, co., S.C.	24,383	E8	188
Dorchester, cape, N.W.Ter., Can.		D11	48
Dorcyville, Iberville, La.	400	B5	180
Dordogne, dept., Fr.	377,870	*E4	278
Dordrecht, Neth.	74,541 (*101,000)	C3	282
Dordrecht, U.S.Afr.	3,126	F5	420
Doré, lake, Ont., Can.		O23	64
Doré, lake, Sask., Can.		C4	58
Doré, riv., Sask., Can.		C4	58
Dorena, Mississippi, Mo.	400	E8	150
Dorena, Lane, Oreg.	225	D4	96
Dorena, dam, Oreg.		D4	96
Dorenlee, Alta., Can.	50	D6	54
Dores, Scot.	607	D8	272
Dores do Indaiá, Braz.	5,475	D1	258
Dorgali, It.	6,900	E2	302
Dori, Upper Volta	3,600	D4	408
Dorion (Vaudreuil), Que., Can.	3,089	S15	66
Dormont, Allegheny, Pa.	13,098	A3	214
Dornbirn, Aus.	22,532	C1	313
Dornoch, Scot.	900	D8	272
Dornoch, firth, Scot.		D9	272
Dorogobuzh, Sov.Un.	17,900	E9	332
Dorohoi, Rom.	14,771	A4	321
Dorotea, Swe.		D7	290
Dorothy, Alta., Can.	25	E6	54
Dorothy, Red Lake, Minn.	100	D2	148
Dorothy, Atlantic, N.J.	450	E3	210
Dorothy, Raleigh, W.Va.	350	D6	194
Dorr, Allegan, Mich.	275	G6	146
Dorrance, Russell, Kans.	331	D5	144
Dorre, isl., Austl.		D2	432
Dorris, Siskiyou, Calif.	973	B3	94
Dorset, Ont., Can.	145	O22	64
Dorset, Bennington, Vt.	300 (1,150▴)	E2	218
Dorset, co., Eng.	304,100	K10	273
Dorset, mtn., Vt.		E2	218
Dorset, peak, Vt.		E2	218
Dorsey, Anne Arundel and Howard, Md.	500	B6	182
Dorsey, Itawamba, Miss.	130	A4	184
Dortmund, Ger.	618,300 (*835,000)	C2	286
Dorton, Pike, Ky.	900	C8	178
Dörtyol, Tur.	5,720	C7	307
Doruma, Con.L.		B4	414
Dorval, Que., Can.	14,055	S15	66
Dory, Southampton, Va.		D7	192
Dos Cabezas, Cochise, Ariz.	72	F6	124
Dos Hermanas, Sp.	17,274	D4	298
Doshi, Afg.	10,000	B5	374
Dos Palos, Merced, Calif.	2,028	D3	94
Dosquet, Que., Can.	585	R13	66
Dosso, Niger	1,900	D5	408
Dossville, Leake, Miss.	200	C3	184
Dothan, Houston, Ala.	31,440	D4	168
Dothan, Fayette, W.Va.	500	D7	194
Dotsero, Eagle, Colo.		C4	106
Dott, Mercer, W.Va.	950	D3	194
Doty, Lewis, Wash.	260	C3	98
Doty, isl., Wis.		A5	160
Douai, Fr.	43,380	B5	278
Douala, Cam.	80,000	F6	409
Douarnenez, Fr.	20,089	C1	278
Double, mtn., Ala.		E5	168
Double Beach, New Haven, Conn.	300	D4	202
Double Mer, lake, Newf., Can.		C6	72
Double Oak, mtn., Ala.		E5	168
Double Run, Wilcox, Ga.	250	E3	176
Double Springs, Winston, Ala.	811	A2	168
Double Springs, Rutherford, Tenn.	400	*C5	190
Doubletop, peak, Wyo.		C2	116
Doubs, dept., Fr.	327,187	*D7	278
Doubs, Frederick, Md.	200	B5	182
Doubs, riv., Fr.		D7	278
Doubs, riv., Switz.		A2	312
Doubtful, sound, N.Z.		F1	437
Douds, Van Buren, Iowa	250	D5	142
Doué [-la-Fontaine], Fr.		D3	278
Douenza, Mali	2,250	D4	408
Doughboy, Cherry, Nebr.		B4	152
Dougherty, Cerro Gordo, Iowa	398	B4	142
Dougherty, Murray, Okla.	294	D6	128
Dougherty, co., Ga.	75,680	E2	176
Douglas, Marshall, Ala.	25	A3	168
Douglas, Alsk.	1,042	D8	84
		I14	
Douglas, Cochise, Ariz.	11,925	G6	124
Douglas, Ont., Can.	525	O24	64
Douglas, Coffee, Ga.	8,736	E4	176
Douglas, I. of Man	20,361	G8	273
Douglas, Worcester, Mass.	397 (2,559▴)	B4	206
Douglas, Allegan, Mich.	602	G5	146
Douglas, Olmsted, Minn.	126	G6	148
Douglas, Otoe, Nebr.	197	D9	152
Douglas, Ward, N.Dak.	210	C4	154
Douglas, Garfield, Okla.	74	B6	128
Douglas, U.S.Afr.	3,333	E4	420
Douglas, Converse, Wyo.	2,822	D7	116
Douglas, co., Colo.	4,816	C5	106
Douglas, co., Ga.	16,741	C2	176
Douglas, co., Ill.	19,243	D5	138
Douglas, co., Kans.	43,720	D8	144
Douglas, co., Minn.	21,313	F3	148
Douglas, co., Mo.	9,653	E5	150
Douglas, co., Nebr.	343,490	C9	152
Douglas, co., Nev.	3,481	E2	112
Douglas, co., Oreg.	68,458	D3	96
Douglas, co., S.Dak.	5,113	D7	158
Douglas, co., Wash.	14,890	B7	98
Douglas, co., Wis.	45,008	B2	160
Douglas, chan., B.C., Can.		D8	52
Douglas, creek, Colo.		C2	106
Douglas, lake, Mich.		D7	146
Douglas, lake, Tenn.		C8	190
Douglas, pt., Ont., Can.		P19	64
Douglas Lake, B.C., Can.		E12	52
Douglass, Butler, Kans.	1,058	B7	144
		E6	
Douglass, Fairfield, S.C.	120	C6	188
Douglas Station, Man., Can.	160	F3	60
Douglastown, N.B., Can.	500	B4	70
Douglasville, Baldwin, Ala.		E2	168
Douglasville, Douglas, Ga.	4,462	C2	176
Doullens, Fr.	5,513	B5	278
Doumé, Cam.	1,644	F7	409
Douna, Mali		D3	408
Dour, Bel.	11,640	D2	282
Dourada, mts., Braz.		C1	258
Douro (Duero), riv., Port.		B2	298
Douro Litoral, prov., Port.	1,240,149	*B2	298
Dousman, Waukesha, Wis.	410	E5	160
Douthat, Ottawa, Okla.	250	*B9	128
Douz, Tun.	4,993	B5	402
Dove Creek, Dolores, Colo.	986	E2	106
Dover, Pope, Ark.	525	B3	170
Dover, Kent, Del.	7,250	D3	172
Dover, Eng.	35,400	J14	273
Dover, Hillsborough, Fla.	350	C8	174
Dover, Screven, Ga.	150	D5	176
Dover, Bonner, Idaho	250	A2	108

Dover, Shawnee, Kans.	150	D8	144
Dover, Mason, Ky.	718	B7	178
Dover, Norfolk, Mass.	1,400	D2	206
	(2,846▲)		
Dover, Olmsted, Minn.	312	H6	148
Dover, Lafayette, Mo.	172	B4	150
Dover, Strafford, N.H.	19,131	E5	208
Dover, Morris, N.J.	13,034	B3	210
Dover, Craven, N.C.	651	B8	186
Dover, Tuscarawas, Ohio	11,300	B5	156
Dover, Kingfisher, Okla.	350	C6	128
Dover, York, Pa.	975	D5	214
Dover, Stewart, Tenn.	736	B4	190
Dover, Windham, Vt.	35	*F3	218
	(370▲)		
Dover, riv., Alta., Can.		B6	54
Dover, strait, Eng., Fr.		K13	273
		B4	278
Dover-Foxcroft, Piscataquis, Maine	2,481	C3	204
	(4,173▲)		
Doverhill, Martin, Ind.	100	D3	140
Dover Plains, Dutchess, N.Y.	950	D8	212
Dovesville, Darlington, S.C.	200	C9	188
Dovetail, Petroleum, Mont.		C8	110
Dovey, Muhlenberg, Ky.	500	C3	178
Dovray, Murray, Minn.	113	G3	148
Dovrefjell, mts., Nor.		F3	291
Dow, Pittsburg, Okla.	300	D8	128
Dow, lake, Bech.		D5	420
Dowa, Rh. & Nya.	1,085	B6	421
Dowagiac, Cass, Mich.	7,208	H5	146
Dow City, Crawford, Iowa	531	C2	142
Dowdell Knob, mtn., Ga.		D2	176
Dowdy, Independence, Ark.	25	B5	170
Dowell, Jackson, Ill.	453	F4	138
Dowelltown, De Kalb, Tenn.	279	B6	190
Dowling, Alta., Can.		E7	54
Dowling, lake, Alta., Can.		E6	54
Dowling Park, Suwannee, Fla.	110	A7	174
Down, co., N.Ire.	242,700	G7	273
Downer, Clay, Minn.	125	E2	148
Downers Grove, Du Page, Ill.	21,154	F2	138
Downey, Los Angeles, Calif.	82,505	C5	94
		F4	
Downey, Bannock, Idaho	726	G6	108
Downieville, Sierra, Calif.	400	C3	94
Downing, Schuyler, Mo.	463	A5	150
Downing, Dunn, Wis.	241	C1	160
Downingtown, Chester, Pa.	5,598	D6	214
Downpatrick, N.Ire.	3,878	*G7	273
Downs, Macon, Ala.	100	C4	168
Downs, McLean, Ill.	497	C5	138
Downs, Osborne, Kans.	1,206	C5	144
Downs, mtn., Wyo.		C3	116
Downs Chapel, Kent, Del.	20	D3	172
Downsville, Union, La.	150	B3	180
Downsville, Washington, Md.	125	A4	182
Downsville, Delaware, N.Y.	400	C7	212
Downsville, Dunn, Wis.	275	D2	160
Downton, mtn., B.C., Can.		D10	52
Dows, Wright, Iowa	882	B4	142
Doyhof, Alsk.	100	J14	84
Doyle, Lassen, Calif.	150	C3	94
Doyle, White, Tenn.	500	C6	190
Doyles, Newf., Can.	150	G6	72
Doylestown, Wayne, Ohio	1,873	B5	156
Doylestown, Bucks, Pa.	5,917	C6	214
Doylestown, Columbia, Wis.	249	E4	160
Doyleville, Gunnison, Colo.	35	D4	106
Doyline, Webster, La.	1,061	B2	180
Doyon, Ramsey, N.Dak.	90	B7	154
Dozier, Crenshaw, Ala.	335	D3	168
Dra, riv., Alg.		C2	402
Drachten, Neth.	9,800	A5	282
Dracut, Middlesex, Mass.	10,000	A5	206
	(13,674▲)		
Drăgănești, Rom.	3,965	B3	321
Draganovo, Bul.	5,465	B2	317
Drăgășani, Rom.	9,963	B3	321
Dragerton, Carbon, Utah	2,959	D5	114
Dragoon, Cochise, Ariz.	200	F5	124
Draguignan, Fr.	11,388	F7	278
Drain, Douglas, Oreg.	1,052	D3	96
Drake, Yavapai, Ariz.	12	D3	124
Drake, Sask., Can.	232	E5	58
Drake, Larimer, Colo.	40	B5	106
Drake, McHenry, N.Dak.	752	C5	154
Drake, Marlboro, S.C.	176	C9	188
Drake, creek, Ky.		D4	178
Drakensberg, mts., U.S.Afr.		F5	420
Drake Passage, strait, Ant.		I4	251
Drakesboro, Muhlenberg, Ky.	832	C3	178
Drakes Branch, Charlotte, Va.	759	D6	192
Drakestown, Morris, N.J.		*B3	210
Drakesville, Davis, Iowa	197	D5	142
Draketown, Haralson, Ga.	100	C1	176
Dráma, Grc.	29,498	A5	306
Dráma, prov., Grc.	120,492	*A5	306
Drammen, Nor.	30,050	B1	292
	(*52,000)		
Drams, fjord, Nor.		B1	292
Drancy, Fr.	50,654	I10	278
Dranesville, Fairfax, Va.		A6	192
Dranka, Sov.Un.		D18	329
Draper, Rockingham, N.C.	3,382	A6	186
Draper, Jones, S.Dak.	215	D5	158
Draper, Salt Lake, Utah	1,000	C4	114
Draper, Pulaski, Va.	233	*D4	192
Draperstown, N.Ire.		G6	272
Draperville, Linn, Oreg.	250	*C4	96
Dras, India		B1	368
Drasco, Cleburne, Ark.	75	B5	170
Drau, riv., Aus.		D5	313
Dráva, riv., Hung.		D2	320
Drava, riv., Yugo.		B4	316
Dravograd, Yugo.	1,701	A2	316
Dravosburg, Allegheny, Pa.	3,458	A4	214
Drawsko, Pol.	3,504	B2	325
Drayden, St. Marys, Md.	75	D7	182
Drayton, Ont., Can.	573	Q20	64
Drayton, Pembina, N.Dak.	940	B8	154
Drayton, Spartanburg, S.C.	1,128	B5	188
Drayton Plains, Oakland, Mich.	6,000	G8	146
Drayton Valley, Alta., Can.	2,588	D5	54
Drebkau, Ger.	2,518	C6	286
Drechu (Chinsha), riv., China		E7	346
Drennen, Nicholas, W.Va.	250	C7	194
Drente, prov., Neth.	293,759	B5	282
Dresbach, Winona, Minn.	350	H7	148
Dresden, Ont., Can.	2,260	R18	64
Dresden, Ger.	496,500	C5	286
	(*680,000)		
Dresden, Decatur, Kans.	134	C3	144
Dresden, Lincoln, Maine	150	D3	204
	(766▲)		
Dresden, Cavalier, N.Dak.	65	B7	154
Dresden, Muskingum, Ohio	1,338	B4	156
Dresden, Weakley, Tenn.	1,510	B3	190
Dresden Village, Macomb, Mich.	5,500	*G8	146
Dresser, Polk, Wis.	498	C1	160
Dreux, Fr.	16,818	C4	278
Drew, Ouachita, La.		B3	180
Drew (Town of), Penobscot, Maine	(43▲)	C4	204
Drew, Sunflower, Miss.	2,143	B2	184
Drew, Douglas, Oreg.	25	E4	96
Drew, co., Ark.	15,213	D5	170
Drewry, Monroe, Ala.	72	D2	168
Drewrys Bluff, Chesterfield, Va.	250	B9	192
		C7	
Drewryville, Southampton, Va.	200	D7	192
Drews, res., Oreg.		E6	96
Drewsey, Harney, Oreg.	39	D8	96
Drewsville, Cheshire, N.H.	100	E2	208
Drexel, Pasco, Fla.	175	C8	174
Drexel, Mineral, Mont.	14	C1	110
Drexel, Cass, Mo.	651	C3	150
Drexel, Burke, N.C.	1,146	B4	186
Drexel, Montgomery, Ohio	2,500	C2	156
Drexel Gardens, Marion, Ind.	1,000	D4	140
Drexel Hill, Delaware, Pa.	39,000	A6	214
Dreyfus, Forrest, Miss.	150	D3	184
Drezna, Sov.Un.	18,000	N19	332
Driffield, Eng.	6,900	H12	273
Drift, creek, Oreg.		C2	96
Driftpile, Alta., Can.		C5	54
Driftpile, riv., Alta., Can.		C5	54
Driftwood, Alfalfa, Okla.	32	B5	128
Driggs, Teton, Idaho	824	F7	108
Drin, gulf, Alb.		D4	316
Drin, riv., Alb.		C5	316
Drina, riv., Yugo.		B4	316
Drinkwater, Sask., Can.	163	E5	58
Driscoll, Burleigh, N.Dak.	220	D5	154
Driscoll, Nueces, Tex.	669	F7	130
Driskill, mtn., La.		B3	180
Drissa, Sov.Un.	6,600	E7	332
Driver, Mississippi, Ark.	150	B6	170
Driver, Nansemond, Va.	160	A8	192
Dröbak, Nor.	2,212	B1	292
Drogheda, Ire.	17,008	H6	273
Drogobych, Sov.Un.	42,000	H4	332
Drôme, dept., Fr.	275,280	*E6	278
Drôme, riv., Fr.		E6	278
Dronninglund, Den.	1,458	D1	292
Dropmore, Man., Can.	50	E2	60
Druid, Sask., Can.	60	E3	58
Druid Hills, De Kalb, Ga.	2,000	*C2	176
Druid Hills, Jefferson, Ky.	444	*B5	178
Druid Hills, Henderson, N.C.	1,207	*B3	186
Drum, isl., S.C.		F4	188
Drumbo, Ont., Can.	475	Q20	64
Drumcliffe, Ire.		G4	273
Drumheller, Alta., Can.	2,632	E6	54
Drummond, Fremont, Idaho	31	E7	108
Drummond, Granite, Mont.	577	D3	110
Drummond, Garfield, Okla.	281	B5	128
Drummond, Bayfield, Wis.	450	B2	160
Drummond, co., Que., Can.	55,565	S12	66
Drummond, isl., Mich.		D8	146
Drummond, lake, Va.		D8	192
Drummond Island, Chippewa, Mich.	150	C8	146
Drummonds, Tipton, Tenn.	300	C2	190
Drummondville, Que., Can.	26,284	S12	66
	(*39,500)		
Drummondville Ouest, Que., Can.	1,606	*S12	66
Drummore, Scot.		G8	273
Drumod, Ire.	156	H5	273
Drumright, Creek, Okla.	4,190	C7	128
Drumshambo, Ire.	540	G4	273
Drury, Sumner, Kans.	45	*E6	144
Drury, Berkshire, Mass.	150	*A1	206
Druzhina, Sov.Un.		C16	329
Druzhkovka, Sov.Un.	39,800	R21	332
Dry, Sov.Un.		C6	336
Dry, creek, Kans.		B5	144
Dry, fork, W.Va.		B5	194
Dry, fork, W.Va.		D3	194
Dry, fork, Wyo.		C7	116
Dry, hill, Mass.		A3	206
Dry, lake, Ariz.		C1	124
Dry, lake, Ariz.		F6	124
Dryad, Lewis, Wash.		C3	98
Dryanovo, Bul.	5,400	B2	317
Dry Branch, Bibb, Ga.	200	D3	176
Drybranch, Kanawha, W.Va.	800	C6	194
Dry Creek, Beauregard, La.	50	D2	180
Dry Creek, Raleigh, W.Va.	490	D6	194
Dryden, Craighead, Ark.	18	*B6	170
Dryden, Ont., Can.	4,428	R23	64
Dryden, Franklin, Maine	625	D2	204
Dryden, Lapeer, Mich.	531	G8	146
Dryden, Tompkins, N.Y.	1,263	C5	212
Dryden, Josephine, Oreg.		E3	96
Dryden, Chelan, Wash.	300	B6	98
Dry Falls, dam, Wash.		B7	98
Dry Fork, Pittsylvania, Va.	250	D5	192
Dryfork, Randolph, W.Va.	50	C5	194
Dry Lake, Clark, Nev.	25	G7	112
Dry Mills, Cumberland, Maine	500	E5	204
Drypond, Jackson, Ga.	350	B3	176
Dry Prong, Grant, La.	360	C3	180
Dry Ridge, Grant, Ky.	802	B6	178
Drysdale, riv., Austl.		A5	432
Dschang, Cam.	1,553	E7	409
Duarte, Los Angeles, Calif.	13,962	C5	94
Dubach, Lincoln, La.	1,013	B3	180
Dubawnt, lake, N.W.Ter., Can.		E8	48
Du Bay, res., Wis.		D4	160
Dubayy, Tr. Coast	20,000	B6	383
Dubberly, Webster, La.	249	B2	180
Dubbo, Austl.	12,009	E9	432
Dublin, Alameda, Calif.	275	B6	94
Dublin, Ont., Can.	275	Q19	64
Dublin, Laurens, Ga.	13,814	D4	176
Dublin, Wayne, Ind.	1,021	C4	140
Dublin (Baile Átha Cliath), Ire.	539,476	H6	273
	(*649,338)		
Dublin, Graves, Ky.	200	D2	178
Dublin, Harford, Md.	150	A7	182
Dublin, Coahoma, Miss.	200	A2	184
Dublin, Cheshire, N.H.	225	F2	208
	(684▲)		
Dublin, Bladen, N.C.	366	C7	186
Dublin, Franklin, Ohio	552	*B3	156
Dublin, Erath, Tex.	2,443	C6	130
Dublin, Pulaski, Va.	1,427	C4	192
Dublin, co., Ire.	705,781	H6	273
Dublin Gulch, Silver Bow, Mont.	2,450	*D4	110
Dublin Hill, Sussex, Del.		E3	172
Dublin Shore, N.S., Can.	215	E5	70
Dublon, isl., Truk		A3	436
Dubois, Clark, Idaho	447	E6	108
Dubois, Dubois, Ind.	510	D3	140
Du Bois, Pawnee, Nebr.	218	D9	152
Du Bois, Clearfield, Pa.	10,667	B3	214
Dubois, Fremont, Wyo.	574	C3	116
Dubois, co., Ind.	27,463	D3	140
Duboistown, Lycoming, Pa.	1,358	B4	214
Du Bose Park, Kershaw, S.C.	900	*C7	188
Dubossary, Sov.Un.	10,300	I7	332
Dubovka, Sov.Un.	12,300	C3	336
Dubrovnik, Yugo.	19,400	C4	316
Dubuc, Sask., Can.	200	E6	58
Dubulu, Con.L.		B3	414
Dubuque, Dubuque, Iowa	56,606	B7	142
Dubuque, co., Iowa	80,048	B7	142
Duce, Desha, Ark.	35	D5	170
Duchcov, Czech.	8,229	A1	324
Duchesne, Duchesne, Utah	770	C5	114
Duchesne, co., Utah	7,179	C5	114
Duchess, Austl.	52	C7	432
Duchess, Alta., Can.	177	E7	54
Du Chien, bayou, Ky.		D1	178
Duck, creek, Del.		C4	172
Duck, creek, Ohio		C5	156
Duck, creek, Wis.		A5	160
Duck, lake, Man., Can.		C3	60
Duck, lake, Maine		C4	204
Duck, mtn., Man., Can.		E2	60
Duck, riv., Tenn.		C4	190
Duck Creek, Brown, Wis. (part of Howard)		A6	160
		D5	
Duckers, Woodford, Ky.	400	B6	178
Duck Hill, Montgomery, Miss.	674	B3	184
Duck Lake, Sask., Can.	585	D4	58
Duck Mountain, prov. park, Sask., Can.		E7	58
Duck River, Hickman, Tenn.	100	C4	190
Ducktown, Polk, Tenn.	741	C7	190
Ducktrap, Waldo, Maine	100	D4	204
Duckwater, Nye, Nev.	20	E6	112
Ducor, Tulare, Calif.	150	E4	94
Dudhi, India		D3	368
Dudinka, Sov.Un.	17,000	C10	328
Dudley, Laurens, Ga.	360	D3	176
Dudley, Worcester, Mass.	200	B4	206
	(6,510▲)		
Dudley, Stoddard, Mo.	287	E7	150
Dudley, Chesterfield, S.C.	200	B8	188
Duékoué, I.C.	300	E3	408
Duenweg, Jasper, Mo.	529	D3	150
Duero (Douro), riv., Sp.		B4	298
Due West, Abbeville, S.C.	1,166	C4	188
Duff, Sask., Can.	102	E6	58
Duff, Rock, Nebr.		*B6	152
Duff, Campbell, Tenn.	200	B7	190
Duffee, Mitchell, Ga.	150	E2	176
Duffee, Newton, Miss.	50	C4	184
Dufferin, co., Ont., Can.	15,569	P20	64
Duffield, Alta., Can.	25	D5	54
Duffield, Scott, Va.	97	*D2	192
Dufftown, Scot.	1,500	D9	272
Dufrost, Man., Can.	135	F4	60
Dufur, Wasco, Oreg.	488	B5	96
Dugdemona, bayou, La.		B3	180
Dugdown, mtn., Ga.		C1	176
Dugger, Sullivan, Ind.	1,062	C2	140
Dug Hill, ridge, Md.		A6	182
Dugi, isl., Yugo.		B2	316
Dugway, Tooele, Utah		C3	114
Dugway, range, Utah		C2	114
Duisburg, Ger.	479,000	C2	286
Duitama, Col.	7,723	B2	244
Duiwelskloof, U.S.Afr.		D6	421
Duke, Calhoun, Ala.	250	B4	168
Duke, Jackson, Okla.	333	D4	128
Duke, isl., Alsk.		K15	84
Duke Center, McKean, Pa.	800	B3	214
Dukedom, Weakley, Tenn.	125	B3	190
Dukes, Union, Fla.	75	B8	174
Dukes, co., Mass.	5,829	D6	206
Duk Fadiat, Sud.		D3	398
Duki, Pak.		D6	375
Dukla, pass, Czech.		B5	324
Dukla, pass, Pol.		D5	325
Dulac, Terrebonne, La.	160	E5	180
Dulce, Rio Arriba, N.Mex.	500	B4	126
Dulce, riv., Arg.		A3	252
Dull Center, Converse, Wyo.		C8	116
Duluth, Gwinnett, Ga.	1,483	A5	176
		B2	
Duluth, Pottawatomie, Kans.	60	*C7	144
Duluth, St. Louis, Minn.	106,884	E6	148
	(*165,200)		
Dumaguete, Phil.	9,366	C6	358
Dumaran, isl., Phil.		B5	358
Dumas, Desha, Ark.	3,540	D5	170
Dumas, Tippah, Miss.	200	A4	184
Dumas, Moore, Tex.	8,477	B5	130
Dumba, Con.L.		C3	414
Dumbarton, Scot.	25,900	F8	272
Dumbarton (Dunbarton), co., Scot.	171,700	E8	272
Dumbier, mtn., Czech.		B4	324
Dumboa, Nig.		D7	409
Dumbrăveni, Rom.	5,367	A3	321
Dum-Dum, India	61,391	I9	366
Dumfries, Scot.	26,700	F9	272
Dumfries, Prince William, Va.	1,368	B7	192
Dumfries, co., Scot.	87,200	F9	272
Dumiât (Damietta), Eg., U.A.R.	53,631	A3	395
		D6	
Dumka, India		D4	368
Dummer, Sask., Can.	125	F5	58
Dummer (Town of), Coos, N.H.	(202▲)	B4	208
Dummerston, Windham, Vt.	40	*F3	218
	(872▲)		
Dumont, Butler, Iowa	719	B5	142
Dumont, Traverse, Minn.	226	F2	148
Dumont, Bergen, N.J.	18,882	A2	210
		B5	
Duna (Danube), riv., Czech., Hung.		C3	324
Dunaföldvár, Hung.	9,621	C3	320
Dunany, pt., Ire.		H6	273
Dunapataj, Hung.	5,389	C3	320
Dunărea (Danube), riv., Rom.		B4	321
Dunav (Danube), riv., Yugo.		B5	316
Dunayevtsy, Sov.Un.	17,600	H6	332
Dunbar, Otoe, Nebr.	232	D9	152
		E3	
Dunbar, Pushmataha, Okla.		D8	128
Dunbar, Fayette, Pa.	1,536	D2	214
Dunbar, Scot.	4,200	F10	272
Dunbar, Marlboro, S.C.	150	B9	188
Dunbar, Kanawha, W.Va.	11,006	C3	194
		C5	
Dunbar, Marinette, Wis.	75	C5	160
Dunbarton, Concordia, La.	50	C4	180
Dunbarton, Merrimack, N.H.	85	E3	208
	(632▲)		
Dunbeath, Scot.		C9	272
Dunblane, Sask., Can.	132	E4	58
Duncan, Greenlee, Ariz.	862	F6	124
Duncan, B.C., Can.	3,247	C14	52
		F11	
Duncan, Mercer, Ky.	50	C6	178
Duncan, Bolivar, Miss.	465	A2	184
Duncan, Platte, Nebr.	294	C8	152
Duncan, Stephens, Okla.	20,009	D6	128
Duncan, Umatilla, Oreg.		B8	96
Duncan, Spartanburg, S.C.	1,186	B4	188
Duncan, Spokane, Wash.		D8	98
Duncan, Fremont, Wyo.		C3	116
Duncan, riv., B.C., Can.		E14	52
Duncan Falls, Muskingum, Ohio	779	C5	156
Duncannon, Perry, Pa.	1,800	C4	214
Duncans Bridge, Monroe, Mo.	125	B5	150
Duncansby, head, Scot.		C9	272
Duncansville, Blair, Pa.	1,396	C3	214
Duncanville, Tuscaloosa, Ala.	100	B2	168
Duncanville, Dallas, Tex.	3,774	B8	130
Duncombe, Webster, Iowa	355	B4	142
Dundalk, Ont., Can.	847	P20	64
Dundalk, Ire.	20,154	G6	273
Dundalk, Baltimore, Md.	82,428	B6	182
		C5	
Dundalk, bay, Ire.		H6	273
Dundas, Ont., Can.	9,507	Q21	64
Dundas, Rice, Minn.	488	G5	148
Dundas, Lunenburg, Va.	200	D6	192
Dundas, Calumet, Wis.	60	A5	160
Dundas, co., Ont., Can.	16,978	O25	64
Dundas, isl., B.C., Can.		C7	52
Dundas, lake, Austl.		E4	432
Dundas, strait, Austl.		A6	432
Dundas Harbour, N.W.Ter., Can.		C10	48
Dundee, Polk, Fla.	1,554	C9	174
Dundee (West Dundee), Kane, Ill.	2,530	A5	138
		E2	
Dundee, Delaware, Iowa	185	B6	142
Dundee, Ohio, Ky.	150	C4	178
Dundee, Monroe, Mich.	2,377	H8	146
Dundee, Nobles, Minn.	148	H3	148
Dundee, Tunica, Miss.	200	A2	184
Dundee, Yates, N.Y.	1,468	C5	212
Dundee, Yamhill, Oreg.	318	B1	96
Dundee, Scot.	178,500	E10	272
Dundee, U.S.Afr.	8,819	E6	420
Dundee, Fond du Lac, Wis.	100	E5	160
Dundern, mtn., Swe.		A3	292
Dundonald, chan., Bermuda		A12	233
Dundrum, bay, N.Ire.		G7	273
Dundurn, Sask., Can.	421	E4	58
Dundy, co., Nebr.	3,570	D4	152
Dune Acres, Porter, Ind.	238	*A2	140
Dunean, Greenville, S.C.	3,950	*B4	188
Dunedin, Pinellas, Fla.	8,444	C5	174
		C8	
Dunedin, N.Z.	71,277	F3	437
	(*99,400)		
Dunellen, Middlesex, N.J.	6,840	B4	210
Dunes Park, see Beach, Ill.			
Dunfanaghy, Ire.	343	F5	272
Dunfermline, Sask., Can.	30	D4	58
Dunfermline, Scot.	45,700	E9	272
Dungannon, Ont., Can.	440	Q19	64
Dungannon, N.Ire.	5,674	G6	273
Dungannon, Scott, Va.	444	D2	192
Dungarpur, India		E1	368
Dungarvan, Ire.	5,394	I5	273
Dungarvon, riv., N.B., Can.		C3	70
Dungeness, Clallam, Wash.	75	A3	98
Dungeness, pt., Eng.		K13	273
Dungeness, riv., Wash.		B3	98
Dungu, Con.L.		B4	414
Dunham, Que., Can.	399	S12	66
Dunjee Park, Oklahoma, Okla.	550	*C6	128
Dunkard, creek, W.Va.		B4	194
Dunkerque, Fr.	21,136	B5	278
Dunkerton, Black Hawk, Iowa	507	B5	142
Dunkirk, Sask., Can.	50	E5	58
Dunkirk, Jay, Ind.	3,117	B4	140
Dunkirk, Calvert, Md.	70	C6	182
Dunkirk, Toole, Mont.	14	B5	110
Dunkirk, Chautauqua, N.Y.	18,205	C2	212
Dunkirk, Hardin, Ohio	1,006	B3	156
Dunklin, co., Mo.	39,139	E7	150
Dunkwa, Ghana	6,827	E4	408
Dun Laoghaire, Ire.	47,553	H6	273
Dunlap, Peoria, Ill.	564	C4	138
Dunlap, Elkhart, Ind.	1,935	A4	140
Dunlap, Harrison, Iowa	1,254	C2	142
Dunlap, Morris, Kans.	134	D7	144
Dunlap, Dawes, Nebr.	19	B3	152
Dunlap, Sequatchie, Tenn.	1,026	C6	190
Dunleer, Ire.	536	H6	273

Dunlo, Cambria, Pa. 982 C3 214
Dunloup, creek, W.Va. D7 194
Dunmor, Muhlenberg, Ky. 158 C4 178
Dunmore, Ire. 524 H4 273
Dunmore, Lackawanna, Pa. 18,917 A5 214
B6
Dunmore, lake, Vt. D2 218
Dunn, Richland, La. 200 B4 180
Dunn, Harnett, N.C. 7,566 B7 186
Dunn, co., N.Dak. 6,350 C3 154
Dunn, co., Wis. 26,156 D2 160
Dunn Center, Dunn, N.Dak. 250 C3 154
Dunnegan, Polk, Mo. 150 D4 150
Dunnell, Martin, Minn. 260 H4 148
Dunnellon, Marion, Fla. 1,079 B8 174
Dunnet, head, Scot. C9 272
Dunnfield, Warren, N.J. B2 210
Dunning, Blaine, Nebr. 210 C5 152
Dunn Loring, Fairfax, Va. 1,500 *B7 192
Dunnothar, Man., Can. 170 E4 60
Dunns Bridge, Jasper, Ind. 150 A3 140
Dunns Corners, Washington, R.I. 300 D1 216
Dunnsville, Essex, Va. 50 C8 192
Dunnville, Ont., Can. 4,776 R21 64
Dunnville, Casey, Ky. 240 C6 178
Dunrea, Man., Can. 260 F3 60
Dunreith, Henry, Ind. 236 *C4 140
Dunrobin, Ont., Can. 125 024 64
P25
Duns, Scot. 2,000 F10 272
Dunseith, Rolette, N.Dak. 1,017 B5 154
Dunsmuir, Siskiyou, Calif. 2,873 B2 94
Dunstable, Middlesex, Mass. 300 A5 206
(824▲)
Dun-sur-Auron, Fr. D5 278
Dunton, Dolores, Colo. E2 106
Duntroon, Ont., Can. 200 P20 64
Dunvegan, Georgetown, S.C. 160 D10 188
Dunville, Newf., Can. 275 G9 72
Dunwoody, DeKalb, Ga. 300 A5 176
Duong Dong, Viet. E4 362
Du Page, co., Ill. 313,459 B5 138
Du Page, riv., Ill. F2 138
Duplessis, Ascension, La. 150 B5 180
Duplin, co., N.C. 40,270 C8 186
Dupo, St. Clair, Ill. 2,937 E3 138
Dupont, Adams, Colo. 350 C6 106
Dupont, Kent, Del. D3 172
Du Pont, Clinch, Ga. 210 E4 176
Dupont, Jefferson, Ind. 375 D4 140
Dupont, Pointe Coupee, La. 150 D4 180
Dupont, Luzerne, Pa. 3,669 A5 214
Dupont, Charleston, S.C. (part of St. Andrews) F3 188
Du Pont, Pierce, Wash. 354 B4 98
Dupont, bayou, La. C7 180
Dupontonia, Davidson, Tenn. 1,896 *B5 190
Dupree, Ziebach, S.Dak. 548 B4 158
Dupuyer, Pondera, Mont. 115 B4 110
Duque de Bragança, Ang. 2,037 A3 420
Duquesne, Allegheny, Pa. 15,019 A4 214
C2
Du Quoin, Perry, Ill. 6,558 E4 138
Dūrā, Jordan 10,000 C6 382
Durance, riv., Fr. F6 278
Durand, Meriwether, Ga. 195 D2 176
Durand, Winnebago, Ill. 797 A4 138
Durand, Shiawassee, Mich. 3,312 G8 146
Durand, Pepin, Wis. 2,039 D2 160
Durango, La Plata, Colo. 10,530 E3 106
Durango, Dubuque, Iowa 37 *B7 142
Durango, Mex. 59,496 C5 224
Durango, state, Mex. 629,874 C4 224
Durant, Cedar, Iowa 1,266 C7 142
Durant, Holmes, Miss. 2,617 B3 184
Durant, Bryan, Okla. 10,467 D7 128
Durants Neck, Perquimans, N.C. 150 A9 186
Duratón, riv., Sp. B5 298
Durazno, Ur. 27,000 B4 252
Durazno, dept., Ur. 95,148 B4 252
Durban, Man., Can. 81 E2 60
Durban, U.S.Afr. 527,400 E6 421
(*612,800)
Durbin, Pocahontas, W.Va. 431 C5 194
Durbin, creek, Fla. B10 174
Düren, Ger. 43,800 C2 286
Durfee, hill, R.I. B1 216
Dürge, lake, Mong. B6 346
Durham, Butte, Calif. 603 C3 94
Durham, Ont., Can. 2,067 P20 64
Durham, Middlesex, Conn. 700 D5 202
(3,096▲)
Durham, Eng. 20,500 G11 272
Durham, Marion, Kans. 183 D6 144
Durham, Androscoggin, Maine 75 D5 204
(1,086▲)
Durham, Strafford, N.H. 4,688 E5 208
(5,504▲)
Durham, Durham, N.C. 78,302 B7 186
(*106,200)
Durham, Roger Mills, Okla. 75 C4 128
Durham, Washington, Oreg. 350 *B1 96
Durham, Waukesha, Wis. 130 *F1 160
Durham, Laramie, Wyo. 20 E8 116
Durham, co., Ont., Can. 35,827 P22 64
Durham, co., Eng. 1,481,000 G11 272
Durham, co., N.C. 111,995 A7 186
Durham Bridge, N.B., Can. 40 C3 70
Durham Center, Middlesex, Conn. 350 D5 202
Durham Downs, Austl. D8 432
Durkee, Baker, Oreg. 65 C9 96
Durmitor, mtn., Yugo. C4 316
Durness, Scot. 413 C8 272
Durnford, pt., Sp. Sahara B1 408
Durrells, Newf., Can. 500 F8 72
Durrës, Alb. 25,579 D4 316
Durrës, pref., Alb. 92,000 *A2 306
Dursey, isl., Ire. J2 273
Duru, Con.L. B4 414
Duruss Heights, New Castle, Del. 240 B3 172
D'Urville, cape, Neth.N.Gui. E9 359
D'Urville, isl., N.Z. D4 437
Duryea, Luzerne, Pa. 5,626 A5 214
B6
Dusky, sound, N.Z. F1 437
Dušniky, Czech. 1,880 *A2 324
Duson, Lafayette, La. 1,033 D3 180
Düsseldorf, Ger. 645,400 C2 286
(*900,000)
Dustin, Hughes, Okla. 457 C7 128
Dusty, Socorro, N.Mex. 41 E3 126
Dutch, creek, Ark. C3 170
Dutch, isl., R.I. C3 216
Dutch Bayou, St. John the Baptist, La. 400 *D5 180
Dutchess, co., N.Y. 176,008 D8 212
Dutch Fork, Richland, S.C. 300 *C6 188
Dutch Harbor, Alsk. 3 E5 84
Duthie, Shoshone, Idaho 75 B3 108
Dutton, Jackson, Ala. 300 A4 168
Dutton, Ont., Can. 784 R19 64
Dutton, Teton, Mont. 504 C5 110
Dutton, mtn., Utah E3 114
Duty, Catahoula, La. C4 180
Duval, Sask., Can. 218 E5 58
Duval, Duval, Fla. 200 A10 174
Duval, co., Fla. 455,411 A9 174
Duval, co., Tex. 13,398 F6 130
Duvall, King, Wash. 345 *B5 98
Duvergé, Dom. Rep. 4,876 C9 233
Duvno, Yugo. 1,610 C3 316
Duwadami, Sau.Ar. C3 383
Duxbury, Washington, Vt. (546▲) *C3 218
Duxbury, Plymouth, Mass. 1,069 B6 206
(4,727▲)
Düzce, Tur. 12,810 A4 307
Dvina, riv., Sov.Un. E7 332
Dvůr Králové nad Labem, Czech. 15,179 A2 324
Dwarkeswar (Dhalkisor), riv., India H8 366
Dwight, Teton, Idaho F7 108
Dwight, Livingston, Ill. 3,086 B5 138
Dwight, Morris, Kans. 281 D7 144
Dwight, Hampshire, Mass. B3 206
Dwight, Butler, Nebr. 209 C8 152
Dwight, Richland, N.Dak. 101 D9 154
Dwyer, Platte, Wyo. 20 D8 116
Dyakovo, Sov.Un. T23 332
Dybyn, Sov.Un. C14 329
Dycusburg, Crittenden, Ky. 99 C2 178
Dye, Kimball, Nebr. 33 *C2 152
Dyer, Crawford, Ark. 450 B2 170
Dyer, Lake, Ind. 3,993 A2 140
Dyer, Esmeralda, Nev. 20 F3 112
Dyer, Gibson, Tenn. 1,909 B3 190
Dyer, co., Tenn. 29,537 B2 190
Dyer, bay, Ont., Can. 019 64
Dyer Brook, Aroostook, Maine 100 B4 204
(180▲)
Dyers Bay, Ont., Can. 85 019 64
Dyersburg, Dyer, Tenn. 12,499 B2 190
Dyersville, Dubuque, Iowa 2,818 B6 142
Dyess, Mississippi, Ark. 185 B6 170
Dyje, riv., Aus. B7 313
Dyje, riv., Czech. B3 324
Dysart, Sask., Can. 341 E5 58
Dysart, Tama, Iowa 1,197 B5 142
Dzerzhinsk, Sov.Un. 163,000 A2 336
Dzerzhinsk, Sov.Un. 13,660 F6 332
Dzerzhinsk, Sov.Un. 26,000 S21 332
Dzhabhan, riv., Mong. B6 346
Dzhalal Abad, Sov.Un. 24,900 D8 336
Dzhambul, Sov.Un. 67,000 D8 336
Dzhankoy, Sov.Un. 15,000 J10 332
Dzhesey, Sov.Un. B13 329
Dzhetygara, Sov.Un. 18,000 B6 336
Dzhezkazgan, Sov.Un. 29,000 C7 336
Dzhugdzhur, mts., Sov.Un. D15 329
Dzhulfa, Iran A1 379
Dzhusaly, Sov.Un. 2,800 C6 336
Działdowo, Pol. 5,139 B5 325
Działoszyce, Pol. 2,306 C5 325
Dzierżoniów, Pol. 24,700 C3 325
Dzilam González, Mex. 1,930 C8 225
Dzioua, Alg. B5 402
Dzitbalché, Mex. 3,617 C7 225
Dzungarian, basin, China B5 346

E

Eads, Kiowa, Colo. 929 D8 106
Eads, Shelby, Tenn. 250 C2 190
Eadston (Hays Crossing), Rowan, Ky. 250 B7 178
Eadytown, Berkeley, S.C. E8 188
Eagan, Claiborne, Tenn. 500 B8 190
Eagar, Apache, Ariz. 873 D6 124
Eagle, Alsk. 92 C7 84
Eagle, Eagle, Colo. 546 C4 106
Eagle, Ada, Idaho 500 F2 108
Eagle, Clinton, Mich. 141 *G7 146
Eagle, Cass, Nebr. 302 D9 152
E2
Eagle, Fayette, W.Va. 250 C3 194
D6
Eagle, Waukesha, Wis. 620 F5 160
Eagle, co., Colo. 4,677 C4 106
Eagle, cave, Wis. E3 160
Eagle, cliff, Mont. C1 110
Eagle, creek, Ind. D4 140
Eagle, creek, Ky. B6 178
Eagle, key, Fla. F10 174
Eagle, lake, Calif. B3 94
Eagle, lake, Maine A4 204
Eagle, lake, Maine B3 204
Eagle, lake, Wis. C4 160
Eagle, mtn., Tex. D3 130
Eagle, peak, Calif. B3 94
Eagle, riv., Newf., Can. D6 72
Eagle Bend, Todd, Minn. 611 E3 148
Eagle Butte, Dewey, S.Dak. 495 B4 158
Eagle City, Blaine, Okla. 70 C5 128
Eagle Cliff, mtn., Idaho B3 108
Eagle Creek, Clackamas, Oreg. 100 *B4 96
Eagle Creek, Benton, Tenn. 35 C4 190
Eagledale, Kitsap, Wash. 500 *D2 98
Eagle Grove, Wright, Iowa 4,381 B4 142
Eagle Harbor, Prince Georges, Md. 15 *C6 182
Eagle Harbor, Keweenaw, Mich. B3 146
Eaglehill, creek, Sask. Can. E3 58
Eagle Lake, Polk, Fla. 1,364 D9 174
Eagle Lake, Aroostook, Maine 900 A4 204
(1,138▲)
Eagle Lake, Blue Earth, Minn. 506 G5 148
Eagle Lake, Colorado, Tex. 3,565 E7 130
Eagle Mills, Ouachita, Ark. 200 D4 170
Eagle Mountain, lake, Tex. B8 130
Eagle Nest, Colfax, N.Mex. 300 B5 126
Eagle Pass, Maverick, Tex. 12,094 E5 130
Eagle Point, Jackson, Oreg. 752 E4 96
Eagle River, Alsk. 100 *C7 84
Eagle River, Keweenaw, Mich. 60 B3 146
Eagle River, Vilas, Wis. 1,367 C4 160
Eagle Rock, Botetourt, Va. 450 C5 192
Eaglesham, Alta., Can. 300 C4 54
Eagle Tail, mts., Ariz. E2 124
Eagleton, Chouteau, Mont. C7 110
Eagleton Village, Blount, Tenn. 5,068 *C8 190
Eagletown, McCurtain, Okla. 400 D9 128
Eagleville, Modoc, Calif. 75 B3 94
Eagleville, Tolland, Conn. 200 B6 202
Eagleville, Harrison, Mo. 341 A4 150
Eagleville, Rutherford, Tenn. 363 C5 190
Eakly, Caddo, Okla. 217 C5 128
Eardley, lake, Man., Can. D4 60
Earl, Las Animas, Colo. E6 106
Earl, isl., Newf., Can. D7 72
Earle, Crittenden, Ark. 2,391 B6 170
Earl Grey, Sask., Can. 258 E5 58
Earlham, Madison, Iowa 788 C3 142
Earlimart, Tulare, Calif. 2,897 E4 94
Earling, Shelby, Iowa 431 C2 142
Earling, Logan, W.Va. 600 D5 194
Earlington, Hopkins, Ky. 2,786 C3 178
Earl Park, Benton, Ind. 551 B2 140
Earlsboro, Pottawatomie, Okla. 257 C7 128
Earlton, Neosho, Kans. 104 E8 144
Earlville, La Salle, Ill. 1,420 B5 138
Earlville, Delaware, Iowa 668 B6 142
Earlville, Madison, N.Y. 1,004 C6 212
Early, Sac, Iowa 824 B2 142
Early, Brown, Tex. 819 *D6 130
Early, co., Ga. 13,151 E2 176
Early Branch, Hampton, S.C. 200 F7 188
Earth, Lamb, Tex. 1,104 B4 130
Easley, Pickens, S.C. 8,283 B3 188
East, bay, Tex. F8 130
East, butte, Mont. B5 110
East, cape, Fla. F9 174
East, cape, N.Z. B7 437
East, chan., Man., Can. C4 60
East, fork, Wyo. D3 116
East, mtn., Mass. A1 206
East, pass, Fla. B6 174
East, pt., P.E.I., Can. C8 70
East, pt., Mass. B6 206
East, pt., N.J. E2 210
East, riv., Ont., Can. 021 64
East, riv., N.Y. E2 212
East, riv., Wis. A6 160
East, riv., Wyo. D3 116
Eastaboga, Talladega, Ala. 700 B3 168
Eastabutchie, Jones, Miss. 200 D3 184
East Acton, Middlesex, Mass. 200 C1 206
East Alburgh, Grand Isle, Vt. 75 B2 218
East Alliance, Mahoning, Ohio 1,275 *B5 156
East Alstead, Cheshire, N.H. 75 E2 208
East Alton, Madison, Ill. 7,630 E3 138
East Andover, Oxford, Maine 150 D2 204
East Andover, Merrimack, N.H. 250 E3 208
East Angus, Que., Can. 4,239 S13 66
East Arlington, Bennington, Vt. 500 E2 218
Eastatoe, Pickens, S.C. 75 B3 188
East Aurora, Erie, N.Y. 6,791 C3 212
East Baldwin, Cumberland, Maine 150 E2 204
East Bangor, Northampton, Pa. 970 C6 214
Eastbank, Kanawha, W.Va. 1,023 C6 194
East Barnet, Caledonia, Vt. 100 C4 218
East Barre, Washington, Vt. 550 C4 218
East Barre, res., Vt. C4 218
East Barrington, Strafford, N.H. 100 E5 208
East Baton Rouge, par., La. 230,058 D4 180
East Bend, Yadkin, N.C. 446 A5 186
East Berkshire, Franklin, Vt. 200 B3 218
East Berlin, Hartford, Conn. 400 C5 202
East Berlin, Ger. 1,139,900 B5 286
East Berlin, Adams, Pa. 1,037 D5 214
East Bernard, Wharton, Tex. 900 E7 130
East Bernstadt, Laurel, Ky. 594 C6 178
East Berwick, Luzerne, Pa. 1,258 *B5 214
East Bethel, Anoka, Minn. 1,408 *F5 148
East Bethel, Windsor, Vt. 50 D3 218
East Billerica, Middlesex, Mass. 200 *A5 206
East Blackstone, Worcester, Mass. 150 *B4 206
East Blue Hill, Hancock, Maine 200 D4 204
East Bonne Terre, St. Francois, Mo. 150 D7 150
East Boothbay, Lincoln, Maine 500 E3 204
Eastborne, Eng. 57,900 K13 273
Eastborough, Sedgwick, Kans. 1,001 B6 144
Eastbourne, N.Z. 2,724 J11 437
East Boxford, Essex, Mass. 200 A6 206
East Brady, Clarion, Pa. 1,282 C2 214
East Braintree, Man., Can. 50 F5 60
East Braintree, Norfolk, Mass. D3 206
East Braintree, Orange, Vt. 75 D3 218
East Brewster, Barnstable, Mass. 165 C7 206
East Brewton, Escambia, Ala. 2,511 D2 168
East Bridgewater, Plymouth, Mass. (6,139▲) B6 206
East Brimfield, Hampden, Mass. 150 *B3 206
Eastbrook, Hancock, Maine 100 D4 204
(167▲)
East Brookfield, Worcester, Mass. 1,150 B3 206
(1,533▲)
East Brooklyn, Windham, Conn. 1,213 B8 202
East Broughton, Que., Can. 1,060 R13 66
East Broughton Station, Que., Can. 215 R13 66
East Brownfield, Oxford, Maine 200 E2 204
East Brunswick, Middlesex, N.J. 12,000 *C4 210
East Burke, Caledonia, Vt. 110 B5 218
East Butler, Butler, Pa. 1,007 C2 214
East Byars, McClain, Okla. (part of Byars) D6 128
East Calais, Washington, Vt. 110 C4 218
East Canaan, Litchfield, Conn. 570 A2 202
East Candia, Rockingham, N.H. 200 E4 208
East Canon, Fremont, Colo. 1,101 D5 106
East Canton, Stark, Ohio 1,521 B5 156
East Carondelet, St. Clair, Ill. 463 *E3 138
East Carroll, par., La. 14,433 B4 180
East Carver, Plymouth, Mass. 175 C6 206
East Chain, Martin, Minn. 150 H4 148
East Charlemont, Franklin, Mass. 180 *A2 206
East Charleston, Orleans, Vt. 60 B5 218
East Chelmsford, Middlesex, Mass. 1,500 A5 206
Eastchester, Alsk. *C7 84
Eastchester, Westchester, N.Y. 12,000 *E8 212
East Chicago, Lake, Ind. 57,669 A2 140
East Chicago Heights, Cook, Ill. 3,270 *B6 138
East China, sea, China J12 349
East Chop, pt., Mass. D6 206
East Cleveland, Cuyahoga, Ohio 37,991 B1 156
East Cleveland, Bradley, Tenn. 1,452 *C7 190
East Clifton, Que., Can. 670 S13 66
East Concord, Essex, Vt. 250 C5 218
East Conemaugh (Conemaugh), Cambria, Pa. 3,224 C3 214
East Conway, Carroll, N.H. 100 C4 208
East Corinth, Penobscot, Maine 250 C3 204
East Corinth, Orange, Vt. 200 C4 218
East Cote Blanche, bay, La. E4 180
East Coulée, Alta., Can. 1,200 E6 54
East Dennis, Barnstable, Mass. 200 C7 206
East Dereham, Eng. 6,700 I13 273
East Derry, Rockingham, N.H. 200 F4 208
East Des Moines, riv., Iowa A3 142
East Detroit, Macomb, Mich. 45,756 B9 146
East Dixmont, Penobscot, Maine 100 D3 204
East Dorset, Bennington, Vt. 140 E2 218
East Douglas, Worcester, Mass. 1,695 B4 206
East Dover, Piscataquis, Maine 70 C3 204
East Dublin, Laurens, Ga. 1,677 D4 176
East Dubuque, Jo Daviess, Ill. 2,082 A3 138
East Dummerston, Windham, Vt. 85 F3 218
East Dundee, Kane, Ill. 2,221 A5 138
E2
East Eddington, Penobscot, Maine 300 D4 204
East Ellijay, Gilmer, Ga. 501 B2 176
East Ely, White Pine, Nev. 1,796 D7 112
Eastend, Sask., Can. 706 F3 58
East Enterprise, Switzerland, Ind. 300 D5 140
Easter, see Rapa Nui, isl., Pac.O.
Eastern, prov., Lib. *E3 408
Eastern, prov., Rh.&Nya. B6 421
Eastern, prov., Tan. 1,084,484 D6 414
Eastern, prov., Ug. B5 414
Eastern, reg., Nig. 7,218,000 E6 408
Eastern (Östlandet), reg., Nor. 1,599,301 *F3 291
Eastern, bay, Md. C7 182
Eastern, isl., Newf., Can. E8 72
Eastern, isl., Midway E3 436
Eastern, pt., Mass. C4 206
Eastern Ghats, mts., India E4 366
Eastern Neck, isl., Md. B7 182
Eastern Region, ter., Ghana E4 408
Eastern Valley, Jefferson, Ala. 1,000 *B3 168
East Etowah, McMinn, Tenn. 800 C7 190
East Fairfield, Franklin, Vt. 150 B3 218
East Fairview, McKenzie, N.Dak. 200 C1 154
East Falmouth, Barnstable, Mass. 1,655 C6 206
East Farmington, Polk, Wis. 100 C1 160
East Farmington Heights, Hartford, Conn. 1,800 C4 202
East Farms, Spokane, Wash. D9 98
East Fayetteville, Cumberland, N.C. 2,797 *B7 186
East Feliciana, par., La. 20,198 D4 180
East Flat Rock, Henderson, N.C. 1,700 B3 186
East Florenceville, N.B., Can. 500 C2 70
Eastford, Windham, Conn. 350 B7 202
(746▲)
East Foxboro, Norfolk, Mass. 950 B5 206
East Freetown, Bristol, Mass. 800 C6 206
East Frisian, is., Ger. B2 286
East Fultonham, Muskingum, Ohio 600 C4 156
East Gaffney, Cherokee, S.C. 4,779 A5 188
East Galesburg, Knox, Ill. 660 C3 138
East Gary, Lake, Ind. 9,309 A2 140
East Gastonia, Gaston, N.C. 3,326 *B4 186
East Gate, Churchill, Nev. 12 D4 112
Eastgate, King, Wash. 3,000 *B4 98
East Germantown, see Pershing, Ind.
East Glacier Park, Glacier, Mont. 300 B3 110
East Glastonbury, Hartford, Conn. 375 C5 202
East Grafton, Grafton, N.H. 100 D3 208
East Granby, Hartford, Conn. 200 B5 202
(2,434▲)
East Grand Forks, Polk, Minn. 6,998 D2 148
East Grand Rapids, Kent, Mich. 10,924 G6 146
East Granville, Addison, Vt. 75 C3 218
East Greenville, Montgomery, Pa. 1,931 C6 214
East Greenwich, Kent, R.I. 6,100 C3 216
East Griffin, Spaulding, Ga. 1,715 *C2 176
East Grinstead, Eng. J12 273
Eastgulf, Raleigh, W.Va. 500 *D3 194
East Gull Lake, Cass, Minn. 311 E4 148
East Haddam, Middlesex, Conn. 500 D6 202
(3,637▲)
Eastham, Barnstable, Mass. 300 C8 206
(1,200▲)
East Hampden, Penobscot, Maine 1,500 *D4 204
East Hampton, Middlesex, Conn. 3,000 C5 202
(5,403▲)
Easthampton, Hampshire, Mass. 12,326 B2 206

Easthampton, Hampshire, Mass. 12,326 B2 206
East Hampton, Suffolk, N.Y. 1,772 D5 212
East Hanover Township, see Hanover, N.J.
East Hardwick, Caledonia, Vt. 195 B4 218
East Harpswell, Cumberland, Maine 50 E5 204
East Hartford, Hartford, Conn. 43,977 B5 202
East Hartland, Hartford, Conn. 330 B4 202
East Harwich, Barnstable, Mass. 500 C7 206
East Haven, New Haven, Conn. 21,388 D4 202
East Haven, Essex, Vt. 30 (164▲) B5 218
East Haverhill, Grafton, N.H. 75 C3 208
East Hazelcrest, Cook, Ill. 1,457 *B6 138
East Helena, Lewis and Clark, Mont. 1,490 D5 110
East Highgate, Franklin, Vt. 110 B3 218
East Hills, Nassau, N.Y. 7,184 *E8 212
East Holden, Penobscot, Maine 200 D4 204
East Holliston, Middlesex, Mass. 121 D1 206
East Hope, Bonner, Idaho 154 A2 108
East Islip, Suffolk, N.Y. 7,000 *E3 212
East Jamestown, Fentress, Tenn. B6 190
East Jordan, N.S., Can. 160 F4 70
East Jordan, Charlevoix, Mich. 1,919 D6 146
East Juliette, Jones, Ga. 201 C3 176
East Keansburg, Monmouth, N.J. 3,000 *C4 210
East Kelowna, B.C., Can. 500 F13 52
East Killingly, Windham, Conn. 560 B8 202
East Kingsford, Dickinson, Mich. 1,063 D3 146
East Kingston, Rockingham, N.H. 300 (574▲) F4 208
Eastlake, Adams, Colo. 200 C6 106
Eastlake, Manistee, Mich. 436 E5 146
Eastlake, Lake, Ohio 12,467 A5 156
Eastland, Eastland, Tex. 3,292 C6 130
Eastland, co., Tex. 19,526 C6 130
East Lansdowne, Delaware, Pa. 3,224 *D6 214
East Lansing, Ingham, Mich. 30,198 G7 146
East Laurinburg, Scotland, N.C. 695 C6 186
Eastlawn, Washtenaw, Mich. 2,510 *G8 146
East Layton, Davis, Utah 444 *B4 114
East Lebanon, York, Maine 40 E2 204
East Lee, Berkshire, Mass. 400 B1 206
Eastleigh, Eng. 32,900 K11 273
East Lempster, Sullivan, N.H. 150 E2 208
East Lexington, Middlesex, Mass. C2 206
East Liberty, Logan, Ohio 400 B3 156
East Litchfield, Litchfield, Conn. 75 B3 202
East Livermore, Androscoggin, Maine 150 D2 204
East Liverpool, Columbiana, Ohio 22,306 B6 156
East London, U.S.Afr. 105,000 (*106,100) F5 420
East Longmeadow, Hampden, Mass. 10,294 B2 206
East Lothian, co., Scot. 51,500 F10 272
East Lumberton, Robeson, N.C. (part of Lumberton) C7 186
East Lyme, New London, Conn. 850 (6,782▲) D7 202
East Lynn, Wayne, W.Va. 200 C2 194
East Lynne, Cass, Mo. 243 C3 150
East Machias, Washington, Maine 700 (1,198▲) D5 204
East McKeesport, Allegheny, Pa. 3,470 *C2 214
Eastman, Que., Can. 681 S12 66
Eastman, Dodge, Ga. 5,118 D3 176
Eastman, Crawford, Wis. 348 E2 160
East Mansfield, Bristol, Mass. 75 B5 206
East Marion, Plymouth, Mass. 400 *C6 206
East Marion, McDowell, N.C. 2,442 *B4 186
East Massapequa, Nassau, N.Y. 6,000 *E8 212
East Meadow, Nassau, N.Y. 46,036 E3 212
East Middleboro, Plymouth, Mass. 130 *C6 206
East Middlebury, Addison, Vt. 320 D2 218
East Middletown, Orange, N.Y. 1,752 *D7 212
East Millbury, Worcester, Mass. 350 *B4 206
East Millcreek, Salt Lake, Utah 6,000 C4 114
East Millinocket, Penobscot, Maine 2,392 C4 204
East Millstone, Somerset, N.J. 700 B3 210
East Milton, Norfolk, Mass. D3 206
East Missoula, Missoula, Mont. 600 *D2 110
East Moline, Rock Island, Ill. 16,732 B3 138
East Montpelier, Washington, Vt. 200 (1,200▲) C4 218
East Morris, Litchfield, Conn. 125 C3 202
East Newark, Hudson, N.J. 1,872 B1 210
East New Market, Dorchester, Md. 225 C8 182
East Newnan, Coweta, Ga. 500 C2 176
East Newport, Waldo, Maine 200 D3 204
East New Portland, Somerset, Maine 70 D2 204
East Nishnabotna, riv., Iowa C2 142
East Norriton, Montgomery, Pa. 7,773 *C6 214
East Northfield, Franklin, Mass. 800 A3 206
East Northport, Suffolk, N.Y. 8,381 *D3 212
East Norton, Bristol, Mass. 300 C5 206
East Norwich, Nassau, N.Y. 2,500 *E8 212
East Olympia, Thurston, Wash. 500 C4 98
East Omaha, Douglas, Nebr. 684 D3 152
Easton, Fairfield, Conn. 600 (3,407▲) D2 202
Easton, Mason, Ill. 361 C4 138
Easton, Leavenworth, Kans. 320 *C8 144
Easton, Aroostook, Maine 550 (1,389▲) B5 204
Easton, Talbot, Md. 6,337 C7 182
Easton, Bristol, Mass. 100 (9,078▲) B5 206
Easton, Faribault, Minn. 411 H5 148
Easton, Buchanan, Mo. 198 B3 150
Easton, Grafton, N.H. 50 (74▲) C3 208
Easton, Northampton, Pa. 31,955 C6 214
Easton, Kittitas, Wash. 250 B5 98
Easton, res., Conn. D2 202
Easton Center, Aroostook, Maine 55 B5 204
Eastondale, Bristol, Mass. 600 *B5 206
Eastonville, El Paso, Colo. 5 C6 106
East Orange, Essex, N.J. 77,259 B1 B4 210
East Orange, Orange, Vt. 60 C4 218
East Orland, Hancock, Maine 140 D4 204
East Orleans, Barnstable, Mass. 300 C8 206
East Orrington, Penobscot, Maine 600 D4 204
East Otis, Berkshire, Mass. 96 B1 206
Eastover, Richland, S.C. 713 D7 188
East Pakistan, prov., Pak. 42,062,610 *K16 375
East Palatka, Putnam, Fla. 1,133 B9 174
East Palestine, Columbiana, Ohio 5,232 B6 156
East Palo Alto, San Mateo, Calif. 12,000 B5 94
East Parsonfield, York, Maine 100 E2 204
East Patchogue, Suffolk, N.Y. 5,500 *D4 212
East Paterson, Bergen, N.J. 19,344 A1 210
East Pea Ridge, Cabell, W.Va. 1,500 *C2 194
East Pembroke, Plymouth, Mass. 180 *B6 206
East Peoria, Tazewell, Ill. 12,310 C4 138
East Pepperell, Middlesex, Mass. 1,200 A4 206
East Peru, Madison, Iowa 173 C4 142
East Peru, Oxford, Maine 75 D2 204
East Petersburg, Lancaster, Pa. 2,053 C5 214
East Pine, B.C., Can. C12 52
East Pines, Prince Georges, Md. 1,800 C4 182
East Pittsburgh, Allegheny, Pa. 4,122 A4 214
East Pittston, Kennebec, Maine 100 D3 204
Eastpoint, Franklin, Fla. 550 B6 174
East Point, Fulton, Ga. 35,633 B5 C2 176
East Point, Red River, La. 100 B2 180
East Poland, Androscoggin, Maine 100 D2 204
Eastport, Newf., Can. 900 F9 72
Eastport, Boundary, Idaho 100 A2 108
Eastport, Washington, Maine 2,537 D6 204
Eastport, Suffolk, N.Y. 950 D4 212
East Portal, Gilpin, Colo. 32 C5 106
East Port Orchard, Kitsap, Wash. 300 *B4 98
East Poultney, Rutland, Vt. 300 D2 218
East Prairie, Mississippi, Mo. 3,449 E8 150
East Princeton, Worcester, Mass. 150 B4 206
East Providence, Providence, R.I. 41,955 B3 216
East Rainelle, Greenbrier, W.Va. 1,244 D4 194
East Randolph, Cattaraugus, N.Y. 594 C3 212
East Randolph, Orange, Vt. 130 D3 218
East Redmond, King, Wash. 203 *D3 98
East Richford, see Missisquoi, Vt.
East Ridge, Hamilton, Tenn. 19,570 E8 190
East Rindge, Cheshire, N.H. 225 F3 208
East River, New Haven, Conn. 200 D5 202
East River, mtn., Va. C3 192
East Rochester, Monroe, N.Y. 8,152 B4 212
East Rochester, Beaver, Pa. 1,025 *C1 214
East Rockaway, Nassau, N.Y. 10,721 E3 212
East Rockingham, Richmond, N.C. 3,211 *C6 186
East Rockwood, Wayne, Mich. 1,000 *G8 146
East Rutherford, Bergen, N.J. 7,769 A1 210
East Ryegate, Caledonia, Vt. 170 C4 218
East St. Johnsbury, Caledonia, Vt. 150 C5 218
East St. Louis, St. Clair, Ill. 81,712 E3 138
East Salt, creek, Colo. C2 106
East Sandwich, Barnstable, Mass. 300 C7 206
East Saugus, Essex, Mass. C3 206
East Sebago, Cumberland, Maine 75 E2 204
East Selkirk, Man., Can. 400 E4 60
East Setauket, Suffolk, N.Y. 1,127 *D4 212
East Siberian, sea, Sov.Un. B17 329
Eastside, Jackson, Miss. 800 E2 184
Eastside, Rankin, Miss. 4,318 *C2 184
Eastside, Coos, Oreg. 1,380 D2 96
Eastside Galesburg, Knox, Ill. 1,147 *C3 138
East Somerset, Pulaski, Ky. 3,645 *D6 178
Eastsound, San Juan, Wash. 150 A4 98
East Sparta, Stark, Ohio 961 B5 156
East Spencer, Rowan, N.C. 2,171 B5 186
East Spokane, Spokane, Wash. 6,000 *B9 98
East Stanwood, Snohomish, Wash. 477 A4 98
East Stoneham, Oxford, Maine 160 D2 204
East Streator, La Salle, Ill. 1,517 *B5 138
East Stroudsburg, Monroe, Pa. 7,674 C6 214
East Sudbury, Middlesex, Mass. 250 D1 206
East Sullivan, Hancock, Maine 250 D4 204
East Sullivan, Cheshire, N.H. 75 F2 208
East Sumner, Oxford, Maine 100 D2 204
East Swanzey, Cheshire, N.H. 250 F2 208
East Syracuse, Onondaga, N.Y. 4,708 B5 212
East Tallassee, Tallapoosa, Ala. (part of Tallassee) C4 168
East Taunton, Bristol, Mass. C5 206
East Tavaputs, plat., Utah D6 114
East Tawas, Iosco, Mich. 2,462 E8 146
East Templeton, Worcester, Mass. 900 A3 206
East Thermopolis, Hot Springs, Wyo. 281 C4 116
East Thetford, Orange, Vt. 100 D4 218
East Thomaston, Upson, Ga. 2,237 D2 176
East Thompson, Windham, Conn. 170 A8 202
East Tohopekaliga, lake, Fla. C9 174
East Toronto, Hancock, W.Va. A2 194
East Troy, Walworth, Wis. 1,455 F5 160
East Tulare, Tulare, Calif. 1,342 *D4 94
East Uniontown, Fayette, Pa. 2,424 *D2 214
East Vandergrift, Westmoreland, Pa. 1,388 *C2 214
East Vaughn, Guadalupe, N.Mex. 423 D5 126
East Vernonia, Columbia, Oreg. 400 *B3 96
Eastview, Ont., Can. 19,283 P25 64
East View, Harrison, W.Va. 1,704 *B4 194
Eastville, Oconee, Ga. 107 *C3 176
Eastville, Northampton, Va. 261 C9 192
East Walker, riv., Nev. E2 112
East Walla Walla, Walla Walla, Wash. C8 98
East Wallingford, Rutland, Vt. 150 E3 218
East Walpole, Norfolk, Mass. 2,000 D2 206
East Wareham, Plymouth, Mass. 950 C6 206
East Washington, Sullivan, N.H. 100 E2 208
East Washington, Washington, Pa. 2,483 C1 214
East Waterboro, York, Maine 180 E2 204
East Waterford, Oxford, Maine 75 D2 204
East Weare, Hillsboro, N.H. E3 208
East Weissport, Carbon, Pa. 200 *C6 214
East Wellington, B.C., Can. 165 B13 52
East Wenatchee, Douglas, Wash. 383 B6 98
East Wenatchee Bench, Douglas, Wash. 2,327 *B6 98
East Weymouth, Norfolk, Mass. D3 206
East Whately, Franklin, Mass. 400 B2 206
East Whittier, Los Angeles, Calif. 19,884 *F5 94
East Williston, Nassau, N.Y. 2,940 *D3 212
East Wilmington, New Hanover, N.C. 5,520 *C8 186
East Wilton, Franklin, Maine 250 D2 204
East Windsor (Town of), Hartford, Conn. (7,500▲) B5 202
East Windsor Hill, Hartford, Conn. 900 B5 202
East Winn, Penobscot, Maine 100 C4 204
Eastwood, Jefferson, Ky. 250 A5 178
East Woodstock, Windham, Conn. 150 B8 202
East York, York, Pa. 1,800 *D5 214
Eaton, Weld, Colo. 1,267 B6 106
Eaton, Delaware, Ind. 1,529 B4 140
Eaton, Preble, Ohio 5,034 C2 156
Eaton, Washington, Maine 75 C5 204
Eaton, see Eaton Center, N.H.
Eaton, Gibson, Tenn. 125 C2 190
Eaton, co., Mich. 49,684 G7 146
Eaton Center (Eaton), Carroll, N.H. 75 (151▲) D4 208
Eatonia, Sask., Can. 565 E3 58
Eaton Rapids, Eaton, Mich. 4,052 G7 146
Eatons Neck, pt., N.Y. D3 212
Eatonton, Putnam, Ga. 3,612 C3 176
Eatontown, Monmouth, N.J. 10,334 C4 210
Eatonville, Orange, Fla. 857 *C9 174
Eatonville, Pierce, Wash. 896 C4 98
Eau Claire, Berrien, Mich. 562 H5 146
Eau Claire, Eau Claire, Wis. 37,987 D2 160
Eau Claire, co., Wis. 58,300 D2 160
Eau Claire, riv., Wis. D2 160
Eau Galle, Dunn, Wis. 235 D1 160
Eau Gallie, Brevard, Fla. 12,300 C10 174
Eau Pleine, riv., Wis. D3 160
Ebadon, isl., Kwajalein A1 436
Ebb, Madison, Fla. 200 A7 174
Ebb and Flow, lake, Man., Can. E3 60
Ebeltoft, Den. 2,202 E1 292
Ebelyakh, Sov.Un. B13 329
Ebenezer, Sask., Can. 151 E6 58
Ebenezer, Holmes, Miss. 75 C2 184
Ebenezer, Florence, S.C. 298 C9 188
Ebenezer, York, S.C. (part of Rock Hill) B6 188
Ebenezer, Knox, Tenn. E9 190
Eben Junction, Alger, Mich. 75 C5 146
Ebensburg, Cambria, Pa. 4,111 C3 214
Ebensee, Aus. 10,327 C5 313
Eberswalde, Ger. 32,300 B5 286
Ebingen, Ger. 20,300 D3 286
Eboli, It. 17,800 E5 302
Ebolowa, Cam. 2,976 F7 409
Ebon, atoll, Marshall B4 436
Ebro, Washington, Fla. 350 A5 174
Ebro, riv., Sp. B6 298
Eburne, B.C., Can. 1,000 B14 52
Eccles, Raleigh, W.Va. 1,145 D3 D6 194
Echigawa, Jap. 8,749 L12 354
Echo, Dale, Ala. 135 D4 168
Echo, Rapides, La. 350 C3 180
Echo, Yellow Medicine, Minn. 459 G3 148
Echo, Umatilla, Oreg. 456 B7 96
Echo, Summit, Utah 130 C4 114
Echo, lake, Maine D2 204
Echo, pond, Vt. B5 218
Echoing, riv., Man., Can. C7 60
Echols, co., Ga. 1,876 F4 176
Echota, Gordon, Ga. 800 B2 176
Echt, Neth. 3,844 C4 282
Echternach, Lux. 3,141 E5 282
Echuca, Austl. 5,405 F8 432
Écija, Sp. 30,303 D4 298
Eckelson, Barnes, N.Dak. 90 D7 154
Eckerman, Chippewa, Mich. 200 C6 146
Eckernförde, Ger. 20,200 A3 286
Eckert (Orchard City), Delta, Colo. 1,021 D3 106
Eckerty, Crawford, Ind. 150 D3 140
Eckhart Mines, Allegany, Md. 900 A2 182
Eckley, Yuma, Colo. 207 B8 106
Eckman, Bottineau, N.Dak. 5 B4 154
Eckman, McDowell, W.Va. 1,125 *D3 194
Eckville, Alta., Can. 456 D5 54
Eclectic, Elmore, Ala. 926 C3 168
Eclipse, Nansemond, Va. 290 A8 D8 192
Econfina, riv., Fla. A7 174
Economy, Wayne, Ind. 280 C4 140
Ecorces, riv., Que., Can. P13 66
Ecorse, Wayne, Mich. 17,328 B8 146
Ecru, Pontotoc, Miss. 442 A3 184
Ector, co., Tex. 90,995 D4 130
Ecuador, country, S.A. 4,127,000 D4 236 245
Ecum Secum, N.S., Can. 290 E7 70
Ed, Swe. 3,326 C2 292
Edam, Sask., Can. 264 D3 58
Edam, Neth. B4 282
Eday, isl., Scot. B10 272
Edberg, Alta., Can. 167 D6 54
Edcouch, Hidalgo, Tex. 2,814 F7 130
Edd, Eth. C5 398
Ed Damer, Sud. 5,458 B3 398
Ed Debba, Sud. B3 398
Ed Debdaba, Tun. B5 402
Eddiceton, Franklin, Miss. 300 D2 184
Eddington, Penobscot, Maine 130 (958▲) D4 204
Ed Dirr, Eg., U.A.R. 1,126 C3 395
Eddiville, Kootenai, Idaho 16 *B2 108
Ed Dueim, Sud. 12,319 C3 398
Eddy, Sanders, Mont. 26 C1 110
Eddy, co., N.Mex. 50,783 F6 126
Eddy, co., N.Dak. 4,936 C7 154
Eddy, mt., Calif. B2 94
Eddystone, Delaware, Pa. 3,006 A6 214
Eddyville, Wapello, Iowa 1,014 C5 142
Eddyville, Lyon, Ky. 1,858 C2 178
Eddyville, Dawson, Nebr. 119 C6 152
Ede, Neth. 18,000 B4 282
Edéa, Cam. 11,000 F7 409
Eden, St. Clair, Ala. (part of Pell City) B3 168
Eden, Graham, Ariz. 45 F6 124
Eden, Man., Can. 150 E3 60
Eden, Effingham, Ga. 400 D5 176
Eden, Jerome, Idaho 426 G4 108
Eden, Hancock, Maine 140 D4 204
Eden, Somerset, Md. 105 D8 182
Eden, Yazoo, Miss. 218 C2 184
Eden, Cascade, Mont. 6 C5 110
Eden, Erie, N.Y. 2,366 C3 212
Eden, Marshall, S.Dak. 136 B8 158
Eden, Concho, Tex. 1,486 D6 130
Eden, Lamoille, Vt. 65 (430▲) B3 218
Eden, Fond du Lac, Wis. 312 E5 160
Eden, Sweetwater, Wyo. 220 D3 116
Eden, lake, Man., Can. B2 60
Edenborn, Fayette, Pa. 800 D2 214
Edenbower, Douglas, Oreg. (part of Roseburg) D3 96
Edenderry, Ire. 2,627 H5 273
Eden Park Gardens, New Castle, Del. 500 *A1 172
Edenton, Chowan, N.C. 4,458 A9 186
Eden Valley, Meeker, Minn. 793 F4 148
Edenwold, Sask., Can. 190 E5 58
Edenwold, Davidson, Tenn. 500 B5 E7 190
Eder, riv., Ger. C3 286
Edesville, Kent, Md. 210 B7 182
Edet, Swe. C3 292
Edgar, Carbon, Mont. 178 E8 110
Edgar, Clay, Nebr. 730 D8 152
Edgar, Marathon, Wis. 803 *D4 160
Edgar, co., Ill. 22,550 D6 138
Edgard, St. John the Baptist, La. 750 B6 D5 180
Edgar Springs, Phelps, Mo. 150 D6 150
Edgarton, Mingo, W.Va. 400 *D2 194
Edgartown, Dukes, Mass. 1,181 (1,474▲) D6 206
Edgecomb, Lincoln, Maine 150 (453▲) *E3 204
Edgecombe, co., N.C. 54,226 B8 186
Edgecumbe, cape, Alsk. J14 84
Edgefield, Edgefield, S.C. 2,876 D5 188
Edgefield, co., S.C. 15,735 D5 188
Edge Hill, Kent, Del. 600 *D3 172
Edgeley, Sask., Can. 200 E6 58
Edgeley, LaMoure, N.Dak. 992 D7 154
Edgely, Bucks, Pa. 950 *C7 214
Edgemere, Bonner, Idaho 10 *A2 108
Edgemere, Baltimore, Md. 2,200 B7 182
Edgemont, Cleburne, Ark. 40 *B4 170
Edgemont, Riverside, Calif. 1,628 *F5 94
Edgemont, Jefferson, Colo. 2,500 C5 106
Edgemont, Fall River, S.Dak. 1,772 D2 158
Edgemont, Utah, Utah 300 *C4 114
Edgemoor, Montgomery, Md. (part of Bethesda) C3 182
Edgemoor, Chester, S.C. 275 B6 188
Edgemoor, Anderson, Tenn. 50 E9 190
Edgerly, Calcasieu, La. 350 D2 180
Edgerton, Alta., Can. 292 D7 54
Edgerton, Johnson, Kans. 414 D8 144
Edgerton, Pipestone, Minn. 1,019 H2 148
Edgerton, Platte, Mo. 449 B3 150
Edgerton, Williams, Ohio 1,566 A2 156
Edgerton, Rock, Wis. 4,000 F4 160
Edgerton, Natrona, Wyo. 512 C6 116
Edgewater, Jefferson, Ala. 1,200 E4 168
Edgewater, Jefferson, Colo. 4,314 C5 106
Edgewater, Volusia, Fla. 2,051 C10 174
Edgewater, Anne Arundel, Md. 3,000 C6 182
Edgewater, Bergen, N.J. 4,113 B2 210
Edgewater, Snohomish, Wash. 350 *B4 98
Edgewater Beach, Porter, Ind. 150 A2 140
Edgewater Park, Harrison, Miss. 750 E1 184
Edgewater Park, Burlington, N.J. 2,866 C3 210
Edgewood, B.C., Can. 215 F13 52
Edgewood, Orange, Fla. 436 *C9 174
Edgewood, Effingham, Ill. 515 E5 138
Edgewood, Madison, Ind. 2,119 B4 140
Edgewood, Clayton and Delaware, Iowa 767 B6 142
Edgewood, Kenton, Ky. 1,100 *A6 178
Edgewood, Harford, Md. 2,240 B7 182
Edgewood, Sante Fe, N.Mex. 25 C4 H7 126
Edgewood, Allegheny, Pa. 5,124 A4 214

Edgewood, Van Zandt, Tex.	887	*C8	130
Edgewood, Roanoke, Va.	500	C4	192
Edgewood, Pierce, Wash.	100	D2	98
Edgeworth, Allegheny, Pa.	2,030	A3	214
Edgmont, chan., Fla.		C6	174
Edgmont, key, Fla.		C6	174
Édhessa, Grc.	14,935	A4	306
Edina, Hennepin, Minn.	28,501	F6	148
Edina, Knox, Mo.	1,457	A5	150
Edinboro, Erie, Pa.	1,703	B1	214
Edinburg, Christian, Ill.	1,003	D4	138
Edinburg, Johnson and Bartholomew, Ind.	3,664	C4	140
Edinburg, Leake, Miss.	425	C3	184
Edinburg, Walsh, N.Dak.	330	B8	154
Edinburg, Hidalgo, Tex.	18,706	F6	130
Edinburg, Shenandoah, Va.	517	B6	192
Edinburgh, Scot.	466,900	F9	272
Edirne, Tur.	33,591	A2	307
Edirne, prov., Tur.	253,319	*A2	307
Edison, El Paso, Colo.		D6	106
Edison, Calhoun, Ga.	1,232	E2	176
Edison, Furnas, Nebr.	249	D6	152
Edison, Middlesex, N.J.	11,000	B4	210
Edison, Morrow, Ohio	559	B4	156
Edison, Skagit, Wash.	150	A4	98
Edison Laboratory, natl. mon., N.J.		B1	210
Edisto, isl., S.C.		F8	188
Edisto, riv., S.C.		E7	188
Edisto Island, Charleston, S.C.	500	F8	188
		G2	
Edistone, Orangeburg, S.C.	240	*E7	188
Edith, Clinch, Ga.	300	F4	176
Edith, Woods, Okla.		B4	128
Edler, Baca, Colo.	30	E8	106
Edmeston, Otsego, N.Y.	500	C6	212
Edmond, Lawrence, Ala.	200	A2	168
Edmond, Norton, Kans.	91	C4	144
Edmond, Oklahoma, Okla.	8,577	C6	128
Edmond, Fayette, W.Va.	425	*C3	194
Edmonds, Madison, Idaho		*F7	108
Edmonds, Snohomish, Wash.	8,016	B4	98
Edmondson, Crittenden, Ark.	288	B6	170
Edmonson, co., Ky.	8,085	C4	178
Edmonston, Prince Georges, Md.	1,197	*C6	182
Edmonton, Alta., Can.	226,002	D6	54
	(*251,000)	F3	
Edmonton, Metcalfe, Ky.	749	C5	178
Edmore, Montcalm, Mich.	1,234	F6	146
Edmore, Ramsey, N.Dak.	405	B7	154
Edmund, lake, Man., Can.		C6	60
Edmunds, Stutsman, N.Dak.	50	C7	154
Edmunds, co., S.Dak.	6,079	B6	158
Edmundson, St. Louis, Mo.	1,428	*C7	150
Edmundston, N.B., Can.	11,997	B1	70
Edna, Labette, Kans.	442	E8	144
Edna, Creek, Okla.	30	C7	128
Edna, Jackson, Tex.	5,038	E7	130
Edna Bay, Alsk.	41	D8	84
		K14	
Edon, Williams, Ohio	757	A2	156
Édouard, lake, Que., Can.		Q12	66
Edrans, Man., Can.		F3	60
Edsbyn, Swe.		F6	291
Edson, Alta., Can.	2,560	D4	54
Edson, Sherman, Kans.	64	C2	144
Edson, Carbon, Wyo.	15	*E6	116
Eduardo Castex, Arg.	4,020	C3	252
Eduni, mtn., N.W.Ter., Can.		E6	48
Edwall, Lincoln, Wash.	165	B9	98
Edwand, Alta., Can.	125	C6	54
Edward, lake, Con.L.		C4	414
Edwards, Kern, Calif.	800	E5	94
Edwards, Ont., Can.	125	Q26	64
Edwards, Eagle, Colo.	10	C4	106
Edwards, Hinds, Miss.	1,206	C2	184
Edwards, St. Lawrence, N.Y.	658	A6	212
Edwards, co., Ill.	7,940	E5	138
Edwards, co., Kans.	5,118	E4	144
Edwards, co., Tex.	2,317	E5	130
Edwards, butte, Oreg.		B3	96
Edwards, plat., Tex.		D5	130
Edwardsburg, Cass, Mich.	902	H5	146
Edwardsport, Knox, Ind.	533	D2	140
Edwardsville, Cleburne, Ala.	168	B4	168
Edwardsville, Madison, Ill.	9,996	E4	138
Edwardsville, Wyandotte, Kans.	513	B7	144
Edwardsville, Luzerne, Pa.	5,711	A5	214
Edwardsville, Northumberland, Va.	60	*C8	192
Edwight, Raleigh, W.Va.	70	D6	194
Edwin, Henry, Ala.	100	D4	168
Edzell, Scot.	946	E10	272
Eek, Alsk.	141	C5	84
Eekloo, Bel.	17,970	C2	282
Eel, riv., Calif.		B2	94
Eel, riv., Ind.		B4	140
Eel, riv., Ind.		C2	140
Eferding, Aus.	3,465	B6	313
Effie, Avoyelles, La.	100	C3	180
Effie, Itasca, Minn.	195	D5	148
Effigy Mounds, natl. mon., Iowa		A6	142
Effingham, Effingham, Ill.	8,172	D5	138
Effingham, Atchison, Kans.	564	C8	144
Effingham, Carroll, N.H.	40	D4	208
	(329▲)		
Effingham, Florence, S.C.	100	C9	188
Effingham, co., Ga.	10,144	D5	176
Effingham, co., Ill.	23,107	D5	138
Efland, Orange, N.C.	500	A6	186
Eforie, Rom.	428	B5	321
Ega, riv., Sp.		A5	298
Egadi, is., It.		F4	302
Egan, Acadia, La.	300	*D3	180
Egan, Moody, S.Dak.	310	C9	158
Eganville, Ont., Can.	1,598	O23	64
Egavik, Alsk.	5	C5	84
Egbert, Laramie, Wyo.	85	E8	116
Egegik, Alsk.	119	D6	84
Egeland, Towner, N.Dak.	190	B6	154
Eger, Hung.	34,000	B5	320
Egersund, Nor.	4,078	G1	291
Egg, lake, Sask., Can.		C5	58
Eggbornsville, Culpeper, Va.		B6	192
Eggenburg, Aus.	3,714	B7	313
Eggertsville, Erie, N.Y. (part of Amherst)		C3	212
Egg Harbor, Door, Wis.	150	C6	160
Egg Harbor City, Atlantic, N.J.	4,416	D3	210
Egg Island, pt., N.J.		E2	210
Eggleston, Giles, Va.	300	C4	192
Egilsstadhir, Ice.	83	L22	290
Egin, Fremont, Idaho		*F7	108
Eglantine, Van Buren, Ark.	50	B4	170
Égletons, Fr.		E4	278
Egmond aan Zee, Neth.	3,679	B3	282
Egmont, bay, P.E.I., Can.		C5	70
Egmont, cape, N.Z.		C4	437
Egmont, mtn., N.Z.		C4	437
Egremont, Alta., Can.	110	C6	54
Egremont, Berkshire, Mass.	100	B1	206
	(895▲)		
Egremont, Sharkey, Miss.	30	C2	184
Eğridir, Tur.	5,766	C4	307
Eğridir, lake, Tur.		B4	307
Egypt, Craighead, Ark.	225	B6	170
Egypt, Effingham, Ga.	200	D5	176
Egypt, Plymouth, Mass.	300	B6	206
		D4	
Egypt, Chickasaw, Miss.	110	B4	184
Egypt, Lehigh, Pa.	1,500	C6	214
Egypt, prov., U.A.R.	25,032,000	D9	388
			395
Eholt, B.C., Can.	60	F13	52
Ehrenberg, Yuma, Ariz.	50	E1	124
Ehrenfeld, Cambria, Pa.	566	C3	214
Ehrhardt, Bamberg, S.C.	482	E6	188
Eibar, Sp.	8,729	A5	298
Eichstätt, Ger.	11,300	D4	286
Eid, Nor.		F2	291
Eider, riv., Ger.		A3	286
Eidfjord, Nor.		F2	291
Eidson, Hawkins, Tenn.	30	B8	190
Eidsvoll, Nor.	11,456	A2	292
Eifel, mts., Ger.		C2	286
Eigg, isl., Scot.		E6	272
Eightmile, Morrow, Oreg.		B7	96
Eighty Mile, beach, Austl.		B4	432
Eil, Som.	2,000	D6	398
Eileen, lake, N.W.Ter., Can.		E8	48
Eilenburg, Ger.	18,800	C5	286
Eil Malk, isl., Palau		A6	436
Einbeck, Ger.	17,400	C3	286
Eindhoven, Neth.	149,460	C4	282
Ein Gev, Isr.	494	B6	382
Ein Harod, Isr.	1,276	B6	382
Ein Netafim, Isr.		E5	382
Ein Scilleme, hill, Libya		C4	394
Einsiedeln, Switz.	8,000	A4	312
Eirunepé, Braz.	1,714	G3	256
Eisenach, Ger.	50,000	C4	286
Eisenerz, Aus.	12,948	C6	313
Eisenstadt, Aus.	5,464	C8	313
Eisleben, Ger.	30,100	C4	286
Eitzen, Houston, Minn.	181	H7	148
Ejea de los Caballeros, Sp.	11,772	A6	298
Ejeda, Malag.		D8	421
Ejutla de Crespo, Mex.	4,288	D6	225
Ekalaka, Carter, Mont.	738	E12	110
Ekeia, riv., Cen. Afr. Rep.		E8	409
Ekeren, Bel.	19,418	C3	282
Ekhinos, Grc.	4,005	A5	306
Ekimchan, Sov.Un.	700	D15	329
Eklo, Baltimore, Md.	125	A6	182
Eklutna, Alsk.	53	C7	84
		G11	
Eknö, isl., Swe.		D7	292
Ekonda, Sov.Un.		C12	329
Ekron, Meade, Ky.	205	C4	178
Eksjö, Swe.	10,065	D5	292
Ekuk (Ukak), Alsk.	30	*D6	84
Ekumaketo, Con.L.		C3	414
Ekwak (Ekwok), Alsk.	131	D6	84
El Aboid Sidi Cheikh, Alg.		B4	402
El Ahmar, sand dunes, Alg.		C3	402
El Ahmar, sand dunes, Mali		B3	408
Elaine, Phillips, Ark.	898	C6	170
El Alamein, Eg., U.A.R.		A2	395
El Alia, Alg.		B5	402
El Allâqi, Eg., U.A.R.		C3	395
El Amiriya, Eg., U.A.R.	3,814	A2	395
Elamsville, Patrick, Va.		D4	192
Elamton, Morgan, Ky.	200	C7	178
Elamville, Barbour, Ala.	110	D4	168
Eland, Shawano, Wis.	213	D4	160
El Arahal, Sp.	13,517	D4	298
El Aricha, Alg.		B3	402
El Arish, Eg., U.A.R.	10,791	A3	395
El Arish, wadi, Eg., U.A.R.		D5	382
Elassón, Grc.	5,755	B4	306
El 'Atate, mtn., Jordan		D6	382
Elath (Eilat), Isr.		E5	382
El 'Atrun (Oasis), Sud.		B2	398
El 'Aujā, Isr.		D5	382
Elâzig, Tur.	41,915	B8	307
Elâzig, prov., Tur.	240,842	*B8	307
Elba, Coffee, Ala.	4,321	D3	168
Elba, Van Buren, Ark.	11	B4	170
Elba, Washington, Colo.	10	C7	106
Elba, Cassia, Idaho	70	G5	108
Elba, Winona, Minn.	152	G6	148
Elba, Howard, Nebr.	184	C7	152
Elba, Genesee, N.Y.	739	B3	212
Elba, dam, Ala.		D3	168
Elba, isl., It.		D3	302
El Bahnasa, Eg., U.A.R.		B3	395
El Bar, cape, Eg., U.A.R.		C2	382
El Barco, Sp.	2,499	A3	298
Elbasan, Alb.	23,616	D5	316
Elbasan, pref., Alb.	115,000	*A3	306
El Baúl, Ven.	838	B4	240
Elbe, riv., Ger.		B4	286
Elberfeld, Warrick, Ind.	485	D2	140
Elberon, Tama, Iowa	211	B5	142
Elberon, Monmouth, N.J.		C5	210
Elbert, Elbert, Colo.	250	C6	106
Elbert, McDowell, W.Va.	950	D3	194
Elbert, co., Colo.	3,708	C6	106
Elbert, co., Ga.	17,835	B4	176
Elbert, mtn., Colo.		C4	106
Elberta, Baldwin, Ala.	384	E2	168
Elberta, Houston, Ga.	644	D3	176
Elberta, Benzie, Mich.	552	E5	146
Elberta, Utah, Utah	50	D4	114
Elberton, Elbert, Ga.	7,107	B4	176
Elberton, Whitman, Wash.	66	C9	98
Elbeuf, Fr.	17,293	C4	278
Elbing, Butler, Kans.	105	*D6	144
Elbing, see Elbląg, Pol.			
Elbistan, Tur.	7,477	B7	307
Elbląg, Pol.	65,000	A4	325
El Bolsón, Arg.		F3	251
El Bonillo, Sp.	5,187	C5	298
El Boquerón, pass, Peru		B2	245
El Bordo, Col.	1,475	C1	244
Elbow, Sask., Can.	281	E4	58
Elbow, lake, Man., Can.		C2	60
Elbow, riv., Alta., Can.		E5	54
Elbow Lake, Grant, Minn.	1,521	F3	148
Elbowoods, McLean, N.Dak.	175	C3	154
Elbridge, Obion, Tenn.	65	B2	190
El Brûk, wadi, Eg., U.A.R.		D4	382
El Bur, Som.	2,300	E6	398
Elburg, Neth.	3,052	B4	282
El Burgo de Osma, Sp.	2,937	B5	298
Elburn, Kane, Ill.	960	B5	138
Elburz, Elko, Nev.	16	C6	112
Elburz, mts., Iran		B3	379
El Cajon, San Diego, Calif.	37,618	F5	94
El Callao, Ven.	4,097	C8	240
El Campo, Wharton, Tex.	7,700	E7	130
El Campo North, Wharton, Tex.	1,086	*E7	130
El Campo South, Wharton, Tex.	1,884	*E7	130
El Capitan, mtn., Mont.		D2	110
El Carito, Ven.		B6	240
El Carmen, Bol.		C3	246
El Carmen, Col.	9,647	B1	244
El Carre, Eth.		D5	398
El Carrizo, Mex.	163	B4	224
El Centro, Imperial, Calif.	16,811	F6	94
El Cerrito, Contra Costa, Calif.	25,437	A5	94
El Cerro, Bol.	117	C2	246
El Chaparro, Ven.	1,186	B6	240
Elche, Sp.	46,596	C6	298
Elcho, Langlade, Wis.	525	C4	160
El Coyote, Mex.		A3	224
El Cuarto, Mex.		G9	224
El Cuervo, butte, N.Mex.		H7	126
El Cuyo, Mex.		C8	225
El Daba, Eg., U.A.R.		A2	395
El Dar el Beda, ruins, Eg., U.A.R.		D2	382
Elde, riv., Ger.		B4	286
Elderon, Marathon, Wis.	177	D4	160
Eldersburg, Carroll, Md.	150	B6	182
Eldersley, Sask., Can.	98	D6	58
El Diviso, Col.		C1	244
Eldon, Wapello, Iowa	1,386	D5	142
Eldon, Miller, Mo.	3,158	C5	150
Eldora, Hardin, Iowa	3,225	B4	142
Eldora, Cape May, N.J.		E3	210
Eldorado, Alsk.	12	*C7	84
El Dorado, Union, Ark.	25,292	D4	170
Eldorado, Ont., Can.	60	P23	64
Eldorado, Saline, Ill.	3,573	F5	138
Eldorado, Fayette, Iowa	100	A6	142
El Dorado, Butler, Kans.	12,523	E7	144
Eldorado, Dorchester, Md.	80	C8	182
El Dorado, Mex.		C4	224
Eldorado, Clay, Nebr.	20	*D8	152
Eldorado, Preble, Ohio	449	C2	156
Eldorado, Jackson, Okla.	708	D4	128
Eldorado, Schleicher, Tex.	1,815	D5	130
El Dorado, Ven.		C8	240
El Dorado, co., Calif.	29,390	C3	94
Eldorado, mtn., Wash.		A5	98
El Dorado Springs, Cedar, Mo.	2,864	D3	150
Eldoret, Ken.	8,193	B6	414
Eldred, Sullivan, N.Y.	625	D7	212
Eldred, McKean, Pa.	1,107	B3	214
Eldridge, Walker, Ala.	500	B2	168
Eldridge, Scott, Iowa	583	C7	142
		D7	
Eldridge, Stutsman, N.Dak.	67	D7	154
Eleanor, Lincoln, Wash.		B9	98
Eleanor, Putnam, W.Va.	700	C3	194
Electra, Wichita, Tex.	4,759	B6	130
Electra, lake, Colo.		E3	106
Electric, peak, Mont., Wyo.		E6	110
		B2	116
Electric City, Grant, Wash.	404	B7	98
Electric Mills, Kemper, Miss.	100	C4	184
Eleele, Kauai, Haw.	950	B2	86
Elektrogorsk, Sov.Un.	18,900	N19	332
Elektrostal, Sov.Un.	50,000	N19	332
Elenora, mtn., Utah		F2	114
Elephant, mtn., Maine		D2	204
Elephant, range, Camb.		E4	362
Elephant Butte, Sierra, N.Mex.	15	*E3	126
Elephant Butte, res., N.Mex.		E3	126
Elephant Point, see Buckland, Alsk.			
El Escorial, Sp.	2,742	*B5	298
Eleuthera, isl., W.I.		A6	232
Eleva, Trempealeau, Wis.	548	D2	160
Eleven Mile Canyon, res., Colo.		D5	106
Eleven Point, riv., Ark., Mo.		A5	170
		E6	150
El Faiyûm, Eg., U.A.R.	73,642	B3	395
El Fasher, Sud.	26,161	C2	398
El Ferrol, Sp.	47,388	A2	298
Elfin Cove, Alsk.	65	I13	84
Elfrida, Cochise, Ariz.	300	G6	124
Elfros, Sask., Can.	308	E6	58
El Fud, Eth.		D5	398
El Fuerte, Mex.	3,551	B4	224
El Galhak, Sud.		C3	398
El Geteina, Sud.		C3	398
El Giddi, mtn., Eg., U.A.R.		D4	382
Elgin, Lauderdale, Ala.	250	A2	168
Elgin, Santa Cruz, Ariz.	20	G5	124
Elgin, Man., Can.	400	F2	60
Elgin, N.B., Can.	310	D4	70
Elgin, Kane, Ill.	49,447	A5	138
		E2	
Elgin, Fayette, Iowa	1,123	B6	142
Elgin, Chautauqua, Kans.	148	E7	144
Elgin, Wabasha, Minn.	521	G6	148
Elgin, Antelope, Nebr.	881	C7	152
Elgin, Lincoln, Nev.	25	F7	112
Elgin, Grant, N.Dak.	944	D4	154
Elgin, Comanche, Okla.	540	D5	128
Elgin, Union, Oreg.	1,315	B9	96
Elgin, Scot.	11,300	D9	272
Elgin, Lancaster, S.C.	300	B7	188
Elgin, Scott, Tenn.	200	B7	190
Elgin, Bastrop, Tex.	3,511	D7	130
Elgin, Page, Va.		B6	192
Elgin, co., Ont., Can.	59,114	R19	64
Elgin Mills, Ont., Can.	200	R22	64
El Giza, Eg., U.A.R.	66,156	B3	395
Elgol, Scot.		D6	272
El-Golea, Alg.	7,452	B4	402
	(12,486▲)		
Elgon, mtn., Ug., Ken.		B5	414
El Grullo, Mex.	6,989	*D5	224
El Hamurre, Som.		D6	398
El Hasaheisa, Sud.	6,000	C3	398
El Haseke, Syr., U.A.R.	12,206	A4	378
El Hawata, Sud.	3,921	C3	398
El Higo, Mex.		K14	225
El Huecú, Arg.		C1	252
El Huerfanito, peak, N.Mex.		B3	126
Eli, Cherry, Nebr.	15	B4	152
Elida, Roosevelt, N.Mex.	534	E7	126
Elida, Allen, Ohio	1,215	B2	156
Elila, riv., Con.L.		C4	414
Elim, Alsk.	154	C5	84
Elimer, Pike, Ky.	900	C8	178
Eliot, York, Maine	1,730	E2	204
	(3,133▲)		
Elis, see Ilia, prov., Grc.			
Elisabethville, Con.L.	128,600	E4	414
El Iskandariyah, see Alexandria, Eg., U.A.R.			
Elista, Sov.Un.	22,000	C2	336
Elizabeth, Fulton, Ark.	20	A4	170
Elizabeth, Elbert, Colo.	326	C6	106
Elizabeth, Cobb, Ga.	1,620	A4	176
		C2	
Elizabeth, Jo Daviess, Ill.	729	A3	138
Elizabeth, Harrison, Ind.	214	D4	140
Elizabeth, Allen, La.	1,030	D3	180
Elizabeth, Otter Tail, Minn.	168	E2	148
Elizabeth, Washington, Miss.	250	B2	184
Elizabeth, Union, N.J.	107,698	B1	210
		B4	
Elizabeth, Allegheny, Pa.	2,597	C2	214
Elizabeth, Wirt, W.Va.	727	B3	194
Elizabeth, cape, Maine		E5	204
Elizabeth, cape, Wash.		B2	98
Elizabeth, is., Mass.		D6	206
Elizabeth City, Pasquotank, N.C.	14,062	A9	186
Elizabeth Lake Estates, Oakland, Mich.	2,000	*G8	146
Elizabeth Park, Norfolk, Va. (part of Norfolk)		A9	192
Elizabethton, Carter, Tenn.	10,896	B9	190
Elizabethtown, Hardin, Ill.	524	F5	138
Elizabethtown, Bartholomew, Ind.	417	C4	140
Elizabethtown, Hardin, Ky.	9,641	C5	178
Elizabethtown, Essex, N.Y.	779	A8	212
Elizabethtown, Bladen, N.C.	1,625	C7	186
Elizabethtown, Lancaster, Pa.	6,780	C5	214
Elizabethville, Dauphin, Pa.	1,455	C5	214
El Jebelein, Sud.		C3	398
El Judio, peak, Mex.		G9	224
Elk, Chaves, N.Mex.	90	F5	126
Elk, Pol.	16,900	B6	325
Elk, Spokane, Wash.	75	A9	98
Elk, Teton, Wyo.	15	C2	116
Elk, co., Kans.	5,048	E7	144
Elk, co., Pa.	37,328	B3	214
Elk, creek, Okla.		C4	128
Elk, creek, S.Dak.		C2	158
Elk, isl., Man., Can.		E4	60
Elk, mtn., N.Mex.		E2	126
Elk, mtn., Okla.		D5	128
Elk, mtn., S.Dak.		D1	158
Elk, mtn., Wyo.		E6	116
Elk, riv., B.C., Can.		F15	52
Elk, riv., Colo.		B4	106
Elk, riv., Kans.		E7	144
Elk, riv., Md.		B8	182
Elk, riv., Tenn.		C5	190
Elk, riv., W.Va.		C6	194
Elk, riv., Wis.		C3	160
El Ka'ab, Eg., U.A.R.		D3	382
Elkader, Clayton, Iowa	1,526	B6	142
El Kamlin, Sud.	4,341	B3	398
Elkatawa, Breathitt, Ky.	200	C7	178
Elk Basin, Park, Wyo.		B4	116
Elk City, Idaho, Idaho	300	D3	108
Elk City, Montgomery, Kans.	498	E8	144
Elk City, Douglas, Nebr.	48	D2	152
Elk City, Beckham, Okla.	8,196	C4	128
Elk Creek, Johnson, Nebr.	170	D9	152
Elkeren, riv., Nor.		B1	292
Elk Falls, Elk, Kans.	179	E7	144
Elk Garden, Russell, Va.	200	D3	192
Elk Garden, Mineral, W.Va.	329	B5	194
Elk Grove, Sacramento, Calif.	2,205	C3	94
Elk Grove Village, Cook, Ill.	6,608	*A6	138
El Khandaq, Sud.	11,995	B3	398
El Khârga, Eg., U.A.R.	11,155	B3	395
Elkhart, Logan, Ill.	418	C4	138
Elkhart, Elkhart, Ind.	40,274	A4	140
Elkhart, Polk, Iowa	260	A7	142
Elkhart, Morton, Kans.	1,780	E2	144
Elkhart, Anderson, Tex.	780	D8	130
Elkhart, co., Ind.	106,790	A4	140
Elkhart Lake, Sheboygan, Wis.	651	B6	160
		E5	
Elkhorn, Man., Can.	673	F2	60
Elk Horn, Shelby, Iowa	679	C2	142
Elkhorn, Douglas, Nebr.	749	D2	152
Elkhorn, McDowell, W.Va.	900	D3	194
Elkhorn, Walworth, Wis.	3,586	F5	160
Elkhorn, peaks, Idaho		F7	108
Elkhorn, ranch site, N.Dak.		C2	154
Elkhorn, riv., Nebr.		B7	152
Elkhorn City, Pike, Ky.	1,085	C8	178
Elkhovo, Bul.	10,339	B3	317
Elkin, Surry, N.C.	2,868	A5	186
Elkins, Washington, Ark.		B2	170
Elkins, Merrimack, N.H.	165	E3	208
Elkins, Chaves, N.Mex.	42	E6	126
Elkins, Randolph, W.Va.	8,307	C5	194
Elkins Park, Montgomery, Pa.	12,000	A6	214
Elk Island, natl. park, Alta., Can.		D6	54
Elk Lake, Deschutes, Oreg.		D5	96
Elkland, Webster, Mo.	200	D4	150
Elkland, Tioga, Pa.	2,189	B4	214
Elk Mills, Cecil, Md.	500	A8	182
Elkmont, Limestone, Ala.	169	A3	168
Elk Mound, Dunn, Wis.	379	D2	160
Elk Mountain, Carbon, Wyo.	190	E6	116

Elko, B.C., Can. 230 F15 52
Elko, Houston, Ga. 165 D3 176
Elko, Scott, Minn. 116 *G5 148
Elko, Elko, Nev. 6,298 C6 112
Elko, Barnwell, S.C. 194 E6 188
Elko, Henrico, Va. 20 C7 192
Elko, co., Nev. 12,011 B6 112
Elkol, Lincoln, Wyo. 25 E2 116
Elk Park, Jefferson, Mont. D4 110
Elk Park, Avery, N.C. 460 A4 186
Elk Point, Alta., Can. 594 D7 54
Elk Point, Union, S.Dak. 1,378 E9 158
Elkport, Clayton, Iowa 100 *B6 142
Elk Ranch, Carroll, Ark. 35 A3 170
Elk Rapids, Antrim, Mich. 1,015 E6 146
Elkridge, Howard, Md. 2,000 B6 182
C4
Elkridge, Fayette, W.Va. 250 D6 194
Elk River, Clearwater, Idaho 382 C2 108
Elk River, Sherburne, Minn. 1,763 F5 148
Elk River, res., Tenn. C5 190
Elk Springs, Moffat, Colo. 6 B2 106
Elkrun, Fauquier, Va. 35 *B7 192
Elk Run Heights, Blackhawk, Iowa 1,124 B5 142
Elkton, Teller, Colo. D5 106
Elkton, Saint Johns, Fla. 400 B9 174
Elkton, Todd, Ky. 1,448 D3 178
Elkton, Cecil, Md. 5,989 A8 182
Elkton, Huron, Mich. 1,014 F8 146
Elkton, Mower, Minn. 147 H6 148
Elkton, Douglas, Oreg. 146 D3 96
Elkton, Brookings, S.Dak. 621 C9 158
Elkton, Giles, Tenn. 199 C5 190
Elkton, Rockingham, Va. 1,506 B6 192
El Kubri, Eg., U.A.R. E7 395
El Kuntilla, Eg., U.A.R. B3 395
Elk Valley, Campbell, Tenn. 250 B7 190
Elkview, Kanawha, W.Va. 600 *C3 194
Elkville, Jackson, Ill. 743 F4 138
Elkwater, Randolph, W.Va. 125 C4 194
Ellabell, Bryan, Ga. 175 D5 176
El Ladhiqiya (Latakia), Syr., U.A.R. 52,041 B1 378
Ellamar, Alsk. 46 G11 84
Ellamore, Randolph, W.Va. 450 C4 194
Ellaville, Madison, Fla. 50 A7 174
Ellaville, Schley, Ga. 905 D2 176
Ellef Ringnes, isl., N.W.Ter., Can. B8 48
Ellen, mtn., Utah E5 114
Ellen, mtn., Vt. C3 218
Ellenboro, Rutherford, N.C. 492 B4 186
Ellenboro, Ritchie, W.Va. 340 B3 194
Ellendale, Sussex, Del. 370 E4 172
Ellendale, Terrebonne, La. 300 C6 180
E5
Ellendale, Steele, Minn. 501 H5 148
Ellendale, Dickey, N.Dak. 1,800 E7 154
Ellendale, Shelby, Tenn. 1,000 C2 190
Ellensburg, Kittitas, Wash. 8,625 C6 98
Ellenton, Manatee, Fla. 800 C6 174
D8
Ellenton, Colquitt, Ga. 385 E3 176
Ellenville, Ulster, N.Y. 5,003 D7 212
Ellenwood, Clayton, Ga. 220 B5 176
Ellerbe, Richmond, N.C. 843 B6 186
Ellerslie, Harris, Ga. 350 D2 176
Ellerslie, Allegany, Md. 560 A2 182
Ellesmere, isl., N.W.Ter., Can. A10 48
Ellettsville, Monroe, Ind. 1,222 C3 140
Ellice, is., Pac.O. C3 436
Ellicott City, Howard, Md. 2,000 B6 182
Ellicottville, Cattaraugus, N.Y. 1,150 C3 212
Ellijay, Gilmer, Ga. 1,320 B2 176
El Limón, Mex. 1,225 D7 225
Ellington, Tolland, Conn. 400 (5,580▲) B6 202
Ellington, Reynolds, Mo. 812 D7 150
Ellinor, Chase, Kans. 28 *D7 144
Ellinwood, Barton, Kans. 2,729 D5 144
Elliott, Ouachita, Ark. 100 D4 170
Elliott, Montgomery, Iowa 459 C2 142
Elliott, Dorchester, Md. 150 D7 182
Elliott, Grenada, Miss. 250 B3 184
Elliott, Ransom, N.Dak. 62 D8 154
Elliott, Lee, S.C. 270 C8 188
Elliott, co., Ky. 6,330 B7 178
Elliott, bay, Wash. D2 98
Elliott, key, Fla. F10 174
Elliott, lake, Man., Can. D5 60
Ellis, Baxter, Ark. 250 A4 170
Ellis, Custer, Idaho 10 E4 108
Ellis, Ellis, Kans. 2,218 D4 144
Ellis, Gage, Nebr. 55 *D9 152
Ellis, co., Kans. 21,270 D4 144
Ellis, co., Okla. 5,457 B4 128
Ellis, co., Tex. 43,395 C7 130
Ellis, pond, Maine D2 204
Ellis, riv., N.H. C4 208
Ellisdale, Monmouth, N.J. 50 C3 210
Ellison, Humboldt, Nev. 10 C4 112
Ellison Bay, Door, Wis. 150 C6 160
Elliston, Austl. 154 E6 432
Elliston, Newf., Can. 150 F9 72
Elliston, Powell, Mont. 200 D4 110
Elliston, Montgomery, Va. 600 C4 192
Ellistown, Union, Miss. 300 A4 184
Ellisville, Nicholas, Ky. 20 B6 178
Ellisville, Plymouth, Mass. 150 *C6 206
Ellisville, Jones, Miss. 4,592 D3 184
Ellisville, St. Louis, Mo. 2,732 *C7 150
Elloam, Blaine, Mont. B7 110
Ellon, Scot. 1,500 D10 272
Elloree, Orangeburg, S.C. 1,031 D7 188
Ellport, Lawrence, Pa. 1,458 C1 214
Ells, riv., Alta., Can. B6 54
Ellscott, Alta., Can. 15 C6 54
Ellsinore, Carter, Mo. 311 E7 150
Ellston, Ringgold, Iowa 116 D3 142
Ellsworth, Hamilton, Iowa 493 B4 142
Ellsworth, Ellsworth, Kans. 2,361 D5 144
Ellsworth, Hancock, Maine 4,444 D4 204
Ellsworth, Antrim, Mich. 386 D6 146
Ellsworth, Nobles, Minn. 634 H3 148
Ellsworth, Sheridan, Nebr. 11 B3 152
Ellsworth (Town of), Grafton, N.H. (3▲) D3 208
Ellsworth, Washington, Pa. 1,456 C1 214
Ellsworth, Pierce, Wis. 1,701 D1 160
Ellsworth, co., Kans. 7,677 D5 144
Ellsworth, mtn., Conn. B2 202
Ellwangen, Ger. 10,700 D4 286
Ellwood City, Lawrence and Beaver, Pa. 12,413 C1 214
Ellzey, Levy, Fla. 135 B8 174
Elm, Camden, N.J. D3 210
Elm, creek, Minn. H4 148
Elma, Howard, Iowa 706 A5 142
Elma, Erie, N.Y. 4,000 *C3 212
Elma, Grays Harbor, Wash. 1,811 B3 98
El Mahmoudia, Eg., U.A.R. 13,610 *A3 395
El Manteco, Ven. 645 C7 240
Elm City, Wilson, N.C. 729 B8 186
Elm Creek, Man., Can. 425 F4 60
Elm Creek, Buffalo, Nebr. 778 D6 152
Elmcrest, Genesee, Mich. 1,000 F8 146
Elmdale, Chase, Kans. 114 D7 144
Elmdale, Morrison, Minn. 88 F4 148
Elmdale Village, St. Louis, Mo. 712 *C7 150
El Memrhar, Maur. C1 408
Elmendorf, Socorro, N.Mex. 16 E4 126
El Mene, Ven. 3,097 A3 240
Elmer, Macon, Mo. 266 B5 150
Elmer, Salem, N.J. 1,505 D2 210
Elmer, Jackson, Okla. 120 D4 128
Elmer City, Okanogan, Wash. 265 *A8 98
El Mesellemiya, Sud. 3,131 C3 398
Elm Grove, Bossier, La. 300 B2 180
Elm Grove, Waukesha, Wis. 4,994 E1 160
Elmhurst, Du Page, Ill. 36,991 B6 138
F2
El Minya, Eg., U.A.R. 70,298 B3 395
Elmira, Ont., Can. 2,916 Q20 64
Elmira, P.E.I., Can. 90 C7 70
Elmira, Bonner, Idaho 20 A2 108
Elmira, Otsego, Mich. 145 D7 146
Elmira, Ray, Mo. 123 B3 150
Elmira, Chemung, N.Y. 46,517 C5 212
Elmira, Lane, Oreg. 500 C3 96
Elmira, Braxton, W.Va. 74 C4 194
El Mirage, Maricopa, Ariz. 1,723 H1 124
Elmira Heights, Chemung, N.Y. 5,157 C5 212
El Misti, vol., Peru D3 245
Elmo, Dickinson, Kans. 50 D6 144
Elmo, Nodaway, Mo. 213 A2 150
Elmo, Lake, Mont. 213 C2 110
Elmo, Emery, Utah 175 D5 114
Elmo, Carbon, Wyo. 91 E6 116
Elmodel, Baker, Ga. 100 E2 176
El Mojib, Jordan C6 382
Elmont, Shawnee, Kans. 75 *C8 144
Elmont, Nassau, N.Y. 42,000 E3 212
Elmont, Hanover, Va. 150 C7 192
El Monte, Contra Costa, Calif. 4,186 *D2 94
El Monte, Los Angeles, Calif. 13,163 C5 94
Elmora (Bakerton), Cambria, Pa. 1,057 C3 214
Elmore, Elmore, Ala. 200 C3 168
Elmore, Ottawa, Ohio 1,302 A3 156
Elmore, Faribault, Minn. 1,078 H4 148
Elmore, Lamoille, Vt. (237▲) *B3 218
Elmore, co., Ala. 30,524 C3 168
Elmore, co., Idaho 16,719 F3 108
Elmore City, Garvin, Okla. 982 D6 128
El Morro, Valencia, N.Mex. 10 C2 126
El Morro, natl. mon., N.Mex. C2 126
El Mraïti, well, Mali C4 408
El Mreïti, well, Maur. B3 408
El Mreyer, well, Maur. B3 408
Elmsdale, N.S., Can. 280 E6 70
Elmsford, Westchester, N.Y. 3,795 D2 212
Elmshorn, Ger. 34,400 B3 286
Elm Springs, Washington, Ark. 238 A2 170
Elm Springs, Meade, S.Dak. 35 C3 158
Elmsta, Swe. B9 292
Elmvale, Ont., Can. 897 P21 64
Elmville, Windham, Conn. 350 B8 202
Elmwood, Ont., Can. 460 P19 64
Elmwood, Peoria, Ill. 1,882 C4 138
Elmwood, Plymouth, Mass. 300 B6 206
Elmwood, Cass, Nebr. 481 D9 152
E2
Elmwood, Beaver, Okla. 25 B3 128
Elmwood, Smith, Tenn. 60 B6 190
Elmwood, Pierce, Wis. 776 D1 160
Elmwood Park, Cook, Ill. 23,866 F2 138
Elmwood Place, Knox, Ohio 3,813 D1 156
Elna, Morgan, Ky. 150 C8 178
Elne, Fr. F5 278
Elnora, Alta., Can. 177 E6 54
Elnora, Daviess, Ind. 824 D2 140
El Nûbâriya, canal, Eg., U.A.R. A2 395
El Obeid, Sud. 52,372 C3 398
El Odaiya, Sud. 11,913 C2 398
Eloise, Polk, Fla. 3,256 D9 174
Elon College, Alamance, N.C. 1,284 A6 186
Elora, Ont., Can. 1,457 Q20 64
Elora, Lincoln, Tenn. 300 C5 190
El Oro, Mex. 4,283 B5 224
Elorza, Ven. C4 240
El Oued, Alg. 13,001 (86,092▲) B5 402
Eloy, Pinal, Ariz. 4,899 F4 124
El Palmito, Mex. 640 B4 224
El Pao, Ven. B7 240
El Paraíso, Hond. 2,805 D4 228
El Pardo, Sp. (part of Madrid) 3,255 *B5 298
El Paso, White, Ark. 120 B4 170
El Paso, Woodford, Ill. 1,964 C4 138
El Paso, El Paso, Tex. 276,687 (*306,800) D2 130
El Paso, co., Colo. 143,742 D6 106
El Paso, co., Tex. 314,070 D2 130
Elphinstone, Man., Can. 300 E2 60
El Portal, Mariposa, Calif. 200 D4 94
El Portal, Dade, Fla. 2,079 E6 174
El Prado, Taos, N.Mex. 100 B5 126
El Pueblo, San Miguel, N.Mex. 116 *C5 126
El Puerto de Santa María, Sp. 28,368 D3 298
El Puesto, Mex. K13 225
El Qâhira, see Cairo, Eg., U.A.R.
Elqui, riv., Chile A1 252
Elrama, Washington, Pa. 823 C2 214
El Rastro, Ven. B5 240
El Real, Pan. 860 F9 228
El Reno, Canadian, Okla. 11,015 C5 128
El Rio, Ventura, Calif. 6,966 E4 94
El Rito, Rio Arriba, N.Mex. 50 B4 126
El Roboré, Bol. 3,715 C3 246
Elrod, Tuscaloosa, Ala. 200 B2 168
Elrod, Clark, S.Dak. 20 C8 158
Elrosa, Stearns, Minn. 205 F4 148
Elrose, Sask., Can. 538 E3 58
Elroy, Juneau, Wis. 1,505 E3 160
El Rucio, Mex. C5 225
Elsa, Hidalgo, Tex. 3,847 F6 130
El Salto, Mex. 5,638 C4 224
El Samán, Ven. 1,018 C4 240
Elsanor, Baldwin, Ala. 250 E2 168
El Sauce, Nic. 1,780 D4 228
Elsberry, Lincoln, Mo. 1,491 B7 150
El Segundo, Los Angeles, Calif. 14,219 C5 94
El Shatt, Eg., U.A.R. E3 382
Elsie, Clinton, Mich. 933 F7 146
Elsie, Perkins, Nebr. 198 D4 152
Elsie, Clatsop, Oreg. 25 B3 96
Elsinore, Riverside, Calif. 2,432 F5 94
Elsinore, Sevier, Utah 483 E3 114
Elsmere, New Castle, Del. 7,319 B3 172
Elsmere, Kenton, Ky. 4,607 A8 178
B6
Elsmere, Cherry, Nebr. 53 B5 152
Elsmere, Albany, N.Y. (part of Delmar) C8 212
Elsmore, Allen, Kans. 128 E8 144
El Sombrero, Ven. 2,947 B5 240
Elsterwerda, Ger. 9,749 C5 286
Elstow, Sask., Can. 111 E4 58
El Sufiya, Eg., U.A.R. D2 382
El Themed, Eg., U.A.R. 3,000 B3 395
El Tigre, Ven. 19,863 B6 240
El Tigre, Ven. D8 240
El Tigrito, Ven. 10,052 B6 240
Eltih, plat., Eg., U.A.R. B3 395
El Tocuyo, Ven. 5,586 B4 240
Elton, Jefferson Davis, La. 1,595 D3 180
Elton, Langlade, Wis. 50 C5 160
Eltopia, Franklin, Wash. 70 C7 98
El Toro, Orange, Calif. 300 D6 94
El Transito, Chile A1 252
El Triunfo, Hond. 1,160 D4 228
El Triunfo, Mex. 520 C3 224
El Uach, Som. E5 398
Eluru, India 87,213 E4 366
Elva, Man., Can. 81 F2 60
El Vado, res., N.Mex. B4 126
Elvas, Port. 10,821 C3 298
El Verano, Sonoma, Calif. 1,236 *C2 94
Elverum, Nor. 12,649 A2 292
El Viejo, Nic. 4,358 D4 228
El Vigia, Ven. 1,688 B3 240
Elvins, St. Francois, Mo. 1,818 D7 150
El Vista, Peoria, Ill. 2,000 C4 138
El Wak, Ken. B7 414
Elwha, riv., Wash. B3 98
Elwood, Will, Ill. 746 B5 138
F2
Elwood, Madison, Ind. 11,793 B4 140
Elwood, Doniphan, Kans. 1,191 C9 144
Elwood, Clarke, Miss. 100 C4 184
Elwood, Gosper, Nebr. 581 D6 152
Elwood, Atlantic, N.J. 400 D3 210
Elwood, Suffolk, N.Y. 2,000 *E8 212
Elwood, Box Elder, Utah 345 B3 114
Elwyn, Delaware, Pa. 1,500 *D6 214
Ely, Eng. 9,900 I13 273
Ely, Linn, Iowa 226 C6 142
Ely, St. Louis, Minn. 5,438 D7 148
Ely, White Pine, Nev. 4,018 D7 112
Elyria, McPherson, Kans. 100 D6 144
Elyria, Valley, Nebr. 89 C6 152
Elyria, Lorain, Ohio 43,782 A4 156
Elysburg, Northumberland, Pa. 1,100 C5 214
Elysian, Le Sueur, Minn. 382 G5 148
Emanuel, co., Ga. 17,815 D4 176
Emba, Sov.Un. 2,900 C5 336
Emba, riv., Sov.Un. C5 336
Embarcación, Arg. 3,303 B5 250
Embarrass, St. Louis, Minn. 210 D6 148
Embarrass, Waupaca, Wis. 306 D5 160
Embarrass, riv., Ill. E6 138
Embarrass, riv., Wis. D5 160
Embden, Somerset, Maine 25 (321▲) *D3 204
Embden, Cass, N.Dak. 61 D8 154
Embden, pond, Maine D3 204
Embetsu, Jap. 8,804 B8 354
Emblem, Big Horn, Wyo. 5 B4 116
Embreeville, Washington, Tenn. 150 B9 190
Embreeville Junction, Washington, Tenn. 1,204 *B9 190
Embro, Ont., Can. 529 Q20 64
Embrun, Ont., Can. 485 O25 64
Embu, Ken. C6 414
Emden, Ger. 42,800 B2 286
Emden, Logan, Ill. 502 C4 138
Emden, Shelby, Mo. 200 B6 150
Emelle, Sumter, Ala. 318 C1 168
Emerado, Grand Forks, N.Dak. 328 C8 154
Emerald, Austl. 1,633 C9 432
Emerald, Lancaster, Nebr. 27 *D9 152
Emerald, St. Croix, Wis. 150 C1 160
Emerald Bay, El Dorado, Calif. 500 C3 94
Emerson, Columbia, Ark. 350 D3 170
Emerson, Man., Can. 896 F4 60
Emerson, Bartow, Ga. 666 B2 176
Emerson, Mills, Iowa 521 C2 142
Emerson, Dakota, Dixon and Thurston, Nebr. 803 B9 152
Emerson, Merrimack, N.H. E3 208
Emerson, Bergen, N.J. 6,849 A1 210
Emery, Hanson, S.Dak. 502 D8 158
Emery, Emery, Utah 326 E4 114
Emery, co., Utah 5,546 E4 114
Emery Mills, York, Maine 100 E2 204
Emery Park, Pima, Ariz. 250 F5 124
Emeryville, Alameda, Calif. 2,686 *D2 94
Emet, Johnston, Okla. 65 D7 128
Emida, Benewah, Idaho 125 B2 108
Emigrant, Park, Mont. 28 E6 110
Emi Koussi, vol., Chad C8 409
Emiliano Zapata, Mex. 2,897 D7 225
Emilia-Romagna, reg., It. 3,625,000 C3 302
Emily, Crow Wing, Minn. 351 E5 148
Emily, lake, Minn. F3 148
Emine, cape, Bul. B3 317
Eminence, Morgan, Ind. 200 C3 140
Eminence, Henry, Ky. 1,958 B5 178
Eminence, Shannon, Mo. 516 D6 150
Emirdağ, Tur. 6,224 B4 307
Emlenton, Venango, Pa. 844 B2 214
Emlyn, Whitley, Ky. 600 D6 178
Emma, Dawson, Ga. 135 B2 176
Emma, Lagrange, Ind. 100 A4 140
Emma, Saline, Mo. 202 C4 150
Emma, lake, Sask., Can. D5 58
Emmaboda, Swe. 2,695 E6 292
Emmaus, Lehigh, Pa. 10,262 C6 214
Emmen, Neth. 6,900 B5 282
Emmerich, Ger. 14,300 C2 286
Emmet, Nevada, Ark. 474 D3 170
Emmet, Holt, Nebr. 66 B7 152
Emmet, co., Iowa 14,871 A3 142
Emmet, co., Mich. 15,904 D7 146
Emmetsburg, Palo Alto, Iowa 3,887 A3 142
Emmett, Gem, Idaho 3,769 F2 106
Emmett, Pottawatomie, Kans. 128 C7 144
Emmett, St. Clair, Mich. 283 G9 146
Emmett, McLean, N.Dak. 100 C4 154
Emmitsburg, Frederick, Md. 1,369 A5 182
Emmons, Freeborn, Minn. 408 H5 148
Emmons, co., N.Dak. 8,462 D5 154
Emory, Rains, Tex. 559 C8 130
Emory, Summit, Utah B4 114
Emory Gap, Roane, Tenn. 500 C7 190
Emory University, De Kalb, Ga. 4,200 B5 176
Empalme, Mex. B3 224
Empangeni, U.S.Afr. 4,144 E6 421
Empedrado, Arg. 3,715 A4 252
Empire, Walker, Ala. 774 B2 168
Empire, Stanislaus, Calif. 1,635 *D3 94
Empire, Clear Creek, Colo. 110 C5 106
Empire, Dodge, Ga. 125 D3 176
Empire, Butler, Kans. B7 144
Empire, Plaquemines, La. 450 E6 180
Empire, Leelanau, Mich. 448 E5 146
Empire, Washoe, Nev. 375 C2 112
Empire, Jefferson, Ohio 551 B6 156
Empire, Coos, Oreg. 3,781 D2 96
Empire, res., Colo. B6 106
Empire City, Stephens, Okla. 25 D5 128
Empoli, It. 17,800 D3 302
Emporia, Lyon, Kans. 18,190 D7 144
Emporia, Greensville, Va. 5,535 D7 192
Emporium, Cameron, Pa. 3,397 B3 214
Empress, Alta., Can. 480 E7 54
Empress Augusta, bay, Solomon D1 436
Emptinne, Bel. 716 D4 282
Ems, riv., Ger. B2 286
Emsdale, Ont., Can. 210 O21 64
Emsdetten, Ger. 23,700 B2 286
Emsworth, Allegheny, Pa. 3,341 A3 214
Ena (Nakatsu), Jap. 31,621 L13 354
Enard, bay, Scot. C7 272
Ena-San, peak, Jap. L13 354
Enaville, Shoshone, Idaho 50 *B2 108
Encampment, Carbon, Wyo. 333 E6 116
Encarnación, Par. 13,321 E5 247
Encarnación de Diaz, Mex. 7,649 C5 225
K12
Enchant, Alta., Can. 100 E6 54
Enchi, Ghana 2,064 E4 408
Encinas, Mex. K12 225
Encinitas, San Diego, Calif. 2,786 F5 94
Encino, Torrance, N.Mex. 346 D5 126
Encontrados, Ven. 3,961 B2 240
Encounter, bay, Austl. F7 432
Endako, B.C., Can. 55 C10 52
Endako, riv., B.C., Can. C10 52
Endau, Mala. 2,675 G4 362
Ende, Indon. 7,226 F6 358
Endeavor, Marquette, Wis. 280 E4 160
Endeavour, Sask., Can. 208 D6 58
Enderby, B.C., Can. 965 E13 52
Enderlin, Ransom, N.Dak. 1,596 D8 154
Enders, Chase, Nebr. 100 D4 152
Enders, res., Nebr. D4 152
Endiang, Alta., Can. 150 E6 54
Endicott, Jefferson, Nebr. 166 D8 152
Endicott, Broome, N.Y. 18,775 C5 212
Endicott, Franklin, Va. 300 D4 192
Endicott, Whitman, Wash. 369 C9 98
Endicott, mts., Alsk. B6 84
Endless, lake, Maine C4 204
Endville, Pontotoc, Miss. 400 A4 184
Endwell, Broome, N.Y. 12,000 C5 212
Ene, riv., Peru C3 245
Energy, Williamson, Ill. 507 *F4 138
Enetal, see Bremerton East, Wash.
Enez, Tur. 566 A2 307
Enfield, N.S., Can. 175 E6 70
Enfield, Hartford, Conn. 3,000 (31,464▲) B5 202
Enfield, White, Ill. 791 E5 138
Enfield, Eng. 109,000 J12 273
Enfield, Penobscot, Maine 120 (1,098▲) C4 204
Enfield, Grafton, N.H. 1,121 (1,867▲) D2 208
Enfield, Halifax, N.C. 2,978 A8 186
Enfield Center, Grafton, N.H. 200 D2 208
Engadine, Mackinac, Mich. 240 C6 146
Engaño, cape, Dom.Rep. C10 233
Engaru, Jap. 18,082 B9 354
Engebi, isl., Eniwetok B1 436
Engelberg, Randolph, Ark. A6 170
Engelberg, Switz. 2,544 B4 312
Engelhard, Hyde, N.C. 600 B10 186
Engels, Sov.Un. 90,000 B3 336
Enghien, Bel. 4,213 D3 282
England, Lonoke, Ark. 2,861 C5 170
D7
England & Wales, reg., United Kingdom 45,244,000 C4 266
Engle, Sierra, N.Mex. 90 E4 126
Englee, Newf., Can. 677 E7 72
E10
Englefeld, Sask., Can. 153 D5 58
Englehart, Ont., Can. 1,705 *S25 64
Englevale, Ransom, N.Dak. 85 D8 154
Engleville, Las Animas, Colo. 30 *E6 106
Englewood, B.C., Can. 150 E9 52
Englewood, Arapahoe, Colo. 33,398 C6 106
Englewood, Sarasota, Fla. 2,877 E8 174
Englewood, Lawrence, Ind. 1,232 *D3 140
Englewood, Clark, Kans. 243 E4 144
Englewood, Bergen, N.J. 26,057 A2 210
Englewood, Montgomery, Ohio 1,515 C2 156

Englewood, Coos, Oreg.	1,382	*D2	96
Englewood, McMinn, Tenn.	1,574	C7	190
Englewood Cliffs, Bergen, N.J.	2,913	*B4	210
English, Crawford, Ind.	698	D3	140
English, McDowell, W.Va.	700	*D3	194
English, chan., Eng., Fr.		L8	273
		C2	278
English, riv., Iowa		C5	142
English Bazar, India		D5	368
English Creek, Atlantic, N.J.	400	E3	210
English Harbour West, Newf., Can.	350	G8	72
English Lake, Starke, Ind.	200	A3	140
Englishtown, Monmouth, N.J.	1,143	C4	210
Enguera, Sp.	4,764	C6	298
Enid, Tallahatchie, Miss.	128	A3	184
Enid, Richland, Mont.	6	C12	110
Enid, Garfield, Okla.	38,859	B6	128
Enid, res., Miss.		A3	184
Enigma, Berrien, Ga.	525	E3	176
Enilda, Alta., Can.	225	C4	54
Eniwetok, isl., Eniwetok		C1	436
Eniwetok Islands, U.S. trust., Pac.O.		B1	436
Enka, Buncombe, N.C.	1,400	B3	186
Enkeldoorn, Rh. & Nya.	800	C6	421
Enkhuizen, Neth.	10,682	B4	282
Enköping, Swe.	11,959	B8	292
Enna, It.	28,200	G5	302
Enna, prov., It.	249,100	*G5	302
Ennadai, lake, N.W.Ter., Can.		E8	48
En Nahud, Sud.	16,499	C2	398
Ennedi, reg., Chad		C9	409
Enning, Meade, S.Dak.	17	C3	158
Ennis, Ire.	5,741	I4	273
Ennis, Madison, Mont.	525	E5	110
Ennis, Ellis, Tex.	9,347	B9	130
		C7	
Enniscorthy, Ire.	5,445	I6	273
Ennis Creek, Walla Walla, Wash.		A3	98
Enniskillen, N.Ire.	6,318	G5	273
Ennistymon, Ire.	1,215	I3	273
Enns, Aus.	8,446	B6	313
Enns, riv., Aus.		B6	313
Ennylabegan, isl., Kwajalein		A1	436
Enoch, Iron, Utah	465	F2	114
Enoch, Clay, W.Va.	78	C7	194
Enochsburg, Franklin, Ind.	80	C4	140
Enola, Faulkner, Ark.	100	B4	170
Enola, Madison, Nebr.	30	C8	152
Enola, Cumberland, Pa.	4,500	C5	214
Enon, see Zona, La.			
Enon, Walthall, Miss.	300	D2	184
Enon, Moniteau, Mo.	110	C5	150
Enon, Clark, Ohio	1,227	C3	156
Enontekiö, Fin.		B10	290
Enoree, Spartanburg, S.C.	950	B5	188
Enoree, riv., S.C.		B4	188
Enosburg Falls (Enosburg), Franklin, Vt.	1,321	*B3	218
	(1,966▲)		
Enosdale, Washington, Kans.	11	*C6	144
Enotah, see Brasstown Bald, mtn., Ga.			
Enrich, riv., Scot.		D8	272
Enriquillo, Dom.Rep.	2,160	D9	233
Enriquillo, lake, Dom.Rep.		C9	233
Enrose, Canyon, Idaho		*F2	108
Enschede, Neth.	113,513	B5	282
Ensenada, Mex.	18,140	A2	224
Ensenada, Rio Arriba, N.Mex.	125	B4	126
Enshih, China	25,000	J4	349
Ensign, Alta., Can.	50	E6	54
Ensign, Gray, Kans.	255	E3	144
Ensign, Delta, Mich.	50	D5	146
Ensley, Escambia, Fla.	1,836	A3	174
Entebbe, Ug.	7,932	B5	414
Enterprise, Coffee, Ala.	11,410	D4	168
Enterprise, Shasta, Calif.	4,946	*B2	94
Enterprise, Ont., Can.	480	P24	64
Enterprise, Dickinson, Kans.	1,015	D6	144
Enterprise, Clarke, Miss.	532	C4	184
Enterprise, Haskell, Okla.	100	C8	128
Enterprise, Wallowa, Oreg.	1,932	B9	96
Enterprise, Morgan, Utah		B4	114
Enterprise, Washington, Utah	859	F2	114
Enterprise, Harrison, W.Va.	900	A7	194
		B4	
Entiat, Chelan, Wash.	357	B6	98
Entrance, Alta., Can.	35	D4	54
Entre Minho e Douro, reg., Port.	1,879,310	B2	298
Entre Rios, see Malema, Moz.			
Entre Rios, prov., Arg.	957,000	D6	250
Entroncamento, Moz.		C6	421
Entwistle, Alta., Can.	354	D5	54
Enugu, Nig.	62,764	E6	409
Enumclaw, King, Wash.	3,269	B5	98
		D3	
Enville, Chester, Tenn.	250	C3	190
Enz, riv., Ger.		D3	286
Enzan, Jap.	30,279	L14	354
Eola, Avoyelles, La.	250	D3	180
Eola, Yamhill, Oreg.	300	*B3	96
Eolia, Pike, Mo.	400	B6	150
Eoline, Bibb, Ala.	300	C2	168
Epe, Neth.	4,000	B4	282
Epéna, Con.B.		F8	409
Épernay, Fr.	21,222	C5	278
Epes, Sumter, Ala.	337	C1	168
Ephraim, Sanpete, Utah	1,801	D4	114
Ephraim, Door, Wis.	221	C6	160
Ephrata, Lancaster, Pa.	7,688	C5	214
Ephrata, Grant, Wash.	6,548	B7	98
Épila, Sp.	5,462	B6	298
Épinal, Fr.	28,688	C7	278
Épinay [-sur-Seine], Fr.	17,611	I10	278
Epirus (Ípiros), reg., Grc.	330,543	B3	306
Epoufette, Mackinac, Mich.	50	C6	146
Epperson, Geneva, Ala.	250	D4	168
Epperson, Monroe, Tenn.	50	C7	190
Epping, Rockingham, N.H.	980	E4	208
	(2,006▲)		
Epping, Williams, N.Dak.	151	B2	154
Epping, dam, N.Dak.		B2	154
Epps, West Carroll, La.	411	B4	180
Epsie, Powder River, Mont.	4	E11	110
Epsom, Merrimack, N.H.	35	E4	208
	(1,002▲)		
Epworth, Dubuque, Iowa	698	B7	142

Epworth, Fannin, Ga.	500	B2	176
Equality, Coosa, Ala.	196	C3	168
Equality, Gallatin, Ill.	665	F5	138
Equator, prov., Con.L.	1,673,400	B2	414
Equatoria, prov., Sud.	903,503	D3	398
Équeurdreville, Fr.	8,615	C3	278
Eram, Okmulgee, Okla.		C8	128
Erath, Vermilion, La.	2,019	E3	180
Erath, co., Tex.	16,236	C6	130
Erba, mtn., Sud.		A4	398
Erbacon, Webster, W.Va.	300	C4	194
Erciş, Tur.	5,536	B10	307
Erciyas, mt., Tur.		B6	307
Ercsi, Hung.	5,406	B3	320
Erd, Hung.	16,514	B3	320
Erda, Tooele, Utah		C3	114
Erdenheim, Montgomery, Pa.	3,700	A6	214
Erdeni Dzuz, Mong.		B8	346
Erding, Ger.	8,800	D4	286
Erechim, Braz.	14,418	K6	257
Ereğli, Tur.	6,965	A4	307
Ereğli, Tur.	24,098	C6	307
Eressós, Grc.	3,301	B5	306
Erfurt, Ger.	188,100	C4	286
Ergene, riv., Tur.		A2	307
Erg Er Raoui, sand dunes, Alg.		C3	402
Erhard, Otter Tail, Minn.	150	E2	148
Erhchiang (Charklik), China	5,000	D5	346
Eria, riv., Sp.		A3	298
Erice, It.	1,500	F4	302
Ericht, lake, Scot.		E8	272
Erick, Beckham, Okla.	1,342	C4	128
Erickson, Man., Can.	488	E3	60
Ericsburg, Koochiching, Minn.	140	C5	148
Ericson, Wheeler, Nebr.	157	C7	152
Erie, Weld, Colo.	875	B5	106
Erie, Whiteside, Ill.	1,215	B3	138
Erie, Neosho, Kans.	1,309	E8	144
Erie, Monroe, Mich.	500	H8	146
Erie, Clark, Nev.	8	H6	112
Erie, Cass, N.Dak.	150	C8	154
Erie, Erie, Pa.	138,440	A1	214
	(*212,000)		
Erie, Loudon, Tenn.	25	C7	190
Erie, co., N.Y.	1,064,688	C3	212
Erie, co., Ohio	68,000	A4	156
Erie, co., Pa.	250,682	B1	214
Erie, lake, Can., U.S.		I10	48
		C10	77
Erieau, Ont., Can.	475	R19	64
Erigavo, Som.		C6	398
Erigayo, pol. dist., Som.		C6	398
Eriksdale, Man., Can.	290	E3	60
Erimanthos, mtn., Grc.		C3	306
Erimo, cape, Jap.		G6	354
Erin, Ont., Can.	885	Q20	64
Erin, Houston, Tenn.	1,097	B4	190
Erin Springs, Garvin, Okla.	200	D6	128
Eriskay, isl., Scot.		D5	272
Erisort, bay, Scot.		C6	272
Erithraí, Grc.	3,495	B4	306
Eritrea, fed. auton. unit, Eth.	1,100,000	B4	398
Erlangen, Ger.	62,100	D4	286
Erlanger, Kenton, Ky.	7,072	A6	178
		A8	
Erlton, Camden, N.J.	1,000	*D2	210
Ermelo, Neth.	5,000	B4	282
Ermelo, U.S.Afr.	9,604	E5	420
Ermenek, Tur.	6,930	C5	307
Erne, lake, N.Ire.		G5	273
Ernée, Fr.		C3	278
Ernest, Indiana, Pa.	950	C2	214
Ernestville, Unicoi, Tenn.	40	B9	190
Ernfold, Sask., Can.	156	E4	58
Eros, Jackson, La.	176	B3	180
Er Rahad, Sud.	6,706	C3	398
Er Rāma, Isr.	2,621	B6	382
Errata, Jones, Miss.		D3	184
Erriboll, bay, Scot.		C8	272
Er Rif, mts., Mor.		B3	402
Errol, Coos, N.H.	130	B4	208
	(220▲)		
Errol, isl., La.		E7	180
Errol Heights, Multnomah, Oreg.	10,000	*A2	96
Er Roseires, Sud.	3,927	C3	398
Erskine, Alta., Can.	172	D6	54
Erskine, Polk, Minn.	614	D3	148
Erskine, Passaic, N.J.		A4	210
Erstein, Fr.	5,747	C7	278
Erstfeld, Switz.	3,747	B4	312
Erving, Franklin, Mass.	400	A3	206
	(1,272▲)		
Erwin, Harnett, N.C.	3,183	B7	186
Erwin, Kingsbury, S.Dak.	157	C8	158
Erwin, Unicoi, Tenn.	3,210	B9	190
Erwin, Preston, W.Va.	150	B5	194
Erwinville, West Baton Rouge, La.	350	D4	180
Erwood, Sask., Can.	135	D6	58
Erzgebirge, see Ore, mts., Ger.			
Erzincan, Tur.	26,664	B8	307
Erzincan, prov., Tur.	216,413	D8	307
Erzurum, Tur.	69,499	B9	307
Erzurum, prov., Tur.	521,836	*B9	307
Esan, cape, Jap.		D8	354
Esashi, Jap.	11,511	B8	354
Esashi, Jap.	15,084	D8	354
Esbjerg, Den.		I3	291
Esbon, Jewell, Kans.	237	C5	144
Escalante, Garfield, Utah	702	F4	114
Escalante, des., Utah		F2	114
Escalante, riv., Utah		F4	114
Escalon, San Joaquin, Calif.	1,763	D3	94
Escalón, Mex.	1,270	B5	224
Escambia, co., Ala.	33,511	D2	168
Escambia, co., Fla.	173,829	A3	174
Escambia, riv., Fla.		A3	174
Escanaba, Delta, Mich.	15,391	D4	146
Escanaba, riv., Mich		C4	146
Escárcega, Mex.		D7	225
Escarceo, pt., Ven.		A6	240
Escatawpa, Jackson, Miss.	1,464	E2	184
		E4	
Escatawpa, riv., Ala., Miss.		E1	168
		D4	184
Eschwege, Ger.	23,800	C4	286
Eschweiler, Ger.	38,500	C2	286
Escocesa, bay, Dom. Rep.		C10	233

Escoheag, Kent, R.I.	35	C1	216
Escondida, pt., Mex.		D6	225
Escondidas, Mex.		C6	225
Escondido, San Diego, Calif.	16,377	F5	94
Escondido, riv., Nic.		D5	228
Escoublac-La-Baule, Fr.	13,166	D2	278
Escoumains, riv., Que., Can.		P15	66
Escuela, Pima, Ariz.	150	F5	124
Escuinapa, Mex.	9,029	C4	224
Escuintla, Guat.	9,746	C2	228
Escuminac, pt., N.B., Can.		B5	70
Eséka, Cam.	3,851	F7	409
Eşfahān, Iran	254,876	C3	379
Esgueva, riv., Sp.		B4	298
Esh, cape, Eg., U.A.R.		D7	395
Eshimba, Con.L.		D3	414
Eshowe, U.S.Afr.		E6	421
Esh Sham, see Damascus, Syr., U.A.R.			
Eskbank, Sask., Can.	102	E4	58
Eskdale, Kanawha, W.Va.	800	C3	194
		D6	
Eskilstuna, Swe.	57,089	B7	292
Eskimo, Alsk.	50	*C7	84
Eskimo, lakes, N.W.Ter., Can.		D5	48
Eskişehir, Tur.	122,755	B4	307
Eskişehir, prov., Tur.	324,614	*B4	307
Esko, Carlton, Minn.	240	E6	148
Eskridge, Wabaunsee, Kans.	519	D7	144
Esla, riv., Sp.		B4	298
Eslava, riv., Mex.		G10	224
Eslöv, Swe.	8,995	F4	292
Esmeralda, Ven.		E6	240
Esmeralda, co., Nev.	619	F4	112
Esmeraldas, Ec.	13,169	A2	245
Esmond, Benson, N.Dak.	420	B6	154
Esmond, Providence, R.I.	4,500	B2	216
Esmond, Kingsbury, S.Dak.	19	C8	158
Esmont, Albemarle, Va.	100	C6	192
Esom Hill, Polk, Ga.	200	C1	176
Espanola, Ont., Can.	4,100	S25	64
Espanola, Flagler, Fla.	150	B9	174
Espanola, Rio Arriba, N.Mex.	1,976	B4	126
Espanola, Spokane, Wash.	25	D8	98
Espanong, see Lake Hopatcong, N.J.			
Esparto, Yolo, Calif.	300	C2	94
Esperance, Austl.	706	E4	432
Esperanza, Arg.		B3	252
Esperanza, Pontotoc, Miss.	250	A3	184
Espichel, cape, Port.		C2	298
Espinal, Col.	9,389	C2	244
Espinal, Mex.	1,365	K15	225
Espinhaço, mts., Braz.		D2	258
Espirito Santo, Braz.	9,701	E2	258
Espirito Santo, state, Braz.	938,000	J8	257
Espiritu Santo, isl., Pac.O.		D3	436
Espita, Mex.	4,946	C8	225
Esposende, Port.	1,760	B2	298
Espy, Columbia, Pa.	1,375	B5	214
Esquatzel, coulee, Wash.		C7	98
Esquel, Arg.	5,584	F3	251
Esquimalt, B.C., Can.	10,384	C14	52
		F11	
Esquina, Arg.	5,878	B4	252
Esschen, Bel.	9,505	C3	282
Essen, Ger.	690,900	C2	286
	(*3,700,000)		
Essequibo, riv., Br.Gu.		E5	256
Essex, Ont., Can.	3,348	R18	64
Essex, Middlesex, Conn.	1,470	D6	202
	(4,057▲)		
Essex, Page, Iowa	767	D2	142
Essex, Baltimore, Md.	35,205	B7	182
Essex, Essex, Mass.	700	A6	206
	(2,238▲)		
Essex, Quitman, Miss.	20	A2	184
Essex, Stoddard, Mo.	511	E8	150
Essex, Flathead, Mont.	100	B3	110
Essex, Chittenden, Vt.	300	B2	218
	(7,090▲)		
Essex, co., Ont., Can.	246,901	R18	64
Essex, co., Eng.	2,165,000	J13	273
Essex, co., Mass.	568,831	A5	206
Essex, co., N.J.	923,545	B4	210
Essex, co., N.Y.	35,300	A8	212
Essex, co., Vt.	6,083	B5	218
Essex, co., Va.	6,690	C8	192
Essex Fells, Essex, N.J.	2,174	*B4	210
Essex Junction, Chittenden, Vt.	5,340	C2	218
Essexvale, Rh.&Nya.		D5	420
Essexville, Bay, Mich.	4,590	F8	146
Esslingen [am Neckar], Ger.	77,500	D3	286
Es Suki, Sud.	7,388	C3	398
Estacada, Clackamas, Oreg.	957	B4	96
Estación Superi, Arg.		A2	252
Estados, isl., Arg.		H5	251
Estância, Braz.	14,051	C3	258
Estancia, Torrance, N.Mex.	797	D4	126
Estarreja, Port.	2,450	B2	298
Estcourt, U.S.Afr.	6,027	E5	420
Este, It.	10,600	C3	302
Este, pt., Ur.		B5	252
Este Crespo, Arg.		B3	252
Esteli, Nic.	5,557	D4	228
Estella, Sp.	7,290	A5	298
Estelle, Jefferson, La.	500	*D5	180
Estelline, Hamlin, S.Dak.	722	C9	158
Estell Manor, Atlantic, N.J.	496	E3	210
Estelville, Atlantic, N.J.		E3	210
Estepa, Sp.	9,534	D4	298
Estepona, Sp.	10,935	D4	298
Ester, Alsk.		C7	84
Esterbrook, Converse, Wyo.		D7	116
Esterhazy, Sask., Can.	748	E6	58
Estero, Lee, Fla.	213	E9	174
Estero, bay, Calif.		E3	94
Estero, isl., Fla.		E9	174
Estes, Winston, Miss.		B3	184
Estes Park, Larimer, Colo.	1,175	B5	106
Estevan, Sask., Can.	5,264	F6	58
Estevan, isl., B.C., Can.		D8	52
Estevan Point, B.C., Can.		F9	52
Esther, Alta., Can.		E7	54
Esther, St. Francois, Mo.	1,033	*D7	150
Estherville, Emmet, Iowa	7,927	A3	142
Estherwood, Acadia, La.	639	D3	180

Estill, Hampton, S.C.	1,865	F6	188
Estill, co., Ky.	12,466	C6	178
Estillfork, Jackson, Ala.	250	A3	168
Estill Springs, Franklin, Tenn.	734	C5	190
Estlin, Sask., Can.	63	E5	58
Esto, Holmes, Fla.	148	A5	174
Eston, Sask., Can.	1,625	E3	58
Eston, Eng.	34,500	G11	273
Estonia, rep., Sov.Un.	1,196,000	D4	328
Estral Beach, Monroe, Mich.	254	*H8	146
Estrêla, mts., Port.		B3	298
Estremadura, prov., Port.	1,592,858	C2	298
Estremadura, reg., Port.	2,404,300	C2	298
Estremadura (Extremadura), reg., Sp.	1,365,959	C3	298
Estrondo, mts., Braz.		B1	258
Estuary, Sask., Can.	90	E3	58
Esztergom, Hung.	19,000	B3	320
Etah, Grnld.	20	O28	290
Etah, India		D2	368
Étampes, Fr.	11,890	C5	278
Étang Saumâtre, lake, Hai.		C9	233
Étaples, Fr.	7,758	B4	278
Etawah, India	59,986	D2	368
Ethan, Davison, S.Dak.	297	D8	158
Ethel, Attala, Miss.	566	B3	184
Ethel, Ont., Can.	265	Q19	64
Ethel, Macon, Mo.	149	B5	150
Ethel, Lewis, Wash.	90	C4	98
Ethel, Logan, W.Va.	650	D5	194
Ethel, mtn., Colo.		B4	106
Ethelbert, Man., Can.	505	E2	60
Ethelsville, Pickens, Ala.	62	B1	168
Ethelton, Sask., Can.	95	D5	58
Ether, Montgomery, N.C.	150	B6	186
Ethete, Fremont, Wyo.	30	C4	116
Ethiopia, country, Afr.	21,600,000	F10	388
			398
Ethridge, Toole, Mont.	51	B5	110
Ethridge, Lawrence, Tenn.	550	C4	190
Etive, inlet, Scot.		E7	272
Etlan, Madison, Va.	100	B6	192
Etna, Siskiyou, Calif.	596	B2	94
Etna, Whitley, Ind.	125	A4	140
Etna, Penobscot, Maine	175	D3	204
	(486▲)		
Etna, Grafton, N.H.	150	D2	208
Etna, Licking, Ohio	343	C4	156
Etna, Allegheny, Pa.	5,519	A4	214
Etna, Box Elder, Utah		B2	114
Etna, Lincoln, Wyo.	100	C1	116
Etna, vol., It.		G5	302
Etna Green, Kosciusko, Ind.	483	A3	140
Etnedal, Nor.		F3	291
Etolin, isl., Alsk.		J14	84
Etolin, strait, Alsk.		C5	84
Eton, Murray, Ga.	275	B2	176
Etosha, lake, S.W.Afr.		C3	420
Etowah, Mississippi, Ark.	100	B6	170
Etowah, Henderson, N.C.	75	B3	186
Etowah, McMinn, Tenn.	3,223	C7	190
Etowah, co., Ala.	96,980	A3	168
Etowah, riv., Ga.		B2	176
Etra, Mercer, N.J.	50	C3	210
Et Taiyiba, Jordan		B6	382
Ettington, Sask., Can.	23	F4	58
Et Tira, Isr.		B5	382
Ettlbruck, Lux.	4,452	E5	282
Ettrick, Chesterfield, Va.	2,998	B9	192
		C7	
Ettrick, Trempealeau, Wis.	479	D2	160
Etzikom, Alta., Can.	100	F7	54
Eu, Fr.	6,343	B4	278
Eubank, Pulaski, Ky.	303	C6	178
Euboea, see Évvoia, prov., Grc.			
Eucha, Delaware, Okla.	150	B9	128
Eucla, Austl.		E5	432
Euclid, Polk, Minn.	200	D2	148
Euclid, Cuyahoga, Ohio	62,998	A5	156
		B1	
Euclid Center, Berrien, Mich.	2,343	*H5	146
Euclid Heights, Garland, Ark.	2,080	*C3	170
Eucutta, Wayne, Miss.	50	D4	184
Eudora, Chicot, Ark.	3,598	D5	170
Eudora, Douglas, Kans.	1,526	D8	144
Eudora, De Soto, Miss.	50	A2	184
Eufaula, Barbour, Ala.	8,357	D4	168
Eufaula, McIntosh, Okla.	2,382	C8	128
Eugena, pt., Mex.		B2	224
Eugene, Vermillion, Ind.	300	C2	140
Eugene, Cole, Mo.	151	C5	150
Eugene, Lane, Oreg.	50,977	C3	96
	(*122,200)		
Euharlee, Bartow, Ga.	200	B2	176
Euless, Tarrant, Tex.	2,062	*C7	130
Eulonia, McIntosh, Ga.	200	E5	176
Eunice, St. Landry, La.	11,326	D3	180
Eunice, Lea, N.Mex.	3,531	F7	126
Eunola, Geneva, Ala.	124	*D4	168
Eupen, Bel.	14,048	D4	282
Euphrates, riv., Asia		F6	340
Eupora, Webster, Miss.	1,468	B3	184
Eure, dept., Fr.	332,514	*C4	278
Eure, riv., Fr.		C4	278
Eure-et-Loir, dept., Fr.	261,035	*C4	278
Eureka, Humboldt, Calif.	28,137	B1	94
Eureka, San Juan, Colo.		*E3	106
Eureka, Marion, Fla.	43	B9	174
Eureka, Woodford, Ill.	2,538	C4	138
Eureka, Greenwood, Kans.	4,055	E7	144
Eureka, St. Louis, Mo.	1,134	B7	150
Eureka, Lincoln, Mont.	1,229	B1	110
Eureka, Eureka, Nev.	470	D6	112
Eureka, Wayne, N.C.	246	B8	186
Eureka, see Hemlock, S.C.			
Eureka, McPherson, S.Dak.	1,555	B6	158
Eureka, Juab, Utah	771	D3	114
Eureka, Walla Walla, Wash.	25	C8	98
Eureka, Pleasants, W.Va.	100	B3	194
Eureka, Winnebago, Wis.	300	D5	160
Eureka, co., Nev.	767	D5	112
Eureka Springs, Carroll, Ark.	1,437	A3	170
Europa, isl., Afr.		D8	420
Europe, cont.	573,353,000		19
			20
Eurytania, see Evritanía, prov., Grc.			
Euskirchen, Ger.	18,900	C2	286
Eustace, Henderson, Tex.	351	C8	130
Eustis, Lake, Fla.	6,189	C9	174

Eustis, Franklin, Maine 100 (666▲) C2 204
Eustis, Frontier, Nebr. 386 D5 152
Eutaw, Greene, Ala. 2,784 C2 168
Eutawville, Orangeburg, S.C. 468 E8 188
Eutsuk, lake, B.C., Can. D9 52
Eva, Morgan, Ala. 150 A3 168
Eva, Concordia, La. 80 C4 180
Eva, Texas, Okla. 10 B2 128
Eva, Benton, Tenn. 200 B3 190
Evale, Ang. C3 420
Evan, Brown, Minn. 153 G4 148
Evangeline, Acadia, La. 950 D3 180
Evangeline, par., La. 31,639 D3 180
Evanger, Nor. 1,487 F2 291
Evans, Weld, Colo. 1,453 B6 106
Evans, Columbia, Ga. 600 C4 176
Evans, Vernon, La. 100 C2 180
Evans, Cascade, Mont. C5 110
Evans, Jackson, W.Va. 200 C3 194
Evans, co., Ga. 6,952 D5 176
Evans, straits, N.W.Ter., Can. E10 48
Evans, mtn., Colo. C5 106
Evans, mtn., N.Z. E3 437
Evansburg, Alta., Can. 358 D5 54
Evans City, Butler, Pa. 1,825 C1 214
Evansdale, Black Hawk, Iowa 5,738 B5 142
Evans Mills, Jefferson, N.Y. 618 A6 212
Evanston, Cook, Ill. 79,283 A6 E3 138
Evanston, Breathitt, Ky. 300 C7 178
Evanston, Uinta, Wyo. 4,901 E2 116
Evansville, Washington, Ark. 25 B2 170
Evansville, Randolph, Ill. 829 E4 138
Evansville, Vanderburgh, Ind. 141,543 (*200,300) E2 140
Evansville, Douglas, Minn. 411 F3 148
Evansville, Tunica, Miss. 15 A2 184
Evansville, Rock, Wis. 2,858 F4 160
Evansville, Natrona, Wyo. 678 D6 116
Evant, Coryell, Tex. 480 D6 130
Evaro, Missoula, Mont. 40 *D2 110
Evart, Osceola, Mich. 1,775 F6 146
Evarts, Harlan, Ky. 1,473 D7 178
Eveleth, St. Louis, Minn. 5,721 D6 148
Evendale, Hamilton, Ohio 773 *C2 156
Evening Shade, Sharp, Ark. 232 A5 170
Evenquén, Ven. D7 240
Everard, lake, Austl. E6 432
Everard, mtn., B.C., Can. E10 52
Everard, ranges, Austl. D6 432
Everest, Brown, Kans. 348 C8 144
Everest, mtn., Nep., China C4 368
Everets, Nansemond, Va. 25 A8 192
Everett, Ont., Can. 210 P21 64
Everett, Glynn, Ga. 150 E5 176
Everett, Middlesex, Mass. 43,544 C3 206
Everett, Bedford, Pa. 2,279 C3 214
Everett, Snohomish, Wash. 40,304 B4 98
Everett, mtn., Mass. B1 206
Everetts, Martin, N.C. 225 *B8 186
Everettville, Monongalia, W.Va. 724 A7 194
Evergem, Bel. 10,845 C2 282
Everglades, Collier, Fla. 552 F9 174
Everglades, nat. park, Fla. F9 174
Everglades, swamp, Fla. F10 174
Evergreen, Conecuh, Ala. 3,703 D3 168
Evergreen, Jefferson, Colo. 596 C5 106
Evergreen, Avoyelles, La. 325 D3 180
Evergreen, Itawamba, Miss. 100 A4 184
Evergreen, Columbus, N.C. 300 C7 186
Evergreen, Florence, S.C. 125 C9 188
Evergreen, Appomattox, Va. 150 C6 192
Evergreen Park, Cook, Ill. 24,178 F3 138
Everly, Clay, Iowa 668 A2 142
Everman, Tarrant, Tex. 1,076 *C7 130
Everson, Fayette, Pa. 1,304 C2 214
Everson, Whatcom, Wash. 431 A4 98
Everton, Boone, Ark. 118 A4 170
Everton, Fayette, Ind. 500 C4 140
Everton, Dade, Mo. 261 D4 150
Evesham, Sask., Can. 90 D3 58
Evinayong, Rio Muni 870 F7 409
Evington, Campbell, Va. 200 C5 192
Evje, Nor. G2 291
Évora, Port. 25,678 C3 298
Évreux, Fr. 23,647 C4 278
Evritania (Eurytania), prov., Grc. 39,678 *B3 306
Évros (Hevros), prov., Grc. 141,340 *A5 306
Evrótas, riv., Grc. C4 306
Evstratios, isl., Grc. B6 306
Évvoia (Euboea), prov., Grc. 164,542 *B4 306
Évvoia (northern), gulf, Grc. B4 306
Évvoia, isl., Grc. B4 306
Ewa, Honolulu, Haw. 3,257 B3 G9 86
Ewa, beach, Haw. G9 86
Ewab, is., Indon. F8 359
Ewa Beach, Honolulu, Haw. 2,459 G9 86
Ewan, Whitman, Wash. 70 B9 98
Ewell, Somerset, Md. 380 E7 182
Ewen, Ontonagon, Mich. 500 C2 146
Ewing, Jackson, Ind. 500 D3 140
Ewing, Fleming, Ky. 525 B7 178
Ewing, Lewis, Mo. 324 A6 150
Ewing, Holt, Nebr. 583 B7 152
Ewing, Lee, Va. 500 D1 192
Ewing Township, see West Trenton, N.J.
Ewingville, Mercer, N.J. (part of Ewing Township) C3 210
Ewo, Con.B. G7 409
Exaltación, Bol. 405 B1 246
Excel, Monroe, Ala. 313 D2 168
Excel, Alta., Can. 75 E7 54
Excello, Macon, Mo. 100 B5 150
Excello, Butler, Ohio 1,000 C2 156
Excelsior, Hennepin, Minn. 2,020 G5 148
Excelsior, Richland, Wis. 150 E3 160
Excelsior, mtn., Calif. C4 94
Excelsior, mts., Nev. E3 112
Excelsior Springs, Clay and Ray, Mo. 6,473 B3 D2 150
Exchange, Braxton, W.Va. 250 C4 194
Excursion Inlet, Alsk. 100 I14 84
Exe, riv., Eng. K9 273
Exeland, Sawyer, Wis. 214 C2 160
Exeter, Tulare, Calif. 4,264 D4 94
Exeter, Ont., Can. 2,655 Q19 64
Exeter, Penobscot, Maine 130 (707▲) D3 204
Exeter, Barry, Mo. 294 E4 150
Exeter, Fillmore, Nebr. 745 D8 152
Exeter, Rockingham, N.H. 7,243 F5 208
Exeter, Luzerne, Pa. 4,747 A5 B6 214
Exeter, Washington, R.I. 80 (2,298▲) C2 216
Exeter, riv., Eng. K9 273
Exeter, riv., N.H. E5 208
Exira, Audubon, Iowa 1,111 C3 142
Exline, Appanoose, Iowa 223 D5 142
Exmoor, moor, Eng. J9 273
Exmore, Northampton, Va. 1,566 C9 192
Exmouth, Eng. 17,800 K9 273
Exmouth, gulf, Austl. C2 432
Expanse, Sask., Can. 55 F5 58
Experiment, Spalding, Ga. 2,497 C2 176
Exploits, bay, Newf., Can. F8 72
Exploits, riv., Newf., Can. F7 72
Export, Westmoreland, Pa. 1,518 C2 214
Exshaw, Alta., Can. 262 E5 54
Extension, B.C., Can. 100 B13 52
Extinct Volcanoes and Lava Beds, Ariz. D6 124
Eya, riv., Sov.Un. I12 332
Eyak, Alsk. 178 C7 G12 84
Eyasi, lake, Tan. C5 414
Eye, pen., Scot. C6 272
Eyebrow, Sask., Can. 286 E4 58
Eyehill, creek, Sask., Can. D3 58
Eyemouth, Scot. 2,100 F10 272
Eyja, fjord, Ice. K20 290
Eyota, Olmsted, Minn. 558 H6 148
Eyre, Austl. E5 432
Eyre, lake, Austl. D7 432
Eyre, peninsula, Austl. E7 432
Eyrecourt, Ire. 383 H4 273
Ezine, Tur. 3,813 B2 307

F

Faaborg, Den. 5,150 I4 291
Fabens, El Paso, Tex. 3,134 D2 130
Faber, Nelson, Va. 80 C6 192
Faber, lake, N.W.Ter., Can. E7 48
Fabius, Jackson, Ala. 300 A4 168
Fabius, Onondaga, N.Y. 378 C6 212
Fabriano, It. 12,700 D4 302
Fabyan, Windham, Conn. 170 A8 202
Facatativá, Col. 13,479 C2 244
Faceville, Decatur, Ga. 100 F2 176
Fachi, well, Niger C7 409
Fackler, Jackson, Ala. 250 A4 168
Factoryville, Wyoming, Pa. 991 B6 214
Fada, Chad C9 409
Fada-Ngourma, Upper Volta 4,100 D5 408
Faddeyev, isl., Sov.Un. B16 329
Faejo, isl., Den. G2 292
Faemö, isl., Den. G2 292
Faenza, It. 52,400 C3 302
Faeroe Islands, Dan. poss., Eur. 31,781 B4 266
Fafa, Mali C5 408
Fafan, riv., Eth. D5 398
Fafe, Port. 5,855 B2 298
Făgăraș, Rom. 17,256 B3 321
Fagernes, Nor. 982 F3 291
Fagersta, Swe. 14,437 A6 292
Făget, Rom. 3,800 B2 321
Fagnano, lake, Arg. H4 251
Faguibine, lake, Mali C4 408
Fahraj, Iran D5 379
Faifo, Viet. 16,000 D6 362
Fair, isl., Scot. B11 272
Fairbank, Cochise, Ariz. 41 G5 124
Fairbank, Buchanan, Iowa 650 B5 142
Fairbank, Talbot, Md. 175 C7 182
Fairbank, Fayette, Pa. 760 *D2 214
Fairbanks, Alsk. 13,311 C7 84
Fairbanks, Alachua, Fla. 100 B8 174
Fairbanks, Ouachita, La. 300 B3 180
Fairbanks, Franklin, Maine 50 D2 204
Fair Bluff, Columbus, N.C. 1,030 C6 186
Fairborn, Greene, Ohio 19,453 C2 156
Fairburn, Fulton, Ga. 2,470 B4 C2 176
Fairburn, Custer, S.Dak. 47 D2 158
Fairbury, Livingston, Ill. 2,937 C5 138
Fairbury, Jefferson, Nebr. 5,572 D8 152
Fairchance, Fayette, Pa. 2,120 D2 214
Fairchild, Eau Claire, Wis. 594 D3 160
Fairdale, Bibb, Ala. 400 *C2 168
Fairdale, Wyandotte, Kans. 200 *B7 144
Fairdale, Jefferson, Ky. 6,000 A5 B5 178
Fairdale, Walsh, N.Dak. 126 B7 154
Fairdale, Raleigh, W.Va. 300 D6 194
Fairfax, Chambers, Ala. 3,107 C4 168
Fairfax, Marin, Calif. 5,813 C2 94
Fairfax, Man., Can. 75 F2 60
Fairfax, New Castle, Del. 1,000 *B3 172
Fairfax, Ware, Ga. 150 E4 176
Fairfax, Linn, Iowa 528 C6 142
Fairfax, Renville, Minn. 1,489 G4 148
Fairfax, Atchison, Mo. 736 A2 150
Fairfax, Hamilton, Ohio 2,430 *C2 156
Fairfax, Osage, Okla. 2,076 B7 128
Fairfax, Allendale, S.C. 1,814 F6 188
Fairfax, Gregory, S.Dak. 253 D7 158
Fairfax, Fairfax, Va. 13,585 A6 B7 192
Fairfax, Franklin, Vt. 350 (1,244▲) B2 218
Fairfax, co., Va. 275,002 B7 192
Fairfax Station, Fairfax, Va. 175 A6 192
Fairfield, Jefferson, Ala. 15,816 B3 E4 168
Fairfield, Solano, Calif. 14,968 C2 94
Fairfield, Fairfield, Conn. 46,183 E2 202
Fairfield, Camas, Idaho 474 F4 108
Fairfield, Wayne, Ill. 6,362 E5 138
Fairfield, Franklin, Ind. 175 C5 140
Fairfield, Jefferson, Iowa 8,054 C6 142
Fairfield, Nelson, Ky. 290 C5 178
Fairfield, Somerset, Maine 3,776 (5,829▲) D3 204
Fairfield, Teton, Mont. 752 C5 110
Fairfield, Clay, Nebr. 495 D7 152
Fairfield (Caldwell Township), Essex, N.J. 3,310 *B4 210
Fairfield, Hyde, N.C. 250 B9 186
Fairfield, Butler, Ohio 9,734 C1 156
Fairfield, Marion, Oreg. 2,000 *C3 96
Fairfield, Freestone, Tex. 1,781 D7 130
Fairfield, Franklin, Vt. 100 (1,225▲) B3 218
Fairfield, Spokane, Wash. 367 B9 E9 98
Fairfield, co., Conn. 653,589 D2 202
Fairfield, co., Ohio 63,912 C4 156
Fairfield, co., S.C. 20,713 C6 188
Fairfield, pond, Vt. B2 218
Fairfield Highlands, Jefferson, Ala. 4,500 E4 168
Fairford, Washington, Ala. 35 D1 168
Fairford, Eng. J11 273
Fairforest, Spartanburg, S.C. 950 *B4 188
Fairground, Neshoba, Miss. 230 C3 184
Fair Grove, Greene, Mo. 275 D4 150
Fair Grove, Davidson, N.C. 1,500 B5 186
Fairhaven, Bristol, Mass. 14,339 C6 206
Fair Haven, St. Clair, Mich. 225 G9 146
Fairhaven, Stearns, Minn. 200 F4 148
Fair Haven, Monmouth, N.J. 5,678 C4 210
Fair Haven, Cayuga, N.Y. 764 B5 212
Fair Haven, Rutland, Vt. 2,378 D2 218
Fair Hill, Cecil, Md. 60 A8 182
Fairholme, Sask., Can. 96 D3 58
Fairhope, Baldwin, Ala. 4,858 E2 168
Fairhope, Somerset, Pa. 1,700 D3 214
Fairland, Shelby, Ind. 750 C4 140
Fairland, Montgomery, Md. 85 B6 182
Fairland, Ottawa, Okla. 646 B9 128
Fair Lawn, Bergen, N.J. 36,421 A1 210
Fairlawn, Pulaski, Va. 1,325 *C4 192
Fairlea, Greenbrier, W.Va. 900 *D4 194
Fairlee, Kent, Md. 200 B7 182
Fairlee, Orange, Vt. 400 (569▲) D4 218
Fairless Hills, Bucks, Pa. 8,000 C7 214
Fairlight Station, Sask., Can. 194 F7 58
Fairmeade, Jefferson, Ky. 368 *B5 178
Fairmont City, St. Clair, Ill. 2,688 *E4 138
Fairmont, Will, Ill. 2,000 F2 138
Fairmont, Martin, Minn. 9,745 H4 148
Fairmont, Fillmore, Nebr. 829 D8 152
Fairmont, Robeson, N.C. 2,286 C6 186
Fairmont, Garfield, Okla. 115 B6 128
Fairmont, Spartanburg, S.C. 300 B4 188
Fairmont, Snohomish, Wash. 1,227 *B4 98
Fairmont, Marion, W.Va. 27,477 A7 B4 194
Fairmount, Sussex, Del. 100 F5 172
Fairmount, Gordon, Ga. 619 B2 176
Fairmount, Vermilion, Ill. 725 C6 138
Fairmount, Grant, Ind. 3,080 B4 140
Fairmount, Somerset, Md. 800 D8 182
Fairmount, Jackson, Mo. (part of Independence) E2 150
Fairmount, Onondaga, N.Y. 3,000 *B5 212
Fairmount, Richland, N.Dak. 503 D9 154
Fairmount Heights, Prince Georges, Md. 2,308 C4 182
Fairmount Station, Sask., Can. 192 E3 58
Fairoaks, Cross, Ark. 150 B5 170
Fair Oaks, Cobb, Ga. 7,969 A5 176
Fair Oaks, Jasper, Ind. 200 A2 140
Fairoaks, Allegheny, Pa. 1,239 A3 214
Fair Plain, Berrien, Mich. 7,998 *G5 146
Fairplain, Jackson, W.Va. 54 C3 194
Fairplay, Park, Colo. 404 C5 106
Fair Play, Washington, Md. A4 182
Fair Play, Polk, Mo. 335 D4 150
Fair Play, Oconee, S.C. 240 B3 188
Fairpoint, Belmont, Ohio 600 B6 156
Fairport, Muscatine, Iowa 150 C7 142
Fairport, Russell, Kans. 30 *C4 144
Fairport, Delta, Mich. 150 D5 146
Fairport, Monroe, N.Y. 5,507 B4 212
Fair Port, Northumberland, Va. 650 C8 192
Fairport Harbor, Lake, Ohio 4,267 A5 156
Fairton, Cumberland, N.J. 975 E2 210
Fairvalley, Woods, Okla. B4 128
Fairview, Dallas, Ark. 50 D4 170
Fairview, Marion, Ark. 80 A4 170
Fairview, Alta., Can. 1,260 B3 54
Fairview, Walker, Ga. 2,000 *B1 176
Fairview, Franklin, Idaho 350 G7 108
Fairview, Fulton, Ill. 544 C3 138
Fairview, St. Clair, Ill. 850 *E3 138
Fairview, Brown, Kans. 272 C8 144
Fairview, Todd, Ky. 200 D3 178
Fairview, Oscoda, Mich. 250 E7 146
Fairview, Newton, Mo. 249 *E3 150
Fairview, Richland, Mont. 1,006 C12 110
Fairview, Burlington, N.J. 350 D3 210
Fairview, Bergen, N.J. 9,399 B1 210
Fairview, Monmouth, N.J. 4,500 *C4 210
Fairview, Rio Arriba, N.Mex. 900 *B4 126
Fairview, Dutchess, N.Y. 8,626 *D8 212
Fairview, Major, Okla. 2,213 B5 128
Fairview, Coos, Oreg. 500 *D2 96
Fairview, Multnomah, Oreg. 578 B4 96
Fairview, Tillamook, Oreg. 400 *B3 96
Fairview, Northampton, Pa. 1,146 *C6 214
Fairview, Northumberland, Pa. 2,100 *B5 214
Fairview, Erie, Pa. 1,399 A1 214
Fairview, Lincoln, S.Dak. 101 D9 158
Fairview, Williamson, Tenn. 1,017 C4 190
Fairview, Sanpete, Utah 655 D4 114
Fairview, Yakima, Wash. 2,758 *C6 98
Fairview, Marion, W.Va. 653 A7 B4 194
Fairview, Sheboygan, Wis. 600 *E6 160
Fairview, Lincoln, Wyo. 100 D2 116
Fairview Park, Vermillion, Ind. 1,039 C2 140
Fairview Park, Cuyahoga, Ohio 14,624 B1 156
Fairview Shores, Orange, Fla. 900 *C9 174
Fair Water, Fond du Lac, Wis. 330 E5 160
Fairway, Johnson, Kans. 5,398 B8 144
Fairweather, mtn., Alsk. D8 84
Fairy Glen, Sask., Can. 119 D5 58
Fairyland, Walker, Ga. 1,000 *B1 176
Faison, Duplin, N.C. 666 B7 186
Faith, Rowan, N.C. 494 B5 186
Faith, Mead, S.Dak. 591 B3 158
Faithorn, Menominee, Mich. 35 D4 146
Faizābād, Afg. 25,770 A6 374
Faizabad, India 76,582 (*82,498) D3 368
Fajardo, P.R. 15,336 C12 233
Fakiragram, India D5 368
Fakse, bay, Den. F3 292
Faku, China 45,000 D11 348
Falabeguets, isl., Truk A3 436
Falaise, Fr. 5,715 C3 278
Fălciu, Rom. 5,124 A5 321
Falcon, Nevada, Ark. 35 D3 170
Falcon, El Paso, Colo. 35 *D6 106
Falcon, Quitman, Miss. 200 A2 184
Falcon, Cumberland, N.C. 235 B7 186
Falcón, state, Ven. 258,759 A3 240
Falcon, res., Tex. F6 130
Falconer, Chautauqua, N.Y. 3,343 C2 212
Falcon Heights, Ramsey, Minn. 5,927 F7 148
Falealili, harbor, Samoa E4 436
Falémé, riv., Sen. D2 408
Falerum, Swe. C7 292
Falfurrias, Brooks, Tex. 6,515 F6 130
Falher, Alta., Can. 802 C4 54
Falkenberg, Ger. 7,831 C5 286
Falkenberg, Swe. 10,141 E3 292
Falkenburg Station, Ont., Can. 50 O21 64
Falkirk, Scot. 37,100 E9 272
Falkland, B.C., Can. 210 E13 52
Falkland Islands, Br. poss., S.A. 2,230 I5 236
Falkner, Tippah, Miss. 200 A4 184
Falköping, Swe. 12,824 C4 292
Falkville, Morgan, Ala. 682 A3 168
Fall, creek, Ind. D5 140
Fall, riv., Kans. E7 144
Fall Branch, Washington, Tenn. 1,000 B9 190
Fallbrook, San Diego, Calif. 4,814 F5 94
Fall City, King, Wash. 560 B5 D3 98
Fall Creek, San Miguel, Colo. 6 D2 106
Fall Creek, Lane, Oreg. 150 *D4 96
Fall Creek, Eau Claire, Wis. 710 D2 160
Falling, creek, Va. B9 192
Falling, creek, W.Va. C6 194
Falling Creek, Chesterfield, Va. B9 192
Falling Water, Hamilton, Tenn. 500 E8 190
Falling Waters, Berkeley, W.Va. 100 B7 194
Fallis, Lincoln, Okla. 42 C6 128
Fallon, Prairie, Mont. 300 D11 110
Fallon, Churchill, Nev. 2,734 D3 112
Fallon, co., Mont. 3,997 D12 110
Fall River, Greenwood, Kans. 226 E7 144
Fall River, Bristol, Mass. 99,942 (*139,200) C5 206
Fall River, Columbia, Wis. 584 E4 160
Fall River, co., S.Dak. 10,688 D2 158
Fall River, res., Kans. E7 144
Fall River Mills, Shasta, Calif. 500 B3 94
Fall Rock, Clay, Ky. 500 C7 178
Falls, co., Tex. 21,263 D7 130
Falls, riv., R.I. C1 216
Falls, riv., Wyo. B2 116
Fallsburg, Lawrence, Ky. 200 B8 178
Falls Church (Independent City), Va. 10,192 A7 192
Falls City, Jerome, Idaho *G4 108
Falls City, Richardson, Nebr. 5,598 D10 152
Falls City, Polk, Oreg. 653 C3 96
Falls Creek, Clearfield and Jefferson, Pa. 1,344 B3 214
Fallsington, Bucks, Pa. 1,000 *C6 214
Falls Mills, Tazewell, Va. 500 C3 192
Falls of Rough, Grayson, Ky. 40 C4 178
Fallston, Harford, Md. 100 A7 182
Fallston, Cleveland, N.C. 500 B4 186
Falls View, Fayette, W.Va. 525 *C3 194
Falls Village, Litchfield, Conn. 500 B2 202
Falmouth, Eng. 16,500 K7 273
Falmouth, Suwannee, Fla. 100 A7 174
Falmouth, Jam. 2,840 C6 232
Falmouth, Pendleton, Ky. 2,568 B6 178
Falmouth, Cumberland, Maine 5,976 E2 E5 204
Falmouth, Barnstable, Mass. 3,308 (13,037▲) C6 206
Falmouth, Missaukee, Mich. 250 E6 146
Falmouth, Stafford, Va. 1,478 B7 192
Falmouth, bay, Eng. K7 273
Falmouth Heights, Barnstable, Mass. 160 C6 206
Falo, isl., Truk A3 436
Faloma, Washington, Oreg. A2 96
False, bay, U.S.Afr. F3 420
False, cape, Fla. C10 174
False, cape, Va. D9 192
False Pass, Alsk. 42 E5 84
Falster, isl., Den. G2 292
Falsterbo, Swe. 383 F3 292
Falta, India I9 366
Fălticeni, Rom. 13,305 A4 321
Falun, Saline, Kans. 100 D6 144
Falun, Swe. 18,389 A6 292
Falun, Burnett, Wis. 100 C1 160
Famagusta, Cyp. 26,763 D5 307
Famatina, mts., Arg. A2 252
Fame, McIntosh, Okla. 100 C8 128
Family, lake, Man., Can. E5 60
Famous Ice, beds, Vt. E3 218
Fancy Farm, Graves, Ky. 375 D2 178
Fangcheng, China 6,000 I6 349
Fanghsien, China 9,000 I5 349
Fangshen, China D9 348
Fannie, Montgomery, Ark. C3 170
Fannin, Levy and Gilchrist, Fla. 100 B8 174
Fannin, Rankin, Miss. 200 C3 184
Fannin, co., Ga. 13,620 B2 176
Fannin, co., Tex. 23,880 C7 130
Fannūj, Iran D5 379
Fanny Bay, B.C., Can. 150 F10 52
Fannystelle, Man., Can. 160 F4 60
Fano, It. 21,200 D4 302
Fanshawe, Le Flore, Okla. 150 D9 128
Fan Si Pan, mtn., Viet. B4 362
Fanudah, Sau.Ar. B3 383

Name	Pop.	Key	Page
Fanwood, Union, N.J.	7,963	B4	210
Fao, Iraq	2,916	E8	378
Faqûs, Eg., U.A.R.	16,263	E6	395
Faradje, Con.L.		B4	414
Farafangana, Malag.	7,300	D9	421
Farâfra, oasis, Eg., U.A.R.		B2	395
Farah, Afg.	15,258	C2	374
Farah, prov., Afg.		*D2	374
Farah, riv., Afg.		C2	374
Farallones, gulf, Calif.		A4	94
Faramana, Upper Volta		D4	408
Farana, Guinea	2,550	D2	408
Faranuf, Valley, Mont.		C9	110
Farasan, is., Sau.Ar.		D3	383
Farber, Audrain, Mo.	451	B6	150
Fareham, Eng.	50,000	K11	273
Farewell, Alsk.	30	*C6	84
Farewell, cape, N.Z.		D4	437
Färgelanda, Swe.	2,602	C3	292
Fargo, Monroe, Ark.	100	C5	170
Fargo, Clinch, Ga.	1,000	F4	176
Fargo, Richardson, Nebr.	12	*D10	152
Fargo, Cass, N.Dak.	46,662	D9	154
Fargo, Ellis, Okla.	291	B4	128
Far Hills, Somerset, N.J.	702	B3	210
Fari, Mali		D2	408
Faribault, Rice, Minn.	16,926	G5	148
Faribault, co., Minn.	23,685	H4	148
Faridpur, Pak.	25,556	L16	375
Farilhoes, is., Port.		C2	298
Farina, Austl.		E7	432
Farina, Fayette, Ill.	692	E5	138
Farisita, Huerfano, Colo.	5	E5	106
Fariskûr, Eg., U.A.R.	11,913	D6	395
Fariston, Laurel, Ky.	150	C6	178
Farjestaden, Swe.		E7	292
Farley, Dubuque, Iowa	920	B6	142
Farley, Franklin, Mass.	138	A3	206
Farley, Colfax, N.Mex.	60	B6	126
Farlington, Crawford, Kans.	100	*E9	144
Farlinville, Linn, Kans.	100	*D9	144
Farm, pond, Mass.		D2	206
Farmer, Hanson, S.Dak.	95	D8	158
Farmer City, DeWitt, Ill.	1,838	C5	138
Farmers, Rowan, Ky.	236	B7	178
Farmers Branch, Dallas, Tex.	13,441	*C7	130
Farmersburg, Sullivan, Ind.	1,027	C2	140
Farmersburg, Clayton, Iowa	250	B6	142
Farmers Exchange, Hickman, Tenn.	15	C4	190
Farmersville, Lowndes, Ala.	80	C3	168
Farmersville, Tulare, Calif.	3,101	*D4	94
Farmersville, Montgomery, Ill.	495	D4	138
Farmersville, Montgomery, Ohio	797	*C2	156
Farmersville, Collin, Tex.	2,021	C7	130
Farmerville, Union, La.	2,727	B3	180
Farmhaven, Madison, Miss.	125	C3	184
Farmingdale, Kennebec, Maine	700 (1,941▲)	*D3	204
Farmingdale, Monmouth, N.J.	959	C4	210
Farmingdale, Nassau, N.Y.	6,128	*E3	212
Farmingdale, Pennington, S.Dak.	68	D3	158
Farmington, Washington, Ark.	216	A2	170
Farmington, Hartford, Conn.	2,500 (10,813▲)	C4	202
Farmington, Kent, Del.	142	E3	172
Farmington, Oconee, Ga.	151	*C3	176
Farmington, Fulton, Ill.	2,831	C3	138
Farmington, Van Buren, Iowa	902	D6	142
Farmington, Reno, Kans.	367	D6	144
Farmington, Franklin, Maine	2,749 (5,001▲)	D2	204
Farmington, Oakland, Mich.	6,881	B7	146
Farmington, Dakota, Minn.	2,300	G5 G7	148
Farmington, St. Francois, Mo.	5,618	D7	150
Farmington, Teton, Mont.	12	C4	110
Farmington, Stafford, N.H.	2,241 (3,287▲)	E4	208
Farmington, San Juan, N.Mex.	23,786	B2	126
Farmington, Washington, Oreg.		B1	96
Farmington, Fayette, Pa.	800	D2	214
Farmington, Marshall, Tenn.	100	C5	190
Farmington, Davis, Utah	1,951	C4	114
Farmington, Whitman, Wash.	176	B9	98
Farmington, Marion, W.Va.	709	A7	194
Farmington, riv., Conn.		B4	202
Farmingville, Suffolk, N.Y.	2,134	*D4	212
Farmland, Randolph, Ind.	1,102	B4	140
Farmville, Pitt, N.C.	3,997	B8	186
Farmville, Prince Edward, Va.	4,293	C6	192
Farnam, Dawson, Nebr.	258	D5	152
Farnams, Berkshire, Mass.	250	A1	206
Farner, Polk, Tenn.	150	C7	190
Farnham, Que., Can.	5,843	S12	66
Farnham, Erie, N.Y.	422	C2	212
Farnham, Richmond, Va.	300	C8	192
Farnham, mtn., B.C., Can.		E14	52
Farnhamville, Calhoun, Iowa	409	B3	142
Farnhurst, New Castle, Del.	350	B3	172
Farnumsville, Worcester, Mass. (part of South Grafton)		B4	206
Faro, Port.	17,631	D3	298
Färön, isl., Swe.		D10	292
Fårösund, Swe.	3,234	D10	292
Farragut, Fremont, Iowa	495	D2	142
Farrans Point, Ont., Can.	275	P25	64
Farrar, riv., Scot.		D8	272
Farrāshband, Iran		D2	379
Farrell, Coahoma, Miss.	300	A2	184
Farrell, Mercer, Pa.	13,793	B1	214
Farrellton, Que., Can.	320	S9	66
Farris, Atoka, Okla.	25	D8	128
Farrukhabad, India	74,205 (*80,332)	D2	368
Fars, prov., Iran	1,655,984	*D3	379
Fars, reg., Iran		D3	379
Fársala, Grc.	5,768	B4	306
Farsi, Afg.	10,000	C2	374
Farson, Sweetwater, Wyo.	20	D3	116
Farsund, Nor.	1,902	G2	291
Fartak, cape, Aden		D5	383
Farur, isl., Iran		D4	379
Farwell, Clare, Mich.	737	F7	146
Farwell, Pope, Minn.	106	F3	148
Farwell, Howard, Nebr.	137	C7	152
Farwell, Parmer, Tex.	1,009	B4	130

Name	Pop.	Key	Page
Fasā, Iran	9,907	D3	379
Fasano, It.	16,100	E6	302
Fassett, Que., Can.	460	S10	66
Fastov, Sov.Un.	29,300	G7	332
Fatehpur, India	24,301	D3	368
Fatsa, Tur.	5,024	A7	307
Fatshan, see Nanhai, China			
Fatuvalu, Samoa	117	E4	436
Faucett, Buchanan, Mo.	150	B3	150
Faulk, co., S.Dak.	4,397	B6	158
Faulkner, co., Ark.	24,303	B4	170
Faulkton, Faulk, S.Dak.	1,051	C6	158
Faunsdale, Marengo, Ala.	124	C2	168
Fauquier, B.C., Can.	625	F13	52
Fauquier, co., Va.	24,066	B7	192
Faussepointe, lake, La.		D4	180
Faust, Franklin, N.Y.	880	A7	212
Favara, It.	26,600	G4	302
Favorita, Flagler, Fla.	200	B9	174
Fawcett, Alta., Can.		C5	54
Fawnie, range, B.C., Can.		D10	52
Fawnie Nose, mtn., B.C., Can.		D10	52
Faxaflói, bay, Ice.		L18	290
Faxon, Comanche, Okla.	137	D5	128
Faxon, Lycoming, Pa.	1,841	*B4	214
Faxon, Benton, Tenn.	100	B3	190
Fay, Dewey, Okla.	150	C5	128
Fayd, Sau.Ar.		B3	383
Fayette, Fayette, Ala.	4,227	B2	168
Fayette, Boone, Ind.	80	C3	140
Fayette, Fayette, Iowa	1,591	B6	142
Fayette, Kennebec, Maine	200 (328▲)	*D3	204
Fayette, Jefferson, Miss.	1,626	D1	184
Fayette, Howard, Mo.	3,294	B5	150
Fayette, Fulton, Ohio	1,090	A2	156
Fayette, Sanpete, Utah	161	D4	114
Fayette, co., Ala.	16,148	B2	168
Fayette, co., Ga.	8,199	C2	176
Fayette, co., Ill.	21,946	D4	138
Fayette, co., Ind.	24,454	C4	140
Fayette, co., Iowa	28,581	B6	142
Fayette, co., Ky.	131,906	B6	178
Fayette, co., Ohio	24,775	C3	156
Fayette, co., Pa.	169,340	D2	214
Fayette, co., Tenn.	24,577	C2	190
Fayette, co., Tex.	20,384	E7	130
Fayette, co., W.Va.	61,731	C3	194
Fayette City, Fayette, Pa.	1,159	C2	214
Fayetteville, Talladega, Ala.	400	B3	168
Fayetteville, Washington, Ark.	20,274	A2	170
Fayetteville, Fayette, Ga.	1,389	C2	176
Fayetteville, Lawrence, Ind.	150	D3	140
Fayetteville, Onondaga, N.Y.	4,311	B5	212
Fayetteville, Cumberland, N.C.	47,106 (*132,000)	B7	186
Fayetteville, Brown, Ohio	389	C3	156
Fayetteville, Franklin, Pa.	810	D4	214
Fayetteville, Lincoln, Tenn.	6,804	C5	190
Fayetteville, Fayette, W.Va.	1,848	C3 D7	194
Fayetteville North, Cumberland, N.C.	1,541	*B7	186
Fâyid, Eg., U.A.R.		E7	395
Fayston, Washington, Vt.	75 (158▲)	*C3	218
Fayville, Worcester, Mass.	200	D1	206
Faywood, Grant, N.Mex.	30	F2	126
Fazilka, India		C1	368
Fazzan (Fezzān), prov., Libya		B2	394
Feagaville, Frederick, Md.	80	B5	182
Fear, cape, N.C.		D8	186
Fearns Springs, Winston, Miss.		B4	184
Feasterville, Bucks, Pa.	6,000	A7	214
Feather, riv., Calif.		C3	94
Feather Falls, Butte, Calif.	900	C3	94
Featherston, Pittsburg, Okla.	50	C8	128
Featherville, Elmore, Idaho		F3	108
Fécamp, Fr.	18,201	C4	278
Feché, Eth.		D4	398
Fédala, Mor.	25,247	B2	402
Federal, Ont., Can.		Q25	64
Federal, Laramie, Wyo.	10	E7	116
Federal Capital, Pak.	1,126,417	*G5	375
Federal Dam, Cass, Minn.	185	D4	148
Federal Heights, Adams, Colo.	391	*C6	106
Federal Point, Putnam, Fla.	275	B9	174
Federalsburg, Caroline, Md.	2,060	C8	182
Federal Way, King, Wash.	7,000	*B4	98
Fedora, Miner, S.Dak.	150	C8	158
Fedscreek, Pike, Ky.	500	C8	178
Feeding Hills, Hampden, Mass.	5,000	B2	206
Fefan, isl., Truk		A3	436
Fegen, lake, Swe.		D4	292
Fehmarn, isl., Ger.		A4	286
Fehmarn, strait, Den., Ger.		G2 A4	292 286
Feia, lake, Braz.		E2	258
Feijó, Braz.		G2	256
Feilding, N.Z.	6,784	D5	437
Feira de Santana, Braz.	26,559	C3	258
Feira Zumbo, Moz.		C6	421
Fejér, co., Hung.	350,000	B3	320
Felanitx, Sp.	7,387	C8	298
Felch, Dickinson, Mich.	150	C4	146
Felda, Hendry, Fla.	250	E9	174
Feldbach, Aus.	3,382	D7	313
Feldberg, mtn., Ger.		E3	286
Feldkirch, Aus.	15,115	C1	313
Felicity, Clermont, Ohio	878	D2	156
Felipe Carrillo Puerto, Mex.	595	D8	225
Felixstowe, Eng.	15,600	J14	273
Felixville, East Feliciana, La.	35	D5	180
Fellowship, Burlington, N.J.	200	D3	210
Fellsmere, Indian River, Fla.	732	D10	174
Felsenthal, Union, Ark.	250	D4	170
Felt, Teton, Idaho	20	F7	108
Felt, Cimarron, Okla.	70	B1	128
Feltar, isl., Scot.		A12	272
Felton, Santa Cruz, Calif.	1,380	*D2	94
Felton, Kent, Del.	422	D3	172
Felton, Haralson, Ga.	160	C1	176
Felton, Clay, Minn.	201	D2	148
Feltre, It.	8,500	B3	302
Felts, Shelby, Tenn. (part of Memphis)		E6	190
Femund, lake, Nor.		E4	291
Fence, Florence, Wis.	250	C5	160

Name	Pop.	Key	Page
Fence, lake, Wis.		C4	160
Fence, riv., Mich.		C3	146
Fence Lake, Valencia, N.Mex.	55	D2	126
Fender, Tift, Ga.	150	E3	176
Fenelon Falls, Ont., Can.	1,137	P22	64
Fénérive, Malag.		C9	421
Fengchen, China		E6	348
Fengcheng, China	45,000	E11	348
Fengcheng, China	4,000	K8	349
Fengchieh, China		J4	349
Fenghsiang, China		H3	348
Fenghsien, China	5,000	H3	348
Fengning, China	3,000	E8	348
Fengshan, China	2,000	B14	348
Fengshan, For.		N10	349
Fengtu, China		K3	349
Fenholloway, Taylor, Fla.	75	A7	174
Fenick, isl., S.C.		G2	188
Fenn, Idaho, Idaho	25	D2	108
Fennimore, Grant, Wis.	1,747	F3	160
Fennville, Allegan, Mich.	705	G5	146
Fenton, Sask., Can.	20	D5	58
Fenton, Kossuth, Iowa	440	A3	142
Fenton, Trigg, Ky.	92	D2	178
Fenton, Jefferson, La.	429	D3	180
Fenton, Genesee, Mich.	6,142	G8	146
Fenton, St. Louis, Mo.	207	B8	150
Fentress, Norfolk, Va.	350	D8	192
Fentress, co., Tenn.	13,288	B7	190
Fenwick, Ont., Can.	280	Q21	64
Fenwick, Middlesex, Conn.	36	*D6	202
Fenwick, Nicholas, W.Va.	505	C4	194
Fenwick Island, Sussex, Del.	48	G5	172
Fenwood, Sask., Can.	191	E6	58
Fenwood, Marathon, Wis.	147	*D3	160
Fenyang, China	65,000	G5	348
Fenyang, China		I8	349
Feodosiya, Sov.Un.	43,600	J10	332
Ferbane, Ire.	708	H5	273
Ferdig, Toole, Mont.	150	B5	110
Ferdinand, Idaho, Idaho	176	C2	108
Ferdinand, Dubois, Ind.	1,427	D3	140
Ferdows, Iran		B5	379
Ferentino, It.	7,522	E4	302
Fergana, Sov.Un.	80,000	D8	336
Fergana, mts., Sov.Un.		D8	336
Fergus, Ont., Can.	3,677	Q20	64
Fergus, Fergus, Mont.	6	C7	110
Fergus, co., Mont.	14,018	C7	110
Fergus Falls, Otter Tail, Minn.	13,733	E2	148
Ferguson, B.C., Can.	35	E14	52
Ferguson, Marshall, Iowa	186	C5	142
Ferguson, Pulaski, Ky.	468	C6	178
Ferguson, Bossier, La.		B2	180
Ferguson, St. Louis, Mo.	22,149	A8 C7	150
Ferguson, Wayne, W.Va.	150	C2	194
Ferguson Creek, Pike, Ky.	300	*C8	178
Ferintosh, Alta., Can.	195	D6	54
Fermanagh, co., N.Ire.	53,000	G5	273
Fermeuse, Newf., Can.		G9	72
Fermo, It.	11,400	D4	302
Fermoselle, Port.		B3	298
Fermoselle, Sp.	4,268	B3	298
Fermoy, Ire.	3,427	I4	273
Fern, creek, Ky.		A5	178
Fernandez Village, Honolulu, Haw. (part of Ewa)	609	G9	86
Fernandina Beach, Nassau, Fla.	7,276	A9 A10	174
Fernando de Noronha, ter., Braz.	1,000	*D8	236
Fernando Póo, overseas prov., Sp.	45,330	F6	409
Fernan Lake, Kootenai, Idaho	134	*B2	108
Fernán-Núñez, Sp.	11,436	D4	298
Fernão Velosa, bay, Moz.		B8	421
Fernbank, Lamar, Ala.	80	B1	168
Ferndale, Pulaski, Ark.	60	D6	170
Ferndale, Humboldt, Calif.	1,116	B1	94
Ferndale, Anne Arundel, Md.	2,500	B6	182
Ferndale, Oakland, Mich.	31,347	B8	146
Ferndale, Umatilla, Oreg.		B8	96
Ferndale, Cambria, Pa.	2,717	C3	214
Ferndale, Northumberland, Pa.	1,900	*B5	214
Ferndale, Whatcom, Wash.	1,442	A4	98
Ferney, Brown, S.Dak.	104	B7	158
Fernie, B.C., Can.	2,808	F15	52
Fernley, Lyon, Nev.	500	D2	112
Fern Park, Seminole, Fla.	407	C9	174
Fern Ridge, dam, Oreg.		C3	96
Ferns, Ire.	588	I6	273
Fernwood, Benewah, Idaho	250	B2	108
Fernwood, Pike, Miss.	600	D2	184
Fernwood, Saratoga, N.Y.	2,108	*B8	212
Ferozepur, India	40,703 (*79,487)	C1	368
Ferrara, It.	73,300 (139,500▲)	C3	302
Ferrara, prov., It.	427,800	*C3	302
Ferreira do Alentejo, Port.	5,205	D2	298
Ferrellsburg, Lincoln, W.Va.	150	C2	194
Ferrelo, cape, Oreg.		E2	96
Ferreñafe, Peru	8,812	B2	245
Ferriday, Concordia, La.	4,563	C4	180
Ferrier, Alta., Can.		D5	54
Ferris, Ellis, Tex.	1,807	B9 C7	130
Ferris, mts., Wyo.		D5	116
Ferrisburg, Addison, Vt.	170 (1,426▲)	C2	218
Ferron, Emery, Utah	386	D4	114
Ferros, Braz.	1,745	D2	258
Ferrum, Franklin, Va.	400	D4	192
Ferry, Alsk.	15	C7	84
Ferry, Oceana, Mich.	100	F5	146
Ferry, co., Wash.	3,889	A8	98
Ferryland, Newf., Can.	500	G9	72
Ferrysburg, Ottawa, Mich.	2,590	F5	146
Ferryville, Crawford, Wis.	194	E2	160
Ferstikla, Ice.		L19	290
Fertile, Worth, Iowa	386	A4	142
Fertile, Polk, Minn.	968	D2	148
Fertilia, It.		E2	302
Fertő, lake, Hung.		B1	320
Feshi, Con.L.		D2	414
Fessenden, Wells, N.Dak.	920	C6	154

Name	Pop.	Key	Page
Festina, Winneshiek, Iowa	150	A6	142
Festiniog, Wales	6,500	I9	273
Festus, Jefferson, Mo.	7,021	B8 C7	150
Fet, Nor.		B2	292
Feteşti, Rom.	15,383	B4	321
Fethard, Ire.	992	I5	273
Fethiye, Tur.	4,364	C3	307
Fetisovo, Sov.Un.		D4	336
Feurs, Fr.	5,381	E6	278
Feversham, Ont., Can.	230	P20	64
Fez, Mor.	179,372	B3	402
Fezzān, see Fazzan, Libya			
Fiambala, Arg.		A2	252
Fianarantsoa, Malag.	18,200	D9	421
Fianarantsoa, prov., Malag.		D9	421
Fianga, Chad		E8	409
Fibre, Chippewa, Mich.	20	C7	146
Fich, Eth.		D5	398
Fichot, isl., Newf., Can.		E8	72
Ficksburg, U.S.Afr.	7,147	E5	420
Fidalgo, isl., Wash.		A4	98
Fidenza, It.	9,800	C3	302
Field, B.C., Can.	365	E14	52
Field, Curry, N.Mex.	25	D7	126
Field, Socorro, N.Mex.	25	D3	126
Field, lake, La.		E5	180
Fieldale, Henry, Va.	1,499	D5	192
Fielding, Sask., Can.	78	D4	58
Fielding, Box Elder, Utah	270	B3	114
Fields, Harney, Oreg.	10	E8	96
Fieldsboro, Burlington, N.J.	583	C3	210
Fierro, Grant, N.Mex.	600	F2	126
Fiesole, It.	4,300	D3	302
Fife, Pierce, Wash.	1,463	D2	98
Fife, co., Scot.	317,300	E9	272
Fife, lake, Sask., Can.		F5	58
Fife Lake, Sask., Can.	166	F5	58
Fife Lake, Grand Traverse, Mich.	218	E6	146
Fife Ness, cape, Scot.		E10	272
Fifield, Price, Wis.	300	C3	160
Fifteen Mile, creek, Wyo.		B4	116
Fifteen Mile Falls, res., N.H.		C3	208
Fifty Lakes, Crow Wing, Minn.	143	*E4	148
Figeac, Fr.	5,933	E5	278
Figeholm, Swe.		D7	292
Figtree, Rh.&Nya.		D5	420
Figueira da Foz, Port.	10,486	B2	298
Figueras, Sp.	15,396	A8	298
Figuig, Alg.		B3	402
Figure Five, Crawford, Ark.	50	B2	170
Fiji Islands, Br. poss., Pac.O.		E6	436
Filbert, York, S.C.	250	A6	188
Filbert, McDowell, W.Va.	950	D3	194
File, lake, Man., Can.		C2	60
Filer, Twin Falls, Idaho	1,249	G4	108
Filer City, Manistee, Mich.	400	E5	146
Filey, Eng.	4,800	G12	273
Filiaşi, Rom.		B2	321
Filiatrá, Grc.	9,209	C3	306
Filicudi, isl., It.		F5	302
Filingue, Niger		D5	408
Filipstad, Swe.	7,085	B5	292
Filley, Gage, Nebr.	149	D9	152
Fillmore, Ventura, Calif.	4,808	E4	94
Fillmore, Sask., Can.	342	F6	58
Fillmore, Montgomery, Ill.	360	D4	138
Fillmore, Putnam, Ind.	550	C3	140
Fillmore, Andrew, Mo.	254	A3	150
Fillmore, Allegany, N.Y.	522	C3	212
Fillmore, Benson, N.Dak.	125	B6	154
Fillmore, Johnston, Okla.	100	D7	128
Fillmore, Millard, Utah	1,602	E3	114
Fillmore, co., Minn.	23,768	H6	148
Fillmore, co., Nebr.	9,425	D8	152
Fimi, riv., Con.L.		C2	414
Final, pt., Mex.		B3	224
Fina Susu, mtn., Saipan		B7	436
Fincastle, Lee, Ky.	150	C7	178
Fincastle, Botetourt, Va.	403	C5	192
Finch, Ont., Can.	389	O25	64
Finderne, Somerset, N.J.	1,100	*B3	210
Findhorn, Scot.		D9	272
Findlater, Sask., Can.	95	E5	58
Findlay, Man., Can.		F2	60
Findlay, Shelby, Ill.	759	D5	138
Findlay, Hancock, Ohio	30,344	A3	156
Findley, mtn., B.C., Can.		E14	52
Findon, Meagher, Mont.		D6	110
Finesville, Warren, N.J.	275	B2	210
Fingal, Ont., Can.		R19	64
Fingal, Barnes, N.Dak.	190	D8	154
Finger, McNairy, Tenn.	150	C3	190
Fingerville, Spartanburg, S.C.	350	A5	188
Fingoe, Moz.		C6	421
Finike, Tur.	1,382	C4	307
Finistère, dept., Fr.	727,847	*C2	278
Finisterre, cape, Sp.		A2	298
Finke, riv., Austl.		D7	432
Finksburg, Carroll, Md.	385	B6	182
Finland, Lake, Minn.	200	D7	148
Finland, country, Eur.	4,065,027	B7 E11	266 290
Finland, gulf, Eur.		B7	266
Finlay, riv., B.C., Can.		B10	52
Finlay Forks, B.C., Can.		C11	52
Finlayson, Pine, Minn.	213	E6	148
Finley, Steele, N.Dak.	808	C8	154
Finley, Pushmataha, Okla.	250	D8	128
Finley, Dyer, Tenn.	600	B2	190
Finmoore, B.C., Can.	100	D11	52
Finna, fjord, Ice.		K22	290
Finnegan, Alta., Can.		E6	54
Finney, co., Kans.	16,093	D3	144
Finneytown, Hamilton, Ohio	5,000	*C2	156
Finnmark, co., Nor.	66,267	*B10	290
Finn Rock, Lane, Oreg.	200	C4	96
Finspang, Swe.	13,632	C6	292
Finsteraarhorn, mtn., Switz.		B4	312
Finsterwalde, Ger.	20,600	C5	286
Fionn, lake, Scot.		D7	272
Fir, riv., Sask., Can.		D6	58
Fircrest, Pierce, Wash.	3,565	D2	98
Fire, isl., N.Y.		E4	212
Firebaugh, Fresno, Calif.	2,070	D3	94
Firebrick, Lewis, Ky.	366	B7	178
Firenze (Florence), It.	392,600	D3	302
Firenze, prov., It.	944,100	*D3	302
Firenzuola, It.	743	C3	302

Fire River, Ont., Can. 50 R24 64
Firesteel, Dewey, S.Dak. 150 B4 158
Firestone, Weld, Colo. 276 B6 106
Firinya, Ven. D6 240
Firmat, Arg. 4,051 B3 252
Firminy, Fr. 21,161 E6 278
Fir Mountain, Sask., Can. 122 F4 58
Firozabad, India 65,438 D2 368
First, fork, Pa. B3 214
First Cataract, Nile riv., Eg., U.A.R. C3 395
First Connecticut, lake, N.H. A4 208
First Creek, Phillips, Mont. 40 C9 110
Firstview, Cheyenne, Colo. 12 D8 106
Firth, Bingham, Idaho 322 F6 108
Firth, Lancaster, Nebr. 277 D9 152
Firuzabad, Iran 23,382 D3 379
Firuzkuh, Iran 5,874 B3 379
Fish, creek, W.Va. B4 194
Fish, mtn., Oreg. D4 96
Fish, riv., Maine A4 204
Fish, riv., S.W.Afr. E3 420
Fish Cove, pt., Newf., Can. C7 72
Fish Creek, Door, Wis. 180 C6 160
Fishheating, creek, Fla. E9 174
Fisher, Poinsett, Ark. 303 B6 170
Fisher, Champaign, Ill. 1,155 C5 138
Fisher, Sabine, La. 300 C2 180
Fisher, Polk, Minn. 326 D2 148
Fisher, Tulsa, Okla. 150 *B7 128
Fisher, Hardy, W.Va. 50 B5 194
Fisher, co., Tex. 7,865 C5 130
Fisher, bay, Man., Can. E4 60
Fisher, peak, Va. D4 192
Fisher, riv., Man., Can. E4 60
Fisher, strait, N.W.Ter., Can. E10 48
Fisher Branch, Man., Can. 500 E4 60
Fishers, Hamilton, Ind. 344 C3 D5 140
Fishers, lake, N.S., Can. E4 70
Fishers, peak, Colo. E6 106
Fishers Island, Suffolk, N.Y. 600 E6 212
Fishers Island, sound, Conn. D7 202
Fishersville, Augusta, Va. 700 B6 192
Fisherville, Ont., Can. 225 R21 64
Fisherville, Worcester, Mass. (part of South Grafton) B4 206
Fishguard [& Goodwick], Wales 4,800 J8 273
Fish Haven, Bear Lake, Idaho 130 G7 108
Fishhook, Alsk. 50 B7 84
Fishing, bay, Md. D7 182
Fishing, creek, N.C. A8 186
Fishing, creek, S.C. B6 188
Fishing, creek, W.Va. B4 194
Fishing, lake, Man., Can. D5 60
Fishing Brook, mtn., N.Y. B7 212
Fishing Creek, Dorchester, Md. 544 D7 182
Fishing Creek, Cape May, N.J. 300 E3 210
Fishing Creek, reservoir, S.C. B7 188
Fishing Ship Harbour, Newf., Can. D8 72
Fishkill, Dutchess, N.Y. 1,033 D8 212
Fish River, lake, Maine B4 204
Fish Springs, range, Utah D2 114
Fishtail, Stillwater, Mont. 50 *E7 110
Fishtrap, Lincoln, Wash. B9 98
Fishville, Grant, La. 150 C3 180
Fisk, Butler, Mo. 498 E7 150
Fiskburg, Kenton, Ky. 40 A8 B6 178
Fiskdale, Worcester, Mass. 950 B3 206
Fiske, Sask., Can. 153 E3 58
Fiskeville, Providence, R.I. 300 C2 216
Fitch Bay, Que., Can. 265 S12 66
Fitchburg, Worcester, Mass. 43,021 A4 206
Fitchville, New London, Conn. 500 C7 202
Fithian, Vermilion, Ill. 495 C6 138
Fitler, Issaquena, Miss. 150 C1 184
Fittstown, Pontotoc, Okla. 200 D7 128
Fitzgerald, Ben Hill, Ga. 8,781 E3 176
Fitzhugh, Woodruff, Ark. 45 B5 170
Fitzhugh, Pontotoc, Okla. 150 D7 128
Fitzhugh, sound, B.C., Can. E9 52
Fitzpatrick, Bullock, Ala. 78 C4 168
Fitzpatrick, Que., Can. 315 Q12 66
Fitz Roy, Arg. G4 251
Fitzroy, Austl. B5 432
Fitzroy, bay, N.Z. J11 437
Fitz Roy, mtn., Chile G3 251
Fitzroy, riv., Austl. C10 432
Fitzroy, riv., Austl. B4 432
Fitzroy Harbor, Ont., Can. 135 O24 64
Fitzwilliam, Cheshire, N.H. 300 (966▲) F2 208
Fitzwilliam, isl., Ont., Can. O19 64
Fitzwilliam Depot, Cheshire, N.H. 200 F2 208
Fiume, see Rijeka, Yugo.
Fiumicino, It. (part of Rome) 5,981 *E4 302
Five Corners, Bristol, Mass. 125 *B5 206
Five Islands, N.S., Can. 385 D5 70
Fivemile, creek, Wyo. C4 116
Fivemiletown, N.Ire. 426 G5 273
Five Points, Chambers, Ala. 285 B4 168
Five Points, Dougherty, Ga. 1,400 E2 176
Five Points, Marion, Ind. 200 D5 140
Five Points, Bernalillo, N.Mex. 2,500 *C4 126
Five Points, Lawrence, Tenn. 115 C4 190
Fizi, Con.L. C4 414
Fjällbacka, Swe. C2 292
Fjärdhunda, Swe. 4,104 B7 292
Fjellsjokampen, mtn., Nor. A1 292
Fjotland, Nor. G2 291
Flackville, Marion, Ind. 600 D4 140
Flaga, Ice. M20 290
Flagler, Kit Carson, Colo. 693 C7 106
Flagler, co., Fla. 4,566 B9 174
Flagler Beach, Flagler, Fla. 970 B9 174
Flag Pond, Unicoi, Tenn. 75 B9 190
Flagstaff, Coconino, Ariz. 18,214 C4 124
Flagstaff, lake, Maine C2 204
Flagstaff, lake, Oreg. E7 96
Flagtown, Somerset, N.J. 250 B3 210
Flamand, lake, Que., Can. Q11 66
Flambeau, res., Wis. B3 160
Flambeau, riv., Wis. C2 160
Flamborough, head, Eng. G12 273
Flanagan, Livingston, Ill. 841 C5 138
Flanders, Morris, N.J. 500 B3 210
Flanders (Flandre), former prov., Fr. 2,099,000 B5 278
Flandreau, Moody, S.Dak. 2,129 C9 158
Flanigan, Washoe, Nev. 23 C2 112
Flannan, is., Scot. C5 272
Flären, lake, Swe. E5 292
Flasher, Morton, N.Dak. 515 D4 154
Flåsjön, lake, Swe. D6 290
Flat, Alsk. 95 C6 84
Flat, Wolfe, Ky. 74 C7 178
Flat, brook, N.J. A3 210
Flat, is., Newf., Can. D8 72
Flat, isl., Newf., Can. E7 72
Flat, lake, La. C5 180
Flat, mtn., N.Z. F1 437
Flat, riv., Mich. F6 146
Flat Bay, Newf., Can. 100 F6 72
Flatbrookville, Sussex, N.J. 60 A3 210
Flatbush, Alta., Can. 100 C5 54
Flat Creek, Walker, Ala. 800 B2 E4 168
Flatcreek, Bedford, Tenn. 100 C5 190
Flateyri, Ice. K18 290
Flat Gap, Wise, Va. C2 192
Flathead, co., Mont. 32,965 B2 110
Flathead, lake, Mont. C2 110
Flathead, mts., Mont. B2 110
Flathead, range, Mont. B3 110
Flathead, riv., Mont. B2 110
Flathead, valley, Mont. C2 110
Flatlands, N.B., Can. 300 B3 70
Flat Lick, Knox, Ky. 500 D7 178
Flatonia, Fayette, Tex. 1,009 E7 130
Flatridge, Grayson, Va. 50 D3 192
Flat River, St. Francois, Mo. 4,515 D7 150
Flat River, res., R.I. C2 216
Flat Rock, Jackson, Ala. 500 A4 168
Flat Rock, Crawford, Ill. 497 E6 138
Flat Rock, Shelby, Ind. 250 C4 140
Flat Rock, Wayne, Mich. 4,696 G8 146
Flat Rock, Henderson, N.C. 1,808 B3 186
Flat Rock, Seneca, Ohio 360 A4 156
Flatrock, creek, Ind. C4 140
Flatrock, lake, Man., Can. C2 60
Flats, McPherson, Nebr. 4 C4 152
Flats, Macon, N.C. B2 186
Flattery, cape, Wash. A2 98
Flattop, Jefferson, Ala. 350 E4 168
Flat Top, Mercer, W.Va. 250 D3 194
Flattop, Platte, Wyo. D8 116
Flatts, Bermuda A13 233
Flatwillow, Petroleum, Mont. D8 110
Flat Willow, creek, Mont. D7 110
Flatwood, Wilcox, Ala. 300 *C3 168
Flatwoods, Greenup, Ky. 3,741 B8 178
Flatwoods, Rapides, La. 150 C3 180
Flat Woods, Perry, Tenn. 150 C4 190
Flat Woods, Braxton, W.Va. 248 C4 194
Flawil, Switz. 6,502 A5 312
Flaxcombe, Sask., Can. 147 E3 58
Flaxton, Burke, N.Dak. 375 B3 154
Flaxville, Daniels, Mont. 262 B11 110
Fleet, Alta., Can. 100 D7 54
Fleet, Eng. 9,700 J12 273
Fleeton, Northumberland, Va. C8 192
Fleetwing, Bucks, Pa. 450 *C6 214
Fleetwood, Eng. 28,000 H9 273
Fleetwood, Jefferson, Okla. 30 E6 128
Fleetwood, Berks, Pa. 2,647 C6 214
Fleischmanns, Delaware, N.Y. 450 C7 212
Flekkefjord, Nor. 2,864 G2 291
Fleming, Sask., Can. 193 E7 58
Fleming, Logan, Colo. 384 B8 106
Fleming, Letcher, Ky. 670 C8 178
Fleming, co., Ky. 10,890 B7 178
Fleming, pt., Calif. A5 94
Flemingsburg, Fleming, Ky. 2,067 B7 178
Flemington, Liberty, Ga. 149 E5 176
Flemington, Polk, Mo. 142 D4 150
Flemington, Hunterdon, N.J. 3,232 B3 210
Flemington, Clinton, Pa. 1,608 B4 214
Flemington, Taylor, W.Va. 478 B7 194
Flen, Swe. 4,863 B7 292
Flensburg, Ger. 94,300 A3 286
Flensburg, Morrison, Minn. 280 F4 148
Flensburger, fjord, Ger. A3 286
Flers [-de-l'Orne], Fr. 11,213 C3 278
Flesherton, Ont., Can. 471 P20 64
Fletcher, Ont., Can. 210 R18 64
Fletcher, Dixie, Fla. 50 B7 174
Fletcher, Henderson, N.C. 800 B3 186
Fletcher, Miami, Ohio 569 B2 156
Fletcher, Comanche, Okla. 884 D5 128
Fletcher, Franklin, Vt. 125 (399▲) B3 218
Fletcher, mtn., Vt. B3 218
Fletcher, pond, Mich. E8 146
Fleur de Lys, Newf., Can. 300 E7 E10 72
Fleurier, Switz. 3,412 B2 312
Flinders, isl., Austl. E6 432
Flinders, isl., Austl. F9 432
Flinders, range, Austl. E7 432
Flinders, riv., Austl. B8 432
Flin Flon, Man., Can. 10,234 C2 E5 60
Flint, Morgan, Ala. 432 A3 168
Flint, Genesee, Mich. 196,940 (*379,900) F8 146
Flint, Wales 14,200 H9 273
Flint, co., Eng. 146,000 H9 273
Flint, isl., Pac.O. D4 436
Flint, riv., Ga. E2 176
Flint, run, W.Va. A6 194
Flint Creek, range, Mont. D3 110
Flint Hill, Rappahannock, Va. 200 B6 192
Flintoft, Sask., Can. 56 F4 58
Flinton, Ont., Can. 215 P23 64
Flintridge, Los Angeles, Calif. 5,000 C5 94
Flintstone, Allegany, Md. 125 A2 182
Flintville, Lincoln, Tenn. 175 C5 190
Flippen, Henry, Ga. 400 C2 176
Flippin, Marion, Ark. 433 A4 170
Flippin, Monroe, Ky. 150 D5 178
Flomaton, Escambia, Ala. 1,454 D2 168
Floodwood, St. Louis, Minn. 677 E6 148
Flora, Clay, Ill. 5,331 E5 138
Flora, Carroll, Ind. 1,742 B3 140
Flora, Natchitoches, La. 250 C2 180
Flora, Madison, Miss. 743 C2 184
Flora, Wallowa, Oreg. 75 B9 96
Florahome, Putnam, Fla. 400 B9 174
Florala, Covington, Ala. 3,011 D3 168
Floral City, Citrus, Fla. 600 C8 174
Floral Park, Silver Bow, Mont. 4,079 *E4 110
Floral Park, Nassau, N.Y. 17,499 E3 212
Flora Vista, San Juan, N.Mex. 40 B2 126
Flordell Hills, St. Louis, Mo. 1,119 *C7 150
Florence, Lauderdale, Ala. 31,649 A2 168
Florence, Pinal, Ariz. 2,143 E4 124
Florence, Drew, Ark. 350 D5 170
Florence, Fremont, Colo. 2,821 D5 106
Florence, Switzerland, Ind. 150 D5 140
Florence, see Firenze, It.
Florence, Marion, Kans. 853 D7 144
Florence, Boone, Ky. 5,837 A6 A8 178
Florence, Hampshire, Mass. B2 206
Florence, Lyon, Minn. 87 G2 148
Florence, Rankin, Miss. 360 C2 184
Florence, Ravalli, Mont. 150 D2 110
Florence, Burlington, N.J. 4,215 C3 210
Florence, Pamlico, N.C. 170 B9 186
Florence, Lane, Oreg. 1,642 D2 96
Florence, Florence, S.C. 24,722 C9 188
Florence, Codington, S.Dak. 216 B8 158
Florence, Williamson, Tex. 610 D7 130
Florence, Rutland, Vt. 80 D2 218
Florence, Snohomish, Wash. A4 98
Florence, Florence, Wis. 700 C5 160
Florence, co., S.C. 84,438 C9 188
Florence, co., Wis. 3,437 C5 160
Florenceville, N.B., Can. 500 C2 70
Florencia, Col. 27,050 C1 244
Florenville, Bel. 2,187 E4 282
Flores, Guat. 1,574 B3 228
Flores, dept., Ur. 36,125 B4 252
Flores, isl., B.C., Can. F9 52
Flores, isl., Indon. F6 358
Flores, sea, Indon. F5 358
Floresta, Braz. 2,134 B3 258
Floresville, Wilson, Tex. 2,126 B7 E6 130
Florham Park, Morris, N.J. 7,222 B4 210
Floriano, Braz. 9,101 B2 258
Florianópolis, Braz. 48,264 K7 257
Florida, Cuba 21,159 B5 232
Florida, Berkshire, Mass. 80 (569▲) A1 206
Florida, Socorro, N.Mex. 175 D4 126
Florida, Orange, N.Y. 1,550 D7 212
Florida, Ur. 15,000 B4 252
Florida, dept., Ur. 106,495 B4 252
Florida, state, U.S. 4,951,560 F10 77 174
Florida, bay, Fla. G10 174
Florida, cape, Fla. F10 174
Florida, isl., Solomon E2 436
Florida, keys, Fla. G10 174
Florida, mts., N.Mex. F3 126
Florida, straits, N.A. G10 77
Florida City, Dade, Fla. 4,114 F5 F10 174
Florien, Sabine, La. 496 C2 180
Florin, Lancaster, Pa. 1,518 C5 214
Flórina, Grc. 12,270 A3 306
Flórina (Phlorina), prov., Grc. 69,391 *A3 306
Floris, Davis, Iowa 187 D5 142
Floris, Fairfax, Va. 75 A6 192
Florissant, Teller, Colo. 40 D5 106
Florissant, St. Louis, Mo. 38,166 A8 150
Florö, Nor. 1,934 F1 291
Flossmoor, Cook, Ill. 4,624 F3 138
Flourtown, Montgomery, Pa. 4,000 A6 214
Flovilla, Butts, Ga. 284 C3 176
Flower, riv., Vt. E2 218
Floweree, Chouteau, Mont. 20 C5 110
Flower Hill, Nassau, N.Y. 4,594 *D3 212
Flowers Cove, Newf., Can. 700 E7 72
Flower Station, Ont., Can. 20 O24 64
Flowery Branch, Hall, Ga. 741 B3 176
Flowood, Rankin, Miss. 486 C2 184
Floyd, Floyd, Iowa 401 A5 142
Floyd, Roosevelt, N.Mex. 200 D7 126
Floyd, Floyd, Va. 487 D4 192
Floyd, co., Ga. 69,130 B1 176
Floyd, co., Ind. 51,397 D4 140
Floyd, co., Iowa 21,102 A5 142
Floyd, co., Ky. 41,642 C8 178
Floyd, co., Tex. 12,369 B5 130
Floyd, co., Va. 10,462 D4 192
Floyd, mtn., Ariz. C3 124
Floyd, riv., Iowa B1 142
Floydada, Floyd, Tex. 3,769 B5 130
Floyd Dale, Dillon, S.C. 125 C10 188
Floyds, canyon, Nev. C4 112
Floyds, fork, Ky. B5 178
Floydsburg, Oldham, Ky. 75 A5 178
Floyds Knobs, Floyd, Ind. 300 D4 140
Fluessenmeer, lake, Neth. B4 282
Flumendosa, riv., It. F2 302
Flums, Switz. 4,833 A5 312
Flushing, Genesee, Mich. 3,761 F8 146
Flushing, Belmont, Ohio 1,189 B5 156
Fluvanna, co., Va. 7,227 C6 192
Flying H, Chaves, N.Mex. 30 E5 126
Foam Lake, Sask., Can. 841 E6 58
Foard, co., Tex. 3,125 B6 130
Foča, Yugo. 3,992 C4 316
Fochimi, well, Chad C8 409
Focşani, Rom. 28,244 B4 321
Foggia, It. 109,100 E5 302
Foggia, prov., It. 687,900 *E5 302
Foggo, Nig. D6 409
Fogliano, It. *E4 302
Fogo, Newf., Can. 1,184 F8 72
Fogo, cape, Newf., Can. F8 72
Fogo, isl., Newf., Can. F8 72
Fohnsdorf, Aus. 11,170 C6 313
Föhr, isl., Ger. A3 286
Foix, Fr. 6,466 F4 278
Foix, former prov., Fr. 81,000 *F4 278
Fokang, China 12,000 N6 349
Fokis (Phocis), prov., Grc. 51,472 *B4 306
Folcroft, Delaware, Pa. 7,013 *D6 214
Foley, Baldwin, Ala. 2,889 E2 168
Foley, Taylor, Fla. 200 A7 174
Foley, Benton, Minn. 1,112 F5 148
Foley, Lincoln, Mo. 183 B7 150
Foley, isl., N.W.Ter., Can. D11 48
Foleyet, Ont., Can. 485 R25 64
Foley Junction, Taylor, Fla. 200 A7 174
Foligno, It. 20,400 D4 302
Folkestone, Eng. 44,900 J14 273
Folkston, Charlton, Ga. 1,810 F4 176
Follansbee, Brooke, W.Va. 4,052 A4 B2 194
Föllinge, Swe. E6 290
Follonica, It. 6,706 D3 302
Folly, hill, Mass. C3 206
Folly, isl., S.C. F9 G4 188
Folly Beach, Charleston, S.C. 1,137 F9 G4 188
Follyfarm, Harney, Oreg. D8 96
Folsom, Sacramento, Calif. 3,925 C3 94
Folsom, St. Tammany, La. 225 D5 180
Folsom, Atlantic, N.J. 482 D3 210
Folsom, Union, N.Mex. 142 B7 126
Folsom, Delaware, Pa. 5,000 *D6 214
Folsom, Wetzel, W.Va. 300 A6 B4 194
Folsom, res., Calif. C3 94
Folsomville, Warrick, Ind. 130 D2 140
Fomento, Cuba 7,852 A5 232
Fonda, Pocahontas, Iowa 1,026 B3 142
Fonda, Montgomery, N.Y. 1,004 C7 212
Fond du Lac, Fond du Lac, Wis. 32,719 B5 E5 160
Fond du Lac, co., Wis. 75,085 E5 160
Fonde, Bell, Ky. 200 D7 178
Fondi, It. 13,700 E4 302
Fonesca, gulf, Sal. D3 228
Fonsagrada, Sp. 950 A3 298
Fontainebleau, Fr. 19,915 C5 278
Fontainebleau, Jackson, Miss. 75 E2 184
Fontana, San Bernardino, Calif. 14,659 *E5 94
Fontana, Miami, Kans. 138 D9 144
Fontana, Walworth, Wis. 1,326 F5 160
Fontana Dam, Graham, N.C. 250 B2 186
Fontanelle, Adair, Iowa 729 C3 142
Fontanet, Vigo, Ind. 200 C2 140
Fonte Boa, Braz. 752 F3 256
Fontenay [-sous-Bois], Fr. 36,739 I10 278
Fontenay-le-Comte, Fr. 9,519 D3 278
Fontenelle, mtn., Wyo. D2 116
Fonthill, Ont., Can. 1,872 Q21 64
Fontibón, Col. 13,871 C2 244
Foochow, see Fuchou, China
Foothill, Spokane, Wash. D9 98
Foothills, Alta., Can. D4 54
Footville, Rock, Wis. 675 F4 160
Foping, China 1,000 I3 348
Forada, Douglas, Minn. 98 F3 148
Foraker, Osage, Okla. 74 B7 128
Foraker, mtn., Alsk. F10 84
Forbach, Fr. 21,591 C7 278
Forbes, Austl. 6,514 E9 432
Forbes, Dickey, N.Dak. 138 E7 154
Forbes, mtn., Alta., Can. E4 54
Forbesganj, India D4 368
Forbing, Caddo, La. 500 B2 180
Forbing Park, Yavapai, Ariz. 300 D3 124
Forcados, Nig. 3,001 E6 408
Forchheim, Ger. 19,300 D4 286
Ford, Ford, Kans. 252 E4 144
Ford, Clark, Ky. 350 C6 178
Ford, Jackson, Miss. (part of Moss Point) E2 184
Ford, Scot. E7 272
Ford, co., Ill. 16,606 C5 138
Ford, co., Kans. 20,938 E4 144
Ford, riv., Mich. D4 146
Ford City, Kern, Calif. 3,926 E4 94
Ford City, Armstrong, Pa. 5,440 C2 214
Forder, Lincoln, Colo. D7 106
Fordland, Webster, Mo. 338 D5 150
Fordlândia, Braz. F5 256
Fordoche, Pointe, La. 400 D4 180
Fords, Middlesex, N.J. 10,000 B4 210
Fords Ferry, Crittenden, Ky. 60 C2 178
Fordson, Mex. D8 225
Fords Prairie, Lewis, Wash. 1,404 *C4 98
Fordsville, Ohio, Ky. 524 C4 178
Fordville, Walsh, N.Dak. 367 B8 154
Fordwich, Ont., Can. 410 Q19 64
Fordwick, Augusta, Va. 150 B5 192
Fordyce, Dallas, Ark. 3,890 D4 170
Fordyce, Cedar, Nebr. 143 B8 152
Forékaria, Guinea, 4,350 E2 408
Forel, mt., Grnld. Q31 290
Foreman, Little River, Ark. 1,001 D2 170
Foremost, Alta., Can. 456 F7 54
Foresman, Newton, Ind. 100 B2 140
Forest, Bel. 49,716 D3 282
Forest, Ont., Can. 2,035 Q18 64
Forest, Clinton, Ind. 400 B3 140
Forest, West Carroll, La. 160 B4 180
Forest, Scott, Miss. 3,917 C3 184
Forest, Hardin, Ohio 1,314 B3 156
Forest, Bedford, Va. 250 C5 192
Forest, co., Pa. 4,485 B2 214
Forest, co., Wis. 7,542 C5 160
Forest Acres, Richland, S.C. 3,842 C7 188
Forestburg, Alta., Can. 552 D6 54
Forestburg, Sanborn, S.Dak. 150 C7 158
Forest City, Winnebago, Iowa 2,930 A4 142
Forest City, Washington, Maine 25 C5 204
Forest City, Holt, Mo. 425 B2 150
Forest City, Rutherford, N.C. 6,556 B4 186
Forest City, Susquehanna, Pa. 2,651 B6 214
Forestdale, Barnstable, Mass. 130 *C6 206
Forestdale, Providence, R.I. 400 B2 216
Forest Dale, Rutland, Vt. 450 D2 218
Forester, Scott, Ark. *C3 170
Forest Glen, Montgomery, Md. 214 *B5 182
Forestgrove, Fergus, Mont. 20 D7 110
Forest Grove, Washington, Oreg. 5,628 B1 B3 96
Forest Heights, New Haven, Conn. 250 E3 202
Forest Heights, Prince Georges, Md. 3,524 C3 C5 182
Forest Hill, Ont., Can. 19,480 R22 64

Forest Hill, Rapides, La. 302 C3 180
Forest Hill, Harford, Md. 200 A7 182
Forest Hill, Tarrant, Tex. 3,221 *C7 130
Forest Hills, Pike, Ky. 180 *A6 178
Forest Hills, Allegheny, Pa. 8,796 A4 214
Forest Hills, Davidson, Tenn. 2,101 E7 190
Forest Home, Butler, Ala. 125 D3 168
Forest Homes, Madison, Ill. 2,025 *E3 138
Forest Junction, Calumet, Wis. 200 A6 160
Forest Knolls, Marin, Calif. 800 *C2 94
Forest Lake, Alger, Mich. 60 C5 146
Forest Lake, Washington, Minn. 2,347 F6 F7 148
Forest Lake, Richland, S.C. 243 *C7 188
Forest Lawn, Alta., Can. 3,150 E6 54
Foreston, Mille Lacs, Minn. 266 F5 148
Foreston, Clarendon, S.C. 210 D8 188
Forest Park, New Castle, Del. 225 B3 172
Forest Park, Clayton, Ga. 14,201 B5 176
Forest Park, Cook, Ill. 14,452 F2 138
Forest Park, Oklahoma, Okla. 766 *C6 128
Forest River, Walsh, N.Dak. 191 B8 154
Forest Station, Washington, Maine 35 C5 204
Forest View, Cook, Ill. 1,042 *B6 138
Forest View, Greenville, S.C. 1,000 *B4 188
Forestville, Prince Georges, Md. 1,500 C6 182
Forestville, Marquette, Mich. 121 *F9 146
Forestville, Chautauqua, N.Y. 905 C2 212
Forestville, Schuylkill, Pa. 200 *C5 214
Forestville, Door, Wis. 300 D6 160
Forez, mts., Fr. E5 278
Forfar, Scot. 10,000 E10 272
Forgan, Sask., Can. 100 E4 58
Forgan, Beaver, Okla. 532 B3 128
Forget, Sask., Can. 166 F6 58
Forge Village, Middlesex, Mass. 1,191 A5 C1 206
Fork, Dillon, S.C. 168 C10 188
Fork, creek, W.Va. C5 194
Fork, lake, Colo. D3 106
Forked Deer, riv., Tenn. C2 190
Forked Island, Vermilion, La. 180 E3 180
Forked River, Ocean, N.J. 800 D4 210
Forkland, Greene, Ala. 300 C2 168
Fork Mountain, Anderson, Tenn. 150 B7 190
Fork Ridge, Claiborne, Tenn. 200 B8 190
Fork River, Man., Can. 180 E2 60
Forks, Phillips, Mont. B9 110
Forks, Clallam, Wash. 1,156 B2 98
Forks of Elkhorn, Franklin, Ky. 172 B6 178
Fork Shoals, Greenville, S.C. 200 B4 188
Fork Union, Fluvanna, Va. 200 C6 192
Forkville, Scott, Miss. 150 C3 184
Forli, It. 48,100 C4 302
Forli, prov., It. 496,500 *C4 302
Forman, Sargent, N.Dak. 530 D8 154
Formello, It. 1,800 *D4 302
Formentera, isl., Sp. C7 298
Formiga, Braz. 11,782 E1 258
Formosa, Arg. 16,506 C6 250
Formosa, Van Buren, Ark. 100 B4 170
Formosa, Braz. 3,631 D1 258
Formosa, Ont., Can. 290 P19 64
Formosa, prov., Arg. 192,900 B5 250
Formosa (Taiwan), rep. (Nationalist China) 7,600,000 G14 N10 340 349
Formosa, bay, Ken. C7 414
Formosa, strait, China M9 349
Formoso, Jewell, Kans. 192 C6 144
Forney, Lemhi, Idaho E4 108
Forney, Horry, S.C. 100 D10 188
Forney, Kaufman, Tex. 1,544 B9 C7 130
Fornfelt, Scott, Mo. D8 150
Forrest, Austl. 61 E5 432
Forrest, Livingston, Ill. 1,220 C5 138
Forrest, Quay, N.Mex. 140 D7 126
Forrest, co., Miss. 52,722 D3 184
Forrest, lakes, Austl. D5 432
Forrest City, St. Francis, Ark. 10,544 B6 170
Forreston, Ogle, Ill. 1,153 A4 138
Forrest Station, Man., Can. 75 F3 60
Forsayth, Austl. 80 B8 432
Forshaga, Swe. 4,387 B4 292
Forst, Ger. 29,700 C6 286
Forsyth, Monroe, Ga. 3,697 C3 176
Forsyth, Macon, Ill. 424 D5 138
Forsyth, Marquette, Mich. 200 C4 146
Forsyth, Taney, Mo. 489 E4 150
Forsyth, Rosebud, Mont. 2,032 D10 110
Forsyth, co., Ga. 12,170 B2 176
Forsyth, co., N.C. 189,428 A5 186
Fort Adams, Wilkinson, Miss. 100 D1 184
Fort Albany, Ont., Can. R25 64
Fortaleza, Braz. 360,466 A3 258
Fortaleza, Braz. D2 258
Fort Ann, Washington, N.Y. 453 B8 212
Fort Anne, natl. hist. park, N.S., Can. E4 70
Fort Apache, Navajo, Ariz. 400 E6 124
Fort Archambault, Chad E8 409
Fort Ashby, Mineral, W.Va. 700 B6 194
Fort Assiniboine, Alta., Can. C5 54
Fort Atkinson, Winneshiek, Iowa 353 A6 142
Fort Atkinson, Jefferson, Wis. 7,908 F5 160
Fort Augustus, Scot. D7 272
Fort Banya, Ken. B6 414
Fort Barnwell, Craven, N.C. 300 B8 186
Fort Bayard, see Hsiying, China
Fort Beaufort, U.S.Afr. 8,293 F5 420
Fort Beausejour, natl. hist. park, N.B., Can. D5 70
Fort Belknap, Blaine, Mont. 200 B8 110
Fort Belknap Agency, Blaine, Mont. 195 B8 110
Fort Bend, co., Tex. 40,527 E8 130
Fort Benton, Chouteau, Mont. 1,887 C6 110
Fort Bidwell, Modoc, Calif. 300 B3 94
Fort Blackmore, Scott, Va. 250 D2 192
Fort Bragg, Mendocino, Calif. 4,433 C2 94
Fort Branch, Gibson, Ind. 1,983 D2 140
Fort Bridger, Uinta, Wyo. 150 E2 116
Fort Calhoun, Washington, Nebr. 458 C9 D3 152
Fort Charlet, see Djanet, Alg.
Fort Cobb, Caddo, Okla. 687 C5 128
Fort Coffee, Le Flore, Okla. 200 *C9 128
Fort Collins, Larimer, Colo. 25,027 B5 106
Fort Collinson, N.W.Ter., Can. C7 48
Fort Collins West, Larimer, Colo. 1,569 *B5 106
Fort Covington, Franklin, N.Y. 976 A7 212
Fort Crampel, Cen.Afr.Rep. E8 409
Fort Crook, Sarpy, Nebr. 75 E3 152
Fort-Dauphin, Malag. 7,100 E9 241
Fort Davis, Macon, Ala. 350 C4 168
Fort Davis, Jeff Davis, Tex. 900 D4 130
Fort Defiance, Apache, Ariz. 500 C6 124
Fort-de-France, Mart. 60,648 E14 233
Fort Delaware, New Castle, Del. B3 172
Fort Deposit, Lowndes, Ala. 1,466 D3 168
Fort Des Moines, Polk, Iowa 3,500 A7 C4 142
Fort Dick, Del Norte, Calif. 150 B1 94
Fort Dodge, Webster, Iowa 28,399 B3 142
Fort Dodge, Ford, Kans. 500 E4 144
Fort Drum, Okeechobee, Fla. 40 D10 174
Fort Duchesne, Uintah, Utah 200 C6 114
Fort Dupont, New Castle, Del. B3 172
Forteau Bay, Newf., Can. 200 E7 72
Fort Edward, Washington, N.Y. 3,737 B8 212
Fort Erie, Ont., Can. 8,632 R22 64
Fortescue, Holt, Mo. 78 A2 150
Fortescue, Cumberland, N.J. 200 E2 210
Fortescue, riv., Austl. C3 432
Fort Fairfield, Aroostook, Maine 3,082 (5,876▲) B5 204
Fort Flatters, Alg. C5 402
Fort-Foureau, Cam. 1,004 D8 409
Fort Frances, Ont., Can. 9,005 R23 64
Fort Fraser, B.C., Can. C10 52
Fort Fred Steele, Carbon, Wyo. 40 *E6 116
Fort Fremont, Beaufort, S.C. 200 *G7 188
Fort Gaines, Clay, Ga. 1,320 E1 176
Fort Garland, Costilla, Colo. 621 E5 106
Fort Garry, Man., Can. 50 F4 60
Fort Gay, Wayne, W.Va. 739 C2 194
Fort George, B.C., Can. 300 D11 52
Fort George, Duval, Fla. 200 A10 174
Fort George, riv., Que., Can. Q9 66
Fort Gibson, Muskogee, Okla. 1,407 C8 128
Fort Gibson, lake, Okla. B8 128
Fort Good Hope, N.W.Ter., Can. D6 48
Fort-Gouraud, Maur. B2 408
Fort Grahame, B.C., Can. B10 52
Fort Grant, Graham, Ariz. 150 F6 124
Fort Green, Hardee, Fla. 175 D9 174
Forth, firth, Scot. E10 272
Forth, riv., Scot. E8 272
Fort Hall, Bingham, Idaho 700 F6 108
Fort Hall, Ken. C6 414
Fort Hancock, Hudspeth, Tex. 600 D3 130
Fort Harrison, Lewis and Clark, Mont. 350 D4 110
Fort Henry, Stewart, Tenn. 50 B4 190
Fort Hill, Rh. & Nya. A6 421
Fort Hope, Ont., Can. R24 64
Fort Howard, Baltimore, Md. 375 B7 182
Fort Huachuca, Cochise, Ariz. 250 G5 124
Fortierville, Que., Can. 600 R12 66
Fortine, Lincoln, Mont. 150 B2 110
Fortin Uno, Arg. C2 252
Fort Jameson, Rh.&Nya. 3,500 B6 421
Fort Jefferson, natl. mon., Fla. G8 174
Fort Jennings, Putnam, Ohio 436 B2 156
Fort Johnson, Rh.&Nya. 950 B7 421
Fort Jones, Siskiyou, Calif. 483 B2 94
Fort Kent, Aroostook, Maine 2,787 (4,701▲) A4 204
Fort Keogh, Custer, Mont. 265 D11 110
Fort Klamath, Klamath, Oreg. 400 E4 96
Fort Knox, Hardin, Ky. C5 178
Fort Knox, federal depository, Ky. C5 178
Fort Lallemand, Alg. B5 402
Fort Lamy, Chad 23,470 D8 409
Fort Langley, B.C., Can. 500 B15 52
Fort Laperrine (Tamanrasset), Alg. 1,714 (10,089▲) D5 402
Fort Laramie, Goshen, Wyo. 233 D8 116
Fort Laramie, natl. mon., Wyo. D8 116
Fort Lauderdale, Broward, Fla. 83,648 D6 E10 174
Fort Lawn, Chester, S.C. 192 B7 188
Fort Lee, Bergen, N.J. 21,815 A2 210
Fort Leonard Wood, Pulaski, Mo. 500 D5 150
Fort Liard, N.W.Ter., Can. E6 48
Fort-Liberté, Hai. 6,604 C9 233
Fort Lincoln, Burleigh, N.Dak. 150 D5 154
Fort Logan, Meagher, Mont. D5 110
Fort Loramie, Shelby, Ohio 687 B2 156
Fort Loudoun, lake, Tenn. C7 190
Fort Lupton, Weld, Colo. 2,194 B6 106
Fort Lynn, Miller, Ark. 25 D3 170
Fort Lyon, Bent, Colo. 260 D7 106
Fort McDowell, Maricopa, Ariz. 226 G3 124
Fort McHenry, natl. mon. and historical shrine, Md. C4 182
Fort MacLeod, Alta., Can. 2,103 F6 54
Fort MacMahon, Alg. C4 402
Fort McPherson, N.W.Ter., Can. D5 48
Fort Madison, Lee, Iowa 15,247 D6 142
Fort Manning, Rh.&Nya. B6 421
Fort Matanzas, natl. mon., Fla. B9 174
Fort Meade, Polk, Fla. 4,014 D9 174
Fort Meade, Meade, S.Dak. 250 C2 158
Fort Meadow, res., Mass. D1 206
Fort Mill, York, S.C. 3,315 A7 188
Fort Missoula, Missoula, Mont. 400 D2 110
Fort Mitchell, Russell, Ala. 80 C4 168
Fort Mitchell, Kenton, Ky. 525 *B6 178
Fort Mitchell, Lunenburg, Va. 150 D6 192
Fort Monroe (Old Point Comfort), Va. (part of Hampton) A9 192
Fort Morgan, Morgan, Colo. 7,379 B7 106
Fort Motte, Calhoun, S.C. 386 D7 188
Fort Myers, Lee, Fla. 22,523 E9 174
Fort Myers Beach, Lee, Fla. 2,463 E9 174
Fort Necessity, Franklin, La. 75 B4 180
Fort Nelson, B.C., Can. 300 E7 52
Fort Norman, N.W.Ter., Can. E6 48
Fort Ogden, De Soto, Fla. 300 D9 174
Fort Oglethorpe, Catoosa and Walker, Ga. 2,251 B1 176
Fort Payne, De Kalb, Ala. 7,029 A4 168
Fort Peck, Valley, Mont. 950 B10 110
Fort Peck, res., Mont. C10 110
Fort Pierce, Saint Lucie, Fla. 22,256 D10 174
Fort Pierce, inlet, Fla. D10 174
Fort Pierre, Stanley, S.Dak. 2,649 C5 158
Fort Pierre Bordes, Alg. E4 402
Fort Plain, Montgomery, N.Y. 2,809 C7 212
Fort Polignac, Alg. C5 402
Fort Portal, Ug. B5 414
Fort Providence, N.W.Ter., Can. E7 48
Fort Pulaski, natl. mon., Ga. D6 176
Fort Qu'Appelle, Sask., Can. 1,130 E6 58
Fort Randall, dam, S.Dak. D7 158
Fort Randall, res., S.Dak. D7 158
Fort Ransom, Ransom, N.Dak. 200 D8 154
Fort Recovery, Mercer, Ohio 1,336 B2 156
Fort Reno, Canadian, Okla. 50 C5 128
Fort Resolution, N.W.Ter., Can. E7 48
Fortress of Louisbourg, natl. hist. park, N.S., Can. D10 70
Fort Riley, Geary, Kans. C7 144
Fort Ripley, Crow Wing, Minn. 55 E4 148
Fort Ritner, Lawrence, Ind. 120 D3 140
Fort Robinson, Dawes, Nebr. 40 B2 152
Fort Robinson, Sullivan, Tenn. 700 *B9 190
Fort Rock, Lake, Oreg. 15 D5 96
Fortrose, N.Z. 136 G2 437
Fort Rosebery, Rh.&Nya. 2,600 B5 420
Fort Ross, N.W.Ter., Can. C9 48
Fort Rousset, Con.B. G8 409
Fort St. James, B.C., Can. 615 C10 52
Fort St. John, B.C., Can. 1,908 B12 52
Fort Sandeman, Pak. 6,001 D6 375
Fort Saskatchewan, Alta., Can. 2,582 D6 54
Fort Scott, Bourbon, Kans. 9,410 E9 144
Fort Selkirk, Yukon, Can. E5 48
Fort Severn, Ont., Can. Q24 D13 64
Fort Shaw, Cascade, Mont. 85 C5 110
Fort Shevchenko, Sov.Un. 18,800 D4 336
Fort Sibut, Cen.Afr.Rep. E8 409
Fort Simpson, N.W.Ter., Can. E6 48
Fort Smith, Sebastian, Ark. 52,991 B2 170
Fort Smith, N.W.Ter., Can. 250 E7 48
Fort Smith, lake, Ark. B2 170
Fort Spring, Fayette, Ky. 60 B6 178
Fort Stanton, Lincoln, N.Mex. 100 E5 126
Fort Steele, B.C., Can. 300 F15 52
Fort Stockton, Pecos, Tex. 6,373 D4 130
Fort Sumner, De Baca, N.Mex. 1,809 D6 126
Fort Sumter, natl. mon., S.C. F9 188
Fort Supply, Woodward, Okla. 394 B4 128
Fort Supply, res., Okla. B4 128
Fort Thomas, Graham, Ariz. 150 E6 124
Fort Thomas, Campbell, Ky. 14,896 A8 178
Fort Thompson, Buffalo, S.Dak. 150 C6 158
Fort Totten, Benson, N.Dak. 200 C7 154
Fort Towson, Choctaw, Okla. 474 D8 128
Fortuna, Humboldt, Calif. 3,523 B1 94
Fortuna, Moniteau, Mo. 155 C5 150
Fortuna, Divide, N.Dak. 185 B2 154
Fortuna Ledge, Alsk. 95 C5 84
Fortune, Newf., Can. 1,194 G8 72
Fortune, bay, Newf., Can. G8 72
Fortune Harbour, Newf., Can. 250 F8 72
Fort Union, Roosevelt, Mont. B12 110
Fort Union, natl. mon., N.Mex. C5 126
Fort Valley, Peach, Ga. 8,310 D3 176
Fort Vancouver, natl. mon., Wash. D4 98
Fort Vermilion, Alta., Can. 300 E3 54
Fort Victoria, Rh.&Nya. 8,300 (*8,700) D6 421
Fortville, Hancock, Ind. 2,209 C4 140
Fort Walton Beach, Okaloosa, Fla. 12,147 A4 174
Fort Washakie, Fremont, Wyo. 130 C4 116
Fort Washington, Prince Georges, Md. C5 182
Fort Washington, Montgomery, Pa. 2,500 A6 214
Fort Washington Forest, Prince Georges, Md. 900 *C5 182
Fort Wayne, Allen, Ind. 161,776 (*215,400) A4 140
Fort White, Columbia, Fla. 425 B8 174
Fort William, Ont., Can. 39,464 (*84,500) R24 64
Fort William, Scot. 2,900 E7 272
Fort Wingate, McKinley, N.Mex. 100 C2 126
Fort Worden, Jefferson, Wash. A4 98
Fort Worth, Tarrant, Tex. 356,268 (*505,100) B8 C7 130
Fort Wright, Kenton, Ky. 2,184 *B6 178
Fort Yates, Sioux, N.Dak. 806 D5 154
Forty Fort, Luzerne, Pa. 6,431 B6 214
Forty Four, Izard, Ark. 25 A4 170
Fort Yukon, Alsk. 446 B7 84
Forward, Sask., Can. 23 F5 58
Foshan, China A14 348
Foshan, see Chaoyang, China
Foshee, Escambia, Ala. 25 D2 168
Foss, Washita, Okla. 289 C4 128
Fossano, It. 11,000 C1 302
Fossil, Wheeler, Oreg. 672 B6 96
Fossil, lake, Oreg. D6 96
Fossombrone, It. 4,659 D4 302
Fosston, Sask., Can. 130 D6 58
Fosston, Polk, Minn. 1,704 D3 148
Foster, Que., Can. 436 S12 66
Foster, Bracken, Ky. 114 B8 178
Foster, Bates, Mo. 153 C3 150
Foster, Pierce, Nebr. 60 B8 152
Foster, Garvin, Okla. 25 D6 128
Foster, Linn, Oreg. 250 C4 96
Foster, see Foster Center, R.I.
Foster, King, Wash. D3 98
Foster, Boone, W.Va. 120 D5 194
Foster, Eau Claire, Wis. 80 D2 160
Foster, co., N.Dak. 5,361 C7 154
Foster, riv., Sask., Can. B5 58
Foster Center (Foster), Providence, R.I. 80 (2,097▲) B2 216
Foster City, Dickinson, Mich. 200 D4 146
Fosters, Tuscaloosa, Ala. 950 B2 168
Fosters, pond, Mass. C2 206
Fosters Corners, Cumberland, Maine 25 E4 204
Fosters Falls, Wythe, Va. 200 D4 192
Foster Village, Honolulu, Haw. 2,300 *G10 86
Fosterville, Rutherford, Tenn. 150 C5 190
Fostoria, Lowndes, Ala. 200 C3 168
Fostoria, Clay, Iowa 167 A2 142
Fostoria, Pottawatomie, Kans. 90 C7 144
Fostoria, Tuscola, Mich. 300 F8 146
Fostoria, Seneca and Hancock, Ohio 15,732 A3 156
Fostoria, Montgomery, Tex. 666 D8 130
Fougamou, Gabon G7 409
Fougères, Fr. 23,151 C3 278
Fouhsin, China 188,600 D10 348
Fouke, Miller, Ark. 394 D3 170
Foul, bay, Eg., U.A.R. C4 395
Foula, isl., Scot. A10 272
Fouliang, China 65,000 K8 349
Fouling, China K3 349
Foulness, isl., Eng. J13 273
Foulwind, cape, N.Z. D3 437
Foumban, Cam. 18,000 E7 409
Founing, China 85,000 I9 348
Fount, Knox, Ky. 700 C7 178
Fountain, Monroe, Ala. 164 D2 168
Fountain, El Paso, Colo. 1,602 D6 106
Fountain, Bay, Fla. 250 A5 174
Fountain, Mason, Mich. 194 E5 146
Fountain, Fillmore, Minn. 297 H6 148
Fountain, Duplin, N.C. 300 C8 186
Fountain, Pitt, N.C. 496 B8 186
Fountain, co., Ind. 18,706 B2 140
Fountain, creek, Colo. D6 106
Fountain City, Wayne, Ind. 833 C5 140
Fountain City, Knox, Tenn. 10,365 B8 E9 190
Fountain City, Buffalo, Wis. 934 D2 160
Fountain Green, Sanpete, Utah 544 D4 114
Fountain Head, Washington, Md. 950 A4 182
Fountain Head, Sumner, Tenn. 207 B5 190
Fountain Hill, Ashley, Ark. 230 D5 170
Fountain Hill, Lehigh, Pa. 5,428 C6 214
Fountain Inn, Greenville, S.C. 2,385 B4 188
Fountain Place, East Baton Rouge, La. 5,000 *D4 180
Fountain Run, Monroe, Ky. 298 D5 178
Fountaintown, Shelby, Ind. 300 C4 140
Fountain Valley, Orange, Calif. 2,068 *F5 94
Fouping, China 2,000 F7 348
Four Buttes, Daniels, Mont. 45 B11 110
Fourchambault, Fr. 5,197 D5 278
Fourche, Perry, Ark. 51 *B4 170
Fourche, mts., Ark. C3 170
Fourche La Favre, riv., Ark. C3 170
Fourche Maline, creek, Okla. D8 128
Fourchu, N.S., Can. 355 D9 70
Four Corners, Toole, Mont. B5 110
Four Corners, Marion, Oreg. 4,743 *C4 96
Four Corners, Weston, Wyo. 5 B8 116
Four Holes, Orangeburg, S.C. 300 E8 188
Four Lakes, Spokane, Wash. 250 B9 D8 98
Fourmies, Fr. 13,414 B6 278
Fourmile, Bell, Ky. 700 D7 178
Fourmile, creek, Iowa A7 142
Four Mountains, is., Alsk. E5 84
Fournier, Ont., Can. 240 O26 64
Fournier, Aroostook, Maine 100 A4 204
Four Oaks, Johnston, N.C. 1,010 B7 186
Four Points, Dougherty, Ga. 1,200 *E2 176
Four States, Marion, W.Va. 700 A7 B4 194
Fouta Djallon, mts., Guinea D2 408
Foutou, bay, China N8 349
Fouyang, China 65,000 I7 349
Foveaux, strait, N.Z. G1 437
Fowblesburg, Baltimore, Md. 100 A6 182
Fowler, Fresno, Calif. 1,892 D4 94
Fowler, Otero, Colo. 1,240 D6 106
Fowler, Benton, Ind. 2,491 B2 140
Fowler, Meade, Kans. 717 E3 144
Fowler, Clinton, Mich. 854 F7 146
Fowler, Pondera, Mont. 37 B5 110
Fowler, point, Austl. E6 432
Fowlerton, Grant, Ind. 297 B4 140
Fowlerville, Livingston, Mich. 1,674 G7 146
Fowlkes, Dyer, Tenn. 250 C2 190
Fowlstown, Decatur, Ga. 400 F2 176
Fox, Stone, Ark. 100 B4 170
Fox, Carter, Okla. 400 D6 128
Fox, Grant, Oreg. 10 C7 96
Fox, Grayson, Va. 30 D3 192
Fox, isl., Alsk. E5 84
Fox, isl., Wash. D2 98
Fox, lake, Ill. A5 138
Fox, ridge, S.Dak. C4 158
Fox, riv., Man., Can. C6 60
Fox, riv., Ill., Wis. B5 F1 138 160
Fox, riv., Mich. C5 146
Fox, riv., Mo. A6 150
Fox, riv., Wis. D5 160
Foxboro, Ont., Can. 325 P23 64
Foxboro (Foxborough), Norfolk, Mass. 5,000 (10,136▲) B5 206
Foxboro, Douglas, Wis. 150 B1 160
Foxborough, see Foxboro, Mass.
Fox Chapel, Allegheny, Pa. 3,302 *C2 214
Foxe, basin, N.W.Ter., Can. D11 48
Foxe, chan., N.W.Ter., Can. D10 48
Foxe, pen., N.W.Ter., Can. D11 48
Foxen, lake, Swe. B2 292
Fox Farm, Laramie, Wyo. 1,371 *E8 116
Foxford, Sask., Can. 70 D5 58
Fox Harbour, Newf., Can. 50 D8 72
Fox Hill, Va. (part of Hampton) C8 192
Foxholm, Ward, N.Dak. 200 B4 154
Foxhome, Wilkin, Minn. 181 E2 148
Fox Lake, Lake, Ill. 3,700 A5 E2 138
Fox Lake, Dodge, Wis. 1,181 E5 160
Foxpark, Albany, Wyo. 150 E6 116

Fox Point, Milwaukee, Wis.	7,315	E2	160
		E6	
Fox River Grove, McHenry, Ill.	1,866	E2	138
Fox River Heights, Kane, Ill.	700	E2	138
Foxton, N.Z.	2,525	D5	437
Fox Town, Crawford, Kans.	25	*E9	144
Foxvale, Norfolk, Mass.	200	*B5	206
Fox Valley, Sask., Can.	395	E3	58
Foxville, Orange, Vt.	100	C4	218
Foxwarren, Man., Can.	270	E2	60
Foxworth, Marion, Miss.	2,000	D3	184
Foyil, Rogers, Okla.	127	B8	128
Foyle, riv., N.Ire.		F5	272
Foynes, Ire.	720	I3	273
Frametown, Braxton, W.Va.	500	C4	194
Framingham, Middlesex, Mass.	44,526	B5	206
Foz do Iguaçu, Braz.	3,000	K6	257
Frackville, Schuylkill, Pa.	5,654	C5	214
Fraga, Sp.	6,817	B7	298
		D1	
Franca, Braz.		C2	258
Franca, Braz.	26,629	E1	258
Francavilla Fontana, It.	25,500	E6	302
France, country, Eur.	44,847,000	D5	266
			278
Frances, Crittenden, Ky.	200	C2	178
Frances, Pacific, Wash.	100	C3	98
Francestown, Hillsboro, N.H.	180	F3	208
	(495▲)		
Francesville, Pulaski, Ind.	1,002	B3	140
Franceville, Gabon		G7	409
Franche-Comté, former prov., Fr.	757,000	D6	278
Francis, Sask., Can.	179	E6	58
Francis, Gallatin, Mont.	10	D5	110
Francis, Pontotoc, Okla.	286	D7	128
Francis, Summit, Utah	252	C4	114
Francis, Harrison, W.Va.	150	A7	194
Francis, lake, N.H.		A4	208
Francisco, Gibson, Ind.	565	D2	140
Francis Creek, Manitowoc, Wis.	400	A6	160
Francistown, Bech.	10,000	D5	420
Francois, Newf., Can.	275	G7	72
Francois, lake, B.C., Can.		C9	52
Franconia, Grafton, N.H.	300	C3	208
	(491▲)		
Franconia, Fairfax, Va.	3,000	*B7	192
Franconia (Franken), reg., Ger.		*D4	286
Franconia, range, N.H.		C3	208
Franeker, Neth.	9,083	A4	282
Frank, Alta., Can.		F5	54
Frank, Pocahontas, W.Va.	350	C5	194
Frankenberg [Eder], Ger.	7,500	C3	286
Frankenmuth, Saginaw, Mich.	1,728	F8	146
Frankenthal, Ger.	28,700	D3	286
Frankewing, Giles, Tenn.	100	C5	190
Frankford, Ont., Can.	1,491	P23	64
Frankford, Sussex, Del.	558	F5	172
Frankford, Pike, Mo.	474	B6	150
Frankford, Greenbrier, W.Va.	225	D4	194
Frankfort, Will, Ill.	1,135	F2	138
Frankfort, Clinton, Ind.	15,302	B3	140
Frankfort, Marshall, Kans.	1,106	C7	144
Frankfort, Franklin, Ky.	18,365	B6	178
Frankfort, Waldo, Maine	300	D4	204
	(692▲)		
Frankfort, Benzie, Mich.	1,690	E5	146
Frankfort, Herkimer, N.Y.	3,872	B6	212
Frankfort, Ross, Ohio	871	C3	156
Frankfort, Spink, S.Dak.	240	C7	158
Frankfort, U.S.Afr.		E5	420
Frankfurt [am Main], Ger.	640,000	C3	286
	(*975,000)		
Frankfurt [an der Oder], Ger.	57,200	B6	286
Franklin, Macon, Ala.		C4	168
Franklin, Monroe, Ala.	100	D2	168
Franklin, Alsk.	5	C7	84
Franklin, Greenlee, Ariz.	150	F6	124
Franklin, Izard, Ark.	75	A5	170
Franklin, Man., Can.	150	E3	60
Franklin, New London, Conn.	50	C7	202
	(974▲)		
Franklin, Heard, Ga.	603	C1	176
Franklin, Ada, Idaho	7,222	*F2	108
Franklin, Franklin, Idaho	446	G7	108
Franklin, Morgan, Ill.	500	D3	138
Franklin, Johnson, Ind.	9,453	C3	140
Franklin, Lee, Iowa	174	D6	142
Franklin, Crawford, Kans.	620	E9	144
Franklin, Simpson, Ky.	5,319	D4	178
Franklin, St. Mary, La.	8,673	E4	180
Franklin, Hancock, Maine	300	D4	204
	(627▲)		
Franklin, Norfolk, Mass.	6,391	B5	206
	(10,530▲)		
Franklin, Oakland, Mich.	2,262	B8	146
Franklin, Renville, Minn.	548	G4	148
Franklin, Howard, Mo.	355	B5	150
Franklin, Franklin, Nebr.	1,194	D7	152
Franklin, Merrimack, N.H.	6,742	E3	208
Franklin, Sussex, N.J.	3,624	A3	210
Franklin, Delaware, N.Y.	525	C6	212
Franklin, Macon, N.C.	2,173	B2	186
Franklin, Warren, Ohio	7,917	C2	156
Franklin, Cleveland, Okla.	40	C6	128
Franklin, Cambria, Pa.	1,352	*C3	214
Franklin, Venango, Pa.	9,586	B2	214
Franklin, Williamson, Tenn.	6,977	C5	190
Franklin, Robertson, Tex.	1,065	D7	130
Franklin, Franklin, Vt.	185	B3	218
	(796▲)		
Franklin, Southampton, Va.	7,264	D8	192
Franklin, Pendleton, W.Va.	758	C5	194
Franklin, Milwaukee, Wis.	10,000	*F5	160
Franklin, Sheboygan, Wis.	25	B6	160
Franklin, co., Ala.	21,988	A2	168
Franklin, co., Ark.	10,213	B3	170
Franklin, co., Fla.	6,576	B6	174
Franklin, co., Ga.	13,274	B3	176
Franklin, co., Idaho	8,457	G7	108
Franklin, co., Ill.	39,281	E4	138
Franklin, co., Ind.	17,015	C4	140
Franklin, co., Iowa	15,472	B4	142
Franklin, co., Kans.	19,548	D8	144
Franklin, co., Ky.	29,421	B6	178
Franklin, co., Maine	20,069	C2	204
Franklin, co., Mass.	54,864	A2	206
Franklin, co., Miss.	9,286	D2	184
Franklin, co., Mo.	44,566	C6	150
Franklin, co., Nebr.	5,449	D6	152
Franklin, co., N.Y.	44,742	A7	212
Franklin, co., N.C.	28,755	A7	186
Franklin, co., Ohio	682,962	B3	156
Franklin, co., Pa.	88,172	D4	214
Franklin, co., Tenn.	25,528	C5	190
Franklin, co., Tex.	5,101	C8	130
Franklin, co., Vt.	29,474	B3	218
Franklin, co., Va.	25,925	D5	192
Franklin, co., Wash.	23,342	C7	98
Franklin, dist., N.W.Ter., Can.	4,408	C9	48
Franklin, par., La.	26,088	B4	180
Franklin, isl., Ont., Can.		O20	64
Franklin, lake, N.W.Ter., Can.		D9	48
Franklin, lake, Nev.		C6	112
Franklin, mtn., N.Z.		E4	437
Franklin, mts., N.W.Ter., Can.		D6	48
Franklin D. Roosevelt, lake, Wash.		A8	98
Franklin Furnace, Scioto, Ohio	975	D4	156
Franklin Grove, Lee, Ill.	773	B4	138
Franklin Lakes, Bergen, N.J.	3,316	*B4	210
Franklin Mine, Houghton, Mich.	550	B3	146
Franklin Park, Cook, Ill.	18,322	F2	138
Franklin Park, Somerset, N.J.	750	C3	210
Franklin Park, Fairfax, Va.	1,300	*B7	192
Franklin Springs, Franklin, Ga.	278	*B3	176
Franklin Square, Nassau, N.Y.	32,483	*E3	212
Franklinton, Washington, La.	3,141	D5	180
Franklinton, Franklin, N.C.	1,513	A7	186
Franklintown, Nassau, Fla.	75	A10	174
Franklinville, Gloucester, N.J.	900	D2	210
Franklinville, Cattaraugus, N.Y.	2,124	C3	212
Franklinville, Randolph, N.C.	686	B6	186
Franks, peak, Wyo.		C3	116
Frankston, Anderson, Tex.	953	C8	130
Franksville, Racine, Wis.	400	F2	160
Frankton, Madison, Ind.	1,445	B4	140
Franktown, Douglas, Colo.	50	C6	106
Frankville, Washington, Ala.	500	D1	168
Frankville, Garrett, Md.		A1	182
Frannie, Big Horn, Wyo.	171	B4	116
Franz Josef Land, reg., Sov.Un.		A7	328
Frascati, It.	11,500	E4	302
Fraser, Grand, Colo.	253	C5	106
Fraser, Boone, Iowa	134	B4	142
Fraser, Macomb, Mich.	7,027	B9	146
Fraser, St. Louis, Minn.	95	D6	148
Fraser (Great Sandy), isl., Austl.		D10	432
Fraser, lake, B.C., Can.		C10	52
Fraser, mtn., Alta., B.C., Can.		D3	54
		D13	52
Fraser, reach, B.C., Can.		D8	52
Fraser, riv., B.C., Can.		E11	52
Fraser, riv., Newf., Can.		D9	72
Fraserburg, U.S.Afr.		F4	420
Fraserburgh, Scot.	10,500	D10	272
Fraserdale, Ont., Can.	135	R25	64
Fraserwood, Man., Can.	105	E4	60
Frauenfeld, Switz.	11,800	A4	312
Fray Bentos, Ur.	20,000	B4	252
Frayle Muerto, Ur.		B5	252
Frayser, Shelby, Tenn. (part of Memphis)		C1	190
		E6	
Frazee, Becker, Minn.	1,083	E3	148
Frazer, Valley, Mont.	378	B10	110
Frazeysburg, Muskingum, Ohio	842	B4	156
Frazier, mtn., Calif.		E4	94
Frazier Park, Kern, Calif.	250	E4	94
Frazier Well, Coconino, Ariz.	10	C2	124
Frederic, Crawford, Mich.	400	E7	146
Frederic, Polk, Wis.	857	C1	160
Frederica, Kent, Del.	863	D4	172
Fredericia, Den.		I3	291
Frederick, Weld, Colo.	595	B6	106
Frederick, Rice, Kans.	48	*D5	144
Frederick, Frederick, Md.	21,744	B5	182
Frederick, Tillman, Okla.	5,879	D5	128
Frederick, Brown, S.Dak.	381	B7	158
Frederick, co., Md.	71,930	B4	182
Frederick, co., Va.	21,941	A6	192
Frederick, sound, Alsk.		J14	84
Frederick Junction, Frederick, Md.	11	B5	182
Fredericksburg, Washington, Ind.	207	D3	140
Fredericksburg, Chickasaw, Iowa	797	B5	142
Fredericksburg, Wayne, Ohio	565	B5	156
Fredericksburg, Crawford, Pa.	1,169	*B1	214
Fredericksburg, Gillespie, Tex.	4,629	D6	130
Fredericksburg (Independent City), Va.	13,639	B7	192
Fredericks Hall, Louisa, Va.	60	C7	192
Fredericktown, see Georgetown, Md.			
Fredericktown, Madison, Mo.	3,848	D7	150
Fredericktown, Knox, Ohio	1,531	B4	156
Fredericktown, Washington, Pa.	1,270	C1	214
Fredericton, N.B., Can.	18,303	D3	70
Fredericton Junction, N.B., Can.	200	D3	70
Frederika, Bremer, Iowa	249	B5	142
Frederik Hendrik, isl., Neth.N.Gui.		F9	359
Frederiksborg, co., Den.	162,889	*I5	291
Frederikshaab, Grnld.	594	R29	290
Frederikshavn, Den.	19,253	D1	292
Frederiksted, Vir.Is.	1,961	D12	233
Frederiksvaerk, Den.	4,184	F3	292
Fredon, Sussex, N.J.	30	A3	210
Fredonia, Chambers, Ala.	200	C4	168
Fredonia, Coconino, Ariz.	643	B3	124
Fredonia, Prairie, Ark.	350	C5	170
Fredonia, Louisa, Iowa	147	C6	142
Fredonia, Wilson, Kans.	3,233	E8	144
Fredonia, Caldwell, Ky.	427	C2	178
Fredonia, Chautauqua, N.Y.	8,477	C2	212
Fredonia, Logan, N.Dak.	141	D6	154
Fredonia, Ozaukee, Wis.	710	E6	160
Fredonyer, peak, Calif.		B3	94
Fredriksberg, Swe.		A5	292
Fredrikstad, Nor.	14,393	B1	292
	(*40,600)		
Freeborn, Freeborn, Minn.	314	H5	148
Freeborn, co., Minn.	37,891	H5	148
Freeburg, St. Clair, Ill.	1,908	E4	138
Freeburg, Osage, Mo.	399	C6	150
Freeburn, Pike, Ky.	377	C8	178
Freedom, Santa Cruz, Calif.	4,206	*D3	94
Freedom, Owen, Ind.	190	C3	140
Freedom, Barren, Ky.	100	D5	178
Freedom, Waldo, Maine	150	*D3	204
	(406▲)		
Freedom, Frontier, Nebr.		D5	152
Freedom, Carroll, N.H.	250	D4	208
	(363▲)		
Freedom, Woods, Okla.	268	B4	128
Freedom, Beaver, Pa.	2,895	C1	214
Freedom, Outagamie, Wis.	300	A5	160
Freedom, Lincoln, Wyo.	25	D2	116
Freehold, Monmouth, N.J.	9,140	C4	210
Freeland, Saginaw, Mich.	850	F7	146
Freeland, Brunswick, N.C.	200	C7	186
Freeland, Luzerne, Pa.	5,068	B6	214
Freelandville, Knox, Ind.	720	D2	140
Freels, cape, Newf., Can.		F9	72
Freelton, Ont., Can.	265	Q20	64
Freeman, Cass, Mo.	391	C3	150
Freeman, Hutchinson, S.Dak.	1,140	D8	158
Freeman, Spokane, Wash.	55	D9	98
Freeman, lake, Ind.		B3	140
Freemansburg, Northampton, Pa.	1,652	C6	214
Freeman Spur, Williamson and Franklin, Ill.	406	*E5	138
Freemanville, Escambia, Ala.	450	D2	168
Freemason, is., La.		E7	180
Freemen, riv., Alta., Can.		C5	54
Freemount, McPherson, Kasns.	18	*D6	144
Freeport, N.S., Can.	675	E3	70
Freeport, Walton, Fla.	350	A4	174
Freeport, Stephenson, Ill.	26,628	A4	138
Freeport, Harper, Kans.	31	E6	144
Freeport, Cumberland, Maine	1,801	E2	204
	(4,055▲)	E5	
Freeport, Barry, Mich.	495	G6	146
Freeport, Stearns, Minn.	615	F4	148
Freeport, Nassau, N.Y.	34,419	E3	212
Freeport, Harrison, Ohio	503	B5	156
Freeport, Armstrong, Pa.	2,439	C2	214
Freeport, Brazoria, Tex.	11,619	E8	130
		G8	
Freer, Duval, Tex.	2,724	F6	130
Free Soil, Mason, Mich.	209	E5	146
Freestone, co., Tex.	12,525	D7	130
Freetown, P.E.I., Can.	295	C6	70
Freetown, Jackson, Ind.	450	D3	140
Freetown (Town of), Bristol, Mass.	(3,039▲)	*C5	206
Freetown, S.L.	77,420	E2	408
Free Union, Albemarle, Va.	60	B6	192
Freeville, Tompkins, N.Y.	471	C5	212
Freezeout, mts., Wyo.		D6	116
Fregenal de la Sierra, Sp.	10,806	C3	298
Fregene, It. (part of Rome)	1,202	*E4	302
Freiberg [in Sachsen], Ger.	45,800	C5	286
Freiburg [im Breisgau], Ger.	129,000	E2	286
Freienwalde, see Bad Freienwalde, Ger.			
Freirina, Chile	1,504	A1	252
Freising, Ger.	26,000	D4	286
Freistadt, Aus.	5,136	B6	313
Freistatt, Lawrence, Mo.	172	*D4	150
Fréjus, Fr.	6,101	F7	278
Frelighsburg, Que., Can.	331	S12	66
Fremantle, Austl.	22,795	E3	432
Fremont, Alameda, Calif.	43,790	D2	94
Fremont, Steuben, Ind.	937	A5	140
Fremont, Mahaska, Iowa	461	C5	142
Fremont, Newaygo, Mich.	3,384	F6	146
Fremont, Carter, Mo.	131	E6	150
Fremont, Dodge, Nebr.	19,698	C9	152
		D2	
Fremont, Rockingham, N.H.	300	F4	208
	(783▲)		
Fremont, Wayne, N.C.	1,609	B8	186
Fremont, Sandusky, Ohio	17,573	A3	156
Fremont, Wayne, Utah	125	E4	114
Fremont, Waupaca, Wis.	575	D5	160
Fremont, co., Colo.	20,196	D5	106
Fremont, co., Idaho	8,679	E7	108
Fremont, co., Iowa	10,282	D2	142
Fremont, co., Wyo.	26,168	C4	116
Fremont, isl., Utah		B3	114
Fremont, lake, Wyo.		D3	116
Fremont, peak, Wyo.		C3	116
Fremont, riv., Utah		E4	114
French, Colfax, N.Mex.	15	B6	126
French, creek, Pa.		B1	214
French, pt., Newf., Can.		E8	72
French, prairie, Oreg.		B1	96
French, riv., Ont., Can.		O20	64
French Broad, riv., N.C., Tenn.		B2	186
		C9	190
Frenchburg, Menifee, Ky.	296	C7	178
French Camp, Choctaw, Miss.	123	B3	184
French Creek, Idaho, Idaho		D2	108
French Creek, Upshur, W.Va.	500	C4	194
French Frigate, shoal, Haw.		A6	86
Frenchglen, Harney, Oreg.	20	E8	96
French Guiana, poss., S.A.	30,000	C6	236
			257
French Gulch, Shasta, Calif.	300	B2	94
French Lick, Orange, Ind.	1,954	D3	140
Frenchman, bay, Maine		D4	204
Frenchman, creek, Colo.		B8	106
Frenchman, creek, Nebr.		D4	152
Frenchman, riv., Sask., Can.		F3	58
Frenchman Butte, Sask., Can.	110	D3	58
Frenchman Knob, peak, Ky.		C5	178
Frenchman's Cove, Newf., Can.	150	F6	72
Frenchmans Island, Newf., Can.		D8	72
French River, Ont., Can.		O20	64
French Settlement, Livingston, La.	350	B6	180
		D5	
French Somaliland, poss., Afr.	69,000	E11	388
			398
Frenchton, Upshur, W.Va.	275	C4	194
Frenchtown, Missoula, Mont.	100	C2	110
Frenchtown, Hunterdon, N.J.	1,340	B2	210
French Village, N.S., Can.	150	E6	70
Frenchville, Aroostook, Maine	875	B4	204
	(1,421▲)		
Frenda, Alg.	9,635	A4	402
	(13,567▲)		
Freneau, Monmouth, N.J.		C4	210
Frenier, St. John the Baptist, La.	25	B6	180
Freshfield, mtn., Alta., B.C., Can.		E4	54
		E14	52
Freshford, Ire.	626	I5	273
Freshwater, Park, Colo.		*D5	106
Fresko, I.C.		E3	408
Fresnillo, Mex.	29,908	C5	224
Fresno, Fresno, Calif.	133,929	D4	94
	(*228,000)		
Fresno, Hill, Mont.	10	B7	110
Fresno, co., Calif.	365,945	D3	94
Fresno, dam, Mont.		B7	110
Freudenstadt, Ger.	13,200	D3	286
Frèvent, Fr.		B5	278
Frewen, Sweetwater, Wyo.	10	E4	116
Frewsburg, Chautauqua, N.Y.	1,623	C2	212
Freycinet's, pen., Austl.		G9	432
Friant, Fresno, Calif.	300	D4	94
Friant, dam, Calif.		D4	94
Friars Point, Coahoma, Miss.	1,029	A2	184
Frías, Arg.	7,941	A2	252
Fribourg, Switz.	31,000	B3	312
Fribourg (Freiburg), canton, Switz.	162,200	B3	312
Friday Harbor, San Juan, Wash.	706	A3	98
Fridley, Anoka, Minn.	15,173	F7	148
Friedberg, Ger.	17,100	C3	286
Friedland, Ger.	8,357	B5	286
Friedrichshafen, Ger.	31,700	E3	286
Friend, Finney, Kans.	50	D3	144
Friend, Saline, Nebr.	1,069	D8	152
Friend, Wasco, Oreg.	15	B5	96
Friendly, Tyler, W.Va.	195	*B4	194
Friendship, Hot Spring, Ark.	162	C4	170
Friendship, Ripley, Ind.	125	D4	140
Friendship, Knox, Maine	350	E3	204
	(806▲)		
Friendship, Anne Arundel, Md.	87	C6	182
Friendship, Burlington, N.J.	15	D3	210
Friendship, Allegany, N.Y.	1,231	C3	212
Friendship, Scioto, Ohio	500	D3	156
Friendship, Jackson, Okla.	50	D4	128
Friendship, Crockett, Tenn.	399	C2	190
Friendship, Adams, Wis.	560	E4	160
Friendsville, Garrett, Md.	580	A1	182
Friendsville, Blount, Tenn.	606	C7	190
		E9	
Friendswood, Hendricks, Ind.	120	E4	140
Frierson, De Soto, La.	200	B2	180
Fries, Grayson, Va.	1,039	D4	192
Friesach, Aus.	3,471	D6	313
Friesland, Columbia, Wis.	308	E4	160
Friesland, prov., Neth.	469,943	A4	282
Fries Mills, Gloucester, N.J.	50	D2	210
Frillesås, Swe.		D3	292
Frink, Calhoun, Fla.		A5	174
Frio, co., Tex.	10,112	E6	130
Frio, cape, S.W.Afr.		C2	420
Frio, riv., Tex.		E6	130
Friona, Parmer, Tex.	2,048	B4	130
Fripps, inlet, S.C.		G8	188
Fripps, isl., S.C.		G8	188
Frisco, Summit, Colo.	316	*C4	106
Frisco, Pontotoc, Okla.		D7	128
Frisco, Beaver, Pa.	900	*C1	214
Frisco, Collin, Tex.	1,184	*C7	130
Frisco, mtn., Utah		E2	114
Frisco City, Monroe, Ala.	1,177	D2	168
Frissell, mtn., Mass.		A2	202
Fristoe, Benton, Mo.	100	C4	150
Fritch, Hutchinson, Tex.	1,846	B5	130
Fritsla, Swe.	3,120	D3	292
Fritzlar, Ger.	6,900	C3	286
Friuli-Venezia Giulia, reg., It.	940,000	*B4	302
Frizzelburg, Carroll, Md.	150	A5	182
Frobisher, Sask., Can.	315	F6	58
Frog, mtn., Tenn.		C7	190
Frogmore, Concordia, La.	85	C4	180
Frogmore, Beaufort, S.C.	50	G7	188
Frohna, Perry, Mo.	216	D8	150
Froid, Roosevelt, Mont.	418	B12	110
Fromberg, Carbon, Mont.	367	E8	110
Frome, Eng.	11,400	J10	273
Frome, lake, Austl.		E8	432
Frompton, inlet, S.C.		G2	188
Front, range, Colo.		B5	106
Frontenac, Crawford, Kans.	1,713	E9	144
Frontenac, Goodhue, Minn.	168	G6	148
Frontenac, St. Louis, Mo.	3,089	*C7	150
Frontenac, co., Ont., Can.	76,534	P24	64
Frontenac, co., Que., Can.	31,433	S13	66
Fronteras, Mex.		A4	224
Frontier, Sask., Can.	306	F3	58
Frontier, Lincoln, Wyo.	500	E2	116
Frontier, co., Nebr.	4,311	D5	152
Frontignan, Fr.	5,341	F5	278
Front Royal, Warren, Va.	7,949	B6	192
Frosinone, It.	15,500	E4	302
Frosinone, prov., It.	479,700	*E4	302
Froso, Swe.		E6	290
Frost, Livingston, La.	30	B6	180
Frost, Faribault, Minn.	381	H5	148
Frostburg, Allegany, Md.	6,722	A2	182
Frostproof, Polk, Fla.	2,664	D9	174
Frostviken, lake, Swe.		D6	290
Frouard, Fr.	5,950	C7	278
Froude, Sask., Can.	42	F6	58
Fröya, isl., Nor.		E3	290
Frozen, Calhoun, W.Va.	50	C3	194
Frozen Creek, Breathitt, Ky.	50	C7	178
Fruita, Mesa, Colo.	1,830	C2	106
Fruitdale, Washington, Ala.	757	D1	168
Fruitdale, Josephine, Oreg.	2,158	*E3	96
Fruitdale, Butte, S.Dak.	79	C2	158
Fruitdale, Dallas, Tex.	1,418	*C7	130
Fruit Heights, Davis, Utah	175	*B4	114
Fruithurst, Cleburne, Ala.	255	B4	168
Fruitland, Payette, Idaho	804	E2	108
Fruitland, Wicomico, Md.	1,147	D8	182
Fruitland, San Juan, N.Mex.	150	B2	126

Fruitland, Gibson, Tenn. 150 C3 190
Fruitland, Duchesne, Utah 10 C5 114
Fruitland Park, Lake, Fla. 774 C9 174
Fruitland Park, Forrest, Miss. 57 E3 184
Fruitport, Muskegon, Mich. 1,037 F5 146
Fruitvale, B.C., Can. 870 F14 52
Fruitvale, Adams, Idaho 100 E2 108
Fruitvale, Yakima, Wash. 3,345 *C6 98
Fruitville, Sarasota, Fla. 2,131 D6 174
Frunze, Sov.Un. 217,000 D8 336
Frutal, Braz. 2,948 D1 258
Fry, Fannin, Ga. 175 B2 176
Fryazevo, Sov.Un. N19 332
Fryburg, Billings, N.Dak. 75 D2 154
Frýdek-Místek, Czech. 24,736 B4 324
Frýdlant, Czech. 4,308 A2 324
Frye, Oxford, Maine 100 D2 204
Fryeburg, Bienville, La. 100 B2 180
Fryeburg, Oxford, Maine 975 D2 204
(1,874▲)
Frys, Sask., Can. 75 F7 58
Fryštát, Czech. (part of Karviná) *B4 324
Frývaldov, Czech. 5,873 A3 324
Fthiótis (Phthiotis), prov., Grc. 148,322 *B4 306
Fu, China 5,000 G4 348
Fuan, China 8,000 L9 349
Fuching, China 5,000 M9 349
Fuchou (Foochow), China 553,000 L9 349
Fuchou, China N4 349
Fuencarral, Sp. (part of Madrid) 7,078 *B5 298
Fuente-Álamos, Sp. 470 D6 298
Fuente de Cantos, Sp. 10,354 C3 298
Fuente el Saz, Sp. 740 *B5 298
Fuenteovejuna, Sp. 8,278 C4 298
Fuentesaúco, Sp. 3,055 B4 298
Fuentes [de Andalucía], Sp. 11,640 D4 298
Fuerte Olimpo, Par. B3 247
Fuerte, riv., Mex. B4 224
Fuerteventura, Mor. C1 402
Fuerteventura, isl., Can.Is. F12 298
Fuhsien, China 5,000 F10 348
Fuhsien, lake, China G8 346
Fuishikiya, Okinawa D1 436
Fujayrah, Tr. Coast B6 383
Fuji, mtn., Jap. G7 354
Fujieda, Jap. 61,466 *G7 354
Fujinomiya, Jap. 57,307 L14 354
Fujisawa, Jap. 109,101 *L15 354
Fujiyoshida, Jap. 39,116 L14 354
Fukien, prov., China 14,650,000 F11 346
Fukou, China 15,000 H7 348
Fukuchiyama, Jap. 62,602 G5 354
L11
Fukue, Jap. 26,736 M13 354
Fukui, Jap. 125,301 F6 354
Fukuoka, Jap. 25,391 D8 354
Fukuoka, Jap. 544,312 H3 354
Fukushima, Jap. 127,259 F8 354
Fukushima, Jap. 9,083 G6 354
Fukuyama, Jap. 76,484 G4 354
Fulanga, passage, Fiji E7 436
Fulda, Ger. 45,900 C3 286
Fulda, Spencer, Ind. 150 D3 140
Fulda, Murray, Minn. 1,202 H3 148
Fulda, riv., Ger. C3 286
Fullarton, Ont., Can. 150 Q19 64
Fullerton, Orange, Calif. 56,180 C6 94
Fullerton, Greenup, Ky. 1,082 B8 178
Fullerton, Baltimore, Md. 3,000 B6 182
Fullerton, Nance, Nebr. 1,475 C8 152
Fullerton, Dickey, N.Dak. 181 D7 154
Fullerville, Carroll, Ga. C2 176
Fulton, Clarke, Ala. 688 D2 168
Fulton, Hempstead, Ark. 309 D3 170
Fulton, Whiteside, Ill. 3,387 B3 138
Fulton, Fulton, Ind. 410 B3 140
Fulton, Bourbon, Kans. 207 D9 144
Fulton, Fulton, Ky. 3,265 D2 178
Fulton, Howard, Md. 140 B6 182
Fulton, Kalamazoo, Mich. 225 G6 146
Fulton, Keweenaw, Mich. 400 B3 146
Fulton, Itawamba, Miss. 1,706 A4 184
Fulton, Callaway, Mo. 11,131 C6 150
Fulton, Oswego, N.Y. 14,261 B5 212
Fulton, Hanson, S.Dak. 135 D8 158
Fulton, Lauderdale, Tenn. 85 C2 190
Fulton, co., Ark. 6,657 A5 170
Fulton, co., Ga. 556,326 C2 176
Fulton, co., Ill. 41,954 C3 138
Fulton, co., Ind. 16,957 A3 140
Fulton, co., Ky. 11,256 D1 178
Fulton, co., N.Y. 51,304 B7 212
Fulton, co., Ohio 29,301 A2 156
Fulton, co., Pa. 10,597 D3 214
Fultondale, Jefferson, Ala. 2,001 E4 168
Fulton Heights, Pueblo, Colo. 500 D6 106
Fumay, Fr. 4,837 C6 278
Funabashi, Jap. 114,921 L16 354
Funakawa, see Oga, Jap.
Funasdalen, Swe. E5 291
Fundación, Col. 6,620 A2 244
Fundão, Port. 3,777 B3 298
Fundy, bay, Can. E3 70
Fundy, natl. park, N.B., Can. D4 70
Funhalouro, Moz. D6 421
Funing, bay, China L10 349
Funk, Phelps, Nebr. 141 D6 152
Funk, isl., Newf., Can. F9 72
Funkley, Beltrami, Minn. 28 D4 148
Funkstown, Washington, Md. 968 A4 182
Funston, Colquitt, Ga. 293 E3 176
Funston, De Soto, La. 50 B2 180
Funtua, Nig. D6 408
Fuquay Springs, Wake, N.C. 3,389 B7 186
Furancungo, Moz. B6 421
Furano, Jap. 21,743 C9 354
Fūrg, Iran D4 379
Furilden, isl., Swe. D10 292
Furka, pass, Switz. B4 312
Furlow, Lonoke, Ark. 30 D7 170
Furman, Hampton, S.C. 244 F6 188
Furmanov, Sov.Un. 37,300 D13 332
Furman University, Greenville, S.C. 1,500 *B4 188
Furnace, Worcester, Mass. 44 B3 206
Furnace, brook, Vt. D3 218
Furnas, co., Nebr. 7,711 D5 152
Furneaux, is., Austl. G9 432
Furness, Sask., Can. 78 D3 58
Furrs, Pontotoc, Miss. 50 A4 184
Fürstenberg [an der Oder], Ger. 5,259 B6 286
Fürstenfeld, Aus. 6,616 C8 313
Fürstenwalde [an der Spree], Ger. 32,700 B6 286
Fürth, Ger. 101,000 D4 286
Furth im Wald, Ger. 9,453 D5 286
Furu, mtn., Iwo A7 436
Furukawa, Jap. 8,873 F6 354
K13
Fusagasugá, Col. 8,345 C2 244
Fusan, see Pusan, Kor.
Fuse, Jap. 176,052 G5 354
M11
Fushih, China G4 348
Fushun, China 985,000 E11 348
Fusilier, Sask., Can. 250 E3 58
Füssen, Ger. 10,200 E4 286
Futamata, Jap. 11,442 M13 354
Futatsune, reef, Iwo A7 436
Futing, China 5,000 L10 349
Fûwa, Eg., U.A.R. 18,975 *A3 395
Fuyang, China 15,000 J9 349
Fuyü, China 57,065 C12 348
Fyffe, De Kalb, Ala. 230 A4 168
Fyn, reg., Den. 399,565 *I4 291
Fyn, isl., Den. F1 292
Fyne, inlet, Scot. E7 272
Fyresdal, Nor. G3 291
Fyzabad, see Faizabad, India

G

Gaastra, Iron, Mich. 582 C3 146
Gabarouse, N.S., Can. 775 D9 70
Gabarus, bay, N.S., Can. D10 70
Gabbs, Nye, Nev. 770 E4 112
Gaberones, Bech. 10,000 D5 420
Gabès, Tun. 24,420 B6 402
Gabès, gulf, Tun. B6 402
Gąbin, Pol. 3,108 B4 325
Gable, Clarendon, S.C. 130 D8 188
Gabon, country, Afr. 421,000 G8 388
409
Gabriel, mtn., Ire. J3 273
Gabriels, Franklin, N.Y. 450 A7 212
Gabriola, B.C., Can. 35 B14 52
Gabriola, isl., B.C., Can. B14 52
Gabrovo, Bul. 33,049 B2 317
Gabrovski, prov., Bul. *B2 317
Gackle, Logan, N.Dak. 523 D6 154
Gacko, Yugo. 1,227 C4 316
Gadag, India 65,509 E3 366
Gaddede, Swe. D6 290
Gaddistown, Union, Ga. 159 B2 176
Gaddy, Pottawatomie, Okla. 50 *C7 128
Gadsby, Alta., Can. 145 D6 54
Gadsden, Etowah, Ala. 58,088 A3 168
Gadsden, Yuma, Ariz. 140 F1 124
Gadsden, Richland, S.C. 200 D7 188
Gadsden, Crockett, Tenn. 222 C3 190
Gadsden, co., Fla. 41,989 A6 174
Gadyach, Sov.Un. 23,600 G9 332
Găeşti, Rom. 7,179 B3 321
Gaeta, It. 18,900 E4 302
Gaeta, gulf, It. E4 302
Gaffney, Cherokee, S.C. 10,435 A5 188
Gafour, Tun. 6,696 A5 402
Gafsa, Tun. 24,345 B5 402
Gagan, isl., Kwajalein A1 436
Gage, Musselshell, Mont. 10 D8 110
Gage, Ellis, Okla. 482 B4 128
Gage, co., Nebr. 26,818 D9 152
Gage, cape, P.E.I., Can. C5 70
Gages Lake, Lake, Ill. 3,395 *A5 138
Gagetown, N.B., Can. 320 D3 70
Gagetown, Tuscola, Mich. 376 F8 146
Gagliano del Capo, It. 3,418 F7 302
Gagnoa, I.C. E3 408
Gagny, Fr. 17,255 I11 278
Gahanna, Franklin, Ohio 2,717 C1 156
Gaharwargaon, India D3 368
Gahmar, India D3 368
Gaibandha, Pak. 14,310 K16 375
Gaighata, India I9 366
Gaillac [-sur-Tarn], Fr. 6,205 F4 278
Gaillard, lake, Conn. D4 202
Gaines, Genesee, Mich. 387 G8 146
Gaines, co., Tex. 12,267 C4 130
Gaines, creek, Okla. C8 128
Gainesboro, Jackson, Tenn. 1,021 B6 190
Gainesville, Sumter, Ala. 214 C1 168
Gainesville, Greene, Ark. 15 A6 170
Gainesville, Alachua, Fla. 29,701 B8 174
Gainesville, Cotton Mills, Ga. 16,523 B3 176
Gainesville, Hancock, Miss. 300 E3 184
Gainesville, Ozark, Mo. 266 E5 150
Gainesville, Cooke, Tex. 13,083 C7 130
Gainesville, Prince William, Va. 150 A6 192
Gainesville North, Alachua, Fla. 4,290 *B8 174
Gainesville West, Alachua, Fla. 2,725 *B8 174
Gainford, Alta., Can. D5 54
Gainsari, India D3 368
Gainsborough, Sask., Can. 400 F7 58
Gainsborough, Eng. 17,400 H12 273
Gairdner, lake, Austl. E7 432
Gaither, Carroll, Md. 150 B6 182
Gaithersburg, Montgomery, Md. 3,847 B5 182
Gakona, Alsk. 50 C7 84
F12
Gakuch, India A1 368
Galahad, Alta., Can. 215 D7 54
Galap, Palau A6 436
Galashiels, Scot. 12,200 F10 272
Galata, Toole, Mont. 43 B5 110
Galatea, Kiowa, Colo. D7 106
Galați, Rom. 95,646 B5 321
Galatia, Saline, Ill. 830 F5 138
Galatia, Barton, Kans. 73 D5 144
Galatina, It. 18,200 E7 302
Galax (Independent City), Va. 5,254 D4 192
Galaxidhion, Grc. 2,240 B4 306
Galbraith, Natchitoches, La. 125 C3 180
Galchutt, Richland, N.Dak. 50 D9 154
Gáldar, Sp. 6,165 F12 298
Galeana, Mex. 744 A4 224
Galeana, Mex. C5 225
Galen, Deer Lodge, Mont. 100 *D4 110
Galen, Macon, Tenn. 80 B6 190
Galena, Alsk. 176 C6 84
Galena, Cochise, Ariz. 280 G6 124
Galena, Jo Daviess, Ill. 4,410 A3 138
Galena, Cherokee, Kans. 3,827 E9 144
Galena, Kent, Md. 299 B8 182
Galena, Stone, Mo. 389 E4 150
Galena, Delaware, Ohio 411 B4 156
Galena, Grant, Oreg. C8 96
Galena Park, Harris, Tex. 10,852 F8 130
Galesburg, Knox, Ill. 37,243 C3 138
Galesburg, Neosho, Kans. 128 E8 144
Galesburg, Kalamazoo, Mich. 1,410 G6 146
Galesburg, Traill, N.Dak. 166 C8 154
Gales Creek, Washington, Oreg. 200 B3 96
Gales Ferry, New London, Conn. 450 D7 202
Galestown, Dorchester, Md. 151 *C8 182
Galesville, Anne Arundel, Md. 625 C6 182
Galesville, Trempealeau, Wis. 1,199 D2 160
Galeton, Weld, Colo. 200 B6 106
Galeton, Potter, Pa. 1,646 B4 214
Galetta, Ont., Can. 180 O24 64
Galeville, Onondaga, N.Y. 1,500 *B5 212
Galiano, isl., B.C., Can. F11 52
Galich, Sov.Un. 14,700 A2 336
Galicia, reg., Pol. D5 325
Galicia, reg., Sp. 2,701,803 A2 298
Galien, Berrien, Mich. 750 H5 146
Galilee, Washington, R.I. 50 *D2 216
Galilee, reg., Isr. B6 382
Galilee, lake, Austl. C9 432
Galion, Crawford, Ohio 12,650 B4 156
Galisteo, Santa Fe, N.Mex. 125 C4 126
H7
Galisteo, creek, N.Mex. H7 126
Galiuro, mts., Ariz. F5 124
Galivants Ferry, Horry, S.C. 25 C10 188
Gallabat, Sud. C4 398
Gallaher, Curry, N.Mex. 30 D7 126
Gallan, head, Scot. C5 272
Gallant, Etowah, Ala. 400 B3 168
Gallarate, It. 31,000 C2 302
Gallatin, Daviess, Mo. 1,658 B4 150
Gallatin, Sumner, Tenn. 7,901 B5 190
Gallatin, co., Ill. 7,638 F5 138
Gallatin, co., Ky. 3,867 B6 178
Gallatin, co., Mont. 26,045 E5 110
Gallatin, range, Mont., Wyo. E5 110
B2 116
Gallatin, riv., Mont. E5 110
Gallatin Gateway, Gallatin, Mont. 160 E5 110
Gallaway, Fayette, Tenn. 100 C2 190
Galle, Cey. 55,848 G4 366
Gallego, riv., Sp. A6 298
Gallegos, riv., Arg. H3 251
Galley, head, Ire. J3 273
Gallia, co., Ohio 26,120 D4 156
Galliano, Lafourche, La. 950 E5 180
Gallicano nel Lazio, It. 1,644 *E4 302
Gallinas, Lincoln, N.Mex. 15 D5 126
Gallinas, mts., N.Mex. D3 126
Gallinas, pt., Col. A2 244
Gallion, Hale, Ala. 175 C2 168
Gallion, Morehouse, La. 75 B4 180
Gallipoli, It. 16,200 E6 302
Gallipoli, pen., Tur. A2 307
Gallipolis, Gallia, Ohio 8,775 D4 156
Gallipolis Ferry, Mason, W.Va. 150 C2 194
Gallitzin, Cambria, Pa. 2,783 C3 214
Gällivare, Swe. 3,966 C9 290
Gallman, Copiah, Miss. 100 D2 184
Gallo, Mex. C5 225
Gällö, Swe. E6 290
Gallo, cape, Grc. C4 306
Gallo, mts., N.Mex. D2 126
Gallo, riv., Sp. B6 298
Galloway, Pulaski, Ark. D7 170
Galloway, Franklin, Ohio 300 C1 156
Galloway, Barbour, W.Va. 815 B4 194
Galloway, Marathon, Wis. 100 D4 160
Gallup, McKinley, N.Mex. 14,089 C2 126
Galt, Sacramento, Calif. 1,868 C3 94
Galt, Ont., Can. 23,738 Q20 64
Galt, Wright, Iowa 75 B4 142
Galt, Rice, Kans. 100 D5 144
Galt, Grundy, Mo. 373 A4 150
Galtasen, mtn., Swe. D4 292
Galty, mts., Ire. I4 273
Galva, Henry, Ill. 3,060 B3 138
Galva, Ida, Iowa 469 B2 142
Galva, McPherson, Kans. 442 D6 144
Galvarino, Chile 1,209 C1 252
Gälve-Bukten, bay, Swe. A8 292
Galveston, Cass, Ind. 1,111 B3 140
Galveston, Galveston, Tex. 67,175 E8 130
(*138,700) G8
Galveston, co., Tex. 140,364 E8 130
Galveston, bay, Tex. E8 130
Galveston, isl., Tex. E8 130
Gálvez, Arg. B3 252
Galvin, Lewis, Wash. 200 C3 98
Galway, Ire. 21,219 H3 273
Galway, co., Ire. 155,533 H3 273
Galway, bay, Ire. H3 273
Gamagōri, Jap. 51,900 M13 354
Gamaliel, Baxter, Ark. 150 A4 170
Gamaliel, Monroe, Ky. 868 D5 178
Gamarra, Col. 2,576 B2 244
Gamba, Con.L. C3 414
Gambaga, Ghana 1,952 D4 408
Gambela, Eth. D3 398
Gambell, Alsk. 309 C4 84
Gamber, Carroll, Md. 180 B6 182
Gambia, Br. poss., Afr. 292,000 E5 388
409
Gambia, riv., Sen. D2 408
Gambier, Knox, Ohio 1,148 B4 156
Gambo, Newf., Can. 500 F8 72
Gamboma, Con.B. G8 409
Gambrills, Anne Arundel, Md. 600 B6 182
Gameleira, Braz. 3,336 B3 258
Gamerco, McKinley, N.Mex. 600 C2 126
Gamina, Chile A4 250
Gamleby, Swe. 6,084 D7 292
Gammon, riv., Man., Can. E5 60
Gamo-Gofa, prov., Eth. 900,000 D4 398
Ganado, Apache, Ariz. 493 C6 124
Ganado, Jackson, Tex. 1,626 E7 130
Ganālē Doryā, riv., Eth. D5 398
Gananoque, Ont., Can. 4,981 P24 64
Gandajika, Con.L. D3 414
Gandak, riv., India D4 368
Gandamak, Afg. 10,000 B6 374
Gandeeville, Roane, W.Va. 350 C3 194
Gander, Newf., Can. 3,000 F8 72
Gander, lake, Newf., Can. F8 72
Gander, riv., Newf., Can. F8 72
Gander Bay, Newf., Can. 350 F8 72
Gandia, Sp. 15,812 C16 298
Gandy, Logan, Nebr. 41 C5 152
Gandy, Millard, Utah D2 114
Ganedidalem, Indon. E7 359
Gangapur, India D2 368
Gangara, Niger D6 409
Gangaw, Bur. 3,800 B2 362
Ganges, B.C., Can. 375 C14 52
Ganges, Fr. 4,262 F5 278
Ganges, canal, India D2 368
Ganges, riv., India C2 368
Ganges, riv., Pak. K15 375
Ganges, riv. mouths, Pak. M16 375
Gangri Karpo, pass, India, China C7 368
Gangtok, Sikkim 2,744 D5 368
Ganju-San, peak, Jap. E8 354
Gannat, Fr. 5,204 D5 278
Gannet, Blaine, Idaho 20 F4 108
Gannet, is., Newf., Can. D7 72
Gannet, peak, Wyo. C3 116
Gannett, hill, N.Y. C4 212
Gannon, Allegany, Md. 450 A1 182
Gannvalley, Buffalo, S.Dak. 102 C7 158
Gano, Payne, Okla. B7 128
Ganongga, isl., Solomon E1 436
Gans, Sequoyah, Okla. 234 C9 128
Ganta, Lib. E3 408
Gantt, Covington, Ala. 500 D3 168
Gantt, Greenville, S.C. 50 B4 188
Gantt, dam, Ala. D3 168
Gantts Quarry, Talledega, Ala. 238 B3 168
Gao, Mali 10,000 C5 408
Gaoua, Upper Volta 2,600 D4 408
Gaoual, Guinea 4,600 D2 408
Gap, Fr. 14,315 E7 278
Gap, Atoka, Okla. D8 128
Gap, Lancaster, Pa. 815 D5 214
Gapland, Washington, Md. 200 B4 182
Gap Mills, Monroe, W.Va. 125 D4 194
Gapville, Magoffin, Ky. 183 C8 178
Gara, lake, Ire. H4 273
Garachiné, Pan. 1,158 F8 228
Garachiné, pt., Pan. F8 228
Garad, Som. D6 398
Garanhuns, Braz. 20,550 B3 258
Garapan, Saipan 2,977 B7 436
Garashiyoo, Palau A6 436
Garäter, Iran E5 379
Garay, riv., Mex. G10 224
Garber, Clayton, Iowa 148 B6 142
Garber, Garfield, Okla. 905 B6 128
Garberville, Humboldt, Calif. 900 B2 94
Garça, Braz. 12,433 E1 258
Garcia, Costilla, Colo. 160 E5 106
Garciasville, Starr, Tex. 900 F6 130
Gard, Cherry, Nebr. B5 152
Gard, dept., Fr. 396,742 *F6 278
Garda, lake, It. C3 302
Gardān, sand reg., Afg. D1 374
Gardanne, Fr. F6 278
Gardar, Pembina, N.Dak. 92 B8 154
Gardelegen, Ger. 12,800 B4 286
Garden, Bartholomew, Ind. 250 C4 140
Garden, Delta, Mich. 380 D5 146
Garden, co., Nebr. 3,472 C3 152
Garden, isl., Mich. D6 146
Gardena, Los Angeles, Calif. 35,943 C5 94
Gardena, Boise, Idaho 25 F2 108
Gardena, Bottineau, N.Dak. 113 B5 154
Garden City, Cullman, Ala. 536 A3 168
Garden City, Weld, Colo. 129 B6 106
Garden City, Duval, Fla. 900 A10 174
Garden City, Okaloosa, Fla. 50 A4 174
Garden City (Chatham City), Chatham, Ga. 5,451 D5 176
Garden City, Ada, Idaho 1,681 F2 108
Garden City, Finney, Kans. 11,811 E3 144
Garden City, St. Mary, La. 300 E4 180
Garden City, Wayne, Mich. 38,017 B8 146
Garden City, Blue Earth, Minn. 300 G4 148
Garden City, Franklin, Miss. 100 D1 184
Garden City, Cass, Mo. 600 C3 150
Garden City, Nassau, N.Y. 23,948 E3 212
Garden City, Tulsa, Okla. (part of Tulsa) *B7 128
Garden City, Clark, S.Dak. 226 C8 158
Garden City, Rich, Utah 168 B4 114
Garden City Park, Nassau, N.Y. 15,364 *E8 212
Gardendale, Jefferson, Ala. 4,712 B3 168
E4
Garden Grove, Orange, Calif. 84,238 C6 94
Garden Grove, Decatur, Iowa 335 D4 142
Garden Home, Washington, Oreg. 2,000 B1 96
Garden Lakes, Floyd, Ga. 1,300 *B1 176
Garden Plain, Sedgwick, Kans. 560 E6 144
Gardenton, Man., Can. 450 F4 60
Garden Valley, Boise, Idaho 10 E3 108
Garden View, Lycoming, Pa. 2,418 *B4 214
Gardez, Afg. 17,540 C5 374
Gardhur, Ice. K21 290
Gardi, Wayne, Ga. 275 E5 176
Gardiner, Kennebec, Maine 6,897 D3 204
Gardiner, Park, Mont. 425 E6 110
Gardiner, Douglas, Oreg. 550 D2 96
Gardiners, bay, N.Y. D6 212
Gardiners, isl., N.Y. D6 212
Gardner, Garland, Ark. 750 C6 170
Gardner, Huerfano, Colo. 200 E5 106
Gardner, Hardee, Fla. 45 D9 174
Gardner, Grundy, Ill. 1,041 B5 138

Gardner, Johnson, Kans. 1,619 D9 144
Gardner, Rapides, La. 65 C3 180
Gardner, Worcester, Mass. 19,038 A4 206
Gardner, Cass, N.Dak. 107 C9 154
Gardner, Weakley, Tenn. 40 B3 190
Gardner, canal, B.C., Can. D8 52
Gardner, lake, Conn. C7 202
Gardner, lake, Maine D5 204
Gardner, mtn., N.H. C2 208
Gardner Pinnacles, isl., Haw. A6 86
Gardners, Washington, Ga. 350 D4 176
Gardnersville, Pendleton, Ky. 58 B8 178
Gardnerville, Douglas, Nev. 600 E2 112
Gardo, Som. D7 398
Gardulä, Eth. D4 398
Garešnica, Yugo. 2,326 B3 316
Garfield, Benton, Ark. 48 A3 170
Garfield, Emanuel, Ga. 225 D4 176
Garfield, Pawnee, Kans. 278 D4 144
Garfield, Douglas, Minn. 240 *F3 148
Garfield, Bergen, N.J. 29,253 A1 210
Garfield, Dona Ana, N.Mex. 100 F3 126
Garfield, Salt Lake, Utah C3 114
Garfield, Whitman, Wash. 607 B9 98
Garfield, co., Colo. 12,017 C2 106
Garfield, co., Mont. 1,981 C9 110
Garfield, co., Nebr. 2,699 C6 152
Garfield, co., Okla. 52,975 B6 128
Garfield, co., Utah 3,577 F3 114
Garfield, co., Wash. 2,976 C9 98
Garfield, mtn., Mont. F4 110
Garfield Heights, Cuyahoga, Ohio 38,455 B1 156
Gargaliánoi, Grc. 7,658 C3 306
Garibaldi, Tillamook, Oreg. 1,163 B3 96
Garibaldi, mtn., B.C., Can. F11 52
Garibaldi, prov. park, B.C., Can. F11 52
Garies, U.S.Afr. 791 F3 420
Garissa, Ken. C6 414
Garland, Butler, Ala. 307 D3 168
Garland, Miller, Ark. 377 D3 170
Garland, Bourbon, Kans. 250 E9 144
Garland, Penobscot, Maine 200 (568▴) C3 204
Garland, Anne Arundel, Md. 1,200 *B6 182
Garland, Custer, Mont. 4 D11 110
Garland, Seward, Nebr. 198 D9 152
Garland, Sampson, N.C. 642 C7 186
Garland, Tipton, Tenn. 168 C2 190
Garland, Dallas, Tex. 38,501 B9 130
Garland, Box Elder, Utah 1,119 B3 114
Garland, Park, Wyo. 50 B4 116
Garland, co., Ark. 46,697 C3 170
Garlandville, Jasper, Miss. 300 C3 184
Garmisch-Partenkirchen, Ger. 25,800 E4 286
Garmouth, Scot. D9 272
Garnavillo, Clayton, Iowa 662 B6 142
Garneill, Fergus, Mont. 32 D7 110
Garner, White, Ark. 120 B5 170
Garner, Hancock, Iowa 1,990 A4 142
Garner, Wake, N.C. 3,451 B7 186
Garnet, Granite, Mont. 3 D3 110
Garnet, range, Mont. D3 110
Garnett, Anderson, Kans. 3,034 D8 144
Garnish, Newf., Can. 550 G8 72
Garo, Park, Colo. C5 106
Garonne, riv., Fr. E3 278
Garou, lake, Mali C4 408
Garoua, Cam. 7,050 E7 409
Garrard, Clay, Ky. 450 C7 178
Garrard, co., Ky. 9,747 C6 178
Garret Park, Montgomery, Md. 965 B3 182
B5
Garretson, Minnehaha, S.Dak. 850 D9 158
Garrett, De Kalb, Ind. 4,364 A4 140
Garrett, Floyd, Ky. 938 C8 178
Garrett, see Walla Walla West, Wash.
Garrett, Albany, Wyo. 5 D7 116
Garrett, co., Md. 20,420 A1 182
Garrett Park Estates, Montgomery, Md. 2,000 *B5 182
Garrettsville, Portage, Ohio 1,662 A5 156
Garrick, Sask., Can. 400 D5 58
Garrison, Benton, Iowa 421 B5 142
Garrison, Lewis, Ky. 350 B7 178
Garrison, Baltimore, Md. 570 B6 182
Garrison, Crow Wing, Minn. 118 E5 148
Garrison, Powell, Mont. 60 D4 110
Garrison, Butler, Nebr. 82 *C8 152
Garrison, Putnam, N.Y. 900 D8 212
Garrison, McLean, N.Dak. 1,794 C4 154
Garrison, Nacogdoches, Tex. 951 D8 130
Garrison, Millard, Utah 100 E1 114
Garrison, dam, N.Dak. C4 154
Garrison, res., N.Dak. C3 154
Garrisonville, Stafford, Va. 200 B7 192
Garristown, Ire. 90 H6 273
Garrovillas, Sp. 6,345 C3 298
Garruk, Pak. E4 375
Garry, lake, N.W.Ter., Can. D9 48
Garryowen, Big Horn, Mont. 4 E9 110
Garson, lake, Alta., Can. B7 54
Garson Quarry, Man., Can. 270 E4 60
Garstand, Eng. 1,439 H10 273
Garten, Fayette, W.Va. 500 C3 194
Garthby Station, Que., Can. 497 S13 66
Gartok, China 5,000 E4 346
Garton Road, Cumberland, N.J. E2 210
Garve, Scot. D8 272
Garvellachs, isl., Scot. E6 272
Garvin, Lyon, Minn. 205 G3 148
Garvin, McCurtain, Okla. 109 E9 128
Garvin, co., Okla. 28,290 D6 128
Garwa, India D3 368
Garwin, Tama, Iowa 546 B5 142
Garwolin, Pol. 5,315 C5 325
Garwood, Union, N.J. 5,426 B4 210
Gary, Lake, Ind. 178,320 A2 140
Gary, Hidalgo, N.Mex. 20 F2 126
Gary, Norman, Minn. 262 D2 148
Gary, Deuel, S.Dak. 471 C9 158
Gary, McDowell, W.Va. 1,393 D3 194
Garysburg, Northampton, N.C. 181 A8 186
Garyton, Porter, Ind. (part of Portage) A2 140
Garyville, St. John the Baptist, La. 2,389 B6 180
D5
Garza, co., Tex. 6,611 C5 130
Garza Little Elm, res., Tex. A8 130
Garzón, Col. 5,750 C1 244
Gas, Allen, Kans. 342 E8 144
Gasan-Kuli, Sov.Un. F7 328
Gasburg, Brunswick, Va. 100 D7 192
Gas City, Grant, Ind. 4,469 B4 140
Gas City, Stephens, Okla. D5 128
Gasconade, Gasconade, Mo. 333 C6 150
Gasconade, co., Mo. 12,195 C6 150
Gasconade, riv., Mo. C6 150
Gascony (Gascogne), former prov., Fr. 996,000 E3 278
Gascoyne, Bowman, N.Dak. 50 D2 154
Gascoyne, riv., Austl. D2 432
Gashaka, Br.Cam. 1,088 E7 409
Gas Hills, Fremont, Wyo. 400 *C4 116
Gashland, Clay, Mo. 325 B3 150
E2
Gashua, Nig. 10,000 D7 409
Gasmata, Bis.Arch. F12 359
Gasparilla, pass, Fla. E8 174
Gaspé, Que., Can. 2,194 Q10 66
Gaspé, pen., Que., Can. Q10 66
Gaspé East, co., Que., Can. 41,319 *Q10 66
Gaspé West, co., Que., Can. 19,021 *Q10 66
Gasport, Niagara, N.Y. 700 B3 212
Gassaway, Cannon, Tenn. 70 C6 190
Gassaway, Braxton, W.Va. 1,223 C4 194
Gassol, Nig. E7 409
Gassville, Baxter, Ark. 233 A4 170
Gaston, Delaware, Ind. 801 B4 140
Gaston, Northampton, N.C. 1,214 A8 186
Gaston, Washington, Oreg. 320 *B3 96
Gaston, Lexington, S.C. 175 D6 188
Gaston, co., N.C. 127,074 B4 186
Gastonia, Gaston, N.C. 37,276 B4 186
Gastre, Arg. F4 251
Gästrikland, prov., Swe. 136,675 *F7 291
Gata, cape, Cyp. D5 307
Gata, cape, Sp. D5 298
Gata, mts., Sp. B3 298
Gatchina, Sov.Un. 47,900 C8 332
Gate, Beaver, Okla. 130 B3 128
Gate City, Scott, Va. 2,142 D2 192
Gates, Custer, Nebr. 14 C6 152
Gates, Marion, Oreg. 189 C4 96
Gates, Lauderdale, Tenn. 291 C2 190
Gates, co., N.C. 9,254 A9 186
Gateshead, Eng. 111,900 G11 272
Gates Mills, Cuyahoga, Ohio 1,588 *A5 156
Gatesville, Copiah, Miss. 90 C2 184
Gatesville, Gates, N.C. 460 A9 186
Gatesville, Coryell, Tex. 4,626 D7 130
Gateway, Benton, Ark. 63 *A3 170
Gateway, Mesa, Colo. 110 D2 106
Gateway, Lincoln, Mont. B1 110
Gateway, Jefferson, Oreg. C5 96
Gatineau, Que., Can. 8,423 S9 66
Gatineau, co., Que., Can. 40,754 S9 66
Gatineau, riv., Que., Can. R9 66
S8
Gatliff, Whitley, Ky. 250 D6 178
Gatliff, Racine, Wis. F2 160
Gatlinburg, Sevier, Tenn. 1,764 C8 190
Gatooma, Rh.&Nya. 7,800 (*8,200) C5 420
Gattman, Monroe, Miss. 145 B4 184
Gaud-i-Zirreh, salt plain, Afg. E2 374
Gauer, lake, Man., Can. B4 60
Gauhati, India 43,615 D5 368
Gauko-Otavi, S.W.Afr. C2 420
Gauley, riv., W.Va. C4 194
Gauley Bridge, Fayette, W.Va. 950 C3 194
D7
Gauley Mills, Webster, W.Va. 300 C4 194
Gaurela, India E3 368
Gaurhati, India I8 366
Gausta, mtn., Nor. G3 291
Gautier, Jackson, Miss. 800 E2 184
Gaveh, riv., Iran B2 379
Gavins Point, dam, Nebr., S.Dak. B8 152
E8 158
Gaviota, Santa Barbara, Calif. 50 E3 94
Gavkhaneh, lake, Iran C3 379
Gävle, Swe. 50,662 A8 292
Gävleborg, co., Swe. 292,541 A7 292
Gavrilov Posad, Sov.Un. 6,800 D13 332
Gavrilovka, Sov.Un. H11 332
Gawler, ranges, Austl. E7 432
Gay, Meriwether, Ga. 194 C2 176
Gay, Keweenaw, Mich. 240 B3 146
Gaya, India 133,700 D4 368
Gaya, Nig. 12,996 D6 409
Gaya, Niger 3,100 D5 408
Gay Head, Dukes, Mass. 80 (103▴) D6 206
Gay Head, pt., Mass. D6 206
Gaylesville, Cherokee, Ala. 144 A4 168
Gaylord, Smith, Kans. 239 C5 144
Gaylord, Otsego, Mich. 2,568 D7 146
Gaylord, Sibley, Minn. 1,631 G4 148
Gaylord, Coos, Oreg. 25 E2 96
Gaylordsville, Litchfield, Conn. 200 C2 202
Gaysin, Sov.Un. 26,700 H7 332
Gays Mills, Crawford, Wis. 634 E3 160
Gaysville, Windsor, Vt. 100 D3 218
Gayville, Yankton, S.Dak. 261 E8 158
Gaza, prov., Moz. D6 421
Gazak, Iran D5 379
Gaziantep, Tur. 97,144 C7 307
Gaziantep, prov., Tur. 370,808 *C7 307
Gdańsk (Danzig), Pol. 240,000 (*440,000) A4 325
Gdańsk, pol. div., Pol. 1,074,000 *A4 325
Gdov, Sov.Un. 7,900 C6 332
Gdynia, Pol. 129,000 A4 325
Gearhart, Clatsop, Oreg. 725 A3 96
Gearhart, mtn., Oreg. E6 96
Geary, Blaine and Canadian, Okla. 1,416 C5 128
Geary, co., Kans. 28,779 D7 144
Geauga, co., Ohio 47,573 A5 156
Gebeit Mines, Sud. A4 398
Gebo, Hot Springs, Wyo. 80 C4 116
Ged, Calcasieu, La. 30 D2 180
Gedaref, Sud. 17,537 C4 398
Geddes, Charles Mix, S.Dak. 380 D7 158
Gedinne, Bel. 955 E3 282
Gediz, Tur. 5,976 B3 307
Gediz, riv., Tur. B2 307
Gedser, Den. 1,090 G2 292
Geel, Bel. 25,333 C4 282
Geelong, Austl. 20,034 F8 432
Geelvink, bay, Neth.N.Gui. E9 359
Geeraardsbergen, Bel. 10,067 D2 282
Gees Bend, Wilcox, Ala. 50 C2 168
Geetbets, Bel. 3,113 D4 282
Geff, Wayne, Ill. 330 E5 138
Geidam, Nig. 11,032 D7 409
Geiger, Sumter, Ala. 104 C1 168
Geislingen [an der Steige], Ger. 24,200 D3 286
Geismar, Ascension, La. 100 B5 180
Geist, res., Ind. C4 140
Geistown, Cambria, Pa. 3,186 C3 214
Geita, Tan. 365 C5 414
Gela, It. 47,200 G5 302
Gelderland, prov., Neth. 1,149,102 B4 282
Geldermalsen, Neth. 1,752 C4 282
Geldrop, Neth. 6,833 C4 282
Gelert, Ont., Can. 200 P22 64
Geliashin, mtn., Tur. C10 307
Gelib, Som. 3,000 (10,000▴) E5 398
Gelibolu (Gallipoli), Tur. 12,481 A2 307
Gellinam, isl., Kwajalein A1 436
Gelsenkirchen, Ger. 371,700 C2 286
Gem, Alta., Can. 25 E6 54
Gem, Shoshone, Idaho 350 B3 108
Gem, Thomas, Kans. 116 C3 144
Gem, Braxton, W.Va. 247 C4 194
Gem, co., Idaho 9,127 E2 108
Gemas, Mala. 4,873 G4 362
Gembloux, Bel. 5,812 D3 282
Gemena, Con.L. B2 414
Gemert, Neth. 5,212 C4 282
Gem Lake, Ramsey, Minn. 305 *F5 148
Gemlik, Tur. 10,403 A3 307
Gemsbok Kalahari, natl. park, Bech. E4 420
Gemünden, Ger. 3,700 C3 286
Gene Autry, Carter, Okla. 110 D6 128
Geneina, Sud. 11,817 C1 398
General Acha, Arg. 4,709 C3 252
General Alvarado, Arg. C4 252
General Alvear, Arg. B2 252
General Alvear, Arg. 2,548 C4 252
General Artigas, Par. 2,574 E4 247
General Belgrano, Arg. 3,789 C4 252
General Cepeda, Mex. B5 225
General Conesa, Arg. D3 252
General La Madrid, Arg. 3,572 C3 252
General Lavalle, Arg. C4 252
General Madariaga, Arg. 7,073 C4 252
General Paz, Arg. A4 252
General Pico, Arg. 11,121 C3 252
General Pinedo, Arg. 2,198 A3 252
General Roca, Arg. 7,449 C2 252
General Toshevo, Bul. 2,102 B4 317
General Triás, Mex. B4 224
General Viamonte, Arg. 5,342 C3 252
General Villegas, Arg. 4,738 C3 252
Genesee, Latah, Idaho 535 C2 108
Genesee, Genesee, Mich. 700 F8 146
Genesee, Waukesha, Wis. 160 E1 160
Genesee, co., Mich. 374,313 F8 146
Genesee, co., N.Y. 53,994 B3 212
Genesee, riv., N.Y. C3 212
Genesee Depot, Waukesha, Wis. 160 E1 160
Geneseo, Henry, Ill. 5,169 B3 138
Geneseo, Rice, Kans. 558 D5 144
Geneseo, Livingston, N.Y. 3,284 C4 212
Geneseo, Sargent, N.Dak. 106 D8 154
Geneva, Geneva, Ala. 3,840 D4 168
Geneva, Talbot, Ga. 261 D2 176
Geneva, Bear Lake, Idaho 10 *G7 108
Geneva, Kane, Ill. 7,646 B5 138
F1
Geneva, Adams, Ind. 1,053 B5 140
Geneva, Franklin, Iowa 219 B4 142
Geneva, Henderson, Ky. 150 C3 178
Geneva, Freeborn, Minn. 347 *H5 148
Geneva, Fillmore, Nebr. 2,352 D8 152
Geneva, Ontario, N.Y. 17,286 C5 212
Geneva, Ashtabula, Ohio 5,677 A6 156
Geneva, see Genève, Switz.
Geneva, Whatcom, Wash. 500 *A4 98
Geneva, co., Ala. 22,310 D4 168
Geneva, see Léman, lake, Switz.
Geneva, lake, Wis. F5 160
Geneva-on-the-Lake, Ashtabula, Ohio 631 *A6 156
Genève (Geneva), Switz. 157,000 (*178,900) B2 312
Genève (Genf), canton, Switz. 227,600 B2 312
Genevia, Pulaski, Ark. 600 C4 170
D7
Genf, see Genève, Switz.
Genichesk, Sov.Un. 21,200 I10 332
Genil, riv., Sp. D4 298
Génissiat, dam, Fr. D6 278
Genk, Bel. 46,497 D4 282
Gennep, Neth. 3,006 C4 282
Gennevilliers, Fr. 33,137 I10 278
Genoa, Miller, Ark. 90 D3 170
Genoa, Lincoln, Colo. 185 C7 106
Genoa, Hamilton, Fla. 50 A8 174
Genoa, De Kalb, Ill. 2,330 A5 138
Genoa, see Genova, It.
Genoa, Nance, Nebr. 1,009 C8 152
Genoa, Douglas, Nev. 125 D2 112
Genoa, Ottawa, Ohio 1,957 A1 156
A3
Genoa, Harris, Tex. 200 E8 130
Genoa, Vernon, Wis. 325 E2 160
Genoa, gulf, It. C2 302
Genoa City, Walworth, Wis. 1,005 F1 160
F5
Genola, Morrison, Minn. 108 *F4 148
Genola, Utah, Utah 380 *D4 114
Genou, Chouteau, Mont. 46 B5 110
Genova (Genoa), It. 711,500 C2 302
Genova, prov., It. 953,200 *C2 302
Gensan, see Wonsan, Kor.
Gent (Ghent), Bel. 161,382 (*288,100) C2 282
Gentbrugge, Bel. 21,207 C2 282
Genthin, Ger. 18,400 B5 286
Gentian, Muscogee, Ga. 800 D2 176
Gentilly, Que., Can. 672 R12 66
Gentilly, Fr. 17,497 I10 278
Gentilly, Polk, Minn. 100 D2 148
Gentry, Benton, Ark. 686 A2 170
Gentry, Gentry, Mo. 98 A3 150
Gentry, co., Mo. 8,793 A3 150
Gentryville, Spencer, Ind. 297 D2 140
Genzano di Roma, It. 11,000 *E4 302
Geographe, bay, Austl. E3 432
Geographe, chan., Austl. C2 432
Geographic Center of North America, N.Dak. B5 154
George, Lyon, Iowa 1,200 *A2 142
George, U.S.Afr. 13,538 F4 420
George, co., Miss. 11,098 E4 184
George, bay, N.S., Can. D8 70
George, cape, N.S., Can. D8 70
George, hill, Md. A1 182
George, isl., Newf., Can. C7 72
George, lake, N.S., Can. E3 70
George, lake, Fla. B9 174
George, lake, N.Y. B8 212
George, riv., Que., Can. P10 66
Georges Mills, Sullivan, N.H. 100 E2 208
Georgetown, White, Ark. 200 B5 170
Georgetown, Br. Gu. 92,000 D5 256
Georgetown, Ont., Can. 5,942 Q21 64
Georgetown, P.E.I., Can. 754 C7 70
Georgetown, Cayman Is. 1,462 C4 232
Georgetown, Clear Creek, Colo. 307 C5 106
Georgetown, Fairfield, Conn. 1,100 D2 202
Georgetown, Sussex, Del. 1,765 F4 172
Georgetown, Putnam, Fla. 500 B9 174
Georgetown, Gam. D2 408
Georgetown, Quitman, Ga. 554 E1 176
George Town, Great Exuma Isl. 229 A7 232
Georgetown, Bear Lake, Idaho 551 G7 108
Georgetown, Vermilion, Ill. 3,544 D6 138
Georgetown, Floyd, Ind. 643 D4 140
Georgetown, Scott, Ky. 6,986 B6 178
Georgetown, Grant, La. 321 C3 180
Georgetown, Sagadahoc, Maine 120 (790▴) *E3 204
George Town, see Penang, Mala.
Georgetown, Kent, Md. 50 B8 182
Georgetown, Essex, Mass. 2,005 (3,755▴) A6 206
Georgetown, Clay, Minn. 178 D2 148
Georgetown, Copiah, Miss. 285 D2 184
Georgetown, Deer Lodge, Mont. 50 *D4 110
Georgetown, Brown, Ohio 2,674 D3 156
Georgetown, Luzerne, Pa. 2,200 A5 214
Georgetown, Georgetown, S.C. 12,261 E10 188
Georgetown, Hamilton, Tenn. 75 C7 190
Georgetown, Williamson, Tex. 5,218 D7 130
Georgetown, co., S.C. 34,798 E10 188
Georgeville, Que., Can. 320 S12 66
George Washington Birthplace, natl. mon., Va. B8 192
George Washington Carver, natl. mon., Mo. E3 150
George West, Live Oak, Tex. 1,878 E6 130
Georgia, rep., Sov.Un. 4,049,000 E6 328
Georgia, state, U.S. 3,943,116 E10 77
176
Georgia, mtn., Vt. B2 218
Georgia Center (Georgia), Franklin, Vt. 100 (1,079▴) B2 218
Georgian, bay, Ont., Can. O19 64
S25
Georgiana, Butler, Ala. 2,093 D3 168
Georgian Bay Islands, natl. park, Ont., Can. O19 64
P21
Georgiaville, Providence, R.I. B2 216
Georgina, riv., Austl. C7 432
Gera, Ger. 98,000 C5 286
Gera, King George, Va. B7 192
Geraia, wadi, Eg., U.A.R. D5 382
Gerald, Sask., Can. 98 E7 58
Gerald, Franklin, Mo. 474 C6 150
Geral de Goias, mts., Braz. C1 258
Geraldine, De Kalb, Ala. 340 A4 168
Geraldine, Chouteau, Mont. 364 C6 110
Geraldton, Austl. 8,309 D2 432
Geraldton, Ont., Can. 3,263 R24 64
Gerard, Somerset, Maine C2 204
Gerber, Tehama, Calif. 600 B2 94
Gerber, res., Oreg. E5 96
Gercüş, Tur. 2,411 C9 307
Gerdine, mtn., Alsk. G10 84
Gerede, Tur. 4,145 A5 307
Gérgal, Sp. 1,689 D5 298
Gering, Scotts Bluff, Nebr. 4,585 C2 152
Gerlach, Washoe, Nev. 110 C2 112
Gerlachovka, mtn., Czech. B5 324
Germania, Yazoo, Miss. 75 C2 184
Germania, Atlantic, N.J. D3 210
Germansen, lake, B.C., Can. C10 52
Germantown, N.B., Can. 75 D5 70
Germantown, Fairfield, Conn. 2,893 *D2 202
Germantown, Clinton, Ill. 983 E4 138
Germantown, Bracken, Ky. 251 B7 178
Germantown, Montgomery, Md. 125 B5 182
Germantown, Montgomery, Ohio 3,399 C2 156
Germantown, Shelby, Tenn. 1,104 C2 190
Germantown, Washington, Wis. 622 E1 160
E5
Germany, country, Eur. 71,737,000 C6 266
286
Germany, East, country, Eur. 17,363,000 B5 286
Germany, West, country, Eur. 54,374,000 C3 286
Germfask, Schoolcraft, Mich. 125 C6 146
Germiston, U.S.Afr. 140,600 E5 420
Gernsheim, Ger. 6,481 D3 286
Gero, Jap. 16,163 L13 354
Gerona, Sp. 26,163 B8 298
Gerona, prov., Sp. 322,371 *B8 298
Geronimo, Graham, Ariz. 30 E5 124
Geronimo, Comanche, Okla. 199 D5 128
Gerrard, B.C., Can. 50 E14 52
Gerrard, Bonneville, Idaho *F6 108
Gerrardstown, Berkeley, W.Va. 250 B6 194

Glen Ullin, Morton, N.Dak.	1,210	D4	154
Glenview, San Diego, Calif.	250	D6	94
Glenview, Cook, Ill.	18,132	E2	138
Glenvil, Clay, Nebr.	323	D7	152
Glenville, Nevada, Ark.		D3	170
Glenville, Freeborn, Minn.	643	H5	148
Glenville, Jackson, N.C.	250	B2	186
Glenville, Gilmer, W.Va.	1,828	C4	194
Glen Whappen Rig, mtn., Scot.		F9	272
Glen White, Raleigh, W.Va.	800	D3	194
Glenwillard (Shousetown), Allegheny, Pa.	1,100	*C1	214
Glenwillow, Cuyahoga, Ohio	359	*A5	156
Glen Wilton, Botetourt, Va.	300	C5	192
Glenwood, Crenshaw, Ala.	416	D3	168
Glenwood, Pike, Ark.	840	C3	170
Glenwood, Newf., Can.	800	F8	72
Glenwood, Wheeler, Ga.	682	D4	176
Glenwood, Hawaii, Haw.	90	D6	86
Glenwood, Idaho, Idaho		C3	108
Glenwood, Cook, Ill.	882	*F3	138
Glenwood, Fayette and Rush, Ind.	382	C4	140
Glenwood, Mills, Iowa	4,783	C2	142
Glenwood (Plantation of), Aroostook, Maine	(30▲)	C4	204
Glenwood, Howard, Md.	25	B5	182
Glenwood, Cass, Mich.	115	G5	146
Glenwood, Pope, Minn.	2,631	F3	148
Glenwood, Schuyler, Mo.	242	A5	150
Glenwood, Sussex, N.J.	200	A4	210
Glenwood, Catron, N.Mex.	150	E2	126
Glenwood Landing, Nassau, N.Y.	3,400	*E8	212
Glenwood, Washington, Oreg.	950	*B3	96
Glenwood, Sevier, Utah	277	E4	114
Glenwood, Pittsylvania, Va.	1,857	*D5	192
Glenwood, Klickitat, Wash.	300	C5	98
Glenwood, Mason, W.Va.	200	C2	194
Glenwood City, St. Croix, Wis.	835	C1	160
Glenwood Springs, Garfield, Colo.	3,637	C3	106
Glenwoodville, Alta., Can.	75	F6	54
Glergad, head, Ire.		F5	272
Glezen, Pike, Ind.	180	D2	140
Glidden, Sask., Can.	131	E3	58
Glidden, Carroll, Iowa	993	B3	142
Glidden, Ashland, Wis.	700	B3	160
Glide, Douglas, Oreg.	200	D3	96
Glimåkra, Swe.	2,920	E5	292
Glines Canyon, dam, Wash.		B3	98
Gliwice, Pol.	134,000	C4	325
Globe, Gila, Ariz.	6,217	E5	124
Globino, Sov.Un.	20,400	H9	332
Glocester (Town of), Providence, R.I.	(3,397▲)	B2	216
Głogów, Pol.	1,681	C3	325
Glomawr, Perry, Ky.	750	C7	178
Glommerstrask, Swe.		D8	290
Glorenza, It.	800	B3	302
Glória, Braz.		B3	258
Gloria, Plaquemines, La.	5	C7	180
Glorieta, Santa Fe, N.Mex.	500	C5	126
		G7	
Glorieuses, is., Afr.		B9	421
Gloster, De Soto, La.	250	B2	180
Gloster, Amite, Miss.	1,369	D1	184
Gloucester, Ont., Can.		Q26	64
Gloucester, Eng.	67,300	J10	273
Gloucester, Essex, Mass.	25,789	A6	206
		C4	
Gloucester, Gloucester, Va.	500	C8	192
Gloucester, co., N.B., Can.	64,119	B4	70
Gloucester, co., Eng.	963,300	J10	273
Gloucester, co., N.J.	134,840	D2	210
Gloucester, co., Va.	11,919	C8	192
Gloucester City, Camden, N.J.	15,511	D2	210
Glouster, Athens, Ohio	2,255	C4	156
Glover, De Soto, Miss.	307	A2	184
Glover, Dickey, N.Dak.	75	D7	154
Glover, McCurtain, Okla.	75	*D9	128
Glover, Orleans, Vt.	230 (683▲)	B4	218
Glover, isl., Newf., Can.		F7	72
Glovergap, Marion, W.Va.	150	A6	194
Gloversville, Fulton, N.Y.	21,741	B7	212
Glovertown, Newf., Can.	604	F8	72
Gloverville, Aiken, S.C.	1,551	D5	188
Głubczyce, Pol.	5,020	C3	325
Glubokoye, Sov.Un.	18,600	E6	332
Głuchołazy, Pol.	17,658	C3	325
Gluck, Anderson, S.C. (part of Anderson)		C3	188
Gluckstadt, Madison, Miss.	150	C2	184
Glukhov, Sov.Un.	37,100	G9	332
Glussk, Sov. Un.	10,000	F7	332
Glyndon, Baltimore, Md.	915	B6	182
Glyndon, Clay, Minn.	489	E2	148
Glyngöre, Den.	750	H3	291
Glynn, co., Ga.	41,954	E5	176
Gmünd, see Schwäbisch Gmünd, Ger.			
Gmunden, Aus.	12,894	C5	313
Gnadenhutten, Tuscarawas, Ohio	1,257	B5	156
Gnesta, Swe.	3,191	B8	292
Gniezno, Pol.	42,000	B3	325
Gnjilane, Yugo.	9,250	C5	316
Gnosjö, Swe.	6,712	D4	292
Gôa (Port. India), poss., Asia	578,000	E2	366
		H9	340
Goalpara, India		D5	368
Goat, mtn., Mont.		C3	110
Goat, riv., B.C., Can.		D12	52
Goat River, B.C., Can.		D12	52
Goat Rock, dam, Ala., Ga.		C4	168
		D1	176
Goba, Eth.		D5	398
Gobabis, S.W.Afr.	1,997	D3	420
Goback, mtn., N.H.		B3	208
Gobardanga, India		I9	366
Gobey, Morgan, Tenn.	95	B7	190
Gob Gordillo, Arg.		B2	252
Gobi, des., Mong.		C8	346
Goble, Columbia, Oreg.	70	*B3	96
Gobles, Van Buren, Mich.	816	G6	146
Goch, Ger.	14,000	C2	286
Gochungomba, China		E8	346
Godār-i-Shāh, Afg.	5,000	E1	374
Godavari, riv., India		E3	366
Godavari, riv. mouths, India		E4	366
Goddard, Sedgwick, Kans.	533	B5	144
		E6	
Goddua, Libya		B2	394
Goderich, Ont., Can.	5,886	Q19	64
Godfrey, Ont., Can.	75	P24	64
Godfrey, Morgan, Ga.	181	C3	176
Godfrey, Madison, Ill.	1,231	E3	138
Godhavn, Grnld.	457	Q28	290
Godhra, India		E1	368
Gödöllö, Hung.	12,216	B4	320
Gods, lake, Man., Can.		C5	60
Gods, riv., Man., Can.		B6	60
Gods Lake, Man., Can.	160	C5	60
Godthaab, Grnld.	1,389	R28	290
Godwin Austen, mtn., India		B2	368
Godwin Heights, Kent, Mich., (part of Southkent)		G6	146
Godwinsville, Dodge, Ga.	150	D3	176
Goehner, Seward, Nebr.	106	*D8	152
Goes, Neth.	14,024	C2	282
Goessel, Marion, Kans.	327	D6	144
Goff, Nemaha, Kans.	259	C8	144
Goffstown, Hillsboro, N.H.	1,052 (7,230▲)	E3	208
Gogebic, co., Mich.	24,370	C2	146
Gogebic, lake, Mich.		C2	146
Gogra, riv., India		D3	368
Goiâna, Braz.	13,744	B4	258
Goiandira, Braz.	2,652	D1	258
Goiânia, Braz.	39,871	D1	258
Goiás, Braz.	5,606	I6	257
Goiás, state, Braz.	1,537,000	H7	257
Gojām, prov., Eth.	1,600,000	C4	398
Gojō, Jap.	13,596	M11	354
Göksun, Tur.	2,856	B7	307
Gokwe, Rh. & Nya.		C5	420
Gol, Nor.	2,767	F3	291
Gola, India		C3	368
Golaghat, India		D6	368
Golchikha, Sov.Un.	1,300	B10	328
Golconda, Pope, Ill.	864	F5	138
Golconda, Humboldt, Nev.	300	C4	112
Gold Acres, Lander, Nev.	100	C5	112
Gołdap, Pol.	632	A6	325
Goldbar, Snohomish, Wash.	315	B5	98
Gold Beach, Curry, Oreg.	1,765	E2	96
Goldboro, N.S., Can.	365	D8	70
Gold Bridge, B.C., Can.	380	E11	52
Goldbutte, Toole, Mont.		B5	110
Gold City, Simpson, Ky.	25	D4	178
Goldcreek, Powell, Mont.	60	*D4	110
Golddust, Lauderdale, Tenn.	25	C2	190
Golden, Crenshaw, Ala.	500	D3	168
Golden, B.C., Can.	595	E14	52
Golden, Jefferson, Colo.	7,118	C5	106
Golden, Idaho, Idaho	50	D3	108
Golden, Adams, Ill.	491	C2	138
Golden, Tishomingo, Miss.	121	A4	184
Golden, Santa Fe, N.Mex.	30	C4	126
		H7	
Golden, McCurtain, Okla.	70	D9	128
Golden, Okanogan, Wash.		A7	98
Golden, bay, N.Z.		D4	437
Golden Beach, Dade, Fla.	413	E6	174
Golden City, Logan, Ark.		B3	170
Golden City, Barton, Mo.	714	D3	150
Goldendale, Klickitat, Wash.	2,536	D6	98
Golden Gate, chan., Calif.		A4	94
Golden Grove, Greenville, S.C.	300	B4	188
Golden Hill, Dorchester, Md.	300	D7	182
Golden Hill, Olmstead, Minn.	2,190	*G6	148
Golden Hinde, mtn., B.C., Can.		F10	52
Golden Lake, Ont., Can.	110	O23	64
Golden Meadow, Lafourche, La.	3,097	E5	180
Golden Prairie, Sask., Can.	244	E3	58
Golden Spike, natl. historical site, Utah		B3	114
Golden Valley, Hennepin, Minn.	14,559	F6	148
Goldenvalley, Mercer, N.Dak.	286	C3	154
Golden Valley, co., Mont.	1,203	D7	110
Golden Valley, co., N.Dak.	3,100	D2	154
Goldenville, N.S., Can.	785	D7	70
Goldfield, Teller, Colo.	75	D5	106
Goldfield, Wright, Iowa	682	B4	142
Goldfield, Esmeralda, Nev.	300	F4	112
Goldfield, mts., Ariz.		H3	124
Gold Hill, Jackson, Oreg.	608	E3	96
Gold Hill, Tooele, Utah		C2	114
Gold Hill, Buckingham, Va.		C6	192
Goldonna, Natchitoches, La.	292	B3	180
Gold Point, Esmeralda, Nev.	150	F4	112
Goldpoint, Hamilton, Tenn.		E8	190
Goldsand, lake, Man., Can.		B2	60
Goldsboro, Caroline, Md.	204	B8	182
Goldsboro, Wayne, N.C.	28,873	B8	186
Goldsmith, Tipton, Ind.	200	B3	140
Goldsmith, Ector, Tex.	670	D4	130
Goldston, Chatham, N.C.	374	B6	186
Gold Stone, Hill, Mont.	12	B6	110
Goldstone, mtn., Idaho		D5	108
Goldthwaite, Mills, Tex.	1,383	D6	130
Goleen, Ire.	89	J3	273
Golela, U.S.Afr.		E6	421
Goleniów, Pol.	1,713	B2	325
Goleta, Santa Barbara, Calif.	4,000	E4	94
Golf, Cook, Ill.	409	*A6	138
Golf Manor, Hamilton, Ohio	4,648	*D1	156
Golfview, Palm Beach, Fla.	131	*E10	174
Goliad, Goliad, Tex.	1,782	E7	130
Goliad, co., Tex.	5,429	E7	130
Gollans, riv., N.Z.		J11	437
Golovin, Alsk.	94	C5	84
Golpāyegān, Iran	20,844	C3	379
Goltry, Alfalfa, Okla.	313	B5	128
Golts, Kent, Md.	100	B8	182
Golva, Golden Valley, N.Dak.	162	D2	154
Golyamo Konare, Bul.	7,577	B2	317
Goma, Con.L.		C4	414
Gombari, Con.L.		B4	414
Gombe, Nig.	18,483	D7	409
Gomel, Sov.Un.	166,000	F8	332
Gomera, isl., Can.Is.		F11	298
Gomez, Martin, Fla.	150	D10	174
Gómez Palacio, Mex.	45,873	B5	224
Gonaïves, Hai.	13,634	C8	233
Gonaïves, gulf, Hai.		C8	232
Gonâve, isl., Hai.		C8	232
Gonbad-e-Kāvūs, Iran	9,637	B4	379
Gonda, India	32,566	D3	368
Gondar, Eth.		C4	398
Gondia, India		E3	368
Gönen, Tur.	9,985	A2	307
Gongogi, mts., Braz.		C2	258
Gongola, riv., Nig.		D7	409
Gonvick, Clearwater, Minn.	363	D3	148
Gonzales, Monterey, Calif.	2,138	D3	94
Gonzales, Ascension, La.	3,252	B5	180
		D5	
Gonzales, Gonzales, Tex.	5,829	E7	130
Gonzales, co., Tex.	17,845	E7	130
Gonzalez, Escambia, Fla.	150	A3	174
González, Mex.	1,913	C6	225
González Chaves, Arg.	4,718	C3	252
Goochland, Goochland, Va.	200	C7	192
Goochland, co., Va.	9,206	C7	192
Goode, mtn., Alsk.		G11	84
Goodell, Hancock, Iowa	231	B4	142
Gooderham, Ont., Can.	115	P22	64
Goodes, Bedford, Va.	250	C5	192
Goodeve, Sask., Can.	211	E6	58
Goodfellow Terrace, St. Louis, Mo.	824	*C7	150
Good Hart, Emmet, Mich.	50	D6	146
Good Hope, Elmore, Ala.	200	C3	168
Good Hope, Walton, Ga.	165	C3	176
Good Hope, McDonough, Ill.	394	C3	138
Good Hope, St. Charles, La. (part of Norco)		B7	180
Good Hope, Fayette, Ohio	350	C3	156
Good Hope, cape, U.S.Afr.		F3	420
Goodhope, mtn., B.C., Can.		E10	52
Goodhue, Goodhue, Minn.	566	G6	148
Goodhue, co., Minn.	33,035	G6	148
Gooding, Gooding, Idaho	2,750	G4	108
Gooding, co., Idaho	9,544	F4	108
Goodland, Collier, Fla.	100	F9	174
Goodland, Newton, Ind.	1,202	B2	140
Goodland, Sherman, Kans.	4,459	C2	144
Goodland, Choctaw, Okla.	50	E8	128
Goodlands, Man., Can.	125	F2	60
Goodlettsville, Davidson, Tenn.	3,163	B5	190
		E7	
Goodman, Holmes, Miss.	932	C3	184
Goodman, McDonald, Mo.	540	E3	150
Goodman, Marinette, Wis.	550	C5	160
Goodman Heights, McDonald, Mo.	822	*E3	150
Goodnews Bay (Mumtrak), Alsk.	100	D5	84
Good Pine, LaSalle, La.	800	C3	180
Goodrich, Morgan, Colo.	10	B6	106
Goodrich, Adams, Idaho		E2	108
Goodrich, Linn, Kans.	35	D9	144
Goodrich, Genesee, Mich.	701	*G8	146
Goodrich, Sheridan, N.Dak.	392	C5	154
Goodrich, Charleston, S.C.		F3	188
Goodrich, Polk, Tex.	800	D8	130
Goodridge, Pennington, Minn.	134	C3	148
Good Spirit, prov. park, Sask., Can.		E6	58
Goodsprings, Walker, Ala.	900	*B2	168
Goodsprings, Clark, Nev.	113	H6	112
Good Thunder, Blue Earth, Minn.	468	G4	148
Goodview, Winona, Minn.	1,348	G7	148
Goodwater, Coosa, Ala.	2,023	B3	168
Goodwater, Sask., Can.	76	F6	58
Goodwater, Clarke, Miss.	102	D4	184
Goodwater, McCurtain, Okla.	100	E9	128
Goodway, Monroe, Ala.	150	D2	168
Goodwell, Texas, Okla.	771	B2	128
Goodwin, Aroostook, Maine		B5	204
Goodwin, Deuel, S.Dak.	113	C9	158
Goodyear, Maricopa, Ariz.	1,654	H1	124
Goodyear, Pearl River, Miss. (part of Picayune)		E3	184
Goor, Neth.	6,214	B5	282
Goose, bay, Newf., Can.		D6	72
Goose, creek, Idaho		G5	108
Goose, creek, Va.		C5	192
Goose, creek, Wyo.		B6	116
Goose, isl., B.C., Can.		E8	52
Goose, lake, Calif., Oreg.		B3	94
		F6	96
Goose, lake, Man., Can.		C2	60
Goose, lake, Sask., Can.		E4	58
Goose, pt., Del.		D4	172
Goose, pond, N.H.		D2	208
Goose, riv., Newf., Can.		E9	72
Goose, riv., N.Dak.		C8	154
Goose Bay, Newf., Can.	1,800	D6	72
		E9	
Gooseberry, creek, Wyo.		B4	116
Goose Creek, Berkeley, S.C.	150	E3	188
		F8	
Goose Creek, res., S.C.		E3	188
Goose Egg, Natrona, Wyo.		D6	116
Gooselake, Clinton, Iowa	191	C7	142
Goose Rocks Beach, York, Maine	90	E2	204
Goosport, Calcasieu, La.	16,778	*D2	180
Gopalganj, India		D4	368
Goplo, lake, Pol.		B4	325
Göppingen, Ger.	45,500	D3	286
Góra, Pol.	3,526	C3	325
Góra Kalwaria, Pol.	3,687	C5	325
Gorakhpur, India	123,844 (*132,436)	D3	368
Gordo, Pickens, Ala.	1,714	B2	168
Gordon, Houston, Ala.	222	D4	168
Gordon, Huerfano, Colo.	15	*E6	106
Gordon, Wilkinson, Ga.	1,793	D3	176
Gordon, Butler, Kans.	100	B7	144
Gordon, Sheridan, Nebr.	2,223	B3	152
Gordon, Douglas, Wis.	350	B2	160
Gordon, co., Ga.	19,228	B2	176
Gordon, lake, Alta., Can.		B7	54
Gordonhorne, peak, B.C., Can.		E13	52
Gordonsburg, Lewis, Tenn.	315	C4	190
Gordonsville, Smith, Tenn.	249	B6	190
Gordonsville, Orange, Va.	1,109	B6	192
Gordonville, Cape Girardeau, Mo.	92	D8	150
Gore, N.S., Can.	145	D6	70
Gorē, Eth.	10,000	D4	398
Gore, N.Z.	6,567	G2	437
Gore, Hocking, Ohio	350	C4	156
Gore, Sequoyah, Okla.	334	C8	128
Gore, Frederick, Va.	200	A6	192
Gore, mtn., Vt.		B5	218
Gore, pt., Alsk.		H10	84
Gore Bay, Ont., Can.	731	O18	64
Goree, Knox, Tex.	543	C6	130
Gorelova, Sov.Un.		C17	329
Gore Springs, Grenada, Miss.	100	B3	184
Goreville, Johnson, Ill.	625	F5	138
Gorey, Ire.	2,816	I6	273
Gorgān (Asterābād), Iran	28,380	B4	379
Gorgas, Walker, Ala.	950	B2	168
Gorge, dam, Wash.		A5	98
Gorgona, isl., Col.		C1	244
Gorham, Jackson, Ill.	378	F4	138
Gorham, Russell, Kans.	429	D4	144
Gorham, Cumberland, Maine	2,322 (5,767▲)	E2	204
		E4	
Gorham, Coos, N.H.	1,945 (3,039▲)	C4	208
Gorham, Ontario, N.Y.	500	C4	212
Gori, Sov.Un.	33,000	D2	336
Gorin, Scotland, Mo.	410	A5	150
Gorinchem, Neth.	17,879	C4	282
Gorizia, It.	42,100	C4	302
Gorizia, prov., It.	137,600	*C4	302
Gorki, see Gorkiy, Sov.Un.			
Gorkiy (Gorki), Sov.Un.	942,000 (*1,250,000)	A2	336
Gorlice, Pol.	6,100	D5	325
Görlitz, Ger.	96,100	C6	286
Gorlovka, Sov.Un.	293,000	H12	332
		S22	
Gorman, Garrett, Md.	83	B1	182
Gorman, Humphreys, Tenn.	50	B4	190
Gorman, Eastland, Tex.	1,142	C6	130
Gormania, Grant, W.Va.	307	B5	194
Gormley, Ont., Can.	85	R22	64
Gorna Dzhumaya, see Blagoevgrad, Bul.			
Gorna Oryakhovitsa, Bul.	18,907	B2	317
Gornji Milanovac, Yugo.	3,402	B5	316
Gorno-Altaysk, Sov.Un.	27,000	B11	336
Gorodenka, Sov.Un.	26,300	H5	332
Gorodets (Gorki), res., Sov.Un.		A2	336
Gorodishche, Sov.Un.		R23	332
Gorodnya, Sov.Un.	11,700	G8	332
Gorodok, Sov.Un.	11,800	E7	332
Gorodok, Sov.Un.	19,300	H4	332
Gorong, is., Indon.		E8	359
Gorontalo, Indon.	15,603	D6	358
Gorrie, Ont., Can.	485	Q19	64
Gorst, Kitsap, Wash.	950	*B4	98
Gort, Ire.	1,094	H4	273
Gorumna, isl., Ire.		H3	273
Goryachinsk, Sov.Un.		D12	329
Goryn, riv., Sov.Un.		G6	332
Góry Swiętokrzyskie, mts., Pol.		C5	325
Gorzów [Wielkopolski], Pol.	44,000	B2	325
Goshen, Pike, Ala.	260	D3	168
Goshen, Tulare, Calif.	1,061	*D4	94
Goshen, N.S., Can.	145	D8	70
Goshen, Litchfield, Conn.	400 (1,288▲)	B3	202
Goshen, Bingham, Idaho		F6	108
Goshen, Elkhart, Ind.	13,718	A4	140
Goshen, Oldham, Ky.	50	A5	178
Goshen, Hampshire, Mass.	250 (385▲)	B2	206
Goshen, Sullivan, N.H.	125 (351▲)	E2	208
Goshen, Cape May, N.J.	500	E3	210
Goshen, Orange, N.Y.	3,906	D7	212
Goshen, Clermont, Ohio	500	C2	156
Goshen, Lane, Oreg.	300	D3	96
Goshen, Utah, Utah	426	D4	114
Goshen, Addison, Vt.	30 (76▲)	*D2	218
Goshen, Rockridge, Va.	99	C5	192
Goshen, co., Wyo.	11,941	D8	116
Goshen Springs, Rankin, Miss.	250	C3	184
Goshute, Juab, Utah	75	*C2	114
Goslar, Ger.	40,200	C4	286
Gosnell, Mississippi, Ark.	800	B7	170
Gosnold (Town of), Dukes, Mass.	(66▲)	*D6	206
Gosper, co., Nebr.	2,489	D6	152
Gospić, Yugo.	5,127	B2	316
Gosport, Clarke, Ala.	25	D2	168
Gosport, Eng.	63,200	K11	273
Gosport, Owen, Ind.	646	C3	140
Goss, Marion, Miss.	100	D3	184
Gossburg, Coffee, Tenn.	100	C5	190
Gossville, Merrimack, N.H.	155	E4	208
Gostivar, Yugo.	9,509	D5	316
Gostyń, Pol.	8,021	C3	325
Gostynin, Pol.	7,357	B4	325
Göta, Swe.		C3	292
Götaland, reg., Swe.	3,466,318	*H6	291
Gotebo, Kiowa, Okla.	538	C5	128
Göteborg, Swe.	380,442	D2	292
Göteborg Och Bohus, co., Swe.	588,055	C2	292
Gotel, mts., Br.Cam.		E7	409
Gotemba, Jap.	38,796	L14	354
Gotene, Swe.	5,011	C4	292
Gotha, Ger.	57,800	C4	286
Gotham, Richland, Wis.	250	E3	160
Gothenburg, Dawson, Nebr.	3,050	D5	152
Gothic, mesas, Ariz.		B6	124
Gotland, reg., Swe.	56,927	*H8	291
Gotland, co., Swe.	56,927	D9	292
Gotland, isl., Swe.		D9	292
Gotō, is., Jap.		H2	354
Gotse Delchev, Bul.	12,526	C1	317
Gotska Sandön, isl., Swe.		C10	292
Gott, peak, B.C., Can.		E11	52
Göttingen, Ger.	80,200	C3	286
Gottne, Swe.		E8	290
Gottwaldov (Zlín), Czech.	57,974	B3	324
Gottwaldovský, co., Czech.	655,207	*B3	324
Gouda, Neth.	40,104	B3	282
Goudeau, Avoyelles, La.	130	D3	180
Goudiri, Sen.		D2	408
Goudswaard, Neth.	730	C3	282
Gough, Burke, Ga.	300	C4	176
Gough, lake, Alta., Can.		D6	54
Gouin, res., Que., Can.		Q9	66
Goulburn, Austl.	19,183	E9	432
Gould, Lincoln, Ark.	1,210	D5	170
Gould, Jackson, Colo.	80	B4	106

Gould, Harmon, Okla.	241	D4	128
Gould City, Mackinac, Mich.	100	C6	146
Goulding, Escambia, Fla.	900	*A3	174
Goulds, Dade, Fla.	5,121	E6	174
Goulds, Washington, R.I.		D2	216
Gouldsboro, Hancock, Maine	280 (1,100▲)	D4	204
Goulimine, Mor.		C2	402
Goundam, Mali	6,400	C4	408
Gourdin, Williamsburg, S.C.		E9	188
Gouré, Niger	800	D7	409
Gourma-Rarous, Mali		C4	408
Gournay [-en-Bray], Fr.		C4	278
Gouro, Chad		C8	409
Gouverneur, Sask., Can.	70	F4	58
Gouverneur, St. Lawrence, N.Y.	4,946	A6	212
Govan, Sask., Can.	442	E5	58
Govan, Bamberg, S.C.	138	E6	188
Gove, Gove, Kans.	228	D3	144
Gove, co., Kans.	4,107	D3	144
Govenlock, Sask., Can.	176	F3	58
Governador Valadares, Braz.	20,357	D2	258
Government Camp, Clackamas, Oreg.	40	B5	96
Government Village, Flathead, Mont.	200	*B2	110
Gowan, riv., Man., Can.		C5	60
Gowanda, Cattaraugus, N.Y.	3,352	C3	212
Gowdey, Hinds, Miss. (part of Jackson)		C2	184
Gowen, Montcalm, Mich.	200	F6	146
Gowen, Latimer, Okla.	350	D8	128
Gowensville, Greenville, S.C.	50	A4	188
Gower, Clinton, Mo.	406	B3	150
Gowk, Iran	6,285	D4	379
Gowrie, Webster, Iowa	1,127	B3	142
Goya, Arg.	20,804	A4	252
Goz Beida, Chad		D9	409
Göz Regeb, Sud.		B4	398
Graaff-Reinet, U.S.Afr.	14,136	F4	420
Grabham, Montgomery, Kans.	40	*E8	144
Grabill, Allen, Ind.	495	A5	140
Gračac, Yugo.	2,308	B2	316
Gračanica, Yugo.	5,620	B4	316
Grace, Caribou, Idaho	725	G7	108
Grace, Presque Isle, Mich.		D7	146
Grace, Issaquena, Miss.	300	C2	184
Graceham, Frederick, Md.	165	A5	182
Gracemont, Caddo, Okla.	306	C5	128
Graceville, Jackson, Fla.	2,307	A5	174
Graceville, Big Stone, Minn.	823	F2	148
Gracewood, Richmond, Ga.	500	C4	176
Gracey, Christian, Ky.	234	D3	178
Gracias, Hond.	1,589	C3	228
Gradačac, Yugo.	4,602	B4	316
Gradaus, mts., Braz.		G6	256
Gradefes, Sp.	522	A4	298
Gradizhsk, Sov.Un.	28,300	H9	332
Grado, Sp.	3,671	A3	298
Grady, Montgomery, Ala.	150	D3	168
Grady, Lincoln, Ark.	622	C5	170
Grady, Curry, N.Mex.	100	D7	126
Grady, Jefferson, Okla.	25	D6	128
Grady, co., Ga.	18,015	F2	176
Grady, co., Okla.	29,590	C6	128
Graefenberg, Shelby, Ky.	100	B5	178
Graehl, Alsk.	1,200	*C7	84
Graested, Den.	1,038	E3	292
Graettinger, Palo Alto, Iowa	879	A3	142
Graf, Dubuque, Iowa	47	*B7	142
Graf, Johnson, Nebr.	80	*D10	152
Graford, Palo Pinto, Tex.	448	C6	130
Grafton, Austl.	9,759 (*14,201)	D10	432
Grafton, Ont., Can.	465	Q22	64
Grafton, Jersey, Ill.	1,084	E3	138
Grafton, Worth, Iowa	273	A4	142
Grafton, Worcester, Mass.	2,200 (10,627▲)	B4	206
Grafton, Fillmore, Nebr.	171	D8	152
Grafton, Rensselaer, N.Y.	820	C8	212
Grafton, Walsh, N.Dak.	5,885	B8	154
Grafton, Lorain, Ohio	1,683	A4	156
Grafton, York, Va.	200	A8	192
Grafton, Windham, Vt.	150 (426▲)	E3	218
Grafton, Taylor, W.Va.	5,791	B4 B7	194
Grafton, Ozaukee, Wis.	3,748	E2 E6	160
Grafton, co., N.H.	48,857	D3	208
Grafton Center, Grafton, N.H.	40	D3	208
Graham, Randolph, Ala.	75	B4	168
Graham, Appling, Ga.	130	E4	176
Graham, Muhlenberg, Ky.	895	C3	178
Graham, Nodaway, Mo.	215	A2	150
Graham, Alamance, N.C.	7,723	A6	186
Graham, Carter, Okla.	350	D6	128
Graham, Hickman, Tenn.	25	C4	190
Graham, Young, Tex.	8,505	C6	130
Graham, Pierce, Wash.	75	B4	98
Graham, co., Ariz.	14,045	F5	124
Graham, co., Kans.	5,586	C3	144
Graham, co., N.C.	6,432	B2	186
Graham, creek, Ind.		D4	140
Graham, isl., B.C., Can.		D6	52
Graham, lake, Maine		D4	204
Graham, mtn., Ariz.		F6	124
Graham, reach, B.C., Can.		D8	52
Graham, riv., B.C., Can.		B11	52
Grahamstown, U.S.Afr.	23,789	F5	420
Grahamville, Jasper, S.C.		G7	188
Grahn, Carter, Ky.	500	B7	178
Graian Alps, mts., Eur.		E7 C1	278 302
Grainfield, Gove, Kans.	389	C3	144
Grainger, Alta., Can.	25	E6	54
Grainger, co., Tenn.	12,506	B8	190
Grainola, Osage, Okla.	67	B7	128
Grainton, Perkins, Nebr.	35	D4	152
Grain Valley, Jackson, Mo.	552	*B3	150
Grajaú, Braz.	2,377	B1	258
Grajaú, riv., Braz.		A1	258
Grajewo, Pol.	6,171	B6	325
Gram, isl., Thai.		D4	362
Gramada, Bul.	4,662	B1	317
Gramalote, Col.	2,776	B2	244
Gramastetten, Aus.	2,151	B6	313
Grambling, Lincoln, La.	3,144	B3	180
Gramercy, St. James, La.	2,094	B6	180
Gramling, Spartanburg, S.C.	200	A4	188
Grammer, Bartholomew, Ind.	200	C4	140
Grammichele, It.	14,400	G5	302
Grampian, mts., Scot.		E8	272
Gramsh, Alb.	650	A3	306
Granada, Prowers, Colo.	593	D8	106
Granada, Martin, Minn.	418	H4	148
Granada, Nic.	21,035	E5	228
Granada, Sp.	153,715	D5	298
Granada, prov., Sp.	793,338	*D5	298
Granbury, Hood, Tex.	2,227	C7	130
Granby, Que., Can.	27,095	S12	66
Granby, Grand, Colo.	503	B5	106
Granby, Hartford, Conn.	700 (4,968▲)	B4	202
Granby, Hampshire, Mass.	1,700 (4,221▲)	B2	206
Granby, Newton, Mo.	1,808	E3	150
Granby, Essex, Vt.	15 (56▲)	B5	218
Granby, res., Colo.		B5	106
Gran Canaria, isl., Can.Is.		G12	298
Gran Chaco, plains, Arg., Par.		F5	236
Grand, co., Colo.	3,557	B4	106
Grand, co., Utah	6,345	E6	114
Grand, bayou, La.		B5	180
Grand, canal, China		G8	348
Grand, canal, Ire.		H5	273
Grand, canyon, Ariz.		B3	124
Grand, caverns, Tenn.		C7	190
Grand, des., Mex.		A3	224
Grand, falls, Newf., Can.		E9	72
Grand, falls, Maine		C5	204
Grand, isl., La.		E6	180
Grand, isl., La., Miss.		D6 E3	180 184
Grand, isl., Mich.		C5	146
Grand, isl., N.Y.		B3	212
Grand, isl, Vt.		B2	218
Grand, lake, N.B., Can.		D4	70
Grand, lake, Newf., Can.		D6	72
Grand, lake, Newf., Can.		F7	72
Grand, lake, Colo.		B5	106
Grand, lake, La.		E6	180
Grand, lake, La.		E4	180
Grand, lake, La.		E3	180
Grand, lake, Maine		B4	204
Grand, lake, Maine		C5	204
Grand, lake, Mich.		D8	146
Grand, lake, Ohio		B2	156
Grand, riv., Ont., Can.		Q20	64
Grand, riv., La.		D4	180
Grand, riv., Mich.		F6	146
Grand, riv., Mo.		A3	150
Grand, riv., Ohio		A5	156
Grand, riv., S.Dak.		B4	158
Grand Atlas, mts., Mor.		B2	402
Grand Bank, Newf., Can.	2,430	G8	72
Grand-Bassam, I.C.	4,650	E4	408
Grand Bay, Mobile, Ala.	500	E1	168
Grand Bay, N.B., Can.	210	D3	70
Grand Bayou, Red River, La.		B2	180
Grand Beach, Man., Can.	62	E4	60
Grand Beach, Berrien, Mich.	86	*H5	146
Grand Bend, Ont., Can.	953	Q19	64
Grand Blanc, Genesee, Mich.	1,565	G8	146
Grand Bostonnais, lake, Que., Can.		Q12	66
Grand-Bourg, Guad.	2,019 (6,042▲)	D14	233
Grand Bruit, Newf., Can.	200	G6	72
Grand Cane, De Soto, La.	322	B2	180
Grand Canyon, Coconino, Ariz.	595	B3	124
Grand Canyon, natl. mon., Ariz.		B3	124
Grand Canyon, natl. park, Ariz.		B3	124
Grand Cayman, isl., Cayman Is.		C4	232
Grand Cess, Lib.		F3	408
Grand Chenier, Cameron, La.	200	E3	180
Grand Coteau, St. Landry, La.	1,165	D3	180
Grand Coulee, Grant, Wash.	1,058	B7	98
Grand Coulee, dam, Wash.		B8	98
Grand Crossing, Duval, Fla.	300	A10	174
Grand Detour, Ogle, Ill.	425	B4	138
Grande, bay, Arg.		H4	251
Grande, riv., Arg.		B4	250
Grande, riv., Arg.		C2	252
Grande, riv., Bol.		C2	246
Grande, riv., Braz.		E1	258
Grande, riv., Nic.		D5	228
Grande, riv. mouth, Ven.		B8	240
Grande-Anse, N.B., Can.	390	B4	70
Grande Catwick, is., Viet.		E6	362
Grande Comore, isl., Afr.		B8	421
Grand Ecore, Natchitoches, La.	55	C2	180
Grande-Digue, N.B., Can.	215	C5	70
Grande Ligne, Que., Can.	590	S11	66
Grande Miquelon, isl., N.A.		G7	72
Grande Prairie, Alta., Can.	6,302	C3	56
Grand Erg Occidental, sand dunes, Alg.		C3	402
Grand Erg Oriental, sand dunes, Alg.		C5	402
Grande Rivière, Que., Can.	1,024	*Q10	66
Grande Ronde, riv., Oreg., Wash.		B9 C9	96 98
Grandes-Bergeronnes, Que., Can.	810	P15	66
Grandes Piles, Que., Can.	670	R12	66
Grand-Etang, N.S., Can.	315	C8	70
Grand Falls, Newf., Can.	6,000	F8	72
Grandfalls, Ward, Tex.	1,012	D4	130
Grand Falls, lake, Maine		C5	204
Grandfather, mtn., N.C.		A4	186
Grandfield, Tillman, Okla.	1,606	D5	128
Grand Forks, B.C., Can.	1,995	F13	52
Grand Forks, Grand Forks, N.Dak.	34,451	C8	154
Grand Forks, co., N.Dak.	48,677	C8	154
Grandglaise, Jackson, Ark.	150	B5	170
Grand Gorge, Delaware, N.Y.	600	C7	212
Grand Harbour, N.B., Can.	215	E3	70
Grand Haven, Ottawa, Mich.	11,066	F5	146
Grandin, Carter, Mo.	259	E7	150
Grandin, Cass, N.Dak.	147	C8	154
Grand Island, Hall, Nebr.	25,742	D7	152
Grand Island, Erie, N.Y.	1,700	C3	212
Grand Isle, Jefferson, La.	2,074	E6	180
Grand Isle, Aroostook, Maine	500 (978▲)	A4	204
Grand Isle, Grand Isle, Vt.	100 (624▲)	B2	218
Grand Isle, co., Vt.	2,927	B2	218
Grand Junction, Mesa, Colo.	18,694	C2	106
Grand Junction, Greene, Iowa	949	B3	142
Grand Junction, Hardeman, Tenn.	446	C2	190
Grand Junction, Van Buren, Mich.	300	G5	146
Grand-Lahou, I.C.	4,700	E3	408
Grand Lake, Grand, Colo.	170	B5	106
Grand Lake, Cameron, La.		D2	180
Grand Lake Stream, Washington, Maine	270 (219▲)	C5	204
Grand Ledge, Eaton, Mich.	5,165	G7	146
Grand Lieu, lake, Fr.		D3	278
Grand Manan, chan., Can., U.S.		E2	70
Grand Manan, chan., Maine		D5	204
Grand Manan, isl., N.B., Can.		E3	70
Grand Marais, Alger, Mich.	600	C6	146
Grand Marais, Cook, Minn.	1,301	D8	148
Grand Marsh, Adams, Wis.	130	E4	160
Grand Meadow, Mower, Minn.	837	H6	148
Grand' Mère, Que., Can.	14,023	R12	66
Grand Mound, Clinton, Iowa	565	C7	142
Grândola, Port.	3,936	C2	298
Grand Pass, Saline, Mo.	120	B4	150
Grand-Popo, Dah.	3,100	E5	408
Grand Portage, Cook, Minn.	136	D9	148
Grand Prairie, Dallas, Tex.	30,386	B8	130
Grand Rapids, Man., Can.		D3	60
Grand Rapids, Kent, Mich.	177,313 (*367,300)	G6	146
Grand Rapids, Itasca, Minn.	7,265	D5	148
Grand Rapids, La Moure, N.Dak.	150	D7	154
Grand Rapids, Wood, Ohio	670	A1 A3	156
Grand Ridge, Jackson, Fla.	415	A5	174
Grand Ridge, La Salle, Ill.	659	B5	138
Grand River, Decatur, Iowa	284	D4	142
Grand River, Lake, Ohio	477	*A5	156
Grand River, valley, Colo., Utah		D6	114
Grand Rivers, Livingston, Ky.	378	D2	178
Grand Ronde, Polk, Oreg.	350	B3	96
Grand St. Bernard, pass, Switz.		C3	312
Grand Saline, Van Zandt, Tex.	2,006	C8	130
Grand Seboeis, lake, Maine		B4	204
Grand Terre, isl., La.		E6	180
Grand Teton, mtn., Wyo.		C2	116
Grand Teton, natl. park, Wyo.		C2	116
Grand Tower, Jackson, Ill.	847	F4	138
Grand Traverse, co., Mich.	33,490	E6	146
Grand Traverse, bay, Mich.		D6	146
Grand Valley, Ont., Can.	655	Q20	64
Grand Valley, Garfield, Colo.	245	C2	106
Grandview, Man., Can.	963	E2	60
Grandview, Edgar, Ill.	2,214	D6	138
Grand View, Owyhee, Idaho	200	G2	108
Grand View, Spencer, Ind.	599	E3	140
Grandview, Louisa, Iowa	300	C6	142
Grandview, Jackson, Mo.	6,027	C3 E2	150
Grandview, Cherokee, N.C.	30	B1	186
Grandview, Jefferson, Oreg.		C5	96
Grandview, Rhea, Tenn.	300	C7	190
Grandview, Johnson, Tex.	961	C7	130
Grandview, Yakima, Wash.	3,366	C7	98
Grandview, Bayfield, Wis.	150	B2	160
Grandview Heights, Franklin, Ohio	8,270	C1	156
Grandville, Kent, Mich.	7,975	G6	146
Grand Wash, cliffs, Ariz.		B2	124
Grand Wash, riv., Ariz.		B2	124
Grandy, Isanti, Minn.	175	F5	148
Grandy, Currituck, N.C.	400	A10	186
Grandy, isl., Newf., Can.		D8	72
Grange, Sharp, Ark.	35	B5	170
Grangeburg, Houston, Ala.	200	D4	168
Grangemont, Clearwater, Idaho		C3	108
Grangemouth, Scot.	16,400	E9	272
Granger, St. Joseph, Ind.	125	A3	140
Granger, Dallas, Iowa	468	A7 C4	142
Granger, Scotland, Mo.	146	A6	150
Granger, Williamson, Tex.	1,339	D7	130
Granger, Salt Lake, Utah	1,300	*C4	114
Granger, Yakima, Wash.	1,424	C6	98
Granger, Sweetwater, Wyo.	159	E3	116
Granges, see Grenchen, Switz.			
Grangeville, Idaho, Idaho	3,642	D2	108
Grangeville, Saint Helena, La.	40	D5	180
Grangeville, York, Pa.	1,100	*D5	214
Granite, Chaffee, Colo.	40	C4	106
Granite, Bonner, Idaho		B2	108
Granite, Baltimore, Md.	170	B6	182
Granite, Greer, Okla.	952	D4	128
Granite, Grant, Oreg.	3	*C7	96
Granite, Salt Lake, Utah	100	*C4	114
Granite, co., Mont.	3,014	D3	110
Granite, mtn., Ark.		D7	170
Granite, mts., Ariz.		F2	124
Granite, pass, Wyo.		B5	116
Granite, peak, Mont.		D4	110
Granite, peak, Mont.		E7	110
Granite, peak, Wyo.		D4	116
Granite, pt., Newf., Can.		E7	72
Granite, range, Nev.		C2	112
Granite Canon, Laramie, Wyo.	30	E7	116
Granite City, Madison, Ill.	40,073	E3	138
Granite Falls, Yellow Medicine and Chippewa, Minn.	2,728	G3	148
Granite Falls, Caldwell, N.C.	2,644	B4	186
Granite Falls, Snohomish, Wash.	599	A5	98
Granite Quarry, Rowan, N.C.	1,059	B5	186
Granite Reef, dam, Ariz.		H3	124
Graniteville, Middlesex, Mass.	677	C1	206
Graniteville, Iron, Mo.	300	D7	150
Graniteville, Providence R.I. (part of Johnston)		B2	216
Graniteville, Aiken, S.C.	3,000	D5	188
Graniteville, Washington, Vt.	860	C4	218
Granja, Braz.	3,790	A2	258
Granja de Torrehermosa, Sp.	7,997	C4	298
Granna, Swe.	3,259	C5	292
Grannis, Polk, Ark.	185	C2	170
Grano, Renville, N.Dak.	14	B4	154
Granollers, Sp.	13,960	B8	298
Gran Quivira, Torrance, N.Mex.	20	D4	126
Gran Quivira, natl. mon., N.Mex.		D4	126
Gran Sabana, plat., Ven.		D7	240
Grant, Marshall, Ala.	274	A3	168
Grant, Park, Colo	35	*C5	106
Grant, Brevard, Fla.	100	D10	174
Grant, Jefferson, Idaho		F6	108
Grant, Montgomery, Iowa	180	C3	142
Grant, Boone, Ky.	175	A7	178
Grant, Allen, La.	150	D3	180
Grant, Newaygo, Mich.	732	F6	146
Grant, Beaverhead, Mont.	5	E3	110
Grant, Perkins, Nebr.	1,166	D4	152
Grant, Choctaw, Okla.	286	E8	128
Grant, co., Ark.	8,294	C4	170
Grant, co., Ind.	75,741	B4	140
Grant, co., Kans.	5,269	E2	144
Grant, co., Ky.	9,489	B6	178
Grant, co., Minn.	8,870	F2	148
Grant, co., Nebr.	1,009	C4	152
Grant, co., N.Mex.	18,700	F2	126
Grant, co., N.Dak.	6,248	D4	154
Grant, co., Okla.	8,140	B6	128
Grant, co., Oreg.	7,726	C7	96
Grant, co., S.Dak.	9,913	B9	158
Grant, co., Wash.	46,477	B7	98
Grant, co., W.Va.	8,304	B5	194
Grant, co., Wis.	44,419	F3	160
Grant, par., La.	13,330	C3	180
Grant City, Worth, Mo.	1,061	A3	150
Grantham, Eng.	23,700	I12	273
Grantham, Sullivan, N.H.	170 (332▲)	E2	208
Granton, Ont., Can.	315	Q19	64
Granton, Clark, Wis.	278	D3	160
Grant Orchards, Grant, Wash.		B7	98
Grant Park, Kankakee, Ill.	757	B6	138
Grants, Valencia, N.Mex.	10,274	C3	126
Grantsburg, Crawford, Ind.	85	D3	140
Grantsburg, Burnett, Wis.	900	C1	160
Grantsdale, Ravalli, Mont.	150	D2	110
Grants Lick, Campbell, Ky.	50	A8	178
Grants Mills, Providence, R.I.	60	A3	216
Grants Pass, Josephine, Oreg.	10,118	E3	96
Grantsville, Garrett, Md.	446	A1	182
Grantsville, Tooele, Utah	2,166	C3	114
Grantsville, Calhoun, W.Va.	866	C3	194
Grant Town, Marion, W.Va.	1,105	A7 B4	194
Grantville, Coweta, Ga.	1,158	C2	176
Grantville, Jefferson, Kans.	120	*C8	144
Grantwood, St. Louis, Mo.	676	*C7	150
Granum, Alta., Can.	322	F6	54
Granville, Fr.	10,368	C3	278
Granville, Putnam, Ill.	1,048	B4	138
Granville, Sioux, Iowa	381	B2	142
Granville, Hampden, Mass.	250 (874▲)	B2	206
Granville, Washington, N.Y.	2,715	B8	212
Granville, McHenry, N.Dak.	400	B5	154
Granville, Licking, Ohio	2,868	B4	156
Granville, Jackson, Tenn.	150	B6	190
Granville, Addison, Vt.	110 (215▲)	D3	218
Granville, Milwaukee, Wis. (part of Brown Deer)		E1	160
Granville, see Mona, W.Va.			
Granville, co., N.C.	33,110	A7	186
Granville, lake, Man., Can.		B2 E5	60
Granville Ferry, N.S., Can.	365	E4	70
Grão Mogal, Braz.	929	D2	258
Grapeland, Houston, Tex.	1,113	D8	130
Grapeview, Mason, Wash.	200	B4	98
Grapeville, Westmoreland, Pa.	1,600	*C2	214
Grapevine, Tarrant, Tex.	2,821	B8 C7	130
Grapevine, res., Tex.		A8	130
Gras, lake, N.W.Ter., Can.		E7	48
Grasmere, Owyhee, Idaho	5	G3	108
Grasmere, Hillsboro, N.H.	400	E3	208
Gräsö, Swe.		A9	292
Grasonville, Queen Annes, Md.	925	C7	182
Grass, isl., Fla.		B7	174
Grass, riv., Man., Can.		C3	60
Grass, riv., N.Y.		A6	212
Grasscreek, Fulton, Ind.	125	B3	140
Grass Creek, Hot Springs, Wyo.	60	C4	116
Grasse, Fr.	14,667	F7	278
Grasselli, Jefferson, Ala.	25	E4	168
Grassflat, Clearfield, Pa.	845	C3	214
Grassington, Eng.		G11	273
Grass Lake, Jackson, Mich.	1,037	G7	146
Grassrange, Fergus, Mont.	222	C8	110
Grasston, Kanabec, Minn.	146	F5	148
Grass Valley, Nevada, Calif.	4,876	C3	94
Grass Valley, Sherman, Oreg.	234	B6	96
Grassy, knob, Mo.		D8	150
Grassy, Butte, McKenzie, N.Dak.	80	C2	154
Grassy, bay, Bermuda		A12	233
Grassy, lake, La.		C5	180
Grassy Cove, Cumberland, Tenn.		C7	190
Grassy Creek, Ashe, N.C.	25	A4	186
Grassy Lake, Alta., Can.	282	F7	54
Grates, pt., Newf., Can.		F9	72
Grates Cove, Newf., Can.	450	F9	72
Gratiot, Lafayette, Wis.	294	F3	160
Gratiot, co., Mich.	37,012	F7	146
Gratis, Preble, Ohio	586	C2	156
Graton, Sonoma, Calif.	1,055	*C2	94
Gratz, Owen, Ky.	125	B6	178
Graubünden (Grisons), canton, Switz.	142,600	B5	312
Graulhet, Fr.	6,671	F4	278
Gravarne, Swe.		C2	292
Gravatá, Braz.	10,816	B3	258
Grave, creek, W.Va.		B2	194
Grave, peak, Idaho		C4	108
Gravelbourg, Sask., Can.	1,434	F4	58
Gravelly, Yell, Ark.	300	C3	170
Gravelly, brook, Del.		F3	172
Gravelridge, Bradley, Ark.		D4	170
Gravelton, Kosciusko, Ind.	80	A4	140
Gravenhurst, Ont., Can.	3,014	P21	64
Graves, Terrell, Ga.	150	E2	176
Graves, Georgetown, S.C.	60	E10	188
Graves, co., Ky.	30,021	D2	178

Gravesend, Eng. 47,700 J13 273
Gravesville, Calumet, Wis. 200 B6 160
Gravette, Benton, Ark. 855 A2 170
Gravina [in Puglia], It. 32,300 E6 302
Gravity, Taylor, Iowa 275 D3 142
Gravleeton, Walker, Ala. 200 *B2 168
Gravois, pt., Hai. D7 232
Grawn, Grand Traverse, Mich. 150 E6 146
Gray, Sask., Can. 78 E5 58
Gray, Fr. 6,632 D6 278
Gray, Jones, Ga. 1,320 C3 176
Gray, Bonneville, Idaho 10 F7 108
Gray, Audubon, Iowa 152 C3 142
Gray, Knox, Ky. 800 D6 178
Gray, Terrebonne, La. 400 C6 180
Gray, Cumberland, Maine 400 E2 204
(2,184▲) E5
Gray, Beaver, Okla. 10 B3 128
Gray, Sussex, Va. 40 D7 192
Gray, co., Kans. 4,380 E3 144
Gray, co., Tex. 31,535 B5 130
Gray Court, Laurens, S.C. 473 B4 188
Graydon, Fayette, W.Va. 200 D7 194
Gray Gables, Barnstable, Mass. 500 *C6 206
Gray Horse, Osage, Okla. 200 B7 128
Grayland, Grays Harbor, Wash. 550 C2 98
Grayling, Crawford, Mich. 2,015 E7 146
Grayling, Gallatin, Mont. 10 F5 110
Graymoor, Jefferson, Ky. 535 *B5 178
Grayridge, Stoddard, Mo. 300 E8 150
Grays, Jasper, S.C. 100 F6 188
Grays, hbr., Wash. C2 98
Grays, lake, Idaho F7 108
Grays, peak, Colo. C5 106
Grays Branch, Greenup, Ky. 102 B8 178
Grays Chapel, Jackson, Ala. 100 A3 168
Grays Harbor, co., Wash. 54,465 B2 98
Grayslake, Lake, Ill. 3,762 A5 138
E2
Grayson, Winston, Ala. 510 A2 168
Grayson, Sask., Can. 355 E6 58
Grayson, Gwinnett, Ga. 282 A6 176
C3
Grayson, Carter, Ky. 1,692 B8 178
Grayson, Caldwell, La. 428 B3 180
Grayson, Okmulgee, Okla. 100 *C8 128
Grayson, co., Ky. 15,834 C4 178
Grayson, co., Tex. 73,043 C7 130
Grayson, co., Va. 17,390 D3 192
Grays River, Wahkiakum, Wash. 100 C3 98
Gray Summit, Franklin, Mo. 200 B7 150
Graysville, Jefferson, Ala. 2,870 E4 168
Graysville, Catoosa, Ga. 138 *B1 176
Graysville, Rhea, Tenn. 838 C6 190
Grayton, Charles, Md. 320 D5 182
Grayville, White, Ill. 2,280 E3 138
Graz, Aus. 226,453 C7 313
Graznyy, Sov.Un. D3 336
Gready Harbour, Newf., Can. D7 72
E10
Great, basin, U.S. D3 77
Great, bay, N.H. E5 208
Great, bay, N.J. D4 210
Great, chan., India G6 366
Great, falls, Tenn. C6 190
Great, isl., Mass. C7 206
Great, isl., N.C. B9 186
Great, lake, Austl. G9 432
Great, pt., Mass. D7 206
Great, pond, Maine D3 204
Great, pond, Mass. D3 206
Great, sound, Bermuda A12 233
Great, val., Pa., Va. D4 214
D3 192
Great Arber, mtn., Ger. D5 286
Great Artesian, basin, Austl. C8 432
Great Australian, bight, Austl. E5 432
Great Averill, pond, Vt. B5 218
Great Barre, mtn., Conn. C2 202
Great Barrier, isl., N.Z. B5 437
Great Barrier, reef, Austl. B9 432
Great Barrington, Berkshire, Mass. 4,000 B1 206
(6,624▲)
Great Bear, lake, N.W.Ter., Can. D6 48
Great Bend, Barton, Kans. 16,670 D5 144
Great Bend, Richland, N.Dak. 164 D9 154
Great Bitter, lake, Eg., U.A.R. E7 395
Great Bridge, Norfolk, Va. 800 D8 192
Great Burnt, lake, Newf., Can. F8 72
Great Cacapon, Morgan, W.Va. 600 B6 194
Great Combin, mtn., Switz. C3 312
Great Divide, Moffat, Colo. B3 106
Great Divide, basin, Wyo. E4 116
Great Dividing, range, Austl. B8 432
E9
Great Duck, isl., Ont., Can. O18 64
Great East, pond, Maine, N.H. E2 204
D5 208
Great Egg, bay, N.J. E3 210
Great Egg, inlet, N.J. E3 210
Great Egg Harbor, riv., N.J. D3 210
Greater Antilles, is., N.A. B4 236
Greater Khingan, mts., China C10 348
Greaterville, Pima, Ariz. 30 G5 124
Great Exuma, isl., W.I. A7 232
Great Falls, Man., Can. 150 E4 60
Great Falls, Cascade, Mont. 55,357 C5 110
Great Falls, Chester, S.C. 3,030 B7 188
Great Guana, isl., W.I. A6 232
Great Inagua, isl., W.I. B8 232
Great Karroo, plat., U.S.Afr. F4 420
Great Meadows, Warren, N.J. 250 B3 210
Great Mercury, isl., N.Z. B5 436
Great Mills, St. Marys, Md. 200 D6 182
Great Misery, isl., Mass. C4 206
Great Natuna, isl., Indon. D3 358
Great Neck, Nassau, N.Y. 10,171 D2 212
Great Neck Estates, Nassau, N.Y. 3,262 *D3 212
Great Neck Plaza, Nassau, N.Y. 4,948 *D2 212
Great Nicobar, isl., India G6 366
Great Paternoster, is., Indon. F5 358
Great Pond, Hancock, Maine 37 D4 204
Great St. Bernard, pass, It. C1 302
Great Salt, lake, Utah B3 114
Great Salt, pond, R.I. E2 216
Great Salt Lake, des., Utah C2 114
Great Salt Plains, res., Okla. B5 128
Great Sand, hills, Sask., Can. E3 58
Great Sand Dunes, natl. mon., Colo. E5 106
Great Sand Sea, reg., Eg., U.A.R. B2 395
Great Sandy, desert, Austl. C4 432
Great Sea, reef, Fiji E6 436
Great Seneca, creek, Md. B5 182
Great Slave, lake, N.W.Ter., Can. E7 48
Great Smoky, mts., N.C., Tenn. B2 186
C8 190
Great Smoky Mts., natl. park., N.C., Tenn. B2 186
C8 190
Great South, bay, N.Y. E4 212
Great Stone Face (Old Man of the Mountain), mtn., N.H. C3 208
Great Victoria, des., Austl. D5 432
Great Village, N.S., Can. 670 D6 70
Great Wall, wall, China D8 346
Great Wass, isl., Maine D5 204
Great Whale, riv., Que., Can. Q9 66
Great Yarmouth, Eng. 51,500 I14 273
Great Zab, riv., Iraq A5 378
Grebbestad, Swe. C2 292
Greco, cape, Cyp. D6 307
Gredos, mts., Sp. B4 298
Greece, country, Eur. 8,216,000 D7 266
306
Greeley, Weld, Colo. 26,314 B6 106
Greeley, Delaware, Iowa 367 B6 142
Greeley, Anderson, Kans. 415 D8 144
Greeley, Reynolds, Mo. 175 D6 150
Greeley, Greeley, Nebr. 656 C7 152
Greeley, co., Kans. 2,087 D2 144
Greeley, co., Nebr. 4,595 C7 152
Greeleyville, Williamsburg, S.C. 504 D9 188
Green, Clay, Kans. 190 C7 144
Green, Ontonagon, Mich. C2 146
Green, co., Ky. 11,249 C5 178
Green, co., Wis. 25,851 F4 160
Green, bay, Wis. D6 160
Green, is., Solomon D1 436
Green, lake, B.C., Can. E12 52
Green, lake, Sask., Can. C4 58
Green, lake, Maine D4 204
Green, lake, Minn. F4 148
Green, lake, Wis. E5 160
Green, mts., Vt. F2 218
Green, mts., Wyo. D5 116
Green, pond, N.J. A4 210
Green, riv., N.B., Can. B1 70
Green, riv., Ill. B4 138
Green, riv., Ky. C3 178
Green, riv., U.S. D5 77
Green, riv., Vt. F3 218
Green, riv., Wash. D3 98
Green, swamp, N.C. C7 186
Green, valley, Tex. E4 130
Green Acres, Nassau, N.Y. 2,500 *E8 212
Greenacres, Spokane, Wash. 2,074 B9 98
D9
Greenacres City, Palm Beach, Fla. 1,026 E10 174
Greenback, Loudon, Tenn. 285 C7 190
E9
Greenbackville, Accomack, Va. 300 B9 192
Green Bank, Burlington, N.J. 100 D3 210
Green Bank, Pocahontas, W.Va. 100 C5 194
Green Bay, Prince Edward, Va. 100 C6 192
Green Bay, Brown, Wis. 62,888 A6 160
(*105,300) D6
Greenbelt, Prince Georges, Md. 7,479 B6 182
Green Bottom, Cabell, W.Va. C2 194
Greenbrier, Limestone, Ala. 150 A3 168
Greenbrier, Faulkner, Ark. 401 B4 170
Greenbrier, Fairfield, S.C. 300 *C6 188
Green Brier, Robertson, Tenn. 1,238 B5 190
Greenbrier, co., W.Va. 34,446 D4 194
Greenbrier, riv., W.Va. D4 194
Green Brook, Somerset, N.J. 3,622 *B4 210
Greenbush, Penobscot, Maine 50 *C4 204
(565▲)
Greenbush, Plymouth, Mass. 250 D4 206
Greenbush, Alcona, Mich. 70 E8 146
Greenbush, Roseau, Minn. 706 C2 148
Greenbush, Sheboygan, Wis. 150 B6 160
Green Camp, Marion, Ohio 492 B3 156
Greencastle, Putnam, Ind. 8,506 C3 140
Green Castle, Sullivan, Mo. 250 A5 150
Greencastle, Franklin, Pa. 2,988 D4 214
Green City, Sullivan, Mo. 628 A5 150
Green Court, Alta., Can. 50 C5 54
Green Cove, Washington, Va. 200 D3 192
Green Cove Springs, Clay, Fla. 4,233 B9 174
B10
Greencreek, Idaho, Idaho 50 *C2 108
Green Creek, Cape May, N.J. 350 E3 210
Greendale, Dearborn, Ind. 2,861 C5 140
Greendale, St. Louis, Mo. 1,107 *C7 150
Greendale, Milwaukee, Wis. 6,843 E2 160
F6
Greendell, Sussex, N.J. 100 B3 210
Greene, Butler, Iowa 1,427 B5 142
Greene, Androscoggin, Maine 100 D2 204
(1,226▲)
Greene, Chenango, N.Y. 2,051 C6 212
Greene, Kent, R.I. 100 C2 216
Greene, co., Ala. 13,600 C1 168
Greene, co., Ark. 25,198 A6 170
Greene, co., Ga. 11,192 C3 176
Greene, co., Ill. 17,460 D3 138
Greene, co., Ind. 26,327 C3 140
Greene, co., Iowa 14,379 B3 142
Greene, co., Miss. 8,366 D4 184
Greene, co., Mo. 126,276 D4 150
Greene, co., N.Y. 31,372 C7 212
Greene, co., N.C. 16,741 B8 186
Greene, co., Ohio 94,642 C3 156
Greene, co., Pa. 39,424 D1 214
Greene, co., Tenn. 42,163 B9 190
Greene, co., Va. 4,715 B6 192
Greeneville, Greene, Tenn. 11,759 B9 190
Greenfield, Monterey, Calif. 1,207 D3 94
Greenfield, Greene, Ill. 1,064 D3 138
Greenfield, Hancock, Ind. 9,049 C4 140
Greenfield, Adair, Iowa 2,243 C3 142
Greenfield, Penobscot, Maine 50 C4 204
(100▲)
Greenfield, Franklin, Mass. 17,690 A2 206
Greenfield, Hennepin, Minn. 639 *F5 148
Greenfield, Dade, Mo. 1,172 D4 150
Greenfield, Hillsboro, N.H. 200 F3 208
(538▲)
Greenfield, Chaves, N.Mex. 100 E6 126
Greenfield, Highland, Ohio 5,422 C3 156
Greenfield, Blaine, Okla. 128 C5 128
Greenfield, Weakley, Tenn. 1,779 B3 190
Greenfield, Nelson, Va. 40 C6 192
Greenfield, Milwaukee, Wis. 17,636 *F5 160
Greenfield Park, Que., Can. 4,417 S16 66
Green Forest, Carroll, Ark. 1,038 A3 170
Green Garden, Marquette, Mich. C4 146
Green Harbor, Plymouth, Mass. 400 *B6 206
Green Haven, Anne Arundel, Md. 1,302 *B6 182
Greenhill, Lauderdale, Ala. 150 A2 168
Greenhill, Warren, Ind. 200 B2 140
Greenhills, Hamilton, Ohio 5,407 D1 156
Green Hills, Maury, Tenn. 14,000 *C4 190
Greenhorn, mtn., Colo. E5 106
Green Island, Jackson, Iowa 97 B7 142
Green Island, Albany, N.Y. 4,016 *C8 212
Green Isle, Sibley, Minn. 331 G5 148
Green Lake, Sask., Can. 50 C4 58
Green Lake, Hancock, Maine 60 D4 204
Green Lake, Green Lake, Wis. 953 E5 160
Green Lake, co., Wis. 15,418 E4 160
Greenland, Washington, Ark. 127 B2 170
Greenland, Douglas, Colo. 5 C6 106
Greenland, Ontonagon, Mich. 360 C2 146
Greenland, Rockingham, N.H. 375 E5 208
(1,196▲)
Greenland, Dan. poss., N.A. 24,118 P28 290
Greenland, sea, Arc.O. K19 290
Greenlawn, Suffolk, N.Y. 5,422 *D3 212
Greenleaf, Canyon, Idaho 200 F2 108
Greenleaf, Washington, Kans. 562 C7 144
Greenleaf, Wayne, N.C. (part of Goldsboro) B8 186
Greenleaf, Brown, Wis. 250 A6 160
D5
Greenlee, co., Ariz. 11,509 E6 124
Green Lowther, mtn., Scot. F9 272
Greenmanorville, Hartford, Conn. 1,200 *B5 202
Green Meadows, Prince Georges, Md. 1,500 C3 182
Green Mountain, Marshall, Iowa 200 B5 142
Greenmountain, Yancey, N.C. 250 B3 186
Green Mountain, res., Colo. C4 106
Green Mountain Falls, El Paso and Teller, Colo. 179 D5 106
Greenmount, Carroll, Md. 150 A6 182
Greenock, Allegheny, Pa. 1,500 C2 214
Greenock, Scot. 77,700 F8 272
Greenough, Missoula, Mont. 35 D3 110
Greenough, pt., Ont., Can. P19 64
Green Pond, Bibb, Ala. 500 *B2 168
Green Pond, Colleton, S.C. 285 F7 188
Green Pond, mtn., N.J. B3 210
Greenport, Suffolk, N.Y. 2,608 D5 212
Green Ridge, Pettis, Mo. 375 C4 150
Green Ridge, Delaware, Pa. 3,500 *D6 214
Green River, Emery, Utah 1,075 E5 114
Green River, Windham, Vt. 60 F3 218
Green River, Sweetwater, Wyo. 3,497 E3 116
Green Rock, Henry, Ill. 2,677 *B3 138
Greens, peak, Ariz. D6 124
Greensboro, Hale, Ala. 3,081 C2 168
Greensboro, Gadsden, Fla. 709 A6 174
Greensboro, Greene, Ga. 2,773 C3 176
Greensboro, Henry, Ind. 232 C4 140
Greensboro, Caroline, Md. 1,160 C8 182
Greensboro, Guilford, N.C. 119,574 A6 186
(*156,800)
Greensboro, Orleans, Vt. 115 B4 218
(600▲)
Greensboro Bend, Orleans, Vt. 100 B4 218
Greensburg, Decatur, Ind. 6,605 C4 140
Greensburg, Kiowa, Kans. 1,988 E4 144
Greensburg, Green, Ky. 2,334 C5 178
Greensburg, St. Helena, La. 512 D5 180
Greensburg, Westmoreland, Pa. 17,383 C2 214
Greens Creek, Jackson, N.C. B2 186
Greens Fork, Wayne, Ind. 474 C4 140
Green Sea, Horry, S.C. 100 C11 188
Greenspond, Newf., Can. 784 F9 72
Green Spring, New Castle, Del. C3 172
Green Spring, Hampshire, W.Va. 120 B6 194
Green Springs, Seneca and Sandusky, Ohio 1,262 A3 156
Greenstone, pt., Scot. D7 272
Green Sulphur Springs, Summers, W.Va. 300 D4 194
Greensville, co., Va. 16,155 D7 192
Greentop, Schuyler, Mo. 311 A5 150
Greentown, Howard, Ind. 1,266 B4 140
Green Tree (Ruidoso Downs), Lincoln, N.Mex. 407 E5 126
Green Tree, Allegheny, Pa. 5,226 *C1 214
Greenup, Cumberland, Ill. 1,477 D5 138
Greenup, Greenup, Ky. 1,240 B8 178
Greenup, co., Ky. 29,238 B7 178
Greenvale, Nassau, N.Y. 1,650 *E8 212
Green Valley, Tazewell, Ill. 552 C4 138
Green Valley, Lyon, Minn. 130 G3 148
Green Valley, Shawano, Wis. 100 D5 160
Greenview, Menard, Ill. 796 C4 138
Greenview, Boone, W.Va. 400 D5 194
Greenville, Butler, Ala. 6,894 D3 168
Greenville, Plumas, Calif. 1,140 B3 94
Greenville, New Castle, Del. A3 172
Greenville, Madison, Fla. 1,318 A7 174
Greenville, Meriwether, Ga. 726 C2 176
Greenville, Bond, Ill. 4,569 E4 138
Greenville, Floyd, Ind. 453 D4 140
Greenville, Clay, Iowa 173 A2 142
Greenville, Muhlenberg, Ky. 3,198 C3 178
Greenville, Lib. F3 408
Greenville, Piscataquis, Maine 1,400 C3 204
(2,025▲)
Greenville, Montcalm, Mich. 7,440 F6 146
Greenville, Washington, Miss. 41,502 B1 184
Greenville, Wayne, Mo. 282 D7 150
Greenville, Hillsboro, N.H. 1,251 F3 208
Greenville, Greene, N.Y. 2,800 C7 212
Greenville, Pitt, N.C. 22,860 B8 186
Greenville, Darke, Ohio 10,585 B2 156
Greenville, Mercer, Pa. 8,765 B1 214
Greenville, Providence, R.I. 3,000 B2 216
Greenville, Greenville, S.C. 66,188 B4 188
(*164,500)
Greenville, Hunt, Tex. 19,087 C7 130
Greenville, Beaver, Utah 10 E3 114
Greenville, Augusta, Va. 400 B5 192
Greenville, Monroe, W.Va. 975 D4 194
Greenville, Outagamie, Wis. 200 A5 160
Greenville, co., S.C. 209,776 B4 188
Greenville, chan., B.C., Can. D8 52
Greenville, creek, Ohio B2 156
Greenville Junction, Piscataquis, Maine 500 C3 204
Greenville North, Washington, Miss. 2,516 *B1 184
Greenwald, Stearns, Minn. 266 F4 148
Green Water Lake, prov. park, Sask., Can. D6 58
Greenway, Clay, Ark. 179 A6 170
Greenway, Man., Can. 130 F3 60
Greenway, McPherson, S.Dak. 101 B6 158
Greenwell Springs, East Baton Rouge, La. 75 D5 180
Greenwich, Fairfield, Conn. 53,793 E1 202
Greenwich, Sedgwick, Kans. 55 A6 144
Greenwich, Cumberland, N.J. 450 E2 210
Greenwich, Washington, N.Y. 2,263 B8 212
Greenwich, Huron, Ohio 1,371 A4 156
Greenwich, Prince William, Va. 100 A6 192
Greenwich, bay, R.I. C3 216
Greenwich, pt., Conn. E1 202
Greenwich Heights, Sedgwick, Kans. 350 *E6 144
Greenwood, Jefferson, Ala. 535 E4 168
Greenwood, Sebastian, Ark. 1,558 B2 170
Greenwood, B.C., Can. 815 F13 52
Greenwood, Sussex, Del. 768 E3 172
Greenwood, Jackson, Fla. 354 A5 174
Greenwood, Johnson, Ind. 7,169 C3 140
E5
Greenwood, McCreary, Ky. 200 D6 178
Greenwood, Caddo, La. 500 B2 180
Greenwood, Terrebonne, La. C5 180
Greenwood, Oxford, Maine 75 D2 204
(601▲)
Greenwood, Hennepin, Minn. 520 *F5 148
Greenwood, Leflore, Miss. 20,436 B2 184
Greenwood, Jackson, Mo. 488 C3 150
E2
Greenwood, Cass, Nebr. 403 D9 152
E2
Greenwood, Steuben, N.Y. 600 C4 212
Greenwood, Blair, Pa. 1,500 C3 214
Greenwood, Kent, R.I. (part of Warwick) C3 216
Greenwood, Greenwood, S.C. 16,644 C4 188
Greenwood, Charles Mix, S.Dak. 120 E7 158
Greenwood, Clark, Wis. 1,041 D3 160
Greenwood, co., Kans. 11,253 E7 144
Greenwood, co., S.C. 44,346 C4 188
Greenwood, lake, Minn. D7 148
Greenwood, lake, N.J. A4 210
Greenwood, lake, S.C. C5 188
Greenwood Mountain, Oxford, Maine 200 D2 204
Greenwood Village, Arapahoe, Colo. 572 *C6 106
Greer, Apache, Ariz. 30 D6 124
Greer, Clearwater, Idaho 70 C2 108
Greer, Greenville, S.C. 8,967 B4 188
Greer, co., Okla. 8,877 D4 128
Greeson, lake, Ark. C3 170
Gregg, Man., Can. 30 F3 60
Gregg, co., Tex. 69,436 C8 130
Greggton, Gregg, Tex. (part of Longview) C8 130
Gregory, Woodruff, Ark. 200 B5 170
Gregory, Livingston, Mich. 300 G7 146
Gregory, Gregory, S.Dak. 1,478 D6 158
Gregory, San Patricio, Tex. 1,970 *E7 130
Gregory, co., S.Dak. 7,399 D6 158
Gregory, lake, Austl. D7 432
Gregory, range, Austl. B8 432
Gregory, riv., Austl. B7 432
Greifswald, Ger. 45,800 A5 286
Grein, Aus. 2,519 B6 313
Greiz, Ger. 40,800 C5 286
Greinwich Terrace, Calcasieu, La. 2,000 *D2 180
Grenaa, Den. 8,535 E1 292
Grenada, Siskiyou, Calif. 300 B2 94
Grenada, Grenada, Miss. 7,914 B3 184
Grenada, co., Miss. 18,409 B3 184
Grenada, ter., W.I.Fed. 86,000 E14 233
Grenada, res., Miss. B3 184
Grenadines, is., W.I. E14 233
Grenagh, Ire. I4 273
Grenchen, Switz. 14,200 A3 312
Grenfell, Sask., Can. 1,080 E6 58
Grenloch, Gloucester, N.J. 975 D2 210
Grenoble, Fr. 116,440 E6 278
Grenola, Elk, Kans. 349 E7 144
Grenora, Williams, N.Dak. 448 B2 154
Grenville, Que., Can. 1,277 S10 66
Grenville, Union, N.Mex. 55 B7 126
Grenville, Day, S.Dak. 151 B8 158
Grenville, co., Ont., Can. 20,563 P25 64
Grenville, cape, Austl. A8 432
Grenville, pt., Wash. B2 98
Gresham, York, Nebr. 239 C8 152
Gresham, Multnomah, Oreg. 3,944 B2 96
B4
Gresham, Marion, S.C. 200 D10 188
Gresham, Shawano, Wis. 458 D5 158
Greshamville, Greene, Ga. 180 C3 176
Gressitt, King and Queen, Va. 300 C8 192

Gretna, Man., Can. 603 F4 60
Gretna, Gadsden, Fla. 647 A6 174
Gretna, Jefferson, La. 21,967 C7 180
E5
Gretna, Sarpy, Nebr. 745 C9 152
E2
Gretna, Pittsylvania, Va. 900 D5 192
Grevená, Grc. 5,191 A3 306
Grey, co., Ont., Can. 60,971 P20 64
Grey, is., Newf., Can. E8 72
Grey, range, Austl. D8 432
Grey, riv., N.Z. E3 437
Greybull, Big Horn, Wyo. 2,286 B4 116
Greybull, riv., Wyo. B4 116
Greycliff, Sweet Grass, Mont. 85 E7 110
Grey Eagle, Todd, Minn. 372 F4 148
Grey Islands Harbour, Newf., Can. E8 72
Greylock, mtn., Mass. A1 206
Greymouth, N.Z. 9,948 E3 436
Greys, riv., Wyo. C2 116
Greystone, Moffat, Colo. 2 *B2 106
Greystone, Litchfield, Conn. 100 C3 202
Greytown, N.Z. 1,429 D5 437
Greytown, U.S.Afr. E6 420
Gribbell, isl., B.C., Can. D8 52
Gridley, Butte, Calif. 3,343 C3 94
Gridley, McLean, Ill. 889 C5 138
Gridley, Coffey, Kans. 321 D8 144
Grieskirchen, Aus. 4,030 B5 313
Griffin, Union, Ark. 20 D4 170
Griffin, Sask., Can. 125 F6 58
Griffin, Spalding, Ga. 21,735 C2 176
Griffin, Posey, Ind. 212 D2 140
Griffing Park, Jefferson, Tex. 2,267 *E8 130
Griffith, Mohave, Ariz. 20 C1 124
Griffith, Austl. 6,608 E9 432
Griffith, Lake, Ind. 9,483 A2 140
Griffith, Clay, Miss. 100 B4 184
Griffith, isl., Ont., Can. P20 64
Griffithsville, Lincoln, W.Va. 200 C3 194
Griffithville, White, Ark. 172 B5 170
Grifton, Pitt, N.C. 1,816 B8 186
Griggs, Cimarron, Okla. 15 B1 128
Griggs, co., N.Dak. 5,023 C7 154
Griggsville, Pike, Ill. 1,240 D3 138
Grigston, Scott, Kans. 30 *D3 144
Grim, cape, Austl. G8 432
Grimari, Cen.Afr.Rep. E9 409
Grimes, Dale, Ala. 100 D4 168
Grimes, Polk, Iowa 697 A7 142
C4
Grimes, East Carroll, La. B4 180
Grimes, Roger Mills, Okla. 15 C4 128
Grimes, co., Tex. 12,709 D7 130
Grimesland, Pitt, N.C. 362 B8 186
Grimes Mill, Aroostook, Maine 50 B5 204
Grimma, Ger. 16,000 C5 286
Grimms, Manitowoc, Wis. 75 B6 160
Grimms Landing, Mason, W.Va. 350 C3 194
Grimsby, Ont., Can. 3,805 Q21 64
Grimsby, Eng. 95,400 H12 273
Grimsey, isl., Ice. K21 290
Grimshaw, Alta., Can. 904 B4 54
Grimsley, Fentress, Tenn. 600 B7 190
Grimstad, Nor. 2,294 G3 291
Grimsthorpe, Ont., Can. 110 O18 64
Grindavik, Ice. M18 290
Grindelwald, Switz. 3,053 B4 312
Grindsted, Den. 3,659 I3 291
Grindstone, Penobscot, Maine 60 C4 204
Grindstone, Fayette, Pa. 1,094 *D2 214
Grind Stone City, Huron, Mich. E9 146
Grinnell, Poweshiek, Iowa 7,367 C5 142
Grinnell, Gove, Kans. 396 C3 144
Grinter Heights, Wyandotte, Kans. B7 144
Griquatown, U.S.Afr. 2,002 E4 420
Grisdella, Garfield, Mont. C10 110
Gris-Nez, cape, Fr. *B4 278
Griswold, Man., Can. 255 F2 60
Griswold (Town of), New London, Conn. (6,472▲) C8 202
Griswold, Cass, Iowa 1,207 C2 142
Griswoldville, Franklin, Mass. 630 A2 206
Grizzly, Jefferson, Oreg. C6 96
Grizzly, creek, Colo. B4 106
Grizzly, mtn., Oreg. C6 96
Grizzly, mtn., Oreg. E4 96
Grizzly Bear, mtn., N.W.Ter., Can. D6 48
Groais, isl., Newf., Can. E8 72
Grodków, Pol. 2,953 C3 325
Grodno, Sov.Un. 72,000 F4 332
Grodzisk, Pol. 6,015 B3 325
Groenlo, Neth. 4,022 B5 282
Groesbeck, Hamilton, Ohio 9,000 D1 156
Groesbeck, Limestone, Tex. 2,498 D7 130
Groix, isl., Fr. D2 278
Grójec, Pol. 6,841 C5 325
Gronau [in Westfalen], Ger. 24,900 B2 286
Grong, Nor. D5 290
Groningen, Neth. 140,456 A5 282
Groningen, prov., Neth. 465,411 A5 282
Gronknuten, mtn., Nor. A1 292
Gronlid, Sask., Can. 475 D5 58
Groom, Carson, Tex. 679 B5 130
Groom Creek, Yavapai, Ariz. 100 D3 124
Groos, Delta, Mich. D4 146
Groote Eylandt, isl., Austl. A7 432
Grootfontein, S.W.Afr. 1,525 C3 420
Groot Vloer, lake, U.S.Afr. E4 420
Groscap, Mackinac, Mich. D7 146
Gros Morne, mtn., Newf., Can. F7 72
Gros Pate, mtn., Newf., Can. E7 72
Gross, Boyd, Nebr. 17 B7 152
Grossenhain [im Bezirk Dresden], Ger. 8,700 C5 286
Grosse Pointe, Wayne, Mich. 6,631 B9 146
Grosse Pointe Farms, Wayne, Mich. 12,172 B9 146
Grosse Pointe Park, Wayne, Mich. 15,457 B9 146
Grosse Pointe Shores, Wayne, Mich. 2,301 B9 146
Grosse Pointe Woods, Wayne, Mich. 18,580 B9 146
Grosser Priel, mtn., Aus. C6 313
Grosse Tete, Iberville, La. 768 D4 180
Grosseto, It. 26,900 D3 302
Grosseto, prov., It. 219,400 *D3 302
Gross Glockner, mtn., Aus. C4 313
Grosvenor Dale, Windham, Conn. 530 B8 202
Gros Ventre, range, Wyo. C2 116
Gros Ventre, riv., Wyo. C2 116
Groton, New London, Conn. 10,111 D7 202
(29,937▲)
Groton, Middlesex, Mass. 1,178 A4 206
(3,904▲) C1
Groton, Grafton, N.H. 80 D3 208
(99▲)
Groton, Tompkins, N.Y. 2,123 C5 212
Groton, Brown, S.Dak. 1,063 B7 158
Groton, Caledonia, Vt. 387 C4 218
(631▲)
Groton Long Point, New London, Conn. 350 D7 202
Grottaferrata, It. 5,123 *E4 302
Grottaglie, It. 21,100 E6 302
Grottoes, Rockingham and Augusta, Va. 969 B6 192
Grouard, Alta., Can. 347 C4 54
Grouse (Lost River), Custer, Idaho 58 F5 108
Grouse, creek, Kans. E7 144
Grouse, creek, Utah B2 114
Grouse Creek, Box Elder, Utah 49 B2 114
Grouse Creek, mts., Utah B2 114
Grovania, Houston, Ga. 186 D3 176
Grove, Shawnee, Kans. 150 *C8 144
Grove, Washington, Maine 35 D5 204
Grove, Delaware, Okla. 975 B9 128
Grove, York, Va. A8 192
Grove, pt., Md. B7 182
Grove City, Meeker, Minn. 466 F4 148
Grove City, Franklin, Ohio 8,107 C1 156
C3
Grove City, Mercer, Pa. 8,368 B1 214
Grove Hill, Clarke, Ala. 1,834 D2 168
Groveland, Tuolumne, Calif. 350 D3 94
Groveland, Lake, Fla. 1,747 C9 174
Groveland, Bryan, Ga. 100 D5 176
Groveland, Essex, Mass. 1,600 A5 206
(3,297▲)
Groveland, Meagher, Mont. D6 110
Groveland, Livingston, N.Y. 400 C4 212
Groveport, Franklin, Ohio 2,043 C1 156
C4
Grover, Weld, Colo. 133 B6 106
Grover, Cleveland, N.C. 538 B4 186
Grover, Wayne, Utah E4 114
Grover, Lincoln, Wyo. 120 D2 116
Grover City, San Luis Obispo, Calif. 5,210 E3 94
Grover Hill, Paulding, Ohio 547 A2 156
Grovertown, Starke, Ind. 175 A3 140
Groves, Jefferson, Tex. 17,304 E9 130
Grovespring, Wright, Mo. 92 D5 150
Groveton, Coos, N.H. 2,004 B3 208
Groveton, Allegheny, Pa. 1,300 *C1 214
Groveton, Trinity, Tex. 1,148 D8 130
Groveton, Fairfax, Va. 400 A7 192
Grovetown, Columbia, Ga. 1,396 C4 176
Groveville, Mercer, N.J. (part of Hamilton Township) C3 210
Growler, Yuma, Ariz. 20 F2 124
Growmore, Yakima, Wash. C6 98
Grubbs, Jackson, Ark. 360 B5 170
Grudovo, Bul. 3,928 B3 317
Grudziądz, Pol. 56,000 B4 325
Grues, isl., Que., Can. Q14 66
Gruetli, Grundy, Tenn. 400 C6 190
Gruinard, bay, Scot. D7 272
Grulla, Starr, Tex. 1,436 F6 130
Grums, Swe. 5,639 B4 292
Grundy, Buchanan, Va. 2,287 C2 192
Grundy, co., Ill. 22,350 B5 138
Grundy, co., Iowa 14,132 B5 142
Grundy, co., Mo. 12,220 A4 150
Grundy, co., Tenn. 11,512 C6 190
Grundy Center, Grundy, Iowa 2,403 B5 142
Grunthal, Man., Can. 900 F4 60
Gruver, Emmet, Iowa 140 A3 142
Gruver, Hansford, Tex. 1,030 A5 130
Gryazi, Sov.Un. 16,000 F13 332
Gryazovets, Sov.Un. 12,500 C13 332
Grycksbo, Swe. A6 292
Gryfice, Pol. 10,100 B2 325
Gryfino, Pol. 1,347 B2 325
Grygla, Marshall, Minn. 192 C3 148
Gstaad, Switz. B3 312
Gua, India E4 368
Guacanyabo, gulf, Cuba B6 232
Gu Achi, Pima, Ariz. 380 F3 124
Guachochic, Mex. B4 224
Guadalajara, Mex. 377,928 C5 224
K12
Guadalajara, Sp. 18,748 B5 298
Guadalajara, prov., Sp. 208,652 *B5 298
Guadalcanal, Sp. 6,058 C4 298
Guadalcanal, isl., Solomon E2 436
Guadalhorce, riv., Sp. D4 298
Guadalope, riv., Sp. B6 298
Guadalquivir, riv., Sp. D3 298
Guadalupe, Maricopa, Ariz. 646 H2 124
Guadalupe, Santa Barbara, Calif. 2,614 E3 94
Guadalupe, Mex. 1,864 A4 224
Guadalupe, Mex. 6,083 B4 224
Guadalupe, co., N.Mex. 5,610 D6 126
Guadalupe, co., Tex. 29,017 E6 130
Guadalupe, isl., Mex. B2 224
Guadalupe, mts., N.Mex. F5 126
Guadalupe, mts., Sp. C4 298
Guadalupe, peak, Tex. D3 130
Guadalupe, riv., Tex. B7 130
Guadalupita, Mora, N.Mex. 480 B5 126
Guadarrama, mts., Sp. B5 298
Guadeloupe, Fr. poss., N.A. 251,000 E14 232
Guadeloupe, isl., Le.Is. B5 236
Guadeloupe, passage, W.I. D14 233
Guadiana, riv., Port. C3 298
Guadiana, riv., Sp. C4 298
Guadiana Menor, riv., Sp. D5 298
Guadiela, riv., Sp. B5 298
Guadix, Sp. 22,886 D5 298
Guafo, isl., Chile F3 251
Guainía, riv., Col. C3 244
Guairá, dept., Par. 90,308 D4 247
Guajará Mirim, Braz. 2,582 H4 257
Guajira, La, intendencia, Col. 112,190 A2 244
Gualaceo, Ec. 3,166 A2 245
Gualán, Guat. 2,898 C3 228
Gualaquizo, Ec. 261 A2 245
Gualeguay, Arg. 23,517 B4 252
Gualeguaychú, Arg. 37,109 B4 252
Gualicho, salt flat, Arg. E4 251
Gualicho, salt flat, Arg. D2 252
Guam, U.S. poss., Pac.O. 59,498 C3 436
Guam, isl., Pac.O. D7 436
Guama, riv., Braz. F7 256
Guaminí, Arg. 2,273 C3 252
Guamote, Ec. 2,567 A2 245
Guamúchil, Mex. 5,865 B4 224
Guanabacoa, Cuba 32,490 A3 232
Guanabara, state, Braz. 2,852,000 *J8 257
Guanacaste, mts., C.R. E5 228
Guanahacabibes, gulf, Cuba A2 232
Guanajay, Cuba 12,908 A3 232
Guanajuato, Mex. 23,389 C5 225
K13
Guanajuato, state, Mex. 1,328,712 C5 225
Guanambi, Braz. 2,077 C2 258
Guanare, Ven. 13,000 B4 240
Guandacol, Arg. A2 252
Guane, Cuba 2,248 A2 232
Guanillos del Norte, Chile B3 250
Guano, lake, Oreg. E7 96
Guantánamo, Cuba 64,671 B7 232
Guapí, Col. 1,882 C1 244
Guaporé, riv., Bol. B2 246
Guaporé, riv., Braz. H4 257
Guaporé, ter., Braz. 52,000 H4 257
Guaqui, Bol. 2,266 C1 246
Guará, Braz. 2,570 E1 258
Guara, mts., Sp. A6 298
Guarabira, Braz. 9,425 B3 258
Guaranda, Ec. 7,299 A2 245
Guarapuava, Braz. 5,489 K6 257
Guaratinguetá, Braz. 20,811 E1 258
Guarda, Port. 7,704 B3 298
Guardafui, cape, Som. C7 398
Guardatinajas, Ven. B5 240
Guareña, Sp. 8,556 C3 298
Guárico, state, Ven. 164,523 B5 240
Guárico, riv., Ven. B5 240
Guasave, Mex. 8,505 B4 224
Guasdualito, Ven. 3,211 C3 240
Guasipati, Ven. 2,859 C8 240
Guastalla, It. 6,416 C3 302
Guasti, San Bernardino, Calif. 500 C6 94
Guasuba, riv., India J9 366
Guata, Hond. 873 C4 228
Guatemala, Guat. 284,922 C2 228
Guatemala, country, N.A. 3,546,000 C2 228
Guateque, Col. 2,408 C2 244
Guatimozin, Arg. B3 252
Guatisimiña, Ven. D7 240
Guaviare, riv., Col. C2 244
Guaxupé, Braz. 9,227 E1 258
Guayabal, Cuba 5,889 B6 232
Guayabero, riv., Col. C2 244
Guayama, P.R. 19,408 D11 233
Guayaquil, Ec. 290,000 A2 245
Guayaquil, gulf, Ec. A1 245
Guaymas, Mex. 18,813 B3 224
Guazacapán, Guat. 3,366 C2 228
Gubakha, Sov.Un. 53,800 A5 336
Gubbio, It. 8,600 D4 302
Guben, Ger. 24,000 C6 286
Gubin, Pol. 3,040 C2 325
Gúdar, mts., Sp. B6 298
Gudermes, Sov.Un. D3 336
Gudhjem, Den. F5 292
Gudinge, isl., Swe. D7 292
Gudur, India 20,056 F3 366
Guebwiller, Fr. 10,414 D7 278
Guecho, Sp. 7,852 A5 298
Guékédou, Guinea E2 408
Guelma, Alg. 17,225 A5 402
(21,587▲)
Guelph, Ont., Can. 33,860 Q20 64
Guelph, Dickey, N.Dak. 300 D7 154
Güemes, Arg. 5,688 B5 250
Guéret, Fr. 10,131 D4 278
Guerette, Aroostook, Maine 160 A4 204
Guernica [y Luno], Sp. 3,381 A5 298
Guernsey, Sask., Can. 94 E5 58
Guernsey, Poweshiek, Iowa 108 C5 142
Guernsey, Platte, Wyo. 800 D8 116
Guernsey, co., Ohio 38,579 B5 156
Guernsey, Br.poss., Eur. 45,496 L10 273
Guerrara, Alg. B4 402
Guerrero, state, Mex. 919,386 D5 225
Gueugnon, Fr. 5,702 D6 278
Gueydan, Vermilion, La. 2,156 D3 180
Guffey, Park, Colo. 15 D5 106
Guffie, McLean, Ky. 75 C3 178
Gugē, mtn., Eth. D4 398
Guh Kuh, mtn., Iran D5 379
Guiana, highlands, Braz. E4 256
Guider, Cam. E7 409
Guide Rock, Webster, Nebr. 441 D7 152
Guidonia, It. 3,545 E4 302
Guiglo, I.C. E3 408
Guild, Sullivan, N.H. 250 E2 208
Guild, Marion, Tenn. 400 C6 190
Guildford, Eng. 50,600 J12 273
Guildhall, Essex, Vt. 100 B5 218
(248▲)
Guilford, New Haven, Conn. 2,420 D5 202
(7,913▲)
Guilford, Dearborn, Ind. 250 C5 140
Guilford, Piscataquis, Maine 1,372 C3 204
(1,880▲)
Guilford, Howard, Md. 175 B6 182
Guilford, Nodaway, Mo. 125 A3 150
Guilford, Chenango, N.Y. 420 C6 212
Guilford, Windham, Vt. 100 F3 218
(823▲)
Guilford, co., N.C. 246,520 A6 186
Guilford College, Guilford, N.C. 1,700 A6 186
Guimarães, Port. 18,294 B2 298
Guin, Marion, Ala. 1,462 B2 168
Guinea, Caroline, Va. 75 B7 192
Guinea, country, Afr. 2,800,000 E5 388
409
Guinea, gulf, Afr. F5 408
Güines, Cuba 29,226 A3 232
Guingamp, Fr. 8,117 C2 278
Guion, Izard, Ark. 222 B5 170
Guipúzcoa, prov., Sp. 371,024 *A4 298
Güira de Melena, Cuba 13,715 A3 232
Güiria, Ven. 7,367 A7 240
Guisborough, Eng. 9,500 G11 273
Guise, Fr. 6,091 C5 278
Guists, creek, Ky. B5 178
Guitiriz, Sp. 1,006 A3 298
Gujan [-et-Mestras], Fr. E3 278
Gujranwala, Pak. 120,860 C9 375
Gujrat, Pak. 46,986 C9 375
Gu Komelik, Pinal, Ariz. 83 F4 124
Gulbarga, India 77,189 E3 366
Gulde, Rankin, Miss. 150 C3 184
Gulen, Nor. F1 291
Gulf, co., Fla. 9,937 B5 174
Gulf, creek, Okla. B2 128
Gulf Breeze, Santa Rosa, Fla. 150 A3 174
Gulf Coastal, plain, Ark. D3 170
Gulf Crest, Mobile, Ala. 250 D1 168
Gulf Hammock, Levy, Fla. 617 B8 174
Gulfport, Pinellas, Fla. 9,730 C6 174
D8
Gulfport, Harrison, Miss. 30,204 E1 184
(*124,200) E3
Gulf Shores, Baldwin, Ala. 356 E2 168
Gulf Stream, Palm Beach, Fla. 176 *E10 174
Gulkana, Alsk. 65 C7 84
F12
Gull, isl., N.C. B10 186
Gull, lake, Alta., Can. D6 54
Gull, lake, Minn. E4 148
Gullänget, Swe. E8 290
Gullivan, bay, Fla. F9 174
Gulliver, Schoolcraft, Mich. 75 D5 146
Gull Lake, Sask., Can. 1,052 E3 58
Gull Lake, Alta., Can. 32 D6 54
Gullmarn, fjord, Swe. C2 292
Gull Point, Escambia, Fla. 200 A3 174
Gullringen, Swe. D6 292
Gullrock, lake, Ont., Can. R23 64
Gullspang, Swe. B5 292
Güllük, Tur. 826 C2 307
Gully, Polk, Minn. 168 D3 148
Gulu, Ug. B5 414
Gulya, Sov.Un. D14 329
Gulyantsi, Bul. 4,741 B2 317
Gulyay-Pole, Sov.Un. 25,000 I11 332
Gum, brook, Del. E3 172
Gumba, Con.L. B3 414
Gumboro, Sussex, Del. 150 G4 172
Gumel, Nig. 10,406 D6 409
Gummersbach, Ger. 31,500 C2 286
Gum Neck, Tyrrell, N.C. B9 186
Gum Spring, Louisa, Va. 40 C7 192
Gum Spring, Monongalia, W.Va. 50 A7 194
Gum Spring, mtn., Tenn. C6 190
Gumti, riv., India D3 368
Gümüsane, Tur. 4,173 A8 308
Gümüsane, prov., Tur. 212,376 *A8 307
Guna, Eth. C4 398
Guna, India D2 368
Guna, mtn., Eth. C4 398
Gunflint, range, Minn. C8 148
Gungu, Con.L. D2 414
Gungung Api, vol., Indon. F6 358
Gunisao, lake, Man., Can. D4 60
Gunisao, riv., Man., Can. D4 60
Gunlock, Washington, Utah. 90 F2 114
Gunn, Smith, Miss. C3 184
Gunnison, Gunnison, Colo. 3,477 C4 106
Gunnison, Bolivar, Miss. 448 B2 184
Gunnison, Sanpete, Utah 1,059 D4 114
Gunnison, co., Colo. 5,477 D3 106
Gunnison, riv., Colo. D2 106
Gunnworth, Sask., Can. 55 E3 58
Gunpowder, creek, Ky. A7 178
Gunpowder, riv., Md. B7 182
Gunpowder Falls, riv., Md. A6 182
Guntersville, Marshall, Ala. 6,592 A3 168
Guntersville, dam, Ala. A3 168
Guntersville, lake, Ala. A3 168
Gunton, Man., Can. 180 E4 60
Guntown, Lee, Miss. 269 A4 184
Guntown, Hawkins, Tenn. B9 190
Guntur, India 125,255 E4 366
Günzburg, Ger. 8,933 D4 286
Gura-Humorului, Rom. 7,216 A3 321
Gurdon, Clark, Ark. 2,166 D3 170
Gurgan, riv., Iran B4 379
Gurgueia, riv., Braz. B2 258
Gurk, riv., Aus. D6 313
Gurley, Madison, Ala. 750 A3 168
Gurley, Cheyenne, Nebr. 329 C3 152
Gurley, Horry, S.C. 30 C11 188
Gurleyville, Tolland, Conn. 100 B7 202
Gurnee, lake, Ill. 1,831 E2 138
Gurnet, pt., Mass. B6 206
Gurney, Iron, Wis. 100 B3 160
Gurskøy, isl., Nor. E1 290
Gurupá, Braz. 629 F6 256
Gurupi, mts., Braz. A1 258
Gurupi, riv., Braz. F7 256
Guryev, Sov.Un. 78,000 C4 336
Gurž (part of Dubrovnik), Yugo. C4 316
Gusau, Nig. 40,202 D6 408
Gusher, Uintah, Utah 65 C6 114
Gusinje, Yugo. 2,555 C4 316
Gus-Khrustalnyy, Sov.Un. 53,000 E13 332
Gustavsberg, Swe. 4,602 B9 292
Gustavus, Alsk. 82 D8 84
I14
Gustine, Merced, Calif. 2,300 D3 94
Güstrow, Ger. 37,100 B5 286
Gusum, Swe. C7 292
Gütersloh, Ger. 48,500 C3 286
Guthrie, Todd, Ky. 1,211 D3 178
Guthrie, Logan, Okla. 9,502 C6 128
Guthrie, co., Iowa 13,607 C3 142
Guthrie Center, Guthrie, Iowa 2,071 C3 142
Guttenberg, Clayton, Iowa 2,087 B6 142
Guttenberg, Hudson, N.J. 5,118 B1 210
Gu Vo, Pima, Ariz. 100 F3 124
Gu-Win, Marion, Ala. 80 *B2 168

Guy, Faulkner, Ark. 300 B4 170
Guyandot, mtn., W.Va. D6 194
Guyandot, riv., W.Va. C2 194
Guyenne, former prov., Fr. 2,061,000 E3 278
Guymon, Texas, Okla. 5,768 B2 128
Guyot, mtn., Tenn. C8 190
Guys, McNairy, Tenn. 100 C3 190
Guysborough, N.S., Can. 815 D8 70
Guysborough, co., N.S., Can. 13,802 D8 70
Guyton, Effingham, Ga. 670 D5 176
Guzar, Sov.Un. F8 328
Gwa, Bur. C2 362
Gwaai, Rh.&Nya. C5 420
Gwadar, Pak. 15,000 G3 375
Gwalior, India 241,577 D2 368
Gwanda, Rh.&Nya. 1,600 D5 420
Gwane, Con.L. B4 414
Gweebarra, bay, Ire. G4 272
Gweesalia, Ire. G3 273
Gwelo, Rh.&Nya. 18,500 (*21,500) C5 420
Gwendolen, Gilliam, Oreg. B6 96
Gwin, Holmes, Miss. 150 B2 184
Gwinn, Marquette, Mich. 1,009 C4 146
Gwinner, Sargent, N.Dak. 242 D8 154
Gwinnett, co., Ga. 43,541 C2 176
Gwinville, Jefferson Davis, Miss. 150 D3 184
Gwynn, Mathews, Va. 400 C8 192
Gwynne, Alta., Can. 100 D6 54
Gwynneville, Shelby, Ind. 300 C4 140
Gwynns Falls, riv., Md. C4 182
Gyangtse, China 20,000 F5 346
Gydan, mts., Sov.Un. C17 329
Gydanskiy, pen., Sov.Un. B9 328
Gympie, Austl. 10,500 D10 432
Gyoma, Hung. 12,242 C5 320
Gyöngyös, Hung. 27,000 B4 320
Györ, Hung. 68,000 B2 320
Györ-Sopron, co., Hung. 390,000 *B2 320
Gypsum, Eagle, Colo. 358 C4 106
Gypsum, Saline, Kans. 593 D6 144
Gypsum, Ottawa, Ohio 408 A4 156
Gypsum Mills, Washoe, Nev. 350 C2 112
Gypsumville, Man., Can. 200 E3 60
Gypsy, Creek, Okla. C7 128
Gypsy, Harrison, W.Va. 500 A7 194
Gyula, Hung. 20,000 C6 320
Gzhatsk, Sov.Un. 16,000 E10 332

H

Haakon, co., S.Dak. 3,303 C4 158
Haaksbergen, Neth. 4,785 B5 282
Haamstede, Neth. 1,601 C2 282
Haapajärvi, Fin. E11 290
Haapsalu, Sov.Un. 9,100 C4 332
Ha Arava (Wadi el 'Araba), depression, Isr. D6 382
Haarlem, Neth. 165,142 (*225,000) B3 282
Haarlemmermeer, Neth. 3,392 B3 282
Hab, riv., Pak. F5 375
Habana, prov., Cuba 1,538,803 A3 232
Habauna, wadi, Sau.Ar. D3 383
Habersham, Habersham, Ga. 800 B3 176
Habersham, co., Ga. 18,116 B3 176
Habiganj, Pak. 10,882 K17 375
Habo, Swe. 4,538 D5 292
Haboro, Jap. 24,270 B8 354
Hachiman, Jap. 22,954 L12 354
Hachinohe, Jap. 141,771 D8 354
Hachiōji, Jap. 133,447 G7 354 L15
Hachita, Grant, N.Mex. 200 G2 126
Hacienda, Broward, Fla. 125 *E10 174
Hackberry, Mohave, Ariz. 100 C2 124
Hackberry, Cameron, La. 800 E2 180
Hackberry, creek, Kans. D3 144
Hackensack, Cass, Minn. 204 E4 148
Hackensack, Bergen, N.J. 30,521 A1 210 B4
Hackensack, riv., N.J. B1 210
Hacker Valley, Webster, W.Va. 150 C4 194
Hackett, Sebastian, Ark. 328 B2 170
Hackett, Alta., Can. D6 54
Hackettstown, Warren, N.J. 5,276 B3 210
Hackleburg, Marion, Ala. 527 A2 168
Hackney, Cowley, Kans. 35 *E6 144
Haco, isl., Truk A3 436
Hacoda, Geneva, Ala. 40 D3 168
Hadar, Pierce, Nebr. 100 B8 152
Haddam, Middlesex, Conn. 350 (3,466▲) D5 202
Haddam, Washington, Kans. 311 C6 144
Haddock, Jones, Ga. 600 C3 176
Haddonfield, Camden, N.J. 13,201 D2 210
Haddon Heights, Camden, N.J. 9,260 D2 210
Hadejia, Nig. 10,453 D7 409
Hadera, Isr. 23,000 B5 382
Haderslev, Den. 18,706 I3 291
Haderslev, co., Den. 71,715 *I3 291
Hadhramaut, reg., Aden E4 383
Hadimkoy, Tur. F12 307
Haditha, Iraq 5,434 B5 378
Hadiyah, Sau.Ar. B2 383
Hadley, Hampshire, Mass. 1,000 (3,099▲) B2 206
Hadley, Murray, Minn. 151 G3 148
Hadley, Saratoga, N.Y. 500 B8 212
Hadley, lake, Maine D5 204
Hadlock, Jefferson, Wash. 300 A4 98
Hadlyme, New London, Conn. 302 D6 202
Hadsund, Den. 3,504 H4 291
Haeju (Kaishu), Kor. 82,135 F12 348
Haena, Kauai, Haw. 76 A2 86
Hafford, Sask., Can. 453 D4 58
Hafizabad, Pak. 30,082 C8 375
Hafnarnes, Ice. L23 290
Hafun, cape, Som. C7 398
Hagaman, Montgomery, N.Y. 1,292 *C7 212
Hagan, Evans, Ga. 552 D5 176
Hagari, riv., India F3 366
Hagar Shores (Lake Michigan Beach), Berrien, Mich. 1,092 *H5 146
Hagarville, Johnson, Ark. 150 B3 170
Hagemeister, isl., Alsk. D5 84
Hagen, Sask., Can. 100 D5 58
Hagen [in Westfalen], Ger. 179,200 C2 286
Hagenow, Ger. 11,000 B4 286
Hager, Klamath, Oreg. E5 96
Hagerman, Gooding, Idaho 430 G4 108
Hagerman, Chaves, N.Mex. 1,144 E6 126
Hagermans Corners, Ont., Can. 175 R22 64
Hagerstown, Wayne, Ind. 1,730 C4 140
Hagerstown, Washington, Md. 36,660 A4 182
Hagersville, Ont., Can. 1,964 R20 64
Hagfors, Swe. 7,472 A4 292
Haggard, Gray, Kans. 35 E3 144
Hagginwood, Sacramento, Calif. 11,469 *C3 94
Hagi, Jap. 57,621 G3 354
Ha Giang, Viet. 25,000 B5 362
Hagood, Sumter, S.C. 200 C7 188
Hags, head, Ire. I3 273
Hague, Sask., Can. 413 D4 58
Hague, The ('s Gravenhage), see The Hague, Neth.
Hague, Alachua, Fla. 120 B8 174
Hague, Emmons, N.Dak. 197 D6 154
Hague, cape, Fr. C3 278
Haguenau, Fr. 19,531 C7 278
Hagues, peak, Colo. B5 106
Hahira, Lowndes, Ga. 1,297 F3 176
Hahns Peak, Routt, Colo. B4 106
Hahnstown, Lancaster, Pa. 800 *C5 214
Hahnville, St. Charles, La. 1,297 C6 180 E5
Haianshih, China O5 349
Haicheng, China 80,000 E11 348
Haichow, bay, China H9 348
Hai Duong, Viet. 21,650 B5 362
Haifa, Isr. 158,000 B5 382
Haifa, dist., Isr. 290,813 *B5 382
Haig, Scotts Bluff, Nebr. 80 *C2 152
Haig, lake, Alta., Can. B4 54
Haig, mtn., Alta., Can. F5 54
Haigler, Dundy, Nebr. 268 D4 152
Ḥa'il, Sau.Ar. 15,000 B3 383
Hailar, see Hulun, China
Haile, Union, La. 160 B3 180
Hailesboro, St. Lawrence, N.Y. 385 A6 212
Hailey, Blaine, Idaho 1,185 F4 108
Haileybury, Ont., Can. 2,654 R25 64
Haileyville, Pittsburg, Okla. 922 D8 128
Hailing, isl., China O5 349
Hailstone, Wasatch, Utah 15 C4 114
Hailun, China 47,648 B13 348
Hailung, China 20,000 D12 348
Hailuto, isl., Fin. D11 290
Haimen, China 5,000 J10 349
Haimen, cape, China N8 349
Hainan, isl., China P4 349
Hainan, strait, China O5 349
Hainaut, prov., Bel. 1,279,063 D2 282
Haines, Alsk. 392 D8 84 I14
Haines, Baker, Oreg. 331 C9 96
Hainesburg, Warren, N.J. 200 B2 210
Haines City, Polk, Fla. 9,135 C9 174
Haines Falls, Greene, N.Y. 600 C7 212
Hainesport, Burlington, N.J. 2,000 D3 210
Hainesville, Sussex, N.J. 70 A3 210
Haining, China 5,000 J10 349
Haiphong, Viet. 188,600 B5 362
Hairy Hill, Alta., Can. 183 D7 54
Haiti, country, N.A. 3,097,220 C8 232
Haiya, Sud. B4 398
Haiyang, China 5,000 G10 348
Haiyüan, China 5,000 G2 348
Hajar, mts., Sau.Ar. B2 383
Hajdu-Bihar, co., Hung. 380,000 *B6 320
Hajduböszörmény, Hung. 24,000 B6 320
Hajduhadház, Hung. 9,070 B6 320
Hajdunánás, Hung. 15,000 B6 320
Hajduszoboszló, Hung. 17,000 B6 320
Hajibad Kavir, salt flats, Iran C5 379
Hajiki, cape, Jap. E7 354
Hajipur, India 25,149 I8 366
Hakalau, Hawaii, Haw. 800 D6 86
Hakâri, Tur. 2,664 C10 307
Hake Fjorden, fjord, Swe. D2 292
Hakkâri, prov., Tur. 54,604 *C10 307
Hakkas, Swe. C9 290
Hakken San, peak, Jap. G5 354
Hakodate, Jap. 242,582 D8 354
Haku-San, peak, Jap. K12 354
Halabja, Iraq B6 378
Halaib, Eg., U.A.R. C4 395
Halal, mtn., Eg., U.A.R. D4 382
Halaula, Hawaii, Haw. 600 C6 86
Halawa, Maui, Haw. 25 B5 86
Halawa, riv., Haw. G10 86
Halawa Heights, Honolulu, Haw. 2,000 *G10 86
Halberstadt, Ger. 45,500 C4 286
Halbrite, Sask., Can. 214 F6 58
Halbturn, Aus. 1,951 C8 313
Halbur, Carroll, Iowa 214 B3 142
Halcyon Hot Springs, B.C., Can. 50 E14 52
Haldeman, Rowan, Ky. 250 B7 178
Halden, Nor. 9,924 B2 292
Haldensleben, see Neuhaldensleben, Ger.
Halder, Marathon, Wis. 40 D4 160
Haldimand, co., Ont., Can. 26,067 R21 64
Haldwani, India C2 368
Hale, Yuma, Colo. 8 *C8 106
Hale, Iosco, Mich. 450 E8 146
Hale, Clarke, Miss. 200 D4 184
Hale, Carroll, Mo. 504 B4 150
Hale, co., Ala. 19,537 C2 168
Hale, co., Tex. 36,798 B5 130
Haleaha, Honolulu, Haw. 180 *G10 86
Haleakala, crater, Haw. C5 86
Haleb, see Aleppo, Syr., U.A.R.
Haleburg, Henry, Ala. 75 D4 168
Hale Center, Hale, Tex. 2,196 B5 130
Haledon, Passaic, N.J. 6,161 A1 210 B4
Haleiwa, Honolulu, Haw. 2,504 B3 86 F9
Hales Bar, res., Tenn. C6 190
Hales Corners, Milwaukee, Wis. 5,549 E1 160
Halesite, Suffolk, N.Y. 2,857 *D3 212
Halethorpe, Baltimore, Md. 22,402 C4 182
Haley, Bowman, N.Dak. 112 E2 154
Haleyville, Winston, Ala. 3,740 A2 168
Haleyville, Cumberland, N.J. 150 E2 210
Half Moon, Flathead, Mont. 150 B2 110
Half Moon, bay, Calif. B5 94
Half Moon Bay, San Mateo, Calif. 1,957 B5 94
Half-Moon Bay (Oban), N.Z. 278 G2 437
Half Mound, Jefferson, Kans. 30 *C8 144
Halfway, Washington, Md. 4,256 A4 182
Half Way, Polk, Mo. 150 D4 150
Halfway, Baker, Oreg. 505 C9 96
Halfway, riv., B.C., Can. B11 52
Halhul, Jordan 4,000 C6 382
Haliburton, Ont., Can. 975 O22 64
Haliburton, co., Ont., Can. 8,012 O22 64
Halibut, pt., Mass. A6 206
Halifax, N.S., Can. 93,301 (*164,200) E6 70
Halifax, Eng. 96,400 H11 273
Halifax, Plymouth, Mass. (1,599▲) C6 206
Halifax, Halifax, N.C. 370 A8 186
Halifax, Dauphin, Pa. 824 C5 214
Halifax, Windham, Vt. 100 (268▲) F3 218
Halifax, Halifax, Va. 792 D6 192
Halifax, co., N.S., Can. 197,943 E7 70
Halifax, co., N.C. 58,956 A8 186
Halifax, co., Va. 33,637 D6 192
Halifax, bay, Austl. B9 432
Haliimaile, Maui, Haw. 600 C5 86
Halileh, cape, Iran D3 379
Halin, Som. D6 398
Haliri, riv., Iran D5 379
Halkirk, Alta., Can. 209 D6 54
Hall, Morgan, Ind. 120 C3 140
Hall, see Schwäbisch Hall, Ger.
Hall, Granite, Mont. 100 D3 110
Hall, co., Ga. 49,739 B3 176
Hall, co., Nebr. 35,757 D7 152
Hall, co., Tex. 7,322 B5 130
Hall, mtn., Wash. A9 98
Hall, pen., N.W.Ter., Can. E12 48
Halladale, riv., Scot. C9 272
Hallam, Lancaster, Nebr. 264 D9 152
Halland, co., Swe. 166,433 D3 292
Halland, reg., Swe. 166,433 *H5 291
Hallandale, Broward, Fla. 10,483 E6 174 F10
Hallandsåsen, mts., Swe. E3 292
Hallboro, Man., Can. 90 E3 60
Hall Creek, Sumter, Ala. C2 168
Halle, Bel. 18,159 D3 282
Halle [an der Saale], Ger. 289,700 C4 286
Hällefors, Swe. 6,335 B5 292
Hallein, Aus. 14,828 C5 313
Hallett, Pawnee, Okla. 132 B7 128
Hallettsville, Lavaca, Tex. 2,808 E7 130
Halley, Desha, Ark. 213 D5 170
Halli, Fin. F11 291
Halliday, Dunn, N.Dak. 509 C3 154
Hall Meadow, brook, Conn. B3 202
Hallock, Kittson, Minn. 1,527 C2 148
Hallonquist, Sask., Can. 110 E4 58
Hallowell, Cherokee, Kans. 225 E9 144
Hallowell, Kennebec, Maine 3,169 D3 204
Halls, Lauderdale, Tenn. 1,890 C2 190
Halls, stream, N.H. A4 208
Hallsberg, Swe. 5,179 B6 292
Hallsboro, Columbus, N.C. 250 C7 186
Halls Crossroads, Knox, Tenn. 50 E9 190
Hall's Creek, Austl. 74 B5 432
Halls Summit, Coffey, Kans. 40 D8 144
Hallstahammer, Swe. 10,470 B7 292
Hallstavik, Swe. A9 292
Hallstead, Susquehanna, Pa. 1,580 B6 214
Hall Summit, Red River, La. 170 B2 180
Hallville, New London, Conn. 100 C7 202
Hallsville, Boone, Mo. 363 B5 150
Hallsville, Harrison, Tex. 684 C8 130
Hallwil, lake, Switz. A4 312
Hallwood, Accomack, Va. 269 C9 192
Hallwood, Mason, W.Va. 263 C2 194
Halma, Kittson, Minn. 115 C2 148
Halmahera, isl., Indon. D7 359
Halmstad, Swe. 37,335 E3 292
Halsell, Choctaw, Ala. 300 C1 168
Halsey, Thomas, Nebr. 111 C5 152
Halsey, Sussex, N.J. A3 210
Halsey, Linn, Oreg. 404 C3 96
Halsingborg, Swe. 74,380 E3 292
Hälsingland, prov., Swe. 156,295 *F7 291
Halstad, Norman, Minn. 639 D2 148
Halstead, Eng. 6,300 J13 273
Halstead, Harvey, Kans. 1,598 D6 144
Halsua, Fin. E11 290
Haltom City, Tarrant, Tex. 23,133 B8 130
Halton, co., Ont., Can. 68,297 Q21 64
Haltwhistle, Eng. G10 272
Hamā, Syr., U.A.R. 167,507 B2 378
Hamada, Jap. 45,638 G4 354
Hamada Zegher, plain, Libya B2 394
Hamadān, Iran B2 379
Hamadān, reg., Iran B2 379
Hamakuapoko, Maui, Haw. 335 C5 86
Hamamatsu, Jap. 268,792 G6 354 M13
Hamar, Eddy, N.Dak. 84 C7 154
Hamar, Nor. 11,587 A2 292
Hamaröy, Nor. B6 290
Hamata, mtn., Eg., U.A.R. C3 395
Hamatombetsu, Jap. B9 354
Hambantota, Cey. 4,299 G4 366
Hamber, prov. park, B.C., Can. D13 52
Hamberg, Wells, N.Dak. 64 C6 154
Hamblen, co., Tenn. 33,092 B8 190
Hambleton, Tucker, W.Va. 275 *B5 194
Hamburg, Ashley, Ark. 2,904 D5 170
Hamburg, New London, Conn. 150 D6 202
Hamburg, Ger. 1,781,500 (*1,950,000) B4 286
Hamburg, state, Ger. 1,781,500 *E3 286
Hamburg, Fremont, Iowa 1,647 D2 142
Hamburg, Carver, Minn. 288 *G5 148
Hamburg, Franklin, Miss. 60 D1 184
Hamburg, Sussex, N.J. 1,532 A3 210
Hamburg, Erie, N.Y. 9,145 C3 212
Hamburg, Berks, Pa. 3,747 C6 214
Hamburg, Aiken, S.C. 150 E5 188
Hamburg, Hardin, Tenn. C3 190
Hamburg, Marathon, Wis. 200 C4 160
Hamden, New Haven, Conn. 41,056 D4 202
Hamden, Vinton, Ohio 1,035 C4 156
Hamdh, wadi, Sau.Ar. B2 383
Häme, dept., Fin. 596,500 *F11 291
Hämeenlinna, Fin. 22,911 F11 291
Hamel (Medina), Hennepin, Minn. 1,472 *F5 148
Hameln, Ger. 50,300 B3 286
Hamer, Jefferson, Idaho 144 F6 108
Hamer, Dillon, S.C. 170 C10 188
Hamersley, range, Austl. C3 432
Hamersville, Brown, Ohio 524 D3 156
Hamhŭng (Kanko), Kor. 112,184 F13 348
Hami (Kumul), China 28,590 C6 346
Hamill, Tripp, S.Dak. 40 D6 158
Hamilton, Marion, Ala. 1,934 A2 168
Hamilton (Old Hamilton), Alsk. 43 C5 84
Hamilton, Austl. 8,507 F8 432
Hamilton, Bermuda 3,000 A12 233
Hamilton, Ont., Can. 239,625 (*327,831) Q21 64
Hamilton, Moffat, Colo. 22 B3 106
Hamilton, Harris, Ga. 396 D2 176
Hamilton, Hancock, Ill. 2,228 C2 138
Hamilton, Steuben, Ind. 380 A5 140
Hamilton, Marion, Iowa 197 C5 142
Hamilton, Greenwood, Kans. 400 E7 144
Hamilton, Boone, Ky. A7 178
Hamilton, Essex, Mass. 350 (5,488▲) A6 206 C4
Hamilton, Allegan, Mich. 700 G5 146
Hamilton, Monroe, Miss. 115 B4 184
Hamilton, Caldwell, Mo. 1,701 B4 150
Hamilton, Ravalli, Mont. 2,475 D2 110
Hamilton, Madison, N.Y. 3,348 C6 212
Hamilton, N.Z. 35,941 (*40,600) B5 437
Hamilton, Martin, N.C. 565 B8 186
Hamilton, Pembina, N.Dak. 217 B8 154
Hamilton, Butler, Ohio 72,354 (*103,200) C1 156 C2
Hamilton, Grant, Oreg. 20 C7 96
Hamilton, Washington, R.I. C3 216
Hamilton, Scot. 41,200 F8 272
Hamilton, Hamilton, Tex. 3,106 D6 130
Hamilton, Loudoun, Va. 403 A7 192
Hamilton, Skagit, Wash. 271 A5 98
Hamilton, co., Fla. 7,705 A7 174
Hamilton, co., Ill. 10,010 E5 138
Hamilton, co., Ind. 40,132 B3 140
Hamilton, co., Iowa 20,032 B4 142
Hamilton, co., Kans. 3,144 E2 144
Hamilton, co., Nebr. 8,714 D7 152
Hamilton, co., N.Y. 4,267 B7 212
Hamilton, co., Ohio 864,121 C2 156
Hamilton, co., Tenn. 237,905 C6 190
Hamilton, co., Tex. 8,488 D6 130
Hamilton, inlet, Newf., Can. C7 72
Hamilton, lake, Ark. C3 170
Hamilton, mtn., Alsk. C6 84
Hamilton, mtn., N.Y. B7 212
Hamilton, res., Mass. B3 206
Hamilton, riv., Newf., Can. E9 72
Hamilton Acres, Alsk. 960 *C7 84
Hamilton City, Glenn, Calif. 700 C2 94
Hamilton Dome, Hot Springs, Wyo. 150 C4 116
Hamilton Park, New Castle, Del. 400 *B3 172
Hamilton Park, Fayette, Ky. 800 *B6 178
Hamiltons Fort, Iron, Utah 47 F2 114
Hamilton Square (Hamilton Township), Mercer, N.J. 65,035 C3 210
Hamīm, wadi, Libya A4 394
Hamina, Fin. 7,184 F12 291
Hamiota, Man., Can. 690 F2 60
Hamirpur, India 8,469 D3 368
Hamler, Henry, Ohio 588 A2 156
Hamlet, Starke, Ind. 688 A3 140
Hamlet, Hayes, Nebr. 113 D4 152
Hamlet, Richmond, N.C. 4,460 C6 186
Hamlin, Audubon, Iowa 150 C3 142
Hamlin, Brown, Kans. 99 C8 144
Hamlin, Aroostook, Maine 60 (374▲) A5 204
Hamlin, Jones and Fisher, Tex. 3,791 C5 130
Hamlin, Lincoln, W.Va. 850 C2 194
Hamlin, co., S.Dak. 6,303 C8 158
Hamlin, lake, Mich. E5 146
Hamm [in Westfalen], Ger. 66,900 (*125,000) C2 286
Ḥammādat Tinghert, plat., Libya, Alg. B1 394
Hammār, Iraq D7 378
Hammarö, Swe. 9,401 B4 292
Hamme, Bel. 16,771 C3 282
Hammer, Roberts, S.Dak. 65 B8 158
Hammerdal, Swe. E6 290
Hammerfest, Nor. 4,362 A10 290
Hammett, Elmore, Idaho 75 G3 108
Hamm-i-Helmand, lake, Iran C5 379
Hammon, Roger Mills, Okla. 656 C4 128
Hammonasset, pt., Conn. E5 202
Hammonasset, riv., Conn. D5 202
Hammond, Piatt, Ill. 471 D5 138
Hammond, Lake, Ind. 111,698 A2 140
Hammond, Bourbon, Kans. 50 *E9 144
Hammond, Tangipahoa, La. 10,563 A6 180 D5
Hammond, Wabasha, Minn. 205 G6 148
Hammond, Carter, Mont. 13 E12 110
Hammond, Clatsop, Oreg. 480 A3 96
Hammond, Horry, S.C. 100 D11 188
Hammond, St. Croix, Wis. 645 D1 160
Hammond, bay, Mich. D7 146
Hammond East, Tangipahoa, La. 1,462 *D5 180
Hammondsport, Steuben, N.Y. 1,176 C4 212
Hammondville, De Kalb, Ala. 134 *A4 168
Hammonton, Atlantic, N.J. 9,854 D3 210
Ham Nord, Que., Can. 785 S13 66
Hamoyet, mtn., Eth. B4 398
Hampden, Newf., Can. 200 F7 72
Hampden, Penobscot, Maine 800 (4,583▲) D4 204

Hampden, Hampden, Mass.	400	B3	206
	(2,345▲)		
Hampden, N.Z.	307	F3	437
Hampden, Ramsey, N.Dak.	71	B7	154
Hampden, co., Mass.	429,353	B2	206
Hampden Highlands, Penobscot, Maine	1,000	D4	204
Hampden Sydney, Prince Edward, Va.	200	C6	192
Hampshire, Kane, Ill.	1,309	A5	138
Hampshire, Maury, Tenn.	150	C4	190
Hampshire, co., Eng.	1,363,100	J11	273
Hampshire, co., Mass.	103,229	B2	206
Hampshire, co., W.Va.	11,705	B6	194
Hampstead, Que., Can.	4,355	*S15	66
Hampstead, Carroll, Md.	696	A6	182
Hampstead, Rockingham, N.H.	300	F4	208
	(1,261▲)		
Hampstead, N.B., Can.	215	D3	70
Hampstead, Pender, N.C.	350	C8	186
Hampton, Calhoun, Ark.	1,011	D4	170
Hampton, N.B., Can.	560	D4	70
Hampton, Windham, Conn.	300	B7	202
	(934▲)		
Hampton, Bradford, Fla.	386	B8	174
Hampton, Henry, Ga.	1,253	C2	176
Hampton, Rock Island, Ill.	742	*B3	138
Hampton, Franklin, Iowa	4,501	B4	142
Hampton, Livingston, Ky.	100	C2	178
Hampton, Dakota, Minn.	305	G6	148
Hampton, Washington, Miss.		B1	184
Hampton, Hamilton, Nebr.	331	D8	152
Hampton, Rockingham, N.H.	3,281	F5	208
Hampton, Hunterdon, N.J.	1,135	B3	210
Hampton, Washington, N.Y.	870	B8	212
Hampton, Lampton, Oreg.	10	D6	96
Hampton, Hampton, S.C.	2,486	F6	188
Hampton, Carter, Tenn.	1,048	B9	190
Hampton (Independent City), Va.	89,258	A8	192
		C8	
Hampton, Uinta, Wyo.		E2	116
Hampton, co., S.C.	17,425	F6	188
Hampton, butte, Oreg.		D6	96
Hampton Bays, Suffolk, N.Y.	2,000	D5	212
Hampton Beach, Rockingham, N.H.	700	F5	208
Hampton Falls, Rockingham, N.H.	885	F5	208
Hampton Roads, harbor, Va.		A8	192
Hampton Springs, Taylor, Fla.	60	A7	174
Hamrarne, strait, Swe.		F5	292
Hams, fork, Wyo.		E2	116
Ham Sud, Que., Can.	165	S13	66
Hamtramck, Wayne, Mich.	34,137	B8	146
Hamûl el Barari, Eg., U.A.R.		C3	382
Hamundarstadhir, Ice.		L22	290
Hamun-i-Helmand, lake, Afg.		D1	374
Hamun-i-Jaz Murian, lake, Iran		D5	379
Hamun-i-Lora, lake, Pak.		E3	375
Hamun-i-Mashkel, lake, Pak.		E3	375
Hamun-i-Murgho, lake, Pak.		F4	375
Hämün-i-Püzak, lake, Afg.		D1	374
Hamyang, Kor.		H13	348
Han, riv., China		J6	349
Han, riv., China		M8	349
Hana, Maui, Haw.	547	C3	86
Hanahan, Berkeley, S.C.	4,000	*F3	188
Hanaipoe, Hawaii, Haw.		D6	86
Hanalei, Kauai, Haw.	364	A2	86
Hanalei, bay, Haw.		A2	86
Hanamaki, Jap.	61,728	*E8	354
Hanamaulu, Kauai, Haw.	950	B2	86
Hanapepe, Kauai, Haw.	1,383	B2	86
Hanau [am Main], Ger.	43,500	C3	286
Hanceville, Cullman, Ala.	1,174	A3	168
Hanceville, B.C., Can.	50	E11	52
Hancock, Pottawattamie, Iowa	252	C2	142
Hancock, Hancock, Maine	350	D4	204
	(806▲)		
Hancock, Washington, Md.	2,004	A3	182
Hancock, Berkshire, Mass.	200	A1	206
	(455▲)		
Hancock, Houghton, Mich.	5,022	B3	146
Hancock, Stevens, Minn.	942	F3	148
Hancock, Hillsboro, N.H.	300	F3	208
	(722▲)		
Hancock, Delaware, N.Y.	1,830	D6	212
Hancock, Addison, Vt.	160	D3	218
	(323▲)		
Hancock, Morgan, W.Va.	136	B6	194
Hancock, Waushara, Wis.	367	D4	160
Hancock, co., Ga.	9,979	C3	176
Hancock, co., Ill.	24,574	C2	138
Hancock, co., Ind.	26,665	C4	140
Hancock, co., Iowa	14,604	A4	142
Hancock, co., Ky.	5,330	C4	178
Hancock, co., Maine	32,293	D4	204
Hancock, co., Miss.	14,039	E3	184
Hancock, co., Ohio	53,686	A3	156
Hancock, co., Tenn.	7,757	B8	190
Hancock, co., W.Va.	39,615	A4	194
Hancock, mtn., N.H.		C4	208
Hancock, pond, Maine		E2	204
Hancocks Bridge, Salem, N.J.	300	D2	210
Hand, co., S.Dak.	6,712	C6	158
Handa, Jap.	67,827	M12	354
Handel, Sask., Can.	115	D3	58
Handeni, Tan.		D6	414
Handley, Kanawha, W.Va.	900	C6	194
Handrung, Nep.		D4	368
Handsboro, Harrison, Miss.	1,577	E1	184
		E3	
Handsom, Southampton, Va.	90	D7	192
Haney, B.C., Can.	2,000	B15	52
		F11	
Hanford, Kings, Calif.	10,133	D4	94
Hanford, Benton, Wash.		C7	98
Hanford Northwest, Kings, Calif.	1,364	*D4	94
Hangchou, China	518,000	J10	349
Hangchow, bay, China		J10	349
Hanging Rock, Lawrence, Ohio	352	D4	156
Hangingstone, riv., Alta., Can.		B7	54
Hangö, Fin.	6,751	G10	291
Hanita, Isr.		A6	382
Hankinson, Claiborne, Miss.	100	C2	184
Hankinson, Richland, N.Dak.	1,285	D9	154
Hankou, see Wuhan, China			
Hanks, Williams, N.Dak.	78	B2	154
Hanksville, Wayne, Utah	100	E5	114
Hanley, Sask., Can.	425	E4	58
Hanley Falls, Yellow Medicine, Minn.	334	G3	148
Hanley Hills, St. Louis, Mo.	3,308	*C7	150
Hanlontown, Worth, Iowa	193	A4	142
Hann, mtn., Austl.		B5	432
Hanna, Alta., Can.	2,327	E7	54
Hanna, La Porte, Ind.	500	A3	140
Hanna, McIntosh, Okla.	233	C8	128
Hanna, Duchesne, Utah	165	C5	114
Hanna, Carbon, Wyo.	625	E6	116
Hanna City, Peoria, Ill.	1,056	C4	138
Hannaford, Griggs, N.Dak.	277	C7	154
Hannagan, Greenlee, Ariz.	10	E6	124
Hannah, Cavalier, N.Dak.	253	B7	154
Hannawa Falls, St. Lawrence, N.Y.	400	A7	212
Hannibal, Marion, and Ralls, Mo.	20,028	B6	150
Hannibal, Oswego, N.Y.	611	B5	212
Hannibal, Monroe, Ohio	375	C6	156
Hannon, Macon, Ala.	350	C4	168
Hannover, Ger.	532,200	B3	286
Hannoversch Münden, see Münden, Ger.			
Hanö, isl., Swe.		E5	292
Hanöbukten, bay, Swe.		F5	292
Hanoi, Viet.	297,900	B5	362
Hanover, Stone, Ark.	10	B4	170
Hanover, Ont., Can.	3,943	P19	64
Hanover, New London, Conn.	250	C7	202
Hanover (Hannover), reg., Ger.		B2	286
Hanover, Jo Daviess, Ill.	1,396	A3	138
Hanover, Jefferson, Ind.	1,170	D4	140
Hanover, Washington, Kans.	773	C7	144
Hanover, Oxford, Maine	170	D2	204
	(240▲)		
Hanover, Plymouth, Mass.	600	B6	206
	(5,923▲)	E4	
Hanover, Jackson, Mich.	449	G7	146
Hanover, Wright and Hennepin, Minn.	263	*F5	148
Hanover, Fergus, Mont.	125	C7	110
Hanover, Grafton, N.H.	5,649	D2	208
	(7,329▲)		
Hanover, Grant, N.Mex.	800	F2	126
Hanover, Licking, Ohio	267	B4	156
Hanover, York, Pa.	15,538	D5	214
Hanover, Hanover, Va.	250	C7	192
Hanover, Wyoming, W.Va.	300	D3	194
Hanover, co., Va.	27,550	C7	192
Hanover, isl., Chile		H2	251
Hanover Center, Plymouth, Mass.	177	E4	206
Hanover (East Hanover Township), Morris, N.J.	4,379	*B4	210
Hanover Green, Luzerne, Pa.	1,000	*B5	214
Hanover Park, Cook, Ill.	451	*B5	138
Hanoverton, Columbiana, Ohio	442	B6	156
Hansard, B.C., Can.		C12	52
Hansboro, Towner, N.Dak.	143	B6	154
Hansell, Franklin, Iowa	168	B4	142
Hansen, Twin Falls, Idaho	427	G4	108
Hansen, Adams, Nebr.	35	D7	152
Hansford, Kanawha, W.Va.	900	*C3	194
Hansford, co., Tex.	6,208	A5	130
Hanska, Brown, Minn.	491	G4	148
Hanson, Madison, Fla.	100	A7	174
Hanson, Hopkins, Ky.	376	C3	178
Hanson, Plymouth, Mass.	800	B6	206
	(4,370▲)		
Hanson, Sequoyah, Okla.	187	C9	128
Hanson, co., S.Dak.	4,584	D8	158
Hanson, lake, Sask., Can.		C6	58
Hansonville, Russell, Va.	80	D2	192
Hansted, Den.		H3	291
Hanston, Hodgeman, Kans.	279	D4	144
Hantan, China		G7	348
Hants, co., N.S., Can.	24,889	D6	70
Hant's Harbour, Newf., Can.	550	F9	72
Hantsport, N.S., Can.	1,298	D5	70
Haoching, China		F8	346
Haofeng, China	1,000	K4	349
Haoli, China	90,000	B15	348
Haparanda, Swe.	3,194	D10	290
Hapeville, Fulton, Ga.	10,082	B5	176
		C2	
Happy, Swisher and Randall, Tex.	624	B5	130
Happy Camp, Siskiyou, Calif.	500	B2	94
Happy Inn, Lincoln, Mont.	8	B1	110
Happy Jack, Coconino, Ariz.	350	D4	124
Happy Jack, Plaquemines, La.	100	E6	180
Happy Valley, Newf., Can.		E9	72
Happy Valley, India		D5	368
Hapsu, Kor.		E14	348
Hapur, India		C2	368
Hara Usa, lake, Mong.		B6	346
Harads, Swe.		C9	290
Harahan, Jefferson, La.	9,275	C7	180
Haralson, Coweta, Ga.	141	C2	176
Haralson, co., Ga.	14,543	C1	176
Harar, Eth.		D5	398
Harardera, Som.	500	E6	398
Hararge, prov., Eth.	1,600,000	D5	398
Haraze, Chad		E9	409
Harbeson, Sussex, Del.	142	F4	172
Harbin (Pinchiang), China	1,163,000	C13	348
Harbine, Jefferson, Nebr.	58	*D8	152
Harbor, Curry, Oreg.	40	E2	96
Harbor Beach, Huron, Mich.	2,282	F9	146
Harbor Springs, Emmet, Mich.	1,433	D7	146
Harborton, Accomack, Va.	350	C9	192
Harbor View, Lucas, Ohio	273	A1	156
Harbour Breton, Newf., Can.	989	G8	72
Harbour Buffett, Newf., Can.	425	G8	72
Harbour Deep, Newf., Can.	200	E7	72
Harbour Grace, Newf., Can.	2,545	G9	72
Harbour Main, Newf., Can.	600	G9	72
Harbour Mille, Newf., Can.	350	G8	72
Harbourton, Mercer, N.J.	50	C3	210
Harbourville, N.S., Can.	188	D5	70
Harcourt, N.B., Can.	235	C4	70
Harcourt, Webster, Iowa	268	B3	142
Harcuvar, Yuma, Ariz.	10	E2	124
Harcuvar, mts., Ariz.		E2	124
Harda, India		E2	368
Hardangerfjord, fjord, Nor.		G1	291
Hardangerjökelem, mtn., Nor.		F2	291
Hardaway, Macon, Ala.	100	C4	168
Hardburly, Perry, Ky.	650	C7	178
Hardee, Issaquena, Miss.	40	C2	184
Hardee, co., Fla.	12,370	D9	174
Hardeeville, Jasper, S.C.	700	G6	188
Hardeman, co., Tenn.	21,517	C2	190
Hardeman, co., Tex.	8,275	B6	130
Hardenberg, Neth.	1,957	B5	282
Harden City, Pontotoc, Okla.	150	D7	128
Harderwijk, Neth.	7,947	B4	282
Hardesty, Texas, Okla.	187	B2	128
Hardin, Calhoun, Ill.	356	D3	138
Hardin, Marshall, Ky.	458	D2	178
Hardin, Ray, Mo.	727	B4	150
Hardin, Big Horn, Mont.	2,789	E9	110
Hardin, co., Ill.	5,879	F5	138
Hardin, co., Iowa	22,533	B4	142
Hardin, co., Ky.	67,789	C4	178
Hardin, co., Ohio	29,633	B3	156
Hardin, co., Tenn.	17,397	C3	190
Hardin, co., Tex.	24,629	D8	130
Harding, Man., Can.		F2	60
Harding, Bourbon, Kans.	50	*E9	144
Harding, Norfolk, Mass.	200	B5	206
		D2	
Harding, Morrison, Minn.	111	E4	148
Harding, Harding, S.Dak.	15	B2	158
Harding, Randolph, W.Va.	250	C5	194
Harding, co., N.Mex.	1,874	C7	126
Harding, co., S.Dak.	2,371	B2	158
Harding, lake, Ala., Ga.		C4	168
		D1	176
Hardingville, Gloucester, N.J.		D2	210
Hardinsburg, Washington, Ind.	218	D3	140
Hardinsburg, Breckinridge, Ky.	1,377	C4	178
Hardisty, Alta., Can.	628	D7	54
Hardisty, lake, N.W.Ter., Can.		E7	48
Hardman, Morrow, Oreg.	30	B7	96
Hardoi, India		D3	368
Hardtner, Barber, Kans.	372	E5	144
Hardwar, India	56,175	C2	368
	(*57,338)		
Hardwick (Midway), Baldwin, Ga.	3,500	C3	176
Hardwick, Wayne, Ky.	300	D6	178
Hardwick, Worcester, Mass.	200	B3	206
	(2,340▲)		
Hardwick, Rock, Minn.	328	H2	148
Hardwick, Caledonia, Vt.	1,521	B4	218
	(2,349▲)		
Hardwicke, N.B., Can.	135	B5	70
Hardy, Alg.	1,002	A4	402
Hardy, Sharp, Ark.	555	A5	170
Hardy, Sask., Can.	75	F5	58
Hardy, Humboldt, Iowa	110	B3	142
Hardy, Pike, Ky.	854	C8	178
Hardy, Grenada, Miss.	125	B3	184
Hardy, Nuckolls, Nebr.	285	D8	152
Hardy, Kay, Okla.	6	B7	128
Hardy, co., W.Va.	9,308	B6	194
Hare, bay, Newf., Can.		E8	72
Hare, hill, Newf., Can.		G8	72
Hare Bay, Newf., Can.	450	F8	72
Harelson, East Baton Rouge, La.	150	B5	180
Haren, Neth.	3,787	A5	282
Harfleur, Fr.	7,495	C4	278
Harford, co., Md.	76,722	A7	182
Hargeisa, Som.	53,000	D5	398
Hargeisa, pol. dist., Som.		D5	398
Harghitei, mts., Rom.		A3	321
Hargill, Hidalgo, Tex.	750	F6	130
Hargrave, Man., Can.	78	F2	60
Hargrave, lake, Man., Can.		C3	60
Hargrave, riv., Man., Can.		C3	60
Hari, riv., Afg.		B2	374
Hari, riv., Iran, Sov.Un.		B5	379
Hariabhanga, riv., India		J9	366
Harihar, India	8,422	F3	366
Harisal, India		E2	368
Härjedalen, prov., Swe.	14,269	*E5	290
Harkers Island, Carteret, N.C.	1,362	C9	186
Harlan, Allen, Ind.	500	A5	140
Harlan, Shelby, Iowa	4,350	C2	142
Harlan, Smith, Kans.	125	C5	144
Harlan, Harlan, Ky.	4,177	D7	178
Harlan, co., Ky.	51,107	D7	178
Harlan, co., Nebr.	5,081	D6	152
Harlan, res., Nebr.		D6	152
Hârläu, Rom.	4,172	A4	321
Harlem, Hendry, Fla.	1,256	*E9	174
Harlem, Columbia, Ga.	1,423	C4	176
Harlem, Blaine, Mont.	1,267	B8	110
Harley Dome, Grand, Utah	5	D6	114
Harleyville, Dorchester, S.C.	561	E8	188
Harlingen, Neth.	11,275	A4	282
Harlingen, Somerset, N.J.	130	C3	210
Harlingen, Cameron, Tex.	41,207	F7	130
Harlow, Benson, N.Dak.	90	B6	154
Harlowton, Wheatland, Mont.	1,734	D7	110
Harman, Buchanan, Va.	700	C2	192
Harman, Randolph, W.Va.	128	C5	194
Harmancik, Tur.	594	B3	307
Harmans, Anne Arundel, Md.	300	B6	182
Harmarville, Allegheny, Pa.	2,000	A4	214
Harmersville, Salem, N.J.	300	E2	210
Harmon, Red River, La.	80	B2	180
Harmon, Ellis, Okla.	15	B4	128
Harmon, co., Okla.	5,852	D4	128
Harmon, creek, W.Va.		A2	194
Harmon, riv., Alta., Can.		B4	54
Harmony, Clay, Ind.	700	C2	140
Harmony, Somerset, Maine	350	D3	204
	(712▲)		
Harmony, Fillmore, Minn.	1,214	H7	148
Harmony, Warren, N.J.		B2	210
Harmony, Iredell, N.C.	322	B5	186
Harmony, Butler, Pa.	1,142	C1	214
Harmony, Providence, R.I.	950	B2	216
Harmony, Halifax, Va.	40	D6	192
Harms, Lincoln, Tenn.	65	C5	190
Harned, Breckinridge, Ky.	375	C4	178
Harnett, co., N.C.	48,236	B6	186
Harney, Carroll, Md.	200	A5	182
Harney, Harney, Oreg.	5	*D7	96
Harney, co., Oreg.	6,744	D7	96
Harney, lake, Fla.		C10	174
Harney, lake, Oreg.		D7	96
Harney, peak, S.Dak.		D2	158
Härnösand, Swe.	16,332	E7	290
Haro, Sp.	8,539	A5	298
Haro, cape, Mex.		B3	224
Haro, strait, B.C., Can.		C14	52
Harold, Santa Rosa, Fla.	400	A4	174
Harper, Keokuk, Iowa	177	C5	142
Harper, Harper, Kans.	1,899	E5	144
Harper, Lib.	5,000	F3	408
Harper, Malheur, Oreg.	100	D9	96
Harper, Kitsap, Wash.	500	D2	98
Harper, co., Kans.	9,541	E5	144
Harper, co., Okla.	5,956	B4	128
Harper, lake, Que., Can.		Q11	66
Harpers Ferry, Allamakee, Iowa	211	A6	142
Harpers Ferry, Jefferson, W.Va.	572	B7	194
Harpersville, Shelby, Ala.	667	B3	168
Harperville, Scott, Miss.	400	C3	184
Harper Woods, Wayne, Mich.	19,995	*G8	146
Harpeth, riv., Tenn.		B5	190
Harpster, Idaho, Idaho		D3	108
Harpster, Wyandot, Ohio	302	B3	156
Harpswell, see Harpswell Center, Maine			
Harpswell Center (Harpswell), Cumberland, Maine	50	E5	204
	(2,032▲)		
Harquahala, mts., Ariz.		E2	124
Harrah, Oklahoma, Okla.	934	C6	128
Harrah, Yakima, Wash.	284	C6	98
Harrell, Calhoun, Ark.	267	D4	170
Harrells, Sampson, N.C.	259	*C7	186
Harricanaw, riv., Que., Can.		Q8	66
Harrietta, Wexford, Mich.	119	E6	146
Harriman, Klamath, Oreg.		E4	96
Harriman, Roane, Tenn.	5,931	C7	190
Harriman, Laramie, Wyo.	25	*E7	116
Harrington, Kent, Del.	2,495	E3	172
Harrington, Washington, Maine	500	D5	204
	(717▲)		
Harrington, Lincoln, Wash.	575	B8	98
Harrington, lake, Maine		C3	204
Harrington Park, Bergen, N.J.	3,581	A2	210
Harris, Washington, Ark.		A2	170
Harris, Sask., Can.	282	E4	58
Harris, Osceola, Iowa	258	*A2	142
Harris, Anderson, Kans.	36	D8	144
Harris, Chisago, Minn.	552	F6	148
Harris, Sullivan, Mo.	171	A4	150
Harris, McCurtain, Okla.	110	E9	128
Harris, Kent, R.I.	500	C2	216
Harris, Scot.		E6	272
Harris, Greenwood, S.C.	850	*C4	188
Harris, Obion, Tenn.	120	B3	190
Harris, co., Ga.	11,167	D2	176
Harris, co., Tex.	1,243,158	E8	130
Harris, hill, Mass.		A3	206
Harris, lake, Fla.		C9	174
Harris, sound, Scot.		D5	272
Harrisburg, Poinsett, Ark.	1,481	B6	170
Harrisburg, Saline, Ill.	9,171	F5	138
Harrisburg, Boone, Mo.	124	B5	150
Harrisburg, Banner, Nebr.	100	C2	152
Harrisburg, Franklin and Pickaway, Ohio	359	*C3	156
Harrisburg, Linn, Oreg.	939	C3	96
Harrisburg, Dauphin, Pa.	79,697	C5	214
	(*257,600)		
Harrisburg, Lincoln, S.Dak.	313	D9	158
Harris Grove, York, Va.	100	A8	192
Harris Hill, Erie, N.Y.	3,944	*C3	212
Harrismith, U.S.Afr.	12,954	E5	420
Harrison, Boone, Ark.	6,580	A3	170
Harrison, Washington, Ga.	209	D4	176
Harrison, Kootenai, Idaho	249	B2	108
Harrison, Cumberland, Maine	550	D2	204
	(1,014▲)		
Harrison, Clare, Mich.	1,072	E7	146
Harrison, Madison, Mont.	151	E5	110
Harrison, Sioux, Nebr.	448	B2	152
Harrison, Hudson, N.J.	11,743	B1	210
Harrison, Westchester, N.Y.	19,201	D3	212
Harrison, Hamilton, Ohio	3,878	C2	156
Harrison (Natrona Heights), Allegheny, Pa.	15,710	C2	214
Harrison, Douglas, S.Dak.	80	D7	158
Harrison, Hamilton, Tenn.	200	E8	190
Harrison, co., Ind.	19,207	D3	140
Harrison, co., Iowa	17,600	C2	142
Harrison, co., Ky.	13,704	B6	178
Harrison, co., Miss.	119,489	E3	184
Harrison, co., Mo.	11,603	A3	150
Harrison, co., Ohio	17,995	B5	156
Harrison, co., Tex.	45,594	C8	130
Harrison, co., W.Va.	77,856	B4	194
Harrison, cape, Newf., Can.		D10	72
Harrison, lake, B.C., Can.		F12	52
Harrisonburg, Catahoula, La.	594	C4	180
Harrisonburg (Independent City), Va.	11,916	B6	192
Harrison Hot Springs, B.C., Can.	613	B16	52
Harrisonville, Baltimore, Md.	215	B6	182
Harrisonville, Cass, Mo.	3,510	C3	150
Harrisonville, Gloucester, N.J.	250	D2	210
Harriston, Ont., Can.	1,592	Q20	64
Harriston, Jefferson, Miss.	200	D1	184
Harrisville, Alcona, Mich.	487	E8	146
Harrisville, Simpson, Miss.	165	D2	184
Harrisville, Cheshire, N.H.	250	F2	208
	(459▲)		
Harrisville, Lewis, N.Y.	842	A6	212
Harrisville, Harrison, Ohio		*B6	156
Harrisville, Providence, R.I.	1,024	B2	216
Harrisville, Weber, Utah	425	B3	114
Harrisville, Ritchie, W.Va.	1,428	B3	194
Harrisville, Marquette, Wis.	100	E4	160
Harrod, Allen, Ohio	563	B3	156
Harrods, creek, Ky.		A5	178
Harrodsburg, Monroe, Ind.	500	C3	140
Harrodsburg, Mercer, Ky.	6,061	C6	178
Harrogate, Eng.	51,900	H11	273
Harrogate, Claiborne, Tenn.	800	B8	190

Harrold, Hughes, S.Dak.	255	C6	158
Harrop, lake, Man., Can.		D5	60
Harrow, Ont., Can.	1,851	R18	64
Harrow, Eng.	216,200	J12	273
Harrowby, Man., Can.	72	E2	60
Harrowsmith, Ont., Can.	415	P24	64
Harrys, riv., Newf., Can.		F6	72
Harry Strunk, lake, Nebr.		D5	152
Harshaw, Santa Cruz, Ariz.	50	G5	124
Harshaw, Oneida, Wis.	20	C4	160
Hârşova, Rom.	4,761	B4	321
Harstad, Nor.	4,214	B7	290
Hart, Sask., Can.	45	F5	58
Hart, Oceana, Mich.	1,990	F5	146
Hart, co., Ga.	15,229	B4	176
Hart, co., Ky.	14,119	C5	178
Hart, lake, Fla.		C9	174
Hart, lake, Oreg.		E7	96
Hart, mtn. Man., Can.		D2	60
Hartell, Alta., Can.	350	E5	54
Hartfield, Middlesex, Va.	200	C8	192
Hartford, Geneva, Ala.	1,956	D4	168
Hartford, Sebastian, Ark.	531	B2	170
Hartford, Hartford, Conn.	162,178	B5	202
	(*763,700)		
Hartford, Pulaski, Ga.	200	D3	176
Hartford, Madison, Ill.	2,355	E3	138
Hartford, Warren, Iowa	271	B7	142
		C4	
Hartford, Lyon, Kans.	337	D8	144
Hartford, Ohio, Ky.	1,618	C4	178
Hartford, Oxford, Maine	50	D2	204
	(325▲)		
Hartford, Van Buren, Mich.	2,305	G5	146
Hartford, Burlington, N.J.	300	D3	210
Hartford, Minnehaha, S.Dak.	688	D9	158
Hartford, Cocke, Tenn.	100	C8	190
Hartford, Windsor, Vt.	450	D4	218
	(6,355▲)		
Hartford, Mason, W.Va.	376	C3	194
Hartford, Washington, Wis.	5,627	E1	160
		E5	
Hartford, co., Conn.	689,555	B4	202
Hartford City, Blackford, Ind.	8,053	B4	140
Hartington, Cedar, Nebr.	1,648	B8	152
Hartland, N.B., Can.	1,022	C2	70
Hartland (Town of), Hartford, Conn.	(1,040▲)	B4	202
Hartland, Somerset, Maine	1,016	D3	204
	(1,447▲)		
Hartland, Livingston, Mich.	200	G8	146
Hartland, Freeborn, Minn.	330	H5	148
Hartland, Windsor, Vt.	200	D4	218
	(1,592▲)		
Hartland, Waukesha, Wis.	2,088	E1	160
		E5	
Hartland, pt., Eng.		J8	273
Hartland Four Corners, Windsor, Vt.	116	D4	218
Hartley, O'Brien, Iowa	1,738	A2	142
Hartley, Rh.&Nya.	2,900	C6	421
Hartley, co., Tex.	2,171	B4	130
Hartline, Grant, Wash.	206	B7	98
Hartly, Kent, Del.	164	D3	172
Hartman, Johnson, Ark.	299	B3	170
Hartman, Prowers, Colo.	164	D8	106
Hartney, Man., Can.	554	F2	60
Harts, pond, N.H.		D2	208
Hartsburg, Boone, Mo.	158	C5	150
Hartsdale, Westchester, N.Y.	9,000	D2	212
Hartsel, Park, Colo.	30	C5	106
Hartselle, Morgan, Ala.	5,000	A3	168
Hartshorn, Texas, Mo.	135	D6	150
Hartshorne, Pittsburg, Okla.	1,903	D8	128
Harts Location (Town of), Carroll, N.H.	(7▲)	*C4	208
Harts Range, Austl.	56	C6	432
Hartsville, Bartholomew, Ind.	399	C4	140
Hartsville, Darlington, S.C.	6,392	C8	188
Hartsville, Trousdale, Tenn.	1,712	B5	190
Hartville, Wright, Mo.	486	D5	150
Hartville, Stark, Ohio	1,353	B5	156
Hartville, Platte, Wyo.	177	D8	116
Hartwell, Hart, Ga.	4,599	B4	176
Hartwick, Poweshiek, Iowa	126	C5	142
Hartwick, Otsego, N.Y.	600	C6	212
Harūt, riv., Afg.		C1	374
Harvard, Latah, Idaho	50	C2	108
Harvard, McHenry, Ill.	4,248	A5	138
Harvard, Wayne, Iowa	150	D4	142
Harvard, Worcester, Mass.	350	A4	206
	(2,563▲)	C1	
Harvard, Clay, Nebr.	1,261	D7	152
Harvard, mtn., Colo.		D4	106
Harvest, Madison, Ala.	500	A3	168
Harvey, Scott, Ark.	50	C3	170
Harvey, N.B., Can.	210	D5	70
Harvey, Cook, Ill.	29,071	B6	138
		F3	
Harvey, Marion, Iowa	270	C5	142
Harvey, Jefferson, La.	10,000	C7	180
		E5	
Harvey, Marquette, Mich.	350	C4	146
Harvey, Wells, N.Dak.	2,365	C6	154
Harvey, co., Kans.	25,865	D6	144
Harvey, creek, Pa.		A4	214
Harvey, lake, Pa.		A4	214
Harvey, mtn., Mass.		B1	206
Harvey Cedars, Ocean, N.J.	134	*D4	210
Harveysburg, Warren, Ohio	514	C2	156
Harvey Station, N.B., Can.	215	D3	70
Harveyton, Perry, Ky.	300	C7	178
Harveytown, Spartanburg, S.C.	200	*B4	188
Harveyville, Wabaunsee, Kans.	204	D8	144
Harviell, Butler, Mo.	177	E7	150
Harwich, Eng.	15,100	J14	273
Harwich, Barnstable, Mass.	800	C7	206
	(3,447▲)		
Harwich Port, Barnstable, Mass.	950	C7	206
Harwick, Allegheny, Pa.	1,500	*C1	214
Harwinton, Litchfield, Conn.	500	B3	202
	(3,344▲)		
Harwood, Ont., Can.	215	P22	64
Harwood, Anne Arundel, Md.	125	C6	182
Harwood, Vernon, Mo.	89	D3	150
Harwood, Cass, N.Dak.	100	D9	154
Harwood Heights, Cook, Ill.	5,688	*B6	138
Harz, mts., Ger.		C4	286
Hasa, reg., Sau.Ar.		B4	383
Hasan Kiādeh, Iran		B2	379
Hasan, mt., Tur.		B6	307
Hasbrouck Heights, Bergen, N.J.	13,046	A1	210
Hasdo, riv., India		E3	368
Hase, riv., Ger.		B2	286
Haselünne, Ger.	4,800	B2	286
Hashimoto, Jap.	32,449	M11	354
Hasi Duaiheb, well, Sp.Sahara		A2	408
Hasi Zegdov, Alg.		C3	402
Haskell, Saline, Ark.	215	C4	170
Haskell, Passaic, N.J. (part of Wanaque)		A4	210
Haskell, Muskogee, Okla.	1,887	C8	128
Haskell, Haskell, Tex.	4,016	C6	130
Haskell, co., Kans.	2,990	E2	144
Haskell, co., Okla.	9,121	C8	128
Haskell, co., Tex.	11,174	C6	130
Haskins, Wood, Ohio	521	A1	156
		A3	
Hasle, Den.	1,596	F5	292
Haslemere, Eng.	11,700	J12	273
Haslett, Ingham, Mich.	1,500	*G7	146
Haslev, Den.	5,468	F2	292
Hassan, India	24,869	F3	366
Hassayampa, creek, Ariz.		E3	124
Hasselt, Bel.	34,486	D4	282
Hasselt, Neth.	2,425	B5	282
Hassfurt, Ger.	6,350	C4	286
Hassi Inifel, Alg.		C4	402
Hässleholm, Swe.	12,169	E4	292
Hasslö, isl., Swe.		E6	292
Hastings, Ont., Can.	816	P23	64
Hastings, Eng.	64,600	K13	273
Hastings, St. John, Fla.	617	B9	174
Hastings, Mills, Iowa	260	C2	142
Hastings, Barry, Mich.	6,375	G6	146
Hastings, Dakota, Minn.	8,965	G6	148
		G7	
Hastings, Adams, Nebr.	21,412	D7	152
Hastings, N.Z.	19,183	C6	437
	(*27,800)		
Hastings, Barnes, N.Dak.	106	D7	154
Hastings, Jefferson, Okla.	200	D5	128
Hastings, Cambria, Pa.	1,751	C3	214
Hastings, Wetzel, W.Va.	300	A6	194
Hastings, co., Ont., Can.	83,745	P23	64
Hastings-on-Hudson, Westchester, N.Y.	8,979	D2	212
Hasty, Newton, Ark.	65	A3	170
Hasty, Bent, Colo.	180	D8	106
Haswell, Kiowa, Colo.	169	D7	106
Hat, creek, S.Dak.		E2	158
Hatay, prov., Tur.	364,992	*C7	307
Hatboro, Montgomery, Pa.	7,315	C6	214
Hatch, Dona Ana, N.Mex.	888	F3	126
Hatch, Garfield, Utah	198	F3	114
Hatchechubbee, Russell, Ala.	250	C4	168
Hatches, Sabine, La.		C2	180
Hatches Creek, Austl.	63	C6	432
Hatchet, creek, Ala.		C3	168
Hatchie, riv., Tenn.		C2	190
Hatchineha, lake, Fla.		C9	174
Hatchville, Barnstable, Mass.	200	C6	206
Hat Creek, Niobrara, Wyo.	5	D8	116
Hațeg, Rom.	3,853	B2	321
Hateruma, isl., Ryūkyū Is., Jap.		M11	349
Hatfield, Polk, Ark.	337	C2	170
Hatfield, Sask., Can.	15	E5	58
Hatfield, Spencer, Ind.	500	E2	140
Hatfield, Pike, Ky.	600	C8	178
Hatfield, Hampshire, Mass.	1,330	B2	206
	(2,350▲)		
Hatfield, Pipestone, Minn.	95	H2	148
Hatfield, Montgomery, Pa.	1,941	C6	214
Hatfield, Rh.&Nya.	8,500	C6	421
Hathaway, Jefferson Davis, La.	50	D3	180
Hathaway, Rosebud, Mont.	27	D10	110
Hatherley Beach, Plymouth, Mass.	320	*D4	206
Hathorn, Marion, Miss.		D3	184
Hathorne, Essex, Mass.		C3	206
Hathras, India	56,619	D2	368
Hatiba, cape, Sau.Ar.		C2	383
Ha Tien, Viet.	5,000	E5	362
Ha Tinh, Viet.	5,000	C5	362
Hatley, Monroe, Miss.	100	B4	184
Hatley, Marathon, Wis.	306	D4	160
Hatnarfjördhur, Ice.		L18	290
Hato Mayor, Dom. Rep.	3,911	C10	233
Hatta, India		D2	368
Hattem, Neth.	3,825	B5	282
Hatteras, Dare, N.C.	700	B10	186
Hatteras, cape, N.C.		B10	186
Hatteras, inlet, N.C.		B10	186
Hattiesburg, Forrest, Miss.	34,988	D3	184
Hattieville, Conway, Ark.	120	B4	170
Hattjeldal, Nor.	159	D5	290
Hatton, Lawrence, Ala.	200	A2	168
Hatton, Polk, Ark.	100	C2	170
Hatton, Sask., Can.	76	E3	58
Hatton, Traill, N.Dak.	856	C8	154
Hatton, Millard, Utah	59	E3	114
Hatton, Adams, Wash.	65	*B8	98
Hatton Fields, Monterey, Calif.	2,362	*D3	94
Hatvan, Hung.	19,000	B4	320
Hatzic, B.C., Can.	395	B16	52
Haubstadt, Gibson, Ind.	1,029	D2	140
Haud, reg., Som.		D6	398
Haugan, Mineral, Mont.	100	C1	110
Haugen, Barron, Wis.	265	C2	160
Haugesund, Nor.	18,924	G1	291
Haughton, Bossier, La.	611	B2	180
Haukivesi, lake, Fin.		E13	291
Haultain, riv., Sask., Can.		B4	58
Hauraki, gulf, N.Z.		B5	437
Haus, Nor.		F1	291
Hauser, Coos, Oreg.	250	D2	96
Hauser, dam, Mont.		D5	110
Hauser Lake, Kootenai, Idaho	127	*B2	108
Haut, isl. Maine		D4	204
Haute-Garonne, dept., Fr.	525,669	*F4	278
Haute-Loire, dept., Fr.	215,577	*E5	278
Haute-Marne, dept., Fr.	197,147	*C6	278
Hautes-Alpes, dept., Fr.	85,067	*E7	278
Haute-Saône, dept., Fr.	209,303	*D7	278
Haute-Savoie, dept., Fr.	293,852	*E7	278
Hautes-Pyrénées, dept., Fr.	203,544	*F4	278
Haute-Vienne, dept., Fr.	324,429	*E4	278
Hautmont, Fr.	15,978	B5	278
Haut-Rhin, dept., Fr.	509,647	*C7	278
Hauts Plateaux, plat., Mor.		B3	402
Hauula, Honolulu, Haw.	950	B4	86
		F10	
Havana, Hale, Ala.	142	C2	168
Havana, Yell, Ark.	277	B3	170
Havana, Cuba	785,455	A3	232
	(*1,217,674)		
Havana, Gadsden, Fla.	2,090	A6	174
Havana, Mason, Ill.	4,363	C3	138
Havana, Montgomery, Kans.	162	E8	144
Havana, Sargent, N.Dak.	206	E8	154
Havasu, creek, Ariz.		B3	124
Havasu, lake, Ariz., Calif.		D1	124
Havel, riv., Ger.		B5	286
Havelock, Ont., Can.	1,205	P23	64
Havelock, Pocahontas, Iowa	289	B3	142
Havelock, Craven, N.C.	2,433	C9	186
Haven, Reno, Kans.	982	E6	144
Haven, Sheboygan, Wis.	50	B6	160
Havensville, Pottawatomie, Kans.	166	C7	144
Haverford, Montgomery and Delaware, Pa.	5,000	A6	214
Haverhill, Palm Beach, Fla.	442	*E10	174
Haverhill, Marshall, Iowa	150	C5	142
Haverhill, Essex, Mass.	46,346	A5	206
Haverhill, Grafton, N.H.	300	C2	208
	(3,127▲)		
Haversham, Washington, R.I.	200	D2	216
Haverstraw, Rockland, N.Y.	5,771	D8	212
Havertown, Delaware, Pa.	35,000	A6	214
Haviland, Kiowa, Kans.	725	E4	144
Havlickův Brod, Czech.	14,068	B2	324
Havre, Hill, Mont.	10,740	B7	110
Havre Boucher, N.S., Can.	310	D8	70
Havre de Grace, Harford, Md.	8,510	A7	182
Havsterns, fjord, Swe.		C2	292
Havza, Tur.	5,155	A6	307
Haw, knob, N.C., Tenn.		C7	190
Haw, riv., N.C.		B6	186
Hawaii, co., Haw.	61,332	D5	86
Hawaii, state, U.S.	632,772	K21	77
			86
Hawaii, isl., Haw.		D6	86
Hawaii, natl. park, Haw.		C5	86
		D6	
Hawarden, Sask., Can.	174	E4	58
Hawarden, Sioux, Iowa	2,544	B1	142
Hawea, lake, N.Z.		F2	437
Hawera, N.Z.	5,620	C5	437
Hawes, Garland, Ark.	100	C6	170
Hawesville, Hancock, Ky.	882	C4	178
Hawi, Hawaii, Haw.	800	C6	86
Hawick, Scot.	16,800	F10	272
Hawke, bay, N.Z.		C6	437
Hawke, isl., Newf., Can.		D8	72
Hawke, riv., Newf., Can.		D7	72
Hawke Harbour, Newf., Can.	15	D8	72
		E10	
Hawkesbury, Ont., Can.	7,929	O26	64
Hawkesbury, isl., B.C., Can.		D8	52
Hawkestone, Ont., Can.	175	P21	64
Hawkeye, Fayette, Iowa	516	B6	142
Hawkins, Bannock, Idaho		G6	108
Hawkins, Wood, Tex.	868	*C8	130
Hawkins, Rusk, Wis.	402	C3	160
Hawkins, co., Tenn.	30,468	B9	190
Hawkins, peak, Utah		F2	114
Hawkinsville, Pulaski, Ga.	3,967	D3	176
Hawk Point, Lincoln, Mo.	270	C6	150
Hawksbill, mtn., Va.		B6	192
Hawkshaw, N.B., Can.	145	D2	70
Hawk Springs, Goshen, Wyo.	125	E8	116
Hawley, Otero, Colo.		E7	106
Hawley, Franklin, Mass.	35	A2	206
	(251▲)		
Hawley, Clay, Minn.	1,270	E2	148
Hawley, Wayne, Pa.	1,433	B6	214
Hawleyville, Fairfield, Conn.	150	D2	202
Haworth, Bergen, N.J.	3,215	A2	210
Haworth, McCurtain, Okla.	351	E9	128
Haw River, Alamance, N.C.	1,410	A6	186
Hawthorn, Washington, Ala.	35	D1	168
Hawthorne, Los Angeles, Calif.	33,035	C5	94
Hawthorne, Alachua, Fla.	1,167	B8	174
Hawthorne, Mineral, Nev.	2,838	E3	112
Hawthorne, Passaic, N.J.	17,735	A1	210
		B4	
Hawthorne, Westchester, N.Y.	4,000	D2	212
Hawthorne, Douglas, Wis.	70	B2	160
Haxby, Garfield, Mont.	5	C10	110
Haxtun, Phillips, Colo.	990	B8	106
Hay, Austl.	3,009	E8	432
Hay, Wales	1,400	I9	273
Hay, Whitman, Wash.	75	C9	98
Hay, isl., Ont., Can.		P20	64
Hay, riv., Austl.		C7	432
Hay, riv., Alta., Can.		D3	54
Hay, riv., N.W.Ter., Can.		F7	48
Hayachine-San, peak, Jap.		E8	354
Hayange, Fr.	11,060	C7	278
Haybro, Routt, Colo.		B4	106
Haycock, Alsk.	16	B5	84
Hayden, Blount, Ala.	187	B3	168
Hayden, Gila, Ariz.	1,760	E5	124
Hayden, Routt, Colo.	764	B3	106
Hayden, Kootenai, Idaho	901	*B2	108
Hayden, Jennings, Ind.	275	D4	140
Hayden, Union, N.Mex.	15	C7	126
Hayden, Uintah, Utah	95	C6	114
Hayden, lake, Idaho		B2	108
Hayden, lake, Maine		D3	204
Haydenburg, Jackson, Tenn.	50	B6	190
Hayden Junction, Pinal, Ariz.	55	F5	124
Hayden Lake, Kootenai, Idaho	247	B2	108
Hayden Rowe, Middlesex, Mass.	600	D1	206
Haydens, Hartford, Conn.	125	B5	202
Haydenville, Hampshire, Mass.	750	B2	206
Haydenville, Hocking, Ohio	661	C4	156
Hayes, Calcasieu, La.	800	D3	180
Hayes, Stanley, S.Dak.	21	C4	158
Hayes, co., Nebr.	1,919	D4	152
Hayes, mtn., Alsk.		C7	84
Hayes, riv., Man., Can.		C6	60
		E6	
Hayes Center, Hayes, Nebr.	283	D4	152
Hayesville, Keokuk, Iowa	122	*C5	142
Hayesville, Clay, N.C.	428	B2	186
Hayesville, Ashland, Ohio	435	B4	156
Hayesville, Marion, Oreg.	4,568	*C4	96
Hayfield, Man., Can.	90	F2	60
Hayfield, Hancock, Iowa	150	A4	142
Hayfield, Dodge, Minn.	889	H6	148
Hayfield, Frederick, Va.	150	A6	192
Hayfield Junction, Hancock, Iowa	150	A4	142
Hayford, Spokane, Wash.	350	D8	98
Hayfork, Trinity, Calif.	400	B2	94
Hay Lakes, Alta., Can.	193	D6	54
Haymana, Tur.	2,420	B5	307
Haymarket, Prince William, Va.	257	A6	192
		B7	
Haymock, lake, Maine		B3	204
Haymond, Franklin, Ind.	120	C4	140
Haynes, Lee, Ark.	200	C6	170
Haynes, Alta., Can.	65	D6	54
Haynes, Adams, N.Dak.	111	E3	154
Haynesville, Claiborne, La.	3,031	B2	180
Haynesville, Aroostook, Maine	100	C5	204
	(187▲)		
Hayneville, Lowndes, Ala.	990	C3	168
Hay River, N.W.Ter., Can.	942	E7	48
Hays, Ellis, Kans.	11,947	D4	144
Hays, Blaine, Mont.	400	C8	110
Hays, Yemen		D3	383
Hays, co., Tex.	19,934	D6	130
Hays Crossing, see Eadston, Ky.			
Haysi, Dickenson, Va.	485	C2	192
Hay Springs, Sheridan, Nebr.	823	B3	152
Haystack, mtn., Okla.		C4	128
Haystack, mtn., Vt.		B3	218
Haystack, mtn., Vt.		F3	218
Haystack, peak, Utah		D2	114
Haysville, Dubois, Ind.	500	D3	140
Haysville, Sedgwick, Kans.	5,836	B5	144
Hayter, Alta., Can.	75	D7	54
Hayti, Pemiscot, Mo.	3,737	E8	150
Hayti, Hamlin, S.Dak.	425	C8	158
Hayton, Calumet, Wis.	95	B6	160
Hayward, Alameda, Calif.	72,700	B5	94
Hayward, Freeborn, Minn.	258	*H5	148
Hayward, Garfield, Okla.	40	B6	128
Hayward, Sawyer, Wis.	1,540	B2	160
Haywood, Man., Can.	125	F3	60
Haywood, Chatham, N.C.	713	B6	186
Haywood, Pittsburg, Okla.	150	D8	128
Haywood, Harrison, W.Va.	950	A6	194
Haywood, co., N.C.	39,711	B2	186
Haywood, co., Tenn.	23,393	C2	190
Hazard, Perry, Ky.	5,958	C7	178
Hazard, Sherman, Nebr.	104	C6	152
Hazardville, Hartford, Conn.	4,000	B5	202
Hazaribagh, India		D4	368
Hazebrouck, Fr.	13,301	B5	278
Hazel, Calloway, Ky.	342	D2	178
Hazel, Hamlin, S.Dak.	128	C8	158
Hazel Crest, Cook, Ill.	6,205	F3	138
Hazel Dell, Clark, Wash.	2,500	*D4	98
Hazel Green, Madison, Ala.	150	A3	168
Hazel Green, Wolfe, Ky.	259	C7	178
Hazel Green, Grant, Wis.	807	F3	160
Hazelhurst, Jeff Davis, Ga.	3,699	E4	176
Hazelhurst, Copiah, Miss.	3,400	D2	184
Hazelhurst, Oneida, Wis.	225	C4	160
Hazel Park, Oakland, Mich.	25,631	B8	146
Hazelridge, Man., Can.	92	*F4	60
Hazel Run, Yellow Medicine, Minn.	115	G3	148
Hazelton, B.C., Can.	279	C9	52
Hazelton, Jerome, Idaho	433	G4	108
Hazelton, Gibson, Ind.	507	D2	140
Hazelton, Barber, Kans.	246	E5	144
Hazelton, Emmons, N.Dak.	451	D5	154
Hazelton, peak, Wyo.		B5	116
Hazelwood, St. Louis, Mo.	6,045	*C7	150
Hazelwood, Haywood, N.C.	1,925	B2	186
Hazelwood, King, Wash.		D3	98
Hazen, Prairie, Ark.	1,456	C5	170
Hazen, Churchill, Nev.	50	D2	112
Hazen, Mercer, N.Dak.	1,222	C4	154
Hazen, strait, N.W.Ter., Can.		B7	48
Hazenmore, Sask., Can.	186	F4	58
Hazle Patch, Laurel, Ky.	200	C6	178
Hazlet, Sask., Can.	200	E3	58
Hazlet, Monmouth, N.J.	9,000	*C4	210
Hazleton, Buchanan, Iowa	665	B6	142
Hazleton, Luzerne, Pa.	32,056	C6	214
Hazlettville, Kent, Del.	35	D3	172
Hazy, Raleigh, W.Va.	750	D6	194
Headford, Ire.	520	H3	273
Head Harbor, isl., Maine		D5	204
Headland, Henry, Ala.	2,650	D4	168
Headlee, White, Ind.	175	B3	140
Head of Island, Livingston, La.	150	B6	180
Headquarters, Clearwater, Idaho	300	C3	108
Headrick, Jackson, Okla.	152	D4	128
Heads, cape, Oreg.		E2	96
Heafford Junction, Lincoln, Wis.	100	C4	160
Healdsburg, Sonoma, Calif.	4,816	C2	94
Healdton, Carter, Okla.	2,898	D6	128
Healdville, Rutland, Vt.	150	E3	218
Healing Springs, Bath, Va.	200	C5	192
Healy, Lane, Kans.	228	D3	144
Healy Fork (Healy), Alsk.	102	C7	84
Heard, co., Ga.	5,333	C1	176
Heardmont, Elbert, Ga.	175	B4	176
Hearne, Sask., Can.	53	E5	58
Hearne, Robertson, Tex.	5,072	D7	130
Hearst, Ont., Can.	2,214	R25	64
Heart, hill, Sask., Can.		F6	58
Heart, lake, Wyo.		B2	116
Heart, riv., Alta., Can.		C4	54
Heart, riv., N.Dak.		D4	154
Heart Butte, Pondera, Mont.	100	B4	110
Hearts Content, Newf., Can.	1,000	G9	72
Heartstone, mtn., Md.		A4	182
Heartwell, Kearney, Nebr.	113	D7	152
Heaters, Braxton, W.Va.	180	C4	194
Heath, Covington, Ala.	125	*D3	168

Heath, Franklin, Mass. 100 (304▲) A2 206
Heath, Fergus, Mont. 11 C7 110
Heath, Licking, Ohio 2,426 B4 156
Heath Springs, Lancaster, S.C. 832 B7 188
Heathsville, Northumberland, Va. 225 C8 192
Heaton, Wells, N.Dak. 100 C6 154
Heavener, Le Flore, Okla. 1,891 D9 128
Hebardsville, Ware, Ga. 2,758 E4 176
Hebbronville, Jim Hogg, Tex. 3,987 F6 130
Hebel, Austl. 65 D9 432
Heber, Navajo, Ariz. 300 D5 124
Heber, Wasatch, Utah 2,936 C4 114
Heber Springs, Cleburne, Ark. 2,265 B4 170
Hebert, Caldwell, La. 70 B4 180
Hébertville, Que., Can. 1,542 P13 66
Hébertville Station, Que., Can. 1,214 *P13 66
Hebgen, res., Mont. F5 110
Hebo, Tillamook, Oreg. B3 96
Hebrides, sea, Scot. D6 272
Hebron, Newf., Can. 150 D9 72
Hebron, N.S., Can. 477 F3 70
Hebron, Tolland, Conn. 200 (1,819▲) C6 202
Hebron, McHenry, Ill. 701 A5 138
Hebron, Porter, Ind. 1,401 A2 140
Hebron, Boone, Ky. 300 A8 178
Hebron, Oxford, Maine 115 (465▲) *D2 204
Hebron, Wicomico, Md. 754 D8 182
Hebron, Jefferson Davis, Miss. 100 D3 184
Hebron, Thayer, Nebr. 1,920 D8 152
Hebron, Grafton, N.H. 30 (153▲) D3 208
Hebron, Morton, N.Dak. 1,340 D3 154
Hebron, Licking, Ohio 1,260 C4 156
Hebron, Dinwiddie, Va. 20 C7 192
Hebron, Pleasants, W.Va. B3 194
Heby, Swe. 1,240 B7 292
Hecate, strait, B.C., Can. D7 52
Hecelchakán, Mex. 3,399 C7 225
Hechingen, Ger. 10,200 D3 286
Hechtel, Bel. 3,560 C4 282
Hecla, Lawrence, Ohio 700 D4 156
Hecla, Man., Can. 25 E4 60
Hecla, Worcester, Mass. 250 B4 206
Hecla, Hooker, Nebr. 4 B4 152
Hecla, Brown, S.Dak. 444 B7 158
Hecla, isl., Man., Can. E4 60
Hector, Pope, Ark. 200 B4 170
Hector, Renville, Minn. 1,297 G4 148
Hede, Swe. 940 E5 291
Hedemora, Swe. 5,359 A6 292
He Devil, mtn., Idaho D2 108
Hedges, Nassau, Fla. 150 A10 174
Hedgesville, Wheatland, Mont. 40 D7 110
Hedgesville, Berkeley, W.Va. 342 B6 194
Hedley, B.C., Can. 500 F12 52
Hedley, Donley, Tex. 494 B5 130
Hedmark, co., Nor. 174,396 *F4 291
Hedo, pt., Okinawa C1 437
Hedona, Okinawa C1 436
Hedrick, Keokuk, Iowa 762 C5 142
Hedwig Village, Harris, Tex. 1,182 *E8 130
Heeia, Honolulu, Haw. 500 G10 86
Heel, pt., Wake A5 437
Heeney, Summit, Colo. 30 C4 106
Heerde, Neth. 2,232 B5 282
Heerenveen, Neth. 7,621 B4 282
Heerlen, Neth. 64,127 D4 282
Heflin, Cleburne, Ala. 2,400 B4 168
Heflin, Webster, La. 289 B2 180
Hefner, lake, Okla. C6 128
Hegeler, Vermilion, Ill. 1,640 *C6 138
Heglar, Cassia, Idaho G5 108
Hegra, Nor. E4 290
Hegyalja, mts., Hung. A6 320
Heiberger, Perry, Ala. 100 C2 168
Heide, Ger. 20,600 A3 286
Heidelberg, Ger. 128,300 D3 286
Heidelberg, Jasper, Miss. 1,049 D4 184
Heidelberg, Allegheny, Pa. 2,118 *C2 214
Heidelberg, U.S.Afr. 7,677 F4 420
Heiden, Switz. 3,094 A5 312
Heidenheim, Ger. 46,600 D4 286
Heijo, see Pyŏngyang, Kor.
Heil, Grant, N.Dak. 100 D4 154
Heilbron, U.S.Afr. 5,279 E5 420
Heilbronn, Ger. 79,100 D3 286
Heiligenblut, Aus. 1,211 C4 313
Heiligenstadt, Ger. 12,700 C4 286
Heilman, Warrick, Ind. 75 D2 140
Heilungkiang, prov., China 14,860,000 B13 346
Heimdal, Wells, N.Dak. 130 C6 154
Heinävesi, Fin. E13 290
Heinola, Fin. F12 291
Heinsburg, Alta., Can. 100 D7 54
Heirnkut (Ft. Keary), Bur. A2 362
Heise, Jefferson, Idaho 64 *F6 108
Heiskell, Knox, Tenn. 175 E9 190
Heisler, Alta., Can. 140 D6 54
Heislerville, Cumberland, N.J. 600 E3 210
Hejaz, reg., Sau.Ar. 2,000,000 B2 383
Hekla, vol., Ice. L20 290
Hekura, isl., Jap. F6 354
Helagsfjället, mtn., Swe. E5 290
Helem, India D6 368
Helemano Camp, Honolulu, Haw. 64 F9 86
Helen, White, Ga. 227 *B3 176
Helen, Raleigh, W.Va. 700 *D3 194
Helena, Shelby, Ala. 523 B3 168
Helena, Phillips, Ark. 11,500 C6 170
Helena, Telfair, Ga. 1,290 D4 176
Helena, Andrew, Mo. 166 B3 150
Helena, Lewis and Clark, Mont. 20,227 D5 110
Helena, Sandusky, Ohio 281 A3 156
Helena, Alfalfa, Okla. 580 B5 128
Helena, Newberry, S.C. 497 C5 188
Helensburgh, Scot. 8,600 E8 272
Helenwood, Scott, Tenn. 30 B7 190
Helgasjon, lake, Swe. E5 292
Helgoland, isl., Ger. A2 286
Heliopolis, Eg., U.A.R. 165,132 D2 382
Helix, Umatilla, Oreg. 148 B8 96
Hellam, York, Pa. 1,234 D5 214
Hellertown, Northampton, Pa. 6,716 C6 214
Hellier, Pike, Ky. 104 C8 178
Hellín, Sp. 14,341 C6 298
Hellville, Malag. 4,046 B9 421
Helm, Fresno, Calif. 125 D3 94
Helm, Washington, Miss. B2 184
Helmand, riv., Afg. D2 374
Helmer, Fayette, Ga. 300 C2 176
Helmer, Latah, Idaho 30 C2 108
Helmeringhausen, S.W.Afr. E3 420
Helmetta, Middlesex, N.J. 779 C4 210
Helmond, Neth. 38,678 C4 282
Helmsburg, Brown, Ind. 180 C3 140
Helmsdale, Scot. C9 272
Helmstedt, Ger. 29,000 B4 286
Helmville, Powell, Mont. *D4 110
Heloise, Dyer, Tenn. B2 190
Helper, Carbon, Utah 2,459 D5 114
Helsingfors, see Helsinki, Fin.
Helsingör, Den. 22,607 E3 292
Helsinki (Helsingfors), Fin. 376,554 F11 291
Helston, Eng. 6,100 K7 273
Heltonville, Lawrence, Ind. 400 D3 140
Helvecia, Arg. 3,390 B3 252
Heman, Fremont, Idaho *F7 108
Hemaruka, Alta., Can. 40 E7 54
Hematheia, see Imathia, prov., Grc.
Hematite, Jefferson, Mo. 204 C7 150
Hemet, Riverside, Calif. 5,416 F5 94
Hemingford, Box Butte, Nebr. 904 B2 152
Hemingway, Williamsburg, S.C. 951 D10 188
Hemlock, Howard, Ind. 150 B3 140
Hemlock, Saginaw, Mich. 900 F7 146
Hemlock, Ashe, N.C. A4 186
Hemlock, Chester, S.C. 1,423 B6 188
Hemlock, res., Conn. E2 202
Hemmingford, Que., Can. 682 S11 66
Hemne, Nor. E3 290
Hemnes, Nor. C5 290
Hemphill, Sabine, Tex. 913 D9 130
Hemp Hill, McDowell, W.Va. 800 *D3 194
Hemphill, co., Tex. 3,185 B5 130
Hempstead, Nassau, N.Y. 34,641 E3 212
Hempstead, Waller, Tex. 1,505 D7 130
Hempstead, co., Ark. 19,661 D3 170
Hemp-Wallace, Garland, Ark. 50 D6 170
Hemse, Swe. 3,837 D9 292
Henagar, De Kalb, Ala. 240 A4 168
Henares, riv., Sp. B5 298
Hendaye, Fr. 6,933 F3 278
Hendek, Tur. 6,661 A4 307
Henderson, Pike, Ala. 150 D3 168
Henderson, Arg. 3,928 C3 252
Henderson, Baxter, Ark. 250 A4 170
Henderson, Adams, Colo. 280 C6 106
Henderson, Mills, Iowa 191 C2 142
Henderson, Henderson, Ky. 16,892 C3 178
Henderson, Saint Martin, La. 500 *D4 180
Henderson, Caroline, Md. 129 B8 182
Henderson, Shiawassee, Mich. 250 F7 146
Henderson, Le Sueur, Minn. 728 G5 148
Henderson, York, Nebr. 730 D8 152
Henderson, Clark, Nev. 12,525 G7 112
Henderson, N.Z. 2,623 H8 437
Henderson, Vance, N.C. 12,740 A7 186
Henderson, Chester, Tenn. 2,691 C3 190
Henderson, Rusk, Tex. 9,666 C8 130
Henderson, Mason, W.Va. 601 C2 194
Henderson, co., Ill. 8,237 C2 138
Henderson, co., Ky. 33,519 C3 178
Henderson, co., N.C. 36,163 B3 186
Henderson, co., Tenn. 16,115 C3 190
Henderson, co., Tex. 21,786 C8 130
Henderson, bay, Wash. D2 98
Henderson, pt., Miss. E1 184
Hendersonville, Henderson, N.C. 5,911 B3 186
Hendersonville, Colleton, S.C. 200 F7 188
Hendersonville, Sumner, Tenn. 950 B5 190
E7
Hendijān, Iran 2,000 C3 379
Hendley, Furnas, Nebr. 79 D6 152
Hendon, Sask., Can. 92 D6 58
Hendon, Bledsoe, Tenn. C6 190
Hendricks, Lincoln, Minn. 797 G2 148
Hendricks, Tucker, W.Va. 407 B5 194
Hendricks, co., Ind. 40,896 C3 140
Hendrix, Wilkes, N.C. A4 186
Hendrix (Kemp City), Bryan, Okla. 142 E7 128
Hendrum, Norman, Minn. 305 D2 148
Hendry, co., Fla. 8,119 E9 174
Henefer, Summit, Utah 408 B4 114
Hengchun, For. N10 349
Hengelo, Neth. 53,580 B5 282
Henghsein, China 18,000 N4 349
Heng Sha, isl., China I18 346
Hengshan, China 1,000 G4 348
Hengshan, China 20,000 L6 349
Hengyang, China 235,000 L6 349
Henlawson, Logan, W.Va. 1,670 D5 194
Henley, Klamath, Oreg. E5 96
Henley Harbour, Newf., Can. 50 D8 72
Henlopen, cape, Del. E5 172
Hennebont, Fr. 6,072 D2 278
Hennepin, Putnam, Ill. 391 B4 138
Hennepin, Garvin, Okla. 325 D6 128
Hennepin, co., Minn. 842,854 F5 148
Hennessey, Kingfisher, Okla. 1,228 B6 128
Henniker, Merrimack, N.H. 850 (1,636▲) E3 208
Henning, Otter Tail, Minn. 980 E3 148
Henning, Lauderdale, Tenn. 466 C2 190
Henpan, cape, Solomon D1 436
Henribourg, Sask., Can. 79 D5 58
Henrico, co., Va. 117,339 C7 192
Henrietta, Ray, Mo. 497 B4 150
Henrietta, Rutherford, N.C. 900 B4 186
Henrietta, Clay, Tex. 3,062 C6 130
Henrietta Maria, cape, Ont., Can. Q25 64
Henrietta Northeast, Monroe, N.Y. 6,403 *B4 212
Henrieville, Garfield, Utah 152 F4 114
Henrique de Carvalho, Ang. A4 420
Henry, Caribou, Idaho G7 108
Henry, Marshall, Ill. 2,278 B4 138
Henry, Scotts Bluff, Nebr. 138 C1 152
Henry, Elko, Nev. 10 B7 112
Henry, Williamsburg, S.C. 100 D10 188
Henry, Codington, S.Dak. 276 C8 158
Henry, Henry, Tenn. 178 B3 190
Henry, Franklin, Va. 125 D5 192
Henry, Grant, W.Va. B5 194
Henry, co., Ala. 15,286 D4 168
Henry, co., Ga. 17,619 C2 176
Henry, co., Ill. 49,317 B3 138
Henry, co., Ind. 48,899 C4 140
Henry, co., Iowa 18,187 C6 142
Henry, co., Ky. 10,987 B5 178
Henry, co., Mo. 19,226 C4 150
Henry, co., Ohio 25,392 A2 156
Henry, co., Tenn. 22,275 B3 190
Henry, co., Va. 40,335 D5 192
Henry, cape, Va. D9 192
Henry, mtn., Mont. B1 110
Henry, mts., Utah E5 114
Henryetta, Okmulgee, Okla. 6,551 C8 128
Henry Kater, cape, N.W.Ter., Can. D12 48
Henrys, fork, Wyo. E2 116
Henry's, lake, Idaho E7 108
Henryville, Que., Can. 644 S11 66
Henryville, Clark, Ind. 400 D4 140
Henryville, Nicholas, Ky. 125 B6 178
Henryville, Lawrence, Tenn. 150 C4 190
Hensall, Ont., Can. 829 Q19 64
Hensel, Pembina, N.Dak. 130 B8 154
Henshaw, Union, Ky. 200 C2 178
Hensley, Pulaski, Ark. 350 C4 170
Henson, creek, Md. C3 182
Henteyn Nuruu, mts., Mong. B9 346
Henzada, Bur. 61,972 C2 362
Hepburn, Sask., Can. 286 D4 58
Hepburn, Page, Iowa 49 D2 142
Hephzibah, Richmond, Ga. 676 C4 176
Hepler, Crawford, Kans. 178 E9 144
Heppner, Morrow, Oreg. 1,661 B7 96
Hepworth, Ont., Can. 387 P19 64
Hepzibah, Harrison, W.Va. 400 B6 194
Herakleion, see Iráklion, prov., Grc.
Herāt, Afg. 75,642 B2 374
Herāt, prov., Afg. *C2 374
Herault, dept., Fr. 471,429 *F5 278
Herbert, Sask., Can. 958 E4 58
Herbert, peak, N.Z. E4 437
Herbertsville, Ocean, N.J. 50 C4 210
Herbesthal, Bel. 2,248 D4 282
Herb Lake, Man., Can. C3 60
Herblet, lake, Man., Can. C3 60
Herbster, Bayfield, Wis. 25 B2 160
Herceg Novi, Yugo. 1,873 C4 316
Herculaneum, Jefferson, Mo. 1,767 B8 150
C7
Herd, Osage, Okla. 100 B7 128
Heredia, C.R. 11,967 E5 228
Hereford, Cochise, Ariz. 150 G5 124
Hereford, Weld, Colo. 50 B6 106
Hereford, Eng. 33,200 I10 273
Hereford, Baltimore, Md. 380 A6 182
Hereford, Baker, Oreg. 35 C8 96
Hereford, Deaf Smith, Tex. 7,652 B4 130
Hereford, co., Eng. 127,400 I10 273
Hereford, inlet, N.J. E3 210
Herelen, riv., Mong. B10 346
Herencia, Sp. 8,989 C5 298
Herendeen Bay, Alsk. 22 D5 84
Herentals, Bel. 17,053 C3 282
Herford, Ger. 54,000 B3 286
Herington, Dickinson, Kans. 3,702 D7 144
Heriot, Lee, S.C. 105 C8 188
Herisau, Switz. 14,000 A5 312
Herkimer, Marshall, Kans. 110 C7 144
Herkimer, Herkimer, N.Y. 9,396 B7 212
Herkimer, co., N.Y. 66,370 B6 212
Herman, Baraga, Mich. 55 C3 146
Herman, Grant, Minn. 764 F2 148
Herman, Washington, Nebr. 335 C9 152
Herma Ness, isl., Scot. A12 272
Hermann, Gasconade, Mo. 2,536 C6 150
Hermano, peak, Colo. E2 106
Hermanos, is., Ven. A6 240
Hermansville, Menominee, Mich. 750 D4 146
Hermantown, St. Louis, Minn. 700 E6 148
Hermanville, Claiborne, Miss. 200 D2 184
Herminie, Westmoreland, Pa. 1,571 C2 214
Hermiston, Umatilla, Oreg. 4,402 B7 96
Hermitage, Bradley, Ark. 379 D4 170
Hermitage, Newf., Can. 350 G8 72
Hermitage, Hickory, Mo. 328 D4 150
Hermitage, Davidson, Tenn. 100 E7 190
Hermitage, Weber, Utah 60 *B4 114
Hermitage, bay, Newf., Can. G7 72
Hermitage Springs, Clay, Tenn. 150 B6 190
Hermleigh, Scurry, Tex. 650 C5 130
Hermon, Penobscot, Maine 230 (2,087▲) *D4 204
Hermon, St. Lawrence, N.Y. 612 A6 212
Hermosa, Custer, S.Dak. 126 D2 158
Hermosa Beach, Los Angeles, Calif. 16,115 C5 94
Hermosillo, Mex. 43,516 B3 224
Hernād, riv., Hung. A6 320
Hernandarias, Par. D5 247
Hernandez, Rio Arriba, N.Mex. 12 B4 126
Hernando, Citrus, Fla. 301 C8 174
Hernando, De Soto, Miss. 1,898 A3 184
Hernando, co., Fla. 11,205 C8 174
Herndon, Rawlins, Kans. 339 C3 144
Herndon, Christian, Ky. 150 D3 178
Herndon, Fairfax, Va. 1,960 A6 192
B7
Herndon, Wyoming, W.Va. 600 D3 194
Herne, Ger. 116,100 *C2 286
Herning, Den. 21,218 H3 291
Hernshaw, Kanawha, W.Va. 900 C6 194
Hero, Jasper, Miss. 100 C3 184
Herod, Terrell, Ga. 100 E2 176
Heron, Sanders, Mont. 50 B1 110
Heron Bay, Mobile, Ala. 250 *E1 168
Heron Bay, Ont., Can. 200 R24 64
Heron Lake, Jackson, Minn. 852 H3 148
Herouxville, Que., Can. 485 R12 66
Herreid, Campbell, S.Dak. 767 B5 158
Herrick, Shelby, Ill. 440 D5 138
Herrick, Gregory, S.Dak. 160 D6 158
Herrick, creek, B.C., Can. C12 52
Herrick, mtn., Vt. D2 218
Herrin, Williamson, Ill. 9,474 F4 138
Herring, bay, Md. C6 182
Herring, run, Md. C4 182
Herrington, La Crosse, Wis. 2,405 *E2 160
Herrington, lake, Ky. C6 178
Herrljunga, Swe. 4,093 C4 292
Hersbruck, Ger. 8,945 D4 286
Herschel, Sask., Can. 203 E3 58
Herscher, Kankakee, Ill. 658 B5 138
Hersey (Town of), Aroostook, Maine (106▲) *C4 204
Hersey, Osceola, Mich. 246 F6 146
Hersfeld, Ger. 23,400 C3 286
Hershey, Lincoln, Nebr. 504 C5 152
Hershey, Dauphin, Pa. 6,851 C5 214
Herstal, Bel. 29,330 D4 282
Hertel, Burnett, Wis. 30 C1 160
Herten, Ger. 49,500 *C2 286
Hertford, Eng. 14,800 J12 273
Hertford, Perquimans, N.C. 2,068 A9 186
Hertford, co., Eng. 715,000 J12 273
Hertford, co., N.C. 22,718 A8 186
Hervás, Sp. 4,868 B4 298
Hervey, bay, Austl. C10 432
Herzliya, Isr. 21,000 B5 382
Herzogenbuchsee, Switz. 3,790 A3 312
Hespeler, Ont., Can. 3,876 Q20 64
Hesper, Winneshiek, Iowa 142 A6 142
Hesper, Yellowstone, Mont. 21 E8 110
Hesperia, San Bernardino, Calif. 950 E5 94
Hesperia, Oceana, Mich. 822 F5 146
Hesperus, La Plata, Colo. 47 E2 106
Hesperus, peak, Colo. E2 106
Hess, Jackson, Okla. 50 D4 128
Hesse (Hessen), reg., Ger. C3 286
Hessel, Mackinac, Mich. 240 C7 146
Hesselö, isl., Den. E2 292
Hessen (Hesse), state, Ger. 4,577,200 *C3 286
Hesse-Nassau (Hessen-Nassau), reg., Ger. *C3 286
Hessmer, Avoyelles, La. 433 C3 180
Hesston, Harvey, Kans. 1,103 D6 144
Hester, Greer, Okla. 22 D4 128
Hetch Hetchy, aqueduct, Calif. D3 94
Hetch Hetchy, res., Calif. D4 94
Heth, St. Francis, Ark. 55 B6 170
Hetland, Kingsbury, S.Dak. 107 C8 158
Hettinger, Adams, N.Dak. 1,769 E3 154
Hettinger, co., N.Dak. 6,317 D3 154
Heuvelton, St. Lawrence, N.Y. 810 A6 212
Heves, Hung. 8,865 B5 320
Heves, co., Hung. 320,000 *B5 320
Hevros, see Evros, prov., Grc.
Heward, Sask., Can. 134 F6 58
Hewett, Boone, W.Va. 800 D5 194
Hewins, Chautauqua, Kans. 110 E7 144
Hewitt, Todd, Minn. 267 E3 148
Hewitt, Passaic, N.J. 200 A4 210
Hewitt, Wood, Wis. 150 D3 160
Hewlett, Nassau, N.Y. 7,500 *E8 212
Hewlett, Hanover, Va. 200 C7 192
Hexham, Eng. 9,400 G10 272
Heyburn, Minidoka, Idaho 829 G5 108
Heyburn, res., Okla. C7 128
Heydalir, Ice. L22 290
Heyworth, McLean, Ill. 1,196 C5 138
Hialeah, Dade, Fla. 66,972 E6 174
F10
Hialeah Gardens, Dade, Fla. 172 *F10 174
Hiattville, Bourbon, Kans. 125 E9 144
Hiawassee, Towns, Ga. 455 B3 176
Hiawatha, Linn, Iowa. 1,336 B6 142
Hiawatha, Brown, Kans. 3,391 C8 144
Hiawatha, Schoolcraft, Mich. C5 146
Hiawatha, Carbon, Utah 439 D4 114
Hibbard, Navajo, Ariz. 10 D5 124
Hibbard, Madison, Idaho F7 108
Hibbard, Marshall, Ind. 150 A3 140
Hibbing, St. Louis, Minn. 17,731 D6 148
Hibernia, Morris, N.J. 450 B4 210
Hickeytown, Johnson, Ark. B3 170
Hickiwan, Pima, Ariz. 52 F3 124
Hickman, Kent, Del. 100 E3 172
Hickman, Fulton, Ky. 1,537 D1 178
Hickman, Lancaster, Nebr. 288 D9 152
Hickman, co., Ky. 6,747 D1 178
Hickman, co., Tenn. 11,862 C4 190
Hickman Mills, Jackson, Mo. C3 150
E2
Hickmans Harbour, Newf., Can. 400 F9 72
Hickok, Grant, Kans. 45 E2 144
Hickory, Graves, Ky. 170 D2 178
Hickory, Harford, Md. 100 A7 182
Hickory, Newton, Miss. 539 C3 184
Hickory, Catawba, N.C. 19,328 B4 186
Hickory, Murray, Okla. 112 D7 128
Hickory, Norfolk, Va. 100 D8 192
Hickory, co., Mo. 4,516 D4 150
Hickory Corners, Barry, Mich. 200 G6 146
Hickory East, Catawba, N.C. 3,274 *B4 186
Hickory Flat, Benton, Miss. 344 A3 184
Hickory Grove, York, S.C. 287 B6 188
Hickory Hills, Cook, Ill. 2,707 *F2 138
Hickory North, Catawba, N.C. 1,541 *B4 186
Hickory Plains, Prairie, Ark. 300 C5 170
Hickory Point, Montgomery, Tenn. B4 190
Hickory Ridge, Cross, Ark. 364 B6 170
Hickory Valley, Hardeman, Tenn. 179 C2 190
Hickory Withe, Fayette, Tenn. 100 C2 190
Hickox, Brantley, Ga. 71 E4 176
Hicks, Vernon, La. 25 C2 180
Hickson, Ont., Can. 235 Q20 64
Hickson, Cass, N.Dak. 52 D9 154
Hickson, lake, Sask., Can. B5 58
Hicksville, Nassau, N.Y. 50,405 D3 212
E8
Hicksville, Defiance, Ohio 3,116 A2 156
Hico, Hamilton, Tex. 1,020 D6 130
Hico, Fayette, W.Va. 800 *C4 194
Hicoria, Highlands, Fla. 75 D9 174
Hicrest (Highland Park), Shawnee, Kans. (part of Topeka) C8 144
Hidalgo, Hidalgo, Tex. 1,078 *F6 130
Hidalgo, co., N.Mex. 4,961 F2 126
Hidalgo, co., Tex. 180,904 F6 130
Hidalgo, state, Mex. 850,394 C6 225
Hidalgo del Parral, Mex. 32,061 B4 224
Hidden Inlet, Alsk. K15 84
Hiddenite, Alexander, N.C. 500 B4 186

Hieflau, Aus.	1,766	C6	313
Hierro, isl., Can.Is.		G10	298
Higashi (Dōgo), isl., Jap.		F4	354
Higbee, Otero, Colo.		E7	106
Higbee, Randolph, Mo.	646	B5	150
Higby, Roan, W.Va.	158	C3	194
Higden, Cleburne, Ark.	40	B4	170
Higdon, Jackson, Ala.	300	A4	168
Higganum, Middlesex, Conn.	900	D5	202
Higgin, lake, Mich.		E7	146
Higgins, Lipscomb, Tex.	711	A5	130
Higgins, pond, Md.		C8	182
Higginson, White, Ark.	183	B5	170
Higginsport, Brown, Ohio	412	D3	156
Higginsville, Lafayette, Mo.	4,003	B4	150
Higgston, Montgomery, Ga.	151	*D4	176
High, des., Oreg.		D6	96
High, isl., Mich.		D6	146
High Bluff, Man., Can.	90	E3	60
High Bridge, Jessamine, Ky.	100	C6	178
High Bridge, Hillsboro, N.H.	125	F3	208
High Bridge, Hunterdon, N.J.	2,148	B3	210
Highcoal, Boone, W.Va.	350	D6	194
Highest Point in Ala.		B4	168
Highest Point in Alsk. and N.A.		C6	84
Highest Point in Ariz.		C4	124
Highest Point in Ark.		B3 C2	170
Highest Point in Calif.		D4	94
Highest Point in Colo.		C4	106
Highest Point in Conn.		A2	202
Highest Point in Del.		A3	172
Highest Point in Fla.		A4	174
Highest Point in Ga.		B3	176
Highest Point in Haw.		D6	86
Highest Point in Idaho		E5	108
Highest Point in Ill.		A3	138
Highest Point in Ind.		B5	140
Highest Point in Iowa		*A2	142
Highest Point in Kans.		D1	144
Highest Point in Ky.		D8	178
Highest Point in La.		B3	180
Highest Point in Maine		C4	204
Highest Point in Md.		B1	182
Highest Point in Mass.		A1	206
Highest Point in Mich.		C3	146
Highest Point in Minn.		D8	148
Highest Point in Miss.		A4	184
Highest Point in Mo.		D7	150
Highest Point in Mont.		E7	110
Highest Point in Nebr.		C1	152
Highest Point in Nev.		F3	112
Highest Point in N.H.		C4	208
Highest Point in N.J.		A3	210
Highest Point in N.Mex.		B5	126
Highest Point in N.Y.		A8	212
Highest Point in N.C.		B3	186
Highest Point in N.Dak.		D2	154
Highest Point in Ohio		B3	156
Highest Point in Okla.		B1	128
Highest Point in Oreg.		B5	96
Highest Point in Pa.		D2	214
Highest Point in R.I.		B1	216
Highest Point in S.C.		A3	188
Highest Point in S.Dak.		D2	158
Highest Point in Tenn.		C8	190
Highest Point in Tex.		D3	130
Highest Point in Utah		C5	114
Highest Point in Vt.		B3	218
Highest Point in Va.		D3	192
Highest Point in Wash.		C5	98
Highest Point in W.Va.		C5	194
Highest Point in Wis.		D4	160
Highest Point in Wyo.		C3	116
High Falls, res., Wis.		C5	160
Highfield, Washington, Md.	500	A5	182
Highfill, Benton, Ark.	92	*A2	170
Highgate, Ont., Can.	378	R19	64
Highgate Center (Highgate), Franklin, Vt.	300 (1,608▲)	B2	218
Highgate Falls, Franklin, Vt.	125	B2	218
Highgate Springs, Franklin, Vt.	125	B2	218
High Hill, Montgomery, Mo.	173	C6	150
High Hill, lake, Man., Can.		C5	60
High Hill, riv., Alta., Can.		B7	54
High Island, Galveston, Tex.	800	E8	130
High Knob, mtn., Md.		B5	182
High Knob, mtn., Va., W.Va.		A6 B6	192 194
High Knob, mtn., W.Va.		C5	194
Highland, Pike, Ark.	50	C3	170
Highland, Madison, Ill.	4,943	E4	138
Highland, Lake, Ind.	16,284	A2	140
Highland, Doniphan, Kans.	755	C8	144
Highland, Howard, Md.	100	B6	182
Highland, Ulster, N.Y.	2,931	D8	212
Highland, Iowa, Wis.	741	E3	160
Highland, co., Ohio	29,716	C3	156
Highland, co., Va.	3,221	B5	192
Highland, lake, Maine		E5	204
Highland, peak, Calif.		C4	94
Highland, pt., Fla.		F9	174
Highland Beach, Palm Beach, Fla.	65	*E10	174
Highland Beach, Anne Arundel, Md.	5	*C7	182
Highland Beach, Oklahoma, Okla.	35	*C6	128
Highland Boy, Salt Lake, Utah	290	*B3	114
Highland City, Polk, Fla.	1,020	D9	174
Highland Creek, Ont., Can.	1,300	Q21	64
Highlandale, Leflore, Miss.	210	B2	184
Highland Falls, Orange, N.Y.	4,469	D8	212
Highland Grove, Ont., Can.	65	022	64
Highland Heights, Campbell, Ky.	3,491	A8	178
Highland Heights, Cuyahoga, Ohio	2,929	*A5	156
Highland Home, Crenshaw, Ala.	75	D3	168
Highland Park, Lake, Ill.	25,532	A6 E2	138
Highland Park, Kalamazoo, Mich.	38,063	B8	146
Highland Park, Middlesex, N.J.	11,049	C4	210
Highland Park, Tulsa, Okla. (part of Tulsa)		B8	128
Highland Park, Dallas, Tex.	10,411	B8	130
Highland Park, Norfolk, Va.	2,500	*D8	192
Highlands, Monmouth, N.J.	3,536	C5	210
Highlands, Macon, N.C.	597	B2	186
Highlands, Harris, Tex.	4,336	F8	130
Highlands, co., Fla.	21,338	D9	174
Highland Springs, Henrico, Va.	5,000	B9 C7	192
Highland View, Gulf, Fla.	700	B5	174
Highmore, Hyde, S.Dak.	1,078	C6	158
Highpoint, Winston, Miss.	75	B3	184
High Point, Guilford, N.C.	62,063 (*100,600)	B6	186
High Point, King, Wash.	100	D3	98
High Point, mtn., N.J.		A3	210
High Point, mtn., W.Va.		C5	194
High Prairie, Alta., Can.	1,743	C4	54
High Ridge, Jefferson, Mo.	250	B7	150
High River, Alta., Can.	2,102	E6	54
Highrock, lake, Man., Can.		C2	60
High Rock, mtn., Md.		A1	182
High Rock, res., N.C.		B5	186
High Shoals, Morgan and Oconee, Ga.	217	C3	176
Highshoals, Gaston, N.C.	900	B4	186
Highsmiths, Sampson, N.C.	30	C7	186
Highspire (High Spire), Dauphin, Pa.	2,999	C5	214
Highsplint, Harlan, Ky.	500	D7	178
High Springs, Alachua, Fla.	2,329	B8	174
Hight, Greer, Okla.	75	*D4	128
High Tatra, mts., Czech.		B4	324
Hightstown, Mercer, N.J.	4,317	C3	210
High Veld, plain, U.S.Afr.		E5	420
Highway Village, Nueces, Tex.	1,927	*F7	130
Highwood, Lake, Ill.	4,499	A6 E2	138
Highwood, Chouteau, Mont.	200	C6	110
Highwood, mts., Mont.		C6	110
Highwood, peak, Mont.		C6	110
High Wycombe, Eng.	43,400	J12	273
Higley, Maricopa, Ariz.	160	E4 H2	124
Higüey, Dom.Rep.	5,208	C10	233
Hiiumaa, isl., Sov.Un.		C4	332
Hijaz, mts., Sau.Ar.		D3	383
Hika, Manitowoc, Wis.	150	B6	160
Hiko, Lincoln, Nev.	15	F6	112
Hikone, Jap.	51,613	L12	354
Hikurangi, mtn., N.Z.		B7	437
Hiland, Natrona, Wyo.	10	C5	116
Hilbert, Calumet, Wis.	736	B5 D5	160
Hilcrest Heights, Polk, Fla.		*D9	174
Hilda, Alta., Can.	225	E7	54
Hilda, Jackson, Miss.	50	E2	184
Hilda, Barnwell, S.C.	259	E6	188
Hildburghausen, Ger.	7,870	C4	286
Hildebran, Burke, N.C.	518	*B4	186
Hildebrand, Klamath, Oreg.		E5	96
Hildesheim, Ger.	85,800	B3	286
Hildreth, Franklin, Nebr.	305	D6	152
Hiles, Forest, Wis.	125	C5	160
Hilgard, Union, Oreg.	15	B8	96
Hilger, Fergus, Mont.	60	C7	110
Hilham, Overton, Tenn.	164	B6	190
Hill, Liberty, Mont.		B5	110
Hill, Merrimack, N.H.	190 (396▲)	D3	208
Hill, co., Mont.	18,653	B6	110
Hill, co., Tex.	23,650	D7	130
Hill, lake, Ark.		D7	170
Hilla, Iraq	46,441	C6	378
Hillburn, Rockland, N.Y.	1,114	*D7	212
Hill City, Camas, Idaho	30	F3	108
Hill City, Graham, Kans.	2,421	C4	144
Hill City, Aitkin, Minn.	429	E5	148
Hill City, Pennington, S.Dak.	419	D2	158
Hillcrest, New Castle, Del.	300	A3	172
Hillcrest, Mercer, N.J.	1,922	*C5	210
Hillcrest, Broome, N.Y.	1,500	*C6	212
Hillcrest, Rockland, N.Y.	1,800	*D7	212
Hillcrest, Sullivan, Tenn.	1,000	B9	190
Hillcrest Heights, Polk, Fla.	138	*D9	174
Hillcrest Heights, Prince Georges, Md.	15,295	*C6	182
Hillcrest Mines, Alta., Can.	850	F5	54
Hillegom, Neth.	10,832	B3	282
Hiller, Fayette, Pa.	1,746	*D2	214
Hilleröd, Den.	10,640	F3	292
Hillhead, Marshall, S.Dak.	75	B8	158
Hilliard, Alta., Can.	130	D6	54
Hilliard, Nassau, Fla.	1,075	A9	174
Hilliards, Franklin, Ohio	5,633	C1	156
Hillier, Ont., Can.	85	Q23	64
Hillisburg, Clinton, Ind.	245	B3	140
Hillman, Montmorency, Mich.	445	D8	146
Hillman, Morrison, Minn.	80	E5	148
Hillman Gardens, Jefferson, Ala.	900	*B3	168
Hillrose, Morgan, Colo.	157	B7	106
Hills, Johnson, Iowa	310	C6	142
Hills, Rock, Minn.	516	H2	148
Hills and Dales, Stark, Ohio	320	*B5	156
Hillsboro, Lawrence, Ala.	218	A2	168
Hillsboro, Jasper, Ga.	150	C3	176
Hillsboro, Montgomery, Ill.	4,232	D4	138
Hillsboro, Fountain, Ind.	517	B2	140
Hillsboro, Henry, Iowa	218	D6	142
Hillsboro, Marion, Kans.	2,441	D6	144
Hillsboro, Fleming, Ky.	125	*B7	178
Hillsboro, Caroline, Md.	201	C8	182
Hillsboro, Scott, Miss.	200	C3	184
Hillsboro, Jefferson, Mo.	457	B7 C7	150
Hillsboro, Carbon, Mont.	25	E8	110
Hillsboro (Hillsborough), Hillsboro, N.H.	1,645 (2,310▲)	E3	208
Hillsboro, Sierra, N.Mex.	250	F3	126
Hillsboro, Orange, N.C.	1,349	A6	186
Hillsboro, Traill, N.Dak.	1,278	C8	154
Hillsboro, Highland, Ohio	5,474	C3	156
Hillsboro, Washington, Oreg.	8,232	B1 B4	96
Hillsboro, Coffee, Tenn.	200	C6	190
Hillsboro, Hill, Tex.	7,402	C7	130
Hillsboro, Loudoun, Va.	124	*A7	192
Hillsboro, Pocahontas, W.Va.	210	C4	194
Hillsboro, Vernon, Wis.	1,366	E3	160
Hillsboro, co., N.H.	178,161	F3	208
Hillsboro, bay, Fla.		C6	174
Hillsboro, canal, Fla.		E10	174
Hillsboro, riv., Fla.		C8	174
Hillsboro Beach, Broward, Fla.	437	*E10	174
Hillsboro Lower Village, Hillsboro, N.H.	100	E3	208
Hillsboro Upper Village, Hillsboro, N.H.	75	E3	208
Hillsborough, San Mateo, Calif.	7,554	B5	94
Hillsborough, N.B., Can.	1,050	D5	70
Hillsborough, co., Fla.	397,788	C8	174
Hillsborough, bay, P.E.I., Can.		C6	70
Hillsburgh, Ont., Can.	490	Q20	64
Hillsdale, Ont., Can.	395	P21	64
Hillsdale, Rock Island, Ill.	490	B3	138
Hillsdale, Vanderburgh, Ind.	250	D2	140
Hillsdale, Vermillion, Ind.	250	C2	140
Hillsdale, Miami, Kans.	142	D9	144
Hillsdale, Hillsdale, Mich.	7,629	H7	146
Hillsdale, Pearl River, Miss.		E3	184
Hillsdale, St. Louis, Mo.	2,788	*C7	150
Hillsdale, Bergen, N.J.	8,734	*A4	210
Hillsdale, Columbia, N.Y.	400	C8	212
Hillsdale, Garfield, Okla.	60	B6	128
Hillsdale, Macon, Tenn.	25	B5	190
Hillsdale, Barron, Wis.	125	C2	160
Hillsdale, Laramie, Wyo.	100	E8	116
Hillsdale, co., Mich.	34,742	H7	146
Hills Grove, Kent, R.I. (part of Warwick)		C3	216
Hillside, Cook, Ill.	7,794	*B6	138
Hillside, Union, N.J.	22,304	B1	210
Hillside Gardens, Jackson, Mich.	450	*G7	146
Hills Point, Dorchester, Md.	75	C7	182
Hillsview, McPherson, S.Dak.	44	B6	158
Hillsville, Lawrence, Pa.	800	B1	214
Hillsville, Carroll, Va.	905	D4	192
Hilltonia, Screven, Ga.	353	D5	176
Hiltons, Scott, Va.	250	D2	192
Hilltop, Cochise, Ariz.	20	G6	124
Hilltop, Fleming, Ky.	75	B7	178
Hill Top, McCreary, Ky.	475	D6	178
Hilltop, Anoka, Minn.	607	*F5	148
Hilltop, Camden, N.J.	1,000	*D2	210
Hilltop, Fayette, W.Va.	765	D7	194
Hillview, Greene, Ill.	305	D3	138
Hillville, Haywood, Tenn.	30	C2	190
Hillwood, Coosa, Ala.	10	C3	168
Hilo, Hawaii, Haw.	25,966	B7 D6	86
Hilo, bay, Haw.		D6	86
Hilpsford, pt., Eng.		G9	273
Hilton, Monroe, N.Y.	1,334	B4	212
Hiltonhead, Beaufort, S.C.	985	G7	188
Hilton Head, isl., S.C.		G7	188
Hilts, Siskiyou, Calif.	470	B2	94
Hilversum, Neth.	93,020	B4	282
Hima, Clay, Ky.	500	C7	178
Himachal Pradesh, ter., India	1,109,466	*B3	366
Himalaya, mts., Asia		B2	368
Himeji, Jap.	252,315	G5	354
Himes, Big Horn, Wyo.		B4	116
Himi, Jap.	68,611	*F6	354
Himlerville, see Beauty, Ky.			
Hinche, Hai.	5,234	C9	233
Hinchinbrook, isl, Austl.		B9	432
Hinchinbrook, isl., Alsk.		G11	84
Hinckley, Eng.	40,000	I11	273
Hinckley, De Kalb, Ill.	940	B5	138
Hinckley, Somerset, Maine	200	D3	204
Hinckley, Pine, Minn.	851	E6	148
Hinckley, Medinah, Ohio	796	A5	156
Hinckley, Millard, Utah	397	D3	114
Hinckley, res., N.Y.		B6	212
Hindaun, India		D2	368
Hindenburg, see Zabrze, Pol.			
Hindiya, Iraq	11,077	C6	378
Hindman, Knott, Ky.	793	C8	178
Hinds, co., Miss.	187,045	C2	184
Hinds, hill, Newf., Can.		F7	72
Hinds, lake, Newf., Can.		F7	72
Hindsboro, Douglas, Ill.	376	D5	138
Hindsville, Madison, Ark.	150	A3	170
Hindubagh, Pak.		D5	375
Hindu Kush, mts., Afg.		B5	374
Hi-Nella, Camden, N.J.	474	*D3	210
Hines, Dixie, Fla.	400	B7	174
Hines, Harney, Oreg.	1,207	D7	96
Hines, riv., Alta., Can.		B3	54
Hinesburg, Chittenden, Vt.	200 (1,180▲)	C2	218
Hinesburg, pond, Vt.		C2	218
Hines Creek, Alta., Can.	360	B3	54
Hinesville, Liberty, Ga.	3,174	E5	176
Hingham, Plymouth, Mass.	10,500 (15,378▲)	B6 D3	206
Hingham, Hill, Mont.	254	B6	110
Hingham, bay, Mass.		D3	206
Hinis, Tur.	2,631	B9	307
Hinkle, Alcorn, Miss.	75	A4	184
Hinkley, San Bernardino, Calif.	75	E5	94
Hinojosa [del Duque], Sp.		C4	298
Hinnoy, isl., Nor.		B6	290
Hinsdale, Du Page, Ill.	12,859	F2	138
Hinsdale, Berkshire, Mass.	990 (1,414▲)	B1	206
Hinsdale, Valley, Mont.	350	B9	110
Hinsdale, Cheshire, N.H.	1,235 (2,187▲)	F2	208
Hinsdale, co., Colo.	208	E3	106
Hinson, Gadsden, Fla.	950	A6	174
Hinton, Pickens, Ga.	400	B2	176
Hinton, Plymouth, Iowa	403	B1	142
Hinton, Caddo, Okla.	907	C5	128
Hinton, Summers, W.Va.	5,197	D4	194
Hintonville, Perry, Miss.	150	D4	184
Hinze, Winston, Miss.		B3	184
Hinzir, cape, Tur.		C6	307
Hirado, isl., Jap.		H2	354
Hiram, Paulding, Ga.	358	C2	176
Hiram, Oxford, Maine	110 (699▲)	E2	204
Hiram, Portage, Ohio	1,011	A5	156
Hirara, Ryūkyū Isl., Jap.	28,504	M12	349
Hiratsuka, Jap.	67,022	G7 L15	354
Hiraya, Jap.		L11	354
Hire, Cherry, Nebr.		B4	152
Hirgis, lake, Mong.		B6	346
Hirosaki, Jap.	138,953	D8	354
Hiroshima, Jap.	357,287	G4	354
Hirschberg, see Jelenia, Pol.			
Hirson, Fr.	11,134	C6	278
Hirtshals, Den.	2,532	H3	291
Hisarönü, Tur.	1,103	A5	307
Hiseville, Barren, Ky.	196	C5	178
Hispaniola, isl., Dom.Rep.		B9	233
Hissar, India	35,297	C1	368
Hit, Iraq	4,830	C5	378
Hita, Jap	69,256	*H3	354
Hitachi, Jap.	131,011	F8	354
Hitchcock, Sask., Can.	78	F6	58
Hitchcock, Blaine, Okla.	134	C5	128
Hitchcock, Beadle, S.Dak.	193	C7	158
Hitchcock, Galveston, Tex.	5,216	G8	130
Hitchcock, co., Nebr.	4,829	D4	152
Hitchins, Carter, Ky.	900	B8	178
Hitchita, McIntosh, Okla.	120	C8	128
Hiteman, Monroe, Iowa	200	C5	142
Hitoyoshi, Jap.	47,877	H3	354
Hitra, Nor.		E3	290
Hitra, isl., Nor.		E3	290
Hitterdal, Clay, Minn.	235	E2	148
Hivonnait, Arg.		A4	252
Hiwannee, Wayne, Miss.	300	D4	184
Hiwasse, Benton, Ark.	200	A2	170
Hiwassee, Pulaski, Va.	400	D4	192
Hiwassee, lake, N.C.		B1	186
Hiwassee, riv., Tenn.		C7	190
Hixson, Hamilton, Tenn.	2,000	C6 E8	190
Hixton, Jackson, Wis.	310	D2	160
Hjälmaren, lake, Swe.		B6	292
Hjardharholt, Ice.		L19	290
Hjelmeland, Nor.		G2	291
Hjo, Swe.	4,738	C5	292
Hjörring, Den.	14,313	H3	291
Hjörring, co., Den.	173,233	*H3	291
Hlohovec, Czech.	11,108	B3	324
Hlomsak, Thai.	5,000	C4	362
Ho, China	5,000	G5	348
Hoa Binh, Viet.	25,000	B5	362
Hoagland, Allen, Ind.	500	B5	140
Hoback, riv., Wyo.		C2	116
Hobart, Austl.	69,016	G9	432
Hobart, Lake, Ind.	18,680	A2	140
Hobart, Delaware, N.Y.	585	C7	212
Hobart, Kiowa, Okla.	5,132	C4	128
Hobart, King, Wash.	300	*B5	98
Hobbema, Alta., Can.	95	D6	54
Hobbieville, Greene, Ind.	150	D3	140
Hobbs, Tipton, Ind.	250	B4	140
Hobbs, Lea, N.Mex.	26,275	F7	126
Hobbs Island, Madison, Ala.	50	A3	168
Hobdo, riv., Mong.		B6	346
Hobe Sound, Martin, Fla.	900	D10	174
Hobgood, Halifax, N.C.	630	A8	186
Hoboken, Bel.	30,552	C3	282
Hoboken, Brantley, Ga.	552	E4	176
Hoboken, Hudson, N.J.	48,441	B1	210
Hobro, Den.	8,344	H3	291
Hobson, Judith Basin, Mont.	207	D7	110
Hobson, Nansemond, Va.	250	A8	192
Hobson, lake, B.C., Can.		D12	52
Hobson City, Calhoun, Ala.	770	B4	168
Hobsonville, N.Z.	921	H8	437
Hobucken, Pamlico, N.C.	500	B9	186
Hoburgen, pt., Swe.		E9	292
Hochatown, McCurtain, Okla.	100	D9	128
Hochfeld, S.W.Afr.		D3	420
Hochgolling, mtn., Aus.		C5	313
Hochien, China		F8	348
Hochih, China		M4	349
Höchst (part of Frankfurt), Ger.		C3	286
Hochstetter, Grnld.		034	290
Hockerville, Ottawa, Okla.	300	B9	128
Hockessin, New Castle, Del.	305	A3	172
Hocking, co., Ohio	20,168	C4	156
Hocking, riv., Ohio		C4	156
Hockinson, Clark, Wash.	50	D4	98
Hockley, Harris, Tex.	200	F7	130
Hockley, co., Tex.	22,340	C4	130
Hodgdon, Aroostook, Maine	225 (926▲)	B5	204
Hodge, Jackson, La.	878	B3	180
Hodgeman, Hodgeman, Kans.		D4	144
Hodgeman, co., Kans.	3,115	E3	144
Hodgen, Le Flore, Okla.	140	*D9	128
Hodgenville, Larue, Ky.	1,985	C5	178
Hodges, Franklin, Ala.	194	A2	168
Hodges, Dawson, Mont.	50	D12	110
Hodges, Greenwood, S.C.	209	C4	188
Hodges Hill, mtn., Newf., Can.		F8	72
Hodgeville, Sask., Can.	312	E4	58
Hodgewood, Choctaw, Ala.	30	D1	168
Hodgkins, Cook, Ill.	1,126	*F2	138
Hodgson, Man., Can.	550	E4	60
Hódmezövásárhely, Hung.	38,000 (54,000▲)	C5	320
Hodonín, Czech.	16,141	B3	324
Hoea Mill, Hoea, Haw.	170	C6	86
Hoehne, Las Animas, Colo.	290	E6	106
Hoek van Holland, Neth.	2,425	C3	282
Hoeryŏng, Kor.	24,330	D14	348
Hoey, Sask., Can.	130	D5	58
Hof, Ger.	57,800	C4	286
Hof, Ice.		L22	290
Hof, Ice.		M21	290
Hofei, China	183,600	J8	349
Hoffman, Grant, Minn.	605	F3	148
Hoffman, Richmond, N.C.	344	B6	186
Hoffman, Okmulgee, Okla.	248	C8	128
Hofn, Ice.		L22	290
Hofors, Swe.	10,901	A7	292
Hofsa, riv., Ice.		L22	290
Hofsjökull, glacier, Ice.		L20	290
Hofsos, Ice.		L20	290
Hofstadhir, Ice.		L20	290
Hofteigur, Ice.		L22	290
Höfu, Jap.	96,821	G3	354
Hog, isl., Fla.		B7	174
Hog, isl., Mich.		D6	146
Hog, isl., N.C.		B9	186
Hog, isl., R.I.		C3	216
Hog, isl., Va.		C9	192
Höganäs, Swe.	7,182	E3	292
Hogansville, Troup, Ga.	3,658	C2	176
Hogatza, Alsk.	40	*B6	84

Hogback, mtn., Mont.		F4	110
Hog Back, mtn., Nebr.		C2	152
Hogback, mtn., Vt.		C2	218
Hogeland, Blaine, Mont.	125	D8	110
Hogem, pass, B.C., Can.		C10	52
Hogglesville, Hale, Ala.	75	C2	168
Högsby, Swe.	8,084	D7	292
Hogsett, Mason, W.Va.	15	C2	194
Hoh, Jefferson, Wash.		B2	98
Hoh, head, Wash.		B2	98
Hoh, riv., Wash.		B2	98
Hohenlinden, Webster, Miss.	50	B3	184
Hohen Solms, Ascension, La.	200	B5	180
Hohenwald, Lewis, Tenn.	2,194	C4	190
Hohenzollern, reg., Ger.		*D3	286
Hohe Tauern, mts., Aus.		C4	313
Hohe Venn, plat., Bel.		D5	282
Hohokus, Passaic, N.J.	3,988	A4	210
Hohsien, China	15,000	M5	349
Hohultslatt, Swe.		E6	292
Hoima, Ug.		B5	414
Hoisington, Barton, Kans.	4,248	D5	144
Hoi Xuan, Viet.		B5	362
Hoka, isl., China		M11	349
Hokah, Houston, Minn.	685	H7	148
Hoke, co., N.C.	16,356	B6	186
Hökensås, mts., Swe.		C5	292
Hokes Bluff, Etowah, Ala.	1,619	B4	168
Hokitika, N.Z.	3,032	E3	437
Hokkaidō, isl., Jap.		C7	354
Hokota, Jap.	29,720	K16	354
Holabird, Hyde, S.Dak.	35	C6	158
Hólar, Ice.		L20	290
Holbaek, Den.	14,946	F2	292
Holbaek, co., Den.	127,127	*I4	291
Holbeach, Eng.	4,805	I13	273
Holbrook, Navajo, Ariz.	3,438	D5	124
Holbrook, Oneida, Idaho	10	G6	108
Holbrook, Norfolk, Mass.	6,000 (10,104▲)	B5 D3	206
Holbrook, Furnas, Nebr.	354	D5	152
Holbrook, Suffolk, N.Y.	3,441	*D4	212
Holcomb, Finney, Kans.	270	E3	144
Holcomb, Grenada, Miss.	97	B3	184
Holcomb, Dunklin, Mo.	436	E7	150
Holcomb, Pacific, Wash.		C3	98
Holcombe, Chippewa, Wis.	275	C2	160
Holcombe, res., Wis.		C2	160
Holcut, Tishomingo, Miss.	100	A4	184
Holden, Alta., Can.	544	D6	54
Holden, Livingston, La.	75	A6	180
Holden, Penobscot, Maine	300 (1,375▲)	*D4	204
Holden, Worcester, Mass.	2,000 (10,117▲)	B4	206
Holden, Johnson, Mo.	1,951	C4	150
Holden, Millard, Utah	388	D3	114
Holden, Chelan, Wash.		A6	98
Holden, Logan, W.Va.	1,900	D2	194
Holdenville, Hughes, Okla.	5,712	C7	128
Holderness, Grafton, N.H.	300 (749▲)	D3	208
Holdfast, Sask., Can.	303	E5	58
Holdingford, Stearns, Minn.	526	F4	148
Holdman, Umatilla, Oreg.		B8	96
Holdrege, Phelps, Nebr.	5,226	D6	152
Holeb, Somerset, Maine	25	C2	204
Hölen, Nor.	334	B1	292
Holgate, Ocean, N.J.	70	D4	210
Holgate, Henry, Ohio	1,374	A2	156
Holguín, Cuba	57,573	B6	232
Holikachuk, Alsk.	98	C6	84
Hollabrunn, Aus.	6,084	B7	313
Holladay, Benton, Tenn.	175	C3	190
Holladay, Salt Lake, Utah	28,000	C4	114
Holland, Faulkner, Ark.	100	B4	170
Holland, Man., Can.	400	F3	60
Holland, Chattooga, Ga.	110	B1	176
Holland, Dubois, Ind.	661	D2	140
Holland, Grundy, Iowa	264	B5	142
Holland, Allen, Ky.	150	D4	178
Holland, Hampden, Mass.	150 (561▲)	B3	206
Holland, Ottawa, Mich.	24,777	G5	146
Holland, Pipestone, Minn.	264	G2	148
Holland, Pemiscot, Mo.	403	E8	150
Holland, Lancaster, Nebr.	110	*D9	152
Holland, Erie, N.Y.	950	C3	212
Holland, Lucas, Ohio	924	A1 A3	156
Holland, Josephine, Oreg.	25	E3	96
Holland, Bell, Tex.	653	D7	130
Holland, Nansemond, Va.	338	D8	192
Holland, Orleans, Vt.	15 (376▲)	*B4	218
Holland, isl., Md.		D7	182
Holland, pt., Md.		C6	182
Holland, straits, Md.		D7	182
Hollandale, Freeborn, Minn.	363	H5	148
Hollandale, Washington, Miss.	2,646	B2	184
Hollandale, Iowa, Wis.	275	F4	160
Holland Center, Ont., Can.	310	P20	64
Hollandia, Neth.N.Gui.		E10	359
Holland Patent, Oneida, N.Y.	538	B6	212
Hollandville, Kent, Del.		E3	172
Hollansburg, Darkes, Ohio	311	C2	156
Hollenberg, Washington, Kans.	55	C7	144
Holley, Orleans, N.Y.	1,788	B3	212
Holley, Linn, Oreg.	100	C4	96
Holliday, Johnson, Kans.	80	B7	144
Holliday, Monroe, Mo.	181	B5	150
Holliday, Archer, Tex.	1,139	C6	130
Hollidaysburg, Blair, Pa.	6,475	C3	214
Hollinger, Furnas, Nebr.	20	*D6	152
Hollins, Clay, Ala.	500	B3	168
Hollins, Baltimore, Md.		C4	182
Hollins, Roanoke, Va.	1,000	C5	192
Hollis, Alsk.	200	D8 K14	84
Hollis, Perry, Ark.	15	C3	170
Hollis, Cloud, Kans.	75	C6	144
Hollis, Hillsboro, N.H.	175 (1,720▲)	F3	208
Hollis, Harmon, Okla.	3,006	D4	128
Hollis Center, York, Maine	75 (1,195▲)	E2	204
Hollister, San Benito, Calif.	6,071	D3	94
Hollister, Twin Falls, Idaho	60	G4	108
Hollister, Taney, Mo.	600	E4	150
Hollister, Halifax, N.C.	450	A8	186
Hollister, Tillman, Okla.	166	D5	128
Hollister, Langlade, Wis.	200	C5	160
Holliston, Middlesex, Mass.	2,447 (6,222▲)	D1	206
Holloway, Swift, Minn.	242	F3	148
Holloway, Belmont, Ohio	541	*B5	156
Holloway Terrace, New Castle, Del.	1,500	*B3	172
Hollow Rock, Carroll, Tenn.	568	B3	190
Hollum, Neth.	878	A4	282
Holly, Prowers, Colo.	1,108	D8	106
Holly, Oakland, Mich.	3,269	G8	146
Holly Bluff, Yazoo, Miss.	250	C2	184
Hollydale, Los Angeles, Calif.	18,000	C5	94
Holly Grove, Monroe, Ark.	672	C5	170
Holly Hill, Volusia, Fla.	4,182	B9	174
Holly Hill, Orangeburg, S.C.	1,235	E8	188
Hollyoak, New Castle, Del.	1,000	A4	172
Holly Park, Ocean, N.J.	500	D4	210
Holly Pond, Cullman, Ala.	193	A3	168
Holly Ridge, Richland, La.	300	B4	180
Holly Ridge, Onslow, N.C.	731	C8	186
Holly Shelter, swamp, N.C.		C8	186
Holly Springs, Dallas, Ark.	100	D4	170
Holly Springs, Cherokee, Ga.	475	B2	176
Holly Springs, Marshall, Miss.	5,621	A3	184
Holly Springs, Wake, N.C.	558	B7	186
Hollyvilla, Jefferson, Ky.	464	*B5	178
Hollyville, Sussex, Del.		F5	172
Hollywood, Jackson, Ala.	246	A4	168
Hollywood, Graham, Ariz.	110	F6	124
Hollywood, Clark, Ark.	25	C3	170
Hollywood, Los Angeles, Calif. (part of Los Angeles)		C5	94
Hollywood, Broward, Fla.	35,237	D6 E10	174
Hollywood, Habersham, Ga.	150	B3	176
Hollywood, Calcasieu, La.	1,750	D2	180
Hollywood, St. Marys, Md.	260	D6	182
Hollywood, Tunica, Miss.	147	A2	184
Hollywood, Lincoln, N.Mex.	100	E5	126
Hollywood, Charleston, S.C.	334	F2	188
Hollywood Park, Bexar, Tex.	783	*E6	130
Hollywood Ridge Farms, Broward, Fla.	108	*E10	174
Holman, Mora, N.Mex.	25	B5	126
Holmavik, Ice.		L19	290
Holmdel Garden, Reno, Kans.	1,437	*E5	144
Holmen, La Crosse, Wis.	635	E2	160
Holmes, Albany, Wyo.	15	E6	116
Holmes, co., Fla.	10,844	A5	174
Holmes, co., Miss.	27,096	B2	184
Holmes, co., Ohio	21,591	B5	156
Holmes, mtn., Wyo.		B2	116
Holmes Beach, Manatee, Fla.	1,143	C6	174
Holmeson, Monmouth, N.J.		C4	210
Holmes Run Acres, Fairfax, Va.	1,000	*B7	192
Holmes Run Park, Fairfax, Va.	1,000	*B7	192
Holmestrand, Nor.	2,320	B1	292
Holmesville, N.B., Can.	350	C2	70
Holmesville, Pike, Miss.	60	D2	184
Holmesville, Gage, Nebr.	120	*D9	152
Holmesville, Holmes, Ohio	422	B5	156
Holmfield, Man., Can.	200	F3	60
Holmquist, Day, S.Dak.	35	B8	158
Holmsbu, Nor.		B1	292
Holmsund, Swe.	5,379	E9	290
Holon, Isr.	30,500	B5	382
Holopaw, Osceola, Fla.	100	C9	174
Holstebro, Den.	16,147	H3	291
Holstein, Ont., Can.	295	P20	64
Holstein, Ida, Iowa	1,413	B2	142
Holstein, Warren, Mo.	150	C6	150
Holstein, Adams, Nebr.	205	D7	152
Holsteinsborg, Grnld.	1,052	Q28	290
Holston, riv., Tenn.		B9	190
Holston High Knob, mtn., Tenn.		B9	190
Holt, Tuscaloosa, Ala.	2,800	B2	168
Holt, Okaloosa, Fla.	600	A4	174
Holt, Ingham, Mich.	4,818	G7	146
Holt, Marshall, Minn.	114	C2	148
Holt, Clay and Clinton, Mo.	281	B3	150
Holt, co., Mo.	7,885	A2	150
Holt, co., Nebr.	13,722	B7	152
Holtland, Marshall, Tenn.	100	C5	190
Holton, Ripley, Ind.	500	C4	140
Holton, Jackson, Kans.	3,028	C8	144
Holton, Muskegon, Mich.	250	F5	146
Holtville, Elmore, Ala.	400	C3	168
Holtville, Imperial, Calif.	3,080	F6	94
Holualoa, Hawaii, Haw.	475	D6	86
Holy, isl., Eng.		F11	272
Holy, isl., Wales		H8	273
Holy Cross, Alsk.	157	C6	84
Holy Cross, Dubuque, Iowa	157	B6	142
Holy Cross, mtn., Colo.		C4	106
Holyhead, Wales	10,300	H8	273
Holyoke, Phillips, Colo.	1,555	B8	106
Holyoke, Hampden, Mass.	52,689	B2	206
Holyoke, range, Mass.		B2	206
Holyrood, Ellsworth, Kans.	737	D5	144
Holy Trinity, Russell, Ala.	300	C4	168
Holzminden, Ger.	23,600	C3	286
Homalin, Bur.		A2	362
Homathko, riv., B.C., Can.		E10	52
Hombori, Mali		C4	408
Homburg, see Bad Homburg (vor der Höhe), Ger.			
Home, Marshall, Kans.	188	C7	144
Home, Baker, Oreg.		C9	96
Home, Pierce, Wash.	600	*D2	98
Home, bay, N.W.Ter., Can.		D12	48
Home Croft, Marion, Ind.	659	E5	140
Home Corner, Grant, Ind.	2,636	*B4	140
Homécourt, Fr.	8,048	C6	278
Homedale, Owyhee, Idaho	1,381	F2	108
Homedale, Franklin, Ohio	670	C1	156
Home Gardens, Riverside, Calif.	1,541	*F5	94
Homelake, Rio Grande, Colo.		E4	106
Homeland, Polk, Fla.	350	D9	174
Homeland, Charlton, Ga.	508	F4	176
Home Place, Hamilton, Ind.	600	C3 D5	140
Homer, Alsk.	1,247	D6 H10	84
Homer, Banks, Ga.	612	B3	176
Homer, Champaign, Ill.	1,276	C6	138
Homer, Logan, Ky.	30	D4	178
Homer, Claiborne, La.	4,665	B2	180
Homer, Calhoun, Mich.	1,629	G7	146
Homer, Winona, Minn.	150	G7	148
Homer, Dakota, Nebr.	370	B9	152
Homer, Cortland, N.Y.	3,622	C5	212
Homer City, Indiana, Pa.	2,471	C2	214
Homerville, Clinch, Ga.	2,634	E4	176
Homestead, Dade, Fla.	9,152	F5 F10	174
Homestead, Iowa, Iowa	150	C6	142
Homestead, Sheridan, Mont.	100	B12	110
Homestead, Blaine, Okla.	75	B5	128
Homestead, Baker, Oreg.	50	B10	96
Homestead, Allegheny, Pa.	7,502	A4	214
Homestead, natl. mon., Nebr.		D9	152
Hometown, Putnam, W.Va.	750	*C3	194
Homewood, Jefferson, Ala.	20,289	B3 E4	168
Homewood, Cook, Ill.	13,371	B6 F3	138
Homewood, Franklin, Kans.	60	*D8	144
Homewood, Anne Arundel, Md. (part of Annapolis)		C6	182
Homewood, Scott, Miss.	100	C3	184
Homeworth, Columbiana, Ohio	600	B5	156
Hominy, Osage, Okla.	2,866	B7	128
Hominy, creek, Okla.		B7	128
Hominy Falls, Nicholas, W.Va.	430	C4	194
Homochitto, riv., Miss.		D1	184
Homosassa, Citrus, Fla.	700	C8	174
Homosassa, pt., Fla.		C8	174
Homosassa Springs, Citrus, Fla.	150	C8	174
Homs, Syr., U.A.R.	132,637	B2	378
Hon, Scott, Ark.	100	C2	170
Honaker, Russell, Va.	851	C3	192
Honan, prov., China	48,670,000	E10	346
Honaunau, Hawaii, Haw.	250	D6	86
Honaz, mt., Tur.		C3	307
Hon Chuoi, isl., Viet.		E4	362
Honda, Col.	16,051	B2	244
Honda, bay, Phil.		C5	358
Hondo, Lincoln, N.Mex.	100	E5	126
Hondo, Medina, Tex.	4,992	E6	130
Hondo, riv., Mex.		G9	224
Hondo, riv., N.Mex.		E6	126
Hondos, riv., Br.Hond.		B3	228
Honduras, country, N.A.	1,888,000	C4	228
Honduras, cape, Hond.		B4	228
Honduras, gulf, Br.Hond.		B4	228
Honea Path, Anderson, S.C.	3,453	C4	188
Hönefoss, Nor.	3,698	A1	292
Honeoye Falls, Monroe, N.Y.	2,143	C4	212
Honesdale, Wayne, Pa.	5,569	B6	214
Honey, lake, Calif.		B3	94
Honey Brook, Chester, Pa.	1,023	C6	214
Honey Creek, Walworth, Wis.	140	F1	160
Honey Grove, Fannin, Tex.	2,071	C8	130
Honeyville, Box Elder, Utah	646	B3	114
Honfleur, Que., Can.	375	P13	66
Honfleur, Fr.	8,661	C4	278
Honga, riv., Md.		D7	182
Hon Gay, Viet.	25,000	B5	362
Hong Kong, Br. poss., Asia	2,748,000	G13 N7	340 349
Hongwŏn, Kor.	25,663	E13	348
Honiara, Solomon	15,000	E2	436
Hon Me, isl., Viet.		C5	362
Hönö, Swe.		D2	292
Honobia, LeFlore, Okla.	30	D9	128
Honohina, Hawaii, Haw.	250	*D6	86
Honokaa, Hawaii, Haw.	1,247	C6	86
Honokahua, Maui, Haw.	475	B5	86
Honokohau, Hawaii, Haw.	35	D6	86
Honokohau, Maui, Haw.	100	B5	86
Honolulu, Honolulu, Haw.	294,179 (*486,400)	B4 B7 G10	86
Honolulu, co., Haw.	500,409	B3	86
Honomu, Hawaii, Haw.	800	D6	86
Honouliuli, Honolulu, Haw.	300	*G9	86
Honor, Benzie, Mich.	278	E5	146
Honoraville, Crenshaw, Ala.	100	D3	168
Hon Quan, Viet.		E5	362
Honshū, isl., Jap.		F5	354
Honuapo, Hawaii, Haw.	22	D6	86
Hood, co., Tex.	5,443	C7	130
Hood, canal, Wash.		B3	98
Hood, mtn., Oreg.		E3	96
Hood, point, Austl.		E3	432
Hoodoo, Coffee, Tenn.	50	C5	190
Hood River, Hood River, Oreg.	3,657	B5	96
Hood River, co., Oreg.	13,395	B5	96
Hoodsport, Mason, Wash.	580	B3	98
Hoogeveen, Neth.	9,059	B5	282
Hoogezand, Neth.	3,040	A5	282
Hooghly, riv., India		J9	366
Hooghly, riv. mouth, India		J8	366
Hook, head, Ire.		I6	273
Hookena, Hawaii, Haw.	15	D6	86
Hooker, Dade, Ga.	300	B1	176
Hooker, Texas, Okla.	1,684	B2	128
Hooker, co., Nebr.	1,130	C4	152
Hooker, mtn., Alta., B.C., Can.		D3 D13	54 52
Hookers Point, Hendry, Fla.	300	*E9	174
Hookerton, Greene, N.C.	358	B8	186
Hooks, Bowie, Tex.	2,048	C8	130
Hooksett, Merrimack, N.H.	900 (3,713▲)	E4	208
Hoolehua, Maui, Haw.	973	B4	86
Hoonah, Alsk.	686	D8 I14	84
Hoopa, Humboldt, Calif.	500	B2	94
Hooper, Alamosa, Colo.	58	E5	106
Hooper, Dodge, Nebr.	832	C9	152
Hooper, Weber, Utah	75	B3	114
Hooper, Adams, Wash.	55	C8	98
Hooper, creek, Nebr.		E2	152
Hooper, isl., Md.		D7	182
Hooper, strait, Md.		D7	182
Hooper Bay, Alsk.	307	C5	84
Hoopersville, Dorchester, Md.	230	D7	182
Hoopeston, Vermilion, Ill.	6,606	C6	138
Hooping Harbour, Newf., Can.	150	E7	72
Hoople, Walsh, N.Dak.	334	B8	154
Höör, Swe.	3,360	F4	292
Hoorn, Neth.	15,372	B4	282
Hoosac, range, Mass.		A1	206
Hoosac, tunnel, Mass.		A2	206
Hoosac Tunnel, Franklin, Mass.	150	A2	206
Hopeton, Woods, Okla.	70	B5	128
Hopetoun, Austl.	55	E4	432
Hopetown, U.S.Afr.	2,696	E4	420
Hoosic, riv., N.Y., Mass., Vt.		C8 A1 F2	212 206 218
Hoosick Falls, Rensselaer, NY.	4,023	C8	212
Hoosier, Sask., Can.	40	E3	58
Hooven, Hamilton, Ohio	500	D1	156
Hoover, dam, Ariz., Nev.		B1 G7	124 112
Hoover, res., Ohio		B4	156
Hooverson Heights, Brooke, W.Va.	1,800	*A4	194
Hooversville, Somerset, Pa.	1,120	C3	214
Hop, riv., Conn.		C6	202
Hopa, Tur.	4,388	A9	307
Hopatcong, Sussex, N.J.	3,391	B3	210
Hopatcong, lake, N.J.		B3	210
Hope, Alsk.	63	C7 G11	84
Hope, Hempstead, Ark.	8,399	D3	170
Hope, B.C., Can.	2,226	F12	52
Hope, Bonner, Idaho	96	A2	108
Hope, Bartholomew, Ind.	1,489	C4	140
Hope, Dickinson, Kans.	463	D6	144
Hope, Knox, Maine	100 (525▲)	D3	204
Hope, Midland, Mich.	80	F7	146
Hope, Neshoba, Miss.	200	C3	184
Hope, Warren, N.J.	300	B3	210
Hope, Eddy, N.Mex.	108	F6	126
Hope, Steele, N.Dak.	390	C8	154
Hope, Malheur, Oreg.		D9	96
Hope, Providence, R.I.	500	C2	216
Hope, isl., B.C., Can.		E9	52
Hope, isl., R.I.		C3	216
Hope, mtn., Scot.		C8	272
Hope, pt., Alsk.		B5	84
Hopedale, Newf., Can.	200	D9	72
Hopedale, Tazewell, Ill.	737	C4	138
Hopedale, Saint Bernard, La.	720	*E6	180
Hopedale, Worcester, Mass.	3,987	B4 E1	206
Hopedale, Harrison, Ohio	932	B6	156
Hope Hull, Montgomery, Ala.	300	C3	168
Hopei, prov., China	44,720,000	D11	346
Hopelawn, Middlesex, N.J.	2,000	*B4	210
Hopelchén, Mex.	2,037	D8	225
Hope Mills, Cumberland, N.C.	1,109	C7	186
Hopemont, Preston, W.Va.	650	B5	194
Hope Valley, Washington, R.I.	900	C2	216
Hopeville, Ont., Can.	110	P20	64
Hopewell, Cleburne, Ala.	50	B4	168
Hopewell, N.S., Can.	374	D7	70
Hopewell, Somerset, Md.		D8	182
Hopewell, Copiah, Miss.	100	D2	184
Hopewell, Mercer, N.J.	1,928	C3	210
Hopewell, Davidson, Tenn.	500	B5 E7	190
Hopewell (Independent City), Va.	17,895	B9 C7	192
Hopewell, Marion, W.Va.	1,230	*B4	194
Hopewell Junction, Dutchess, N.Y.	500	D8	212
Hopi, buttes, Ariz.		C5	124
Hoping, China	3,000	M7	349
Hopkins, Allegan, Mich.	556	G6	146
Hopkins, Hennepin, Minn.	11,370	F6	148
Hopkins, Nodaway, Mo.	710	A3	150
Hopkins, Richland, S.C.	125	D7	188
Hopkins, co., Ky.	38,458	C3	178
Hopkins, co., Tex.	18,594	C8	130
Hopkinsville, Christian, Ky.	19,465	D3	178
Hopkinton, Delaware, Iowa	768	B6	142
Hopkinton, Middlesex, Mass.	2,754 (4,932▲)	B4 D1	206
Hopkinton, Merrimack, N.H.	500 (2,225▲)	E3	208
Hopkinton, Washington, R.I.	120 (4,174▲)	D1	216
Hopland, Mendocino, Calif.	600	C2	94
Hopp, Chouteau, Mont.		C7	110
Hopu, China	80,000	O4	349
Hopwood, Fayette, Pa.	1,615	D2	214
Hoquiam, Grays Harbor, Wash.	10,762	C3	98
Horace, Greeley, Kans.	195	D2	144
Horace, Cass, N.Dak.	178	D9	154
Hor al Hammer, lake, Iraq		D7	378
Horatio, Sevier, Ark.	722	D2	170
Horatio, Sumter, S.C.	500	C7	188
Horburg, Alta., Can.	20	D5	54
Horby, Swe.	3,356	F4	292
Horconcitos, Pan.	1,046	F6	228
Hordaland, co., Nor.	204,141	*F1	291
Hordio, Som.		C7	398
Hordville, Hamilton, Nebr.	128	C8	152
Hořice, Czech.	7,100	A2	324
Horicon, Dodge, Wis.	2,996	E5	160
Horizon, Sask., Can.	70	F5	58
Hormigas, Mex.		B4	224
Hormuz, isl., Iran		D4	379
Hormuz, strait, Iran		D4	379
Horn, Aus.	4,316	B7	313
Horn, Dawes, Nebr.	15	*B2	152
Horn, Swe.		D6	292
Horn, cape, Chile		I4	251
Horn, head, Ire.		F5	272
Horn, isl., Miss.		E4	184
Horn, lake, Miss.		A2	184
Horn, mtn., Ala.		B3	168
Horn, mts., N.W.Ter., Can.		E7	48
Horn, pond, Mass.		C2	206
Hornavan, lake, Swe.		C7	290
Hornbeak, Obion, Tenn.	307	B2	190
Hornbeck, Vernon, La.	374	C2	180
Horncastle, Eng.	3,900	H12	273
Horndal, Swe.		A7	292
Hörnefors, Swe.		E8	290

Hornell, Steuben, N.Y.	13,907	C4	212
Hornepayne, Ont., Can.	1,500	R24	64
Hornerstown, Monmouth, N.J.	145	C3	210
Hornersville, Dunklin, Mo.	752	E7	150
Hornick, Woodbury, Iowa	275	B1	142
Horni Litvinov, Czech.	19,284	A1	324
Hornings Mills, Ont., Can.	295	P20	64
Horni Počernice, Czech.	7,579	*A2	324
Horn Island, pass, Miss.		E2	184
Horn Lake, De Soto, Miss.	300	A2	184
Hornsby, Hardeman, Tenn.	228	C3	190
Hornsbyville, York, Va.	525	A8	192
Hornsea, Eng.	5,400	H12	273
Hörnum, Ger.	1,900	A3	286
Horqueta, Par.	2,817	C4	247
Horrel Hill, Richland, S.C.	200	D7	188
Horry, co., S.C.	68,247	D10	188
Hor Sanniya, lake, Iraq		C7	378
Horse, creek, Colo.		D7	106
Horse, creek, Mo.		D3	150
Horse, creek, Wyo.		E8	116
Horse, peak, N.Mex.		E2	126
Horse, riv., Alta., Can.		B6	54
Horseback Knob, hill, Ohio		C3	156
Horse Branch, Ohio, Ky.	300	C4	178
Horse Cave, Hart, Ky.	1,780	C5	178
Horse Creek, Laramie, Wyo.	100	E7	116
Horsefly, B.C., Can.	20	D12	52
Horsefly, lake, B.C., Can.		D12	52
Horse Head, lake, N.Dak.		C6	154
Horseheads, Chemung, N.Y.	7,207	C5	212
Horse Heaven, Jefferson, Oreg.		C6	96
Horse Heaven, hills, Wash.		C6	98
Horse Island, Newf., Can.		E8	72
Horseneck Beach, Bristol, Mass.	25	C5	206
Horse Nose, butte, N.Dak.		C3	154
Horsens, Den.	36,211	I3	291
Horseshoe, cove, Fla.		B7	174
Horseshoe, lake, Man., Can.		D5	60
Horseshoe, pt., Fla.		B7	174
Horseshoe, res., Ariz.		D4	124
Horseshoe Beach, Dixie, Fla.	150	B7	174
Horse Shoe Bend, Boise, Idaho	480	F2	108
Horse Springs, Catron, N.Mex.	100	E2	126
Horsham, Austl.	7,767	F8	432
Horsham, Eng.	17,800	J12	273
Horsham, Montgomery, Pa.	3,500	*C6	214
Horten, Nor.	11,975	G4	291
Hortense, Brantley, Ga.	380	E5	176
Horton, Marshall, Ala.	140	A3	168
Horton, Hamilton, Ind.	150	B3	140
Horton, Brown, Kans.	2,361	C8	144
Horton, Custer, Mont.	29	D10	110
Hortonia, lake, Vt.		D2	218
Hortonville, Outagamie, Wis.	1,366	D5	160
Hoschton, Jackson, Ga.	378	B3	176
Hosford, Liberty, Fla.	700	A6	174
Hoshab, Pak.		F3	375
Hoshan, China	10,000	J8	349
Hoshangabad, India		E2	368
Hoshiarpur, India	45,291	C1	368
Hoskins, Wayne, Nebr.	179	B8	152
Hoskins, Benton, Oreg.	100	C3	96
Hosmer, B.C., Can.	125	F15	52
Hosmer, Edmunds, S.Dak.	433	B6	158
Hospers, Sioux, Iowa	600	A2	142
Hospitalet, Sp.	14,844	B8	298
Hosston, Caddo, La.	400	B2	180
Hosta, butte, N.Mex.		C2	126
Hoste, isl., Chile		I3	251
Hostomice, Czech.	1,609	*B2	324
Hotchkiss, Delta, Colo.	626	D3	106
Hotevilla, Navajo, Ariz.	560	C5	124
Hotien (Khotan), China	20,000	D3	346
Hoting, Swe.	905	D7	290
Hot Lake, Union, Oreg.		B9	96
Hotse, China	5,000	H7	348
Hot Spring, co., Ark.	21,893	C3	170
Hot Springs, Alsk.	20	B6	84
Hot Springs (Hot Springs Natl. Park), Garland, Ark.	28,337	C3	170
		C7	
Hot Springs, Jefferson, Mont.	50	*D4	110
Hot Springs, Sanders, Mont.	585	C2	110
Hot Springs, see Truth or Consequences, New Mexico			
Hot Springs, Madison, N.C.	723	B3	186
Hot Springs, Fall River, S.Dak.	4,943	D2	158
Hot Springs, Bath, Va.	200	C5	192
Hot Springs, co., Wyo.	6,365	C4	116
Hot Springs, natl. park, Ark.		C3	170
Hot Springs, peak, Calif.		B3	94
Hot Sulphur Springs, Grand, Colo.	237	B4	106
Hottah, lake, N.W.Ter., Can.		D7	48
Hotte, mts., Hai.		C8	232
Hou, riv., Laos		B4	362
Houck, Apache, Ariz.	10	C6	124
Houffalize, Bel.	1,254	D4	282
Houghton, Houghton, Mich.	3,393	B3	146
Houghton, Allegany, N.Y.	1,200	C3	212
Houghton, Brown, S.Dak.	90	B7	158
Houghton, King, Wash.	2,426	D3	98
Houghton, co., Mich.	35,654	C3	146
Houghton, lake, Mich.		E7	146
Houghton Lake, Roscommon, Mich.	150	E7	146
Houghton Lake Heights, Roscommon, Mich.	1,195	E7	146
Houilles, Fr.	22,974	I9	278
Houlka, Chickasaw, Miss.	547	A3	184
Houlton, Aroostook, Maine	5,976 (8,289▲)	B5	204
Houltonville, St. Tammany, La.	200	B7	180
Houma, Terrebonne, La.	22,561	C6	180
		E5	
Houndé, Upper Volta	1,200	D4	408
Hourn, inlet, Scot.		D7	272
Housatonic, Berkshire, Mass.	1,370	B1	206
Housatonic, riv., Conn., Mass.		D3	202
		B1	206
House, Quay, N.Mex.	125	D7	126
House, range, Utah		D2	114
House, riv., Alta., Can.		B6	54
House Rock, Coconino, Ariz.	24	B3	124
House Springs, Jefferson, Mo.	375	B7	150
Houston, Alsk.	8	*C7	84
Houston, Perry, Ark.	206	B4	170
Houston, B.C., Can.	150	C9	52
Houston, Kent, Del.	421	E3	172
Houston, Suwannee, Fla.	50	A8	174
Houston, Houston, Minn.	1,082	H7	148
Houston, Chickasaw, Miss.	2,577	B3	184
Houston, Texas, Mo.	1,660	D6	150
Houston, Washington, Pa.	1,865	C1	214
Houston, Harris, Tex.	938,219 (*1,251,700)	E8	130
		F8	
Houston, co., Ala.	50,718	D4	168
Houston, co., Ga.	39,154	D3	176
Houston, co., Minn.	16,588	H7	148
Houston, co., Tenn.	4,794	B4	190
Houston, co., Tex.	19,376	D8	130
Houston, lake, Tex.		F8	130
Houston Acres, Jefferson, Ky.	723	*B5	178
Houstonia, Pettis, Mo.	261	C4	150
Houston Lake, Platte, Mo.	289	*B3	150
Houstonville, Baldwin, Ala.	250	*E2	168
Houtzdale, Clearfield, Pa.	1,239	C3	214
Hova, Swe.	4,652	C5	292
Hove, Eng.	69,700	K12	273
Hoven, Potter, S.Dak.	568	B6	158
Hovenweep, natl. mon., Colo.		E1	106
Hovenweep, natl. mon., Utah		F6	114
Hoveyzen, Iran		C2	379
Hovfjallen, mtn., Swe.		A4	292
Hovland, Cook, Minn.	150	D9	148
Hovmantorp, Swe.	2,729	E6	292
Howar, wadi, Sud.		B2	398
Howard, Fayette, Ala.	50	B2	168
Howard, Dade, Fla.	350	E6	174
Howard, Fremont, Colo.	43	D5	106
Howard, Taylor, Ga.	200	D2	176
Howard, Elk, Kans.	1,017	E7	144
Howard, Holmes, Miss.	100	B2	184
Howard, Providence, R.I. (part of Cranston)		C3	216
Howard, Miner, S.Dak.	1,208	C8	158
Howard, Brown, Wis.	3,485	*D5	160
Howard, co., Ark.	10,878	C3	170
Howard, co., Ind.	69,509	B3	140
Howard, co., Iowa	12,734	A5	142
Howard, co., Md.	36,152	B5	182
Howard, co., Mo.	10,859	B5	150
Howard, co., Nebr.	6,541	C7	152
Howard, co., Tex.	40,139	C5	130
Howard City, Montcalm, Mich.	1,004	F6	146
Howard City, see Boelus, Nebr.			
Howard Hill, Sullivan, Tenn.	200	B9	190
Howard Lake, Wright, Minn.	1,007	F4	148
Howards Grove, Sheboygan, Wis.	350	B6	160
		E6	
Howe, Butte, Idaho	25	F5	108
Howe, Lagrange, Ind.	550	A4	140
Howe, Nemaha, Nebr.	10	*C3	152
Howe, Le Flore, Okla.	390	D9	128
Howe, Grayson, Tex.	680	*C7	130
Howe, cape, Austl.		F10	432
Howe, sound, B.C., Can.		F11	52
Howe Brook, Aroostook, Maine	25	B4	204
Howell, Woodruff, Ark.	200	B5	170
Howell, Echols, Ga.	141	F3	176
Howell, Livingston, Mich.	4,861	G8	146
Howell, Lincoln, Tenn.	125	C5	190
Howell, Box Elder, Utah	188	B3	114
Howell, co., Mo.	22,027	E6	150
Howells, Colfax, Nebr.	694	C8	152
Howesville, Preston, W.Va.	100	B5	194
Howey-in-the-Hills, Lake, Fla.	402	*C9	174
Howick, Que., Can.	560	S11	66
Howison, Harrison, Miss.		E3	184
Howland, Penobscot, Maine	1,362	C4	204
Howland, isl., Pac.O.		C4	436
Howland Station, Penobscot, Maine		*C4	204
Howley, Newf., Can.	500	F7	72
Howley, mtn., Newf., Can.		F6	72
Howrah, India	433,630	I9	366
Howser, B.C., Can.	45	E14	52
Howson, peak, B.C., Can.		C9	52
Hoxie, Lawrence, Ark.	1,886	A6	170
Hoxie, Sheridan, Kans.	1,289	C3	144
Hoxsie, Kent, R.I. (part of Warwick)		C3	216
Hoy, isl., Scot.		C9	272
Hoya, Ger.	4,400	B3	286
Hoyang, China	15,000	H5	348
Hoyerswerda, Ger.	7,274	C6	286
Hoyleton, Washington, Ill.	475	E4	138
Hoyt, Jackson, Kans.	283	C8	144
Hoyt, Haskell, Okla.	320	C8	128
Höytiäinen, lake, Fin.		E14	290
Hoyt Lakes, St. Louis, Minn.	3,186	D6	148
Hoytsville, Summit, Utah	250	C4	114
Hoytville, Wood, Ohio	334	A3	156
Hoyüan, China	20,000	N7	349
Hradec Králové, Czech.	55,250	A2	324
Hradecký, co., Czech.	583,868	*A2	324
Hranice, Czech.	10,786	B3	324
Hriňová, Czech.	6,831	B4	324
Hron, riv., Czech.		B4	324
Hrubieszów, Pol.	11,300	C6	325
Hsi, China		G5	348
Hsiachiang, China	5,000	L7	349
Hsiaching, China	15,000	G7	348
Hsiamen, see Amoy, China			
Hsian, China		D12	348
Hsian (Sian), China		H4	348
Hsiang, riv., China		K6	349
Hsianghsiang, China	3,000	L6	349
Hsiangyang, China	5,000	I6	349
Hsiapu, China		L10	349
Hsichang, China	25,000	F8	346
Hsienning, China	2,000	K7	349
Hsienyang, China	28,000	H4	348
Hsifeng, China	25,000	D12	348
Hsinchang, China		J16	346
Hsinchiang, China	8,000	H5	348
Hsinchu, For.	52,370	M10	349
Hsinfeng, China	7,000	M7	349
Hsingan, China	10,000	M5	349
Hsingan, mtn., China		E8	348
Hsingcheng, China	5,000	E10	348
Hsinghua, bay, China		M9	349
Hsingning, China	8,000	M7	349
Hsingshanchen, China		B15	348
Hsingtai, China	70,000	G7	348
Hsinhsien, China		F6	348
Hsinhsing, China	1,000	N6	349
Hsinhua, China	10,000	L5	349
Hsining, China	93,700	D8	346
Hsinking, see Changchun, China			
Hsinmin, China	55,000	D11	348
Hsinning, China		L5	349
Hsinpin, China	15,000	E12	348
Hsintai, China	5,000	H8	348
Hsintsai, China	9,000	I7	349
Hsinyang, China	50,000	I7	349
Hsinyeh, China	10,000	I6	349
Hsipaw, Bur.		B3	362
Hsiushui, China	6,000	K7	349
Hsiying (Fort Bayard), China		O5	349
Hstang, riv., China		L6	349
Hsüancheng, China	3,000	J9	349
Hsüanhua, China	114,100	E7	348
Hsüchang, China	58,000	H6	348
Hsuchou (Suchow), China	340,000	H8	348
Hsüi, China	10,000	I9	349
Hsüpu, China		L5	349
Htawgaw, Bur.		A3	362
Huacho, Peru	19,332	C2	245
Huachuca City, Cochise, Ariz.	1,330	*G5	124
Huacrachuco, Peru	723	B2	245
Huaian, China	45,000	I9	349
Huailai, China	10,000	E7	348
Huaiyango, China		I7	348
Huaiyin, China	100,000	I9	349
Huaiyüan, China	40,000	I8	349
Huajuapan, Mex.		L14	225
Huajuapan de León, Mex.	6,684	D6	225
		M15	
Hualalai, mtn., Haw.		D6	86
Hualgayoc, Peru	1,173	B2	245
Hualiche, Mex.		L13	225
Hualien, For.	22,838	M10	349
Huallaga, riv., Peru		B2	245
Huallanca, Peru		B2	245
Hualpai, mts., Ariz.		D2	124
Hualpai, peak, Ariz.		C2	124
Huamantla [de Juárez], Mex.	8,525	L15	225
Huambo, dist., Ang.	567,062	B3	420
Huan, China		G3	348
Huancabamba, Peru	2,443	B2	245
Huancané, Peru	2,236	D4	245
Huancavelica, Peru	11,220	C2	245
Huancavelica, dept., Peru	368,237	C2	245
Huancayo, Peru	43,357	C2	245
Huanchaca, Bol.		D1	246
Huangan, China	2,000	J7	349
Huangchuan, China	25,000	I7	349
Huangkang, China		J7	349
Huangmei, China		J7	349
Huangping, China		L3	349
Huangyen, China	1,000	K10	349
Huangyuan, China		D8	346
Huanta, Peru	4,439	C3	245
Huánuco, Peru	17,700	B2	245
Huánuco, dept., Peru	349,140	B2	245
Huanuni, Bol.	5,696	C1	246
Huara, Chile	1,794	A4	250
Huaral, Peru	5,012	C2	245
Huarás, Peru	16,600	132	245
Huari, Bol.	1,070	C1	246
Huarica, Peru	1,593	C2	245
Huarina, Bol.	1,151	C1	246
Huarmey, Peru	1,333	C2	245
Huascarán, mtn., Peru		B2	245
Huasco, Chile	1,537	A1	252
Huasco, riv., Chile		A1	252
Huatabampo, Mex.	7,702	B4	224
Huatusco, Mex.	6,561	L15	225
Huauchinango, Mex.	9,080	K14	225
Huautla, Mex.		L15	225
Huayllay, Peru	593	C2	245
Huaytará, Peru	718	C2	245
Hub, Marion, Miss.	375	D3	184
Hubbard, Sask., Can.	187	E6	58
Hubbard, Hardin, Iowa	806	B4	142
Hubbard, Dakota, Nebr.	138	*B9	152
Hubbard, Trumbull, Ohio	7,137	A6	156
Hubbard, Marion, Oreg.	526	B1	96
		B4	
Hubbard, Hill, Tex.	1,628	D7	130
Hubbard, co., Minn.	9,962	D3	148
Hubbard, lake, Mich.		E8	146
Hubbard Lake, Alpena, Mich.	150	E8	146
Hubbards, N.S., Can.	442	E5	70
Hubbardston, Worcester, Mass.	500 (1,217▲)	B3	206
Hubbardston, Ionia, Mich.	381	F7	146
Hubbardton, Rutland, Vt.	25 (238▲)	D2	218
Hubbardton, riv., Vt.		D2	218
Hubbell, Houghton, Mich.	1,429	B3	146
Hubbell, Thayer, Nebr.	126	D8	152
Huberdeau, Que., Can.	890	S10	66
Hubli, India	129,609	E3	366
Huckleberry, mtn., Oreg.		D4	96
Huckleberry, mts., Wash.		A9	98
Huckleberry Corner, Plymouth, Mass.	75	C6	206
Huddersfield, Eng.	127,600	H11	273
Huddleston, Bedford, Va.	85	C5	192
Hudiksvall, Swe.	10,605	F7	291
Hudin, Som.		D6	398
Hudson, Que., Can.	1,549	S10	66
		S15	
Hudson, Weld, Colo.	430	B6	106
Hudson, McLean, Ill.	493	*C5	138
Hudson, Steuben, Ind.	428	A4	140
Hudson, Black Hawk, Iowa	1,085	B5	142
Hudson, Stafford, Kans.	201	D5	144
Hudson, Penobscot, Maine	130 (542▲)	*C4	204
Hudson, Dorchester, Md.	125	C7	182
Hudson, Middlesex, Mass.	9,666	B4	206
		D1	
Hudson, Lenawee, Mich.	2,546	H7	146
Hudson, Hillsboro, N.H.	3,651 (5,876▲)	F4	208
Hudson, Columbia, N.Y.	11,075	C8	212
Hudson, Caldwell, N.C.	1,536	B4	186
Hudson, Summit, Ohio	2,438	A5	156
Hudson, Lincoln, S.Dak.	455	D9	158
Hudson, St. Croix, Wis.	4,325	D1	160
Hudson, Fremont, Wyo.	369	D4	116
Hudson, co., N.J.	610,734	B4	210
Hudson, bay, Can.		E10	48
Hudson, mtn., Maine		B3	204
Hudson, riv., N.Y.		C8	212
Hudson, strait, Can.		E11	48
Hudson Bay, Sask., Can.	1,421	D6	58
Hudson Falls, Washington, N.Y.	7,752	B8	212
Hudson Heights, Que., Can.	1,289	S15	66
Hudson Hope, B.C., Can.		B12	52
Hudson Lake, La Porte, Ind.	800	A3	140
Hudsonville, Ottawa, Mich.	2,649	G6	146
Hudsonville, Marshall, Miss.	40	A3	184
Hudspeth, co., Tex.	3,343	D3	130
Hudwin, lake, Man., Can.		D5	60
Hue, Viet.	96,388	C5	362
Hueco, mts., Tex.		D3	130
Huedin, Rom.	5,134	A2	321
Huehuetenango, Guat.	6,188	C2	228
Huejutla, Mex.	3,682	C6	225
		K14	
Huelma, Sp.	6,365	D5	298
Huelva, Sp.	56,427	D3	298
Huelva, prov., Sp.	369,722	*D3	298
Huentelauquén, Chile		B1	252
Huércal-Overa, Sp.	4,676	D6	298
Huerfano, co., Colo.	7,867	E5	106
Huerfano, riv., Colo.		E6	106
Huerva, riv., Sp.		B6	298
Huesca, Sp.	17,730	A6	298
Huesca, prov., Sp.	237,681	*A6	298
Huéscar, Sp.	5,499	D5	298
Huetamo de Núñez, Mex.	5,633	D5	225
		L13	
Huete, Sp.	3,433	B5	298
Huetter, Kootenai, Idaho	114	*B2	108
Hueysville, Floyd, Ky.	650	C8	178
Hueytown, Jefferson, Ala.	5,997	E4	168
Huff, Independence, Ark.	70	B5	170
Huffakers, Washoe, Nev.	300	D2	112
Huffman, Jefferson, Ala. (part of Birmingham)		E5	168
Huffman, Mississippi, Ark.	200	B7	170
Huger, Berkeley, S.C.	500	E4	188
Hughenden, Austl.	1,772	C8	432
Hughenden, Alta., Can.	212	D7	54
Hughes, Alsk.	49	B6	84
Hughes, St. Francis, Ark.	1,960	C6	170
Hughes, Austl.		E5	432
Hughes, Latimer, Okla.		D9	128
Hughes, co., Okla.	15,144	C7	128
Hughes, co., S.Dak.	12,725	C5	158
Hughes, range, B.C., Can.		F15	52
Hughes, riv., Man., Can.		B2	60
Hughes, riv., W.Va.		B3	194
Hughesdale, Providence, R.I.		B3	216
Hughes Springs, Cass, Tex.	1,813	*C8	130
Hugheston, Kanawha, W.Va.	600	*C6	194
Hughestown, Luzerne, Pa.	1,615	*B5	214
Hughesville, Charles, Md.	160	C6	182
Hughesville, Pettis, Mo.	134	C4	150
Hughesville, Judith Basin, Mont.	7	C6	110
Hughesville, Lycoming, Pa.	2,218	B5	214
Hughson, Stanislaus, Calif.	1,898	*D3	94
Hughton, Sask., Can.	100	E4	58
Hugo, Lincoln, Colo.	811	C7	106
Hugo, Washington, Minn.	538	F7	148
Hugo, Choctaw, Okla.	6,287	D8	128
Hugo, Josephine, Oreg.		E3	96
Hugoton, Stevens, Kans.	2,912	E2	144
Huguley, Chambers, Ala.	2,189	*C4	168
Huhehot (Kueisui), China	148,400	E5	348
Huhucunya, Ven.		D6	240
Huichang, China	5,000	M7	349
Huichapan, Mex.	2,197	K14	225
Hüichŏn, Kor.	14,619	E13	348
Huila, dept., Col.	330,270	C1	244
Huila, dist., Ang.	503,605	C2	420
Huilai, China	10,000	N8	349
Huili, China		F8	346
Huimin, China	5,000	G8	348
Huinan, China	1,000	D13	348
Huipulco, Mex.		G10	224
Huitzuco, Mex.	4,667	D6	225
		L14	
Huitzuco [de los Figueroa], Mex.	4,667	L14	225
Huixtla, Mex.	10,208	D7	225
Huiyang, China	30,000	N7	349
Huizen, Neth.	13,104	B4	282
Hukou, China	25,000	K8	349
Hukuntsi, Bech.	1,423	D4	420
Hulah, Osage, Okla.	50	B7	128
Hulah, res., Okla.		B7	128
Hulan, China	49,423	B13	348
Hulbert, Crittenden, Ark.	500	B6	170
Hulbert, Chippewa, Mich.	300	C6	146
Hulbert, Cherokee, Okla.	500	C8	128
Hulda, Isr.		C5	382
Huleh, lake, Isr.		A6	382
Hulett, Crook, Wyo.	335	B8	116
Hull, Tuscaloosa, Ala.	150	B2	168
Hull, Que., Can.	49,243	S9	66
Hull, Eng.	300,200	H12	273
Hull, Madison, Ga.	119	B3	176
Hull, Pike, Ill.	535	D2	138
Hull, Sioux, Iowa	1,289	A1	142
Hull, Plymouth, Mass.	7,055	B6	206
		D3	
Hull, co., Que., Can.	69,079	S9	66
Hulls Cove, Hancock, Maine	350	D4	204
Hullt, Marion, Oreg.		C2	96
		C4	
Hultsfred, Swe.	4,005	D6	292
Hulun (Hailar), China	16,000	A9	348
Hulutao, China	20,000	E10	348
Humacao, P.R.	10,851	C12	233
Humahuaca, Arg.	2,094	B4	250
Humaitá, Braz.	781	G4	256
Humansdorp, U.S.Afr.	2,560	F4	420
Humansville, Polk, Mo.	745	D4	150
Humarock, Plymouth, Mass.	250	E4	206
Humbe, Ang.		C2	420
Humber, riv., Eng.		H12	273
Humbermouth, Newf., Can. (part of Corner Brook)		F7	72
Humbird, Clark, Wis.	300	D3	160
Humble, Harris, Tex.	1,711	E8	130
		F8	
Humble City, Lea, N.Mex.	33	F7	126

Humboldt, Yavapai, Ariz.	450	D3	124
Humboldt, Sask., Can.	2,916	D5	58
Humboldt, Humboldt, Iowa	4,031	B3	142
Humboldt, Allen, Kans.	2,285	E8	144
Humboldt, Marquette, Mich.		C4	146
Humboldt, Kittson, Minn.	169	C1	148
Humboldt, Richardson, Nebr.	1,322	D10	152
Humboldt, Pershing, Nev.	30	C3	112
Humboldt, Minnehaha, S.Dak.	446	D8	158
Humboldt, Gibson, Tenn.	8,482	C3	190
Humboldt, co., Calif.	104,892	B1	94
Humboldt, co., Iowa	13,150	B3	142
Humboldt, co., Nev.	5,708	B3	112
Humboldt, range, Nev.		C3	112
Humboldt, riv., Nev.		C3	112
Hume, Edgar, Ill.	449	D6	138
Hume, Bates, Mo.	369	C3	150
Hume, Fauquier, Va.	130	B7	192
Humeston, Wayne, Iowa	638	D4	142
Hummelstown, Dauphin, Pa.	4,474	*C5	214
Hummels Wharf, Snyder, Pa.	900	C5	214
Humnoke, Lonoke, Ark.	319	C5	170
Humpata, Ang.	490	C2	420
Humphrey, Arkansas and Jefferson, Ark.	649	C5	170
Humphrey, Clark, Idaho	25	E6	108
Humphrey, Platte, Nebr.	801	C8	152
Humphreys, Sullivan, Mo.	163	A4	150
Humphreys, Jackson, Okla.	50	D4	128
Humphreys, co., Miss.	19,093	B2	184
Humphreys, co., Tenn.	11,511	B4	190
Humphreys, mtn., Calif.		D4	94
Humphreys, peak, Ariz.		C4	124
Humpolec, Czech.	5,083	B2	324
Humptulips, Grays Harbor, Wash.	110	B3	98
Hūn, Libya		B3	394
Húnaflói, bay, Ice.		L19	290
Hunan, prov., China	36,220,000	F10	346
Hunchun, China	13,974	D15	348
Hundested, Den.	3,001	F2	292
Hundred, Wetzel, W.Va.	475	B4	194
Hunedoara, Rom.	36,498	B2	321
Hungary, country, Eur.	9,911,000	D6	266
			320
Hunger, mtn., Mass.		B1	206
Hunger, mtn., Vt.		C3	218
Hungerford, Austl.	39	D8	432
Hŭnghae, Kor.		G14	348
Hungnam, Kor.	143,600	F13	348
Hungry Horse, Flathead, Mont.	500	B2	110
Hungry Horse, res., Mont.		B3	110
Hungtze, lake, China		I9	349
Hunnebostrand, Swe.		C2	292
Hunnewell, Sumner, Kans.	83	E6	144
Hunnewell, Shelby, Mo.	284	B6	150
Hunsrück, mts., Ger.		D2	286
Hunstanton, Eng.	4,100	I13	273
Hunt, Johnson, Ark.	50	B3	170
Hunt, co., Tex.	39,399	C7	130
Hunt, mtn., Yukon, Can.		E6	48
Hunt, mtn., Wyo.		B5	116
Hunte, riv., Ger.		B3	286
Hunter, Montgomery, Ala.	1,500	*C3	168
Hunter, Woodruff, Ark.	286	B5	170
Hunter, Mitchell, Kans.	229	C5	144
Hunter, Carter, Mo.	105	E7	150
Hunter, Greene, N.Y.	457	C7	212
Hunter, Cass, N.Dak.	446	C8	154
Hunter, Garfield, Okla.	203	B6	128
Hunter, cape, Solomon		E2	436
Hunter, isl., B.C., Can.		E8	52
Hunter, is., Austl.		G8	432
Hunter, mtn., N.Y.		C7	212
Hunterdon, co., N.J.	54,107	B2	210
Hunters, Stevens, Wash.	220	A8	98
Hunters, hot springs, Oreg.		E6	96
Hunters Creek, Harris, Tex.	2,478	*E8	130
Huntersfield, mtn., N.Y.		C7	212
Hunters River, P.E.I., Can.	390	C6	70
Huntersville, Mecklenburg, N.C.	1,004	B5	186
Huntersville, Madison, Tenn.		C3	190
Huntersville, Pocahontas, W.Va.	100	C4	194
Huntertown, Allen, Ind.	400	A4	140
Hunting, creek, Md.		C6	182
Hunting, isl., S.C.		G8	188
Huntingburg, Dubois, Ind.	4,146	D3	140
Huntingdon, B.C., Can.	200	C15	52
Huntingdon, Que., Can.	2,995	S10	66
Huntingdon, Huntingdon, Pa.	7,234	C3	214
Huntingdon, Carroll, Tenn.	2,119	B3	190
Huntingdon, co., Que., Can.	14,278	S10	66
Huntingdon, co., Eng.	75,300	I12	273
Huntingdon, co., Pa.	39,457	C3	214
Huntingdon, isl., Newf., Can.		D7	72
Hunting Hill, Montgomery, Md.	150	B5	182
Huntington, Sebastian, Ark.	560	B2	170
Huntington, Huntington, Ind.	16,185	B4	140
Huntington, Hampshire, Mass.	900	B2	206
	(1,392▲)		
Huntington, Warren, N.J.	1,879	*B2	210
Huntington, Suffolk, N.Y.	11,255	D3	212
		E8	
Huntington, Baker, Oreg.	689	C9	96
Huntington, Angelina, Tex.	1,009	D8	130
Huntington, Emery, Utah	787	D5	114
Huntington, Chittenden, Vt.	118	C3	218
	(518▲)		
Huntington, Cabell, W.Va.	83,627	C2	194
	(*231,100)		
Huntington, co., Ind.	33,814	B4	140
Huntington Beach, Orange, Calif.	11,492	D5	94
Huntington Center, Chittenden, Vt.	100	C3	218
Huntington Park, Los Angeles, Calif.	29,920	C5	94
Huntington Station, Suffolk, N.Y.	23,438	D3	212
Huntington Woods, Oakland, Mich.	8,746	B8	146
Huntingtown, Calvert, Md.	165	C6	182
Hunting Valley, Cuyahoga and Geauga, Ohio	629	*A5	156
Huntland, Franklin, Tenn.	500	C5	190
Huntleigh, St. Louis, Mo.	375	*C7	150
Huntley, McHenry, Ill.	1,143	A5	138
Huntley, Faribault, Minn.	136	H4	148
Huntley, Yellowstone, Mont.	278	E8	110
Huntley, Harlan, Nebr.	91	D6	152
Huntley, Goshen, Wyo.	75	E8	116
Huntly, Scot.	4,000	D10	272
Huntly, Rappahannock, Va.	25	B6	192
Huntsman, Cheyenne, Nebr.	10	*C3	152
Hunts Point, King, Wash.	428	*D3	98
Huntsville, Madison, Ala.	72,365	A3	168
Huntsville, Madison, Ark.	1,050	A3	170
Huntsville, Ont., Can.	3,051	O21	64
		S25	
Huntsville, Madison, Ind.	300	C4	140
Huntsville, Butler, Ky.	150	C4	178
Huntsville, Randolph, Mo.	1,526	B5	150
Huntsville, Logan, Ohio	511	*B3	156
Huntsville, Scott, Tenn.	500	B7	190
Huntsville, Walker, Tex.	11,999	D8	130
Huntsville, Weber, Utah	552	B4	114
Huntsville, Columbia, Wash.	100	C8	98
Hunucmá, Mex.	5,533	C8	225
Hupei, prov., China	30,790,000	E10	346
Hurd, cape, Ont., Can.		O19	64
Hurdland, Knox, Mo.	205	A5	150
Hurdsfield, Wells, N.Dak.	183	C6	154
Hurffville, Gloucester, N.J.	200	D2	210
Hurghada, Eg., U.A.R.	2,727	B3	395
Hurley, Jackson, Miss.	300	E4	184
Hurley, Stone, Mo.	117	E4	150
Hurley, Grant, N.Mex.	1,851	F2	126
Hurley, Turner, S.Dak.	450	D8	158
Hurley, Buchanan, Va.	400	C2	192
Hurley, Iron, Wis.	2,763	B3	160
Hurleyville, Sullivan, N.Y.	800	D7	212
Hurliness, Scot.		C9	272
Hurlock, Dorchester, Md.	1,035	C8	182
Hurmagai, Pak.		E4	375
Huron, Fresno, Calif.	1,269	D3	94
Huron, Lawrence, Ind.	225	D3	140
Huron, Atchison, Kans.	119	C8	144
Huron, Erie, Ohio	5,197	A4	156
Huron, Beadle, S.Dak.	14,180	C7	158
Huron, co., Ont., Can.	51,728	Q19	64
Huron, co., Mich.	34,006	F8	146
Huron, co., Ohio	47,326	A4	156
Huron, lake, Can., U.S.		I10	48
		C10	77
Huron, mts., Mich.		C4	146
Huron, riv., Ohio		A4	156
Hurricane, Baldwin, Ala.	300	E2	168
Hurricane, Washington, Utah	1,251	F2	114
Hurricane, Putnam, W.Va.	1,970	C2	194
Hurricane, cliffs, Ariz.		B2	124
Hurricane, creek, Ark.		C4	170
Hurricane, creek, Ga.		E4	176
Hurricane Mills, Humphreys, Tenn.	15	C4	190
Hurst, Williamson, Ill.	863	F4	138
Hurst, Tarrant, Tex.	10,165	*C7	130
Hurstville, Jackson, Iowa	105	*B7	142
Hurt, Pittsylvania, Va.	800	C5	192
Hurtsboro, Russell, Ala.	1,056	C4	168
Húsavik, Ice.	1,364	K21	290
Húsavik, Ice.		L23	290
Huşi, Rom.	18,055	A5	321
Huskerville, Lancaster, Nebr.	550	D9	152
Huskvarna, Swe.	13,179	D5	292
Huslia, Alsk.	65	B6	84
Huson, Missoula, Mont.	5	C2	110
Hussar, Alta., Can.	168	E6	54
Husser, Tangipahoa, La.	35	D5	180
Hustberg, Humphreys, Tenn.	150	C4	190
Hustisford, Dodge, Wis.	708	E5	160
Hustle, Essex, Va.	65	B7	192
Hustler, Juneau, Wis.	177	*E3	160
Huston, Canyon, Idaho	50	*F2	108
Hustonville, Lincoln, Ky.	387	C6	178
Husum, Ger.	22,700	A3	286
Husum, Klickitat, Wash.	15	D5	98
Hutch, isl., S.C.		G2	188
Hutchins, Dallas, Tex.	1,100	B8	130
Hutchinson, Reno, Kans.	37,574	D6	144
Hutchinson, McLeod, Minn.	6,207	G4	148
Hutchinson, co., S.Dak.	11,085	D8	158
Hutchinson, co., Tex.	34,419	B5	130
Hutchinsons, isl., Fla.		D10	174
Huto, riv., China		F6	348
Hutsonville, Crawford, Ill.	583	D6	138
Huttig, Union, Ark.	936	D4	170
Hutton, Vernon, La.	50	C2	180
Hutton, Garrett, Md.	175	B1	182
Huttonsville, Randolph, W.Va.	242	C5	194
Hutton Valley, Howell, Mo.	125	E6	150
Huu, Indon.		F5	358
Huxford, Escambia, Ala.	92	D2	168
Huxley, Alta., Can.	116	E6	54
Huxley, Story, Iowa	486	A7	142
		C4	
Huy, Bel.	13,188	D4	282
Hvalbykampen, mtn., Nor.		A1	292
Hvammstangi, Ice.		L19	290
Hvar, isl., Yugo.		C3	316
Hveravellir, Ice.		L20	290
Hvitá, riv., Ice.		L20	290
Hvitsten, Nor.	188	B1	292
Hwainan, China	286,900	I8	349
Hwai Yan, mtn., China		J6	349
Hwang Ho (Yellow), riv., China		G8	348
Hwangling, China		H4	348
Hyak, Kittitas, Wash.	30	B5	98
Hyannis, Barnstable, Mass.	5,139	C7	206
Hyannis, Grant, Nebr.	373	B4	152
Hyannis Port, Barnstable, Mass.	300	C7	206
Hyas, Sask., Can.	267	E6	58
Hyattstown, Montgomery, Md.	120	B5	182
Hyattsville, Prince Georges, Md.	15,168	C3	182
		C6	
Hyattville, Big Horn, Wyo.	50	B5	116
Hybart, Monroe, Ala.	150	D2	168
Hybla, Ont., Can.	20	O23	64
Hybla Valley, Fairfax, Va.	1,500	*B7	192
Hyco, riv., Va.		D5	192
Hydaburg, Alsk.	251	D8	84
		K14	
Hyde, co., N.C.	5,765	B9	186
Hyde, co., S.Dak.	2,602	C6	158
Hyden, Austl.	261	E3	432
Hyden, Leslie, Ky.	348	C7	178
Hyde Park, Dutchess, N.Y.	1,979	D8	212
Hyde Park, Cache, Utah	696	B4	114
Hyde Park, Lamoille, Vt.	474	B3	218
	(1,219▲)		
Hyder, Alsk.	30	D8	84
		K15	
Hyder, Yuma, Ariz.	30	E2	124
Hyderabad, India	860,366	E3	366
	(*1,175,000)		
Hyderabad, Pak.	229,412	G6	375
	(241,801▲)		
Hydes, Baltimore, Md.	100	B6	182
Hyde Villa, Berks, Pa.	1,300	*C5	214
Hydeville, Tolland, Conn.	100	B6	202
Hydeville, Rutland, Vt.	300	D2	218
Hydra, see Ídhra, isl., Grc.			
Hydro, Caddo, Okla.	697	C5	128
Hyères, Fr.	20,843	F7	278
Hyesanjin, Kor.		E14	348
Hygiene, Boulder, Colo.	125	B5	106
Hylo, Alta., Can.		C6	54
Hyltebruk, Swe.		D4	292
Hyman, Florence, S.C.	60	C9	188
Hymel, St. James, La.	250	B6	180
Hymera, Sullivan, Ind.	1,015	C2	140
Hyndman, Bedford, Pa.	1,124	D3	214
Hyndman, peak, Idaho		F4	108
Hynish, bay, Scot.		E6	272
Hyŏpchŏn, Kor.		H14	348
Hypoluxo, Palm Beach, Fla.	114	E10	174
Hyrum, Cache, Utah	1,728	B4	114
Hyrynsalmi, Fin.	4,719	D13	290
Hysham, Treasure, Mont.	494	D9	110
Hythe, Alta., Can.	481	C3	54
Hytop, Jackson, Ala.	252	A3	168
Hyvinkää, Fin.		F11	291

I

Iables, sand dunes, Alg.		C3	402
Iaeger, McDowell, W.Va.	930	D3	194
Ialomita, riv., Rom.		B4	321
Iamonia, lake, Fla.		A6	174
Iantha, Barton, Mo.	147	D3	150
Iaşi, Rom.	112,989	A4	321
Iatt, lake, La.		C3	180
Ibadan, Nig.	459,196	E5	408
Ibanda, Ug.		C5	414
Ibapah, Tooele, Utah	25	C2	114
Ibaqué, Col.	119,400	C1	244
Ibar, riv., Yugo.		C5	316
Ibarra, Ec.	14,031	A2	245
Ibb, Yemen	25,000	E3	383
Ibbenbüren, Ger.	14,619	B2	286
Iberá, lake, Arg.		A4	252
Iberia, Miller, Mo.	694	C5	150
Iberia, par., La.	51,657	E4	180
Iberville, Que., Can.	6,270	S11	66
Iberville, Iberville, La.	150	D4	180
Iberville, co., Que., Can.	15,724	S11	66
Iberville, par., La.	29,939	D4	180
Ibi, Nig.	6,183	E6	409
Ibiá, Braz.	4,616	D1	258
Ibiapaba, mts., Braz.		A2	258
Ibicuy, Arg.		B4	252
Ibitinga, Braz.	6,113	E1	258
Ibiza, Sp.	9,644	C7	298
Ibiza, isl., Sp.		C7	298
Ibo, Moz.	5,000	B8	421
'Ibri, Om.		C6	383
Ica, Peru	30,900	C2	245
Ica, dept., Peru	199,795	C2	245
Içana, riv., Braz.		E3	256
Ice, cave, Iowa		A6	142
Ice, mtn., B.C., Can.		C12	52
Ice, mtn., W.Va.		B6	194
Içel, prov., Tur.	372,932	*C6	307
Iceland, country, Eur.	148,938	B3	266
			291
Icha, Sov.Un.		D17	329
Ichang, China	81,000	J5	349
Ichāpur, India		I9	366
Icheng, China	5,000	J6	349
Ichikawa, Jap.	129,700	L15	354
Ichinomiya, Jap.	157,025	L12	354
Ichinoseki, Jap.	58,292	E8	354
Ichnya, Sov.Un.	25,000	G9	332
Ichuan, China	5,000	G5	348
Ichun, China		B14	348
Ichun, China	5,000	L7	349
Ichun, Sov.Un.		C19	329
Icicle, creek, Wash.		B5	98
Icó, Braz.	3,953	B3	258
Icy, strait, Alsk.		I14	84
Ida, Caddo, La.	300	A2	180
Ida, Monroe, Mich.	700	H8	146
Ida, co., Iowa	10,269	B2	142
Ida, lake, Minn.		F3	148
Ida, mtn., Grc.		D6	306
Idabel, McCurtain, Okla.	4,967	E9	128
Ida Grove, Ida, Iowa	2,265	B2	142
Idah, Nig.	7,334	E6	408
Idaho, co., Idaho	13,542	D3	108
Idaho, state, U.S.	667,191	B3	77
			108
Idaho City, Boise, Idaho	188	F3	108
Idaho Falls, Bonneville, Idaho	33,161	F6	108
Idahome, Cassia, Idaho		*G5	108
Idaho Springs, Clear Creek, Colo.	1,480	C5	106
Idalia, Yuma, Colo.	75	C8	106
Idalou, Lubbock, Tex.	1,274	C5	130
Idamay, Lee, Ky.	100	C7	178
Idamay, Marion, W.Va.	800	A7	194
Idana, Clay, Kans.	100	C6	144
Idanha, Marion, Oreg.	295	C4	96
Idar-Oberstein, Ger.	26,984	D2	286
Idaville, White, Ind.	600	B3	140
Idaville, Tillamook, Oreg.	200	*B3	96
Iddan, Som.		D6	398
'Iddel Ghanam, Sud.		C1	398
Iddesleigh, Alta., Can.	50	E7	54
Ideal, Macon, Ga.	432	D2	176
Ideal, Tripp, S.Dak.	30	D6	158
Idehan, des., Libya		B2	394
Idell, Hunterdon, N.J.		C2	210
Ider, De Kalb, Ala.	132	A4	168
Iderlin, riv., Mong.		B7	346
Idfina, Eg., U.A.R.	4,816	*A3	395
Idfū, Eg., U.A.R.	18,404	C3	395
Ídhra, Grc.	2,843	C4	306
Ídhra (Hydra), isl., Grc.		C4	306
Idi, Indon.		C1	358
Idiofa, Con.L.		D2	414
Idku, Eg., U.A.R.	27,321	*A3	395
Idledale, Jefferson, Colo.	475	*C5	106
Idlewild, Gibson, Tenn.	100	B3	190
Idlewilde, Alleghany, Va. (part of Covington)		C4	192
Idleyld Park, Douglas, Oreg.	100	D3	96
Idlib, Syr., U.A.R.	30,970	B2	378
Idnah, Jordan	3,000	C5	382
Idre, Swe.		F5	291
Idrigill, pt., Scot.		D6	272
Idrija, Yugo.	5,013	A2	316
Idritsa, Sov.Un.	7,000	D7	332
Idzhim, Sov.Un.		D11	329
Ie, isl., Okinawa		C1	436
Ieper (Ypres), Bel.	17,682	D1	282
Ierápetra, Grc.	5,516	D5	306
Ierissós, Grc.	2,768	A4	306
Ierwukungli, China		B10	348
Iesi, It.	21,900	D4	302
Ifakara, Tan.		D6	414
Ifantas, Col.		B2	244
Ife, Nig.	111,000	E5	408
Iférouane, Niger		C6	409
Ifni, overseas prov., Spain	38,300	*C1	402
Iganga, Ug.		B5	414
Igara-Paraná, riv., Col.		D2	244
Igarapava, Braz.	5,792	E1	258
Igarka, Sov.Un.	33,800	C10	328
Iğdir, Tur.	7,801	B11	307
Iggesund, Swe.		F7	291
Igin, Tur.	5,484	B4	307
Igiugig, Alsk.	30	D6	84
Iglesia, Arg.		B2	252
Iglesias, It.	17,700	F2	302
Igloo, Alsk.	64	*B5	84
Igloo, Fall River, S.Dak.	750	D2	158
Ignace, Ont., Can.	315	R23	64
Ignacio, Marin, Calif.	150	C2	94
Ignacio, La Plata, Colo.	609	E3	106
Iğneada, Tur.	713	A2	307
Igny, Fr.		J9	278
Igoumenítsa, Grc.	2,448	B3	306
Igra, Sov.Un.		A4	336
Iguaçu, Braz.		K6	257
Iguaçu, riv., Braz.		K6	257
Iguala, Mex.	19,414	D6	225
		L14	
Igualada, Sp.	15,603	B7	298
Iguape, Braz.	3,780	J7	257
Iguidi, sand dunes, Alg., Mauritania		C2	402
Iguidi, sand dunes, Maur.		A3	408
Igurin, isl., Eniwetok		C1	436
Igushik, Alsk.	60	D6	84
Ihosy, Malag.		D9	421
Ihsien, China	20,000	E10	348
Ihsien, China	15,000	G9	348
Ihsien, China	5,000	H8	348
Ihsing, China	20,000	J9	349
Iida, Jap.	34,052	G6	354
		L13	
Iide-San, peak, Jap.		F7	354
Iijima, Jap.	8,189	L13	354
Iijoki, riv., Fin.		D12	290
Iisvesi, lake, Fin.		E12	290
Iizuka, Jap.	61,650	*H3	354
Ijamsville, Frederick, Md.	120	B5	182
Ijebu Ode, Nig.	27,558	E5	408
IJmuiden, Neth.	26,900	B3	282
IJssel, riv., Neth.		B5	282
IJsselmeer (Zuider Zee), sea, Neth.		B4	282
Ikaalinen, Fin.	537	F10	291
Ikaría, isl., Grc.		C6	306
Ikatan, Alsk.	29	E5	84
Ikeda, Jap.	50,073	M11	354
Ikela, Con.L.		C3	414
Ikhtiman, Bul.	9,123	B1	317
Iki, isl., Jap.		H2	354
Ila, Madison, Ga.	216	B3	176
Ilagan, Phil.	7,436	A6	358
Ilan (Sanhsing), China	37,301	B14	348
Ilan, For.	33,943	M10	349
Ilanz, Switz.	1,590	B5	312
Iława, Pol.	2,220	B4	325
Ilbunga, Austl.		D7	432
Ilchester, Howard, Md.	60	B6	182
Ilderton, Ont., Can.	180	Q19	64
Île Bizard, Que., Can.	750	S15	66
Île-de-France, former prov., Fr.	7,733,000	C5	278
Île Perrot, Que., Can.	2,600	*D8	66
Ilesha, Nig.	72,029	E5	408
Ilford, Man., Can.	110	B5	60
Ilfracombe, Eng.	8,800	J8	273
Ilgachuz, range, B.C., Can.		D10	52
Ilhavo, Port.	6,969	B2	298
Ilhéus, Braz.	22,593	C3	258
Ili, Sov.Un.		D9	336
Ili, riv., Sov.Un.		D9	336
Ilia, Rom.		B2	321
Ilía (Elis), prov., Grc.	188,274	*C3	306
Iliamna, Alsk.	44	D6	84
Iliamna, lake, Alsk.		D6	84
Iliamna, vol., Alsk.		G10	84
Iliff, Logan, Colo.	204	B7	106
Ilinskaya, Sov.Un.	29,600	J13	332
Iliodhrómia, isl., Grc.		B4	306
Ilion, Herkimer, N.Y.	10,199	B6	212
Ill, riv., Aus.		C1	313
Illampu, mts., Bol.		C1	246
Illana, bay, Phil.		C6	358
Illapel, Chile	8,266	B1	252
Ille-et-Vilaine, dept., Fr.	586,812	*C3	278
Iller, riv., Ger.		D4	286
Ille[-sur-la-Têt], Fr.	3,957	F5	278
Illinois, state, U.S.	10,081,158	C9	77
			138
Illinois, bayou, Ark.		B3	170
Illinois, peak, Idaho, Mont.		B3	108
		C1	110
Illinois, riv., Ill.		D3	138
Illinois, riv., Ark., Okla.		A2	170
		C8	128
Illinois, riv., Oreg.		E3	96
Illinois and Mississippi, canal, Ill.		B3	138
Illiopolis, Sangamon, Ill.	995	D4	138

Illmo, Scott, Mo.	1,774	D8	150
Illo, Nig.		D5	408
Íllora, Sp.	5,516	D5	298
Ilmen, lake, Sov.Un.		C8	332
Ilmenau, Ger.	17,100	C4	286
Ilmenau, riv., Ger.		B4	286
Ilo, Peru	1,043	D3	245
Iloilo, Phil.	46,416 (*85,000)	B6	358
Ilomantsi, Fin.		E14	290
Ilorin, Nig.	40,994	E5	408
Ilovinskaya, Sov.Un.		C2	336
Ilubabor, prov., Eth.	1,300,000	D4	398
Ilwaco, Pacific, Wash.	518	C2	98
Ilwaki, Indon.		F7	358
Iłża, Pol.	3,813	C5	325
Imabari, Jap.	96,654	G4	354
Imambaba, Sov.Un.		F8	328
Im Amguel, Alg.		D5	402
Iman, Sov.Un.	18,000	E15	329
Imari, Jap.	81,625	*H2	354
Imathia (Hematheia), prov., Grc.	96,439	*A4	306
Imatra, Fin.		F13	291
Imazu, Jap.	11,682	L12	354
Imbâba, Eg., U.A.R.	50,100	D2	382
Imbler, Union, Oreg.	137	B9	96
Imboden, Lawrence, Ark.	400	A5	170
Ime, mtn., Scot.		E8	272
Imes, Franklin, Kans.	25	*D8	144
Imgyt, marsh, Sov.Un.		A8	336
Imias, Cuba		B7	232
Imilac, Chile		B4	250
Imlay, Pershing, Nev.	300	C3	112
Imlay City, Lapeer, Mich.	1,968	F8	146
Imlaystown, Monmouth, N.J.	150	C3	210
Immeln, lake, Swe.		E5	292
Immenstadt [in Allgäu], Ger.	9,700	E4	286
Immokalee, Collier, Fla.	3,224	E9	174
Imnaha, Wallowa, Oreg.	30	B10	96
Imnaha, riv., Oreg.		B10	96
Imogene, Fremont, Iowa	264	D2	142
Imola, It.	24,900	C3	302
Imotski, Yugo.	3,591	C3	316
Imperatriz, Braz.	1,152	B1	258
Imperia, It.	26,400	D2	302
Imperia, prov., It.	173,000	*D2	302
Imperial, Imperial, Calif.	2,658	F6	94
Imperial, Sask., Can.	566	E5	58
Imperial, Jefferson, Mo.	250	B8 C7	150
Imperial, Chase, Nebr.	1,423	D4	152
Imperial, Allegheny, Pa.	2,000	A3	214
Imperial, Pecos, Tex.	750	D4	130
Imperial, co., Calif.	72,105	F6	94
Imperial, diversion dam, Ariz.		F1	124
Imperial, valley, Calif.		*F6	94
Imperial Beach, San Diego, Calif.	17,773	D6	94
Imperoyal, N.S., Can.	1,040	E6	70
Impfondo, Con.B.		F8	409
Imphal, India	2,862	D6	368
Impienpo, China	7,000	C14	348
Imst, Aus.	3,983	C2	313
Ina, Jefferson, Ill.	332	E5	138
Ina, Jap.	45,783	L13	354
In Ahmar, well, Maur.		C3	408
Inajá, Braz.	773	B3	258
In Alay, Mali		C4	408
Inanwatan, Neth.N.Gui.		E8	359
Iñapari, Peru	131	C4	245
Inarajan, Guam	812	D7	436
Inari, Fin.		B12	290
Inari, lake, Fin.		B12	290
Inatori, Jap.	7,990	M15	354
Inavale, Webster, Nebr.	150	D7	152
In Azaoua (Oasis), Alg.		D5	402
In Azaoua (Oasis), Niger		B6	409
In Belbel, Alg.		C4	402
In Beriem, well, Mali		C4	408
Inca, Sp.	12,174	C8	298
İnce, cape, Tur.		A6	307
İncesu, Tur.	4,780	B6	307
Inchelium, Ferry, Wash.	100	A8	98
Inchŏn, Kor.	321,072	G13	348
Inda, Stone, Miss.	200	E3	184
Indaal, inlet, Scot.		F6	272
Indalsälven, riv., Swe.		E6	290
Indaparapeo, Mex.	3,066	L13	225
Indaw, Bur.	2,138	A3	362
Indawgyi, riv., Bur.		A3	362
Independence, Autauga, Ala.	80	C3	168
Independence, Inyo, Calif.	875	D4	94
Independence, Warren, Ind.	170	B2	140
Independence, Buchanan, Iowa	5,498	B6	142
Independence, Montgomery, Kans.	11,222	E8	144
Independence, Kenton, Ky.	309	A8 B6	178
Independence, Tangipahoa, La.	1,941	D5	180
Independence, Hennepin, Minn.	1,446	*F5	148
Independence, Tate, Miss.	159	A3	184
Independence, Jackson, Mo.	62,328	B3 E2	150
Independence, Cuyahoga, Ohio	6,868	B1	156
Independence, Polk, Oreg.	1,930	C3	96
Independence, Grayson, Va.	679	D3	192
Independence, Trempealeau, Wis.	954	D2	160
Independence, co., Ark.	20,048	B5	170
Independence, mts., Nev.		C5	112
Independence, riv., N.Y.		B6	212
Independence Hill, Lake, Ind.	1,824	A2	140
Independencia, Bol.	1,742	C1	246
Inderagiri, riv., Indon.		E2	358
Inderborskiy, Sov.Un.		C4	336
Inderöy, Nor.		E4	290
Index, Snohomish, Wash.	158	B5	98
Index, peak, Wyo.		B3	116
India, country, Asia	438,000,000	G9	340 368
Indiahoma, Comanche, Okla.	378	D5	128
Indialantic, Brevard, Fla.	1,653	C10	174
Indian, bay, Fla.		C8	174
Indian, cave, Tenn.		B8	190
Indian, creek, Ind.		D3	140
Indian, creek, Kans.		B8	144
Indian, creek, Md.		C6	182
Indian, creek, Ohio		C2	156
Indian, creek, S.Dak.		B2	158
Indian, creek, Tenn.		C3	190
Indian, creek, W.Va.		D4	194
Indian, isl., N.C.		B9	186
Indian, lake, Mich.		D5	146
Indian, lake, N.Y.		B7	212
Indian, lake, Ohio		B3	156
Indian, mtn., Conn.		B2	202
Indian, ocean			19
Indian, peak, Utah		E2	114
Indian, peak, Wyo.		B3	116
Indian, pond, Maine		B3	204
Indian, pond, Maine		C3	204
Indian, riv., Ont., Can.		O23	64
Indian, riv., Del.		F4	172
Indian, riv., Fla.		C10	174
Indian, riv., N.Y.		A6	212
Indian, stream, N.H.		A4	208
Indiana, Indiana, Pa.	13,005	C2	214
Indiana, co., Pa.	75,366	C2	214
Indiana, state, U.S.	4,662,498	D9	77 140
Indianapolis, Marion, Ind.	476,258 (*806,900)	C3 D5	140
Indianapolis, Custer, Okla.		C5	128
Indian Bay, Man., Can.		F5	60
Indian Brook, N.S., Can.	57	C9	70
Indian Cove, Owyhee, Idaho		G3	108
Indian Creek, Dade, Fla.	60	*F10	174
Indian Grave, mtn., Ga.		C2	176
Indian Harbour, Newf., Can.		C7 D10	72
Indian Head, Sask., Can.	1,721	E6	58
Indian Head, Charles, Md.	780	C5	182
Indian Hill, Hamilton, Ohio	4,526	D1	156
Indian Hills, Jefferson, Colo.	600	C5	106
Indian Hills, Jefferson, Ky.	601	*B5	178
Indian Lake, Hamilton, N.Y.	600	B7	212
Indian Mills, Burlington, N.J.		D3	210
Indian Mound, Stewart, Tenn.		B4	190
Indian Mound Beach, Plymouth, Mass.	300	*C6	206
Indian Neck, New Haven, Conn.	1,000	D4	202
Indianola, Vermilion, Ill.	295	D6	138
Indianola, Warren, Iowa	7,062	C4	142
Indianola, Sunflower, Miss.	6,714	B2	184
Indianola, Red Willow, Nebr.	754	D5	152
Indianola, Pittsburg, Okla.	234	C8	128
Indianola, Allegheny, Pa.	1,000	*C1	214
Indianola, Kitsap, Wash.	700	*B4	98
Indianola, creek, Kans.		A6	144
Indian Prairie, canal, Fla.		D9	174
Indian River, Ont., Can.	50	P22	64
Indian River, Washington, Maine	100	D5	204
Indian River, Cheboygan, Mich.	300	D7	146
Indian River, co., Fla.	25,309	D10	174
Indian River, bay, Del.		F5	172
Indian River City, Brevard, Fla.	350	C10	174
Indian Rocks Beach, Pinellas, Fla.	1,940	C5	174
Indian Rocks Beach South Shore, Pinellas, Fla.	296	*C5	174
Indian Springs, Butts, Ga.	250	C3	176
Indian Springs, Martin, Ind.	120	D3	140
Indian Springs, Clark, Nev.	100	G6	112
Indiantown, Martin, Fla.	1,411	D10	174
Indian Trail, Union, N.C.	364	B5	186
Indian Valley, Adams, Idaho	30	E2	108
Indian Valley, Floyd, Va.	75	D4	192
Indian Village, Alsk.	64	*C7	84
Indian Village, St. Joseph, Ind.	82	*A3	140
Indian Village, Allen, La.	200	D3	180
Indian Village, Iberville, La.		D4	180
Indian Wells, Navajo, Ariz.	5	C5	124
Indiga, Sov.Un.	800	C6	328
Indigirka, riv., Sov.Un.		C16	329
Indio, Riverside, Calif.	9,745	F5	94
Indispensable, strait, Solomon		E2	436
Indochina, reg., Asia		B4	362
Indonesia, country, Asia	84,000,000	J14	340 359
Indore, India	310,859	E1	368
Indravati, riv., India		E4	366
Indre, dept., Fr.	247,436	*D4	278
Indre-et-Loire, dept., Fr.	364,706	*D4	278
Indus, Koochiching, Minn.	10	C5	148
Indus, riv., India		B2	368
Indus, riv., Pak.		D7	375
Industrial, York, S.C.	900	*B7	188
Industrial City, Jefferson, Ala.	1,000	*E4	168
Industrial City, Buchanan, Mo.	1,350	B3	150
Industry, Butler, Ala.	100	D3	168
Industry, McDonough, Ill.	514	C3	138
Industry, Clay and Dickinson, Kans.	7	C6	144
Industry (Town of), Franklin, Maine	(262▲)	*D2	204
Ine, Jap.	7,653	L11	354
İnebolu, Tur.	4,521	A5	307
Inez, Martin, Ky.	566	C8	178
Infantes, Sp.	9,953	C5	298
Infiesto, Sp.	1,650	A4	298
Inga, Chouteau, Mont.		B6	110
In-Gall, Niger		C6	408
Ingalls, Bradley, Ark.	100	D4	170
Ingalls, Madison, Ind.	873	C4	140
Ingalls, Gray, Kans.	174	E3	144
Ingalls, Menominee, Mich.	200	D4	146
Ingalls Park, Will, Ill.	5,000	*B6	138
Ingallston, Menominee, Mich.		D4	146
Ingarölandet, isl., Swe.		B9	292
Ingels, Swe.		A6	292
Ingelstad, Swe.		E5	292
Ingende, Con.L.		C2	414
Ingeniero Jacobacci, Arg.	2,257	F4	251
Ingeniero Luiggi, Arg.		C3	252
Ingenika, riv., B.C., Can.		B10	52
Ingersoll, Ont., Can.	6,811	Q20	64
Ingersoll, Alfalfa, Okla.	30	B5	128
Ingham, Austl.	3,943	B9	432
Ingham, Lincoln, Nebr.		D5	152
Ingham, co., Mich.	211,296	G7	146
Ingleford, Spokane, Wash.		D8	98
Ingleside, Queen Annes, Md.	110	B8	182
Ingleside, Adams, Nebr.	300	D7	152
Ingleside, San Patricio, Tex.	3,022	F7	130
Inglewood, Los Angeles, Calif.	63,390	C5	94
Inglewood, Ont., Can.	325	Q21	64
Inglewood, Dodge, Nebr.	805	*C9	152
Inglewood, N.Z.	1,682	C5	437
Inglewood, Davidson, Tenn.	26,527	*B5	190
Inglis, Man., Can.	215	E2	60
Inglis, Levy, Fla.	250	B8	174
Ingoldsby, Ont., Can.		P22	64
Ingolstadt, Ger.	46,800	D4	286
Ingomar, Union, Miss.	262	A3	184
Ingomar, Rosebud, Mont.	80	D9	110
Ingomar, Allegheny, Pa.	1,500	*C1	214
Ingonish, N.S., Can.	387	C9	70
Ingornachoix, bay, Newf., Can.		E7	72
Ingraham, lake, Fla.		F9	174
Ingram, Allegheny, Pa.	4,730	A3	214
Ingram, Rusk, Wis.	99	C3	160
Ingram Branch, Fayette, W.Va.	500	D6	194
Ingul, riv., Sov.Un.		I9	332
Ingulets, riv., Sov.Un.		I9	332
Inhambane, Moz.	3,266	D7	421
Inhambane, prov., Moz.		D6	421
Inhambane, bay, Moz.		D7	421
Inhambupe, Braz.	3,245	C3	258
Inhaminga, Moz.		C6	421
Inharrime, Moz.	10,000	D7	421
Inhuçu, Braz.	1,145	A2	258
Inhumas, Braz.	3,254	D1	258
Iniesta, Sp.	4,755	C6	298
Inirida, riv., Col.		C3	244
Inishbofin, isl., Ire.		H2	273
Inishcrone, Ire.		G3	273
Inisheer, isl., Ire.		H3	273
Inishmaan, isl., Ire.		H3	273
Inishmore, isl., Ire.		H3	273
Inishowen, head, Ire.		F6	272
Inishturk, isl., Ire.		H2	273
Ink, Polk, Ark.	100	C2	170
Inkerman, N.B., Can.	285	B5	70
Inkerman, Luzerne, Pa.	1,000	*B5	214
Inkerman, Hardy, W.Va.	50	B6	194
Inkeromen, Fin.		F12	291
Inkom, Bannock, Idaho	528	G6	108
Inkster, Wayne, Mich.	39,097	B7	146
Inkster, Grand Forks, N.Dak.	282	B8	154
Inland, Clay, Nebr.	85	*D7	152
Inland, dam, Ala.		B3	168
Inman, Fayette, Ga.	175	C2	176
Inman, McPherson, Kans.	729	D6	144
Inman, Holt, Nebr.	192	B7	152
Inman, Spartanburg, S.C.	1,714	A4	188
Inman, Wise, Va.	650	*D2	192
Inman Mills, Spartanburg, S.C.	1,769	A4	188
Inn, riv., Aus.		B5	313
Inn, riv., Ger.		D5	286
Inn, riv., Switz.		B5	312
Innamincka, Austl.		D8	432
Inner, sound, Scot.		D7	272
Inner Hebrides, is., Scot.		E6	272
Inner Mongolia, reg., China	9,200,000	B10	346
Inner Rhoden (Rhodes Intérieures), sub-canton, Switz.	13,600	*A5	312
Innisfail, Austl.	6,649	B9	432
Innisfail, Alta., Can.	1,883	D6	54
Innisfree, Alta., Can.	318	D7	54
Innsbruck, Aus.	95,055	C3	313
Inola, Rogers, Okla.	584	B8	128
Inongo, Con.L.	2,061	C2	414
Inowrocław, Pol.	43,000	B4	325
In Salah, Alg.	330 (17,511▲)	C4	402
Insch, Scot.	1,421	D10	272
Insein, Bur.	27,030	C3	362
Insinger, Sask., Can.	135	E6	58
Inskip, Knox, Tenn. (part of Fountain City)		B8	190
Inspiration, Gila, Ariz.	500	E5	124
Institute, Kanawha, W.Va.	2,500	C3	194
Instow, Sask., Can.	45	F3	58
Intake, Dawson, Mont.	14	C12	110
Interburg, see Chernyakhovsk, Sov.Un.			
Intercession City, Osceola, Fla.	150	C9	174
Intercity, Snohomish, Wash.	1,475	*B4	98
Interior, Jackson, S.Dak.	179	D4	158
Interior, Giles, Va.	40	C4	192
Interlachen, Putnam, Fla.	349	B9	174
Interlachen, Multnomah, Oreg.	150	*B4	96
Interlaken, Berkshire, Mass.	250	*B1	206
Interlaken, Monmouth, N.J.	1,168	*C4	210
Interlaken, Seneca, N.Y.	780	C5	212
Interlaken, Switz.	4,368	B3	312
Interlochen, Grand Traverse, Mich.	50	E6	146
International Peace Garden, park, Man., Can.		F2	60
Interprise, Union, Miss.	100	A3	184
Intersection, mtn., B.C., Can.		D12	52
Intervale, Carroll, N.H.	200	C4	208
Intiyaco, Arg.		A3	252
Intracoastal Waterway, Fla., La., S.C.		D10 E3 D11	174 180 188
Intsy, Sov.Un.		C6	328
Inubō, cape, Jap.		G8	354
Inútil, bay, Chile		H3	251
Inuvik, N.W.Ter., Can.		D5	48
Inverbervie, Scot.	900	E10	272
Invercargill, N.Z.	29,094 (*35,100)	G2	437
Inverell, Austl.	7,514	D10	432
Invergarry, Scot.		D7	272
Invermay, Sask., Can.	300	E6	58
Invermere, B.C., Can.	543	E14	52
Inverness, Bullock, Ala.	100	C4	168
Inverness, Marin, Calif.	450	C2	94
Inverness, B.C., Can.	15	C7	52
Inverness, N.S., Can.	2,026	C8	70
Inverness, Que., Can.	321	R13	66
Inverness, Citrus, Fla.	1,878	C8	174
Inverness, Cook, Ill.	1,500	*B6	138
Inverness, Sunflower, Miss.	1,039	B2	184
Inverness, Hill, Mont.	175	B6	110
Inverness, Scot.	28,300	D8	272
Inverness, co., N.S., Can.	18,235	C8	70
Inverness, co., Scot.	84,800	D7	272
Inwood, Man., Can.	100	E4	60
Inwood, Ont., Can.	415	R18	64
Inwood, Marshall, Ind.	165	A3	140
Inwood, Lyon, Iowa	638	A1	142
Inwood, Nassau, N.Y.	10,362	E2	212
Inwood, Berkeley, W.Va.	480	B6	194
Inya, Sov.Un.		B11	336
Inyanga, Rh. & Nya.		C6	421
Inyankara, creek, Wyo.		B8	116
Inyo, co., Calif.	11,684	D5	94
Inyokern, Kern, Calif.	450	E5	94
Inza, Sov.Un.	7,000	F16	332
Inzano, lake, B.C., Can.		C10	52
Ioánnina, Grc.	32,315	B3	306
Ioánnina, prov., Grc.	153,748	*B3	306
Ioka, Duchesne, Utah		C5	114
Iola, Allen, Kans.	6,885	E8	144
Iola, Waupaca, Wis.	831	D4	160
Iona, N.S., Can.	154	D9	70
Iona, Bonneville, Idaho	702	F7	108
Iona, Gloucester, N.J.	200	D2	210
Iona, Murray, Okla.		D6	128
Iona, Lyman, S.Dak.	25	D6	158
Iona, isl., Scot.		E6	272
Ione, Amador, Calif.	1,118	C3	94
Ione, Weld, Colo.	100	B6	106
Ione, Nye, Nev.	10	E4	112
Ione, Morrow, Oreg.	350	B7	96
Ione, Pend Oreille, Wash.	648	A9	98
Ionia, Chickasaw, Iowa	265	A5	142
Ionia, Jewell, Kans.	100	C5	144
Ionia, Ionia, Mich.	6,754	G6	146
Ionia, Benton, Mo.	114	C4	150
Ionia, co., Mich.	43,132	G6	146
Ionian, sea, Grc.		B2	306
Ionian Islands (Iónioi Nésoi), reg., Grc.	228,597	B2	306
Íos, isl., Grc.		C5	306
Iosco, co., Mich.	16,505	E8	146
Iosegun, riv., Alta., Can.		C4	54
Iosepa, Tooele, Utah	15	C3	114
Iota, Acadia, La.	1,245	D3	180
Iowa, Calcasieu, La.	1,857	D2	180
Iowa, co., Iowa	16,396	C5	142
Iowa, co., Wis.	19,631	E3	160
Iowa, state, U.S.	2,757,537	C8	77 142
Iowa, lake, Iowa		A3	142
Iowa, riv., Iowa		C6	142
Iowa City, Johnson, Iowa	33,443	C6	142
Iowa Falls, Hardin, Iowa	5,565	B4	142
Iowa Park, Wichita, Tex.	3,295	C6	130
Iowa Point, Doniphan, Kans.	100	C8	144
Ipameri, Braz.	7,234	D1	258
Ipava, Fulton, Ill.	623	C3	138
Ipel, riv., Czech.		B4	324
Iphigenia, sound, Alsk.		K14	84
Ipiales, Col.	11,569	C1	244
Ipin, China	177,500	F8	346
Ipirá, Braz.	2,232	C3	258
Ipoh, Mala.	125,855	F4	362
Ipoly, riv., Hung.		B3	320
Ipotureima, Ven.		D7	240
Ippy, Cen.Afr.Rep.		E9	409
Ipswich, Austl.	42,300	D10	432
Ipswich, Eng.	110,300	I14	273
Ipswich, Essex, Mass.	5,400 (8,544▲)	A6	206
Ipswich, Edmunds, S.Dak.	1,131	B6	158
Ipswich, riv., Mass.		A5	206
Ipu, Braz.	5,874	A2	258
Ipueiras, Braz.	1,999	A2	258
Iquatú, Braz.		B3	258
Iquique, Chile	39,576	B3	250
Iquitos, Peru	49,200	A3	245
Ira, Rutland, Vt.	50 (220▲)	D2	218
Iraan, Pecos, Tex.	1,255	D5	130
Iracoubo, Fr.Gu.	423	D6	256
Iráklion (Candia), Grc.	51,144	D5	306
Iráklion (Herakleion), prov., Grc.	189,637	*D5	306
Iran (Persia), country, Asia	20,042,000	F7	340 379
Iran, mts., Indon.		D4	358
Iran, plat., Iran		B3	379
Irang, riv., India		D6	368
Irapa, Ven.	3,663	A7	240
Irapuato, Mex.	49,443	C5 K13	225
Iraq, country, Asia	6,700,000	F6	340 378
Irasburg, Orleans, Vt.	200 (711▲)	B4	218
Irbil, Iraq	34,313	A6	378
Irby, Marlboro, S.C.	75	B9	188
Irebu, Con.L.		C2	414
Iredell, co., N.C.	62,526	B5	186
Ireland, Dubois, Ind.	340	D3	140
Ireland (Eire), country, Eur.	2,846,000	C4	266 273
Ireland, isl., Bermuda		A12	233
Ireland, pt., Bermuda		A12	233
Irene, Clay, S.Dak.	399	D8	158
Irerrer, riv., Alg.		D5	402
Ireton, Sioux, Iowa	510	B1	142
Irgiz, Sov.Un.	1,900	C6	336
Irgiz, riv., Sov.Un.		C6	336
Iringa, Tan.	9,587	D6	414
Iriomote, isl., Ryūkyū Is.		M11	349
Irion, co., Tex.	1,183	D5	130
Iriri, riv., Braz.		F6	256
Irish, sea, Eur.		H7	273
Irkutsk, Sov.Un.	365,000	D12	329
Irma, Alta., Can.	421	D7	54
Irma, Crittenden, Ky.	17	C2	178
Irma, Lincoln, Wis.	75	D4	160
Irmo, Lexington, S.C.	359	C6	188
Iro, cape, Jap.		G7	354
Iron, co., Mich.	17,184	C3	146
Iron, co., Mo.	8,041	D7	150
Iron, co., Utah	10,795	F2	114
Iron, co., Wis.	7,830	B3	160
Iron, mtn., Ariz.		E4	124
Iron, mtn., Fla.		D9	174

J

K

Kaiwi, chan., Haw. B4 86
Kaiyüan, China 35,000 D12 348
Kaizuka, Jap. 56,166 M11 354
Kaj, riv., Afg. C3 374
Kajaani, Fin. 11,208 D12 290
Kajan, mtn., Indon. D5 358
Kajiado, Ken. C6 414
Kajikazawa, Jap. 7,757 L14 354
Kajmakčalan, mtn., Grc. A3 306
Kaka, Sud. C3 398
Kaka, pt., Haw. C5 86
Kakaiga, isl., Jap. J3 354
Kakamas, U.S.Afr. E4 420
Kakamega, Ken. B5 414
Kake, Alsk. 455 D8 84, J14
Kakegawa, Jap. 37,301 M14 354
Kakhonak, Alsk. 39 D6 84
Kakhovka, res., Sov.Un. I9 332
Kakhtana, Sov.Un. D17 329
Kakinada, India 99,952 E4 366
Kakogawa, Jap. 71,517 *G5 354
Kakumaa, Ken. B5 414
Kakwa, riv., Alta., Can. C3 54
Kalabagh, Pak. 10,523 C7 375
Kalabakan, N.Bor. D5 358
Kalabana, Mali D3 408
Kalabo, Rh.&Nya. 1,710 B4 420
Kalābsha, Eg., U.A.R. C3 395
Kalach, Sov.Un. 16,900 B2 336
Kalach [-na-Donu], Sov.Un. 16,300 H14 332
Kaladan, riv., Bur. B2 362
Kaladar, Ont., Can. 200 P23 64
Ka Lae (South Cape), cape, Haw. E6 86
Kalahari, des., Bech. D4 420
Kalaheo, Kauai, Haw. 1,185 B2 86
Kalajoki, Fin. D10 290
Kalak, Iran E5 379
Kalama, Cowlitz, Wash. 1,088 C4 98
Kalámai, Grc. 37,781 C4 306
Kalamazoo, Kalamazoo, Mich. 82,089 (*170,000) G6 146
Kalamazoo, co., Mich. 169,712 G6 146
Kalamazoo, riv., Mich. G6 146
Kalambo, falls, Tan. D5 414
Kalaoa, Hawaii, Haw. 200 *D6 86
Kalaotoa, isl., Indon. F6 358
Kalapana, Hawaii, Haw. 60 D7 86
Kälarne, Swe. E7 290
Kalasin, prov., Thai. 307,793 *C4 362
Kalat, Pak. 2,009 E5 375
Kalāteh Minar, Iran B5 379
Kalāt-i-Ghilzai, Afg. 5,000 C4 374
Kalauao, Honolulu, Haw. 240 *G10 86
Kalaupapa, Kalawao, Haw. 446 B5 86
Kalávrita, Grc. 2,208 B4 306
Kalawao, Maui, Haw. 340 *B5 86
Kalecik, Tur. 4,095 A5 307
Kaleden, B.C., Can. 75 F13 52
Kalegauk, isl., Bur. D3 362
Kalehe, Con.L. C4 414
Kaleva, Manistee, Mich. 348 E5 146
Kalewa, Bur. 2,263 B2 362
Kalfafell, Ice. M21 290
Kalfafellsstadhur, Ice. L22 290
Kalgan, see Changchiakou, China
Kalgin, isl., Alsk. G10 84
Kalgoorlie, Austl. 9,962 (*22,837) E4 432
Kalida, Putnam, Ohio 705 B2 156
Kali Gandaki, riv., Nep. C3 368
Kalima, Con.L. C4 414
Kálimnos, Grc. 9,683 C6 306
Kálimnos, isl., Grc. C6 306
Kalinin, Sov.Un. 261,000 A1 336
Kaliningrad, Sov.Un. 30,000 N18 332
Kaliningrad (Königsberg), Sov.Un. 202,000 E3 332
Kalinkovichi, Sov.Un. 15,200 F7 332
Kal-i-Shur, salt lake, Iran B5 379
Kalispell, Flathead, Mont. 10,151 B2 110
Kalisz, Pol. 66,000 C4 325
Kaliua, Tan. D5 414
Kalix, Swe. D10 290
Kalixälven, riv., Swe. C10 290
Kalkaska, Kalkaska, Mich. 1,321 E6 146
Kalkaska, co., Mich. 4,382 E6 146
Kalkfeld, S.W.Afr. D3 420
Kallandso, isl., Swe. C4 292
Kallavesi, lake, Fin. E12 290
Kallinge, Swe. E6 292
Kallsjön, lake, Swe. E5 290
Kalmalo, Nig. D6 408
Kalmar, Swe. 29,152 E7 292
Kalmar, co., Swe. 237,256 D7 292
Kalmare, Pap. F10 359
Kalmar Sund, sound, Swe. E7 292
Kalmykovo, Sov.Un. C4 336
Kalo, Webster, Iowa 150 B3 142
Kalocsa, Hung. 12,000 C3 320
Kalohi, chan., Haw. C4 86
Kaloli, pt., Haw. D7 86
Kalomo, Rh. & Nya. 1,185 C4 420
Kalona, Washington, Iowa 1,235 C6 142
Kalpi, India D2 368
Kalskag, Alsk. 139 C5 84
Kaltag, Alsk. 121 C6 84
Kaluaihakoko, Maui, Haw. 270 *C5 86
Kaluga, Sov.Un. 133,000 E11 332
Kalundborg, Den. 8,950 F2 292
Kalush, Sov.Un. 21,600 H5 332
Kałuszyn, Pol. 2,554 B5 325
Kalvesta, Finney, Kans. 52 D3 144
Kama, Con.L. C4 414
Kama, res., Sov.Un. A5 336
Kama, riv., Sov.Un. A4 336
Kamadia, well, Niger B7 409
Kamaee, Hawaii, Haw. 302 *D6 86
Kamaing, Bur. 608 A3 362
Kamaishi, Jap. 81,006 E8 354
Kamakura, Jap. 91,328 L15 354
Kamalo, Maui, Haw. 50 B5 86
Kamananui, riv., Haw. F9 86
Kamaniskeg, lake, Ont., Can. O23 64
Kamarod, Pak. F3 375
Kamas, Summit, Utah 749 C4 114
Kambara, isl., Fiji E7 436
Kambove, Con.L. E4 414
Kamchatka, pen., Sov.Un. D17 329
Kamela, Union, Oreg. 10 B8 96
Kamenets-Podolskiy, Sov. Un. 55,200 H6 332
Kamenjak, cape, Yugo. B1 316
Kamenka, Sov.Un. 3,700 H7 332
Kamen-na-Obi, Sov.Un. 37,000 B10 336
Kamenskoye, Sov.Un. C18 329
Kamensk-Shakhtinskiy, Sov.Un. 58,000 H13 332
Kamensk-Uralskiy, Sov.Un. 141,000 A6 336
Kamenz, Ger. 15,000 C6 286
Kameoka, Jap. 38,049 L11 354
Kamet, mtn., India C2 368
Kamganka, Bhu. D5 368
Kami, isl., Jap. G2 354
Kamiah, Lewis, Idaho 1,245 C2 108
Kamiak, mtn., Wash. C9 98
Kamichli, Syr., U.A.R. 24,321 A4 378
Kamień Pomorski, Pol. 1,576 B2 325
Kamina, Con.L. D4 414
Kamioka, Jap. 26,871 *K13 354
Kamla, riv., India D6 368
Kamloops, B.C., Can. 9,096 E12 52, F8
Kamouraska, Que., Can. 506 Q15 66
Kamouraska, co., Que., Can. 27,817 Q15 66
Kampala, Ug. 22,094 (*40,000) B5 414
Kampar, Mala. 24,583 F4 362
Kampar, riv., Indon. D2 358
Kampen, Neth. 25,248 B4 282
Kampeska, lake, S.Dak. C8 158
Kamphaeng Phet, Thai. C3 362
Kamphaeng Phet, prov., Thai. 65,742 *C3 362
Kampong Thom, Camb. 25,000 D5 362
Kampot, Camb. 5,000 E5 362
Kampsville, Calhoun, Ill. 453 D3 138
Kampungbaru, Indon. D6 358
Kamrar, Hamilton, Iowa 268 B4 142
Kamsack, Sask., Can. 2,843 E7 58
Kamuchawie, lake, Man., Can. B1 60
Kamuela, Hawaii, Haw. 950 C6 86
Kamuli, Ug. B5 414
Kamuri-Yama, peak, Jap. G4 354
Kamuri-Yama, peak, Jap. L12 354
Kamyshin, Sov.Un. 55,000 B3 336
Kamyshlov, Sov.Un. 25,700 A6 336
Kan, riv., China L7 349
Kanab, Kane, Utah 1,645 F3 114
Kanab, creek, Ariz. B3 124
Kanabec, co., Minn. 9,007 F5 148
Kanaga, isl., Alsk. E4 84
Kanaio, Maui, Haw. 12 C5 86
Kanaiwa, Jap. (part of Kanazawa) *F6 354
Kanakanak, Alsk. 54 D6 84
Kanalaksiorvik, fiord, Newf., Can. C9 72
Kananaskis, riv., Alta., Can. E5 54
Kanapou, bay, Haw. C5 86
Kanarraville, Iron, Utah 236 F2 114
Kanash, Sov.Un. 29,000 A3 336
Kanaskat, King, Wash. 100 D3 98
Kanatak, Alsk. D6 84
Kanathea, isl., Fiji E7 436
Kanauga, Gallia, Ohio 500 D4 156
Kanauj, India D2 368
Kanawha, Hancock, Iowa 735 B4 142
Kanawha, co., W.Va. 252,925 C3 194
Kanawha, riv., W.Va. C3 194
Kanayama, Jap. 3,326 L13 354
Kanayis, cape, Eg., U.A.R. A2 395
Kanayyen, Sov.Un. C19 329
Kanazawa, Jap. 277,283 F6 354
Kanburi, prov., Thai. 140,198 *D3 362
Kanchalon, Sov.Un. C19 329
Kanchanaburi, Thai. 10,000 D3 362
Kancheepuram (Conjeeveram), India 84,810 F3 366
Kanchenjunga, mtn., Sikkim, Nep. D5 368
Kanchumiao, China A9 358
Kanchussu, China A8 348
Kanda, Sweetwater, Wyo. E3 116
Kandagach, Sov.Un. C5 336
Kandahār, Afg. 77,186 D3 374
Kandahar, prov., Afg. *D3 374
Kandahar, Sask., Can. 98 E5 58
Kandalaksha, Sov.Un. 37,500 C5 328
Kandangan, Indon. 9,774 E5 358
Kandavu, isl., Fiji E6 436
Kandersteg, Switz. 913 B3 312
Kandi, Dah. 5,900 D5 408
Kandira, Tur. 4,007 A4 307
Kandiyohi, co., Minn. 29,987 F3 148
Kandreho, Malag. 180 C9 421
Kandy, Cey. 57,200 G4 366
Kane, Greene, Ill. 469 D3 138
Kane, McKean, Pa. 5,380 B3 214
Kane, Big Horn, Wyo. 20 B4 116
Kane, co., Ill. 208,246 B5 138
Kane, co., Utah 2,667 F3 114
Kane, basin, N.W.Ter., Can. B12 48
Kanen, China 1,000 P4 349
Kaneohe, Honolulu, Haw. 14,414 B4 86, G10
Kaneohe, bay, Haw. F10 86
Kangal, Tur. 2,430 B7 307
Kangaroo, isl., Austl. F7 432
Kangasniemi, Fin. F12 291
Kangean, is., Indon. F5 358
Kanggye, Kor. 30,013 E13 348
Kanghwa, bay, Kor. G12 348
Kangley, La Salle, Ill. 267 B5 138
Kangnung, Kor. 50,991 G14 348
Kango, Gabon F7 409
Kangos, Swe. C10 290
Kangting, China 25,934 E8 346
Kanhsien, China M6 349
Kanhsien, China 98,600 M7 349
Kani, Bur. B2 362
Kani, I.C. E3 408
Kaniama, Con.L. D3 414
Kaniapiskau, lake, Que., Can. Q9 66
Kaniapiskau, riv., Que., Can. Q9 66
Kanin, cape, Sov.Un. C6 328
Kanjiža, Yugo. 11,290 A5 316
Kankaanpää, Fin. F10 291
Kankakee, Kankakee, Ill. 27,666 B6 138
Kankakee, co., Ill. 92,063 B5 138
Kankakee, riv., Ill., Ind. B5 138, A3 140
Kankan, Guinea 17,500 D3 408
Kanker, India 5,173 D4 366
Kanko, see Hamhüng, Kor.
Kannan, China 15,000 B11 348
Kannapolis, Cabarrus and Rowan, N.C. 34,647 B5 186
Kannus, Fin. E10 290
Kano, Nig. 93,016 (*130,173) D6 409
Kanona, Decatur, Kans. 25 C3 144
Kanona, Rh.&Nya. B6 421
Kanopolis, Ellsworth, Kans. 732 D5 144
Kanorado, Sherman, Kans. 245 C1 144
Kanosh, Millard, Utah 499 E3 114
Kanoya, Jap. 75,488 I3 354
Kanpur, India 636,443 (*705,383) D3 368
Kanrach, Pak. G4 375
Kansas, Walker, Ala. 211 B2 168
Kansas, Edgar, Ill. 815 D6 138
Kansas, Seneca, Ohio 350 A3 156
Kansas, Delaware, Okla. 300 B9 128
Kansas, state, U.S. 2,178,611 D7 77, 144
Kansas, riv., Kans. D7 144
Kansas City, Wyandotte, Kans. 121,901 B8 144, C9
Kansas City, Jackson and Clay, Mo. 475,539 (*1,025,900) B3 150, E2
Kansasville, Racine, Wis. 100 F1 160
Kansk, Sov.Un. 74,000 D11 329
Kansŏng, Kor. F14 348
Kansu, prov., China 12,800,000 D8 346
Kantang, Thai. F3 362
Kantunilkin, Mex. 872 C8 225
Kanuma, Jap. 80,771 *F7 354
Kanye, Bech. 22,922 D5 420
Kanyü, China 5,000 H9 348
Kaoan, China 10,000 K7 349
Kaohsiung (Takao), For. 334,636 N10 349
Kaokiao, China I17 346
Kaolack, Sen. 42,976 D1 408
Kao Tao, is., Viet. B5 362
Kaouar, oasis, Niger C7 409
Kaoyao, China 55,000 N6 349
Kaoyu, China 25,000 I9 349
Kaoyu, lake, China I9 349
Kapaa, Kauai, Haw. 3,439 A2 86
Kapanga, Con.L. D3 414
Kapapa, isl., Haw. G10 86
Kapehu, Hawaii, Haw. 181 *D6 86
Kapela, mts., Yugo. B2 316
Kapenguria, Ken. B6 414
Kapfenberg, Aus. 23,761 C7 313
Kapiri Mposhi, Rh.&Nya. 184 B5 420
Kapit, Sar. 1,398 D4 358
Kaplan, Vermilion, La. 5,267 D3 180
Kapoeta, Sud. E3 398
Kapoho, Hawaii, Haw. 250 D7 86
Kapos, riv., Hung. C3 320
Kaposvár, Hung. 43,000 C2 320
Kaposvar, creek, Sask., Can. E6 58
Kapowsin, Pierce, Wash. 180 C4 98
Kapsan, Kor. E14 348
Kapterko, well, Chad C9 409
Kapuas, riv., Indon. E4 358
Kapulena, Hawaii, Haw. 235 *C6 86
Kapurthala, India C1 368
Kapuskasing, Ont., Can. 5,643 R25 64
Kapustin Yar, Sov.Un. C3 336
Kapuvár, Hung. 10,315 B2 320
Kara, Sov.Un. C8 328
Kara, mtn., Tur. C5 307
Kara, sea, Sov.Un. B8 328
Kara-Bogaz-Gol, Sov.Un. D4 336
Kara-Bogaz-Gol, gulf, Sov.Un. D4 336
Karaburun, Tur. F12 307
Karachev, Sov.Un. 27,200 F10 332
Karachi, Pak. 905,781 (*1,009,438) G5 375
Karaga, Sov.Un. D18 329
Karagan, Sov.Un. D11 329
Karaganda, Sov.Un. 398,000 E9 282
Karagin, isl., Sov.Un. D18 329
Karaisali, Tur. 1,098 C6 307
Karakelong, isl., Indon. D7 358
Karakoram, pass, India B2 368
Karakoram, range, Tibet, India A1 368
Karaköse, Tur. 17,022 B10 307
Karakum, des., Sov.Un. D5 336
Karaman, Tur. 17,209 C5 307
Karamea, N.Z. 162 D4 437
Karamea, bight, N.Z. D3 437
Karamürsel, Tur. 3,150 A3 307
Karand, Iran 15,000 B2 379
Karanganla, India D6 368
Karapinar, Tur. 7,426 C5 307
Karas, mts., S.W.Afr. E3 420
Kara Shahr, see Yenchi, China
Karasjok, Nor. B11 290
Karasu, Tur. 3,388 A4 307
Karasuk, Sov.Un. 17,300 B9 336
Karatal, riv., Sov.Un. C9 336
Karatas, cape, Tur. C6 307
Kara Tau, range, Sov.Un. D7 336
Karatsu, Jap. 76,899 H2 354
Karauli, India D2 368
Karaul Keldy, Sov.Un. C5 336
Karawanken, mts., Aus. D6 313
Karawanken, mts., Yugo. A2 316
Karbalā, Iraq 44,600 C5 378
Karcag, Hung. 20,000 B5 320
Kardeljevo, Yugo. 57 C3 316
Kardhista, Grc. 18,543 B3 306
Kardhista, prov., Grc. 138,736 *B3 306
Karelian A.S.S.R., Sov.Un. 649,000 C6 328
Karema, Pap. F11 359
Karema, Tan. 882 D5 414
Karen Park, Oklahoma, Okla. 6 *C6 128
Karesuando, Swe. 263 B10 290
Kargasok, Sov.Un. 900 A10 336
Karghalik, see Yehch'eng, China
Kargopol, Sov.Un. 7,400 B12 332
Karguiri, Niger D7 409
Karhula, Fin. F12 291
Kariai, Grc. 453 A5 306
Kariba, Rh.&Nya. 6,170 C5 420
Kariba-Yami, peak, Jap. C7 354
Karibib, S.W.Afr. 835 D3 420
Karigasniemi, Fin. B11 290
Karikal, India 24,600 F3 366
Karikari, cape, N.Z. A4 437
Karima, Sud. 5,989 B3 398
Karimata, arch., Indon. E3 358
Karimata, strait, Indon. E3 358
Karimganj, India D6 368
Karimundjawa, is., Indon. F4 358
Karin, Som. C6 398
Karisimbi, vol., Con.L., Ruanda-Urundi C4 414
Káristos, Grc. 3,118 B5 306
Kāriz, Iran B5 379
Karjaa, Fin. F10 291
Karkaralinsk, Sov.Un. 12,200 C9 336
Karkheh, riv., Iran C2 379
Karkinitskiy, bay, Sov.Un. J9 332
Karkkila, Fin. F11 291
Karkur, Isr. 3,000 B5 382
Karl-Marx-Stadt (Chemnitz), Ger. 290,200 C5 286
Karlobag, Yugo. 403 B2 316
Karlovac, Yugo. 32,400 B2 316
Karlovarsky, co., Czech. 337,890 *A1 324
Karlóvasi, Grc. 5,024 C6 306
Karlovy Vary, Czech. 42,639 A1 324
Karlsborg, Swe. 4,205 C5 292
Karlshamn, Swe. 11,333 E5 292
Karlskoga, Swe. 33,885 B5 292
Karlskrona, Swe. 33,514 E6 292
Karlsruhe, Ger. 222,600 D3 286
Karlsruhe, McHenry, N.Dak. 221 B5 154
Karlstad, Swe. 38,689 B4 292
Karluk, Alsk. 144 D6 84
Karmakuly, Sov.Un. B7 328
Karmarly, mts., Sov.Un. C9 336
Karmöy, isl., Nor. G1 291
Karmutzen, mtn., B.C., Can. E9 52
Karnak, Pulaski, Ill. 667 F5 138
Karnal, India 57,906 C2 368
Karnali, riv., Nep. C3 368
Karnes, co., Tex. 14,995 E7 130
Karnes City, Karnes, Tex. 2,693 E7 130
Karnten (Carinthia), state, Aus. 474,764 *D5 313
Karoi, Rh.&Nya. C5 420
Karong, India D6 368
Karonga, Rh.&Nya. A6 421
Karora, Sud. B4 398
Karori, riv., N.Z. J10 437
Kárpathos, isl., Grc. D6 306
Karpenísion, Grc. 3,700 B3 306
Kars, Tur. 30,920 A10 307
Kars, prov., Tur. 488,406 *A10 307
Karsakpay, Sov.Un. 12,000 C7 336
Karshi, Sov.Un. 19,000 F8 328
Karsts Kamp, Gallatin, Mont. 100 *E5 110
Karstula, Fin. E11 290
Karsun, Sov.Un. 12,800 E16 332
Kartal, Tur. 4,513 G13 307
Kartaly, Sov.Un. 33,400 B6 336
Kartuzy, Pol. 5,991 A4 325
Karun, riv., Iran C2 379
Karunki, Fin. C11 290
Karup, Den. 720 H3 291
Karval, Lincoln, Colo. 80 D7 106
Karvia, Fin. E10 291
Karviná, Czech. 44,190 B4 324
Karwar, India 19,764 F2 366
Karwi, India D3 368
Kas, Sud. C1 398
Kaş, Tur. 649 C3 307
Kasaan, Alsk. 47 K14 84
Kasai, prov., Con.L. 1,997,400 C3 B14
Kasai, riv., Ang., Con.L. B3 420, D3 414
Kasai, riv., India I8 366
Kasaji, Con.L. E3 414
Kasama, Rh.&Nya. 3,700 A6 421
Kasanga, Tan. 5,369 D5 414
Kasaoka, Jap. 69,926 *H8 354
Kasaragod, India 22,708 F2 366
Kasatori-Yama, peak, Jap. H4 354
Kasba, India D4 368
Kasba, lake, N.W.Ter., Can. E8 48
Kasempa, Rh.&Nya. 225 B5 420
Kasenga, Con.L. E4 414
Kasese, Ug. C5 414
Kasganj, India D2 368
Kāshān, Iran 45,955 C3 379
Kashega, Alsk. E5 84
Kashgar, see Sufu, China
Kashima, Jap. 16,407 L16 354
Kashipur, India C2 368
Kashira, Sov.Un. 18,800 E12 332
Kashirka, riv., Sov.Un. O19 332
Kashiwazaki, Jap. 59,275 F7 354
Kāshmar (Turshiz), Iran 12,052 B5 379
Kashō, isl., China N10 349
Kasiglook, Alsk. 111 C5 84
Kasilof, Alsk. 62 C6 84, G10
Kasimov, Sov.Un. 33,500 B2 336
Kaskaskia, riv., Ill. D5 138
Kaskmor, Pak. E6 375
Kaskö, Fin. 1,663 E9 291
Kas Kong, Camb. E4 362
Kaslo, B.C., Can. 669 F14 52
Kasongo, Con.L. C4 414
Kasongo-Lunda, Con.L. D2 414
Kásos, isl., Grc. D6 306
Kassala, Sud. 35,621 B4 398
Kassala, prov., Sud. 941,039 B4 398
Kassandra, gulf, Grc. A4 306
Kassel, Ger. 192,500 C3 286
Kastamonu, Tur. 15,695 A5 307
Kastamonu, prov., Tur. 394,299 *A5 307
Kastélli, Grc. 2,205 D4 306
Kastoria, Grc. 9,468 A3 306
Kastoria, prov., Grc. 46,407 *A3 306
Kástron, Grc. 3,497 B5 306
Kasugai, Jap. 53,311 *L12 354
Kasukabe, Jap. 32,517 L15 354
Kasumi, Jap. 17,356 G5 354
Kasumiga-Ura, bay, Jap. F8 354
Kasungu, Rh.&Nya. B6 421
Kasur, Pak. 63,086 D9 375
Kata, Sov.Un. D12 329

Kataghan, prov., Afg. *A5 374
Katahdin, mtn., Maine C4 204
Katako-Kombe, Con.L. C3 414
Katalla, Alsk. 12 C7 84
Katanga, prov., Con.L. 1,451,800 D3 414
Katanning, Austl. 2,864 E3 432
Katata, Jap. 16,757 L11 354
Katerini, Grc. 24,605 A4 306
Kat Gusheh, Iran C5 379
Katha, Bur. 7,714 A3 362
Katherina, mtn., Eg., U.A.R. B3 395
Katherine, Austl. 555 A6 432
Kathiawar, pen., India D1 366
Kathleen, Polk, Fla. 650 C8 174
Kathryn, Alta., Can. 55 E6 54
Kathryn, Barnes, N.Dak. 142 D8 154
Kathua, India B1 368
Kathwood, Aiken, S.C. 2,000 *D6 188
Katie, Garvin, Okla. 75 D6 128
Katihar, India D4 368
Katimik, lake, Man., Can. D3 60
Katiola, I.C. 7,200 E3 408
Katire, Sud. 699 E3 398
Katmai, natl. mon., Alsk. D6 84
Katmai, vol., Alsk. D6 84
Katmandu, Nep. 106,579 D4 368
Katni, India 33,884 E3 368
Katokhi, Grc. 1,750 B3 306
Katombe, Con.L. D3 414
Katonah, Westchester, N.Y. 3,000 D8 212
Katong, dist., Singapore 204,056 *G4 362
Katopasa, mtn., Indon. E6 358
Katoúna, Grc. 3,176 B3 306
Katowice (Stalinogród), Pol. 198,000 (▲1,600,000) C4 325
Katrine, lake, Scot. E8 272
Katrineholm, Swe. 16,613 C7 292
Katsina, Nig. 52,672 D6 409
Katsina Ala, riv., Nig., Br.Cam. E6 409
Katsuyama, Jap. 37,556 K12 354
Kattegat, chan., Den. E2 292
Katun, riv., Sov.Un. B11 336
Katwijk aan Zee, Neth. 20,800 B3 282
Katy, Harris, Fort Bend, and Waller, Tex. 1,569 F7 130
Kauai, co., Haw. 28,176 B1 86
Kauai, chan., Haw. B3 86
Kauai, isl., Haw. A2 86
Kaufbeuren, Ger. 28,900 E4 286
Kaufman, Kaufman, Tex. 3,087 C7 130
Kaufman, co., Tex. 29,931 C7 130
Kauhava, Fin. E10 290
Kaukauna, Outagamie, Wis. 10,096 A5 160, D5
Kaukau Veld, plain, S.W.Afr. D4 420
Kaula, isl., Haw. B6 86
Kaulakahi, chan., Haw. A1 86
Kaumakani, Kauai, Haw. 950 B2 86
Kaumalapau, Maui, Haw. 100 C5 86
Kauna, pt., Haw. D6 86
Kaunakakai, Maui, Haw. 900 B4 86
Kaunas, Sov.Un. 214,000 E4 332
Kaupo, Maui, Haw. 20 C5 86
Kaura Namoda, Nig. 19,146 D6 408
Kautokeino, Nor. 1,601 B10 290
Kauttua, Fin. F10 291
Kavacha, Sov.Un. C18 329
Kavaje, Alb. 12,757 D4 316
Kavali, India 15,516 F3 366
Kavála, Grc. 42,102 A5 306
Kavála, prov., Grc. 136,337 *A5 306
Kavála, gulf, Grc. A5 306
Kavarna, Bul. 7,112 B4 317
Kavieng, Bis.Arch. E12 359
Kavir, salt flat, Iran C3 379
Kavir-i-Namak, salt lake, Iran B4 379
Kaw, Kay, Okla. 457 B7 128
Kawagama, lake, Ont., Can. O22 64
Kawagoe, Jap. 104,612 L15 354
Kawaguchi, Jap. 130,599 L15 354
Kawaihae, Hawaii, Haw. 100 C6 86
Kawaihae, bay, Haw. C6 86
Kawaihoa, pt., Haw. B1 86
Kawaikini, peak, Haw. A2 86
Kawailoa, Honolulu, Haw. 391 F9 86
Kawailoa Beach, Honolulu, Haw. 400 F9 86
Kawambwa, Rh.&Nya. 610 A6 420
Kawanui, Hawaii, Haw. 250 *D6 86
Kawardha, India E3 368
Kawasaki, Jap. 445,420 G7 354, L15
Kawata, Okinawa C1 436
Kawela, Honolulu, Haw. 60 B3 86, F9
Kawhia, harbor, N.Z. C5 437
Kawinaw, lake, Man., Can. D3 60
Kawkareik, Bur. C3 362
Kawkawlin, Bay, Mich. 300 F8 146
Kawlin, Bur. B2 362
Kay, co., Okla. 51,042 B6 128
Kaya, Upper Volta 3,600 D4 408
Kayangel, is., Palau A6 436
Kayar, Iran D3 379
Kaycee, Johnson, Wyo. 284 C6 116
Kayenta, Navajo, Ariz. 35 B5 124
Kayes, Con.B. G7 409
Kayes, Mali 28,617 D2 408
Kayford, Kanawha, W.Va. 400 C3 194, D6
Kayjay, Knox, Ky. 400 D7 178
Kaylor, Hutchinson, S.Dak. 165 D8 158
Kayseri, Tur. 81,127 B6 307
Kayseri, prov., Tur. 423,189 *B6 307
Kaysville, Davis, Utah 3,608 B4 114
Kayville, Sask., Can. 110 F5 58
Kazachye, Sov.Un. 900 B15 329
Kazakh S.S.R., Sov.Un. 9,301,000 E7 328
Kazan, Sov.Un. 643,000 A3 336
Kazan, riv., N.W.Ter., Can. E8 48
Kazankh, hills, Sov.Un. C7 336
Kazanlük, Bul. 31,133 B2 317
Kazan-retto (Volcano), is., Pac.O. C3 436
Kazbek, mtn., Sov.Un. D2 336
Kāzerūn, Iran 30,641 D3 379
Kazhim, Sov.Un. A4 336
Kazi-Magomed, Sov.Un. 10,000 D3 336
Kazimierz, Pol. 2,929 C5 325
Kâzim Paşa (Saray), Tur. 3,860 B11 307
Kazincbarcika, Hung. A5 320
Kazumba, Con.L. D3 414
Kéa, Grc. 2,201 C5 306
Kéa, isl., Grc. C5 306
Keaau, Honolulu, Haw. 24 B3 86, F9
Keaau, see Olaa, Haw.
Keahole, pt., Haw. D5 86
Keahua, Maui, Haw. 250 *C5 86
Kealaikahiki, chan., Haw. C5 86
Kealaikahiki, pt., Haw. C5 86
Kealakekua, Hawaii, Haw. 325 D6 86
Kealakekua, bay, Haw. D6 86
Kealia, Hawaii, Haw. 100 D6 86
Kealia, Kauai, Haw. 100 A2 86
Keams Canyon, Navajo, Ariz. 500 C5 124
Keamuku, Hawaii, Haw. 12 D6 86
Keanae, Maui, Haw. 54 C5 86
Keansburg, Monmouth, N.J. 6,854 C4 210
Keaoi, isl., Haw. D6 86
Kearney, Pinal, Ariz. 902 *E5 124
Kearney, Ont., Can. 454 O21 64
Kearney, Clay, Mo. 678 B3 150, D2
Kearney, Buffalo, Nebr. 14,210 D6 152
Kearney, co., Nebr. 6,580 D7 152
Kearneysville, Jefferson, W.Va. 700 B7 194
Kearns, Salt Lake, Utah 17,172 C3 114
Kearny, Hudson, N.J. 37,472 B1 210
Kearny, co., Kans. 3,108 D2 144
Kearsarge, Houghton, Mich. 400 B3 146
Kearsarge, Carroll, N.H. 150 C4 208
Kearsarge, mtn., N.H. E3 208
Keasbey, Middlesex, N.J. 1,500 *B4 210
Keatchie, De Soto, La. 345 B2 180
Keating, Baker, Oreg. 10 C9 96
Keats, Riley, Kans. 85 C7 144
Keauhou, Hawaii, Haw. 200 D6 86
Keaukaha, Hawaii, Haw. (part of Hilo) 2,500 D6 86
Keawekaheka, pt., Haw. D6 86
Kebbi, Nig. D5 408
Kebnekaise, mtn., Swe. C8 290
Kebock, head, Scot. C6 272
Kecel, Hung. 11,622 C4 320
Kechi, Sedgwick, Kans. 245 A6 144, E6
Kecskemét, Hung. 39,000 (67,000▲) C4 320
Kedah, state, Mala. 701,486 *F4 362
Kedavom, Sov.Un. C7 328
Keddie, Plumas, Calif. 300 B3 94
Kedges, straits, Md. D7 182
Kedgwick, N.B., Can. 475 B2 70
Kedgwick, riv., N.B., Can. B2 70
Kedleston, Sask., Can. 65 E5 58
Kédougou, Sen. 800 D2 408
Kedron, Cleveland, Ark. 30 C4 170
Keedysville, Washington, Md. 433 B4 182
Keefers, B.C., Can. 100 E12 52
Keefeton, Muskogee, Okla. 80 C8 128
Keegan, Aroostook, Maine 800 A5 204
Keego Harbor, Oakland, Mich. 2,761 *G8 146
Keele, peak, Yukon, Can. E5 48
Keeler, Inyo, Calif. 200 D5 94
Keeler, Sask., Can. 90 E5 58
Keeline, Niobrara, Wyo. 30 D8 116
Keeling, Pittsylvania, Va. 30 D5 192
Keels, Newf., Can. 250 F9 72
Keelung, see Chilung, For.
Keene, Kern, Calif. 120 E4 94
Keene, Ont., Can. 350 P22 64
Keene, Jessamine, Ky. 500 C6 178
Keene, Kearney, Nebr. 30 *D6 152
Keene, Cheshire, N.H. 17,562 F2 208
Keene, Johnson, Tex. 1,532 B8 130
Keener, Etowah, Ala. 100 A4 168
Keenesburg, Weld, Colo. 409 B6 106
Keene Valley, Essex, N.Y. 500 A8 212
Keeney Knob, mtn., W.Va. D4 194
Keeper, hill, Ire. I4 273
Keeseville, Essex, N.Y. 2,213 A8 212
Keetley, Wasatch, Utah 60 C4 114
Keetmanshoop, S.W.Afr. 4,410 E3 420
Keevil, Monroe, Ark. C5 170
Keewatin, Ont., Can. 1,949 *S25 64
Keewatin, Itasca, Minn. 1,651 D5 148
Keewatin, dist., N.W.Ter., Can. 2,413 E9 48
Keewatin, riv., Man., Can. B2 60
Keezletown, Rockingham, Va. 175 B6 192
Kefallinia (Cephalonia), prov., Grc. 47,369 *B3 306
Kefallinia (Cephalonia), isl., Grc. B3 306
Keflavik, Ice. 3,924 M18 290
Kegley, Mercer, W.Va. 800 *D3 194
Keheili, Sud. B3 398
Kehoe, Greenup, Ky. 200 B7 178
Kehsi Mansam, Bur. B3 362
Keijo, see Seoul, Kor.
Keilberg, mtn., Czech. A1 324
Keimoes, U.S.Afr. 2,629 E4 420
Keip'ing, China N5 349
Keiser, Mississippi, Ark. 516 B6 170
Keiser (Marion Heights), Northumberland, Pa. 1,132 C5 214
Keishū, see Kyŏngju, Kor.
Keith, co., Nebr. 7,958 C4 152
Keithley Creek, B.C., Can. 15 D12 52
Keithsburg, Cherokee, Ga. 300 B2 176
Keithsburg, Mercer, Ill. 963 B3 138
Keithville, Caddo, La. 100 B2 180
Keizer, Marion, Oreg. 5,288 *C1 96
Kekaha, Kauai, Haw. 2,082 B2 86
Kekoskee, Dodge, Wis. 247 *E5 160
Kel, India B1 368
Kelantan, state, Mala. 505,171 *F4 362
Keldron, Corson, S.Dak. 23 B4 158
Kelfield, Sask., Can. 60 E3 58
Kelford, Bertie, N.C. 362 A8 186
Kelheim, Ger. 11,951 D4 286
Kelkit, riv., Tur. A7 307
Kellé, Con.B. G7 409
Keller, Tarrant, Tex. 827 B8 130
Keller, Accomack, Va. 263 C9 192
Keller, Ferry, Wash. 25 A8 98
Kellerman, Tuscaloosa, Ala. 500 B2 168
Kellerton, Ringgold, Iowa 341 D3 142
Kellet, cape, N.W.Ter., Can. C6 48
Kelley, Story, Iowa 239 C4 142
Kelleys, isl., Ohio A4 156
Kelleys Island, Erie, Ohio 171 A4 156
Kelliher, Sask., Can. 461 E6 58
Kelliher, Beltrami, Minn. 297 D4 148
Kellnersville, Manitowoc, Wis. 350 A6 160, D6
Kelloe, Man., Can. 80 E2 60
Kellogg, Shoshone, Idaho 5,061 B2 108
Kellogg, Jasper, Iowa 623 C5 142
Kellogg, Wabasha, Minn. 446 G7 148
Kelly, Nemaha, Kans. 65 *C7 144
Kelly, Christian, Ky. 175 D3 178
Kelly, Caldwell, La. 450 C3 180
Kelly, Petroleum, Mont. D8 110
Kelly, Socorro, N.Mex. 20 D3 126
Kelly, Teton, Wyo. 20 C2 116
Kelly, isl., Del. D4 172
Kelly Brook, mtn., Maine A3 204
Kelly Lake, St. Louis, Minn. 900 D5 148
Kellyton, Coosa, Ala. 299 C3 168
Kellyville, Sullivan, N.H. 140 E2 208
Kellyville, Creek, Okla. 501 C7 128
Kélo, Chad E8 409
Kelona, Jasper, Miss. 100 D3 184
Kelowna, B.C., Can. 9,181 F13 52
Kelsey, Alta., Can. 70 D6 54
Kelsey, lake, Man., Can. D2 60
Kelsey, mtn., N.H. B4 208
Kelsey Bay, B.C., Can. E9 52
Kelso, Desha, Ark. 95 *D5 170
Kelso, San Bernardino, Calif. 100 E6 94
Kelso, Scott, Mo. 258 D8 150
Kelso, Scot. 4,200 F10 272
Kelso, Cowlitz, Wash. 8,379 C4 98
Kelso Station, Sask., Can. 110 F7 58
Kelton, Union, S.C. 62 B5 188
Keltonburg, De Kalb, Tenn. 60 C6 190
Keltys, Angelina, Tex. 1,056 D8 130
Kelvington, Sask., Can. 819 D6 58
Kelwood, Man., Can. 225 E3 60
Kem, Sov.Un. 26,300 C5 328
Ké-Macina, Mali 1,000 D3 408
Kemah, Galveston, Tex. 950 F8 130
Kembé, Cen.Afr.Rep. F9 409
Kemerburgaz, Tur. F12 307
Kemerovo, Sov.Un. 277,000 A11 336
Kemi, Fin. 23,203 D11 290
Kemijärvi, Fin. 2,871 C12 290
Kemijärvi, lake, Fin. C13 290
Kemijoki, riv., Fin. C13 290
Kemme, well, Libya C3 394
Kemmerer, Lincoln, Wyo. 2,028 E2 116
Kemnay, Man., Can. 60 F2 60
Kemoo Camps (Thompson Corner), Honolulu, Haw. 250 *F9 86
Kemp, Bryan, Okla. 153 E7 128
Kemp, Kaufman, Tex. 816 C7 130
Kemp, lake, Tex. C6 130
Kemp City, see Hendrix, Okla.
Kempen, heath, Bel. C4 282
Kemper, co., Miss. 12,277 C4 184
Kempsey, Austl. 7,489 E10 432
Kempster, Langlade, Wis. 35 C4 160
Kempsville, Princess Anne, Va. 40 A9 192
Kempten [in Allgäu], Ger. 41,400 E4 286
Kempton, Tipton, Ind. 480 B3 140
Kempton, Grand Forks, N.Dak. 58 C8 154
Kemptown, Frederick, Md. 100 B5 182
Kemptville, Ont., Can. 1,730 O25 64
Ken, riv., India D3 368
Kenadsa, Alg. B3 402
Kenai, Alsk. 321 C6 84, G10
Kenai, lake, Alsk. G11 84
Kenai, mts., Alsk. H10 84
Kenai, pen., Alsk. H10 84
Kenamu, riv., Newf., Can. D6 72
Kenansville, Osceola, Fla. 300 D10 174
Kenansville, Duplin, N.C. 724 C8 186
Kenaston, Sask., Can. 385 E4 58
Kenberma, Plymouth, Mass. D3 206
Kenbridge, Lunenburg, Va. 1,188 D6 192
Kenbro, Greenwood, Kans. 64 D7 144
Kendal, Eng. 18,500 G10 273
Kendal Green, Middlesex, Mass. D2 206
Kendall, Dade, Fla. 2,500 E6 174
Kendall, Hamilton, Kans. 250 E2 144
Kendall, Monroe, Wis. 528 E3 160
Kendall, co., Ill. 17,540 B5 138
Kendall, co., Tex. 5,889 E6 130
Kendallville, Noble, Ind. 6,765 A4 140
Kendal Station, Sask., Can. 162 E6 58
Kendari, Indon. E6 358
Kendrapara, India 11,880 D5 366
Kendrick, Marion, Fla. 900 B8 174
Kendrick, Latah, Idaho 443 C2 108
Kendrick, Alcorn, Miss. A4 184
Kendrick, Lincoln, Okla. 155 C7 128
Kenduskeag, Penobscot, Maine 300 (584▲) D4 204
Kenedy, Karnes, Tex. 4,301 E7 130
Kenedy, co., Tex. 884 F7 130
Kenefic, Bryan, Okla. 125 D7 128
Kenel, Corson, S.Dak. 75 B5 158
Kenema, S.L. E2 408
Kenesaw, Adams, Nebr. 546 D7 152
Ken Gar, Montgomery, Md. (part of Wheaton) B5 182
Kenge, Con.L. C2 414
Keng Kabao, Laos C5 362
Keng Tung, Bur. 5,508 B3 362
Kenhardt, U.S.Afr. 2,305 E4 420
Kenhorst, Berks, Pa. 2,815 *C6 214
Kéniéba, Mali D2 408
Kenilworth, Cook, Ill. 2,959 E3 138
Kenilworth, Chouteau, Mont. B6 110
Kenilworth, Union, N.J. 8,379 *B4 210
Kenilworth, Carbon, Utah 933 D5 114
Kenitra, Mor. B2 402
Kenly, Johnston, N.C. 1,147 B7 186
Kenmare, Ire. 1,054 J3 273
Kenmare, Ward, N.Dak. 1,696 B3 154
Kenmare, riv., Ire. J3 273
Kenmore, Erie, N.Y. 21,261 C3 212
Kenmore, King, Wash. 1,000 B4 98
Kenna, Roosevelt, N.Mex. 80 E7 126
Kenna, Jackson, W.Va. 50 C3 194
Kennaday, peak, Wyo. E6 116
Kennan, Price, Wis. 162 C3 160
Kennard, Henry, Ind. 466 C4 140
Kennard, Washington, Nebr. 331 C9 152, D2
Kennebago, lake, Maine C2 204
Kennebec, Lyman, S.Dak. 372 D6 158
Kennebec, co., Maine 89,150 D3 204
Kennebec, riv., Maine D3 204
Kennebunk, York, Maine 2,804 (4,551▲) E2 204
Kennebunk Beach, York, Maine 40 *E2 204
Kennebunk Lower Village, York, Maine 600 *E2 204
Kennebunkport, York, Maine 700 (1,851▲) E2 204
Kennecott, Alsk. C7 84
Kennedale, Tarrant, Tex. 1,521 B8 130
Kennedy, Lamar, Ala. 379 B2 168
Kennedy, Sask., Can. 268 E6 58
Kennedy, Kittson, Minn. 458 C2 148
Kennedy, Cherry, Nebr. 11 B5 152
Kennedy, Chautauqua, N.Y. 526 C2 212
Kennedy, lake, Sask., Can. D6 58
Kennedyville, Kent, Md. 350 B8 182
Kenner, Jefferson, La. 17,037 C7 180, E5
Kennesaw, Cobb, Ga. 1,507 A4 176, B2
Kennesaw, mtn., Ga. C2 176
Kennetcook, N.S., Can. 195 D6 70
Kenneth, Johnson, Kans. 75 *D9 144
Kenneth, Rock, Minn. 111 H2 148
Kenneth City, Pinellas, Fla. 2,114 *D8 174
Kennett, Dunklin, Mo. 9,098 E7 150
Kennett Square, Chester, Pa. 4,355 D6 214
Kennewick, Benton, Wash. 14,244 C7 98
Kenney, De Witt, Ill. 400 C4 138
Kennington Cove, N.S., Can. 97 D9 70
Kennisis, lake, Ont., Can. O22 64
Kennydale, King, Wash. 3,500 D3 98
Keno, Klamath, Oreg. 175 E5 96
Kenogami, Que., Can. 11,309 P13 66
Kenogami, lake, Que., Can. P13 66
Kenora, Ont., Can. 10,728 R23 64
Kenora, dist., Ont., Can. 47,156 Q24 64
Kenosha, Kenosha, Wis. 67,899 F2 160, F6
Kenosha, co., Wis. 100,615 F5 160
Kenova, Wayne, W.Va. 4,577 C2 194
Kensal, Stutsman, N.Dak. 334 C7 154
Kensett, White, Ark. 905 B5 170
Kensett, Worth, Iowa 409 A4 142
Kensico, res., N.Y. D2 212
Kensington, P.E.I., Can. 854 C6 70
Kensington, Hartford, Conn. 4,500 C4 202
Kensington, Smith, Kans. 619 C4 144
Kensington, Montgomery, Md. 2,175 B3 182, B5
Kensington, Douglas, Minn. 324 F3 148
Kensington, Rockingham, N.H. 50 (708▲) F5 208
Kensington, Columbiana, Ohio 450 B6 156
Kensington Estates, Montgomery, Md. 1,600 *B5 182
Kensington Park, Chatham, Ga. 1,000 *D5 176
Kenspur, Ravalli, Mont. 74 D2 110
Kent, Elmore, Ala. 500 C4 168
Kent, Litchfield, Conn. 400 (1,686▲) C2 202
Kent, Union, Iowa 94 D3 142
Kent, Wilkin, Minn. 134 E2 148
Kent, Portage, Ohio 17,836 A5 156
Kent, Sherman, Oreg. 65 B6 96
Kent, King, Wash. 9,017 B4 98, D3
Kent, co., N.B., Can. 27,492 C4 70
Kent, co., Ont., Can. 85,362 R18 64
Kent, co., Del. 65,651 D3 172
Kent, co., Eng. 1,631,000 J13 273
Kent, co., Md. 15,481 B7 182
Kent, co., Mich. 363,187 F6 146
Kent, co., R.I. 112,619 C2 216
Kent, co., Tex. 1,727 C5 130
Kent, dam, R.I. C2 216
Kent, isl., Del. D4 172
Kent, isl., Md. C7 182
Kent, pt., Md. C7 182
Kent Acres, Kent, Del. 500 *D3 172
Kent Bridge, Ont., Can. 180 R18 64
Kent City, Kent, Mich. 617 F6 146
Kentfield, Marin, Calif. 4,000 A4 94
Kent Junction, N.B., Can. 85 C4 70
Kentland, Newton, Ind. 1,783 B2 140
Kentland, Prince Georges, Md. 1,800 *C6 182
Kenton, Man., Can. 125 F2 60
Kenton, Kent, Del. 249 D3 172
Kenton, Kenton, Ky. 240 A8 178
Kenton, Hardin, Ohio 8,747 B3 156
Kenton, Cimarron, Okla. 100 B1 128
Kenton, Obion, Tenn. 1,095 B2 190
Kenton, co., Ky. 120,700 B6 178
Kents Store, Fluvanna, Va. 20 C6 192
Kentucky, state, U.S. 3,038,156 D9 77, 178
Kentucky, dam, Ky. C2 178
Kentucky, lake, Ky., Tenn. D2 178, B3 190
Kentucky, ridge, Ky. D7 178
Kent Village, Prince Georges, Md. 2,500 C6 182
Kentville, N.S., Can. 4,937 D5 70
Kentwood, Tangipahoa, La. 2,607 D5 180
Kenvil, Morris, N.J. 2,000 B3 210
Kenville, Man., Can. 150 E2 60
Kenvir, Harlan, Ky. 950 D7 178
Kenwood, Delaware, Okla. 75 B9 128
Kenya, Br. poss., Afr. 6,450,000 F10 388, 414
Kenya, mt., Ken. C6 414
Kenyon, Goodhue, Minn. 1,624 G6 148
Kenyon, Washington, R.I. 250 D2 216
Keo, Lonoke, Ark. 237 C4 170, D7
Keokuk, Lee, Iowa 16,316 D6 142
Keokuk, co., Iowa 15,492 C5 142
Keokuk, lake, Iowa C6 142
Keoma, Alta., Can. 25 E6 54
Keonjhargarh, India E4 368
Keosauqua, Van Buren, Iowa 1,023 D6 142
Keota, Weld, Colo. 13 B6 106
Keota, Keokuk, Iowa 1,096 C6 142

Keota, Haskell, Okla. 579 C9 128
Kep, Camb. E5 362
Kępno, Pol. 7,810 C3 325
Keppel, Sask., Can. 95 D4 58
Kerala, state, India 13,549,118 G3 366
Kerang, Austl. 3,227 F8 432
Kerava, Fin. F11 291
Kerby, Josephine, Oreg. 600 E3 96
Kerby, peak, Oreg. E3 96
Kerch, Sov.Un. 99,000 J11 332
Kerch, strait, Sov.Un. J11 332
Keremeos, B.C., Can. 500 F13 52
Kerempe, cape, Tur. A5 307
Kerens, Navarro, Tex. 1,123 C7 130
Kerhonkson, Ulster, N.Y. 690 D7 212
Kericho, Ken. C6 414
Kerintji, mtn., Indon. E2 358
Keriya, China D4 346
Kerkennah, isl., Tun. B6 402
Kerkhoven, Swift, Minn. 645 F3 148
Kerki, Sov.Un. 21,600 F8 328
Kérkira, Grc. 27,431 B2 306
Kérkira (Corfu, Corcyra), prov., Grc. 105,414 *B2 306
Kérkira (Corfu), isl., Grc. B2 306
Kerkrade, Neth. 45,351 D5 282
Kermadec, is., Pac.O. D4 436
Kerman, Fresno, Calif. 1,970 D3 94
Kermān, Iran 62,157 C4 379
Kermān, prov., Iran 1,301,335 *C4 379
Kermān, reg., Iran D4 379
Kermānshāh, Iran 125,439 B2 379
Kermānshāh, prov., Iran 2,244,885 *B2 379
Kermānshāh, reg., Iran B2 379
Kermit, Winkler, Tex. 10,465 D4 130
Kermit, Mingo, W.Va. 743 D2 194
Kermode, mtn., B.C., Can. D7 52
Kern, Alsk. 6 *C7 84
Kern, co., Calif. 291,984 E4 94
Kern, riv., Calif. E4 94
Kernersville, Forsyth, N.C. 2,942 A5 186
Kernville, Kern, Calif. 600 E4 94
Kernville, Lincoln, Oreg. 15 C3 96
Kerr, co., Tex. 16,800 D6 130
Kerr, lake, Fla. B9 174
Kerrera, isl., Scot. E7 272
Kerrick, Pine, Minn. 110 E6 148
Kerrobert, Sask., Can. 1,037 E3 58
Kerrs Creek, Rockbridge, Va. C5 192
Kerrville, Shelby, Tenn. 150 C2 190
Kerrville, Kerr, Tex. 8,901 D6 130
Kerry, co., Ire. 122,072 I3 273
Kerry, head, Ire. I3 273
Kersey, Weld, Colo. 378 B6 106
Kershaw, Kershaw, S.C. 1,567 B7 188
Kershaw, co., S.C. 33,585 C7 188
Kersley, B.C., Can. D11 52
Kerteminde, Den. 3,884 F1 292
Kerza, Alg. C3 402
Keşan, Tur. 11,089 A2 307
Kesarya (Sdot Yam), Isr. 405 B5 382
Kesch, peak, Switz. B5 312
Kesennuma, Jap. 53,715 E8 354
Kesh, N.Ire. 202 G5 273
Keshena, Shawano, Wis. 200 D5 160
Keswick, Ont., Can. 225 P21 64
Keswick, Keokuk, Iowa 265 C5 142
Keswick, Albemarle, Va. 300 B6 192
Keszthely, Hung. 15,000 C2 320
Ket, riv., Sov.Un. A11 336
Keta, Ghana 11,380 E5 408
Keta, Ice. K19 290
Ketapang, Indon. 4,385 E4 358
Ketchikan, Alsk. 6,483 D8 84
K15
Ketchum, Blaine, Idaho 746 F4 108
Ketchum, Craig, Okla. 255 B8 128
Ketchum, mts., Tex. D5 130
Keton, Sov.Un. E16 329
Ketona, Jefferson, Ala. 150 E5 168
Kętrzyn, Pol. 13,900 A5 325
Kettering, Eng. 37,000 I12 273
Kettering, Montgomery, Ohio 54,462 C2 156
Kettle, creek, Pa. B4 214
Kettle, riv., B.C., Can., Wash. F13 52
A8 98
Kettle, riv., Minn. E6 148
Kettle Falls, Stevens, Wash. 905 A8 98
Kettle Island, Bell, Ky. 375 D7 178
Kettleman City, Kings, Calif. 400 E4 94
Kettle River, Carlton, Minn. 234 E6 148
Kettle River, range, Wash. A8 98
Kettlewell, Eng. G10 273
Kęty, Pol. 6,581 D4 325
Keuka, lake, N.Y. C4 212
Keuruu, Fin. E11 291
Keuterville, Idaho, Idaho 30 C2 108
Kevil, Ballard, Ky. 231 C2 178
Kevin, Toole, Mont. 375 B5 110
Kewanee, Henry, Ill. 16,324 B4 138
Kewanee, Lauderdale, Miss. 225 C4 184
Kewanee, New Madrid, Mo. 200 E8 150
Kewanna, Fulton, Ind. 683 A3 140
Kewaskum, Washington, Wis. 1,572 E5 160
Kewaunee, Kewaunee, Wis. 2,772 D6 160
Kewaunee, co., Wis. 18,282 D6 160
Keweenaw, co., Mich. 2,417 B3 146
Keweenaw, bay, Mich. C3 146
Keweenaw, pt., Mich. B4 146
Keweenaw Bay, Baraga, Mich. 75 C3 146
Key, lake, Ire. G4 273
Keya Paha, Tripp, S.Dak. 19 D5 158
Keya Paha, co., Nebr. 1,672 B6 152
Keya Paha, riv., Nebr., S.Dak. A5 152
D5 158
Keyes, Stanislaus, Calif. 1,546 *D3 94
Keyes, Man., Can. 65 E3 60
Keyes, Cimarron, Okla. 627 B1 128
Keyesport, Clinton, Ill. 412 E4 138
Keyhole, res., Wyo. B8 116
Key Junction, Ont., Can. 55 O20 64
Key Largo, Monroe, Fla. 250 F10 174
Keymar, Carroll, Md. 150 A5 182
Keyport, Monmouth, N.J. 6,440 C4 210
Keyport, Kitsap, Wash. 500 *B4 98
Keysburgh, Logan, Ky. 100 D3 178
Keyser, Mineral, W.Va. 6,192 B6 194
Keystone, Wells, Ind. 260 B4 140
Keystone, Benton, Iowa 522 C5 142
Keystone, Keith, Nebr. 50 C4 152
Keystone, Pawnee, Okla. 151 B7 128
Keystone, Pennington, S.Dak. 500 D2 158
Keystone, McDowell, W.Va. 1,457 D3 194
Keystone Heights, Clay, Fla. 655 B8 174
Keystown, Sask., Can. 85 E5 58
Keysville, Hillsborough, Fla. 385 D8 174
Keysville, Burke, Ga. 250 C4 176
Keysville, Charlotte, Va. 733 C6 192
Keytesville, Chariton, Mo. 644 B5 150
Key West, Monroe, Fla. 33,956 G9 174
Key West, Dubuque, Iowa 85 B7 142
Kezar, lake, Maine D2 204
Kezar, pond, Maine D2 204
Kezar Falls, Oxford, Maine 600 E2 204
Kezhma, Sov.Un. 3,000 D12 329
Kežmarok, Czech. 7,372 B5 324
Kfar Ata, Isr. 10,300 B6 382
Kfar Blum, Isr. A6 382
Kfar Sava, Isr. 16,000 B5 382
Kfar Vitkin, Isr. B5 382
Khabarovsk, Sov.Un. 322,000 E15 329
Khabis, see Shahdad, Iran
Khabour, riv., Syr., U.A.R. B4 378
Khabura, Om. C6 383
Khachmas, Sov.Un. D3 336
Khadar Khel, Afg. 5,000 C5 374
Khairpur, Pak. 18,186 F6 375
Khalaf, Om. C6 383
Khalafābād, Iran C2 379
Khalesavoy, Sov.Un. C9 328
Khalij Surt, see Sidra, gulf, Libya
Khalki, isl., Grc. C6 306
Khalkidhiki (Chalcidice), prov., Grc. 75,735 *A4 306
Khalkidhiki, pen., Grc. A4 306
Khalkis, Grc. 23,786 B4 306
Khalsi, India B2 368
Khambhaliya, India 15,194 D1 366
Khānābād, Afg. 18,042 A5 374
Khānaqīn, Iraq 10,090 B6 378
Khandwa, India 51,940 E2 368
Khanh An, Viet. E5 362
Khaniá (Canea), Grc. 33,211 D4 306
Khaniá (Canea), prov., Grc. 126,524 *D4 306
Khaniá, gulf, Grc. D4 306
Khaniadhana, India D2 368
Khanpur, Pak. 13,484 E7 375
(15,224▲)
Khanty-Mansiysk, Sov.Un. 19,000 A7 336
Khanyangda, Sov.Un. D16 329
Khanzi, Bech. D4 420
Khapcheranga, Sov.Un. E13 329
Kharagpur, India 129,636 I8 366
Kharalakh, Sov.Un. C14 329
Kharānaq, Iran C4 379
Kharan Kalat, Pak. 2,589 E4 375
Khardyu, mtn., Grnld. Q33 290
Kharg, isl., Iran D3 379
Khargon, India E1 368
Khari, riv., India D1 368
Kharīt, riv., Eg., U.A.R. C3 395
Kharkov, Sov.Un. 930,000 G11 332
(*1,125,000)
Kharmanli, Bul. 12,577 C2 317
Kharovšk, Sov.Un. 6,100 A2 336
Kharstan, Sov.Un. B16 329
Khartoum, Sud. 93,103 B3 398
(*260,000)
Khartoum, prov., Sud. 504,923 B3 398
Khartoum North, Sud. 39,082 B3 398
Khartsyzsk, Sov.Un. 26,500 S22 332
Khāsh, Afg. 5,000 D2 374
Khāsh, Iran 9,291 D5 379
Khāsh, riv., Afg. D2 374
Khaskovo, Bul. 39,066 C2 317
Khaskovski, prov., Bul. *C2 317
Khatanga, Sov.Un. B12 329
Khatanga, riv., Sov.Un. C12 329
Khatanye, Sov.Un. D15 329
Khatatba, Eg., U.A.R. D1 382
Khatyrka, Sov.Un. C19 329
Khedive, Sask., Can. 153 *F5 58
Khemmarat, Thai. C5 362
Khenchela, Alg. 11,051 A5 402
(12,196▲)
Khenifra, Mor. 11,549 B2 402
Kherson, Sov.Un. 157,000 I9 332
Kheta, riv., Sov.Un. B11 329
Khieo, mtn., Thai. D4 362
Khilchipur, India D2 368
Khilok, Sov.Un. 18,600 D12 329
Khimki, Sov.Un. 43,000 N18 332
Khios, Grc. 24,361 B6 306
Khios (Chios), prov., Grc. 66,823 *B6 306
Khios (Chios), isl., Grc. B5 306
Khirpai, India I8 366
Khiva, Sov.Un. 19,000 D6 336
Khlebarovo, Bul. 5,614 B3 317
Khmelnik, Sov.Un. 14,300 H6 332
Khmelnitskiy, Sov.Un. 62,000 H6 332
Khodzheyli, Sov.Un. 15,000 D5 336
Khokhropar, Pak. G7 375
Kholm, Sov.Un. 11,600 D8 332
Kholmsk, Sov.Un. 33,000 E16 329
Khonak, Afg. 5,000 B4 374
Khong, Laos 10,000 D5 362
Khong, riv., Laos D5 362
Khongor Ula, Mong. 1,000 B10 346
Khong Sedone, Laos 1,000 D5 362
Khon Kaen, Thai. C4 362
Khon Kaen, prov., Thai. 590,664 *C4 362
Khonu, Sov.Un. C16 329
Khoper, riv., Sov.Un. F14 332
Khor Anghar, Fr.Som. C5 398
Khóra Sfakíon, Grc. 382 D5 306
Khorog, Sov.Un. 8,000 F9 328
Khorol, Sov.Un. 19,400 H9 332
Khorramabād, Iran 38,676 C2 379
Khorramshahr, Iran 43,850 C2 379
Khotan, see Hotien, China
Khotin, Sov.Un. 13,100 H6 332
Khouribga, Mor. 26,000 B2 402
Khowai, India D5 368
Khrisoúpolis, Grc. 5,041 A5 306
Khrom-Tau, Sov.Un. B5 336
Khu Khan, Thai. 5,000 D5 362
Khulna, Pak. 42,225 L16 375
Khurasan, prov., Iran 2,460,147 *B5 379
Khurasan, reg., Iran B5 379
Khurja, India C2 368
Khushab, Pak. 20,476 C8 375
Khust, Sov.Un. 33,900 H4 332
Khuzdar, Pak. F5 375
Khuzistan, prov., Iran 1,807,460 *C2 379
Khuzistan, reg., Iran C2 379
Khvāf, Iran B5 379
Khvor, Iran C4 379
Khvormūj, Iran 2,500 D3 379
Khvoy, Iran 34,491 A1 379
Khyber, pass, Afg. B6 374
Khyber, pass, Pak. B7 375
Kia, Solomon E1 436
Kiamichi, Pushmataha, Okla. 75 D8 128
Kiamichi, mtn., Okla. D8 128
Kiamichi, riv., Okla. D8 128
Kiamika, Que., Can. 420 R9 66
Kiana, Alsk. 181 B5 84
Kiangsi, prov., China 18,610,000 F11 346
Kiangsu, prov., China 45,230,000 E12 346
Kiantajärvi, lake, Fin. E13 290
Kiantojärvi, lake, Fin. D13 290
Kiask, lake, Man., Can. B4 60
Kiawah, isl., S.C. F8 188
G3
Kibangou, Con.B. G7 409
Kibau, Tan. D6 414
Kibbee, Montgomery, Ga. 155 D4 176
Kiberege, Tan. D6 414
Kiblah, Miller, Ark. 10 D3 170
Kibombo, Con.L. C4 414
Kibondo, Tan. C5 414
Kibwezi, Ken. C6 414
Kičevo, Yugo. 9,567 D5 316
Kickapoo, Leavenworth, Kans. 30 *C9 144
Kickapoo, creek, Ill. C4 138
Kickapoo, lake, Tex. C6 130
Kickapoo, riv., Wis. E3 160
Kicking Horse, pass, Alta., B.C., Can. E4 54
E14 52
Kidal, Mali 750 C5 408
Kidder, Caldwell, Mo. 224 B3 150
Kidder, Marshall, S.Dak. 142 B8 158
Kidder, co., N.Dak. 5,386 C6 154
Kidderminster, Eng. 39,000 I10 273
Kidira, Sen. D2 408
Kidnappers, cape, N.Z. C6 437
Kidugalo, Tan. D6 414
Kief, McHenry, N.Dak. 97 C5 154
Kiefer, Creek, Okla. 489 C7 128
Kiel, Ger. 257,300 A4 286
Kiel, Manitowoc, Wis. 2,524 B6 160
E5
Kiel, bay, Ger. A4 286
Kiel, canal, Ger. A3 286
Kielce, Pol. 74,000 C5 325
Kielce, pol.div., Pol. 1,761,000 *C5 325
Kieler, Grant, Wis. 91 F3 160
Kiesling, Spokane, Wash. D8 98
Kiester, Faribault, Minn. 741 H5 148
Kieta, Solomon D1 436
Kiev, Sov.Un. 1,102,000 G8 332
Kiffa, Maur. C2 408
Kifri, Iraq 4,760 B6 378
Kigali, Ruanda-Urundi 5,000 C5 414
Kiği, Tur. 1,136 B9 307
Kiglapait, mtn., Newf., Can. D9 72
Kigoma, Tan. 4,244 C4 414
Kihei, Maui, Haw. 95 C5 86
Kiheki, Osage, Okla. B7 128
Kiholo, Hawaii, Haw. 2 D6 86
Kiholo, bay, Haw. D6 86
Kii, strait, Jap. G5 354
Kikinda, Yugo. 29,570 B5 316
Kikládhes (Cyclades), prov., Grc. 125,959 *C5 306
Kikongo, Con.L. C2 414
Kikori, Pap. F10 359
Kikwit, Con.L. D2 414
Kil, Swe. B4 292
Kila, Flathead, Mont. 73 B2 110
Kila Saifullah, Pak. D6 375
Kilauea, Kauai, Haw. 800 A2 86
Kilauea, crater, Haw. D6 86
Kilbaha, Ire. I3 273
Kilbeggan, Ire. 832 H5 273
Kilbourne, Mason, Ill. 352 C3 138
Kilbourne, West Carroll, La. 227 B4 180
Kilbrannan, sound, Scot. F7 272
Kilburn, N.B., Can. 185 C2 70
Kilchrenan, Scot. 349 E7 272
Kilchu, Kor. 30,026 E14 348
Kilconnell, Ire. 119 H4 273
Kilcoole, Ire. 605 H6 273
Kildare, Que., Can. 465 R11 66
Kildare, Kay, Okla. 124 B6 128
Kildare, Ire. 2,617 H6 273
Kildare, co., Ire. 65,915 H6 273
Kildare, cape, P.E.I., Can. C6 70
Kilembe, Con.L. D2 414
Kilgore, Clark, Idaho 20 E7 108
Kilgore, Cherry, Nebr. 157 B5 152
Kilgore, Gregg and Rusk, Tex. 10,092 C8 130
Kilgore East, Gregg, Tex. 1,236 *C8 130
Kilifi, Ken. C6 414
Kilimanjaro, mt., Tan. C6 414
Kilis, Tur. 30,247 C7 307
Kiliya, Sov.Un. 26,700 J7 332
Kilkee, Ire. 1,565 I3 273
Kilkeel, N.Ire. 2,329 G6 273
Kilkenny, Ire. 10,607 I5 273
Kilkenny, Le Sueur, Minn. 221 G5 148
Kilkenny, co., Ire. 64,089 I5 273
Kilkerrin, Ire. 197 H3 273
Kilkieran, bay, Ire. H3 273
Kilkis, Grc. 9,702 A4 306
Kilkis, prov., Grc. 89,475 *A4 306
Killadoon, Ire. H3 273
Killala, bay, Ire. G3 273
Killaloe, Ont., Can. O23 64
Killaloe, Ire. 888 I4 273
Killaloe Station, Ont., Can. 854 O23 64
Killaly, Sask., Can. 206 E6 58
Killam, Alta., Can. 524 D7 54
Killarney, Man., Can. 1,434 F3 60
Killarney, Ire. 6,464 I3 278
Killarney, Raleigh, W.Va. 712 D3 194
Killbuck, Holmes, Ohio 865 B5 156
Killdeer, Dunn, N.Dak. 765 C3 154
Killdeer, mts., N.Dak. C3 154
Kill Devil Hills, Dare, N.C. 268 A10 186
Killeen, Bell, Tex. 23,377 D7 130
Killen, Lauderdale, Ala. 620 A2 168
Killen, Clay, Ga. 100 E1 176
Killeter, N.Ire. C5 273
Killian, Livingston, La. 22 B6 180
Killin, Scot. 1,199 E8 272
Killinek, isl., Newf., Can. C8 72
Killingly (Town of), Windham, Conn. (11,298▲) B8 202
Killington, peak, Vt. D3 218
Killingworth, Middlesex, Conn. 150 D5 202
(1,098▲)
Killini, Grc. 744 C3 306
Killisnoo, Alsk. 10 J14 84
Killona, Saint Charles, La. 650 B6 180
Killorglin, Ire. 1,106 I3 273
Killucan, Ire. 318 H5 273
Kill Van Kull, chan., N.J. B1 210
Killybegs, Ire. 990 G4 273
Killyleagh, N.Ire. 1,461 G7 273
Kilmallock, Ire. 1,238 I4 273
Kilmanagh, Huron, Mich. 50 F8 146
Kilmarnock, Scot. 43,900 F8 272
Kilmarnock, Lancaster, Va. 927 C8 192
Kilmatinde, Tan. D5 414
Kilmichael, Montgomery, Miss. 532 B3 184
Kiln, Hancock, Miss. 450 E3 184
Kilosa, Tan. 3,743 D6 414
Kilpatrick, De Kalb, Ala. 500 A3 168
Kilpisjärvi, Fin. B9 290
Kilrush, Ire. 3,000 I3 273
Kilsbergen, mts., Swe. B4 292
Kilsyth, Scot. 10,300 F8 272
Kilwa, Con.L. D4 414
Kilwa, Tan. D6 414
Kilworthy, Ont., Can. 125 P21 64
Kilyos, Tur. F13 307
Kim, Las Animas, Colo. 400 E7 106
Kimajärvi, lake, Fin. E11 290
Kimamba, Tan. 1,330 D6 414
Kimball, Stearns, Minn. 535 F4 148
Kimball, Kimball, Nebr. 4,384 C2 152
Kimball, Brule, S.Dak. 912 D7 158
Kimball, Marion, Tenn. 250 C6 190
Kimball, McDowell, W.Va. 1,175 D3 194
Kimball, co., Nebr. 7,975 C2 152
Kimball Junction, Summit, Utah C4 114
Kimballton, Audubon, Iowa 380 C2 142
Kimballton, Giles, Va. 350 C4 192
Kimbasket, lake, B.C., Can. E13 52
Kimberley, Pike, Ark. 30 *C3 170
Kimberley, B.C., Can. 5,774 F14 52
Kimberley, Ont., Can. P20 64
Kimberley, U.S.Afr. 58,771 E4 420
(*62,439)
Kimberling, Mingo, W.Va. 600 *D2 194
Kimberlin Heights, Knox, Tenn. 75 E10 190
Kimberly, Jefferson, Ala. 763 B3 168
Kimberly, Twin Falls, Idaho 1,298 G4 108
Kimberly, White Pine, Nev. 120 D6 112
Kimberly, Grant, Oreg. 10 C7 96
Kimberly, Fayette, W.Va. 900 D6 194
Kimberly, Outagamie, Wis. 5,322 A5 160
Kimble, co., Tex. 3,943 D6 130
Kimbrough, Wilcox, Ala. 65 C2 168
Kim Chaek (Sŏngjin), Kor. 67,778 E14 348
Kimes, mtn., Ark. B2 170
Kimi, Grc. 4,071 B5 306
Kimiwan, lake, Alta., Can. C4 54
Kimmell, Noble, Ind. 350 A4 140
Kimmins, Lewis, Tenn. 50 C4 190
Kimmswick, Jefferson, Mo. 303 B8 150
Kimowin, riv., Alta., Can. B8 54
Kimry, Sov.Un. 40,000 D11 332
Kimshan Cove, Alsk. 10 D8 84
J13
Kimsquit, B.C., Can. 25 D9 52
Kinabalu, mtn., N.Bor. C5 358
Kinard, Calhoun, Fla. 150 A5 174
Kinards, Newberry, S.C. 234 C5 188
Kinbrace, Scot. C8 272
Kinbrae, Nobles, Minn. 55 H3 148
Kinburn, Ont., Can. 200 O24 64
Kincaid, Sask., Can. 306 F4 58
Kincaid, Christian, Ill. 1,544 D4 138
Kincaid, Anderson, Kans. 220 D8 144
Kincaid, Fayette, W.Va. 600 D6 194
Kincardine, Ont., Can. 2,667 P19 64
Kincardine, co., Scot. 27,800 E10 272
Kinchafonee, riv., Ga. E2 176
Kincorth, Sask., Can. 59 F3 58
Kinde, Huron, Mich. 624 F9 146
Kinder, Allen, La. 2,299 D3 180
Kinderhook, Columbia, N.Y. 1,078 C8 212
Kindersley, Sask., Can. 2,572 E3 58
Kindia, Guinea 13,900 D2 408
Kindred, Cass, N.Dak. 580 D8 154
Kindu, Con.L. C4 414
Kineo, mtn., Maine C3 204
Kineshma, Sov.Un. 84,000 A2 336
King, Sevier, Ark. 45 C2 170
King, Gibson, Ind. 100 D2 140
King, Stokes, N.C. 1,000 A5 186
King, co., Tex. 640 C5 130
King, co., Wash. 935,014 B5 98
King, isl., Alsk. C5 84
King, isl., Austl. F8 432
King, isl., Bur. D3 362
King, isl., B.C., Can. D9 52
King, mtn., Oreg. D8 96
King, sound, Austl. B4 432
King and Queen, co., Va. 5,889 C8 192
King and Queen Court House, King and Queen, Va. 65 C8 192
King Christian IX Land, reg., Grnld. Q31 290
King Christian X Land, reg., Grnld. O33 290
King City, Monterey, Calif. 2,937 D3 94
King City, Ont., Can. 360 R22 64
King City, Gentry, Mo. 1,009 A3 150
King Cove, Alsk. 290 D5 84
Kingfield, Franklin, Maine 700 D2 204
(864▲)
Kingfisher, Kingfisher, Okla. 3,249 C6 128
Kingfisher, co., Okla. 10,635 C5 128
King Frederik VI, coast, Grnld. R30 290

King Frederik VIII Land, reg., Grnld.		O33	290
King George, King George, Va.	240	B7	192
King George, co., Va.	7,243	B7	192
King George, sound, Austl.		F3	432
King George IV, lake, Newf., Can.		F7	72
King Hill, Elmore, Idaho	200	F3	108
King Hill, Natchitoches, La.	100	C2	180
King Island, Alsk.	208	C5	84
King Lear, peak, Nev.		B3	112
King Leopold, range, Austl.		B5	432
Kingman, Mohave, Ariz.	4,525	C1	124
Kingman, Alta., Can.	75	D6	54
Kingman, Fountain, Ind.	461	C2	140
Kingman, Kingman, Kans.	3,582	E5	144
Kingman, Penobscot, Maine	250 (358▲)	C4	204
Kingman, co., Kans.	9,958	E5	144
Kings, co., Calif.	49,954	D4	94
Kings, co., N.B., Can.	24,267	D4	70
Kings, co., N.S., Can.	37,816	E5	70
Kings, co., P.E.I., Can.	17,853	C7	70
Kings, co., N.Y.	2,627,319	E2	212
Kings, peak, Utah		C5	114
Kings, ridge, Tex.		B6	130
Kings, riv., Ark.		A3	170
Kings, riv., Calif.		D4	94
Kings, riv., Nev.		B3	112
King Salmon, Alsk.	100	*D6	84
Kingsbridge, Eng.	3,100	K9	273
Kingsburg, Fresno, Calif.	3,093	D4	94
Kingsbury, La Porte, Ind.	281	A3	140
Kingsbury, Piscataquis, Maine	5 (8▲)	C3	204
Kingsbury, co., S.Dak.	9,227	C8	158
Kings Canyon, Jackson, Colo.	10	B4	106
Kings Canyon, natl. park, Calif.		D4	94
Kingscote, Austl.	739	F7	432
Kings Creek, Caldwell, N.C.	100	A4	186
Kings Creek, Cherokee, S.C.	200	A6	188
Kingsdown, Ford, Kans.	100	E4	144
Kingsey Falls, Que., Can.	596	S12	66
Kingsford Heights, La Porte, Ind.	1,276	A3	140
Kingsford, Dickinson, Mich.	5,084	D3	146
Kings Gardens, Reno, Kans.	400	*D6	144
Kingsgate, B.C., Can.	50	F14	52
Kingsland, Cleveland, Ark.	249	D4	170
Kingsland, Camden, Ga.	1,536	F5	176
Kings Landing, Dallas, Ala.	300	C2	168
Kingsley, Plymouth, Iowa	1,044	B2	142
Kingsley, Jefferson, Ky.	508	*B5	178
Kingsley, Grand Traverse, Mich.	586	E6	146
Kingsley, dam, Nebr.		C4	152
King's Lynn, Eng.	26,200	I13	273
Kingsmere, lake, Sask., Can.		C4	58
Kings Mills, Warren, Ohio	700	C1	156
		C2	
Kings Mountain, Lincoln, Ky.	500	C6	178
Kings Mountain, Cleveland, N.C.	8,008	B4	186
Kings Park, Suffolk, N.Y.	4,949	D3	212
Kings Point, Newf., Can.	250	F7	72
Kings Point, Nassau, N.Y.	5,410	D2	212
Kingsport, Sullivan, Tenn.	26,314	B9	190
Kingston, Madison, Ark.	150	A3	170
Kingston, Austl.	907	F7	432
Kingston, N.S., Can.	487	E5	70
Kingston, Ont., Can.	48,618	P24	64
Kingston, Bartow, Ga.	695	B2	176
Kingston, Shoshone, Idaho	500	B2	108
Kingston, De Kalb, Ill.	406	A5	138
Kingston, Jam.	137,700 (*289,245)	D6	232
Kingston, Madison, Ky.	200	C6	178
Kingston, Somerset, Md.	5	D8	182
Kingston, Plymouth, Mass.	2,000 (4,302▲)	C6	206
Kingston, Tuscola, Mich.	456	F8	146
Kingston, Meeker, Minn.	125	F4	148
Kingston, Caldwell, Mo.	311	B3	150
Kingston, Frontier, Nebr.	3	*D5	152
Kingston, Rockingham, N.H.	600 (1,672▲)	F4	208
Kingston, Somerset, N.J.	850	C3	210
Kingston, Ulster, N.Y.	29,260	D7	212
Kingston, Ross, Ohio	1,066	C4	156
Kingston, Marshall, Okla.	639	E7	128
Kingston, Linn, Oreg.		C1	96
Kingston, Luzerne, Pa.		A5	214
		B6	
Kingston, Washington, R.I.	2,616	D2	216
Kingston, Roane, Tenn.	2,010	C7	190
Kingston, Piute, Utah	143	E3	114
Kingston, Kitsap, Wash.	475	B4	98
Kingston, Fayette, W.Va.	400	D3	194
		D6	
Kingston, Green Lake, Wis.	343	E4	160
Kingston Springs, Cheatham, Tenn.	400	B4	190
Kingstown, St. Vincent, Windward Is., B.W.I.	6,500	E14	233
Kingstree, Williamsburg, S.C.	3,847	D9	188
Kings Valley, Benton, Oreg.	250	C3	96
Kingsville, Ont., Can.	2,884	R18	64
Kingsville, Johnson, Mo.	225	C3	150
Kingsville, Ashtabula, Ohio	900	A6	156
Kingsville, Kleberg, Tex.	25,297	F7	130
Kingswood, Breckenridge, Ky.	248	C4	178
Kingurutik, lake, Newf., Can.		D9	72
Kingussie, Scot.	1,100	D8	272
Kingville, Lamar, Ala.	125	B1	168
Kingville, Richland, S.C.	200	D7	188
King William, King William, Va.	40	C7	192
King William, co., Va.	7,563	C7	192
King William, isl., N.W.Ter., Can.		D9	48
King William's Town, U.S.Afr.	12,480	F5	420
Kingwood, Hunterdon, N.J.		C2	210
Kingwood, Preston, W.Va.	2,530	B5	194
Kinistino, Sask., Can.	654	D5	58
Kinkala, Con.B.		G7	409
Kinkora, P.E.I., Can.	266	C6	70
Kinley, Sask., Can.	116	D4	58
Kinloch, St. Louis, Mo.	6,501	A8	150
Kinlochewe, Scot.		D7	272
Kinmount, Ont., Can.	500	P22	64
Kinmundy, Marion, Ill.	813	E5	138
Kinn, Ice.		K21	290
Kinna, Swe.	5,340	D3	292
Kinnaird, B.C., Can.	1,305	F14	52
Kinnairds, head, Scot.		D11	272
Kinnared, Swe.		D4	292
Kinnear, Fremont, Wyo.	50	C4	116
Kinnelon, Morris, N.J.	4,431	B4	210
Kinney, St. Louis, Minn.	240	D6	148
Kinney, co., Tex.	2,452	E5	130
Kinniconick, Lewis, Ky.	100	B7	178
Kinomoto, Jap.	12,629	L12	354
Kinosaki, Jap.	5,922	G5	354
Kinpoku, peak, Jap.		E7	354
Kinrooi, Bel.	1,884	C4	282
Kinross, Keokuk, Iowa	103	C6	142
Kinross, Scot.	2,500	E9	272
Kinross, co., Scot.	7,200	E9	272
Kinsale, Ire.	1,612	J4	273
Kinsale, Westmoreland, Va.	250	B8	192
Kinsella, Alta., Can.	110	D7	54
Kinsey, Houston, Ala.	283	*D4	168
Kinsey, Custer, Mont.	5	D11	110
Kinsley, Edwards, Kans.	2,263	E4	144
Kinsman, Trumbull, Ohio	990	A6	156
Kinston, Coffee, Ala.	470	D3	168
Kinston, Lenoir, N.C.	24,819	B8	186
Kinta, Haskell, Okla.	233	C8	128
Kintampo, Ghana	2,829	E4	408
Kintinku, Tan.		D6	414
Kinton, St. Francis, Ark.		B6	170
Kintyre, Emmons, N.Dak.	102	D6	154
Kintyre, head, Scot.		F7	272
Kinuso, Alta., Can.	306	C5	54
Kinvara, Ire.	363	H4	273
Kinyangiri, Tan.	1,540	C5	414
Kinyeti, mtn., Sud.		E3	398
Kinzel Springs, Blount, Tenn.	30	E9	190
Kinzua, Wheeler, Oreg.	300	C6	96
Kiona, Benton, Wash.	150	C7	98
Kiowa, Elbert, Colo.	195	C6	106
Kiowa, Barber, Kans.	1,674	E5	144
Kiowa, Pittsburg, Okla.	607	D8	128
Kiowa, co., Colo.	2,425	D8	106
Kiowa, co., Kans.	4,626	E4	144
Kiowa, co., Okla.	14,825	D4	128
Kiowa, creek, Colo.		C6	106
Kiowa, creek, Okla.		B3	128
Kipahigan, lake, Man., Sask., Can.		C2	60
		C7	58
Kipahulu, Maui, Haw.	25	C5	86
Kiparissia, Grc.	5,032	C3	306
Kiparissia, gulf, Grc.		C3	306
Kipili, Tan.		D5	414
Kipini, Ken.		C7	414
Kipling, Delta, Mich.	350	D4	146
Kipling Station, Sask., Can.	684	E6	58
Kipnuk, Alsk.	185	D5	84
Kipp, Alta., Can.		F6	54
Kipp, Saline, Kans.	100	D6	144
Kippen, Toole, Mont.	40	*B5	110
Kiptopeke, Northampton, Va.		A9	192
Kipushi, Con.L.		E4	414
Kirakira, Solomon		E2	436
Kirby, Pike, Ark.	300	C3	170
Kirby, Big Horn, Mont.	2	E10	110
Kirby, Bexar, Tex.	680	*E6	130
Kirby, Caledonia, Vt.	(235▲)	*C5	218
Kirby, Hot Springs, Wyo.	82	C4	116
Kirby Lonsdale, Eng.	1,240	G10	273
Kirbyville, Jasper, Tex.	1,660	D9	130
Kirchdorf, Aus.	2,606	C6	313
Kirdâsa, Eg., U.A.R.		D2	382
Kirensk, Sov.Un.	12,500	D12	329
Kirghiz S.S.R., Sov.Un.	2,063,000	E9	328
Kirghiz, range, Sov.Un.		D8	336
Kiri, Con.L.		C2	414
Kirin, see Chilin, China			
Kirin, prov., China	12,550,000	C13	346
Kirinian, isl., Eniwetok		B1	436
Kirk, Yuma, Colo.	75	C8	106
Kirk, Klamath, Oreg.	20	E5	96
Kirkağaç, Tur.	9,000	B2	307
Kirkcaldy, Alta.' Can.	60	E6	54
Kirkcaldy, Scot.	51,500	E9	272
Kirkcudbright, Scot.	2,500	G8	272
Kirkcudbright, co., Scot.	30,200	F8	272
Kirkella, Man., Can.	60	E2	60
Kirkfield, Ont., Can.	420	P21	64
Kirkfield Park, Man., Can.	800	F4	60
Kirkjubaer, Ice.		L22	290
Kirkland, Escambia, Ala.	75	D2	168
Kirkland, Yavapai, Ariz.	18	D3	124
Kirkland, Atkinson, Ga.	150	E4	176
Kirkland, De Kalb, Ill.	928	A5	138
Kirkland, Williamson, Tenn.		C5	190
Kirkland, King, Wash.	6,025	B4	98
		D3	
Kirkland Junction, Yavapai, Ariz.	15	D3	124
Kirkland Lake, Ont., Can.	17,766	R25	64
Kirklareli, Tur.	19,312	A2	307
Kirklareli, prov., Tur.	213,843	*A2	307
Kirklin, Clinton, Ind.	767	B3	140
Kirkman, Shelby, Iowa	92	C2	142
Kirkmansville, Todd, Ky.	150	C3	178
Kirkoswald, Eng.	528	G10	273
Kirköy, Nor.		B1	292
Kirkpatrick, lake, Alta., Can.		E7	54
Kirksey, Calloway, Ky.	180	D2	178
Kirksey, Greenwood, S.C.	35	C4	188
Kirksville, Madison, Ky.	100	C6	178
Kirksville, Adair, Mo.	13,123	A5	150
Kirkton, Ont., Can.	245	Q19	64
Kirkük, Iraq	89,917	B6	378
Kirkville, Wapello, Iowa	203	C5	142
Kirkville, Itawamba, Miss.	250	A4	184
Kirkwall, Scot.	4,300	B10	272
Kirkwood, New Castle, Del.	430	B3	172
Kirkwood, Warren, Ill.	771	C3	138
Kirkwood, Prince Georges, Md.	2,500	*C6	182
Kirkwood, St. Louis, Mo.	29,421	B8	150
Kirkwood, U.S.Afr.		F4	420
Kirn, Ger.	9,700	D2	286
Kiron, Crawford, Iowa	271	B2	142
Kirov, Sov.Un.	252,000	A3	336
Kirovabad, Sov.Un.	116,000	D3	336
Kirovgrad, Sov.Un.	21,500	A5	336
Kirovograd, Sov.Un.	127,000	H9	332
Kirovsk, Sov.Un.	52,800	C5	328
Kirovskiy, Sov.Un.		D17	329
Kirriemuir, Alta., Can.	100	E7	54
Kirriemuir, Scot.	3,500	E10	272
Kirsanov, Sov.Un.	38,900	F14	332
Kirşehir, Tur.	16,606	B6	307
Kirşehir, prov., Tur.	149,000	*B6	307
Kirthar, range, Pak.		F5	375
Kirtland, San Juan, N.Mex.	300	B2	126
Kirtland, Lake, Ohio	1,500	*A5	156
Kirtley, Niobrara, Wyo.		D8	116
Kiruna, Swe.	22,374	C9	290
Kirundu, Con.L.		C4	414
Kirva Palanke, Yugo.	2,539	C6	316
Kirwin, Phillips, Kans.	356	C4	144
Kirwin, res., Kans.		C4	144
Kiryū, Jap.	116,935	F7	354
		K15	
Kisa, Swe.		D6	292
Kisaki, Tan.		D6	414
Kisalaya, Nic.		C5	228
Kisanga, Con.L.		D4	414
Kisarazu, Jap.	51,741	*L15	354
Kisatchie, Natchitoches, La.	30	C2	180
Kisbey, Sask., Can.	276	F6	58
Kiselevsk, Sov.Un.	130,000	B11	336
Kisengi, Con.L.		E3	414
Kisengwa, Con.L.		D4	414
Kisenyi, Ruanda-Urundi		C4	414
Kishanganga, riv., India		B1	368
Kishanganj, India		D4	368
Kishangarh, India		C2	366
Kishi, Nig.		E5	408
Kishinev, Sov.Un.	214,000	I7	332
Kishiwada, Jap.	107,640 (*165,000)	M11	354
Kishon, riv., Isr.		B6	382
Kishorganj, Pak.	19,067	K17	375
Kisii, Ken.		C5	414
Kisiju, Tan.		D6	414
Kisiwani, Tan.		C6	414
Kiska, isl., Alsk.		E3	84
Kiskatinaw, riv., B.C., Can.		C12	52
Kiskitto, lake, Man., Can.		C3	60
Kiskittogisu, lake, Man., Can.		C3	60
Kiskörös, Hung.	9,154	C4	320
Kiskundorozsma, Hung.	6,530	C5	320
Kiskunfélegyháza, Hung.	22,000 (32,000▲)	C4	320
Kiskunhalas, Hung.	16,000	C4	320
Kiskunmajsa, Hung.	7,809	C4	320
Kislovodsk, Sov.Un.	79,000	D2	336
Kismet, Seward, Kans.	150	E3	144
Kiso-Sammyaku, mts., Jap.		L13	354
Kisseynew, lake, Man., Can.		C2	60
Kissidougou, Guinea		E2	408
Kissimmee, Osceola, Fla.	6,845	D9	174
Kissimmee, lake, Fla.		D9	174
Kissimmee, riv., Fla.		D9	174
Kissimmee Park, Osceola, Fla.	75	C9	174
Kississing, Man., Can.	350	C2	60
Kississing, lake, Man., Can.		C2	60
Kississing, riv., Man., Can.		C2	60
Kistigan, lake, Man., Can.		C6	60
Kistler, Logan, W.Va.	1,084	D3	194
		D5	
Kistna, riv., India		E3	366
Kistrand, Nor.	3,347	A11	290
Kisújszállás, Hung.	11,000	B5	320
Kisumu, Ken.	10,899	C5	414
Kisvárda, Hung.	13,055	A7	320
Kita, Iwo		A7	436
Kita, Mali	3,150	D3	408
Kitale, Ken.	6,338	B5	414
Kitamaki, Jap.	5,223	K14	354
Kitami, Jap.	52,988	C9	354
Kitangari, Tan.		E6	414
Kit Carson, Cheyenne, Colo.	356	D8	106
Kit Carson, co., Colo.	6,957	C8	106
Kitchener, Ont., Can.	59,562	Q20	64
Kitchen's Creek, falls, Pa.		B5	214
Kitchings Mill, Aiken, S.C.	150	D6	188
Kite, Johnson, Ga.	424	D4	176
Kitega, Ruanda-Urundi	5,000	C5	414
Kitgum, Ug.		B5	414
Kithira, Grc.	997	C4	306
Kithira (Cythera), isl., Grc.		C4	306
Kithnos, isl., Grc.		C5	306
Kitimat, B.C., Can.	9,676	C8	52
Kitnen, riv., Fin.		C12	290
Kitsap, co., Wash.	84,176	B4	98
Kitscoty, Alta., Can.	283	D7	54
Kittanning, Armstrong, Pa.	6,793	C2	214
Kittatinny, mts., N.J.		B2	210
Kittery, York, Maine	8,051 (10,689▲)	E2	204
Kittery Point, York, Maine	1,259	E2	204
Kittilä, Fin.	1,266	C11	290
Kittitas, Kittitas, Wash.	536	C6	98
Kittitas, co., Wash.	20,467	B6	98
Kittredge, Jefferson, Colo.	400	*C5	106
Kittrell, Perry, Miss.	100	D4	184
Kitts, Harlan, Ky.	950	D7	178
Kitts Hummock, Kent, Del.	15	D4	172
Kittson, co., Minn.	8,343	C2	148
Kitty Hawk, Dare, N.C.	250	A10	186
Kittyhawk, bay, N.C.		A10	186
Kitui, Ken.		C6	414
Kitwe, Rh.&Nya.	19,975	B5	420
Kitzbühel, Aus.	7,211	C4	313
Kitzingen, Ger.	17,600	D4	286
Kitzmiller, Garrett, Md.	535	B1	182
Kiukiang, China	125,000	K8	349
Kiuruvesi, Fin.		E12	290
Kivalina, Alsk.	117	B5	84
Kivijärvi, lake, Fin.		F12	291
Kivik, Swe.	5,052	F5	292
Kivu, prov., Con.L.	1,895,000	C4	414
Kivu, lake, Con.L.		C4	414
Kiwalik, Alsk.		B5	84
Kiya, Sov.Un.		C6	328
Kiyiu, lake, Sask., Can.		E3	58
Kizel, Sov.Un.	60,000	A5	336
Kizil, riv., Tur.		A6	307
Kizlyar, Sov.Un.	33,200	D3	336
Kizyl-Su, Sov.Un.		E4	336
Kizyl-Arvat, Sov.Un.	26,000	F7	328
Kjelvik, Nor.		A11	290
Kjøllefjord, Nor.		A12	290
Kladno, Czech.	49,701	A2	324
Klagenfurt, Aus.	62,782	D6	313
Klaipėda (Memel), Sov.Un.	89,000	E3	332
Klamath, Del Norte, Calif.	500	B1	94
Klamath, co., Oreg.	47,475	E5	96
Klamath, riv., Calif., Oreg.		B2	94
		F4	91
Klamath, mts., Oreg.		E2	96
Klamath Agency, Klamath, Oreg.	200	E5	96
Klamath Falls, Klamath, Oreg.	16,949	E5	96
Klang, Mala.	75,678	G4	362
Klarälven, riv., Swe.		A4	292
Klasma, riv., Sov.Un.		A1	336
Klatovy, Czech.	14,333	B1	324
Klawock (Klawak), Alsk.	251	D8	84
		K14	
Kleberg, Dallas, Tex.	3,572	B9	130
Kleberg, co., Tex.	30,052	F7	130
Klecany, Czech.	1,700	*A2	324
Kleena Kleene, B.C., Can.		E10	52
Klein, Musselshell, Mont.	400	D8	110
Kleinburg, Ont., Can.	235	R21	64
Kleine Scheidegg, Switz.		B3	312
Klemme, Hancock, Iowa	615	A4	142
Klerksdorp, U.S.Afr.	24,277	E5	420
Kletnya, Sov.Un.	3,800	F9	332
Kletsk, Sov.Un.	13,300	F6	332
Kleve (Cleve), Ger.	19,500	C2	286
Klevshult, Swe.	2,901	D5	292
Klickitat, Klickitat, Wash.	850	D5	98
Klickitat, co., Wash.	13,455	D5	98
Klickitat, creek, Wash.		D5	98
Klickitat, riv., Wash.		C5	98
Klimovsk, Sov.Un.	30,000	O18	332
Klinaklini, riv., B.C., Can.		E10	52
Kline, Barnwell, S.C.	213	E6	188
Klintehamn, Swe.	4,650	D9	292
Klintsy, Sov.Un.	49,200	F9	332
Klippan, Swe.	8,074	E4	292
Ključ, Yugo.	1,514	B3	316
Kłobuck, Pol.	6,533	C4	325
Kloch, lake, B.C., Can.		C10	52
Klock, Ont., Can.	75	*O22	64
Kłodzko, Pol.	20,200	C3	325
Klondike, Knox, Tenn.		E9	190
Klondike Lotus Point, Lake, Ill.	1,402	*A5	138
Klondyke, Graham, Ariz.	100	F5	124
Klosterneuburg, Aus.	23,683	B8	313
Kloten, Nelson, N.Dak.	120	C7	154
Kloten, Switz.	3,429	A4	312
Klotzville, Assumption, La.	300	B5	180
Klövsjö, Swe.		E6	291
Kluane, lake, Yukon, Can.		E5	48
Kluang, Mala.	32,457	G4	362
Kluczbork, Pol.	11,800	C4	325
Klukwan, Alsk.	91	I14	84
Klyuchevskaya, vol., Sov.Un.		D17	329
Knapp, Dunn, Wis.	374	D1	160
Knapp, creek, W.Va.		C5	194
Knaresborough, Eng.	8,500	G11	273
Knebel, Den.		E1	292
Knee, lake, Man., Can.		C5	60
Knee, lake, Sask., Can.		C4	58
Knezha, Bul.	13,856	B2	317
Knierim, Calhoun, Iowa	153	B3	142
Knife, riv., N.Dak.		C3	154
Knife River, Lake, Minn.	350	E7	148
Knifley, Adair, Ky.	250	C5	178
Knight, inlet, B.C., Can.		E10	52
Knightdale, Wake, N.C.	622	B7	186
Knighton, Wales	1,800	I9	273
Knights Landing, Yolo, Calif.	725	C3	94
Knightstown, Henry, Ind.	2,496	C4	140
Knightsville, Clay, Ind.	722	C2	140
Knightsville, dam, Mass.		B2	206
Knik, Alsk.	15	C7	84
		G11	
Kniman, Jasper, Ind.	100	A2	140
Knin, Yugo.	3,543	B3	316
Knislinge, Swe.	3,523	E5	292
Knittelfeld, Aus.	13,123	C6	313
Knob, creek, Ky.		A5	178
Knobel, Clay, Ark.	339	A6	170
Knob Hill, El Paso, Colo.		D6	106
Knob Lake (Schefferville), Que., Can.		D8	72
Knob Lick, Metcalfe, Ky.	100	C5	178
Knob Lick, St. Francois, Mo.	150	D7	150
Knobly, mtn., W.Va.		B5	194
Knob Noster, Johnson, Mo.	2,292	C4	150
Knobs, Fallon, Mont.		E12	110
Knobs, mtn., Pa.		B3	214
Knockadoon, head, Ire.		J5	273
Knockanefune, mtn., Ire.		I3	273
Knokke, Bel.	12,917	C2	282
Knolls, Tooele, Utah	10	C2	114
Knollwood, Greene, Ohio	2,500	C2	156
Knollwood Park, Jackson, Mich.	2,100	*G7	146
Knops, pond, Mass.		C1	206
Knott, co., Ky.	17,362	C7	178
Knotts Island, Currituck, N.C.	140	A10	186
Knottsville, Daviess, Ky.	350	C4	178
Knowles, Beaver, Okla.	62	B3	128
Knowlton, Que., Can.	1,328	S12	66
Knowlton, Custer, Mont.		D11	110
Knowlton, Marathon, Wis.	75	D4	160
Knox, Starke, Ind.	3,458	A3	140
Knox (Town of), Waldo, Maine	(439▲)	*D3	204
Knox, Benson, N.Dak.	122	B6	154
Knox, Clarion, Pa.	1,247	B2	214
Knox, co., Ill.	61,280	B3	138
Knox, co., Ind.	41,561	D2	140
Knox, co., Ky.	25,258	D7	178
Knox, co., Maine	28,575	E3	204
Knox, co., Mo.	6,558	A5	150
Knox, co., Nebr.	13,300	B7	152
Knox, co., Ohio	38,808	B4	156
Knox, co., Tenn.	250,523	B8	190
Knox, co., Tex.	7,857	C6	130
Knox, cape, B.C., Can.		C6	52
Knox City, Knox, Mo.	330	A5	150
Knox City, Knox, Tex.	1,805	C6	130
Knoxville, Greene, Ala.	100	C2	168
Knoxville, Johnson, Ark.	300	B3	170
Knoxville, Crawford, Ga.	385	D3	176
Knoxville, Knox, Ill.	2,560	C3	138
Knoxville, Marion, Iowa	7,817	C4	142
Knoxville, Frederick, Md.	400	B4	182
Knoxville, Franklin, Miss.	150	D1	184
Knoxville, Ray, Mo.	103	B3	150

Knoxville, Knox, Tenn.	111,827	C8	190
	(*286,000)	E9	
Knysna, U.S.Afr.	8,880	F4	420
Knyszyn, Pol.	2,780	B6	325
Ko, isl., Jap.		D7	354
Koae, Hawaii, Haw.	20	D7	86
Koa Mill, Hawaii, Haw.	55	D6	86
Kobdo, see Jirgalanta, Mong.			
Kōbe, Jap.	979,305	G5	354
		M11	
Kobelyaki, Sov.Un.	14,500	H10	332
København, co., Den.	398,227	*I5	291
København, see Copenhagen, Den.			
Kobi Uotsuri, isl., Ryūkyū Is.		M11	349
Koblenz, Ger.	87,000	C2	286
Kobrin, Sov.Un.	23,000	F5	332
Kobroor, isl., Indon.		F8	359
Kobuk, Alsk.	38	B6	84
Kobuk, riv., Alsk.		B6	84
Kocaeli, see İzmit, Tur.			
Kocaeli, prov., Tur.	254,263	*A4	307
Kočani, Yugo.	8,034	D6	316
Kočevje, Yugo.	4,447	B2	316
Koch, St. Louis, Mo.	900	B8	150
		C7	
Koch, mtn., Mont.		E5	110
Kocher, riv., Ger.		D3	286
Kōchi, Jap.	180,146	H4	354
Kochiu, China	159,700	G8	346
Kochumdek, Sov.Un.		C11	329
Kock, Pol.	2,381	C6	325
Kodak, Sevier, Tenn.	200	C8	190
Kodiak, Alsk.	2,628	D6	84
Kodiak, isl., Alsk.		D6	84
Kodok, Sud.		D3	398
Koehler, Colfax, N.Mex.	300	B6	126
Koen, Prowers, Colo.		D8	106
Koes, S.W.Afr.		E3	420
Kofa, mts., Ariz.		E2	124
Koffiefontein, U.S.Afr.		E5	420
Koforidua, Ghana	17,806	E4	408
Kōfu, Jap.	154,494	G7	354
		L14	
Koga, Jap.	40,206	K15	354
Köge, Den.	10,975	F3	292
Köge, bay, Den.		F3	292
Kohala, Hawaii, Haw.	950	C6	86
Kohat, Pak.	30,719	C7	375
	(40,841*)		
Kohatk, Pinal, Ariz.	75	F3	124
Kohima, India	4,125	D6	368
Kohler, Sheboygan, Wis.	1,524	B6	160
		E6	
Kohls Ranch, Gila, Ariz.	25	D4	124
Kohlu, Pak.		E6	375
Koitere, lake, Fin.		E14	290
Koje, isl., Kor.		H14	348
Kokadjo, Piscataquis, Maine	10	C3	204
Kokadjo, lake, Maine		C3	204
Kokand, Sov.Un.	105,000	D8	336
Kokanee Glacier, prov. park, B.C., Can.		F14	52
Kokchetav, Sov.Un.	40,000	B7	336
Kokkola, Fin.	13,499	E10	290
Koko, Nig.	7,624	D5	408
Koko, head, Haw.		B4	86
Kokomo (Recen), Summit, Colo.	74	C4	106
Kokomo, Maui, Haw.	250	C5	86
Kokomo, Howard, Ind.	47,197	B3	140
Kokomo, Marion, Miss.	250	D2	184
Koko Nor, see Chinghai, lake, China		D7	346
Kokonselka, lake, Fin.		F13	291
Kokopo, Bis.Arch.		E12	359
Kokosing, riv., Ohio		B4	156
Kokrines, Alsk.	68	C6	84
Koksilah, B.C., Can.	225	C14	52
Koksoak, riv., Que., Can.		P9	66
Kokstad, U.S.Afr.	7,533	F5	420
Kokura, Jap.	242,240	H3	354
Kola, Sov.Un.	1,900	C5	328
Kola, pen., Sov.Un.		C5	328
Kolan, China	1,000	F5	348
Kolar, India	27,176	F3	366
Kolari, Fin.		C10	290
Kolarovgrad (Shumen), Bul.	41,670	B3	317
Kolarovgradski, prov., Bul.		*B3	317
Kolárovo, Czech.	12,592	C3	324
Kolbäcksån, riv., Swe.		B7	292
Kolbano, Austl.		A4	432
Kolbano, Indon.		F6	358
Kolbio, Som.		F5	398
Kolbuszowa, Pol.	2,124	C5	325
Kolda, Sen.	4,000	D2	408
Kolding, Den.	32,474	I3	291
Kole, Con.L.		C3	414
Koleč, Czech.	974	*A2	324
Kolguyev, isl., Sov.Un.		C6	328
Kolhapur, India	136,835	E2	366
Kolimbine, riv., Maur.		C2	408
Kolin, Czech.	21,743	A2	324
Kolin, Judith Basin, Mont.	9	C7	110
Kolmarden, mts., Swe.		C7	292
Köln (Cologne), Ger.	715,900	C2	286
	(*1,275,000)		
Kolno, Pol.	3,295	B5	325
Koło, Pol.	10,600	B4	325
Koloa, Kauai, Haw.	1,426	B2	86
Kolob, canyon, Utah		F2	114
Kołobrzeg, Pol.	2,816	A2	325
Kolokani, Mali		D3	408
Kolombangara, isl., Solomon		E1	436
Kolomna, Sov.Un.	100,000	A1	336
Kolomyya, Sov.Un.	45,000	H5	332
Kolonodale, Indon.		E6	358
Kolosib, India		D6	368
Kolp, riv., Sov.Un.		C11	332
Kolpashevo, Sov.Un.	32,100	A10	336
Kolva, riv., Sov.Un.		A5	336
Kolwa, Pak.		F4	375
Kolwezi, Con.L.	37,600	E4	414
Kolyberovo, Sov.Un.	18,000	O19	332
Kolyma, riv., Sov.Un.		C17	329
Komádi, Hung.	10,577	B6	320
Komadugu, riv., Nig.		D7	409
Komandorskiye, is., Sov.Un.		D18	329
Komarno, Man., Can.	130	E4	60
Komárno, Czech.	23,996	C4	324
Komarno, marsh, Sov.Un.		A10	336
Komárom, Hung.	10,000	B3	320
Komárom, co., Hung.	250,000	*B3	320
Komatipoort, U.S.Afr.	1,835	E6	421
Komatke, Maricopa, Ariz.	100	E3	124
		H2	
Komatsu, Jap.	72,378	F6	354
Komatsushima, Jap.	32,013	G5	354
Kōm el Tawil, Eg., U.A.R.	24,610	C2	382
Kom Hamada, Eg., U.A.R.	3,671	*A3	395
Komi, A.S.S.R. Sov.Un.	804,000	C8	328
Kominato, Jap.	12,591	L16	354
Komodo, isl., Indon.		F5	358
Kōm Ombo, Eg., U.A.R.		C3	395
Komono, Con.B.		G7	409
Komoran, isl., Neth.N.Gui.		F9	359
Komotini, Grc.	29,734	A5	306
Kompong Cham, Camb.	25,000	D5	362
Kompong Chhnang, Camb.	25,000	D5	362
Kompong Kleang, Camb.	10,000	D5	362
Kompong Som, bay, Camb.		E4	362
Kompong Speu, Camb.	5,000	E5	362
Komrat, Sov.Un.	16,700	I7	332
Komsomolets, isl., Sov.Un.		A11	329
Komsomolsk, Sov.Un.	177,000	D15	329
Kona Shahr, China		C4	346
Konawa, Seminole, Okla.	1,555	C7	128
Kondinskoye, Sov.Un.		C8	328
Kondoa, Tan.	2,816	C6	414
Kondopoga, Sov.Un.	26,800	A10	332
Kong, prov., I.C.		E4	408
Kong, isl., Camb.		E4	362
Kongju, Kor.		G13	348
Kongolo, Con.L.		D4	414
Kongsberg, Nor.	8,545	G3	291
Kongsvinger, Nor.	2,242	A3	292
Königsberg, see Kaliningrad, Sov.Un.			
Konin, Pol.	13,500	B4	325
Kónista, Grc.	3,716	A3	306
Konjic, Yugo.	4,272	C3	316
Konnarock, Washington, Va.	400	D3	192
Konnevesi, lake, Fin.		E12	290
Konolfingen, Switz.	3,565	B3	312
Konomoc, lake, Conn.		D7	202
Konosha, Sov.Un.	18,300	B13	332
Konotop, Sov.Un.	53,000	G9	332
Końskie, Pol.	7,386	C5	325
Konstantinovka, Sov.Un.	89,000	R21	332
Konstanz (Constance), Ger.	49,800	E3	286
Kontagora, Nig.	5,665	D6	408
Kontcha, Cam.		E7	409
Kontich, Bel.	10,391	C3	282
Kontiomaki, Fin.		D13	290
Kontum, Viet.		D6	362
Konya, Tur.	93,125	C5	307
Konya, prov., Tur.	849,771	*C5	307
Konyang, Kor.		H13	348
Konzhakovskiy Kamen, mtn. Sov.Un.		A5	336
Koochiching, co., Minn.	18,190	C4	148
Koolau, range, Haw.		F10	86
Koontz Lake, Starke, Ind.	900	A3	140
Koosharem, Sevier, Utah	148	E4	114
Kooskia, Idaho, Idaho	801	C3	108
Kootenai, Bonner, Idaho	180	A2	108
Kootenai, co., Idaho	29,556	B2	108
Kootenai, riv., Idaho, Mont.		A3	108
		B1	110
Kootenay, lake, B.C., Can.		F14	52
Kootenay, natl. park, B.C., Can.		E14	52
Kootenay, riv., B.C., Can.		E15	52
Kopasker, Ice.		K21	290
Kopervik, Nor.	1,764	G1	291
Kopeysk, Sov.Un.	160,000	A6	336
Köping, Swe.	15,630	B6	292
Köpmanholmen, Swe.		E8	290
Koppány, riv., Hung.		C3	320
Kopparberg, Swe.	2,685	B6	292
Kopparberg, co., Swe.	279,041	A5	292
Koppel, Beaver, Pa.	1,389	C1	214
Kopperston, Wyoming, W.Va.	950	D6	194
Koprivnica, Yugo.	1,329	A3	316
Kopychintsy, Sov.Un.	17,700	H5	332
Korab, mtn., Alb.		D5	316
K'orahē, Eth.		D5	398
Koraluk, riv., Newf., Can.		D9	72
Koram, Eth.		C4	398
Korarou, lake, Mali		C4	408
Korbu, mtn., Mala.		F4	362
Korçë, Alb.	31,833	A3	306
Korçë, pref., Alb.	175,000	*A3	306
Korčula, isl., Yugo.		C3	316
Kordofan, prov., Sud.	1,761,968	C2	398
Korea, country, Asia	30,882,000	F14	340
		F13	348
Korea, North, country, Asia	8,046,000	F12	348
Korea, South, country, Asia	22,836,000	G12	348
Korea, bay, China		F11	348
Korea, strait, Jap.		H2	354
Korea, strait, Kor.		H14	348
Korets, Sov.Un.		G6	332
Korf, Sov.Un.		C18	329
Korhogo, I.C.	5,700	E3	408
Korinthia (Corinthia), prov. Grc.	113,358	*C4	306
Kórinthos (Corinth), Grc.	17,728	C4	306
Kōriyama, Jap.	91,119	F8	354
Korkudeli, Tur.	4,037	C4	307
Korla, see Kuerhlo, China			
Kormatiki, cape, Cyp.		D5	307
Körmend, Hung.	7,269	B1	320
Kornat, isl., Yugo.		C2	316
Korneuburg, Aus.	7,872	B8	313
Koro, isl., Fiji		E7	436
Koromo, Jap.	34,010	L13	354
Koronis, lake, Minn.		F3	148
Körös, riv., Hung.		C6	320
Körös, riv., Rom.		A2	321
Korosten, Sov.Un.	33,800	G7	332
Korotoyak, Sov.Un.	11,500	G12	332
Korovin, vol., Alsk.		E4	84
Korpfjallen, mtn., Swe.		A5	292
Korsakov, Sov.Un.	43,800	E16	329
Korsnäs, Fin.		E9	290
Korsnas, Swe.		A6	292
Korsör, Den.	12,361	F2	292
Korti, Sud.		B3	398
Kortrijk (Courtrai), Bel.	41,779	D2	282
Korumburra, Austl.	2,858	F9	432
Korville, Harris, Tex.	75	*D8	130
Koryak, mts., Sov.Un.		C18	329
Kós, Grc.	8,863	C6	306
Kós, isl., Grc.		C6	306
Koschagyl, Sov.Un.		C4	336
Kościan, Pol.	12,900	B3	325
Kościerzyna, Pol.	7,820	A3	325
Kosciusko, Attala, Miss.	6,800	B3	184
Kosciusko, co., Ind.	40,373	A4	140
Kosciusko, mtn., Austl.		F9	432
Koshan, China	20,918	A12	348
Koshiki, isl., Jap.		I2	354
Koshkonong, Oregon, Mo.	478	E6	150
Koshkonong, lake, Wis.		F5	160
Košice, Czech.	79,460	B5	324
Košický, co., Czech.	541,359	*B5	324
Košiře, Czech. (part of Prague)	17,715	*A2	324
Koskaecodde, lake, Newf., Can.		G8	72
Köslin, see Koszalin, Pol.			
Kosmos, Lewis, Wash.	200	C4	98
Kosöng, Kor.	14,842	F14	348
Kosovë, pref., Alb.	53,000	*C5	316
Kosovska Mitrovica, Yugo.	17,195	C5	316
Kossol, passage, Palau		A6	436
Kossol, reef, Palau		A6	436
Kossuth, Alcorn, Miss.	178	A4	184
Kossuth, co., Iowa	25,314	A3	142
Kosta, Swe.		E7	292
Kostelec, Czech.	2,704	*A2	324
Kostelec nad Černými Lesy, Czech.	3,341	*B2	324
Kosterfjord, fjord, Swe.		C2	292
Kosti, Sud.	22,688	C3	398
Kosti, riv., Nep.		D4	368
Kostino, Sov.Un.		C10	328
Kostroma, Sov.Un.	171,000	A2	336
Kostryń, Pol.	635	B2	325
Koszalin, Pol.	37,000	A3	325
Koszalin, pol.div., Pol.	628,000	*A3	325
Kőszeg, Hung.	9,000	B1	320
Koszta, Iowa, Iowa	160	C5	142
Kota Bharu, Mala.	38,075	F4	362
Kotah, India	65,107	D1	368
Kota Kota, Rh.&Nya.		B6	421
Kotel, Bul.	5,881	B3	317
Kotelnich, Sov.Un.	27,000	A3	336
Kotelnikovskiy, Sov.Un.	19,300	C2	336
Kotelny, isl., Sov.Un.		B15	329
Köthen, Ger.	39,100	C4	286
Kotido, Ug.		B5	414
Kotka, Fin.	24,024	F12	291
Kotlas, Sov.Un.	37,000	C6	328
Kotlik, Alsk.	53	C5	84
Kōtō, isl., China		N10	349
Kotonkoro, Nig.		D6	408
Kotor, Yugo.	3,814	C4	316
Kotor Varoš, Yugo.	2,700	B3	316
Kotovsk, Sov.Un.	30,000	I7	332
Kotri, Pak.	15,154	G6	375
Kotto, riv., Cen.Afr.Rep.		E9	409
Kotung, China	10,000	B13	348
Kotzebue, Alsk.	1,290	B5	84
Kotzebue, sound, Alsk.		B5	84
Kouango, Cen.Afr.Rep.		E9	409
Kouchibouguacis, riv., N.B., Can.		C4	70
Koudougou, Upper Volta	25,900	D4	408
Koula-Moutou, Gabon		G7	409
Koulikoro, Mali	4,350	D3	408
Kounradskiy, Sov.Un.		C9	336
Kountze, Hardin, Tex.	1,768	D8	130
Koupangtzu, China	5,000	E10	348
Kourémalé, Mali		D3	408
Kourou, Fr.Gu.	217	D6	256
Kouroussa, Guinea	5,550	D3	408
Koutiala, Mali	2,900	D3	408
Kouts, Porter, Ind.	1,007	A2	140
Kouvola, Fin.	10,824	F12	291
Ko Vaya, Pima, Ariz.	35	F4	124
Kovel, Sov.Un.	42,600	G5	332
Kovrov, Sov.Un.	100,000	A2	336
Kōwa, Jap.	9,347	M12	354
Kowloon, Hong Kong	547,000	N7	349
Kowŏn, Kor.		F13	348
Koylyukyu, Sov.Un.		B15	329
Koyuk, Alsk.	134	C5	84
Koyukuk, Alsk.	79	C6	84
Koyukuk, riv., Alsk.		B6	84
Kozan, Tur.	11,382	C6	307
Kozáni, Grc.	17,651	A3	306
Kozáni, prov., Grc.	177,838	*A3	306
Kozelsk, Sov.Un.	12,600	E10	332
Kozhikode, India	158,724	F3	366
Kozienice, Pol.	4,099	C5	325
Koźle, Pol.	8,277	C4	325
Kozloduy, Bul.	7,773	B1	317
Kōzu, isl., Jap.		G7	354
Kożuchów, Pol.	2,385	C2	325
Kpandu, Ghana	4,040	E5	408
Kra, isth., Thai.		E3	362
Krabi, prov., Thai.	59,483	*E3	362
Kraemer, Lafourche, La.	450	C6	180
Krafton, Mobile, Ala. (part of Prichard)		E1	168
Kragerö, Nor.	4,351	G3	291
Kragujevac, Yugo.	41,700	B5	316
Kraków, Pol.	423,000	C4	325
Krakow, Shawano, Wis.	200	D5	160
Kraków, pol.div., Pol.	2,350,000	*D5	325
Kraljevo, Yugo.	15,152	C5	316
Královské Vinohrady, Czech. (part of Prague)		*A2	324
Kralupy nad Vltavou, Czech.	9,167	*A2	324
Králův Dvůr, Czech.	3,390	*B2	324
Kramatorsk, Sov.Un.	115,000	H11	332
		R21	
Kramer, Warren, Ind.	150	B2	140
Kramer, Lancaster, Nebr.	30	*D9	152
Kramer, Bottineau, N.Dak.	175	B5	154
Kramfors, Swe.		E7	290
Kränge, Swe.		E7	290
Kranidhion, Grc.	4,385	C4	306
Kranj, Yugo.	5,553	A2	316
Kranzburg, Codington, S.Dak.	156	C9	158
Krasburg, S.W.Afr.		E3	420
Kraslice, Czech.	6,294	A1	324
Krasnaya Sloboda, Sov.Un.		C3	336
Kraśnik Lubelski, Pol.	9,158	C6	325
Krasnoarmeysk, Sov.Un.	31,300	G15	332
Krasnoarmeysk, Sov.Un.	11,500	H15	332
Krasnodar, Sov.Un.	312,000	J12	332
Krasnodon, Sov.Un.	10,000	S23	332
Krasnograd, Sov.Un.	24,500	H10	332
Krasnokamsk, Sov.Un.	54,000	A5	336
Krasnoselkup, Sov.Un.		C10	328
Krasnoselye, Sov.Un.	14,700	H9	332
Krasnoslobodsk, Sov.Un.	19,300	E14	332
Krasnoufimsk, Sov.Un.	31,300	A5	336
Krasnovishersk, Sov.Un.	28,300	A5	336
Krasnovodsk, Sov.Un.	38,000	D4	336
Krasnoyarsk, Sov.Un.	409,000	D11	329
Krasnoznamenskiy, Sov.Un.		B7	336
Krasnystaw, Pol.	10,300	C6	325
Krasnyy Chikoy, Sov.Un.		D12	329
Krasnyy Kholm, Sov.Un.	11,700	C11	332
Krasnyy Kut, Sov.Un.	10,000	S22	332
Krasnyy Liman, Sov.Un.	21,000	R21	332
Krasnyy Luch, Sov.Un.	94,000	S22	332
Krasnyy Sulin, Sov.Un.	66,600	I13	332
Krasnyy Yar, Sov.Un.	18,300	G15	332
Kratie, Camb.	25,000	D5	362
Kratovo, Yugo.	1,993	C6	316
Krebs, Pittsburg, Okla.	1,342	D8	128
Krefeld, Ger.	198,100	C2	286
Kremenchug, Sov.Un.	86,000	H9	332
Kremenets, Sov.Un.	36,000	G5	332
Kremennaya, Sov.Un.	18,600	Q22	332
Kremlin, Hill, Mont.	125	B6	110
Kremlin, Garfield, Okla.	128	B6	128
Kremmling, Grand, Colo.	576	B4	106
Krems [an der Donau], Aus.	20,353	B7	313
Kreole, Jackson, Miss.	1,870	E2	184
		E4	
Kresson, Camden, N.J.		D3	210
Kreuzlingen, Switz.	10,700	A5	312
Kribi, Cam.	3,055	F6	409
Krichev, Sov.Un.	15,900	F8	332
Krider, Roosevelt, N.Mex.	12	D7	126
Kriens, Switz.	9,821	A4	312
Krishnagar, India	50,042	E5	368
Krishnagiri, India	19,774	F3	366
Kristdala, Swe.	2,695	D7	292
Kristiansand, Nor.	26,270	G3	291
	(*32,700)		
Kristianstad, Swe.	24,896	E5	292
Kristianstad, co., Swe.	259,047	E4	292
Kristiansund, Nor.	15,350	E2	290
Kristinehamn, Swe.	20,029	B4	292
Kristinestäd, Fin.	2,829	E9	291
Krivoy Rog, Sov.Un.	386,000	I9	332
Križevci, Yugo.	5,591	A3	316
Krk, isl., Yugo.		B2	316
Krka, riv., Yugo.		C3	316
Krnov, Czech.	22,029	A3	324
Krokeai, Grc.	3,012	C4	306
Krokom, Swe.		E6	290
Kroměříž, Czech.	21,014	B3	324
Kromy, Sov.Un.	12,800	F10	332
Kron, lake, Swe.		D6	292
Kronau, Sask., Can.	78	E5	58
Kronborg, Hamilton, Nebr.	23	*D8	152
Kronoberg, co., Swe.	159,482	E5	292
Kronshtadt, Sov.Un. (part of Leningrad)	59,000	C7	332
Kroonstad, U.S.Afr.	26,612	E5	420
Kropotkin, Sov.Un.	54,000	J13	332
Kroppefjäll, mts., Swe.		C3	292
Krosno, Pol.	18,500	D5	325
Krosno Odrzańskie, Pol.	2,249	B2	325
Krotoszyn, Pol.	16,300	C3	325
Krotz Springs, St. Landry, La.	1,057	D4	180
Krško, Yugo.	629	B2	316
Kruger, natl. park, U.S.Afr.		D6	421
Krugersdorp, U.S.Afr.	75,738	E5	420
Krujë, Alb.	5,107	D4	316
Krumovgrad, Bul.	2,232	C2	317
Krung Thep, see Bangkok, Thai.			
Krusenstern Rock, reef, Haw.		B5	86
Kruševac, Yugo.	16,638	C5	316
Kruševo, Yugo.	3,846	D5	316
Kruszwica, Pol.	4,822	B4	325
Krydanyy, Sov.Un.		C14	329
Krydor, Sask., Can.	169	D4	58
Krym (Crimea), pen., Sov.Un.		J9	332
Krymskaya, Sov.Un.	36,200	J11	332
Krynica, Pol.	2,649	D5	325
Ksar es Souk, Mor.	5,484	B3	402
Kuala Dungun, Mala.	12,504	F4	362
Kuala Krau, Mala.	1,271	G4	362
Kualakurun, Indon.		E4	358
Kuala Lipis, Mala.	8,758	F4	362
Kuala Lumpur, Mala.	315,040	G4	362
Kualapuu, Maui, Haw.	607	B4	86
Kuala Trengganu, Mala.	29,441	F4	362
Kuan, China	10,000	G7	348
Kuandang, Indon.		D6	358
Kuangan, China		J2	349
Kuangchang, China	10,000	L8	349
Kuangchou, see Canton, China			
Kuanghua, China	5,000	I5	349
Kuangning, China	1,000	N6	349
Kuangte, China	15,000	J9	349
Kuangyüan, China	1,000	I3	349
Kuansienshih, China		O5	349
Kuantan, Mala.	23,025	G4	362
Kuanti, China		D14	348
Kuantien, China	8,000	E12	348
Kuba, Okinawa		D1	436
Kuban, riv., Sov.Un.		J13	332
Kubrat, Bul.	6,559	B3	317
Kubyshev, Sov.Un.		A9	336
Kucha, China	103,865	C4	346
Kuchen, China	5,000	I8	349
Kucheng, China	5,000	I5	349
Kuchêng, see Chitai, China			
Kuching, Sar.	37,949	D4	358
Kuchino, isl., Jap.		I2	354
Kuchino Erabu, isl., Jap.		I2	354
Kudat, N.Bor.	3,800	C5	358
Kudymkar, Sov.Un.	20,000	A4	336
Kuei, China	5,000	N4	349
Kuei, riv., China		M5	349
Kueichi, China		K8	349
Kueichih, China	10,000	J8	349
Kueichou, China		J5	349
Kueilin, China	145,100	M5	349
Kueisui, see Huhehot, China			
Kueite, China		D8	346
Kueitung, China		L6	349
Kueiyang, China	270,900	L3	349
Kuerhlo (Korla), China	10,000	C5	346
Kufstein, Aus.	11,007	C4	313

L

Lanai, isl., Haw. C4 86
Lanai City, Maui, Haw. 2,056 C5 86
Lanark, Ont., Can. 879 O24 64
Lanark, Franklin, Fla. 250 B6 174
Lanark, Carroll, Ill. 1,473 A4 138
Lanark, Scot. 8,100 F9 272
Lanark, Raleigh, W.Va. 400 D3 194 D7
Lanark, co., Ont., Can. 38,025 O24 64
Lanark, co., Scot. 1,621,300 F8 272
Lanarote, Mor. C1 402
Lancashire, co., Eng. 5,099,000 H10 273
Lancaster, Los Angeles, Calif. 26,012 E4 94
Lancaster, Ont., Can. 594 O26 64
Lancaster, Eng. 49,500 G10 273
Lancaster, Atchison, Kans. 196 C8 144
Lancaster, Garrard, Ky. 3,021 C6 178
Lancaster, Worcester, Mass. 750 B4 206 (3,958▲)
Lancaster, Kittson, Minn. 462 C2 148
Lancaster, Schuyler, Mo. 740 A5 150
Lancaster, Coos, N.H. 2,392 C3 208 (3,138▲)
Lancaster, Erie, N.Y. 12,254 C3 212
Lancaster, Fairfield, Ohio 29,916 C4 156
Lancaster, Lancaster, Pa. 61,055 C5 214 (*125,100)
Lancaster, Lancaster, S.C. 7,999 B7 188
Lancaster, Smith, Tenn. 150 B6 190
Lancaster, Dallas, Tex. 7,501 B8 130
Lancaster, Lancaster, Va. 100 C8 192
Lancaster, Grant, Wis. 3,703 F3 160
Lancaster, co., Nebr. 155,272 D9 152
Lancaster, co., Pa. 278,359 D5 214
Lancaster, co., S.C. 39,352 B7 188
Lancaster, co., Va. 9,174 C8 192
Lancaster, sound, N.W.Ter., Can. C10 48
Lancaster Mills, Lancaster, S.C. 6,255 *B7 188
Lance Creek, Niobrara, Wyo. 500 C8 116
Lance, creek, Wyo. C8 116
Lance, pt., Newf., Can. G8 72
Lancer, Sask., Can. 215 E3 58
Lanchi, China 10,000 K9 349
Lanchou, China 699,000 D8 346
Lanciano, It. 13,300 D5 302
Lancing, Morgan, Tenn. 250 B7 190
Łancut, Pol. 9,106 C6 325
Landa, Bottineau, N.Dak. 110 B5 154
Landaff, Grafton, N.H. 100 C3 208 (289▲)
Landana, Ang. 819 D1 414
Landau [an der Isar], Ger. 5,900 D5 286
Landau [in der Pfalz], Ger. 26,500 D3 286
Landeck, Aus. 5,615 C2 313
Landen, Bel. 4,674 D4 282
Lander, Fremont, Wyo. 4,182 D4 116
Lander, co., Nev. 1,566 C4 112
Landerneau, Fr. 10,950 C1 278
Landes, dept., Fr. 248,943 *F3 278
Landes, Grant, W.Va. 150 C5 194
Landes, heath, Fr. E3 278
Landess, Grant, Ind. 200 B4 140
Landfall, Washington, Minn. 437 *F6 148
Landgrove, Bennington, Vt. 30 *E3 218 (49▲)
Landing (Shore Hills), Morris, N.J. 1,068 *B3 210
Landing, lake, Man., Can. C4 60
Landis, Searcy, Ark. 80 B4 170
Landis, Sask., Can. 240 D3 58
Landis, Rowan, N.C. 1,763 B5 186
Landisville, Atlantic, N.J. D3 210
Landisville, Lancaster, Pa. 1,690 *D5 214
Landivisiau, Fr. C1 278
Lando, Chester, S.C. 732 B7 188
Land O'Lakes, Pasco, Fla. 700 C8 174
Land O'Lakes, Vilas, Wis. 500 B4 160
Landon, Harrison, Miss. E1 184 E3
Landover Hills, Prince Georges, Md. 1,850 *C6 182
Landrum, Spartanburg, S.C. 1,930 A4 188
Landsberg, Ger. 12,000 D4 286
Landsdown, Hunterdon, N.J. 30 B3 210
Land's End, pt., Eng. K7 273
Landshut, Ger. 48,000 D5 286
Landskrona, Swe. 26,596 F3 292
Landsman, creek, Colo. C8 106
Landusky, Phillips, Mont. 300 C8 110
Lane, Kootenai, Idaho B2 108
Lane, Franklin, Kans. 282 D8 144
Lane, Douglas, Nebr. 20 *C9 152
Lane, Williamsburg, S.C. 497 D9 188
Lane, Jerauld, S.Dak. 99 C7 158
Lane, Dyer, Tenn. 65 B2 190
Lane, co., Kans. 3,060 D3 144
Lane, co., Oreg. 162,890 D3 96
Laneburg, Nevada, Ark. 125 D3 170
La Negra, Chile B3 250
Laneheart, Wilkinson, Miss. D1 184
Lanesboro, Carroll, Iowa 258 B3 142
Lanesboro, Berkshire, Mass. 400 A1 206 (2,933▲)
Lanesboro, Fillmore, Minn. 1,063 H7 148
Lanesville, Harrison, Ind. 346 D4 140
Lanett, Chambers, Ala. 7,674 C4 168
Lanfine, Alta., Can. 75 E7 54
Lanford, Laurens, S.C. 300 B5 188
Lang, Sask., Can. 281 F5 58
Langadhás, Grc. 7,660 A4 306
Langak, lake, China E4 346
Langa Langa, Con.L. C2 414
Langbank, Sask., Can. 100 E6 58
Langchung, China 70,000 J3 349
Langdale, Chambers, Ala. 2,528 C4 168
Langdale, dam, Ala. C4 168
Langdale, dam, Ga. D1 176
Langdon, Alta., Can. 128 E6 54
Langdon, Reno, Kans. 97 E5 144
Langdon, Sullivan, N.H. 80 E2 208 (338▲)
Langdon, Cavalier, N.Dak. 2,151 B7 154
Langeac, Fr. E5 278
L'Ange Gardien, Que., Can. 350 R16 66
Langeland, is., Den. I4 291
Längelmävesi, lake, Fin. F11 291
Langeloth, Washington, Pa. 1,112 C1 214
Langenburg, Sask., Can. 668 E7 58
Langensalza, Ger. 16,800 C4 286
Langenthal, Switz. 8,933 A3 312
Langeoog, isl., Ger. B2 286
Langes Corner, Brown, Wis. 100 A6 160
Langesund, Nor. 2,169 G3 291
Langevin, Que., Can. 540 R14 66
Langford, Marshall, S.Dak. 397 B8 158
Langford Station, B.C., Can. 385 C14 52
Langham, Sask., Can. 390 D4 58
Langholm, Scot. 2,400 F9 272
Langhorne, Bucks, Pa. 1,461 *C6 214
Langhorne Manor, Bucks, Pa. 1,506 *C6 214
Langjokull, glacier, Ice. L19 290
Langkawi, isl., Mala. F3 362
Langkha Tuk, mtn., Thai. E3 362
Langlade, co., Wis. 19,916 C4 160
Langley, Pike, Ark. 25 C3 170
Langley, B.C., Can. 2,131 C15 52
Langley, Mayes, Okla. 205 B8 128
Langley, Aiken, S.C. 1,216 D5 188
Langley, Fairfax, Va. 500 A7 192
Langley, Island, Wash. 448 A4 98
Langley Park, Prince Georges, Md. 11,510 *C5 182
Langlois, Curry, Oreg. 300 E2 96
Langma, China E5 346
Langnau in Emmental, Switz. 9,105 B3 312
Langogne, Fr. E5 278
Langon, Fr. E3 278
Langoy, isl., Nor. B6 290
Langreo, Sp. 7,138 A4 298
Langres, Fr. 6,205 D6 278
Langres, plat., Fr. D6 278
Langruth, Man., Can. 175 E3 60
Langsa, Indon. 4,749 D1 358
Langsdale, Clarke, Miss. 40 D4 184
Langshyttan, Swe. A7 292
Langstaff, Ont., Can. 515 R22 64
Langston, Jackson, Ala. 275 A3 168
Langston, Logan, Okla. 136 C6 128
Langton, Ont., Can. 255 R20 64
Languedoc, former prov., Fr. 2,413,000 F4 278
L'Anguille, riv., Ark. B6 170
Langvik, Swe. B9 292
Lanham, Prince Georges, Md. 2,500 C6 182
Lanham, Jones, Miss. 100 D3 184
Lanham, Gage, Nebr. 125 D9 152
Lanhsi, China 10,000 B13 348
Lanier, co., Ga. 5,097 E3 176
Lanigan, Sask., Can. 462 E5 58
Lanigan, creek, Sask., Can. E5 58
Lanikai, Honolulu, Haw. (part of Kailua) *G11 86
Lanin, vol., Arg. C1 252
Lankin, Walsh, N.Dak. 303 B8 154
Lanklaar, Bel. 2,785 C4 282
Lannion, Fr. 6,734 C2 278
Lannon, Waukesha, Wis. 1,084 E1 160
L'Annonciation, Que., Can. 783 R10 66
Lanoka Harbor, Ocean, N.J. 100 D4 210
Lanoraie, Que., Can. 890 S11 66
Lansdale, Montgomery, Pa. 12,612 C6 214
Lansdowne, Ont., Can. 520 P24 64
Lansdowne, Baltimore, Md. 13,134 B6 182 C4
Lansdowne, Delaware, Pa. 12,601 A6 214
Lansdowne House, Ont., Can. R24 64
L'Anse, Baraga, Mich. 2,397 C3 146
L'Anse St. Jean, Que., Can. 265 P14 66
Lansford, Bottineau, N.Dak. 382 B4 154
Lansford, Carbon, Pa. 5,958 C6 214
Lansing, Crittenden, Ark. B6 170
Lansing, Ont., Can. 4,000 R22 64
Lansing, Cook, Ill. 18,098 B6 138 F3
Lansing, Allamakee, Iowa 1,325 A6 142
Lansing, Leavenworth, Kans. 1,264 *C9 144
Lansing, Ingham, Mich. 107,807 G7 146 (*209,100)
Lansing, Ashe, N.C. 278 A4 186
Lansing, Belmont, Ohio 1,200 B6 156
Lansing, Fayette, W.Va. 472 D7 194
Lanta, isl., Thai. F3 362
Lantana, Palm Beach, Fla. 5,021 E10 174
Lantana, Cumberland, Tenn. C6 190
Lantern, hill, Conn. D8 202
Lantry, Dewey, S.Dak. 22 B4 158
Lantsang, China G7 346
Lanty, Conway, Ark. B4 170
Lantz, Barbour, W.Va. 30 C4 194
Lanusei, It. 5,000 F2 302
Lanuvio, It. 2,389 *E4 302
Lanzarote, isl., Can.Is. F12 298
Laoag, Phil. 22,218 A6 358
Laoighis, co., Ire. 47,087 I5 273
Lao Kay, Viet. 25,000 B5 362
Laon, Fr. 21,931 C5 278
Laona, Forest, Wis. 950 C5 160
La Oroya, Peru 20,496 C2 245
Laos, country, Asia 1,690,000 G12 340 362
Laotto, Noble, Ind. 300 A4 140
Lap, isl., Truk A3 436
La Palma, Mex. 386 K12 225
La Palma, Pan. F8 228
La Palma, Sp. 8,037 D3 298
La Pampa, prov., Arg. 190,900 E4 250
La Paragua, Ven. 313 C7 240
La Passe, Ont., Can. 150 O24 64
La Patrie, Que., Can. 535 S13 66
La Paz, Arg. B2 252
La Paz, Arg. 15,006 B4 252
La Paz, Bol. 321,073 C1 246
La Paz, dept., Bol. C1 246
La Paz, Col. A2 244
La Paz, Hond. 3,877 C4 228
Lapaz, Marshall, Ind. 545 A3 140
La Paz, Mex. 13,081 C3 224
La Paz, Mex. 3,330 C5 225
La Paz, bay, Mex. C2 224
La Pedrera, Col. D3 244
Lapeer, Lapeer, Mich. 6,160 F8 146
Lapeer, co., Mich. 41,920 F8 146
Lapel, Madison, Ind. 1,772 B4 140
La Pena, Mex. K15 225
La Perade, Que., Can. 1,282 R12 66
La Petite-Rivière St. François, Que., Can. 440 Q14 66
La Piedad, Mex. 17,841 K12 225
Lapine, Montgomery, Ala. 300 D3 168
La Pine, Deschutes, Oreg. 450 D5 96
Lapinlahti, Fin. E12 290
La Place, Macon, Ala. C4 168
Laplace, St. John the Baptist, La. 3,541 B6 180
Lapland, reg., Eur. B9 290
La Plant, Dewey, S.Dak. 40 B5 158
La Plata, Arg. 207,031 B4 252 (*275,000)
La Plata, Col. 2,416 C1 244
La Plata, Charles, Md. 1,214 C6 182
La Plata, Macon, Mo. 1,365 A5 150
Laplata, San Juan, N.Mex. 15 B2 126
La Plata, co., Colo. 19,225 E3 106
La Plata, peak, Colo. C4 106
La Platte, Sarpy, Nebr. 125 E3 152
La Platte, riv., Vt. C2 218
La Pobla de Lillet, Sp. 2,164 A7 298
La Poile, bay, Newf., Can. G6 72
Lapoint, Uintah, Utah 25 C6 114
La Pointe, Ashland, Wis. 300 B3 160
Lapointe Station, Que., Can. 215 Q15 66
La Pola, Sp. 920 A4 298
Laporte, Sask., Can. 105 E3 58
Laporte, Larimer, Colo. 300 B5 106
La Porte, La Porte, Ind. 21,157 A3 140
Laporte, Hubbard, Minn. 155 D4 148
Laporte, Sullivan, Pa. 195 B5 214
La Porte, Harris, Tex. 4,512 F8 130
La Porte, co., Ind. 95,111 A3 140
La Porte City, Black Hawk, Iowa 1,953 B5 142
La Porte, Plumas, Calif. 50 C3 94
Lappäjärvi, lake, Fin. E10 290
Lappeenranta, Fin. 17,410 F13 291
Lappi, dept., Fin. 189,200 *C11 290
Lappland, prov., Swe. 136,401 *C9 290
Laprairie, Que., Can. 5,372 S11 66 S16
La Prairie, Itasca, Minn. 243 *D5 148
Laprairie, co., Que., Can. 24,620 S11 66 S16
Laprida, Arg. 3,261 C3 252
La Providence, Que., Can. 3,826 *S12 66
La Pryor, Zavala, Tex. 900 E6 130
Lapseki, Tur. 2,387 A2 307
Laptev, sea, Sov.Un. B14 329
Lapua, Fin. E10 290
Lapuanjoki, riv., Fin. E10 290
La Puebla, Sp. 10,147 C8 298
La Puebla de Montalbán, Sp. 6,581 C4 298
La Puente, Los Angeles, Calif. 24,723 *E5 94
La Puente, Rio Arriba, N.Mex. 150 B4 126
La Purísima, Mex. 557 B3 224
Lapurucuara, Braz. F3 256
Lapush, Clallam, Wash. 250 B2 98
Lapwai, Nez Perce, Idaho 500 C2 108
Laqiya Arba'in, Sud. B2 398
La Quiaca, Arg. B4 250
L'Aquila, It. 25,600 D4 302
L'Aquila, prov., It. 368,900 *D4 302
Lār, Iran 13,010 D4 379
Lara, state, Ven. 368,169 B3 240
Larache, Mor. 41,898 A2 402
Larak, isl., Iran D4 379
Laramie, Albany, Wyo. 17,520 E7 116
Laramie, co., Wyo. 60,149 E8 116
Laramie, basin, Wyo. D6 116
Laramie, mts., Wyo. D6 116
Laramie, peak, Wyo. D7 116
Laramie, riv., Colo., Wyo. A5 106 E7 116
Laranjeiras, Braz. 4,149 C3 258
Larantuka, Indon. F6 358
Larb, Valley, Mont. B9 110
Lärbro, Swe. 2,540 D9 292
Larchmont, Westchester, N.Y. 6,789 D2 212
Larchwood, Lyon, Iowa 531 A1 142
Lardeau, B.C., Can. 200 E14 52
Lardo, Valley, Idaho 75 *E2 108
L'Ardoise, N.S., Can. 436 D9 70
Laredo, Grundy, Mo. 370 A4 150
Laredo, Hill, Mont. 7 B7 110
Laredo, Sp. 5,838 A5 298
Laredo, Webb, Tex. 60,678 F6 130 (*61,500)
Laredo, sound, B.C., Can. D8 52
La Réole, Fr. E3 278
Largeau, Chad C8 409
Largent, Morgan, W.Va. 75 B6 194
Largo, Pinellas, Fla. 5,302 C5 174 D8
Largo, key, Fla. F10 174
Largo Canyon, riv., N.Mex. B3 126
Largs, Scot. 7,700 F8 272
Lariat, Rio Grande, Colo. *E4 106
La Ricamarie, Fr. 10,915 E6 278
Larimer, Westmoreland, Pa. 1,500 *C2 214
Larimer, co., Colo. 53,343 B5 106
Larimore, Grand Forks, N.Dak. 1,714 C8 154
Larino, It. 6,019 E5 302
La Rioja, Arg. 23,809 A2 252
La Rioja, Cuba B6 232
La Rioja, prov., Arg. 126,500 C4 250
Lárisa, Grc. 41,016 B4 306
Lárisa (Larissa), prov., Grc. 208,120 B4 306
Larissa, see Lárisa, prov., Grc.
Laristan, reg., Iran D3 379
La Riviere, Man., Can. 260 F3 60
Lark, Salt Lake, Utah 700 *C3 114
Larkana, Pak. 33,414 F6 375
Lark Harbour, Newf., Can. 375 F6 72
Larkinburg, Jackson, Kans. 51 *C8 144
Larkinsville, Jackson, Ala. 275 A3 168
Larkspur, Marin, Calif. 5,710 A4 94
Larkspur, Douglas, Colo. 175 C6 106
Larksville, Luzerne, Pa. 4,390 A5 214
Larnaca, Cyp. D5 307
Larne, N.Ire. 11,976 G7 272
Larned, Pawnee, Kans. 5,001 D4 144
La Robla, Sp. 9,002 A4 298
La Rochelle, Fr. 58,799 D3 278
La Roche-sur-Yon, Fr. 19,576 D3 278
La Roda, Sp. 11,602 C5 298
La Romana, Dom. Rep. 14,074 C10 233
La Ronge, Sask., Can. 639 C5 58
Larose, Lafourche, La. 2,796 E5 180
Larrabee, Cherokee, Iowa 167 B2 142
Larrabee, Washington, Maine 125 D5 204
Larrey, pt., Austl. B3 432
Larrys River, N.S., Can. 385 D8 70
Larsen Bay, Alsk. 53 D6 84
Larslan, Valley, Mont. 5 B10 110
Larsmont, Lake, Minn. 203 E7 148
Larson, Burke, N.Dak. 62 B3 154
Larto, Catahoula, La. 125 C4 180
La Rubia, Arg. B3 252
La Rue, Marion, Ohio 842 B3 156
Larue, co., Ky. 10,346 C5 178
Larvik, Nor. 10,382 B1 292 (*17,000)
Larwill, Whitley, Ind. 994 A4 140
La Sabana, Ven. A5 240
La Sal, San Juan, Utah 200 E6 114
La Sal, mts., Utah E6 114
La Salle, Man., Can. 115 F4 60
La Salle, Ont., Can. 2,703 R18 64
La Salle, Que., Can. 18,973 *S16 66
La Salle, Weld, Colo. 1,070 B6 106
La Salle, La Salle, Ill. 11,897 B4 138
La Salle, Watonwan, Minn. 147 G4 148
La Salle, Flathead, Mont. 50 B2 110
La Salle, co., Ill. 110,800 B4 138
La Salle, co., Tex. 5,972 E6 130
La Salle, par., La. 13,011 C3 180
Las Animas, Bent, Colo. 3,402 D7 106
Las Animas, co., Colo. 19,983 E6 106
Las Anod, Som. D6 398
Las Anod, pol. dist., Som. D6 398
Lasauses, Conejos, Colo. 200 E5 106
Las Cabras, Chile 1,032 B1 252
Lascahobas, Haw. 2,191 C9 86
Lascano, Ur. B5 252
Lascar, Huerfano, Colo. 10 *E6 106
Lascassas, Rutherford, Tenn. 100 C5 190
L'Ascension, Que., Can. 285 P13 66
La Scie, Newf., Can. 400 E8 72
Las Coloradas, Arg. C1 252
Las Cruces, Mex. L12 225
Las Cruces, Dona Ana, N.Mex. 29,367 F4 126
La Serena, Chile 37,618 A1 252
La Seyne [-sur-Mer], Fr. 26,672 F6 278
Las Flores, Arg. 9,287 C4 252
Lashburn, Sask., Can. 394 D3 58
Lashio, Bur. 4,638 B3 362
Lashkar, India D2 368
La Sierra, Riverside, Calif. 7,000 *F5 94
Lasithi, prov., Grc. 73,784 D5 306
Łask, Pol. 3,819 C4 325
Las Lajas, Arg. C1 252
Las Lomitas, Arg. B5 250
Las Matas, Dom. Rep. 1,818 C9 233
Las Mercedes, Ven. B5 240
Las Mesitas, Conejos, Colo. 200 *E4 106
Las Nutrias, Socorro, N.Mex. 149 D4 126
La Solana, Sp. 13,462 C5 298
Las Palmas, Can. Is. 180,074 D5 388
Las Palmas, Pan. F7 228
Las Palmas, prov., Sp. 379,977 *F12 298
Las Palomas, Sierra, N.Mex. 14 E3 126
La Spezia, It. 114,400 C2 302
La Spezia, prov., It. 236,100 *C2 302
Las Piedras, Ur. 10,000 B4 252
Las Pipinas, Arg. C4 252
Las Plumas, Arg. F4 251
Las Rosas, Arg. 6,153 B3 252
Las Rosas de Madrid, Sp. 1,196 *B5 298
Lassen, co., Calif. 13,597 B3 94
Lassen, peak, Calif. B3 94
Lassen Volcanic, natl. park, Calif. B3 94
Lasso, mtn., Tinian B7 436
L'Assomption, Que., Can. 3,683 S11 66
L'Assomption, co., Que., Can. 28,642 S11 66
Last, mtn., Sask., Can. E5 58
Las Tablas, Rio Arriba, N.Mex. 100 B4 126
Las Tablas, Pan. 2,662 G7 228
Last Chance, creek, Utah F4 114
Las Termas, Arg. 4,699 A3 252
Last Mountain, lake, Sask., Can. E5 58
Lastoursville, Gabon G7 409
Lastovo, isl., Yugo. C3 316
Lastrup, Morrison, Minn. 138 E4 148
Las Varas, Mex. B4 224
Las Varillas, Arg. 5,950 B3 252
Las Vegas, Clark, Nev. 64,405 G6 112 (*119,300)
Las Vegas (City), San Miguel, N.Mex. 7,790 C5 126
Las Vegas (Town), San Miguel, N. Mex. 6,028 C5 126
Las Vigas, Mex. 4,857 L15 225
Las Villas, prov., Cuba 1,030,162 A4 232
Latacunga, Ec. 10,389 A2 245
La Tagua, Col. D2 244
Latah, Spokane, Wash. 190 B9 98
Latah, co., Idaho 21,170 C2 108
Latah, creek, Wash. B9 98
Laterriere, Que., Can. 658 P13 66
La Teste-de-Buch, Fr. 8,009 E3 278
Latham, Baldwin, Ala. 113 D2 168
Latham, Logan, Ill. 389 D4 138
Latham, Butler, Kans. 203 E7 144
Latham, Albany, N.Y. 5,000 *C8 212
Latham, Sweetwater, Wyo. 25 E5 116
Lathrop, San Joaquin, Calif. 1,123 *D3 94
Lathrop, Delta, Mich. 25 C4 146
Lathrop, Clinton, Mo. 1,006 B3 150
Lathrop Wells, Nye, Nev. 20 G5 112
Lathrup Village, Oakland, Mich. 3,556 B8 146
Latimer, Franklin, Iowa 445 B4 142
Latimer, Morris, Kans. 40 D7 144
Latimer, co., Okla. 7,738 D8 128
Latina, It. 16,700 E4 302
Latina, prov., It. 302,000 *E4 302
Latium (Lazio), reg., It. 3,626,000 D4 302
La Toma, Ec. A2 245
Laton, Fresno, Calif. 1,052 D4 94
Latonia Lakes, Kenton, Ky. 585 *A6 178
Latouche, Alsk. 7 G11 84
La Tour-du-Pin, Fr. E6 278

La Tremblade, Fr. E3 278
Latrobe, Westmoreland, Pa. 11,932 C2 214
Latrūn, Jordan 1,000 C5 382
Latta, Dillon, S.C. 1,901 C10 188
Lattan, lake, Thai. C5 362
Lattimore, Cleveland, N.C. 257 B4 186
Latuda, Carbon, Utah 100 D4 114
La Tuque, Que., Can. 11,096 Q12 66
Latvia, rep., Sov.Un. 2,094,000 D4 328
Lau, Nig. E7 409
Lauban, see Luban, Pol.
Lauca, riv., Bol. C1 246
Laud, Whitley, Ind. 150 A4 140
Lauder, Man., Can. 215 F2 60
Lauderdale, Ramsey, Minn. 1,676 F7 148
Lauderdale, Lauderdale, Miss. 500 C4 184
Lauderdale, co., Ala. 61,622 A2 168
Lauderdale, co., Miss. 67,119 C4 184
Lauderdale, co., Tenn. 21,844 C2 190
Lauderdale-by-the-Sea, Broward, Fla. 1,327 *E10 174
Lauderhill, Broward, Fla. 132 *E10 174
Lauenburg, see Lębork, Pol.
Laughery, creek, Ind. C4 140
Laughlin, peak, N.Mex. B6 126
Lauitsala, Fin. F13 291
Laulau, Saipan B7 436
Launceston, Austl. 37,120 G9 432
Launceston, Eng. 4,700 K8 273
La Unión, Arg. C2 252
La Unión, Chile 9,830 F3 251
La Unión, Col. 2,796 C1 244
La Unión, Mex. 1,336 D5 225
La Union, Dona Ana, N.Mex. 350 G4 126
La Unión, Peru 1,672 B2 245
La Unión, Sal. 7,890 D4 228
La Unión, Sp. 10,079 D6 298
Lau or Eastern Group, is., Fiji E7 436
Laupahoehoe, Hawaii, Haw. 500 C6 86
Laupheim, Ger. 8,200 D3 286
Laura, Austl. 56 B8 432
Laura, Sask., Can. 90 E4 58
Laura, Miami, Ohio 526 C2 156
Laurel, Ont., Can. 145 Q20 64
Laurel, Sussex, Del. 2,709 F3 172
Laurel, Sarasota, Fla. 700 D8 174
Laurel, Franklin, Ind. 848 C4 140
Laurel, Marshall, Iowa 223 C5 142
Laurel, Prince Georges, Md. 8,503 B6 182
Laurel, Jones, Miss. 27,889 D3 184
Laurel, Yellowstone, Mont. 4,601 E8 110
Laurel, Cedar, Nebr. 922 B8 152
Laurel, Washington, Oreg. B1 96
Laurel, Henrico, Va. 500 C7 192
Laurel, Whatcom, Wash. A4 98
Laurel, Klickitat, Wash. 5 D5 98
Laurel, fork, W.Va. C5 194
Laurel, co., Ky. 24,901 C6 178
Laurel, creek, W.Va. D6 194
Laurel, creek, W.Va. D7 194
Laurel, ridge, W.Va. B5 194
Laurel, riv., Del. F3 172
Laurel, riv., Ky. D6 178
Laurel, riv., Md. C8 182
Laurel Bloomery, Johnson, Tenn. 100 B10 190
Laureldale, Atlantic, N.J. 400 D3 210
Laureldale, Berks, Pa. 4,051 C6 214
Laureles, Ur. B4 252
Laurel Fork, Carroll, Va. 25 D4 192
Laurel Gardens, Allegheny, Pa. 1,500 *C1 214
Laurel Grove, Lafourche, La. 150 C6 180
Laurel Heights, Snohomish, Wash. 900 B4 98
Laurel Hill, Okaloosa, Fla. 411 A4 174
Laurel Hill, Scotland, N.C. 900 C6 186
Laurel Park, Henderson, N.C. 421 *B3 186
Laurel Ridge, Iberville, La. 107 B5 180
Laurel Run, Luzerne, Pa. 855 A5 214
Laurel Springs, Camden, N.J. 2,028 *D3 210
Laurelton, Ocean, N.J. 212 C4 210
Laurelville, Hocking, Ohio 539 C4 156
Laurelwood Academy, Washington, Oreg. 400 *B3 96
Laurens, Pocahontas, Iowa 1,799 B3 142
Laurens, Laurens, S.C. 9,598 B4 188
Laurens, co., Ga. 32,313 D4 176
Laurens, co., S.C. 47,609 C4 188
Laurentides, Que., Can. 1,513 S11 66
Laurentides, prov. park, Que., Can. Q13 66
Lauria Inferiore, It. 4,530 E5 302
Laurie, lake, Man., Can. B2 60
Laurie, riv., Man., Can. B2 60
Laurier, Man., Can. 230 E3 60
Laurierville, Que., Can. 767 R13 66
Laurin, Madison, Mont. 101 E4 110
Laurinburg, Scotland, N.C. 8,242 C6 186
Laurium, Houghton, Mich. 3,058 B3 146
Laurot, is., Indon E5 358
Lausanne, Switz. 113,200 (*130,900) B2 312
Lauscha, Ger. 6,506 C4 286
Laut, isl., Indon. E5 358
Lautaro, Chile 9,255 C1 252
Lauterbach, Ger. 9,436 C3 286
Lauterbrunnen, Switz. 2,876 B3 312
Lauthala, isl., Fiji E7 436
Lautoka, Fiji E6 436
Lauzon, Que., Can. 10,255 R13 R16 66
Lava, beds, Idaho F5 108
Lava, flow, N.Mex. C3 126
Lava Beds, natl. mon., Calif. B3 94
Lavaca, Sebastian, Ark. 392 B2 170
Lavaca, co., Tex. 20,174 E7 130
Lava Hot Springs, Bannock, Idaho 593 G6 108
Laval (des Rapides), Que., Can. 11,248 S15 66
Laval, Fr. 34,597 C3 278
Laval, co., Que., Can. 69,410 S11 S15 66
La Vale, Allegany, Md. 4,031 A2 182
Lavalle, Arg. B2 252
La Valle, Sauk, Wis. 417 E3 160
La Valleja, dept., Ur. 115,864 B4 252
Lavallette, Ocean, N.J. 832 D4 210
Lavalley, Costilla, Colo. 50 E5 106
Lavaltrie, Que., Can. 917 S11 66
Lavant, riv., Aus. D6 313
Lavant Station, Ont., Can. 45 O24 64
Lavapie, pt., Chile C1 252
Lavar Maidan, salt lake, Iran C4 379
Lavaur, Fr. F4 278
Laveen, Maricopa, Ariz. 300 E3 H2 124
La Vega, Dom.Rep. 14,200 C9 233
La Vela, Ven. 2,086 A4 240
Lavelanet, Fr. 6,820 F4 278
Lavello, It. 15,300 E5 302
La Vergne, Rutherford, Tenn. 800 B5 E7 190
La Verkin, Washington, Utah 365 F2 114
La Verne, Los Angeles, Calif. 6,516 *E5 94
Laverne, Harper, Okla. 1,937 B4 128
La Vernia, Wilson, Tex. 600 B7 E6 130
Laverton, Austl. 179 D4 432
La Veta, Huerfano, Colo. 632 E5 106
La Veta, pass, Colo. E5 106
Laviana, Sp. 38,462 A4 298
La Victoria, Ven. 12,004 A5 240
Lavieille, lake, Ont., Can. O22 64
La Villa, Hidalgo, Tex. 1,261 *F6 130
Lavina, Golden Valley, Mont. 212 D8 110
Lavinia, Carroll, Tenn. 100 C3 190
La Vista, DeKalb, Ga. 3,000 *C2 176
Lavon, res., Tex. A9 130
Lavonia, Franklin, Ga. 2,088 B3 176
Lavoy, Alta., Can. 127 D7 54
Lavras, Braz. 12,257 E1 258
Lavras da Mangabeira, Braz. 2,192 B3 258
Lávrion, Grc. 6,842 C5 306
Lawagan, Bis.Arch. E12 359
Lawai, Kauai, Haw. 145 B2 86
Lawen, Harney, Oreg. 15 D8 96
Lawers, mtn., Scot. E8 272
Lawford, lake, Man., Can. C4 60
Lawhon, Bienville, La. 100 B2 180
Lawley, Bibb, Ala. 250 C3 168
Lawn, Newf., Can. 634 G8 72
Lawndale, Los Angeles, Calif. 21,740 C5 94
Lawndale, Cleveland, N.C. 723 B4 186
Lawnside, Camden, N.J. 2,155 *D3 210
Lawra, Ghana D4 408
Lawrence, Marion, Ind. 10,103 C3 D5 140
Lawrence, Douglas, Kans. 32,858 D8 144
Lawrence, Essex, Mass. 70,933 (*196,500) A5 206
Lawrence, Van Buren, Mich. 773 G5 146
Lawrence, Newton, Miss. 250 C3 184
Lawrence, Nuckolls, Nebr. 338 D7 152
Lawrence, Nassau, N.Y. 5,907 *E2 212
Lawrence, N.Z. 589 F2 437
Lawrence, Pontotoc, Okla. 100 D7 128
Lawrence (Lawrence Hills), Washington, Pa. 1,048 C1 214
Lawrence, co., Ala. 24,501 A2 168
Lawrence, co., Ark. 17,267 A5 170
Lawrence, co., Ill. 18,540 E6 138
Lawrence, co., Ind. 36,564 D3 140
Lawrence, co., Ky. 12,134 B8 178
Lawrence, co., Miss. 10,215 D2 184
Lawrence, co., Mo. 23,260 D4 150
Lawrence, co., Ohio 55,438 D4 156
Lawrence, co., Pa. 112,965 B1 214
Lawrence, co., S.Dak. 17,075 C2 158
Lawrence, co., Tenn. 28,049 C4 190
Lawrenceburg, Dearborn, Ind. 5,004 C5 140
Lawrenceburg, Anderson, Ky. 2,523 B6 178
Lawrenceburg, Lawrence, Tenn. 8,042 C4 190
Lawrence Harbor, Middlesex, N.J. 3,000 C4 210
Lawrence Hills, see Lawrence, Pa.
Lawrence Park, Erie, Pa. 4,403 A1 214
Lawrenceport, Lawrence, Ind. 200 D3 140
Lawrence Station, N.B., Can. 175 D2 70
Lawrencetown, N.S., Can. 615 E4 70
Lawrenceville, Henry, Ala. 60 D4 168
Lawrenceville, Que., Can. 347 S12 66
Lawrenceville, Gwinnett, Ga. 3,804 A6 C3 176
Lawrenceville, Lawrence, Ill. 5,492 E6 138
Lawrenceville, Mercer, N.J. 2,000 C3 210
Lawrenceville, Brunswick, Va. 1,941 D7 192
Lawing, Alsk. 35 G11 84
Lawler, Chickasaw, Iowa 532 A5 142
Laws, Inyo, Calif. 75 D4 94
Lawson, Union, Ark. 200 D4 170
Lawson, Sask., Can. 77 E4 58
Lawson, Ray, Mo. 778 B3 150
Lawsonia, Somerset, Md. 500 E8 182
Lawsonville, Stokes, N.C. 70 A5 186
Lawtell, St. Landry, La. 500 D3 180
Lawtey, Bradford, Fla. 623 A8 174
Lawton, Woodbury, Iowa 324 B1 142
Lawton, Cherokee, Kans. 150 *E9 144
Lawton, Van Buren, Mich. 1,402 G6 146
Lawton, Ramsey, N.Dak. 159 B7 154
Lawton, Comanche, Okla. 61,697 D5 128
Lawton, Fayette, W.Va. 500 D4 D7 194
Lawyers, Campbell, Va. 15 C5 192
Laxå, Swe. 4,770 B5 292
Lay, Moffat, Colo. 15 B3 106
Lay, cape, Viet. C5 362
Lay, dam, Ala. C3 168
Lay, lake, Ala. B3 168
Layland, Fayette, W.Va. 400 D7 194
Layman, Montgomery, Va. C4 192
Laysan, isl., Haw. A5 86
Laysville, New London, Conn. 275 D6 202
Layton, Sussex, N.J. 200 A3 210
Layton, Davis, Utah 9,027 B4 114
Laytonsville, Montgomery, Md. 196 *B5 182
Lazear, Delta, Colo. 75 D3 106
Lea, Lea, N.Mex. 50 F7 126
Lea, co., N.Mex. 53,429 E7 126
Leaburg, Lane, Oreg. 100 *C4 96
Leach, Delaware, Okla. 35 B9 128
Leachville, Mississippi, Ark. 1,507 B6 170
Leacross, Sask., Can. 75 D5 58
Lead, Lawrence, S.Dak. 6,211 C2 158
Leadbetter, pt., Wash. C2 98
Leader, Sask., Can. 1,085 E3 58
Lead Hill, Boone, Ark. 102 A4 170
Leadhills, Scot. 1,362 F9 272
Leadington, St. Francois, Mo. 365 *D7 150
Lead Mountain, ponds, Maine D5 204
Leadore, Lemhi, Idaho 112 E5 108
Leadpoint, Stevens, Wash. 25 A9 98
Leadville, Lake, Colo. 4,008 C4 106
Leadwood, St. Francois, Mo. 1,343 D7 150
Leaf, White, Ga. 400 B3 176
Leaf, Greene, Miss. 350 D4 184
Leaf, lake, Sask., Can. D6 58
Leaf, riv., Que., Can. P9 66
Leaf, riv., Miss. D3 184
Leaf River, Ogle, Ill. 546 A4 138
League City, Galveston, Tex. 2,622 *E8 130
Leah, Columbia, Ga. 300 C4 176
Leake, co., Miss. 18,660 C3 184
Leakesville, Greene, Miss. 1,014 D4 184
Leakey, Real, Tex. 587 E6 130
Leaksville, Rockingham, N.C. 6,427 A6 186
Leal, Barnes, N.Dak. 70 C7 154
Leamington, Ont., Can. 7,856 R18 64
Leamington, Eng. 38,200 I11 273
Leamington, Millard, Utah 190 D3 114
Leander, Vernon, La. 75 C3 180
Leando, Van Buren, Iowa 150 D5 142
Leapwood, McNairy, Tenn. C3 190
Learned, Hinds, Miss. 96 C2 184
Leary, Calhoun, Ga. 848 E2 176
Leasburg, Crawford, Mo. 176 C6 150
Leaside, Ont., Can. 16,538 R22 64
Leask, Sask., Can. 412 D4 58
Leatherman, Macon, N.C. B2 186
Leatherwood, Perry, Ky. 1,283 C7 178
Leatherwood, Henry, Va. D5 192
Leatherwood, creek, W.Va. C7 194
Leavenworth, Crawford, Ind. 387 D3 140
Leavenworth, Leavenworth, Kans. 22,052 C9 144
Leavenworth, Chelan, Wash. 1,480 B6 98
Leavenworth, co., Kans. 48,524 C8 144
Leavittsburg, Trumbull, Ohio 3,300 A6 156
Leawood, Johnson, Kans. 7,466 B8 D9 144
Łeba, Pol. 3,021 A3 325
Lebam, Pacific, Wash. 400 C3 98
Lebanon, New London, Conn. 300 (2,434▲) C7 202
Lebanon, Kent, Del. 110 D3 172
Lebanon, Levy, Fla. 125 B8 174
Lebanon, St. Clair, Ill. 2,863 E4 138
Lebanon, Boone, Ind. 9,523 B3 140
Lebanon, Smith, Kans. 583 C5 144
Lebanon, Marion, Ky. 4,813 C5 178
Lebanon (Town of), York, Maine (1,533▲) *E2 204
Lebanon, Laclede, Mo. 8,220 D5 150
Lebanon, Red Willow, Nebr. 143 D5 152
Lebanon, Grafton, N.H. 9,299 D2 208
Lebanon, Hunterdon, N.J. 880 B3 210
Lebanon, Warren, Ohio 5,993 C2 156
Lebanon, Marshall, Okla. 100 E7 128
Lebanon, Linn, Oreg. 5,858 C4 D1 96
Lebanon, Lebanon, Pa. 30,045 C5 214
Lebanon, Potter, S.Dak. 198 B6 158
Lebanon, Wilson, Tenn. 10,512 B5 190
Lebanon, Russell, Va. 2,085 D2 192
Lebanon, co., Pa. 90,853 C5 214
Lebanon, country, Asia, 1,719,000 F5 340 378
Lebanon Junction, Bullitt, Ky. 1,527 C5 178
Lebanon Station, Levy, Fla. 125 B8 174
Lebeau, St. Landry, La. 100 D4 180
Lebec, Kern, Calif. 400 E4 94
Lebedyan, Sov.Un. 16,700 F12 332
Lebesby, Nor. A12 290
Le Blanc, Fr. 5,279 D4 278
Le Blanc-Mesnil, Fr. 25,363 I10 278
Lebo, Con.L. B3 414
Lebo, Coffey, Kans. 498 D8 144
Lebo, Meagher, Mont. 40 D6 110
Lebo, well, Chad B8 409
Lębork, Pol. 17,800 A3 325
Le Bourget, Fr. 8,404 I10 278
Le Bouscat, Fr. 19,558 E3 278
Lebret, Sask., Can. 335 E6 58
Lebrija, Sp. 12,297 D3 298
Lebu, Chile 3,827 C1 252
Lebyazhye, Sov.Un. A7 336
Le Cateau, Fr. 8,457 B5 278
Lecce, It. 58,400 (67,400▲) E7 302
Lecce, prov., It. 645,000 *E7 302
Lecco, It. 43,800 C2 302
Le Center, Le Sueur, Minn. 1,597 G5 148
Lech, riv., Ger. D4 286
Le Chambon-Feugerolles, Fr. 17,695 E6 278
Le Châtelard-Montreux, see Montreux, Switz.
Le Chesnay, Fr. 9,259 I9 278
Le Claire, Scott, Iowa 1,546 C7 D7 142
Leclercville, Que., Can. 517 R13 66
Lecompte, Rapides, La. 1,485 C3 180
Lecompton, Douglas, Kans. 304 C8 144
Léconi, Gabon G7 409
Le Conte, mtn., Tenn. C8 190
Le Coteau, Fr. 6,222 D6 278
Le Creusot, Fr. 28,663 D6 278
Le Croisic, Fr. D2 278
Łęczyca, Pol. 6,755 B4 325
Ledčice, Czech. 709 *A2 324
Ledesma, Arg. 4,476 B5 250
Ledesma, Sp. 2,869 B4 298
Ledger, Pondera, Mont. 10 B5 110
Ledgewood, Morris, N.J. 800 B3 210
Ledo, India D6 368
Ledoux, Mora, N.Mex. 100 C5 126
Leduc, Alta., Can. 2,008 D6 54
Ledyard, New London, Conn. 250 (5,395▲) D7 202
Ledyard, Kossuth, Iowa 289 A3 142
Lee, Madison, Fla. 243 A7 174
Lee, Penobscot, Maine 300 (555▲) C4 204
Lee, Berkshire, Mass. 3,078 (5,271▲) B1 206
Lee, Strafford, N.H. 50 (931▲) E4 208
Lee, co., Ala. 49,754 C4 168
Lee, co., Ark. 21,001 C6 170
Lee, co., Fla. 54,539 E9 174
Lee, co., Ga. 6,204 E2 176
Lee, co., Ill. 38,749 B4 138
Lee, co., Iowa 44,207 D6 142
Lee, co., Ky. 7,420 C7 178
Lee, co., Miss. 40,589 A4 184
Lee, co., N.C. 26,561 B6 186
Lee, co., S.C. 21,832 C8 188
Lee, co., Tex. 8,949 D7 130
Lee, co., Va. 25,824 D1 192
Lee, creek, Ark., Okla. B2 170 C9 128
Lee, riv., Ire. E3 273
Lee, lake, Miss. B1 184
Lee Center, Oneida, N.Y. 500 B6 212
Lee City, Wolfe, Ky. 97 *C7 178
Leedon Estates, Delaware, Pa. 1,800 *D6 214
Leech, lake, Sask., Can. E6 58
Leech, lake, Minn. D4 148
Leechburg, Armstrong, Pa. 3,545 C2 214
Leedey, Dewey, Okla. 451 C4 128
Leeds, Jefferson, Ala. 6,162 B3 E5 168
Leeds, Eng. 508,600 (*1,100,000) H11 273
Leeds, Androscoggin, Maine 50 (807▲) *D2 204
Leeds, Hampshire, Mass. B2 206
Leeds, Greene, N.Y. 500 C8 212
Leeds, Benson, N.Dak. 797 B6 154
Leeds, Chester, S.C. 120 B6 188
Leeds, Washington, Utah 109 F2 114
Leeds, co., Ont., Can. 43,077 P24 64
Leeds Junction, Androscoggin, Maine 40 D2 204
Leeds Point, Atlantic, N.J. 350 E4 210
Leeds Village, Que., Can. 475 R13 66
Leedy, Tishomingo, Miss. 60 A4 184
Lee Heights, Rapides, La. 450 *C3 180
Leek, Eng. 19,000 H10 273
Leelanau, co., Mich. 9,321 E6 146
Leelanau, lake, Mich. D6 146
Leenane, Ire. 122 H3 273
Leeper, Wayne, Mo. 350 D7 150
Leer, Ger. 21,600 B2 286
Leesburg, Cherokee, Ala. 100 A4 168
Leesburg, Lake, Fla. 11,172 C9 174
Leesburg, Lee, Ga. 774 E2 176
Leesburg, Kosciusko, Ind. 427 A4 140
Leesburg, Rankin, Miss. 100 C3 184
Leesburg, Cumberland, N.J. 625 E3 210
Leesburg, Highland, Ohio 932 C3 156
Leesburg, Loudoun, Va. 2,869 A7 192
Lee's Summit, Jackson, Mo. 8,267 C3 E2 150
Leesville, Vernon, La. 4,689 C2 180
Leesville, Lexington, S.C. 1,619 D5 188
Leesville, res., Ohio B5 156
Leetes Island, New Haven, Conn. 400 D5 202
Leeton, Johnson, Mo. 371 C4 150
Leetonia, Columbiana, Ohio 2,543 B6 156
Leetsdale, Allegheny, Pa. 2,153 A3 214
Leeuwarden, Neth. 80,928 A4 282
Leeuwin, cape, Austl. E2 432
Lee Valley, Hawkins, Tenn. B8 190
Lee Vining, Mono, Calif. 350 D4 94
Leeward, is., N.A. B5 236
Leeward Islands, Br. poss., W.I. 108,838 D13 233
Leewood, Kanawha, W.Va. 250 D6 194
Le Ferriere, It. *E4 302
Leflore, Le Flore, Okla. 250 D9 128
Leflore, co., Miss. 47,142 B2 184
Le Flore, co., Okla. 29,106 D9 128
Lefor, Stark, N.Dak. 175 D3 154
Lefors, Gray, Tex. 864 B5 130
Le François, Mart. 2,189 (10,639▲) E14 233
Lefroy, Ont., Can. 300 P21 64
Lefroy, lake, Austl. E4 432
Legal, Alta., Can. 457 D6 54
Leganés, Sp. 4,713 *B5 298
Legaspi, Phil. 18,987 B6 358
Legau, Ger. 2,700 E4 286
Legg, Phillips, Mont. 30 C9 110
Leghorn, see Livorno, It.
Legion, Kerr, Tex. 1,691 *D6 130
Legler, Ocean, N.J. 200 C4 210
Legnano, It. 38,900 C2 302
Legnica, Pol. 51,000 C3 325
Le Gore, Frederick, Md. 80 A5 182
Le Grand, Merced, Calif. 769 D3 94
Le Grand, Marshall, Iowa 465 B5 142
Leh, India 3,372 B2 368
Le Havre, Fr. 139,810 C4 278
Lehi, Utah, Utah 4,377 C4 114
Lehigh, Webster, Iowa 846 B3 142
Lehigh, Marion, Kans. 178 D6 144
Lehigh, Coal, Okla. 296 D7 128
Lehigh, co., Pa. 227,536 C6 214
Lehigh, riv., Pa. C6 214
Lehighton, Carbon, Pa. 6,318 C6 214
Lehliu, Rom. B4 321
Lehman Caves, nat. mon., Nev. E7 112
Lehman Hot Springs, Umatilla, Oreg. B8 96
Lehr, Logan and McIntosh, N.Dak. 381 D6 154
Lehrte, Ger. 20,300 B3 286
Lehua, isl., Haw. A1 86
Leiah, Pak. 14,914 D7 375
Leibnitz, Aus. 5,722 D7 313
Leicester, Eng. 284,000 I11 273
Leicester, Worcester, Mass. 1,750 (8,177▲) B4 206
Leicester, Livingston, N.Y. 365 C4 212
Leicester, Addison, Vt. 50 (551▲) D2 218
Leicester, co., Eng. 648,600 I11 273
Leicester Junction, Addison, Vt. 100 D2 218
Leichhardt, riv., Austl. B8 432
Leichou, China O5 349
Leichu, pen., China O4 349
Leiden, Neth. 92,734 (*125,000) B3 282
Leigh, Colfax, Nebr. 502 C8 152
Leighton, Colbert, Ala. 1,158 A2 168

Liberty, Union, Ind. 1,745 C5 140
Liberty, Montgomery, Kans. 233 E8 144
Liberty, Casey, Ky. 1,578 C6 178
Liberty, Waldo, Maine 150 D3 204
(458▲)
Liberty, Amite, Miss. 642 D2 184
Liberty, Clay, Mo. 8,909 B3 150
E2
Liberty, Gage, Nebr. 174 D9 152
Liberty, Sullivan, N.Y. 4,704 D7 212
Liberty, Randolph, N.C. 1,438 B6 186
Liberty, Bryan, Okla. 20 E7 128
Liberty, Allegheny, Pa. 3,624 *C3 214
Liberty, Pickens, S.C. 2,657 B3 188
Liberty, De Kalb, Tenn. 293 C6 190
Liberty, Liberty, Tex. 6,127 D8 130
F8
Liberty, Kittitas, Wash. 30 B6 98
Liberty, Putnam, W.Va. 50 C3 194
Liberty, co., Fla. 3,138 A6 174
Liberty, co., Ga. 14,487 E5 176
Liberty, co., Mont. 2,624 B5 110
Liberty, co., Tex. 31,595 D8 130
Liberty Center, Wells, Ind. 275 B4 140
Liberty Center, Henry, Ohio 867 A2 156
Liberty Corner, Somerset, N.J. 800 B3 210
Liberty Grove, Cecil, Md. 55 A7 182
Liberty Hill, Kershaw, S.C. 350 C7 188
Liberty Hill, Grainger, Tenn. 50 B8 190
Liberty Lake, Spokane, Wash. 800 D9 98
Liberty Mills, Wabash, Ind. 300 B4 140
Liberty Pole, Vernon, Wis. 40 E3 160
Libertytown, Frederick, Md. 650 B5 182
Libertytown, Worcester, Md. 75 D9 182
Libertyville, Lake, Ill. 8,560 E2 138
Libertyville, Jefferson, Iowa 368 D5 142
Libertyville, Sussex, N.J. A3 210
Libiron, isl., Eniwetok C1 436
Libong, isl., Thai. F3 362
Libourne, Fr. 15,654 E3 278
Libramont, Bel. 2,429 E4 282
Library, Allegheny, Pa. 3,000 *C3 214
Libreville, Gabon 19,692 F6 409
Libušín, Czech. 3,584 *A2 324
Libya, country, Afr. 1,153,000 D8 388
394
Libyan, des., Libya, Eg., U.A.R. B4 394
Libyan, plat., Libya, Eg., U.A.R. A4 394
A1 395
Licantén, Chile C1 252
Licata, It. 39,200 G4 302
Lice, Tur. 6,441 B9 307
Licenza, It. 1,309 *D4 302
Lichfield, Eng. 11,100 I11 273
Lichiang, China F8 346
Liching, China 15,000 G9 348
Lichtenburg, U.S.Afr. 10,189 E5 420
Lichtenfels, Ger. 10,526 C4 286
Lick, creek, Ind. D5 140
Lick, creek, Ky. A8 178
Lick, creek, Tenn. B9 190
Licking, Texas, Mo. 954 D6 150
Licking, co., Ohio 90,242 B4 156
Licking, creek, Md. A3 182
Licking, riv., Ky. B7 178
Licking, riv., Ohio B4 156
Licosa, cape, It. E5 302
Lida, Esmeralda, Nev. 16 F4 112
Lida, Sov. Un. 28,000 F5 332
Lida, lake, Minn. E3 148
Lidderdale, Carroll, Iowa 201 B3 142
Lidgerwood, Richland, N.Dak. 1,081 D8 154
Lidhult, Swe. 2,477 E4 292
Lidingo, Swe. 24,338 B9 292
Lidköping, Swe. 15,767 C4 292
Lido di Roma (Lido di Ostia)
(part of Rome), It. 13,730 *E4 W02
Lidzbark Warmiński, Pol. 10,000 A5 325
Liebenthal, Rush, Kans. 191 D4 144
Liechtenstein, country,
Eur. 16,000 D6 266
312
Liège, Bel. 155,670 D4 282
Liège, prov., Bel. 1,005,849 D4 282
Liege, riv., Alta., Can. B6 54
Liegnitz, see Legnica, Pol.
Lieksa, Fin. 3,550 E14 290
Lienchiang, China 10,000 O5 349
Lienhua, China 5,000 L6 349
Lienping, China 5,000 M7 349
Lienyün, China 85,000 H9 348
Lienz, Aus. 10,096 D4 313
Liepāja, Sov.Un. 71,000 D3 332
Lier (Lierre), Bel. 29,060 C3 282
Lierena, Sp. 4,778 C3 298
Lierneux, Bel. 2,943 D4 282
Lierre, see Lier, Bel.
Liestal, Switz. 8,449 A3 312
Lièvre, riv., Que., Can. S9 66
Lièvres, isl., Que., Can. Q15 66
Liezen, Aus. 4,802 C6 313
Liftwood, New Castle, Del. 800 *A1 172
Liggett, Harlan, Ky. 350 *D7 178
Light, Greene, Ark. 75 A6 170
Lightfoot, James City, Va. 300 C8 192
Lighthouse, inlet, S.C. G4 188
Lighthouse, pt., Fla. B6 174
Lighthouse, pt., La. E3 180
Lighthouse, pt., Mich. D6 146
Lighthouse Point,
Broward, Fla. 2,453 *E10 174
Lightning, creek, Wyo. C8 116
Lignite, Burke, N.Dak. 355 B3 154
Lignum, Culpeper, Va. 120 B7 192
Ligon, Floyd, Ky. 697 C8 178
Ligonha, riv., Moz. C7 421
Ligonia, Cumberland, Maine E5 204
Ligonier, Noble, Ind. 2,595 A4 140
Ligonier, Westmoreland, Pa. 2,276 C2 214
Liguria, reg., It. 1,633,000 C2 302
Ligurian, sea, It. D2 302
Ligurta, Yuma, Ariz. 10 F1 124
Lihua, China F8 346
Lihue, Kauai, Haw. 3,908 B2 86
Likely, Modoc, Calif. 100 B3 94
Likhoslavl, Sov.Un. 7,600 D10 332
Likino-Dulevo, Sov.Un. 18,600 N19 332
Lilbourn, New Madrid, Mo. 1,216 E8 150
Lilburn, Gwinnett, Ga. 753 A5 176
Lilburn, Powhatan, Va. C7 192
Lilesville, Anson, N.C. 635 C6 186

Liling, China 5,000 L6 349
Lilla Karlsö, isl., Swe. D9 292
Lillard Park, Oklahoma, Okla. 250 C6 128
Lille, Fr. 194,616 B5 278
Lille, Aroostook, Maine 125 A4 204
Lille Belt, strait, Den. I3 291
Lillesand, Nor. 1,079 G3 291
Lilleström, Nor. 8,388 B2 292
Lillhärdal, Swe. F6 291
Lillian, Baldwin, Ala. 180 E2 168
Lillian, Scott, Miss. 150 C3 184
Lillie, Union, La. 85 B3 180
Lillington, Harnett, N.C. 1,242 B7 186
Lillis, Marshall, Kans. 60 C7 144
Lillooet, B.C., Can. 1,083 E12 52
Lillooet, range, B.C., Can. F12 52
Lillooet, riv., B.C., Can. E11 52
Lilly, Dooly, Ga. 136 D3 176
Lilly, Cambria, Pa. 1,642 C3 214
Lilly, fork, W.Va. C7 194
Lilly Grove, Mercer, W.Va. 1,255 *D3 194
Lilongwe, Rh.&Nya. 6,660 B6 421
Lily, Laurel, Ky. 450 C6 178
Lily, Day, S.Dak. 119 B8 158
Lily, Langlade, Wis. 60 C5 160
Lilydale, Dakota, Minn. 116 *G5 148
Lily Lake, see Lakemoor, Ill.
Lima, Beaverhead, Mont. 397 F4 110
Lima, Livingston, N.Y. 1,366 C4 212
Lima, Allen, Ohio 51,037 B2 156
Lima, (New Lima),
Seminole, Okla. 100 C7 128
Lima, Par. C4 247
Lima, Peru 1,086,250 C2 245
Lima, dept., Peru 1,625,848 C2 245
Lima, res., Mont. F4 110
Lima, riv., Port. B2 298
Lima Duarte, Braz. 2,788 E2 258
Limanowa, Pol. 1,963 D5 325
Limassol, Cyp. 36,536 D5 307
Limavady, N.Ire. 3,179 *F6 272
Limay, riv., Arg. C2 252
Limay Mahuida, Arg. C2 252
Limbé, Hai. 3,744 C8 233
Limbe, Rh.&Nya. C7 421
Limberg, dam, Aus. C4 W13
Limburg [an der Lahn], Ger. 15,900 C3 286
Limburg, prov., Bel. 546,877 C4 282
Limburg, prov., Neth. 785,732 C4 282
Lime, Pueblo, Colo. 50 D6 106
Lime, Baker, Oreg. 75 C9 96
Lime, creek, Iowa A4 142
Limeil-Brévannes, Fr. 7,547 J10 278
Limeira, Braz. 27,552 E1 258
Lime Kiln, Frederick, Md. 175 B5 182
Limerick, Sask., Can. 239 F4 58
Limerick, Ire. 50,886 I4 273
Limerick, York, Maine 450 E2 204
(907▲)
Limerick, co., Ire. 137,881 I3 273
Limeridge, Saulk, Wis. 152 *E4 160
Lime Rock, Litchfield, Conn. 220 B2 202
Lime Rock, Providence, R.I. 80 B3 216
Lime Spring, Howard, Iowa 581 A5 142
Limestone, Newton, Ark. 100 B3 170
Limestone, Hardee, Fla. 100 D9 174
Limestone, Aroostook, Maine 1,772 B5 204
(13,102▲)
Limestone, Stillwater, Mont. E7 110
Limestone, Cattaraugus, N.Y. 539 C3 212
Limestone, Washington, Tenn. 500 B9 190
Limestone, Marshall, W.Va. 100 B2 194
Limestone, co., Ala. 36,513 A2 168
Limestone, co., Tex. 20,413 D7 130
Limestone, bay, Man., Can. D3 60
Limestone, pt., Man., Can. D3 60
Limestone, riv., Man., Can. B5 60
Limeton, Warren, Va. 100 B6 192
Limfjorden, fjord, Den. E1 292
Limingen, lake, Nor. D5 290
Limington, York, Maine 125 E2 204
(839▲)
Liminka, Fin. D11 290
Limmared, Swe. 1,316 D4 292
Limmen, bight, Austl. A7 432
Limni, Grc. 3,398 B4 306
Limnos, isl., Grc. A5 W06
Limoeiro, Braz. 14,122 B3 258
Limoeiro do Norte, Braz. 4,647 B3 258
Limoges, Ont., Can. W55 O25 64
Limoges, Fr. 105,990 E4 278
Limon, Lincoln, Colo. 1,811 C7 106
Limón, C.R. 11,310 E6 228
Limón, Hond. 475 C5 228
Limousin, former prov., Fr. 487,000 E4 278
Limousin, plat., Fr. E4 278
Limoux, Fr. 8,334 F5 278
Limpio, Par. D4 247
Limpopo, riv., Moz. D6 421
Linah, Sau.Ar. B3 383
Linares, Chile 1M,624 C1 252
Linares, Col. 732 C1 244
Linares, Mex. 13,489 CU 225
Linares, Sp. 47,5U2 C5 298
Linares, prov., Chile 146,257 E3 250
Linaro, cape, It. D3 302
Linch, Johnson, Wyo. 600 C6 116
Linching, China 50,000 G7 348
Linchuan, China 10,000 L8 349
Lincoln, Talladega, Ala. 629 B3 168
Lincoln, Arg. 12,695 B3 252
Lincoln, Washington, Ark. 820 B2 170
Lincoln, Placer, Calif. 3,197 C3 94
Lincoln, Sussex, Del. 400 E4 172
Lincoln, Eng. 70,500 H12 273
Lincoln, Bonneville, Idaho 300 F6 108
Lincoln, Logan, Ill. 16,890 C4 138
Lincoln, Cass, Ind. 200 B3 140
Lincoln, Tama, Iowa 183 B5 142
Lincoln, Lincoln, Kans. 1,717 C5 144
Lincoln, Penobscot, Maine 3,616 C4 204
(4,541▲)
Lincoln, Middlesex, Mass. 1,700 C2 206
(5,613▲)
Lincoln, Alcona, Mich. 441 E8 146
Lincoln, Benton, Mo. 446 C4 150
Lincoln, Lewis and Clark, Mont. 260 D4 110
Lincoln, Lancaster, Nebr. 128,521 D9 152
(*145,400) E2
Lincoln, Grafton, N.H. 900 C3 208
(1,228▲)

Lincoln, Lincoln, N.Mex. 150 E5 126
Lincoln, Richland, Ohio 8,004 *B4 156
Lincoln, Allegheny, Pa. 1,686 *C1 214
Lincoln, Providence, R.I. 8,000 B3 216
(13,551▲)
Lincoln, Lincoln, Tenn. 100 D5 190
Lincoln, Addison, Vt. 250 C3 218
(481▲)
Lincoln, Loudoun, Va. 150 A7 192
Lincoln, Lincoln, Wash. 140 B8 98
Lincoln, co., Ark. 14,447 D5 170
Lincoln, co., Ont., Can. 111,740 Q21 64
Lincoln, co., Colo. 5,310 D7 106
Lincoln, co., Eng. 717,400 H12 273
Lincoln, co., Ga. 5,906 C4 176
Lincoln, co., Idaho 3,686 G4 108
Lincoln, co., Kans. 5,556 C5 144
Lincoln, co., Ky. 16,503 C6 178
Lincoln, co., Maine 18,497 D3 204
Lincoln, co., Minn. 9,651 G2 148
Lincoln, co., Miss. 26,759 D2 184
Lincoln, co., Mo. 14,783 B6 150
Lincoln, co., Mont. 12,537 B1 110
Lincoln, co., Nebr. 28,491 D4 152
Lincoln, co., Nev. 2,431 F6 112
Lincoln, co., N.Mex. 7,744 E5 126
Lincoln, co., N.C. 28,814 B4 186
Lincoln, co., Okla. 18,783 C7 128
Lincoln, co., Oreg. 24,635 C3 96
Lincoln, co., S.Dak. 12,371 D9 158
Lincoln, co., Tenn. 23,829 C5 190
Lincoln, co., Wash. 10,919 B8 98
Lincoln, co., W.Va. 20,267 C2 194
Lincoln, co., Wis. 22,338 C4 160
Lincoln, co., Wyo. 9,018 D2 116
Lincoln, par., La. 28,535 B3 180
Lincoln, mtn., Colo. C4 106
Lincoln, mtn., Mass. B3 206
Lincoln, mtn., N.H. C3 208
Lincoln, tomb, Ill. D4 138
Lincoln, natl. historical park, Ky. C5 178
Lincoln Beach, Lincoln, Oreg. 125 *C2 96
Lincoln Center, Penobscot,
Maine 200 C4 204
Lincoln City, Spencer, Ind. 150 D3 140
Lincoln Heights, Hamilton,
Ohio 7,798 D1 156
Lincoln Highway,
Lincoln, Nebr. 950 *C5 152
Lincoln Park,
Fremont, Colo. 2,085 D5 106
Lincoln Park, Upson, Ga. 1,840 *D2 176
Lincoln Park, Wayne, Mich. 53,933 B8 146
Lincoln Park, Morris, N.J. 6,048 B4 210
Lincoln Park, Ulster, N.Y. 1,100 *D7 212
Lincoln Park, Berks, Pa. 1,500 *C5 214
Lincoln Park, Delaware, Pa. 1,500 *D6 214
Lincolnshire, Lake, Ill. 555 *A6 138
Lincolnshire, Jefferson, Ky. 223 *B5 178
Lincolnton, Lincoln, Ga. 1,450 C4 176
Lincolnton, Lincoln, N.C. 5,699 B4 186
Lincoln Valley, Sheridan,
N.Dak. 90 C5 154
Lincolnville, Marion, Kans. 244 D7 144
Lincolnville, Waldo, Maine 200 D3 204
(867▲)
Lincolnville, Charleston, S.C. 420 E3 188
Lincolnville Center, Waldo,
Maine 185 D3 204
Lincoln Wolds,
highlands, Eng. H12 273
Lincolnwood, Cook, Ill. 11,744 E3 138
Lincroft, Monmouth, N.J. 4,000 C4 210
Lind, Adams, Wash. 697 C8 98
Linda, Yuba, Calif. 6,129 *C3 94
Lindale, Floyd, Ga. 2,600 B1 176
Lindale, Smith, Tex. 1,285 C8 130
Lindau [am Bodensee], Ger. 22,400 E3 286
Linden, Marengo, Ala. 2,516 C2 168
Linden, Navajo, Ariz. 160 D5 124
Linden, Montgomery, Ind. 619 B3 140
Linden, Dallas, Iowa 258 C3 142
Linden, Genesee, Mich. 1,146 G8 146
Linden, Clay, Mo. 6,000 E2 150
Linden, Union, N.J. 39,931 B1 210
Linden, Perry, Tenn. 1,086 C4 190
Linden, Cass, Tex. 1,832 C8 130
Linden, Iowa, Wis. 418 F3 160
Lindenhurst, Lake, Ill. 1,256 *A6 138
Lindenhurst, Suffolk, N.Y. 20,905 E3 212
Lindenwold, Camden, N.J. 7,335 D3 210
Linderödsåsen, mts., Swe. F4 292
Lindesberg, Swe. 5,540 B6 292
Lindhos, Grc. C7 360
Lindi, Tan. 10,315 D6 414
Lindi, riv., Con.L. B4 414
Lindon, Washington, Colo. 20 C7 106
Lindon, Utah, Utah 1,150 C4 114
Lindsay, Tulare, Calif. 5,397 D4 94
Lindsay, Ont., Can. 10,110 P22 64
Lindsay, Dawson, Mont. 60 C11 110
Lindsay, Platte, Nebr. 218 C8 152
Lindsay, Garvin, Okla. 4,258 D6 128
Lindsborg, McPherson, Kans. 2,609 D6 128
Lindsey, Sandusky, Ohio 581 A3 156
Lindstrom, Chisago, Minn. 835 F6 148
Lindy, Knox, Nebr. 60 *B8 152
Line, mtn., N.Mex. F2 126
Lineboro, Carroll, Md. 240 A6 182
Linefork, Letcher, Ky. 65 C8 178
Linesville, Crawford, Pa. 1,255 B1 214
Lineville, Clay, Ala. 1,612 B4 168
Lineville, Wayne, Iowa 452 D4 142
Linfen, China G5 348
Linganore, creek, Md. B5 182
Lingayen, Phil. 6,350 A6 358
Lingbo, Swe. A7 292
Lingen, Ger. 22,400 B2 286
Lingga, arch., Indon. E3 358
Linghed, Swe. A6 292
Lingle, Goshen, Wyo. 437 D8 116
Lingling (Yungchow),
China 25,000 L5 349
Lingshan, China N4 349
Lingshire, Meagher, Mont. D5 110
Linguère, Sen. 1,300 C1 408
Lingwu, China 5,000 F3 348
Lingyüan, China 20,000 E9 348
Linhai, China 72,000 K10 W49
Linhares, Braz. 2,939 D2 258
Linho, China 5,000 E3 348

Linhsi, China 10,000 E9 348
Lini, China 100,000 H9 348
Linière, Que., Can. 1,149 R14 66
Linju, China 5,000 H6 348
Linkao, China 3,000 P4 349
Linköping, Swe. 60,989 C6 292
Linkwood, Dorchester, Md. 85 C8 182
Linn, Washington, Kans. 466 C6 144
Linn, Osage, Mo. 1,050 C6 150
Linn, co., Iowa 136,899 B6 142
Linn, co., Kans. 8,274 D9 144
Linn, co., Mo. 16,815 B4 150
Linn, co., Oreg. 58,867 C4 96
Linn, mtn., Calif. B2 94
Linn Creek, Camden, Mo. 174 C5 150
Linnekleppen, mtn., Nor. B2 292
Linneus, Aroostook, Maine 250 B5 204
(607▲)
Linneus, Linn, Mo. 471 B4 150
Linn Grove, Adams, Ind. 250 B4 140
Linn Grove, Buena Vista, Iowa 330 B2 142
Linnhe, inlet, Scot. E7 272
Linnsburg, Montgomery, Ind. 100 B3 140
Linntown, Union, Pa. 1,628 *C4 214
Lino Lakes, Anoka, Minn. 2,329 *F7 148
Lins, Braz. 23,737 E1 258
Lintan, China E8 346
Linth, riv., Switz. A5 312
Linthicum Heights, Anne
Arundel, Md. 6,000 B6 182
C4
Lintien, China 20,000 B12 348
Lintlaw, Sask., Can. 338 D6 58
Linton, Hancock, Ga. 150 C4 176
Linton, Greene, Ind. 5,736 C2 140
Linton, Trigg, Ky. 90 D3 178
Linton, Emmons, N.Dak. 1,826 D5 154
Linton, Davidson, Tenn. 45 B4 190
Lintung, China 5,000 C9 348
Linville, Union, La. 50 B3 180
Linville, Avery, N.C. 500 A4 186
Linville, Rockingham, Va. 180 B6 192
Linwood, Pike, Ala. 100 D4 168
Linwood, Jefferson, Ark. C5 170
Linwood, Ont., Can. 515 Q20 64
Linwood, Bartow, Ga. 760 B2 176
Linwood, Scott, Iowa 300 C7 142
D7
Linwood, Leavenworth, Kans. 375 *D8 144
Linwood, Worcester, Mass. 950 B4 206
Linwood, Bay, Mich. 400 F8 146
Linwood, Butler, Nebr. 151 C9 152
Linwood, Atlantic, N.J. 3,847 E3 210
Linwood, Davidson, N.C. 150 B5 186
Linwood (Lower Chichester),
Delaware, Pa. 4,460 *C6 214
Linwood, Daggett, Utah 30 C6 114
Linworth, Franklin, Ohio 350 C1 156
Linwu, China 10,000 M6 349
Linwushih, China O5 349
Linyü, China 35,000 E9 348
Linz, Aus. 184,685 B6 313
Lions, St. John the
Baptist, La. 450 B6 180
Lions, gulf, Fr. F5 278
Lions Head, Ont., Can. 413 P19 64
Lipa, Phil. 8,663 B6 358
Lipari, It. 3,731 F5 302
Lipari, is., It. F5 302
Lipari, isl., It. F5 302
Lipetsk, Sov.Un. 156,000 B1 336
Lipik, Yugo. 1,562 B3 316
Liping, China L4 349
Lipno, Pol. 8,389 B4 325
Lipova, Rom. 10,064 A1 321
Lippe, reg., Ger. *C3 286
Lippe, riv., Ger. C3 286
Lippstadt, Ger. 34,800 C3 286
Lipscomb, Jefferson, Ala. 2,811 B3 168
E4
Lipscomb, co., Tex. 3,406 A5 130
Lipsos, isl., Grc. C6 306
Lipton, Sask., Can. 412 E6 58
Lipu, China 15,000 M5 349
Lira, Ug. B5 414
Lircay, Peru 2,012 C3 245
Liri, riv., It. E4 302
Liria, Sp. 9,327 C6 298
Li Ringu, Sud. 2,971 E2 398
Lisafa, Con.L. C2 414
Lisala, Con.L. 1,682 B3 414
Lisbon (Town of),
New London, Conn. (2,019▲) C7 202
Lisbon, Linn, Iowa 1,227 C6 142
Lisbon, Claiborne, La. 229 B3 180
Lisbon, Androscoggin, Maine 1,542 D2 204
(5,042▲) D5
Lisbon, Howard, Md. 109 B5 182
Lisbon, Grafton, N.H. 1,220 C3 208
(1,788▲)
Lisbon, Ransom, N.Dak. 2,093 D8 154
Lisbon, Columbiana, Ohio 3,579 B6 156
Lisbon (Lisboa), Port. 783,226 C2 298
(*1,100,000)
Lisbon Center,
Androscoggin, Maine 350 D5 204
Lisbon Falls,
Androscoggin, Maine 2,640 D5 204
E2
Lisburn, N.Ire. 14,778 G6 273
Lisburne, cape, Alsk. B5 84
Liscarney, Ire. H3 273
Lisco, Garden, Nebr. 150 C3 152
Liscomb, N.S., Can. 217 D8 70
Liscomb, Marshall, Iowa 296 B4 142
Lishih, China 15,000 G5 348
Lishu, China 20,000 D12 348
Lishui, China 5,000 K9 349
Lishukou, China 10,000 C15 348
Lisianski, isl., Haw. A5 86
Lisichansk, Sov.Un. 34,000 R22 332
Lisieux, Sask., Can. 96 F5 58
Lisieux, Fr. 15,342 C4 278
Lisle, Ont., Can. 165 P21 64
Lisle, Du Page, Ill. 4,219 F2 138
L'Islet, Que., Can. 823 Q14 66
L'Islet, co., Que., Can. 24,047 Q14 66
Lisman, Choctaw, Ala. 909 C1 168
Lismore, Austl. 17,372 D10 432
Lismore, N.S., Can. 164 D7 70
Lismore, Ire. 893 I5 273

Lismore, Concordia, La. C4 180
Lismore, Nobles, Minn. 306 H3 148
Lismore, isl., Scot. E7 272
Lisnaskea, N.Ire. 836 G5 273
Lister, B.C., Can. F14 52
Listowel, Ont., Can. 3,644 Q20 64
Listowel, Ire. 3,144 I3 273
Litchfield, Lassen, Calif. 55 B3 94
Litchfield, Litchfield, Conn. 1,363 C3 202
Litchfield, Montgomery, Ill. 7,330 D4 138
Litchfield, Kennebec, Maine 100 (1,011▴) *D3 204
Litchfield, Hillsdale, Mich. 993 G7 146
Litchfield, Meeker, Minn. 5,078 F4 148
Litchfield, Sherman, Nebr. 264 C6 152
Litchfield, Hillsboro, N.H. 100 (721▴) F4 208
Litchfield, co., Conn. 119,856 B2 202
Litchfield Park, Maricopa, Ariz. 1,000 H1 124
Litchville, Barnes, N.Dak. 345 D7 154
Liteň, Czech. 936 *B2 324
Lithgow, Austl. 15,128 E10 432
Lithia Springs, Douglas, Ga. 222 B4 176
Lithinon, cape, Grc. D5 306
Lithonia, De Kalb, Ga. 1,667 B5 176
C2
Lithopolis, Fairfield, Ohio 411 C1 156
Lithuania, rep., Sov.Un. 2,713,000 D4 328
Lititz, Lancaster, Pa. 5,987 C5 214
Litókhoron, Grc. 5,032 A4 306
Litoměřice, Czech. 14,491 A2 324
Litomyšl, Czech. 6,384 B3 324
Little, Breathitt, Ky. 150 C7 178
Little, Seminole, Okla. 25 C7 128
Little, butte, Idaho F6 108
Little, lake, La. E5 180
Little, riv., Ark. B6 170
Little, riv., Ark., Okla. D2 170
D8 128
Little (or Gray), riv., Newf., Can. G7 72
Little, riv., Conn. C7 202
Little, riv., Ga. C3 176
Little, riv., Ga. C4 176
Little, riv., Ga. E3 176
Little, riv., Ky. D3 178
Little, riv., La. C3 180
Little, riv., N.C. B7 186
Little, riv., Okla. C7 128
Little, riv., S.C. C3 188
Little, riv., Tenn. E9 190
Little, riv., Va. D4 192
Little Acres, Gila, Ariz. 300 E5 124
Little Allemands, lake, La. C7 180
Little America, Sweetwater, Wyo. 75 E3 116
Little Andaman, isl., India F6 366
Little Antietam, creek, Md. B5 182
Little Arkansas, riv., Kans. D6 144
Little Assawoman, bay, Del. G5 172
Little Bay Islands, Newf., Can. 534 F8 72
Little Beaver, creek, Colo. C8 106
Little Beaver, creek, Kans. C2 144
Little Belt, mts., Mont. D6 110
Little Bighorn, riv., Mont. E9 110
Little Birch, Braxton, W.Va. 500 C4 194
Little Bitter, lake, Eg., U.A.R. E7 395
Little Black, riv., Maine A3 204
Little Blue, riv., Kans. B6 144
Little Blue, riv., Nebr. E8 152
Little Bow, riv., Alta., Can. E6 54
Little Britain, Ont., Can. 275 P22 64
Little Brook, N.S., Can. 387 E3 70
Little Bullhead, Man., Can. 15 E4 60
Little Cadotte, riv., Alta., Can. B4 54
Little Canada, Ramsey, Minn. 3,512 *F5 148
Little Carpathians, mts., Czech. B3 324
Little Catalina, Newf., Can. 550 F9 72
Little Cayman, isl., Cayman Is. C4 232
Little Cedar, riv., Iowa A5 142
Little Chief, Osage, Okla. 150 B7 128
Little Churchill, riv., Man., Can. B5 60
Little Chute, Outagamie, Wis. 5,099 A5 160
D5
Little City, Marshall, Okla. 102 D7 128
Little Coal, riv., W.Va. D5 194
Little Colorado, riv., Ariz. B4 124
Little Compton, Newport, R.I. 275 (1,702▴) C4 216
Little Creek, Kent, Del. 306 D4 172
Little Creek, peak, Utah F3 114
Little Current, Ont., Can. 1,514 O19 64
S25
Little Cypress, creek, Tex. F7 130
Little Deer Isle, Hancock, Maine 200 D4 204
Little Diomede, isl., Alsk. B5 84
Little Eagle, Corson, S.Dak. 125 B5 158
Little Egg, harbor, N.J. D4 210
Little Egg, inlet, N.J. E4 210
Little Falls, Morrison, Minn. 7,551 F4 148
Little Falls, Passaic, N.J. 9,730 A1 210
B4
Little Falls, Herkimer, N.Y. 8,935 B7 212
Little Farms Park, Jefferson, La. 500 *E5 180
Little Ferry, Bergen, N.J. 6,175 A1 210
Littlefield, Mohave, Ariz. 20 B2 124
Littlefield, Lamb, Tex. 7,236 C4 130
Little Fishing, creek, W.Va. A6 194
Littlefork, Koochiching, Minn. 805 C5 148
Little Fork, riv., Minn. C5 148
Little Frog, mtn., Tenn. C7 190
Little Grand, lake, Newf., Can. F7 72
Little Gunpowder Falls, riv., Md. A6 182
Little Harbour Deep, Newf., Can. 40 E7 72
Little Humboldt, riv., Nev. B4 112
Little Inagua, isl., W.I. B8 232
Little Juniper, mtn., Oreg. D7 96
Little Kanawha, riv., W.Va. B3 194
Little Laramie, riv., Wyo. E6 116
Little Lynches, riv., S.C. C8 188
Little Manatee, riv., Fla. C6 174
Little Manitou, lake, Sask., Can. E5 58
Little Mazarn, creek, Ark. D6 170
Little Miami, riv., Ohio C2 156
Little Minch, chan., Scot. D6 272
Little Missouri, riv., Ark. D3 170
Little Missouri, riv., U.S. B6 77
Little Moose, mtn., N.Y. B7 212
Little Mountain, Newberry, S.C. 238 C6 188
Little Muddy, riv., Ill. E4 138
Little Nicobar, isl., India F2 362
Little Ocmulgee, riv., Ga. D3 176
Little Orleans, Allegany, Md. 70 A3 182
Little Osage, riv., Kans. E9 144
Little Otter, creek, Vt. C2 218
Little Owyhee, riv., Nev. B4 112
Little Paternoster, is., Indon. E5 358
Little Pee Dee, riv., S.C. C10 188
Little Pend Oreille, riv., Wash. A9 98
Little Pigeon, riv., Ind. E2 140
Little Pine, creek, Pa. B4 214
Little Pipe, creek, Md. A5 182
Littleport, Clayton, Iowa 119 B6 142
Little Powder, riv., Mont., Wyo. E11 110
B7 116
Little Prairie, B.C., Can. C12 52
Little Rapids, Brown, Wis. 80 A6 160
Little Red, riv., Ark. B5 170
Little River, Baldwin, Ala. 300 D2 168
Little River, N.S., Can. 235 E3 70
Little River, Rice, Kans. 552 D5 144
Little River, Horry, S.C. 25 D11 188
Little River, co., Ark. 9,211 D2 170
Little River, inlet, S.C. D11 188
Little River, res., Vt. C3 218
Little Rock, Pulaski, Ark. 107,813 (*238,500) C4 170
D6
Little Rock, Lyon, Iowa 564 *A1 142
Little Rock, Bourbon, Ky. 300 B6 178
Little Rock, Dillon, S.C. 500 C10 188
Littlerock, Thurston, Wash. 250 C3 98
Little Sable, pt., Mich. F5 146
Little St. Bernard, pass, It. C1 302
Little Salt, lake, Utah F3 114
Little Sandy, creek, Wyo. D3 116
Little Sandy, riv., Ky. B7 178
Little Satilla, riv., Ga. E4 176
Little Sebago, lake, Maine E4 204
Little Sevier, riv., Utah F3 114
Little Silver, Monmouth, N.J. 5,202 C4 210
Little Sioux, Harrison, Iowa 295 C1 142
Little Sioux, riv., Iowa B2 142
Little Smoky, riv., Alta., Can. C4 54
Little Snake, riv., Colo., Wyo. A3 106
E5 116
Little South West Miramichi, riv., N.B., Can. B3 70
Little Spokane, riv., Wash. B9 98
Littlestown, Adams, Pa. 2,756 D4 214
Little Suamico, Oconto, Wis. 100 D6 160
Little Sugar, riv., N.H. E2 208
Little Tallapoosa, riv., Ala., Ga. B4 168
C1 176
Little Tenmile, creek, W.Va. A6 194
Little Tennessee, riv., Tenn. C7 190
Little Texas, Macon, Ala. 250 C4 168
Little Texas, Assumption, La. 350 C5 180
Littleton, Jefferson, Ala. 400 E4 168
Littleton, Arapahoe, Colo. 13,670 C5 106
Littleton, Buchanan, Iowa 250 B5 142
Littleton, Aroostook, Maine 180 (982▴) B5 204
Littleton, Middlesex, Mass. 700 (5,109▴) C1 206
Littleton, Grafton, N.H. 3,355 (5,003▴) C3 208
Littleton, Halifax and Warren, N.C. 1,024 A8 186
Littleton, Sussex, Va. 40 D7 192
Littleton, Wetzel, W.Va. 339 B4 194
C2
Littleton Common, Middlesex, Mass. 2,277 C1 206
Little Traverse, bay, Mich. D6 146
Little Tucson, Pima, Ariz. 208 G4 124
Little Valley, Cattaraugus, N.Y. 1,244 C3 212
Littleville, Colbert, Ala. 460 A2 168
Little Wabash, riv., Ill. E5 138
Little White, riv., S.Dak. D5 158
Little Wolf, riv., Wis. D4 160
Little Wood, riv., Idaho F4 108
Little York, P.E.I., Can. 215 C6 70
Little York, Washington, Ind. 180 D4 140
Little York, Hunterdon, N.J. 120 B2 210
Little Zab, riv., Iraq B5 378
Lituhi, Tan. E5 414
Liuan, China 28,000 J8 349
Liucheng, China M4 349
Liuchow, China 158,800 M4 349
Liucura, Chile 1,094 C1 252
Liuho, China 15,000 I16 346
Liuhsu, China N4 349
Liupa, China I3 348
Liu Panshan, mts., China G2 348
Liu Pen, mts., China L3 349
Liuyang, China 20,000 K6 349
Livelong, Sask., Can. 135 D3 58
Lively, Ont., Can. 2,840 *S25 64
Lively, Lancaster, Va. 350 C8 192
Livengood, Alsk. 40 B7 84
Live Oak, Sutter, Calif. 2,276 C3 94
Live Oak, Suwannee, Fla. 6,544 A8 174
Live Oak, co., Tex. 7,846 E6 130
Livermore, Alameda, Calif. 16,058 B6 94
Livermore, Larimer, Colo. 20 B5 106
Livermore, Humboldt, Iowa 545 B3 142
Livermore, McLean, Ky. 1,506 C3 178
Livermore, Androscoggin, Maine 200 (1,363▴) D2 204
Livermore, peak, Tex. D3 130
Livermore Falls, Androscoggin, Maine 2,882 (3,343▴) D2 204
Livermore Falls, Grafton, N.H. 75 D3 208
Liverpool, Macon, Ala. 200 C4 168
Liverpool, N.S., Can. 3,500 E5 70
Liverpool, Eng. 773,700 (*1,470,000) H10 273
Liverpool, St. Helena, La. 140 D5 180
Liverpool, Onondaga, N.Y. 3,487 B5 212
Liverpool, Jackson, W.Va. 75 C3 194
Liverpool, bay, Eng. H9 273
Liverpool, bay, N.W.Ter., Can. C5 48
Liverpool, lake, Bol. B2 246
Livinda, riv., Gabon, Con.B. F7 409
Living Springs, Wheatland, Mont. D7 110
Livingston, Sumter, Ala. 1,544 C1 168
Livingston, Merced, Calif. 2,188 D3 94
Livingston, Madison, Ill. 964 *E4 138
Livingston, Rockcastle, Ky. 419 C6 178
Livingston, Livingston, La. 1,183 A6 180
D5
Livingston, Park, Mont. 8,229 E6 110
Livingston, Essex, N.J. 23,124 B4 210
Livingston, Orangeburg, S.C. 208 D6 188
Livingston, Overton, Tenn. 2,817 B6 190
Livingston, Polk, Tex. 3,398 D8 130
Livingston, Grant, Wis. 488 F3 160
Livingston, co., Ill. 40,341 C5 138
Livingston, co., Ky. 7,029 C2 178
Livingston, co., Mich. 38,233 G7 146
Livingston, co., Mo. 15,771 B4 150
Livingston, co., N.Y. 44,053 C4 212
Livingston, par., La. 26,974 D5 180
Livingstone, Rh.&Nya. 24,500 C5 420
Livingstone, range, Alta., Can. E5 54
Livingstone Cove, N.S., Can. 163 D8 70
Livingstonia, Rh.&Nya. B6 421
Livingston Manor, Sullivan, N.Y. 2,080 D7 212
Livno, Yugo. 3,672 C3 316
Livny, Sov.Un. 33,200 F11 332
Livonia, Washington, Ind. 150 D3 140
Livonia, Pointe Coupee, La. 430 D4 180
Livonia, Wayne, Mich. 66,702 B7 146
Livonia, Putnam, Mo. 154 A5 150
Livonia, Livingston, N.Y. 946 C4 212
Livorno (Leghorn), It. 148,300 D3 302
Livorno, prov., It. 294,100 *D3 302
Livramento, Braz. 29,099 L5 257
Livry-Gargan, Fr. 25,322 I11 278
Liwale, Tan. 2,898 D6 414
Liyang, China 25,000 J9 349
Lizard, creek, Iowa B3 142
Lizard Head, pass, Colo. E3 106
Lizard Head, peak, Wyo. D3 116
Lizella, Bibb, Ga. 450 D3 176
Lizemores, Clay, W.Va. 521 C3 194
C7
Lizton, Hendricks, Ind. 366 C3 140
Ljubljana, Yugo. 138,981 A2 316
Ljubuški, Yugo. 1,817 C3 316
Ljungan, riv., Swe. E6 291
Ljungaverk, Swe. E7 291
Ljungby, Swe. 7,996 E4 292
Ljungsbro, Swe. C6 292
Ljungskile, Swe. C2 292
Ljusdal, Swe. 4,315 F7 291
Ljusnan, riv., Swe. E6 291
Ljusne Ala, Swe. F7 291
Ljusterö, isl., Swe. B9 292
Llandovery, Wales 1,900 J9 273
Llandudno, Wales 16,700 H9 273
Llanelly, Wales 31,900 J8 273
Llanfyllin, Wales 1,300 I9 273
Llang East, mtn., Mala. G4 362
Llangollen, Wales 3,200 I9 273
Llangynog, Wales I9 273
Llanidloes, Wales 2,300 I9 273
Llano, Mex. K15 225
Llano, Taos, N.Mex. 45 B5 126
Llano, Llano, Tex. 2,656 D6 130
Llano, co., Tex. 5,240 D6 130
Llano Estacado, plain, Tex. C4 130
Llano Estacado, plat., N.Mex. D7 126
Llanquihue, prov., Chile 139,986 F3 251
Llanquihue, lake, Chile F3 251
Llata, Peru 1,741 B2 245
Llaves, Rio Arriba, N.Mex. 70 B4 126
Llerena, pt., C.R. F5 228
Lleyn, pen., Wales I8 273
Llgachuz, range, B.C., Can. D10 52
Llico, Chile B1 252
Llio, point, Haw. B4 86
Llobregat, riv., Sp. B7 298
Lloyd, Jefferson, Fla. 300 A6 174
Lloyd, Blaine, Mont. 5 B7 110
Lloyd, pt., N.Y. D3 212
Lloydminster, Alta. and Sask., Can. 5,077 D3 58
D7 54
Lloyd Place, Nansemond, Va. 2,282 *D8 192
Llullaillaco, vol., Arg., Chile B4 250
Loa, Wayne, Utah 359 E4 114
Loa, riv., Chile B4 250
Loachapoka, Lee, Ala. 400 C4 168
Loami, Sangamon, Ill. 450 D4 138
Loan, lake, Maine B3 204
Loange, riv., Con.L. D3 414
Lobatos, Conejos, Colo. E5 106
Löbau, Ger. 17,700 C6 286
Lobaye, riv., Cen.Afr.Rep. F8 409
Lobelville, Perry, Tenn. 449 C4 190
Lobería, Arg. 7,916 C4 252
Lobito, Ang. 31,630 B2 420
Lobos, Arg. 8,372 C4 252
Lobos, pt., Calif. B4 94
Lobos, pt., Mex. B3 224
Lobos de Tierra, isl., Peru B1 245
Lobosti, Bech. E5 420
Lobster, lake, Maine C3 204
Lobstick, lake, Newf., Can. D9 72
Locarno, Switz. 7,767 (*14,700) B4 312
Locate, Custer, Mont. 25 D11 110
Lochaline, Scot. E7 272
Loch Arbour, Monmouth, N.J. 297 *C4 210
Lochdale, B.C., Can. 900 B15 52
Lochearn, Baltimore, Md. 2,000 *B6 182
Lochem, Neth. 5,621 B5 282
Loches, Fr. 4,316 D4 278
Loching, China 10,000 K10 349
Lochinver, Scot. C7 272
Loch Lynn Heights, Garrett, Md. 476 B1 182
Lochmere, Belknap, N.H. 225 E3 208
Lochnagar, mtn., Scot. E9 272
Lochranza, Scot. F7 272
Loch Raven, Baltimore, Md. 23,278 *B6 182
Loch Raven, res., Md. B6 182
Lochsa, riv., Idaho C3 108
Lochuan, China H4 348
Lockbourne, Franklin, Ohio 460 C1 156
Locke, Elkhart, Ind. 80 A3 140
Locke, Cayuga, N.Y. 550 C5 212
Locke, Shelby, Tenn. 50 C1 190
E6
Locke, Pend Oreille, Wash. A9 98
Locke Mills, Oxford, Maine 160 D2 204
Lockeport, N.S., Can. 1,207 F4 70
Lockesburg, Sevier, Ark. 511 D2 170
Lockhart, Covington, Ala. 799 D3 168
Lockhart, Orange, Fla. 950 C9 174
Lockhart, Lauderdale, Miss. C4 184
Lockhart, Union, S.C. 128 B6 188
Lockhart, Caldwell, Tex. 6,084 A7 130
E7
Lock Haven, Clinton, Pa. 11,748 B4 214
Lockland, Hamilton, Ohio 5,292 D1 156
Lockney, Floyd, Tex. 2,141 B5 130
Lockport, Man., Can. 235 E4 60
Lockport, Will, Ill. 7,560 B5 138
F2
Lockport, Henry, Ky. 82 B6 178
Lockport, Lafourche, La. 2,221 C6 180
E5
Lockport, Niagara, N.Y. 26,443 B3 212
Lockridge, Jefferson, Iowa 206 D6 142
Lock Springs, Daviess, Mo. 117 B4 150
Lockwood, Sask., Can. 113 E5 58
Lockwood, Dade, Mo. 835 D4 150
Lockwood, Nicholas, W.Va. 300 C3 194
C7
Loc Ninh, Viet. E5 362
Loco, Stephens, Okla. 268 D6 128
Loco Hills, Eddy, N.Mex. 500 F7 126
Locumba, Peru 634 D3 245
Locust, Monmouth, N.J. 350 C4 210
Locust, Stanly, N.C. 211 *B5 186
Locust, creek, Mo. B4 150
Locust, fork, Ala. B3 168
Locust, pt., Md. B7 182
Locust Bayou, Calhoun, Ark. 150 D4 170
Locust Fork, Blount, Ala. 250 *A3 168
Locust Gap, Northumberland, Pa. 700 C5 214
Locust Grove, Henry, Ga. 369 C2 176
Locust Grove, Mayes, Okla. 828 B8 128
Locust Hill, Ont., Can. 100 R22 64
Locust Valley, Nassau, N.Y. 3,700 *D3 212
Lod (Lydda), Isr. 18,000 C5 382
Loda, Iroquois, Ill. 585 C5 138
Lodève, Fr. 6,426 F5 278
Lodeynoye Pole, Sov.Un. 22,500 B9 332
Lodge, Colleton, S.C. 181 E7 188
Lodge, creek, Mont., Sask., Can. B7 110
F3 58
Lodge Grass, Big Horn, Mont. 687 E9 110
Lodgepole, Cheyenne, Nebr. 492 C3 152
Lodgepole, Perkins, S.Dak. 35 B3 158
Lodgepole, creek, Nebr., Wyo. C3 152
E8 116
Lodhran, Pak. 4,890 E7 375
Lodi, San Joaquin, Calif. 22,229 C3 94
Lodi, Con.L. C3 414
Lodi, Bergen, N.J. 23,502 A1 210
Lodi, Seneca, N.Y. 396 C5 212
Lodi, Medina, Ohio 2,213 A4 156
Lodi, Washington, Va. 35 D3 192
Lodi, Columbia, Wis. 1,620 E4 160
Lodja, Con.L. C3 414
Łódź, Pol. 671,000 (*800,000) C4 325
Łódź, pol. div., Pol. 1,533,000 *C4 325
Loeches, Sp. 847 *B5 298
Loei, Thai. 25,000 C4 362
Loei, prov., Thai. 134,202 *C4 362
Loelli, Sud. D3 398
Loeriesfontein, U.S.Afr. 1,812 F3 420
Loesch, Powder River, Mont. E11 110
Lofer, Aus. 1,438 C4 313
Lofgreen, Tooele, Utah 20 C3 114
Lofoten, is., Nor. B5 290
Lofton, Heard, Ga. 200 C1 176
Logan, Harrison, Iowa 1,605 C2 142
Logan, Phillips, Kans. 846 C4 144
Logan, Gallatin, Mont. 207 E5 110
Logan, Logan, Nebr. C5 152
Logan, Quay, N.Mex. 400 C7 126
Logan, Hocking, Ohio 6,417 C4 156
Logan, Beaver, Okla. 10 B3 128
Logan, Cache, Utah 18,731 B4 114
Logan, Logan, W.Va. 4,185 D3 194
D5
Logan, co., Ark. 15,957 B3 170
Logan, co., Colo. 20,302 B7 106
Logan, co., Ill. 33,656 C4 138
Logan, co., Kans. 4,036 D2 144
Logan, co., Ky. 20,896 D4 178
Logan, co., Nebr. 1,108 C5 152
Logan, co., N.Dak. 5,369 D6 154
Logan, co., Ohio 34,803 B3 156
Logan, co., Okla. 18,662 C6 128
Logan, co., W.Va. 61,570 D3 194
Logan, creek, Nebr. B9 152
Logan, mtn., Ariz. B2 124
Logan, mtn., Yukon, Can. E4 48
Logan, mtn., Wash. A6 98
Logan, pass, Mont. B3 110
Logan, peak, Ala. A3 168
Logandale, Clark, Nev. 35 G7 112
Logansport, Cass, Ind. 21,106 B3 140
Logansport, Butler, Ky. 125 C4 178
Logansport, De Soto, La. 1,371 C2 180
Loganville, Walton and Gwinnett, Ga. 926 C3 176
Loganville, Sauk, Wis. 220 E3 160
Logcabin, Larimer, Colo. B5 106
Logdeälven, riv., Swe. D8 290
Logdell, Grant, Oreg. C7 96
Loge, riv., Ang. A2 420
Log Lane Village, Morgan, Colo. 310 *B7 106
Logone, riv., Chad D8 409
Logroño, Sp. 50,080 A5 298
Logroño, prov., Sp. 231,010 *A5 298
Logrosán, Sp. 5,839 C4 298
Logsden, Lincoln, Oreg. 200 *C3 96
Logtown, Hancock, Miss. 250 E3 184
Lohals, Den. 646 F1 292
Lohardaga, India 7,400 E4 368
Loharu, India C1 368
Lohja, Fin. F11 291
Lohjanjärvi, lake, Fin. F10 291
Lohman, Blaine, Mont. 63 B7 110
Lohr, Ger. 11,114 C3 286
Lohrville, Calhoun, Iowa 653 B3 142
Lohrville, Waushara, Wis. 225 *D4 160
Loimaa, Fin. F10 291

Loi Mai, mtn., Bur. B3 362
Loir, riv., Fr. D4 278
Loire, dept., Fr. 654,482 *E6 278
Loire, riv., Fr. D3 278
Loire-Atlantique, dept., Fr. 733,575 *D3 278
Loiret, dept., Fr. 360,523 *D4 278
Loir-et-Cher, dept., Fr. 239,824 *D4 278
Lois, Moore, Tenn. C5 190
Loja, Ec. 15,399 A2 245
Loja, Sp. 12,439 D4 298
Lojar, cape, Indon. E5 358
Lokandu, Con.L. C4 414
Lokeren, Bel. 25,926 C2 282
Lokhvitsa, Sov.Un. 12,500 G9 332
Lokichar, Ken. B6 414
Lokichoggio, Ken. B5 414
Lokitaung, Ken. B6 414
Lokoja, Nig. 12,606 E6 408
Lokoro, riv., Con.L. C3 414
Lokossa, Dah. E5 408
Lokwei, China P5 349
Lol, riv., Sud. D2 398
Lola, Livingston, Ky. 400 C2 178
Lolland, isl., Den. G2 292
Lolland-Falster, reg., Den. 135,421 *I4 291
Lollie, Laurens, Ga. 147 D4 176
Lolo, Missoula, Mont. 200 D2 110
Lolo, pass, Idaho C4 108
Lolo Hot Springs, Missoula, Mont. 25 D2 110
Lom, Bul. 23,015 B1 317
Lom, Nor. F3 291
Loma, Mesa, Colo. 100 C2 106
Loma, Chouteau, Mont. 110 C6 110
Loma, Butler, Nebr. 50 *C9 152
Loma, Cavalier, N.Dak. 20 B7 154
Loma, mts., S.L. E2 408
Loma, pt., Calif. *F5 94
Lomami, riv., Con.L. D4 414
Lomas, Peru 500 D3 245
Lomas de Zamora, Arg. 125,943 B4 252
Lomax, Henderson, Ill. 535 C2 138
Lombard, Du Page, Ill. 22,561 F2 138
Lombardy (Lombardia), reg., It. 6,880,000 C2 302
Lomblen, isl., Indon. F6 358
Lombok, isl., Indon. F5 358
Lombok, strait, Indon. F5 358
Lomé, Togo 39,000 E5 408
Lomela, Con.L. C3 414
Lomela, riv., Con.L. C3 414
Lometa, Lampasas, Tex. 817 D6 130
Lomiphsu, China O4 349
Lomira, Dodge, Wis. 807 E5 160
Lomita, Los Angeles, Calif. 14,983 C5 94
Lommel, Bel. 16,445 C4 282
Lomond, Alta., Can. 189 E6 54
Lomond, Newf., Can. 120 F7 72
Lomond, lake, Scot. E8 272
Lomonosovskaya, Sov.Un. B7 336
Lompoc, Santa Barbara, Calif. 14,415 E3 94
Łomża, Pol. 17,000 B6 325
Lonaconing, Allegany, Md. 2,077 A2 182
Loncoche, Chile 5,061 C1 252
Londesborough, Ont., Can. 210 Q19 64
London, Pope, Ark. 282 B3 170
London, Ont., Can. 101,693 (*154,453) R19 64
London, Eng. 3,273,000 (Greater London 8,270,400) (*10,450,000) J12 273
London, Laurel, Ky. 4,035 C6 178
London, Madison, Ohio 6,379 C3 156
London, Kanawha, W.Va. 500 C6 194
London, co., Eng. 3,273,000 J12 273
Londonbridge, Princess Anne, Va. 1,061 A9 192
Londonderry, N.S., Can. 632 D6 70
Londonderry, Rockingham, N.H. 500 (2,457▲) F4 208
Londonderry, N.Ire. 50,300 G5 272
Londonderry, Ross, Ohio 400 C4 156
Londonderry, Windham, Vt. 200 (898▲) E3 218
Londonderry, co., N.Ire. 107,700 G5 272
Londonderry, cape, Austl. A5 432
Londonderry, isl., Chile I3 251
London Mills, Fulton, Ill. 170 C3 138
Londrina, Braz. 33,095 J6 257
Lone Elm, Anderson, Kans. 69 D8 144
Lone Grove, Carter, Okla. 500 D6 128
Lonely, isl., Ont., Can. O19 64
Lone Mountain, Claiborne, Tenn. 200 B8 190
Lone Oak, Meriwether, Ga. 122 C2 176
Loneoak, McCracken, Ky. 2,104 C2 178
Lone Oak, see Southern Shops, S.C.
Lonepine, Sanders, Mont. 16 C2 110
Lone Pine, Brown, Nebr. 487 B6 152
Lone Rock, Sask., Can. 75 D3 58
Lone Rock, Kossuth, Iowa 185 A3 142
Lonerock, Gilliam, Oreg. 31 B7 96
Lone Rock, Richland, Wis. 563 E3 160
Lone Star, Douglas, Kans. 31 *D8 144
Lone Star, Calhoun, S.C. 350 D7 188
Lone Star, Morris, Tex. 1,513 *C8 130
Lone Tree, Johnson, Iowa 717 C6 142
Lonetree, Uinta, Wyo. 5 E2 116
Lone Tree, creek, Colo. B6 106
Lone Wolf, Kiowa, Okla. 617 D4 128
Long, Alsk. 8 C6 84
Long, Sequoyah, Okla. C9 128
Long, co., Ga. 3,874 E5 176
Long, bay, N.C. D7 186
Long, creek, Ark. A3 170
Long, creek, Sask., Can. F5 58
Long, isl., N.S., Can. E3 70
Long, isl., Fla. G10 174
Long, isl., Maine D4 204
Long, isl., Mass. D3 206
Long, isl., N.Y. D3 212
Long, isl., W.I. A7 232
Long, key, Fla. D8 174
Long, key, Fla. G10 174
Long, lake, Maine A4 204
Long, lake, Maine D2 204
Long, lake, Mich. D8 146
Long, lake, Mich. E6 146
Long, lake, N.Y. A7 212
Long, lake, N.Dak. D6 154
Long, lake, Wash. D2 98
Long, lake, Wis. C2 160
Long, mtn., N.H. B4 208
Long, pt., Man., Can. D3 60
Long, pt., Newf., Can. F6 72
Long, pt., Ont., Can. R20 64
Long, pond, Fla. B8 174
Long, pond, Maine C3 204
Long, pond, Mass. C6 206
Long, strait, Sov.Un. B19 329
Longa, riv., Ang. B2 420
Longá, riv., Braz. A2 258
Long Beach, Los Angeles, Calif. 344,168 C5 94
F4
Longbeach, Manatee, Fla. 300 D6 174
Long Beach, La Porte, Ind. 2,007 A3 140
Long Beach, Calvert, Md 100 D7 182
Long Beach, Pope, Minn. 236 F3 148
Long Beach, Harrison, Miss. 4,770 E1 184
E3
Long Beach, Nassau, N.Y. 26,473 E3 212
E8
Long Beach, Brunswick, N.C. 50 D7 186
Long Beach, Pacific, Wash. 665 C2 98
Longboat, inlet, Fla. D6 174
Longboat, key, Fla. D8 174
Longboat Key, Manatee and Sarasota, Fla. 1,000 *D8 174
Long Branch, Ont., Can. 10,249 S22 64
Long Branch, Monmouth, N.J. 26,228 C5 210
Longbranch, Pierce, Wash. 150 B4 98
D2
Longbridge, Avoyelles, La. 75 C3 180
Long Bridge, Warren, N.J. B3 210
Long Corner, Howard, Md. 150 B5 182
Longcreek, Pender, N.C. 115 C7 186
Long Creek, Grant, Oreg. 295 C7 96
Longcreek, Oconee, S.C. 200 B2 188
Longdale, Blaine, Okla. 218 B5 128
Long Eaton, Eng. 29,700 I11 273
Longford, Ire. 3,716 H5 273
Longford, Clay, Kans. 146 C6 144
Longford, co., Ire. 32,969 H5 273
Longford Mills, Ont., Can. 400 P21 64
Longfork, Dickenson, Va. C2 192
Long Grove, Lake, Ill. 640 *A6 138
Long Grove, Scott, Iowa 182 C7 142
Long Harbour, Newf., Can. 450 G9 72
Long Hill, Fairfield, Conn. (part of Trumbull) D3 202
Longhurst, Person, N.C. 1,546 A7 186
Longiram, Indon. 5,000 E4 358
Long Island, Jackson, Ala. 200 A4 168
Long Island, Phillips, Kans. 229 C4 144
Long Island, Cumberland, Maine (part of Portland) E5 204
Long Island, Hancock, Maine (97▲) *E5 204
Long Island, Sullivan, Tenn. 1,925 *B9 190
Long Island, Campbell, Va. 75 C5 192
Long Island, sound, N.Y. D4 212
Long Key, Monroe, Fla. 50 G10 174
Long Lake, Lake, Ill. 3,502 E2 138
Long Lake, Iasco, Mich. 125 E8 146
Long Lake, Hennepin, Minn. 996 *F5 148
Long Lake, Hamilton, N.Y. 700 B7 212
Longlake, McPherson, S.Dak. 109 B6 158
Long Lake, Florence, Wis. 175 C5 160
Long Lake, dam, Wash. B7 98
Long Lane, Dallas, Mo. 110 D5 150
Longleaf, Rapides, La. 725 C3 180
Longmeadow, Hampden, Mass. 10,565 B2 206
Longmeadow, Kent, R.I. (part of Warwick) C3 216
Longmont, Boulder, Colo. 11,489 B5 106
Long Park, Montrose, Colo. 70 *D2 106
Long Pine, Inyo, Calif. 1,310 D4 94
Long Plain, Bristol, Mass. 100 C6 206
Long Point, N.S., Can. 89 D8 70
Long Pond, Newf., Can. 850 G9 72
Long Pond, Somerset, Maine 70 C2 204
Longport, Atlantic, N.J. 1,077 E3 210
Long Prairie, Todd, Minn. 2,414 F4 148
Long Range, mts., Newf., Can. G6 72
Long Rapids, Alpena, Mich. 90 D8 146
Longreach, Austl. 3,350 C8 432
Long Run, Doddridge, W.Va. 120 B4 194
B6
Longs, Horry, S.C. 50 D11 188
Longs, peak, Colo. B5 106
Long Savannah, Hamilton, Tenn. E8 190
Longstreet, DeSoto, La. 283 B2 180
Longton, Elk, Kans. 401 E7 144
Longtown, Eng. 2,577 F10 272
Longtown, Perry, Mo. 113 D8 150
Longu, Solomon E2 436
Longueuil, Que., Can. 14,332 S11 66
S16
Longuyon, Fr. 5,926 C6 278
Longvale, Mendocino, Calif. 130 C2 94
Long Valley, Morris, N.J. 1,220 B3 210
Long Valley Junction, Kane, Utah F3 114
Longview, Alta., Can. 1,100 E5 54
Longview, Oktibbeha, Miss. 227 B4 184
Longview, Catawba, N.C. 2,997 B4 186
Longview, Gregg, Tex. 40,050 C8 130
Longview, Isle of Wight, Va. A8 192
Longview, Cowlitz, Wash. 23,349 C4 98
Longville, Beauregard, La. 140 D2 180
Longville, Cass, Minn. 159 E4 148
Longwood, Seminole, Fla. 1,689 *C9 174
Longwood, Washington, Miss. B1 184
Longwood Park, Richmond, N.C. 1,144 *C6 186
Longwoods, Talbot, Md. 60 C7 182
Longwy, Fr. 16,578 C6 278
Long Xuyen, Viet. 28,560 E5 362
Loning, China 10,000 H5 348
Lonkin, Bur. A3 362
Lonoke, Lonoke, Ark. 2,359 C5 170
D7
Lonoke, co., Ark. 24,551 C5 170
Lönsdal, Nor. C6 290
Lonsdale, Garland, Ark. 95 C4 170
Lonsdale, Ont., Can. 165 P23 64
Lonsdale, Rice, Minn. 541 G5 148
Lonsdale, Providence, R.I. B3 216
Lonsdale Mill, see Utica, S.C.
Lons-le-Saunier, Fr. 15,030 D6 278
Looe, Eng. 3,700 K8 273
Loogootee, Martin, Ind. 2,858 D3 140
Lookeba, Caddo, Okla. 158 C5 128
Lookout, Modoc, Calif. 125 B3 94
Lookout, Pike, Ky. 900 C8 178
Lookout, Woods, Okla. 5 B4 128
Lookout, Fayette, W.Va. 350 C4 194
D7
Lookout, Albany, Wyo. 20 E7 116
Lookout, cape, N.C. C9 186
Lookout, mtn., Ala., Ga. A4 168
B1 176
Lookout, mtn., Oreg. C6 96
Lookout, mtn., Oreg. C8 96
Lookout, mtn., Oreg. C9 96
Lookout, mtn., Wash. D4 98
Lookout, pass, Mont. C1 110
Lookout, pt., Md. D7 182
Lookout, pt., Mich. E8 146
Lookout Heights, Kenton, Ky. 776 *B6 178
Lookout Mountain, Hamilton, Tenn. 1,817 E8 190
Lookout Point, res., Oreg. D4 96
Looma, Alta., Can. 15 D6 54
Loomis, Sask., Can. 75 F3 58
Loomis, Phelps, Nebr. 299 D6 152
Loomis, Davison, S.Dak. 75 D7 158
Loomis, Okanogan, Wash. 190 A7 98
Loon, creek, Sask., Can. E5 58
Loon, lake, Alta., Can. B5 54
Loon, riv., Alta., Can. B5 54
Loon, riv., Man., Can. B2 60
Loon Bay, Newf., Can. 125 F8 72
Loon Lake, Stevens, Wash. 50 A9 98
Loon Lake, mts., N.Y. A7 212
Loop, creek, W.Va. D6 194
Loop, head, Ire. I3 273
Loosahatchie, riv., Tenn. C2 190
Looxahoma, Tate, Miss. 450 A3 184
Lop, lake, China C6 346
Lopatka, cape, Sov.Un. D17 329
Lopburi, prov., Thai. 203,313 *D4 362
Lopei, China 5,000 B15 348
Lopez, cape, Gabon G6 409
Lopez, isl., Wash. A4 98
Loping, China 28,000 K8 349
Lopori, riv., Con.L. B3 414
Loppa, Nor. A9 290
Lora (del Rio), Sp. 11,465 D4 298
Lorado, Logan, W.Va. 700 D3 194
D6
Lorain, Lorain, Ohio 68,932 A4 156
Lorain, Cambria, Pa. 1,324 *C3 214
Lorain, co., Ohio 217,500 A4 156
Loraine, Adams, Ill. 303 C2 138
Loraine, Renville, N.Dak. 54 B4 154
Loraine, Mitchell, Tex. 837 C5 130
Loralai, Pak. 4,437 D6 375
Loramie, res., Ohio B2 156
Loranger, Tangipahoa, La. 60 D5 180
Lorca, Sp. 21,057 D6 298
Lord Howe, is., Pac.O. D3 436
Lordsburg, Hidalgo, N.Mex. 3,436 F2 126
Loreauville, Iberia, La. 655 D4 180
Loreburn, Sask., Can. 197 E4 58
Lore City, Guernsey, Ohio 458 C5 156
Lorena, Braz. 16,033 E1 258
Lorenço Marques, prov., Moz. E6 421
Lorentz, Upshur, W.Va. 500 B4 194
Lorenzo, Jefferson, Idaho 200 F7 108
Lorenzo, Cheyenne, Nebr. 36 *C2 152
Lorenzo, Crosby, Tex. 1,188 C5 130
Loreto, Arg. A3 252
Loreto, Braz. 625 B1 258
Loreto, Col. D2 244
Loreto, It. 4,300 D4 302
Loreto, Mex. 1,409 B3 224
Loreto, Mex. C3 224
Loreto, Par. C4 247
Loreto, dept., Peru 251,440 A2 245
Loretta, Rush, Kans. 45 *D4 144
Loretta, Sawyer, Wis. 110 C3 160
Lorette, Man., Can. 400 F4 60
Loretteville, Que., Can. 4,957 R13 66
R15
Loretto, Duval, Fla. 200 B10 174
Loretto, Marion, Ky. 500 C5 178
Loretto, Dickinson, Mich. 250 D4 146
Loretto, Hennepin, Minn. 271 *F5 148
Loretto, Boone, Nebr. 100 C7 152
Loretto, Cambria, Pa. 1,338 C3 214
Loretto, Lawrence, Tenn. 929 C4 190
Lorica, Col. 8,420 B1 244
Lorida, Highlands, Fla. 300 D9 174
Lorient, Fr. 47,095 D2 278
L'Orignal, Ont., Can. 1,067 O26 64
Lorimor, Union, Iowa 460 C3 142
Loring, Madison, Miss. 60 C3 184
Loring, Wright, Mo. 125 D5 150
Loring, Phillips, Mont. 50 B9 110
Loris, Horry, S.C. 1,702 C11 188
Lorlie, Sask., Can. 105 E6 58
Lorman, Jefferson, Miss. 200 D1 184
Lorne, Caroline, Va. 100 C7 192
Lorne, firth, Scot. E7 272
Lorne Park, Ont., Can. 555 S21 64
Lorneville, Ont., Can. 200 P21 64
Lörrach, Ger. 28,100 E2 286
Lorraine, Ellsworth, Kans. 157 D5 144
Lorraine, Harrison, Miss. 100 E1 184
Lorraine, former prov., Fr. 1,956,000 C6 278
Lorraine, plat., Fr. C7 278
Lorton, Otoe, Nebr. 58 *D9 152
Lorton, Fairfax, Va. 25 A7 192
Los, Swe. F6 291
Los, mts., Guat. C2 228
Los Alamitos, Orange, Calif. 4,312 C5 94
Los Alamos, Santa Barbara, Calif. 500 E3 94
Los Alamos, Los Alamos, N.Mex. 13,037 C4 126
G6
Los Alamos, co., N.Mex. 13,037 C4 126
Los Aldamas, Mex. B6 225
Los Altos, Santa Clara, Calif. 19,696 *D2 94
Los Altos Hills, Santa Clara, Calif. 3,412 *D2 94
Los Amatos, Guat. 628 C3 228
Los Andes, Chile 19,162 B1 252
Los Angeles, Los Angeles, Calif. 2,479,015 (*6,565,000) C5 94
E4
Los Angeles, Chile 25,071 C1 252
Los Angeles, co., Calif. 6,038,771 E4 94
Los Angeles, aqueduct, Calif. E4 94
Los Angeles, riv., Calif. C4 94
Losantville (Bronson), Randolph, Ind. 868 B4 140
Los Banos, Merced, Calif. 5,272 D3 94
Los Barrios, Sp. 3,583 D4 298
Los Blancos, Arg. B5 250
Los Cerrillos, Arg. B2 252
Los Ebanos, Hidalgo, Tex. 750 F6 130
Los Fresnos, Cameron, Tex. 1,289 F7 130
Los Gatos, Santa Clara, Calif. 9,036 D3 94
Loshan, China 5,000 F8 346
Loshan, China 60,000 I7 349
Los Hornos, Mex. L14 225
Lošinj, isl., Yugo. B2 316
Los Lunas, Valencia, N.Mex. 1,186 D4 126
Los Mochis, Mex. 21,491 B4 224
Los Molinos, Tehama, Calif. 800 B2 94
Los Nietos, Los Angeles, Calif. 9,000 C5 94
Losombo, Con.L. B2 414
Los Palacios, Cuba 5,250 A3 232
Los Palacios, Sp. 11,163 D4 298
Los Pinos, Rio Arriba, N.Mex. 130 B4 126
Los Pinos, riv., Colo. E3 106
Los Pozos, Chile A1 252
Los Reyes, Mex. 1,494 G10 224
Los Reyes, Mex. 3,045 G10 224
Los Reyes, Mex. 2,177 G11 224
Los Reyes (de Salgado), Mex. 7,775 D5 225
L12
Los Santos, Pan. 2,608 G7 228
Los Santos, Sp. 8,711 C3 298
Los Sarmientos, Arg. A2 252
Los Sauces, Chile 2,158 C1 252
Lossiemouth (& Branderburgh), Scot. 5,200 D9 272
Lost, creek, Wyo. D4 116
Lost, riv., Ind. D3 140
Lost, riv., Minn. D3 148
Lost, riv., W.Va. B6 194
Lost, riv., Wash. A6 98
Lostant, La Salle, Ill. 460 B4 138
Los Taques, Ven. 1,283 A3 240
Lost Cabin, Fremont, Wyo. 47 C5 116
Lost City, Hardy, W.Va. 125 C6 194
Lost Creek, Harrison, W.Va. 128 B4 194
Los Teques, Ven. 22,000 A5 240
Lost Hills, Kern, Calif. 200 E4 94
Lostine, Wallowa, Oreg. 240 B9 96
Lost Nation, Clinton, Iowa 567 C7 142
Lost River, Alsk. 25 B5 84
Lost River, see Grouse, Idaho
Lost River, Hardy, W.Va. 50 C6 194
Lost River, cave, Ky. D4 178
Lost River Glacial, caverns, N.H. C3 208
Lost Springs, Marion, Kans. 139 D7 144
Lost Springs, Converse, Wyo. 5 D8 116
Lost Trail, pass, Mont. E3 110
Los Vilos, Chile 1,305 B1 252
Lot, Ponape A2 436
Lot, dept., Fr. 147,754 *E4 278
Lot, riv., Fr. E4 278
Lota, Chile 40,475 C1 252
Lotbinière, Que., Can. 582 R13 66
Lotbinière, co., Que., Can. 30,116 R13 66
S15
Lot-et-Garonne, dept., Fr. 265,549 *E4 278
Lothair, Perry, Ky. 1,082 C7 178
Lothair, Liberty, Mont. 50 B5 110
Lothian, Anne Arundel, Md. 300 C6 182
Lothrop, Alta., Can. C3 54
Lotien, China I16 346
Loting, China 10,000 N5 349
Loto, Con.L. C3 414
Lotofaga, Samoa E4 436
Lotschberg, tunnel, Switz. B3 312
Lott, Falls, Tex. 924 D7 130
Lotung, For. M10 349
Louann, Ouachita, Ark. 261 D4 170
Loudenville, Marshall, W.Va. 42 B2 194
Loudima, Con.B. G7 409
Loudon, Merrimack, N.H. 350 (1,194▲) E4 208
Loudon, Loudon, Tenn. 3,812 C7 190
Loudon, co., Tenn. 23,757 C7 190
Loudonville, Albany, N.Y. 5,500 *C8 212
Loudonville, Ashland, Ohio 2,611 B4 156
Loudoun, co., Va. 24,549 A7 192
Loudun, Fr. 5,501 D4 278
Louellen, Harlan, Ky. 300 D7 178
Louga, Sen. 4,100 C1 408
Lough, riv., N.Ire. F5 272
Loughborough, Eng. 36,000 I11 273
Lougheed, Alta., Can. 201 D7 54
Loughman, Polk, Fla. 350 C9 174
Louin, Jasper, Miss. 389 C3 184
Louisa, Lawrence, Ky. 2,071 B8 178
Louisa, St. Mary, La. 100 E4 180
Louisa, Louisa, Va. 576 B7 192
Louisa, co., Iowa 10,290 C6 142
Louisa, co., Va. 12,959 C7 192
Louisa, lake, Fla. C9 174
Louisbourg, N.S., Can. 1,314 D10 70
Louisburg, Miami, Kans. 862 D9 144
Louisburg, Dallas, Mo. 176 D4 150
Louisburg, Franklin, N.C. 2,862 A7 186
Louisburg, Lac qui Parle, Minn. 91 F2 148
Louisdale, N.S., Can. 295 D8 70
Louise, Troup, Ga. 120 C2 176
Louise, Humphreys, Miss. 481 C2 184
Louise, Wharton, Tex. 900 E7 130
Louise, Brooke, W.Va. 140 B2 194
Louise, isl., B.C., Can. D7 52
Louise, lake, Alsk. F11 84
Louiseville, Que., Can. 4,392 R12 66

Louis Gentil, Mor. 4,835 B2 402
Louisiana, Pike, Mo. 4,286 B6 150
Louisiana, state, U.S. 3,257,022 E8 77, 180
Louisiana, pt., La. E2 180
Louis Trichardt, U.S.Afr. 7,146 D5 420
Louisville, Barbour, Ala. 890 D4 168
Louisville, Boulder, Colo. 2,073 C5 106
Louisville, Jefferson, Ga. 2,413 C4 176
Louisville, Clay, Ill. 906 E5 138
Louisville, Pottawatomie, Kans. 204 C7 144
Louisville, Jefferson, Ky. 390,639 (*735,800) A5 178, B5
Louisville, Winston, Miss. 5,066 B3 184
Louisville, Cass, Nebr. 1,194 D9 152, E3
Louisville, Stark, Ohio 5,116 B5 156
Louisville, Blount, Tenn. 200 C7 190, E9
Loukhi, Sov.Un. 2,500 C5 328
Loulé, Port. 6,479 D2 298
Louny, Czech. 12,004 A1 324
Loup, co., Nebr. 1,097 C6 152
Loup, riv., Que., Can. Q15 66
Loup, riv., Que., Can. R11 66
Loup, riv., Nebr. C8 152
Loup City, Sherman, Nebr. 1,415 C7 152
Lourdes, Newf., Can. 450 F6 72
Lourdes, Que., Can. 315 R13 66
Lourdes, Fr. 15,829 F3 278
Lourenço Marques, Moz. 99,000 E6 421
Lousã, Port. 8,922 B2 298
Lousana, Alta., Can. 100 D6 54
Louth, Eng. 11,400 H12 273
Louth, Ire. 211 H6 273
Louth, co., Ire. 69,194 H6 273
Loutrá Aidhipsoú, Grc. 5,028 B4 306
L'Outre, bayou, La. B3 180
Louvain, see Leuven, Bel.
Louvale, Stewart, Ga. 300 D2 176
Louviers, Douglas, Colo. 500 C6 106
Louviers, Fr. 10,746 C4 278
Louzi, Con.L. C1 414
Lovat, riv., Sov.Un. D8 332
Love, Sask., Can. 148 D5 58
Love, DeSoto, Miss. A3 184
Love, co., Okla. 5,862 E6 128
Love, pt., Md. B7 182
Lovech, Bul. 17,963 B2 317
Lovejoy, see Brooklyn, Ill.
Lovejoy, Clayton, Ga. 191 C2 176
Lovelaceville, Ballard, Ky. 200 D2 178
Loveland, Larimer, Colo. 9,734 B5 106
Loveland, Clermont, Hamilton and Warren, Ohio 5,008 C2 156, D1
Loveland, Tillman, Okla. 90 D5 128
Loveland, pass, Colo. C5 106
Lovell, Oxford, Maine 165 (588▲) D2 204
Lovell, Logan, Okla. 27 B6 128
Lovell, Big Horn, Wyo. 2,451 B4 116
Lovelock, Pershing, Nev. 1,948 C3 112
Loverna, Sask., Can. 129 E3 58
Loveshki, prov., Bul. *B2 317
Loves Park, Winnebago, Ill. 9,086 A4 138
Lovettsville, Loudoun, Va. 217 A7 192
Loveville, St. Marys, Md. 100 D6 182
Lovewell, pond, Maine D2 204
Lovick, Jefferson, Ala. 225 E5 168
Lovilia, Monroe, Iowa 630 C5 142
Loving, Eddy, N.Mex. 1,646 F6 126
Loving, co., Tex. 226 D4 130
Lovingston, Nelson, Va. 375 C6 192
Lovington, Moultrie, Ill. 1,200 D5 138
Lovington, Lea, N.Mex. 9,660 F7 126
Lovisa, Fin. 4,268 F12 291
Lovsta-Bukten, bay, Swe. A8 292
Low, Que., Can. 450 S9 66
Low, cape, N.W.Ter., Can. E10 48
Low, pen., B.C., Can. F10 52
Lowa, Con.L. C4 414
Lowa, riv., Con.L. C4 414
Lowden, Cedar, Iowa 641 C7 142
Lowe Farm, Man., Can. 150 F4 60
Lowell, Cochise, Ariz. (part of Bisbee) G6 124
Lowell, Benton, Ark. 277 A2 170
Lowell, Idaho, Idaho C3 108
Lowell, Bartholomew, Ind. 2,270 A2 140
Lowell, Middlesex, Mass. 92,107 (*147,000) A5 206
Lowell, Kearney, Nebr. 84 D7 152
Lowell, Gaston, N.C. 2,784 B4 186
Lowell, Washington, Ohio 783 C5 156
Lowell, Lane, Oreg. 503 D4 96
Lowell, Orleans, Vt. 135 (617▲) B4 218
Lowell, Snohomish, Wash. 1,086 B4 98
Lowell, Summers, W.Va. 250 D4 194
Lowell, Dodge, Wis. 341 E5 160
Lowell, isl., Mass. C4 206
Lowell, mts., Vt. B4 218
Lowellville, Mahoning, Ohio 2,055 A6 156
Lower Arrow, lake, B.C., Can. F13 52
Lower Bank, Burlington, N.J. 110 D3 210
Lower Brule, Lyman, S.Dak. 150 C6 158
Lower Burrell, Westmoreland, Pa. 11,952 *C2 214
Lower Cabot, Washington, Vt. 150 C4 218
Lower Chichester, see Linwood, Pa.
Lower Egypt, reg., Eg., U.A.R. 9,162,838 *A3 395
Lower Hutt, N.Z. 47,813 J11 437
Lower Island Cove, Newf., Can. 500 F9 72
Lower Kalskag, Alsk. 103 *C5 84
Lower Lake, Lake, Calif. 550 C2 94
Lower Marlboro, Calvert, Md. 75 C6 182
Lower Matecumbe, key, Fla. G10 174
Lower Paia, Maui, Haw. 950 C5 86
Lower Peach Tree, Wilcox, Ala. 900 D2 168
Lower Red, lake, Minn. D3 148
Lower Salmon, dam, Idaho G4 108
Lower Village, Lamoille, Vt. 75 C3 218
Lowery, Larimer, Colo. 25 *B5 106
Lowes, Graves, Ky. 200 D2 178
Lowes Crossroads, Sussex, Del. 50 F4 172
Lowestoft, Eng. 43,700 I14 273
Lowgap, Newton, Ark. 10 A3 170
Lowgap, Surry, N.C. 250 A5 186
Łowicz, Pol. 14,400 B4 325
Lowland, Pamlico, N.C. 500 B9 186
Lowland, Hamblen, Tenn. 100 C8 190
Lowman, Boise, Idaho 100 E3 108
Lowmansville, Lawrence, Ky. 800 C8 178
Low Moor, Clinton, Iowa 343 C7 142
Lowmoor, Alleghany, Va. 900 C5 192
Lowndes, Wayne, Mo. 150 D7 150
Lowndes, co., Ala. 15,417 C3 168
Lowndes, co., Ga. 49,270 F3 176
Lowndes, co., Miss. 46,639 B4 184
Lowndesboro, Lowndes, Ala. 250 C3 168
Lowndesville, Abbeville, S.C. 274 C3 188
Lowry, Cameron, La. 35 D3 180
Lowry, Pope, Minn. 294 F3 148
Lowry, Walworth, S.Dak. 44 B6 158
Lowry City, St. Clair, Mo. 437 C4 150
Lowrys, Chester, S.C. 298 B6 188
Low Tatra, mts., Czech. B4 324
Lowville, Lewis, N.Y. 3,616 B6 212
Loxahatchee, Palm Beach, Fla. 500 E10 174
Loxicha, Mex. 2,869 D6 225
Loxley, Baldwin, Ala. 831 E2 168
Loyal, Kingfisher, Okla. 87 C5 128
Loyal, Clark, Wis. 1,146 D3 160
Loyalhanna, Westmoreland, Pa. 1,000 *C2 214
Loyalist, Alta., Can. 86 E7 54
Loyall, Harlan, Ky. 1,260 D7 178
Loyalsock, creek, Pa. B5 214
Loyalton, Sierra, Calif. 936 C3 94
Loyalton, Edmunds, S.Dak. 34 B6 158
Loyalty, is., Pac.O. D3 436
Loyang, China 171,200 H6 348
Loyd, Moffat, Colo. 60 B3 106
Loyd, Calhoun, Miss. 150 B3 184
Lozeau, Mineral, Mont. 18 C2 110
Lozère, dept., Fr. 82,391 *E5 278
Loznica, Yugo. 5,031 B4 316
Lozovatko, Sov.Un. H9 332
Lualaba, riv., Con.L. C4 414
Lualualei, Honolulu, Haw. 450 *G9 86
Luama, riv., Con.L. C4 414
Luampa, Rh.&Nya. C4 420
Luan, riv., China E9 348
Luana, Clayton, Iowa 276 A6 142
Luanda, Ang. 189,590 A2 420
Luanda, dist., Ang. 281,791 A2 420
Luang Prabang, Laos 25,000 C4 362
Luang, lake, Thai. F4 362
Luang, mtn., Thai. E3 362
Luanguinga, riv., Ang. B4 420
Luanshya, Rh.&Nya. 16,000 (*48,000) B5 420
Luarca, Sp. 4,233 A3 298
Luashi, Con.L. E3 414
Lubaczów, Pol. 4,986 C6 325
Luban, Pol. 11,100 C2 325
Lubang, is., Phil. B6 358
Lubartów, Pol. 5,542 C6 325
Lubawa, Pol. 4,679 B4 325
Lübben, Ger. 9,433 C5 286
Lubbock, Lubbock, Tex. 128,691 (*144,300) C5 130
Lubbock, co., Tex. 156,271 C5 130
Lubec, Washington, Maine 1,289 (2,684▲) D6 204
Lübeck, Ger. 228,800 B4 286
Lübeck, bay, Ger. A4 286
Lubefu, Con.L. C3 414
Lubero, Con.L. C4 414
Lubicon, lake, Alta., Can. B5 54
Lubilash, riv., Con.L. D3 414
Lubin, Pol. 1,769 C3 325
Lublin, Pol. 130,000 C6 325
Lublin, Taylor, Wis. 160 C3 160
Lublin, pol. div., Pol. 1,713,000 *C6 325
Lubliniec, Pol. 12,400 C5 325
Lubny, Sov.Un. 30,000 G9 332
Lubrin, Sp. 1,247 D5 298
Lubsko, Pol. 2,689 C2 325
Lubudi, Con.L. D4 414
Lubudi, riv., Con.L. E3 414
Lubue, Con.L. C2 414
Lubutu, Con.L. C4 414
Lucama, Wilson, N.C. 498 B7 186
Lucan, Ont., Can. 924 Q19 64
Lucan, Redwood, Minn. 216 G3 148
Lucas, Lucas, Iowa 357 C4 142
Lucas, Russell, Kans. 559 C5 144
Lucas, Missaukee, Mich. 100 E6 146
Lucas, Jefferson Davis, Miss. 100 D3 184
Lucas, Richland, Ohio 719 B4 156
Lucas, Gregory, S.Dak. 24 D6 158
Lucas, co., Iowa 10,923 C4 142
Lucas, co., Ohio 456,931 A3 156
Lucas, chan., Ont., Can. O19 64
Lucasville, Scioto, Ohio 1,277 D4 156
Lucca, It. 42,300 (86,800▲) D3 302
Lucca, prov., It. 368,700 *D3 302
Luce, co., Mich. 7,827 C6 146
Luce, bay, Scot. G8 273
Lucea, Jam. 1,950 C5 232
Lucedale, George, Miss. 1,977 E4 184
Luce Farms, George, Miss. E4 184
Lucena, Phil. 18,085 B6 358
Lucena, Sp. 24,866 D4 298
Lucena del Cid, Sp. 1,379 B6 298
Lučenec, Czech. 15,083 B4 324
Lucera, It. 23,100 E5 302
Lucerne, Lake, Calif. 420 C2 94
Lucerne, Weld, Colo. 75 B6 106
Lucerne, Cass, Ind. 215 B3 140
Lucerne, Putnam, Mo. 157 A4 150
Lucerne, see Luzern, Switz.
Lucerne, Hot Springs, Wyo. 25 C4 116
Lucerne, lake, Switz. A4 312
Lucernemines, Indiana, Pa. 1,524 C2 214
Lucerne Valley, San Bernardino, Calif. 900 E5 94
Luceville, Que., Can. 1,265 P16 66
Luchi, China 10,000 K5 349
Luchmayor, Sp. 10,041 C8 298
Luchuan, China 5,000 N5 349
Lucien, Franklin, Miss. 150 D2 184
Lucien, Noble, Okla. 100 B6 128
Lucile, Idaho, Idaho 20 D2 108
Lucin, Box Elder, Utah 75 B2 114
Lucipara, is., Indon. F7 359
Lucira, Ang. B2 420
Luck, Polk, Wis. 853 C1 160
Luckau, Ger. 6,145 C6 286
Luckenwalde, Ger. 29,600 B5 286
Luckey, Wood, Ohio 946 A1 156, A3
Lucknow, Ont., Can. 962 Q19 64
Lucknow, India 444,711 (*496,861) D3 368
Lucknow, Richland, La. B4 180
Lucknow, Lee, S.C. 60 C8 188
Lucky Lake, Sask., Can. 432 E4 58
Luckyshot, Alsk. 1 G11 84
Lucky Strike, Alta., Can. 25 F7 54
Luçon, Fr. 7,839 D3 278
Lucrecia, cape, Cuba B7 232
Lucy, St. John the Baptist, La. 725 B6 180
Lucy, Shelby, Tenn. 130 C2 190, E6
Luda Kamchiya, riv., Bul. B3 317
Ludden, Dickey, N.Dak. 59 E7 154
Ludden, riv., Swe. C7 292
Ludell, Rawlins, Kans. 105 C3 144
Lüdenscheid, Ger. 55,700 C2 286
Lüderitz, S.W.Afr. 2,836 E3 420
Lüderitz, bay, S.W.Afr. E2 420
Ludgate, Ont., Can. O20 64
Ludhiana, India 153,795 C1 368
Ludington, Mason, Mich. 9,421 F5 146
Ludlow, San Bernardino, Calif. 250 E5 94
Ludlow, N.B., Can. 95 C3 70
Ludlow, Las Animas, Colo. 9 E6 106
Ludlow, Champaign, Ill. 460 C5 138
Ludlow, Kenton, Ky. 6,233 A8 178
Ludlow, Aroostook, Maine 25 (274▲) B4 204
Ludlow, Hampden, Mass. 8,000 (13,805▲) B3 206
Ludlow, Scott, Miss. 300 C3 184
Ludlow, Livingston, Mo. 235 B4 150
Ludlow, Windsor, Vt. 1,658 (2,386▲) E3 218
Ludlow, mtn., Vt. E3 218
Ludlow-Asbury, Hunterdon, N.J. 300 B2 210
Ludlow Center, Hampden, Mass. 325 B3 206
Ludowici, Long, Ga. 1,578 E5 176
Luduș, Rom. A3 321
Ludvika, Swe. 11,352 A6 292
Ludwig, canal, Ger. D4 286
Ludwigsburg, Ger. 65,800 D3 286
Ludwigshafen [am Rhein], Ger. 150,200 D3 286
Ludwigslust, Ger. 12,500 B4 286
Luebo, Con.L. D3 414
Lueders, Jones, Tex. 654 C6 130
Luella, Henry, Ga. 300 C2 176
Luepa, Ven. D8 240
Lufkin, Angelina, Tex. 17,641 D8 130
Lufuna, Con.L. D2 414
Luga, Sov.Un. 43,000 C7 332
Luga, riv., Sov.Un. C7 332
Lugan, riv., Sov.Un. R23 332
Luganchik, riv., Sov.Un. R23 332
Lugano, Switz. 18,400 (*28,100) B4 312
Lugano, lake, Switz. C4 312
Lugansk, Sov.Un. 274,000 H12 332, R23
Lugela, riv., Moz. C7 421
Lugenda, riv., Moz. B7 421
Lugert, Kiowa, Okla. 25 D4 128
Lugerville, Price, Wis. 30 C3 160
Lugh Ferrandi, Som. 2,800 E5 398
Lugnaquilla, mtn., Ire. I6 273
Lugo, It. 12,800 C3 302
Lugo, Sp. 43,800 (62,310▲) A3 298
Lugo, prov., Sp. 521,213 *A3 298
Lugoff, Kershaw, S.C. 200 C7 188
Lugoj, Rom. 30,258 B1 321
Luho, China E8 346
Luho, China D12 348
Luirojoki, riv., Fin. C12 290
Luis Gomes, Braz. 1,082 B3 258
Luis Lopez, Socorro, N.Mex. 25 E4 126
Luiza, Con.L. D3 414
Luiz Correia, Braz. 1,450 A2 258
Luján, Arg. 3,542 B2 252
Lukachukai, Apache, Ariz. 20 B6 124
Lukchek, Sov.Un. D15 329
Luke, Allegany, Md. 587 B1 182
Lukenie, riv., Con.L. C2 414
Lukeville, Pima, Ariz. 49 G3 124
Lukolela, Con.L. C2 414
Lukovit, Bul. 8,812 B2 317
Łuków, Pol. 8,513 C6 325
Lukoyanov, Sov.Un. 14,800 E15 332
Lukuga, riv., Con.L. D4 414
Lukulu, Rh. & Nya. B4 420
Lula, Hall, Ga. 557 B3 176
Lula, Coahoma, Miss. 484 A2 184
Lula, Pontotoc, Okla. 50 D7 128
Luleå, Swe. 27,767 D10 290
Luleälven, riv., Swe. C9 290
Lüleburgaz, Tur. 8,355 A2 307
Luling, St. Charles, La. 2,122 C7 180
Luling, Caldwell, Tex. 4,412 B7 130, E7
Lulu, Columbia, Fla. 152 A8 174
Lulua, riv., Con.L. D3 414
Luluabourg, Con.L. D3 414
Lulung, China 5,000 F9 348
Lum, Lapeer, Mich. 265 F8 146
Lumba, Con.L. B2 414
Lumber, riv., N.C. C7 186
Lumber City, Telfair, Ga. 1,360 E4 176
Lumberport, Harrison, W.Va. 1,031 A6 194, B4
Lumberton, Lamar, Miss. 2,108 D3 184
Lumberton, Burlington, N.J. 600 D3 210
Lumberton, Rio Arriba, N.Mex. 250 B4 126
Lumberton, Robeson, N.C. 15,305 C7 186
Lumbo, Moz. B8 421
Lumby, B.C., Can. 786 E13 52
Lumding, India D6 368
Lumpkin, Stewart, Ga. 1,348 D2 176
Lumpkin, co., Ga. 7,241 B2 176
Lumsden, Newf., Can. 450 F9 72
Lumsden, Sask., Can. 512 E5 58
Lumsden, N.Z. 592 F2 437
Lumut, pt., Indon. E3 358
Luna, Catron, N.Mex. 220 E2 126
Luna, Lincoln, N.Mex. 15 E5 126
Luna, co., N.Mex. 9,839 F3 126
Luna Pier, Monroe, Mich. 1,815 H8 146
Lund, Caribou, Idaho 10 G7 108
Lund, White Pine, Nev. 375 E6 112
Lund, Swe. 36,920 F4 292
Lund, Iron, Utah 50 E2 114
Lunde, dist., Ang. 266,087 A3 420
Lundale, Logan, W.Va. 500 D3 194, D5
Lundar, Man., Can. 650 E3 60
Lundarbrekka, Ice. L21 290
Lundazi, Rh.&Nya. 915 B6 421
Lundbreck, Alta., Can. 131 F5 54
Lundby, Den. 526 F2 292
Lundell, Phillips, Ark. 150 C6 170
Lundu, Sar. 768 D3 358
Lundville, Roosevelt, Mont. B11 110
Lundy, isl, Eng. J8 273
Lüneburg, Ger. 57,400 B4 286
Lunel, Fr. 7,758 F6 278
Lünen, Ger. 68,400 *C2 286
Lunenburg, N.S., Can. 2,859 E5 70
Lunenburg, Worcester, Mass. 990 (6,334▲) A4 206
Lunenburg, Essex, Vt. 250 (1,237▲) C5 218
Lunenburg, Lunenburg, Va. 40 D6 192
Lunenburg, co., N.S., Can. 34,207 E5 70
Lunenburg, co., Va. 12,523 D6 192
Lunéville, Fr. 22,690 C7 278
Lung, China 5,000 H3 348
Lungchen, China 2,000 A13 348
Lungchi, China 81,200 M8 349
Lungchuan, China 5,000 K9 349
Lungchuchai, China 8,000 I5 348
Lunghsi, China E8 346
Lungkou, China 5,000 G10 348
Lunglitai, China O4 349
Lungnan, China M7 349
Lungping, China G7 348
Lungué-Bungo, riv., Ang. B4 420
Lungyen, China M8 349
Luni, riv., India C2 366
Luning, Mineral, Nev. 75 E3 112
Lunino, Sov.Un. 6,200 F15 332
Lunita, Calcasieu, La. D2 180
Lunyama, Con.L. D4 414
Lup, Thai. C4 362
Lupani, Rh.&Nya. C5 420
Lupei, China 1,000 C10 348
Lupeni, Rom. 21,188 B2 321
Lupin (Nanchouli), China 7,882 A8 348
Lupton, Apache, Ariz. 150 C6 124
Lupton, Ogemaw, Mich. 100 E7 146
Lupton City, Hamilton, Tenn. 250 E8 190
Luqsor (Luxor), Eg., U.A.R. 24,118 B3 395
Luque, Par. 6,867 D4 247
Luray, Russell, Kans. 328 C5 144
Luray, Clark, Mo. 154 A6 150
Luray, Hampton, S.C. 102 F6 188
Luray, Henderson, Tenn. 100 C3 190
Luray, Page, Va. 3,014 B6 192
Lure, Fr. 6,723 D7 278
Lurgan, N.Ire. 16,181 G6 273
Luribay, Bol. 392 C1 246
Lurich, Giles, Va. 50 C4 192
Lurín, Peru 2,141 C2 245
Lúrio, Moz. B8 421
Luristan, reg., Iran C2 379
Luröy, Nor. C5 290
Lurton, Newton, Ark. 100 B3 170
Lusaka, Rh.&Nya. 52,500 (*59,500) C5 420
Lusako, Con.L. C4 414
Lusambo, Con.L. C3 414
Lusby, Calvert, Md. 75 D7 182
Luscar, Alta., Can. 400 D4 54
Luseland, Sask., Can. 591 D3 58
Lushan, China 10,000 I6 348
Lushnje, Alb. 8,585 A2 306
Lushoto, Tan. 1,270 C6 414
Lushton, York, Nebr. 45 *D8 152
Lüshun (Port Arthur), China 126,000 F10 348
Lusk, Niobrara, Wyo. 1,890 D8 116
Lustenau, Aus. 10,292 C1 313
Luster, Nor. F2 291
Lustre, Valley, Mont. 4 B11 110
Lutcher, St. James, La. 3,274 B6 180, D5
Lutesville, Bollinger, Mo. 658 D8 150
Luther, Boone, Iowa 147 C4 142
Luther, Lake, Mich. 325 E6 146
Luther, Carbon, Mont. 20 E7 110
Luther, Oklahoma, Okla. 517 C6 128
Luthersville, Meriwether, Ga. 282 C2 176
Lutherville, Johnson, Ark. 35 B3 170
Lutherville, Baltimore, Md. 12,265 B6 182
Lutie, Latimer, Okla. 300 *D8 128
Luting, China F8 346
Luton, Eng. 114,500 J12 273
Lutsk, Sov.Un. 49,000 G5 332
Luttrell, Union, Tenn. 600 B8 190
Lutts, Wayne, Tenn. 350 C4 190
Lutugino, Sov.Un. 3,600 S23 332
Lutz, Hillsborough, Fla. 700 B6 174, C8
Luverne, Crenshaw, Ala. 2,238 D3 168
Lu Verne, Kossuth, Iowa 468 B3 142
Luverne, Rock, Minn. 4,249 H2 148
Luverne, Steele, N.Dak. 109 C8 154
Luvua, riv., Con.L. D4 414
Luwingu, Rh.&Nya. 540 B6 421
Luwuk, Indon. E6 358
Luxapalila, creek, Ala., Miss. B1 168, B4 184
Luxembourg, Lux. 61,996 E5 282
Luxembourg, prov., Bel. 216,364 D4 282
Luxembourg, country, Eur. 322,000 D5 266, 282
Luxemburg, Dubuque, Iowa 159 B6 142
Luxemburg, Kewaunee, Wis. 730 D6 160

Luxeuil-les-Bains, Fr. 6,691 D7 278
Luxomni, Gwinnett, Ga. 180 A5 176
Luxor, see Luqsor, Eg., U.A.R.
Luxora, Mississippi, Ark. 1,236 B7 170
Luz, Braz. 3,255 D1 258
Luza, Sov.Un. 12,200 A3 336
Luza, riv., Sov.Un. A3 336
Luzern, Switz. 63,600 (*101,500) A4 312
Luzerne, Benton, Iowa 136 C5 142
Luzerne, Oscoda, Mich. 75 E7 146
Luzerne, Luzerne, Pa. 5,118 A5 214
Luzerne, co., Pa. 346,972 B5 214
Lužnice, riv., Czech. B2 324
Luzon, isl., Phil. A6 358
Lvov, Sov.Un. 410,000 H5 332
Lvungbyån, riv., Swe. E6 292
Lwówek Slaski, Pol. 3,364 C2 325
Lyall, bay, N.Z. J11 437
Lyall, mtn., B.C., Can. E15 52
Lyall, mtn., N.Z. F1 437
Lyallpur, Pak. 179,144 D8 375
Lyaskovets, Bul. 6,418 B2 317
Lybgt, mtn., Swe. A4 292
Lybster, Scot. C9 272
Lyckeby, Swe. 5,446 E6 292
Lycksele, Swe. 4,307 D8 290
Lycoming, co., Pa. 109,367 B4 214
Lycoming, creek, Pa. B4 214
Lyden, Rio Arriba, N.Mex. 50 B4 126
Lydenburg, U.S.Afr. 4,653 E6 421
Lydia, Wichita, Kans. D2 144
Lydia, Darlington, S.C. 200 C8 188
Lydia Mills, Laurens, S.C. 1,177 *C5 188
Lydiatt, Man., Can. 50 *F4 60
Lydick, St. Joseph, Ind. 1,217 A3 140
Lyell, isl., B.C., Can. D7 52
Lyell, mtn., Alta., B.C., Can. E4 52, E14 52
Lyerly, Chattooga, Ga. 409 B1 176
Lyford, Parke, Ind. 400 C2 140
Lyford, Willacy, Tex. 1,554 F7 130
Lygnern, lake, Swe. D3 292
Lykens, Dauphin, Pa. 2,527 C5 214
Lykesland, Richland, S.C. 150 D7 188
Lyle, Mower, Minn. 607 H6 148
Lyle, Klickitat, Wash. 400 D5 98
Lyles, Hickman, Tenn. 500 C4 190
Lyleton, Man., Can. 165 F2 60
Lyman, Madison, Idaho 50 *F7 108
Lyman (Town of), York, Maine (529▲) *E2 204
Lyman, Harrison, Miss. 225 E1 184, E3
Lyman, Scotts Bluff, Nebr. 626 C1 152
Lyman, Grafton, N.H. 25 (201▲) C3 208
Lyman, Osage, Okla. 30 B7 128
Lyman, Spartanburg, S.C. 1,261 B4 188
Lyman, Wayne, Utah 255 E4 114
Lyman, Skagit, Wash. 400 A4 98
Lyman, Uinta, Wyo. 425 E2 116
Lyman, co., S.Dak. 4,428 D5 158
Lyman, res., Ariz. D6 124
Lymantown, Price, Wis. 300 C3 160
Lyme (Town of), New London, Conn. (1,183▲) D6 202
Lyme, Grafton, N.H. 250 (1,026▲) D2 208
Lyme, bay, Eng. K9 273
Lyme Center, Grafton, N.H. 75 D2 208
Lymington, Eng. 24,200 K11 273
Lyna, riv., Pol. A5 325
Lynas, pt., Wales H8 273
Lynbrook, Nassau, N.Y. 19,881 E3 212
Lynch, Harlan, Ky. 3,810 D8 178
Lynch, Kent, Md. 150 B7 182
Lynch, Boyd, Nebr. 409 B7 152
Lynchburg, Highland, Ohio 1,022 C3 156
Lynchburg, Lee, S.C. 544 C8 188
Lynchburg, Moore, Tenn. 396 C5 190
Lynchburg (Independent City), Va. 54,790 C5 192
Lynches, riv., S.C. D9 188
Lynch Point, Baltimore, Md. (part of Edgemere) B7 182
Lynch Station, Campbell, Va. 400 C5 192
Lynd, Lyon, Minn. 259 G3 148
Lyndeboro (Lyndeborough), Hillsboro, N.H. 25 (594▲) F3 208
Lyndeborough, see Lyndeboro, N.H.
Lynden, Ont., Can. 475 Q20 64
Lynden, Whatcom, Wash. 2,542 A4 98
Lyndes, neck, Conn. D6 202
Lyndhurst, Ont., Can. 310 P24 64
Lyndhurst, Bergen, N.J. 21,867 B1 210
Lyndhurst, Cuyahoga, Ohio 16,805 B1 156
Lyndon, Whiteside, Ill. 677 B4 138
Lyndon, Osage, Kans. 953 D8 144
Lyndon, Jefferson, Ky. 5,000 A5 178
Lyndon, Caledonia, Vt. 250 (3,425▲) B4 218
Lyndon Center, Caledonia, Vt. 274 B4 218
Lyndon Station, Juneau, Wis. 335 E4 160
Lyndonville, Orleans, N.Y. 755 B3 212
Lyndonville, Caledonia, Vt. 1,477 B4 218
Lyndora, Butler, Pa. 5,700 C2 214
Lyngby, Den. F3 292
Lyngdal, Nor. G2 291
Lyngen, Nor. B9 290
Lyngsfjord, fjord, Nor. B9 290
Lynhurst, Marion, Ind. 183 D4 140
Lynn, Winston, Ala. 531 A2 168
Lynn, Lawrence, Ark. 200 A5 170
Lynn, Randolph, Ind. 1,260 B5 140
Lynn, Essex, Mass. 94,478 B6 206, C3
Lynn, Polk, N.C. 500 B3 186
Lynn, Box Elder, Utah B2 114
Lynn, co., Tex. 10,914 C5 130
Lynn, canal, Alsk. I14 84
Lynn, lake, W.Va. B5 194
Lynn Addition, Osage, Okla. 600 B7 128
Lynn Camp, Marshall, W.Va. 50 C2 194
Lynn Creek, B.C., Can. 850 B15 52
Lynn Creek, Noxubee, Miss. 64 B4 184
Lynndale, Montgomery, Ala. 400 *C3 168
Lynndyl, Millard, Utah 145 D3 114
Lynnfield, Essex, Mass. 8,398 C3 206
Lynn Garden, Sullivan, Tenn. 5,261 *B9 190
Lynn Grove, Calloway, Ky. 200 D2 178
Lynn Haven, Bay, Fla. 3,078 A5 174
Lynnhaven, Princess Anne, Va. 350 A9 192, D8
Lynnhaven Roads, harbor, Va. A9 192
Lynn Lake, Man., Can. 600 B2 60
Lynn Lane, Tulsa, Okla. 100 B8 128
Lynnville, Warrick, Ind. 409 D2 140
Lynnville, Jasper, Iowa 411 C5 142
Lynnville, Graves, Ky. 1,711 D2 178
Lynnville, Giles, Tenn. 362 C5 190
Lynnwood, Snohomish, Wash. 7,207 *B4 98
Lynwood, Los Angeles, Calif. 31,614 C5 94
Lynxville, Crawford, Wis. 183 E2 160
Lyon, Fr. 471,270 E6 278
Lyon, Coahoma, Miss. 393 A2 184
Lyon, co., Iowa 14,468 A1 142
Lyon, co., Kans. 26,928 D7 144
Lyon, co., Ky. 5,924 C2 178
Lyon, co., Minn. 22,655 G3 148
Lyon, co., Nev. 6,143 D2 112
Lyon Mountain, Clinton, N.Y. 950 A8 212
Lyonnais, former prov., Fr. 1,621,000 E6 278
Lyons, Boulder, Colo. 706 B5 106
Lyons, Toombs, Ga. 3,219 D4 176
Lyons, Cook, Ill. 9,936 F2 138
Lyons, Greene, Ind. 651 D2 140
Lyons, Rice, Kans. 4,592 D5 144
Lyons, Ionia, Mich. 687 G7 146
Lyons, Burt, Nebr. 974 C9 152
Lyons, Somerset, N.J. 140 B3 210
Lyons, Wayne, N.Y. 4,673 B5 212
Lyons, Fulton, Ohio 590 A2 156
Lyons, Linn, Oreg. 463 C2 96, C4
Lyons, Walworth, Wis. 400 F1 160
Lyons Falls, Lewis, N.Y. 887 B6 212
Lyons Point, Acadia, La. 50 D3 180
Lyons View, Knox, Tenn. (part of Bearden) E9 190
Lys, riv., Bel. D2 282
Lysá nad Labem, Czech. 6,500 *A2 324
Lysaya Gora, Sov.Un. 19,500 H8 332
Lysekil, Swe. 7,830 C2 292
Lysite, Fremont, Wyo. 70 C5 116
Lyss, Switz. 4,133 A3 312
Lyster Station, Que., Can. 1,010 R13 66
Lysva, Sov.Un. 73,000 A5 336
Lytham [St. Anne's], Eng. 30,900 H10 273
Lytle, Atascosa, Tex. 798 E6 130
Lytton, B.C., Can. 329 E12 52
Lytton, Sac, Iowa 376 B3 142
Lyubar, Sov.Un. 19,300 H6 332
Lyubertsy, Sov.Un. 93,000 N18 332
Lyublino, Sov.Un. 86,000 N18 332
Lyung, Mong. 10,000 B9 346

M

Ma'ād, Jordan 1,000 B6 382
Maādi, Eg., U.A.R. E2 382
Maalaea, Maui, Haw. 200 C5 86
Maalaea, bay, Haw. C5 86
Ma'ale Aqrabim (Scorpion Pass), pass, Isr. D6 382
Ma'an, Jordan 4,509 D1 378
Ma'aqala, Sau.Ar. B4 383
Maas, Ire. G4 272
Maas, riv., Neth. C3 282
Maaseik, Bel. 7,823 C4 282
Maastricht, Neth. 83,644 D4 282
Mabana, Island, Wash. 75 A4 98
Mabank, Kaufman, Tex. 944 C7 130
Mabber, cape, Som. D7 398
Mabel, Fillmore, Minn. 815 H7 148
Mabel, lake, B.C., Can. E13 52
Mabelvale, Pulaski, Ark. 550 D6 170
Maben, Jefferson, Ala. 30 E4 168
Maben, Oktibbeha and Webster, Miss. 696 B3 184
Maberly, Ont., Can. 90 P24 64
Mabie, Randolph, W.Va. 750 C5 194
Mableton, Cobb, Ga. 7,127 A4 176
Mabote, Moz. D6 421
Mabou, N.S., Can. 589 C8 70
Mabrous, well, Niger B7 409
Mabscott, Raleigh, W.Va. 1,591 D3 194, D7
Mabton, Yakima, Wash. 958 C6 98
Mabuni, Okinawa D1 436
Macachin, Arg. C3 252
McAdam, N.B., Can. 2,000 D2 70
McAdams, Attala, Miss. 200 B3 184
McAdenville, Gaston, N.C. 748 *B4 186
McAdoo, Schuylkill, Pa. 3,560 C5 214
Macaé, Braz. 10,664 E2 258
McAfee, De Kalb, Ga. 3,000 *C2 176
McAfee, Leake, Miss. 556 C3 184
McAfee, Sussex, N.J. 250 A3 210
McAlester, Pittsburg, Okla. 17,419 D8 128
McAlester, lake, Okla. C8 128
McAllaster, Logan, Kans. 39 *C2 144
McAllen, Hidalgo, Tex. 32,728 F6 130
McAllister, Madison, Mont. 20 E5 110
McAllister, Marinette, Wis. 25 C6 160
McAlmont, Pulaski, Ark. D7 170
McAlpin, Suwannee, Fla. 200 A8 174
McAlpin, Raleigh, W.Va. 600 *D3 194
McAndrews, Pike, Ky. 533 C8 178
Macao, Port. poss., Asia 210,000 G13 340, N6 349
Macapá, Braz. 9,748 E6 256
Macará, Ec. 3,330 A2 245
McArthur, Vinton, Ohio 1,529 C4 156
MacArthur, Raleigh, W.Va. 1,418 *D3 194
Macas, Ec. 976 A2 245
Macáu, Braz. 7,661 B3 258
McAuley, Man., Can. 160 E2 60
McBain, Missaukee, Mich. 551 E6 146
McBean, Richmond, Ga. 100 C5 176
McBee, Chesterfield, S.C. 512 C8 188
Macbeth, Berkeley, S.C. 80 E9 188
McBride, B.C., Can. 582 D12 52
McBride, Jefferson, Miss. 45 D2 184
McBride, Montcalm, Mich. 265 *F6 146
McBride, Marshall, Okla. 14 *D7 128
McCabe, Roosevelt, Mont. 45 B12 110
McCall, Valley, Idaho 1,423 E2 108
McCall, Ascension, La. 130 B5 180, D4
McCalla, Jefferson, Ala. 500 E4 168
McCall Creek, Franklin, Miss. 169 D2 184
McCallsburg, Story, Iowa 272 B4 142
McCamey, Upton, Tex. 3,375 D4 130
McCammon, Bannock, Idaho 557 G6 108
Maccan, N.S., Can. 412 D5 70
McCanna, Grand Forks, N.Dak. 80 B8 154
Maccarese, It. (part of Rome) 815 E4 302
McCarley, Carroll, Miss. 200 B3 184
McCarthy, Alsk. 12 C7 84
McCarthy, mtn., Mont. E4 110
McCartys, Valencia, N.Mex. 25 C3 126
McCaskill, Hempstead, Ark. 62 D3 170
McCauley, isl., B.C., Can. D7 52
McCausland, Scott, Iowa 173 C7 142
McCaysville, Fannin, Ga. 1,871 B2 176
McChesneytown, Westmoreland, Pa. 1,140 *C2 214
McClain, co., Okla. 12,740 D6 128
McClave, Bent, Colo. 90 D8 106
McCleary, Grays Harbor, Wash. 1,115 B3 98
McClelland, Woodruff, Ark. 65 B5 170
McClelland, Pottawattamie, Iowa 150 C2 142
McClellanville, Charleston, S.C. 324 E10 188
Macclenny, Baker, Fla. 2,671 A8 174
Macclesfield, Eng. 36,300 H10 273
Macclesfield, Edgecombe, N.C. 473 B8 186
McClintock, chan., N.W.Ter., Can. C8 48
McCloud, Siskiyou, Calif. 2,140 B2 94
Maccluer, gulf, Neth. N.Gui. E8 359
McClure, Alexander, Ill. 400 F4 138
McClure, Henry, Ohio 651 A3 156
McClure, Snyder, Pa. 1,001 C4 214
McClure, Dickenson, Va. 500 C2 192
M'Clure, strait, N.W.Ter., Can. C7 48
McClusky, Sheridan, N.Dak. 751 C5 154
McColl, Marlboro, S.C. 2,479 B9 188
McComas, Mercer, W.Va. 950 D3 194
McComb, Pike, Miss. 12,020 D2 184
McComb, Hancock, Ohio 1,176 A3 156
McConaughy, lake, Nebr. C4 152
McCondy, Chickasaw, Miss. 111 B4 184
McCone, co., Mont. 3,321 C11 110
McConnell, Logan, W.Va. 950 D5 194
McConnells, York, S.C. 266 B6 188
McConnellsburg, Fulton, Pa. 1,245 D3 214
McConnelsville, Morgan, Ohio 2,257 C5 156
McCook, Cook, Ill. 441 *B6 138
McCook, Red Willow, Nebr. 8,301 D5 152
McCook, Union, S.Dak. 300 E9 158
McCook, co., S.Dak. 8,268 D8 158
McCool, Porter, Ind. (part of Portage) A2 140
McCool, Attala, Miss. 211 B3 184
McCoole, Allegany, Md. 368 A2 182
McCool Junction, York, Nebr. 246 D8 152
McCord, Sask., Can. 145 F4 58
McCordsville, Hancock, Ind. 350 C4 140
McCorkle, Lincoln, W.Va. 300 C3 194, C5
McCormick, McCormick, S.C. 1,998 D4 188
McCormick, co., S.C. 8,629 D4 188
McCracken, Rush, Kans. 406 D4 144
McCracken, co., Ky. 57,306 C2 178
McCrary, Lowndes, Miss. 100 B4 184
McCreary, Man., Can. 325 E3 60
McCreary, co., Ky. 12,463 D6 178
McCrory, Woodruff, Ark. 1,053 B5 170
McCulloch, co., Tex. 8,815 D6 130
McCullom Lake, McHenry, Ill. 759 *A5 138
McCullough, Escambia, Ala. 350 D2 168
McCune, Crawford, Kans. 433 E8 144
McCurtain, Haskell, Okla. 528 C9 128
McCurtain, co., Okla. 25,851 D9 128
McDaniel, Talbot, Md. 50 C7 182
McDaniel Heights, New Castle, Del. 486 *B4 172
McDavid, Escambia, Fla. 600 A3 174
McDermitt, Humboldt, Nev. 250 B4 112
McDermott, Scioto, Ohio 700 D3 156
Macdhui, mtn., Scot. D9 272
MacDonald, Man., Can. 190 E3 60
McDonald, Rawlins, Kans. 323 C2 144
McDonald, Neshoba, Miss. 150 C3 184
McDonald, Trumbull, Ohio 2,727 A6 156
McDonald, Washington and Allegheny, Pa. 3,141 A3 214
McDonald, Bradley, Tenn. 125 C7 190, E9
MacDonald, Fayette, W.Va. 400 D3 194, D7
McDonald, co., Mo. 11,798 E3 150
McDonald, creek, Mont. C8 110
Macdonald, lake, Austl. C5 432
McDonald, peak, Mont. C3 110
MacDonald, range, B.C., Can. F15 52
MacDonnell, ranges, Austl. C6 432
McDonogh, Baltimore, Md. 600 B6 182
McDonough, New Castle, Del. 15 C3 172
McDonough, Henry, Ga. 2,224 C2 176
McDonough, co., Ill. 28,928 C3 138
McDougal, Clay, Ark. 200 A6 170
McDougal, mtn., Wyo. D2 116
McDowell, Sumter, Ala. 250 C2 168
McDowell, Floyd, Ky. 700 C8 178
McDowell, Highland, Va. 127 B5 192
McDowell, McDowell, W.Va. 400 *D3 194
McDowell, co., N.C. 26,742 B3 186
McDowell, co., W.Va. 71,359 D3 194
McDowell, peak, Ariz. G2 124
Macduff, Scot. 3,300 D10 272
McDuffie, co., Ga. 12,627 C4 176
Mace, Shoshone, Idaho 75 *B3 108
Macedon, Wayne, N.Y. 645 B4 212
Macedonia, Litchfield, Conn. 130 C2 202
Macedonia, Pottawattamie, Iowa 290 C2 142
Macedonia, Summit, Ohio 800 A5 156, B1
Macedonia (Makedhonia) reg., Grc., Yugo. 1,700,835 A3 306
Macedonia (Makedonija), rep., Yugo. 1,304,514 D5 316
Maceió, Braz. 149,039 B3 258
McElroy, creek, W.Va. A6 194
Macenta, Guinea E3 408
Maceo, Daviess, Ky. 200 C4 178
Macerata, It. 20,600 D4 302
Macerata, prov., It. 299,500 *D4 302
McEwen, Baker, Oreg. C8 96
McEwen, Humphreys, Tenn. 979 B4 190
McFadden, Jackson, Ark. B5 170
McFadden, Carbon, Wyo. 150 E6 116
McFall, Gentry, Mo. 206 A3 150
Macfarlan, Ritchie, W.Va. 500 B3 194
McFarland, Kern, Calif. 3,686 E4 94
McFarland, Wabaunsee, Kans. 256 C7 144
McFarland, Dane, Wis. 1,272 E4 160
McGaffey, McKinley, N.Mex. 50 C2 126
McGaheysville, Rockingham, Va. 250 B6 192
McGee, Sask., Can. 50 E3 58
McGehee, Desha, Ark. 4,448 D5 170
McGill, White Pine, Nev. 2,195 D7 112
MacGillicuddy's Reeks, mts., Ire. J3 273
McGillivray Falls, B.C., Can. E11 52
McGillivray, range, B.C., Can. F15 52
McGirts, creek, Fla. A10 174
McGivney Junction, N.B., Can. 145 C3 70
McGrann, Armstrong, Pa. 800 *C2 214
McGrath, Alsk. 175 C6 84
McGrath, Aitkin, Minn. 96 E5 148
McGraw, Cortland, N.Y. 1,276 C5 212
McGraws, Wyoming, W.Va. 85 D3 194
MacGregor, Man., Can. 611 F3 60
McGregor, Montgomery, Ga. 200 D4 176
McGregor, Clayton, Iowa 1,040 A6 142
McGregor, Aitkin, Minn. 283 E5 148
McGregor, Williams, N.Dak. 125 B3 154
McGregor, McLennan, Tex. 4,642 D7 130
McGregor, lake, Alta., Can. E6 54
McGregor, riv., B.C., Can. C12 52
McGrew, Scotts Bluff, Nebr. 90 C2 152
McGuffey, Hardin, Ohio 647 B3 156
McGuire, mtn., Idaho D4 108
McGuires, Kootenai, Idaho B2 108
Mach, Pak. 3,211 E5 375
Machachi, Ec. 2,584 A2 245
Machado, Braz. 6,042 E1 258
Machakos, Ken. C6 414
Machala, Ec. 7,549 A2 245
Machanao, mtn., Guam C7 436
Machar, lake, Ont., Can. O21 64
Macheke, Rh.&Nya. C6 421
Macheng, China 1,000 J7 349
McHenry, McHenry, Ill. 3,336 A5 138, E2
McHenry, Ohio, Ky. 446 C4 178
McHenry, Garrett, Md. 60 A1 182
McHenry, Stone, Miss. 500 E3 184
McHenry, Foster, N.Dak. 155 C7 154
McHenry, co., Ill. 84,210 C5 138
McHenry, co., N.Dak. 11,099 B5 154
Machias, Washington, Maine 1,523 (2,614▲) D5 204
Machias, Cattaraugus, N.Y. 610 C3 212
Machias, bay, Maine D5 204
Machias, lakes, Maine C5 204
Machias, riv., Maine B4 204
Machias, riv., Maine D5 204
Machiasport, Washington, Maine 280 (980▲) D5 204
Machiques, Ven. 6,923 A2 240
Machovec, Moore, Tex. A5 130
McHue, Independence, Ark. 25 B5 170
Machum, India D7 368
Machu Picchu, Peru C3 245
Machynlleth, Wales I9 273
Macia, Moz. E6 421
Măcin, Rom. 6,533 B5 321
McIndoe Falls, Caledonia, Vt. 155 C4 218
McIntire, Mitchell, Iowa 270 A5 142
McIntosh, Washington, Ala. 400 D1 168
McIntosh, Marion, Fla. 258 B8 174
McIntosh, Liberty, Ga. 150 E5 176
McIntosh, Polk, Minn. 785 D3 148
McIntosh, Corson, S.Dak. 568 B4 158
McIntosh, co., Ga. 6,364 E5 176
McIntosh, co., N.Dak. 6,702 D6 154
McIntosh, co., Okla. 12,371 C8 128
McIntosh, lake, Sask., Can. C5 58
McIntosh, run, Md. D6 182
McIntyre, Wilkinson, Ga. 316 D3 176
Mack, Mesa, Colo. 150 C2 106
McKague, Sask., Can. 155 D6 58
Mackay, Austl. 15,100 C9 432
Mackay, Custer, Idaho 652 F5 108
Mackay, lake, Austl. C5 432
MacKay, lake, N.W.Ter., Can. E7 48
Mackay, riv., Alta., Can. B6 54
Mackayville, Que., Can. 9,958 *S16 66
McKean, co., Pa. 54,517 B3 214
McKee, Jackson, Ky. 234 C7 178
McKee City, Atlantic, N.J. 300 E3 210
McKeefrey, Marshall, W.Va. 140 B1 194
McKeesport, Allegheny, Pa. 45,489 C2 214
McKees Rocks, Allegheny, Pa. 13,185 A3 214, C1
Mackenna, Arg. B3 252
McKenna, Pierce, Wash. 250 *C4 98
McKenney, Dinwiddie, Va. 519 D7 192
McKenzie, Butler, Ala. 558 D3 168
Mackenzie, St. Louis, Mo. 283 *C7 150
McKenzie, Fallon, Mont. D12 110
McKenzie, Burleigh, N.Dak. 100 D5 154
McKenzie, Carroll and Weakley, Tenn. 3,780 B3 190
McKenzie, co., N.Dak. 7,296 C2 154
Mackenzie, dist., N.W.Ter., Can. 12,492 E8 48
Mackenzie, bay, N.W.Ter., Can. D5 48
Mackenzie, mts., N.W.Ter., Can. E5 48
McKenzie, pass, Oreg. C5 96
Mackenzie, riv., N.W.Ter., Can. D6 48
McKenzie Bridge, Lane, Oreg. 315 C4 96
Mackey, Gibson, Ind. 98 *D2 140
McKey, Sequoyah, Okla. 50 C9 128
Mackinac, co., Mich. 10,853 C6 146
Mackinac, isl., Mich. D7 146
Mackinac, straits, Mich. D7 146
Mackinac Island, Mackinac, Mich. 942 D7 146
Mackinaw, Tazewell, Ill. 1,163 C4 138

Mackinaw, riv., Ill. C4 138
Mackinaw City, Cheboygan, Mich. 934 D7 146
McKinley, Marengo, Ala. 100 C2 168
McKinley, Hancock, Maine 300 D4 204
McKinley, St. Louis, Minn. 408 D6 148
McKinley, Coos, Oreg. 120 *D2 96
McKinley, Converse, Wyo. 35 D7 116
McKinley, co., N.Mex. 37,209 C2 126
McKinley, mtn., Alsk. C6 84
McKinley Park, Alsk. 59 C7 84
McKinleyville, Humboldt, Calif. 3,000 B1 94
McKinney, Lincoln, Ky. 300 C6 178
McKinney, Collins, Tex. 13,763 C7 130
McKinney, lake, Kans. E2 144
McKinnon, Houston, Tenn. 150 B4 190
McKinnon, Sweetwater, Wyo. 10 E3 116
Mackinnon Road, Ken. C6 414
McKittrick, Kern, Calif. 135 E4 94
McKittrick, summit, Calif. E4 94
Macklin, Sask., Can. 661 D3 58
McKnight, lake, Man., Can. B2 60
McKownville, Albany, N.Y. 2,000 *C8 212
Macksburg, Madison, Iowa 174 C3 142
Macksburg, Washington, Ohio C5 156
Macks Creek, Camden, Mo. 123 D5 150
Macksville, Stafford, Kans. 546 E5 144
Mackville, Washington, Ky. 400 C5 178
Mackville, Outagamie, Wis. 50 A5 160
McLain, Greene, Miss. 600 D4 184
McLaughlin Alta., Can. 75 D7 54
McLaughlin, Corson, S.Dak. 983 B5 158
McLaughlin, riv., Man., Can. D4 60
McLaurin, Forrest, Miss. 800 D3 184
McLean, Sask., Can. 148 E5 58
McLean, McLean, Ill. 758 C4 138
McLean, Pierce, Nebr. 73 B8 152
McLean, Gray, Tex. 1,330 B5 130
McLean, Fairfax, Va. 2,000 A7 192
B7
McLean, co., Ill. 83,877 C4 138
McLean, co., Ky. 9,355 C3 178
McLean, co., N.Dak. 14,030 C4 154
McLean, mtn., Maine A4 204
Maclean, strait, N.W.Ter., Can. B8 48
McLeansboro, Hamilton, Ill. 2,951 E5 138
Maclear, U.S.Afr. 2,372 F5 420
McLemore, Oklahoma, Okla. 528 *C6 128
McLemoresville, Carroll, Tenn. 285 C3 190
McLennan, Alta., Can. 1,092 C4 54
McLennan, co., Tex. 150,091 D7 130
McLeod, Sweet Grass, Mont. 15 E6 110
McLeod, Ransom, N.Dak. 300 D8 154
McLeod, co., Minn. 24,401 G4 148
McLeod, lake, B.C., Can. C11 52
McLeod, peak, Mont. C3 110
McLeod, riv., Alta., Can. D4 54
McLeod Lake, B.C., Can. C11 52
McLoud, Pottawatomie, Okla. 837 C6 128
McLoughlin, mtn., Oreg. E4 96
McLouth, Jefferson, Kans. 494 C8 144
McMahon, Sask., Can. 165 E4 58
McMan, Carter, Okla. 100 D6 128
McMasterville, Que., Can. 1,738 *S11 66
McMechen, Marshall, W.Va. 2,999 B2 194
B4
McMillan, Luce, Mich. 300 C6 146
McMillan, Marshall, Okla. 10 D7 128
McMillan, Knox, Tenn. E9 190
McMillan, lake, N.Mex. F6 126
McMillan Manor, Ventura, Calif. 1,193 *E4 94
McMinn, co., Tenn. 33,662 C7 190
McMinnville, Yamhill, Oreg. 7,656 B3 96
McMinnville, Warren, Tenn. 9,013 C6 190
McMullen, co., Tex. 1,116 E6 130
McMunn, Man., Can. 20 F5 60
McMurray, Alta., Can. 1,110 B7 54
McMurray, Skagit, Wash. 75 A4 98
McNab, Hempstead, Ark. 142 D3 170
McNair, Jefferson, Miss. 60 D1 184
McNair, Harris, Tex. 1,880 *E8 130
McNairy, McNairy, Tenn. 100 C3 190
McNairy, co., Tenn. 18,085 C3 190
McNary, Apache, Ariz. 1,608 D6 124
McNary, Rapides, La. 250 D3 180
McNary, Umatilla, Oreg. 350 B7 96
McNary, dam, Oreg., Wash. B7 96
D7 98
McNary Junction, Navajo, Ariz. 15 D6 124
McNeal, Cochise, Ariz. 40 G6 124
McNeal, Calhoun, Fla. 250 *A5 174
McNeil, Columbia, Ark. 746 D3 170
McNeil, isl., Wash. D2 98
McNeill, Pearl River, Miss. 350 E3 184
McNeill, mtn., B.C., Can. C7 52
MacNutt, Sask., Can. 228 E7 58
McNutt, isl., N.S., Can. F4 70
Maco, Bol. B1 246
Macocola, Ang. A3 420
Macomb, McDonough, Ill. 12,135 C3 138
Macomb, Pottawatomie, Okla. 76 C6 128
Macomb, co., Mich. 405,804 G9 146
Mâcon, Fr. 22,393 D6 278
Macon, Bibb, Ga. 69,764 D3 176
(*170,700)
Macon, Macon, Ill. 1,229 D5 138
Macon, Noxubee, Miss. 2,432 B4 184
Macon, Macon, Mo. 4,547 B5 150
Macon, Franklin, Nebr. 30 *D7 152
Macon, Fayette, Tenn. 50 C2 190
Macon, co., Ala. 26,717 C4 168
Macon, co., Ga. 13,170 D2 176
Macon, co., Ill. 118,257 D4 138
Macon, co., Mo. 16,473 B5 150
Macon, co., N.C. 14,935 B2 186
Macon, co., Tenn. 12,197 B5 190
Macon, bayou, Ark. D5 170
Macon, bayou, La. B4 180
Macopin, Passaic, N.J. A4 210
Macoun, Sask., Can. 191 F6 58
Macoun, lake, Sask., Can. B6 58
Macoupin, co., Ill. 43,524 D3 138
Macoupin, creek, Ill. D3 138
Macouria, Fr.Gu. 77 E6 256
Macovane, Moz. D7 421
McPhail, riv., Man., Can. D4 60
McPhee, Montezuma, Colo. E2 106
McPherson, McPherson, Kans. 9,996 D6 144
McPherson, co., Kans. 24,285 D6 144
McPherson, co., Nebr. 735 C4 152
McPherson, co., S.Dak. 5,821 B6 158
McQuady, Breckenridge, Ky. 100 C4 178
Macquarie, riv., Austl. E9 432
McQueeney, Guadalupe, Tex. 900 B7 130
McRae, White, Ark. 428 B5 170
McRae, Telfair, Ga. 2,738 D4 176
McRae, Big Horn, Mont. E9 110
McRoberts, Letcher, Ky. 1,363 C8 178
Macroom, Ire. 2,186 J4 273
Macrorie, Sask., Can. 152 E4 58
McShan, Pickens, Ala. 75 B1 168
McSherrystown, Adams, Pa. 2,839 D4 214
McTaggart, Sask., Can. 73 F5 58
McTavish, Man., Can 120 F4 60
MacTier, Ont., Can. 515 O21 64
Macuelizo, Hond. 913 C3 228
Macungie, Lehigh, Pa. 1,266 C6 214
McVeigh, Pike, Ky. 800 C8 178
McVille, Attala and Leake, Miss. 50 C3 184
McVille, Nelson, N.Dak. 551 C7 154
Macwahoc, Aroostook, Maine 100 C4 204
(165*)
McWilliams, Wilcox and Monroe, Ala. 550 D2 168
Macy, Miami, Ind. 328 B3 140
Macy, Thurston, Nebr. 203 B9 152
Mad, riv., Calif. B2 94
Mad, riv., N.H. D3 208
Mad, riv., Ohio C3 156
Mad, riv., Vt. C3 218
Madaba, Tan. D6 414
Madagascar, isl., Afr. C9 421
Mada'in Ṣāliḥ, Sau.Ar. B2 383
Madan, Bul. 5,858 C2 317
Madang, N.Gui. 379 F11 359
Madaoua, Niger 2,100 D6 408
Madari Hat, India D5 368
Madaripur, Pak. 21,693 L17 375
Madawaska, Ont., Can. 425 O23 64
Madawaska, Aroostook, Maine 4,035 A4 204
(5,507*)
Madawaska, co., N.B., Can. 36,988 B1 70
Madawaska, lake, Maine A4 204
Madawaska, riv., Ont., Can. O23 64
Madawaska, riv., Que., Can. Q16 66
Madaya, Bur. B3 362
Madbury, Strafford, N.H. 35 E5 208
(556*)
Maddaket, Nantucket, Mass. 250 *D7 206
Madden, Leake, Miss. 150 C3 184
Madden, Natrona, Wyo. C5 116
Maddens, Laurens, S.C. 50 C4 188
Maddock, Benson, N.Dak. 740 C6 154
Madeira, Hamilton, Ohio 6,744 D1 156
Madeira (Archipelago), prov., Port. 269,769 *C5 388
Madeira, isl., Atl.O. C5 388
Madeira, riv., Braz. G4 256
Madeira Beach, Pinellas, Fla. 3,943 *D8 174
Madelia, Watonwan, Minn. 2,190 G4 148
Madeline, Lassen, Calif. 60 B3 94
Madeline, isl., Wis. B3 160
Madera, Madera, Calif. 14,430 D3 94
Madera, Mex. 5,145 B4 224
Madera, Clearfield, Pa. 808 C3 214
Madera, co., Calif. 40,468 D4 94
Madhupur, India D4 368
Madhya Pradesh, state, India 26,071,637 D3 366
Madill, Marshall, Okla. 3,084 D7 128
Madimba, Con.L. D2 414
Madingou, Con.B. G7 409
Madison, Madison, Ala. 1,435 A3 168
Madison, St. Francis, Ark. 750 B6 170
Madison, Sask., Can. 107 E3 58
Madison, New Haven, Conn. 1,416 D5 202
(4,567*)
Madison, Madison, Fla. 3,239 A7 174
Madison, Morgan, Ga. 2,680 C3 176
Madison, Madison, Ill. 6,861 E3 138
Madison, Jefferson, Ind. 10,097 D4 140
Madison, Greenwood, Kans. 1,105 D7 144
Madison, Somerset, Maine 2,761 D3 204
(3,935*)
Madison, Dorchester, Md. 200 C7 182
Madison, Lac qui Parle, Minn. 2,380 F2 148
Madison, Madison, Miss. 703 C2 184
Madison, Monroe, Mo. 528 B5 150
Madison, Madison, Nebr. 1,513 C8 152
Madison, Carroll, N.H. 130 D4 208
(429*)
Madison, Essex, N.J. 15,122 B4 210
Madison, Rockingham, N.C. 1,912 A6 186
Madison, Lake, Ohio 1,347 A5 156
Madison, Oconee, S.C. (part of Graniteville) B2 188
Madison, Lake, S.Dak. 5,420 C8 158
Madison, Davidson, Tenn. 13,583 B5 190
E7
Madison, Madison, Va. 510 B6 192
Madison, Boone, W.Va. 2,215 C3 194
D5
Madison, Dane, Wis. 126,706 E4 160
(*179,200)
Madison, co., Ala. 117,348 A3 168
Madison, co., Ark. 9,068 B3 170
Madison, co., Fla. 14,154 A7 174
Madison, co., Ga. 11,246 B3 176
Madison, co., Idaho 9,417 F7 108
Madison, co., Ill. 224,689 E4 138
Madison, co., Ind. 125,819 B4 140
Madison, co., Iowa 12,295 C3 142
Madison, co., Ky. 33,482 C6 178
Madison, co., Miss. 32,904 C2 184
Madison, co., Mo. 9,366 D7 150
Madison, co., Mont. 5,211 E4 110
Madison, co., Nebr. 25,145 C8 152
Madison, co., N.Y. 54,635 C6 212
Madison, co., N.C. 17,217 B3 186
Madison, co., Ohio 26,454 C3 156
Madison, co., Tenn. 60,655 C3 190
Madison, co., Tex. 6,749 D8 130
Madison, co., Va. 8,187 B6 192
Madison, par., La. 16,444 B4 180
Madison, range, Mont. E5 110
Madison, riv., Mont., Wyo. E5 110
B2 116
Madison College, Davidson, Tenn. 700 E7 190
Madison Heights, Oakland, Mich. 33,343 *G8 146
Madison Heights, Amherst, Va. 3,000 C5 192
Madison Lake, Blue Earth, Minn. 477 G5 148
Madisonville, Hopkins, Ky. 13,110 C3 178
Madisonville, St. Tammany, La. 860 B7 180
D5
Madisonville, Monroe, Tenn. 1,812 C7 190
Madisonville, Madison, Tex. 2,324 D8 130
Madjene, Indon. E5 358
Madoc, Ont., Can. 1,325 P23 64
Madoc, Daniels, Mont. 23 B11 110
Madona, Sov.Un. 5,500 D6 332
Madraka, cape, Om. D6 383
Madras, Coweta, Ga. 200 C2 176
Madras, India 1,416,056 F4 366
Madras, Jefferson, Oreg. 1,515 C5 96
Madras, state, India 29,974,936 F3 366
Madre, mts., Mex. D7 225
Madre de Dios, dept., Peru 7,286 C3 245
Madre de Dios, isl., Chile H2 251
Madre de Dios, riv., Bol., Peru B1 246
C3 245
Madre Occidental, mts., Mex. B4 224
Madre Oriental, mts., Mex. B5 225
Madrid, Houston, Ala. 245 D4 168
Madrid, Boone, Iowa 2,286 A7 142
C4
Madrid, Breckinridge, Ky. 45 C4 178
Madrid, Perkins, Nebr. 271 D4 152
Madrid, Santa Fe, N.Mex. 474 C4 126
H7
Madrid, St. Lawrence, N.Y. 644 A6 212
Madrid, Sp. 1,848,901 B5 298
(*1,875,000)
Madrid, prov., Sp. 1,823,410 *B5 298
Madrideios, Sp. 8,227 C5 298
Madrūsah, Libya C2 394
Madura, India 361,781 G3 366
Madura, isl., Indon. F4 358
Maebashi, Jap. 171,265 F7 354
K15
Mae, Grant, Wash. B7 98
Mae Hong Son, Thai. 5,000 C3 362
Mae Hong Son, prov., Thai. 66,280 *C3 362
Maelamun, mtn., Thai. D3 362
Maelifell, Ice. L20 290
Maella, Sp. 3,005 B7 298
Maengsan, Kor. F13 348
Maeser, Uintah, Utah 929 C6 114
Maestra, mts., Cuba B6 232
Maevatanana, Malag. 6,660 C9 421
Ma'fan, Libya B2 394
Mafeking, Man., Can. 250 D2 60
Mafeking, U.S.Afr. 6,965 E5 420
Maffitt Village, New Hanover, N.C. 2,238 *C8 186
Mafia, isl., Tan. D6 414
Mafra, Braz. 8,603 K7 257
Mafra, Port. 3,096 C2 298
Maga, mtn., Tinian B7 436
Magadan, Sov.Un. 62,000 D17 329
Magadi, Ken. C6 414
Magadi, lake, Ken. C6 414
Magaguadavic, lake, N.B., Can. D2 70
Magalia, Butte, Calif. 125 C3 94
Magallanes, prov., Chile 55,119 H3 251
Maganga, Con.L. B4 414
Magangué, Col. 17,114 B2 244
Maganja da Costa, Moz. C7 421
Magaria, Niger D6 409
Magazine, Mobile, Ala. E1 168
Magazine, Logan, Ark. 463 B3 170
Magazine, mtn., Ark. B3 170
Magdalen, isl., Que., Can. Q10 66
Magdalena, Arg. 4,114 C4 252
Magdalena, Bol. 1,724 B2 246
Magdalena, Mex. 6,116 A3 224
Magdalena, Mex. K12 225
Magdalena, Socorro, N.Mex. 1,211 D3 126
Magdalena, dept., Col. 450,920 A2 244
Magdalena, isl., Chile F3 251
Magdalena, isl., Mex. C3 224
Magdalena, lake, Mex. C5 224
Magdalena, riv., Col. B2 244
Magdalena, riv., Mex. G9 224
Magdalen Islands, co., Que., Can. 11,556 *Q10 66
Magdeburg, Ger. 261,400 B4 286
Magee, Simpson, Miss. 2,039 D3 184
Magelang, Indon. 78,800 F4 358
Magellan, strait, Chile H3 251
Magenta, It. 16,000 C2 302
Mageröy, isl., Nor. A11 290
Maggard, Magoffin, Ky. 500 C7 178
Maggia, riv., Switz. B4 312
Maggie, Craig, Va. 25 C4 192
Maggiore, lake, It., Switz. B2 302
B4 312
Maghera, N.Ire. 1,345 G6 272
Magherafelt, N.Ire. 1,866 G6 272
Magic, res., Idaho F4 108
Magicienne, bay, Saipan B7 436
Maglaj, Yugo. 2,498 B4 316
Maglic, Yugo. 1,157 C5 316
Maglie, It. 12,800 E7 302
Magna, Salt Lake, Utah 6,442 C3 114
Magnesia, see Magnisia, prov., Grc.
Magness, Independence, Ark. 140 B5 170
Magnet, Hot Spring, Ark. 200 C4 170
D7
Magnet, Man., Can. 45 E3 60
Magnet, Rockdale, Ga. 300 B6 176
Magnet, Cedar, Nebr. 116 B8 152
Magnetawan, Ont., Can. 197 O21 64
Magnetawan, riv., Ont., Can. O20 64
Magnetic Springs, Union, Ohio 344 B3 156
Magnisia (Magnesia), prov., Grc. 153,808 B4 306
Magnitogorsk, Sov.Un. 311,000 B5 336
Magnolia, Marengo, Ala. 75 C2 168
Magnolia, Columbia, Ark. 10,651 D3 170
Magnolia, Kent, Del. 310 D4 172
Magnolia, Harrison, Iowa 215 C2 142
Magnolia, Larue, Ky. 300 C5 178
Magnolia, East Feliciana, La. D5 180
Magnolia, Harford, Md. 450 B7 182
Magnolia, Essex, Mass. A6 206
C4
Magnolia, Rock, Minn. 280 H2 148
Magnolia, Pike, Miss. 2,083 D2 184
Magnolia, Gloucester, N.J. 4,199 D2 210
Magnolia, Duplin, N.C. 629 C7 186
Magnolia, Stark and Carroll, Ohio 1,596 B5 156
Magnolia, Montgomery, Tex. 800 D8 130
Magnolia, Nansemond, Va. 160 A8 192
Magnolia, Morgan, W.Va. B6 194
Magnolia Springs, Baldwin, Ala. 225 E2 168
Magoari, cape, Braz. F7 256
Magoffin, co., Ky. 11,156 C7 178
Magog, Que., Can. 12,720 S12 66
Magomaj, lake, Swe. D6 290
Magothy, riv., Md. B6 182
Magou, Niger D5 408
Magra, India I9 366
Magrath, Alta., Can. 1,382 F6 54
Magruder, mtn., Nev. F4 112
Magude, Moz. D6 421
Magwe, Bur. 13,270 B2 362
Mahābad (Saujbulagh), Iran 12,858 B1 379
Mahabo, Malag. 1,840 D8 421
Mahagi, Con.L. B5 414
Mahaicony, Br.Gu. 1,179 D5 256
Mahajan, India C1 368
Mahakam, riv., Indon. E5 358
Mahalapye, Bech. 2,453 D4 420
Mahalla el Kobra, Eg., U.A.R. 115,758 A3 395
Mahameru, mtn., Indon. F4 358
Mahan, Fayette, W.Va. 800 *C3 194
Mahanadi, riv., India D4 366
Mahanoro, Malag. 3,436 C9 421
Mahanoy City, Schuylkill, Pa. 8,536 C5 214
Maha Sarakham, Thai. C4 362
Maha Sarakham, prov., Thai. 390,294 *C4 362
Mahaska, Washington, Kans. 160 C6 144
Mahaska, co., Iowa 23,602 C5 142
Mahbubnagar, India 23,827 E3 366
Mahd'adh Dhahab, Sau.Ar. C3 383
Mahe, India 19,600 F3 366
Mahenge, Tan. 1,180 D6 414
Mahgara, isl., Eg., U.A.R. C2 382
Mahi, riv., India D2 366
Mahia, pen., N.Z. C6 437
Mahiganj, Pak. K16 375
Mahitahi, N.Z. 19 E2 437
Mahmutbey, Tur. F12 307
Mahnomen, Mahnomen, Minn. 1,462 D3 148
Mahnomen, co., Minn. 6,341 D3 148
Mahoba, India D2 368
Mahola, Sussex, N.J. A3 210
Mahomet, Champaign, Ill. 1,367 C5 138
Mahón, Sp. 15,732 C9 298
Mahone, bay, N.S., Can. E5 70
Mahone Bay, N.S., Can. 1,109 E5 70
Mahoning, co., Ohio 300,480 B6 156
Mahoosuc, range, Maine, N.H. D1 204
C4 208
Mahopac, Putnam, N.Y. 1,337 D8 212
Mahsama, Eg., U.A.R. D3 382
Mahtomedi, Washington, Minn. 2,127 F7 148
Mahukona, Hawaii, Haw. 100 C6 86
Mahunda, Moz. B7 421
Mahuta, Tan. E6 414
Mahwah, Bergen, N.J. 3,200 A4 210
Maidan Gil, salt lake, Iran D4 379
Maiden, Catawba, N.C. 2,039 B4 186
Maidenhead, Eng. 29,500 J12 273
Maiden Rock, Pierce, Wis. 189 D1 160
Maidstone, Sask., Can. 555 D3 58
Maidstone, Eng. 55,500 J13 273
Maidstone, Essex, Vt. 50 *B5 218
(78*)
Maidstone, lake, Vt. B5 218
Maidsville, Monongalia, W.Va. 750 B5 194
Maiduguri, Nig. 54,646 D7 409
Maigualide, mts., Ven. D6 240
Maihar, India D3 368
Maikala, range, India E3 368
Maiko, riv., Con.L. C4 414
Maikoor, isl., Indon. F8 359
Maili, pt., Haw. G9 86
Maillot, Alg. A4 402
Maimana, Afg. 25,698 B3 374
Maimana, prov., Afg. *A3 374
Main, entrance, N.Z. J11 437
Main, pass, La. E6 180
Main, riv., Ger. D3 286
Main à Dieu, N.S., Can. 210 C10 70
Main Centre, Sask., Can. 65 E4 58
Maine, Broome, N.Y. 600 C5 212
Maine, former prov., Fr. 682,000 C3 278
Maine, state, U.S. 969,265 B13 77
204
Maine-et-Loire, dept., Fr. 518,241 *D3 278
Mainé-Soroa, Nig. D7 409
Mainland (Orkney Is.), isl., Scot. B9 272
Mainland (Shetland Is.), isl., Scot. A11 272
Mainland, riv., Man., Can. D5 60
Mainpur, India E3 368
Mainpuri, India D2 368
Main South West Miramichi, riv., N.B., Can. C3 70
Maintirano, Malag. 2,594 C8 421
Main Topsail, mtn., Newf., Can. F7 72
Mainz (Mayence), Ger. 117,000 D3 286
Maipú, Arg. 5,469 C4 252
Maiquetia, Ven. 38,568 A5 240
Maire, strait, Arg. I4 251
Mairum, Pak. E3 375

Maisi, cape, Cuba		B7	232
Maisons-Alfort, Fr.	40,358	I10	278
Maisons-Laffitte, Fr.	15,481	I9	278
Mait, Som.		C6	398
Maitland, Austl.	21,331	E10	432
Maitland, N.S., Can.	397	D6	70
Maitland, Ont., Can.	200	P25	64
Maitland (Lake Maitland), Orange, Fla.	3,570	C9	174
Maitland, Holt, Mo.	427	A2	150
Maitland, McDowell, W.Va.	200	*D3	194
Maize, Sedgwick, Kans.	623	A5	144
Maizuru, Jap.	92,839	G5	354
		L11	
Majagual, Col.	1,516	B2	244
Majel, Kiowa, Kans.	25	*E4	144
Majestic, Pike, Ky.	503	C8	178
Maji, Eth.		D4	398
Majijo, peak, Ponape		A2	436
Majmaah, Sau.Ar.		B4	383
Major, Sask., Can.	131	E3	58
Major, co., Okla.	7,808	B5	128
Majorsville, Marshall, W.Va.	100	B2	194
Majra, Afg.	5,000	B3	374
Majunga, Malag.	32,200	C9	421
Majunga, prov., Malag.		C9	421
Makaha, Honolulu, Haw.	2,720	G9	86
Makahuena, pt., Haw.		B2	86
Makalado, Con.L.		C4	414
Mak'alē, Eth.		C4	398
Makanalua, pen., Haw.		B5	86
Makapala, Hawaii, Haw.	100	C6	86
Makapuu, pt., Haw.		B4	86
Makarska, Yugo.	2,547	C3	316
Makaryev, Sov.Un.	10,200	D14	332
Makasar, Indon.	360,000	F5	358
Makassar, strait, Indon.		E6	358
Makat, Sov.Un.	3,500	C4	336
Makawao, Maui, Haw.	950	C5	86
Makaweli, Kauai, Haw.	600	B2	86
Mak'edalā, Eth.		C4	398
Makena, Maui, Haw.	20	C5	86
Makeyevka, Sov.Un.	358,000	H11	332
		S21	
Makhachkala, Sov.Un.	119,000	D3	336
Makhfar al Quwayrah, Jordan		E6	382
Makhlata, Bul.	6,679	B2	317
Makin, isl., Pac.O.		C3	436
Makinak, Man., Can.	135	E3	60
Makinsk, Sov.Un.		B8	336
Makkah, see Mecca, Sau.Ar.			
Makkinga, Neth.	443	B5	282
Makkovik, Newf., Can.	75	D10	72
Makkum, Neth.	2,086	A4	282
Makläppen, pt., Swe.		F4	292
Maknassy, Tun.	6,028	B5	402
Makó, Hung.	34,000	C5	320
Makokou, Gabon		F7	409
Makongai, isl., Fiji		E6	436
Makoti, Ward, N.Dak.	214	C4	154
Makoua, Con.B.		G8	409
Maków, Pol.	2,642	B5	325
Makran, range, Pak.		F4	375
Makrana, India		D1	368
Makri, India		E4	366
Makteïr, sand dunes, Maur.		B2	408
Mākū, Iran	10,687	A1	379
Makumbi, Con.L.		D3	414
Makump, S.L.		E2	408
Makung, Pescadores Is., For.		N10	349
Makurazaki, Jap.	35,546	I3	354
Makurdi, Nig.	16,713	E6	409
Makushin, vol., Alsk.		E5	84
Mal, bay, Ire.		I3	273
Mala, pt., Pan.		G8	228
Malabar, Brevard, Fla.	169	D10	174
Malabar, coast, India		F2	366
Mal Abrigo, Ur.		B4	252
Malacca, Mala.	69,865	G4	362
Malacca, state, Mala.	291,233	*G4	362
Malacca, strait, Asia		D2	358
Malad City, Oneida, Idaho	2,274	G6	108
Málaga, Col.	6,022	B2	244
Malaga, Gloucester, N.J.	200	D2	210
Malaga, Eddy, N.Mex.	50	F6	126
Málaga, Sp.	274,847	D4	298
Málaga, prov., Sp.	756,083	*D4	298
Málaga, bay, Sp.		D4	298
Malagasy, country, Afr.	4,918,000	H11	388
			421
Malagón, Sp.	9,795	C5	298
Malaimbandy, Malag.		D9	421
Malaita, isl., Solomon		E2	436
Malakal, Sud.	9,680	D3	398
Malakoff, Fr.	28,876	I10	278
Malakoff, Henderson, Tex.	1,657	C7	130
Malang, Indon.	281,700	F4	358
Malange, Ang.	12,815	A3	420
Malange, dist., Ang.	461,653	A3	420
Malanzán, Arg.		B2	252
Mälaren, riv., Swe.		B8	292
Malargüe, Arg.		C2	252
Malaspina, Arg.		F4	251
Malaspina, glacier, Alsk.		C7	84
Malåträsk, Swe.		D8	290
Malatya, Tur.	64,880	B8	307
Malatya, prov., Tur.	341,925	*B8	307
Malay, pen., Asia		E4	362
Malaya, Br. poss., Asia	6,276,915	I12	340
			362
Malaya Vishera, Sov.Un.	14,000	C9	332
Malaybalay, Phil.	2,267	C7	358
Malāyer, Iran	32,357	B2	379
Malazgirt, Tur.	1,931	B10	307
Malbaie, riv., Que., Can.		Q14	66
Malbon, Austl.		C8	432
Malbork, Pol.	20,000	A4	325
Malchin, Ger.	6,825	B5	286
Malcolm, Austl.		D4	432
Malcolm, Charles, Md.	90	C6	182
Malcolm, Lancaster, Nebr.	116	*D9	152
Malcom, Poweshiek, Iowa	416	C5	142
Malden, Porter, Ind.	100	A2	140
Malden, Middlesex, Mass.	57,676	C3	206
Malden, Dunklin, Mo.	5,007	E8	150
Malden, Whitman, Wash.	292	B9	98
Malden, Kanawha, W.Va.	1,000	C6	194
Malden, isl., Pac.O.		C4	436
Maldive Islands, Br. poss., Asia	85,000	G2	366
Maldonado, Ur.	8,000	B5	252
Maldonado, dept., Ur.	67,015	B4	252
Maléa, cape, Grc.		C4	306
Malehow, Ger.	8,049	B5	286
Malema (Entre Rios), Moz.		B7	421
Malemba-Nkulu, Con.L.		D4	414
Maler Kotla, India	32,575	C1	368
Malesherbes, Fr.		C5	278
Malesus, Madison, Tenn.	350	C3	190
Malha, Sud.		B2	398
Malheur, Malheur, Oreg.		C9	96
Malheur, co., Oreg.	22,764	D9	96
Malheur, lake, Oreg.		D8	96
Malheur, riv., Oreg.		D9	96
Mali, Guinea		D2	408
Mali, country, Afr.	3,650,000	E6	388
			409
Malibu, Los Angeles, Calif.	2,000	C4	94
		E4	
Maligne, lake, Alta., Can.		D4	54
Målillå, Swe.	3,048	D6	292
Malin, Ire.	105	F5	272
Malin, Klamath, Oreg.	568	E5	96
Malin, head, Ire.		F5	272
Malina de Segura, Sp.	8,578	C6	298
Malinau, Indon.		D5	358
Malin Beg, Ire.		G4	273
Malindi, Ken.	3,292	C7	414
Málinec, Czech.	6,551	B4	324
Malino, Sov.Un.	1,000	O19	332
Malinta, Henry, Ohio	339	A2	156
Maliseet, N.B., Can.		C2	70
Maliwun, Bur.		E3	362
Maljamar, Lea, N.Mex.	350	F7	126
Malkara, Tur.	6,025	A2	307
Malko Tŭrnovo, Bul.	3,746	C3	317
Mallaig, Alta., Can.		C7	54
Mallaig, Scot.		E7	272
Mallanwan, India		D3	368
Mallard, Palo Alto, Iowa	431	B3	142
Malleco, prov., Chile	159,419	E3	250
Mallet Creek, Medina, Ohio	305	A5	156
Malletts, bay, Vt.		B2	218
Mallorca, isl., Sp.		C8	298
Mallory, Logan, W.Va.	1,133	D3	194
Mallorytown, Ont., Can.		P25	64
Mallow, Ire.	5,729	I4	273
Mallow, Alleghany, Va.	300	*C5	192
Malmberget, Swe.	5,116	C9	290
Malmedy, Bel.	5,977	D5	282
Malmesbury, U.S.Afr.	6,391	F3	420
Malmkoping, Swe.	3,772	B7	292
Malmo, Saunders, Nebr.	135	C9	152
		D1	
Malmö, Swe.	209,473	F4	292
	(*208,107)		
Malmöhus, co., Swe.	601,974	F4	292
Maloarkhangelsk, Sov.Un.	13,300	F11	332
Maloelap, atoll, Marshall		A4	436
Maloja, pass, Switz.		B5	312
Malone, Randolph, Ala.	100	B4	168
Malone, Ont., Can.	50	P23	64
Malone, Jackson, Fla.	661	A5	174
Malone, Marshall, Miss.		A3	184
Malone, Franklin, N.Y.	8,737	A7	212
Malone, Grays Harbor, Wash.	250	C3	98
Malone, Fond du Lac, Wis.	50	B5	160
Maloneyville, Knox, Tenn.	250	E9	190
Malonton, Man., Can.	50	E4	60
Malott, Okanogan, Wash.	350	A7	98
Maloy, Ringgold, Iowa	68	D3	142
Maloyaroslavets, Sov.Un.	18,000	E11	332
Malpeque, bay, PEI., Can.		C6	70
Malpura, India		D1	368
Målsely, Nor.		B8	290
Malshaya Uzen, riv., Sov.Un.		C3	336
Malta, Lake, Colo.	25	*C4	106
Malta, Cassia, Idaho	250	G5	108
Malta, De Kalb, Ill.	782	B5	138
Malta, Phillips, Mont.	2,239	B9	110
Malta, Morgan, Ohio	983	C5	156
Malta, Br. poss., Eur.	305,991	E6	266
Malta Bend, Saline, Mo.	338	B4	150
Maltahöhe, S.W.Afr.	700	D3	420
Malton, Ont., Can.	1,400	Q21	64
		R21	
Malung, Swe.	1,396	A4	292
Malungstors, Swe.		F5	291
Malvern, Geneva, Ala.	213	D4	168
Malvern, Hot Spring, Ark.	9,566	C4	170
		D7	
Malvern, Eng.	24,600	I10	273
Malvern, Mills, Iowa	1,193	C2	142
Malvern, Carroll, Ohio	1,320	B5	156
Malvern, Chester, Pa.	2,268	A6	214
		C6	
Malverne, Nassau, N.Y.	9,968	*E3	212
Malwood, Ont., Can.		P25	64
Malyy, isl., Sov.Un.		B16	329
Malyye Derbety, Sov.Un.	900	I15	332
Mamala, bay, Haw.		G9	86
Mamanguape, Braz.	6,334	B3	258
Mamantel, Mex.	89	D7	225
Mamanutha, is., Fiji		E6	436
Mamaroneck, Westchester, N.Y.	17,673	D2	212
Mamba, Jap.	6,635	K14	354
Mambasa, Con.L.		B4	414
Mamberamo, riv., Neth. N.Gui.		E9	359
Mambone, Moz.		D7	421
Mamche Bazar, Nep.		D4	368
Ma-Me-O Beach, Alta., Can.	137	D6	54
Mamers, Fr.	5,086	C4	278
Mamers, Harnett, N.C.	150	B7	186
Mamfe, Br.Cam.	5,107	E6	409
Mamie, Currituck, N.C.	100	A10	186
Mamina, Chile		B4	250
Mammoth, Pinal, Ariz.	1,913	F5	124
Mammoth Spring, Fulton, Ark.	825	A5	170
Mammoth, Kanawha, W.Va.	800	C3	194
		C6	
Mammoth Cave, natl. park, Ky.		C4	178
Mammoth, Juab, Utah	100	D3	114
Mamor, India		B2	368
Mamoré, riv., Bol.		B1	246
Mamou, Guinea	6,700	D2	408
Mamou, Evangeline, La.	2,928	D3	180
Mampawah, Indon.		D3	358
Mampong, Ghana	3,948	E4	408
Mamry, lake, Pol.		A5	325
Mam Soul, mtn., Scot.		D8	272
Mamudju, Indon.		E5	358
Man, I.C.	4,600	E3	408
Man, Logan, W.Va.	1,486	D3	194
		D5	
Man, riv., Sask., Can.		D6	58
Mana, Fr.Gu.	700	D6	256
Mana, Kauai, Haw.	225	A2	86
Manacapuru, Braz.	1,695	F4	256
Manacor, Sp.	18,702	C8	298
Manado, Indon.	62,000	D6	358
Managua, Nic.	109,352	D4	228
Managua, lake, Nic.		D5	228
Manahawkin, Ocean, N.J.	400	D4	210
Manakara, Malag.	6,200	D9	421
Manakin, Goochland, Va.	330	C7	192
Manalapan, Monmouth, N.J.	50	C4	210
Manama, Bahrain	39,648	B5	383
Mañana, Pan.		F8	228
Manana, isl., Haw.		G11	86
Mananara, Malag.	2,852	C9	421
Mananara, riv., Malag.		D9	421
Mananjary, Malag.	9,200	D9	421
Manantenina, Malag.	750	D9	421
Manantico, creek, N.J.		E3	210
Manaoba, isl., Solomon		E2	436
Manapire, riv., Ven.		B5	240
Manas, see Suilai, China			
Manasquan, Monmouth, N.J.	4,022	C4	210
Manasquan, riv., N.J.		C4	210
Manassa, Conejos, Colo.	831	E5	106
Manassas, Tattnall, Ga.	154	D4	176
Manassas, Prince William, Va.	3,555	A6	192
		B7	
Manassas Park, Prince William, Va.	5,342	*B7	192
Manatee, co., Fla.	69,168	D8	174
Manatee, riv., Fla.		D8	174
Manati, P.R.	10,092	C11	233
Manaus, Braz.	89,612	F4	256
Manavgat, Tur.	1,265	C4	307
Manawa, Waupaca, Wis.	1,037	D5	160
Manawan, lake, Sask., Can.		C6	58
Mancelona, Antrim, Mich.	1,141	E6	146
Mancha, reg., Sp.		C5	298
Manchac, bayou, La.		B5	180
Mancha Real, Sp.	9,534	D5	298
Manchaug, Worcester, Mass.	900	B4	206
Manche, dept., Fr.	446,860	*C3	278
Manchester, Walker, Ala.	175	B2	168
Manchester, Hartford, Conn.	42,102	B5	202
Manchester, Eng.	686,000	H10	273
	(*1,975,000)		
Manchester, Meriwether, Ga.	4,115	D2	176
Manchester, Scott, Ill.	282	D3	138
Manchester, Delaware, Iowa	4,402	B6	142
Manchester, Dickinson, Kans.	153	C6	144
Manchester, Clay, Ky.	1,868	C7	178
Manchester, Kennebec, Maine	300	D3	204
	(1,068▲)		
Manchester, Carroll, Md.	1,108	A6	182
Manchester, Essex, Mass.	3,932	A6	206
		C4	
Manchester, Washtenaw, Mich.	1,568	G7	146
Manchester, Freeborn, Minn.	131	*H5	148
Manchester, St. Louis, Mo.	2,021	B7	150
Manchester, Hillsboro, N.H.	88,282	F4	208
	(*111,900)		
Manchester, Ontario, N.Y.	1,344	C4	212
Manchester, Adams, Ohio	2,172	D3	156
Manchester, Grant, Okla.	162	B5	128
Manchester, York, Pa.	1,454	C5	214
Manchester, Kingsbury, S.Dak.	70	C8	158
Manchester, Coffee, Tenn.	3,930	C5	190
Manchester, Bennington, Vt.	403	E2	218
	(2,470▲)		
Manchester, Kitsap, Wash.	700	B4	98
Manchester Center, Bennington, Vt.	600	E2	218
Manchester Depot, Bennington, Vt.	800	E2	218
Manchuria, reg., China	46,342,000	B13	346
Manco, Pike, Ky.	300	C8	178
Mancos, Montezuma, Colo.	832	E2	106
Mancos, riv., Colo.		E2	106
Mandabe, Malag.		D8	421
Mandaguari, Braz.	6,387	J6	257
Mandal, Afg.	10,000	C1	374
Mandal, Nor.	4,514	G2	291
Mandalay, Bur.	190,000	B3	362
Mandali, Iraq	9,722	C6	378
Mandan, Morton, N.Dak.	10,525	D5	154
Mandar, gulf, Indon.		E5	358
Mandara, mts., Cam.		E7	409
Mandarin, Duval, Fla.	400	A9	174
		B10	
Mandera, Ken.		B7	414
Manderfeld, Bel.	1,276	D5	282
Manderfield, Beaver, Utah	70	E3	114
Manderson, Shannon, S.Dak.	55	D3	158
Manderson, Big Horn, Wyo.	167	B5	116
Mandeville, Miller, Ark.	350	D3	170
Mandeville, Que., Can.	380	R11	66
Mandeville, St. Tammany, La.	1,740	B7	180
		D5	
Mandi, India		C2	368
Mandimba, Rh.&Nya.		B6	421
Mandla, India		E3	368
Mándra, Grc.	3,594	B4	306
Mandritsara, Malag.		C9	421
Mandsaur, India	34,541	D1	368
Manduria, It.	22,500	E6	302
Mandvi, India	29,305	D1	366
Manfalût, Eg., U.A.R.	20,939	B3	395
Manfred, Wells, N.Dak.	79	C6	154
Manfredonia, It.	30,000	E5	302
Manfredonia, gulf, It.		E6	302
Manga, Braz.		C2	258
Mangaldai, India		D6	368
Mangalia, Rom.	4,792	C5	321
Mangalore, India	117,083	F2	366
Mangas, mtn., N.Mex.		E2	126
Mangham, Richland, La.	521	B4	180
Mangkalihat, cape, Indon.		D5	358
Mangohick, King William, Va.	50	C7	192
Mangoky, riv., Malag.		D8	421
Mangole, isl., Indon.		E7	358
Mangonia Park, Palm Beach, Fla.	594	*E10	174
Mangrove, pt., Fla.		C6	174
Mangrove, swamp, Fla.		F10	174
Mangualde, Port.	3,093	B3	298
Manguéni, plat., Niger		B7	409
Mangum, Greer, Okla.	3,950	D4	128
Mangyshlak, pen., Sov.Un.		D4	336
Manhasset, Nassau, N.Y.	10,000	D3	212
Manhattan, Will, Ill.	1,117	B6	138
		F2	
Manhattan, Riley, Kans.	22,993	C7	144
Manhattan, Gallatin, Mont.	889	E5	110
Manhattan, Nye, Nev.	40	E4	112
Manhattan, see New York, co., N.Y.			
Manhattan Beach, Los Angeles, Calif.	33,934	C5	94
Manhattan Beach, Tillamook, Oreg.	150	*B3	96
Manheim, Lancaster, Pa.	4,790	C5	214
Manheim, Preston, W.Va.	285	B5	194
Manhica, Moz.		E6	421
Manhuaçu, Braz.	6,050	E2	258
Manica E Sofala, prov., Moz.		C6	421
Manicoré, Braz.	2,099	G4	256
Manicuare, Ven.		A6	240
Manigotagan, Man., Can.	20	E4	60
Manigotagan, lake, Man., Can.		E5	60
Manigotagan, riv., Man., Can.		E4	60
Manihiki, is., Pac.O.		D4	436
Manila, Navajo, Ariz.	25	D5	124
Manila, Mississippi, Ark.	1,753	B6	170
Manila, Phil.	983,906	B6	358
	(*1,510,000)		
Manila, Daggett, Utah	329	C6	114
Manila, Boone, W.Va.	300	D5	194
Manila, bay, Phil.		B6	358
Manilla, Rush, Ind.	400	C4	140
Manilla, Crawford, Iowa	939	C2	142
Manipur, ter., India	577,635	*D6	366
Manipur, riv., India		D6	368
Manisa, Tur.	45,484	B2	307
Manisa, prov., Tur.	564,457	*B3	307
Manistee, Manistee, Mich.	8,324	E5	146
Manistee, co., Mich.	19,042	E5	146
Manistee, riv., Mich.		E6	146
Manistique, Schoolcraft, Mich.	4,875	D5	146
Manistique, lake, Mich.		C6	146
Manistique, riv., Mich.		C5	146
Manito, Mason, Ill.	1,093	C4	138
Manito, lake, Sask., Can.		D3	58
Manitoba, prov., Can.	894,000	F9	48
			60
Manitoba, lake, Man., Can.		E3	60
		F6	
Manitou, Man., Can.	795	F3	60
Manitou, Tillman, Okla.	269	D5	128
Manitou, isl., Mich.		B4	146
Manitou Beach, Sask., Can.	164	E5	58
Manitou Beach, Lenawee, Mich.	1,544	*H7	146
Manitoulin, dist., Ont., Can.	11,060	O18	64
Manitoulin, isl., Ont., Can.		O18	64
Manitou Springs, El Paso, Colo.	3,626	D6	106
Manitowaning, Ont., Can.	700	O19	64
Manitowish, Iron, Wis.	50	B3	160
Manitowish Waters, Vilas, Wis.	200	B4	160
Manitowoc, Manitowoc, Wis.	32,275	B6	160
		D6	
Manitowoc, co., Wis.	75,215	D6	160
Manitowoc, riv., Wis.		B6	160
Manitowoc Rapids, Manitowoc, Wis.	400	B6	160
Maniwaki, Que., Can.	5,399	R9	66
Maniya (Oasis), Iraq		D5	378
Manizales, Col.	147,210	B1	244
Manja, Malag.	2,253	D8	421
Manjacaze, Moz.		D6	421
Manjimup, Austl.	2,223	E3	432
Manjra, riv., India		E3	366
Mankato, Jewell, Kans.	1,231	C5	144
Mankato, Blue Earth, Minn.	23,797	G5	148
Mankono, I.C.	7,200	E3	408
Mankota, Sask., Can.	461	F4	58
Mankoya, Rh.&Nya.	2,500	B4	420
Manley, Cass, Nebr.	113	E3	152
Manlius, Bureau, Ill.	374	B4	138
Manlius, Onondaga, N.Y.	1,997	B6	212
Manlléu, Sp.	6,396	A8	298
Manly, Worth, Iowa	1,425	A4	142
Manly, Moore, N.C.	239	B6	186
Mann, ranges, Austl.		D5	432
Mannar, Cey.	7,000	G3	366
Mannar, gulf, India		G3	366
Mannboro, Amelia, Va.	25	C7	192
Mannford, Creek, Okla.	358	B7	128
Mannheim, Ger.	290,700	D3	286
	(*550,000)		
Manning, Dallas, Ark.	300	C4	170
Manning, Alta., Can.	726	B4	54
Manning, Carroll, Iowa	1,676	C2	142
Manning, Dunn, N.Dak.	50	C3	154
Manning, Washington, Oreg.	40	*B3	96
Manning, Clarendon, S.C.	3,917	D8	188
Manning, Angelina, Tex.	715	D8	130
Manning, strait, Solomon		E1	436
Mannington, Christian, Ky.	500	C3	178
Mannington, Marion, W.Va.	2,996	A6	194
		B4	
Manns, creek, W.Va.		D7	194
Mannsville, Taylor, Ky.	150	C5	178
Mannsville, Jefferson, N.Y.	446	B5	212
Mannsville, Johnston, Okla.	297	D7	128
Mannu, riv., It.		F2	302
Mannville, Alta., Can.	599	D7	54
Manokin, Somerset, Md.	80	D8	182
Manokin, riv., Md.		D8	182
Manokotak, Alsk.	120	*D6	84
Manokwari, Neth.N.Gui.		E8	359
Manombo, Malag.		D8	421
Manomet, pt., Mass.		C6	206
Manono, Con.L.	29,700	D4	414
Manor, Sask., Can.	275	F6	58
Manor, Ware, Ga.	500	E4	176
Manor, Westmoreland, Pa.	1,136	*C2	214
Manor, Travis, Tex.	766	D7	130
Manor, Clark, Wash.		D4	98

Marmora, Ont., Can. 1,428 P23 64
Marmora, Cape May, N.J. 500 E3 210
Marmora, pt., It. E2 302
Marne, Cass, Iowa 205 C2 142
Marne, Ottawa, Mich. 450 F6 146
Marne, dept., Fr. 415,141 *C6 278
Maro, reef, Haw. A5 86
Maroa, Macon, Ill. 1,235 C5 138
Maroantsetra, Malag. 4,412 C9 421
Maromokotro, mtn., Malag. B9 421
Maroni, riv., Sur. E6 256
Maros, riv., Hung. C5 320
Maroua, Cam. 30,000 D7 409
Marovoay, Malag. 12,200 C9 421
Marpi, mtn., Saipan B7 436
Marpleton, Braxton, W.Va. C4 194
Marpo, pt., Tinian C7 436
Marquam, Clackamas, Oreg. 100 B2 96
B4
Marquand, Madison, Mo. 392 D7 150
Marquesas, is., Pac.O. C5 436
Marquesas, keys, Fla. G8 174
Marquette, Man., Can. 60 E4 60
Marquette, Clayton, Iowa 572 A6 142
Marquette, McPherson, Kans. 607 D6 144
Marquette, Marquette, Mich. 19,824 C4 146
Marquette, Hamilton, Nebr. 210 D7 152
Marquette, Green Lake, Wis. 162 *E4 160
Marquette, co., Mich. 56,154 C4 146
Marquette, co., Wis. 8,516 E4 160
Marquette Heights, Tazewell, Ill. 2,517 *C4 138
Marquez, Valencia, N.Mex. 35 C3 126
Marquis, Sask., Can. 157 E5 58
Marra, mtn., Sud. C1 398
Marrakech, Mor. 215,312 B2 402
Marree, Austl. 206 D7 432
Marrero, Jefferson, La. 19,000 C7 180
Marromeu, Moz. 5,000 C7 421
Marroqui, pt., Sp. D4 298
Marrowbone, Cumberland, Ky. 200 D5 178
Mars, Butler, Pa. 1,522 C1 214
Mars, hill, Maine. B5 204
Mars, riv., Que., Can. P14 66
Marsá al 'Uwayjah (Anchorage), Libya A3 394
Marsabit, Ken. B6 414
Marsala, It. 31,700 (77,300▲) G4 302
Mars Bluff, Florence, S.C. C9 188
Marsden, Sask., Can. 176 D3 58
Marseillan, Fr. F5 278
Marseille, Fr. 661,492 F6 278
Marseilles, La Salle, Ill. 4,347 B5 138
Marsh, Pima, Ariz. 15 F5 124
Marsh, Dawson, Mont. 75 D12 110
Marsh, creek, Calif. A6 94
Marsh, creek, Mich. C5 146
Marsh, fork, W.Va. D6 194
Marsh, isl., La. E4 180
Marsh, lake, Minn. F2 148
Marshall, Searcy, Ark. 1,095 B4 170
Marshall, Sask., Can. 138 D3 58
Marshall, Clark, Ill. 3,270 D6 138
Marshall, Parke, Ind. 360 C2 140
Marshall, Lib. E2 408
Marshall, Calhoun, Mich. 6,736 G7 146
Marshall, Lyon, Minn. 6,681 G3 148
Marshall, Saline, Mo. 9,572 B4 150
Marshall, Madison, N.C. 926 B3 186
Marshall (New Marshall), Logan, Okla. 363 B6 128
Marshall, Harrison, Tex. 23,846 C8 130
Marshall, Fauquier, Va. 500 B7 192
Marshall, Spokane, Wash. 100 D8 98
Marshall, Dane, Wis. 736 E4 160
Marshall, Albany, Wyo. D7 116
Marshall, co., Ala. 48,018 A3 168
Marshall, co., Ill. 13,334 B4 138
Marshall, co., Ind. 32,443 A3 140
Marshall, co., Iowa 37,984 C4 142
Marshall, co., Kans. 15,598 C7 144
Marshall, co., Ky. 16,736 D2 178
Marshall, co., Minn. 14,262 C2 148
Marshall, co., Miss. 24,503 A3 184
Marshall, co., Okla. 7,263 D7 128
Marshall, co., S.Dak. 6,663 B8 158
Marshall, co., Tenn. 16,859 C5 190
Marshall, co., W.Va. 38,041 B4 194
Marshall, is., Pac.O. A4 436
Marshallberg, Carteret, N.C. 600 C9 186
Marshall Hall, Charles, Md. 20 C5 182
Marshall Islands, U.S. trust., Pac.O. 16,000 A4 436
Marshall Northeast, Harrison, Tex. 1,192 *C8 130
Marshallton, New Castle, Del. 1,800 B3 172
Marshallton, Chester, Pa. 2,316 *B5 214
Marshalltown, Marshall, Iowa 22,521 B5 142
Marshallville, Macon, Ga. 1,308 D3 176
Marshallville, Wayne, Ohio 611 B5 156
Marshes Siding, McCreary, Ky. 500 D6 178
Marshfield, Warren, Ind. 100 B2 140
Marshfield, Washington, Maine 100 (267▲) *D5 204
Marshfield, Plymouth, Mass. 1,500 (6,748▲) B6 206
Marshfield, Webster, Mo. 2,221 D5 150
Marshfield, Washington, Vt. 313 (891▲) C4 218
Marshfield, Wood, Wis. 14,153 D3 160
Marshfield Center, Plymouth, Mass. 100 E4 206
Marshfield Hills, Plymouth, Mass. 265 B6 206
E4
Mars Hill, Marion, Ind. 1,000 C3 140
D4
Mars Hill, Aroostook, Maine 1,458 (2,062▲) B5 204
Mars Hill, Madison, N.C. 1,574 B3 186
Marshland, Buffalo, Wis. 35 D2 160
Marsh Valley, Bannock, Idaho G6 108
Marshville, Union, N.C. 1,360 C5 186
Marshyhope, creek, Md. C8 182
Marsing, Owyhee, Idaho 555 F2 108
Marsland, Dawes, Nebr. 39 B2 152
Marstal, Den. 1,996 G1 292
Marsteller, Cambria, Pa. 958 C3 214
Marston, New Madrid, Mo. 631 E8 150
Marston, Richmond, N.C. 75 C6 186
Marstons Mills, Barnstable, Mass. 550 C7 206
Marstrand, Swe. 1,205 D2 292
Mart, McLennan, Tex. 2,197 D7 130
Martaban, Bur. 5,639 C3 362
Martaban, gulf, Bur. C3 362
Martapura, Indon. E4 358
Martel, Que., Can. 891 P13 66
Martel, Loudon, Tenn. 65 C7 190
Martelange, Bel. 1,593 E4 282
Martell, Lancaster, Nebr. 104 D9 152
Martell, Pierce, Wis. 150 D1 160
Martelle, Jones, Iowa 247 B6 142
Martensdale, Warren, Iowa 316 C4 142
Martha, Jackson, Okla. 243 D4 128
Marthasville, Warren, Mo. 339 C6 150
Martha's Vineyard, isl., Mass. D6 206
Marthaville, Natchitoches, La. 181 C2 180
Martigny-Ville, Switz. 3,487 B3 312
Martigues, Fr. 9,852 F6 278
Martin, Stephens, Ga. 209 B3 176
Martin, Floyd, Ky. 992 C8 178
Martin, Allegan, Mich. 483 G6 146
Martin, Sheridan, N.Dak. 146 C5 154
Martin, Allendale, S.C. 150 E6 188
Martin, Bennett, S.Dak. 1,184 D4 158
Martin, Weakley, Tenn. 4,750 B3 190
Martin, co., Fla. 16,932 D10 174
Martin, co., Ind. 10,608 D3 140
Martin, co., Ky. 10,201 C8 178
Martin, co., Minn. 26,986 H4 148
Martin, co., N.C. 27,139 B8 186
Martin, co., Tex. 5,068 C4 130
Martin, bay, Newf., Can. D8 72
Martin, dam, Ala. C4 168
Martin, lake, Ala. C4 168
Martin, pt., Alsk. A7 84
Martina [Franca], It. 25,100 E6 302
Martina, Missoula, Mont. 5 C2 110
Martin City, Flathead, Mont. 500 *B2 110
Martinez, Contra Costa, Calif. 9,604 C2 94
Martinez, Columbia, Ga. 2,000 C4 176
Martinique, Fr. poss., N.A. 258,000 E14 233
Martinique, isl., Win.Is. B5 236
Martinique, passage, W.I. E14 233
Martinniemi, Fin. D11 290
Martins, pond, Mass. C2 206
Martinsburg, Washington, Ind. 100 D3 140
Martinsburg, Keokuk, Iowa 172 C5 142
Martinsburg, see Sandy Hook, Ky.
Martinsburg, Montgomery, Md. 100 B5 182
Martinsburg Audrain, Mo. 330 B6 150
Martinsburg, Dixon, Nebr. 68 B9 152
Martinsburg, Blair, Pa. 1,772 C3 214
Martinsburg, Berkeley, W.Va. 15,179 B7 194
Martinsdale, Meagher, Mont. 150 D6 110
Martins Ferry, Belmont, Ohio 11,919 B6 156
Martins Pond, Middlesex, Mass. C2 206
Martin Springs, Marion, Tenn. C6 190
Martinsville, Clark, Ill. 1,351 D6 138
Martinsville, Morgan, Ind. 7,525 C3 140
Martinsville, Wayne, Mich. 2,100 G8 146
Martinsville, Copiah, Miss. 100 D2 184
Martinsville, Somerset, N.J. 1,700 B3 210
Martinsville, Clinton, Ohio 488 C3 156
Martinsville (Independent City), Va. 18,798 D5 192
Martinville, Faulkner, Ark. 25 B4 170
Martos, Sp. 21,552 D5 298
Martre, lake, N.W.Ter., Can. E7 48
Martwick, Muhlenberg, Ky. 300 C3 178
Marty, Charles Mix, S.Dak. 50 E7 158
Marūchāk, Afg. 5,000 B2 374
Mārūf, Afg. 5,000 D4 374
Marugame, Jap. 59,329 G4 354
Marum, Neth. 1,264 A5 282
Marumsco, creek, Md. E8 182
Marvast, Iran C4 379
Marvejols, Fr. E5 278
Marvel, Bibb, Ala. 500 B3 168
Marvel, La Plata, Colo. 100 E2 106
Marvel, cave, Mo. E4 150
Marvell, Phillips, Ark. 1,690 C6 170
Marvin, Grant, S.Dak. 93 B9 158
Marvin Terrace, St. Louis, Mo. 1,260 *C7 150
Marvine, mtn., Utah E4 114
Marvyn, Lee, Ala. 75 C4 168
Marwayne, Alta., Can. 337 D7 54
Mary, Sov.Un. 48,000 F8 328
Mary, lake, Minn. F3 148
Mary, lake, Miss. D1 184
Maryborough, Austl. 6,827 F8 432
Maryborough, Austl. 18,900 D10 432
Marydel, Caroline and Kent, Del., Md. 130 B8 182
Mary Esther, Okaloosa, Fla. 780 A4 174
Maryfield, Sask., Can. 456 F7 58
Maryhill, Klickitat, Wash. 75 D6 98
Maryland, state, U.S. 3,100,689 D11 77
182
Maryland, pt., Md. D5 182
Maryland Heights, St. Louis, Mo. 2,000 A8 150
Maryland Line, Baltimore, Md. 165 A6 182
Maryland Park, Prince Georges, Md. 1,000 C4 182
Marylhurst, Clackamas, Oreg. 875 *B2 96
Maryport, Eng. 12,500 G9 273
Mary Ridge, St. Louis, Mo. 631 *C7 150
Marys, riv., Nev. B6 112
Marystown, Newf., Can. 1,460 G8 72
Marysvale, Piute, Utah 354 E3 114
Marysville, Yuba, Calif. 9,553 C3 94
Marysville, B.C., Can. 930 F15 52
Marysville, N.B., Can. 2,538 D3 70
Marysville, Ont., Can. 125 P23 64
Marysville, Calhoun, Fla. 100 A5 174
Marysville, Fremont, Idaho 201 E7 108
Marysville, Marion, Iowa 113 C5 142
Marysville, Marshall, Kans. 4,143 C7 144
Marysville, St. Clair, Mich. 4,065 *G9 146
Marysville, Lewis and Clark, Mont. 79 D4 110
Marysville, Union, Ohio 4,952 B3 156
Marysville, Perry, Pa. 2,580 C5 214
Marysville, Snohomish, Wash. 3,117 A4 98
Marytown, McDowell, W.Va. 100 D3 194
Marytown, Fond du Lac, Wis. 130 B5 160
Maryus, Gloucester, Va. 200 C8 192
Maryville, Madison, Ill. 675 *E4 138
Maryville, Nodaway, Mo. 7,807 A3 150
Maryville, Charleston, S.C. 500 F3 188
Maryville, Georgetown, S.C. 600 E10 188
Maryville, Blount, Tenn. 10,348 C8 190
E9
Marzūq, Libya 2,853 B2 394
Marzūq, des., Libya C2 394
Masai Steppe, plat., Tan. C6 414
Masaka, Ug. C5 414
Masalembo-Besar, isl., Indon. F4 358
Masan, Kor. 129,986 H14 348
Masardis, Aroostook, Maine 250 (408▲) B4 204
Masaryktown, Hernando, Fla. 400 C8 174
Masash el Sirr (Oasis), Eg., U.A.R. D4 382
Masasi, Tan. 2,720 E6 414
Masatepe, Nic. 4,231 E4 228
Masaya, Nic. 16,743 E4 228
Masbate, Phil. 5,817 B6 358
Mascara, Alg. 39,830 A4 402
Mascoma, lake, N.H. D2 208
Mascoma, riv., N.H. D2 208
Mascot, Harlan, Nebr. 40 *D6 152
Mascot, Knox, Tenn. 1,500 B8 190
E10
Mascota, Mex. 4,711 C5 224
Mascotte, Lake, Fla. 702 *C9 174
Mascouche, Que., Can. 950 S11 66
Mascoutah, St. Clair, Ill. 3,625 E4 138
Maseru, Bas. 5,599 E5 420
Mashaki, Afg. 5,000 C5 374
Masham, Eng. 894 G11 273
Mashapaug, pond, Conn. A7 202
Mashhad, Iran 241,989 B5 379
Mashiz, Iran D4 379
Mashkel, riv., Iran D5 379
Mashkel, riv., Pak. F2 375
Mashonaland, prov., Rh.&Nya. C6 421
Mashpee, Barnstable, Mass. 250 (867▲) C7 206
Mashriqi, prov., Afg. *B6 374
Mashulaville, Noxubee, Miss. 150 B4 184
Masi-Manimba, Con.L. C2 414
Masindi, Ug. B5 414
Masira, gulf, Om. D6 383
Masira, isl., Om. C6 383
Masisea, Peru 1,742 B3 245
Masisi, Con.L. C4 414
Mask, lake, Ire. H3 273
Maskell, Dixon, Nebr. 54 B9 152
Maskinonge, Que., Can. 800 R11 66
Maskinonge, co., Que., Can. 20,870 R11 66
Masoala, cape, Malag. C10 421
Mason, Ingham, Mich. 4,522 G7 146
Mason, Lyon, Nev. 200 E2 112
Mason, Hillsboro, N.H. 50 (349▲) F3 208
Mason, Warren, Ohio 4,727 C1 156
C2
Mason, Okfuskee, Okla. 50 C7 128
Mason, Tipton, Tenn. 407 C2 190
Mason, Mason, Tex. 1,910 D6 130
Mason, Mason, W.Va. 1,005 B2 194
Mason, Bayfield, Wis. 100 B2 160
Mason, co., Ill. 15,193 C3 138
Mason, co., Ky. 18,454 B7 178
Mason, co., Mich. 21,929 E5 146
Mason, co., Tex. 3,780 D6 130
Mason, co., Wash. 16,251 B3 98
Mason, co., W.Va. 24,459 C3 194
Mason, range, B.C., Can. C10 52
Mason City, Mason, Ill. 2,160 C4 138
Mason City, Cerro Gordo, Iowa 30,642 A4 142
Mason City, Custer, Nebr. 277 C6 152
Mason City, Okanogan, Wash. (part of Coulee Dam) B8 98
Masonhall, Obion, Tenn. 200 B2 190
Masontown, Fayette, Pa. 4,730 D2 214
Masontown, Preston, W.Va. 841 B5 194
Masonville, Desha, Ark. 50 D5 170
Masonville, Larimer, Colo. 200 B5 106
Masonville, Delaware, Iowa 168 B6 142
Mass, Ontonagon, Mich. 500 C2 146
Massa, It. 39,800 C3 302
Massabesic, lake, N.H. F4 208
Massac, co., Ill. 14,341 F5 138
Massa-Carrara, prov., It. 205,800 *C3 302
Massachusetts, state, U.S. 5,148,578 C12 77
206
Massachusetts, bay, Mass. B6 206
Massacre, bay, Samoa E5 436
Massacre, lake, Nev. B2 112
Massafra, It. 18,000 E6 302
Massakori, Chad D8 409
Massa Marittima, It. 5,700 D3 302
Massangena, Moz. D7 421
Massanutten, mtn., Va. B6 192
Massapá, Braz. 4,601 A2 258
Massapequa, Nassau, N.Y. 30,000 E3 212
Massapequa Park, Nassau, N.Y. 19,904 *E3 212
Massapoag, pond, Mass. E2 206
Massaua, Eth. 17,000 B4 398
Massena, Cass, Iowa 456 C3 142
Massena, St. Lawrence, N.Y. 15,478 A7 212
Massénia, Chad D8 409
Masset, inlet, B.C., Can. D6 52
Massett, B.C., Can. 500 C6 52
Massey, Ont., Can. 1,068 S25 64
Massey, Kent, Md. 75 B8 182
Massif Central, mts., Fr. E5 278
Massillon, Stark, Ohio 31,236 B5 156
Massinga, Moz. D7 421
Massive, mtn., Colo. C4 106
Masson, Que., Can. 1,656 S9 66
Massy, Fr. J10 278
Masten, Kent, Del. 18 E3 172
Masters, Weld, Colo. 3 B6 106
Masterton, N.Z. 13,000 D5 437
Mastic, Suffolk, N.Y. 1,600 *D4 212
Mastic Beach, Suffolk, N.Y. 3,035 D4 212
Mastuj, Pak. A8 375
Mastung, Pak. 2,792 E5 375
Mastūrah, Sau.Ar. C2 383
Masuda, Jap. 57,883 G3 354
Masulipatnam, India 77,953 E4 366
Masuria, reg., Pol. B5 325
Masury, Trumbull, Ohio 5,900 A6 156
Mata Armilla, Arg. G3 251
Mata, Con.L. D3 414
Matabeleland, prov., Rh.&Nya. C5 420
Mataboor, Neth.N.Gui. E9 359
Matachewan, Ont., Can. R25 64
Mata de São João, Braz. 4,766 C3 258
Matadi, Con.L. 55,100 D1 414
Matador, Motley, Tex. 1,217 B5 130
Matagalpa, Nic. 10,323 D5 228
Matagorda, Coahoma, Miss. A2 184
Matagorda, co., Tex. 25,744 E8 130
Matagorda, bay, Tex. E7 130
Matagorda, isl., Tex. E7 130
Mataliele, U.S.Afr. F5 420
Matam, Sen. 2,400 C2 408
Matamā, Eth. C4 398
Matamoras, Pike, Pa. 2,087 B7 214
Matamoros, Mex. 10,156 B5 224
Matamoros, Mex. 45,737 B6 224
Matane, Que., Can. 8,069 *Q10 66
Matane, co., Que., Can. 34,957 *Q10 66
Matanuska, Alsk. 41 G11 84
Matanuska, riv., Alsk. G11 84
Matanuska, val., Alsk. G11 84
Matanzas, Cuba 63,916 A4 232
Matanzas, prov., Cuba 395,780 A4 232
Matanzas, inlet, Fla. B9 174
Matapan, cape, Grc. C4 306
Matapédia, co., Que., Can. 36,085 *Q10 66
Matara, Cey. 27,641 G4 366
Mataram, Indon. F5 358
Matarani, Peru D3 245
Mataria, Eg., U.A.R. 18,682 A3 395
D7
Mataria, Eg., U.A.R. 30,004 D2 382
Mataró, Sp. 29,920 B8 298
Matawan, Monmouth, N.J. 5,097 C4 210
Matehuala, Mex. 14,177 C5 225
Mateko, Con.L. C2 414
Matera, It. 32,800 E6 302
Matera, prov., It. 190,800 *E6 302
Mátészalka, Hung. 11,055 B7 320
Matewan, Mingo, W.Va. 896 D2 194
Matfield, Plymouth, Mass. 500 *B5 206
Matfield Green, Chase, Kans. 95 D7 144
Mathelo, Pak. F6 375
Mather, Man., Can. 145 F3 60
Mather, Greene, Pa. 1,033 D1 214
Mather, Juneau, Wis. 65 D3 160
Mather, peak, Wyo. B5 116
Matherville, Mercer, Ill. 612 B3 138
Matherville, Wayne, Miss. 250 D4 184
Matheson, Elbert, Colo. 150 C7 106
Matheson Island, Man., Can. E4 60
Mathews, Montgomery, Ala. 114 C3 168
Mathews, Lafourche, La. 200 C6 180
E5
Mathews, Mathews, Va. 500 C8 192
Mathews, co., Va. 7,121 C8 192
Mathews, mtn., Mo. D7 150
Mathias, Hardy, W.Va. 50 C6 194
Mathis, San Patricio, Tex. 6,075 E7 130
Mathiston, Webster and Choctaw, Miss. 597 B3 184
Mathura, India 98,552 (*105,773) D2 368
Matiakouali, Upper Volta D5 408
Matias Romera, Mex. D6 225
Matinicus, Knox, Maine 75 (100▲) E4 204
Matinicus, isl., Maine E4 204
Matjan, isl., Indon. F6 358
Matla, riv., India I9 366
Matlock, Eng. 18,300 H11 273
Matlock, Sioux, Iowa 103 A2 142
Mato, pt., Braz. B4 258
Matoaca, Chesterfield, Va. 2,000 B9 192
C7
Matoaka, Mercer, W.Va. 613 D3 194
Mato Grosso, Braz. 433 H5 257
Mato Grosso, state, Braz. 595,000 H5 257
Mato Grosso, plat., Braz. I6 257
Mátra, mts., Hung. B4 320
Matrah, Om. 8,500 C6 383
Matruh, Eg., U.A.R. 3,047 A2 395
Matsqui, B.C., Can. 175 C16 52
Matsudo, Jap. 68,363 *L15 354
Matsue, Jap. 97,857 G4 354
Matsuida, Jap. 24,136 K14 354
Matsumae, Jap. 20,072 D8 354
Matsumoto, Jap. 145,228 F6 354
K13
Matsuyama, Jap. 213,457 H4 354
Matsuzaka, Jap. 93,573 G6 354
M12
Matsuzaki, Jap. 8,576 M14 354
Mattamiscontis, lake, Maine C4 204
Mattamuskeet, lake, N.C. B9 186
Mattancheri, India 73,904 G3 366
Mattapoisett, Plymouth, Mass. 1,640 (3,117▲) C6 206
Mattaponi, riv., Va. C7 192
Mattawa, Ont., Can. 3,208 S25 64
Mattawa, Grant, Wash. 394 *C7 98
Mattawamkeag, Penobscot, Maine 750 (945▲) C4 204
Mattawamkeag, lake, Maine C4 204
Mattawamkeag, riv., Maine C4 204
Mattawin, riv., Que., Can. R11 66
Mattawoman, creek, Md. C5 182
Matterhorn, mtn., It., Switz. C1 302
C3 312
Mattese, St. Louis, Mo. 900 *C7 150
Matteson, Cook, Ill. 3,225 F3 138
Matthews, Jefferson, Ga. 106 C4 176
Matthews, Grant, Ind. 627 B4 140
Matthews, New Madrid, Mo. 450 E8 150
Matthews, Mecklenburg, N.C. 609 B5 186
Matthew Town, Great Inagua 995 B8 232
Mattice, Ont., Can. 245 R25 64
Mattighofen, Aus. 3,572 B5 313

Mattituck, Suffolk, N.Y. 1,274 D5 212
Mattoon, Coles, Ill. 19,088 D5 138
Mattoon, Shawano, Wis. 435 C4 160
Mattson, Coahoma, Miss. 400 A2 184
Mattydale, Onondaga, N.Y. 9,000 B5 212
Matucana, Peru 1,746 C2 245
Matuku, isl., Fiji E7 436
Matūn, Afg. 5,000 C5 374
Matunuck, Washington, R.I. 50 D2 216
Matundu, Con.L. B3 414
Maturín, Ven. 42,000 B7 240
Mau, Fiji E6 436
Mau, India D3 368
Maúa, Moz. B7 421
Maubeuge, Fr. 24,215 B5 278
Maubin, Bur. C2 362
Mauch Chunk, see Jim Thorpe, Pa.
Mauckport, Harrison, Ind. 107 D3 140
Maud, Tunica, Miss. 100 A2 184
Maud, Seminole and Pottawatomie, Okla. 1,137 C7 128
Maud, Bowie, Tex. 951 C8 130
Maudaha, India D3 368
Maud, Butler, Ohio 350 C1 156 / C2
Maués, Braz. 1,974 F5 256
Mauganj, India D3 368
Maugansville, Washington, Md. 625 A4 182
Maugerville, N.B., Can. D3 70
Maughold, head, Isle of Man G8 273
Maui (incl. Kalawao), co., Haw. 42,855 C5 86 / B4
Maui, isl., Haw. C6 86
Mauldin, Greenville, S.C. 1,462 B4 188
Maule, prov., Chile 72,181 E3 250
Mauléon-Soule, Fr. F3 278
Maumee, Lucas, Ohio 12,063 A1 156 / A3
Maumee, bay, Ohio A1 156
Maumee, riv., Ind., Ohio A5 140 / A2 156
Maun, Bech. 500 C4 420
Mauna Kea, vol., Haw. D6 86
Maunaloa, Maui, Haw. 950 B4 86
Mauna Loa, vol., Haw. D6 86
Maunalua, bay, Haw. G10 86
Maunawai, Honolulu, Haw. 570 F9 86
Maungdaw, Bur. 3,846 B2 362
Maunie, White, Ill. 363 E5 138
Maupin, Wasco, Oreg. 381 B5 96
Maurepas, Livingston, La. 50 B6 180
Maurepas, lake, La. D5 180
Maurertown, Shenandoah, Va. 225 B6 192
Maurice, Sioux, Iowa 237 B1 142
Maurice, Vermilion, La. 411 D3 180
Maurice, Lawrence, S.Dak. 25 C2 158
Maurice, riv., N.J. E2 210
Maurice River, Cumberland, N.J. 40 E2 210
Mauricetown, Cumberland, N.J. 250 E3 210
Mauritania, country, Afr. 725,000 D5 388 / 409
Maury, Greene, N.C. 285 B8 186
Maury, co., Tenn. 41,699 C4 190
Maury, isl., Wash. D2 98
Maury City, Crockett, Tenn. 624 C2 190
Mauston, Juneau, Wis. 3,531 E3 160
Mauterndorf, Aus. 1,651 C5 313
Maverick, co., Tex. 14,508 E5 130
Mavinga, Ang. C4 420
Mawer, Sask., Can. 84 E4 58
Mawkmai, Bur. B3 362
Mawlaik, Bur. 3,042 B2 362
Max, Talbot, Ga. 400 D2 176
Max, Dundy, Nebr. 150 D4 152
Max, McLean, N.Dak. 410 C4 154
Maxbass, Bottineau, N.Dak. 218 B4 154
Maxcanú, Mex. 4,271 C7 225
Maxeys, Oglethorpe, Ga. 149 C3 176
Maxie, Forrest, Miss. 60 E3 184
Maxie, Buchanan, Va. 370 C2 192
Maxim, Monmouth, N.J. C4 210
Max Meadows, Wythe, Va. 900 D4 192
Maxton, Robeson, N.C. 1,755 C6 186
Maxville, Ont., Can. 782 O26 64
Maxville, Duval, Fla. 350 A8 174
Maxville, Granite, Mont. 40 D3 110
Maxwell, Colusa, Calif. 800 C2 94
Maxwell, Hancock, Ind. 280 C4 140
Maxwell, Story, Iowa 773 A8 142 / C4
Maxwell, Lincoln, Nebr. 324 C5 152
Maxwell, Colfax, N.Mex. 392 B6 126
Maxwell, Franklin, Tenn. 50 C5 190
Maxwell, Carbon, Utah 150 *D5 114
Maxwelton, Greenbrier, W.Va. 100 D4 194
May, Lemhi, Idaho 60 E5 108
May, Harper, Okla. 114 B4 128
May, Brown, Tex. 400 D6 130
May, cape, N.J. E3 210
May, isl., Scot. E10 272
Maya, mts., Br. Hond. B3 228
Mayaguana, isl., W.I. A8 232
Mayaguana, passage, W.I. A8 232
Mayagüez, P.R. 58,944 C11 233
Mayama, Con.B. G7 409
Mayarí, Cuba 6,386 B7 232
Maybee, Monroe, Mich. 459 G8 146
Mayberry, Carroll, Md. 100 A5 182
Maybeury, McDowell, W.Va. 900 D3 194
Maybrook, Orange, N.Y. 1,348 D7 212
Mayday, La Plata, Colo. 35 *E2 106
Maydee, Tipton, Tenn. 100 C2 190
Maydi, Yemen D3 383
Mayen, Ger. 16,000 C2 286
Mayence, see Mainz, Ger.
Mayenne, Fr. 9,705 C3 278
Mayenne, dept., Fr. 251,522 *C3 278
Mayer, Yavapai, Ariz. 250 D3 124
Mayer, Carver, Minn. 179 *G5 148
Mayersville, Issaquena, Miss. 136 C1 184
Mayerthorpe, Alta., Can. 563 D5 54
Mayes, co., Okla. 20,073 B8 128
Mayesville, Sumter, S.C. 750 D8 188
Mayetta, Jackson, Kans. 218 C8 144
Mayetta, Ocean, N.J. 150 D4 210
Mayfair, Sask., Can. 90 D4 58
Mayfair, Greenville, S.C. 5,000 *B4 188
Mayfield, Hancock, Ga. 100 C4 176
Mayfield, Sumner, Kans. 119 E6 144
Mayfield, Graves, Ky. 10,762 D2 178
Mayfield, Fulton, N.Y. 818 B7 212
Mayfield, Butler, Ohio 2,747 *C2 156
Mayfield, Beckham, Okla. 25 C4 128
Mayfield, Lackawanna, Pa. 1,996 B6 214
Mayfield, Sanpete, Utah 329 D4 114
Mayfield, Lewis, Wash. 45 C4 98
Mayfield Heights, Cuyahoga, Ohio 13,478 A5 156
Mayflower, Faulkner, Ark. 355 C4 170
Mayhew, Lowndes, Miss. 300 B4 184
Mayhill, Otero, N.Mex. 90 F5 126
Maykain, Sov.Un. B9 336
Maykop, Sov.Un. 82,000 J13 332
Mayland, Cumberland, Tenn. 450 B6 190
Maymakan, Sov.Un. D15 329
Maymont, Sask., Can. 197 D4 58
Maymyo, Bur. 22,287 B3 362
Mayna, Catahoula, La. 40 C4 180
Maynard, Randolph, Ark. 201 A6 170
Maynard, Fayette, Iowa 515 B6 142
Maynard, Middlesex, Mass. 7,695 B5 206 / C1
Maynard, Chippewa, Minn. 429 G3 148
Maynardville, Union, Tenn. 620 B8 190
Mayne, B.C., Can. 100 C14 52
Maynooth, Ont., Can. 310 O23 64
Maynooth, Ire. 1,722 H6 273
Mayo, Lafayette, Fla. 687 A7 174
Mayo, Anne Arundel, Md. 500 C6 182
Mayo, Spartanburg, S.C. 500 A5 188
Mayo, Halifax, Va. 50 D6 192
Mayo, co., Ire. 133,052 H3 273
Mayo, mts., Ire. G3 273
Mayo, riv., Arg. G3 251
Mayodan, Rockingham, N.C. 2,366 A6 186
Mayo Landing, Yukon, Can. 249 E5 48
Mayo Mills, Spartanburg, S.C. 200 *A5 188
Mayon, vol., Phil. B6 358
Mayotte, isl., Afr. B9 421
May Pen, Jam. 6,950 D6 232
Mayport, Duval, Fla. 1,100 A9 174 / A10
Mayrhofen, Aus. 2,351 C3 313
Mays, Rush, Ind. 200 C4 140
Mays Landing, Atlantic, N.J. 1,404 E3 210
Mays Lick, Mason, Ky. 400 B7 178
Maysville, Madison, Ala. 175 A3 168
Maysville, Benton, Ark. 200 A2 170
Maysville, Banks and Jackson, Ga. 553 B3 176
Maysville, Daviess, Ind. 100 D2 140
Maysville, Scott, Iowa 126 *C7 142
Maysville, Mason, Ky. 8,484 B7 178
Maysville, De Kalb, Mo. 942 B3 150
Maysville, Jones, N.C. 892 C8 186
Maysville, Garvin, Okla. 1,530 D6 128
Maysville, Grant, W.Va. 120 B5 194
Mayton, Rankin, Miss. 190 C3 184
Maytown, Jefferson, Ala. 297 *B3 168
Mayumba, Gabon G7 409
May Valley, Prowers, Colo. D8 106
Mayview, Lafayette, Mo. 270 *B4 150
Mayville, Tuscola, Mich. 896 F8 146
Mayville, Cape May, N.J. 315 E3 210
Mayville, Chautauqua, N.Y. 1,619 C2 212
Mayville, Traill, N.Dak. 2,168 C8 154
Mayville, Gilliam, Oreg. 50 B6 96
Mayville, Dodge, Wis. 3,607 E5 160
Maywood, Los Angeles, Calif. 14,588 C5 94
Maywood, Cook, Ill. 27,330 F2 138
Maywood, Marion, Ind. 400 D4 140
Maywood, Lewis, Mo. 158 B6 150
Maywood, Frontier, Nebr. 337 D5 152
Maywood, Bergen, N.J. 11,460 A1 210
Maywood, Albany, N.Y. 1,500 *C8 212
Maza, Arg. C3 252
Maza, Towner, N.Dak. 31 B6 154
Mazabuka, Rh.&Nya. 4,400 C5 420
Mazagan, Mor. 34,781 B2 402
Mazagão, Braz. 601 F6 256
Mazamet, Fr. 13,969 F5 278
Mazán, Arg. A2 252
Mazanderan, reg., Iran B3 379
Mazapil, Mex. 1,742 C5 225
Mazar, prov., Afg. *A4 374
Mazar, Eg., U.A.R. 343 A3 395
Mazara del Vallo, It. 34,700 G4 302
Mazār-i-Sharif, Afg. 41,960 A4 374
Mazarn, creek, Ark. C6 170
Mazarrón, Sp. 2,483 D6 298
Mazarrón, gulf, Sp. D6 298
Mazaruni, riv., Br.Gu. D5 256
Mazatenango, Guat. 11,032 C2 228
Mazatlán, Mex. 41,459 C4 224
Mazatzal, mts., Ariz. D4 124
Mazatzal, peak, Ariz. D4 124
Mažeikiai, Sov.Un. 8,900 D4 332
Mazenod, Sask., Can. 173 F4 58
Mazeppa, Alta., Can. 35 E6 54
Mazeppa, Wabasha, Minn. 444 G6 148
Mazgirt, Tur. 1,033 B8 307
Mazie, Mayes, Okla. 100 B8 128
Mazomanie, Dane, Wis. 1,069 E4 160
Mazon, Grundy, Ill. 683 B5 138
Mazzarino, It. 19,200 G5 302
Mba, Fiji 94,004 E6 436
Mbabane, Swaz. 3,428 E6 421
Mbaïki, Cen.Afr.Rep. F8 409
Mbale, Ug. B5 414
Mbalmayo, Cam. 6,242 F7 409
Mbamba Bay, Tan. E5 414
Mbarara, Ug. C5 414
M'bari, riv., Cen.Afr.Rep. E9 409
Mbenga, pass, Fiji E6 436
Mbeya, Tan. 6,932 D5 414
Mbour, Sen. D1 408
Mbout, Maur. C2 408
Mburucuyá, Arg. 2,555 A4 252
Mbya, bay, Fiji E6 436
Mchinja, Tan. D6 414
Mdandu, Tan. D5 414
Meacham, Sask., Can. 193 D5 58
Meachem, Umatilla, Oreg. 120 B8 96
Mead, Weld, Colo. 192 B6 106
Mead, Saunders, Nebr. 428 C9 152 / D2
Mead, Bryan, Okla. 250 E7 128
Mead, Spokane, Wash. 800 B9 98 / D8
Mead, lake, Ariz., Nev. B1 124 / G7 112
Meade, Meade, Kans. 2,019 E3 144
Meade, co., Kans. 5,505 E3 144
Meade, co., Ky. 18,938 C4 178
Meade, co., S.Dak. 12,044 C3 158
Meade, peak, Idaho G7 108
Meade River, Alsk. 50 A6 84
Meaderville, Silver Bow, Mont. 1,345 *E4 110
Meadow, Sarpy, Nebr. E3 152
Meadow, Perkins, S.Dak. 35 B3 158
Meadow, Millard, Utah 244 E3 114
Meadow, creek, W.Va. D7 194
Meadow, mtn., Md. A1 182
Meadow, riv., W.Va. C4 194
Meadow Bridge, Fayette, W.Va. 426 D4 194 / D7
Meadowbrook, Allen, Ind. 1,500 *A4 140
Meadowbrook, Montgomery, Pa. 1,500 *C6 214
Meadowbrook, Harrison, W.Va. 975 A7 194
Meadowbrook Downs, St. Louis, Mo. 659 *C7 150
Meadow Creek, Boundary, Idaho 15 A2 108
Meadow Creek, Summers, W.Va. 325 D4 194 / D7
Meadowdale, Marion, W.Va. 300 *B4 194
Meadow Grove, Madison, Nebr. 430 B8 152
Meadowlands, St. Louis, Minn. 176 D6 148
Meadow Lands, Washington, Pa. 1,967 C1 214
Meadows, Adams, Idaho 250 E2 108
Meadows of Dan, Patrick, Va. 30 D4 192
Meadowview, Washington, Va. 750 D3 192
Meadowview Estates, Jefferson, Ky. 131 *B5 178
Meadville, Franklin, Miss. 611 D2 184
Meadville, Linn, Mo. 447 B4 150
Meadville, Keya Paha, Nebr. 29 B6 152
Meadville, Crawford, Pa. 16,671 B1 214
Meaford, Ont., Can. 3,643 P20 64
Meagher, co., Mont. 2,616 D6 110
Meaghers Grant, N.S., Can. 157 E6 70
Mealy, mts., Newf., Can. D6 72
Meandarra, Austl. 251 D9 432
Means, Menifee, Ky. 160 C7 178
Meansville, Pike, Ga. 335 *C2 176
Mearim, riv., Braz. B1 258
Mears, Oceana, Mich. 250 F5 146
Meath, co., Ire. 66,762 H6 273
Meath Park Station, Sask., Can. 198 D5 58
Meaux, Fr. 16,767 C5 278
Mebane, Alamance and Orange, N.C. 2,364 A6 186
Mecaha, Garfield, Mont. C9 110
Mecca, Riverside, Calif. 300 F5 94
Mecca, Parke, Ind. 500 C2 140
Mecca (Makkah), Sau.Ar. 80,000 C2 383
Mechanic Falls, Androscoggin, Maine 2,195 D2 204
Mechanicsburg, Sangamon, Ill. 428 *D4 138
Mechanicsburg, Henry, Ind. 120 B3 140
Mechanicsburg, Champaign, Ohio 1,810 B3 156
Mechanicsburg, Cumberland, Pa. 8,123 C4 214
Mechanicsville, Windham, Conn. 130 B8 202
Mechanicsville, Cedar, Iowa 1,010 C6 142
Mechanicsville, St. Marys, Md. 175 D6 182
Mechanicsville, Hanover, Va. 500 C7 192
Mechanicville, Saratoga, N.Y. 6,831 C8 212
Mechant, lake, La. E5 180
Mechelen, Bel. 63,298 C3 282
Mecheria, Alg. 5,290 B3 402 / (39,347▲)
Mecklenburg, co., N.C. 272,111 B5 186
Mecklenburg, co., Va. 31,428 D6 192
Mecklenburg, reg., Ger. B4 286
Meckling, Clay, S.Dak. 93 E8 158
Meconta, Moz. B7 421
Mecosta, Mecosta, Mich. 303 F6 146
Mecosta, co., Mich. 21,051 F6 146
Mecsek, mts., Hung. C3 320
Mecúfi, Moz. B8 421
Medan, Indon. 310,600 D1 358
Medano, Mex. A2 224
Médanos, Arg. 2,229 C3 252
Medart, Wakulla, Fla. 403 A6 174
Medaryville, Pulaski, Ind. 758 A3 140
Meddybemps, lake, Maine C5 204
Médéa, Alg. 7,638 A4 402 / (26,350▲)
Medellín, Col. 485,250 B1 244
Medelpad, prov., Swe. 116,242 *E7 290
Medemblik, Neth. 5,056 B4 282
Médenine, Tun. 5,350 B6 402
Méderdra, Maur. C1 408
Medfield, Norfolk, Mass. 2,424 D2 206 / (6,021▲)
Medford, Piscataquis, Maine C4 204
Medford, Middlesex, Mass. 64,971 B5 206 / C3
Medford, Steele, Minn. 567 G5 148
Medford, Burlington, N.J. 1,480 *D3 210
Medford, Grant, Okla. 1,223 B6 128
Medford, Jackson, Oreg. 24,425 E4 96
Medford, Taylor, Wis. 3,260 C3 160
Medford Lakes, Burlington, N.J. 2,876 D3 210
Medford Station, Suffolk, N.Y. 951 D4 212
Medfra, Alsk. 25 C6 84
Medgidia, Rom. 17,943 B5 321
Media, Delaware, Pa. 5,803 A6 214 / D6
Mediapolis, Des Moines, Iowa 1,040 D6 142
Medias, Rom. 32,503 A3 321
Medical Lake, Spokane, Wash. 4,765 B9 98 / D8
Medicinal, springs, Ark. B4 170
Medicine, butte, N.Dak. C4 154
Medicine, creek, Mo. B4 150
Medicine, creek, Nebr. D5 152
Medicine Bow, Carbon, Wyo. 392 E6 116
Medicine Bow, mts., Wyo. E6 116
Medicine Bow, peak, Wyo. E6 116
Medicine Bow, riv., Wyo. D6 116
Medicine Hat, Alta., Can. 20,826 E7 54 / F4
Medicine Lake, Hennepin, Minn. 323 *F5 148
Medicine Lake, Sheridan, Mont. 452 B12 110
Medicine Lodge, Barber, Kans. 3,072 E5 144
Medicine Lodge, riv., Kans. E4 144
Medicine Park, Comanche, Okla. 800 D5 128
Medill, Clark, Mo. 140 A6 150
Medimont, Kootenai, Idaho 50 *B2 108
Medina, Orleans, N.Y. 6,681 B3 212
Medina, see Hamel, Minn.
Medina, Stutsman, N.Dak. 545 D6 154
Medina, Medina, Ohio 8,235 A5 156
Medina, see Al Madīnah, Sau.Ar.
Medina, Gibson, Tenn. 722 C3 190
Medina, King, Wash. 2,285 D3 98
Medina, co., Ohio 65,315 A4 156
Medina, co., Tex. 18,904 E6 130
Medina, riv., Tex. B7 130
Medina del Campo, Sp. 13,154 B4 298
Medina de Rioseco, Sp. 4,763 B4 298
Medina Sidonia, Sp. 8,704 D4 298
Mediterranean, sea, Afr., Eur. E5 266
Medium, lake, Iowa A3 142
Medley, Dade, Fla. 112 *F10 174
Mednogorsk, Sov.Un. 32,400 B5 336
Medomak, Lincoln, Maine 125 D3 204
Medon, Madison, Tenn. 97 C3 190
Medora, Man., Can. 150 F2 60
Medora, Macoupin, Ill. 447 D3 138
Medora, Jackson, Ind. 716 D3 140
Medora, Reno, Kans. 75 D6 144
Medora, Billings, N.Dak. 133 D2 154
Medstead, Sask., Can. 202 D3 58
Meductic, N.B., Can. 112 D2 70
Medulla, Polk, Fla. 300 D9 174
Meduxnekeag, riv., Maine B5 204
Medveditsa, riv., Sov.Un. B2 336
Medvedovskaya, Sov.Un. J12 332
Medvezhi, isl., Sov.Un. B18 329
Medvezhyegorsk, Sov.Un. 19,200 C5 328
Medway, Penobscot, Maine 150 C4 204 / (1,266▲)
Medway, Norfolk, Mass. 1,602 B5 206 / (5,168▲) E1
Medway, Clark, Ohio 950 C2 156
Medzhibozh, Sov.Un. 22,400 H6 332
Meehan, Lauderdale, Miss. 100 C4 184
Meek, Holt, Nebr. B7 152
Meekatharra, Austl. 585 D3 432
Meeker, Rio Blanco, Colo. 1,655 B3 106
Meeker, Lincoln, Okla. 664 C7 128
Meeker, co., Minn. 18,887 F4 148
Meeks, Johnson, Ga. 100 F4 176
Meelpaeg, lake, Newf., Can. F7 72
Meenen, Bel. 21,663 D2 282
Meerane, Ger. 25,900 C5 286
Meerut, India 158,407 C2 368 / (*233,183)
Meeteetse, Park, Wyo. 514 B4 116
Meeting, lake, Sask., Can. D4 58
Meeting Creek, Alta., Can. 125 D6 54
Mēga, Eth. E4 398
Megalópolis, Grc. 2,893 C4 306
Mégantic, co., Que., Can. 53,028 R13 66
Mégantic, lake, Que., Can. S14 66
Mégantic, mtn., Que., Can. S13 66
Mégara, Grc. 13,863 B4 306
Megargel, Monroe, Ala. 400 D2 168
Meggett, Charleston, S.C. 188 F2 188 / F8
Mehama, Marion, Oreg. 200 C2 96 / C4
Mehar, Pak. F5 375
Meherpur, Pak. 7,174 L16 375
Meherrin, Lunenburg, Va. 300 C6 192
Meherrin, riv., Va. D6 192
Mehun-sur-Yèvre, Fr. 4,735 D5 278
Meia Ponte, riv., Braz. D1 258
Meiganga, Cam. 2,998 E7 409
Meighen, isl., N.W.Ter., Can. B8 48
Meigs, Thomas and Mitchell, Ga. 1,236 E2 176
Meigs, co., Ohio 22,159 C4 156
Meigs, co., Tenn. 5,160 C7 190
Meihsien, China M8 349
Meiktila, Bur. 25,180 B2 362
Meilap, Ponape A2 436
Meilen, Switz. 5,992 A1 312
Meilleur, lake, Que., Can. P11 66
Meiners Oaks, Ventura, Calif. 3,513 *E4 94
Meiningen, Ger. 23,600 C4 286
Meire Grove, Stearns, Minn. 167 *F4 148
Meiringen, Switz. 3,640 B4 312
Meissen, Ger. 49,900 C5 286
Meitan, China 5,000 L3 349
Mejicana, mtn., Arg. A2 252
Mejillones, Chile 1,056 B3 250
Mejit, isl., Marshall A4 436
Mékambo, Gabon F7 409
Mekerrhane, lake, Alg. C4 402
Mekhtar, Pak. D6 375
Mekinac, lake, Que., Can. R12 66
Mekinock, Grand Forks, N.Dak. 100 B8 154
Meknes, Mor. 140,380 B2 402
Mekong, riv., Asia H12 340
Mekong, riv. mouths, Viet. E5 362
Mekoryuk, Alsk. 156 C5 84
Mélambes, Grc. 1,414 D5 306
Melaval, Sask., Can. 110 F4 58
Melba, Canyon, Idaho 197 F2 108
Melber, McCracken, Ky. 219 D2 178
Melbeta, Scotts Bluff, Nebr. 118 C2 152
Melbourne, Izard, Ark. 571 A5 170
Melbourne, Austl. 128,820 F9 432
Melbourne, Ont., Can. 400 R19 64
Melbourne, Brevard, Fla. 11,982 C10 174
Melbourne, Marshall, Iowa 517 C4 142
Melbourne, Campbell, Ky. 250 A8 178
Melbourne, Harrison, Mo. 70 A4 150
Melbourne, Grays Harbor, Wash. 50 C3 98
Melbourne Beach, Brevard, Fla. 1,004 C10 174
Melbourne Village, Brevard, Fla. 458 *C10 174
Melcher, Marion, Iowa 867 C4 142
Meldrim, Effingham, Ga. 220 D5 176
Meldrum Bay, Ont., Can. 60 O17 64

Meleb, Man., Can. 85 E4 60
Melekeiok, Palau A6 436
Melenki, Sov.Un. 24,200 E13 332
Melfa, Accomack, Va. 409 C9 192
Melfi, Chad D8 409
Melfi, It. 18,600 E5 302
Melfort, Sask., Can. 3,322 D5 58
Melhus, Nor. E4 290
Melik, wadi, Sud. B3 398
Melilla, Mor. 76,247 A3 402
Melipilla, Chile 11,525 B1 252
Melita, Man., Can. 926 F2 60
Melito di Porto Salvo, It. 4,342 G5 302
Melitopol, Sov.Un. 95,000 I10 332
Melitota, Kent, Md. 75 B7 182
Mellan Fryken, lake, Swe. B4 292
Mellen, Ashland, Wis. 1,182 B3 160
Mellerud, Swe. 4,156 C3 292
Mellette, Spink, S.Dak. 208 B7 158
Mellette, co., S.Dak. 2,664 D5 158
Mellit, Sud. C2 398
Mellott, Fountain, Ind. 312 B2 140
Mellow Valley, Clay, Ala. B4 168
Mellville, Newport, R.I. C3 216
Mellwood, Phillips, Ark. 300 C6 170
Mělník, Czech. 11,998 A2 324
Melo, Ur. 23,000 B5 252
Melocheville, Que., Can. 1,422 S15 66
Melouprey, Camb. 10,000 D5 362
Meloy, Nor. C5 290
Melrhir, salt lake, Alg. B5 402
Melrose, N.B., Can. 200 C6 70
Melrose, N.S., Can. 140 D7 70
Melrose, Alachua, Fla. 619 B8 174
Melrose, Nez Perce, Idaho *C2 108
Melrose, Monroe, Iowa 214 D4 142
Melrose, Cherokee, Kans. 80 *E9 144
Melrose, Natchitoches, La. 200 C3 180
Melrose, Middlesex, Mass. 29,619 B5 206
C3
Melrose, Stearns, Minn. 2,135 F4 148
Melrose, Silver Bow, Mont. 150 E4 110
Melrose, Curry, N.Mex. 698 D7 126
Melrose, Douglas, Oreg. D3 96
Melrose, Jackson, Wis. 516 D2 160
Melrose Park, Cook, Ill. 22,291 F2 138
Melrose Park, Cayuga, N.Y. 2,058 *C5 212
Melsetter, Rh.&Nya. 400 C6 421
Melstone, Musselshell, Mont. 266 D9 110
Melstrand, Alger, Mich. 100 C5 146
Melun, Fr. 20,219 C5 278
Melvern, Osage, Kans. 376 D8 144
Melvich, Scot. C9 272
Melville, Sask., Can. 4,948 E6 58
Melville, St. Landry, La. 1,939 D4 180
Melville, Sweet Grass, Mont. 20 D7 110
Melville, bay, Grnld. O28 290
Melville, cape, Austl. A8 432
Melville, isl., Austl. A6 432
Melville, isl., N.W.Ter., Can. B7 48
Melville, lake, Newf., Can. D6 72
Melville, pen., N.W.Ter., Can. D10 48
Melvin, Choctaw, Ala. 300 D1 168
Melvin, Ford, Ill. 559 C5 138
Melvin, Osceola, Iowa 364 A2 142
Melvin, Sanilac, Mich. 196 *F9 146
Melvin, McCulloch, Tex. 401 D6 130
Melvina, Monroe, Wis. 111 E3 160
Melvindale, Wayne, Mich. 13,089 *B8 146
Melvine, Bledsoe, Tenn. 60 C6 190
Melvin Village, Carroll, N.H. 270 D4 208
Mélykút, Hung. 6,312 C4 320
Memba, Moz. B8 421
Memel, see Klaipeda, Sov.Un.
Memmingen, Ger. 28,600 E4 286
Memorial, Clay, Tenn. B6 190
Memphis, Manatee, Fla. 2,647 *D8 174
Memphis, Clark, Ind. 200 D4 140
Memphis, St. Clair, Mich. 996 G9 146
Memphis, Scotland, Mo. 2,106 A5 150
Memphis, Saunders, Nebr. 77 E2 152
Memphis, Shelby, Tenn. 497,524 C1 190
(*628,100) E6
Memphis, Hall, Tex. 3,332 B5 130
Memphis, ruins, Eg., U.A.R. B3 395
Memphremagog, lake, Que., Can., Vt. S12 66
B4 218
Memramcook, N.B., Can. 395 C5 70
Mena, Polk, Ark. 4,388 C2 170
Menahga, Wadena, Minn. 799 E3 148
Ménaka, Mali 400 C5 408
Menam, see Chao Phraya, riv., Thai.
Menan, Jefferson, Idaho 497 F7 108
Menands, Albany, N.Y. 2,314 C8 212
Menard, Menard, Tex. 1,914 D6 130
Menard, co., Ill. 9,248 C4 138
Menard, co., Tex. 2,964 D6 130
Menasha, Winnebago, Wis. 14,647 A5 160
D5
Menchalville, Manitowoc, Wis. 60 A6 160
Menche, Guat. B2 228
Mencheng, China 5,000 I8 349
Mendawi, riv., Indon. E4 358
Mende, Fr. 7,752 E5 278
Mendenhall, Simpson, Miss. 1,946 D3 184
Mendes, Tattnall, Ga. 150 E5 176
Méndez, Ec. 915 A2 245
Méndez, Mex. 207 B6 225
Mendham, Sask., Can. 211 E3 58
Mendham, Morris, N.J. 2,371 B3 210
Mendip, hills, Eng. J10 273
Mendjalutung, Indon. D5 358
Mendocino, Mendocino, Calif. 669 C2 94
Mendocino, co., Calif. 51,059 C2 94
Mendocino, cape, Calif. B1 94
Mendon, Adams, Ill. 784 C2 138
Mendon, Worcester, Mass. 900 B4 206
(2,068▲) E1
Mendon, St. Joseph, Mich. 867 G6 146
Mendon, Chariton, Mo. 287 B4 150
Mendon, Mercer, Ohio 663 B2 156
Mendon, Cache, Utah 345 B4 114
Mendon, Rutland, Vt. 35 D3 218
(461▲)
Mendota, Fresno, Calif. 2,099 D3 94
Mendota, La Salle, Ill. 6,154 B4 138
Mendota, Dakota, Minn. 259 F7 148
Mendota, lake, Wis. E4 160
Mendota Heights, Dakota, Minn. 5,028 *G5 148
Mendoza, Arg. 97,496 B2 252
(*200,000)
Mendoza, prov., Arg. 787,800 D4 250
Mendrisio, Switz. 4,602 C4 312
Menemsha, Dukes, Mass. 50 D6 206
Menfi, It. 12,100 G4 302
Menggala, Indon. E3 358
Menglien, China G7 346
Mengtzu, China 9,000 G8 346
Menifee, Conway, Ark. 300 B4 170
Menifee, co., Ky. 4,276 C7 178
Menihek, lakes, Newf., Can. D8 72
Menindee, Austl. 644 E8 432
Meningie, Austl. 556 F7 432
Menlo, Chattooga, Ga. 466 B1 176
Menlo, Guthrie, Iowa 421 C3 142
Menlo, Thomas, Kans. 99 C3 144
Menlo, Pacific, Wash. 100 C3 98
Menlo Park, San Mateo, Calif. 26,957 B5 94
Menlo Park, Middlesex, N.J. 400 B4 210
Menlo Park Terrace, Middlesex, N.J. 2,500 *B4 210
Menno, Hamilton, Kans. E2 144
Menno, Hutchinson, S.Dak. 837 D8 158
Meno, Major, Okla. 118 B5 128
Menoken, Burleigh, N.Dak. 60 D5 154
Menominee, Menominee, Mich. 11,289 D4 146
Menominee, Cedar, Nebr. 25 *B8 152
Menominee, co., Mich. 24,685 D4 146
Menominee, riv., Mich., Wis. D4 146
C6 160
Menomonee, riv., Wis. E1 160
Menomonee Falls, Waukesha, Wis. 18,276 E1 160
E5
Menomonie, Dunn, Wis. 8,624 D2 160
Menorca, isl., Sp. C9 298
Mentana, It. 3,102 *D4 302
Mentawai, is., Indon. E1 358
Mentmore, McKinley, N.Mex. 90 C2 126
Menton, Fr. 17,109 F7 278
Mentone, De Kalb, Ala. 250 A4 168
Mentone, Kosciusko, Ind. 813 A3 140
Mentor, Campbell, Ky. 350 A8 178
Mentor, Polk, Minn. 281 D2 148
Mentor, Lake, Ohio 4,354 A5 156
Mentor, Blount, Tenn. 350 E9 190
Mentor-on-the-Lake, Lake, Ohio 3,290 *A5 156
Menzies, Austl. 147 D4 432
Menziken, Switz. 3,377 A4 312
Meoqui, Mex. 6,736 B4 224
Meota, Sask., Can. 240 D3 58
Meppel, Neth. 16,869 B5 282
Meppen, Ger. 13,100 B2 286
Mequon, Ozaukee, Wis. 8,543 E2 160
Merabéllo, gulf, Grc. D5 306
Meramec, caverns, Mo. C6 150
Meramec, riv., Mo. C7 150
Merano, It. 29,400 B3 302
Merasheen, Newf., Can. 325 G8 72
Merasheen, isl., Newf., Can. G8 72
Merauke, Neth.N.Gui. F10 359
Meraux, St. Bernard, La. 500 C7 180
Merca, Som. 15,000 E6 398
(59,000▲)
Mercara, India 10,117 F3 366
Merced, Merced, Calif. 20,068 D3 94
Merced, co., Calif. 90,446 D3 94
Merced, riv., Calif. D3 94
Mercedes, Arg. 14,813 A4 252
Mercedes, Arg. 25,912 B2 252
Mercedes, Arg. 16,932 B4 252
Mercedes, Hidalgo, Tex. 10,943 F7 130
Mercedes, Ur. 25,000 B4 252
Mercer, Muhlenberg, Ky. 500 C3 178
Mercer, Somerset, Maine 140 D3 204
(272▲)
Mercer, Mercer, Mo. 368 A4 150
Mercer, McLean, N.Dak. 154 C5 154
Mercer, Mercer, Pa. 2,800 B1 214
Mercer, Madison, Tenn. 400 C2 190
Mercer, Iron, Wis. 950 B3 160
Mercer, co., Ill. 17,149 B3 138
Mercer, co., Ky. 14,596 C6 178
Mercer, co., Mo. 5,750 A4 150
Mercer, co., N.J. 266,392 C3 210
Mercer, co., N.Dak. 6,805 C4 154
Mercer, co., Ohio 32,559 B2 156
Mercer, co., Pa. 127,519 B1 214
Mercer, co., W.Va. 68,206 D3 194
Mercer, isl., Wash. D3 98
Mercer Island, King, Wash. 500 B4 98
D3
Mercersburg, Franklin, Pa. 1,759 D4 214
Mercerville, Mercer, N.J. (part of Hamilton Township) C3 210
Merchantville, Camden, N.J. 4,075 *D3 210
Mercoal, Alta., Can. 500 D4 54
Mercury, Nye, Nev. 308 G5 112
Mercury, bay, N.Z. B5 437
Mercy, cape, N.W.Ter., Can. D12 48
Meredith, Belknap, N.H. 950 D3 208
(2,434▲)
Meredith, King, Wash. D3 98
Meredith, lake, Colo. D7 106
Meredith Center, Belknap, N.H. 100 D3 208
Meredith College, Wake, N.C. 600 B7 186
Meredithville, Brunswick, Va. 60 D7 192
Meredosia, Morgan, Ill. 1,034 D3 138
Merefa, Sov.Un. 25,200 H11 332
Meregh, Som. E6 398
Mergen (Nenchiang), China 5,000 A12 348
Mergui, Bur. 33,697 D3 362
Mergui, arch., Bur. E2 362
Merid, Sask., Can. 45 E3 58
Mérida, Mex. 142,838 C8 225
Mérida, Sp. 22,134 C3 298
Mérida, Ven. 34,000 B3 240
Mérida, state, Ven. 211,110 B3 240
Meriden, New Haven, Conn. 51,850 C4 202
Meriden, Cherokee, Iowa 192 B2 142
Meriden, Jefferson, Kans. 402 C8 144
Meriden, Sullivan, N.H. 175 D2 208
Meriden, Laramie, Wyo. 5 E8 116
Meridian, McIntosh, Ga. 150 E5 176
Meridian, Ada, Idaho 2,081 F2 108
Meridian, Lauderdale, Miss. 49,374 C4 184
Meridian, Cayuga, N.Y. 379 B5 212
Meridian, Logan, Okla. 160 C6 128
Meridian, Butler, Pa. 1,649 C2 214
Meridian, Bosque, Tex. 993 D7 130
Meridian Hills, Marion, Ind. 1,807 D5 140
Meridiano, Arg. C3 252
Meridianville, Madison, Ala. 750 A3 168
Merigold, Bolivar, Miss. 602 B2 184
Merikarvia, Fin. F9 291
Merino, Logan, Colo. 200 B7 106
Merino, Judith Basin, Mont. C6 110
Merino Village, Worcester, Mass. 3,099 B4 206
Merioneth, co., Wales 40,580 I9 273
Meriso, pt., Guam D7 436
Merit, Simpson, Miss. 100 D3 184
Meriwether, McCormick, S.C. 150 D4 188
Meriwether, co., Ga. 19,756 C2 176
Meriwether Lewis, natl. mon., Tenn. C4 190
Merkel, Taylor, Tex. 2,312 C5 130
Merkis, riv., Sov.Un. E5 332
Merksem, Bel. 33,026 C3 282
Merksplas, Bel. 4,672 C3 282
Merlin, Ont., Can. 490 R18 64
Merlin, Josephine, Oreg. 300 E3 96
Mermentau, Acadia, La. 334 D3 180
Mermentau, riv., La. E2 180
Merna, Custer, Nebr. 349 C6 152
Merna, Sublette, Wyo. D2 116
Merom, Sullivan, Ind. 352 *C2 140
Merowe, Sud. 1,620 B3 398
Merriam, Noble, Ind. 125 A4 140
Merriam, Johnson, Kans. 5,084 B8 144
Merrick, Nassau, N.Y. 18,789 E3 212
Merrick, co., Nebr. 8,363 C7 152
Merrick, mtn., Scot. F8 272
Merrickville, Ont., Can. 859 P25 64
Merricourt, Dickey, N.Dak. 66 D7 154
Merridin, Austl. 2,342 E3 432
Merrifield, Crow Wing, Minn. 200 E4 148
Merrifield, Fairfax, Va. 1,000 A7 192
Merrill, Plymouth, Iowa 645 B1 142
Merrill (Town of), Aroostook, Maine (337▲) *B4 204
Merrill, Saginaw, Mich. 963 F7 146
Merrill, George, Miss. 150 E4 184
Merrill, Klamath, Oreg. 804 E5 96
Merrill, Lincoln, Wis. 9,451 C4 160
Merrillan, Jackson, Wis. 591 D3 160
Merrillville, Thomas, Ga. 111 F3 176
Merrillville, Lake, Ind. 3,120 A2 140
Merrimac, Taylor, Ky. 250 C5 178
Merrimac, Essex, Mass. 1,800 A5 206
(3,261▲)
Merrimac, Sauk, Wis. 297 E4 160
Merrimack, Hillsboro, N.H. 500 F4 208
Merrimack, co., N.H. 67,785 E3 208
Merrimack, riv., Mass., N.H. A5 206
E3 208
Merrimacport, Essex, Mass. 200 A6 206
Merriman, Cherry, Nebr. 285 B4 152
Merrimon, Carteret, N.C. 200 C9 186
Merrionette Park, Cook, Ill. 2,354 *B6 138
Merritt, B.C., Can. 1,790 E12 52
Merritt, Pamlico, N.C. 100 B9 186
Merritt Island, Brevard, Fla. 3,554 C10 174
Merritton, Ont., Can. 5,404 Q21 64
Merriweather, Ontonagon, Mich. 90 C2 146
Mer Rouge, Morehouse, La. 853 B4 180
Merrymeeting, lake, N.H. E4 208
Merryville, Beauregard, La. 1,232 D2 180
Mersa Fatma, Eth. B5 398
Merseburg, Ger. 41,600 C4 286
Mers-el-Kébir, Alg. 4,332 A3 402
(11,138▲)
Mershon, Pierce, Ga. 300 E4 176
Mersin, Tur. 51,251 C6 307
Mersing, Mala. 7,229 G4 362
Merta Road, India D1 368
Merthyr Tydfil, Wales 59,500 J9 273
Merti, Ken. B6 414
Mértola, Port. 6,439 D3 298
Merton, Waukesha, Wis. 407 E1 160
Mertzon, Irion, Tex. 584 D5 130
Méru, Fr. 5,076 C5 278
Meru, Ken. B6 414
Meru, mtn., Tan. C6 414
Mervin, Sask., Can. 207 D3 58
Merwin, dam, Wash. D4 98
Merzifon, Tur. 20,012 A6 307
Mesa, Maricopa, Ariz. 33,772 E4 124
H2
Mesa, Mesa, Colo. 60 C2 106
Mesa, Adams, Idaho 30 E2 108
Mesa, Franklin, Wash. 263 *C7 98
Mesa, co., Colo. 50,715 D2 106
Mesa, falls, Idaho E7 108
Mesa, peak, Colo. E4 106
Mesagne, It. 20,700 E6 302
Mesa Verde, natl. park, Colo. E2 106
Mescal, Cochise, Ariz. 20 G5 124
Mescalero, Otero, N.Mex. 370 E5 126
Mesena, Warren, Ga. 200 C4 176
Meservey, Cerro Gordo, Iowa 331 B4 142
Meshack, Monroe, Ky. 20 D5 178
Meshcherskoye, Sov.Un. O18 332
Meshchovsk, Sov.Un. 6,800 E10 332
Meshik, Alsk. 30 D6 84
Meshkovskaya, Sov.Un. H13 332
Meshomasic, mtn., Conn. C5 202
Meshra' er Req, Sud. D2 398
Mesic, Pamlico, N.C. 350 B9 186
Mesick, Wexford, Mich. 304 E6 146
Mesilinka, riv., B.C., Can. B10 52
Mesilla, Dona Ana, N.Mex. 1,264 F4 126
Mesilla Park, Dona Ana, N.Mex. 2,400 F4 126
Mesita, Costilla, Colo. 25 E5 106
Meskéné, Syr., U.A.R. A3 378
Mesocco, Switz. 1,150 B5 312
Mesolóngion, Grc. 12,179 B3 306
Mesquite, Clark, Nev. 750 G7 112
Mesquite, Dona Ana, N.Mex. 210 F4 126
Mesquite, Dallas, Tex. 27,526 B9 130
Messalonskee, lake, Maine D3 204
Messenia, see Messinia, prov., Grc.
Messex, Washington, Colo. 20 B7 106
Messias Lopes, Braz. B2 258
Messick, York, Va. (part of Poquoson) A8 192
C8
Messina, It. 176,600 F5 302
(231,600▲)
Messina, U.S.Afr. 9,349 D6 421
Messina, prov., It. 683,000 *F5 302
Messina, strait, It. G5 302
Messini, Grc. 7,722 C3 306
Messini, gulf, Grc. C3 306
Messinia (Messenia), prov., Grc. 227,871 C4 306
Mesta, riv., Bul. C1 317
Mestre, It. (part of Venezia) 73,435 C4 302
Mesudiye, Tur. 1,940 A7 307
Meta, Osage, Mo. 360 C5 150
Meta, intendencia, Col. 74,780 C2 244
Meta, pond, Newf., Can. F8 72
Meta, riv., Col. B3 244
Meta, riv., Ven. C4 240
Métabetchouan, Que., Can. 1,505 P13 66
Métabetchouan, riv., Que., Can. P13 66
Metairie, Jefferson, La. 65,000 C7 180
Metaline, Pend Oreille, Wash. 299 A9 98
Metaline Falls, Pend Oreille, Wash. 469 A9 98
Metalton, Carroll, Ark. 25 A3 170
Metamora, Woodford, Ill. 1,808 C4 138
Metamora, Franklin, Ind. 400 C4 140
Metamora, Lapeer, Mich. 452 G8 146
Metamora, Fulton, Ohio 598 A3 156
Metán, Arg. 6,915 C5 250
Metangula, Moz. B7 421
Metapán, Sal. 2,811 C3 228
Metaponto, It. 293 E6 302
Metarica, Moz. B7 421
Metascouac, lake, Que., Can. Q13 66
Metcalf, Thomas, Ga. 241 F3 176
Metcalfe, Ont., Can. 425 O25 64
Metcalfe, Washington, Miss. 500 B1 184
Metcalfe, co., Ky. 9,367 D5 178
Metchosin, B.C., Can. 35 C14 52
Meteghan, N.S., Can. 730 E3 70
Meteghan River, N.S., Can. 385 E3 70
Meteghan Station, N.S., Can. 215 E4 70
Meteor, crater, Ariz. D4 124
Methóni, Grc. 2,087 C3 306
Methow, Okanogan, Wash. 75 A6 98
Methow, riv., Wash. A6 98
Methuen, Essex, Mass. 28,114 A5 206
Methy, lake, Alta., Can. B8 54
Metiskow, Alta., Can. 50 D7 54
Metković, Yugo. 3,606 C3 316
Metlakatla, Alsk. 817 D8 84
K15
Metlakatla, B.C., Can. 20 C7 52
Meto, bayou, Ark. C5 170
Metolius, Jefferson, Oreg. 270 C5 96
Metonga, lake, Wis. C5 160
Metropolis, Massac, Ill. 7,339 F5 138
Metropolitan, Dickinson, Mich. 100 D4 146
Métsovon, Grc. 2,798 B3 306
Mettawee, riv., Vt. E2 218
Metter, Candler, Ga. 2,362 D4 176
Mettet, Bel. 3,150 D3 282
Metuchen, Middlesex, N.J. 14,041 B4 210
Metulla, Isr. 178 A6 382
Metz, Fr. 85,701 C7 278
Metz, Steuben, Ind. 200 A5 140
Metz, Presque Isle, Mich. 60 D8 146
Metz, Vernon, Mo. 137 C3 150
Metz, Marion, W.Va. 300 A6 194
Metzger, Washington, Oreg. B1 96
Meudon, Fr. 24,729 I9 278
Meurthe-et-Moselle, dept., Fr. 607,022 *C7 278
Meuse, dept., Fr. 207,106 *C6 278
Meuse, hills, Fr. C6 278
Meuse, riv., Bel. D4 282
Meuse, riv., Fr. C6 278
Mexia, Monroe, Ala. 150 D2 168
Mexia, Limestone, Tex. 6,121 D7 130
Mexicali, Mex. 64,658 A2 224
Mexican Hat, San Juan, Utah 250 *F5 114
Mexican Springs, McKinley, N.Mex. 30 C2 126
Mexico, Miami, Ind. 600 B3 140
Mexico, Crittenden, Ky. 300 C2 178
Mexico, Oxford, Maine 5,043 D2 204
Mexico, Audrain, Mo. 12,889 B6 150
Mexico, Oswego, N.Y. 1,465 B5 212
México, country, N.A. 32,347,698 225
México, state, Mex. 1,392,623 D5 225
Mexico, gulf, U.S. F8 77
Mexico Beach, Bay, Fla. 500 B5 174
México City, Mex. 2,233,914 D6 225
(*3,015,000) G10
Meyädin, Syr., U.A.R. 8,012 B4 378
Meyer, Muskogee, Okla. C8 128
Meyers, Garland, Ark. 75 C6 170
Meyersdale, Somerset, Pa. 2,901 D2 214
Meyronne, Sask., Can. 220 F4 58
Mezdra, Bul. 6,514 B1 317
Mèze, Fr. 4,403 F5 278
Mezen, Sov.Un. 7,300 C6 328
Mezen, riv., Sov.Un. C6 328
Mézenc, mtn., Fr. E6 278
Meziadin, lake, B.C., Can. B8 52
Mézières, Fr. 11,073 C6 278
Mezöberény, Hung. 14,578 C6 320
Mezökövesd, Hung. 18,075 B5 320
Mezötúr, Hung. 16,000 B5 320
(24,000▲)
Mezquital, Mex. 832 C5 224
Mezquite, Mex. B5 225
Mglin, Sov.Un. 15,400 F9 332
Mhor, lake, Scot. D8 272
Mhow, India E1 368
Mi, isl., Jap. G3 354
Miahuatlán, Mex. 5,539 D6 225
Miajadas, Sp. 8,302 C4 298
Miami, Gila, Ariz. 3,350 E5 124
Miami, Man., Can. 350 F3 60

Miami, Dade, Fla. 291,688 (*1,212,000) E6 F10 174
Miami, Miami, Ind. 300 B3 140
Miami, Saline, Mo. 156 B4 150
Miami, Colfax, N.Mex. 150 B6 126
Miami, Ottawa, Okla. 12,869 B9 128
Miami, Rh.&Nya. C5 420
Miami, Roberts, Tex. 656 B5 130
Miami, Kanawha, W.Va. 450 D6 194
Miami, co., Ind. 38,000 B3 140
Miami, co., Kans. 19,884 D9 144
Miami, co., Ohio 72,901 B2 156
Miami, canal, Fla. E10 174
Miami, riv., Ohio C2 156
Miami Beach, Dade, Fla. 63,145 E6 F10 174
Miamisburg, Montgomery, Ohio 9,893 C2 156
Miami Shores, Dade, Fla. 8,865 E6 F10 174
Miami Shores, Montgomery, Ohio 1,200 *C2 156
Miami Springs, Dade, Fla. 11,229 E6 F10 174
Miamitown, Hamilton, Ohio 500 D1 156
Miāndasht, Iran B4 379
Miandrivazo, Malag. 1,505 C9 421
Miāneh, Iran 14,758 B2 379
Mianwali, Pak. 23,341 C7 375
Miaoli, For. 50,000 M10 349
Miarinarivo, Malag. C9 421
Miass, Sov.Un. 35,000 B6 336
Miass, riv., Sov.Un. A6 336
Miastko, Pol. 3,417 A3 325
Mica, Spokane, Wash. 75 B9 D9 98
Micanopy, Alachua, Fla. 658 B8 174
Micay, Col. C1 244
Micco, Brevard, Fla. 300 D10 174
Miccosukee, Leon, Fla. 175 A6 174
Miccosukee, lake, Fla. A7 174
Michael, lake, Newf., Can. C6 72
Michaga, mtn., Bol. C1 246
Michalovce, Czech. 15,167 B5 324
Michaud, Aroostook, Maine A4 204
Michaud, pt., N.S., Can. D9 70
Michaudville, Que., Can. 205 S11 66
Michel, B.C., Can. 770 F15 52
Michel, lake, Newf., Can. E7 72
Michelson, mtn., Alsk. B7 84
Michiana, Berrien, Mich. 135 *H5 146
Michiana Shores, La Porte, Ind. 229 *A3 140
Michichi, Alta., Can. 100 E6 54
Michie, McNairy, Tenn. 200 C3 190
Michigamme, Marquette, Mich. 250 C3 146
Michigamme, lake, Mich. C3 146
Michigan, Nelson, N.Dak. 451 B7 154
Michigan, state, U.S. 7,823,194 C9 77 146
Michigan, creek, Colo. B4 106
Michigan, isl., Wis. B3 160
Michigan, lake, U.S. C9 77
Michigan, prairie, Wash. C8 98
Michigan Center, Jackson, Mich. 4,611 G7 146
Michigan City, La Porte, Ind. 36,653 A3 140
Michigan City, Benton, Miss. 50 A3 184
Michigantown, Clinton, Ind. 513 B3 140
Michikamau, lake, Newf., Can. D9 72
Michipicoten Harbour, Ont., Can. 200 R24 64
Michoacán, state, Mex. 1,422,717 D5 225
Michurin, Bul. 2,794 B3 317
Michurinsk, Sov.Un. 80,000 B2 336
Mickleyville, Marion, Ind. 950 D4 140
Micoud, St. Lucia 1,350 *E14 233
Micro, Johnston, N.C. 350 B7 186
Midale, Sask., Can. 703 F6 58
Midas, Bonner, Idaho 50 *A2 108
Midas, Elko, Nev. 25 B5 112
Middelburg, Neth. 21,805 C2 282
Middelfart, Den. 8,863 I3 291
Middelharnis, Neth. 5,014 C3 282
Middelkerke, Bel. 4,610 C1 282
Middle, fork, Idaho E4 108
Middle, fork, Kans. C2 144
Middle, fork, Wyo. D5 116
Middle, fork, Wyo. C6 116
Middle, riv., B.C., Can. C10 52
Middle, riv., Iowa C3 142
Middle, riv., Minn. C2 148
Middle Alkali, lake, Nev. B2 112
Middle Amana, Iowa, Iowa 250 C6 142
Middle Andaman, isl., India F6 366
Middleberg, Grady, Okla. 50 C6 128
Middleboro, Plymouth, Mass. 6,003 (11,065▲) C6 206
Middlebourne, Tyler, W.Va. 711 B4 194
Middlebranch, Holt, Nebr. B7 152
Middlebranch, Stark, Ohio 500 B5 156
Middlebro, Man., Can. F5 60
Middle Brook, Newf., Can. 500 F8 72
Middlebrook, Augusta, Va. 140 B5 192
Middleburg, Clay, Fla. 250 A9 174
Middleburg, Casey, Ky. 150 C6 178
Middleburg, Schoharie, N.Y. 1,317 C7 212
Middleburg, Logan, Ohio 350 B3 156
Middleburg, Snyder, Pa. 1,366 C4 214
Middleburg, Hardeman, Tenn. 25 C2 190
Middleburg, U.S.Afr. 6,193 F4 420
Middleburg, Loudoun, Va. 761 B7 192
Middleburg Heights, Cuyahoga, Ohio 7,282 B1 156
Middlebury, New Haven, Conn. 2,000 (4,785▲) C3 202
Middlebury, Elkhart, Ind. 917 A4 140
Middlebury, Addison, Vt. 3,688 C2 218
Middlebury, riv., Vt. D2 218
Middledam, Oxford, Maine D2 204
Middlefield, Middlesex, Conn. 400 (3,255▲) C5 202
Middlefield, Hampshire, Mass. 100 (315▲) B1 206
Middlefield, Geauga, Ohio 1,467 A5 156
Middle Grandville, Washington, N.Y. 869 B8 212
Middle Ground, isl., Midway E3 436
Middle Haddam, Middlesex, Conn. 500 C5 202
Middle Inlet, Marinette, Wis. 75 C5 160
Middle Island, Suffolk, N.Y. 950 D4 212
Middle Island, creek, W.Va. B3 194
Middle Lake, Sask., Can. 150 D5 58
Middle Loup, riv., Nebr. C6 152
Middle Nodaway, riv., Iowa C3 142
Middle Park, basin, Colo. B4 106
Middle Patuxent, riv., Md. B6 182
Middle Point, Van Wert, Ohio 571 B2 156
Middleport, Niagara, N.Y. 1,882 B3 212
Middleport, Meigs, Ohio 3,373 C4 156
Middle Racoon, riv., Iowa C3 142
Middle Ridge, mts., Newf., Can. F8 72
Middle River, Baltimore, Md. 10,825 B7 182
Middle River, Marshall, Minn. 414 C2 148
Middlesboro, Bell, Ky. 12,607 D7 178
Middlesbrough, Eng. 149,900 G11 273
Middlesex, Br. Hond. B3 228
Middlesex, Middlesex, N.J. 10,520 B4 210
Middlesex, Nash, N.C. 588 B7 186
Middlesex, Washington, Vt. 80 (770▲) C3 218
Middlesex, co., Ont., Can. 190,897 Q19 64
Middlesex, co., Conn. 88,865 D5 202
Middlesex, co., Eng. 2,251,000 J12 273
Middlesex, co., Mass. 1,238,742 A5 206
Middlesex, co., N.J. 433,856 C4 210
Middlesex, co., Va. 6,319 C8 192
Middle Sister, mtn., Oreg. C5 96
Middleton, N.S., Can. 1,769 E4 70
Middleton, Elbert, Ga. 106 B4 176
Middleton, Canyon, Idaho 541 F2 108
Middleton, Essex, Mass. 2,200 (3,718▲) A5 C3 206
Middleton, Gratiot, Mich. 550 F7 146
Middleton, Strafford, N.H. 100 (349▲) E4 208
Middleton, Hardeman, Tenn. 461 C3 190
Middleton, Dane, Wis. 4,410 E4 160
Middleton, isl., Alsk. D7 84
Middletown, Lake, Calif. 450 C2 94
Middletown, Middlesex, Conn. 33,250 C5 202
Middletown, New Castle, Del. 2,191 C3 172
Middletown, Logan, Ill. 543 C4 138
Middletown, Henry, Ind. 2,033 B4 140
Middletown, Des Moines, Iowa 245 D6 142
Middletown, Jefferson, Ky. 2,764 A5 178
Middletown, Frederick, Md. 1,036 B4 182
Middletown, Montgomery, Mo. 199 B6 150
Middletown, Monmouth, N.J. 3,500 C4 210
Middletown, Orange, N.Y. 23,475 D7 212
Middletown, Hyde, N.C. 200 B9 186
Middletown, Butler, Ohio 42,115 C2 156
Middletown, Dauphin, Pa. 11,182 C5 214
Middletown, Newport, R.I. 12,675 C3 216
Middletown, Frederick, Va. 378 A6 192
Middletown Heights, Delaware, Pa. 1,000 *D6 214
Middletown Springs, Rutland, Vt. 275 (381▲) E2 218
Middle Valley, Morris, N.J. 250 B3 210
Middle Village, Honolulu, Haw. (part of Ewa) 128 G9 86
Middleville, Ont., Can. 210 O24 64
Middleville, Barry, Mich. 1,196 G6 146
Middleville, Sussex, N.J. 75 A3 210
Middleville, Herkimer, N.Y. 648 B7 212
Middleway, Jefferson, W.Va. 760 B7 194
Midfield, Jefferson, Ala. 3,556 E4 168
Midgic Station, N.B., Can. 310 D5 70
Midhdalur, Ice. L19 290
Midhurst, Ont., Can. 175 P21 64
Midian, Butler, Kans. E7 144
Midi d'Ossau, peak, Fr. F3 278
Midkiff, Lincoln, W.Va. 200 C2 194
Midland, Sebastian, Ark. 261 B2 170
Midland, Riverside, Calif. 500 F6 94
Midland, Ont., Can. 8,250 P21 64
Midland, Greene, Ind. 475 C2 140
Midland, Acadia, La. 500 D3 180
Midland, Allegany, Md. 737 A2 182
Midland, Midland, Mich. 27,779 F7 146
Midland, Cabarrus, N.C. 750 B5 186
Midland, Clinton, Ohio 367 C3 156
Midland, Beaver, Pa. 6,425 C1 214
Midland, Washington, Pa. 1,317 *C1 214
Midland, Haakon, S.Dak. 401 C4 158
Midland, Midland, Tex. 62,625 C4 130
Midland, Fauquier, Va. 100 B7 192
Midland, Pierce, Wash. 4,000 *B4 98
Midland, co., Mich. 51,450 F7 146
Midland, co., Tex. 67,717 D4 130
Midland Acres, Clark, Wash. 900 *D4 98
Midland City, Dale, Ala. 854 D4 168
Midland Park, Bergen, N.J. 7,543 A1 B4 210
Midland Park, Charleston, S.C. F3 188
Midlandvale, Alta., Can. 685 E6 54
Midleton, Ire. 2,784 J4 273
Midlothian, Cook, Ill. 6,605 F3 138
Midlothian, Allegany, Md. 525 A2 182
Midlothian, Lincoln, Okla. 50 C7 128
Midlothian, Ellis, Tex. 1,521 B8 C7 130
Midlothian, Chesterfield, Va. 400 B8 C7 192
Midlothian, co., Scot. 574,000 F9 272
Midnapore, Alta., Can. 27 E5 54
Midnapore, India 45,476 I8 366
Midnight, Humphreys, Miss. 150 B2 184
Midongy du Sud, Malag. D9 421
Mid River Farms, Broward, Fla. 400 D6 174
Midstate Mill, Robeson, N.C. 1,090 *C6 186
Midvale, New Castle, Del. 500 *A1 172
Midvale, Washington, Idaho 211 E2 108
Midvale, Tuscarawas, Ohio 683 B5 156
Midvale, Salt Lake, Utah 5,802 C4 114
Midville, Burke, Ga. 676 D4 176
Midway, Bullock, Ala. 594 C4 168
Midway, Baxter, Ark. 70 A4 170
Midway, B.C., Can. 250 F13 52
Midway, Sussex, Del. 250 F5 172
Midway, Gadsden, Fla. 150 A6 174
Midway, Liberty, Ga. 240 E5 176
Midway, Bingham, Idaho *F6 108
Midway, Woodford, Ky. 1,044 B6 178
Midway, La Salle, La. 400 C3 180
Midway, Multnomah, Oreg. 19,000 *A2 96
Midway, Adams, Pa. 1,012 D4 214
Midway, Bamberg, S.C. 100 E7 188
Midway, Greene, Tenn. B8 190
Midway, Wasatch, Utah 713 C4 114
Midway, King, Wash. 1,000 D3 98
Midway, Raleigh, W.Va. 500 *D3 194
Midway, range, B.C., Can. F13 52
Midway City, Orange, Calif. 2,500 C5 94
Midway Island, Stafford, Va. B7 192
Midway Islands, U.S. poss., Pac.O. 416 E3 436
Midway Park, Onslow, N.C. 4,164 C8 186
Midway Village, Oklahoma, Okla. 2,292 C6 128
Midwest, Natrona, Wyo. 1,000 C6 116
Midwest City, Oklahoma, Okla. 36,058 C6 128
Midwest Heights, Natrona, Wyo. 60 *D6 116
Midyat, Tur. 8,210 C9 307
Midye, Tur. 1,318 A3 307
Midzhur, mtn., Bul. B1 317
Midzhur, mtn., Yugo. C6 316
Miechów, Pol. 6,878 C5 325
Międzychód, Pol. 4,632 B2 325
Międzyrzec, Pol. 8,696 C6 325
Międzyrzecz, Pol. 4,385 B2 325
Międzyzdroje, Pol. 1,949 B2 325
Mielec, Pol. 18,100 C5 325
Mien, lake, Swe. E5 292
Mienning, China F8 346
Mienyang, China E8 346
Mienyang, China 5,000 J6 349
Miercurea-Ciuc, Rom. 11,996 A3 321
Mieres, Sp. 14,137 A4 298
Mieso, Eth. D5 398
Miesville, Dakota, Minn. 126 G6 148
Mieves, Mex. C5 224
Mifflin, Juniata, Pa. 745 C4 214
Mifflin, Chester, Tenn. 50 C3 190
Mifflin, co., Pa. 44,348 C4 214
Mifflinburg, Union, Pa. 2,476 C4 214
Mifflintown, Juniata, Pa. 887 C4 214
Mifflinville, Columbia, Pa. 1,027 B5 214
Miflin, Baldwin, Ala. E2 168
Migdal, Isr. 295 B6 382
Migdal Ashgelon, Isr. 14,400 C5 382
Migennes, Fr. 5,226 D5 278
Migiurtinia, pol. dist., Som. 82,653 D6 398
Mignon, Talladega, Ala. 2,271 B3 168
Miguel Alves, Braz. 4,426 A2 258
Miguel Anza, Mex. 6,538 C5 224
Mihaileni, Rom. 3,807 A4 321
Mihai-Viteazu, Rom. 2,598 B5 321
Mihara, Jap. 70,650 *G4 354
Mijares, riv., Sp. B6 298
Mikado, Sask., Can. 179 E6 58
Mikado, Alcona, Mich. 125 E8 146
Mikana, Barron, Wis. 120 C2 160
Mike Horse, Lewis and Clark, Mont. C4 110
Mikhaylov, Sov.Un. 23,600 E12 332
Mikhaylovgrad, Bul. 13,434 B1 317
Mikhaylovgradski, prov., Bul. *B1 317
Mikhaylovka, Sov.Un. 31,100 B2 336
Mikhaylovka, Sov.Un. 24,000 I10 332
Mikhaylovskiy, Sov.Un. B9 336
Mikindani, Tan. 4,807 E7 414
Mikkalo, Gilliam, Oreg. 15 B6 96
Mikkeli, Fin. 16,359 F12 291
Mikkeli, dept., Fin. 246,900 *F12 291
Mikonos, isl., Grc. C5 306
Mikope, Con.L. D3 414
Mikulov, Czech. 5,220 B3 324
Mikura, isl., Jap. H7 354
Mila, Northumberland, Va. 25 C8 192
Milaca, Mille Lacs, Minn. 1,821 F5 148
Milagro, Arg. B2 252
Milagro, Ec. 16,081 A2 245
Milam, Hardy, W.Va. 65 C5 194
Milam, co., Tex. 22,263 D7 130
Milan, Que., Can. 200 S13 66
Milan, Telfair and Dodge, Ga. 786 D3 176
Milan, Rock Island, Ill. 3,065 B3 138
Milan, Ripley, Ind. 1,174 C4 140
Milan, see Milano, It.
Milan, Sumner, Kans. 144 E6 144
Milan, Washtenaw, Mich. 3,616 G8 146
Milan, Chippewa, Minn. 482 F3 148
Milan, Sullivan, Mo. 1,670 A4 150
Milan, Coos, N.H. 100 (661▲) B4 208
Milan, Valencia, N.Mex. 2,658 *C3 126
Milan, Erie, Ohio 1,309 A4 156
Milan, Gibson, Tenn. 5,208 C3 190
Milan, Spokane, Wash. 70 B9 98
Milan, Marathon, Wis. 150 D3 160
Milano (Milan), It. 1,305,400 (*1,640,000) C2 302
Milano, Milam, Tex. 600 D7 130
Milano, prov., It. 2,598,500 *C2 302
Milazzo, It. 12,900 F5 302
Milbank, Grant, S.Dak. 3,500 B9 158
Milbanke, sound, B.C., Can. D8 52
Milbridge, Washington, Maine 675 (1,101▲) D5 204
Milburn, Carlisle, Ky. 400 D2 178
Milburn, Custer, Nebr. 16 C6 152
Milburn, Johnston, Okla. 228 D7 128
Milburn, Fayette, W.Va. 700 D6 194
Milden, Sask., Can. 390 E4 58
Mildmay, Ont., Can. 870 P19 64
Mildred, Sask., Can. 100 D4 58
Mildred, Allen, Kans. 60 D8 144
Mildred, Prairie, Mont. 50 D12 110
Mildred, Sullivan, Pa. 800 B5 214
Mildura, Austl. 10,972 E8 432
Miléai, Grc. 1,983 B4 306
Miles, Austl. 1,193 D10 432
Miles, Jackson, Iowa 376 B7 142
Miles, Runnels, Tex. 626 D5 130
Miles City, Custer, Mont. 9,665 D11 110
Milestone, Sask., Can. 488 F5 58
Milesville, Haakon, S.Dak. 20 C4 158
Miley, Hampton, S.C. 450 F6 188
Milfay, Creek, Okla. 130 C7 128
Milford, New Haven, Conn. 41,662 E3 202
Milford, Sussex, Del. 5,795 E4 172
Milford, Iroquois, Ill. 1,699 C6 138
Milford, Decatur, Ind. 197 C4 140
Milford, Kosciusko, Ind. 1,167 A4 140
Milford, Dickinson, Iowa 1,476 A2 142
Milford, Geary, Kans. 318 C7 144
Milford, Bracken, Ky. 100 B6 178
Milford, Penobscot, Maine 800 (1,572▲) D4 204
Milford, Worcester, Mass. 15,749 B4 E1 206
Milford, Oakland, Mich. 4,323 B7 G8 146
Milford, Seward, Nebr. 1,462 D8 152
Milford, Hillsboro, N.H. 3,916 (4,863▲) F3 208
Milford, Hunterdon, N.J. 1,114 B2 210
Milford, Otsego, N.Y. 548 C7 212
Milford, Clermont and Hamilton, Ohio 4,131 C2 156
Milford, Pike, Pa. 1,198 B7 214
Milford, Beaver, Utah 1,471 E3 114
Milford, Caroline, Va. 250 B7 192
Milford, sound, N.Z. F1 437
Milford Center, Union, Ohio 794 B3 156
Milford Haven, Wales 12,000 J7 273
Milford Lawns, New Haven, Conn. 575 E3 202
Milford Mills, Baltimore, Md. 5,000 *B6 182
Milford Station, N.S., Can. 312 D6 70
Milhurst, Monmouth, N.J. 100 C4 210
Miliana, Alg. 5,983 (15,666▲) A4 402
Milicz, Pol. 2,929 C3 325
Miling, Austl. 384 E3 432
Milk, riv., Alta., Can., Mont. F7 B8 54 110
Milkovo, Sov.Un. D17 329
Milk River, Alta., Can. 642 F6 54
Mil Kūh, mtn., Afg. C2 374
Mill, Winn, La. B3 180
Mill, brook, Vt. B5 218
Mill, creek, Ind. C3 140
Mill, creek, Kans. B7 144
Mill, creek, Kans. C6 144
Mill, creek, Kans. D7 144
Mill, creek, N.J. D4 210
Mill, creek, Ohio B3 156
Mill, creek, Tenn. E7 190
Mill, creek, W.Va. C3 194
Milladore, Wood, Wis. 239 D4 160
Millard, Pike, Ky. 300 C8 178
Millard, Pearl River, Miss. 15 E3 184
Millard, Adair, Mo. 250 A5 150
Millard, Douglas, Nebr. 1,014 D3 152
Millard, Walworth, Wis. 100 F5 160
Millard, co., Utah 7,866 D2 114
Millau, Fr. 19,209 E5 278
Millbank, Ont., Can. 495 Q20 64
Millboro, Tripp, S.Dak. 34 D6 158
Millboro, Bath, Va. 300 C5 192
Millbrae, San Mateo, Calif. 15,873 B5 94
Mill Bridge, Ont., Can. P23 64
Millbrook, Elmore, Ala. 1,000 *C3 168
Millbrook, Ont., Can. 807 P22 64
Millbrook, Plymouth, Mass. 200 B6 206
Millbrook, Mecosta, Mich. 100 F6 146
Millbrook, Morris, N.J. 900 *B3 210
Millbrook, Dutchess, N.Y. 1,717 D8 212
Millburn, Essex, N.J. 18,799 B4 210
Millbury, Worcester, Mass. 6,000 (9,623▲) B4 206
Millbury, Wood, Ohio 730 A1 A3 156
Mill City, Pershing, Nev. 20 C3 112
Mill City, Marion, Oreg. 1,289 C4 96
Mill Creek, La Porte, Ind. 150 A3 140
Mill Creek, Deer Lodge, Mont. 200 *D4 110
Mill Creek, Johnston, Okla. 287 D7 128
Mill Creek, Randolph, W.Va. 817 C5 194
Milldale, Hartford, Conn. 950 C4 202
Mille, atoll, Marshall A4 436
Milledgeville, Baldwin, Ga. 11,117 C3 176
Milledgeville, Carroll, Ill. 1,208 B4 138
Milledgeville, McNairy, Tenn. 300 C3 190
Millegan, Cascade, Mont. C5 110
Mille Lacs, co., Minn. 14,560 E5 148
Mille Lacs, lake, Minn. E5 148
Millen, Jenkins, Ga. 3,633 D5 176
Miller, Lyon, Kans. 75 D8 144
Miller, De Soto, Miss. 150 A3 184
Miller, Lawrence, Mo. 601 D4 150
Miller, Buffalo, Nebr. 137 D6 152
Miller, Sherman, Oreg. B6 96
Miller, Hand, S.Dak. 2,081 C7 158
Miller, co., Ark. 31,686 D3 170
Miller, co., Ga. 6,908 E2 176
Miller, co., Mo. 13,800 C5 150
Miller, isl., Md. B7 182
Miller, mtn., Alsk. C7 84
Miller, peak, Ariz. G5 124
Miller Heights, Northampton, Pa. 1,500 *C6 214
Mille-Roches, Ont., Can. 740 O26 64
Millerovo, Sov.Un. 32,400 H13 332
Miller Run, riv., Vt. B4 218
Millers, Carroll, Md. 160 A6 182
Millers, riv., Mass. A3 206
Millersburg, Elkhart, Ind. 489 A4 140
Millersburg, Iowa, Iowa 186 C5 142
Millersburg, Bourbon, Ky. 913 B6 178
Millersburg, Presque Isle., Mich. 280 D7 146
Millersburg, Holmes, Ohio 3,101 B5 156
Millersburg, Linn, Oreg. C1 96
Millersburg, Dauphin, Pa. 2,984 C5 214
Millers Falls, Franklin, Mass. 1,199 A3 206
Millers Ferry, Washington, Fla. 50 A5 174
Millersport, Fairfield, Ohio 752 C4 156
Millersville, Anne Arundel, Md. 250 B6 182
Millersville, Lancaster, Pa. 3,883 D5 214
Millerton, N.B., Can. 325 C4 70
Millerton, Wayne, Iowa 90 D4 142
Millerton, Dutchess, N.Y. 1,027 D8 212

Millerton, McCurtain, Okla. 150 E8 128
Millertown, Newf., Can. 350 F7 72
Millertown Junction, Newf., Can. 150 F7 72
Millerville, Clay, Ala. 90 B4 168
Millerville, Worcester, Mass. 1,200 B4 206
Millerville, Douglas, Minn. 119 E3 148
Milles Iles, riv., Que., Can. S15 66
Millet, Alta., Can. 427 D6 54
Millett, Nye, Nev. 10 D4 112
Millett, Allendale, S.C. 50 E5 188
Milleur, pt., Scot. F7 272
Mille Vaches, pt., Que., Can. P15 66
Mill Fork, Utah, Utah 7 D4 114
Millgrove, Blackford, Ind. 130 B4 140
Mill Grove, Mercer, Mo. 139 A4 150
Mill Hall, Clinton, Pa. 1,891 B4 214
Millhousen, Decatur, Ind. 212 C4 140
Millicent, Alta., Can. 109 E7 54
Milligan, Okaloosa, Fla. 750 A4 174
Milligan, Fillmore, Nebr. 323 D8 152
Milligan, mtn., B.C., Can. C10 52
Milligan College, Carter, Tenn. 200 B9 190
Milliken, Weld, Colo. 630 B6 106
Millikin, East Carroll, La. 100 B4 180
Millington, Kent and Queen Annes, Md. 408 B8 182
Millington, Tuscola, Mich. 1,159 F8 146
Millington, Morris, N.J. 1,182 *B3 210
Millington, Coos, Oreg. 300 D2 96
Millington, Shelby, Tenn. 6,059 C2 190
Millinocket, Penobscot, Maine 7,453 C4 204
Millinocket, lake, Maine B4 204
Mill Iron, Carter, Mont. 5 E12 110
Millom, Eng. 7,116 G9 273
Mill Plain, Fairfield, Conn. 170 D1 202
Mill Point, Pocahontas, W.Va. 150 C4 194
Millport, Lamar, Ala. 943 B1 168
Millport, Chemung, N.Y. 425 C5 212
Mill River, Franklin, Mass. 250 B1 206
Millry, Washington, Ala. 645 D1 168
Mills, Keya Paha, Nebr. 37 B6 152
Mills, Harding, N.Mex. 136 B6 126
Mills, see Cotton Mills, Tex.
Mills, Juab, Utah D3 114
Mills, Natrona, Wyo. 1,477 D6 116
Mills, co., Iowa 13,050 C2 142
Mills, co., Tex. 4,467 D6 130
Mills, lake, N.W.Ter., Can. E7 48
Millsboro, Sussex, Del. 536 F4 172
Millsboro, Washington, Pa. 1,179 D1 214
Mill Shoals, White, Ill. 322 E5 138
Millside, New Castle, Del. 1,000 *A1 172
Mill Spring, Wayne, Mo. 226 D7 150
Millstadt, St. Clair, Ill. 1,830 E3 138
Millston, Jackson, Wis. 200 D3 160
Millstone, New London, Conn. 125 D7 202
Millstone, Letcher, Ky. 900 C8 178
Millstone, Somerset, N.J. 409 B3 210
Millstone, riv., N.J. C3 210
Mill Stream, Austl. C3 432
Milltown, Chambers, Ala. 200 B4 168
Milltown, N.B., Can. 1,975 D2 70
Milltown, Crawford and Harrison, Ind. 793 D3 140
Mill Town, Madison, Miss. 300 C2 184
Milltown, Missoula, Mont. 650 D3 110
Milltown, Middlesex, N.J. 5,435 C4 210
Milltown, Hutchinson, S.Dak. 52 D8 158
Milltown, Polk, Wis. 608 C1 160
Millvale, Allegheny, Pa. 6,624 A4 214
Mill Valley, Marin, Calif. 10,411 A4 94
Millview, Escambia, Fla. 200 A3 174
Mill Village, N.S., Can. 145 E5 70
Millville, N.B., Can. 365 C2 70
Millville, Sussex, Del. 231 F5 172
Millville, Wabasha, Minn. 171 G6 148
Millville, Cumberland, N.J. 19,096 E2 210
Millville, Butler, Ohio 676 C1 156
Millville, Columbia, Pa. 952 B5 214
Millville, Cache, Utah 364 *B4 114
Millville, Jefferson, W.Va. 500 B7 194
Millwood, Ware, Ga. 900 E4 176
Millwood, Clarke, Va. 400 A6 192
Millwood, Spokane, Wash. 1,776 D9 98
Millwood, Jackson, W.Va. 150 C3 194
Milmay, Atlantic, N.J. 450 E3 210
Milner, B.C., Can. 425 B15 52
Milner, Routt, Colo. 100 B3 106
Milner, Lamar, Ga. 305 C2 176
Milner, dam, Idaho G5 108
Milner Ridge, Man., Can. E4 60
Milnor, Sargent, N.Dak. 658 D8 154
Milo, Alta., Can. 167 E6 54
Milo, Warren, Iowa 468 C4 142
Milo, Piscataquis, Maine 1,802 C4 204
(2,756▲)
Milo, Vernon, Mo. 108 D3 150
Milo, Carter, Okla. 40 D6 128
Milo, Douglas, Oreg. 500 *E3 96
Milo, Bledsoe, Tenn. C7 190
Milolii, Hawaii, Haw. 95 D6 86
Milos, isl., Grc. C5 306
Milpalta, Mex. L14 225
Milparinka, Austl. 38 D8 432
Milpitas, Santa Clara, Calif. 6,572 B6 94
Milroy, Rush, Ind. 690 C4 140
Milroy, Redwood, Minn. 268 G3 148
Milroy, Mifflin, Pa. 1,666 C4 214
Milstead, Rockdale, Ga. 1,047 B6 176
C3
Milton, N.S., Can. 990 E5 70
Milton, Sussex, Del. 1,617 E4 172
Milton, Santa Rosa, Fla. 4,108 A3 174
Milton, Pike, Ill. 309 D2 138
Milton, Wayne, Ind. 700 C4 140
Milton, Van Buren, Iowa 609 D5 142
Milton, Sumner, Kans. 150 E6 144
Milton, Trimble, Ky. 365 B5 178
Milton, Lafayette, La. 150 D3 180
Milton, Norfolk, Mass. 26,375 B5 206
D3
Milton, Strafford, N.H. 650 E5 208
(1,418▲)
Milton, Morris, N.J. 400 A3 210
Milton, Ulster, N.Y. 800 D8 212
Milton, N.Z. 1,904 G2 437
Milton, Caswell, N.C. 235 A6 186
Milton, Cavalier, N.Dak. 264 B7 154
Milton, Le Flore, Okla. 100 *C8 128
Milton, Northumberland, Pa. 7,972 B5 214
Milton, Morgan, Utah B4 114
Milton, Chittenden, Vt. 817 B2 218
(2,022▲)
Milton, Pierce, Wash. 2,218 D2 98
Milton, Cabell, W.Va. 1,714 C2 194
Milton, Rock, Wis. 1,671 F5 160
Milton, res., Colo. B6 106
Milton, res., Ohio A6 156
Miltona, Douglas, Minn. 163 E3 148
Miltona, lake, Minn. E3 148
Milton-Freewater, Umatilla, Oreg. 4,110 B8 96
Milton Junction, Rock, Wis. 1,433 F5 160
Milton Mills, Strafford, N.H. 275 D5 208
Miltonvale, Cloud, Kans. 814 C6 144
Milton West, Ont., Can. 4,294 Q21 64
Milverton, Ont., Can. 1,070 Q20 64
Milwaukee, Northampton, N.C. 311 A8 186
Milwaukee, Milwaukee, Wis. 741,324 E2 160
(*1,240,700) E6
Milwaukee, co., Wis. 1,036,041 E5 160
Milwaukee, riv., Wis. E2 160
Milwaukie, Clackamas, Oreg. 9,099 B2 96
B4
Mimbres, Grant, N.Mex. 75 F2 126
Mimbres, mts., N.Mex. F3 126
Mimico, Ont., Can. 13,687 Q21 64
S22
Mimongo, Gabon G7 409
Mims, Brevard, Fla. 1,307 C10 174
Mina, Mineral, Nev. 300 E3 112
Mina, Edmunds, S.Dak. 50 B7 158
Mināb, Iran D4 379
Minabetsu, Sov.Un. E16 329
Mina el Qamh, Eg., U.A.R. 13,829 *A3 395
Mina el Qamh, Eg., U.A.R. 18,829 D2 382
Minago, riv., Man., Can. C3 60
Minam, Wallowa, Oreg. 75 B9 96
Minamata, Jap. 46,233 H3 354
Minami, Iwo A7 436
Minas, Cuba 3,305 B6 232
Minas, Ur. 30,000 B4 252
Minas, basin, N.S., Can. D5 70
Minas, chan., N.S., Can. D5 70
Minas de Oro, Hond. 1,601 C4 228
Minas de Riotinto, Sp. 2,224 D3 298
Minas Gerais, state, Braz. 8,404,000 I7 257
Minatare, Scotts Bluff, Nebr. 894 C2 152
Minatitlán, Mex. 22,425 D7 225
Minato, Jap. K16 354
Minato, Jap. 4,824 L15 354
Minbu, Bur. 9,096 B2 362
Minburn, Alta., Can. 150 D7 54
Minburn, Dallas, Iowa 357 C3 142
Minch, chan., Scot. C7 272
Minchin, China D8 346
Minco, Grady, Okla. 1,021 C6 128
Mindanao, isl., Phil. C6 358
Mindanao, sea, Phil. C6 358
Mindemoya, Ont., Can. O18 64
Minden, Ont., Can. 570 P22 64
Minden, Ger. 47,500 B3 286
Minden, Pottawattamie, Iowa 355 C2 142
Minden, Webster, La. 12,785 B2 180
Minden, Kearney, Nebr. 2,383 D7 152
Minden, Douglas, Nev. 240 E2 112
Minden, Fayette, W.Va. 1,114 D3 194
D7
Minden City, Sanilac, Mich. 369 F9 146
Mindenmines, Barton, Mo. 356 D3 150
Mindoro, La Crosse, Wis. 200 D2 160
Mindoro, isl., Phil. B6 358
Mindoro, strait, Phil. B6 358
Mine, head, Ire. J5 273
Minechoag, mtn., Mass. B3 206
Minehead, Eng. 7,400 J9 273
Mine Hill, Morris, N.J. 3,362 *B3 210
Mineiros, Braz. 2,382 I6 257
Mineola, Mills, Iowa 150 C2 142
Mineola, Clark, Kans. 679 E3 144
Mineola, Nassau, N.Y. 20,519 E3 212
E8
Mineola, Wood, Tex. 3,810 C8 130
Miner, Scott, Mo. 548 *E8 150
Miner, Park, Mont. 5 E6 110
Miner, co., S.Dak. 5,398 D8 158
Mineral, Louisa, Va. 366 B7 192
Mineral, Lewis, Wash. 400 C4 98
Mineral, co., Colo. 424 E4 106
Mineral, co., Mont. 3,037 C1 110
Mineral, co., Nev. 6,329 E3 112
Mineral, co., W.Va. 22,354 B6 194
Mineral, mts., Utah E3 114
Mineral Bluff, Fannin, Ga. 149 *B2 176
Mineral City, Tuscarawas, Ohio 917 B5 156
Mineral del Oro, Mex. 4,283 L13 225
Mineral Hills, Iron, Mich. 311 C3 146
Mineral Hot Springs, Saguache, Colo. 10 *D5 106
Mineral Park, Bradley, Tenn. 25 E8 190
Mineral Point, Washington, Mo. 332 D7 150
Mineral Point, Iowa, Wis. 2,385 F3 160
Mineral Springs, Howard, Ark. 616 D3 170
Mineral Wells, De Soto, Miss. 210 A3 184
Mineral Wells, Palo Pinto, Tex. 11,053 C6 130
Minersville, Meigs, Ohio 500 C5 156
Minersville, Schuylkill, Pa. 6,606 C5 214
Minersville, Beaver, Utah 580 E3 114
Minerva, Stark and Carroll, Ohio 3,833 B5 156
Minerva Park, Franklin, Ohio 1,169 *B4 156
Minervino Murge, It. 21,300 E6 302
Minetto, Oswego, N.Y. 800 B5 212
Mineville, Essex, N.Y. 1,181 A8 212
Mingechaur, res., Sov. Un. D3 336
Mingenew, Austl. 633 D3 432
Mingo, Jasper, Iowa 260 C4 142
Mingo, Thomas, Kans. 10 C3 144
Mingo, Tulsa, Okla. 450 *B8 128
Mingo, co., W.Va. 39,742 D2 194
Mingo, creek, S.C. D10 188
Mingo Junction, Jefferson, Ohio 4,987 B6 156
Mingoyo, Tan. E6 414
Mingshui, China C7 346
Minho, prov., Port. 825,788 *B2 298
Minicoy, isl., India G2 366
Minidoka, Minidoka, Idaho 154 G5 108
Minidoka, co., Idaho 14,394 G5 108
Minidoka, dam, Idaho G5 108
Minier, Tazewell, Ill. 847 C4 138
Miniota, Man., Can. 325 E2 60
Minipi, lake, Newf., Can. E9 72
Minisink, isl., N.J. A3 210
Minitonas, Man., Can. 663 D2 60
Minkcreek, Franklin, Idaho 109 G7 108
Minna, Nig. 12,810 E6 408
Minneapolis, Ottawa, Kans. 2,024 C6 144
Minneapolis, Hennepin, Minn. 482,872 F7 148
(*1,441,700) G5
Minneapolis, Avery, N.C. 200 A4 186
Minnedosa, Man., Can. 2,306 E3 60
Minnedosa, riv., Man., Can. E2 60
Minneha, Sedgwick, Kans. B6 144
Minnehaha, Clark, Wash. 2,000 *D4 98
Minnehaha, co., S.Dak. 86,573 D9 158
Minneiska, Wabasha, Minn. 110 G7 148
Minneola, Lake, Fla. 684 *C9 174
Minneota, Lyon, Minn. 1,297 G3 148
Minnequa, Pueblo, Colo. 900 D6 106
Minnesota, state, U.S. 3,413,864 B8 77
148
Minnesota, riv., Minn. G3 148
Minnesota City, Winona, Minn. 190 *G7 148
Minnesota Lake, Faribault, Minn. 697 H5 148
Minnetonka, Hennepin, Minn. 25,037 *G5 148
Minnetonka, lake, Minn. G5 148
Minnetonka Beach, Hennepin, Minn. 544 *F5 148
Minnetrista, Hennepin, Minn. 2,076 *G5 148
Minnewanka, lake, Alta., Can. E5 54
Minnewaska, lake, Minn. F3 148
Minnewaukan, Benson, N.Dak. 420 B6 154
Minnie Maud, creek, Utah D5 114
Minnora, Calhoun, W.Va. 500 C3 194
Mino, Jap. 31,188 L12 354
Miño, riv., Port. A2 298
Miño, riv., Sp. A3 298
Minoa, Onondaga, N.Y. 1,838 *C5 212
Minocqua, Oneida, Wis. 700 C4 160
Minokamo, Jap. 31,144 L12 354
Minong, Washburn, Wis. 348 B2 160
Minonk, Woodford, Ill. 2,001 C4 138
Minooka, Grundy, Ill. 539 B5 138
Minor Hill, Giles, Tenn. 400 C4 190
Minor Lane Heights, Jefferson, Ky. 152 *B5 178
Minot, Androscoggin, Maine 200 *D2 204
(780▲)
Minot, Ward, N.Dak. 30,604 B4 154
Minotola, Atlantic, N.J. D3 210
Minquadale, New Castle, Del. 1,200 B3 172
Minsk, Sov.Un. 509,000 F6 332
Mińsk Mazowiecki, Pol. 14,300 B5 325
Minster, Auglaize, Ohio 2,193 B2 156
Minter, Dallas, Ala. 50 C3 168
Minter City, Leflore, Miss. 250 B2 184
Minto, Alsk. 152 C7 84
Minto, Man., Can. 180 F2 60
Minto, N.B., Can. 835 C3 70
Minto, Walsh, N.Dak. 642 B8 154
Minto, lake, Que., Can. P9 66
Minto, pass, Oreg. C5 96
Minton, Sask., Can. 191 F5 58
Mintons Corner, Brevard, Fla. 3,000 C10 174
Minturn, Lawrence, Ark. 61 B5 170
Minturn, Eagle, Colo. 662 C4 106
Minturn, Hancock, Maine 120 D4 204
Minturno, It. 3,125 E4 302
Minûf, Eg., U.A.R. 30,289 A3 395
Minûf, Eg., U.A.R. 36,900 D1 382
Minusinsk, Sov.Un. 44,600 D11 329
Minvoul, Gabon F7 409
Minya Konka, mtn., China F8 346
Minzong, India D7 368
Mio, Oscoda, Mich. 500 E7 146
Miquelon, cape, Miquelon Isl. G7 72
Miquihuana, Mex. C6 225
Mira, Caddo, La. 75 B2 180
Mira, Port. 2,258 B2 298
Mira, bay, N.S., Can. C10 70
Mira, riv., Port. D2 298
Miracle Hot Springs, Kern, Calif. 100 E4 94
Mirador, Braz. 734 B2 258
Miraflores, Col. C2 244
Miraflores, Peru 16,146 D3 245
Miragoâne, Hai. 2,499 C8 232
Miraj, India 40,224 E2 366
Mira Loma, Riverside, Calif. 3,982 C6 94
Miramar, Broward, Fla. 5,485 *E10 174
Miramichi, bay, N.B., Can. B4 70
Miranda, Braz. 1,593 J5 257
Miranda, Col. 4,082 C1 244
Miranda, Faulk, S.Dak. 65 B7 158
Miranda, state, Ven. 351,938 A5 240
Miranda de Ebro, Sp. 15,116 A5 298
Miranda do Douro, Port. 1,331 B3 298
Mirandela, Port. 3,418 B3 298
Mirando City, Webb, Tex. 600 F6 130
Mirassol, Braz. 7,620 E1 258
Mirebalais, Hai. 1,835 C8 232
Mirecourt, Fr. 7,939 C7 278
Mirgorod, Sov.Un. 24,500 H9 332
Miri, Sar. 8,810 D4 358
Miriánské Lázně, Czech. 8,417 B1 324
Mirim, lagoon, Braz. L6 257
Mirimire, Ven. A4 240
Mirond, lake, Sask., Can. C6 58
Mirpur, India B1 368
Mirpur-Khas, Pak. 40,420 G6 375
Mirror, Alta., Can. 591 D6 54
Mirror Lake, King, Wash. 500 *B4 98
Mirror Landing, Alta., Can. 300 C5 54
Mirzapur, India 86,528 D3 368
Misaki, see Miura, Jap.
Misakubo, Jap. 10,947 L13 354
Misantla, Mex. 4,903 D6 225
L15
Miscou, isl., N.B., Can. B5 70
Miscou, pt., N.B., Can. A5 70
Misery, pt., Newf., Can. D8 72
Mishawaka, St. Joseph, Ind. 33,361 A3 140
Misheguk, mtn., Alsk. B5 84
Mishicot, Manitowoc, Wis. 762 A7 160
D6
Mishima, Jap. 58,179 G7 354
L14
Misiones, dept., Par. 43,449 E4 247
Misiones, prov., Arg. 357,900 C7 250
Miskish, mts., Ire. J3 273
Miskito, is., Nic. C6 228
Miskolc, Hung. 150,000 A5 320
Misoöl, is., Neth.N.Gui. E7 359
Mispillion, riv., Del. E4 172
Misquamicut, Washington, R.I. 250 D1 216
Misrātah, Libya 59,902 A3 394
Missaukee, co., Mich. 6,784 E6 146
Missaukee, lake, Mich. E6 146
Mission, Johnson, Kans. 4,626 B8 144
Mission, Todd, S.Dak. 611 D5 158
Mission, Hidalgo, Tex. 14,081 F6 130
Mission, bay, Calif. D6 94
Mission, range, Mont. C3 110
Missionary, Caddo, La. B2 180
Mission City, B.C., Can. 3,010 B15 52
F11
Mission Hill, Yankton, S.Dak. 165 E8 158
Mission Hills, Johnson, Kans. 3,621 B8 144
Mission Woods, Johnson, Kans. 243 *D9 144
Missisquoi, Franklin, Vt. 100 B3 218
Missisquoi, co., Que., Can. 26,773 S11 66
Missisquoi, riv., Vt. B3 218
Mississinewa, riv., Ind. B4 140
Mississippi, co., Ark. 70,174 B6 170
Mississippi, co., Mo. 20,695 E8 150
Mississippi, state, U.S. 2,178,141 E9 77
184
Mississippi, delta, La. E6 180
Mississippi, riv., U.S. E8 77
Mississippi, sound, Ala., Miss. E1 168
E4 184
Mississippi City, Harrison, Miss. 4,169 E1 184
E3
Missoula, Missoula, Mont. 27,090 D2 110
Missoula Southwest, Missoula, Mont. 3,817 *D2 110
Missoula, co., Mont. 44,663 D2 110
Missouri, state, U.S. 4,319,813 D8 77
150
Missouri, buttes, Wyo. B8 116
Missouri, caverns, Mo. C6 150
Missouri, riv., U.S. C7 77
Missouri City, Clay, Mo. 404 E2 150
Missouri City, Fort Bend and Harris, Tex. 604 F8 130
Missouri Valley, Harrison, Iowa 3,567 C2 142
Mist, Columbia, Oreg. 100 *A3 96
Mistaken, pt., Newf., Can. G9 72
Mistassini, lake, Que., Can. Q9 66
Mistatim, Sask., Can. 187 D6 58
Mistatin, lake, Newf., Can. D9 72
Mistelbach [an der Zaya], Aus. 5,250 B8 313
Miston, Dyer, Tenn. 100 B2 190
Mistretta, It. 11,400 G5 302
Mita, pt., Mex. C4 224
Mitaka, Jap. 69,466 *L15 354
Mitake, Jap. 15,930 G6 354
L13
Mitchell, Bullock, Ala. C4 168
Mitchell, Ont., Can. 2,146 Q19 64
Mitchell, Glascock, Ga. 184 C4 176
Mitchell, Lawrence, Ind. 3,552 D3 140
Mitchell, Mitchell, Iowa 237 A5 142
Mitchell, Sabine, La. 300 C2 180
Mitchell, Scotts Bluff, Nebr. 1,920 C2 152
Mitchell, Wheeler, Oreg. 236 C6 96
Mitchell, Davison, S.Dak. 12,555 D7 158
Mitchell, co., Ga. 19,652 E2 176
Mitchell, co., Iowa 14,043 A5 142
Mitchell, co., Kans. 8,866 C5 144
Mitchell, co., N.C. 13,906 A3 186
Mitchell, co., Tex. 11,255 C5 130
Mitchell, dam, Ala. C3 168
Mitchell, isl., La. E6 180
Mitchell, lake, Ala. C3 168
Mitchell, lake, Mich. E6 146
Mitchell, mtn., N.C. B3 186
Mitchell, plain, Ind. *D3 140
Mitchell, riv., Austl. B8 432
Mitchell Heights, Logan, W.Va. 290 *D3 194
Mitchelltown, Bath, Va. 400 B5 192
Mitchellville, Polk, Iowa 957 A8 142
C4
Mitchellville, Sumner, Tenn. 184 B5 190
Mitchelstown, Ire. 2,674 I4 273
Mit Fâris, Eg., U.A.R. C2 382
Mit Ghamr, Eg., U.A.R. 34,400 D2 382
Mitilini, Grc. 25,518 B6 306
Mitishto, riv., Man., Can. C3 60
Mitkof, isl., Alsk. J14 84
Mitla, pass, Eg., U.A.R. D3 382
Mito, Jap. 110,436 F8 354
K16
Mitre, mtn., N.Z. D5 437
Mitsinjo, Malag. C9 421
Mittelland, canal, Ger. B4 286
Mitterteich, Ger. 6,700 D5 286
Mittie, Allen, La. 15 D3 180
Mittweida, Ger. 20,800 C5 286
Mitú, Col. 9,750 C2 244
Mitûbis, Eg., U.A.R. 6,732 *A3 395
Mitumba, mts., Con.L. E4 414
Mitwaba, Con.L. D4 414
Mitzic, Gabon F7 409
Miura (Misaki), Jap. 36,358 L15 354
Mixcoac, Mex. G10 224
Mixquiahuala, Mex. 5,564 K14 225
Mixville, New Haven, Conn. 400 C4 202
Miyake, isl., Jap. G7 354

Miyako, Jap. 53,623 E8 354
Miyako, isl., Ryūkyū Is., Jap. M12 349
Miyakonojō, Jap. 81,203 I3 354
Miyan Kaleh, pen., Iran B3 379
Miyazaki, Jap. 140,782 I3 354
Miyazu, Jap. 33,897 L11 354
Mizdah, Libya A2 394
Mize, Smith, Miss. 371 D3 184
Mizil, Rom. 7,460 B4 321
Mizpah, Koochiching, Minn. 140 D4 148
Mizpah, Custer, Mont. D11 110
Mizpah, Atlantic, N.J. 350 E3 210
Mizpah, creek, Mont. E11 110
Mizque, Bol. 870 C1 246
Mjällom, Swe. E8 290
Mjölby, Swe. 9,860 C6 292
Mjörn, lake, Swe. D3 292
Mjösa, lake, Nor. F4 291
Mjösa, riv., Nor. A1 292
Mkalama, Tan. C5 414
Mkushi, Rh.&Nya. B5 420
Mladá Boleslav, Czech. 24,389 A2 324
Mlanje, Rh.&Nya. C7 421
Mława, Pol. 14,100 B5 325
Mljet, isl., Yugo. C3 316
Mo, Nor. 5,263 C6 290
Moa, isl., Indon. F7 359
Moab, Grand, Utah 4,682 E6 114
Moala, isl., Fiji E7 436
Moamba, Moz. E6 421
Moapa, Clark, Nev. 20 G7 112
Moar, lake, Man., Can. E5 60
Moark, Clay, Ark. 130 A6 170
Mobara, Jap. 34,189 L16 354
Mobaye, Cen.Afr.Rep. F9 409
Moberly, Randolph, Mo. 13,170 B5 150
Moberly, lake, B.C., Can. C12 52
Mobile, Mobile, Ala. 202,779 E1 168
(*304,000)
Mobile, Maricopa, Ariz. 50 E3 124
Mobile, Newf., Can. 100 G9 72
Mobile, co., Ala. 314,301 E1 168
Mobile, bay, Ala. E1 168
Mobile, riv., Ala. E1 168
Mobridge, Walworth, S.Dak. 4,391 B5 158
Mobula, Con.L. B4 414
Moca, Dom.Rep. 9,589 C9 233
Mocajuba, Braz. 687 A1 258
Mocambique, Moz. 9,222 C8 421
Mocambique, prov., Moz. B7 421
Moçâmedes, Ang. 7,185 C2 420
Moçâmedes, dist., Ang. 44,940 C2 420
Mocanaqua, Luzerne, Pa. 1,104 B5 214
Moccasin, Mohave, Ariz. 50 B3 124
Moccasin, Judith Basin, Mont. 150 *C6 110
Mocha, isl., Chile C1 252
Mochudi, Bech. 11,767 D5 420
Mocimboa da Praia, Moz. B8 421
Möckeln, lake, Swe. E5 292
Mockingbird Valley,
Jefferson, Ky. 169 *B5 178
Mocksville, Davie, N.C. 2,379 B5 186
Moclips, Grays Harbor, Wash. 500 B2 98
Mocoa, Col. 1,698 C1 244
Mocóca, Braz. 7,893 E1 258
Mocomoco, Bol. 977 C1 246
Mocorito, Mex. 2,472 B4 224
Moçoró, Braz. B3 258
Moctezuma, Mex. 2,151 B4 224
Moctezuma, riv., Mex. K14 225
Mocuba, Moz. C7 421
Modale, Harrison, Iowa 276 C1 142
Modamin, Harrison, Iowa 436 C1 142
Model, Las Animas, Colo. 25 E6 106
Model, Stewart, Tenn. 100 B4 190
Model, res., Colo. E6 106
Modello, Dade, Fla. 150 F6 174
Modena, It. 78,500 C3 302
(116,100▲)
Modena, Ulster, N.Y. 450 D7 212
Modena, Iron, Utah 62 F2 114
Modena, Buffalo, Wis. 125 D2 160
Modena, prov., It. 501,300 *C3 302
Modeste, Ascension, La. 250 B5 180
Modesto, Stanislaus,
Calif. 36,585 D3 94
Modica, It. 30,400 G5 302
Mödling, Aus. 17,076 B8 313
Modoc, Randolph, Ind. 238 B4 140
Modoc, Scott, Kans. 73 D2 144
Modoc, McCormick, S.C. 200 D4 188
Modoc, co., Calif. 8,308 B3 94
Modoc Point, Klamath, Oreg. 75 E5 96
Modřany, Czech. 8,948 A2 324
Moeajuba, Braz. F7 256
Moecherville, Kane, Ill. 1,200 *B5 138
Möen, isl., Den. G3 292
Moenkopi, Coconino, Ariz. 600 B4 124
Moenkopi, wash, Ariz. B5 124
Moerbeke, Bel. 5,267 C2 282
Moffat, Saguache, Colo. 104 D5 106
Moffat, Scot. 2,100 F9 272
Moffat, co., Colo. 7,061 B2 106
Moffett, Sequoyah, Okla. 357 C9 128
Moffit, Burleigh, N.Dak. 97 D5 154
Moga, Con.L. C4 414
Moga, India C1 368
Mogadiscio, Som. 77,000 E6 398
Mogador, Mor. 22,291 B8 402
Mogadore, Summit, Ohio 3,851 A5 156
Mogaung, Bur. 2,940 A3 362
Mogfog, Guam C7 437
Mogi das Cruzes, Braz. 31,300 E1 258
Mogielnica, Pol. 4,667 C5 325
Mogilev, Sov.Un. 121,000 F8 332
Mogilev-Podolskiy, Sov.Un. 46,300 H6 332
Mogilno, Pol. 5,193 B3 325
Mogi Mirim, Braz. 10,913 E1 258
Mogincual, Moz. C8 421
Mogocha, Sov.Un. 18,000 D13 329
Mogochin, Sov.Un. 3,500 A10 336
Mogok, Bur. 8,369 B3 362
Mogollon, Catron, N.Mex. 24 E2 126
Mogollon, plat., Ariz. D4 124
Mogote, Conejos, Colo. 30 E4 106
Mogotes, pt., Arg. C4 252
Moguer, Sp. 6,821 D3 298
Mogzon, Sov.Un. D13 329
Mohács, Hung. 14,000 D3 320
Mohaleshoek, Bas. F5 420
Mohall, Renville, N.Dak. 956 B4 154
Mohave, co., Ariz. 7,736 C1 124
Mohave, lake, Ariz., Nev. C1 124
H7 112
Mohave, mts., Ariz. D1 124
Mohawk, Yuma, Ariz. 27 F2 124
Mohawk, Keweenaw, Mich. 650 B3 146
Mohawk, Herkimer, N.Y. 3,533 B6 212
Mohawk, Lane, Oreg. 100 C4 96
Mohawk, lake, N.J. A3 210
Mohawk, mtn., Conn. B2 202
Mohawk, riv., N.H. B4 208
Mohawk, riv., N.Y. C7 212
Moheda, Swe. 4,555 D5 292
Mohegan, New London, Conn. 300 D7 202
Mohegan Lake,
Westchester, N.Y. 1,500 *D8 212
Moheli, isl., Afr. B8 421
Mohican, riv., Ohio B4 156
Mohler, Lewis, Idaho 20 *C2 108
Mohler, Lincoln, Wash. 30 B8 98
Mohnton, Berks, Pa. 2,223 C6 214
Moholm, Swe. 4,081 C5 292
Mohon, Fr. 7,706 C6 278
Mohoro, Tan. 1,160 D6 414
Mohrland, Emery, Utah D4 114
Mohulu, Con.L. C4 414
Moiese, Lake, Mont. 7 C2 110
Moinești, Rom. 12,934 A4 321
Mointy, Sov.Un. C8 336
Moira, Franklin, N.Y. 500 A7 212
Moissac, Fr. 4,770 E4 278
Moïssala, Chad E8 409
Mojave, Kern, Calif. 1,845 E4 94
Mojave, des., Calif. E5 94
Mojave, riv., Calif. E5 94
Moji, Jap. 145,027 H3 354
Mojo, Eth. D4 398
Mokameh, India D4 368
Mokami, hill, Newf., Can. D6 72
Mokane, Callaway, Mo. 419 C6 150
Mokapu, pt., Haw. G11 86
Mokelumne, riv., Calif. C3 94
Mokelumne Hill,
Calaveras, Calif. 425 C3 94
Mokena, Will, Ill. 1,332 F2 138
Mokepa, Con.L. B4 414
Mokhotlong, Bas. E5 420
Mokokchung, India D6 368
Mokolo, Cam. 1,610 D7 409
Mokpo, Kor. 113,636 H13 348
Moksha, riv., Sov.Un. E14 332
Mokuaweoweo, crater, Haw. D6 86
Mokuleia, Honolulu, Haw. 200 B3 86
F9
Moku Manu, isl., Haw. G11 86
Mol, Bel. 22,741 C4 282
Mol, Yugo. 8,121 B5 316
Mola [di Bari], It. 23,000 E6 302
Molalla, Clackamas, Oreg. 1,501 B2 96
B4
Molalla, riv., Oreg. B2 96
Molango, Mex. 1,577 K14 225
Moláoi, Grc. 3,026 C4 306
Molasses, pond, Maine D4 204
Mold, Wales 6,600 H9 273
Moldavia, prov., Rom. 2,598,258 *B8 321
Moldavia (Moldova), reg., Rom. A4 321
Moldavia, rep., Sov.Un. 2,880,000 E4 328
Molde, Nor. 6,599 E2 290
Moldova, riv., Rom. A4 321
Moldova-Nouă, Rom. 3,582 B1 321
Moldovenu, peak, Rom. B3 321
Moledet, Isr. B6 382
Moleen, Elko, Nev. 20 C6 112
Mole Hill, see Mountain, W.Va.
Molena, Pike, Ga. 279 C2 176
Molengraaff, mts., Indon. E5 358
Molepolole, Bech. 14,805 D4 420
Môle St. Nicholas, Hai. 1,700 C8 232
Molfetta, It. 57,500 E6 302
Molina, Chile 6,123 C1 252
Molina de Aragón, Sp. 3,131 B6 298
Moline, Rock Island, Ill. 42,705 B3 138
Moline, Elk, Kans. 698 E7 144
Moline, Allegan, Mich. 550 G6 146
Moline Acres, St. Louis,
Mo. 3,132 *C7 150
Molino, Escambia, Fla. 400 A3 174
Molinos, Arg. C4 250
Moliro, Con.L. D5 414
Moliterno, It. 4,983 E5 302
Molkom, Swe. B4 292
Mollendo, Peru 17,479 D3 245
Mollusk, Lancaster, Va. 325 C8 192
Mölndal, Swe. 22,783 D3 292
Moloaa Camp, Kauai, Haw. 176 *A2 86
Molodechno, Sov.Un. 26,000 E6 332
Molokai, isl., Haw. B5 86
Molokini, isl., Haw. C5 86
Molopo, riv., U.S.Afr. E4 420
Molotovsk, Sov.Un. 79,000 *C5 328
Molotovskoye, Sov.Un. 28,000 J13 332
Moloundou, Cam. F8 409
Molson, Man., Can. 100 E4 60
Molson, Okanogan, Wash. 80 A7 98
Molson, lake, Man., Can. C4 60
Molson, riv., Man., Can. D4 60
Molt, Stillwater, Mont. 5 E8 110
Molteno, U.S.Afr. 3,395 F5 420
Molucca, is., Indon. E7 359
Molucca, passage, Indon. D7 358
Molucca, sea, Indon. D7 358
Molucca Islands, reg.,
Indon. 700,000 E7 339
Molunkus, Aroostook, Maine 35 C4 204
Moma, Moz. C7 421
Mombango, Con.L. B3 414
Mombasa, Ken. 84,746 C6 414
Mombetsu, Jap. 37,388 B9 354
Momboyo, riv., Con.L. C3 414
Momchilgrad, Bul. 4,307 C2 317
Momence, Kankakee, Ill. 2,949 B6 138
Momostenango, Guat. 4,986 C2 228
Mompono, Con.L. B3 414
Mompós, Col. 9,192 B2 244
Mon, India D6 368
Mona, Richland, Mont. 5 B12 110
Mona, Juab, Utah 347 D4 114
Mona, Monongalia, W.Va. 806 A7 194
Mona, isl., P.R. C11 233
Mona, passage, W.I. C11 233
Monaca, Beaver, Pa. 8,394 C1 214
Monaco, Monaco 1,860 F7 278
(*20,442)
Monaco, country, Eur. 21,000 D5 266
278
Monadhliath, mts., Scot. D8 272
Monadnock, mtn., N.H. F2 208
Monagas, state, Ven. 175,560 B7 240
Monaghan, Ire. 4,701 G6 273
Monaghan, Greenville, S.C. 1,200 B4 188
Monaghan, co., Ire. 52,064 G5 273
Monahans, Ward, Tex. 8,567 D4 130
Monamolin, Ire. I6 273
Monango, Dickey, N.Dak. 133 D7 154
Mona ó Carreta, pt., C.R. F6 228
Monarch, Alta., Can. 100 F6 54
Monarch, Chaffee, Colo. 2 *D4 106
Monarch, Cascade, Mont. 20 C6 110
Monarch, Union, S.C. 1,990 B5 188
Monarch, mtn., B.C., Can. E10 52
Monarch, pass, Colo. D4 106
Monarda, Aroostook, Maine 50 C4 204
Monashee, mts., B.C., Can. E13 52
Monastyrshchina, Sov.Un. 5,300 E8 332
Mona Vatu, mtn., Fiji E6 436
Monaville, Logan, W.Va. 825 D5 194
Monção, Braz. 585 F7 256
Moncayo, mtn., Sp. B6 298
Mönchen-Gladbach, Ger. 144,800 C2 286
(*250,000)
Monchique, Port. 2,169 D2 298
Monchique, mts., Port. D2 298
Moncks Corner, Berkeley,
S.C. 2,030 E8 188
Monclo, Logan, W.Va. 721 D3 194
D5
Monclova, Mex. 19,048 B5 225
Moncton, N.B., Can. 36,003 C5 70
(*50,018)
Moncure, Chatham, N.C. 400 B6 186
Mondego, cape, Port. B2 298
Mondego, riv., Port. B2 298
Mondoñedo, Sp. 8,145 A3 298
Mondorf-les-Bains, Lux. 1,087 E5 282
Mondovi, It. 8,800 C1 302
(20,700▲)
Mondovi, Buffalo, Wis. 2,320 D2 160
Mondsee, Aus. 2,675 C5 313
Monee, Will, Ill. 646 B6 138
F3
Monemvasia, Grc. 638 C4 306
Monero, Rio Arriba, N.Mex. 500 B4 126
Monessen, Westmoreland,
Pa. 18,424 C2 214
Moneta, O'Brien, Iowa 76 *A2 142
Moneta, Bedford, Va. 170 C5 192
Moneta, Fremont, Wyo. 10 C5 116
Monett, Barry and
Lawrence, Mo. 5,359 E4 150
Monetta, Saluda, S.C. 242 D5 188
Monette, Craighead, Ark. 981 B6 170
Money, Leflore, Miss. 100 B2 184
Monfalcone, It. 25,800 C4 302
Monford, Butler, Ky. 25 C4 178
Monforte de Lemos, Sp. 13,502 A3 298
Monga, Con.L. B3 414
Mongala, riv., Con.L. B3 414
Mongalla, Sud. D3 398
Mong Hpayak, Bur. B3 362
Mong Hsat, Bur. B3 362
Monghyr, India 74,348 D4 368
Mong Mit, Bur. B3 362
Mong Nai, Bur. B3 362
Mongo, Chad D8 409
Mongo, Lagrange, Ind. 225 A4 140
Mongolia, Ont., Can. R22 64
Mongolia, country,
Asia 1,040,000 E12 340
346
Mongolia, plat., Mong. B8 346
Mong Pan, Bur. B3 362
Mongu, Rh.&Nya. 3,000 C4 420
Monhegan, isl., Maine E3 204
Moniac, Charlton, Ga. 425 F4 176
Moniaive, Scot. 1,219 F9 272
Monico, Oneida, Wis. 150 C4 160
Monida, pass, Idaho, Mont. E6 108
F4 110
Monie, Somerset, Md. 70 D8 182
Moniquirá, Col. 3,230 B2 244
Moniteau, co., Mo. 10,500 C5 150
Monitor, Alta., Can. 82 E7 54
Monitor, Marion, Oreg. 100 B1 96
Monitor, Chelan, Wash. 400 B6 98
Monitor, range, Nev. E5 112
Monkey River, Br. Hond. 421 B3 228
Monkman, pass, B.C., Can. C12 52
Monkoto, Con.L. C3 414
Monkton, Ont., Can. 365 Q19 64
Monkton, Baltimore, Md. 75 A6 182
Monkton, Addison, Vt. 130 C2 218
(551▲)
Monktonridge, Addison, Vt. 75 C2 218
Mon Louis, Mobile, Ala. 300 *E1 168
Monmouth, Wales 5,700 J10 273
Monmouth, Warren, Ill. 10,372 C3 138
Monmouth, Jackson, Iowa 291 B7 142
Monmouth, Kennebec, Maine 500 D2 204
(1,884▲)
Monmouth, Polk, Oreg. 2,229 C3 96
Monmouth, co., N.J. 334,401 C4 210
Monmouth, co., Wales 428,300 J9 273
Monmouth, mtn., B.C., Can. E11 52
Monmouth Beach,
Monmouth, N.J. 1,363 C5 210
Monmouth Junction,
Middlesex, N.J. 700 C3 210
Monnikendam, Neth. 2,296 B4 282
Mono, co., Calif. 2,213 D4 94
Mono, lake, Calif. D4 94
Monocracy, riv., Md. B5 182
Monolith, Kern, Calif. 450 E4 94
Monomoy, isl., Mass. C7 206
Monomoy, pt., Mass. C7 206
Monon, White, Ind. 1,417 B3 140
Monona, Clayton, Iowa 1,346 A6 142
Monona, Dane, Wis. 8,178 E4 160
Monona, co., Iowa 13,916 B1 142
Monongah, Marion, W.Va. 1,321 A7 194
B4
Monongahela, Washington, Pa. 8,388 C2 214
Monongahela, riv., Pa., W.Va. D2 214
A7 194
Monongalia, co., W.Va. 55,617 B4 194
Monopoli, It. 23,100 E6 302
Monor, Hung. 11,567 B4 320
Monos, Mex. D8 225
Monóvar, Sp. 7,640 C6 298
Monoville, Smith, Tenn. 65 B6 190
Monowi, Boyd, Nebr. 40 B7 152
Monponsett, Plymouth, Mass. 500 B6 206
Monreale, It. 17,500 F4 302
Monroe, Monroe, Ark. 150 C5 170
Monroe, Fairfield, Conn. 1,000 D3 202
(6,402▲)
Monroe, Walton, Ga. 6,826 C3 176
Monroe, Tippecanoe, Ind. 499 B3 140
Monroe, Jasper, Iowa 1,366 C4 142
Monroe, Ouachita, La. 52,219 B3 180
Monroe, Waldo, Maine 180 D3 204
(497▲)
Monroe (Town of), Franklin,
Mass. (206▲) *A2 206
Monroe, Monroe, Mich. 22,968 H8 146
Monroe, Franklin, Miss. 120 D2 184
Monroe, Platte, Nebr. 261 C8 152
Monroe, Grafton, N.H. 150 C2 208
(421▲)
Monroe, Sussex, N.J. 110 A3 210
Monroe, Orange, N.Y. 3,323 D7 212
Monroe, Union, N.C. 10,882 C5 186
Monroe, Butler, Ohio 1,475 C2 156
Monroe, Le Flore, Okla. 135 D9 128
Monroe, Benton, Oreg. 374 C3 96
Monroe, Turner, S.Dak. 156 D8 158
Monroe, Overton, Tenn. 69 B6 190
Monroe, Sevier, Utah 955 E3 114
Monroe, Amherst, Va. 800 C5 192
Monroe, Snohomish, Wash. 1,901 B5 98
Monroe, Green, Wis. 8,050 F4 160
Monroe, co., Ala. 22,372 D2 168
Monroe, co., Ark. 17,327 C5 170
Monroe, co., Fla. 47,921 G9 174
Monroe, co., Ga. 10,495 D3 176
Monroe, co., Ill. 15,507 E3 138
Monroe, co., Ind. 59,225 C3 140
Monroe, co., Iowa 10,463 D5 142
Monroe, co., Ky. 11,799 D5 178
Monroe, co., Mich. 101,120 H8 146
Monroe, co., Miss. 33,953 B4 184
Monroe, co., Mo. 10,688 B5 150
Monroe, co., N.Y. 586,387 B4 212
Monroe, co., Ohio 15,268 C5 156
Monroe, co., Pa. 39,567 B6 214
Monroe, co., Tenn. 23,316 C7 190
Monroe, co., W.Va. 11,584 D4 194
Monroe, co., Wis. 31,241 E3 160
Monroe Bridge, Franklin,
Mass. 360 A2 206
Monroe Center, Ogle, Ill. 300 A5 138
Monroe Center, Adams, Wis. 30 D4 160
Monroe City, Knox, Ind. 505 D2 140
Monroe City, Monroe and
Marion, Mo. 2,337 B6 150
Monroeville, Monroe, Ala. 3,632 D2 168
Monroeville, Allen, Ind. 1,294 B5 140
Monroeville, Salem, N.J. 200 D2 210
Monroeville, Huron, Ohio 1,371 A4 156
Monrovia, Los Angeles,
Calif. 27,079 C5 94
Monrovia, Morgan, Ind. 450 C3 140
Monrovia, Lib. 41,829 E2 408
Mons, Bel. 26,049 D2 282
Monsarás, pt., Braz. D3 258
Monsey, Rockland, N.Y. 3,000 *D7 212
Monson, Piscataquis, Maine 700 C3 204
(852▲)
Monson, Hampden, Mass. 2,413 B3 206
(6,712▲)
Monsteras, Swe. 4,377 D7 292
Montagne Tremblante, see
Mont-Tremblant, prov. park, Que., Can.
Montague, Siskiyou, Calif. 782 B2 94
Montague, P.E.I., Can. 1,152 C7 70
Montague, Franklin, Mass. 700 A2 206
(7,836▲)
Montague, Muskegon, Mich. 2,366 F5 146
Montague, Chouteau, Mont. 16 C6 110
Montague, co., Tex. 14,893 C7 130
Montague, isl., Alsk. D7 84
Montague, isl., Mex. A3 224
Montague City, Franklin, Mass. 600 A2 206
Montalbán, Sp. 2,200 B6 298
Montalegre, Port. 1,799 B3 298
Mont Alto, Franklin, Pa. 1,039 D4 214
Montalvo, Ventura, Calif. 2,028 *E4 94
Montana, Johnson, Ark. 25 B3 170
Montana, state, U.S. 674,767 B4 77
110
Montánchez, Sp. 5,056 C3 298
Montara, San Mateo, Calif. 500 B4 94
Montara, pt., Calif. B4 94
Montargis, Fr. 15,117 C5 278
Montauban, Que., Can. 634 R12 66
Montauban, Fr. 26,860 E4 278
Montauban-les-Mines,
Que., Can. 356 R12 66
Montauk, Suffolk, N.Y. 900 D6 212
Mont-aux-Sources, mtn., U.S.Afr. E5 420
Montbard, Fr. 4,871 D6 278
Montbéliard, Fr. 17,023 D7 278
Mont Belvieu, Chambers, Tex. 950 E8 130
F8
Montblanch, Sp. 3,773 B7 298
Montbrison, Fr. 8,521 E6 278
Montcalm, Mercer, W.Va. 800 *D3 194
Montcalm, co., Que., Can. 18,670 R10 66
Montcalm, co., Mich. 35,795 F6 146
Montcalm, peak, Fr. F4 278
Mont Carmel, Que., Can. 840 Q15 66
Montceau-les-Mines, Fr. 28,308 D6 278
Montcerf, Que., Can. 150 R8 66
Montchanin [-les-Mines], Fr. 5,452 D6 278
Montclair, San Bernardino,
Calif. 13,546 *E5 94
Montclair, Essex, N.J. 43,129 B1 210
B4
Mont Clare, Montgomery, Pa. 1,124 A6 214
Mont Clare, Darlington, S.C. 200 C9 188
Montcoal, Raleigh, W.Va. 450 D3 194
D6
Mont-de-Marsan, Fr. 17,120 F3 278

Montdidier, Fr.	4,557	C5	278
Monteagle, Grundy, Tenn.	700	C6	190
Monteagudo, Arg.		A5	252
Monte Alto, Braz.		C2	258
Monte Azul, Braz.	2,231	D2	258
Montebello, Los Angeles, Calif.	32,097	C5	94
Monte Bello, Que., Can.	1,287	S10	66
Montebello, Nelson, Va.	50	C5	192
Monte Bello, is., Austl.		C3	432
Montebello Gardens, Los Angeles, Calif.	2,000	C5	94
Monte Carlo, Monaco	8,484	*F7	278
Monte Carmelo, Braz.	4,122	D1	258
Monte Caseros, Arg.	11,409	B4	252
Montecatini Terme, It.	15,700	*D3	302
Montecelio, It.	3,816	*D4	302
Monte Coman, Arg.		B2	252
Monte Creek, B.C., Can.		E12	52
Montecristi, Dom.Rep.	4,600	C9	233
Monte Cristo, Bol.		B2	246
Montecristo, isl., It.		D3	302
Montefrio, Sp.	5,137	D4	298
Montego Bay, Jam.	13,200	C6	232
Montegut, Terrebonne, La.	588	E5	180
Monteiro, Braz.	3,787	B3	258
Monteith, mtn., B.C., Can.		C11	52
Montélimar, Fr.	11,983	E6	278
Monte Lindo, riv., Par.		C2	247
Monte Lindo Grande, riv., Arg.		C6	250
Montellano, Sp.	11,022	D4	298
Montello, Elko, Nev.	125	B7	112
Montello, Marquette, Wis.	1,021	E4	160
Montemayor, plat., Arg.		F4	251
Montemorelos, Mex.	7,580	B6	225
Monte Ne, Benton, Ark.	200	A2	170
Montenegro, Braz.	8,123	K6	257
Montenegro (Crna Gora), rep., Yugo.	419,873	C4	316
Monte Patria, Chile		B1	252
Monte Plata, Dom.Rep.	1,474	C10	233
Monte Porzio Catone, It.	2,367	*E4	302
Montepuez, Moz.		B7	421
Montepulciano, It.	3,300	D3	302
Monte Quemado, Arg.		C5	250
Montereau [-faut-Yonne], Fr.	10,119	C5	278
Monterey, Butler, Ala.	50	D3	168
Monterey, Monterey, Calif.	22,618	D3	94
Monterey, Pulaski, Ind.	278	A3	140
Monterey, Owen, Ky.	211	B6	178
Monterey, Concordia, La.	40	C4	180
Monterey, Berkshire, Mass.	100	B1	206
	(480▲)		
Monterey, Cuming, Nebr.	15	*C9	152
Monterey, Putnam, Tenn.	2,069	B6	190
Monterey, Highland, Va.	270	B5	192
Monterey, co., Calif.	198,351	D3	94
Monterey, bay, Calif.		D3	94
Monterey Park, Los Angeles, Calif.	37,821	C5	94
Monteria, Col.	88,640	B1	244
Monteros, Arg.	7,745	A2	252
Monterotondo, It.	6,841	*D4	302
Monterrey, Mex.	333,422	B5	225
Montesano, Grays Harbor, Wash.	2,486	C3	98
Monte Sant' Angelo, It.	21,300	E5	302
Monte Santo, Braz.	1,595	C3	258
Monte Santu, cape, It.		E2	302
Montes Claros, Braz.	20,370	D2	258
Monte Sereno, Santa Clara, Calif.	1,506	*D3	94
Montevallo, Shelby, Ala.	2,755	B3	168
Montevarchi, It.	9,100	D3	302
Montevideo, Chippewa, Minn.	5,693	G3	148
Montevideo, Ur.	845,000	B4	252
Montevideo, dept., Ur.	541,042	*B4	252
Monteview, Jefferson, Idaho	10	F6	108
Monte Vista, Rio Grande, Colo.	3,385	E4	106
Monte Vista, Pierce, Wash.	1,500	*B4	98
Montevue, Frederick, Md.	100	B5	182
Montezuma, Summit, Colo.	17	*C4	106
Montezuma, Macon, Ga.	3,744	D2	176
Montezuma, Parke, Ind.	1,231	C2	140
Montezuma, Poweshiek, Iowa	1,416	C5	142
Montezuma, Gray, Kans.	543	E3	144
Montezuma, San Miguel, N.Mex.	100	*C5	126
Montezuma, Chester, Tenn.	100	C3	190
Montezuma, co., Colo.	14,024	E2	106
Montezuma, creek, Utah		F6	114
Montezuma Castle, natl. mon., Ariz.		D4	124
Montfort, Que., Can.	230	S10	66
Montfort, Grant, Wis.	538	F3	160
Montgomery, Montgomery, Ala.	134,393	C3	168
	(*155,200)		
Montgomery, Chatham, Ga.	350	E5	176
Montgomery, Kane, Ill.	2,122	F1	138
Montgomery, Daviess, Ind.	446	D2	140
Montgomery, Trigg, Ky.	5	D3	178
Montgomery, Grant, La.	866	C3	180
Montgomery, Hampden, Mass.	80	B2	206
	(333▲)		
Montgomery, Hillsdale, Mich.	362	H7	146
Montgomery, Le Sueur, Minn.	2,118	G5	148
Montgomery, Somerset, N.J.		C3	210
Montgomery, Orange, N.Y.	1,312	D7	212
Montgomery, Hamilton, Ohio	3,075	*C2	156
Montgomery, Pak.	50,158	D8	375
Montgomery, Lycoming, Pa.	2,150	B5	214
Montgomery, Franklin, Vt.	250	B3	218
	(876▲)		
Montgomery, Fayette and Kanawha, W.Va.	3,000	C3	194
		C6	
Montgomery, co., Ala.	169,210	C3	168
Montgomery, co., Ark.	5,370	C3	170
Montgomery, co., Ga.	6,284	D4	176
Montgomery, co., Ill.	31,244	D4	138
Montgomery, co., Ind.	32,089	B3	140
Montgomery, co., Iowa	14,467	C2	142
Montgomery, co., Kans.	45,007	E8	144
Montgomery, co., Ky.	13,461	B7	178
Montgomery, co., Md.	340,928	B5	182
Montgomery, co., Miss.	13,320	B3	184
Montgomery, co., Mo.	11,097	C6	150
Montgomery, co., N.Y.	57,240	C7	212
Montgomery, co., N.C.	18,408	B6	186
Montgomery, co., Ohio	527,080	C2	156
Montgomery, co., Pa.	516,682	C6	214
Montgomery, co., Tenn.	55,645	B4	190
Montgomery, co., Tex.	26,839	D8	130
Montgomery, co., Va.	32,923	C4	192
Montgomery, co., Wales	44,940	I9	273
Montgomery, peak, Calif.		D4	94
Montgomery Center, Franklin, Vt.	375	B3	218
Montgomery City, Montgomery, Mo.	1,918	C6	150
Monthey, Switz.	5,608	B2	312
Monticello, Drew, Ark.	4,412	D5	170
Monticello, Jefferson, Fla.	2,490	A7	174
Monticello, Jasper, Ga.	1,931	C3	176
Monticello, Piatt, Ill.	3,219	C5	138
Monticello, White, Ind.	4,035	B3	140
Monticello, Jones, Iowa	3,190	B6	142
Monticello, Wayne, Ky.	2,940	D6	178
Monticello, Aroostook, Maine	625	B5	204
	(1,109▲)		
Monticello, Wright, Minn.	1,477	F5	148
Monticello, Lawrence, Miss.	1,432	D2	184
Monticello, Lewis, Mo.	159	A6	150
Monticello, Sierra, N.Mex.	150	E3	126
Monticello, Sullivan, N.Y.	5,222	D7	212
Monticello, Fairfield, S.C.	200	C6	188
Monticello, San Juan, Utah	1,845	F6	114
Monticello, Green, Wis.	789	F4	160
Mont Ida, Anderson, Kans.	50	D8	144
Montigny [-lès-Metz], Fr.	19,271	C7	278
Montijo, Port.	13,306	C2	298
Montijo, Sp.	11,113	C3	298
Montilla, Sp.	19,755	D4	298
Montivilliers, Fr.	7,137	C4	278
Mont Joli, Que., Can.	6,179	*Q10	66
Mont Laurier, Que., Can.	5,486	R9	66
Montluçon, Fr.	48,743	D5	278
Montmagny, Que., Can.	6,405	R14	66
Montmagny, co., Que., Can.	25,969	R14	66
Montmartre, Sask., Can.	425	E6	58
Montmorenci, Tippecanoe, Ind.	100	B2	140
Montmorenci, Aiken, S.C.	150	D5	188
Montmorency, Que., Can.	6,077	R13	66
		R16	
Montmorency No. 1, co., Que., Can.	19,863	Q13	66
Montmorency No. 2, co., Que., Can.	4,735	*R14	66
Montmorency, co., Mich.	4,424	D7	146
Montmorency, riv., Que., Can.		Q13	66
Montmorillon, Fr.	4,766	D4	278
Montney, B.C., Can.		B12	52
Montone, riv., It.		C3	302
Montoro, Sp.	14,278	C4	298
Montour, Gem, Idaho	75	*F2	108
Montour, Tama, Iowa	452	C5	142
Montour, co., Pa.	16,730	B5	214
Montour Falls, Schuyler, N.Y.	1,533	C5	212
Montoursville, Lycoming, Pa.	5,211	B5	214
Montoya, Quay, N.Mex.	70	C6	126
Montpelier, Bear Lake, Idaho	3,146	G7	108
Montpelier, Blackford, Ind.	1,954	B4	140
Montpelier, St. Helena, La.	197	D5	180
Montpelier, Clay, Miss.	230	B4	184
Montpelier, Stutsman, N.Dak.	97	D7	154
Montpelier, Williams, Ohio	4,131	A2	156
Montpelier, Washington, Vt.	8,782	C3	218
Montpelier, Hanover, Va.	125	C7	192
Montpelier Station, Orange, Va.	150	B6	192
Montpellier, Que., Can.	230	S9	66
Montpellier, Fr.	97,501	F5	278
Montreal, Sebastian, Ark.	50	B2	170
Montréal, Que., Can.	1,109,439	S11	66
	(*1,620,758)	S16	
Montreal, Iron, Wis.	1,361	B3	160
Montreal, lake, Sask., Can.		C5	58
Montreal, riv., Sask., Can.		C5	58
Montreal, riv., Wis.		B3	160
Montréal-Est, Que., Can.	4,607	*S16	66
Montréal-Nord, Que., Can.	25,407	S16	66
Montréal-Ouest, Que., Can.	4,370	*S16	66
Montréal-Sud, Que., Can.	5,319	*S16	66
Montreuil [-sous-Bois], Fr.	76,252	I10	278
Montreux, Switz.	10,600	B2	312
	(*16,400)		
Mont-Rolland, Que., Can.	975	S10	66
Montrose, Baldwin, Ala.	500	*E2	168
Montrose, Ashley, Ark.	399	D5	170
Montrose, Los Angeles, Calif.	6,000	C5	94
Montrose, Montrose, Colo.	5,044	D3	106
Montrose, Laurens, Ga.	236	D3	176
Montrose, Lee, Iowa	632	D6	142
Montrose, Jewell, Kans.	105	C5	144
Montrose, Genesee, Mich.	1,466	F8	146
Montrose, Wright, Minn.	360	*F4	148
Montrose, Jasper, Miss.	169	C3	184
Montrose, Henry, Mo.	526	C4	150
Montrose, Sioux, Nebr.		B2	152
Montrose, Westchester, N.Y.	1,800	*D8	212
Montrose, Susquehanna, Pa.	2,363	B6	214
Montrose, Scot.	10,800	E10	272
Montrose, McCook, S.Dak.	430	D8	158
Montrose, Randolph, W.Va.	114	*C5	194
Montrose, co., Colo.	18,286	D2	106
Montross, Westmoreland, Va.	394	B8	192
Montrouge, Fr.	36,298	I10	278
Mont Royal, Que., Can.	16,990	*S16	66
Mont-St. Martin, Fr.	5,811	C6	278
Montserrat, Johnson, Mo.	150	C4	150
Montserrat, ter., W.I.Fed.	1,400	D13	233
Montserrat, isl., W.I.Fed.		D13	233
Montserrat, peak, Sp.		B7	298
Mont-Tremblant, Que., Can.	300	R10	66
Mont-Tremblant, prov. park, Que., Can.		R10	66
Montvale, Bergen, N.J.	3,699	A4	210
Montvale, Bedford, Va.	500	C5	192
Montverde, Lake, Fla.	374	*C9	174
Mont Vernon, Hillsboro, N.H.	150	F3	208
	(585▲)		
Montville, New London, Conn.	1,060	D7	202
	(7,759▲)		
Montville, see Center Montville, Maine			
Montville, Berkshire, Mass.	85	B1	206
Montville, Morris, N.J.	1,200	B4	210
Montz, St. Charles, La.	350	*D5	180
Montzen, Bel.	2,477	D4	282
Monument, El Paso, Colo.	204	C6	106
Monument, Logan, Kans.	150	C2	144
Monument, Lea, N.Mex.	62	F7	126
Monument, Grant, Oreg.	214	C7	96
Monument, peak, Colo.		C3	106
Monument, peak, Idaho		D2	108
Monument, peak, Oreg.		C4	96
Monumental, buttes, Idaho		B3	108
Monument Beach, Barnstable, Mass.	400	C6	206
Monywa, Bur.	26,172	B2	362
Monza, It.	73,800	C2	302
Monze, Rh.&Nya.	1,800	C5	420
Monzón, Peru	514	B2	245
Monzón, Sp.	4,657	B7	298
Moodus, Middlesex, Conn.	1,103	D6	202
Moodus, lake, Conn.		C6	202
Moody, McLennan, Tex.	1,074	D7	130
Moody, co., S.Dak.	8,810	C9	158
Moodys, Cherokee, Okla.	40	B9	128
Mooers, Clinton, N.Y.	543	A8	212
Moon, lake, Miss.		A2	184
Moonachie, Bergen, N.J.	3,052	*B4	210
Moon Crest, Allegheny, Pa.	1,500	*C1	214
Moon Run, Allegheny, Pa.	650	A3	214
Moonshine, hill, Mass.		A2	206
Moonta, Austl.	1,220	E7	432
Moora, Austl.	829	E3	432
Moorcroft, Crook, Wyo.	826	B8	116
Moore, Butte, Idaho	358	F5	108
Moore, Fergus, Mont.	216	*D7	110
Moore, Cleveland, Okla.	1,783	C6	128
Moore, Spartanburg, S.C.	150	B5	188
Moore, Frio, Tex.	600	E6	130
Moore, Emery, Utah	25	E4	114
Moore, Tucker, W.Va.		B5	194
Moore, co., N.C.	36,733	B6	186
Moore, co., Tenn.	3,454	C5	190
Moore, co., Tex.	14,773	B5	130
Moore, lake, Austl.		E3	432
Moorefield, Ont., Can.	430	Q20	64
Moorefield, Nicholas, Ky.	200	B7	178
Moorefield, Frontier, Nebr.	55	D5	152
Moorefield, Hardy, W.Va.	1,434	B6	194
Moorefield, riv., W.Va.		C5	194
Moore Haven, Glades, Fla.	790	E9	174
Mooreland, Henry, Ind.	477	C4	140
Mooreland, Woodward, Okla.	871	B4	128
Mooreland Heights, Knox, Tenn.	900	*C8	190
Moorepark, Man., Can.	150	E3	60
Moores Bridge, Tuscaloosa, Ala.	400	B2	168
Mooresburg, Hawkins, Tenn.	200	B8	190
Moores Corner, Franklin, Mass.	102	B3	206
Moores Hill, Dearborn, Ind.	476	C4	140
Moore's Mills, N.B., Can.	155	D2	70
Moorestown, Missaukee, Mich.	65	E6	146
Moorestown, Burlington, N.J.	12,497	D3	210
Mooresville, Limestone, Ala.	93	A3	168
Mooresville, Morgan, Ind.	3,856	C3	140
Mooresville, Livingston, Mo.	117	B4	150
Mooresville, Iredell, N.C.	6,918	B5	186
Mooresville, Marshall, Tenn.	50	C5	190
Mooreton, Richland, N.Dak.	164	D9	154
Mooreville, Lee, Miss.	200	A4	184
Moorewood, Custer, Okla.	35	C4	128
Moorhead, Monona, Iowa	313	C2	142
Moorhead, Clay, Minn.	22,934	E2	148
Moorhead, Sunflower, Miss.	1,754	B2	184
Moorhead, Powder River, Mont.	5	E11	110
Mooring, Lake, Tenn.	100	B2	190
Mooringsport, Caddo, La.	864	B2	180
Moor Lake Station, Ont., Can.	80	O23	64
Moorland, Webster, Iowa	281	B3	142
Moorman, Muhlenberg, Ky.	250	C3	178
Moorpark, Ventura, Calif.	2,902	E4	94
Moors, The, moors, Scot.		G8	272
Moose, Teton, Wyo.	15	C2	116
Moose, creek, Wyo.		E2	116
Moose, hill, Mass.		B5	206
Moose, isl., Man., Can.		E4	60
Moose, lake, Man., Can.		C2	60
Moose, mtn., N.H.		D2	208
Moose, mtn., N.Y.		B7	212
Moose, pond, Maine		D3	204
Moose, riv., Maine		C2	204
Moose, riv., N.H.		C4	208
Moose, riv., N.Y.		B6	212
Moose, riv., Vt.		B5	218
Moose Creek, Ont., Can.	625	O26	64
Moose Creek, buttes, Idaho		C3	108
Moosehead, Piscataquis, Maine	15	C3	204
Moosehead, lake, Maine		C3	204
Mooseheart, Kane, Ill.	995	B5	138
		F1	
Moosehorn, Man., Can.	200	E3	60
Moose Jaw, Sask., Can.	29,603	E5	58
Moosejaw, creek, Sask., Can.		E5	58
Moose Lake, Man., Can.		D2	60
Moose Lake, Carlton, Minn.	1,514	E6	148
Moose Lake, res., Wis.		B3	160
Mooseleuk, stream, Maine		B4	204
Mooselookmeguntic, lake, Maine		D2	204
Moose Mountain, creek, Sask., Can.		F6	58
Moose Mountain, prov. park, Sask., Can.		F6	58
Moose Pass, Alsk.	70	C7	84
		G11	
Moose River, Somerset, Maine	180	C2	204
	(205▲)		
Moosic, Lackawanna, Pa.	4,243	A5	214
Moosic, mts., Pa.		A5	214
Moosilauke, mtn., N.H.		C3	208
Moosomin, Sask., Can.	1,390	E7	58
Moosonee, Ont., Can.	290	R25	64
Moosup, Windham, Conn.	2,760	C8	202
Moosup, riv., R.I.		C1	216
Mopang, lakes, Maine		D5	204
Mopeia, Moz.		C7	421
Mopti, Mali	12,000	D4	408
Moquegua, Peru	5,500	D3	245
Moquegua, dept., Peru	49,457	D3	245
Mor, Hung.	9,997	B3	320
Mora, Cam.	3,833	D7	409
Mora, Atkinson, Ga.	150	E4	176
Mora, Natchitoches, La.	30	C3	180
Mora, Kanabec, Minn.	2,329	F5	148
Mora, Mora, N.Mex.	750	C5	126
Mora, Sp.	10,441	C5	298
Mora, co., N.Mex.	6,028	B6	126
Mora, riv., N.Mex.		C6	126
Morada, San Joaquin, Calif.	2,156	*D3	94
Moradabad, India	154,018	C2	368
	(*161,854)		
Morada Nova, Braz.	1,496	B3	258
Mora de Ebro, Sp.	3,059	B7	298
Morafenobe, Malag.		C8	421
Morąg, Pol.	2,746	B4	325
Moraga, Contra Costa, Calif.	450	*A5	94
Moraine, Montgomery, Ohio	2,262	*C2	156
Morales, Guat.	2,143	C3	228
Moramanga, Malag.	3,750	C9	421
Moran, Crawford, Ga.	300	D3	176
Moran, Allen, Kans.	549	E8	144
Moran, Mackinac, Mich.	180	C7	146
Moran, Shackelford, Tex.	392	C6	130
Moran, Teton, Wyo.	10	C2	116
Morant Bay, Jam.	3,250	D6	232
Morastrand, Swe.	3,686	A5	292
Morat, lake, Switz.		B3	312
Morata de Tajuña, Sp.	3,670	*B5	298
Moratalla, Sp.	5,879	C6	298
Morattico, Lancaster, Va.	250	C8	192
Morava, riv., Aus.		B8	313
Morava, riv., Czech.		B3	324
Morava, riv., Yugo.		C6	316
Moravia, Boundary, Idaho		A2	108
Moravia, Appanoose, Iowa	621	D5	142
Moravia, Cayuga, N.Y.	1,575	C5	212
Moravia (Morava), reg., Czech.		B3	324
Moravian Falls, Wilkes, N.C.	250	A4	186
Morawhanna, Br.Gu.	305	D5	256
Moray, co., Scot.	49,600	D9	272
Moray, firth, Scot.		D9	272
Moraya, Bol.		D1	246
Morbihan, dept., Fr.	520,978	*D2	278
Mörbylånga, Swe.		E7	292
Morco, see Devonia, Tenn.			
Morden, Man., Can.	2,237	F3	60
More, mtn., Scot.		D5	272
More, mtn., Scot.		E6	272
More, mtn., Scot.		E8	272
More Assynt, mtn., Scot.		C8	272
Moreau, Dewey, S.Dak.	70	B5	158
Moreau, riv., S.Dak.		B3	158
Moreauville, Avoyelles, La.	815	C4	180
Morecambe [& Heysham], Eng.	36,700	G10	273
Morecambe, bay, Eng.		G10	273
Moree, Austl.	5,502	D9	432
Morehead, Rowan, Ky.	4,170	B7	178
Morehead City, Carteret, N.C.	5,583	C9	186
Morehouse, New Madrid, Mo.	1,417	E8	150
Morehouse, par., La.	33,709	B4	180
Moreland, Pope, Ark.	55	B4	170
Moreland, Coweta, Ga.	329	C2	176
Moreland, Bingham, Idaho	250	F6	108
Moreland, Lincoln, Ky.	300	C6	178
Moreland Hills, Cuyahoga, Ohio	2,188	*A5	156
Morelia, Mex.	63,245	D5	225
		L13	
Morell, P.E.I., Can.	309	C7	70
Morella, Sp.	2,488	B6	298
Morelos, state, Mex.	272,842	D6	225
Morelos, dam, Ariz.		F1	124
Morena, mts., Sp.		D4	298
Morenci, Greenlee, Ariz.	2,431	E6	124
Morenci, Lenawee, Mich.	2,053	H7	146
Moreni, Rom.	11,687	B3	321
Moreno, pt., Fla.		A4	174
Möre og Romsdal, co., Nor.	196,913	*E2	290
Moresby, isl., B.C., Can.		D6	52
Moreton, isl., Austl.		D10	432
Moretown, Washington, Vt.	150	C3	218
	(788▲)		
Morewood, Ont., Can.	215	O25	64
Morez, Fr.	5,588	D7	278
Morgan, Calhoun, Ga.	293	E2	176
Morgan, Pendleton, Ky.	65	B6	178
Morgan, Redwood, Minn.	975	G4	148
Morgan, Phillips, Mont.	4	B9	110
Morgan, Morrow, Oreg.		B7	96
Morgan, Morgan, Utah	1,299	B4	114
Morgan, Orleans, Vt.	45	B4	218
	(260▲)		
Morgan, co., Ala.	60,454	A3	168
Morgan, co., Colo.	21,192	B7	106
Morgan, co., Ga.	10,280	C3	176
Morgan, co., Ill.	36,571	D3	138
Morgan, co., Ind.	33,875	C3	140
Morgan, co., Ky.	11,056	C7	178
Morgan, co., Mo.	9,476	C5	150
Morgan, co., Ohio	12,747	C5	156
Morgan, co., Tenn.	14,304	B7	190
Morgan, co., Utah	2,837	B4	114
Morgan, co., W.Va.	8,376	B6	194
Morgan, isl., S.C.		G7	188
Morgan, pt., Conn.		E4	202
Morgana, Edgefield, S.C.	122	D4	188
Morgan Center, Orleans, Vt.	80	B5	218
Morgan City, Morgan, Ala.	350	*A3	168
Morgan City, St. Mary, La.	13,540	C5	180
		E4	
Morgan City, Leflore, Miss.	350	B2	184
Morganfield, Union, Ky.	3,741	C3	178
Morgan Hill, Santa Clara, Calif.	3,151	D3	94
Morganton, Van Buren, Ark.	75	B4	170
Morganton, Fannin, Ga.	211	B2	176
Morganton, Burke, N.C.	9,186	B4	186
Morgantown, Morgan, Ind.	971	C3	140
Morgantown, Butler, Ky.	1,318	C4	178
Morgantown, Marion, Miss.	310	D3	184
Morgantown, Rhea, Tenn.	550	C6	190
Morgantown, Monongalia, W.Va.	22,487	A7	194
		B5	
Morganville, Clay, Kans.	226	C6	144
Morganville, Monmouth, N.J.	400	C4	210
Morganza, Pointe Coupee, La.	937	D4	180
Morges, Switz.	6,456	B2	312
Morghāb, Iran		C3	379
Morgongåva, Swe.		B7	292
Mori, Jap.	22,076	C8	354
Moriah, Essex, N.Y.	540	A8	212
Moriah, mtn., N.H.		C4	208

Moriarty, Torrance, N.Mex.	720	D4	126
Morice, lake, B.C., Can.		C9	52
Morice, riv., B.C., Can.		C9	52
Moriguchi, Jap.	28,204	*M11	354
Morin Heights, Que., Can.	590	S10	66
Morinville, Alta., Can.	957	D6	54
Morioka, Jap.	142,875	E8	354
Morjarv, Swe.	457	C10	290
Morkill, riv., B.C., Can.		D12	52
Morlaix, Fr.	15,037	C2	278
Morland, Graham, Kans.	317	C3	144
Morley, Las Animas, Colo.	300	E6	106
Morley, Jones, Iowa	124	B6	142
Morley, Mecosta, Mich.	445	F6	146
Morley, Scott, Mo.	472	D8	150
Mörlunda, Swe.	4,114	D6	292
Mormon, range, Nev.		G7	112
Mormon Lake, Coconino, Ariz.	25	D4	124
Morning, Shoshone, Idaho		B3	108
Morningdale, Worcester, Mass.	600	*B4	206
Morningside, New Haven, Conn.	375	E3	202
Morningside, Prince Georges, Md.	1,708	C6	182
Morningside, Hennepin, Minn.	1,981	*F5	148
Morning Star, Garland, Ark.	100	C7	170
Morning Sun, Louisa, Iowa	875	C6	142
Mornington, isl., Chile		G2	251
Morning View, Kenton, Ky.	150	A8	178
Moro, Lee, Ark.	182	C6	170
Moro, Sherman, Oreg.	327	B6	96
Moro, creek, Ark.		D4	170
Moro, gulf, Phil.		C6	358
Morobay, Bradley, Ark.	40	D4	170
Morobe, N.Gui.		F11	359
Morocco, Newton, Ind.	1,341	B2	140
Morocco, country, Afr.	10,330,000	C6	388 402
Morococha, Peru	1,522	C2	245
Morogoro, Tan.	14,507	D6	414
Moroleón, Mex.	13,808	K13	225
Morombe, Malag.		D8	421
Morón, Cuba	18,629	A5	232
Morona, riv., Peru		A2	245
Morondava, Malag.	5,300	D8	421
Morón de la Frontera, Sp.	22,091	D4	298
Moroni, Sanpete, Utah	879	D4	114
Morotai, isl., Indon.		D7	359
Moroto, Ug.		B5	414
Moroubas, Cen.Afr.Rep.		E9	409
Morozovsk, Sov.Un.	28,000	C2	336
Morpeth, Ont., Can.	225	R19	64
Morpeth, Eng.	10,800	F11	272
Morphou, Cyp.	6,097	D5	307
Morral, Marion, Ohio	493	B3	156
Morrice, Shiawassee, Mich.	530	G7	146
Morrill, Brown, Kans.	299	C8	144
Morrill, Waldo, Maine	150 (355▲)	*D3	204
Morrill, Scotts Bluff, Nebr.	884	C2	152
Morrill, co., Nebr.	7,057	C2	152
Morrilton, Conway, Ark.	5,997	B4	170
Morrinhos, Braz.	4,696	D1	258
Morrinsville, N.Z.	3,652	B5	437
Morris, Jefferson, Ala.	638	*B3	168
Morris, Man., Can.	1,260	F4	60
Morris, Litchfield, Conn.	150 (1,190▲)	C3	202
Morris, Quitman, Ga.	150	E2	176
Morris, Grundy, Ill.	7,935	B5	138
Morris, Ripley, Ind.	400	C4	140
Morris, Wyandotte, Kans.	50	B7	144
Morris, Stevens, Minn.	4,199	F3	148
Morris, Otsego, N.Y.	677	C6	212
Morris, Okmulgee, Okla.	982	C8	128
Morris, co., Kans.	7,392	D7	144
Morris, co., N.J.	261,620	B3	210
Morris, co., Tex.	12,576	C8	130
Morris, isl., S.C.		F4 F9	188
Morris, mtn., N.Y.		A7	212
Morris, res., Calif.		C6	94
Morrisburg, Ont., Can.	2,131	P25	64
Morris Chapel, Hardin, Tenn.	100	C3	190
Morris Jessup, cape, Grnld.		O33	290
Morrison, Jefferson, Colo.	426	*C5	106
Morrison, Whiteside, Ill.	4,159	B4	138
Morrison, Grundy, Iowa	139	B5	142
Morrison, Gasconade, Mo.	232	C6	150
Morrison, Noble, Okla.	256	B6	128
Morrison, Warren, Tenn.	294	C6	190
Morrison, Brown, Wis.	125	A6	160
Morrison, co., Minn.	26,641	E4	148
Morrison, hill, Conn.		A4	202
Morrison Bluff, Logan, Ark.		B3	170
Morrison City, Sullivan, Tenn.	2,426	*B9	190
Morrisonville, Christian, Ill.	1,129	D4	138
Morrisonville, Clinton, N.Y.	540	A8	212
Morris Plains, Morris, N.J.	4,703	B4	210
Morriston, Levy, Fla.	150	B8	174
Morristown, Maricopa, Ariz.	25	E3	124
Morristown, Winnebago, Ill.	402	*A4	138
Morristown, Shelby, Ind.	704	C4	140
Morristown, Rice, Minn.	616	G5	148
Morristown, Morris, N.J.	17,712	B4	210
Morristown, St. Lawrence, N.Y.	541	A6	212
Morristown, Corson, S.Dak.	219	B4	158
Morristown, Hamblen, Tenn.	21,267	B8	190
Morristown, Lamoille, Vt.	65 (3,347▲)	B3	218
Morristown, natl. historical park, N.J.		B3	210
Morrisville, Polk, Mo.	228	D4	150
Morrisville, Madison, N.Y.	1,304	C6	212
Morrisville, Wake, N.C.	222	*B7	186
Morrisville, Bucks, Pa.	7,790	C7	214
Morrisville, Lamoille, Vt.	2,047	B3	218
Morrisville, Fauquier, Va.	100	B7	192
Morrito, Nic.	387	E5	228
Morro, Ec.		A1	245
Morro, pt., Chile		A1	252
Morro, pt., Chile		C3	250
Morro Bay, San Luis Obispo, Calif.	3,692	E3	94
Morro Beach (Del Mar Heights), San Luis Obispo, Calif.	1,907	*E3	94
Morro do Chapéu, Braz.	1,230	C2	258
Morro Furo Mantilla, Arg.		A4	252
Morropón, Peru	3,909	B2	245
Morros, pt., Mex.		D7	225
Morrosquillo, gulf, Col.		B1	244
Morrow, Clayton, Ga.	580	B5 C2	176
Morrow, St. Landry, La.	400	D3	180
Morrow, Warren, Ohio	1,477	C2	156
Morrow, co., Ohio	19,405	B4	156
Morrow, co., Oreg.	4,871	B7	96
Morrowville, Washington, Kans.	195	C6	144
Morrum, Swe.	4,156	E5	292
Mors, isl., Den.		H3	291
Morse, Sask., Can.	459	E4	58
Morse, Acadia, La.	682	D3	180
Morse, Ashland, Wis.	45	B3	160
Morse Bluff, Saunders, Nebr.	119	C9	152
Morses, creek, N.J.		B1	210
Morshansk, Sov.Un.	48,000	B2	336
Mortagne [-au-Perche], Fr.		C4	278
Mortara, It.	10,500	C2	302
Morteau, Fr.	4,670	D7	278
Morteros, Arg.	5,593	B3	252
Mortlach, Sask., Can.	251	E4	58
Morton, Bonner, Idaho		A2	108
Morton, Tazewell, Ill.	5,325	C4	138
Morton, Renville, Minn.	624	G4	148
Morton, Scott, Miss.	2,260	C3	184
Morton, Delaware, Pa.	2,207	*D6	214
Morton, Cochran, Tex.	2,731	C4	130
Morton, Lewis, Wash.	1,183	C4	98
Morton, Fremont, Wyo.	15	C4	116
Morton, co., Kans.	3,354	E2	144
Morton, co., N.Dak.	20,992	D4	154
Morton Grove, Cook, Ill.	20,533	E3	138
Mortons Gap, Hopkins, Ky.	1,308	C3	178
Morvan, mts., Fr.		D6	278
Morven, Brooks, Ga.	476	F3	176
Morven, Anson, N.C.	518	C5	186
Morven, mtn., Scot.		C9	272
Moryakovskiy Zaton, Sov.Un.		A10	336
Morzhovoi, Alsk.	30	E5	84
Mosalsk, Sov.Un.		E10	332
Mosby, Clay, Mo.	293	D2	150
Mosby, Garfield, Mont.	5	D9	110
Mosca, Alamosa, Colo.	150	E5	106
Moscos, is., Bur.		D3	362
Moscow, Jefferson, Ark.	100	C5	170
Moscow, Latah, Idaho	11,183	C2	108
Moscow, Rush, Ind.	180	C4	140
Moscow, Muscatine, Iowa	208	C6	142
Moscow, Stevens, Kans.	211	E2	144
Moscow, Hickman, Ky.	100	D1	178
Moscow (Town of), Somerset, Maine	(559▲)	*C3	204
Moscow, Clermont, Ohio	438	D2	156
Moscow, Lackawanna, Pa.	1,212	A5	214
Moscow (Moskva), Sov.Un.	5,032,000 (*7,800,000)	E11 N18	332
Moscow, Fayette, Tenn.	368	C2	190
Moscow, Lamoille, Vt.	100	C3	218
Moscow, Hancock, W.Va.	30	A2	194
Moscow Mills, Lincoln, Mo.	360	C7	150
Mosel, riv., Ger.		D2	286
Moseley, Powhatan, Va.	100	C7	192
Moselle, Jones, Miss.		D3	184
Moselle, dept., Fr.	769,388	*C7	278
Moselle, riv., Fr.		C7	278
Moselle, riv., Lux.		E5	282
Mosers River, N.S., Can.	235	E7	70
Moses, coulee, Wash.		B7	98
Moses, lake, Wash.		B7	98
Moses Lake, Grant, Wash.	11,299	B7	98
Mosgiel, N.Z.	4,050	F3	437
Mosheim, Greene, Tenn.	300	B9	190
Mosher, Mellette, S.Dak.	25	D5	158
Mosherville, N.S., Can.	200	D6	70
Moshi, Tan.	13,726	C6	414
Moshupa, Bech.		D5	420
Mosier, Wasco, Oreg.	252	B5	96
Mosinee, Marathon, Wis.	2,067	D4	160
Mosjöen, Nor.	3,530	D5	290
Moskee, Crook, Wyo.	15	B8	116
Moskva, see Moscow, Sov.Un.			
Moskva, riv., Sov.Un.		O19	332
Mosley, creek, B.C., Can.		E10	52
Mosonmagyaróvár, Hung.	21,000	B2	320
Mosos, plains, Bol.		C2	246
Mosquera, Col.	318	C1	244
Mosquero, Harding and San Miguel, N.Mex.	310	C7	126
Mosquito, Newf., Can.	70	G9	72
Mosquito, creek, Iowa		C2	142
Mosquito, lagoon, Fla.		C10	174
Mosquito Coast, reg., Hond., Nic.		D6	228
Mosquito Creek, res., Ohio		A6	156
Mosquitos, gulf, Pan.		F7	228
Moss, Jasper, Miss.	125	D3	184
Moss, Nor.	18,848	B1	292
Moss, Clay, Tenn.	200	B6	190
Moss, mtn., Ark.		C4	170
Mossaka, Con.B.		G8	409
Mossbank, Sask., Can.	593	F5	58
Mossbank, Scot.		A11	272
Moss Beach, San Mateo, Calif.	500	B4	94
Moss Bluff, Calcasieu, La.	700	*D2	180
Mossel Bay, U.S.Afr.	9,307	F4	420
Mossendjo, Con.B.		G7	409
Moss Glen, falls and chasm, Vt.		C3	218
Mossleigh, Alta., Can.		E6	54
Mossmain, Yellowstone, Mont.		E8	110
Moss Point, Jackson, Miss.	6,631	E2 E4	184
Mossville, Newton, Ark.	40	B3	170
Mossville, Calcasieu, La.	1,500	*D2	180
Mossy, Fayette, W.Va.	50	D6	194
Mossy, pt., Man., Can.		D3	60
Mossy, riv., Man., Can.		E3	60
Mossy, riv., Sask., Can.		C6	58
Mossy Head, Walton, Fla.	100	A4	174
Mossyrock, Lewis, Wash.	344	C4	98
Most, Czech.	35,770	A1	324
Mostaganem, Alg.	60,186	A4	402
Mostar, Yugo.	32,400	C3	316
Móstoles, Sp.	1,819	*B5	298
Mosul, Iraq	140,245	A5	378
Mösvatn, lake, Nor.		G3	291
Moswansicut, res., R.I.		B2	216
Motagua, riv., Guat.		C3	228
Motala, Swe.	26,043	C6	292
Motatán, Ven.	2,653	B3	240
Motbridge, Sumter, S.C.	150	D9	188
Motherwell [& Wishaw], Scot.	70,700	F9	272
Motihari, India		D4	368
Motilla del Palancar, Sp.	3,878	C6	298
Motley, Morrison, Minn.	430	E4	148
Motley, co., Tex.	2,870	B5	130
Moto, see Oshima, Jap.			
Moto, mtn., Iwo		A7	436
Motocurunya, Ven.		D6	240
Motril, Sp.	19,185	D5	298
Motrul, riv., Rom.		B2	321
Mott, Hettinger, N.Dak.	1,463	D3	154
Motueka, N.Z.	2,824	D4	437
Motuhora, N.Z.	117	C6	437
Motul, Mex.	7,789	C8	225
Motupe, Peru	4,396	B2	245
Moturiki, isl., Fiji		E6	436
Mouat Mine, Stillwater, Mont.	250	*E7	110
Mouchoir, passage, W.I.		B9	233
Moúdhros, Grc.	1,720	B5	306
Moudjéria, Maur.		C2	408
Moudon, Switz.	2,476	B2	312
Mouila, Gabon		G7	409
Moujärvi, lake, Fin.		D13	290
Moulins, Fr.	24,437	D5	278
Moulmein, Bur.	102,777	C3	362
Moulton, Lawrence, Ala.	1,716	A2	168
Moulton, Appanoose, Iowa	773	D5	142
Moulton, Fergus, Mont.		C7	110
Moulton, Lavaca, Tex.	646	*E7	130
Moulton, val., Ala.		A2	168
Moultonboro (Moultonborough), Carroll, N.H.	150 (840▲)	D4	208
Moultonville, Carroll, N.H.	215	D4	208
Moultrie, Saint Johns, Fla.	500	B9	174
Moultrie, Colquitt, Ga.	15,764	E3	176
Moultrie, co., Ill.	13,635	D5	138
Moultrie, lake, S.C.		E8	188
Mound, Madison, La.	107	B4	180
Mound, Hennepin, Minn.	5,440	G5	148
Mound Bayou, Bolivar, Miss.	1,354	B2	184
Mound City, Pulaski, Ill.	1,669	F4	138
Mound City, Linn, Kans.	661	D9	144
Mound City, Holt, Mo.	1,249	A2	150
Mound City, Campbell, S.Dak.	144	B5	158
Mound City Group, natl. mon., Ohio		C3	156
Moundou, Chad		E8	409
Moundridge, McPherson, Kans.	1,214	D6	144
Mounds, Pulaski, Ill.	1,835	F4	138
Mounds, Creek, Okla.	674	C7	128
Mounds View, Ramsey, Minn.	6,416	*F5	148
Moundsville, Marshall, W.Va.	15,163	B1 B4	194
Mound Valley, Labette, Kans.	481	E8	144
Moundville, Hale, Ala.	922	B2	168
Moundville, Vernon, Mo.	136	D3	150
Mounier, mtn., Fr.		E7	278
Mountain, Pembina, N.Dak.	218	B8	154
Mountain, Ritchie, W.Va.	200	B4	194
Mountain, Oconto, Wis.	400	C5	160
Mountain, lake, Sask., Can.		C5	58
Mountainair, Torrance, N.Mex.	1,605	D4	126
Mountain Ash, Whitley, Ky.	275	D6	178
Mountain Brook, Jefferson, Ala.	12,680	E5	168
Mountainburg, Crawford, Ark.	402	B2	170
Mountain City, Rabun, Ga.	550	B3	176
Mountain City, Elko, Nev.	100	B6	112
Mountain City, Johnson, Tenn.	1,379	B10	190
Mountain Creek, Chilton, Ala.	300	C3	168
Mountain Dale, Sullivan, N.Y.	800	D7	212
Mountain Fork, riv., Okla.		D9	128
Mountain Grove, Ont., Can.	225	P24	64
Mountain Grove, Wright, Mo.	3,176	D5	150
Mountain Grove, Bath, Va.	25	B5	192
Mountain Home, Baxter, Ark.	2,105	A4	170
Mountain Home, Elmore, Idaho	9,344	F3	108
Mountain Iron, St. Louis, Minn.	1,808	D6	148
Mountain Lake, Cottonwood, Minn.	1,943	H4	148
Mountain Lake Park, Garrett, Md.	975	B1	182
Mountain Lakes, Morris, N.J.	4,037	B4	210
Mountain Park, Alta., Can.	415	D4	54
Mountain Park, Kiowa, Okla.	403	D5	128
Mountain Pine, Garland, Ark.	1,279	C3 C6	170
Mountain Point, Alsk.	109	*K15	84
Mountainside, Union, N.J.	6,325	B4	210
Mountaintop, Luzerne, Pa.	1,600	B6	214
Mountaintown, Gilmer, Ga.	150	B2	176
Mountain Valley, Garland, Ark.	150	C3	170
Mountain Valley, Henry, Va.		D5	192
Mountain View, Alsk. (part of Anchorage)		G11	84
Mountain View, Stone, Ark.	983	B4	170
Mountain View, Santa Clara, Calif.	30,889	B5	94
Mountain View, Alta., Can.	100	F6	54
Mountain View, Jefferson, Colo.	826	*C5	106
Mountain View, Clayton, Ga.	1,500	*C2	176
Mountainview, Hawaii, Haw.	747	D6	86
Mountain View, Ada, Idaho	4,898	*F2	108
Mountain View, Howell, Mo.	936	D6	150
Mountain View, Passaic, N.J. (part of Wayne)		A1	210
Mountain View, Kiowa, Okla.	864	C5	128
Mountain View, Asotin, Wash.	25	C9	98
Mountain View, Natrona, Wyo.	1,721	*D6	116
Mountain View, Uinta, Wyo.	400	E2	116
Mountain Village, Alsk.	221	C5	84
Mount Airy, Habersham, Ga.	417	B3	176
Mount Airy, St. John the Baptist, La.	500	B6	180
Mount Airy, Carroll and Frederick, Md.	1,352	B5	182
Mount Airy, Hunterdon, N.J.	60	C3	210
Mount Airy, Surry, N.C.	7,055	A5	186
Mountairy, Sequatchie, Tenn.	25	C6	190
Mount Airy, Pittsylvania, Va.	45	D5	192
Mount Albert, Ont., Can.	650	P21	64
Mount Albert, N.Z.	25,644	H8	438
Mount Andrew, Barbour, Ala.	25	D4	168
Mount Angel, Marion, Oreg.	1,428	B1 B4	96
Mount Arlington, Morris, N.J.	1,246	B3	210
Mount Athos, see Áyion Óros, prov., Grc.			
Mount Auburn, Christian, Ill.	502	D4	138
Mount Auburn, Wayne, Ind.	144	*C4	140
Mount Auburn, Benton, Iowa	186	B5	142
Mount Ayr, Newton, Ind.	186	B2	140
Mount Ayr, Ringgold, Iowa	1,738	D3	142
Mount Berry, Floyd, Ga.	1,000	B1	176
Mount Bethel, Somerset, N.J.	150	B3	210
Mount Blanchard, Hancock, Ohio	432	B3	156
Mount Brydges, Ont., Can.	610	R19	64
Mount Calvary, Fond du Lac, Wis.	650	B5 E5	160
Mount Carmel, Newf., Can.	350	G9	72
Mount Carmel, Wabash, Ill.	8,594	E6	138
Mount Carmel, Franklin, Ind.	142	C5	140
Mount Carmel, Fleming, Ky.	162	B7	178
Mount Carmel, Northumberland, Pa.	10,760	C5	214
Mount Carmel, McCormick, S.C.	109	C4	188
Mount Carmel, Kane, Utah	110	F3	114
Mount Carmel Junction, Kane, Utah	9	F3	114
Mount Carroll, Carroll, Ill.	2,056	A4	138
Mount Cenis, pass, Fr.		E7	278
Mount Cenis, pass, It.		C1	302
Mount Chase (Plantation of), Penobscot, Maine	(179▲)	*B4	204
Mount Clare, Harrison, W.Va.	900	B4	194
Mount Clemens, Macomb, Mich.	21,016	B9 G9	146
Mount Clinton, Rockingham, Va.	170	B6	192
Mount Crawford, Rockingham, Va.	247	*B6	192
Mount Croghan, Chesterfield, S.C.	145	B8	188
Mount Darwin, Rh.&Nya.	485	C6	421
Mount Desert, Hancock, Maine	100 (1,663▲)	*D4	204
Mount Desert, isl., Maine		D4	204
Mount Desert Ferry, Hancock, Maine	50	D4	204
Mount Dora, Lake, Fla.	3,756	C9	174
Mount Dora, Union, N.Mex.	55	B7	126
Mount Eden, Spencer, Ky.	350	B5	178
Mount Eden, N.Z.	18,629	H9	437
Mount Edgecumbe, Alsk.	1,884	D8 J14	84
Mount Elgin, Ont., Can.	215	R20	64
Mount Enterprise, Rusk, Tex.	400	D8	130
Mount Ephraim, Camden, N.J.	5,447	*D3	210
Mount Etna, Huntington, Ind.	192	B4	140
Mount Forest, Ont., Can.	2,438	Q20	64
Mountforest, Bay, Mich.	35	F7	146
Mount Freedom, Morris, N.J.	100	*B3	210
Mount Gambier, Austl.	10,331	F8	432
Mount Gay, Logan, W.Va.	3,386	D2	194
Mount Gilead, Montgomery, N.C.	1,229	B6	186
Mount Gilead, Morrow, Ohio	2,788	B4	156
Mount Harris, Routt, Colo.	730	B3	106
Mount Healthy, Hamilton, Ohio	6,553	D1	156
Mount Hebron, Greene, Ala.	125	C1	168
Mount Hebron, Siskiyou, Calif.	150	B2	94
Mount Hermon, Washington, La.	90	D5	180
Mount Hermon, Franklin, Mass.	600	A3	206
Mount Heron, Buchanan, Va.	100	C2	192
Mount Holly, Union, Ark.	300	D4	170
Mount Holly, Burlington, N.J.	13,271	D3	210
Mount Holly, Gaston, N.C.	4,037	B4	186
Mount Holly, Berkeley, S.C.	150	E8 E3	188
Mount Holly, Rutland, Vt.	70 (517▲)	E3	218
Mount Holly Springs, Cumberland, Pa.	1,840	C4	214
Mount Hood, Hood River, Oreg.	50	B5	96
Mount Hope, Lawrence, Ala.	300	A2	168
Mount Hope, Ont., Can.	340	Q21	64
Mount Hope, Sedgwick, Kans.	539	E6	144
Mount Hope, Morris, N.J.	500	B3	210
Mount Hope, Spokane, Wash.		D9	98
Mount Hope, Fayette, W.Va.	2,000	D3 D7	194
Mount Hope, Grant, Wis.	218	F3	160
Mount Hope, bay, R.I.		C4	216
Mount Hope, riv., Conn.		B7	202
Mount Horeb, Dane, Wis.	1,991	E4	160
Mount Ida, Montgomery, Ark.	564	C3	170
Mount Ida, Grant, Wis.	55	F3	160
Mount Idaho, Idaho, Idaho	90	D2	108
Mount Isa, Austl.	7,433	C7	432
Mount Jackson, Shenandoah, Va.	372	B6	192
Mount Jewett, McKean, Pa.	1,226	B3	214
Mount Joy, Lancaster, Pa.	3,292	C5	214
Mount Judea, Newton, Ark.	60	B3	170
Mount Juliet, Wilson, Tenn.	750	B5	190
Mount Kisco, Westchester, N.Y.	6,805	D8	212
Mountlake Terrace, Snohomish, Wash.	9,122	B4	98
Mount Laurel, Burlington, N.J.	200	D3	210
Mount Lebanon, Allegheny, Pa.	35,361	C1	214
Mount Lemmon, Pima, Ariz.	30	F5	124
Mount Lookout, Nicholas, W.Va.	404	C4 D7	194
Mount McKinley, natl. park, Alsk.		C6	84
Mount Magnet, Austl.	648	D3	432
Mount Meigs, Montgomery, Ala.	400	C3	168
Mount Misery, pt., N.Y.		D4	212
Mount Montgomery, Mineral, Nev.	10	E3	112

Mount Morgan, Austl. 4,152 C10 432
Mount Moriah, Harrison, Mo. 225 A4 150
Mount Morris, Ogle, Ill. 3,075 A4 138
Mount Morris, Genesee, Mich. 3,484 F8 146
Mount Morris, Livingston, N.Y. 3,250 C4 212
Mount Olive, Jefferson, Ala. 1,800 B3 168, E4
Mount Olive, Izard, Ark. 50 B4 170
Mount Olive, Macoupin, Ill. 2,295 D4 138
Mount Olive, Covington, Miss. 841 D3 184
Mount Olive, Wayne, N.C. 4,673 B7 186
Mount Olive, Knox, Tenn. 500 E9 190
Mount Oliver, Allegheny, Pa. 5,980 A4 214
Mount Olivet, Robertson, Ky. 386 B6 178
Mount Orab, Brown, Ohio 1,058 C3 156
Mount Penn, Berks, Pa. 3,574 *C6 214
Mount Pleasant, Izard, Ark. 250 B5 170
Mount Pleasant, New Castle, Del. 65 B3 172
Mount Pleasant, Gadsden, Fla. 300 A6 174
Mount Pleasant, Henry, Iowa 7,339 D6 142
Mount Pleasant, Frederick, Md. 100 B5 182
Mount Pleasant, Isabella, Mich. 14,875 F7 146
Mount Pleasant, Marshall, Miss. 150 A3 184
Mount Pleasant, Hunterdon, N.J. 145 B2 210
Mount Pleasant, Cabarrus, N.C. 1,041 B5 186
Mount Pleasant, Jefferson, Ohio 656 *B6 156
Mount Pleasant, Westmoreland, Pa. 6,107 C2 214
Mount Pleasant, Charleston, S.C. 5,116 F4 188, F9
Mount Pleasant, Maury, Tenn. 2,921 C4 190
Mount Pleasant, Titus, Tex. 8,027 C8 130
Mount Pleasant, Sanpete, Utah 1,572 D4 114
Mount Pleasant Church, Lincoln, Miss. 500 D2 184
Mount Prospect, Cook, Ill. 18,906 A6 138, E2
Mount Pulaski, Logan, Ill. 1,689 C4 138
Mountrail, co., N.Dak. 10,077 B3 154
Mount Rainier, Prince Georges, Md. 9,855 C3 182
Mount Rainier, natl. park, Wash. C5 98
Mount Robson, prov. park, B.C., Can. D13 52
Mount Roskill, N.Z. 25,555 H9 437
Mount Royal, Gloucester, N.J. 800 D2 210
Mount Rushmore, natl. memorial, S.Dak. D2 158
Mount St. George, Tobago 1,300 E14 233
Mount Savage, Allegany, Md. 1,639 A2 182
Mount Shasta, Siskiyou, Calif. 1,936 B2 94
Mount Sherman, Newton, Ark. A3 170
Mount Sidney, Augusta, Va. 500 B6 192
Mount Solon, Augusta, Va. 140 B5 192
Mount Sterling, Choctaw, Ala. 150 C1 168
Mount Sterling, Brown, Ill. 2,262 D3 138
Mount Sterling, Van Buren, Iowa 86 D6 142
Mount Sterling, Montgomery, Ky. 5,370 B7 178
Mount Sterling, Gasconade, Mo. 821 C6 150
Mount Sterling, Madison, Ohio 1,338 C3 156
Mount Sterling, Crawford, Wis. 161 E3 160
Mount Stewart, P.E.I., Can. 439 C7 70
Mount Storm, Grant, W.Va. 200 B5 194
Mount Summit, Henry, Ind. 424 B4 140
Mount Tabor, Rutland, Vt. 45 (165▲) E3 218
Mount Uniacke, N.S., Can. 245 E6 70
Mount Union, Henry, Iowa 176 C6 142
Mount Union, Huntingdon, Pa. 4,091 C4 214
Mount Upton, Chenango, N.Y. 400 C6 212
Mount Vernon, Mobile, Ala. 553 D1 168
Mount Vernon, Faulkner, Ark. 200 B4 170
Mount Vernon, Montgomery, Ga. 1,166 D4 176
Mount Vernon, Jefferson, Ill. 15,566 E5 138
Mount Vernon, Posey, Ind. 5,970 E2 140
Mount Vernon, Linn, Iowa 2,593 C6 142
Mount Vernon, Rockcastle, Ky. 1,177 C6 178
Mount Vernon, Kennebec, Maine 225 (596▲) D3 204
Mount Vernon, Somerset, Md. 250 D8 182
Mount Vernon, Lawrence, Mo. 2,381 D4 150
Mount Vernon, Westchester, N.Y. 76,010 D2 212
Mount Vernon, Knox, Ohio 13,284 B4 156
Mount Vernon, Lucas, Ohio 1,000 A1 156
Mount Vernon, Grant, Oreg. 502 C7 96
Mount Vernon, Davison, S.Dak. 379 D7 158
Mount Vernon, Monroe, Tenn. C7 190
Mount Vernon, Franklin, Tex. 1,338 C8 130
Mount Vernon, Fairfax, Va. 101 A7 192, B7
Mount Vernon, Skagit, Wash. 7,921 A4 98
Mount Victory, Pulaski, Ky. 500 C6 178
Mount Victory, Hardin, Ohio 598 B3 156
Mountville, Troup, Ga. 139 C2 176
Mountville, Lancaster, Pa. 1,411 *D5 214
Mountville, Laurens, S.C. 139 C5 188
Mount Washington, Bullitt, Ky. 1,173 A5 178, B5
Mount Washington, Berkshire, Mass. 25 (34▲) B1 206
Mount Washington, Jackson, Mo. 950 E2 150
Mount Willing, Lowndes, Ala. 350 C3 168
Mount Wilson, Baltimore, Md. 600 B6 182
Mount Wolf, York, Pa. 1,514 C5 214
Mount Zion, Carroll, Ga. 211 C1 176
Mount Zion, Macon, Ill. 925 *D5 138
Moura, Braz. 62 F4 256
Moura, Port. 9,509 C3 298
Mourne, mts., N.Ire. G6 273
Mouscron, Bel. 36,562 D2 282
Mousie, Knott, Ky. 500 C8 178
Mouth of Keswick, N.B., Can. D3 70
Moutier, Switz. 5,916 A3 312
Mouton, isl., N.S., Can. F5 70
Mouzon, Williamsburg, S.C. 300 D9 188
Moville, Woodbury, Iowa 1,156 B1 142
Moville, Ire. 1,093 F5 272
Mowbray, Man., Can. 70 F3 60
Moweaqua, Shelby, Ill. 1,614 D4 138
Mower, co., Minn. 48,498 H6 148
Mowich, Klamath, Oreg. D5 96
Mowrystown, Highland, Ohio 416 C3 156
Moxee City, Yakima, Wash. 499 C6 98
Moxico, dist., Ang. 251,675 B4 420
Moxie, mtn., Maine C3 204
Moxie, pond, Maine C3 204
Moyalē, Eth. E4 398
Moyale, Ken. B6 414
Moyamba, S.L. E2 408
Moyen Atlas, mts., Mor. B2 402
Moyers, Pushmataha, Okla. 150 D8 128
Moyeuvre [-Grande], Fr. 10,707 C7 278
Moyie, B.C., Can. 225 F15 52
Moyie, range, B.C., Can. F14 52
Moyie Springs, Boundary, Idaho 196 A2 108
Moylan, Delaware, Pa. 1,000 *D6 214
Moyobamba, Peru 10,700 B2 245
Moyock, Currituck, N.C. 350 A9 186
Moyuta, Guat. 1,478 C2 228
Mozambique, Port. poss., Afr. 6,234,000 H10 388, 421
Mozambique, chan., Afr. C8 421
Mozart, Sask., Can. 81 E5 58
Mozdok, Sov.Un. 32,000 D2 336
Mozhaysk, Sov.Un. 15,000 E11 332
Mozyr, Sov.Un. 25,000 F7 332
Mpanda, Tan. D5 414
Mpika, Rh.&Nya. 117 B6 421
Mporokoso, Rh.&Nya. A6 421
Mpouia, Con.B. G8 409
Mpulungu, Rh.&Nya. A6 421
Mpwapwa, Tan. 1,612 D6 414
Mrągowo, Pol. 3,254 B5 325
M'Raïer, Alg. 6,935 B5 402
Mrewa, Rh.&Nya. 790 C6 421
Mšec, Czech. 1,007 *A2 324
Mšeně, Czech. 886 *A2 324
M'Sila, Alg. 8,645 (71,627▲) A4 402
Msta, riv., Sov.Un. C9 332
Mtakuja, Tan. D5 414
Mtoko, Rh.&Nya. 975 C6 421
Mtorashanga, Rh.&Nya. 2,270 C6 421
Mtsensk, Sov.Un. 23,300 F11 332
Mtubatuba, U.S.Afr. E6 421
Mtwara, Tan. 10,459 E7 414
Muang Fang, Thai. 5,000 C3 362
Muang Hot, Thai. 10,000 C3 362
Muang Nan, Thai. 25,000 C4 362
Muang Ubon, Thai. 10,000 D5 362
Muar, see Bandar Maharani, Mala.
Mubi, Br.Cam. D7 409
Muchkap, Sov.Un. 17,000 G14 332
Muck, isl., Scot. E6 272
Muckalee, creek, Ga. D2 176
Mucuburi, Moz. B7 421
Mucuri, Braz. D3 258
Mucuri, riv., Braz. D2 258
Mucusso, Ang. C4 420
Mud, creek, Ala. E4 168
Mud, creek, Ga. B5 176
Mud, creek, Iowa A8 142
Mud, creek, Okla. D6 128
Mud, lake, Maine A4 204
Mud, lake, Minn D5 148
Mud, lake, Wash. D3 98
Mud, riv., Minn. C3 148
Mud, riv., W.Va. C2 194
Muddo Gashi, Ken. B6 414
Muddy, creek, Colo. D3 106
Muddy, creek, Colo. B4 106
Muddy, creek, Ky. D3 178
Muddy, creek, Wyo. C4 116
Muddy, creek, Wyo. D6 116
Muddy, creek, Wyo. E2 116
Muddy, creek, Wyo. E5 116
Muddy, lake, Sask., Can. D3 58
Muddy, mts., Nev. G7 112
Muddy, riv., Utah E4 114
Muddy Boggy, creek, Okla. D8 128
Muddy Creek, mtn., Ark. C3 170
Muddy Creek, res., Colo. E7 106
Muddy Gap, Carbon, Wyo. 15 D5 116
Mudjatik, riv., Sask., Can. B4 58
Mud Lake, Jefferson, Idaho 187 F6 108
Mud Lick, Monroe, Ky. 55 D5 178
Mud Mountain, dam, Wash. B5 98
Mudon, Bur. 20,123 C3 362
Mud Tavern, Davidson, Tenn. 25 E7 190
Mudugh, pol. dist., Som. 141,120 D6 398
Mueda, Moz. B7 421
Muenster, Sask., Can. 147 D5 58
Muenster, Cooke, Tex. 1,190 C7 130
Mufulira, Rh.&Nya. 11,000 (*40,000) B5 420
Mugia, Sp. 1,148 A2 298
Muğla, Tur. 12,081 C3 307
Muğla, prov., Tur. 266,789 *C3 307
Muglad, Sud. 3,735 C2 398
Mugodzhary, mts., Sov.Un. C5 336
Mugu Karnali, riv., Nep. C3 368
Mugwump, lake, Oreg. E7 96
Muharraq, Bahrain 22,577 B5 383
Muheza, Tan. D6 414
Muhinga, Ruanda-Urundi C5 414
Mühldorf, Ger. 10,700 D5 286
Muhlenberg, co., Ky. 27,791 C3 178
Muhlenberg Park, Berks, Pa. 1,000 *C5 214
Mühlhausen [in Thüringen], Ger. 47,100 C4 286
Muhutwe, Tan. C5 414
Mui, isl., Eniwetok C1 436
Muir, Ionia, Mich. 610 F7 146
Muirkirk, Prince Georges, Md. 100 B6 182
Muirkirk, Scot. 3,721 F8 272
Mui Ron, cape, Viet. C5 362
Muir Woods, natl. mon., Calif. A4 94
Mujeres, isl., Mex. C8 225
Mukachevo, Sov.Un. 33,000 H4 332
Mukah, Sar. 4,701 D4 358
Mukalla, Aden E4 383
Mukden (Shenyang), China 2,213,000 E11 348
Mukeru, Palau A6 436
Mukhtuya, Sov.Un. C13 329
Mukilteo, Snohomish, Wash. 1,128 *B4 98
Mukutawa, riv., Man., Can. D4 60
Mukwonago, Waukesha, Wis. 1,877 F1 160, F5
Mula, Sp. 9,874 C6 298
Mulat, isl., Yugo. B2 316
Mulberry, Crawford, Ark. 934 B2 170
Mulberry, Butte, Calif. 2,643 *C3 94
Mulberry, Polk, Fla. 2,922 D9 174
Mulberry, Clinton, Ind. 1,062 B3 140
Mulberry, Crawford, Kans. 642 E9 144
Mulberry, Clermont, Ohio 349 C2 156
Mulberry, Lincoln, Tenn. 200 C5 190
Mulberry, fork, Ala. B3 168
Mulberry, gap, N.C. A4 186
Mulberry, mtn., Ark. B4 170
Mulberry, riv., Ark. B3 170
Mulberry Grove, Bond, Ill. 745 E4 138
Mulchén, Chile 7,324 C1 252
Mulde, riv., Ger. C5 286
Muldon, Monroe, Miss. 40 B4 184
Muldoon, Fayette, Tex. 600 E7 130
Muldraugh, Meade, Ky. 1,743 C5 178
Muldrow, Sequoyah, Okla. 1,137 C9 128
Mule, creek, Kans. E4 144
Mule Creek, Niobrara, Wyo. 30 C8 116
Mulegé, Mex. 945 B3 224
Muleng, China 20,000 C15 348
Muleng, riv., China C15 348
Muleshoe, Bailey, Tex. 3,871 B4 130
Mulford, Alameda, Calif. 1,400 B5 94
Mulga, Jefferson, Ala. 482 B3 168, E4
Mulga Mine, Jefferson, Ala. 950 *B3 168
Mulgrave, N.S., Can. 1,227 D8 70
Mulgrave, isl., Austl. A8 432
Mulhacén, mts., Sp. D5 298
Mulhall, Logan, Okla. 253 B6 128
Mülheim [an der Ruhr], Ger. 168,300 C2 286
Mulhouse, Fr. 99,079 D7 278
Muliama, Bis. Arch. E12 359
Mulino, Clackamas, Oreg. 250 B2 96, B4
Mulitapuili, cape, Samoa E4 436
Mull, Marion, Ark. A4 170
Mull, head, Scot. C10 272
Mull, isl., Scot. E6 272
Mull, sound, Scot. E7 272
Mullaghareik, mts., Ire. I3 273
Mullan, Shoshone, Idaho 1,477 B3 108
Mullan, pass, Mont. D4 110
Mullen, Hooker, Nebr. 811 B4 152
Mullens, Wyoming, W.Va. 3,544 D3 194
Müller, mts., Indon. E4 358
Mullet, key, Fla. C6 174
Mullet, lake, Mich. D7 146
Mullet, pen., Ire. G2 273
Mullet, riv., Wis. B6 160
Mullewa, Austl. 806 D3 432
Müllheim, Ger. 6,400 E2 286
Mullica, riv., N.J. D3 210
Mullica Hill, Gloucester, N.J. 750 D2 210
Mulliken, Eaton, Mich. 484 G7 146
Mullinger, Ire. 5,884 H5 273
Mullins, Marion, S.C. 6,229 C10 188
Mullinville, Kiowa, Kans. 385 E4 144
Mullsjo, Swe. 3,879 D4 292
Mulobezi, Rh. & Nya. C4 420
Mulrany, Ire. 149 H3 273
Multan, Pak. 175,429 (*190,122) D7 375
Multnomah, Multnomah, Oreg. B1 96
Multnomah, co., Oreg. 522,813 B4 96
Mulvane, Sumner and Sedgwick, Kans. 2,981 E6 144
Mulvihill, Man., Can. 175 E3 60
Mumbwa, Rh. & Nya. 700 B5 420
Mumper, Garden, Nebr. C3 152
Mumtrak, see Goodnews Bay, Alsk.
Muna, Mex. 3,966 C8 225
München (Munich), Ger. 968,200 (*1,100,000) D4 286
München-Gladbach, see Mönchen-Gladbach, Ger.
Muncie, Delaware, Ind. 68,603 (*100,500) B4 140
Muncie, Wyandotte, Kans. 1,000 *C9 144
Muncy, Lycoming, Pa. 2,830 B5 214
Mundare, Alta., Can. 650 D6 54
Munday, Knox, Tex. 1,978 C6 130
Mundelein, Lake, Ill. 10,526 A5 138, E2
Mundell, Carroll, Ark. A3 170
Münden, Ger. 19,200 C3 286
Munden, Republic, Kans. 177 C6 144
Munden, Princess Anne, Va. 35 D8 192
Mundi Mundi, Solomon E1 436
Munford, Talladega, Ala. 549 B4 168
Munford, Tipton, Tenn. 1,014 C2 190
Munfordville, Hart, Ky. 1,157 C5 178
Mungana, Austl. B8 432
Mungari, Moz. D6 421
Mungbere, Con.L. B4 414
Munger, Bay, Mich. 200 F8 146
Mungindi, Austl. 962 D9 432
Munhall, Allegheny, Pa. 17,312 A4 214
Munich, see München, Ger.
Munich, Cavalier, N.Dak. 213 B7 154
Munising, Alger, Mich. 4,228 C5 146
Munith, Jackson, Mich. 250 G7 146
Munjor, Ellis, Kans. 150 D4 144
Munkedal, Swe. 4,833 C2 292
Munkfors, Swe. 6,257 B4 292
Munksund, Swe. D9 290
Munnsville, Madison, N.Y. 391 C6 212
Muñoz Gamero, pen., Chile H3 251
Munroe Falls, Summit, Ohio 1,828 *A5 156
Munsan, Kor. G13 348
Munsey Park, Nassau, N.Y. 2,847 *E8 212
Münsingen, Switz. 5,250 B3 312
Munson, Alta., Can. 82 E6 54
Munson, Santa Rosa, Fla. 75 A4 174
Munsonville, Cheshire, N.H. 100 E2 208
Munster, Fr. 4,974 C7 278
Munster, Ger. 7,700 B4 286
Munster, Lake, Ind. 10,313 A2 140
Munster, prov., Ire. 332,584 I3 273
Münster [in Westfalen], Ger. 155,700 (*177,000) C2 286
Munsungan, lake, Maine B3 204
Muntenia, prov., Rom. 4,991,289 *C8 321
Muntenia, reg., Rom. B3 321
Muntok, Indon. 6,929 E3 358
Munugudzhak, Sov.Un. C17 329
Munuscong, lake, Mich. C7 146
Muong Hou Nua, Laos 10,000 B4 362
Muong Hou Tai, Laos B4 362
Muong Hun Xieng Hung, Laos B4 362
Muong Lane, Laos C4 362
Muong May, Laos D5 362
Muong Phalane, Laos C5 362
Muong Sing, Laos 10,000 B4 362
Muong Soui, Laos C4 362
Muong Sung, Laos B4 362
Muonio, Fin. C10 290
Muonio, riv., Fin. C10 290
Muqdadiyah, Iraq 4,203 C6 378
Mur, riv., Aus. C7 313
Mura, riv., Yugo. A3 316
Murakami, Jap. 33,014 E7 354
Murashi, Sov.Un. 12,900 A3 336
Murat, mtn., Tur. B3 307
Murat, riv., Tur. B9 307
Murau, Aus. 2,768 C6 313
Muravera, It. 3,001 F2 302
Murbat, Om. D5 383
Mürcheh Khvort, Iran C3 379
Murchison, N.Z. 580 D4 437
Murchison, falls, Ug. B5 414
Murchison, riv., Austl. D3 432
Murcia, Sp. 120,000 (*236,049) D6 298
Murcia, prov., Sp. 755,850 *D6 298
Murcia, reg., Sp. 1,156,581 C5 298
Murderkill, riv., Del. D4 172
Murdo, Jones, S.Dak. 783 D5 158
Murdoch, Charlotte, Fla. 50 D8 174
Murdock, Kingman, Kans. 100 E6 144
Murdock, Swift, Minn. 381 F3 148
Murdock, Cass, Nebr. 247 E2 152
Mureşul, riv., Rom. A3 321
Murfreesboro, Pike, Ark. 1,096 C3 170
Murfreesboro, Hertford, N.C. 2,643 A8 186
Murfreesboro, Rutherford, Tenn. 18,991 C5 190
Murgab, Sov.Un. F9 328
Murghab, bay, Iran B2 379
Murghab, riv., Afg. B3 374
Murgha Kibzai, Pak. D6 375
Muri, Nig. E7 409
Muriaé, Braz. 11,437 E2 258
Murit, mtn., Tur. B8 307
Müritz, lake, Ger. B5 286
Murmansk, Sov.Un. 226,000 C5 328
Murom, Sov.Un. 73,000 A2 336
Muroran, Jap. 123,533 C8 354
Muros, Sp. 2,420 A2 298
Muroto, cape, Jap. H5 354
Murphy, Owyhee, Idaho 50 F2 108
Murphy, Jefferson, Mo. 200 B7 150
Murphy, Cherokee, N.C. 2,235 B1 186
Murphy, Josephine, Oreg. 150 E3 96
Murphy, isl., S.C. E10 188
Murphy, lake, B.C., Can. D12 52
Murphysboro, Jackson, Ill. 8,673 F4 138
Murphytown, Wood, W.Va. 200 B3 194
Murray, Newton, Ark. 100 B3 170
Murray, Shoshone, Idaho 100 B3 108
Murray, Clarke, Iowa 613 C4 142
Murray, Calloway, Ky. 9,303 D2 178
Murray, Cass, Nebr. 279 D10 152, E3
Murray, Salt Lake, Utah 16,806 C4 114
Murray, co., Ga. 10,447 B2 176
Murray, co., Minn. 14,743 G3 148
Murray, co., Okla. 10,622 D6 128
Murray, head, P.E.I., Can. C7 70
Murray, lake, Okla. D6 128
Murray, lake, S.C. C6 188
Murray, res., Calif. D6 94
Murray, riv., Austl. F8 432
Murray, riv., B.C., Can. C12 52
Murray City, Hocking, Ohio 717 C4 156
Murray Harbour, P.E.I., Can. 405 D7 70
Murray River, P.E.I., Can. 450 D7 70
Murraysville, Jackson, W.Va. 115 B3 194
Murrayville, B.C., Can. 295 C15 52
Murrayville, Hall, Ga. 300 B3 176
Murrayville, Morgan, Ill. 442 D3 138
Murrells, inlet, S.C. D10 188
Murrells Inlet, Georgetown, S.C. 750 D10 188
Mürren, Switz. B3 312
Murrieta, Riverside, Calif. 500 F5 94
Murrumbidgee, riv., Austl. E9 432
Murrupula, Moz. C7 421
Murrysville, Westmoreland, Pa. 1,200 A4 214
Murska Sobota, Yugo. 5,346 A3 316
Murtaugh, Twin Falls, Idaho 214 G4 108
Murtle, lake, B.C., Can. D13 52
Murud, India 9,744 E2 366
Murukta, Sov.Un. C12 329
Mürz, riv., Aus. C7 313
Mürzzuschlag, Aus. 11,176 C7 313
Muş, Tur. 10,487 B9 307
Muş, prov., Tur. 136,248 *B9 307
Musala, mtn., Bul. B1 317
Musan, Kor. 20,717 D14 348
Musangoi, Con.L. D3 414
Mūsā Qal'a, Afg. 5,000 C3 374
Musashino, Jap. 94,948 *L15 354
Muscat, Om. 6,000 C6 383
Muscatatuck, riv., Ind. D4 140
Muscatine, Muscatine, Iowa 20,997 C6 142
Muscatine, co., Iowa 33,840 C6 142
Muscle Shoals, Colbert, Ala. 4,084 A2 168
Musclow, mtn., B.C., Can. D9 52
Muscoda, Jefferson, Ala. 500 *B3 168
Muscoda, Grant, Wis. 927 E3 160
Muscogee, co., Ga. 158,623 D2 176
Musconetcong, mtn., N.J. B2 210
Muscotah, Atchison, Kans. 228 C8 144
Muse, Le Flore, Okla. 100 D9 128
Muse, Washington, Pa. 1,386 C1 214
Musgrave, ranges, Austl. D6 432
Musgrave Harbour, Newf., Can. 350 F9 72

Name	Population	Key	Page
Mushie, Con.L.		C2	414
Mushketovo, Sov.Un.	5,800	T21	332
Musi, riv., Indon.		E2	358
Music, mtn., Ariz.		C2	124
Muskeget, chan., Mass.		D7	206
Muskeget, isl., Mass.		D7	206
Muskego, Waukesha, Wis.	2,000	F1	160
Muskego, lake, Wis		F1	160
Muskegon, Muskegon, Mich.	46,485 (*167,400)	F5	146
Muskegon, co., Mich.	149,943	F5	146
Muskegon, lake, Mich.		F5	146
Muskegon, riv., Mich.		F5	146
Muskegon Heights, Muskegon, Mich.	19,552	F5	146
Muskingum, co., Ohio	79,159	B4	156
Muskingum, riv., Ohio		C5	156
Muskogee, Muskogee, Okla.	38,059	C8	128
Muskogee, co., Okla.	61,866	C8	128
Muskoka, dist., Ont., Can.	25,134	O21	64
Muskoka, lake, Ont., Can.		P21	64
Muskrat, creek, Wyo.		C5	116
Muskwa, riv., Alta., Can.		B5	54
Musoma, Tan.	7,207	C5	414
Musquacook, lakes, Maine		B3	204
Musquaro, lake, Que., Can.		Q10	66
Musquash, N.B., Can.	200	D3	70
Musquash, mtn., Maine		C5	204
Musquodoboit Harbour, N.S., Can.	485	E6	70
Musselburgh, Scot.	18,100	F9	272
Musselshell, Musselshell, Mont.	350	D8	110
Musselshell, co., Mont.	4,888	D8	110
Musselshell, riv., Mont.		D9	110
Mussende, Ang.		B3	420
Mussolinia, see Arborea, It.			
Mustafa Kemalpaşa, Tur.	16,867	A3	307
Mustajiddah, Sau.Ar.		B3	383
Mustang, Canadian, Okla.	198	C6	128
Mustang, draw, Tex.		C4	130
Mustèr, see Disentis, Switz.			
Musters, lake, Arg.		G4	251
Mustinka, riv., Minn.		F2	148
Mustree, Sov.Un.	3,000	C6	332
Musumusu, Samoa	881	E5	436
Muswellbrook, Austl.	5,635	E10	432
Mût, Eg., U.A.R.	2,529	B2	395
Mut, Tur.	2,916	C5	307
Muta, pt., Braz.		C3	258
Mutan, riv., China		C14	348
Mutanchiang, China	151,400	C14	348
Mutarara, Moz.		C6	421
Mutayyin, Yemen		D3	383
Mutena, Con.L.		D3	414
Mutombo-Mukulu, Con.L.		D3	414
Mutsu, bay, Jap.		D8	354
Muttra, see Mathura, India			
Mutual, Woodward, Okla.	84	B4	128
Mutual, Carbon, Utah	52	*D5	114
Muxima, Ang.	143	A2	420
Muyak, Sov.Un.		D5	336
Muyunkum, des., Sov.Un.		D7	336
Muzaffarabad, India		B1	368
Muzaffargarh, Pak.	11,271	D7	375
Muzaffarnagar, India	64,213	C2	368
Muzaffarpur, India	73,594	D4	368
Muzon, cape, Alsk.		K14	84
Muztagh Ata, mtn., China		D3	346
Mwambo, Tan.		E7	414
Mwanza, Tan.	19,877	C5	414
Mwaya, Tan.	2,270	D5	414
Mwene-Ditu, Con.L.		D3	414
Mwenga, Con.L.		C4	414
Mweru, lake, Rh.&Nya., Con.L.		D4	414
Mwimba, Con.L.		D3	414
Mwinilunga, Rh.&Nya.	145	B4	420
Mya, riv., Alg.		B4	402
Myakka, riv., Fla.		D8	174
Myakka City, Manatee, Fla.	200	D8	174
Myaungmya, Bur.		C2	362
Mycenae, ruins, Grc.		C4	306
Myers, Treasure, Mont.	20	D9	110
Myers, Charleston, S.C.	1,000	F4	188
Myers Chuck, Alsk.	51	K14	84
Myerstown, Lebanon, Pa.	3,268	C5	214
Myersville, Frederick, Md.	355	A4	182
Myingyan, Bur.	36,536	B2	362
Myitkyina, Bur.	12,833	A3	362
Myitnge, riv., Bur.		B3	362
Myjava, Czech.	9,935	B3	324
Myllymäki, Fin.		E11	290
Mylo, Rolette, N.Dak.	103	B6	154
Mymensingh, Pak.	45,315	K17	375
Mynämäki, Fin.		F9	291
Myn-Aral, Sov.Un.		C8	336
Mynard, Cass, Nebr.	60	*D10	152
Myrdal, Nor.		F2	91
Myrick, Jones, Miss.	120	D4	184
Myrnam, Alta., Can.	440	D7	54
Myrtis, Caddo, La.	100	B1	180
Myrtle, Man., Can.	125	F4	60
Myrtle, Ont., Can.	145	P22	64
Myrtle, Freeborn, Minn.	89	H5	148
Myrtle, Union, Miss.	313	A3	184
Myrtle, Nansemond, Va.	25	A8	192
Myrtle Beach, Horry, S.C.	7,834	D11	188
Myrtle Creek, Douglas, Oreg.	2,231	D3	96
Myrtle Grove, Escambia, Fla.	800	A3	174
Myrtle Grove, Plaquemines, La.	50	C7	180
Myrtle Point, Coos, Oreg.	2,033	D2	96
Myrtlewood, Marengo, Ala.	403	C2	168
Mysen, Nor.	2,563	B2	292
Myślenice, Pol.	6,520	D4	325
Myślibórz, Pol.	3,887	B2	325
Mysore, India	244,323	F3	366
Mysore, state, India	19,401,193	F3	366
Mystic, New London, Conn.	2,536	D8	202
Mystic, Irwin, Ga.	274	E3	176
Mystic, Appanoose, Iowa	761	D5	142
Mystic, Pennington, S.Dak.	13	C2	158
Mystic, cavern, Ark.		A3	170
Mystic, lakes, Mass.		C2	206
My Tho, Viet.	53,500	E5	362
Mytilene, see Mitilini, Grc.			
Mytishchi, Sov.Un.	99,000	N18	332
Myton, Duchesne, Utah	329	C5	114
Myvatn, lake, Ice.		L21	290
Mzimba, Rh.&Nya.	1,355	B6	421
Mzuzu, Rh.&Nya.		B6	421

N

Name	Population	Key	Page
Naab, riv., Ger.		D5	286
Naalehu, Hawaii, Haw.	950	D6	86
Naaman, New Castle, Del.		A4	172
Naantali, Fin.	1,988	F9	291
Naas Harbour, B.C., Can.	100	C8	52
Nabadwip, India	56,298	E5	368
Nabberu, lake, Austl.		D4	432
Nabesna, Alsk.	28	C7	84
Nabnasset, Middlesex, Mass.	1,381	*A5	206
Naboomspruit, U.S.Afr.		D5	421
Nābulus, Jordan	42,499	B6	382
Nacala, Moz.		B8	421
Nacaome, Hond.	3,429	D4	228
Nacfa, Eth.		B4	398
Na Cham, Viet.		B5	362
Nachang, China		O3	349
Naches, Yakima, Wash.	680	C6	98
Naches, riv., Wash.		B5	98
Nachingwea, Tan.	1,693	E6	414
Náchod, Czech.	18,620	A3	324
Nachvak, Newf., Can.		D9	72
Nacimiento, Chile	2,815	C1	252
Nacional, Mex.		M15	225
Nacmine, Alta., Can.	400	E6	54
Naco, Cochise, Ariz.	300	G6	124
Nacogdoches, Nacogdoches, Tex.	12,674	D8	130
Nacogdoches, co., Tex.	28,046	D8	130
Nacozari, Mex.	3,562	A4	224
Nada, Beaver, Utah		E2	114
Nadeau, Menominee, Mich.	220	D4	146
Naden, hbr., B.C., Can.		C6	52
Nadina River, B.C., Can.		D9	52
Nădlac, Rom.	12,284	A1	321
Nadudvar, Hung.	10,491	B6	320
Nadvornaya, Sov.Un.	19,600	H5	332
Nady, Arkansas, Ark.		C5	170
Naerbo, Nor.		G1	291
Naesŏng, Kor.		G14	348
Naestved, Den.	18,478	F2	292
Naf, Cassia, Idaho	10	G5	108
Nafada, Nig.		D7	409
Nafutan, pt., Saipan		B7	436
Naga, Phil.	8,136	B6	358
Nagahama, Jap.	46,903	*L12	354
Nagano, Jap.	152,547	F7	354
Nagaoka, Jap.	130,785	F7	354
Nagar, India		B2	368
Nagarote, Nic.	3,197	D4	228
Nagar-Parkar, Pak.		G7	375
Nagasaki, Jap.	303,724	H2	354
Nagaur, India		D1	368
Nagchhu Dzong, China		E6	346
Nagelê, Eth.		D4	398
Nagercoil, India	79,284	G3	366
Nag' Hammâdi, Eg., U.A.R.	8,022	B3	395
Nago, Okinawa	13,820	C1	436
Nago, bay, Okinawa		C1	436
Nagod, India		D3	368
Nagog, pond, Mass.		C1	206
Nagornyy, Sov.Un.		D14	329
Nagoya, Jap.	1,336,780	G6 L12	354
Nagpur, India	449,099	D3	366
Nagykanizsa, Hung.	32,000	C2	320
Nagykáta, Hung.	10,764	B4	320
Nagykörös, Hung.	19,000 (27,000*)	B4	320
Naha, Ryūkyū Is., Jap.	63,630	L13	349
Naha, Okinawa	63,630	D1	436
Nahant, Essex, Mass.	3,960	C3	206
Nahariya, Isr.	5,000	A6	382
Nahcotta, Pacific, Wash.	250	*C2	98
Nahe, riv., Ger.		D2	286
Nahiku, Maui, Haw.	15	C5	86
Nahma, Delta, Mich.	300	D5	146
Nahmakanta, lake, Maine		C3	204
Nahuatzen, Mex.		L12	225
Nahuatzen, Mex.		L13	225
Nahuel Huapi, Arg.		F3	251
Nahuel Huapi, lake, Arg.		F3	251
Nahuel Niyeu, Arg.		F4	251
Nahuelquir, Arg.		F4	251
Nahunta, Brantley, Ga.	952	E5	176
Naicam, Sask., Can.	529	D5	58
Naihati, India	55,313	I9	366
Nailenut'u, China		A10	348
Nain, Newf., Can.	300	D9	72
Na'in, Iran	6,790	C3	379
Nairai, isl., Fiji		E7	436
Nairn, Plaquemines, La.	125	E6	180
Nairn, Scot.	4,700	D9	272
Nairn, co., Scot.	8,300	D9	272
Nairobi, Ken.	210,000	C6	414
Nairobi, prov. dist., Ken.		*C6	414
Naivasha, Ken.		C6	414
Najibabad, India		C2	368
Najin (Rashin), Kor.	34,338	D15	348
Nakadomari, Okinawa		C1	436
Nakagusuku, bay, Okinawa		D1	436
Nakalau, Fiji		E6	436
Nak'amet, Eth.		D4	398
Nakaminato, Jap.	34,665	*K16	354
Nakamura, Jap.	40,086	H4	354
Nakano, isl., Jap.		J2	354
Nakatsu, Jap.	66,918	*H3	354
Nakatsu, see Ena, Jap.			354
Nakhichevan, Iran		A1	379
Nakhichevan na Arakse, Sov.Un.	25,000	E3	336
Nakhon Nayok, prov., Thai.	117,547	*D4	362
Nakhon Pathom, Thai.	10,000	D4	362
Nakhon Pathom, prov., Thai.	268,958	*D4	362
Nakhon Phanom, prov., Thai.	307,172	*C4	362
Nakhon Ratchasima, Thai.	25,000	D4	362
Nakhon Ratchasima, prov., Thai.	723,393	*D4	362
Nakhon Sawan, Thai.		D4	362
Nakhon Sawan, prov., Thai.	371,898	*D4	362
Nakhon Si Thammarat, Thai.	10,000	E3	362
Nakhon Si Thammarat, prov., Thai.	494,261	*E3	362
Nakhrachi, Sov.Un.		A7	336
Nakiri, Jap.	7,129	M12	354
Nakło, Pol.	12,000	B3	325
Naknek, Alsk.	174	D6	84
Naknek, lake, Alsk.		D6	84
Nakskov, Den.	16,568	G2	292
Nakuri, India		C2	368
Nakuru, Ken.	17,625	C6	414
Nakusp, B.C., Can.	1,500	E14	52
Nal, riv., Pak.		F4	375
Nalchik, Sov.Un.	87,000	D2	336
Nalhati, India		D4	368
Nallen, Fayette, W.Va.	350	C4 D7	194
Nalón, riv., Sp.		A3	298
Naloto, Fiji		E6	436
Nālūt, Libya	4,850	A2	394
Nam (Tengri), lake, China		E6	346
Namaka, Alta., Can.	68	E6	54
Namakan, lake, Minn.		C6	148
Namaland, reg., S.W.Afr.		*E3	420
Namangan, Sov.Un.	122,000	D8	336
Namanock, isl., N.J.		A3	210
Namanyere, Tan.		D5	414
Namapa, Moz.		B7	421
Namasgali, Ug.		B5	414
Namatanai, Bis. Arch.		E12	359
Nambe, Santa Fe, N.Mex.	350	C5 G7	126
Nam Dinh, Viet.	60,580	B5	362
Namekagon, lake, Wis.		B2	160
Namekagon, riv., Wis.		B2	160
Nametil, Moz.		C7	421
Namew, lake, Man., Sask., Can.		C2	60
		C7	58
Namib, des., S.W.Afr.		D2	420
Namiquipa, Mex.	489	B4	224
Namlan, Bur.		B3	362
Namlea, Indon.		E7	358
Namoi, riv., Austl.		E9	432
Namoli, Fiji		E6	436
Nampa, Alta., Can.		B4	54
Nampa, Canyon, Idaho	18,013	F2	108
Nampala, Mali		C3	408
Nampo (Chinnampo), Kor.	82,162	F12	348
Nampula, Moz.	2,561	C7	421
Namsen, riv., Nor.		D5	290
Namsos, Nor.	4,703	D4	290
Namu, atoll, Marshall		A4	437
Namua, isl., Samoa		E5	436
Namur, Bel.	32,848	D3	282
Namur, Que., Can.	315	S10	66
Namur, prov., Bel.	367,475	D3	282
Namuruputh, Eth.		D4	398
Namutoni, S.W.Afr.		C3	420
Namwala, Rh.&Nya.	500	C5	420
Namwŏn, Kor.	24,736	H13	348
Namysłów, Pol.	4,095	C3	325
Nan, prov., Thai.	204,599	*C4	362
Nan, riv., Thai.		C4	362
Nana, riv., Cen.Afr.Rep.		E8	409
Nanachehaw, Warren, Miss.		C2	184
Nanafalia, Marengo, Ala.	500	C2	168
Nanaimo, B.C., Can.	12,705	B14 F10	52
Nanakuli, Honolulu, Haw.	2,745	B3 G9	86
Nanam, Kor.		E14	348
Nanao, Jap.	50,698	F6	354
Nanatsu, isl., Jap.		F6	354
Nanawan, riv., Man., Can.		D4	60
Nance, co., Nebr.	5,635	C7	152
Nanchang, China		J5	349
Nanchang, China	398,200	K7	349
Nancheng, China	55,000	I3	349
Nancheng, China	10,000	L8	349
Nanchouli, see Lupin, China			
Nanchuan, China	1,000	K3	349
Nanchung, China	164,700	J3	349
Nancowry, isl., India		E2	362
Nancy, Fr.	124,797	C7	278
Nancy, Pulaski, Ky.	300	C6	178
Nancy, creek, Ga.		A5	176
Nanda Devi, mtn., India		C2	368
Nandurbar, India		E1	368
Nanfeng, China	5,000	L8	349
Nanga Eboko, Cam.	3,030	F7	409
Nang Rong, Thai.		D4	362
Nanhai (Fatshan), China		N6	349
Nanhsiang, China		I16	346
Nanhsiung, China	38,000	M7	349
Nanhwei, China		J18	346
Nani, Afg.	5,000	C5	374
Nanjemoy, Charles, Md.	50	D5	182
Nankapenparam, reef, Ponape		A2	437
Nankin, Ashland, Ohio	400	B4	156
Nanking, China	1,091,600	I9	349
Nankou, China		E8	348
Nankung, China	30,000	G7	348
Nannine, Austl.		D3	432
Nanning, China	194,600	N4	349
Nanoose Bay, B.C., Can.	100	B13	52
Nan P'eng (Lamock), is., China			
Nanping, China	130,000	L9	349
Nansemond, Nansemond, Va.	120	A8	192
Nansemond, co., Va.	31,366	D8	192
Nansemond, riv., Va.		A8	192
Nan Shan, mts., China		D7	346
Nansio, Tan.		C5	414
Nantasket Beach, Plymouth, Mass.		B6 D3	206
Nanterre, Fr.	53,037	I9	278
Nantes, Fr.	222,790	D3	278
Nanticoke, Ont., Can.	125	R20	64
Nanticoke, Wicomico, Md.	450	D8	182
Nanticoke, Luzerne, Pa.	15,601	A4 B6	214
Nantien, China		K10	349
Nanton, Alta., Can.	1,047	E6	54
Nantucket, Nantucket, Mass.	2,804 (3,559*)	D7	206
Nantucket, co., Mass.	3,559	D7	206
Nantucket, isl., Mass.		D7	206
Nantucket, sound, Mass.		C7	206
Nantung, China	260,400	I10	349
Nantuxent, pt., N.J.		E2	210
Nanty Glo, Cambria, Pa.	4,608	C3	214
Nanuet, Rockland, N.Y.	5,000	D2	212
Nanuku, passage, Fiji		E7	436
Nanvarnarluk, Alsk.	116	*C5	84
Nanyang, China	50,000	I6	349
Nanyuki, Ken.	4,090	B6	414
Nao, cape, Sp.		C7	298
Naola, Amherst, Va.	50	C5	192
Naoma, Raleigh, W.Va.	600	D6	194
Naomi, Plaquemines, La.	50	C7	180
Napa, Napa, Calif.	22,170	C2	94
Napa, co., Calif.	65,890	C2	94
Napaiskak, Alsk.	121	C5	84
Napakiak, Alsk.	139	C5	84
Napamute, Alsk.	44	C6	84
Napanee, Ont., Can.	4,273	P24	64
Napanoch, Ulster, N.Y.	950	D7	212
Napartokh, bay, Newf., Can.		C9	72
Napatree, pt., R.I.		D1	216
Napavine, Lewis, Wash.	314	C4	98
Nape, Laos		C5	362
Naper, Boyd, Nebr.	198	B6	152
Naperville, Du Page, Ill.	12,933	B5 F2	138
Napier, N.Z.	21,270 (*27,500)	C6	437
Napierville, Que., Can.	1,510	S11	66
Napierville, co., Que., Can.	10,140	S11 S16	66
Napinka, Man., Can.	181	F2	60
Naplate, La Salle, Ill.	738	*B5	138
Naples, Collier, Fla.	4,655	E9	174
Naples, Boundary, Idaho	100	A2	108
Naples, see Napoli, It.			
Naples, Cumberland, Maine	350 (735*)	E2	204
Naples, Ontario, N.Y.	1,237	C4	212
Naples, Clark, S.Dak.	36	C8	158
Naples, Morris, Tex.	1,692	C8	130
Naples, Uintah, Utah		C6	114
Naples, bay, It.		E5	302
Napo, riv., Ec.		A2	245
Napo, riv., Peru		A3	245
Napoleon, Ripley, Ind.	290	C4	140
Napoleon, Lafayette, Mo.	215	*B3	150
Napoleon, Logan, N.Dak.	1,078	D6	154
Napoleon, Henry, Ohio	6,739	A2	156
Napoleonville, Assumption, La.	1,148	C5 E4	180
Napoli (Naples), It.	1,059,100 (*1,275,000)	E5	302
Napoli, prov., It.	2,188,500	*E5	302
Naponee, Franklin, Nebr.	206	D6	152
Napoopoo, Hawaii, Haw.	90	D6	86
Nappanee, Elkhart, Ind.	3,895	A4	140
Naptowne, see Sterling, Alsk.			
Napudogan, N.B., Can.	200	C3	70
Nara, Jap.	115,674	M11	354
Nara, Mali	2,200	C3	408
Nara, canal, Pak.		F6	375
Naracoorte, Austl.	3,329	F8	432
Narai, Jap.	5,505	L13	354
Naramata, B.C., Can.	500	F13	52
Naranja, Dade, Fla.	2,509	E6 F10	174
Naranjas, pt., Pan.		G7	228
Naranjos, Mex.		K15	225
Nararu, mtn., Fiji		E6	436
Narathiwat, prov., Thai.	166,565	*F4	362
Nara Visa, Quay, N.Mex.	100	C7	126
Narayanganj, Pak.	72,517	L17	375
Narbada, riv., India		E1	368
Narberth, Montgomery, Pa.	5,109	A6 C6	214
Narbonne, Fr.	32,060	F5	278
Narcissa, Ottawa, Okla.	25	B9	128
Narcisse, Man., Can.	50	E4	60
Narcoossee, Osceola, Fla.	50	C9	174
Nardin, Kay, Okla.	142	B6	128
Nardò, It.	22,200	E7	302
Nares, pt., Ont., Can.		O20	64
Narew, riv., Pol.		B5	325
Nāri, hills, Libya		C4	394
Nariño, dept., Col.	606,940	C1	244
Narita, Jap.	44,969	L16	354
Narka, Republic, Kans.	166	C6	144
Närke, prov., Swe.	156,838	*G6	291
Narnaul, India		C2	368
Narodnaya, mtn., Sov.Un.		C8	328
Naro-Fominsk, Sov.Un.	32,000	E11	332
Narok, Ken.		C6	414
Narrabri, Austl.	3,722	E9	432
Narragansett, Washington, R.I.	1,741 (3,444*)	D3	216
Narragansett, bay, R.I.		C3	216
Narraguagus, riv., Maine		D5	204
Narrandera, Austl.	4,418	E9	432
Narraway, riv., Alta., Can.		C3	54
Narrogin, Austl.	3,768	E3	432
Narrow Lake, Ont., Can.		R23	64
Narrows, Harney, Oreg.		D8	96
Narrows, Giles, Va.	2,508	C4	192
Narrows, strait, Wash.		D2	98
Narrowsburg, Sullivan, N.Y.	525	D6	212
Narrows Park, Allegany, Md. (part of La Vale)		A2	182
Narsinghpur, India		E2	368
Naruna, Campbell, Va.	250	C5	192
Narva, Sov.Un.	43,600	C7	332
Narvik, Nor.	11,414	B7	290
Naryan-Mar, Sov.Un.	11,400	C7	328
Naryilco, Austl.		D8	432
Naryn, Sov.Un.	15,000	D9	336
Naryn, riv., Sov.Un.		D9	336
Nasala, Fiji		E6	436
Nasarawa, Nig.		E6	409
Năsăud, Rom.	5,725	A3	321
Naschitti, San Juan, N.Mex.	50	B2	126
Naseby, N.Z.	189	F3	437
Naselle, Pacific, Wash.	350	C3	98
Nash, Grant, Okla.	230	B5	128
Nash, Bowie, Tex.	1,124	C8	130
Nash, co., N.C.	61,002	A8	186
Nash, pt., Wales		J8	273
Nash, stream, N.H.		B4	208
Nashawena, isl., Mass.		D6	206
Nashoba, Pushmataha, Okla.	100	D8	128
Nashoba, hill, Mass.		C1	206
Nashotah, Waukesha, Wis.	321	*E5	160
Nashua, Chickasaw, Iowa	1,737	B5	142
Nashua, Wilkin, Minn.	146	E2	148
Nashua, Clay, Mo.	300	E2	150

Nashua, Valley, Mont. 796 B10 110
Nashua, Hillsboro, N.H. 39,096 F4 208
Nashua, riv., Mass., N.H. A4 206; F3 208
Nashville, Howard, Ark. 3,579 D3 170
Nashville, Berrien, Ga. 4,070 E3 176
Nashville, Washington, Ill. 2,606 E4 138
Nashville, Brown, Ind. 489 C3 140
Nashville, Kingman, Kans. 137 E5 144
Nashville, Barry, Mich. 1,525 G6 146
Nashville, Nash, N.C. 1,423 B8 186
Nashville, Davidson, Tenn. 170,874 B5 190 (*411,500) E7
Nashwaak, riv., N.B., Can. C3 70
Nashwauk, Itasca, Minn. 1,712 D5 148
Našice, Yugo. 3,383 B4 316
Nasielsk, Pol. 4,028 B5 325
Näsijärvi, lake, Fin. F10 291
Nasik, India 97,042 E2 366
Nasir, Sud. D3 398
Nasirabad, India D1 368
Nāsiri, see Ahvāz, Iran
Naskaupi, riv., Newf., Can. D9 72
Naslini, Apache, Ariz. 125 B6 124
Nasonville, Providence, R.I. 600 B2 216
Nass, riv., B.C., Can. C8 52
Nassau, Ba.Is. 6,000 A6 232 (*46,125)
Nassau, Sussex, Del. 100 E5 172
Nassau, Lac qui Parle, Minn. 182 F2 148
Nassau, Rensselaer, N.Y. 1,248 C7 212
Nassau, co., Fla. 17,189 A9 174
Nassau, co., N.Y. 1,300,171 D3 212
Nassau, gulf, Chile I4 251
Nassau, range, Neth. N.Gui. E9 359
Nassau, riv., Fla. A10 174
Nassau, sound, Fla. A9 174
Nassauville, Nassau, Fla. 60 A9 174; A10
Nassawadox, Northampton, Va. 650 C9 192
Nässjö, Swe. 16,228 D5 292
Nasu-Dake, peak, Jap. F7 354
Nasukoin, mtn., Mont. B2 110
Nata, China 14,000 P4 349
Natá, Pan. 1,481 F7 228
Natagaima, Col. 4,107 C1 244
Natal, Braz. 161,917 B3 258
Natal, B.C., Can. 1,100 F15 52
Natal, prov., U.S.Afr. 2,415,318 E6 421
Natalbany, Tangipahoa, La. 350 D5 180
Natalia, Medina, Tex. 1,154 E6 130
Natanes, plat., Ariz. E5 124
Natanya, Isr. 31,000 B5 382
Natawahunan, lake, Man., Can. C4 60
Natchaug, riv., Conn. B7 202
Natchez, Natchitoches, La. 100 C2 180
Natchez, Adams, Miss. 23,791 D1 184
Natchitoches, Natchitoches, La. 13,924 C2 180
Natchitoches, par., La. 35,653 C2 180
Natewa, bay, Fiji E7 436
Nathalie, Halifax, Va. 125 D6 192
Nathrop, Chaffee, Colo. 25 D4 106
Natick, Middlesex, Mass. 28,831 D2 206
Nation, lakes, B.C., Can. C10 52
Nation, riv., B.C., Can. C10 52
National, Pierce, Wash. 60 C4 98
National, Monongalia, W.Va. 60 A7 194; B4
National City, San Diego, Calif. 32,771 D6 94; F5
National City, Iosco, Mich. 90 E8 146
National Gardens, Volusia, Fla. 150 B9 174
National Park, Gloucester, N.J. 3,380 *D2 210
Natitingou, Dah. 1,850 D5 408
Natividade, Braz. 800 C1 258
Nativitas, Mex. 1,872 H10 224
Natoma, Osborne, Kans. 778 C4 144
Natron, lake, Tan. C6 414
Natrona, Natrona, Wyo. 5 C6 116
Natrona, co., Wyo. 49,623 D6 116
Natrona Heights, Allegheny, Pa. 15,710 *C1 214
Natrona Heights, see Harrison, Pa.
Nattaung, mtn., Bur. C3 362
Natuna, is., Indon. D3 358
Natural, bridge, Ohio C5 156
Natural, bridge, Utah F3 114
Natural, bridge, Va. C5 192
Natural Bridge, Winston, Ala. 400 A2 168
Natural Bridge, Jefferson, N.Y. 500 A6 212
Natural Bridge, Rockbridge, Va. 600 C5 192
Natural Bridges, natl. mon., Utah F6 114
Naturaliste, cape, Austl. E2 432
Natural Steps, Pulaski, Ark. 60 D6 170
Naturita, Montrose, Colo. 979 D2 106
Naubinway, Mackinac, Mich. 100 C6 146
Naucalpan de Juárez, Mex. 3,862 G10 224
Nauders, Aus. 1,089 D2 313
Naudville, Que., Can. 2,894 *P13 66
Nauen, Ger. 13,100 B5 286
Naugatuck, New Haven, Conn. 19,511 D3 202
Naugatuck, riv., Conn. D3 202
Naumburg [an der Saale], Ger. 39,300 C4 286
Naupe, Peru B2 245
Nauru, Austl. trust., Pac.O. 3,473 C3 436
Nauru, is., Pac.O. C3 436
Naushon, isl., Mass. D6 206
Nautanwa, India D3 368
Nautla, Mex. 1,437 C6 225; K15
Nauvoo, Walker, Ala. 318 B2 168
Nauvoo, Hancock, Ill. 1,039 C2 138
Nauwigewauk, N.B., Can. 140 D4 70
Nava, lake, Sp. A4 298
Navahermosa, Sp. 4,632 C4 298
Navajo, Apache, Ariz. 15 C6 124
Navajo, Daniels, Mont. 5 B11 110
Navajo, co., Ariz. 37,994 C5 124
Navajo, mtn., Utah F5 114
Navajo, natl. mon., Ariz. B5 124
Navajo, riv., Colo. E4 106
Naval Academy, Md. C7 182
Navalcarnero, Sp. 4,783 B4 298
Navalmoral de la Mata, Sp. 7,336 C4 298
Naval Training Station, Newport, R.I. (part of Newport) C3 216
Navan, Ont., Can. 200 O25 64; P26
Navarin, cape, Sov.Un. C19 329
Navarino, Shawano, Wis. 110 D5 160
Navarino, isl., Chile I4 251
Navarra, prov., Sp. 383,354 *A6 298
Navarre, Dickinson, Kans. 84 *D6 144
Navarre, Stark, Ohio 1,698 B5 156
Navarre (Navarra), reg., Sp. 383,354 A6 298
Navarro, Arg. 2,547 C4 252
Navarro, co., Tex. 34,423 D7 130
Navas de Tolosa, Sp. 1,134 C5 298
Navasota, Grimes, Tex. 4,937 D7 130
Navassa, Brunswick, N.C. 500 C7 186
Navassa, isl., W.I. C7 232
Naver, lake, Scot. C7 272
Naver, riv., Scot. C8 272
Navesink, Monmouth, N.J. 2,000 C4 210
Navia, Arg. B2 252
Navia, riv., Sp. A3 298
Navidad, Chile B1 252
Navina, Logan, Okla. 11 C6 128
Naviti, isl., Fiji E6 436
Navojoa, Mex. 17,342 B4 224
Navola, Fiji E6 436
Navolato, Mex. 7,119 C4 224
Navouzensk, Sov.Un. B3 336
Návpaktos, Grc. 6,561 B3 306
Návplion, Grc. 8,466 C4 306
Navrongo, Ghana 1,170 D4 408
Navy Yard, Charleston, S.C. F3 188
Navy Yard City, Kitsap, Wash. 3,341 *B4 98
Nawabshah, Pak. 34,205 F6 375
Nawada, India D4 368
Nawakot, Nep. D4 368
Naxera, Gloucester, Va. 250 C8 192
Náxos, Grc. 2,547 C5 306
Náxos, isl., Grc. C5 306
Nay, Fr. F3 278
Nayarit, state, Mex. 290,124 C4 224
Nay Band, Iran C4 379
Näy Band, Iran D3 379
Naylor, Lowndes, Ga. 272 F3 176
Naylor, Ripley, Mo. 499 E7 150
Nayoro, Jap. 33,339 B9 354
Naytahwaush, Mahnomen, Minn. 300 D3 148
Nazaré, Braz. 11,205 C3 258
Nazaré, Port. 9,241 C2 298
Nazareth, Isr. 22,000 B6 382
Nazareth, Kalamazoo, Mich. 400 G6 146
Nazareth, Northampton, Pa. 6,209 C6 214
Nazas, Mex. 2,294 B5 224
Nazas, riv., Mex. B5 224
Nazca, Peru 2,175 C3 245
Naze, headland, Eng. J14 273
Nāzerābād, Iran D5 379
Nāzik, Iran A1 379
Nazilli, Tur. 31,386 C3 307
Nazko, riv., B.C., Can. D11 52
Nazla, Isr. 4,000 C5 382
Nazreth (Adāmā), Eth. D4 398
Nazyvayevsk, Sov.Un. 10,000 A8 336
Ncheu, Moz. B6 421
Ndala, Tan. C5 414
Ndélé, Cen.Afr.Rep. E9 409
Ndendé, Gabon G7 409
Ndjolé, Gabon G7 409
Ndola, Rh.&Nya. 52,000 B5 420
Ndravuni, isl., Fiji E6 436
Nea, riv., Nor. E4 291
Neagh, lake, N.Ire. G6 273
Neah Bay, Clallam, Wash. 900 A2 98
Neal, Greenwood, Kans. 122 E7 144
Neales, riv., Austl. D7 432
Neals Run, Hampshire, W.Va. 50 B6 194
Neápolis, Grc. 2,060 C4 306
Neápolis, Grc. 3,930 D5 306
Near, is., Alsk. E3 84
Neavitt, Talbot, Md. 312 C7 182
Neba, Jap. L13 354
Nebit-Dag, Sov.Un. 30,000 F7 328
Nebo, Pike, Ill. 441 D3 138
Nebo, Hopkins, Ky. 338 C3 178
Nebo, LaSalle, La. 150 C3 180
Nebo, mtn., Utah D4 114
Nebraska, Jennings, Ind. 120 C4 140
Nebraska, state, U.S. 1,411,330 C6 77; 152
Nebraska City, Otoe, Nebr. 7,252 D10 152; E3
Nebužely, Czech. 465 *A2 324
Necedah, Juneau, Wis. 691 D3 160
Nechako, mts., B.C., Can. D10 52
Nechako, riv., B.C., Can. D10 52
Neche, Pembina, N.Dak. 545 B8 154
Nechi, Col. B2 244
Nechi, riv., Col. B2 244
Neckar, riv., Ger. D3 286
Neck City, Jasper, Mo. 110 D3 150
Necker, isl., Haw. A6 86
Necochea, Arg. 17,808 C4 252
Nederburgh, cape, Indon. E6 358
Nederland, Boulder, Colo. 272 C5 106
Nederland, Jefferson, Tex. 12,036 E9 130
Neder Rijn, riv., Neth. C4 282
Nedesundafjärdarna, lake, Swe. A8 292
Nedrow, Onondaga, N.Y. 2,000 C5 212
Nee, res., Colo. D8 106
Needham, Norfolk, Mass. 25,793 D2 206
Needham Heights, Norfolk, Mass. D2 206
Needle, mtn., Wyo. B3 116
Needle or Mountain Home, mts., Utah E2 114
Needles, San Bernardino, Calif. 4,590 E6 94
Needmore, Lawrence, Ind. 150 D3 140
Needmore, Hardy, W.Va. 600 B6 194
Needville, Fort Bend, Tex. 861 E8 130; F7
Neel, gap, Ga. B3 176
Neeley, Power, Idaho 40 *G6 108
Neelin, Man., Can. 95 F3 60
Neely, Greene, Miss. 400 D4 184
Neelyville, Butler, Mo. 385 E7 150
Ñeembucu, dept., Par. 50,861 E4 247
Neenah, Winnebago, Wis. 18,057 A5 160; D5
Neepawa, Man., Can. 3,109 E3 60
Neerpelt, Bel. 6,975 C4 282
Neeses, Orangeburg, S.C. 347 D6 188
Neffs, Belmont, Ohio 950 B6 156
Neffsville, Lancaster, Pa. 975 C5 214
Nefta, Tun. B5 402
Nefud Dahi, des., Sau.Ar. C4 383
Negapattinam, India 57,854 F3 366
Negaunee, Marquette, Mich. 6,126 C4 146
Negev, reg., Isr. D5 382
Negley, Columbiana, Ohio 600 B6 156
Negoi, mtn., Rom. B3 321
Negotin, Yugo. 6,982 B6 316
Negra, pt., Peru B1 245
Negrais, cape, Bur. C2 362
Negreira, Sp. 1,173 A2 298
Negrine, Alg. B5 402
Negri Sembilan, state, Mala. 365,045 *G4 362
Negrita, C.R. E6 228
Negro, mtn., Md. A1 182
Negro, riv., Arg. C3 252
Negro, riv., Bol. B2 246
Negro, riv., Braz. F4 256
Negro, riv., Ur. B4 252
Negros, isl., Phil. C6 358
Negru Vodă, Rom. 3,154 C5 321
Neguac, N.B., Can. 165 B4 70
Nehalem, Tillamook, Oreg. 233 B3 96
Nehalem, riv., Oreg. B3 96
Nehawka, Cass, Nebr. 262 D10 152; E3
Nehbandān, Iran C5 379
Neichiang, China 190,200 F8 346
Neidpath, Sask., Can. 210 E4 58
Neihart, Cascade, Mont. 150 D6 110
Neihsiang, China 18,000 I5 349
Neihuang, China H7 348
Neilburg, Sask., Can. 264 D3 58
Neill, pt., Wash. D2 98
Neillsville, Clark, Wis. 2,728 D3 160
Neisse, see Nysa, Pol.
Neisse, riv., Ger. C6 286
Neiva, Col. 62,730 C1 244
Nejd, reg., Sau.Ar. 5,000,000 B3 383
Nekhl, Eg., U.A.R. B3 395
Nekoma, Rush, Kans. 3,830 D4 144
Nekoma, Cavalier, N.Dak. 143 B7 154
Nekoosa, Wood, Wis. 2,515 D4 160
Nekso, Den. 3,305 F6 292
Nelagoney, Osage, Okla. 138 B7 128
Nelbi, Sen. C2 408
Nelemnoye, Sov.Un. C17 329
Neligh, Antelope, Nebr. 1,776 B7 152
Nellie, Wilcox, Ala. 75 D2 168
Nellis, Boone, W.Va. 550 D5 194
Nelliston, Montgomery, N.Y. 729 C7 212
Nellore, India 81,480 F3 366
Nellysford, Nelson, Va. 140 C6 192
Nelscott, Lincoln, Oreg. 400 C2 96
Nelson, Yavapai, Ariz. 85 C2 124
Nelson, B.C., Can. 7,226 F14 52
Nelson, Pickens and Cherokee, Ga. 658 B2 176
Nelson, Muhlenberg, Ky. 510 C3 178
Nelson, Douglas, Minn. 150 *F3 148
Nelson, Saline, Mo. 126 B4 150
Nelson, Nuckolls, Nebr. 695 D7 152
Nelson, Clark, Nev. 50 H7 112
Nelson, Cheshire, N.H. 75 F2 208
Nelson, N.Z. (222▲) 17,707 D4 437 (*22,500)
Nelson, Buffalo, Wis. 250 D1 160
Nelson, co., Ky. 22,168 C5 178
Nelson, co., N.Dak. 7,034 C7 154
Nelson, co., Va. 12,752 C6 192
Nelson, lake, Man., Can. C2 60
Nelson, riv., Man., Can. B5 60; E6
Nelsonville, Nelson, Ky. 160 C5 178
Nelsonville, Athens, Ohio 4,834 C4 156
Nelsonville, Portage, Wis. 170 *D4 160
Nelspruit, U.S.Afr. E6 421
Néma, Maur. 3,000 C3 408
Nemacolin, Greene, Pa. 1,404 D2 214
Nemadji, riv., Minn., Wis. E6 148; B1 160
Nemaha, Sac, Iowa 151 B2 142
Nemaha, Nemaha, Nebr. 232 D10 152
Nemaha, co., Kans. 12,897 C7 144
Nemaha, co., Nebr. 9,099 D10 152
Nemaha, riv., Nebr. D10 152
Neman, riv., Sov.Un. F5 332
Nemeiben, lake, Sask., Can. C5 58
Nemi, lake, It. *E4 302
Nemo, Lawrence, S.Dak. 100 C2 158
Nemours, Alg. 6,148 A3 402 (13,245▲)
Nemours, Fr. 5,594 C5 278
Nemu, Sov.Un. D15 329
Nemunas (Niemen), riv., Sov.Un. E4 332
Nemuro, Jap. 24,659 C10 354
Nemuro, strait, Jap. B10 354
Nen, riv., China B11 348
Nenagh, Ire. 4,450 I4 273
Nenana, Alsk. 286 C7 84
Nenchiang, see Mergen, China
Nene, riv., Eng. I13 273
Nenzel, Cherry, Nebr. 43 B4 152
Neodesha, Wilson, Kans. 3,594 E8 144
Neoga, Cumberland, Ill. 1,145 D5 138
Neola, Pottawattamie, Iowa 870 C2 142
Neola, Duchesne, Utah 600 C5 114
Neon, Letcher, Ky. 766 C8 178
Neopit, Shawano, Wis. 1,359 D5 160
Neosho, Newton, Mo. 7,452 E3 150
Neosho, Dodge, Wis. 345 E5 160
Neosho, co., Kans. 19,455 E8 144
Neosho, riv., Kans., Okla. D7 144; C8 128
Neosho Falls, Woodson, Kans. 222 D8 144
Neosho Rapids, Lyon, Kans. 178 D8 144
Neotsu, Lincoln, Oreg. 200 *B3 96
Nepal, country, Asia 9,044,000 G10 340; 368
Nepalganj, Nep. 10,813 C3 368
Nepaug, res., Conn. B4 202
Nephi, Juab, Utah 2,566 D4 114
Neponset, Bureau, Ill. 495 B4 138
Neponset, riv., Mass. D2 206
Nepton, Fleming, Ky. 300 B7 178
Neptune, Sask., Can. 55 F5 58
Neptune, Monmouth, N.J. 16,000 *C4 210
Neptune Beach, Duval, Fla. 2,868 A9 174; A10
Neptune City, Monmouth, N.J. 4,013 C4 210
Nequasset, Sagadahoc, Maine 60 E3 204
Nera, riv., It. D4 302
Nérac, Fr. E4 278
Nerchinsk, Sov.Un. 28,700 D13 329
Nerekhta, Sov.Un. 19,900 D13 332
Neretva, riv., Yugo. C4 316
Neris, riv., Sov.Un. E6 332
Nerja, Sp. 6,022 D5 298
Nero, Plaquemines, La. 210 C8 180; E6
Nero, mtn., It. C2 302
Nerstrand, Rice, Minn. 584 G5 148
Neruteaila, China B9 348
Nerva, Sp. 11,002 D3 298
Nes, Ice. L21 290
Nesbit, DeSoto, Miss. 200 A2 184
Nesbitt, Man., Can. 100 F3 60
Nesco, Atlantic, N.J. 300 D3 210
Nesconset, Suffolk, N.Y. 1,964 *D4 212
Nescopeck, Luzerne, Pa. 1,934 B5 214
Nesebur, Bul. 2,340 B3 317
Neshanic, riv., N.J. C3 210
Neshanic Station, Somerset, N.J. 400 B3 210
Nesher, Isr. 1,700 B6 382
Neshkoro, Marquette, Wis. 368 E4 160
Neshoba, Neshoba, Miss. 250 C3 184
Neshoba, co., Miss. 20,927 C3 184
Nesika Beach, Curry, Oreg. 150 *E2 96
Neskaupstadhur, Ice. 1,340 L23 290
Neskowin, Tillamook, Oreg. 50 B3 96
Nesmith, Williamsburg, S.C. 85 D9 188
Nesodden, Nor. 4,839 B1 292
Nesom, East Feliciana, La. D5 180
Nes op Ameland, Neth. 782 A4 282
Nespelem, Okanogan, Wash. 358 A8 98
Nesquehoning, Carbon, Pa. 2,714 C6 214
Ness, co., Kans. 5,470 D3 144
Ness City, Ness, Kans. 1,653 D4 144
Nesslau, Switz. 2,073 A5 312
Nestoria, Baraga, Mich. 20 C3 146
Nestórion, Grc. 3,197 A3 306
Nestorville, Barbour, W.Va. 250 B5 194
Néstos, riv., Grc. A5 306
Nesvizh, Sov.Un. 11,000 F6 332
Netarts, Tillamook, Oreg. 600 B3 96
Netawaka, Jackson, Kans. 225 C8 144
Netcong, Morris, N.J. 2,765 B3 210
Netherhill, Sask., Can. 111 E3 58
Netherlands, country, Eur. 11,334,000 C5 266; 282
Netherlands Guiana, see Surinam
Netherlands Indies, see Indonesia
Netherlands New Guinea, poss., Asia 700,000 J15 340; 359
Nethy Bridge, Scot. D9 272
Netrakona, Pak. 12,924 K17 375
Nett, lake, Minn. C5 148
Nettie, Nicholas, W.Va. 600 C4 194
Nettilling, lake, N.W.Ter., Can. D11 48
Nett Lake, St. Louis, Minn. 250 C5 148
Nettleboro, Clarke, Ala. D2 168
Nettleridge, Patrick, Va. D4 192
Nettleton, Craighead, Ark. (part of Jonesboro) B6 170
Nettleton, Lee and Monroe, Miss. 1,389 A4 184
Nettuno, It. 14,100 *E4 302
Netvořice, Czech. 619 *B2 324
Neubert, Knox, Tenn. 600 C8 190; E9
Neubrandenburg, Ger. 27,000 B5 286
Neuburg [an der Donau], Ger. 12,900 D4 286
Neuchâtel, Switz. 30,000 B2 312 (*39,100)
Neuchâtel, lake, Switz. B2 312
Neudorf, Aus. B8 313
Neudorf, Sask., Can. 442 E6 58
Neuenburg, see Neuchâtel, Switz.
Neufchâteau, Bel. 2,702 E4 282
Neufchâteau, Fr. 4,350 C6 278
Neufchâtel [-en-Bray], Fr. 4,838 C4 278
Neufelden, Aus. 1,054 B5 313
Neuhaldensleben (Haldensleben), Ger. 22,000 B4 286
Neuilly [-sur-Marne], Fr. 12,798 I11 278
Neuilly [-sur-Seine], Fr. 66,095 I10 278
Neukirchen am Grossvenediger, Aus. 1,800 C4 313
Neumarkt [in der Oberpfalz], Ger. 14,300 D4 286
Neumarkt-Sankt Viet, Ger. 3,514 D5 286
Neumünster, Ger. 72,400 A3 286
Neunkirchen, Aus. 9,767 C8 313
Neuquén, Arg. 7,498 C2 252
Neuquén, prov., Arg. 117,600 E3 250
Neuquén, riv., Arg. C2 252
Neurara, Chile B4 250
Neuruppin, Ger. 23,500 B5 286
Neusalz, see Nowa Sól, Pol.
Neuse, riv., N.C. B7 186
Neusiedler, lake, Aus. C8 313
Neuss, Ger. 79,200 *C2 286
Neustadt, Ont., Can. 490 P19 64
Neustadt [an der Aisch], Ger. 9,000 D4 286
Neustadt [an der Dosse], Ger. 2,152 B5 286
Neustadt [an der Weinstrasse], Ger. 31,300 D3 286
Neustadt [bei Coburg], Ger. 13,200 C4 286

Neustadt [im Schwarzwald], Ger. 6,900 E3 286
Neustadt [in Holstein], Ger. 15,200 A4 286
Neustrelitz, Ger. 27,900 B5 286
Neu-Ulm, Ger. 21,300 D4 286
Neuville, Que., Can. 727 R13 66
R15
Neuwied, Ger. 27,100 C2 286
Neva, Johnson, Tenn. 75 B10 190
Nevada, Story, Iowa 4,227 B4 142
Nevada, Vernon, Mo. 8,416 D3 150
Nevada, Wyandot, Ohio 919 B3 156
Nevada, co., Ark. 10,700 D3 170
Nevada, co., Calif. 20,911 C3 94
Nevada, state, U.S. 285,278 D3 77
112
Nevada, mts., Sp. D5 298
Nevada City, Nevada, Calif. 2,353 C3 94
Nevada del Illimani, mtn., Bol. C1 246
Nevada de Santa Marta, mts., Col. A2 244
Nevadaville, Gilpin, Colo. 6 *C5 106
Nevado, mtn., Arg. C2 252
Nevado Sajama, mtn., Bol. C2 246
Nevel, Sov.Un. 27,700 D7 332
Nevers, Fr. 35,183 D5 278
Neversink, res., N.Y. D7 212
Neversink, riv., N.Y. D7 212
Nevesinje, Yugo. 1,798 C4 316
Neville, Sask., Can. 199 F4 58
Nevils, Bulloch, Ga. 250 D5 176
Nevin, Wales I8 273
Nevinnomyssk, Sov.Un. 27,400 J13 332
Nevis, Hubbard, Minn. 344 E4 148
Nevis, ter., W.I.Fed. 13,910 D13 233
Nevis, bay, Scot. D7 272
Nevis, mtn., Scot. E7 272
Nevşehir, Tur. 16,820 B6 307
Nevşehir, prov., Tur. 239,608 *B6 307
New, inlet, Fla. B6 174
New, inlet, N.C. D8 186
New, isl., India J9 366
New, riv., Ariz. G1 124
New, riv., N.C. C8 186
New, riv., Va., W.Va. C4 192
C3 194
Newala, Tan. 3,000 E6 414
New Albany, N.S., Can. 218 E4 70
New Albany, Floyd, Ind. 37,812 D4 140
New Albany, Wilson, Kans. 104 E8 144
New Albany, Union, Miss. 5,151 A3 184
New Albin, Allamakee, Iowa 643 A6 142
Newald, Forest, Wis. 175 C5 160
New Alexandria, Fairfax, Va. 1,500 *B7 *192
Newalla, Oklahoma, Okla. 200 C6 128
New Almelo, Norton, Kans. 90 *C3 144
New Alsace, Dearborn, Ind. 200 C4 140
New Amsterdam, Br.Gu. 9,567 D5 256
New Amsterdam, La Crosse, Wis. 40 E2 160
Newark, Independence, Ark. 728 B5 170
Newark, Alameda, Calif. 9,884 B5 94
Newark, New Castle, Del. 11,404 B3 172
Newark, Eng. 23,600 H12 273
Newark, Kendall, Ill. 489 B5 138
Newark, Greene, Ind. 100 C3 140
Newark, Worcester, Md. 175 D9 182
Newark, Knox, Mo. 116 B6 150
Newark, Kearney, Nebr. 13 *D7 152
Newark, Essex, N.J. 405,220 B1 210
B4
Newark, Wayne, N.Y. 12,868 B4 212
Newark, Licking, Ohio 41,790 B4 156
Newark, Marshall, S.Dak. 39 B8 158
Newark, Caledonia, Vt. 50 *B5 218
(151▲)
Newark, bay, N.J. B1 210
Newark Valley, Tioga, N.Y. 1,234 C5 212
New Ashford, Berkshire, Mass. 50 *A1 206
New Athens, St. Clair, Ill. 1,923 E4 138
New Athens, Harrison, Ohio 472 B5 156
New Auburn, Sibley, Minn. 299 G4 148
New Auburn, Chippewa, Wis. 383 C2 160
New Augusta, Marion, Ind. 225 D4 140
New Augusta, Perry, Miss. 275 D3 184
Newaygo, Newaygo, Mich. 1,447 F6 146
Newaygo, co., Mich. 24,160 F6 146
New Baden, Clinton, Ill. 1,464 E4 138
New Baltimore, Macomb, Mich. 3,159 G9 146
New Baltimore, Greene, N.Y. 500 C8 212
New Bedford, Bureau, Ill. 166 B4 138
New Bedford, Bristol, Mass. 102,477 C6 206
(*146,400)
Newberg, Yamhill, Oreg. 4,204 B1 96
B4
New Berlin, Duval, Fla. 100 A10 174
New Berlin, Sangamon, Ill. 627 D4 138
New Berlin, Chenango, N.Y. 1,262 C6 212
New Berlin, Waukesha, Wis. 15,788 E1 160
New Berlinville, Berks, Pa. 1,151 *C6 214
Newbern, Hale, Ala. 316 C2 168
New Bern, Craven, N.C. 15,717 B8 186
Newbern, Dyer, Tenn. 1,695 B2 190
Newberry, San Bernardino, Calif. 200 E5 94
Newberry, Alachua, Fla. 1,105 B8 174
Newberry, Greene, Ind. 256 D2 140
Newberry, Luce, Mich. 2,612 C6 146
Newberry, Newberry, S.C. 8,208 C5 188
Newberry, co., S.C. 29,416 C5 188
New Bethlehem, Clarion, Pa. 1,599 B2 214
New Blaine, Logan, Ark. 200 B3 170
New Bloomfield, Callaway, Mo. 359 C5 150
New Bloomfield, Perry, Pa. 987 C4 214
Newborn, Newton, Ga. 283 C3 176
Newboro, Ont., Can. 270 P24 64
Newboro, Wheeler, Nebr. B7 152
New Boston, Mercer, Ill. 726 B3 138
New Boston, Berkshire, Mass. 150 B1 206
New Boston, Hillsboro, N.H. 300 F3 208
(925▲)
New Boston, Scioto, Ohio 3,984 D4 156
New Boston, Bowie, Tex. 2,773 C8 130
New Braintree, Worcester, Mass. 400 B3 206
(509▲)
New Braunfels, Comal, Tex. 15,631 A7 130
E6
New Bremen, Auglaize, Ohio 1,972 B2 156
Newbridge, Ire. H4 273
New Bridge, Baker, Oreg. 75 C9 96
New Brigden, Alta., Can. 75 E7 54
New Brighton, Ramsey, Minn. 6,448 F5 148
F7
New Brighton, Beaver, Pa. 8,397 C1 214
New Britain, Hartford, Conn. 82,201 C4 202
New Britain, Bucks, Pa. 1,109 *C6 214
New Britain, isl., Bis. Arch. F12 359
New Brockton, Coffee, Ala. 1,093 D4 168
Newbrook, Alta., Can. 100 C6 54
New Brunswick, Middlesex, N.J. 40,139 C4 210
New Brunswick, prov., Can. 554,616 H12 48
C4 70
New Brunswick Heights, Middlesex, N.J. 1,000 *C4 210
New Buffalo, Berrien, Mich. 2,128 H5 146
Newburg, Franklin, Ala. 200 A2 168
Newburg, Charles, Md. 400 D6 182
Newburg, Phelps, Mo. 844 D6 150
Newburg, Bottineau, N.Dak. 158 B5 154
Newburg, Preston, W.Va. 494 B5 194
Newburg Center, Penobscot, Maine 80 D4 204
Newburgh, Ont., Can. 603 P24 64
Newburgh, Warrick, Ind. 1,450 E2 140
Newburgh, Penobscot, Maine 75 D3 204
(636▲)
Newburgh, Orange, N.Y. 30,979 D7 212
(*104,000)
Newburgh, Scot. D10 272
Newburgh Heights, Cuyahoga, Ohio 3,512 B1 156
New Burlington, Clinton, Ohio 318 C3 156
Newbury, Ont., Can. 331 R19 64
Newbury, Eng. 19,300 J11 273
Newbury (Town of), Essex, Mass. (2,519▲) *A6 206
Newbury, Merrimack, N.H. 100 E2 208
(342▲)
Newbury, Orange, Vt. 391 C4 218
(1,452▲)
Newbury Old Town, Essex, Mass. 355 *A6 206
Newburyport, Essex, Mass. 14,004 A6 206
New Caledonia, Fr. poss., Pac.O. 64,000 D3 436
New Caledonia, isl., Pac.O. D3 436
New Cambria, Saline, Kans. 187 D6 144
New Cambria, Macon, Mo. 270 B5 150
New Canaan, Fairfield, Conn. 13,466 E2 202
New Canada (Plantation of), Aroostook, Maine (288▲) *A4 204
New Canton, Pike, Ill. 449 D2 138
New Canton, Buckingham, Va. 350 C6 192
New Carlisle, Que., Can. 985 *Q10 66
New Carlisle, St. Joseph, Ind. 1,376 A3 140
New Carlisle, Clark, Ohio 4,107 C2 156
New Cassel, Nassau, N.Y. 7,000 *E8 212
New Castile (Castilla la Nueva), reg., Sp. 3,482,338 C4 298
New Castle, Jefferson, Ala. 950 B3 168
E5
Newcastle, Austl. 140,853 E10 432
Newcastle, Placer, Calif. 670 C3 94
Newcastle, N.B., Can. 4,670 B4 70
Newcastle, Ont., Can. 1,098 Q22 64
New Castle, Garfield, Colo. 447 C3 106
New Castle, New Castle, Del. 4,469 B3 172
New Castle, Henry, Ind. 20,349 C4 140
New Castle, Henry, Ky. 699 B5 178
Newcastle, Lincoln, Maine 430 D3 204
(1,101▲)
Newcastle, Dixon, Nebr. 357 B9 152
New Castle, Rockingham, N.H. 823 E5 208
Newcastle, N.Ire. 3,076 *C6 272
Newcastle, McClain, Okla. 80 C6 128
New Castle, Lawrence, Pa. 44,790 B1 214
Newcastle, Young, Tex. 617 C6 130
Newcastle, U.S.Afr. 13,281 E5 420
Newcastle, Iron, Utah 100 F2 114
New Castle, Craig, Va. 200 C4 192
Newcastle, Weston, Wyo. 4,345 C8 116
New Castle, co., Del. 307,446 B3 172
Newcastle Bridge, N.B., Can. 110 C3 70
Newcastle Mine, Alta., Can. 900 E6 54
Newcastle-on-Tyne, Eng. 277,100 G11 272
(*841,700)
Newcastle-under-Lyme, Eng. 73,200 H10 273
Newcastle Waters, Austl. B6 432
New Centerville, St. Croix, Wis. 30 D1 160
New Chicago, Lake, Ind. 2,312 A2 140
New Church, Accomack, Va. 250 C9 192
New City, Rockland, N.Y. 4,000 D2 212
D8
New Coeln, Milwaukee, Wis. (part of Milwaukee) E2 160
Newcomb, Essex, N.Y. 575 B7 212
Newcomb, Campbell, Tenn. 288 B7 190
Newcomerstown, Tuscarawas, Ohio 4,273 B5 156
New Concord, Calloway, Ky. 75 D2 178
New Concord, Muskingum, Ohio 2,127 C5 156
New Cordell, see Cordell, Okla.
New Cumberland, Cumberland, Pa. 9,257 C5 214
New Cumberland, Hancock, W.Va. 2,076 A2 194
A4
New Cumnock, Scot. 3,871 F8 272
Newdale, Man., Can. 350 E2 60
Newdale, Fremont, Idaho 272 F7 108
New Dayton, Alta., Can. 130 F6 54
Newdegate, Austl. 222 E3 432
New Delhi, India 276,314 C2 368
New Denmark, N.B., Can. 100 B2 70
New Denver, B.C., Can. 736 F14 52
New Diggings, Lafayette, Wis. 85 F3 160
New Durham, Strafford, N.H. 200 E4 208
(474▲)
New Eagle, Washington, Pa. 2,670 *C1 214
New Edinburg, Cleveland, Ark. 300 D4 170
New Effington, Roberts, S.Dak. 280 B9 158
New Egypt, Ocean, N.J. 1,737 C3 210
Newell, Randolph, Ala. 100 B4 168
Newell, Union, Ark. 150 D4 170
Newell, Buena Vista, Iowa 893 B2 142
Newell, Butte, S.Dak. 797 C2 158
Newell, Hancock, W.Va. 1,842 A2 194
A4
Newell, lake, Alta., Can. E7 54
New Ellenton, Aiken, S.C. 2,309 E5 188
New Elliott, Lake, Ind. 900 *A2 140
Newellton, Tensas, La. 1,453 B4 180
New England, Hettinger, N.Dak. 1,095 D3 154
Newenham, cape, Alsk. D5 84
New Era, Concordia, La. 30 C4 180
New Era, Oceana, Mich. 403 F5 146
New Fairfield, Fairfield, Conn. 200 D2 202
(3,355▲)
Newfane, Niagara, N.Y. 1,423 B3 212
Newfane, Windham, Vt. 146 F3 218
(714▲)
Newfield, York, Maine 150 E2 204
(319▲)
Newfield, Gloucester, N.J. 1,299 D2 210
Newfield, Tompkins, N.Y. 500 C5 212
Newfields, Rockingham, N.H. 400 E5 208
(737▲)
New Florence, Montgomery, Mo. 616 C6 150
New Florence, Westmoreland, Pa. 958 C2 214
Newfolden, Marshall, Minn. 370 C2 148
Newfound, gap, N.C., Tenn. B2 186
C8 190
Newfound, lake, N.H. D3 208
Newfoundland, Passaic, N.J. 450 A4 210
Newfoundland, prov., Can. 415,074 H13 48
72
Newfoundland, mts., Utah C2 114
New Franken, Brown, Wis. 150 A6 160
D6
New Franklin, Howard, Mo. 1,096 B5 150
New Freedom, York, Pa. 1,395 D5 214
Newgate, B.C., Can. 75 F15 52
New Georgia, isl., Solomon E1 436
New Germany, N.S., Can. 890 E5 70
New Germany, Carver, Minn. 274 *G5 148
New Glarus, Green, Wis. 1,468 F4 160
New Glasgow, N.S., Can. 9,998 D7 70
New Gloucester, Cumberland, Maine, 200 D5 204
(3,047▲) E2
New Goshen, Vigo, Ind. 500 C2 140
New Gretna, Burlington, N.J. 800 D4 210
New Guinea, Ter. of, Austl. trust., Pac.O. 1,210,000 C3 436
New Guinea, isl., Pac.O. C3 436
Newgulf, Wharton, Tex. 1,419 E8 130
Newhalem, Alsk. 48 D6 84
Newhalem, Whatcom, Wash. 400 A5 98
Newhall, Los Angeles, Calif. 4,705 E4 94
Newhall, Benton, Iowa 495 C6 142
Newhall, Cumberland, Maine 250 E4 204
Newhall McDowell, W.Va. 500 D3 194
New Hamburg, Ont., Can. 1,939 Q20 64
New Hampshire, state, U.S. 606,921 C12 77
208
New Hampton, Chickasaw, Iowa 3,456 A5 142
New Hampton, Harrison, Mo. 289 A3 150
New Hampton, Belknap, N.H. 862 D3 208
New Hanover, co., N.C. 71,742 C8 186
New Harbor, Lincoln, Maine 300 E3 204
New Harbour, Newf., Can. 650 G9 72
New Harmony, Posey, Ind. 1,121 D2 140
New Harmony, Washington, Utah 105 F2 114
New Hartford, Litchfield, Conn. 1,034 B4 202
(3,033▲)
New Hartford, Butler, Iowa 649 B5 142
New Hartford, Oneida, N.Y. 2,468 *B6 212
New Haven, New Haven, Conn. 152,048 D4 202
(*320,800)
New Haven, Gallatin, Ill. 642 F5 138
New Haven, Allen, Ind. 3,396 A4 140
New Haven, Nelson, Ky. 1,009 C5 178
New Haven, Macomb, Mich. 1,198 G9 146
New Haven, Franklin, Mo. 1,223 C6 150
New Haven, Huron, Ohio 340 A4 156
New Haven, Addison, Vt. 150 C2 218
(922▲)
New Haven, Mason, W.Va. 1,314 C3 194
New Haven, Crook, Wyo. 15 B8 116
New Haven, co., Conn. 660,315 D3 202
New Haven, hbr., Conn. D4 202
New Haven, riv., Vt. C2 218
New Hazelton, B.C., Can. 150 C9 52
New Hebrides, Br. and Fr. poss., Pac.O. 53,000 D3 436
New Hebrides, is., Pac.O. D3 436
Newhebron, Lawrence, Miss. 271 D3 184
New Holland, Hall, Ga. 1,000 B3 176
New Holland, Pickaway and Fayette, Ohio 798 C3 156
New Holland, Lancaster, Pa. 3,425 C5 214
New Holland, Douglas, S.Dak. 110 D7 158
New Holland Crossroads, Aiken, S.C. 100 D6 188
New Holstein, Calumet, Wis. 2,401 B6 160
E5
New Hope, Madison, Ala. 953 A3 168
Newhope, Pike, Ark. 70 C3 170
New Hope, Nelson, Ky. 250 C5 178
New Hope, Hennepin, Minn. 3,552 *F5 148
New Hope, Bucks, Pa. 958 C7 214
New Hope, mtn., Ala. E4 168
New Hudson, Oakland, Mich. 450 B7 146
New Hyde Park, Nassau, N.Y. 10,808 *E3 212
New Iberia, Iberia, La. 29,062 D4 180
Newington, Hartford, Conn. 17,664 C5 202
Newington, Screven, Ga. 399 D5 176
Newington, Rockingham, N.H. 125 E5 208
(2,499▲)
Newington, Fairfax, Va. 180 A7 192
New Ipswich, Hillsboro, N.H. 300 F3 208
(1,455▲)
New Ireland, isl., Bis.Arch. E12 359
New Jersey, state, U.S. 6,066,782 C12 77
210
New Johnsonville, Humphreys, Tenn. 559 B4 190
New Kensington, Westmoreland, Pa. 23,485 A4 214
C2
New Kent, New Kent, Va. 25 C8 192
New Kent, co., Va. 4,504 C8 192
Newkirk, Kay, Okla. 2,092 B6 128
Newkirk, Guadalupe, N.Mex. 150 C6 126
New Knock Hock, Alsk. 122 *C5 84
New Knoxville, Auglaize, Ohio 792 B2 156
Newktok, Alsk. 90 *C5 84
Newland, Avery, N.C. 564 A4 186
Newland, Richmond, Va. 90 B8 192
New Lebanon, Sullivan, Ind. 130 C2 140
New Lebanon, Montgomery, Ohio 1,459 *C2 156
New Leipzig, Grant, N.Dak. 390 D4 154
New Lenox, Will, Ill. 1,750 B6 138
F2
New Lexington, Tuscaloosa, Ala. 75 B2 168
New Lexington, Perry, Ohio 4,514 C4 156
New Liberty, Scott, Iowa 145 C7 142
New Liberty, Owen, Ky. 250 B6 178
New Liberty, Beckham, Okla. C4 128
Newlight, Tensas, La. B4 180
New Lima, see Lima, Okla.
New Limerick, Aroostook, Maine 200 B5 204
(394▲)
New Lisbon, Henry, Ind. 300 C4 140
New Lisbon, Burlington, N.J. 200 D3 210
New Lisbon, Juneau, Wis. 1,337 E3 160
New Liskeard, Ont., Can. 4,619 R25 64
Newllano, Vernon, La. 264 C2 180
Newlon, Upshur, W.Va. 136 C4 194
New London, New London, Conn. 34,182 D7 202
(*104,600)
New London, Howard, Ind. 240 B3 140
New London, Henry, Iowa 1,694 D6 142
New London, Kandiyohi, Minn. 721 F4 148
New London, Ralls, Mo. 875 B6 150
New London, Merrimack, N.H. 1,007 E3 208
(1,738▲)
New London, Stanly, N.C. 223 B5 186
New London, Huron, Ohio 2,392 A4 156
New London, Waupaca, Wis. 5,288 D5 160
New London, co., Conn. 185,745 C7 202
New Lothrop, Shiawassee, Mich. 510 F7 146
New Lowell, Ont., Can. 320 P21 64
New Lynn, N.Z. 7,547 H8 437
New Madison, Darke, Ohio 910 C2 156
New Madrid, New Madrid, Mo. 2,867 E8 150
New Madrid, co., Mo. 31,350 E8 150
Newman, Stanislaus, Calif. 2,148 D3 94
Newman, Douglas, Ill. 1,097 D6 138
Newman, Otero, N.Mex. 25 F4 126
Newman, lake, Wash. B9 98
Newman Grove, Madison, Nebr. 880 C8 152
Newmans, lake, Fla. B8 174
Newmanstown, Lebanon, Pa. 1,200 C5 214
New Marion, Ripley, Ind. 150 C4 140
New Market, Madison, Ala. 500 A3 168
Newmarket, Ont., Can. 7,368 P21 64
Newmarket, Eng. 10,600 I13 273
New Market, Montgomery, Ind. 578 C3 140
New Market, Taylor, Iowa 506 D3 142
New Market, Frederick, Md. 358 B5 182
New Market, Scott, Minn. 211 G5 148
Newmarket, Rockingham, N.H. 2,745 E5 208
(3,153▲)
New Market, Middlesex, N.J. 3,500 B4 210
New Market, Jefferson, Tenn. 750 B8 190
New Market, Shenandoah, Va. 783 B6 192
New Marlboro, Berkshire, Mass. 75 B1 206
(1,083▲)
New Marshall, see Marshall, Okla.
New Marshfield, Athens, Ohio 400 C4 156
New Martinsville, Wetzel, W.Va. 5,607 B4 194
New Matamoras, Washington, Ohio 925 C5 156
New Meadows, Adams, Idaho 647 E2 108
New Melle, St. Charles, Mo. 300 C7 150
New Mexico, state, U.S. 951,023 E5 77
126
New Miami, Butler, Ohio 2,360 C2 156
New Middleton, Smith, Tenn. 100 B5 190
New Middletown, Harrison, Ind. 132 D3 140
New Middletown, Mahoning, Ohio 500 *B6 156
New Milford, Litchfield, Conn. 3,023 C2 202
(8,318▲)
New Milford, Bergen, N.J. 18,810 A1 210
New Milford, Susquehanna, Pa. 1,129 B6 214
New Mills, N.B., Can. 265 B3 70
New Milton, Doddridge, W.Va. 45 B4 194
New Monmouth, Monmouth, N.J. 400 C4 210
New Munich, Stearns, Minn. 296 F4 148
New Munster, Kenosha, Wis. 250 F1 160
Newnan, Coweta, Ga. 12,169 C2 176
Newnata, Stone, Ark. 60 B4 170
New Norfolk, Austl. 4,900 G9 432
New Norway, Alta., Can. 273 D6 54
New Offenburg, Ste. Genevieve, Mo. 200 D7 150
New Orleans, Orleans, La. 627,525 C7 180
(*885,200) E5
New Osgoode, Sask., Can. 125 D6 58
New Oxford, Adams, Pa. 1,407 D4 214
New Palestine, Hancock, Ind. 725 C4 140
New Paltz, Ulster, N.Y. 3,041 D7 212
New Paris, Elkhart, Ind. 900 *A4 140
New Paris, Preble, Ohio 1,679 C2 156
New Perlican, Newf., Can. 600 G9 72
New Philadelphia, Tuscarawas, Ohio 14,241 B5 156
New Philadelphia, Schuylkill, Pa. 1,702 C5 214

New Pine Creek, Lake, Oreg. 150 E6 96
New Plymouth, Payette, Idaho 940 F2 108
New Plymouth, N.Z. 24,071 (*28,300) C5 437
New Point, Decatur, Ind. 319 C4 140
New Point, Mathews, Va. 100 C8 192
New Point Comfort, Charlotte, Fla. 104 E8 174
New Point Comfort, point, Va. C8 192
Newport, Jackson, Ark. 7,007 B5 170
Newport, N.S., Can. 355 E5 70
Newport, New Castle, Del. 1,239 B3 172
Newport, Eng. 20,200 K11 273
Newport, Wakulla, Fla. 225 A6 174
Newport, Vermillion, Ind. 627 C2 140
Newport, Campbell, Ky. 30,070 A6 A8 178
Newport, Penobscot, Maine 1,589 (2,322▲) D3 204
Newport, Charles, Md. 90 D6 182
Newport, Monroe, Mich. 650 H8 146
Newport, Washington, Minn. 2,349 F7 148
Newport, Rock, Nebr. 162 B6 152
Newport, Sullivan, N.H. 3,222 (5,458▲) E2 208
Newport, Cumberland, N.J. 980 E2 210
Newport, Herkimer, N.Y. 827 B6 212
Newport, Carteret, N.C. 861 C9 186
Newport, Washington, Ohio 450 C5 156
Newport, Lincoln, Oreg. 5,344 C2 96
Newport, Perry, Pa. 1,861 C4 214
Newport, Newport, R.I. 47,049 D3 216
New Port, York, S.C. 50 B6 188
Newport, Cocke, Tenn. 6,448 C8 190
Newport, Orleans, Vt. 5,019 B4 218
Newport (Town of), Orleans, Vt. (1,010▲) *B4 218
Newport, Giles, Va. 100 C4 192
Newport, Wales 104,900 J10 273
Newport, Pend Oreille, Wash. 1,513 A9 98
Newport, co., R.I. 81,891 C3 216
Newport Beach, Orange, Calif. 26,564 D6 F5 94
Newport Center, Orleans, Vt. 288 B4 218
Newport News (Independent City), Va. 113,662 (*219,200) A8 D8 192
New Portland, Somerset, Maine 175 (620▲) D2 204
New Port Richey, Pasco, Fla. 3,520 C8 174
New Prague, Le Sueur, Minn. 2,533 G5 148
New Preston, Litchfield, Conn. 900 C2 202
New Prospect, Spartanburg, S.C. 375 A4 188
New Providence, see Borden, Ind.
New Providence, Hardin, Iowa 206 B4 142
New Providence, Union, N.J. 10,243 *B4 210
New Providence, Montgomery, Tenn. 4,451 B4 190
New Quay, Eng. 1,000 K7 273
New Raymer, Weld, Colo. 91 B7 106
New Richland, Waseca, Minn. 1,046 H5 148
New Richmond, Montgomery, Ind. 394 B3 140
New Richmond, Clermont, Ohio 2,834 D2 156
New Richmond, Summers, W.Va. 800 *D3 194
New Richmond, St. Croix, Wis. 3,316 C1 160
New Riegel, Seneca, Ohio 349 A3 156
New River, Maricopa, Ariz. 75 E3 124
New River, Bradford, Fla. 50 B8 174
New River, Scott, Tenn. 300 B7 190
New River, Pulaski, Va. 600 C4 192
New River, gorge, W.Va. D7 194
New River, inlet, Fla. D6 174
New River, inlet, N.C. C8 186
New Roads, Pointe Coupee, La. 3,965 D4 180
New Rochelle, Westchester, N.Y. 76,812 D2 212
New Rockford, Eddy, N.Dak. 2,177 C6 154
New Rocky Comfort, see Foreman, Ark.
New Ross, N.S., Can. 510 E5 70
New Ross, Montgomery, Ind. 332 C3 140
Newry, Oxford, Maine (260▲) D2 204
Newry, N.Ire. 13,264 G6 273
Newry, Oconee, S.C. 762 B3 188
New Salem, Rush, Ind. 250 C4 140
New Salem, Cowley, Kans. 60 E7 144
New Salem, Franklin, Mass. 250 (397▲) A3 206
New Salem, Morton, N.Dak. 986 D4 154
New Salem, Fayette, Pa. 1,100 D2 214
New Salisbury, Harrison, Ind. 200 D3 140
New Sarpy, St. Charles, La. 1,259 C7 180
New Sharon, Mahaska, Iowa 1,063 C5 142
New Sharon, Franklin, Maine 250 (712▲) D2 204
New Shoreham, Newport, R.I. E2 216
New Shrewsbury, Monmouth, N.J. 7,313 *C4 210
Newsite, Tallapoosa, Ala. 100 B4 168
New Site, Prentiss, Miss. 7 A4 184
New Smyrna Beach, Volusia, Fla. 8,781 B10 174
Newsom, Davidson, Tenn. E7 190
Newsoms, Southampton, Va. 423 D7 192
New South Wales, state, Austl. 3,622,906 E9 432
New Straitsville, Perry, Ohio 1,019 C4 156
New Stuyahok, Alsk. 141 *C5 84
New Sweden, Aroostook, Maine 250 (713▲) B4 204
New Tazewell, Claiborne, Tenn. 768 B8 190
Newton, Dale, Ala. 958 D4 168
Newton, Baker, Ga. 529 E2 176
Newton, Jasper, Ill. 2,901 E5 138
Newton, Jasper, Iowa 15,381 C4 142
Newton, Harvey, Kans. 14,877 D6 144
Newton, Calcasieu, La. (part of Moss Bluff) D2 180
Newton, Middlesex, Mass. 92,384 B5 D2 206
Newton, Newton, Miss. 3,178 C3 184
Newton, Catawba, N.C. 6,658 B4 186
Newton, N.Ire. G6 272
Newton, Rockingham, N.H. 175 (1,419▲) F4 208
Newton, Sussex, N.J. 6,563 A3 210
Newton, Newton, Tex. 1,233 D9 130
Newton, Cache, Utah 480 B4 114
Newton, Roan, W.Va. 350 C3 194
Newton, Manitowoc, Wis. 60 B6 160
Newton, co., Ark. 5,963 B3 170
Newton, co., Ga. 20,999 C3 176
Newton, co., Ind. 11,502 A2 140
Newton, co., Miss. 19,517 C3 184
Newton, co., Mo. 30,093 E3 150
Newton, co., Tex. 10,372 D9 130
Newton Abbot, Eng. 17,100 K9 273
Newton Brook, Ont., Can. 1,600 R22 64
Newton Falls, St. Lawrence, N.Y. 664 A7 212
Newton Falls, Trumbull, Ohio 5,038 A6 156
Newton Grove, Sampson, N.C. 477 B7 186
Newtonia, Newton, Mo. 153 *E3 150
Newton Junction, Rockingham, N.H. 225 F4 208
Newton Station, B.C., Can. 550 B15 52
Newton Stewart, Scot. 2,000 G8 272
Newtonville, Fayette, Ala. 80 B2 168
Newtonville, Ont., Can. Q22 64
Newtonville, Spencer, Ind. 125 D3 140
Newtonville, Atlantic, N.J. 350 D3 210
New Toronto, Ont., Can. 11,560 Q21 S22 64
Newtown, Newf., Can. 590 F9 72
Newtown, Fairfield, Conn. 1,261 (11,373▲) D2 202
Newtown, Fountain, Ind. 321 B2 140
Newtown, Sullivan, Mo. 265 A4 150
New Town, Mountrail, N.Dak. 1,586 C3 154
Newtown, Hamilton, Ohio 1,750 C2 D1 156
Newtown, Bucks, Pa. 2,323 C7 214
Newtown, Luzerne, Pa. 2,400 A5 214
Newtown, Polk, Tenn. 400 C7 190
Newtown, King and Queen, Va. 65 C7 192
Newtownards, N.Ire. 12,237 G7 273
New Town Village, Dillon, S.C. 633 *C10 188
New Trenton, Franklin, Ind. 150 C5 140
New Trier, Dakota, Minn. 106 *G6 148
New Ulm, Brown, Minn. 11,114 G4 148
New Underwood, Pennington, S.Dak. 462 C3 158
New Upton, Gloucester, Va. C8 192
New Vienna, Dubuque, Iowa 265 B6 142
New Vienna, Clinton, Ohio 858 C3 156
New Village, Warren, N.J. 350 B2 210
Newville, Henry, Ala. 546 D4 168
Newville, N.S., Can. 125 D5 70
Newville, Cumberland, Pa. 1,656 C4 214
Newville, Braxton, W.Va. 75 C4 194
New Vineyard, Franklin, Maine 250 (357▲) D2 204
New Virginia, Warren, Iowa 381 C4 142
New Washington, Clark, Ind. 700 D4 140
New Washington, Crawford, Ohio 1,162 B4 156
New Waterford, N.S., Can. 10,381 C9 70
New Waterford, Columbiana, Ohio 711 B6 156
New Waverly, Cass, Ind. 200 B3 140
New Westminster, B.C., Can. 31,665 B15 F11 52
New Whiteland, Johnson, Ind. 3,488 C3 140
New Wilmington, Lawrence, Pa. 2,203 B1 214
New Windsor, Mercer, Ill. 658 B3 138
New Windsor, Carroll, Md. 738 A5 182
New Windsor, Orange, N.Y. 4,041 *D7 212
New Witten, Tripp, S.Dak. 146 D5 158
New Woodstock, Madison, N.Y. 375 C6 212
New Woodville, see Woodville, Okla.
New World, isl., Newf., Can. F8 72
New Year, lake, Nev. B2 112
New York, N.Y. 7,781,984 (*15,404,300) D2 E8 212
New York, co., N.Y. 1,698,281 D2 212
New York, state, U.S. 16,782,304 C11 77 212
New York, peak, Calif. E6 94
New York Mills, Otter Tail, Minn. 828 E3 148
New York Mills, Oneida, N.Y. 3,788 *B6 212
New Zealand, country, Pac.O. 2,174,062 D3 436
New Zion, Clarendon, S.C. 200 D8 188
Ney, lake, Man., Can. C6 60
Neya, Sov.Un. A2 336
Neyriz, Iran 19,439 D4 379
Neyshābūr, Iran 25,820 B5 379
Nezhin, Sov.Un. 59,000 G8 332
Nezperce, Lewis, Idaho 667 C2 108
Nez Perce, co., Idaho 27,066 C2 108
Nez Perce, pass, Idaho, Mont. D4 108, E2 110
Nezpique, bayou, La. D3 180
Ngabang, Indon. D3 358
Ngabé, Con.B. G8 409
Ngala, Br.Cam. D7 409
Ngaloa, bay, Fiji E6 436
Ngaloa, harbor, Fiji E6 436
Ngami, lake, Bech. D4 420
Nganglaring, lake, China E4 346
Ngaoundéré, Cam. 10,090 E7 409
Ngara, Tan. C5 414
Ngardmau, Palau A6 436
Ngaruawahia, N.Z. 2,703 B5 437
Ngatapa, N.Z. 230 C6 437
Ngele Levu, isl., Fiji D7 436
Ngemelis, is., Palau A6 436
Ngidinga, Con.L. D2 414
Ngnau, isl., Fiji E7 436
Ngong, Ken. C6 414
Ngounié, riv., Gabon G7 409
Nguigmi, Nig. 2,400 D7 409
Nguru, Nig. 23,084 D7 409
Nha Trang, Viet. 25,000 D6 362
Niafounké, Mali 4,100 C4 408
Niagara, Grand Forks, N.Dak. 157 C8 154
Niagara, Marinette, Wis. 2,098 C5 160
Niagara, co., N.Y. 242,269 B3 212
Niagara, cave, Minn. H6 148
Niagara, falls, N.Y., Ont., Can. *B2 212, *Q21 64
Niagara, riv., N.Y. B2 212
Niagara Falls, Ont., Can. 23,563 Q21 64
Niagara Falls, Niagara, N.Y. 102,394 B2 212
Niagara-on-the-Lake, Ont., Can. 2,740 Q21 64
Niagara University, Niagara, N.Y. 1,500 *B3 212
Niamey, Niger 8,967 D5 408
Niangara, Con.L. B4 414
Niangua, Webster, Mo. 287 D5 150
Niangua, riv., Mo. D5 150
Niantic, New London, Conn. 2,788 D7 202
Niantic, Macon, Ill. 629 D4 138
Niarada, Sanders, Mont. 5 C2 110
Nias, isl., Indon. D1 358
Niassa, prov., Moz. B7 421
Nibbe, Yellowstone, Mont. 25 E8 110
Nibe, Den. 2,491 H3 291
Nibley, Cache, Utah 333 *B4 114
Nicaragua, country, N.A. 1,399,000 D4 228
Nicaragua, lake, Nic. E5 228
Nicastro, It. 21,200 F6 302
Nicatous, lake, Maine C4 204
Nice, Fr. 244,360 F7 278
Nice, former prov., Fr. 339,000 *F7 278
Niceville, Okaloosa, Fla. 4,517 A4 174
Nichicun, lake, Que., Can. Q9 66
Nicholas, co., Ky. 6,677 B6 178
Nicholas, co., W.Va. 25,414 C4 194
Nicholas, chan., Cuba A4 232
Nicholasville, Jessamine, Ky. 4,275 C6 178
Nicholls, Coffee, Ga. 930 E4 176
Nichols, Fairfield, Conn. (part of Trumbull) E3 202
Nichols, Muscatine, Iowa 329 C6 142
Nichols, Greene, Mo. 100 D4 150
Nichols, Tioga, N.Y. 663 C5 212
Nichols, Marion, S.C. 617 C10 188
Nichols Hills, Oklahoma, Okla. 4,897 C6 128
Nicholson, Jackson, Ga. 359 B3 176
Nicholson, Trigg, Ky. 375 C3 178
Nicholson, Pearl River, Miss. 500 E3 184
Nicholson, Wyoming, Pa. 942 B6 214
Nicholson, riv., Austl. B7 432
Nicholsville, Marengo, Ala. 250 C2 168
Nicholville, St. Lawrence, N.Y. 400 A7 212
Nickelsville, Scott, Va. 291 D2 192
Nickerson, Reno, Kans. 1,091 D5 144
Nickerson, Dodge, Nebr. 168 C9 152
Nickerson, hill, Conn. D6 202
Nickwall, McCone, Mont. B11 110
Nicobar, is., India G6 366
Nicodemus, Graham, Kans. 300 C4 144
Nicola, B.C., Can. 125 E12 52
Nicola, riv., B.C., Can. E12 52
Nicolet, Que., Can. 3,771 R12 66
Nicolet, co., Que., Can. 31,248 R12 66
Nicolet, lake, Mich. C7 146
Nicolet, riv., Que., Can. R12 66
Nicollet, Nicollet, Minn. 493 G4 148
Nicollet, co., Minn. 23,196 G4 148
Nicoma Park, Oklahoma, Okla. 1,263 *C6 128
Nicosia, Cyp. 48,864 (*81,741) D5 307
Nicosia [Sicilia], It. 17,600 G5 302
Nicotera, It. 4,761 F5 302
Nicoya, C.R. 1,625 E5 228
Nicoya, gulf, C.R. F5 228
Nicoya, pen., C.R. E5 228
Nictaux Falls, N.S., Can. 255 E5 70
Nicuadala, Moz. C7 421
Nicut, Sequoyah, Okla. 40 C9 128
Nida, Johnston, Okla. 40 D7 128
Nidan, rock, Iwo A7 436
Nidwalden (Nidwald), subcanton, Switz. 20,600 *B4 312
Nidzica, Pol. 2,852 B5 325
Niedere Tauern, mts., Aus. C5 313
Niederösterreich (Lower Austria), state, Aus. 1,400,471 *B6 313
Niedersachsen (Lower Saxony), state, Ger. 6,548,100 *B3 286
Nielsville, Polk, Minn. 183 D2 148
Niemodlin, Pol. 2,580 C3 325
Nienburg [an der Weser], Ger. 21,800 B3 286
Nieszawa, Pol. 2,403 B4 325
Niete, mtn., Lib. E3 408
Nieuw Amsterdam, Sur. D6 256
Nieuweroord, Neth. 753 B5 282
Nieuwpoort, Bel. 6,548 C1 282
Nièvre, dept., Fr. 240,078 *D5 278
Nifisha, Eg., U.A.R. D3 382
Nigadoo, N.B., Can. 50 B4 70
Niğde, Tur. 14,693 C6 307
Niğde, prov., Tur. 285,824 *C6 307
Nigei, isl., B.C., Can. E9 52
Niger, country, Afr. 2,800,000 E7 388 409
Niger, riv., Guinea D3 408
Niger, riv., Mali D3 408
Niger, riv., Niger D5 408
Niger, riv., Nig. E6 408
Niger, riv. mouths, Nig. F6 408
Nigeria, country, Afr. 29,600,000 F7 388 409
Nighthawk, Okanogan, Wash. 15 A7 98
Nightingale, isl., Viet. B5 362
Nigrita, Grc. 8,335 A4 306
Nigtu, China L7 349
Nihing, riv., Pak. F3 375
Nihoa, isl., Haw. B6 86
Nii, isl., Jap. G7 354
Niigata, Jap. 261,758 F7 354
Niihama, Jap. 107,234 H4 354
Niihau, isl., Haw. B1 86
Niijimahon, Jap. M15 354
Niimi, Jap. 39,155 G4 354
Nijar, Sp. 2,052 D5 298
Nijkerk, Neth. 6,652 B4 282
Nijmegen, Neth. 116,989 C4 282
Nikep, Allegany, Md. 215 A2 182
Nikitinka, Sov.Un. E9 332
Nikitovka, Sov.Un. 20,000 S22 332
Nikki, Dah. E5 408
Nikko, Jap. 33,490 F7 354
Nikolayev, Sov.Un. 224,000 I9 332
Nikolayevsk, Sov.Un. 30,000 D16 329
Nikolayevskiy, Sov.Un. 30,000 G15 332
Nikolsk, Sov.Un. A3 336
Nikolski, Alsk. 64 E5 84
Nikonovskoye, Sov.Un. O19 332
Nikopol, Bul. 5,788 B2 317
Nikopol, Sov.Un. 81,000 I10 332
Niksar, Tur. 7,640 A7 307
Nikshahr, Iran D5 379
Nikšić, Yugo. 14,900 C4 316
Nilakka, lake, Fin. E11 290
Niland, Imperial, Calif. 700 F6 94
Nile, riv., Eg., U.A.R. B3 395
Nile, riv., Sud. A3 398
Niles, Alameda, Calif. (part of Fremont) B6 94
Niles, Cook, Ill. 20,393 E2 138
Niles, Ottawa, Kans. 105 D6 144
Niles, Berrien, Mich. 13,842 H5 146
Niles, Trumbull, Ohio 19,545 A6 156
Nilsiä, Fin. E13 290
Nimaj, India D1 368
Nimba, mts., Guinea E3 408
Nimburg, Butler, Nebr. 10 *C9 152
Nimes, Fr. 89,130 F6 278
Nimmons, Clay, Ark. 154 A6 170
Nimpkish, riv., B.C., Can. E9 52
Nimrod, Perry, Ark. C3 170
Nimrod, Wadena, Minn. 60 E4 148
Nimrod, res., Ark. C3 170
Nimule, Sud. E3 398
Ninemile, hill, Tenn. E7 190
Nine Mile, pt., Mich. D7 146
Nine Mile Falls, Spokane, Wash. 80 D8 98
Nine Times, Pickens, S.C. B3 188
Ninette, Man., Can. 170 F3 60
Ninety Mile, beach, Austl. F9 432
Ninety Six, Greenwood, S.C. 1,435 C4 188
Nineveh, ruins, Iraq A5 378
Nineveh, Johnson, Ind. 300 C3 140
Ninga, Man., Can. 310 F3 60
Ningan (Ninguta), China 35,093 C14 348
Ningchiang, China 5,000 I3 349
Ningchin, China 15,000 G7 348
Ningching, China F7 346
Ningerh, China G8 346
Ninghai, China 10,000 K10 349
Ninghsia, see Yinchuan, China
Ninghsien, China 5,000 H3 348
Ninghsien (Ningpo), China 237,500 K10 349
Ninghua, China 5,000 L8 349
Ningpo, see Ninghsien, China
Ningte, China 60,000 L9 349
Ninguta, see Ningan, China
Ningwa, China F6 348
Ningyüan, China 1,000 M5 349
Ninh Binh, Viet. 25,000 B5 362
Ninigret, pond, R.I. D2 216
Ninilchik, Alsk. 97 C6 G10 84
Ninnekah, Grady, Okla. 300 D6 128
Ninnescah, riv., Kans. E6 144
Ninole, Hawaii, Haw. 112 D6 86
Ninove, Bel. 11,882 D3 282
Nioaque, Braz. 1,279 J5 257
Niobe, Ward, N.Dak. 67 B3 154
Niobrara, Knox, Nebr. 736 B7 152
Niobrara, co., Wyo. 3,750 C8 116
Niobrara, riv., Nebr. B7 152
Nioki, Con.L. C2 414
Nioro, Mali 8,000 C3 408
Nioro, Sen. D1 408
Niort, Fr. 33,167 D3 278
Niota, McMinn, Tenn. 679 C7 190
Niotaze, Chautauqua, Kans. 124 E7 144
Nipawin, Sask., Can. 3,337 D5 58
Nipigon, lake, Ont., Can. R24 64
Nipishish, lake, Newf., Can. D9 72
Nipisiguit, bay, N.B., Can. B4 70
Nipisiguit, riv., N.B., Can. B3 70
Nipissing, dist., Ont., Can. 60,452 O22 64
Nipissing Junction, Ont., Can. O21 64
Nipmuck Pond, Worcester, Mass. 150 *B4 206
Nipomo, San Luis Obispo, Calif. 550 E3 94
Nipper's Harbour, Newf., Can. 250 F8 72
Niquelândia, Braz. C1 258
Niquero, Cuba 7,204 B6 232
Nirasaki, Jap. 31,698 L14 354
Niš, Yugo. 62,100 C5 316
Nisa, Port. 5,617 C3 298
Nišava, riv., Yugo. C6 316
Nishi, Iwo A7 436
Nishinomiya, Jap. 210,179 *M11 354
Nishio, Jap. 66,143 *M13 354
Nishnabotna, riv., Iowa D2 142
Nisiros, isl., Grc. C6 306
Nisko, Pol. 6,590 C6 325
Nisku, Alta., Can. D6 54
Nisland, Butte, S.Dak. 211 C2 158
Nisqually, Thurston, Wash. 300 *B4 98
Nisqually, riv., Wash. C4 98
Nisservatn, lake, Nor. G3 291
Nisswa, Crow Wing, Minn. 742 E4 148
Nistowiak, lake, Sask., Can. C5 58
Nisula, Houghton, Mich. 45 C3 146
Niterói, Braz. 255,585 E2 258
Nitra, Czech. 29,238 B4 324
Nitra, riv., Czech. B4 324
Nitriansky, co., Czech. 743,787 *B4 324
Nitro, Kanawha, W.Va. 6,894 C3 194

Nitta Yuma, Sharkey, Miss. 125 B2 184
Niulii (Niulii Plantation), Hawaii, Haw. 250 *C6 86
Niulii Plantation, see Niulii, Hawaii, Haw.
Niut, range, B.C., Can. E10 52
Niuyen, China N3 349
Nivala, Fin. E11 290
Nive Island, N.Z. poss., Pac.O. 4,950 *D4 436
Nivelles, Bel. 13,440 D3 282
Nivernais, former prov., Fr. 236,000 D5 278
Nivernais, hills, Fr. D5 278
Niverville, Man., Can. 500 F4 60
Niwot, Boulder, Colo. 150 B5 106
Nixa, Christian, Mo. 944 D4 150
Nixburg, Coosa, Ala. 200 C3 168
Nixon, Washoe, Nev. 25 D2 112
Nixon, Middlesex, N.J. 14,000 C4 210
Nixon, Gonzales, Tex. 1,751 B7 130, E7
Nizhne-Chirskaya, Sov.Un. 17,200 H14 332
Nizhne-Kolymsk, Sov.Un. C18 329
Nizhneudinsk, Sov.Un. 35,900 D11 329
Nizhneye, Sov.Un. 12,700 R22 332
Nizhniy Lomov, Sov.Un. 9,500 F14 332
Nizhniy Pesha, Sov.Un. C6 328
Nizhniy Tagil, Sov.Un. 338,000 A5 336
Nizhnyaya Tunguska, riv., Sov.Un. C11 329
Njardhvik, Ice. L23 290
Njombe, Tan. 7,560 D5 414
Njurunda, Swe. 1,000 E7 291
Nkai, Rh. & Nya. C5 420
Nkata Bay, Rh. & Nya. B6 421
Nkongsamba, Cam. 12,000 F6 409
Nmai Hka, riv., Bur. A3 362
Noakhali, Pak. 16,677 L17 375
Noank, New London, Conn. 1,116 D8 202
Noatak, Alsk. 326 B5 84
Noatak, riv., Alsk. B5 84
Nobel, Ont., Can. 550 O20 64
Nobeoka, Jap. 116,762 H3 354
Noble, Walker, Ga. 200 B1 176
Noble, Richland, Ill. 761 E5 138
Noble, Rice, Kans. D5 144
Noble, Sabine, La. 206 C2 180
Noble, Cleveland, Okla. 995 C6 128
Noble, co., Ind. 28,162 A4 140
Noble, co., Ohio 10,982 C5 156
Noble, co., Okla. 10,376 B6 128
Nobleboro, Lincoln, Maine 75 (679▲) D3 204
Nobleford, Alta., Can. 263 F6 54
Noble Lake, Jefferson, Ark. 100 C5 170
Nobles, co., Minn. 23,365 H3 148
Noblestown, Allegheny, Pa. 700 *C2 214
Noblesville, Hamilton, Ind. 7,664 B3 140
Noboribetsu, Jap. C8 354
Nobscot, hill, Mass. D1 206
Nocatee, De Soto, Fla. 627 D9 174
Nochistlán, Mex. 4,561 K12 225
Nochixtlán, Mex. 2,571 M15 225
Nocona, Montague, Tex. 3,127 C7 130
Nodaway, Adams, Iowa 204 D3 142
Nodaway, co., Mo. 22,215 A3 150
Nodaway, riv., Iowa, Mo. D2 142, A2 150
Node, Niobrara, Wyo. 15 D8 116
Noel, McDonald, Mo. 736 E3 150
Noel Pauls, brook, Newf., Can. F7 72
Noelville, Ont., Can. 275 O20 64
Noemfoor, isl., Neth.N.Gui. E9 359
Nogal, Lincoln, N.Mex. 40 E5 126
Nogal, riv., Som. D6 398
Nogales, Santa Cruz, Ariz. 7,286 G5 124
Nogales, Mex. 24,480 A3 224
Nogales, Mex. 7,524 L15 225
Nōgata, Jap. 62,250 *H3 354
Nogent-en-Bassigny, Fr. C6 278
Nogent-le-Rotrou, Fr. 8,765 C4 278
Nogent [-sur-Marne], Fr. 23,581 I10 278
Noginsk, Sov.Un. 93,000 E12 332, N19
Nogliki, Sov.Un. D16 329
Nogoyá, Arg. 12,051 B4 252
Nógrád, co., Hung. 230,000 *A4 320
Nogueira, Sp. 317 A3 298
Nohar, India 10,836 C1 368
Noheji, Jap. 16,945 D8 354
Nohili, pt., Haw. A2 86
Nohly, Richland, Mont. 9 C12 110
Noho, China 20,000 A12 348
Noire, riv., Upper Volta D4 408
Noisy-le-Sec, Fr. 22,337 L10 278
Nojima, cape, Jap. G7 354
Nokesville, Prince William, Va. 100 B7 192
Nokia, Fin. F10 291
Nok Kundi, Pak. E3 375
Nokomis, Sask., Can. 516 E5 58
Nokomis, Sarasota, Fla. 2,253 E8 174
Nokomis, Montgomery, Ill. 2,476 D4 138
Nokomis, lake, Wis. C4 160
Nola, Cen.Afr.Rep. F8 409
Nola, Scott, Ark. 25 C3 170
Nola, It. 16,400 E5 302
Nola, Lawrence, Miss. 125 D2 184
Nolan, Mingo, W.Va. 787 D2 194
Nolan, co., Tex. 18,963 C5 130
Nolensville, Williamson, Tenn. 400 C5 190, E7
Nolin, riv., Ky. C4 178
Nolinsk, Sov.Un. 9,600 A3 336
Noma, Holmes, Fla. 344 A5 174
Noma, cape, Jap. I2 354
No Mans Land, isl., Mass. D6 206
Nome, Alsk. 2,316 C5 84
Nome, Barnes, N.Dak. 145 D8 154
Nominingue, Que., Can. 738 R9 66
Non, Hughes, Okla. 45 D7 128
Nonacho, lake, N.W.Ter., Can. E8 48
Nonconnah, creek, Tenn. E6 190
Nondalton, Alsk. 103 C6 84
Nong Khai, Thai. C4 362
Nong Khai, prov., Thai. 144,201 *C4 362
Nongoma, U.S.Afr. 992 E6 421
Nonoava, Mex. 1,582 B4 224
Nonquit, pond, R.I. C4 216
Nontburi, prov., Thai. 135,537 *D4 362
Nooksack, Whatcom, Wash. 318 A4 98
Nooksack, riv., Wash. A4 98
Noon, hill, Mass. D2 206
Noonan, Divide, N.Dak. 625 B2 154
Noord-Brabant, prov., Neth. 1,332,033 C3 282
Noord-Holland, prov., Neth. 1,929,620 B3 282
Noord-Oost Polder, reg., Neth. 15,938 B4 282
Noordwijk-Binnen, Neth. 6,734 B3 282
Noorvik, Alsk. 248 B5 84
Nooseneck Hill, Kent, R.I. 100 C2 216
Nootka, isl., B.C., Can. F9 52
Nootka, sound, B.C., Can. F9 52
Nopala, Mex. 799 L15 225
No Point, pt., Md. D7 182
Noquebay, lake, Wis. C6 160
Noqui, Ang. A2 420
Nora, Marion, Ind. 200 D5 140
Nora, Nuckolls, Nebr. 60 D8 152
Nora, Swe. 3,730 B6 292
Nora, Dickenson, Va. 200 C2 192
Nora Springs, Floyd, Iowa 1,275 A5 142
Norborne, Carroll, Mo. 965 B4 150
Norbourne Estates, Jefferson, Ky. 507 *B5 178
Norcatur, Decatur, Kans. 302 C3 144
Norco, Riverside, Calif. 4,964 C6 94
Norco, St. Charles, La. 4,682 B6 180, D5
Norcross, Gwinnett, Ga. 1,605 A5 176, C2
Norcross, Penobscot, Maine 30 C4 204
Norcross, Grant, Minn. 153 F2 148
Nord, dept., Fr. 2,098,545 *B5 278
Nord, mts., Hai. C8 232
Nordegg, Alta., Can. 1,000 D4 54
Nordegg, riv., Alta., Can. D5 54
Norden, Ger. 17,000 B2 286
Norden, Keya Paha, Nebr. 32 B5 152
Nordenham, Ger. 26,500 B3 286
Norderney, isl., Ger. B2 286
Nordfjord, fjord, Nor. F1 291
Nordhausen, Ger. 39,200 C4 286
Nordhlingafljot, riv., Ice. L19 290
Nordhorn, Ger. 38,400 B2 286
Nordhtunga, Ice. L19 290
Nordhue, mtn., Nor. A2 292
Nordland, Jefferson, Wash. 100 A4 98
Nordland, co., Nor. 225,394 *C6 290
Nordli, Nor. D5 290
Nördlingen, Ger. 14,200 D4 286
Nordmaling, Swe. 910 E8 290
Nordman, Bonner, Idaho 25 A2 108
Nordrhein-Westfalen (North Rhine-Westphalia), state, Ger. 14,856,100 *C2 286
Nordstrand, isl., Ger. A3 286
Nord-Tröndelag, co., Nor. 112,185 *D5 290
Nordvik, Sov.Un. 2,500 B13 329
Nore, Nor. F3 291
Nore, riv., Ire. I5 273
Norene, Wilson, Tenn. 70 B5 190
Norfield, Lincoln, Miss. 50 D2 184
Norfolk, Baxter, Ark. 283 A4 170
Norfolk, Litchfield, Conn. 850 (1,827▲) B3 202
Norfolk, Norfolk, Mass. 350 (3,471▲) E2 206
Norfolk, Madison, Nebr. 13,111 B8 152
Norfolk, St. Lawrence, N.Y. 1,353 A6 212
Norfolk (Independent City), Va. 305,872 (*574,900) A9 192, D8
Norfolk, co., Ont., Can. 46,122 R20 64
Norfolk, co., Eng. 551,700 I13 273
Norfolk, co., Mass. 510,256 B5 206
Norfolk, co., Va. 51,612 D8 192
Norfolk, isl., Pac.O. D3 436
Norfolk, lake, Ark. A4 170
Norfolk Highlands, Norfolk, Va. 1,000 *D8 192
Norfolk Island, Austl. poss., Pac.O. 938 D3 436
Norge, Grady, Okla. 60 D6 128
Norheim, Blaine, Mont. B7 110
Norikura-Dake, peak, Jap. K13 354
Norilsk, Sov.Un. 108,000 C10 328
Norland, Ont., Can. 100 P22 64
Norland, Dickenson, Va. C2 192
Norlina, Warren, N.C. 927 A7 186
Norma, Salem, N.J. 700 E2 210
Norma, Renville, N.Dak. 84 B4 154
Norma, Scott, Tenn. 250 B7 190
Normal, Madison, Ala. 1,500 A3 168
Normal, McLean, Ill. 13,357 C5 138
Normalville, Fayette, Pa. 900 D2 214
Norman, Montgomery, Ark. 482 C3 170
Norman, riv., Austl. B8 432
Norman, Jackson, Ind. 130 D3 140
Norman, Kearney, Nebr. 57 D7 152
Norman, Richmond, N.C. 220 B6 186
Norman, Cleveland, Okla. 33,412 C6 128
Norman, co., Minn. 11,253 D2 148
Norman, upland, Ind. *D3 140
Normanby, riv., Austl. A8 432
Normandy, St. Louis, Mo. 4,452 A8 150
Normandy, Bedford, Tenn. 119 C5 190
Normandy (Normandie), former prov., Fr. 2,407,000 C3 278
Normandy, hills, Fr. C3 278
Normandy Beach, Ocean, N.J. 300 C4 210
Normandy Park, King, Wash. 3,224 *B4 98
Normangee, Leon and Madison, Tex. 718 D7 130
Norman Park, Colquitt, Ga. 891 E3 176
Normanton, Austl. 238 B8 432
Norman Wells, N.W.Ter., Can. 600 D6 48
Nornalup, Austl. E3 432
Norphlet, Union, Ark. 459 D4 170
Norquay, Sask., Can. 448 E6 58
Ñorquincó, Arg. F3 251
Norrbotten, co., Swe. 251,031 *C7 290
Norrbotten, prov., Swe. 176,651 *D9 290
Norridge, Cook, Ill. 14,087 *B6 138
Norridgewock, Somerset, Maine 850 (1,634▲) D3 204
Norrie, Marathon, Wis. 65 D4 160
Norris, Madison, Mont. 185 E5 110
Norris, Pickens, S.C. 594 B3 188
Norris, Mellette, S.Dak. 100 D4 158
Norris, Anderson, Tenn. 1,389 B7 190
Norris, dam, Tenn. B7 190
Norris, lake, Tenn. B8 190
Norris Arm, Newf., Can. 1,050 F8 72
Norris City, White, Ill. 1,243 F5 138
Norris Point, Newf., Can. 450 F7 72
Norristown, Emanuel, Ga. 200 D4 176
Norristown, Montgomery, Pa. 38,925 A6 214, C6
Norrisville, Harford, Md. 75 A6 182
Norrköping, Swe. 88,762 C7 292
Norrland, Swe. E7 290
Norrland, reg., Swe. 1,213,910 *D8 290
Norrsundet, Swe. A8 292
Norrtälje, Swe. 7,968 B9 292
Norseman, Austl. 2,539 E4 432
Norsholm, Swe. 2,940 C7 292
Norsholmen, pt., Swe. D10 292
Norsjö, Swe. D8 290
Norte, chan., Braz. E6 256
Norte, pt., Arg. F5 251
Norte de Santander, dept., Col. 403,420 B2 244
North, Orangeburg, S.C. 1,047 D6 188
North, Mathews, Va. 150 C8 192
North, brook, Vt. B3 218
North, cape, N.S., Can. B9 70
North, cape, Ice. K18 290
North, cape, N.Z. A4 437
North, cape, Nor. A11 290
North, chan., Ont., Can. O18 64
North, chan., Scot. F6 272
North, creek, Ga. B5 176
North, dam, Wash. B7 98
North, fork, Wash. A5 98
North, head, Newf., Can. F6 72
North, inlet, S.C. E10 188
North, isl., N.Z. B4 437
North, isl., Pac.O. D4 436
North, isl., S.C. E10 188
North, is., La. E7 180
North, mtn., Okla. D5 128
North, mtn., Pa. B5 214
North, park, Pa. A3 214
North, pass, La. E6 180
North, plains, N.Mex. D2 126
North, pt., Calif. A5 94
North, pt., P.E.I., Can. B6 70
North, pt., Md. B7 182
North, pt., Mich. D8 146
North, pt., R.I. C3 216
North, pond, Maine D3 204
North, pond, Mass. D1 206
North, riv., Ala. B2 168
North, riv., Newf., Can. D7 72
North, riv., Fla. B10 174
North, riv., Iowa B7 142
North, riv., Mass. E4 206
North, riv., Vt. F3 218
North, sea, Eur. C5 266
North, sound, Ire. H3 273
North Abington, Plymouth, Mass. 4,900 B6 206, E3
North Acton, Middlesex, Mass. 600 C1 206
North Adams, Berkshire, Mass. 19,905 A1 206
North Adams, Hillsdale, Mich. 494 H7 146
North Agawam, Hampden, Mass. 2,000 *B2 206
North Albany, Benton, Oreg. C1 96
Northallerton, Eng. 6,100 G11 273
Northam, Austl. 5,725 E3 432
North America, cont. 251,054,000 18, 43
North Amherst, Hampshire, Mass. 1,009 B2 206
North Amity (Amity), Aroostook, Maine 50 (206▲) C5 204
North Amityville, Suffolk, N.Y. 6,000 *E3 212
Northampton, Austl. 992 D2 432
Northampton, Eng. 101,800 I12 273
Northampton, Hampshire, Mass. 30,058 B2 206
Northampton, Northampton, Pa. 8,866 C6 214
Northampton, co., Eng. 442,350 I11 273
Northampton, co., N.C. 26,811 A8 186
Northampton, co., Pa. 201,412 C6 214
Northampton, co., Va. 16,966 C9 192
North Andaman, isl., India F6 366
North Andover, Essex, Mass. 10,908 A5 206
North Anson, Somerset, Maine 700 D3 204
North Apollo, Armstrong, Pa. 1,741 C2 214
North Arlington, Bergen, N.J. 17,477 B1 210
North Asheboro, Randolph, N.C. 3,805 B6 186
North Atlanta, De Kalb, Ga. 12,661 A5 176
North Attleboro, Bristol, Mass. 14,777 C5 206
North Augusta, Ont., Can. 485 P25 64
North Augusta, Aiken, S.C. 10,348 D5 188
North Aulatsivik, isl., Newf., Can. C9 72
North Aurora, Kane, Ill. 2,088 F1 138
North Avondale, Pueblo, Colo. 102 D6 106
North Babylon, Suffolk, N.Y. 12,000 *E3 212
North Baltimore, Wood, Ohio 3,011 A3 156
North Bangor, Franklin, N.Y. 570 A7 212
North Battleford, Sask., Can. 8,924 C3 58, D3
North Bay, Ont., Can. 21,020 S25 64
North Bay, Dade, Fla. 2,006 *F10 174
North Bay, Racine, Wis. 264 *F6 160
North Bay, riv., Newf., Can. G8 72
North Beach, Calvert, Md. 606 C6 182
North Belgrade, Kennebec, Maine 200 D3 204
North Belle Vernon, Westmoreland, Pa. 3,148 *C2 214
North Bellingham, Norfolk, Mass. 495 E1 206
North Bellmore, Nassau, N.Y. 19,639 *E8 212
North Bellport, Suffolk, N.Y. 2,000 *D4 212
North Belmont, Gaston, N.C. 3,000 B4 186
North Bend, B.C., Can. 315 F12 52
North Bend, Dodge, Nebr. 1,174 C9 152
North Bend, Hamilton, Ohio 622 D1 156
North Bend, Coos, Oreg. 7,512 D2 96
North Bend, Clinton, Pa. 900 B4 214
North Bend, King, Wash. 945 B5 98
North Bend, Jackson, Wis. 100 D2 160
North Bennington, Bennington, Vt. 1,437 F2 218
North Bergen, Hudson, N.J. 42,387 B1 210
North Berwick, York, Maine 1,295 (1,844▲) E2 204
North Berwick, Scot. 3,800 E10 272
North Billerica, Middlesex, Mass. 3,000 A5 206, C2
North Bonneville, Skamania, Wash. 494 D5 98
North Borneo, Br. poss., Asia 334,141 I13 340, 359
Northboro, Page, Iowa 135 D2 142
North Braddock, Allegheny, Pa. 13,204 A4 214
North Bradford, Penobscot, Maine 100 C4 204
North Bradley, Midland, Mich. 220 F7 146
Northbranch, Jewell, Kans. 60 *C5 144
North Branch, Allegany, Md. 250 A2 182
North Branch, Lapeer, Mich. 901 F8 146
North Branch, Chisago, Minn. 949 F6 148
North Branch, Somerset, N.J. 250 B3 210
North Branford, New Haven, Conn. 450 (6,771▲) D4 202
North Brentwood, Prince Georges, Md. 864 *C6 182
Northbridge Center, Worcester, Mass. 300 *B4 206
North Bridgton, Cumberland, Maine 300 D2 204
North Brook, Ont., Can. 95 P23 64
Northbrook, Cook, Ill. 11,635 E2 138
North Brookfield, Worcester, Mass. 2,615 (3,616▲) B3 206
North Brooksville, Hancock, Maine 100 D4 204
North Brother, mtn., Maine C4 204
North Brunswick, Middlesex, N.J. 10,099 *C4 210
North Buena Vista, Clayton, Iowa 150 B7 142
North Caldwell, Essex, N.J. 4,163 A1 210, B4
North Canaan (Town of), Litchfield, Conn. (2,836▲) A2 202
North Canadian, riv., Okla. B3 128
North Canton, Hartford, Conn. 250 B4 202
North Canton, Cherokee, Ga. 1,996 *B2 176
North Canton, Stark, Ohio 7,727 B5 156
North Cape, Racine, Wis. 200 F1 160
North Carolina, state, U.S. 4,556,155 D11 77, 186
Northcarrollton, Carroll, Miss. 521 B3 184
North Carver, Plymouth, Mass. 360 C6 206
North Catasauqua, Northampton, Pa. 2,805 *C6 214
North Charleroi, Washington, Pa. 2,259 *C2 214
North Charleston, Charleston, S.C. 22,339 F9 188, F3
North Charlestown, Sullivan, N.H. 75 E2 208
North Chatham, Barnstable, Mass. 200 *C8 206
North Chelmsford, Middlesex, Mass. 3,500 A5 206
North Chicago, Lake, Ill. 20,517 A6 138, E2
North Chili, Monroe, N.Y. 2,000 *B4 212
North Chillicothe, Peoria, Ill. 2,259 C4 138
North City, King, Wash. 2,000 *B4 98
North Clarendon, Rutland, Vt. 200 D3 218
North Cohasset, Norfolk, Mass. 150 D4 206
North College Hill, Hamilton, Ohio 12,035 D1 156
North Collins, Erie, N.Y. 1,574 C3 212
North Conway, Carroll, N.H. 1,104 C4 208
North Corbin, Laurel, Ky. 950 *C6 178
Northcote, N.Z. 3,777 H9 437
North Creede, Mineral, Colo. 2 E4 106
North Creek, Warren, N.Y. 703 B8 212
Northcrest, Del Norte, Calif. 1,945 *B1 94
North Crossett, Ashley, Ark. 950 D5 170
North Crows Nest, Marion, Ind. 60 *C3 140
North Dakota, state, U.S. 632,446 B6 77, 154
North Danville, Caledonia, Vt. 80 C4 218
North Dartmouth, Bristol, Mass. 4,000 C6 206
North Decatur, De Kalb, Ga. 10,000 *C2 176
North Derby, Orleans, Vt. 81 A4 218
North Dighton, Bristol, Mass. 1,167 C5 206
North Dixmont, Penobscot, Maine 100 D3 204
North Downs, hills, Eng. J13 273
North Druid Hills, De Kalb, Ga. 4,000 *C2 176
North East, Cecil, Md. 1,628 A8 182
North East, Erie, Pa. 4,217 A2 214
North East, is., Truk A3 436
Northeast, pass, La. E6 180
Northeast, pond, N.H. E5 208
Northeast, riv., Md. B8 182
Northeast Cape Fear, riv., N.C. C8 186
North East Carry, Piscataquis, Maine 9 C3 204
Northeast Foreland, reg., Grnld. O34 290
North Eastham, Barnstable, Mass. 200 C8 206
Northeast Harbor, Hancock, Maine 750 D4 204
North Easton, Bristol, Mass. 4,000 B5 206

North Edmonton, Alta., Can. 1,200 D6 54
North Egremont, Berkshire, Mass. 170 B1 206
Northeim, Ger. 19,400 C3 286
North Ellsworth, Hancock, Maine D4 204
North Englewood, Prince Georges, Md. 380 *C6 182
North English, Iowa, Iowa 1,004 C5 142
North Enid, Garfield, Okla. 286 B6 128
Northern, Clay, Kans. 20 *C6 144
Northern, dist., Isr. 302,245 *B6 382
Northern, prov., Ken. B6 414
Northern (N.Rh.), prov., Rh.&Nya. B6 421
Northern (Nya.), prov., Rh.&Nya. B6 421
Northern, prov., Sud. 873,059 B2 398
Northern, prov., Tan. 771,426 C6 414
Northern, prov., Ug. B5 414
Northern, reg., Nig. 16,840,479 D6 408
Northern, reg., Nor. 407,351 *B10 290
Northern, head, N.B., Can. E3 70
Northern Bight, Newf., Can. 40 F8 72
Northern Dvina, riv., Sov.Un. C6 328
Northern Indian, lake, Man., Can. B4 60
Northern Ireland, reg., United Kingdom 1,384,100 G6 272
Northern Region, ter., Ghana D4 408
Northern Rhodesia, prot., Rh.&Nya. 2,108,000 C5 420
Northern Sporades, is., Grc. B5 306
Northern Territory, ter., Austl. 19,170 B6 432
North Etowah, McMinn, Tenn. 200 C7 190
North Fairfield, Huron, Ohio 547 A4 156
North Falmouth, Barnstable, Mass. 500 C6 206
North Fayette, Kennebec, Maine 220 D2 204
North Ferrisburg, Addison, Vt. 200 C2 218
Northfield, B.C., Can. 150 B13 52
Northfield, Litchfield, Conn. 350 C3 202
Northfield, Cook, Ill. 4,005 E3 138
Northfield, Washington, Maine 50 D5 204 (79▲)
Northfield, Franklin, Mass. 1,179 A3 206 (2,320▲)
Northfield, Rice, Minn. 8,707 G5 148
Northfield, Merrimack, N.H. 1,243 E3 208 (1,784▲)
Northfield, Atlantic, N.J. 5,849 E3 210
Northfield (Northfield Center), Summit, Ohio 2,427 *A5 156
Northfield, Summit, Ohio 1,055 B1 156
Northfield, Washington, Vt. 2,159 C3 218 (4,511▲)
Northfield, Jackson, Wis. 50 D2 160
Northfield, mts., Vt. C3 218
Northfield Center, Washington, Vt. 100 C3 218
Northfield Falls, Washington, Vt. 325 C3 218
North Fond du Lac, Fond du Lac, Wis. 2,549 B5 E5 160
Northford, New Haven, Conn. 300 D4 202
North Foreland, cape, Eng. J14 273
North Fork, Madera, Calif. 200 D4 94
North Fork, Lemhi, Idaho 30 D5 108
Northfork, McDowell, W.Va. 798 *D3 194
North Fox, isl., Mich. D6 146
North Franklin, New London, Conn. 202 C7 202
North Freedom, Sauk, Wis. 579 E4 160
North Frisian, is., Den. I3 291
North Frisian, is., Ger. A2 286
North Fryeburg, Oxford, Maine 150 D2 204
North Galiano, B.C., Can. 20 C14 52
North Gamboa, Can.Z. 3,074 F8 228
Northgate, Sask., Can. 30 F6 58
Northgate, Burke, N.Dak. 65 B3 154
North Girard, see Lake City, Pa.
North Gorham, Cumberland, Maine 100 E4 204
North Gower, Ont., Can. 500 O25 64
North Grafton, Worcester, Mass. 2,600 B4 206
North Granby, Hartford, Conn. 200 B4 202
North Great River, Suffolk, N.Y. 1,500 *E3 212
North Grosvenor Dale, Windham, Conn. 1,874 B8 202
North Grove, Miami, Ind. 127 *B4 140
North Gulfport, Harrison, Miss. 3,323 *E3 184
North Hadley, Hampshire, Mass. 300 *B2 206
North Haledon, Passaic, N.J. 6,026 A1 210
North Hampton, Rockingham, N.H. 678 F5 208 (1,910▲)
North Hampton, Clark, Ohio 495 C3 156
North Hanover, Plymouth, Mass. 300 E3 206
North Harpswell, Cumberland, Maine 80 E5 204
North Hartland, Windsor, Vt. 150 D4 218
North Hartsville, Darlington, S.C. 1,899 *C8 188
North Harwich, Barnstable, Mass. 220 *C7 206
North Hatfield, Hampshire, Mass. 450 B2 206
North Hatley, Que., Can. 671 S13 66
North Haven, New Haven, Conn. 15,935 D4 202
North Haven, Knox, Maine 330 D4 204 (384▲)
North Haven, Suffolk, N.Y. 450 D5 212
North Haverhill, Grafton, N.H. 300 C2 208
North Havre, Hill, Mont. 1,168 *B7 110
North Head, N.B., Can. 790 E3 70
North Henderson, Mercer, Ill. 210 B3 138
North Henderson, Vance, N.C. 1,995 *A7 186
North Hero, Grand Isle, Vt. 50 B2 218 (328▲)
North Highlands, Sacramento, Calif. 21,271 *C3 94
North Highlands, Caddo, La. 900 *B2 180
North High Shoals, Oconee, Ga. 122 *C3 176
North Hills, New Castle, Del. 400 *B3 172
North Hodge, Jackson, La. 680 B3 180
North Holtson, Smyth, Va. 200 D3 192
North Horn, lake, Tenn. E6 190
North Horr, Ken. B6 414
North Hudson, St. Croix, Wis. 1,019 *C1 160
North Hyde Park, Lamoille, Vt. 230 B3 218
North Industry, Stark, Ohio 1,800 B5 156
North Irwin, Westmoreland, Pa. 1,143 *C2 214
North Island, reg., N.Z. 1,497,364 B4 437
North Isleboro, Waldo, Maine 50 D4 204
North Jackson, Mahoning, Ohio 402 A6 156
North Jay, Franklin, Maine 500 D2 204
North Judson, Starke, Ind. 1,942 A3 140
North Kamloops, B.C., Can. 4,398 E12 52
North Kansas City, Clay, Mo. 5,657 B3 E2 150
North Kennebunkport, York, Maine E2 204
North Kingstown (Town of), Washington, R.I. (18,977▲) C3 216
North Kingsville, Ashtabula, Ohio 1,854 A6 156
North Kvaloy, isl., Nor. A8 290
North La Junta, Otero, Colo. 950 D7 106
Northlake, Cook, Ill. 12,318 *B6 138
North Lake, Marquette, Mich. 400 C4 146
North Lake, Waukesha, Wis. 300 E1 160
North Lakhimpur, India D6 368
North Lancaster, Worcester, Mass. 250 *B4 206
Northland, Marquette, Mich. 45 C4 146
North Laramie, riv., Wyo. D7 116
North Larchmont, Westchester, N.Y. 9,000 *D8 212
North Las Vegas, Clark, Nev. 18,422 G6 112
North Laurel, Sussex, Del. F3 172
North Lawrence, St. Lawrence, N.Y. 400 A7 212
North Leominster, Worcester, Mass. A4 206
North Lewisburg, Champaign, Ohio 879 B3 156
North Liberty, St. Joseph, Ind. 1,241 A3 140
North Liberty, Johnson, Iowa 334 C6 142
North Lilbourn, New Madrid, Mo. 301 *E8 150
North Lima, Allen, Ohio 600 B2 156
North Lima, Mahoning, Ohio 350 B6 156
North Lindenhurst, Suffolk, N.Y. 10,000 *E3 212
North Linkhorn Park, Princess Anne, Va. 300 *D8 192
North Little Rock, Pulaski, Ark. 58,032 C4 D7 170
North Littleton, Middlesex, Mass. 150 *C1 206
North Logan, Cache, Utah 741 *B4 114
North Loup, Valley, Nebr. 453 C7 152
North Loup, riv., Nebr. B5 152
North Lovell, Oxford, Maine 70 D2 204
North Lubec, Washington, Maine 250 D5 204
North Magnetic Pole, N.W.Ter., Can. C8 48
North Mam, peak, Colo. C3 106
North Manchester, Wabash, Ind. 4,377 B4 140
North Manitou, isl., Mich. D5 146
North Mankato, Nicollet, Minn. 5,927 G4 148
North Marshfield, Plymouth, Mass. 130 E4 206
North Matewan, Mingo, W.Va. 900 *D2 194
North Merrick, Nassau, N.Y. 12,976 *E8 212
North Miami, Dade, Fla. 28,708 E6 F10 174
North Miami, Ottawa, Okla. 472 B9 128
North Miami Beach, Dade, Fla. 21,405 E6 174
North Middleboro, Plymouth, Mass. 400 *C6 206
North Middletown, Bourbon, Ky. 291 B6 178
North Monmouth, Kennebec, Maine 300 D2 204
North Monson, Hampden, Mass. 400 B3 206
North Montpelier, Washington, Vt. 140 C4 218
Northmoor, Platte, Mo. 696 E2 150
North Mullins, Marion, S.C. (part of Mullins) C10 188
North Muskegon, Muskegon, Mich. 3,855 F5 146
North New Castle, Lincoln, Maine D3 204
North New Hyde Park, Nassau, N.Y. 9,930 *E8 212
North Newport, Penobscot, Maine D3 204
North Newport, Sullivan, N.H. 100 E2 208
North New Portland, Somerset, Maine 300 D2 204
North New River, canal, Fla. E10 174
North Newton, Harvey, Kans. 890 *D6 144
North Norway, Oxford, Maine 100 D2 204
North Oaks, Ramsey, Minn. 803 *F5 148
North Ogden, Weber, Utah 2,621 B4 114
North Olmsted, Cuyahoga, Ohio 16,290 B1 156
Northome, Koochiching, Minn. 291 D4 148
North Orange, Franklin, Mass. 100 A3 206
North Oxford, Worcester, Mass. 1,466 B4 206
North Palm Beach, Palm Beach, Fla. 2,684 *E10 174
North Parsonfield, York, Maine 100 E2 204
North Patchogue, Suffolk, N.Y. 8,000 *D4 212
North Pekin, Tazewell, Ill. 2,025 C4 138
North Pelham, Westchester, N.Y. 5,326 *D8 212
North Pembroke, Plymouth, Mass. 250 *B6 206
North Penobscot, Hancock, Maine 125 D4 204
North Perry, Washington, Maine 100 C5 204
North Perry, Lake, Ohio 658 *A5 156
North Plainfield, Somerset, N.J. 16,992 B4 210
North Plains, Washington, Oreg. 500 A1 B3 96
North Platte, Lincoln, Nebr. 17,184 C5 152
North Platte, riv., Nebr., Wyo. C3 D7 152 116
North Pleasanton, Atascosa, Tex. 1,018 *E6 130
North Pleasureville, Henry, Ky. 313 *B5 178
North Plymouth, Plymouth, Mass. (part of Plymouth) C6 206
North Pocatello, Bannock, Idaho (part of Alameda) G6 108
North Pole, Alsk. 615 *C7 84
North Pole, mtn., Idaho D3 108
Northport, Tuscaloosa, Ala. 5,245 B2 168
Northport, Waldo, Maine 100 D4 204 (648▲)
Northport, Leelanau, Mich. 530 D6 146
Northport, Morrill, Nebr. 110 C2 152
Northport, Suffolk, N.Y. 5,972 D3 212
Northport, Stevens, Wash. 482 A9 98
Northport, Waupaca, Wis. 250 D5 160
North Portal, Sask., Can. 253 F6 58
North Port Charlotte, Sarasota, Fla. 178 *E8 174
North Powder, Union, Oreg. 399 B9 96
North Pownal, Cumberland, Maine 55 E5 204
North Pownal, Bennington, Vt. 275 F2 218
North Prairie, Waukesha, Wis. 489 F5 160
North Princeton, Mercer, N.J. 4,506 *C3 210
North Providence, Providence, R.I. 18,220 B3 216
North Pulaski, Pulaski, Va. 1,156 *C4 192
North Puyallup, Pierce, Wash. 650 *B4 98
North Quincy, Adams, Ill. 2,256 *D2 138
North Randall, Cuyahoga, Ohio 688 *A5 156
North Ravenswood, Jackson, W.Va. C3 194
North Reading, Middlesex, Mass. 8,331 C3 206
North Redington Beach, Pinellas, Fla. 346 *C8 174
North Redwood, Redwood, Minn. 179 G3 148
North Richland Hills, Tarrant, Tex. 8,662 *C7 130
North Ridgeville, Lorain, Ohio 825 A4 B1 156
North Riverside, Cook, Ill. 7,989 *B6 138
North Rockville Centre, Nassau, N.Y. 1,500 *D4 212
North Ronaldsay, isl., Scot. B10 272
Northrop, Martin, Minn. 189 H4 148
North Rose, Wayne, N.Y. 462 B5 212
North Royalton, Cuyahoga, Ohio 9,290 B1 156
North Rustico, P.E.I., Can. 814 C6 70
North Sacramento, Sacramento, Calif. 12,922 *C3 94
North St. Paul, Ramsey, Minn. 8,520 F7 148
North Salem, Hendricks, Ind. 626 C3 140
North Salem, Rockingham, N.H. 400 F4 208
North Salt Lake, Davis, Utah 1,655 C4 114
North Santee, riv., S.C. E10 188
North Saskatchewan, riv., Alta., Sask., Can. D7 D4 54 58
North Scarboro, Cumberland, Maine 75 E2 E4 204
North Scituate, Plymouth, Mass. 3,421 D4 206
North Scituate, Providence, R.I. 500 B2 216
North Seaford, Nassau, N.Y. 3,000 *E8 212
North Searsmont, Waldo, Maine 50 D3 204
North Seekonk, Bristol, Mass. 800 *C5 206
North Shreveport, Caddo, La. 7,701 *B2 180
North Side, Marion, Oreg. 200 *B4 96
North Sioux City, Union, S.Dak. 736 E9 158
North Sister, mtn., Oreg. C5 96
North Slidell, Saint Tammany, La. (part of Slidell) B8 180
North Smithfield (Town of), Providence, R.I. (7,632▲) B2 216
North Springfield, Windsor, Vt. 600 E3 218
North Springfield, Fairfax, Va. 5,000 *B7 192
Northstar, Gratiot, Mich. 200 F7 146
North Stonington, New London, Conn. 800 D8 202 (1,982▲)
North Stradbroke, isl., Austl. D10 432
North Stratford, Coos, N.H. 600 *B3 208
North Street, St. Clair, Mich. 50 F9 146
North Sudbury, Middlesex, Mass. 250 C1 206
North Sunderland, Eng. F11 272
North Sutton, Merrimack, N.H. 160 E3 208
North Swansea, Bristol, Mass. 150 C5 206
North Swanzey, Cheshire, N.H. 800 *F2 208
North Sydney, N.S., Can. 8,125 C9 70
North Syracuse, Onondaga, N.Y. 7,412 B5 212
North Taranaki, bight, N.Z. C5 437
North Tarrytown, Westchester, N.Y. 8,818 D8 212
North Tazewell, Tazewell, Va. 713 C3 192
North Terre Haute, Vigo, Ind. 1,100 C2 140
North Thetford, Orange, Vt. 100 D4 218
North Thompson, riv., B.C., Can. E13 52
North Tisbury, Dukes, Mass. 130 *D6 206
North Tiverton, Newport, R.I. 2,800 C4 216
North Tonawanda, Niagara, N.Y. 34,757 B3 212
North Troy, Orleans, Vt. 961 B4 218
North Truro, Barnstable, Mass. 250 B7 206
North Tunica, Tunica, Miss. 1,025 *A2 184
North Turlock, Stanislaus, Calif. 2,535 *D3 94
North Turner, mtn., Maine C4 204
North Twin, lake, Newf., Can. F7 72
North Twin, lake, Wis. B4 160
North Uist, isl., Scot. D5 272
Northumberland, Coos, N.H. 100 B3 208 (2,586▲)
Northumberland, Northumberland, Pa. 4,156 C5 214
Northumberland, co., N.B., Can. 47,223 B3 70
Northumberland, co., Ont., Can. 38,018 P22 64
Northumberland, co., Eng. 804,600 F10 272
Northumberland, co., Pa. 104,138 B5 214
Northumberland, co., Va. 10,185 C8 192
Northumberland, isl., Austl. C10 432
Northumberland, strait, Can. C5 70
North Umpqua, riv., Oreg. D4 96
North Uxbridge, Worcester, Mass. 1,882 B4 206
Northvale, Bergen, N.J. 2,892 A5 210
North Valley Stream, Nassau, N.Y. 5,000 *E8 212
North Vancouver, B.C., Can. 19,951 B15 F11 52
North Vandergrift, Armstrong, Pa. 1,827 *C2 214
North Vassalboro, Kennebec, Maine 778 D3 204
North Vernon, Jennings, Ind. 4,062 C4 140
Northview, Webster, Mo. 200 D4 150
Northville, Litchfield, Conn. 155 C2 202
Northville, Wayne, Mich. 3,967 B7 146
Northville, Fulton, N.Y. 1,156 B7 212
Northville, Spink, S.Dak. 153 B7 158
North Virginia Beach, Princess Anne, Va. 2,587 A8 D8 192
North Wabiskaw, lake, Alta., Can. B6 54
North Waldoboro, Lincoln, Maine 262 D3 204
North Wales, Montgomery, Pa. 3,673 C6 214
North Walpole, Cheshire, N.H. 950 E2 208
North Walsham, Eng. 4,800 I14 273
North Warren, Knox, Maine 75 D3 204
North Warren, Warren, Pa. 1,458 B2 214
North Washington, Chickasaw, Iowa 156 A5 142
North Waterford, Oxford, Maine 300 D2 204
Northway, Alsk. 196 C7 84
North Weare, Hillsboro, N.H. E3 208
North Webster, Kosciusko, Ind. 494 A4 140
North West, cape, Austl. C2 432
Northwest, pt., Newf., Can. D6 72
North Western, prov., Rh. & Nya. B4 420
Northwest Hardeeville, Jasper, S.C. 200 *G6 188
North Westminster, Windham, Vt. 368 E4 218
North West Miramichi, riv., N.B., Can. B3 70
Northwest Park Apartments, Montgomery, Md. 3,000 *C5 182
North Westport, Bristol, Mass. 3,000 C5 206
North West River, Newf., Can. 400 D6 E9 72
Northwest Territories, ter., Can. 21,000 D8 48
North Weymouth, Norfolk, Mass. D3 206
Northwich, Eng. 19,500 H10 273
North Wichita, Sedgwick, Kans. A5 144
North Wilbraham, Hampden, Mass. 2,000 B3 206
North Wildwood, Cape May, N.J. 3,598 E3 210
North Wilkesboro, Wilkes, N.C. 4,197 A4 186
North Wilmington, Middlesex, Mass. 900 C2 206
North Windham, Windham, Conn. 250 C7 202
North Windham, Cumberland, Maine 900 E2 E4 204
North Woburn Junction, Middlesex, Mass. C2 206
Northwood, Worth, Iowa 1,768 A4 142
Northwood, Kalamazoo, Mich. 3,000 *G6 146
Northwood, Rockingham, N.H. 150 E4 208 (1,034▲)
Northwood, Grand Forks, N.Dak. 1,195 C8 154
North Woodbury, Litchfield, Conn. 150 C3 202
Northwood Center, Rockingham, N.H. 120 E4 208
Northwood Narrows, Rockingham, N.H. 200 E4 208
Northwood Ridge, Rockingham, N.H. 125 E4 208
Northwoods, De Kalb, Ga. 1,000 *C2 176
Northwoods, St. Louis, Mo. 4,701 *C7 150
North Woodstock, Windham, Conn. 350 B8 202
North Woodstock, Grafton, N.H. 600 C3 208
North Worcester, Worcester, Mass. B4 206
Northwye, Phelps, Mo. 183 *D6 150
North Yarmouth, Cumberland, Maine 150 E5 204 (1,140▲)
North York, York, Pa. 2,290 D5 214
North York, moors, Eng. G12 273
Norton, N.B., Can. 530 D4 70
Norton, Eng. 4,800 G12 273
Norton, Norton, Kans. 3,345 C4 144
Norton, Bristol, Mass. 1,501 C5 206 (6,818▲)
Norton, Rh. & Nya. C6 421
Norton, Essex, Vt. 100 A5 218 (241▲)
Norton (Independent City), Va. 4,996 D2 192
Norton, Randolph, W.Va. 600 C5 194
Norton, co., Kans. 8,035 C3 144
Norton, bay, Alsk. C5 84
Norton, pond, Vt. B5 218
Norton, sound, Alsk. C5 84
Norton Grove, Bristol, Mass. 500 *C5 206
Nortonville, Jefferson, Kans. 595 C8 144
Nortonville, Hopkins, Ky. 755 C3 178
Nortonville, La Moure, N.Dak. 105 D7 154
Norvell, Crittenden, Ark. 362 B6 170
Norvello, Mecklenburg, Va. 75 D6 192
Norvelt, Westmoreland, Pa. 1,211 *C2 214
Norwalk, Los Angeles, Calif. 88,739 C5 F4 94
Norwalk, Fairfield, Conn. 67,775 E2 202

Oakwood (Oakwood Village), Cuyahoga, Ohio	3,283	B1	156
Oakwood (Far Hills), Montgomery, Ohio	10,493	C2	156
Oakwood, Paulding, Ohio	686	A2	156
Oakwood, Dewey, Okla.	122	C5	128
Oakwood, Leon, Tex.	716	D8	130
Oakwood, Buchanan, Va.	250	C3	192
Oakwood, Milwaukee, Wis. (part of Oak Creek)		F2	160
Oakwood College, Madison, Ala.	400	*A3	168
Oamaru, N.Z.	9,801	F3	437
Ōami, Jap.	24,933	L16	354
Oa Mull, head, Scot.		F6	272
Oark, Johnson, Ark.	100	*B3	170
Oasis, Elko, Nev.	12	B7	112
Oasis, Millard, Utah	102	D3	114
Oasis, dept., Alg.		C5	402
Oatman, Mohave, Ariz.	60	C1	124
Oats, Darlington, S.C.	125	C8	188
Oatville, Sedgwick, Kans.	5	B5	144
Oaxaca, Mex.	46,741	D6	225
Oaxaca, state, Mex.	1,421,313	D6	225
Ob, bay, Sov.Un.		C9	328
Ob, riv., Sov.Un.		C8	328
Obadiah, Lauderdale, Miss.	125	C4	184
Obama, Jap.	38,058	L11	354
Oban, see Half-moon Bay, N.Z.			
O'Bannon, Jefferson, Ky.	300	A5	178
Oban Station, Sask., Can.	35	D3	58
Obbia, Som.	1,700	D6	398
Obed, Alta., Can.		D4	54
Obed, riv., Tenn.		B7	190
Obeh, Afg.		B2	374
Oberammergau, Ger.	4,800	*E4	286
Oberdrauburg, Aus.	785	D4	313
Oberhausen, Ger.	239,100	C2	286
Oberlin, Decatur, Kans.	2,337	C3	144
Oberlin, Allen, La.	1,794	D3	180
Oberlin, Lorain, Ohio	8,198	A4	156
Oberlin, Bryan, Okla.		E8	128
Oberlin, Dauphin, Pa.	2,500	*C5	214
Obernai, Fr.	4,389	C7	278
Oberon, Benson, N.Dak.	248	C6	154
Oberösterreich (Upper Austria), state, Aus.	1,108,720	*B5	313
Oberstdorf, Ger.	8,200	E4	286
Obert, Cedar, Nebr.	42	B8	152
Oberwald, Switz.	321	B4	312
Obetz, Franklin, Ohio	1,984	C1	156
		C4	
Obi, is., Indon.		E7	359
Obi, is., Viet.		E5	362
Obidos, Braz.	3,419	F5	256
Obihiro, Jap.	70,027	C9	354
Obion, Obion, Tenn.	1,097	B2	190
Obion, co., Tenn.	26,957	B2	190
Obion, creek, Ky.		D2	178
Obion, riv., Tenn.		B2	190
Oblong, Crawford, Ill.	1,817	E6	138
Obluchye, Sov.Un.	15,000	E15	329
Obo, Cen.Afr.Rep.		E10	409
Obock, Fr.Som.	250	C5	398
Obong, mtn., Sar.		D5	358
Oborniki, Pol.	5,266	B3	325
Öbör Sumun, Mong.		B8	346
Oboyan, Sov.Un.	15,000	G11	332
O'Brien, Suwannee, Fla.	300	A8	174
O'Brien, Miami, Kans.	25	*D8	144
O'Brien, Josephine, Oreg.	325	E3	96
O'Brien, co., Iowa	18,840	A2	142
Observation, isl., Fla.		E10	174
Observation, peak, Calif.		B3	94
Observation, peak, Oreg.		E4	96
Obsidian, Custer, Idaho	5	E4	108
Obuasi, Ghana	15,876	E4	408
Obubra, Nig.		E6	409
Obwalden (Obwald), subcanton, Switz.	22,800	*B4	312
Ocala, Marion, Fla.	13,598	B8	174
Ocampo, Arg.		A4	252
Ocampo, Mex.	373	B4	224
Ocaña, Col.	15,214	B2	244
Ocaña, Sp.	6,864	C5	298
Occoquan, Prince William, Va.	301	B7	192
Ocean, co., N.J.	108,241	D4	210
Oceana, Princess Anne, Va.	2,448	A9	192
Oceana, Wyoming, W.Va.	1,303	D3	194
Oceana, co., Mich.	16,547	F5	146
Ocean Bluff, Plymouth, Mass.	100	B6	206
		E4	
Ocean City, Worcester, Md.	983	D9	182
Ocean City, Cape May, N.J.	7,618	E3	210
Ocean Drive Beach, Horry, S.C.	313	D11	188
Ocean Falls, B.C., Can.	2,400	D9	52
Ocean Gate, Ocean, N.J.	706	D4	210
Ocean Grove, Bristol, Mass.	1,200	C5	206
Ocean Grove, Monmouth, N.J.	5,000	C4	210
Oceanlake, Lincoln, Oreg.	1,342	C2	96
Oceano, San Luis Obispo, Calif.	1,317	E3	94
Ocean Park, Pacific, Wash.	750	C2	98
Oceanport, Monmouth, N.J.	4,937	C4	210
Ocean Ridge, Palm Beach, Fla.	209	*E10	174
Oceanside, San Diego, Calif.	24,971	F5	94
Oceanside, Nassau, N.Y.	30,448	E3	212
Oceanside, Tillamook, Oreg.	225	*B3	96
Ocean Springs, Jackson, Miss.	5,025	E2	184
		E4	
Ocean View, Sussex, Del.	422	F5	172
Ocean View, Cape May, N.J.	150	E3	210
Oceanville, Atlantic, N.J.	500	E4	210
Oceanway, Duval, Fla.	1,271	A9	174
		A10	
Ochakov, Sov.Un.	13,000	I8	332
Ochamchire, Sov.Un.	15,000	E6	328
Ocheda, lake, Minn.		H3	148
Ochelata, Washington, Okla.	312	B7	128
Ocheltree, Johnson, Kans.	100	D9	144
Ocheyedan, Osceola, Iowa	662	*A2	142
Ocheyedan, riv., Iowa		A2	142
Ochil, hills, Scot.		E9	272
Ochiltree, co., Tex.	9,380	A5	130
Ochina, riv., China		C8	346
Ochlochnee, Thomas, Ga.	502	F2	176
Ochlockonee, riv., Fla., Ga.		A6	174
		F2	176
Ochoco, res., Oreg.		C6	96
Ochopee, Collier, Fla.	300	F9	174
Ochre River, Man., Can.	315	E3	60
Ocilla, Irwin, Ga.	3,217	E3	176
Ocmulgee, natl. mon., Ga.		D3	176
Ocmulgee, riv., Ga.		D3	176
Ocna Sibiului, Rom.	3,752	B3	321
Ocnele Mari, Rom.	4,420	B3	321
Ocoee, Orange, Fla.	2,628	C9	174
Ocoee, Polk, Tenn.	300	C7	190
Ocoee, lake, Tenn.		C7	190
Ocoña, Peru	932	D3	245
Oconee, Washington, Ga.	500	D4	176
Oconee, co., Ga.	6,304	C3	176
Oconee, co., S.C.	40,204	B2	188
Oconee, riv., Ga.		D4	176
Oconomowoc, Waukesha, Wis.	6,682	E5	160
Oconomowoc Lake, Waukesha, Wis.	414	*E5	160
Oconto, Custer, Nebr.	219	C6	152
Oconto, Oconto, Wis.	4,805	D6	160
Oconto, co., Wis.	25,110	D5	160
Oconto, riv., Wis.		D5	160
Oconto Falls, Oconto, Wis.	2,331	D5	160
Ocós, Guat.	340	C1	228
Ocotal, Nic.	2,672	D4	228
Ocotepeque, Hond.	4,170	C3	228
Ocotillo, Maricopa, Ariz.	250	H2	124
Ocotlán, Mex.	16,853	C5	224
		K12	
Ocracoke, Hyde, N.C.	600	B10	186
Ocracoke, inlet, N.C.		B9	186
Ocracoke, isl., N.C.		B10	186
Ocros, Peru	1,321	C2	245
Octagon, Marengo, Ala.		C2	168
Octavia, Butler, Nebr.	94	*C8	152
Octavia, Le Flore, Okla.	25	D9	128
Octoraro, creek, Pa.		D5	214
Ocumare del Tuy, Ven.	9,549	A5	240
Ocussi, reg., Port. Timor		F6	358
Oda, Ghana	8,374	E4	408
Odanah, Ashland, Wis.	300	B3	160
Odawara, Jap.	113,099	G7	354
		L15	
Odda, Nor.	8,983	F2	291
Oddur, Som.	2,600	E5	398
Odebolt, Sac, Iowa	1,331	B2	142
Odei, riv., Man., Can.		B4	60
Odell, Livingston, Ill.	936	B5	138
Odell, Gage, Nebr.	358	D9	152
Odell, McCurtain, Okla.		E9	128
Odell, Hood River, Oreg.	350	*B5	96
Odell, Kanawha, W.Va.		C6	194
Odell, lake, Oreg.		D5	96
Odem, San Patricio, Tex.	2,088	F7	130
Odemira, Port.	2,266	D2	298
Ödemiş, Tur.	25,560	B2	307
Oden, Montgomery, Ark.	90	C3	170
Odendaalsrus, U.S.Afr.	11,009	E5	420
Odense, Den.	104,344 (*116,200)	F1	292
Odense, co., Den.	196,213	*I4	291
Odenton, Anne Arundel, Md.	1,914	B6	182
Odenville, St. Clair, Ala.	300	B3	168
Odenwald, mts., Ger.		D3	286
Oder, riv., Ger.		B6	286
Ödeshög, Swe.	4,587	C5	292
Odessa, Ont., Can.	590	P24	64
Odessa, Sask., Can.	252	E6	58
Odessa, New Castle, Del.	526	C3	172
Odessa, Pasco, Fla.	150	C8	174
Odessa, Big Stone, Minn.	234	F2	148
Odessa, Lafayette, Mo.	2,034	C4	150
Odessa, Buffalo, Nebr.	150	D6	152
Odessa, Schuyler, N.Y.	573	C5	212
Odessa, Sov.Un.	667,000	I8	332
Odessa, Ector, Tex.	80,338	D4	130
Odessa, Lincoln, Wash.	1,231	B8	98
Odessadale, Meriwether, Ga.	142	*C2	176
Odiel, riv., Sp.		D3	298
Odienné, I.C.	6,500	E3	408
Odin, Marion, Ill.	1,242	E4	138
Odin, Barton, Kans.	150	D5	144
Odin, Watonwan, Minn.	184	H4	148
Odin, mtn., B.C., Can.		E13	52
Odobeşti, Rom.	4,977	B4	321
Odon, Daviess, Ind.	1,192	D3	140
O'Donnell, Lynn and Dawson, Tex.	1,356	C5	130
Odorhei, Rom.	14,162	A3	321
Odra (Oder), riv., Pol.		B2	325
Odum, Wayne, Ga.	404	E4	176
Odweina, Som.		D6	398
Odzi, Rh.&Nya.		C6	421
Oeiras, Braz.	3,748	B2	258
Oella, Baltimore, Md.	860	B6	182
Oelrichs, Fall River, S.Dak.	132	D2	158
Oels, see Oleśnica, Pol.			
Oelsnitz [im Erzgebirge], Ger.	17,100	C5	286
Oelsnitz [im Vogtland], Ger.	20,100	C5	286
Oelwein, Fayette, Iowa	8,282	B6	142
Oeyŏn, isl., Kor.		G13	348
Ofahoma, Leake, Miss.	300	C3	184
O'Fallon, St. Clair, Ill.	4,018	E4	138
O'Fallon, St. Charles, Mo.	3,770	C7	150
O'Fallon, creek, Mont.		D12	110
Ofanto, riv., It.		E5	302
Offaly, co., Ire.	51,970	H5	273
Offenbach [am Main], Ger.	104,400	C3	286
Offenburg, Ger.	27,300	D2	286
Offerle, Edwards, Kans.	208	E4	144
Offerman, Pierce, Ga.	483	E4	176
Ofotfjord, fjord, Nor.		B7	290
Ōfunato, Jap.	33,715	E8	354
Oga (Funakawa), Jap.	48,563	E7	354
Oga, pen., Jap.		E7	354
Ōgaki, Jap.	94,128	G6	354
		L12	
Ogallah, Trego, Kans.	251	D4	144
Ogallala, Keith, Nebr.	4,250	C4	152
Ogasawara Islands (Bonin), U.S. occ. area, Pac.O.	7,361	B3	436
Ogasawara (Bonin Is.), is., Pac.O.		B3	436
Ogbomosho, Nig.	139,535	E5	408
Ogburntown, Forsyth, N.C. (part of Winston-Salem)		A5	186
Ogden, Little River, Ark.	282	D2	170
Ogden, Champaign, Ill.	515	C6	138
Ogden, Boone, Iowa	1,525	B3	142
Ogden, Riley, Kans.	1,780	C7	144
Ogden, Delaware, Pa.	1,600	*D6	214
Ogden, Weber, Utah	70,197 (*141,400)	B4	114
Ogden Dunes, Porter, Ind.	947	A2	140
Ogdensburg, Sussex, N.J.	1,212	A3	210
Ogdensburg, St. Lawrence, N.Y.	16,122	A6	212
Ogdensburg, Waupaca, Wis.	181	*D5	160
Ogeechee, riv., Ga.		D5	176
Ogema, Sask., Can.	455	F5	58
Ogema, Becker, Minn.	224	D3	148
Ogema, Price, Wis.	250	C3	160
Ogemaw, Ouachita, Ark.	125	D3	170
Ogemaw, co., Mich.	9,680	E7	146
Ogilvie, Kanabec, Minn.	376	F5	148
Ogilvie, range, Yukon, Can.		E5	48
Oglala, Shannon, S.Dak.	45	D3	158
Ogle, co., Ill.	38,106	A4	138
Oglesby, La Salle, Ill.	4,215	B4	138
Oglesby, Washington, Okla.	80	B8	128
Oglesby, Davidson, Tenn.	50	E7	190
Oglethorpe, Macon, Ga.	1,169	D2	176
Oglethorpe, co., Ga.	7,926	C3	176
Ogletown, New Castle, Del.	2,500	*B3	172
Oglio, riv., It.		C3	302
Ogoamas, mtn., Indon.		D6	358
Ogoja, Nig.		E6	409
Ogoki, Ont., Can.		R24	64
Ogoki, riv., Ont., Can.		R24	64
Ogontz, Somerset, Maine	30	C3	204
Ogooué, riv., Gabon		G7	409
Ogosta, riv., Bul.		B1	317
Ogulin, Yugo.	2,232	B2	316
Ogunquit, York, Maine	800	E2	204
Ogur, Ice.		K18	290
Ohakune, N.Z.	1,626	C5	437
Ōhara, Jap.	25,579	L16	354
Ohatchee, Calhoun, Ala.	437	B3	168
Ohaton, Alta., Can.	53	D6	54
Ohau, bay, N.Z.		J10	437
Ohau, pt., N.Z.		J10	437
O'Higgins, prov., Chile	224,593	D3	250
Ohio, Gunnison, Colo.	35	D4	106
Ohio, Bureau, Ill.	489	B4	138
Ohio, co., Ind.	4,165	D5	140
Ohio, co., Ky.	17,725	C3	178
Ohio, co., W.Va.	68,437	A4	194
Ohio, state, U.S.	9,706,397	C10	77
			156
Ohio, caverns, Ohio		B3	156
Ohio, peak, Colo.		D3	106
Ohio, riv., U.S.		D9	77
Ohio Brush, creek, Ohio		D3	156
Ohio Camp, Toole, Mont.	45	*B5	110
Ohio City, Van Wert, Ohio	851	B2	156
Ohiowa, Fillmore, Nebr.	195	D8	152
Ohogamute, Alsk.	27	C5	84
Ohoopee, riv., Ga.		D4	176
Ohopoho, S.W.Afr.		C2	420
Ohře, riv., Czech.		A1	324
Ohrid, Yugo.	12,640	D5	316
Ohrid, lake, Alb., Yugo.		D5	316
Ohrigstad, U.S.Afr.		D6	421
Oiapoque, riv., Braz.		E6	256
Oich, riv., Scot.		D8	272
Oil, creek, Pa.		B2	214
Oil Center, Lea, N.Mex.	100	F7	126
Oil City, Caddo, La.	1,430	B2	180
Oil City, Yazoo, Miss.		C2	184
Oil City, Carter, Okla.		D6	128
Oil City, Venango, Pa.	17,692	B2	214
Oildale, Kern, Calif.	19,000	E4	94
Oil Hill, Butler, Kans.	375	E7	144
Oilmont, Toole, Mont.	250	B5	110
Oil Springs, Ont., Can.	481	R18	64
Oilton, Creek, Okla.	1,100	B7	128
Oil Trough, Independence, Ark.	237	B5	170
Oise, dept., Fr.	435,308	*C4	278
Oise, riv., Fr.		C5	278
Oiseau, riv., Man., Can.		E5	60
Ōita, Jap.	112,429	H3	354
Oizula, Moz.		B7	421
Ojai, Ventura, Calif.	4,495	E4	94
Ojaren, lake, Swe.		A7	292
Ojinaga, Mex.	4,608	B5	224
Ojo Caliente, Mex.	902	A4	224
Ojocaliente, Mex.	5,531	C5	225
Ojo Caliente, Rio Arriba, N.Mex.	25	B4	126
Ojo de Agua, Arg.		A3	252
Ojo Feliz, Mora, N.Mex.	250	B5	126
Ojos del Salado, mtn., Arg.		C4	250
Ojus, Dade, Fla.	3,000	E6	174
		F10	
Oka, Que., Can.	995	S10	66
		S15	
Oka, riv., Sov.Un.		A2	336
Okaba, Neth.N.Gui.		F9	359
Okabena, Jackson, Minn.	244	H3	148
Okahandja, S.W.Afr.	1,634	D3	420
Okahola, Lamar, Miss.	100	D3	184
Okak, Newf., Can.		D9	72
Okak, is., Newf., Can.		D9	72
Okaloosa, co., Fla.	61,175	A4	174
Okanagan, lake, B.C., Can.		E13	52
Okanagan, range, B.C., Can.		F12	52
Okanagan Centre, B.C., Can.	100	E13	52
Okanagan Falls, B.C., Can.	150	F13	52
Okanagan Landing, B.C., Can.	160	E13	52
Okanogan, Okanogan, Wash.	2,001	A7	98
Okanogan, co., Wash.	25,520	A6	98
Okanogan, riv., Wash.		A7	98
Okapilco, creek, Ga.		E3	176
Okarche, Kingfisher and Canadian, Okla.	584	C6	128
Okatibbee, creek, Miss.		C4	184
Okatoma, creek, Miss.		D3	184
Okaton, Jones, S.Dak.	75	D5	158
Okauchee, Waukesha, Wis.	1,879	E5	160
Okaukuejo, S.W.Afr.		C3	420
Okawville, Washington, Ill.	931	E4	138
Okay, Howard, Ark.	150	D3	170
Okay, Wagoner, Okla.	419	C8	128
Okaya, Jap.	46,420	F7	354
		K14	
Okayama, Jap.	235,754	G4	354
Okazaki, Jap.	155,902	M13	354
O'Kean, Randolph, Ark.	137	A6	170
Okeechobee, Okeechobee, Fla.	2,947	D10	174
Okeechobee, co., Fla.	6,424	D9	174
Okeechobee, lake, Fla.		E10	174
Okeene, Blaine, Okla.	1,164	B5	128
Okefenokee, swamp, Ga.		F4	176
Okehampton, Eng.	3,900	K8	273
Okemah, Okfuskee, Okla.	2,836	C7	128
Okemos, Ingham, Mich.	1,000	*G7	146
Okesa, Osage, Okla.	75	B7	128
Oketo, Marshall, Kans.	128	C7	144
Okfuskee, co., Okla.	11,706	C7	128
Okha, India	6,176	D1	366
Okha, Sov.Un.	35,000	D16	329
Okhotsk, Sov.Un.	2,000	D16	329
Okhotsk, sea, Sov.Un.		D16	329
Oki, isl., Jap.		F4	354
Okinawa, is., Pac.O.		C1	436
Okinawa, isl., Ryūkyū Is., Jap.		L13	349
Oklahoma, co., Okla.	439,506	C6	128
Oklahoma, state, U.S.	2,328,284	D7	77
			128
Oklahoma City, Oklahoma, Cleveland and Canadian, Okla.	324,253 (*448,300)	C6	128
Oklawaha, Marion, Fla.	478	B9	174
Oklee, Red Lake, Minn.	529	D3	148
Okmulgee, Okmulgee, Okla.	15,951	C8	128
Okmulgee, co., Okla.	36,945	C7	128
Okoboji, Dickinson, Iowa	330	A2	142
Okobojo, creek, S.Dak.		C5	158
Okoe, Hawaii, Haw.	10	D6	86
Okolona, Clark, Ark.	344	C3	170
Okolona, Jefferson, Ky.	5,000	A5	178
Okolona, Chickasaw, Miss.	2,622	B4	184
Okondja, Gabon		G7	409
Okotoks, Alta., Can.	764	E6	54
Okovanggo, basin, Bech.		C4	420
Okovanggo, riv., S.W.Afr.		C3	420
Okreek, Todd, S.Dak.	120	D5	158
Öksnes, Nor.		B6	290
Oktaha, Muskogee, Okla.	199	C8	128
Oktibbee, co., Miss.	26,175	B3	184
Oktyabrskiy, Sov.Un.	40,000	B4	336
Oktyabrskoy Revolyutsii, isl., Sov.Un.		B12	329
Oku, Okinawa		C1	436
Okushiri, isl., Jap.		C7	354
Ola, Yell, Ark.	805	B3	170
Ola, Gem, Idaho	20	E2	108
Oladsfjördhur, Ice.	896	K20	290
Olafsvik, Ice.	627	L18	290
Olalla, Kitsap, Wash.	125	D2	98
Olamon, Penobscot, Maine	150	C4	204
Olancha, Inyo, Calif.	75	D5	94
Olancha, peak, Calif.		D4	94
Olanchito, Hond.	3,256	C4	228
Öland, isl., Swe.		E7	292
Öland, reg., Swe.	24,937	*H7	291
Ölands Norra, cape, Swe.		D8	292
Ölands Södra, cape, Swe.		E7	292
Olanta, Florence, S.C.	568	D9	188
Olar, Bamberg, S.C.	467	E6	188
Olascoaga, Arg.		C3	252
Olathe, Montrose, Colo.	773	D3	106
Olathe, Johnson, Kans.	10,987	D9	144
Olavarría, Arg.	24,204	C3	252
Oława, Pol.	6,410	C3	325
Olberg, Pinal, Ariz.	20	E4	124
		H3	
Olbia, It.	11,000	E2	302
Olcott, Niagara, N.Y.	1,215	B3	212
Olcott, Kanawha, W.Va.	150	C3	194
		C6	
Old, chan., Sask., Can.		D6	58
Old, riv., Calif.		A6	94
Old Bahama, chan., Cuba		A5	232
Old Bennington, Bennington, Vt.	205	F2	218
Old Bethpage, Nassau, N.Y.	3,000	*E8	212
Old Blight, Cat Island	574	A7	232
Old Bridge, Middlesex, N.J.	3,500	C4	210
Old Castile (Castilla la Vieja), reg., Sp.	2,238,278	B4	298
Oldcastle, Ire.	697	H5	273
Old Chatanika, Alsk.	20	*B7	84
Oldeant, Tan.		C6	414
Oldenburg, Franklin, Ind.	694	C4	140
Oldenburg, reg., Ger.		*B3	286
Oldenburg [in Holstein], Ger.	8,200	A4	286
Oldenburg [in Oldenburg], Ger.	120,800	B3	286
Oldenzaal, Neth.	14,214	B5	282
Old Faithful, Yellowstone Natl. Park, Wyo.		B2	116
Old Faithful, geyser, Wyo.		B2	116
Old Forge, Herkimer, N.Y.	950	B7	212
Old Forge, Lackawanna, Pa.	8,928	A5	214
		B6	
Old Fort, McDowell, N.C.	787	B3	186
Oldham, Eng.	119,500	H10	273
Oldham, Kingsbury, S.Dak.	291	C8	158
Oldham, co., Ky.	13,388	B5	178
Oldham, co., Tex.	1,928	B4	130
Old Hamilton, see Hamilton, Alsk.			
Old Harbor, Alsk.	121	D6	84
Old Harbor, pt., R.I.		E2	216
Old Head of Kinsale, pt., Ire.		J4	273
Old Hickory, Davidson, Tenn.	5,000	B5	190
		E7	
Old Hickory, res., Tenn.		B5	190
Old Hometown, Shelby, Tenn.	2,500	*B1	190
Old Jenny Lind, Sebastian, Ark.	100	*B2	170
Old Lyme, New London, Conn.	800 (3,068*)	D6	202
Oldman, riv., Alta., Can.		F6	54
Oldmans, creek, N.J.		D2	210
Old Meldrum, Scot.	1,100	D10	272
Old Mines, Washington, Mo.	400	C7	150
Old Monroe, Lincoln, Mo.	290	A7	150
		C7	
Old Mystic, New London, Conn.	500	D8	202
Old Orchard Beach, York, Maine	4,580	E2	204
		E5	
Old Perlican, Newf., Can.	700	F9	72

Old Point Comfort, pt., Va. A9 192
Old Rhodes, key, Fla. F10 174
Old River, lake, Ark. D7 170
Olds, Alta., Can. 1,980 E5 54
Olds, Henry, Iowa 189 C6 142
Olds, Chelan, Wash. B6 98
Old Saybrook, Middlesex, Conn. 1,671 (5,274▲) D6 202
Old Shawneetown, Gallatin, Ill. 433 *F5 138
Oldsmar, Pinellas, Fla. 878 B6 174
Old Spec, mtn., Maine D2 204
Old Tampa, bay, Fla. C6 174
Old Tappan, Bergen, N.J. 2,330 *B4 210
Old Tati, Bech. D5 420
Old Topsail, inlet, N.C. C8 186
Old Town, Lafayette, Ark. 100 D3 170
Old Town, Dixie, Fla. 150 B8 174
Oldtown, Bonner, Idaho 211 A2 108
Old Town, Dickinson, Iowa 27 *A2 142
Old Town, Penobscot, Maine 8,626 D4 204
Oldtown, Allegany, Md. 200 A2 182
Old Trap, Camden, N.C. 300 A9 186
Old Waco, Sedgwick, Kans. 30 *E6 144
Old Washington, Guernsey, Ohio 369 B5 156
Old Westbury, Nassau, N.Y. 2,064 *E8 212
Oldwick, Hunterdon, N.J. 250 B3 210
Olean, Miller, Mo. 135 C5 150
Olean, Cattaraugus, N.Y. 21,868 C3 212
O'Leary Station, P.E.I., Can. 639 C5 70
Olecko, Pol. 1,413 A6 325
Oleiros, Sp. 76 A2 298
Olekma, riv., Sov.Un. D14 329
Olekminsk, Sov.Un. 5,500 C14 329
Olenek, Sov.Un. C13 329
Olenek, riv., Sov.Un. C13 329
Olentangy, riv., Ohio B3 156
Oleomoana, Hawaii, Haw. 55 D6 86
Oleśnica, Pol. 14,300 C3 325
Olesno, Pol. 6,058 C4 325
Olex, Gilliam, Oreg. 15 B6 96
Olga, Cavalier, N.Dak. 96 B7 154
Olga, Sov.Un. 5,000 E15 329
Olgopol, Sov.Un. 13,900 H7 332
Olhão, Port. 16,592 D3 298
Olifants, riv., U.S.Afr. D6 421
Olimpia, Braz. 9,245 E1 258
Olimpo, dept., Par. 2,705 B3 247
Olin, Jones, Iowa 703 B6 142
Olinda, Braz. 38,169 B4 258
Oling, lake, China E7 346
Oliva, Sp. 13,472 C6 298
Oliva de Jerez, Sp. 12,899 C3 298
Olive, Powder River, Mont. 5 E11 110
Olive, Creek, Okla. 50 B7 128
Olive, Norfolk, Va. 7,000 *D8 192
Olive Branch, Alexander, Ill. 500 F4 138
Olive Branch, De Soto, Miss. 642 A3 184
Olivebridge, Ulster, N.Y. 387 D7 212
Olive Hill, Carter, Ky. 1,398 B7 178
Olivehill, Hardin, Tenn. 75 C3 190
Olivehurst, Yuba, Calif. 4,835 C3 94
Oliveira, Braz. 7,832 E2 258
Olivenza, Sp. 11,469 C3 298
Oliver, Lauderdale, Ala. 49 A2 168
Oliver, B.C., Can. 1,147 F13 52
Oliver, Gunnison, Colo. 30 D3 106
Oliver, Screven, Ga. 192 D5 176
Oliver, Posey, Ind. 75 D2 140
Oliver, Fayette, Pa. 1,250 D2 214
Oliver, Douglas, Wis. 222 B1 160
Oliver, co., N.Dak. 2,610 C4 154
Oliver Beach, Baltimore, Md. 500 *B7 182
Oliverian, see East Haverhill, N.H.
Oliver Springs, Roane and Anderson, Tenn. 1,163 B7 190
Olivet, Osage, Kans. 116 D8 144
Olivet, Calvert, Md. 125 D7 182
Olivet, Eaton, Mich. 1,187 G7 146
Olivet, Hutchinson, S.Dak. 135 D8 158
Olivette, St. Louis, Mo. 8,257 *C7 150
Olivia, Renville, Minn. 2,355 G4 148
Olivia, Harnett, N.C. 200 B6 186
Olivier, Iberia, La. 400 E4 180
Olivone, Switz. 707 B4 312
Olla, La Salle, La. 1,246 C3 180
Ollague, Chile B4 250
Ollague, vol., Bol. D1 246
Ollague, vol., Chile B4 250
Ollie, Keokuk, Iowa 291 C5 142
Ollie, Fallon, Mont. 15 D12 110
Ollita, range, Arg. B1 252
Olmito, Cameron, Tex. 600 F7 130
Olmitz, Barton, Kans. 141 D5 144
Olmos, Peru 2,163 B2 245
Olmos Park, Bexar, Tex. 2,457 B6 130
Olmstead, Pulaski, Ark. 50 C4 170
Olmstead, Logan, Ky. 120 D3 178
Olmsted, Pulaski, Ill. 475 F4 138
Olmsted, Cuyahoga, Ohio 4,773 *A5 156
Olmsted, co., Minn. 65,532 H6 148
Olmsted Falls, Cuyahoga, Ohio 2,144 B1 156
Olney, Richland, Ill. 8,780 E5 138
Olney, Montgomery, Md. 650 B5 182
Olney, Flathead, Mont. 225 B2 110
Olney, Coal, Okla. 60 D7 128
Olney, Young, Tex. 3,872 C6 130
Olney Springs, Crowley, Colo. 263 D7 106
Olof, Wheatland, Mont. D6 110
Olofström, Swe. 4,543 E5 292
Olomouc, Czech. 73,899 B3 324
Olomoucký, co., Czech. 650,646 *B3 324
Oloron-Ste. Marie, Fr. 9,915 F3 278
Olot, Sp. 13,654 A8 298
Olowalu, Maui, Haw. 75 C5 86
Olpe, Lyon, Kans. 722 D7 144
Olsburg, Pottawatomie, Kans. 137 C7 144
Olshany, Sov.Un. 20,000 G10 332
Olst, Neth. 2,083 B5 282
Olsztyn, Pol. 54,000 B5 325
Olsztyn, pol. div., Pol. 805,000 *B5 325
Olten, Switz. 17,900 (*26,200) A3 312
Oltenia, prov., Rom. 1,717,982 *C6 321
Oltenia, reg., Rom. B2 321
Oltenita, Rom. 14,111 B4 321
Oltetul, riv., Rom. B2 321
Olton, Lamb, Tex. 1,917 B4 130
Oltre Giuba, pol.dist., Som. 362,234 E5 398
Oltu, Tur. 2,677 A9 307
Oltul, riv., Rom. B3 321
Olustee, Baker, Fla. 400 A8 174
Olustee, Jackson, Okla. 463 D4 128
Olvera, Sp. 8,341 D4 298
Olvey, Boone, Ark. 25 A4 170
Olympia, Bath, Ky. 250 B7 178
Olympia, Thurston, Wash. 18,273 B4 98
Olympia, ruins, Grc. C3 306
Olympia Fields, Cook, Ill. 1,503 *F3 138
Olympia Mills, Richland, S.C. 900 *C6 188
Olympic, mts., Wash. B2 98
Olympic, natl. park, Wash. B3 98
Olympic, natl. park ocean strip, Wash. B2 98
Olympus, mtn., Grc. A4 306
Olympus, mtn., Ky. B7 178
Olympus, mtn., Wash. B3 98
Olyphant, Lackawanna, Pa. 5,864 A5 214, B6
Olyutorskiy, cape, Sov.Un. D19 329
Om, riv., Sov.Un. A9 336
Oma, Lawrence, Miss. 100 D2 184
Oma, Sov.Un. C6 328
Omae, cape, Jap. M14 354
Om Ager, Eth. C4 398
Omagh, N.Ire. 6,762 G5 273
Omaguas, Peru A3 245
Omaha, Boone, Ark. 195 A3 170
Omaha, Stewart, Ga. 174 D2 176
Omaha, Gallatin, Ill. 312 F5 138
Omaha, Douglas, Nebr. 301,598 (*434,800) C10 152, D3
Omaha, Morris, Tex. 854 *C8 130
Omak, Okanogan, Wash. 4,068 A7 98
Omak, lake, Wash. A7 98
Oman, country, Asia 550,000 D6 383, G7 340
Oman, gulf, Asia C6 383
Omar, Logan, W.Va. 900 D3 194, D5
Omarama, N.Z. 211 F2 437
Omaruru, S.W.Afr. D3 420
Omas, Peru 278 C2 245
Omboue, Gabon G6 409
Ombrone, riv., It. D3 302
Omdurman, Sud. 113,551 B3 398
Omega, Bullock, Ala. 60 D4 168
Omega, Tift, Ga. 940 E3 176
Omega, Catron, N.Mex. 20 D2 126
Omega, Kingfisher, Okla. 35 C5 128
Omemee, Ont., Can. 837 P22 64
Omemee, Bottineau, N.Dak. 11 B5 154
Omer, Arenac, Mich. 322 E8 146
Ometepe, Nic. E5 228
Ometepec, Mex. 4,820 D6 225
Omigawa, Jap. 23,715 L16 354
Ominato, Jap. 14,861 D8 354
Omineca, range, B.C., Can. B9 52
Omineca, riv., B.C., Can. C10 52
Ōmiya, Jap. 144,540 G7 354, L15
Ommaney, cape, Alsk. J14 84
Ommen, Neth. 2,287 B5 282
Omo, isl., Den. F2 292
Omo, riv., Eth. D4 398
Omolon, riv., Sov.Un. C17 329
Ompompanoosuc, riv., Vt. D4 218
Omro, Winnebago, Wis. 1,991 D5 160
Omsk, Sov.Un. 579,000 A8 336
Ōmura, Jap. 61,230 *H2 354
Ōmuta, Jap. 201,737 H3 354
Ona, Hardee, Fla. 134 *D9 174
Ona, Cabell, W.Va. 100 C2 194
Onaga, Pottawatomie, Kans. 850 C7 144
Onaka, Faulk, S.Dak. 85 B6 158
Onalaska, Lewis, Wash. 250 C4 98
Onalaska, La Crosse, Wis. 3,161 E2 160
Onamia, Mille Lacs, Minn. 645 E5 148
Onancock, Accomack, Va. 1,759 C9 192
Onarga, Iroquois, Ill. 1,397 C5 138
Onawa, Monona, Iowa 3,176 B1 142
Onawa, Piscataquis, Maine 30 C3 204
Onawa, lake, Maine C3 204
Onaway, Latah, Idaho 191 C2 108
Onaway, Presque Isle, Mich. 1,388 D7 146
Onda, Sp. 7,184 C6 298
Ondangua, S.W.Afr. C3 420
Ondava, riv., Czech. B5 324
Ondo, Nig. 36,233 E5 408
Öndör Haan, Mong. 10,000 B10 346
Ondverdharnes, cape, Ice. L17 290
Oneco, Windham, Conn. 300 C8 202
Oneco, Manatee, Fla. 1,530 D6 174, D8
Onega, Sov.Un. 17,000 C5 328
Onega, lake, Sov.Un. B10 328
100 Mile House, B.C., Can. 150 E12 52
150 Mile House, B.C., Can. 175 D12 52
Onehunga, N.Z. 16,702 H9 437
Oneida, Phillips, Ark. 275 C6 170
Oneida, Franklin, Idaho 40 *G7 108
Oneida, Knox, Ill. 672 B3 138
Oneida, Delaware, Iowa 76 B6 142
Oneida, Nemaha, Kans. 119 C8 144
Oneida, Clay, Ky. 500 C7 178
Oneida, Madison, N.Y. 11,677 B6 212
Oneida, Butler, Ohio 4,000 *C2 156
Oneida, Scott, Tenn. 2,480 B7 190
Oneida, Outagamie, Wis. 125 A5 160
Oneida, co., Idaho 3,603 G6 108
Oneida, co., N.Y. 264,401 B6 212
Oneida, co., Wis. 22,112 C4 160
Oneida, lake, N.Y. B6 212
Oneill, Custer, Mont. D11 110
O'Neill, Holt, Nebr. 3,181 B7 152
Onekama, Manistee, Mich. 469 E5 146
Onekotan, isl., Sov.Un. E17 329
Onemak, isl., Kwajalein A1 436
Oneonta, Blount, Ala. 4,136 B3 168
Oneonta, Otsego, N.Y. 13,412 C6 212
One Tree Hill, N.Z. 12,889 H9 437
Ong, Clay, Nebr. 128 D8 152
Ongea Levu, is., Fiji E7 436
Ongin, Mong. B8 346
Ongoin, riv., Mong. B8 346
Ongonhororusumu, China C7 348
Onia, Stone, Ark. 100 B4 170
Onida, Sully, S.Dak. 843 C5 158
Onilahy, riv., Malag. D8 421
Onion Lake, Sask., Can. 72 D3 58
Onitsha, Nig. E6 408
Onley, Accomack, Va. 415 C9 192
Only, Hickman, Tenn. 50 C4 190
Ōno, Jap. 44,185 L12 354
Onoda, Jap. 54,627 *H3 354
Onojo, Ven. F5 240
Onomea, Hawaii, Haw. 485 *D6 86
Onomichi, Jap. 84,882 G4 354
Onondaga, Ingham, Mich. 300 G7 146
Onondaga, co., N.Y. 423,028 C5 212
Onondaga, cave, Mo. C6 150
Onota, lake, Mass. B1 206
Onoway, Alta., Can. 190 D5 54
Onset, Plymouth, Mass. 1,714 C6 206
Onslow, Austl. 242 C3 432
Onslow, Jones, Iowa 269 B6 142
Onslow, co., N.C. 82,706 C8 186
Onslow, bay, N.C. C8 186
Onsong, Kor. 10,116 D14 348
Onsted, Lenawee, Mich. 526 G7 146
Ontake-San, peak, Jap. L13 354
Ontario, San Bernardino, Calif. 46,617 C6 94, E5
Ontario, Lagrange, Ind. 150 A4 140
Ontario, Wayne, N.Y. 654 B4 212
Ontario, Richland, Ohio 3,049 B4 156
Ontario, Malheur, Oreg. 5,101 C10 96
Ontario, Charlotte, Va. 100 D6 192
Ontario, Vernon, Wis. 448 E3 160
Ontario, co., Ont., Can. 108,440 P21 64
Ontario, co., N.Y. 68,070 C4 212
Ontario, prov., Can. 6,040,000 G10 48, 64
Ontario, lake, Can., U.S. I11 48, C11 77
Onteniente, Sp. 13,564 C6 298
Ontojärvi, lake, Fin. D13 290
Onton, Webster, Ky. 150 C3 178
Ontonagon, Ontonagon, Mich. 2,358 C2 146
Ontonagon, co., Mich. 10,584 C2 146
Ontonagon, riv., Mich. C2 146
Onward, Cass, Ind. 153 B3 140
Onyx, caverns, Mo. E6 150
Oodnadatta, Austl. 126 D7 432
Ookala, Hawaii, Haw. 662 C6 86
Ooldea, Austl. E6 432
Oolitic, Lawrence, Ind. 1,140 D3 140
Oologah, Rogers, Okla. 299 B8 128
Ooltewah, Hamilton, Tenn. 900 C6 190, E8
Ooltgensplaat, Neth. 2,135 C3 282
Oostburg, Neth. 2,313 C2 282
Oostburg, Sheboygan, Wis. 1,065 E6 160
Oostende (Ostend), Bel. 54,297 C1 282
Oosterend, Neth. 908 A3 282
Oosterend, Neth. 120 A4 282
Oosterhout, Neth. 15,200 C3 282
Oostmahorn, Neth. 130 A5 282
Oost Vlaanderen, prov., Bel. 1,257,002 C2 282
Oostvoorne, Neth. 2,421 C3 282
Ootacamund, India 41,370 F3 366
Ootsa, lake, B.C., Can. D9 52
Ootsa, riv., B.C., Can. D10 52
Ootsa Lake, B.C., Can. 25 D9 52
Opaeula Camp, Honolulu, Haw. 150 F9 86
Opal, Alta., Can. 115 D6 54
Opal, Lincoln, Wyo. 55 E2 116
Opala, Con.L. C3 414
Opal Cliffs, Santa Cruz, Calif. 3,825 *D2 94
Opa-locka, Dade, Fla. 9,810 E6 174
Opatów, Pol. 5,459 C5 325
Opava, Czech. 42,308 B3 324
Opdal, Nor. E3 290
Opelika, Lee, Ala. 15,678 C4 168
Opelousas, St. Landry, La. 17,417 D3 180
Opeongo, lake, Ont., Can. O22 64
Opeongo, riv., Ont., Can. O22 64
Opequon, creek, W.Va. B6 194
Opheim, Valley, Mont. 457 B10 110
Ophir, Alsk. 18 C6 84
Ophir, San Miguel, Colo. *E2 106
Ophir, Curry, Oreg. 250 E2 96
Ophir, Tooele, Utah 36 C3 114
Ophir, mtn., Mala. G4 362
Opihikao, Hawaii, Haw. 116 D7 86
Opochka, Sov.Un. 16,500 D7 332
Opoczno, Pol. 7,433 C5 325
Opole, Pol. 55,000 C3 325
Opole, pol. div., Pol. 883,000 *C3 325
Oporto, see Pôrto, Port.
Opotiki, N.Z. 2,346 C6 437
Opp, Covington, Ala. 5,535 D3 168
Oppeln, see Opole, Pol.
Oppelo, Conway, Ark. 100 B4 170
Oppkuven, mtn., Nor. A1 292
Oppland, co., Nor. 162,519 *F3 291
Opportunity, Deer Lodge, Mont. D4 110
Opportunity, Holt, Nebr. B7 152
Opportunity, Spokane, Wash. 12,465 B9 98, D9
Oppy, Martin, Ky. 150 C8 178
Optima, Texas, Okla. 64 B2 128
Oputo, Mex. A4 224
Oquawka, Henderson, Ill. 1,090 C3 138
Oquossoc, Franklin, Maine 100 D2 204
Ora, Starke, Ind. 170 A3 140
Ora, Covington, Miss. 200 D3 184
Ora, Okinawa C1 436
Ora, Laurens, S.C. 300 B5 188
Oraba, Ug. B5 414
Oracle, Pinal, Ariz. 600 F5 124
Oradea, Rom. 99,007 A1 321
Oradell, Bergen, N.J. 7,487 A1 210
Oradell, res., N.J. A1 210
Oraefajökull, peak, Ice. L21 290
Orafino, Frontier, Nebr. D5 152
Orai, India D2 368
Oraibi, Navajo, Ariz. 300 C5 124
Oraibi, wash, Ariz. B5 124
Oral, Fall River, S.Dak. 60 D2 158
Oran, Alg. 299,008 A3 402
Orán, Arg. 6,706 B5 250
Oran, Scott, Mo. 1,090 D8 150
Orange, Austl. 18,247 E9 432
Orange, Orange, Calif. 26,444 C6 94
Orange, New Haven, Conn. 8,547 D3 202
Orange, Fr. 12,643 E6 278
Orange, Fayette, Ind. 200 C4 140
Orange, Franklin, Mass. 4,000 (6,154▲) A3 206
Orange, Grafton, N.H. 50 (83▲) D3 208
Orange, Essex, N.J. 35,789 B1 210, B4
Orange, Cuyahoga, Ohio 2,006 A5 156
Orange, Orange, Va. 2,955 B6 192
Orange, Orange, Vt. 35 (430▲) C4 218
Orange, Orange, Tex. 25,605 D9 130
Orange, co., Calif. 703,925 F5 94
Orange, co., Fla. 263,540 C9 174
Orange, co., Ind. 16,877 D3 140
Orange, co., N.Y. 183,734 D7 212
Orange, co., N.C. 42,970 A6 186
Orange, co., Tex. 60,357 D9 130
Orange, co., Vt. 16,014 D4 218
Orange, co., Va. 12,900 B6 192
Orange, bay, Newf., Can. E7 72
Orange, cape, Braz. E6 256
Orange, cliffs, Utah E5 114
Orange, lake, Fla. B8 174
Orange Beach, Baldwin, Ala. 58 E2 168
Orangeburg, Orangeburg, S.C. 13,852 E7 188
Orangeburg, co., S.C. 68,559 E7 188
Orange City, Volusia, Fla. 1,598 C9 174
Orange City, Sioux, Iowa 2,707 B1 142
Orange Cove, Fresno, Calif. 2,885 *D4 94
Orangedale, N.S., Can. 250 D8 70
Orange Free State, prov., U.S.Afr. 1,016,570 E5 420
Orange Grove, Jackson, Miss. E2 184, E4
Orange Grove, Jim Wells, Tex. 1,109 F7 130
Orange Lake, Marion, Fla. 500 B8 174
Orange Park, Clay, Fla. 2,624 A9 174, B10
Orangeville, Ont., Can. 3,887 Q20 64
Orangeville, Stephenson, Ill. 491 A4 138
Orangeville, Orange, Ind. 100 D3 140
Orangeville, Emery, Utah 571 D4 114
Orange Walk, Br.Hond. 1,395 A3 228
Oranienburg, Ger. 20,800 B5 286
Oranje, canal, Neth. B5 282
Oranje, mts., Neth.N.Gui. E10 359
Oranjemund, S.W.Afr. E3 420
Oranmore, Ire. 341 H4 273
Orăştie, Rom. 10,488 B2 321
Oraşul-Stalin (Braşov), Rom. 123,882 B3 321
Oratia, mtn., Alsk. C6 84
Oraville, St. Marys, Md. 100 D6 182
Oraviţa, Rom. 8,175 B1 321
Orbetello, It. 7,100 D3 302
Orbigo, riv., Sp. A4 298
Örbyhus, Swe. A8 292
Orcas, San Juan, Wash. 250 *A4 98
Orcas, isl., Wash. A4 98
Orchard, Morgan, Colo. 100 B6 106
Orchard, Ada, Idaho 50 F2 108
Orchard, Mitchell, Iowa 116 A5 142
Orchard, Antelope, Nebr. 421 B7 152
Orchard Avenue, Spokane, Wash. 5,000 *B9 98
Orchard Beach, Anne Arundel, Md. 1,691 B6 182
Orchard City, see Eckert, Colo.
Orchard Hill, Spalding, Ga. 105 *C2 176
Orchard Homes, Missoula, Mont. 2,019 *D2 110
Orchard Lake, Oakland, Mich. 1,127 *G8 146
Orchard Mesa, Mesa, Colo. 4,956 *C2 106
Orchard Park, Chaves, N.Mex. 350 *E6 126
Orchard Park, Erie, N.Y. 3,278 C3 212
Orchards, Clark, Wash. 250 D4 98
Orchard Valley, Laramie, Wyo. 1,449 E8 116
Orchilla, isl., Ven. A5 240
Orcotuna, Peru 3,400 C2 245
Orcutt, Santa Barbara, Calif. 1,414 E3 94
Ord, Valley, Nebr. 2,413 C7 152
Ordenes, Sp. 1,311 A2 298
Orderville, Kane, Utah 398 F3 114
Ordoqui, Arg. C3 252
Ordoz, mtn., China F4 348
Ordu, Tur. 14,962 A7 307
Ordu, prov., Tur. 409,891 *A7 307
Orduña, Sp. 2,665 A5 298
Ordville, Cheyenne, Nebr. 950 C2 152
Ordway, Crowley, Colo. 1,254 D7 106
Ordzhonikidze, Sov.Un. 164,000 D2 336
Ordzhonikidzegrad, see Bezhitsa, Sov.Un.
Ore (Erzgebirge), mts., Ger. C5 286
Öre, sound, Swe. F3 292
Oreälven, riv., Swe. D8 290
Oreana, Owyhee, Idaho 10 *F2 108
Oreana, Macon, Ill. 464 *D5 138
Oreana, Pershing, Nev. 15 C3 112
Oreapolis, Cass, Nebr. 10 *C10 152
Orebank, Sullivan, Tenn. 400 B9 190
Ore Bank, Buckingham, Va. (part of Arvonia) C6 192
Örebro, Swe. 71,418 B6 292
Örebro, co., Swe. 256,174 B5 292
Ore City, Upshur, Tex. 819 C8 130
Oregench, Sov.Un. D6 336
Oregon, Ogle, Ill. 3,732 A4 138
Oregon, Holt, Mo. 887 B2 150
Oregon, Lucas, Ohio 13,319 *A3 156
Oregon, Dane, Wis. 1,701 F4 160
Oregon, co., Mo. 9,845 E6 150
Oregon, state, U.S. 1,768,687 C2 77, 96
Oregon Caves, Josephine, Oreg. E3 96
Oregon Caves, natl. mon., Oreg. E3 96
Oregon City, Clackamas, Oreg. 7,996 B2 96, B4
Öregrund, Swe. 2,240 A9 292

Oregrunds-Grepen, bay, Swe. A9 292
Orekhov, Sov.Un. 17,200 I10 332
Orekhovo-Zuyevo, Sov.Un. 108,000 E12 332; N19
Orel, Sov.Un. 152,000 F11 332
Orella, Sioux, Nebr. B2 152
Orem, Utah, Utah 18,394 C4 114
Orenburg, Sov.Un. 260,000 B5 336
Orenco, Washington, Oreg. 200 B1 96
Orense, Sp. 50,000 (71,511▲) A3 298
Orense, prov., Sp. 494,283 *A3 298
Öresjön, lake, Swe. D3 292
Orestes, Madison, Ind. 507 B4 140
Oreti, riv., N.Z. G2 437
Oretown, Tillamook, Oreg. B3 96
Orford, Grafton, N.H. 175 (667▲) D2 208
Orford, mtn., Que., Can. S12 66
Orfordville, Grafton, N.H. 150 D2 208
Orfordville, Rock, Wis. 665 F4 160
Organ, Dona Ana, N.Mex. 110 F4 126
Organ, cave, W.Va. D4 194
Organ Pipe Cactus, natl. mon., Ariz. F3 124
Orgas, Boone, W.Va. 200 D6 194
Orgaz, Sp. 3,397 C5 298
Orgeyev, Sov.Un. 13,000 I7 332
Orhon, riv., Mong. B8 346
Orick, Humboldt, Calif. 800 B1 94
Orient, Franklin, Ill. 588 F5 138
Orient, Adair, Iowa 341 C3 142
Orient, Aroostook, Maine 30 (124▲) C5 204
Orient, Faulk, S.Dak. 133 C6 158
Orient, Ferry, Wash. 150 A8 98
Orienta, Major, Okla. 20 B5 128
Oriental, Burlington, N.J. D3 210
Oriental, Pamlico, N.C. 522 B9 186
Oriental, Mex. 4,089 D6 225
Oriental, prov., Con.L. 2,280,700 B3 414
Orient Bay, Ont., Can. 45 R24 64
Oriente, prov., Cuba 1,797,606 B6 232
Orihuela, Sp. 14,335 C6 298
Orillia, Ont., Can. 13,857 P21 64
Orillia, King, Wash. 75 D3 98
Orimattila, Fin. F11 291
Orin, Converse, Wyo. 5 D7 116
Orinda, Contra Costa, Calif. 10,280 A5 94
Orinoco, riv., Ven. B7 240
Oriole, Somerset, Md. 200 D8 182
Orion, Pike, Ala. 100 D3 168
Orion, Alta., Can. 75 F7 54
Orion, Henry, Ill. 1,269 B3 138
Oriska, Barnes, N.Dak. 148 D8 154
Oriskany, Oneida, N.Y. 1,580 B6 212
Oriskany, Botetourt, Va. 110 C5 192
Oriskany Falls, Oneida, N.Y. 972 C6 212
Orissa, state, India 14,645,946 D5 366
Orissa Coast, canal, India J8 366
Oristano, It. 14,300 F2 302
Oristano, gulf, It. F2 302
Orivesi, Fin. F11 291
Orivesi, lake, Fin. E13 290
Orizaba, Mex. 55,531 D6 225; L15
Örje, Nor. B2 292
Orkdal, Nor. E3 290
Orkla, riv., Nor. E3 290
Orkney, Sask., Can. 121 F4 58
Orkney, co., Scot. 20,100 B9 272
Orkney Islands, Br. poss., Eur. 21,000 B9 272
Orkney, is., Scot. B9 272
Orland, Glenn, Calif. 2,534 C2 94
Orland, Steuben, Ind. 424 A4 140
Orland, Hancock, Maine 380 (1,195▲) D4 204
Örland, Nor. E3 290
Orlando, Orange, Fla. 88,135 (*255,800) C9 174
Orlando, Logan, Okla. 194 B6 128
Orland Park, Cook, Ill. 2,592 F2 138
Orlavá, Czech. B4 324
Orleães, Braz. 2,184 K7 257
Orléanais, former prov., Fr. 782,000 D4 278
Orleans, Humboldt, Calif. 300 B2 94
Orléans, Ont., Can. 325 P26 64
Orléans, Fr. 76,439 D4 278
Orleans, Orange, Ind. 1,659 D3 140
Orleans, Dickinson, Iowa 280 A2 142
Orleans, Barnstable, Mass. 900 (2,342▲) C8 206
Orleans, Kittson, Minn. 56 C2 148
Orleans, Harlan, Nebr. 608 D6 152
Orleans, Orleans, Vt. 1,240 B4 218
Orleans, co., N.Y. 34,159 B3 212
Orleans, co., Vt. 20,143 B4 218
Orleans, par., La. 627,525 E6 180
Orleans, isl., Que., Can. R13 66
Orleans Road, Morgan, W.Va. 35 B6 194
Orléansville, Alg. 40,432 A4 402
Orlinda, Robertson, Tenn. 450 B5 190
Orlovo, Sov.Un. 9,000 E16 329
Orlyak, Bul. 3,072 B3 317
Orman, dam, S.Dak. C2 158
Ormara, Pak. G4 375
Orme, Marion, Tenn. 171 *C6 190
Ormhöjden, mtn., Swe. A3 292
Ormiston, Sask., Can. 110 F5 58
Ormond Beach, Volusia, Fla. 8,658 B9 174
Ormond-by-the-Sea, Volusia, Fla. 3,476 *B9 174
Ormsby, Ont., Can. 65 P23 64
Ormsby, Martin and Watonwan, Minn. 221 H4 148
Ormsby, co., Nev. 8,063 D2 112
Ormstown, Que., Can. 1,347 S10 66
Orne, dept., Fr. 274,862 *C3 278
Orne, riv., Fr. C3 278
Orneta, Pol. 2,109 A5 325
Ornö, isl., Swe. B9 292
Ornsköldsvik, Swe. 7,549 E8 290
Orocué, Col. 645 C2 244
Orofino, Clearwater, Idaho 2,471 C2 108
Oro Grande, San Bernardino, Calif. 685 E5 94
Orogrande, Idaho, Idaho 10 D3 108
Orogrande, Otero, N.Mex. 40 F4 126
Oromocto, N.B., Can. 661 D3 70
Oromocto, lake, N.B., Can. D3 70
Orongorongo, riv., N.Z. J11 437
Orono, Ont., Can. 790 Q22 64
Orono, Penobscot, Maine 8,341 D4 204
Orono, Hennepin, Minn. 5,643 F6 148
Oronoco, Olmsted, Minn. 250 G6 148
Oronogo, Jasper, Mo. 513 D3 150
Oronoque, Norton, Kans. 15 *C3 144
Oronsay, passage, Scot. F6 272
Oropeo, Mex. L13 225
Oroquieta, Phil. 7,233 C6 358
Orós, Braz. B3 258
Orosei, gulf, It. E2 302
Orosháza, Hung. 22,000 (32,000▲) C5 320
Orosi, Tulare, Calif. 1,048 *D4 94
Orovada, Humboldt, Nev. 15 B4 112
Oroville, Butte, Calif. 6,115 C3 94
Oroville, Okanogan, Wash. 1,437 A7 98
Orpha, Converse, Wyo. 15 D7 116
Orr, St. Louis, Minn. 361 C6 148
Orr, Grand Forks, N.Dak. 65 B8 154
Orr, Love, Okla. 65 D6 128
Orrick, Ray, Mo. 800 B3 150
Orrin, Pierce, N.Dak. 175 B5 154
Orrington, Penobscot, Maine 200 (2,539▲) *D4 204
Orrs Island, Cumberland, Maine 450 E3 204; E5
Orrville, Dallas, Ala. 422 C2 168
Orrville, Ont., Can. O21 64
Orrville, Wayne, Ohio 6,511 B5 156
Orsa, Swe. 1,415 A5 292
Orsha, Sov.Un. 64,000 E8 332
Orsières, Switz. 2,286 B3 312
Orsino, Brevard, Fla. 100 C10 174
Orsk, Sov.Un. 176,000 B5 336
Orşova, Rom. 6,527 B2 321
Örsted, Den. 912 H4 291
Örsundsbro, Swe. 316 B8 292
Örsunduån, riv., Swe. B8 292
Ortegal, cape, Sp. A3 298
Ortel, mtn., It. B3 302
Orthez, Fr. 5,125 F3 278
Ortigueira, Sp. 1,590 A7 298
Orting, Pierce, Wash. 2,697 B4 98
Ortin Heights, Putnam, W.Va. 160 *C3 194
Ortiz, Conejos, Colo. 30 E4 106
Ortiz, Mex. 524 B3 224
Ortiz, mts., N.Mex. H7 126
Ortly, Roberts, S.Dak. 127 B8 158
Ortona a Mare, It. 10,700 D5 302
Ortonville, Oakland, Mich. 771 G8 146
Ortonville, Big Stone, Minn. 2,674 F2 148
Örudden, isl., Swe. C8 292
Orukuizu, isl., Palau A6 436
Orum, Washington, Nebr. 30 *C9 152
Oruro, Bol. 62,975 C1 246
Oruro, dept., Bol. C1 246
Orvieto, It. 9,600 D4 302
Orwell, Ashtabula, Ohio 819 A6 156
Orwell, Addison, Vt. 250 (826▲) D2 218
Orwigsburg, Schuylkill, Pa. 2,131 C5 214
Oryakhovo, Bul. 8,136 B1 317
Os, Nor. F1 291
Osa, pen., C.R. F5 228
Osage, Sask., Can. 102 F6 58
Osage, Mitchell, Iowa 3,753 A5 142
Osage, Becker, Minn. 150 E3 148
Osage, Osage, Okla. 220 B7 128
Osage, Monongalia, W.Va. 614 *B5 194
Osage, Weston, Wyo. 350 C8 116
Osage, co., Kans. 12,886 D8 144
Osage, co., Mo. 10,867 C6 150
Osage, co., Okla. 32,441 B7 128
Osage, riv., Mo. C5 150
Osage City, Osage, Kans. 2,213 D8 144
Osage City, Cole, Mo. 235 C5 150
Osage, creek, Ark. A3 170
Ōsaka, Jap. 2,547,316 G5 354; M11
Osaka, Jap. 6,477 L13 354
Osaka, Wise, Va. 100 *D2 192
Ōsaka, bay, Jap. M11 354
Osaka, mtn., Iwo A7 436
Osakis, Douglas, Minn. 1,396 F3 148
Osakis, lake, Minn. F3 148
Osam, riv., Bul. B2 317
Osawatomie, Miami, Kans. 4,622 D9 144
Osborn, Oktibbeha, Miss. 100 B4 184
Osborn, De Kalb and Clinton, Mo. 274 B3 150
Osborn, Charleston, S.C. 60 F2 188
Osborne, Osborne, Kans. 2,049 C5 144
Osborne, co., Kans. 7,506 C5 144
Osbornsville, Ocean, N.J. 900 C4 210
Osburn, Shoshone, Idaho 1,788 B3 108
Osby, Swe. 4,667 E4 292
Oscar, Pointe Coupee, La. 150 D4 180
Oscarville, Forsyth, Ga. 275 B3 176
Osceola, Mississippi, Ark. 6,189 B7 170
Osceola, St. Joseph, Ind. 1,350 A3 140
Osceola, Clarke, Iowa 3,350 C4 142
Osceola, St. Clair, Mo. 1,066 C4 150
Osceola, Polk, Nebr. 951 C8 152
Osceola, Polk, Wis. 942 C1 160
Osceola, co., Fla. 19,029 C9 174
Osceola, co., Iowa 10,064 A2 142
Osceola, co., Mich. 13,595 F6 146
Osceola Mills, Clearfield, Pa. 1,777 C3 214
Osceola Park, Broward, Fla. 400 *E10 174
Oschatz, Ger. 15,800 C5 286
Oschersleben, Ger. 19,700 B4 286
Oscoda, Iosco, Mich. 700 E8 146
Oscoda, co., Mich. 3,447 E7 146
Oscura, peak, N.Mex. E4 126
Osgood, Ripley, Ind. 1,434 C4 140
Osgood, Sullivan, Mo. 135 A4 150
Osgoode Station, Ont., Can. 410 O25 64
Osh, Sov.Un. 65,000 D8 336
Oshamambe, Jap. 14,667 C8 354
Oshawa, Ont., Can. 50,412 Q22 64
Oshima (Moto), Jap. 12,434 M15 354
Ō Shima, isl., Jap. G7 354
Oshkosh, Garden, Nebr. 1,025 C3 152
Oshkosh, Winnebago, Wis. 45,110 B5 160; D5
Oshogbo, Nig. 122,728 E5 408
Oshoto, Crook, Wyo. 10 B8 116
Oshwe, Con.L. C2 414
Osierfield, Irwin, Ga. 82 E3 176
Osijek, Yugo. 58,600 B4 316
Osilinka, riv., B.C., Can. B10 52
Osinniki, Sov.Un. 68,000 B11 336
Osipenko, Sov.Un. 65,000 I11 332
Oskaloosa, Mahaska, Iowa 11,053 C5 142
Oskaloosa, Jefferson, Kans. 807 C8 144
Oskaloosa, Barton, Mo. 150 D3 150
Oskarshamn, Swe. 11,754 D7 292
Oskarström, Swe. 2,963 E4 292
Oskol, riv., Sov.Un. H11 332
Osler, Sask., Can. 215 D4 58
Oslo, Indian River, Fla. 50 D10 174
Oslo, Marshall, Minn. 372 C1 148
Oslo, Nor. 440,674 (*520,000) B1 292
Oslofjord, fjord, Nor. B1 292
Osma, Sp. 1,212 B5 298
Osmancik, Tur. 4,673 A6 307
Osmaniye, Tur. 19,701 C7 307
Osmond, Pierce, Nebr. 719 B8 152
Osmond, Lincoln, Wyo. D2 116
Osnabrock, Cavalier, N.Dak. 289 B7 154
Osnabrück, Ger. 126,600 B3 286
Osorno, Chile 40,120 F3 251
Osorno, prov., Chile 123,059 F3 251
Osov, Czech. 398 *A2 324
Osowaw, Okeechobee, Fla. 55 D10 174
Osoyoos, B.C., Can. 860 F13 52
Osoyoos, lake, Wash. A7 98
Ospakseyri, Ice. L19 290
Ospika, riv., B.C., Can. B11 52
Osprey, Sarasota, Fla. 350 D8 174
Oss, Neth. 20,500 C4 282
Ossabaw, isl., Ga. E5 176
Ossabaw, sound, Ga. E5 176
Ossakmamuan, lake, Newf., Can. E9 72
Osseo, Hennepin, Minn. 2,104 F6 148
Osseo, Trempealeau, Wis. 1,144 D2 160
Ossian, Wells, Ind. 1,108 B4 140
Ossian, Winneshiek, Iowa 827 A6 142
Ossineke, Alpena, Mich. 100 E8 146
Ossining, Westchester, N.Y. 18,662 D2 212; D8
Ossipee, Carroll, N.H. 125 (1,409▲) D4 208
Ossipee, lake, N.H. D4 208
Ossipee, mts., N.H. D4 208
Ossipee, riv., N.H. D5 208
Ossjöen, lake, Nor. F4 291
Ostashkov, Sov.Un. 29,000 D9 332
Oste, riv., Ger. B3 286
Osteen, Volusia, Fla. 400 C9 174
Ostend, see Oostende, Bel.
Österbyburk, Swe. A8 292
Österbymo, Swe. D6 292
Österdalälven, riv., Swe. F5 291
Osterdock, Clayton, Iowa 45 *B6 142
Östergarnsholm, isl., Swe. D9 292
Östergötland, co., Swe. 355,344 C6 292
Östergötland, reg., Swe. 354,746 *G6 291
Osterode, see Ostróda, Pol.
Östersund, Swe. 23,518 E6 290
Osterville, Barnstable, Mass. 1,094 C7 206
Östfold, co., Nor. 189,154 *G4 291
Östhammar, Swe. 1,500 A9 292
Ostia Antica, It. (part of Rome) 1,398 *E4 302
Ostrander, Delaware, Ohio 438 B3 156
Ostrander, Fillmore, Minn. 216 H6 148
Ostrava, Czech. 199,206 B4 324
Ostravský, co., Czech. 948,225 *B4 324
Ostróda, Pol. 15,200 B4 325
Ostrogozhsk, Sov.Un. 36,500 G12 332
Ostrołęka, Pol. 11,700 B5 325
Ostrov, Rom. 4,015 B4 321
Ostrov, Sov.Un. 12,000 D7 332
Ostrowiec [Świętokrzyski], Pol. 32,000 C5 325
Ostrów [Mazowiecka], Pol. 12,900 B5 325
Ostrów [Wielkopolski], Pol. 39,000 C3 325
Ostrów Lubelski, Pol. 2,604 C6 325
Ostrzeszów, Pol. 5,403 C3 325
Ostuni, It. 24,100 E6 302
O'Sullivan, dam, Wash. C7 98
Osum, riv., Alb. A3 306
Osumi, isl., Jap. I3 354
Ōsumi (Van Diemen), strait, Jap. I3 354
Osuna, Sp. 19,569 D4 298
Oswegatchie, riv., N.Y. A6 212
Oswego, Kendall, Ill. 1,510 B5 138; F1
Oswego, Labette, Kans. 2,027 E8 144
Oswego, Valley, Mont. 75 B11 110
Oswego, Oswego, N.Y. 22,155 B5 212
Oswego, Clackamas, Oreg. 8,906 B2 96
Oswego, Sumter, S.C. 100 C8 188
Oswego, Campbell, Tenn. 100 B7 190
Oswego, co., N.Y. 86,118 B5 212
Oswego, riv., N.Y. B5 212
Oswestry, Eng. 11,000 I9 273
Oswichee, Russell, Ala. 400 C5 168
Oświęcim, Pol. 14,400 C4 325
Osyka, Pike, Miss. 712 D2 184
Otago, hbr., N.Z. F3 437
Otago, pen., N.Z. F3 437
Ōtahuhu, N.Z. 8,555 H9 437
Ōtaki, Jap. 18,379 L16 354
Otaki, N.Z. 2,722 D5 437
Otar, Sov.Un. D9 336
Otari, mtn., N.Z. J11 437
Otaru, Jap. 188,488 C8 354
Otaru, bay, Jap. C8 354
Otavalo, Ec. 8,425 A2 245
Otavi, S.W.Afr. C3 420
Otay, San Diego, Calif. 1,500 D6 94
Otay, riv., Calif. D6 94
Otchinjau, Ang. C2 420
Oteen, Buncombe, N.C. 1,000 B3 186
Otego, Jewell, Kans. 9 C5 144
Otego, Otsego, N.Y. 875 C6 212
Otero, co., Colo. 24,128 E7 106
Otero, co., N.Mex. 36,976 F4 126
Othello, Adams, Wash. 2,669 C7 98
Otho, Webster, Iowa 593 B3 142
Othris, mts., Grc. B4 306
Oti, riv., Ghana E5 408
Otis, Washington, Colo. 568 B8 106
Otis, La Porte, Ind. 200 A3 140
Otis, Rush, Kans. 362 D4 144
Otis, Berkshire, Mass. 300 (473▲) B1 206
Otis, Eddy, N.Mex. 600 F6 126
Otis, res., Mass. B1 206
Otisco, Clark, Ind. 250 D4 140
Otisfield, Cumberland, Maine 100 (549▲) D2 204
Otis Orchards, Spokane, Wash. 750 D9 98
Otisville, Genesee, Mich. 701 F8 146
Otjiwarongo, S.W.Afr. 2,383 D3 420
Otley, Marion, Iowa 177 C4 142
Oto, Woodbury, Iowa 221 B2 142
Otočac, Yugo. 3,055 B2 316
Otoe, Otoe, Nebr. 225 D9 152; E3
Otoe, co., Nebr. 16,503 D9 152
Otok, isl., Yugo. C2 316
Otra, riv., Nor. G2 291
Otranto, It. 3,600 E7 302
Otsego, Allegan, Mich. 4,142 G6 146
Otsego, co., Mich. 7,545 D7 146
Otsego, co., N.Y. 51,942 C6 212
Otsego, lake, N.Y. C7 212
Otsego Lake, Otsego, Mich. E7 146
Ōtsu, Jap. 107,498 M11 354
Ottauquechee, riv., Vt. D3 218
Ottawa, Ont., Can. 222,129 (*345,000) O25 64; P25; S26
Ottawa, La Salle, Ill. 19,408 B5 138
Ottawa, Franklin, Kans. 10,673 D8 144
Ottawa, Putnam, Ohio 3,245 A2 156
Ottawa, Boone, W.Va. 400 D5 194
Ottawa, co., Kans. 6,779 C6 144
Ottawa, co., Mich. 98,719 G5 146
Ottawa, co., Ohio 35,323 A3 156
Ottawa, co., Okla. 28,301 B9 128
Ottawa, is., N.W.Ter., Can. F10 48
Ottawa, riv., Ont., Que., Can. O23 64; S9 66
Ottawa Hills, Lucas, Ohio 3,870 A1 156; A3
Ottawa Lake, Monroe, Mich. 250 H8 146
Ottenby, Swe. 3,165 E7 292
Otter, Powder River, Mont. 50 E10 110
Otter, brook, N.H. E2 208
Otter, creek, Utah E4 114
Otter, creek, Vt. C2 218
Otter, lake, Sask., Can. C5 58
Otter, riv., Va. C5 192
Otterbein, Benton, Ind. 788 B2 140
Otterburn, Eng. 624 F10 272
Otterburne, Man., Can. 300 F4 60
Otter Creek, Levy, Fla. 800 B8 174
Otter Creek, Hancock, Maine 300 D4 204
Otter Lake, Ont., Can. O21 64
Otter Lake, Lapeer, Mich. 562 F8 146
Otter River, Worcester, Mass. 498 A3 206
Otter Rock, Lincoln, Oreg. 150 *C2 96
Ottertail, Otter Tail, Minn. 164 E3 148
Otter Tail, co., Minn. 48,960 E2 148
Otter Tail, lake, Minn. E3 148
Otter Tail, riv., Minn. E2 148
Otterville, Ont., Can. 520 R20 64
Otterville, Cooper, Mo. 416 C5 150
Otthon, Sask., Can. 38 E6 58
Ottignies, Bel. 4,621 D3 282
Otto, Big Horn, Wyo. 50 B4 116
Ottosen, Humboldt, Iowa 92 B3 142
Ottoville, Putnam, Ohio 793 B2 156
Ottumwa, Wapello, Iowa 33,871 C5 142
Ottumwa, Coffey, Kans. 49 D8 144
Ottway, Greene, Tenn. B9 190
Oturkpo, Nig. 1,367 E6 409
Otuzco, Peru 3,534 B2 245
Otway, Carteret, N.C. 350 C9 186
Otway, cape, Austl. F8 432
Otway, sound, Chile H3 251
Otwell, Craighead, Ark. 90 B6 170
Otwell, Pike, Ind. 550 D2 140
Ouachita, Dallas, Ark. 65 D4 170
Ouachita, co., Ark. 31,641 D4 170
Ouachita, par., La. 101,663 B3 180
Ouachita, lake, Ark. C3 170
Ouachita, mts., Ark., Okla. C2 170; D8 128
Ouachita, riv., Ark., La. D4 170; B3 180
Ouadaï, reg., Chad D9 409
Ouadi Rimé, Chad D8 409
Ouagadourou, Upper Volta 37,678 D4 408
Ouahigouya, Upper Volta 7,000 D4 408
Ouaka, riv., Cen.Afr.Rep. E9 409
Ouakoro, Mali D3 408
Oualata, Maur. C3 408
Ouallam, Niger D5 408
Ouanda Djallé, Cen.Afr.Rep. E9 409
Ouarane, sand dunes, Maur. B2 408
Ouargla, Alg. 6,456 (27,360▲) B5 402
Ouchina, well, Mali C5 408
Ouddorp, Neth. 2,680 C2 282
Oudenaarde, Bel. 6,639 D2 282
Oude-Pekela, Neth. 5,702 A6 282
Oudtshoorn, U.S.Afr. 18,729 F4 420
Ouedea Daoura, riv., Mor. B3 402
Oued Moulouya, riv., Mor. B3 402
Oued Oum er Rbia, riv., Mor. B3 402
Oued Sebou, riv., Mor. B2 402
Oued Tensift, riv., Mor. B2 402
Oueïba, well, Chad C9 409
Ouelle, I.C. E4 408
Ouelle, riv., Que., Can. Q15 66
Ouesso, Con.B. F8 409
Ougarta, Alg. C3 402
Oughter, lake, Ire. G5 273
Oughterard, Ire. 618 H3 273

Palmer, Merrick, Nebr.	418	C7	152
Palmer, Grundy, Tenn.	1,069	C6	190
Palmer, Ellis, Tex.	613	B9	130
Palmer, King, Wash.	25	D3	98
Palmerdale, Jefferson, Ala.	700	*B3	168
Palmer Lake, El Paso, Colo.	542	C6	106
Palmer Park, Prince Georges, Md.	4,000	*C6	182
Palmerston, Ont., Can.	1,550	Q20	64
Palmerston, N.Z.	878	F3	437
Palmerston North, N.Z.	35,632 (*37,800)	D5	437
Palmersville, Weakley, Tenn.	150	B3	190
Palmerton, Carbon, Pa.	5,942	C6	214
Palmerville, Austl.		B8	432
Palmetto, Pickens, Ala.	100	B2	168
Palmetto, Manatee, Fla.	5,556	C6 D8	174
Palmetto, Fulton and Coweta, Ga.	1,466	C2	176
Palmetto, St. Landry, La.	430	D4	180
Palm Harbor, Pinellas, Fla.	950	B6	174
Palmi, It.	15,400	F5	302
Palmillas, Mex.	191	K13	225
Palmira, Col.	54,293	C1	244
Palmira, Cuba	6,261	A4	232
Palmira, Ec.		A2	245
Palms, Sanilac, Mich.	50	F9	146
Palms, isl., S.C.		F9	188
Palm Springs, Riverside, Calif.	13,468	F5	94
Palm Springs, Palm Beach, Fla.	2,503	*E10	174
Palmyra, Lincoln, Ark.	25	*D5	170
Palmyra, Macoupin, Ill.	811	D4	138
Palmyra, Harrison, Ind.	470	D3	140
Palmyra, Somerset, Maine	100 (1,009▲)	D3	204
Palmyra, Marion, Mo.	2,933	B6	150
Palmyra, Otoe, Nebr.	377	D9 E2	152
Palmyra, Burlington, N.J.	7,036	C2	210
Palmyra, Wayne, N.Y.	3,476	B4	212
Palmyra, Lebanon, Pa.	6,999	C5	214
Palmyra, Syr., U.A.R.		B3	378
Palmyra, Montgomery, Tenn.	100	B4	190
Palmyra, Fluvanna, Va.	350	C6	192
Palmyra, Jefferson, Wis.	1,000	F5	160
Palmyra, is., Pac.O.		D4	436
Palo, Linn, Iowa	387	B6	142
Palo (Alsium), It.	136	*E4	302
Palo, Ionia, Mich.	250	F7	146
Palo Alto, Santa Clara, Calif.	52,287	B5 D2	94
Palo Alto, Schuylkill, Pa.	1,445	*C5	214
Palo Alto, co., Iowa	14,736	A3	142
Palo Blanco, Mex.		B5	225
Palo Duro, canyon, Tex.		B5	130
Paloich, Sud.		C3	398
Palomar, mtn., Calif.		F5	94
Palombara Sabina, It.	4,983	*D4	302
Palo Pinto, co., Tex.	20,516	C6	130
Palopo, Indon.	4,208	E6	358
Palos, cape, Sp.		D6	298
Palos Heights, Cook, Ill.	3,775	F2	138
Palos Hills, Cook, Ill.	3,766	*B6	138
Palos Park, Cook, Ill.	2,169	F2	138
Palos Verdes Estates, Los Angeles, Calif.	9,564	C5	94
Palourde, lake, La.		C5	180
Palouse, Whitman, Wash.	926	C9	98
Palouse, riv., Wash.		C8	98
Palo Verde, Maricopa, Ariz.	50	E3 H1	124
Palpa, Peru	2,171	C3	245
Palua, Ven.		B7	240
Palung, China		D7	346
Palwal, India		C2	368
Pama, Upper Volta		D5	408
Pambrun, Sask., Can.	25	F4	58
Pamekasan, Indon.	13,403	F4	358
Pamiers, Fr.	12,822	F4	278
Pamir, mts., China, Sov. Un.		F9	328
Pamlico, co., N.C.	9,850	B9	186
Pamlico, riv., N.C.		B9	186
Pamlico, sound, N.C.		B9	186
Pampa, Gray, Tex.	24,664	B5	130
Pampa Grande, Bol.	727	C2	246
Pampa Peñon, Chile		B4	250
Pampas, Peru	1,622	C3	245
Pampilhosa do Botão, Port.	2,779	B2	298
Pamplico, Florence, S.C.	988	C9	188
Pamplin, Appomattox and Prince Edward, Va.	312	C6	192
Pamplona, Col.	16,396	B2	244
Pamplona, Sp.	68,288	A6	298
Pamunkey, riv., Va.		C7	192
Pana, Christian, Ill.	6,432	D4	138
Panaca, Lincoln, Nev.	450	F7	112
Panacea, Wakulla, Fla.	900	A6	174
Panagyurishte, Bul.	14,038	B2	317
Panaitan, isl., Indon.		F3	358
Panama, Montgomery, Ill.	487	D4	138
Panama, Shelby, Iowa	257	C2	142
Panama, Lancaster, Nebr.	155	D9	152
Panama, Chautauqua, N.Y.	450	C2	212
Panama, Le Flore, Okla.	937	C9	128
Panamá, Pan.	158,500 (*221,200)	F8	228
Panama, country, N.A.	1,024,000	F7	228
Panama, bay, Pan.		F8	228
Panama, gulf, Pan.		G8	228
Panama Canal Zone, see Canal Zone, U.S. poss., N.A.			
Panama City, Bay, Fla.	33,275	A5	174
Panama City Beach, Bay, Fla.	36	A5	174
Panang, isl., Mala.		F4	362
Panao, Peru	954	B2	245
Panarea, isl., It.		F5	302
Panaro, riv., It.		C3	302
Panay, isl., Phil.		B6	358
Pancake, range, Nev.		E5	112
Pančevo, Yugo.	30,103	B5	316
Pancheco, Mex.		C5	225
Panciu, Rom.	7,679	B4	321
Panda, Moz.		D6	421
Pandharpur, India	40,514	E3	366
Pandhurna, India		E2	368
Pando, Eagle, Colo.	14	C4	106
Pando, Ur.	9,600	B4	252
Pando, dept., Bol.		B1	246
Pandora, Putnam, Ohio	782	B3	156
Pandu, Con.L.		B2	414
Panevėžys, Sov.Un.	37,000	E5	332
Pangala, Con.B.		G7	409
Pangang, lake, China		E3	346
Pangburn, White, Ark.	489	B5	170
Pang Hoei, mtn., Thai.		D4	362
Pangi, Con.L.		C4	414
Pangkalanbuun, Indon.		E4	358
Pangkalangresik, Indon.		E2	358
Pangkalpinang, Indon.	11,970	E3	358
Pangman, Sask., Can.	231	F5	58
Pangnirtung, N.W.Ter., Can.		D12	48
Pango, India		C6	368
Pangong, lake, India		B2	368
Pangsau, pass, India, Bur.		D7 A3	368 362
Panguitch, Garfield, Utah	1,435	F3	114
Panhandle, Carson, Tex.	1,958	B5	130
Panipat, India	54,981	C2	368
Panjang, isl., Viet.		E4	362
Panjao, Afg.	10,000	B4	374
Panjgur, Pak.	754	F4	375
Panjim, Goa	14,213	E2	366
Panjpai, Pak.		E5	375
Pankakoski, Fin.		E14	290
Pankshin, Nig.	5,654	E6	409
Panmure, N.Z.	141	H9	437
Panna, India	13,375	D3	368
Panola, Sumter, Ala.	300	C1	168
Panola, Latimer, Okla.	90	*D8	128
Panola, co., Miss.	28,791	A2	184
Panola, co., Tex.	16,870	C8	130
Panora, Guthrie, Iowa	1,019	C3	142
Panorama Park, Scott, Iowa	140	C7	142
Pansey, Houston, Ala.	165	D4	168
Panshan, China	15,000	E10	348
Panshiho, China		D12	348
Pantano, Pima, Ariz.	20	G5	124
Pantar, isl., Indon.		F6	358
Pantego, Beaufort, N.C.	262	B9	186
Pantelleria, It.		G3	302
Pantelleria, isl., It.		G4	302
Panther, mtn., N.Y.		B7	212
Pantin, Fr.	36,963	I10	278
Panton, Addison, Vt.	35 (352▲)	C2	218
Pantsyan, China	1,000	D6	348
Pánuco, Mex.	6,661	C6 J14	225
Pánuco, riv., Mex.		J14	225
Panulcillo, Chile		B1	252
Panzi, Con.L.		D2	414
Panzós, Guat.	573	C3	228
Paochang, China	5,000	E7	348
Paocheng, China	10,000	I3	348
Paochi, China	130,000	H3	348
Pão de Açúcar, Braz.	3,221	B3	258
Paokang, China	5,000	J7	349
Paokuotu, China	1,000	D10	348
Paola, It.	9,197	F6	302
Paola, Miami, Kans.	4,784	D9	144
Paoli, Phillips, Colo.	81	B8	106
Paoli, Orange, Ind.	2,754	D3	140
Paoli, Garvin, Okla.	358	D6	128
Paoli, Chester, Pa.	5,000	A6	214
Paonia, Delta, Colo.	1,083	D3	106
Paoshan, China		F7	346
Paoshan, China		I16	346
Paote, China	5,000	F5	348
Paoti, China	12,000	F8	348
Paoting, China	197,000	F7	348
Paotow, China	400,000	E5	348
Paoua, Cen.Afr.Rep.		E8	409
Pap, mtn., Scot.		E7	272
Papa, Hawaii, Haw.	35	D6	86
Pápa, Hung.	24,000	B2	320
Papaaloa, Hawaii, Haw.	500	D6	86
Papagayo, gulf, C.R.		E4	228
Papaikou, Hawaii, Haw.	1,591	D6	86
Papantla [de Olarte], Mex.	11,361	C6 K15	225
Papa Stour, isl., Scot.		A11	272
Papatoetoe, N.Z.	11,031	H9	437
Papenburg, Ger.	15,300	B2	286
Papeton, El Paso, Colo.	400	D6	106
Paphos, Cyp.	7,283	D5	307
Papillion, Sarpy, Nebr.	2,235	C9 E3	152
Papillion, creek, Nebr.		E2	152
Papineau, co., Que., Can.	30,175	S9	66
Papineau, lake, Ont., Can.		O23	64
Papineauville, Que., Can.	1,141	S9	66
Paposo, Chile		C3	250
Papua, Austl. poss., Pac.O.	495,000	C3	436
Papudo, Chile		B1	252
Papun, Bur.	1,881	C3	362
Papy, pt., Fla.		C6	174
Paquetville, N.B., Can.	245	B4	70
Pará, state, Braz.	1,266,000	F6	256
Pará, riv., Braz.		F7	256
Parabati, riv., India		D2	368
Parabel, Sov.Un.		A10	336
Paracatú, Braz.	5,909	D1	258
Paracatú, riv., Braz.		D1	258
Parachilna, Austl.		E7	432
Parachinar, Pak.		C7	375
Paraćin, Yugo.	11,590	C5	316
Paracurú, Braz.	1,007	A3	258
Paradis, St. Charles, La.	800	C6	180
Paradise, Cochise, Ariz.	10	G6	124
Paradise, Butte, Calif.	8,268	C3	94
Paradise, Russell, Kans.	134	C5	144
Paradise, Sanders, Mont.	280	C2	110
Paradise, Wallowa, Oreg.		B9	96
Paradise, Cache, Utah	368	*B4	114
Paradise Hill, Sask., Can.	251	D3	58
Paradise Valley, Alta., Can.	175	D7	54
Paradox, Montrose, Colo.	50	D2	106
Paragon, Morgan, Ind.	560	C3	140
Paragonah, Iron, Utah	300	F3	114
Paragould, Greene, Ark.	9,947	A6	170
Paragua, riv., Ven.		C7	240
Paraguacú, riv., Braz.		C3	258
Paraguai, riv., Bol.		C3	246
Paraguaná, pen., Ven.		A3	240
Paraguarí, Par.	4,658	D4	247
Paraguarí, dept., Par.	159,161	E4	247
Paraguay, country, S.A.	1,677,000	F6	236 247
Paraguay, riv., Braz., Par.		J5 D4	257 247
Paraíba, state, Braz.	1,919,000	G9	256
Paraíba, riv., Braz.		E2	258
Paraíbal, see João Pessoa, Braz.			
Paraiso, Mex.	2,804	D7	225
Paraisópolis, Braz.	5,341	E1	258
Parakhino-Poddubye, Sov.Un.	20,000	C9	332
Parakou, Dah.	5,000	E5	408
Paraloma, Sevier, Ark.	94	D2	170
Param, isl., Ponape		A2	436
Paramã, riv., Braz.		C1	258
Paramaribo, Sur.	71,496	D5	256
Paramé, Fr.	8,515	C3	278
Paramirim, Braz.	1,271	C2	258
Paramithia, Grc.	2,950	B3	306
Paramonga, Peru		C2	245
Paramount, Los Angeles, Calif.	27,249	C5	94
Paramount, Washington, Md.	200	A4	182
Paramus, Bergen, N.J.	23,238	A1	210
Paramushir, isl., Sov.Un.		D17	329
Paraná, Arg.	84,153	B3	252
Paranã, Braz.		C1	258
Paraná, state, Braz.	2,967,000	J6	257
Paraná, riv., Arg., Braz., Par.		B3 G4 D5	252 256 247
Paranaguá, Braz.	16,046	K7	257
Paranaíba, Braz.	1,324	I6	257
Paranaíba, riv., Braz.		I6	257
Paranapanema, riv., Braz.		J6	257
Paranatinga, riv., Braz.		H5	257
Parapeti, riv., Bol.		C2	246
Paray-le-Monial, Fr.	8,499	D6	278
Parchim, Ger.	19,600	B4	286
Parchman, Sunflower, Miss.	750	B2	184
Parchment, Kalamazoo Mich.	1,565	G6	146
Parczew, Pol.	6,173	C6	325
Pardee, Wise, Va.	200	C2	192
Pardeeville, Columbia, Wis.	1,331	E4	160
Pardess Hanna, Isr.	5,800	B5	382
Pardo, riv., Braz.		D2	258
Pardo, riv., Braz.		E1	258
Pardoo, Austl.		C3	432
Pardubice, Czech.	54,077	A2	324
Pardubický, co., Czech.	456,819	*A2	324
Parecis, mts., Braz.		H4	257
Paredes de Nava, Sp.	4,766	A4	298
Parent, Aroostook, Maine		A4	204
Parepare, Indon.	6,273	E5	358
Parfuri, U.S.Afr.		D6	421
Párga, Grc.	1,722	B3	306
Pargas, Fin.		F10	291
Parhams, Catahoula, La.	35	C4	180
Paria, gulf, Ven.		A7	240
Paria, pen., Ven.		A7	240
Paria, riv., Ariz., Utah		A4 F4	124 114
Pariaguán, Ven.	4,507	B6	240
Paricutín, vol., Mex.		L12	225
Parigi, Indon.		E6	358
Parikkala, Fin.		F13	291
Parima, mts., Braz., Ven.		E4 E6	256 240
Pariñas, pt., Peru		A1	245
Parintins, Braz.	5,855	F5	256
Paris, Logan, Ark.	3,007	B3	170
Paris, Ont., Can.	5,504	Q20	64
Paris, Fr.	2,850,189 (*6,650,000)	C5 I10	278
Paris, Bear Lake, Idaho	746	G7	108
Paris, Edgar, Ill.	9,823	D6	138
Paris, Bourbon, Ky.	7,791	B6	178
Paris, Oxford, Maine	200 (3,601▲)	D2	204
Paris, Calvert, Md.	100	C6	182
Paris, Mecosta, Mich.	180	F6	146
Paris, Lafayette, Miss.	102	A3	184
Paris, Monroe, Mo.	1,393	B5	150
Paris, Greenville, S.C.	1,000	*B4	188
Paris, Henry, Tenn.	9,325	B3	190
Paris, Lamar, Tex.	20,977	C8	130
Paris, Fauquier, Va.	100	A7	192
Paris Crossing, Jennings, Ind.	135	D4	140
Parish, Oswego, N.Y.	567	B5	212
Parishville, St. Lawrence, N.Y.	400	A7	212
Parisville, Que., Can.	510	R12	66
Park, Latah, Idaho		C2	108
Park, Gove, Kans.	218	C3	144
Park, co., Colo.	1,822	C5	106
Park, co., Mont.	13,168	E6	110
Park, co., Wyo.	16,874	B3	116
Park, range, Colo., Wyo.		B4 E5	106 116
Parkano, Fin.		F10	291
Parkbeg, Sask., Can.	86	E4	58
Park City, Lake, Ill.	1,408	*A6	138
Park City, Sedgwick, Kans.	2,687	*E6	144
Park City, Barren, Ky.	497	C4	178
Park City, Stillwater, Mont.	350	E8	110
Park City, Summit, Utah	1,366	C4	114
Park Court, Alta., Can.		D5	54
Parkdale, Ashley, Ark.	448	D5	170
Parkdale, Fremont, Colo.	30	*D5	106
Parkdale, Hood River, Oreg.	400	B5	96
Parke, co., Ind.	14,804	C2	140
Park East, Sedgwick, Kans.	100	*E6	144
Parkell, Pontotoc, Okla.		D7	128
Parker, Yuma, Ariz.	1,642	D1	124
Parker, Douglas, Colo.	100	C6	106
Parker, Bay, Fla.	2,669	*A5	174
Parker, Fremont, Idaho	284	F7	108
Parker, Randolph, Ind.	1,181	B4	140
Parker, Linn, Kans.	181	D9	144
Parker, Polk, Oreg.		*C3	96
Parker, Armstrong, Pa.	945	B2	214
Parker, Turner, S.Dak.	1,142	D8	158
Parker, Spotsylvania, Va.	100	B7	192
Parker, Yakima, Wash.	300	C6	98
Parker, co., Tex.	22,880	C7	130
Parker, dam, Ariz.		D1	124
Parker, peak, S.Dak.		D2	158
Parker Dam, San Bernardino, Calif.	250	E6	94
Parker Head, Sagadahoc, Maine	100	E6	204
Parkersburg, Butler, Iowa	1,468	B5	142
Parkersburg, Wood, W.Va.	44,797	B3	194
Parkers Ferry, Charleston, S.C.		F2	188
Parkers Prairie, Otter Tail, Minn.	884	E3	148
Parkerton, Converse, Wyo.	50	D7	116
Parkertown, Ocean, N.J.	400	D4	210
Parkerville, Morris, Kans.	59	D7	144
Parkesburg, Chester, Pa.	2,759	D6	214
Park Falls, Price, Wis.	2,919	C3	160
Park Forest, Cook, Ill.	29,993	F3	138
Park Grove, Valley, Mont.	20	B10	110
Park Hall, St. Marys, Md.	300	D7	182
Park Head, Ont., Can.	110	P19	64
Park Hill, Cherokee, Okla.	150	C9	128
Park Hill, Ont., Can.	1,043	Q19	64
Park Hills, Kenton, Ky.	4,076	A8	178
Parkin, Cross, Ark.	1,489	B6	170
Parkland, Alta., Can.	109	E6	54
Parkland, Lincoln, Okla.	50	C7	128
Parkland, Bucks, Pa.	1,200	*C7	214
Parkland, Pierce, Wash.	15,000	D2	98
Parkland Beach, Plymouth, Mass.	200	*C6	206
Parklawn, Fairfax, Va.	1,000	*B7	192
Parkman, Sask., Can.	70	F7	58
Parkman, Piscataquis, Maine	65 (530▲)	C3	204
Parkman, Sheridan, Wyo.	25	B5	116
Park Place, Clackamas, Oreg.	100	B2	96
Park Place, Greenville, S.C.	1,600	*B4	188
Park Rapids, Hubbard, Minn.	3,047	E3	148
Park Ridge, Cook, Ill.	32,659	E2	138
Park Ridge, Bergen, N.J.	6,389	*A4	210
Park Ridge, Portage, Wis.	504	D4	160
Park River, Walsh, N.Dak.	1,813	B8	154
Parkrose, Multnomah, Oreg.	24,000	A2	96
Parks, Coconino, Ariz.	100	C4	124
Parks, St. Martin, La.	413	D4	180
Parks, Dundy, Nebr.	120	D4	152
Parkside, Sask., Can.	125	D4	58
Parkside, Jefferson, Ky.	333	*B5	178
Parkside, Delaware, Pa.	2,426	*D6	214
Parksley, Accomack, Va.	850	C9	192
Parkston, Hutchinson, S.Dak.	1,514	D8	158
Parksville, B.C., Can.	1,112	F10	52
Parksville, Boyle, Ky.	200	C6	178
Parksville, McCormick, S.C.	164	D4	188
Parkton, Baltimore, Md.	180	A6	182
Parkton, Robeson, N.C.	906	C6	186
Park Valley, Box Elder, Utah	25	B2	114
Park View, Rio Arriba, N.Mex.	300	B4	126
Parkview, Cuyahoga, Ohio	2,018	*A5	156
Parkville, Baltimore, Md.	27,236	C5	182
Parkville, Platte, Mo.	1,229	B3 E2	150
Parkville, York, Pa.	1,500	*D5	214
Parkway, Franklin, Mo.	222	*C6	150
Parkway Village, Jefferson, Ky.	949	A5	178
Parkwood, Montgomery, Md.	1,400	*B5	182
Parla, Sp.	1,049	B5	298
Parlier, Fresno, Calif.	1,366	D4	94
Parlin, Gunnison, Colo.	5	D4	106
Parlin, Middlesex, N.J.		C4	210
Parma, Canyon, Idaho	1,295	F2	108
Parma, It.	89,300 (121,800▲)	C3	302
Parma, Jackson, Mich.	770	G7	146
Parma, New Madrid, Mo.	1,060	E8	150
Parma, Cuyahoga, Ohio	82,845	A5 B1	156
Parma, prov., It.	393,000	*C3	302
Parmachenee, lake, Maine		C2	204
Parma Heights, Cuyahoga, Ohio	18,100	B1	156
Parmele, Martin, N.C.	323	B8	186
Parmelee, Todd, S.Dak.	140	D4	158
Parmer, co., Tex.	9,583	B4	130
Parnaguá, Braz.	348	C2	258
Parnaíba, Braz.	30,174	A2	258
Parnaíba, riv., Braz.		F8	256
Parnassós, mtn., Grc.		B4	306
Parnell, Iowa, Iowa	200	C6	142
Parnell, Nodaway, Mo.	260	A3	150
Pärnu, Sov.Un.	43,000	C5	332
Parole, Anne Arundel, Md. (part of Annapolis)		C6	182
Paron, Saline, Ark.	100	C4	170
Paron, India		B2	368
Paroo, riv., Austl.		E8	432
Paropamisus, range, Afg.		B3	374
Páros, Grc.	3,174	C5	306
Páros, isl., Grc.		C5	306
Parowan, Iron, Utah	1,486	F3	114
Parr, Jasper, Ind.	90	A2	140
Parr, Fairfield, S.C.	100	C6	188
Parral, Chile	10,717	C1	252
Parramore, isl., Va.		C9	192
Parran, Calvert, Md.	200	C6	182
Parras de la Fuente, Mex.	18,546	B5	225
Parrish, Walker, Ala.	1,608	B2	168
Parrish, Manatee, Fla.	517	C6 D8	174
Parrish, Langlade, Wis.	50	C4	160
Parris Island, Beaufort, S.C.		G7	188
Parrott, Terrell, Ga.	280	E2	176
Parrott, Pulaski, Va.	650	C4	192
Parrottsville, Cocke, Tenn.	91	B8	190
Parrs, ridge, Md.		B5	182
Parrsboro, N.S., Can.	1,849	D5	70
Parry, Sask., Can.	75	F5	58
Parry, cape, N.W.Ter., Can.		C6	48
Parry, isl., Ont., Can.		O20	64
Parry, is., N.W.Ter.,Can.		B7	48
Parry, isl., Eniwetok		B1	436
Parry, mtn., B.C., Can.		D8	52
Parry Sound, Ont., Can.	5,378	O20 S25	64
Parry Sound, dist., Ont., Can.	28,095	O20	64
Parsberg, Ger.	2,500	D4	286
Parshall, Mountrail, N.Dak.	1,216	C3	154

Parsippany, Morris, N.J.	3,500	B4	210
Parsnip, riv., B.C., Can.		C11	52
Parsonfield, York, Maine	35 (869▲)	*E2	204
Parsons, Labette, Kans.	13,929	E8	144
Parsons, Decatur, Tenn.	1,859	C3	190
Parsons, Tucker, W.Va.	1,798	B5	194
Parsonsburg, Wicomico, Md.	500	D9	182
Parsons Pond, Newf., Can.	200	E7 E10	72
Partabgarh, India		D1	368
Partabpur, India		E4	366
Parthenay, Fr.	8,350	D3	278
Parthenen, Aus.	624	D2	313
Parthenon, Newton, Ark.	125	B3	170
Partinico, It.	25,100	F4	302
Partlow, Spotsylvania, Va.	30	B7	192
Partridge, Reno, Kans.	221	E5	144
Partridge, pt., Newf., Can.		E7	72
Partridgeberry, hills, Newf., Can.		F8	72
Parú, riv., Braz.		F6	256
Parvān, Afg.	5,000	B2	374
Parwan, prov., Afg.		*B4	374
Parwan, riv., India		D2	368
Pasadena, Los Angeles, Calif.	116,407	C5 E4	94
Pasadena, Newf., Can.	468	F7	72
Pasadena, Pinellas, Fla.	500	C6	174
Pasadena, Anne Arundel, Md.	2,000	B6	182
Pasadena, Ocean, N.J.		D4	210
Pasadena, Harris, Tex.	58,737	F8	130
Pasadena Hills, St. Louis, Mo.	1,315	*C7	150
Pasadena Park, St. Louis, Mo.	680	*C7	150
Pasadena Park, Spokane, Wash.	2,000	*B9	98
Pasado, cape, Ec.		A1	245
Pasay, Phil.	88,728	B6	358
Pasayton, riv., Wash.		A6	98
Pascagoula, Jackson, Miss.	17,139	E2 E4	184
Pascagoula, bay, Miss.		E2	184
Pascagoula, riv., Miss.		E4	184
Paşcani, Rom.	15,008	A4	321
Paschall, Warren, N.C.		A7	186
Pasco, Franklin, Wash.	14,522	C7	98
Pasco, co., Fla.	36,785	C8	174
Pasco, dept., Peru	134,306	C2	245
Pascoag, Providence, R.I.	2,983	B2	216
Pascoag, res., R.I.		B2	216
Pascola, Pemiscot, Mo.	228	E8	150
Pas de Calais, dept., Fr.	1,276,833	*B5	278
Paseley, cape, Austl.		E4	432
Pasewalk, Ger.	12,600	B6	286
Pasighat, India		C6	368
Pasión, riv., Guat.		B2	228
Pasłąk, Pol.	3,278	A4	325
Pasni, Pak.	6,168	G3	375
Paso del Limay, Arg.		F3	251
Paso de los Indios, Arg.		F4	251
Paso de los Libres, Arg.	11,665	A4	252
Paso Robles, San Luis Obispo, Calif.	6,677	E3	94
Pasqua, Sask., Can.	60	E5	58
Pasque, isl., Mass.		D6	206
Pasqueira, Braz.		B3	258
Pasquia, hills, Sask., Can.		D6	58
Pasquia, riv., Man., Sask., Can.		D2 D7	60 58
Pasquo, Davidson, Tenn.	50	E7	190
Pasquotank, co., N.C.	25,630	A9	186
Pasrur, Pak.	9,403	C9	375
Passaconaway, mtn., N.H.		D4	208
Passadumkeag, Penobscot, Maine	300 (355▲)	C4	204
Passage East, Ire.	461	I6	273
Passadumkeag, mtn., Maine		C4	204
Pass-a-Grille Beach, Pinellas, Fla. (part of St. Petersburg Beach)		C6	174
Passaic, Passaic, N.J.	53,963	A1 B4	210
Passaic, co., N.J.	406,618	A4	210
Passamaquoddy, bay, Maine		C6	204
Passau, Ger.	33,500	D5	286
Pass Christian, Harrison, Miss.	3,881	E1 E3	184
Passekeag, N.B., Can.	75	D4	70
Passero, cape, It.		G5	302
Passo Fundo, Braz.	24,395	K6	257
Passos, Braz.	14,044	E1	258
Passumpsic, Caledonia, Vt.	180	C4	218
Passumpsic, riv., Vt.		C4	218
Pastaza, riv., Ec.		A2	245
Pastaza, riv., Peru		A2	245
Pasto, Col.	98,790	C1	244
Pastolik, Alsk.	19	C5	84
Pastora, peak, Ariz.		B6	124
Pastorn, Mex.		J13	225
Pastura, Guadalupe, N.Mex.	105	D6	126
Pasuruan, Indon.	36,973	F4	358
Paswegin, Sask., Can.	110	E6	58
Patagonia, Santa Cruz, Ariz.	540	G5	124
Patan, Nep.	42,183	D4	368
Patapsco, Carroll, Md.	120	A6	182
Patapsco, res., Md.		B6	182
Patapsco, riv., Md.		B6	182
Pataskala, Licking, Ohio	1,046	C4	156
Pataz, Peru	214	B2	245
Patch Grove, Grant, Wis.	208	*F3	160
Patchogue, Suffolk, N.Y.	8,838	D4	212
Patea, N.Z.	1,898	C5	437
Paternò, It.	38,200	G5	302
Pateros, Okanogan, Wash.	673	A7	98
Paterson, Passaic, N.J.	143,663	A1 B4	210
Paterson, Benton, Wash.	45	D7	98
Patesville, Hancock, Ky.	75	C4	178
Pathfinder, res., Wyo.		D6	116
Pathlow, Sask., Can.	90	D5	58
Pathumthani, prov., Thai.	139,336	*D4	362
Pati, pt., Guam		C7	436
Patia, riv., Col.		C1	244
Patiala, India	97,869	C2	368
Patience, isl., R.I.		C3	216
Patkai, range, Bur., India		D6	368
Patmos, Hempstead, Ark.	120	D3	170
Pátmos, is., Grc.		C6	306
Patna, India	283,479	D4	368
Patoka, Marion, Ill.	601	E4	138
Patoka, Gibson, Ind.	579	D2	140
Patoka, riv., Ind.		D2	140
Patom, plat., Sov.Un.		D13	329
Paton, Greene, Iowa	370	B3	142
Patos, Braz.	13,889	B3	258
Patos, lagoon, Braz.		L6	257
Patos de Minas, Braz.	11,414	D1	258
Patquia, Arg.		B2	252
Pátrai (Patras), Grc.	79,014	B3	306
Pátrai, gulf, Grc.		B3	306
Patras, see Pátrai, Grc.			
Patricia, Alta., Can.	100	E7	54
Patrick, Chesterfield, S.C.	393	B8	188
Patrick, co., Va.	15,282	D4	192
Patricksburg, Owen, Ind.	350	C3	140
Patrick Springs, Patrick, Va.	500	D4	192
Patriot, Switzerland, Ind.	277	D5	140
Patrocínio, Braz.	6,905	D1	258
Patsaltiga, creek, Ala.		D3	168
Patsburg, Crenshaw, Ala.	85	D3	168
Patsua, Solomon Is.		F13	359
Pattani, Thai.	10,000	F4	362
Pattani, prov., Thai.	199,253	*F4	362
Pattani, pt., Mala.		F4	362
Pattani, riv., Thai.		F4	362
Pattaquattie, hill, Mass.		B3	206
Patten, Penobscot, Maine	1,099 (1,312▲)	C4	204
Pattenburg, Hunterdon, N.J.	250	B2	210
Pattenville, Middlesex, Mass.	350	*A5	206
Patterson, Woodruff, Ark.	324	B5	170
Patterson, Stanislaus, Calif.	2,246	*D3	94
Patterson, Pierce, Ga.	719	E4	176
Patterson, Lemhi, Idaho	24	E5	108
Patterson, Madison, Iowa	157	C4	142
Patterson, St. Mary, La.	2,923	E4	180
Patterson, Wayne, Mo.	125	D7	150
Patterson, Putnam, N.Y.	800	D8	212
Patterson, Caldwell, N.C.	265	A4	186
Patterson, Latimer, Okla.	50	D8	128
Patterson, Buchanan, Va.	400	C3	192
Patterson, creek, W.Va.		B5	194
Patterson, knob, Tenn.		E7	190
Patterson, mtn., Calif.		C4	94
Patterson Creek, mtn., W.Va.		B6	194
Patterson Gardens, Monroe, Mich.	1,747	*H8	146
Pattison, Claiborne, Miss.	300	D2	184
Patton, Bollinger, Mo.	108	D7	150
Patton, Cambria, Pa.	2,880	C3	214
Pattonsburg, Daviess, Mo.	753	A3	150
Patú, Braz.	1,531	B3	258
Patuakhali, Pak.	10,289	L17	375
Patuca, pt., Hond.		C5	228
Patuca, riv., Hond.		C5	228
Patung, China	1,000	J5	349
Patupatuai Mission, Solomon Is.		F13	359
Patuxent, Anne Arundel, Md.	60	B6	182
Patuxent, riv., Md.		D6	182
Patzau, Douglas, Wis.	50	B1	160
Pátzcuaro, Mex.	10,331	D5 L13	225
Pátzcuaro, lake, Mex.		L13	225
Patzicia, Guat.	5,021	C2	228
Patzún, Guat.	5,103	C2	228
Pau, Fr.	48,320	F3	278
Paucarbamba, Peru	1,738	C3	245
Paucartambo, riv., Peru		C3	245
Paudalho, Braz.	5,360	B3	258
Pau dos Ferros, Braz.	2,629	B3	258
Paugh Lake, Ont., Can.		O23	64
Pauk, Bur.		B2	362
Paukaa, Hawaii, Haw.	365	*D6	86
Paul, Minidoka, Idaho	701	G5	108
Paul, Otoe, Nebr.	25	*D10	152
Paul, isl., Newf., Can.		D9	72
Paul, stream, Vt.		B5	218
Paulden, Yavapai, Ariz.	25	D3	124
Paulding, Ontonagon, Mich.	75	C2	146
Paulding, Jasper, Miss.	180	C3	184
Paulding, Paulding, Ohio	2,936	A2	156
Paulding, co., Ga.	13,101	C2	176
Paulding, co., Ohio	16,792	A2	156
Paulette, Noxubee, Miss.	350	B4	184
Paulina, St. James, La.	1,014	B6	180
Paulina, Warren, N.J.	75	B3	210
Paulina, Crook, Oreg.	30	C7	96
Paulina, mts., Oreg.		D5	96
Paulina, peak, Oreg.		D5	96
Pauline, Shawnee, Kans.	125	D8	144
Pauline, Adams, Nebr.	85	D7	152
Pauline, Spartanburg, S.C.	200	B5	188
Pauline, mtn., Alta., B.C., Can.		D3 D13	54 52
Paulins, kill, N.J.		A3	210
Paulis, Con.L.		B4	414
Paulista, Braz.	1,017	B2	258
Paull, lake, Sask., Can.		B5	58
Paull, riv., Sask., Can.		C5	58
Paullina, O'Brien, Iowa	1,329	B2	142
Paulo Afonso, falls, Braz.		B3	258
Pauloff Harbor (Pavlof), Alsk.	68	D5	84
Paulsboro, Gloucester, N.J.	8,121	D2	210
Paul Spur, Cochise, Ariz.	150	G6	124
Pauls Valley, Garvin, Okla.	6,856	D6	128
Paumalu, Honolulu, Haw.	60	F9	86
Paungde, Bur.	17,286	C2	362
Pauwela, Maui, Haw.	300	C5	86
Pavia, It.	67,100	C2	302
Pavia, prov., It.	514,100	*C2	302
Pavilion, Genesee, N.Y.	538	C3	212
Pavilion, key, Fla.		F9	174
Pavillion, Fremont, Wyo.	190	C4	116
Pavlikeni, Bul.	9,265	B2	317
Pavlodar, Sov.Un.	90,000	B9	336
Pavlof, vol., Alsk.		D5	84
Pavlograd, Sov.Un.	36,000	H10	332
Pavlovo, Sov.Un.	38,000	E14	332
Pavlovsk, Sov.Un.	10,000	G13	332
Pavlovskiy Posad, Sov.Un.	55,000	N19	332
Pavo, Thomas and Brooks, Ga.	817	F3	176
Pawan, riv., Indon.		E4	358
Pawcatuck, New London, Conn.	6,000	D8	202
Pawcatuck, riv., R.I.		D2	216
Paw Creek, Mecklenburg, N.C.	2,000	B5	186
Pawhuska, Osage, Okla.	5,414	B7	128
Pawlet, Rutland, Vt.	165 (1,112▲)	E2	218
Pawleys Island, Georgetown, S.C.	500	E10	188
Pawling, Dutchess, N.Y.	1,734	D8	212
Pawnee, Sangamon, Ill.	1,517	D4	138
Pawnee, Pawnee, Okla.	2,303	B7	128
Pawnee, co., Kans.	10,254	D4	144
Pawnee, co., Nebr.	5,356	D9	152
Pawnee, co., Okla.	10,884	B7	128
Pawnee, creek, Colo.		B7	106
Pawnee, riv., Kans.		D3	144
Pawnee City, Pawnee, Nebr.	1,343	D9	152
Pawnee Rock, Barton, Kans.	380	D5	144
Pawpaw, Lee, Ill.	725	B5	138
Paw Paw, Van Buren, Mich.	2,970	G6	146
Paw Paw, Morgan, W.Va.	789	B6	194
Pawpaw, creek, W.Va.		A7	194
Paw Paw, lake, Mich.		G5	146
Paw Paw, riv., Mich.		G5	146
Paw Paw Lake, Berrien, Mich.	3,518	*G5	146
Pawtuckaway, pond, N.H.		E4	208
Pawtucket, Providence, R.I.	81,001	B3	216
Pawtuxet, riv., R.I.		C3	216
Pax, Fayette, W.Va.	408	D6	194
Paxico, Wabaunsee, Kans.	276	C7	144
Paxoí, isl., Grc.		B2	306
Paxtang, Dauphin, Pa.	1,916	*C5	214
Paxton, Walton, Fla.	215	A4	174
Paxton, Ford, Ill.	4,370	C5	138
Paxton, Sullivan, Ind.	275	C2	140
Paxton, Worcester, Mass.	600 (2,399▲)	B4	206
Paxton, Keith, Nebr.	566	C4	152
Paxville, Clarendon, S.C.	216	D8	188
Payen, China	30,000	B13	348
Payenhala, China		B11	348
Payerne, Switz.	5,649	B2	312
Payette, Payette, Idaho	4,451	E2	108
Payette, co., Idaho	12,363	E2	108
Payette, lake, Idaho		E2	108
Payette, riv., Idaho		F2	108
Payintala, see Tungliao, China			
Payne, Paulding, Ohio	1,287	A2	156
Payne, co., Okla.	44,231	B6	128
Payne, lake, Que., Can.		P9	66
Paynes, Bibb, Ga.	346	D3	176
Paynes, Tallahatchie, Miss.	115	B2	184
Paynesville, Ontonagon, Mich.	55	C2	146
Paynesville, Stearns, Minn.	1,754	F4	148
Paynesville, Pike, Mo.	150	B7	150
Payneville, Meade, Ky.	113	C4	178
Paynton, Sask., Can.	241	D3	58
Paysandú, Ur.	65,000	B4	252
Paysandú, dept., Ur.	84,265	B4	252
Payson, Gila, Ariz.	750	D4	124
Payson, Adams, Ill.	502	D2	138
Payson, Lincoln, Okla.	30	C7	128
Payson, Utah, Utah	4,237	C4	114
Pazardzhik, Bul.	39,520	B2	317
Pazardzhishki, prov., Bul.		*B2	317
Pazin, Yugo.	2,450	B1	316
Pea, riv., Ala.		D4	168
Peabody, Marion, Kans.	1,309	D6	144
Peabody, Essex, Mass.	32,202	A6 C3	206
Peabody, riv., N.H.		C4	208
Peace, riv., Alta., B.C., Can.		B4 B11	54 52
Peace, riv., Fla.		D9	174
Peace Dale, Washington, R.I.	2,000	D3	216
Peace River, Alta., Can.	2,034	B4 E3	54
Peach, co., Ga.	13,846	D3	176
Peacham, Caledonia, Vt.	75 (433▲)	C4	218
Peachburg, Bullock, Ala.	300	C4	168
Peach Creek, Logan, W.Va.	700	D5	194
Peache, pt., Mass.		C4	206
Peachland, B.C., Can.	575	F13	52
Peachland, Anson, N.C.	563	C5	186
Peach Orchard, Clay, Ark.	348	A6	170
Peach Orchard, knob, Ky.		C4	178
Peach Springs, Mohave, Ariz.	500	C2	124
Peachtree, Cherokee, N.C.	60	B2	186
Peacock, Lake, Mich.	20	E6	146
Peacock, mts., Ariz.		C2	124
Peacock, pt., Wake		A5	436
Peak, Newberry, S.C.	86	C6	188
Peake, Hanover, Va.		C7	192
Peaked, mtn., Maine		B4	204
Peak Hill, Austl.		D3	432
Peale, isl., Wake Isl.		A5	436
Peale, mtn., Utah		E6	114
Pea Patch, isl., Del.		B3	172
Pearce, Cochise, Ariz.	25	G6	124
Pearce, Alta., Can.	41	F6	54
Pearcy, Garland, Ark.	100	C3 D6	170
Pea Ridge, Shelby, Ala.	500	*B3	168
Pea Ridge, Benton, Ark.	380	A2	170
Pearisburg, Giles, Va.	2,268	C4	192
Pearl, Gem, Idaho	24	*F2	108
Pearl, Pike, Ill.	348	D3	138
Pearl, Rankin, Miss.	5,081	C2	184
Pearl, hbr., Haw.		B3	86
Pearl, riv., Miss.		C2	184
Pearland, Brazoria, Tex.	1,497	*E8	130
Pearl and Hermes, reef, Haw.		A5	86
Pearl Beach, St. Clair, Mich.	1,224	*G9	146
Pearl City, Honolulu, Haw.	8,200	B4 G10	86
Pearl City, Stephenson, Ill.	488	A4	138
Pearlington, Hancock, Miss.	500	E3	184
Pearl River, St. Tammany, La.	964	D6	180
Pearl River, Rockland, N.Y.	9,000	D2	212
Pearl River, co., Miss.	22,411	E3	184
Pear Ridge, Jefferson, Tex.	3,470	*E9	130
Pearsall, Frio, Tex.	4,957	E6	130
Pearsoll, peak, Oreg.		E3	96
Pearson, Cleburne, Ark.	40	B4	170
Pearson, Atkinson, Ga.	1,615	E4	176
Pearson, Rankin, Miss.	225	C2	184
Pearson, Pottawatomie, Okla.	50	C7	128
Pearson, Langlade, Wis.	80	C4	160
Peary, chan., N.W.Ter., Can.		B9	48
Peary Land, reg., Grnld.		O31	290
Pease, Mille Lacs, Minn.	191	F5	148
Peavine, Cumberland, Tenn.		B7	190
Pebane, Moz.	5,000	C7	421
Pebworth, Owsley, Ky.	200	C7	178
Peć, Yugo.	21,058	C5	316
Pecan, Jackson, Miss.	200	E2	184
Peçanha, Braz.	2,840	D2	258
Pecatonica, Winnebago, Ill.	1,659	A4	138
Pecatonica, riv., Wis.		F3	160
Pechenga, Sov.Un.	13,200	C5	328
Pechora, riv., Sov.Un.		C7	328
Peck, Nez Perce, Idaho	186	C2	108
Peck, Sedgwick and Sumner, Kans.	105	E6	144
Peck, Casey, Ky.	157	C6	178
Peck, Catahoula, La.		C4	180
Peck, Sanilac, Mich.	548	F9	146
Peckerwood, lake, Ark.		C5	170
Peckham, Weld, Colo.	50	*B6	106
Peckham, Kay, Okla.	100	B6	128
Peckville, Lackawanna, Pa.	6,374	A5	214
Peconic, bay, N.Y.		D5	212
Pecos, San Miguel, N.Mex.	584	C5 G7	126
Pecos, Reeves, Tex.	12,728	D4	130
Pecos, co., Tex.	11,957	D4	130
Pecos, riv., N.Mex., Tex.		E6 D5	126 130
Pécs, Hung.	110,000	C3	320
Peculiar, Cass, Mo.	458	C3	150
Pedasí, Pan.	856	G7	228
Peddocks, isl., Mass.		D3	206
Pedernal, peak, N.Mex.		D5	126
Pedlar Mills, Amherst, Va.	35	C5	192
Pedley, Riverside, Calif.	1,600	*E5	94
Pedregal, Pan.	309	F6	228
Pedregal, Ven.	1,696	A3	240
Pedricktown, Salem, N.J.	645	D2	210
Pedro, Marion, Fla.	50	C8	174
Pedro, is., W.I.		D6	232
Pedro Afonso, Braz.	1,683	B1	258
Pedro Avelino, Braz.	1,536	B3	258
Pedro de Valdivia, Chile	10,989	B4	250
Pedro Juan Caballero, Par.	3,968	C5	247
Pedro Luro, Arg.		C3	252
Peebinga, Austl.	54	E8	432
Peebles, Sask., Can.	40	E6	58
Peebles, Adams, Ohio	1,601	D3	156
Peebles, Scot.	5,700	F8	272
Peebles, Fond du Lac, Wis.	150	B5	160
Peebles, co., Scot.	14,300	F8	272
Pee Dee, riv., N.C., S.C.		B5 B9	186 188
Peekaboo, mtn., Maine		C5	204
Peekskill, Westchester, N.Y.	18,737	D8	212
Peel, N.B., Can.	135	C2	70
Peel, Isle of Man	2,612	G8	273
Peel, co., Ont., Can.	83,108	Q21	64
Peel, riv., Yukon, Can.		D5	48
Peel Fell, mtn., Scot.		F10	272
Pe Ell, Lewis, Wash.	593	C3	98
Peene, riv., Ger.		B5	286
Peer, Bel.	5,379	C4	282
Peerless, Daniels, Mont.	110	B11	110
Peerless, lake, Alta., Can.		B5	54
Peers, Alta., Can.	75	D5	54
Peesane, Sask., Can.	122	D6	58
Peetz, Logan, Colo.	218	B7	106
Peever, Roberts, S.Dak.	208	B9	158
Pefferlaw, Ont., Can.	200	P21	64
Pegan, hill, Mass.		D2	206
Pegasus, bay, N.Z.		E4	436
Peggs, Cherokee, Okla.	28	B8	128
Pegnitz, Ger.	7,392	D4	286
Pegnitz, riv., Ger.		D4	286
Pego, Sp.	9,736	C6	298
Pegram, Bear Lake, Idaho		G7	108
Pegram, Cheatham, Tenn.	400	B4	190
Pegu, Bur.	47,378	C3	362
Pegu Yona, riv., Bur.		C2	362
Pehčevo, Yugo.	1,750	D6	316
Pehuajó, Arg.	13,537	C3	252
Pei, China	5,000	H8	348
Pei, riv., China		M6	349
Peian, China	18,000	A13	348
Peichiao, China		J16	346
Peihai, China	50,000	O4	349
Peili, China	1,000	P4	349
Peilintzu, see Suihua, China			
Peine, Ger.	28,600	B4	286
Peiping, see Peking, China			
Peipus, lake, Sov.Un.		C6	332
Peixe, Braz.		C1	258
Pei Ya Shih, bay, China		N7	349
Pejepscot, Sagadahoc, Maine	200	E2 E5	204
Pekalongan, Indon.	55,406	F3	358
Pekan, Mala.	2,070	G4	362
Pekin, Tazewell, Ill.	28,146	C4	138
Pekin, Washington, Ind.	661	D3	140
Pekin, Nelson, N.Dak.	180	C7	154
Peking (Peiping), China	4,060,000	F8	348
Peking, prov., China		*D11	346
Pélagos, isl., Grc.		B4	306
Pelahatchie, Rankin, Miss.	1,066	C3	184
Pelaihari, Indon.		E4	358
Pelat, mtn., Fr.		E7	278
Pelee, isl., Ont., Can.		S18	64
Peleliu, isl., Palau		A6	436
Pelew, see Palau, is., Pac.O.			
Pelham, Shelby, Ala.	450	B3	168
Pelham, Mitchell, Ga.	4,609	E2	176
Pelham, Hampshire, Mass.	150 (805▲)	B3	206
Pelham, Hillsboro, N.H.	150 (2,605▲)	F4	208
Pelham, Westchester, N.Y.	1,964	*D8	212
Pelham, Caswell, N.C.	200	A6	186
Pelham, Greenville, S.C.	500	B4	188
Pelham, Grundy, Tenn.	300	C6	190
Pelham Manor, Westchester, N.Y.	6,114	D2	212
Pelhřimov, Czech.	6,191	B2	324
Pelican (Pelican City), Alsk.	135	I13	84
Pelican, De Soto, La.	250	C2	180
Pelican, bay, Man., Can.		D2	60
Pelican, butte, Oreg.		E4	96
Pelican, lake, Man., Can.		D2	60
Pelican, lake, Sask., Can.		C6	58
Pelican, lake, Minn.		C6	148

Pelican, lake, Minn. E3 148
Pelican, lake, Minn. E4 148
Pelican, lake, Minn. F5 148
Pelican, lake, Wis. C4 160
Pelican, mts., Alta., Can. C6 54
Pelican Lake, Palm Beach, Fla. 300 E10 174
Pelican Lake, Oneida, Wis. 300 C4 160
Pelican Lakes, Crow Wing, Minn. 134 E4 148
Pelican Rapids, Man., Can. D2 60
Pelican Rapids, Otter Tail, Minn. 1,693 E2 148
Pelion, Lexington, S.C. 233 D6 188
Pelkosenniemi, Fin. C12 290
Pell, Lincoln, Nebr. 750 *C5 152
Pella, Marion, Iowa 5,198 C5 142
Pélla, prov., Grc. 116,969 A4 306
Pell City, St. Clair, Ala. 4,165 B3 168
Pellettown, Sussex, N.J. A3 210
Pellez, Webster, Miss. 45 B3 184
Pell Lake, Walworth, Wis. 1,000 F1 160
Pello, Fin. C11 290
Pellston, Emmet, Mich. 429 D7 146
Pellville, Hancock, Ky. 119 C4 178
Pellworm, isl., Ger. A3 286
Pelly, Sask., Can. 477 E7 58
Pelly, lake, N.W.Ter., Can. D8 48
Pelly, mts., Yukon, Can. E5 48
Pelly, riv., Yukon, Can. E5 48
Pelly Crossing, Yukon, Can. E5 48
Peloncillo, mts., Ariz., N.Mex. F6 124
F2 126
Peloponnesos (Peloponnesus), reg., Grc. 1,130,505 C3 306
Pelotas, Braz. 78,014 L6 257
Pelotas, riv., Braz. K6 257
Pelusium, bay, Eg., U.A.R. A3 395
Pelzer, Anderson, S.C. 106 B4 188
Pelzer North, Anderson, S.C. 1,400 *B4 188
Pemadumcook, lake, Maine C4 204
Pemanggil, isl., Mala. G5 362
Pemaquid, Lincoln, Maine 200 E3 204
Pemba, Rh.&Nya. 189 C5 420
Pemberton, B.C., Can. 75 E11 52
Pemberton, Blue Earth, Minn. 177 G5 148
Pemberton, Burlington, N.J. 1,250 D3 210
Pemberville, Wood, Ohio 1,237 A1 156
A3
Pembina, Pembina, N.Dak. 625 B8 154
Pembina, co., N.Dak. 12,946 B8 154
Pembina, mts., N.Dak. B8 154
Pembina, riv., Alta., Can. D5 54
Pembina, riv., Man., Can., N.Dak. F3 60
A7 154
Pembine, Marinette, Wis. 550 C6 160
Pembroke, Ont., Can. 15,434 O23 64
S25
Pembroke, Broward, Fla. 569 *E10 174
Pembroke, Bryan, Ga. 1,450 D5 176
Pembroke, Christian, Ky. 517 D3 178
Pembroke, Washington, Maine 500 D5 204
(871▲)
Pembroke, Plymouth, Mass. 1,300 B6 206
(4,919▲)
Pembroke (Town of), Merrimack, N.H. (3,514▲) E4 208
Pembroke, Robeson, N.C. 1,372 C6 186
Pembroke, Giles, Va. 1,038 C4 192
Pembroke, Wales 13,800 I8 273
Pembroke, co., Wales 94,260 J8 273
Pembroke Pines, Broward, Fla. 1,429 *E10 174
Pemigewasset, riv., N.H. D3 208
Pemiscot, co., Mo. 38,095 E8 150
Pemuco, Chile 1,703 C1 252
Penablanca, Sandoval, N.Mex. 120 C4 126
G6
Penafiel, Port. 4,361 B2 298
Penafiel, Sp. 8,527 B4 298
Peñalara, mtn., Sp. B5 298
Penalosa, Kingman, Kans. 84 E5 144
Penamacor, Port. 2,740 B3 298
Peña Negra, mts., Sp. A3 298
Peña Negra, pt., Peru A1 245
Penang, Mala. 234,855 F4 362
Penang, state, Mala. 571,923 *F4 362
Penápolis, Braz. 8,832 E1 258
Pen Argyl, Northampton, Pa. 3,693 C6 214
Peña Roya, mtn., Sp. B6 298
Peñarroya-Pueblonuevo, Sp. 27,728 C4 298
Peñas, cape, Sp. A4 298
Peñas, gulf, Chile G2 251
Peñas, pt., Ven. A8 240
Penasco, Taos, N.Mex. 627 B5 126
Penasco, riv., N.Mex. F5 126
Penawawa, Whitman, Wash. 30 C9 8
Penbrook, Dauphin, Pa. 3,671 C5 214
Pence, Warren, Ind. 100 B2 140
Pence, Iron, Wis. 450 B3 160
Penchi, China 449,000 E11 348
Pencil Bluff, Montgomery, Ark. 130 C3 170
Pendembu, S.L. E2 408
Pender, B.C., Can. C14 52
Pender, Thurston, Nebr. 1,165 B9 152
Pender, co., N.C. 18,508 C8 186
Pender, isl., B.C., Can. C14 52
Pendergrass, Jackson, Ga. 215 B3 176
Pendle, hill, Eng. H10 273
Pendleton, Madison, Ind. 2,472 C4 140
Pendleton, Umatilla, Oreg. 14,434 B8 96
Pendleton, Anderson, S.C. 2,358 B3 188
Pendleton, co., Ky. 9,968 B6 178
Pendleton, co., W.Va. 8,093 C5 194
Pend Oreille, co., Wash. 6,914 A9 98
Pend Oreille, lake, Idaho A2 108
Pend Oreille, riv., Idaho, Wash. A1 108
A9 98
Pendroy, Teton, Mont. 60 B4 110
Penedo, Braz. 14,222 C3 258
Penetanguishene, Ont., Can. 5,420 P21 64
Penfield, Greene, Ga. 105 C3 176
Penfield, Monroe, N.Y. 3,500 *B4 212
Penfield Junction, Lorain, Ohio 2,300 *A4 56
Pengan, China 5,000 J3 349
Penge, Co.L. D3 414
Penghu, see Pescadores, is., For.
Pengilly, Itasca, Minn. 300 D5 148
Penglai (Tengchow), China 15,000 G10 348
Pengpu, China 253,000 I8 349
Pengshui, China 10,000 K4 349
Penguin, is., Newf., Can. G7 72
Penhold, Alta., Can. 213 D6 54
Penhook, Franklin, Va. 45 D5 192
Penicuik, Scot. 5,800 F9 272
Peninsula, Summit, Ohio 644 A5 156
Penitas, Hidalgo, Tex. 700 F6 130
Penitente, mts., Braz. B1 258
Penitentiary, mtn., Ala. A2 168
Pénjamo, Mex. 9,433 K13 225
Penn, Ramsey, N.Dak. 70 B6 154
Pennant, pt., N.S., Can. E6 70
Pennant Station, Sask., Can. 306 E3 58
Pennask, mtn., B.C., Can. F12 52
Penne, It. 5,054 D4 302
Pennell, mtn., Utah F5 114
Penner, riv., India F3 366
Penney Farms, Clay, Fla. 545 B9 174
Pennfield, N.B., Can. 215 D3 70
Penniac, N.B., Can. 150 C3 70
Pennine Alps, mts., Switz. B3 312
Pennine Chain, mts., Eng. G11 273
Pennington, Choctaw, Ala. 40 C1 168
Pennington, Mercer, N.J. 2,063 C3 210
Pennington, co., Minn. 12,468 C2 148
Pennington, co., S.Dak. 58,195 D2 158
Pennington, mtn., Maine B4 204
Pennington Gap, Lee, Va. 1,799 D1 192
Pennock, Kandiyohi, Minn. 257 F3 148
Pennsauken, Camden, N.J. 33,771 D2 210
Pennsboro, Ritchie, W.Va. 1,660 B4 194
Pennsburg, Montgomery, Pa. 1,698 C6 214
Penns Grove, Salem, N.J. 6,176 D2 210
Pennsuco, Dade, Fla. 117 E6 174
Pennsville, Salem, N.J. 7,000 D1 210
Pennsylvania, state, U.S. 11,319,366 C11 77
214
Pennville, Jay, Ind. 730 B4 140
Penn Yan, Yates, N.Y. 5,770 C4 212
Penny Highland, mts., N.W.Ter., Can. D12 48
Penny Hill, New Castle, Del. 1,000 *B3 172
Penobscot, Hancock, Maine 150 D4 204
(706▲)
Penobscot, co., Maine 126,346 C4 204
Penobscot, bay, Maine D4 204
Penobscot, lake, Maine C2 204
Penobscot, riv., Maine C4 204
Penobsquis, N.B., Can. 140 D4 70
Penokee, Graham, Kans. 92 C4 144
Penola, Caroline, Va. 25 C7 192
Penong, Austl. 98 E6 432
Penonomé, Pan. 3,515 F7 228
Penrith, Eng. 10,600 G10 273
Penrose, Fremont, Colo. 200 D5 106
Pensacola, Escambia, Fla. 56,752 A3 174
(*165,400)
Pensacola, Mayes, Okla. 55 B8 128
Pensacola, dam, Okla. B8 128
Pensaukee, Oconto, Wis. 250 D6 160
Pense, Sask., Can. 301 E5 58
Pentagon, mtn., Mont. C3 110
Pentecoste, Braz. 869 A3 258
Penticton, B.C., Can. 11,894 F13 52
Pentland, firth, Scot. C9 272
Pentland, hills, Scot. F9 272
Penton, Salem, N.J. 150 D2 210
Pentwater, Oceana, Mich. 1,030 F5 146
Peñuelas, Mex. K12 225
Penza, Sov.Un. 254,000 F15 332
Penzance, Navajo, Ariz. 12 D5 124
Penzance, Sask., Can. 122 E5 58
Penzance, Eng. 19,800 K7 273
Penzberg, Ger. 10,100 E4 286
Penzhina, riv., Sov.Un. C18 329
Penzhino, Sov.Un. 600 C18 329
Peoa, Summit, Utah 203 C4 114
Peonan, pt., Man., Can. E3 60
Peone, Spokane, Wash. D9 98
Peonia, Grayson, Ky. 30 C4 178
Peoples, Jackson, Ky. 200 C6 178
Peoria, Maricopa, Ariz. 2,593 E3 124
H1
Peoria, Peoria, Ill. 103,162 C4 138
(*265,000)
Peoria, Franklin, Kans. 50 *D8 144
Peoria, Amite, Miss. 100 D2 184
Peoria, Ottawa, Okla. 156 B9 128
Peoria, co., Ill. 189,044 C4 138
Peoria Heights, Peoria, Ill. 7,064 C4 138
Peosta, Dubuque, Iowa 50 *B7 142
Peotone, Will, Ill. 1,788 B6 138
Pepacton, res., N.Y. C7 212
Pepeekeo, Hawaii, Haw. 750 D6 86
Pepin, Pepin, Wis. 825 D1 160
Pepin, co., Wis. 7,332 D2 160
Pepita, Chile B4 250
Pepper, Sussex, Del. 25 F4 172
Pepperell, Lee, Ala. (part of Opelika) C4 168
Pepperell, Middlesex, Mass. 700 A4 206
(4,336▲)
Pepper Pike, Cuyahoga, Ohio 3,217 B1 156
Pepperton, Butts, Ga. 523 C3 176
Peppertown, Franklin, Ind. 100 C4 140
Peqin, Alb. 3,069 D4 316
Pequabuck, Litchfield, Conn. 300 C4 202
Pequaming, Baraga, Mich. C3 146
Pequannock, Morris, N.J. 4,600 B4 210
Pequest, riv., N.J. B3 210
Pequiri, riv., Braz. J6 257
Pequot Lakes, Crow Wing, Minn. 461 E4 148
Perak, state, Mala. 1,220,633 *F4 362
Perak, riv., Mala. F4 362
Perales de Tajuña, Sp. 1,874 *B5 298
Peralta, Valencia, N.Mex. 573 D4 126
Percé, Que., Can. 675 *Q10 66
Perche, hills, Fr. D4 278
Percival, Fremont, Iowa 300 D2 142
Percy, Randolph, Ill. 810 E4 138
Percy, Washington, Miss. 100 B2 184
Percy, peaks, N.H. B4 208
Perdido, Baldwin, Ala. 350 D2 168
Perdido, bay, Ala., Fla. E2 168
A3 174
Perdido, mtn., Sp. A7 298
Perdido, riv., Ala., Fla. E2 168
A3 174
Perdue, Sask., Can. 413 D4 58
Pereira, Col. 76,262 C1 244
Perekop, Sov.Un. I9 332
Pere Marquette, riv., Mich. F5 146
Perené, riv., Peru C3 245
Pereslavl-Zalesskiy, Sov.Un. 22,200 D12 332
Pereyaslav-Khmelnitskiy, Sov.Un. 27,500 G8 332
Pergamino, Arg. 32,382 B3 252
Pergine Valsugana, It. 3,879 B3 302
Perham, Aroostook, Maine 125 B4 204
(512▲)
Perham, Otter Tail, Minn. 2,019 E3 148
Peridot, Gila, Ariz. 25 E5 124
Périgueux, Fr. 40,785 E4 278
Perija, mts., Col. B2 244
Perija, mts., Ven. B2 240
Perim, isl., Aden E3 383
Perister, mtn., Yugo. D5 316
Perkasie, Bucks, Pa. 4,650 C6 214
Perkins, Jenkins, Ga. 250 D5 176
Perkins, Delta, Mich. 250 D4 146
Perkins, Payne, Okla. 769 C6 128
Perkins, co., Nebr. 4,189 D4 152
Perkins, co., S.Dak. 5,977 B3 158
Perkinston, Stone, Miss. 350 E3 184
Perkinsville, Windsor, Vt. 167 E3 218
Perla, Hot Spring, Ark. 200 C4 170
D7
Perlas, arch., Pan. F8 228
Perlas, lagoon, Nic. D6 228
Perleberg, Ger. 13,600 B4 286
Perley, Norman, Minn. 165 D2 148
Perlis, state, Mala. 90,834 *F4 362
Perm, Sov.Un. 628,000 A5 336
Perma, Sanders, Mont. 60 *C1 110
Përmet, Alb. 2,302 A3 306
Pernambuco, state, Braz. 3,916,000 G9 256
Pernambuco, see Recife, Braz.
Pernell, Garvin, Okla. 150 D6 128
Pernik, see Dimitrovo, Bul.
Perniö, Fin. F10 291
Péronne, Fr. C5 278
Perote, Bullock, Ala. 65 D4 168
Perovo, Sov.Un. 143,000 N18 332
Perpignan, Fr. 70,051 F5 278
Perquimans, co., N.C. 9,178 A9 186
Perrin, Gloucester, Va. 300 C8 192
Perrine, Dade, Fla. 6,424 E6 174
F10
Perrineville, Monmouth, N.J. 250 C4 210
Perrinton, Gratiot, Mich. 424 *F7 146
Perris, Riverside, Calif. 2,950 F5 94
Perros-Guirec, Fr. C2 278
Perrot, isl., Que., Can. S15 66
Perry, Perry, Ark. 224 B4 170
Perry, Taylor, Fla. 8,030 A7 174
Perry, Houston, Ga. 6,032 D3 176
Perry, Pike, Ill. 483 D3 138
Perry, Dallas, Iowa 6,442 C3 142
Perry, Jefferson, Kans. 495 C8 144
Perry, Vermilion, La. 150 E3 180
Perry, Washington, Maine 125 D5 204
(564▲)
Perry, Shiawassee, Mich. 1,370 G7 146
Perry, Ralls, Mo. 802 B6 150
Perry, Wyoming, N.Y. 4,629 C3 212
Perry, Lake, Ohio 885 A5 156
Perry, Noble, Okla. 5,210 B6 128
Perry, Aiken, S.C. 196 D6 188
Perry, Box Elder, Utah 587 B3 114
Perry, co., Ala. 17,358 C2 168
Perry, co., Ark. 4,927 C4 170
Perry, co., Ill. 19,184 E4 138
Perry, co., Ind. 17,232 D3 140
Perry, co., Ky. 34,961 C7 178
Perry, co., Miss. 8,745 D3 184
Perry, co., Mo. 14,642 D8 150
Perry, co., Ohio 27,864 C4 156
Perry, co., Pa. 26,582 C4 214
Perry, co., Tenn. 5,273 C4 190
Perry, peak, Mass. B1 206
Perry, stream, N.H. A4 208
Perrydale, Jackson, Oreg. E4 96
Perrydale, Polk, Oreg. 125 B3 96
Perrygo Place, Rock, Wis. 4,475 *F4 160
Perryman, Harford, Md. 700 B7 182
Perryopolis, Fayette, Pa. 1,799 *D2 214
Perry Point, Cecil, Md. 700 A7 182
Perrysburg, Cattaraugus, N.Y. 434 C2 212
Perrysburg, Wood, Ohio 5,519 A1 156
A3
Perry's Victory and International Peace Memorial, natl. mon., Ohio A4 156
Perrysville, Vermillion, Ind. 497 B2 140
Perrysville, Ashland, Ohio 769 B4 156
Perrysville, Allegheny, Pa. (part of McKnight) A3 214
Perryton, Ochiltree, Tex. 7,903 A5 130
Perryvale, Alta., Can. 14 C6 54
Perryville, Alsk. 130 D6 84
Perryville, Maricopa, Ariz. 50 H1 124
Perryville, Perry, Ark. 719 B4 170
Perryville, Boyle, Ky. 715 C6 178
Perryville, Ouachita, La. 100 B4 180
Perryville, Cecil, Md. 674 A7 182
Perryville, Perry, Mo. 5,117 D8 150
Perryville, Washington, R.I. 125 D2 216
Perryville, Decatur, Tenn. 250 C3 190
Pershing (East Germantown), Wayne, Ind. 367 C4 140
Pershing, Marion, Iowa 275 C5 142
Pershing, Gasconade, Mo. 165 C6 150
Pershing, Osage, Okla. 62 B7 128
Pershing, co., Nev. 3,199 C3 112
Persia, Harrison, Iowa 322 C2 142
Persia, see Iran
Persia, Hawkins, Tenn. 150 B8 190
Persian, gulf, Asia G7 340
Persinger, Nicholas, W.Va. 400 C4 194
Person, co., N.C. 26,394 A6 186
Perstorp, Swe. 5,359 E4 292
Pertek, Tur. 2,583 B8 307
Perth, Austl. 119,320 E3 432
Perth, N.B., Can. 715 C2 70
Perth, Ont., Can. 5,145 P24 64
Perth, Sumner, Kans. 100 E6 144
Perth, Jefferson, Miss. 150 D2 184
Perth Amboy, Middlesex, N.J. 38,007 B4 210
C1
Perth, Towner, N.Dak. 73 B6 154
Perth, Scot. 41,100 E9 272
Perth, co., Ont., Can. 55,057 Q19 64
Perth, co., Scot. 127,600 E8 272
Perthshire, Bolivar, Miss. 500 B2 184
Pertuis, Fr. 4,611 F6 278
Peru, La Salle, Ill. 10,460 B4 138
Peru, Miami, Ind. 14,453 B3 140
Peru, Madison, Iowa 265 C4 142
Peru, Chautauqua, Kans. 340 E7 144
Peru, Oxford, Maine 60 *D2 204
(1,229▲)
Peru, Berkshire, Mass. 50 B1 206
(197▲)
Peru, Nemaha, Nebr. 1,151 D10 152
Peru, Clinton, N.Y. 900 A8 212
Peru, Bennington, Vt. 40 E3 218
(194▲)
Peru, Hardy, W.Va. C5 194
Peru, Sweetwater, Wyo. 5 E3 116
Peru, country, S.A. 10,524,000 D4 236
245
Perugia, It. 41,500 D4 302
(99,000▲)
Perugia, prov., It. 588,900 *D4 302
Péruwelz, Bel. 7,757 D2 282
Pervomaysk, Sov.Un. 40,000 H8 332
Pervomaysk, Sov.Un. R22 332
Pervouralsk, Sov.Un. 90,000 A5 336
Pesaro, It. 35,900 D4 302
Pesaro e Urbino, prov., It. 335,100 *D4 302
Pesca, Mex. C6 225
Pescadero, San Mateo, Calif. 354 D2 94
Pescadores (Penghu), is., For. N10 349
Pescara, It. 71,500 D5 302
Pescara, prov., It. 246,500 *D5 302
Pescara, riv., It. D4 302
Pescia, It. D3 302
Peshastin, Chelan, Wash. 600 B6 98
Peshawar, Pak. 109,715 C7 375
(*151,776)
Peshkopi, Alb. 2,524 D5 316
Peshtera, Bul. 13,921 B2 317
Peshtigo, Marinette, Wis. 2,504 C6 160
Peshtigo, riv., Wis. C5 160
Peski, Sov.Un. B7 336
Peski, Sov.Un. 25,000 G14 332
Peski, Sov.Un. 5,000 O19 332
Peso da Régua, Port. 5,623 B3 298
Pesotum, Champaign, Ill. 468 D5 138
Pest, co., Hung. 750,000 *B4 320
Petaca, Rio Arriba, N.Mex. 150 B5 126
Petacas, Mex. L12 225
Petah Tiqva, Isr. 37,500 B5 382
Petal, Forrest, Miss. 4,007 D3 184
Petaluma, Sonoma, Calif. 14,035 C2 94
Pétange, Lux. 10,456 E4 282
Petatlán, Mex. 3,630 D5 225
Petauke, Rh.&Nya. 1,410 B6 421
Petawawa, Ont., Can. 290 O23 64
Petawawa, riv., Ont., Can. O23 64
Petenwell, res., Wis. D4 160
Peterborough, Austl. 3,473 E7 432
Peterborough, Ont., Can. 42,698 P22 64
Peterborough, Eng. 54,400 I12 273
Peterborough, Hillsboro, N.H. 1,931 F3 208
(2,963▲)
Peterborough, co., Ont., Can. 67,981 P22 64
Peterhead, Scot. 12,700 D11 272
Peterman, Monroe, Ala. 600 D2 168
Peters, Dade, Fla. 100 E6 174
Peters, Sheridan, Nebr. B3 152
Peters, creek, W.Va. C7 194
Peters, mtn., Va., W.Va. C4 192
D4 194
Petersburg, Alsk. 1,502 D8 84
J14
Petersburg, Menard, Ill. 2,359 C4 138
Petersburg, Pike, Ind. 2,939 D2 140
Petersburg, Boone, Ky. 390 A7 178
Petersburg, Monroe, Mich. 1,018 H8 146
Petersburg, Boone, Nebr. 400 C7 152
Petersburg, Cape May, N.J. 200 E3 210
Petersburg, Rensselaer, N.Y. 445 C8 212
Petersburg, Nelson, N.Dak. 272 B8 154
Petersburg, Mahoning, Ohio 700 B6 156
Petersburg, Jefferson, Okla. E6 128
Petersburg, Lincoln and Marshall, Tenn. 423 C5 190
Petersburg, Hale, Tex. 1,400 C5 130
Petersburg (Independent City), Va. 36,750 B9 192
(*100,300) C7
Petersburg, Grant, W.Va. 2,079 B5 194
Petersfield, Man., Can. 165 E4 60
Petersham, Worcester, Mass. 450 B3 206
(890▲)
Peters Landing, Perry, Tenn. 25 C4 190
Peterson, Tuscaloosa, Ala. 500 *B2 168
Peterson, Maricopa, Ariz. 10 H2 124
Peterson, Clay, Iowa 565 B2 142
Peterson, Fillmore, Minn. 283 H7 148
Peterstown, Monroe, W.Va. 616 D4 194
Petersville, Lauderdale, Ala. 750 *A2 168
Petersville, Lewis, Ky. 50 B7 178
Petersville, Frederick, Md. 150 B4 182
Peter the Great, bay, Sov.Un. E15 329
Peterton, Osage, Kans. 50 *D8 144
Petilia Policastro, It. 8,662 F6 302
Pétionville, Hai. 9,477 C8 233
Petit, lake, La. C8 180
Petit Bois, isl., Miss. E4 184
Petitcodiac, N.B., Can. 850 D4 70
Petite Amite, riv., La. B6 180
Petite Miquelon, isl., N.A. G7 72
Petit Jean, mtn., Ark. B4 170
Petit Jean, mtn., Ark. C3 170
Petite Rivière Bridge, N.S., Can. 337 E5 70
Petit-Étang, N.S., Can. 345 C9 70
Petit-Goâve, Hai. 5,378 C8 232
Petit Rocher, N.B., Can. 490 B4 70
Petlalcatl, peak, Mex. F10 224

Petlalcingo, Mex. 3,055 L15 225
Peto, Mex. 5,787 C8 225
Petone, N.Z. 10,288 J11 437
Petorca, Chile 1,098 B1 252
Petoskey, Emmet, Mich. 6,138 D7 146
Petra, ruins, Jordan D6 382
Petrey, Crenshaw, Ala. 165 D3 168
Petrich, Bul. 16,462 C1 317
Petrified, forest, Miss. C2 184
Petrified, forest, S.Dak. D2 158
Petrified Forest, natl. mon., Ariz. C6 124
Petrified Wood, park, S.Dak. B3 158
Petrikov, Sov.Un. 15,600 F7 332
Petrinja, Yugo. 5,461 B3 316
Petrohué, Chile F3 251
Petrokrepost, Sov.Un. 30,000 C8 332
Petrolândia, Braz. 1,971 B3 258
Petroleum, Wells, Ind. 300 B4 140
Petroleum, Allen, Ky. 100 D4 178
Petroleum, co., Mont. 894 C8 110
Petrolia, Ont., Can. 3,426 R18 64
Petrolia, Allen, Kans. 125 E8 144
Petrolia, Clay, Tex. 631 B6 130
Petrolina, Braz. 7,478 B2 258
Petropavlovka, Sov.Un. S23 332
Petropavlovsk, Sov.Un. 86,000 B7 336
Petropavlovsk, Sov.Un. 131,000 D17 329
Petrópolis, Braz. 61,011 E2 258
Petros, Morgan, Tenn. 850 B7 190
Petroşeni, Rom. 23,052 B2 321
Petrovgrad, see Zrenjanin, Yugo.
Petrovsk, Sov.Un. 40,000 F15 332
Petrovskoye, Sov.Un. 29,000 C2 336
Petrovskoye, Sov.Un. 5,000 J14 332
Petrovsk-Zabaykalskiy, Sov.Un. 59,000 D12 329
Petrozavodsk, Sov.Un. 135,000 B10 332
Pettaquamscutt, riv., R.I. D3 216
Pettibone, Kidder, N.Dak. 205 C6 154
Pettigrew, Madison, Ark. 150 B3 170
Pettis, co., Mo. 35,120 C4 150
Pettisville, Fulton, Ohio 310 A2 156
Pettus, Lonoke, Ark. C5 D7 170
Pettus, Bee, Tex. 450 E7 130
Pettusville, Limestone, Ala. 100 A3 168
Petty Harbour, Newf., Can. 800 G9 72
Petukhovo, Sov.Un. 12,300 A7 336
Pevek, Sov.Un. C19 329
Pevely, Jefferson, Mo. 416 B8 150
Pewano, Ionia, Mich. 415 F7 146
Pewaukee, Waukesha, Wis. 2,484 E1 E5 160
Pewee Valley, Oldham, Ky. 881 A5 B5 178
Peyton, El Paso, Colo. 110 C6 106
Peytona, Boone, W.Va. 150 D6 194
Pézenas, Fr. 6,530 F5 278
Pfaffenhofen, Ger. 7,715 D4 286
Pfäffikon, Switz. 4,784 A4 312
Pfarrkirchen, Ger. 6,000 D5 286
Pfeifer, Ellis, Kans. 200 D4 144
Pforzheim, Ger. 70,800 D3 286
Pfunds, Aus. 1,766 D2 313
Phalodi, India 15,224 C2 366
Phangan, isl., Thai. E4 362
Phang-Nga, prov., Thai. 61,014 *E3 362
Phan Rang, Viet. 39,524 E6 362
Phan Thiet, Viet. 11,762 E6 362
Pharoah, Okfuskee, Okla. 250 C7 128
Pharr, Hidalgo, Tex. 14,106 F6 130
Phatthalung, Thai. F4 362
Phatthalung, prov., Thai. 149,469 *F4 362
Pheba, Clay, Miss. 351 B4 184
Phelps, Pike, Ky. 725 C8 178
Phelps, Ontario, N.Y. 1,887 C4 212
Phelps, Vilas, Wis. 500 B4 160
Phelps, co., Mo. 25,396 D6 150
Phelps, co., Nebr. 9,800 D6 152
Phelps, lake, N.C. B9 186
Phelps City, Atchison, Mo. 81 A2 150
Phenix, Kent, R.I. (part of Warwick) C2 216
Phenix, Charlotte, Va. 259 C6 192
Phenix City, Russell, Ala. 27,630 C4 168
Phet Buri, Thai. 10,000 D3 362
Phet Buri, prov., Thai. 180,467 *D3 362
Phetchabun, Thai. 25,000 C4 362
Phetchabun, prov., Thai. 162,730 *C4 362
Phichit, Thai. 25,000 C4 362
Phichit, prov., Thai. 237,241 *C4 362
Philadelphia, Neshoba, Miss. 5,017 C3 184
Philadelphia, Marion, Mo. 166 B6 150
Philadelphia, Jefferson, N.Y. 868 A6 212
Philadelphia, Philadelphia, Pa. 2,002,512 (*3,969,500) A6 D6 214
Philadelphia, Loudon, Tenn. 500 C7 190
Philadelphia, co., Pa. 2,002,512 D6 214
Phil Campbell, Franklin, Ala. 898 A2 168
Philip, Haakon, S.Dak. 1,114 C4 158
Philipp, Tallahatchie, Miss. 250 B2 184
Philippeville, Alg. 70,406 A5 402
Philippeville, Bel. 1,570 D3 282
Philippi, Barbour, W.Va. 2,228 B4 194
Philippine, sea, Phil. B6 358
Philippines, country, Asia 19,234,182 A6 358, H14 340
Philippolis, U.S.Afr. 2,027 F5 420
Philipsburg, Granite, Mont. 1,107 D3 110
Philipsburg, Centre, Pa. 3,872 C3 214
Philipsville, Ont., Can. 200 P24 64
Philleo, lake, Wash. D8 98
Phillippy, Lake, Tenn. 100 B2 190
Phillips, Franklin, Maine 600 (1,021▲) D2 204
Phillips, Phillips, Mont. B8 110
Phillips, Hamilton, Nebr. 192 D7 152
Phillips, Coal, Okla. 91 D7 128
Phillips, Hutchinson, Tex. 3,605 B5 130
Phillips, Price, Wis. 1,524 C3 160
Phillips, co., Ark. 43,997 C6 170
Phillips, co., Colo. 4,440 B8 106
Phillips, co., Kans. 8,709 C4 144
Phillips, co., Mont. 6,027 B8 110
Phillips, brook, N.H. B4 208
Phillips, isl., S.C. G7 188
Phillipsburg, Que., Can. 412 S11 66
Phillipsburg, Tift, Ga. 2,037 E3 176
Phillipsburg, Phillips, Kans. 3,233 C4 144
Phillipsburg, Laclede, Mo. 142 D5 150
Phillipsburg, Warren, N.J. 18,502 B2 210
Phillipsburg, Montgomery, Ohio 715 *C2 156
Phillips Hill, Sussex, Del. F4 172
Phillipston, Worcester, Mass. 100 (695▲) A3 206
Phillips Village, Saline, Kans. 350 *D6 144
Phillipsville, Haywood, N.C. 1,311 *B3 186
Philmont, Columbia, N.Y. 1,750 C8 212
Philo, Champaign, Ill. 740 C5 138
Philo, Muskingum, Ohio 913 C5 156
Philomath, Oglethorpe, Ga. 550 C4 176
Philomath, Benton, Oreg. 1,359 C3 96
Philpott, res., Va. D4 192
Philrich, Hutchinson, Tex. 2,067 *B5 130
Phippen, Sask., Can. 60 D3 58
Phippsburg, Routt, Colo. 150 B4 106
Phippsburg, Sagadahoc, Maine 100 (1,121▲) E3 E6 204
Phitsanulok, Thai. C4 362
Phitsanulok, prov., Thai. 202,249 *C4 362
Phlorina, see Flórina, prov., Grc.
Phlox, Langlade, Wis. 150 C4 160
Phnom Penh, Cam. 123,883 E5 362
Phocis, see Fokis, prov., Grc.
Phoebus, Va. (part of Hampton) A8 192
Phoenicia, Ulster, N.Y. 475 C7 212
Phoenix, Maricopa, Ariz. 439,170 (*619,600) E3 H2 124
Phoenix, Cook, Ill. 4,203 F3 138
Phoenix, Plaquemines, La. 400 C7 180
Phoenix, Baltimore, Md. 200 A6 182
Phoenix, Oswego, N.Y. 2,408 B5 212
Phoenix, Jackson, Oreg. 769 E4 96
Phoenix, is., Pac.O. C4 436
Phoenixville, Chester, Pa. 13,797 A6 C6 214
Phong Saly, Laos. 10,000 B4 362
Phosphate, Powell, Mont. 75 *D4 110
Phrae, Thai. 25,000 C4 362
Phrae, prov., Thai. 213,351 *C4 362
Phra Nakhon (Bangkok), prov., Thai. 884,197 *D4 362
Phthiotis, see Fthiótis, prov., Grc.
Phuket, Thai. 5,000 F3 362
Phuket, prov., Thai. 49,324 *F3 362
Phuket, isl., Thai. F3 362
Phu Lai Leng, mtn., Laos C5 362
Phu Quoc, isl., Viet. E5 362
Phutthaisong, Thai. D4 362
Phyllis, Pike, Ky. 900 C8 178
Piaanu, pass, Truk A3 436
Piacenza, It. 62,400 (75,600▲) C2 302
Piacenza, prov., It. 299,300 *C2 302
Pianosa, isl., It. D3 302
Pianosa, isl., It. D5 302
Piapot, Sask., Can. 268 F3 58
Piatra-Neamţ, Rom. 32,648 A4 321
Piatt, co., Ill. 14,960 D5 138
Piaui, state, Braz. 1,215,000 G8 256
Piaui, mts., Braz. B2 258
Piaui, riv., Braz. B2 258
Piave, Greene, Miss. 80 D4 184
Piave, riv., It. B4 302
Piaxtla, pt., Mex. C4 224
Piazza Armerina, It. 27,900 G5 302
Pibor, riv., Sud. D3 398
Pibor Post, Sud. D3 398
Pibroch, Alta., Can. 100 C6 54
Pica, Yavapai, Ariz. 29 C2 124
Picabo, Blaine, Idaho 75 F4 108
Picacho, Pinal, Ariz. 500 F4 124
Picacho, Imperial, Calif. 50 F6 94
Picacho, Lincoln, N.Mex. 75 E5 126
Picacho, peak, Calif. F6 94
Picadome, Fayette, Ky. 900 *B6 178
Picardy (Picardie), former prov., Fr. 1,051,000 C5 278
Picayune, Pearl River, Miss. 7,834 E3 184
Piccadilly, Newf., Can. 200 F6 72
Piceance, creek, Colo. C2 106
Pichan, see Shanshan, China
Pichanal, Arg. B5 250
Picher, Ottawa, Okla. 2,553 B9 128
Pichilemu, Chile B1 252
Pichilingue, Mex. C3 224
Pickard, pt., Mass. C4 206
Pickardville, Alta., Can. 400 C6 54
Pickaway, co., Ohio 35,855 C3 156
Pick City, Mercer, N.Dak. 101 C4 154
Pickens, Desha, Ark. 100 D5 170
Pickens, Holmes, Miss. 727 C3 184
Pickens, McCurtain, Okla. 150 D8 128
Pickens, Pickens, S.C. 2,198 B3 188
Pickens, Randolph, W.Va. 500 C4 194
Pickens, co., Ala. 21,882 B1 168
Pickens, co., Ga. 8,903 B2 176
Pickens, co., S.C. 46,030 B3 188
Pickensville, Pickens, Ala. 160 B1 168
Pickerel, Ont., Can. 75 O20 64
Pickerel, lake, Wis. C5 160
Pickerel, riv., Ont., Can. O20 64
Pickering, Ont., Can. 1,150 Q21 64
Pickering, Nodaway, Mo. 234 A3 150
Pickerington, Fairfield, Ohio 634 C1 C4 156
Pickett, co., Tenn. 4,431 B6 190
Pickford, Chippewa, Mich. 650 C7 146
Pickleville, Rich, Utah 94 B4 114
Pickrell, Gage, Nebr. 130 D9 152
Pickstown, Charles Mix, S.Dak. 600 D7 158
Pickwick, Winona, Minn. 150 H7 148
Pickwick, lake, Ala., Miss., Tenn. A1 168, A4 184, C3 190
Pickwick Dam, Hardin, Tenn. 25 C3 190
Pico, Los Angeles, Calif. 18,000 C5 94
Pico Rivera, Los Angeles, Calif. 49,150 *E4 94
Picos, Braz. 4,568 B2 258
Pictograph, rocks, Ariz. E2 124
Picton, Ont., Can. 4,998 P23 64
Picton, N.Z. 2,079 D5 437
Pictou, N.S., Can. 4,564 D7 70
Pictou, Huerfano, Colo. E6 106
Pictou, co., N.S., Can. 44,566 D7 70
Pictou, isl., N.S., Can. D7 70
Picture Butte, Alta., Can. 881 F6 54
Pictured, cave, Wis. E2 160
Pictured, rocks, Ariz. F4 124
Pictured, rocks, Mich. C5 146
Picún-Leufú, Arg. C2 252
Pidcock, Brooks, Ga. 250 F3 176
Pidurutalagala, mtn., Cey. G4 366
Piedmont, Calhoun, Ala. 4,794 B4 168
Piedmont, Alameda, Calif. 11,117 *A5 94
Piedmont, Que., Can. 325 S10 66
Piedmont, Greenwood, Kans. 250 E7 144
Piedmont, Wayne, Mo. 1,555 D7 150
Piedmont, Canadian, Okla. 146 C6 128
Piedmont, Greenville, S.C. 2,108 B4 188
Piedmont, Meade, S.Dak. 200 C2 158
Piedmont, Mineral, W.Va. 2,307 B5 194
Piedmont, Uinta, Wyo. 10 E2 116
Piedmont (Piemonte), reg., It. 3,686,300 C1 302
Piedmont, plat., Va. D5 192
Piedmont, res., Ohio B5 156
Piedra, Maricopa, Ariz. 25 F2 124
Piedrabuena, Sp. 9,490 C4 298
Piedra Negra, pt., Mex. D6 225
Piedras, pt., Arg. C4 252
Piedras, riv., Peru C3 245
Piedras Blancas, pt., Calif. E3 94
Piedras Negras, Guat. B2 228
Piedras Negras, Mex. 27,578 B5 225
Piedra Sola, Ur. B4 252
Pieksämäki, Fin. 8,041 E12 291
Piélagos, Sp. 1,328 A5 298
Pielavesi, Fin. E12 290
Pielien, lake, Fin. E13 290
Piendamó, Col. 1,615 C1 244
Pienkuan, China 1,000 F5 348
Pierce, Weld, Colo. 424 B6 106
Pierce, Polk, Fla. 937 D9 174
Pierce, Clearwater, Idaho 522 C3 108
Pierce, Pierce, Nebr. 1,216 B8 152
Pierce, Tucker, W.Va. 215 B5 194
Pierce, co., Ga. 9,678 E4 176
Pierce, co., Nebr. 8,722 B8 152
Pierce, co., N.Dak. 7,394 B5 154
Pierce, co., Wash. 321,590 C4 98
Pierce, co., Wis. 22,503 D1 160
Pierce, lake, Man., Can. C6 60
Pierce, lake, Fla. D9 174
Pierce, pond, Maine C2 204
Pierce City, Lawrence, Mo. 1,006 E3 150
Pierces, Cape May, N.J. 175 E3 210
Pierceton, Kosciusko, Ind. 1,186 A4 140
Pierceville, Finney, Kans. 175 E3 144
Pieria, prov., Grc. 86,161 A4 306
Piermont, Grafton, N.H. 125 (477▲) D2 208
Piermont, Rockland, N.Y. 1,906 D2 D8 212
Piermont, mtn., N.H. D3 208
Pierowall, Scot. B9 272
Pierpont, Ashtabula, Ohio 500 A6 156
Pierpont, Day, S.Dak. 258 B8 158
Pierre, Hughes, S.Dak. 10,088 C5 158
Pierre, bayou, Miss. D2 184
Pierrefitte [-sur-Seine], Fr. 12,867 I10 278
Pierre Part, Assumption, La. 500 C5 180
Pierreville, Que., Can. 1,589 R12 66
Pierron, Bond, Ill. 451 E4 138
Pierson, Man., Can. 220 F2 60
Pierson, Volusia, Fla. 716 B9 174
Pierson, Woodbury, Iowa 425 B2 142
Pierson, Montcalm, Mich. 219 *F6 146
Pierz, Morrison, Minn. 816 F4 148
Piešťany, Czech. 19,215 B3 324
Pietermaritzburg, U.S.Afr. 73,273 (*74,493) E5 420
Pietersburg, U.S.Afr. 20,341 D5 420
Pie Town, Catron, N.Mex. 120 D2 126
Pietrasanta, It. 6,600 *D3 302
Piet Retief, U.S.Afr. 5,999 E6 421
Pietrosu, mtn., Rom. A3 321
Pieve di Cadore, It. 3,900 B4 302
Pigeon, Huron, Mich. 1,191 F8 146
Pigeon, bay, Man., Can. D4 60
Pigeon, creek, Ala. D3 168
Pigeon, creek, Ind. D2 140
Pigeon, lake, Alta., Can. D5 54
Pigeon, mtn., Ga. B1 176
Pigeon, mtn., N.Y. B7 212
Pigeon, pt., Calif. D2 94
Pigeon, pt., Minn. D9 148
Pigeon, riv., Man., Can. D4 60
Pigeon, riv., Ind. A4 140
Pigeon, riv., Minn. C9 148
Pigeon Cove, Essex, Mass. 1,064 A6 206
Pigeon Creek, Butler, Ala. 25 D3 168
Pigeon Falls, Trempealeau, Wis. 207 D2 160
Pigeon Forge, Sevier, Tenn. 950 C8 190
Pigeon Key, Monroe, Fla. 150 G9 174
Pigg, riv., Va. D4 192
Piggott, Clay, Ark. 2,776 A6 170
Pihtipudas, Fin. E11 290
Piippola, Fin. D11 290
Piirai, isl., Eniwetok B1 436
Pijijiapan, Mex. 3,307 D7 225
Pikangikum, Ont., Can. R23 64
Pike, Pike, Ark. 50 C3 170
Pike, Brown, Nebr. B6 152
Pike, Grafton, N.H. 200 C2 208
Pike, Yamhill, Oreg. *B3 96
Pike, co., Ala. 25,987 D4 168
Pike, co., Ark. 7,864 C3 170
Pike, co., Ga. 7,138 C2 176
Pike, co., Ill. 20,552 D2 138
Pike, co., Ind. 12,797 D2 140
Pike, co., Ky. 68,264 C8 178
Pike, co., Miss. 35,063 D2 184
Pike, co., Mo. 16,706 B6 150
Pike, co., Ohio 19,380 C3 156
Pike, co., Pa. 9,158 B6 214
Pike, riv., Wis. C5 160
Piker Springs, Sweetwater, Wyo. 5 E5 116
Pikes, peak, Colo. D5 106
Pikes Peak, St. James, La. 200 C6 180
Pikes Rocks, mtn., Pa. B2 214
Pikesville, Baltimore, Md. 18,737 C4 182
Piketberg, U.S.Afr. F3 420
Piketon, Pike, Ohio 1,244 C3 156
Pikeview, El Paso, Colo. 200 D6 106
Pikeville, Pike, Ky. 4,754 C8 178
Pikeville, Wayne, N.C. 525 B8 186
Pikeville, Bledsoe, Tenn. 951 C6 190
Pikwitonei, Man., Can. 15 C4 60
Piła, Pol. 27,000 B3 325
Pilar, Braz. 6,826 B3 258
Pilar, Taos, N.Mex. 127 B5 126
Pilar, Par. 5,061 E3 247
Pilar de Goias, Braz. 232 C1 258
Pilatus, mtn., Switz. B4 312
Pilcomayo, riv., Arg. B5 250
Pilcomayo, riv. Bol. D2 246
Pilcomayo, riv., Par. C2 247
Pilger, Sask., Can. 200 D5 58
Pilger, Stanton, Nebr. 491 B8 152
Pilgrim, Martin, Ky. 600 C8 178
Pilgrim Knob, Buchanan, Va. 100 C3 192
Pilibhit, India C2 368
Pilica, riv., Pol. C4 325
Pillager, Cass, Minn. 338 E4 148
Pillar, pt., Calif. B4 94
Pillaro, Ec. 2,792 A2 245
Pilley's Island, Newf., Can. 400 F8 72
Pillsbury, Barnes, N.Dak. 76 C8 154
Pilos, Grc. 3,314 C3 306
Pilot, knob, Ark. B3 170
Pilot, knob, Ark. C2 170
Pilot, knob, Idaho D3 108
Pilot, knob, Mo. E4 150
Pilot, knob, Tenn. B6 190
Pilot, peak, Nev. B7 112
Pilot, range, N.H. B4 208
Pilot Butte, Sask., Can. 120 E5 58
Pilot Grove, Cooper, Mo. 680 C5 150
Pilot Knob, Iron, Mo. 524 D7 150
Pilot Mound, Man., Can. 785 F3 60
Pilot Mound, Boone, Iowa 196 B3 142
Pilot Mountain, Surry, N.C. 1,310 A5 186
Pilot Point, Alsk. 67 D6 84
Pilot Point, Denton, Tex. 1,254 C7 130
Pilot Rock, Umatilla, Oreg. 1,695 B8 96
Pilot Station, Alsk. 52 C5 84
Pilottown, Sussex, Del. E5 172
Pilottown, Plaquemines, La. 150 E6 180
Pilsen, Marion, Kans. 55 *D6 144
Pilsen, Kewaunee, Wis. 30 A6 160
Pima, Graham, Ariz. 806 F6 124
Pima, co., Ariz. 265,660 F3 124
Pimba, Austl. 92 E7 432
Pimento, Vigo, Ind. 100 C2 140
Pimmet Hills, Fairfax, Va. 1,000 *B7 192
Pinal, co., Ariz. 62,673 F4 124
Pinal, mts., Ariz. E5 124
Pinarbaşi, Tur. 3,865 B7 307
Pinar del Rio, Cuba 38,885 A3 232
Pinar del Rio, prov., Cuba 448,422 A3 232
Pinardville, Hillsboro, N.H. 1,500 *F4 208
Pinás, Arg. B2 252
Pincher, Alta., Can. 150 F6 54
Pincher Creek, Alta., Can. 1,729 F6 54
Pinchiang, see Harbin, China
Pinchi Lake, B.C., Can. C10 52
Pinckard, Dale, Ala. 578 D4 168
Pinckney, Livingston, Mich. 732 G8 146
Pinckney, isl., S.C. G7 188
Pinckneyville, Perry, Ill. 3,085 E4 138
Pinconning, Bay, Mich. 1,329 F8 146
Pincourt, Que., Can. 1,437 S15 66
Pińczów, Pol. 3,701 C5 325
Pindall, Searcy, Ark. 100 A4 170
Pindamonhangaba, Braz. 13,397 E1 258
Pindaré, riv., Braz. A1 258
Pindus, mts., Grc. B3 306
Pine, Gila, Ariz. 120 D4 124
Pine, Jefferson, Colo. 5 C5 106
Pine, Ripley, Mo. 150 E6 150
Pine, San Miguel, N.Mex. 100 C5 126
Pine, co., Minn. 17,004 E6 148
Pine, cape, Newf., Can. G9 72
Pine, creek, Nev. C5 112
Pine, creek, Pa. B4 214
Pine, creek, Wash. B9 98
Pine, hill, Conn. C3 202
Pine, key, Fla. C6 174
Pine, lake, Ind. A3 140
Pine, lake, Minn. E3 148
Pine, lake, Wis. C4 160
Pine, mtn., Conn. B4 202
Pine, mtn., Conn. D2 202
Pine, mtn., Ga. D2 176
Pine, mtn., Ky., Tenn. D6 178, B7 190
Pine, mtn., Mass. B3 206
Pine, mtn., Okla. D8 128
Pine, mtn., Oreg. D6 96
Pine, pass, B.C., Can. C11 52
Pine, pt., Fla. B7 174
Pine, ridge, Nebr., Wyo. B2 152, D8 116
Pine, riv., Man., Can. E2 60
Pine, riv., Mich. E6 146
Pine, riv., N.H. D4 208
Pine, riv., Wis. C4 160
Pine Apple, Wilcox, Ala. 355 D3 168
Pine Bank, Greene, Pa. 20 D1 214
Pine Barren, Escambia, Fla. 150 A3 174
Pine Beach, Ocean, N.J. 985 D4 210
Pine Bluff, Jefferson, Ark. 44,037 C4 170
Pinebluff, Clay, Miss. 200 B4 184
Pinebluff, Moore, N.C. 509 B6 186
Pinebluff, lake, Sask., Can. C6 58
Pine Bluffs, Laramie, Wyo. 1,121 E8 116
Pine Bluff Southeast, Jefferson, Ark. 2,679 *C5 170
Pine Bush, Orange, N.Y. 1,016 D7 212
Pine Castle, Orange, Fla. 2,500 C9 174
Pine City, Monroe, Ark. 125 C5 170
Pine City, Pine, Minn. 1,972 F6 148
Pine City, Whitman, Wash. 50 B9 98
Pinecraft, Sarasota, Fla. 1,200 D6 174
Pine Creek, Austl. 83 A6 432
Pinecreek, Roseau, Minn. 34 C3 148
Pine Creek, gorge, Pa. B4 214
Pine Crest, El Paso, Colo. 30 *C6 106
Pinecroft, Spokane, Wash. D9 98
Pinedale, Navajo, Ariz. 25 D5 124

Pinedale, Fresno, Calif. 3,202 D4 94
Pinedale, Sublette, Wyo. 965 D3 116
Pine Falls, Man., Can. 525 E4 60
Pine Flat, res., Calif. D4 94
Pine Forest, mts., Nev. B3 112
Pine Grove, Dallas, Ark. D4 170
Pine Grove, Appling, Ga. 100 E4 176
Pine Grove, St. Helena, La. 150 D5 180
Pine Grove, Schuylkill, Pa. 2,267 C5 214
Pine Grove, Wetzel, W.Va. 760 A6 194, B4
Pine Grove, Brown, Wis. 25 A6 160
Pine Hall, Stokes, N.C. 400 A5 186
Pine Harbor, McIntosh, Ga. 125 E5 176
Pine Hill, Wilcox, Ala. 367 D2 168
Pine Hill, Rockcastle, Ky. 600 C6 178
Pine Hill, Camden, N.J. 3,939 D3 210
Pine Hills, Harrison, Miss. 100 E1 184
Pinehurst, Dooly, Ga. 457 D3 176
Pinehurst, Shoshone, Idaho 1,432 B2 108
Pinehurst, Middlesex, Mass. 1,991 C2 206
Pinehurst, Moore, N.C. 1,124 B6 186
Pinehurst, Dorchester, S.C. 200 *E8 188
Pinehurst, Orange, Tex. 1,703 *D9 130
Pinehurst, Snohomish, Wash. 3,000 B4 98
Pine Island, Goodhue, Minn. 1,308 G6 148
Pine Island, sound, Fla. E8 174
Pineknob, Raleigh, W.Va. 300 D6 194
Pine Knot, McCreary, Ky. 750 D6 178
Pine Lake, De Kalb, Ga. 738 B5 176
Pine Lake, La Porte, Ind. 1,400 A3 140
Pine Lake, Middlesex, Mass. 400 *D1 206
Pineland, Jasper, S.C. 82 F6 188
Pineland, Sabine, Tex. 1,236 D9 130
Pine Lawn, St. Louis, Mo. 5,943 A8 150
Pine Level, Montgomery, Ala. C3 168
Pine Level, Johnston, N.C. 833 B7 186
Pinellas, co., Fla. 374,665 C8 174
Pinellas, pt., Fla. C6 174
Pinellas Park, Pinellas, Fla. 10,848 C6 174, D8
Pine Log, Bartow, Ga. 150 B2 176
Pine Meadow, Litchfield, Conn. 400 B4 202
Pine Mount, Suwannee, Fla. 125 A8 174
Pine Mountain, Harris, Ga. 790 D2 176
Pineora, Effingham, Ga. 210 D5 176
Pine Park, York, Maine E2 204
Pine Plains, Dutchess, N.Y. 665 D8 212
Pine Point, Cumberland, Maine 800 E2 204, E5
Pine Point, Becker, Minn. 150 E3 148
Pine Prairie, Evangeline, La. 387 D3 180
Pine Rest, Middlesex, Mass. 250 *D1 206
Pine Ridge, Montgomery, Ark. 100 C3 170
Pine Ridge, Wolfe, Ky. 300 C7 178
Pine Ridge, Adams, Miss. 50 D1 184
Pine Ridge, Dawes, Nebr. B2 152
Pineridge, Lexington, S.C. 329 *D6 188
Pine Ridge, Shannon, S.Dak. 1,256 D3 158
Pine River, Man., Can. 160 E2 60
Pine River, Cass, Minn. 775 E4 148
Pine River, Waushara, Wis. 125 D4 160
Pinerolo, It. 20,000 C1 302
Pinesburg, Washington, Md. 350 A4 182
Pine Springs, Ramsey, Minn. 142 *F5 148
Pinetop, Navajo, Ariz. 400 D6 124
Pinetops, Edgecombe, N.C. 1,372 B8 186
Pinetown, Beaufort, N.C. 215 B9 186
Pine Tree Park, Broward, Fla. 600 *E10 174
Pinetta, Madison, Fla. 200 A7 174
Pine Valley, San Diego, Calif. 150 F5 94
Pine Valley, Hillsboro, N.H. 100 F3 208
Pine Valley, Camden, N.J. 20 *D3 210
Pine Valley, Le Flore, Okla. D9 128
Pineview, Wilcox, Ga. 369 D3 176
Pineview, Fremont, Idaho E7 108
Pine Village, Warren, Ind. 309 B2 140
Pineville, Bell, Ky. 3,181 D7 178
Pineville, Rapides, La. 8,636 C3 180
Pineville, Smith, Miss. 300 C3 184
Pineville, McDonald, Mo. 545 E3 150
Pineville, Mecklenburg, N.C. 1,514 B5 186
Pineville, Berkeley, S.C. 100 E8 188
Pineville, Wyoming, W.Va. 1,137 D3 194
Pinewald, Ocean, N.J. 400 D4 210
Pinewood, Sumter, S.C. 570 D8 188
Piney, Man., Can. 300 F5 60
Piney, buttes, Mont. C10 110
Piney, fork, W.Va. A6 194
Piney, pt., Fla. B7 174
Piney Flats, Sullivan, Tenn. 300 B9 190
Piney Fork, Jefferson, Ohio 870 B6 156
Piney Point, St. Marys, Md. 200 D6 182
Piney Point, Harris, Tex. 1,790 *E8 130
Piney River, Nelson, Va. 300 C5 192
Piney Swamp, knob, W.Va. B5 194
Piney View, Raleigh, W.Va. 800 D7 194
Piney Woods, Rankin, Miss. 480 C2 184
Ping, riv., Thai. C3 362
Pingchou, China M3 349
Pingchüan, China 20,000 E9 348
Pingham, China N5 349
Pingho, China 10,000 M8 349
Pinghsiang, China 25,000 L6 349
Pingliang, China 55,000 H3 348
Pinglo, China 5,000 F3 348
Pinglo, China 10,000 M5 349
Pingree, Bingham, Idaho 100 F6 108
Pingree, Stutsman, N.Dak. 151 C7 154
Pingtan, China 10,000 M9 349
Pingting, China 20,000 G6 348
Pingtingshan, China 50,000 I6 348
Pingtu, China 10,000 G9 348
Pingtung, For. 110,000 N10 349
Pingwu, China E8 346
Pinhal, Braz. 10,103 E1 258
Pinhead, buttes, Oreg. C5 96
Pinheiro, Braz. 4,477 F7 256
Pinhel, Port. 3,312 B3 298
Pinhsien, China 25,000 C13 348
Pinhsien, China 1,000 H4 348
Pini, isl., Indon. D1 358
Piniós, riv., Grc. B3 306
Pink, Pottawatomie, Okla. C6 128
Pink, cliffs, Utah F3 114
Pinkey, Gaston, N.C. 3,762 *B4 186
Pinkham, Sask., Can. 91 E3 58
Pink Hill, Lenoir, N.C. 457 B8 186
Pinkstaff, Lawrence, Ill. 300 E6 138
Pinnacle, Pulaski, Ark. 25 C4 170, D6
Pinnacle, Stokes, N.C. 400 A5 186
Pinnacle, butte, Wyo. C3 116
Pinnacle, mtn., Mo. B7 150
Pinnacle, peak, Wyo. C2 116
Pinnacles, natl. mon., Calif. D3 94
Pinnebog, Huron, Mich. 110 F8 146
Pinó Hachado, pass, Arg. C1 252
Pinola, Simpson, Miss. 116 D3 184
Pinole, Contra Costa, Calif. 6,064 *C2 94
Pinon, Otero, N.Mex. 40 F5 126
Pinopolis, Berkeley, S.C. 311 E8 188
Pinopolis, dam, S.C. E9 188
Pinos, Mex. 3,327 C5 225, J13
Pinos, isl., Cuba B3 232
Pinos, pt., Calif. D3 94
Pinos Altos, Grant, N.Mex. 150 F2 126
Pinoso, Sp. 3,943 C6 298
Pinos-Puente, Sp. 8,652 D5 298
Pinsk, Sov.Un. 39,000 F6 332
Pinsk, marshes, Sov.Un. F6 332
Pinson, Jefferson, Ala. 1,121 E5 168
Pinson, Madison, Tenn. 240 C3 190
Pinsonfork, Pike, Ky. 800 C8 178
Pintados, Chile B4 250
Pintendre, Que., Can. 300 R16 66
Pinto, Allegany, Md. 150 A2 182
Pinto, Sp. 3,258 *B5 298
Pinto, butte, Sask., Can. F4 58
Pinto, creek, Sask., Can. F4 58
Pintura, Washington, Utah 5 F2 114
Pinware, riv., Newf., Can. E7 72
Pinyon, peak, Idaho E4 108
Pioche, Lincoln, Nev. 900 F7 112
Piombino, It. 28,700 D3 302
Pioneer, Humboldt, Iowa 448 B3 142
Pioneer, West Carroll, La. 154 B4 180
Pioneer, Williams, Ohio 855 A2 156
Pioneer, Campbell, Tenn. 90 B7 190
Pioneer, mts., Mont. E3 110
Pioneer Mine, B.C., Can. 350 E11 52
Piotrków [Trybunalski], Pol. 48,000 C4 325
Pipe, Fond du Lac, Wis. 90 B5 160
Pipe, creek, Ind. B4 140
Piper, Bibb, Ala. 20 B2 168
Piper, Wyandotte, Kans. 240 B7 144
Piper City, Ford, Ill. 807 C5 138
Piperi, isl., Grc. B5 306
Pipers Gap, Carroll, Va. 25 D4 192
Pipestone, Ont., Can. Q26 64
Pipe Spring, natl. mon., Ariz. B3 124
Pipestem, Summers, W.Va. 250 D4 194
Pipe Stem, creek, N.Dak. C6 154
Pipestone, Man., Can. 245 F2 60
Pipestone, Pipestone, Minn. 5,324 H2 148
Pipestone, co., Minn. 13,605 G2 148
Pipestone, creek, Man., Sask., Can. F2 60, E7 58
Pipestone, natl. mon., Minn. H2 148
Pipestone, pass, Mont. E4 110
Pipmuacan, lake, Que., Can. Q9 66
Piqua, Woodson, Kans. 258 E8 144
Piqua, Robertson, Ky. 25 B6 178
Piqua, Miami, Ohio 19,219 B2 156
Piqüe, Arg. C3 252
Piracanjuba, Braz. 2,473 D1 258
Piracicaba, Braz. 45,782 E1 258
Piraçununga, Braz. 12,546 E1 258
Piracuruca, Braz. 3,402 A2 258
Piraiévs, Grc. 186,014 C4 306
Pirajú, Braz. 5,980 E1 258
Pirajui, Braz. 5,654 E1 258
Piramida, mtn., Sov.Un. D11 329
Pirane, Arg. 3,561 C6 250
Piranga, Braz. 1,808 E2 258
Pirano, Yugo. 31,280 B1 316
Pirapóra, Braz. 8,531 D2 258
Pirdop, Bul. 5,570 B2 317
Pirgos, Grc. 17,996 C3 306
Piriápolis, Ur. 8,600 B4 252
Pirin, mts., Bul. C1 317
Piripiri, Braz. 4,357 A2 258
Piritu, Ven. A6 240
Pirmasens, Ger. 51,400 D2 286
Pirna, Ger. 40,400 C5 286
Pirot, Yugo. 3,175 C6 316
Pirtleville, Cochise, Ariz. 898 G6 124
Piru, Indon. E7 359
Piryatin, Sov.Un. 26,600 G9 332
Pisa, It. 81,100 D3 302
Pisa, prov., It. 354,700 *D3 302
Pisagua, Chile A3 250
Piscataqua, riv., N.H. E5 208
Piscataquis, co., Maine 17,379 C3 204
Piscataquis, riv., Maine C3 204
Piscataquog, riv., N.H. E3 208
Piscataway, Prince Georges, Md. 77 *C6 182
Piscataway, creek, Md. C6 182
Pisciotta, It. 1,488 E5 302
Pisco, Peru 20,698 C2 245
Piseco, lake, N.Y. B7 212
Pisek, Czech. 20,297 B2 324
Pisek, Walsh, N.Dak. 176 B8 154
Pisgah, Jackson, Ala. 214 A4 168
Pisgah, Harrison, Iowa 343 C2 142
Pisgah, Augusta, Va. B6 192
Pisgah, mtn., Wyo. C8 116
Pisgah Forest, Transylvania, N.C. 700 B3 186
Pishin, Pak. 3,106 D5 375
Pishin Lora, riv., Afg., Pak. E3 374, E4 375
Pishukan, cape, Pak. G3 375
Pismo Beach, San Luis Obispo, Calif. 1,762 E3 94
Pistoia, It. 34,100 (79,100▲) D3 302
Pistoia, prov., It. 222,900 *D3 302
Pistol River, Curry, Oreg. 50 E2 96
Pistolet, bay, Newf., Can. E8 72
Pisuerga, riv., Sp. A4 298
Pisz, Pol. 1,028 B5 325
Pit, riv., Calif. B3 94
Pita, Guinea D2 408
Pital, Mex. K15 225
Pitalito, Col. 3,616 C1 244
Pitangui, Braz. 5,367 D2 258
Pitcairn, Allegheny, Pa. 5,383 A4 214
Pitcairn, Br. poss., Pac.O. 125 D5 436
Pitcairn, isl., Pac.O. D5 436
Pitea, Swe. 6,466 D9 290
Piteälven, riv., Swe. D8 290
Pitești, Rom. 38,333 B3 321
Pithiviers, Fr. 6,944 C5 278
Piti, Guam 777 C7 436
Pitkas Point, Alsk. 84 C5 84
Pitkin, Gunnison, Colo. 94 D4 106
Pitkin, Vernon, La. 400 D3 180
Pitkin, co., Colo. 2,381 C4 106
Pitman, Gloucester, N.J. 8,644 D2 210
Pito, Pan. F9 228
Pitreville, St. Landry, La. 30 D3 180
Pitrufquén, Chile 4,982 C1 252
Pitsburg, Darke, Ohio 394 C2 156
Pitt, co., N.C. 69,942 B8 186
Pitt, cape, Solomon E1 436
Pitt, isl., B.C., Can. D8 52
Pittman, Alsk. 6 *C7 84
Pittman, Clark, Nev. 250 G7 112
Pittman Center, Sevier, Tenn. 45 C8 190
Pitts, Wilcox, Ga. 388 E3 176
Pitts, Estill, Ky. 54 C7 178
Pittsboro, Hendricks, Ind. 826 C3 140
Pittsboro, Calhoun, Miss. 205 B3 184
Pittsboro, Chatham, N.C. 1,215 B6 186
Pittsburg, Contra Costa, Calif. 19,062 *C3 94
Pittsburg, Williamson, Ill. 485 F5 138
Pittsburg, Carroll, Ind. 250 B3 140
Pittsburg, Crawford, Kans. 18,678 E9 144
Pittsburg, Laurel, Ky. 810 C6 178
Pittsburg, Hickory, Mo. 104 D4 150
Pittsburg, Coos, N.H. 200 (639▲) A4 208
Pittsburg, Pittsburg, Okla. 195 D8 128
Pittsburg, Columbia, Oreg. 50 B3 96
Pittsburg, Camp, Tex. 3,796 C8 130
Pittsburg, co., Okla. 34,360 D8 128
Pittsburgh, Allegheny, Pa. 604,332 (*1,957,700) A4 214, C1
Pittsburg Landing, Hardin, Tenn. 100 C3 190
Pittsfield, Pike, Ill. 4,089 D3 138
Pittsfield, Somerset, Maine 3,232 (4,010▲) D3 204
Pittsfield, Berkshire, Mass. 57,879 B1 206
Pittsfield, Washtenaw, Mich. 1,500 *G8 146
Pittsfield, Merrimack, N.H. 1,407 (2,419▲) E4 208
Pittsfield, Warren, Pa. 500 B2 214
Pittsfield, Rutland, Vt. 100 (254▲) D3 218
Pittsford, Hillsdale, Mich. 450 H7 146
Pittsford, Monroe, N.Y. 1,749 B4 212
Pittsford, Rutland, Vt. 671 (2,225▲) D2 218
Pittsford Mills, Rutland, Vt. 200 D2 218
Pittston, Kennebec, Maine 150 (1,311▲) *D3 204
Pittston, Luzerne, Pa. 12,407 A5 214, B6
Pittston Farm, Somerset, Maine 30 C3 204
Pittstown, Hunterdon, N.J. 230 B3 210
Pittsview, Russell, Ala. 200 C4 168
Pittsville, Wicomico, Md. 488 D9 182
Pittsville, Wood, Wis. 661 D3 160
Pittsylvania, co., Va. 58,296 D5 192
Pitzuwo, China 5,000 F11 348
Piuka, Jap. 13,876 B9 354
Piura, Peru 29,700 B1 245
Piura, dept., Peru 598,157 B1 245
Piute, co., Utah 1,436 E3 114
Piuthan, Nep. 1,350 C3 368
Pixley, Tulare, Calif. 1,327 E4 94
Piyang, China 5,000 I6 349
Pizzo, It. 9,900 F6 302
Placentia, Orange, Calif. 5,861 *F5 94
Placentia, Newf., Can. 1,233 G9 72
Placentia, bay, Newf., Can. G8 72
Placer, Josephine, Oreg. 125 E3 96
Placer, co., Calif. 56,998 C3 94
Placerville, El Dorado, Calif. 4,439 C3 94
Placerville, San Miguel, Colo. 50 D2 106
Placerville, Boise, Idaho 12 F3 108
Placetas, Cuba 25,226 A5 232
Placid, lake, N.Y. A8 212
Placita, Sierra, N.Mex. 55 E3 126
Placitas, Sandoval, N.Mex. 60 C4 126, H6
Plage Laval, Que., Can. 3,818 *S15 66
Plain, Sauk, Wis. 677 E3 160
Plain City, Madison and Union, Ohio 2,146 B3 156
Plain City, Weber, Utah 1,152 B3 114
Plain Dealing, Bossier, La. 1,357 B2 180
Plainfield, Columbia, Ark. D3 170
Plainfield, Windham, Conn. 2,044 (8,884▲) C8 202
Plainfield, Will, Ill. 2,183 B5 138, F2
Plainfield, Hendricks, Ind. 5,460 C3 140
Plainfield, Bremer, Iowa 445 B5 142
Plainfield, Hampshire, Mass. 100 (237▲) A2 206
Plainfield, Sullivan, N.H. 125 (1,071▲) D2 208
Plainfield, Union, N.J. 45,330 B4 210
Plainfield, Blount, Tenn. 2,127 *C8 190
Plainfield, Washington, Vt. 507 (966▲) C4 218
Plainfield, Waushara, Wis. 660 D4 160
Plainfield Heights, Kent, Mich. 1,000 *G6 146
Plains, Sumter, Ga. 572 D2 176
Plains, Meade, Kans. 780 E3 144
Plains, Sanders, Mont. 769 C2 110
Plains, Luzerne, Pa. 8,500 A5 214
Plains, Yoakum, Tex. 1,195 C4 130
Plainsboro, Middlesex, N.J. 600 C3 210
Plainview, Yell, Ark. 548 C3 170
Plain View, Scott, Iowa 37 *C7 142
Plainview, Wabasha, Minn. 1,833 G6 148
Plainview, Pierce, Nebr. 1,467 B8 152
Plainview, Nassau, N.Y. 27,710 D3 212
Plainview, Hale, Tex. 18,735 B5 130
Plainville, Hartford, Conn. 13,149 C4 202
Plainville, Gordon, Ga. 161 *B2 176
Plainville, Daviess, Ind. 545 D2 140
Plainville, Rooks, Kans. 3,104 C4 144
Plainville (Town of), Norfolk, Mass. (3,810▲) B5 206
Plainwell, Allegan, Mich. 3,125 G6 146
Plaisance, Que., Can. 525 S9 66
Plaisance, Hai. 1,692 C8 233
Plaisted, Aroostook, Maine 200 A4 204
Plaistow, Rockingham, N.H. 1,500 (2,915▲) F4 208
Plamondon, Alta., Can. 62 C6 54
Planada, Merced, Calif. 1,704 *D3 94
Planaltina, Braz. 1,385 D1 258
Plandome, Nassau, N.Y. 1,379 *E8 212
Plankinton, Aurora, S.Dak. 644 D7 158
Plano, Madison, Idaho F7 108
Plano, Kendall, Ill. 3,343 B5 138
Plano, Appanoose, Iowa 87 D4 142
Plano, Collin, Tex. 3,695 A9 130, C7
Plantagenet, Ont., Can. 600 O25 64
Plantation, Broward, Fla. 4,772 *E10 174
Plantation No. 14, Washington, Maine (63▲) *D5 204
Plant City, Chambers, Ala. 950 *C4 168
Plant City, Hillsborough, Fla. 15,711 C8 174
Plantersville, Dallas, Ala. 550 C3 168
Plantersville, Lee, Miss. 572 A4 184
Plantersville, Georgetown, S.C. 750 D10 188
Plantsite, Greenlee, Ariz. 1,552 *E6 124
Plantsville, Hartford, Conn. 2,793 C4 202
Plaquemine, Iberville, La. 7,689 B5 180, D4
Plaquemines, par., La. 22,545 E6 180
Plaquemine Southwest, Iberville, La. 1,272 *D4 180
Plasencia, Sp. 16,255 B3 298
Plaster Rock, N.B., Can. 875 C2 70
Platanar, Mex. C4 224
Plateau City, Mesa, Colo. 60 C3 106
Plate Cove, Newf., Can. 400 F9 72
Platinum, Alsk. 72 D5 84
Platner, Washington, Colo. 40 B7 106
Plato, Sask., Can. 185 E3 58
Plato, Col. 8,039 B2 244
Plato, McLeod, Minn. 280 G4 148
Plato, Texas, Mo. 140 D5 150
Platt, natl. park, Okla. D7 128
Platte, Charles Mix, S.Dak. 1,167 D7 158
Platte, co., Mo. 23,350 B3 150
Platte, co., Nebr. 23,992 C8 152
Platte, co., Wyo. 7,195 D7 116
Platte, riv., Iowa, Mo. D3 142, B3 150
Platte, riv., Minn. E4 148
Platte, riv., Nebr. D6 152
Platte Arkansas, divide, Colo. C6 106
Platte Center, Platte, Nebr. 402 C8 152
Platte City, Platte, Mo. 1,188 B3 150, D1
Plattenville, Assumption, La. 300 B5 180
Platter, Bryan, Okla. 200 E7 128
Platteville, Weld, Colo. 582 B6 106
Platteville, Grant, Wis. 6,957 F3 160
Platte Woods, Platte, Mo. 393 *B3 150
Plattling, Ger. 8,316 D5 286
Plattsburg, Winston, Miss. 100 C3 184
Plattsburg, Clinton, Mo. 1,663 B3 150
Plattsburgh, Clinton, N.Y. 20,172 A8 212
Plattsmouth, Cass, Nebr. 6,244 C10 152, E3
Plattsville, Ont., Can. 685 Q20 64
Plattsville, Fairfield, Conn. 400 E2 202
Plaucheville, Avoyelles, La. 228 D4 180
Plauen [im Vogtland], Ger. 82,000 C5 286
Playa Azul, Mex. D5 225
Playa de Candela, Ven. E5 240
Playas, Hidalgo, N.Mex. 25 G2 126
Playgreen, lake, Man., Can. C3 60
Plaza, Mountrail, N.Dak. 385 B4 154
Plaza del Moro Almanzor, mtn., Sp. B4 298
Pleasant, bay, Maine D5 204
Pleasant, lake, Ariz. E3 124
Pleasant, lake, Maine C5 204
Pleasant, mtn., N.B., Can. D3 70
Pleasant, mtn., Maine D4 204
Pleasant, pond, Maine B4 204
Pleasant, pond, Maine C3 204
Pleasant, pond, N.H. E4 208
Pleasant, riv., Maine C3 204
Pleasant Beach, Kitsap, Wash. (part of Port Blakely) D2 98
Pleasant City, Guernsey, Ohio 491 C5 156
Pleasantdale, Sask., Can. 175 D5 58
Pleasant Dale, Seward, Nebr. 190 *D8 152
Pleasant Gap, Centre, Pa. 1,389 C4 214
Pleasant Garden, Guilford, N.C. 1,000 B6 186
Pleasant Green, Phillips, Kans. 35 *C4 144
Pleasant Grove, Jefferson, Ala. 3,097 E4 168
Pleasant Grove, Pickens, Ala. 22 B2 168
Pleasant Grove, Panola, Miss. 60 A2 184
Pleasant Grove, Utah, Utah 4,772 C4 114
Pleasant Hill, Dale, Ala. D4 168
Pleasant Hill, Dallas, Ala. 300 C3 168
Pleasant Hill, Contra Costa, Calif. 23,844 *D2 94
Pleasant Hill, Pike, Ill. 950 D3 138
Pleasant Hill, Sabine, La. 907 C2 180
Pleasant Hill, De Soto, Miss. 150 A3 184
Pleasant Hill, Cass, Mo. 2,689 C3 150
Pleasant Hill, Miami, Ohio 1,060 B2 156
Pleasant Hill, McCurtain, Okla. 100 E9 128
Pleasant Hill, Lancaster, S.C. 150 B7 188
Pleasant Hill, Cumberland, Tenn. 267 *C6 190
Pleasant Hill, Nansemond, Va. 2,636 *D8 192

Pleasant Hills, Allegheny, Pa.	8,573	C1	214
Pleasant Home, Multnomah, Oreg.	200	*B2	96
Pleasant Hope, Polk, Mo.	216	D4	150
Pleasant Lake, Steuben, Ind.	600	A4	140
Pleasant Lake, Barnstable, Mass.	100	C7	206
Pleasant Mills, Adams, Ind.	160	B5	140
Pleasanton, Alameda, Calif.	4,203	B6	94
Pleasanton, Decatur, Iowa	103	D4	142
Pleasanton, Linn, Kans.	1,098	D9	144
Pleasanton, Buffalo, Nebr.	199	D6	152
Pleasanton, Atascosa, Tex.	3,467	E6	130
Pleasant Plain, Jefferson, Iowa	147	C6	142
Pleasant Plains, Independence, Ark.	112	B5	170
Pleasant Plains, Sangamon, Ill.	518	D4	138
Pleasant Prairie, Spokane, Wash.		D8	98
Pleasant Prairie, Kenosha, Wis.	400	F2	160
Pleasant Ridge, Daviess, Ky.	100	C4	178
Pleasant Ridge, Oakland, Mich.	3,807	B8	146
Pleasant Ridge, Princess Anne, Va.	200	D8	192
Pleasants, co., W.Va.	7,124	B3	194
Pleasant Shade, Smith, Tenn.	125	B6	190
Pleasant Site, Franklin, Ala.	200	A1	168
Pleasant Valley, Litchfield, Conn.		B4	202
Pleasant Valley, Scott, Iowa	700	D7	142
Pleasant Valley, Carroll, Md.	150	A5	182
Pleasant Valley, Clay, Mo.	1,109	*B3	150
Pleasant Valley, Flathead, Mont.		B2	110
Pleasant Valley, Dutchess, N.Y.	650	D8	212
Pleasant Valley, Baker, Oreg.	25	C9	96
Pleasant Valley, Fairfax, Va.		A6	192
Pleasant View, Montezuma, Colo.	75	E2	106
Pleasant View, Shelby, Ind.	100	E5	140
Pleasant View, Whitley, Ky.	500	D6	178
Pleasant View, Cheatham, Tenn.	150	B4	190
Pleasant View, Weber, Utah	927	B3	114
Pleasant View, Walla Walla, Wash.		C8	98
Pleasantville, Sullivan, Ind.	175	D2	140
Pleasantville, Marion, Iowa	1,025	C4	142
Pleasantville, Atlantic, N.J.	15,172	E3	210
Pleasantville, Westchester, N.Y.	5,877	D2	212
Pleasantville, Fairfield, Ohio	741	C4	156
Pleasure Beach, New London, Conn.	1,264	D7	202
Pleasure Ridge Park, Jefferson, Ky.	10,612	A5	178
Pleasureville, Henry and Shelby, Ky.	466	B5	178
Pleasureville, York, Pa.	1,000	*D5	214
Plebo, Lib.		F3	408
Pleiku, Viet.		D5	362
Plenița, Rom.	6,735	B2	321
Plenty, Sask., Can.	212	E3	58
Plenty, bay, N.Z.		B6	437
Plenty River, Austl.	60	C7	432
Plentywood, Sheridan, Mont.	2,121	B12	110
Plessisville, Que., Can.	5,829	R13	66
Pleszew, Pol.	8,760	C3	325
Pletcher, Chilton, Ala.	75	C3	168
Pletipi, lake, Que.. Can.		Q9	66
Pleven, Bul.	57,758	B2	317
Plevenski, prov., Bul.		*B2	317
Plevlja, Yugo.	6,883	C4	316
Plevna, Reno, Kans.	117	E5	144
Plevna, Knox, Mo.	110	B5	150
Plevna, Fallon, Mont.	263	D12	110
Pliny, range, N.H.		C4	208
Płock, Pol.	37,000	B4	325
Ploërmel, Fr.		D2	278
Ploești, Rom.	114,560	B4	321
Plomárion, Grc.	5,887	B6	306
Płońsk, Pol.	7,758	B5	325
Plovdiv, Bul.	162,518	B2	317
Plovdiv, prov., Bul.		*B2	317
Plovdivski, prov., Bul.		*B2	317
Plover, Pocahontas, Iowa	182	B3	142
Plover, Portage, Wis.	950	D4	160
Plover, riv., Wis.		D4	160
Pluck, Ire.		G5	272
Plum, bayou, Ark.		D7	170
Plum, creek, Nebr.		B5	152
Plum, creek, Nebr.		D5	152
Plum, isl., Mass.		A6	206
Plum, isl., N.Y.		D5	212
Plumas, Man., Can.	375	E3	60
Plumas, co., Calif.	11,620	B3	94
Plum Bayou, Jefferson, Ark.		C4	170
Plum Branch, McCormick, S.C.	139	D4	188
Plum City, Pierce, Wis.	384	D1	160
Plum Coulee, Man., Can.	498	F4	60
Plumerville, Conway, Ark.	586	B4	170
Plummer, Benewah, Idaho	344	B2	108
Plummer, Red Lake, Minn.	283	D2	148
Plumpoint, Calvert, Md.	550	C6	182
Plum Point, New Kent, Va.	200	C8	192
Plumtree, Rh.&Nya.	1,200	D5	420
Plunkett, Sask., Can.	117	E5	58
Plunkettville, McCurtain, Okla.	50	D9	128
Plush, Lake, Oreg.	40	E7	96
Plymouth, Amador, Calif.	489	*C3	94
Plymouth, Litchfield, Conn.	950 (8,981▲)	C3	202
Plymouth, Eng.	216,200	K8	273
Plymouth, Orange, Fla.	250	C9	174
Plymouth, Hancock, Ill.	781	C3	138
Plymouth, Marshall, Ind.	7,558	A3	140
Plymouth, Cerro Gordo, Iowa	422	A4	142
Plymouth, Penobscot, Maine	170 (494▲)	D3	204
Plymouth, Plymouth, Mass.	11,000 (14,445▲)	C6	206
Plymouth, Hennepin, Minn.	9,576	F6	148
Plymouth, Wayne, Mich.	8,766	B7	146
Plymouth, Montserrat	1,350	D13	233
Plymouth, Jefferson, Nebr.	372	D9	152
Plymouth, Grafton, N.H.	2,244 (3,210▲)	D3	208
Plymouth, Washington, N.C.	4,666	B9	186
Plymouth, Richland and Huron, Ohio	1,822	B4	156
Plymouth, Luzerne, Pa.	10,401	B6	214
Plymouth, Box Elder, Utah	231	B3	114
Plymouth, Windsor, Vt.	25 (308▲)	*D3	218
Plymouth, Sheboygan, Wis.	5,128	B6 E6	160
Plymouth, Putnam, W.Va.	200	C3	194
Plymouth, co., Iowa	23,906	B1	142
Plymouth, co., Mass.	248,449	C6	206
Plymouth, bay, Mass.		C6	206
Plymouth, rock, Mass.		C6	206
Plymouth Union, Windsor, Vt.	75	D3	218
Plymouth Village, Jefferson, Ky.	311	*B5	178
Plympton, N.S., Can.	295	E4	70
Plympton, Plymouth, Mass.	300 (821▲)	C6	206
Plymptonville, Clearfield, Pa.	1,220	*B3	214
Plzeň, Czech.	134,273	B1	324
Plzeňský, co., Czech.	578,085	*B1	324
Po, China	90,000	I7	348
Pô, Upper Volta		D4	408
Po, riv., It.		C3	302
Po, riv., Va.		B7	192
Po, riv. mouths, It.		C4	302
Poamoho, riv., Haw.		F10	86
Poamoho Camp, Honolulu, Haw.	368	F9	86
Pobé, Dah.	3,900	E5	408
Poca, Putnam, W.Va.	607	C3	194
Pocahontas, Randolph, Ark.	3,665	A6	170
Pocahontas, Bond, Ill.	718	E4	138
Pocahontas, Pocahontas, Iowa	2,011	B3	142
Pocahontas, Hinds, Miss.	400	C2	184
Pocahontas, Hardeman, Tenn.	50	C3	190
Pocahontas, Tazewell, Va.	1,313	C3	192
Pocahontas, co., Iowa	14,234	B3	142
Pocahontas, co., W.Va.	10,136	C4	194
Pocasset, Barnstable, Mass.	365	C6	206
Pocasset, Grady, Okla.	180	C6	128
Pocatalico, riv., W.Va.		C3	194
Pocataligo, Jasper, S.C.	150	F7	188
Pocatello, Bannock and Power, Idaho	28,534	G6	108
Pochep, Sov.Un.	25,000	F9	332
Pochutla, Mex.	3,084	D6	225
Pocito Casas, Mex.		B3	224
Pocitos, Arg.		B4	250
Pocklington, reef, Solomon		E1	437
Pocola, Le Flore, Okla.		C9	128
Pocomoke, riv., Del., Md.		F4 D9	172 182
Pocomoke, sound, Md., Va.		E8	182
Pocomoke City, Worcester, Md.	3,329	D8	182
Poconé, Braz.	3,054	I5	257
Pocono, mts., Pa.		*B6	214
Poços de Caldas, Braz.	19,109	E1	258
Pocotalico, Kanawha, W.Va.	100	C3	194
Pocotopaug, lake, Conn.		C5	202
Poděbrady, Czech.	10,799	A2	324
Podhořany, Czech.	149	*A2	324
Podkamennaya Tunguska, riv., Sov.Un.		C11	329
Podmokly, Czech. (part of Děčín)		A2	324
Podolsk, Sov.Un.	124,000	A1	336
Podor, Sen.	4,000	C2	408
Poe, Allen, Ind.	150	B4	140
Poe, Greenville, S.C.	1,000	*B4	188
Pofadder, U.S.Afr.		E3	420
Poge, cape, Mass.		D7	206
Poggibonsi, It.	7,236	D3	302
Pöggstall, Aus.	895	B7	313
Pogradec, Alb.	5,643	A3	306
Pohai, see Chihli, gulf, China			
Pohakapu, Honolulu, Haw.	1,133	*G11	86
Pohang, Kor.	52,473	G14	348
Poindexter, Louisa, Va.		B6	192
Poinsett, co., Ark.	30,834	B6	170
Poinsett, lake, Fla.		C10	174
Poinsett, lake, S.Dak.		C8	158
Point, lake, N.W.Ter., Can.		D7	48
Point Agassiz, Alsk.	6	J14	84
Point Arena, Mendocino, Calif.	596	C2	94
Point Blue, Evangeline, La.	100	D3	180
Point Cedar, Hot Spring, Ark.	150	C3 D6	170
Point Clear, Baldwin, Ala.	600	E2	168
Point Comfort, Calhoun, Tex.	1,453	E7	130
Pointe a la Hache, Plaquemines, La.	600	E6	180
Pointe-à-Pitre, Guad.	26,160	D14	233
Pointe-au-Baril, Ont., Can.		O20	64
Pointe-au-Baril-Station, Ont., Can.	215	O20	64
Pointe-au-Pic, Que., Can.	1,220	Q14	66
Pointe-aux-Trembles, Que., Can.	11,981	S16	66
Pointe-Bleue, Que., Can.	290	P12	66
Pointe-Claire, Que., Can.	15,208	S11 S15	66
Pointe Coupee, par., La.	22,488	D4	180
Pointe-du-Bois, Man., Can.	200	E5	60
Pointe du Chene, N.B., Can.	265	C5	70
Pointe-du-Lac, Que., Can.	560	R12	66
Point Edward, Ont., Can.	2,558	Q18	64
Pointe Noire, Con.B.	31,199	G7	409
Pointe Verte, N.B., Can.	365	B4	70
Point Hope (Tigara), Alsk.	264	B5	84
Point Isabel, Grant, Ind.	120	B4	140
Point Judith, Washington, R.I.	200	D3	216
Point Judith, pond, R.I.		D3	216
Point Lay, Alsk.	75	B5	84
Point Leamington, Newf., Can.	500	F8	72
Point Lookout, St. Marys, Md.	102	D7	182
Point Marion, Fayette, Pa.	1,853	D2	214
Point of Rocks, Frederick, Md.	326	B4	182
Point of Rocks, Sweetwater, Wyo.	55	E4	116
Point Pelee, natl. park, Ont., Can.		S18	64
Point Peter, Oglethorpe, Ga.	200	C4	176
Point Pleasant, Ocean, N.J.	10,182	C4	210
Point Pleasant, Bland, Va.		C3	192
Point Pleasant, Mason, W.Va.	5,785	C2	194
Point Pleasant Beach, Ocean, N.J.	3,873	C4	210
Point Sapin, N.B., Can.	250	C5	70
Point Washington, Walton, Fla.	275	A4	174
Poison, creek, Wyo.		C5	116
Poissy, Fr.	15,046	C5	278
Poitiers, Fr.	52,633	D4	278
Poitou, former prov., Fr.	1,037,000	D3	278
Pojo, Bol.	1,047	C2	246
Pojoaque, Santa Fe, N.Mex.	250	C4 G7	126
Pok, Ponape		A2	436
Pokaran, India	5,117	C2	366
Pokegama, lake, Minn.		D5	148
Pokegama, lake, Wis.		C2	160
Pokhara, Nep.	3,732	C3	368
Poko, Con.L.		B4	414
Pokotu, China	5,000	A10	348
Pokrov, Sov.Un.	8,000	N20	332
Pokrovskoye, Sov.Un.		I12	332
Po Kuang, is., China		O7	349
Pokusagyr, Sov.Un.		B12	329
Polacca, Navajo, Ariz.	600	C5	124
Polān, Iran		E5	379
Poland, Androscoggin, Maine	175 (1,537▲)	*D2	204
Poland, Herkimer, N.Y.	564	B6	212
Poland, Mahoning, Ohio	2,766	*B6	156
Poland, country, Eur.	28,783,000	C6	266 325
Poland Spring, Androscoggin, Maine	100	D2	204
Polar, Langlade, Wis.	110	C5	160
Polar, caves, N.H.		D3	208
Polaris, Shoshone, Idaho (part of Osburn)		B3	108
Polaris, Beaverhead, Mont.	20	E3	110
Polathane, see Akçaabat, Tur.			
Polbain, Scot.		C7	272
Polcura, Chile		C1	252
Pole, mtn., Wyo.		E7	116
Polebridge, Flathead, Mont.	5	B2	110
Polecat, creek, Okla.		C7	128
Polgár, Hung.	7,573	B6	320
Poli, Cam.		E7	409
Poli, China	37,527	C15	348
Policastro, gulf, It.		F5	302
Poligny, Fr.		D6	278
Polikhnitos, Grc.	6,071	B6	306
Polillo, is., Phil.		B6	358
Polis, Cyp.	1,727	D5	307
Poliyiros, Grc.	4,389	A4	306
Polk, Crawford, Kans.	60	*E9	144
Polk, Polk, Nebr.	433	C8	152
Polk, Ashland, Ohio	358	B4	156
Polk, Venango, Pa.	3,574	B2	214
Polk, Obion, Tenn.	50	B2	190
Polk, co., Ark.	11,981	C2	170
Polk, co., Fla.	195,139	D9	174
Polk, co., Ga.	28,015	C1	176
Polk, co., Iowa	266,315	C4	142
Polk, co., Minn.	36,182	D2	148
Polk, co., Mo.	13,753	D4	150
Polk, co., Nebr.	7,210	C8	152
Polk, co., N.C.	11,395	B3	186
Polk, co., Oreg.	26,523	C3	96
Polk, co., Tenn.	12,160	C7	190
Polk, co., Tex.	13,861	D8	130
Polk, co., Wis.	24,968	C1	160
Polkan, mtn., Sov.Un.		C11	329
Polk City, Polk, Fla.	203	C9	174
Polk City, Polk, Iowa	567	A7 C4	142
Polkton, Anson, N.C.	530	B5	186
Polkville, Smith, Miss.	300	C3	184
Polkville, Cleveland, N.C.	400	B4	186
Pollard, Escambia, Ala.	210	D2	168
Pollard, Clay, Ark.	170	A6	170
Pollensa, Sp.	7,241	C8	298
Pollock, Idaho, Idaho	40	*D2	108
Pollock, Grant, La.	366	C3	180
Pollock, Sullivan, Mo.	202	A4	150
Pollock, Campbell, S.Dak.	417	B5	158
Pollocksville, Jones, N.C.	416	B8	186
Pollockville, Alta., Can.	42	E7	54
Polo, Ogle, Ill.	2,551	B4	138
Polo, Caldwell, Mo.	469	B3	150
Polotsk, Sov.Un.	35,000	E7	332
Polson, Lake, Mont.	2,314	C2	110
Poltava, Sov.Un.	141,000	H10	332
Poltimore, Que., Can.	410	S9	66
Poluinkin, Mex.		D8	225
Polunochnoye, Sov.Un.		A6	336
Polvadera, Socorro, N.Mex.	300	D4	126
Polvijärvi, Fin.		E13	290
Polyanovgrad, Bul.	14,551	B3	317
Polytechnic, Yellowstone, Mont.	300	E8	110
Pomabamba, Peru	2,346	B2	245
Pomaria, Newberry, S.C.	230	C6	188
Pombal, Braz.	4,867	B3	258
Pombal, Braz.		C3	258
Pombal, Port.	2,541	C2	298
Pombetsu, Jap.	17,507	C9	354
Pomerania, (Pommern) reg., Ger.		*B6	286
Pomerania, reg., Pol.		B2	325
Pomeray, N.Ire.	367	G6	273
Pomerene, Cochise, Ariz.	150	F5	124
Pomeroy, Calhoun, Iowa	816	B3	142
Pomeroy, Meigs, Ohio	3,345	C4	156
Pomeroy, Chester, Pa.	1,085	*D6	214
Pomeroy, Garfield, Wash.	1,677	C9	98
Pomezia, It.		*E4	302
Pomfret, Windham, Conn.	600 (2,136▲)	B8	202
Pomfret, Charles, Md.	300	C5	182
Pomfret, Windsor, Vt.	20 (600▲)	D3	218
Pomme de Terre, riv., Minn.		F3	148
Pomme de Terre, riv., Mo.		C4	150
Pomona, Los Angeles, Calif.	67,157 (*212,000)	C6 E5	94
Pomona, Franklin, Kans.	489	D8	144
Pomona, Howell, Mo.	300	E6	150
Pomona, Atlantic, N.J.	400	E3	210
Pomona Park, Putnam, Fla.	516	B9	174
Pomonkey, Charles, Md.	400	C5	182
Pomorie, Bul.	6,020	B3	317
Pompano Beach, Broward, Fla.	15,992	D6 E10	174
Pompeii, ruins, It.		E5	302
Pompeys Pillar, Yellowstone, Mont.	104	E9	110
Pompton Lakes, Passaic, N.J.	9,445	A4	210
Pompton Plains, Morris, N.J.	5,800	B4	210
Ponaganset, res., R.I.		B2	216
Ponaganset, riv., R.I.		B2	216
Ponape, Ponape		A2	436
Ponape, is., Pac.O.		A2	436
Ponca, Dixon, Nebr.	924	B9	152
Ponca, creek, Nebr.		A6	152
Ponca, lake, Okla.		B6	128
Ponca City, Kay, Okla.	24,411	B6	128
Ponca Creek, riv., S.Dak.		E7	158
Ponce, P.R.	99,492	D11	233
Ponce de Leon, Holmes, Fla.	400	A5	174
Ponce de Leon, bay, Fla.		F9	174
Ponce de Leon, inlet, Fla.		B10	174
Poncha, pass, Colo.		D4	106
Poncha Springs, Chaffee, Colo.	201	D4	106
Ponchatoula, Tangipahoa, La.	4,727	B6 D5	180
Pond, creek, Colo.		D7	106
Pond, creek, Ky.		A4	178
Pond, creek, Okla.		C5	128
Pond, fork, W.Va.		D3	194
Pond, riv., Ky.		C3	178
Pondcreek, Grant, Okla.	935	B6	128
Pondera, co., Mont.	7,653	B4	110
Ponderay, Bonner, Idaho	231	A2	108
Ponderosa, Sandoval, N.Mex.	100	C4 G6	126
Pond Gap, Kanawha, W.Va.	100	C6	194
Pondicherry, India	58,600 (*130,000)	F3	366
Pond Inlet, N.W.Ter., Can.		C11	48
Pond Meadow, Middlesex, Conn.	150	D6	202
Pondosa, Siskiyou, Calif.	310	B3	94
Pondosa, Union, Oreg.	160	B9	96
Pond Point, New Haven, Conn.	350	E3	202
Ponds, isl., Newf., Can.		D8	72
Ponds, lake, Newf., Can.		E7	72
Pone, isl., Md.		D7	182
Poneloya, Nic.		D4	228
Poneto, Wells, Ind.	289	B4	140
Ponferrada, Sp.	13,008	A3	298
Pongo de Manseriche, gorge, Peru		A2	245
Ponhook, lake, N.S., Can.		E5	70
Ponkapog, pond, Mass.		D3	206
Ponoka, Alta., Can.	3,387	D6	54
Pons, Isle of Wight, Va.		A8 C8	192
Ponsford, Becker, Minn.	150	E3	148
Ponta de Pedras, Braz.	1,486	F7	256
Ponta Grossa, Braz.	42,875	K6	257
Pont-à-Mousson, Fr.	11,416	C7	278
Ponta Porã, Braz.	5,152	J5	257
Pontarlier, Fr.	13,768	D7	278
Pontchartrain, lake, La.		D5	180
Pontedera, It.	12,400	D3	302
Ponte de Sôr, Port.	3,827	C2	298
Ponteix, Sask., Can.	794	F4	58
Ponte Nova, Braz.	15,056	E2	258
Pontevedra, Sp.	17,733	A2	298
Pontevedra, prov., Sp.	714,666	*A2	298
Ponte Vedra Beach, Saint Johns, Fla.	800	A9 A10	174
Ponthierville, Con.L.		C4	414
Pontiac, Livingston, Ill.	8,435	C5	138
Pontiac, Oakland, Mich.	82,233	G8	146
Pontiac, co., Que., Can.	20,995	*R8	66
Pontianak, Indon.	121,000	E3	358
Pontine, is., It.		E4	302
Pontivy, Fr.	7,700	C2	278
Pont-l'Abbé, Fr.	5,541	D1	278
Pontoise, Fr.	14,139	C5	278
Pontoosuc, lake, Mass.		B1	206
Pontotoc, Pontotoc, Miss.	2,108	A3	184
Pontotoc, Johnston, Okla.	60	D7	128
Pontotoc, co., Miss.	17,232	A3	184
Pontotoc, co., Okla.	28,089	D7	128
Pontotoc, ridge, Miss.		A4	184
Pontremoli, It.	4,839	C2	302
Pontresina, Switz.	774	B5	312
Pontrilas, Sask., Can.	125	D5	58
Pont Rouge, Que., Can.	2,631	R13 R15	66
Pont-St. Esprit, Fr.		E6	278
Pont Viau, Que., Can.	8,218	*S15	66
Pontypool, Ont., Can.	215	P22	64
Pontypool, Wales	41,300	J9	273
Pony, Madison, Mont.	154	E5	110
Ponza, isl., It.		E4	302
Poole, Eng.	86,000	K11	273
Poole, Webster, Ky.	300	C3	178
Poole, Buffalo, Nebr.	19	D7	152
Pooler, Chatham, Ga.	1,073	D5	176
Pooles, isl., Md.		B7	182
Poolesville, Montgomery, Md.	298	B5	182
Pooleville, Carter, Okla.	50	D6	128
Poona, India	480,982 (*590,000)	E2	366
Pooncarie, Austl.	157	E8	432
Poopó, Bol.	736	C1	246
Poopó, lake, Bol.		C1	246
Poor Knights, is., N.Z.		A5	437
Poorman, Alsk.	2	C6	84
Popasnaya, Sov.Un.	28,000	R22	332
Popayán, Col.	52,620	C1	244
Pope, Marengo, Ala.	300	C2	168
Pope, Man., Can.	35	E2	60
Pope, Panola, Miss.	246	A3	184
Pope, co., Ark.	21,177	B3	170
Pope, co., Ill.	4,061	F5	138
Pope, co., Minn.	11,914	F3	148
Popejoy, Franklin, Iowa	190	B4	142
Poperinge, Bel.	12,411	D1	282
Popham, pt., Ont., Can.		O19	64
Popham Beach, Sagadahoc, Maine	35	E3	204
Poplar, Tulare, Calif.	1,478	*D4	94
Poplar, Roosevelt, Mont.	1,565	B11	110
Poplar, Mitchell, N.C.	275	A3	186
Poplar, Douglas, Wis.	475	B2	160
Poplar, isl., Md.		C7	182
Poplar, mtn., Ky.		D5	178
Poplar, riv., Man., Can.		D4	60
Poplar, riv., Sask., Can., Mont.		F4 B11	58 110
Poplar Bluff, Butler, Mo.	15,926	E7	150

Poplar Branch, Currituck, N.C. 290 A10 186
Poplar Creek, B.C., Can. 50 E14 52
Poplar Creek, Montgomery, Miss. 75 B3 184
Poplarfield, Man., Can. 26 E4 60
Poplar Grove, Phillips, Ark. 169 C6 170
Poplar Grove, Boone, Ill. 460 A5 138
Poplar Grove, Owen, Ky. 35 B6 178
Poplar Heights, Fairfax, Va. 1,000 *B7 192
Poplar Plains, Fleming, Ky. 200 B7 178
Poplar Point, Man., Can. 100 E4 60
Poplars, Calvert, Md. 150 *C6 182
Poplar Springs, Howard, Md. 100 B5 182
Poplarville, Pearl River, Miss. 2,136 E3 184
Popocatepetl, vol., Mex. L14 225
Popokabaka, Con.L. D2 414
Popovka, Sov.Un. 15,000 I11 332
Popovo, Bul. 10,650 B3 317
Poppel, Bel. 2,009 C4 282
Popple, riv., Wis. C5 160
Poquetanuck, New London, Conn. 200 D7 202
Poquonock, Hartford, Conn. 400 B5 202
Poquonock Bridge, New London, Conn. 3,000 D7 202
Poquoson, York, Va. 4,278 A8 192
C8
Porali, riv., Pak. F5 375
Porbandar, India 58,824 D1 366
Porcher, isl., B.C., Can. D7 52
Porcuna, Sp. 12,492 D4 298
Porcupine, cape, Newf., Can. D7 72
Porcupine, mtn., Man., Sask., Can. D2 60
D7 58
Porcupine, mts., Mich. C2 146
Porcupine, riv., Alsk., Can. B8 84
D4 48
Porcupine Plain, Sask., Can. 572 D6 58
Pordenone, It. 23,200 C4 302
Poreč, Yugo. 2,488 B1 316
Pori, Fin. 43,578 F9 291
Porjus, Swe. 1,197 C8 290
Porlamar, Ven. 14,769 A7 240
Poroma, Bol. 171 C1 246
Poronaysk, Sov.Un. 33,000 E16 329
Porong, riv., Camb. D5 362
Poroshiri-Dake, peak, Jap. C9 354
Porpoise, pt., Fla. F9 174
Porrentruy, Switz. 6,523 A3 312
Porsangerfjord, fjord, Nor. A11 290
Porsgrunn, Nor. 9,902 G3 291
Portachuelo, Bol. 2,456 C2 246
Portacloy, Ire. G3 273
Port Adelaide, Austl. 38,377 E7 432
Portadown, N.Ire. 17,202 G6 273
Portaferry, N.Ire. 1,275 G7 273
Portage, Alsk. 34 G11 84
Portage, P.E.I., Can. 35 C5 70
Portage, Porter, Ind. 11,822 *A2 140
Portage, Aroostook, Maine 450 B4 204
(458▲)
Portage, Kalamazoo, Mich. 6,000 *G6 146
Portage, Cascade, Mont. 20 C5 110
Portage, Cambria, Pa. 3,933 C3 214
Portage, Box Elder, Utah 189 B3 114
Portage, Columbia, Wis. 7,822 E4 160
Portage, co., Ohio 91,798 A5 156
Portage, co., Wis. 36,964 D4 160
Portage, bay, Man., Can. E3 60
Portage, head, Wash. A2 98
Portage, isl., N.B., Can. B5 70
Portage, lake, Maine B4 204
Portage, riv., Ohio A3 156
Portage Des Sioux, St. Charles, Mo. 371 A8 150
Portage Lakes, Summit, Ohio 10,000 A5 156
Portage la Prairie, Man., Can. 10,525 F3 60
Portageville, New Madrid, Mo. 2,505 E8 150
Portageville, Wyoming, N.Y. 450 C3 212
Portal, Cochise, Ariz. 35 G6 124
Portal, Bulloch, Ga. 494 D5 176
Portal, Burke, N.Dak. 351 B3 154
Port Alberni, B.C., Can. 10,373 F10 52
Portalegre, Port. 10,510 C3 298
Portales, Roosevelt, N.Mex. 9,695 D7 126
Port Alexander, Alsk. 18 D8 84
J14
Port-Alfred, Que., Can. 7,968 P14 66
Port Alfred, U.S.Afr. 5,733 F5 420
Port Alice, B.C., Can. 300 E9 52
Port Allegany, McKean, Pa. 2,742 B3 214
Port Allen, West Baton Rouge, La. 5,026 B5 180
D4
Port Angeles, Clallam, Wash. 12,653 A3 98
Port Angeles East, Clallam, Wash. 1,283 *A3 98
Port Anson, Newf., Can. 300 F8 72
Port Antonio, Jam. 5,860 C6 232
Port Aransas, Nueces, Tex. 824 F7 130
Portarlington, Ire. 2,720 H5 273
Port Arthur, Ont., Can. 38,136 R24 64
Port Arthur, see Lüshun, China
Port Arthur, Jefferson, Tex. 66,676 E9 130
Port Augusta, Austl. 6,704 E7 432
Port au Port, Newf., Can. 400 F6 72
Port au Port, bay, Newf., Can. F6 72
Port au Port, pen., Newf., Can. F6 72
Port-au-Prince, Hai. 134,117 C8 233
Port Austin, Huron, Mich. 706 E9 146
Port Barre, St. Landry, La. 1,876 D4 180
Port Bergé, Malag. 1,538 C9 421
Port Birmingham, Jefferson, Ala. 150 E4 168
Port Blair, India 3,496 F6 366
Port Blakely, Kitsap, Wash. 400 D2 98
Port Blandford, Newf., Can. 550 F8 72
Port Boca Grande, Lee, Fla. 112 E8 174
Port Bolivar, Galveston, Tex. 600 E8 130
F8
Port Borden, P.E.I., Can. 712 C6 70
Port Burwell, Ont., Can. 722 R20 64
Port Byron, Rock Island, Ill. 1,153 B3 138
Port Byron, Cayuga, N.Y. 1,201 B5 212
Port Canning, India I9 366
Port Carbon, Schuylkill, Pa. 2,775 *C5 214
Port Carling, Ont., Can. 510 O21 64
Port Chalmers, N.Z. 3,012 F3 437
Port Charlotte, Charlotte, Fla. 3,197 *E8 174
Port Chester, Westchester, N.Y. 24,960 D3 212
E8
Port Chicago, Contra Costa, Calif. 1,746 *C2 94
Port Chilkoot, Alsk. 120 D8 84
I14
Port Clements, B.C., Can. D6 52
Port Clinton, Ottawa, Ohio 6,870 A4 156
Port Clyde, N.S., Can. 215 F4 70
Port Clyde, Knox, Maine 350 E3 204
Port Colborne, Ont., Can. 14,028 R21 64
Port Colden, Warren, N.J. 200 B3 210
Port Coquitlam, B.C., Can. 4,632 B15 52
F11
Port Crane, Broome, N.Y. 700 C6 212
Port Credit, Ont., Can. 6,350 Q21 64
S21
Port Dalhousie, Ont., Can. 3,087 Q21 64
Port-de-Bouc, Fr. 8,551 F6 278
Port-de-Paix, Hai. 6,405 C8 232
Port Deposit, Cecil, Md. 953 A7 182
Port Dickinson, Broome, N.Y. 2,295 C6 212
Port Dickson, Mala. 4,422 G4 362
Port Discovery, Jefferson, Wash. A4 98
Port Douglas, Austl. 216 B9 432
Port Dover, Ont., Can. 2,790 R20 64
Port Edwards, Wood, Wis. 1,849 D4 160
Portel, Braz. 456 F6 256
Port Elgin, N.B., Can. 717 C5 70
Port Elgin, Ont., Can. 1,597 P19 64
Port Elizabeth, Cumberland, N.J. 300 E3 210
Port Elizabeth, U.S.Afr. 203,700 F5 420
(*239,600)
Port Ellen, Scot. F6 272
Porteña, Arg. B3 252
Porter, Jefferson, Ala. 500 E4 168
Porter, New Castle, Del. 20 B3 172
Porter, Porter, Ind. 2,189 A2 140
Porter, Oxford, Maine 150 E2 204
(975▲)
Porter, Yellow Medicine, Minn. 261 G2 148
Porter, Wagoner, Okla. 492 C8 128
Porter, Montgomery, Tex. 900 D8 130
Porter, Grays Harbor, Wash. 200 C3 98
Porter, co., Ind. 60,279 A2 140
Porter, lake, Sask., Can. B4 58
Porterdale, Newton, Ga. 2,365 C3 176
Port Erin, Isle of Man 1,435 G8 273
Porterfield, Marinette, Wis. 55 C6 160
Porterville, Tulare, Calif. 7,991 D4 94
Porterville, Kemper, Miss. 120 C4 184
Port Essington, B.C., Can. 275 C7 52
Port Étienne, Maur. 1,300 B1 408
Port Ewen, Ulster, N.Y. 2,622 D8 212
Port Fouad, Eg., U.A.R. 3,804 C3 382
Port Francqui, Con.L. 3,553 C3 414
Port Gamble, Kitsap, Wash. 400 B4 98
Port-Gentil, Gabon 5,342 G6 409
Port Gibson, Claiborne, Miss. 2,861 D2 184
Port Glasgow, Scot. 23,000 F8 272
Port Graham, Alsk. 92 D6 84
H10
Port Greville, N.S., Can. 357 D5 70
Port Hammond, B.C., Can. 1,800 B15 52
Port Harcourt, Nig. 71,634 F6 408
Port Hardy, B.C., Can. 100 E9 52
Port Hawkesbury, N.S., Can. 1,078 D8 70
Port Hedland, Austl. 613 C3 432
Port Henry, Essex, N.Y. 1,767 A8 212
Port Herald, Rh.&Nya. C7 421
Porthill, Boundary, Idaho 65 A2 108
Port Hood, N.S., Can. 647 C8 70
Port Hope, Ont., Can. 7,522 Q22 64
Port Hope, Huron, Mich. 349 F9 146
Port Hope Simpson, Newf., Can. 300 D7 72
Port Hudson, East Baton Rouge, La. 200 D4 180
Port Hueneme, Ventura, Calif. 11,067 E4 94
Port Huron, St. Clair, Mich. 36,084 G9 146
(*62,700)
Portia, Lawrence, Ark. 333 A5 170
Portillo, Cuba B6 232
Portimão, Port. 12,066 D2 298
Portis, Osborne, Kans. 232 C5 144
Port Isabel, Cameron, Tex. 3,575 F7 130
Port Jefferson, Shelby, Ohio 438 B2 156
Port Jefferson, Suffolk, N.Y. 2,336 D4 212
Port Jervis, Orange, N.Y. 9,268 D7 212
Portland, Ashley, Ark. 566 D5 170
Portland, Austl. 4,759 F8 432
Portland, Ont., Can. 220 P24 64
Portland, Fremont, Colo. 73 D5 106
Portland, Ouray, Colo. 76 *D3 106
Portland, Middlesex, Conn. 7,496 C5 202
Portland, Eng. 15,000 K10 273
Portland, Walton, Fla. 250 A4 174
Portland, Jay, Ind. 6,999 B5 140
Portland, Cumberland, Maine 72,566 E2 204
(*142,700) E5
Portland, Ionia, Mich. 3,330 G7 146
Portland, Callaway, Mo. 125 C6 150
Portland, Chautauqua, N.Y. 400 C2 212
Portland, Traill, N.Dak. 606 C8 154
Portland, Multnomah, Oreg. 372,676 B2 96
(*731,200) B4
Portland, Sumner, Tenn. 2,424 B5 190
Portland, San Patricio, Tex. 2,538 F7 130
Portland, Dodge, Wis. 100 E5 160
Portland, canal, Alsk., B.C., Can. K15 84
C7 52
Portland, inlet, B.C., Can. C7 52
Portland, promontory, Que., Can. P9 66
Portland Bill, pt., Eng. K10 273
Portland Creek, pond, Newf., Can. E7 72
Portlaoighise, Ire. 3,196 H5 273
Port Lavaca, Calhoun, Tex. 8,864 E7 130
Portlaw, Ire. 1,120 I5 273
Port Leyden, Lewis, N.Y. 898 B6 212
Port Lincoln, Austl. 5,871 E7 432
Portlock, Alsk. 12 D6 84
H10
Port-Lokko, S.L. G2 408
Port Loring, Ont., Can. O21 64
Port Louis, Fr. D2 278
Port Ludlow, Jefferson, Wash. 300 B4 98
Port McNicoll, Ont., Can. 932 P21 64
Port Macquarie, Austl. 4,408 E10 432
Portmagee, Ire. 149 J2 273
Portmahomack, Scot. D9 272
Port Maitland, N.S., Can. 515 F3 70
Port Maitland, Ont., Can. 475 R21 64
Port Maria, Jam. 3,250 C6 232
Port Mayaca, Martin, Fla. 50 E10 174
Port Medway, N.S., Can. 375 E5 70
Port Mellon, B.C., Can. F11 52
Port Moller, Alsk. 33 D5 84
Port Monmouth, Monmouth, N.J. 4,000 C4 210
Port Moody, B.C., Can. 2,713 B15 52
F11
Port Moresby, Pap. 14,250 F11 359
Port-Morien, N.S., Can. 807 C10 70
Port Morris, Morris, N.J. 900 B3 210
Port Mouton, N.S., Can. 212 F5 70
Port Murray, Warren, N.J. 300 B3 210
Port Musgrave, bay, Austl. A8 432
Portnahaven, Scot. F6 272
Port Neches, Jefferson, Tex. 8,696 D9 130
Port Nelson, Man., Can. B6 60
Portneuf, Que., Can. 1,251 R13 66
Portneuf, co., Que., Can. 46,098 R12 66
R15
Port Nicholson, hbr., N.Z. J11 437
Port Nolloth, U.S.Afr. 1,943 E3 420
Port Norris, Cumberland, N.J. 1,789 E2 210
Pôrto (Oporto), Port. 281,406 B2 298
(*650,000)
Pôrto Alegre, Braz. 375,049 L6 257
Pôrto Alexandre, Ang. 2,874 C2 420
Pôrto Amboim, Ang. 1,537 B2 420
Pôrto Amélia, Moz. 10,000 B8 421
Portobelo, Pan. 510 F7 228
Pôrto Calvo, Braz. 2,309 B3 258
Pôrto de Moz, Braz. 959 F6 256
Pôrto Esperança, Braz. 1,174 I5 257
Pôrto Feliz, Braz. 9,112 E1 258
Portoferraio, It. 6,000 D3 302
Portofino, It. 1,100 *C2 302
Port of Ness, Scot. C6 272
Port-of-Spain, Trin. 114,150 E14 233
(*186,300)
Portogruaro, It. 7,100 C4 302
Pôrto Guaíra, Braz. J6 257
Portola, Plumas, Calif. 1,874 C3 94
Portomaggiore, It. 4,300 C3 302
Pôrto Mendes, Braz. J6 257
Pôrto Murtinho, Braz. 2,806 J5 257
Pôrto Nacional, Braz. 2,889 C1 258
Porto-Novo, Dah. 28,763 E5 408
Port Orange, Volusia, Fla. 1,801 B10 174
Port Orchard, Kitsap, Wash. 2,778 B4 98
D2
Port Orford, Curry, Oreg. 1,171 E2 96
Portoscuso, It. 1,887 F2 302
Pôrto Seguro, Braz. 1,888 D3 258
Portotorres, It. 8,500 E2 302
Pôrto União, Braz. 5,405 K6 257
Porto-Vecchio, Fr. E2 302
Pôrto Velho, Braz. 10,036 G4 256
Portoviejo, Ec. 16,330 A1 245
Portpatrick, Scot. 1,063 G7 272
Port Penn, New Castle, Del. 271 B3 172
Port Perry, Ont., Can. 2,121 P22 64
Port Phillip, bay, Austl. F8 432
Port Pirie, Austl. 14,223 E7 432
Port Radium, N.W.Ter., Can. 300 D7 48
Port Reading, Middlesex, N.J. 3,000 C1 210
Portreeve, Sask., Can. 128 E3 58
Port Renfrew, B.C., Can. 100 F10 52
Port Republic, Atlantic, N.J. 561 D4 210
Port Republic, Rockingham, Va. 500 B6 192
Port Rexton, Newf., Can. 650 F9 72
Port Richey, Pasco, Fla. 1,931 C8 174
Port Rowan, Ont., Can. 766 R20 64
Port Royal, Henry, Ky. 90 B5 178
Port Royal, Juniata, Pa. 805 C4 214
Port Royal, Beaufort, S.C. 686 G7 188
Port Royal, Caroline, Va. 128 B7 192
Port Royal, bay, Bermuda A12 233
Port Royal, isl., S.C. G7 188
Port Royal, natl. hist. park, N.S., Can. E4 70
Port Royal, sound, S.C. G7 188
Port Said, Eg., U.A.R. 190,300 A3 95
Port St. Joe, Gulf, Fla. 4,217 B5 174
Port St. Johns, U.S.Afr. 1,024 F5 420
Port St. Louis [-du-Rhône], Fr. 4,262 F6 278
Port Sanilac, Sanilac, Mich. 361 F9 146
Port Saunders, Newf., Can. 325 E7 72
E10
Port Shepstone, U.S.Afr. 4,216 F6 420
Port Simpson, B.C., Can. 600 C7 52
Portsmouth, Ont., Can. P24 64
Portsmouth, Dominica 1,725 E14 233
Portsmouth, Eng. 231,000 K11 273
(*385,000)
Portsmouth, Shelby, Iowa 232 C2 142
Portsmouth, Rockingham, N.H. 25,833 E5 208
Portsmouth, Scioto, Ohio 33,637 D4 156
Portsmouth, Newport, R.I. 3,000 C4 216
(8,251▲)
Portsmouth (Independent City), Va. 114,773 A8 192
D8
Portsoy, Scot. 1,700 D10 272
Port Stanley, Ont., Can. 1,480 R19 64
Port Sudan, Sud. 47,562 B4 398
Port Sulphur, Plaquemines, La. 2,868 E6 180
Portsville, Sussex, Del. 50 F3 172
Port Sydney, Ont., Can. 185 O21 64
Port Talbot, Wales 47,100 J9 273
Port Tampa, Hillsborough, Fla. 1,764 C6 174
D8
Port Taufiq, Eg., U.A.R. B3 395
F7
Port Tobacco, Charles, Md. 75 C5 182
Port Townsend, Jefferson, Wash. 5,074 A4 98
Portugal, country, Eur. 8,510,240 E4 266
298
Portugal Cove South, Newf., Can. 200 G9 72
Portugalete, Sp. 10,612 A5 298
Portugalia, Ang. A4 420
Portuguesa, state, Ven. 122,153 B4 240
Portuguesa, riv., Ven. B5 240
Portuguese Guinea, poss., Afr. 559,000 E5 388
409
Portuguese Timor, poss., Asia 442,378 F7 358
Port Union, Newf., Can. 600 F9 72
Port Union, Ont., Can. R22 64
Port-Vendres, Fr. F5 278
Portville, Cattaraugus, N.Y. 1,336 C3 212
Port Vincent, Livingston, La. 340 B6 180
D5
Port Vue, Allegheny, Pa. 6,635 *C2 214
Port Wakefield, Austl. 478 E7 432
Port Washington, Nassau, N.Y. 15,657 D3 212
Port Washington, Tuscarawas, Ohio 526 B5 156
Port Washington, Ozaukee, Wis. 5,984 E6 160
Port Wentworth, Chatham, Ga. 3,705 D5 176
Port William, Clinton, Ohio 360 C3 156
Port Wing, Bayfield, Wis. 250 B2 160
Porum, Muskogee, Okla. 573 C8 128
Porvenir, Chile H3 251
Porvenir, Mex. A4 224
Posadas, Arg. 37,588 A4 252
Posadas, Sp. 7,350 D4 298
Poschiavo, Switz. 4,034 B6 312
Posen, Cook, Ill. 4,517 F3 138
Posen, Presque Isle, Mich. 341 D8 146
Posen, see Farwell, Nebr.
Posey, co., Ind. 19,214 D2 140
Poseyville, Posey, Ind. 997 D2 140
Poshan, China 20,000 G8 348
Poshekhonye-Volodarsk, Sov.Un. 7,500 C12 332
Posio, Fin. C13 290
Poslovo, cape, Sov.Un. B9 328
Poso, Indon. 2,875 E6 358
Posse, Braz. 1,109 C1 258
Post, Crook, Oreg. 5 C6 96
Post, Garza, Tex. 4,663 C5 130
Posta, LaPlata, Colo. E3 106
Post Falls, Kootenai, Idaho 1,983 B2 108
Postmasburg, U.S.Afr. 2,813 E4 420
Post Mills, Orange, Vt. 200 D4 218
Postojna, Yugo. 4,081 B2 316
Poston, Florence, S.C. 250 D10 188
Postville, Allamakee, Iowa 1,554 A6 142
Posyet, Sov.Un. E15 329
Potapovo, Sov.Un. C10 328
Potaro Landing, Br.Gu. 353 D5 256
Potash, Plaquemines, La. (part of Port Sulphur) E6 180
Potchefstroom, U.S.Afr. 32,058 E5 420
Poteau, Le Flore, Okla. 4,428 C9 128
Poteau, mtn., Ark., Okla. C2 170
D9 128
Poteau, riv., Okla. C9 128
Potecasi, Northampton, N.C. 200 A8 186
Poteet, Atascosa, Tex. 2,811 E6 130
Potenza, It. 23,700 E5 302
Potenza, prov., It. 457,000 *E5 302
Potgietersus, U.S.Afr. 7,011 D5 420
Poth, Wilson, Tex. 1,119 E6 130
Potherie, lake, Que., Can. Q11 66
Potholes, res., Wash. B7 98
Poti, Sov.Un. 43,000 E6 328
Poti, riv., Braz. B2 258
Potiskum, Nig. 14,692 D7 409
Potlatch, Latah, Idaho 880 C2 108
Poto, Peru 247 C4 245
Potomac, Vermilion, Ill. 661 C6 138
Potomac, Montgomery, Md. 150 B5 182
Potomac, Missoula, Mont. 40 D3 110
Potomac, riv., U.S. D11 77
Potomac Park, Allegany, Md. 1,016 *A2 182
Potosí, Bol. 45,758 C1 246
Potosi, Washington, Mo. 2,805 D7 150
Potosi, Grant, Wis. 589 F3 160
Potosí, dept., Bol. D1 246
Potowomut, riv., R.I. C3 216
Potrerillos, Chile A2 252
Potrerillos, Hond. 1,430 C4 228
Potro, mtn., Arg. A2 252
Potsdam, Ger. 117,600 B5 286
Potsdam, St. Lawrence, N.Y. 7,765 A7 212
Pottawatomie, co., Kans. 11,957 C7 144
Pottawatomie, co., Okla. 41,486 C7 128
Pottawatomie, creek, Kans. D8 144
Pottawattamie, co., Iowa 83,102 C2 142
Pottawattamie Park, La Porte, Ind. 292 *A3 140
Potter, Polk, Ark. 120 C2 170
Potter, Atchison, Kans. 109 C8 144
Potter, Cheyenne, Nebr. 554 C2 152
Potter, Calumet, Wis. 225 B6 160
Potter, co., Pa. 16,483 B3 214
Potter, co., S.Dak. 4,926 B5 158
Potter, co., Tex. 115,580 B5 130
Potter, pond, R.I. D2 216
Potter Hill, Washington, R.I. 175 D1 216
Potters Fork, Letcher, Ky. 150 *C8 178
Pottersville, Somerset, N.J. 200 B3 210
Pottersville, Warren, N.Y. 500 B8 212
Potter Valley, Mendocino, Calif. 220 C2 94
Potterville, Taylor, Ga. 400 D2 176
Potterville, Eaton, Mich. 1,028 *G7 146

Name	Pop.	Key	Page
Potts, creek, Va.		C4	192
Potts, mtn., Va.		C4	192
Pottsboro, Grayson, Tex.	640	*C7	130
Potts Camp, Marshall, Miss.	429	A3	184
Pottstown, Montgomery, Pa.	26,144	C6	214
Pottsville, Pope, Ark.	250	B3	170
Pottsville, Schuylkill, Pa.	21,659	C5	214
Potwin, Butler, Kans.	635	E6	144
Pouce Coupé, B.C., Can.	585	C12	52
Pouch Cove, Newf., Can.	1,100	G9	72
Poughkeepsie, Sharp, Ark.	250	A5	170
Poughkeepsie, Dutchess, N.Y.	38,330 (*124,700)	D8	212
Poulan, Worth, Ga.	736	E3	176
Poulo Condore, is., Viet.		E5	362
Poulsbo, Kitsap, Wash.	1,505	B4	98
Poultney, Rutland, Vt.	1,810 (3,009▲)	D2	218
Poultney, riv., Vt.		D2	218
Pound, Wise, Va.	1,135	C2	192
Pound, Marinette, Wis.	273	C5	160
Pound, gap, Ky., Va.		C8 / C2	178 / 192
Pouso Alegre, Braz.	12,509	E1	258
Poverty, bay, N.Z.		C7	437
Póvoa de Varzim, Port.	16,913	B2	298
Povorino, Sov.Un.	24,000	B2	336
Powassan, Ont., Can.	935	O21	64
Poway, San Diego, Calif.	1,921	*F5	94
Powder, riv., Oreg.		C9	96
Powder, riv., Mont., Wyo.		D11 / C6	110 / 116
Powderhorn, Gunnison, Colo.	5	D3	106
Powderly Hills, Jefferson, Ala.	900	*B3	168
Powder River, Sheridan, Wyo.	50	C6	116
Powder River, co., Mont.	2,485	E11	110
Powder River, pass, Wyo.		B6	116
Powder Springs, Cobb, Ga.	746	A4	176
Powder Springs, Grainger, Tenn.	200	B8	190
Powderville, Powder River, Mont.	1	E11	110
Powell, Mohave, Ariz.	20	D1	124
Powell, Coahoma, Miss.	150	A2	184
Powell, McDonald, Mo.	300	E3	150
Powell, Jefferson, Nebr.	75	*D8	152
Powell, Delaware, Ohio	390	B3	156
Powell, Marshall, Okla.	90	E7	128
Powell, Knox, Tenn.	500	E9	190
Powell, Park, Wyo.	4,740	B4	116
Powell, co., Ky.	6,674	C7	178
Powell, co., Mont.	7,002	D3	110
Powell, mtn., Colo.		C4	106
Powell, mtn., N.Mex.		C2	126
Powell, mtn., Tenn., Va.		B8 / D1	190 / 192
Powell, peak, Ariz.		D1	124
Powell, riv., Tenn., Va.		B8 / D1	190 / 192
Powell Butte, Crook, Oreg.	40	C5	96
Powell River, B.C., Can.	9,969	F10	52
Powellsville, Bertie, N.C.	259	A9	186
Powellton, Fayette, W.Va.	1,256	C3 / D6	194
Powellville, Wicomico, Md.	500	D9	182
Power, Teton, Mont.	5	C5	110
Power, Brooke, W.Va.	750	A4 / B2	194
Power, co., Idaho	4,111	G6	108
Power, head, Ire.		J5	273
Powers, Menominee, Mich.	383	D4	146
Powers, Coos, Oreg.	1,366	E2	96
Powers Lake, Burke, N.Dak.	633	B3	154
Powersville, Putnam, Mo.	189	A4	150
Powerview, Man., Can.	1,078	E4	60
Poweshiek, co., Iowa	19,300	C5	142
Powhatan, Jefferson, Ala.	620	B2 / E4	168
Powhatan, Lawrence, Ark.	136	A5	170
Powhatan, Natchitoches, La.	300	C2	180
Powhatan, Powhatan, Va.	300	C7	192
Powhatan, McDowell, W.Va.	600	*D3	194
Powhatan, co., Va.	6,747	C7	192
Powhatan Point, Belmont, Ohio	2,147	C6	156
Powhattan, Brown, Kans.	128	C8	144
Pownal, Cumberland, Maine	50 (778▲)	E5	204
Pownal, Bennington, Vt.	325 (1,509▲)	F2	218
Pownal Center, Bennington, Vt.	75	F2	218
Poyang, China	55,000	K8	349
Poyang, lake, China		K8	349
Poydras, St. Bernard, La.	200	C8	180
Poyen, Grant, Ark.	312	C4	170
Poygan, lake, Wis.		D5	160
Poynette, Columbia, Wis.	1,090	E4	160
Poyntzpass, N.Ire.		G6	273
Poy Sippi, Waushara, Wis.	450	D5	160
Požarevac, Yugo.	18,529	B5	316
Poza Rica, Mex.	14,906	C6	225
Poznań, Pol.	372,000	B3	325
Poznań, pol.div., Pol.	2,298,000	*B3	325
Pozo Almonte, Chile		B4	250
Pozoblanca, Sp.	14,733	C4	298
Pozo Redondo, mts., Ariz.		F3	124
Pozuelo de Alarcón, Sp.	2,517	*B5	298
Pozuzo, Peru	132	C2	245
Pozzallo, It.	12,500	G5	302
Pozzuoli, It.	36,800	E5	302
Praag, Buffalo, Wis.	45	D2	160
Prachin Buri, Thai.	10,000	D4	362
Prachin Buri, prov., Thai.	217,395	*D4	362
Prachuap Khiri, prov., Thai.	72,343	*E3	362
Prachuap Khiri Khan, Thai.	10,000	E3	362
Praco, Jefferson, Ala.	900	E4	168
Practicos, pt., Cuba		B6	232
Prades, Fr.	5,393	F5	278
Prado, basin, Calif.		C6	94
Praestö, Den.	1,578	F3	292
Praestö, co., Den.	123,382	*I4	291
Prague (Praha), Czech.	978,634	A2	324
Prague, Saunders, Nebr.	372	C9	152
Prague, Lincoln, Okla.	1,545	C7	128
Praha, see Prague, Czech.			
Prairie, Wilcox, Ala.	100	C2	168
Prairie, Elmore, Idaho		F3	108
Prairie, Monroe, Miss.	112	B4	184
Prairie, co., Ark.	10,515	C5	170
Prairie, co., Mont.	2,318	D11	110
Prairie, bayou, Ark.		D7	170
Prairie, riv., Minn.		D5	148
Prairie, riv., Wis.		C4	160
Prairieburg, Linn, Iowa	226	B6	142
Prairie City, McDonough, Ill.	613	C3	138
Prairie City, Jasper, Iowa	943	C4	142
Prairie City, Grant, Oreg.	801	C8	96
Prairie Creek, Vigo, Ind.	240	C2	140
Prairie Dog, creek, Nebr.		E5	152
Prairie Dog Town, fork, Okla.		D4	128
Prairie du Chien, Crawford, Wis.	5,649	E2	160
Prairie du Rocher, Randolph, Ill.	679	E3	138
Prairie du Sac, Sauk, Wis.	1,676	E4	160
Prairie Farm, Barron, Wis.	350	C2	160
Prairie Grove, Washington, Ark.	1,056	B2	170
Prairie Hill, Chariton, Mo.	84	B5	150
Prairie Home, Cooper, Mo.	213	C5	150
Prairie Home, Lancaster, Nebr.	29	E2	152
Prairie Point, Noxubee, Miss.	75	B4	184
Prairie River, Sask., Can.	100	D6	58
Prairieton, Vigo, Ind.	250	C2	140
Prairie View, Logan, Ark.	165	B3	170
Prairie View, Phillips, Kans.	188	C4	144
Prairie View, Waller, Tex.	2,326	D7	130
Prairie Village, Johnson, Kans.	25,356	B8	144
Prairieville, Ascension, La.	150	B5	180
Praise, see Elkhorn City, Ky.			
Pran Buri, Thai.	5,000	D3	362
Praszka, Pol.	3,013	C4	325
Prata, Braz.	2,948	D1	258
Pratas, isl., China		O8	349
Prato, It.	48,100 (83,700▲)	D3	302
Pratt, Man., Can.		F3	60
Pratt, Pratt, Kans.	8,156	E5	144
Pratt, Kanawha, W.Va.	602	*C3	194
Pratt, co., Kans.	12,122	E5	144
Prattmont, Autauga, Ala.		C3	168
Prattsburg, Steuben, N.Y.	690	C4	212
Prattsville, Grant, Ark.	150	C4	170
Prattsville, Greene, N.Y.	600	C7	212
Prattville, Autauga, Ala.	6,616	C3	168
Prattville, Hillsdale, Mich.	175	H7	146
Prattville, Tulsa, Okla.	2,530	*B7	128
Pratum, Marion, Oreg.	100	C1	96
Pravia, Sp.	1,804	A3	298
Prawle, pt., Eng.		K9	273
Pray, Park, Mont.	5	E6	110
Pražský, co., Czech.	2,128,221	*A2	324
Preble, Adams, Ind.	170	B4	140
Preble, Brown, Wis.	12,245	A6	160
Preble, co., Ohio	32,498	C2	156
Precept, Furnas, Nebr.	16	*D6	152
Predeal, Rom.	5,121	B3	321
Preeceville, Sask., Can.	807	E6	58
Pregel, riv., Sov.Un.		E3	332
Pregnall, Dorchester, S.C.	100	E8	188
Prelate, Sask., Can.	632	E3	58
Premier, B.C., Can.	450	B7	52
Premier, McDowell, W.Va.	700	*D3	194
Premont, Jim Wells, Tex.	3,049	F6	130
Prenter, Boone, W.Va.	400	C3 / D6	194
Prentice, Price, Wis.	427	C3	160
Prentiss, Penobscot, Maine	200 (227▲)	C4	204
Prentiss, Jefferson Davis, Miss.	1,321	D3	184
Prentiss, co., Miss.	17,949	A4	184
Prenzlau, Ger.	20,000	B5	286
Přerov, Czech.	24,730	B3	324
Prescott, Yavapai, Ariz.	12,861	D3	124
Prescott, Nevada, Ark.	3,533	D3	170
Prescott, Ont., Can.	4,920	P25	64
Prescott, Adams, Iowa	331	C3	142
Prescott, Linn, Kans.	278	D9	144
Prescott, Ogemaw, Mich.	308	E8	146
Prescott, Columbia, Oreg.	129	A4	96
Prescott, Walla Walla, Wash.	269	C8	98
Prescott, Pierce, Wis.	1,536	D1	160
Prescott, co., Ont., Can.	26,291	O26	64
Presho, Lyman, S.Dak.	881	D5	158
Presidencia Roque Sãenz Peña, Arg.	23,100	A3	252
Presidente Hayes, dept., Par.	23,490	C3	247
Presidente Prudente, Braz.	26,790	J6	257
Presidential, range, N.H.		C4	208
Presidents, isl., Tenn.		E6	190
Presidio, Presidio, Tex.	1,062	E3	130
Presidio, co., Tex.	5,460	D3	130
Preslav, Bul.	5,507	B3	317
Prešov, Czech.	31,100	B5	324
Presovský, co., Czech.	448,319	*B5	324
Prespa, lake, Alb.		A3	306
Prespa, lake, Yugo.		D5	316
Presque Isle, Aroostook, Maine	12,886	B4	204
Presque Isle, Presque Isle, Mich.	60	D8	146
Presque Isle, Vilas, Wis.	200	B4	160
Presque Isle, co., Mich.	13,117	D7	146
Pressmens Home, Hawkins, Tenn.	400	B8	190
Prestbakki, Ice.		M20	290
Prestebakka, Nor.		B2	292
Presteign, Wales	1,300	I9	273
Preston, Ont., Can.	9,387	Q20	64
Preston, New London, Conn.	200 (4,992▲)	C8	202
Preston, Eng.	117,200	H10	273
Preston, Webster, Ga.	232	D2	176
Preston, Franklin, Idaho	3,640	G7	108
Preston, Jackson, Iowa	819	B7	142
Preston, Pratt, Kans.	278	E5	144
Preston, Caroline, Md.	469	C8	182
Preston, Fillmore, Minn.	1,491	H6	148
Preston, Kemper, Miss.	300	C4	184
Preston, Hickory, Mo.	117	D4	150
Preston, Richardson, Nebr.	66	*D9	152
Preston, Okmulgee, Okla.	200	C8	128
Preston, King, Wash.	250	D3	98
Preston, co., W.Va.	27,233	B5	194
Preston, lake, S.Dak.		C8	158
Preston, peak, Calif.		B2	94
Prestonsburg, Floyd, Ky.	3,133	C8	178
Prestonville, Carroll, Ky.	211	*B5	178
Prestwick, Washington, Ala.	200	D2	168
Prestwick, Scot.	11,400	F8	272
Presumpscot, riv., Maine		E4	204
Prêto, riv., Braz.		C2	258
Pretoria, U.S.Afr.	265,900 (*335,300)	E5	420
Pretty Boy, res., Md.		A6	182
Prettyman Mill, Dorchester, S.C.	250	*E8	188
Pretty Prairie, Reno, Kans.	525	E5	144
Préveza, Grc.	11,008	B3	306
Préveza, prov., Grc.	56,779	B3	306
Prewitt, res., Colo.		B7	106
Prey Veng, Camb.	5,000	E5	362
Pribilof, is., Alsk.		D4	84
Priboj, Yugo.	1,902	C4	316
Příbram, Czech.	14,653	B2	324
Price, Que., Can.	3,140	*Q10	66
Price, Queen Annes, Md.	126	B8	182
Price, Rusk, Tex.	800	C8	130
Price, Carbon, Utah	6,802	D5	114
Price, Lincoln, W.Va.	165	C2	194
Price, co., Wis.	14,370	C3	160
Price, isl., B.C., Can.		D8	52
Price, riv., Utah		D5	114
Price Creek, Moffat, Colo.		B2	106
Pricedale, Pike, Miss.	250	D2	184
Pricedale, Westmoreland, Pa.	1,300	*C2	214
Price Hill, Raleigh, W.Va.	300	D3 / D7	194
Priceville, Ont., Can.	250	P20	64
Prichard, Mobile, Ala.	47,371	E1	168
Prichard, Tunica, Miss.	225	A2	184
Prichard, Wayne, W.Va.	400	C2	194
Pride, Union, Ky.	50	C3	178
Prides Crossing, Essex, Mass.		C4	206
Priego, Sp.	13,801	D4	298
Prieska, U.S.Afr.	4,827	E4	420
Priest, lake, Idaho		A2	108
Priest, riv., Idaho		A2	108
Priestly, mtn., B.C., Can.		C8	52
Priestly, mtn., Maine		B3	204
Priest River, Bonner, Idaho	1,749	A2	108
Prijedor, Yugo.	10,464	B3	316
Prijepolje, Yugo.	3,274	C4	316
Prikumsk, Sov.Un.	10,000	D2	336
Prilep, Yugo.	32,614	D5	316
Priluki, Sov.Un.	40,000	G9	332
Prim, pt., P.E.I., Can		C6	70
Primate, Sask., Can.	120	D3	58
Primera, Cameron, Tex.	1,066	*F7	130
Primero, riv., Arg.		B3	252
Primghar, O'Brien, Iowa	1,131	A2	142
Primorsk, Sov.Un.	8,000	B7	332
Primorsko-Akhtarsk, Sov.Un.	25,000	I12	332
Primos, Delaware, Pa.	1,000	*D6	214
Primrose, Lee, Ky.	50	C7	178
Primrose, Boone, Nebr.	117	C7	152
Primrose, Providence, R.I.	75	B2	216
Primrose, lake, Alta., Can.		C8	54
Prince, Sask., Can.	55	D3	58
Prince, Lincoln, Nev.	25	F7	112
Prince, co., P.E.I., Can.	38,007	C5	70
Prince, inlet, S.C.		F5	188
Prince, lake, Va.		A8	192
Prince Albert, Sask., Can.	20,366	C3 / D5	58
Prince Albert, cape, N.W.Ter., Can.		C6	48
Prince Albert, natl. park, Sask., Can.		C4	58
Prince Albert, sound, N.W.Ter., Can.		C7	48
Prince Charles, isl., N.W.Ter., Can.		D11	48
Prince Edward, co., Ont., Can.	21,145	P23	64
Prince Edward, co., Va.	14,121	C6	192
Prince Edward, isl., Can.		C6	70
Prince Edward Island, prov., Can.	103,000	H12 / C6	48 / 70
Prince Edward Island, natl. park, P.E.I., Can.		C7	70
Prince Frederick, Calvert, Md.	500	C6	182
Prince George, B.C., Can.	10,563	D11 / F7	52
Prince George, Prince George, Va.	80	B9 / C7	192
Prince George, co., Va.	20,270	C7	192
Prince Georges, co., Md.	357,395	C6	182
Prince of Wales, cape, Alsk.		B5	84
Prince of Wales, isl., Alsk.		K14	84
Prince of Wales, isl., Austl.		A8	432
Prince of Wales, isl., N.W.Ter., Can.		C9	48
Prince Patrick, isl., N.W.Ter., Can.		B6	48
Prince Regent, inlet, N.W.Ter., Can.		C9	48
Prince Rupert, B.C., Can.	10,498	C7 / F7	52
Princesa Isabel, Braz.	3,306	B3	258
Princes Lake, Ont., Can.		O22	64
Prince's Lakes, Johnson, Ind.	374	*C3	140
Princess Anne, Somerset, Md.	1,351	D8	182
Princess Anne, Princess Anne, Va.	250	A9 / D8	192
Princess Anne, co., Va.	76,124	D8	192
Princess Charlotte, bay, Austl.		A8	432
Princess Royal, isl., B.C., Can.		D8	52
Princeton, Jackson, Ala.	125	A3	168
Princeton, Dallas, Ark.	57	D4	170
Princeton, Colusa, Calif.	800	C2	94
Princeton, B.C., Can.	2,245	F12	52
Princeton, Newf., Can.	125	F9	72
Princeton, Ont., Can.	480	Q20	64
Princeton, Dade, Fla.	1,719	E6 / F10	174
Princeton, Latah, Idaho	90	C2	108
Princeton, Bureau, Ill.	6,250	B4	138
Princeton, Gibson, Ind.	7,906	D2	140
Princeton, Scott, Iowa	580	C7	142
Princeton, Franklin, Kans.	174	D8	144
Princeton, Caldwell, Ky.	5,618	C3	178
Princeton, Bossier, La.	250	B2	180
Princeton, Washington, Maine	600 (829▲)	C5	204
Princeton, Worcester, Mass.	400 (1,360▲)	B4	206
Princeton, Marquette, Mich.	180	C4	146
Princeton, Mille Lacs, Minn.	2,353	F5	148
Princeton, Mercer, Mo.	1,443	A4	150
Princeton, Lancaster, Nebr.	75	*D9	152
Princeton, Mercer, N.J.	11,890	C3	210
Princeton, Johnston, N.C.	948	B7	186
Princeton, Harney, Oreg.	10	D8	96
Princeton, Laurens, S.C.	167	B4	188
Princeton, Mercer, W.Va.	8,393	D3	194
Princeton, Green Lake, Wis.	1,509	E4	160
Princeton, mtn., Colo.		D4	106
Princeton Depot, Worcester, Mass.		*B4	206
Princeton Junction, Mercer, N.J.	450	C3	210
Princeville, Que., Can.	2,841	R13	66
Princeville, Peoria, Ill.	1,281	C4	138
Princeville, Edgecombe, N.C.	797	B8	186
Prince William, co., Va.	50,164	B7	192
Prince William, sound, Alsk.		G11	84
Principális, canal, Hung.		C1	320
Principe, chan., B.C., Can.		D8	52
Principe, isl., Afr.		F6	408
Prineville, Crook, Oreg.	3,263	C6	96
Prineville Southeast, Crook, Oreg.	1,299	*C6	96
Pringle, Luzerne, Pa.	1,418	*B5	214
Pringle, Custer, S.Dak.	145	D2	158
Prinsburg, Kandiyohi, Minn.	462	G3	148
Prinzapolca, Nic.	4,887	D6	228
Prinzapolca, riv., Nic.		D5	228
Prior Lake, Scott, Minn.	848	G5 / G6	148
Priozersk, Sov.Un.	32,800	B8	332
Pripyat (Pripet), riv., Sov.Un.		G7	332
Prismatic, Kemper, Miss.	80	C4	184
Priština, Yugo.	25,100	C5	316
Pritchard, isl., S.C.		G8	188
Pritchardville, Beaufort, S.C.	50	G7	188
Pritchett, Baca, Colo.	247	E8	106
Pritzwalk, Ger.	9,416	B5	286
Privas, Fr.	7,558	E6	278
Privolnoye, Sov.Un.		I9	332
Prizren, Yugo.	22,997	C5	316
Prizzi, It.	10,600	G4	302
Probolinggo, Indon.	63,400	F4	358
Procious, Clay, W.Va.	300	C7	194
Procter, B.C., Can.	175	F14	52
Proctor, Logan, Colo.	35	B8	106
Proctor, Lee, Ky.	150	C7	178
Proctor, St. Louis, Minn.	2,963	E6	148
Proctor, Lake, Mont.	6	C2	110
Proctor, Elko, Nev.	10	C7	112
Proctor, Adair, Okla.	65	C9	128
Proctor, Rutland, Vt.	1,978 (2,102▲)	D2	218
Proctor, Wetzel, W.Va.	500	C1	194
Proctorsville, Windsor, Vt.	476	E3	218
Proctorville, Lawrence, Ohio	831	D4	156
Progreso, Hond.	9,150	C4	228
Progreso, Mex.	13,334	C8	225
Progress, Pike, Miss.	150	D2	184
Progress, Dauphin, Pa.	1,700	*C5	214
Project City, Shasta, Calif.	950	B2	94
Prokhladnyy, Sov.Un.	28,000	D2	336
Prokopyevsk, Sov.Un.	260,000	B11	336
Prokuplje, Yugo.	10,050	C5	316
Proletarsk, Sov.Un.	10,000	R22	332
Proletarskaya, Sov.Un.	24,800	I13	332
Prome, Bur.	36,997	C2	362
Promise, Wallowa, Oreg.		B9	96
Promise City, Wayne, Iowa	161	D4	142
Promised Land, Mississippi, Ark.		B7	170
Promontory, Box Elder, Utah		B3	114
Promontory, pt., Utah		B3	114
Promontory Point, Box Elder, Utah		B3	114
Prophetstown, Whiteside, Ill.	1,802	B4	138
Propriá, Braz.	12,654	C3	258
Prospect, New Haven, Conn.	4,367	C4	202
Prospect, Sedgwick, Kans.		B5	144
Prospect, Jefferson, Ky.	100	A5	178
Prospect, Waldo, Maine	75 (412▲)	*D4	204
Prospect, Marion, Ohio	1,067	B3	156
Prospect, Jackson, Oreg.	350	E4	96
Prospect, Giles, Tenn.	200	C4	190
Prospect, Prince Edward, Va.	125	C6	192
Prospect, Waukesha, Wis. (part of New Berlin)		E1	160
Prospect, hill, Mass.		D2	206
Prospect, hill, Mass.		D4	206
Prospect, hill, Mass.		D6	206
Prospect, hill, Oreg.		C1	96
Prospect, mtn., Oreg.		C2	96
Prospect Harbor, Hancock, Maine	350	D4	204
Prospect Heights, Fremont, Colo.	39	*D5	106
Prospect Heights, Cook, Ill.	1,700	E2	138
Prospect Park, Passaic, N.J.	5,201	B4	210
Prospect Park, Delaware, Pa.	6,596	A6	214
Prospect Plains, Middlesex, N.J.	100	C4	210
Prosperity, Newberry, S.C.	752	C5	188
Prosperity, Raleigh, W.Va.	900	D7	194
Prosser, Adams, Nebr.	70	D7	152
Prosser, Benton, Wash.	2,763	C7	98
Prostějov, Czech.	33,853	B3	324
Protection, Comanche, Kans.	780	E4	144
Protivin, Howard, Iowa	302	A5	142
Proton Station, Ont., Can.	150	P20	64
Provadiya, Bul.	12,426	B3	317
Provadiya, riv., Bul.		B3	317
Pröven, Grnld.	248	P28	290
Provencal, Natchitoches, La.	570	C2	180
Provence, former prov., Fr.	1,750,000	F6	278
Providence, Union, Fla.	150	B8	174
Providence, Webster, Ky.	3,771	C3	178
Providence, Cecil, Md.	85	A8	182
Providence, Caswell, N.C.	300	A6	186
Providence, Providence, R.I.	207,498 (*804,300)	B2	216
Providence, Davidson, Tenn.	3,830	*B5	190
Providence, Cache, Utah	1,189	B4	114

Quemado de Güines, Cuba	3,276	A4	232
Quemoy (Chinmen), China		M9	349
Quemú Quemú, Arg.		C3	252
Quenemo, Osage, Kans.	434	D8	144
Quentin, Franklin, Miss.	250	D2	184
Que Que, Rh.&Nya.	5,000 (*9,500)	C5	420
Quequén, Arg.	4,760	C4	252
Querétaro, Mex.	49,209	C5 K13	225
Querétaro, state, Mex.	286,238	C5	225
Querobavi, Mex.		A3	224
Quesada, Sp.	7,609	D5	298
Quesnel, B.C., Can.	4,384	D11	52
Quesnel, lake, B.C., Can.		D12	52
Quesnel, riv., B.C., Can.		D11	52
Questa, Taos, N.Mex.	900	B5	126
Quetena, Bol.	183	D1	246
Quetico, prov. park, Ont., Can.		R23	64
Quetta, Pak.	56,249 (*84,343)	D5	375
Quevedo, Ec.	4,146	A2	245
Quezaltenango, Guat.	27,696	C2	228
Quezaltepeque, Sal.	6,433	D3	228
Quezon City, Phil.	107,977	B6	358
Quezzane, Mor.		B2	402
Quibala, Ang.	263	B2	420
Quibdó, Col.	39,520	B1	244
Quiberon, Fr.		D2	278
Quiberon, pen., Fr.		D2	278
Quick, Frontier, Nebr.		D5	152
Quick, Kanawha, W.Va.	450	C6	194
Quicksand, pond, R.I.		C4	216
Quicksburg, Shenandoah, Va.	150	B6	192
Quidnick, Kent, R.I.	800	C2	216
Quidnick, res., R.I.		C2	216
Quietus, Big Horn, Mont.	5	E10	110
Quigilinook, see Kwigillingok, Alsk.			
Quigley, Union, La.		B3	180
Quiindy, Par.	2,150	D4	247
Quilá, Mex.	1,290	C4	224
Quilán, cape, Chile		F3	251
Quilcene, Jefferson, Wash.	600	B4	98
Quilengues, Ang.	472	B2	420
Quilino, Arg.	2,547	B3	252
Quill, Gilmer, Ga.	126	B2	176
Quill, lakes, Sask., Can.		E5	58
Quillaga, Chile		B4	250
Quillan, Fr.		F5	278
Quill Lake, Sask., Can.	458	D5	58
Quillota, Chile	22,640	B1	252
Quilon, India	66,126	G3	366
Quilpie, Austl.	860	D8	432
Quilpué, Chile	16,332	B1	252
Quilty, Ire.	149	I3	273
Quimbele, Ang.		A3	420
Quimby, Cherokee, Iowa	369	B2	142
Quimby, Aroostook, Maine	200	B4	204
Quimby, Accomack, Va.	200	C9	192
Quimilí, Arg.	3,686	A3	252
Quimper, Fr.	19,352	D1	278
Quimperlé, Fr.	7,845	D2	278
Quinaby, Marion, Oreg.	50	B4 C1	96
Quinapoxet, Worcester, Mass.	100	B4	206
Quinault, Grays Harbor, Wash.	300	B3	98
Quinault, lake, Wash.		B3	98
Quinault, riv., Wash.		B2	98
Quincy, Plumas, Calif.	1,700	C3	94
Quincy, Gadsden, Fla.	8,874	A6	174
Quincy, Adams, Ill.	43,793	D2	138
Quincy, Owen, Ind.	150	C3	140
Quincy, Greenwood, Kans.	90	E8	144
Quincy, Lewis, Ky.	300	B7	178
Quincy, Norfolk, Mass.	87,409	B5 D3	206
Quincy, Branch, Mich.	1,602	H7	146
Quincy, Monroe, Miss.	125	B4	184
Quincy, Grafton, N.H.	85	D3	208
Quincy, Logan, Ohio	668	B3	156
Quincy, Columbia, Oreg.	200	A3	96
Quincy, Grant, Wash.	3,269	B7	98
Quincy, bay, Mass.		D3	206
Quindaro, Wyandotte, Kans.	500	A8	144
Quinebaug, Windham, Conn.	350	A8	202
Quinebaug, riv., Conn.		C8	202
Quines, Arg.	3,038	B2	252
Quinhagak (Kwinhagak), Alsk.	194	D5	84
Qui Nhon, Viet.	10,000	D6	362
Quinlan, Woodward, Okla.	75	B4	128
Quinlan, Hunt, Tex.	621	C7	130
Quinn, Pennington, S.Dak.	162	D3	158
Quinn, riv., Nev.		B4	112
Quinnesec, Dickinson, Mich.	400	D4	146
Quinney, Calumet, Wis.	50	B5	160
Quinnipiac, riv., Conn.		D4	202
Quinsett, Barnstable, Mass.	65	C6	206
Quintana de la Serena, Sp.	9,098	C4	298
Quintana Roo, ter., Mex.	26,967	D8	225
Quintanar, Sp.	9,498	C5	298
Quinter, Gove, Kans.	776	C3	144
Quintero, Chile	5,563	B1	252
Quinton, Sask., Can.	184	E5	58
Quinton, Pulaski, Ky.	200	D6	178
Quinton, Salem, N.J.	600	D2	210
Quinton, Pittsburg, Okla.	898	C8	128
Quinwood, Greenbrier, W.Va.	506	C4	194
Quipapá, Braz.	2,226	B3	258
Quipungo, Ang.		B2	420
Quiraug, mtn., Md.		A4	182
Quiroga, Sp.	624	A3	298
Quirpon, isl., Newf., Can.		E8	72
Quissanga, Moz.		B8	421
Quitaque, Briscoe, Tex.	586	B5	130
Quita Sueño Bank, shoals, Caribbean Sea		C7	228
Quithlook, see Kwethluk, Alsk.			
Quitman, Cleburne, Ark.	305	B4	170
Quitman, Brooks, Ga.	5,071	F3	176
Quitman, Jackson, La.	185	B3	180
Quitman, Clarke, Miss.	2,030	C4	184
Quitman, Nodaway, Mo.	113	A2	150
Quitman, Wood, Tex.	1,237	C8	130
Quitman, co., Ga.	2,432	E1	176
Quitman, co., Miss.	21,019	A2	184
Quitman, mts., Tex.		D3	130
Quito, Ec.	232,000	A2	245
Quitovac, Mex.		A3	224
Quivera, lake, Kans.		B7	144
Quivira Lake, Wyandotte and Johnson, Kans.	450	*C9	144
Quixadá, Braz.	5,417	A3	258
Quixeramobim, Braz.	3,052	B3	258
Qulin, Butler, Mo.	587	E7	150
Qum, riv., Iran		C3	379
Quogue, Suffolk, N.Y.	692	D5	212
Quoi, isl., Truk		A3	436
Quonochontaug, Washington, R.I.	50	D2	216
Quonochontaug, pond, R.I.		D2	216
Quonset Point, Washington, R.I.		C3	216
Quoyness, Scot.		C9	272
Qûs, Eg., U.A.R.	19,530	B3	395
Qusaiba, Iraq		B4	378
Qusaima, Eg., U.A.R.		A3	395
Quseir, Eg., U.A.R.		B3	395
R			
Raab, riv., Aus.		C7	313
Raabs [an der Thaya], Aus.	1,281	B7	313
Raahe, Fin.	4,508	D11	290
Raalte, Neth.	3,301	B5	282
Raasay, isl., Scot.		D6	272
Rab, isl., Yugo.		B2	316
Raba, Indon.	6,781	F5	358
Rába, riv., Hung.		B2	320
Rabat, Mor.	171,000	B2	402
Rabaul, Bis. Arch.		E12	359
Rabbit, creek, S.Dak.		B3	158
Rabbit Ear, pass, Colo.		B4	106
Rabbit Hash, Boone, Ky.	50	A7	178
Rabbit Lake, Sask., Can.	197	D4	58
Rabch, riv., Iran		E5	379
Rābigh, Sau.Ar.		C2	383
Rabun, Baldwin, Ala.	250	*D2	168
Rabun, co., Ga.	7,456	B3	176
Rabun, gap, Ga.		B3	176
Rabun Bald, mtn., Ga.		B3	176
Rača Kragujevačka, Yugo.	1,000	B5	316
Răcari, Rom.		B3	321
Raccoon, creek, Ohio		D4	156
Raccoon, mtn., Ala.		B3	168
Raccoon, riv., Iowa		C3	142
Raccourci, isl., La.		D4	180
Race, cape, Newf., Can.		G9	72
Race, pt., Mass.		B7	206
Raceland, Greenup, Ky.	1,115	B8	178
Raceland, Lafourche, La.	3,666	C6 E5	180
Racepond, Charlton, Ga.	250	F4	176
Rachel, Marion, W.Va.	950	A7	194
Rach Gia, Viet.	24,000	E5	362
Racho de Santana, Braz.		C2	258
Racibórz, Pol.	30,000	C4	325
Racine, Mower, Minn.	180	H6	148
Racine, Newton, Mo.	150	E3	150
Racine, Meigs, Ohio	499	D5	156
Racine, Boone, W.Va.	975	C3 D6	194
Racine, Racine, Wis.	89,144 (*113,500)	F2 F6	160
Racine, co., Wis.	141,781	F5	160
Račiněves, Czech.	626	*A2	324
Rackett, Garden, Nebr.		C3	152
Rackwick, Scot.		C9	272
Raco, Chippewa, Mich.	100	C7	146
Rădăuti, Rom.	15,949	A3	321
Radcliff, Hardin, Ky.	3,384	C5	178
Radcliffe, Hardin, Iowa	615	B4	142
Radeberg, Ger.	16,600	C5	286
Radersburg, Broadwater, Mont.	100	D5	110
Radford (Independent City), Va.	9,371	C4	192
Radiant Valley, Prince Georges, Md.	1,500	*C6	182
Radisson, Sask., Can.	500	D4	58
Radisson, Sawyer, Wis.	179	C2	160
Radium, Stafford, Kans.	64	D5	144
Radium Hot Springs, B.C., Can.	100	E14	52
Radium Springs, Dona Ana, N.Mex.	30	F4	126
Radley, Crawford, Kans.	235	E9	144
Radnor, co., Wales	19,210	I9	273
Radnor, forest, Wales		I9	273
Radom, Pol.	117,000	C5	325
Radomir, Bul.	6,709	B1	317
Radomsko, Pol.	21,300	C4	325
Radomyshl, Sov.Un.	25,000	G7	332
Radoviš, Yugo.	5,255	D6	316
Radstadt, Aus.	3,403	C5	313
Radville, Sask., Can.	1,087	F5	58
Radwah, mtn., Sau.Ar.		C2	383
Radway, Alta., Can.	203	C6	54
Radzymin, Pol.	4,356	B5	325
Radzyń, Pol.	4,694	C6	325
Rae Bareli, India	24,958	D3	368
Raeford, Hoke, N.C.	3,058	C6	186
Raeside, lake, Austl.		E4	432
Raeville, Boone, Nebr.	80	C7	152
Rafaela, Arg.	23,665	B3	252
Rafai, Cen.Afr.Rep.		E9	409
Rafḥā, Sau.Ar.		B3	383
Raft, riv., Idaho		G5	108
Raft River, mts., Utah		B2	114
Rag, mtn., Tenn.		C8	190
Raga, Sud.		D2	398
Ragan, Harlan, Nebr.	90	D6	152
Ragged, isl., Maine		E4	204
Ragged, lake, Maine		C3	204
Ragged, pt., Md.		C7	182
Ragged Top, mtn., Wyo.		E7	116
Raggon, isl., S.C.		G2	188
Raghunathpali, India		E4	368
Raghunathpur, India		D4	368
Ragland, St. Clair, Ala.	1,166	B3	168
Ragland, Mingo, W.Va.	800	D2	194
Ragley, Beauregard, La.	25	D2	180
Rago, Kingman, Kans.	50	E5	144
Ragsdale, Knox, Ind.	210	D2	140
Ragusa, It.	42,000	G5	302
Ragusa, prov., It.	248,100	*G5	302
Rahab el Berdi, Sud.		C1	398
Rahimyar-Khan, Pak.	14,919	E7	375
Rahway, Union, N.J.	27,699	B1 B4	210
Rahway, riv., N.J.		B1	210
Raices, Arg.		B4	252
Raichur, India	54,032	E3	366
Raiford, Union, Fla.	500	A8	174
Raigarh, India	29,684	E3	368
Raimangal, riv., India		I10	366
Raimund, Jefferson, Ala.	250	*B3	168
Rainbow, Hartford, Conn.	250	B5	202
Rainbow, falls, Tenn.		C8	190
Rainbow, lake, Maine		C3	204
Rainbow, pt., Fla.		C8	174
Rainbow, res., Wis.		C4	160
Rainbow Bridge, natl. mon., Utah		F5	114
Rainbow City, Etowah, Ala.	1,625	*A3	168
Rainelle, Greenbrier, W.Va.	649	D4	194
Raines, Shelby, Tenn. (part of Whitehaven)		C1 E6	190
Rainier, Columbia, Oreg.	1,152	A4	96
Rainier, Thurston, Wash.	245	C4	98
Rainier, mtn., Wash.		C5	98
Rains, Marion, S.C.	200	C10	188
Rains, co., Tex.	2,993	C8	130
Rainsville, De Kalb, Ala.	398	*A4	168
Rainy, lake, Minn., Ont., Can.		C5 R23	148 64
Rainy, mtn., Okla.		D4	128
Rainy, riv., Minn.		C4	148
Rainy River, Ont., Can.	1,354	R23	64
Rainy River, co., Ont., Can.	25,483	R23	64
Raipur, India	89,804	D4	366
Ra'is, Sau.Ar.		C2	383
Raith, Ont., Can.	75	R24	64
Raja, Solomon Is.		F13	359
Raja, mtn., Indon.		E4	358
Rajahmundry, India	105,276	E4	366
Rajang, riv., Sar.		D4	358
Rajasthan, state, India	15,970,774	C2	366
Rajgarh, India		C1	368
Rajkot, India	132,069	D2	366
Rajpur, India		E1	368
Rajuna, Ven.		D6	240
Rakaia, riv., N.Z.		E3	437
Rakaposhi, mtn., India		A1	368
Rake, Winnebago, Iowa	328	A4	142
Rakovník, Czech.	12,445	A1	324
Rakvere, Sov.Un.	21,500	C6	332
Raleigh, Newf., Can.	250	E8	72
Raleigh, Levy, Fla.	156	B8	174
Raleigh, Rush, Ind.	120	C4	140
Raleigh, Smith, Miss.	614	C3	184
Raleigh, Wake, N.C.	93,931 (*130,200)	B7	186
Raleigh, Grant, N.Dak.	125	D4	154
Raleigh, Shelby, Tenn.	6,000	C2 E6	190
Raleigh, Raleigh, W.Va.	750	D7	194
Raleigh, co., W.Va.	77,826	D3	194
Raleigh, bay, N.C.		C9	186
Raleigh Hills, Washington, Oreg.	1,100	*B4	96
Raley, Alta., Can.	15	F6	54
Ralik Chain, is., Marshall		A4	437
Rallouia, well, Maur.		B2	408
Ralls, Crosby, Tex.	2,229	C5	130
Ralls, co., Mo.	8,078	B6	150
Ralph, Tuscaloosa, Ala.	500	B2	168
Ralph, Sussex, Del.		G3	172
Ralph, Dickinson, Mich.	40	C4	146
Ralph, Harding, S.Dak.	20	B2	158
Ralston, Carroll, Iowa	143	B3	142
Ralston, Douglas, Nebr.	2,977	D3	152
Ralston, Morris, N.J.	90	B3	210
Ralston, Pawnee, Okla.	411	B7	128
Ralston, Weakley, Tenn.	50	B3	190
Ralston, Park, Wyo.	20	B4	116
Ram, riv., Alta., Can.		D5	54
Rama, Sask., Can.	262	E6	58
Rama, Nic.	581	E5	228
Ramadan, see Turabah, Sau.Ar.			
Ramādi, Iraq	12,020	C5	378
Ramah, Newf., Can.		D9	72
Ramah, El Paso, Colo.	109	C6	106
Ramah, McKinley, N.Mex.	175	C2	126
Rām Allāh, Jordan	17,145	C6	382
Ramapo, mts., N.J.		A4	210
Ramat Gan, Isr.	58,000	B5	382
Rambaultown, Houghton, Mich.	900	*B3	146
Rambervillers, Fr.	5,214	C7	278
Rambouillet, Fr.	8,923	C4	278
Ramburg, Blaine, Mont.		B7	110
Ramea, Newf., Can.	931	G7	72
Ramea, is., Newf., Can.		G7	72
Ramelau, mtn., Port. Timor		F7	358
Ramenskoye, Sov.Un.	42,000	E12 N19	332
Ramer, Montgomery, Ala.	750	C3	168
Ramer, McNairy, Tenn.	358	C3	190
Rameshk, Iran		D5	379
Rāmhormoz, Iran	17,267	C2	379
Ramhurst, Murray, Ga.	100	B2	176
Ramiriqui, Col.	881	B2	244
Ramle, Isr.	21,500	C5	382
Ramnäs, Swe.	1,103	B7	292
Râmnicu-Sărat, Rom.	19,095	B4	321
Râmnicu-Vâlcea, Rom.	18,984	B3	321
Ramon, mtn., Isr.		D5	382
Ramona, San Diego, Calif.	2,449	F5	94
Ramona, Marion, Kans.	132	D6	144
Ramona, Washington, Okla.	546	B8	128
Ramona, Lake, S.Dak.	247	C8	158
Rampart, Alsk.	94	B6	84
Rampur, India	134,277	C2	368
Rampur, India		E1	368
Rampur Boalia, Pak.	39,993	K16	375
Ramree, isl., Bur.		C2	362
Ramsay, Gogebic, Mich.	1,158	C1	146
Ramsay, Silver Bow, Mont.	125	D4	110
Ramsayville, Ont., Can.		Q26	64
Ramsele, Swe.		E7	290
Ramseur, Randolph, N.C.	1,258	B6	186
Ramsey, Dallas, Ark.	25	*D4	170
Ramsey, Eng.	5,700	I12	273
Ramsey, Fayette, Ill.	815	D4	138
Ramsey, Isle of Man	4,621	G8	273
Ramsey, Bergen, N.J.	9,527	A4	210
Ramsey, Shelby, Tenn.		C1 E6	190
Ramsey, Carbon, Wyo.	15	*E6	116
Ramsey, co., Minn.	422,525	F5	148
Ramsey, co., N.Dak.	13,443	B7	154
Ramsgate, Eng.	36,000	J14	273
Ramshorn, mtn., Wyo.		C3	116
Ranaghat, India	28,064	H9	366
Ranau, lake, Indon.		E2	358
Ranburne, Cleburne, Ala.	317	B4	168
Rancagua, Chile	39,972	B1	252
Ranchcreek, Powder River, Mont.	3	E11	110
Rancherie, rock, Oreg.		C6	96
Ranches of Taos, Taos, N.Mex.	1,668	B5	126
Ranchester, Sheridan, Wyo.	235	B5	116
Ranchi, India	106,849	E4	368
Rancho Cordova, Sacramento, Calif.	7,429	*C3	94
Ranco, Chile		F3	251
Ranco, lake, Chile		F3	251
Rancocas, Burlington, N.J.	300	C3	210
Rancocas, creek, N.J.		D3	210
Rand, Jackson, Colo.	12	B4	106
Rand, Kanawha, W.Va.	3,000	C6	194
Randalia, Fayette, Iowa	114	B6	142
Randall, Hamilton, Iowa	201	B4	142
Randall, Jewell, Kans.	201	C5	144
Randall, Morrison, Minn.	516	E4	148
Randall, co., Tex.	33,913	B5	130
Randallstown, Baltimore, Md.	2,000	B6	182
Randers, Den.	41,177	H4	291
Randers, co., Den.	170,802	*H4	291
Randijaur, lake, Swe.		C8	290
Randle, Lewis, Wash.	100	C5	98
Randleman, Randolph, N.C.	2,232	B6	186
Randles, Cape Girardeau, Mo.	169	D8	150
Randlett, Cotton, Okla.	356	D5	128
Randlett, Uintah, Utah	10	C6	114
Randolph, Bibb, Ala.	250	C3	168
Randolph, Pinal, Ariz.	245	F4	124
Randolph, Fremont, Iowa	257	D2	142
Randolph, Riley, Kans.	35	*C7	144
Randolph, Kennebec, Maine	1,724	D3	204
Randolph, Norfolk, Mass.	18,900	B5 D3	206
Randolph, Dakota, Minn.	315	G5	148
Randolph, Pontotoc, Miss.	131	A3	184
Randolph, Clay, Mo.	219	*B3	150
Randolph, Cedar, Nebr.	1,063	B8	152
Randolph, Coos, N.H.	25 (140▲)	C4	208
Randolph, Cattaraugus, N.Y.	1,414	C3	212
Randolph, Portage, Ohio	700	A5	156
Randolph, Tipton, Tenn.		C2	190
Randolph, Rich, Utah	537	B4	114
Randolph, Orange, Vt.	2,122 (3,414▲)	D3	218
Randolph, Columbia, Wis.	1,507	E5	160
Randolph, co., Ala.	19,477	B4	168
Randolph, co., Ark.	12,520	A5	170
Randolph, co., Ga.	11,078	E2	176
Randolph, co., Ill.	29,988	E4	138
Randolph, co., Ind.	28,434	B4	140
Randolph, co., Mo.	22,014	B5	150
Randolph, co., N.C.	61,497	B6	186
Randolph, co., W.Va.	26,349	C5	194
Randolph Center, Orange, Vt.	140	D3	218
Randolph Hills, Montgomery, Md.	2,000	*B5	182
Random, isl., Newf., Can.		F9	72
Random Lake, Sheboygan, Wis.	858	E6	160
Randow, riv., Ger.		B6	286
Randsburg, Kern, Calif.	300	E5	94
Randsfjord, lake, Nor.		F3	291
Rånea, Swe.		D10	290
Ranfjord, fjord, Nor.		C5	290
Ranfurly, Alta., Can.	129	D7	54
Rangaunu, bay, N.Z.		A4	437
Range, Grant, Oreg.		C7	96
Rangeley, Franklin, Maine	749 (1,087▲)	D2	204
Rangeley, lake, Maine		D2	204
Rangely, Rio Blanco, Colo.	1,464	B2	106
Ranger, Gordon, Ga.	161	B2	176
Ranger, Eastland, Tex.	3,313	C6	130
Ranger, Lincoln, W.Va.	150	C2	194
Ranger, lake, N.Mex.		E7	126
Rangia, India		D5	368
Rangiora, N.Z.	3,150	E4	437
Rangitata, riv., N.Z.		E3	437
Rangitoto, channel, N.Z.		H9	437
Rangitoto, isl., N.Z.		H9	437
Rangoon, Bur.	752,000	C3	362
Rangoon, Barbour, W.Va.	100	B4	194
Rangpur, Pak.	31,759	K16	375
Ranier, Koochiching, Minn.	262	C5	148
Raniganj, India	25,939	E4	368
Rankin, Vermilion, Ill.	761	C6	138
Rankin, Rankin, Miss.	150	C3	184
Rankin, Allegheny, Pa.	5,164	A4	214
Rankin, Upton, Tex.	1,214	D5	130
Rankin, co., Miss.	34,322	C2	184
Ranlo, Gaston, N.C.	2,000	*B4	186
Rannoch, lake, Scot.		E8	272
Ranong, prov., Thai.	21,488	*E3	362
Ransfjord, lake, Nor.		A2	292
Ranshaw, Northumberland, Pa.	1,078	*B5	214
Ransom, La Salle, Ill.	415	B5	138
Ransom, Ness, Kans.	387	D4	144
Ransom, co., N.Dak.	8,078	D8	154
Ransomville, Niagara, N.Y.	950	B3	212
Ranson, Jefferson, W.Va.	1,974	B7	194
Rantem, Newf., Can.	15	G9	72
Rantemario, mtn., Indon.		E6	358
Rantoul, Champaign, Ill.	22,116	C5	138
Rantoul, Franklin, Kans.	157	D8	144
Rantowles, Charleston, S.C.	100	F7	188
Ranua, Fin.		D12	290
Rapallo, It.	11,900	C2	302
Rapa Nui (Easter), isl., Pac.O.		D5	436
Rapelje, Stillwater, Mont.	115	E7	110
Raphine, Rockbridge, Va.	300	C5	192
Rapid, riv., Minn.		C4	148
Rapidan, Culpeper, Va.	220	B6	192
Rapid City, Man., Can.	434	E2	60
Rapid City, Kalkaska, Mich.	300	E6	146
Rapid City, Pennington, S.Dak.	42,399	C2	158
Rapides, Rapides, La.		C3	180
Rapides, par., La.	111,351	C3	180

Rapid River, Delta, Mich.	550	D5	146
Rapids City, Rock Island, Ill.	675	B3	138
Rappahannock, co., Va.	5,368	B6	192
Rappahannock, riv., Va.		B7	192
Rappahannock Academy, Caroline, Va.	5	B7	192
Rapperswil, Switz.	5,597	A4	312
Rapson, Huron, Mich.		F9	146
Rapti, riv., Nep.		D3	368
Raqah, Sau.Ar.		D3	383
Raqqah, Syr., U.A.R.	11,411	B3	378
Raquette, lake, N.Y.		B7	212
Raquette, riv., N.Y.		A7	212
Rara Avis, Itawamba, Miss.	103	A4	184
Raritan, Somerset, N.J.	6,137	B3	210
Raritan, bay, N.J.		C4	210
Rarous, well, Niger		C6	408
Rasa, pt., Arg.		F5	251
Ras al Khaymah, Tr. Coast		B6	383
Ra's an Naqb, Jordan		E6	382
Rasar, Blount, Tenn.		C8	190
Ra's at Tannūrah, Sau.Ar.		B5	383
Rasdajan, mtn., Eth.		C4	398
Ras el 'Ain, Syr., U.A.R.		A4	378
Ras el Esh, Eg., U.A.R.		C3	382
Rashad, Sud.	1,683	C3	398
Rashid (Rosetta), Eg., U.A.R.	23,996	A3	395
Rashin, see Najin, Kor.			
Rasht, Iran	109,491	B2	379
Raška, Yugo.	1,832	C5	316
Raška, riv., Yugo.		C5	316
Raso, cape, Braz.		E6	256
Raspberry, peak, Ark.		C2	170
Rasskazovo, Sov.Un.	43,500	F13	332
Rastatt, Ger.	22,700	D3	286
Rat, is., Alsk.		E3	84
Rat, riv., Man., Can.		B3	60
Rat, riv., Man., Can.		F4	60
Ratakahöjden, mtn., Swe.		B3	292
Ratak Chain, is., Marshall		A4	436
Ratangarh, India	27,431	C1	368
Ratangarh, India		D1	368
Rat Buri, Thai.	10,000	D3	362
Rat Buri, prov., Thai.	295,534	*D3	362
Ratcliff, Logan, Ark.	147	B3	170
Rath, India		D2	368
Rathbun, Appanoose, Iowa	203	D5	142
Rathdrum, Kootenai, Idaho	710	B2	108
Rathdrum, Ire.	1,269	I6	273
Rathenow, Ger.	29,400	B5	286
Rathlin, isl., N.Ire.		F6	272
Rathlin, sound, N.Ire.		F6	272
Rathowen, Ire.	147	H5	273
Rathwell, Man., Can.	245	F3	60
Ratibor, see Racibórz, Pol.			
Ratlam, India	63,403	E1	368
Ratliff City, Carter, Okla.	150	*D6	128
Ratnagiri, India	27,082	E2	366
Ratner, Sask., Can.	60	D5	58
Raton, Colfax, N.Mex.	8,146	B6	126
Raton, pass, Colo.		E6	106
Rattan, Pushmataha, Okla.	300	D8	128
Rattenberg, Aus.	879	C3	313
Rattlesnake, butte, N.Dak.		D2	154
Rattlesnake, creek, Kans.		E4	144
Rattlesnake, creek, Ohio		C3	156
Rattlesnake, creek, Wash.		C7	98
Rattlesnake, flat, Wash.		C8	98
Rattlesnake, hill, Conn.		A6	202
Rattlesnake, mtn., Conn.		C4	202
Rattlesnake, range, Wyo.		D5	116
Rattling Brook, Newf., Can.	100	F7	72
Rattray, head, Scot.		D11	272
Rättvik, Swe.	1,368	A6	292
Raub, Benton, Ind.	100	B2	140
Rauch, Arg.	5,274	C4	252
Raufarhöfn, Ice.	414	K22	290
Rauma, Fin.	15,639	F9	291
Rausu-Dake, peak, Jap.		B10	354
Ravalli, Lake, Mont.	50	C2	110
Ravalli, co., Mont.	12,341	D2	110
Ravanna, Mercer, Mo.	127	A4	150
Rāvar, Iran	5,074	C4	379
Rava-Russkaya, Sov.Un.	24,000	G4	332
Raven, Tazewell, Va.	900	C3	192
Ravena, Albany, N.Y.	2,410	C8	212
Ravenden, Lawrence, Ark.	231	A5	170
Ravenden Springs, Randolph, Ark.	126	A5	170
Ravenel, Charleston, S.C.	527	F2	188
Ravenglass, Eng.	417	G9	273
Ravenna, It.	36,100 (94,900▲)	C4	302
Ravenna, Estill, Ky.	921	C7	178
Ravenna, Muskegon, Mich.	801	F6	146
Ravenna, Buffalo, Nebr.	1,417	C7	152
Ravenna, Portage, Ohio	10,918	A5	156
Ravenna, prov., It.	301,400	*C4	302
Raven Rock, Hunterdon, N.J.		C2	210
Ravensburg, Ger.	29,200	E3	286
Ravenscrag, Sask., Can.	115	F3	58
Ravensdale, King, Wash.	250	D3	98
Ravensthorpe, Austl.	158	E4	432
Ravenswood, Marion, Ind.	618	D5	140
Ravenswood, Jackson, W.Va.	3,410	C3	194
Ravensworth, Ont., Can.	65	O21	64
Ravenwood, Nodaway, Mo.	282	A3	150
Ravi, riv., Pak.		D8	375
Ravia, Johnston, Okla.	307	D7	128
Ravinia, Charles Mix, S.Dak.	164	D7	158
Rawalpindi, Pak.	153,070 (237,219▲)	C8	375
Rawa Mazowiecka, Pol.	6,908	C5	325
Rawdon, Que., Can.	2,049	R11	66
Rawhide, creek, Wyo.		D8	116
Rawicz, Pol.	11,600	C3	325
Rawles Springs, Forrest, Miss.	180	D3	184
Rawlings, Allegany, Md.	180	A2	182
Rawlings, Brunswick, Va.	50	D7	192
Rawlinna, Austl.	89	E5	432
Rawlins, Carbon, Wyo.	8,968	E5	116
Rawlins, co., Kans.	5,279	C2	144
Rawlins, hill, Wyo.		D5	116
Rawson, Arg.	2,425	F4	251
Rawson, McKenzie, N.Dak.	28	C2	154
Rawson, Hancock, Ohio	407	B3	156
Ray, Pinal, Ariz.	1,468	E5	124
Ray, Steuben, Ind.	200	A5	140
Ray, Williams, N.Dak.	1,049	B2	154
Ray, Koochiching, Minn.	55	C5	148
Ray, co., Mo.	16,075	B3	150
Ray, cape, Newf., Can.		G6	72
Ray-Aleksandrovka, Sov.Un.		R21	332
Raybon, Brantley, Ga.	250	E5	176
Ray Brook, Essex, N.Y.	546	A7	212
Ray City, Berrien, Ga.	713	E3	176
Rayford, Murray, Okla.		D6	128
Raygorodka, Sov.Un.		R23	332
Rayland, Jefferson, Ohio	694	*B6	156
Rayle, Wilkes, Ga.	200	C4	176
Raymond, Los Angeles, Calif.	300	D4	94
Raymond, Alta., Can.	2,399	F6	54
Raymond, Coweta, Ga.	300	C2	176
Raymond, Bear Lake, Idaho	35	*G7	108
Raymond, Montgomery, Ill.	871	D4	138
Raymond, Black Hawk, Iowa	378	B5	142
Raymond, Rice, Kans.	143	D5	144
Raymond, Cumberland, Maine	300 (732▲)	E4	204
Raymond, Kandiyohi, Minn.	608	F3	148
Raymond, Hinds, Miss.	1,381	C2	184
Raymond, Sheridan, Mont.	40	B12	110
Raymond, Lancaster, Nebr.	223	D9	152
Raymond, Rockingham, N.H.	800 (1,867▲)	E4	208
Raymond, Clark, S.Dak.	168	C8	158
Raymond, Pacific, Wash.	3,301	C3	98
Raymondville, Texas, Mo.	202	D6	150
Raymondville, Willacy, Tex.	9,385	F7	130
Raymore, Sask., Can.	434	E5	58
Raymore, Cass, Mo.	268	C3	150
Rayne, Acadia, La.	8,634	D3	180
Raynesford, Judith Basin, Mont.	41	C6	110
Raynham, Bristol, Mass.	350 (4,150▲)	C5	206
Raynham Center, Bristol, Mass.	900	C5	206
Raynor, Isle of Wight, Va.		A8	192
Rayón, Mex.	1,351	B3	224
Rayong, Thai.	10,000	D4	362
Rayong, prov., Thai.	84,197	*D4	362
Rayon Terrace, Va. (part of Covington)		C4	192
Raystown, branch, Pa.		C3	214
Raytown, Jackson, Mo.	17,083	E2	150
Rayville, Richland, La.	4,052	B4	180
Rayville, Ray, Mo.	200	B3	150
Raywick, Marion, Ky.	175	C5	178
Raywood, Pocahontas, W.Va.	700	C5	194
Razan, Iran	3,195	B2	379
Razelm, lake, Rom.		B5	321
Razgrad, Bul.	18,416	B3	317
Razgradski, prov., Bul.		*B3	317
Razlog, Bul.	8,652	C1	317
Razmak, Pak.		C6	375
Razorback, mtn., B.C., Can.		E10	52
Ré, isl., Fr.		D3	278
Rea, Andrew, Mo.	90	A3	150
Reader, Ouachita, Ark.	86	D3	170
Reader, Wetzel, W.Va.	500	A6 B4	194
Reader, lake, Man., Can.		D2	60
Readfield, Kennebec, Maine	200 (1,029▲)	D3	204
Reading, Eng.	117,900	J12	273
Reading, Lyon, Kans.	249	D8	144
Reading, Middlesex, Mass.	19,259	A5 C3	206
Reading, Hillsdale, Mich.	1,128	H7	146
Reading, Nobles, Minn.	160	H3	148
Reading, Hamilton, Ohio	12,832	C2 D1	156
Reading, Berks, Pa.	98,177 (*192,500)	C6	214
Reading, Windsor, Vt.	165 (472▲)	E3	218
Readland, Chicot, Ark.	100	D5	170
Readlyn, Sask., Can.	120	F5	58
Readlyn, Bremer, Iowa	547	B5	142
Readsboro, Bennington, Vt.	577 (783▲)	F3	218
Reads Landing, Wabasha, Minn.	250	G6	148
Readstown, Vernon, Wis.	469	E3	160
Ready, Grayson, Ky.	48	C4	178
Readyville, Cannon, Tenn.	100	C5	190
Reagan, Johnston, Okla.	50	D7	128
Reagan, Henderson, Tenn.	150	C3	190
Reagan, co., Tex.	3,782	D5	130
Real, co., Tex.	2,079	E6	130
Real, range, Bol.		C1	246
Realicó, Arg.		C3	252
Realitos, Duval, Tex.	400	F6	130
Real Morelos, Mex.		B4	224
Ream, Camb.	5,000	E4	362
Ream, McDowell, W.Va.	800	*D3	194
Reamstown, Lancaster, Pa.	950	C5	214
Reardan, Lincoln, Wash.	474	B9	98
Reasnor, Jasper, Iowa	324	C4	142
Reata, Mex.	208	B5	225
Reaville, Hunterdon, N.J.	75	C3	210
Rebecca, Turner, Ga.	278	E3	176
Rebel Creek, Humboldt, Nev.	10	B4	112
Rebiana, oasis, Libya		C4	394
Rebiana, sand sea, Libya		C3	394
Rebun, isl., Jap.		B8	354
Recalde, Arg.		C3	252
Recanati, It.	6,288	D4	302
Recherche, arch., Austl.		E4	432
Rechitsa, Sov.Un.	33,800	F8	332
Recife, Braz.	703,726	B4	258
Recinto, Chile		C1	252
Reck, Carter, Okla.		D6	128
Recklinghausen, Ger.	123,500	C2	286
Recluse, Campbell, Wyo.	15	B7	116
Recogne, Bel.	717	E4	282
Reconnaissance, mtn., Guam		C7	436
Recreo, Arg.	2,656	A2	252
Rector, Clay, Ark.	1,757	A6	170
Rectortown, Fauquier, Va.	250	B7	192
Red, creek, Miss.		E3	184
Red, isl., Newf., Can.		G8	72
Red, mtn., Ala.		E4	168
Red, mtn., Calif.		B2	94
Red, mtn., Mont.		C4	110
Red, peak, Colo.		C4	106
Red, peak, Idaho		E3	108
Red, riv., Man., Can.		F4	60
Red, riv., Ky.		C7	178
Red, riv., Tenn.		B4	190
Red, riv., U.S.		E8	77
Red, riv., Viet.		B5	362
Red, sea, Sau.Ar.		C2	383
Redan, De Kalb, Ga.	250	B5	176
Redang, isl., Mala.		F4	362
Redange, Lux.	823	E4	282
Red Ash, Tazewell, Va.	500	C3	192
Red Bank, Monmouth, N.J.	12,482	C4	210
Red Bank, Lexington, S.C.	350	D6	188
Red Banks, Marshall, Miss.	250	A3	184
Redbank Village, Cumberland, Maine		E2	204
Red Bank-White Oak, Hamilton, Tenn.	10,777	C6 E8	190
Red Bay, Franklin, Ala.	1,954	A1	168
Red Bay, Newf., Can.	150	E7 E10	72
Redbay, Walton, Fla.	500	A5	174
Redberry, lake, Sask., Can.		D4	58
Redbird, Holt, Nebr.	55	B7	152
Redbird, Wagoner, Okla.	310	C8	128
Red Bird, creek, Ky.		C7	178
Red Bluff, Tehama, Calif.	7,202	B2	94
Red Bluff, res., Tex.		D3	130
Red Boiling Springs, Macon, Tenn.	597	B6	190
Redbud, Harlan, Ky.	500	*D7	178
Red Bud, Randolph, Ill.	1,942	E4	138
Red Buttes, Albany, Wyo.	15	E7	116
Redby, Beltrami, Minn.	300	D4	148
Redcar, Eng.	28,100	G11	273
Red Cedar, lake, Wis.		C2	160
Red Cedar, riv., Wis.		D2	160
Redcliff, Alta., Can.	2,001	E7	54
Redcliff, Eagle, Colo.	586	C4	106
Red Cliff, Bayfield, Wis.	100	B3	160
Red Cloud, Webster, Nebr.	1,525	D7	152
Red Cloud, peak, Colo.		E3	106
Red Creek, Wayne, N.Y.	689	B5	212
Red Deer, Alta., Can.	12,338	D6	54
Red Deer, lake, Man., Can.		D2	60
Red Deer, riv., Alta., Can.		E6	54
Red Deer, riv., Sask, Can.		D6	58
Reddell, Evangeline, La.	500	D3	180
Redden, Sussex, Del.	34	F4	172
Redden, Atoka, Okla.	10	D8	128
Red Desert, Sweetwater, Wyo.	30	E4	116
Reddick, Marion, Fla.	594	B8	174
Redding, Jefferson, Ala.	600	E4	168
Redding, Shasta, Calif.	12,773	B2	94
Redding, Fairfield, Conn.	200 (3,359▲)	D2	202
Redding, Ringgold, Iowa	129	D3	142
Redding Ridge, Fairfield, Conn.	325	D2	202
Redditch, Eng.	31,400	I11	273
Redenção, Braz.	1,822	A3	258
Redeye, riv., Minn.		E3	148
Red Feather Lakes, Larimer, Colo.	150	B5	106
Redfield, Jefferson, Ark.	242	C4	170
Redfield, Dallas, Iowa	966	C3	142
Redfield, Bourbon, Kans.	133	E9	144
Redfield, Spink, S.Dak.	2,952	C7	158
Redford Heights, Wayne, Mich.	71,276	G8	146
Redgranite, Waushara, Wis.	588	D4	160
Red Hill, Franklin, Ga.	600	B3	176
Red Hill, Montgomery, Pa.	1,086	*C6	214
Red Hook, Dutchess, N.Y.	1,719	D8	212
Redhouse, Madison, Ky.	250	C6	178
Red House, Humboldt, Nev.	50	C4	112
Red House, Charlotte, Va.	50	C6	192
Red House, Putnam, W.Va.	250	C3	194
Red Indian, lake, Newf., Can.		F7	72
Redings Mill, Newton, Mo.	202	*E3	150
Redington, Morrill, Nebr.	14	C2	152
Redington Beach, Pinellas, Fla.	1,368	*D8	174
Redington Shores, Pinellas, Fla.	917	*D8	174
Red Jacket, Mingo, W.Va.	950	D2	194
Red Key, Jay, Ind.	1,746	B4	140
Red Lake, Ont., Can.	1,200	*R23	64
Redlake, Beltrami, Minn.	400	D3	148
Red Lake, co., Minn.	5,830	D2	148
Red Lake, riv., Minn.		C3	148
Red Lake Falls, Red Lake, Minn.	1,520	D2	148
Redland, Dade, Fla.	437	E5 F10	174
Redlands, San Bernardino, Calif.	26,829	E5	94
Redlawn, Mecklenburg, Va.	40	D6	192
Red Level, Covington, Ala.	327	D3	168
Red Lick, Jefferson, Miss.	250	D2	184
Red Lion, Burlington, N.J.		D3	210
Red Lion, York, Pa.	5,594	D5	214
Red Lion, creek, Del.		B3	172
Red Lodge, Carbon, Mont.	2,278	E7	110
Redmesa, La Plata, Colo.	135	E2	106
Redmond, Deschutes, Oreg.	3,340	C5	96
Redmond, Sevier, Utah	413	E4	114
Redmond, King, Wash.	1,426	D3	98
Red Mountain, San Bernardino, Calif.	350	E5	94
Red Mountain, pass, Colo.		E3	106
Rednitz, riv., Ger.		D4	286
Red Oak, Fulton, Ga.	800	B5	176
Red Oak, Montgomery, Iowa	6,421	C2	142
Red Oak, Latimer, Okla.	453	D8	128
Redoak, Charlotte, Va.	50	D6	192
Redon, Fr.	6,444	D2	278
Redonda, isl., B.C., Can.		E10	52
Redondela, Sp.	3,261	A2	298
Redondo Beach, Los Angeles, Calif.	46,986	C5 E5	94
Redondo, King, Wash.	600	D2	98
Redondo, peak, N.Mex.		G6	126
Redoubt, mtn., Alsk.		G10	84
Red Pass, B.C., Can.	50	D13	52
Red Rapids, N.B., Can.	200	C2	70
Red River (Celriver), York, S.C.	255	B7	188
Red River, co., Tex.	15,682	C8	130
Red River, par., La.	9,978	B2	180
Red River Hot Springs, Idaho, Idaho		D3	108
Red River of the North, riv., U.S.		B7	77
Red Rock, Apache, Ariz.	50	F4	124
Redrock, Newton, Ark.		B3	170
Redrock, Noble, Okla.	262	B6	128
Red Rock, pass, Idaho, Mont.		E7 F5	108 110
Red Rock, riv., Mont.		F4	110
Red Sea Coast, reg., Eg., U.A.R.	15,929	*B3	395
Red Slate, mtn., Calif.		D4	94
Red Springs, Robeson, N.C.	2,767	C6	186
Red Star, Madison, Ark.	10	B3	170
Redstone, B.C., Can.	25	D11	52
Redstone, Sheridan, Mont.	150	B12	110
Redstone, Carroll, N.H.	150	C4	208
Redstone Park, Madison, Ala.	1,000	*A3	168
Red Sucker, riv., Man., Can.		C6	60
Red Top, Charleston, S.C.		F3	188
Redvale, Montrose, Colo.	10	D2	106
Redvers, Sask., Can.	561	F7	58
Redwater, Alta., Can.	1,065	D6	54
Redwater, creek, Mont.		C11	110
Red Willow, Alta., Can.	75	D6	54
Red Willow, co., Nebr.	12,940	D5	152
Red Willow, creek, Colo.		B8	106
Red Willow, creek, Nebr.		D5	152
Red Willow, riv., B.C., Can.		C12	52
Redwine, Morgan, Ky.	88	B7	178
Red Wing, Goodhue, Minn.	10,528	G6	148
Redwood, Jefferson, N.Y.	524	A6	212
Redwood, co., Minn.	21,718	G3	148
Redwood, riv., Minn.		G3	148
Redwood City, San Mateo, Calif.	46,290	B5 D2	94
Redwood Falls, Redwood, Minn.	4,285	G3	148
Redwood Valley, Mendocino, Calif.	727	C2	94
Ree, lake, Ire.		H5	273
Reece, Greenwood, Kans.	400	E7	144
Reece City, Etowah, Ala.	470	*A3	168
Reed, Henderson, Ky.	225	C3	178
Reed, Aroostook, Maine	25 (325▲)	*C4	204
Reed, Greer, Okla.	100	D4	128
Reed, Lane, Oreg.		C3	96
Reed, Kanawha, W.Va.		C6	194
Reed, lake, Man., Can.		C2	60
Reed City, Osceola, Mich.	2,184	F6	146
Reeder, Adams, N.Dak.	321	D3	154
Reedley, Fresno, Calif.	5,850	D4	94
Reedpoint, Stillwater, Mont.	130	E7	110
Reeds, Jasper, Mo.	185	*D3	150
Reedsburg, Sauk, Wis.	4,371	E3	160
Reeds Ferry, Hillsboro, N.H.	300	F4	208
Reeds Lake, see East Grand Rapids, Mich.			
Reedsport, Douglas, Oreg.	2,998	D2	96
Reeds Spring, Stone, Mo.	327	E4	150
Reedsville, Meigs, Ohio	325	C5	156
Reedsville, Mifflin, Pa.	950	C4	214
Reedsville, Preston, W.Va.	398	B5	194
Reedsville, Manitowoc, Wis.	830	A6 D6	160
Reedville, Northumberland, Va.	400	C8	192
Reedy, Roane, W.Va.	352	C3	194
Reedy, creek, W.Va.		C3	194
Reedy, isl., Del.		B3	172
Reedy, lake, Fla.		D9	174
Reedy, pt., Del.		B3	172
Reedy, riv., S.C.		B4	188
Reef, point, N.Z.		A4	437
Reefton, N.Z.	1,787	E3	437
Reega, Atlantic, N.J.		E3	210
Ree Heights, Hand, S.Dak.	188	C6	158
Reelfoot, lake, Tenn.		B2	190
Reelsville, Putnam, Ind.	100	C3	140
Reeman, Newaygo, Mich.	120	F5	146
Reengus, India		D1	368
Rees, Franklin, Ohio	600	C1	156
Reese, Tuscola, Mich.	711	F8	146
Reese, Weber, Utah		B3	114
Reese, riv., Nev.		D4	112
Reese River, Nye, Nev.	100	D4	112
Reese Village, Lubbock, Tex.	1,433	*C5	130
Reeseville, Etowah, Ala.	500	*A3	168
Reeseville, Dodge, Wis.	491	E5	160
Reeves, Allen, La.	151	D2	180
Reeves, co., Tex.	17,644	D4	130
Reevesville, Dorchester, S.C.	268	E7	188
Reform, Pickens, Ala.	1,241	B1	168
Reform, Saline, Ark.		C4	170
Reform, Choctaw, Miss.	300	B3	184
Refresco, Chile		C4	250
Refuge, harbor, Del.		E5	172
Refuge Cove, B.C., Can.		E10	52
Refugio, Refugio, Tex.	4,944	E7	130
Refugio, co., Tex.	10,975	E7	130
Rega, riv., Pol.		B2	325
Reg Aftout, sand dunes, Alg.		C3	402
Regan, Burleigh, N.Dak.	104	C5	154
Regen, riv., Ger.		D5	286
Regensburg, Ger.	124,100	D5	286
Regent, Man., Can.	65	F2	60
Regent, Hettinger, N.Dak.	388	D3	154
Reger, Sullivan, Mo.	77	A4	150
Reggane, Alg.		C4	402
Reggio, Saint Bernard, La.	180	C8	180
Reggio di Calabria, It.	83,300 (144,500▲)	F5	302
Reggio di Calabria, prov., It.	650,500	*F5	302
Reggio nell'Emilia, It.	66,500 (108,200▲)	C3	302
Reggio nell'Emilia, prov., It.	388,600	*C3	302
Reghin, Rom.	18,091	A3	321
Regina, Sask., Can.	89,755	C3 E5	58
Regina, Phillips, Mont.	13	C9	110
Regina, Sandoval, N.Mex.	30	B4	126
Regina Beach, Sask., Can.	301	E5	58
Register, Bulloch, Ga.	300	D5	176
Regla, Cuba	26,755	A3	232
Regocijo, Mex.		C4	224
Regong, India		C6	368
Rehoboth, Wilcox, Ala.	35	C2	168
Rehoboth, Bristol, Mass.	250 (4,953▲)	C5	206
Rehoboth, McKinley, N.Mex.	100	C2	126
Rehoboth, S.W.Afr.		D3	420

Rehoboth, bay, Del.		F5	172
Rehoboth Beach, Sussex, Del.	1,507	F5	172
Rehovot, Isr.	26,000	C5	382
Reï Bouba, Cam.		E7	409
Reichenbach [im Vogtland], Ger.	31,400	C5	286
Reichert, Le Flore, Okla.	25	D9	128
Reid, Calhoun, Miss.	75	A3	184
Reidland, McCracken, Ky.	300	D2	178
Reids Grove, Dorchester, Md.	25	C8	182
Reidsville, Tattnall, Ga.	1,229	D4	176
Reidsville, Rockingham, N.C.	14,267	A6	186
Reidville, Spartanburg, S.C.	242	B4	188
Reidy Manor, Wyandotte, Kans.	230	*C9	144
Reigate, Eng.	48,700	J12	273
Reims, Fr.	121,145	C6	278
Reina Adélaida, arch., Chile		H2	251
Reinach, Switz.	4,891	A9	312
Reinbeck, Grundy, Iowa	1,621	B5	142
Reindeer, isl., Man., Can.		D4	60
Reindeer, lake, Man., Sask., Can.		B1 B6	60 58
Reindeer, riv., Sask., Can.		C6	58
Reinosa, Sp.	8,481	A4	298
Reipetown, White Pine, Nev.	75	D6	112
Reisterstown, Baltimore, Md.	3,300	B6	182
Reitz, U.S.Afr.		E5	421
Rejkjanes, cape, Ice.		M18	290
Rejmyre, Swe.		C6	292
Rekinniki, Sov.Un.		C18	329
Relay, Baltimore, Md. (part of Halethorpe)		B6	182
Relee, Coffee, Ga.	200	E4	176
Reliance, N.W.Ter., Can.		E8	48
Reliance, Sussex, Del.	40	F3	172
Reliance, Lyman, S.Dak.	201	D6	158
Reliance, Polk, Tenn.	400	C7	190
Reliance, Sweetwater, Wyo.	300	E3	116
Relizane, Alg.	27,120	A4	402
Rema, mtn., Aden		E3	383
Remada, Tun.	1,866	B6	402
Remagen, Ger.	6,800	*C2	286
Remanso, Braz.	4,073	B2	258
Rembert, Sumter, S.C.	400	C7	188
Rembertów, Pol.	22,000	B5	325
Rembrandt, Buena Vista, Iowa	265	B2	142
Remecó, Arg.		C3	252
Remedios, Cuba	10,602	A5	232
Remedios, Pan.	968	F6	228
Remer, Cass, Minn.	492	D5	148
Remerton, Lowndes, Ga.	571	F3	176
Remington, Jasper, Ind.	1,207	B2	140
Remington, Fauquier, Va.	288	B7	192
Remiremont, Fr.	9,799	C7	278
Remlap, Blount, Ala.	122	B3	168
Remmel, dam, Ark.		D7	170
Remmel, mtn., Wash.		A6	98
Remote, Coos, Oreg.	150	*D3	96
Remscheid, Ger.	117,300	C2	286
Remsen, Plymouth, Iowa	1,338	B2	142
Remsen, Oneida, N.Y.	567	B6	212
Remus, Mecosta, Mich.	600	F6	146
Remy, St. James, La. (part of Paulina)		B6	180
Ren, Sov.Un.		C19	329
Rena, Nor.		F4	291
Rena, riv., Nor.		F4	291
Renault, Alg.	2,578 (36,718▲)	A4	402
Rencontre East, Newf., Can.	300	G8	72
Rendova, harbor, Solomon		E1	436
Rendova, isl., Solomon		E1	436
Rendsburg, Ger.	34,800	A3	286
Renews, Newf., Can.	400	G9	72
Renfrew, Ont., Can.	8,634	O24 S25	64
Renfrew, Greenville, S.C.	200	B4	188
Renfrew, co., Ont., Can.	78,245	O23	64
Renfrew, co., Scot.	331,400	F8	272
Renfrow, Grant, Okla.	38	B6	128
Rengo, Chile	9,115	B1	252
Renick, Randolph, Mo.	190	B5	150
Renick (Falling Springs), Greenbrier, W.Va.	265	C4	194
Renish, pt., Scot.		D6	272
Renk, Sud.		C3	398
Renmark, Austl.	1,979	E7	432
Renner, Minnehaha, S.Dak.	100	D9	158
Rennes, Fr.	124,122	C3	278
Rennie, Man., Can.	125	F5	60
Renno, Laurens, S.C.	200	C5	188
Reno, Lemhi, Idaho		E6	108
Reno, Washoe, Nev.	51,470	D2	112
Reno, Venango, Pa.	866	B2	214
Reno, co., Kans.	59,055	E5	144
Reno, lake, Minn.		F3	148
Reno, riv., It.		C3	302
Reno Beach, Lucas, Ohio	674	A3	156
Renous, riv., N.B., Can.		C3	70
Renovo, Clinton, Pa.	3,316	B4	214
Renown, Sask., Can.	75	E5	58
Rensselaer, Jasper, Ind.	4,740	B2	140
Rensselaer, Rensselaer, N.Y.	10,506	C8	212
Rensselaer, co., N.Y.	142,585	C8	212
Rensselaer Falls, St. Lawrence, N.Y.	375	A6	212
Rentiesville, McIntosh, Okla.	122	C8	128
Renton, King, Wash.	18,453	B4 D3	98
Rentz, Laurens, Ga.	307	D4	176
Renville, Renville, Minn.	1,373	G3	148
Renville, co., Minn.	23,249	G3	148
Renville, co., N.Dak.	4,698	B4	154
Renwick, Humboldt, Iowa	477	B4	142
Repton, Conecuh, Ala.	314	D2	168
Republic, Jefferson, Ala.	500	*B3	168
Republic, Republic, Kans.	333	C6	144
Republic, Marquette, Mich.	950	C4	146
Republic, Greene, Mo.	1,519	D4	150
Republic, Seneca, Ohio	729	A3	156
Republic, Fayette, Pa.	1,921	D2	214
Republic, Ferry, Wash.	1,064	A8	98
Republic, co., Kans.	9,768	C6	144
Republican, riv., U.S.		D6	77
Republican City, Harlan, Nebr.	189	D6	152
Repulse, bay, Austl.		C9	432
Repulse Bay, N.W.Ter., Can.		D10	48
Requa, Del Norte, Calif.	150	B1	94
Requena, Sp.	8,228	C6	298
Resaca, Gordon, Ga.	325	B2	176
Reşadiye, Tur.	1,703	A7	307
Rescue, Isle of Wight, Va.	325	A8 D8	192
Reserve, Sask., Can.	45	D6	58
Reserve, Brown, Kans.	138	C8	144
Reserve, St. John the Baptist, La.	5,297	B6	180
Reserve, Sheridan, Mont.	250	B12	110
Reserve, Catron, N.Mex.	200	E2	126
Reserve, Sawyer, Wis.	140	C2	160
Reservoir, pond, Mass.		D2	206
Resistencia, Arg.	52,385	A4	252
Reşiţa, Rom.	41,241	B1	321
Resko, Pol.	1,314	B2	325
Resolution, isl., N.W.Ter., Can.		E12	48
Rest Haven, Gwinnett, Ga.	167	*B3	176
Resthaven, mtn., Alta., Can.		D3	54
Restigouche, co., N.B., Can.	39,720	B2	70
Reston, Man., Can.	420	F2	60
Reszel, Pol.	846	A5	325
Retalhuleu, Guat.	9,209	C2	228
Retamito, Arg.		B2	252
Rethel, Fr.	5,686	C6	278
Rethimni (Rethymne), prov., Grc.	72,179	D5	306
Réthimnon, Grc.	11,057	D5	306
Rethymne, see Rethimni, prov., Grc.			
Reti, Pak.		E6	375
Retie, Bel.	5,420	C4	282
Retlaw, Alta., Can.	75	E6	54
Retreat, Luzerne, Pa.	890	B5	214
Retrop, Beckham and Washita, Okla.	40	C4	128
Retsil, Kitsap, Wash.		D2	98
Reubens, Lewis, Idaho	113	C2	108
Reus, Sp.	32,285	B7	298
Reusens, Va. (part of Lynchburg)		C5	192
Reutlingen, Ger.	61,400	D3	286
Reutte, Aus.	3,478	C2	313
Revda, Sov.Un.	55,000	A5	336
Revel, Fr.		F4	278
Revelstoke, B.C., Can.	3,469	E13	52
Revelstoke, natl. park, B.C., Can.		E13	52
Reventazón, Peru		B1	245
Revenue, Sask., Can.	120	D3	58
Revere, Suffolk, Mass.	40,080	C3	206
Revere, Redwood, Minn.	201	G3	148
Revere, Clark, Mo.	190	A6	150
Reverie, Tipton, Tenn.	150	C2	190
Revillagigedo, isl., Alsk.		K15	84
Revillo, Grant, S.Dak.	202	B9	158
Revin, Fr.	8,498	C6	278
Revivim, Isr.		C5	382
Revloc, Cambria, Pa.	900	C3	214
Řevnice, Czech.	3,033	*B2	324
Revsundsjön, lake, Swe.		E6	290
Rewa, India	29,623	D3	368
Rewari, India	34,082	C2	368
Rewey, Iowa, Wis.	219	F3	160
Rex, Eagle, Colo.		C4	106
Rexburg, Madison, Idaho	4,767	F7	108
Rexford, Thomas, Kans.	245	C3	144
Rexford, Lincoln, Mont.	300	B1	110
Rexford, Carter, Tenn.		B9	190
Rexroat, Carter, Okla.	60	D6	128
Rexton, N.B., Can.	415	C5	70
Rexton, Mackinac, Mich.	90	C6	146
Reyburn, Hot Spring, Ark.		D7	170
Reydell, Jefferson, Ark.	50	C5	170
Reydhar, fjord, Ice.		L23	290
Reydon, Roger Mills, Okla.	183	C4	128
Reyes, pt., Calif.		C2	94
Reykjahlidh, Ice.		L21	290
Reykjavik, Ice.	65,305	L19 R34	290
Reynaud, Sask., Can.	175	D5	58
Reyno, Randolph, Ark.	348	A6	170
Reynolds, Taylor, Ga.	1,087	D2	176
Reynolds, Owyhee, Idaho		F2	108
Reynolds, Rock Island, Ill.	494	B3	138
Reynolds, White, Ind.	547	B3	140
Reynolds, Jefferson, Nebr.	131	D8	152
Reynolds, Grand Forks, N.Dak.	269	C8	154
Reynolds, co., Mo.	5,161	D6	150
Reynoldsburg, Franklin, Ohio	7,793	C1 C4	156
Reynolds Corners, Lucas, Ohio	7,000	A1	156
Reynolds Knob, mtn., W.Va.		C5	194
Reynoldsville, Jefferson, Pa.	3,158	B3	214
Reynosa, Mex.	34,076	B6	225
Rezāīyeh (Urmia), Iran	67,605	B1	379
Rezé, Fr.	19,000	D3	278
Rēzekne, Sov.Un.	27,000	D6	332
Rhaetian Alps, mts., It.		B2	302
Rhaetian Alps, mts., Switz.		B5	312
Rhame, Bowman, N.Dak.	254	D2	154
Rhea, co., Tenn.	15,863	C7	190
Rheatown, Greene, Tenn.	91	*B9	190
Rheden, Neth.	3,787	B5	282
Rhein, Sask., Can.	384	E6	58
Rheine, Ger.	43,000	B2	286
Rheinfelden, Switz.	4,550	A3	312
Rheinhausen, Ger.	62,300	*C2	286
Rheinland-Pfalz (Rhineland-Palatinate), state, Ger.	3,304,900	*D2	286
Rheinwaldhorn, mtn., Switz.		B5	312
Rhenen, Neth.	5,012	C4	282
Rheydt, Ger.	88,700	*C2	286
Rhin, canal, Ger.		B5	286
Rhine, Dodge, Ga.	485	E3	176
Rhine, riv., Ger.		C2	286
Rhine, riv., Switz.		B5	312
Rhinebeck, Dutchess, N.Y.	2,093	D8	212
Rhineland, Montgomery, Mo.	190	*C6	150
Rhineland (Rheinland), reg., Ger.		C2	286
Rhinelander, Oneida, Wis.	8,790	C4	160
Rhode Island, state, U.S.	859,488	C12	77 216
Rhode Island, sound, R.I.		D3	216
Rhodell, Raleigh, W.Va.	626	D3	194
Rhodes, Marshall, Iowa	358	C4	142
Rhodes, Gladwin, Mich.	75	F7	146
Rhodes, see Ródhos, isl., Grc.		C7	306
Rhodes, peak, Idaho		C4	108
Rhodesia & Nyasaland, Fed. of, Br. poss., Afr.	7,990,000	H9	388 421
Rhodes Point, Somerset, Md.	97	E7	182
Rhodhiss, Caldwell and Burke, N.C.	837	B4	186
Rhododendron, Clackamas, Oreg.	200	*B5	96
Rhodope, see Rodhópi, prov., Grc.			
Rhodope, mts., Bul.		C2	317
Rhondda, Wales	107,400	J9	273
Rhône, dept., Fr.	966,782	*E6	278
Rhône, riv., Switz.		B3	312
Rhyne, Lincoln, N.C.	645	*B4	186
Rialto, San Bernardino, Calif.	18,567	*E5	94
Rianjo, Sp.	1,580	A2	298
Riasi, India		B1	368
Riazo, riv., Sp.		B5	298
Rib, mtn., Wis.		D4	160
Rib, riv., Wis.		C3	160
Ribadavia, Sp.	3,029	A2	298
Ribadeo, Sp.	3,230	A3	298
Ribadesella, Sp.	2,531	A4	298
Ribas do Rio Pardo, Braz.	658	J6	257
Ribatejo, prov., Port.	464,874	*C2	298
Ribáue, Moz.		B7	421
Ribble, riv., Eng.		H10	273
Ribe, Den.	7,484	I3	291
Ribe, co., Den.	178,501	*I3	291
Ribeauville, Fr.	4,764	C7	278
Ribeira, riv., Braz.		J7	257
Ribeirão Prêto, Braz.	63,312	E1	258
Ribera, It.	18,800	G4	302
Riberalta, Bol.	6,549	B1	246
Rib Falls, Marathon, Wis.	80	D4	160
Rib Lake, Taylor, Wis.	794	C3	160
Ribstone, Alta., Can.	100	D7	54
Ribstone, creek, Alta., Can.		D7	54
Říčany, Czech.	6,376	B2	324
Riccarton, N.Z.	7,914	E4	437
Riccione, It.	10,600	*C4	302
Rice, San Bernardino, Calif.	50	E6	94
Rice, Benton, Minn.	387	F4	148
Rice, Prince Edward, Va.	300	C6	192
Rice, co., Kans.	13,909	D5	144
Rice, co., Minn.	38,988	G5	148
Rice, creek, Minn.		F7	148
Rice, lake, Ont., Can.		P22	64
Rice, lake, Minn.		D3	148
Rice, lake, Minn.		E5	148
Rice, mtn., N.H.		B4	208
Riceboro, Liberty, Ga.	259	E5	176
Rice Lake, Barron, Wis.	7,303	C2	160
Riceton, Sask., Can.	165	E5	58
Riceville, Mitchell, Iowa	898	A5	142
Riceville, McMinn, Tenn.	500	C7	190
Rich, co., Utah	1,685	B4	114
Rich, cape, Ont., Can.		P20	64
Rich, mtn., Ark., Okla.		C2 D9	170 128
Rich, mtn., Va.		C3	192
Rich, mtn., W.Va.		C4	194
Rich, mtn., W.Va.		C5	194
Richard, Sask., Can.	101	D4	58
Richard City, Marion, Tenn.	224	C6	190
Richards, Vernon, Mo.	133	D3	150
Richards (Richards Spur), Comanche, Okla.	100	D5	128
Richards, Grimes, Tex.	500	D8	130
Richards, lake, Ariz.		D5	124
Richard's Harbour, Newf., Can.	100	G7	72
Richardson, Alsk.	8	C7	84
Richardson, Leavenworth, Kans.	100	*C9	144
Richardson, Lawrence, Ky.	125	C8	178
Richardson, Dallas, Tex.	16,810	B8	130
Richardson, co., Nebr.	13,903	D10	152
Richardson, lakes, Maine		D2	204
Richardson, mts., Alsk.		B7	84
Richardson, mts., Yukon, Can.		D5	48
Richardson, riv., Alta., Can.		*E4	54
Richardson Station, Sask., Can.	43	E5	58
Richardsville, Warren, Ky.	200	C4	178
Richardton, Stark, N.Dak.	792	D3	154
Richburg, Allegany, N.Y.	493	C3	212
Richburg, Chester, S.C.	235	B6	188
Rich Creek, Giles, Va.	748	C4	192
Richdale, Alta., Can.	60	E7	54
Riche, cape, Austl.		E3	432
Riche, pt., Newf., Can.		E7	72
Richelieu, co., Que., Can.	36,086	S11	66
Richer, Man., Can.	490	F4	60
Richey, Dawson, Mont.	480	C11	110
Richfield, Lincoln, Idaho	329	F4	108
Richfield, Morton, Kans.	122	E2	144
Richfield, Hennepin, Minn.	42,523	F7	148
Richfield, Sarpy, Nebr.	48	E3	152
Richfield, Stanly, N.C.	293	B5	186
Richfield, Sevier, Utah	4,412	E3	114
Richfield, Washington, Wis.	250	E1	160
Richfield Springs, Otsego, N.Y.	1,630	C7	212
Richford, Franklin, Vt.	1,663 (2,316▲)	B3	218
Rich Fountain, Osage, Mo.	150	C6	150
Rich Hill, Bates, Mo.	1,699	C3	150
Richibucto, N.B., Can.	1,200	C5	70
Rich Lake, Alta., Can.		C7	54
Richland, Stewart, Ga.	1,472	D2	176
Richland, Rush, Ind.	100	C4	140
Richland, Spencer, Ind.	600	E2	140
Richland, Keokuk, Iowa	546	C6	142
Richland, Shawnee, Kans.	200	D8	144
Richland, Kalamazoo, Mich.	511	*G6	146
Richland, Pulaski, Mo.	1,622	D5	150
Richland, Valley, Mont.	95	B10	110
Richland, Colfax, Nebr.	139	C8	152
Richland, Atlantic, N.J.	500	E3	210
Richland, Baker, Oreg.	228	C9	96
Richland, Lebanon, Pa.	1,276	*C5	214
Richland, Oconee, S.C.	150	B2	188
Richland, Union, S.Dak.	55	E9	158
Richland, Benton, Wash.	23,548	C7	98
Richland, co., Ill.	16,299	E5	138
Richland, co., Mont.	10,504	C12	110
Richland, co., N.Dak.	18,824	D9	154
Richland, co., Ohio	117,761	B4	156
Richland, co., S.C.	200,102	D7	188
Richland, co., Wis.	17,684	E3	160
Richland, par., La.	23,824	B4	180
Richland, creek, Tenn.		C5	190
Richland Center, Richland, Wis.	4,746	E3	160
Richland Hills, Tarrant, Tex.	7,804	*C7	130
Richlands, Onslow, N.C.	1,079	C8	186
Richlands, Tazewell, Va.	4,963	C3	192
Richland Springs, San Saba, Tex.	331	D6	130
Richlawn, Jefferson, Ky.	649	*B5	178
Richlea, Sask., Can.	120	E3	58
Richmond, Little River, Ark.	100	D2	170
Richmond, Austl.	806	C8	432
Richmond, Contra Costa, Calif.	71,854	A5	94
Richmond, Ont., Can.	794	O25	64
Richmond, P.E.I., Can.	120	C6	70
Richmond, Que., Can.	3,849	S12	66
Richmond, Eng.	6,000	G11	273
Richmond, McHenry, Ill.	855	A5 D1	138
Richmond, Wayne, Ind.	44,149	C5	140
Richmond, Washington, Iowa	150	C6	142
Richmond, Franklin, Kans.	352	D8	144
Richmond, Madison, Ky.	12,168	C6	178
Richmond, Sagadahoc, Maine	1,412 (2,185▲)	D3 D6	204
Richmond, Berkshire, Mass.	130 (890▲)	B1	206
Richmond, Macomb, Mich.	2,667	G9	146
Richmond, Stearns, Minn.	751	F4	148
Richmond, Ray, Mo.	4,604	B4	150
Richmond, Cheshire, N.H.	70 (295▲)	F2	208
Richmond, N.Z.	2,515	D4	437
Richmond, Jefferson, Ohio	728	*B6	156
Richmond, Wheeler, Oreg.		C7	96
Richmond (Town of), Washington, R.I.	(1,986▲)	C2	216
Richmond, Fort Bend, Tex.	3,668	E8 F7	130
Richmond, U.S.Afr.	2,025	E6	420
Richmond, U.S.Afr.		F4	420
Richmond, Cache, Utah	977	B4	114
Richmond, Chittenden, Vt.	765 (1,303▲)	C3	218
Richmond (Independent City), Va.	219,958 (*409,100)	B9 C7	192
Richmond, co., N.S., Can.	10,961	D9	70
Richmond, co., Que., Can.	38,641	S12	66
Richmond, co., Ga.	135,601	C4	176
Richmond, co., N.Y.	221,991	E2	212
Richmond, co., N.C.	39,202	B6	186
Richmond, co., Va.	6,375	C8	192
Richmond, pt., Calif.		A5	94
Richmond Beach, King, Wash.	2,000	B4	98
Richmond Dale, Ross, Ohio	600	C4	156
Richmond Furnace, Berkshire, Mass.	150 (890▲)	B1	206
Richmond Heights, Dade, Fla.	4,311	*F10	174
Richmond Heights, St. Louis, Mo.	15,622	B8	150
Richmond Heights, Cuyahoga, Ohio	5,068	B1	156
Richmond Heights, Henrico, Va.	100	B9	192
Richmond Highlands, King, Wash.	6,000	B4	98
Richmond Hill, Ont., Can.	6,677	Q21 R22	64
Richmond Hill, Bryan, Ga.	1,000	E5	176
Richmond Hill, Alamance, N.C.	2,943	*A6	186
Richmondville, Tuscola, Mich.		F9	146
Richmondville, Schoharie, N.Y.	743	C7	212
Richmound, Sask., Can.	196	E3	58
Rich Mountain, Polk, Ark.		C2	170
Rich Square, Northampton, N.C.	1,134	A8	186
Richthofen, mtn., Colo.		B5	106
Richton, Perry, Miss.	1,089	D4	184
Richton Park, Cook, Ill.	933	*B6	138
Richvalley, Wabash, Ind.	150	B4	140
Richview, Washington, Ill.	255	E4	138
Richville, Sanilac, Mich.	400	F8	146
Richville, Otter Tail, Minn.	91	E3	148
Richville, St. Lawrence, N.Y.	292	A6	212
Richwood, Boone, Ky.	100	A8	178
Richwood, Union, Ohio	2,137	B3	156
Richwood, Nicholas, W.Va.	4,110	C4	194
Richwoods, Washington, Mo.	250	C7	150
Richwood Village, Brazoria, Tex.	649	*E8	130
Ricketts, Crawford, Iowa	133	B2	142
Rickman, Overton, Tenn.	400	B6	190
Rickreall, Polk, Oreg.	150	C3	96
Rico, Dolores, Colo.	353	E2	106
Rico, Fulton, Ga.	200	C2	176
Riddle, Owyhee, Idaho	20	G2	108
Riddle, Douglas, Oreg.	992	E3	96
Riddleville, Washington, Ga.	111	D4	176
Riderwood, Choctaw, Ala.	100	C1	168
Ridge, Carter, Mont.	5	E12	110
Ridge, Henrico, Va.	20,000	*C7	192
Ridgebury, Fairfield, Conn.	175	D1	202
Ridgecrest, Kern, Calif.	5,099	E5	94
Ridgecrest, Buncombe, N.C.	300	B3	186
Ridgecrest, King, Wash.	3,000	*B4	98
Ridgedale, Sask., Can.	208	D5	58
Ridgedale, Oneida, Idaho		G6	108
Ridge Farm, Vermilion, Ill.	894	D6	138
Ridgefield, Fairfield, Conn.	2,954 (8,165▲)	D2	202
Ridgefield, Bergen, N.J.	10,788	A1	210
Ridgefield, Clark, Wash.	823	D4	98
Ridgefield Park, Bergen, N.J.	12,701	A1 B4	210
Ridgeland, Madison, Miss.	875	C2	184
Ridgeland, Jasper, S.C.	1,192	G6	188
Ridgeland, Dunn, Wis.	288	C2	160
Ridgeley, Mineral, W.Va.	1,229	B6	194
Ridgely, Caroline, Md.	886	C8	182
Ridgely, Lake, Tenn.	1,464	B2	190

Ridgeside, Hamilton, Tenn. 448 E8 190
Ridge Spring, Saluda, S.C. 649 D5 188
Ridgetop, Robertson, Tenn. 372 B5 190
Ridgetown, Ont., Can. 2,483 R19 64
Ridgeview, Miami, Ind. 439 B3 140
Ridgeview, Dewey, S.Dak. 40 B5 158
Ridgeview, Boone, W.Va. 350 C3 194
D5
Ridgeville, Man., Can. 450 F4 60
Ridgeville, McIntosh, Ga. 187 E5 176
Ridgeville, Randolph, Ind. 950 B4 140
Ridgeville, Frederick, Md. 200 B5 182
Ridgeville, Dorchester, S.C. 611 E8 188
E2
Ridgeway, Ont., Can. 850 R21 64
Ridgeway, Winneshiek, Iowa 267 A6 142
Ridgeway, Lenawee, Mich. 180 H8 146
Ridgeway, Harrison, Mo. 470 A4 150
Ridgeway, Hardin and Logan, Ohio 448 B3 156
Ridgeway, Fairfield, S.C. 417 C7 188
Ridgeway, Henry, Va. 524 D5 192
Ridgeway, Iowa, Wis. 455 E4 160
Ridgeway, branch, N.J. C4 210
Ridgewood, Will, Ill. 5,500 *B6 138
Ridgewood, Bergen, N.J. 25,391 B4 210
Ridgewood Park, New London, Conn. 280 D7 202
Ridgway, Ouray, Colo. 254 D3 106
Ridgway, Gallatin, Ill. 1,055 F5 138
Ridgway, Carter, Mont. 5 E12 110
Ridgway, Elk, Pa. 6,387 B3 214
Riding, mtn., Man., Can. E2 60
Riding Mountain, natl. park, Man., Can. E2 60
Ridley Farms, Delaware, Pa. 1,500 *D6 214
Ridley Park, Delaware, Pa. 7,387 A6 214
Ridotta Capuzzo, Libya 1,983 A4 394
Ridpath, Sask., Can. 65 E3 58
Ried [im Innkreis], Aus. 10,099 B5 313
Riegelsville, Warren, N.J. 300 B2 210
Rienzi, Alcorn, Miss. 375 A4 184
Riesa, Ger. 36,700 C5 286
Riesco, isl., Chile H3 251
Rieth, Umatilla, Oreg. 300 B8 96
Rieti, It. 18,500 D4 302
Rieti, prov., It. 179,400 *D4 302
Riffe, Lewis, Wash. 250 C4 98
Riffle, Braxton, W.Va. 75 C4 194
Rifle, Garfield, Colo. 2,135 C3 106
Rift Valley, prov., Ken. B6 414
Riga, Sov.Un. 605,000 D5 332
Riga, gulf, Sov.Un. D4 332
Rigaud, Que., Can. 1,784 S10 66
Rigby, Jefferson, Idaho 2,281 F7 108
Riggins, Idaho, Idaho 588 D2 108
Rigi, mtn., Switz. A4 312
Rigili, isl., Eniwetok B1 436
Rigo, Pap. F11 359
Rigolet, Newf., Can. 40 C6 72
D10
Rijeka (Fiume), Yugo. 75,328 B2 316
Rijssen, Neth. 13,014 B5 282
Riley, Vigo, Ind. 248 C2 140
Riley, Riley, Kans. 575 C7 144
Riley, Marion, Ky. 150 C5 178
Riley, see Suntex, Oreg.
Riley, co., Kans. 41,714 C7 144
Riley, mtn., N.Mex. G3 126
Rileyville, Page, Va. 250 B6 192
Rillito, Pima, Ariz. 250 F4 124
Rimavská Sobota, Czech. 10,175 B5 324
Rimbey, Alta., Can. 980 D5 54
Rimbo, Swe. 1,253 B9 292
Rimersburg, Clarion, Pa. 1,323 B2 214
Rimforsa, Swe. C6 292
Rimini, It. 53,400 (82,300*) C4 302
Rimini, Lewis and Clark, Mont. 35 D4 110
Rimmy Jims, Coconino, Ariz. 10 C4 124
Rimouski, Que., Can. 14,630 P16 66
Rimouski, co., Que., Can. 61,357 P16 66
Rimouski, riv., Que., Can. P16 66
Rinard, Calhoun, Iowa 99 B3 142
Rinchhen Ling (Jenchinli), China F6 346
Rincon, Effingham, Ga. 1,057 D5 176
Rincon, Dona Ana, N.Mex. 300 F3 126
Rinconada, Arg. B4 250
Rincón de Romos, Mex. 4,257 C5 225
J12
Rindge, Cheshire, N.H. 100 (941*) F2 208
Rindjani, mtn., Indon. F5 358
Riner, Montgomery, Va. 125 C4 192
Riner, Sweetwater, Wyo. 15 E5 116
Rineyville, Hardin, Ky. 350 C5 178
Ringana, Solomon E1 436
Ringchiang, China K6 349
Ringe, Den. 2,627 I4 291
Ringebu, Nor. F4 291
Ringgold, Catoosa, Ga. 1,311 B1 176
Ringgold, Bienville, La. 953 B2 180
Ringgold, Washington, Md. 75 A4 182
Ringgold, McPherson, Nebr. 23 C5 152
Ringgold, Pittsylvania, Va. 150 D5 192
Ringgold, co., Iowa 7,910 D3 142
Ringgold, is., Fiji E7 436
Ringim, Nig. D6 409
Ringköbing, Den. 4,721 H3 291
Ringköbing, co., Den. 198,389 *H3 291
Ringkollen, mtn., Nor. A1 292
Ringling, Meagher, Mont. 65 D6 110
Ringling, Jefferson, Okla. 1,170 D6 128
Ringo, Crawford, Kans. 120 *E9 144
Ringoes, Hunterdon, N.J. 550 C3 210
Ringold, McCurtain, Okla. 50 D8 128
Ringos Mills, Fleming, Ky. 45 B7 178
Ringsaker, Nor. 15,948 F4 291
Ringsoön, lake, Swe. F4 292
Ringsted, Den. 9,069 F2 292
Ringsted, Emmet, Iowa 559 A3 142
Ringvassöy, isl., Nor. B8 290
Ringwood, Passaic, N.J. 4,182 A4 210
Ringwood, Major, Okla. 232 B5 128
Rinnes, mtn., Scot. D9 272
Rio, St. Lucie, Fla. 100 D10 174
Rio, Hampshire, W.Va. 156 B6 194
Rio, Columbia, Wis. 788 E4 160
Rio Arriba, co., N.Mex. 24,193 B3 126
Río Balsas, Mex. 814 D6 225
L14
Riobamba, Ec. 29,830 A2 245
Rio Blanco, co., Colo. 5,150 C2 106
Rio Branco, Braz. 9,371 G3 256
Rio Branco, Braz. C2 258
Rio Branco, Braz. E2 258
Rio Branco, Ur. B5 252
Rio Branco, ter., Braz. 23,000 E4 256
Rio Bueno, Chile 6,259 F3 251
Rio Caribe, Ven. 6,633 A7 240
Rio Chico, Ven. 1,753 A6 240
Rio Claro, Braz. 34,618 E1 258
Rio Colorado, Arg. 3,304 C3 252
Rio Cuarto, Arg. 48,706 B3 252
Rio de Janeiro, Braz. 2,940,045 E2 258
Rio de Janeiro, state, Braz. 2,623,000 J8 257
Rio de Jesús, Pan. 1,022 G7 228
Río de la Plata, estuary, Arg. B4 252
Rio Dell, Humboldt, Calif. 3,222 B1 94
Rio de Oro, Col. 1,679 B2 244
Rio de Oro, reg., Sp. Sahara B2 408
Rio Gallegos, Arg. 5,880 H4 251
Rio Grande, Arg. H4 251
Rio Grande, Braz. 63,235 L6 257
Rio Grande, Mex. 6,806 C5 224
Rio Grande, Cape May, N.J. 950 E3 210
Rio Grande, Nic. 173 D6 228
Rio Grande, Gallia, Ohio 333 D4 156
Rio Grande, co., Colo. 11,160 E4 106
Rio Grande, res., Colo. E3 106
Rio Grande, riv., U.S. F6 77
Rio Grande (Rio Bravo del Norte), riv., U.S., Mex. B5 225
Rio Grande City, Starr, Tex. 5,835 F6 130
Rio Grande do Norte, state, Braz. 1,115,000 G9 256
Rio Grande do Sul, state, Braz. 4,782,000 K6 257
Riohacha, Col. 12,660 A2 244
Rio Hato, Pan. 1,754 F7 228
Rio Hondo, Mex. 1,718 G9 224
Rio Hondo, Cameron, Tex. 1,344 F7 130
Rioja, Peru 3,694 B2 245
Rio Linda, Sacramento, Calif. 6,000 *C3 94
Riom, Fr. 12,664 E5 278
Rio Maior, Port. 3,055 C2 298
Rio Mulato, Bol. 381 C1 246
Rio Muni, overseas prov., Sp. 169,670 F6 409
Rion, Fairfield, S.C. 500 C6 188
Rio Negro, Braz. 7,653 K7 257
Rio Negro, dept., Ur. 47,586 B4 252
Rio Negro, prov., Arg. 190,900 E4 251
Rionero in Vulture, It. 14,900 E5 302
Rio Pardo, Braz. 8,322 D2 258
Rio Piedras, P.R. 81,921 C11 233
(pop. inc. in San Juan)
Rio Primero, Arg. B3 252
Rio Seco, Arg. A3 252
Rio Seco, Chile B3 250
Riosucio (Caldas dept.), Col. 7,363 B1 244
Riosucio (Choco dept.), Col. 847 B1 244
Rio Tercero, Arg. 10,683 B3 252
Riouw, arch., Indon. D2 358
Rio Verde, Braz. 5,395 I6 257
Rio Verde, Mex. 10,100 K13 225
Rio Vista, Solano, Calif. 2,616 C3 94
Ripley, Ont., Can. 472 P19 64
Ripley, Somerset, Maine 125 (317*) D3 204
Ripley, Tippah, Miss. 2,668 A4 184
Ripley, Chautauqua, N.Y. 1,247 C2 212
Ripley, Brown, Ohio 2,174 D3 156
Ripley, Payne, Okla. 263 B7 128
Ripley, Lauderdale, Tenn. 3,782 C2 190
Ripley, Jackson, W.Va. 2,756 C3 194
Ripley, co., Ind. 20,641 C4 140
Ripley, co., Mo. 9,096 E7 150
Riplinger, Clark, Wis. 100 D3 160
Ripogenus, lake, Maine C3 204
Ripoll, Sp. 6,991 A8 298
Ripon, San Joaquin, Calif. 1,894 *D3 94
Ripon, Que., Can. 549 S9 66
Ripon, Eng. 10,100 G11 273
Ripon, Fond du Lac, Wis. 6,163 E5 160
Rippey, Greene, Iowa 331 C3 142
Ripton, Addison, Vt. 70 (1,310*) D2 218
Ririe, Jefferson and Bonneville, Idaho 560 F7 108
Risco, New Madrid, Mo. 502 E8 150
Rishiri, isl., Jap. B8 354
Rishon-le-Zion, Isr. 22,000 C5 382
Rising, Berkshire, Mass. 130 *B1 206
Rising City, Butler, Nebr. 308 C8 152
Rising Star, Eastland, Tex. 997 C6 130
Rising Sun, Kent, Del. 110 D3 172
Rising Sun, Ohio, Ind. 2,230 D5 140
Rising Sun, Cecil, Md. 824 A7 182
Risingsun, Wood, Ohio 815 A3 156
Rison, Cleveland, Ark. 889 D4 170
Rison, Charles, Md. 330 C5 182
Risör, Nor. 2,941 G3 291
Ristiina, Fin. F12 291
Ristijärvi, Fin. D13 290
Ritchie, co., W.Va. 10,877 B3 194
Ritter, Grant, Oreg. 15 C7 96
Ritter, mtn., Calif. D4 94
Rittman, Wayne, Ohio 5,410 B5 156
Ritzville, Adams, Wash. 2,173 B8 98
Riva, It. 6,839 C3 302
Riva, Anne Arundel, Md. 600 C6 182
Rivadavia, Arg. B5 250
Rivadavia, Arg. B2 252
Rivadavia, Arg. C3 252
Rivadavia, Chile A1 252
Rivaköy, Tur. F13 307
Rivanna, riv., Va. B6 192
Rivare, Adams, Ind. 100 B5 140
Rivas, Nic. 4,793 E5 228
Rive-de-Gier, Fr. 15,118 E6 278
River, Huntington, Ind. 75 B4 140
Rivera, Arg. C3 252
Rivera, Los Angeles, Calif. 30,000 C5 94
Rivera, Ur. 10,000 B4 252
Rivera, dept., Ur. 75,464 B4 252
Riverbank, Stanislaus, Calif. 2,786 D3 94
River Cess, Lib. E3 408
Riverdale, Sebastian, Ark. *B2 170
Riverdale, Fresno, Calif. 1,012 D4 94
Riverdale, Clayton, Ga. 1,045 B5 176
Riverdale, Cook, Ill. 12,008 F3 138
Riverdale, Scott, Iowa 477 C7 142
D7
Riverdale, Sumner, Kans. 102 E6 144
Riverdale, Prince Georges, Md. 4,389 C4 182
C6
Riverdale, Essex, Mass. A6 206
Riverdale, Worcester, Mass. 300 E1 206
Riverdale, Gratiot, Mich. 380 F7 146
Riverdale, Buffalo, Nebr. 144 D6 152
Riverdale, Morris, N.J. 2,596 B4 210
Riverdale, McLean, N.Dak. 1,055 C4 154
Riverdale, Multnomah, Oreg. 1,500 *A2 96
Riverdale, Knox, Tenn. 1,000 *B8 190
Riverdale, Weber, Utah 1,848 *B3 114
Riverdale Heights, Prince Georges, Md. 1,800 *C6 182
River Edge, Bergen, N.J. 13,264 A1 210
River Falls, Covington, Ala. 401 D3 168
River Falls, Pierce, Wis. 4,857 D1 160
River Falls, dam, Ala. D3 168
River Forest, Cook, Ill. 12,695 F2 138
River Grove, Cook, Ill. 8,464 F2 138
Riverhead, Suffolk, N.Y. 5,830 D4 212
River Hébert, N.S., Can. 1,050 D5 70
River Heights, Cache, Utah 880 *B4 114
River Hills, Milwaukee, Wis. 1,257 E2 160
Riverhurst, Sask., Can. 251 E4 58
Riverina, reg., Austl. E8 432
River John, N.S., Can. 715 D6 70
River Jordan, B.C., Can. C13 52
F10
Riverland Terrace, Charleston, S.C. 2,400 F3 188
Riverlea, Franklin, Ohio 625 C1 156
Rivermines, St. Francois, Mo. 449 *D7 150
Rivermoor, Plymouth, Mass. 225 D4 206
River Oaks, Tarrant, Tex. 8,444 B8 130
River of Ponds, Newf., Can. 120 E7 72
River Pines, Middlesex, Mass. 1,000 C2 206
River Plaza, Monmouth, N.J. 3,000 *C4 210
River Point, Kent, R.I. (part of West Warwick) C2 216
Riverport, N.S., Can. 195 E5 70
River Rouge, Wayne, Mich. 18,147 B8 146
Rivers, Man., Can. 1,422 E2 60
Rivers, inlet, B.C., Can. E9 52
Riversdale, N.S., Can. 75 D6 70
Riverside, St. Clair, Ala. 159 B3 168
Riverside, Riverside, Calif. 84,332 F5 94
Riverside, Ont., Can. 13,335 R18 64
Riverside, Colquitt, Ga. 329 E3 176
Riverside, Cook, Ill. 9,750 F2 138
Riverside, Washington, Iowa 656 C6 142
Riverside, Charles, Md. 100 D5 182
Riverside, Franklin, Mass. 300 *A2 206
Riverside, Jackson, Mich. 600 *G7 146
Riverside, Platte, Mo. 1,315 *B3 150
Riverside, Burlington, N.J. 8,474 C3 210
Riverside, Malheur, Oreg. 5 D8 96
Riverside, Northumberland, Pa. 1,580 C5 214
Riverside, Providence, R.I. (part of East Providence) B3 216
Riverside, Greenville, S.C. 1,200 *B4 188
Riverside, Box Elder, Utah 150 B3 114
Riverside, Okanogan, Wash. 201 A7 98
Riverside, Monongalia, W.Va. B4 194
Riverside, Carbon, Wyo. 87 E6 116
Riverside, co., Calif. 306,191 F5 94
Riverside, res., Colo. B6 106
Riverside Park, Burlington, N.J. 800 C3 210
River Sioux, Harrison, Iowa 150 C1 142
Riverton, Colbert, Ala. 50 A1 168
Riverton, Man., Can. 795 E4 60
Riverton, Litchfield, Conn. 240 B3 202
Riverton, Sangamon, Ill. 1,536 D4 138
Riverton, Fremont, Iowa 399 D2 142
Riverton, Cherokee, Kans. 250 E9 144
Riverton, Wicomico, Md. 100 C8 182
Riverton, Crow Wing, Minn. 121 E4 148
Riverton, Franklin, Nebr. 303 D7 152
Riverton, Burlington, N.J. 3,324 C2 210
Riverton, N.Z. 1,171 G1 437
Riverton, Coos, Oreg. 200 D2 96
Riverton, Salt Lake, Utah 1,993 C4 114
Riverton, Washington, Vt. 100 C3 218
Riverton, Warren, Va. 250 B6 192
Riverton, Pendleton, W.Va. 300 C5 194
Riverton, Fremont, Wyo. 6,845 C4 116
Riverton Heights, King, Wash. 19,000 *B4 98
Rivervale, Bergen, N.J. 5,616 *B4 210
Riverview, Chambers, Ala. 1,171 C4 168
Riverview, Hillsborough, Fla. 150 C6 174
Riverview, Wayne, Mich. 7,237 C8 146
Riverview, St. Louis, Mo. 3,706 *C7 150
Riverview, Keya Paha, Nebr. 20 B6 152
Riverview (Pasco West), Franklin, Wash. 2,894 *C7 98
Riverview, dam, Ala. C4 168
Riverville, Amherst, Va. 50 C6 192
Rives, Obion, Tenn. 291 B2 190
Rivesaltes, Fr. 5,860 F5 278
Rives Junction, Jackson, Mich. 300 G7 146
Rivesville, Marion, W.Va. 1,191 A7 194
B4
Riviera, Kleberg, Tex. 600 F7 130
Riviera Beach, Palm Beach, Fla. 13,046 E10 174
Riviera Beach, Anne Arundel, Md. 4,902 B6 182
Rivière-à-Pierre, Que., Can. 800 R12 66
Rivière-Bleue, Que., Can. 1,481 Q15 66
Rivière-des-Prairies, Que., Can. 6,806 *S16 66
Rivière-du-Loup, Que., Can. 9,964 Q15 66
Rivière-du-Loup, co., Que., Can. 39,461 Q15 66
Rivière-du-Moulin, Que., Can. 4,138 P13 66
Rivière-Ouelle, Que., Can. 575 Q14 66
Rivière-Raquette, Que., Can. 200 R14 66
Rivière-Trois-Pistoles, Que., Can. 375 P15 66
Rivière-Verte, N.B., Can. 685 B1 70
Rivière-Verte, Que., Can. 715 Q15 66
Rivulet, Mineral, Mont. 30 C2 110
Rize, Tur. 17,868 A9 307
Rize, prov., Tur. 213,075 *A9 307
Rizokarpaso, Cyp. 3,667 D6 307
Rizzuto, cape, It. F6 302
Rjukan, Nor. 5,677 G3 291
Roachdale, Putnam, Ind. 927 C3 140
Road Forks, Hidalgo, N.Mex. 24 F2 126
Roads End, Lincoln, Oreg. 200 *C2 96
Roadstown, Cumberland, N.J. 130 E2 210
Road Town, Vir.Is. 706 C12 233
Roan, mtn., Tenn. B9 190
Roane, co., Tenn. 39,133 C7 190
Roane, co., W.Va. 15,720 C3 194
Roan High Knob, mtn., N.C., Tenn. B9 190
Roan Mountain, Carter, Tenn. 800 B9 190
Roann, Wabash, Ind. 478 B4 140
Roanne, Fr. 46,501 D6 278
Roanoke, Randolph, Ala. 5,288 B4 168
Roanoke, Woodford, Ill. 1,821 C4 138
Roanoke, Huntington, Ind. 935 B4 140
Roanoke, Jefferson Davis, La. 600 D3 180
Roanoke (Independent City), Va. 97,110 (*160,400) C5 192
Roanoke, Lewis, W.Va. 300 C4 194
Roanoke, co., Va. 61,693 C4 192
Roanoke, isl., N.C. B10 186
Roanoke, riv., N.C., Va. A8 186
C5 192
Roanoke Rapids, Halifax, N.C. 13,320 A8 186
Roan or Brown, cliffs, Utah D6 114
Roaring Bulls, is., Mass. D4 206
Roaring Fork, riv., Colo. C4 106
Roaring Spring, Blair, Pa. 2,937 C3 214
Roaring Springs, Greene, Tenn. B9 190
Roaringwater, bay, Ire. J3 273
Roark, Leslie, Ky. 500 C7 178
Roatán, Hond. 870 B4 228
Roba, Macon, Ala. 100 C4 168
Robanna, Gloucester, N.J. D2 210
Robards, Henderson, Ky. 375 C3 178
Robāt-E'Khān, Iran C4 379
Robb, Alta., Can. D4 54
Robbins, Cook, Ill. 7,511 F3 138
Robbins, Moore, N.C. 1,294 B6 186
Robbins, Scott, Tenn. 550 B7 190
Robbins, Oneida, Wis. 100 C4 160
Robbins, pt., Md. B7 182
Robbinsdale, Hennepin, Minn. 16,381 F5 148
F6
Robbinston, Washington, Maine 250 (476*) C5 204
Robbinsville, Mercer, N.J. 300 C3 210
Robbinsville, Graham, N.C. 587 B2 186
Robbs, Pontotoc, Miss. 75 A3 184
Robeline, Natchitoches, La. 308 C2 180
Roberdel, Richmond, N.C. 379 C6 186
Robersonville, Martin, N.C. 1,684 B8 186
Robert, Tangipahoa, La. 150 A7 180
D5
Robert, cape, Ont., Can. O18 64
Roberta, Crawford, Ga. 714 D3 176
Roberta, Bryan, Okla. 30 E7 128
Robert Lee, Coke, Tex. 990 D5 130
Roberts, Escambia, Ala. 75 D3 168
Roberts, Jefferson, Idaho 422 F6 108
Roberts, Ford, Ill. 504 C5 138
Roberts, Newton, Miss. 25 C3 184
Roberts, Carbon, Mont. 240 E7 110
Roberts, St. Croix, Wis. 308 D1 160
Roberts, co., S.Dak. 13,190 B8 158
Roberts, co., Tex. 1,075 B5 130
Roberts, pt., Wash. A3 98
Robertsdale, Baldwin, Ala. 1,474 E2 168
Robertsdale, Huntingdon, Pa. 975 C3 214
Robertsfors, Swe. D9 290
Robertson, St. Louis, Mo. 549 A8 150
Robertson, U.S.Afr. 6,970 F4 420
Robertson, Uinta, Wyo. 15 E2 116
Robertson, co., Ky. 2,443 B6 178
Robertson, co., Tenn. 27,335 B5 190
Robertson, co., Tex. 16,157 D7 130
Robertsonville, Que., Can. 1,030 R13 66
Robertsport, Lib. E2 408
Robertstown, White, Ga. 400 B3 176
Roberval, Que., Can. 6,648 P12 66
Robeson, co., N.C. 89,102 C6 186
Robesonia, Berks, Pa. 1,579 *C5 214
Robinette, Baker, Oreg. C9 96
Robinette, Logan, W.Va. 800 *D3 194
Robins, Linn, Iowa 426 B6 142
Robins, Guernsey, Ohio 400 C5 156
Robinson, Crawford, Ill. 7,226 D6 138
Robinson, Brown, Kans. 317 C8 144
Robinson, Kidder, N.Dak. 155 C6 154
Robinson, Indiana, Pa. 875 C2 214
Robinson, McLennan, Tex. 2,111 *D7 130
Robinson, fork, W.Va. A6 194
Robinson, fork, W.Va. C7 194
Robinson, mtn., Wash. A6 98
Robinsons, Aroostook, Maine 125 B5 204
Robinsons Station, Newf., Can. 225 F6 72
Robinsonville, Escambia, Ala. 300 D2 168
Robinsonville, Tunica, Miss. 300 A2 184
Robinwood, Jefferson, Ala. 1,000 *B3 168
Robinwood, Lawrence, Miss. 100 D2 184
Roblin, Man., Can. 1,173 E2 60
Robsart, Sask., Can. 115 F3 58
Robson, B.C., Can. 150 F14 52
Robson, mtn., B.C., Can. D13 52
Robstown, Nueces, Tex. 10,266 F7 130
Roby, Fisher, Tex. 913 C5 130
Roca, Lancaster, Nebr. 123 E2 152
Rocafuerte, Peru A2 245
Rocanville, Sask., Can. 491 E7 58
Rocca Littorio (Galcaio), Som. 8,400 D6 398
Rocca Massima, It. 967 *E4 302
Roccastrada, It. 3,109 D3 302
Rocha, Ur. 25,000 B5 252
Rocha, dept., Ur. 82,814 B5 252
Rochdale, Worcester, Mass. 1,058 B4 206
Rochdale, Dutchess, N.Y. 1,800 *D8 212
Rochefort, Bel. 3,956 D4 282

Roscoe, Stearns, Minn.	168	F4	148
Roscoe, St. Clair, Mo.	125	D4	150
Roscoe, Carbon, Mont.	45	E7	110
Roscoe, Keith, Nebr.	90	C4	152
Roscoe, Sullivan, N.Y.	900	D7	212
Roscoe, Coshocton, Ohio (part of Coshocton)		B5	156
Roscoe, Washington, Pa.	1,315	C2	214
Roscoe, Edmunds, S.Dak.	532	B6	158
Roscoe, Nolan, Tex.	1,490	C5	130
Roscommon, co., Ire.	63,710	H4	273
Roscommon, Roscommon, Mich.	867	E7	146
Roscommon, co., Mich.	7,200	E7	146
Roscrea, Ire.	3,095	I6	273
Rose, Rock, Nebr.	200	B6	152
Rose, Mayes, Okla.	45	B8	128
Rose, peak, Ariz.		E6	124
Rose, pt., B.C., Can.		C7	52
Roseau, Dominica	9,752	E14	233
Roseau, Roseau, Minn.	2,146	C3	148
Roseau, co., Minn.	12,154	C2	148
Roseau, riv., Man., Can., Minn.		F4 B2	60 148
Roseberry, Valley, Idaho		E2	108
Rosebery, B.C., Can.	145	E14	52
Rose Blanche, Newf., Can.	900	G6	72
Rosebloom, Tallahatchie, Miss.	125	B3	184
Roseboro, Sampson, N.C.	1,354	C7	186
Rose Bud, White, Ark.	120	B4	170
Rosebud, Alta., Can.	130	E6	54
Rosebud, Gasconade, Mo.	288	C6	150
Rosebud, Rosebud, Mont.	250	D10	110
Rosebud, Todd, S.Dak.	600	D5	158
Rosebud, Falls, Tex.	1,644	D7	130
Rosebud, co., Mont.	6,187	D10	110
Rosebud, creek, Mont.		E10	110
Rosebud, riv., Alta., Can.		E5	54
Roseburg, Douglas, Oreg.	11,467	D3	96
Rosebush, Isabella, Mich.	400	F7	146
Rose City, Ogemaw, Mich.	435	E7	146
Rosecrans, Manitowoc, Wis.	25	A6	160
Rose Creek, Mower, Minn.	351	H6	148
Rosedale, Tuscaloosa, Ala.		*B2	168
Rosedale, B.C., Can.	300	B16	52
Rosedale, Weld, Colo.	70	*B6	106
Rosedale, Manatee, Fla.	4,085	*D8	174
Rosedale, Parke, Ind.	726	C2	140
Rosedale, Iberville, La.	674	D4	180
Rosedale, Bolivar, Miss.	2,339	B1	184
Rosedale, Mercer, N.J.	75	C3	210
Rosedale, Atlantic, N.J.		D3	210
Rosedale, McClain, Okla.	88	D6	128
Rosedale, Anderson, Tenn.	150	B7	190
Rosedale, Gilmer, W.Va.	175	C4	194
Rosedale, Pierce, Wash.	30	D2	98
Rosedale-Abbey, Eng.		G12	273
Rosedale Station, Alta., Can.	1,200	E6	54
Rose Hill, Covington, Ala.	75	D3	168
Rose Hill, New Castle, Del.	500	*B3	172
Rose Hill, Mahaska, Iowa	223	C5	142
Rose Hill, Butler, Kans.	273	B6	144
Rose Hill, Jasper, Miss.	100	C3	184
Rosehill, Duplin, N.C.	1,292	C7	186
Rose Hill, Lee, Va.	600	D1	192
Roseisle, Man., Can.	165	F3	60
Rose Lake, Kootenai, Idaho		B2	108
Roseland, Mississippi, Ark.	25	B6	170
Roseland, St. Joseph, Ind.	971	A3	140
Roseland, Cherokee, Kans.	100	*E9	144
Roseland, Tangipahoa, La.	1,254	D5	180
Roseland, Adams, Nebr.	163	D7	152
Roseland, Essex, N.J.	2,804	*B4	210
Roseland, Richland, Ohio	8,204	*B4	156
Roselawn, Newton, Ind.	150	A2	140
Rosella, Lawrence, Miss.	150	D2	184
Roselle, Du Page, Ill.	3,581	E2	138
Roselle, Union, N.J.	21,032	B1	210
Roselle Park, Union, N.J.	12,546	B1	210
Rose Lodge, Lincoln, Oreg.	150	*B3	96
Rose Lynn, Alta., Can.	10	E7	54
Rosemark, Shelby, Tenn.	250	C2	190
Rosemary, Alta., Can.	158	E6	54
Rosemead, Los Angeles, Calif.	15,476	C5	94
Rosemere, Que., Can.	3,500	S15	66
Rosemont, Cook, Ill.	978	*A6	138
Rosemont, Baltimore, Md.	212	C4	182
Rosemont, Webster, Nebr.	50	*D7	152
Rosemont, Hunterdon, N.J.	90	C3	210
Rosemont, Taylor, W.Va.	250	B7	194
Rosemount, Dakota, Minn.	1,068	G5 G7	148
Rosenberg, Fort Bend, Tex.	9,698	F7	130
Rosenburg, Platte, Nebr.	25	*C8	152
Rosendaël, Fr.	17,678	B5	278
Rosendale, Andrew, Mo.	234	A3	150
Rosendale, Fond du Lac, Wis.	415	E5	160
Roseneath, Ont., Can.	210	P22	64
Rosenfeld, Man., Can.	190	F4	60
Rosenhayn, Cumberland, N.J.	600	E2	210
Rosenheim, Ger.	31,500	E5	286
Rosepine, Vernon, La.	414	D2	180
Rose Prairie, B.C., Can.		B12	52
Roseto, Northampton, Pa.	1,630	C6	214
Rosetown, Sask., Can.	2,262	E4	58
Rosetta, Johnson, Ark.		B3	170
Rosetta, see Rashid, Eg., U.A.R.			
Rosetta, Wilkinson, Miss.	129	D1	184
Rosetta, branch, Eg., U.A.R.		D1	382
Rosette, Box Elder, Utah		B2	114
Rose Valley, Sask., Can.	537	D6	58
Rosevear, Alta., Can.	15	D4	54
Roseville, Placer, Calif.	13,421	C3	94
Roseville, Warren, Ill.	1,065	C3	138
Roseville, Macomb, Mich.	50,195	B9	146
Roseville, Ramsey, Minn.	23,997	F7	148
Roseville, Muskingum and Perry, Ohio	1,749	C4	156
Roseville, Stafford, Va.	30	B7	192
Rosewood, Muhlenberg, Ky.	80	*C3	178
Rosewood, Champaign, Ohio	700	B3	156
Rosewood Heights, Madison, Ill.	4,572	*E3	138
Roseworth, Twin Falls, Idaho		G4	108
Rosholt, Roberts, S.Dak.	423	B9	158
Rosholt, Portage, Wis.	497	D4	160
Rosh Pina, Isr.	575	B6	382
Rosiclare, Hardin, Ill.	1,700	F5	138
Rosie, Independence, Ark.	150	B5	170
Rosignol, Br.Gu.	1,204	D5	256
Rosillo, peak, Tex.		E4	130
Rosine, Ohio, Ky.	350	C4	178
Roşiorii-de-Vede, Rom.	17,320	B3	321
Rosken, lake, Swe.		D5	292
Roskilde, Den.	27,894	F3	292
Roskilde, co., Den.	82,223	*I5	291
Roslavl, Sov.Un.	36,000	F9	332
Roslin, Fentress, Tenn.	50	B7	190
Roslyn, Nassau, N.Y.	2,681	D3	212
Roslyn, Montgomery, Pa.	8,500	*C6	214
Roslyn, Day, S.Dak.	256	B8	158
Roslyn, Kittitas, Wash.	1,283	B6	98
Roslyn Heights, Nassau, N.Y.	4,000	*E8	212
Rosman, Transylvania, N.C.	419	B3	186
Rosny-sous-Bois, Fr.	16,491	I10	278
Ross, Marin, Calif.	2,551	*D2	94
Ross, N.Z.	549	E3	437
Ross, Mountrail, N.Dak.	167	B3	154
Ross, Butler, Ohio	350	C1 C2	156
Ross, co., Ohio	61,215	C3	156
Ross, dam, Wash.		A5	98
Ross, isl., Bur.		D3	362
Ross, isl., Man., Can.		C4	60
Ross, lake, Wash.		A5	98
Ross, mtn., N.Z.		D5	437
Ross and Cromarty, co., Scot.	59,400	D8	272
Rossano, It.	12,400	F6	302
Rossburn, Man., Can.	589	E2	60
Rosseau, Ont., Can.	223	O21	64
Rossendale, Man., Can.	150	F3	60
Rosses, bay, Ire.		F4	272
Rossford, Wood, Ohio	4,406	A1 A3	156
Ross Fork, Fergus, Mont.	10	C7	110
Rossie, Clay, Iowa	102	A2	142
Rossignol, lake, N.S., Can.		E4	70
Rossiter, Indiana, Pa.	950	C3	214
Rossland, B.C., Can.	4,344	F14	52
Rosslare, Ire.	468	I6	273
Rossmore, Logan, W.Va.	500	*D5	194
Rossmoyne, Hamilton, Ohio	2,000	D1	156
Rosso, Maur.		C1	408
Rossön, Swe.		E7	290
Ross-on-Wye, Eng.	5,300	J10	273
Rossosh, Sov.Un.	28,500	G12	332
Rosston, Nevada, Ark.	250	D3	170
Rosston, Harper, Okla.	58	B4	128
Rossville, Walker, Ga.	4,665	B1	176
Rossville, Vermilion, Ill.	1,470	C6	138
Rossville, Clinton, Ind.	831	B3	140
Rossville, Shawnee, Kans.	797	C8	144
Rossville, Fayette, Tenn.	183	C2	190
Rosthern, Sask., Can.	1,268	D4	58
Rostock, Ger.	150,000	A5	286
Rostov, Sov.Un.	29,200	D12	332
Rostov [-na-Donu], Sov.Un.	597,000 (*675,000)	I12	332
Roşul, pass, Rom.		B2	321
Röstavn, lake, Nor.		D6	290
Roswell, Fulton, Ga.	2,983	A5 B2	176
Roswell, Canyon, Idaho	100	F2	108
Roswell, Chaves, N.Mex.	39,593	E6	126
Roswell, Miner, S.Dak.	39	C8	158
Rota, Sp.	10,353	D3	298
Rotan, Fisher, Tex.	2,788	C5	130
Rotenburg, Ger.	13,900	B3	286
Rothaar, mts., Ger.		C3	286
Rothbur, Eng.		F11	272
Rothbury, Oceana, Mich.	200	F5	146
Rothenburg [ob der Tauber], Ger.	11,400	D4	286
Rother, riv., Eng.		K13	273
Rotherham, Eng.	82,900	H11	273
Rothesay, N.B., Can.	802	D4	70
Rothesay, Scot.	9,400	F7	272
Rothiemay, Golden Valley, Mont.		D7	110
Rothsay, Wilkin, Minn.	457	E2	148
Rothschild, Marathon, Wis.	2,550	D4	160
Rothville, Chariton, Mo.	138	B4	150
Roti, isl., Austl.		A4	432
Roto, Austl.	158	E9	432
Rotondella, It.	4,025	E6	302
Rotorua, N.Z.	12,302	C6	437
Rottenmann, Aus.	4,074	C6	313
Rotterdam, Neth.	704,646 (*915,000)	C3	282
Rotterdam, Schenectady, N.Y.	16,871	*C7	212
Rotterdam Junction, Schenectady, N.Y.	756	C7	212
Rottumeroog, isl., Neth.		A5	282
Rottweil, Ger.	17,400	D3	286
Rotuma, isl., Pac.O.		D3	436
Roubaix, Fr.	11,067	B5	278
Roudnice, Czech.	8,683	*A2	324
Rouen, Fr.	116,540	C4	278
Rouge, riv., Que., Can.		S10	66
Rougemont, Durham, N.C.	400	A7	186
Rough, riv., Ky.		C4	178
Rougon, Pointe Coupee, La.	375	D4	180
Rouleau, Sask., Can.	402	E5	58
Roulers, see Roeselare, Bel.			
Roulette, Potter, Pa.	850	B3	214
Round, hill, Conn.		E1	202
Round, isl., Miss.		E2	184
Round, lake, N.Dak.		B5	154
Round, lake, Ont., Can.		O23	64
Round, lake, Wis.		B2	160
Round, mtn., Kans.		D4	144
Round, pond, Newf., Can.		F8	72
Round Bay, Anne Arundel, Md.	600	B6	182
Round Butte, Lake, Mont.		C2	110
Round Harbour, Newf., Can.	90	F8	72
Round Hill, Alta., Can.	190	D6	54
Round Hill, Loudoun, Va.	430	A7	192
Round House, mtn., Kans.		D4	144
Round Island, passage, Fiji		E6	436
Round Knob, mtn., Tenn.		B7	190
Round Lake, Jackson, Fla.	225	A5	174
Round Lake, Lake, Ill.	997	E2	138
Round Lake, Nobles, Minn.	449	H3	148
Roundlake, Bolivar, Miss.	206	A2	184
Round Lake, Saratoga, N.Y.	750	C8	212
Round Lake Beach, Lake, Ill.	5,011	E2	138
Round Lake Park, Lake, Ill.	2,565	E2	138
Round Mountain, Nye, Nev.	75	E4	112
Round O, Colleton, S.C.	75	F7	188
Round Oak, Jones, Ga.	200	C3	176
Round Pond, St. Francis, Ark.	50	B6	170
Round Pond, Lincoln, Maine	300	E3	204
Round Rock, Williamson, Tex.	1,878	D7	130
Rounds, B.C., Can.		F10	52
Round Spring, caverns, Mo.		D6	150
Roundstone, Ire.	269	H3	273
Roundup, Musselshell, Mont.	2,842	D8	110
Round Valley, Custer, Nebr.		C6	152
Rousay, isl., Scot.		B9	272
Rouse, Huerfano, Colo.	35	E6	106
Rouses Point, Clinton, N.Y.	2,160	A8	212
Rouseville, Venango, Pa.	923	B2	214
Roussillon, former prov., Fr.	217,000	F5	278
Routalampi, Fin.		E12	290
Routt, co., Colo.	5,900	B3	106
Rouville, co., Que., Can.	22,083	S11	66
Rouyn, Que., Can.	17,076	R25	64
Rovaniemi, Fin.	13,485	C11	290
Rovato, It.	6,288	C2	302
Rovenki, Sov.Un.	23,000	H12	332
Rovenki, Sov.Un.	11,000	H12 S23	332
Rover, Yell, Ark.	200	C3	170
Rovereto, It.	17,300	C3	302
Rovigo, It.	17,600	C3	302
Rovigo, prov., It.	344,300	*C3	302
Rovinj, Yugo.	5,712	B1	316
Rovno, Sov.Un.	57,000	G6	332
Rovnoye, Sov.Un.	13,500	G16	332
Rowan, Wright, Iowa	273	B4	142
Rowan, co., Ky.	12,808	B7	178
Rowan, co., N.C.	82,817	B5	186
Rowan Mill, Rowan, N.C.	1,089	*B5	186
Rowe, Franklin, Mass.	130 (231▲)	A2	206
Rowe, San Miguel, N.Mex.	475	C5 H7	126
Rowe, Buchanan, Va.	125	C2	192
Rowell, Chester, S.C.	200	B7	188
Rowena, Wasco, Oreg.	175	*B5	96
Rowes Run, Fayette, Pa.	950	*D2	214
Rowesville, Orangeburg, S.C.	398	E7	188
Rowland, Lincoln, Ky.	200	C6	178
Rowland, Robeson, N.C.	1,408	C6	186
Rowlesburg, Preston, W.Va.	970	B5	194
Rowlett, Dallas, Tex.	1,015	*C7	130
Rowletts, Hart, Ky.	275	C5	178
Rowley, Alta., Can.	115	E6	54
Rowley, Buchanan, Iowa	234	B6	142
Rowley, Essex, Mass.	1,223 (2,783▲)	A6	206
Roxana, Sussex, Del.	100	G5	172
Roxana, Madison, Ill.	2,090	E3	138
Roxas, Phil.	11,673	B6	358
Roxboro, Person, N.C.	5,147	A7	186
Roxburgh, N.Z.	794	F2	437
Roxburgh, co., Scot.	45,400	F10	272
Roxbury, Litchfield, Conn.	225 (912▲)	C2	202
Roxbury, McPherson, Kans.	135	D6	144
Roxbury, Oxford, Maine	250 (344▲)	D2	204
Roxbury, Cheshire, N.H.	50 (137▲)	F2	208
Roxbury, Delaware, N.Y.	475	C7	212
Roxbury, Washington, Vt.	225 (364▲)	C3	218
Roxen, lake, Swe.		C6	292
Roxie, Franklin, Miss.	585	D1	184
Roxobel, Bertie, N.C.	452	A8	186
Roxton, Lamar, Tex.	950	C8	130
Roxton Falls, Que., Can.	1,023	S12	66
Roxton Pond, Que., Can.	735	S12	66
Roy, Flagler, Fla.	350	B9	174
Roy, Power, Idaho		G6	108
Roy, Bienville, La.	250	B2	180
Roy, Fergus, Mont.	175	C8	110
Roy, Harding, N.Mex.	633	C6	126
Roy, Weber, Utah	9,239	B3	114
Roy, Pierce, Wash.	264	B4	98
Roy, knob, Tenn.		C7	190
Royal, Garland, Ark.	25	C3 C6	170
Royal, Clay, Iowa	475	A2	142
Royal, Antelope, Nebr.	93	B7	152
Royal, Bedford, Tenn.	900	C5	190
Royal, Carbon, Utah	100	D5	114
Royal, canal, Ire.		H6	273
Royal, riv., Maine		E5	204
Royal Center, Cass, Ind.	966	B3	140
Royal Cotton Mills, Wake, N.C.	600	A7	186
Royale, isl., Mich.		B3	146
Royal Gorge, Fremont, Colo.	10	*D5	106
Royal Oak, B.C., Can.		C14	52
Royal Oak, Talbot, Md.	500	C7	182
Royal Oak, Oakland, Mich.	80,612	B8	146
Royal Oak Township, Oakland, Mich.	8,147	*G8	146
Royal Palm Hammock, Collier, Fla.	69	F9	174
Royalston, Worcester, Mass.	350 (800▲)	*A3	206
Royalties, Alta., Can.	700	E5	54
Royalton, Franklin, Ill.	1,225	F4	138
Royalton, Magoffin, Ky.	300	C7	178
Royalton, Morrison, Minn.	580	F4	148
Royalton, Windsor, Vt.	150 (1,388▲)	D3	218
Royalton, Waupaca, Wis.	300	D5	160
Royan, Fr.	12,289	E3	278
Royce, Greene, Miss.	100	D4	184
Roye, Fr.	4,635	C5	278
Royersford, Montgomery, Pa.	3,969	C6	214
Royerton, Delaware, Ind.	100	B4	140
Roy Hill, Austl.		C3	432
Royse City, Rockwall and Collin, Tex.	1,274	C7	130
Royston, Franklin, Hart and Madison, Ga.	2,333	B3	176
Roysville, Lib.		E2	408
Royville, Russell, Ky.	295	*C5	178
Roza, dam, Wash.		C6	98
Rozel, Pawnee, Kans.	207	D4	144
Rozet, Campbell, Wyo.	15	B7	116
Rožňava, Czech.	6,991	B5	324
Rtishcheva, Sov.Un.	32,000	B2	336
Rtishchevo, Sov.Un.	32,000	F14	332
Ruaha, Tan.		D6	414
Ruanda-Urundi, Bel. trust., Afr.	3,389,187	G9	388 414
Ruapehu, mtn., N.Z.		C5	437
Ru'ays, wadi, Libya		B3	394
Rub 'Al Khali, des., Sau.Ar.		D4	383
Rubezhnoye, Sov.Un.	55,000	Q22	332
Rubio, Ven.		C2	240
Rubonia, Manatee, Fla.	100	C6	174
Rubtsovsk, Sov.Un.	111,000	B10	336
Ruby, Alsk.	132	C6	84
Ruby, Rapides, La.	25	C3	180
Ruby, Seward, Nebr.	9	*D8	152
Ruby, Chesterfield, S.C.	284	B8	188
Ruby, lake, Nev.		C6	112
Ruby, mts., Nev.		C6	112
Ruby, range, Mont.		E4	110
Rubys Inn, Garfield, Utah	50	F3	114
Ruby Valley, Elko, Nev.	35	C6	112
Rucio, Mex.		C5	225
Ruda, Swe.		D7	292
Rudauli, India		D3	368
Rūdbār, Afg.	5,000	D2	374
Rudd, Floyd, Iowa	436	A5	142
Ruddell, Sask., Can.	61	D4	58
Rüdesheim, Ger.		D2	286
Rudha Hunish, isl., Scot.		D6	272
Rudköbing, Den.	4,520	G1	292
Rudnichnyy, Sov.Un.		A4	336
Rudog, China	5,000	E3	346
Rudolf, lake, Ken., Eth.		B6	414
Rudolph, Wood, Ohio	450	A3	156
Rudolstadt, Ger.	27,000	C4	286
Rūd Sar, Iran		B3	379
Rudy, Crawford, Ark.	113	*B2	170
Rudyard, Chippewa, Mich.	600	C7	146
Rudyard, Hill, Mont.	650	B6	110
Rueil-Malmaison, Fr.		I9	278
Ruelle [-sur-Touvre], Fr.	5,366	E4	278
Rufa'a, Sud.	9,137	C3	398
Rufe, McCurtain, Okla.	80	D8	128
Ruffec, Fr.		D4	278
Ruffin, Colleton, S.C.	250	E7	188
Rufiji, riv., Tan.		D6	414
Rufino, Arg.	10,987	B3	252
Rufisque, Sen.	38,179	D1	408
Rufus, Sherman, Oreg.	150	B6	96
Rugby, Las Animas, Colo.		E6	106
Rugby, Pierce, N.Dak.	2,972	B6	154
Rügen, isl., Ger.		A5	286
Rugged, mtn., B.C., Can.		E9	52
Rugless, Lewis, Ky.	150	B7	178
Ruhr, riv., Ger.		C3	286
Rui, Afg.	5,000	B4	374
Ruidoso, Lincoln, N.Mex.	1,557	E5	126
Ruidoso Downs, see Green Tree, N.Mex.			
Rujen, mtn., Bul.		B1	317
Rukwa, lake, Tan.		D5	414
Rulac, isl., Truk		A3	436
Rule, Haskell, Tex.	1,347	C6	130
Ruleton, Sherman, Kans.	50	C2	144
Ruleville, Sunflower, Miss.	1,902	B2	184
Rulo, Richardson, Nebr.	412	D10	152
Rum, creek, W.Va.		D5	194
Rum, is., W.I.		A7	232
Rum, isl., Scot.		D6	272
Rum, riv., Minn.		F5	148
Rum, sound, Scot.		E6	272
Ruma, Yugo.	15,619	B4	316
Rumaitha, Iraq	4,468	D6	378
Rumbek, Sud.	2,944	D2	398
Rumbley, Somerset, Md.	105	D8	182
Rumburk, Czech.	6,759	A2	324
Rumely, Alger, Mich.	25	C4	146
Rumford, Oxford, Maine	7,233 (10,005▲)	D2	204
Rumford, Providence, R.I. (part of East Providence)		B3	216
Rumford Corner, Oxford, Maine	60	D2	204
Rum Jungle, Austl.		A6	432
Rumney, Grafton, N.H.	200 (820▲)	D3	208
Rumney Depot, Grafton, N.H.	110	D3	208
Rumoe, Jap.	35,797	C8	354
Rump, mtn., Maine		C1	204
Rumpi, Rh.&Nya.		B6	421
Rumsey, Alta., Can.	104	E6	54
Rumsey, McLean, Ky.	252	C3	178
Rumson, Monmouth, N.J.	6,405	C4	210
Rundvik, Swe.		E8	290
Runge, Karnes, Tex.	1,036	E7	130
Rungwa, Tan.		D5	414
Runn, lake, Swe.		F6	291
Runnells, Polk, Iowa	322	A8 C4	142
Runnels, co., Tex.	15,016	D5	130
Runnelstown, Perry, Miss.	125	D3	184
Runnemede, Camden, N.J.	8,396	D2	210
Running, creek, Colo.		C6	106
Runnö, isl., Swe.		D7	292
Runnymede, Sask., Can.	90	E7	58
Runtu, S.W.Afr.		C3	420
Rupanco, Chile		F3	251
Rupar, India		C2	368
Rupea, Rom.	4,691	B3	321
Rupert, riv., Que., Can.		Q9	66
Rupert, Minidoka, Idaho	4,153	G5	108
Rupert, Bennington, Vt.	150 (603▲)	E2	218
Rupert, Greenbrier, W.Va.	921	D4	194
Rupnarayan, riv., India		I8	366
Rural, Pike, Ky.	200	C8	178
Rural Hall, Forsyth, N.C.	1,503	A5	186
Rural Hill, Winston, Miss.	112	B3	184
Rural Retreat, Wythe, Va.	413	D3	192
Rurrenabaque, Bol.	1,225	B1	246
Rusapi, Rh.&Nya.	2,200	C6	421
Ruse, Bul.	83,472	B2	317
Rusenski, prov., Bul.		*B3	317
Rusera, India		D4	368
Rush, Marion, Ark.		A4	170

Rush, El Paso, Colo. 25 D6 106
Rush, Boyd, Ky. 300 B8 178
Rush, co., Ind. 20,393 C4 140
Rush, co., Kans. 6,160 D4 144
Rush, creek, Colo. D7 106
Rush, creek, Nebr. C3 152
Rush, creek, Ohio B3 156
Rush, creek, Okla. D6 128
Rush, lake, Sask., Can. E4 58
Rush, lake, Minn. E3 148
Rush, lake, Minn. F5 148
Rush, lake, Wis. E5 160
Rush, riv., Wis. D1 160
Rush, val., Utah C3 114
Rush Center, Rush, Kans. 278 D4 144
Rush City, Chisago, Minn. 1,108 F6 148
Rushford, Fillmore, Minn. 1,335 H7 148
Rushford (Village), Fillmore, Minn. 581 *H7 148
Rushford, Allegany, N.Y. 400 C3 212
Rush Hill, Audrain, Mo. 132 B6 150
Rush Lake, Sask., Can. 186 E4 58
Rushmere, Isle of Wight, Va. 125 A8 192
Rushmore, Nobles, Minn. 382 H3 148
Rush Springs, Grady, Okla. 1,303 D6 128
Rushsylvania, Logan, Ohio 601 B3 156
Rushville, Schuyler, Ill. 2,819 C3 138
Rushville, Rush, Ind. 7,264 C4 140
Rushville, Buchanan, Mo. 253 B2 150
Rushville, Sheridan, Nebr. 1,228 B3 152
Rushville, Yates, N.Y. 465 C4 212
Rusk, Cherokee, Tex. 4,900 D8 130
Rusk, co., Tex. 36,421 C8 130
Rusk, co., Wis. 14,794 C2 160
Ruskin, B.C., Can. B15 52
F11
Ruskin, Hillsborough, Fla. 1,894 C6 174
D8
Ruskin, Nuckolls, Nebr. 203 D8 152
Ruso, McLean, N.Dak. 31 C5 154
Russas, Braz. 5,531 A3 258
Russell, White, Ark. 203 B5 170
Russell, Alameda, Calif. 1,150 B5 94
D2
Russell, Man., Can. 1,227 E2 60
Russell, Ont., Can. 570 025 64
Russell, Costilla, Colo. E5 106
Russell, Clay, Fla. 108 B10 174
Russell, Barrow, Ga. 163 C3 176
Russell, Lucas, Iowa 577 D4 142
Russell, Russell, Kans. 6,113 D5 144
Russell, Greenup, Ky. 1,458 B8 178
Russell, Hampden, Mass. 600 B2 206
(1,366▲)
Russell, Lyon, Minn. 449 G3 148
Russell, Chouteau, Mont. B5 110
Russell, Saint Lawrence, N.Y. 500 A6 212
Russell, N.Z. A5 437
Russell, Bottineau, N.Dak. 25 B5 154
Russell, Greer, Okla. 100 D4 128
Russell, co., Ala. 46,351 C4 168
Russell, co., Ont., Can. 18,994 025 64
Russell, co., Kans. 11,348 D5 144
Russell, co., Ky. 11,076 C5 178
Russell, co., Va. 26,290 D2 192
Russell, fork, Ky. C8 178
Russell, isl., Solomon E2 436
Russell, lake, Alta., Can. B5 54
Russell, lake, Man., Can. B2 60
Russell, mtn., Alsk. F10 84
Russells Point, Logan, Ohio 1,111 B3 156
Russell Springs, Logan, Kans. 93 D2 144
Russell Springs, Russell, Ky. 1,125 C5 178
Russellton, Allegheny, Pa. 1,613 *A4 214
Russellville, Franklin, Ala. 6,628 A2 168
Russellville, Pope, Ark. 8,921 B3 170
Russellville, Putnam, Ind. 372 C3 140
Russellville, Logan, Ky. 5,861 D4 178
Russellville, Cole, Mo. 442 *C5 150
Russellville, Brown, Ohio 412 D3 156
Russellville, Berkeley, S.C. 100 E9 188
Russellville, Hamblen, Tenn. 750 B8 190
Russett, Johnston, Okla. 75 D7 128
Russian, riv., Calif. C2 94
Russian Soviet Federated Socialist Republic, rep., Sov.Un. 117,494,000 C7 328
Russiaville, Howard, Ind. 1,064 B3 140
Russum, Claiborne, Miss. 50 D1 184
Rustburg, Campbell, Va. 350 C5 192
Ruston, Lincoln, La. 13,991 B3 180
Ruston, Pierce, Wash. 694 B4 98
D2
Rutana, Ruanda-Urundi C5 414
Rutba, Iraq C4 378
Rute, Sp. 10,077 D4 298
Ruteng, Indon. F6 358
Ruth, Huron, Mich. 210 F9 146
Ruth, Lincoln, Miss. 300 D2 184
Ruth, White Pine, Nev. 800 D7 112
Ruth, Rutherford, N.C. 529 B4 186
Ruthdale, Nowata, Okla. B8 128
Rutherford, Russell, Ala. 150 C4 168
Rutherford, Bergen, N.J. 20,473 A1 210
B4
Rutherford, Gibson, Tenn. 983 B3 190
Rutherford, co., N.C. 45,091 B4 186
Rutherford, co., Tenn. 52,368 C5 190
Rutherford, fork, Tenn. B3 190
Rutherford Heights, Dauphin, Pa. 17,500 *C5 214
Rutherfordton, Rutherford, N.C. 3,392 B4 186
Rutherglen, Scot. 24,600 F8 272
Rutheron, Rio Arriba, N.Mex. 50 B4 126
Ruthilda, Sask., Can. 92 E3 58
Ruthin, Wales 3,700 H9 273
Ruthton, Pipestone, Minn. 476 G2 148
Ruthton, Sullivan, Tenn. 50 B9 190
Ruthven, Wilcox, Ala. 400 D2 168
Ruthven, Ont., Can. R18 64
Ruthven, Palo Alto, Iowa 712 A3 142
Ruthville, Charles City, Va. 150 C7 192
Rüti, Switz. 6,647 A4 312
Rutland, B.C., Can. 425 F13 52
Rutland, La Salle, Ill. 509 C4 138
Rutland, Humboldt, Iowa 221 B3 142
Rutland, Worcester, Mass. 1,774 B4 206
(3,253▲)
Rutland, Sargent, N.Dak. 308 D8 154
Rutland, Meigs, Ohio 687 C4 156
Rutland, Lake, S.Dak. 100 C9 158
Rutland, Rutland, Vt. 18,325 D3 218
Rutland (Town of), Rutland, Vt. (1,542▲) *D3 218
Rutland, co., Eng. 22,250 I12 273
Rutland, co., Vt. 46,719 D2 218
Rutland Heights, Worcester, Mass. 450 B4 206
Rutland Station, Sask., Can. 115 D3 58
Rutledge, Crenshaw, Ala. 276 D3 168
Rutledge, Morgan, Ga. 478 C3 176
Rutledge, Pine, Minn. 146 E6 148
Rutledge, Scotland, Mo. 158 A5 150
Rutledge, Grainger, Tenn. 793 B8 190
Rutledge Springs, Jefferson, Ala. 300 *B3 168
Rutshuru, Con.L. C4 414
Rutter, Ont., Can. 75 020 64
Ruukki, Fin. D11 290
Ruunitto, isl., Eniwetok B1 436
Ruvo [di Puglia], It. 26,100 E6 302
Ruvu, Tan. D6 414
Ruvuma, riv., Moz. B7 421
Ruvuma, riv., Tan., Moz. E6 414
Ruwāndiz, Iraq 3,320 A6 378
Ruweiha, ruins, Jordan D6 382
Ruwenzori, mts., Afr. B4 414
Ruxton, Baltimore, Md. 2,100 C4 182
Ruza, Sov.Un. 7,000 E11 332
Ruzayevka, Sov.Un. 34,500 B3 336
Ružomberok, Czech. 22,483 B4 324
Ryan, Delaware, Iowa 347 B6 142
Ryan, Jefferson, Okla. 978 D6 128
Ryan, riv., Ala. B2 168
Ryan, peak, Idaho F4 108
Ryan Park, Carbon, Wyo. 100 E6 116
Ryans Slough, Humboldt, Calif. 3,634 *B1 94
Ryazan, Sov.Un. 213,000 B1 336
Ryazhsk, Sov.Un. 37,300 F13 332
Rybachye, Sov.Un. D9 336
Rybinsk (Shcherbakov), Sov.Un. 181,000 A1 336
Rybinsk, res., Sov.Un. A1 336
Rybnik, Pol. 29,100 C4 325
Rybnovsk, Sov.Un. D16 329
Rycroft, Alta., Can. 424 C3 54
Rydal, Montgomery, Pa. 1,500 *C6 214
Ryder, Ward, N.Dak. 264 C4 154
Ryderwood, Cowlitz, Wash. 380 C3 98
Rye, Cleveland, Ark. 50 D5 170
Rye, Pueblo, Colo. 179 E6 106
Rye, Eng. 4,600 K13 273
Rye, Rockingham, N.H. 450 E5 208
Rye, Westchester, N.Y. 14,225 D3 212
Rye Beach, Rockingham, N.H. 165 F5 208
Ryegate, Golden Valley, Mont. 314 D7 110
Ryegate, Caledonia, Vt. 30 C4 218
(894▲)
Rye Patch, res., Nev. C3 112
Ryerson, Sask., Can. 15 F7 58
Ryley, Alta., Can. 495 D6 54
Rylsk, Sov.Un. 26,000 G10 332
Ryndon, Elko, Nev. 20 C6 112
Ryōzu, Jap. 30,048 *E7 354
Rypin, Pol. 7,350 B4 325
Ryūkyū, is., Asia B3 436
Ryūkyū Islands (Southern), U.S. occ. area, Asia 745,194 B3 436
Rzepin, Pol. 1,543 B2 325
Rzeszów, Pol. 52,000 C6 325
Rzeszów, pol. div., Pol. 1,524,000 *D6 325
Rzhev, Sov.Un. 42,000 D10 332

S

Saa, Solomon E2 436
Saale, riv., Ger. C4 286
Saalfeld, Ger. 27,200 C4 286
Saalfelden [am Steinernen Meer], Aus. 8,315 C4 313
Saar (Saarland), reg., Ger. D2 286
Saarbrücken, Ger. 121,600 D2 286
(*230,000)
Saaremaa, isl., Sov.Un. C4 332
Saarijärvi, Fin. E11 290
Saarland (Saar), state, Ger. 996,200 *D2 286
Saarlouis (Saarlautern), Ger. 33,500 D2 286
Saavedra, Arg. 2,130 C3 252
Saavedra, Chile C1 252
Sabá, Hond. C4 228
Saba, isl., W.I. D13 233
Sabac, Yugo. 19,894 B4 316
Sabadell, Sp. 47,831 B8 298
Sab'ah, hill, Libya B3 394
Sabalana, is., Indon. F5 358
Sabalgarh, India D2 368
Sabana de la Mar, Dom.Rep. 2,780 C10 233
Sabanagrande, Hond. 1,580 D4 228
Sabanalarga, Col. 13,982 A2 244
Sabará, Braz. 9,183 D2 258
Sabarmati, riv., India D2 366
Sabattus, Androscoggin, Maine 850 D2 204
Sabattus, pond, Maine D2 204
Sabaudia, It. 2,552 E4 302
Sabbathday, pond, Maine D5 204
Sabderat, Eth. B4 398
Sabetha, Nemaha, Kans. 2,318 C8 144
Sabhah, Libya 3,640 B2 394
Sabillasville, Frederick, Md. 300 A5 182
Sabin, Clay, Minn. 251 E2 148
Sabina, Clinton, Ohio 2,313 C3 156
Sabinal, Uvalde, Tex. 1,747 E6 130
Sabinas, Mex. 11,253 B5 225
Sabinas Hidalgo, Mex. 8,629 B5 225
Sabine, Wyoming, W.Va. 440 D3 194
Sabine, co., Tex. 7,302 D9 130
Sabine, par., La. 18,564 C2 180
Sabine, lake, La. E2 180
Sabine, pass, La. E2 180
Sabine, riv., La., Tex. D2 180
D9 130
Sabinópolis, Braz. 1,799 D2 258
Sabkhat al Bardawil, lagoon, Eg., U.A.R. A3 395
Sable, cape, Fla. F9 174
Sablé [-sur-Sarthe], Fr. 6,511 D3 278
Sabon Birni, Nig. D6 408
Sabor, riv., Port. B3 298
Sabraton, Monongalia, W.Va. 1,810 A7 194
Sabula, Jackson, Iowa 894 B7 142
Sabula, Clearfield, Pa. 80 B3 214
Şabyā, Sau.Ar. 10,000 D3 383
Sabzawar, Afg. 10,000 C2 374
Sabzevār, Iran 28,151 B4 379
Sac, co., Iowa 17,007 B2 142
Sac, riv., Mo. D4 150
Sacaba, Bol. 2,752 C1 246
Sacajawea, peak, Oreg. B9 96
Sacandaga, lake, N.Y. B7 212
Sacandaga, res., N.Y. B7 212
Sacaton, Pinal, Ariz. 584 E4 124
Sac City, Sac, Iowa 3,354 B2 142
Sachuest, pt., R.I. D4 216
Sackets Harbor, Jefferson, N.Y. 1,279 B5 212
Sackville, N.B., Can. 2,849 D5 70
Saco, Pike, Ala. 150 D4 168
Saco, York, Maine 10,515 E2 204
E4
Saco, Phillips, Mont. 490 B9 110
Saco, riv., Maine, N.H. E2 204
C4 208
Sacramento, Sacramento, Calif. 191,667 C3 94
(*536,000)
Sacramento, McLean, Ky. 429 C3 178
Sacramento, Phelps, Nebr. 17 *D6 152
Sacramento, co., Calif. 502,778 C3 94
Sacramento, mts., N.Mex. F5 126
Sacramento, riv., Calif. C3 94
Sacramento, riv., N.Mex. F5 126
Sacré-Coeur Saguenay, Que., Can. 896 P15 66
Sacred Heart, Renville, Minn. 696 G3 148
Sacred Heart, Pottawatomie, Okla. 35 C7 128
Sacrofano, It. 1,700 *D3 302
Săcueni, Rom. A2 321
Sá da Bandeira, Ang. 13,867 B2 420
Şa'dah, Yemen 25,000 D3 383
Saddle, mtn., Colo. D5 106
Saddle, mtn., Oreg. B3 96
Saddle, riv., N.J. A1 210
Saddleback, mtn., Maine B4 204
Saddleback, mtn., Maine D2 204
Saddle Ball, mtn., Mass. A1 206
Saddle Brook, Bergen, N.J. 13,834 A1 210
Saddle Bunch, keys, Fla. G9 174
Saddle Mountain, Kiowa, Okla. D5 128
Saddle River, Bergen, N.J. 1,776 A4 210
Saddlerock, mtn., Maine C3 204
Saddlestring, Johnson, Wyo. 5 B6 116
Sadieville, Scott, Ky. 276 B6 178
Sadiya, India 2,056 D6 368
Sado, isl., Jap. E7 354
Sado, riv., Port. C2 298
Sadská, Czech. 3,047 *A2 324
Saegertown, Crawford, Pa. 1,131 B1 214
Saeki, Jap. 51,226 H3 354
Saengchŏn, Kor. F13 348
Safad, Isr. 7,000 B6 382
Safety Harbor, Pinellas, Fla. 1,787 C6 174
D8
Safety Valve, entrance, Fla. F10 174
Saffell, Lawrence, Ark. 150 B5 170
Saffle, Swe. 10,182 B3 292
Safford, Dallas, Ala. 200 C2 168
Safford, Graham, Ariz. 4,648 F6 124
Saffordville, Chase, Kans. 40 D7 144
Saffron Walden, Eng. 7,300 I13 273
Safi, Mor. 66,751 B2 402
Safidābeh, Iran C5 379
Safranbolu, Tur. 5,374 A5 307
Saga, Jap. 126,432 H3 354
Sagadahoc, co., Maine 22,793 E3 204
Sagaing, Bur. 15,439 B2 362
Sagamihara, Jap. 83,841 *L15 354
Sagamore, Barnstable, Mass. 987 C6 206
Sagamore, Armstrong, Pa. 800 C2 214
Sagamore Beach, Barnstable, Mass. 150 *C6 206
Sagamore Hills, Summit, Ohio 3,848 B1 156
Sagån, riv., Swe. B7 292
Saganaga, lake, Minn. C8 148
Sagar, isl., India J9 366
Sagara, Fiji E6 436
Sagara, Jap. 29,596 M14 354
Sage, Izard, Ark. 50 A5 170
Sage, Lincoln, Wyo. 35 E2 116
Sageville, Dubuque, Iowa 110 B7 142
Sag Harbor, Suffolk, N.Y. 2,346 D5 212
Saginaw, Shelby, Ala. 350 B3 168
Saginaw, Saginaw, Mich. 98,265 F8 146
(*160,900)
Saginaw, Newton, Mo. 188 *D3 150
Saginaw, Lane, Oreg. 100 D3 96
Saginaw, Tarrant, Tex. 1,001 B8 130
Saginaw, co., Mich. 190,752 F7 146
Saginaw, bay, Mich. F8 146
Saginaw, riv., Mich. F8 146
Sagiz, Sov.Un. C4 336
Sagiz, riv., Sov.Un. C5 336
Sagle, Bonner, Idaho 100 *A2 108
Saglek, bay, Newf., Can. D9 72
Sagola, Dickinson, Mich. 150 C3 146
Sagra, mts., Sp. D5 298
Sagsag, Bis.Arch. F11 359
Saguache, Saguache, Colo. 722 D4 106
Saguache, co., Colo. 4,473 D4 106
Saguache, creek, Colo. D4 106
Sagua de Tánamo, Cuba 7,604 B7 232
Sagua la Grande, Cuba 26,187 A4 232
Saguaro, natl. mon., Ariz. F5 124
Saguenay, co., Que., Can. 57,364 P15 66
Saguenay, riv., Que., Can. P14 66
Saguia Hamra, reg., Sp. Sahara A2 408
Sagunto, Sp. 12,123 C6 298
Sahaba, wadi, Sau.Ar. C4 383
Sahagún, Col. 5,910 B1 244
Sahara, des., Afr. C2 394
Saharanpur, India 142,665 C2 368
(*148,435)
Sahibganj, India D4 368
Sahragt el Kubra, Eg., U.A.R. D2 382
Sahuaripa, Mex. 3,836 B4 224
Sahuarita, Pima, Ariz. 250 G5 124
Sahuayo, Mex. 12,511 K12 225
Sai, riv., India D3 368
Saïda, Alg. 22,651 B4 402
Saida (Sidon), Leb. 18,488 C1 378
Sa'īdābād, Iran 8,074 D4 379
Saidpur, Pak. 61,369 K16 375
Saigō, Jap. 16,199 F4 354
Saigon, Viet. 1,614,200 E5 362
Saihut, Aden D5 383
Saijō, Jap. 48,241 *G4 354
Saimaa, lake, Fin. F12 291
St. Abb's, head, Scot. F10 272
Ste. Adèle, Que., Can. 1,309 S10 66
St. Adelphe-de-Champlain, Que., Can. 775 R12 66
St. Adolphe, Que., Can. 410 S13 66
St. Affrique, Fr. 5,591 F5 278
St. Agapit, Que., Can. 1,079 R13 66
St. Agatha, Aroostook, Maine 500 A4 204
(1,137▲)
Ste. Agathe, Man., Can. 450 F4 60
Ste. Agathe, Que., Can. 559 R13 66
Ste. Agathe-des-Monts, Que., Can. 5,173 R10 66
St. Aimé, Que., Can. 644 S12 66
St. Alban, Que., Can. 815 R12 66
St. Alban's, Newf., Can. 1,334 G8 72
St. Albans, Eng. 46,700 J12 273
St. Albans, Somerset, Maine 350 D3 204
(927▲)
St. Albans, Franklin, Vt. 8,806 B2 218
St. Albans (Town of), Franklin, Vt. (2,303▲) *B2 218
St. Albans, Kanawha, W.Va. 15,103 C3 194
St. Albans, bay, Vt. B2 218
St. Albans, head, Eng. K11 273
St. Albans Bay, Franklin, Vt. 350 B2 218
St. Albert, Alta., Can. 1,320 D6 54
St. Alexandre, Que., Can. 900 *Q15 66
St. Alexandre, Que., Can. 375 S11 66
St. Alexis-des-Monts, Que., Can. 690 R11 66
St. Alphonse, Que., Can. 521 S12 66
St. Amand-Mont-Rond, Fr. 10,765 D5 278
St. Amant, Ascension, La. 100 B6 180
St. Ambroise, Que., Can. 1,305 P13 66
St. Anaclet, Que., Can. 810 P16 66
St. André [de Kamouraska], Que., Can. 539 Q15 66
St. André, cape, Malag. C8 421
St. Andrew, Bay, Fla. 2,500 *A5 174
St. Andrew, bay, Fla. A5 174
St. Andrew, bay, Scot. E10 272
St. Andrew, sound, Ga. F5 176
St. Andrews, N.B., Can. 1,534 D2 70
St. Andrews, Newf., Can. 225 G6 72
St. Andrews, Scot. 9,600 E10 272
St. Andrews, Charleston, S.C. 15,000 F3 188
St. Andrews, Franklin, Tenn. 250 C6 190
St. Andrews East, Que., Can. 800 S10 66
Ste. Angèle, Que., Can. 570 S11 66
St. Anicet, Que., Can. 310 S10 66
St. Ann, St. Louis, Mo. 12,155 A8 150
St. Ann, Frontier, Nebr. 5 D5 152
St. Anna, Stearns, Minn. 215 F4 148
St. Anna, Calumet, Wis. 100 B6 160
Ste. Anne, Que., Can. 900 S11 66
Ste. Anne, Guad. 2,384 D14 233
(9,859▲)
St. Anne, Kankakee, Ill. 1,378 B6 138
St. Anne, lake, Alta., Can. D5 54
Ste. Anne, riv., Que., Can. Q14 66
Ste. Anne, riv., Que., Can. R13 66
Ste. Anne-de-Beaupré, Que., Can. 1,865 Q14 66
Ste. Anne [de Bellevue], Que., Can. 3,647 S15 66
Ste. Anne-de-la-Pérade, see La Pérade, Que., Can.
Ste. Anne-de-la-Pocatière, Que., Can. 325 Q14 66
Ste. Anne-des-Chênes, Man., Can. 700 F4 60
Ste. Anne-des-Monts, Que., Can. 950 *Q10 66
St. Anns, N.S., Can. 115 C9 70
St. Ann's, bay, N.S., Can. C9 70
St. Ann's Bay, Jam. 3,500 C6 232
St. Anselme, Que., Can. 1,086 R14 66
St. Ansgar, Mitchell, Iowa 1,014 A5 142
St. Anthony, Newf., Can. 1,761 E8 72
St. Anthony, Fremont, Idaho 2,700 F7 108
St. Anthony, Dubois, Ind. 165 D3 140
St. Anthony, Marshall, Iowa 130 B4 142
St. Anthony, Hennepin, Minn. 5,084 *F5 148
St. Anthony, Morton, N.Dak. 88 D5 154
St. Antoine, Que., Can. 290 R13 66
R15
St. Antoine, Que., Can. 435 S11 66
St. Antoine de Kent, N.B., Can. 315 C5 70
St. Antoine-des-Laurentides, Que., Can. 2,092 *S10 66
St. Antonin, Que., Can. 450 Q15 66
St. Apollinaire, Que., Can. 822 R13 66
Ste. Apolline, Que., Can. 600 R14 66
St. Arsène, Que., Can. 375 Q15 66
St. Athanase, Que., Can. 235 Q15 66
St. Aubert, Que., Can. 525 Q14 66
St. Augustin, Que., Can. 540 R15 66
St. Augustin, Que., Can. 393 S15 66
St. Augustin, riv., Newf., Can. D6 72
St. Augustine, Saint Johns, Fla. 14,734 B9 174
B10
St. Augustine Beach, Saint Johns, Fla. 396 *B9 174
St. Austell, Eng. 23,400 K8 273

St. Avold, Fr.	11,244	C7	278
St. Barbe, is., Newf., Can.		E8	72
St. Barnabé, Que., Can.	310	S12	66
St. Barnabé-Nord, Que., Can.	620	R12	66
St. Barthélémi, Que., Can.	875	R11	66
St. Barthélemy, isl., W.I.		D13	233
St. Basile, Que., Can.	675	S11	66
St. Basile [de Portneuf], Que., Can.	1,050	R13	66
St. Basile Station, Que., Can.	1,635	*R13	66
Ste. Béatrix, Que., Can.	360	R11	66
St. Bee's, head, Eng.		G9	273
St. Benedict, Sask., Can.	230	D5	58
St. Benedict, St. Tammany, La.	250	D5	180
St. Benedict, Marion, Oreg.	450	C1	96
St. Benoit, Que., Can.	467	S15	66
St. Benoit Labre, Que., Can.	555	R14	66
St. Bernard, Cullman, Ala.	450	A3	168
St. Bernard, Que., Can.	435	R13	66
St. Bernard, St. Bernard, La.	350	C8 E6	180
St. Bernard, Platte, Nebr.	35	*C8	152
St. Bernard, Hamilton, Ohio	6,778	D1	156
St. Bernard, par., La.	32,186	E6	180
St. Bernice, Vermillion, Ind.	800	C2	140
St. Bethlehem, Montgomery, Tenn.	200	B4	190
Ste. Blandine, Que., Can.	490	P16	66
St. Bonaventure, Que., Can.	510	S12	66
St. Bonaventure, Cattaraugus, N.Y.	2,000	*C3	212
St. Boniface, Man., Can.	28,851	F4	60
St. Bonifacius, Hennepin, Minn.	576	*F5	148
St. Boswells, Sask., Can.	95	E4	58
St. Brendan's, Newf., Can.	829	F9	72
St. Bride, mtn., Alta., Can.		E5	54
St. Brides, Newf., Can.	275	G8	72
St. Brides, Norfolk, Va.	130	D8	192
St. Brides, bay, Wales		J7	273
St. Brieuc, Fr.	37,670	C2	278
St. Brieux, Sask., Can.	411	D5	58
Ste. Brigide, Que., Can.	250	S11	66
Ste. Brigitte, Que., Can.	375	R12	66
St. Bruno, Que., Can.	913	Q15	66
St. Calixte, Que., Can.	375	S11	66
St. Camille, Que., Can.	625	R14	66
St. Camille, Que., Can.	360	S13	66
St. Casimir, Que., Can.	1,447	R12	66
St. Catharine, Washington, Ky.	200	C5	178
St. Catharines, Ont., Can.	39,708 (*85,000)	Q21	64
Ste. Catherine, Que., Can.	430	R13 R15	66
St. Catherine, lake, Vt.		E2	218
St. Catherines, isl., Ga.		E5	176
St. Catherine's, pt., Bermuda		A13	233
St. Catherines, pt, Eng.		K11	273
St. Catherines, sound, Ga.		E5	176
Ste. Cécile, Que., Can.	360	S14	66
St. Célestin, Que., Can.	394	R12	66
St. Césaire, Que., Can.	1,739	S12	66
St. Chamond, Fr.	15,580	E6	278
St. Charles, Arkansas, Ark.	255	C5	170
St. Charles, Bear Lake, Idaho	300	G7	108
St. Charles, Kane, Ill.	9,269	B5 F1	138
St. Charles, Madison, Iowa	355	C4	142
St. Charles, Hopkins, Ky.	421	C3	178
St. Charles, Saginaw, Mich.	1,959	F7	146
St. Charles, Winona, Minn.	1,882	H6	148
St. Charles, St. Charles, Mo.	21,189	A7 C7	150
St. Charles, Lee, S.C.	150	C8	188
St. Charles, Gregory, S.Dak.	58	D6	158
St. Charles, Lee, Va.	368	D1	192
St. Charles, par., La.	21,219	E5	180
St. Charles, co., Mo.	52,970	C7	150
St. Charles, cape, Newf., Can.		D8	72
St. Charles [de Bellechasse], Que., Can.	946	R14	66
St. Chély-d'Apcher, Fr.		E5	278
Ste. Christine, Que., Can.	630	S12	66
St. Chrysostôme, Que., Can.	866	S11	66
St. Clair, St. Clair, Mich.	4,538	G9	146
St. Clair, Blue Earth, Minn.	373	G5	148
St. Clair, Franklin, Mo.	2,711	C7	150
St. Clair, Schuylkill, Pa.	5,159	C5	214
St. Clair, co., Ala.	25,388	B3	168
St. Clair, co., Ill.	262,509	E3	138
St. Clair, co., Mich.	107,201	G9	146
St. Clair, co., Mo.	8,421	C4	150
St. Clair, lake, Ont., Can.		R18	64
St. Clair, lake, Mich.		G9	146
St. Clair, riv., Ont., Can.		R18	64
St. Clair Bottom, Smyth, Va.	200	D3	192
Ste. Claire, Que., Can.	810	R14	66
St. Claire Shores, Macomb, Mich.	76,657	B9	146
St. Clairsville, Belmont, Ohio	3,865	B6	156
St. Claude, Man., Can.	315	F3	60
St. Claude, Que., Can.	250	S13	66
St. Claude [-sur-Bienne], Fr.	11,301	D6	278
St. Clément, Que., Can.	490	Q15	66
St. Cléophas, Que., Can.	220	R11	66
Ste. Clothilde, Que., Can.	460	S12	66
St. Cloud, Osceola, Fla.	4,353	C9	174
St. Cloud, Fr.	20,671	I9	278
St. Cloud, Stearns, Minn.	33,815	F4	148
St. Cloud, Fond du Lac, Wis.	530	B5 E5	160
St. Columbans, Sarpy, Nebr.	85	*C10	152
St. Côme, Que., Can.	515	R11	66
St. Constant, Que., Can.	455	S16	66
Ste. Croix, N.B., Can.	85	D2	70
Ste. Croix, Que., Can.	1,241	R13 S15	66
St. Croix, Perry, Ind.	100	D3	140
Ste. Croix, Switz.	6,575	B2	312
St. Croix, co., Wis.	29,164	C1	160
St. Croix, isl., Vir.Is.		D12	233
St. Croix, lake, N.S., Can.		E5	70
St. Croix, lake, Wis.		D1	160
St. Croix, riv., N.B., Can.		D2	70
St. Croix, riv., Maine		C5	204
St. Croix, riv., Minn., Wis.		F6 C1	148 160
St. Croix, stream, Maine		B4	204
St. Croix Falls, Polk, Wis.	1,249	C1	160
St. Cuthbert, Que., Can.	585	R11	66
St. Cyprien, Que., Can.	550	Q15	66
St. Cyrille [de L'Islet], Que., Can.	675	Q14	66
St. Cyrille [de Wendover], Que., Can.	1,198	S12	66
St. Damase, Que., Can.	737	Q14	66
St. Damase, Que., Can.	435	S11	66
St. Damien, Que., Can.	385	R11	66
St. Damien, Que., Can.	475	R14	66
St. David, Cochise, Ariz.	400	G5	124
St. David, Que., Can.	410	R16	66
St. David, Que., Can.	790	S12	66
St. David, Fulton, Ill.	862	C3	138
St. David, Aroostook, Maine	80	A4	204
St. David's, Newf., Can.	250	F6	72
St. Davids, Delaware, Pa.	1,200	*D6	214
St. David's, head, Wales		J7	273
St. David's, isl., Bermuda		A13	233
St. Denis, Que., Can.	944	Q15	66
St. Denis, Que., Can.	822	S11	66
St. Denis, Fr.	80,705	C5 I10	278
St. Didace, Que., Can.	465	R11	66
St. Dié, Fr.	20,952	C7	278
St. Dizier, Fr.	25,515	C6	278
St. Dominique, Que., Can.	483	S12	66
St. Dominique, Que., Can.	180	S15	66
St. Donat, Que., Can.	740	R10	66
St. Edouard, Que., Can.	345	S11	66
St. Edward, Boone, Nebr.	777	C8	152
Ste. Edwidge, Que., Can.	435	S13	66
St. Eleuthère, Que., Can.	635	Q15	66
St. Elias, cape, Alsk.		D7	84
St. Elias, mtn., Alsk.		C7	84
St. Elias, mts., Alsk.		C7	84
Ste. Elizabeth, Que., Can.	525	R11	66
St. Elmo, Mobile, Ala.	600	E1	168
St. Elmo, Fayette, Ill.	1,503	D5	138
St. Eloi, Que., Can.	630	P15	66
St. Elzéar, Que., Can.	2,589	S15	66
St. Elzéar [de Témiscouata], Que., Can.	372	Q15	66
Ste. Emélie, Que., Can.	655	R11	66
St. Emile-de-Suffolk, Que., Can.	430	S10	66
St. Éphrem, Que., Can.	831	R14	66
Saintes, Fr.	23,768	E3	278
St. Esprit, Que., Can.	825	S11	66
St. Étienne, Que., Can.	235	R16	66
St. Étienne, Que., Can.	155	S15	66
St. Étienne, Fr.	181,730	E6	278
Ste. Eulalie, Que., Can.	500	R12	66
Ste. Euphémie, Que., Can.	490	R14	66
St. Eusèbe, Que., Can.	300	Q16	66
St. Eustache, Que., Can.	3,740	S11 S15	66
St. Eustache-sur-le-Lac, Que., Can.	5,830	S15	66
St. Eustatius, isl., W.I.		D13	233
St. Fabien, Que., Can.	1,000	P16	66
Ste. Famille, Que., Can.	310	R14	66
Ste. Famille-d'Aumond, Que., Can.	265	R9	66
St. Félicien, Que., Can.	4,152	P12	66
St. Félix-de-Valois, Que., Can.	1,323	R11	66
St. Ferdinand, Que., Can.	2,431	*R13	66
St. Féréol, Que., Can.	350	Q14	66
St. Fidèle, Que., Can.	375	Q14	66
St. Fintan's, Newf., Can.	90	F6	72
St. Flavien, Que., Can.	634	R13	66
Ste. Flore, Que., Can.	480	R12	66
St. Florent [-sur-Cher], Fr.		D5	278
St. Florian, Lauderdale, Ala.	350	A2	168
St. Flour, Fr.	5,763	E5	278
St. Fortunat, Que., Can.	415	S13	66
Ste. Foy, Que., Can.	14,615	R16	66
Ste. Foy-la-Grande, Fr.		E4	278
St. Francis, Clay, Ark.	224	A6	170
St. Francis, Cheyenne, Kans.	1,594	C2	144
St. Francis, Aroostook, Maine	450 (1,058▲)	A4	204
St. Francis, Anoka, Minn.	175	F5	148
St. Francis, Todd, S.Dak.	421	D5	158
St. Francis, Milwaukee, Wis.	10,065	E2	160
St. Francis, co., Ark.	33,303	B6	170
St. Francis, cape, Newf., Can.		G9	72
St. Francis, lake, Que., Can.		S13	66
St. Francis, riv., Ark., Mo.		C6 E7	170 150
St. Francis, riv., Que., Can.		S12	66
St. Francis, riv., Maine		A3	204
St. Francisville, Lawrence, Ill.	1,040	E6	138
St. Francisville, West Feliciana, La.	1,661	D4	180
St. Francois, co., Mo.	36,516	D7	150
St. Francois, mts., Mo.		D7	150
St. François [du Lac], Que., Can.	826	R12	66
Ste. Françoise, Que., Can.	595	P15	66
St. François [Montmagny], Que., Can.	610	R14	66
St. François Xavier, Que., Can.	290	S12	66
St. Frédéric, Que., Can.	350	R14	66
St. Froid, lake, Maine		B4	204
St. Fulgence, Que., Can.	1,054	P14	66
St. Gabriel, Iberville, La.	75	B5	180
St. Gabriel [de Brandon], Que., Can.	3,265	R11	66
St. Gall, see St. Gallen, Switz.			
St. Gallen, Switz.	71,300	A5	312
St. Gallen (Sankt Gallen) (St. Gall), canton, Switz.	327,600	A5	312
St. Gaudens, Fr.	5,755	F4	278
St. Gédéon, Que., Can.	857	S14	66
Ste. Geneviève, Que., Can.	525	R12	66
Ste. Genevieve, Ste. Genevieve, Mo.	4,443	D7	150
Ste. Genevieve, co., Mo.	12,116	D7	150
Ste. Geneviève [de Pierrefonds], Que., Can.	2,041	S15	66
St. George, Alsk.	187	D5	84
St. George, Austl.	1,698	D9	432
St. George, Bermuda	1,500	A13	233
St. George, N.B., Can.	1,322	D3	70
St. George, Ont., Can.	580	Q20	64
St. George, Charlton, Ga.	582	F4	176
St. George, Pottawatomie, Kans.	259	C7	144
St. George, Knox, Maine	200 (1,588▲)	*D3	204
St. George, St. Louis, Mo.	1,323	*C7	150
St. George, Richmond, N.Y.		E2	212
St. George, Dorchester, S.C.	1,833	E7	188
St. George, Washington, Utah	5,130	F2	114
St. George, Burlington, Vt.	(108▲)	*C2	218
St. George, Greene, Va.	5	B6	192
St. George, cape, Newf., Can.		F6	72
St. George, cape, Fla.		B5	174
St. George, isl., Alsk.		D5	84
St. George, isl., Fla.		B6	174
St. George, pt., Calif.		B1	94
St. George Island, St. Marys, Md.	200	D7	182
St. Georges, Bel.	5,937	D4	282
St. George's, Newf., Can.	700	F6	72
St. Georges, Que., Can.	1,454	R12	66
St. Georges, Que., Can.	385	S13	66
St. Georges, New Castle, Del.	339	B3	172
St. Georges, Fr.Gu.	465	E6	256
St. George's, Grenada	20,900	E14	233
St. Georges, bay, Newf., Can.		F6	72
St. George's, chan., Wales		J6	273
St. George's, isl., Bermuda		A13	233
St. Georges [de Clarenceville], Que., Can.	275	S11	66
St. Georges-Ouest, Que., Can.	3,643	*R14	66
St. Gérard, Que., Can.	665	S13	66
St. Germain, Que., Can.	265	Q15	66
St. Germain [de Grantham], Que., Can.	919	S12	66
St. Germain, Vilas, Wis.	350	C4	160
St. Germain, forest, Fr.		I9	278
Ste. Germaine, Que., Can.	300	R14	66
St. Germain-en-Laye, Fr.	29,429	I9	278
Ste. Gertrude, Que., Can.	376	R12	66
St. Gertrude, St. Tammany, La.	75	*D5	180
St. Gervais, Que., Can.	975	R14	66
St. Giles, Que., Can.	420	R13	66
St. Gilles [-du-Gard], Fr.	4,791	F6	278
St. Girons, Fr.	5,752	F4	278
St. Gotthard, tunnel, Switz.		B4	312
St. Govan's, head, Wales		I8	273
St. Gregoire, Que., Can.	625	R12	66
St. Gregor, Sask., Can.	170	D5	58
St. Gregory, mtn., Newf., Can.		F6	72
St. Guillaume, Que., Can.	802	S12	66
St. Helen, lake, Mich.		E7	146
St. Helena, Napa, Calif.	2,722	C2	94
St. Helena, Cedar, Nebr.	63	B8	152
St. Helena, Pender, N.C.	150	C8	186
St. Helena, par., La.	9,162	D5	180
St. Helena, Br. poss., Afr.	5,032	H6	388
St. Helena, bay, U.S.Afr.		F3	420
St. Helena, isl., S.C.		G7	188
St. Helena, sound, S.C.		G8	188
Ste. Hélène, Que., Can.	810	Q15	66
St. Helens, Eng.	110,900	H10	273
St. Helens, Columbia, Oreg.	5,022	B4	96
St. Helens, mtn., Wash.		C4	98
St. Helier, Jersey	25,364 (*36,100)	L10	273
Ste. Hénédine, Que., Can.	590	R14	66
St. Henri, Que., Can.	661	R13 R16	66
St. Henry, Mercer, Ohio	978	B2	156
St. Hermas, Que., Can.	375	S15	66
St. Herménégilde, Que., Can.	236	S13	66
St. Hilaire, Que., Can.	2,000	S11	66
St. Hilaire, Pennington, Minn.	270	C2	148
St. Hilarion, Que., Can.	385	Q14	66
St. Honoré, Que., Can.	480	Q15	66
St. Honoré, Que., Can.	635	S14	66
St. Hubert, Bel.	3,100	D4	282
St. Hubert, Que., Can.	825	Q15	66
St. Hugues, Que., Can.	487	S12	66
St. Hyacinthe, Que., Can.	20,439	S12	66
St. Hyacinthe, co., Que., Can.	40,302	S11	66
St. Ignace, Mackinac, Mich.	3,334	D7	146
St. Ignatius, Lake, Mont.	940	C2	110
St. Imier, Switz.	5,972	A3	312
St. Inigoes, St. Marys, Md.	125	D7	182
St. Irénée, Que., Can.	475	Q14	66
St. Isidore, Que., Can.	450	S13	66
St. Isidore, Que., Can.	290	S16	66
St. Isidore-de-Prescott, Ont., Can.	480	026	64
St. Ives, Eng.	8,500	K7	273
St. Jacob, Madison, Ill.	529	E4	138
St. Jacobs, Ont., Can.	600	Q20	64
St. Jacques, Que., Can.	1,979	S11	66
St. Jacques, cape, Viet.		E5	362
St. Jacques-le-Mineur, Que., Can.	240	S16	66
St. James, Stone, Ark.	30	B5	170
St. James, Man., Can.	26,502	F4	60
St. James, St. James, La.	280	B6	180
St. James, Charlevoix, Mich.	180	D6	146
St. James, Watonwan, Minn.	4,174	H4	148
St. James, Phelps, Mo.	2,384	D6	150
St. James, Suffolk, N.Y.	3,524	D4	212
St. James, par., La.	18,369	D5	180
St. James, cape, B.C., Can.		E7	52
St. James City, Lee, Fla.	75	E8	174
St. Janvier, Que., Can.	630	S11 S15	66
St. Jean, Que., Can.	24,367	S11	66
St. Jean, co., Que., Can.	34,054	S11	66
St. Jean, riv., Que., Can.		P14	66
St. Jean Baptiste, Man., Can.	1,000	F4	60
St. Jean-Chrysostôme, Que., Can.	485	R16	66
St. Jean-d'Angély, Fr.	7,929	E3	278
St. Jean-de-Dieu, Que., Can.	950	P15	66
St. Jean-de-Luz, Fr.	9,672	F3	278
St. Jean-de-Matha, Que., Can.	995	R11	66
St. Jean-Eudes, Que., Can.	2,560	*P14	66
St. Jean Port Joli, Que., Can.	895	Q14	66
St. Jérôme, Que., Can.	20,645	S10	66
St. Jo, Montague, Tex.	977	C7	130
St. Joachim, Que., Can.	550	Q14	66
St. Joe, Searcy, Ark.	150	A4	170
St. Joe, Benewah, Idaho	50	B2	108
St. Joe, De Kalb, Ind.	499	A5	140
St. Joe, riv., Idaho		B3	108
St. John, N.B., Can.	52,491 (*86,015)	D3	70
St. John, Lake, Ind.	1,128	A2	140
St. John, Stafford, Kans.	1,753	E5	144
St. John, St. Louis, Mo.	7,342	*C7	150
St. John, Whitman, Wash.	545	B9	98
St. John, Aroostook, Maine	400 (407▲)	A4	204
St. John, Rolette, N.Dak.	420	B6	154
St. John, Tooele, Utah		C3	114
St. John, co., N.B., Can.	81,392	D4	70
St. John, bay, Newf., Can.		E7	72
St. John, cape, Newf., Can.		F8	72
St. John, isl., Newf., Can.		E7	72
St. John, isl., Vir.Is.		C12	233
St. John, lake, Newf., Can.		F8	72
St. John, lake, Que., Can.		P12	66
St. John, riv., N.B., Can.		C2	70
St. John, riv., Que., Can.		R14	66
St. John, riv., Maine		B3	204
St. John's, Antigua	10,965	D14	233
St. Johns, Apache, Ariz.	1,318	D6	124
St. John's, Newf., Can.	57,078 (*77,991)	G9	72
St. Johns, Clinton, Mich.	5,629	G7	146
St. Johns, co., Fla.	30,034	B9	174
St. John's, pt., Ire.		G4	273
St. Johns, riv., Fla.		A9	174
St. Johnsbury, Caledonia, Vt.	6,809 (8,869▲)	C4	218
St. Johnsbury Center, Caledonia, Vt.	300	C4	218
St. Johns River, entrance, Fla.		A10	174
St. Johnsville, Montgomery, N.Y.	2,196	B7	212
St. John the Baptist, par., La.	18,439	D5	180
St. Jones, riv., Del.		D3	172
St. Joseph, N.B., Can.	390	D5	70
St. Joseph, Dominica	3,050	E14	233
St. Joseph, Pasco, Fla.	250	C8	174
St. Joseph, Champaign, Ill.	1,210	C5	138
St. Joseph, Daviess, Ky.	30	C3	178
St. Joseph, Tensas, La.	1,653	C4	180
St. Joseph, Berrien, Mich.	11,755	G5	146
St. Joseph, Stearns, Minn.	1,487	F4	148
St. Joseph, Buchanan, Mo.	79,673	B3	150
Saint Joseph, Lawrence, Tenn.	547	C4	190
St. Joseph, co., Ind.	238,614	A3	140
St. Joseph, co., Mich.	42,332	H6	146
St. Joseph, bay, Fla.		B5	174
St. Joseph, isl., Tex.		E7	130
St. Joseph, lake, Ont., Can.		R24	64
St. Joseph, lake, Que., Can.		R15	66
St. Joseph, pt., Fla.		B5	174
St. Joseph, riv., Ind., Mich.		A5	140
Ohio		A2	156
St. Joseph [de Beauce], Que., Can.	2,484	R14	66
St. Joseph-de-St.-Hyacinthe, Que., Can.	2,708	*S12	66
St. Joseph-de-Sorel, Que., Can.	3,571	*R11	66
St. Joseph-du-Lac, Que., Can.	410	S15	66
St. Joseph's, Newf., Can.	300	G9	72
St. Josephs, sound, Fla.		B5	174
St. Jovite, Que., Can.	1,613	R10	66
St. Jovite-Station, Que., Can.	225	R10	66
St. Jude, Que., Can.	690	S12	66
Ste. Julie, Que., Can.	240	R13	66
Ste. Julienne, Que., Can.	710	S11	66
St. Junien, Fr.	8,039	E4	278
Ste. Justine, Que., Can.	495	S10	66
St. Kilda, N.Z.	6,946	F3	437
St. Kilda, isl., Scot.		D4	272
St. Kitts (St. Christopher), ter., W.I.Fed.	33,550	D14	233
St. Lambert, Que, Can.	520	R13	66
St. Lambert, Que., Can.	12,224	S16	66
St. Landry, Evangeline, La.	425	D3	180
St. Landry, par., La.	81,493	D3	180
St. Laurent, Man., Can.	280	E4	60
St. Laurent, Que., Can.	38,291	S16	66
St. Laurent, Fr.Gu.	2,185	D6	256
St. Lawrence, Austl.	290	C9	432
St. Lawrence, Newf., Can.	1,837	G8	72
St. Lawrence, Hand, S.Dak.	290	C7	158
St. Lawrence, co., N.Y.	111,239	A6	212
St. Lawrence, cape, N.S., Can.		B9	70
St. Lawrence, gulf, Newf., Can.		E9	72
St. Lawrence, gulf, Que., Can.		Q10	66
St. Lawrence, isl., Alsk.		C4	84
St. Lawrence, riv., Can., U.S.		H12 B13	48 77
St. Lazare, Man., Can.	323	E2	60
St. Lazare, Que., Can.	345	S15	66
St. Leo, Pasco, Fla.	278	C8	174
St. Leo, Yellow Medicine, Minn.	129	G2	148
St. Léon, Que., Can.	230	R12	66
St. Leon, Dearborn, Ind.	319	C5	140
St. Leonard, N.B., Can.	1,593	B2	70
St. Léonard, Que., Can.	650	R13	66
St. Leonard, Calvert, Md.	140	D6	182
St. Léonard [d'Aston], Que., Can.	751	R12	66
St. Léonard [-de-Noblat], Fr.		E4	278
St. Lewis, riv., Newf., Can.		D7	72
St. Lewis, sound, Newf., Can.		D8	72
St. Liboire, Que., Can.	613	S12	66
St. Libory, Howard, Nebr.	150	C7	152
St. Lô, Fr.	11,778	C3	278
St. Louis, P.E.I., Can.	215	C5	70
St. Louis, Que., Can.	550	S12	66
St. Louis, Sask., Can.	165	D5	58
St. Louis, Iberville, La.		B5	180

St. Louis, Gratiot, Mich. 3,808 F7 146
St. Louis (Independent City), Mo. 750,026 B8 150 (*2,050,800) C7
St. Louis, Pottawatomie, Okla. 76 C7 128
St. Louis, Sen. 65,278 C1 408
St. Louis, co., Minn. 231,588 D6 148
St. Louis, co., Mo. 703,532 C7 150
St. Louis, bay, Miss. E1 184
St. Louis, lake, Que., Can. S15 66
St. Louis, riv., Minn. E6 148
St. Louis [de Gonzague], Que., Can. 575 S11 66
St. Louis de Kent, N.B., Can. 485 C5 70
St. Louis-du-Ha-Ha, Que., Can. 780 Q15 66
Ste. Louise, Que., Can. 550 Q14 66
St. Louis Park, Hennepin, Minn. 43,310 F6 148
St. Louisville, Licking, Ohio 349 B4 156
St. Lucas, Fayette, Iowa 211 A6 142
St. Lucia, ter., W.I.Fed. 86,000 E14 233
St. Lucia, cape, U.S.Afr. E6 421
St. Lucia, chan., W.I. E14 233
Ste. Lucie, Que., Can. 475 R10 66
St. Lucie, St. Lucie, Fla. 350 D10 174
St. Lucie, co., Fla. 39,294 D10 174
St. Lucie, canal, Fla. D10 174
St. Lucie, inlet, Fla. D10 174
Ste. Lucie [de Beauregard], Que., Can. R14 66
St. Ludger, Que., Can. 301 S14 66
Ste. Madeleine, Que., Can. 825 S11 66
St. Magloire, Que., Can. 795 R14 66
St. Magnu, bay, Scot. A11 272
St. Maixent-l'École, Fr. 7,288 D3 278
St. Malachie, Que., Can. 525 R14 66
St. Malo, Fr. 14,339 C2 278
St. Malo, gulf, Fr. C2 278
St. Mandé, Fr. 24,522 I10 278
St. Marc, Que., Can. 330 S11 66
St. Marc, Hai. 9,401 C8 233
St. Marc [des Carrières], Que., Can. 2,457 R12 66
St. Marcel, Que., Can. 500 R14 66
St. Marcellin, Fr. E6 278
St. Margaret, bay, Newf., Can. E7 72
St. Margarets, Anne Arundel, Md. 75 B7 182
St. Margaret's, bay, N.S., Can. E6 70
St. Margrethen, see Sankt Margrethen, Switz.
Ste. Marguerite, Que., Can. 340 R14 66
Ste. Marguerite, riv., Que., Can. P14 66
Ste. Marie, Que., Can. 265 R12 66
Ste. Marie, Que., Can. 3,094 R13 66
Ste. Marie, cape, Malag. E8 421
Ste. Marie, isl., Malag. C9 421
St. Maries, Benewah, Idaho 2,435 B2 108
St. Mark, Sedgwick, Kans. 35 A5 144
St. Marks, Wakulla, Fla. 350 A6 174
Ste. Marthe, Que., Can. 264 S10 66
St. Martin, Que., Can. 6,440 *S15 66
St. Martin, Stearns, Minn. 215 F4 148
St. Martin, par., La. 29,063 D4 180
St. Martin, isl., Mich. D5 146
St. Martin, isl., W.I. C13 233
St. Martin, riv., Md. D9 182
Ste. Martine, Que., Can. 580 S11 66 S15
St. Martins, N.B., Can. 555 D4 70
St. Martins, Milwaukee, Wis. (part of Franklin) F1 160
St. Martins College, Thurston, Wash. 700 *B4 98
St. Martin Station, Man., Can. 65 E3 60
St. Martinville, St. Martin, La. 6,468 D4 180
St. Mary, Marion, Ky. 250 C5 178
St. Mary, Johnson, Nebr. 62 *D9 152
St. Mary, par., La. 48,833 E4 180
St. Mary, bay, N.S., Can. E3 70
St. Mary, cape, N.S., Can. E3 70
St. Mary, riv., Alta., Can. F6 54
St. Mary-of-the-Woods, Vigo, Ind. 700 C2 140
St. Marys (Andreafski), Alsk. 258 *C5 84
St. Mary's, Newf., Can. 600 G9 72
St. Marys, Ont., Can. 4,185 Q19 64
St. Marys, Camden, Ga. 3,272 F5 176
St. Marys, Warren, Iowa 91 *C4 142
St. Marys, Pottawatomie, Kans. 1,509 C7 144
St. Marys, Ste. Genevieve, Mo. 620 D8 150
St. Marys, Auglaize, Ohio 7,737 B2 156
St. Marys, Elk, Pa. 8,065 B3 214
St. Marys, Pleasants, W.Va. 2,443 B3 194
St. Marys, co., Md. 38,915 D6 182
St. Mary's, bay, Newf., Can. G9 72
St. Mary's, cape, Newf., Can. G8 72
St. Mary's, entrance, Fla., Ga. A9 174 F5 176
St. Marys, riv., N.S., Can. D8 70
St. Marys, riv., Fla., Ga. A9 174 F5 176
St. Marys, riv., Ind., Ohio B5 140 B2 156
St. Marys, riv., Md. D6 182
St. Marys College, Contra Costa, Calif. 700 A5 94
St. Mary's Point, Washington, Minn. 271 *G6 148
St. Mathieu, Que., Can. 545 P15 66
St. Matthew, isl., Alsk. C4 84
St. Matthew, isl., Bur. E3 362
St. Matthews, Jefferson, Ky. 8,738 A5 178 B5
St. Matthews, Calhoun, S.C. 2,433 D7 188
St. Maur-des-Fossés, Fr. 64,387 I10 278
St. Maurice, Que., Can. 600 R12 66
St. Maurice, Switz. 2,728 B3 312
St. Maurice, co., Que., Can. 102,050 R11 66
St. Maurice, riv., Que., Can. R12 66 Q11
St. Maxime, Que., Can. 210 R13 66
St. Meinrad, Spencer, Ind. 850 D3 140
Ste. Mélanie, Que., Can. 300 R11 66
Ste. Menehould, Fr. C6 278
St. Méthode, Que., Can. 650 R13 66
St. Michael, Alsk. 157 C5 84
St. Michael, Alta., Can. 250 D6 54
St. Michael, Wright, Minn. 707 F5 148
St. Michael, Buffalo, Nebr. 17 *D7 152
St. Michael, Cambria, Pa. 1,292 *C3 214
St. Michaels, Apache, Ariz. 400 C6 124
St. Michaels, Talbot, Md. 1,484 C7 182
St. Michaels, bay, Newf., Can. D8 72
St. Michel, Que., Can. 675 R14 66
St. Michel, Que., Can. 315 S16 66
St. Michel-de-l'Atalaye, Hai. 2,236 C8 233
St. Mihiel, Fr. 5,035 C6 278
St. Modeste, Que., Can. 295 Q15 66
Ste. Monique, Que., Can. 201 R12 66
St. Moritz, see Sankt Moritz, Switz.
St. Nazaire, Que., Can. 485 S12 66
St. Nazaire, Fr. 39,350 D2 278
St. Nazianz, Manitowoc, Wis. 669 B6 160 D6
St. Nérée, Que., Can. 510 R14 66
St. Nicholas, Que., Can. 340 R15 66
St. Noël, Que., Can. 1,027 *Q10 66
St. Norbert, Man., Can. 750 F4 60
St. Norbert [d'Arthabaska], Que., Can. 275 R13 66
St. Odilon, Que., Can. 435 R14 66
St. Olaf, Clayton, Iowa 169 B6 142
St. Omer, Fr. 19,280 B5 278
St. Onge, Lawrence, S.Dak. 100 C2 158
Saintonge, former prov., Fr. 286,000 E3 278
St. Ouen, Fr. 48,112 I10 278
St. Ours, Que., Can. 691 S11 66
St. Pacôme, Que., Can. 1,283 Q15 66
St. Pamphile, Que., Can. 975 R15 66
St. Paris, Champaign, Ohio 1,460 B3 156
St. Pascal, Que., Can. 1,962 Q15 66
St. Paul, Alsk. 359 D4 84
St. Paul, Madison, Ark. 118 B3 170
St. Paul, Alta., Can. 2,229 C7 54
St. Paul, Que., Can. 575 Q15 66
St. Paul, Que., Can. 835 R14 66
St. Paul, Decatur and Shelby, Ind. 702 C4 140
St. Paul, Lee, Iowa 128 D6 142
St. Paul, Neosha, Kans. 675 E8 144
St. Paul, Ramsey, Minn. 313,411 F7 148 G5
St. Paul, Howard, Nebr. 1,714 C7 152
St. Paul, Marion, Oreg. 254 B1 96
St. Paul, Clarendon, S.C. 75 D8 188
St. Paul, Wise, Va. 1,156 D2 192
St. Paul, isl., Alsk. D4 84
St. Paul, isl., N.S., Can. B9 70
St. Paul, riv., Newf., Can. E10 72
St. Paul, riv., Lib. E2 408
St. Paul du Nord, Que., Can. 320 P15 66
St. Paulin, Que., Can. 943 R11 66
St. Paul Park, Washington, Minn. 3,267 G6 148 G7
St. Pauls, Blaine, Mont. 75 C8 110
St. Pauls, Robeson, N.C. 2,249 C7 186
Ste. Perpétue, Que., Can. 515 Q15 66
Ste. Perpétue, Que., Can. 475 R12 66
St. Peter, Graham, Kans. 60 C3 144
St. Peter, Nicollet, Minn. 8,484 G5 148
St. Peter, Cascade, Mont. 75 C5 110
St. Peter, lake, Que., Can. R12 66
St. Peter Port, Guernsey 16,800 *L10 273
St. Peters, N.S., Can. 800 D9 70
St. Peters, Logan, Colo. B8 106
St. Peters, St. Charles, Mo. 404 A7 150 C7
St. Peters Bay, P.E.I., Can. 308 C7 70
St. Petersburg, Pinellas, Fla. 181,298 C6 174 (*355,200) D8
St. Petersburg Beach, Pinellas, Fla. 6,268 *D8 174
Ste. Pétronille, Que., Can. 409 R16 66
St. Philémon, Que., Can. 490 R14 66
St. Philip, Posey, Ind. 100 E2 140
St. Philippe, Que., Can. 510 S11 66 S16
St. Philippe de Néri, Que., Can. 650 Q15 66
St. Phillips, Wibaux, Mont. 30 D12 110
Ste. Philomène, Que., Can. 595 S11 66 S15
St. Pie, Que., Can. 1,228 S12 66
St. Pierre, Que., Can. 350 R14 66
St. Pierre, Mart. 3,942 E14 233 (5,498▲)
St. Pierre, St. Pierre & Miquelon 3,997 G7 72
St. Pierre, isl., N.A. G7 72
St. Pierre & Miquelon, Fr. poss., N.A. 4,606 G7 72
St. Pierre-Jolys, Man., Can. 838 F4 60
St. Pierre [les Becquets], Que., Can. 388 R12 66
St. Pius, Stark, N.Dak. 75 D3 154
St. Placide, Que., Can. 305 S14 66
St. Pol [-de-Léon], Fr. 6,037 C2 278
St. Pol [-sur-Ternoise], Fr. 5,087 B5 278
St. Prime, Que., Can. 629 P12 66
St. Prosper, Que., Can. 425 R12 66
St. Prosper, Que., Can. 990 R14 66
St. Quentin, N.B., Can. 935 B2 70
St. Quentin, Fr. 53,866 C5 278
St. Raphaël, Que., Can. 1,059 R14 66
St. Raphaël, Fr. 7,044 F7 278
St. Raymond, Que., Can. 3,502 R13 66
St. Rédempteur, Que., Can. 872 R16 66
St. Regis, Mineral, Mont. 600 C1 110
St. Regis, riv., N.Y. A7 212
St. Regis Falls, Franklin, N.Y. 400 A7 212
St. Regis Park, Jefferson, Ky. 1,179 *B5 178
St. Rémi, Que., Can. 2,303 S11 66 S16
St. Rémi, Que., Can. 425 S13 66
St. Rémi d'Amherst, Que., Can. 740 R10 66
St. Robert, Que., Can. 475 S11 66
St. Robert, Pulaski, Mo. 860 *D5 150
St. Roch, Que., Can. 510 S11 66
St. Roch-des-Aulnaies, Que., Can. 335 Q14 66
St. Romain, Que., Can. 600 S13 66
St. Romuald, Que., Can. 4,000 R13 66 R16
Ste. Rosalie, Que., Can. 1,142 *S12 66
Ste. Rose, Que., Can. 5,378 S11 66 S15
Ste. Rose, Guad. 1,288 D14 233 (8,184▲)
St. Rose, St. Charles, La. 1,099 C7 180
Ste. Rose-de-Lima, Que., Can. 2,475 S9 66
Ste. Rose-du-Dégelé, Que., Can. 1,380 Q16 66
Ste. Rose-du-Lac, Man., Can. 740 F3 60
Ste. Sabine, Que., Can. 390 R14 66
St. Samuel, Que., Can. 535 S14 66
St. Sauveur [des Montagnes], Que., Can. 1,316 S10 66
Ste. Savine, Fr. 10,947 C6 278
Ste. Scholastique, Que., Can. 865 S10 66 S15
St. Sébastien, Que., Can. 473 S14 66
St. Sébastien, cape, Malag. B9 421
St. Servan [-sur-Mer], Fr. 13,763 C3 278
St. Séverin, Que., Can. 265 R13 66
St. Shotts, Newf., Can. 140 G9 72
St. Siméon, Que., Can. 1,114 Q15 66
St. Simon, Que., Can. 535 P15 66
St. Simons, isl., Ga. E5 176
St. Simons, sound, Ga. E5 176
St. Simons Island, Glynn, Ga. 3,199 E5 176
Ste. Sophie, Que., Can. 445 R12 66
Ste. Sophie, Que., Can. 560 R13 66
St. Stanislas [de Champlain], Que., Can. 628 R12 66
St. Stephen, N.B., Can. 3,491 D2 70
St. Stephen, Berkeley, S.C. 1,462 E9 188
St. Stephens, Stearns, Minn. 276 F4 148
St. Stephens, Fremont, Wyo. 5 D4 116
St. Sylvestre, Que., Can. 476 R13 66
St. Tammany, St. Tammany, La. 50 B8 180 D6
St. Tammany, par., La. 38,643 D5 180
Ste. Thècle, Que., Can. 1,499 R12 66
St. Théodore, Que., Can. 315 R11 66
St. Théophile, Que., Can. 400 S14 66
Ste. Thérèse [de Blainville], Que., Can. 8,266 S11 66 S15
St. Thomas, Ont., Can. 19,129 R19 64
St. Thomas, Que., Can. 475 *R11 66
St. Thomas, Las Animas, Colo. 450 E6 106
St. Thomas, Cole, Mo. 180 C5 150
St. Thomas, Pembina, N.Dak. 660 B8 154
St. Thomas, isl., Vir.Is. C12 233
St. Thuribe, Que., Can. 510 R12 66
St. Timothée, Que., Can. 688 S15 66
St. Tite, Que., Can. 3,183 R12 66
St. Tite-des-Caps, Que., Can. 625 Q14 66
St. Tropez, Fr. 3,988 F7 278
St. Ubald, Que., Can. 775 R12 66
St. Urbain, Que., Can. 680 Q14 66
St. Urbain, Que., Can. 315 S15 66
St. Valère, Que., Can. 290 R12 66
St. Valérien, Que., Can. 355 S12 66
St. Vallier, Que., Can. 525 R14 66
St. Vallier, Fr. E6 278
St. Victor [de Beauce], Que., Can. 684 R14 66
St. Vincent, Kittson, Minn. 217 C1 148
St. Vincent, ter., W.I.Fed. 75,000 E14 233
St. Vincent, cape, Malag. D8 421
St. Vincent, cape, Port. D2 298
St. Vincent, gulf, Austl. F7 432
St. Vincent, isl., Fla. B5 174
St. Vincent, passage, W.I. E14 233
St. Vincent-de-Paul, Que., Can. 6,784 S16 66
St. Vincent's, Newf., Can. 400 G9 72
St. Vith, Bel. 2,688 D5 282
St. Vrain, Curry, N.Mex. 15 D7 126
St. Walburg, Sask., Can. 618 D3 58
St. Wendel, Manitowoc, Wis. 100 B6 160
St. Wendells, Posey and Vanderburgh, Ind. 160 D2 140
St. Williams, Ont., Can. 390 R20 64
St. Xavier, Big Horn, Mont. 75 E9 110
St. Yrieix-la-Perche, Fr. 4,368 E4 278
St. Zacharie, Que., Can. 385 R14 66
St. Zéphirin, Que., Can. 415 R12 66
Saipan, chan., Saipan B7 436
Saipan, isl., Pac.O. B7 436
Sa'ir, Jordan 3,000 C6 382
Saishū, isl., Kor. I13 348
Saishū, see Cheju, isl., Kor.
Saito Grande, Braz. E1 258
Saiun, Aden 9,707 D4 383
Saiyidābād, Afg. 10,000 B5 374
Sajó, riv., Hung. A5 320
Saka, Ken. C6 414
Sakai, Jap. 251,793 M11 354
Sakākā, Sau.Ar. 10,000 B3 383
Sakania, Con.L. 25,095 E4 414
Sakaraha, Malag. D8 421
Sakarya, prov., Tur. 298,488 *A4 307
Sakarya, riv., Tur. A4 307
Sakashita, Jap. 6,376 L13 354
Sakata, Jap. 96,735 E7 354
Sakchu, Kor. 13,568 E12 348
Sakhalin, isl., Sov.Un. D16 329
Sakimotobu, Okinawa 20,409 C1 436
Sakishima, is., Ryūkyū Is., Jap. M12 349
Sakmara, riv., Sov.Un. B5 336
Sakon Nakhon, Thai. 103,198 C4 362
Sakon Nakhon, prov., Thai. 273,262 *C4 362
Sakonnet, Newport, R.I. 100 D4 216
Sakonnet, pt., R.I. D4 216
Sakonnet, riv., R.I. C4 216
Sak'ot'a, Eth. C4 398
Sakripe, Lib. E3 408
Sakskøbing, Den. 2,578 G2 292
Sakti, India 4,187 E3 368
Sakyany, Sov.Un. E3 336
Säkylä, Fin. F10 291
Sal, pt., Calif. E3 94
Sal, riv., Sov.Un. C2 336
Sala, Swe. 10,638 B7 292
Sala Consilina, It. 6,897 E5 302
Saladas, Arg. 3,900 A4 252
Saladillo, Arg. 7,586 C4 252
Salado, Independence, Ark. 250 B5 170
Salado, riv., Arg. B2 252
Salado, riv., Arg. B3 252
Salado, riv., Arg. F4 251
Salado, riv., Mex. B5 225
Salado, riv., N.Mex. D3 126
Salaga, Ghana 3,156 E4 408
Salajar, is., Indon. F6 358
Salala, Om. D5 383
Salamá, Guat. 2,760 C2 228
Salamá, Hond. 1,261 C4 228
Salamanca, Chile 2,819 B1 252
Salamanca, Mex. 20,586 C5 225 K13
Salamanca, Cattaraugus, N.Y. 8,480 C3 212
Salamanca, Sp. 74,223 B4 298
Salamanca, prov., Sp. 415,127 *B4 298
Salamava, N.Gui. 270 F11 359
Salamina, Col. 7,940 B1 244
Salamis, Grc. 8,347 C4 306
Salamonia, Jay, Ind. 142 B5 140
Salamonie, riv., Ind. B4 140
Salangen, Nor. B8 290
Salas, Sp. 2,522 A3 298
Salaverry, Peru 3,403 B2 245
Salavina, Arg. A3 252
Salawati, is., Neth.N.Gui. E8 359
Sala y Gómez, isl., Pac.O. D5 436
Salbani, India I8 366
Saldanha, U.S.Afr. 1,806 F3 420
Saldus, Sov.Un. 8,400 D4 332
Sale City, Mitchell, Ga. 275 E2 176
Sale Creek, Hamilton, Tenn. 700 C6 190
Salekhard, Sov.Un. 16,000 C8 328
Salem, Lee, Ala. 300 C4 168
Salem, Fulton, Ark. 713 A5 170
Salem, Saline, Ark. 25 D6 170
Salem, New London, Conn. 300 D6 202 (925▲)
Salem, Taylor, Fla. 200 B7 174
Salem, Madison, Idaho F7 108
Salem, Marion, Ill. 6,165 E5 138
Salem, India 202,335 F3 366
Salem, Washington, Ind. 4,546 D3 140
Salem, Henry, Iowa 442 D6 142
Salem, Livingston, Ky. 480 C2 178
Salem, Franklin, Maine 50 D2 204 (67▲)
Salem, Essex, Mass. 39,211 A6 206 C3
Salem, Washtenaw, Mich. 250 B7 146
Salem, Dent, Mo. 3,870 D6 150
Salem, Richardson, Nebr. 261 D10 152
Salem, Rockingham, N.H. 950 F4 208 (9,210▲)
Salem, Salem, N.J. 8,941 D2 210
Salem, Dona Ana, N.Mex. 175 F3 126
Salem, Washington, N.Y. 1,076 B8 212
Salem, Columbiana, Ohio 13,854 B6 156
Salem, Marion, Oreg. 49,142 C1 96 C4
Salem, Oconee, S.C. 206 B3 188
Salem, McCook, S.Dak. 1,188 D8 158
Salem, Utah, Utah 920 C4 114
Salem, Roanoke, Va. 16,058 C4 192
Salem, Harrison, W.Va. 2,366 B4 194 B6
Salem, Kenosha, Wis. 500 F1 160
Salem, co., N.J. 58,711 D2 210
Salem, fork, W.Va. B6 194
Salem, plat., Mo. D6 150
Salem, pond, Vt. B4 218
Salem, riv., N.J. D2 210
Salemburg, Sampson, N.C. 569 B7 186
Salem Depot, Rockingham, N.H. 2,523 F4 208
Salem Heights, Marion, Oreg. 10,770 *C4 96
Salemi, It. 13,300 G4 302
Salen, Scot. E7 272
Salen, lake, Swe. E5 292
Salerno, Martin, Fla. 867 D10 174
Salerno, It. 76,200 E5 302 (95,200▲)
Salerno, prov., It. 868,200 *E5 302
Salerno, gulf, It. E5 302
Sales, point, Eng. J13 273
Salfit, Jordan 2,000 B6 382
Salgótarján, Hung. 25,000 A4 320
Salgueiro, Braz. 3,523 B3 258
Salhia, Eg., U.A.R. 8,190 E6 395
Salida, Stanislaus, Calif. 1,109 D3 94
Salida, Chaffee, Colo. 4,560 D5 106
Salima, Rh.&Nya. 1,450 B6 421
Salin, Bur. B2 362
Salina, Saline, Kans. 43,202 D6 144
Salina, Mayes, Okla. 972 B8 128
Salina, Sevier, Utah 1,618 E4 114
Salina, isl., It. F5 302
Salina Cruz, Mex. 8,243 D6 225
Salinas, Braz. 3,523 D2 258
Salinas, Monterey, Calif. 28,957 D3 94
Salinas, Ec. 2,672 A1 245
Salinas, cape, Sp. C8 298
Salinas, pampa, Arg. B2 252
Salinas, peak, N.Mex. E4 126
Salinas, pt., Ang. B2 420
Salinas, riv., Calif. D3 94
Salinas de Garci Mendoza, Bol. 635 C1 246
Salinas Grandes, salt flat, Arg. B2 252
Saline, Bienville, La. 329 B3 180
Saline, Washtenaw, Mich. 2,334 G8 146
Saline, co., Ark. 28,956 C4 170
Saline, co., Ill. 26,227 F5 138
Saline, co., Kans. 54,715 D6 144
Saline, co., Mo. 25,148 B4 150
Saline, co., Nebr. 12,542 D8 152
Saline, bayou, La. B3 180
Saline, lake, La. C3 180
Saline, riv., Ark. D4 170

Saline, riv., Ill. F5 138
Saline, riv., Kans. C4 144
Saline City, Clay, Ind. 90 C2 140
Salineville, Columbiana, Ohio 1,898 B6 156
Salins-les-Bains, Fr. 4,930 D6 278
Salisbury, N.B., Can. 325 C4 70
Salisbury, Litchfield, Conn. 368 (3,309▲) B2 202
Salisbury, Eng. 34,000 J11 273
Salisbury, Wicomico, Md. 16,302 D8 182
Salisbury, Essex, Mass. 950 (3,154▲) A6 206
Salisbury, Chariton, Mo. 1,787 B5 150
Salisbury, Merrimack, N.H. 100 (415▲) E3 208
Salisbury, Rowan, N.C. 21,297 B5 186
Salisbury, Somerset, Pa. 862 D2 214
Salisbury, Rh.&Nya. 140,000 (*210,000) C6 421
Salisbury, Addison, Vt. 130 (575▲) D2 218
Salisbury, isl., N.W.Ter., Can. E11 48
Salisbury, plain, Eng. J11 273
Salisbury Beach, Essex, Mass. 350 *A6 206
Salisbury West, Rowan, N.C. 1,323 *B5 186
Salitpa, Clarke, Ala. 425 D1 168
Salix, Woodbury, Iowa 394 B1 142
Salkehatchie, riv., S.C. E6 188
Salkum, Lewis, Wash. 200 C4 98
Salla, Fin. C13 290
Salley, Aiken, S.C. 403 D6 188
Salliqueló, Arg. 3,938 C3 252
Sallis, Attala, Miss. 223 B3 184
Sallisaw, Sequoyah, Okla. 3,351 C9 128
Salmo, B.C., Can. 846 F14 52
Salmon, Lemhi, Idaho 2,944 D5 108
Salmon, mtn., N.H. A4 208
Salmon, peak, Tex. E5 130
Salmon, res., N.Y. B6 212
Salmon, riv., B.C., Can. C11 52
Salmon, riv., N.B., Can. C4 70
Salmon, riv., Idaho D3 108
Salmon, riv., N.Y. A7 212
Salmon Arm, B.C., Can. 1,344 E13 52
Salmon Creek, Clark, Wash. 175 D4 98
Salmon Falls, Strafford, N.H. 1,210 E5 208
Salmon Falls, creek, Nev. B7 112
Salmon Falls, riv., Idaho G4 108
Salmon Falls, riv., N.H. E5 208
Salmon Gums, Austl. 172 E4 432
Salmon River, mts., Idaho D3 108
Salmon River, res., Idaho G4 108
Salmon Valley, B.C., Can. C11 52
Salo, Fin. 9,398 F10 291
Salome, Yuma, Ariz. 400 E2 124
Salon-de-Provence, Fr. 12,455 F6 278
Salonika, see Thessaloníki, Grc.
Salonika, see Thessaloníki, prov., Grc.
Salonika, gulf, Grc. A4 306
Salonta, Rom. 16,276 A1 321
Salpi, lake, It. E6 302
Salsacate, Arg. B2 252
Salsk, Sov.Un. 18,500 I13 332
Salsomaggiore, It. 8,600 C2 302
Salt, creek, Ind. D3 140
Salt, creek, Nebr. E2 152
Salt, creek, Wyo. C6 116
Salt, fork, Okla. D4 128
Salt, fork, Okla. B5 128
Salt, lake, Austl. C2 432
Salt, lake, Sask., Can. D7 58
Salt, lake, Haw. G10 86
Salt, lake, N.Mex. D7 126
Salt, lake, N.Mex. F7 126
Salt, marsh, Kans. D5 144
Salt, riv., Ariz. E4 124
Salt, riv., India I9 366
Salt, riv., Ky. C5 178
Salt, riv., Mo. A5 150
Salta, Arg. 67,403 B4 250
Salta, prov., Arg. 402,600 C4 250
Saltair, Salt Lake, Utah 60 C3 114
Saltash, Eng. 7,500 K8 273
Salt Ash, mtn., Vt. D3 218
Saltburn [-& Marske]-by-the-Sea, Eng. 9,100 G12 273
Saltcoats, Sask., Can. 506 E6 58
Saltdal, Nor. C6 290
Saltee, is., Ire. I6 273
Salter, Butler, Kans. B6 144
Salter Path, Carteret, N.C. 135 C9 186
Salters, Williamsburg, S.C. 100 D9 188
Saltese, Mineral, Mont. 87 C1 110
Saltfjord, fjord, Nor. C6 290
Saltfork, Grant, Okla. 35 B6 128
Salt Fork, creek, Kans. E4 144
Salt Fork, riv., Okla. B6 128
Saltholm, isl., Den. F3 292
Saltillo, Washington, Ind. 121 D3 140
Saltillo, Mex. 69,869 B5 225
Saltillo, Lee, Miss. 536 A4 184
Saltillo, Hardin, Tenn. 397 C3 190
Salt Lake, co., Utah 383,035 C3 114
Salt Lake City, Salt Lake, Utah 189,454 (*410,200) C4 114
Salt Lick, Bath, Ky. 370 B7 178
Salto, Ur. 55,000 B4 252
Salto, dept., Ur. 100,840 B4 252
Salton, sea, Calif. F6 94
Saltonstall, lake, Conn. D4 202
Salt Peter, cave, Ga. B2 176
Saltpond, Ghana 6,968 E4 408
Salt River, mts., Ariz. H2 124
Salt River, range, Wyo. C2 116
Salt Rock, Cabell, W.Va. 150 C2 194
Saltrou, Hai. 1,106 C8 233
Saltsburg, Indiana, Pa. 1,054 C2 214
Saltsjuöbaden, Swe. 5,041 B9 292
Saltspring, isl., B.C., Can. F11 52
Saltville, Smyth and Washington, Va. 2,844 D3 192
Saluda, Polk, N.C. 570 B3 186
Saluda, Saluda, S.C. 2,089 C5 188
Saluda, Middlesex, Va. 300 C8 192
Saluda, co., S.C. 14,554 C5 188
Saluda, riv., S.C. C4 188
C5
Saluda Gardens, Lexington, S.C. 2,000 *D6 188
Salûm, Eg., U.A.R. 1,011 A2 395
Salur, India 24,405 E4 366
Saluzzo, It. 11,100 C1 302
Salvador, Braz. 532,619 C3 258
Salvador, Sask., Can. 145 D3 58
Salvador, El, see El Salvador, N.A.
Salvador, lake, La. E5 180
Salvage, Newf., Can. 150 F9 72
Salvatierra, Mex. 13,250 K13 225
Salvisa, Mercer, Ky. 500 C6 178
Salween, riv., Bur. C3 362
Salyersville, Magoffin, Ky. 1,173 C7 178
Salym, marsh, Sov.Un. A8 336
Salzach, riv., Aus. C5 313
Salzburg, Aus. 102,927 C5 313
Salzburg, state, Aus. 327,232 *C4 313
Salzgitter, Ger. 99,500 B4 286
Salzwedel, Ger. 21,800 B4 286
Samaipata, Bol. 1,656 C2 246
Samalá, riv., Guat. C2 228
Samaná, Dom.Rep. 2,477 C10 233
Samaná, bay, Dom.Rep. C10 233
Samana, isl., W.I. A8 232
Samandira, Tur. G13 307
Samaniego, Col. 2,303 C1 244
Samannûd, Eg., U.A.R. 23,300 D2 382
Samantha, Tuscaloosa, Ala. 187 B2 168
Samar, isl., Pac.O. C2 436
Samar, isl., Phil. B7 358
Samara, riv., Sov.Un. B4 336
Samarai, Pap. G12 359
Samaria, Oneida, Idaho 150 G6 108
Samarinda, Indon. 11,086 E5 358
Samarkand, Sov.Un. 195,000 F8 328
Sāmarrā, Iraq 8,867 B5 378
Samastipur, India D4 368
Samata, Samoa 469 E4 436
Samāwa, Iraq 19,018 D6 378
Sambalpur, India 23,525 D4 366
Sambar, cape, Indon. E4 358
Sambas, Indon. 12,000 D3 358
Sambava, Malag. B10 421
Sambhal, India 61,429 C2 368
Sambhar, India D1 368
Sambor, Sov.Un. 41,200 H4 332
Samborombón, bay, Arg. C4 252
Sambre, riv., Bel. D3 282
Samburg, Obion, Tenn. 451 B2 190
Same, Tan. 4,428 C6 414
Sameden, Switz. 1,685 B5 312
Samit, Camb. E4 362
Sammamish, lake, Wash. D3 98
Sam Neua, Laos B4 362
Samnū, Libya B2 394
Samoa, Humboldt, Calif. 600 B1 94
Samoa Islands, U.S. poss., Pac.O. 18,937 D4 436
Samoa, is., Pac.O. D4 436
Samokov, Bul. 16,919 B1 317
Sámos, prov., Grc. 59,709 C6 306
Sámos, isl., Grc. C6 306
Samoset, Manatee, Fla. 4,824 *D8 174
Samosir, isl., Indon. D1 358
Samothráki, isl., Grc. A5 306
Sampacho, Arg. 3,554 B3 252
Sampit, Indon. E4 358
Sampit, riv., S.C. E10 188
Sample, Breckinridge, Ky. 300 C4 178
Sampson, Saint Johns, Fla. 50 B10 174
Sampson, co., N.C. 48,013 C7 186
Sampwe, Con.L. D4 414
Samrong, Camb. D4 362
Samsö, isl., Den. I4 291
Samsö Belt, strait, Den. F1 292
Samson, Geneva, Ala. 1,932 D3 168
Samstown, Iberville, La. B5 180
Samsun, Tur. 62,648 A7 307
Samsun, prov., Tur. 551,125 *A6 307
Sams Valley, Jackson, Oreg. E4 96
Samthar, India D2 368
Samtown, Rapides, La. 4,008 *C3 180
Samū', Jordan 3,000 C6 382
Samuel, hill, Ky. A5 178
Samuels, Bonner, Idaho 10 A2 108
Samuels, Nelson, Ky. 250 C5 178
Samui, isl., Thai. E4 362
Samutprakan, prov., Thai. 164,227 *D4 362
Samutsakhon, prov., Thai. 112,052 *D4 362
Samutsongkhram, prov., Thai. 125,328 *D4 362
Samwari, Pak. E5 375
San, Mali 6,900 D4 408
San, riv., Camb. D5 362
San, riv., Pol. C6 325
San'a, Yemen 60,000 D3 383
San Acacio, Costilla, Colo. 150 E5 106
Sanaga, riv., Cam. F7 409
San Agustín, Arg. B2 252
San Agustín, Col. 2,493 C1 244
Sanak, Alsk. 7 E5 84
Sanak, isl., Alsk. E5 84
San Ambrosia, isl., Pac.O. D6 436
Sanana, isl., Indon. E7 358
Sanandaj, Iran 40,641 B2 379
San Andreas, Calaveras, Calif. 1,416 C3 94
San Andrés, Mex. 1,999 G10 224
San Andrés, isl., Col. D7 228
San Andres, mts., N.Mex. F4 126
San Andrés Tetepilco, Mex. 11,266 G10 224
San Andrés Tomatlan, Mex. G10 224
San Andrés Tuxtla, Mex. 15,116 D6 225
San Angelo, Tom Green, Tex. 58,815 D5 130
San Anselmo, Marin, Calif. 11,584 *C2 94
San Antioco, isl., It. F2 302
San Antonio, Arg. B4 250
San Antonio, Chile A1 252
San Antonio, Chile 18,394 B1 252
San Antonio, Pasco, Fla. 479 C8 174
San Antonio, Socorro, N.Mex. 100 E4 126
San Antonio, Bernalillo, N.Mex. 108 H6 126
San Antonio, Bexar, Tex. 587,718 (*689,700) B6 E6 130
San Antonio, Ven. C2 240
San Antonio, bay, Tex. E7 130
San Antonio, cape, Arg. C4 252
San Antonio, cape, Cuba B2 232
San Antonio, creek, Calif. B6 94
San Antonio, peak, Calif. B6 94
San Antonio, pt., Mex. B2 224
San Antonio Abad, Sp. 2,665 C7 298
San Antonio de los Baños, Cuba 17,783 A3 232
San Antonio de los Cobres, Arg. B4 250
San Antonio Oeste, Arg. 3,847 F5 251
San Antonito, Bernalillo, N.Mex. 90 H6 126
Sanarate, Guat. 2,936 C2 228
San Ardo, Monterey, Calif. 500 D3 94
Sanariapo, Ven. D5 240
Sanator, Custer, S.Dak. 21 D2 158
Sanatorium, Simpson, Miss. 200 D3 184
Sanatorium, Tom Green, Tex. D5 130
San Augustine, San Augustine, Tex. 2,584 D8 130
San Augustine, co., Tex. 7,722 D8 130
San Bartolo Ameyalco, Mex. G9 224
San Bartolomeo [in Galdo], It. 10,300 E5 302
San Benedetto del Tronto, It. 18,600 D4 302
San Benito, Cameron, Tex. 16,422 F7 130
San Benito, co., Calif. 15,396 D3 94
San Benito, mtn., Calif. D3 94
San Bernabe, Mex. G9 224
San Bernardino, San Bernardino, Calif. 91,922 (*460,000) E5 94
San Bernardino, co., Calif. 503,591 E5 94
San Bernardino, mts., Calif. *E5 94
San Bernardo, Chile 37,221 B1 252
San Blas, Mex. 1,597 B4 224
San Blas, cape, Fla. B5 174
San Blas, mts., Pan. F8 228
San Blas, pt., Pan. F8 228
San Borja, Bol. 708 B1 246
San Borja, riv., Mex. G10 224
Sanborn, O'Brien, Iowa 1,323 A2 142
Sanborn, Redwood, Minn. 521 G3 148
Sanborn, Barnes, N.Dak. 263 D7 154
Sanborn, Ashland, Wis. 100 B3 160
Sanborn, co., S.Dak. 4,641 D7 158
Sanbornton, Belknap, N.H. 100 (857▲) E3 208
Sanbornville, Carroll, N.H. 400 D4 208
San Bruno, San Mateo, Calif. 29,063 B5 D2 94
San Bruno, pt., Calif. B5 94
San Buenaventura, see Ventura, Calif.
San Carlos, Arg. B2 252
San Carlos, Arg. 6,562 F3 251
San Carlos, Gila, Ariz. 100 E5 124
San Carlos, San Mateo, Calif. 21,370 B5 94
San Carlos, Chile 11,094 C1 252
San Carlos, Mex. 832 B5 225
San Carlos, Nic. 1,238 E5 228
San Carlos, Ur. 10,700 B5 252
San Carlos, Ven. 10,000 B4 240
San Carlos, res., Ariz. E5 124
San Carlos, [del Zulia], Ven. 10,000 B3 240
San Carlos [de Rio Negro], Ven. 607 F5 240
San Cataldo, It. 23,900 G4 302
Sánchez, Dom.Rep. 3,135 C10 233
Sánchez Roman, Mex. 4,413 C5 224
Sanchiang, China 5,000 M4 349
San Clemente, Orange, Calif. 8,527 F5 94
San Clemente, Sp. 6,530 C5 298
San Clemente, isl., Calif. F4 94
San Cristóbal, Arg. 9,071 B3 252
San Cristóbal, Dom.Rep. 9,723 C9 233
San Cristóbal, Pan. 66 F7 228
San Cristóbal, Ven. 73,000 C2 240
San Cristobal, isl., Solomon E2 436
Sancti-Spíritus, Cuba 37,741 B5 232
Sand, Nor. G2 291
Sand, creek, Colo. B7 106
Sand, creek, Ind. C4 140
Sand, creek, Wyo. C7 116
Sand, isl., Haw. G10 86
Sand, isl., Midway E3 436
Sand, isl., Wis. B3 160
Sand, islet, Midway E3 436
Sand, mtn., Colo. B3 106
Sand, riv., Alta., Can. C7 54
Sand, riv., Minn. E6 148
Sanda, Jap. 8,005 M11 354
Sandakan, N.Bor. 15,000 C5 358
Sandani, Tan. D6 414
Sandanski, Bul. 10,554 C1 317
Sanday, isl., Scot. B10 272
Sanday, sound, Scot. B10 272
Sandborn, Knox, Ind. 547 D2 140
Sandbluff, Choctaw, Okla. D8 128
Sand Brook, Hunterdon, N.J. 150 C3 210
Sandcoulee, Cascade, Mont. 385 C5 110
Sand Creek, McCone, Mont. 15 C11 110
Sand Creek, Grant, Okla. 15 B5 128
Sand Creek, Dunn, Wis. 150 C2 160
Sand Draw, Fremont, Wyo. 80 D4 116
Sandefjord, Nor. 6,720 B1 292
Sänderborg, Den. I3 291
Sanders, Apache, Ariz. 250 C6 124
Sanders, Benewah, Idaho 10 B2 108
Sanders, Monroe, Ind. 350 C3 140
Sanders, Carroll, Ky. 203 B6 178
Sanders, Treasure, Mont. 35 D9 110
Sanders, co., Mont. 6,880 C1 110
Sanderson, Terrell, Tex. 2,189 D4 130
Sandersville, Washington, Ga. 5,425 D4 176
Sandersville, Jones, Miss. 657 D3 184
Sandfly, lake, Sask., Can. C4 58
Sandfontein, Bech. D4 420
Sand Fork (Layopolis), Gilmer, W.Va. 237 C4 194
Sandgate, Bennington, Vt. 25 (93▲) *E2 218
Sandhammaren, cape, Swe. F5 292
Sandhill, Rankin, Miss. 150 C3 184
Sand Hill, riv., Newf., Can. D7 72
Sand Hill, riv., Minn. D2 148
Sandhills, Plymouth, Mass. 800 D4 206
Sandia, Peru 1,482 C4 245
Sandia, Jim Wells, Tex. 200 E7 130
Sandia, peak, N.Mex. H6 126
Sandia Park, Bernalillo, N.Mex. 100 H6 126
San Diego, San Diego, Calif. 573,224 (*890,000) D6 F5 94
San Diego, Duval and Jim Wells, Tex. 4,351 F6 130
San Diego, co., Calif. 1,033,011 F5 94
San Diego, aqueduct, Calif. F5 94
San Diego, bay, Calif. D6 94
San Diego, riv., Calif. D6 94
Sandiki, Tur. 8,073 B4 307
Sandila, India 17,400 D3 368
Sandilands, Man., Can. 25 F4 60
San Dimas, Los Angeles, Calif. 7,200 *E5 94
San Dimas, Mex. 190 C4 224
San Dimas, Mex. D7 225
San Dimas, res., Calif. C6 94
Sand Lake, Kent, Mich. 394 F6 146
Sandlake, Tillamook, Oreg. B3 96
Sandlick, creek, W.Va. D6 194
Sandnes, Nor. 4,138 G1 291
Sandoa, Con.L. D3 414
Sandomierz, Pol. 8,357 C5 325
Sandon, B.C., Can. 150 F14 52
Sandoña, Col. 4,767 C1 244
San Donà, di Piave, It. 11,100 C4 302
Sandoval, Marion, Ill. 1,356 E4 138
Sandoval, Sandoval, N.Mex. 600 C4 H6 126
Sandoval, co., N.Mex. 14,201 C3 126
Sandoway, Bur. 5,172 C2 362
Sandown, Rockingham, N.H. 40 (366▲) F4 208
Sandown [-Shanklin], Eng. 12,600 K11 273
Sand Point, Alsk. 107 D5 84
Sand Point, Ont., Can. 200 O24 64
Sandpoint, Bonner, Idaho 4,355 A2 108
Sand Point, Allen, Ind. (part of Fort Wayne) A4 140
Sands, Marquette, Mich. C4 146
Sands, key, Fla. E6 174
Sandspit, B.C., Can. D7 52
Sands Point, Nassau, N.Y. 2,161 *D3 212
Sand Springs, Garfield, Mont. 10 C9 110
Sand Springs, Tulsa, Okla. 7,754 B7 128
Sandston, Henrico, Va. 4,500 B9 C7 192
Sandstone, Austl. 59 D3 432
Sandstone, Pine, Minn. 1,552 E6 148
Sandstone, Summers, W.Va. 500 D4 D7 194
Sandusky, Sanilac, Mich. 2,066 F9 146
Sandusky, Erie, Ohio 31,989 A4 156
Sandusky, co., Ohio 56,486 A3 156
Sandusky, bay, Ohio A4 156
Sandusky, riv., Ohio A3 156
Sandusky South, Erie, Ohio 4,724 *A4 156
Sandviken, Swe. 21,157 A7 292
Sandwich, De Kalb, Ill. 3,842 B5 138
Sandwich, Barnstable, Mass. 1,099 (2,082▲) C7 206
Sandwich, Carroll, N.H. 50 (620▲) D4 208
Sandwich, bay, Newf., Can. D7 72
Sandwich, range, N.H. D3 208
Sandy, Clackamas, Oreg. 1,147 B4 96
Sandy, Clearfield, Pa. 2,070 *B3 214
Sandy, Salt Lake, Utah 3,322 C4 114
Sandy, brook, Conn. A3 202
Sandy, cape, Austl. C10 432
Sandy, creek, Ohio B5 156
Sandy, creek, W.Va. C3 194
Sandy, creek, Wyo. D3 116
Sandy, hook, N.J. C5 210
Sandy, isl., S.C. D10 188
Sandy, lake, Newf., Can. F7 72
Sandy, lake, Ont., Can. Q23 64
Sandy, lake, Minn. E5 148
Sandy, neck, Mass. C7 206
Sandy, pt., Md. B7 182
Sandy, pond, Mass. C2 206
Sandy, ridge, Va. C2 192
Sandy, riv., Maine D2 204
Sandy Bay, mtn., Maine C2 204
Sandy Creek, Oswego, N.Y. 697 B5 212
Sandy Hook, Fairfield, Conn. 950 D2 202
Sandy Hook, Washington, Md. 250 B4 182
Sandy Hook, Marion, Miss. 175 D3 184
Sandy Lake, Man., Can. 290 E2 60
Sandy Level, Pittsylvania, Va. 20 D5 192
Sandy Point, Waldo, Maine 200 D4 204
Sandy Ridge, Lowndes, Ala. 250 *C3 168
Sandy Spring, Montgomery, Md. 200 B5 182
Sandy Springs, Fulton, Ga. 5,000 A5 176
Sandy Springs, Anderson, S.C. 174 B3 188
Sandyville, Warren, Iowa 115 *C4 142
Sandyville, Carroll, Md. 130 A6 182
Sandyville, Jackson, W.Va. 175 C3 194
San Elizario, El Paso, Tex. 1,064 D2 130
San Enrique, Arg. C3 252
San Estanislao, Par. 2,209 D4 247
San Esteban, Hond. 1,733 C5 228
San Felipe, Chile 15,476 B1 252
San Felipe, Mex. 995 A3 224
San Felipe, Mex. D7 225
San Felipe, Sandoval, N.Mex. 1,034 C4 H6 126
San Felipe, Ven. 20,000 A4 240
San Felipe, pt., Mex. A3 224
San Feliu de Guixols, Sp. 7,583 B8 298
San Felix, isl., Pac.O. D6 436
San Fernando, Arg. B4 252
San Fernando, Los Angeles, Calif. 16,093 B4 94
San Fernando, Chile 17,598 B1 252
San Fernando, Mex. 1,886 C6 225
San Fernando, Phil. 6,636 A6 358
San Fernando, Sp. 12,093 D3 298
San Fernando, Trin. 36,050 E14 233
San Fernando, res., Calif. B4 94
San Fernando de Apure, Ven. 17,000 C5 240
San Fernando de Atabapo, Ven. 397 D5 240
San Fernando de Henares, Sp. *B5 298

San Fidel, Valencia, N.Mex. 77 C3 126
Sanfjallet, mtn., Swe. E5 291
Sanford, Covington, Ala. 247 D3 168
Sanford, Man., Can. 100 F4 60
Sanford, Conejos, Colo. 679 E5 106
Sanford, Seminole, Fla. 19,175 C9 174
Sanford, Vigo, Ind. 350 C2 140
Sanford, York, Maine 10,936 E2 204
(14,962*)
Sanford, Midland, Mich. 450 F7 146
Sanford, Covington, Miss. 250 D3 184
Sanford, Lee, N.C. 12,253 B6 186
Sanford, Hutchinson, Tex. 400 B5 130
Sanford, mtn., Alsk. F12 84
Sanford, mtn., Conn. D4 202
Sanfordtown, Kenton, Ky. 100 A8 178
San Francisco, Arg. 24,354 B3 252
San Francisco, San Francisco, Calif. 742,855 B5 94
(*3,275,000) D2
San Francisco, Col. C1 244
San Francisco, Mex. 514 L13 225
San Francisco, Sal. 2,883 D3 228
San Francisco, Ven. A3 240
San Francisco, co., Calif. 742,855 D2 94
San Francisco, bay, Calif. B5 94
San Francisco, pass, Arg. C4 250
San Francisco, riv., Ariz., N.Mex. E7 124
E2 126
San Francisco de Borja, Mex. 1,015 B4 224
San Francisco del Oro, Mex. 11,459 B4 224
San Francisco del Rincón, Mex. 18,197 K13 225
San Francisco de Macorís, Dom.Rep. 16,083 C9 233
San Francisco Solano, pt., Col. B1 244
Sangabar, Afg. 5,000 B3 374
San Gabriel, Los Angeles, Calif. 22,561 C5 94
San Gabriel, Ec. 6,269 A2 245
San Gabriel, mts., Calif. B5 94
San Gabriel, pt., Mex. B3 224
San Gabriel, res., Calif. C6 94
San Gabriel, riv., Calif. C5 94
San Gabriel Chilac, Mex. 5,790 D6 225
L15
Sangallan, isl., Peru C2 245
Sangamon, co., Ill. 146,539 D4 138
Sangamon, riv., Ill. C3 138
Sangau, India E6 368
Sangélima, Cam. F7 409
Sanger, Fresno, Calif. 8,072 D4 94
Sanger, Sov.Un. C14 329
Sanger, Denton, Tex. 1,190 C7 130
Sangerhausen, Ger. 21,400 C4 286
San Germán, P.R. 8,872 C11 233
Sangerville, Piscataquis, Maine 600 C3 204
(1,157*)
Sanggau, Indon. D4 358
Sangha, riv., Con.B. F8 409
Sangihe, isl., Indon. D7 358
San Gil, Col. 10,149 B2 244
Sang-i-Māsha, Afg. 10,000 C4 374
San Gimignano, It. 3,500 D3 302
San Giovanni in Fiore, It. 17,400 F6 302
Sangju, Kor. 43,760 G14 348
Sangonera, riv., Sp. D5 298
San Gorgonio, mtn., Calif. E5 94
Sangre de Cristo, range, Colo., N.Mex. D5 106
C5 126
San Gregorio, Chile B4 250
San Gregorio Atlapulco, Mex. 5,555 H10 224
Sangre Grande, Trin. E14 233
Sangro, riv., It. E5 302
Sangrur, India C1 368
Sangudo, Alta., Can. 331 D5 54
Sangüesa, Sp. 3,878 A6 298
Sangwin, Lib. E3 408
Sanhedrin, mtn., Calif. C2 94
Sanhsing, see Ilan, China
Sanibel, Lee, Fla. 125 E8 174
Sanibel, isl., Fla. E8 174
San Ignacio, Bol. 1,819 C2 246
San Ignacio, Bol. 1,757 B1 246
San Ignacio, Mex. 898 B3 224
San Ignacio, Par. 3,030 E4 247
Sanilac, co., Mich. 32,314 F9 146
San Ildefonso, Santa Fe, N.Mex. 500 C4 126
G7
San Ildefonso, Sp. 1,816 B4 298
San Ildefonso, pen., Phil. A6 358
San Isabel, Custer, Colo. 20 E5 106
Sanish, Mountrail, N.Dak. 63 *C3 154
San Isidro, Mex. K13 225
San Jacinto, Riverside, Calif. 2,553 F5 94
San Jacinto, Elko, Nev. 8 B7 112
San Jacinto, co., Tex. 6,153 D8 130
San Jacinto, riv., Tex. F8 130
San Jaime, Arg. B4 252
San Javier, Arg. 2,961 B3 252
San Javier, Bol. 564 C2 246
San Javier, Chile 7,006 C1 252
San Javier, riv., Arg. B3 252
San Jerónimo, Mex. 3,009 G10 224
San Jerónimo, mts., Col. B1 244
Sanjō, Jap. 68,570 F7 354
San Joaquin, Fresno, Calif. 879 *D3 94
San Joaquín, Mex. 721 K14 225
San Joaquín, Par. D4 247
San Joaquin, co., Calif. 249,989 C3 94
San Joaquin, riv., Calif. D3 94
San Jon, Quay, N.Mex. 411 C7 126
San Jorge, gulf, Arg. G4 251
San Jorge, gulf, Sp. B7 298
San José, Bol. 1,933 C2 246
San Jose, Br.Hond. B3 228
San Jose, Santa Clara, Calif. 204,196 D3 94
San José, C.R. 86,909 F5 228
(*142,000)
San José, Ec. 2,218 A2 245
San José, Guat. 2,789 D2 228
San Jose, Mason, Ill. 1,093 C4 138
San Jose, San Miguel, N.Mex. 175 C5 126
San Jose, Phil. 2,259 B6 358
San José, Ur. 15,000 B4 252
San José, Ven. D5 240
San José, dept., Ur. 97,687 B4 252
San José, isl., Mex. B3 224
San Jose, riv., B.C., Can. E12 52
San José Boquerón, Arg. C5 250
San José de Amacuro, Ven. B8 240
San José de Feliciano, Arg. 7,643 B4 252
San José de Gracia, Mex. K12 225
San José de Guaribe, Ven. B6 240
San José del Cabo, Mex. 1,838 C4 224
San José del Guaviare, Col. C2 244
San José de los Molinos, Peru 1,221 C2 245
San Josef Bay, B.C., Can. 25 E8 52
San Juan, Arg. 82,410 B2 252
San Juan, Dom.Rep. 9,920 C9 233
San Juan, Grant, N.Mex. 98 F3 126
San Juan, P.R. 357,205 C11 233
San Juan, Hidalgo, Tex. 4,371 F6 130
San Juan, Ven. A4 240
San Juan, co., Colo. 849 E3 106
San Juan, co., N.Mex. 53,306 B2 126
San Juan, co., Utah 9,040 F6 114
San Juan, co., Wash. 2,872 A3 98
San Juan, prov., Arg. 349,800 D4 250
San Juan, isl., Wash. A3 98
San Juan, mts., Colo., N.Mex. E3 106
A4 126
San Juan, riv., Arg. B2 252
San Juan, riv., B.C., Can. C13 52
San Juan, riv., Col. C1 244
San Juan, riv., Nic. E5 228
San Juan, riv., U.S. D4 77
San Juan Bautista, San Benito, Calif. 1,046 *D3 94
San Juan Bautista, Par. 4,602 E4 247
San Juan Capistrano, Orange, Calif. 1,120 F5 94
San Juan de Aragón, Mex. 3,098 G10 224
San Juan de Colón, Ven. 5,874 B2 240
San Juan de Guía, cape, Col. A2 244
San Juan de Lima, pt., Mex. D5 224
San Juan del Norte, Nic. 307 E6 228
San Juan del Norte, bay, Nic. E6 228
San Juan de los Lagos, Mex. 7,795 K12 225
San Juan de los Morros, Ven. 15,000 B5 240
San Juan del Río, Mex. 7,507 K13 225
San Juan del Sur, Nic. 1,025 E5 228
San Juanico, Mex. 2 G10 224
San Juanico, pt., Mex. B3 224
San Juan Nepomuceno, Col. 5,832 B1 244
San Juan Nepomuceno, Par. 2,452 D4 247
San Juan y Martínez, Cuba 4,142 A3 232
San Julián, Arg. 3,050 G4 251
San Julio, Mex. B2 224
San Justo, Arg. 6,571 B3 252
Sankarani, riv., Mali D3 408
Sankh, riv., India E4 368
Sankt Gallen, see St. Gallen, Switz.
Sankt Margrethen, Switz. 3,371 A5 312
Sankt Moritz, Switz. 2,558 B5 312
Sankt Pölten, Aus. 40,203 B7 313
Sankt Veit [an der Glan], Aus. 9,219 D6 313
Sankurru, riv., Con.L. C3 414
San Leandro, Alameda, Calif. 65,962 B5 94
San Lorenzo, Arg. 11,109 B3 252
San Lorenzo, Alameda, Calif. 23,773 B5 94
San Lorenzo, Ec. A2 245
San Lorenzo, Hond. 2,742 D4 228
San Lorenzo, Mex. G9 224
San Lorenzo, Grant, N.Mex. 200 F3 126
San Lorenzo, Ven. B3 240
San Lorenzo del Escorial, Sp. 6,357 B4 298
San Lorenzo Tezonco, Mex. 3,208 G10 224
Sanlúcar, Sp. 29,773 D3 298
San Lucas, Bol. 925 D1 246
San Lucas, Mex. 548 C4 224
San Lucas, Mex. C5 224
San Lucas, Mex. 1,459 F10 224
San Lucas, Mex. 538 L13 225
San Lucas, cape, Mex. C3 224
San Luis, Arg. 25,147 B2 252
San Luis, Pima, Ariz. 27 F4 124
San Luis, Yuma, Ariz. 50 F1 124
San Luis, Costilla, Colo. 800 E5 106
San Luis, Cuba 11,110 B7 232
San Luis, Guat. 562 B3 228
San Luis, Mex. 4,085 A3 224
San Luis, prov., Arg. 186,300 D4 250
San Luis, creek, Colo. D5 106
San Luis, lake, Bol. B2 246
San Luis, lake, Colo. E5 106
San Luis, pass, Tex. G8 130
San Luis, peak, Colo. E4 106
San Luis, pt., Calif. E3 94
San Luis, val., Colo. E4 106
San Luis Acatlán, Mex. D6 225
San Luis de la Paz, Mex. 7,215 K13 225
San Luis Jilotepeque, Guat. 4,136 C3 228
San Luis Obispo, San Luis Obispo, Calif. 20,437 E3 94
San Luis Obispo, co., Calif. 81,044 E3 94
San Luis Potosí, Mex. 125,640 C5 225
J13
San Luis Potosí, state, Mex. 856,066 C5 225
San Luis Tlaxialtemalco, Mex. G10 224
San Manuel, Pinal, Ariz. 4,524 F5 124
San Marcial, Socorro, N.Mex. 25 E4 126
San Marco [in Lamis], It. 22,000 E5 302
San Marcos, Col. 3,966 B1 244
San Marcos, Guat. 4,703 C2 228
San Marcos, Hays, Tex. 12,713 A7 130
E7
San Marcos, riv., Tex. A7 130
San Marcos de Colón, Hond. 3,197 D4 228
San Marino, Los Angeles, Calif. 13,658 C5 94
San Marino, San Marino 2,410 D4 302
San Marino, country, Eur. 15,000 D6 266
302
San Martín, Arg. 8,748 B2 252
San Martin, Santa Clara, Calif. 1,162 *D3 94
San Martín, Col. 3,094 C2 244
San Martín, Mex. 1,782 K14 225
San Martín, dept., Peru 139,921 B2 245
San Martín, lake, Chile G3 251
San Martín, riv., Bol. B2 246
San Martín de la Vega, Sp. 2,435 *B5 298
San Martín de los Andes, Arg. 2,366 F3 251
San Mateo, San Mateo, Calif. 69,870 B5 94
San Mateo, Putnam, Fla. 850 B9 174
San Mateo, Valencia, N.Mex. 230 C3 126
San Mateo, Sp. 2,890 B7 298
San Mateo, Ven. 1,490 B6 240
San Mateo, co., Calif. 444,387 D2 94
San Mateo, cape, Ec. A1 245
San Mateo, mts., N.Mex. E3 126
San Mateo, pt., Calif. B5 94
San Mateo Tlaltenango, Mex. G9 224
San Matías, Bol. 887 C3 246
San Matías, gulf, Arg. F5 251
Sanmen, bay, China K10 349
San Miguel, Pima, Ariz. 256 G4 124
San Miguel, San Luis Obispo, Calif. 500 E3 94
San Miguel, Dona Ana, N.Mex. 150 F4 126
San Miguel, Pan. 1,328 F8 228
San Miguel, Sal. 26,702 D3 228
San Miguel, co., Colo. 2,944 E2 106
San Miguel, co., N.Mex. 23,468 C5 126
San Miguel, isl., Calif. E3 94
San Miguel, pt., Pan. F8 228
San Miguel, riv., Bol. C2 246
San Miguel, riv., Colo. D2 106
San Miguel de Allende, Mex. 11,638 K13 225
San Miguel de Salcedo, Ec. 2,596 A2 245
San Morcas, Mex. D6 225
San Nicolás, Arg. 25,926 B3 252
San Nicolás, Mex. 2,971 G10 224
San Nicolas, isl., Calif. F4 94
Sânnicolaul-Mare, Rom. 9,956 A1 321
Sano, Jap. 69,412 *K15 354
Sanok, Pol. 13,800 D6 325
San Onofre, Col. 4,668 B1 244
San Pablo, Contra Costa, Calif. 19,687 *D2 94
San Pablo, Costilla, Colo. 75 E5 106
San Pablo, Mex. 124 G10 224
San Pablo, pt., Mex. B3 224
San Pablo, res., Calif. A5 94
San Patricio, bayou, La. C2 180
San Patricio, Lincoln, N.Mex. 75 E5 126
San Patricio, co., Tex. 45,021 E7 130
San Pedro, Arg. 12,798 B4 252
San Pedro, Arg. 6,105 B5 250
San Pedro, Bol. 262 B2 246
San Pedro, Bol. 1,094 C1 246
San Pedro, Los Angeles, Calif. (part of Los Angeles) C5 94
San Pedro, Mex. 19 G10 224
San Pedro, Par. 2,464 D4 247
San Pedro, Nueces, Tex. 7,634 *F7 130
San Pedro, Ven. C7 240
San Pedro, dept., Par. 64,534 C4 247
San Pedro, mtn., N.Mex. B4 126
San Pedro, pt., Calif. B4 94
San Pedro, pt., Chile C3 250
San Pedro, riv., Ariz. F5 124
San Pedro, riv., Mex. C5 224
San Pedro de las Colonias, Mex. 19,262 B5 225
San Pedro de Lloc, Peru 5,286 B2 245
San Pedro del Paraná, Par. 2,233 E4 247
San Pedro de Macorís, Dom.Rep. 19,876 C10 233
San Pedro Sula, Hond. 21,139 C3 228
Sanpete, co., Utah 11,053 D4 114
San Pierre, Starke, Ind. A3 140
San Pietro, isl., It. F2 302
Sanpoil, riv., Wash. A8 98
San Quentin, Marin, Calif. 500 A4 94
San Quintín, Mex. A2 224
San Rafael, Arg. 28,847 B2 252
San Rafael, Marin, Calif. 20,460 D2 94
San Rafael, Mex. A2 224
San Rafael, Mex. D7 225
San Rafael, Valencia, N.Mex. 300 C3 126
San Rafael, Ven. 3,901 A3 240
San Rafael, knob, Utah E5 114
San Rafael, riv., Utah D5 114
San Rafael, swell, Utah E5 114
San Rafael, valley, Utah E5 114
San Rafael del Norte, Nic. 810 D4 228
San Ramon, Contra Costa, Calif. 50 A6 94
San Ramón, Peru 1,275 C2 245
San Remo, It. 29,500 D1 302
San Remo, Suffolk, N.Y. 2,000 *E3 212
San Roque, Sp. 13,676 D4 298
San Rosendo, Chile 3,315 C1 252
San Saba, San Saba, Tex. 2,728 D6 130
San Saba, co., Tex. 6,381 D6 130
San Salvador, Arg. B4 252
San Salvador, Mex. 2,780 L15 225
San Salvador, Sal. 161,951 D3 228
San Salvador (Watling), isl., W.I. A7 233
Sansanné-Mango, Togo D5 408
San Sebastián, Mex. G10 224
San Sebastián, Sp. 110,687 A6 298
San Sebastián, Ven. B5 240
San Sebastián, cape, Arg. H4 251
San Sebastián de los Reyes, Sp. 1,775 B5 298
San Sepolcro, It. 7,242 D4 302
San Severo, It. 50,700 E5 302
Sanshui, China 9,000 N6 349
San Simon, Cochise, Ariz. 100 F6 124
San Simon, creek, Ariz. F6 124
Sansom Park Village, Tarrant, Tex. 4,175 *C7 130
San Souci Beach, Mobile, Ala. 400 *E1 168
Sans Souci, Greenville, S.C. 7,000 *B4 188
Santa, Benewah, Idaho 100 B2 108
Santa, Peru 1,089 B2 245
Santa, riv., Peru B2 245
Santa Ana, Bol. 2,225 B1 246
Santa Ana, Bol. 171 C1 246
Santa Ana, Orange, Calif. 100,350 C6 94
F5
Santa Ana, Mex. 3,976 A3 224
Santa Ana, Mex. K13 225
Santa Ana, Sandoval, N.Mex. 300 C4 126
H6
Santa Ana, Peru 201 C3 245
Santa Ana, Sal. 51,702 D3 228
Santa Ana, Ven. 2,351 B6 240
Santa Ana, mts., Calif. C6 94
Santa Ana, riv., Calif. C6 94
Santa Anita, Mex. 4,441 G10 224
Santa Anna, Coleman, Tex. 1,320 D6 130
Santa Bárbara, Braz. 3,358 E2 258
Santa Barbara, Santa Barbara, Calif. 58,768 E4 94
Santa Bárbara, Chile 2,292 C1 252
Santa Bárbara, Hond. 3,218 C3 228
Santa Bárbara, Mex. 14,805 B4 224
Santa Barbara, co., Calif. 168,962 E3 94
Santa Barbara, chan., Calif. E3 94
Santa Barbara, isl., Calif. F4 94
Santa Catalina, Arg. B4 250
Santa Catalina, gulf, Calif. F5 94
Santa Catalina, isl., Calif. F4 94
Santa Catalina, mts., Ariz. F5 124
Santa Catarina, Mex. G11 224
Santa Catarina, state, Braz. 1,852,000 K6 257
Santa Catarina, isl., Braz. K7 257
Santa Clara, Santa Clara, Calif. 58,880 D3 94
Santa Clara, Cuba 77,398 A5 232
Santa Clara, Franklin, N.Y. 110 A7 212
Santa Clara, Lane, Oreg. 950 *C3 96
Santa Clara, Ur. 10,000 B5 252
Santa Clara, Washington, Utah 291 F2 114
Santa Clara, co., Calif. 642,315 D3 94
Santa Clara, riv., Calif. E4 94
Santa Claus, Spencer, Ind. 50 D3 140
Santa Coloma de Farnés, Sp. 4,240 B8 298
Santa Croce, cape, It. G5 302
Santa Cruz, Arg. G4 251
Santa Cruz, Bol. 34,837 C2 246
Santa Cruz, Braz. 3,197 B3 258
Santa Cruz, Santa Cruz, Calif. 25,596 D2 94
Santa Cruz, Chile 4,303 B1 252
Santa Cruz, C.R. 1,986 E5 228
Santa Cruz, Santa Fe, N.Mex. 600 C4 126
Santa Cruz, co., Ariz. 10,808 G5 124
Santa Cruz, co., Calif. 84,219 D2 94
Santa Cruz, dept., Bol. C2 246
Santa Cruz, prov., Arg. 58,700 G3 251
Santa Cruz, isl., Calif. F4 94
Santa Cruz, riv., Arg. H4 251
Santa Cruz, riv., Ariz. F4 124
Santa Cruz Barillas, Guat. 1,296 C2 228
Santa Cruz de la Palma, Sp. 8,835 F11 298
Santa Cruz de la Zarza, Sp. 5,947 C5 298
Santa Cruz del Quiché, Guat. 4,210 C2 228
Santa Cruz del Sur, Cuba 2,571 B6 232
Santa Cruz de Tenerife, Sp. 130,501 F11 298
Santa Cruz de Tenerife, prov., Sp. 427,796 *F12 298
Santa Cruz do Rio Pardo, Braz. 8,293 E1 258
Santa Cruz Village, Pinal, Ariz. E3 124
H2
Santa Elena, Ec. 2,775 A1 245
Santa Elena, Starr, Tex. 250 F6 130
Santa Elena, bay, Ec. A1 245
Santa Elena, cape, C.R. E4 228
Santa Elena [de Uairén], Ven. 699 D8 240
Santa Eugenia [de Ribeira], Sp. 4,543 A2 298
Santa Eulalia del Río, Sp. 2,644 C7 298
Santa Fe, Arg. 168,791 B3 252
Santa Fe, Cuba 1,098 B4 232
Santa Fe, Mex. 3,706 G10 224
Santa Fe, Santa Fe, N.Mex. 34,676 C5 126
G7
Santafé, Sp. 8,387 D5 298
Santa Fe, Maury, Tenn. 125 C4 190
Santa Fe, co., N.Mex. 44,970 C4 126
Santa Fe, prov., Arg. 2,035,400 D5 250
Santa Fe, lake, Kans. B6 144
Santa Fe, riv., N.Mex. G7 126
Santa Fe Baldy, mtn., N.Mex. C5 126
Santa Felicia, res., Calif. E4 94
Santa Fe Springs, Los Angeles, Calif. 16,342 C5 94
Santa Filomena, Braz. 544 B1 258
Santa Inés, Ven. B6 240
Santa Inés, isl., Chile H3 251
Santa Inés Ahuatempan, Mex. 2,465 L14 225
Santa Isabel, Arg. C2 252
Santa Isabel, Ec. 1,186 A2 245
Santa Isabel, Fernando Póo 11,098 F6 409
Santa Isabel, Ur. B4 252
Santa Isabel, isl., Solomon E2 436
Santa Isabel de Siguas, Peru 80 D3 245
Santa Lucía, Cuba 1,969 B7 232
Santa Lucía, Ur. 27,000 B4 252
Santa Margarita, San Luis Obispo, Calif. 600 E3 94
Santa Margarita, isl., Mex. C3 224
Santa María, Arg. 2,052 A2 252
Santa Maria, Braz. 44,949 K6 257
Santa Maria, Santa Barbara, Calif. 20,027 E3 94
Santa Maria, Santa Rosa, Fla. 100 A4 174
Santa Maria, mts., Ariz. D3 124
Santa María, riv., Arg. C4 250
Santa Maria, riv., Ariz. D2 124
Santa María, riv., Mex. K14 225
Santa Maria [Capua Vetere], It. 29,900 E5 302
Santa María del Oro, Mex. 3,246 B4 224
Santa María del Río, Mex. 4,848 C5 225

Santa Maria di Leuca, cape, It. F7 302
Santa María Hastahuacán, Mex. G10 224
Santa Maria Madalena, Braz. 1,101 E2 258
Santa Marta, Col. 54,590 A2 244
Santa Marta, Mex. G10 224
Santa Marta, Sp. 5,501 C3 298
Santa Marta Grande, cape, Braz. K7 257
Santa Monica, Los Angeles, Calif. 83,249 C4 94
Santan, Pinal, Ariz. 15 E4 124
Santan, mtn., Ariz. H3 124
Santana, Braz. 3,059 C2 258
Santana do Ipanema, Braz. 3,222 B3 258
Santander, Col. 5,669 C1 244
Santander, Sp. 100,069 A5 298
Santander, dept., Col. 804,490 B2 244
Santander, prov., Sp. 405,420 *A5 298
Santander Jiménez, Mex. 1,358 C6 225
Sant'Angelo Romano, It. 2,000 *D4 302
Santanoni, peak, N.Y. A7 212
Santanópole, Braz. 1,704 B2 258
Santañy, Sp. 2,990 C8 298
Santa Paula, Ventura, Calif. 13,279 E4 94
Santaquin, Utah, Utah 1,183 D4 114
Santa Quitéria, Braz. A2 258
Santarém, Braz. 14,061 F6 256
Santarém, Port. 13,114 C2 298
Santaren, chan., Cuba A5 232
Santa Rita, Braz. 12,362 B4 258
Santa Rita, Guam 1,410 D7 436
Santa Rita, Glacier, Mont. 110 B4 110
Santa Rita, Grant, N.Mex. 1,772 F2 126
Santa Rita, Ven. 4,111 A3 240
Santa Rosa, Arg. B2 252
Santa Rosa, Arg. 3,564 B2 252
Santa Rosa, Arg. 2,999 B3 252
Santa Rosa, Arg. 14,623 C3 252
Santa Rosa, Bol. B1 246
Santa Rosa, Braz. 4,816 H3 257
Santa Rosa, Sonoma, Calif. 31,027 C2 94
Santa Rosa, Col. 4,668 B1 244
Santa Rosa, Ec. 4,776 A2 245
Santa Rosa, Guadalupe, N.Mex. 2,220 D6 126
Santa Rosa, Cameron, Tex. 1,572 *F7 130
Santa Rosa, Ven. B6 240
Santa Rosa, co., Fla. 29,547 A3 174
Santa Rosa, isl., Calif. F3 94
Santa Rosa, isl., Fla. A4 174
Santa Rosa, mtn., Guam C7 436
Santa Rosa, range, Nev. B4 112
Santa Rosa Beach, Walton, Fla. 250 A4 174
Santa Rosa de Aguán, Hond. 680 C5 228
Santa Rosa de Copán, Hond. 6,417 C3 228
Santa Rosa de Sucumbíos, Ec. 210 A2 245
Santa Rosalía, Mex. 6,950 B3 224
Santa Rosalía, Ven. C6 240
Santa Rosalía, pt., Mex. B3 224
Santa Susana, Ventura, Calif. 2,310 *E4 94
Santa Teresa, Mex. B6 225
Santa Teresa, Ven. D8 240
Santa Teresa Gallura, It. 1,674 E2 302
Santa Úrsula, Mex. 3,570 G10 224
Santa Venetia, Marin, Calif. 3,000 *D2 76
Santa Ynez, Santa Barbara, Calif. 400 E3 94
Santee, San Diego, Calif. 2,500 D6 94
Santee, Knox, Nebr. 65 B8 152
Santee, Orangeburg, S.C. 105 D8 188
Santee, dam, S.C. E8 188
Santee, riv., S.C. E9 188
Sant'Eufemia, gulf, It. F5 302
Santiago, Bol. 218 C1 246
Santiago, Braz. 9,469 K6 257
Santiago, Chile 794,900 (*1,546,884) B1 252
Santiago, Dom.Rep. 56,558 C9 233
Santiago, Mex. 635 C4 224
Santiago, Pan. 5,886 F7 228
Santiago, Par. E4 247
Santiago, Sp. 31,140 A2 298
Santiago, prov., Chile 1,754,954 D3 250
Santiago, creek, Calif. C6 94
Santiago, mts., Bol. C2 246
Santiago, mts., Tex. E4 130
Santiago, peak, Calif. C6 94
Santiago, res., Calif. C6 94
Santiago, riv., Peru A2 245
Santiago Cahualtepec, Mex. G11 224
Santiago de Cao, Peru 957 B2 245
Santiago de Cuba, Cuba 163,237 B7 232
Santiago del Estero, Arg. 60,039 A3 252
Santiago del Estero, prov., Arg. 596,100 C5 250
Santiago Ixcuintla, Mex. 9,161 C4 224
Santiago Papasquiaro, Mex. 4,137 B4 224
Santiago Tepalcatlalpan, Mex. 2,766 H10 224
Santiam, riv., Oreg. C1 96
Santipur, India E5 368
Santisteban del Puerto, Sp. 6,248 C5 298
Santo Amaro, Braz. 12,258 C3 258
Santo Ângelo, Braz. 13,573 K6 257
Santo Antônio, Braz. 2,440 C3 258
Santo Antônio, pt., Braz. D3 258
Santo António do Zaire, Ang. 528 A2 420
Santo Domingo, Nic. 3,105 D5 228
Santo Domingo de la Calzada, Sp. 4,631 A5 298
Santo Domingo de los Colorados, Ec. A2 245
Santo Domingo Pueblo, Sandoval, N.Mex. 900 C4 126
G6
Santoña, Sp. 8,271 A5 298
Santos, Braz. 198,405 E1 258
Santos Dumont, Braz. 13,599 E2 258
Santo Tomas, Dona Ana, N.Mex. 300 F4 126
Santo Tomás, Peru 877 C3 245
Santo Tomé, Arg. 8,348 A4 252
Santuao, China L9 349
Santuck, Union, S.C. 40 B5 188
Santuit, Barnstable, Mass. 300 *C7 206
San Valentín, mtn., Chile G3 251
Sanvic, Fr. 19,160 C4 278
San Vicente, Mex. K12 225
San Vicente, Sal. 10,950 D3 228
San Vicente de Alcántara, Sp. 8,212 C3 298
San Vicente de la Barquera, Sp. 3,002 A4 298
San Vicente [de Caguán], Col. 1,002 C2 244
San Vincent, res., Calif. F5 94
San Vito al Tagliamento, It. 5,065 C4 302
Sanya, China 5,000 P4 349
Sanyati, riv., Rh.&Nya. C5 420
San Ygnacio, Zapata, Tex. 900 F6 130
San Ysidro, San Diego, Calif. (part of San Diego) D6 94
F5
San Ysidro, Sandoval, N.Mex. 26 C4 126
G6
Sanza Pombo, Ang. 269 A3 420
São Antônio, Braz. B3 258
São Bernardo [do Campo], Braz. 19,960 E1 258
São Carlos, Braz. 30,830 E1 258
São Cristóvão, Braz. 6,742 C3 258
São Domingos, Braz. C1 258
São Fidélis, Braz. 4,473 E2 258
São Francisco, Braz. 2,903 D2 258
São Francisco, riv., Braz. C2 258
São Francisco do Sul, Braz. 9,825 K7 257
São Gotardo, Braz. 2,724 D1 258
São João da Barra, Braz. 2,777 E2 258
São João da Boa Vista, Braz. 15,837 E1 258
São João del Rei, Braz. 24,560 E2 258
São João do Cariri, Braz. 1,188 B3 258
São João do Piauí, Braz. 1,467 B2 258
São João Nepomuceno, Braz. 6,797 E2 258
São José do Rio Prêto, Braz. 36,942 E1 258
São José dos Campos, Braz. 25,892 E1 258
São Leopoldo, Braz. 18,380 K6 257
São Lourenço, Braz. 8,692 E1 258
São Luís, Braz. 79,731 F8 256
São Luís Gonzaga, Braz. 7,767 K6 257
São Manuel, Braz. 6,280 E1 258
São Manuel ou das Tres Barras, riv., Braz. G5 256
São Mateus, Braz. 3,023 D3 258
Saona, isl., Dom.Rep. C10 233
Saône, riv., Fr. D6 278
Saône-et-Loire, dept., Fr. 511,182 *D6 278
São Paulo, Braz. 3,417,208 E1 258
São Paulo, state, Braz. 11,450,673 J6 257
São Paulo de Olivença, Braz. 948 F3 256
São Pedro do Piauí, Braz. 1,653 B2 258
São Raimundo Nonato, Braz. 2,663 B2 258
São Roque, cape, Braz. B3 258
São Salvador, Ang. 2,965 A2 420
São Sebastião, cape, Moz. D7 421
São Sebastião, isl., Braz. E2 258
São Sebastião do Paraíso, Braz. 10,532 E1 258
São Simão, Braz. 3,450 E1 258
São Tomé, São Tomé 7,817 F6 408
São Tomé, cape, Braz. E2 258
São Tomé, isl., Afr. F6 408
São Tomé e Príncipe, Port. poss., Afr. 60,159 F6 408
Saoura, riv., Alg. B3 402
Sápai, Grc. 5,713 A5 306
Sapatu, isl., Viet. E6 362
Sapele, Nig. 33,638 E6 408
Sapelo, isl., Ga. E5 176
Sapelo, sound, Ga. E5 176
Sapinero, Gunnison, Colo. 10 D3 106
Saponac, Penobscot, Maine 20 C4 204
Saposoa, Peru 3,243 B2 245
Sapozhok, Sov.Un. 21,500 F13 332
Sappa, creek, Kans. C3 144
Sappemeer, Neth. 4,565 A5 282
Sapphire, mts., Mont. D3 110
Sappho, Clallam, Wash. 100 A2 98
Sapporo, Jap. 426,620 C8 354
Sapps Still, Coffee, Ga. 200 E4 176
Sapri, It. 4,431 E5 302
Sapulpa, Creek, Okla. 14,282 C7 128
Saqqara, Eg., U.A.R. 8,230 *B3 395
Saqqez, Iran 10,479 B2 379
Saquarema, Braz. E2 258
Saquisilí, Ec. 3,217 A2 245
Sara, dune, Libya C4 394
Sara Buri, Thai. 10,000 D4 362
Sara Buri, prov., Thai. 203,562 *D4 362
Sarabyum, Eg., U.A.R. E7 395
Saragossa, Walker, Ala. 100 B2 168
Sarah, Tate, Miss. 125 A2 184
Sarajevo, Yugo. 136,283 C4 316
Sara Kaeo, Thai. 25,000 D4 362
Saraland, Mobile, Ala. 4,595 E1 168
Saranac, Ionia, Mich. 1,081 G6 146
Saranac, Clinton, N.Y. 400 A8 212
Saranac, lakes, N.Y. A7 212
Saranac, riv., N.Y. A8 212
Saranac Lake, Franklin, N.Y. 6,421 A7 212
Saranap, Contra Costa, Calif. 6,450 A5 94
Sarande, Alb. 3,444 B3 306
Sarandí del Yi, Ur. 5,600 B4 252
Sarandí Grande, Ur. 5,000 B4 252
Sarangani, bay, Phil. C6 358
Sarangpur, India E2 368
Saransk, Sov.Un. 90,000 B3 336
Sarapul, Sov.Un. 68,000 A4 336
Sarasota, Sarasota, Fla. 34,083 D6 174
D8
Sarasota, co., Fla. 76,895 D8 174
Sarasota, bay, Fla. D8 174
Saratoga, Howard, Ark. 62 D3 170
Saratoga, Santa Clara, Calif. 14,861 *D2 94
Saratoga, Randolph, Ind. 363 B5 140
Saratoga, Wilson, N.C. 409 B8 186
Saratoga, Hardin, Tex. 800 D8 130
Saratoga, Carbon, Wyo. 1,133 E6 116
Saratoga, co., N.Y. 89,096 B8 212
Saratoga, lake, N.Y. B8 212
Saratoga Place, Nansemond, Va. 1,478 *D8 192
Saratoga Springs, Saratoga, N.Y. 16,630 B8 212
Saratov, Sov.Un. 581,000 (*685,000) B3 336
Saravane, Laos 25,000 D5 362
Sarawak, Br. poss., Asia 546,385 I13 340
359
Saray, see Kâzim Paşa, Tur.
Sarayköy, Tur. 5,292 C3 307
Sarbāz, Iran D5 379
Sarben, Keith, Nebr. 105 C4 152
Sarbhang, Bhu. D5 368
Sárbogárd, Hung. 5,058 C3 320
Sarcoxie, Jasper, Mo. 1,056 D3 150
Sarda, riv., India, Nep. C3 368
Sardalas, Libya B2 394
Sardarshahr, India C1 368
Sardinia, Decatur, Ind. 170 C4 140
Sardinia (Sardegna), reg., It. 1,383,000 E1 302
Sardinia, Brown, Ohio 799 C3 156
Sardinia, Clarendon, S.C. 100 D8 188
Sardinia, isl., It. E2 302
Sardis, Dallas, Ala. 500 C3 168
Sardis, Saline, Ark. C4 170
Sardis, B.C., Can. 600 C16 52
Sardis, Burke, Ga. 829 D5 176
Sardis, Mason, Ky. 190 B7 178
Sardis, Panola, Miss. 2,098 A3 184
Sardis, Monroe, Ohio 400 C6 156
Sardis, Pushmataha, Okla. 103 D8 128
Sardis, Henderson, Tenn. 274 C3 190
Sardis, res., Miss. A3 184
Sarektjakko, mtn., Swe. C7 290
Sarepta, Webster, La. 737 B2 180
Sarepta, Calhoun, Miss. 126 A3 184
Sar-e-Yazd, Iran C4 379
Sargans, Switz. 2,075 A5 312
Sargeant, Mower, Minn. 113 H6 148
Sargent, Coweta, Ga. 950 C2 176
Sargent, Custer, Nebr. 876 C6 152
Sargent, co., N.Dak. 6,856 D8 154
Sargents, Saguache, Colo. 60 D4 106
Sargodha, Pak. 78,463 C8 375
Sarhad, Afg. 5,000 A7 374
Sārī, Iran 23,990 B3 379
Sária, isl., Grc. D6 306
Sarikamis, Tur. 17,566 A10 307
Sarine, riv., Switz. B3 312
Sariñena, Sp. 2,893 B6 298
Sar-i-Pul, Afg. 5,000 A3 374
Sariwŏn, Kor. 42,957 F12 348
Sariyer, Tur. F13 307
Sark, isl., Guernsey L10 273
Şarkişla, Tur. 4,578 B7 307
Şarköy, Tur. 3,313 A2 307
Sarlat, Fr. 5,251 E4 278
Sarles, Cavalier and Towner, N.Dak. 225 B7 154
Sarmiento, mtn., Chile H3 251
Särna, Swe. 1,393 F5 291
Sarnen, Switz. 6,199 B4 312
Sarnen, lake, Switz. B4 312
Sarnia, Ont., Can. 43,447 R18 64
Sarny, Sov.Un. 18,600 G6 332
Sarona, Washburn, Wis. 90 C2 160
Saronic, gulf, Grc. C4 306
Saronno, It. 22,000 C2 302
Saronville, Clay, Nebr. 71 *D7 152
Sárospatak, Hung. 8,733 A6 320
Şarova, Sov.Un. 900 E14 332
Šar Planina, mts., Yugo. D5 316
Sarpsborg, Nor. 13,499 (*29,400) B2 292
Sarpy, Big Horn, Mont. E10 110
Sarpy, co., Nebr. 31,281 C9 152
Sarra, well, Libya C4 394
Sarreguemines, Fr. 14,947 C7 278
Sarria, Sp. 3,935 A3 298
Sarstún, riv., Guat. C3 228
Sartell, Stearns, Minn. 791 F4 148
Sartène, Fr. D2 302
Sarthe, dept., Fr. 420,393 *D4 278
Sartrouville, Fr. 21,743 I9 278
Sarufutsu, Jap. B9 354
Sarur, Om. C6 383
Sárvár, Hung. 10,025 B1 320
Sarvestan, Iran D3 379
Sárviz, canal, Hung. C3 320
Sary-Ishikotrau, desert, Sov.Un. C9 336
Sary-Ozek, Sov.Un. D9 336
Sarysa, riv., Sov.Un. C7 336
Sarzana, It. 8,600 C2 302
Sasabe, Pima, Ariz. 70 G4 124
Sasaginnigak, lake, Man., Can. E5 60
Sasakwa, Seminole, Okla. 253 D7 128
Sasaram, India 29,265 D3 368
Sasebo, Jap. 258,221 H2 354
Sashiki, Okinawa D1 436
Saskatchewan, prov., Can. 906,000 F8 48
58
Saskatchewan, riv., Man., Sask., Can. D2 60
D6 58
Saskatoon, Sask., Can. 72,858 C3 58
D4
Saskeram, riv., Sask., Can. D7 58
Saskylakh, Sov.Un. B13 329
Sasovo, Sov.Un. 26,000 B2 336
Sassafras, Knott, Ky. 500 *C7 178
Sassafras, mtn., S.C. A3 188
Sassafras, riv., Md. B7 182
Sassandra, I.C. 4,200 F3 408
Sassandra, riv., I.C. E3 408
Sassari, It. 62,400 (76,200*) E2 302
Sassari, prov., It. 365,500 *E2 302
Sasser, Terrell, Ga. 382 E2 176
Sassnitz, Ger. 12,000 A5 286
Sastre, Arg. 2,308 B3 252
Sasuri, Kor. E13 348
Sasykkol, lake, Sov.Un. C10 336
Satan, mtn., B.C., Can. D10 52
Satanta, Haskell, Kans. 686 E3 144
Satapuala, Samoa 637 E4 436
Satartia, Yazoo, Miss. 105 C2 184
Satellite Beach, Brevard, Fla. 825 *C10 174
Säter, Swe. 4,193 A6 292
Saticoy, Ventura, Calif. 2,283 E4 94
Satilla, riv., Ga. E5 176
Satipo, Peru C3 245
Satka, Sov.Un. 38,900 A5 336
Satna, India D3 368
Satolah, Rabun, Ga. 200 B3 176
Sátoraljaújhely, Hung. 16,000 A6 320
Satpura, range, India D3 366
Satsop, Grays Harbor, Wash. 150 B3 98
Satsuma, Mobile, Ala. 1,491 E1 168
Satsuma, Putnam, Fla. 500 B9 174
Sattahip, Thai. D4 362
Satu-Mare, Rom. 52,099 A2 321
Satun, Thai. F4 362
Satun, prov., Thai. 46,514 *F3 362
Satupaitea, Samoa 1,047 E4 436
Saturna, isl., B.C., Can. F11 52
Satus, creek, Wash. C6 98
Sauce, Arg. 3,017 B4 252
Sauceda, mts., Ariz. F3 124
Saucier, Harrison, Miss. 300 E3 184
Saucillo, Mex. 4,457 B4 224
Saudhárkrókur, Ice. 1,075 L20 290
Saudi Arabia, country, Asia 6,159,000 G6 340
383
Saugatuck, Allegan, Mich. 927 G5 146
Saugatuck, riv., Conn. D2 202
Saugerties, Ulster, N.Y. 4,286 C8 212
Saugor, India 66,442 E2 368
Saugus, Essex, Mass. 20,666 B5 206
C3
Saugus, riv., Mass. C3 206
Saujbulagh, see Mahābād, Iran
Sauk, co., Wis. 36,179 E4 160
Sauk, riv., Minn. F4 148
Sauk, riv., Wash. A5 98
Sauk Centre, Stearns, Minn. 3,573 F4 148
Sauk City, Sauk, Wis. 2,095 E4 160
Sauk Rapids, Benton, Minn. 4,038 F4 148
Sauk Village, Cook, Ill. 4,687 *B6 138
Saukville, Ozaukee, Wis. 1,038 E6 160
Saulsbury, Hardeman, Tenn. 141 C2 190
Sault-au-Mouton, Que., Can. 873 P15 66
Sault Ste. Marie, Ont., Can. 37,329 S24 64
Sault Ste. Marie, Chippewa, Mich. 18,722 C7 146
Saumlakki, Indon. F8 359
Saumur, Fr. 18,169 D3 278
Saunders, Alta., Can. 145 D5 54
Saunders, co., Nebr. 17,270 C9 152
Saunderstown, Washington, R.I. 300 C3 216
Saundersville, Worcester, Mass. 750 *B4 206
Saundersville, Sumner, Tenn. 100 E7 190
Sauquoit, Oneida, N.Y. 1,715 B6 212
Sausalito, Marin, Calif. 5,331 A5 94
D2
Sautee, White, Ga. 300 B3 176
Sava, riv., Yugo. B4 316
Savage, Howard, Md. 1,341 B6 182
Savage, Scott, Minn. 1,094 G5 148
G6
Savage, Tate, Miss. 75 A2 184
Savage, Richland, Mont. 275 C12 110
Savage, riv., Md. A1 182
Savaii, isl., Samoa E4 436
Savalou, Dah. 3,800 E5 408
Savanna, Carroll, Ill. 4,950 A3 138
Savanna, Pittsburg, Okla. 620 D8 128
Savannah, Chatham, Ga. 149,245 (*189,200) D5 176
Savannah, Andrew, Mo. 2,455 B3 150
Savannah, Wayne, N.Y. 602 B5 212
Savannah, Ashland, Ohio 409 B4 156
Savannah, Hardin, Tenn. 4,315 C3 190
Savannah, lake, Md. D8 182
Savannah, riv., Ga., S.C. D5 176
C3 188
Savannah Beach, Chatham, Ga. 1,385 E6 176
Savannakhet, Laos C5 362
Savanna-la-Mar, Jam. 4,450 C5 232
Savant Lake, Ont., Can. 115 R23 64
Savé, Dah. 5,100 E5 408
Save, riv., Moz. D6 421
Savedge, Surry, Va. 60 C7 192
Saveh, Iran 15,365 B3 379
Säven, riv., Swe. D4 292
Săveni, Rom. 6,470 A4 321
Saverne, Fr. 8,682 C7 278
Saverton, Ralls, Mo. 135 B6 150
Savery, Carbon, Wyo. 25 E5 116
Savigliano, It. 14,800 C1 302
Savo, isl., Solomon E2 436
Savoie, dept., Fr. 252,192 *E6 278
Savolinna, Fin. 11,649 F13 291
Savona, B.C., Can. 225 E12 52
Savona, It. 68,300 C2 302
Savona, Steuben, N.Y. 904 C4 212
Savona, prov., It. 242,600 *C2 302
Savonburg, Allen, Kans. 131 E8 144
Savoonga, Alsk. 249 C4 84
Savoy (Savoie), former prov., Fr. 546,000 E7 278
Savoy, Berkshire, Mass. 100 (277*) A1 206
Savoy, Blaine, Mont. 12 B8 110
Savran, Sov.Un. H8 332
Sävsjö, Swe. 4,900 D5 292
Sävsjöström, Swe. D6 292
Savu, isl., Austl. A4 432
Savu, sea, Indon. F6 358
Savukoski, Fin. C13 290
Savur, Tur. 3,129 C9 307
Savusavu, bay, Fiji E7 436
Sawai Madhopur, India D2 368
Sawankhalok, Thai. 25,000 C3 362
Sawbuck, range, Alta., Can. E5 54
Sawdy, Alta., Can. 95 C6 54
Sawmill, Apache, Ariz. 300 C6 124
Saw Pit, San Miguel, Colo. 30 *E3 106
Sawtooth, ridge, Wash. A6 98
Sawyer, Pratt, Kans. 192 E5 144
Sawyer, McCreary, Ky. 500 D6 178
Sawyer, Berrien, Mich. 1,300 H5 146
Sawyer, Ward, N.Dak. 390 B4 154
Sawyer, Choctaw, Okla. 235 D8 128
Sawyer, co., Wis. 9,475 C2 160
Sawyer, lake, Wash. D3 98
Sawyers, hill, Newf., Can. G9 72
Sawyerville, Que., Can. 823 S13 66

Saxapahaw, Alamance, N.C. 600 B6 186
Saxe, Charlotte, Va. 125 D6 192
Saxis, Accomack, Va. 577 C9 192
Saxman, Alsk. 167 K15 84
Saxman, Nicholas, W.Va. 29 C4 194
Saxon, Spartanburg, S.C. 3,917 B5 188
Saxon, Raleigh, W.Va. 225 D3 194
D6
Saxon, Iron, Wis. 250 B3 160
Saxonville, Middlesex, Mass. D1 206
Saxony, Prussian (Preussisch Sachsen), reg., Ger. *B4 286
Saxony (Sachsen), reg., Ger. C5 286
Saxton, Whitley, Ky. 650 D6 178
Saxton, Bedford, Pa. 977 C3 214
Saxton Falls, Warren, N.J. B3 210
Saxtons, riv., Vt. E3 218
Saxtons River, Windham, Vt. 725 E3 218
Say, Niger 2,200 D5 408
Sayabec, Que., Can. 2,281 *Q10 66
Sayán, Peru 1,229 C2 245
Sayan, mts., Sov.Un. D11 329
Saybrook, McLean, Ill. 859 C5 138
Saybrook Manor, Middlesex, Conn. 300 D6 202
Saybrook Point, Middlesex, Conn. 500 D6 202
Sayer, is., Thai. E3 362
Sayle, Powder River, Mont. 7 E11 110
Saylesville, Providence, R.I. B3 216
Sayner, Vilas, Wis. 350 B4 160
Sayr Usa, Mong. C9 346
Sayre, Jefferson, Ala. 950 B3 168
Sayre, Beckham, Okla. 2,913 C4 128
Sayre, Bradford, Pa. 7,917 B5 214
Sayreton, Jefferson, Ala. 1,000 E4 168
Sayreville, Middlesex, N.J. 22,553 C4 210
Sayula, Mex. 10,095 D5 224
Sayville, Suffolk, N.Y. 6,500 D4 212
Sazan, isl., Alb. A2 306
Sázava, Czech. 1,435 *B2 324
Sázava, riv., Czech. B2 324
Sazin, Pak. B8 375
Sazliyka, riv., Bul. B2 317
Scafell Pike, mtn., Eng. G9 273
Scaggsville, Howard, Md. 150 B6 182
Scalby, Eng. 6,300 G12 273
Scalp Level, Cambria, Pa. 1,445 C3 214
Scaly, Macon, N.C. 100 B2 186
Scammon, Cherokee, Kans. 429 E9 144
Scammon Bay, Alsk. 103 C5 84
Scandia, Alta., Can. E6 54
Scandia, Republic, Kans. 643 C6 144
Scandia, Washington, Minn. 150 F8 148
Scandinavia, Waupaca, Wis. 266 D4 160
Scanlon, Carlton, Minn. 1,126 E6 148
Scansano, It. 1,839 D3 302
Scanterbury, Man., Can. 75 E4 60
Scanzano, It. 392 E6 302
Scapa, Alta., Can. E7 54
Scapa, flow, Scot. C9 272
Scapegoat, mtn., Mont. C4 110
Scappoose, Columbia, Oreg. 923 B4 96
Scarba, isl., Scot. E7 272
Scarboro, Jenkins, Ga. 150 D5 176
Scarboro, Cumberland, Maine 500 E5 204
(6,418▲)
Scarborough, Ont., Can. 900 R22 64
Scarborough, Eng. 43,900 G12 273
Scarborough Junction, Ont., Can. 450 R22 64
Scarbro, Fayette, W.Va. 900 D7 194
Scarsdale, Westchester, N.Y. 17,968 D2 212
Scarth, Man., Can. 80 F2 60
Scarville, Winnebago, Iowa 105 A4 142
Scauri, It. G3 302
Sceaux, Fr. 10,601 I10 278
Scebeli, riv., Som. E5 398
Scenic, Pennington, S.Dak. 83 D3 158
Sceptre, Sask., Can. 254 E3 58
Sceui Ghimira, Eth. D4 398
Schaal, Howard, Ark. 200 D3 170
Schaffer, Delta, Mich. 130 D4 146
Schaffhausen, Switz. 26,800 A4 312
(*40,400)
Schaffhausen (Schaffhouse), subcanton, Switz. 62,000 A4 312
Schaffhouse, see Schaffhausen, Switz.
Schagen, Neth. 3,889 B3 282
Schaghticoke, Rensselaer, N.Y. 720 C8 212
Schaller, Sac, Iowa 896 B2 142
Scharding, Aus. 5,864 B5 313
Schaumberg, Cook, Ill. 986 E2 138
Schefferville (Knob Lake), Que., Can. 1,632 D8 72
Scheibbs, Aus. 3,155 C7 313
Scheldt, riv., Bel. C3 282
Schell City, Vernon, Mo. 343 C3 150
Schenectady, Schenectady, N.Y. 81,682 C8 212
Schenectady, co., N.Y. 152,896 C7 212
Schenevus, Otsego, N.Y. 493 C7 212
Schererville, Lake, Ind. 2,875 A2 140
Schertz, Guadalupe, Tex. 2,281 B7 130
Scheveningen, Neth. (part of The Hague) B3 282
Schiedam, Neth. 75,568 C3 282
Schiermonnikoog, isl., Neth. A5 282
Schiller Park, Cook, Ill. 5,687 E2 138
Schiltigheim, Fr. 22,798 C7 278
Schio, It. 18,300 C3 302
Schladming, Aus. 2,690 C5 313
Schlater, Leflore, Miss. 300 B2 184
Schleicher, co., Tex. 2,791 D5 130
Schleswig, Ger. 33,600 A3 286
Schleswig, Crawford, Iowa 785 B2 142
Schleswig-Holstein, reg., Ger. A3 286
Schleswig-Holstein, state, Ger. 2,277,300 *A3 286
Schley, Gloucester, Va. 175 C8 192
Schley, co., Ga. 3,256 D2 176
Schlüchtern, Ger. 5,800 C3 286
Schmalkalden, Ger. 13,100 C4 286
Schneekoppe, mtn., Czech. A2 324
Schneider, Lake, Ind. 405 A2 140
Schochoh, Logan, Ky. 100 D4 178
Schoenchen, Ellis, Kans. 188 D4 144
Schofield, Marathon, Wis. 3,038 D4 160
Schofield Barracks, Honolulu, Haw. B3 86
G9
Schoharie, Schoharie, N.Y. 1,168 C7 212
Schoharie, co., N.Y. 22,616 C7 212
Schoharie, creek, N.Y. C7 212
Scholls, Washington, Oreg. 200 B1 96
Schönbach, Aus. 716 B7 313
Schönebeck, Ger. 45,900 B4 286
Schongau, Ger. 7,700 E4 286
Schoodic, lake, Maine C4 204
Schoolcraft, Kalamazoo, Mich. 1,205 G6 146
Schoolcraft, co., Mich. 8,953 C5 146
Schoonhoven, Neth. 567 C3 282
Schoten, Bel. 23,275 C3 282
Schouten, is., Neth. N.Gui. E9 359
Schramberg, Ger. 17,700 D3 286
Schram City, Montgomery, Ill. 698 D4 138
Schreiber, Ont., Can. 1,800 *R24 64
Schriever, Terrebonne, La. 650 C6 180
E5
Schrobenhausen, Ger. 8,200 D4 286
Schroon Lake, Essex, N.Y. 532 B8 212
Schroon, lake, N.Y. B8 212
Schuchk, Pima, Ariz. 38 F4 124
Schuermann Heights, St. Louis, Mo. 288 *C7 150
Schulenburg, Fayette, Tex. 2,207 E7 130
Schuler, Alta., Can. 150 E7 54
Schuls, see Scuol, Switz.
Schulte, Sedgwick, Kans. 50 B5 144
Schulter, Okmulgee, Okla. 500 C8 128
Schüpfheim, Switz. 3,763 B4 312
Schurz, Mineral, Nev. 171 E3 112
Schuyler, Colfax, Nebr. 3,096 C8 152
Schuyler, Nelson, Va. 450 C6 192
Schuyler, co., Ill. 8,746 C3 138
Schuyler, co., Mo. 5,052 A5 150
Schuyler, co., N.Y. 15,044 C5 212
Schuylerville, Saratoga, N.Y. 1,361 B8 212
Schuylkill, co., Pa. 173,027 C5 214
Schuylkill, riv., Pa. A6 214
Schuylkill Haven, Schuylkill, Pa. 6,470 C5 214
Schwabach, Ger. 20,600 D4 286
Schwäbisch Gmünd, Ger. 35,900 D3 286
Schwäbisch Hall, Ger. 19,900 D3 286
Schwandorf [in Bayern], Ger. 14,500 D5 286
Schwaner, mts., Indon. E4 358
Schwarzwald, see Black Forest, mts., Ger.
Schwaz, Aus. 8,898 C3 313
Schwedt, Ger. 5,961 B6 286
Schweidnitz, see Swidnica, Pol.
Schweinfurt, Ger. 53,700 C4 286
Schwenningen [am Neckar], Ger. 29,900 D3 286
Schwerin, Ger. 94,200 B4 286
Schwerin, see Skwierzyna, Pol.
Schweriner See, lake, Ger. B4 286
Schwyz, Switz. 10,300 A4 312
Schwyz, canton, Switz. 74,600 A4 312
Sciacca, It. 23,400 G4 302
Science Hill, Pulaski, Ky. 463 C6 178
Scilly, is., Eng. L6 273
Scio, Allegany, N.Y. 600 C4 212
Scio, Harrison, Ohio 1,135 B5 156
Scio, Linn, Oreg. 441 C1 96
C4
Scioto, co., Ohio 84,216 D3 156
Scioto, riv., Ohio B3 156
Sciotodale, Scioto, Ohio 800 *D4 156
Scioto Furnace, Scioto, Ohio 375 D4 156
Scipio, Jennings, Ind. 200 C4 140
Scipio, Pittsburg, Okla. 75 C8 128
Scipio, Millard, Utah 328 D3 114
Scitico, Hartford, Conn. 225 B5 202
Scituate, Plymouth, Mass. 3,229 B6 206
(11,214▲) D4
Scituate (Town of), Providence, R.I. (5,210▲) B2 216
Scituate, res., R.I. B2 216
Scituate Center, Plymouth, Mass. 350 D4 206
Scobey, Yalobusha, Miss. 100 B3 184
Scobey, Daniels, Mont. 1,726 B11 110
Scofield, Carbon, Utah 158 D4 114
Scollard, Alta., Can. 50 E6 54
Scooba, Kemper, Miss. 513 C4 184
Scotch Plains, Union, N.J. 18,491 B4 210
Scotia, Humboldt, Calif. 1,122 B1 94
Scotia, Ont., Can. O21 64
Scotia, Greeley, Nebr. 350 C7 152
Scotia, Schenectady, N.Y. 7,625 C8 212
Scotia, Hampton, S.C. 102 F6 188
Scotland, Van Buren, Ark. 150 B4 170
Scotland, Ont., Can. 435 Q20 64
Scotland, Windham, Conn. 250 C7 202
(684▲)
Scotland, Telfair and Wheeler, Ga. 236 D4 176
Scotland, Greene, Ind. 100 D3 140
Scotland, St. Marys, Md. 100 D7 182
Scotland, Plymouth, Mass. 130 *C6 206
Scotland, Franklin, Pa. 800 D4 214
Scotland, Bon Homme, S.Dak. 1,077 D8 158
Scotland, co., Mo. 6,484 A5 150
Scotland, co., N.C. 25,183 C6 186
Scotland, reg., United Kingdom 5,144,700 E8 272
Scotland Neck, Halifax, N.C. 2,974 A8 186
Scotlandville, East Baton Rouge, La. 10,000 A5 180
Scotsguard, Sask., Can. 80 F3 58
Scotstown, Que., Can. 1,347 S13 66
Scott, Pulaski and Lonoke, Ark. 240 C4 170
D7
Scott, Sask., Can. 339 D3 58
Scott, Johnson, Ga. 149 D4 176
Scott, Lafayette, La. 902 D3 180
Scott, Bolivar, Miss. 350 B1 184
Scott, Van Wert and Paulding, Ohio 365 B2 156
Scott, co., Ark. 7,297 C2 170
Scott, co., Ill. 6,377 D3 138
Scott, co., Ind. 14,643 D4 140
Scott, co., Iowa 119,067 C7 142
Scott, co., Kans. 5,228 D2 144
Scott, co., Ky. 15,376 B6 178
Scott, co., Minn. 21,909 G5 148
Scott, co., Miss. 21,187 C3 184
Scott, co., Mo. 32,748 D8 150
Scott, co., Tenn. 15,413 B7 190
Scott, co., Va. 25,813 D2 192
Scott, cape, B.C., Can. E8 52
Scott, isl., B.C., Can. E8 52
Scott, mtn., Okla. D5 128
Scott City, Scott, Kans. 3,555 D3 144
Scott City (Fornfelt), Scott, Mo. 1,963 *D8 150
Scottdale, De Kalb, Ga. 4,000 B5 176
Scottdale, Westmoreland, Pa. 6,244 C2 214
Scottish, sea, Scot. E5 272
Scotts, Kalamazoo, Mich. 280 G6 146
Scotts, mtn., N.J. B2 210
Scottsbluff, Scotts Bluff, Nebr. 13,377 C2 152
Scotts Bluff, co., Nebr. 33,809 C2 152
Scotts Bluff, natl. mon., Nebr. C2 152
Scottsboro, Jackson, Ala. 6,449 A3 168
Scottsburg, Scott, Ind. 3,810 D4 140
Scottsburg, Douglas, Oreg. 200 D3 96
Scottsburg, Halifax, Va. 188 D6 192
Scottsdale, Maricopa, Ariz. 10,026 E4 124
H2
Scotts Hill, Henderson, Tenn. 298 C3 190
Scotts Mills, Marion, Oreg. 155 B4 96
C2
Scottsmoor, Brevard, Fla. 125 C10 174
Scott Station, Perry, Ala. 15 C2 168
Scottsville, Pope, Ark. 145 B3 170
Scottsville, Mitchell, Kans. 60 C6 144
Scottsville, Allen, Ky. 3,324 D4 178
Scottsville, Monroe, N.Y. 1,863 B4 212
Scottsville, Albemarle and Fluvanna, Va. 353 C6 192
Scottville, Mason, Mich. 1,245 F5 146
Scourie, Scot. C7 272
Scout Lake, Sask., Can. 100 F5 58
Scraggly, lake, Maine B4 204
Scranton, Logan, Ark. 229 B3 170
Scranton, Greene, Iowa 865 B3 142
Scranton, Osage, Kans. 576 D8 144
Scranton, Menifee, Ky. 127 C7 178
Scranton, Bowman, N.Dak. 358 D2 154
Scranton, Lackawanna, Pa. 111,443 A5 214
(*215,600) B6
Scranton, Florence, S.C. 613 D9 188
Scraper, Kane, Ill. 700 *B5 138
Scraper, Cherokee, Okla. B9 128
Screven, Wayne, Ga. 1,010 E4 176
Screven, co., Ga. 14,919 D5 176
Scribner, Dodge, Nebr. 1,021 C9 152
Scridain, bay, Scot. E7 272
Scullin, Murray, Okla. 27 *D7 128
Scullville, Atlantic, N.J. 350 E3 210
Scullyville, Le Flore, Okla. 200 C9 128
Scunthorpe, Eng. 58,800 H12 273
Scuol (Schuls), Switz. 1,384 B6 312
Scurry, co., Tex. 20,369 C5 130
Scusciuban, Som. C7 398
Scutari, lake, Alb. C4 316
Scutari, lake, Yugo. C4 316
Scyrene, Clarke, Ala. 200 D2 168
Sdom, Isr. C6 382
Seabeck, Kitsap, Wash. 400 D2 98
Seaboard, Northampton, N.C. 624 A8 186
Seabra, Braz. 1,962 G2 256
Sea Bright, Monmouth, N.J. 1,138 C5 210
Seabrook, Liberty, Ga. 150 E5 176
Seabrook, Prince Georges, Md. 3,000 *C6 182
Seabrook (Seabrook Farms), Cumberland, N.J. 1,798 E2 210
Seabrook, Rockingham, N.H. 700 F5 208
(2,209▲)
Seabrook, Beaufort, S.C. 500 F7 188
Seabrook, isl., S.C. F8 188
G3
Seaby, Den. 3,482 D1 292
Sea Cliff, Nassau, N.Y. 5,669 *D3 212
Seadrift, Calhoun, Tex. 1,082 E7 130
Seaford, Sussex, Del. 4,430 F3 172
Seaford, Nassau, N.Y. 14,718 *E3 212
Seaford, York, Va. 1,000 A8 192
C8
Seaforth, Ont., Can. 2,128 Q19 64
Seaforth, Redwood, Minn. 131 G3 148
Sea Girt, Monmouth, N.J. 1,798 C4 210
Seagoville, Dallas, Tex. 3,745 B9 130
Seagram, lake, Sask., Can. D3 58
Seagrave, Ont., Can. 150 P22 64
Seagraves, Gaines, Tex. 2,307 C4 130
Seagrove, Randolph, N.C. 323 B6 186
Seaham, Eng. 25,900 G11 272
Seahurst, King, Wash. 2,500 D2 98
Sea Island, Glynn, Ga. 300 E5 176
Sea Isle City, Cape May, N.J. 1,393 E3 210
Seal, lake, Newf., Can. D9 72
Seal Beach, Orange, Calif. 6,994 C5 94
Seal Cove, N.B., Can. 110 E3 70
Seal Cove, Newf., Can. 225 F7 72
Seal Cove, Hancock, Maine 130 D4 204
Seale, Russell, Ala. 350 C4 168
Sealevel, Carteret, N.C. 500 C9 186
Seal Harbor, Hancock, Maine 200 D4 204
Seal Rock, Lincoln, Oreg. 250 C2 96
Sealston, King George, Va. 150 B7 192
Sealy, Austin, Tex. 2,328 E7 130
Seama, Valencia, N.Mex. 447 C3 126
Seaman, Adams, Ohio 714 D3 156
Sea Ranch Lakes, Broward, Fla. 170 *E10 174
Searchlight, Clark, Nev. 180 H7 112
Searcy, White, Ark. 7,272 B5 170
Searcy, co., Ark. 8,124 B4 170
Searight, Crenshaw, Ala. 64 D3 168
Searles, Tuscaloosa, Ala. 400 B2 168
Searles, lake, Calif. E5 94
Sears, Osceola, Mich. 60 F6 146
Sears, falls, Nebr. B5 152
Searsboro, Poweshiek, Iowa 165 C5 142
Searsburg, Bennington, Vt. 50 F3 218
(73▲)
Searsmont, Waldo, Maine 150 D3 204
(628▲)
Searsport, Waldo, Maine 783 D4 204
(1,838▲)
Searston, Newf., Can. 150 G6 72
Seaside, Monterey, Calif. 19,353 *D3 94
Seaside, Clatsop, Oreg. 3,877 B3 96
Seaside Heights, Ocean, N.J. 954 D4 210
Seaside Park, Ocean, N.J. 1,054 D4 210
Seatack, Princess Anne, Va. 3,120 A9 192
Seaton, Eng. 3,000 K9 273
Seaton, Mercer, Ill. 235 B3 138
Seat Pleasant, Prince Georges, Md. 5,365 C4 182
C6
Seattle, King, Wash. 557,087 B4 98
(*938,400) D2
Seattle Heights, Snohomish, Wash. 300 *B4 98
Sea View, Plymouth, Mass. 200 E4 206
Seaview, Pacific, Wash. 600 C2 98
Seaview, mtn., Austl. E10 432
Seaville, Cape May, N.J. 100 E3 210
Seba Beach, Alta., Can. 141 D5 54
Sébaco, Nic. 1,338 D4 228
Sebago, Cumberland, Maine 50 *E2 204
(546▲)
Sebago, lake, Maine E2 204
Sebago Lake, Cumberland, Maine 350 E2 204
Sebasco Estates, Sagadahoc, Maine 250 E3 204
E6
Sebastian, Indian River, Fla. 698 D10 174
Sebastian, co., Ark. 66,685 B2 170
Sebastian, cape, Oreg. E2 96
Sebastian, inlet, Fla. D10 174
Sebastian Vizcaino, bay, Mex. B3 224
Sebasticook, lake, Maine D3 204
Sebastopol, Sonoma, Calif. 2,694 C2 94
Sebastopol, Scott, Miss. 343 C3 184
Sebatik, isl., Indon. D5 358
Sebec, Piscataquis, Maine 150 C3 204
(384▲)
Sebec, lake, Maine C3 204
Sebeka, Wadena, Minn. 823 E3 148
Sebeş, Rom. 11,628 B2 321
Sebewaing, Huron, Mich. 2,026 F8 146
Şebinkarahisar, Tur. 7,588 A8 307
Sebnitz, Ger. 15,400 C6 286
Seboeis, Penobscot, Maine 60 C4 204
(77▲)
Seboeis, riv., Maine B4 204
Seboois, lake, Maine C4 204
Seboomook, Somerset, Maine 10 C3 204
Seboomook, lake, Maine C3 204
Seboyeta, Valencia, N.Mex. 167 C3 126
Sebree, Webster, Ky. 1,139 C3 178
Sebrell, Southampton, Va. 200 D7 192
Sebring, Highlands, Fla. 6,939 D9 174
Sebring, Mahoning, Ohio 4,439 B5 156
Sebringville, Ont., Can. 555 Q19 64
Secaucus, Hudson, N.J. 12,154 B1 210
Secchia, riv., It. C3 302
Secession, lake, S.C. C3 188
Sechelt, B.C., Can. 439 F11 52
Sechura, Peru 3,826 B1 245
Sechura, bay, Peru B1 245
Seco, Letcher, Ky. 531 C8 178
Second, lake, Maine B4 204
Second Connecticut, lake, N.H. C4 208
Second Mesa, Navajo, Ariz. 400 C5 124
Secor, Woodford, Ill. 427 C4 138
Secretan, Sask., Can. 60 E4 58
Secretary, Dorchester, Md. 351 C8 182
Section, Jackson, Ala. 595 A4 168
Secunderabad, India 161,807 E3 366
Security, El Paso, Colo. 7,000 *D6 106
Sedalia, Alta., Can. 50 E7 54
Sedalia, Douglas, Colo. 202 C6 106
Sedalia, Clinton, Ind. 170 B3 140
Sedalia, Graves, Ky. 258 D2 178
Sedalia, Pettis, Mo. 23,874 C4 150
Sedalia, Union, S.C. B5 188
Sedan, Fr. 17,637 C6 278
Sedan, Chautauqua, Kans. 1,677 E7 144
Sedan, Pope, Minn. 91 F3 148
Sedan, Nuckolls, Nebr. 35 *D8 152
Sedan, Union, N.Mex. 45 B7 126
Sedberg, Eng. 2,049 G10 273
Sédérog, Niger. C5 408
Sedgewick, Alta., Can. 608 D7 54
Sedgwick, Lawrence, Ark. 206 B6 170
Sedgwick, Sedgwick, Colo. 299 B8 106
Sedgwick, Harvey, Kans. 1,095 E6 144
Sedgwick, Hancock, Maine 150 D4 204
(574▲)
Sedgwick, co., Colo. 4,242 B8 106
Sedgwick, co., Kans. 343,231 E6 144
Sédhiou, Sen. D1 408
Sedley, Sask., Can. 352 E5 58
Sedley, Southampton, Va. 500 D8 192
Sedona, Coconino, Ariz. 280 D4 124
Sedro Woolley, Skagit, Wash. 3,705 A4 98
Seebe, Alta., Can. E5 54
Seebert, Pocahontas, W.Va. 100 C4 194
Seeheim, S.W.Afr. E3 420
Seeis, S.W.Afr. D3 420
Seekonk, Bristol, Mass. 8,399 C5 206
Seekonk, riv., R.I. B3 216
Seeley, Imperial, Calif. 600 F6 94
Seeley Lake, Missoula, Mont. 200 C3 110
Seeleys Bay, Ont., Can. 300 P24 64
Seely, Crook, Wyo. 5 B8 116
Seelyville, Vigo, Ind. 1,114 C2 140
Sefadu, S.L. E2 408
Seffner, Hillsborough, Fla. 500 C8 174
Sefid, riv., Iran B2 379
Segamat, Mala. 18,454 G4 362
Segargea, Rom. B2 321
Segesta, ruins, It. G4 302
Sego, Grand, Utah 20 D6 114
Segorbe, Sp. 6,502 C6 298
Ségou, Mali 22,000 D3 408
Segovia, Sp. 24,977 B4 298
Segovia, prov., Sp. 203,488 *B4 298
Segré, Fr. 5,108 D3 278
Segre, riv., Sp. B7 298
Segreganset, Bristol, Mass. 300 C5 206
Seguedine, well, Niger B7 409

Séguéla, I.C. 4,200 E3 408
Seguin, Guadalupe, Tex. 14,299 B7 130
E7
Seguin Falls, Ont., Can. 65 O21 64
Segundo, Las Animas, Colo. 175 E6 106
Segura, riv., Sp. C5 298
Sehan (Sarus), riv., Tur. C6 307
Sehkuheh, Iran C5 379
Sehore, India E2 368
Sehwan, Pak. 3,827 F5 375
Seibert, Kit Carson, Colo. 210 C8 106
Seibo, Dom. Rep. 3,164 C10 233
Seigling, Allendale, S.C. 143 E6 188
Seiland, isl., Nor. A10 290
Seiling, Dewey, Okla. 910 B5 128
Seinäjoki, Fin. 7,493 E10 290
Seine, dept., Fr. 5,154,834 *C5 278
Seine, bay, Fr. C3 278
Seine, riv., Fr. C4 278
Seine-et-Marne, dept., Fr. 453,438 *C5 278
Seine-et-Oise, dept., Fr. 1,708,791 *C4 278
Seine-Inférieure, see Seine-Maritime, dept., Fr.
Seine-Maritime, dept., Fr. 941,684 *C4 278
Seishin, see Chŏngjin, Kor.
Sejerö, isl., Den. F2 292
Sekenke, Tan. C5 414
Seki, Jap. 8,554 M12 354
Sekibi, isl., Ryukyu Is., Jap. M12 349
Sekiu, Clallam, Wash. 150 A2 98
Sekondi, Ghana 26,757 (*44,557) F4 408
Selah, Yakima, Wash. 2,824 C6 98
Selangor, state, Mala. 1,012,047 *G4 362
Selanovtsi, Bul. 6,842 B2 317
Selardalur, Ice. L17 290
Selaru, isl., Indon. F8 359
Selatan, cape, Indon. E4 358
Selawik, Alsk. 273 B5 84
Selawik, lake, Alsk. B5 84
Selb, Ger. 19,100 C5 286
Selbu, Nor. 4,560 E4 290
Selby, Walworth, S.Dak. 979 B5 158
Selbyville, Sussex, Del. 1,080 G5 172
Selbyville, Upshur, W.Va. 93 C4 194
Selden, Sheridan, Kans. 347 C3 144
Selden, Aroostook, Maine 25 C5 204
Selden, Suffolk, N.Y. 1,604 D4 212
Seldovia, Alsk. 460 D6 84
H10
Selenge, riv., Mong. B8 346
Selenicë, Alb. 3,182 A2 306
Sélestat, Fr. 11,705 C7 278
Seletytengiz, lake, Sov.Un. B8 336
Selfridge, Sioux, N.Dak. 371 D5 154
Selibaby, Maur. 22,000 C2 408
Selidovka, Sov.Un. S21 332
Seligman, Yavapai, Ariz. 764 C3 124
Seligman, Barry, Mo. 387 E4 150
Selima (Oasis), Sud. A2 398
Selinsgrove, Snyder, Pa. 3,948 C5 214
Selinunte, ruins, It. G4 302
Selizharovo, Sov.Un. 5,000 D9 332
Selkirk, Man., Can. 7,413 E4 60
Selkirk, Ont., Can. 500 R21 64
Selkirk, Wichita, Kans. 60 D2 144
Selkirk, Scot. 5,800 F10 272
Selkirk, co., Scot. 21,200 F9 272
Selkirk, mts., B.C., Can. E14 52
Selleck, King, Wash. 100 B5 98
D3
Seller, lake, Man., Can. C5 60
Sellers, Montgomery, Ala. 150 C3 168
Sellers, Hancock, Miss. 160 E3 184
Sellers, Marion, S.C. 431 C10 188
Sellersburg, Clark, Ind. 2,679 D4 140
Sellersville, Bucks, Pa. 2,497 C6 214
Sells, Pima, Ariz. 789 G4 124
Selma, Dallas, Ala. 28,385 C2 168
Selma, Drew, Ark. 150 D5 170
Selma, Fresno, Calif. 6,934 D4 94
Selma, Delaware, Ind. 562 B4 140
Selma, Adams, Miss. 250 D1 184
Selma, Johnston, N.C. 3,102 B7 186
Selma, Josephine, Oreg. 30 E3 96
Selma, Alleghany, Va. 850 C5 192
Selman, Harper, Okla. 60 B4 128
Selmer, McNairy, Tenn. 1,897 C3 190
Selukwe, Rh.&Nya. 3,500 C6 421
Selva, Arg. A3 252
Selvas, forest, Braz. G5 256
Selvin, Warrick, Ind. 150 D2 140
Selway, riv., Idaho C3 108
Selwyn, Austl. C8 432
Selwyn, lake, N.W.Ter., Can. E8 48
Selwyn, mtn., B.C., Can. C11 52
Selz, Pierce, N.Dak. 150 C6 154
Seman, Elmore, Ala. 103 C3 168
Seman, riv., Alb. A2 306
Semans, Sask., Can. 402 E5 58
Semarang, Indon. 373,900 F4 358
Semenovka, Sov.Un. 15,000 F9 332
Seminary, Covington, Miss. 288 D3 184
Seminoe, res., Wyo. E6 116
Seminoe Dam, Carbon, Wyo. 55 D6 116
Seminole, Baldwin, Ala. 150 E2 168
Seminole, Pinellas, Fla. 600 C6 174
Seminole, Seminole, Okla. 11,464 C7 128
Seminole, Gaines, Tex. 5,737 C4 130
Seminole, co., Fla. 54,947 C9 174
Seminole, co., Ga. 6,802 F2 176
Seminole, co., Okla. 28,066 C7 128
Semipalatinsk, Sov.Un. 155,000 B9 336
Semitau, Sar. D4 358
Semiway, McLean, Ky. 200 C3 178
Semiyarskoye, Sov.Un. B9 336
Semliki, riv., Con.L. B4 414
Semmens, lake, Man., Can. G5 60
Semmering, pass, Aus. C7 313
Semmes, Mobile, Ala. 300 *E1 168
Semnān, Iran 23,078 B3 379
Semora, Caswell, N.C. 75 A6 186
Semoy, riv., Bel. E3 282
Sempacher, lake, Switz. A4 312
Semur-en-Auxois, Fr. D6 278
Sen, riv., Camb. D5 362
Sena, San Miguel, N.Mex. 45 C5 126
Senachwine, lake, Ill. B4 138
Senador Pompeu, Braz. 5,158 B3 258
Sena Madureira, Braz. 1,663 G3 256
Senanga, Rh.&Nya. 2,785 C4 420
Senate, Sask., Can. 75 F3 58
Senath, Dunklin, Mo. 1,369 E7 150
Senatobia, Tate, Miss. 3,259 A3 184
Sendai (Kagoshima pref.), Jap. 49,106 I3 354
Sendai (Miyagi pref.), Jap. 375,844 E8 354
Sendai, bay, Jap. E8 354
Sendhwa, India E1 368
Seneca, La Salle, Ill. 1,719 B5 138
Seneca, Nemaha, Kans. 2,072 C7 144
Seneca, Montgomery, Md. 150 B5 182
Seneca, Newton, Mo. 1,478 E3 150
Seneca, Thomas, Nebr. 160 B5 152
Seneca, Union, N.Mex. 15 B7 126
Seneca, Lane, Oreg. 400 C8 96
Seneca, Venango, Pa. 800 B2 214
Seneca, Oconee, S.C. 5,227 B3 188
Seneca, Faulk, S.Dak. 161 B6 158
Seneca, Crawford, Wis. 180 E3 160
Seneca, co., N.Y. 31,984 C5 212
Seneca, co., Ohio 59,326 A3 156
Seneca, caverns, W.Va. C5 194
Seneca, lake, N.Y. C5 212
Seneca, rocks, W.Va. C5 194
Seneca Falls, Seneca, N.Y. 7,439 C5 212
Seneca Gardens, Jefferson, Ky. 928 *B5 178
Senecaville, Guernsey, Ohio 575 C5 156
Senecaville, res., Ohio C5 156
Seneffe, Bel. 3,061 D3 282
Senegal, country, Afr. 2,250,000 E5 388
409
Sénégal, riv., Maur. C2 408
Senekal, U.S.Afr. 5,430 E5 420
Seney, Schoolcraft, Mich. 80 C6 146
Senftenberg, Ger. 19,400 C6 286
Senga Hill, Rh.&Nya. A6 421
Senhōshi, Jap. 3,403 B8 354
Senigallia, It. 16,700 D4 302
Senkaku, is., Ryukyu Is., Jap. L11 349
Senj, Yugo. 3,093 B2 316
Senja, isl., Nor. B7 290
Senlac, Sask., Can. 121 D3 58
Senlis, Fr. 7,992 C5 278
Sennar, Sud. 8,093 C3 398
Senoia, Coweta, Ga. 782 C2 176
Sens, Fr. 18,612 C5 278
Senta, Yugo. 25,524 B5 316
Sentery, Con.L. D4 414
Sentinel, Maricopa, Ariz. 75 F2 124
Sentinel, Washita, Okla. 1,154 C4 128
Sentinel, butte, N.Dak. D2 154
Sentinel Butte, Golden Valley, N.Dak. 160 D2 154
Senzu, Jap. L14 354
Seo de Urgel, Sp. 4,194 A7 298
Seoni, India E2 368
Seoul (Keijo), Kor. 1,574,868 G13 348
Separ, Grant, N.Mex. 44 F2 126
Sept Îles (Seven Islands), Que., Can. 5,592 Q10 66
E8 72
Sępolno, Pol. 4,214 B3 325
Sepulga, riv., Ala. D3 168
Sequatchie, Marion, Tenn. 400 C6 190
Sequatchie, co., Tenn. 5,915 C6 190
Sequatchie, riv., Tenn. C6 190
Sequim, Clallam, Wash. 1,164 A3 98
Sequoia, natl. park, Calif. D4 94
Sequoyah, co., Okla. 18,001 C9 128
Serafimovich, Sov.Un. 8,800 C2 336
Seragaki, Okinawa C1 436
Seraing, Bel. 42,534 D4 282
Serakhs, Sov.Un. 3,000 F8 328
Serampore, India 74,324 I9 366
Seran, lake, Sov.Un. D3 336
Serang, Indon. 11,163 F3 358
Serangoon, dist., Singapore 218,275 *G4 362
Serape, Maricopa, Ariz. 24 H2 124
Serbia (Srbija), rep., Yugo. 6,979,154 C5 316
Serdobsk, Sov.Un. 35,000 F15 332
Sered, Czech. 6,208 B3 324
Şereflikoçhisar, Tur. 4,458 B5 307
Seremban, Mala. 52,038 G4 362
Serengeti, plain, Tan. C5 414
Serenje, Rh.&Nya. 510 B6 421
Serenli, Som. E5 398
Sergeant Bluff, Woodbury, Iowa 813 B1 142
Sergeantsville, Hunterdon, N.J. 165 C3 210
Sergipe, state, Braz. 716,000 H9 257
Seria, Bru. 5,525 D4 358
Sérifos, Grc. 2,372 C5 306
Sérifos, isl., Grc. C5 306
Seringapatam, India 7,678 F3 366
Serles, Hardeman, Tenn. 25 C3 190
Seroei, Neth.N.Gui. E9 359
Serón, Sp. 1,894 D5 298
Serov, Sov.Un. 98,000 A6 336
Serowe, Bech. 15,935 D5 420
Serpa, Port. 7,273 D3 298
Serpentine, lakes, Austl. D6 432
Serpentine, mts., N.B., Can. B3 70
Serpukhov, Sov.Un. 105,000 B1 336
Serra dos Aimorés, reg., Braz. 160,915 *I8 257
Sérrai, Grc. 36,760 A4 306
Sérrai, prov., Grc. 222,549 A4 306
Serrana Bank, shoals, Caribbean Sea C8 228
Serranilla Bank, shoals, Caribbean Sea C8 228
Serra Talhada, Braz. 5,353 B3 258
Serrezuela, Arg. B2 252
Sêrro, Braz. 3,746 D2 258
Sertã, Port. 7,281 C2 298
Sertânia, Braz. 5,170 B3 258
Serua, isl., Indon. F8 359
Seruli, Bech. D5 420
Sérvia, Grc. 3,236 A4 306
Servia, Wabash, Ind. 150 B4 140
Service, Choctaw, Ala. 200 D1 168
Service, buttes, Oreg. B7 96
Service Creek, Wheeler, Oreg. C6 96
Sese, is., Ug. C5 414
Sesheke, Rh.&Nya. 124 C4 420
Sesia, riv., It. C2 302
Sesser, Franklin, Ill. 1,764 E4 138
Sessums, Oktibbeha, Miss. 150 B4 184
Sesto [Fiorentino], It. 14,100 D3 302
Sestri Levante, It. 9,100 C2 302
Sestroretsk, Sov.Un. (part of Leningrad) 34,000 B7 332
Setana, Jap. 6,023 C7 354
Setauket, Suffolk, N.Y. 1,207 *D4 212
Setberg, Ice. L18 290
Sète (Cette), Fr. 33,454 F5 302
Sete Lagoas, Braz. 18,438 D2 258
Seth, Boone, W.Va. 800 C3 194
D6
Seth Ward, Hale, Tex. 1,328 B5 130
Seti, riv., Nep. C3 368
Sétif, Alg. 53,057 A5 402
Seto, Jap. 64,681 G6 354
L13
Seton Portage, B.C., Can. 50 E11 52
Settat, Mor. 25,205 B2 402
Setté-Cama, Gabon G6 409
Settee, lake, Sask., Can. C5 58
Setting, lake, Man., Can. C3 60
Settle, Eng. 2,297 G10 273
Settle, Allen, Ky. 928 D4 178
Setúbal, Port. 44,235 C2 298
Setúbal, bay, Port. C2 298
Seul, lake, Ont., Can. R23 64
Seul Choix, pt., Mich. D6 146
Sevastopol, Sov.Un. 148,000 J9 332
Seven, heads, Ire. J4 273
Seven Harbors, Oakland, Mich. 2,748 *G8 146
Seven Hills, Cuyahoga, Ohio 57,081 B1 156
Seven Mile, Butler, Ohio 690 C2 156
Seven Mile, beach, N.J. E3 210
Seven Persons, Alta., Can. 125 F7 54
Seven Sisters, mtn., B.C., Can. C8 52
Seven Springs, Maricopa, Ariz. 100 E4 124
Seven Springs, Wayne, N.C. 207 B8 186
70 Mile House, B.C., Can. E12 52
Severance, Weld, Colo. 70 B6 106
Severance, Doniphan, Kans. 146 C8 144
Severka, riv., Sov.Un. O19 332
Severn, Anne Arundel, Md. 280 B6 182
Severn, Northampton, N.C. 310 A8 186
Severn, Gloucester, Va. 300 C8 192
Severn, mouth, Eng. J9 273
Severn, riv., Ont., Can. Q24 64
Severn, riv., Eng. I10 273
Severn, riv., Md. B6 182
Severna Park, Anne Arundel, Md. 3,100 B6 182
Severnaya, Sov.Un. C6 328
Severnaya Zemlya, is., Sov.Un. B11 329
Severo-Yeniseyskiy, Sov.Un. C11 329
Severy, Greenwood, Kans. 492 E7 144
Sevier, Sevier, Utah 10 E3 114
Sevier, co., Ark. 10,156 D2 170
Sevier, co., Tenn. 24,251 C8 190
Sevier, co., Utah 10,565 D4 114
Sevier, des., Utah D2 114
Sevier, lake, Utah E2 114
Sevier, riv., Utah D3 114
Sevierville, Sevier, Tenn. 2,890 C8 190
Sevilla, Col. 17,210 C1 244
Sevilla, Sp. 374,138 D4 298
Sevilla, prov., Sp. 1,101,595 *D4 298
Seville, Volusia, Fla. 623 B9 174
Seville, Wilcox, Ga. 179 E3 176
Seville, Medina, Ohio 1,190 A5 156
Sevlievo, Bul. 14,420 B2 317
Sevogle, riv., N.B., Can. B3 70
Sevran, Fr. 12,956 I11 278
Sèvre, riv., Fr. D3 278
Sèvre Niortaise, riv., Fr. D3 278
Sèvres, Fr. 17,109 I9 278
Sewalls Point, Martin, Fla. 151 *D10 174
Sewanee, Franklin, Tenn. 1,464 C6 190
Seward, Alsk. 1,891 C7 84
G11
Seward, Stafford, Kans. 92 D5 144
Seward, Seward, Nebr. 4,208 D8 152
Seward, Logan, Okla. 49 C6 128
Seward, Westmoreland, Pa. 754 C2 214
Seward, co., Kans. 15,930 E3 144
Seward, co., Nebr. 13,581 D8 152
Seward, pen., Alsk. B5 84
Seward Roads, chan., Midway E3 436
Sewaren, Middlesex, N.J. 1,500 C1 210
Sewell, Chile 2,009 B1 252
Sewell, Gloucester, N.J. 900 D2 210
Sewickley, Allegheny, Pa. 6,157 A3 214
C1
Sextonville, Richland, Wis. 250 E3 160
Sexsmith, Alta., Can. 345 C3 54
Seydhisfjordhur, Ice. 708 L22 290
Seydişehir, Tur. 4,523 C4 307
Seym, riv., Sov.Un. G9 332
Seymchan, Sov.Un. C17 329
Seymour, New Haven, Conn. 10,100 D3 202
Seymour, Jackson, Ind. 11,629 D4 140
Seymour, Wayne, Iowa 1,117 D4 142
Seymour, Harrison, Miss. (part of D'Iberville) E1 184
E4
Seymour, Webster, Mo. 1,046 D5 150
Seymour, Sevier, Tenn. 40 C8 190
E10
Seymour, Baylor, Tex. 3,789 C6 130
Seymour, Outagamie, Wis. 2,045 A5 160
D5
Seymour, inlet, B.C., Can. E9 52
Seymour, lake, Vt., B4 218
Seymour, range, B.C., Can. C13 52
Seymour, riv., B.C., Can. E9 52
Seymourville, Iberville, La. 1,788 B5 180
Sézanne, Fr. 5,186 C5 278
Sezimbra, Port. 6,957 C2 298
Sezze, It. 7,544 E4 302
Sfântul-Gheorghe, Rom. 17,638 B3 321
Sfax, Tun. 65,645 B6 402
Šfkofja Loka, Yugo. 3,360 A2 316
's Gravenhage, see The Hague, Neth.
Sgurr Mor, mtn., Scot. D7 272
Sha, China L8 349
Shabani, Rh.&Nya. 11,000 D6 421
Shabbona, De Kalb, Ill. 690 B5 138
Shabrakhit, Eg., U.A.R. 5,609 C1 382
Shabunda, Con.L. C4 414
Shabwa, Aden D4 383
Shackelford, co., Tex. 3,990 C6 130
Shackleton, Sask., Can. 105 E3 58
Shade, riv., Ohio C5 156
Shadehill, Perkins, S.Dak. 20 B3 158
Shadehill, res., S.Dak. B3 158
Shades, creek, Ala. E4 168
Shades, mtn., Ala. E4 168
Shadrinsk, Sov.Un. 52,000 A6 336
Shady Cove, Jackson, Oreg. 875 E4 96
Shady Dale, Jasper, Ga. 201 C3 176
Shady Grove, Pike, Ala. 125 D3 168
Shady Grove, Taylor, Fla. 300 A7 174
Shady Grove, Crittenden, Ky. 100 C3 178
Shadygrove, Franklin, Pa. 800 D4 214
Shady Grove, Hamilton, Tenn. 100 E8 190
Shadypoint, Le Flore, Okla. 300 C9 128
Shady Side, Anne Arundel, Md. 749 C6 182
Shadyside, Belmont, Ohio 5,028 C6 156
Shady Spring, Raleigh, W.Va. 850 D3 194
Shady Valley, Johnson, Tenn. 50 B10 190
Shafer, lake, Ind. B3 140
Shafer, Chisago, Minn. 147 *F6 148
Shafter, Kern, Calif. 4,576 E4 94
Shafter, Elko, Nev. 20 C7 112
Shafter, Presidio, Tex. 50 E3 130
Shaftesbury, Eng. 3,400 K11 273
Shaftsbury, Bennington, Vt. 55 (1,939▲) *F2 218
Shageluk, Alsk. 100 C6 84
Shag Harbour, N.S., Can. 197 F4 70
Shahabad, India D2 368
Shahdad (Khabis), Iran C4 379
Shahdadkot, Pak. 8,994 F5 375
Shāh Fuladi, mtn., Afg. B4 374
Shahgarh, India C1 366
Shaḩḩat, Libya, 4,149 A4 394
Shāhi, isl., Iran B1 379
Shahjahanpur, India 98,949 (104,835▲) D2 368
Shāhjui, Afg. 5,000 C4 374
Shaho, China N4 349
Shāhpūr (Dilmān), Iran 13,161 A1 379
Shahpur, Pak. E6 375
Shahpura, India D1 368
Shahr-e Bābak, Iran C4 379
Shahrezā, Iran 23,980 C3 379
Shāhrūd, Iran 23,132 B4 379
Shahsavār, Iran 5,046 B3 379
Shaikh Shu'aib, isl., Iran D3 379
Shailerville, Middlesex, Conn. 230 D6 202
Shaker Heights, Cuyahoga, Ohio 36,460 A5 156
B1
Shakhty, Sov.Un. 196,000 I13 332
Shakhunya, Sov.Un. A3 336
Shaki, Nig. 22,983 E5 408
Shakopee, Scott, Minn. 5,201 G5 148
G6
Shakotan, cape, Jap. C8 354
Shaktoolik, Alsk. 127 C5 84
Shalalth, B.C., Can. 200 E11 52
Shalimar, Okaloosa, Fla. 754 A4 174
Shallmar, Garrett, Md. 100 B1 182
Shallotte, Brunswick, N.C. 480 D7 186
Shallotte, inlet, N.C. D7 186
Shallow Lake, Ont., Can. 366 P19 64
Shallow Water, Scott, Kans. 125 D3 144
Shallowater, Lubbock, Tex. 1,001 C4 130
Shallufa, Eg., U.A.R. E7 395
Shalym, Sov.Un. B11 336
Shambat, Sud. 6,611 B3 398
Shambaugh, Page, Iowa 206 D2 142
Shambe, Sud. D3 398
Shamokin, Northumberland, Pa. 13,674 C5 214
Shamokin Dam, Snyder, Pa. 1,093 C5 214
Shamrock, Sask., Can. 95 E4 58
Shamrock, Dixie, Fla. 600 B7 174
Shamrock, Creek, Okla. 211 C7 128
Shamrock, Wheeler, Tex. 3,113 B5 130
Shamva, Rh.&Nya. C6 421
Shana (Kurilsk), Sov.Un. E16 329
Shandaken, Ulster, N.Y. 450 C7 212
Shandon, San Luis Obispo, Calif. 500 E3 94
Shandon, Butler, Ohio 350 C1 156
Shanesville, Tuscarawas, Ohio 510 *B5 156
Shang, China I4 348
Shangchiu, China 134,400 H7 348
Shangchuan, isl., China O6 349
Shanghai, China 7,100,000 J16 346
Shanghai, prov., China *E12 346
Shangjao, China 50,000 K9 349
Shangnan, China 5,000 I5 348
Shangssu, China N3 349
Shangtu, China 10,000 E6 348
Shaniko, Wasco, Oreg. 39 B6 96
Shannock, Washington, R.I. 375 D2 216
Shannon, Jefferson, Ala. 547 E4 168
Shannon, Floyd, Ga. 1,629 B1 176
Shannon, Carroll, Ill. 766 A4 138
Shannon, Lee, Miss. 554 A4 184
Shannon, co., Mo. 7,087 D6 150
Shannon, co., S.Dak. 6,000 D3 158
Shannon, airport, Ire. I3 273
Shannon, dam, Wash. A5 98
Shannon, isl., Grnld. P34 290
Shannon, lake, Wash. *A5 98
Shannon, mouth, Ire. I3 273
Shannon, riv., Ire. I3 273
Shannon City, Union, Iowa 127 D3 142
Shannontown, Sumter, S.C. 7,064 *D8 188
Shanshan (Pichan), China C6 346
Shansi, prov., China 15,960,000 D10 346
Shantar, Sov.Un. D15 329
Shantar, isl., Sov.Un. D15 329
Shantou, see Swatow, China
Shantung, prov., China 54,030,000 D11 346
Shantung, pen., China G10 348
Shantung, pt., China G11 348
Shanwa, Tan. C5 414
Shaohsing, China 130,600 J10 349
Shaopo, China 20,000 I9 349
Shaowu, China 5,000 L8 349
Shaoyang, China 117,700 L5 349
Shaping, China N4 349
Shapinsay, isl., Scot. B10 272
Shapio, lake, Newf., Can. D9 72
Shapleigh, York, Maine 120 (515▲) E2 204
Shaqrā', Sau.Ar. 10,000 B4 383

Sharafkhāneh

Sharafkhāneh, Iran	1,260	A1	379
Sharbot Lake, Ont., Can.	550	P24	64
Shåre, Swe.		B4	292
Shari, Jap.	17,468	C10	354
Sharja, Tr.Coast	4,000	B6	383
Shark, bay, Austl.		D2	432
Shark, pt., Fla.		F9	174
Sharkey, co., Miss.	10,738	C2	184
Sharkh, Om.		C6	383
Sharon, Litchfield, Conn.	800	B2	202
	(2,141▲)		
Sharon, Taliaferro, Ga.	264	C4	176
Sharon, Bear Lake, Idaho	40	*G7	108
Sharon, Barber, Kans.	272	E5	144
Sharon, Norfolk, Mass.	10,070	B5	206
		E2	
Sharon, Kalkaska, Mich.		E6	146
Sharon, Hillsboro, N.H.	50	F3	208
	(78▲)		
Sharon, Steele, N.Dak.	251	C8	154
Sharon, Woodward, Okla.	97	B4	128
Sharon, Mercer, Pa.	25,267	B1	214
Sharon, York, S.C.	280	B6	188
Sharon, Weakley, Tenn.	966	B3	190
Sharon, Windsor, Vt.	155	D4	218
	(485▲)		
Sharon, Spokane, Wash.		D8	98
Sharon, Kanawha, W.Va.	612	D6	194
Sharon, Walworth, Wis.	1,167	F5	160
Sharon Grove, Todd, Ky.	100	D3	178
Sharon Hill, Delaware, Pa.	7,123	A6	214
Sharon Springs, Wallace, Kans.	966	D2	144
Sharon Springs, Schoharie, N.Y.	351	C7	212
Sharonville, Hamilton, Ohio	3,890	D1	156
Sharp, Burlington, N.J.	900	C3	210
Sharp, Okmulgee, Okla.		C7	128
Sharp, co., Ark.	6,319	A5	170
Sharpe, lake, Man., Can.		C6	60
Sharpes, Brevard, Fla.	300	C10	174
Sharples, Logan, W.Va.	500	D3	194
		D5	
Sharps, Richmond, Va.	100	C8	192
Sharpsburg, Coweta, Ga.	155	*C2	176
Sharpsburg, Taylor, Iowa	130	D3	142
Sharpsburg, Bath, Ky.	311	B7	178
Sharpsburg, Washingbn, Md.	861	B4	182
Sharpsburg, Edgecombe, Nash and Wilson, N.C.	490	B8	186
Sharpsburg, Allegheny, Pa.	6,096	A4	214
Sharps Chapel, Union, Tenn.	25	B8	190
Sharpsville, Tipton, Ind.	663	B3	140
Sharpsville, Mercer, Pa.	6,061	B1	214
Sharp Top, mtn., Ark.		C3	170
Sharptown, Wicomico, Md.	620	C8	182
Sharptown, Salem, N.J.	220	D2	210
Sharr, mtn., Sau.Ar.		B2	383
Sharya, Sov.Un.	21,700	A3	336
Shashamani, Eth.		D4	398
Shashi, riv., Bech.		D5	420
Shashih, China	85,800	J6	349
Shashke, Sov.Un.		B7	336
Shasta, co., Calif.	59,468	B3	94
Shasta, lake, Calif.		B2	94
Shasta, mtn., Calif.		B2	94
Shatra, Iraq	9,543	D7	378
Shatsk, Sov.Un.	24,500	E13	332
Shatt al Arab, riv., Iraq		D7	378
Shattuck, Ellis, Okla.	1,625	B4	128
Shattuckville, Franklin, Mass.	150	A2	206
Shatura, Sov.Un.	20,000	*E12	332
Shaunavon, Sask., Can.	1,959	F3	58
Shavano, mtn., Colo.		D4	106
Shavers, fork, W.Va.		C5	194
Shavers, mtn., W.Va.		C5	194
Shaw, Lincoln, Colo.		C7	106
Shaw, Concordia, La.		C4	180
Shaw, Bolivar, Miss.	2,062	B2	184
Shaw, Marion, Oreg.	100	C1	96
Shaw, Mineral, W.Va.	225	B5	194
Shawa, prov., Eth.	2,100,000	D4	398
Shawan, Baltimore, Md.	96	A6	182
Shawanaga, Ont., Can.	75	O20	64
Shawanee, Claiborne, Tenn.	200	B8	190
Shawangunk, mts., N.Y.		D7	212
Shawano Plantation, Palm Beach, Fla.	60	E10	174
Shawano, Shawano, Wis.	6,103	D5	160
Shawano, co., Wis.	34,351	D5	160
Shawano, lake, Wis.		D5	160
Shawatun, China		E10	348
Shawbridge, Que., Can.	680	S10	66
Shawhan, Bourbon, Ky.	250	B6	178
Shawinigan-Est, Que., Can.	2,451	*R12	66
Shawinigan Falls, Que., Can.	28,597	R12	66
	(*58,500)		
Shawinigan Lake, B.C., Can.	275	C14	52
Shawinigan-Sud, Que., Can.	10,947	R12	66
Shawmut, Chambers, Ala.	1,898	C4	168
Shawmut, Pike, Ark.		C3	170
Shawmut, Somerset, Maine	225	D3	204
Shawnee, Wilcox, Ala.	400	D2	168
Shawnee, Johnson, Kans.	9,072	B8	144
Shawnee, Perry, Ohio	1,000	C4	156
Shawnee, Pottawatomie, Okla.	24,326	C7	128
Shawnee, Converse, Wyo.	18	D8	116
Shawnee, co., Kans.	141,286	D8	144
Shawnee, res., Okla.		C6	128
Shawneetown, Gallatin, Ill.	1,280	F5	138
Shawnut, Wheatland, Mont.	65	D7	110
Shawomet, Kent, R.I. (part of Warwick)		C3	216
Shawsheen, riv., Mass.		C2	206
Shawsheen Village, Essex, Mass.	3,000	A5	206
Shawsville, Harford, Md.	250	A6	182
Shawsville, Montgomery, Va.	300	C4	192
Shawver Mill, Tazewell, Va.		C3	192
Shayang, China	10,000	J5	349
Shayib Al Banāt, mtn., Eg., U.A.R.		B3	395
Shchelkovo, Sov.Un.	38,000	N19	332
Shcherbakov, see Rybinsk, Sov.Un.			
Shchetovo, Sov.Un.	2,000	S23	332
Shchigry, Sov.Un.	16,800	G11	332
Shchors, Sov.Un.	15,000	G8	332
Shchuchinsk, Sov.Un.	10,000	B8	336
Shchurovo, Sov.Un.	15,000	O19	332
Shearer Dale, B.C., Can.		B12	52
Sheaville, Malheur, Oreg.		D9	96
Sheboygan, Sheboygan, Wis.	45,747	B6	160
		E6	
Sheboygan, co., Wis.	86,484	E6	160
Sheboygan, riv., Wis.		B6	160
Sheboygan Falls, Sheboygan, Wis.	4,061	B6	160
		E6	
Shebshi, mts., Br.Cam.		E7	409
Shechichen, China	5,000	I6	349
Shedd, Linn, Oreg.	150	C3	96
Shedden, Ont., Can.	215	R19	64
Shediac, N.B., Can.	2,173	C5	70
Sheelin, lake, Ire.		H5	273
Sheenjek, riv., Alsk.		B7	84
Sheep, creek, Alta., Can.		D3	54
Sheep, mtn., Ariz.		F1	124
Sheep, mtn., Wyo.		C3	116
Sheep, range, Nev.		G6	112
Sheep Creek, B.C., Can.	250	F14	52
Sheep Haven, bay, Ire.		F5	272
Sheerness, Alta., Can.	80	E7	54
Sheet Harbour, N.S., Can.	1,400	E7	70
Sheffield, Colbert, Ala.	13,491	A2	168
Sheffield, Eng.	499,000	H11	273
	(*660,000)		
Sheffield, Bureau, Ill.	1,078	B4	138
Sheffield, Franklin, Iowa	1,156	B4	142
Sheffield, Berkshire, Mass.	700	B1	206
	(2,138▲)		
Sheffield, Custer, Mont.		D10	110
Sheffield, N.Z.	151	E4	437
Sheffield, Lorain, Ohio	1,664	A4	156
Sheffield, Warren, Pa.	1,971	B2	214
Sheffield, Caledonia, Vt.	225	B4	218
	(342▲)		
Sheffield, lake, Newf., Can.		F7	72
Sheffield Lake, Lorain, Ohio	6,884	A4	156
Shefford, co., Que., Can.	48,665	S12	66
Shefford, mtn., Que., Can.		S12	66
Sheguiandah, Ont., Can.	85	O19	64
Sheho, Sask., Can.	407	E6	58
Shehsien, China	5,000	K9	349
Shehuen, riv., Arg.		G3	251
Sheikh, Som.		D6	398
Shelagyote, peak, B.C., Can.		C9	52
Shelbiana, Pike, Ky.	800	C8	178
Shelbina, Shelby, Mo.	2,067	B5	150
Shelburn, Sullivan, Ind.	1,299	C2	140
Shelburn, East Carroll, La.	75	B4	180
Shelburn, Linn, Oreg.	40	C1	96
		C4	
Shelburne, N.S., Can.	2,337	F4	70
Shelburne, Ont., Can.	1,245	P20	64
Shelburne, Franklin, Mass.	100	A2	206
	(1,739▲)		
Shelburne, Coos, N.H.	50	C4	208
	(226▲)		
Shelburne, Chittenden, Vt.	250	C2	218
	(1,805▲)		
Shelburne, co., N.S., Can.	14,604	F4	70
Shelburne, pond, Vt.		C2	218
Shelburne Falls, Franklin, Mass.	2,097	A2	206
Shelby, Shelby, Ala.	750	B3	168
Shelby, Lake, Ind.	500	A2	140
Shelby, Shelby, Iowa	533	C2	142
Shelby, Oceana, Mich.	1,603	F5	146
Shelby, Bolivar, Miss.	2,384	B2	184
Shelby, Toole, Mont.	4,017	B5	110
Shelby, Polk, Nebr.	613	C8	152
Shelby, Cleveland, N.C.	17,698	B4	186
Shelby, Richland, Ohio	9,106	B4	156
Shelby, co., Ala.	32,132	B3	168
Shelby, co., Ill.	23,404	D5	138
Shelby, co., Ind.	34,093	C4	140
Shelby, co., Iowa	15,825	C2	142
Shelby, co., Ky.	18,493	B5	178
Shelby, co., Mo.	9,063	B5	150
Shelby, co., Ohio	33,586	B2	156
Shelby, co., Tenn.	627,019	C2	190
Shelby, co., Tex.	20,479	D8	130
Shelby City, Boyle, Ky.	500	C6	178
Shelby Village, Macomb, Mich.	1,900	*G8	146
Shelbyville, Sharp, Ark.		B5	170
Shelbyville, Shelby, Ill.	4,821	D5	138
Shelbyville, Shelby, Ind.	14,317	C4	140
Shelbyville, Shelby, Ky.	4,525	B5	178
Shelbyville, Shelby, Mo.	657	B5	150
Shelbyville, Bedford, Tenn.	10,466	C5	190
Sheldahl, Polk, Iowa	279	A7	142
Sheldon, Iroquois, Ill.	1,137	C6	138
Sheldon, O'Brien, Iowa	4,251	A2	142
Sheldon, Vernon, Mo.	434	D3	150
Sheldon, Ransom, N.Dak.	221	D8	154
Sheldon, Beaufort, S.C.	200	F7	188
Sheldon, Franklin, Vt.	300	B3	218
	(1,281▲)		
Sheldon, Rusk, Wis.	240	C3	160
Sheldon Point, Alsk.	137	*C5	84
Sheldon Springs, Franklin, Vt.	250	B3	218
Sheldonville, Norfolk, Mass.	450	B5	206
Shelekhov, gulf, Sov.Un.		C17	329
Shelikof, strait, Alsk.		D6	84
Shell, Horry, S.C.	150	D11	188
Shell, Big Horn, Wyo.	50	B5	116
Shell, bay, Scot.		D6	272
Shell, creek, Wyo.		B5	116
Shell, lake, Minn.		E3	148
Shell, lake, Wis.		C2	160
Shell, riv., Man., Can.		E2	60
Shell Beach, San Luis Obispo, Calif.	1,820	*E3	94
Shell Beach, St. Bernard, La.	125	E6	180
Shellbrook, Sask., Can.	907	D4	58
Shell Camp, Gregg, Tex.	500	*C8	130
Shell Creek, range, Nev.		D7	112
Shell Creek, Carter, Tenn.	400	C9	190
Shelley, Bingham, Idaho	2,612	F6	108
Shell Lake, Sask., Can.	258	D4	58
Shell Lake, Washburn, Wis.	1,016	C2	160
Shellman, Randolph, Ga.	1,050	E2	176
Shellmouth, Man., Can.	90	E2	60
Shell Point, see West Pittsburg, Calif.			
Shell Rock, Butler, Iowa	1,112	B5	142
Shellrock, riv., Iowa		B5	142
Shellsburg, Benton, Iowa	625	B6	142
Shelly, Norman, Minn.	310	D2	148
Shelter Island, Suffolk, N.Y.	900	D5	212
Shelton, Fairfield, Conn.	18,190	D3	202
Shelton, Buffalo, Nebr.	904	D7	152
Shelton, Fairfield, S.C.	100	C6	188
Shelton, Mason, Wash.	5,651	B3	98
Shemogue, N.B., Can.	140	C5	70
Shenandoah, Page, Iowa	6,567	D2	142
Shenandoah, Schuylkill, Pa.	11,073	C5	214
Shenandoah, Page, Va.	1,839	B6	192
Shenandoah, co., Va.	21,825	B6	192
Shenandoah, mtn., Va.		B5	192
Shenandoah, natl. park, Va.		B6	192
Shenandoah, riv., Va.		B6	192
Shenandoah, valley, Va.		B5	192
Shenandoah Heights, Schuylkill, Pa.	1,721	*C5	214
Shenandoah Tower, mtn., Va., W.Va.		B5	192
		C5	194
Shenchiu, China	10,000	I7	349
Shendi, Sud.	11,031	B3	398
Shenipsit, lake, Conn.		B6	202
Shenmu, China	10,000	F5	348
Shensi, prov., China	18,130,000	D9	346
Shenyang, see Mukden, China			
Sheopur, India		D2	368
Shepard, Alta., Can.	90	E6	54
Shepardsville, Vigo, Ind.	350	C2	140
Shepaug, riv., Conn.		C2	202
Shepetovka, Sov.Un.	28,400	G6	332
Shepherd, Isabella, Mich.	1,293	F7	146
Shepherd, Yellowstone, Mont.	100	E8	110
Shepherd, San Jacinto, Tex.	800	D8	130
Shepherd Brook, mtn., Maine		B3	204
Shepherdstown, Jefferson, W.Va.	1,328	B7	194
Shepherdsville, Bullitt, Ky.	1,525	B5	178
		C5	
Sheppard Park, Dorchester, S.C.	150	*E8	188
Sheppards, Buckingham, Va.		C6	192
Shepparton, Austl.	10,848	F9	432
Sheppey, isl., Eng.		J13	273
Sherard, Coahoma, Miss.	60	A2	184
Sherborn, Middlesex, Mass.	500	D2	206
	(1,806▲)		
Sherborne, Eng.	7,300	K10	273
Sherbrooke, N.S., Can.	512	D8	70
Sherbrooke, Que., Can.	58,668	S13	66
Sherbrooke, co., Que., Can.	70,568	S13	66
Sherbrooke, lake, N.S., Can.		E5	70
Sherburn, Martin, Minn.	1,227	H4	148
Sherburne, Fleming, Ky.	80	*B7	178
Sherburne, Chenango, N.Y.	1,647	C6	212
Sherburne, see Sherburne Center, Vt.			
Sherburne, co., Minn.	12,861	F5	148
Sherburne Center (Sherburne), Rutland, Vt.	60	D3	218
	(266▲)		
Shereik, Sud.		B3	398
Sheridan, Grant, Ark.	1,938	C4	170
Sheridan, Arapahoe, Colo.	3,559	C6	106
Sheridan, La Salle, Ill.	704	B5	138
Sheridan, Hamilton, Ind.	2,165	B3	140
Sheridan, Aroostook, Maine	350	B4	204
Sheridan, Montcalm, Mich.	606	F6	146
Sheridan, Worth, Mo.	277	A3	150
Sheridan, Madison, Mont.	539	E4	110
Sheridan, Yamhill, Oreg.	1,763	B3	96
Sheridan, Sheridan, Wyo.	11,651	B6	116
Sheridan, co., Kans.	4,267	C3	144
Sheridan, co., Mont.	6,458	B12	110
Sheridan, co., Nebr.	9,049	B3	152
Sheridan, co., N.Dak.	4,350	C5	154
Sheridan, co., Wyo.	18,989	B5	116
Sheridan, mtn., Wyo.		B2	116
Sheridan Beach, King, Wash.	1,500	*B4	98
Sheridan Lake, Kiowa, Colo.	90	D8	106
Sheringham, Eng.	4,600	I14	273
Sherkaly, Sov.Un.		C8	328
Sherman, Fairfield, Conn.	250	C2	202
	(825▲)		
Sherman, Aroostook, Maine	100	C4	204
	(1,034▲)		
Sherman, Pontotoc and Union, Miss.	403	A4	184
Sherman, St. Louis, Mo.	300	B7	150
Sherman, Chautauqua, N.Y.	873	C2	212
Sherman, Minnehaha, S.Dak.	116	D9	158
Sherman, Grayson, Tex.	24,988	C7	130
Sherman, co., Kans.	6,682	C2	144
Sherman, co., Nebr.	5,382	C6	152
Sherman, co., Oreg.	2,446	B6	96
Sherman, co., Tex.	2,605	A5	130
Sherman, mtn., Ark.		A3	170
Sherman Mills, Aroostook, Maine	450	C4	204
Sherman Station, Penobscot, Maine	375	C4	204
Sherpur, Pak.	19,312	K16	375
Sherrard, Mercer, Ill.	574	B3	138
Sherridon, Man., Can.	1,300	C2	60
Sherrill, Jefferson, Ark.	241	C5	170
Sherrill, Dubuque, Iowa	174	B7	142
Sherrill, Oneida, N.Y.	2,922	B6	212
Sherrodsville, Carroll, Ohio	480	B5	156
's Hertogenbosch, Neth.	63,330	C5	282
Sherwood, Pulaski, Ark.	1,222	C4	170
		D7	
Sherwood, Talbot, Md.	100	C7	182
Sherwood, Branch, Mich.	356	*H6	146
Sherwood, Renville, N.Dak.	360	B4	154
Sherwood, Defiance, Ohio	578	A2	156
Sherwood, McCurtain, Okla.	100	D9	128
Sherwood, Washington, Oreg.	680	B1	96
Sherwood, Franklin, Tenn.	650	C6	190
Sherwood, Calumet, Wis.	300	A5	160
Shetek, lake, Minn.		G3	148
Shetland, see Zetland, co., Scot.			
Shetland, is., Scot.		A12	272
Shetland Islands, Br. poss., Eur.	19,000	A12	272
Shetucket, riv., Conn.		C7	202
Shevlin, Clearwater, Minn.	203	D3	148
Shevlin, Klamath, Oreg.		D5	96
Sheyenne, Eddy, N.Dak.	423	C6	154
Sheyenne, riv., N.Dak.		D8	154
Shfaram, Isr.	3,905	B6	382
Shiawassee, co., Mich.	53,446	G7	146
Shibam, Aden	7,500	D4	383
Shibarghān, Afg.	22,464	A3	374
Shibata, Jap.	68,146	*E7	354
Shibetsu, Jap.	15,000	B9	354
	(39,191▲)		
Shibin el Kōm, Eg., U.A.R.	47,100	D2	382
Shibin el Qanātir, Eg., U.A.R.	11,610	D2	382
Shickley, Fillmore, Nebr.	371	D8	152
Shickshinny, Luzerne, Pa.	1,843	B5	214
Shideler, Delaware, Ind.	240	B4	140
Shiderty, riv., Sov.Un.		B8	336
Shidler, Osage, Okla.	870	B7	128
Shiel, inlet, Scot.		E7	272
Shields, Lane, Kans.	50	D3	144
Shields, Harlan, Ky.	900	*D7	178
Shields, Saginaw, Mich.	450	F7	146
Shields, Grant, N.Dak.	99	D4	154
Shigaki, isl., Ryūkyū Is., Jap.		M12	349
Shihchiachuang, China	598,000	F7	348
Shihchuan, China		I4	349
Shihmen, China	5,000	K5	349
Shihtaokuo, China	5,000	G11	348
Shikarpur, Pak.	45,376	F6	375
Shikokou, isl., Jap.		H4	354
Shilka, Sov.Un.	23,000	D13	329
Shilka, riv., Sov.Un.		D13	329
Shillington, Berks, Pa.	5,639	C6	214
Shillong, India	53,756	D5	368
Shiloh, Marengo, Ala.	100	C2	168
Shiloh, Cleburne, Ark.	6	*B4	170
Shiloh, Harris, Ga.	250	D2	176
Shiloh, St. Clair, Ill.	701	*E4	138
Shiloh, Cumberland, N.J.	554	E2	210
Shiloh, Camden, N.C.	400	A9	186
Shiloh, Richland, Ohio	724	B4	156
Shiloh, York, Pa.	1,500	*D5	214
Shiloh, Montgomery, Tenn.	40	B4	190
Shiloh, natl. military park and cemetery, Tenn.		C3	190
Silver Bank, passage, W.I.		B9	233
Shimabara, Jap.	46,184	H3	354
Shimada, Jap.	51,238	M14	354
Shimanovsk, Sov.Un.	17,000	D14	329
Shimizu, Jap.	126,586	G7	354
		L14	
Shimo, Jap.		K15	354
Shimo, isl., Jap		G2	354
Shimo, isl., Jap.		H3	354
Shimoda, Jap.	27,369	M14	354
Shimodate, Jap.	52,850	K16	354
Shimoga, India	46,524	F3	366
Shimonoseki, Jap.	230,503	G3	354
Shimotsuma, Jap.	31,951	*K15	354
Shin, lake, Scot.		C8	272
Shiner, Lavaca, Tex.	1,945	E7	130
Shinewell, McCurtain, Okla.	50	E9	128
Shingbwiyang, Bur.		A3	362
Shinglehouse, Potter, Pa.	1,298	B3	214
Shingler, Worth, Ga.	300	E3	176
Shingleton, Alger, Mich.	450	C5	146
Shingū, Jap.	37,267	H5	354
Shinjō, Jap.	38,603	E8	354
Shinkolobwe, Con.L.		E4	414
Shinlung, China		N6	349
Shinnston, Harrison, W.Va.	2,724	A7	194
		B4	
Shin Pond, Penobscot, Maine	40	B4	204
Shinshiro, Jap.	35,560	M13	354
Shinshou, China		K6	349
Shinyanga, Tan.	2,907	C5	414
Shio, cape, Jap.		H5	354
Shiocton, Outagamie, Wis.	685	A5	160
		D5	
Shiogama, Jap.	50,960	E8	354
Shiojiri, Jap.	13,863	K13	354
Shioya, cape, Jap.		F8	354
Ship, isl., Miss.		E4	184
Ship Bottom, Ocean, N.J.	717	D4	210
Ship Cove, Newf., Can.	50	G8	72
Ship Harbour, N.S., Can.	485	E7	70
Shipiskan, lake, Newf., Can.		D9	72
Ship Island, pass, Miss.		E1	184
Shipka, pass, Bul.		B2	317
Shipman, Macoupin, Ill.	417	D3	138
Shipman, Nelson, Va.	500	C6	192
Shippensburg, Cumberland and Franklin, Pa.	6,138	C4	214
Shippigan, N.B., Can.	1,362	B5	70
Shippigan, isl., N.B., Can.		B5	70
Shiprock, San Juan, N.Mex.	125	B2	126
Shipshewana, Lagrange, Ind.	312	A4	140
Shipunskiy, cape, Sov.Un.		D18	329
Shirāz, Iran	170,659	D3	379
Shirbin, Eg., U.A.R.	13,293	A3	395
Shire, riv., Rh.&Nya.		C6	421
Shiremanstown, Cumberland, Pa.	1,212	*C4	214
Shire Nor, China		E6	346
Shiretoko, cape, Jap.		B10	354
Shireza, Pak.		F4	375
Shiriya, cape, Jap.		D8	354
Shir Kuh, mtn., Iran		C4	379
Shirley, Van Buren, Ark.	197	B4	170
Shirley, Henry and Hancock, Ind.	1,038	C4	140
Shirley, Middlesex, Mass.	1,762	A4	206
	(5,202▲)		
Shirley, Salem, N.J.		D2	210
Shirley, Tyler, W.Va.	137	A6	194
Shirley, Brown, Wis.	50	A6	160
Shirley, basin, Wyo.		D6	116
Shirley Center, Middlesex, Mass.	150	A4	206
Shirley Mills, Piscataquis, Maine	200	C3	204
	(214▲)		
Shirotori, Jap.	6,043	*L12	354
Shishaldin, vol., Alsk.		E5	84
Shishido, Jap.	11,018	K16	354
Shishmaref, Alsk.	194	B5	84
Shively, Humboldt, Calif.	100	B2	94
Shively, Jefferson, Ky.	15,153	A5	178
		B5	
Shivers, Simpson, Miss.	10	D2	184
Shivpuri, India		D2	368
Shivwits, Washington, Utah	40	F2	114

Shizuoka, Jap.	295,172	G7 M14	354
Shkodër, Alb.	38,564	C4	316
Shkodër, pref., Alb.	150,000	*C4	316
Shoal, creek, Tenn.		C4	190
Shoal, lake, Man., Can.		F5	60
Shoal, lakes, Man., Can.		E4	60
Shoal, riv., Man., Can.		D2	60
Shoal Creek Drive, Newton, Mo.	277	*E3	150
Shoal Harbour, Newf., Can.	400	F9	72
Shoal Lake, Man., Can.	751	E2	60
Shoals, Martin, Ind.	1,022	D3	140
Shoals Junction, Greenwood, S.C.	100	C4	188
Shoalwater, cape, Wash.		C2	98
Shobankazgan, Sov.Un.		D6	336
Shoe, pt., Newf., Can.		F9	72
Shoe Cove, Newf., Can.	120	F8	72
Shoeheel, creek, S.C.		B10	188
Shoemakersville, Berks, Pa.	1,464	C6	214
Shoffner, Jackson, Ark.	25	B5	170
Shokuy, Sov.Un.		E12	329
Shola, lake, Eth.		D4	398
Sholapur, India	266,050 (*277,087)	E3	366
Sholes, Wayne, Nebr.	26	B8	152
Shona, isl., Scot.		E7	272
Shongaloo, Webster, La.	200	B2	180
Shongopovi, Navajo, Ariz.	150	C5	124
Shonkin, Chouteau, Mont.	11	C6	110
Shooks, Sevier, Tenn.		E9 C8	190
Shop Spring, Wilson, Tenn.	175	B5	190
Shore Acres, Contra Costa, Calif.	3,093	*C3	94
Shoreacres, B.C., Can.	350	F14	52
Shore Acres, Bristol, Mass.	980	D4	206
Shoreham, Berrien, Mich.	443	G5	146
Shoreham, Addison, Vt.	130 (786▲)	D2	218
Shore Hills, see Landing, N.J.			
Shoreview, Ramsey, Minn.	7,157	*G5	148
Shorewood, Rock, Wis.	15,990	E2 E6	160
Shorewood Hills, Dane, Wis.	2,320	E4	160
Shorey, Shawnee, Kans.		C8	144
Short, mtn., Tenn.		B8	190
Short, mtn., Tenn.		C6	190
Short Beach, New Haven, Conn.	950	D4	202
Short Creek, Mohave, Ariz.	200	B3	124
Short Creek, Brooke, W.Va.	500	B2	194
Shorter, Macon, Ala.	500	C4	168
Shorterville, Henry, Ala.	300	D4	168
Short Falls, Merrimack, N.H.	100	E4	208
Shortland, isl., Solomon		E1	436
Shortleaf, Marengo, Ala.	325	C2	168
Shortly, Sussex, Del.		F4	172
Shorts Creek, Carroll, Va.	50	D4	192
Shortsville, Ontario, N.Y.	1,382	C4	212
Shoshone, Garfield, Colo.	5	*C3	106
Shoshone, Lincoln, Idaho	1,416	G4	108
Shoshone, Eureka, Nev.	12	E7	112
Shoshone, co., Idaho	20,876	B3	108
Shoshone, basin, Wyo.		C4	116
Shoshone, falls, Idaho		G4	108
Shoshone, lake, Wyo.		B2	116
Shoshone, mtn., Nev.		G5	112
Shoshone, mts., Nev.		D4	112
Shoshone, mts., Wyo.		C3	116
Shoshone, riv., Wyo.		B4	116
Shoshoni, Fremont, Wyo.	766	C4	116
Shottsville, Marion, Ala.	200	A1	168
Shou, China	27,000	I8	349
Shouldice, Alta., Can.		E6	54
Shouns, Johnson, Tenn.	250	B10	190
Shoup, Lemhi, Idaho	10	D4	108
Shover Springs, Hempstead, Ark.		D3	170
Showak, Sud.	2,171	C4	398
Showell, Worcester, Md.	200	D9	182
Show Low, Navajo, Ariz.	1,625	D5	124
Shpola, Sov.Un.	26,300	H8	332
Shreve, Wayne, Ohio	1,617	B4	156
Shreveport, Caddo, La.	164,372 (*215,600)	B2	180
Shrewsbury, Eng.	46,900	I10	273
Shrewsbury, Jefferson, La. (part of Jefferson)		C7	180
Shrewsbury, Worcester, Mass.	16,622	B4	206
Shrewsbury, St. Louis, Mo.	4,730	*C7	150
Shrewsbury, Monmouth, N.J.	3,222	C4	210
Shrewsbury, Rutland, Vt.	35 (445▲)	*D3	218
Shrewsbury, riv., N.J.		C5	210
Shrewsbury Township, see Vail Homes, N.J.			
Shriver, Carbon, Mont.		E8	110
Shropshire, co., Eng.	298,000	I10	273
Shrub Oak, Westchester, N.Y.	1,874	*D8	212
Shuangcheng, China	81,000	C13	348
Shuangchiang, China		G7	346
Shuangliao, China	120,000	D11	348
Shuangshan, China		D11	348
Shuangyang, China		D12	348
Shuangyashan, China	50,000	B15	348
Shubenacadie, N.S., Can.	800	D6	70
Shubert, Richardson, Nebr.	231	D10	152
Shubuta, Clarke, Miss.	718	*D4	184
Shucheng, China	5,000	J8	349
Shujabad, Pak.	14,602	E7	375
Shuksan, mtn., Wash.		A5	98
Shulan, China		C13	348
Shulaps, peak, B.C., Can.		E11	52
Shulerville, Berkeley, S.C.	250	E9	188
Shullsburg, Lafayette, Wis.	1,324	F3	160
Shumagin, is., Alsk.		D5	84
Shuman House, Alsk.	20	B7	84
Shumaykh, Libya		A2	394
Shumen, see Kolarovgrad, Bul.			
Shumerlya, Sov.Un.	26,800	A3	336
Shumikha, Sov.Un.		A6	336
Shumway, Navajo, Ariz.	10	D6	124
Shunan, China	15,000	K9	349
Shunchang, China	5,000	L8	349
Shungnak, Alsk.	141	B6	84
Shunner Fell, mtn., Eng.		G10	273
Shunning, China		G7	346
Shuo, China	55,000	F6	348
Shuqra, Aden		E4	383
Shuqualak, Noxubee, Miss.	550	C4	184
Shur, riv., Iran		B3	379
Shur, riv., Iran		C4	379
Shur, riv., Iran		C5	379
Shur, riv., Iran		D4	379
Shūrāb, Iran		D5	379
Shūsh, Iran		C2	379
Shushan, Washington, N.Y.	275	B8	212
Shushong, Bech.		D4	420
Shūshtar, Iran	23,654	C2	379
Shusht el Maghara, mtn., Eg., U.A.R.		D4	382
Shuswap, B.C., Can.	125	E13	52
Shuswap, lake, B.C., Can.		E13	52
Shuswap, riv., B.C., Can.		E13	52
Shutesbury, Franklin, Mass.	150 (265▲)	B3	206
Shuya, Sov.Un.	64,000	A2	336
Shūzenji, Jap.	7,921	M14	354
Shwebo, Bur.	17,842	B2	362
Shwegyin, Bur.		C3	362
Shyok, India		B2	368
Shyok, riv., India		B2	368
Si, riv., China		N5	349
Siahan, range, Pak.		F3	375
Siāh Band, mtn., Afg.		C2	374
Sialkot, Pak.	135,401 (167,543▲)	C9	375
Sialum, N.Gui.		F11	359
Siam, see Thailand, country, Asia			
Siam, gulf, Asia		E4	362
Sian, see Hsian, China			
Siangtan, China	183,600	L6	349
Siapa, riv., Ven.		F6	240
Siasconset, Nantucket, Mass.	150	D8	206
Siátista, Grc.	4,980	A3	306
Siau, isl., Indon.		D7	358
Šiauliai, Sov.Un.	60,000	E4	332
Sibay, Sov.Un.		B5	336
Sibbald, Alta., Can.	100	E7	54
Šibenik, Yugo.	18,899	C2	316
Siberut, isl., Indon.		E1	358
Sibi, Pak.	11,842	E5	375
Sibiti, Con.B.		G7	409
Sibiu, Rom.	90,478	B3	321
Sibley, Osceola, Iowa	2,852	*A2	142
Sibley, Webster, La.	595	B2	180
Sibley, Jackson, Mo.	177	E3	150
Sibley, Adams, Miss.	50	D1	184
Sibley, co., Minn.	16,228	G4	148
Sibley, Barnes, N.Dak.	22	*C7	154
Sibolga, Indon.	36,000	D1	358
Sibsagar, India	7,559	D6	368
Sibu, Sar.	9,983	D4	358
Sibutu, isl., Phil.		D5	358
Sibuyan, sea, Phil.		B6	358
Sicamous, B.C., Can.	150	E13	52
Sicard, Ouachita, La.	2,000	*B3	180
Sicily (Sicilia), reg., It.	4,721,000	G4	302
Sicily, isl., It.		G4	302
Sicily Island, Catahoula, La.	761	C4	180
Sicklerville, Camden, N.J.	350	D3	210
Sickles, Caddo, Okla.		C5	128
Sico, riv., Hond.		C5	228
Sicuani, Peru	7,036	C3	245
Sidādah, Libya		A2	394
Sidāmo, prov., Eth.	1,250,000	E4	398
Sideling, hill, Md., W.Va.		B3 B6	182 194
Sideling Hill, creek, Md.		A3	182
Sidell, Vermilion, Ill.	614	D6	138
Siderno Marina, It.	6,915	F6	302
Siderovsk, Sov.Un.		C10	328
Sidewood, Sask., Can.	58	E3	58
Sidheros, cape, Grc.		D6	306
Sidhirókastron, Grc.	7,754	A4	306
Sidi Abdallah Ben Ali, Alg.		C4	402
Sidi Abd el Hakem, Alg.		C4	402
Sidi Barrâni, Eg., U.A.R.	3,308	A2	395
Sidi-bel-Abbès, Alg.	80,632	A3	402
Sidi bou Haous, Alg.		B4	402
Sidi Hadjed Dine, Alg.		B4	402
Sidi Ifni, Ifni	7,991	C1	402
Sidikalang, Indon.		D1	358
Sidi Salim, Eg., U.A.R.		C1	382
Sidlaw, hills, Scot.		E9	272
Sidnaw, Houghton, Mich.	200	C3	146
Sidney, Sharp, Ark.	97	A5	170
Sidney, B.C., Can.	1,371	C14 F11	52
Sidney, Man., Can.	160	F3	60
Sidney, Routt, Colo.		B4	106
Sidney, Champaign, Ill.	686	C5	138
Sidney, Kosciusko, Ind.	208	A4	140
Sidney, Fremont, Iowa	1,057	D2	142
Sidney, Kennebec, Maine	50 (988▲)	D3	204
Sidney, Richland, Mont.	4,564	C12	110
Sidney, Cheyenne, Nebr.	8,004	C3	152
Sidney, Delaware, N.Y.	5,157	C6	212
Sidney, Shelby, Ohio	14,663	B2	156
Sidney Center, Delaware, N.Y.	475	C6	212
Sidney Lanier, lake, Ga.		B2	176
Sidon, White, Ark.	90	B5	170
Sidon, see Saida, Leb.			
Sidon, Leflore, Miss.	410	B2	184
Sidonia, Weakley, Tenn.	120	B3	190
Sidra (Khalīj Surt), gulf, Libya		A3	394
Siedlce, Pol.	29,000	B6	325
Sieg, riv., Ger.		C2	286
Siegburg, Ger.	28,900	C2	286
Siegen, Ger.	46,000	C3	286
Siemiatycze, Pol.	4,106	B6	325
Siem Reap, Camb.	10,000	D4	362
Siena, It.	40,600	D3	302
Siena, prov., It.	279,400	*D3	302
Sieper, Rapides, La.	150	C3	180
Sieradz, Pol.	11,700	C4	325
Siero, Sp.	2,554	A4	298
Sierpc, Pol.	10,200	B4	325
Sierra, co., Calif.	2,247	C3	94
Sierra, co., N.Mex.	6,409	E3	126
Sierra Ancha, mts., Ariz.		E4	124
Sierra Blanca, Hudspeth, Tex.	800	D3	130
Sierra Blanca, mtn., N.Mex.		E5	126
Sierra City, Sierra, Calif.	150	C3	94
Sierra Colorado, Arg.		F4	251
Sierra del Carmen, mts., Tex.		E4	130
Sierra Diablo, mts., Tex.		D3	130
Sierra Estrella, Ariz.		H1	124
Sierra Gordo, Chile		B4	250
Sierra Leone, country, Afr.	2,260,000	F5	388 409
Sierra Madre, Los Angeles, Calif.	9,732	C5	94
Sierra Madre, mts., Guat.		C2	228
Sierra Madre, mts., Wyo.		E6	116
Sierra Mojada, Mex.	954	B5	224
Sierra Nevada, mts., Calif.		C3	94
Sierra Vista, Cochise, Ariz.	3,121	G5	124
Sierre, Switz.	7,161	B3	312
Siesta, key, Fla.		D8	174
Sifnos, isl., Grc.		C5	306
Sifton, Man., Can.	950	E2	60
Sigdal, Nor.		F3	291
Sigel, Shelby, Ill.	387	D5	138
Sighet, Rom.	22,361	A2	321
Sighişoara, Rom.	20,363	A3	321
Sighty Crag, mtn., Eng.		F10	272
Sigli, Indon.	3,327	C1	358
Siglufjördhur, Ice.	2,756	K20	290
Signal, Mohave, Ariz.	25	D2	124
Signal, mtn., Va.		A6	192
Signal Hill, Los Angeles, Calif.	4,627	C5	94
Signal Mountain, Hamilton, Tenn.	3,413	C6 E8	190
Sigourney, Keokuk, Iowa	2,387	C5	142
Sigsig, Ec.	1,662	A2	245
Sigtuna, Swe.	2,647	B8	292
Siguatepeque, Hond.	4,599	C4	228
Sigüenza, Sp.	4,541	B5	298
Siguiri, Guinea	11,200	D3	408
Sigurd, Sevier, Utah	339	E4	114
Sihora, India		E3	368
Siikajok, Fin.		D11	290
Siikajoki, riv., Fin.		D11	290
Siirt, Tur.	20,895	C9	307
Siirt, prov., Tur.	191,657	*C10	307
Sikar, India	44,140	D1	368
Sikasso, Mali	15,000	D3	408
Sikes, Winn, La.	233	B3	180
Sikeston, Scott and New Madrid, Mo.	13,765	E8	150
Sikhote-Alin, mts., Sov.Un.		E15	329
Sikiá, Grc.	2,547	A4	306
Sikinos, isl., Grc.		C5	306
Sikionía, Grc.	5,113	B4	306
Sikkim, country, Asia	150,000	D5	368
Siklós, Hung.	5,926	D3	320
Sil, riv., Sp.		A3	298
Silandro, It.	1,727	B3	302
Silao, Mex.	18,460	K13	225
Silas, Choctaw, Ala.	353	D1	168
Silchar, India	34,059	D6	368
Sile, Sandoval, N.Mex.	60	G6	126
Sile, Tur.	2,012	A3	307
Silen, lake, Swe.		B3	292
Siler City, Chatham, N.C.	4,455	B6	186
Silerton, Hardeman, Tenn.	84	C3	190
Silesia, Prince Georges, Md.	60	C5	182
Silesia, Carbon, Mont.	50	E8	110
Silesia (Schlesien), reg., Ger.		*C6	286
Silesia, reg., Pol.		C3	325
Siletz, Lincoln, Oreg.	583	C3	96
Silex, Lincoln, Mo.	176	B6	150
Silgarhi Doti, Nep.	1,461	C3	368
Silghat, India		D6	368
Silhuas, Peru	1,432	B2	245
Silica, Deer Lodge, Mont.	50	*D4	110
Silica, Randolph, W.Va.		C4	194
Silifke, Tur.	6,303	C5	307
Silistra, Bul.	20,491	A3	317
Silistrenski, prov., Bul.		*B3	317
Silivri, Tur.	4,182	A3	307
Siljan, lake, Swe.		F6	291
Silkeborg, Den.	23,878	H3	291
Sillery, Que., Can.	13,154	R16	66
Sillimans Fossil, mtn., N.W.Ter., Can.		E11	48
Silloth, Eng.	3,081	G9	272
Sil Nakya, Pima, Ariz.	40	F4	124
Silo, Bryan, Okla.	100	D7	128
Siloam, Greene, Ga.	321	C3	176
Siloam Springs, Benton, Ark.	3,953	A2	170
Silos, Mex.		C5	225
Silsbee, Hardin, Tex.	6,277	D8	130
Silsby, lake, Man., Can.		C5	60
Silt, Garfield, Colo.	384	C3	106
Silton, Sask., Can.	93	E5	58
Siltou, Chad		C8	409
Siluria, Shelby, Ala.	736	B3	168
Silva, Pierce, N.Dak.	56	B6	154
Silver, Clarendon, S.C.	50	D8	188
Silver, creek, Nebr.		D2	152
Silver, creek, Oreg.		C2	96
Silver, creek, Oreg.		D7	96
Silver, lake, Iowa		A3	142
Silver, lake, Maine		C3	204
Silver, lake, N.H.		D4	208
Silver, lake, N.H.		F2	208
Silver, lake, Oreg.		D6	96
Silver, lake, Oreg.		D7	96
Silver, lake, Wash.		D8	98
Silver, riv., N.S., Can.		E4	70
Silver Bay, Lake, Minn.	3,723	D7	148
Silver Beach, Barnstable, Mass.	700	*C6	206
Silver Bell, Pima, Ariz.	500	F4	124
Silver Bow, co., Mont.	46,454	E4	110
Silver Bow Park, Silver Bow, Mont.	4,798	*E4	110
Silver City, C.Z.	5,726	F8	228
Silver City, Owyhee, Idaho		F2	108
Silver City, Mills, Iowa	281	C2	142
Silver City, Humphreys, Miss.	431	B2	184
Silver City, Lyon, Nev.	125	D2	112
Silver City, Grant, N.Mex.	6,972	F2	126
Silver City, Pennington, S.Dak.	150	C2	158
Silver City, Juab, Utah	16	D3	114
Silver Cliff, Custer, Colo.	153	D5	106
Silver Creek, Floyd, Ga.	200	B1	176
Silver Creek, Lawrence, Miss.	229	D2	184
Silver Creek, Chautauqua, N.Y.	3,310	C2	212
Silver Creek, Merrick, Nebr.	431	C8	152
Silverdale, Cowley, Kans.	50	E7	144
Silverdale, Onslow, N.C.		C8	186
Silverdale, Kitsap, Wash.	950	B4 D2	98
Silver Gate, Park, Mont.	15	E7	110
Silver Grove, Campbell, Ky.	1,207	A8	178
Silverhill, Baldwin, Ala.	417	E2	168
Silver Hill, Prince Georges, Md. (part of Suitland)		C3	182
Silver Hill, Middlesex, Mass.	200	D2	206
Silver Lake, Kosciusko, Ind.	514	A4	140
Silver Lake, Shawnee, Kans.	392	C8	144
Silver Lake, Middlesex, Mass.	4,654	C2	206
Silver Lake, Plymouth, Mass.	140	*C6	206
Silver Lake, McLeod, Minn.	646	G4	148
Silver Lake, Carroll, N.H.	150	D4	208
Silver Lake, Summit, Ohio	2,655	A5	156
Silver Lake, Lake, Oreg.	97	D5	96
Silverlake, Cowlitz, Wash.	300	C4	98
Silverlake, Kenosha, Wis.	1,077	F1 F5	160
Silver Mine, Madison, Mo.	148	D7	150
Silverpeak, Esmeralda, Nev.	50	F4	112
Silver Plume, Clear Creek, Colo.	86	*C5	106
Silver Point, Putnam, Tenn.	150	B6	190
Silver River, mtn., Newf., Can.		F7	72
Silver Run, Carroll, Md.	125	A5	182
Silver Spring, Montgomery, Md.	66,348	C3 C5	182
Silver Springs, Marion, Fla.	375	B8	174
Silver Springs, Lyon, Nev.	60	D2	112
Silver Springs, Wyoming, N.Y.	726	C3	212
Silver Star, Madison, Mont.	50	E4	110
Silver Star, mtn., Wash.		A6	98
Silverstreet, Newberry, S.C.	181	C5	188
Silverthrone, mtn., B.C., Can.		E9	52
Silvertip, mtn., Mont.		C3	110
Silverton, B.C., Can.	347	F14	52
Silverton, San Juan, Colo.	822	E3	106
Silverton, Shoshone, Idaho	700	B3	108
Silverton, Ocean, N.J.	600	C4	210
Silverton, Hamilton, Ohio	6,682	D1	156
Silverton, Marion, Oreg.	3,081	B4 C1	96
Silverton, Briscoe, Tex.	1,098	B5	130
Silverton, Snohomish, Wash.	25	A5	98
Silvertown, Upson, Ga.		D2	176
Silves, Port.	4,361	D2	298
Silvia, Col.	2,499	C1	244
Silvies, Grant, Oreg.		C8	96
Silvies, riv., Oreg.		D7	96
Silview, New Castle, Del.	519	B3	172
Silvis, Rock Island, Ill.	3,973	B3	138
Silvo Pôrto, Ang.	12,146	B3	420
Simanggang, Sar.	2,449	D4	358
Simav, Tur.	5,415	B3	307
Simcoe, Ont., Can.	8,078	R20	64
Simcoe, co., Ont., Can.	127,016	P20	64
Simcoe, creek, Wash.		C5	98
Simcoe, lake, Ont., Can.		P21	64
Simcoe, mtn., Wash.		C6	98
Simeon, Cherry, Nebr.		B5	152
Simeulue, is., Indon.		D1	358
Simferopol, Sov.Un.	189,000	J10	332
Simi, Ventura, Calif.	2,107	*E4	94
Simi, isl., Grc.		C6	306
Simití, Col.	1,742	B2	244
Simla, Elbert, Colo.	450	C6	106
Simla, India	46,150	C2	368
Şimleul-Silvaniei, Rom.	8,560	A2	321
Simmesport, Avoyelles, La.	2,125	D4	180
Simmie, Sask., Can.	135	F3	58
Simmons, cave, Mo.		D5	150
Simms, Cascade, Mont.	100	C5	110
Simnasho, Wasco, Oreg.	40	C5	96
Simo, Fin.		D11	290
Simoda, Pendelton, W.Va.	70	C5	194
Simojärvi, lake, Fin.		C12	290
Simola, Fin.		F13	291
Simonette, riv., Alta., Can.		C3	54
Simonhouse, lake, Man., Can.		C2	60
Simonton Lake, Elkhart, Ind.	900	A4	140
Simoom Sound, B.C., Can.	250	E9	52
Simplicio Mendes, Braz.	1,243	B2	258
Simplon, pass, Switz.		B4	312
Simplon, tunnel, It., Switz.		B2 B4	302 312
Simpson, Sask., Can.	371	E5	58
Simpson, Adams, Colo.		C7	106
Simpson, Mitchell and Cloud, Kans.	154	C6	144
Simpson, Vernon, La.	400	C2	180
Simpson, Hill, Mont.	5	B6	110
Simpson, Pitt, N.C.	302	*B8	186
Simpson, Marshall, Okla.	25	D7	128
Simpson, Lackawanna, Pa.	1,800	B6	214
Simpson, Taylor, W.Va.	400	B7	194
Simpson, co., Ky.	11,548	D4	178
Simpson, co., Miss.	20,454	D2	184
Simpson, creek, W.Va.		B7	194
Simpson, des., Aust.		D7	432
Simpson, pen., N.W.Ter., Can.		D10	48
Simpsonville, Shelby, Ky.	220	B5	178
Simpsonville, Greenville, S.C.	2,282	B4	188
Simrishamn, Swe.	7,272	F5	292
Sims, Wayne, Ill.	376	E5	138
Sims, Grant, Ind.	225	B4	140
Sims, Wilson, N.C.	205	B7	186
Simsboro, Lincoln, La.	363	B3	180
Simsbury, Hartford, Conn.	2,745 (10,138▲)	B4	202
Sims Chapel, Washington, Ala.	300	D1	168
Simunjan, Sar.	1,679	D4	358
Simushir, isl., Sov.Un.		E17	329
Sinai, Brookings, S.Dak.	166	C9	158
Sinai, reg., Eg., U.A.R.	37,670	*B3	395
Sinai, pen., Eg., U.A.R.		B3	395
Sinaia, Rom.	9,006	B3	321
Sinai Gebel Musa, mtn., Eg., U.A.R.		B3	395
Sinajana, Guam	3,069	C7	437
Sinaloa, Mex.	1,284	B4	224
Sinaloa, state, Mex.	635,681	B4	224
Sinamaica, Ven.		A3	240
Sināwan, Libya	609	A2	394
Sinawi, Afg.	10,000	B6	374
Sinbillawēn, Eg., U.A.R.	29,700	D2	382
Sincé, Col.	7,112	B1	244
Sincelejo, Col.	21,625	B1	244
Sinclair, Man., Can.	100	F2	60
Sinclair, Carbon, Wyo.	621	E5	116
Sinclair, lake, Ga.		C3	176
Sinclair Head, cape, N.Z.		J10	437
Sinclairville, Chautauqua, N.Y.	726	C2	212
Sind, riv., India		D2	368
Sindara, Gabon		G7	409

Smyrna, Rutherford, Tenn. 3,612 C5 E7 190
Smyrna, see İzmir, Tur.
Smyrna, riv., Del. C3 172
Smyrna Mills, Aroostook, Maine 200 (331▲) B4 204
Smyth, co., Va. 31,066 D3 192
Snaefell, mtn., Isle of Man G8 273
Snake, creek, Nebr. B2 152
Snake, creek, Nebr. B4 152
Snake, falls, Nebr. B5 152
Snake, lake, Sask., Can. C4 58
Snake, mtn., N.C. A4 186
Snake, range, Nev. D7 112
Snake, riv., Minn. C1 148
Snake, riv., Minn. F5 148
Snake, riv., U.S. C3 77
Snake Indian, riv., Alta., Can. D3 54
Snake River, range, Wyo. C1 116
Snåsavatn, lake, Nor. D5 290
Sneads, Jackson, Fla. 1,399 A6 174
Sneads Ferry, Onslow, N.C. 500 C8 186
Sneedville, Hancock, Tenn. 799 B8 190
Sneek, Neth. 19,627 A4 282
Snell, Clarke, Miss. C4 184
Snelling, Barnwell, S.C. 100 E6 188
Snellville, Gwinnett, Ga. 468 A6 176
Snellville, Worcester, Mass. 100 *B3 206
Snezhnoye, Sov.Un. 22,000 S22 332
Snezhnyy, peak, Sov.Un. D13 329
Sniardwy, lake, Pol. B5 325
Snider, Sanders, Mont. 110 *C1 110
Snipe, keys, Fla. G9 174
Snipe, lake, Alta., Can. C4 54
Snizort, bay, Scot. D6 272
Snodgrass, Claiborne, Tenn. B8 190
Snohetta, mtn., Nor. E3 291
Snohomish, Snohomish, Wash. 3,894 B4 98
Snohomish, co., Wash. 172,199 A5 98
Snomac, Seminole, Okla. 100 C7 128
Snoqualmie, King, Wash. 1,216 B5 98
Snoqualmie Falls, King, Wash. 800 B5 98
Snov, riv., Sov.Un. G8 332
Snover, Sanilac, Mich. 250 F9 146
Snow, Pushmataha, Okla. 20 D8 128
Snow, mtn., Maine C2 204
Snow, peak, Wash. A8 98
Snowball, Searcy, Ark. 124 B4 170
Snowbank, lake, Minn. C7 148
Snow Camp, Alamance, N.C. 130 B6 186
Snowden, Sask., Can. 260 D5 58
Snowdon, mts., Wales H8 273
Snowdoun, Montgomery, Ala. 250 C3 168
Snowfield, peak, Wash. A5 98
Snowflake, Navajo, Ariz. 982 D5 124
Snowflake, Man., Can. 100 F3 60
Snow Hill, Wilcox, Ala. 250 D2 168
Snow Hill, Ouachita, Ark. 50 D4 170
Snow Hill, Worcester, Md. 2,311 D9 182
Snow Hill, Greene, N.C. 1,043 B8 186
Snowking, mtn., Wash. A5 98
Snow Lake, Desha, Ark. 119 C5 170
Snowmass, Pitkin, Colo. 8 C4 106
Snowmass, mtn., Colo. C3 106
Snow Road Station, Ont., Can. 150 P24 64
Snowshoe, lake, Maine B4 204
Snowshoe, peak, Mont. B1 110
Snowtown, Jefferson, Ala. 350 *B2 168
Snowville, Box Elder, Utah 159 B3 114
Snowville, Pulaski, Va. 100 C4 192
Snyder, Ashley, Ark. 75 D5 170
Snyder, Morgan, Colo. 95 B7 106
Snyder, Dodge, Nebr. 325 C9 152
Snyder, Erie, N.Y. 9,500 C3 212
Snyder, Kiowa, Okla. 1,663 D5 128
Snyder, Scurry, Tex. 13,850 C5 130
Snyder, co., Pa. 25,922 C4 214
Snyder Knob, mtn., W.Va. C5 194
Snyderville, Summit, Utah 25 C4 114
Soai Rieng, Camb. 5,000 E5 362
Soalala, Malag. 759 C9 421
Soap Lake, Grant, Wash. 1,591 B7 98
Soatá, Col. 3,116 B2 244
Soay, isl., Scot. D4 272
Sobat, riv., Sud. D3 398
Sobieski, Morrison, Minn. 190 F4 148
Sobieski, Oconto, Wis. 80 D5 160
Sobinka, Sov.Un. 32,000 E13 332
Sobol, Pushmataha, Okla. 10 D8 128
Sobral, Braz. 22,628 A2 258
Sobti, well, Mali B4 408
Sochaczew, Pol. 13,300 B5 325
Soche (Yarkand), China 80,000 D3 346
Social Circle, Walton, Ga. 1,780 C3 176
Social Hill, Hot Spring, Ark. 100 D7 170
Society, is., Pac.O. D4 436
Society Hill, Darlington, S.C. 677 B9 188
Socompa, pass., Arg., Chile B4 250
Socorro, Col. 11,842 B2 244
Socorro, Socorro, N.Mex. 4,334 D4 126
Socorro, El Paso, Tex. 1,500 D2 130
Socorro, co., N.Mex. 10,168 D3 126
Socotra, isl., Indian O. H7 340
Socotra Island, Aden 12,000 H7 340
Socrum, Polk, Fla. 512 C8 174
Soc Trang, Viet. 16,890 E5 362
Socuéllamos, Sp. 11,890 C5 298
Soda, lake, Calif. E5 94
Soda Creek, B.C., Can. 65 D11 52
Sodankylä, Fin. 1,641 C12 290
Soda Springs, Caribou, Idaho 2,424 G7 108
Sodaville, Mineral, Nev. 20 E3 112
Sodaville, Linn, Oreg. 145 C4 96
Soddy, Hamilton, Tenn. 2,206 C6 E8 190
Söderfors, Swe. 2,785 A8 292
Söderhamn, Swe. 12,224 F7 291
Söderköping, Swe. 5,451 C7 292
Södermanland, co., Swe. 220,946 B7 292
Södermanland, prov., Swe. 744,167 *G7 291
Södertälje, Swe. 28,641 B8 292
Sodiri, Sud. 1,804 C2 398
Sodo, Eth. D4 398
Södra Kvarken, gulf, Swe. A9 292
Sodus, Wayne, N.Y. 1,645 B4 212

Sodus Point, Wayne, N.Y. 868 B5 212
Soest, Ger. 31,900 C3 286
Sofádhes, Grc. 4,046 B4 306
Sofia (Sofiya), Bul. 612,270 (*725,756) B1 317
Sofia, prov., Bul. *B1 317
Sofia, riv., Malag. C9 421
Sofiya, see Sofia, Bul.
Sofiyevka, Sov.Un. H9 332
Sofiyski, prov., Bul. *B1 317
Sofre, Pan. 787 F7 228
Sogamoso, Col. 13,574 B2 244
Sogndal, Nor. F2 291
Sogndal, Nor. G2 291
Sognefjord, fjord, Nor. F1 291
Sogn og Fjordane, co., Nor. 98,263 *F2 291
Sohâg, Eg., U.A.R. 43,168 B3 395
Sohagpur, India E3 368
Sohano, Solomon D1 436
Sohar, Om. C6 383
Soignies, Bel. 10,926 D3 282
Sointula, B.C., Can. 500 E9 52
Soissons, Fr. 20,484 C5 278
Sokal, Sov.Un. 25,000 G5 332
Sokalov, Czech. A1 324
Soke, Okinawa C1 436
Sokh Bulak, India A1 368
Sokhondg, mtn., Sov.Un. D13 329
Sokol, Sov.Un. 36,000 C13 332
Sokółka, Pol. 4,879 B6 325
Sokolo, Mali D3 408
Sokłów, Pol. 7,515 B6 325
Sokoto, Nig. 47,643 D6 408
Solana, Charlotte, Fla. 1,309 *E8 174
Solander, isl., N.Z. G1 437
Solano, Harding, N.Mex. 75 C6 126
Solano, co., Calif. 134,597 C2 94
Solano Beach, San Diego, Calif. 3,000 F5 94
Solbad Hall (in Tirol), Aus. 10,016 C3 313
Soldatna, Alsk. 200 C6 G10 84
Soldier, Monona, Iowa 284 C2 142
Soldier, Jackson, Kans. 171 C8 144
Soldier, Carter, Ky. 150 B7 178
Soldier, key, Fla. E6 174
Soldier, riv., Iowa C2 142
Soldier Pond, Aroostook, Maine 500 A4 204
Soldiers Grove, Crawford, Wis. 663 E3 160
Soldier Summit, Wasatch, Utah 33 D4 114
Soledad, Monterey, Calif. 2,837 D3 94
Soledad, Col. 20,158 A2 244
Soledad, Mex. L15 225
Soledad, Ven. 3,358 B7 240
Soleduck, riv., Wash. B2 98
Solen, Sioux, N.Dak. 250 D5 154
Soleure, see Solothurn, Switz.
Solgen, lake, Swe. D5 292
Solgohachia, Conway, Ark. 80 *B4 170
Soligalich, Sov.Un. 5,500 C14 332
Solihull, Eng. 78,900 I11 273
Solikamsk, Sov.Un. 35,000 A5 336
Sol-Iletsk, Sov.Un. 19,100 B5 336
Solingen, Ger. 162,800 C2 286
Solitario, mtn., Tex. B6 130
Sollas, Scot. D5 272
Sollebrunn, Swe. C3 292
Sollefteå, Swe. 9,656 E7 290
Sollentuna, Swe. 21,534 B8 292
Sóller, Sp. 6,817 C8 298
Sollyu-Bong, mts., Kor. F12 348
Solna, Swe. 44,303 B8 292
Solok, Indon. 6,214 E2 358
Solomea, Samoa E4 436
Solomon, Alsk. 93 C5 84
Solomon, Graham, Ariz. 375 F6 124
Solomon, Dickinson, Kans. 1,008 D6 144
Solomon, is., Pac.O. D3 436
Solomon, riv., Kans. C6 144
Solomon, sea, Solomon E1 436
Solomon Islands (Austl.), reg., N.Gui. 66,000 *D1 436
Solomon Islands, Br. poss., Pac.O. 100,000 D1 436
Solomons, Calvert, Md. 183 D7 182
Solon, Johnson, Iowa 604 C6 142
Solon, Somerset, Maine 500 (669▲) D3 204
Solon, Cuyahoga, Ohio 6,333 A5 156
Solon Springs, Douglas, Wis. 530 B2 160
Solothurn, Switz. 17,400 (*27,000) A3 312
Solothurn (Soleure), canton, Switz. 187,000 A3 312
Solsberry, Greene, Ind. 150 C3 140
Solsgirth, Man., Can. 100 E2 60
Šolta, isl., Yugo. C3 316
Soltau, Ger. 14,200 B3 286
Solun, China 5,000 B10 348
Solund, isl., Nor. F1 291
Solvang, Santa Barbara, Calif. 1,325 *E3 94
Solvay, Onondaga, N.Y. 8,732 B5 212
Sölvesborg, Swe. 5,880 E5 292
Solway, Beltrami, Minn. 100 D3 148
Solway, firth, Scot. G9 273
Solwezi, Rh.&Nya. B5 420
Somalia, country, Afr. 1,980,000 F11 388 398
Sombor, Yugo. 26,637 B4 316
Sombra, Ont., Can. 400 R18 66
Sombrerete, Mex. 5,976 C5 224
Sombrero, chan., India G6 366
Sombrero Butte, Pinal, Ariz. 10 F5 124
Somerdale, Camden, N.J. 4,839 D2 210
Somero, Fin. F10 291
Somers, Tolland, Conn. 950 (3,702▲) B6 202
Somers, Calhoun, Iowa 203 B3 142
Somers, Flathead, Mont. 700 B2 110
Somers, Kenosha, Wis. 200 F2 F6 160
Somerset, Man., Can. 250 F3 60
Somerset, Gunnison, Colo. 200 D3 106
Somerset, Wabash, Ind. 250 B4 140
Somerset, Miami, Kans. 100 D9 144
Somerset, Pulaski, Ky. 7,112 C6 178
Somerset, Montgomery, Md. 1,444 *B5 182
Somerset, Bristol, Mass. 12,196 C5 206

Somerset, Perry, Ohio 1,361 C4 156
Somerset, Somerset, Pa. 6,347 C2 214
Somerset, Bexar, Tex. 700 B6 130
Somerset, St. Croix, Wis. 729 C1 160
Somerset, co., Eng. 571,400 J10 273
Somerset, co., Maine 39,749 C2 204
Somerset, co., Md. 19,623 D8 182
Somerset, co., N.J. 143,913 B3 210
Somerset, co., Pa. 77,450 D2 214
Somerset, isl., Bermuda A12 233
Somerset, isl., N.W.Ter., Can. C9 48
Somerset, res., Vt. F3 218
Somerset Bridge, Bermuda A12 233
Somerset East, U.S.Afr. 8,053 F4 420
Somers Point, Atlantic, N.J. 4,504 E3 210
Somersville, Tolland, Conn. 500 B6 202
Somersworth, Stafford, N.H. 8,529 E5 208
Somerton, Yuma, Ariz. 1,613 F1 124
Somerton, Nansemond, Va. 35 D8 192
Somervell, co., Tex. 2,577 C7 130
Somerville, Morgan, Ala. 166 A3 168
Somerville, Gibson, Ind. 317 D2 140
Somerville, Lincoln, Maine 25 (254▲) *D3 204
Somerville, Middlesex, Mass. 94,697 B5 D3 206
Somerville, Somerset, N.J. 12,458 B3 210
Somerville, Butler, Ohio 478 C2 156
Somerville, Fayette, Tenn. 1,820 C2 190
Somes, isl., N.Z. J11 437
Someşul, riv., Rom. A2 321
Somme, dept., Fr. 464,153 *C5 278
Somme, riv., Fr. B4 278
Sommen, lake, Swe. D6 292
Sommerville, Burleson, Tex. 1,177 D7 130
Somogy, co., Hung. 360,000 *C2 320
Somonauk, De Kalb, Ill. 899 B5 138
Somosomo, strait, Fiji E7 436
Somoto, Nic. 2,313 D4 228
Somuncura, plat., Arg. F4 251
Son, Nor. B1 292
Son, riv., India D3 368
Soná, Pan. 2,037 F7 228
Sonai, riv., India E6 368
Sonar, riv., India D2 368
Sŏnchŏn, Kor. 22,725 F12 348
Sönderborg, Den. 16,822 I3 291
Sönderborg, co., Den. 49,604 *I3 291
Sondershausen, Ger. 19,000 C4 286
Sondheimer, East Carroll, La. 350 B4 180
Sondrio, It. 11,100 B2 302
Sondrio, prov., It. 156,100 *B2 302
Song, Nig. E7 409
Song Cau, Viet. D6 362
Sŏngchŏn, Kor. 9,148 F13 348
Songea, Tan. 1,401 E6 414
Songjin, see Kim Chaek, Kor.
Songkhla, Thai. 106,410 F4 362
Songkhla, prov., Thai. 351,847 *F4 362
Songololo, Con.L. D1 414
Songor, Iran 12,126 B2 379
Songpekmun, India D6 368
Sonhat, India E3 368
Son La, Viet. 10,000 B4 362
Sonmiani, Pak. G5 375
Sonmiani, bay, Pak. G5 375
Sonneberg, Ger. 29,100 C4 286
Sonnette, Powder River, Mont. 3 E11 110
Sonningdale, Sask., Can. 240 D4 58
Sono, riv., Braz. B1 258
Sonobe, Jap. 15,734 L11 354
Sonoita, Mex. 1,275 A3 224
Sonoma, Sonoma, Calif. 3,023 C2 94
Sonoma, co., Calif. 147,375 C2 94
Sonoma, peak, Nev. C4 112
Sonora, Pinal, Ariz. 1,244 E4 124
Sonora, Tuolumne, Calif. 2,725 D3 94
Sonora, Hardin, Ky. 268 C5 178
Sonora, Sutton, Tex. 2,619 D5 130
Sonora, state, Mex. 510,607 B3 224
Sonpur Raj, India 9,065 D4 366
Sonsón, Col. 10,913 B1 244
Sonsonate, Sal. 17,949 D3 228
Sontag, Lawrence, Miss. 200 D2 184
Son Tay, Viet. 16,640 B5 362
Sonyea, Livingston, N.Y. 500 C4 212
Soo, locks, Mich. C7 146
Soochow, see Suchou, China
Soo Junction, Luce, Mich. C6 146
Sooke, B.C., Can. 350 C14 F11 52
Sopchoppy, Wakulla, Fla. 450 A6 174
Soper, Choctaw, Okla. 309 D8 128
Soperton, Treutlen, Ga. 2,317 D4 176
Soperton, Forest, Wis. (part of Wabeno) C5 160
Sophia, Raleigh, W.Va. 1,284 D3 194
Sopot, Pol. 40,000 A4 325
Sopris, Las Animas, Colo. 653 E6 106
Sopron, Hung. 37,000 B1 320
Sop's Arm, Newf., Can. 85 F7 72
Sör, riv., Port. C2 298
Sora, It. 9,000 E4 302
Söraker, Swe. E7 291
Sorak San, peak, Kor. F14 348
Sorata, Bol. 2,087 C1 246
Sorau, see Zary, Pol.
Sorbas, Sp. 1,551 D5 298
Sorel, Que., Can. 16,476 R11 66
Sorell, cape, Austl. G8 432
Sorento, Bond, Ill. 681 E4 138
Soresina, It. 9,100 C2 302
Sörfold, Nor. C6 290
Soria, Sp. 13,054 B5 298
Soria, prov., Sp. 164,575 *B5 298
Soriano, dept., Ur. 93,490 B4 252
Sorö, Den. 5,592 F2 292
Sorö, co., Den. 128,176 *I4 291
Sorocaba, Braz. 68,811 E1 258
Sorochinsk, Sov.Un. 18,400 B4 336
Soroki, Sov.Un. 16,000 H7 332
Sorong, Neth. N. Gui. E8 359
Soroti, Ug. B5 414
Söröy, isl., Nor. A10 290
Sorraia, riv., Port. C2 298
Sorrento, Lake, Fla. 350 C9 174
Sorrento, It. 7,900 E5 302

Sorrento, Ascension, La. 1,151 B6 D5 180
Sorrento, Hancock, Maine 100 (196▲) *D4 204
Sorris Sorris, S.W.Afr. D2 420
Sorsele, Swe. D7 290
Sorsogon, Phil. 9,971 B6 358
Sortavala, Sov.Un. 16,400 B8 332
Sör-Tröndelag, co., Nor. 199,958 *E4 290
Sosnovka, Sov.Un. F13 332
Sosnowiec, Pol. 124,000 C4 325
Soso, Jones, Miss. 150 D3 184
Sotjernöy, isl., Nor. A9 290
Sotkamo, Fin. D13 290
Sotra, isl., Nor. F1 291
Sotteville [-lès-Rouen], Fr. 25,625 C4 278
Souanke, Con.B. F7 409
Soubré, I.C. 300 E3 408
Soudan, St. Louis, Minn. 810 D6 148
Souderton, Montgomery, Pa. 5,381 C6 214
Souflion, Grc. 7,435 A6 306
Soufriere, St. Lucia 3,550 E14 233
Souhegan, riv., N.H. F3 208
Souk Ahras, Alg. 17,444 (22,761▲) A5 402
Soulanges, co., Que., Can. 9,736 S10 S15 66
Soumussalmi, Fin. D13 290
Sound Beach, Suffolk, N.Y. 1,625 D4 212
Sounding, creek, Alta., Can. E7 54
Sounne, lake, Fin. F12 291
Sourdnahunk, lake, Maine B3 204
Soure, Braz. 1,286 C3 258
Soure, Braz. 5,264 F7 256
Soure, Port. 9,317 B2 298
Souris, Man., Can. 1,759 F2 60
Souris, Bottineau, N.Dak. 213 B5 154
Souris, riv., N.Dak., Man., Can. B4 F2 154 60
Souris East, P.E.I., Can. 1,449 C7 70
Sourlake, Hardin, Tex. 1,602 D8 130
Sousa, Braz. 4,555 B3 258
Sousse, Tun. 48,185 A6 402
South, cape, N.Z. G1 437
South, fork, Wash. A4 98
South, fork, Wyo. B3 116
South, fork, Wyo. C6 116
South, isl., N.Z. F3 437
South, isl., S.C. E10 188
South, isl., Truk B3 436
South, mtn., Md. B4 182
South, mts., N.C. B4 186
South, pass, Kwajalein A1 436
South, pass, La. F6 180
South, pass, Wyo. D4 116
South, pt., Md. D9 182
South, pt., Mich. E8 146
South, riv., Ont., Can. O21 64
South, riv., Ga. B5 176
South, riv., Iowa C4 142
South, riv., Md. C6 182
South, sound, Ire. H3 273
South Acton, Middlesex, Mass. 1,700 C1 206
South Acworth, Sullivan, N.H. 100 E2 208
South Addison, Washington, Maine 150 D5 204
South Africa (Union of South Africa), country, Afr. 14,673,000 I9 388 421
South Amana, Iowa, Iowa 215 C6 142
South Amboy, Middlesex, N.J. 8,422 C4 210
South America, cont. 137,847,000 18 236
South Amherst, Lorain, Ohio 1,657 A4 156
Southampton, Ont., Can. 1,640 P19 64
Southampton, Eng. 196,400 K11 273
Southampton, Hampshire, Mass. 400 (2,192▲) B2 206
Southampton, Suffolk, N.Y. 4,582 D5 212
Southampton, Bucks, Pa. 4,500 *C6 214
Southampton, co., Va. 27,195 D7 192
Southampton, cape, N.W.Ter., Can. E10 48
Southampton, isl., N.W.Ter., Can. E10 48
South Andaman, isl., India F6 366
South Anna, riv., Va. C7 192
South Apopka, Orange, Fla. 2,484 *C9 174
Southard, Monmouth, N.J. 120 C4 210
Southard, Blaine, Okla. 385 B5 128
South Ashburnham, Worcester, Mass. 700 A4 206
South Ashfield, Franklin, Mass. 200 A2 206
South Athol, Worcester, Mass. 500 A3 206
South Attleboro, Bristol, Mass. C5 206
South Aulatsivik, isl., Newf., Can. D9 72
South Australia, state, Austl. 873,123 D6 432
South Baker, Baker, Oreg. (part of Baker) C9 96
Southbank, B.C., Can. D10 52
South Barre, Worcester, Mass. 900 B3 206
South Barre, Washington, Vt. 300 C3 218
South Bay, Palm Beach, Fla. 1,631 E10 174
Southbeach, Lincoln, Oreg. 300 C2 96
South Bellingham, Norfolk, Mass. 2,300 B5 206
South Belmar, Monmouth, N.J. 1,537 C4 210
South Belmont, Gaston, N.C. 2,286 *B4 186
South Beloit, Winnebago, Ill. 3,781 A4 138
South Bend, St. Joseph, Ind. 132,445 (*265,100) A3 140
South Bend, Cass, Nebr. 86 E2 152
South Bend, Pacific, Wash. 1,671 C3 98
South Bennettsville, Marlboro, S.C. 1,025 *B9 188
South Bentinck Arm, chan., B.C., Can. D9 52
South Bernam, riv., Mala. G4 362
South Berwick, York, Maine 1,773 (31,120▲) E2 204
South Bethlehem, Albany, N.Y. 400 C8 212
South Boardman, Kalkaska, Mich. 175 E6 146
South Boise, Ada, Idaho 1,452 *F2 108
South Bolton, Que., Can. 275 S12 66

Southboro, Worcester, Mass. 1,114 (3,996▲) B4 D1 206
South Boston (Independent City), Va. 5,974 D6 192
South Bound Brook, Somerset, N.J. 3,626 B3 210
South Braintree, Norfolk, Mass. D3 206
South Branch, Newf., Can. 250 G6 72
Southbranch, Ogenaw, Mich. 80 E8 146
South Branch, lake, Maine C4 204
South Branch, mtn., W.Va. B6 194
Southbridge, Worcester, Mass. 16,523 B3 206
South Bristol, Lincoln, Maine 550 (610▲) E3 204
South Britain, New Haven, Conn. 300 D3 202
South Broadway, Yakima, Wash. 3,661 *C6 98
South Brooksville, Hancock, Maine 90 D4 204
South Burlington, Chittenden, Vt. 6,903 C2 218
Southbury, New Haven, Conn. 800 (5,186▲) D3 202
South Byfield, Essex, Mass. 40 A6 206
South Canon, Fremont, Colo. (part of Canon City) D5 106
South Carolina, state, U.S. 2,382,594 E10 77 188
South Carrollton, Muhlenberg, Ky. 234 *C3 178
South Carthage, Smith, Tenn. 500 B6 190
South Carver, Plymouth, Mass. 300 C6 206
South Chaplin, Windham, Conn. 150 B7 202
South Charleston, Clark, Ohio 1,505 C3 156
South Charleston, Kanawha, W.Va. 19,180 C3 C6 194
South Charlestown, Sullivan, N.H. 100 E2 208
South Chatham, Barnstable, Mass. 279 C7 206
South Chaves, McKinley, N.Mex. 12 C2 126
South Chelmsford, Middlesex, Mass. 1,500 C1 206
South Cheney, Spokane, Wash. D8 98
South Chicago Heights, Cook, Ill. 4,043 F3 138
South China, Kennebec, Maine 115 D3 204
South China, sea 37
South City, Leon, Fla. 650 *A6 174
South Cle Elum, Kittitas, Wash. 383 B6 98
South Clement, creek, Md. D6 182
South Cleveland, Bradley, Tenn. 1,512 C7 190
South Clinton, Anderson, Tenn. 1,356 *B7 190
South Coatesville, Chester, Pa. 2,032 *D6 214
South Coffeyville, Nowata, Okla. 622 B8 128
South Colby, Kitsap, Wash. 350 D2 98
South Colton, St. Lawrence, N.Y. 660 A7 212
South Congaree, Lexington, S.C. 650 *D6 188
South Connellsville, Fayette, Pa. 2,434 D2 214
South Coventry, Tolland, Conn. B6 202
South Covington, Alleghany, Va. (part of Covington) C4 192
South Dakota, state, U.S. 680,514 C6 77 158
South Danville, Rockingham, N.H. 100 F4 208
South Dartmouth, Bristol, Mass. 6,000 C6 206
South Dayton, Cattaraugus, N.Y. 696 C2 212
South Daytona, Volusia, Fla. 1,954 B9 174
South Decatur, De Kalb, Ga. 15,000 *C2 176
South Deerfield, Franklin, Mass. 1,253 B2 206
South Deerfield, Rockingham, N.H. 50 E4 208
South Deer Isle, Hancock, Maine 115 D4 204
South Dennis, Barnstable, Mass. 300 *C7 206
South Dennis, Cape May, N.J. 365 E3 210
South Dorset, Bennington, Vt. 160 E2 218
Southdown, Terrebonne, La. 130 C6 180
South Downs, hills, Eng. K12 273
South Durham, Que., Can. 419 *S12 66
South Durham, Androscoggin, Maine E2 E5 204
South Duxbury, Plymouth, Mass. 900 B6 206
South Dyersburg, Dyer, Tenn. 500 B2 190
Southeast, pass, La. E6 180
Southeast, pt., Jam. D6 232
South Easton, Bristol, Mass. 795 B5 206
South Effingham, Carroll, N.H. 80 D5 208
South Egremont, Berkshire, Mass. 250 B1 206
South Elgin, Kane, Ill. 2,624 E2 138
South Eliot, York, Maine E2 204
South El Monte, Los Angeles, Calif. 4,850 *E5 94
South Elwood, Madison, Ind. 400 B4 140
Southend-on-Sea, Eng. 155,800 J13 273
South English, Keokuk, Iowa 217 C5 142
Southern, dist., Isr. 96,432 *D5 382
Southern, prov., Ken. C6 414
Southern (N.Rh.), prov., Rh.&Nya. C5 420
Southern (Nya.), prov., Rh.&Nya. C6 421
Southern, prov., Tan. 1,014,265 E6 414
Southern, reg., Nor. 173,771 *G3 291
Southern, uplands, Scot. F8 272
Southern Alps, mtn., N.Z. E3 437
Southern and Western Deserts, reg., Eg., U.A.R. 162,415 *B2 395
Southern Bug., riv., Sov.Un. I8 332
Southern Cross, Austl. 625 E3 432
Southern Cross, Deer Lodge, Mont. 25 D3 110
Southern Highlands, prov., Tan. 1,030,041 D5 414
Southern Indian, lake, Man., Can. B3 E6 60
Southern Islands, dist., Singapore 14,628 *G4 362
Southern Pines, Moore, N.C. 5,198 B6 186
Southern Rhodesia, colony, Rh.&Nya. 2,480,000 C5 420
Southern Shops (Lone Oak), Spartanburg, S.C. 1,435 *B5 188
Southern View, Sangamon, Ill. 1,485 *D4 138
South Essex, Essex, Mass. 700 A6 206
South Etowah, McMinn, Tenn. 150 C7 190
South Euclid, Cuyahoga, Ohio 27,569 B1 156
Southey, Sask., Can. 460 E5 58
South Fallsburg, Sullivan, N.Y. 1,290 D7 212
South Farmingdale, Nassau, N.Y. 16,318 *E8 212
South Fayetteville, Cumberland, N.C. 3,411 *B7 186
Southfield, Oakland, Mich. 31,501 *G8 146
South Flomaton, Escambia, Fla. 462 *A3 174
Southford, New Haven, Conn. 262 D3 202
South Fork, Sask., Can. 100 F3 58
South Fork, Rio Grande, Colo. 175 E4 106
South Fork, Cambria, Pa. 2,053 C3 214
South Fort Mitchell, Kenton, Ky. 4,086 A8 178
South Foster, Providence, R.I. 90 B2 216
South Freeport, Cumberland, Maine 350 E5 204
South Fulton, Obion, Tenn. 2,512 B3 190
South Gate, Los Angeles, Calif. 53,831 C5 94
Southgate, Campbell, Ky. 2,070 A8 178
Southgate, Wayne, Mich. 29,404 *G8 146
South Georgia Island, Br.poss., Atl.O. 300 I8 236
South Gifford, Macon, Mo. 93 A5 150
South Glastonbury, Hartford, Conn. 1,000 C5 202
South Glens Falls, Saratoga, N.Y. 4,129 *B8 212
South Gorin, Scotland, Mo. 279 *A5 150
South Grafton, Worcester, Mass. 3,000 *B4 206
South Grand, riv., Mo. C3 150
South Gray, Cumberland, Maine 70 E5 204
South Greenfield, Dade, Mo. 179 D4 150
South Greensburg, Westmoreland, Pa. 3,058 C2 214
South Greenwood, Greenwood, S.C. 2,520 C4 188
South Groveland, Essex, Mass. 700 A5 206
South Hackensack, Bergen, N.J. 1,841 *B4 210
South Hadley, Hampshire, Mass. 5,000 (14,956▲) B2 206
South Hadley Falls, Hampshire, Mass. 3,100 B2 206
South Hamilton, Essex, Mass. 2,000 A6 C3 206
South Hampton, Rockingham, N.H. 100 (443▲) F5 208
South Hanover, Plymouth, Mass. 500 E4 206
South Harpswell, Cumberland, Maine 500 E5 204
South Harriman, Roane, Tenn. 2,884 *C7 190
South Harwich, Barnstable, Mass. 500 *C7 206
South Haven, Sumner, Kans. 408 E6 144
South Haven, Van Buren, Mich. 6,149 G5 146
South Haven, Wright, Minn. 328 *F4 148
South Heart, Stark, N.Dak. 97 D3 154
South Hempstead, Nassau, N.Y. 3,000 *E8 212
South Henderson, Vance, N.C. 2,017 *A7 186
South Hero, Grand Isle, Vt. 70 (614▲) B2 218
South Hill, Mecklenburg, Va. 2,569 D6 192
South Hills, Kenton, Ky. 752 *B6 178
South Hingham, Plymouth, Mass. 545 B6 D3 206
South Holland, Cook, Ill. 10,412 *B6 138
South Holston, lake, Tenn. B9 190
South Holston, lake, Va. D3 192
South Hooksett, Merrimack, N.H. 1,700 E4 208
South Hopkinton, Washington, R.I. 350 *D2 216
South Houston, Harris, Tex. 7,523 F8 130
South Humboldt, riv., Nev. C6 112
South Huntington, Suffolk, N.Y. 7,084 *D3 212
South Hutchinson, Reno, Kans. 1,672 *D6 144
South Hyannis, Barnstable, Mass. 200 *C7 206
Southington, Hartford, Conn. 14,000 (22,797▲) C4 202
South International Falls, Koochiching, Minn. 2,479 C5 148
South Island, reg., N.Z. 676,698 F3 437
South Jacksonville, Morgan, Ill. 2,340 D3 138
South Jordan, Salt Lake, Utah 1,354 C4 114
South Junction, Man., Can. 18 F5 60
South Junction, Wasco, Oreg. 35 C5 96
South Kent, Litchfield, Conn. 150 C2 202
Southkent, Kent, Mich. 15,000 *G6 146
South Killingly, Windham, Conn. 150 B8 202
South Kingston, Rockingham, N.H. 100 F4 208
South Kingstown (Town of) Washington, R.I. (11,942▲) D2 216
South Klamath, Klamath, Oreg. *E5 96
South Kvalöy, isl., Nor. B8 290
South Lagrange, Penobscot, Maine 100 C4 204
South Laguna, Orange, Calif. 2,000 *F5 94
Southlake, Tarrant, Tex. 1,023 *C7 130
South Lancaster, Worcester, Mass. 1,891 B4 206
Southland, Lenawee, Mich. 2,000 *H8 146
South Lebanon, Warren, Ohio 2,720 C2 156
South Lee, Berkshire, Mass. 500 B1 206
South Liberty, Waldo, Maine 100 D3 204
South Lincoln, Middlesex, Mass. 525 C2 206
South Londonderry, Windham, Vt. 250 E3 218
South Loup, riv., Nebr. C6 152
South Lubec, Washington, Maine 230 D6 204
South Lunenburg, Essex, Vt. 100 C5 218
South Lyme, New London, Conn. 250 D6 202
South Lynchburg, Lee, S.C. 150 C8 188
South Lyndeboro, Hillsboro, N.H. 150 F3 208
South Lynnfield, Essex, Mass. (part of Lynnfield) C3 206
South Lyon, Oakland, Mich. 1,753 B6 146
South Macon, Bibb, Ga. 9,000 *D3 176
Southmag, Ont., Can. 020 64
South Manitou, isl., Mich. D5 146
South Mansfield, De Soto, La. 616 B2 180
South Marsh, isl., Md. D7 182
South Medford, Jackson, Oreg. 2,306 *E4 96
South Merrimack, Hillsboro, N.H. 125 F3 208
South Miami, Dade, Fla. 9,846 E6 F10 174
South Middleboro, Plymouth, Mass. 200 C6 206
South Milford, Lagrange, Ind. 350 A4 140
South Milford, Worcester, Mass. 600 B4 E1 206
South Mills, Camden, N.C. 479 A9 186
South Milwaukee, Milwaukee, Wis. 20,307 F2 F6 160
South Modesto, Stanislaus, Calif. 9,000 *D3 94
South Monroe, Monroe, Mich. 2,919 *H8 146
South Monson, Hampden, Mass. *B3 206
Southmont, Davidson, N.C. 700 B5 186
Southmont, Cambria, Pa. 2,857 C3 214
South Mound, Neosho, Kans. 75 *E8 144
South Mount Vernon, Knox, Ohio 1,420 *B4 156
South Muda, riv., Mala. F4 362
South Naknek, Alsk. 75 D6 84
South Natick, Middlesex, Mass. D2 206
South Natuna, isl., Indon. D3 358
South Negril, pt., Jam. C5 232
South New Berlin, Chenango, N.Y. 421 C6 212
South Newfane, Windham, Vt. 100 F3 218
South Newport, McIntosh, Ga. 150 E5 176
South New River, canal, Fla. D5 174
South Norfolk (Independent City), Va. 22,035 A9 192
South Northfield, Washington, Vt. 65 C3 218
South Nyack, Rockland, N.Y. 3,113 *D7 212
South Ogden, Weber, Utah 7,405 B4 114
Southold, Suffolk, N.Y. 950 D5 212
South Orange, Essex, N.J. 16,175 B1 B4 210
South Orleans, Barnstable, Mass. 185 C8 206
South Oroville, Butte, Calif. 3,704 *C3 94
South Orrington, Penobscot, Maine 600 D4 204
South Otselic, Chenango, N.Y. 450 C6 212
South Palm Beach, Palm Beach, Fla. 113 *E10 174
South Paris, Oxford, Maine 2,063 D2 204
South Park, Kane, Ill. 2,000 *B5 138
South Park, Johnson, Kans. 753 B8 144
South Park, Jefferson, Ky. 600 A5 178
South Park, basin, Colo. C5 106
South Parkersburg, Wood, W.Va. (part of Parkersburg) B3 194
South Pasadena, Los Angeles, Calif. 19,706 C5 94
South Pasadena, Pinellas, Fla. 651 *D8 174
South Pass City, Fremont, Wyo. 15 D4 116
South Peabody, Essex, Mass. C3 206
South Pekin, Tazewell, Ill. 1,007 C4 138
South Penobscot, Hancock, Maine 100 D4 204
South Pittsburg, Marion, Tenn. 4,130 C6 190
South Plainfield, Middlesex, N.J. 17,879 B4 210
South Platte, riv., Colo., Nebr. B6 D3 106 152
South Point, Lawrence, Ohio 1,663 D4 156
South Pomfret, Windsor, Vt. 150 D3 218
South Pond, mtn., N.Y. B7 212
South Ponte Vedra Beach, Saint Johns, Fla. 150 B10 174
South Porcupine, Ont., Can. R25 64
Southport, Austl. 23,700 D10 432
Southport, Eng. 82,100 H10 273
Southport, Bay, Fla. 980 A5 174
Southport, Marion, Ind. 892 C3 E5 140
Southport, Jefferson, La. (part of Jefferson) C7 180
Southport, Lincoln, Maine 150 (416▲) *E3 204
Southport, Chemung, N.Y. 6,698 C5 212
Southport, Brunswick, N.C. 2,034 D7 186
South Portland, Cumberland, Maine 22,788 E2 E5 204
South Portsmouth, Greenup, Ky. 378 B7 178
South Pottstown, Chester, Pa. 1,850 *C6 214
South Poultney, Rutland, Vt. 100 E2 218
South Prairie, Pierce, Wash. 214 B4 98
South Range, Houghton, Mich. 760 B3 146
South Range, Douglas, Wis. 100 *B2 160
South Renovo, Clinton, Pa. 777 B4 214
South River, Ont., Can. 995 021 64
South River, Middlesex, N.J. 13,397 C4 210
South Rockwood, Monroe, Mich. 1,337 G8 146
South Ronaldsay, isl., Scot. C10 272
South Roxana, Madison, Ill. 2,010 *E3 138
South Roxton, Que., Can. 475 S12 66
South Royalston, Worcester, Mass. 350 A3 206
South Royalton, Windsor, Vt. 450 D3 218
South Russell, Geauga, Ohio 1,276 *A5 156
South Ryegate, Caledonia, Vt. 346 C4 218
South St. Paul, Dakota, Minn. 22,032 F7 G5 148
South Salisbury, Rowan, N.C. 3,065 *B5 186
South Salt Lake, Salt Lake, Utah 9,520 C4 114
South Sandwich, Barnstable, Mass. 120 *C7 206
South San Francisco, San Mateo, Calif. 39,418 B5 94
South San Gabriel, Los Angeles, Calif. 26,213 C5 94
South Saskatchewan, riv., Alta., Can. E7 54
South Seabrook, Rockingham, N.H. F5 208
South Seaville, Cape May, N.J. 350 E3 210
South Shaftsbury, Bennington, Vt. 600 F2 218
South Shields, Eng. 108,100 G11 272
South Shore, Greenup, Ky. 658 *B8 178
South Shore, Codington, S.Dak. 259 B9 158
Southside, Independence, Ark. 436 *A3 168
Southside, Montgomery, Tenn. 100 B4 190
South Side Place, Harris, Tex. 1,282 F8 130
South Sioux City, Dakota, Nebr. 7,200 B9 152
South Sioux Falls, Minnehaha, S.Dak. (part of Sioux Falls) D9 158
South Sister, mtn., Oreg. C5 96
South Slocan, B.C., Can. 230 F14 52
South Solon, Madison, Ohio 414 C3 156
South Spencer, Worcester, Mass. 125 B3 206
South Spring, Chaves, N.Mex. 25 E6 126
South Springfield, Penobscot, Maine 55 C4 204
South Strafford, Orange, Vt. 75 D4 218
South Streator, Livingston, Ill. 1,923 *C5 138
South Superior, Sweetwater, Wyo. 401 E4 116
South Sutton, Merrimack, N.H. 100 E3 208
South Swansea, Bristol, Mass. 1,100 C5 206
South Taft, Kern, Calif. 1,910 *E4 94
South Tamworth, Carroll, N.H. 160 D4 208
South Taranaki, bight, N.Z. C5 437
South Temple, Berks, Pa. 1,500 *C6 214
South Tent, mtn., Utah D4 114
South Thomaston, Knox, Maine 350 (732▲) D3 204
South Toms River, Ocean, N.J. 1,603 *D4 210
South Torrington, Goshen, Wyo. 1,000 D8 116
South Trail, Sarasota, Fla. 5,471 *D8 174
South Truro, Barnstable, Mass. 12 C7 206
South Tucson, Pima, Ariz. 7,004 F5 124
South Tunnel, Sumner, Tenn. 200 B5 190
South Twin, lake, Newf., Can. F8 72
South Twin, mtn., N.H. C3 208
South Uist, isl., Scot. D5 272
South Union, Logan, Ky. 150 D4 178
South Union, Knox, Maine 100 D3 204
South Uniontown, Fayette, Pa. 3,603 *D2 214
South Vernon, Franklin, Mass. 716 A3 206
South Vienna, Clark, Ohio 440 C3 156
Southville, Worcester, Mass. 245 D1 206
South Vineland, Cumberland, N.J. E2 210
South Wabiskaw, lake, Alta., Can. C6 54
South Wadesboro, Anson, N.C. 189 C5 186
South Wallingford, Rutland, Vt. 120 E3 218
South Walpole, Norfolk, Mass. 700 E2 206
South Wareham, Plymouth, Mass. 445 C6 206
South Waterford, Oxford, Maine 230 D2 204
South Wausau, Marathon, Wis. 4,105 *D4 160
South Waverly, Bradford, Pa. 1,382 B5 214
South Wayne, Lafayette, Wis. 354 F4 160
South Weber, Davis, Utah 382 B4 114
South Webster, Scioto, Ohio 803 D4 156
South Wellfleet, Barnstable, Mass. 17 C8 206
South Wellington, B.C., Can. 210 B14 52
South Wenatchee, see Appleyard, Wash.
South Wenatchee, Chelan, Wash. B6 98
Southwest, Westmoreland, Pa. 800 C2 214
Southwest, cape, Austl. G8 432
Southwest, chan., Fla. D8 174
Southwest, head, N.B., Can. E3 70
Southwest, pass, La. E3 180
Southwest, pass, La. F6 180
Southwest, pt., R.I. E2 216
South West Africa, U.S.Afr. mandate, Afr. 554,000 I8 388 421
South Westbury, Nassau, N.Y. 11,977 *E8 212

South West City, McDonald, Mo.	504	E3	150
South West Fargo, Cass, N.Dak.	3,328	D9	154
Southwest Greensburg, Westmoreland, Pa.	3,264	*C2	214
Southwest Harbor, Hancock, Maine	900 (1,480▲)	D4	204
Southwest Lanett, Chambers, Ala.	1,631	*C4	168
South Westminster, B.C., Can.	500	B15	52
South Weymouth, Norfolk, Mass.		B6 D3	206
South Whitley, Whitley, Ind.	1,325	A4	140
Southwick, Nez Perce, Idaho	50	C2	108
Southwick, Hampden, Mass.	1,242 (5,139▲)	B2	206
South Williamson, Pike, Ky.	1,097	C8	178
South Williamsport, Lycoming, Pa.	6,972	B4	214
South Willington, Tolland, Conn.	300	B6	202
South Wilmington, Grundy, Ill.	730	B5	138
South Windermere, Charleston, S.C.	1,500	*F9	188
South Windham, Windham, Conn.	380	C7	202
South Windham, Cumberland, Maine	1,142	E2 E4	204
South Windsor, Hartford, Conn.	900 (9,460▲)	B5	202
Southwold, Eng.	2,400	I14	273
South Wolf, isl., Newf., Can.		D8	72
South Woodstock, Windham, Conn.	400	B8	202
South Woodstock, Windsor, Vt.	85	D3	218
South Woodstown, Salem, N.J.		D2	210
South Worthington, Hampshire, Mass.	45	B2	206
South Yarmouth, Barnstable, Mass.	2,029	C7	206
South Zanesville, Muskingum, Ohio	1,557	C4	156
Soverato, It.	3,006	F6	302
Sovereign, Sask., Can.	161	E4	58
Sovetsk (Tilsit), Sov.Un.	85,900	E3	332
Sovetskaya Gavan, Sov.Un.	60,000	E15	329
Soviet Union (U.S.S.R.), country, Eur., Asia	208,826,000	C9 D10	266 340 329
Sōya, cape, Jap.		B8	354
Sōya, strait, Jap.		B8	354
Sōya, strait, Sov.Un.		E16	329
Sozh, riv., Sov.Un.		F8	332
Sozopol, Bul.	3,265	B3	317
Spa, Bel.	8,710	D4	282
Spadra, Johnson, Ark.	300	B3	170
Spain, country, Eur.	29,894,000	D4	266 298
Spalding, Sask., Can.	378	D5	58
Spalding, Eng.	14,600	I12	273
Spalding, Nez Perce, Idaho	200	C2	108
Spalding, Greeley, Nebr.	683	C7	152
Spalding, co., Ga.	35,404	C2	176
Spanaway, Pierce, Wash.	2,500	B4	98
Spangle, Spokane, Wash.	208	B9 D8	98
Spangler, Cambria, Pa.	2,658	C3	214
Spangler, hill, Ohio		C1	156
Spaniard's Bay, Newf., Can.	1,400	G9	72
Spanish, head, Isle of Man		G8	273
Spanishburg, Mercer, W.Va.	400	D3	194
Spanish Fork, Utah, Utah	6,472	C4	114
Spanish Fort, Sharkey, Miss.	150	C2	184
Spanish Guinea, reg., Afr.		F7	388
Spanish Ranch, Plumas, Calif.	150	C3	94
Spanish Sahara, overseas prov., Sp.	19,000	D5	388 409
Spanish Town, Jam.	13,600	D6	232
Spanish West Africa, reg., Sp. Sahara		A1	408
Sparkman, Dallas, Ark.	787	D4	170
Sparkman, Charlotte, Fla.	60	E9	174
Sparks, Cook, Ga.	1,158	E3	176
Sparks, Doniphan, Kans.	150	*C8	144
Sparks, Cherry, Nebr.	5	B5	152
Sparks, Washoe, Nev.	16,618	D2	112
Sparks, Lincoln, Okla.	186	C7	128
Sparksville, Jackson, Ind.	100	D3	140
Sparksville, Adair, Ky.	150	C5	178
Sparland, Marshall, Ill.	534	B4	138
Sparlingville, St. Clair, Mich.	1,877	G9	146
Sparr, Marion, Fla.	400	B8	174
Sparr, Otsego, Mich.		D7	146
Sparrow Lake, Ont., Can.	90	P21	64
Sparrows Point, Baltimore, Md.	3,300	B7	182
Sparta, Hancock, Ga.	1,921	C4	176
Sparta, see Spárti, Grc.			
Sparta, Randolph, Ill.	3,452	E4	138
Sparta, Gallatin, Ky.	235	B6	178
Sparta, Christian, Mo.	272	E4	150
Sparta, Sussex, N.J.	500	A3	210
Sparta, Alleghany, N.C.	1,047	A4	186
Sparta, Baker, Oreg.		C9	96
Sparta, Kent, Mich.	2,749	F6	146
Sparta, White, Tenn.	4,510	C6	190
Sparta, Monroe, Wis.	6,080	E3	160
Sparta, mts., N.J.		B3	210
Spartanburg, Randolph, Ind.	200	B5	140
Spartanburg, Spartanburg, S.C.	44,352	B5	188
Spartanburg, co., S.C.	156,830	B4	188
Spárti, Grc.	7,900	C4	306
Spartivento, cape, It.		F2	302
Spartivento, cape, It.		G6	302
Spas-Demensk, Sov.Un.	4,000	E10	332
Spassk-Ryazanskiy, Sov.Un.	14,500	E13	332
Spátha, cape, Grc.		D4	306
Spaulding, Jefferson, Ala.	800	E4	168
Spaulding, Hughes, Okla.	150	C7	128
Spavinaw, Mayes, Okla.	319	B8	128
Spavinaw, creek, Okla.		B9	128
Spear, Avery, N.C.	170	A3	186
Spear, cape, Newf., Can.		G9	72
Spearfish, Lawrence, S.Dak.	3,682	C2	158
Spearhill, Man., Can.		E3	60
Spearman, Hansford, Tex.	3,555	A5	130
Spearville, Ford, Kans.	602	E4	144
Spearsville, Union, La.	90	B3	180
Spectacle, pond, Maine		D4	204
Speculator, Hamilton, N.Y.	372	B7	212
Spedden, Alta., Can.	135	C7	54
Spedromartir, mts., Mex.		A2	224
Speed, Clark, Ind.	950	D4	140
Speed, Phillips, Kans.	75	C4	144
Speedway, Marion, Ind.	9,624	C3 D4	140
Speedwell, Claiborne, Tenn.	75	B8	190
Speedwell, Wythe, Va.	200	D3	192
Speer, Choctaw, Okla.	50	D8	128
Speers, Sask., Can.	155	D4	58
Speers, Washington, Pa.	1,479	*C1	214
Speigner, Elmore, Ala.	300	C3	168
Spelter, Harrison, W.Va.	500	B4 B6	194
Spelter City, Okmulgee, Okla.	250	*C8	128
Spenard, Alsk.	9,074	C7 G11	84
Spencer, Clark, Idaho	100	E6	108
Spencer, Owen, Ind.	2,557	C3	140
Spencer, Clay, Iowa	8,864	A2	142
Spencer, Worcester, Mass.	5,593 (7,838▲)	B4	206
Spencer, Boyd, Nebr.	671	B7	152
Spencer, Tioga, N.Y.	767	C5	212
Spencer, Rowan, N.C.	2,904	B5	186
Spencer, Oklahoma, Okla.	1,189	*C6	128
Spencer, Medina, Ohio	742	A4	156
Spencer, McCook, S.Dak.	460	D8	158
Spencer, Van Buren, Tenn.	870	C6	190
Spencer, Henry, Va.	200	D4	192
Spencer, Roane, W.Va.	2,660	C3	194
Spencer, Marathon, Wis.	897	D3	160
Spencer, co., Ind.	16,074	D3	140
Spencer, co., Ky.	5,680	B5	178
Spencer, butte, Oreg.		D3	96
Spencer, cape, Alsk.		I13	84
Spencer, gulf, Austl.		E7	432
Spencer, lake, Maine		C2	204
Spencer, mts., Maine		C3	204
Spencer, pond, Maine		C3	204
Spencerport, Monroe, N.Y.	2,461	B4	212
Spencerville, De Kalb, Ind.	340	A5	140
Spencerville, Montgomery, Md.	900	B6	182
Spencerville, Allen, Ohio	2,061	B2	156
Spencerville, Choctaw, Okla.	100	D8	128
Spences Bridge, B.C., Can.	300	E12	52
Sperkhiós, riv., Grc.		B4	306
Sperling, Man., Can.	175	F4	60
Sperry, Tulsa, Okla.	883	B7	128
Sperryville, Rappahannock, Va.	300	B6	192
Spesutie, isl., Md.		B7	182
Spey, riv., Scot.		D9	272
Speyer, Ger.	35,600	D3	286
Spiceland, Henry, Ind.	863	C4	140
Spicer, Kandiyohi, Minn.	589	F4	148
Spicer, is., N.W.Ter., Can.		D10	48
Spickard, Grundy, Mo.	450	A4	150
Spicket, hill, Mass.		A5	206
Spider, lake, Wis.		B2	160
Spiekeroog, isl., Ger.		B2	286
Spielman, Washington, Md.	75	A4	182
Spiess, Santa Fe, N.Mex.	150	H7	126
Spiez, Switz.	6,536	B3	312
Spillville, Winneshiek, Iowa	389	A6	142
Spilsby, Eng.	1,486	H13	273
Spinazzola, It.	13,500	E6	302
Spindale, Rutherford, N.C.	4,082	B4	186
Spink, co., S.Dak.	11,706	C7	158
Spirit, lake, Iowa		A2	142
Spirit, lake, Wash.		C4	98
Spirit, res., Wis.		C4	160
Spirit Lake, Kootenai, Idaho	693	B2	108
Spirit Lake, Dickinson, Iowa	2,685	A2	142
Spirit River, Alta., Can.	743	C3	54
Spiritwood, Sask., Can.	488	D4	58
Spiritwood, Stutsman, N.Dak.	90	D7	154
Spiro, Le Flore, Okla.	1,450	C9	128
Spišská Nová Ves, Czech.	18,017	B5	324
Spiti, riv., India		B2	368
Spitsbergen, see Svalbard, Nor.			
Spittal [an der Drau], Aus.	8,798	D5	313
Spivey, Kingman, Kans.	98	E5	144
Split, Yugo.	75,695	C3	316
Split, cape, N.S., Can.		D5	70
Split, lake, Man., Can.		B5	60
Split, mtn., Calif.		D4	94
Split Rock, creek, Minn.		H2	148
Splügen, Switz.	387	B5	312
Splügen, pass, Switz.		B5	312
Splunge, Monroe, Miss.		B4	184
Spocari, Marengo, Ala.		C2	168
Spofford, Cheshire, N.H.	300	F2	208
Spofford, lake, N.H.		F2	208
Spokane, Concordia, La.	200	C4	180
Spokane, Spokane, Wash.	181,608 (*252,000)	B9 D8	98
Spokane, co., Wash.	278,333	B9	98
Spokane, lake, Wash.		D8	98
Spokane, mtn., Wash.		B9	98
Spokane, riv., Wash.		B8	98
Spokane, val., Wash.		D9	98
Spoleto, It.	14,000	D4	302
Spondin, Alta., Can.		E7	54
Spoon, butte, Wyo.		D8	116
Spoon, riv., Ill.		C3	138
Spooner, Washburn, Wis.	2,398	C2	160
Spooner, lake, Wis.		C2	160
Spooners Mill, Penobscot, Maine	25	D3	204
Sporades (Dodecanese), is., Grc.		C6	306
Spotswood, Middlesex, N.J.	5,788	C4	210
Spotsylvania, Spotsylvania, Va.	150	B7	192
Spotsylvania, co., Va.	13,819	B7	192
Spotted, isl., Newf., Can.		D8	72
Spotted Horse, Campbell, Wyo.	10	B7	116
Spottsville, Henderson, Ky.	463	C3	178
Spout Spring, Appomattox, Va.	100	C6	192
Sprague, Montgomery, Ala.	100	C3	168
Sprague, Man., Can.	355	F5	60
Sprague (Town of), New London, Conn.	(2,509▲)	C7	202
Sprague, Lancaster, Nebr.	120	D9	152
Sprague, Lincoln, Wash.	597	B9	98
Sprague, Raleigh, W.Va.	3,073	D7	194
Sprague, lake, Wash.		B8	98
Sprague, riv., Oreg.		E5	96
Sprague River, Klamath, Oreg.	150	E5	96
Spragueville, Jackson, Iowa	100	B7	142
Spragueville, Providence, R.I.	400	B2	216
Spray, Rockingham, N.C.	4,565	A6	186
Spray, Wheeler, Oreg.	194	C7	96
Spread Eagle, Florence, Wis.	150	C5	160
Spreckelsville, Maui, Haw.	950	C5	86
Spree, riv., Ger.		B6	286
Spremberg [in der Niederlausitz], Ger.	22,500	C6	286
Sprigg, Mingo, W.Va.	350	D2	194
Spring, Harris, Tex.	950	F8	130
Spring, brook, Pa.		A5	214
Spring, creek, Kans.		B5	144
Spring, isl., S.C.		G7	188
Spring, lake, Maine		C2	204
Spring, mts., Nev.		G6	112
Spring, riv., Ark.		A5	170
Spring, riv., Mo.		D4	150
Spring Arbor, Jackson, Mich.	700	G7	146
Springbok, U.S.Afr.	1,812	E3	420
Springboro, Warren, Ohio	917	C2	156
Spring Brook, Ont., Can.	190	P23	64
Springbrook, Jackson, Iowa	139	B7	142
Spring Brook, Williams, N.Dak.	35	B2	154
Springbrook, Washburn, Wis.	100	C2	160
Spring Canyon, Carbon, Utah	250	D5	114
Spring City, Chester, Pa.	3,162	C6	214
Spring City, Rhea, Tenn.	1,800	C7	190
Spring City, Sanpete, Utah	463	D4	114
Spring Coulee, Alta., Can.	100	F6	54
Springcreek, Madison, Tenn.	100	C3	190
Springdale, Washington, Ark.	10,076	A2	170
Springdale, Newf., Can.	900	F7	72
Springdale, Park, Mont.	75	E6	110
Springdale, Hamilton, Ohio	3,556	D1	156
Springdale, Multnomah, Oreg.	150	B4	96
Springdale, Allegheny, Pa.	5,602	A4 C2	214
Springdale, Lancaster, S.C.	1,002	*B7	188
Springdale, Washington, Utah	248	F3	114
Springdale, Stevens, Wash.	254	A9	98
Spring Dale, Fayette, W.Va.	950	D4	194
Springdell, Utah, Utah	55	*C4	114
Springer, Colfax, N.Mex.	1,564	B6	126
Springer, Carter, Okla.	212	D6	128
Springerton, White, Ill.	232	E5	138
Springerville, Apache, Ariz.	719	D6	124
Springfield, Conway, Ark.	125	B4	170
Springfield, N.S., Can.	212	E5	70
Springfield, Ont., Can.	482	R20	64
Springfield, Baca, Colo.	1,791	E8	106
Springfield, Bay, Fla.	4,628	A5	174
Springfield, Effingham, Ga.	858	D5	176
Springfield, Bingham, Idaho	80	F6	108
Springfield, Sangamon, Ill.	83,271 (*122,700)	D4	138
Springfield, Washington, Ky.	2,382	C5	178
Springfield, Livingston, La.	350	B6 D5	180
Springfield, Penobscot, Maine	75 (426▲)	C4	204
Springfield, Hampden, Mass.	174,463 (*429,400)	B2	206
Springfield, Calhoun, Mich.	4,605	*G6	146
Springfield, Brown, Minn.	2,701	G4	148
Springfield, Greene, Mo.	95,865 (*108,700)	D4	150
Springfield, Sarpy, Nebr.	506	C9 E3	152
Springfield, Sullivan, N.H.	50 (283▲)	D2	208
Springfield, Union, N.J.	14,467	B4	210
Springfield, Clark, Ohio	82,723 (*112,100)	C3	156
Springfield, Lane, Oreg.	19,616	C3	96
Springfield, Delaware, Pa.	26,733	A6	214
Springfield, Orangeburg, S.C.	787	D6	188
Springfield, Bon Homme, S.Dak.	1,194	E8	158
Springfield, Robertson, Tenn.	9,221	B5	190
Springfield, Windsor, Vt.	6,600 (9,934▲)	E4	218
Springfield, Fairfax, Va.	10,783	A7	192
Springfield, Hampshire, W.Va.	300	B6	194
Springfield, lake, Ill.		D4	138
Springfield, plat., Mo.		D4	150
Springfield Place, Calhoun, Mich.	5,136	*G6	146
Springfontein, U.S.Afr.	2,583	F5	420
Spring Gap, Allegany, Md.	75	A2	182
Spring Garden, Cherokee, Ala.	200	B4	168
Spring Garden, Pittsylvania, Va.	100	D5	192
Spring Glen, Carbon, Utah	500	*D5	114
Spring Green, Sauk, Wis.	1,146	E3	160
Spring Grove, Wayne, Ind.	471	C5	140
Spring Grove, Houston, Minn.	1,342	H7	148
Spring Grove, York, Pa.	1,675	D5	214
Spring Hill, Barbour, Ala.	125	C4	168
Spring Hill, Mobile, Ala.		E1	168
Springhill, Pike, Ala.	80	D4	168
Springhill, Faulkner, Ark.	100	B4	170
Spring Hill, Hempstead, Ark.	200	D3	170
Springhill, N.S., Can.	7,348	D5	70
Spring Hill, Que., Can.	300	S13	66
Spring Hill, Warren, Iowa	111	*C4	142
Spring Hill, Johnson, Kans.	909	D9	144
Springhill, Washington, La.	6,437	A2	180
Spring Hill, Stearns, Minn.	105	*F4	148
Spring Hill, Cambria, Pa.	1,127	*C3	214
Spring Hill, Maury, Tenn.	689	C5	190
Spring Hope, Nash, N.C.	1,336	B7	186
Springhouse, B.C., Can.	25	E11	52
Spring Lake, Hernando, Fla.	150	C8	174
Springlake, Kenton, Ky.	250	A8	178
Spring Lake, Ottawa, Mich.	2,063	F5	146
Spring Lake, Monmouth, N.J.	2,922	C4	210
Spring Lake, Cumberland, N.C.	4,110	B7	186
Spring Lake, Klamath, Oreg.		E5	96
Spring Lake, Utah, Utah		C4	114
Spring Lake Heights, Monmouth, N.J.	3,309	C4	210
Spring Lake Park, Hancock, Ind.	206	*C4	140
Spring Lake Park, Anoka and Ramsey, Minn.	3,260	*F5	148
Springlake Park, Oklahoma, Okla.	11	*C6	128
Springlee, Jefferson, Ky.	987	*B5	178
Spring Lick, Grayson, Ky.	125	C4	178
Spring Mill, Montgomery, Pa.	300	*C6	214
Spring Mills, Centre, Pa.	800	C4	214
Spring Mills, Lancaster, S.C.	1,069	*B7	188
Springmont, Berks, Pa.	1,000	*D5	214
Spring Place, Murray, Ga.	194	B2	176
Springport, Henry, Ind.	253	*B4	140
Springport, Jackson, Mich.	693	G7	146
Springs, U.S.Afr.	129,500	E5	420
Springside, Sask., Can.	308	E6	58
Springside, Burlington, N.J.	700	*C3	210
Springstead, Iron, Wis.	40	B3	160
Springston, Kootenai, Idaho	25	*B2	108
Springsure, Austl.	728	C9	432
Springtown, Benton, Ark.	82	*A2	170
Springtown, Parker, Tex.	859	*C7	130
Springvale, York, Maine	2,379	E2	204
Spring Valley, Colbert, Ala.	100	A2	168
Spring Valley, San Diego, Calif.	4,000	D6	94
Spring Valley, Sask., Can.	115	F5	58
Spring Valley, Bureau, Ill.	5,371	B4	138
Spring Valley, Fillmore, Minn.	2,628	H6	148
Spring Valley, Rockland, N.Y.	6,538	D2	212
Spring Valley, Greene, Ohio	678	C2	156
Spring Valley, Harris, Tex.	3,004	E8	130
Spring Valley, Grayson, Va.	25	D3	192
Spring Valley, Manitowoc, Wis.	40	B6	160
Spring Valley, Pierce, Wis.	977	D1	160
Springview, Keya Paha, Nebr.	281	B6	152
Springville, St. Clair, Ala.	822	B3	168
Springville, Lawrence, Ind.	150	C3	140
Springville, Linn, Iowa	785	B6	142
Springville, Livingston, La.	60	B6 D5	180
Springville, Pontotoc, Miss.	25	A3	184
Springville, Erie, N.Y.	3,852	C3	212
Springville, Henry, Tenn.	40	B3	190
Springville, Utah, Utah	7,913	C4	114
Springwater, Sask., Can.	118	E3	58
Springwater, Livingston, N.Y.	475	C4	212
Sprott, Perry, Ala.	62	C2	168
Spruce, fork, W.Va.		D5	194
Spruce, mtn., Nev.		C7	112
Spruce, peak, Vt.		E2	218
Spruce, pond, Newf., Can.		F7	72
Spruce, riv., Sask., Can.		D5	58
Spruce Brook, Newf., Can.	90	F6	72
Sprucedale, Ont., Can.	275	O21	64
Spruce Grove, Alta., Can.	309	D6	54
Spruce Head, Knox, Maine	175	D3	204
Spruce Knob, mtn., W.Va.		C5	194
Spruce Lake, Sask., Can.	104	D3	58
Spruce Pine, Franklin, Ala.	400	A2	168
Spruce Pine, Mitchell, N.C.	2,504	B3	186
Spry, Garfield, Utah	25	F3	114
Spud Rock, mtn., Ariz.		F5	124
Spungabera, Moz.		D6	421
Spur, Dickens, Tex.	2,170	C5	130
Spurfield, Alta., Can.		C5	54
Spurgeon, Pike, Ind.	269	D2	140
Spurn, head, Eng.		H13	273
Spurr, mtn., Alsk.		G10	84
Spurrier Gardens, Sedgwick, Kans.	400	B6	144
Spy Hill, Sask., Can.	172	E7	58
Squak, mtn., Wash.		D3	98
Squam, butte, Oreg.		D7	96
Squam, lake, N.H.		D3	208
Squam, mts., N.H.		D3	208
Squamish, B.C., Can.	1,292	F11	52
Squa Pan, Aroostook, Maine	50	B4	204
Squapan, lake, Maine		B4	204
Square, lake, Maine		A4	204
Square Butte, Chouteau, Mont.	85	C6	110
Square Island Harbour, Newf., Can.		D8 E10	72
Squatteck, Que., Can.	250	Q16	66
Squaw, mtn., Maine		C3	204
Squaw, val., Calif.		C3	94
Squaw Lake, Itasca, Minn.	129	D4	148
Squibnocket, pt., Mass.		D6	206
Squillace, gulf, It.		F6	302
Squire, McDowell, W.Va.	900	D3	194
Squirrel, Fremont, Idaho	5	*E7	108
Srbobran, Yugo.	13,635	B4	316
Sredinnyy, mts., Sov.Un.		D18	329
Sredne-Kolymsk, Sov.Un.	3,000	C17	329
Sredneye, Sov.Un.		D17	329
Śrem, Pol.	8,308	B3	325
Sremska Mitrovica, Yugo.	15,456	B4	316
Sremski Karlovci, Yugo.	5,618	B4	316
Srepok, riv., Camb.		D5	362
Sretensk, Sov.Un.	24,600	D13	329
Srinagar, India	207,787	B1	368
Srisaket, prov., Thai	451,576	*D5	362
Środa, Pol.	11,700	B3	325
Środa Śląska, Pol.	4,301	C3	325
Ssu, China	5,000	I8	349
Ssumao, China		G8	346
Ssunan, China		L4	349
Ssupingkai, China	76,000	D12	348
Ssushui, China	5,000	H8	348
Staalberg Huk, pt., Ice.		L17	290
Staatsburg, Dutchess, N.Y.	450	D8	212
Stab, Pulaski, Ky.	300	C6	178
Stacey, Powder River, Mont.	6	E11	110
Stacks, mts., Ire.		I3	273
Stacy, Chisago, Minn.	211	F5	148
Stacyville, Mitchell, Iowa	588	A5	142
Stacyville, Penobscot, Maine	130 (673▲)	C4	204
Stade, Ger.	29,100	B3	286
Stadharfell, Ice.		L18	290
Stadhur, Ice.		L18	290
Stadhurhraun, Ice.		L18	290
Stadskanaal, Neth.	6,234	B5	282
Stafflin, Scot.		D6	272
Stafford, Pickens, Ala.	20	B1	168

Stafford, Tolland, Conn.	350 (7,476▲)	B6	202
Stafford, Eng.	41,400	I10	273
Stafford, Stafford, Kans.	1,862	E5	144
Stafford, Holt, Nebr.	3	B7	152
Stafford, Custer, Okla.	25	C4	128
Stafford, Fort Bend, Tex.	1,485	*F8	130
Stafford, Stafford, Va.	500	B7	192
Stafford, co., Eng.	1,657,000	I10	273
Stafford, co., Kans.	7,451	D5	144
Stafford, co., Va.	16,876	B7	192
Stafford, pond, R.I.		C4	216
Stafford Springs, Tolland, Conn.	3,322	B6	202
Stafford Springs, Jasper, Miss.		D4	184
Staffordville, Tolland, Conn.	400	B6	202
Staffordville, Ocean, N.J.	75	D4	210
Staines, Eng.	44,200	J12	273
Stains, Fr.	19,028	I10	278
Stalactite, cavern, Mo.		E6	150
Staley, Randolph, N.C.	260	B6	186
Stalin, see Varna, Bul.			
Stalin, peak, Sov.Un.		F9	328
Stalinabad, Sov.Un.	224,000	F8	328
Stalingrad, Sov.Un.	591,000 (*680,000)	C2	336
Stalingrad, res., Sov.Un.		C3	336
Staliniri, Sov.Un.	22,000	D2	336
Stalino, Sov.Un.	701,000 (*1,525,000)	I11 T21	332
Stalinogorsk, Sov.Un.	107,000	B1	336
Stalinogród, see Katowice, Pol.			
Stalinogród, pol.div., Pol.	3,024,000	*C4	325
Stalinsk, Sov.Un.	377,000	B11	336
Stallo, Neshoba, Miss.	200	C3	184
Stalwart, Sask., Can.	110	E5	58
Stalwart, Chippewa, Mich.	15	C7	146
Stambaugh, Iron, Mich.	1,876	C3	146
Stamford, Fairfield, Conn.	92,713	E1	202
Stamford, Harlan, Nebr.	220	D6	152
Stamford, Delaware, N.Y.	1,166	C7	212
Stamford, Jackson, S.Dak.	50	D4	158
Stamford, Jones, Tex.	5,259	C6	130
Stamford, Bennington, Vt.	150 (600▲)	F2	218
Stamford, lake, Tex.		C6	130
Stamping Ground, Scott, Ky.	353	B6	178
Stampried, S.W.Afr.		D3	420
Stamps, Lafayette, Ark.	2,591	D3	170
Stanaford, Raleigh, W.Va.	950	D3 D7	194
Stanardsville, Greene, Va.	283	B6	192
Stanberry, Gentry, Mo.	1,409	A3	150
Stanchfield, Isanti, Minn.	150	F5	148
Standale, Kent, Mich.	1,000	*G6	146
Standard, Alta., Can.	230	E6	54
Standard, La Salle, La.	150	C3	180
Standard, Westmoreland, Pa.	700	*C2	214
Standerton, U.S.Afr.	11,616	E5	420
Standing Rock, Chambers, Ala.	150	B4	168
Standish, Cumberland, Maine	200 (2,095▲)	E2	204
Standish, Plymouth, Mass.	103	E4	206
Standish, Arenac, Mich.	1,214	F8	146
Standrod, Box Elder, Utah		B2	114
Standsville, Dorchester, S.C.	75	E2	188
Stånevik, Nor.		G1	291
Stanfield, Pinal, Ariz.	150	F3	124
Stanfield, Harlan, Ky.	125	*D7	178
Stanfield, Stanly, N.C.	471	B5	186
Stanfield, Umatilla, Oreg.	745	B7	96
Stanford, Santa Clara, Calif.	9,000	B5	94
Stanford, McLean, Ill.	479	C4	138
Stanford, Monroe, Ind.	100	C3	140
Stanford, Lincoln, Ky.	2,019	C6	178
Stanford, Judith Basin, Mont.	615	C6	110
Stangelville, Kewaunee, Wis.	100	A7 D6	160
Stanger, U.S.Afr.	5,585	E6	421
Stanhope, Hamilton, Iowa	461	B4	142
Stanhope, Sussex, N.J.	1,814	B3	210
Stanislaus, co., Calif.	157,294	D3	94
Stanislaus, riv., Calif.		D3	94
Stanislav, Sov.Un.	66,000	H5	332
Stanke Dimitrov, Bul.	25,137	B1	317
Stanley, N.B., Can.	285	C3	70
Stanley, Custer, Idaho	35	E4	108
Stanley, Buchanan, Iowa	156	B6	142
Stanley, Johnson, Kans.	330	D9	144
Stanley, Daviess, Ky.	170	C3	178
Stanley, De Soto, La.	234	C2	180
Stanley, Santa Fe, N.Mex.	51	C4 H7	126
Stanley, Gaston, N.C.	1,980	B4	186
Stanley, Mountrail, N.Dak.	1,795	B3	154
Stanley, Pushmataha, Okla.	5	D8	128
Stanley, Page, Va.	1,039	B6	192
Stanley, Chippewa, Wis.	2,014	D3	160
Stanley, co., S.Dak.	4,085	C5	158
Stanley, falls, Con.L.		B3	414
Stanleytown, Henry, Va.	500	D5	192
Stanleyville, Con.L.	53,400	B4	414
Stanleyville, Forsyth, N.C.	1,138	*A5	186
Stanly, co., N.C.	40,873	B5	186
Stanmore, Alta., Can.	75	E7	54
Stann Creek, Br.Hond.	3,414	B3	228
Stans, Switz.	3,992	B4	312
Stansbury, Sweetwater, Wyo.	50	E3	116
Stanstead, co., Que., Can.	35,319	S12	66
Stanton, Chilton, Ala.	302	C3	168
Stanton, Orange, Calif.	11,163	C5	94
Stanton, New Castle, Del.	2,000	B3	172
Stanton, Montgomery, Iowa	514	D2	142
Stanton, Powell, Ky.	753	C7	178
Stanton, Montcalm, Mich.	1,139	F6	146
Stanton, Adams, Miss.	250	D1	184
Stanton, Franklin, Mo.	163	C6	150
Stanton, Stanton, Nebr.	1,317	C8	152
Stanton, Hunterdon, N.J.	200	B3	210
Stanton, Mercer, N.Dak.	409	C4	154
Stanton, Haywood, Tenn.	458	C2	190
Stanton, Martin, Tex.	2,228	C5	130
Stanton, co., Kans.	2,108	E2	144
Stanton, co., Nebr.	5,783	C8	152
Stantonsburg, Wilson, N.C.	897	B8	186
Stantonville, McNairy, Tenn.	125	C3	190
Stanwood, Cedar, Iowa	598	C6	142
Stanwood, Mecosta, Mich.	205	F6	146
Stanwood, Snohomish, Wash.	1,123	A4	98
Staplehurst, Seward, Nebr.	240	D8	152
Staples, Todd, Minn.	2,706	E4	148
Stapleton, Baldwin, Ala.	600	E2	168
Stapleton, Jefferson, Ga.	356	C4	176
Stapleton, Logan, Nebr.	359	C5	152
Star, Ada, Idaho	400	F2	108
Star, Rankin, Miss.	300	C2	184
Star, Montgomery, N.C.	745	B6	186
Stara Boleslav, Czech.	4,744	*A2	324
Starachowice, Pol.	30,200	C5	325
Staraya Russa, Sov.Un.	35,400	D8	332
Stara Zagora, Bul.	55,322	B2	317
Stara Zagorski, prov., Bul.		*B2	317
Starbuck, Man., Can.	250	F4	148
Starbuck, Pope, Minn.	1,099	F3	148
Starbuck, Columbia, Wash.	161	C8	98
Starbuck, isl., Pac.O.		C4	436
Star City, Lincoln, Ark.	1,573	D5	170
Star City, Sask., Can.	619	D5	58
Star City, Pulaski, Ind.	500	B3	140
Star City, Monongalia, W.Va.	1,236	B5	194
Stargard [Szczecinski], Pol.	23,500	B2	325
Stargo, Greenlee, Ariz.	1,075	*E6	124
Staritsa, Sov.Un.	7,500	D10	332
Star Junction, see Starjunction, Pa.			
Starjunction (Star Junction), Fayette, Pa.	1,142	*D2	214
Stark, Neosho, Kans.	96	E8	144
Stark, Missoula, Mont.	12	C2	110
Stark, Coos, N.H.	35 (327▲)	B4	208
Stark, co., Ill.	8,152	B4	138
Stark, co., N.Dak.	18,451	D3	154
Stark, co., Ohio	340,345	B5	156
Starke, Bradford, Fla.	4,806	B8	174
Starke, co., Ind.	17,911	A3	140
Starkey, Union, Oreg.		B8	96
Starkey, Roanoke, Va.	800	C4	192
Starks, Calcasieu, La.	500	D2	180
Starks, Somerset, Maine	150 (306▲)	D3	204
Starksboro, Addison, Vt.	150 (502▲)	C2	218
Starkville, Las Animas, Colo.	261	E6	106
Starkville, Oktibbena, Miss.	9,041	B4	184
Starkweather, Ramsey, N.Dak.	223	B7	154
Star Lake, Minn.		E3	148
Starobelsk, Sov.Un.	33,000	H12	332
Starodub, Sov.Un.	28,700	F9	332
Starogard [Gdanski], Pol.	19,400	B4	325
Starominskaya, Sov.Un.		I12	332
Star Prairie, St. Croix, Wis.	331	C1	160
Starr, Anderson, S.C.	243	C3	188
Starr, co., Tex.	17,137	F6	130
Starrsville, Newton, Ga.	100	C3	176
Start, bay, Eng.		K9	273
Startex, Spartanburg, S.C.	950	B4	188
Startup, Snohomish, Wash.	250	B5	98
Stary Sącz, Pol.	4,586	D5	325
Staryy Oskol, Sov.Un.	32,000	G11	332
Stassfurt, Ger.	26,800	C4	286
Staszów, Pol.	4,586	C5	325
State, lake, Kans.		C6	144
Stateburg, Sumter, S.C.	200	D7	188
State Center, Marshall, Iowa	1,142	B4	142
State College, Oktibbeha, Miss.	6,000	B4	184
State College, Centre, Pa.	22,409	C4	214
State Hospital, Saline, Ark.	500	C4	170
Stateline, Kootenai, Idaho	33	*B2	108
State Line, Warren, Ind.	171	B2	140
State Line, Berkshire, Mass.	80	B1	206
State Line, Green and Wayne, Miss.	653	D4	184
State Line, Douglas, Nev.	125	E2	112
Staten, isl., N.Y.		E2	212
Statenville, Echols, Ga.	400	F3	176
State Park, Richland, S.C.	250	*C7	188
State Road, Aroostook, Maine	65	B4	204
State Sanatorium, Logan, Ark.		B3	170
State Sanatorium, see Cullen, Md.			
Statesboro, Bulloch, Ga.	8,356	D5	176
State Schools, Drew, Ark.	500	D5	170
Statesville, Iredell, N.C.	19,844	B5	186
Statham, Barrow, Ga.	711	C3	176
Station No. 6, Sud.		A3	398
Statue of Liberty, natl. mon., N.Y.		E2	212
Stauffer, Lake, Oreg.		D6	96
Staunton, Macoupin, Ill.	4,228	D4	138
Staunton, Clay, Ind.	490	C2	140
Staunton (Independent City), Va.	22,232	B5	192
Stavanger, Nor.	51,321 (*76,000)	G1	291
Stave, Wyoming, W.Va.	900	*D3	194
Stave, lake, B.C., Can.		B16	52
Stavelot, Bel.	4,729	D4	282
Stavely, Alta., Can.	338	E6	54
Stavenisse, Neth.	1,416	C3	282
Staveren, Neth.	839	B4	282
Stavropol, Sov.Un.	140,000	J13	332
Stavsnäs, Swe.		B9	292
Stayner, Ont., Can.	1,429	P20	64
Stayton, Marion, Oreg.	2,108	C1 C4	96
Steamboat, Washoe, Nev.	100	D2	112
Steamboat, mtn., Mont.		C4	110
Steamboat Rock, Hardin, Iowa	426	B4	142
Steamboat Springs, Routt, Colo.	1,843	B4	106
Stearns, McCreary, Ky.	950	D6	178
Stearns, co., Minn.	80,345	F4	148
Stearns, lake, Fla.		D9	174
Stebbins, Alsk.	115	C5	84
Stebbins, Aroostook, Maine	70	B5	204
Steblev, Sov.Un.	14,300	H8	332
Štěchovice, Czech.	1,086	*B2	324
Stecker, Caddo, Okla.	100	D5	128
Stedman, Cumberland, N.C.	458	B7	186
Steel, mtn., Idaho		F3	108
Steele, St. Clair, Ala.	625	B3	168
Steele, Pemiscot, Mo.	2,301	E8	150
Steele, Kidder, N.Dak.	847	D6	154
Steele, co., Minn.	25,029	G5	148
Steele, co., N.Dak.	4,719	C8	154
Steele, mtn., Wyo.		E6	116
Steele City, Jefferson, Nebr.	173	D8	152
Steeleville, Randolph, Ill.	1,569	E4	138
Steelmanville, Atlantic, N.J.	200	E3	210
Steelton, Dauphin, Pa.	11,266	C5	214
Steelville, Crawford, Mo.	1,127	D6	150
Steen, Rock, Minn.	198	H2	148
Steenbergen, Neth.	4,484	C3	282
Steenburg, Ont., Can.		P23	64
Steens, Lowndes, Miss.	120	B4	184
Steens, mtn., Oreg.		E8	96
Steenwijk, Neth.	9,561	B5	282
Steep, point, Austl.		D2	432
Steep Falls, Cumberland, Maine	450	E2	204
Steephill, lake, Sask., Can.		C6	58
Steep Rock, Man., Can.	75	E3	60
Steep Rock Lake, Ont., Can.	1,460	R23	64
Ştefăneşti, Rom.	7,770	A4	321
Steffenville, Lewis, Mo.	200	B6	150
Stegall, Jackson, Ark.		B5	170
Stege, Den.	2,679	G3	292
Steger, Cook, Ill.	6,432	B6 F3	138
Stegi, Swaz.		E6	421
Stehekin, Chelan, Wash.	45	A6	98
Steiermark (Styria), state, Aus.	1,109,335	*C6	313
Steilacoom, Pierce, Wash.	1,569	B4 E2	98
Stein, Ger.		E3	286
Steinach, Aus.	2,015	C3	313
Steinauer, Pawnee, Nebr.	124	D9	152
Steinbach, Man., Can.	2,688	F4	60
Steinfort, Lux.	1,082	E4	282
Steinhatchee, Taylor, Fla.	800	B7	174
Steinhatchee, riv., Fla.		B7	174
Steinhausen, S.W.Afr.		D3	420
Steinkjer, Nor.	3,670	E4	290
Steins, Hidalgo, N.Mex.	25	F2	126
Stella, Izard, Ark.		A5	170
Stella, Ont., Can.	215	P24	64
Stella, Newton, Mo.	166	E3	150
Stella, Richardson, Nebr.	262	D10	152
Stellarton, N.S., Can.	5,445	D7	70
Stem, Granville, N.C.	221	A7	186
Stemmers Run, Baltimore, Md.	827	B7	182
Stendal, Ger.	39,100	B4	286
Stendal, Pike, Ind.	180	D2	140
Stenen, Sask., Can.	301	E6	58
Stensan, riv., Swe.		E4	292
Stensele, Swe.	600	D7	290
Stenungsund, Swe.	5,065	C2	292
Stepanakert, Sov.Un.	20,000	E3	336
Stephan, Hyde, S.Dak.	300	C6	158
Stephen, Marshall, Minn.	858	C2	148
Stephens, Ouachita, Ark.	1,275	D3	170
Stephens, Oglethorpe, Ga.	150	C3	176
Stephens, co., Ga.	18,391	B3	176
Stephens, co., Okla.	37,990	D6	128
Stephens, co., Tex.	8,885	C6	130
Stephens, passage, Alsk.		J14	84
Stephensburg, Morris, N.J.	200	B3	210
Stephens City, Frederick, Va.	876	A6	192
Stephenson, Menominee, Mich.	820	D4	146
Stephenson, Wyoming, W.Va.	600	*D3	194
Stephenson, co., Ill.	46,207	A4	138
Stephensport, Breckinridge, Ky.	150	C4	178
Stephenville, Newf., Can.	3,762	F6	72
Stephenville, Erath, Tex.	7,359	C6	130
Stephenville Crossing, Newf., Can.	600	F6	72
Stepney Depot, Fairfield, Conn.	700	D3	202
Stepnoy, Sov.Un.	22,000	I15	332
Stepnyak, Sov.Un.	20,000	B8	336
Steptoe, Whitman, Wash.	100	B9	98
Sterco, Alta., Can.	125	D4	54
Stereá Ellás Kai Évvoia, see Central Greece and Euboea, reg., Grc.			
Sterkstroom, U.S.Afr.	3,544	F5	420
Sterling (Naptowne), Alsk.	99	*C6	84
Sterling, Logan, Colo.	10,751	B7	106
Sterling, Windham, Conn.	450 (1,397▲)	C8	202
Sterling, Bingham, Idaho	70	F6	108
Sterling, Whiteside, Ill.	15,688	B4	138
Sterling, Fountain, Ind.	300	B2	140
Sterling, Rice, Kans.	2,303	D5	144
Sterling, Worcester, Mass.	700 (3,193▲)	B4	206
Sterling, Arenac, Mich.	470	E7	146
Sterling, Johnson, Nebr.	471	D9	152
Sterling, Burleigh, N.Dak.	100	D5	154
Sterling, Comanche, Okla.	562	D5	128
Sterling, Sanpete, Utah	137	D4	114
Sterling, Loudoun, Va.	300	A6 A7	192
Sterling, co., Tex.	1,177	D5	130
Sterling, res., Colo.		B7	106
Sterling City, Sterling, Tex.	854	D5	130
Sterling Junction, Worcester, Mass.	350	*B4	206
Sterlington, Ouachita, La.	1,200	B3	180
Sterlitamak, Sov.Un.	111,000	B5	336
Šternberk, Czech.	10,973	B3	324
Sterrett, Shelby, Ala.	500	B3	168
Stetson, Penobscot, Maine	150 (420▲)	D3	204
Stetson, mtn., Maine		C4	204
Stetsonville, Taylor, Wis.	319	C3	160
Stettin, see Szczecin, Pol.			
Stettin, lagoon, Ger.		B5	286
Stettin, lagoon, Pol.		B2	325
Stettler, Alta., Can.	3,359	D6	54
Steuben, Washington, Maine	350 (673▲)	D5	204
Steuben, Schoolcraft, Mich.	15	C5	146
Steuben, Crawford, Wis.	193	E3	160
Steuben, co., Ind.	17,184	A4	140
Steuben, co., N.Y.	97,691	C4	212
Steubenville, Steuben, Ind.	50	A4	140
Steubenville, Jefferson, Ohio	34,495 (*121,300)	B6	156
Steve, Yell, Ark.	10	C3	170
Stevens, Catron, N.Mex.	45	E2	126
Stevens, co., Kans.	4,400	E2	144
Stevens, co., Minn.	11,262	F2	148
Stevens, co., Wash.	17,884	A8	98
Stevens, peak, Mont.		C1	110
Stevenson, Jackson, Ala.	1,456	A4	168
Stevenson, Fairfield, Conn.	200	D3	202
Stevenson, Skamania, Wash.	927	D5	98
Stevenson, lake, Man., Can.		D4	60
Stevenson, riv., Man., Can.		D5	60
Stevenson, mtn., Ark.		B2	170
Stevens Point, Portage, Wis.	17,837	D4	160
Stevens Pottery, Baldwin, Ga.	300	D3	176
Stevens Village, Alsk.	84	B7	84
Stevensville, Queen Annes, Md.	400	C7	182
Stevensville, Berrien, Mich.	697	G5	146
Stevensville, Ravalli, Mont.	784	D2	110
Steveston, B.C., Can.	950	B14	52
Stewardson, Shelby, Ill.	656	D5	138
Stewart, Hale, Ala.	187	C2	168
Stewart, B.C., Can.	435	C8	52
Stewart, McLeod, Minn.	676	G4	148
Stewart, Montgomery, Miss.	162	B3	184
Stewart, Ormsby, Nev.	500	D2	112
Stewart, Houston, Tenn.	150	B4	190
Stewart, co., Ga.	7,371	D2	176
Stewart, co., Tenn.	7,851	B4	190
Stewart, isl., N.Z.		G1	437
Stewart Manor, Nassau, N.Y.	2,422	*E8	212
Stewartstown, Coos, N.H.	125 (918▲)	B4	208
Stewartstown, York, Pa.	1,164	D5	214
Stewartsville, Coosa, Ala.		B3	168
Stewartsville, Posey, Ind.	235	D2	140
Stewartsville, De Kalb, Mo.	466	B3	150
Stewartsville, Warren, N.J.	875	B2	210
Stewartsville, Bedford, Va.	150	C5	192
Stewart Valley, Sask., Can.	135	E4	58
Stewartville, Olmsted, Minn.	1,670	H6	148
Stewiacke, N.S., Can.	1,024	D6	70
Steynsburg, U.S.Afr.		F5	420
Steyr, Aus.	36,818	B6	313
Stibnite, Valley, Idaho	25	E3	108
Stickney, Cook, Ill.	6,239	B6	138
Stickney, Aurora, S.Dak.	456	D7	158
Stidham, McIntosh, Okla.	88	C8	128
Stier, Craighead, Ark.		B6	170
Stig, fjord, Swe.		C2	292
Stigen, Swe.		C2	292
Stigler, Haskell, Okla.	1,923	C8	128
Stigtomta, Swe.	2,474	C7	292
Stikine, riv., Alsk.		D8 J15	84
Stilesboro, Bartow, Ga.	650	B2	176
Stilesville, Hendricks, Ind.	361	C3	140
Stilis, Grc.	3,606	B4	306
Stillaguamish, riv., Wash.		A5	98
Stillman Valley, Ogle, Ill.	596	A4	138
Stillmore, Emanuel, Ga.	354	D4	176
Still Pond, Kent, Md.	350	B7	182
Still River, Worcester, Mass.	132	B4	206
Stillwater, B.C., Can.	100	F10	52
Stillwater, Washington, Minn.	8,310	F6 F7	148
Stillwater, Sussex, N.J.	200	A3	210
Stillwater, Saratoga, N.Y.	1,398	C8	212
Stillwater, Payne, Okla.	23,965	B6	128
Stillwater, Providence, R.I.	75	B2	216
Stillwater, co., Mont.	5,526	E7	110
Stillwater, range, Nev.		D3	112
Stillwell, La Porte, Ind.	225	A3	140
Stilson, Bulloch, Ga.	160	D5	176
Stiltner, Wayne, W.Va.	400	C2	194
Stilwell, Johnson, Kans.	162	D9	144
Stilwell, Adair, Okla.	1,916	C9	128
Stimson, mtn., Mont.		B3	110
Stinesville, Monroe, Ind.	288	C3	140
Stinnett, Hutchinson, Tex.	2,695	B5	130
Stinson Beach, Marin, Calif.	700	D2	94
Štip, Yugo.	13,845	D6	316
Stirling, Alta., Can.	430	F6	54
Stirling, Ont., Can.	1,191	P23	64
Stirling, Morris, N.J.	1,382	B4	210
Stirling, Scot.	26,800	E9	272
Stirling, co., Scot.	190,500	E8	272
Stirling City, Butte, Calif.	350	C3	94
Stirrat, Logan, W.Va.	900	*D3	194
Stirum, Sargent, N.Dak.	80	D8	154
Stites, Idaho, Idaho	299	C3	108
Stittsville, Ont., Can.	260	O25	64
Stockaryo, Swe.		D5	292
Stockbridge, Henry, Ga.	1,201	C2	176
Stockbridge, Berkshire, Mass.	900 (2,161▲)	B1	206
Stockbridge, Ingham, Mich.	1,097	G7	146
Stockbridge, Calumet, Wis.	476	B5 D5	160
Stockdale, Riley, Kans.	40	*C7	144
Stockdale, Wilson, Tex.	1,111	B7 E7	130
Stockerau, Aus.	11,182	B8	313
Stockett, Cascade, Mont.	400	C5	110
Stockham, Hamilton, Nebr.	69	D8	152
Stockholm, Sask., Can.	199	E6	58
Stockholm, Aroostook, Maine	500 (649▲)	A4	204
Stockholm, Sussex, N.J.	200	A3	210
Stockholm, Grant, S.Dak.	155	B9	158
Stockholm, Swe.	785,945 (*1,015,390)	B9	292
Stockholm, Pepin, Wis.	106	D1	160
Stockholm, co., Swe.	397,127	B9	292
Stockhorn, mtn., Switz.		B3	312
Stockley, Sussex, Del.	10	F4	172
Stockport, Eng.	140,900	H10	273
Stockport, Van Buren, Iowa	342	D6	142
Stockport, Morgan, Ohio	458	C5	156
Stockton, Baldwin, Ala.	950	E2	168
Stockton, San Joaquin, Calif.	86,321 (*160,000)	D3	94
Stockton, Man., Can.	100	F3	60
Stockton, Lanier, Ga.	500	F4	176
Stockton, Jo Daviess, Ill.	1,800	A3	138
Stockton, Muscatine, Iowa	164	C7	142
Stockton, Rooks, Kans.	2,073	C4	144
Stockton, Worcester, Md.	300	D9	182
Stockton, Winona, Minn.	242	G7	148
Stockton, Cedar, Mo.	838	D4	150
Stockton, Hunterdon, N.J.	520	C3	210
Stockton, Tooele, Utah	362	C3	114

Stockton, isl., Wis.		B3	160
Stockton-on-Tees, Eng.	75,700	G11	273
Stockton Springs, Waldo, Maine	400 (980▲)	D4	204
Stockville, Frontier, Nebr.	91	D5	152
Stockwell, Tippecanoe, Ind.	400	B3	140
Stoddard, Cheshire, N.H.	100 (146▲)	E2	208
Stoddard, Vernon, Wis.	552	E2	160
Stoddard, co., Mo.	29,490	E7	150
Stöde, Swe.		E7	291
Stoeckl, mtn., B.C., Can.		B7	52
Stoer, pt., Scot.		C7	272
Stoke Centre, Que., Can.	330	S13	66
Stoke-on-Trent, Eng.	273,000 (*425,000)	H10	273
Stokes, Pitt, N.C.	195	B8	186
Stokes, co., N.C.	22,314	A5	186
Stokes, mtn., N.Z.		D5	437
Stokes Bridge, Lee, S.C.	200	C8	188
Stokesdale, Guilford, N.C.	900	A6	186
Stokesland, Va. (part of Danville)		D5	192
Stokkseyri, Ice.		M19	290
Stolac, Yugo.	2,271	C3	316
Stolberg, Ger.	35,600	C2	286
Stolbovaya, Sov.Un.		C17	329
Stolbovaya, Sov.Un.		O18	332
Stollings, Logan, W.Va.	900	D5	194
Stolp, see Słupsk, Pol.			
Stone, Oneida, Idaho	20	G6	108
Stone, Pike, Ky.	728	C8	178
Stone, Gage, Nebr.	120	*D9	152
Stone, co., Ark.	6,294	B4	170
Stone, co., Miss.	7,013	E3	184
Stone, co., Mo.	8,176	E4	150
Stone, mtn., Ga.		C2	176
Stone, mtn., Tenn.		C8	190
Stone, mtn., Vt.		B5	218
Stone, mts., Tenn.		B10	190
Stonebluff, Fountain, Ind.	170	B2	140
Stoneboro, Mercer, Pa.	1,267	B1	214
Stoneboro, Kershaw, S.C.	100	B7	188
Stone Canyon, res., Calif.		C4	94
Stone City, Pueblo, Colo.	35	D6	106
Stone City, Jones, Iowa	200	B6	142
Stonecoal, Wayne, W.Va.	300	D2	194
Stone Corral, lake, Oreg.		E7	96
Stonefort, Saline, Ill.	349	F5	138
Stonega, Wise, Va.	800	D2	192
Stoneham, Que., Can.	500	R13	66
Stoneham, Weld, Colo.	80	B7	106
Stoneham, Middlesex, Mass.	17,821	C3	206
Stone Harbor, Cape May, N.J.	834	E3	210
Stonehaven, Scot.	4,500	E10	272
Stone Lake, Washburn, Wis.	175	C2	160
Stoneleigh, Baltimore, Md.	8,000	*B6	182
Stone Mountain, De Kalb, Ga.	1,976	B5 C2	176
Stone Park, Cook, Ill.	3,038	*B6	138
Stoner, Montezuma, Colo.	30	E2	106
Stones, riv., Tenn.		B5	190
Stones River, Rutherford, Tenn.	1,800	*C5	190
Stoneville, Worcester, Mass.		B4	206
Stoneville, Washington, Miss.	350	B2	184
Stoneville, Rockingham, N.C.	951	A6	186
Stonewall, Greene, Ark.	25	A6	170
Stonewall, Man., Can.	1,100	E4	60
Stonewall, Fulton, Ga.	800	B4	176
Stonewall, De Soto, La.	100	B2	180
Stonewall, Clarke, Miss.	1,126	C4	184
Stonewall, Pamlico, N.C.	214	*B9	186
Stonewall, Pontotoc, Okla.	584	D7	128
Stonewall, co., Tex.	3,017	C5	130
Stonewood, Harrison, W.Va.	2,202	B7	194
Stoney, isl., Newf., Can.		D8	72
Stoney Creek, Ont., Can.	4,506	Q21	64
Stonington, Baca, Colo.	36	E8	106
Stonington, New London, Conn.	1,622 (13,969▲)	D8	202
Stonington, Christian, Ill.	1,076	D4	138
Stonington, Hancock, Maine	800 (1,408▲)	D4	204
Stono, inlet, S.C.		F9 G3	188
Stono, riv., S.C.		G3	188
Stony, brook, N.J.		C3	210
Stony, creek, Va.		C7	192
Stony, isl., N.Y.		B5	212
Stony, lake, Ont., Can.		P22	64
Stony, riv., W.Va.		B5	194
Stony Beach, Sask., Can.	90	E5	58
Stony Brook, Suffolk, N.Y.	3,548	*D4	212
Stony Creek, Warren, N.Y.	450	B8	212
Stony Creek, Sussex, Va.	437	D7	192
Stony Creek Mills, Berks, Pa.	1,500	*C5	214
Stonyford, Colusa, Calif.	125	C2	94
Stony Mountain, Man., Can.	150	E4	60
Stony Plain, Alta., Can.	1,098	D5	54
Stony Point, Le Flore, Okla.	50	*C9	128
Stony Point, Rockland, N.Y.	3,330	D8	212
Stony Point, Alexander, N.C.	1,015	B4	186
Stör, riv., Ger.		B3	286
Storå, Swe.		B6	292
Stora Gla, lake, Swe.		B3	292
Stora Karlsö, isl., Swe.		D9	292
Stora Le, riv., Nor.		B2	292
Stora Lulevatten, lake, Swe.		C8	290
Stora Möja, isl., Swe.		B9	292
Storavan, lake, Swe.		D8	290
Stord, isl., Nor.		G1	291
Storden, Cottonwood, Minn.	390	G3	148
Store Belt, strait, Den.		I4	291
Store Heddinge, Den.	2,244	F3	292
Stor-Elvdal, Nor.		F4	291
Støren, Nor.		E4	290
Storey, co., Nev.	568	D2	112
Storfjord, fjord, Nor.		E2	290
Storfors, Swe.	4,068	B5	292
Stori As, Ice.		L19	290
Storinupur, Ice.		L19	290
Storkerson, cape, N.W.Ter., Can.		C8	48
Storlien, Swe.		E5	290
Storm, lake, Iowa		B2	142
Storm Lake, Buena Vista, Iowa	7,728	B2	142
Stormont, co., Ont., Can.	56,452	O26	64
Stornoway, Sask., Can.	115	E6	58
Stornoway, Scot.	5,200	C6	272
Storozhinets, Sov.Un.	15,800	H5	332
Storr, mtn., Scot.		D6	272
Storrs, Tolland, Conn.	6,054	B7	202
Storsjö, Swe.		E5	290
Storsjö, lake, Nor.		A2	292
Storsjön, lake, Swe.		E5	290
Storsjön, riv., Swe.		A7	292
Storthoaks, Sask., Can.	234	F7	58
Storuman, Swe.		D7	290
Storuman, lake, Swe.		D7	290
Storvik, Swe.	1,932	A7	292
Storvik, Swe.		F7	291
Story, Sheridan, Wyo.	200	B6	116
Story, co., Iowa	49,327	B4	142
Story City, Story, Iowa	1,773	B4	142
Story Prairie, Sandusky, Ohio	1,720	*A3	156
Stotesbury, Raleigh, W.Va.	300	*D3	194
Stotts City, Lawrence, Mo.	221	D4	150
Stouffville, Ont., Can.	2,307	Q21	64
Stoughton, Sask., Can.	562	F6	58
Stoughton, Norfolk, Mass.	16,328	B5 E3	206
Stoughton, Dane, Wis.	5,555	F4	160
Stour, riv., Eng.		J13	273
Stour, riv., Eng.		K10	273
Stourbridge, Eng.	38,600	I10	273
Stout, Grundy, Iowa	145	B5	142
Stoutland, Camden, Mo.	172	D5	150
Stoutsville, Monroe, Mo.	109	B6	150
Stoutsville, Fairfield, Ohio	560	C4	156
Stovall, Meriwether, Ga.	250	D2	176
Stovall, Granville, N.C.	570	A7	186
Stover, Tallahatchie, Miss.	150	A2	184
Stover, Morgan, Mo.	757	C5	150
Stow, Oxford, Maine	75 (108▲)	D2	204
Stow, Middlesex, Mass.	800 (2,573▲)	B4 C1	206
Stow, Summit, Ohio	12,194	A5	156
Stow, creek, N.J.		E2	210
Stowe, Allegheny, Pa.	11,730	A3	214
Stowe, Montgomery, Pa.	3,501	C6	214
Stowe, Lamoille, Vt.	534 (1,901▲)	C3	218
Stowmarket, Eng.	7,600	I14	273
Stoyoma, mtn., B.C., Can.		F12	52
Strabane, N.Ire.	6,620	G5	272
Strabane, Washington, Pa.	1,940	C1	214
Strachur, Scot.	578	E7	272
Stradone, Ire.	127	H5	237
Strafford, Strafford, N.H.	135 (722▲)	E4	208
Strafford, Orange, Vt.	100 (548▲)	D4	218
Strafford, co., N.H.	59,799	E4	208
Straffordville, Ont., Can.	280	R20	64
Straight, Texas, Okla.	300	B2	128
Strakonice, Czech.	13,421	B1	324
Straldzha, Bul.	5,972	B3	317
Stralhy, pt., Scot.		C8	272
Stralsund, Ger.	65,300	A5	286
Strandarkirkja, Ice.		M19	290
Strandburg, Grant, S.Dak.	105	B9	158
Strandquist, Marshall, Minn.	160	C2	148
Strang, Fillmore, Nebr.	68	D8	152
Strang, Mayes, Okla.	176	B8	128
Strangeville, Orangeburg, S.C.		E7	188
Strangford, N.Ire.	372	G7	273
Strängnäs, Swe.	7,922	B8	292
Strangvik, Nor.		E3	290
Stranraer, Sask., Can.	106	E3	58
Stranraer, Scot.	8,700	G7	272
Strasbourg, Fr.	200,921	C7	278
Strasbourg Station, Sask., Can.	589	E5	58
Strasburg, Arapahoe, Colo.	439	C6	106
Strasburg, Shelby, Ill.	467	D5	138
Strasburg, Cass, Mo.	213	C3	150
Strasburg, Emmons, N.Dak.	612	D5	154
Strasburg, Tuscarawas, Ohio	1,687	B5	156
Strasburg, Lancaster, Pa.	1,416	D5	214
Strasburg, Shenandoah, Va.	2,428	B6	192
Strass [bei Jenbach], Aus.	437	C3	313
Stratford, Kings, Calif.	500	D4	94
Stratford, Ont., Can.	19,972	Q20	64
Stratford, Fairfield, Conn.	45,012	E3	202
Stratford, Hamilton, Iowa	703	B4	142
Stratford, Coos, N.H.	130 (1,029▲)	B3	208
Stratford, Camden, N.J.	4,308	D2	210
Stratford, N.Z.	4,811	C5	437
Stratford, Garvin, Okla.	1,058	D7	128
Stratford, Brown, S.Dak.	109	B7	158
Stratford, Sherman, Tex.	1,380	A4	130
Stratford, Marathon, Wis.	1,106	D3	160
Stratford, pt., Conn.		E3	202
Stratford Center, Que., Can.	485	S13	66
Stratford Hills, Chesterfield, Va.	2,500	*C7	192
Stratham, Rockingham, N.H.	160 (1,033▲)	E5	208
Strathclair, Man., Can.	215	E2	60
Strathcona, Ont., Can.	140	P24	64
Strathcona, Roseau, Minn.	64	C2	148
Strathcona, prov. park, B.C., Can.		F10	52
Strathlorne, N.S., Can.	93	C8	70
Strathmere, Cape May, N.J.	100	E3	210
Strathmoor Gardens, Jefferson, Ky.	329	*B5	178
Strathmoor Manor, Jefferson, Ky.	434	*B5	178
Strathmoor Village, Jefferson, Ky.	498	*B5	178
Strathmore, Tulare, Calif.	1,095	D4	94
Strathmore, Alta., Can.	727	E6	54
Strathnaver, B.C., Can.	35	D11	52
Strathroy, Ont., Can.	4,240	R19	64
Stratton, Kit Carson, Colo.	680	C8	106
Stratton, Franklin, Maine	500	C2	204
Stratton, Newton, Miss.	127	C3	184
Stratton, Hitchcock, Nebr.	492	D4	152
Stratton, Jefferson, Ohio	311	B6	156
Straubing, Ger.	36,600	D5	286
Straughn, Henry, Ind.	349	C4	140
Straw, Fergus, Mont.	20	D7	110
Strawberry, Lawrence, Ark.	200	B5	170
Strawberry, mtn., Oreg.		C8	96
Strawberry, mts., Oreg.		C8	96
Strawberry, peak, Utah		C4	114
Strawberry, pt., Mass.		B6	206
Strawberry, res., Utah		C4	114
Strawberry, riv., Ark.		A5	170
Strawberry, riv., Utah		C4	114
Strawberry Plains, Jefferson, Tenn.	400	B8	190
Strawberry Point, Clayton, Iowa	1,303	B6	142
Strawn, Coffey, Kans.	105	D8	144
Strawn, Palo Pinto, Tex.	817	C6	130
Strayhorn, Tate, Miss.	150	A2	184
Strážnice, Czech.	4,989	B3	324
Streamstown, Alta., Can.	65	D7	54
Streamwood, Cook, Ill.	4,821	*A5	138
Streator, La Salle, Ill.	16,868	B5	138
Streeter, Stutsman, N.Dak.	491	D6	154
Streetsboro, Portage, Ohio	1,000	*A5	156
Streetsville, Ont., Can.	2,648	S21	64
Strehaia, Rom.	8,545	B2	321
Strelka, Sov.Un.		D11	329
Stretka, Sov.Un.		C12	329
Stribling, Stewart, Tenn.		B4	190
Strike, J. C., dam and res., Idaho		G3	108
Strimón, gulf, Grc.		A4	306
Strimón, riv., Grc.		A4	306
Stringer, Jasper, Miss.	150	D3	184
Stringtown, Lake, Colo.	500	C4	106
Stringtown, Bolivar, Miss.	150	B2	184
Stringtown, Atoka, Okla.	414	D7	128
Strofádhes, isl., Grc.		C3	306
Stroh, Lagrange, Ind.	475	A4	140
Stromboli, isl., It.		F5	302
Strome, Alta., Can.	306	D6	54
Strome Ferry, Scot.		D7	272
Stromness, Scot.	1,500	C9	272
Stromsburg, Polk, Nebr.	1,244	C8	152
Strömsnäsbruk, Swe.		E4	292
Strömstad, Swe.	3,798	C2	292
Strömsund, Swe.		E6	290
Stronach, Manistee, Mich.	350	E5	146
Stroner, Crook, Wyo.	5	B7	116
Strong, Union, Ark.	741	D4	170
Strong, Franklin, Maine	300 (976▲)	D2	204
Strong, Monroe, Miss.	300	B4	184
Strong, riv., Miss.		C3	184
Strong City, Chase, Kans.	659	D7	144
Strong City, Roger Mills, Okla.	51	C4	128
Strongfield, Sask., Can.	164	E4	58
Stronghurst, Henderson, Ill.	815	C3	138
Strongs, Chippewa, Mich.	225	C7	146
Strongsville, Cuyahoga, Ohio	8,504	A5 B1	156
Stronsay, firth, Scot.		B10	272
Stronsay, isl., Scot.		B10	272
Strontian, Scot.		E6	272
Strontia Springs, Douglas, Colo.	162	C5	106
Stroud, Chambers, Ala.	75	*C4	168
Stroud, Eng.	16,000	J10	273
Stroud, Lincoln, Okla.	2,456	C7	128
Stroudsburg, Monroe, Pa.	6,070	C6	214
Stroudsburg West, Monroe, Pa.	1,569	*B6	214
Struble, Plymouth, Iowa	74	B1	142
Struer, Den.	7,895	H3	291
Strum, Trempealeau, Wis.	663	D2	160
Struma, riv., Bul.		C1	317
Strumica, Yugo.	12,149	D6	316
Strunk, McCreary, Ky.	450	D6	178
Struthers, Mahoning, Ohio	15,631	A6	156
Stryama, riv., Bul.		B2	317
Stryker, Lincoln, Mont.	57	B2	110
Stryker, Williams, Ohio	1,205	A2	156
Strykersville, Wyoming, N.Y.	360	C3	212
Stryy, Sov.Un.	47,000	H4	332
Strzegom, Pol.	7,137	C3	325
Strzelce Krajeńskie, Pol.	1,552	B2	325
Strzelce [Opolskie], Pol.	10,300	C4	325
Strzelecki, creek, Austl.		D8	432
Strzelin, Pol.	7,334	C3	325
Strzelno, Pol.	5,264	B4	325
Stuart, Martin, Fla.	4,791	D10	174
Stuart, Guthrie, Iowa	1,486	C3	142
Stuart, Holt, Nebr.	794	B6	152
Stuart, Hughes, Okla.	271	D7	128
Stuart, Patrick, Va.	974	D4	192
Stuart, lake, B.C., Can.		C10	52
Stuart, mtn., Wash.		B6	98
Stuart, range, Austl.		D7	432
Stuart, riv., B.C., Can.		C11	52
Stuartburn, Man., Can.	440	F4	60
Stuarts Draft, Augusta, Va.	600	B5	192
Stub, hill, N.H.		A4	208
Stubbeköbing, Den.	2,204	G3	292
Stuckey, Williamsburg, S.C.	199	*D10	188
Studley, Sheridan, Kans.	60	C3	144
Stull, riv., Man., Can.		C6	60
Stump, lake, N.Dak.		C7	154
Stumptown, Gilmer, W.Va.	66	C3	194
Stung Treng, Camb.	10,000	D5	362
Stupart, riv., Man., Can.		C5	60
Sturbridge, Worcester, Mass.	400 (3,604▲)	B3	206
Sturgeon, Boone, Mo.	619	B5	150
Sturgeon, Allegheny, Pa.	1,000	*C1	214
Sturgeon, bay, Man., Can.		D4	60
Sturgeon, riv., Sask., Can.		D4	58
Sturgeon Bay, Door, Wis.	7,353	D6	160
Sturgeon Falls, Ont., Can.	5,874	S25	64
Sturgeon Lake, Pine, Minn.	151	E6	148
Sturgeon Landing, Sask., Can.	20	C7	58
Sturgeon-weir, riv., Sask., Can.		C6	58
Sturgis, Sask., Can.	729	E6	58
Sturgis, Union, Ky.	2,209	C3	178
Sturgis, St. Joseph, Mich.	8,915	H6	146
Sturgis, Oktibbeha, Miss.	358	B3	184
Sturgis, Meade, S.Dak.	4,639	C2	158
Sturkö, isl., Swe.		E6	292
Sturmill, Dallas, Ark.		D4	170
Sturtevant, Racine, Wis.	1,488	F2 F6	160
Stutsman, co., N.Dak.	25,137	C7	154
Stutterheim, U.S.Afr.	6,610	F5	420
Stuttgart, Arkansas, Ark.	9,661	C5	170
Stuttgart, Ger.	602,900 (*825,000)	D3	286
Stuttgart, Phillips, Kans.	100	C4	144
Stykkisholmur, Ice.	908	L18	290
Styr, riv., Sov.Un.		G5	332
Su, China	50,000	I8	349
Suakin, Sud.	4,228	B4	398
Suao, For.		M10	349
Suapure, riv., Ven.		C5	240
Suaqui, Mex.		B4	224
Subansiri, riv., India		C6	368
Subiaco, Logan, Ark.	290	B3	170
Sublett, Cassia, Idaho		G5	108
Sublette, Haskell, Kans.	1,077	E3	144
Sublette, co., Wyo.	3,778	D2	116
Subligna, Chattooga, Ga.	150	B1	176
Sublimity, Marion, Oreg.	490	C1 C4	96
Subotica, Yugo.	115,342	A4	316
Subric, Phil.	1,839	B6	358
Sucarnoochee, Kemper, Miss.	100	C4	184
Sucarnoochee, creek, Ala., Miss.		C1 / C4	168 / 184
Succasunna, Morris, N J.	2,500	B3	210
Success, Clay, Ark.	226	A6	170
Success, Sask., Can.	98	E3	58
Suceava, Rom.	20,949	A4	321
Suceava, riv., Rom.		A4	321
Sucha, Pol.	5,866	D4	325
Suchan, Sov.Un.	47,200	E15	329
Suchdol, Czech.	3,730	*A2	324
Suches, Union, Ga.	600	B2	176
Suchitoto, Sal.	3,521	D3	228
Suchou (Soochow), China	474,000	J10	349
Suchow, see Chiuchuan, China			
Suchow, see Hsuchou, China			
Sucre, Bol.	40,128	C1	246
Sucre, state, Ven.	333,607	A7	240
Sucuriú, riv., Braz.		I6	257
Sucy-en-Brie, Fr.	8,570	I11	278
Sudan, Lamb, Tex.	1,235	B4	130
Sudan, country, Afr.	11,037,000	E9	388 398
Sudan, reg., Afr.		D3	408
Sudbury, Ont., Can.	46,482 (*95,500)	S25	64
Sudbury, Eng.	6,300	I13	273
Sudbury, Middlesex, Mass.	1,800 (7,447▲)	D1	206
Sudbury, dist., Ont., Can.	141,975	R25	64
Sudbury, res., Mass.		D1	206
Sudbury, riv., Mass.		B5	206
Sudd, swamp, Sud.		D2	398
Sudetes, mts., Czech.		A2	324
Sudetes, mts., Pol.		C3	325
Sudlersville, Queen Annes, Md.	394	B8	182
Sudley, Anne Arundel, Md.	80	C6	182
Sudogda, Sov.Un.	10,500	E13	332
Sudzha, Sov.Un.	15,400	G10	332
Sueca, Sp.	19,890	C6	298
Sueville, Fairfield, S.C.	150	C6	188
Suez, Eg., U.A.R.	107,244	B3 F7	395
Suez, bay, Eg., U.A.R.		F7	395
Suez, canal, Eg., U.A.R.		A3	395
Suez, gulf, Eg., U.A.R.		B3	395
Suez Canal, reg., Eg., U.A.R.	353,176	*A3	395
Suffern, Rockland, N.Y.	5,094	D2 D7	212
Suffield, Alta., Can.	90	E7	54
Suffield, Hartford, Conn.	1,069 (6,779▲)	B5	202
Suffolk, Fergus, Mont.	10	C7	110
Suffolk, (Independent City), Va.	12,609	A8 D8	192
Suffolk, co., Eng.	456,300	I13	273
Suffolk, co., Mass.	791,329	B5	206
Suffolk, co., N.Y.	666,784	D4	212
Sufu (Kashgar), China	91,000	D3	346
Sugar, creek, Ind.		C2	140
Sugar, creek, Pa.		B5	214
Sugar, isl., Mich.		C7	146
Sugar, riv., N.H.		E2	208
Sugar, riv., Wis.		F4	160
Sugar Bush, Outagamie, Wis.	30	D5	160
Sugar City, Crowley, Colo.	409	D7	106
Sugar City, Madison, Idaho	584	F7	108
Sugar Creek, Jackson, Mo.	2,663	E2	150
Sugarcreek, Tuscarawas, Ohio	982	B5	156
Sugar Grove, Logan, Ark.	100	B3	170
Sugar Grove, Fairfield, Ohio	479	C4	156
Sugar Grove, Watauga, N.C.	500	A4	186
Sugar Grove, Smyth, Va.	800	D3	192
Sugar Grove, Pendleton, W.Va.	75	C5	194
Sugar Hill, Gwinnett, Ga.	1,175	B2	176
Sugar Hill, Grafton, N.H.	100	C3	208
Sugar Land, Fort Bend, Tex.	2,802	E8 F7	130
Sugar Loaf, Boone, Ark.	49	*A3	170
Sugarloaf, hill, Ohio		A5	156
Sugarloaf, mtn., Maine		C2	204
Sugarloaf, mtn., Md.		B5	182
Sugarloaf, mtn., Mont.		C4	110
Sugarloaf, mtn., N.H.		B4	208
Sugarloaf, mts., Okla.		C9	128
Sugar Notch, Luzerne, Pa.	1,524	A5	214
Sugarpine, mtn., Oreg.		D5	96
Sugartown, Beauregard, La.	125	D2	180
Sugar Tree, Decatur, Tenn.	40	C3	190
Sugar Valley, Gordon, Ga.	165	B1	176
Sugden, Jefferson, Okla.	68	D6	128
Suggi, lake, Sask., Can.		C6	58
Suggsville, Clarke, Ala.	200	D2	168
Suhinya, Ven.		D6	240
Suhl, Ger.	25,200	C4	286
Sui, China	15,000	H7	348
Suiattle, riv., Wash.		A5	98
Suichiang, China		F8	346
Suichuan, China	15,000	L7	349
Suichung, China	45,000	E10	348
Suifenho, China	1,000	C15	348
Suihsien, China	10,000	J6	349
Suihua (Peilintzu), China	25,000	B13	348
Suilai (Manas), China	10,000	C5	348
Suileng, China	5,000	B13	348
Suilu, China		N3	349
Suipacha, Bol.		D1	246
Suipin, China	5,000	B15	348

Suir, riv., Ire. I5 273
Suisun City, Solano, Calif. 2,470 *C2 94
Suita, Jap. 88,458 *M11 354
Suite, China 15,000 G5 348
Suiter, Bland, Va. C3 192
Suitland, Prince Georges, Md. 10,300 C4 182
Suitung, China 1,000 D10 348
Sujangarh, India D1 368
Sukabumi, Indon. 66,000 F3 358
Sukadana, Indon. E3 358
Sukhona, riv., Sov.Un. A2 336
Sukhothai, prov., Thai. 194,856 *C3 362
Sukkur, Pak. 77,057 F6 375
Sukunka, riv., B.C., Can. C12 52
Sul, chan., Braz. F7 256
Sula, Ravalli, Mont. 27 E3 110
Sula, is., Indon. E6 358
Sula, riv., Sov.Un. G9 332
Sulaiman, range, Pak. E6 375
Sulaimāniya, Iraq 35,352 B6 378
Sula Sgeir, isl., Scot. B6 272
Sulęcin, Pol. 2,566 B2 325
Sulgen, Switz. 1,212 A5 312
Sulina, Rom. 3,622 B5 321
Sulitjelma, mtn., Swe. C7 290
Sulkava, Fin. F13 291
Sullana, Peru 33,100 A1 245
Sulligent, Lamar, Ala. 1,346 B1 168
Sullivan, Moultrie, Ill. 3,946 D5 138
Sullivan, Sullivan, Ind. 4,979 C2 140
Sullivan, Union, Ky. 250 C3 178
Sullivan, Hancock, Maine 150 *D4 204
(709▲)
Sullivan, Franklin and Crawford, Mo. 4,098 C6 150
Sullivan, Cheshire, N.H. 35 E2 208
(261▲)
Sullivan, Ashland, Ohio 348 A4 156
Sullivan, Jefferson, Wis. 418 E5 160
Sullivan, co., Ind. 21,721 C2 140
Sullivan, co., Mo. 8,783 A4 150
Sullivan, co., N.H. 28,067 E2 208
Sullivan, co., N.Y. 45,272 D7 212
Sullivan, co., Pa. 6,251 B5 214
Sullivan, co., Tenn. 114,139 B9 190
Sullivan, isl., Bur. E3 362
Sullivan, lake, Alta., Can. D7 54
Sullivan Gardens, Sullivan, Tenn. 950 *B9 190
Sullivans Island, Charleston, S.C. 1,358 F4 188
Sully, Jasper, Iowa 508 C5 142
Sully, co., S.Dak. 2,607 C5 158
Sulmona, It. 18,400 D4 302
Sulphide, Ont., Can. 210 P23 64
Sulphur, Henry, Ky. 275 B5 178
Sulphur, Calcasieu, La. 11,429 D2 180
Sulphur, Murray, Okla. 4,737 D7 128
Sulphur, fork, Tenn. B4 190
Sulphur, riv., Ark. D2 170
Sulphur, riv., Alta., Can. D3 54
Sulphur, riv., Tex. C8 130
Sulphur Rock, Independence, Ark. 225 B5 170
Sulphur South, Calcasieu, La. 1,351 *D2 180
Sulphur Spring, val., Ariz. F6 124
Sulphur Springs, Benton, Ark. 460 A2 170
Sulphur Springs, Montgomery, Ark. C3 170
Sulphur Springs, Henry, Ind. 400 C4 140
Sulphur Springs, Buena Vista, Iowa 150 B2 142
Sulphur Springs, Douglas, Oreg. D3 96
Sulphur Springs, Hopkins, Tex. 9,160 C8 130
Sultan, Snohomish, Wash. 821 B5 98
Sultanpur, India D3 368
Sulu, arch., Phil. C6 358
Sulu, riv., China C7 346
Sulu, sea, Phil. C5 358
Sulūq, Libya 1,000 A4 394
Sumach, Yakima, Wash. 1,345 *C6 98
Sumas, Whatcom, Wash. 629 A4 98
Sumatra, Liberty, Fla. 138 A6 174
Sumatra, Rosebud, Mont. 45 D9 110
Sumatra, reg., Indon. 12,100,000 D1 358
Sumatra, isl., Indon. D1 358
Sumava Resorts, Newton, Ind. 200 A2 140
Sumay, Guam C7 436
Sumba, isl., Austl. A3 432
Sumba, isl., Indon. F6 358
Sumbawa, Indon. F5 358
Sumbawa, isl., Indon. F5 358
Sumbawanga, Tan. 4,590 D5 414
Sumbay, Peru D3 245
Sumburgh, head, Scot. A11 272
Sümeg, Hung. 5,398 C2 320
Sumenep, Indon. 17,824 F4 358
Sumiton, Walker, Ala. 1,287 B2 168
Summan Dahama, des., Sau. Ar. B4 383
Summer, isl., Mich. D5 146
Summer, lake, Oreg. E6 96
Summerberry, Sask., Can. 95 E6 58
Summerberry, riv., Man., Can. D2 60
Summerdale, Baldwin, Ala. 533 E2 168
Summerdale, Cumberland, Pa. 1,200 *C4 214
Summerfield, Marion, Fla. 350 B8 174
Summerfield, Marshall, Kans. 237 C7 144
Summerfield, Claiborne, La. 200 B3 180
Summerfield, Guilford, N.C. 700 A6 186
Summerfield, Noble, Ohio 352 C5 156
Summerford, Newf., Can. 200 F8 72
Summerhaven, Pima, Ariz. 25 F5 124
Summer Lake, Lake, Oreg. 5 E6 96
Summerland, B.C., Can. 2,500 F13 52
Summerland, Smith, Miss. D3 184
Summerlee, Fayette, W.Va. 747 D7 194
Summers, Washington, Ark. 100 B2 170
Summers, co., W.Va. 15,640 D4 194
Summer Shade, Metcalfe, Ky. 250 D5 178
Summerside, P.E.I., Can. 7,242 C6 70
Summersville, Green, Ky. 350 C5 178
Summersville, Texas, Mo. 356 D6 150
Summersville, Nicholas, W.Va. 2,008 C4 194
C7
Summerton, Clarendon, S.C. 1,504 D8 188
Summertown, Emanuel, Ga. 100 D4 176
Summertown, Lawrence, Tenn. 700 C4 190
Summerville, Chattooga, Ga. 4,706 B1 176
Summerville, La Salle, La. 75 C3 180
Summerville, Union, Oreg. 76 B8 96
Summerville, Jefferson, Pa. 895 B2 214
Summerville, Dorchester, S.C. 3,633 E8 188
E3
Summit, Marion, Ark. 239 A4 170
Summit, Cook, Ill. 10,374 F2 138
Summit, Pike, Miss. 1,663 D2 184
Summit, Union, N.J. 23,677 B4 210
Summit, Muskogee, Okla. 200 C8 128
Summit, Benton, Oreg. 50 C3 96
Summit, Kent, R.I. 100 C2 216
Summit, Lexington, S.C. 108 D6 188
Summit, Roberts, S.Dak. 283 B9 158
Summit, Hamilton, Tenn. 200 E8 190
Summit, Iron, Utah 150 F3 114
Summit, co., Colo. 2,073 C4 106
Summit, co., Ohio 513,569 A5 156
Summit, co., Utah 5,673 C4 114
Summit, lake, Iowa C3 142
Summit, mtn., Nev. D5 112
Summit, mtn., N.Z. D6 437
Summit, peak, Colo. E4 106
Summit Bridge, New Castle, Del. 65 B3 172
Summit-Graymont, see Twin City, Ga.
Summit Hill, Carbon, Pa. 4,386 C6 214
Summit Point, Jefferson, W.Va. 250 B7 194
Summitville, Rio Grande, Colo. E4 106
Summitville, Madison, Ind. 1,048 B4 140
Summitville, Coffee, Tenn. 400 C6 190
Sumner, Levy, Fla. 147 B8 174
Sumner, Worth, Ga. 193 E3 176
Sumner, Lawrence, Ill. 1,035 E6 138
Sumner, Bremer, Iowa 2,170 B5 142
Sumner, Oxford, Maine 25 *D2 204
(481▲)
Sumner, Gratiot, Mich. 85 F7 146
Sumner, Tallahatchie, Miss. 551 B2 184
Sumner, Chariton, Mo. 234 B4 150
Sumner, Dawson, Nebr. 254 D6 152
Sumner, Noble, Okla. 27 B6 128
Sumner, Pierce, Wash. 5,874 B4 98
D3
Sumner, co., Kans. 25,316 E6 144
Sumner, co., Tenn. 36,217 B5 190
Sumner, strait, Alsk. J14 84
Sumoto, Jap. 49,358 G5 354
Šumperk, Czech. 21,595 B3 324
Sumprabum, Bur. A3 362
Sumpter, Baker, Oreg. 96 C8 96
Sumrall, Lamar, Miss. 797 D3 184
Sumter, Sumter, S.C. 23,062 D8 188
Sumter, co., Ala. 20,041 C1 168
Sumter, co., Fla. 11,869 C8 174
Sumter, co., Ga. 24,652 D2 176
Sumter, co., S.C. 74,941 D8 188
Sumterville, Sumter, Ala. 250 C1 168
Sumy, Sov.Un. 97,000 G10 332
Sun, St. Tammany, La. 1,125 D6 180
Sun, Fayette, W.Va. 585 D7 194
Sun, riv., Mont. C4 110
Suna, Tan. D5 414
Sunabi, Okinawa D1 436
Sunagawa, Jap. 30,057 C8 354
Sunapee, Sullivan, N.H. 700 E2 208
(1,164▲)
Sunapee, lake, N.H. E2 208
Sunapee, mtn., N.H. E2 208
Sunart, inlet, Scot. E7 272
Sunbeam, Duval, Fla. 250 A10 174
Sunbeam, Custer, Idaho 5 E4 108
Sunbright, Morgan, Tenn. 550 B7 190
Sunbright, Scott, Va. D2 192
Sunburg, Kandiyohi, Minn. 161 F3 148
Sunburst, Toole, Mont. 882 B5 110
Sunbury, Delaware, Ohio 1,360 B4 156
Sunbury, Northumberland, Pa. 13,687 C5 214
Sunbury, co., N.B., Can. 10,547 D3 70
Sunchales, Arg. B3 252
Suncho Corral, Arg. A3 252
Sunchōn, Kor. 61,647 F13 348
Sunchōn, Kor. 20,682 H13 348
Sun City, Hillsborough, Fla. 280 C6 174
Sun City, Barber, Kans. 188 E5 144
Suncook, Merrimack, N.H. 3,807 E4 208
Suncook, lakes, N.H. E4 208
Suncook, riv., N.H. E4 208
Suncrest, Randolph, W.Va. C4 194
Sunda, strait, Indon. F3 358
Sundance, Crook, Wyo. 908 B8 116
Sundance, mtn., Wyo. B8 116
Sunday, strait, Austl. B4 432
Sundbyberg, Swe. 26,082 B8 292
Sunderland, Ont., Can. 775 P21 64
Sunderland, Eng. 182,800 G11 272
Sunderland, Calvert, Md. 25 C6 182
Sunderland, Franklin, Mass. 400 B2 206
(1,279▲)
Sundial, Raleigh, W.Va. 250 D6 194
Sundown, Man., Can. 500 F4 60
Sundown, Hockley, Tex. 1,186 C4 130
Sundre, Alta., Can. 923 E5 54
Sundridge, Ont., Can. 697 O21 64
Sundsvall, Swe. 27,674 E7 291
Sunfield, Eaton, Mich. 626 G6 146
Sunfish Lake, Dakota, Minn. 181 *G5 148
Sunflower, Maricopa, Ariz. 40 E4 124
Sunflower, Johnson, Kans. 900 D8 144
Sunflower, Sunflower, Miss. 662 B2 184
Sunflower, co., Miss. 45,750 B2 184
Sunflower, riv., Miss. B2 184
Sungaiguntung, Indon. D2 358
Sungari, res., China D13 348
Sungari, riv., China B15 348
Sungchiang, China 67,000 J10 349
Sungei Patani, Mala. 22,897 F4 362
Sunghsien, China H5 348
Sungkan, China 5,000 K3 349
Sunglow, Cochise, Ariz. 50 G6 124
Sungtao, China 5,000 K4 349
Sungurlu, Tur. 6,461 A6 307
Sunland Gardens, Saint Lucie, Fla. 570 *D10 174
Sunlight, creek, Wyo. B3 116
Sunman, Ripley, Ind. 446 C4 140
Sunnan, Nor. D4 290
Sunnansjö, Swe. A5 292
Sunne, Swe. 3,173 B4 292
Sunniland, Collier, Fla. 60 E9 174
Sunny Acres, Kenton, Ky. 844 *A6 178
Sunnybrae, N.S., Can. 275 D7 70
Sunnybrook, Alta., Can. 95 D5 54
Sunnydell, Madison, Idaho F7 108
Sunny Hill, Washington, La. D5 180
Sunnyland, Tazewell, Ill. 1,200 C4 138
Sunnyland, Sarasota, Fla. 4,761 *D8 174
Sunnylven, Nor. E2 291
Sunnymead, Riverside, Calif. 3,404 *F5 94
Sunnynook, Alta., Can. 115 E7 54
Sunnyside, San Diego, Calif. 175 D6 94
Sunnyside, Newf., Can. 350 G9 72
Sunnyside, Bay, Fla. 250 A5 174
Sunny Side, Spalding, Ga. 190 *C2 176
Sunnyside, Leflore, Miss. 50 B2 184
Sunnyside, Nye, Nev. 20 E6 112
Sunnyside, Carbon, Utah 1,740 D5 114
Sunnyside, Yakima, Wash. 6,208 C6 98
Sunnyslope, Maricopa, Ariz. (part of Phoenix) H2 124
Sunnyslope, Alta., Can. 125 E6 54
Sunny South, Wilcox, Ala. 250 D2 168
Sunnyvale, Santa Clara, Calif. 52,898 *D2 94
Sunnyvale, Dallas, Tex. 969 *C7 130
Sunny Valley, Josephine, Oreg. 65 E3 96
Sunol, Alameda, Calif. 700 B6 94
Sunol, Cheyenne, Nebr. 100 C3 152
Sun Prairie, Dane, Wis. 4,008 E4 160
Sunray, Stephens, Okla. 100 *D6 128
Sunray, Moore, Tex. 1,967 A5 130
Sunrise, El Paso, Tex. 1,708 *D2 130
Sunrise, Platte, Wyo. 300 D8 116
Sunrise Heights, Calhoun, Mich. 1,569 *G6 146
Sun River, Cascade, Mont. 104 C5 110
Sunset, St. Landry, La. 1,307 D3 180
Sunset, Hancock, Maine 150 D4 204
Sunset, Pickens, S.C. 150 A3 188
Sunset, Montague, Tex. 150 C7 130
Sunset, Davis, Utah 4,235 B3 114
Sunset Beach, Orange, Calif. 1,000 C5 94
Sunset Beach, Clatsop, Oreg. 150 *A3 96
Sunset Crater, natl. mon., Ariz. C4 124
Sunset Hills, Saint Louis, Mo. 3,525 *C7 150
Sunset Hills, Fairfax, Va. 100 A6 192
Sunset Mill Village, Dallas, Ala. 500 *C2 168
Sunshine, Coconino, Ariz. 100 C4 124
Sunshine, Iberville, La. 500 B5 180
Sunshine, Hancock, Maine 120 D4 204
Sunshine, Park, Wyo. B4 116
Suntar, Sov.Un. C13 329
Suntaug, lake, Mass. C3 206
Suntex (Riley), Harney, Oreg. 5 D7 96
Suntrana, Alsk. 130 C7 84
Sun Valley, Blaine, Idaho 317 F4 108
Sunwui, China 49,000 N6 349
Sunyani, Ghana 4,570 E4 408
Suo, sea, Jap. H3 354
Suolahti, Fin. E11 290
Suonejoki, Fin. E12 290
Suoyarvi, Sov.Un. A9 332
Supai, Coconino, Ariz. 150 B3 124
Superb, Sask., Can. 90 E3 58
Superior, Pinal, Ariz. 4,875 E4 124
Superior, Boulder, Colo. 173 C5 106
Superior, Dickinson, Iowa 190 A3 142
Superior, Mineral, Mont. 1,242 C2 110
Superior, Nuckolls, Nebr. 2,935 D7 152
Superior, Lawrence, Ohio 500 D4 156
Superior, Douglas, Wis. 33,563 B1 160
Superior, McDowell, W.Va. 900 *D3 194
Superior, Sweetwater, Wyo. 241 E4 116
Superior, lake, Can., U.S. H10 48
B9 77
Superior Village, Douglas, Wis. 374 *B2 160
Suphan, mt., Tur. B10 307
Suphan Buri, Thai. 10,000 D4 362
Suphan Buri, prov., Thai. 340,872 *D3 362
Supi Oidak, Pima, Ariz. 40 G4 124
Suplee, Crook, Oreg. C7 96
Supply, Randolph, Ark. A6 170
Supreme, Assumption, La. 250 C5 180
Sūq ash Shuyukh, Iraq 7,735 D7 378
Suquamish, Kitsap, Wash. 950 B4 98
Sur, Om. 12,000 C6 383
Sur, pt., Calif. D3 94
Sura, riv., Sov.Un. E16 332
Surabaja, Indon. 935,700 F4 358
Surahammar, Swe. B7 292
Surakarta, Indon. 369,800 F4 358
Surakhany, Sov.Un. D4 336
Šurany, Czech. 5,381 B4 324
Surat, India 223,182 D2 366
Suratgarh, India C1 368
Surat Thani, Thai. 10,000 E3 362
Surat Thani, prov., Thai. 208,390 *E3 362
Surazh, Sov.Un. 13,700 F9 332
Suresnes, Fr. 37,149 I9 278
Suretka, C.R. F6 228
Surette Island, N.S., Can. 156 F4 70
Surf, Santa Barbara, Calif. 50 E3 94
Surf City, Ocean, N.J. 419 D4 210
Surfside, Dade, Fla. 3,157 E6 174
Surfside Beach, Horry, S.C. 350 *D11 188
Surgères, Fr. D3 278
Surgoinsville, Hawkins, Tenn. 914 B9 190
Surgut, Sov.Un. 3,500 A8 336
Suri, India 15,867 E4 368
Suribachi, mtn., Iwo A7 436
Surigao, Phil. 12,870 C7 358
Surin, prov., Thai. 435,382 *D5 362
Surinam (Netherlands Guiana), poss., S.A. 241,000 C6 236
257
Suriname, riv., Sur. E5 256
Suring, Oconto, Wis. 513 D5 160
Surprise, Butler, Nebr. 79 C8 152
Surrency, Appling, Ga. 312 E4 176
Surrey, Ward, N.Dak. 309 B4 154
Surrey, co., Eng. 1,655,000 J12 273
Surry, Hancock, Maine 180 D4 204
(547▲)
Surry, Cheshire, N.H. 200 E2 208
(362▲)
Surry, Surry, Va. 288 A7 192
C8
Surry, co., N.C. 48,205 A5 186
Surry, co., Va. 6,220 C8 192
Sursee, Switz. 4,265 A4 312
Surt (Sirte), Libya 890 A3 394
Sürüç, Tur. 4,217 C8 307
Surud Ad, mtn., Som. C6 398
Suruga, bay, Jap. M14 354
Surveyor, Raleigh, W.Va. 120 D6 194
Surville, cape, Solomon E2 436
Susa, It. 4,359 C1 302
Sušac, isl., Yugo. C3 316
Sušak, Yugo. (part of Rijeka) B2 316
Sušak, isl., Yugo. B2 316
Susan, Mathews, Va. 350 C8 192
Susank, Barton, Kans. 87 D5 144
Susanville, Lassen, Calif. 5,598 B3 94
Susanville, Grant, Oreg. C8 96
Sušice, Czech. 6,793 B1 324
Susitna, Alsk. 15 G10 84
Susitna, riv., Alsk. C7 84
Susquehanna, Susquehanna, Pa. 2,591 B6 214
Susquehanna, co., Pa. 33,137 B5 214
Susquehanna, riv., N.Y., Pa. C6 212
D5 214
Susques, Arg. B4 250
Sussex, N.B., Can. 3,403 D4 70
Sussex, Sussex, N.J. 1,656 A3 210
Sussex, Sussex, Va. 75 D7 192
Sussex, Waukesha, Wis. 1,087 E1 160
Sussex, Johnson, Wyo. 5 C6 116
Sussex, co., Del. 73,195 F4 172
Sussex, co., Eng. 986,800 K12 273
Sussex, co., N.J. 49,255 A3 210
Sussex, co., Va. 12,411 D7 192
Sustut, riv., B.C., Can. B9 52
Susung, China 5,000 J8 349
Susurluk, Tur. 10,068 B3 307
Sutcliffe, Washoe, Nev. 10 D2 112
Sutherland, U.S.Afr. 1,497 F4 420
Sutherland, O'Brien, Iowa 883 B2 142
Sutherland, Lincoln, Nebr. 867 C4 152
Sutherland, Dinwiddie, Va. 65 B9 192
C7
Sutherland, co., Scot. 13,300 C8 272
Sutherland, res., Nebr. C5 152
Sutherlin, Douglas, Oreg. 2,452 D3 96
Sutlej, riv., China, India, Pak. E4 346
D8 375
Sutter, Sutter, Calif. 1,219 *C3 94
Sutter, co., Calif. 33,380 C3 94
Sutter Creek, Amador, Calif. 1,161 C3 94
Suttle, Perry, Ala. 256 C2 168
Sutton, Alsk. 200 G11 84
Sutton, Nevada, Ark. 70 D3 170
Sutton, Que., Can. 1,407 S12 66
Sutton, Worcester, Mass. 200 B4 206
(3,638▲)
Sutton, Clay, Nebr. 1,252 D8 152
Sutton, Merrimack, N.H. 200 E3 208
(487▲)
Sutton, Griggs, N.Dak. 150 C7 154
Sutton, Caledonia, Vt. 125 B4 218
(476▲)
Sutton, Braxton, W.Va. 967 C4 194
Sutton, co., Tex. 3,738 D5 130
Sutton Coldfield, Eng. 52,510 I11 273
Sutton-in-Ashfield, Eng. 40,300 H11 273
Suttons Bay, Leelanau, Mich. 421 G8 146
Sutton West, Ont., Can. 1,310 P21 64
Suttsu, Jap. 10,794 C8 354
Suva, Fiji 11,398 E6 436
(*23,513)
Suvasvesi, lake, Fin. E13 290
Suver, Polk, Oreg. *C3 96
Süveydiye, Tur. C6 307
Suwa, Jap. 42,740 K14 354
Suwałki, Pol. 18,600 A6 325
Suwanee, Gwinnett, Ga. 541 A5 176
B2
Suwanee, mtn., Ga. B2 176
Suwannee, Dixie, Fla. 150 B7 174
Suwannee, co., Fla. 14,961 A7 174
Suwannee, riv., Fla., Ga. B8 174
F4 176
Suwannee, sound, Fla. B7 174
Suwanose, isl., Jap. J2 354
Suyo, Peru 744 A1 245
Suzu, cape, Jap. F6 354
Suzuka, Jap. 80,741 M12 354
Suzuka-Sammyaku, mts., Jap. M12 354
Svalbard (Spitsbergen), Nor.poss., Eur. 1,200 B4 328
(no permanent pop.)
Svalbardh, Ice. K22 290
Svaneke, Den. 1,191 F6 292
Svängsta, Swe. E5 292
Svatovo, Sov.Un. 20,000 H12 332
Svealand, reg., Swe. 2,609,884 *G6 291
Svedala, Swe. 5,172 F4 292
Sveg, Swe. 2,010 F6 291
Svelvik, Nor. B1 292
Svendborg, Den. 23,652 F1 292
Svendborg, co., Den. 150,365 *I4 291
Svenljunga, Swe. 2,511 D4 292
Svensen, Clatsop, Oreg. 50 A3 96
Sverdlovsk, Sov.Un. 777,000 A6 336
(*900,000)
Sverdrup, is., N.W.Ter., Can. B8 48
Svetlaya, Sov.Un. E15 329
Svetlyy, Sov.Un. D13 329
Svilajnac, Yugo. 5,049 B5 316
Svilengrad, Bul. 11,001 C3 317
Svir, riv., Sov.Un. B9 332
Svirstroy, Sov.Un. 15,000 B9 332
Svishtov, Bul. 18,357 B2 317
Svitavy, Czech. 8,983 B3 324
Svoboday, Sov.Un. D14 329
Svyatoy, cape, Sov.Un. B16 329
Swabia (Schwaben), reg., Ger. *D4 286
Swain, co., N.C. 8,387 B2 186

Swain, mtn., Ark.		A3	170
Swain, reefs, Austl.		C10	432
Swains, isl., Pac.O.		D4	436
Swainsboro, Emanuel, Ga.	5,943	D4	176
Swainton, Cape May, N.J.	75	E3	210
Swakopmund, S.W.Afr.		D2	420
Swale, riv., Eng.		G11	273
Swaledale, Cerro Gordo, Iowa	217	B4	142
Swallows, Pueblo, Colo.	10	D6	106
Swalwell, Alta., Can.	114	E6	54
Swampers, Franklin, La.	20	B4	180
Swampscott, Essex, Mass.	13,294	B6 C3	206
Swan, Marion, Iowa	168	C4	142
Swan, creek, Ohio		A1	156
Swan, falls, Idaho		F2	108
Swan, isl., Caribbean Sea		B6	228
Swan, lake, Man., Can.		D2	60
Swan, lake, Maine		D4	204
Swan, lake, Nebr.		C3	152
Swan, lake, Wash.		D3	98
Swan, peak, Mont.		C3	110
Swan, pt., Md.		B7	182
Swan, range, Mont.		B3	110
Swan, riv., Austl.		E3	432
Swan, riv., Man., Sask., Can.		E2 D6	60 58
Swanage, Eng.	7,200	K11	273
Swandale, Clay, W.Va.	350	C4 C7	194
Swan Hill, Austl.	5,197	F8	432
Swanington, Benton, Ind.	150	B2	140
Swan Lake, Man., Can.	275	F3	60
Swanlake, Bannock, Idaho	150	G6	108
Swan Lake, Lake, Mont.	88	C3	110
Swanlinbar, Ire.	290	G5	273
Swannanoa, Buncombe, N.C.	2,189	B3	186
Swanquarter, Hyde, N.C.	200	B9	186
Swan River, Man., Can.	2,644	D2	60
Swan River, Itasca, Minn.	150	D5	148
Swans, isl., Maine		D4	204
Swansboro, Onslow, N.C.	1,104	C8	186
Swansea, Ont., Can.	8,595	S22	64
Swansea, St. Clair, Ill.	3,018	E4	138
Swansea, Bristol, Mass.	1,000 (9,916▲)	C5	206
Swansea, Lexington, S.C	776	D6	188
Swansea, Wales	161,700	J9	273
Swansea, bay, Wales		J9	273
Swans Island, Hancock, Maine	300 (402▲)	D4	204
Swanson, Sask., Can.	40	E4	58
Swanson, N.Z.	416	H8	437
Swanson, lake, Nebr.		D4	152
Swanton, Garrett, Md.	100	B1	182
Swanton, Saline, Nebr.	190	D8	152
Swanton, Fulton, Ohio	2,306	A3	156
Swanton, Franklin, Vt.	2,390 (3,946▲)	B2	218
Swan Valley, Bonneville, Idaho	217	F7	108
Swanville, Waldo, Maine	100 (514▲)	*D3	204
Swanville, Morrison, Minn.	342	F4	148
Swanzey, Cheshire, N.H.	150 (3,626▲)	F2	208
Swanzey Center, Cheshire, N.H.	700	*F2	208
Swarthmore, Delaware, Pa.	5,753	A6	214
Swartswood, Sussex, N.J.	100	A3	210
Swartswood, lake, N.J.		A3	210
Swartz, Ouachita, La.	300	B4	180
Swartz Creek, Genesee, Mich.	3,006	G8	146
Swatow (Shantou), China	280,400	N8	349
Swayzee, Grant, Ind.	863	B4	140
Swaziland, Br. poss., Afr.	267,000	I10	388 421
Swea City, Kossuth, Iowa	805	A3	142
Sweatman, Montgomery, Miss.	25	B3	184
Swedeborg, Pulaski, Mo.	175	D5	150
Swedeburg, Saunders, Nebr.	65	E2	152
Swedehome, Polk, Nebr.	23	*C8	152
Swedeland, Montgomery, Pa.	950	A6	214
Sweden (Town of), Oxford, Maine	(119▲)	*D2	204
Sweden, country, Eur.	7,436,000	B6	266 291
Swedesboro, Gloucester, N.J.	2,449	D2	210
Swedesburg, Montgomery, Pa.	950	*C6	214
Sweeny, Brazoria, Tex.	3,087	G7	130
Sweet, Gem, Idaho	100	*F2	108
Sweet Briar, Amherst, Va.	850	C5	192
Sweetgrass, Toole, Mont.	205	B5	110
Sweet Grass, co., Mont.	3,290	E7	110
Sweet Hall, King William, Va.	50	C8	192
Sweet Home, Pulaski, Ark.	900	C4 D7	170
Sweet Home, Linn, Oreg.	3,353	C4	96
Sweetsburg, Que., Can.	879	S12	66
Sweetsers, Grant, Ind.	896	B4	140
Sweet Springs, Saline, Mo.	1,452	C4	150
Sweetsprings, Monroe, W.Va.	500	D4	194
Sweet Water, Marengo, Ala.	400	C2	168
Sweetwater, B.C., Can.		C12	52
Sweetwater, Dade, Fla.	645	*F10	174
Sweetwater, Buffalo, Nebr.	15	*C6	152
Sweetwater, Roger Mills and Beckham, Okla.	50	C4	128
Sweetwater, Monroe, Tenn.	4,145	C7	190
Sweetwater, Nolan, Tex.	13,914	C5	130
Sweetwater, co., Wyo.	17,920	E3	116
Sweet Water, canyon, Utah		D6	114
Sweetwater, res., Calif.		D6	94
Sweetwater, riv., Wyo.		D4	116
Swepsonville, Alamance, N.C.	800	A6	186
Świdnica, Pol.	34,000	C3	325
Świdwin, Pol.	6,098	B2	325
Świebodzice, Pol.	6,078	C3	325
Świebodzin, Pol.	11,200	B2	325
Świecie, Pol.	8,358	B4	325
Swift, co., Minn.	14,936	F3	148
Swift, creek, N.C.		B8	186
Swift, creek, Va.		B8	192
Swift, riv., N.H.		C4	208
Swift, riv., N.H.		D4	208
Swift Current, Sask., Can.	10,612	C3 E4	58
Swiftcurrent, creek, Sask., Can.		E3	58
Swift Diamond, riv., N.H.		B4	208
Swifton, Jackson, Ark.	601	B5	170
Swiftown, Leflore, Miss.	200	B2	184
Swifts Beach, Plymouth, Mass.	200	*C6	206
Swilly, lake, Ire.		F5	272
Swinburne, cape, N.W.Ter., Can.		C8	48
Swindle, isl., B.C., Can.		D8	52
Swindon, Eng.	74,000	J11	273
Swinemünde, see Swinoujście, Pol.			
Swink, Otero, Colo.	348	D7	106
Swink, Choctaw, Okla.	86	D8	128
Swinoujście, Pol.	10,600	B2	325
Swisher, Johnson, Iowa	271	C6	142
Swisher, co., Tex.	10,607	B5	130
Swiss, Nicholas, W.Va.	325	C3 C7	194
Swissvale, Allegheny, Pa.	15,089	A4	214
Switchback, McDowell, W.Va.	525	*D3	194
Switz City, Greene, Ind.	339	C2	140
Switzer, Spartanburg, S.C.	125	B4	188
Switzer, Logan, W.Va.	1,131	*D3	194
Switzerland, Saint Johns, Fla.	250	B10	174
Switzerland, Jasper, S.C.	50	G6	188
Switzerland, co., Ind.	7,092	D4	140
Switzerland, country, Eur.	5,230,000	D5	266 312
Swords, Morgan, Ga.	200	C3	176
Swords, Ire.	1,629	H6	273
Swoyersville, Luzerne, Pa.	6,751	A5 B6	214
Sycamore, Talladega, Ala.	900	B3	168
Sycamore, Sussex, Del.		F4	172
Sycamore, Turner, Ga.	501	E3	176
Sycamore, De Kalb, Ill.	6,961	B5	138
Sycamore, Montgomery, Kans.	187	E8	144
Sycamore, Wyandot, Ohio	998	B3	156
Sycamore, Allendale, S.C.	401	E6	188
Sycamore, Pittsylvania, Va.		C5	192
Sycamore, creek, Tenn.		B4	190
Sycamore, creek, W.Va.		C7	194
Sycamore Hills, St. Louis, Mo.	972	*C7	150
Sychevka, Sov.Un.		E10	332
Syców, Pol.	2,108	C3	325
Sydenham, Ont., Can.	525	P24	64
Sydney, Austl.	230,330	E10	432
Sydney, N.S., Can.	32,162	C9	70
Sydney, hbr., Austl.		E10	432
Sydney Mines, N.S., Can.	8,731	C9	70
Sydnorsville, Franklin, Va.	10	D5	192
Sykeston, Wells, N.Dak.	236	C6	154
Sykesville, Carroll, Md.	1,196	B6	182
Sykesville, Burlington, N.J.	100	C3	210
Sykesville, Jefferson, Pa.	1,479	B3	214
Syktyvkar, Sov.Un.	64,000	C7	328
Sylacauga, Talladega, Ala.	12,857	B3	168
Sylamore, Izard, Ark.	45	B4	170
Sylhet, Pak.	33,124	K17	375
Sylt, isl., Ger.		A3	286
Sylva, Jackson, N.C.	1,564	B2	186
Sylvan, Multnomah, Oreg.	600	B1	96
Sylvan, Franklin, Pa.	20	D3	214
Sylvan, Pierce, Wash. (part of Fox Island)		D2	98
Sylvan Beach, Oneida, N.Y.	800	B6	212
Sylvan Grove, Lincoln, Kans.	400	C5	144
Sylvan Hills, Pulaski, Ark.	2,000	D7	170
Sylvania, De Kalb, Ala.	350	A4	168
Sylvania, Sask., Can.	190	D5	58
Sylvania, Screven, Ga.	3,469	D5	176
Sylvania, Jefferson, Ky.	1,200	*B5	178
Sylvania, Lucas, Ohio	5,187	A1 A3	156
Sylvan Lake, Alta., Can.	1,114	D5	54
Sylvan Lake, Oakland, Mich.	2,004	*G8	146
Sylvan Shores, Lake, Fla.	1,214	*C9	174
Sylvan Springs, Jefferson, Ala.	245	*B2	168
Sylvarena, Smith, Miss.	69	C3	184
Sylvatus, Carroll, Va.	100	D4	192
Sylvester, Worth, Ga.	3,610	E3	176
Sylvester, Boone, W.Va.	316	D6	194
Sylvester, mtn., Newf., Can.		F8	72
Sylvia, Reno, Kans.	402	E5	144
Sylvia, Dickson, Tenn.	100	B4	190
Symmes, creek, Ohio		D4	156
Symsonia, Graves, Ky.	400	D2	178
Syosset, Nassau, N.Y.	14,000	D3	212
Syracuse, Kosciusko, Ind.	1,595	A4	140
Syracuse, see Siracusa, It.			
Syracuse, Hamilton, Kans.	1,888	E2	144
Syracuse, Morgan, Mo.	180	C5	150
Syracuse, Otoe, Nebr.	1,261	D9 E2	152
Syracuse, Onondaga, N.Y.	216,038 (*442,300)	B5	212
Syracuse, Meigs, Ohio	731	C5	156
Syracuse, Davis, Utah	1,061	B3	114
Syr Darya, riv., Sov.Un.		D7	336
Syria, prov., U.A.R.	4,421,000	F5	340 378
Syriam, Bur.		C3	362
Syrian, des., Arabian Pen.		C3	378
Sysladobsis, lake, Maine		C4	204
Sysmä, Fin.		F11	291
Sysola, riv., Sov.Un.		A4	336
Sysslebäck, Swe.		A3	292
Syväri, lake, Fin.		E13	290
Syzran, Sov.Un.	148,000	B3	336
Szabadszállás, Hung.	4,598	C4	320
Szabolcs-Szatmár, co., Hung.	560,000	*B6	320
Szamos, riv., Hung.		B7	320
Szamotuły, Pol.	10,800	B3	325
Szarvas, Hung.	11,357 (22,728▲)	C5	320
Szczebrzeszyn, Pol.	5,122	C6	325
Szczecin (Stettin), Pol.	223,000	B2	325
Szczecin, pol. div., Pol.	650,000	*B2	325
Szczecinek, Pol.	19,600	B3	325
Szczuczyn Białostocki, Pol.	2,479	B6	325
Szczytno, Pol.	3,645	B5	325
Szechwan, prov., China	72,160,000	E8	346
Szeged, Hung.	100,000	C5	320
Szeghalom, Hung.	10,712	B6	320
Székesfehérvár, Hung.	52,000	B4	320
Szekszárd, Hung.	18,000	C3	320
Szengen, China		N3	349
Szentendre, Hung.	7,000	B4	320
Szentes, Hung.	26,000 (34,000▲)	C5	320
Szigetvár, Hung.	6,544	C2	320
Szolnok, Hung.	43,000	B5	320
Szombathely, Hung.	53,000	B1	320
Szprotawa, Pol.	2,672	C2	325
Sztálinváros, Hung.	34,000	C3	320
Sztum, Pol.	3,111	B4	325
Szubin, Pol.	3,742	B3	325
Szydłowiec, Pol.	4,010	C5	325

T

Taaveti, Fin.		F12	291
Tab, Warren, Ind.	100	B2	140
Tābah, Sau.Ar.		B3	383
Tabarka, Tun.	857	A5	402
Tabas, Iran	17,743	C4	379
Tabas, Iran		C5	379
Tabasco, state, Mex.	362,716	D7	225
Tabatinga, mts., Braz.		C1	258
Tabelbala, Alg.		C3	402
Taber, Alta., Can.	3,688	F6	54
Taber, Bingham, Idaho		F6	108
Taberg, Oneida, N.Y.	375	B6	212
Tabernacle, Burlington, N.J.	100	D3	210
Tabernas, Sp.	3,507	D5	298
Tabernash, Grand, Colo.	275	C5	106
Tabiona, Duchesne, Utah	167	C5	114
Tablas, cape, Chile		B1	252
Tablas, isl., Phil.		B6	358
Table, bay, Newf., Can.		D7	72
Table, bay, U.S.Afr.		F3	420
Table, head, Newf., Can.		D8	72
Table, mtn., Ariz.		F5	124
Table, mtn., Newf., Can.		G6	72
Table, rock, Oreg.		C4	96
Table Grove, Fulton, Ill.	500	C3	138
Table Rock, Pawnee, Nebr.	422	D9	152
Table Rock, Jackson, Oreg.		E4	96
Table Rock, Sweetwater, Wyo.	5	E4	116
Table Rock, lake, Mo.		E4	150
Table Top, mtn., Ariz.		F3	124
Taboada, Sp.	733	A3	298
Tábor, Czech.	19,585	B2	324
Tabor, Fremont and Mills, Iowa	909	D2	142
Tabor, Morris, N.J.	1,000	*B4	210
Tabor, Bon Homme, S.Dak.	378	E8	158
Tabor, Sov.Un.		B16	329
Tabora, Tan.	15,361	D5	414
Tabor City, Columbus, N.C.	2,338	C7	186
Tabou, I.C.	1,400	F3	408
Tabrīz, Iran	290,195	A2	379
Tabūk, Sau.Ar.	10,000	B2	383
Tabusintac, riv., N.B., Can.		B4	70
Täby, Swe.	13,787	B9	292
Tacámbaro de Codallos, Mex.	5,954	L13	225
Tachang, China		I16	346
Tachang, China		I17	346
Tachiang, China		E13	348
Tachie, riv., B.C., Can.		C10	52
Tachikawa, Jap.	63,644	L15	354
Táchira, state, Ven.	304,181	C2	240
Tacloban, Phil.	31,155	B7	358
Tacna, Yuma, Ariz.	100	F1	124
Tacna, Peru	16,000	D3	245
Tacna, dept., Peru	51,920	D3	245
Tacoma, La Plata, Colo.	17	E3	106
Tacoma, Pierce, Wash.	147,979 (*298,000)	B4 D2	98
Taconic, Litchfield, Conn.	200	A2	202
Taconic, range, Mass.		A1	206
Taconite, Itasca, Minn.	376	D5	148
Tacoronte, Sp.	10,020	F11	298
Tacuarembó, Ur.	24,000	B4	252
Tacuarembó, dept., Ur.	105,939	B4	252
Tacuati, Par.		C4	247
Tacuato, Ven.		A4	240
Tacuba, Mex.		G10	224
Tacubaya, Mex.		G10	224
Tad, Kanawha, W.Va.	654	C6	194
Tademaït, plat., Alg.		C4	402
Tadent, riv., Alg.		D5	402
Tadjoura, Fr.Som.	1,150	C5	398
Tadoussac, Que., Can.	1,066	P15	66
Tadzhik S.S.R., Sov.Un.	1,989,000	F10	328
Taecheng, China		F8	348
Taegu (Taikyū), Kor.	488,690	H14	348
Taejŏn, Kor.	173,143	G13	348
Taeyudong, Kor.		E12	348
Tafalla, Sp.	6,303	A6	298
Taft, Kern, Calif.	3,822	E4	94
Taft, B.C., Can.	50	E13	52
Taft, Orange, Fla.	1,214	C9	174
Taft, St. Charles, La.	260	B6	180
Taft, Muskogee, Okla.	386	C8	128
Taft, Lincoln, Oreg.	557	C2	96
Taft, Lincoln, Tenn.	200	C5	190
Taft, San Patricio, Tex.	3,463	F7	130
Taft Heights, Kern, Calif.	2,661	*E4	94
Taft Southwest, San Patricio, Tex.	1,927	*E7	130
Taftsville, Windsor, Vt.	100	D4	218
Taganrog, Sov.Un.	201,000	I12	332
Taganrog, gulf, Sov.Un.		I12	332
Tagawa, Jap.	100,071	*H3	354
Tagbilaran, Phil.	5,879	C6	358
Taghrifat, Libya		B3	394
Tagolo, pt., Phil.		C6	358
Taguatinga, Braz.	1,027	C1	258
Taguay, Ven.		B5	240
Taguchi, Jap.	5,243	L13	354
Tagur, Sov.Un.		D15	329
Tagus, Mountrail, N.Dak.	72	B4	154
Tahan, mtn., Mala.		F4	362
Tahat, mtn., Alg.		D5	402
Tahawas, Essex, N.Y.	700	A7	212
Tahiti, isl., Pac.O.		D4	436
Tahlequah, Cherokee, Okla.	5,840	C9	128
Tahoe, lake, Calif., Nev.		C3 D1	94 112
Tahoe City, Placer, Calif.	350	C3	94
Tahoka, Lynn, Tex.	3,012	C5	130
Taholah, Grays Harbor, Wash.	400	B2	98
Tahoma, Placer, Calif.	50	C3	94
Tahona, Le Flore, Okla.	35	C9	128
Tahoua, Niger	12,600	D6	408
Tahquamenon, falls, Mich.		C6	146
Tahquamenon, riv., Mich.		C6	146
Tahsien, China	70,000	J3	349
Tahta, Eg., U.A.R.	36,125	B3	395
Tahtsa, lake, B.C., Can.		D9	52
Tahtsa, peak, B.C., Can.		D9	52
Tahtsa, riv., B.C., Can.		D9	52
Tahungopo, China		B8	348
Tahuya, Mason, Wash.	150	B3	98
Tai, China	15,000	F6	348
Tai, China	5,000	I9	349
Taï, I.C.		E3	408
Taian, China	15,000	E11	348
Taian, China	25,000	G8	348
Taiban, De Baca, N.Mex.	120	D6	126
Taichao, China		E6	346
Taichintata, China	5,000	C10	348
Taichung, For.	231,169	M10	349
Taihape, N.Z.	2,464	C5	437
Taihoku, see Taipei, For.			
Taikang, China	10,000	B12	348
Taiku, China	15,000	G6	348
Taikyū, see Taegu, Kor.			
Tailai, China	25,000	B11	348
Tailem Bend, Austl.	1,952	F7	432
Tain, Scot.	1,600	D8	272
Tainan, For.	264,783	N10	349
Taining, China	18,000	L8	349
Taipei (Taihoku), For.	704,124	M10	349
Taiping, Mala.	48,199	F4	362
Taira, Jap.	70,808	F8	354
Taishan, China	25,000	N6	349
Taishun, China	5,000	L9	349
Taitao, pen., Chile		G2	251
Taitiarato, Pap.		F10	359
Taitung, For.		N10	349
Taivalkoski, Fin.		D13	290
Taiwan, see Formosa, rep. (Nationalist China)			
Taiwara, see Qal'a-i-Ghor, Afg.			
Taiyüan, China	720,700	G6	348
Taiyüan, see Yangkü, China			
Ta'izz, Yemen		E3	383
Tajarḥī, Libya		C2	394
Tajimi, Jap.	47,405	G6 L13	354
Tajique, Torrance, N.Mex.	115	D4	126
Tajo (Tagus), riv., Sp.		C4	298
Tajumulco, peak, Guat.		C2	228
Tajuna, riv., Sp.		B5	298
Tājūrā', Libya	2,670	A2	394
Tak, Thai.	5,000	C3	362
Tak, prov., Thai.	102,193	*C3	362
Taka Banare, isl., Okinawa		D1	436
Takabba, Ken.		B7	414
Takada, Jap.	71,432	F7	354
Takaka, N.Z.	739	D4	437
Takamatsu, Jap.	144,812	G5	354
Takangbesi, is., Indon.		F6	358
Takao, see Kaohsiung, For.			
Takaoka, Jap.	131,531	F6	354
Takapuna, N.Z.	18,724	H9	437
Takasaki, Jap.	125,195	F7 K15	354
Takata, Jap.	23,025	F7	354
Takatō, Jap.	4,872	L14	354
Takatsuki, Jap.	54,028	M11	354
Takaw, Bur.		B3	362
Takayama, Jap.	49,708	F6 K13	354
Takazé, riv., Eth.		C4	398
Take, isl., Jap.		F3	354
Takee, Okinawa		C1	436
Takefu, Jap.	54,137	L12	354
Takeo, Camb.	5,000	E5	362
Tåkern, lake, Swe.		C5	292
Takestān, Iran	10,534	B2	379
Takhta-Bazar, Sov.Un.	5,400	F8	328
Takhta-Kupyr, Sov.Un.		D6	336
Takht-i-Sulaiman, mtn., Iran		B3	379
Taki, India		I9	366
Taki, Solomon Is.		F13	359
Takihara, Jap.	4,364	M12	354
Takilma, Josephine, Oreg.	50	E3	96
Takla, lake, B.C., Can.		C9	52
Takla Makan, des., China		D4	346
Takoma Park, Montgomery, Md.	16,799	C3	182
Takoradi, Ghana	17,800 (*44,557)	F4	408
Takotna, Alsk.	42	C6	84
Takouchen, China	5,000	E8	348
Takou Ho, riv., China		M3	349
Taku, China	25,000	F8	348
Taku, riv., Alsk.		I14	84
Takua Pa, Thai.		E3	362
Takut, Bur.		B3	362
Tala, Mex.	9,003	C5	224
Tala, Eg., U.A.R.	21,200	D1	382
Tala, Ur.	10,000	B4	252
Talache, Bonner, Idaho	15	*A2	108
Talagante, Chile	7,966	B1	252
Talai, China	5,000	C12	348
Talakmau, mtn., Indon.		D1	358
Talala, Rogers, Okla.	147	B8	128
Talamanca, mts., C.R.		F6	228
Talanga, Hond.	2,460	C4	228
Talara, Peru	12,985	A1	245
Talas, Sov.Un.	10,000	D8	336
Talasea, N.Gui.		F11	359
Talaud, is., Indon.		D7	358
Talavera de la Reina, Sp.	18,631	C4	298
Talbot, Benton, Ind.	100	B2	140
Talbot, Marion, Oreg.	65	C1	96
Talbot, co., Ga.	7,127	D2	176
Talbot, co., Md.	21,578	C7	182
Talbot, isl., Fla.		A9	174
Talbot, lake, Man., Can.		C3	60
Talbott, Jefferson, Tenn.	250	B8	190
Talbotton, Talbot, Ga.	1,163	D2	176
Talca, Chile	55,059	C1	252
Talca, prov., Chile	173,693	E3	250
Talcahuano, Chile	54,782	C1	252
Talcher, India	6,002	D5	366
Talco, Titus, Tex.	1,024	C8	130
Talcott, Summers, W.Va.	600	D4	194
Talcottville, Tolland, Conn.	670	B6	202
Talcottville, Lewis, N.Y.	700	B6	212
Taldy-Kurgan, Sov.Un.	41,000	C9	336
Talence, Fr.	22,695	E3	278
Talent, Jackson, Oreg.	868	E4	96
Talha, Chad		B9	409
Tali, China		F8	346

Tali, China	80,000	H5	348
Taliabu, isl., Indon		E6	358
Taliaferro, co., Ga.	3,370	C4	176
Talien (Darien), China	595,000	F10	348
Talihina, Le Flore, Okla.	1,048	D8	128
Tali Post, Sud.		D3	398
Talitsa, Sov.Un.	17,300	A6	336
Talkeetna, Alsk.	106	C7	84
		F10	
Talkeetna, mts., Alsk.		F11	84
Talkha, Eg., U.A.R.	13,216	C2	382
Talladega, Talladega, Ala.	17,742	B3	168
Talladega, co., Ala.	65,495	B3	168
Talladega Springs, Talladega, Ala.	177	B3	168
Tallahala, creek, Miss.		D3	184
Tallahassee, Leon, Fla.	48,174	A6	174
Tallahatchie, co., Miss.	24,081	B2	184
Tallahatchie, riv., Miss.		B2	184
Tallant, Osage, Okla.	25	B7	128
Tallapoosa, Haralson, Ga.	2,744	C1	176
Tallapoosa, New Madrid, Mo.	225	E8	150
Tallapoosa, co., Ala.	35,007	C4	168
Tallapoosa, riv., Ala.		B4	168
		C3	
Tallåsen, Swe.		F6	291
Tallassee, Elmore and Tallapoosa, Ala.	4,934	C4	168
Tallassee, Blount, Tenn.	100	C7	190
Tallaweka, Elmore, Ala. (part of Tallassee)	609	C4	168
Tall el Kebir, Eg., U.A.R.		E6	395
Tallevast, Manatee, Fla.	200	D6	174
		D8	
Talleyville, New Castle, Del.	1,000	A3	172
Tallinn, Sov.Un.	208,000	C5	332
Tallmadge, Summit, Ohio	10,246	A5	156
Tallula, Menard, Ill.	547	D4	138
Tallula, Issaquena, Miss.	200	C1	184
Tallulah, Madison, La.	9,413	B4	180
Tallulah, mts., Ga.		B3	176
Tallulah Falls, Rabun and Habersham, Ga.	225	*B3	176
Talma, Fulton, Ind.	800	A3	140
Talmage, Sask., Can.	75	F6	58
Talmage, Dickinson, Kans.	200	C6	144
Talmage, Otoe, Nebr.	361	D9	152
Talmage, Duchesne, Utah	10	C5	114
Talmo, Jackson, Ga.	162	*B3	176
Talnoye, Sov.Un.	22,800	H8	332
Talo, mtn., Eth.		C4	398
Talodi, Sud.	2,736	C3	398
Talofofo, Guam	618	D7	436
Talofofo, bay, Guam		D7	436
Taloga, Dewey, Okla.	322	B5	128
Talpa, Taos, N.Mex.	500	B5	126
Talquin, lake, Fla.		A6	174
Talsi, Sov.Un.	8,400	D4	332
Taltal, Chile	4,901	C3	250
Talvik, Nor.		A10	290
Tama, Tama, Iowa	2,925	C5	142
Tama, co., Iowa	21,413	B5	142
Tamaha, Haskell, Okla.	80	C9	128
Tamaki, riv., N.Z.		H9	437
Tamalameque, Col.	1,843	B2	244
Tamale, Ghana	16,164	E4	408
Taman, Sov.Un.		J11	332
Tamanar, Mor.		B2	402
Tamano, Jap.	62,365	G4	354
Tamanrasset, see Fort Laperrine, Alg.			
Tamanrasset, riv., Alg.		D4	402
Tamaqua, Schuylkill, Pa.	10,173	C6	214
Tamarack, Adams, Idaho	50	E2	108
Tamarack, Aitkin, Minn.	112	E5	148
Tamarite, Sp.	3,581	B7	298
Tamaroa, Perry, Ill.	696	E4	138
Tamassee, Oconee, S.C.	350	B2	188
Tamatave, Malag.	28,700	C9	421
Tamatave, prov., Malag.		C9	421
Tamaulipas, state, Mex.	718,167	C6	225
Tamazula de Gordiano, Mex.	7,837	L12	225
Tamazunchale, Mex.	5,817	C6	225
		K14	
Tambach, Ken.		B6	414
Tambacounda, Sen.	3,700	D2	408
També, Braz.	2,891	B3	258
Tambelan, is., Indon.		D3	358
Tambellaga, well, Niger		C6	409
Tambo, Austl.	481	C9	432
Tambo, riv., Peru		C3	245
Tambo, riv., Peru		D3	245
Tambo Grande, Peru	4,078	A1	245
Tambov, Sov.Un.	170,000	B2	336
Tambre, riv., Sp.		A2	298
Tambura, Sud.		D2	398
Tamchakett, Maur.		C2	408
Tamdy-Bulak, Sov.Un.		D6	336
Tame, Col.	1,383	B2	244
Tamega, riv., Port.		B3	298
Tamel Aike, Arg.		G3	251
Tamgué, mtn., Guinea		D2	408
Tamiahua, Mex.	4,055	C6	225
		K15	
Tamiahua, lagoon, Mex.		C6	225
		K15	
Tamiami, canal, Fla.		F10	174
Tamiao, China		D5	348
Taming, China	20,000	G7	348
Tamiš, riv., Yugo.		B5	316
Tam Ky, Viet.		D6	362
Tamluk, India		I8	366
Tamms, Alexander, Ill.	548	F4	138
Ṭammūn, Jordan	2,000	B6	382
Tämnarån, riv., Swe.		A8	292
Tamney, Ire.		F5	272
Tamo, Jefferson, Ark.	100	C5	170
Tamora, Seward, Nebr.	88	*D8	152
Tamora, Ponape		A2	436
Tamoroi, Ponape		A2	436
Tampa, Hillsborough, Fla.	274,970 (*356,200)	C6	174
		D8	
Tampa, Marion, Kans.	145	D6	144
Tampa, bay, Fla.		D8	174
Tampasak, N.Bor.		C5	358
Tampere, Fin.	101,509	F10	291
Tampico, Whiteside, Ill.	790	B4	138
Tampico, Mex.	94,342 (*140,000)	C6	225
		J15	
Tampico, Valley, Mont.	30	B10	110
Tampico, Grainger, Tenn.		B8	190
Tamrau, mtn., Neth.N.Gui.		E8	359
Tams, Raleigh, W.Va.	500	D3	194
Tamworth, Austl.	13,641	E10	432
Tamworth, Ont., Can.	475	P24	64
Tamworth, Carroll, N.H.	250 (1,016▲)	D4	208
Tan, China	5,000	P4	349
Tana, Chile		A4	250
Tana, Nor.		A13	290
Tana, lake, Eth.		C4	398
Tana, riv., Fin., Swe.		B11	290
Tana, riv., Ken.		C7	414
Tana, riv., Nor.		B11	290
Tanabe, Jap.	48,368	H5	354
Tanacross, Alsk.	137	C7	84
Tanafjord, fjord, Nor.		A13	290
Tanaga, isl., Alsk.		E4	84
Tanahbata, isl., Indon.		E1	358
Tanahgrogot, Indon.		E5	358
Tanahmasa, isl., Indon.		E1	358
Tanakpur, India		C3	368
Tanami, Austl.		C5	432
Tanana, Alsk.	228	B6	84
Tanana, riv., Alsk.		C7	84
Tananarive, Malag.	181,205	C9	421
Tananarive, prov., Malag.		C9	421
Tanapag, Saipan		B7	436
Tanaro, riv., It.		C2	302
Tanaunella, It.	328	E2	302
Tancheng, China	10,000	H9	348
Tanchŏn, Kor.	32,761	E14	348
Tancook Island, N.S., Can.	300	E6	70
Tanda, India		D3	368
Tăndărei, Rom.	2,353	B4	321
Tandil, Arg.	32,309	C4	252
Tandjung, Indon.		E5	358
Tandjungbalai, Indon.	10,200	D1	358
Tandjungpandan, Indon.	15,708	E3	358
Tandjungselor, Indon.	10,000	D5	358
Tando-Adam, Pak.	21,275	G6	375
Tandovala, mtn., Swe.		A4	292
Tanega, isl., Jap.		I3	354
Tanega, strait, Jap.		I3	354
Taney, co., Mo.	10,238	E4	150
Taneycomo, lake, Mo.		E5	150
Taneytown, Carroll, Md.	1,519	A5	182
Taneyville, Taney, Mo.	134	E4	150
Tanezrouft, des., Mali		B4	408
Tanga, Tan.	38,053	D6	414
Tanga, prov., Tan.	687,846	D6	414
Tangancícuaro, Mex.	6,541	L12	225
Tanganyika, Br. poss., Afr.	9,077,000	G10	388
		D5	414
Tanganyika, lake, Tan., Con.L.		D4	414
Tangchiaochen, China		J17	346
Tangent, Linn, Oreg.	150	C3	96
		D1	
Tangermünde, Ger.	14,600	B4	286
Tangho, China	10,000	I6	349
Tangier, N.S., Can.	295	E7	70
Tangier, Parke, Ind.	95	C2	140
Tangier, Mor.	162,000	A2	402
Tangier, Woodward, Okla.		B4	128
Tangier, Accomack, Va.	876	C9	192
Tangier, isl., Va.		C8	192
Tangier, sound, Md.		D8	182
Tangipahoa, Tangipahoa, La.	465	D5	180
Tangipahoa, par., La.	59,434	D5	180
Tangipahoa, riv., La.		D5	180
Tango, Lincoln, W.Va.	100	C3	194
		C5	
Tangra, lake, China		E5	346
Tangshan, China		F9	348
Tangshan, China		H8	248
Tangtu, China	20,000	J9	349
Tanguiéta, Dah.		D5	408
Tangwang, riv., China		B14	348
Tangyang, China		J5	349
Tangyüan, China	25,000	B14	348
Tanimbar, is., Indon.		F8	359
Tanjore, India	100,680	F3	366
Tank, Pak.	6,899	C7	375
Tanlajás, Mex.		K14	225
Tanner, Limestone, Ala.	450	A3	168
Tanner, Gilmer, W.Va.	86	C4	194
Tannis, bay, Den.		D1	292
Tannu-Ola, mts., Sov.Un., Mong.		D11	329
Tanout, Niger		D6	409
Tanque Verde, Pima, Ariz.	1,053	*F5	124
Tanshui, For.		M10	349
Tansing, Nep.		D3	368
Tanta, Eg., U.A.R.	139,926	A3	395
Tanta, Eg., U.A.R.	151,700	D1	382
Tantallon, Sask., Can.	132	E7	58
Tantoyuca, Mex.	4,571	K14	225
Tanunak (Tununak), Alsk.	161	C5	84
Tao, China	10,000	M5	349
Taoan, China	1,000	C11	348
Taoerh, riv., China		C11	348
Taoerhshan, China		C10	348
Taokou, China	20,000	H7	348
Taolin, China		E6	348
Taonan, China	47,888	C11	348
Taopi, Mower, Minn.	92	H6	148
Taormina, It.	5,100	G5	302
Taos, Taos, N.Mex.	2,163	B5	126
Taos, co., N.Mex.	15,934	B5	126
Taos Pueblo, Taos, N.Mex.	911	B5	126
Taoudenni, Mali		B4	408
Taoyüan, China	10,000	K5	349
Tapa, mts., China		J5	349
Tapacarí, Bol.	980	C1	246
Tapachula, Mex.	30,027	E7	225
Tapajós, riv., Braz.		G5	256
Tapak, Ponape		A2	436
Tapaktuan, Indon.		D1	358
Tapalqué, Arg.	3,018	C3	252
Tapanahoni, riv., Sur.		E5	256
Tapanshang, China	5,000	D9	348
Tapanui, N.Z.	409	F2	437
Tapati, riv., India		E1	368
Tapauá, riv., Braz.		G3	256
Tapehualapa, Mex.		M14	225
Tapicitoes, Rio Arriba, N.Mex.	10	B3	126
Tápiószele, Hung.	10,165	B4	320
Tapis, mtn., Mala.		F4	362
Tapi Town, Lib.		E3	408
Tapotchau, mtn., Saipan		B7	436
Tappahannock, Essex, Va.	1,086	C8	192
Tappan, Rockland, N.Y.	2,100	D2	212
Tappan, res., Ohio		B5	156
Tappen, Kidder, N.Dak.	326	D6	154
Tapti, riv., India		D2	366
Tapuaenuku, mtn., N.Z.		D4	437
Tapuhsing, China		E7	346
Taquara, Braz.	7,274	K6	257
Taquari, riv., Braz.		I5	257
Tar, riv., N.C.		B8	186
Tara, Ont., Can.	540	P19	64
Tara, Sov.Un.	20,400	A8	336
Tara, riv., Sov.Un.		A9	336
Tarabuco, Bol.	2,833	C1	246
Tarabulus (Tripoli), Leb.	70,842	B1	378
Ṭarābulus, see Tripoli, Libya			
Ṭarābulus, see Tripolitania, Libya			
Tarague, Guam		C7	437
Tarakan, Indon.	11,589	D5	358
Tarama, isl., Ryūkyū Is.		M12	349
Tarancón, Sp.	6,769	B5	298
Taransay, isl., Scot.		D5	272
Taranto, It.	180,500	E6	302
Taranto, prov., It.	444,500	*E6	302
Taranto, gulf, It.		E6	302
Tarapaca, prov., Chile	102,789	A4	250
Tarapaca, Col.		D3	244
Tarapoto, Peru	9,249	B2	245
Tarare, Fr.	11,364	E6	278
Tarascon [-sur-Rhône], Fr.	5,643	F6	278
Tarata, Bol.	3,016	C1	246
Tarata, Peru	2,827	D3	245
Tarauacá, riv., Braz.		G2	256
Tarawa, isl., Pac.O.		C3	436
Tarawera, N.Z.	117	C6	437
Tarazit, plat., Niger		B6	409
Tarazona, Sp.	11,237	B6	298
Tarazona, Sp.	6,714	C6	298
Tarbagatay Range, mts., Sov.Un.		C10	336
Tarbat Ness, cape, Scot.		D9	272
Tarbert, Scot.		D6	272
Tarbert, Scot.		F7	272
Tarbes, Fr.	40,242	F4	278
Tarboro, Camden, Ga.	185	F5	176
Tarboro, Edgecombe, N.C.	8,411	B8	186
Tarbū, Libya		B3	394
Tarcoola, Austl.	157	E6	432
Tarentum, Pike, Ala.	350	D4	168
Tarentum, Allegheny, Pa.	8,232	A4	214
		C2	
Tarfaya, Mor.		C1	402
Targana, Sov.Un.		C15	329
Targhee, pass, Idaho, Mont.		E7	108
		F5	110
Târgovişte, Rom.	24,360	B3	321
Târgul-Frumos, Rom.	4,665	A4	321
Târgul-Jiu, Rom.	19,618	B2	321
Târgul-Neamt, Rom.	10,373	A4	321
Târgul-Ocna, Rom.	11,227	A4	321
Târgul-Săcuesc, Rom.	7,500	A4	321
Târgu-Mureş, Rom.	65,194	A3	321
Tarifa, Sp.	7,736	D4	298
Tariffville, Hartford, Conn.	650	B4	202
Tarija, Bol.	16,869	D2	246
Tarija, dept., Bol.		D2	246
Tarija, riv., Bol.		D2	246
Tarim Darya, riv., China		C4	346
Tarimoro, Mex.	5,080	K13	225
Tarkiln, Providence, R.I.	100	B2	216
Tarkiln, hill, Maine		E4	204
Tarkio, Atchison, Mo.	2,160	A2	150
Tarkio, Mineral, Mont.	24	C2	110
Tarko-sale, Sov.Un.		C9	328
Tarkwa, Ghana	7,840	E4	408
Tarlac, Phil.	20,818	A6	358
Tarlton, Pickaway, Ohio	377	C4	156
Tarma, Peru	7,876	C2	245
Tarn, dept., Fr.	308,197	*F5	278
Tarn, riv., Fr.		E5	278
Tarna, riv., Hung.		B5	320
Tärnaby, Swe.		D6	290
Târnava Mică, riv., Rom.		A3	321
Târnăveni, Rom.	14,883	A3	321
Tarn-et-Garonne, dept., Fr.	172,379	*E4	278
Tarnobrzeg, Pol.	4,140	C5	325
Tarnopol, Sask., Can.	110	D5	58
Tarnov, Platte, Nebr.	70	C8	152
Tarnów, Pol.	58,000	C5	325
Tarnowskie Góry, Pol.	25,500	C4	325
Tärnsjö, Swe.		A7	292
Taro, riv., It.		C3	302
Tarom, Iran		D4	379
Taroudant, Mor.	12,877	B2	402
Tarpon Springs, Pinellas, Fla.	6,768	B6	174
		C8	
Tarqui, Peru		A2	245
Tarquinia, It.	7,900	D3	302
Tarragona, Sp.	35,648	B7	298
Tarragona, prov., Sp.	356,864	*B7	298
Tarrant, Jefferson, Ala.	7,810	B3	168
		E5	
Tarrant, co., Tex.	538,495	C7	130
Tarrasa, Sp.	45,081	B8	298
Tárrega, Sp.	6,059	B7	298
Tarry, Lincoln, Ark.	50	C5	170
Tarryall, creek, Colo.		C5	106
Tarrytown, Montgomery, Ga.	191	D4	176
Tarrytown, Westchester, N.Y.	11,109	D2	212
Tarshiha, Isr.	639	A6	382
Tarso Ahon, mtn., Chad		B8	409
Tarsus, Tur.	39,622	C6	307
Tartagal, Arg.	8,539	B5	250
Tartu, Sov.Un.	74,000	C6	332
Tartūs, Syr., U.A.R.	12,764	B1	378
Tarutao, isl., Thai.		F3	362
Tarver, Echols, Ga.	178	F4	176
Tasajara, creek, Calif.		B6	94
Tasāwah, Libya		B2	394
Taseko, lake, B.C., Can.		E11	52
Taseko, mtn., B.C., Can.		E11	52
Taseko, riv., B.C., Can.		E11	52
Tashauz, Sov.Un.	37,000	D5	336
Tashkent, Sov.Un.	911,000 (*1,025,000)	D7	336
Tashkumyr, Sov.Un.	12,000	D8	336
Tāshkurghān, Afg.	20,000	A4	374
Taskan, Sov.Un.		C16	329
Taşköprü, Tur.	4,601	A6	307
Tasman, bay, N.Z.		D4	437
Tasman, sea, Austl.		F10	432
Tasman, sea, N.Z.		C3	437
Tasmania, state, Austl.	327,895	G8	432
Tassili-N-Ajjer, plat., Alg.		C5	402
Tassili Oua-N-Ahaggar, plat., Alg.		D5	402
Tasso, Bradley, Tenn.	150	C7	190
Taswell, Crawford, Ind.	125	D3	140
Tata, Hung.	12,328	B3	320
Tatabánya, Hung.	48,000	B3	320
Tatamagouche, N.S., Can.	900	D6	70
Tatar A.S.S.R., Sov.Un.	2,847,000	D6	328
Tatar, strait, Sov.Un.		D16	329
Tatarsk, Sov.Un.	31,100	A9	336
Tate, Sask., Can.	30	E5	58
Tate, Pickens, Ga.	900	B2	176
Tate, Pawnee, Nebr.	10	*D9	152
Tate, co., Miss.	18,138	A2	184
Tateville, Pulaski, Ky.	500	D6	178
Tateyama, Jap.	59,416	G7	354
		M15	
Tathlina, lake, N.W.Ter., Can.		E6	48
Tatien, China	1,000	M8	349
Tatitlek, Alsk.	89	C7	84
		G11	
Tatla, lake, B.C., Can.		D10	52
Tatlayoka Lake, B.C., Can.		E10	52
Tatta, Pak.	9,716	G5	375
Tattnall, co., Ga.	15,837	D4	176
Tatuí, Braz.	13,244	E1	258
Tatuk, lake, B.C., Can.		D10	52
Tatum, Lea, N.Mex.	1,168	E7	126
Tatum, Marlboro, S.C.	132	B9	188
Tatums, Carter, Okla.	300	D6	128
Tatung, China	228,500	E6	348
Tatung, China	5,000	J8	349
Tatvan, Tur.	3,179	B10	307
Tau, isl., Thai.		E3	362
Tauá, Braz.	2,780	B2	258
Taubaté, Braz.	35,149	E1	258
Tauern, tunnel, Aus.		C5	313
Taum Sauk, mtn., Mo.		D7	150
Taung, U.S.Afr.	1,496	E4	420
Taungdwingyi, Bur.	16,233	C2	362
Taunggyi, Bur.	8,652	B3	362
Taunton, Eng.	34,100	J9	273
Taunton, Bristol, Mass.	41,132	C5	206
Taunton, Lyon, Minn.	233	G2	148
Taunton, Burlington, N.J.	200	D3	210
Taunton, riv., Mass.		C5	206
Taunus, mts., Ger.		C3	286
Taupaki, N.Z.	382	H8	437
Taupo, lake, N.Z.		C5	437
Taurage, Sov.Un.	18,600	E4	332
Tauranga, N.Z.	9,572	B6	437
Taurianova, It.	14,300	F6	302
Tauste, Sp.	6,214	B6	298
Tauu, is., Solomon		D1	436
Tauysk, Sov.Un.		D16	329
Tavares, Lake, Fla.	2,724	C9	174
Tavda, Sov.Un.	40,800	A7	336
Tavda, riv., Sov.Un.		A6	336
Tavernier, Monroe, Fla.	196	G10	174
Taveuni, isl., Fiji		E7	436
Taviche, Mex.	1,085	D6	225
Tavira, Port.	7,496	D3	298
Tavistock, Ont., Can.	1,155	Q20	64
Tavistock, Eng.	6,200	K8	273
Tavistock, Camden, N.J.	10	*D3	210
Tavolzhan, Sov.Un.		B9	336
Tavoy, Bur.	40,312	D3	362
Tavoy, isl., Bur.		D3	362
Tavoy, pt., Bur.		D3	362
Tavua, Fiji		E6	436
Tawa Flat, N.Z.	4,015	F11	437
Tawan, China		N3	349
Tawar, riv., Eng.		K8	273
Tawas, lake, Mich.		E8	146
Tawas City, Iosco, Mich.	1,810	E8	146
Tawatinaw, Alta., Can.	100	C6	54
Tawitawi, isl., Phil.		C5	358
Tawitawi Group, is., Phil.		D5	358
Tāwurghā', Libya		A3	394
Taxco de Alarcón, Mex.	10,025	L14	225
Tay, firth, Scot.		E9	272
Tay, lake, Scot.		E8	272
Tayabamba, Peru	1,179	B2	245
Taycheedah, Fond du Lac, Wis.	400	B5	160
Tayga, Sov.Un.	34,800	A11	336
Taygetus, mts., Grc.		C4	306
Taylor, Navajo, Ariz.	10	D5	124
Taylor, Columbia, Ark.	734	D3	170
Taylor, Baker, Fla.	200	A8	174
Taylor, Wayne, Mich.	49,658	*G8	146
Taylor, Lafayette, Miss.	122	A3	184
Taylor, Loup, Nebr.	280	C6	152
Taylor, Stark, N.Dak.	215	D3	154
Taylor, Lackawanna, Pa.	6,148	A5	214
		B6	
Taylor, Williamson, Tex.	9,434	D7	130
Taylor, Jackson, Wis.	334	D2	160
Taylor, co., Fla.	13,168	A7	174
Taylor, co., Ga.	8,311	D2	176
Taylor, co., Iowa	10,288	D3	142
Taylor, co., Ky.	16,285	C5	178
Taylor, co., Tex.	101,078	C6	130
Taylor, co., W.Va.	15,010	B4	194
Taylor, co., Wis.	17,843	C3	160
Taylor, dam, Nev.		C3	112
Taylor, knob, Tenn.		E7	190
Taylor, mtn., Idaho		E4	108
Taylor, mtn., N.Mex.		C3	126
Taylor, mtn., N.Z.		E3	437
Taylor, ridge, Ga.		B1	176
Taylor, riv., Man., Can.		C3	60
Taylor, riv., Colo.		D4	106
Taylor Mill, Kenton, Ky.	710	*A6	178
Taylor Park, res., Colo.		D4	106
Taylors, Greenville, S.C.	1,071	B4	188
Taylors, isl., Md.		D7	182

Taylors Bridge, New Castle, Del. C3 172
Taylors Falls, Chisago, Minn. 546 F6 148
Taylors Island, Dorchester, Md. 50 D7 182
Taylors Island, pt., Md. B7 182
Taylor Springs, Montgomery, Ill. 550 D4 138
Taylorsville, Bartow and Polk, Ga. 226 B2 176
Taylorsville, Bartholomew, Ind. 350 C4 140
Taylorsville, Spencer, Ky. 937 B5 178
Taylorsville, Smith, Miss. 1,132 D3 184
Taylorsville, Alexander, N.C. 1,470 B4 186
Taylorsville, Salt Lake, Utah 500 *C4 114
Taylortown, Moore, N.C. 500 B6 186
Taylorville, Christian, Ill. 8,801 D4 138
Taylorville, Vigo, Ind. 550 C2 140
Taymā', Sau.Ar. B2 383
Taymouth, N.B., Can. 100 C3 70
Taymya, pen., Sov.Un. B12 329
Taymyr, lake, Sov.Un. B11 329
Tayncha, Sov.Un. B7 336
Tayshet, Sov.Un. 28,900 D11 329
Taytay, Phil. 506 B6 358
Tayü, China M7 349
Tayung, China 5,000 K5 349
Taz, riv., Sov.Un. C10 328
Taza, Mor. 21,966 B3 402
Tazerbo, oasis, Libya B4 394
Tazewell, Marion, Ga. 112 D2 176
Tazewell, Claiborne, Tenn. 1,264 B8 190
Tazewell, Tazewell, Va. 3,000 C3 192
Tazewell, co., Ill. 99,789 C4 138
Tazewell, co., Va. 44,791 C3 192
Tazrouk, Alg. D5 402
Tbilisi, Sov.Un. 694,000 D2 336
Tchepone, Laos C5 362
Tchibanga, Gabon G7 409
Tchula, Holmes, Miss. 882 B2 184
Tczew, Pol. 31,000 A4 325
Te, China 35,000 G8 348
Tea, Lincoln, S.Dak. 188 *D9 158
Teague, Freestone, Tex. 2,728 D7 130
Teana-Katuku, mtn., N.Z. H8 437
Te Anau, lake, N.Z. F1 437
Teanaway, Kittitas, Wash. B6 98
Teaneck, Bergen, N.J. 42,085 A1 210
Teapa, Mex. 2,793 D7 225
Teasdale, Wayne, Utah 200 E4 114
Teaticket, Barnstable, Mass. 387 C6 206
Te Awamutu, N.Z. 4,614 C5 437
Tebbetts, Callaway, Mo. 211 C6 150
Tebèssa, Alg. 24,966 A5 402
Tebicuary, riv., Par. E4 247
Teche, bayou, La. D4 180
Teching, China E7 346
Techirghiol, Rom. 2,705 B5 321
Techny, Cook, Ill. 600 E2 138
Tecka, Arg. F3 251
Tecolote, Lincoln, N.Mex. 15 D5 126
Tecolutla, riv., Mex. K15 225
Tecopa, Inyo, Calif. 100 E5 94
Tecozautla, Mex. 2,522 K14 225
Tecpan de Galeana, Mex. 4,601 D5 225
Tecuala, Mex. 8,973 C4 224
Tecuci, Rom. 23,400 B4 321
Tecumseh, Ont., Can. 4,209 R18 64
Tecumseh, Shawnee, Kans. 100 *C8 144
Tecumseh, Lewanee, Mich. 7,045 H8 146
Tecumseh, Johnson, Nebr. 1,887 D9 152
Tecumseh, Pottawatomie, Okla. 2,630 C7 128
Tecumseh, mtn., N.H. D3 208
Ted, Som. E5 398
Tedzhen, Sov.Un. 3,800 F8 328
Teedee, Carter, Mont. D12 110
Teegarden, Marshall, Ind. 150 A3 140
Tees, Alta., Can. 75 D6 54
Teeswater, Ont., Can. 866 Q19 64
Tefé, Braz. 2,073 F4 256
Tefft, Jasper, Ind. 130 A3 140
Tegelen, Neth. 15,663 C5 282
Teges, Clay, Ky. 300 C7 178
Teghin, India A1 368
Tegucigalpa, Hond. 72,385 C4 228
Teguise, Sp. 1,065 F13 298
Tehachapi, Kern, Calif. 3,161 E4 94
Tehama, Tehama, Calif. 261 *B2 94
Tehama, co., Calif. 25,305 B2 94
Tehrān, Iran 1,513,164 (*1,590,000) B3 379
Tehrān, prov., Iran 3,327,502 *B3 379
Tehri, India C2 368
Tehsing, China 5,000 K8 349
Tehua, China 10,000 M9 349
Tehuacán, Mex. 23,212 D6 225 L15
Tehuagui, Mex. L13 225
Tehuantepec, Mex. 10,087 D6 225
Tehuantepec, gulf, Mex. D6 225
Tehuantepec, isth., Mex. D7 225
Tehuipango, Mex. L15 225
Tehuitzingo, Mex. 2,930 L14 225
Teide, peak, Can.Is. F11 298
Teifi, riv., Wales I8 273
Teigen, Petroleum, Mont. 2 C8 110
Tejas, Mex. K13 225
Tejo (Tagus), riv., Port. C2 298
Tejo, riv., Port. C3 298
Tejo, riv., Sp. C3 298
Tekamah, Burt, Nebr. 1,788 C9 152
Tekapo, lake, N.Z. E3 437
Tekax de Alvaro Obregón, Mex. 6,337 C8 225
Tekirdağ, Tur. 17,804 A2 307
Tekirdağ, prov., Tur. 251,920 *A2 307
Tekoa, Whitman, Wash. 911 B9 98
Tekoa, mtn., Wash. B9 98
Tekonsha, Calhoun, Mich. 744 G7 146
Tekouiat ta Middeh, riv., Alg. D4 402
Tekro, well, Chad C9 409
Te Kuiti, N.Z. 3,871 C5 437
Tel, riv., India D4 366
Tela, Hond. 12,614 C4 228
Tel Abiad, Syr., U.A.R. A3 378
Tel 'Afar, Iraq 19,806 A5 378
Telahsi, China E6 346
Telavi, Sov.Un. 22,600 D3 336
Tel Aviv, dist., Isr. 571,632 *B5 382
Tel Aviv-Jaffa, Isr. 363,500 B5 382
Telde, Sp. 10,328 F12 298
Telegraph, range, B.C., Can. D11 52
Tel el Farama, ruins, Eg., U.A.R. C3 382
Telemark, co., Nor. 139,172 *G3 291
Telén, Arg. C2 252
Teleño, mt., Sp. A3 298
Teleorman, riv., Rom. B3 321
Telerhteba, mtn., Alg. D5 402
Telescope, peak, Calif. D5 94
Teletskoye, riv., Sov.Un. B11 336
Telfair, co., Ga. 11,715 E4 176
Telford, Montgomery, Pa. 2,763 C6 214
Telford, Washington, Tenn. 100 B9 190
Telfs, Aus. 4,786 C3 313
Télimélé, Guinea D2 408
Telkwa, B.C., Can. 580 C9 52
Tell City, Perry, Ind. 6,609 E3 140
Teller, Alsk. 269 B5 84
Teller, co., Colo. 2,495 D5 106
Telli, lake, China B5 346
Tellico Plains, Monroe, Tenn. 794 C7 190
Telluride, San Miguel, Colo. 677 E3 106
Tel Mond, Isr. 741 B5 382
Telocaset, Union, Oreg. 45 B9 96
Telogia, Liberty, Fla. 100 A6 174
Telok Anson, Mala. 36,986 F4 362
Teloloapan, Mex. 7,297 D6 225 L14
Telos, lake, Maine B3 204
Tel Rak, Eg., U.A.R. E6 395
Telsen, Arg. F4 251
Telukbetung, Indon. 88,900 F3 358
Temascaltepec, Mex. 1,062 L14 225
Temax, Mex. 3,804 C8 225
Tembo, Con.L. D2 414
Temecula, Riverside, Calif. 500 F5 94
Temerloh-Mentekab, Mala. 12,302 G4 362
Temir-Tau, Sov.Un. 54,000 B8 336
Temiscouata, co., Que., Can. 28,901 Q16 66
Temiscouata, lake, Que., Can. Q16 66
Temósachic, Mex. 1,164 B4 224
Tempe, Maricopa, Ariz. 24,897 E4 124 H2
Tempe Downs, Austl. C6 432
Temperance, Telfair, Ga. 125 E3 176
Temperance, Monroe, Mich. 2,215 H8 146
Temperance, riv., Minn. D8 148
Temperanceville, Accomack, Va. 400 C9 192
Tempio Pausania, It. 8,300 E2 302
Temple, Carroll, Ga. 788 C1 176
Temple, Franklin, Maine 140 (314▲) *D2 204
Temple, Clare, Mich. 100 E6 146
Temple, Hillsboro, N.H. 65 (361▲) F3 208
Temple, Cotton, Okla. 1,282 D5 128
Temple, Berks, Pa. 1,633 C6 214
Temple, Bell, Tex. 30,419 D7 130
Temple City, Los Angeles, Calif. 31,838 C5 94
Temple Hill, Barren, Ky. 55 D5 178
Temple Terrace, Hillsborough, Fla. 3,812 B6 174
Templeton, Benton, Ind. 130 B2 140
Templeton, Carroll, Iowa 354 C3 142
Templeton, Worcester, Mass. 900 (5,371▲) A3 206
Templeton, Armstrong, Pa. 900 C2 214
Templeville, Queen Annes and Caroline, Md. 98 B8 182
Templin, Ger. 11,100 B5 286
Tempoal, riv., Mex. K14 225
Temryuk, Sov.Un. 30,000 J11 332
Temuco, Chile 102,331 C1 252
Temuka, N.Z. 2,254 F3 437
Tena, Ec. 351 A2 245
Tenafly, Bergen, N.J. 14,264 A2 210 B5
Tenaha, Shelby, Tex. 1,097 D8 130
Tenakee Springs, Alsk. 140 D8 84 J14
Tenakihi, range, B.C., Can. B10 52
Tenancingo, Mex. 8,249 D6 225 L14
Tenango del Valle, Mex. 6,100 L14 225
Tenant, mtn., N.Y. B7 212
Tenants Harbor, Knox, Maine 400 E3 204
Tenasserim, Bur. 1,194 D3 362
Tenasserim, riv., Bur. D3 362
Tenbridge, Hamilton, Tenn. E8 190
Tendal, Madison, La. 75 B4 180
Ten Degree, chan., India G6 366
Tendelti, Sud. 7,555 C3 398
Tendoy, Lemhi, Idaho 20 E5 108
Tendoy, mts., Mont. F4 110
Tendre, mtn., Switz. B2 312
Ténéré, des., Niger B7 409
Tenerife, isl., Can.Is. F11 298
Ténès, Alg. 7,266 (12,372▲) A4 402
Teng, China 20,000 H8 348
Tengchow, see Penglai, China
Tengchung, China 82,951 F7 346
Tenggol, isl., Mala. F4 362
Tengiz, lake, Sov.Un. B7 336
Tengkou, China 1,000 F3 348
Tengrela, I.C. D3 408
Tengri, see Nam, lake, China
Tenino, Thurston, Wash. 836 C4 98
Tenke, Con.L. E4 414
Tenkiller Ferry, res., Okla. C9 128
Tenkodogo, Upper Volta D4 408
Ten Mile, Meigs, Tenn. 100 C7 190
Tenmile, Upshur, W.Va. 50 C4 194
Tenmile, creek, W.Va. A6 194
Ten Mile, lake, Newf., Can. E7 72
Tenmile, lake, Minn. E4 148
Tennant Creek, Austl. 662 B6 432
Tennant, Shelby, Iowa 95 C2 142
Tennent, Monmouth, N.J. 150 C4 210
Tennessee, state, U.S. 3,567,089 D9 77 190
Tennessee, cave, Tenn. C6 190
Tennessee, pass, Colo. C4 106
Tennessee, riv., U.S. E9 77
Tennessee City, Dickson, Tenn. 175 B4 190
Tennessee Ridge, Houston, Tenn. 324 B4 190
Tennga, Murray, Ga. 250 B2 176
Tennga, Polk, Tenn. C7 190
Tennille, Washington, Ga. 1,837 D4 176
Tennis, Finney, Kans. 18 D3 144
Tennyson, Warrick, Ind. 312 D2 140
Tennyson, Grant, Wis. 314 *F3 160
Tenosique, Mex. 4,750 D7 225
Tensas, par., La. 11,796 B4 180
Tensas, basin, La. *B4 180
Tensas, riv., La. B4 180
Tensaw, Baldwin, Ala. 200 D2 168
Tensed, Benewah, Idaho 184 B2 108
Ten Sleep, Washakie, Wyo. 314 B5 116
Tenstrike, Beltrami, Minn. 147 D4 148
Tenterfield, Austl. 3,268 D10 432
Ten Thousand, is., Fla. F9 174
Teocaltiche, Mex. 9,582 C5 224 K12
Teófilo Otoni, Braz. 19,790 D2 258
Teotihuacán, Mex. 1,766 L14 225
Tepa, Indon. F7 359
Tepalcatepec, Mex. 2,555 L12 225
Tepalcatepec, riv., Mex. L12 225
Tepatitlán, Mex. 15,072 C5 224 K12
Tepehuanes, Mex. B4 224
Tepelenë, Alb. 1,100 A3 306
Tepenahauc, Mex. K15 225
Tepepan, Mex. 3,163 G10 224
Tepeyahualco, Mex. 1,186 L15 225
Tepic, Mex. 24,600 C5 224
Teplice, Czech. 37,940 A1 324
Tepoca, cape, Mex. A3 224
Tequesta, Palm Beach, Fla. 199 *E10 174
Ter, riv., Sp. A8 298
Téra, Niger D5 408
Teramo, It. 21,200 D4 302
Teramo, prov., It. 275,500 *D4 302
Tercan, Tur. 1,720 B9 307
Tercero, riv., Arg. B3 252
Terebovlya, Sov.Un. H5 332
Terence, Man., Can. 50 F2 60
Terence Bay, N.S., Can. 165 E6 70
Teresina, Braz. 111,811 B2 258
Teresita, Shannon, Mo. 250 E6 150
Teresita, Cherokee, Okla. 30 B9 128
Teresópolis, Braz. 14,651 E2 258
Teressa, isl., India G6 366
Terhune, Boone, Ind. 80 B3 140
Terlingua, creek, Tex. E4 130
Terlton, Pawnee, Okla. 90 B7 128
Termet, Niger C7 409
Termez, Sov.Un. 22,000 F8 328
Terminal, Salt Lake, Utah 65 *C4 114
Termini Imerese, It. 25,900 G4 302
Términos, lagoon, Mex. D7 225
Termoli, It. 9,000 E5 302
Termon, Ire. F5 272
Termoncarragh, Ire. G2 273
Ternate, Indon. 21,200 D7 359
Ternate, isl., Indon. D7 359
Terneuzen, Neth. 9,378 C2 282
Terni, It. 55,900 (88,800▲) D4 302
Terni, prov., It. 227,600 *D4 302
Ternitz, Aus. 8,366 C8 313
Ternopol, Sov.Un. 52,000 H5 332
Terpeniya, cape, Sov.Un. E16 329
Terra Alta, Preston, W.Va. 1,504 B5 194
Terrace, B.C., Can. 1,473 C8 52
Terrace, mts., Utah B2 114
Terra Ceia, Manatee, Fla. 600 C6 174
Terra Ceia, isl., Fla. C6 174
Terrace Park, Hamilton, Ohio 2,023 *C2 156
Terracina, It. 17,300 E4 302
Terra Heights, Shawnee, Kans. 350 *C8 144
Terral, Jefferson, Okla. 585 E6 128
Terra Nova, Newf., Can. 100 F8 72
Terra Nova, natl. park, Newf., Can. F8 72
Terraville, Lawrence, S.Dak. 200 C2 158
Terrebonne, Que., Can. 4,097 S11 66 S16
Terrebonne, Red Lake, Minn. 100 D2 148
Terrebonne, Deschutes, Oreg. 275 C5 96
Terrebonne, co., Que., Can. 81,329 R10 66
Terrebonne, par., La. 60,771 E5 180
Terrebonne, bay, La. E5 180
Terrebonne, bayou, La. E5 180
Terre Haute, Vigo, Ind. 72,500 C2 140
Terre Hill, Lancaster, Pa. 1,129 C5 214
Terrell, Kaufman, Tex. 13,803 C7 130
Terrell, co., Ga. 12,742 E2 176
Terrell, co., Tex. 2,600 D4 130
Terrell Hills, Bexar, Tex. 5,572 B7 130
Terrenceville, Newf., Can. 350 G8 72
Terreton, Jefferson, Idaho 10 F6 108
Terrible, mtn., Switz. A3 312
Terrible, mtn., Vt. E3 218
Terril, Dickinson, Iowa 382 A3 142
Terrill, mtn., Utah E4 114
Terry, Hinds, Miss. 585 C2 184
Terry, Prairie, Mont. 1,140 D11 110
Terry, peak, S.Dak. C2 158
Terry, co., Tex. 16,286 C4 130
Terrytown, Jefferson, La. 5,000 *E5 180
Terrytown, Scotts Bluff, Nebr. 164 *C2 152
Terryville, Litchfield, Conn. 5,231 C3 202
Tersakkan, riv., Sov.Un. B7 336
Terschelling, isl., Neth. A4 282
Terskey Alat, range, Sov.Un. D9 336
Teruel, Col. 1,099 C1 244
Teruel, Sp. 16,172 B6 298
Teruel, prov., Sp. 243,269 *B6 298
Tervola, Fin. C11 290
Terwagne, Bel. 347 D4 282
Tes, riv., Mong. B7 346
Tešanj, Yugo. 3,032 B3 316
Tescott, Ottawa, Kans. 396 C6 144
Teshekpuk, lake, Alsk. A6 84
Teshio, Jap. 10,019 B8 354
Teslin, Yukon, Can. E5 48
Tessalit, Mali B5 408
Tessaoua, Niger 4,000 D6 409
Tessenei, Eth. B4 398
Tessier, Sask., Can. 104 E4 58
Tessner, Marion, Ala. 100 A2 168
Testeboån, riv., Swe. A7 292
Testigos, is., Ven. A7 240
Tesuque, Santa Fe, N.Mex. 500 C5 126 G7
Tesuque Pueblo, Santa Fe, N.Mex. 300 G7 126
Tetachuk, lake, B.C., Can. D10 52
Tetagouche, riv., N.B., Can. B3 70
Tetas, pt., Chile B3 250
Tetbury, Eng. 2,501 J10 273
Tete, Moz. 1,670 C6 421
Tete, prov., Moz. C6 421
Tête Jaune Cache, B.C., Can. D13 52
Teterboro, Bergen, N.J. 22 *B4 210
Teterow, Ger. 11,300 B5 286
Teteven, Bul. 7,799 B2 317
Tetipari, isl., Solomon E1 436
Tetlin, Alsk. 73 C7 84
Teton, Fremont, Idaho 399 F7 108
Teton, co., Idaho 2,639 F7 108
Teton, co., Mont. 7,295 C4 110
Teton, co., Wyo. 3,062 C2 116
Teton, mts., Wyo. C2 116
Teton, riv., Mont. C5 110
Tetonia, Teton, Idaho 194 F7 108
Tetovo, Yugo. 20,209 D5 316
Tetu, China 5,000 A13 348
Tetuán, Mor. 93,658 A2 402
Teufen, Switz. 4,318 A5 312
Teulada, It. 4,229 F2 302
Teulon, Man., Can. 634 E4 60
Teutopolis, Effingham, Ill. 1,140 D5 138
Tevere (Tiber), riv., It. D4 302
Tevriz, Sov.Un. A8 336
Te Waewae, bay, N.Z. G1 437
Tewksbury, Middlesex, Mass. 1,800 (15,902▲) A5 206 C2
Texada, isl., B.C., Can. F10 52
Texanna, McIntosh, Okla. 10 C8 128
Texarkana, Miller, Ark. 19,788 D2 170
Texarkana, Bowie, Tex. 30,218 C8 130
Texas, Baltimore, Md. 853 B6 182
Texas, co., Mo. 17,758 D5 150
Texas, co., Okla. 14,162 B2 128
Texas, state, U.S. 9,579,677 E7 77 130
Texas City, Galveston, Tex. 32,065 E8 130 F8
Texcaltitlán, Mex. 3,404 L14 225
Texcoco, Mex. 7,451 L14 225
Texcoco, lake, Mex. G10 224
Texel, isl., Neth. A3 282
Texhoma, Texas, Okla. 911 B2 128
Texico, Curry, N.Mex. 889 D7 126
Texmelucán, Mex. 11,343 L14 225
Texola, Beckham, Okla. 202 C4 128
Texoma, lake, Okla., Tex. E7 128 C7 130
Teziutlán, Mex. 13,583 D6 225 L15
Tezontepec, Mex. 2,114 L14 225
Tezontle, riv., Mex. G10 224
Tezpur, India 11,879 D6 368
Tezzeron, lake, B.C., Can. C10 52
Thabeikkyin, Bur. B3 362
Thacker, Mingo, W.Va. 500 D2 194
Thackerville, Love, Okla. 185 E6 128
Tha Hin, Thai. 10,000 D4 362
Thailand (Siam), country, Asia 21,881,000 H12 340 362
Thain Road (Lewiston Orchards), Nez Perce, Idaho 9,680 C2 108
Thakhek, Laos C5 362
Thakuran (Jamira), riv., India J9 366
Thal, Pak. 5,757 C7 375
Thaltenango, Mex. K12 225
Thalwil, Switz. 8,787 A4 312
Thamad Hassān, Libya A3 394
Thames, N.Z. 5,001 B5 437
Thames, firth, N.Z. B5 437
Thames, riv., Ont., Can. R19 64
Thames, riv., Conn. D7 202
Thames, riv., Eng. J11 273
Thames, riv. mouth, Eng. J13 273
Thamesville, Ont., Can. 1,074 R18 64
Thamilet Suweilma (Oasis), Eg., U.A.R. D5 382
Thāmit, wadi, Libya A3 394
Thane, Alsk. 81 I14 84
Thanglhari, mts., China E6 346
Thanh Hoa, Viet. 25,000 C5 362
Thann, Fr. 6,473 D7 278
Thano-Bulakhan, Pak. G5 375
Thaon [-les-Vosges], Fr. 8,181 C7 278
Thaple, pass, China, Nep. C4 368
Thar or Indian, des., India, Pak. C2 366 G6 375
Thargomindah, Austl. 108 D8 432
Tharptown (Uniontown), Northumberland, Pa. 1,085 *C5 214
Tharrawaddy, Bur. 8,977 C2 362
Thásos, Grc. 1,749 A5 306
Thásos, isl., Grc. A5 306
Thatcher, Graham, Ariz. 1,581 F6 124
Thatcher, Las Animas, Colo. 10 E6 106
Thatcher, Franklin, Idaho 100 G7 108
Thatcher, Box Elder, Utah 160 B3 114
Thaton, Bur. 38,047 C3 362
Thaxton, Pontotoc, Miss. 200 A3 184
Thaxton, Bedford, Va. 150 C5 192
Thayer, Sangamon, Ill. 649 D4 138
Thayer, Newton, Ind. 200 A2 140
Thayer, Union, Iowa 101 C3 142
Thayer, Neosho, Kans. 396 E8 144
Thayer, Oregon, Mo. 1,713 E6 150

Thayer, York, Nebr. 78 D8 152
Thayer Apartments, Eddy, N.Mex. 300 F6 126
Thayer, Fayette, W.Va. 300 D7 194
Thayer, co., Nebr. 9,118 D8 152
Thayer Junction, Sweetwater, Wyo. 20 E4 116
Thayetmyo, Bur. C2 362
Thayne, Lincoln, Wyo. 214 D2 116
Thazi, Bur. B3 362
Thealka, Johnson, Ky. 662 C8 178
Theba, Maricopa, Ariz. 200 F3 124
The Backway, bay, Newf., Can. C6 72
Thebes, see Thivai, Grc.
Thebes, Alexander, Ill. 471 F4 138
Thebes, ruins, Eg., U.A.R. B3 395
The Cedars, New Castle, Del. 800 *A3 172
The Dalles, Wasco, Oreg. 10,493 B5 96
The Dells, cliffs, Wis. E4 160
Thedford, Ont., Can. 717 Q19 64
Thedford, Thomas, Nebr. 303 C5 152
The Farms, Berkeley, S.C. 600 F3 188
The Forks, Somerset, Maine 40 (53▲) C3 204
The Graves, is., Mass. D4 206
The Hague ('s Gravenhage), Neth. 590,755 B3 282
The Hollow, Patrick, Va. 25 D4 192
The Hummocks, Newport, R.I. 200 *C4 216
Thélepte, Tun. A5 402
Thelon, riv., N.W.Ter., Can. E8 48
Thenzawl, India E6 368
Theodore, Mobile, Ala. 500 E1 168
Theodore, Austl. 595 C10 432
Theodore, Sask., Can. 418 E6 58
Theodore Roosevelt, natl. memorial park, N.Dak. C2 154
The Pas, Man., Can. 3,971 D2 F5 60
The Plains, Athens, Ohio 1,148 C4 156
The Plains, Fauquier, Va. 484 B7 192
The Range, N.B., Can. 60 C4 70
The Raven, pt., Ire. I6 273
Theresa, Jefferson, N.Y. 956 A6 212
Theresa, Dodge, Wis. 576 E5 160
Theressa, Bradford, Fla. 180 B8 174
Thérien, Alta., Can. 450 C7 54
Theriot, Terrebonne, La. 110 E5 180
Thérmon, Grc. 2,665 B3 306
Thermopolis, Hot Springs, Wyo. 3,955 C4 116
The Rock, Upson, Ga. 115 D2 176
The Slot, strait, Solomon E1 436
Thesprotia, prov., Grc. 47,299 B3 306
Thessalon, Ont., Can. 1,716 S25 64
Thessaloníki, Grc. 217,049 A4 306
Thessaloníki (Salonika), prov., Grc. 459,956 A4 306
Thessaly (Thessalia), reg., Grc. 628,195 B3 306
Theta, Maury, Tenn. 250 C4 190
Thetford, Eng. 4,700 I13 273
Thetford, Orange, Vt. 100 (1,049▲) D4 218
Thetford Center, Orange, Vt. 150 D4 218
Thetford Mines, Que., Can. 19,511 R13 66
The Thimbles, is., Conn. E5 202
The Village, Oklahoma, Okla. 12,118 C6 128
Thibaudeau, Man., Can. B5 60
Thibodaux, Lafourche, La. 13,403 C6 E5 180
Thida, Independence, Ark. 50 B5 170
Thief, riv., Minn. C2 148
Thief, lake, Minn. C3 148
Thief River Falls, Pennington, Minn. 7,151 C2 148
Thielson, mtn., Oreg. D4 96
Thiensville, Ozaukee, Wis. 2,507 E2 E6 160
Thiers, Fr. 12,673 E5 278
Thiès, Sen. 34,984 D1 408
Thika, Ken. C6 414
Thingmuli, Ice. L22 290
Thingvallavatn, lake, Ice. L19 290
Thingvellir, Ice. L19 290
Thio, Eth. C5 398
Thionville, Fr. 23,054 C7 278
Thira, isl., Grc. C5 306
Third, lake, N.H. A4 208
Thirsk, Eng. 2,670 G11 273
Thirty One Mile, lake, Que., Can. R9 66
Thisted, Den. 9,026 H3 291
Thisted, co., Den. 86,703 *H3 291
Thistil, fjord, Ice. K22 290
Thistle, Utah, Utah 150 D4 114
Thithia, isl., Fiji E7 436
Thivai, Grc. 12,582 B4 306
Thjórsá, riv., Ice. L20 290
Thoeny, Valley, Mont. B10 110
Tholen, Neth. 3,285 C3 282
Thomas, Dorchester, Md. 190 C7 182
Thomas, Custer, Okla. 1,211 C5 128
Thomas, King, Wash. 300 D3 98
Thomas, Tucker, W.Va. 830 B5 194
Thomas, co., Ga. 34,319 F3 176
Thomas, co., Kans. 7,358 C2 144
Thomas, co., Nebr. 1,078 C5 152
Thomas, creek, Fla. A10 174
Thomas, creek, Oreg. C1 96
Thomas, lake, Tex. C5 130
Thomas, range, Utah D2 114
Thomasboro, Champaign, Ill. 458 C5 138
Thomaston, Marengo, Ala. 857 C2 168
Thomaston, Litchfield, Conn. 3,579 (5,850▲) C3 202
Thomaston, Upson, Ga. 9,336 D2 176
Thomaston, Knox, Maine 2,780 D3 204
Thomaston, Nassau, N.Y. 2,767 *E8 212
Thomastown, Leake, Miss. 200 C3 184
Thomasville, Clarke, Ala. 3,182 D2 168
Thomasville, Thomas, Ga. 18,246 F3 176
Thomasville, Davidson, N.C. 15,190 B5 186
Thomlinson, mtn., B.C., Can. C9 52
Thompson, Bullock, Ala. 50 C4 168
Thompson, Man., Can. 500 C4 60
Thompson, Windham, Conn. 500 (6,217▲) B8 202
Thompson, Winnebago, Iowa 689 A4 142
Thompson, Fayette, Ky. 1,186 *B6 178
Thompson, Schoolcraft, Mich. 60 D5 146
Thompson, Jefferson, Nebr. 30 *D8 152
Thompson, Grand Forks, N.Dak. 211 C8 154
Thompson, Grand, Utah 100 D6 114
Thompson, creek, Miss. D4 184
Thompson, isl., Mass. D3 206
Thompson, lake, Maine D2 204
Thompson, lake, S.Dak. C8 158
Thompson, peak, N.Mex. G7 126
Thompson, res., Calif. C6 94
Thompson, res., Oreg. E5 96
Thompson, riv., B.C., Can. E12 52
Thompson, riv., Iowa, Mo. C3 142, A4 150
Thompson Corner, see Kemoo Camps, Honolulu, Haw.
Thompson Corners, Penobscot, Maine C4 204
Thompson Falls, Sanders, Mont. 1,274 C1 110
Thompsons Station, Williamson, Tenn. 300 C5 190
Thompsonville, Hartford, Conn. 19,000 B5 202
Thompsonville, Franklin, Ill. 428 *F5 138
Thompsonville, Benzie, Mich. 243 E6 146
Thomson, McDuffie, Ga. 4,522 C4 176
Thomson, Carroll, Ill. 543 B3 138
Thomson, Carlton, Minn. 179 E6 148
Thomson, riv., Austl. C8 432
Thomson's Falls, Ken. B6 414
Thonburi, prov., Thai. 289,352 *D4 362
Thor, Humboldt, Iowa 234 B3 142
Thorburn, N.S., Can. 1,100 D7 70
Thoreau, McKinley, N.Mex. 200 C2 126
Thorhild, Alta., Can. 288 C6 54
Thorisvatn, lake, Ice. L20 290
Thorn, Chickasaw, Miss. 435 B3 184
Thornburg, Perry, Ark. 60 C4 170
Thornburg, Keokuk, Iowa 101 C5 142
Thornbury, Ont., Can. 1,037 P20 64
Thorndale, Ont., Can. 310 Q19 64
Thorndale, Milam, Tex. 995 D7 130
Thorndike, Waldo, Maine 150 (457▲) D3 204
Thorndike, Hampden, Mass. 850 B3 206
Thorne, Mineral, Nev. 8 E3 112
Thornegrove, Knox, Tenn. 350 E10 190
Thornhill, Man., Can. 150 F3 60
Thornhill, Ont., Can. 875 Q21 R22 64
Thornhill, Scot. 1,161 F9 272
Thornhill, Orange, Va. B7 192
Thornton, Calhoun, Ark. 658 D4 170
Thornton, Ont., Can. 300 *P21 64
Thornton, Adams, Colo. 11,306 *C6 106
Thornton, Madison, Idaho 200 *F7 108
Thornton, Cook, Ill. 2,895 *B6 138
Thornton, Cerro Gordo, Iowa 449 B4 142
Thornton, Grafton, N.H. 30 (480▲) *D3 208
Thornton, Providence, R.I. (part of Cranston) B3 216
Thornton, Limestone, Tex. 504 D7 130
Thornton, Whitman, Wash. 220 B9 98
Thornton, Taylor, W.Va. 300 A7 194
Thornton, Weston, Wyo. B8 116
Thorntown, Boone, Ind. 1,486 B3 140
Thornville, Perry, Ohio 521 C4 156
Thornville, Perry, Ohio 521 C4 156
Thornwood, Pocahontas, W.Va. C5 194
Thorny, mtn., Mo. D6 150
Thorofare, Gloucester, N.J. 1,100 D2 210
Thorold, Ont., Can. 8,053 Q21 64
Thorp, Kittitas, Wash. 430 B6 98
Thorp, Clark, Wis. 1,496 D3 160
Thorpe, McDowell, W.Va. 1,102 *D3 194
Thorsby, Chilton, Ala. 968 C3 168
Thorsby, Alta., Can. 411 D5 54
Thórshöfn, Ice. K22 290
Thouars, Fr. 10,626 D3 278
Thoubal, India D6 368
Thoune, see Thun, Switz.
Thousand, is., N.Y., Ont., Can. A5 212, P24 64
Thousand Lake, mtn., Utah E4 114
Thousand Oaks, Ventura, Calif. 2,934 *E4 94
Thousand Spring, creek, Nev. B7 112
Thousandsticks, Leslie, Ky. 600 C7 178
Thrace (Thráki), reg., Grc. 336,754 A5 306
Thrall, Williamson, Tex. 631 D7 130
Thrashers, Prentiss, Miss. 100 A4 184
Three Bridges, Hunterdon, N.J. 750 B3 210
Three Creek, Owyhee, Idaho G3 108
Three Fingered Jack, mtn., Oreg. C5 96
Threeforks, Martin, Ky. 500 C8 178
Three Forks, Gallatin, Mont. 1,161 E5 110
Three Hills, Alta., Can. 1,095 E6 54
Three Kings, is., N.Z. A4 437
Three Lakes, Oneida, Wis. 800 C4 160
Three Oaks, Berrien, Mich. 1,763 H5 146
Threepoint, lake, Man., Can. C3 60
Three Points, cape, Ghana F4 408
Three Rivers, Hampden, Mass. 3,082 B3 206
Three Rivers, St. Joseph, Mich. 7,092 H6 146
Three Rivers, Jackson, Miss. 300 E4 184
Three Rivers, Live Oak, Tex. 1,932 E6 130
Three Rock Cove, Newf., Can. 90 F6 72
Three Sisters, mtn., Oreg. C5 96
Threet, Lauderdale, Ala. 400 A2 168
Throckmorton, Throckmorton, Tex. 1,299 C6 130
Throckmorton, co., Tex. 2,767 C6 130
Throop, Lackawanna, Pa. 4,732 A5 214
Thu Da Mot, Viet. 9,500 E5 362
Thule, Grnld. 142 O28 290
Thun, Switz. 25,600 (*38,000) B3 312
Thun, lake, Switz. B3 312
Thunder, bay, Mich. D8 146
Thunder, butte, S.Dak. B4 158
Thunder Bay, dist., Ont., Can. 122,890 R24 64
Thunder Bay, riv., Mich. E7 146
Thunderbolt, Chatham, Ga. 1,925 D5 176
Thunder Butte, Ziebach, S.Dak. 50 B4 158
Thunder Hawk, Corson, S.Dak. 70 B4 158
Thune, McPherson, Nebr. C4 152
Thungsong, Thai. E3 362
Thurgau (Thurgovie), canton, Switz. 157,800 A5 312
Thuringer Wald, mts., Ger. C4 286
Thuringia (Thuringen), reg., Ger. C4 286
Thurles, Ire. 6,363 I5 273
Thurlow, Rosebud, Mont. D10 110
Thurlow, dam, Ala. C4 168
Thurman, Washington, Colo. C7 106
Thurman, Fremont, Iowa 268 D2 142
Thurmond, Fayette, W.Va. 189 *C3 194
Thurmont, Frederick, Md. 2,802 A5 182
Thursday, isl., Austl. A8 432
Thurso, Que., Can. 2,324 S9 66
Thurso, Scot. 3,600 C9 272
Thurso, riv., Scot. C9 272
Thurston, Thurston, Nebr. 140 B9 152
Thurston, Fairfield, Ohio 429 C4 156
Thurston, Lane, Oreg. 500 *C4 96
Thurston, co., Nebr. 7,237 B9 152
Thurston, co., Wash. 55,049 C4 98
Thuvu, Fiji E6 436
Thyanboche, Nep. D4 368
Thykkvibaer, Ice. M19 290
Thysville, Con.L. D1 414
Tiahuanaco, Bol. 1,127 C1 246
Tiaret, Alg. 24,830 A4 402
Tiawah, Rogers, Okla. B8 128
Tibasti, des., Libya C3 394
Tibati, Cam. 5,411 E7 409
Tibbee, Clay, Miss. 100 B4 184
Tibbie, Washington, Ala. 300 D1 168
Tibé, peak, Guinea E3 408
Tibeghim, Alg. D4 402
Tiber, res., Mont. B5 110
Tiber Dam, Liberty, Mont. B5 110
Tiberias, Isr. 18,000 B6 382
Tiberias (Sea of Galilee), lake, Isr. B6 382
Tibesti, reg., Chad B8 409
Tibesti, plat., Chad B8 409
Tibet, reg., China 1,270,000 E5 346
Tibet, plat., China E5 346
Tibro, Swe. 7,221 C5 292
Tiburon, Marin, Calif. 1,200 A5 94
Tiburón, isl., Mex. B3 224
Tice, Lee, Fla. 4,377 E9 174
Tichborne, Ont., Can. 135 P24 64
Tichfield, Sask., Can. 65 E4 58
Tichinane, well, Maur. C2 408
Tichit, Maur. C3 408
Tichnor, Arkansas, Ark. 100 C5 170
Ticino (Tessin), canton, Switz. 181,000 B4 312
Ticino, riv., It. C2 302
Ticino, riv., Switz. B4 312
Tickfaw, Tangipahoa, La. 317 D5 180
Tickfaw, riv., La. D5 180
Ticonderoga, Essex, N.Y. 3,568 B8 212
Tidaholm, Swe. 6,150 C5 292
Tidan, riv., Swe. C4 292
Tiddim, Bur. B2 362
Tide Head, N.B., Can. 145 B3 70
Tidewater, Lincoln, Oreg. 200 *C3 96
Tidewater, Richmond, Va. 170 C8 192
Tidioute, Warren, Pa. 860 B2 214
Tidjikja, Maur. 5,700 C2 408
Tiehling, China 55,000 D11 348
Tieh Shan Chang, peak, China M8 349
Tiel, Neth. 15,128 C4 282
Tiel, Sen. D1 408
Tielmes de Tajuña, Sp. 4,626 *B5 298
Tielt, Bel. 13,185 D2 282
Tienchen, China E7 348
Tienching, China 5,000 J3 349
Tienen, Bel. 22,656 D3 282
Tienmen, China 38,000 J6 349
Tienpai, China 10,000 O5 349
Tientsin, China 3,024,147 F8 348
Tien Yen, Viet. 5,000 B5 362
Tie Plant, Pulaski, Ark. (part of North Little Rock) D7 170
Tie Plant, Grenada, Miss. 1,491 B3 184
Tiernan, Lane, Oreg. 150 *C3 96
Tierp, Swe. 3,750 A8 292
Tierra Amarilla, Chile 1,086 A1 252
Tierra Amarilla, Rio Arriba, N.Mex. 300 B4 126
Tierra Blanca, Mex. 12,007 D6 L15 225
Tierra Blanca, Mex. K13 225
Tierra del Fuego, ter., Arg. 10,800 H4 251
Tierra del Fuego, isl., Chile H4 251
Tierra Vieja, mts., Tex. D3 130
Tie Siding, Albany, Wyo. 50 E7 116
Tiétar, riv., Sp. C4 298
Tieté, Braz. 7,187 E1 258
Tieté, riv., Braz. E1 258
Tieton, Yakima, Wash. 479 C6 98
Tieton, dam, Wash. C5 98
Tieton, peak, Wash. C5 98
Tieton, res., Wash. C5 98
Tieton, riv., Wash. C5 98
Tieul, Mex. 10,233 C8 225
Tiffany, La Plata, Colo. 80 E3 106
Tiffany, mtn., Wash. A7 98
Tiffin, Johnson, Iowa 311 C6 142
Tiffin, Seneca, Ohio 21,478 A3 156
Tiffin, riv., Ohio A2 156
Tift, co., Ga. 23,487 E3 176
Tifton, Tift, Ga. 9,903 E3 176
Tiftona, Hamilton, Tenn. 3,520 *C6 190
Tigara, see Point Hope, Alsk.
Tigard, Washington, Oreg. 5,000 B1 96
Tiger, Rabun, Ga. 277 B3 176
Tiger, Pend Oreille, Wash. 10 A9 98
Tigerton, Shawano, Wis. 781 D4 160
Tigerville, Greenville, S.C. 105 A4 188
Tigil, Sov.Un. 1,200 D17 329
Tignall, Wilkes, Ga. 556 C4 176
Tignère, Cam. E7 409
Tignish, P.E.I., Can. 914 C5 70
Tigre, prov., Eth. 1,000,000 C4 398
Tigre, isl., Viet. C5 362
Tigre, pt., La. E3 180
Tigre, riv., Peru A2 245
Tigres, pen., Ang. C2 420
Tigrett, Dyer, Tenn. 150 C2 190
Tigris, riv., Iraq B5 378
Tiguabos, Cuba 1,148 B7 232
Tihuatlán, Mex. 2,636 K15 225
Tijeras, Bernalillo, N.Mex. 150 H6 126
Tiji, Libya 1,270 A2 394
Tijuana, Mex. 59,950 A2 224
Tikal, ruins, Guat. B3 228
Tikamgarh, India D2 368
Tikhoretsk, Sov.Un. 43,800 J13 332
Tikhvin, Sov.Un. 34,300 C9 332
Tikicheo, Mex. L13 225
Tikrit, Iraq 5,788 B5 378
Tiksi, Sov.Un. 1,000 B15 329
Tila, riv., Nep. C3 368
Tilamuta, Indon. D6 358
Tilburg, Neth. 126,939 C4 282
Tilbury, Ont., Can. 3,138 R18 64
Tilcara, Arg. B4 250
Tilden, Randolph, Ill. 808 E4 138
Tilden, Madison and Antelope, Nebr. 917 B8 152
Tilden, McMullen, Tex. 250 E6 130
Tilden, Chippewa, Wis. 50 C2 160
Tilemsi, val., Mali C4 408
Tilford, Meade, S.Dak. 75 C2 158
Tilghman, Talbot, Md. 800 C7 182
Tilghman, isl., Md. C7 182
Tillabéri, Niger 1,000 D5 408
Tillamook, Tillamook, Oreg. 4,244 B3 96
Tillamook, co., Oreg. 18,955 B3 96
Tillamook, bay, Oreg. B3 96
Tillamook, head, Oreg. B2 96
Tillar, Drew, Ark. 232 D5 170
Tillatoba, Yalobusha, Miss. 102 B3 184
Tiller, Douglas, Oreg. 120 E4 96
Tillery, lake, N.C. B5 186
Tilley, Alta., Can. 240 E7 54
Tillicum, Pierce, Wash. 1,500 B4 98
Tillman, Claiborne, Miss. 200 D2 184
Tillman, Jasper, S.C. 500 G6 188
Tillman, co., Okla. 14,654 D4 128
Tillne, Livingston, Ky. 100 C2 178
Tillson, Ulster, N.Y. 900 D7 212
Tillsonburg, Ont., Can. 6,216 R20 64
Tillyfourie, Scot. D10 272
Tilos, isl., Grc. C6 306
Tilremt, Alg. B4 402
Tilsit, see Sovetsk, Sov.Un.
Tilston, Man., Can. 125 F2 60
Tilting, Newf., Can. 375 F8 72
Tilton, Vermilion, Ill. 2,598 C6 138
Tilton, Belknap, N.H. 1,129 (2,137▲) E3 208
Tiltonsville, Jefferson, Ohio 2,454 B6 156
Tim, Sov.Un. 4,800 G11 332
Timaná, Col. 2,439 C1 244
Timaru, N.Z. 23,308 (*24,700) F3 437
Timashevskaya, Sov.Un. 34,800 J12 332
Timbalier, bay, La. E5 180
Timbalier, isl., La. E5 180
Timbédra, Maur. C3 408
Timber, Washington, Oreg. 250 B3 96
Timbered, knob, Mo. E5 150
Timberlake, Lake, Ohio 670 *A5 156
Timber Lake, Dewey, S.Dak. 624 B4 158
Timberlake, Campbell, Va. 2,400 *C5 192
Timber Ridge, Rockbridge, Va. 40 C5 192
Timberville, Rockingham, Va. 412 B6 192
Timbo, Stone, Ark. 75 B4 170
Timbuktu, see Tombouctou, Mali
Timerzit, Mor. B3 402
Times Beach, St. Louis, Mo. 986 *C7 150
Timimoun, Alg. 3,038 (29,002▲) C4 402
Timimoun, lake, Alg. C4 402
Timiskaming, co., Que., Can. 57,661 *Q8 66
Timiskaming, dist., Ont., Can. 50,264 R25 64
Timişoara, Rom. 142,257 B1 321
Timken, Rush, Kans. 147 D4 144
Timkerdat, well, Sp. Sahara B2 408
Timmins, Ont., Can. 27,551 R25 64
Timmonsville, Florence, S.C. 2,178 C9 188
Timnath, Larimer, Colo. 150 B6 106
Timok, riv., Yugo. C6 316
Timon, Natchitoches, La. C2 180
Timonium, Baltimore, Md. (part of Lutherville) B6 182
Timor, isl., Indon. F6 358
Timor, sea, Austl. A3 432
Timor, sea, Indon. G7 358
Timpanogos Cave, natl. mon., Utah C4 114
Timpas, Otero, Colo. 50 E7 106
Timpie, Tooele, Utah 10 C3 114
Timpson, Shelby, Tex. 1,120 D8 130
Timrå, Swe. 10,554 E7 291
Timsa, lake, Eg., U.A.R. D3 382
Tin, cape, Libya A4 394
Tina, Eg., U.A.R. D7 395
Tina, Carroll, Mo. 199 B4 150
Tina (Pelusium), bay, Eg., U.A.R. C3 382
Tinaca, pt., Phil. C7 358
Tinahely, Ire. 375 I6 273
Tinajas, Mex. C6 225
Tin Amzi, riv., Alg. D4 402
Tinaquillo, Ven. 5,726 B4 240
Tindall, Garfield, Mont. C9 110
Tindouf, Alg. 1,356 (22,372▲) C2 402
Tindouf, lake, Alg. C2 402
Tineo, Sp. 1,930 A3 298
Tinghsien, China F7 348
Tinghsin, China C7 346
Tinghsing, China 10,000 F7 348

Tingjegaon, Nep.		C3	368
Tinglev, Den.	1,350	I3	291
Tingley, Ringgold, Iowa	278	D3	142
Tingmerkpuk, mtn., Alsk.		B5	84
Tingo Maria, Peru		B2	245
Tingpien, China		G3	348
Tingsryd, Swe.	3,064	E6	292
Tingwick, Que., Can.	475	S13	66
Tingyüanying, China		F2	348
Tinian, Tinian		C7	436
Tinian, isl., Pac.O.		B7	436
Tinkisso, riv., Guinea		D2	408
Tinley Park, Cook, Ill.	6,392	F2	138
Tinn, Nor.		G3	291
Tinnie, Lincoln, N.Mex.	20	E5	126
Tinniswood, mtn., B.C., Can.		E11	52
Tinnoset, Nor.		G3	291
Tinogasta, Arg.	2,169	A2	252
Tinos, Grc.	2,758	C5	306
Tinos, isl., Grc.		C5	306
Tinquipaya, Bol.	766	C1	246
Tin Rerhoh (Oasis), Alg.		D4	402
Tinrh'ert, plat., Alg.		B5	402
Tinsley, Yazoo, Miss.	100	C2	184
Tinsman, Calhoun, Ark.	100	D4	170
Tinsukia, India	8,338	D6	368
Tintah, Traverse, Minn.	228	E2	148
Tintigny, Bel.	1,157	E4	282
Tintina, Arg.	2,219	A3	252
Tin Zaouatene (Oasis), Alg.		E4	402
Tioga, Huerfano, Colo.		E6	106
Tioga, Rapides, La.	250	C3	180
Tioga, Williams, N.Dak.	2,087	B3	154
Tioga, Nicholas, W.Va.	350	C4	194
Tioga, co., N.Y.	37,802	C5	212
Tioga, co., Pa.	36,614	B4	214
Tioga, riv., Pa.		B4	214
Tiogue, lake, R.I.		C2	216
Tioman, isl., Mala.		G5	362
Tionesta, Forest, Pa.	778	B2	214
Tionesta, creek, Pa.		B2	214
Tioughnioga, riv., N.Y.		C5	212
Tipler, Florence, Wis.	300	C5	160
Tiplersville, Tippah, Miss.	105	A4	184
Tippah, co., Miss.	15,093	A4	184
Tipp City, Miami, Ohio	4,267	C2	156
Tippecanoe, Marshall, Ind.	350	A3	140
Tippecanoe, co., Ind.	89,122	B3	140
Tippecanoe, riv., Ind.		B3	140
Tipperary, Ire.	4,790	I4	273
Tipperary, co., Ire.	129,415	I4	273
Tippo, Tallahatchie, Miss.	85	B2	184
Tipton, Tulare, Calif.	980	D4	94
Tipton, Tipton, Ind.	5,604	B3	140
Tipton, Cedar, Iowa	2,862	C6	142
Tipton, Mitchell, Kans.	252	C5	144
Tipton, Moniteau, Mo.	1,639	C5	150
Tipton, Tillman, Okla.	1,117	D4	128
Tipton, Sweetwater, Wyo.	35	E4	116
Tipton, co., Ind.	15,856	B3	140
Tipton, co., Tenn.	28,564	C2	190
Tipton, mtn., Ariz.		C1	124
Tiptonville, Lake, Tenn.	2,068	B2	190
Tip Top, Magoffin, Ky.	300	C7	178
Tiptop, Tazewell, Va.	100	C3	192
Tiranë, Alb.	108,183	D4	316
Tiranë, pref., Alb.	57,000	*D4	316
Tirano, It.	5,609	B3	302
Tiraque Chico, Bol.	1,390	C1	246
Tiraspol, Sov.Un.	62,000	I7	332
Tirat Carmel, Isr.	13,000	B5	382
Tirat Zvi, Isr.		B6	382
Tire, Tur.	23,721	B2	307
Tirebolu, Tur.	4,246	A8	307
Tiree, isl., Scot.		E6	272
Tirenno, Chad		B8	409
Tirich Mir, mtn., Pak.		A7	375
Tiriro, Guinea		D3	408
Tirnavos, Grc.	10,662	B4	306
Tiro, Crawford, Ohio	334	B4	156
Tirol (Tyrol), state, Aus.	427,465	*C2	313
Tirso, riv., It.		E2	302
Tiruchirappalli, India	218,921	F3	366
Tirunelveli, India	73,476	G3	366
Tirzah, York, S.C.		B6	188
Tisa, riv., Yugo.		B5	316
Tisch Mills, Manitowoc, Wis.	200	A7	160
Tisdale, Sask., Can.	2,104	D5	58
Tishomingo, Tishomingo, Miss.	415	A4	184
Tishomingo, Johnston, Okla.	2,381	D7	128
Tishomingo, co., Miss.	13,889	A4	184
Tiskilwa, Bureau, Ill.	951	B4	138
Tisonia, Duval, Fla.	30	A10	174
Tisza, riv., Hung.		B5	320
Tiszafüred, Hung.	9,165	B5	320
Tiszakécske, Hung.	6,596	C5	320
Titagarh, India	71,622	I9	366
Titicaca, lake, Bol., Peru		C1	246
		D4	245
Titirangi, N.Z.	1,599	H8	437
Titograd, Yugo.	17,000	C4	316
Titonka, Kossuth, Iowa	647	A3	142
Titovo, Užice, Yugo.	13,255	C4	316
Titov Veles, Yugo.	19,373	D5	316
Titule, Con.L.		B4	414
Titus, Elmore, Ala.	100	C3	168
Titus, co., Tex.	16,785	C8	130
Titus, mtn., Conn.		B2	202
Titusville, Brevard, Fla.	6,410	C10	174
Titusville, Mercer, N.J.	1,000	C3	210
Titusville, Crawford, Pa.	8,356	B2	214
Tiuggi, isl., Mala.		G5	362
Tivaouane, Sen.		C1	408
Tiveden, mts., Swe.		C5	292
Tiverton, N.S., Can.	355	E3	70
Tiverton, Ont., Can.	261	P19	64
Tiverton, Eng.	11,700	K9	273
Tiverton, Newport, R.I.	2,000 (9,461▲)	C4	216
Tiverton Four Corners, Newport, R.I.	250	C4	216
Tiverton Station, Newport, R.I.		C4	216
Tivoli, Dutchess, N.Y.	732	C8	212
Tivoli, It.	23,000	E4	302
Tivoli, Refugio, Tex.	800	E7	130
Tixtla, Mex.	7,093	M14	225
Tizafoldvár, Hung.	12,096	C5	320
Tizapán, Mex.	5,620	G10	224
Tizimin, Mex.	10,651	C8	225
Tizi-Ouzou, Alg.	5,772 (55,497▲)	A4	402
Tiznit, Mor.	6,476	C2	402
Tizu, riv., India		D6	368
Tjeggelvas, lake, Swe.		C7	290
Tjeukemeer, lake, Neth.		B4	282
Tjilatjap, Indon.	28,309	F3	358
Tjina, cape, Indon.		F2	358
Tjirebon, Indon.	106,700	F3	358
Tjorn, Ice.		L19	290
Tjörn, Ice.		L20	290
Tlacolula, Mex.	5,831	D6	225
Tlacotalpan, Mex.	5,777	D6	225
Tlacotepec, Mex.	2,433	M14	225
Tláhuac, Mex.	4,802	G11	224
Tlahuaililo, Mex.		B5	224
Tlahualilo de Zaragoza, Mex.	3,201	B5	224
Tlalnepantla, Mex.	10,330	F10	224
Tlalnepantla, riv., Mex.		F9	224
Tlalpan, Mex.	18,141	G10	224
Tlalpujahua, Mex.	2,283	L13	225
Tlaltenco, Mex.	3,950	G10	224
Tlapa, Mex.	3,067	D6	225
		M14	
Tlapacoyan, Mex.	6,311	L15	225
Tlapaneco, riv., Mex.		M14	225
Tlaquepaque, Mex.	20,824	K12	225
Tlaxcala, Mex.	5,071	D6	225
		L14	
Tlaxcala, state, Mex.	284,551	D6	225
Tlaxco, Mex.	4,124	L14	225
Tlaxiaco, Mex.	8,228	D6	225
Tlemcés, well, Niger		C5	408
Tmassah, Libya	3,225	B3	394
To, isl., Jap.		G7	354
Toadlena, San Juan, N.Mex.	49	B2	126
Toano, James City, Va.	250	C8	192
Toast, Surry, N.C.	2,023	A5	186
Toay, Arg.		C3	252
Toba, Jap.	30,121	M12	354
Toba, inlet, B.C., Can.		E10	52
Toba, lake, Indon.		D1	358
Toba, riv., B.C., Can.		E10	52
Tobaccoport, Stewart, Tenn.		B4	190
Tobacco Root, mts., Mont.		E4	110
Tobago, ter., W.I. Fed.	34,310	E14	233
Tobarra, Sp.	8,243	C6	298
Tobaru, Okinawa		D1	436
Tobata, Jap.		*H3	354
Tobe, Las Animas, Colo.	5	*E7	106
Tobermory, Ont., Can.	420	O19	64
Tobi, isl., Jap.		E7	354
Tobias, Saline, Nebr.	202	D8	152
Tobin Harbor, Keweenaw, Mich.		B3	146
Tobique, riv., N.B., Can.		B2	70
Tobol, Sov.Un.		B6	336
Tobol, riv., Sov.Un.		B6	336
Tobolsk, Sov.Un.	46,700	A7	336
Tobruk (Tubruq), Libya	4,995	A4	394
Tobyhanna, Monroe, Pa.	900	B6	214
Tobys Rock, mtn., Conn.		D3	202
Tocansa, isl., Braz.		F8	256
Tocantinópolis, Braz.	3,531	B1	258
Tocantins, riv., Braz.		F7	256
Toccoa, Stephens, Ga.	7,303	B3	176
Toccopola, Pontotoc, Miss.	198	A3	184
Tochcha, lake, B.C., Can.		C10	52
Tochigi, Jap.	67,924	F7	354
		K15	
Töcksmark, Swe.	2,947	B2	292
Tocoa, Hond.	1,226	C4	228
Tocopilla, Chile	19,353	B3	250
Tocra, see Tukrah, Libya			
Tocsin, Wells, Ind.	175	B4	140
Tocuyo, riv., Ven.		A4	240
Todi, It.	4,600	D4	302
Todd, co., Ky.	11,364	D3	178
Todd, co., Minn.	23,119	E4	148
Todd, co., S.Dak.	4,661	D5	158
Todd, fork, Ohio		C3	156
Todd, mtn., B.C., Can.		F10	52
Todd, mtn., N.B., Can.		C3	70
Todd, riv., Austl.		C7	432
Toddville, Linn, Iowa	138	B6	142
Toddville, Dorchester, Md.	325	D7	182
Toddville, Horry, S.C.	180	D10	188
Toddy, pond, Maine		D4	204
Tödi, mtn., Switz.		B4	312
Todoga, cape, Jap.		E9	354
Todos os Santos, bay, Braz.		C3	258
Todos Santos, Bol.	408	C1	246
Todos Santos, Mex.	1,886	C3	224
Tod Park, Tooele, Utah	700	C3	114
Toe, head, Ire.		J3	273
Tofield, Alta., Can.	800	D6	54
Tofino, B.C., Can.	389	F10	52
Toga, Buckingham, Va.	100	C6	192
Togba, well, Sp. Sahara		B1	408
Togiak, Alsk.	108	D5	84
Togian, is., Indon.		E6	358
Togo, Sask., Can.	302	E7	58
Togo, country, Afr.	1,100,000	F7	388
			409
Tohatchi, McKinley, N.Mex.	200	C2	126
Tohopekaliga, lake, Fla.		C9	174
Toi, cape, Jap.		I3	354
Toijala, Fin.		F10	291
Toivola, Houghton, Mich.	80	C3	146
Toiyabe, range, Nev.		E4	112
Tokaj, Hung.	5,074	A6	320
Tokar, Sud.	16,802	B4	398
Tokara, isl., Jap.		J2	354
Tokara, is., Jap.		J2	354
Tokara, strait, Jap.		I3	354
Tokat, Tur.	26,716	A7	307
Tokat, prov., Tur.	388,724	*A7	307
Tokeland, Pacific, Wash.	150	C3	98
Tokelau (Union), is., Pac.O.		D4	436
Tokelau Islands (Union), N.Z. poss., Pac.O.	1,580	D4	436
Toki, pt., Wake		A5	436
Tokio, Hempstead, Ark.	90	C3	170
Tokio, Benson, N.Dak.	100	C7	154
Tok Junction, Alsk.	104	C7	84
Tokmak, Sov.Un.	30,000	D9	336
Tokoto, China	5,000	E5	348
Tokuno, isl., Ryūkyū Is., Jap.		L14	349
Tokushima, Jap.	171,419	G5	354
Tokuyama, Jap.	70,987	G3	354
Tokyō, Jap.	7,900,000	G7	354
	(*12,500,000)	L15	
Tōkyō, bay, Jap.		L15	354
Tolar, Roosevelt, N.Mex.	20	D7	126
Tolbukhin (Dobrich), Bul.	42,815	B3	317
Tolbukhinski, prov., Bul.		*B4	317
Tolchester Beach, Kent, Md.	50	B7	182
Toleak, pt., Wash.		B2	98
Toledo, Ont., Can.	250	P24	64
Toledo, Charlton, Ga.	81	F4	176
Toledo, Cumberland, Ill.	998	D5	138
Toledo, Tama, Iowa	2,850	C5	142
Toledo, Lucas, Ohio	318,000	A1	156
	(*514,200)	A3	
Toledo, Lincoln, Oreg.	3,053	C3	96
Toledo, Sp.	34,592	C4	298
Toledo, Lewis, Wash.	499	C4	98
Toledo, prov., Sp.	533,654	*C4	298
Toledo, mts., Sp.		C4	298
Tolerville, Sedgwick, Kans.		A6	144
Tolima, dept., Col.	788,030	C1	244
Tolima, vol., Col.		C1	244
Tolimán, Mex.	717	K14	225
Tolland, Tolland, Conn.	400 (2,950▲)	B6	202
Tolland, Hampden, Mass.	35 (101▲)	B1	206
Tolland, co., Conn.	68,737	B6	202
Tollarp, Swe.	4,235	F4	292
Tollesboro, Lewis, Ky.	480	B7	178
Tolleson, Maricopa, Ariz.	3,886	H1	124
Tollette, Howard, Ark.	350	D3	170
Tolley, Renville, N.Dak.	189	B4	154
Tolloche, Arg.		C5	250
Töllöse, Den.		F2	292
Tollville, Prairie, Ark.		C5	170
Tolmezzo, It.	4,190	B4	302
Tolmin, Yugo.	1,638	A1	316
Tolna, Nelson, N.Dak.	291	C7	154
Tolna, Hung.	8,627	C3	320
Tolo, Jackson, Oreg.		E4	96
Tolo, gulf, Indon.		E6	358
Tolocolme, peak, Ponape		A2	436
Tolono, Champaign, Ill.	1,539	D5	138
Tolosa, Sp.	11,248	A5	298
Tolovana, Alsk.	15	C7	84
Tolovana Park, Clatsop, Oreg.	150	B3	96
Tolsta, head, Scot.		C6	272
Tolstoi, Man., Can.	500	F4	60
Tolstoy, Potter, S.Dak.	142	B6	158
Toltec, Pinal, Ariz.	75	F4	124
Toltec, Lonoke, Ark.		D7	170
Tolten, Chile	1,014	C1	252
Tolú, Col.	5,415	B1	244
Tolu, Crittenden, Ky.	325	C2	178
Toluca, Marshall, Ill.	1,352	B4	138
Toluca (de Lerdo), Mex.	52,968	D6	225
		L14	
Tolun, China	10,000	D8	348
Tom, McCurtain, Okla.	300	E9	128
Tom, mtn., Mass.		B2	206
Tom, riv., Sov.Un.		B11	336
Tomah, Monroe, Wis.	5,321	E3	160
Tomahawk, Lincoln, Wis.	3,348	C4	160
Tomahawk, lake, Wis.		C4	160
Tomakomai, Jap.	51,319	C8	354
Tomakovka, Sov.Un.		I10	332
Tomales, Marin, Calif.	150	*C2	94
Tomar, Port.	8,034	C2	298
Tomari, Sov.Un.	16,600	E16	329
Tomaszów Lubelski, Pol.	7,338	C6	325
Tomaszów Mazowiecki, Pol.	43,000	C5	325
Tomatlán, Mex.	1,059	D4	224
Tomato, Mississippi, Ark.	150	B7	170
Tomave, Bol.	201	D1	246
Tombador, mts., Braz.		H5	257
Tomball, Harris, Tex.	1,713	D8	130
Tomberlins, Lonoke, Ark.	175	C5	170
Tombigbee, riv., Ala., Miss.		D1	168
		B4	184
Tombouctou (Timbuktu), Mali	7,000	C4	408
Tombstone, Cochise, Ariz.	1,283	G5	124
Tomé, Chile	18,228	C1	252
Tomelilla, Swe.	6,511	F4	292
Tomelloso, Sp.	28,982	C5	298
Tom Green, co., Tex.	64,630	D5	130
Tomichi, creek, Colo.		D4	106
Tomini, gulf, Indon.		D6	358
Tommot, Sov.Un.	4,800	D14	329
Tom Nevers, head, Mass.		D7	206
Tomnolen, Webster, Miss.	165	B3	184
Tomo, riv., Col.		B3	244
Tompa, Sov.Un.		D13	329
Tompkins, Newf., Can.	125	G6	72
Tompkins, Sask., Can.	399	E3	58
Tompkins, co., N.Y.	66,164	C5	212
Tompkinsville, Monroe, Ky.	2,091	D5	178
Tompkinsville, Charles, Md.	140	D6	182
Toms, riv., N.J.		C4	210
Toms Brook, Shenandoah, Va.	244	B6	192
Toms Creek, Wise, Va.	250	D2	192
Tomsk, Sov.Un.	249,000	A11	336
Toms River, Ocean, N.J.	6,062	D4	210
Tomtabacken, mtn., Swe.		D5	292
Tomtor, Sov.Un.		C15	329
Tonalá, Mex.	10,497	D7	225
Tonasket, Okanogan, Wash.	958	A7	98
Tonawanda, Erie, N.Y.	21,561	B3	212
Tondano, Indon.	15,007	D6	358
Tönder, Den.	7,288	I3	291
Tönder, co., Den.	42,842	*I3	291
Toney, Madison, Ala.	118	A3	168
Tonga, is., Pac.O.		D4	436
Tonga Islands, Br. poss., Pac.O.	56,000	D4	436
Tonganoxie, Leavenworth, Kans.	1,354	C8	144
Tongeren, Bel.	15,396	D4	282
Tongjosŏn, bay, Kor.		F13	348
Tongoy, Chile		B1	252
Tongue, Scot.	827	C8	272
Tongue, riv., Mont.		E10	110
Tonica, La Salle, Ill.	750	B4	138
Tónichi, Mex.	315	B4	224
Tonj, Sud.	2,071	D2	398
Tonk, India		D1	368
Tonka Bay, Hennepin, Minn.	1,204	*G5	148
Tonkawa, Kay, Okla.	3,415	B6	128
Tonkin, gulf, Asia		C5	362
Tonle Sap, lake, Camb.		D4	362
Tonneins, Fr.	4,775	E4	278
Tonnerre, Fr.	4,345	D5	278
Tono, Thurston, Wash.		C4	98
Tonoloway, ridge, Md.		A3	182
Tonopah, Maricopa, Ariz.	30	E2	124
Tonopah, Nye, Nev.	1,679	E4	112
Tonosí, Pan.	351	G7	228
Tonquin, Washington, Oreg.		B1	96
Tons, riv., India		C2	368
Tönsberg, Nor.	12,261 (*32,000)	B1	292
Tontitown, Washington, Ark.	209	A2	170
Tonto, natural bridge, Ariz.		D4	124
Tonto, natl. mon., Ariz.		E4	124
Tonto, riv., Mex.		L15	225
Tonto Basin, Gila, Ariz.	30	E4	124
Tontogany, Wood, Ohio	380	A1	156
Tony, Rusk, Wis.	162	C3	160
Tooele, Tooele, Utah	9,133	C3	114
Tooele, co., Utah	17,868	C2	114
Toole, co., Mont.	7,904	B5	110
Toombs, co., Ga.	16,837	D4	176
Toomsboro, Wilkinson, Ga.	764	D3	176
Toomsuba, Lauderdale, Miss.	300	C4	184
Toone, Hardeman, Tenn.	202	C3	190
Toowoomba, Austl.	46,600	D10	432
Top, Grant, Oreg.		C7	96
Top, pond, Newf., Can.		G7	72
Topawa, Pima, Ariz.	304	G4	124
Topaz, Pinal, Ariz.	10	F4	124
Topeka, Lagrange, Ind.	600	A4	140
Topeka, Shawnee, Kans.	119,484 (*135,800)	C8	144
Topia, Mex.		B4	224
Topinabee, Cheboygan, Mich.	200	D7	146
Topki, Sov.Un.	28,000	A11	336
Topley, B.C., Can.	35	C9	52
Toplica, riv., Yugo.		C5	316
Toplița, Rom.	8,944	A3	321
Topocalma, pt., Chile		B1	252
Topock, Mohave, Ariz.	50	D1	124
Topol'čany, Czech.	10,189	B4	324
Topolnitsa, riv., Bul.		B2	317
Topolobampo, Mex.	1,738	B4	224
Topolovgrad, Bul.	6,970	B3	317
Toponas, Routt, Colo.	70	B4	106
Toppenish, Yakima, Wash.	5,667	C6	98
Topsfield, Washington, Maine	130 (231▲)	C5	204
Topsfield, Essex, Mass.	2,000 (3,351▲)	A6	206
Topsham, Sagadahoc, Maine	2,240	E3	204
	(3,818▲)	E5	
Topsham, Orange, Vt.	150 (638▲)	C4	218
Topsy, Delaware, Okla.	25	B9	128
Topsy, Wayne, Tenn.		C4	190
Topton, Lauderdale, Miss.	35	C4	184
Topton, Berks, Pa.	1,684	C6	214
Toquerville, Washington, Utah	197	F2	114
Toquima, range, Nev.		E4	112
Tor, bay, N.S., Can.		D8	70
Torbat-e-Heydariyeh, Iran	23,816	B5	379
Torbat-e-Jām, Iran	8,870	B5	379
Torbay, Newf., Can.	1,450	G9	72
Torbert, mtn., Alsk.		G10	84
Torch, lake, Mich.		E6	146
Torch, riv., Sask., Can.		D6	58
Töre, Swe.		D10	290
Töreboda, Swe.	5,619	C5	292
Toreva, Navajo, Ariz.	500	C5	124
Torgau, Ger.	20,400	C5	286
Torhout, Bel.	12,950	C2	282
Toride, Jap.	21,233	L16	354
Torino (Turin), It.	783,100 (*910,000)	C1	302
Torino, prov., It.	1,513,200	*C1	302
Torit, Sud.	2,353	E3	398
Torko, Solomon		E1	436
Tormes, riv., Sp.		B3	298
Tornado, peak, Alta., B.C., Can.		F5	54
		F15	52
Torneälven, riv., Swe.		C9	290
Tornetrask, lake, Swe.		B9	290
Torngat, mts., Que., Newf., Can.		C9	72
Tornio, Fin.	3,359	D11	290
Tornquist, Arg.	2,782	C3	252
Toro, Sabine, La.	35	C2	180
Toro, Sp.	8,346	B4	298
Toro, lake, Que., Can.		R11	66
Toro, peak, Calif.		F5	94
Törökszentmiklós, Hung.	17,000 (24,000▲)	B5	320
Toronto, Ont., Can.	667,706	Q21	64
	(*1,450,000)	S22	
Toronto, Clinton, Iowa	144	C7	142
Toronto, Woodson, Kans.	524	E8	144
Toronto, Jefferson, Ohio	7,780	B6	156
Toronto, Deuel, S.Dak.	268	C9	158
Toropets, Sov.Un.	24,700	D8	332
Tororo, Ug.		B5	414
Toros, mts., Tur.		C4	307
Torquay, Sask., Can.	526	F6	58
Torquay, Eng.	50,000	K9	273
Torrance, Los Angeles, Calif.	100,991	C5	94
Torrance, Ont., Can.	125	P21	64
Torrance, co., N.Mex.	6,497	D5	126
Torre Annunziata, It.	54,800	E5	302
Torre de Cerredo, mt., Sp.		A4	298
Torre del Greco, It.	53,500 (68,700▲)	E5	302
Torredonjimeno, Sp.	15,530	D5	298
Torrejoncillo, Sp.	5,118	C3	298
Torrejón de Ardoz, Sp.	2,718	B5	298
Torrelavega, Sp.	11,395	A4	298
Torremaggiore, It.	18,900	E5	302
Torrens, lake, Austl.		E7	432
Torrente, Sp.	13,586	C6	298
Torreón, Mex.	128,976 (*195,000)	B5	224
Torre Pacheco, Sp.	731	D6	298
Torres, Las Animas, Colo.		E5	106
Torres, strait, Pap.		F10	359
Tôrres Novas, Port.	7,291	C2	298
Tôrres Vedras, Port.	5,151	C2	298
Torrevieja, Sp.	9,143	D6	298
Torrey, Wayne, Utah	128	E4	114
Torrey, mtn., Mont.		E4	110

Name	Population	Key	Page
Torridge, riv., Eng.		K8	273
Torrington, Alta., Can.	115	E6	54
Torrington, Litchfield, Conn.	30,045	B3	202
Torrington, Eng.	2,800	K8	273
Torrington, Goshen, Wyo.	4,188	D8	116
Torrox, Sp.	5,377	D5	298
Torsås, Swe.	2,284	E6	292
Torsby, Swe.		A4	292
Tors Cove, Newf., Can.	250	G9	72
Torshälla, Swe.	5,424	B7	292
Torsö, isl., Swe.		C4	292
Tortola, isl., Vir. Is.		C12	233
Tortona, It.	16,100	C2	302
Tortosa, Sp.	15,150	B7	298
Tortosa, cape, Sp.		B7	298
Tortuga, isl., Ven.		A6	240
Tortugas, Dona Ana, N.Mex.	400	F4	126
Torture, isl., Hai.		C8	233
Torūd, Iran		B4	379
Toruń, Pol.	92,000	B4	325
Torup, Swe.	4,296	E4	292
Tory, isl., Ire.		F4	272
Tory, sound, Ire.		F4	272
Tory Hill, Ont., Can.	65	P22	64
Torysa, riv., Czech.		B5	324
Torzhok, Sov.Un.	32,000	D10	332
Tosno, Sov.Un.	24,600	C8	332
Tosson, hill, Eng.		F11	272
Tostado, Arg.	5,234	A3	252
Toston, Broadwater, Mont.	100	D5	110
Tosya, Tur.	11,693	A6	307
Totagatic, riv., Wis.		B2	160
Totana, Sp.	9,949	D6	298
Toteng, Bech.		D4	420
Totes Gebirge, mts., Aus.		C5	313
Tótkomlós, Hung.	9,314	C5	320
Totma, Sov.Un.		A2	336
Totnes, Eng.	5,500	K9	273
Toto, Ang.		A2	420
Toto, Guam	526	C7	436
Tōtōmi, sea, Jap.		M13	354
Totopicapán, Guat.	6,403	C2	228
Totorapalca, Bol.		C1	246
Totowa, Passaic, N.J.	10,847	A1 B4	210
Totoya, isl., Fiji		E7	436
Tottenham, Ont., Can.	702	P21	64
Tottori, Jap.	104,880	G5	354
Totzke, Sask., Can.	55	D5	58
Touba, I.C.		E3	408
Touba, Sen.		D1	408
Touchet, Walla Walla, Wash.	250	C8	98
Touchet, riv., Wash.		C8	98
Touchstone, Simpson, Miss.	250	D2	184
Touchwood, hills, Sask., Can.		E5	58
Touchwood, lake, Man., Can.		C5	60
Toufourine (Oasis), Mali		B4	408
Tougaloo, Hinds, Miss.	1,000	C2	184
Tougan, Upper Volta		D4	408
Touggourt, Alg.	17,305 (83,752▲)	D5	402
Touggourt, dept., Alg.		B5	402
Touisset, Bristol, Mass.	380	*C5	206
Toul, Fr.	12,134	C6	278
Toulépleu, I.C.		E3	408
Toulon, Fr.	141,117	F6	278
Toulon, Stark, Ill.	1,213	B4	138
Toulon, Pershing, Nev.	30	C3	112
Toulouse, Fr.	268,863	F4	278
Toummo, well, Niger		B7	409
Toungo, Br.Cam.		E7	409
Toungoo, Bur.	31,589	C3	362
Tounin, Alg.	299 (5,466▲)	A4	402
Touraine, former prov., Fr.	392,000	D4	278
Tourane, Viet.	57,395	C6	362
Tourcoing, Fr.	83,416	B5	278
Tourlaville, Fr.	9,600	C3	278
Tournai, Bel.	33,342	D2	282
Tournon [-sur-Rhône], Fr.	5,970	E6	278
Tournus, Fr.		D6	278
Touros, Braz.	1,446	B3	258
Tours, Fr.	83,618	D4	278
Tourville, Que., Can.	700	Q15	66
Tousidé, peak, Chad		B8	409
Toussain, creek, Ohio		A1	156
Toutle, riv., Wash.		C4	98
Touy-Khaya, Sov.Un.		C13	329
Tovar, Ven.	6,136	B3	240
Tovey, Christian, Ill.	646	D4	138
Towaco, Morris, N.J.	1,200	B4	210
Towada, lake, Jap.		D8	354
Towanda, McLean, Ill.	586	C5	138
Towanda, Butler, Kans.	1,031	A7 E7	144
Towanda, Bradford, Pa.	4,293	B5	214
Towanda, creek, Pa.		B5	214
Towaoc, Montezuma, Colo.	60	E2	106
Towar Gardens, Ingham, Mich.	1,500	*G7	146
Tower, Cheboygan, Mich.	300	D7	146
Tower, St. Louis, Minn.	878	D6	148
Tower City, Cass, N.Dak.	300	D8	154
Tower City, Schuylkill, Pa.	1,968	C5	214
Tower Hill, Shelby, Ill.	700	D5	138
Town, creek, Md.		A2	182
Town, hill, Md.		A3	182
Town and Country, St. Louis, Mo.	1,440	*C7	150
Town Creek, Lawrence, Ala.	810	A2	168
Towner, Kiowa, Colo.	10	D8	106
Towner, McHenry, N.Dak.	948	B5	154
Towner, co., N.Dak.	5,624	B6	154
Townley, Walker, Ala.	649	B2	168
Town of Pines, Porter, Ind.	939	*A3	140
Town Point, Cecil, Md.	30	B8	182
Towns, co., Ga.	4,538	B3	176
Townsend, New Castle, Del.	434	C3	172
Townsend, McIntosh, Ga.	100	E5	176
Townsend, Middlesex, Mass.	1,100 (3,650▲)	A4	206
Townsend, Broadwater, Mont.	1,528	D5	110
Townsend, Blount, Tenn.	283	C8 E10	190
Townsend, Northampton, Va.	120	C9	192
Townsend Harbor, Middlesex, Mass.		A4	206
Townsends Inlet, Cape May, N.J.		E3	210
Townshend, Windham, Vt.	170 (643▲)	E3	218
Townsville, Austl.	43,800	B9	432
Townsville, Vance, N.C.	195	*A7	186
Townville, Anderson, S.C.	200	B3	188
Towson, Baltimore, Md.	17,000	B6 C4	182
Towuti, lake, Indon.		E6	358
Toxey, Choctaw, Ala.	157	D1	168
Toyama, Jap.	170,495	F6	354
Toyama, bay, Jap.		F6	354
Toyohashi, Jap.	202,985	G6 M13	354
Toyokawa, Jap.		*M13	354
Toyonaka, Jap.	127,628	M11	354
Tozeur, Tun.	11,820	B5	402
Tozghi Koh, mtn., Pak.		E3	375
Trabancos, riv., Sp.		B4	298
Trabzon, Tur.	42,273	A8	307
Trabzon, prov., Tur.	463,918	*A8	307
Tracadie, N.B., Can.	1,400	B5	70
Tracadie, N.S., Can.	212	D8	70
Tracadie, riv., N.B., Can.		B4	70
Tracy, San Joaquin, Calif.	11,289	D3	94
Tracy, Que., Can.	6,542	R11	66
Tracy, New Haven, Conn.	300	C4	202
Tracy, Marion, Iowa	300	C5	142
Tracy, Barren, Ky.	50	D5	178
Tracy, Lyon, Minn.	2,862	G3	148
Tracy, Platte, Mo.	208	B3 D1	150
Tracy, brook, Md.		C6	182
Tracy City, Grundy, Tenn.	1,577	C6	190
Tracys Landing, Anne Arundel, Md.	300	C6	182
Tracyton, Kitsap, Wash.	300	D2	98
Trade, Cullman, Ala.	25	A2	168
Trade, Johnson, Tenn.	40	B10	190
Trade, lake, Sask., Can.		C6	58
Trade Lake, Burnett, Wis.	40	C1	160
Tradesville, Lancaster, S.C.	75	B7	188
Tradewater, riv., Ky.		C3	178
Traer, Tama, Iowa	1,623	B5	142
Traer, Decatur, Kans.	52	C3	144
Trafalgar, Johnson, Ind.	459	C3	140
Trafalgar, cape, Sp.		D3	298
Trafford, Jefferson, Ala.	529	*B3	168
Trafford, Westmoreland and Allegheny, Pa.	4,330	A4	214
Trafford, lake, Fla.		E9	174
Traiguén, Chile	8,806	C1	252
Trail, B.C., Can.	11,395	F14	52
Trail, Polk, Minn.	100	D3	148
Trail, Jackson, Oreg.	40	E4	96
Trail, ridge, Ga.		F4	176
Trail City, Dewey, S.Dak.	100	B5	158
Trail Creek, La Porte, Ind.	1,552	A3	140
Trailcreek, Flathead, Mont.		B2	110
Trailer Estates, Manatee, Fla.	1,562	*D8	174
Traill, co., N.Dak.	10,583	C8	154
Traill, isl., Grnld.		P33	290
Trainer, Delaware, Pa.	2,358	*D6	214
Traipú, Braz.	1,866	B3	258
Tralee, Ire.	10,928	I3	273
Tramelan, Switz.	3,516	A3	312
Trammel, Allen, Ky.	15	D4	178
Trammel, Dickenson, Va.	900	C2	192
Tramping, lake, Sask., Can.		D3	58
Tramping Lake, Sask., Can.	262	D3	58
Tranås, Swe.	14,571	C5	292
Trancoso, Port.	3,537	B3	298
Tranebjerg, Den.	864	F1	292
Tranemo, Swe.	4,677	D4	292
Trang, Thai.	5,000	F3	362
Trang, prov., Thai.	148,591	*F3	362
Trangan, is., Indon.		F8	359
Trani, It.	36,000	E6	302
Tran Ninh, plat., Laos		C4	362
Tranquility, Sussex, N.J.	100	B3	210
Tranquillity, Fresno, Calif.	650	D3	94
Transcona, Man., Can.	8,312	F4	60
Trans-Ili Alatau, mts., Sov.Un.		D9	336
Transtrands-Fjallen, mtn., Swe.		A4	292
Transvaal, prov., U.S.Afr.	4,818,838	E5	420
Trans-Volta Togoland, reg., Ghana		E5	408
Transylvania, East Carroll, La.	50	B4	180
Transylvania, co., N.C.	16,372	B3	186
Transylvania, prov., Rom.	3,420,859	*B6	321
Transylvania (Transilvania), reg., Rom.		A2	321
Transylvanian Alps, mts., Rom.		B3	321
Trap, mtn., Ark.		D6	170
Trapani, It.	75,000	F4	302
Trapani, prov., It.	422,700	*F4	302
Trapiche, Guat.		B2	228
Trappe, Talbot, Md.	358	C7	182
Trappe, Montgomery, Pa.	1,264	*C6	214
Trappe, creek, Md.		D9	182
Trapper, peak, Mont.		E2	110
Traralgon, Austl.	8,845	F9	432
Traryd, Swe.	5,716	E4	292
Trasimeno, lake, It.		D4	302
Traskwood, Saline, Ark.	205	C4	170
Trás-os-Montes, reg., Port.	547,781	B3	298
Trás-os-Montes e Alto Douro, prov., Port.	639,846	*B3	298
Trat, Thai.		D4	362
Trat, prov., Thai.	44,819	*D4	362
Traun, Aus.	9,655	B6	313
Traun, lake, Aus.		C5	313
Traun, riv., Aus.		B5	313
Traunik, Alger, Mich.	50	C5	146
Traunstein, Ger.	14,700	E5	286
Travannes, Switz.	3,650	A3	312
Travelers Rest, Greenville, S.C.	1,973	B4 B2	188
Travers, Alta., Can.	75	E6	54
Traverse, co., Minn.	7,503	F2	148
Traverse, isl., Mich.		B3	146
Traverse, lake, Minn.		F2	148
Traverse City, Grand Traverse, Mich.	18,432	E6	146
Tra Vinh, Viet.	39,700	E5	362
Travis, Tyrrell, N.C.		B9	186
Travis, co., Tex.	212,136	D7	130
Travnik, Yugo.	8,163	B3	316
Tray, mtn., Ga.		B3	176
Treadway, Hancock, Tenn.	75	B8	190
Treasure, co., Mont.	1,345	D9	110
Treasure, isl., Calif.		A5	94
Treasure, isl., Fla.		D8	174
Treasure Island, Pinellas, Fla.	3,506	*D8	174
Treasury, is., Solomon		E1	436
Třebíč, Czech.	19,149	B2	324
Trebinje, Yugo.	3,445	C4	316
Trebišov, Czech.	7,627	B5	324
Treble, mtn., B.C., Can.		C8	52
Trebloc, Chickasaw, Miss.	500	B4	184
Třeboň, Czech.	4,172	B2	324
Treece, Cherokee, Kans.	280	E9	144
Tregaron, Wales	1,243	I9	273
Tregarva, Sask., Can.	50	E5	58
Trego, Lincoln, Mont.	12	B2	110
Trego, Washburn, Wis.	175	C2	160
Trego, co., Kans.	5,473	D3	144
Tréguier, Fr.		C2	278
Treherne, Man., Can.	551	F3	60
Treinta y Tres, Ur.	18,500	B5	252
Treinta y Tres, dept., Ur.	68,850	B5	252
Treknatten, mtn., Nor.		A1	292
Trélazé, Fr.	6,934	D3	278
Trelew, Arg.	5,880	F4	251
Trelleborg, Swe.	17,924	F4	292
Tremador, bay, Wales		I8	273
Tremblant, mtn., Que., Can.		R10	66
Trembleur, lake, B.C., Can.		C10	52
Tremiti, is., It.		D5	302
Tremont, Tazewell, Ill.	1,558	C4	138
Tremont, Hancock, Maine	150 (1,044▲)	*D4	204
Tremont, Itawamba, Miss.	300	A4	184
Tremont, Schuylkill, Pa.	1,893	C5	214
Tremont City, Clark, Ohio	414	B3	156
Tremonton, Box Elder, Utah	2,115	B3	114
Tremp, Sp.	3,521	A7	298
Trempealeau, Trempealeau, Wis.	704	D2	160
Trempealeau, co., Wis.	23,377	D2	160
Trempealeau, riv., Wis.		D2	160
Trenary, Alger, Mich.	180	C5	146
Trenche, riv., Que., Can.		Q12	66
Trenčín, Czech.	22,970	B4	324
Trengganu, state, Mala.	278,147	*F4	362
Trenque Lauquén, Arg.	10,887	C3	252
Trent, see Trento, It.			
Trent, Lane, Oreg.	40	D4	96
Trent, Moody, S.Dak.	232	D9	158
Trent, riv., Eng.		H12	273
Trent, riv., N.C.		B8	186
Trentino-Alto Adige, reg., It.	765,000	*B3	302
Trento, It.	40,800 (64,800▲)	B3	302
Trento, prov., It.	401,700	*B3	302
Trenton, Jackson, Ala.	200	A3	168
Trenton, Phillips, Ark.	50	*C6	170
Trenton, N.S., Can.	3,420	D7	70
Trenton, Ont., Can.	11,492	P23	64
Trenton, Gilchrist, Fla.	941	B8	174
Trenton, Dade, Ga.	1,301	B1	176
Trenton, Clinton, Ill.	1,866	E4	138
Trenton, Todd, Ky.	542	D3	178
Trenton, Hancock, Maine	65 (373▲)	*D4	204
Trenton, Wayne, Mich.	18,439	C8 G8	146
Trenton, Smith, Miss.	100	C3	184
Trenton, Grundy, Mo.	6,262	A4	150
Trenton, Hitchcock, Nebr.	914	D4	152
Trenton, Mercer, N.J.	114,167 (*279,800)	C3	210
Trenton, Jones, N.C.	404	B8	186
Trenton, Williams, N.Dak.	125	B2	154
Trenton, Butler, Ohio	3,064	C2	156
Trenton, Edgefield, S.C.	314	D5	188
Trenton, Gibson, Tenn.	4,225	C3	190
Trenton, Fannin, Tex.	712	C7	130
Trenton, Cache, Utah	448	B4	114
Trenton, dam, Nebr.		D4	152
Trentville, Knox, Tenn.	400	E10	190
Trentwood, Spokane, Wash.	1,387	*B9	98
Trent Woods, Craven, N.C.	517	*B8	186
Trepassey, Newf., Can.	550	G9	72
Trepassey, bay, Newf., Can.		G9	72
Tres Algarrobos, Arg.		C3	252
Tres Arboles, Ur.		B4	252
Tres Arroyos, Arg.	29,996	C3	252
Tres Cerros, Arg.		G4	251
Tresckow, Carbon, Pa.	1,145	C6	214
Três Corações, Braz.	10,025	E1	258
Tres Esquinas, Col.		C1	244
Treshnish, pt., Scot.		E6	272
Três Lagoas, Braz.	7,650	J6	257
Tres Lomas, Arg.	3,425	C3	252
Tres Marias, is., Mex.		C4	224
Tres Matas, Ven.		B6	240
Tres Piedras, Taos, N.Mex.	150	B5	126
Tres Puntas, cape, Arg.		G4	251
Trestle Creek, Bonner, Idaho	50	*A2	108
Tretten, Nor.		F4	291
Treutlen, co., Ga.	5,874	D4	176
Trevett, Lincoln, Maine	100	E3	204
Treviglio, It.	16,600	C2	302
Treviño, Sp.	397	A5	298
Treviso, It.	56,300 (67,300▲)	C4	302
Treviso, prov., It.	614,800	*C4	302
Trevor, Kenosha, Wis.	250	F1	160
Trevorton, Northumberland, Pa.	2,597	C5	214
Trevose, head, Eng.		K7	273
Trevose Heights, Bucks, Pa.	1,500	*C6	214
Treynor, Pottawattamie, Iowa	368	C2	142
Trezevant, Carroll, Tenn.	944	B3	190
Triadelphia, Ohio, W.Va.	600	A4 B2	194
Triadelphia, res., Md.		B5	182
Triangle, Owyhee, Idaho		G2	108
Triangle, Prince William, Va.	2,948	B7	192
Triangle Lake, Lane, Oreg.	100	C3	96
Tribbett, Washington, Miss.	200	B2	184
Tribbey, Pottawatomie, Okla.	150	C6	128
Tribble, Mason, W.Va.	161	C3	194
Tribune, Sask., Can.	129	F6	58
Tribune, Greeley, Kans.	1,036	D2	144
Tricca, see Trikkala, Grc.			
Trichur, India	69,515	F3	366
Tri City, Graves, Ky.	150	D2	178
Tridell, Uintah, Utah	310	C6	114
Trident, peak, Nev.		B3	112
Trier, Ger.	86,700	D2	286
Trieste, It.	270,900	C4	302
Trieste, reg., It.	310,000	*C4	302
Trieste, gulf, It.		C4	302
Trigg, co., Ky.	8,870	D3	178
Triglav, mtn., Yugo.		A1	316
Trigo, mts., Ariz.		E1	124
Trigueros, Sp.	6,188	D3	298
Trikkala, Grc.	23,385	B3	306
Trikkala, prov., Grc.	127,481	B3	306
Tri Lakes, Whitley, Ind.	1,089	A4	140
Trilby, Pasco, Fla.	500	C8	174
Trilby, Lucas, Ohio	5,000	A1	156
Trillick, N.Ire.	203	G5	273
Trim, Ire.	1,342	H6	273
Trimble, Clinton, Mo.	185	B3	150
Trimble, Athens, Ohio	481	C4	156
Trimble, Dyer and Obion, Tenn.	581	B2	190
Trimble, co., Ky.	5,102	B5	178
Trimble, isl., Wash.		D2	98
Trimont, Martin, Minn.	942	H4	148
Trimountain, Houghton, Mich.	400	B3	146
Trinchera, Las Animas, Colo.	150	E6	106
Trinchera, creek, Colo.		E5	106
Trinchera, peak, Colo.		E5	106
Trincomalee, Cey.	26,356	G4	366
Trine, Phillips, Mont.		C8	110
Tring-Jonction, Que., Can.	1,083	R14	66
Trinidad, Bol.	8,695	B2	246
Trinidad, Humboldt, Calif.	289	*B2	94
Trinidad, Las Animas, Colo.	10,691	E6	106
Trinidad, Cuba	16,756	B5	232
Trinidad, Mex.		B4	224
Trinidad, Henderson, Tex.	786	C7	130
Trinidad, Ur.	15,700	B4	252
Trinidad, ter., W.I.Fed.	686,140	E14	233
Trinidad, isl., Arg.		C3	252
Trinité, Mart.	2,584 (7,378▲)	E14	233
Trinity, Morgan, Ala.	454	A2	168
Trinity, Newf., Can.	700	F9	72
Trinity, Randolph, N.C.	881	B6	186
Trinity, Trinity, Tex.	1,787	D8	130
Trinity, co., Calif.	9,706	B2	94
Trinity, co., Tex.	7,539	D8	130
Trinity, bay, Newf., Can.		F9	72
Trinity, is., Alsk.		D6	84
Trinity, mtn., Idaho		F3	108
Trinity, range, Nev.		C3	112
Trinity, riv., Calif.		B2	94
Trinity, riv., Tex.		D8	130
Trinity Center, Trinity, Calif.	100	B2	94
Trinity Springs, Martin, Ind.	125	D3	140
Trino, It.	8,100	C2	302
Trinway, Muskingum, Ohio	500	B4	156
Trio, Williamsburg, S.C.	174	E9	188
Trion, Chattooga, Ga.	2,227	B1	176
Triplet, Brunswick, Va.	250	D7	192
Triplett, Chariton, Mo.	231	B4	150
Triplett, Roane, W.Va.		C3	194
Tripoli, Bremer, Iowa	1,179	B5	142
Tripoli, see Tarabulus, Leb.			
Tripoli (Ţarābulus), Libya	129,728	A2	394
Tripoli, Oneida, Wis.	45	C4	160
Tripolis, Grc.	17,585	C4	306
Tripolitania (Ţarābulus), prov., Libya		B2	394
Tripp, Hutchinson, S.Dak.	837	D8	158
Tripp, co., S.Dak.	8,761	D5	158
Tripura, ter., India	639,029	*D6	366
Trischen, isl., Ger.		A3	286
Triste, gulf, Ven.		A4	240
Tritle, mtn., Ariz.		D3	124
Triumph, Blaine, Idaho		F4	108
Triumph, Plaquemines, La.	900	E6	180
Triune, Williamson, Tenn.	50	C5	190
Triunfo, Braz.	2,364	B3	258
Trivandrum, India	186,931	G3	366
Trnava, Czech.	32,507	B3	324
Trochu, Alta., Can.	680	E6	54
Trogir, Yugo.	4,348	C3	316
Trois-Pistoles, Que., Can.	4,039	P15	66
Trois-Rivières, Que., Can.	50,483	R12	66
Troisvierges, Lux.	1,912	D5	282
Troitsk, Sov.Un.	76,000	B6	336
Troitsko-Pechorsk, Sov.Un.		C7	328
Trollhättan, Swe.	28,446	C3	292
Trombetas, riv., Braz.		F5	256
Trombly, Delta, Mich.		C4	146
Trommald, Crow Wing, Minn.	101	*E4	148
Troms, co., Nor.	119,774	*B8	290
Tromsö, Nor.		B8	290
Trona, San Bernardino, Calif.	1,138	E5	94
Tronador, mtn., Chile		F3	251
Tröndelag, reg., Nor.	309,755	*E3	290
Trondheim, Nor.	58,344 (*82,000)	E4	290
Trondheimsfjorden, fjord, Nor.		E4	290
Tropea, It.	5,732	F5	302
Trophy, mtn., B.C., Can.		E13	52
Tropic, Garfield, Utah	382	F3	114
Trosa, Swe.	1,360	C8	292
Trosky, Pipestone, Minn.	122	H2	148
Trossachs, Sask., Can.	225	F5	58
Trostan, mtn., N.Ire.		F6	272
Trotwood, Montgomery, Ohio	4,992	C2	156
Troup, Smith and Cherokee, Tex.	1,667	C8	130
Troup, co., Ga.	47,189	D1	176
Trousdale, Edwards, Kans.	83	E4	144
Trousdale, Pottawatomie, Okla.	10	C6	128
Trousdale, co., Tenn.	4,914	B5	190
Trout, La Salle, La.	500	C3	180
Trout, creek, Fla.		A10	174
Trout, lake, B.C., Can.		E14	52
Trout, lake, Minn.		C6	148
Trout, lake, Wis.		B4	160
Trout, peak, Wyo.		B3	116
Trout, riv., Alta., Can.		B5	54
Trout, riv., Vt.		B3	218

Tuttle, lake, Iowa		A3	142
Tuttlingen, Ger.	23,900	E3	286
Tutubu, Tan.		D5	414
Tutuila, isl., Samoa		E5	436
Tutwiler, Tallahatchie, Miss.	912	A2	184
Tuusniemi, Fin.		E13	290
Tuvek, Pol.	7,179	B4	325
Tuwaiq, mts., Sau.Ar.		C4	383
Tuxedo, Man., Can.	1,163	F4	60
Tuxedo, Henderson, N.C.	900	B3	186
Tuxedo Park, Orange, N.Y.	723	D7	212
Tuxford, Sask., Can.	133	E5	58
Tuxpán, Mex.	11,649	C4	225
Tuxpán, Mex.	15,691	C6	225
		K15	
Tuxpán, Mex.	8,211	D5	224
Tuxpán, Mex.	2,502	L13	225
Tuxpán, riv., Mex.		K15	225
Tuxtepec, Mex.	5,850	L15	225
Tuxtepec, riv., Mex.		L15	225
Tuxtla Gutiérrez, Mex.	28,260	D7	225
Túy, Sp.	2,779	A2	298
Tuyen Quang, Viet.	6,000	B5	362
Tuyün, China		L3	349
Tuz, lake, Tur.		B5	307
Tuzigoot, natl. mon., Ariz.		D4	124
Tuz Khurmati, Iraq	6,381	B6	378
Tuzla, Yugo.	32,400	B4	316
Tuzlu, lake, Iran		B3	379
Tvaa, Swe.		D3	292
Tvedestrand, Nor.		G3	291
Tweed, Ont., Can.	1,634	P23	64
Tweed, riv., Scot.		F9	272
Tweedsmuir, prov. park, B.C., Can.		D9	52
Twelve Mile, Cass, Ind.	225	B3	140
Twelve Mile, Multnomah, Oreg.	700	*B4	96
Twelve Pins, mts., Ire.		H3	273
Twelvepole, creek, W.Va.		C2	194
Twentymile, creek, W.Va.		C3	194
Twentynine Palms, San Bernardino, Calif.	1,000	E5	94
Twiggs, co., Ga.	7,935	D3	176
Twila, Harlan, Ky.	200	D7	178
Twillingate, Newf., Can.	1,800	F8	72
Twillingate, is., Newf., Can.		F8	72
Twin, buttes, Oreg.		C4	96
Twin, creek, Ohio		C2	156
Twin, lakes, Conn.		A2	202
Twin, lakes, Iowa		B3	142
Twin, lakes, Maine		C4	204
Twin, mts., Wyo.		E7	116
Twin, peaks, Idaho		E4	108
Twin, peaks, Mont.		E5	110
Twin Beach, Oakland, Mich.	900	*B7	146
Twin Bridges, Madison, Mont.	509	E4	110
Twin Brooks, Grant, S.Dak.	86	B9	158
Twin City, Emanuel, Ga.	1,095	D4	176
Twin Creek, Izard, Ark.	10	*B4	170
Twin Falls, Twin Falls, Idaho	20,126	G4	108
Twin Falls, co., Idaho	41,842	G4	108
Twin Groves, Fremont, Idaho		E7	108
Twining, Arenac, Mich.	199	E8	146
Twin Lake, Muskegon, Mich.	300	F5	146
Twin Lakes, Santa Cruz, Calif.	1,849	*D2	94
Twin Lakes, Lake, Colo.	30	C4	106
Twin Lakes, Lowndes, Ga.	200	F3	176
Twin Lakes, Kootenai, Idaho		B2	108
Twin Lakes, Freeborn, Minn.	153	*H5	148
Twin Lakes, Kenosha, Wis.	1,497	F1	160
Twin Mountain, Coos, N.H.	200	C3	208
Twin Oaks, St. Louis, Mo.	206	*C7	150
Twin Oaks, Delaware, Okla.	85	B9	128
Twin River Beach, Baltimore, Md.	50	*B7	182
Twin Rocks, Tillamook, Oreg.	250	B3	96
Twin Rocks, Cambria, Pa.	900	C3	214
Twinsburg, Summit, Ohio	4,098	A5	156
Twin Springs, Boise, Idaho		F3	108
Twinton, Overton, Tenn.	125	B6	190
Twin Valley, Norman, Minn.	841	D2	148
Twisp, Okanogan, Wash.	750	A6	98
Twist, Cross, Ark.	150	B6	170
Two Butte, creek, Colo.		E8	106
Two Buttes, Baca, Colo.	111	E8	106
Two Buttes, res., Colo.		E8	106
Two Creeks, Man., Can.	110	E2	60
Twodot, Wheatland, Mont.	65	D6	110
Twoforks, riv., Sask., Can.		C4	58
Two Harbors, Lake, Minn.	4,695	D7	148
Two Hearted, riv., Mich.		C6	146
Two Hills, Alta., Can.	713	D7	54
Two Mile, beach, N.J.		E3	210
Two Mountains, co., Que., Can.	26,595	S10	66
		S15	
Two Mountains, lake, Que., Can.		S15	66
Two Prairie, bayou, Ark.		D7	170
Two Rivers, Manitowoc, Wis.	12,393	B7	160
		D6	
Two Rivers, riv., Minn.		C2	148
Tyaskin, Wicomico, Md.	125	D8	182
Tyborön, Den.	1,708	H3	291
Tye River, Nelson, Va.	130	C6	192
Tyerlton, Somerset, Md.	200	E7	182
Tygart, res., W.Va.		B4	194
Tygart, riv., W.Va.		B4	194
Tygart River, falls, W.Va.		A7	194
Tygarts, creek, Ky.		B7	178
Tygda, Sov.Un.		D14	329
Tyger, riv., S.C.		B5	188
Tygh Valley, Wasco, Oreg.	270	B5	96
Tyhee, Bannock, Idaho	100	G6	108
Tyler, Dallas, Ala.	400	C3	168
Tyler, Cleburne, Ark.		B5	170
Tyler, Sedgwick, Kans.		B5	144
Tyler, Lincoln, Minn.	1,138	G2	148
Tyler, Smith, Tex.	51,230	C8	130
Tyler, Spokane, Wash.	30	D8	98
Tyler, co., Tex.	10,666	D8	130
Tyler, co., W.Va.	10,026	B4	194
Tyler, brook, Vt.		B3	218
Tyler Heights, Kanawha, W.Va.	1,500	*C3	194
Tyler Park, Fairfax, Va.	1,000	*B7	192
Tylertown, Walthall, Miss.	1,532	D2	184
Tylöskog, mts., Swe.		C6	292
Tynagh, Ire.		H4	273
Tyndall, Man., Can.	300	E4	60
Tyndall, Bon Homme, S.Dak.	1,262	E8	158
Tyndinskiy, Sov.Un.		D14	329
Týnec, Czech.	1,146	*B2	324
Tynemouth, Eng.	67,700	G11	272
Tyner, Marshall, Ind.	200	A3	140
Tyner, Jackson, Ky.	500	C7	178
Tyner, Hamilton, Tenn.	1,000	C6	190
		E8	
Tyne Valley, P.E.I., Can.	190	C6	70
Tyngsboro, Middlesex, Mass.	150	A5	206
	(3,302▲)		
Tynset, Nor.	4,324	E4	291
Tyonek, Alsk.	132	C6	84
		G10	
Tyringham, Berkshire, Mass.	175	B1	206
	(197▲)		
Tyro, Lincoln, Ark.	50	D5	170
Tyro, Montgomery, Kans.	289	E8	144
Tyro, Tate, Miss.	350	A3	184
Tyrone, Las Animas, Colo.	30	E6	106
Tyrone, Anderson, Ky.	240	B6	178
Tyrone, Fayette, Ga.	124	*C2	176
Tyrone, Grant, N.Mex.	200	F2	126
Tyrone, Texas, Okla.	456	B2	128
Tyrone, Blair, Pa.	7,792	C3	214
Tyrone, co., N.Ire.	133,000	G6	273
Tyronza, Poinsett, Ark.	601	B6	170
Tyrrell, co., N.C.	4,520	B9	186
Tyrrhenian, sea, It.		E3	302
Tysfjord, Nor.		B7	290
Tysnes, Nor.		F1	291
Tyson, Windsor, Vt.	75	E3	218
Ty Ty, Tift, Ga.	461	E3	176
Tyukalinsk, Sov.Un.		A8	336
Tyumen, Sov.Un.	150,000	A7	336
Tyumyati, Sov.Un.		B14	329
Tyvan, Sask., Can.	98	E6	58
Tzeliutsing, China	223,000	F8	346
Tzucacab, Mex.	3,296	C8	225
Tzuli, China	5,000	K5	349
Tzuyang, China	25,000	H8	348
Tzuyang, China	5,000	I4	349
Tzuyüan, China		L5	349

U

U, cape, Ponape		A2	436
Uardere, Eth.		D6	398
Uaupés, Braz.	465	F3	256
Uaupés, riv., Braz.		E3	256
Ubá, Braz.	14,022	E2	258
Ubaira, Braz.	2,217	C3	258
Ubangi, riv., Con.B.		F8	409
Ubangi, riv., Afr.		B2	414
Ube, Jap.	160,020	H3	354
Ubeda, Sp.	30,379	C5	298
Uberaba, Braz.	42,481	D1	258
Uberlândia, Braz.	34,866	D1	258
Überlingen, Ger.	9,500	E3	286
Ubiaja, Nig.	6,034	E6	408
Ubly, Huron, Mich.	819	F9	146
Ubombo, U.S.Afr.	273	E6	421
Ubonratchthani, prov., Thai.	850,526	*D5	362
Ubort, riv., Sov.Un.		G6	332
Ubrique, Sp.	7,599	D4	298
Ucayali, riv., Peru		B3	245
Uccen Jargga, mtn., Nor.		B8	290
Uccle, Bel.	68,256	D3	282
Uch-Aral, Sov.Un.	3,700	C10	336
Uchee, Russell, Ala.	50	C4	168
Uchisa, Peru	259	B2	245
Uchiura, bay, Jap.		C8	354
Ücker, riv., Ger.		B5	286
Ucluelet, B.C., Can.	520	F10	52
Ucon, Bonneville, Idaho	532	F7	108
Ucross, Sheridan, Wyo.	25	B6	116
Udaipur, India	89,621	D1	368
Udall, Cowley, Kans.	600	E6	144
Udáquiola, Arg.		C4	252
Uddevalla, Swe.	28,234	C2	292
Uddjaur, lake, Swe.		D7	290
Udell, Appanoose, Iowa	76	D5	142
Uden, Neth.	4,644	C4	282
Udhampur, India	4,666	B1	368
Udine, It.	76,400	B4	302
Udine, prov., It.	801,900	*B4	302
Udon Thani, Thai.	10,000	C4	362
Udon Thani, prov., Thai.	382,564	*C4	362
Uebi Scebeli, pol. dist., Som.	176,528	E6	398
Ueckermünde, Ger.	12,000	B6	286
Ueda, Jap.	51,572	F7	354
		K14	
Uehling, Dodge, Nebr.	231	C9	152
Uélé, riv., Con.L.		B3	414
Uelen, Sov.Un.	800	C20	329
Uelkal, Sov.Un.	800	C19	329
Uelzen, Ger.	24,200	B4	286
Ueno, Jap.	62,355	M12	354
Ufa, Sov.Un.	546,000	B5	336
Ufa, riv., Sov.Un.		A5	336
Uga, Okinawa		C1	436
Ugab, riv., S.W.Afr.		D3	420
Ugalla, riv., Tan.		D5	414
Uganda, reg., Con.L.		*B5	414
Uganda, country, Afr.	5,868,000	F10	388
			414
Ugar, Sov.Un.		D11	329
Ugashik, Alsk.	48	D6	84
Ugashik, lakes, Alsk.		D6	84
Uglich, Sov.Un.	25,600	A1	336
Ugolnyy, Sov.Un.		C19	329
Ugra, riv., Sov.Un.		E10	332
Ugumun, Sov.Un.		C13	329
Ugürchin, Bul.	6,862	B2	317
Uherské Hradiště, Czech.	10,884	B3	324
Uhrichsville, Tuscarawas, Ohio	6,201	B5	156
Uhříněves, Czech.	4,581	*A2	324
Uhu, Solomon		E2	436
Uig, Scot.		C6	272
Uiju (Gishū), Kor.	27,378	E12	348
Uil, Sov.Un.	2,500	C4	336
Uil, riv., Sov.Un.		C4	336
Uinamarca, lake, Bol.		C1	246
Uinta, co., Wyo.	7,484	E2	116
Uinta, mts., Utah		C5	114
Uinta, riv., Utah		C5	114
Uintah, Weber, Utah	344	*B4	114
Uintah, co., Utah	11,582	D6	114
Uitenhage, U.S.Afr.	38,748	F4	420
Uithuizen, Neth.	3,353	A5	282
Uivuk, cape, Newf., Can.		D9	72
Ujae, atoll, Marshall		A4	436
Ujfehértó, Hung.	15,154	B6	320
Uji, isl., Jap.		I2	354
Ujiji, Tan.	12,011	C4	414
Ujiyamada, Jap.	97,223	G6	354
		M12	
Ujjain, India	129,817	E1	368
Uka, Sov.Un.		D18	329
Ukak, see Ekuk, Alsk.			
Ukerewe, isl., Tan.		C5	414
Ukhta, Sov.Un.	15,000	C7	328
Ukiah, Mendocino, Calif.	9,900	C2	94
Ukiah, Umatilla, Oreg.	200	B8	96
Ukmerge, Sov.Un.	19,800	E5	332
Ukraine, rep., Sov.Un.	41,983,000	E4	328
Ukusu, Jap.	3,417	M14	354
Ulaan Goom, Mong.	5,000	B6	346
Ulalu, isl., Truk		A3	436
Ulan Bator (Urga), Mong.	70,000	B9	346
Ulan-Ude, Sov.Un.	174,000	D12	329
Ulchin, Kor.		G14	348
Ulcinj, Yugo.	4,919	D4	316
Uldza, riv., Mong.		B10	346
Ulen, Boone, Ind.	130	B3	140
Ulen, Clay, Minn.	481	D2	148
Ulety, Sov.Un.		D13	329
Ulfborg, Den.	1,166	H3	291
Uliassutai, see Jibhalanta, Mong.			
Ulifauro, pass, Truk		A3	436
Ulindi, riv., Con.L.		C4	414
Ulithi, is., Pac.O.		C3	436
Ulla, Sov.Un.	5,500	E7	332
Ulla, riv., Sp.		A2	298
Ullapool, Scot.		D8	272
Ullared, Swe.	1,843	D3	292
Ullensvang, Nor.		F2	291
Ullin, Pulaski, Ill.	577	F4	138
Ullsfjord, fjord, Nor.		B8	290
Ullswater, lake, Eng.		G10	273
Ullvattern, lake, Swe.		B5	292
Ulm, Prairie, Ark.	140	C5	170
Ulm, Ger.	89,800	D3	286
Ulm, Cascade, Mont.	75	*C5	110
Ulm, Sheridan, Wyo.	25	B6	116
Ulmers, Allendale, S.C.	168	E6	188
Ulricehamn, Swe.	7,885	D5	292
Ulsan, Kor.		H14	348
Ulster, co., N.Y.	118,804	D7	212
Ulster, prov., Ire.	27,316	G4	273
Ulster, canal, Ire.		G5	273
Ulu, mtn., Tur.		A3	307
Uluborlu, Tur.	4,276	B4	307
Ulukisla, Tur.	3,664	C6	307
Ulva, isl., Scot.		E6	272
Ulverston, Eng.	10,400	G9	273
Ulverstone, Austl.	5,361	G9	432
Ulvik, Nor.		F2	291
Ulyanovsk, Sov.Un.	205,000	B3	336
Ulysses, Grant, Kans.	3,157	E2	144
Ulysses, Butler, Nebr.	357	C8	152
Uman, Sov.Un.	63,000	H8	332
Umanak, fjord, Grnld.		P28	290
Umaria, India		E3	368
Umarkot, Pak.	5,142	G6	375
Umatilla, Lake, Fla.	1,717	C9	174
Umatilla, Umatilla, Oreg.	617	B7	96
Umatilla, co., Oreg.	44,352	B8	96
Umatilla, riv., Oreg.		B7	96
Umbagog, lake, Maine		D1	204
Umbagog, lake, N.H.		B4	208
Umbria, reg., It.	822,000	D4	302
Umbuzeiro, Braz.		B3	258
Umcolcus, lake, Maine		B4	204
Umeå, Swe.	19,092	E9	290
Umeälven, riv., Swe.		D8	290
Umiat, Alsk.		B6	84
Umm al 'Abid, Libya		B3	394
Umm al Qaiwain, Tr. Coast		B6	383
Umm el Fahm, Isr.	4,861	B6	382
Umm Keddada, Sud.		C2	398
Umm Lajj, Sau.Ar.		C2	383
Umm Rakh, Sau.Ar.		B2	383
Umm Ruwāba, Sud.	7,805	C3	398
Umnak, isl., Alsk.		E5	84
Umpire, Howard, Ark.	64	C2	170
Umpqua, Douglas, Oreg.	20	D3	96
Umpqua, riv., Oreg.		D3	96
Umsaskis, lake, Maine		B3	204
Umtali, Rh. & Nya.	26,500	C6	421
	(*28,000)		
Umtata, U.S.Afr.	9,185	F5	420
Umuahia, Nig.		E6	409
Umvuma, Rh. & Nya.	600	C6	421
Umzinto, U.S.Afr.	3,811	F6	420
Una, Spartanburg, S.C.	1,500	*B5	188
Una, Davidson, Tenn.	100	E7	190
Una, riv., Yugo.		B3	316
Unadilla, Dooly, Ga.	1,304	D3	176
Unadilla, Otoe, Nebr.	254	E2	152
Unadilla, Otsego, N.Y.	1,586	C6	212
Unadilla, riv., N.Y.		C6	212
Unadshdalur, Ice.		K18	290
Unalakleet, Alsk.	469	C5	84
Unalaska, Alsk.	218	E5	84
Unalaska, isl., Alsk.		E5	84
Unango, Moz.		B7	421
Unao, India		D3	368
Unare, lake, Ven.		A6	240
'Unayzah, Sau.Ar.		B3	383
Uncas, Kay, Okla.	100	B7	128
Uncasville, New London, Conn.	1,381	D7	202
Uncompahgre, peak, Colo.		D3	106
Uncompahgre, plat., Colo.		D2	106
Uncompahgre, riv., Colo.		D3	106
Unden, lake, Swe.		C5	292
Underhill, Chittenden, Vt.	225	B3	218
	(730▲)		
Underhill, Oconto, Wis.	80	D5	160
Underhill Center, Chittenden, Vt.	150	B3	218
Underwood, Shelby, Ala.	250	B3	168
Underwood, Clark, Ind.	200	D4	140
Underwood, Pottawattamie, Iowa	337	C2	142
Underwood, Otter Tail, Minn.	314	E3	148
Underwood, McLean, N.Dak.	819	C4	154
Underwood, Skamania, Wash.	350	D5	98
Undirfell, Ice.		L19	290
Unecha, Sov.Un.	16,600	F9	332
Uneeda, Boone, W.Va.	250	D5	194
Unga, Alsk.	107	D5	84
Ungava, bay, Que., Can.		P9	66
Unggi, Kor.	20,882	D15	348
Unhošt, Czech.	3,063	*A2	324
União, Braz.	3,198	A2	258
União dos Palmares, Braz.	6,917	B3	258
Unica, Bol.	4,507	C1	246
Unicoi, Unicoi, Tenn.	500	B9	190
Unicoi, co., Tenn.	15,082	B9	190
Unicoi, mts., N.C., Tenn.		B1	186
		C7	190
Unije, isl., Yugo.		B2	316
Unimak, isl., Alsk.		E5	84
Unimak, pass, Alsk.		E5	84
Union, Fulton, Ark.	50	A5	170
Union, Tolland, Conn.	70	B7	202
	(383▲)		
Union, McHenry, Ill.	480	A5	138
Union, Pike, Ind.	150	D2	140
Union, Hardin, Iowa	534	B4	142
Union, Boone, Ky.	135	A8	178
Union, St. James, La.	640	B5	180
		D5	
Union, Knox, Maine	300	D3	204
	(1,196▲)		
Union, Newton and Neshoba, Miss.	1,726	C3	184
Union, Franklin, Mo.	3,937	C6	150
Union, Cass, Nebr.	303	D10	152
		E3	
Union, Carroll, N.H.	300	E4	208
Union, Union, N.J.	51,499	B1	210
		B4	
Union, Hertford, N.C.	306	A8	186
Union, Montgomery, Ohio	1,072	*C2	156
Union, Canadian, Okla.	329	C6	128
Union, Union, Oreg.	1,490	B9	96
Union, Union, S.C.	10,191	B5	188
Union, Salt Lake, Utah	500	*C4	114
Union, Mason, Wash.	500	B3	98
Union, Monroe, W.Va.	411	D4	194
Union, co., Ark.	49,518	D4	170
Union, co., Fla.	6,043	A8	174
Union, co., Ga.	6,510	B2	176
Union, co., Ill.	17,645	F4	138
Union, co., Ind.	6,457	C5	140
Union, co., Iowa	13,712	C3	142
Union, co., Ky.	14,537	C2	178
Union, co., Miss.	18,904	A3	184
Union, co., N.J.	504,255	B4	210
Union, co., N.Mex.	6,068	B7	126
Union, co., N.C.	44,670	B5	186
Union, co., Ohio	22,853	B3	156
Union, co., Oreg.	18,180	B8	96
Union, co., Pa.	25,646	C4	214
Union, co., S.C.	30,015	B5	188
Union, co., S.Dak.	10,197	E9	158
Union, co., Tenn.	8,498	B8	190
Union, par., La.	17,624	B3	180
Union, see Tokelau, isl., Pac.O.			
Union, lake, N.J.		E2	210
Union, riv., Maine		D4	204
Union Bay, B.C., Can.	500	F10	52
Union Beach, Monmouth, N.J.	5,862	C4	210
Union Bleachery, Greenville, S.C.	600	*B4	188
Union Bridge, Carroll, Md.	833	A5	182
Union Center, Juneau, Wis.	252	E3	160
Union Church, Jefferson, Miss.	125	D2	184
Union City, Alameda, Calif.	6,618	*B5	94
Union City, Fulton, Ga.	2,118	B4	176
		C2	
Union City, Randolph, Ind.	4,047	B5	140
Union City, Branch, Mich.	1,669	G6	146
Union City, Hudson, N.J.	52,180	B1	210
Union City, Darke, Ohio	1,657	B2	156
Union City, Erie, Pa.	3,819	B2	214
Union City, Obion, Tenn.	8,837	B2	190
Union Creek, Jackson, Oreg.	25	E4	96
Uniondale, Wells, Ind.	311	B4	140
Uniondale, Nassau, N.Y.	20,041	*E8	212
Unión de Reyes, Cuba	5,351	A4	232
Unión de Tula, Mex.	4,807	D5	224
Union Flat, creek, Wash.		C9	98
Union Furnace, Hocking, Ohio	875	C4	156
Union Gap, Douglas, Oreg.	200	*D3	96
Union Gap, Yakima, Wash.	2,100	C6	98
Union Grove, Racine, Wis.	1,970	F1	160
		F5	
Union Hall, Franklin, Va.	50	C5	192
Unionhill, Independence, Ark.	25	B5	170
Union Hill, Davidson, Tenn.	100	B5	190
Union Lake, Oakland, Mich.	2,000	*G8	146
Union Mill, Hawaii, Haw.	250	*C6	86
Union Mills, La Porte, Ind.	450	A3	140
Union Mills, Carroll, Md.	60	A5	182
Union Mills, Rutherford, N.C.	120	B4	186
Union of South Africa, see South Africa			
Union of Soviet Socialist Republics, country, Eur., Asia	208,826,000	C9	266
		D10	340
			329
Union Pier, Berrien, Mich.	700	H5	146
Union Point, Man., Can.	100	F4	60
Union Point, Greene, Ga.	1,615	C3	176
Union Springs, Bullock, Ala.	3,704	C4	168
Union Springs, Cayuga, N.Y.	1,066	C5	212
Union Star, Breckinridge, Ky.	36	C4	178
Union Star, De Kalb, Mo.	392	B3	150
Uniontown, Perry, Ala.	1,993	C2	168
Uniontown, Bourbon, Kans.	211	E9	144
Uniontown, Union, Ky.	1,255	C3	178
Uniontown, Perry, Mo.	125	D8	150
Uniontown, Stark, Ohio	1,668	B5	156
Uniontown, Fayette, Pa.	17,942	D2	214
Uniontown (Tharptown), Northumberland, Pa.	1,085	*C5	214
Uniontown, Whitman, Wash.	242	C9	98
Union Village, Providence, R.I.		B2	216
Union Village, Orange and Windsor, Vt.	75	D4	218
Unionville, Ont., Can.	570	Q21	64
		R22	
Unionville, Hartford, Conn.	2,246	B4	202
Unionville, Tift, Ga.	1,607	*E3	176

Unionville, Bibb, Ga. 1,000 *D3 176
Unionville, Monroe, Ind. 100 C3 140
Unionville, Appanoose, Iowa 185 D5 142
Unionville, Frederick, Md. 125 B5 182
Unionville, Norfolk, Mass. B5 206
Unionville, Tuscola, Mich. 629 F8 146
Unionville, Putnam, Mo. 1,896 A4 150
Unionville, Lewis and Clark, Mont. 125 *D4 110
Unionville, Orange, N.Y. 511 D7 212
Unionville, Ashtabula, Ohio 480 A6 156
Unionville, Bedford, Tenn. 100 C5 190
Unionville, Orange, Va. 250 B7 192
United, Westmoreland, Pa. 2,044 C2 214
United Arab Republic, country, Afr., Asia 29,453,000 D9 388
F5 340
United Kingdom of Great Britain & Northern Ireland, country, Eur. 52,029,000 C4 266
273
United States, country, N.A. 179,323,175 77
United States Naval Ammunition Depot, Mineral, Nev. E3 112
Unity, Sask., Can. 1,607 D3 58
Unity, Waldo, Maine 400 D3 204
(983▲)
Unity, Montgomery, Md. 125 B5 182
Unity, Sullivan, N.H. 50 E2 208
(708▲)
Unity, Baker, Oreg. 150 C8 96
Unity, Allegheny, Pa. 900 A4 214
Unity, Clark and Marathon, Wis. 386 D3 160
Unity, dam, Oreg. C8 96
Unity, pond, Maine D3 204
Unity Village, Jackson, Mo. 153 *C3 150
Unityville, McCook, S.Dak. 66 D8 158
Universal, Vermillion, Ind. 424 C2 140
Universal, Allegheny, Pa. (part of Penn Hills) A4 214
C2
Universales, mts., Sp. B6 298
University, Lafayette, Miss. 3,597 A3 184
University City, St. Louis, Mo. 51,249 A8 150
C7
University Gardens, Prince Georges, Md. 1,000 *C6 182
University Heights, Johnson, Iowa 841 C6 142
University Heights, Cuyahoga, Ohio 16,641 B1 156
University Hills, Montgomery, Md. 1,700 *C5 182
University Park, Mahaska, Iowa 569 C5 142
University Park, Prince Georges, Md. 3,098 *C6 182
University Park, Dona Ana, N.Mex. 2,400 *F4 126
University Park, Dallas, Tex. 23,202 B8 130
Unsan, Kor. F12 348
Unst, isl., Scot. A12 272
Unstrut, riv., Ger. C4 286
Unterwalden (Unterwald), canton, Switz. 43,400 B4 312
Unuk, riv., B.C., Can. B7 52
Unuwhao, mtn., N.Z. A4 437
Unwin, Sask., Can. 60 D3 58
Ünye, Tur. 8,532 A7 307
Unzha, riv., Sov.Un. A2 336
Uonám, Ven. D7 240
Uondo, Eth. D4 398
Uorra Ilu, Eth. C4 398
Upalco, Duchesne, Utah 10 C5 114
Upata, Ven. 6,999 B7 240
Upemba, lake, Con.L. D4 414
Upernavik, Grnld. 419 P28 290
Upham, McKenry, N.Dak. 333 B5 154
Upheim, Nor. F2 291
Upia, riv., Col. C2 244
Upington, U.S.Afr. 13,303 E4 420
Upland, San Bernardino, Calif. 15,918 C6 94
E5
Upland, Grant, Ind. 1,999 B4 140
Upland, Franklin, Nebr. 237 D7 152
Upland, Delaware, Pa. 4,081 *D6 214
Uplands Park, St. Louis, Mo. 549 *C7 150
Upolu, isl., Samoa E5 436
Upolu, pt., Haw. C6 86
Upper, bay, N.J. B1 210
Upper Ammonoosuc, riv., N.H. B4 208
Upper Anton Chico, Guadalupe, N.Mex. 120 C5 126
Upper Arlington, Franklin, Ohio 28,486 B3 156
C1
Upper Arrow, lake, B.C., Can. E14 52
Upper Blackville, N.B., Can. 215 C4 70
Upperco, Baltimore, Md. 150 A6 182
Upper Darby, Delaware, Pa. 44,000 A6 214
D6
Upper Des Lacs, lake, N.Dak. B3 154
Upper Egypt, reg., Eg., U.A.R. 9,289,812 *B3 395
Upper Erne, lake, N.Ire. G4 273
Upper Fairmount, Somerset, Md. 550 D8 182
Upper Falls, Baltimore, Md. 160 B7 182
Upper Frenchville, Aroostook, Maine 200 A4 204
Upper Gagetown, N.B., Can. 225 D3 70
Upper Gloucester, Cumberland, Maine 150 D5 204
E2
Upper Hill, Somerset, Md. 200 D8 182
Upper Humber, riv., Newf., Can. F7 72
Upper Hutt, N.Z. 12,226 D5 437
Upper Indian, lake, Newf., Can. F7 72
Upper Iowa, riv., Iowa A6 142
Upper Island Cove, Newf., Can. 800 G9 72
Upper Kapuas, mts., Indon. D4 358
Upper Kent, N.B., Can. 95 C2 70
Upper Klamath, lake, Oreg. E4 96
Upper Lake, Lake, Calif. 400 C2 94
Upper Marlboro, Prince Georges, Md. 673 C6 182
Upper Musquodoboit, N.S., Can. 500 D7 70
Upper Nile, prov., Sud. 888,611 D3 398
Upper Nyack, Rockland, N.Y. 1,833 *D7 212
Upper Red, lake, Minn. C4 148
Upper Saddle River, Bergen, N.J. 3,570 A4 210
Upper Sandusky, Wyandot, Ohio 4,941 B3 156
Upper San Fernando, res., Calif. B4 94
Upper Tract, Pendleton, W.Va. 117 C5 194
Upper Tygart, Carter, Ky. B7 178
Upperville, Fauquier, Va. 350 B7 192
Upper Volta, country, Afr. 4,000,000 E6 388
409
Upper Wilson, pond, Maine C3 204
Uppland, prov., Swe. 849,190 *G7 291
Uppsala, Swe. 70,244 B8 292
Uppsala, co., Swe. 161,383 A8 292
Upsala, Ont., Can. 205 R23 64
Upsala, Morrison, Minn. 356 F4 148
Upsalquitch, N.B., Can. 85 B3 70
Upsalquitch, riv., N.B., Can. B3 70
Upshur, co., Tex. 19,793 C8 130
Upshur, co., W.Va. 18,292 C4 194
Upson, Iron, Wis. 150 B3 160
Upson, co., Ga. 23,800 D2 176
Uptergrove, Ont., Can. 90 P21 64
Upton, Que., Can. 754 S12 66
Upton, Hardin, Ky. 547 C5 178
Upton, Oxford, Maine 30 D1 204
(35▲)
Upton, Worcester, Mass. 1,000 B4 206
(3,127▲) D1
Upton, Summit, Utah C4 114
Upton, Weston, Wyo. 1,224 B8 116
Upton, co., Tex. 6,239 D4 130
Uracoa, Ven. 994 B7 240
Urakawa, Jap. 15,993 C9 354
Ural, Lincoln, Mont. 5 B1 110
Ural, mts., Sov.Un. B5 336
Ural, riv., Sov.Un. C4 336
Uralsk, Sov.Un. 105,000 B4 336
Urandi, Braz. 1,585 C2 258
Urania, La Salle, La. 1,063 C3 180
Uranium City, Sask., Can. 3,636 B2 58
Uraricoera, riv., Braz. E4 256
Uravan, Montrose, Colo. 1,005 D2 106
Urawa, Jap. G7 354
L15
Urban, Clay, Ky. 300 C7 178
Urbana, Union, Ark. 400 D4 170
Urbana, Champaign, Ill. 27,294 C5 138
Urbana, Wabash, Ind. 350 B4 140
Urbana, Benton, Iowa 544 B6 142
Urbana, Frederick, Md. 100 B5 182
Urbana, Dallas, Mo. 348 D4 150
Urbana, Champaign, Ohio 10,461 B3 156
Urbancrest, Franklin, Ohio 1,029 C1 156
Urbandale, Polk, Iowa 5,821 A7 142
C4
Urbanette, Carroll, Ark. 60 *A3 170
Urbank, Otter Tail, Minn. 177 E3 148
Urbanna, Middlesex, Va. 512 C8 192
Urbino, It. 6,400 D4 302
Urbo, Newton, Miss. C3 184
Urcos, Peru 2,096 C3 245
Urdhir, Ice. L20 290
Urdzhar, Sov.Un. 3,500 C10 336
Ures, Mex. 3,456 B3 224
Urfa, Tur. 48,013 C8 307
Urfa, prov., Tur. 347,712 *C8 307
Urga, see Ulan Bator, Mong.
Urga, Sov.Un. D5 336
Urgun, Afg. 5,000 C5 374
Uri, canton, Switz. 29,900 B4 312
Uriah, Monroe, Ala. 800 D2 168
Uriba, Col. 1,101 A2 244
Urica, Ven. B6 240
Urich, Henry, Mo. 408 C4 150
Uriondo, Bol. 860 D2 246
Urique, Mex. 256 B4 224
Urirantariña, Ven. D7 240
Urk, Neth. 5,067 B4 282
Urmia, salt lake, Iran B1 379
Urne, Buffalo, Wis. 100 D2 160
Urrao, Col. 5,958 B1 244
Ursatyevskaya, Sov.Un. D7 336
Ursine, Lincoln, Nev. 60 F7 112
Urton Kuytun, Mong. B9 346
Uruapan, Mex. 31,409 D5 225
L13
Urubamba, Peru 3,481 C3 245
Urubamba, riv., Peru C3 245
Uruçui, Braz. 1,764 B2 258
Urucuia, riv., Braz. D1 258
Uruguai, riv., Braz. K6 257
Uruguaiana, Braz. 32,639 K5 257
Uruguay, country, S.A. 2,700,000 B4 252
G6 236
Uruguay, riv., Arg., Ur. B4 252
Urukthapel, isl., Palau A6 436
Urumchi, China 140,700 C5 346
Urungu, riv., China B5 346
Urup, isl., Sov.Un. E17 329
Uryupinsk, Sov.Un. 29,900 B2 336
Urzhum, Sov.Un. 11,200 A3 336
Urziceni, Rom. 6,061 B4 321
Uşak, Tur. 23,366 B3 307
Uşak, prov., Tur. 166,271 *B3 307
Usakos, S.W.Afr. 2,355 D3 420
Usalgin, Sov.Un. D15 329
'Usfān, Sau.Ar. C2 383
'Ushayrah, Sau.Ar. C3 383
Usher, Levy, Fla. 70 B8 174
Ushi, pt., Tinian B7 436
Ush-Tobe, Sov.Un. 16,300 C9 336
Ushturinan Kuh, mtn., Iran C2 379
Ushuaia, Arg. 1,950 H4 251
Usk, B.C., Can. 100 C8 52
Usk, Pend Oreille, Wash. 300 A9 98
Üsküdar, Tur. (pop. inc. in İstanbul) 69,671 A3 307
F13
Usman, Sov.Un. 23,800 F12 332
Usolye-Sibirskoye, Sov.Un. 33,500 D12 329
Uspallata, pass, Arg. B1 252
Usquepaugh, Washington, R.I. 110 C2 216
Ussel, Fr. 6,146 E5 278
Ussuri, riv., Sov.Un. E15 329
Ust-Aldal, Sov.Un. C14 329
Ust-Bolsheretsk, Sov.Un. D17 329
Ústecký, co., Czech. 675,907 *A2 324
Uster, Switz. 13,300 A4 312
Ustica, isl., It. F4 302
Ustick, Ada, Idaho 125 F2 108
Ústí nad Labem, Czech. 64,798 A2 324
Ústí nad Orlici, Czech. 10,399 B3 324
Ust-Ishim, Sov.Un. A8 336
Ustka, Pol. 2,807 A3 325
Ust-Kamchatsk, Sov.Un. 800 D18 329
Ust-Kamenogorsk, Sov.Un. 117,000 C10 336
Ust'Karsk, Sov.Un. D13 329
Ust-Kozhva, Sov.Un. C7 328
Ust-Kulom, Sov.Un. A4 336
Ust-Kut, Sov.Un. 21,900 D12 329
Ust-Maya, Sov.Un. 2,300 C15 329
Ust-Nem, Sov.Un. A5 336
Ust-Olenek, Sov.Un. B13 329
Ust-Port, Sov.Un. C10 328
Ust-Srednikan, Sov.Un. 800 C17 329
Ust-Tsilma, Sov.Un. 7,900 C7 328
Ust-Tym, Sov.Un. A9 336
Ust-Usa, Sov.Un. 2,500 C7 328
Ustyurt, plat., Sov.Un. D4 336
Ustyuzhna, Sov.Un. 12,600 C11 332
Usulután, Sal. 9,481 D3 228
Usumbura, Ruanda-Urundi 47,327 C4 414
Utah, co., Utah 106,991 C4 114
Utah, state, U.S. 890,627 D4 77
114
Utah, lake, Utah C4 114
Utajarvi, Fin. D12 290
Ute, Monona, Iowa 511 B2 142
Ute, creek, N.Mex. B7 126
Utete, Tan. 970 D6 414
Uthai-Thani, prov., Thai. 104,852 *D3 362
Utholmen, isl., Swe. D9 292
Utica, La Salle, Ill. 1,014 B4 138
Utica, Clark, Ind. 800 D4 140
Utica, Ness, Kans. 322 D3 144
Utica, Daviess, Ky. 300 C3 178
Utica, Macomb, Mich. 1,454 G8 146
Utica, Winona, Minn. 218 H7 148
Utica, Hinds, Miss. 764 C2 184
Utica, Livingston, Mo. 450 B4 150
Utica, Judith Basin, Mont. 60 D6 110
Utica, Seward, Nebr. 564 D8 152
Utica, Oneida, N.Y. 100,410 B6 212
(*160,400)
Utica, Licking, Ohio 1,854 B4 156
Utica, Bryan, Okla. 100 E7 128
Utica (Lonsdale Mill), Oconee, S.C. 1,294 B3 188
Utica, Yankton, S.Dak. 70 E8 158
Utica Heights, Macomb, Mich. 2,700 *G8 146
Utica Institute, Copiah, Miss. 500 C2 184
Utiel, Sp. 10,076 C6 298
Utik, lake, Man., Can. C5 60
Utikuma, lake, Alta., Can. C5 54
Utirik, atoll, Marshall A4 437
Utkholok, Sov.Un. D17 329
Utlängan, isl., Swe. E6 292
Utö, isl., Swe. C9 292
Utopia, Uvalde, Tex. 500 E6 130
Utopia, lake, N.B., Can. D3 70
Utrecht, Neth. 241,635 B4 282
Utrecht, prov., Neth. 608,972 B4 282
Utrera, Sp. 29,975 D4 298
Utsjoki, Fin. B12 290
Utsunomiya, Jap. 227,153 F7 354
Uttaradit, Thai. 25,000 C4 362
Uttaradit, prov., Thai. 170,844 *C4 362
Uttar Pradesh, state, India 63,215,742 C3 366
Utterson, Ont., Can. 290 O21 64
Utting, Yuma, Ariz. 20 E2 124
Utvalnäs, Swe. A8 292
Uusikaupunki, Fin. 4,276 F9 291
Uusimaa, dept., Fin. 767,000 *F11 291
Uusi Värtsilä, Fin. E14 290
Uvalda, Montgomery, Ga. 589 D4 176
Uvalde, Uvalde, Tex. 10,293 E6 130
Uvalde, co., Tex. 16,814 E6 130
Úvaly, Czech. 4,706 *A2 324
Uvat, Sov.Un. A7 336
Uvinza, Tan. 1,880 D5 414
Uvria, Con.L. C4 414
Uwajima, Jap. 66,154 H4 354
Uwaynāt, mtn., Sud. A2 398
Uxbridge, Ont., Can. 2,065 P21 64
Uxbridge, Eng. 59,600 J12 273
Uxbridge, Worcester, Mass. 3,377 B4 206
(7,789▲)
Uxmal, ruins, Mex. C8 225
Uyak, Alsk. 11 D6 84
Uyega, Sov.Un. C16 329
Uyuni, Bol. 6,968 D1 246
Uyuni, salt flat, Bol. D1 246
Uzbek S.S.R., Sov.Un. 8,113,000 E8 328
Uzes, Fr. 4,390 E6 278
Uzh, riv., Sov.Un. G7 332
Uzhgorod, Sov.Un. 47,000 H4 332
Uzhur, Sov.Un. A11 336
Uzlovaya, Sov.Un. 54,000 F12 332
Uzunköprü, Tur. 15,455 A2 307

V

Vaal, riv., U.S.Afr. E5 420
Vaals, Neth. 5,956 D4 282
Vaasa, Fin. 35,157 E9 290
Vaasa, dept., Fin. 630,800 *E9 290
Vác, Hung. 23,000 B4 320
Vaca, key, Fla. G9 174
Vacaville, Solano, Calif. 10,898 C2 94
Vacherie, St. James, La. 950 C6 180
Vader, Lewis, Wash. 380 C4 98
Väderöfjorden, fjord, Swe. C2 292
Vadis, Lewis, W.Va. 125 B4 194
Vadnais Heights, Ramsey, Minn. 2,459 *F5 148
Vado, Dona Ana, N.Mex. 190 F4 126
Vadsö, Nor. 2,622 A13 290
Vadstena, Swe. 4,235 C5 292
Vaduz, Liech. 2,735 A5 312
Vågan, Nor. B6 290
Vagay, Sov.Un. A7 336
Vaggeryo, Swe. D5 292
Vågsfjord, fjord, Nor. B7 290
Váh, riv., Czech. B3 324
Vaiden, Carroll, Miss. 475 B3 184
Vaigai, riv., India G3 366
Vaigalu, Samoa 802 E5 436
Vail, Crawford, Iowa 473 B2 142
Vail Homes (Shrewsbury Township), Monmouth, N.J. 1,204 *C4 210
Vails, Warren, N.J. 50 B2 210
Väja, Swe. E7 290
Vakfikebir (Büyükliman), Tur. 1,394 A8 307
Vakh, riv., Sov.Un. A9 336
Valais (Wallis), canton, Switz. 29,900 B3 312
Valašské Meziříčí, Czech. 10,636 B4 324
Valatie, Columbia, N.Y. 1,237 C8 212
Val Barrette, Que., Can. 568 R9 66
Vålbergsrös, mtn., Swe. A4 292
Valcartier, Que., Can. 775 R13 66
R15
Valcartier Village, Que., Can. 785 R15 66
Valcheta, Arg. F4 251
Valcourt, Que., Can. 753 S12 66
Val David, Que., Can. 1,016 R10 66
Valday, Sov.Un. 14,400 D9 332
Valday, hills, Sov.Un. D9 332
Valdemarsvik, Swe. 3,366 C7 292
Valdemorillo, Sp. 1,541 *B4 298
Valdepeñas, Sp. 26,000 C5 298
Valders, Manitowoc, Wis. 622 B6 160
D6
Valdes, isl., B.C., Can. B14 52
Valdés, pen., Arg. F5 251
Val des Bois, Que., Can. 200 S9 66
Valdese, Burke, N.C. 2,941 B4 186
Valdez, Alsk. 555 C7 84
G11
Valdez, Las Animas, Colo. 400 E6 106
Valdilecha, Sp. 1,547 *B5 298
Valdivia, Chile 45,128 C1 252
Valdivia, Col. 1,169 B1 244
Valdivia, prov., Chile 232,647 E3 251
Valdosta, Lowndes, Ga. 30,652 F3 176
Vale, Malheur, Oreg. 1,491 D9 96
Vale, Butte, S.Dak. 108 C2 158
Vale, Carroll, Tenn. 125 B3 190
Valemount, B.C., Can. D13 52
Valença, Braz. 11,492 C3 258
Valença, Braz. E2 258
Valença, Port. 2,825 B2 298
Valença do Piauí, Braz. 1,886 B2 258
Valence [-sur-Rhône], Fr. 41,470 E6 278
Valencia, Shawnee, Kans. 10 C8 144
Valencia, Sp. 15,415 C3 298
Valencia, Sp. 550,969 C6 298
(*660,000)
Valencia, Ven. A2 240
Valencia, Ven. 118,000 A4 240
Valencia, co., N.Mex. 39,085 D2 126
Valencia, prov., Sp. 1,344,365 *C3 298
Valencia, reg., Sp. 2,309,254 C6 298
Valencia, isl., Ire. J2 273
Valenciennes, Fr. 43,434 B5 278
Vălenii [de Munte], Rom. 5,472 B4 321
Valentigney, Fr. 5,723 D7 278
Valentine, Pulaski, Ark. C4 170
D7
Valentine, Mohave, Ariz. 50 C2 124
Valentine, Lagrange, Ind. 80 A4 140
Valentine, La Fourche, La. C6 180
Valentine, Fergus, Mont. 6 C8 110
Valentine, Cherry, Nebr. 2,875 B5 152
Valera, Ven. 20,529 B3 240
Valeria, Jasper, Iowa 76 *C4 142
Valhalla, Westchester, N.Y. 3,000 D2 212
D8
Valhermoso Springs, Morgan, Ala. 400 A3 168
Valier, Franklin, Ill. 649 E4 138
Valier, Pondera, Mont. 724 B4 110
Valjevo, Yugo. 17,977 B4 316
Valka, Sov.Un. 6,600 D6 332
Valkaria, Brevard, Fla. 150 D10 174
Valkeakoski, Fin. 12,321 F11 291
Valkenswaard, Neth. 11,071 C4 282
Valki, Sov.Un. 18,000 H10 332
Valladolid, Mex. 8,168 C8 225
Valladolid, Sp. 119,499 B4 298
Valladolid, prov., Sp. 348,185 *B4 298
Vallauris, Fr. 4,337 F7 278
Vall de Uxó, Sp. 9,630 C6 298
Valle, Nor. G2 291
Vallecas (part of Madrid), Sp. 5,161 B5 298
Vallecito, La Plata, Colo. E3 106
Vallecito, Mex. D5 225
Vallecito, res., Colo. E3 106
Vallecitos, Rio Arriba, N.Mex. 250 B4 126
Valle d'Aosta, reg., It. 99,000 *C1 302
Valle de Bravo, Mex. 4,459 L13 225
Valle de la Pascua, Ven. 12,704 B5 240
Valle del Cauca, dept., Col. 1,396,630 C1 244
Valle de Santiago, Mex. 15,644 K13 225
Valledupar, Col. 9,011 A2 244
Vallée-Jonction, Que., Can. 1,340 R14 66
Valle Grande, Bol. 5,094 C2 246
G6 126
Valle Grande, mts., N.Mex.
Vallejo, Solano, Calif. 60,877 C2 94
Vallenar, Chile 9,677 A1 252
Valles Mines, Jefferson, Mo. 225 C7 150
Valley, Yazoo, Miss. 60 C2 184
Valley, Douglas, Nebr. 1,452 C9 152
D2
Valley, Avery, N.C. A3 186
Valley, Stevens, Wash. 250 A9 98
Valley, Park, Wyo. 15 B3 116
Valley, co., Idaho 3,663 E3 108
Valley, co., Mont. 17,080 B10 110
Valley, co., Nebr. 6,590 C6 152
Valley, creek, Ala. E4 168
Valley, riv., Man., Can. E2 60
Valley Bend, Randolph, W.Va. 350 C5 194
Valley Brook, Oklahoma, Okla. 1,378 *C6 128

Valley Center, Sedgwick, Kans. 2,570 A5 144
E6
Valley Center, Highland, Va. 30 B5 192
Valley Centre, Sask., Can. 110 E4 58
Valley City, Barnes, N.Dak. 7,809 D7 154
Valley Creek, Claiborne, Tenn. 100 B8 190
Valley Falls, Jefferson, Kans. 1,193 C8 144
Valley Falls, Lake, Oreg. E6 96
Valley Falls, Providence, R.I. B3 216
Valley Falls, Spartanburg, S.C. 900 *B5 188
Valley Farms, Pinal, Ariz. 200 F4 124
Valleyfield, Newf., Can. 250 F9 72
Valleyfield, Que., Can. 23,584 S10 66
S15
Valleyford, Spokane, Wash. 100 B9 98
D9
Valley Forge, Chester, Pa. 450 A6 214
C6
Valley Grove, Ohio, W.Va. 548 A4 194
B2
Valley Head, De Kalb, Ala. 424 A4 168
Valley Head, Randolph, W.Va. 800 C4 194
Valley Lee, St.Marys, Md. 300 D6 182
Valley Mills, Marion, Ind. 150 D4 140
Valley Mills, Bosque, Tex. 1,061 D7 130
Valley Park, St.Louis, Mo. 3,452 B7 150
Valley Springs, Boone, Ark. 150 A4 170
Valley Springs, Minnehaha, S.Dak. 472 D9 158
Valley Station, Jefferson, Ky. 10,553 A5 178
B5
Valley Stream, Nassau, N.Y. 38,629 E3 212
Valleyview, Alta., Can. 973 C4 54
Valley View, Kane, Ill. 1,741 *A5 138
Valley View, Madison, Ky. 200 C6 178
Valley View, Cuyahoga, Ohio 1,221 *A5 156
Valley View, Franklin, Ohio 790 *C3 156
Valley View, Schuylkill, Pa. 1,540 C5 214
Valliant, McCurtain, Okla. 477 E8 128
Vallimanca, riv., Arg. C3 252
Vallö, isl., Swe. D7 292
Vallo della Lucania, It. 3,219 E5 302
Vallonia, Jackson, Ind. 500 D3 140
Vallorbe, Switz. 3,896 B2 312
Vallorso, Las Animas, Colo. E6 106
Valls, Sp. 5,000 B7 298
Vallscreek, McDowell, W.Va. 729 D3 194
Val Marie, Sask., Can. 383 F4 58
Valmeyer, Monroe, Ill. 709 E3 138
Valmiera, Sov.Un. 15,200 D5 332
Valmont, Que., Can. 500 R12 66
Valmont, Boulder, Colo. 100 B5 106
Valmontone, It. 4,543 *E4 302
Val Morin, Que., Can. 290 R10 66
Valmy, Humboldt, Nev. 30 C4 112
Valognes, Fr. 3,938 C3 278
Valois, Que., Can. 390 S15 66
Valor, Sask., Can. 65 F4 58
Valparaiso, Sask., Can. 68 D5 58
Valparaíso, Chile 247,212 B1 252
(*353,900)
Valparaiso, Okaloosa, Fla. 5,975 A4 174
Valparaiso, Porter, Ind. 15,227 A2 140
Valparaíso, Mex. 4,428 C5 224
Valparaiso, Saunders, Nebr. 394 C9 152
Valparaíso, prov., Chile 498,254 D3 250
Val Racine, Que., Can. 200 S13 66
Valréas, Fr. E6 278
Valsch, cape, Neth.N.Gui. F9 359
Valsetz, Polk, Oreg. 900 C3 96
Valthjofsstadhir, Ice. L22 290
Valtimo, Fin. E13 290
Value, Rankin, Miss. 300 C2 184
Val Verda, Davis, Utah 600 *C4 114
Valverde, Dom.Rep. 6,600 C9 233
Val Verde, co., Tex. 24,461 D5 130
Valverde del Camino, Sp. 10,350 D3 298
Vama, Rom. 4,580 A3 321
Vamdrup, Den. 2,055 I3 291
Vammala, Fin. F10 291
Vamoosa, Seminole, Okla. 50 *D7 128
Vamori, Pima, Ariz. 127 G4 124
Van, Arkansas, Ark. 10 C5 170
Van, Van Zandt, Tex. 1,103 C8 130
Van, Tur. 17,408 B10 307
Van, prov., Tur. 176,203 *B10 307
Van, Boone, W.Va. 940 D6 194
Van, lake, Tur. B10 307
Vanajanselkä, lake, Fin. F11 291
Van Alstyne, Grayson, Tex. 1,608 C7 130
Vananda, Rosebud, Mont. 125 D10 110
Vanavara, Sov.Un. C12 329
Van Buren, Crawford, Ark. 6,787 B2 170
Van Buren, Grant, Ind. 929 B4 140
Van Buren, Aroostook, Maine 3,589 A5 204
(4,679▲)
Van Buren, Carter, Mo. 575 E7 150
Vanburen, Hancock, Ohio 374 A3 156
Van Buren, co., Ark. 7,228 B4 170
Van Buren, co., Iowa 9,778 D6 142
Van Buren, co., Mich. 48,395 G5 146
Van Buren, co., Tenn. 3,671 C6 190
Van Buskirk, Iron, Wis. 25 B3 160
Vance, Tuscaloosa, Ala. 375 B2 168
Vance, Quitman, Miss. 100 A2 184
Vance, Orangeburg, S.C. 85 E8 188
Vance, co., N.C. 32,002 A7 186
Vanceboro, Washington, Maine 450 C5 204
(389▲)
Vanceboro, Craven, N.C. 806 B8 186
Vanceburg, Lewis, Ky. 1,881 B7 178
Vancleave, Jackson, Miss. 350 E4 184
Vancouver, B.C., Can. 365,844 B14 52
(*665,017) F11
Vancouver, Clark, Wash. 32,464 D4 98
Vancouver, isl., B.C., Can. F9 92
Vandalia, Fayette, Ill. 5,537 E4 138
Vandalia, Cass, Mich. 357 *H6 146
Vandalia, Audrain, Mo. 2,624 B6 150
Vandalia, Valley, Mont. 15 B10 110
Vandalia, Montgomery, Ohio 6,342 C2 156
Vandemere, Pamlico, N.C. 452 B9 186
Vanderbilt, Otsego, Mich. 509 D7 146
Vanderbilt, Fayette, Pa. 826 C2 214
Vanderbilt, Jackson, Tex. 750 E7 130
Vanderburgh, co., Ind. 165,794 D2 140
Vandercook, Jackson, Mich. 4,000 *G7 146
Vandergrift, Westmoreland, Pa. 8,742 C2 214
Vanderhoof, B.C., Can. 1,085 D10 52
Vanderpool, Highland, Va. 25 B5 192
Vandervoort, Polk, Ark. 450 C2 170
Vander Wagen, McKinley, N.Mex. 30 C2 126
Van Deusenville, Berkshire, Mass. 200 B1 206
Vandever, Cumberland, Tenn. C6 190
Van Diemen, cape, Austl. A6 432
Van Diemen, gulf, Austl. A6 432
Vandiver, Shelby, Ala. 700 B3 168
E5
Vanduser, Scott, Mo. 272 E8 150
Vandyke, New Castle, Del. C3 172
Vandyne, Fond du Lac, Wis. 200 B5 160
Vanegas, Mex. 2,246 C5 225
Vänersborg, Swe. 17,338 C3 292
Van Etten, Chemung, N.Y. 507 C5 212
Vang, Nor. F3 291
Vanga, Ken. C6 414
Vangaindrano, Malag. D9 421
Vanguard, Sask., Can. 443 F4 58
Vanguna, isl., Solomon E2 436
Van Hiseville, Ocean, N.J. 110 C4 210
Van Horn, Culberson, Tex. 1,953 D3 130
Van Horne, Benton, Iowa 554 B5 142
Vankarem, Sov.Un. C20 329
Vankleek Hill, Ont., Can. 1,647 026 64
Van Lear, Johnson, Ky. 921 C8 178
Vanleer, Dickson, Tenn. 234 B4 190
Vanlue, Hancock, Ohio 386 B3 156
Van Meter, Dallas, Iowa 385 C4 142
Vanna, Hart, Ga. 152 B3 176
Vännäs, Swe. E8 290
Vanndale, Cross, Ark. 300 B6 170
Vannes, Fr. 28,403 D2 278
Van Norman, Garfield, Mont. 3 C10 110
Vannöy, isl., Nor. A8 290
Vannsjo, lake, Nor. B1 292
Vanoss, Pontotoc, Okla. 100 D7 128
Van Rees, mts., Neth.N.Gui. E9 359
Van Rhynsdorp, U.S.Afr. 1,824 F3 420
Vansant, Buchanan, Va. 850 C2 192
Vansbro, Swe. F6 291
Vanscoy, Sask., Can. 107 E4 58
Vantage, Sask., Can. 60 F4 58
Vantage, Kittitas, Wash. 225 C7 98
Van Tassell, Niobrara, Wyo. 15 D8 116
Vanua Levu, isl., Fiji E7 436
Vanua Mbalavu, isl., Fiji E7 436
Vanves, Fr. 21,743 I10 278
Van Vleck, Matagorda, Tex. 900 G7 130
Van Vleet, Chickasaw, Miss. 300 B4 184
Van Wert, Polk, Ga. 311 C1 176
Van Wert, Decatur, Iowa 253 D4 142
Van Wert, Van Wert, Ohio 11,323 B2 156
Van Wert, co., Ohio 28,840 B2 156
Van Winkle, B.C., Can. D12 52
Van Winkle, Hinds, Miss. 450 C2 184
Van Wyck, Lancaster, S.C. 300 B7 188
Van Wyksvlei, U.S.Afr. 1,318 F4 420
Van Yen, Viet. 10,000 B5 362
Vanylven, Nor. E1 291
Van Zandt, co., Tex. 19,091 C8 130
Var, dept., Fr. 413,012 *F7 278
Vara, Swe. 2,706 C3 292
Varangerfjord, fjord, Nor. B14 290
Varano, lake, It. E5 302
Varaždin, Yugo. 19,341 A3 316
Varazze, It. 9,200 C2 302
Varberg, Swe. 13,693 D3 292
Vardaman, Calhoun, Miss. 637 B3 184
Vardar, riv., Yugo. D5 316
Varde, Den. 8,780 I3 291
Vardö, Nor. 3,316 A13 290
Varel, Ger. 12,600 B3 286
Varella, cape, Viet. D6 362
Varennes, Que., Can. 2,047 S11 66
S16
Vareš, Yugo. 2,966 B4 316
Varese, It. 56,500 C2 302
Varese, prov., It. 502,100 *C2 302
Varf Mandra, mtn., Rom. B2 321
Vårgårda, Swe. 8,074 C3 292
Varginha, Braz. 13,147 E1 258
Varilla, Chile B3 250
Varina, Pocahontas, Iowa 162 B3 142
Varina, Henrico, Va. 100 B9 192
Varkaus, Fin. 18,061 E12 290
Värmdölandet, isl., Swe. B9 292
Värmeln, lake, Swe. B4 292
Värmland, co., Swe. 288,580 B3 292
Värmland, prov., Swe. 331,311 *G5 291
Varna, Bul. 119,769 B3 317
Varna, Ont., Can. 110 Q19 64
Varna, prov., Bul. *B3 317
Varnado, Washington, La. 331 D6 180
Värnamo, Swe. 12,254 D5 292
Varnell, Whitfield, Ga. 400 B2 176
Varnenski, prov., Bul. *B3 317
Varney, Ont., Can. 75 P20 64
Varney, Madison, Mont. E5 110
Varnsdorf, Czech. 15,356 A2 324
Varnville, Hampton, S.C. 1,461 F6 188
Várpalota, Hung. B3 320
Vars, Ont., Can. 315 *Q26 64
Vartoffa, Swe. C4 292
Varysburg, Wyoming, N.Y. 300 C3 212
Vascos, Mex. B3 224
Vashon, King, Wash. 850 B4 98
D2
Vashon, isl., Wash. D2 98
Vashon, pt., Wash. D2 98
Vashon Heights, King, Wash. 350 *B4 98
Vasilkov, Sov.Un. 41,300 G8 332
Vaslui, Rom. 14,850 A4 321
Vasper, Campbell, Tenn. 300 B7 190
Vasquez, Grand, Colo. C5 106
Vass, Moore, N.C. 767 B6 186
Vassalborough, Kennebec, Maine 60 *D3 204
(2,446▲)
Vassar, Man., Can. 115 F5 60
Vassar, Tuscola, Mich. 2,680 F8 146
Vassman, mtn., Swe. A5 292
Vasterås, Swe. 68,197 B7 292
Västerbotten, co., Swe. 238,031 *D6 290
Västerbotten, prov., Swe. 157,319 *D9 290
Västerdalälven, riv., Swe. F5 291
Västergötland, reg., Swe. 984,939 *G5 291
Västernorrland, co., Swe. 289,365 B7 292
Västersjön, lake, Swe. E4 292
Västervik, Swe. 16,800 D7 292
Västmanland, co., Swe. 218,393 *G7 291
Västmanland, prov., Swe. 247,640 *G6 291
Vasto, It. 12,600 D5 302
Vasyugan, riv., Sov.Un. A9 336
Vaternish, pt., Scot. D5 272
Vathí, Grc. 5,052 C6 306
Vatican City, country, Eur. 1,000 *D6 266
Vaticanto, cape, It. F5 302
Vatnajökull, glacier, Ice. L21 290
Vatneyri, Ice. L18 290
Vatomandry, Malag. 2,323 C9 421
Vatra-Dornei, Rom. 10,822 A3 321
Vättern, lake, Swe. C5 292
Vatu Leile, isl., Fiji E6 436
Vatyna, Sov.Un. C19 329
Vaucluse, Aiken, S.C. 490 D5 188
Vaucluse, dept., Fr. 268,318 *F6 278
Vaud (Waadt), canton, Switz. 397,600 B2 312
Vaudreuil, Que., Can. 778 S10 66
S15
Vaudreuil, co., Que., Can. 22,625 S10 66
S15
Vaughan, Yazoo, Miss. 400 C2 184
Vaughan, Nicholas, W.Va. 140 C7 194
Vaughn, Benton, Ark. 75 A2 170
Vaughn, Cascade, Mont. 135 C5 110
Vaughn, Guadalupe, N.Mex. 1,170 D5 126
Vaughn, Lane, Oreg. 180 C3 96
Vaughn, Pierce, Wash. 300 D2 98
Vaughns Gap, Davidson, Tenn. 35 E7 190
Vaughnsville, Putnam, Ohio 312 B2 156
Vaupés, comisaría, Col. 9,750 C2 244
Vaupes, riv., Col. C2 244
Vauxhall, Alta., Can. 713 E6 54
Vavoua, I.C. 600 E3 408
Vawn, Sask., Can. 74 D3 58
Vaxholm, Swe. 3,683 B9 292
Växjö, Swe. 22,142 E5 292
Vay, Bonner, Idaho 10 *A2 108
Vaygach, isl., Sov.Un. B7 328
Vayland, Hand, S.Dak. 14 C7 158
Vazovgrad, Bul. 5,142 B2 317
Veadeiros, plat., Braz. D1 258
Veazie, Penobscot, Maine 1,354 D4 204
Veberöd, Swe. 2,006 F4 292
Veblen, Marshall, S.Dak. 437 B8 158
Vecsés, Hung. 13,805 B4 320
Vedea, riv., Rom. B3 321
Vedia, Arg. 3,676 B3 252
Veedersburg, Fountain, Ind. 1,762 B2 140
Veendam, Neth. 11,165 A5 282
Vega, Oldham, Tex. 658 B4 130
Vega, isl., Nor. D4 290
Vegas Heights, Clark, Nev. 1,200 *G6 112
Vegreville, Alta., Can. 2,574 D6 54
Veguita, Socorro, N.Mex. 170 D4 126
Veinticinco de Mayo, Arg. B2 252
Veinticinco de Mayo, Arg. C2 252
Veinticinco de Mayo, Arg. 9,063 C3 252
Veisali, Solomon E2 436
Vejer, Sp. 10,110 D4 298
Vejle, Den. 30,447 I3 291
Vejle, co., Den. 207,881 *I3 291
Vejprty, Czech. 5,476 A1 324
Velarde, Rio Arriba, N.Mex. 50 B5 126
Velas, cape, C.R. E4 228
Velda, St. Louis, Mo. 524 *C7 150
Velda Village Hills, St. Louis, Mo. 1,365 *C7 150
Velebit, mts., Yugo. B2 316
Velestínon, Grc. 2,984 B4 306
Vélez, Col. 4,305 B2 244
Vélez-Blanco, Sp. 2,501 D5 298
Vélez-Málaga, Sp. 11,835 D4 298
Vélez-Rubio, Sp. 4,484 D5 298
Velhas, riv., Braz. D2 258
Velika, riv., Yugo. D5 316
Velikaya, riv., Sov.Un. D7 332
Velikiye, Luki, Sov.Un. 59,000 D8 332
Velikiy Ustyug, Sov.Un. 41,300 A3 336
Velingara, Sen. D2 408
Velingrad, Bul. 18,240 B1 317
Velizh, Sov.Un. 24,500 E8 332
Velké Meziříčí, Czech. 6,217 B3 324
Vella, gulf, Solomon E1 436
Vella Lavella, isl., Solomon E1 436
Velletri, It. 16,200 E4 302
Vellinge, Swe. 3,440 F4 292
Vellore, India 106,024 F3 366
Velma, Stephens, Okla. 700 D6 128
Velpen, Pike, Ind. 185 D2 140
Velsen, Neth. 1,232 B3 282
Velsk, Sov.Un. 14,300 C6 328
Veltrusy, Czech. 1,883 *A2 324
Velva, McHenry, N.Dak. 1,330 B5 154
Velvary, Czech. 2,169 *A2 324
Ven, isl., Swe. F3 292
Venado, Mex. 2,531 C5 225
Venado Tuerto, Arg. 15,947 B3 252
Venango, Perkins, Nebr. 227 D3 152
Venango, co., Pa. 65,295 B2 214
Venator, Harney, Oreg. D8 96
Venceslau Brás, Braz. E1 258
Vendée, dept., Fr. 395,641 *D3 278
Vendée, hills, Fr. D3 278
Vendelso, Swe. B9 292
Vendôme, Fr. 9,111 D4 278
Vendor, Newton, Ark. 50 *B3 170
Vendrell, Sp. 4,217 B7 298
Veneta, Lane, Oreg. 750 C3 96
Venetia (Veneto), reg., It. 3,910,000 C3 302
Venetian Alps, mts., It. B4 302
Venetian Village, Lake, Ill. 2,084 *A5 138
Venetie, Alsk. 81 B7 84
Venev, Sov.Un. 13,800 E12 332
Venezia (Venice), It. 327,700 C4 302
Venezia, prov., It. 746,500 *C4 302
Venezuela, country, S.A. 6,512,000 C5 236
240
Venezuela, gulf, Ven. A3 240
Veniaminof, vol., Alsk. D6 84
Venice, Alta., Can. 10 C6 54
Venice, Sarasota, Fla. 3,444 D8 174
Venice, Madison, Ill. 5,380 E3 138
Venice, see Venezia, It.
Venice, Plaquemines, La. 500 E6 180
Venice, Douglas, Nebr. 20 D2 152
Venice, Sevier, Utah 250 E3 114
Venice, gulf, It. C4 302
Vénissieux, Fr. 20,374 E6 278
Venlo, Neth. 48,562 C5 282
Venn, Sask., Can. 100 E5 58
Vennachar, Ont., Can. 70 023 64
Venta, riv., Sov.Un. D3 332
Ventimiglia, It. 12,200 D1 302
Ventnor, Ont., Can. 200 P25 64
Ventnor, Eng. 6,800 K11 273
Ventnor (Ventnor City), Atlantic, N.J. 8,688 E4 210
Ventnor City, see Ventnor, N.J.
Venton, Somerset, Md. 60 D8 182
Ventry, Ire. I2 273
Ventspils, Sov.Un. 26,200 D3 332
Ventuari, riv., Ven. D5 240
Ventura, Ventura, Calif. 29,114 E4 94
Ventura, Cerro Gordo, Iowa 280 A4 142
Ventura, co., Calif. 199,138 E4 94
Venturia, McIntosh, N.Dak. 148 E6 154
Venus, Madison, Ark. B3 170
Venus, Highlands, Fla. 250 D9 174
Venus, Knox, Nebr. 10 B7 152
Venus, McDowell, W.Va. 800 *D3 194
Venustiano Carranza, Mex. 6,440 D7 225
Vera, Arg. 7,667 A3 252
Vera, Washington, Okla. 125 B8 128
Vera, Sp. 4,688 D6 298
Verá, lake, Par. E4 247
Vera Cruz, Wells, Ind. 176 B4 140
Veracruz, Mex. 101,469 D6 225
L15
Veracruz, state, Mex. 2,040,231 C6 225
Veradale, Spokane, Wash. 2,000 B9 98
Veraval, India 40,378 D2 366
Verbena, Chilton, Ala. 700 C3 168
Verboort, Washington, Oreg. 100 *B3 96
Vercelli, It. 44,700 C2 302
Vercelli, prov., It. 390,900 *C2 302
Verchères, Que., Can. 1,412 S11 66
Verchères, co., Que., Can. 20,908 S11 66
Verda, Harlan, Ky. 950 D7 178
Verda, Grant, La. 57 C3 180
Verde, pt., Newf., Can. G8 72
Verde, riv., Ariz. D4 124
Verde, riv., Mex. K14 225
Verde, riv., Par. C3 247
Verde Grande, riv., Mex. K12 225
Verdel, Knox, Nebr. 123 B7 152
Verden, Ger. 19,900 B3 286
Verden, Grady, Okla. 405 C5 128
Verdery, Greenwood, S.C. 100 C4 188
Verdi, Lincoln, Minn. 112 G2 148
Verdi, Washoe, Nev. 350 D2 112
Verdigre, Knox, Nebr. 584 B7 152
Verdigris, Rogers, Okla. 40 B8 128
Verdigris, riv., Kans., Okla. E8 144
B8 128
Verdon, Richardson, Nebr. 267 D10 152
Verdon, Brown, S.Dak. 28 B7 158
Verdun, Que., Can. 78,262 S16 66
Verdun, Scott, Tenn. B7 190
Verdun [-sur-Meuse], Fr. 18,831 C6 278
Verdunville, Logan, W.Va. 2,260 D2 194
Vereeniging, U.S.Afr. 109,200 E5 420
(*201,000)
Verendrye, McHenry, N.Dak. 100 B5 154
Verga, Gloucester, N.J. 1,000 *D2 210
Vergara, Sp. 5,150 *A5 298
Vergara, Ur. B5 252
Vergas, Otter Tail, Minn. 292 E3 148
Vergennes, Addison, Vt. 1,921 C2 218
Verigin, Sask., Can. 278 E6 58
Verín, Sp. 3,215 B3 298
Veríssimo Sarmento, Ang. A4 420
Verkhne-Angarsk, Sov.Un. D13 329
Verkhne-Kolymsk, Sov.Un. C17 329
Verkhneye, Sov.Un. 26,300 H12 332
R22
Verkhniy Baskunchak, Sov.Un. C3 336
Verkhniy Ufaley, Sov.Un. 32,700 A6 336
Verkhniy Zub, mtn., Sov.Un. B11 336
Verkhnyaya Tunguska, riv., Sov.Un. D11 329
Verkhoyansk, Sov.Un. 1,200 C15 329
Verkhoyansk, mts., Sov.Un. D14 329
Verlo, Sask., Can. 150 E3 58
Vermilion, Alta., Can. 2,196 D7 54
Vermilion, Erie, Ohio 4,785 A4 156
Vermilion, co., Ill. 96,176 C6 138
Vermilion, par., La. 38,855 E3 180
Vermilion, bay, La. E3 180
Vermilion, lake, Minn. D6 148
Vermilion, pass, Alta., Can. E4 54
Vermilion, range, Minn. D6 148
Vermilion, riv., Alta., Can. D7 54
Vermilion, riv., Ill. B5 138
Vermilion, riv., Ind. B2 140
Vermilion, riv., La. E3 180
Vermilion, riv., Ohio A4 156
Vermilion Heights, Vermilion, Ill. 1,568 *C6 138
Vermilion-on-the-Lake, Lorain, Ohio 1,273 *A4 156
Vermillion, Marshall, Kans. 265 C7 144
Vermillion, Dakota, Minn. 248 G7 148
Vermillion, Clay, S.Dak. 6,102 E9 158
Vermillion, Sevier, Utah 120 E4 114
Vermillion, co., Ind. 17,683 C2 140
Vermillion, riv., Que., Can. Q11 66
Vermont, Fulton, Ill. 903 C3 138
Vermont, state, U.S. 389,881 C12 77
218
Vermontville, Eaton, Mich. 768 G6 146
Verna, Lawrence, Miss. 15 D2 184
Vernal, Uintah, Utah 3,655 C6 114
Verndale, Wadena, Minn. 606 E3 148
Verne, Uinta, Wyo. 20 E2 116
Verner, Mingo, W.Va. 600 D3 194
Verneuil [-sur-Avre], Fr. 4,611 C4 278
Verneuk, lake, U.S.Afr. E4 420
Vernon, Lamar, Ala. 1,492 B1 168

Vernon, Apache, Ariz.	100	D6	124
Vernon, Los Angeles, Calif.	229	*F4	94
Vernon, B.C., Can.	8,998	E13	52
Vernon, Yuma, Colo.	60	C8	106
Vernon, Tolland, Conn.	500	B6	202
	(16,961▲)		
Vernon, Kent, Del.		E3	172
Vernon, Washington, Fla.	624	A5	174
Vernon, Fr.	14,460	C4	278
Vernon, Jennings, Ind.	461	D4	140
Vernon, Jackson, La.	35	B3	180
Vernon, Shiawassee, Mich.	754	*G7	146
Vernon, Sussex, N.J.	150	A4	210
Vernon, McIntosh, Okla.	150	C8	128
Vernon, Hickman, Tenn.	35	C4	190
Vernon, Wilbarger, Tex.	12,141	B6	130
Vernon, Tooele, Utah	511	C3	114
Vernon, Windham, Vt.	130	F3	218
	(865▲)		
Vernon, co., Mo.	20,540	D3	150
Vernon, co., Wis.	25,663	E3	160
Vernon, par., La.	18,301	C2	180
Vernon, lake, Ont., Can.		O21	64
Vernon Center, Blue Earth, Minn.	333	H4	148
Vernon Hill, Halifax, Va.	20	D5	192
Vernonia, Columbia, Oreg.	1,089	B3	96
Vernon Valley, Suffolk, N.Y.	5,998	*D3	212
Vero Beach, Indian River, Fla.	8,849	D10	174
Véroia, Grc.	21,844	A4	306
Verona, Ont., Can.	300	P24	64
Verona, It.	140,800	C3	302
	(186,900▲)		
Verona, Boone, Ky.	225	A8	178
Verona, Hancock, Maine	250	*D4	204
	(435▲)		
Verona, Lee, Miss.	824	A4	184
Verona, Lawrence, Mo.	401	E4	150
Verona, Clay, Nebr.	30	*D8	152
Verona, Essex, N.J.	13,782	B4	210
Verona, La Moure, N.Dak.	162	D7	154
Verona, Preble and Montgomery, Ohio	527	C2	156
Verona, Allegheny, Pa.	4,032	A4	214
Verona, Marshall, Tenn.	30	C5	190
Verona, Augusta, Va.	500	B6	192
Verona, Dane, Wis.	1,471	E4	160
Verona, prov., It.	654,100	*C3	302
Verona Park, Calhoun, Mich.	1,884	*G6	146
Verret, lake, La.		E4	180
Verrières-le-Buisson, Fr.		J10	278
Versailles, New London, Conn.	300	C7	202
Versailles, Fr.	84,445	C5	278
		I9	
Versailles, Brown, Ill.	427	D3	138
Versailles, Ripley, Ind.	1,158	C4	140
Versailles, Woodford, Ky.	4,060	B6	178
Versailles, Morgan, Mo.	2,047	C5	150
Versailles, Darke, Ohio	2,159	B2	156
Versailles, Allegheny, Pa.	2,297	*C2	214
Verse, Converse, Wyo.		C7	116
Versoix, Switz.	2,471	B2	312
Verte, isl., Que., Can.		P15	66
Verte, riv., Que., Can.		Q15	66
Vertrees, Hardin, Ky.	500	C4	178
Verviers, Bel.	37,185	D4	282
Verwood, Sask., Can.	120	F5	58
Veseleyville, Walsh, N.Dak.	150	B8	154
Veseli, Rice, Minn.	135	G5	148
Veseloye, Sov.Un.	18,600	I10	332
Vesoul, Fr.	12,038	D7	278
Vesper, Lincoln, Kans.	100	C5	144
Vesper, Wood, Wis.	351	D4	160
Vessigebro, Swe.	3,622	E3	292
Vesta, C.R.		F6	228
Vesta, Oglethorpe, Ga.	150	C4	176
Vesta, Redwood, Minn.	318	G3	148
Vesta, Johnson, Nebr.	75	*D9	152
Vestaburg, Montcalm, Mich.	450	F7	146
Vestaburg, Washington, Pa.	950	C2	214
Vest-Agder, co., Nor.	99,149	*G2	291
Vestal, Broome, N.Y.	7,000	C5	212
Vestal Center, Broome, N.Y.	400	C5	212
Vestavia Hills, Jefferson, Ala.	4,029	*B3	168
Vesteraalen, is., Nor.		B6	290
Vesteroy, isl., Nor		B1	292
Vestfjorden, fjord, Nor.		B6	290
Vestfold, co., Nor.	159,155	B1	292
Vestmannaeyjar, Ice.	4,224	M19	290
Vestro Havn, Den.	546	D1	292
Vesuvius, Rockbridge, Va.	400	C5	192
Vesuvius, vol., It.		E5	302
Vesyegonsk, Sov.Un.	9,700	C11	332
Veszprém, Hung.	23,000	B2	320
Vésztő, Hung.	8,976	C6	320
Vetal, Bennett, S.Dak.	20	D4	158
Veteran, Alta., Can.	241	D7	54
Veteran, Goshen, Wyo.	40	E8	116
Vetlanda, Swe.	8,733	D6	292
Vetluga, riv., Sov.Un.		A3	336
Vetluzhskiy, Sov.Un.		A3	336
Vetovo, Bul.	4,981	B3	317
Vetren, Bul.	6,326	B2	317
Vetters, hill, Mo.		D3	150
Veurne, Bel.	7,379	C1	282
Vevay, Switzerland, Ind.	1,508	D4	140
Vevey, Switz.	14,600	B2	312
	(*22,500)		
Veynes, Fr.		E6	278
Veyo, Washington, Utah	60	F2	114
Vezirköprü, Tur.	6,266	A6	307
Viacha, Bol.	6,607	C1	246
Viadana, It.	5,587	C3	302
Viamonte, Arg.		B3	252
Vian, Sequoyah, Okla.	930	C9	128
Viana, Braz.	4,995	A2	258
Viana del Bollo, Sp.	1,049	A3	298
Viana do Alentejo, Port.	3,566	C2	298
Viana do Castelo, Port.	14,023	B2	298
Vianen, Neth.	3,346	C4	282
Vianópolis, Braz.	1,588	D1	258
Viareggio, It.	36,500	D3	302
Vibank, Sask., Can.	253	E6	58
Viborg, Den.	22,543	H3	291
Viborg, Turner, S.Dak.	699	D8	158
Viborg, co., Den.	160,018	*H3	291
Vibo Valentia, It.	12,800	F6	302
Viburnum, Iron, Mo.	590	D6	150
Vicálvaro, Sp.	6,615	*B5	298
	(part of Madrid)		
Vicars, Roane, W.Va.	300	C3	194
Vicco, Perry, Ky.	900	C7	178
Vic [-en-Bigorre], Fr.		F4	278
Vicenza, It.	63,700	C3	302
	(83,200▲)		
Vicenza, prov., It.	611,300	*C3	302
Viceroy, Sask., Can.	289	F5	58
Vich, Sp.	12,414	B8	298
Vichada, comisaría, Col.	13,860	C3	244
Vichada, riv., Col.		C3	244
Vichuga, Sov.Un.	51,000	D14	332
Vichuquén, Chile		B1	252
Vichy, Fr.	30,403	D5	278
Vichy, Maries, Mo.	200	C6	150
Vici, Dewey, Okla.	601	B4	128
Vick, Bradley, Ark.	40	*D4	170
Vick, Avoyelles, La.	100	C3	180
Vicksburg, Yuma, Ariz.	15	E2	124
Vicksburg, Greene, Ind.	175	C2	140
Vicksburg, Kalamazoo, Mich.	2,224	G6	146
Vicksburg, Warren, Miss.	29,130	C2	184
Viçosa, Braz.	6,000	B3	258
Viçosa, Braz.	6,424	E2	258
Viçosa [do Ceará], Braz.	2,534	A2	258
Vicovaro, It.	3,012	*D4	302
Victor, Teller, Colo.	434	D5	106
Victor, Teton, Idaho	240	F7	108
Victor, Iowa, Iowa	870	C5	142
Victor, Ravalli, Mont.	360	D2	110
Victor, Ontario, N.Y.	1,180	C4	212
Victor, Roberts, S.Dak.	30	B9	158
Victoria, Coffee, Ala.		D4	168
Victoria, Arg.	17,771	B3	252
Victoria, Mississippi, Ark.	200	B6	170
Victoria, Br.Cam.	8,025	F6	409
Victoria, B.C., Can.	54,584	C14	52
	(*125,500)	F11	
Victoria, Newf., Can.	1,050	G9	72
Victoria, P.E.I., Can.	146	C6	70
Victoria, Chile	10,671	C1	252
Victoria, Hong Kong	1,000,000	N7	349
Victoria, Knox, Ill.	453	B3	138
Victoria, Ellis, Kans.	1,170	D4	144
Victoria, Carver, Minn.	425	*G5	148
Victoria, Marshall, Miss.	500	A3	184
Victoria, Jefferson, Mo.	150	C7	150
Victoria, Gloucester, N.J.	100	D3	210
Victoria, Marion, Tenn.	600	C6	190
Victoria, Victoria, Tex.	33,047	E7	130
Victoria, Lunenburg, Va.	1,737	D6	192
Victoria, co., N.B., Can.	19,020	B2	70
Victoria, co., N.S., Can.	8,185	C9	70
Victoria, co., Ont., Can.	28,248	P22	64
Victoria, co., Tex.	46,475	E7	130
Victoria, state, Austl.	2,673,498	F8	432
Victoria, falls, Rh.&Nya.		C5	420
Victoria, isl., N.W.Ter., Can.		C8	48
Victoria, lake, Afr.		C5	414
Victoria, lake, Newf., Can.		F7	72
Victoria, mtn., Bur.		B2	362
Victoria, riv., Austl.		B6	432
Victoria, riv., Newf., Can.		F7	72
Victoria, strait, N.W.Ter., Can.		D8	48
Victoria Beach, Man., Can.	50	E4	60
Victoria de las Tunas, Cuba	20,431	B6	232
Victoria Falls, Rh.&Nya.	1,455	C5	420
Victoria Harbour, Ont., Can.	1,012	P21	64
Victoria Point, Bur.	1,519	E3	362
Victoria River Downs, Austl.		B6	432
Victoria Road, Ont., Can.	235	P22	64
Victoriaville, Que., Can.	16,031	R13	66
Victoria West, U.S.Afr.	2,948	F4	420
Victorica, Arg.		C2	252
Victorino de la Plaza, Arg.		C3	252
Victor Mills, Spartanburg, S.C.	2,018	*B4	188
Victorville, San Bernardino, Calif.	5,000	E5	94
Victory, Jackson, Okla.	25	D4	128
Victory, Vernon, Wis.	140	E2	160
Victory Gardens, Morris, N.J.	1,085	*B3	210
Victory Heights, Chemung, N.Y.	1,030	*C5	212
Vicuna, Chile	3,415	B1	252
Vida, McCone, Mont.	85	C11	110
Vida, Lane, Oreg.	150	C4	96
Vida, Rom.		B3	321
Vidalia, Toombs, Ga.	7,569	D4	176
Vidalia, Concordia, La.	4,313	C4	180
Vidette, Burke, Ga.	103	C4	176
Vidhirhóll, Ice.		L21	290
Vidin, Bul.	23,984	B1	317
Vidinski, prov., Bul.		*B1	317
Vidor, Orange, Tex.	4,938	D8	130
Vidora, Sask., Can.	65	F3	58
Vidra, Rom.		B4	321
Vidrine, Evangeline, La.	80	D3	180
Viedma, Arg.	4,683	F5	251
Viedma, lake, Arg.		G3	251
Vieja, peak, Tex.		D3	130
Vielsalm, Bel.	3,968	D4	282
Vienna (Wien), Aus.	1,616,125	B8	313
	(*1,900,000)		
Vienna, Ont., Can.	362	R20	64
Vienna, Dooly, Ga.	2,099	D3	176
Vienna, Johnson, Ill.	1,094	F5	138
Vienna, Lincoln, La.	250	B3	180
Vienna, Kennebec, Maine	150	*D3	204
	(160▲)		
Vienna, Dorchester, Md.	420	D8	182
Vienna, Maries, Mo.	536	C6	150
Vienna, Warren, N.J.	250	B3	210
Vienna, Clark, S.Dak.	191	C8	158
Vienna, Fairfax, Va.	11,440	A6	192
		B7	
Vienna, Wood, W.Va.	9,381	B3	194
Vienne, Fr.	25,669	E6	278
Vienne, dept., Fr.	319,208	*D4	278
Vienne, riv., Fr.		D4	278
Vientiane, Laos	25,000	C4	362
Vieques, isl., P.R.		C12	233
Vierzon, Fr.	28,627	D5	278
Viesca, Mex.	3,043	B5	225
Vieste, It.	13,100	E6	302
Vietnam, country, Asia	27,800,000	H12	340
			362
Vietnam, North, country, Asia	14,500,000	C5	362
Vietnam, South, country, Asia,	11,000,000	D6	362
Vigan, Phil.	7,424	A6	358
Viger, Que., Can.	435	Q15	66
Vigevano, It.	38,600	C2	302
Vigo, Sp.	90,000	A2	298
	(140,000▲)		
Vigo, co., Ind.	108,458	C2	140
Vihowa, Pak.	2,827	D7	375
Vihti, Fin.		F11	291
Viinijärvi, Fin.		E13	290
Viiose, riv., Alb.		A3	306
Viitasaari, Fin.		E11	290
Vijayavada, India	161,198	E4	366
Vik, Ice.		M20	290
Vik, Nor.		F2	291
Viken, Swe.	787	E3	292
Viken, lake, Swe.		C5	292
Viking, Alta., Can.	897	D7	54
Viking, Marshall, Minn.	128	C2	148
Vikna, Nor.		D4	290
Vikren, mtn., Bul.		C1	317
Vila Cabral, Moz.		B7	421
Vila Coutinho, Moz.		B6	421
Vila da Feira, Port.		B2	298
Vila da Ponte, Ang.	329	B3	420
Vila de Aljustrel, Ang.		B3	420
Vila de João Belo, Moz.	1,936	E6	421
Vila de Manica, Moz.		C6	421
Vila de Rei, Port.	5,982	C2	298
Vila Fontes, Moz.		C7	421
Vila Gago Contínho, Ang.		B4	420
Vila General Machado, Ang.	2,387	B3	420
Vilaine, riv., Fr.		D2	278
Vila João de Almeida, Ang.		C2	420
Vila Junqueiro, Moz.		C7	421
Vila Luso, Ang.	2,821	B3	420
Vila Macedo de Cavaleiros, Ang.		B3	420
Vila Marechal Carmona, Ang.		A3	420
Vila Mariano Machado, Ang.		B3	420
Vilanculos, Moz.		D6	421
Vilano Beach, St. Johns, Fla.	200	B10	174
Vila Nova de Fozcôa, Port.	3,481	B3	298
Vila Nova de Milfontes, Port.	2,460	D2	298
Vila Nova do Seles, Ang.	1,115	B2	420
Vila Pereira de Eça, Ang.	416	C3	420
Vila Pery, Moz.		C6	421
Vila Real, Port.	9,285	B3	298
Vila Real de Santo António, Port.	6,086	D3	298
Vila Robert Williams, Ang.		B3	420
Vilas, Baca, Colo.	107	E8	106
Vilas, Miner, S.Dak.	49	C8	158
Vilas, co., Wis.	9,332	B4	160
Vila Salazar, Ang.		A2	420
Vila Serpa Pinto, Ang.	387	B3	420
Vila Teixeira da Silva, Ang.		B3	420
Vila Teixeira de Sousa, Ang.	870	B4	420
Vilcanota, mts., Peru		C3	245
Vildo, Hardeman, Tenn.	40	C2	190
Vileyka, Sov.Un.	12,100	E6	332
Vilhelmina, Swe.	2,242	D7	290
Viljandi, Sov.Un.	19,700	C5	332
Vilkovo, Sov.Un.	23,500	J7	332
Villa Abecia, Bol.	539	D1	246
Villa Acuña, Mex.	11,355	B5	225
Villa Ahumada, Mex.	2,489	A4	224
Villa Alhucemas, Mor.	11,257	A3	402
Villa Angela, Arg.	7,345	A3	252
Villa Aroma, Bol.	1,486	C1	246
Villa Azueta, Mex.		D6	225
Villa Bella, Bol.	88	B1	246
Villablino, Sp.	1,204	A3	298
Villacañas, Sp.	9,137	C5	298
Villacarrillo, Sp.	13,090	C5	298
Villach, Aus.	30,066	D5	313
Villacidro, It.	10,600	F2	302
Villa Cisneros, Sp. Sahara		B1	408
Villa Colón, C.R.	310	F5	228
Villa Constitución, Arg.	9,183	B3	252
Villa Cuauhtémoc, Mex.	2,436	J15	225
Villa de Cura, Ven.	10,348	A5	240
Villa del Rosario, Arg.	4,461	B3	252
Villa del Rosario, Ven.		A2	240
Villadolid, Ec.		A2	245
Villa Dolores, Arg.	13,835	B2	252
Villa Federal, Arg.	9,158	B4	252
Villafranca del Bierzo, Sp.	3,081	A3	298
Villafranca de los Barros, Sp.	16,671	C3	298
Villafranca del Panadés, Sp.	10,773	B7	298
Villafranca [di Verona], It.	6,015	C3	302
Villagarcia de Arosa, Sp.	23,705	A2	298
Village, Columbia, Ark.	85	D3	170
Village, Richmond, Va.	140	C8	192
Village, creek, Ala.		E4	168
Village Richelieu, Que., Can.	1,398	*S11	66
Village Springs, Blount, Ala.	250	B3	168
Villaggio Duca degli Abruzzi, Som.	9,000	E6	398
	(15,900▲)		
Villa Grove, Saguache, Colo.	100	D5	106
Villa Grove, Douglas, Ill.	2,308	D5	138
Villaguay, Arg.		B4	252
Villa Hayes, Par.	2,242	D4	247
Villahermosa, Mex.	33,587	D7	225
Villa Huidobro, Arg.		B3	252
Villa Iris, Arg.	2,422	C3	252
Villajoyosa, Sp.	6,963	C6	298
Villa Juárez, Mex.		C5	225
Villa Juárez, Mex.	6,693	C6	225
		K15	
Villalba, Sp.	3,180	A3	298
Villaldama, Mex.	2,529	B5	225
Villalonga, Arg.		C3	252
Villalpando, Sp.	2,825	B4	298
Villa Maria, Arg.	30,362	B3	252
Villamartin, Sp.	8,409	D4	298
Villa Montes, Bol.	3,105	D2	246
Villanueva, Col.	5,830	B2	244
Villanueva, San Miguel, N.Mex.	300	C5	126
Villanueva, Sp.	10,982	D4	298
Villanueva de Córdoba, Sp.	16,037	C4	298
Villanueva del Arzobispo, Sp.	9,712	*C5	298
Villanueva y Geltrú, Sp.	19,555	B7	298
Villa Obregón, Mex.	25,908	G10	224
Villa Oliva, Par.		E4	247
Villa Park, Du Page, Ill.	20,391	F2	138
Villa Pedro Montoya, Mex.	4,443	K14	225
Villaputzu, It.	3,449	F2	302
Villard, Pope, Minn.	235	F3	148
Villard-Bonnot, Fr.	5,810	E6	278
Villa Rica, Carroll and Douglas, Ga.	3,450	C2	176
Villa Ridge, Pulaski, Ill.	550	F4	138
Villa Ridge, Franklin, Mo.	150	C7	150
Villarreal, Sp.	16,778	C6	298
Villarrica, Chile	7,036	C1	252
Villarrica, Par.	14,680	D4	247
Villarrobledo, Sp.	20,362	C5	298
Villarrubia, Sp.	7,907	C5	298
Villas, Cape May, N.J.	2,085	E3	210
Villa Tasso, Walton, Fla.	100	A4	174
Villa Unión, Arg.		A2	252
Villa Unión, Mex.	4,199	C4	224
Villa Unión, Mex.		C5	224
Villa Valeria, Arg.		B3	252
Villaverde, Sp.	7,103	B5	298
Villavicencio, Col.	37,850	C2	244
Villaviciosa, Sp.	2,322	A4	298
Villa Viscarra, Bol.	658	C1	246
Villazón, Bol.	6,261	D1	246
Villazón, Bol.		D2	246
Ville d'Alma, Que., Can.	10,822	P13	66
Villefranche [-de-Rouergue], Fr.	6,530	E5	278
Villefranche [-sur-Saône], Fr.	21,703	E6	278
Villegreen, Las Animas, Colo.	10	E7	106
Villejuif, Fr.	29,280	I10	278
Villemomble, Fr.	21,522	I11	278
Villena, Sp.	15,687	C6	298
Villeneuve, Alt., Can.		D6	54
Villeneuve-le-Roi, Fr.	16,715	J10	278
Villeneuve-St.-Georges, Fr.	21,596	J10	278
Villeneuve-sur-Lot, Fr.	13,786	E4	278
Villeneuve-sur-Yonne, Fr.		C4	278
Ville Platte, Evangeline, La.	7,512	D3	180
Villeroy, Que., Can.	260	R13	66
Villers-Cotterêts, Fr.		C5	278
Villerupt, Fr.	10,111	C6	278
Ville-St.-Georges, Que., Can.	3,197	R14	66
Ville St. Pierre, Que., Can.	5,276	*S16	66
Villeta, Par.	2,526	D4	247
Villeurbanne, Fr.	81,769	E6	278
Villingen [im Schwarzwald], Ger.	26,800	D3	286
Villisca, Montgomery, Iowa	1,690	D3	142
Vilna, Alta., Can.	374	C7	54
Vilnius, Sov.Un.	235,000	E5	332
Vilonia, Faulkner, Ark.	234	B4	170
Vilppula, Fin.	1,563	E11	291
Vilvoorde, Bel.	30,143	D3	282
Vilyuy, riv., Sov.Un.		C14	329
Vilyuysk, Sov.Un.	3,600	C14	329
Vilyuyskiye, mts., Sov.Un.		C13	329
Vimiazo, Sp.	654	A2	298
Vimmerby, Swe.	5,735	D6	292
Vimpeli, Fin.		E10	290
Vimperk, Czech.	2,940	B1	324
Vimy Ridge, Saline, Ark.	300	D6	170
Vina, Franklin, Ala.	184	A1	168
Vina, Tehama, Calif.	200	C2	94
Viña del Mar, Chile	102,206	B1	252
Vinalhaven, Knox, Maine	950	D4	204
	(1,273▲)		
Vinalhaven, isl., Maine		D4	204
Vinaroz, Sp.	9,235	B7	298
Vincennes, Fr.	50,434	I10	278
Vincennes, Knox, Ind.	18,046	D2	140
Vincent, Shelby, Ala.	1,402	B3	168
Vincent, Webster, Iowa	173	B3	142
Vincent, Calcasieu, La.	75	D2	180
Vincent, Washington, Ohio	2,100	C5	156
Vincentown, Burlington, N.J.	545	D3	210
Vinces, Ec.	3,748	A2	245
Vinchina, Arg.		A2	252
Vinco, Payne, Okla.	50	C6	128
Vindelälven, riv., Swe.		D8	290
Vindeln, Swe.		D8	290
Vindex, Garrett, Md.	80	B1	182
Vine, brook, Mass.W		C2	206
Vine Grove, Hardin, Ky.	2,435	C5	178
Vineland, Orange, Fla.	150	C9	174
Vineland, Cumberland, N.J.	37,685	E2	210
Vinemont, Cullman, Ala.	500	A3	168
Vineyard, Lee, Ark.		C6	170
Vineyard, Utah, Utah		C4	114
Vineyard, sound, Mass.		D6	206
Vineyard Haven, Dukes, Mass.	2,169	D6	206
Vingåker, Swe.	3,963	B6	292
Vinh, Viet.	30,000	C5	362
Vinhais, Port.	2,911	B3	298
Vinh Long, Viet.	30,000	E5	362
Vinh Yen, Viet.	3,820	B5	362
Vining, Tama, Iowa	122	C5	142
Vining, Clay and Washington, Kans.	128	C6	144
Vining, Otter Tail, Minn.	136	E3	148
Vinita, Craig, Okla.	6,027	B8	128
Vinita Park, St. Louis, Mo.	2,204	*C7	150
Vinita Terrace, St. Louis, Mo.	382	*C7	150
Vinje, Nor.		G3	291
Vinkovci, Yugo.	19,179	B4	316
Vinnitsa, Sov.Un.	121,000	H7	332
Vinson, Harmon, Okla.	75	D4	128
Vintjärn, Swe.		A7	292
Vinton, Benton, Iowa	4,781	B5	142
Vinton, Calcasieu, La.	2,987	D2	180
Vinton, Gallia, Ohio	374	D4	156
Vinton, Roanoke, Va.	3,432	C5	192
Vinton, Nicholas, W.Va.	20	C4	194
		C7	
Vinton, co., Ohio	10,274	C4	156
Vintondale, Cambria, Pa.	938	C3	214
Viola, Fulton, Ark.	196	A5	170
Viola, Kent, Del.	159	D3	172

Viola, Latah, Idaho	60	*C2	108
Viola, Mercer, Ill.	812	B3	138
Viola, Linn, Iowa	150	B6	142
Viola, Sedgwick, Kans.	203	E6	144
Viola, Warren, Tenn.	206	C6	190
Viola, Richland, Wis.	721	E3	160
Violet, St. Bernard, La.	900	C8	180
Vioöstern, lake, Swe.		D4	292
Virden, Man., Can.	3,225	F2	60
Virden, Macoupin, Ill.	3,309	D4	138
Virden, Hidalgo, N.Mex.	135	F2	126
Vire, Fr.	7,963	C3	278
Vire, riv., Fr.		C3	278
Virgelle, Chouteau, Mont.	5	B6	110
Virgenes, cape, Arg.		H4	251
Virgil, Greenwood, Kans.	229	E7	144
Virgil, Choctaw, Okla.		D8	128
Virgil, Beadle, S.Dak.	81	C7	158
Virgilina, Halifax, Va.	286	D6	192
Virgin, Washington, Utah	124	F2	114
Virgin, mts., Ariz., Nev.		B1	124
		G7	112
Virgin, riv., Ariz., Nev., Utah		B1	124
		G8	112
		G2	114
Virgin Islands, Br.poss., N.A.	8,000	C12	233
Virgin Islands, U.S. poss., N.A.	26,665	C12	233
Virginia, Jefferson, Ala.	500	*B2	168
Virginia, Bannock, Idaho	50	G6	108
Virginia, Cass, Ill.	1,669	D3	138
Virginia, St. Louis, Minn.	14,034	D6	148
Virginia, Gage, Nebr.	88	*D9	152
Virginia, state, U.S.	3,966,949	D11	77
			192
Virginia, peak, Wyo.		D2	116
Virginia Beach (Independent City), Va.	8,091	A9	192
		D9	
Virginia City, Madison, Mont.	194	E5	110
Virginia City, Storey, Nev.	600	D2	112
Virginia Gardens, Dade, Fla.	2,159	*F10	174
Virginia Heights, Kanawha, W.Va.	250	*C3	194
Virkkala, Fin.		F11	291
Viroflay, Fr.	13,292	I9	278
Viroqua, Vernon, Wis.	3,926	E3	160
Virovitica, Yugo.	11,684	B3	316
Vir-Pazar, Yugo.	323	C4	316
Virrat, Fin.	1,187	E10	291
Virserum, Swe.	2,297	D6	292
Virtaniemi, Fin.		B13	290
Virton, Bel.	3,277	E4	282
Virú, Peru	2,573	B2	245
Vis, Yugo.	3,132	C3	316
Vis, isl., Yugo.		C3	316
Visakhapatnam, India	108,042	E4	366
Visalia, Tulare, Calif.	15,791	D4	94
Visalia, Kenton, Ky.	253	A8	178
Visayan, sea, Phil.		B6	358
Visby, Swe.	15,234	D9	292
Viscount, Sask., Can.	302	E5	58
Viscount Melville, sound, N.W.Ter., Can.		C8	48
Vise, Bel.	5,695	D4	282
Višegrad, Yugo.	2,549	C4	316
Viseu, Braz.	1,189	F7	256
Viseu, Port.	13,190	B3	298
Vişeul-de-Sus, Rom.	13,956	A3	321
Vishera, riv., Sov.Un.		A5	336
Visingsö, lake, Swe.		C5	292
Viskan, riv., Swe.		D3	292
Vislanda, Swe.	3,409	E5	292
Viso, Solomon		E2	436
Viso, mtn., Fr.		E7	278
Viso, mtn., It.		C1	302
Visoko, Yugo.	5,845	C4	316
Visonau, Fiji		D7	436
Visp, Switz.	2,727	B3	312
Vista, San Diego, Calif.	14,795	F5	94
Vista, Man., Can.	100	E2	60
Vistillas, Lake, Oreg.		E6	96
Vistonis, lake, Grc.		A5	306
Vistula, lagoon, Pol.		A4	325
Vit, riv., Bul.		B2	317
Vita, Man., Can.	365	F4	60
Vitanovac, Yugo.	1,127	C5	316
Vitava, riv., Czech.		B2	324
Vitebsk, Sov.Un.	148,000	E8	332
Vitemölla, Swe.		F5	292
Viterbo, It.	27,100	D4	302
Viterbo, prov., It.	265,000	*D4	302
Vitichi, Bol.		D1	246
Viti Levu, isl., Fiji		E6	436
Vitim, Sov.Un.	2,300	D13	329
Vitim, riv., Sov.Un.		D13	329
Vito, Solomon		F13	359
Vitor, Peru	2,343	D3	245
Vitória, Braz.	49,735	E2	258
Vitoria, Sp.	48,100	A5	298
	(53,607▲)		
Vitória (de Santo Antão), Braz.	15,720	B3	258
Vitória do Mearim, Braz.	1,217	A2	258
Vitré, Fr.	8,374	C3	278
Vitry-le-François, Fr.	11,131	C6	278
Vittangi, Swe.		C9	290
Vittel, Fr.		C6	278
Vittoria, Ont., Can.	275	R20	64
Vittoria, It.	44,600	G5	302
Vittorio Veneto, It.	14,500	C4	302
Vivero, Sp.	3,628	A3	298
Vivian, Caddo, La.	2,624	B2	180
Vivian, Lyman, S.Dak.	300	D5	158
Vivian, McDowell, W.Va.	900	*D3	194
Vivian Park, Utah, Utah	60	*C4	114
Vivoratá, Arg.		C4	252
Vixen, Caldwell, La.		B3	180
Vizcaino, des., Mex.		B3	224
Vizcaino, mts., Mex.		B3	224
Vizcaya, prov., Sp.	554,302	*A5	298
Vize, Tur.	4,891	A2	307
Vizianagaram, India	67,104	E4	366
Vizille, Fr.	5,977	E6	278
Viziru, Rom.	5,414	B4	321
Vizzini, It.	13,300	G5	302
Vlaardingen, Neth.	54,994	C3	282
Vladimir, Sov.Un.	154,000	A2	336
Vladimirovka, Sov.Un.		C3	336
Vladimir-Volynskiy, Sov.Un.	38,300	G5	332
Vladivostok, Sov.Un.	283,000	E15	329
Vlasenica, Yugo.	2,484	B4	316
Vlašim, Czech.	5,066	B2	324
Vlasotinci, Yugo.	4,977	C6	316
Vlčany, Czech.	4,555	B3	324
Vlieland, Neth.	650	A4	282
Vlieland, isl, Neth.		A3	282
Vliets, Marshall, Kans.	100	C7	144
Vlissingen, Neth.	25,745	C2	282
Vlkava, Czech.	526	*A2	324
Vlonë, Alb.	28,212	A2	306
Vlonë, pref., Alb.	58,000	A2	306
Vöcklabruck, Aus.	8,857	B5	313
Vodlozero, lake, Sov.Un.		A11	332
Voeune Sai, Camb.	10,000	D5	362
Vogelkop, pen., Neth.N.Gui.		E8	359
Voghera, It.	27,300	C2	302
Vohipeno, Malag.		D9	421
Voi, Ken.		C6	414
Voiotia (Boeotia), prov., Grc.	106,838	*B4	306
Voiron, Fr.	10,119	E6	278
Voitsberg, Aus.	5,873	C7	313
Voiviis, lake, Grc.		B4	306
Volborg, Custer, Mont.	8	E11	110
Volchansk, Sov.Un.	33,800	G11	332
Volcour, Lincoln, Mont.	10	B1	110
Volens, Halifax, Va.	50	D6	192
Volga, Clayton, Iowa	361	B6	142
Volga, Brookings, S.Dak.	780	C9	158
Volga, Barbour, W.Va.	139	B4	194
Volga, plat., Sov.Un.		B3	336
Volga, riv., Sov.Un.		C3	336
Volgo-Donskoy, canal, Sov.Un.		H14	332
Volin, Yankton, S.Dak.	171	E8	158
Volkhov, Sov.Un.	16,500	C9	332
Volkhov, riv., Sov.Un.		C8	332
Volkovysk, Sov.Un.	24,000	F5	332
Vollenhove, Neth.	1,918	B4	282
Volney, Grayson, Va.	40	D3	192
Volochanka, Sov.Un.		B11	329
Volochisk, Sov.Un.	14,100	H6	332
Volodarskoye, Sov.Un.		B7	336
Vologda, Sov.Un.	138,000	A1	336
Volokolamsk, Sov.Un.	11,800	D10	332
Vólos, Grc.	51,144	B4	306
Vólos, gulf, Grc.		B4	306
Volsk, Sov.Un.	62,000	B3	336
Volta, riv., Ghana, Upper Volta		D4	408
		E4	
Voltaire, McHenry, N.Dak.	70	B5	154
Volta Redonda, Braz.	32,143	E2	258
Volterra, It.	9,300	D3	302
Voltri, It. (part of Genova)		C2	302
Volturno, riv., It.		E5	302
Voluntown, New London, Conn.	500	C8	202
	(1,028▲)		
Volusia, co., Fla.	125,319	B9	174
Volzhskiy, Sov.Un.	67,000	H15	332
Vona, Kit Carson, Colo.	130	C8	106
Vonda, Sask., Can.	246	D4	58
Von Frank, mtn., Alsk.		C6	84
Vónitsa, Grc.	2,796	B3	306
Vonore, Monroe, Tenn.	525	C7	190
Vopna, fjord, Ice.		L22	290
Vopnafjordhur, Ice.	340	L22	290
Vorarlberg, state, Aus.	193,657	*C1	313
Vordingborg, Den.	11,358	F2	292
Vorkuta, Sov.Un.	55,000	C8	328
Vorma, riv., Nor.		A2	292
Vorona, riv., Sov.Un.		G14	332
Voronezh, Sov.Un.	454,000	B1	336
Voronezh, riv., Sov.Un.		F12	332
Vorontsovka, Sov.Un.		D13	329
Voroshilovsk, Sov.Un.	98,000	H12	332
		S22	
Vorskla, riv., Sov.Un.		H10	332
Vosburg, U.S.Afr.	718	F4	420
Vosges, dept., Fr.	372,523	*C7	278
Vosges, mts., Fr.		C7	278
Voskresensk, Sov.Un.	39,000	O19	332
Voskresenskoye, Sov.Un.	5,100	D15	332
Voss, Nor.	3,134	F2	291
Vossburg, Jasper, Miss.	300	D4	184
Vostok, isl., Pac.O.		D4	436
Votkinsk, Sov.Un.	59,000	A4	336
Vouga, riv., Port.		B2	298
Vouhijärvi, Fin.		F12	291
Voutso, Fin.		B12	290
Vouziers, Fr.		C6	278
Vowells Mill, Natchitoches, La.		C2	180
Vozhega, Sov.Un.	3,600	B13	332
Voznesensk, Sov.Un.	34,600	I8	332
Voznesenye, Sov.Un.	7,100	B10	332
Vrachanski, prov., Bul.		*B2	317
Vrañany, Czech.	659	*A2	324
Vranje, Yugo.	12,072	C5	316
Vratsa, Bul.	26,592	B1	317
Vrbas, Yugo.	15,470	B4	316
Vrbas, riv., Yugo.		B3	316
Vrchlabi, Czech.	10,061	A2	324
Vrede, U.S.Afr.		E5	420
Vredenburgh, Monroe and Wilcox, Ala.	632	D2	168
Vriezenveen, Neth.	6,017	B5	282
Vršac, Yugo.	26,710	B5	316
Vršovice, Czech. (part of Prague)		*A2	324
Vrútky, Czech. (part of Turčiansky Svätý Martin)		B4	324
Vryburg, U.S.Afr.	9,245	E4	420
Vryheid, U.S.Afr.	9,056	E6	421
Všetaty, Czech.	1,636	*A2	324
Vsetin, Czech.	18,451	B4	324
Vsevidof, mtn., Alsk.		E5	84
Vŭcha, riv., Bul.		C2	317
Vukovar, Yugo.	18,705	B4	316
Vulcan, Alta., Can.	1,204	E6	54
Vulcan, Dickinson, Mich.	450	D4	146
Vulcano, isl., It.		F5	302
Vŭlchedrŭm, Bul.	8,371	B1	317
Vuohijärvi, lake, Fin.		F12	291
Vuya, pt., Fiji		E6	436
Vyatka, riv., Sov.Un.		A4	336
Vyatskiye Polyany, Sov.Un.	23,200	A4	336
Vyazma, Sov.Un.	26,700	E10	332
Vyazma, riv., Sov.Un.		N19	332
Vyazniki, Sov. Un.	42,300	D14	332
Vyborg, Sov.Un.	51,000	B7	332
Vyksa, Sov.Un.	28,600	E14	332
Vyshniy Volochek, Sov.Un.	66,000	D10	332
Vyškov, Czech.	12,498	B3	324
Vysočany, Czech. (part of Prague)		*A2	324
Vysoká u Mělnika, Czech.	392	*A2	324
Vysoké Mýto, Czech.	7,983	B3	324
Vytegra, Sov. Un.	11,800	B11	332

W

Wa, Ghana	5,165	D4	408
Waal, riv., Neth.		C4	282
Waalwijk, Neth.	14,969	C4	282
Wabamun, Alta., Can.	200	D5	54
Wabamun, lake, Alta., Can.		D5	54
Wabana (Bell Island), Newf., Can.	7,873	G9	72
Wabash, Phillips, Ark.	115	C6	170
Wabash, Wabash, Ind.	12,621	B4	140
Wabash, Cass, Nebr.	30	E2	152
Wabash, co., Ill.	14,047	E6	138
Wabash, co., Ind.	32,605	B4	140
Wabash, riv., U.S.		D9	77
Wabasha, Wabasha, Minn.	2,500	G6	148
Wabasha, co., Minn.	17,007	G6	148
Wabasso, Indian River, Fla.	400	D10	174
Wabasso, Redwood, Minn.	789	G3	148
Wabaunsee, Wabaunsee, Kans.	97	C7	144
Wabaunsee, co., Kans.	6,648	D7	144
Wabbaseka, Jefferson, Ark.	432	C5	170
Wabek, Mountrail, N.Dak.	14	C4	154
Wabeno, Forest, Wis.	800	C5	160
Wābi Shabalē, riv., Eth.		D5	398
Wabiskaw, riv., Alta., Can.		B5	54
Wabowden, Man., Can.	75	C3	60
Wąbrzeźno, Pol.	9,320	B4	325
Wabuska, Lyon, Nev.	60	D2	112
Waccamaw, riv., N.C., S.C.		D7	186
		D11	188
Waccasassa, bay, Fla.		B8	174
Wachapreague, Accomack, Va.	507	C9	192
Wachusett, mtn., Mass.		B4	206
Wachusett, res., Mass.		B4	206
Waco, Haralson, Ga.	381	C1	176
Waco, Sedgwick, Kans.	20	B5	144
Waco, Madison, Ky.	300	C6	178
Waco, York, Nebr.	166	D8	152
Waco, Cleveland, N.C.	256	B4	186
Waco, McLennan, Tex.	97,808	D7	130
	(*129,000)		
Waconia, Carver, Minn.	2,048	G5	148
Waddān, Libya		B3	394
Waddān, mts., Libya		B3	394
Wadden, sea, Neth.		A4	282
Waddington, mtn., B.C., Can.		E10	52
Waddington, St. Lawrence, N.Y.	921	A6	212
Waddy, Shelby, Ky.	300	B5	178
Waddy, lake, Sask., Can.		B6	58
Wade (Town of), Aroostook, Maine	(220▲)	*B4	204
Wade, Jackson, Miss.	400	E4	184
Wade, Cumberland, N.C.	500	B7	186
Wade, Bryan, Okla.	150	E7	128
Wadena, Sask., Can.	1,154	E6	58
Wadena, Fayette, Iowa	275	B6	142
Wadena, Wadena, Minn.	4,381	E3	148
Wadena, co., Minn.	12,199	E3	148
Wädenswil, Switz.	10,400	A4	312
Wadesboro, Tangipahoa, La.	150	B6	180
Wadesboro, Anson, N.C.	3,744	C5	186
Wadesville, Posey, Ind.	300	D2	140
Wadham, is., Newf., Can.		F9	72
Wādi ar Ratam, Jordan	1,000	E1	378
Wādi Halfa, Sud.	11,006	A3	398
Wading, riv., N.J.		D3	210
Wading River, Burlington, N.J.	90	D4	210
Wading River, Suffolk, N.Y.	600	D4	212
Wadley, Randolph, Ala.	605	B4	168
Wadley, Jefferson, Ga.	1,898	D4	176
Wadmalaw, isl., S.C.		F8	188
Wadmalaw Island, Charleston, S.C.	725	G2	188
Wad Medani, Sud.	47,677	C3	398
Wadowice, Pol.	7,123	D4	325
Wadsworth, Autauga, Ala.	50	C3	168
Wadsworth, Washoe, Nev.	250	D2	112
Wadsworth, Medina, Ohio	10,635	A5	156
Waelder, Gonzales, Tex.	1,270	E7	130
Wagarville, Washington, Ala.	225	*D1	168
Wagener, Aiken, S.C.	614	D6	188
Wages, Yuma, Colo.		B8	106
Wagga, Sud.	4,676	B4	398
Waggaman, Jefferson, La.	800	C7	180
Waggāş, Jordan	1,000	B6	382
Wagga Wagga, Austl.	19,235	F9	432
Wagina, isl., Solomon		E1	436
Waginger, lake, Ger.		D5	286
Wagner, Phillips, Mont.	50	B8	110
Wagner, Charles Mix, S.Dak.	1,586	D7	158
Wagoner, Wagoner, Okla.	4,469	C8	128
Wagoner, co., Okla.	15,673	C8	128
Wagon Mound, Mora, N.Mex.	760	B6	126
Wagontire, mtn., Oreg.		D7	96
Wagontire, Harney, Oreg.		D7	96
Wagonwheel Gap, res., Colo.		E4	106
Wagram, Scotland, N.C.	562	C6	186
Wągrowiec, Pol.	10,800	B3	325
Wahai, Indon.		E7	359
Wahak Hotrontk, Pima, Ariz.	75	F3	124
Wahalak, Kemper, Miss.	145	C4	184
Wāhat Jabrin, Sau.Ar.		C4	383
Wahiawa, Honolulu, Haw.	15,512	B3	86
		F9	
Wahiawa, Kauai, Haw.	568	B2	86
Wahkiakum, co., Wash.	3,426	C3	98
Wahkon, Mille Lacs, Minn.	172	E5	148
Wahneta, Polk, Fla.	1,796	*D9	174
Wahoo, Saunders, Nebr.	3,610	C9	152
		D2	
Wahoo, creek, Nebr.		E2	152
Wahpeton, Dickinson, Iowa	117	*A2	142
Wahpeton, Richland, N.Dak.	5,876	D9	154
Waia, isl., Fiji		E6	436
Waiahole, Honolulu, Haw.		B4	86
		G10	
Waiakoa, Maui, Haw.	450	C5	86
Waialee, Honolulu, Haw.	75	F9	86
Waialua, Honolulu, Haw.	2,689	B3	86
		F9	
Waianae, Honolulu, Haw.	4,120	B3	68
		G9	
Waianae, mts., Haw.		G9	86
Waiau, Honolulu, Haw.		G10	86
Waiawa, riv., Haw.		G10	86
Waidhofen (an der Thaya), Aus.	3,602	B7	313
Waidhofen (an der Ybbs), Aus.	5,201	C6	313
Waigeo, isl., Neth.N.Gui.		D8	359
Waihee, Maui, Haw.	500	C5	86
Waikabubak, Indon.		F5	358
Waikalo, Indon.		F5	358
Waikane, Honolulu, Haw.	40	G10	86
Waikari, N.Z.	360	E4	437
Waikato, riv., N.Z.		B5	437
Waikawa, N.Z.	128	G2	437
Waikii, Hawaii, Haw.	45	D6	86
Waikiki, Honolulu, Haw. (part of Honolulu)		G10	86
Wailangilala, isl., Fiji		E7	436
Wailea, Hawaii, Haw.	250	D6	86
Wailua, Kauai, Haw.	1,129	A2	86
Wailua (Wailua Homesteads), Maui, Haw.	165	*C5	89
Wailua Homesteads, see Wailua, Hawaii, Haw.			
Wailuku, Maui, Haw.	6,969	C5	86
Wailuku, riv., Haw.		D6	86
Waimanalo, Honolulu, Haw.	3,011	B4	86
		G11	
Waimanalo, bay, Haw.		G11	86
Waimanalo Village, Honolulu, Haw.		G9	86
Waimate, N.Z.	3,107	F3	437
Waimea, Kauai, Haw.	1,312	B2	86
Waimea Camp, Honolulu, Haw.	70	F9	86
Wainganga, riv., India		D3	366
Waingapu, Indon.	2,217	F6	358
Waini, pt., Br.Gu.		D5	256
Wainuiomata, riv., N.Z.		J11	437
Wainwright, Alsk.	227	A6	84
Wainwright, Alta., Can.	2,653	D7	54
Wainwright, Tuscarawas, Ohio	500	B5	156
Wainwright, Muskogee, Okla.	114	C8	128
Waiohinu, Hawaii, Haw.	163	D6	86
Waipahu, Honolulu, Haw.	7,650	B3	86
		G9	
Waipara, N.Z.	168	E4	437
Waipawa, N.Z.	1,607	C6	437
Waipio Acres, Honolulu, Haw.	1,158	*G9	86
Waipio Camp, Honolulu, Haw.	500	G9	86
Waipukurau, N.Z.	2,886	D6	437
Wairoa, N.Z.	3,796	C6	437
Waitaki, riv., N.Z.		F3	437
Waitara, N.Z.	3,675	C5	437
Waite, Washington, Maine	65	C5	204
	(73▲)		
Waitemata, hbr., N.Z.		H8	437
Waiteville, Monroe, W.Va.	500	D4	194
Waite Park, Stearns, Minn.	2,016	F4	148
Waits, riv., Vt.		C4	218
Waitsburg, Walla Walla, Wash.	1,010	C8	98
Waitsfield, Washington, Vt.	175	C3	218
	(658▲)		
Waits River, Orange, Vt.	75	C4	218
Waiwo, Neth. N.Gui.		E8	359
Wajima, Jap.	34,052	F6	354
Wajir, Ken.		B7	414
Waka, Con.L.		B3	414
Wakamatsu (Fukuoka pref.), Jap.	97,310	*H3	354
Wakamatsu (Fukushima pref.), Jap.	97,885	F7	354
Wakarusa, Elkhart, Ind.	1,145	A3	140
Wakarusa, Shawnee, Kans.	90	D8	144
Wakasa, bay, Jap.			354
Wakatipu, lake, N.Z.		F2	437
Wakatomika, creek, Ohio		B4	156
Wakaw, Sask., Can.	898	D5	58
Wakayama, Jap.	97,885	G5	354
		M11	
Wake, co., N.C.	169,082	B7	186
Wake, isl., Pac.O.		A5	436
Wa Keeney, Trego, Kans.	2,808	C4	144
Wakefield, Que., Can.	376	S9	66
Wakefield, Eng.	59,700	H11	273
Wakefield, Clay, Kans.	603	C6	144
Wakefield, Middlesex, Mass.	24,295	A5	206
		C3	
Wakefield, Dixon and Wayne, Nebr.	1,068	B9	152
Wakefield, Carroll, N.H.	100	D4	208
	(1,223▲)		
Wakefield, Washington, R.I.	3,570	D3	216
Wakefield, Sussex, Va.	1,015	D8	192
Wake Forest, Wake, N.C.	2,664	B7	186
Wake Island, U.S. poss., Pac.O.	349	A5	436
Wakeman, Huron, Ohio	728	A4	156
Wakenda, Carroll, Mo.	146	B4	150
Wake Village, Bowie, Tex.	1,140	*C8	130
Wakita, Grant, Okla.	452	B6	128
Wakkanai, Jap.	44,751	B8	354
Wakkerstroom, U.S.Afr.	2,398	E6	420
Wakonda, Clay, S.Dak	382	D8	158
Wakopa, Man., Can.	35	F3	60
Wakpala, Corson, S.Dak.	100	B5	158
Wakuach, lake, Newf., Can.		D8	72
Wakulla, co., Fla.	5,257	A6	174
Walachia, reg., Rom.		B3	321
Walagā, prov., Eth.	1,000,000	D4	398
Walapai, Mohave, Ariz.	10	C2	124
Walbridge, Wood, Ohio	2,142	A1	156
Wałbrzych, Pol.	109,000	C3	325
Walcott, Greene, Ark.	75	A6	170
Walcott, Scott, Iowa	664	C7	142
Walcott, Carbon, Wyo.	30	E6	116
Walcz, Pol.	13,600	B3	325
Waldeck, Sask., Can.	128	E4	58
Walden, Jackson, Colo.	809	B4	106
Walden, Orange, N.Y.	4,851	D7	212
Walden, pond, Mass.		C3	206
Walden, ridge, Tenn.		C6	190
Waldenburg, Poinsett, Ark.	113	B6	170
Waldenburg, see Wałbrzych, Pol.			
Waldheim, Sask., Can.	495	D4	58
Waldo, Columbia, Ark.	1,722	D3	170

Waldo, B.C., Can.	109	F15	52
Waldo, Alachua, Fla.	735	B8	174
Waldo, Russell, Kans.	178	C5	144
Waldo, Waldo, Maine	35	*D3	204
	(395▲)		
Waldo, Marion, Ohio	374	B3	156
Waldo, Sheboygan, Wis.	403	E6	160
Waldo, co., Maine	22,632	D3	204
Waldo, hills, Oreg.		C1	96
Waldo, lake, Mass.		E3	206
Waldo, lake, Oreg.		D4	96
Waldoboro, Lincoln, Maine	705	D3	204
	(2,882▲)		
Waldorf, Charles, Md.	1,048	C6	182
Waldorf, Waseca, Minn.	270	H5	148
Waldport, Lincoln, Oreg.	667	C2	96
Waldron, Scott, Ark.	1,619	C2	170
Waldron, Sask., Can.	119	E6	58
Waldron, Shelby, Ind.	700	C4	140
Waldron, Harper, Kans.	38	E5	144
Waldron, Platte, Mo.	200	B3	150
Waldrup, Jasper, Miss.	200	D3	184
Waldshut, Ger.	10,600	E3	286
Waldwick, Bergen, N.J.	10,495	A4	210
Wales, Alsk.	141	B5	84
Wales, Ont., Can.	235	026	64
Wales (Town of), Androscoggin, Maine	(488▲)	*D2	204
Wales, Hampden, Mass.	300	B3	206
	(659▲)		
Wales, Cavalier, N.Dak.	151	B7	154
Wales, Giles, Tenn.	100	C4	190
Wales, Sanpete, Utah	130	D4	114
Wales, Waukesha, Wis.	356	*E5	160
Wales, reg., United Kingdom	2,991,000	I9	273
Waleska, Cherokee, Ga.	479	B2	176
Walford, Benton, Iowa	264	C6	142
Walgett, Austl.	1,348	D9	432
Walhachin, B.C., Can.	100	E12	52
Walhalla, Pembina, N.Dak.	1,432	B8	154
Walhalla, Oconee, S.C.	3,431	B2	188
Walhonding, riv., Ohio		B4	156
Walker, Yavapai, Ariz.	10	D3	124
Walker, Linn, Iowa	584	B6	142
Walker, Ellis, Kans.	100	D4	144
Walker, Livingston, La.	912	A6	180
Walker, Cass, Minn.	1,180	D4	148
Walker, Vernon, Mo.	235	D3	150
Walker, Corson, S.Dak.	20	B4	158
Walker, co., Ala.	54,211	B2	168
Walker, co., Ga.	45,264	B1	176
Walker, co., Tex.	21,475	D8	130
Walker, creek, Wyo.		D7	116
Walker, knob, Tenn.		C6	190
Walker, lake, Man., Can.		C4	60
Walker, lake, Nev.		E3	112
Walker, mtn., Ga.		B3	176
Walker, mtn., Oreg.		D5	96
Walker, mtn., Va.		D3	192
Walker Springs, Clarke, Ala.	450	D2	168
Walkersville, Frederick, Md.	1,020	B5	182
Walkersville, Lewis, W.Va.	190	C4	194
Walkerton, Ont., Can.	3,698	P19	64
Walkerton, St. Joseph, Ind.	2,044	A3	140
Walkertown, Forsyth, N.C.	1,240	A5	186
Walkerville, Silver Bow, Mont.	1,453	D4	110
Wall, Allegheny, Pa.	1,493	*C2	214
Wall, Pennington, S.Dak.	629	D3	158
Wall, lake, Iowa		B4	142
Wallace, Escambia, Ala.	100	D2	168
Wallace, Little River, Ark.		D2	170
Wallace, N.S., Can.	279	D6	70
Wallace, Shoshone, Idaho	2,412	B3	108
Wallace, Fountain, Ind.	122	C2	140
Wallace, Wallace, Kans.	110	D2	144
Wallace, St. John the Baptist, La.	130	B6	180
Wallace, Menominee, Mich.	120	D4	146
Wallace, Lincoln, Nebr.	293	D4	152
Wallace, Steuben, N.Y.	300	C4	212
Wallace, Duplin, N.C.	2,285	C8	186
Wallace, Marlboro, S.C.	350	B9	188
Wallace, Codington, S.Dak.	132	B8	158
Wallace, Washington, Va.	200	D2	192
Wallace, Harrison, W.Va.	525	A6	194
		B4	
Wallace, co., Kans.	2,069	D2	144
Wallace, lake, La.		B2	180
Wallaceburg, Ont., Can.	7,892	R18	64
Wallacetown, Ont., Can.	375	R19	64
Wallagrass (Plantation of), Aroostook, Maine	(818▲)	A4	204
Wallal Downs, Austl.		B4	432
Walland, Blount, Tenn.	250	C8	190
		E9	
Wallaroo, Austl.	2,403	E7	432
Walla Walla, Walla Walla, Wash.	24,536	C8	98
Walla Walla, co., Wash.	42,195	C8	98
Walla Walla, riv., Wash.		C8	98
Walla Walla East, Walla Walla, Wash.	1,557	C8	98
Walla Walla West (Garrett), Walla Walla, Wash.	1,641	*C8	98
Walled Lake, Oakland, Mich.	3,550	B7	146
Wallen, lake, Switz.		A5	312
Wallen, ridge, Va.		D1	192
Wallenpaupack, lake, Pa.		B6	214
Wallenstadt, Switz.	3,349	A5	312
Waller, Waller, Tex.	900	D8	130
Waller, co., Tex.	12,071	E7	130
Wallerville, Union, Miss.		A4	184
Wallingford, New Haven, Conn.	29,920	D4	202
Wallingford, Emmet, Iowa	228	A3	142
Wallingford, Rutland, Vt.	900	E3	218
	(1,439▲)		
Wallington, Bergen, N.J.	9,261	A1	210
Wallins Creek, Harlan, Ky.	468	*D7	178
Wallis, Austin, Tex.	950	E7	130
Wallkill, Ulster, N.Y.	1,215	D7	212
Wallkill, riv., N.Y.		D7	212
Wall Lake, Sac, Iowa	812	B2	142
Wallo, prov., Eth.	1,000,000	C4	398
Walloomsac, riv., Vt.		F2	218
Walloon, lake, Mich.		D7	146
Wallowa, Wallowa, Oreg.	989	B9	96
Wallowa, co., Oreg.	7,102	B9	96
Wallowa, mts., Oreg.		B9	96
Wallpack Center, Sussex, N.J.	25	A3	210
Walls, DeSoto, Miss.	300	A2	184
Walls, Scot.		A11	272
Wallsburg, Wasatch, Utah	180	C4	114
Wallsend, Eng.	49,600	G11	272
Wall Springs, Pinellas, Fla.	180	B6	174
Wallula, Walla Walla, Wash.	150	C8	98
Wallum Lake, Providence, R.I.	75	B2	216
Walney, isl., Eng.		G9	273
Walnut, Los Angeles, Calif.	934	C6	94
Walnut, Bureau, Ill.	1,192	B4	138
Walnut, Pottawattamie, Iowa	777	C2	142
Walnut, Crawford, Kans.	381	E8	144
Walnut, Tippah, Miss.	390	A4	184
Walnut, Knox, Nebr.		B7	152
Walnut, Madison, N.C.	450	B3	186
Walnut, creek, Calif.		A5	94
Walnut, creek, Kans.		D3	144
Walnut, hill, Mass.		B2	206
Walnut, riv., Kans.		E6	144
Walnut Canyon, natl. mon., Ariz.		C4	124
Walnut Cove, Stokes, N.C.	1,288	A5	186
Walnut Creek, Contra Costa, Calif.	9,903	A5	94
Walnut Grove, Etowah, Ala.	237	A3	168
Walnut Grove, Walton, Ga.	119	*C3	176
Walnut Grove, Redwood, Minn.	886	G3	148
Walnut Grove, Leake, Miss.	433	C3	184
Walnut Grove, Greene, Mo.	373	D4	150
Walnut Heights, Contra Costa, Calif.	5,080	*D3	94
Walnut Hill, Lafayette, Ark.	25	D3	170
Walnut Hill, Cumberland, Maine		E5	204
Walnut Park, Los Angeles, Calif.	7,500	C5	94
Walnutport, Northampton, Pa.	1,609	C6	214
Walnut Ridge, Grant, Ark.		C4	170
Walnut Ridge, Lawrence, Ark.	3,547	A6	170
Walnut Springs, Sevier, Ark.	15	*D2	170
Walnut Springs, Bosque, Tex.	490	C7	130
Walnut Valley, Warren, N.J.	25	B2	210
Walpole, Sask., Can.	95	F7	58
Walpole, Norfolk, Mass.	7,000	B5	206
	(14,068▲)	E2	
Walpole, Cheshire, N.H.	800	E2	208
	(2,825▲)		
Walsall, Eng.	114,700	I10	273
Walsen, Huerfano, Colo.	100	E6	106
Walsenburg, Huerfano, Colo.	5,071	E6	106
Walsh, Alta., Can.	125	F7	54
Walsh, Baca, Colo.	856	E8	106
Walsh, co., N.Dak.	17,997	B8	154
Walsingham, cape, N.W.Ter., Can.		D12	48
Walsrode, Ger.	13,260	B3	286
Walston, Wicomico, Md.	120	D9	182
Walter Bathurst, cape, N.W.Ter., Can.		C11	48
Walterboro, Colleton, S.C.	5,417	F7	188
Walterhill, Rutherford, Tenn.	100	C5	190
Walters, Faribault, Minn.	133	H5	148
Walters, Cotton, Okla.	2,825	D5	128
Walters, Isle of Wight, Va.	135	D8	192
Walters Falls, Ont., Can.	200	P20	64
Waltersville, Warren, Miss.	400	C2	184
Walterville, Lane, Oreg.	170	C4	96
Walthall, Webster, Miss.	153	B3	184
Walthall, Chesterfield, Va.		B9	192
Walthall, co., Miss.	13,512	D2	184
Waltham, Hancock, Maine	30	*D4	204
	(153▲)		
Waltham, Middlesex, Mass.	55,413	B5	206
		D2	
Waltham, Mower, Minn.	207	H6	148
Waltham, Chouteau, Mont.	25	C6	110
Walthill, Thurston, Nebr.	844	B9	152
Walthourville, Liberty, Ga.	600	E5	176
Waltman, Natrona, Wyo.	5	C5	116
Walton, N.S., Can.	275	D6	70
Walton, Ont., Can.	175	Q19	64
Walton, Saint Lucie, Fla.	75	D10	174
Walton, Cass, Ind.	1,079	B3	140
Walton, Harvey, Kans.	225	D6	144
Walton, Boone, Ky.	1,530	A8	178
		B6	
Walton, Lancaster, Nebr.	80	E2	152
Walton, Delaware, N.Y.	3,855	C6	212
Walton, Roane, W.Va.	375	C3	194
Walton, co., Fla.	15,576	A4	174
Walton, co., Ga.	20,481	C3	176
Walton Hills, Cuyahoga, Ohio	1,776	*A5	156
Waltonville, Jefferson, Ill.	394	E4	138
Waltreak, Yell, Ark.	50	C3	170
Walville, peak, Wash.		C3	98
Walvis Bay, S.W.Afr.	2,325	D2	420
Walworth, Walworth, Wis.	1,494	F5	160
Walworth, co., S.Dak.	8,097	B5	158
Walworth, co., Wis.	52,368	F5	160
Wama, Afg.	5,000	B6	374
Wamac, Marion, Ill.	1,394	E4	138
Wamba, Con.L.		B4	414
Wamba, Nig.		E6	409
Wamba, riv., Con.L.		D2	414
Wamego, Pottawatomie, Kans.	2,363	C7	144
Wamesit, Middlesex, Mass.	406	A5	206
Wamgumbaug, lake, Conn.		B6	202
Wami, riv., Tan.		D6	414
Wamic, Wasco, Oreg.	125	B5	96
Wampee, Horry, S.C.		D11	188
Wampsville, Madison, N.Y.	564	B6	212
Wampum, Lawrence, Pa.	1,085	C1	214
Wamsutter, Sweetwater, Wyo.	110	E5	116
Wana, Pak.		C6	375
Wanaaring, Austl.	64	D8	432
Wanaka, lake, N.Z.		F2	437
Wanakah, Erie, N.Y.	2,000	C3	212
Wanamaker, Marion, Ind.	600	D5	140
		C3	
Wanamassa, Monmouth, N.J.	3,928	C4	210
Wanamie, Luzerne, Pa.	950	B5	214
Wanamingo, Goodhue, Minn.	540	G6	148
Wanan, China		L7	349
Wananish, Columbus, N.C. (part of Lake Waccamaw)		C7	186
Wanapitei, riv., Ont., Can.		020	64
Wanaque, Passaic, N.J.	7,126	A4	210
Wanaque, res., N.J.		A4	210
Wanatah, La Porte, Ind.	800	A3	140
Wanblee, Washabaugh, S.Dak.	200	D4	158
Wanchese, Dare, N.C.	600	B10	186
Wanda, Redwood, Minn.	160	G3	148
Wanderer, bay, Solomon		E2	436
Wandering River, Alta., Can.		C6	54
Wando, Kor.	15,142	H13	348
Wando, Berkeley, S.C.	100	F4	188
		F9	
Wando, riv., S.C.		F9	188
Waneta, B.C., Can.	67	F14	52
Wanette, Pottawatomie, Okla.	381	D6	128
Wang, riv., Thai.		C3	362
Wanganui, N.Z.	29,671	C5	437
	(*32,100)		
Wangaratta, Austl.	10,715	F9	432
Wangching (Paitsaokou), China	5,000	D14	348
Wangerooge, isl., Ger.		B2	286
Wangkuei, China	5,000	B13	348
Wangmeng, China		M3	349
Wangyehmiao, China	5,000	B11	348
Wanham, Alta., Can.	150	C3	54
Wanhsien, China	50,000	J4	349
Wanipigow, riv., Man., Can.		E5	60
Wankie, Rh.&Nya.	20,000	C5	420
Wankie, natl. park, Rh.&Nya.		C5	420
Wann, Saunders, Nebr.	35	E2	152
Wann, Nowata, Okla.	157	B8	128
Wanne-Eickel, Ger.	101,100	*C2	286
Wantagh, Nassau, N.Y.	34,172	E3	212
Wantsai, China	10,000	K7	349
Wapakoneta, Auglaize, Ohio	6,756	B2	156
Wapanucka, Johnston, Okla.	459	D6	128
Wapato, Yakima, Wash.	3,137	C6	98
Wapawekka, hills, Sask., Can.		C5	58
Wapawekka, lake, Sask., Can.		C5	58
Wapella, Sask., Can.	530	E7	58
Wapella, De Witt, Ill.	526	C5	138
Wapello, Louisa, Iowa	1,745	C6	142
Wapello, co., Iowa	46,126	C5	142
Wapi, Blaine, Idaho		G5	108
Wapisu, lake, Man., Can.		C3	60
Wapiti, Park, Wyo.	15	B3	116
Wapiti, pass, B.C., Can.		C12	52
Wapiti, range, Wyo.		B3	116
Wapiti, riv., Alta., B.C., Can.		C3	54
		C12	52
Wappapello, Wayne, Mo.	150	E7	150
Wappapello, res., Mo.		D7	150
Wappingers Falls, Dutchess, N.Y.	4,447	D8	212
Wapsipinicon, riv., Iowa		B6	142
Wapus, lake, Sask., Can.		B6	58
Waquoit, Barnstable, Mass.	336	C6	206
War, McDowell, W.Va.	3,006	D3	194
War, ridge, W.Va.		D7	194
Waramaug, lake, Conn.		C2	202
Warangal, India	133,130	E3	366
Warba, Itasca, Minn.	162	D5	148
Warburg, Alta., Can.	257	D5	54
Warburg, Ger.	10,071	C3	286
Ward, Sumter, Ala.	100	C1	168
Ward, Lonoke, Ark.	470	B5	170
Ward, Boulder, Colo.	9	*B5	106
Ward, Saluda, S.C.	162	D5	188
Ward, Moody, S.Dak.	74	C9	158
Ward, Kanawha, W.Va.	1,109	C6	194
Ward, co., N.Dak.	47,072	B4	154
Ward, co., Tex.	14,917	D4	130
Ward, isl., N.Z.		J11	437
Ward, mtn., Mont.		D2	110
Wardân, Eg., U.A.R.		D1	382
Wardell, Pemiscot, Mo.	331	E8	150
Warden, Richland, La.	100	B4	180
Warden, Grant, Wash.	949	C7	98
Warden Junction, Alta., Can.	60	D6	54
Wardensville, Hardy, W.Va.	289	B6	194
Wardha, India	39,827	D3	366
Wardha, riv., India		D3	366
Ward Hill, Essex, Mass.		A5	206
Ward Hill, mtn., Scot.		C9	272
Wardlow, Alta., Can.	30	E7	54
Wardner, B.C., Can.	200	F15	52
Wardner, Shoshone, Idaho	577	B2	108
Ward Ridge, Gulf, Fla.	1,886	*B5	174
Wardsboro, Windham, Vt.	125	E3	218
	(322▲)		
Ward Spring, Pittsburg, Okla.		D7	128
Ward's Stone, mtn., Eng.		G10	273
Wardville, Rapides, La.	1,086	*C3	180
Wardville, Atoka, Okla.	150	D7	128
Ware, Hampshire, Mass.	6,650	B3	206
	(7,517▲)		
Ware, Fergus, Mont.	11	C7	110
Ware, co., Ga.	34,219	E4	176
Ware, riv., Mass.		B3	206
Wareagle, Benton, Ark.	40	A3	170
War Eagle, Mingo, W.Va.	300	D3	194
War Eagle, creek, Ark.		A3	170
Ware Center, Hampshire, Mass.	40	B3	206
Wareham, Plymouth, Mass.	1,739	C6	206
	(9,461▲)		
Wareham Center, Plymouth, Mass.		C6	206
Warehouse Point, Hartford, Conn.	1,936	B5	202
Waren, Ger.	19,900	B5	286
Waren, Neth.N.Gui.		E9	359
Waresboro, Ware, Ga.	350	E4	176
Ware Shoals, Greenwood, S.C.	2,671	C4	188
Waretown, Ocean, N.J.	500	D4	210
Warfield, B.C., Can.	2,051	*F14	52
Warfield, Martin, Ky.	295	C8	178
Warfield, Brunswick, Va.	80	D7	192
Warkworth, Ont., Can.	675	P23	64
Warkworth, N.Z.	883	B5	437
Warland, Lincoln, Mont.	40	B1	110
Warman, Sask., Can.	95	D4	58
Warmbad, S.W.Afr.	4,137	E3	420
Warmbad, U.S.Afr.		D5	420
Warm Beach, Snohomish, Wash.	300	A4	98
Warminster, Eng.	8,500	J10	273
Warm River, Fremont, Idaho	20	*E7	108
Warm Springs, Randolph, Ark.	40	A5	170
Warm Springs, Meriwether, Ga.	538	D2	176
Warmsprings, Deer Lodge, Mont.		D4	110
Warm Springs, Nye, Nev.	17	D7	112
Warm Springs, Jefferson, Oreg.	250	C5	96
Warm Springs, Bath, Va.	300	B5	192
Warm Springs, res., Oreg.		D8	96
Warnemünde, Ger. (part of Rostock)		A5	286
Warner, Alta., Can.	450	F6	54
Warner, Merrimack, N.H.	750	E3	208
	(1,004▲)		
Warner, Washington, Ohio	350	C5	156
Warner, Muskogee, Okla.	881	C8	128
Warner, Brown, S.Dak.	135	B7	158
Warner, mtn., Mass.		B1	206
Warner Robins, Houston, Ga.	18,633	D3	176
Warner Springs, San Diego, Calif.	150	F5	94
Warnerton, Washington, La.	35	D5	180
Warnes, Bol.	1,581	C2	246
Warnow, riv., Ger.		B4	286
Warr Acres, Oklahoma, Okla.	7,135	C6	128
Warrego, riv., Austl.		D9	432
Warren, Cochise, Ariz. (part of Bisbee)		G6	124
Warren, Bradley, Ark.	6,752	D4	170
Warren, Litchfield, Conn.	100	C2	202
	(600▲)		
Warren, Idaho, Idaho	30	D3	108
Warren, Jo Daviess, Ill.	1,470	A4	138
Warren, Huntington, Ind.	1,241	B4	140
Warren, Knox, Maine	50	D3	204
	(1,678▲)		
Warren, Worcester, Mass.	1,616	B3	206
	(3,383▲)		
Warren, Macomb, Mich.	89,246	B9	146
Warren, Marshall, Minn.	2,007	C2	148
Warren, Carbon, Mont.	17	E8	110
Warren, Grafton N.H.	400	D3	208
	(548▲)		
Warren, Trumbull, Ohio	59,648	A6	156
Warren, Jackson, Okla.	40	D4	128
Warren, Columbia, Oreg.	150	B4	96
Warren, Warren, Pa.	14,505	B2	214
Warren, Bristol, R.I.	8,750	C3	216
Warren, Washington, Vt.	200	C3	218
	(469▲)		
Warren, co., Ga.	7,360	C4	176
Warren, co., Ill.	21,587	C3	138
Warren, co., Ind.	8,545	B2	140
Warren, co., Iowa	20,829	C4	142
Warren, co., Ky.	45,491	C4	178
Warren, co., Miss.	42,206	C2	184
Warren, co., Mo.	8,750	C6	150
Warren, co., N.J.	63,220	B3	210
Warren, co., N.Y.	44,002	B8	212
Warren, co., N.C.	19,652	A7	186
Warren, co., Ohio	65,711	C2	156
Warren, co., Pa.	45,582	B2	214
Warren, co., Tenn.	23,102	C6	190
Warren, co., Va.	14,655	B6	192
Warren, pt., R.I.		D4	216
Warren Grove, Ocean, N.J.	50	D4	210
Warren Park, Marion, Ind.	852	D5	140
Warrenpoint, N.Ire.	2,798	G6	273
Warrens, Monroe, Wis.	280	D3	160
Warrensburg, Macon, Ill.	681	D4	138
Warrensburg, Johnson, Mo.	9,689	C4	150
Warrensburg, Warren, N.Y.	2,240	B8	212
Warrensburg, Greene, Tenn.	100	B8	190
Warrensville [Heights], Cuyahoga, Ohio	10,609	B1	156
Warrenton, Warren, Ga.	1,770	C4	176
Warrenton, Warren, Mo.	1,869	C6	150
Warrenton, Warren, N.C.	1,124	A7	186
Warrenton, Clatsop, Oreg.	1,717	A3	96
Warrenton, Fauquier, Va.	3,522	B7	192
Warrentown, U.S.Afr.		E4	420
Warrenville, Du Page, Ill.	3,134	F2	138
Warrenville, Aiken, S.C.	1,128	D5	188
Warri, Nig.	10,726	E6	408
Warrick, Chouteau, Mont.	5	B7	110
Warrick, co., Ind.	23,577	D2	140
Warrington, Escambia, Fla.	16,752	A3	174
Warrior, Jefferson, Ala.	2,448	B3	168
Warrior, mtn., Md.		A2	182
Warrior Run, Luzerne, Pa.	833	B6	214
Warrnambool, Austl.	10,850	F8	432
Warroad, Roseau, Minn.	1,309	C3	148
Warsaw, Ont., Can.	250	P22	64
Warsaw, Hancock, Ill.	1,938	C2	138
Warsaw, Kosciusko, Ind.	7,234	A4	140
Warsaw, Gallatin, Ky.	981	B6	178
		B7	
Warsaw, Rice, Minn.	108	G5	148
Warsaw, Benton, Mo.	1,054	C4	150
Warsaw, Wyoming, N.Y.	3,653	C3	212
Warsaw, Duplin, N.C.	2,221	B7	186
Warsaw, Coshocton, Ohio	594	B4	156
Warsaw (Warszawa), Pol.	996,000	B5	319
	(*1,300,000)		
Warsaw, Richmond, Va.	549	C8	192
Warson Woods, St. Louis, Mo.	1,746	*C7	150
Warspite, Alta., Can.	159	C6	54
Warszawa, see Warsaw, Pol.			
Warszawa, pol. div., Pol.	2,237,000	*B5	325
Warta, Pol.	2,896	C4	325
Warta, riv., Pol.		C4	325
Wartburg, Morgan, Tenn.	800	B7	190
Warthen, Washington, Ga.	275	C4	176
Wartime, Sask., Can.	105	E3	58
Wartrace, Bedford, Tenn.	545	C5	190
Warwick, Austl.	9,850	D10	432
Warwick, Ont., Can.	170	Q19	64
Warwick, Que., Can.	2,248	S13	66
Warwick, Worth, Ga.	434	E3	176
Warwick, Cecil, Md.	350	B8	182
Warwick, Franklin, Mass.	150	A3	206
	(426▲)		
Warwick, Orange, N.Y.	3,218	D7	212
Warwick, Benson, N.Dak.	204	C7	154
Warwick, Lincoln, Okla.	250	C7	128
Warwick, Kent, R.I.	68,504	C3	216
Warwick, co., Eng.	1,919,000	I11	273
Warwick Neck, Kent, R.I. (part of Warwick)		C3	216
Wasatch, co., Utah	5,308	C4	114
Wasatch, mts., Utah		C4	114
Wasco, Kern, Calif.	6,841	E4	94
Wasco, Sherman, Oreg.	348	B6	96
Wasco, co., Oreg.	20,205	B5	96
Waseca, Sask., Can.	132	D3	58
Waseca, Waseca, Minn.	5,898	G5	148

Waseca, co., Minn. 16,041 G5 148
Wascott, Douglas, Wis. 55 B2 160
Wash, bay, Eng. I13 273
Washabaugh, co., S.Dak. 1,042 D4 158
Washago, Ont., Can. 300 P21 64
Washakie, Box Elder, Utah 65 *B3 114
Washakie, co., Wyo. 8,883 C5 116
Washakie Needles, mtn., Wyo. C3 116
Washburn, Sebastian, Ark. 100 *B2 170
Washburn, Woodford, Ill. 1,064 C4 138
Washburn, Black Hawk, Iowa 181 B5 142
Washburn, Aroostook, Maine 1,055 (2,083▲) B4 204
Washburn, Barry, Mo. 325 E4 150
Washburn, McLean, N.Dak. 993 C4 154
Washburn, Bayfield, Wis. 1,896 B3 160
Washburn, co., Wis. 10,301 C2 160
Washington, Hempstead, Ark. 321 D3 170
Washington, Litchfield, Conn. 500 (2,603▲) C2 202
Washington, D.C. 763,956 (*2,053,600) B8 192
Washington, Wilkes, Ga. 4,440 C4 176
Washington, Tazewell, Ill. 5,919 C4 138
Washington, Daviess, Ind. 10,846 D2 140
Washington, Washington, Iowa 6,037 C6 142
Washington, Washington, Kans. 1,506 C6 144
Washington, Mason, Ky. 600 B7 178
Washington, St. Landry, La. 1,291 D3 180
Washington, Knox, Maine 250 (636▲) D3 204
Washington, Berkshire, Mass. 80 (290▲) B1 206
Washington, Macomb, Mich. 900 G8 146
Washington, Adams, Miss. 200 D1 184
Washington, Franklin, Mo. 7,961 C6 150
Washington, Washington, Nebr. 44 D2 152
Washington, Sullivan, N.H. 100 (162▲) E2 208
Washington, Warren, N.J. 5,723 B3 210
Washington, Beaufort, N.C. 9,939 B8 186
Washington, McClain, Okla. 278 C6 128
Washington, Washington, Pa. 23,545 C1 214
Washington, Rhea, Tenn. 90 C7 190
Washington, Washington, Utah 445 F2 114
Washington, Orange, Vt. 200 (565▲) C4 218
Washington, Rappahannock, Va. 255 B6 192
Washington, Wood, W.Va. 300 B3 194
Washington, co., Ala. 15,372 D1 168
Washington, co., Ark. 55,797 A2 170
Washington, co., Colo. 6,625 C7 106
Washington, co., Fla. 11,249 A5 174
Washington, co., Ga. 18,903 C4 176
Washington, co., Idaho 8,378 E2 108
Washington, co., Ill. 13,569 E4 138
Washington, co., Ind. 17,819 D3 140
Washington, co., Iowa 19,406 C6 142
Washington, co., Kans. 10,739 C6 144
Washington, co., Ky. 11,168 C5 178
Washington, co., Maine 32,908 D5 204
Washington, co., Md. 91,219 A3 182
Washington, co., Minn. 52,432 F6 148
Washington, co., Miss. 78,638 B1 184
Washington, co., Mo. 14,346 D7 150
Washington, co., Nebr. 12,103 C9 152
Washington, co., N.Y. 48,476 B8 212
Washington, co., N.C. 13,488 B9 186
Washington, co., Ohio 51,689 C5 156
Washington, co., Okla. 42,347 B8 128
Washington, co., Oreg. 92,237 B3 96
Washington, co., Pa. 217,271 C1 214
Washington, co., R.I. 59,054 D2 216
Washington, co., Tenn. 64,832 B9 190
Washington, co., Tex. 19,145 D7 130
Washington, co., Utah 10,271 F2 114
Washington, co., Vt. 42,860 C3 218
Washington, co., Va. 38,076 D3 192
Washington, co., Wis. 46,119 E5 160
Washington, par., La. 44,015 D5 180
Washington, state, U.S. 2,853,214 B2 77, 98
Washington, cape, Fiji E6 436
Washington, isl., Pac.O. C4 436
Washington, isl., Wis. C7 160
Washington, lake, Fla. C10 174
Washington, lake, Minn. F4 148
Washington, lake, Miss. B1 184
Washington, lake, Wash. D3 98
Washington, mtn., N.H. C4 208
Washington, mtn., Oreg. C5 96
Washington C.H., Fayette, Ohio 12,388 C3 156
Washington Crossing, Mercer, N.J. 500 C3 210
Washington Depot, Litchfield, Conn. 503 C2 202
Washington Grove, Montgomery, Md. 576 B5 182
Washington Island, Door, Wis. 300 C7 160
Washington Park, St. Clair, Ill. 6,601 E3 138
Washington Park, Beaufort, N.C. 574 B8 186
Washington Place, Marion, Ind. 2,000 D5 140
Washington Terrace, Weber, Utah 6,441 B4 114
Washington Township, Bergen, N.J. 6,654 *B4 210
Washington Valley, Morris, N.J. 800 *B4 210
Washingtonville, Columbiana, Ohio 810 *B6 156
Washir, Afg. 10,000 C2 374
Washita, co., Okla. 18,121 C4 128
Washita, riv., Okla. C5 128
Washoe, Carbon, Mont. 115 *E7 110
Washoe, co., Nev. 84,743 C2 112
Washougal, Clark, Wash. 2,672 D4 98
Washow, bay, Man., Can. E4 60
Washta, Cherokee, Iowa 310 B2 142
Washtenaw, co., Mich. 172,440 G8 146
Washtucna, Adams, Wash. 331 C8 98
Washunga, Kay, Okla. 60 B7 128
Wasilków, Pol. 3,948 B6 325
Wasilla, Alsk. 97 C7, G11 84
Wasioja, Dodge, Minn. 130 G6 148
Waskada, Man., Can. 357 F2 60
Waskaiowaka, lake, Man., Can. B4 60
Waskana, creek, Sask., Can. E5 58
Waskatenau, Alta., Can. 289 C6 54
Waskesiu, lake, Sask., Can. D4 58
Waskigomog, lake, Ont., Can. O21 64
Waskom, Harrison, Tex. 1,336 C8 130
Wasola, Ozark, Mo. 256 E5 150
Wasque, pt., Mass. D7 206
Wass, lake, Man., Can. D5 60
Wassaw, sound, Ga. E6 176
Wassenaar, Neth. 3,831 B3 282
Wasserburg [am Inn], Ger. 6,500 D5 286
Wassokeag, lake, Maine C3 204
Wassuk, range, Nev. E3 112
Wasta, Pennington, S.Dak. 196 C3 158
Wasta, Eg., U.A.R. 7,311 B3 395
Wataga, Knox, Ill. 570 B3 138
Watampone, Indon. 2,515 F6 358
Wataroa, N.Z. 159 E3 437
Watatic, mtn., Mass. A4 206
Watauga, Corson, S.Dak. 74 B4 158
Watauga, Carter, Tenn. 500 B9 190
Watauga, co., N.C. 17,529 A4 186
Watauga, riv., Tenn. B10 190
Watchaug, pond, R.I. D2 216
Watch Hill, Washington, R.I. 300 D1 216
Watchung, Somerset, N.J. 3,312 B4 210
Waterboro, York, Maine 300 (1,059▲) E2 204
Waterbury, New Haven, Conn. 107,130 (*190,300) C3 202
Waterbury, Dixon, Nebr. 81 B9 152
Waterbury, Washington, Vt. 2,984 (4,303▲) C3 218
Waterbury, riv., Vt. C3 218
Waterbury Center, Washington, Vt. 400 C3 218
Waterdown, Ont., Can. 1,754 Q21 64
Wateree, Richland, S.C. 75 D7 188
Wateree, res., S.C. C7 188
Wateree, riv., S.C. D7 188
Waterflow, San Juan, N.Mex. 15 B2 126
Waterford, Stanislaus, Calif. 1,780 *D3 94
Waterford, Ont., Can. 1,908 R20 64
Waterford, New London, Conn. 5,000 (15,391▲) D7 202
Waterford, La Porte, Ind. 200 A3 140
Waterford, Ire. 28,878 I5 273
Waterford, Spencer, Ky. 60 A5 178
Waterford, Oxford, Maine 160 (834▲) *D2 204
Waterford, Oakland, Mich. 1,000 *G8 146
Waterford, Marshall, Miss. 175 A3 184
Waterford, Saratoga, N.Y. 2,915 C8 212
Waterford, Washington, Ohio 450 C5 156
Waterford, Erie, Pa. 1,390 B2 214
Waterford, Loudoun, Va. 247 A7 192
Waterford, Racine, Wis. 1,500 F1, F5 160
Waterford, co., Ire. 7,403 I5 273
Waterford Mills, Elkhart, Ind. 150 A4 140
Waterford Works, Camden, N.J. 700 D3 210
Waterhen, lake, Man., Can. D3 60
Waterloo, Lauderdale, Ala. 215 A1 168
Waterloo, Nevada, Ark. 200 D3 170
Waterloo, Bel. 10,089 D3 282
Waterloo, Ont., Can. 16,373 Q20 64
Waterloo, Que., Can. 4,266 S12 66
Waterloo, Monroe, Ill. 3,739 E3 138
Waterloo, De Kalb, Ind. 1,432 A4 140
Waterloo, Black Hawk, Iowa 71,755 (*114,300) B5 142
Waterloo, Madison, Mont. 200 E4 110
Waterloo, Douglas, Nebr. 516 D2 152
Waterloo, Seneca, N.Y. 5,098 C5 212
Waterloo, Linn, Oreg. 151 C4 96
Waterloo, S.L. E2 408
Waterloo, Laurens, S.C. 148 C4 188
Waterloo, Overton, Tenn. B6 190
Waterloo, Jefferson, Wis. 1,947 E5 160
Waterloo, co., Ont., Can. 148,774 Q20 64
Waterman, De Kalb, Ill. 916 B5 138
Waterman, Wheeler, Oreg. C7 96
Waterman, res., R.I. B2 216
Waterport, Orleans, N.Y. 200 B3 212
Water Proof, Tensas, La. 1,412 C4 180
Waters, Otsego, Mich. 35 E7 146
Watersmeet, Gogebic, Mich. 500 C2 146
Waterton Glacier, International Peace Park, Can., U.S. B4 77
Waterton Lakes, natl. park, Alta., Can. F5 54
Waterton Park, Alta., Can. 225 F6 54
Watertown, Litchfield, Conn. 5,500 (14,837▲) C3 202
Watertown, Columbia, Fla. 2,109 A8 174
Watertown, Middlesex, Mass. 39,092 D2 206
Watertown, Carver, Minn. 1,046 *G5 148
Watertown, Jefferson, N.Y. 33,306 B6 212
Watertown, Codington, S.Dak. 14,077 C9 158
Watertown, Wilson, Tenn. 919 B5 190
Watertown, Jefferson, Wis. 13,943 E5 160
Watertown, riv., Alta., Can. F6 54
Water Valley, Graves, Ky. 267 D2 178
Water Valley, Yalobusha, Miss. 3,206 A3 184
Water View, Middlesex, Va. 150 C8 192
Waterville, N.S., Can. 415 D5 70
Waterville, Que., Can. 1,373 S13 66
Waterville, Allamakee, Iowa 184 A6 142
Waterville, Marshall, Kans. 700 C7 144
Waterville, Kennebec, Maine 18,695 D3 204
Waterville, Worcester, Mass. 300 A3 206
Waterville, Le Sueur, Minn. 1,623 G5 148
Waterville, Grafton, N.H. 11 (14▲) D3 208
Waterville, Oneida, N.Y. 1,901 C6 212
Waterville, Lucas, Ohio 1,856 A1, A3 156
Waterville, Lamoille, Vt. 250 (332▲) B3 218
Waterville, Douglas, Wash. 1,013 B6 98
Watervliet, Bel. 2,072 C2 282
Watervliet, Berrien, Mich. 1,818 G5 146
Watervliet, Albany, N.Y. 13,917 C8 212
Waterways, Alta., Can. 250 B7 54
Watford, Ont., Can. 1,217 R19 64
Watford, Eng. 72,520 J12 273
Watford City, McKenzie, N.Dak. 1,865 C2 154
Wathena, Doniphan, Kans. 837 C9 144
Watino, Alta., Can. 65 C4 54
Watkins, Adams, Colo. 100 C6 106
Watkins, Meeker, Minn. 744 F4 148
Watkins Glen, Schuyler, N.Y. 2,813 C5 212
Watkinsville, Oconee, Ga. 758 C3 176
Watonga, Blaine, Okla. 3,252 C5 128
Watonwan, co., Minn. 14,460 G4 148
Watonwan, riv., Minn. G4 148
Watou, Bel. 2,841 D1 282
Watova, Nowata, Okla. 80 B8 128
Watrous, Sask., Can. 1,340 E5 58
Watrous, Mora, N.Mex. 150 C6 126
Watsa, Con.L. B4 414
Watseka, Iroquois, Ill. 5,219 C6 138
Watson, Jefferson, Ala. 250 *B3 168
Watson, Desha, Ark. 312 D5 170
Watson, Sask., Can. 783 D5 58
Watson, Clark, Ind. 500 D4 140
Watson, Chippewa, Minn. 267 F3 148
Watson, Marshall, Miss. 100 A3 184
Watson, Atchison, Mo. 181 A2 150
Watson, McCurtain, Okla. 30 D9 128
Watson, Marion, W.Va. 900 A7 194
Watson Chapel, Jefferson, Ark. 250 C4 170
Watson Lake, Yukon, Can. 100 E6 48
Watsontown, Northumberland, Pa. 2,431 B5 214
Watsonville, Santa Cruz, Calif. 13,293 D3 94
Watten, lake, Scot. C9 272
Wattenberg, Weld, Colo. 150 B6 106
Wattensaw, bayou, Ark. C5 170
Wattenscheid, Ger. 75,500 *C2 286
Wattis, Carbon, Utah 100 D4 114
Watton, Eng. 3,104 I13 273
Watton, Baraga, Mich. 70 C3 146
Wattrelos, Fr. 31,993 B5 278
Watts, Adair, Okla. 268 B9 128
Watts Bar, lake, Tenn. C7 190
Watts Bar Dam, Rhea, Tenn. 25 C7 190
Watts Mills, see Wattsville, S.C.
Wattsville, St. Clair, Ala. 700 B3 168
Wattsville (Watts Mills), Laurens, S.C. 1,438 B5 188
Wattwil, Switz. 6,336 A5 312
Watu, Con.L. C3 414
Wau, Sud. 8,009 D2 398
Waubamick, Ont., Can. 95 O20 64
Waubaushene, Ont., Can. 565 P21 64
Waubay, Day, S.Dak. 851 B8 158
Waubay, lake, S.Dak. B8 158
Waubun, Mahnomen, Minn. 350 D3 148
Wauchope, Sask., Can. 78 F7 58
Wauchula, Hardee, Fla. 2,872 D9 174
Waucoma, Fayette, Iowa 364 A5 142
Wauconda, Lake, Ill. 3,227 E2 138
Wauconda, Okanogan, Wash. 15 A7 98
Waukau, Winnebago, Wis. 150 E5 160
Waukee, Dallas, Iowa 687 C4 142
Waukeenah, Jefferson, Fla. 300 A7 174
Waukegan, Lake, Ill. 55,719 A6, E2 138
Waukesha, Waukesha, Wis. 30,004 E1, E5 160
Waukesha, co., Wis. 158,249 F5 160
Waukomis, Garfield, Okla. 516 B6 128
Waukon, Allamakee, Iowa 3,639 A6 142
Waukon, Lincoln, Wash. 25 D8 98
Wauna, Clatsop, Oreg. 175 A3 96
Wauna, Pierce, Wash. 130 D2 98
Waunakee, Dane, Wis. 1,611 E4 160
Wauneta, Chase, Nebr. 794 D4 152
Waupaca, Waupaca, Wis. 3,984 D4 160
Waupaca, co., Wis. 35,340 D5 160
Waupun, Fond du Lac, Wis. 7,935 E5 160
Wauregan, Windham, Conn. 950 C8 202
Waurika, Jefferson, Okla. 1,933 D6 128
Wausa, Knox, Nebr. 724 B8 152
Wausau, Washington, Fla. 325 A5 174
Wausau, Marathon, Wis. 31,943 D4 160
Wausaukee, Marinette, Wis. 608 C6 160
Wauseon, Fulton, Ohio 4,311 A2 156
Waushara, co., Wis. 13,497 D4 160
Wautoma, Waushara, Wis. 1,466 D4 160
Wauwatosa, Milwaukee, Wis. 56,923 E1 160
Wauzeka, Crawford, Wis. 494 E3 160
Wave, Dallas, Ark. C4 170
Wave Hill, Austl. B6 432
Waveland, Yell, Ark. 90 B3 170
Waveland, Montgomery, Ind. 549 C2 140
Waveland, Hancock, Miss. 1,106 E1, E3 184
Waveney, riv., Eng. I13 273
Waverley, N.S., Can. 346 E6 70
Waverley, Middlesex, Mass. D2 206
Waverly, Lee and Chambers, Ala. 250 C4 168
Waverly, Polk, Fla. 1,160 *D9 174
Waverly, Camden, Ga. 165 E5 176
Waverly, Morgan, Ill. 1,375 D4 138
Waverly, Morgan, Ind. 150 C3 140
Waverly, Bremer, Iowa 6,357 B5 142
Waverly, Coffey, Kans. 381 D8 144
Waverly, Union, Ky. 331 C3 178
Waverly, Madison, La. 75 B4 180
Waverly, Wright, Minn. 574 F5 148
Waverly, Lafayette, Mo. 837 B4 150
Waverly, Lancaster, Nebr. 511 D9, E2 152
Waverly, Tioga, N.Y. 5,950 C5 212
Waverly, Pike, Ohio 3,830 C4 156
Waverly, Humphreys, Tenn. 2,891 B4 190
Waverly, Sussex, Va. 1,601 C7 192
Waverly, Spokane, Wash. 108 *D8 98
Waverly, Wood, W.Va. 300 B3 194
Waverly Hall, Harris, Ga. 712 D2 176
Waverly Hills, Jefferson, Ky. 100 A5 178
Wavre, Bel. 9,020 D3 282
Wawaka, Noble, Ind. 300 A4 140
Wāw al Kabīr, Libya B3 394
Wawanesa, Man., Can. 440 F3 60
Wawasee, Kosciusko, Ind. 300 A4 140
Wawasee, lake, Ind. A4 140
Wawayanda, lake, N.J. A4 210
Wawota, Sask., Can. 441 F6 58
Wax, Floyd, Ga. 100 B1 176
Wax, Grayson, Ky. 120 C4 178
Waxahachie, Ellis, Tex. 12,749 B8, C7 130
Waxhaw, Bolivar, Miss. 200 B2 184
Waxhaw, Union, N.C. 729 C5 186
Way, Madison, Miss. 100 C2 184
Way, is., Viet. E4 362
Wayagamack, lake, Que., Can. Q12 66
Wayan, Caribou, Idaho 10 G8 108
Waycross, Ware, Ga. 20,944 E4 176
Wayland, Henry, Iowa 597 C6 142
Wayland, Floyd, Ky. 1,340 C8 178
Wayland, Middlesex, Mass. (10,444▲) D2 206
Wayland, Allegan, Mich. 2,019 G6 146
Wayland, Clark, Mo. 384 A6 150
Wayland, Steuben, N.Y. 2,003 C4 212
Wayland Springs, Lawrence, Tenn. 200 C4 190
Waymansville, Bartholomew, Ind. 110 C3 140
Waymart, Wayne, Pa. 1,106 B6 214
Wayne, Alta., Can. 565 E6 54
Wayne, Republic, Kans. 54 C6 144
Wayne, Kennebec, Maine 175 (498▲) *D2 204
Wayne, Wayne, Mich. 16,034 B7 146
Wayne, Wayne, Nebr. 4,217 B8 152
Wayne, Passaic, N.J. 29,353 *B4 210
Wayne, Schuyler, N.Y. 250 C4 212
Wayne, Wood, Ohio 949 A3 156
Wayne, McClain, Okla. 517 D6 128
Wayne, Delaware, Pa. 10,000 A6, C6 214
Wayne, Wayne, W.Va. 1,274 C2 194
Wayne, co., Ga. 17,921 E5 176
Wayne, co., Ill. 19,008 E5 138
Wayne, co., Ind. 74,039 C4 140
Wayne, co., Iowa 9,800 D4 142
Wayne, co., Ky. 14,700 D6 178
Wayne, co., Mich. 2,666,297 G8 146
Wayne, co., Miss. 16,258 D4 184
Wayne, co., Mo. 8,638 D7 150
Wayne, co., Nebr. 9,959 B8 152
Wayne, co., N.Y. 67,989 B4 212
Wayne, co., N.C. 82,059 B7 186
Wayne, co., Ohio 75,497 B5 156
Wayne, co., Pa. 28,237 B6 214
Wayne, co., Tenn. 11,908 C4 190
Wayne, co., Utah 1,728 E4 114
Wayne, co., W.Va. 38,977 C2 194
Wayne City, Wayne, Ill. 903 E5 138
Waynedale, Allen, Ind. (part of Fort Wayne) A4 140
Waynesboro, Burke, Ga. 5,359 C4 176
Waynesboro, Wayne, Miss. 3,892 D4 184
Waynesboro, Franklin, Pa. 10,427 D4 214
Waynesboro, Wayne, Tenn. 1,343 C4 190
Waynesboro (Independent City), Va. 15,694 B6 192
Waynesburg, Lincoln, Ky. 450 C6 178
Waynesburg, Stark, Ohio 1,442 B5 156
Waynesburg, Greene, Pa. 5,188 D1 214
Waynesfield, Auglaize, Ohio 765 B3 156
Waynesville, Brantley, Ga. 250 E5 176
Waynesville, De Witt, Ill. 510 C4 138
Waynesville, Pulaski, Mo. 2,377 D5 150
Waynesville, Haywood, N.C. 6,159 B3 186
Waynesville, Warren, Ohio 1,298 C2 156
Waynetown, Montgomery, Ind. 933 B2 140
Waynoka, Woods, Okla. 1,794 B5 128
Wayside, Jones, Ga. 130 C3 176
Wayside, Montgomery, Kans. 100 E8 144
Wayside, Washington, Miss. 250 B1 184
Wayside, Dawes, Nebr. 13 B2 152
Wayside, Monmouth, N.J. 200 C4 210
Wayside, Brown, Wis. 130 A6 160
Wayzata, Hennepin, Minn. 3,219 *F5 148
Wazi Khwa (Marjan), Afg. C5 374
Weakley, co., Tenn. 24,227 B3 190
Wealand, Ottawa, Okla. 400 *B9 128
Weare, Hillsboro, N.H. 250 (1,420▲) E3 208
Weatherby, De Kalb, Mo. 450 B3 150
Weatherby Lake, De Kalb, Mo. 376 *B3 150
Weatherford, Custer, Okla. 4,499 C5 128
Weatherford, Parker, Tex. 9,759 C7 130
Weatherly, Carbon, Pa. 2,591 C6 214
Weathers, Pittsburg, Okla. 100 *D8 128
Weathersby, Simpson, Miss. 80 D3 184
Weatogue, Hartford, Conn. 200 B4 202
Weaubleau, Hickory, Mo. 349 D4 150
Weaver, Calhoun, Ala. 1,401 B4 168
Weaver, Wabasha, Minn. 105 G7 148
Weaver, lake, Man., Can. D4 60
Weaver, mts., Ariz. D3 124
Weaverville, Trinity, Calif. 1,736 B2 94
Weaverville, Buncombe, N.C. 1,041 B3 186
Webb, Houston, Ala. 331 D4 168
Webb, Sask., Can. 179 E3 58
Webb, Clay, Iowa 236 B2 142
Webb, Clearwater, Minn. 212 *D3 148
Webb, Tallahatchie, Miss. 686 B2 184
Webb, co., Tex. 64,791 F6 130
Webb, hill, Mass. B3 206
Webb, lake, Maine D2 204
Webb City, Franklin, Ark. 60 B3 170
Webb City, Jasper, Mo. 6,740 D3 150
Webb City, Osage, Okla. 233 B7 128
Webber, Jewell, Kans. 58 C5 144
Webber, lake, Man., Can. C6 60
Webbers Falls, Muskogee, Okla. 441 C8 128
Webberville, Ingham, Mich. 664 G7 146
Webb Lake, Burnett, Wis. 25 B2 160
Webbville, Lawrence, Ky. 225 B8 178
Weber, Berrien, Ga. 125 E3 176
Weber, co., Utah 110,744 B4 114
Weber, mtn., B.C., Can. C8 52
Weber City, Curry, N.Mex. 15 D7 126
Weber City, Scott, Va. 1,274 *D2 192

Weberville, Alta., Can. B4 54
Webhannet, York, Maine E2 204
Webster, Alta., Can. C3 54
Webster, Sumter, Fla. 366 C8 174
Webster, Keokuk, Iowa 137 C5 142
Webster, Rooks, Kans. 110 C4 144
Webster, Androscoggin, Maine 25 (1,302▲) D5 204
Webster, Harford, Md. 150 A7 182
Webster, Worcester, Mass. 13,680 B4 206
Webster, Fallon, Mont. 4 D12 110
Webster, Dodge, Nebr. 12 *C9 152
Webster, Merrimack, N.H. 100 (457▲) E3 208
Webster, Monroe, N.Y. 3,060 B4 212
Webster, Ramsey, N.Dak. 105 B7 154
Webster, Westmoreland, Pa. 898 C2 214
Webster, Day, S.Dak. 2,409 B8 158
Webster, Burnett, Wis. 514 C1 160
Webster, co., Ga. 3,247 D2 176
Webster, co., Iowa 47,810 B3 142
Webster, co., Ky. 14,244 C3 178
Webster, co., Miss. 10,580 B3 184
Webster, co., Mo. 13,753 D5 150
Webster, co., Nebr. 6,224 D7 152
Webster, co., W.Va. 13,719 C4 194
Webster, par., La. 39,701 B2 180
Webster, res., Kans. C4 144
Webster City, Hamilton, Iowa 8,520 B4 142
Webster Groves, St. Louis, Mo. 28,990 B8 150
Webster Springs (Addison), Webster, W.Va. 1,132 C4 194
Websterville, Washington, Vt. 750 C4 218
Wecoma, Lincoln, Oreg. B2 96
Weda, Indon. D7 359
Wedgefield, Sumter, S.C. 500 D7 188
Wedgeport, N.S., Can. 1,327 F4 70
Wedgeworth, Hale, Ala. C2 168
Wedowee, Randolph, Ala. 917 B4 168
Weed, Siskiyou, Calif. 3,223 B2 94
Weed, Otero, N.Mex. 100 F5 126
Weed Heights, Lyon, Nev. 1,092 D2 112
Weedon, Que., Can. 1,287 S13 66
Weedpatch, hill, Ind. C3 140
Weedsport, Cayuga, N.Y. 1,731 B5 212
Weedville, Elk, Pa. 600 B3 214
Weehawken, Hudson, N.J. 13,504 B1 210
Weekapaug, Washington, R.I. 30 D1 216
Weekes, Sask., Can. 286 D6 58
Weeks, Iberia, La. 1,138 E4 180
Weeks, Lyon, Nev. 10 D2 112
Weeksbury, Floyd, Ky. 700 C8 178
Weekstown, Atlantic, N.J. 50 D3 210
Weems, Lancaster, Va. 250 C8 192
Weenusk, Ont., Can. Q24 64
Weeping Water, Cass, Nebr. 1,048 D9 152, E3
Weeping Water, creek, Nebr. E2 152
Weert, Neth. 12,604 C4 282
Weesp, Neth. 9,052 B4 282
Wegdahl, Chippewa, Minn. 125 G3 148
Wegorzewo, Pol. 1,184 A5 325
Wegra, Walker, Ala. 350 *E4 168
Wegrów, Pol. 5,185 B6 325
Wehadkee, Randolph, Ala. B4 168
Wei, riv., China H4 348
Weichang, China 5,000 E9 348
Weiden, Ger. 40,500 D5 286
Weidman, Isabella, Mich. 350 F7 146
Weihaiwei, China 175,000 G11 348
Weihsi, China F7 346
Weihsien, China 180,000 G9 348
Weilheim, Ger. 11,500 E4 286
Weimar, Ger. 66,700 C4 286
Weimar, Colorado, Tex. 2,006 E7 130
Weinan, China 75,000 H4 348
Weiner, Poinsett, Ark. 669 B6 170
Weinfelden, Switz. 5,823 A5 312
Weinheim, Ger. 26,700 D3 286
Weining, China F8 346
Weippe, Clearwater, Idaho 600 C3 108
Weir, Cherokee, Kans. 699 E9 144
Weir, Muhlenberg, Ky. 150 C3 178
Weir, Choctaw, Miss. 522 B3 184
Weir, lake, Fla. B9 174
Weirdale, Sask., Can. 112 D5 58
Weir River, Man., Can. B5 60
Weirsdale, Marion, Fla. 900 C9 174
Weirton, Hancock, W.Va. 28,201 A2 194, A4
Weiser, Washington, Idaho 4,208 E2 108
Weiser, riv., Idaho E2 108
Weishan, lake, China H8 348
Weisner, mtn., Ala. A4 168
Weissenburg [in Bayern], Ger. 13,900 D4 286
Weissenfels, Ger. 46,900 C4 286
Weissert, Custer, Nebr. 19 C6 152
Weisshorn, mtn., Switz. B3 312
Weitchpec, Humboldt, Calif. 100 B2 94
Wejherowo, Pol. 19,900 A4 325
Wekusko, lake, Man., Can. C3 60
Welaka, Putnam, Fla. 526 B9 174
Welasco, Hidalgo, Tex. 15,649 F7 130
Welborn, Wyandotte, Kans. 6,500 *C9 144
Welch, Craig, Okla. 557 B8 128
Welch, McDowell, W.Va. 5,313 D3 194
Welcome, Martin, Minn. 733 H4 148
Welcome, Greenville, S.C. 1,500 *B4 188
Weld, Franklin, Maine 130 (348▲) D2 204
Weld, co., Colo. 72,344 B6 106
Welda, Anderson, Kans. 180 D8 144
Weldon, Jackson, Ark. 150 B5 170
Weldon, Sask., Can. 220 D5 58
Weldon, De Witt, Ill. 449 C5 138
Weldon, Decatur, Iowa 202 D4 142
Weldon, Halifax, N.C. 2,165 A8 186
Weldona, Morgan, Colo. 92 B7 106
Weleetka, Okfuskee, Okla. 1,231 C7 128
Welford, Austl. D8 432
Welland, Ont., Can. 16,405 R21 64
Welland, co., Ont., Can. 149,606 R21 64
Welland, canal, Ont., Can. R21 64
Welland, riv., Eng. I12 273
Wellandport, Ont., Can. 230 Q21 64
Wellborn, Suwannee, Fla. 475 A8 174
Wellesley, Ont., Can. 775 Q20 64
Wellesley, Norfolk, Mass. 26,071 B5 206, D2
Wellesley, is., Austl. B7 432
Wellesley Hills, Norfolk, Mass. B5 206, D2
Wellfleet, Barnstable, Mass. 850 (1,404▲) C7 206
Wellfleet, Lincoln, Nebr. 67 D5 152
Wellford, Spartanburg, S.C. 1,040 B4 188
Wellin, Bel. 1,054 D4 282
Welling, Cherokee, Okla. 150 C9 128
Wellingborough, Eng. 28,800 I12 273
Wellington, Calhoun, Ala. 125 B4 168
Wellington, B.C., Can. 400 B13 52
Wellington, Ont., Can. 1,077 Q23 64
Wellington, Larimer, Colo. 532 B5 106
Wellington, Eng. 13,100 I10 273
Wellington, Eng. 7,400 K9 273
Wellington, Sumner, Kans. 8,809 E6 144
Wellington, Jefferson, Ky. 804 A5 178
Wellington, Piscataquis, Maine 100 (231▲) C3 204
Wellington, Lafayette, Mo. 651 B4 150
Wellington, Lyon, Nev. 50 E2 112
Wellington, N.Z. 122,070 (*224,400) D5 437, J11
Wellington, Lorain, Ohio 3,599 A4 156
Wellington, Collingsworth, Tex. 3,137 B5 130
Wellington, Carbon, Utah 1,066 D5 114
Wellington, Fairfax, Va. 8,000 A7 192, B7
Wellington, co., Ont., Can. 75,691 Q20 64
Wellington, isl., Chile G3 251
Wellman, Washington, Iowa 1,085 C6 142
Wellpinit, Stevens, Wash. 100 B9 98
Wells, B.C., Can. 1,000 D12 52
Wells, Ottawa, Kans. 90 C6 144
Wells, York, Maine 600 (3,528▲) E2 204
Wells, Menominee, Mich. 900 D4 146
Wells, Faribault, Minn. 2,897 H5 148
Wells, Elko, Nev. 1,071 B7 112
Wells, Hamilton, N.Y. 400 B7 212
Wells, Cherokee, Tex. 544 D8 130
Wells, Rutland, Vt. 200 (419▲) E2 218
Wells, co., Ind. 21,220 B4 140
Wells, co., N.Dak. 9,237 C6 154
Wells, harbor, Midway E3 436
Wells, lake, Austl. D4 432
Wells, riv., Vt. C4 218
Wells Beach, York, Maine E2 204
Wellsboro, La Porte, Ind. 100 A3 140
Wellsboro, Tioga, Pa. 4,369 B4 214
Wellsburg, Grundy, Iowa 827 B5 142
Wellsburg, Chemung, N.Y. 643 C5 212
Wellsburg, Brooke, W.Va. 5,514 A4 194, B2
Wellsdale, Benton, Oreg. *C3 96
Wellsford, Kiowa, Kans. 24 E4 144
Wells Gray, prov. park, B.C., Can. D12 52
Wells [-next-the-Sea], Eng. 2,600 I13 273
Wells River, Orange, Vt. 472 C4 218
Wellston, Manistee, Mich. 175 E6 146
Wellston, St. Louis, Mo. 7,979 A8 150
Wellston, Jackson, Ohio 5,728 C4 156
Wellston, Lincoln, Okla. 630 C6 128
Wellsville, Franklin, Kans. 984 D8 144
Wellsville, Montgomery, Mo. 1,523 B6 150
Wellsville, Allegany, N.Y. 5,967 C4 212
Wellsville, Columbiana, Ohio 7,117 B6 156
Wellsville, Cache, Utah 1,106 B4 114
Wellton, Yuma, Ariz. 300 F1 124
Wellwood, Man., Can. 140 E3 60
Wels, Aus. 38,120 B6 313
Welsford, N.B., Can. 310 D3 70
Welsh, Jefferson, La. 3,332 D3 180
Welshire, New Castle, Del. 400 *B3 172
Welshpool, N.B., Can. 385 E3 70
Welshpool, Wales 6,100 I9 273
Welton, Clinton, Iowa 88 C7 142
Welty, Okfuskee, Okla. 50 C7 128
Welwyn, Sask., Can. 224 E7 58
Wema, Con.L. C3 414
Wembere, riv., Tan. C5 414
Wembley, Alta., Can. 272 C3 54
Wemme, Clackamas, Oreg. 150 *B5 96
Wenasoga, Alcorn, Miss. 150 A4 184
Wenatchee, Chelan, Wash. 16,726 B6 98
Wenatchee, lake, Wash. B6 98
Wenatchee, mts., Wash. B5 98
Wenatchee, riv., Wash. B6 98
Wenceslau Braz, Braz. 2,003 J7 257
Wenchang, China 15,000 P5 349
Wenchi, Ghana 3,812 E4 408
Wenchou (Wenchow), China 201,600 L10 349
Wenchow, see Wenchou, China
Wenchuan, see Aerhshan, China
Wendel, Lassen, Calif. 60 B3 94
Wendel, Taylor, W.Va. 300 B7 194
Wendell, Gooding, Idaho 1,232 G4 108
Wendell, Franklin, Mass. 100 (292▲) A3 206
Wendell, Grant, Minn. 253 E2 148
Wendell, Valley, Mont. B10 110
Wendell, Sullivan, N.H. 100 E2 208
Wendell, Wake, N.C. 1,620 B7 186
Wenden, Yuma, Ariz. 250 E2 124
Wendling, Linn, Oreg. C4 96
Wendover, Tooele, Utah 609 C1 114
Wendover, Platte, Wyo. D8 116
Wengen, Switz. B3 312
Wenham, Essex, Mass. 2,798 A6 206, C3
Wenham, lake, Mass. C3 206
Wenham, swamp, Mass. C3 206
Wenlock, riv., Austl. A8 432
Wennington, Eng. G10 273
Wenona, Marshall, Ill. 1,005 B4 138
Wenona, Somerset, Md. 325 D8 182
Wenonah, Jefferson, Ala. 950 *B3 168
Wenonah, Gloucester, N.J. 2,100 D2 210
Wenshan, China G8 346
Wentworth, Austl. 4,034 E7 432
Wentworth, Newton, Mo. 174 E3 150
Wentworth, Grafton, N.H. 275 (300▲) D3 208
Wentworth, Rockingham, N.C. 125 A6 186
Wentworth, Lake, S.Dak. 211 C8 158
Wentworth, Douglas, Wis. 35 B2 160
Wentworth, co., Ont., Can. 316,238 Q20 64
Wentworth, lake, N.H. D4 208
Wentworth Location (Town of), Coos, N.H. (58▲) *B4 208
Wentzville, St. Charles, Mo. 2,742 C7 150
Weogufka, mtn., Ala. C3 168
Weohyakapka, lake, Fla. D9 174
Weona, Poinsett, Ark. 100 B6 170
Weott, Humboldt, Calif. 350 B2 94
Wepener, U.S.Afr. 3,256 E5 420
Werbomont, Bel. 421 D4 282
Werdau [in Sachsen], Ger. 25,400 C5 286
Werfen, Aus. 3,168 C5 313
Wernberg, Ger. 1,070 D5 286
Werner, Dunn, N.Dak. 59 C3 154
Werner, Grundy, Tenn. 40 C6 190
Wernersville, Berks, Pa. 1,462 *C5 214
Werneuchen, Ger. 4,218 B5 286
Wernigerode, Ger. 34,200 C4 286
Werra, riv., Ger. C3 286
Wertach, riv., Ger. D4 286
Wervik, Bel. 12,364 D2 282
Wesel, Ger. 25,800 C2 286
Weser, canal, Ger. B3 286
Weser, riv., Ger. B3 286
Wesermünde, see Bremerhaven, Ger.
Weskan, Wallace, Kans. 240 D2 144
Weslaco North, Hidalgo, Tex. 1,049 *F6 130
Weslemkoon, lake, Ont., Can. O23 64
Wesley, Madison, Ark. 65 A3 170
Wesley, Kossuth, Iowa 514 A4 142
Wesley, Washington, Maine 65 (145▲) D5 204
Wesleyville, Newf., Can. 1,313 F9 72
Wesleyville, Erie, Pa. 3,534 A1 214
Wessel, is., Austl. A7 432
Wessington, Beadle and Hand, S.Dak. 378 C7 158
Wessington Springs, Jerauld, S.Dak. 1,488 C7 158
Wesson, Union, Ark. 250 D4 170
Wesson, Copiah, Miss. 1,157 D2 184
West, Holmes, Miss. 282 B3 184
West, McLennan, Tex. 2,352 D7 130
West, bay, La. E6 180
West, bay, N.C. B9 186
West, bay, Tex. G8 130
West, branch, Pa. B3 214
West, butte, Mont. B5 110
West, channel, Man., Can. D3 60
West, fork, W.Va. D6 194
West, fork, Wyo. B5 116
West, hill, Mass. E1 206
West, isl., Mass. C6 206
West, isl., R.I. D4 216
West, lake, Maine C4 204
West, mtn., Ark. C7 170
West, mtn., Mass. A2 206
West, mtn., N.Y. B7 212
West, mtn., Vt. B5 218
West, pt., P.E.I., Can. C5 70
West, riv., N.S., Can. D7 70
West, riv., Mass. E1 206
West, riv., Vt. E3 218
West, split, Eniwetok B1 436
West Acton, Middlesex, Mass. 950 C1 206
West Alburgh, Grand Isle, Vt. 515 *B2 218
West Alexandria, Preble, Ohio 1,524 C2 156
West Allenhurst, Monmouth, N.J. 900 *C4 210
West Allis, Milwaukee, Wis. 68,157 E2 160
West Alton, St. Charles, Mo. 300 A8 150
West Alton, Belknap, N.H. 100 D4 208
West Andrews, Georgetown, S.C. 200 *E9 188
West Arichat, N.S., Can. 475 D8 70
West Athens, Somerset, Maine 150 D3 204
West Auburn, Androscoggin, Maine D2 204
West Augusta, Augusta, Va. 10 B5 192
West Ausdale, Richland, Ohio 1,354 *B4 156
West Baden Springs, Orange, Ind. 879 D3 140
West Bainbridge, Decatur, Ga. 1,782 F2 176
West Baldwin, Cumberland, Maine 75 E2 204
Westbank, B.C., Can. 450 F13 52
West Baraboo, Sauk, Wis. 613 *E4 160
West Barnet, Caledonia, Vt. 113 C4 218
West Barnstable, Barnstable, Mass. 575 C7 206
West Barrington, Bristol, R.I. 4,000 C3 216
West Bath (Town of), Sagadahoc, Maine (766▲) E6 204
West Baton Rouge, par., La. 14,796 D4 180
West Battle, lake, Minn. E3 148
Westbay, Bay, Fla. 325 A5 174
West Bedford, Middlesex, Mass. C2 206
West Belmar, Monmouth, N.J. 2,511 *C4 210
West Bend, Sask., Can. 95 E6 58
West Bend, Palo Alto, Iowa 910 B3 142
West Bend, Washington, Wis. 9,969 E5 160
West Bengal, state, India *D5 366
West Benson, Douglas, Nebr. 900 *C9 152
West Berkshire, Franklin, Vt. 95 B3 218
West Berlin, Ger. 2,303,300 B5 286
West Berlin (Carters), Worcester, Mass. 250 B4 206
West Berlin (Berlin Township), Camden, N.J. 3,363 *D3 210
West Bethel, Oxford, Maine 160 D2 204
West Billerica, Middlesex, Mass. 200 *A5 206
West Billings, Yellowstone, Mont. 3,500 *E8 110
West Blocton, Bibb, Ala. 1,156 B2 168
West Bloomfield, Ontario, N.Y. 200 C4 212
Westboro, Ont., Can. 3,450 P25 64
Westboro, Worcester, Mass. 4,011 (9,599▲) B4 206, D1
Westboro, Atchison, Mo. 262 A2 150
Westboro, Taylor, Wis. 500 C3 160
West Bountiful, Davis, Utah 945 *C4 114
Westbourne, Man., Can. 125 E3 60
Westbourne, Campbell, Tenn. 100 B7 190
West Bowdoin, Sagadahoc, Maine 50 D5 204
West Boxford, Essex, Mass. 200 *A6 206
West Boylston, Worcester, Mass. 2,000 (5,526▲) B4 206
West Branch, Cedar, Iowa 1,053 C6 142
West Branch, Ogemaw, Mich. 2,025 E7 146
West Brentwood, Rockingham, N.H. 135 F4 208
West Brewster, Barnstable, Mass. 139 C7 206
West Bridgewater, Plymouth, Mass. 2,000 (5,061▲) B5 206
West Bridgewater (Bridgewater), Beaver, Pa. 1,292 *C1 214
West Bridgewater, Rutland and Windsor, Vt. 95 D3 218
West Brimfield, Hampden, Mass. 150 B3 206
West Bromwich, Eng. 90,700 *I11 273
Westbrook, Middlesex, Conn. 950 (2,399▲) D6 202
Westbrook, Cumberland, Maine 13,820 E2 204, E5
Westbrook, Cottonwood, Minn. 1,012 G3 148
West Brookfield, Worcester, Mass. 1,250 (2,053▲) B3 206
Westbrookville, Sullivan, N.Y. 280 D7 212
West Brownsville, Washington, Pa. 1,907 *C1 214
West Brunswick, Somerset, N.J. 2,000 *C4 210
West Buechel, Jefferson, Ky. 504 *B5 178
West Burke, Caledonia, Vt. 369 B5 218
West Burlington, Des Moines, Iowa 2,560 D6 142
West Burra, isl., Scot. A11 272
Westbury, Nassau, N.Y. 14,757 D3 212, E8
West Butler, Choctaw, Ala. 15 C1 168
West Buxton, York, Maine 300 E2 204
Westby, Sheridan, Mont. 309 B12 110
Westby, Vernon, Wis. 1,544 E3 160
West Caldwell, Essex, N.J. 8,314 *B4 210
West Camp, Ulster, N.Y. 275 C8 212
West Campton, Grafton, N.H. 100 D3 208
West Canaan, Grafton, N.H. 95 D2 208
West Canada, creek, N.Y. B7 212
West Cape Howe, cape, Austl. F3 432
West Cape May, Cape May, N.J. 1,030 E3 210
West Carroll, par., La. 14,177 B4 180
West Carrollton, Montgomery, Ohio 4,749 C2 156
West Carry, pond, Maine C2 204
West Carthage, Jefferson, N.Y. 2,167 B6 212
West Charleston, Orleans, Vt. 150 B4 218
West Chatham, Barnstable, Mass. 200 C8 206
West Chazy, Clinton, N.Y. 566 A8 212
West Chelmsford, Middlesex, Mass. 300 C1 206
Westchester, Cook, Ill. 18,092 *B6 138
West Chester, Washington, Iowa 253 C6 142
West Chester, Butler, Ohio 418 C1 156
West Chester, Chester, Pa. 15,705 D6 214
Westchester, co., N.Y. 808,891 D8 212
West Chesterfield, Hampshire, Mass. 125 *B2 206
West Chesterfield, Cheshire, N.H. 175 F1 208
West Chevy Chase Heights, Montgomery, Md. 1,800 *C5 182
West Chicago, Du Page, Ill. 6,854 F2 138
West Chop, pt., Mass. D6 206
West City, Franklin, Ill. 814 E5 138
West Clarkston, Asotin, Wash. 2,851 *C9 98
Westcliffe, Custer, Colo. 306 D5 106
West Clinton, Vermillion, Ind. 200 C2 140
West Coffeyville, Montgomery, Kans. 500 E8 144
West College Corner, Union, Ind. 613 C5 140
West Collingswood, Camden, N.J. 2,000 *D2 210
West Collingswood Heights, Camden, N.J. 1,100 *D3 210
West Columbia, Lexington, S.C. 6,410 D6 188
West Columbia, Brazoria, Tex. 2,947 E8 130, G7
West Concord, Middlesex, Mass. 1,556 B5 206, C1
West Concord, Dodge, Minn. 810 G6 148
West Concord, Cabarrus, N.C. 5,570 *B5 186
Westconnaug, res., R.I. B2 216
West Conshohocken, Montgomery, Pa. 2,254 A6 214
West Cornwall, Litchfield, Conn. 200 B2 202
West Cote Blanche, bay, La. E4 180
Westcott, Kent, R.I. (part of West Warwick) C2 216
West Covina, Los Angeles, Calif. 50,645 C6 94
Westcreek, Douglas, Colo. 5 C5 106
West Creek, Ocean, N.J. 600 D4 210
West Crossett, Ashley, Ark. 255 D5 170
West Cumberland, Cumberland, Maine 200 E2 204, E5
West Cummington, Hampshire, Mass. 40 B2 206
Westdale, Red River, La. 50 B2 180
Westdale, Plymouth, Mass. 200 *B6 206
West Danville, Caledonia, Vt. 85 C4 218
West Decatur, Clearfield, Pa. 900 C3 214
West Deerfield, Franklin, Mass. *A2 206
West Dennis, Barnstable, Mass. 900 C7 206
West Derry, Westmoreland, Pa. 1,000 *C2 214
West Des Moines, Polk, Iowa 11,949 A7 142, C4
West Dudley, Worcester, Mass. 200 B4 206
West Dummerston, Windham, Vt. 90 F3 218
West Dundee, see Dundee, Ill.
West Duxbury, Plymouth, Mass. 300 B6 206
West Easton, Northampton, Pa. 1,228 *C6 214
West Eden, Hancock, Maine D4 204

West Elmira, Chemung, N.Y. 5,763 C5 212
West Elwood, Tipton, Ind. 200 B4 140
West Eminence, Shannon, Mo. 145 D6 150
West Emma, creek, Kans. D6 144
West End, Jefferson, Ark. 2,208 *C4 170
Westend, San Bernardino, Calif. 300 E5 94
West End, Marion, Fla. 3,124 *B8 174
West End, Otsego, N.Y. 1,436 *C6 212
West End Anniston-Cobb Town, Calhoun, Ala. 5,485 *B4 168
West Enfield, Penobscot, Maine 500 C4 204
West Englewood, Bergen, N.J. (part of Teaneck) A1 210
West Enosburg, Franklin, Vt. 75 B3 218
West Enterprise, Clarke, Miss. 691 C4 184
West Epping, Rockingham, N.H. 350 E4 208
Westerham, Sask., Can. 89 E3 58
Westerland, Ger. 9,100 A3 286
Westerlo, Albany, N.Y. 250 C7 212
Westerly, Washington, R.I. 9,698 (14,267▲) D1 216
Western, Saline, Nebr. 351 D8 152
Western, prov., Lib. *E2 408
Western, prov., Rh.&Nya. B5 420
Western, prov., Tan. 955,852 D5 414
Western, prov., Ug. C5 414
Western, reg., Nig. 6,087,000 E5 408
Western, reg., Nor. 820,643 *F2 291
Western, head, Newf., Can. F6 72
Western, head, N.S., Can. F5 70
Western, isl., Newf., Can. E8 72
Western Australia, state, Austl. 691,882 C3 432
Western Downs, hills, Eng. K10 273
Western Ghats, mts., India E2 366
Western Grove, Newton, Ark. 148 A4 170
Westernport, Allegany, Md. 3,559 B1 182
Western Region, ter., Ghana E4 408
Western Samoa, N.Z. trust., Pac.O. 84,909 *D4 436
Western Springs, Cook, Ill. 10,838 F2 138
Westernville, Oneida, N.Y. 340 B6 212
Wester Schelde, chan., Neth. C2 282
Westerville, Custer, Nebr. 40 C6 152
Westerville, Franklin, Ohio 7,011 B1 156 / B4
Westerwald, mts., Ger. C2 286
West Fairlee, Orange, Vt. 185 (333▲) D4 218
West Fairview, Cumberland, Pa. 1,718 C5 214
Westfall, Lincoln, Kans. 100 D5 144
West Falmouth, Cumberland, Maine E5 204
West Falmouth, Barnstable, Mass. 362 C6 206
West Fargo, Cass, N.Dak. 93 D9 154
West Farmington, Franklin, Maine 500 D2 204
West Farmington, Trumbull, Ohio 614 A6 156
West Feliciana, par., La. 12,395 D4 180
Westfield, Jefferson, Ala. 2,000 E4 168
Westfield, N.B., Can. 140 D3 70
Westfield, Clark, Ill. 636 D6 138
Westfield, Hamilton, Ind. 1,217 B3 140
Westfield, Plymouth, Iowa 187 B1 142
Westfield, Aroostook, Maine 350 (569▲) B5 204
Westfield, Hampden, Mass. B2 206
Westfield, Union, N.J. 31,447 B4 210
Westfield, Chautauqua, N.Y. 3,878 C2 212
Westfield, Tioga, Pa. 1,333 B4 214
Westfield, Orleans, Vt. 90 (347▲) B4 218
Westfield, Marquette, Wis. 919 E4 160
Westfield, riv., Mass. B2 206
Westfir, Lane, Oreg. 500 D4 96
Westford, Windham, Conn. 230 B7 202
Westford, Chittenden, Vt. 90 (680▲) B2 218
West Fork, Washington, Ark. 350 B2 170
West Fork, riv., W.Va. B4 194
West Forks (Plantation of), Somerset, Maine (93▲) C3 204
West Frankfort, Franklin, Ill. 9,027 F5 138
West Friendship, Howard, Md. 50 B6 182
West Frisian, is., Neth. A3 282
West Gardiner (Town of), Kennebec, Maine (1,144▲) *D3 204
Westgate, Palm Beach, Fla. 2,500 *E10 174
Westgate, Fayette, Iowa 214 B6 142
West Glacier, Flathead, Mont. 270 B3 110
West Glens Falls, Warren, N.Y. 2,725 *B8 212
West Glocester, Providence, R.I. 50 B1 216
West Gorham, Cumberland, Maine 40 E4 204
West Gouldsboro, Hancock, Maine 90 D4 204
West Granby, Hartford, Conn. 375 B4 202
West Granville, Hampden, Mass. 175 B2 206
West Gravenhurst, Ont., Can. 150 P21 64
West Gray, Cumberland, Maine 75 E2 204 / E5
West Green, Coffee, Ga. 300 E4 176
West Greene, Greene, Ala. 80 C1 168
West Greenville, Greenville, S.C. (part of Greenville) B4 188
West Greenwich (Town of), Kent, R.I. (1,169▲) C2 216
West Groton, Middlesex, Mass. 600 A4 206 / C1
West Grove, Chester, Pa. 1,607 D6 214
West Halifax, Windham, Vt. 100 F3 218
West Ham, Eng. 167,000 J13 273
West Hamlin, Lincoln, W.Va. 788 C2 194
West Hampden, Penobscot, Maine D4 204
West Hampstead, Rockingham, N.H. 150 F4 208
Westhampton, Hampshire, Mass. 175 (583▲) B2 206
Westhampton Beach, Suffolk, N.Y. 1,460 D5 212
West Hanover, Plymouth, Mass. 950 E3 206
West Harpswell, Cumberland, Maine 90 E5 204
West Harrison, Dearborn, Ind. 341 C5 140
West Hartford, Sebastian, Ark. 100 B2 170
West Hartford, Hartford, Conn. 62,382 B5 202
West Hartford, Windsor, Vt. 100 D4 218
West Hartland, Hartford, Conn. 200 A4 202
West Hartlepool, Eng. 73,200 G11 273
West Hartsville, Darlington, S.C. 2,427 *C9 188
West Harwich, Barnstable, Mass. 300 C7 206
West Hatfield, Hampshire, Mass. 200 B2 206
West Haven, New Haven, Conn. 43,002 D4 202
West Haverstraw, Rockland, N.Y. 5,020 *D7 212
West Hazleton, Luzerne, Pa. 6,278 C5 214
West Helena, Phillips, Ark. 8,385 C6 170
West Hempstead, Nassau, N.Y. 15,800 *E8 212
West Highlands, Jefferson, Ala. 500 *B3 168
West Hill, Ont., Can. 1,800 Q21 64 / R22
West Hillsboro, Orange, N.C. 1,065 *A6 186
West Hollywood, Los Angeles, Calif. 28,870 C5 94
West Hollywood, Broward, Fla. 25,750 *E10 174
West Homestead, Allegheny, Pa. 4,155 *C2 214
Westhope, Bottineau, N.Dak. 824 B4 154
West Hyannisport, Barnstable, Mass. 175 *C7 206
West Jefferson, Ashe, N.C. 1,000 A4 186
West Jefferson, Madison, Ohio 2,774 C1 156 / C3
West Jonesport, Washington, Maine 540 D5 204
West Jordan, Salt Lake, Utah 3,009 C4 114
West Junction, Shelby, Tenn. 4,000 C1 190 / E6
West Juneau, Alsk. 325 *D8 84
West Kankakee, Kankakee, Ill. 3,917 B6 138
Westkapelle, Bel. 2,241 C2 282
Westkapelle, Neth. 2,308 C2 282
West Keansburg, Monmouth, N.J. 3,000 *C4 210
West Kennebunk, York, Maine 350 E2 204
West Kingston, Washington, R.I. 350 D2 216
West Kittanning, Armstrong, Pa. 1,101 *C2 214
West La Crosse, La Crosse, Wis. 1,440 E2 160
West Lafayette, Tippecanoe, Ind. 12,680 B3 140
West Lafayette, Coshocton, Ohio 1,476 B5 156
West Lake, Hamilton, Fla. 100 A7 174
Westlake, Idaho, Idaho C2 108
Westlake, Calcasieu, La. 3,311 D2 180
Westlake, Cuyahoga, Ohio 12,906 B1 156
Westlake, Lane, Oreg. 150 D2 96
Westlake, Grant, Wash. 298 *B7 98
West Lake Hills, Travis, Tex. 714 *D7 130
Westlands, Middlesex, Mass. 2,100 A5 206
West Lawn, Berks, Pa. 2,059 C5 214
West Lawn, Fairfax, Va. 1,400 *B7 192
West Lebanon, Warren, Ind. 720 B2 140
West Lebanon, York, Maine 160 E2 204
West Lebanon, Grafton, N.H. (part of Lebanon) D2 208
West Lebanon, Lebanon, Pa. 1,054 *C5 214
West Leechburg, Westmoreland, Pa. 1,323 *C2 214
West Lewistown, Fergus, Mont. 150 *C7 110
West Leyden, Lewis, N.Y. 250 B6 212
West Liberty, Muscatine, Iowa 2,042 C6 142
West Liberty, Morgan, Ky. 1,165 C7 178
West Liberty, Logan, Ohio 1,522 B3 156
West Liberty, Ohio, W.Va. 1,500 B2 194
West Lima, Richland, Wis. 140 E3 160
West Lincoln, Lancaster, Nebr. 507 E1 152
West Lincoln, Addison, Vt. 70 C2 218
West Linn, Clackamas, Oreg. 3,933 B2 96 / B4
Westlock, Alta., Can. 1,136 C6 54
West Logan, Logan, W.Va. 855 *D3 194
West Long Branch, Monmouth, N.J. 5,337 C4 210
West Lorne, Ont., Can. 1,088 R19 64
West Lothian, co., Scot. 91,100 F9 272
West Louisville, Daviess, Ky. 250 C3 178
West Lubec, Washington, Maine 150 D5 204
West Manayunk (Belmont Hills), Montgomery, Pa. 1,900 *C6 214
West Manchester, Preble, Ohio 460 C2 156
West Mansfield, Bristol, Mass. 565 *B5 206
West Mansfield, Logan, Ohio 791 B3 156
West Marion, McDowell, N.C. 1,600 *B4 186
West Marion, Marion, S.C. 45 C10 188
West Mayfield, Beaver, Pa. 2,201 *C1 214
Westmeath, Ont., Can. 400 O24 64
Westmeath, co., Ire. 54,122 H5 273
West Medway, Norfolk, Mass. 1,818 B5 206 / E1
West Melbourne, Brevard, Fla. 2,266 *C10 174
West Memphis, Crittenden, Ark. 19,374 B6 170
West Methow, riv., Wash. A6 98
West Miami, Dade, Fla. 5,296 E6 174
West Middlesex, Mercer, Pa. 1,301 B1 214
West Middleton, Howard, Ind. 280 B3 140
West Mifflin, Allegheny, Pa. 27,289 C2 214
West Milan, Coos, N.H. 100 B4 208
West Milford, Passaic, N.J. 800 A4 210
West Milford, Harrison, W.Va. 367 B4 194
West Millbury, Worcester, Mass. 300 B4 206
West Mills, Franklin, Maine 70 D2 204
West Milton, Miami, Ohio 2,972 C2 156
West Milwaukee, Milwaukee, Wis. 5,043 E2 160
West Mineral, Cherokee, Kans. 262 E9 144
Westminster, Orange, Calif. 25,750 C5 94
Westminster, Adams, Colo. 13,850 C5 106
Westminster, Carroll, Md. 6,123 A6 182
Westminster, Worcester, Mass. 1,047 (4,022▲) A4 206
Westminster, Oconee, S.C. 2,413 B2 188
Westminster, Windham, Vt. 333 (1,602▲) E4 218
Westminster Depot, Worcester, Mass. A4 206
Westminster Station, Windham, Vt. 60 E4 218
Westminster West, Windham, Vt. 60 E3 218
West Monroe, Ouachita, La. 15,215 B3 180
Westmont, Du Page, Ill. 5,997 F2 138
Westmont, Camden, N.J. 14,000 D2 210
Westmont, Cambria, Pa. 6,573 C3 214
Westmore, Fallon, Mont. D12 110
Westmoreland, Pottawatomie, Kans. 460 C7 144
Westmoreland, Cheshire, N.H. 100 (921▲) F2 208
Westmoreland, Sumner, Tenn. 865 B5 190
Westmoreland, co., Pa. 352,629 C2 214
Westmoreland, co., Va. 11,042 B8 192
Westmoreland City, Westmoreland, Pa. 1,300 *C2 214
Westmorland, Imperial, Calif. 1,404 F6 94
Westmorland, co., N.B., Can. 85,415 C5 70
Westmorland, co., Eng. 66,600 G10 273
Westmount, Que., Can. 24,800 *S16 66
West Muncie, Delaware, Ind. 300 B4 140
West Musquash, lake, Maine C5 204
West Mystic, New London, Conn. 3,268 D8 202
West Newbury, Essex, Mass. 800 (1,844▲) A6 206
West Newfield, York, Maine 100 E2 204
West Newton, Marion, Ind. 400 E4 140
West Newton, Westmoreland, Pa. 3,982 C2 214
West New York, Hudson, N.J. 35,547 B1 210
West Nicholson, Rh.&Nya. D5 420
West Nishnabotna, riv., Iowa C2 142
West Norfolk, Norfolk, Va. 500 A8 192
West Okoboji, Dickinson, Iowa 171 A2 142
West Oldtown, Penobscot, Maine D4 204
West Olive, Ottawa, Mich. 60 G5 146
Weston, Ont., Can. 9,543 R22 64
Weston, Las Animas, Colo. 350 E6 106
Weston, Fairfield, Conn. 3,000 (4,039▲) E2 202
Weston, Webster, Ga. 120 E2 176
Weston, Franklin, Idaho 284 G7 108
Weston, Aroostook, Maine 50 (202▲) C5 204
Weston, Middlesex, Mass. 4,000 (8,261▲) D2 206
Weston, Platte, Mo. 1,057 B3 150 / D1
Weston, Saunders, Nebr. 340 C9 152
Weston, Wood, Ohio 1,075 A3 156
Weston, Umatilla, Oreg. 783 B8 96
Weston, Windsor, Vt. 200 (442▲) E3 218
Weston, Lewis, W.Va. 8,754 B4 194
Weston, Dunn, Wis. 40 D1 160
Weston, Campbell, Wyo. 5 B7 116
Weston, co., Wyo. 7,929 C8 116
Weston-super-Mare, Eng. 40,300 J10 273
West Orange, Essex, N.J. 39,895 B4 210
West Orange, Orange, Tex. 4,848 *D9 130
West Ossipee, Carroll, N.H. 100 D4 208
Westover, Shelby, Ala. 750 B3 168 / E5
Westover, Somerset, Md. 250 D8 182
Westover, Madison, Tenn. 300 C3 190
Westover, Monongalia, W.Va. 4,749 A7 194 / B5
West Pakistan, prov., Pak. 32,653,138 *E6 375
West Palm Beach, Palm Beach, Fla. 56,208 (*157,200) E10 174
West Panama City Beach, Bay, Fla. 617 *A5 174
West Paris, Oxford, Maine 600 (1,050▲) D2 204
West Park, Ulster, N.Y. 500 D8 212
West Paterson, Passaic, N.J. 7,602 *B4 210
West Pawlet, Rutland, Vt. 280 E2 218
West Peabody, Essex, Mass. A6 206 / C3
West Pea Ridge, Wayne, W.Va. 750 *C2 194
West Pearl, riv., La. D6 180
West Pelham, Hampshire, Mass. 600 B3 206
West Pelzer, Anderson, S.C. 687 B4 188
West Pembroke, Washington, Maine 400 D5 204
West Pensacola (Brownsville), Escambia, Fla. 25,000 *A3 174
West Peru, Oxford, Maine 350 D2 204
West Peterborough, Hillsboro, N.H. 325 F3 208
West Petersburg, Alsk. 60 J14 84
Westphalia, Knox, Ind. 300 D2 140
Westphalia, Shelby, Iowa 131 C2 142
Westphalia, Anderson, Kans. 249 D8 144
Westphalia, Clinton, Mich. 560 G7 146
Westphalia, Osage, Mo. 316 C5 150
Westphalia (Westfalen), reg., Ger. C2 286
West Pittsburg, Lawrence, Pa. 850 C1 214
West Pittsfield, Berkshire, Mass. B1 206
West Pittston, Luzerne, Pa. 6,998 A5 214
West Plains, see Plains, Kans.
West Plains, Howell, Mo. 5,836 E6 150
West Point, White, Ark. 97 B5 170
West Point, Calaveras, Calif. 950 C3 94
West Point, Troup, Ga. 4,610 D1 176
Westpoint, Tippecanoe, Ind. 350 B2 140
West Point, Lee, Iowa 758 D6 142
West Point, Hardin, Ky. 1,957 C5 178
Westpoint, Sagadahoc, Maine 170 E6 204
West Point, Clay, Miss. 8,550 B4 184
West Point, Cuming, Nebr. 2,921 C9 152
West Point, Orange, N.Y. 4,000 D8 212
Westpoint, Lawrence, Tenn. 300 C4 190
West Point, Davis, Utah 599 *B3 114
West Point, King William, Va. 1,678 C8 192
West Point, mtn., Alsk. C7 84
Westport, Newf., Can. 150 F7 72 / E10
Westport, N.S., Can. 500 E3 70
Westport, Ont., Can. 704 P24 64
Westport, Fairfield, Conn. 20,955 E2 202
Westport, Decatur, Ind. 833 C4 140
Westport, Ire. 2,947 H3 273
Westport, Oldham, Ky. 125 A5 178 / B5
Westport, Lincoln, Maine 35 (133▲) *E3 204
Westport, Bristol, Mass. 600 (6,641▲) C5 206
Westport, Pope, Minn. 87 F3 148
Westport, Cheshire, N.H. 170 F2 208
Westport, Essex, N.Y. 723 A8 212
Westport, N.Z. 5,522 D3 437
Westport, Clatsop, Oreg. 300 A3 96
Westport, Brown, S.Dak. 85 B7 158
Westport, Carroll, Tenn. 125 C3 190
Westport, Grays Harbor, Wash. 976 C2 98
West Portland, Multnomah, Oreg. 2,000 *A1 96
West Portland Park, Multnomah, Oreg. 1,500 *A1 96
Westport Mills, Bristol, Mass. 400 *C5 206
Westport Point, Bristol, Mass. 200 C5 206
West Portsmouth, Scioto, Ohio 3,100 D3 156
West Prairie, riv., Alta., Can. C4 54
West Pubnico, N.S., Can. 215 F4 70
West Quoddy Head, cape, Maine D6 204
Westray, isl., Scot. B9 272
West Reading, Berks, Pa. 4,938 C6 214
West Redding, Fairfield, Conn. 250 D2 202
Westree, Ont., Can. 100 S25 64
West Richland, Benton, Wash. 1,347 *C7 98
West Rindge, Cheshire, N.H. 130 F2 208
West River, Anne Arundel, Md. 100 C6 182
West Riverside, Missoula, Mont. 150 *D3 110
West Road, riv., B.C., Can. D10 52
West Rockingham, Richmond, N.C. 1,128 *C6 186
West Roundup, Musselshell, Mont. 250 *D8 110
West Rumney, Grafton, N.H. 40 D3 208
West Rupert, Bennington, Vt. 160 E2 218
West Rutland, Rutland, Vt. 2,302 D2 218
West Rye, Rockingham, N.H. 150 E5 208
West St. Modeste, Newf., Can. 75 E7 72
West St. Paul, Dakota, Minn. 13,101 F7 148
West Salem, Edwards, Ill. 956 E5 138
West Salem, Wayne, Ohio 1,017 B4 156
West Salem, Polk, Oreg. (part of Salem) C1 96 / C3
West Salem, La Crosse, Wis. 1,707 E2 160
West Salisbury, Addison, Vt. 85 D2 218
West Sayville, Suffolk, N.Y. 3,000 *E4 212
West Scarboro, Cumberland, Maine 900 E2 204 / E4
West Seboois, Penobscot, Maine 50 C4 204
West Selmont, Dallas, Ala. 400 *C2 168
West Shefford, Que., Can. 373 S12 66
West Siberian, plain, Sov.Un. A7 336
Westside, Crawford, Iowa 367 B2 142
West Side, Lake, Oreg. E6 96
West Simsbury, Hartford, Conn. 170 B4 202
West Sioux Falls, Minnehaha, S.Dak. 250 D9 158
West Slope, Washington, Oreg. 9,000 B1 96
West Somerset, Pulaski, Ky. 400 C6 178
West Spanish, peak, Colo. E6 106
West Springfield, Hampden, Mass. 24,924 B2 206
West Stafford, Tolland, Conn. 300 B6 202
West Sterling, Whiteside, Ill. 1,430 *B3 138
West Stewartstown, Coos, N.H. 225 B3 208
West Stockbridge, Berkshire, Mass. 800 (1,244▲) B1 206
West Stoughton, Norfolk, Mass. E2 206
West Suffield, Hartford, Conn. 400 B5 202
West Sullivan, Hancock, Maine 125 D4 204
West Summerland, B.C., Can. 2,500 F13 52
West Sumner, Oxford, Maine 125 D2 204
West Sutton, Worcester, Mass 120 *B4 206
West Swanzey, Cheshire, N.H. 900 F2 208
West Terre Haute, Vigo, Ind. 3,006 C2 140
Westterschelling, Neth. 1,995 A4 282
West Thornton, Grafton, N.H. 130 D2 208
West Tisbury, Dukes, Mass. 350 (360▲) D6 206
West Topsham, Orange, Vt. 100 C4 218
Westtown, Orange, N.Y. 200 D7 212
West Townsend, Middlesex, Mass. 900 A4 206
West Townshend, Windham, Vt. 95 E3 218
West Travaputs, plat., Utah D5 114
West Tremont, Hancock, Maine 200 D4 204
West Trenton (Ewing Township), Mercer, N.J. 26,628 C3 210
West Union, Clark, Ill. 400 D6 138
West Union, Fayette, Iowa 2,551 B6 142
West Union, Todd, Minn. 83 F3 148
West Union, Adams, Ohio 1,762 D3 156
West Union, Oconee, S.C. 443 B2 188
West Union, Doddridge, W.Va. 1,186 B4 194 / B6
West Unity, Williams, Ohio 1,192 A2 156
West University Place, Harris, Tex. 14,628 F8 130
West Upton, Worcester, Mass. 990 B4 206 / D1
Westvaco, Sweetwater, Wyo. 10 E3 116
West Valley, Cattaraugus, N.Y. 350 C3 212
West Van Lear, Johnson, Ky. 900 *C8 178
Westview, B.C., Can. (part of Powell River) F10 52
Westview, Cuyahoga, Ohio 1,303 B1 156
West View, Allegheny, Pa. 8,079 A3 214
Westview Heights, New Haven, Conn. 900 C3 202
West View Park, Sullivan, Tenn. 4,722 *B9 190

Westville, N.S., Can. 4,247 D7 70
Westville, Holmes, Fla. 200 A5 174
Westville, Vermilion, Ill. 3,497 C6 138
Westville, La Porte, Ind. 789 A3 140
Westville, Rockingham, N.H. 400 F4 208
Westville, Gloucester, N.J. 4,951 D2 210
Westville, Adair, Okla. 727 C9 128
Westville, Kershaw, S.C. 200 C7 188
Westville Grove, Gloucester, N.J. 2,500 *D2 210
West Virginia, state, U.S. 1,860,421 D10 77
194
West Vlaanderen, prov., Bel. 1,044,451 C1 282
West Walker, riv., Nev. E2 112
West Wareham, Plymouth, Mass. 200 C6 206
West Warren, Worcester, Mass. 1,124 B3 206
West Warwick, Kent, R.I. 21,414 C2 216
Westwater, Grand, Utah 15 D6 114
Westwego, Jefferson, La. 9,815 C7 180
E5
West Wenatchee, Chelan, Wash. 2,518 *B6 98
West Wildwood, Cape May, N.J. 207 *E3 210
West Willington, Tolland, Conn. 300 B6 202
West Wilton, Hillsboro, N.H. 100 F3 208
West Winfield, Herkimer, N.Y. 960 C6 212
West Winter Haven, Polk, Fla. 5,050 *C9 174
Westwold, B.C., Can. 150 E13 52
Westwood, Lassen, Calif. 1,209 B3 94
Westwood, Henry, Ind. 280 C4 140
Westwood, Johnson, Kans. 2,040 B8 144
Westwood, Boyd, Ky. 6,000 B8 178
Westwood, Norfolk, Mass. 5,800 B5 206
(10,354▲) D2
Westwood, Kalamazoo, Mich. 6,500 *G6 146
Westwood, St. Louis, Mo. 291 *C7 150
Westwood, Bergen, N.J. 9,046 A1 210
B4
Westwood Hills, Johnson, Kans. 495 *D9 144
Westwood Lakes, Dade, Fla. 22,517 *F10 174
West Worthington, Hampshire, Mass. 25 B2 206
Westworth Village, Tarrant, Tex. 3,321 *C7 130
West Wyoming, Luzerne, Pa. 3,166 A5 214
West Yarmouth, Barnstable, Mass. 1,365 C7 206
West Yellowstone, Gallatin, Mont. 300 F5 110
West York, York, Pa. 5,526 D5 214
West Yuma, Yuma, Ariz. 2,781 *F1 124
Wetar, isl., Indon. F7 358
Wetaskiwin, Alta., Can. 4,476 D6 54
Wethersfield, Hartford, Conn. 20,561 C5 202
Wetmore, Custer, Colo. 100 D5 106
Wetmore, Nemaha, Kans. 390 C8 144
Wetmore, Alger, Mich. 200 C5 146
Wetonka, McPherson, S.Dak. 46 B7 158
Wettingen, Switz. 14,200 A4 312
Wetumka, Hughes, Okla. 1,798 C7 128
Wetumpka, Elmore, Ala. 3,672 C3 168
Wetzel, co., W.Va. 19,347 B4 194
Wetzlar, Ger. 32,400 C3 286
Wevelgem, Bel. 12,811 D2 282
Wevok, Alsk. 100 *B5 84
Wewahitchka, Gulf, Fla. 1,436 A5 174
Wewak, N.Gui. 59 F11 359
Wewela, Tripp, S.Dak. 22 D6 158
Wewoka, Seminole, Okla. 5,954 C7 128
Wexford, Ire. 10,838 I6 273
Wexford, co., Ire. 87,259 I6 273
Wexford, co., Mich. 18,466 E6 146
Weyakwin, lake, Sask., Can. C4 58
Weyanoke, West Feliciana, La. 50 D4 180
Weyauwega, Waupaca, Wis. 1,239 D5 160
Weyburn, Sask., Can. 7,684 F6 58
Weyerhauser, Rusk, Wis. 339 C2 160
Weyers Cave, Augusta, Va. 300 B6 192
Weymouth, N.S., Can. 1,350 E4 70
Weymouth, Norfolk, Mass. 48,177 B6 206
D3
Weymouth, Atlantic, N.J. 300 D3 210
Weymouth, bay, Eng. K10 273
Weymouth [& Melcombe Regis], Eng. 37,900 K10 273
Whakatane, N.Z. 5,445 B6 437
Whalan, Fillmore, Minn. 146 H7 148
Whaleysville, Worcester, Md. 240 D9 182
Whaleyville, Nansemond, Va. 402 D8 192
Whalom, Worcester, Mass. 600 A4 206
Whalsay, isl., Scot. A12 272
Whangarei, N.Z. 13,363 A5 437
Whangarei, hbr., N.Z. A5 437
Wharton, Morris, N.J. 5,006 B3 210
Wharton, Wyandot, Ohio 463 B3 156
Wharton, Wharton, Tex. 5,734 E7 130
Wharton, Boone, W.Va. 1,055 D6 194
Wharton, co., Tex. 38,152 E7 130
Wharton West, Wharton, Tex. 1,609 *E7 130
Whatcheer, Alta., Can. 15 E7 54
What Cheer, Keokuk, Iowa 956 C5 142
Whatcom, co., Wash. 70,317 A4 98
Whatcom, lake, Wash. A4 98
Whately, Franklin, Mass. 150 B2 206
(1,037▲)
Whatley, Clarke, Ala. 500 D2 168
Wheatcroft, Webster, Ky. 317 C3 178
Wheatfield, Jasper, Ind. 679 A2 140
Wheatland, Yuba, Calif. 813 C3 94
Wheatland, Knox, Ind. 614 D2 140
Wheatland, Clinton, Iowa 643 C7 142
Wheatland, Hickory, Mo. 305 D4 150
Wheatland, Cass, N.Dak. 112 D8 154
Wheatland, Oklahoma, Okla. (part of Oklahoma City) C6 128
Wheatland, Mercer, Pa. 1,813 B1 214
Wheatland, Kenosha, Wis. 20 F1 160
Wheatland, Platte, Wyo. 2,350 D8 116
Wheatland, co., Mont. 3,026 D7 110
Wheatley, St. Francis, Ark. 443 C5 170
Wheatley, Ont., Can. 1,196 R18 64
Wheaton, Du Page, Ill. 24,312 B5 138
F2
Wheaton, Pottawatomie, Kans. 114 C7 144
Wheaton, Montgomery, Md. 54,635 B3 182
B5
Wheaton, Traverse, Minn. 2,102 F2 148
Wheaton, Barry, Mo. 341 E3 150
Wheat Ridge, Jefferson, Colo. 21,619 C5 106
Wheat Road, Atlantic, N.J. D3 210
Wheeler, Lawrence, Ala. 250 A2 168
Wheeler, Porter, Ind. 500 A2 140
Wheeler, Cheyenne, Kans. 40 C2 144
Wheeler, Prentiss, Miss. 250 A4 184
Wheeler, Valley, Mont. 25 B10 110
Wheeler, Wheeler, Nebr. C7 152
Wheeler, Tillamook, Oreg. 237 B3 96
Wheeler, Wheeler, Tex. 1,174 B5 130
Wheeler, Dunn, Wis. 227 C2 160
Wheeler, co., Ga. 5,342 D4 176
Wheeler, co., Nebr. 1,297 C7 152
Wheeler, co., Oreg. 2,722 C6 96
Wheeler, co., Tex. 7,947 B5 130
Wheeler, dam, Ala. A2 168
Wheeler, peak, Nev. E7 112
Wheeler, peak, N.Mex. B5 126
Wheelersburg, Scioto, Ohio 2,682 D4 156
Wheeless, Cimarron, Okla. 10 B1 128
Wheeling, Cook, Ill. 7,169 E2 138
Wheeling, Livingston, Mo. 302 B4 150
Wheeling, Ohio, W.Va. 53,400 A4 194
(*126,600) B2
Wheeling, creek, W.Va. B2 194
Wheelock, Williams, N.Dak. 82 B2 154
Wheelock, Caledonia, Vt. 70 B4 218
(246▲)
Wheelock, mtn., Vt. B4 218
Wheelwright, Floyd, Ky. 1,518 C8 178
Wheelwright, Worcester, Mass. 250 B3 206
Whelen Springs, Clark, Ark. 155 D3 170
Whernside, mtn, Eng. G10 273
Whetstone, Oconee, S.C. 100 B2 188
Whetstone, riv., S.Dak. F2 148
Whidbey, isl., Wash. A4 98
Whigham, Grady, Ga. 463 F2 176
Whigville, Hartford, Conn. 250 C4 202
Whippany, Morris, N.J. 4,700 B4 210
Whipple, Providence, R.I. 50 B2 216
Whiskey Chitto, creek, La. D2 180
Whiskey Gap, Alta., Can. 75 F6 54
Whispering Hills, Brevard, Fla. 834 *C10 174
Whistler, Mobile, Ala. (part of Prichard) E1 168
Whitaker, Allegheny, Pa. 2,130 *C2 214
Whitakers, Edgecombe and Nash, N.C. 1,004 A8 186
Whitbourne, Newf., Can. 600 G9 72
Whitby, Ont., Can. 9,995 Q22 64
Whitby, Eng. 11,500 G12 273
Whitchurch, Eng. 6,900 I10 273
Whitcomb, mtn., N.H. B4 208
Whitcomb Heights, Vigo, Ind. 300 C2 140
Whitcomb Summit, Berkshire, Mass. 200 *A1 206
White, Bartow, Ga. 439 B2 176
White, Hayes, Nebr. D5 152
White, Brookings, S.Dak. 417 C9 158
White, co., Ark. 32,745 B5 170
White, co., Ga. 6,935 B3 176
White, co., Ill. 19,373 E5 138
White, co., Ind. 19,709 B3 140
White, co., Tenn. 15,577 C6 190
White, bay, Newf., Can. F7 72
White, lake, Ont., Can. O24 64
White, lake, La. E3 180
White, mts., Maine D1 204
White, pt., Newf., Can. E8 72
White, riv., Ariz. E5 124
White, riv., Ark. A3 170
C5
White, riv., Colo. B2 106
White, riv., Ind. D2 140
White, riv., Mich. F5 146
White, riv., Mo. E4 150
White, riv., Nev. E6 112
White, riv., S.Dak. D5 158
White, riv., Tex. C5 130
White, riv., Utah D6 114
White, riv., Vt. D4 218
White, riv., Wash. B5 98
White, rock, Oreg. D3 96
White, sea, Sov.Un. C5 328
White Bear, Sask., Can. 85 E3 58
White Bear, is., Newf., Can. C7 72
White Bear, lake, Newf., Can. C6 72
White Bear, riv., Newf., Can. G7 72
White Bear, riv., Newf., Can. D7 72
White Bear Beach, Ramsey, Minn. 150 F7 148
White Bear Lake, Ramsey, Minn. 12,849 F5 148
F7
White Bird, Idaho, Idaho 253 D2 108
White Bluff, Dickson, Tenn. 486 B4 190
Whitebreast, creek, Iowa D4 142
White Butte, Perkins, S.Dak. 50 B3 158
White Canyon, San Juan, Utah 98 F5 114
White Cap, mtn., Maine C3 204
White Carpathians, mts., Czech. B3 324
White Castle, Iberville, La. 2,253 B5 180
D4
White Church, Wyandotte, Kans. 75 B7 144
White City, St. Lucie, Fla. 500 D10 174
White City, Morris, Kans. 459 D7 144
Whiteclay, Sheridan, Nebr. 80 B3 152
White Clay, creek, Nebr. A3 152
White Cloud, Doniphan, Kans. 238 C8 144
White Cloud, Newaygo, Mich. 1,001 F6 146
Whitecloud, peaks, Idaho E4 108
White Court, Alta., Can. 115 C5 54
Whiteday, creek, W.Va. A7 194
White Deer, Carson, Tex. 1,057 B5 130
White Earth, Becker, Minn. 350 D3 148
White Earth, Mountrail, N.Dak. 208 B3 154
White Earth, lake, Minn. D3 148
White Earth, riv., N.Dak. B3 154
Whiteface, mtn., N.Y. A7 212
White Face, mtn., Vt. B3 218
Whiteface, riv., Minn. D6 148
Whitefield, Lincoln, Maine 150 *D3 204
(1,068▲)
Whitefield, Coos, N.H. 1,244 C3 208
(1,581▲)
Whitefield, Haskell, Okla. 200 C8 128
Whitefish, Flathead, Mont. 2,965 B2 110
Whitefish, bay, Mich. C7 146
Whitefish, lake, Minn. E4 148
Whitefish, pt., Mich. C7 146
Whitefish, pt., Wis. D6 160
Whitefish, range, Mont. B2 110
Whitefish, riv., Mich. C5 146
Whitefish Bay, Milwaukee, Wis. 18,390 E2 160
Whitefish Falls, Ont., Can. 200 O19 64
Whitefish Point, Chippewa, Mich. 100 C7 146
Whiteford, Harford, Md. 300 A7 182
White Fox, Sask., Can. 366 D5 58
Whitefox, riv., Sask., Can. D5 58
White Gull, creek, Sask., Can. D5 58
White Gull, lake, Newf., Can. D9 72
White Hall, Lowndes, Ala. 200 C3 168
Whitehall, Jefferson, Ark. 300 C4 170
Whitehall, Poinsett, Ark. 170 B6 170
White Hall, Clarke, Ga. 409 C3 176
White Hall, Greene, Ill. 3,012 D3 138
Whitehall, Livingston, La. 150 B6 180
D5
White Hall, Baltimore, Md. 115 A6 182
Whitehall, Jefferson, Mont. 898 E4 110
Whitehall, Washington, N.Y. 4,016 B8 212
Whitehall, Franklin, Ohio 20,818 C1 156
Whitehall, Mifflin, Pa. 16,075 *C2 214
White Hall, Colleton, S.C. 130 F7 188
White Hall, Albemarle, Va. 55 B6 192
Whitehall, Trempealeau, Wis. 1,446 D2 160
Whitehall, pond, Mass. B4 206
Whitehaven, Eng. 25,700 G9 273
Whitehaven, Wicomico, Md. 60 D8 182
White Haven, Luzerne, Pa. 1,778 B6 214
Whitehaven, Shelby, Tenn. 13,894 E6 190
Whitehead, Lauderdale, Ala. 150 A2 168
Whitehead, N.Ire. 1,862 G7 272
Whitehorse, Yukon, Can. 2,570 E5 48
White Horse, Mercer, N.J. (part of Hamilton Township) C3 210
Whitehorse, Dewey, S.Dak. 50 B5 158
White Horse Beach, Plymouth, Mass. 112 C6 206
Whitehouse, Duval, Fla. 600 A10 174
Whitehouse, Johnson, Ky. 500 C8 178
Whitehouse, Hunterdon, N.J. 600 B3 210
Whitehouse, Lucas, Ohio 1,135 A1 156
A3
White House, Robertson, Tenn. 450 B5 190
Whitehouse, Smith, Tex. 842 *C8 130
White House Station, Hunterdon, N.J. 700 B3 210
White Lake, Ont., Can. 135 O24 64
White Lake, Aurora, S.Dak. 397 D7 158
White Lake, Langlade, Wis. 325 C5 160
White Lakes, Santa Fe, N.Mex. C5 126
H7
Whiteland, Johnson, Ind. 1,368 C3 140
Whitelaw, Alta., Can. 450 B4 54
Whitelaw, Greeley, Kans. 2 D2 144
Whitelaw, Manitowoc, Wis. 420 B6 160
Whiteleysburg, Kent, Del. E3 172
White Marsh, Baltimore, Md. 300 B7 182
White Mesa, natural bridge, Ariz. B4 124
White Mountain, Alsk. 129 C5 84
White Mountain, peak, Calif. D4 94
Whitemouth, Man., Can. 315 F5 60
Whitemouth, lake, Man., Can. F5 60
Whitemouth, riv., Man., Can. F5 60
Whitemud, riv., Alta., Can. B3 54
White Nile, riv., Sud. C3 398
White Oak, Barbour, Ala. 8 D4 168
White Oak, Camden, Ga. 150 E5 176
Whiteoak, Craig, Okla. 75 B8 128
White Oak, Allegheny, Pa. 9,047 *C2 214
White Oak, Fairfield, S.C. 125 C6 188
White Oak, Gregg, Tex. 1,250 *C8 130
Whiteoak, creek, Ohio D3 156
Whiteoak, creek, Tenn. B4 190
White Oak, mtn., Ark. B4 170
White Oak, mtn., Ark. C3 170
White Oak, mtn., Tenn. E8 190
Whiteoak, swamp, N.C. C8 186
White Pine, Ontonagon, Mich. 950 *B2 146
Whitepine, Sanders, Mont. 11 C1 110
White Pine, Jefferson, Tenn. 1,035 B8 190
White Pine, co., Nev. 9,808 D6 112
White Plains, Calhoun, Ala. 400 B4 168
White Plains, Greene, Ga. 273 C3 176
White Plains, Allen, Ky. 500 D4 178
White Plains, Hopkins, Ky. 359 C3 178
White Plains, Charles, Md. 150 C6 182
White Plains, Westchester, N.Y. 50,485 D2 212
D8
White Plains, Surry, N.C. 500 A5 186
White Plains, Brunswick, Va. 50 D7 192
White Point Beach, N.S., Can. 127 F5 70
White Pond, Aiken, S.C. 150 E6 188
White Post, Clarke, Va. 200 A6 192
Whiteriver, Navajo, Ariz. 450 E6 124
White River, Mellette, S.Dak. 583 D5 158
White River Junction, Windsor, Vt. 2,546 D4 218
White Rock, B.C., Can. 1,800 C15 52
F11
White Rock, Los Alamos, N.Mex. 150 G7 126
White Rock, Washington, R.I. D1 216
White Rock, Richland, S.C. 141 C6 188
White Rock, Roberts, S.Dak. 76 B9 158
White Rock, creek, Kans. C5 144
Whiterocks, Uintah, Utah 170 C6 114
White Rocks, mtn., Ky. D7 178
White Russia, see Byelorussia, Sov.Un.
Whites, Clay, Miss. 200 B4 184
Whites, Grays Harbor, Wash. 55 B3 98
Whites, creek, Tenn. E7 190
Whitesail, lake, B.C., Can. D9 52
White Salmon, Klickitat, Wash. 1,590 D5 98
Whitesand, bay, Eng. K8 273
Whitesand, riv., Sask., Can. E6 58
White Sands, nat. mon., N.Mex. F4 126
Whitesbog, Burlington, N.J. 100 D3 210
Whitesboro, Cape May, N.J. 700 E3 210
Whitesboro, Oneida, N.Y. 4,784 *B6 212
Whitesboro, Le Flore, Okla. 75 D9 128
Whitesboro, Grayson, Tex. 2,485 C7 130
Whites Brook, N.B., Can. B2 70
Whitesburg, Carroll, Ga. 366 C2 176
Whitesburg, Letcher, Ky. 1,774 C8 178
Whites City, Eddy, N.Mex. 175 F6 126
Whites Creek, Davidson, Tenn. 100 E7 190
White Settlement, Tarrant, Tex. 11,513 B8 130
Whiteshield, mtn., Alta., B.C., Can. D3 54
D13 52
Whiteside, Marion, Tenn. 500 C6 190
Whiteside, co., Ill. 59,887 B3 138
Whiteson, Yamhill, Oreg. 100 B3 96
White Springs, Hamilton, Fla. 700 A8 174
Whitestone, Gilmer, Ga. 300 B2 176
White Stone, Spartanburg, S.C. 250 *B5 188
White Stone, Lancaster, Va. 395 C8 192
Whitestone, lake, Man., Can. B4 60
Whitestown, Boone, Ind. 613 B3 140
White Sulphur Springs, Meriwether, Ga. 156 *D2 176
White Sulphur Springs, La Salle, La. C3 180
White Sulphur Springs, Meagher, Mont. 1,519 D6 110
White Sulphur Springs, Greenbrier, W.Va. 2,676 D4 194
Whitesville, Sussex, Del. G4 172
Whitesville, Harris, Ga. 500 D1 176
Whitesville, Daviess, Ky. 713 C4 178
Whitesville, Monmouth, N.J. 300 C4 210
Whitesville, Allegany, N.Y. 600 C4 212
Whitesville, Boone, W.Va. 774 D3 194
D6
White Swan, Yakima, Wash. 300 C6 98
Whitetail, Daniels, Mont. 253 B11 110
White Tail, Otero, N.Mex. 70 E5 126
White Tank, mts., Ariz. G1 124
White Township, Beaver, Pa. 1,437 *C1 214
Whiteville, Columbus, N.C. 4,683 C7 186
Whiteville, Hardeman, Tenn. 757 C2 190
White Volta, riv., Ghana E4 408
Whitewater, Man., Can. 110 F2 60
Whitewater, Mesa, Colo. 170 D2 106
Whitewater, Wayne, Ind. 102 *C5 140
Whitewater, Butler, Kans. 499 E6 144
Whitewater, Cape Girardeau, Mo. 169 D8 150
Whitewater, Phillips, Mont. 90 B9 110
Whitewater, Walworth, Wis. 6,380 F5 160
Whitewater, bay, Fla. F10 174
Whitewater, riv., Ind. C4 140
Whitewater, riv., Kans. E6 144
Whitewater Baldy, mtn., N.Mex. E2 126
White Women, creek, Colo. D8 106
Kans. D2 144
Whitewood, Sask., Can. 789 E6 58
Whitewood, Lawrence, S.Dak. 470 C2 158
Whitewood, lake, S.Dak. C8 158
Whitewright, Grayson, Tex. 1,315 C7 130
Whitfield, Sumter, Ala. 990 C1 168
Whitfield, Rankin, Miss. 300 C2 184
Whitfield Estate, Manatee, Fla. 600 D6 174
Whitfield, co., Ga. 42,109 B2 176
Whithorn, Scot. 1,000 G8 273
Whiting, Lake, Ind. 8,137 A2 140
Whiting, Monona, Iowa 595 B1 142
Whiting, Jackson, Kans. 233 C8 144
Whiting, Washington, Maine 230 D5 204
(339▲)
Whiting, Ocean, N.J. 308 D4 210
Whiting, Addison, Vt. 70 D2 218
(304▲)
Whiting, Portage, Wis. 1,193 D4 160
Whitingham, Windham, Vt. 100 F3 218
(838▲)
Whitingham, res., Vt. F3 218
Whitinsville, Worcester, Mass. 5,102 B4 206
Whitkow, Sask., Can. 100 D4 58
Whitla, Alta., Can. 78 F7 54
Whitlash, Liberty, Mont. 10 B5 110
Whitley, co., Ind. 20,954 A4 140
Whitley, co., Ky. 25,815 D6 178
Whitley City, McCreary, Ky. 1,034 D6 178
Whitlock, Henry, Tenn. 130 B3 190
Whitman, Plymouth, Mass. 10,485 B6 206
Whitman, Grant, Nebr. 150 B4 152
Whitman, Nelson, N.Dak. 100 B7 154
Whitman, co., Wash. 31,263 B9 98
Whitman Knob, mtn., W.Va. C4 194
Whitman, natl. mon., Wash. C8 98
Whitmans, Logan, W.Va. 500 *D2 194
Whitmans, pond, Mass. D3 206
Whitmell, Pittsylvania, Va. 35 D5 192
Whitmer, Randolph, W.Va. 250 C5 194
Whitmire, Newberry, S.C. 2,663 B5 188
Whitmore Village (Whitmore City), Honolulu, Haw. 1,820 F9 86
Whitnel, Caldwell, N.C. 1,232 B4 186
Whitney, St. Clair, Ala. 150 B3 168
Whitney, Ont., Can. 265 O22 64
Whitney, Ada, Idaho 13,603 *F2 108
Whitney, Franklin, Idaho 80 *G7 108
Whitney, Dawes, Nebr. 98 B2 152
Whitney, Clark, Nev. 700 G6 112
Whitney, Baker, Oreg. 3 C8 96
Whitney, Westmoreland, Pa. 775 C2 214
Whitney, Spartanburg, S.C. 2,502 B5 188
Whitney, Hill, Tex. 1,050 D7 130
Whitney, lake, Tex. D7 130
Whitney, mtn., Calif. D4 94
Whitney Point, Broome, N.Y. 1,049 C6 212
Whitney Point, res., N.Y. C6 212
Whitneyville, Washington, Maine 200 D5 204
(229▲)
Whitstable, Eng. 17,400 J14 273
Whittemore, Kossuth, Iowa 741 A3 142
Whittemore, Iosco, Mich. 460 E8 146
Whitten, Hardin, Iowa 184 B4 142
Whittier, Alsk. 627 C7 84
G11
Whittier, Los Angeles, Calif. 33,663 C5 94
F4
Whittier, Linn, Iowa 170 B6 142
Whittlesey, Eng. 8,800 I12 273

Wind Lake, Racine, Wis. 1,305 F1 160
F5
Windmill, pt., Va. C8 192
Windom, McPherson, Kans. 168 D6 144
Windom, Cottonwood, Minn. 3,691 H3 148
Windom, peak, Colo. E3 106
Windorah, Austl. 70 D8 432
Window Rock, Apache, Ariz. 300 C6 124
Wind Point, Racine, Wis. 463 *F6 160
Wind River, Fremont, Wyo. D4 116
Wind River, basin, Wyo. C4 116
Wind River, range, Wyo. C3 116
Windsor, Newf., Can. 4,520 F8 72
Windsor, N.S., Can. 3,651 E5 70
Windsor, Ont., Can. 121,980 R18 64
(*185,865)
Windsor, Que., Can. 5,886 S12 66
Windsor, Weld, Colo. 1,509 B6 106
Windsor, Hartford, Conn. 12,000 B5 202
(19,467▲)
Windsor, Shelby, Ill. 1,021 D5 138
Windsor, Randolph, Ind. 125 B4 140
Windsor, Kennebec, Maine 25 D3 204
(878▲)
Windsor, Berkshire, Mass. 100 A1 206
(384▲)
Windsor, Henry, Mo. 2,714 C4 150
Windsor, Mercer, N.J. 300 C3 210
Windsor, Broome, N.Y. 1,026 C6 212
Windsor, Bertie, N.C. 1,813 B9 186
Windsor, Stutsman, N.Dak. 55 D6 154
Windsor, York, Pa. 1,029 D5 214
Windsor, Aiken, S.C. 151 E5 188
Windsor, Windsor, Vt. 3,256 E4 218
(4,468▲)
Windsor, Isle of Wight, Va. 579 A8 192
D8
Windsor, co., Vt. 42,483 D3 218
Windsor Heights, Polk, Iowa 4,715 A7 142
Windsor Heights, Brooke,
W.Va. 780 B2 194
Windsor Locks, Hartford,
Conn. 11,411 B5 202
Windsorville,
Hartford, Conn. 180 B5 202
Windthorst, Sask., Can. 212 E6 58
Windward, is., N.A. B5 236
Windward, passage, W.I. C7 232
Windward Islands, Br. poss., N.A. E14 233
Windy, Wirt, W.Va. 17 B3 194
Windy, lake, Sask., Can. C6 58
Windy, peak, Wash. A7 98
Windy, pt., Newf., Can. E8 72
Windy Hill, Florence, S.C. 2,201 *C9 188
Windy Hill Beach, Horry, S.C. 150 D11 188
Windy Hills, Jefferson, Ky. 1,371 *B5 178
Wine, isl., La. E5 180
Winefred, lake, Alta., Can. C7 54
Winefred, riv., Alta., Can. C7 54
Winesap, Cumberland, Tenn. C6 190
Winfall, Perquimans, N.C. 269 A9 186
Winfield, Marion, Ala. 2,907 B2 168
Winfield, Alta., Can. 300 D5 54
Winfield, Columbia, Fla. 50 A8 174
Winfield, Du Page, Ill. 1,575 B5 138
Winfield, Henry, Iowa 862 C6 142
Winfield, Cowley, Kans. 11,117 E7 144
Winfield, Carroll, Md. 100 B5 182
Winfield, Lincoln, Mo. 564 A7 150
C7
Winfield, Union, N.J. 2,458 *B4 210
Winfield, Scott, Tenn. 200 B7 190
Winfield, Putnam, W.Va. 318 C3 194
Winfred, Lake, S.Dak. 137 C8 158
Wing, Covington, Ala. 82 *D3 168
Wing, Yell, Ark. 15 *C3 170
Wing, Burleigh, N.Dak. 303 C5 154
Wing, riv., Minn. E3 148
Wingate, Montgomery, Ind. 431 B2 140
Wingate, Dorchester, Md. 400 D7 182
Wingate, Union, N.C. 1,304 C5 186
Winger, Polk, Minn. 292 D3 148
Wingham, Ont., Can. 2,766 Q19 64
Wing Lake, Oakland, Mich. 1,500 *G8 146
Wingo, Graves, Ky. 340 D2 178
Winifred, Fergus, Mont. 220 C7 110
Winifreda, Arg. C3 252
Winifrede, Kanawha, W.Va. 200 D6 194
Winisk, lake, Ont., Can. Q24 64
Winisk, riv., Ont., Can. Q24 64
Wink, Winkler, Tex. 1,863 D4 130
Winkelman, Gila, Ariz. 1,123 F5 124
Winkler, Man., Can. 1,634 F4 60
Winkler, co., Tex. 13,652 D4 130
Winlaw, B.C., Can. 150 F14 52
Winlock, Wheeler, Oreg. C7 96
Winlock, Lewis, Wash. 808 C4 98
Winn, par., La. 16,034 B3 180
Winn, Penobscot, Maine 200 C4 204
(526▲)
Winn, Isabella, Mich. 300 F7 146
Winnabow, Brunswick, N.C. 150 C7 186
Winnapaug, pond, R.I. D1 216
Winneba, Ghana 15,171 E4 408
Winnebago, Winnebago, Ill. 1,059 A4 138
Winnebago, Faribault, Minn. 2,088 H4 148
Winnebago, Thurston, Nebr. 682 B9 152
Winnebago, Winnebago, Wis. 150 B5 160
Winnebago, co., Ill. 209,765 A4 138
Winnebago, co., Iowa 13,099 A6 142
Winnebago, co., Wis. 107,928 D5 160
Winnebago, lake, Wis. D5 160
Winneconne, Winnebago,
Wis. 1,273 D5 160
Winneconnet, Bristol, Mass. 300 *C5 206
Winnegance, Sagadahoc,
Maine 125 E3 204
E6
Winnemucca, Humboldt, Nev. 3,453 C4 112
Winnemucca, lake, Nev. C2 112
Winner, Tripp, S.Dak. 3,705 D6 158
Winneshiek, co., Iowa 21,651 A6 142
Winnetka, Cook, Ill. 13,368 A6 138
E3
Winnetoon, Knox, Nebr. 85 B8 152
Winnett, Petroleum, Mont. 360 C8 110
Winnfield, Winn, La. 7,022 C3 180
Winnibigoshish, lake, Minn. D4 148
Winnie, Chambers, Tex. 1,114 *E8 130
Winnifred, Alta., Can. 125 F7 54
Winning Pool, Austl. C2 432
Winnipeg, Man., Can. 255,093 F4 60
(*409,121) F6
Winnipeg, lake, Man., Can. D3 60
F6
Winnipeg, riv., Man., Can. E5 60
Winnipeg Beach, Man., Can. 805 E4 60
Winnipegosis, Man., Can. 984 E3 60
Winnipegosis, lake, Man., Can. D3 60
F5
Winnipesaukee, lake, N.H. D4 208
Winnisquam, Belknap, N.H. 80 D3 208
Winnisquam, lake, N.H. D3 208
Winnsboro, Franklin, La. 4,437 B4 180
Winnsboro, Fairfield, S.C. 3,479 C6 188
Winnsboro, Wood and
Franklin, Tex. 2,675 C8 130
Winnsboro Mills, Fairfield,
S.C. 2,411 C6 188
Winona, Ont., Can. 575 Q21 64
Winona, Starke, Ind. 100 A3 140
Winona, Logan, Kans. 393 C2 144
Winona, Houghton, Mich. 120 C3 146
Winona, Winona, Minn. 24,895 G7 148
Winona, Montgomery, Miss. 4,282 B3 184
Winona, Shannon, Mo. 562 D6 150
Winona, Whitman, Wash. 100 C9 98
Winona, Fayette, W.Va. 650 C4 194
D7
Winona, co., Minn. 40,937 G7 148
Winona Lake, Kosciusko,
Ind. 1,928 A4 140
Winona Lakes, Orange, N.Y. 1,655 D7 212
Winooski, Chittenden, Vt. 7,420 C2 218
Winooski, riv., Vt. C3 218
Winschoten, Neth. 15,908 A6 282
Winside, Wayne, Nebr. 416 B8 152
Winslow, Navajo, Ariz. 8,862 C5 124
Winslow, Washington, Ark. 183 B2 170
Winslow, Pike, Ind. 1,089 D2 140
Winslow, Kennebec, Maine 3,640 D3 204
(5,891▲)
Winslow, Dodge, Nebr. 136 C9 152
Winslow, Camden, N.J. 400 D3 210
Winslow, Kitsap, Wash. 919 D2 98
Winsper, Clark, Idaho E6 108
Winsted, Litchfield, Conn. 8,136 B3 202
Winsted, McLeod, Minn. 1,163 G4 148
Winston, Douglas, Ga. 125 *C2 176
Winston, Daviess, Mo. 236 B3 150
Winston, Broadwater, Mont. 40 D5 110
Winston, Sierra, N.Mex. 200 E3 126
Winston, Douglas, Oreg. 2,395 D3 96
Winston, co., Ala. 14,858 A2 168
Winston, co., Miss. 19,246 B3 184
Winston Park, Kenton, Ky. 744 *A6 178
Winston-Salem, Forsyth,
N.C. 111,135 A5 186
(*185,700)
Winstonville, Bolivar, Miss. 327 B2 184
Winsum, Neth. 996 A5 282
Winter, Sask., Can. 75 D3 58
Winter, Sawyer, Wis. 500 C2 160
Winter Beach, Indian River, Fla. 150 D10 174
Winter Garden, Orange, Fla. 5,513 C9 174
Winter Harbor,
Hancock, Maine 500 D4 204
(756▲)
Winter Harbour, B.C., Can. E8 52
Winterhaven, Imperial, Calif. 700 F6 94
Winter Haven, Polk, Fla. 16,277 C9 174
Wintering, lake, Man., Can. C4 60
Winter Park, Grand, Colo. 100 C5 106
Winter Park, Orange, Fla. 17,162 C9 174
Winter Park, New Hanover, N.C.
(part of East Wilmington) C8 186
Winterpock, Chesterfield, Va. 130 C7 192
Winterport, Waldo, Maine 900 D4 204
(2,088▲)
Winters, Yolo, Calif. 1,700 C3 94
Winters, Runnels, Tex. 3,266 C6 130
Winterset, Madison, Iowa 3,639 C3 142
Wintersville,
Jefferson, Ohio 3,597 B6 156
Winterswijk, Neth. 12,883 C5 282
Winterthur, New Castle, Del. 275 A3 172
Winterthur, Switz. 70,500 A4 312
Winterton, Newf., Can. 900 G9 72
Winterville, Clarke, Ga. 497 C3 176
Winterville, Aroostook, Maine 100 B4 204
(215▲)
Winterville, Washington, Miss. 300 B1 184
Winterville, Pitt, N.C. 1,418 B8 186
Winthrop, Little River, Ark. 225 D2 170
Winthrop, Buchanan, Iowa 649 B6 142
Winthrop, Kennebec, Maine 2,260 D3 204
(3,537▲)
Winthrop, Suffolk, Mass. 20,303 B6 206
D3
Winthrop, Sibley, Minn. 1,381 G4 148
Winthrop, Okanogan, Wash. 359 A6 98
Winthrop, lake, Mass. D1 206
Winthrop Harbor, Lake, Ill. 3,848 A6 138
D2
Winton, Austl. 1,398 C8 432
Winton, St. Louis, Minn. 182 D7 148
Winton, Hertford, N.C. 835 A9 186
Winton (Jessup), Lackawanna,
Pa. 5,456 A5 214
Winwŏn, Kor. E13 348
Winyah, bay, S.C. E10 188
Wiota, Cass, Iowa 195 C3 142
Wiota, Lafayette, Wis. 140 F4 160
Wirral, N.B., Can. 40 D3 70
Wirt, Carter, Okla. 500 D6 128
Wirt, co., W.Va. 4,391 B3 194
Wirtz, Franklin, Va. 75 C5 192
Wisacky, Lee, S.C. 100 C8 188
Wisbech, Eng. 17,200 I13 273
Wiscasset, Lincoln, Maine 950 D3 204
(1,800▲)
Wiscoal, Knott, Ky. 100 C7 178
Wisconsin, state, U.S. 3,951,777 C9 77
160
Wisconsin, lake, Wis. E4 160
Wisconsin, riv., Wis. E3 160
Wisconsin Dells, Columbia,
Wis. 2,105 E4 160
Wisconsin Rapids, Wood,
Wis. 15,042 D4 160
Wisdom, Beaverhead, Mont. 185 E3 110
Wise, Warren, N.C. 350 A7 186
Wise, Wise, Va. 2,614 D2 192
Wise, co., Tex. 17,012 C7 130
Wise, co., Va. 43,579 C2 192
Wiseman, Alsk. 30 B6 84
Wise River, Beaverhead, Mont. 50 E4 110
Wiseton, Sask., Can. 215 E4 58
Wishart, Sask., Can. 252 E5 58
Wishek, McIntosh, N.Dak. 1,290 D6 154
Wishram, Klickitat, Wash. 750 D6 98
Wisła (Vistula), riv., Pol. B4 325
Wismar, Ger. 54,800 B4 286
Wisner, Franklin, La. 1,254 C4 180
Wisner, Cuming, Nebr. 1,192 C9 152
Wissembourg, Fr. 4,940 C7 278
Wissmann Pool, lake, Con.L. C2 414
Wissota, lake, Wis. D2 160
Wister, Le Flore, Okla. 592 D9 128
Wister, res., Okla. D9 128
Witbank, U.S.Afr. 16,098 E5 420
Witch Hazel, Washington, Oreg. 500 *B4 96
Witch Lake, Marquette, Mich. 50 C3 146
Witham, riv., Eng. H12 273
Withamsville, Clermont, Ohio 2,811 C2 156
D1
Withee, Clark, Wis. 442 D3 160
Witherbee, Essex, N.Y. 800 A8 212
Witherbee, Berkeley, S.C. 50 E9 188
Withernsea, Eng. 5,000 H13 273
Witherspoon, mtn., Alsk. G11 84
Withla, Polk, Fla. 160 C9 174
Withlacoochee, riv., Fla., Ga. A7 174
E3 176
Withrow, Douglas, Wash. 25 B7 98
Witless Bay, Newf., Can. 550 G9 72
Witney, Eng. 7,300 J11 272
Witoka, Winona, Minn. 125 H7 148
Witt, Montgomery, Ill. 1,101 D4 138
Witt, Torrance, N.Mex. 40 D4 126
Witten, Ger. 91,000 *C2 286
Wittenberg (Lutherstadt),
Ger. 48,100 C5 286
Wittenberg, Shawano, Wis. 892 D4 160
Wittenberge (an der
Prignitz), Ger. 32,000 B4 286
Wittengen, Ger. 5,100 B4 286
Witter, Madison, Ark. 40 *B3 170
Wittlich, Ger. 8,900 D2 286
Wittman, Talbot, Md. 370 C7 182
Wittmann, Maricopa, Ariz. 90 G1 124
Wittstock, Ger. 10,200 B5 286
Witvlei, S.W.Afr. D3 420
Wiville, Woodruff, Ark. 40 B5 170
Wixom, Oakland, Mich. 1,531 B7 146
Wixom, lake, Mich. F7 146
Wkra, riv., Pol. B5 325
Włocławek, Pol. 59,000 B4 325
Włodawa, Pol. 4,438 C6 325
Włoszczowa, Pol. 4,683 C4 325
Woburn, Que., Can. 215 S14 66
Woburn, Middlesex, Mass. 31,214 B5 206
C2
Woden, Hancock, Iowa 283 A4 142
Woerden, Neth. 11,609 B3 282
Wohlen, Switz. 6,670 A4 312
Woito, Ont., Can. 55 O23 64
Wokam, isl., Indon. F8 359
Woking, Alta., Can. 100 C3 54
Woking, Eng. 56,800 J12 273
Wolbach, Greeley, Nebr. 382 C7 152
Wolco, Osage, Okla. B7 128
Wolcott, Eagle, Colo. 34 C4 106
Wolcott, New Haven, Conn. 1,500 C4 202
(8,889▲)
Wolcott, White, Ind. 877 B2 140
Wolcott, Wyandotte, Kans. 300 A7 144
Wolcott, Wayne, N.Y. 1,641 B5 212
Wolcott, Lamoille, Vt. 150 B4 218
(633▲)
Wolcottville, Lagrange and
Noble, Ind. 720 A4 140
Wolf, Sheridan, Wyo. 40 B5 116
Wolf, creek, Iowa B5 142
Wolf, creek, Mich. E8 146
Wolf, creek, Mont. C7 110
Wolf, creek, Okla. B4 128
Wolf, creek, W.Va. D7 194
Wolf, lake, Ill. F3 138
Wolf, riv., Miss., Tenn. A3 184
C2 190
Wolf, riv., Miss. E3 184
Wolf, riv., Wis. D5 160
Wolf Bayou, Cleburne, Ark. 50 B5 170
Wolf Coal, Breathitt, Ky. 250 C7 178
Wolf Creek, Arapahoe, Colo. C6 106
Wolf Creek, Lewis and
Clark, Mont. 160 C4 110
Wolf Creek, Josephine, Oreg. 550 E3 96
Wolf Creek, Cocke, Tenn. C9 190
Wolf Creek, pass, Colo. E4 106
Wolfe, Sask., Can. 40 D3 58
Wolfe, co., Que., Can. 18,774 S13 66
Wolfe, co., Ky. 6,534 C7 178
Wolfeboro, Carroll, N.H. 1,557 D4 208
(2,689▲)
Wolfeboro Center,
Carroll, N.H. 125 D4 208
Wolfeboro Falls,
Carroll, N.H. 500 D4 208
Wolfe City, Hunt, Tex. 1,317 C7 130
Wolfe Island, Ont., Can. 265 P24 64
Wolfenbüttel, Ger. 33,900 B4 286
Wolfestown, Que., Can. 295 S13 66
Wolflake, Noble, Ind. 375 A4 140
Wolf Lake, Muskegon, Mich. 2,525 F5 146
Wolf Lake, Becker, Minn. 83 E3 148
Wolford, Pierce, N.Dak. 136 B6 154
Wolf Point, Roosevelt, Mont. 3,585 B11 110
Wolfsberg, Aus. 8,045 D6 313
Wolfsburg, Ger. 44,800 B4 286
Wolf Summit, Harrison, W.Va. 600 B6 194
Wolfsville, Frederick, Md. 20 A4 182
Wolfton, Orangeburg, S.C. 350 D6 188
Wolfville, N.S., Can. 2,497 D5 70
Wolgast, Ger. 13,400 A5 286
Wolhusen, Switz. 3,255 A4 312
Wollaston, is., Chile I4 251
Wollongong, Austl. 90,852 E10 432
Wolmaransstad, U.S.Afr. E5 420
Wołów, Pol. 2,902 C3 325
Wolseley, Sask., Can. 1,001 E6 58
Wolsey, Beadle, S.Dak. 354 C7 158
Wolsztyn, Pol. 4,967 B3 325
Wolverhampton, Eng. 153,100 I10 273
Wolverine, Cheboygan, Mich. 292 D7 146
Wolverine, riv., B.C., Can. C12 52
Wolverine Lake,
Oakland, Mich. 2,404 *G8 146
Wolverton, Eng. 13,500 I12 273
Wolverton, Wilkin, Minn. 204 E2 148
Womack, Red River, La. B2 180
Womack Hill, Choctaw, Ala. D1 168
Womelsdorf, Berks, Pa. 1,471 C5 214
Womelsdorf, see Coalton, W.Va.
Women, lake, Minn. E4 148
Wonder, Josephine, Oreg. 200 E3 96
Wonder, cave, Iowa A6 142
Wonder Lake, McHenry, Ill. 3,543 A5 138
E1
Wonewoc, Juneau, Wis. 878 E3 160
Wŏnsan (Gensan), Kor. 112,952 F13 348
Wonthaggi, Austl. 4,461 F9 432
Wood, Huntingdon, Pa. 800 C3 214
Wood, Mellette, S.Dak. 267 D5 158
Wood, co., Ohio 72,596 A3 156
Wood, co., Tex. 17,653 C8 130
Wood, co., W.Va. 78,331 B3 194
Wood, co., Wis. 59,105 D3 160
Wood, lake, Sask., Can. C6 58
Wood, mtn., Sask., Can. F4 58
Wood, mtn., Mont. E7 110
Wood, pond, Maine C2 204
Wood, riv., B.C., Can. D13 52
Wood, riv., Sask., Can. F4 58
Wood, riv., R.I. C2 216
Wood, riv., Wyo. C3 116
Woodall, mtn., Miss. A4 184
Woodberry, Calhoun, Ark. 44 D4 170
Woodbine, Camden, Ga. 845 F5 176
Woodbine, Harrison, Iowa 1,304 C2 142
Woodbine, Dickinson, Kans. 173 D7 144
Woodbine, Whitley, Ky. 800 D6 178
Woodbine, Carroll, Md. 130 B5 182
Woodbine, Cape May, N.J. 2,823 E3 210
Woodbine, Davidson, Tenn. 11,500 B5 190
E7
Woodbourne, Sullivan, N.Y. 850 D7 212
Woodbridge, Ont., Can. 1,958 Q21 64
R21
Woodbridge, New
Haven, Conn. 5,182 D3 202
Woodbridge, Middlesex, N.J. 17,000 B4 210
C1
Woodbridge, Prince
William, Va. 1,100 B7 192
Wood Buffalo, natl., park,
Alta., Can. E3 54
Woodburn, Allen, Ind. 585 A5 140
Woodburn, Clarke, Iowa 202 C4 142
Woodburn, Warren, Ky. 291 D4 178
Woodburn, Marion, Oreg. 3,120 B1 96
B4
Woodbury, Litchfield, Conn. 1,000 C3 202
(3,910▲)
Woodbury, Meriwether, Ga. 1,230 D2 176
Woodbury, Butler, Ky. 94 C4 178
Woodbury, Gloucester, N.J. 12,453 D2 210
Woodbury, Cannon, Tenn. 1,562 C5 190
Woodbury, Washington, Vt. 250 C4 218
(317▲)
Woodbury, co., Iowa 107,849 B1 142
Woodbury Heights, Gloucester
N.J. 1,723 *D2 210
Woodcliff Lake, Bergen, N.J. 2,742 *A4 210
Wood Creek Farms, Oakland,
Mich. 684 *G8 146
Wood Dale, Du Page, Ill. 3,071 F2 138
Woodfibre, B.C., Can. 500 F11 52
Woodford, Carter, Okla. 30 D6 128
Woodford, Orangeburg, S.C. 172 D6 188
Woodford, co., Ill. 24,579 C4 138
Woodford, co., Ky. 11,913 B6 178
Woodgate, Oneida, N.Y. 200 B6 212
Woodhull, Henry, Ill. 779 B3 138
Woodhull, Steuben, N.Y. 321 C4 212
Woodinville, King, Wash. 650 B4 98
Woodlake, Tulare
Calif. 2,623 D4 94
Wood Lake, Yellow Medicine,
Minn. 506 G3 148
Wood Lake, Cherry, Nebr. 197 B5 152
Woodland, Randolph, Ala. 100 B4 168
Woodland, Yolo, Calif. 13,524 C3 94
Woodland, Sussex, Del. 48 F3 172
Woodland, Talbot, Ga. 720 D2 176
Woodland, Idaho, Idaho 300 C2 108
Woodland, St. Joseph, Ind. 80 A3 140
Woodland (Town of),
Aroostook, Maine (1,372▲) B4 204
Woodland, Washington,
Maine 1,393 C5 204
Woodland, Barry, Mich. 374 G6 146
Woodland, Jackson, Mich. 300 *G7 146
Woodland, Hennepin, Minn. 449 *F5 148
Woodland, Chickasaw, Miss. 100 B3 184
Woodland, Northampton, N.C. 651 A8 186
Woodland, Clearfield, Pa. 900 C3 214
Woodland, Cowlitz, Wash. 1,336 D4 98
Woodland Beach, Kent, Del. 150 C4 172
Woodland Beach, Monroe,
Mich. 1,944 *H8 146
Woodland Heights, Pulaski, Ark. 30 D6 170
Woodland Mills, Obion, Tenn. 200 B2 190
Woodland Park, Teller, Colo. 666 C5 106
Woodlawn, Campbell, Ky. 387 *A6 178
Woodlawn, McCracken, Ky. 1,688 C2 178
Woodlawn, Baltimore, Md. 6,000 C4 182
Woodlawn, Prince Georges,
Md. 3,000 *C6 182
Woodlawn, Hamilton, Ohio 3,007 D1 156
Woodlawn, Carroll, Va. 30 D4 192
Woodlawn Beach, Erie, N.Y. 1,800 C3 212
Woodlawn Heights, Madison,
Ind. 29 *B4 140
Woodlawn Orchards,
Jackson, Mich. 2,000 *G7 146
Woodlawn Park, Jefferson,
Ky. 1,137 *B5 178
Woodlawn Park, Anne
Arundel, Md. 1,200 *B6 182
Woodlawn Park, Oklahoma,
Okla. 129 *C6 128
Woodley Hills, Fairfax, Va. 2,000 *B7 192

X

Y

Z

Zalțan, mts., Libya		B3	394
Zaltbommel, Neth.	5,469	C4	282
Zama, Attala, Miss.	150	C3	184
Zambezi, riv., Ang., Rh.&Nya.		B4	420
		C5	
Zambézia, prov., Moz.		C7	421
Zamboanga, Phil.	17,001	C6	358
Zambrano, Col.	5,863	B2	244
Zambrów, Pol.	4,150	B6	325
Zamora, Ec.	458	A2	245
Zamora, Mex.	23,434	D5	225
		K12	
Zamora, Sp.	32,388	B4	298
Zamora, prov., Sp.	316,493	*B4	298
Zamora, riv., Ec.		A2	245
Zamość, Pol.	26,000	C6	325
Zampa, pt., Okinawa		C1	436
Zamzam, wadi, Libya		A2	394
Zandvoort, Neth.	11,694	B3	282
Zanesville, Wells and Allen, Ind.	400	B4	140
Zanesville, Muskingum, Ohio	39,077	C5	156
Zangla, India		B2	368
Zanjān, Iran	47,159	B2	379
Zante, see Zákinthos, prov., Grc.			
Zanzibar, Br. poss., Afr.	304,000	G10	388
			414
Zap, Mercer, N.Dak.	339	C4	154
Zapadna Morava, riv., Yugo.		C5	316
Zapala, Arg.	3,387	C1	252
Zapata, Zapata, Tex.	2,031	F6	130
Zapata, co., Tex.	4,393	F6	130
Zapata, pen., Cuba		A4	232
Zapatoca, Col.	5,629	B2	244
Zaporozhye, Sov.Un.	435,000	I10	332
Zapotitlán, Mex.	3,248	G10	224
Zaqaziq, Eg., U.A.R.	81,813	A3	395
Zara, Tur.	6,717	B7	307
Zaragoza, Col.	1,732	B2	244
Zaragoza, Mex.	4,055	B5	225
Zaragoza, Mex.	2,464	K13	225
Zaragoza, Sp.	244,015	B6	298
Zaragoza, prov., Sp.	609,393	*B6	298
Zarah, Johnson, Kans.	90	B7	144
Zarand, Iran	4,493	C4	379
Zárate, Arg.	35,197	B4	252
Zaraysk, Sov.Un.	28,600	E12	332
Zaraza, Ven.	5,780	B6	240
Zardeh Kuh, mtn., Iran		C3	379
Zarembo, isl., Alsk.		J14	84
Zaria, Nig.	32,559 (*53,974)	D6	409
Zarqa, Eg., U.A.R.	6,069	C2	382
Zaruma, Ec.	3,922	A2	245
Zarumilla, Peru	1,738	A1	245
Żary, Pol.	18,500	C2	325
Zarzal, Col.	7,395	C1	244
Zashiversk, Sov.Un.	800	C16	329
Zaskar, riv., India		B2	368
Zásmuky, Czech.	1,533	*B2	324
Zastron, U.S.Afr.	4,185	F5	420
Žatec, Czech.	15,114	A1	324
Zavala, co., Tex.	12,696	E6	130
Zavalla, Angelina, Tex.	700	D8	130
Zavitaya, Sov.Un.	14,500	D14	329
Zavodo-Petrovskiy, Sov.Un.		A7	336
Zawiercie, Pol.	31,000	C4	325
Zawilah, Libya	1,409	B3	394
Zāwiyat Masūs, Libya		A4	394
Zaysan, Sov.Un.	15,600	C10	336
Zaysan, lake, Sov.Un.		C10	336
Zaza, riv., Cuba		B5	232
Zbraslav, Czech.	4,643	*B2	324
Zdice, Czech.	3,037	*B2	324
Zdolbunov, Sov.Un.	14,600	G6	332
Zduńska Wola, Pol.	18,500	C4	325
Zealandia, Sask., Can.	186	E4	58
Zearing, Story, Iowa	528	B4	142
Zeba, Baraga, Mich.	75	C3	146
Zeballos, B.C., Can.	154	E9	52
Zebulon, Pike, Ga.	563	C2	176
Zebulon, Pike, Ky.	200	C8	178
Zebulon, Wake, N.C.	1,534	B7	186
Zeebrugge, Bel.	3,000	C2	282
Zeeland, Ottawa, Mich.	3,702	G5	146
Zeeland, McIntosh, N.Dak.	427	E6	154
Zeeland, prov., Neth.	274,244	C2	282
Zehdenick, Ger.	13,300	B5	286
Zeigler, Franklin, Ill.	2,133	F4	138
Zeiglerville, Yazoo, Miss.	50	C2	184
Zeist, Neth.	46,634	B4	282
Zeitz, Ger.	45,900	C5	286
Zekiah, swamp, Md.		D6	182
Zela, Nicholas, W.Va.	250	C7	194
Żelechów, Pol.	3,892	C5	325
Zelenodolsk, Sov.Un.	60,000	A3	336
Zelenogorsk, Sov.Un. (part of Leningrad)	32,000	B7	332
Zelienople, Butler, Pa.	3,284	C1	214
Zell, Faulk, S.Dak.	100	C7	158
Zella-Mehlis, Ger.	16,600	C4	286
Zellwood, Orange, Fla.	300	C9	174
Zelma, Sask., Can.	103	E5	58
Zelzate, Bel.	10,412	C2	282
Zemetchino, Sov.Un.	12,800	F14	332
Zémio, Cen.Afr.Rep.		E10	409
Zena, Delaware, Okla.	150	B9	128
Zenda, Kingman, Kans.	157	E5	144
Zenia, Trinity, Calif.	160	B2	94
Zenica, Yugo.	30,000	B3	316
Zenith, King, Wash.	600	D2	98
Zenon Park, Sask., Can.	411	D6	58
Zenoria, La Salle, La.	100	C3	180
Žepče, Yugo.	2,292	B4	316
Zephyr Cove, Douglas, Nev.	100	E2	112
Zephyrhills, Pasco, Fla.	2,887	C8	174
Zerbst, Ger.	18,100	C5	286
Zerka, riv., Jordan		B6	382
Zermatt, Switz.	1,395	B3	312
Zernez, Switz.	739	B6	312
Zetland (Shetland), co., Scot.	18,600	*A12	272
Zetto, Clay, Ga.	300	E2	176
Zeven, Ger.	6,593	B3	286
Zevenaar, Neth.	3,273	C5	282
Zevgolatió, Grc.	1,089	C3	306
Zewāy, lake, Eth.		D4	398
Zeya, Sov.Un.	15,100	D14	329
Zeya, riv., Sov.Un.		D14	329
Zezere, riv., Port.		B3	298
Zgierz, Pol.	32,000	C4	325
Zhangiz-Tobe, Sov.Un.		C10	336
Zharkamys, Sov.Un.		C5	336
Zhdanov (Mariupol), Sov.Un.	284,000	I11	332
Zhelaniya, cape, Sov.Un.		B8	328
Zhigalovo, Sov.Un.		D12	329
Zhikatse, China	10,000	F5	346
Zhilevo, Sov.Un.		P19	332
Zhitomir, Sov.Un.	105,000	G7	332
Zhizdra, Sov.Un.	21,200	F10	332
Zhmerinka, Sov.Un.	44,600	H7	332
Zhob, riv., Pak.		D6	375
Zhupanova, Sov.Un.		D18	329
Ziā'ābād, Iran		B2	379
Ziebach, co., S.Dak.	2,495	C4	158
Ziel, mtn., Austl.		C6	432
Zielona Góra, Pol.	39,000	C2	325
Zielona Góra, pol. div., Pol.	675,000	*C2	325
Zierikzee, Neth.	6,967	C2	282
Zifta, Eg., U.A.R.	29,700	D2	382
Zifta, Eg., U.A.R.	26,520	A3	395
Ziguinchor, Sen.	15,100	D1	408
Zikhron Ya'aqov, Isr.	4,200	B5	382
Zile, Tur.	21,399	A6	307
Žilina, Czech.	31,123	B4	324
Žilinský, co., Czech.	587,215	*B4	324
Zillah, Yakima, Wash.	1,059	C6	98
Zilwaukee, Saginaw, Mich.	1,400	F8	146
Zima, Sov.Un.	33,200	D12	329
Zimapán, Mex.	2,343	C6	225
		K14	
Zimba, Rh.&Nya.	95	C5	420
Zimmerman, Rapides, La.	500	C3	180
Zimmerman, Sherburne, Minn.	302	F5	148
Zimnicea, Rom.	12,445	C3	321
Zinc, Boone, Ark.	68	A4	170
Zincville, Ottawa, Okla.	65	B9	128
Zindajān, Afg.	10,000	B1	374
Zinder, Niger	13,200	D6	409
Zion, Izard, Ark.	100	A5	170
Zion, Lake, Ill.	11,941	A6	138
		D2	
Zion, Cecil, Md.	360	A8	182
Zion, Somerset, N.J.	50	C3	210
Zion, Marion, S.C.	216	C10	188
Zion, natl. park, Utah		F3	114
Zion Hill, Amite, Miss.	75	D2	184
Zionsville, Boone, Ind.	1,822	C3	140
		D4	
Zipaquirá, Col.	12,708	B2	244
Zipp, Vanderburgh, Ind.	200	D2	140
Zipperer, Beaufort, S.C.	500	*F7	188
Zippori, Isr.	281	B6	382
Zirándaro, Mex.	1,205	D5	225
		L13	
Zirkel, mtn., Colo.		B4	106
Zisterdorf, Aus.	3,070	B8	313
Zitácuaro, Mex.	19,940	D5	225
		L13	
Zitlala, Mex.	3,215	M14	225
Zittau, Ger.	46,100	C6	286
Zlatograd, Bul.	4,522	C2	317
Zlín, see Gottwaldov, Czech.			
Zlitan, Libya		A2	394
Złoczew, Pol.	2,948	C4	325
Zlonice, Czech.	271	*A2	324
Złotów, Pol.	5,275	B3	325
Złtoryja, Pol.	4,613	C2	325
Zlynka, Sov.Un.	17,800	F8	332
Zmeinogorsk, Sov.Un.		B10	336
Znamenka, Sov.Un.	37,300	H9	332
Żnin, Pol.	5,615	B3	325
Znojmo, Czech.	22,681	B3	324
Zoar, Newf., Can.		D9	72
Zofingen, Switz.	7,393	A3	312
Zolfo Springs, Hardee, Fla.	838	D9	174
Zollikofen, Switz.	3,453	A3	312
Zolochev, Sov.Un.	28,600	H5	332
Zolotonosha, Sov.Un.	33,400	H9	332
Zomba, Rh.&Nya.	9,245	C7	421
Zomergem, Bel.	6,128	C2	282
Zona, Roane, W.Va.	111	C3	194
Zongsar, India		B2	368
Zonguldak, Tur.	46,902	A4	307
Zonguldak, prov., Tur.	492,422	*A5	307
Zoquitlán, Mex.	3,354	L15	225
Zorita, Sp.	5,981	C4	298
Zortman, Phillips, Mont.	120	C8	110
Zossen, Ger.	5,958	B5	286
Zottegem, Bel.	6,576	D2	282
Zoug, well, Sp. Sahara		B2	408
Zoug, see Zug, canton, Switz.			
Zoutkamp, Neth.	1,068	A5	282
Zrenjanin (Petrovgrad), Yugo.	45,300	B5	316
Zrmanja, riv., Yugo.		B2	316
Ztatoust, Sov.Un.		A5	336
Zubtsov, Sov.Un.	9,100	D10	332
Zuénoula, I.C.		E3	408
Zuera, Sp.	3,587	B6	298
Zug, Switz.	16,400	A4	312
Zug (Zoug), canton, Switz.	46,500	A4	312
Zug, lake, Switz.		A4	312
Zugspitze, mtn., Aus.		C2	313
Zuhreh, riv., Iran		C3	379
Zuider Zee, see Ijsselmeer, sea, Neth.			
Zuidholland, prov., Neth.	2,506,576	B3	282
Zuidhorn, Neth.	1,863	A5	282
Zulia, state, Ven.	560,336	B2	240
Zulueta, Cuba	4,337	A5	232
Zumbro, riv., Minn.		G6	148
Zumbro Falls, Wabasha, Minn.	164	G6	148
Zumbrota, Goodhue, Minn.	1,830	G6	148
Zumpango (de Ocampo), Mex.	6,545	L14	225
Zumwalt, Lane, Oreg.	1,000	*C3	96
Zuni (Zuni Pueblo), McKinley, N.Mex.	3,585	C2	126
Zuni, Isle of Wight, Va.	155	A7	192
Zuni, mts., N.Mex.		C2	126
Zuni, res., Ariz.		D6	124
Zuni, riv., Ariz., N.Mex.		D6	124
		C2	126
Zurich, Ont., Can.	560	Q19	64
Zurich, Rooks, Kans.	244	C4	144
Zürich, Switz.	414,000 (*438,300)	A4	312
Zürich, canton, Switz.	865,000	A4	312
Zürich, lake, Switz.		A4	312
Zuru, Nig.		D6	408
Zutphen, Neth.	23,793	B5	282
Zuwārah, Libya	2,380	A2	394
Zuyevka, Sov.Un.	18,200	A4	336
Zvenigorodka, Sov.Un.	39,800	H8	332
Zvolen, Czech.	19,921	B4	324
Zvornik, Yugo.	5,197	B4	316
Zwartsluis, Neth.	3,504	B5	282
Zweibrücken, Ger.	31,800	D2	286
Zweisimmen, Switz.	2,599	B3	312
Zwettl, Aus.	3,812	B7	313
Zwickau, Ger.	135,800	C5	286
Zwingle, Dubuque, Iowa	110	B7	142
Zwolle, Sabine, La.	1,326	C2	180
Zwolle, Neth.	52,455	B5	282
Zylks, Caddo, La.	200	A1	180
Żyrardów, Pol.	27,000	B5	325
Zyryanovsk, Sov.Un.	54,000	C10	336
Żywiec, Pol.	17,000	D4	325

TEXT AND INDEX PHOTOCOMPOSED ON PHOTON EQUIPMENT
IN THE EDITORIAL OFFICES OF TIME INCORPORATED, NEW YORK, NEW YORK

COLOR SCANNING BY PRINTING DEVELOPMENTS INCORPORATED, NEW YORK, NEW YORK

COLOR ENGRAVINGS BY GRAPHIC COLOR PLATE, INC., STAMFORD, CONNECTICUT
AND R. R. DONNELLEY & SONS COMPANY, CHICAGO, ILLINOIS

PRINTED BY OFFSET LITHOGRAPHY AND BOUND BY
RAND McNALLY & COMPANY, CHICAGO, ILLINOIS

PAPER BY THE MEAD CORPORATION, DAYTON, OHIO

PICTURE CREDITS

The sources for the photographs and illustrations in this book are shown below. Credits for pictures placed from left to right on a page are separated by commas, top to bottom by dashes.

Photographs of Geo-Physical Globe by David McGowan of Crandall Associates.

10, 11 – Chesley Bonestell – Antonio Petruccelli
12 – U.S. Air Force
13, 14, 15 – Antonio Petruccelli
16 – Kenneth Fagg
17 – Antonio Petruccelli
20, 21 – Kenneth Fagg
24, 25 – Antonio Petruccelli
29 – Francis Pfotenhauer from Shostal – Duncan Edwards from Free Lance Photographers Guild – Bill Gulley from Photo Researchers, Inc. – Dmitri Kessel – Fritz Goro – Tom Hollyman from Photo Researchers, Inc. – Ray Manley from Shostal – Fritz Goro – Dmitri Kessel – Albert Fenn – George Silk – Eliot Elisofon
32, 33 – top: Charting of mineral deficiencies by American Geographical Society
41 – top right: Kenneth Fagg
50, 51 – left: Margaret Bourke-White; right: Andreas Feininger – J. R. Eyerman
56, 57 – Chris Lund from Annan Photo Features
62 – Erich Hartmann from Magnum for FORTUNE
63 – Fritz Goro
68, 69 – Malak
82 – Robert Wenkam
83 – Fritz Goro
90, 91 – left: J. R. Eyerman; center: N. R. Farbman – Ralph Crane; right: J. R. Eyerman
92, 93 – Ansel Adams
102 – Eliot Elisofon
103 – Loomis Dean
104, 105 – Margaret Bourke-White
120, 121 – Chuck Abbott from Rapho-Guillumette
122, 123 – Ray Manley from Shostal
134, 135 – Charles E. Rotkin from Photography for Industry for FORTUNE – William Vandivert
136, 137 – Laurence Lowry from Rapho-Guillumette, Roger Fuhrmeyer from Foto/Find
164, 165 – Margaret Bourke-White – Andreas Feininger
166, 167 – David Preston from Shostal
198 – Dmitri Kessel
199 – Henri Cartier-Bresson from Magnum
200, 201 – Laurence Lowry from Rapho-Guillumette
222, 223 – left: Laurence Lowry from Rapho-Guillumette; right: John Lewis Stage from Lens-group – Patrice Hartley from Rapho-Guillumette
230, 231 – Fritz Goro
238, 239 – Cornell Capa from Magnum
242, 243 – Dmitri Kessel except bottom right Jerry Frank from Alpha Photos
248 – Cornell Capa from Magnum
249 – Rene Burri from Magnum
254, 255 – left: Anthony Linck – Dmitri Kessel; center: David Bergamini; right: Paulo Muniz
260, 261 – bottom: Kenneth Fagg
262, 263 – top: Kenneth Fagg
270, 271 – Rene Burri from Magnum
276 – N. R. Farbman
277 – Gisèle Freund from Monkmeyer Press Photos
280, 281 – left: Thomas McAvoy; right: Jerry Cooke – Maynard Williams from Shostal
284 – Charles E. Rotkin from Photography for Industry
285 – Stephen W. Frisch from Free Lance Photographers Guild
288, 289 – James Whitmore
296, 297 – Dmitri Kessel
300, 301 – Marilyn Silverstone from Nancy Palmer Photo Agency – Gjon Mili
304, 305 – Marc Riboud from Magnum, Burt Glinn from Magnum
310 – Ewing Krainin from Photo Researchers, Inc. – Inge Morath from Magnum
311 – Photo Researchers, Inc.
314 – Peter Schmid from Pix
315 – Edwin A. Nystrom from Free Lance Photographers Guild
318, 319 – Inge Morath from Magnum except top left John P. Taylor from Rapho-Guillumette
322, 323 – Alan Shayne from Photo Researchers, Inc., Erich Lessing from Magnum
330, 331 – Howard Sochurek
334 – Howard Sochurek – Marilyn Silverstone from Nancy Palmer Photo Agency
335 – Howard Sochurek
344 – John Dominis
345 – Marc Riboud from Magnum
352, 353 – Joseph Breitenbach
356, 357 – Philip Lustig from Free Lance Photographers Guild
360, 361 – John Dominis – Howard Sochurek, Dmitri Kessel
364 – Dmitri Kessel
365 – Howard Sochurek
372, 373 – Marc Riboud from Magnum
376, 377 – left: Rene Burri from Magnum; right: Leo Lionni for FORTUNE – George Rodger from Magnum
380, 381 – Dmitri Kessel – Arabian American Oil Company
392, 393 – John G. Ross
396, 397 – Laurence Lowry from Rapho-Guillumette
400 – Jean Boissonnas
401 – Inge Morath from Magnum
406, 407 – Emil Schulthess from Black Star, Pierre Boulat for TIME
412, 413 – Eliot Elisofon
418, 419 – Gordon Douglas from Photo Library
423 – top: Gemological Institute of America, L.A.
426, 427 – bottom: Kenneth Fagg
428, 429 – top: Kenneth Fagg
430, 431 – Fritz Goro
434, 435 – Eliot Elisofon – George Silk
438 – top left: Kenneth Fagg